REFERENCE ONLY

B&T

6/05
mw

HISTORICAL GAZETTEER
of the UNITED STATES

HISTORICAL GAZETTEER
of the UNITED STATES

PAUL T. HELLMANN

ROUTLEDGE

NEW YORK AND LONDON

Published in 2005 by
Routledge
270 Madison Avenue
New York, NY 10016
www.routledge-ny.com

Published in Great Britain by
Routledge
2 Park Square
Milton Park, Abingdon
Oxon, OX14 4RN
www.routledge.co.uk

Routledge is an imprint of Taylor & Francis Books, Inc.

10 9 8 7 6 5 4 3 2 1

Printed on acid-free, 250-year-life paper
Manufactured in the United States of America

Library of Congress Cataloging-in-Publication Data
Hellman, Paul T., 1949-
    Historical gazetteer of the United States / Paul T. Hellman.
        p. cm.
    Includes index.
    ISBN 0-415-93948-8 (acid-free paper)
    1. United States–Gazetteers. 2. United States–Historical geography–
Dictionaries. 3. U.S. States–Dictionaries.
    4. United States–History, Local–Dictionaries. I. Title.
E154.H45 2005
911′.73–dc22   2004011421

Lovingly dedicated to my parents Robert and Ruth Hellmann

Contents

Advisors

ALABAMA
John Hardin, Archivist
Alabama Department of Archives and History
Montgomery

ALASKA
Bruce Merrill, Librarian, Alaska Collection
Anchorage Department of Libraries

ARIZONA
Melanie Sturgeon, Division Director
Arizona History and Archives Division
Arizona State Library
Phoenix

ARKANSAS
Thomas W. Dillard, Curator
The Butler Center for Arkansas Studies
Arkansas Historical Association
Little Rock

CALIFORNIA
Walter Gray, Chief
California State Archives
Sacramento

COLORADO
Madupe Labode, Chief Historian
Colorado Historical Society
Denver

DELAWARE
Brian Page, Historic Preservation Planner
Sussex County Government
Georgetown

DISTRICT OF COLUMBIA
Edward C. Papenfuse, State Archivist
Maryland State Archives
Annapolis

FLORIDA
Boyd Murphree, Archivist
Florida Division of Archives,
Tallahassee

GEORGIA
Sandra Boling, Senior Archivist
The Georgia Archives
Morrow

HAWAII
Robert C. Schmitt, Editorial Board
Hawaiian Journal of History
Hawaiian Historical Society
Honolulu
Retired Director, Hawaii State Data Board

IDAHO
Judy Austin, Publications Coordinator
Idaho Historical Society
Boise

ILLINOIS
Tom Schwartz, State Historian
Illinois State Historical Society
Springfield

INDIANA
Paul Brockman, Senior Archivist
Indiana Historical Society
Indianapolis

IOWA
Loren N. Horton, Retired Historian
State Historical Society of Iowa
Des Moines and Iowa City

KANSAS
Virgil W. Dean, Historian, Editor
Kansas State Historical Society
Topeka

KENTUCKY
Ron D. Bryant, History Specialist
Kentucky Historical Society
Frankfort

LOUISIANA
Carolyn Bennett, Executive Director
Foundation for Historical Louisiana
Baton Rouge

SOUTH CAROLINA
Marion C. Chandler, Retired
Department of Archives and History
Columbia

SOUTH DAKOTA
Richard Popp, State Archivist
South Dakota State Historical Society
Pierre

TENNESSEE
Wayne C. Moore, Assistant State Archivist
Tennessee State Library and Archives
Nashville

TEXAS
Douglas C. Barnett, Editor, *Texas Historian*
Texas State Historical Association
Austin

UTAH
Allen Kent Powell, Public History Coordinator
Utah State Historical Society
Salt Lake City

VERMONT
Gregory Sanford, State Archivist
Vermont State Archives
Montpelier

VIRGINIA
Donald Zeigler, Professor of Geography
Old Dominion University
Norfolk

WASHINGTON
Robert E. Ficken, Historian, Author
Washington State Historical Society

WEST VIRGINIA
Frederick H. Armstrong, Director
West Virginia Archives and History
The Cultural Center
East Charleston

WISCONSIN
Geraldine E. Strey, Map Curator
Reference Librarian
Wisconsin Historical Society
Madison

The advisors for Connecticut and Wyoming prefer to be anonymous.

Introduction

When the European explorers began arriving on the shores of the Americas, they brought with them a systematic means of measuring time and the subsequent means of recording history with relative accuracy. There is such a wide disparity between pre-Columbian and post-Columbian history, in how it is measured and how it has been told, that their stories are best told separately.

Likewise, the share of post-Columbian history within the confines of the United States of America is so disparate from the histories of the remainder of the countries of the Western Hemisphere that it too is best told on its own, as it already has been in countless narratives, chronologies, listings, maps, and pictures, at all levels of geography, for nearly every time period and event. But amid all of these options one option has been lacking.

The editor of the *Historical Gazetteer of the United States* was inspired by a significant void perceived in what was available on the history of the United States. The editor knew that it was possible to draw from one source to find out the birth dates of notable or popular persons, another source for founding dates of colleges, yet other sources for dates of disasters or battles, or individual accounts of significant events, and so on. What was lacking was a quick reference that aggregated American history by place, in which the only common thread was locality.

Encyclopedias fill this void to a limited extent, and some gazetteers offer limited historical information by place. Individual historical narratives or chronologies can be found in libraries or online, or can be obtained through various historical societies. All too often, events of national or general interest are embedded in local detail. Also, having to obtain information on several or numerous places can become a major undertaking if gained through locally produced historical accounts, especially when what is needed are simply a few basic events.

Four years in the making, the *Historical Gazetteer* achieves the goal of aggregating American history by place. The early stages of research revealed the need to report significant events in a basic framework of local history, rather than simply listing the events by themselves, to give the events local relevance. As a gazetteer, this was to become a geographical reference as much as a historical reference, with the historical element subordinate to the geography. So it was important that the local frame of reference emphasize the political and physical geography of each profiled place, including the founding and incorporation dates of places, the formation dates of counties, the dates of construction of dams, bridges, railroads, major buildings, and other man-made features, as well as naturally occurring events that have altered the landscape.

Thoroughness and a desire to develop a document that was interesting to the reader superseded any hope of being comprehensive with this text. While all major and secondary cities are included, what places were covered beyond this was determined more by the amount and content of history rather than the population. On the one hand, there are numerous places profiled that are now ghost towns or have disappeared completely, while other places having tens of thousands of inhabitants have been excluded, especially in urban areas, for having little more than incorporation dates to report. The exception to these are the county seats. So many county seats were covered anyway that it became a goal of the gazetteer to include every county seat regardless of size or historical content. The purpose was to complete the national geographical mosaic of settlement and of county formation.

Comprehensive coverage of every subject proved unrealistic. Limitations of time, resources, and page space made it necessary to settle for an assortment of coverage beyond the core information. For instance, it was possible to report construction dates of railroads for most places, but not for all places. It was possible to include the founding or construction dates of many libraries, but not for all libraries. It was possible to report who or what the place or its county was named for, but not for all places or counties. Again, the fundamental goal of the *Historical Gazetteer* is to report as many significant events of nationwide importance or general interest as possible at the local level by place, within a brief framework of local history, rather than to be comprehensive with the local history itself. Beyond this, only a limited assortment of information was practical. The outcome of this effort is this unique presentation of the history of the United States.

References to Events or Sites Outside Profiled Places

Coverage of events in rural or uninhabited areas or in obscure localities has been assigned to the nearest profiled place. This is often the case, for instance, with construction dates of reservoirs or establishment dates of national park units. Major battles or certain disastrous events may have occurred in remote locations. Wherever necessary, the direction of the site of the event's occurrence from the profiled place is given, "to the west," "to the southwest," etc. In some cases, the actual distance to the site is given.

If an event is relevant to an entire county, it is reported at the county seat or other major city. An event relevant to an entire state is likewise reported at the entry for the state capital or, in some cases, at a major city.

In many cases, the same event is repeated if it is relevant to more than one place. For instance, if a bridge connects two profiled cities, its construction date might be given at both. Or, if a national park, reservoir, or other large feature is dominant to more than one profiled place, the date that it came into being may be repeated.

It should be added that construction dates are reported within the time frame of construction usually when that period is within 2–3 years. When reported as completion dates, the reference is more specific. Where possible, and where space has permitted it, both starting dates and completion dates have been given.

Cross-References

Many events have occurred in obscure localities or in places that are lacking enough history to justify a separate place entry. Where called for, a cross-reference has been added to the text to indicate to the reader what profiled place the event has been assigned to and to locate obscure localities where most other commonly available sources fail. An example is the birthplace of Hawaiian entertainer Don Ho, given as Kakaako, Oahu, now a part of Honolulu, not easily found on maps. A cross-reference refers the reader to Honolulu and to the year of the event within the lengthy Honolulu article. Another example, the official lowest temperature for Utah was recorded at a physical feature named Peter's Sink. A cross-reference gives the mention to Logan, the nearest profiled place.

Cross-references are also used for places that have undergone a relatively recent name change. For instance, the city of Mauch Chunk, Pennsylvania, was renamed Jim Thorpe, for the famed football star, in 1954, and the city of Hot Springs, New Mexico, was renamed Truth or Consequences, for the old Ralph Edwards television show, in 1950. Cross-references are given for the former names of both places.

Municipalities and Incorporation Dates

For every incorporated profiled place at least one incorporation date has been given as part of the core local historical framework, that usually being the earliest date of permanent incorporation. As is true for most subjects touched upon by this gazetteer, complete incorporation histories and accounts of their changes in classification were unattainable within the constraints of this project and for lack of adequate sources on the subject.

Many sources were nonspecific with reporting the municipality's classification along with the incorporation date, while other sources or responses to queries were suspect in their accuracy, often using the term "city" as a synonym for "municipality" instead of specifically as a classification. Classification refers to the official status of a municipality as defined by the state, with the options usually being village, town, or city. Some states have only village and city, others only town and city. Other states use borough as a classification, not to be confused with the five boroughs of New York City, which are merely subdivisions of that one city, or with Alaska's boroughs, which are part of a recently created system of county equivalents. Other states have no classification at all, in which case classifications may be applied informally by the municipality itself. Finally, several states further divide the classification of "city" into two or more classes, including 4th class, 3rd class, 2nd class, 1st class, and/or home rule city in ascending order. While the gazetteer attempts to report most primary classifications and changes in status, this further sub-classification has been ignored for the general purposes of this reference.

When reporting a municipal incorporation with its classification, the statement "incorporated as a (village, town, city, borough)" is employed and is re-employed with changes in classification. When reporting the incorporation date without the municipal classification, the generic statement "town incorporated" is employed.

There is the further complication of a municipality becoming disincorporated, or unincorporated, for periods of time or permanently, usually due to a catastrophe or general decline in population. Some of these changes are covered in the gazetteer. Also, it was possible for sources on incorporations to vary and still be correct. A local source might give the date that the citizens approved the incorporation by popular referendum, while a state source might give the date that the state legislature approved the incorporation a year or more later. Whereas the locally cited date is preferred, for that is usually when the new entity begins to function, both are acceptable.

Townships and New England's Towns

An intermediate level of political geography between the county level and the municipal level are townships. They are civil divisions of the county created much the same way that counties are created within states. Out of the 50 states, only 25 have townships, comprising all of the Midwestern and Northeastern states, plus a few Southern states. Their function varies greatly from having no organized government at all or very limited governments to strong governments, particularly in the Northeast.

In the six New England states—Maine, New Hampshire, Vermont, Massachusetts, Rhode Island, and Connecticut—the townships are called towns, a different use of the term than in most

other states in which "town" is used either generically in reference to a settlement or as a specific municipal classification. New England's townships, or towns, have such strong governments that they take the place of municipalities as defined by other states. In other states, the citizens of a settlement may elect to incorporate a place and draw a corporate limit around it. The New England town boundaries were drawn first, settled later, except where further subdividing was necessitated by growth. The strength of New England town governments have relegated the county governments of these six states to minimal functions or have led to the total abolition of county governments altogether.

Outside of New England, of the few states that have organized, incorporated townships, New Jersey's townships have the strongest governments, equaling municipalities in their status. New York is the only state outside of New England that refers to its townships as towns, using the two terms interchangeably.

Except for New England, the *Historical Gazetteer* has ignored the intermediate township level of political geography for the lack of consistency among the states and since they are rarely found on maps. The aggregation of American history by place has been adequately reported without the use of townships beyond New England.

Within the New England townships, or towns, are one or more villages, settlements more comparable to generic towns in other states. The New England villages remain distinct in rural and suburban areas, each having their own history and identity. In urban areas, the villages have coalesced. But in areas where the villages remain distinct, the gazetteer has focused on them as the most localized level of geography. The central village usually reflects the name of the town (township) that it is located in and usually serves as the center of government for that town. In these cases, the incorporation date is stated as "town incorporated" because the town name is known. Where a profiled village differs from the name from its town, the incorporation statement includes the town name.

Brief introductions are given at the beginning of each state chapter and also for the District of Columbia chapter. At the end of each introduction is a statement pertaining to the counties, townships, and municipalities of that state.

Acknowledgments

Special appreciation is owed to several individuals who provided large amounts of information for this work, all of whom explained that they were just doing their jobs:

Ms. Lynne Mueller, Special Collections Librarian, Mississippi State University

Mrs. Elizabeth Danley, Arkansas State Library, Little Rock

Ms. Tina Arnold, Election Services, Arkansas Secretary of State's office

Ms. Judy Smith, State Library of Louisiana, Baton Rouge

Ms. Sherri Mann, Tulsa City-County Library

Mr. Joe Horton, Kentucky Archives, Frankfort

Ms. Sara Wylie, South Dakota State Library, Pierre

Special thanks to the fifty state advisors and the thousands of state, county, and local contacts, at libraries, historical societies, and government offices, from Maine to Hawaii, some of which probably belong on the above list.

Finally, an extra special note of appreciation goes out to Ed Knappman, Vice President of New England Publishing Associates (NEPA), Higganum, Connecticut, for his support and guidance through the entire course of this project, and to Vicki Harlow, Editor at NEPA, for her part in enlisting the fifty advisors consulted for the gazetteer sections.

HISTORICAL GAZETTEER
of the UNITED STATES

Alabama

Southeastern U.S. Capital: Montgomery. Major cities: Birmingham, Mobile.

Alabama became part of the U.S. as Mississippi Territory in 1798. The extension to the Gulf known as West Florida was annexed by the U.S. in 1813. Alabama Territory was created March 3, 1817. Mississippi separated from the territory on December 10, 1817. Alabama became the 22nd state of the U.S. December 14, 1819. Alabama seceded from the U.S. as a Confederate state January 11, 1861. It was readmitted to the U.S. February 23, 1868.

Alabama has 67 counties. One county, St. Clair County, has two (shared) county seats, Ashville and Pell City. Municipalities have eight classifications based upon population. There are no townships. See Introduction.

Abbeville *Henry County* *Southeastern Alabama, 85 mi/137 km southeast of Montgomery*

1819 Henry County formed, called the "Mother County," eight present counties created from it; **1822** Richmond becomes first county seat; **1826** county seat moved to Columbia, now in Houston County; **1833** town founded as new county seat on Abbey Creek; **1872** town incorporated; **1962** Walter F. George Reservoir formed by dam to northeast on Chattahoocee River, on Georgia boundary; **1966** fourth county courthouse built at Abbeville.

Albertville *Marshall County* *Northern Alabama, 63 mi/101 km northeast of Birmingham*

1881 large store established by L. S. Emmett; town founded as cotton processing center; **Feb. 1891** town incorporated; **Apr. 24, 1908** one of state's worst tornadoes destroys town, 16 killed.

Alexander City *Tallapoosa County* *East central Alabama, 45 mi/72 km northeast of Montgomery*

March 27, 1814 Gen. Andrew Jackson defeats Creek Confederacy in Battle of Horseshoe Bend, on Tallapoosa River to northeast; **1859** town founded, originally named Youngville; **1873** town incorporated, renamed Alexander City; **1927** large Lake Martin reservoir formed to south on Tallapoosa River by Martin Dam; **July 25, 1956** Horseshoe Bend National Military Park authorized; **1965** Central Alabama Community College established.

Andalusia *Covington County* *Southern Alabama, 75 mi/121 km south of Montgomery*

1821 Covington County formed; Montezuma becomes first county seat; **1830s** town founded, originally named New Site; **1842** town renamed Andalusia; county seat moved from Montezuma; **1899** Central of Georgia Railroad depot built; **1901** town incorporated; **1916** county courthouse built; **1920** Andalusia Public Library founded.

Anniston *Calhoun County* *Eastern Alabama, 57 mi/92 km east-northeast of Birmingham*

1832 Calhoun County formed, originally named Benton County for Missouri Sen. Thomas Hart Benton; **1833–1836** Creek Confederacy ends with removal of Creek people to Indian Territory; **1858** in response to Sen. Benton's pro-Union stand, county renamed for South Carolina Cong. John C. Calhoun; **1862** Alabama & Tennessee Railroad built to village of Blue Mountain; Confederates establish supply base here; **1863** Oxford Iron Works established to manufacture war materials for Confederacy; **1865** Union forces under Gen. John H. Croxton destroy iron mill and cotton factories; **1872** Woodstock Iron Company established; town founded by Samuel Noble and Daniel Tyler, originally named Woodstock; **1879** town incorporated; post office overturns town name of Woodstock, used elsewhere in Alabama, Anniston derived from "Annie's Town," in honor of Mrs. Annie Scott Tyler; **1880** textile mill established; **1880s** Anniston Inn built, destroyed by fire 1901; **1882** pig iron furnace built; Alabama Mineral Railroad reaches town; **1883** incorporated as a city; *Anniston Star* newspaper founded; **1885** Grace Episcopal Church built; **1890** St. Michael and All Angels Episcopal Church completed; **1899** county seat moved from Jacksonville; **1891** Temple Beth-El dedicated; **1900** county courthouse built; **1914** Camp McClellan established, becomes Fort McClellan training base 1929, closed 1999; Kirby House mansion built; **1918** Carnegie Library opens; **1927** Wilson Building built; **1937** Anniston Airport established; **Oct. 1944** Regional Medical Center established; **1961** mob attacks buses carrying Freedom Riders; **1966** Harry M. Ayers State Technical College (2-year) established; **1976** Anniston Museum of Natural History opened in Lagarde Park; **1996** Berman Museum of World History established.

Ashland   *Clay County   Eastern Alabama, 53 mi/ 85 km east-southeast of Birmingham*

1866 Clay County formed; post office established; **1867** town founded as county seat; **1871** town incorporated; **Feb. 27, 1886** Supreme Court Justice Hugo Black born in rural Clay County (died 1971); **1906** county courthouse built.

Ashville   *Saint Clair County   North central Alabama, 38 mi/61 km northeast of Birmingham*

1818 St. Clair County formed; **1817** John Ashe becomes first settler; **1821** town founded as county seat; **1822** town incorporated; **1831** Ashville Academy founded; **1844** county courthouse built; **1902** Pell City becomes shared county seat, seat of county's new southern division; Ashville remains seat of county's northern division.

Athens   *Limestone County   Northern Alabama, 92 mi/148 km north of Birmingham*

1814 area first settled; **1816** town founded, originally named Athenson; **1818** Limestone County formed; town incorporated; **1819** town becomes county seat; **1822** Athens State University established, originally Athens Academy; **1846** The Cedars plantation house built by Col. James Malone; **1862** town sacked and occupied by Union troops; **1864** town recaptured by Confederate troops of Gen. Nathan B. Forrest; **1918** county courthouse built; **1934** Athens becomes first Alabama community to purchase power from Tennessee Valley Authority (TVA); **Aug. 17, 1973** first phase of Browns Ferry Nuclear Power Plant begins operation.

Atmore   *Escambia County   Southwestern Alabama, 42 mi/68 km northeast of Mobile*

1866 town founded as agricultural shipping center, originally named Williams Station for early settler William L. Williams; **1876** large lumber mill established by William Marshall Carney; **1895** town renamed Atmore; **1907** town incorporated; **1955** Fountain Correctional Center established to east; **1969** Holman Correctional Center established to east; **1972** Atmore State Work Release Center opened.

Auburn   *Lee County   Eastern Alabama, 50 mi/80 km east-northeast of Montgomery*

1836 town founded by group of Georgians led by Judge John J. Harper; town named from line in Goldsmith's *Deserted Village*; Drake House built; **1839** town incorporated; **1840s** Stage Inn built, becomes Jones Hotel; **1856** East Alabama Male College established, became State Agricultural and Mechanical College 1872, became Auburn University 1960; **Aug. 25, 1916** virologist Frederick Chapman Robbins born, Nobel Prize 1954.

Bay Minette   *Baldwin County   Southwestern Alabama, 20 mi/32 km northeast of Mobile*

1809 Baldwin County formed; **1861** town founded; **1898** plan to move county seat from Daphne to Bay Minette's central location rejected by voters at Daphne; **1900** county seat moved from Daphne by order of state supreme court; **1901** county courthouse built; **1965** James H. Faulkner State Community College established.

Bessemer   *Jefferson County   North central Alabama, 12 mi/19 km southwest of Birmingham*

1869 mineral rights purchased by Woodward Iron Company; **1887** Henry F. De Bardeleben builds first steel furnace, founds town at steel mill, named for Sir Henry Bessemer, British inventor of Bessemer steel making process; **Sept. 1887** incorporated as a city; **Feb. 20, 1905** explosion at Virginia City Coal Mine to west, 108 killed; **Nov. 22, 1922** accident at Dolomite Coal Mine to north, 90 killed; **1966** Bessemer State Technical College (2-year) established.

Birmingham   *Jefferson County   North central Alabama, in Appalachian Mountains*

1813 family of John Jones becomes first settlers in Jones Valley, named for them; Fort Jonesborough built; **1819** Jefferson County formed; town of Carrollsville founded as county seat; **1821** William Ely founds town of Elyton 2 mi/ 3.2 km east of Carrollsville; county seat moved to Elyton; **1842** Arlington mansion built by William S. Mudd; **1845** *Jones Valley Times* becomes county's first newspaper, folds 1847; **1851** *Elyton Herald* newspaper founded; **1854** county courthouse built; **1856** Southern University established; **1860** Beylis E. Grace becomes first to use red iron ore from Red Mountain for industrial purposes; **1863** Shelby Iron Works established; **1865** many industrial plants destroyed by Union forces of James H. Wilson; **1870** South & North Railroad and Alabama & Chattanooga Railroad built through town; **1871** new development platted at rail junction; Birmingham incorporated as city; **1873** county seat moved from Elyton; **Apr. 1882** Sloss Iron Furnace established, closed 1971; **1886** Morris Hotel built; Henry DeBardeleben establishes DeBardeleben Coal and Iron Company; **1887** Lane House built; **1889** First Presbyterian Church built; Howard College, established 1856, moves from Marion, becomes Samford University; **1890** Tennessee Coal, Iron and Railroad Company established builds factory, becomes part of U.S. Steel Corporation 1907; Ensley Steel Works established by Enoch T. Ensley; **1892** Alabama State Fairgrounds established; **1894** National Guard called out during miners' strike; **1898** Birmingham College established; **1901** Shelby Hotel built; **Sept. 20, 1902** church fire kills 115; **1903** Cahaba Power Plant built; **1905** Miles College established; **1910** Lake Purdy formed by dam on Cahaba River to southeast, enlarged 1928; **Jan. 1, 1910** Greater Birmingham created by merger of several municipalities, including Elyton, with Birmingham; **May 5, 1910** explosion at Palos Coal Mine to northwest, 90 killed; **Apr. 8, 1911** explosion at Littleton Coal Mine to northwest, 128 killed; **Feb. 14, 1913** radio announcer Mel Allen born; **Apr. 12, 1913** jazz musician Lionel Hampton born; **1914** Temple Emmanuel synagogue built; **1916** Walker Methodist Church built; **May 28, 1916** novelist Walker Percy born (died 1990); **1918** Birmingham-Southern College established with merger of Southern University and Birmingham College; **1921** *Post* newspaper founded; Post Office built; **1924** Negro Masonic Temple built; **1925** Independent Presbyterian Church built; Ruhama Baptist Church built, founded 1819; **1927** Birmingham Public Library completed; Alabama Theatre built by Paramount Studios, restored 1987 as Alabama Theatre for Performing Arts; **1928** Birmingham Little Theater organized and built; **Dec. 31, 1930** singer Odetta (Gordon) born; **1931** Birmingham Municipal Airport developed; Birmingham Air Carnival established; county courthouse built; **May 6, 1931** Giants baseball player Willie Mays born in suburban Westfield to west; **1932** Civic Symphony Orchestra established; **1933** Alabama Symphony Orchestra founded; **July 22, 1934** actress Louise Fletcher born; **1935** miners' strike lasting months creates bitterness between coal companies and United Mine Workers union; **1936** Vulcan Statue erected atop Red Mountain, originally displayed at St. Louis Exposition 1904, stood neglected at state fairgrounds, Birmingham; **1937** Allan Gray Fish Hatchery established at Lane Park; Smithfield Court low income housing project completed; Swann Company Chemical Research Laboratory built; **Oct. 15, 1937** coal mine accident kills 34; **1945** Birmingham Historical Society founded; **Apr. 2, 1947** country singer Emmylou Harris born; **Sept. 13, 1948** TV actress Nell Carter born (died 2003); **Oct. 19, 1948** TV actress Kate Jackson born; **1951** Birmingham Museum of Art established; **1962** Birmingham Botanical Gardens opened to public; **Apr. 2, 1963** Dr. Martin Luther King opens desegregation campaign, is arrested three weeks later for violation of state court injunction; **May 2–7, 1963** wave of civil rights protests leads to arrests, rioting, and bombing of desegregated motel; **Sept. 10, 1963** Alabama National Guard is Federalized to force integration of five schools in Birmingham, Tuskegee, and Mobile; **Sept. 15, 1963** bomb explodes at 16th Street Baptist Church during service, kills 4 young girls, injures 20; **1965** Lawson State and Jefferson State community colleges established; **1969** University of Alabama at Birmingham established; **Dec. 1971** Birmingham Jefferson Civic Center completed; **Nov. 18, 1977** former KKK member Robert Chambliss, 73,

convicted in 1963 church bombing in which four girls were killed; **1981** Iron and Steel Museum of Alabama founded; **1984** Alabama Mining Museum established; **1986** 34-story Southtrust Tower building completed; **1989** 30-story AmSouth-Harbert Plaza building completed; **March 13–14, 1993** unusual 13-inch snowfall, tornadoes in South, East Coast, 14 killed statewide, total c.200 killed; **Jan. 29, 1998** bomb kills security guard at abortion clinic, injures nurse, Army of God anti-abortion group claims responsibility, suspect Eric Rudolph apprehended June 2003, Murphy, North Carolina; **May 17, 2000** two ex-Klansmen, Thomas Blanton and Bobby Cherry, charged with murder in 1963 church bombing, convicted 2001 and 2002 respectively, convicted bomber Robert Chambliss died in prison 1985, suspect Bobby Cash died 1994 without being charged.

Blountsville *Blount County Northern Alabama, 42 mi/68 km north-northeast of Birmingham*

1814 area opened to settlement following Creek War; **1815** Caleb Friley becomes first settler, occupies deserted cabin of Creek chief; town founded; **1818** Blount County formed; **1820** as county seat; **1827** town incorporated; **1833** county courthouse built, burned 1895; **1835** Barcliff Hotel built as stagecoach stop; **May 2, 1863** Union forces of Col. A. D. Streight pass through area en route to Rome, Georgia, to destroy its supply depots with General Forrest's Confederates in pursuit; Streight sets fire to own supply wagons, Forrest's men salvage contents; **1889** county seat moved to Oneonta; **1890** Blount College established, closed 1895; **1911** cotton mill established.

Boligee *Greene County Western Alabama, 90 mi/145 km southwest of Birmingham*

1735 Fort Tombigbee built to southwest on Tombigbee River under orders from Jean Baptiste Le Moyne de Bienville, Governor of Louisiana; **Apr. 1736** Bienville stops at fort en route to his defeat at hands of Chickasaw people at Ackia, Mississippi, retreats to fort; **1812** Hill of Howth mansion built by John McKee, county's first resident; **1833** Thornhill antebellum house built by James Thornton; **1835** Rosemount plantation house built by slaves for Williamson Allen Glover; **1870** Northeast & Southwest Railroad built; town founded; **1927** town incorporated.

Brewton *Escambia County Southern Alabama, 100 mi/161 km southwest of Montgomery*

1818 Fort Crawford built overlooking Conecuh River, now East Brewton; **1861** Alabama & Florida Railroad built; town founded as pine timber center; **1868** Escambia County formed; **1874** incorporated as a town; **1883** county seat moved from Pollard; **1885** Leigh Place mansion built; **1885** incorporated as a city; **1887** *Brewton Standard* newspaper founded; **July 1888** fire destroys business district; **Dec. 1898** meeting of local political groups leads to violent confrontation; **1902** county courthouse built;

1929 flooding inundates half of town; **1996** city hall completed.

Bridgeport *Jackson County   Northeastern Alabama, 118 mi/190 km northeast of Birmingham*

7000 BC earliest human habitation of Russell Cave, until as late as 1650 AD; **1814** Charles and Delia Smithson of Virginia become first white settlers; town founded near Tennessee River; **fall 1863** Union troops occupy town; **1889** land boom begins spearheaded by financiers led by elder Henry Morgenthau, ends with panic of 1893; **1890** town incorporated; **May 11, 1961** Russell Cave National Monument authorized to west.

Butler *Choctaw County   Western Alabama, 100 mi/161 km north of Mobile, near Tombigbee River*

1847 Choctaw County formed; Barrytown becomes first county seat; town of Butler founded as permanent county seat; town incorporated; **1907** second county courthouse completed, addition built 1985.

Cahaba *Dallas County   Central Alabama, 50 mi/80 km west of Montgomery*

1818 Dallas County formed **1819** town founded on Alabama River as Alabama's first state capital and as county seat; **1825** flooding damages capitol building during legislative session; vote taken to move capital; **Apr. 1825** General Lafayette visits town; **1826** state capital moved to Tuscaloosa; **1830** town incorporated; **1833** flooding forces more residents away; **1840s** town experiences cultural rebirth, ends with Civil War; **1866** county seat moved to Selma.

Camden *Wilcox County   Southern Alabama, 67 mi/108 km west-southwest of Montgomery*

1814 first white settlers arrive; **1819** Wilcox County formed, named for Lt. Joseph M. Wilcox, killed by Creeks June 1814; Canton becomes first county seat; **1832** town founded near Alabama River, named Barbourville; **1833** county seat moved to Barbourville; **1841** town incorporated, renamed Camden; **1859** county courthouse built; **1970** William "Bill" Dannelly Reservoir formed by Millers Ferry Lock & Dam on Alabama River to northwest.

Carrollton *Pickens County   Western Alabama, 80 mi/129 km west-southwest of Birmingham*

1817 first settlers arrive; **1819** Pickens County formed; **c.1825** town founded, named for Charles Carroll, signer of Declaration of Independence; **1830** town incorporated; **1834** county seat moved from Pickensville; **1837** Phoenix Hotel built; **1865** Union troops burn courthouse; **1878** county courthouse built.

Centerville *Conecuh County   See **Evergreen** (1925)*

Centre *Cherokee County   Northeastern Alabama, 80 mi/129 km northeast of Birmingham*

1830 Garrett House built; **1836** Cherokee County formed; **c.1840s** town founded near Coosa River; **1844** county seat moved from Cedar Bluff; **1878** *Coosa River News* newspaper founded; **1937** town incorporated; county courthouse built; **1961** Weiss Dam built on Coosa River forming large Weiss Lake.

Centerville *Bibb County   Central Alabama, 45 mi/72 km southwest of Birmingham*

1818 Cahaba County formed; **1820** county renamed for Gov. William Wyatt Bibb; town founded as county seat on Cahaba River; **1832** town incorporated; **1965** county courthouse built.

Chatom *Washington County   Southwestern Alabama, 55 mi/89 km north-northwest of Mobile*

1800 Washington County formed; McIntosh's Bluff becomes county seat, moved to Wakefield 1804; **1824** St. Stephens becomes county seat for one year, moved to Rodney; **1904** town founded; **1910** county seat moved to Chatom; county courthouse completed; **1949** town incorporated; **1965** new county courthouse built.

Claiborne *Monroe County   Southern Alabama, 93 mi/150 km southwest of Montgomery*

1540 Hernando de Soto visits Native American town of Piache; **1560** settlement of Nanipacana established by Tristan de Luna; **1813** Fort Claiborne built on Alabama River by Gen. F. L. Claiborne; town founded as cotton growing center; **1814** Gen. Andrew Jackson brings his troops through Fort Claiborne; **1939** plaque erected by Colonial Dames of Alabama commemorating De Soto's landing; **1969** Claiborne Lock & Dam built to north on Alabama River.

Clanton *Chilton County   Central Alabama, 38 mi/61 km north-northwest of Montgomery*

1868 Baker County formed; Grantsville becomes first county seat; **1870** town founded as county seat, named for Confederate Gen. James H. Clanton; **1873** town incorporated; **1874** county renamed for Confederate Brig. Gen. James Holt Chilton; **c.1900** depletion of timber reserves forces area to change over to cotton and poultry production; **1914** Lay Dam built on Coosa River to northeast forming Lay Lake; **1923** Mitchell Dam built on Coosa River to east forming Mitchell Lake; **1947** first annual Peach Festival held; **1962** county courthouse completed.

Clayton *Barbour County   Southeastern Alabama, 60 mi/97 km southeast of Montgomery*

1832 Barbour County formed; **1833** town founded as county seat, named for Georgian Augustine G. Clayton; **1836** fort built in response to Indian troubles; **1841** town incorporated; **1852** original section of County Courthouse built; **Feb. 10, 1857** Cong. Henry De Lamar Clayton born in rural Barbour County (died 1929); **1876** Grace Episcopal Church built; **Aug. 25, 1919** Gov. George Corley Wallace born at Clio to southwest (died 1998).

Clio *Barbour County* See **Clayton (1919)**

Columbiana *Shelby County* *Central Alabama, 25 mi/40 km south-southeast of Birmingham*

1818 Shelby County formed; **1825** town settled by Joseph Howard and William Akin; **1826** post office established; town named Columbia; **1832** town renamed Columbiana; **1837** town incorporated; **May 1862** munitions plant here from Corinth, Mississippi, after Union forces overrun Corinth; **1865** Union troops under General Wilson burn munitions plant; **1866** Hamilton Beggs establishes stove foundry at site of munitions plant; **1907** county courthouse completed.

Cullman *Cullman County* *Northern Alabama, 47 mi/76 km north of Birmingham*

1872 land purchased by German immigrant John Cullman; **1873** town founded and platted by Cullman; **1875** town incorporated; **1877** Cullman County formed; town becomes county seat; **1932** Ave Maria Grotto developed by the Right Rev. Bernard Menges, completed by Abbot Ambrose Reger; **1965** county courthouse built.

Dadeville *Tallapoosa County* *East central Alabama, 45 mi/72 km northeast of Montgomery*

March 27, 1814 Andrew Jackson defeats Creeks with aid of Davy Crockett in Battle of Horseshoe Bend on Tallapoosa River to north; **1832** Tallapoosa County formed; Okfuskee becomes county seat; trading post established; Dennis Hotel built; **1836** town platted, named for Maj. Francis Langhorne Dade, killed with his entire force by Seminoles 1835 at Fort King, Florida; **1837** town incorporated; **1838** county seat moved to Dadeville; **June 10, 1855** Texas Sen. Charles Allen Culberson born (died 1925); **1858** incorporated as a city; **Sept. 8, 1900** Florida Cong. Claude Denson Pepper born at rural Dudleyville to northeast (died 1989); **1961** county courthouse built.

Dauphin Island *Mobile County* *Southwestern Alabama, 30 mi/48 km south of Mobile*

1519 Alonzo de Pineda charts Gulf Coast west of Florida; **1699** Pierre le Moyne Sieur d'Iberville establishes base at entrance to Mobile Bay for French, named Ile Dauphine; **1704** 25 young women sent to fort aboard *Pelican* as wives for men, referred to as the Pelican Girls; **1708** settlers arrive from Fort Louis de la Louisiane on Mobile River; **1711** colony raided by British; **1717** hurricane washes away half of island; **1740** hurricane damages buildings, kills 300 head of cattle; **1763** island ceded to England; **1781** island captured by Spanish; **1803** island claimed by U.S. as

part of Louisiana Purchase; **Apr. 1813** island seized by Gen. James Wilkinson for U.S.; **1821** Fort Gaines built on eastern point; **Jan. 5, 1861** fort seized by Alabama militia; **Aug. 8, 1864** Union troops take fort from Confederates; **1873** Sand Island Lighthouse built, discontinued 1970; **1906** severe hurricane hits island, again in 1916; **1955** bridge built to mainland; Audubon Bird Sanctuary established; **Sept. 12–13, 1979** Hurricane Frederic damages island, destroys bridge; **July 1982** new bridge opened; **1988** town incorporated.

Decatur *Morgan County* *Northern Alabama, 80 mi/129 km north of Birmingham, on Tennessee River*

1818 Morgan County formed; Dr. Henry Rhodes establishes ferry on Tennessee River; settlement of Rhodes Ferry founded; **1820** town site chosen by U.S. Surveyor General, named for Commodore Stephen Decatur of War of 1812; **1826** town incorporated; **1829** hemp rope and bag factory built; **1835** Methodist Church built; Hinds-McEntire House built by John Burleson; **1836** Tuscumbia, Courtland & Decatur Railroad (Southern Railway) reaches town; **1838** cotton factory established; **1878** yellow fever epidemic reduces population from 1,400 to 300; **1887** Princess Theatre built as livery stable, becomes vaudeville theater 1919; **1891** county seat moved from Somerville; **1897** Cedar Lake founded to south by Mrs. Ray Nelson as model farm community for black residents; **1927** incorporated as a city; town of Albany annexed by Decatur; **Sept. 12, 1913** Olympic track star Jesse Owens born at rural Oakville to southwest (died 1980); **1928** Keller Memorial Bridge built across Tennessee River, named for engineer William Keller, brother of Helen Keller; **1933** Tennessee Valley Authority launches major hydroelectric project in Tennessee River basin; **1936** Wheeler Dam completed on Tennessee River; Ingalls Shipbuilding Plant established; **1938** Decatur Armory built; **1965** Calhoun Community College established; **Aug. 17, 1973** Browns Ferry Nuclear Power Plant begins operation on north side of river; **1975** county courthouse built.

Demopolis *Marengo County* *Western Alabama, 90 mi/145 km west of Montgomery*

Oct. 15, 1540 battle fought between Native Americans and De Soto's men to north; **1817** town settled by exiles from Napoleonic France; town incorporated; **1832** Bluff Hall house built by Allen Glover; **1842** Gaineswood mansion built by Gen. Nathan Whitfield; **1863** Whitfield Drainage Canal completed; **1869** First Presbyterian Church built; **c.1918** Rooster Bridge built across Tombigbee River; **1955** Demopolis Lock & Dam built to west on Tombigbee River.

Dothan *Houston and Dale counties* *Southeastern Alabama, 97 mi/156 km southeast of Montgomery*

1858 first nine families settle here; town of Dothen founded; **1880s** sawmill built by Brinks brothers; **1885** town incorporated, spelling changed to Dothan; **1890s**

5

Col. W. B. Steele begins large-scale logging, builds narrow gauge railroad to haul timber; **1903** Houston County formed; town becomes county seat; **1938** first National Peanut Festival held; **1941** Napier Army Air Field established, became Dothan Regional Airport 1946; **1949** George C. Wallace Community College established; **1961** Troy State University at Dothan established; **1962** county courthouse built; **Aug. 1, 1977** Farley Nuclear Power Plant begins operation to southeast; **1991** Wiregrass Museum of Art opened.

Double Springs *Winston County* *Northwestern Alabama, 59 mi/95 km northwest of Birmingham*

1850 Winston County formed, originally Hancock County, renamed Winston 1858; Houston becomes first county seat; **1882** town founded as new county seat; **1894** county courthouse completed; **1943** town incorporated; **1961** large Lewis Smith Lake formed by dam to east on Sipsey Fork River.

Dudleyville *Tallapoosa County* See **Dadeville (1900)**

Elba *Coffee County* *Southern Alabama, 70 mi/113 km south-southeast of Montgomery*

c.1840 ferry established on Pea River; town founded, named Bridgeville; **1841** Coffee County formed; **1850** town renamed Bentonville; **1852** town renamed Elba; county seat moved from Wellborn; **1853** county courthouse built, burned by army deserters 1863, rebuilt 1867; **1929** flooding heavily damages town, followed by levee building program; **1903** third county courthouse built; **Oct. 9, 1908** Gov. James "Big Jim" Folsom born (died 1987).

Enterprise *Coffee County* *Southeastern Alabama, 80 mi/129 km south-southeast of Montgomery*

1881 John Henry Carmichael becomes first settler; **1884** town founded as cotton center; **1896** incorporated as a city; **1910** boll weevil infestation forces farmers to change from cotton to peanut production; **1919** Boll Weevil monument erected; **1935** Coffee County Homesteads completed by Resettlement Administration; **1941** Fort Rucker Army Base established to northeast; **1965** Enterprise State Junior College established; **Jan. 13, 1972** tornado hits two trailer parks near Fort Rucker, four killed, over 400 injured.

Eufaula *Barbour County* *Southeastern Alabama, 77 mi/124 km east-southeast of Montgomery*

1820s town founded on Chattahoochee River, originally named Irwinton; **1836** troubles with Creek Tribe reach peak, requiring construction of four forts in county; Hart House built; **1843** town renamed Eufaula, derived from Native American term for beech tree; **1844** town incorporated; **1845** Mary Shorter Thornton House built; **1850s** Maj. Jefferson Buford organizes 500 men to settle in Kansas to counteract effort of Massachusetts to settle Free Soiler abolitionists in that contested state; **1962** Walter F. George Reservoir (Lake Eufaula) formed by dam on Chattahoochee River.

Eutaw *Greene County* *Western Alabama, 80 mi/129 km southwest of Birmingham*

1818 town founded near Black Warrior River, named Mesopotamia; **1819** Greene County formed; **1830s** Wilson House built; **1832** Myrtle Hall house built; **1838** town incorporated, renamed for Battle of Eutaw Springs, South Carolina, 1781; **1839** county seat moved from Erie; county courthouse built, destroyed by fire during Civil War, rebuilt; **1848** St. Stephens Episcopal Church built; **1993** William McKinley Branch Courthouse completed.

Evergreen *Conecuh County* *Southern Alabama, 75 mi/121 km southwest of Montgomery*

1818 Conecuh County formed; **1820** Revolutionary veteran John Cosey settles here, site named Cosey's Old Field; **c.1825** town founded, renamed for abundance of evergreens; **c.1840** Tomlinson's Mill built to west; **1866** county seat moved from Sparta; **1873** town incorporated; **1896** county courthouse built; **Sept. 5, 1925** highest temperature ever recorded in Alabama reached at rural Centerville to southeast, 112°F/44°C.

Fayette *Fayette County* *Western Alabama, 65 mi/105 km west-northwest of Birmingham*

1821 town founded and incorporated, named Frog Level, later renamed Latone; **1824** Fayette County formed; town becomes county seat, renamed Fayette Courthouse, later Lafayette; **1898** town renamed Fayette; **1909** natural gas field discovered, supplies town with gas for nine years; **1911** many of town's businesses destroyed by fire; county courthouse built.

Florence *Lauderdale County* *Northwestern Alabama, 105 mi/169 km northwest of Birmingham*

1779 trading post established on Tennessee River; rapids named Muscle Shoals; **1811** Pope's Tavern built; **1818** town platted by Richard Rapier as base for his fleet of flatboats; **1819** East Tennessee Steamboat Company organized; **1820** Forks of Cypress mansion built by James Jackson; **1824** First Presbyterian Church built; **1826** town incorporated, part of Tri-Cities region with Tuscumbia and Sheffield; **1830** University of North Alabama established, originally La Grange College; **1836** canal built around rapids, closes 1837; **1840** wooden bridge built across Tennessee River, later destroyed by storm; **c.1840** Lambeth House built; **c.1850** Perry House built by Robert Brahan with slave labor; **1854** Courtview house built by planter George Washington Foster; **1855** Florence Synodical College founded; **1858** railroad bridge built, destroyed during Civil War; **1865** Federal troops invade town, inflict minor damage; **1870** second bridge built, known for its narrow width; **Nov. 16, 1873** African-American band leader, songwriter W. C. Handy born (died 1958); **1884** *Florence Herald* newspaper founded; **1903** Confederate Memorial dedicated; **May 13, 1914** heavyweight boxer Joe Louis born at rural Lexington to northeast (died 1981); **1918** Lauderdale County formed; city becomes county seat; Wilson Dam completed on Tennessee River, part of TVA project; **1939** highway bridge built across river; **1966** county courthouse built.

Fort Morgan *Baldwin County Southwestern Alabama, 32 mi/51 km south of Mobile*

1812 Fort Bowyer established on Gulf of Mexico, at entrance to Mobile Bay, during War of 1812; **Sept. 15, 1814** British fleet defeated by garrison at fort; **Feb. 1815** British return, capture fort, withdraw in Apr.; **1837** fort regarrisoned, named Fort Morgan for Gen. John H. Morgan of Mexican War; **1864** fort shelled by Adm. Farragut during Civil War; **1898** fort reactivated during Spanish-American War.

Fort Payne *De Kalb County Northeastern Alabama, 90 mi/145 km northeast of Birmingham*

c.1765 Cherokee chief Sequoyah born at Native American village of Will's Town (died 1843); **1836** De Kalb County formed; **1838** Fort Payne built, named for Lt. John Payne, responsible for removal of Cherokee to western lands; **1840** Lebanon becomes first permanent county seat; **1878** town founded new as county seat; **1885** discovery of iron deposit leads to land boom; **1889** town incorporated; Opera House built; **1906** town's first hosiery mill built; town becomes "Sock Capital of World"; **1950** county courthouse built; **2000** over 150 sock factories remain in business.

Gadsden *Etowah County Northeastern Alabama, 58 mi/93 km northeast of Birmingham*

1835 Hughes House built by part Cherokee John Riley; **1836** village of Double Springs founded on Coosa River; post office established; **1840** Gabriel and Joseph Hughes and John S. Morgan develop plans for large city; Gen. James Gadsden visits area, initial plans for town fail to materialize; **1857** Col. Robert B. Kyle revives city plans; **1863** Union Col. A. D. Streight's troops invade area, sack town; Confederate Capt. John H. Wisdom leaves from Gadsden on night ride to warn Rome, Georgia, of impending invasion, leads to Streight's surrender; **1866** Etowah County formed; town becomes county seat; **1870** county courthouse built; **1871** incorporated as a city; **1896** Dwight Manufacturing Plant opens, maker of textile products; **1906** Alabama Power Company organized by William P. Lay; **1910** Federal Building built; **1914** Lay Dam built on Coosa River; **1923** County Curb Market established; **1925** East Gadsden annexed by Gadsden; **1926** Memorial Bridge built to East Gadsden; **1929** Goodyear Tire and Rubber Plant built; **1932** Alabama City annexed by Gadsden; **1936** Civic Center completed by WPA; **1938** Carnegie Library opens; **1985** Gadsden State Community College established; **1990** Center for Cultural Arts opened.

Geneva *Geneva County Southeastern Alabama, 98 mi/158 km south-southeast of Montgomery*

1820 trading post established on Pea River, near mouth of Chocktawhatchee River; **1868** Geneva County formed; town becomes county seat; **1872** town incorporated; **1929** flooding forces town to build levee; **1969** county courthouse built; **1976** first annual River Festival held.

Georgiana *Butler County See Greenville (1923)*

Greensboro *Hale County West central Alabama, 80 mi/129 km west-northwest of Montgomery*

c.1815 three Russell brothers become first settlers; **1816** town founded; **1823** town incorporated; **1840** Magnolia Grove built by Col. Isaac Croom, later home of Adm. Richmond Hobson; **1856** Southern University established, consolidated with Birmingham College 1918; **1867** Hale County formed; town becomes county seat; **Aug. 17, 1870** naval officer Richmond Pearson Hobson born (died 1937); **1908** county courthouse built.

Greenville *Butler County Southern Alabama, 42 mi/68 km southwest of Montgomery*

1819 Butler County formed; town settled by group from Greenville, South Carolina, founded as county seat; **1820** town incorporated; **1903** county courthouse built; **1907** Lomax-Harmon High and Industrial School for black students established by Bishop J. W. Alstook of African Methodist Episcopal Church; **Sept. 17, 1923** singer, songwriter Hank Williams born at rural Georgiana to south (died 1953); **1980** first annual Hank Williams Festival held.

Grove Hill *Clarke County Southwestern Alabama, 75 mi/121 km north-northeast of Mobile*

1812 Clarke County formed; **1813** Fort White built, town of Fort White founded; **Aug. 30, 1813** Creeks kill 12 settlers in their homes outside Fort Sinquefield to southeast, battle between settlers and Native Americans ensues during burials, 11 more settlers killed, masterminded by Creek leader Josiah Francis, the Prophet; **1820** Clarksville becomes county seat; **1832** county seat moved to Grove Hill; **1929** town incorporated; **1955** county courthouse completed.

Guin *Marion County Northwestern Alabama, 74 mi/119 km northwest of Birmingham*

1818 Marion County formed; **1819** trading post established on Byler Turnpike; town of Pikesville founded as county seat; **1860** railroad reaches town; new town of Guin ("gwin") founded on town site; **1881** county seat moved to Hamilton; **1889** town incorporated; **Apr. 3, 1974** tornado destroys town, 23 killed.

Guntersville *Marshall County* *Northern Alabama, 67 mi/108 km north-northeast of Birmingham*

1790 Gunter's Landing founded on Tennessee River at site of Cherokee village; **1818** town settled; **1820s** advent of steamboats brings boom to town; **1836** Marshall County formed; Claysville becomes first county seat; **1837** Gen. Winfield Scott's troops remove Cherokee people from region to Indian Territory, including great-grandmother of humorist Will Rogers; **1838** county seat moved to Marshall, to Warrenton 1841; **1848** town incorporated as Gunter's Landing; county seat moved from Warrenton; county courthouse built; **1854** town renamed Guntersville; **1937** Guntersville Public Library founded; **1939** Guntersville Lock & Dam built to west on Tennessee River.

Hamilton *Marion County* *Northwestern Alabama, 85 mi/137 km northwest of Birmingham*

1818 Marion County formed; Pikesville (Guin) becomes first county seat, site immediately south of present county seat; **1819** town founded on new Byler Turnpike on land owned by Capt. A. J. Hamilton; **1881** county seat moved to Hamilton; **1896** town incorporated; **1900** county courthouse built; **1998** first annual Pigfest held.

Hayneville *Lowndes County* *South central Alabama, 21 mi/34 km southwest of Montgomery*

1820 town founded, named Big Swamp; **1830** Lowndes County formed; town becomes county seat, renamed Hayneville; **1831** town incorporated; **1854** second county courthouse built; **Sept. 30, 1965** white deputy Tom Coleman acquitted of death of white student Jonathan Daniels of New Hampshire; **Nov. 22, 1965** Klansman Collie Leroy Wilkins, Jr. found not guilty in trial for March 25 murder of civil rights worker Viola Liuzzo.

Heflin *Cleburne County* *Eastern Alabama, 70 mi/113 km east of Birmingham*

1847 regional gold rush reaches peak, overshadowed by California Gold Rush 1848; **1866** Cleburne County formed; Edwardsville becomes first county seat; **1882** Georgia Pacific Railroad reaches site; **1883** town founded, named for Dr. Wilson L. Heflin, father of U.S. Senator Thomas Heflin; **Dec. 1886** town incorporated; **1906** county seat moved to Heflin; county courthouse built.

Heiberger *Perry County* *See* **Marion (1927)**

Huntsville *Madison County* *Northern Alabama, 85 mi/137 km north of Birmingham*

1805 John Hunt of Virginia becomes first settler; **1808** Madison County formed; First Baptist Church founded; **1809** town of Twickenham founded as county seat; Huntsville Textile Mill established, closed 1885; **1811** incorporated as a town, renamed Huntsville; **1812** *Madison Gazette* newspaper founded; **1814** Alabama Territory constitutional convention held; **1815** Green Bottom Inn built by John Connelly, destroyed by fire 1930; **1819** Howard Weeden House built; **July 5, 1819** constitutional convention meets here, adopted Aug. 2; **1821** Neal House built; **June 1, 1825** Confederate Gen. John Hunt Morgan born (died 1864); **1836** First National Bank building completed; **1837** Bibb House built; **c.1840** Steele-Fowler House built; **1844** incorporated as a city; **1851** Memphis & Charleston Railroad reaches town; **1859** Church of the Nativity (Episcopal) completed; **1860** First Presbyterian Church built; **Apr. 1862** Union troops capture city, wreak heavy damage; **1873** State Agricultural and Mechanical Institute established for black students, becomes Alabama A & M University; **1885** Monte Sano Hotel built; **1896** Oakwood College established; **Dec. 20, 1899** Cong., Sen. John Sparkman born (died 1985); **Jan. 31, 1902** actress Tallulah Bankhead born (died 1968); **1935** Monte Sano State Park established to east; **1938** Wheeler National Wildlife Refuge established to southwest; **1941** Redstone Army Arsenal established; **Jan. 30, 1966** lowest temperature ever recorded in Alabama reached, −27°F/−33°C, at New Market to northeast; **1950** University of Alabama at Huntsville established; German rocket scientists led by Werner von Braun arrive at Red Stone Arsenal to conduct rocket and missile research; **1954** Huntsville Symphony Orchestra founded; **1960** George C. Marshall NASA Space Flight Center established; **1966** fourth county courthouse built; **Nov. 15, 1989** tornado strikes, kills 18.

Jacksonville *Calhoun County* *Eastern Alabama, 65 mi/105 km east-northeast of Birmingham*

1822 town settled, originally named Drayton; **1832** Calhoun County formed; **1833** town becomes county seat; **1835** town renamed for Andrew Jackson who fought the Creeks; **1836** town incorporated; **1857** Rowan House built; **1859** Presbyterian Church built, served as Confederate hospital during Civil War; **1862** town damaged by Union forces; **1883** Jacksonville State University established; **1899** county seat moved to Anniston.

Jasper *Walker County* *North central Alabama, 50 mi/80 km northwest of Birmingham*

1815 Native American trading post established; town founded; **1832** Walker County formed; **1834** county seat moved from Hilliard; **1886** Kansas, Memphis & Birmingham and Sheffield & Birmingham railroads reach town; **1889** town incorporated; **c.1890** over 400 coke ovens in operation in area; **c.1895** Sunset house built, home of U.S. Sen. John Hollis Bankhead and son U.S. Sen. John H. Bankhead, Jr.; **1930s** county courthouse built.

Lafayette *Chambers County* *Eastern Alabama, 66 mi/106 km northeast of Montgomery*

1832 Chambers County formed; **1833** town founded as county seat; **1835** town incorporated; **1899** second county courthouse built.

Lexington *Lauderdale County* See **Florence** **(1914)**

Linden *Marengo County* *Western Alabama, 90 mi/ 145 km west of Montgomery*

1818 Marengo County formed; town founded as county seat, originally named Screamersville; **1819** town renamed Marengo; **1823** town incorporated, renamed Hohenlinden, later shortened; **1880** notorious outlaw Rube Burrow shot and killed by posse members after escaping from jail; **1968** fifth county courthouse built.

Livingston *Sumter County* *Western Alabama, 115 mi/185 km west-northwest of Montgomery*

1832 Sumter County formed; **1833** town founded as county seat, named for statesman Edward Livingston; **1835** Livingston State Teachers College established, later becomes University of West Alabama; **1860** Oak Manor house built by Isaac James Lee to east; **1867** town incorporated; **1901** third county courthouse built.

Luverne *Crenshaw County* *Southern Alabama, 45 mi/72 km south of Montgomery*

1866 Crenshaw County formed; Rutledge becomes first county seat; **1888** Montgomery & Florida Railroad built; **1889** town founded; county seat moved from Rutledge; **1890** town incorporated; **1893** county courthouse built.

Marion *Perry County* *Central Alabama, 63 mi/ 101 km west-northwest of Montgomery*

1817 Michael Muckle builds cabin, site named Muckle Ridge; **1819** Perry County formed; town becomes county seat; **1822** incorporated as a town; renamed for Gen. Francis Marion of Revolutionary War; **1829** incorporated as a city; **1837** county courthouse built; **1839** Judson College established; **1840** Pres. Sam Houston of Texas marries Margaret Lea; **1841** Howard College established, moved to Birmingham 1889, becomes Samford University; **1842** Marion Military Institute founded; **1867** Lincoln Normal School established, becomes Alabama State University, moved to Montgomery 1887; **Apr. 27, 1927** Coretta Scott King born at Heiberger to northeast, wife of late Dr. Martin Luther King, Jr.; **1970** Alabama Women's Hall of Fame founded; **1975** Alabama Military Hall of Honor dedicated.

Mobile *Mobile County* *Southwestern Alabama, 160 mi/257 km southwest of Montgomery, on Gulf of Mexico*

1507 earliest depictions of Mobile Bay appear on maps; **1528** explorer Narvaez lands on shores of Mobile Bay;

1559 Tristan de Luna establishes Spanish settlement, abandoned 1561; **1699** Pierre Le Moyne d'Iberville, builds Fort Louis de la Mobile; **1702** town founded when Gov. Jean Baptiste Le Moyne de Bienville, Pierre's brother, establishes seat of government of Louisiana at Fort Louis de la Louisiane (Mobile); **1704** town's first Mardi Gras Festival instituted as the Masque de la St. Louis; **1711** flooding forces town to be moved to higher ground; Fort Conde established; **1720** Louisiana capital moved back to Biloxi before moving to New Orleans 1722; **1721** two ships, the *Africaine* and *Le Duc de Maine*, bring 120 slaves from Africa; **1754** azaleas introduced to Mobile from France; **1763** British occupy area; **1780** Bernardo de Gálvez forces Mobile to surrender to Spanish; **1795** Spanish House built, oldest building in city; **1799** Alabama, then part of Mississippi Territory, ceded to U.S., coastal section including Mobile remains under Spanish rule; **1809** Register Building built; **1810** town becomes part of West Florida; **1812** Mobile County formed; town becomes county seat; **1813** town seized for U.S. by Gen. James Wilkinson during War of 1812; *Mobile Register* newspaper founded; **1814** incorporated as a town; **Feb. 8, 1815** British withdraw from New Orleans, take Mobile; *Mobile Press* newspaper founded, later *Press-Register*; **1819** incorporated as a city; **1825** City Hospital built; **1827** fire destroys large part of city, second fire occurs 1839; **1830** Spring Hill College established; **Sept. 19, 1835** glass manufacturer Ethan Allen Hitchcock born, secretary of interior under President McKinley (died 1909); **1836** Barton Academy built; **1837** Government Street Presbyterian Church built; **1840** Christ Episcopal Church completed, begun 1828; **1842** U.S. Marine Hospital built; **Dec. 1850** Cathedral of the Immaculate Conception dedicated; **1852** state's first public school system established; **1853** city's worst yellow fever epidemic kills 764; **Jan. 17, 1853** suffragist, socialite Alva Belmont born (died 1933); **1855** city hall built; **1859** ship *Clothilde* with load of smuggled slaves runs up Mobile River, scuttled and burned by captain, community of Plateau, in north part of Mobile, settled by escaped slaves, derogatorily referred to as Africky Town by whites; **Aug. 1864** in Battle of Mobile Bay, Union Admiral Farragut exclaims, "Damn the torpedoes! Full speed ahead!" as he attacks Mobile; **Apr. 12, 1865** Mobile captured for Union by Generals Canby and Steel; **May 25, 1865** ordnance stored at Marshall's Warehouse explodes, up to 600 killed; **1866** Mobile National Cemetery established; **1870** boiler explosion on excursion steamer *Ocean Wave* at Point Clear to south kills over 100; **Aug. 27, 1872** boiler on ship *Ocean Wave* explodes in Mobile Bay, 60 killed; **1874** county courthouse built; **1878** yellow fever epidemic kills 87; **July 7, 1906** baseball player Satchel Paige born (died 1982); **1919** fire destroys 40 blocks in city center; **1927** St. Mary's Catholic Church built; Cochrane Bridge causeway built across Mobile Bay; **1928** Mobile Public Library built; **1929** Alabama State Docks built; first Azalea Festival held; **1940** Bankhead Tunnel built under Mobile River; **1941** Brookley Airport established; **1961**

University of Mobile established; **1963** University of South Alabama established; **1964** Museum of Art opened; Municipal Auditorium opened; *USS Alabama* permanently moored in Mobile Bay; **1965** Bishop State Community College established; **1971** Tenn-Tom Waterway opened linking Tennessee and Tombigbee river systems; **1979** Hurricane Frederick damages 75 percent of city's buildings; first oil well drilled in Mobile Bay; **1991** new Cochrane Bridge built across Mobile Bay; **1993** Convention Center opened; **Sept. 22, 1993** Amtrak passenger train derails on swing bridge on Big Bayou Conot to north, 47 killed; **Dec. 1994** Mobile Government Plaza completed by county.

Monroeville   *Monroe County*   *Southern Alabama, 85 mi/137 km southwest of Montgomery*

1815 Monroe County formed; town founded; town and county named for James Monroe; **c.1816** James Dellet House built; **c.1823** Masonic Hall built; **1832** county seat moved from Claiborne; **1899** town incorporated; **1960** Harper Lee's novel "To Kill a Mockingbird" published, town used as setting for fictional Maycomb, wins Pulitzer Prize 1961; **1962** county courthouse built; **1965** Alabama Southern Community College established.

Montevallo   *Shelby County*   *Central Alabama, 28 mi/45 km south of Birmingham*

1815 town settled by James Wilson, veteran of Creek War under Andrew Jackson, names town Wilson's Hill; **c.1823** King Mansion built by early settler Edmund King, first brick house in central Alabama; **1848** town incorporated, renamed Montevallo; **1852** Montevallo Male Institute founded, housed in Reynolds Hall built same year; **1896** Alabama Girls' Industrial School established at Reynolds Hall, becomes University of Montevallo.

Montgomery   *Montgomery County*   *Central Alabama, 83 mi/134 km south-southeast of Birmingham*

Sept. 13, 1540 Hernando de Soto visits Native American town of Tawasa on Alabama River; **1716** Scottish trader James McQueen visits site of Montgomery; **1717** Fort Toulouse built by French at confluence of Tallapoosa and Coosa rivers to north, surrendered to British 1763; **1802** state's first commercial cotton gin established by Abram Mordecai; **1816** Montgomery County formed; **1817** group of New Englanders establish town of Philadelphia, rival group from Georgia establishes town of East Alabama; **1819** rival towns merge, named for Maj. Lemuel P. Montgomery, hero of the American colonial army; incorporated as a city, becomes county seat; **1821** first steamboats arrive from Mobile; *Montgomery Republican* newspaper founded; **1825** General Lafayette visits town; **1828** *Montgomery Advertiser* newspaper founded; **1832** state bank organized by John Gindrat; **1838** Pickett House built for John Figh with slave labor; **Dec. 1847** state capital moved from Tuscaloosa; state capitol built, destroyed by fire 1849, rebuilt 1851; **1851** Montgomery Railroad completed to West Point, Georgia; St. Mary of

Loretto Academy founded; **1852** Sayre House built by William Sayre, used 1861 as First White House of the Confederacy; **1854** Huntingdon College established; **Jan. 6, 1861** Secession Convention convenes, ending with secession of six states Feb. 4; **Feb. 18, 1861** Jefferson Davis inaugurated as President of Confederate States of America; **May 1861** Confederate capital moved to Richmond, Virginia, closer to main battle lines; **Apr. 12, 1865** Gen. James Wilson's Union forces enter city, encounter bonfire of 100,000 bales of cotton set by retreating Confederates; **1881** *Montgomery Journal* newspaper founded; **1885** first wing of state capitol built, completed 1912; **1887** State Normal School and University, established 1867, moved from Marion, later becomes Alabama State University; **1890** large lumber mill founded; **Dec. 29, 1894** Cong., Sen. Lister Hill born (died 1984); **1901** Agriculture and Industries Building built; **1905** Exchange Hotel built on site of hotel built by Abner McGehee 1846; **1910** first flight school in U.S. established by Wright Brothers; **1906** governor's mansion built, acquired by state 1911, demolished 1963; **1911** Alabama Reform School for Juvenile Negroes established at Mount Meigs to east; **March 17, 1919** singer Nat "King" Cole born (died 1965); **1926** Scottish Rite Temple built, converted to state judicial building 1938; **1930** Museum of Fine Arts organized; **1937** state highway building built; Paterson Courts low income housing development built with Public Works Administration (PWA) funding; Riverside Heights development completed by U.S. Housing Authority; **1940** World War Memorial building completed; **1941** Dannelly Field airport established to west; William A. Gunter dies, city's "Permanent Mayor" since 1912; **1942** Montgomery Bible College established, becomes Faulkner University; **May 8, 1943** singer Toni Tennille born; **1948** Maxwell Air Force Base established; **1953** Garrett Coliseum completed; **Dec. 1, 1955** Rosa Parks, 42, arrested after refusing to ride in back of bus; **1956** Dr. Martin Luther King's year-long boycott of bus system results in transit desegregation edict; **1965** Troy State University at Montgomery established; **March 25, 1965** Selma-Montgomery civil rights march ends at Capitol steps with Martin Luther King speech to 25,000 demonstrators; **1967** Auburn University at Montgomery established; **Feb. 7, 1967** fire at Dale's Penthouse Restaurant kills 25; **1969** Kilby State Penitentiary established to east; **1975** Montgomery Zoo founded; **Sept. 20, 1978** Gary Thomas Rowe, Jr. indicted for March 25, 1965, slaying of civil rights worker Viola Liuzzo; **1987** county courthouse built; **Apr. 22, 1993** Gov. Guy Hunt found guilty of using inaugural funds for personal use, removed from office.

Moulton   *Lawrence County*   *Northern Alabama, 75 mi/121 km north-northwest of Birmingham*

1818 Lawrence County formed; town founded and incorporated as county seat; **1840** asphalt deposit discovered to southeast at Oakville; **1936** Black Warrior National Forest established, renamed William B.

Bankhead National Forest 1942; **1940** county courthouse built.

Muscle Shoals *Colbert County Northwestern Alabama, 102 mi/164 km northwest of Birmingham*

c.1917 town founded near Tennessee River as service center for federal nitrate plant reservation to north; **1921** town incorporated; **1941** Listerhill Aluminum Plant built on river; **1961** Northwest-Shoals Community College established; **Sept. 9, 1967** aluminum plant smelter explodes killing four, injuring 40.

New Market *Madison County See* **Huntsville (1966)**

Notasulga *Macon County See* **Tuskegee (1891)**

Oakville *Hale County See* **Decatur (1913)**

Oneonta *Blount County North central Alabama, 37 mi/60 km northeast of Birmingham*

1818 Blount County formed; **1889** town founded; county seat moved from Blountsville; **1891** town incorporated; **1896** county courthouse built; **1934** Nectar Covered Bridge built to west, burned by vandals June 13, 1993; **1984** first Covered Bridge Festival held celebrating county's eleven covered bridges.

Opelika *Lee County Eastern Alabama, 58 mi/ 93 km east-northeast of Montgomery*

1836 first settlers arrive from Georgia; **1840** post office established; town named Opelikan, derivative of Creek word for swamp, spelling corrected to Opelika 1851; **1854** town incorporated; **Jan. 15, 1861** World War I Gen. Robert Lee Bullard born (died 1947); **1866** Lee County formed; town becomes county seat; **1896** county courthouse built.

Ozark *Dale County Southeastern Alabama, 75 mi/ 121 km southeast of Montgomery*

1820 town founded, originally named Woodshop; **1824** Dale County formed; Daleville becomes first county seat, moved to Newton 1846; **1830** Claybank Methodist Church built; **1855** town renamed for Ozark Tribe; **1870** town incorporated; county seat moved to Ozark; **1941** Fort Rucker Army Base established; **1968** county courthouse built.

Palos *Jefferson County See* **Birmingham (1910)**

Pell City *Saint Clair County North central Alabama, 30 mi/48 km east of Birmingham*

1818 St. Clair County formed; Ashville becomes county seat; **1836** William Prater Cook establishes hotel at Cooks Springs to west, gains in popularity by 1860 **1890** town founded by Sumter Caldwell; **1891** town incorporated;

1902 town becomes seat of county's new southern division, with Ashville remaining as seat of county's northern division; county courthouse built, rebuilt 1960s; **1964** Logan Martin Lake formed by dam on Coosa River to south.

Phenix City *Russell and Lee counties Eastern Alabama, 78 mi/126 km east of Montgomery*

1811 Fort Mitchell built to south on Chattahoochee River, large Federal garrison maintained here until 1837; **1832** Russell County formed; **1833** trading post established on Chattachoochee River, town of Girard founded as county seat; **1868** county seat moved to Seale; **1883** neighboring town of Brownsville incorporated; **1889** Brownsville renamed Phoenix City; **1923** spelling altered to Phenix City; Girard annexed by city; **1935** county seat moved to Phenix City; **1939** county courthouse built; **1974** Chattahoochee Valley State Community College established.

Prattville *Autauga County Central Alabama, 10 mi/16 km northwest of Montgomery*

1816 area first settled; **1818** Autauga County formed; Washington becomes county seat; **1830** county seat moved to Kingston; **1833** cotton mill built by Daniel Pratt of New Hampshire; **1839** town platted; **1859** Prattville Academy founded; **1868** county seat moved to Prattville; **1872** town incorporated; **1906** county courthouse completed.

Rockford *Coosa County Central Alabama, 35 mi/ 56 km north of Montgomery*

1832 Coosa County formed; **1834** town founded as county seat on site of Unifulka Native American village; **1860** town incorporated; **1925** county courthouse built, renovated 1970.

Russellville *Franklin County Northwestern Alabama, 90 mi/145 km northwest of Birmingham*

c.1815 town founded, named for Maj. William Russell, commander of Tennessee scouts, War of 1812, who settled here after the war; **1818** Franklin County formed; Cedar Creek Furnace built to southwest by Joseph Heslip, first iron smelter in Alabama, closed 1837; **1819** town incorporated; town becomes county seat; **1887** Southern Railway reaches town; **1891** county courthouse built; **1967** Bear Creek Reservoir formed to west as part of TVA project.

Scottsboro *Jackson County Northeastern Alabama, 93 mi/150 km northeast of Birmingham*

1819 Jackson County formed; Sauta Cave becomes first county seat, moved to Bellefonte 1821; **1856** Memphis & Charleston Railroad reaches town through efforts of Robert Scott; town founded near Tennessee River; **1859** county seat moved to Scottsboro; **1870** town incorporated; **1912** county courthouse built; **1931** nine young black men convicted of raping two white women at Paint Rock in sensational Scottsboro Case, overturned by Supreme Court 1932 for lack of adequate counsel, again 1935 for lack of black participation in jury, five of nine reconvicted, sentenced to Kilby Prison, Montgomery, last survivor pardoned by Gov. Wallace 1976.

Selma   *Dallas County   Central Alabama, 43 mi/ 69 km west of Montgomery, on Alabama River*

1540 Hernando de Soto's expedition arrives, spends 20 days in area; **1702** Jean-Baptiste Le Moyne de Bienville defeats band of Native Americans here; **1732** D'Anville names site Bienville Bluff; **1815** Thomas Moore becomes first permanent settler at town site; **1817** William Rufus King, future U.S. vice president, founds town, names it for Ossian's "Song of Selma"; **1818** Dallas County formed; Cahaba becomes county seat; **1820** town incorporated; **Apr. 5, 1825** General Lafayette visits town; **1826** malaria epidemic follows flooding; **1827** *Selma Courier* newspaper founded; **1840s** St. James Hotel built; **1848** iron casting industry introduced by German immigrants; **c.1848** Pettus House built by Confederate Gen. Edmund Pettus; **1849** Mabry House built; **1853** Sturdivant Hall mansion built; **1861** Confederate Naval Foundry established; **Apr. 2, 1865** Union troops under Gen. James H. Wilson force Confederates under Gen. Nathan B. Forrest to evacuate town; **1866** county seat moved from Cahaba; **1868** Selma, Rome & Dalton Railroad completed to Rome, Georgia; **1869** Our Lady of the Assumption Church built; **1875** St. Paul's Episcopal Church built; **1878** Selma University established; **1891** four-story Hotel Albert completed, begun 1854, work interrupted by Civil War; **1900** county courthouse built; **May 1940** Edmund Pettus Bridge opened on Alabama River; **Feb. 2, 1965** Dr. Martin Luther King Jr. leads voting rights march to Montgomery, King and 770 others arrested in protest over voter literacy test; **March 7, 1965** "Bloody Sunday," 600 civil rights marchers stopped at Edmund Pettus Bridge by Alabama Police wielding billy clubs; **March 9, 1965** second march led by Dr. King; Rev. James Reeb of Boston, two other civil rights ministers, attacked; Reeb died March 11; **1966** George C. Wallace State Community College established; **1992** National Voting Rights Museum opened; **2000** James Perkins elected city's first black mayor.

Sheffield   *Colbert County   Northwestern Alabama, 103 mi/166 km northwest of Birmingham*

1815 trading post established on Tennessee River; **1816** speculative land boom started by Andrew Jackson and John Coffee; **1820** town of York Bluff platted by Coffee, soon abandoned in favor of Tuscumbia; **1883** new town founded by Sheffield Land Development Company; **1885** town incorporated, part of Tri-Cities area including Tuscumbia and Florence; **1918** Wilson Dam built on Tennessee River, named for Pres. Woodrow Wilson; **1921**

Belmont Hospital established, later renamed Helen Keller Hospital; **1941** Listerhill Aluminum Plant built nearby.

Sylacauga   *Talladega County   Central Alabama, 40 mi/64 km southeast of Birmingham*

1836 town founded as Syllacauga, name derived from Shawnee term for "buzzard roost"; **1838** incorporated as a town; **1840** first marble quarry begins production; **1886** Anniston & Atlantic Railroad reaches town; **1887** incorporated as a city, spelling altered to Sylacauga; *Argus* newspaper founded; **March 12, 1932** tornado strikes city, 22 killed, 281 injured; **June 12, 1933** TV actor, comedian Jim Nabors born.

Talladega   *Talladega County   East central Alabama, 40 mi/64 km east of Birmingham*

c.1801 fort built by John Bruner; **c.1805** Aboyne Court residence built, home of Sen. John Tyler Morgan; **c.1810** town founded, originally named Border Town for its location between Cherokee and Creek nations; **Nov. 9, 1813** Andrew Jackson defeats Creek Confederacy in Battle of Talladega; **1820s** Masonic East Alabama Female Institute founded; **1832** Talladega County formed; town becomes county seat; **1835** incorporated as a town; **1836** county courthouse built; **1858** Alabama School for the Deaf founded; **1867** Talladega College established; **1885** incorporated as a city; **1892** Alabama School for the Deaf, Dumb, and Blind founded for blacks; **1964** Logan Martin Lake formed by dam of same name on Coosa River to west; **1969** Talladega Superspeedway auto race track opened.

Tallassee   *Elmore County   Central Alabama, 25 mi/40 km northeast of Montgomery, on Tallapoosa River*

1540 Hernando de Soto stops at Native American town of Huiliwahli; **1766** traders report existence of walled city of Fusihachee; **1811** at Native American town of Tukabatchee, extended 4 mi/6.4 km along river, Shawnee chief Tecumseh urges Creeks to wage war against U.S.; **1820s** Thomas Barnett builds cotton mill; **1838** town founded; **1870** Tallassee Falls Manufacturing Company builds largest cotton mill in Alabama; **1908** town incorporated; **1927** Lake Martin formed by dam to north on Tallapoosa River; **1928** Yates Dam built on Tallapoosa River; **1931** Thurlow Dam built downstream.

Troy   *Pike County   Southern Alabama, 45 mi/72 km south-southeast of Montgomery*

1821 Pike County formed; Louisville becomes first county seat, later moved to Monticello; **1836** in Battle of Hobdy's Bridge, several hundred Creeks massacred by whites under Gen. William Wellborn at Walnut Creek while relocating to Indian Territory (Oklahoma); **1839** town founded as new county seat; **1843** town incorporated; **1887** Troy State University established, originally State Teachers College; **1932** county courthouse built.

Trussville *Jefferson County* *North central Alabama, 13 mi/21 km northeast of Birmingham*

1781 Warren Truss becomes first settler; **1818** log house built by William J. Reed; **1870** Alabama & Chattanooga Railroad completed; **1886** blast furnace established; **1899** Alabama Boys Industrial School established; **1930s** Government Resettlement Administration builds Cahaba Village, 261 homes for needy families; **1937** State Training School for Girls established; **1947** incorporated as a town; **1957** incorporated as a city.

Tuscaloosa *Tuscaloosa County* *West central Alabama, 50 mi/80 km southwest of Birmingham*

1809 Creek people establish village on Black Warrior River; **1813** Creeks revolt against whites, village sacked and burned by Gen. John Coffee, with David Crockett serving as scout; **1816** site settled by Thomas York; **1818** Tuscaloosa County formed; town becomes county seat; **1819** incorporated as a city; *American Mirror* newspaper founded; **1826** state capital moved from Cahaba; *Alabama Sentinel* newspaper founded; **1829** Christ Episcopal Church built; governor's mansion built; **1831** University of Alabama established; **1847** state capital moved to Montgomery; **1853** Bryce Hospital built, unit of Alabama Insane Hospitals system; **Apr. 4, 1865** Union troops under General Croxton capture city; **1870s** Alabama Great Southern Railroad reaches town; **1876** Stillman Institute established for black students, becomes Stillman College; **1898** Mobile & Ohio Railroad built; coal mining begins; **1938** Hargrove Van de Graff Airport founded; **June 11, 1963** Gov. George Wallace confronts Vivian Malone and James Hood at University of Alabama to prevent them from enrolling as first black students; **1964** county courthouse built; **1971** Lake Tuscaloosa Dam built on North River; **Dec. 14, 2000** tornado damages 350 homes, kills 11.

Tuscumbia *Colbert County* *Northwestern Alabama, 103 mi/166 km northwest of Birmingham*

1787 Chickasaw village sacked and burned by Cherokees allied with settlers from Cumberland region led by Col. James Robertson; **1790** ferry established on Tennessee River by George Colbert; **1817** town founded, platted by Gen. John Coffee; **1819** incorporated as a town, named Occocopoosa; **1820** Ivy Green house built, birthplace of Helen Keller; **1821** town renamed Big Spring; **1822** town renamed for local Chief Tuscumbia; Belmont mansion built; **1824** First Presbyterian Church built; **1830** Tuscumbia Railroad built; **1867** Colbert County formed; **1870** town becomes county seat; **June 27, 1880** teacher, author Helen Keller born deaf, blind, and mute, advocate for handicapped (died 1968); **1881** county courthouse built, rebuilt 1909; **1933** Pres. Franklin D. Roosevelt visits area to launch Tennessee Valley Authority hydroelectric project; **Nov. 25, 1940** singer Percy Sledge born at Leighton to east.

Tuskegee *Macon County* *Eastern Alabama, 35 mi/56 km east of Montgomery*

c.1760 area settled by French traders, build blockhouse; **1763** British enter region, take blockhouse; **Jan. 26, 1814** large band of Creeks attacks Georgia Militia of 1,300 under Gen. John Floyd forcing retreat; **1832** Macon County formed; town becomes county seat; **1840** Varner-Alexander House built; **1843** town incorporated; **1881** Tuskegee Institute established by Booker T. Washington, later becomes Tuskegee University; **Jan. 7, 1891** African-American author Zora Neale Hurston born at rural Notasulga to north (died 1960); **1896** George Washington Carver made head of Agricultural Department at Tuskegee Institute; **1905** county courthouse built; **Feb. 4, 1913** civil rights icon Rosa Parks born, arrested for refusing to sit in back of bus at Montgomery Dec. 5, 1955, led to year-long bus boycott; **Feb. 12, 1923** U.S. Negro Veterans Hospital dedicated; **July 1941** Army Air Force begins training program for Tuskegee Airmen, African-American force totaling 992 by end of World War II, 450 saw combat, 150 lost their lives; **June 20, 1950** singer Lionel Richie born; **1960** U.S. Supreme Court rules against town's boundaries drawn to exclude black residents; **Oct. 26, 1974** Tuskegee Institute National Historic Site authorized.

Union Springs *Bullock County* *East central Alabama, 40 mi/64 km east-southeast of Montgomery*

1832 lands ceded to white settlers by Creeks following bitter struggle; **1836** town founded; **1844** town incorporated; **1849** First Baptist Church organized; **1866** Bullock County formed; town becomes county seat; **1872** county courthouse completed; **1880** Josephine Hotel built; **1888** city hall built; **1911** Carnegie Library built; **Feb. 1996** Bird Dog Field Trial Monument (dog statue) dedicated to regional sport of bird dogging.

Vernon *Lamar County* *Western Alabama, 86 mi/138 km west-northwest of Birmingham*

1866 town founded as county seat, named for Edmund Vernon; **1867** Jones County formed; **1868** county renamed Sanford; **July 8, 1872** Sen. John Hollis Bankhead II born in rural Sanford County (died 1946); **Apr. 12, 1874** Cong. William Brockman Bankhead born in rural Sanford County, Speaker of House 1936–1940 (died 1940); **1877** county renamed for Chief Justice L. Q. C. Lamar; **1870** incorporated as a city; **1909** county courthouse built.

Virginia City *Jefferson County* *See **Bessemer** (1905)*

Wedowee *Randolph County* *Eastern Alabama, 78 mi/126 km east of Birmingham*

1832 Randolph County formed; Blake's Ferry becomes county seat; **1834** town founded as new county seat; **1836** incorporated as a town; **1839** town renamed McDonald, reverts to Wedowee 1842; **1941** county courthouse built.

Westfield   *Jefferson County*   *See* **Birmingham (1931)**

Wetumpka   *Elmore County*   *Central Alabama,*
12 mi/19 km north-northeast of Montgomery

1833 town founded on Coosa River; **1834** town incorporated; **1837** Kelly Fitzpatrick House built; **1839** state penitentiary built, used as women's prison 1969 after completion of Kilby State Prison at Montgomery; **1852** Baptist Church dedicated; **1866** Elmore County formed; town becomes county seat; **1929** Jordan Dam built on Coosa River to north; **1931** county courthouse built; bridge built over Coosa River replacing span built late 1800s.

Alaska

Northwestern North America, detached from contiguous U.S. Capital: Juneau. Largest cities: Anchorage, Fairbanks.

Alaska was purchased from Russia by the U.S. October 18, 1867, becoming Alaska Territory. It was admitted to the U.S. as the 49th state January 3, 1959.

Alaska is divided into 25 boroughs, which are county equivalents. 16 boroughs, with 30 percent of the total land area, are organized. In 1975, the City of Anchorage merged with Greater Anchorage Borough to become the Municipality of Anchorage. All municipalities are classified as cities, of which there are two classes. There are no townships. See Introduction.

Adak   *Southwestern Alaska, central Aleutian Islands*

1741 Danish explorer Vitus Bering discovers Aleutian Islands for Russia; **early 1800s** many Aleuts follow Russians eastward during famine, forced to hunt marine mammals for Russians; **1942** air base constructed; **1943** air raids launched against Japanese occupying nearby Attu, Kiska, and Agattu islands; **Sept. 24, 1959** 16 killed as Aleutian Airways DC-4 hits mountain on Great Sitkin Island to east; **Nov. 6, 1971** hydrogen bomb test on Amchitka Island, 160 mi/257 km to west, stirs protests in U.S.; **1997** Naval Air Facility closed; **2001** incorporated as a city.

Anchorage   *Municipality of Anchorage*   *Southern Alaska, on Cook Inlet*

1741 Russian explorer Vitus Bering discovers Alaskan mainland; **June 1778** Captain James Cook explores inlet that bears his name; **1794** George Vancouver returns to area, had been with Cook's party; **1867** U.S. purchases Russian America, renames it Alaska; **1888** gold discovered by Alexander King on Turnagain Arm of Cook Inlet to south; **1902** area mapped by Alfred H. Brooks of U.S. Geological Survey; **1914** town adopts current name with opening of post office; construction begins on Alaska Railroad north to Fairbanks; **1915** first 887 lots auctioned at present site south of Ship Creek; *Anchorage Times* newspaper founded; Oscar Anderson House built; **1918** Alaska Railroad completed from Seward; **1920** federal government foregoes control over town; incorporated as a city; **1923** Alaska Railroad completed to Fairbanks; **1930** Merrill Field airport established, named for aviator Russel Merrill lost in Cook Inlet 1929; **1934** Providence Hospital built; **1935** Matanuska Valley to north opened to farming; **Feb. 1937** first Alaska Fur Rendezvous (the "Rondy")

held; **1942** Elmendorf Air Force Base and Fort Richardson army base built; Glenn Highway built from Tok for military purposes, branch of new Alaska Highway; **1946** Anchorage Symphony Orchestra founded; **1951** Anchorage International Airport opened, renamed Ted Stevens Anchorage International Airport 2000 for Alaska's senior U.S. Senator; **1954** University of Alaska at Anchorage established; **1960** Alaska Methodist University established; **June 14, 1960** crash of Pacific Northern Airlines Constellation into mountain 50 mi/80 km to east kills 14; **1962** Anchorage Opera established; **1964** Greater Anchorage Area Borough incorporated; **March 27, 1964** Good Friday Earthquake strikes at 5:36 p.m., 9.2 on Richter scale, 125 killed; subsequent tsunami (tidal wave) hits Hawaii and California March 28; **Sept. 12, 1966** hotel fire kills 14; **1968** Anchorage Museum of History and Art opened; **1973** first full-length 1,100-mi/1,770-km Anchorage-to-Nome Iditarod Sled Dog Race held; **Sept. 16, 1975** Greater Anchorage Area Borough merges with City of Anchorage as Municipality of Anchorage; **1983** Sullivan Sports Arena opened; **1988** Alaska Center for the Performing Arts opened; **1997** Anchorage Classical Ballet organized; **March 2003** warm weather forces 200 mi/322 km reroute of Iditarod race, coined "Idita-detour."

Angoon   *Southeastern Alaska, 65 mi/105 km south of Juneau, on Admiralty Island*

Oct. 1882 Northwest Company sealing vessel harpoon misfires, killing Tlingit crew member; Tlingits demand payment of 200 blankets; two company men taken hostage by Tlingits to ensure payment, U.S. Navy shells Tlingit village, killing six children; **1928** post office established; **1963** incorporated as a city; **1973** U.S. government pays villagers $90,000 reparations for shelling incident; **1978** Admiralty Island National Monument created; **1989** Greens Creek Mine begins production of silver, zinc, gold, and lead, closed 1993, reopened 1996.

Atka   *Southwestern Alaska, central Aleutian Islands*

1747 Russians explore Aleutian Islands; **1787** Aleut Natives taken to Pribilof Islands as slaves; **1860s** town founded; **1920s** fox farming introduced; **June 1942** Attu and Kiska islands taken by Japanese; residents evacuated to Ketchikan area, returned 1944; **1945** Attu islanders return from Japanese prisons, relocated to Atka; **1988** incorporated as a city.

Attu   *Southwestern Alaska, western Aleutian Islands*

June 1942 occupied by Japanese invaders, its Aleut residents deported to Japan; **May 1943** island retaken by American troops, heavy casualties on both sides; **1944** Long Range Aid to Navigation (LORAN) system becomes operational; **1945** islanders released from Japanese prisons relocated to Atka; **Dec. 22, 1958** crash of Air Force C-54 airplane from Elmendorf Air Base to Shemya Island, to southeast, kills 15; **1997** Attu Dock completed.

Barrow   *North Slope Borough   Northern Alaska, 480 mi/772 km north-northwest of Fairbanks, Arctic Ocean*

c.500 earliest known occupation by Inupiat people; **1826** Capt. John F. W. Beechey plots Arctic coastline for Royal Navy on the H.M.S. *Blossom*, named Point Barrow for Sir John Barrow of British Admiralty; **1881** meteorological station established by U.S. Army; **1893** Cape Smythe Whaling Station established; **1901** post office established, most northerly post office in U.S.; **1930s** outpost attracts Inuit (Eskimo) seeking federal aid; **Aug. 15, 1935** on flight from Fairbanks to Siberia, Wiley Post's airplane crashes in fog 15 mi/24 km to south after making a brief landing to ask directions to Barrow, Post and humorist Will Rogers killed; **1942** town serves as base for oil exploration; **1954** Naval Arctic Research Laboratory (NARL) established, closed 1980; **1957** first long-distance phone call from Barrow made; **1958** incorporated as a city; **1968** oil discovered at Prudhoe Bay 200 mi/322 km to east; **1972** North Slope Borough incorporated; city becomes administrative center; **1973** Barrow Observatory established for climate research; **1982** Will Rogers and Wiley Post monument dedicated; **Feb. 1999** Inupiat Heritage Center dedicated.

Bethel   *Southwestern Alaska, 425 mi/684 km west of Anchorage, on Kuskokwim River, near Bering Sea*

1870s trading post established; **1885** town founded by Moravian Church missionaries William H. Weinland and John H. Kilbuck; **1905** post office established; **1940** hospital built by Bureau of Indian Affairs; **1954** White Alice communication station opened, bringing telephone, telegraph, and teletype service to community; **1957** incorporated as a city; **1972** Kuskokwim Community College established; **1980** first annual Kuskokwim 300 Sled Dog Race held.

Circle   *Eastern Alaska, 130 mi/209 km northeast of Fairbanks, on Yukon River*

1887 L. N. McQuesten establishes trading post on Yukon River; **1893** gold discovered in nearby Birch Creek; town founded, originally named Circle City, assumed closer to Arctic Circle than it actually was (50 mi/80 km south of it); **1896** gold rush swells population, most miners leave within year for Klondike gold rush; **1898** town name shortened; **1902** Fairbanks gold rush turns Circle into virtual ghost town; **1927** Steese Highway completed from Fairbanks.

Copper Center   *Southern Alaska, 70 mi/113 km north-northeast of Valdez, on Copper River*

1884 Lt. William Abercrombie explores Copper River; **1885** Lt. Henry Allen ascends Copper River; **1896** trading post established, first white town in Alaskan interior; **1897** Blix Roadhouse built by Ringwald Blix; **1898–1899** hundreds of Klondike gold rush stampeders winter over here; **1901** post office and telegraph station established; **1932** Copper Center Lodge built on site of Blix Roadhouse; **1942** Chapel on the Hill built of logs by Army volunteers.

Cordova   *Southern Alaska, 150 mi/241 km east-southeast of Anchorage, on Prince William Sound*

1790 Spanish explorer Don Salvador Fidalgo enters Puerto Cordova, later renamed Orca Bay; **1794** area visited by George Vancouver; **1884** Capt. William Abercrombie uses Cordova as starting point for exploration of Copper River valley; **1889** Pacific Steam Whaling Company cannery established at nearby Orca; **1898–1899** copper stampede leads to settlement of area; **1902** gold discovered in area; Katalla Oil Field begins production, ends 1933; **1906** post office established; Copper River & Northwestern Railway built to Kennecott Copper Mine at Kennicott; **1909** incorporated as a city; **1910** Million Dollar Bridge spanning Copper River completed on railroad 50 mi/80 km to east, railroad opened 1911; **1938** rail service ends with closing of copper mine; harbor deepened, breakwater completed; **1940s** fishing becomes primary industry; **1945** construction of Copper River Highway begins on railroad right-of-way; **March 27, 1964** Good Friday Earthquake destroys Million Dollar Bridge, highway abandoned beyond bridge.

Deadhorse   *North Slope Borough   See **Prudhoe Bay***

Delta Junction   *Eastern Alaska, 80 mi/129 km southeast of Fairbanks, on Delta River*

1903 trail built from Valdez to Fairbanks; **1904** McCarthy Telegraph Station established by U.S. Army Signal Corps;

1919 construction camp for Richardson Highway established; **1927** camp becomes known as Buffalo Center with relocation of herds of bison to area from Moise, Montana; **1942** Alaska Highway built; **1946** area's first dairy farm established; **1955** Fort Greely Army Base established to south for northern warfare training; **1960** incorporated as a city; **1978** Delta Agricultural Project I adds 60,000 ac/24,500 ha to 6,500 ac/2,450 ha already under cultivation, mainly barley; **1980** Delta Bison Range established to move herd away from farmland; **1982** Delta Agricultural Project II opens 25,000 ac/10,125 ha to farming; **1984** Delta Agricultural Project III opens 22,000 ac/8,910 ha; **2000** Fort Greely deactivated; **Aug. 2001** site preparation begins on Fort Greely Testbed missile defense system.

Denali Park   *Denali Borough   Central Alaska, 85 mi/137 km south-southwest of Fairbanks*

1794 George Vancouver sights mountain from Cook Inlet; **1896** mountain named by prospector William A. Dickey for Pres. William McKinley; **Apr. 3, 1910** "Sourdough Party" Pete Anderson, Billy Taylor, and Charles McGonagall reach McKinley's North Peak; **June 7, 1913** South Peak, McKinley's true summit (20,320 ft/6,194 m), reached by Hudson Stuck, Walter Harper, Robert Tatum, and Harry Karstens; **Feb. 26, 1917** Mount McKinley National Park established; **1922** Alaska Railroad reaches park; **1926** coyotes first appear in park; **1938** McKinley Park Road built to Wonder Lake; **1972** George Parks Highway completed; **1973** North Face Lodge built; **1980** park expanded and renamed Denali National Park and Preserve, native name of mountain; **1987** Princess Wilderness Lodge built.

Dillingham   *Southwestern Alaska, 350 mi/563 km southwest of Anchorage, on Nushagak River*

1822 Russians establish Alexandrovski Redoubt fortification on opposite side of Nushagak Bay; **1884** salmon cannery in Bristol Bay built; **1904** post office established, named for U.S. Sen. Paul Dillingham of Vermont; **1918–1919** native survivors of influenza epidemic in Nushagak River area relocated to town; **1947** town platted; **1963** incorporated as a city; **Jan. 23, 1971** lowest temperature recorded in Alaska reached at Prospect Creek to southeast, −80°F/−62°C.

Dutch Harbor   *See* **Unalaska**

Eagle   *Eastern Alaska, 175 mi/282 km east of Fairbanks, on Yukon River*

1874 Belle Isle trading post established by François Mercier for Alaska Commercial Company; **1898** discovery of gold on Mission and American creeks swells population; post office established, town named Eagle; **1899** Fort Egbert established; **1901** incorporated as a city; road from Valdez completed by War Department; **1903** telegraph service reaches town; **Dec. 5, 1905** Roald Amundsen emerges out of fog, arriving by dogsled in

one of harshest winters after being first to sail the Northwest Passage, announces feat by telegraph; **1910** windmill built above 60-ft/18-m hand-dug well to draw water for town; **1911** Fort Egbert abandoned; **1950s** Taylor Highway built from Tetlin Junction on Alaska Highway; **1959** population drops to 13; **1976** renovation project includes monument honoring Amundsen; **1979** Fort Egbert restored; **Dec. 2, 1980** Yukon-Charley Rivers National Preserve established to northwest.

Fairbanks   *Fairbanks North Star Borough Central Alaska, 280 mi/451 km north of Anchorage, on Chena River*

1901 Capt. E. T. Barnette sails up Tanana River in the *Lavelle Young*, establishes winter cache and trading post on Chena River; **Sept. 1902** Felix Pedro discovers gold in creek later named for him 12 mi/19 km to north starting stampede; **1903** incorporated as a city; Barnette serves as first mayor; **1904** Immaculate Conception Catholic Church built; **1906** gold boom goes bust due to area's swampy muck; fire starts at Eagle Saloon, destroys three blocks; **1913** road from Valdez reaches city, later named Richardson Highway; **1917** Alaska Agricultural College and School of Mines established at College, west of town, becomes University of Alaska; **1923** Alaska Railroad completed from Anchorage; **1927** Steese Highway completed northeast to Circle; **1933** city hall built; **1936** Elliott Highway completed west to Manley Hot Springs; **1938** Ladd Field airport established, becomes Fort Wainwright Military Base 1942; **1942** Alaska Highway completed from Dawson Creek, British Columbia; **1964** Fairbanks-North Star Borough incorporated; city becomes administrative center; **1966** Creamer's Field Migratory Waterfowl Refuge opened on north side of city at site of Charles Creamer's dairy farm, northernmost dairy in Western Hemisphere; **May 1967** Alaskaland, unofficial World's Fair, opens on south bank of Chena River; **Aug. 15, 1967** city and fairgrounds flooded after 7 in/19 cm of rain, three killed; **1969** Geophysical Institute of University of Alaska builds rocket facility at Chatanika to north to study *aurora borealis*, upper atmosphere; **1971** George Parks Highway from Anchorage opens; **Feb. 2, 1972** hotel fire kills nine; **1974** construction of Alaska Pipeline boosts economy; **1984** Borough Administration Building built; **Feb. 1984** first annual Yukon Quest Sled Dog Race to Dawson and Whitehorse held.

Fort Yukon   *Northeastern Alaska, 140 mi/225 km northeast of Fairbanks, on Yukon River*

1847 trading post established by Alexander Hunter Murray for Hudson's Bay Company; **1869** clarification of U.S.–Canada boundary puts site in U.S. territory, Hudson's Bay post moved to Porcupine River, Yukon Territory; **1898** post office established; **1915** Hudson Stuck Memorial Hospital built; **June 27, 1915** highest temperature ever recorded in Alaska reached, 100°F/38°F; **1949** town destroyed by flooding; **1959** incorporated as a city.

ALASKA

Galena
West central Alaska, 200 mi/322 km west of Fairbanks, on Yukon River

1918 village founded as fishing camp on Yukon River, named Henry's Roost; **1932** post office established; **1942** Galena Army Air Field established, becomes Air Force Base after World War II; **1948** flooding severely damages town; **1950s** new military construction brings growth; **1971** more flooding occurs, new town site founded to east on Alexander Lake; incorporated as a city; **1993** Air Force base relegated to caretaker status, operates under contract.

Gambell
Western Alaska, at western end St. Lawrence Island, Bering Sea

1728 Russian explorer Vitus Bering visits island; **1878–1880** famine decimates population; **1894** village founded with establishment of Presbyterian mission to serve island's Siberian Inuit (Eskimo) people; **1898** mission abandoned when missionary Vene C. Gambell, wife, and daughter are lost at sea; **1900** reindeer introduced as food source; **1903** reindeer reserve established by President Roosevelt; **1963** incorporated as a city.

Haines
Haines Borough Southeastern Alaska, 70 mi/113 km north-northwest of Juneau

1878 George Dickinson of North West Company arrives at end of Lynn Canal estuary; **1879** Presbyterian missionary Rev. Samuel Hall Young and naturalist John Muir arrive; **1881** Rev. Young founds Willard Mission, renamed for Mrs. F. E. Haines, secretary of Presbyterian missions; **1880s** Jack Dalton blazes 305-mi/491-km toll road to the Yukon, exacts $150 toll; **1884** post office established, named Chilkoot; **1900** horticulturist Charles Anway develops Alaskan hybrid strawberry, takes top honors at 1906 Seattle Exposition; **1904** Fort William H. Seward established, only military base in Alaska until 1942; **1910** incorporated as a city; **1922** fort renamed Chilkoot Barracks; **Feb. 25, 1925** Glacier Bay National Monument proclaimed to southwest, became Glacier Bay National Park and Preserve 1980; **1943** Haines Highway (Haines Cut-Off) built to Haines Junction, Yukon, and Alaska Highway, route of Jack Dalton's trail; **1946** base deactivated, Officers' Row homes, other buildings converted to historic site, hotel; **1968** Haines Borough incorporated; city becomes administrative center; **1982** Alaska Chilkat Bald Eagle Preserve established to north.

Healy
Denali Borough Central Alaska, 80 mi/ 129 km south-southwest of Fairbanks

1918 Usibelli Coal Mine established; town founded; **1971** Dall sheep introduced; coal mine reclamation begins; **1980s** Community Center built; **Dec. 1990** Denali Borough incorporated; town becomes borough administrative center.

Homer
Kenai Peninsula Borough Southern Alaska, 120 mi/193 km south-southwest of Anchorage

1898 town founded, named for prospector Homer Pennock; **1899** mining begins in Cook Inlet coal fields; railroad built from coal mine 7 mi/11.3 km to loading facility at end of Homer Spit; **1907** fire damages town; coal mining ends; **1920s** town becomes fishing port; **1952** Sterling Highway completed from Anchorage; **March 27, 1964** in Good Friday Earthquake, Homer Spit sinks 4–6 ft/6–9 m into inlet; **March 31, 1964** incorporated as a city.

Hope
Kenai Peninsula Borough Southern Alaska, 23 mi/37 km south of Anchorage

1888 gold discovered at Resurrection Creek; **1896** town founded with gold rush, named Hope City; **1897** post office established; name shortened; **1940s** mining declines; Hope endures with about 225 people; **March 27, 1964** 7-ft/12-m drop in level of earth's surface along inlet as result of Good Friday Earthquake, parts of town destroyed.

Hydaburg
Southeastern Alaska, 50 mi/80 km west of Ketchikan, on Prince of Wales Island, on Tlevak Strait

1700 Haida Native Americans from Queen Charlotte Islands (Canada) move into area once inhabited by Tlingits; **1911** town founded as site for school to serve three nearby villages on Prince of Wales Island; **1927** incorporated as a city; fish processing plant opened; **1930s** CCC program restores town's totem collection; **1936** town becomes first in Alaska to organize an Indian Recognition Act (IRA) Council; **1983** road from other parts of island extended to Hydaburg.

Hyder
Southeastern Alaska, 110 mi/177 km north of Prince Rupert, B.C., at end of Portland Canal estuary

1794 Capt. George Vancouver transits Portland Canal fjord, four-day journey; **1896** Portland Canal estuary (U.S./Canada boundary) surveyed by David D. Gaillard (Gaillard Cut, Panama Canal, named for him); **1898** town founded by D. J. Raine at same time as neighboring Stewart, British Columbia, named Portland City; gold and silver mining boom begins; **1910** town renamed for geologist F. B. Hyder; **1917** post office established; **1919** Premier Gold and Silver Mine opened; **1948** forest fire destroys town; mine closed; **1956** most remaining mines close; **1972** Cassiar Highway and Stewart-Hyder Road spur opened from Canada; **1978** Misty Fjords National Monument established.

Iliamna
*Lake and Peninsula Borough See **King Salmon** (1968)*

Juneau
City and Borough of Juneau Southeastern Alaska, 600 mi/966 km east-southeast of Anchorage

Oct. 1880 prospectors Joe Juneau and Dick Harris discover coloration in Gold Creek; **1881** town founded

18

as Harrisburg; gold mines established, including the Treadwell and Ready Bullion mines at Douglas, on opposite side of Gastineau Channel; **1882** town renamed Juneau; **1885** Perseverance Gold Mine opened; **1886** Chinese mine laborers sent to Wrangell at insistence of white miners; **1894** St. Nicholas Russian Orthodox Church built; **1900** incorporated as a city; Alaska Historical Society founded, state museum opened 1920; **1906** territorial capital moved from Sitka; **1916** Alaska-Juneau Gold Mine opened, largest gold mine in world; **Apr. 21, 1917** cave-in and flood at Treadwell Mine swallows gymnasium and fire hall, mine closed, $66 million in gold extracted in 36 years; **1921** Perseverance Mine closed; **1931** federal building completed, later becomes state capitol; **1944** A-J (Alaska-Juneau) Mine south of town closes after yielding $80 million in gold since opening prior to Treadwell disaster; **1963** Greater Juneau Borough incorporated; **1970** unified City and Borough of Juneau incorporated; city of Douglas annexed; **Sept. 4, 1971** Alaska Airlines Boeing 727 crashes into mountain killing 111; **1972** University of Alaska Southeast Campus established at Auke Lake to northwest; **1974** Alaskans vote to move state capital, site at Willow chosen 1976; state office building ("S.O.B.") built; state court building built; **1981** new bridge built across Gastineau Channel to Douglas; **1982** proposed move of state capital to Willow canceled with failure to approve funding.

Kake *Southeastern Alaska, 50 mi/80 km east of Sitka, on Kupreanof Island, on Keku Strait*

1856 Kake tribesmen descend coast to Whidby Island, Washington, behead customs officer, return with his skull and scalp, retaliation for death of chief in Puget Sound 1855; **1902** Five Finger Lighthouse built to northeast off Cape Fanshaw, oldest lighthouse in Alaska; **1904** post office established; **1912** cannery built; **1952** incorporated as a city.

Kasaan *Southeastern Alaska, 32 mi/51 km west-northwest of Ketchikan, on Prince of Wales Island*

1892 Copper Queen Mine opened; town founded among Haida people; **1902** salmon cannery established; **Oct. 25, 1916** Kasaan National Monument established to protect town's totems; **1938** Kasaan Totem Park created from former national monument; **1976** incorporated as a city; **1980** cannery buildings removed.

Kenai *Kenai Peninsula Borough Southern Alaska, 65 mi/105 km southwest of Anchorage, on Cook Inlet*

1791 Fort St. Nicholas trading post established by Grigor Konovalof, second Russian settlement in Alaska; **1849** Holy Assumption Russian Orthodox Church founded by Egumen Nicolai; **1850** gold discovered in Kenai River basin; **1869** Fort Kenai established by U.S. Army; **1899** post office established; **1951** road built from Anchorage; **1957** oil discovered to northeast along Swanson River; **1960** incorporated as a city; **March 27, 1964** Good Friday

Earthquake severely damages town. **1965** offshore oil reserves discovered.

Kennicott *See* **McCarthy**

Ketchikan *Ketchikan Gateway Borough*
Southeastern Alaska, 235 mi/378 km south-southeast of Juneau

1793 Capt. George Vancouver explores area, names Revillagigedo Island for Mexican Viceroy Revilla Gigedo; **1885** settlers arrive at site of Tlingit fishing camp; **1887** first salmon cannery opened; **1892** post office established; **1898** gold discovered; **1900** incorporated as a city; **c.1900** notorious Creek Street red light district, including Dolly's House, begins plying its trade, "where salmon and fishermen go upstream to spawn"; **1903** first sawmill opened; **1930s** CCC program restores nearly 30 totems, largest collection in world, at nearby village of Saxman; **1933** Thomas Basin Boat Harbor dredged, breakwater completed; **1938** federal building completed; **1940s** after boasting more than a dozen canneries a decade earlier, catch declines by half due to over-fishing; **1942** as Japanese attack Aleutian Islands, Aleut refugees transferred here to be housed in vacant canneries, returned by 1945; **1945** c.30 "female boardinghouses" line Creek Street district; **1954** large pulp mill opens at Ward Cove to northwest; last of Creek Street brothels closed; **1963** Ketchikan Gateway Borough incorporated; city becomes borough administrative center; **1973** Ketchikan International Airport built on Gravina Island to west, connected by ferry; **1997** pulp mill closed.

King Salmon *Bristol Bay Borough Southwestern Alaska, 280 mi/451 km southwest of Anchorage*

1778 Capt. James Cook enters bay, names it for the Earl of Bristol; **June 2, 1912** Novarupta Volcano erupts to east, one of greatest natural cataclysms on record; **Sept. 24, 1918** Katmai National Monument, with its Valley of Ten Thousand Smokes, established to east; **1942** King Salmon Air Force Base established, closed 1993; **1949** post office established; road built from Naknek; **1956** King Salmon Inn opened; **Feb. 12, 1968** twin-engine plane crashes at Iliamna to northeast, 39 killed; **Dec. 2, 1980** Katmai Monument redesignated Katmai National Park and Preserve; **1989** Lake and Peninsula Borough incorporated; town becomes borough administrative center for its central location, although located in Bristol Bay Borough; **1990** Borough Administrative Building converted from school, built 1983.

Kodiak *Kodiak Island Borough Southern Alaska, 255 mi/410 km south-southwest of Anchorage*

Sept. 8, 1763 Kodiak Island discovered by Russian explorer Stephen Glotov; **1784** first European settlement in Alaska at Three Saints Bay, now Old Harbor, site of massacre of hundreds of Koniag Native Americans on orders from Gregori Shelikof, founder of the Russian

America Company; **1785** island explored and named by Captain James Cook; **1792** town founded as Russian Alaska's first capital; Erskine House built by Alexander Baranof to warehouse otter pelts, converted to residence 1911, declared historic site 1962, now the Baranof Museum; **1794** Father Herman arrives to establish first mission in Alaska, canonized 1970, first North American saint of Russian Orthodox Church; **1804** capital moved to Sitka; Russian explorer Lisianski visits area; **1867** first horses in Alaska brought to Woody Island in Chiniak Bay to work ice harvesting; **1880s** Kodiak and Woody Island flourish as boat-building centers; **1882** first cannery opened; **June 2, 1912** the Novarupta Volcano on Alaska Peninsula to west erupts with twice the volume of Krakatoa 1883, buries town in ash; **1939** Fort Abercrombie military base built, now a state park; **1940** incorporated as a city; **1941** Kodiak National Wildlife Refuge created; **1958** first annual Crab Festival held; **1963** Kodiak Island Borough incorporated; city becomes administrative center; **March 27, 1964** Good Friday earthquake shakes area, tidal wave destroys downtown, canneries, fishing fleet, 150 homes, many killed; **Oct. 9, 1967** freighter *Panoceanic Faith* sinks in storm, 36 killed; **1968** city becomes most productive fishing port in U.S.; state courthouse built; **1973** St. Herman Theological Seminary established; **1979** school converted to Borough Administrative Building.

Kotzebue   *Northwest Arctic Borough*
Northwestern Alaska, 480 mi/772 km northwest of Fairbanks

1816 Polish explorer Otto von Kotzebue arrives on behalf of Russians; **1897** reindeer station established on Arctic Ocean; **1899** post office established; **1958** incorporated as a city; **1968** oil and natural gas discovered in Brooks Range, raises environmental concerns; **Dec. 1, 1978** Bering Land Bridge National Preserve established on Seward Peninsula to southwest; **Dec. 2, 1980** Cape Krusenstern National Monument, Kobuk Valley National Park, and Noatak National Preserve created in Brooks Range, other areas; **1986** Northwest Arctic Borough incorporated; city becomes administrative center; **1990** Red Dog Mine opened 100 mi/161 km to north, largest zinc mine in world.

Manley Hot Springs   *Central Alaska, 85 mi/ 137 km west of Fairbanks, on Tanana River*

1902 hot springs discovered by J. F. Karshner, establishes homestead; **1903** telegraph station established by Army Signal Corps; Sam's Rooms and Meals established; **1906** gold discovered; **1907** Frank Manley builds resort hotel; town of Hot Springs founded; **1908** gold mining begins at Tofty to northwest; **1913** Manley Resort destroyed by fire; **1957** town renamed Manley Hot Springs; **1959** Elliott Highway completed from Fairbanks, **1985** new resort opened.

McCarthy   *Southern Alaska, 120 mi/193 km east-northeast of Valdez, in Chitina River Valley*

1898 copper discovered at base of Wrangell Mountains to north; **1906** Copper River & Northwestern Railway built from Cordova, completed 1911; **1908** Kennecott Copper Mine opened to north at Kennicott (mine officially misspelled Kennecott); **1913** population peaks at 1,300; **1938** copper mine closed; both McCarthy and Kennicott abandoned; **1960s** McCarthy Road built; **Dec. 2, 1980** Wrangell-St. Elias National Park established; **1983** tram built by residents across Kennicott River from end of McCarthy Road; **1997** state builds footbridge, replacing tram.

McKinley Park   *Denali Borough*   See **Denali Park**

Mekoryuk   *Western Alaska, 580 mi/933 km west of Anchorage, on Etolin Strait, Bering Sea*

1 AD Nunivak Island first inhabited by Nuniwarmiut people; **1821** village discovered by Russian American Company; **1874** summer camp established at site; **1900** epidemics diminish population, only four families remain; **1920** reindeer introduced for commercial purposes; **1934** 34 musk ox introduced from Greenland to help save species; **1940** post office established; **1945** reindeer slaughter house built; **1990s** musk ox population reaches 500.

Metlakatla   *Southeastern Alaska, 17 mi/27 km south of Ketchikan, on Annette Island*

1887 Scottish minister William Duncan arrives to organize model community at abandoned Tlingit village; sawmill and cannery built; **1891** title to Annette Island given to Metlakatlas; **1913** public school opens, threatening Duncan's hold on community; **1917** salmon cannery opened, leased to Metlakatla Council; **1918** Duncan dies; **1942** airfield built by military; **1948** 1,000-seat church built by Duncan burns, rebuilt 1954; **1971** Annette Island Reserve remains one of Alaska's few Indian reservations with refusal to join Alaska Native Claims Settlement.

Naknek   *Bristol Bay Borough*   *Southwestern Alaska, 305 mi/491 km southwest of Anchorage*

1778 Bristol Bay, arm of Bering Sea, named by Capt. Cook for Earl of Bristol; **1890** salmon cannery established; town founded on Kvichak Bay, extension of Bristol Bay, near mouth of Naknek River; **1907** post office established; **1949** road built east to town of King Salmon; **1962** Bristol Bay Borough incorporated, first and smallest borough in Alaska; town becomes borough administrative center; Borough Building, built 1952, renovated for government.

Nenana   *Denali Borough*   *Central Alaska, 45 mi/ 72 km west-southwest of Fairbanks*

1902 Jim Duke builds trading post on south side of Tanana River, at confluence of Nenana River; **1908** post office established; 1916 town founded as railroad construction camp; 1917 first Nenana Ice Classic held, offering payoffs for guessing exact time of ice breakup on river; 1921 incorporated as a city; July 5, 1923 Warren G. Harding, first president to visit Alaska, drives golden spike on north end of railroad bridge completing Alaska Railroad, begun 1903 (Harding died Aug. 2 in San Francisco); 1934 steamer *Nenana* launched by railroad for service to Marshall (Fortuna Ledge) on lower Yukon River, dry docked at Fairbanks 1956; 1961 Clear Air Force Station established to southwest; 1967 flooding devastates town; 1968 bridge built on Tanana River; 1971 George Parks Highway completed.

Nome   *Western Alaska, 580 mi/933 km northwest of Anchorage, on Norton Sound, Bering Sea*

1898 gold discovered; Cape Nome Mining District incorporated; town site named Anvil City, after nearby Anvil Creek; 1899 Nome post office established, name attributed to cartographic error, "? name" mistaken for "C. Nome," with "C" standing for "Cape"; gold found lying on beaches of Norton Sound, subsequent rush swells population to 30,000 within year, ends by Oct. 1900; 1901 incorporated as a city; 7-mi/11.3-km Wild Goose Railroad built to mines at Anvil Creek, railroad named for tendency to disappear into thawing tundra; 1902 Judge James Wickersham brings order to town after previous judge is indicted on corruption charges; 1919 system of marked trails and shelters established from Alaskan interior; 1925 diphtheria epidemic necessitates 650-mi/1,046-km delivery of serum by dogsled from Nenana, inspiration for the annual Iditarod sled dog race; May 13, 1926 Roald Amundsen, 13 others, arrive in dirigible *Norge* from Norway at Teller to northwest, first to fly over North Pole; June 29, 1931 Wiley Post and Harold Gatty arrive from Khabarovsk, Russia, two days before reaching New York on 9-day, round-the-world flight; 1934 fire destroys business district; 1938 federal building completed; 1962 gold dredging ceases; 1963 Soviets make reconnaissance flights over Bering Sea, part of Cold War tensions; 1973 first full-length, 1,100-mile/1,770-km Anchorage-to-Nome Iditarod Trail Sled Dog Race held, name derived from Igalik Native American "hidedhod," meaning "distant place"; 1974 buildings on Front Street damaged by storm; Dec. 1, 1978 Bering Land Bridge National Preserve created to north; 1980s gold dredging resumed; 1983 first oil and natural gas leases sold in Norton Sound.

Palmer   *Matanuska-Susitna Borough   Southern Alaska, 40 mi/64 km northeast of Anchorage*

1913 gold miners homestead in Matanuska Valley; 1916 town founded on Alaska Railroad; 1917 experiment station established by U.S. Department of Agriculture; 1935 settlement program begins with 200 families of Scandinavian descent from upper Midwest; 1936 farmers co-op organized; first Alaska State Fair held; 1937 Church of a Thousand Logs completed; 1942 Glenn Highway built; 1951 incorporated as a city; 1958 Matanuska-Susitna (Mat-Su) Community College established; 1964 Matanuska-Susitna Borough incorporated; city becomes administrative center.

Petersburg   *Southeastern Alaska, 120 mi/193 km south-southeast of Juneau, on Frederick Sound*

1897 salmon cannery built by Peter Buschmann; town founded; 1899 sawmill completed; Norwegian settlers arrive; 1910 incorporated as a city; 1912 Sons of Norway Hall built, focal point of annual Little Norway Festival; 1916 shrimp processing plant established; 1937 small boat basin built; 1938 town boasts Alaska's only traffic light.

Platinum   *Southwestern Alaska, 460 mi/740 km west-southwest of Anchorage, on Kuskokwim Bay, Bering Sea*

1926 trading post established; 1927 "white gold" discovered in Fox Gulch by Eskimo Johnnie Kilbuck; platinum production begins; 1935 post office established; large platinum dredge built; 1936 discovery of new layer of platinum begins mining rush; 1957 incorporated as a city; 1960 school opened; 1990 mining activity ceases.

Prospect Creek   *See* Dillingham (1971)

Prudhoe Bay   *North Slope Borough   Northern Alaska, 420 mi/767 km north of Fairbanks, on Arctic Ocean*

Aug. 16, 1826 site named by Royal Navy's John Franklin; 1923 discovery of oil seepages along Arctic Coast prompts creation of Naval Petroleum Reserve; 1968 major oil discovery announced; 1974 Trans-Alaska Pipeline construction begins amid stiff environmental opposition; town of Deadhorse founded as support center; Apr. 1974 construction of North Slope Haul Road begins, parallels pipeline from Livengood, northwest of Fairbanks, completed in five months, renamed Dalton Highway 1981 for oil engineer James B. Dalton; 1977 Trans-Alaska Pipeline completed to Valdez; July 1977 first oil delivered through pipeline; Dec. 2, 1980 Gates of the Arctic National Park established on North Slope to south; 1994 public access on Dalton Highway extended from Mile 211 at Disaster Creek to Deadhorse.

Saint George   *Southwestern Alaska, 745 mi/1,199 km southwest of Anchorage, Pribilof Islands, Bering Sea*

June 12, 1786 St. George Island discovered by Russian Gerasim Pribilof; 1787 Aleuts brought to Pribilof Islands by Russians as slaves; 1870 Pribilof Islands leased to U.S. government for fur seal harvesting; 1910 U.S. Bureau of Fisheries assumes control of islands after overharvesting of seals leads to starvation of Aleut people; 1979 Pribilof Aleuts receive $8.5 million compensation for loss of sealing rights; 1983 incorporated as a city; U.S. Fisheries withdraws from islands; St. George receives $8 million grant; 1985 total ban on sealing implemented.

21

Saint Paul   *Southwestern Alaska, 750 mi/1,207 km southwest of Anchorage, Pribilof Islands, Bering Sea*

June 12, 1786 uninhabited islands discovered by Russian fur trader Gerasim Pribilof, named for himself, uses Aleuts as slaves to harvest seals nearly to extinction; **1900** U.S. Fisheries assumes control of islands after overharvesting of fur seals leads to starvation of Aleuts; **1911** with seal population reduced from millions to c.150,000, treaty banning pelagic (open ocean) sealing signed by U.S., Russia, England, and Japan; **1971** incorporated as a city; **1979** Pribilof Aleuts receive $8.5 million compensation for sealing losses; **1983** Aleuts gain control of islands; St. Paul receives $12 million grant; **1985** total sealing ban implemented; **March 1990** fishing boat *Aleutian Enterprise* capsizes to south, nine killed, 22 rescued; **Apr. 1, 2001** *Arctic Rose* lost in Bering Sea 205 mi/330 km to north with 15 crew.

Sand Point   *Aleutians East Borough*
Southwestern Alaska, 590 mi/950 km southwest of Anchorage

1760s Russians explore south coast of Alaska Peninsula; **1898** town founded on Popof Island, Sumagin Islands, as trading post; **1933** St. Nicholas Russian Orthodox Chapel built; **1946** halibut processing plant established; **1966** incorporated as a city; **1987** Aleutians East Borough incorporated; town becomes administrative center.

Seldovia   *Kenai Peninsula Borough*   *Southern Alaska, 190 mi/308 km south-southwest of Anchorage*

1869 trading post established, name derived from Russian term "seldevoy," meaning "herring bay"; **1882** trading post abandoned; **1898** post office established; **1945** incorporated as a city; **March 27, 1964** Good Friday Earthquake causes subsidence of several feet along waterfront; **1968** municipal dock built to replace facilities damaged by quake.

Seward   *Kenai Peninsula Borough*   *Southern Alaska, 80 mi/129 km south of Anchorage*

1791 Resurrection Bay named by Russian explorer Alexander Baranof; **1884** Frank Lowell becomes first settler; **1902** construction begins on Alaska Central Railroad to Matanuska coal fields; **1903** town founded, named for William H. Seward, U.S. secretary of state responsible for acquisition of Alaska 1867; **1909** railroad suspended with closing of coal fields; **1912** incorporated as a city; **1915** first annual race to summit of Mount Marathon begins with bar bet; **1915** work on Alaska Railroad resumes, completed to Fairbanks 1923; **1935** harbor improvements made; **March 27, 1964** Good Friday Earthquake destroys much of town; **Dec. 2, 1980** Kenai Fjords National Park established to west; **1992** town becomes favored port for cruise ships in place of Whittier; **1998** Alaska Sealife Center opened.

Sitka   *Sitka Borough*   *Southeastern Alaska, 95 mi/153 km south-southwest of Juneau, on Sitka Sound*

July 1741 Capt. Alexei Chirikof sails into Sitka Harbor, two landing parties fail to return to ship; **1799** Redoubt St. Michael built by Alexander Baranof for Russia on land occupied by Tlingits; **1802** fort destroyed by Tlingits, most occupants killed; **1804** Russian warship *Neva* arrives, Tlingits forced to leave; fort rebuilt; settlement renamed New Archangel; **1806** Sitka replaces Kodiak as capital of Russian Alaska; **1816** Sitka's first church (Russian Orthodox) built; **1821** Tlingits invited to return under uneasy truce; Trinity Mission Church built into wall of stockade, entered on both sides of wall; **1835** Baranof's Castle built; **1840** town becomes known as Paris of North Pacific for its library, schools, other institutions; **c.1841** Lutheran Church built; **1842** Russian Bishop's House built for Ivan Veniaminov, oldest building in Sitka; **1848** St. Michael's Cathedral (Russian Orthodox) built; **1855** Native Americans enter stockade through Trinity Church, ensuing battle leaves 20 Russians dead, 60 Native Americans dead; **Oct. 18, 1867** Alaska transferred to U.S. at Baranof Castle overlooking Sitka Harbor, territory purchased for $7,200,000, less than two cents per acre; **1878** Sheldon Jackson College established for native Alaskans; **1884** civilian government assumes control from military; **1888** Sheldon Jackson Museum founded, opened 1897, purchased by state 1985; **1894** Baranof's Castle destroyed by fire; **1899** St. Peter's by the Sea Episcopal Church built; **1906** capital moved to Juneau; **March 23, 1910** Sitka National Monument established to preserve 1855 battle site; **1935** Alaska Pioneers Home completed on harbor, established 1913; **1941** military establishes airport and seaplane base on Japonski Island, west side of harbor; **1960** pulp mill established at Silver Bay, closed 1993; **1966** St. Michael's Cathedral burns, rebuilt 1976; **1971** unified Sitka Borough incorporated; **1972** first Sitka Summer Music Festival held.

Skagway   *Southeastern Alaska, 90 mi/145 km north-northwest of Juneau, at end of Lynn Canal estuary*

1888 Capt. William Moore and son settle on Skagway River; **July 1897** first prospectors of Klondike Gold Rush arrive; **Oct. 1897** tent city quickly surrounds Moore cabin, transformed within months into wood-structured city of 20,000 with saloons, gambling houses, dance halls; **1898** up to 25,000 men pass over Chilkoot Trail to Yukon; Anvil Gold Mine established; **Apr. 3, 1898** many killed in avalanche at Sheep Camp on Chilkoot Trail, buried at Slide Cemetery; **July 1898** "bad guy" con artist Soapy Smith and "good guy" Frank Reid, of town's vigilance committee, killed in gunfight, both buried in Gold Rush Cemetery; **1899** gold rush ends; **1900** incorporated as a city; **July 1900** White Pass & Yukon Railway opened to Whitehorse, Yukon; **1963** Alaska State Ferry System begins service; **1979** Klondike Highway opened to Whitehorse; **May 14, 1980** Klondike Gold Rush National Historical Park established; **1982** gold mine closed; railroad suspends service, reopened 1988 as excursion route to Fraser, British Columbia.

Soldotna *Kenai Peninsula Borough* *Southern Alaska, 65 mi/105 km southwest of Anchorage*

1938 Kenai National Moose Range established, becomes Kenai National Wildlife Refuge 1941; **1947** Sterling Highway completed from Anchorage; town founded on Cook Inlet; **1949** post office established; **1957** oil discovered; **1960** incorporated as a city; **1964** Kenai Peninsula Borough incorporated; city becomes administrative center.

Teller *See* **Nome (1926)**

Tok (Tok Junction) *West central Alaska, 180 mi/290 km southeast of Fairbanks, near Tanana River*

1942 Alaska Highway construction camp established near Tokyo Creek, name shortened due to anti-Japanese sentiment; **1946** town founded; **1947** Army fuel pipeline from Haines to Fairbanks established with main pumping station at Tok, discontinued 1979; **1976** Coast Guard LORAN (Long Range Aid to Navigation) station established; **July 1990** lightning strike starts largest, most costly forest fire in Alaskan history; wind shift spares edge of town.

Unalakleet *Western Alaska, 150 mi/241 km east-southeast of Nome, on Norton Sound, Bering Sea*

200 BC beach site occupied by early peoples; **1964** experimental musk ox raising program begun with small herd moved from Fairbanks, for their underwool, or qiviut, used in making knit goods; **1901** telegraph line built by Army Signal Corps; **1974** incorporated as a city; **1977** success of musk ox breeding experiment leads to expansion of herd.

Unalaska *Southwestern Alaska, on Unalaska Island, eastern Aleutian Islands*

1759 Russians discover Unalaska Island; **1768** Russians found settlement, originally named Iliuliuk; **1778** explorer Capt. James Cook spends six weeks here; **1827** Church of Holy Ascension completed by Aleuts, oldest standing Russian Orthodox church in Alaska; **1880** Methodist Mission founded; **1942** incorporated as a city to stop Navy from building runway, destroying village; Dutch Harbor Naval Base established on Amaknak Island across bay, bridge built; **June 1942** Dutch Harbor attacked by Japanese; Aleuts relocated to camps in abandoned canneries near Ketchikan, 10 percent die from harsh conditions; **1944** Aleuts returned from Ketchikan; **1960s** crab fishing brings growth to community; **1982** crab stock plummets, industry turns to pollock, becomes one of leading seafood ports in nation; **Feb. 14, 1983** fishing boats *Americus* and *Altair* from Port Angeles, Washington, capsize in rough seas, 14 killed.

Valdez *Southern Alaska, 120 mi/193 km east of Anchorage, on Prince William Sound*

1778 Capt. James Cook enters and names Prince William Sound; **1790** harbor named Puerto de Valdez by Spanish explorer Don Salvador Fidalgo; **1792** explored by George Vancouver; **1898** gold and copper discovered in Wrangell Mountains, attracts 10,000 stampeders; town founded, briefly named Copper City, renamed Valdez (val-DEEZ); Capt. William Abercrombie blazes trail north to Fort Egbert at Eagle, now Richardson Highway; **Jan. 1, 1898** Alaska's first hanging takes life of Doc Tanner for murder of two camp mates; **1900** Fort Liscom established; **1901** incorporated as a city; **1904** Fairbanks gold boom brings prospectors through city; **1907** copper rush attracts miners to Kennecott Mine in Chitina Valley; **1915** fire destroys business district; **c.1922** Richardson Highway completed; **March 27, 1964** Good Friday Earthquake and tsunami (tidal wave) severely damage city and waterfront; city center moved to west; **July 29, 1977** first oil reaches port after 38½-day trip through 800 mi/1,287 km Alaska Pipeline from Prudhoe Bay, first shipment made Aug. 1; **March 24, 1989** tanker *Exxon Valdez* runs aground on Bligh Reef 25 mi/40 km to south, spilling over 10 million gal/37 million liters of oil, one of worst environmental disasters in history.

Whittier *Southern Alaska, 50 mi/80 km southeast of Anchorage, on Prince William Sound*

1941 town founded as military port and petroleum transfer center, named for poet John Greenleaf Whittier; **1942** Whittier Rail Tunnel completed to west; **1960** military facility deactivated; **March 27, 1964** Good Friday Earthquake damages town, 13 killed locally; **1969** incorporated as a city; **March 24, 1989** supertanker *Exxon Valdez* strikes nearby reef causing major oil spill; **1992** deteriorating docking facilities and 4 percent sales tax force cruise ships to call at Seward; **2000** Anton Anderson Memorial Tunnel converted from rail traffic to alternating rail and highway traffic.

Willow *Matanuska-Susitna Borough* *See* **Juneau (1974, 1982)**

Wrangell *Southern Alaska, 100 mi/161 km south-southeast of Juneau*

c.6000 BC early inhabitants leave petroglyphs (rock paintings) on Wrangell Island; **1811** Russians begin trade with Stikines; **1834** Redoubt St. Dionysius fort built by Russians; **1840** renamed Fort Stikine by Hudson's Bay Company; **1861** gold rush begins on Stikine River on mainland; **1867** site renamed Fort Wrangell by U.S.; **1869** post office established; **1879** Presbyterian church founded, considered first Protestant church in Alaska; naturalist John Muir visits Stikine Valley; **1903** incorporated as a city; **1906** fire sweeps area; **1936** boat basin dredged, breakwater completed; **1952** town damaged by fire; **1950s** Japanese interests build lumber mill; **1994** pulp mill closed.

Yakutat   *Yakutat Borough*   *Southeastern Alaska, 210 mi/338 km northwest of Juneau, on Gulf of Alaska*

July 16, 1741 Mt. St. Elias (18,008 ft/5,489 m) becomes first part of Alaskan mainland sighted by explorer Vitus Bering; **1795** penal colony established by Russians on Yakutat Bay, destroyed by Native Americans 1803–1804; **1805** Russian fort built, destroyed by Tlingits; **1880s** prospectors and trappers arrive; **1889** Swedish Lutheran Mission established; **1897** Mt. St. Elias first climbed by Italian Prince Luigi; **1903** fish cannery opened, closed 1970; **June 22, 1948** incorporated as a city; **1986** advance of Hubbard Glacier blocks Russell Fjord, traps pod of whales, temporarily changes fjord to freshwater; **Sept. 22, 1992** Yakutat Borough incorporated; town becomes administrative center.

Arizona

Southwestern U.S. Capital: Phoenix. Major cities: Phoenix, Tucson.

The area was acquired by the U.S. in 1848 as a result of the Mexican War. The Territory of New Mexico was formed in December 1850. The Gadsden Purchase added land from Mexico in the far south in 1853. Arizona Territory separated from New Mexico Territory on February 14, 1863. Arizona was admitted to the Union as the 48th state February 14, 1912.

Arizona is divided into 15 counties. The most recently created county was La Paz County in 1983. Municipalities are classified as villages, towns, and cities. There are no townships. See Introduction.

Ajo *Pima County   Southern Arizona, 85 mi/137 km southwest of Phoenix*

1750 Spanish work copper mines; **1854** Ajo Copper Company organized; town founded; **1916** John C. Greenway acquires mines, organizes New Cornelia Copper Company, becomes highly productive entity; **1931** mines acquired by Phelps Dodge Corporation; **Apr. 13, 1937** Organ Pipe Cactus National Monument proclaimed to south.

Apache Junction *Pinal County   Central Arizona, 30 mi/48 km east of Phoenix*

Dec. 1872 Gen. George Crook's troops fight Apaches in Battle of the Caves near Tortilla Flat to northeast, 82 Apaches hiding in cave killed by Crook's bullets deliberately ricocheted off cave ceiling; **1923** town founded by George Cleveland Curtis; Mormon Flat Dam completed to northeast on Salt River; **1927** Horse Mesa Dam completed on Salt River upstream (east) of Mormon Flat Dam; **1978** incorporated as a city.

Benson *Cochise County   Southeastern Arizona, 43 mi/69 km southeast of Tucson*

1690s Spanish visit San Pedro Valley, are impressed by its fertility; **1860** site used as stop on Butterfield Stagecoach Route; **1880** Atchison, Topeka & Santa Fe Railroad built; town founded on San Pedro River, serves as connecting point to Tombstone; **1882** Sonora Railroad built by Santa Fe Railroad south to Morena, Mexico; **1924** incorporated as a city; **Nov. 1974** Kartchner Caverns discovered in Whetstone Mountains to southwest by spelunkers Gary Tenen and Randy Tufts, location held secret until state park established 1988 to protect delicate crystalline formations.

Bisbee *Cochise County   Southeastern Arizona, 81 mi/130 km southeast of Tucson*

1875 silver prospector Hugh Jones discovers copper, walks away from it; **1877** copper ore found by army scouts, George Warren sent to stake claims; town founded, named for shareholder Judge DeWitt Bisbee; **1880** Copper Queen Consolidated Mining Company formed by Copper Queen and Phelps Dodge interests; **1881** Cochise County formed; Tombstone becomes county seat; **1882** Copper Queen Library established; **1902** incorporated as a city; **1908** fire destroys most of business district; **1914** U.S. Highway 80, now State Highway 80, built northwest through Mule Mountains to Tucson by life-term prison inmates; **July 1917** thousands of striking miners rounded up, delivered to middle of desert in Bisbee Deportation; **1929** county seat moved to Bisbee; **1931** Phelps Dodge Corporation achieves dominance through acquisitions; county courthouse completed; *Brewery Gulch Gazette* newspaper founded; **1935** miners' monument dedicated; **1971** Bisbee Mining Museum opened; **1975** mining operations cease.

Bowie *Cochise County   Southeastern Arizona, 90 mi/145 km east of Tucson*

1862 Fort Bowie established to protect emigrants against Apaches at eastern end of Apache Pass, most dangerous point on road to California; **1872** Chiricahua Indian Reservation established to east, revoked 1876; Native Americans moved north to San Carlos Reservation; **1896** fort abandoned, sold 1911; **1964** fort designated a National Historic Site.

Buckeye *Maricopa County* *Central Arizona, 30 mi/48 km west of Phoenix*

1888 town founded on Salt River; **1929** incorporated as a town; **1935** first Helzapoppin Rodeo held; **1958** Buckeye Public Library established; **May 25, 1985** first phase of Palo Verde Nuclear Power Plant begins production to west.

Bullhead City *Mohave County* *Western Arizona, 185 mi/298 km northwest of Phoenix, on Colorado River*

1857 Lt. Edward F. Brule leads camel train with assistance of Syrian camel driver Hadji Ali, nicknamed Hi-Jolly, experiment in desert military transport; **1910** Katherine Gold Mine discovered, closed 1930; **1949** Davis Dam built on Colorado River to north, completed 1953, forming Lake Mohave; town founded with dam construction; **1984** incorporated as a city; **1987** Laughlin Bridge built across Colorado River from Laughlin, Nevada.

Camp Verde *Yavapai County* *Central Arizona, 76 mi/122 km north of Phoenix*

c.1250 Montezuma's Well built to northwest; **1864** Camp Lincoln established by Arizona volunteer militia as Indian defense; town founded; **1886** fort and town renamed Camp Verde; **Dec. 8, 1906** Montezuma Castle National Monument proclaimed, preserves cliff dwellings; **1986** incorporated as a town.

Casa Grande *Pinal County* *Southern Arizona, 43 mi/69 km south-southeast of Phoenix*

1879 town founded; **June 22, 1892** Casa Grande National Monument established to northeast; **1915** town incorporated; **Nov. 4, 2001** man fights with Greyhound bus driver while in motion on I-10 causing crash, narrowly missed by semi truck, 33 injured.

Chandler *Maricopa County* *Central Arizona, suburb 17 mi/27 km southeast of Phoenix*

1891 ranch established in Salt River Valley by veterinarian Dr. Alexander J. Chandler; **1912** town platted by Dr. Chandler; **1915** Hotel San Marcos opened; **1920** incorporated as a town; **1954** incorporated as a city; **1985** Chandler-Gilbert Community College established; **1989** first annual Ostrich Festival held to celebrate new ostrich industry.

Chinle *Apache County* *Northeastern Arizona, 235 mi/378 km northeast of Phoenix*

1863–1864 Navajos gathered into Canyon de Chelly as their new home by Kit Carson; **winter 1864** about 10,000 Navajos subjected to 350 mi/563 km long march to Fort Sumner, southeastern New Mexico, held prisoner there for four years; **1882** trading post established by Denis M. Riordan in Navajo Indian Reservation; town founded around post at entrance to Canyon de Chelly; town name Navajo term for "water outlet"; **1910** Chinle Indian Boarding School established; **Feb. 14, 1931** Canyon de Chelly ("shay") National Monument authorized to east.

Clarkdale *Yavapai County* *Central Arizona, 90 mi/145 km north of Phoenix*

c.1100 Tuzigoot pueblo established, abandoned c.1450; **1895** branch of Atchison, Topeka & Santa Fe Railroad built; **1911** smelter built by United Verde Copper Company, later Phelps-Dodge Corporation; **1912** town founded in Verde Valley, named for U.S. Sen. William A. Clark; **July 25, 1939** Tuzigoot National Monument proclaimed; **1953** mining operations discontinued; **1957** incorporated as a town.

Clifton *Greenlee County* *Eastern Arizona, 163 mi/262 km east-southeast of Phoenix*

1867 group of Mexican placer gold miners arrives; **1872** first copper mining claims made; town founded; **1875** post office established; **1881** Southern Pacific Railroad reaches town; Clifton Cliff Jail built; **1882** Arizona Copper Company mine established; **1891** flash floods damage town; **Dec. 4, 1906** town's worst flood ruins 30 homes, 18 killed; **1909** Greenlee County formed; town incorporated, becomes county seat; **1911** county courthouse built.

Coolidge *Pinal County* *Southern Arizona, 45 mi/72 km southeast of Phoenix*

Aug. 3, 1918 Casa Grande National Monument proclaimed to west, renamed Casa Grande Ruins National Monument 1991; **1924** construction of Coolidge Dam authorized on Gila River 50 mi/80 km to east; **1926** town founded as support base for dam project and irrigated farming area; **1935** Casa Grande Farms agricultural community established by Resettlement Administration for farmers made destitute by economic depression; **1945** town incorporated; **1961** Central Arizona College (2-year) established; **May 6, 1971** plane crashes into cotton field, all 14 on board killed.

Douglas *Cochise County* *Southeastern Arizona, 103 mi/166 km southeast of Tucson, on Mexico border*

Sept. 5, 1886 Apache Chief Geronimo (1829–1909) surrenders to Gen. George Crook's forces in Skeleton Canyon to northeast ending five years of killing and plundering; **1900** site selected for smelter by Phelps Dodge Corporation for copper mines at Nacozari and Pilares, Mexico; **1901** El Paso & Southwestern (Southern Pacific) Railroad reaches town; town founded, named for Phelps Dodge president Dr. James Douglas; **1904** Copper Queen Smelter built; **1905** town incorporated; **1907** Calumet & Arizona Smelter built; **1911** Mexican troops surrender adjoining town of Agua Prieta to Capt. Red Lopez' volunteers to quell violence spilling into streets of Douglas; **Nov. 2, 1915** Agua Prieta attacked by Pancho Villa's rebels, defeated with U.S. assistance; attacks Columbus, New Mexico, March 1916 in retaliation; **1926** Company of Mary Novitiate founded; **1931**

Copper Queen Smelter closed; **1962** Cochise College, Douglas Campus (2-year) established; **1983** Arizona State Prison Complex completed, replacing prison at Florence.

Duncan   *Greenlee County*   *Southeastern Arizona, 112 mi/180 km east-northeast of Tucson*

1883 Arizona & New Mexico Railroad completed; town founded on Gila River; **March 26, 1930** Supreme Court Justice Sandra Day O'Connor born; **1938** incorporated as a town; **1949** Duncan Public Library founded.

Eager   *Apache County*   *Eastern Arizona, 165 mi/ 266 km east-northeast of Phoenix*

1878 homesteaded by the John Eager family; **1888** town founded; **1892** post office established; **1948** incorporated as a town; **Jan. 7, 1971** lowest temperature ever recorded in Arizona reached, −40°F/−40°C.

Flagstaff   *Coconino County*   *North central Arizona, 122 mi/196 km north of Phoenix*

1876 first settler F. F. McMillan builds shack at spring; town founded; **July 4, 1876** settlers strip towering pine tree of its branches, mount American flag at top, landmark for travelers, origin of town's name; **1881** store and saloon opened by Edgar Whipple; **1882** Atlantic & Pacific (Santa Fe) Railroad reaches town; Fort Moroni established to northwest by Mormons led by John W. Young, son of leader Brigham Young; **1891** Coconino County formed; town becomes county seat; **1894** town incorporated; Lowell Observatory founded by Dr. Percival Lowell at western edge of town; county courthouse built; **1899** Arizona State Teachers' College established, becomes Northern Arizona University; **Oct. 7, 1905** actor Andy Devine born (died 1977); **1915** City Library founded; **Nov. 30, 1915** Walnut Canyon National Monument proclaimed to east, preserves Pueblo cliff dwellings dating to 1200 A.D.; **Dec. 9, 1924** Wupatki National Monument proclaimed to northeast, preserves pueblos dating to 1065 A.D.; **1930** Clyde W. Tombaugh discovers planet Pluto at Lowell Observatory, predicted through calculations of Dr. Lowell; **May 26, 1930** Sunset Crater Volcano National Monument proclaimed to northeast; **1934** Museum of Northern Arizona built; **1948** Pulliam Airport established; **1981** Coconino Center for the Arts established; **1991** Coconino Community College established.

Florence   *Pinal County*   *South central Arizona, 50 mi/80 km southeast of Phoenix, near Gila River*

1866 Levi Ruggles becomes first settler; town founded; Ruggles House built; **1875** Pinal County formed; town becomes county seat; Silver King Hotel built, closed 1977; **1879** first county courthouse built, still standing; **1884** Sloan House built by William Clark, later owned by Richard E. Sloan, last territorial governor; **1891** second county courthouse completed; **1908** town incorporated; **1909** Arizona Territorial Prison opened, moved from

Yuma; **1911** Church of the Assumption (Catholic) built; **1921** Ashhurst-Hayden Diversion Dam built on Gila River 12 mi/19 km to east, bringing agriculture to area; **1983** state prison moved to Douglas.

Ganado   *Apache County*   *Northeastern Arizona, 212 mi/341 km northeast of Phoenix*

1870 first trading post established; town founded in Navajo Indian Reservation; **1876** post acquired by J. Lorenzo Hubbell; **Aug. 25, 1965** Hubbell Trading Post National Historic Site authorized; **May 29, 1993** Navajo Reservation in Arizona, New Mexico, and Colorado hit by unidentified illness, ten die, 23 treated at hospitals, later blamed on airborne dust particles containing sheep feces, identified as hantavirus disease.

Glendale   *Maricopa County*   *Central Arizona, suburb 10 mi/16 km northwest of northwest of Phoenix*

1883 irrigation canal built from Salt River by William J. Murphy; **1891** town founded by Murphy; **1906** beet sugar refinery built, closed 1916; **1910** incorporated as a city; **1941** Luke Army Air Base established, becomes Air Force Base 1951; **1965** Glendale Community College established; **2003** Glendale Arena completed, home of NAL Phoenix Coyotes.

Globe   *Gila County*   *East central Arizona, 75 mi/ 121 km east of Phoenix*

1876 nearly pure silver discovered; town founded, named for globe-shaped boulder near silver strike; **1880** silver boom ends; copper interests begin; **1881** Gila County formed; town becomes county seat; George W. P. Hunt, born 1859, arrives by burro from Missouri, becomes leading town merchant, serves as first governor of Arizona 1912 until his death 1934; **1883** Old Dominion Copper Company organized; **1886** capture of Geronimo ends Native American threat; **1895** Lewisohn brothers of New York buy Old Dominion, transform it into major copper producer; **1898** Southern Pacific Railroad reaches town; **1907** incorporated as a city; county courthouse built; **Aug. 6, 1908** tennis player Helen Hall Jacobs born (died 1997); **1909** The Lodge saloon opened; **1917** city's worst labor strike requires call-out of U.S. Cavalry; **1931–1933** mines closed during depression; nearly all miners go to work for WPA.

Grand Canyon   *Coconino County*   *Northern Arizona, 178 mi/286 km north of Phoenix, on Colorado River*

Aug.–Sept. 1869 eight-man expedition of John Wesley Powell passes through Grand Canyon in four rowboats; **1870** Powell makes second journey through canyon, explores side canyons; **Feb. 20, 1893** Grand Canyon Forest Preserve proclaimed; **1905** El Tovar Hotel built by hotelier Fred Harvey; **1907** Atchison, Topeka & Santa Fe Railroad reaches Grand Canyon from Williams; **Jan. 11, 1908** Grand Canyon National Monument proclaimed;

Feb. 26, 1919 Grand Canyon National Park established from national monument; Dec. 22, 1932 separate Grand Canyon National Monument proclaimed west of park, June 30, 1956 TWA Super-Constellation and United DC-7 airplanes collide over canyon, 128 killed; July 26, 1967 sightseeing plane hits canyon wall, seven killed; 1969 rail service ends; Jan. 3, 1975 Grand Canyon National Monument and Marble Canyon National Monument to northeast added to Grand Canyon National Park; 1989 rail service reinstated; Aug. 10, 2001 sightseeing helicopter crashes killing six, one survives.

Holbrook   *Navajo County   Eastern Arizona, 147 mi/237 km northeast of Phoenix*

1879 Juan Padilla becomes first settler at site on Little Colorado River; 1881 Atlantic & Pacific Railroad reaches site; town founded, named for engineer H. R. Holbrook; Sept. 4, 1887 shootout between Sheriff Commodore Owens and cattle rustler Andy Blevins leaves Andy, three others of Blevins family dead; 1895 Navajo County formed; town becomes county seat; 1898 county courthouse built; Dec. 8, 1906 Petrified Forest National Monument proclaimed to east, becomes National Park 1962; 1914 first church built ending notoriety as only county seat in U.S. without a church; 1917 town incorporated; 1927 U.S. Highway 66 reaches town; 1974 Northland Pioneer College (2-year) established.

Humboldt   *Yavapai County   Central Arizona, 72 mi/116 km north of Phoenix*

1899 post office established, originally named Val Verde; 1905 town renamed Humboldt for German explorer Alexander von Humboldt; 1906 copper mining begins; Arizona Smelting Company established; 1928 gold and silver discovered, start of mining boom; 1934 iron mining begins, ceases 1968.

Jerome   *Yavapai County   Central Arizona, 88 mi/ 142 km north of Phoenix*

1886 copper properties purchased by W. A. Clark of Montana; town founded, named for New York investor Eugene Jerome; 1895 Atchison, Topeka & Santa Fe Railroad reaches town; 1899 town incorporated; 1900 J. J. Fisher claims Little Daisy Copper Mine, becomes United Verde Extension Mine 1910; 1916 adobe Douglas Mansion built by James Douglas; 1917 Verde Central Mine established; labor strikes affect most mining operations; July 10, 1917 in Jerome Deportation, 200 pro-union volunteers "clean up" town, deport 75 anarchists comprised largely of itinerant workers; 1920 excavation of the Big Pit copper mine begins; 1938 Extension Mine closed; 1953 copper mining ends.

Kayenta   *Navajo County   Northeastern Arizona, 250 mi/402 km north-northeast of Phoenix*

March 20, 1909 Navajo National Monument proclaimed to west, has three elaborate cliff dwellings; 1910 Indian

school opened; 1910 trading post established; 1929 Kayenta Tuberculosis Indian Sanatorium established; June 29, 1970 Navajos and Hopis awarded 2,000,000 ac (810,000 ha) land claim in Arizona and New Mexico.

Kingman   *Mohave County   Western Arizona, 165 mi/266 km northwest of Phoenix*

1864 Mohave County formed; Mohave City becomes county seat, followed by Hardyville 1867, Cerbat 1873, Mineral Park 1877; 1881 town's first house built, destroyed by fire June 1903; 1882 Atchison, Topeka & Santa Fe Railroad built; town founded; 1883 post office established; 1887 county seat moved to Kingman; 1915 county courthouse completed; 1926 U.S. Highway 66 reaches town; 1936 Boulder (Hoover) Dam completed on Colorado River to northwest creating Lake Mead; March 29, 1939 movie stars Carol Lombard and Clark Gable are wed at St. John's Methodist Church; 1942 Kingman Army Air Field established, closed 1946; 1952 incorporated as a city; 1956 Ford Motor Proving Ground established at Yucca to south; Oct. 8, 1964 Lake Mead National Recreation Area established to north, extends into Nevada; 1971 Mohave Community College established; 1980 Interstate Highway 40 opened.

Lake Havasu City   *Mohave County   Western Arizona, 150 mi/241 km northwest of Phoenix*

1938 Lake Havasu formed on Colorado River by Parker Dam to south; 1963 town founded by Robert P. McCulloch Sr., originally named Site Six; 1971 London Bridge purchased from City of London when it was discovered to be sinking into Thames River, built 1831, rebuilt on arm of Lake Havasu; 1978 incorporated as a city; June 24, 1994 highest temperature ever recorded in Arizona reached, 128°F/53°C.

Litchfield Park   *Maricopa County   Central Arizona, suburb 17 mi/27 km west-northwest of Phoenix*

1903 U.S. Department of Agriculture plants boll-resistant Egyptian cotton in Salt River Valley; 1918 first commercial cotton produced in Arizona; town founded by Southwest Cotton Company, subsidiary of Goodyear Tire Company, manufactures tire cords; town renamed for Paul W. Litchfield, president of Goodyear; 1987 incorporated as a city.

Marana   *Pima County   Southern Arizona, 25 mi/ 40 km northwest of Tucson*

1890 Southern Pacific Railroad built; town founded; 1920 irrigation system developed by Edwin R. Post of Michigan; 1942 Marana Army Air Field established to west, closed after World War II, becomes Marana Northwest Regional Airport 1962; 1977 incorporated as a town; 1979 aggressive annexation expands town's land area to 115 sq mi/298 sq km; Apr. 8, 2000 Osprey tilt-rotor experimental aircraft crashes at Marana Airport killing all 19 Marines on board.

Marble Canyon   *Coconino County*   *Northern Arizona, 230 mi/370 km north of Phoenix, on Colorado River*

1864 ferrying point selected in Marble Canyon by Catholic missionaries, named Crossing of the Fathers; **Aug. 1869** John Wesley Powell expedition passes point in their descent of Colorado River; **1872** Lee's Ferry established by Mormon pioneer John D. Lee, executed 1877 for leading role in Mountain Meadows Massacre, Utah, 1857 [see Enterprise, Utah]; town founded; **1929** Navajo Bridge built, replaces ferry; **Jan. 20, 1969** Marble Canyon National Monument proclaimed; **Jan. 3, 1975** Grand Canyon National Park absorbs Marble Canyon National Monument.

Mesa   *Maricopa County*   *Central Arizona, suburb 12 mi/19 km east of Phoenix*

1878 town founded on Salt River by Mormon settlers; **1883** incorporated as a city; **1906** Mesa Public Library built; **1927** Arizona Mormon Temple built; **1931** city annexes adjacent suburbs; **1965** Mesa Community College established; **1977** Mesa Southwest Museum established; **1978** Mesa Centennial Convention Center opened; **1995** Arizona State University East established.

Miami   *Gila County*   *Central Arizona, 68 mi/109 km east of Phoenix*

1870s first mining claims made; **1907** site purchased by Cleve W. Van Dyke; town founded by settlers from Miami, Ohio; Miami Copper Company begins large-scale mining; **1908** Van Dyke House built; **1909** large reduction plants built at nearby town of Inspiration; **Oct. 11, 1909** Miami Townsite Day declared by Van Dyke; **1915** copper mining reaches peak; **Nov. 13, 1916** actor Jack Elam born (died 2003); **1918** town incorporated; **1923** *Silver Belt* newspaper moved from Globe by Cleve Van Dyke, founded 1878; **1926** Post Office built; **1931** copper production slumps.

Mocassin   *Mohave County*   *Northern Arizona, 240 mi/386 km north-northwest of Phoenix*

1856 party of Mormons, sent by Brigham Young to make peace with Navajo, camp at Pipe Spring; **1868** Mormon bishop S. P. Winsor builds fort called Winsor Castle over spring, only water source within 60 mi/97 km, to prevent it from being poisoned by Native Americans; **1871** first telegraph office in Arizona established; **1873** Kaibab Indian Reservation established; town founded as Indian agency; **May 31, 1923** Pipe Spring National Monument established.

Nogales   *Santa Cruz County*   *Southern Arizona, 62 mi/100 km south of Tucson, on Mexico border*

1691 Father Eusebio Francisco Kino establishes Tumacácori and Tubac missions in area; **1880** trading post established by Jacob Isaacson; town founded opposite Nogales, Mexico; **1882** Southern Pacific Railroad reaches town; **1893** town incorporated; **1897** fort built on Mexican side by Yaqui who raid Nogales, Mexico, driven off with aid of American militia; **1899** Santa Cruz County formed; town becomes county seat; **1904** county courthouse built; **Sept. 15, 1908** Tumacácori National Historical Park established to north; **1911** U.S. troops move in to defend town against Madero rebels in Mexico; Camp Little established, abandoned 1931; **1916** Pancho Villa's army takes Nogales, Mexico, from Madero rebels; National Guard erects barricades on border, many Villa rebels killed in cross-border shootout; **Aug. 26, 1918** border guard shoots and kills Mexican arms smuggler as he crawls under barbed wire, leads to armed conflict between two Nogaleses, c.75 Mexicans killed, 32 Americans killed or wounded; **1929** Nogales, Mexico, bombed during Manso-Topete rebellion, many Mexicans flee to U.S.

Oracle   *Pinal County*   *Southern Arizona, 30 mi/48 km north-northeast Tucson*

1880 Oracle Copper Mine established by Albert Weldon; town founded; **1895** Mountain View Hotel opened by "Curly" Bill Neal; **Dec. 1912** visiting Buffalo Bill Cody plays Santa Claus for miners' children; **1984** Biosphere 2 built at Mt. Lemmon to south, sponsored by philanthropist Edward P. Russ, highly publicized experiment in sustainability of life in enclosed environments, model for living in outer space; **Sept. 26, 1991** mission begins in Biosphere 2 with crew of four men, four women, ends Sept. 26, 1993; **1996** Earth Institute established by Columbia University, New York.

Oraibi   *Navajo County*   *Northeastern Arizona, 185 mi/298 km north-northeast of Phoenix*

c.1100 Oraibi Pueblo built; **1540** Coronado's Lt. Pedro de Tovar discovers Oraibi; **1629** San Francisco Mission established, destroyed during Pueblo revolt 1680; **1776** site visited by Father Garces; **1907** dissenting residents form new pueblos at Hotevilla and Bacavi (Bakabi).

Page   *Coconino County*   *Northern Arizona, 240 mi/386 km north of Phoenix, on Colorado River*

May 30, 1910 Rainbow Bridge National Monument, Utah, established to northeast; **1958** construction on Glen Canyon Dam begins on Colorado River; Glen Canyon Bridge built in front of dam; town founded at east end of bridge; Page Airport established; **1964** dam completed, forming large Lake Powell, extends into Utah; **Oct. 27, 1972** Glen Canyon National Recreation Area established, almost entirely within Utah; **1976** incorporated as a city.

Palo Verde   *Maricopa County*   See **Buckeye (1985)**

Parker *La Paz County* Western Arizona, 135 mi/217 km west-northwest of Phoenix, on Colorado River

1858 Fort Mohave established on Colorado River, abandoned 1861, reestablished 1869; **1864** over 70 dead emigrants from Texas and Arkansas discovered along the trail to east, killed and scalped by Native Americans; **1865** Colorado River Indian Reservation established, extends into California; **1867** irrigation system developed, completed 1871; **1871** Parker post office established at northern end of Colorado River Indian Reservation; **1905** Atchison, Topeka & Santa Fe Railroad built; post office moved 4 mi/6.4 km to railroad; **1908** town platted; **1910** ferry service established by Joe and Nellie Bush; **1934** Governor Moeur sends troops to Parker Dam site to stop its construction, opposed to diversion of water to California, overruled by U.S. Supreme Court; **1937** bridge built, ending ferry service; **1938** Parker Dam completed on Colorado River forming Lake Havasu; **1948** town incorporated; **1980** Parker South annexed; **1983** La Paz County formed from Yuma County; town becomes county seat; **1994** county courthouse built.

Payson *Gila County* Central Arizona, 68 mi/109 km northeast of Phoenix

1878 Bill Burch becomes first settler; **1882** town founded and platted by John H. Hise, Arizona's Surveyor-General, originally named Union Park; **1884** post office established; town renamed for Louis Edwin Payson, U.S. Senator from Illinois, who appointed Hise to his position; **1920s** author Zane Grey resides in cabin outside of town writing his books, cabin burned 1990; **1959** Beeline Highway (State Highway 89) built; **1973** town incorporated.

Peach Springs *Mohave County* Western Arizona, 162 mi/261 km northwest of Phoenix

1776 Franciscan Father Garces camps at springs while traveling to Hopi villages; **1874** Hualapai people subdued by whites, transported to Colorado Valley, where many die; **1882** Atchison, Topeka & Santa Fe Railroad built; town founded as Indian agency; **1883** Hualapai Indian Reservation established; **1915** U.S. government begins issuing cattle to impoverished Hualapai; **Oct. 16, 1971** sightseeing plane crashes to north, all ten on board killed.

Pearce *Cochise County* Southeastern Arizona, 70 mi/113 km east-southeast of Tucson

1872 Apache Chief Cochise captured at Dragoon Mountains hideout to west, on run 12 years, accused of leading raid in 1860 which he had nothing to do with, surrenders peacefully through effort of white "blood brother" stagecoach operator Tom Jeffords; **1894** rancher John Pearce strikes gold; town founded; **1904** gold mine closed following series of cave-ins; **1904** cyanide plant built to tap mine tailings.

Phoenix *Maricopa County* Central Arizona, on Salt River

c.500–1200 AD Hohokam settle area, develop sophisticated canal system; **1863** Arizona Territory created from New Mexico Territory; **1864** John Y. T. Smith arrives at Salt River, establishes hay camp to provide forage for Camp McDowell to northeast; **1867** prospector Jack Swilling builds irrigation canal system; **Oct. 1870** town founded, named for Egyptian Phoenix bird, symbol of immortality; Hancock's Store built, town's first building; **1871** Maricopa County formed; town becomes county seat; **1880** *Arizona Gazette* newspaper founded, becomes *Phoenix Gazette*; **1881** incorporated as a city; **1884** first Arizona Territorial Fair held, predecessor to state fair; **1885** Arizona Canal built for irrigation; **1887** Maricopa & Phoenix Railroad reaches city; **1889** territorial capital moved from Prescott; **1891** U.S. Indian School founded; rains on top of snow in mountains to east flood Salt River Valley, disintegrating city's adobe structures; **1895** Atchison, Topeka & Santa Fe Railroad reaches city from Prescott; **1901** territorial capitol, later state capitol, dedicated; **Jan. 1, 1909** U.S. Sen. Barry Goldwater born, Republican presidential nominee 1964 (died 1998); **1912** U.S. courthouse built; **Feb. 14, 1912** Arizona enters Union as 48th state; **1920** Phoenix College (2-year) established; Trinity Episcopal Cathedral completed; **1926** Southern Pacific Railroad arrives; **1927** Arizona Museum built; **1928** city hall/county courthouse completed; Brophy College established; **1929** Heard Museum founded by Dwight and Maie Heard, displays native culture and art; **1935** Sky Harbor airport established, later renamed Phoenix International Airport, first terminal built 1952; **1940** Desert Botanical Garden established; **May 26, 1948** female rock singer Stevie Nicks born; **1949** Grand Canyon University established; Phoenix Art Museum founded, opened 1959; **July 24, 1951** TV actress Linda Carter born; **June 9, 1954** Evelyn Smith, 23, kidnapped, $75,000 paid, released next day, Daniel Martin charged; **1957** Phoenix Symphony Orchestra founded; **May 9, 1959** actress Mare Winningham born; **June 8, 1959** 16 killed, 32 injured as bus carrying Mexican migrant workers hits tree, explodes; **1962** Phoenix Zoo opened; **1965** Maricopa County Complex completed; **1968** Phoenix Suns NBA basketball team established; Gateway Community College established; **1970** city's land area increases to 247 sq mi/640 sq km from 17 sq mi/44 sq km in 1950; **1972** Phoenix Civic Plaza Convention Center opened; Symphony Hall built; 40-story Bank One Center built; **1976** 31-story Bank of America built; University of Phoenix established; **June 2, 1976** *Arizona Republic* reporter Don Bolles, investigating organized crime and Arizona Racing Commission, killed by car bomb; **Nov. 6, 1977** contractor Max Dunlop and plumber James Robison convicted of plotting to kill state Attorney General Bruce Babbitt; **1978** Western International University established; **1979** South Mountain Community College established; **1984** Arizona State University West established; Arizona Science Center opened; **1985** Paradise Valley Community College established; **1988** Phoenix Cardinals

NFL football team moved from St. Louis, renamed Arizona Cardinals 1994; **June 1992** America West Arena opened; **1995** Central Library opened; **Oct. 9, 1995** saboteurs remove bolts from tracks to southwest causing Amtrak derailment, crewman killed, 100 injured; **1996** Phoenix Coyotes NHL hockey team established, formerly Winnipeg Jets; **July 1, 1996** 12 from Viper Militia paramilitary group arrested for plotting to blow up seven government buildings in city; **Sept. 3, 1997** Gov. Fife Symington found guilty on seven counts involving real estate dealings, resigns Sept. 5; **1998** Arizona Diamondbacks MLB baseball team established; Bank One Ballpark completed.

Picacho   *Pinal County   Southern Arizona, 60 mi/ 97 km south-southeast of Phoenix*

Feb. 1862 Confederate Capt. Sherod Hunter's Texas cavalry travel through Picacho Pass to southeast on way to Tucson; **Apr. 15, 1862** Arizona's only Civil War battle fought at Picacho Pass, Lt. James Barrett's forces ambushed by Capt. Sherod Hunter's band, Hunter's forces retreat, two Union killed, three captured; **1881** town founded.

Prescott   *Yavapai County   Central Arizona, 78 mi/ 126 km north-northwest of Phoenix*

1863 gold discovered by Joe Walker party; Fort Whipple established to north; Territory of Arizona created from New Mexico Territory by President Lincoln to counter Confederate sympathies; **1864** Yavapai County formed; town founded, becomes county seat; territorial capital moved from Chino Valley; governor's mansion built; territorial capitol built; **1867** capital moved to Tucson; **1873** Congress and Crown King gold mines established; **1877** capital returned to Prescott; **1881** Buckey O'Neill arrives from St. Louis, becomes mayor, killed at Battle of San Juan Hill July 2, 1898; **1883** town incorporated; **Dec. 31, 1886** Atchison, Topeka & Santa Fe Railroad reaches town five minutes ahead of contracted deadline; **1888** first Frontier Days Rodeo held; **1889** territorial capital moved to Phoenix; **1893** new route of Santa Fe Railroad built, extended to Phoenix 1895; **July 1900** fire sweeps business district; **1903** Carnegie Library built; **1908** statue of Buckey O'Neill mounted on horse dedicated; **Nov. 14, 1910** actress Rosemary De Camp born (died 2001); **1917** county courthouse built; **1928** Sharlot Hull Museum founded by historian Sharlot M. Hull (1870–1943); Prescott Airport established to north; **1966** Yavapai College (2-year) established.

Quartzsite   *La Paz County   Western Arizona, 121 mi/195 km west of Phoenix*

1856 Fort Tyson built; **1867** town founded, named for local mineral quartzite, "s" added by post office; **Dec. 16, 1902** popular Syrian camel driver Hadji Ali, known as Hi-Jolly, dies, buried at local cemetery, drove camel trains in area (born 1828) [see also Bullhead City]; **1989** incorporated as a town.

Roosevelt   *Gila County   Central Arizona, 55 mi/ 89 km east-northeast of Phoenix*

1300s cliff dwellings built to south by Pueblos; **Dec. 19, 1907** Tonto National Monument proclaimed to south, has ancient cliff dwellings; **1911** Roosevelt Dam completed on Salt River, forming Theodore Roosevelt Lake; town founded; **Oct. 1990** Roosevelt Lake Bridge completed behind dam; **1996** Roosevelt Dam raised, enlarging reservoir.

Safford   *Graham County   Southeastern Arizona, 84 mi/135 km northeast of Tucson*

1872 town founded on north bank Gila River, named for Gov. Anson P. K. Safford; Montezuma Irrigation Canal built; **1874** town relocated to south bank following flood; **1881** incorporated as a town; **1883** Graham County formed; Solomonsville (Solomon) becomes county seat; **1901** incorporated as a city; **1908** Crook National Forest established, later absorbed by Coronado National Forest; **1915** county seat moved to Safford; **1916** county courthouse built.

Saint Johns   *Apache County   Eastern Arizona, 170 mi/274 km northeast of Phoenix*

1874 Sol Barth wins several thousand head of sheep, thousands of dollars in card game with Mexicans; town founded by Barth on Little Colorado River; **1879** Apache County formed; town becomes county seat; **1880** Mormon settlers arrive led by Jesse N. Smith and David K. Udall; **1915** Lyman Lake formed by dam on Little Colorado River to south; **1917** county courthouse built; **Jan. 31, 1920** Cong. Stewart L. Udall born, U.S. secretary of Interior 1961–1969; **June 15, 1922** U.S. Cong. Morris K. Udall born, brother of Stewart Udall (died 1998); **1946** incorporated as a town.

Scottsdale   *Maricopa County   Central Arizona, suburb 7 mi/11.3 km east of Phoenix*

1888 George Washington Scott becomes first settler, plants barley, citrus, joined 1889 by brother Gen. Winfield Scott; town founded on Salt River, originally named Orangedale; **1894** town renamed Scottsdale; **1920** cotton gin established; **1927** Jokake Inn established as town's first resort; **1937** Taliesen West retreat and architectural school built by Frank Lloyd Wright; **1951** incorporated as a city; **1969** Scottsdale Community College established.

Show Low   *Navajo County   Eastern Arizona, 130 mi/209 km northeast of Phoenix*

1870 town founded as farming community; **1875** Corydon E. Cooley wins ranch from Marion Clark in card game of seven-up, Cooley challenged by Clark to "Show low and take the ranch," which he did; **1953** incorporated as a city; **June 2002** Rodeo-Chedeski Woodland Fire, largest forest fire in state's history, reaches edge of town, firefighter Leonard Gregg, 29, charged with setting wildfires which destroyed 400 homes.

Sierra Vista   *Cochise County   Southeastern Arizona, 60 mi/97 km southeast of Tucson*

1877 Camp Huachuca established as defense against Apaches; **1882** Camp Huachuca made permanent base, renamed Fort Huachuca; town founded; **1911** fort used as base camp for border patrols during Madera revolt in Mexico; **1956** incorporated as a city; **1962** Fort Huachuca becomes headquarters for U.S. Army Strategic Communications Command; **1971** fort annexed by city; **1977** Cochise College, Sierra Vista Campus (2-year) established.

Solomon   *Graham County   Southeastern Arizona, 86 mi/138 km northeast of Tucson*

1876 Isador E. Solomon opens general store; town founded by Jewish settlers on Gila River, originally named Solomonsville; **1879** Mormon settlers arrive; **1883** Graham County formed; town becomes county seat; **1915** county seat moved to Safford; **1940s** town name shortened to Solomon.

Superior   *Pinal County   Central Arizona, 55 mi/ 89 km east of Phoenix*

1875 Silver King silver mine opened; town founded; **1902** post office established; **1910** Magma Copper Mine established; **1914** narrow gauge Magma Arizona Railroad built; **1924** copper smelter built; Thompson Southwest Arboretum founded by William Boyce Thompson; **1971** Magma Mine closed; **1976** incorporated as a town.

Tempe   *Maricopa County   Central Arizona, suburb 7 mi/11.3 km east of Phoenix*

1872 trading post founded on Salt River; ferry established by trader Charles Trumbull Hayden; town founded; **1885** Arizona State Teachers College established, becomes Arizona State University; **Oct. 2, 1887** U.S. Sen. Carl Trumbull Hayden born (died 1972); **1894** incorporated as a town; **1908** Tempe Public Library founded; **Oct. 9, 1925** Robert H. Finch born, secretary of health, education, and welfare under President Nixon (died 1995); **1929** incorporated as a city; **1975** Tempe Symphony Orchestra founded; **1978** Rio Salado College (2-year) established.

Thatcher   *Graham County   Southeastern Arizona, 81 mi/130 km northeast of Tucson*

1881 town founded on Gila River by Mormons, named for apostle Moses Thatcher; **1888** St. Joseph Stake Academy founded, changed to Gila Junior College 1933, renamed Eastern Arizona College 1962; **1899** town incorporated.

Tombstone   *Cochise County   Southeastern Arizona, 63 mi/101 km southeast of Tucson*

1877 silver deposits discovered by Ed Schieffelin, establishes Tombstone Mine; **1879** town founded; Crystal Palace Saloon opened; **1880** *Tombstone Epitaph* newspaper founded; Wells-Fargo Office built; **1881** Cochise County formed; town becomes county seat; incorporated as a city; Bird Cage Theater built; Episcopal Church built; feud between shady lawmen of Wyatt Earp clan and Clanton-McLowery clan culminates in shootout at OK Corral; Billy Clanton and Ed and Tom McLowery killed, first to be buried "with boots on" at Boot Hill Cemetery, Earps flee to Colorado; **1882** old county courthouse built; city hall built; **Feb. 22, 1884** mob lynches John Heath from jail accused of killing six in Bisbee store holdup; **1890** large-scale mining activity ends; **1909** final attempt to drain mines fails, water had reached 500 ft/152 m years earlier, effectively ending mining; **1929** county seat moved to Bisbee.

Tortilla Flat   *Maricopa County   See **Apache Junction** (1872)*

Tubac   *Santa Cruz County   Southern Arizona, 42 mi/68 km south of Tucson*

1691 Tumacácori Mission founded to south by Father Kino; **1752** Spanish establish presidio; town founded; **1776** town serves as gathering site for Anzas colonizing party's journey to Pacific Coast; **1852** first Mormon settlers in Arizona arrive; **1859** *Weekly Arizonian* newspaper founded, first in territory; **1861** town abandoned after raids by outlaws, Apaches; **Sept. 15, 1908** Tumacácori National Monument proclaimed to south, becomes National Historical Park 1990; **1959** Tubac Presidio State Historical Park established; **1972** Tubac Center for the Arts founded.

Tucson   *Pima County   Southern Arizona, 105 mi/ 169 km southeast of Phoenix*

10,000 BC first known human habitations of Tucson Valley; **200 AD** Hohokam cultures occupy region, through c.1450; **1690s** first Spanish settlers arrive on Santa Cruz River; **1699** Mission of San Xavier del Bac founded by Father Eusebio Francisco Kino; **1775** San Jose del Tucson Mission (Tucson Presidio) established, "Tucson" Native American word for "dark spring"; **1797** present Mission building completed, begun 1783; **1822** Spanish rule ends in Mexico; **1846** U.S. takes control of New Mexico territory; **1853** Gadsden Purchase added to U.S.; **1856** First U.S. Dragoons occupy town; **1861** town occupied by Confederate troops; **1862** Fort Lowell established to southeast by California Volunteers of Union Army, moved north of Tucson 1873, abandoned 1886; **1863** Arizona Territory created; **1864** Pima County formed; town becomes county seat; **1867** territorial capital moved from Prescott; **1874** San Xavier Indian Reservation established to south; **1877** territorial capital returned to Prescott; incorporated as a city; **June 28, 1877** *Arizona Daily Star* newspaper founded; **1880** Southern Pacific Railroad reaches city; **1883** Tucson Public Library founded; **1885** University of Arizona established; **1888** Indian Training School founded by Presbyterian Church; **1897** San Augustin Roman Catholic Cathedral completed; **1900** Carnegie Library built, later becomes Children's Museum; **1919** Tucson Airport established to south, first commercial service 1928, becomes International Airport 1963; **1924** Tucson Museum of Arts founded, facility opened 1975; **1927** Temple of Music and Art built; **1929** Tucson Mountain Park created by county to west; **March 1, 1933** Saguaro National Monument proclaimed to east, smaller unit to west, becomes National Park 1994; **Jan. 25, 1934** bank robbers John Dillinger, Charles Mackley, Russell Clark, Harry Pierpont arrested with $36,000 loot; **Aug. 23, 1934** TV actress Barbara Eden born; **July 15, 1946** singer Linda Ronstadt born; **Nov. 29, 1949** comedian Garry Shandling born; **1958** Kitt Peak National Observatory established to southwest; **Dec. 20, 1970** fire at Pioneer International Hotel kills 28, injures 27; **1971** Tucson Convention Center opened; **1975** county courthouse built; **March 8, 1985** Thomas Creighton dies after receiving three heart transplants in four days at Arizona Medical Center, Center rebuked by medical professionals.

Wickenburg *Maricopa County* Central Arizona, *52 mi/84 km northwest of Phoenix*

1863 Henry Wickenburg discovers gold at Vulture Mine; town founded; **1866** town loses selection as territorial capital by two votes; **1890** dam under construction on Hassayampa River collapses, c.80 killed; **1905** destitute town founder Henry Wickenburg takes his own life with shotgun on his 85th birthday; **1909** incorporated as a city.

Willcox *Cochise County* Southeastern Arizona, *65 mi/105 km east of Tucson*

1880 Southern Pacific Railroad built; town founded, originally named Maley; **1889** town renamed for U.S Army Gen. Orlando B. Willcox, hero of Battle of Bull Run, Virginia; **Sept. 9, 1899** $10,000 train heist, constable Burt Alvord, deputy W. N. Stiles, and cattleman William Downing arrested, latter a member of Texas' Sam Bass gang; **1915** town incorporated; **Apr. 18, 1924** Chiricahua National Monument proclaimed to southeast, has volcanic rock formations.

Williams *Coconino County* Central Arizona, *124 mi/200 km north of Phoenix*

1878 cattleman Charles T. Rogers becomes first homesteader; **1881** town founded, named for trapper Bill Williams; **1882** Atlantic & Pacific (Santa Fe) Railroad reaches town; **1893** Kaibab National Forest established; large sawmill established; **1901** town incorporated; fire destroys large part of town; **1907** Atchison, Topeka &

Santa Fe Railroad built north to Grand Canyon, ends 1969, resumed 1989; **1927** U.S. Highway 66 reaches town.

Window Rock *Apache County* Northeastern *Arizona, 230 mi/370 km northeast of Phoenix*

1864 Window Rock becomes first stopping point on Navajo Long March from northeastern Arizona to Fort Sumner, eastern New Mexico; **1936** town founded on New Mexico boundary as Navajo Capital, named for sandstone formation; Navajo Administration Buildings built; **1961** Navajo Tribal Museum established, new facility opened 1997; **1963** Navajo Tribal Zoo opened; **July 20, 1989** council member Peter McDonald suspended on bribery charges, attempted to overthrow Tribal Council with 200 supporters (Peter's Patrol), two members killed by tribal police.

Winslow *Navajo County* East central Arizona, *132 mi/212 km northeast of Phoenix*

1882 Atchison, Topeka & Santa Fe Railroad built; town founded on Little Colorado River as railroad division point; **1900** incorporated as a city; **1905** test drilling begun at center of mile-wide Barringer Crater to west, eventually reveals hard mass thought to be remnant of meteor which fell 50,000 years before present; **1926** U.S. Highway 66 reaches town; **1929** Hotel La Posada built by Fred Harvey hotel system, designed by June Coler.

Yuma *Yuma County* Southwestern Arizona, *157 mi/253 km west-southwest of Phoenix, on Colorado River*

1540 navigator for Coronado expedition Hernando de Alarcón passes site on Colorado River; **1683** Father Eusebio Francisco Kino visits region; **1779** two missions founded on either side of river by Father Francisco Tomas Garces; **1781** Native Americans kill nearly all men of 150 colonists attending mass; **1848** region acquired by U.S.; **1849** ferry established by L. J. F. Jaeger; gold seekers pass through on way to California; **1850** Fort Yuma built; **1852** steamboat *Uncle Sam* begins service, ends 1854 when it runs aground below town; **1854** town founded; **1864** Yuma County formed; La Paz becomes county seat; placer gold rush begins on Colorado and Gila rivers; **1870** county seat moved to Yuma; **1873** region annexed by Arizona Territory; **1876** incorporated as a village; Arizona Territorial Prison built, moved to Florence 1909; **1878** Southern Pacific Railroad reaches town from California; **1902** incorporated as a town; **1909** Laguna Dam completed to northeast on Colorado River; last steamboats employed in construction of dam; **1914** incorporated as a city; **1915** highway bridge replaces ferry; **March 31, 1927** farm workers' labor leader Cesar Chavez born (died 1993); **1928** county courthouse built; **1938** Imperial Dam built on Colorado River to northeast; **1962** Arizona Western College (2-year) established; **1973** Yuma Civic and Convention Center opened; **1975** Yuma Art Center established in former railway station, destroyed by fire Apr. 1993; **1986** Yuma Botanical Gardens established.

Arkansas

South central U.S. Capital and largest city: Little Rock.

The region became part of the U.S. with the Louisiana Purchase in 1803. Arkansas Territory was established March 2, 1819. Arkansas was admitted to the U.S. as the 25th state June 15, 1836. It seceded as one of the Confederate states May 6, 1861, and was readmitted to the Union June 22, 1868.

Arkansas is divided into 75 counties, 10 of which have shared (two) county seats, a vestige of an earlier era when a natural feature such as a river or mountain ridge dissected some counties, making it difficult to maintain a single seat of government. The counties are divided into townships, but the townships have no government. Municipalities are classified as towns and cities; there are two classes of cities. See Introduction.

Arkadelphia   *Clark County*   *Central Arkansas, 65 mi/105 km southwest of Little Rock*

c.1807 area on Ouachita River first settled; **1811** John Hemphill arrives from South Carolina, establishes Hemphill Salt Works, abandoned after 1850; **1823** Clark County formed; town founded as county seat; **1857** incorporated as a town; Magnolia Manor house completed; **1874** incorporated as a city; **1886** Ouachita Baptist University established; **1890** Henderson State University established; **1899** county courthouse built; **1903** County Library built.

Arkansas City   *Desha County*   *Southeastern Arkansas, 110 mi/177 km southeast of Little Rock*

1838 Desha County formed, named for early settler Capt. Ben Desha; Napoleon becomes county seat; **1873** town founded on Mississippi River to replace town of Napoleon subject to repeated flooding; **1874** county seat moved from Napoleon; **1881** incorporated as a town; **1896** Desha Bank built; **1900** county courthouse built; **1935** opening of bottom land in Desha and Chicot counties to settlement sparks land rush; **1960** incorporated as a city.

Arkansas Post   *Arkansas County*   *Southeastern Arkansas, 80 mi/129 km southeast of Little Rock*

March 14, 1682 Rene Robert Cavelier de la Salle reaches mouth of Arkansas River in his descent of Mississippi River; **1686** Henri de Tonti descends Mississippi in search of La Salle, establishes Poste de Arkansas here on his return, oldest white settlement in state; **1717** John Law lures immigrants by producing limitless quantity of notes in Mississippi Bubble scheme, acquiring land for himself in area; **1719** boat loaded with 500 African slaves arrives; **1720** 800 immigrants from Alsatia, Germany, arrive; **Dec. 1720** collapse of Bubble scheme sends John Law packing for France, penniless colonists descend upon New Orleans, given land by Louisiana Gov. Bienville along section of river called the German Coast; **1722** shipment of flour from Louisiana saves remaining 47 colonists from starvation; **1727** Catholic mission established; **1763** Spanish take control of Louisiana Territory, rename town Fort Charles III; **1782** St. Mary's Catholic Church built; **1783** town attacked by Chickasaws, allies of British; **1804** town occupied by Americans; **1813** Arkansas County formed; town becomes county seat; **1817** post office established; **1819** capital of Arkansas Territory established; *Arkansas Gazette* newspaper founded by William E. Woodruff, moved to Little Rock 1822; **1821** territorial capital moved to Little Rock; **1855** county seat moved to De Witt; **Jan. 10, 1863** town captured by Union troops under Gen. John A. McClernand; **1880s** town declines with coming of railroads; **1929** Arkansas Post State Park established; **July 6, 1960** Arkansas Post National Memorial established, former state park.

Ash Flat   *Sharp County*   *Northern Arkansas, 123 mi/198 km north-northeast of Little Rock*

1856 town founded; post office established; **1868** Sharp County formed; Hardy becomes county seat, shared with Evening Shade after 1847; **1931** incorporated as a town;

1965 shared county seats at Hardy and Evening Shade abolished for single county seat at Ash Flat; **1967** county courthouse built; **1981** incorporated as a city.

Ashdown   *Little River County*   *Southwestern Arkansas, 140 mi/225 km southwest of Little Rock*

1867 Little River County formed; **1880** county organized; Richmond becomes county seat; **1890** town founded; **1892** incorporated as a town; **1902** county seat moved to Rocky Comfort; **1903** town's saloons abolished; **1906** county seat moved to Ashdown; **1907** county courthouse built; **1920** incorporated as a city; **1966** Millwood Lake formed by dam on Little River to east; **1968** Nekoosa-Edwards Paper Plant established.

Augusta   *Woodruff County*   *East central Arkansas, 75 mi/121 km northeast of Little Rock*

1848 trading post established on White River by Quaker Thomas Hough of Maryland; town founded, named for Hough's niece; **1852** incorporated as a town; **1862** Woodruff County formed; town occupied by Gen. Frederick Steele's Union troops, encamp at courthouse; **1865** town becomes county seat; **1868** militia kills ten carpetbaggers searching for Ku Klux Klansmen, martial law imposed; **1880s** Iron Mountain Railroad built 1 mi/1.6 km to south, town builds short line Augusta Railroad; **1902** county courthouse completed; **1931** incorporated as a city.

Batesville   *Independence County*   *Northern Arkansas, 90 mi/145 km north-northeast of Little Rock*

1812 area on White River first settled by John Reed of Missouri, establishes trading post; **1818** ferry established by Judge James Bates; **1820** Independence County formed; **1821** town founded as county seat; **1831** steamboat *Waverly* first to reach town; **1836** Batesville Academy founded, becomes Arkansas College 1872, renamed Lyon College 1876; **1849** incorporated as a town; **1892** incorporated as a city; **1900** White River Lock & Dam built for flood control; **1939** White River Wharf-Stadium built for water carnivals; **1940** county courthouse built.

Bauxite   *Saline County*   *Central Arkansas, 18 mi/29 km southwest of Little Rock*

1887 bauxite deposits discovered; **1900** town founded; **1896** first shipment of bauxite made for production of aluminum; **1918** bauxite production reaches peak; **1925** incorporated as a town; **1973** incorporated as a city; **1980s** Reynolds and Alcoa mines closed.

Benton   *Saline County*   *Central Arkansas, 20 mi/32 km southwest of Little Rock*

1815 first settlers arrive; **1827** salt works begins operation; **1835** Saline County formed; **1836** town founded on Saline River as county seat; **1838** horse race track established; **1848** incorporated as a town; **c.1895** pottery making becomes important industry; **1902** county courthouse completed; **1916** incorporated as a city; **1931** Benton Colony of Arkansas State Hospital founded; Benton Library founded.

Bentonville   *Benton County*   *Northwestern Arkansas, 170 mi/274 km northwest of Little Rock*

1830 Benton County formed; **1837** town founded as county seat; town and county named for U.S. Senator Thomas Hart Benton (1782–1858) of Missouri; **March 6, 1862** Confederate General Van Dorn encounters Union Gen. Franz Sigel, forces Sigel to retreat to Pea Ridge, preliminary skirmish prior to Battle of Pea Ridge; **March 6–8, 1862** Battle of Pea Ridge to northeast leads to Union victory under Gen. Sam Curtis, c.1,300 killed on each side; **1873** incorporated as a town; **1881** St. Louis, Arkansas & Texas Railroad built 5 mi/8 km to east, rival town of Rogers established; **1888** rail spur reaches town; **c.1890** county's apple industry established; **1905** incorporated as a city; **Feb. 13, 1905** lowest temperature ever recorded in Arkansas reached at Pond, near Gravette to west, −29°F/−34°C; **1915** Bella Vista Resort established by Rev. William S. Baker; **1928** county courthouse built; **1938** Ozark Christian College established; **1969** Wal-Mart Stores incorporated by Sam Walton, opened first store 1962 at nearby Rogers; **1989** North West Arkansas Community College established; **1996** County Administration Buildings completed.

Berryville   *Carroll County*   *Northwestern Arkansas, 145 mi/233 km northwest of Little Rock*

1833 Carroll County formed; **1835** Carrollton becomes county seat; **1850** town founded; **1875** county seat moved to Berryville; **1876** incorporated as a town; **1883** Eureka Springs becomes shared county seat with Berryville; **1902** Missouri & North Arkansas Railroad reaches town; Grand View Hotel built; **1945** incorporated as a city; **1972** County Electric Co-op building renovated as new county courthouse, built 1947.

Billstown   *Pike County*   See **Murfreesboro (1936)**

Blytheville   *Mississippi County*   *Northeastern Arkansas, 175 mi/282km northeast of Little Rock*

500 BC early inhabitants build mounds in region; **1812** Big Lake formed to west on chute of Little River by New Madrid Earthquake; **1833** Mississippi County formed; **1836** Osceola becomes county seat; **1853** Rev. Henry T. Blythe arrives from Virginia, builds house and church; **1879** town founded; **1888** cotton gin established by L. W. Gosnell; **1892** incorporated as a town; **1898** *Blytheville Plain Dealer* newspaper founded; **1901** Jonesboro, Lake City & Eastern Railroad reaches town; Blytheville becomes shared county seat with Osceola; **1902** St. Louis & Memphis Railroad reaches town; **1907** incorporated as a city; town of Chickasawba annexed; **1911** Federal Compress Company established; **1919** county courthouse built; **1921** Public Library organized; **1923** Blytheville Cotton Oil Mill founded; **1928** city hall built; **1929** Blytheville Canning Company founded; **Feb. 1937** Big Lake to west monitored for levee breaks during major flooding, good cotton land spared; **1937** garment factory opened; **1942** Blytheville Air Force Base established, becomes Eaker Air Force Base 1988, closed 1992, reopened as Arkansas International Airport; **1975** Mississippi County Community College established.

Booneville   *Logan County   Western Arkansas, 108 mi/174 km west-northwest of Little Rock*

1825 Walter Calhoun becomes first settler; **1828** post office established; **1873** Sarber County formed, renamed Logan County 1875; town becomes county seat; **1878** incorporated as a town; **1898** Choctaw & Memphis Railroad built; **1899** incorporated as a city; **1910** Arkansas Tuberculosis Sanatorium opened; **Jan. 16, 1911** baseball player Dizzy (Jay Hama) Dean born at rural town of Lucas to southwest (died 1974); **1928** county courthouse built.

Camden   *Ouachita County   Southern Arkansas, 95 mi/153 km south-southwest of Little Rock*

1783 Frenchman named Fabre establishes Ecore Fabre trading post; **1824** town founded, named Fabre's Bluff; **1829** Union County formed; town becomes county seat; **1841** cotton gin established; **1842** Ouachita County formed; town becomes county seat; Union County seat moved to Champagnolle Landing; **1844** town renamed for Camden, South Carolina, home town of Gen. Thomas Woodward; **1860** woolen mill established, Confederate uniforms made; **Apr. 18, 1864** in Battle of Poison Spring, Union supply train captured by Confederates; **1889** incorporated as a city; **1926** lock and dam built on Ouachita River; **1927** Southern Kraft Pulp Mill built; **1933** county courthouse built.

Champagnolle Landing   *Union County
Southern Arkansas, 112 mi/180 km south of Little Rock*

1818 first few settlers arrive on Ouachita River, one of the oldest settlements in Southern Arkansas; town named Scarborough, serves as river port; **1829** Union County formed; Camden becomes county seat; **1842** town becomes new county seat, renamed Union Courthouse; **1844** county seat moved to El Dorado; town renamed Champagnolle Landing; **c.1900** town declines with coming of railroads; **1934** Lion Oil Company shipping station established.

Clarendon   *Monroe County   East central Arkansas, 63 mi/101 km east of Little Rock*

1819 post office established on White River, named Mouth of the Cache; **1823** ferry established by John Maddox; **1829** Monroe County formed; Lawrenceville becomes county seat; **1837** town renamed Clarendon; **1857** county seat moved to Clarendon; **1898**

incorporated as a town; **1899** incorporated as a city; **1911** county courthouse built; **1927** levees give way, inundating town with 18 ft/5.5 m of water; **1937** new levee system completed.

Clarksville   *Johnson County   Northwestern Arkansas, 92 mi/148 km northwest of Little Rock*

1833 Johnson County formed; **1836** town founded on Arkansas River as county seat; **1838** county courthouse built; **1840** coal mining begins; **1848** incorporated as a town; **1891** College of the Ozarks moved from Cane Hill, founded 1834; **1929** natural gas production begins; **1938** first annual Peach Festival held; **1950** incorporated as a city.

Clinton   *Van Buren County   North central Arkansas, 65 mi/105 km north of Little Rock*

1825 first settlers arrive; **1833** Van Buren County formed; Bloomington becomes county seat; **1842** town founded on Little Red River; **1846** county seat moved to Clinton; **1851** incorporated as a town; **1934** county courthouse built; **1938** incorporated as a city.

Combs   *Madison County   See* **Huntsville (1910)**

Conway   *Faulkner County   Central Arkansas, 27 mi/43 km north-northwest of Little Rock*

c.1770 French trading post established at Cadron settlement, on Arkansas River to west; **1820s** Conway family arrives, establishes plantation; **1871** Little Rock & Fort Smith Railroad built; town founded; **1873** Faulkner County formed, named for "Arkansas Traveler" Sanford C. Faulkner; town becomes county seat; **1875** incorporated as a town; **1876** Hendrix College established; **1892** Central Baptist College for women established; **1905** incorporated as a city; **1907** University of Central Arkansas established; **1936** county courthouse built.

Corning   *Clay County   Northeastern Arkansas, 170 mi/274 km northeast of Little Rock*

1873 Clay County formed; town founded on Black River as county seat; **1877** incorporated as a town; county seat moved to Boydsville; **1881** Corning becomes western district county seat, Boydsville remains eastern district county seat; **1888** eastern county seat moved to Piggott; **1939** incorporated as a city; **1966** county courthouse built.

Danville   *Yell County   West central Arkansas, 72 mi/116 km west-northwest of Little Rock*

1840 Yell County formed, named for Archibald Yell, second Arkansas governor; **1842** town founded as county seat; **1872** steamboat service inaugurated on Petit Jean Creek by Captain Howell; **1875** Dardanelle becomes shared county seat; **1899** incorporated as a town; **1944** incorporated as a city; **1975** county courthouse built.

Dardanelle *Yell County* *Central Arkansas, 65 mi/ 105 km northwest of Little Rock*

1819 trading post established here on Arkansas River; **1836** town founded, named for similarity of rock peninsula to strait at entrance to Black Sea; **1840** Yell County formed; **1843** Danville becomes county seat, **1855** incorporated as a town; **1875** Dardanelle becomes shared county seat with Danville; **1914** county courthouse built; **1928** incorporated as a city; Mount Nebo State Park established; **1929** highway bridge built across Arkansas River; **1969** Dardanelle Lake formed by Dardanelle Lock & Dam on Arkansas River, part of project opening barge traffic to Tulsa.

De Queen *Sevier County* *Southwestern Arkansas, 140 mi/225 km southwest of Little Rock*

1828 Sevier County formed; Paraclifta becomes county seat; **1871** county seat moved to Lockesburg; **1896** Kansas City Southern Railroad built; town founded, named for Dutch capitalist De Geoijen, anglicized; **1897** incorporated as a town; *De Queen Bee* newspaper founded; **1904** incorporated as a city; **1907** county seat moved to De Queen; **1933** county courthouse built; **1977** De Queen Lake formed by dam to north on Rolling Fork River.

Des Arc *Prairie County* *East central Arkansas, 55 mi/89 km east-northeast of Little Rock*

1810 first settlers arrive; **1820s** town founded on White River, named Francisville; **1846** Prairie County formed; Brownsville becomes county seat; **1848** town renamed Des Arc; **1854** incorporated as a town; **1868** county seat moved to De Valls Bluff; **1875** Des Arc becomes shared county seat with De Valls Bluff; **1903** rice production begins; **1914** county courthouse built.

De Valls Bluff *Prairie County* *East central Arkansas, 53 mi/85 km east of Little Rock*

1846 Prairie County formed; Brownsville becomes county seat; **1851** town founded on White River; **1862** Memphis & Little Rock Railroad reaches town, work suspended during Civil War, completed 1871; **1866** incorporated as a town; **1868** county seat moved to De Valls Bluff; **1875** Des Arc becomes shared county seat; **1939** county courthouse built; **1965** incorporated as a city.

De Witt *Arkansas County* *Eastern Arkansas, 70 mi/113 km east-southeast of Little Rock*

1813 Arkansas County formed; **1854** town founded near La Grue River; Haliburton House built; **1855** county seat moved from Arkansas Post; **1876** incorporated as a town; **1893** Stuttgart becomes shared county seat with De Witt; **1933** third county courthouse completed; **1933** incorporated as a city.

El Dorado *Union County* *Southern Arkansas, 120 mi/193 km south of Little Rock*

1829 Union County formed; Camden becomes county seat; **1842** county seat moved to Champagnolle Landing; **1843** Matthew Rainey's wagon breaks down, sells possessions, builds cabin; **1844** town founded as new county seat; county courthouse built; **1848** First Presbyterian Church organized; **1851** incorporated as a town; **c.1860** *Union* newspaper begins publication, changed to *True Southern* with Civil War; **1870** town reincorporated; **1891** Camden & Alexander Railroad reaches town; **1903** Little Rock Southern Railroad reaches town; **1905** incorporated as a city; El Dorado Junior College established, becomes South Arkansas Community College 1975; **Jan 10, 1921** first discovery of oil west of town at Busey well, over 400 producing wells established by Oct.; **1922** large oil reserve discovered to north, depleted by 1940; **1928** county courthouse built; **1937** Shuler Oil Field opened; **1943** Goodwin Field airport established to west, becomes South Arkansas Regional Airport 1991; **1956** South Arkansas Symphony Orchestra founded; **1986** Museum of Natural Resources opened at Smackover to north.

Elaine *Phillips County* See **Helena (1919)**

Eureka Springs *Carroll County* *Northwestern Arkansas, 155 mi/249 km northwest of Little Rock*

1833 Carroll County formed; Carrollton becomes county seat; **1856** first settler Dr. Alvah Jackson discovers healing properties of spring waters; **1875** county seat moved to Berryville; **1879** town founded; **1880** incorporated as a town; **1881** incorporated as a city; **1883** Eureka Springs becomes shared county seat with Berryville; **1886** Crescent Hotel opened; **1892** New Orleans Hotel opened; **1901** Palace Bath House built; **1902** Missouri & North Arkansas Railroad built through town; **1905** Basin Park Hotel opened; **1906** St. Elizabeth's Catholic Church built, top of bell tower accessible at street level in steep terrain; **1908** county courthouse completed; **1911** temperance leader Carrie Nation delivers final speech months before her death; **1948** first annual Ozark Folk Festival (Barefoot Ball) held.

Fayetteville *Washington County* *Northwestern Arkansas, 155 mi/249 km northwest of Little Rock*

1828 Washington County formed; town founded as county seat; **1830s** Waxhaws House built by Archibald Yell; **1836** incorporated as a town; **c.1838** Fayetteville Female Seminary founded; **c.1840** George Reed House built; **c.1847** Tibbetts House built, used as headquarters by Union troops 1863; **1854** Quesenbury House built; **1871** University of Arkansas established; **1904** old county courthouse built; **1883** incorporated as a city; **1888** Agricultural Experiment Station of University of Arkansas established; **March 9, 1902** architect Edward Durell Stone born (died 1978); **1916** Fayetteville Public Library established, new library built 1992; **1954** North Arkansas Symphony Orchestra founded; **1986** Arkansas

Air Museum founded; **1990** new county courthouse established in former bank building.

Fordyce   *Dallas County   Southern Arkansas, 70 mi/ 113 km south of Little Rock*

1845 Dallas County formed; Princeton becomes county seat; **1883** town founded near Moro River; **1884** incorporated as a town; **c.1900** lumber industry becomes important; **1907** incorporated as a city; **1908** county seat moved to Fordyce; county courthouse built; **c.1910** A. B. Banks House built.

Forrest City   *Saint Francis County   Eastern Arkansas, 100 mi/161 km east-northeast of Little Rock*

1827 St. Francis County formed; Franklin becomes county seat; **1841** county seat moved to Madison; **1867** town founded as construction camp on Memphis & Little Rock Railroad; town named for Confederate Gen. Nathan B. Forrest; **1871** incorporated as a town; **1875** county seat moved to Forrest City; **1920** peach orchards planted on Crowley's Ridge; **Feb. 14, 1932** country singer Charlie Rich born; **Apr. 13, 1946** singer Al Green born; **1974** East Arkansas Community College established; **1972** county courthouse built.

Fort Smith   *Sebastian County   Northwestern Arkansas, 140 mi/225 km west-northwest of Little Rock*

1817 military post founded on Arkansas River; town founded; **1822** the *Robert Thompson* becomes first steamboat to reach town site; **1838** larger fort begun, work halted 1843 short of completion; **1842** incorporated as a city; **1844** horse racing begins at Race Track Prairie; **1848** town serves as supply point for California Gold Rush; Weaver House built; **1851** Sebastian County formed; Greenwood becomes county seat; **1853** St. Anne's Academy founded; **1857** brewery built by Joseph Knobel; **1861** Fort Smith becomes shared county seat with Greenwood; **1867** Fort Smith National Cemetery established at fort, burial ground originally founded 1832; **1875** Judge Isaac Parker of Missouri, the "hanging judge," appointed to federal bench, responsible for 79 hangings until his death 1896; **1879** Little Rock & Fort Smith Railroad reaches city; **1882** St. Louis, Arkansas & Texas Railroad reaches city; **1887** Opera House built, closed 1911; **1901** natural gas wells drilled to south; **1926** Fort Smith Regional Airport established; **Nov. 9, 1930** actor Charlie Jones born; **Nov. 21, 1934** actor Laurence Luckinbill born; **1936** Lake Fort Smith built in hills to northeast; **1937** county courthouse built; **1941** Fort Chaffee Military Reservation established to southeast; **Sept. 13, 1961** Fort Smith National Historic Site authorized, preserves two frontier forts and federal courthouse; **1969** James W. Trimble Lock & Dam built on Arkansas River to east; **Jan. 2001** Fort Smith Convention Center opened.

Greenwood   *Sebastian County   Western Arkansas, 127 mi/204 km west-northwest of Little Rock*

1851 Sebastian County formed; town founded as county seat and as coal mining center; **1861** county divided into two districts; Fort Smith becomes shared county seat in Northern District, Greenwood becomes shared county seat of Southern District; **1884** incorporated as a town; **1916** county courthouse built; **1941** Fort Chaffee Military Reservation established to north; **1951** incorporated as a city; **Oct. 2000** Coal Miners Memorial dedicated.

Hamburg   *Ashley County   Southeastern Arkansas, 120 mi/193 km south-southeast of Little Rock*

1848 town founded; **1849** Ashley County formed; town becomes county seat; **1854** incorporated as a town; **1931** Overflow National Wildlife Refuge established; **1941** incorporated as a city; **1969** county courthouse completed.

Hampton   *Calhoun County   Southern Arkansas, 95 mi/153 km south of Little Rock*

1848 Nathaniel Hunt becomes town's first settler; **1851** Calhoun County formed; town founded as county seat on land donated by Hunt, named for Col. John R. Hampton; **1853** incorporated as a town; **1860s** Civil War brings total destruction to town, its economy ruined; **1877** town reincorporated following Civil War; **1883** St. Louis, Arkansas & Texas Railroad reaches town; **1910** county courthouse completed; **1944** incorporated as a city.

Harrisburg   *Poinsett County   Northeastern Arkansas, 118 mi/190 km northeast of Little Rock*

1838 Poinsett County formed, named for Joel R. Poinsett of South Carolina, secretary of war under President Van Buren; Bolivar becomes county seat; **1857** town founded as new county seat on land donated by Benjamin Harris; **1883** incorporated as a town; **1918** county courthouse completed; **1949** incorporated as a city.

Harrison   *Boone County   Northern Arkansas, 125 mi/201 km north-northwest of Little Rock*

1830s Cherokee and Osage people removed to Indian Territory; **1860** town founded; **1869** Boone County formed; **1873** town becomes county seat; **1876** incorporated as a town; **1902** Missouri & North Arkansas Railroad built; **1909** county courthouse built; **1910** incorporated as a city; **1974** North Arkansas Community College established.

Heber Springs   *Cleburne County   North central Arkansas, 60 mi/97 km north-northeast of Little Rock*

1881 town founded on Little Red River, originally named Sugar Loaf; **1882** incorporated as a town; **1883** Cleburne County formed; town becomes county seat; **1907** town renamed Heber Springs; **1915** county courthouse complete; **1957** incorporated as a city; **1962** Greers Ferry Lake formed by dam on Little Red River.

ARKANSAS

Helena *Phillips County* *Eastern Arkansas, 110 mi/ 177 km east of Little Rock*

1820 Sylvanus Phillips becomes first settler; town platted on Mississippi River by Phillips, named for daughter; **1820** Phillips County formed; **1830** town becomes county seat; **1831** post office established; **1833** incorporated as a town; **1855** yellow fever epidemic ravages town; **1856** incorporated as a city; **1862** town occupied by Gen. Samuel Curtis' Union forces; **July 4, 1863** in Battle of Helena, Curtis' army attacked by Confederate generals Holmes, Marmaduke, and Walker, strained feelings between latter two leads to duel in which Walker is killed; **1870** Arkansas Central Railroad reaches town from Clarendon to west; **1881** Iron Mountain Railroad reaches town from north; **1890** Helena Ferry established; **1909** Missouri & North Arkansas Railroad reaches town from northwest; **1915** county courthouse completed; **Sept. 30– Oct. 6, 1919** racial unrest centered on town of Elaine to southwest leaves several whites dead, at least 100 blacks killed; **1938** Walridge Knitting Mill founded; **1941** "King Biscuit Time" blues radio program begins on KFFA radio, presented by King Biscuit Flour Company; **1961** highway bridge built across Mississippi River to Lula, Mississippi; **1965** Phillips Community College of University of Arkansas (2-year) established.

Hope *Hempstead County* *Southwestern Arkansas, 115 mi/185 km southwest of Little Rock*

1818 Hempstead County formed; **1824** Washington becomes first permanent county seat; **1872** town founded; **1875** incorporated as a town; **1888** Bruner Ivory Handle Factory founded; **1906** incorporated as a city; **1927** Fruit and Truck Branch Experiment Station established by University of Arkansas; **1938** county seat moved to Hope; **1939** county courthouse built; **Aug. 19, 1946** William Jefferson "Bill" Clinton, 42nd U.S. President, born, house built 1917; **1966** University of Arkansas Community College of Hope established; **1977** first Watermelon Festival held.

Hopefield *Crittenden County* *Eastern Arkansas, 2 mi/3.2 km west of Memphis*

May 1795 Fort San Fernando de las Barrancas built by Spanish at site of Memphis; **1797** Spanish forced to move to west side of Mississippi River under pressure from U.S., built Fort Esperanza; town founded above fort by Benjamin Foy of Holland opposite Chickasaw Bluffs (now Memphis); **1857** Arkansas' first railroad, the Memphis & Little Rock Railroad, establishes eastern terminus here; town founded; **1858** post office established; **1863** Union forces burn town; **Apr. 27, 1865** steamboat *Sultana* explodes upstream killing estimated 1,800 to 2,000 people; **1909** flooding Mississippi sweeps away remainder of town; post office closed.

Hot Springs *Garland County* *Central Arkansas, 50 mi/80 km west-southwest of Little Rock*

Dec. 1804 William Dunbar and Dr. George Hunter commissioned by President Jefferson to explore Ouachita River, discover huts at springs of non-native construction, probably made by trappers; **1807** Jean Emanuel Prudhomme becomes first settler; **1820** Joseph Millard opens first hotel, closed by c.1825; **1828** Ludovicus Belding of Massachusetts arrives with family, opens hotel; **1830** Asa Thompson opens first bathhouses; **Apr. 20, 1832** Hot Springs Reservation created by U.S. government, centered on 47 hot mineral springs; **1851** incorporated as a town; **1873** Garland County formed; town becomes county seat; **1875** "Diamond Jo" Railroad completed from Malvern by Chicago industrialist "Diamond Jo" Reynolds, unhappy with rough road; **1876** incorporated as a city; **1902** Majestic Hotel built; **1904** Oaklawn Jockey Club established; **1905** county courthouse completed, damaged by fire 1913; **Sept. 3, 1913** actor Alan Ladd born (died 1964); **Sept. 5, 1913** fire levels over 1,000 buildings in 50-block area; **March 4, 1921** reservation designated Hot Springs National Park; **1924** Lake Catherine formed by Remmel Dam to southeast on Ouachita River; **1931** Lake Hamilton formed by Carpenter Dam on Ouachita River; **1953** Lake Ouachita formed by dam to northwest on Ouachita River; **1973** Garland County Community College established.

Huntsville *Madison County* *Northwestern Arkansas, 143 mi/230 km northwest of Little Rock*

1836 Madison County formed; town founded as county seat; **1837** post office established; **1877** incorporated as a town; **Jan. 7, 1910** Gov. Orval Eugene Faubus born at rural Combs to southeast, attempted to block Little Rock school desegregation effort 1957 (died 1994); **1924** incorporated as a city; **1939** county courthouse built.

Jacksonville *Pulaski County* *Central Arkansas, 17 mi/27 km northeast of Little Rock*

1850 Russell Beall family become first settlers; **1865** black community of Mount Pisgah developed by Robert Beall, former Beall family slave; **1870** Cairo & Fulton Railroad reaches town; **1934** hail storm strips peach and pear crops, citizens band together in emergency canning operation; **1940** Arkansas Ordnance Plant established, closed 1945; **1941** incorporated as a town; **1949** incorporated as a city; **1952** Little Rock Air Force Base established; **1996** dioxin cleanup begins at ordnance plant site.

Jasper *Newton County* *Northern Arkansas, 112 mi/180 km northwest of Little Rock*

1832 Diamond Cave discovered to west by Sam and Andrew Hudson; Hudson brothers build log cabin; **1842** Newton County formed; town founded as county seat near Buffalo River; **1843** post office established; **1896** incorporated as a town; **1940** county courthouse built; **1947** incorporated as a city.

Jerome *Drew County* *Southeastern Arkansas, 115 mi/185 km southeast of Little Rock*

1900 town founded on Bayou Bartholomew, named Blissville; **1908** incorporated as a town; **1920** town renamed; **1939** entire town purchased by Farm Security Administration for rehabilitation project; **1943** Jerome Relocation Center established as Japanese American internment camp, closed 1944; **1965** incorporated as a city.

Jonesboro *Craighead County* *Northeastern Arkansas, 132 mi/212 km northeast of Little Rock*

1829 Daniel Martin family settles to southwest; **1859** Craighead County formed, named for state Sen. Thomas B. Craighead; town founded as county seat, named for state Sen. William Jones; **1863** Confederates drive Union troops out of town; **1867** *Jonesboro Register* newspaper founded; **1878** Cobb House built; **1882** Texas & St. Louis Railroad reaches town; **1883** St. Louis-San Francisco Railroad reaches town; incorporated as a town; Lake City becomes shared county seat; **1892** incorporated as a city; **1909** Arkansas State University established; **c.1910** rice production begins; **1921** Riceland Rice Mill established, one of largest rice mills in world; **1934** county courthouse built; **March 6, 1942** actor Ben Murphy born; **Feb. 8, 1955** author John Grisham born; **March 24, 1998** Michael Johnson, 13, and Andrew Golden, 11, shoot and kill four fellow students, teacher, wound ten at Westside Middle School.

Kingsland *Cleveland County* *Southern Arkansas, 67 mi/108 km south of Little Rock*

Apr. 25, 1864 in Battle of Marks' Mill to south, Union Gen. Powell Clayton surprised by Confederates under Gen. James F. Fagan, large amount of supplies and prisoners captured; **1882** post office established; **1884** incorporated as a town; **Feb. 26, 1932** country singer Johnny Cash born (died 2003); **1958** incorporated as a city.

Lake City *Craighead County* *Northeastern Arkansas, 145 mi/233 km northeast of Little Rock*

Dec. 16, 1811 first tremors of New Madrid Earthquake, continue for more than a year; **1859** Craighead County formed; Jonesboro becomes county seat; **1878** town founded on St. Francis River; **1883** town becomes shared county seat with Jonesboro; county courthouse built; **1898** incorporated as a town; **1961** incorporated as a city.

Lake Village *Chicot County* *Southeastern Arkansas, 125 mi/201 km southeast of Little Rock*

1823 Chicot County formed; Villemont becomes first county seat; **1847** county seat moved to Columbia; **1857** town founded on Lake Chicot, oxbow lake in old channel of Mississippi River; county seat moved to Lake Village; **June 6–7, 1864** town occupied for one day by Union troops of General A. J. Smith following Battle of Bitch Bayou to south, Confederate General J. S. Marmaduke

forced to retreat, 40 Union killed, 4 Confederates killed; **1895** incorporated as a town; **1910** Confederate Soldier Statue erected; **Apr. 1923** Charles A. Lindbergh stops here en route by plane from Houston to St. Louis, makes first night landing ever made, takes citizens on short rides; **1931** Lake Village Library established; **1935** U.S. opens bottom land in Chicot and Desha counties for settlement sparking land rush; **1937** incorporated as a city; **1940** bridge built across Mississippi River from Greenville, Mississippi; **1956** county courthouse built; **1985** Lake Chicot Pumping Station built to remove silt from lake.

Lewisville *Lafayette County* *Southwestern Arkansas, 135 mi/217 km southwest of Little Rock*

1827 Lafayette County formed; **1842** town founded as county seat; **1850** incorporated as a town; **1882** Texas & St. Louis (St. Louis Southwestern) Railroad built, town site relocated to railroad; **Apr. 4, 1928** writer, poet Maya Angelou born at rural town of Stamps to east; **1937** incorporated as a city; **1942** county courthouse built.

Little Rock *Pulaski County* *Central Arkansas, 145 mi/233 km west-southwest of Memphis, on Arkansas River*

1722 site named *Petite la Roche* by French hunters for small outcrop of rock on south side of Arkansas River; hunter William Lewis becomes first white settler; **1818** Pulaski County formed; **1819** William Russell of St. Louis plats town; **1821** territorial capital moved from Arkansas Post; town becomes county seat; **1822** *Arkansas Gazette* newspaper moved from Arkansas Post; **March 16, 1822** first steamboat *Eagle* arrives; **1831** incorporated as a city; **June 15, 1836** Arkansas enters Union as 25th state; city becomes state capital; **1839** ferry established; **1862** first train arrives on north bank of Arkansas River; **Dec. 6, 1862** Claiborne Jackson, exiled governor of Missouri, dies of pneumonia (born 1807); **Sept. 1863** Confederate Gen. Sterling Price's troops set eight steamboats afire as Union forces of Gen. Frederick Steele advance, capture city Sept. 10; **1873** Baring Cross Bridge built across river, destroyed by flood 1927, rebuilt 1929; **Apr. 1874** two Republican candidates claim victory in governor's race, Rev. Joseph Brooks entrenches himself in Capitol while nominee Elisha Baxter sets up office outside, leads to Brooks-Baxter War, armed tension ends when President Grant declares Baxter winner; **Jan. 26, 1880** World War II Gen. Douglas MacArthur born at U.S. Army Barracks to north (died 1964); **1882** St. Andrew's Cathedral completed; State Hospital for Nervous Diseases built; **Jan. 3, 1886** poet John Gould Fletcher born (died 1950); **1887** county courthouse built, addition built 1915, remodeled 1996; **1889** Arkansas Confederate Home established, closed 1963; **1890s** Pulaski Heights section developed; **1896** Temple B'Nai Israel built; **1909** state capitol completed, begun 1899; **1910** state penitentiary established, closed 1933; **1917** Camp Pike established north of city, later renamed Camp Joseph T. Robinson; **1924** Federal Reserve Bank built; **1926** Adams Field airport established to east, renamed Little Rock National Airport 1937; **1927** Little Rock Junior College established, becomes University of Arkansas at Little Rock; **1931** Thomas C. McRae Sanatorium for black tuberculosis patients opened; Arkansas School for the Deaf built; **1938** Greater Little Rock Stockyards established in North Little Rock; **1939** Robinson Center Music Hall built; Arkansas School for the Blind built; Public Library built; **1940** Robinson Memorial Auditorium built; **1957** Lake Maumelle formed by dam on Big Maumelle River to west; **Sept. 4, 1957** National Guard called out by Gov. Orval Faubus to block integration of schools by nine black students, Sept. 21 court order forces removal of Guard, Federal troops called out by President Eisenhower Sept. 24; **March 5, 1959** fire at Arkansas Negro Boys Industrial School kills 27; **Aug. 12, 1959** integration of four high schools met by jeering mob of 900 segregationists; **1967** Arkansas Symphony Orchestra founded; **1969** Murray Lock & Dam built on Arkansas River, project gives barge access to Tulsa; **Nov. 12, 1971** Air Force cargo training plane crashes on takeoff killing all ten on board; **1973** Arkansas Opera Theatre founded; **1975** 30-story First Commercial Bank completed; **1979** Arkansas State Library established; **1982** I-440 highway bridge built across Arkansas River; Statehouse Convention Center opened, expanded 1999; **1986** 40-story TCBY Towers built; Wildwood Park for the Performing Arts established.

Lonoke   *Lonoke County*   *Central Arkansas, 25 mi/ 40 km east of Little Rock*

1867 town founded; **1871** Memphis & Little Rock Railroad completed; incorporated as a town; **Aug. 26, 1872** U.S. Sen. Joseph T. Robinson born, running mate in Al Smith's 1928 bid for presidency (died 1937); **1873** Lonoke County formed; town becomes county seat; **1928** county courthouse built; **1937** incorporated as a city.

Lucas   *Logan County*   See **Boonsville (1911)**

Magnolia   *Columbia County*   *Southwestern Arkansas, 125 mi/201 km south-southwest of Little Rock*

1852 Columbia County formed; town founded as county seat; **1855** incorporated as a town; **1905** county courthouse built; **1909** Southern Arkansas University established; **1911** incorporated as a city; **1919** oil discovered in area; **1928** Magnolia Cotton Mill opened; **Aug. 2, 1930** train wreck at McNeil to north kills all eight on board, five crew, three hoboes.

Malvern   *Hot Spring County*   *Central Arkansas, 42 mi/68 km southwest of Little Rock, on Ouachita River*

1829 Hot Spring County formed; Rockport becomes county seat; **1870** Cairo & Fulton Railroad reaches site; town founded; **1875** rail line built to Hot Springs by Chicago industrialist "Diamond Jo" Reynolds; **1876** incorporated as a town; **1878** county seat moved to

Malvern; **1936** county courthouse built; **1937** incorporated as a city.

Marianna   *Lee County*   *Eastern Arkansas, 98 mi/ 158 km east of Little Rock*

1790 John Patterson born, considered first white child born in Arkansas (died 1886); **1870** town founded as county seat on L'Anguille River, named for wife of early settler; **1873** Lee County formed; **1878** incorporated as a town; **1890** county courthouse built, addition built 1930s; **1905** incorporated as a city.

Marion   *Crittenden County*   *Eastern Arkansas, 10 mi/16 km northwest of Memphis*

1825 Crittenden County formed, named for War of 1812 veteran and Territorial Secretary Robert Crittenden; **1826** Greenock (east of Clarkedale) becomes county seat; **1836** town founded as new county seat near Mississippi River; **1896** incorporated as a town; **1911** county courthouse completed; **1946** incorporated as a city.

Marked Tree   *Poinsett County*   *Northeastern Arkansas, 133 mi/214 km northeast of Little Rock*

1881 Kansas City, Fort Scott & Memphis Railroad built; **1883** town founded on St. Francis River; **1897** incorporated as a town; **1922** incorporated as a city; **1927** flooding inundates area; Dr. De Kleine and Red Cross nurse Annie Gabriel use yeast against pellagra dietary deficiency; **1934** Southern Tenant Farmers' Union organized.

Marshall   *Searcy County*   *Northern Arkansas, 90 mi/145 km north of Little Rock*

1838 Searcy County formed; Lebanon becomes county seat; **1856** town founded as new county seat, originally named Burrowsville; **1867** town renamed Marshall; **1884** incorporated as a town; **1889** county courthouse built; **1890** incorporated as a city.

McNeil   *Columbia County*   See **Magnolia (1930)**

Melbourne   *Izard County*   *Northern Arkansas, 105 mi/169 km north of Little Rock*

1807 Revolutionary War veteran John Lafferty arrives from North Carolina, builds log cabin; **1825** Izard County formed; Liberty becomes county seat; **1836** county seat moved to Mount Olive; **1840s** county seat moved to Mount Vernon; **1854** town founded, named Mill Creek; **1875** county seat moved to Mill Creek; **1878** incorporated as a town, renamed Melbourne; **1940** county courthouse completed; **1945** incorporated as a city.

Mena   *Polk County*   *Western Arkansas, 123 mi/ 198 km west of Little Rock*

1844 Polk County formed; Dallas becomes county seat; **1851** log cabin built at town site, probably used by guerillas in Civil War; **1896** Kansas City Southern Railroad built through area; town founded; incorporated as a town; **1897** Queen Wilhelmina Inn built at Rich Mtn. to west, burned 1973; **1898** incorporated as a city; county seat moved to Mena; county courthouse built; **1923** Commonwealth College founded to west by Newllano cooperative society, closed 1940; **1927** Will Dilg dies, founder of Izaak Walton League conservation group, spent final years here (born 1869); **1942** Intermountain Municipal Airport established; **1973** Rich Mountain Community College established; **Sept. 27, 1973** Texas International Airlines turboprop hits mountain, all 11 killed.

Monticello   *Drew County   Southeastern Arkansas, 90 mi/145 km south-southeast of Little Rock*

1845 Drew County formed; Rough and Ready becomes county seat; **1849** town founded; **1851** county seat moved to Monticello; **1852** incorporated as a town; **1909** incorporated as a city; **1910** Arkansas Agricultural and Mechanical College established, becomes University of Arkansas at Monticello; **1932** fourth county courthouse completed.

Morrilton   *Conway County   Central Arkansas, 42 mi/68 km northwest of Little Rock*

1825 Conway County formed; Cadron becomes county seat; **1831** Lewisburg founded on Arkansas River as new county seat; **1850** county seat moved to Springfield; **1873** county seat moved back to Lewisburg; Little Rock & Fort Smith Railroad built; new town of Morrilton founded on railroad near Lewisburg; **1879** incorporated as a town; **1883** Morrilton annexes Lewisburg, becomes county seat; **1899** incorporated as a city; **1930** county courthouse built; **1961** Petit Jean College (2-year) established; **1969** Arthur V. Ormond Lock & Dam built on Arkansas River.

Mount Ida   *Montgomery County   Western Arkansas, 85 mi/137 km west-southwest of Little Rock*

1836 Granville Whittington establishes general store; **1842** Montgomery County formed, named for Revolutionary War Gen. Richard Montgomery; **1844** town of Montgomery founded as county seat, later renamed Salem; **1850** town renamed Mount Ida; **1900** incorporated as a town; **1923** county courthouse built; **1938** incorporated as a city.

Mountain Home   *Baxter County   Northern Arkansas, 122 mi/196 km north of Little Rock*

1873 Baxter County formed; town founded as county seat; **1888** incorporated as a town; **1943** county courthouse completed; **1944** Norfork Lake formed by dam to southeast on North Fork White River; **1976** North Arkansas Community College established, becomes Arkansas State University at Mountain Home 1995.

Mountain View   *Stone County   Northern Arkansas, 89 mi/143 km north of Little Rock*

1854 town founded near White River; **1873** Stone County formed; town becomes county seat; **1890** incorporated as a town; **Nov. 14, 1904** actor Dick Powell born (died 1963); **1922** county courthouse built; **1941** incorporated as a city; **1973** Ozark Folk Center State Park opened; **June 12, 2003** Terry Wallis, 39, emerges from coma after 19 years, suffered in car accident 1984.

Murfreesboro   *Pike County   Southwestern Arkansas, 100 mi/161 km southwest of Little Rock*

1833 Pike County formed; **1851** town founded as county seat near Little Missouri River; **1878** incorporated as a town; **1902** first peach seedlings planted in Highland Peach Orchard, beginning of peach production in area; **1906** farmer John M. Huddleston discovers diamonds on part of his farm unsuitable for crop growing; **1908** small diamond mine and processing plant opened, only diamond mine in North America, closed 1925; **1930** cinnabar deposits discovered to northeast; **Apr. 22, 1936** singer Glen Campbell born at Billstown to southeast; **1940** county courthouse built; **1941** incorporated as a city; **1950** Lake Greeson formed by dam to north on Little Missouri River.

Nashville   *Howard County   Southwestern Arkansas, 113 mi/182 km southwest of Little Rock*

1856 town founded; **1873** Howard County formed; town becomes county seat; **1883** incorporated as a town; **1910** incorporated as a city; **1939** county courthouse built.

Newport   *Jackson County   Northeastern Arkansas, 95 mi/153 km northeast of Little Rock*

1829 Jackson County formed; **1832** Litchfield becomes first county seat; **1839** county seat moved to Elizabeth; **1852** county seat moved to Augusta; **1854** county seat moved to Jacksonport; **1870** town founded by Cairo & Fulton Railroad after Jacksonport refuses railroad right of way; **1874** county seat moved to Newport; **1875** incorporated as a town; **1891** incorporated as a city; **1892** county courthouse built; **Feb. 8, 1953** actress Mary Steenburgen born.

North Little Rock   *Pulaski County   Central Arkansas, 1 mi/1.6 km north of Little Rock*

1839 ferry established on Arkansas River to Little Rock; **1862** first train arrives on north bank of river; **1866** town of Argenta founded; **1871** incorporated as a town; Cairo & Fulton Railroad establishes shops here; **1873** Baring Cross Bridge built, destroyed by 1927 flood, replaced 1929; **1880** Temple Cotton Oil Mill founded; **1890** Little Rock annexes section north of river; **1904** incorporated as a city; section previously annexed by Little Rock merges with Argenta; **1917** city renamed North Little Rock; Camp Pike military base established, later renamed Camp Joseph T. Robinson; **1921** U.S. Veterans Administration

Hospital opened; **1936** Seawall levee built; **1938** Greater Little Rock Stockyards opened; **1945** Pulaski Technical College (2-year) established; **Oct. 1999** ALLTEL Arena completed.

Osceola   *Mississippi County   Northeastern Arkansas, 165 mi/266 km northeast of Little Rock*

1830 William B. Edrington purchases site from Indians; **1833** Mississippi County formed; **1836** town founded as county seat on Mississippi River, named Plum Point; **1838** incorporated as a town, renamed for Seminole Chief Osceola; **1871** Great Chicago Fire places demands on area timber; **1872** Reconstruction Era troubles peak when band of whites led by Capt. Billy Erwin organize to oppose black regiment sent by Gov. Powell Clayton, Erwin escapes to New Orleans when $5,000 reward is posted; **1887** first levees built in county; **1901** Blytheville becomes shared county seat with Osceola; **1912** incorporated as a city; county courthouse built; **1927** levees fail when flood waters exceed 60 ft/18 m, worst flood in city's history; **1931** Revetment Fleet of U.S. Engineer Office established.

Ozark   *Franklin County   Northwestern Arkansas, 112 mi/180 km northwest of Little Rock*

1836 town founded on Arkansas River; **1837** Franklin County formed; **1838** town becomes one of two county seats (shared with Charleston); **1855** incorporated as a town; **1904** county courthouse built, altered after 1944 fire; **Aug. 10, 1936** highest temperature ever reached in Arkansas, 120°F/49°C; **1938** incorporated as a city; **1969** Ozark Jeta Taylor Lock & Dam built on Arkansas River.

Paragould   *Greene County   Northeastern Arkansas, 152 mi/245 km northeast of Little Rock*

c.1820 Benjamin Crowley, War of 1812 veteran, builds cabin on north-south ridge which bears his name; **1833** Greene County formed; Gainesville becomes county seat; **1881** town founded on St. Louis Southwestern Railroad, named for railroad men Jay Gould and J. W. Paramore; **1883** incorporated as a town; **1884** county seat moved to Paragould; **1888** old county courthouse built; **1894** incorporated as a city; **1996** new county courthouse completed.

Paris   *Logan County   Western Arkansas, 98 mi/158 km west-northwest of Little Rock*

1873 Sarber County formed, renamed Logan County 1875; Reveille becomes county seat; **1875** town founded as new county seat after two temporary moves; **1879** incorporated as a town; **1908** county courthouse built; **1910s** large-scale coal mining begins in area; **1917** incorporated as a city.

Parkin   *Cross County   Eastern Arkansas, 117 mi/188 km east-northeast of Little Rock*

c.900 AD bands of Mississippian people occupy area along Plum Bayou, through c.1200; **c.1300** Native American village of Casquie established, occupied through 1550, noted for burial mounds; **1887** St. Louis, Iron Mountain & Southern Railroad built; town founded on St. Francis River, named for engineer William Parkin; **1912** incorporated as a town; **1928** incorporated as a city; **1967** Parkin Archaeological State Park established to protect mounds.

Perryville   *Perry County   Central Arkansas, 36 mi/58 km northwest of Little Rock*

1840 Perry County formed; town founded as county seat; **1841** post office established; **1878** incorporated as a town; **1888** county courthouse built; **1950** incorporated as a city.

Piggott   *Clay County   Northeastern Arkansas, 185 mi/298 km northeast of Little Rock*

1873 Clayton County formed; Corning becomes county seat; **1875** renamed Clay County for Henry Clay; **1877** county seat moved to Boydsville; **1881** county divided into two districts with Corning as western county seat, Boydsville as eastern county seat; town of Piggott founded; **1888** eastern county seat moved to Piggott; **1891** incorporated as a town; **1910** Hemingway-Pfeiffer House built, family home of Ernest Hemingway's second wife Pauline Pfeiffer, married 1927, divorced 1940; **1916** incorporated as a city; **1966** county courthouse built.

Pine Bluff   *Jefferson County   Central Arkansas, 42 mi/68 km south-southeast of Little Rock*

1818 French farmer Joseph Bonne signs agreement with Quapaws to serve as interpreter in exchange for right to settle on Arkansas River; **1819** Bonne ascends river from flooded homestead in search of higher ground, lands at pine covered bluff; Mont Marie trading post established; **1829** Jefferson County formed; town becomes county seat; **1832** town renamed Pine Bluff; **1839** incorporated as a town; **1844** Portis House built; **1858** county courthouse built, rebuilt after 1976 fire, completed 1980; **1860** incorporated as a city; **c.1860** Thompson House built; **Apr. 1861** several Union boats halted by Confederate Jefferson Guards, first local military action of Civil War; **1866** Bocage House built; **1870** Little Rock, Pine Bluff & New Orleans Railroad reaches town; **1873** Blanch Normal College established for blacks, becomes University of Arkansas at Pine Bluff; **Apr. 1874** violence breaks out in Brooks-Baxter War resulting from factions in Republican governor's race, seven killed, 30 wounded; **1882** Texas & St. Louis Railroad completed from Gatesville, Texas, its shops established here 1884; **1931** Public Library built; **1957** Southeast Arkansas Livestock Showground established; **1968** Southeast Arkansas Arts and Science Center founded, building opened 1994; **1976** Convention Center opened; **1987** Pine Bluff Symphony Orchestra founded;

1991 Southeast Arkansas College (2-year) established; **1998** Arkansas Entertainers Hall of Fame opened.

Pocahontas   *Randolph County   Northeastern Arkansas, 145 mi/233 km northeast of Little Rock*

1836 Randolph County formed; town founded as county seat on Black River; **1857** incorporated as a town; **1870s** town becomes important river port; **1872** county courthouse built; **1923** incorporated as a city; **1939** new county courthouse built; **1972** Black River Technical College (2-year) established.

Pond   *Benton County   See* **Bentonville (1905)**

Prescott   *Nevada County   Southwestern Arkansas, 97 mi/156 km southwest of Little Rock*

1864 Union Gen. Frederick Steele's troops stopped by Confederates under Gen. T. P. Dockery and Gen. Joe Shelby, prevented from joining Union Gen. N. P. Banks' forces; **1871** Nevada County formed; Rosston becomes county seat; **1873** town founded as new county seat; **1874** incorporated as a town; **1906** incorporated as a city; **1913** county courthouse built.

Rison   *Cleveland County   Southern Arkansas, 60 mi/ 97 km south of Little Rock*

1873 Dorsey County formed; Toledo becomes county seat; **1880** town founded near Saline River; **1885** county renamed Cleveland County for President Grover Cleveland; **1889** county seat moved to Rison; **1890** incorporated as a town; **1944** incorporated as a city; **1967** fourth county courthouse completed.

Rogers   *Benton County   Northwestern Arkansas, 165 mi/266 km northwest of Little Rock*

1858 Elkhorn Tavern built, destroyed by fire, rebuilt 1886; **March 7–8, 1862** in Battle of Pea Ridge, Confederates attack Gen. Samuel Curtis' Union forces, Confederate Generals Ben McCulloch and James I. McIntosh killed, Gen. W. Y. Slack mortally wounded; Union assured control of Missouri; **1881** St. Louis, Arkansas & Texas Railroad reaches site; town founded; **May 1881** incorporated as a town; **1903** incorporated as a city; **July 20, 1956** Pea Ridge National Military Park authorized; **1962** first Wal-Mart store opened by founder Sam Walton [see Bentonville].

Russellville   *Pope County   West central Arkansas, 65 mi/105 km northwest of Little Rock*

1822 Dwight Mission founded by Cephas Washburn on Illinois Bayou among Cherokees, arrived 1817 from Georgia, including chief Sequoyah, who produced Cherokee alphabet by 1825; **1829** Pope County formed; Dwight Mission becomes county seat; **1830** county seat moved to Morristown, to Dover 1840; **1835** British-born Dr. T. J. Russell arrives as first settler; **1855** Cephas

Washburn House built; **1870** incorporated as a town; **1874** Little Rock & Fort Smith Railroad reaches town; **1887** county seat moved to Russellville; **1899** incorporated as a city; **1909** Arkansas Technical University established; **1931** county courthouse built; **1969** Dardenelle Lake formed by lock and dam on Arkansas River; **Aug. 1974** first phase of Arkansas Nuclear Power Plant begins operation.

Salem   *Fulton County   Northern Arkansas, 130 mi/ 209 km north-northeast of Little Rock*

1842 Fulton County formed; town founded as county seat, originally named Pilot Hill; **1872** town renamed Salem; **1892** county courthouse built; **1900** incorporated as a town; **1905** incorporated as a city.

Searcy   *White County   Central Arkansas, 55 mi/ 89 km northeast of Little Rock*

1835 White County formed; **1836** town founded near Little Red River as county seat and health resort, named Sulphur Springs; **1837** town renamed for Richard Searcy; **1854** incorporated as a town; **1867** town reincorporated after Civil War; **1869** county courthouse built; **1877** Methodist Church built; **1889** Galloway College for women established, merged 1932 with Hendrix College at Conway; **1901** incorporated as a city; **May 24, 1909** U.S. Cong. Wilbur Mills born at Kensett to east (died 1992); **1924** Harding University established at site of former Galloway College; **1948** Searcy Airport established; **Aug. 9, 1965** 53 killed in explosion in Titan-2 missile silo.

Sheridan   *Grant County   Central Arkansas, 35 mi/ 56 km south of Little Rock*

1864 Gen. Frederick Steele's Union army overextends its advance from Little Rock, attacked by Confederates at Jenkins Ferry, Saline River, battle indecisive, heavy casualties both sides; **1869** Grant County formed; town founded as county seat; **1887** incorporated as a town; **1938** incorporated as a city; **1964** county courthouse built.

Siloam Springs   *Benton County   Northwestern Arkansas, 175 mi/282 km northwest of Little Rock*

1880 town founded as resort on Sager Creek; **1881** incorporated as a city; **1919** John Brown University established by evangelist John E. Brown.

Springdale   *Washington, Benton counties   Northwestern Arkansas, 160 mi/257 km northwest of Little Rock*

1872 town founded, named Spring-in-the-Dale; **1878** incorporated as a town; **1881** St. Louis, Arkansas & Texas Railroad built through town; town name shortened; **1912** incorporated as a city; **1957** John Tyson establishes his first chicken processing plant, beginnings of Tyson

Foods; **1967** Don and wife Helen Tyson killed in car-train accident.

Stamps *Lafayette County* *See* **Lewisville (1928)**

Star City *Lincoln County* *Southeastern Arkansas, 89 mi/143 km south-southeast of Little Rock*

1871 Lincoln County formed; town founded as county seat; **1876** incorporated as a town; **1889** county courthouse completed; **1945** incorporated as a city.

Stuttgart *Arkansas County* *Central Arkansas, 50 mi/80 km east-southeast of Little Rock*

1813 Arkansas County formed; Arkansas Post becomes county seat; **1855** county seat moved to De Witt; **1880** post office established; **1889** incorporated as a town; **1893** town becomes shared county seat with De Witt; **1897** incorporated as a city; **c.1905** first commercial rice production in Arkansas begins in area; **1927** Rice Branch Experiment Station established by University of Arkansas; **1929** county courthouse built.

Texarkana *Miller County* *Southwestern Arkansas, 148 mi/238 km southwest of Little Rock*

1873 Texas & Pacific Railroad reaches state line from west; **Dec. 1873** town platted on Texas side of state line by railroad; **1874** Miller County formed; Cairo & Fulton Railroad reaches state line from Arkansas; town founded on Arkansas side of state line as county seat; **1876** Texarkana, Texas, incorporated as a town; **1880** Texarkana, Arkansas, incorporated as a town; **1882** Texas & St. Louis Railroad reaches town; **July 12, 1882** heavy rains force pedestrians to seek shelter in Paragon Saloon, storm causes walls to collapse, fire follows, 52 killed; **1887** Texarkana, Arkansas, incorporated as a city; **1897** Kansas City Southern Railroad reaches town; **Apr. 15, 1921** series of tornadoes hit Miller County, other parts of Arkansas and Texas, total 61 killed; **1939** county courthouse built.

Van Buren *Crawford County* *Northwestern Arkansas, 5 mi/8 km north-northeast of Fort Smith*

1818 town founded on Arkansas River, named Phillip's Landing; **1820** Crawford County formed; town becomes county seat; **c.1838** town renamed in honor of President Van Buren; **1842** incorporated as a town; **Sept. 13, 1863** educator Cyrus Adler born, prominent in Jewish affairs (died 1940); **1890** county courthouse built; **1891** incorporated as a city; **Aug. 2, 1896** comic Bob "Bazooka" Burns born (died 1956).

Waldron *Scott County* *Western Arkansas, 112 mi/ 180 km west of Little Rock*

1833 Scott County formed; town founded as county seat, originally named Winfield; **1846** town renamed; **1875**

incorporated as a town; **1934** county courthouse built; **1940** incorporated as a city.

Walnut Ridge *Lawrence County* *Northeastern Arkansas, 135 mi/217 km northeast of Little Rock*

1815 Lawrence County formed; Davidsonville becomes county seat; **1820** county seat moved to Powhatan; **1870** town founded as shared county seat; **1880** incorporated as a town; **1903** Iron Mountain Railroad passes 1.5 mi/2.4 km to south; **1921** incorporated as a city; **1966** town becomes sole county seat; **1967** county courthouse built.

Warren *Bradley County* *Southern Arkansas, 85 mi/137 km south of Little Rock, near Saline River*

1840 Bradley County formed; **1843** town founded as county seat; **1850** incorporated as a town; **c.1900** lumber industry becomes important, declines by 1940; **1903** county courthouse built; **1906** incorporated as a city.

Washington *Hempstead County* *Southwestern Arkansas, 115 mi/185 km southwest of Little Rock*

1818 Hempstead County formed; **1824** Elijah Stuart builds tavern; town founded as county seat; **1830** Travelers' Inn built; **1830s** thousands of Choctaws follow "Trail of Tears" in forced migration from the Southeast to Indian Territory; **1840** *Washington Telegraph* newspaper founded; **1857** A. O. Stuart House built; **1863** during occupation of Little Rock, state government moved to Washington, returned to Little Rock 1865; **1880** incorporated as a town; **1938** county seat moved to Hope; **1956** incorporated as a city.

West Helena *Phillips County* *Eastern Arkansas, 108 mi/174 km east of Little Rock*

1909 town founded near Mississippi River as industrial suburb of Helena; **1917** incorporated as a town; **1920** incorporated as a city; **Jan. 22, 1920** baritone singer, actor William Warfield born, sang "Ole Man River" in movie "Show Boat" (died 2002); **1926** Cotton Branch Experimental Station established by University of Arkansas.

West Memphis *Crittenden County* *Eastern Arkansas, 8 mi/12.9 km west of Memphis*

1890 U.S. Engineer Office established on Mississippi River; **c.1893** town founded as logging camp near Mississippi River, named Bragg's Spur; **1927** incorporated as a town, renamed West Memphis; **1935** incorporated as a city; **1949** highway bridge built across Mississippi River to Memphis; **1955** Southland Greyhound Race Track opened; **1972** I-40 highway bridge built across Mississippi River; **1993** Mid-South Community College established.

Wynne *Cross County* *Eastern Arkansas, 105 mi/ 169 km northeast of Little Rock*

1862 Cross County formed; Pineville becomes county seat; **1863** town founded; **1868** county seat moved to Wittsburg; **1884** county seat moved to Vanndale; **1888** incorporated as a town; **1903** county seat moved to Wynne; **1904** incorporated as a city; county courthouse built; **1930** Summersweet Peach Orchards founded.

Yellville *Marion County* *Northern Arkansas, 115 mi/185 km north-northwest of Little Rock*

1820 town of Shawneetown established on Crooked Creek by Shawnee people; **1836** Marion County formed; town becomes county seat; **1840** town renamed for Col. Archibald Yell, later (1846) led Arkansas cavalry in Battle of Buena Vista, Mexican War, and killed; **1853** James Berry House built; **1855** incorporated as a town; **1862** town occupied by Union troops; **1938** Buffalo River State Park established to south; **1944** county courthouse built; **1946** incorporated as a city; **March 1, 1972** Buffalo National River established, absorbs Buffalo River State Park.

California

Western U.S. Capital: Sacramento. Major cities: Los Angeles, San Francisco, San Diego, Sacramento, San Jose.

The Bear Flag Republic was declared June 14, 1846, following a revolt by the Californians against Mexico. The U.S. assumed control July 7, 1846, and established California Territory. California was admitted to the U.S. as the 31st state September 9, 1850.

California has 58 counties. In San Francisco County, the City of San Francisco is coterminous with the county. The municipalities are classified as towns and cities. There are no townships. See Introduction.

Alameda *Alameda County   Western California, 10 mi/16 km east of San Francisco, on San Francisco Bay*

1853 town founded, Spanish for "poplar grove"; **1884** incorporated as a city; **1893** Pacific Coast Borax Company established, closed c.1930; **1896** city hall built; **Dec. 15, 1896** World War II Gen. James Harold "Jimmy" Doolittle born (died 1993); **Oct. 27, 1911** actor Leif Erickson born (died 1986); **1928** Posey Tube completed, tunnel under Inner Harbor to Oakland replacing Webster Street Bridge; **1940** Alameda Naval Air Station established, closed 1997; **1970** College of Alameda (2-year) established; **Feb. 7, 1973** Navy bomber crashes into apartment building killing 16.

Albany *Alameda County   Western California, 8 mi/ 12.9 km northeast of San Francisco*

1849 powder works established on Fleming Point of San Francisco Bay, support industry for California gold mines; **1883** dynamite plant explosion kills 35; **1905** dynamite industry ceases following series of explosions; **1906** large migrations from San Francisco following earthquake in Apr. swells population; town founded on San Francisco Bay, named Ocean View; **1908** incorporated as a town; **1910** town renamed for mayor's hometown of Albany, New York; **1927** incorporated as a city; **1941** Golden Gate Fields Race Track opened.

Alhambra *Los Angeles County   Southwestern California, 5 mi/8 km east of Los Angeles*

1873 Southern Pacific Railroad built; Alonzo Phillips family become first settlers; **1874** town founded by Don Benito; **1880s** orchards and vineyards established in area; **1889** Ramona Convent built; **1903** incorporated as a city;

1961 city hall built; **1974** $62 million county courthouse built, satellite facility to downtown Los Angeles County courthouse.

Alturas *Modoc County   Northeastern California, 215 mi/346 km north-northeast of Sacramento*

Sept. 26, 1867 Gen. George Crook's forces fight Native Americans in Battle of Infernal Caverns to south, 8 soldiers killed, 14 wounded before natives are routed; **1870** town founded, originally named Dorris Bridge; **1874** Modoc County formed; town becomes county seat, renamed Alturas; **1901** town incorporated; **1914** county courthouse built.

Anaheim *Orange County   Southwestern California, 24 mi/39 km southeast of Los Angeles*

1857 town founded by German settlers; **1876** incorporated as a town; **1880** town becomes major orange producer through 1960; **1887** Santa Fe Railroad reaches town; **1888** incorporated as a city; **1924** first Halloween Parade held; **1952** construction begins on Disneyland theme park, completed 1955; **1963** Anaheim Stadium completed; Los Angeles Angels American League baseball team (established 1961) move from Los Angeles, renamed California Angels; **1965** city receives city charter; **1966** Anaheim Stadium (baseball) built, later renamed Edison International Field at Anaheim; **1957** entertainer Jack Benny named honorary mayor; **Apr. 20, 1982** in Palm Lane Fire, high winds down power lines igniting palm trees, 51 buildings destroyed, 39 injured; **1993** Anaheim Mighty Ducks NHL hockey team established; **1998** Edison International Field stadium opened, home of renamed Anaheim Angels baseball team.

Angels Camp *Calaveras County* *Central California, 64 mi/103 km southeast of Sacramento*

1848 gold discovered by Henry Angell; town founded; **1855** fire destroys town's tents and wooden structures; **1857** Calaveras Hotel built; Stickle Store built; **Feb. 8, 1865** Mark Twain's "Jumping Frog of Calaveras County" said to have originated with story overheard at Hotel Angel, similar claim of Metropolitan Hotel at San Andreas; **1912** incorporated as a city; **1928** first annual Jumping Frog Jubilee held, later becomes part of Calaveras County Fair.

Antioch *Contra Costa County* *Western California, 38 mi/61 km northeast of San Francisco*

1849 twin brothers Rev. Joseph H. and Rev. W. W. Smith arrive from Boston aboard schooner *Rialto*, become first American settlers; **1850** settlers arrive from Maine at inducement of Smith brothers; **1851** town founded at mouths of San Joaquin and Sacramento rivers on Suisun Bay, extension of San Francisco Bay; town given name of Biblical city; Kimball House built by George W. Kimball; **1872** town incorporated.

Arcadia *Los Angeles County* *Southwestern California, 15 mi/24 km northeast of Los Angeles*

1875 town founded by Lucky Baldwin; **1903** incorporated as a city; **1904** Santa Anita Race Track opened; **1914** Ross Field military base established at racetrack site; **1925** Lyon Pony Express Museum opened by Parker Lyon (died 1949), features Western paraphernalia, museum closed 1955; **1934** racetrack reestablished by Charles Strub.

Arcata *Humboldt County* *Northwestern California, 238 mi/383 km north-northwest of San Francisco*

1850 town founded on Arcata Bay, northern extension of Humboldt Bay, Pacific Ocean, named Uniontown; **1853** Humboldt County formed; Orleans (Orleans Bar) becomes county seat; **1854** county seat moved to Arcata; **1856** county seat moved to Eureka; **1857** author Bret Harte writes first published work while working for *Northern Californian* newspaper; **1858** incorporated as a town; **1903** incorporated as a city; **1913** California State Normal School established, now California State University, Humboldt; **1914** Minor Theatre built; **1915** Hotel Arcata built.

Auburn *Placer County* *North central California, 33 mi/53 km northeast of Sacramento*

1848 gold first mined by Claude Chana; **1849** miners arrive from Auburn, New York; town founded; **1851** Placer County formed; **1852** *Auburn Herald* newspaper founded; **1853** town becomes county seat; **1860** town incorporated; **1865** Central Pacific Railroad reaches town; **1898** county courthouse completed; **1913** Hotel Auburn built.

Avalon *Los Angeles County* *Southwestern California, 52 mi/84 km south of Los Angeles, on Pacific Ocean*

Oct. 7, 1542 Santa Catalina Island discovered by Juan Rodriguez Cabrillo; **1811** island's natives massacred by Russians; **1821** unlawful trading ends with Mexico's independence from Spain; **1834** gold discovered on island; **1863** gold rush begins; **Feb. 1, 1864** Federal troops occupy island, foil Confederate plan to establish base here; **1888** town founded at eastern end of island; **1913** town incorporated; **1915** town destroyed by fire; **1919** William Wrigley, Jr. acquires island, guides limited development as resort; **1923** steamship *Catalina* built by Wrigley to ferry visitors from mainland; **1929** Avalon Casino ballroom built at edge of harbor; **May 31, 1950** TV actor Gregory Harrison born.

Azusa *Los Angeles County* *Southwestern California, 20 mi/32 km east-northeast of Los Angeles*

1844 Azusa Rancho established by Henry Dalton; **1854** flour mill built by Dalton; gold discovered in San Gabriel Canyon; **1874** honey production begins when Dalton imports Italian bees; **1887** town founded by Jonathan Slauson, variation of Native American village name Asuksag-na; **1898** incorporated as a city; **1899** Azusa Pacific University established.

Bakersfield *Kern County* *South central California, 107 mi/172 km north-northwest of Los Angeles*

1851 gold discovered on Kern River; **1858** group of homesteaders arrive; **1862** Col. Thomas Baker arrives to direct land reclamation project; **1865** first oil discovered in area; **1866** Kern County formed; Havilah becomes county seat; **1869** town founded; **1873** county seat moved to Bakersfield; town incorporated to legally oust its town marshal Alex Mills; **1876** town disincorporated; **1885** gold discovered in Kern River Canyon to northeast; **1889** fire destroys most of town; **1897** *Bakersfield Californian* newspaper founded; **1898** incorporated as a city; **1899** Kern River Oil Field discovered north of city; **1910** Kern City (East Bakersfield) annexed; **1913** Bakersfield College (2-year) established; **Jan. 19, 1922** TV actor Guy Madison born (died 1996); **Apr. 6, 1937** country singer Merle Haggard born; **1953** Isabella Reservoir formed to northeast on Kern River; **March 1, 1960** fuel truck hit by Santa Fe passenger train at crossing, 14 killed; **1970** California State University, Bakersfield established; **1991** county government center completed.

Baldwin Park *Los Angeles County* *Southwestern California, 16 mi/26 km east of Los Angeles*

1860 grazing lands established for San Gabriel Mission; **1870** town founded on San Gabriel River, named Pleasant View; **1880** town renamed Vineland; **1906** town platted, renamed Baldwin Park for promoter Lucky Baldwin; **1956** incorporated as a city; **Dec. 14, 1963** break in

Baldwin Hills flood control dam damages 250 homes, three killed.

Barstow *San Bernardino County* *Southern California, 95 mi/153 km northeast of Los Angeles*

1847 Old Spanish Trail established; **1883** Atchison, Topeka & Santa Fe Railroad built; town founded as silver mining center; **1947** incorporated as a city; **May 25, 1925** actress Jeanne Crain born; **1931** Mojave River Bridge built; **1951** Camp Irwin army base established to northeast, renamed Fort Irwin 1961; **1959** Barstow College (2-year) established.

Belmont *San Mateo County* *Western California, 20 mi/32 km south of San Francisco*

Nov. 20, 1792 George Vancouver pauses here for lunch during his exploration of San Francisco Bay, first non-Spaniard to visit bay; **1851** roadhouse established by Charles A. Angelo; town founded, named Angelo's Corners; **1864** San Francisco-San Jose Railroad completed; **1865** Good Shepherd Episcopal Church founded; **1868** villa of William Chapman Ralston completed; **1926** incorporated as a city; **1931** Belmont Dog Race Track built.

Benicia *Solano County* *Western California, 24 mi/39 km northeast of San Francisco*

1847 town founded on Carquinez Strait, extension of San Francisco Bay, named for wife of founder Gen. Mariano Vallejo; California House hotel built; Von Pfister Store built; **1849** town becomes port of entry for Sierra Nevada gold miners; U.S. arsenal established; **1850** Solano County formed, named for Francisco Solano (Sem Yoto), chief of Suisunes; town becomes county seat; incorporated as a city; **1851** Masonic Hall built; **1852** state capital moved from Vallejo; Benicia Young Ladies' Seminary founded, moved to Oakland 1860s to become Mills College; **1854** capital moved to Sacramento; **1854** St. Catherine's Catholic Seminary moved from Monterey; St. Dominic's Catholic Church organized; **1859** county seat moved to Fairfield; **1885** St. Paul's Episcopal Church built.

Berkeley *Alameda County* *Western California, 8 mi/12.9 km east-northeast of San Francisco*

1820 Rancho San Antonio granted to Peralta family on eastern shore of San Francisco Bay; **1850s** American squatters develop false survey; landowner José Domingo Peralta jailed for attempting to evict squatters; **1868** town founded; University of California at Berkeley established; **1878** incorporated as a city; **1906** Santa Fe Railroad depot built; **1906** refugees from San Francisco earthquake flock to city; **June 7, 1928** movie director James Ivory born; **Sept. 26, 1962** actress Melissa Sue Anderson born; **1964** student civil rights and antiwar protests overwhelm University of California Berkeley campus, inspiring activities at one-third of U.S. college campuses; **1974** Vista College (2-year) established; **Feb. 4, 1974** publishing

heiress Patty Hearst kidnapped by activist Symbionese Liberation Army.

Beverly Hills *Los Angeles County* *Southwestern California, 6 mi/9.7 km west of Los Angeles*

1907 town founded by Burton Green of Beverly, Massachusetts; **1912** Beverly Hills Hotel opened; **1914** incorporated as a city; **1919** Douglas Fairbanks and Mary Pickford establish Pickfair Estate, first film stars to reside here; **1920** Beverly Hills Speedway established, razed 1925; **1925** humorist Will Rogers named honorary mayor; **March 31, 1935** TV actor Richard Chamberlain born; **May 9, 1946** actress Candice Bergen born to ventriloquist Edgar Bergen; **July 22, 1947** actor Albert Brooks born; **Oct. 21, 1956** actress Carrie Fisher born to singer Eddie Fisher.

Bishop *Inyo County* *Eastern California, 195 mi/314 km southeast of Sacramento*

1861 Samuel A. Bishop drives first herd of cattle into Owens Valley from Fort Tejon [see Lebec]; **1862** Fort Independence built to south as defense against Native Americans; **1863** more settlers arrive; town founded; **1883** Carson and Colorado Railroad reaches town; **1903** incorporated as a city; **1913** Los Angeles Aqueduct completed from Sierra Nevada to deliver water to Los Angeles area; **1966** Laws Railroad Museum opened to northeast.

Blythe *Riverside County* *Southeastern California, 220 mi/354 km east-southeast of Los Angeles*

1877 Thomas Blythe makes land claim on Colorado River, dies before settling on it; **1910** town founded on Blythe estate; **1916** incorporated as a city; **1932** Native American intaglios discovered 20 mi/32 km to north, incised rock figures of humans and animals so extensive that they went unnoticed until seen from air; **1935** completion of Boulder (Hoover) Dam 170 mi/274 km to north ends constant flooding here; **1947** Palo Verde College (2-year) established.

Boca *Nevada County* *See* **Truckee (1937)**

Bodéga Bay *Sonoma County* *Western California, 52 mi/84 km north-northwest of San Francisco*

Sept. 3, 1775 Lt. Juan Francisco de la Bodéga enters bay of Pacific Ocean aboard schooner *Sonora*; **1809** Ivan Kuskof arrives from Alaska with party from Russian-American Fur Company; **1811** Russian trading post established; town founded; **1835** first American land grants made; **1847** warehouse built by Capt. Stephen Smith; **1850** schooner service to San Francisco inaugurated by John Keyes; **1852** hotel built by Smith; **1870s** clear cut logging, agriculture, causes bay to silt, restricting use; **1963** Alfred Hitchcock's movie *The Birds* completed after years of filming here.

Bodie   *Mono County   Eastern California, 140 mi/ 225 km east-southeast of Sacramento*

1859 gold discovered here by W. S. Bodey; town founded; Bodey Mining District established; **1862** town and district renamed Bodie; **1864** Sonora Pass Road diverts travelers from Mono Trail; **1876** Bodie Mine established; population jumps to 12,000; **1880** gold mining dwindles, all but two mines closed by 1883; **1887** remaining mines consolidate; **1895** fire destroys part of town; **June 24, 1932** fire destroys remainder of town; **Oct. 1936** Roseclip Mine reopened; **1942** Roseclip Mine closed; town abandoned; **1964** Bodie State Historic Park established.

Bridgeport   *Mono County   Eastern California, 130 mi/209 km east-southeast of Sacramento*

1833 Bonneville-Walker party of fur trappers pass through area; **1857** gold discovered at Virginia Creek, gold strikes continue into 1860s; **1861** Mono County formed; **1864** county residents surprised to learn that their county seat of Aurora, c.20 mi/32 km to east, is in Nevada; new town founded as county seat; **1880** county courthouse built.

Burbank   *Los Angeles County   Southwestern California, 10 mi/16 km north of Los Angeles*

1867 Dr. David Burbank acquires land; **1886** town founded by Burbank; **1911** incorporated as a city; **1928** Warner Brothers Studios moved from Hollywood; **1940** Walt Disney Studios moved from Hollywood; **March 14, 1946** actor Steve Kanaly born; **Sept. 17, 1948** actor John Ritter born to country singer Tex Ritter (died 2003); **Nov. 8, 1949** singer Bonnie Raitt born to actor John Raitt; **Sept. 2, 1951** actor Mark Harmon born; **Aug. 17, 1960** actor Sean Penn born; **July 29, 1972** actor Wil Wheaton born; **1987** Woodbury University moved from Los Angeles, founded 1884.

Calexico   *Imperial County   Southern California, 195 mi/314 km southeast of Los Angeles*

1900 town founded in Imperial Valley on land owned by irrigation promoter George Chaffey; **1904** Southern Pacific Railroad reaches town; **1908** incorporated as a city; **1919** Carnegie Library opened, replaced by new library 1986; **1940** All American Canal completed, delivers water from Imperial Dam on Colorado River to Imperial Valley.

Calistoga   *Napa County   Western California, 57 mi/92 km north of San Francisco*

1859 area in Napa Valley settled by Mormon Samuel Brannan, noted for hot springs and geysers; **1862** town founded, name conjunction of California and Saratoga; hotel built by Brannan; **1868** Napa Valley Railroad reaches town; **1880** writer Robert Louis Stevenson spends honeymoon at site to north with bride Fannie Van de Grift; **1886** incorporated as a town; **1937** incorporated as a city.

Carmel-by-the-Sea   *Monterey County   Western California, 57 mi/92 km south of San Jose, on Pacific O.*

1602 three Carmelite missionaries accompanying Vizcaino expedition name site for Mt. Carmel, Palestine; **1770** Mission San Carlos Borromeo Del Rio Carmelo founded, church built 1794; **1880** Hotel Del Monte established, rebuilt 1887, 1919, and 1924 following successive fires; **1880s** mission restored; **1881** work begins on 17-Mile Drive, scenic coastal road through Pebble Beach; **1889** Point Sur Lighthouse built at Big Sur to south, automated 1974; **1897** Del Monte Golf Course opened at Pebble Beach, oldest course west of Mississippi River; **1900** town founded; **c.1905** town attracts artists and writers; **1916** incorporated as a city; **1919** Forest Theater founded; **1960s** folk singer Joan Baez leads Cultural Revolution from her Miramonte Ranch; **1966** Spyglass Hill Golf Course opened.

Cerritos   *Los Angeles County   Southern California, 17 mi/27 km southeast of Los Angeles*

c.1950 area becomes urbanized; **1956** incorporated as a city, named Dairy Valley; **1967** city renamed Cerritos for Spanish land grant of Rancho Los Cerritos; **Aug. 31, 1986** Aeromexico DC-9 airplane collides with Piper aircraft killing 82, including 15 on ground; **1993** Center for Performing Arts opened; **2002** Cerritos Public Library opened.

Chatsworth   *Los Angeles County   See Los Angeles (1958)*

Chico   *Butte County   Northern California, 85 mi/ 137 km north of Sacramento*

1841 John Bidwell arrives among first overland emigrant party to cross Sierra Nevada; **1860** town founded by Bidwell; **1865** Bidwell Mansion built by Gen. John Bidwell; **1872** incorporated as a city; **1887** California State Normal School established, becomes California State University, Chico.

Chinese Camp   *Tuolumne County   Central California, 77 mi/124 km southeast of Sacramento*

1850s area's gold mined by 5,000 Chinese; **1854** post office established; **1855** St. Xavier Catholic Church built; **Sept. 26, 1856** "tong war" waged between 900 from Yan Wo Tong (or Tan Woo Tong) faction and 1,200 from Sam Tu Wong (or Sam Yap) faction using pitchforks, knives, clubs, four killed, four wounded [see also Weaverville].

Chula Vista   *San Diego County   Southwestern California, 8 mi/12.9 km south of San Diego*

1887 town founded on San Diego Bay; **1888** orchard industry begins with completion of Sweetwater Dam to northeast; **1911** town incorporated; **1913** severe freeze ruins crops; **Jan. 1916** flash flood caused by break in Lower Otay Dam, over 20 killed; **1941** Rohr Aircraft

Company established; **1961** Southwestern College (2-year) established.

Claremont *Los Angeles County* *Southwestern California, 32 mi/51 km east of Los Angeles*

1887 Atchison, Topeka & Santa Fe Railroad built; town founded; Pomona College established at Pomona, moved here Jan. 1888; **1907** incorporated as a city; **1926** Rancho Santa Ana Botanic Gardens founded; Scripps College for women established; **1946** Claremont McKenna College established.

Cloverdale *Sonoma County* *Western California, 82 mi/132 km north-northwest of San Francisco*

1870s notorious outlaw Black Bart (Charles E. Bolles) strikes region; **1872** Northwestern & Pacific Railroad built; town founded; **1876** incorporated as a city; **Dec. 28, 1876** fire starts at livery stable, destroys town; **1883** Icarian communal society migrates from Corning, Iowa, follows strict controls; town founded on Russian River; **1976** first Old Time Fiddle Contest held; **Dec. 4, 1993** body of 12-year-old Polly Klaas found, abducted Oct. 1 at Petaluma.

Coalinga *Fresno County* *South central California, 122 mi/196 km southeast of San Jose*

1889 town founded with discovery of low-grade coal; **1890** large Coalinga Oil Field discovered in Anticline Ridge to north; **1891** Southern Pacific Railroad reaches site; **1906** incorporated as a city; **Nov. 12, 1917** singer Jo Stafford born; **1928** new oil reserves discovered to southeast in Kettleman Hills; **1932** West Hills (formerly Coalinga) Community College established; **May 2, 1983** business district struck by 6.1 magnitude earthquake, 47 injured, $31 million damage; **Nov. 29, 1991** massive 205-car pileup on Interstate 5 caused by dust storm kills 17, injures over 100.

Coloma *El Dorado County* *North central California, 37 mi/60 km northeast of Sacramento*

July 1845 James Marshall of Missouri hired as carpenter by John Sutter; **Sept. 1847** Sutter's Mill built on American River by Marshall; **Jan. 24, 1848** Marshall discovers gold at Sutter's sawmill; hordes of prospectors overwhelm site; town founded; **1850** El Dorado County formed; town becomes county seat; **1856** St. John Catholic Church built; **1857** county seat moved to Placerville; **1862** Bayley House inn built to west by Alexander Bayley; **Aug. 10, 1885** Marshall dies impoverished (born 1810); **1895** Sutter monument erected; **1980** James Marshall monument erected.

Colton *San Bernardino County* *Southwestern California, 56 mi/90 km east of Los Angeles*

1819 Mission San Gabriel cattle ranch established; **1842** Jose Maria Lugo builds house; **c.1858** Fort Benson built by Jerome Benson as protection against Mormon neigh-

bors; **1875** town founded as terminus for Southern Pacific Railroad; **1887** incorporated as a city; **Feb. 23, 1907** railroad accident, 26 killed.

Columbia *Tuolumne County* *Central California, 72 mi/116 km southeast of Sacramento*

1850 gold diggings operated by Mexican prospectors; Dr. Thaddeus Hildreth, four others, strike gold; town founded; **c.1851** arena built for bull-and-bear fights, reaches newspaper man Horace Greeley, term applied to Wall Street financial markets; **1853** Presbyterian Church built, rebuilt 1864; **1856** St. Ann's Catholic Church built; **1857** Fallon Hotel built; **1858** Pioneer Saloon built; **1862** schoolhouse built; **1945** Columbia State Historic Park established.

Colusa *Colusa County* *North central California, 55 mi/89 km north-northeast of Sacramento*

1850 Colusa County formed; town founded as county seat on Sacramento River; **1861** county courthouse built; **1870** town incorporated; **1876** Southern Pacific Railroad reaches town; **1906** Carnegie Library built.

Compton *Los Angeles County* *Southwestern California, 7 mi/11.3 km south of Los Angeles*

1867 settlers Griffith Compton and William Morton arrive; **1888** incorporated as a city; **Feb. 20, 1907** singer Nadine Conner born (died 2003); **1927** Compton Community College established; **Jan. 18, 1955** actor Kevin Costner born.

Concord *Contra Costa County* *Western California, 25 mi/40 km east-northeast of San Francisco*

1834 land grant made to Salvio Pacheco; **1852** squatters settle on Pacheco's land; **1869** town founded; **1905** incorporated as a town; **Dec. 6, 1920** jazz pianist Dave Brubeck born; **July 17, 1944** ordnance explosion at Navy pier at Port Chicago to north on Suisun Bay, 322 killed, most victims African-American; **1948** incorporated as a city; **Aug. 31, 1964** John Muir National Historic Site authorized to west.

Corona *Riverside County* *Southwestern California, 43 mi/69 km east-southeast of Los Angeles*

1886 town founded, originally named South Riverside; **1896** incorporated as a city; **1913** Ralph de Palma, Barney Oldfield, and Earl Cooper hold 300-mi/483-km automobile race with Cooper winning, averaging 75 mi/121 km per hour; **1952** California Correctional Institution for Women established.

Coronado *San Diego County* *Southwestern California, 3 mi/4.8 km west of San Diego, on Pacific Ocean*

1886 town founded on peninsula separating San Diego Bay from Pacific Ocean; **1888** Hotel Del Coronado built;

1890 incorporated as a city; **1908** Glorietta Bay Inn built; **1917** Coronado U.S. Naval Air Station established; **July 27, 1933** singer Nick Reynolds born, founding member of Kingston Trio; **1943** Coronado Naval Amphibious Base established; **1969** Coronado Bridge built across San Diego Bay, replacing ferry.

Costa Mesa   *Orange County   Southwestern California, 34 mi/55 km south-southeast of Los Angeles*

1810 Spanish land grant made to José Antonio Yorba; **1820** Estancia Adobe built; **c.1880** settlers begin buying land parcels; **1909** town founded on Pacific Ocean, originally named Harper; **1920** town renamed; Vanguard University of Southern California established; **March 10, 1933** Long Beach earthquake damages businesses; **1947** Orange Coast College (2-year) established; **1953** incorporated as a city.

Crescent City   *Del Norte County   Northwestern California, 300 mi/483 km north-northwest of San Francisco*

1852 town founded on Pacific Ocean; **1853** Klamath County formed; town becomes county seat, later moved to Orleans (Orleans Bar); **1854** incorporated as a city; **1856** Battery Point Lighthouse built; **1857** Del Norte County formed from Klamath County, remainder of county becomes Humboldt County; Crescent City becomes Del Norte County seat; **July 30, 1865** steamer *Brother Jonathan* sinks on St. George Reef to northwest, 215 killed, 19 survive; **1882** Point St. George Lighthouse built on St. George Reef, completed 1892, deactivated 1974; **1885** county courthouse built; **March 28, 1964** tsunami (tidal wave) from Good Friday Earthquake, Alaska, kills 12; **Oct. 2, 1968** Redwood National Park established to south; **1990** Smith River National Recreation Area established to east.

Cupertino   *Santa Clara County   Western California, 7 mi/11.3 km west of San Jose*

1850s area settled by squatters driven off Rancho Quito; **1880s** retired sea captains favor town, build New England style cottages; **1898** post office established; **1955** incorporated as a city; **1967** De Anza College (2-year) established; **1976** Steve Wozniak and Steve Jobs ("The Two Steves") develop Apple, first personal computer, in Jobs' garage.

Cypress   *Orange County   Southwestern California, 27 mi/43 km south-southeast of Los Angeles*

1956 town founded, incorporated as a city; **Aug. 19, 1963** actor John Stamos born; **1966** Cypress College (2-year) established; **Dec. 30, 1975** African-Thai-American champion golfer Eldrick "Tiger" Woods born.

Daly City   *San Mateo County   Western California, 7 mi/11.3 km south-southwest of San Francisco*

1859 settlers build fort to fend off land speculators, driven away by speculators; **1866** courts reinstate lands to settlers; **1907** town founded on Pacific Ocean, named for dairyman John D. Daly; area experiences sudden growth following Apr. 1906 San Francisco earthquake; **1911** incorporated as a city; **1948** city annexes Westlake.

Davis   *Yolo County   North central California, 14 mi/23 km west of Sacramento*

1868 town founded, named Davisville for prominent farmer Jerome C. Davis; **1907** town name shortened; **1905** University of California at Davis established; **1917** incorporated as a city; **June 28, 1978** Supreme Court ruling favors white man Alan Bakke for admission to University of California Medical School in reverse discrimination suit.

Death Valley   *Inyo County   Eastern California, 170 mi/274 km east-southeast of Fresno*

1882 Harmony Borax Works opened by W. T. Coleman and F. M. "Borax" Smith, closed 1887; borax hauled out in ten large wagons built by J. W. S. Perry, delivered to town of Mojave; **1903** gold discovered at Keane Wonder Mine to north; **July 10, 1913** highest temperature recorded in California reached at Greenland Ranch, 134°F/57°C; **1914** Ashford Gold Mill built to south; **1920s** Scotty's Castle built to north by prospector Walter E. "Death Valley" Scotty and investor Albert M. Johnson, cost $2 million; **1927** Furnace Creek Inn opened; **Feb. 11, 1933** Death Valley National Monument proclaimed, extends into Nevada, becomes Death Valley National Park Oct. 31, 1994, expanded.

Decoto   *Alameda County   See* **Fremont (1951)**

Delano   *Kern County   South central California, 135 mi/217 km north-northwest of Los Angeles*

1872 Southern Pacific Railroad built; town founded; **1915** incorporated as a city; **July 29, 1970** Cesar Chavez' Grape War, involving 5 years of migrant labor strikes and boycotts, ends with signing of 26 contracts; **1993** North Kern State Prison completed.

Downieville   *Sierra County   Eastern California, 76 mi/122 km north-northeast of Sacramento*

1849 Frank Anderson becomes first gold panner; more gold seekers arrive later in year led by Maj. William Downie; town founded; **1852** Sierra County formed; town becomes county seat; **1853** *Mountain Messenger* newspaper founded; Costa Store built; St. Charles Hotel built; **1940** Yuba Theater built; **1947** county courthouse built.

Dublin *Alameda County* *Western California, 28 mi/45 km east of San Francisco*

1811 José Maria Amador visits area, later brings cattle and sheep of Mission San José to graze; **1834** land grant made to Amador for his services; Amador adobe house built, serves as inn; **1850** Jeremiah Fallon House built; **1852** town founded; **1859** St. Raymond's Catholic Church built; **May 7, 1964** Pacific Airlines F-27 crashes, killing all 44 on board, flight tapes indicate pilot was shot by highly-insured passenger; **1982** incorporated as a city.

El Cajon *San Diego County* *Southwestern California, suburb 10 mi/16 km east of San Diego*

1869 Rancho El Cajon opened to settlers; **1876** hotel built by Samuel Lunkershim; town founded; **1912** incorporated as a city; **1961** Grossmont College (2-year) established; **March 22, 2001** Jason Hoffman, 18, accused of shooting and wounding five at El Cajon High School, commits suicide in jail cell Nov. 29.

El Centro *Imperial County* *Southern California, 188 mi/303 km southeast of Los Angeles*

1900 irrigation canal built from Colorado River through below-sea-level Salton Basin of Imperial Valley; **1905** deliberate levee break sends water out of control into basin creating Salton Sea, stopped Feb. 1907; town founded by W. F. Holt; **1907** Imperial County formed, last of California's 58 counties; **1908** incorporated as a city; **1919** Southern Pacific Railroad reaches city; **1924** county courthouse built; **1928** irrigation project begun; **1934** violence erupts during lettuce-pickers strike; **1940** All American Canal opened from Imperial Dam, Colorado River; **March 28, 1944** actor Ken Howard born; **1946** El Centro Naval Air Station established to west; **May 20, 1946** singer Cher Bono born; **Oct. 27, 1964** Navy Skywarrior bomber crashes killing three crewmen and seven on ground, 26 injured.

Escondido *San Diego County* *Southwestern California, 24 mi/39 km north-northeast of San Diego*

Dec. 1846 in Battle of San Pasqual, Brig. Gen. Stephen W. Kearney attacks the Californios, native Californians who wanted independence, under Gen. Andres Pico, 19 of Kearney's men killed, 17 wounded, virtually no casualties among the Californios; **1886** town founded; **1888** incorporated as a city; **1972** San Diego Wild Animal Park opened.

Eureka *Humboldt County* *Northwestern California, 235 mi/378 km north-northwest of San Francisco*

1850 town founded on Humboldt Bay, Pacific Ocean, by James Ryan; **1853** Klamath County formed; Fort Humboldt built; Orleans becomes county seat; **1854** county seat moved to Arcata; **1856** incorporated as a town; county seat moved to Eureka; **1857** county renamed

Humboldt County; **Feb. 20, 1860** white men go to Indian Island in bay, kill women and children of Native American camp while men are hunting; author Bret Harte forced to return to San Francisco for writing criticisms of massacre; **1865** fort abandoned; incorporated as a city; **Feb. 6, 1885** mobs attack Chinese minority after stray bullet kills councilman, raising anti-Chinese sentiment, Chinese forced to leave; **1888** Carson House built; **1907** Sequoia Park Zoo established; **1959** county courthouse built; **1964** College of the Redwoods (2-year) established; **June 27, 1971** DC-3 airplane clips sewage treatment plant, crashes into Pacific, 16 killed.

Fairfield *Solano County* *Western California, 38 mi/61 km north-northeast of San Francisco*

1850 Solano County formed; Benicia becomes county seat; **1859** town founded by sea captains Robert H. Waterman and Archibald A. Ritchie; county seat moved to Fairfield; **1903** incorporated as a city; **1911** county courthouse built; **1942** Travis Army Air Field established to east, becomes Air Force Base 1950.

Ferndale *Humboldt County* *Northwestern California, 225 mi/362 km north-northwest of San Francisco*

1854 Seth Louis Shaw becomes first settler, names house Fern Dale (Shaw House still stands); town founded near Pacific Ocean; **1893** incorporated as a city, westernmost incorporated city in continental U.S.; **Apr. 25–26, 1992** town badly damaged by 7.1 magnitude earthquake; **1995** flooding inundates town.

Folsom *Sacramento County* *North central California, suburb 18 mi/29 km northeast of Sacramento*

1844 camp established on grant made to William A. Leidesdorff; **1848** Capt. Joseph L. Folsom purchases site; **1849** gold diggings made by black prospectors; **1855** town founded by Theodore D. Judah; **1856** Sacramento Valley Railroad, first steam railroad in California, reaches town; **1866** Folsom Dam built on American River; **1880** Folsom State Prison established; **1946** incorporated as a city; **1956** new Folsom Dam completed, begun 1948.

Fort Bragg *Mendocino County* *Northwestern California, 140 mi/225 km north-northwest of San Francisco*

1856 Mendocino Indian Reservation established; **1857** Fort Bragg established by Lt. Horatio Gates Gibson; **1864** fort abandoned; **1867** reservation opened to white settlement; **1869** first lumber camps established; **1870** Point Arena Lighthouse built to south, destroyed by 1906 earthquake, rebuilt; **1873** town founded as lumber center; **1885** Fort Bragg Railroad built; **1889** town platted, incorporated as a city; **Apr. 18, 1906** city damaged by earthquake, rebuilt.

Fremont *Alameda County* *Western California,
30 mi/48 km southeast of San Francisco*

1797 Mission San José founded by Padre Fermin Lasuen,
sold 1846; **1809** adobe mission church built, replica built
1984; **1850** post office established; **1870** Weibel Vineyards
established by Leland Stanford; **1946** Ohlone College (2-
year) established; **Aug. 24, 1951** United Airlines DC-6B
crashes at Decoto to north, 50 killed; **1956** incorporated as
a city; **Aug. 4, 1967** truck filled with children overturns,
five killed, 60 injured; **Dec. 1984** New United Motor
Manufacturing Incorporated (NUMMI) plant opened,
joint automobile venture between General Motors and
Toyota.

Fresno *Fresno County* *Central California, 215 mi/
346 km north-northwest of Los Angeles*

early 1800s area explored by Spanish; **1830s** fur trappers
visit area; **1850s** first settlers arrive with discovery of gold;
1856 Fresno County formed; Millerton becomes county
seat; **1860s** A. J. Manssen becomes first permanent settler;
1872 Central Pacific Railroad reaches site; town founded;
1874 county seat moved to Fresno; raisin production
begins; **1885** incorporated as a town; **Sept. 9, 1887** baseball
player, manager of Chicago Cubs Frank LeRoy Chance
born (died 1924); **1889** commercial fig production begins
through cross-fertilization efforts of Frank Roeding; **1898**
Raisin Growers Association organized; **1900** incorporated
as a city; **1902** Japanese Buddhist Temple built; **1908**
Roeding Park Zoo established, renamed Chaffee Zoo
1990; **Aug. 31, 1908** novelist William Saroyan born (died
1981); **1910** Fresno City College (2-year) established; **1911**
California State Normal School established, becomes
California State University, Fresno; **1922** *Fresno Bee*
newspaper founded; **Feb. 21, 1925** movie producer Sam
Peckinpah born; **Aug. 15, 1925** TV actor Mike Connors
born; **1928** Chandler Downtown Airport established;
1932 Memorial Auditorium built; **1941** Hammer Army
Air Base established, becomes Fresno Air Terminal
(airport) 1946, renamed Fresno Yosemite International
1990s; **1944** Fresno Pacific University established; **Nov. 17,
1944** baseball pitcher Tom Seaver born; **1948** Fresno Art
Museum founded; **1966** county courthouse dedicated;
Fresno Convention Center opened; **1984** Metropolitan
Museum opened.

Fullerton *Orange County* *Southwestern
California, suburb 23 mi/37 1 km southeast of Los Angeles*

1887 town founded by George and Edward Amerige; **1888**
Atchison, Topeka & Santa Fe Railroad built; **1892** oil
discovered in area; **1904** incorporated as a city; **1913**
Fullerton College (2-year) established; **1927** Fullerton
Airport established; **1950s** Santa Ana Freeway built; **1957**
California State College (now University) at Fullerton
established.

Gilroy *Santa Clara County* *Western California,
30 mi/48 km south-southeast of San Jose*

1814 Scotsman John Cameron deserts scurvy ridden ship,
assumes alias John Gilroy, becomes first settler, acquires
ranch through marriage; **1850** town founded in Santa
Clara Valley; **1858** Henry Miller, born Heinrich Kreiser,
joins with Charles Lux, amass cattle empire in California,
Nevada, and Arizona; **1867** incorporated as a town; **1869**
Southern Pacific Railroad reaches town; **1870** incorporated as a city; **1919** Gavilan College (2-year) established.

Glen Ellen *Sonoma County* *Western California,
42 mi/68 km north of San Francisco*

1880 Northwestern Pacific Railroad built; town
founded; **1889** Sonoma State Hospital established, later
renamed Sonoma Developmental Center; **Nov. 12, 1916**
author Jack London dies at his ranch, established in his
last years as experimental model farm (born 1876); **1926**
House of Happy Walls completed by widow Charmian
London, donated at her death 1955 as memorial to
husband; **1959** Jack London State Historic Park
established.

Glendale *Los Angeles County* *Southwestern
California, 9 mi/14.5 km north of Los Angeles*

1798 Rancho San Rafael created; **c.1865** Casa Adobe de
San Rafael built; **1871** Rancho San Rafael subdivided;
1887 town founded; **1902** Pacific Electric Railroad reaches
town; **1904** mansion built by Leslie C. Brand, converted to
Brand Library and Art Center 1956; **1906** incorporated as
a city; **1917** Forest Lawn Cemetery established, auxiliary
to Forest Lawn Cemetery, Hollywood, Clark Gable,
Jimmy Stewart, Walt Disney, others buried here; **May
11, 1935** actor Doug McClure born (died 1995); **Dec. 31,
1947** actor Tim Matheson born; **1967** Glendale
Community College established.

Greenland Ranch *Inyo County* See **Death Valley**
(1913)

Hanford *Kings County* *South central California,
185 mi/298 km north-northwest of Los Angeles*

1877 town founded, named for railroad paymaster James
Madison Hanford; **1880** Southern Pacific Railroad
reaches town; **May 1880** in Mussell Slough Feud, sheriff's
men engage in shootout with ranchers over taking
property along railroad route as authorized by act of
Congress, five ranchers, two deputies killed; **1891** incorporated as a city; **1893** Kings County formed; city
becomes county seat; **1897** county courthouse built.

Hayward *Alameda County* *Western California,
22 mi/35 km east-southeast of San Francisco*

1852 William Hayward pitches tent on property of
Guillermo Castro; Hayward reaches agreement with
Castro on allowing him to settle; **1854** town founded by

Castro on San Francisco Bay, named for his friend; **1876** incorporated as a city; **1929** San Mateo Bridge (lift) built across San Francisco Bay from San Mateo, rebuilt 1967; **1957** California State University at Hayward established; **1961** Chabot College (2-year) established.

Hollister   *San Benito County   Western California, 45 mi/72 km south-southeast of San Jose*

1797 Mission San Juan Bautista established to west; **1868** town founded by William Welles Hollister; **1872** town incorporated; **1874** San Benito County formed; town becomes county seat; **1962** county courthouse built.

Hollywood   *Los Angeles County   Southwestern California, 4 mi/6.4 km northwest of Los Angeles*

1853 Don Tomas Urquidez builds first adobe house; **1860s** farms established throughout area; **1887** Horace H. Wilcox builds first subdivision, named Hollywood by Wilcox's wife; **1896** film industry begins when T. L. Tally opens Phonograph and Vitascope Parlor; **1903** town incorporated; **1907** Forest Lawn Cemetery established, burial place of numerous film stars, auxiliary unit established at Glendale 1917; **1908** Selig Company makes first film shot entirely in California, *Heart of a Race Tout*, open Hollywood's first studios 1909; **1910** Hollywood annexed by Los Angeles; **1911** Nestor Company, organized by Horsley brothers, establishes film studio in barn at Sunset and Gower streets, makes first film *The Law of the Range*; **1913** Cecil B. De Mille arrives from Eastern U.S., opens studios, makes his first movie, *Squaw Man*, shot at Lake Arrowhead, San Bernardino Mountains; **1913** Paramount Studios established; Japanese Gardens built by Adolph and Eugene Bernheimer; **1918** Grauman's Chinese Theatre opened on Hollywood Boulevard; **1920s** motion picture industry booms; **Nov. 8, 1921** entertainer Jerome Hines born (died 2003); **1922** Hollywood Bowl natural amphitheater opened; Egyptian Theater premiers its first movie *Robin Hood*; **1923** "Hollywoodland" sign erected in prominent letters on Mt. Lee, Hollywood Hills, shortened to "Hollywood" 1945; Warner Brothers Studios established, moved to Burbank 1928; Walt Disney Studios established, moved to Burbank 1940; **Aug. 10, 1923** actress Rhonda Fleming born; **Aug. 8, 1926** actor John Derek born; **1928** Mickey Mouse created by Walt Disney; **July 31, 1929** actor Don Murray born; **July 1, 1932** Peg Entwistle commits suicide by jumping from top of "H" in "Hollywood" sign; **Apr. 15, 1933** TV actress Elizabeth Montgomery born (died 1995); **Nov. 16, 1934** actor Guy Stockwell born (died 2002); **Oct. 8, 1936** actor David Carradine born; **1938** National Broadcasting Company studios opened; Columbia Square Playhouse opened; **Jan. 14, 1938** singer Jack Jones born; **Nov. 12, 1942** actress Stefanie Powers born; **Nov. 19, 1941** actor Dan Haggerty born; **Dec. 9, 1941** actor Beau Bridges born to actor Lloyd Bridges; **Jan. 29, 1942** actress Katherine Ross born; **Aug. 5, 1946** actress Erika Slezak born; **June 6, 1948** actor Robert Englund born; **July 8, 1948** actress Kim Darby

born; **July 17, 1951** actress Lucie Arnaz born to Lucille Ball and Desi Arnaz; **Sept. 7, 1955** actor Corbin Bernsen born at North Hollywood; **March 5, 1956** actor Dean Stockwell born; **Feb. 9, 1960** actress Joanne Woodward becomes first celebrity to receive bronze star on Hollywood's Walk of Fame at Grauman's Chinese Theatre, over 1,550 stars embedded in sidewalk by 2003; **Dec. 14, 1962** Super Constellation aircraft crashes in North Hollywood, nine killed, including five on ground, a dozen buildings burn.

Huntington Beach   *Orange County   Southwestern California, 30 mi/48 km south-southeast of Los Angeles*

1901 town founded on Pacific Ocean; **1904** first Huntington Beach Pier built, rebuilt 1912, 1940, 1983; **1909** incorporated as a city; **1920** oil discovered, companies drill at angle to tap reserves from other properties, avoiding royalty payments; **1925** Pacific Coast Highway built; **March 10, 1933** earthquake damages city; **1939** legislation passed compensating property owners for oil taken from their land; **1966** Golden West College (2-year) established.

Independence   *Inyo County   Eastern California, 90 mi/145 km east of Fresno*

July 1862 Fort Independence established as defense against Paiutes; **1866** Inyo County formed; town founded as county seat; **1877** fort abandoned; **1883** Carson & Colorado Railroad reaches town; **1908** construction begins on Los Angeles Aqueduct to deliver water from Sierra Nevada to Los Angeles, completed 1913; **1917** Mt. Whitney Fish Hatchery opened on Oak Creek to west; **1923** county courthouse built; **1928** Eastern California Museum founded.

Inglewood   *Los Angeles County   Southwestern California, 7 mi/11.3 km southwest of Los Angeles*

1873 town founded by Daniel Freeman; **1908** incorporated as a city; **1938** Hollywood Park Race Track opened; **March 26, 1949** TV actress Vicki Lawrence born; **1994** Hollywood Park Casino opened to limited gambling.

Irvine   *Orange County   Southern California, 40 mi/64 km southeast of Los Angeles*

1893 land acquired by James Irvine, Jr.; **1942** El Toro Marine Corps Air Station established, closed 1993; **c.1950** residential development begun by son Myford Irvine; **1965** University of California at Irvine established; **1972** Concordia University established; **1971** incorporated as a city; **1979** Irvine Valley College established.

Jackson *Amador County* *Central California,*
43 mi/69 km east-southeast of Sacramento

1848 town founded as emigrant camp by Alden Jackson;
1850 Calaveras County formed; Double Springs becomes
county seat; **1851** county seat moved to Jackson; **1852**
county seat moved to Mokelumne Hill; **1854** Amador
County formed from Calaveras County; Jackson becomes
county seat; county courthouse built; **Aug. 1862** fire
destroys business district; **1905** town incorporated; **1929**
Pardee Reservoir formed by dam on Mokelumne River to
southwest.

Jenner *Sonoma County* *Western California, 60 mi/*
97 km north-northwest of San Francisco, on Pacific Ocean

1806 Russian chamberlain Nikolai Rezanof visits area in
search of food for starving colonists in Alaska; **1812** Fort
Rossiya (Russia) built to northwest by Ivan Alexander
Kuskof; **1819** Russians turn to ship building after failing
at farming; **1824** Russians abandon intentions in
California; **1841** fort sold to John Sutter; **1904** lumber
mill established; Jenner Inn built; town founded; **1906** fort
damaged by earthquake, later restored as Fort Ross State
Historic Park.

La Jolla *San Diego County* *Southwestern*
California, 10 mi/16 km north-northwest of San Diego

1834 La Jolla Pueblo established by Mexicans; **1887** town
founded on Pacific Ocean; **1903** Scripps Institute of
Oceanography founded by University of California Prof.
William E. Ritter through endowment of Ellen Browning
Scripps; **Apr. 5, 1916** actor Gregory Peck born (died 2003);
Sept. 9, 1925 TV actor Cliff Robertson born; **1941** La Jolla
Museum of Contemporary Art founded; **c.1950** town
annexed by San Diego; **1951** Scripps Aquarium and
Museum opened, new aquarium completed 1992; **1959**
University of California at San Diego established; **1971**
National University established; **1978** Mingei
International Museum founded.

Lake Tahoe *El Dorado County* *See* **South Lake
Tahoe**

Lakeport *Lake County* *Northwestern California,*
94 mi/151 km north of San Francisco

1861 Lake County formed; town founded as county seat
on Clear Lake, named Forbestown for town site landowner William Forbes, soon renamed Lakeport; **1871**
county courthouse built; **1888** incorporated as a city; **1968**
new county courthouse built.

Lebec *Kern County* *Southwestern California,*
68 mi/109 km north-northwest of Los Angeles

Oct. 17, 1837 Peter Lebecque, exploring area for Hudson's
Bay Company, shoots grizzly bear, killed by wounded
bear, buried by companion with inscription carved on
tree; **1854** Fort Tejon established, abandoned 1864; **1858**

first stagecoach of Butterfield Overland Mail route passes
through Tejon Pass to San Francisco; U.S. Army camel
train passes through, use of camels in U.S. deserts soon
fails, rocky ground unsuitable for camel hoofs; **1919** Ridge
Route completed across San Gabriel Mountains to
southeast; **1933** new Ridge Route (U.S. Highway 99)
completed.

Lee Vining *Mono County* *Eastern California,*
150 mi/241 km southeast of Sacramento

1852 prospector Leroy "Lee" Vining fails to find gold at
southern end of Lake Mono, salt lake with no outlet,
builds sawmill; town founded; **1913** Los Angeles
Aqueduct completed, delivers water to city of Los
Angeles from streams feeding Lake Mono from Sierra
Nevada; **1941** second Los Angeles Aqueduct completed;
1970 third aqueduct built; **1978** legal action initiated to
save shrinking Lake Mono; **1995** lake level reaches 40 ft/
12 m below level of 1940.

Livermore *Alameda County* *Western California,*
40 mi/64 km east of San Francisco

1838 British deserter Robert Livermore establishes
Rancho las Positas; **1851** Livermore House built, rebuilt
by son 1880s; **1869** town founded by William Mendenhall;
1876 incorporated as a city; **1918** first Livermore Rodeo
held; **1952** Lawrence Radiation Laboratory of University
of California established.

Lodi *San Joaquin County* *Central California,*
32 mi/51 km south of Sacramento

1869 town founded by German immigrants Charles O.
Ivory and John M. Burt, originally named Mokelumne;
1874 town renamed Lodi; **1885** Lodi Public Library
founded; first annual Grape Festival held; **c.1900** wine
industry flourishes; **1905** Opera House built; **1906** town
incorporated; **Nov. 7, 1973** Walter Parkin, wife, two
children, parents, babysitter, her boyfriend, brother,
found dead at ranch, sixth mass murder in California in
four years, fugitives Willie Steelman and Douglas Gretzler
apprehended next day.

Loma Linda *San Bernardino County* *Southern*
California, 5 mi/8 km south-southeast of San Bernardino

1900 town founded; **1905** Loma Linda University established by Seventh-day Adventist Church; **March 22, 1959**
actor Matthew Modine born; **1970** incorporated as a city;
Nov. 15, 1984 Baby Fae dies, human baby had received
controversial baboon's heart transplant Oct. 26 at Loma
Linda University Medical Center.

Lompoc *Santa Barbara County* *Southwestern*
California, 140 mi/225 km northwest of Los Angeles

1787 Mission La Purisma Concepción founded, Chunah
term for "lake"; **1812** earthquake destroys mission,
rebuilt; **1874** town founded by California Immigrant

Union, first colonization project in California; **1880s** town leads way in adopting alcohol prohibition; **1888** incorporated as a city; **May 11, 1907** railroad accident, 36 killed; **1941** Camp Cooke Army training facility established, becomes Vandenberg Air Force Base 1957; **1957** first space rocket and missile programs launched here; **Sept. 28, 1962** Canadian Alouette missile launched into polar orbit.

Lone Pine *Inyo County* *Eastern California, 100 mi/161 km east-southeast of Fresno*

1850s town founded as gold mining support center; **1864** Prof. J. D. Whitney of California Geological Society determines Mt. Whitney (14,494 ft/4,417 m) to west as highest point in U.S.; **June 1871** geologist Clarence King attempts to climb Mt. Whitney in adverse weather conditions, leaves marker at supposed summit; **March 16, 1872** earthquake destroys most of town, 26 killed; **1873** W. A. Goodyear climbs neighboring Mt. Langley to south, discovers King's marker on wrong summit; **Aug. 18, 1873** local fishermen A. H. Johnson, C. D. Begole, and John Lucas become first to reach Mt. Whitney summit; **Sept. 19, 1873** Clarence King returns hurriedly from East to climb Mt. Whitney to overcome his error to learn he is one month late; **1883** Carson & Colorado Railroad reaches town.

Long Beach *Los Angeles County* *Southwestern California, 20 mi/32 km south of Los Angeles*

1784 land grant made to Manuel Nieto by King of Spain; **1840** Rancho los Alamitos acquired by John Temple and Abel Stearns of Massachusetts; **1857** Phineas Banning makes harbor improvements, converting Rattlesnake Island into Terminal Island; **1863–1864** drought kills livestock, leads to land foreclosures; town site purchased by Llewellyn Bixby and Benjamin and Dr. Thomas Flint; **1881** first home built by William E. Willmore; town founded on San Pedro Bay, Pacific Ocean, named Willmore City; **1884** Willmore venture fails; **1885** Southern Pacific Railroad reaches site; town refounded as Long Beach; **1888** incorporated as a city; **1902** Pacific Electric Railway reaches city; **1911** Port of Long Beach established; **1921** Signal Hill Oil Field discovered; **1923** Long Beach Airport established; **Aug. 28, 1924** actress Peggy Ryan born; **1927** Long Beach City College (2-year) established; **July 8, 1931** columnist Jack Anderson born; **March 10, 1933** earthquake of 6.2 magnitude levels city, 121 killed; **May 20, 1936** actor Anthony Zerbe born; **1937** Central Public Library completed, replaces library destroyed in 1933 earthquake; **June 2, 1937** TV actress Sally Kellerman born; **1941** Long Beach Naval Base established; **Nov. 22, 1943** tennis player Billie Jean King born; **June 4, 1944** singer Michelle Phillips of the Mamas and the Papas born; **Nov. 2, 1947** only flight of Howard Hughes' *Spruce Goose* wooden seaplane occurs; **1949** California State University, Long Beach, established; **Nov. 20, 1956** actress Bo Derek born; **Jan. 7, 1964** actor Nicolas Cage born; **1967** Cunard Line's *Queen Mary*, launched 1936, permanently docked as tourist center; **1971** Brooks

College (2-year) established; **1989** Greater Los Angeles World Trade Center opened; **1990** Los Angeles Metro light rail Blue Line reaches city; **1995** Aquarium of the Pacific built.

Los Angeles *Los Angeles County* *Southwestern California, on Pacific Ocean*

1542 Spanish explorer Juan Rodriguez Cabrillo sails Los Angeles Harbor in his caravel, names it Bay of Smokes and Fires for the numerous Native American camp fires; **1769** Native American village of Yang-na discovered here by Capt. Gaspar de Portolá; **Sept. 1771** Mission San Gabriel founded; **Sept. 4, 1781** pueblo founded by Father Junipero Serra and Don Felipe de Neve, governor of Spanish California, with 44 settlers at Yang-na, named pueblo Nuestra Senora la Reina de Los Angeles de Porciuncula (Our Lady of the Queen of Angels of Porciuncula); **1805** American ship *Lelia Byrd* anchors at San Pedro; **1817** capital of California Territory alternates between Los Angeles and Monterey; **1818** Joseph (José) Chapman becomes first English-speaking settler; **1822** Church of Our Lady the Queen of the Angels completed; **1840** Lugo House built by Don Vicente Lugo; **March 9, 1842** gold discovered in Placerita Canyon, north of San Fernando Valley; **1846** California seized by U.S.; Commodore R. F. Stockton captures town in bloodless battle; **1850** Los Angeles County established; incorporated as a city; city becomes county seat; **1869** Pico House built by Pio Pico; **1871** accidental killing of white man by Chinese man results in mob action, 19 Chinese killed; **1876** Cathedral of St. Vibiana built; **Sept. 5, 1876** golden spike driven into Southern Pacific Railroad at Lang Station, Soledad Canyon, connecting city with Eastern U.S.; **1880** University of Southern California established; **1884** Woodbury University established, moved to Burbank 1987; **1886** Atchison, Topeka & Santa Fe Railroad reaches city; **1887** Occidental College established; Los Angeles Chamber of Commerce established; **1891** E. L. Doheny and C. A. Canfield strike oil; **March 19, 1891** Chief Supreme Court Justice Earl Warren born (died 1974); **1895** Interurban Rail Line established; **1898** Griffith Park donated by Col. Griffith J. Griffith; **1899** San Pedro Bay expanded into large harbor; **Feb. 5, 1900** U.S. Senator from Illinois Adlai E. Stevenson (the younger) born (died 1965); **1901** Angel's Flight funicular railway built, discontinued 1969, revived 1996; Pacific Electric Railway begins operating distinctive "Red Car" trolleys, last line removed 1961; **1903** *Herald Examiner* newspaper founded as *The Examiner* by William Randolph Hearst; Court Flight cable railway built, discontinued 1943; **Nov. 17, 1904** sculptor Isama Noguchi born (died 1988); **Nov. 26, 1909** actress Frances Dee born (died 2004); **1910** city annexes Hollywood; **Oct. 1, 1910** 20-year labor feud with typographers culminates in dynamite explosion at Los Angeles *Times* building, 21 killed, perpetrators defended by District Attorney Clarence Darrow; **1911** Loyola Marymount University established; **Sept. 5, 1912**

composer John Cage born (died 1992); **Oct. 8, 1912** educator John William Gardner born, secretary of Health, Education and Welfare under Pres. Lyndon Johnson (died 2002); **1913** Los Angeles Aqueduct completed, delivers water from Owens River system on eastern side of Sierra Nevada; Natural History Museum established; **1914** Southwest Museum opened; **July 25, 1914** actor Woody Strode born (died 1994); **Oct. 26, 1914** actor Jackie Coogan born (died 1984); **1915** Universal City Studios opened; **Dec. 13, 1915** mystery writer Ross MacDonald born, pen name Kenneth Miller (died 1983); **May 1, 1917** actor John Beradino born (died 1996); **June 18, 1917** TV actor Richard Boone born (died 1981); **1919** University of California at Los Angeles established; Los Angeles Philharmonic Orchestra founded; **Jan. 13, 1919** TV actor Robert Stack born (died 2003); **c.1920** Simon Rodia begins assembling "Watts Towers" sculpture using odd assortment of objects on his small residential lot, through 1950; **Sept. 1, 1920** actor Richard Farnsworth born, died of self-inflicted gunshot Oct. 6, 2000; **1920s** surge occurs in construction of stucco dwellings; **1921** large Signal Hill Oil Field discovery at Long Beach brings boom to area; **Sept. 15, 1921** actor Jackie Cooper born; **July 6, 1922** actor William Schallert born; **1923** Rosecrans and Athens oil fields opened in southern part of city; Biltmore Hotel completed; **June 1923** Los Angeles Coliseum opened; **Aug. 8, 1923** swimmer, actress Esther Williams born; actor Rory Calhoun born (died 1999); **July 24, 1924** actor Robert Horton born; **1925** Los Angeles Hall of Justice built; Mount St. Mary's College established; Japanese Temple built; St. Vincent de Paul Catholic Church completed; **Jan. 13, 1925** actress Gwen Verdon born (died 2000); **July 23, 1925** actress Gloria De Haven born; **1926** Los Angeles Public Library built; **June 1, 1926** actress Marilyn Monroe born, died of drug overdose Aug. 5, 1962; **Nov. 30, 1926** TV actor Richard Crenna born (died 2003); **1927** 28-story city hall completed, renovated 2002; **Dec. 15, 1927** Marian Parker, 12, kidnapped, $1,500 ransom paid, found dead, William Hackman later hanged; **1928** Los Angeles Airport established near Pacific Ocean in southwest part of city, becomes Los Angeles International Airport (LAX) 1949; **May 9, 1928** tennis player Pancho Gonzalez born (died 1995); **1929** Los Angeles City College (2-year) established; **Jan. 1, 1929** actor Terry Moore born; **1930** Los Angeles Stock Exchange opened; **Jan. 17, 1933** actress Sheree North born; **March 31, 1935** musician Herb Alpert born; **July 13, 1935** U.S. Sen. Jack Kemp born, secretary of Housing and Urban Development under Pres. George H. W. Bush; **Sept. 3, 1935** actress Eileen Brennan born; **1937** Pepperdine University established in Watts district, moved to Malibu 1972; Los Angeles Rams NFL football team established, moved to St. Louis 1994; **Aug. 8, 1937** actor Dustin Hoffman born; **Aug. 11, 1937** ballerina Allegra Kent born; **Nov. 15, 1937** actress Margaret O'Brien born; **Dec. 8, 1937** actor James MacArthur born; **May 5, 1938** singer Michael Murphy born; **Dec. 1, 1939** Diane Lennon of Lennon Sisters

born; **July 18, 1940** actor James Brolin born; **Aug. 19, 1940** actress Jill St. John born; **1941** second Los Angeles Aqueduct completed from Owens River Valley, Sierra Nevada; **Apr. 8, 1941** singer Peggy Lennon of Lennon Sisters born; **Apr. 20, 1941** actor Ryan O'Neal born; **May 22, 1941** actor Paul Winfield born (died 2004); **Jan. 8, 1942** actress Yvette Mimieux born; **June 24, 1942** actress Michelle Lee born; **Aug. 14, 1941** singer David Crosby born; **May 31, 1943** actress Sharon Gless born; **Nov. 28, 1943** singer Randy Newman born; **Feb. 9, 1945** actress Mia Farrow born; **March 12, 1946** performer Liza Minelli born to actress Judy Garland; **July 8, 1946** ballerina Cynthia Gregory born; **July 13, 1946** entertainer Cheech Marin born; **Aug. 14, 1946** actress Susan St. James born; **Nov. 11, 1946** singer Janet Lennon of Lennon Sisters born; **1947** California State University at Los Angeles established; **June 21, 1947** TV actress Meredith Baxter born; **Feb. 5, 1948** actress Barbara Hershey born; **Feb. 4, 1949** actor Jeff Bridges born to actor Lloyd Bridges; **June 22, 1949** actress Lindsay Wagner born; **Sept. 16, 1949** actor Ed Begley, Jr. born; **Feb. 6, 1950** singer Natalie Cole born to singer Nat "King" Cole; **Aug. 25, 1950** actress Anne Archer born; **Feb. 20, 1951** actor Edward Albert born; **Sept. 7, 1951** actress Julie Kavner born; **Jan. 19, 1953** TV actor Desi Arnaz, Jr. born to Lucille Ball and Desi Arnaz; **Jan. 22, 1956** train wreck kills 30; **Jan. 31, 1957** 4 Douglas DC-7B crew members, Air Force Scorpion fighter pilot killed in midair collision, fiery debris crashes into Pacoima Junior High School yard killing three boys, injuring 74; **1958** Los Angeles Dodgers National League baseball team moved from Brooklyn, New York; **1958** central Los Angeles County courthouse built, supplemented by satellite Courthouse at Alhambra built 1974; California State University, Northridge established; **Feb. 1, 1958** C-118 and Navy P2V Neptune aircraft collide over city killing 48; **Aug. 18, 1958** actress Madeleine Stowe born; **Sept. 27, 1958** singer, actor Shaun Cassidy born; **Nov. 22, 1958** actress Jamie Lee Curtis born; **Dec. 10, 1958** dynamite explosion kills ten Fountain of the World cult members, including leader Krishna Ventu, in Box Canyon, suburban Chatsworth, northwestern part of city; **Nov. 17, 1959** actor William Moses born; **Dec. 31, 1959** actor Val Kilmer born; **1960** Los Angeles Lakers NBA basketball team moved from Minneapolis, established 1947; **1961** Los Angeles Angels American League baseball team established, moved to Anaheim and renamed California Angels 1966, renamed Anaheim Angels 1998; **Sept. 25, 1961** actress, model Heather Locklear born; **1962** Dodgers Stadium opened; **Feb. 5, 1962** actress Jennifer Jason Leigh born; **Sept. 11, 1962** actress Kristy McNichol born; **June 15, 1963** actress Helen Hunt born; **Nov. 5, 1963** actress Tatum O'Neal born to actor Ryan O'Neal; **1964** Performing Arts Center opened; **Jan. 13, 1964** actress Penelope Ann Miller born; **Jan. 27, 1964** actress Bridget Fonda born to actor Peter Fonda; **May 8, 1964** TV actress Melissa Gilbert born; **1965** Los Angeles County Museum of Art opened; **June 25, 1965** Air Force C-135 jet transport crashes near Los Angeles killing all 84 on board; **Aug.**

11–16, 1965 race riots devastate Watts district south of downtown, 35 killed, hundreds injured, $200 million in property damage; **1966** Los Angeles Zoo established at Griffith Park; **June 26, 1966** actress Mary Stuart Masterson born; **1967** Los Angeles Kings NHL hockey team established; **Apr. 19, 1968** actress Ashley Judd born to country singer Naomi Judd; **June 4, 1968** Senator and presidential candidate Robert F. Kennedy shot by Sirhan B. Sirhan following campaign speech while exiting through hotel kitchen, dies June 6; **Aug. 9, 1969** pregnant actress Sharon Tate, four others, found murdered; **Jan. 13, 1969** Scandinavian Air jet crashes into Pacific on approach to Los Angeles Airport, 15 of 48 on board killed; **Jan. 18, 1969** United Airlines Boeing 727 crashes into Pacific west of L.A. Airport, killing all 38 on board; **Apr. 17, 1969** Sirhan B. Sirhan found guilty in slaying of Robert F. Kennedy, sentenced to gas chamber, later reduced to life; **Dec. 14, 1969** cult leader Charles Manson indicted for brutal murder of Sharon Tate and four others; **1970** third Los Angeles Aqueduct completed from Mono Lake area; **Aug. 29, 1970** anti-Vietnam riots spread to Mexican-American community, leader Ruben Salazar killed, 60 injured; **Sept. 13, 1970** fire at Ponet Square Apartment-Hotel kills 11, injures 22; **Sept. 26, 1970** brush fires burn for week in northern Los Angeles County and southern Ventura County, 14 killed, 400 homes destroyed; **Oct. 4, 1970** rock singer Janis Joplin found dead of drug overdose in motel room; **1971** Los Angeles Convention Center opened; 52-story Bank of America Tower built; 52-story Atlantic Richfield Tower built; **Feb. 9, 1971** San Fernando Earthquake strikes area, 6.6 on Richter scale, 65 killed; **Dec. 30, 1971** Daniel Ellsberg reindicted for distributing secret documents while at U.S. Defense Department; **Nov. 25, 1972** actress Christina Applegate born; **May 29, 1973** Thomas Bradley defeats incumbent Sam Yorty, becomes first black mayor in Los Angeles; **1974** 62-story First Interstate Bank built; **May 17, 1974** police raid hideout of Symbionese Liberation Army, six SLA members killed, kidnapped Patty Hearst not there; **1975** 55-story Security Pacific Plaza building built; **Feb. 22, 1975** actress Drew Barrymore born; **Feb. 10, 1978** heavy rains, floods, mudslides, and 90 mph winds batter Southern California, 20 killed; **March 1, 1978** Continental Airlines DC-10 blows tire on takeoff, slides off runway in rain, two killed, 50 injured; **March 31, 1978** former head of Columbia Pictures David Begelman charged with embezzling $40,000 by endorsing checks made out to others; **Nov. 25, 1980** brush fires burn 70,000 acres, destroy over 400 homes in 5 counties in 10 days; **Sept. 4, 1982** apartment building fire leaves 24 dead; **1983** 54-story Wells Fargo Tower built; **Feb. 27–March 5, 1983** Pacific storms bring mudslides and flooding, even rare tornadoes to Los Angeles and Pasadena, 13 killed, $200 million in damage, disrupts visit of England's Queen Elizabeth II; **1989** 52-story Sanwa Bank Plaza built; **Sept. 20, 1989** Richard Ramirez, 29, accused of being the "Night Stalker" who roamed Southern California since 1985, convicted of killing 13; **1990** Los Angeles Metrolink Light Rail system's Blue Line opened, Green Line opened 1995, extended to North Hollywood 2000; 52-story 777 Tower built; 55-story Southern California Gas Center built; 73-story Library Tower built; **1992** 52-story Two California Plaza built; **March 3, 1992** African American Rodney King pulled over for speeding, beaten by police, caught on video; **Apr.–May 1992** rioting in Watts and other parts of city leaves 52 dead, reaction to acquittal of police in Rodney King beating; **Jan. 30, 1993** 4.4 mi/7 km subway from Union Station to McArthur Park opens; **Oct. 27, 1993** widespread brush fires from Ventura to Mexico affects five counties, 1,000 homes destroyed; **Apr. 17, 1993** Sgt. Stacey Koon and Officer Laurence Powell found guilty of excessive force in Rodney King beating, originally acquitted Apr. 1992; **Jan. 17, 1994** earthquake 6.8 magnitude centered in Northridge area of San Fernando Valley, 61 killed, over 9,000 injured, 45,000 homes damaged, large part of highway system shut down; **Apr. 19, 1994** Rodney King, victim of videotaped roadside beating by police 1991, awarded $3.8 million in damages; **June 13, 1994** Nicole Simpson Brown and friend Ronald Goldman found stabbed to death at Brentwood home of former football star O. J. Simpson, Simpson leads police on 60 mi/97 km chase in his white Ford Bronco June 17, shown live on TV; **Oct. 4, 1995** O. J. Simpson found not guilty in murders of wife and Ron Goldman, trial began Sept. 26, 1994; **1999** Staples Center arena opened; **July 4, 2002** Egyptian man fires gun at Israeli El Al airlines ticket counter, two killed, four injured, man killed by guards; **Aug. 6, 2002** one-year-old Guatemalan twin girls conjoined at head separated in 11-hour operation at Mattel Children's Hospital; **Sept. 2, 2002** Cathedral of Our Lady of Angels (Catholic) dedicated, cost $195 million; **2003** Chinese-American Museum opened; Walt Disney Concert Hall opened; **July 27, 2003** comedian Bob Hope dies at age 100, born London, England, May 29, 1903; **June 5, 2004** former Pres. Ronald Reagan dies in suburban Bel Air at age 93.

Malibu   *Los Angeles County*   *Southwestern California, 22 mi/35 km west of Los Angeles*

1892 Rindge Estate established by Frederick H. Rindge of Massachusetts; **1903** Rindge House destroyed by brush fire; **1905** Fred Rindge dies at age 48; **1915–1917** bitter feud lasting 30 years between May K. Rindge and railroad interests seeking coastal right-of-way through Rindge Estate peaks with farmers, travelers smashing her gates, overpowering guards; **1926** Malibu Potteries established by Mrs. Rindge, widely distributed, closed 1936 after fire; **1928** Malibu Movie Colony established, beginning of city's development; cottages built by Hollywood notables Harold Lloyd, Jack Warner, Gloria Swanson, others; **1932** work halted on Rindge "Castle," never completed; **1945** Malibu Pier built; **Aug. 16, 1960** actor Timothy Hutton born; **1970** second brush fire destroys Rindge Castle; **1972** Pepperdine University moved from near Watts, Los Angeles, established 1937; **1991** incorporated as a city; **Nov. 2, 1993** brush fires destroy 300 homes

CALIFORNIA

in this exclusive resort community, three killed, dozens injured.

Manzanar *Inyo County* *Eastern California, 93 mi/ 150 km east of Fresno*

1873 John Shepherd builds ranch house, becomes first settler; **1910** town founded as pear and apple growing center; **1935** town abandoned; **March 1942** Japanese Internment Camp established, closed late 1945; **March 3, 1992** Manzanar National Historic Site established.

Mariposa *Mariposa County* *Central California, 112 mi/180 km east of San Jose*

1846 land grant made to John Charles and Jessie Fremont; **1848** gold discovered at Mariposa Mine; **1850** Mariposa County formed; town founded as county seat; **1854** county courthouse built, oldest in state still in use; *Gazette* newspaper founded; **1856** title regranted to Charles and Fremont under new state law, critical to future land claims; **1863** St. Joseph's Catholic Church built; **1866** Schlagster Hotel built; **1902** Yosemite Valley Railroad reaches town.

Markleeville *Alpine County* *Central California, 95 mi/153 km east of Sacramento*

1848–1849 Carson Route through Sierra Nevada used by Mormon Battalion and gold prospectors; **1850s** first settlers arrive; **1861** Jacob Marklee makes claim, town founded at bridge crossing of Markleeville Creek; **1863** Marklee killed in shootout; **1864** Alpine County formed; Silver Mountain City becomes county seat, site 10 mi/ 16 km to south; **1875** county seat moved to Markleeville; Odd Fellows Hall used as county courthouse; **1928** county courthouse built.

Martinez *Contra Costa County* *Western California, 23 mi/37 km northeast of San Francisco*

1836 Ignacio Martinez settles at nearby Rancho El Piñole; **1849** town founded by Col. William M. Smith on Carquinez Strait, northeastern extension of San Francisco Bay; **1850** Contra Costa County formed; town becomes county seat; **1876** Intercontinental Railroad reaches town; incorporated as a town; **1879** Central Pacific Railroad reaches town; train ferry established to Port Costa; **1880s** Christian Brothers Winery established, moved to Napa 1932; **1882** 14-room mansion built by naturalist John Muir, lives here 1890 until his death 1914; **1884** incorporated as a city; **Nov. 25, 1914** baseball legend Joe DiMaggio born (died 1999); **1915** Shell Oil Refinery established; **1930** railroad lift bridge built across Carquinez Strait; **1931** county courthouse built, **Aug. 31, 1964** John Muir National Historic Site established; **May 21, 1976** Yuba City High School choir bus crashes, 28 killed, 20 injured.

Marysville *Yuba County* *North central California, 41 mi/66 km north of Sacramento*

1842 trading post established by Theodore Cordua; **1849** general store opened; town founded on Feather River, named for resident Mary Murphy Covillaud, Donner party survivor; town platted by Stephen J. Field, later appointed to Supreme Court by Pres. Lincoln; **1850** Yuba County formed; town becomes county seat; **1850s** Ramirez House built; **1851** incorporated as a city; **1855** St. Joseph's Roman Catholic Church built; **1857** California Central Railroad reaches town; **Jan. 16, 1864** playwright Frank Bacon born (died 1922); **1905** gold dredging begins on Yuba River to east; **1942** Camp Beale Army Base established, becomes Beale Air Force Base 1948; **1962** county courthouse built.

Merced *Merced County* *Central California, 80 mi/ 129 km east of San Jose*

1855 Merced County formed; Snelling becomes first county seat; **1868** dairying introduced to area; **1872** Southern Pacific Railroad built; town founded as new county seat; **1875** county courthouse built, **1889** incorporated as a city; **July 6, 1927** actress Janet Leigh born; **1962** Merced College (2-year) established.

Mill Valley *Marin County* *Western California, 10 mi/16 km north of San Francisco, near San Francisco Bay*

1834 sawmill built by Juan Reed; **1891** town founded on former Rancho Saucelito; **1896** Mount Tamalpais & Muir Woods Railroad built; **1900** incorporated as a city; **Jan. 9, 1908** Muir Woods National Monument proclaimed to west; **Apr. 30, 1912** actress Eve Arden born (died 1990); **1913** Mountain Theater founded at Mt. Tamalpais to west; **Nov. 21, 1961** actress Mariel Hemingway born to author Ernest Hemingway four months after his suicide.

Milpitas *Santa Clara County* *Western California, suburb 6 mi/9.7 km north of San Jose*

1821 Rancho Tularcitos granted to José Higuera; **1835** Rancho Milpitas granted to José Maria de Jesus Alviso; **1841** Alviso Adobe built; **1952** Ford Assembly Plant built, moved from Richmond; **1954** incorporated as a city to prevent annexation by San Jose; **1993** Elmwood Correctional Facility built.

Modesto *Stanislaus County* *Central California, 55 mi/72 km east-northeast of San Jose*

Nov. 14, 1841 first wagon train to California arrives at Stanislaus River with 47 emigrants from Missouri; **1854** Stanislaus County formed; Adamsville becomes county seat; **1862** county seat moved to Knights Ferry; **1870** Central Pacific Railroad built; town founded on Tuolumne River; **1872** county seat moved to Modesto; **1884** incorporated as a city; **1887** Modesto Irrigation District established; **1912** Modesto Arch erected over intersection of 9th and I streets; **1921** Modesto Junior College established; **May 14, 1944** *Star Wars* movie producer George Lucas born; **Feb. 10, 1950** Olympic swimmer Mark Spitz born; **1959** county courthouse built; **1971** New Don Pedro Dam built to east on Tuolumne River, at edge of Sierra Nevada, forming large Don Pedro Lake, replaces dam built 1923.

Mojave   *Kern County*   *South central California, 72 mi/116 km north of Los Angeles*

1876 Carson & Colorado Railroad reaches site; town founded; Morrissey Hotel built; John W. Searles uses 20-mule-team wagons to haul borax from Lake Searles, four-day journey to northeast; **1882** J. W. S. Perry builds ten large wagons, hauls borax out of Death Valley, through 1889; **1894** gold mining begins at Golden Queen Mine at Soledad Mountain, ends 1942; **1949** Edwards Air Force Base established to southeast; **1940** Mojave Airport established.

Montara   *San Mateo County*   *Western California, 18 mi/29 km south-southwest of San Francisco*

Oct. 31, 1769 Portolá expedition camps at San Pedro Point to north, climb Montara Mtn., become first white men to view San Francisco Bay; **1900** first commercial artichoke plantings made; **1925** everlasting flower industry established; **1928** Montara Point Lighthouse built.

Montebello   *Los Angeles County*   *Southwestern California, suburb 8 mi/12.9 km east of Los Angeles*

1771 Mission San Gabriel established, moved 5 mi/8 km north 1776; **1803** first orange grove in California planted at San Gabriel mission; **Jan. 8, 1847** in Battle of San Gabriel, troops of Gen. Stephen W. Kearney engage forces of Gen. José Flores, two killed on each side; **1899** town founded; **1917** oil boom begins; **1920** incorporated as a city.

Monterey   *Monterey County*   *Western California, 53 mi/85 km south of San Jose, on Pacific Ocean*

1542 Spanish explorer Cabrillo observes Point Piños; **1602** Sebastian Vizcaino sails into Monterey Bay; **1709** Gaspar de Portolá overland expedition camps here twice going and coming from San Francisco; **1770** Presidio of Monterey established; town founded at southern end of Monterey Bay; **Aug. 1775** town becomes capital of California; **1789** presidio chapel damaged by fire, rebuilt 1795; **July 7, 1808** government official Mariano Guadalupe Vallejo born, advocate of U.S. rule over California (died 1890); **1814** Spanish Customhouse built; **1818** French pirate Hypolite Bouchard raids town; **1822** California becomes part of Mexico; **1829** Sanchez Adobe house built by Gil Sanchez; Cooper House built by Capt. John B. R. Cooper; **1835** House of Four Winds built by Thomas O. Larkin; **Nov. 1836** Juan Alvarado, José Castro, and American Isaac Graham overthrow Gov. Nicolas Gutiérrez, Castro becomes

governor; **July 7, 1846** Commodore Sloat takes Monterey from Mexicans, declares California part of U.S.; **1847** Dickinson family builds first brick house in California; **1849** Monterey selected for California Constitutional Convention; Colton Hall residence built by Walter Colton; **1850** Monterey County formed; incorporated as a town, becomes county seat; capital of California moved to San Jose upon admission as a state; **1850s** port becomes important whaling center; **1851** St. Catherine's Catholic Seminary founded, moved to Benicia 1854; **1854** Monterey Jail built; **1855** Point Piños Lighthouse built to northwest, rebuilt 1872; Portuguese Whaling Station built; **1873** county seat moved to Salinas; **1880** Hotel Del Monte built, rebuilt 1887, third structure built 1924; **1889** incorporated as a city; **1892** Hopkins Marine Station of Stanford University founded by Timothy Hopkins; **1934** Few Memorial City Hall built, incorporates adobe house built 1843; **1947** Monterey Peninsula College (2-year) established; **1957** first Monterey Jazz Festival held; **Oct. 17, 1997** singer John Denver killed in crash of light aircraft over bay.

Mount Shasta   *Siskiyou County*   *Northern California, 202 mi/325 km north-northwest of Sacramento*

Feb. 14, 1824 Peter Skene Ogden discovers snowcapped Mt. Shasta (14,162 ft/4,317 m) to northeast; **1854** area first settled; town of Berryvale founded; **Sept. 1854** Capt. E. D. Pearce, merchant from Yreka to north, becomes first known person to climb Mt. Shasta; **Apr. 1875** naturalist John Muir and Jerome Fay spend 13 hours lying next to hot spring during blizzard; **1887** Southern Pacific Railroad reaches town; town platted by J. H. Sisson, first postmaster; town renamed Sisson; **1905** incorporated as a city; **1922** city renamed Mount Shasta, also called Mount Shasta City.

Napa   *Napa County*   *Western California, 35 mi/56 km north-northeast of San Francisco*

1823 Napa Valley, inhabited by Wappos, first explored by Europeans; **1832** first settlers arrive; **1840** Juarez Adobes built by Cayetano Juarez; **1848** saloon built by Nathan Coombs; town founded; **1850** Napa County formed; town becomes county seat; **1858** silver rush begins; **1860s** Napa Valley's first wineries established; **1868** Napa Valley Railroad completed; **1872** town incorporated; **1875** Napa State Hospital built; **1879** county courthouse built; **1932** Christian Brothers Winery moved from Martinez, founded 1880s; **1942** Napa Valley College (2-year) established.

Needles   *San Bernardino County*   *Southeastern California, 222 mi/357 km east-northeast of Los Angeles*

1883 Atchison, Topeka & Santa Fe Railroad built; town founded on Colorado River, named for rock formations on nearby mountain ridges; **1890** Red Rock Cantilever Railroad Bridge built across Colorado River; **1906** railroad station and Harvey House restaurant built, destroyed by fire same year with some loss of life, rebuilt 1908; **1913** incorporated as a town; **1926** National Trail Road designated U.S. Highway 66; **1958** incorporated as a city.

Nevada City   *Nevada County*   *North central California, 56 mi/90 km north-northeast of Sacramento*

1849 first placer gold deposits discovered; **1850** gold rich Lost Hill section discovered; town founded, named Coyoteville, becomes one of wealthiest mining towns in California; Union Hotel built; Empire Mine established by George Roberts; **1851** Nevada County formed; town incorporated, becomes county seat; **1852** National Hotel established; **1856** fire nearly destroys town, again in 1863; **1864** county courthouse built; **1956** Empire Mine closed.

Newport Beach   *Orange County*   *Southwestern California, 35 mi/56 km south-southeast of Los Angeles*

1872 town founded on bay of Pacific Ocean formed by mouth of Santa Ana River; **1898** Newport Pier (McFadden's Wharf) built; **1898** San Pedro surpasses town in importance as a port; **1905** Balboa Pavilion built; **1906** incorporated as a city; **1908** first annual Christmas Boat Parade held in Balboa Harbor; **1916** resort community of Balboa annexed by Newport Beach; **July 19, 1960** Navy destroyers *Ammen* and *Collett* collide killing 11 *Ammen* crewmen.

Northridge   *Los Angeles County*   *See* **Los Angeles (1958, 1994)**

Oakland   *Alameda County*   *Western California, 8 mi/12.9 km east of San Francisco, on San Francisco Bay*

c.1200 Ohlones inhabit area; **1772** Capt. Pedro Fages expedition enters San Francisco Bay; **1820** Sgt. Luis Maria Peralta receives Rancho San Antonio land grant; **1849** Moses Chase arrives at site, builds redwood lumber mill; gold rush in Sierra Nevada brings surge of fortune seekers through region; **1850** first ferry begins operating to San Francisco; Moses Chase House built; **1851** town founded by Horace W. Carpentier; **1852** incorporated as a town; **1853** Alameda County formed; Alameda becomes county seat, seat moved to San Leandro 1856; **1854** incorporated as a city; **1860** St. John's Episcopal Church built; **1860s** Mills College moved from Benicia, established 1852 as women's seminary; **1872** county seat moved to Oakland; **1879** first transcontinental train arrives; **c.1880** First and Last Chance Saloon built; **June 26, 1891** dramatist Sidney Howard born (died 1939); **1898** Lake Merritt formed by infill of unsightly saltwater estuary; **1907** California College of Arts and Crafts founded; **1914** city hall built; **1922** Oakland Zoo established; Snow Museum founded, stuffed animal collection of Henry A. Snow and son Sidney; **Feb. 30, 1922** actress Jo Van Fleet born; **1927** Oakland Municipal Airport established at North Field, replaced by Oakland International Airport at South Field 1962; **1928** Posey Tube completed, tunnel built under Inner Harbor to Alameda, replaces Webster Street Bridge; **March 7, 1930** chemist Stanley Lloyd Miller born; **Aug. 16, 1930** TV actor Robert Culp born; **1931** Paramount Theatre opened; **1936** San Francisco-Oakland Bay Bridge completed; county courthouse completed; **1937** Broadway Tunnel completed through Round Top mountain to east, later replaced by Caldecott Tunnel; **Sept. 25, 1951** actor Mark Hamill born; **1953** Laney College (2-year) established; Merritt College (2-year) established; **July 9, 1956** actor Tom Hanks born; **1960** Oakland Raiders NFL football team established; **March 29, 1962** rap singer MC Hammer born; **1965** Oakland Ballet Company established; **1968** Oakland Athletics American League baseball team moves here from Kansas City; **1969** Oakland Museum opened; **1971** Golden State Warriors NBA basketball team moved from San Francisco; **Dec. 15, 1977** Richard and James Schoenfeld found guilty of 1976 Chowchilla school bus kidnapping, get life sentence without parole; **Apr. 7, 1982** tanker truck explosion in tunnel kills seven; **Oct. 17, 1989** Loma Prieta Earthquake, magnitude 7.1, strikes Bay Area as third game of World Series between Athletics and San Francisco Giants is about to begin, collapsing sections of Nimitz Freeway (I-880) and Bay Bridge, total 62 killed; **1990** Oakland Symphony Orchestra founded; 29-story American President Line building completed; **Oct. 20–21, 1991** brush fires spread through hills above Oakland, 24 killed, 3,000 homes destroyed; **Dec. 18, 1996** school board recognizes black form of English as a distinct language, prompting nationwide debate.

Oceanside   *San Diego County*   *Southwestern California, 30 mi/48 km north of San Diego, on Pacific Ocean*

July 20, 1769 Father Juan Crespi arrives in area; **1798** Mission San Luis Rey de Francia founded to northeast; **1837** Rancho Santa Margarita hacienda built by Pio Pico; **1883** California Southern Railroad reaches site; town founded by J. Chauncey Hayes; **1888** incorporated as a city; first Oceanside Pier built, sixth structure built 1987; **1934** Mira Costa College (2-year) established; **1942** Camp Pendleton Marine Corps Base established to north; **1971** Oceanside Public Library built; **Aug. 28, 1976** TV actress Mary Anissa "Buffy" Jones, 18, dies of drug overdose (born 1958).

Ojai   *Ventura County*   *Southwestern California, 67 mi/108 km west-northwest of Los Angeles*

1872 town founded, named Nordhoff for Charles Nordhoff, columnist for New York *Herald*, helped establish town; **1888** preparatory school founded by Yale graduates S. D. and W. L. Thatcher; **1915** Libbey Mansion built by glass manufacturer Edward D. Libbey; **1916** Libbey persuades town to remodel buildings in Spanish style, compatible with his mansion; The Pergola built, trellis-covered walkway in town center, demolished 1977, rebuilt 1998; **1917** town renamed ("O-hei"),

Chumash term for "nest"; **1921** town incorporated; **1923** Ojai Valley Inn built by Libbey.

Ontario   *San Bernardino County*   *Southwestern California, 36 mi/58 km east of Los Angeles*

1881 Ontario Irrigation Colony established by Canadian brothers George and William B. Chaffey; efficient pipeline plan allows water distribution to every land parcel; town founded; **1883** Chaffey College (2-year) established, moved to nearby Cucamonga (Rancho Cucamonga) 1960; **1886** Chaffey brothers leave for Australia to apply their irrigation methods there; **1891** incorporated as a town; **1904** Guasti Vineyard established to east by Secundo Guasti; **1910** incorporated as a city; **1912** Pacific Electric Railway ("Red Car") line reaches city; **1929** Ontario Airport established, becomes Ontario International Airport 1946; **Sept. 6, 1970** Ontario Motor Speedway opened, closed 1980.

Orange   *Orange County*   *Southwestern California, 30 mi/48 km southeast of Los Angeles*

1869 town founded by Alfred B. Chapman and Andrew Glassell, named Richland; **1875** town renamed by Chapman, uses poker game to decide among Orange, Lemon, Almond, or Olive; **1876** first Valencia orange trees introduced; **1888** incorporated as a city; **1910** Cleveland National Forest created to east; **1950s** Chapman University moved from Whittier, established 1861; **May 21, 1985** septuplets born, mother took fertility drug, one stillborn, two die in June.

Oroville   *Butte County*   *North central California, 67 mi/108 km north of Sacramento*

1849 gold discovered; town founded on Feather River, originally named Ophir City; **1850** Butte County formed; Hamilton becomes county seat; **1853** county seat moved to Bidwell's Bar; **1856** county seat moved to Oroville; **1857** incorporated as a city; **1870s** thousands of Chinese arrive to work the mines; **1898** first successful elevated bucket dredge built by W. P. Hammon and Thomas Couch; **1928** Oroville Theater opened; **1968** Lake Oroville formed by dam to northeast on Feather River, begun 1957; **1971** county courthouse built, addition completed 1996.

Oxnard   *Ventura County*   *Southwestern California, 55 mi/89 km west of Los Angeles*

1898 American Sugar Beet Company plant built; town founded on Pacific Ocean; **1903** incorporated as a city; **1907** Carnegie Library built, becomes Carnegie Art Museum 1988; **1937** Oxnard Harbor District established; **1942** Point Mugu Naval Air Station established to southeast; **1946** Pacific Missile Test Center established, Air Station and Test Center become Naval Air Weapons Station 1992; **1952** Oxnard Air Force Base established; **1975** Oxnard College (2-year) established; **Jan. 31, 2000** Alaska Airlines airliner out of Puerto Vallarta, Mexico, bound for San Francisco, crashes into Santa Barbara Channel while attempting to reach Los Angeles Airport for emergency landing, 78 killed.

Pacoima   *Los Angeles County*   *See* **Los Angeles (1957)**

Palm Springs   *Riverside County*   *Southern California, 103 mi/309 km east-southeast of Los Angeles*

1774 site named Agua Caliente by Spanish for its hot springs; **1862** stagecoach stop established; **1876** Southern Pacific Railroad built; town founded; Agua Caliente Indian Reservation established to west; **1884** McCallum Adobe built by John McCallum, first permanent white settler; **1922** Palm Canyon National Monument authorized to south, fails consent of Agua Caliente tribe, never fully established; **1938** incorporated as a city.

Palo Alto   *Santa Clara County*   *Western California, 16 mi/26 km northwest of San Jose*

Nov. 6–11, 1769 Portolá expedition establishes camp here; **March 1776** Juan Bautista de Anza discovers cross erected by Portolá; **1891** Stanford University established; town founded on San Francisco Bay; **1894** incorporated as a city; **June 19, 1914** Sen. Alan Cranston born (died 2000); **1920** Hoover House built, home of Pres. Herbert Clark Hoover, deeded to Stanford University 1944 after wife Lou Henry Hoover's death; **Nov. 4, 1950** TV actress Markie Post born; **Sept. 10, 1953** actress Amy Irving born; **Apr. 24, 1970** arson fire destroys research lab and work of 10 professors at Stanford University; **1971** journalist Don Hoefler, working for *Electronic News*, becomes first to coin term "Silicon Valley" to region northwest of San Jose for its high concentration of computer-related businesses.

Pasadena   *Los Angeles County*   *Southwestern California, 12 mi/19 km northeast of Los Angeles*

1826 Rancho San Pasqual granted to elderly mission housekeeper Doña Eulalia Perez de Guillen, property passed on with her marriage at age 100, grant later abandoned by step-heirs; **1839** Flores Adobe built for Doña Eulalia; **1843** Don Manuel Garfias receives abandoned grant; **1873** property acquired by Benjamin D. Wilson and Dr. John S. Griffin; Dr. Thomas B. Elliott of Indianapolis purchases land from Griffin, beginning of arrival of wealthy Easterners; **1875** town founded; **1882** Pasadena Public Library founded; **1885** Southern Pacific Railroad reaches town; **1886** incorporated as a city; Raymond Hotel built; **1890** simple flower festival marks beginning of annual Tournament of Roses; **1891** California Institute of Technology (Cal Tech) established; **1904** Mount Wilson Observatory established to north; **c.1905** original Busch Gardens developed as parkland on estate of St. Louis beer baron Adolphus Busch, offer of property for use as park rejected by city 1938, later developed; **Sept. 28, 1911** tennis player H. (Henry) Ellsworth Vines, Jr. born (died 1994); **Nov. 5, 1911** Galbraith Rogers' transcontinental flight from New

York arrives, departed Sept. 17, with stopovers; **Aug. 15, 1912** gourmet Julia Child born (died 2004); **1916** first annual Rose Bowl football game held; **1919** Pasadena (Norton Simon) Museum of Art opened; **Oct. 19, 1921** actor George Nader born (died 2002); **1923** Millard House built for Mrs. George M. Millard, designed by Frank Lloyd Wright; **1924** Pasadena City College (2-year) established; **Aug. 7, 1926** satirist, entertainer Stanley Freberg born; **1927** city hall built; **1929** Pasadena Symphony Orchestra founded; **1930** Art Center College of Design established; **Jan. 13, 1942** actor Richard Moll born; **1944** Jet Propulsion Laboratory established at California Institute of Technology, becomes part of NASA 1958; **Nov. 6, 1946** actress Sally Field born; **Oct. 30, 1951** actor Harry Hamlin born; **June 6, 1971** Air West DC-9 and Navy Phantom F-4 jet collide in San Gabriel Mountains, all 49 passengers, Navy pilot killed, co-pilot survives.

Pebble Beach *Monterey County* See **Carmel-by-the-Sea**

Petaluma *Sonoma County* *Western California, 33 mi/53 km north of San Francisco*

1833 Casa Grande built by Gen. Mariano Vallejo at Rancho Petaluma to northeast; **1850** town founded on Petaluma River; **1852** Americans arrive in region; **1858** incorporated as a city; **1878** Canadian Lyman Byce invents egg incubator, establishes chicken and egg industry; **June 19, 1919** film critic Pauline Kael born (died 2001); **Aug. 13, 1968** first annual National Egg Day established; **Oct. 1, 1993** Polly Klaas, 12, kidnapped, later found dead at Cloverdale to north Dec. 4, drifter Richard Allen Davis charged, sentenced to death.

Pittsburg *Contra Costa County* *Western California, 35 mi/56 km northeast of San Francisco*

1849 town of New York Landing founded by Lt. William Tecumseh Sherman on Suisun Bay, northeastern extension of San Francisco Bay; **1851** coal discovered at Mt. Diablo to south; town renamed Black Diamond; **1903** incorporated as a city; **1906** Columbia Steel Company established; **1911** city renamed for Pittsburgh, Pennsylvania; **1941** Camp Stoneman Army Base established, closed 1954; **1974** Los Medanos College (2-year) established.

Placerville *El Dorado County* *North central California, 40 mi/64 km east-northeast of Sacramento*

1848 placer gold deposits discovered by William Daylor and Perry McCoon; town founded, named Hangtown for local Hangman's Tree; **1850** El Dorado County formed; Coloma becomes county seat; **1852** Catholic church built; **1854** town incorporated, renamed Placerville; **July 6, 1856** fire destroys town, recurs 1864 and 1865; **1856** Bell Tower erected as community fire alarm, bell not installed until 1865; **1857** county seat moved to Placerville; **1859**

Comstock silver rush begins; **1861** Placerville Academy founded, closed 1890s; Methodist church completed; **1865** St. Patrick's Catholic Church built on site of old church; **1900** incorporated as a city; **1912** county courthouse built.

Point Reyes Station *Marin County* *Western California, 29 mi/47 km north-northwest of San Francisco*

June 17, 1759 Sir Francis Drake sails into bay on southern shore of Point Reyes Peninsula, later named Drakes Bay; **1870** Point Reyes Lighthouse built; **1874** North Pacific Coast Railroad reaches site; town founded at end of Tomales Bay, Pacific Ocean, named Olema Station; **1883** town renamed; **1933** hunter's driver discovers metal plate bearing inscription by Francis Drake, rediscovered by motorist 1936, determined authentic by professionals, concluded later an elaborate prank; **1933** railroad abandoned; **Oct. 20, 1972** Point Reyes National Seashore established to west.

Pomona *Los Angeles County* *Southwestern California, 30 mi/48 km east of Los Angeles*

1830 Rancho San José granted to Ygnacio Alvarado and Ricardo Vejar; **1837** Palomares Adobe built; **1875** Southern Pacific Railroad built; town founded, named for Roman goddess of fruit trees; **1888** incorporated as a city; **1922** first Los Angeles County Fair held, "biggest county fair in country"; **1925** W. K. Kellogg Institute of Animal Husbandry founded, becomes part of University of California 1932; **1938** California Polytechnic State University established.

Port Chicago *Contra Costa County* See **Concord (1944)**

Quincy *Plumas County* *Northeastern California, 103 mi/166 km north-northeast of Sacramento*

1851 wagon road built through Sierra Nevada; **1854** Plumas County formed; town founded as county seat by H. J. Bradley; **1921** county courthouse built; **1968** Feather River Community College established.

Red Bluff *Tehama County* *Northern California, 123 mi/198 km north-northwest of Sacramento*

1849 Ide Adobe House built to north by Gen. William B. Ide, served as only president of California Republic (1846–1848); **1856** Tehama County formed; town of Tehama becomes county seat; town of Red Bluff founded on Sacramento River; **1857** county seat moved to Red Bluff; **1864** residents raise money to assist abolitionist John Brown's widow, three daughters residing here; **1876** incorporated as a city; **Apr. 30, 1916** music director Robert Shaw born (died 1999); **1922** county courthouse built; **1964** Red Bluff Diversion Dam built on Sacramento River, sends irrigation water south through Tehama Colusa Canal, 28 mi/45 km long, dam and canal completed 1966.

CALIFORNIA

Redding *Shasta County* *Northern California, 153 mi/246 km north-northwest of Sacramento*

1843 northernmost Mexican land claim of Rancho Buenaventura made to Pierson Barton Reading, establishes area's lumber industry; **1850** Shasta County formed; town of Shasta becomes county seat; **1872** Central Pacific Railroad arrives; town founded on Sacramento River, named for railroad agent B. B. Redding; town incorporated; **1888** county seat moved to Redding; **May 6, 1907** Lassen Peak and Cinder Cone National Monument established to east; **1912** Lassen Peak volcano begins series of eruptions, continue into 1921; **Aug. 9, 1916** Lassen Volcanic National Park established from national monument; **1921** Simpson College established; **1945** Lake Shasta formed by dam to north on Sacramento River; **1956** county courthouse built; **1962** Clair Engle Lake formed by Trinity Dam to northwest on Trinity River; **1963** Whiskeytown Lake formed by dam to west on Clear Creek; **Nov. 8, 1965** Whiskeytown-Shasta-Trinity National Recreation Area proclaimed to north and west.

Redlands *San Bernardino County* *Southwestern California, 63 mi/101 km east of Los Angeles*

1819 Asistencia San Bernardino sub-mission established, razed for orange groves 1857, later reconstructed as historical site; **1881** town founded by Frank E. Brown and Edward G. Judson; **1888** town incorporated; **1894** A. K. Smiley Public Library founded; **1907** University of Redlands established; **1932** Lincoln Memorial erected.

Redondo Beach *Los Angeles County* *Southwestern California, 17 mi/27 km southwest of Los Angeles*

1890 railroad reaches site; town founded on Pacific Ocean; Hotel Redondo built; **1892** incorporated as a city; **1907** five-day real estate boom occurs with announcement by railroad tycoon Henry E. Huntington of plans for vast improvements, plans unfulfilled; **Sept. 18, 1907** physicist Edwin Mattison McMillan born (died 1991); **1912** development of San Pedro Harbor near Long Beach ends city's role as seaport; **1926** rail service suspended.

Redwood City *San Mateo County* *Western California, 25 mi/40 km south-southeast of San Francisco*

1851 town founded on San Francisco Bay as redwood milling center, named Embarcadero; shipbuilding begins; **1856** San Mateo County formed; town becomes county seat; **1858** town renamed Redwood City; **1868** incorporated as a city; **1906** San Francisco Earthquake damages newly completed third county courthouse beyond repair; **1913** construction begins on Hetch-Hetchy Aqueduct from reservoir in Yosemite National Park to east, completed 1923, enlarged 1938; **1958** fifth county courthouse completed; **1968** Cañada College (2-year) established.

Richmond *Contra Costa County* *Western California, 12 mi/19 km north-northeast of San Francisco*

1859 Ellis Landing established by George Ellis; **1873** East Brother Lighthouse built at point separating San Francisco Bay from its northern extension San Pablo Bay; **1899** Atchison, Topeka & Santa Fe Railroad built; town founded on San Francisco Bay; **1900** Santa Fe Railroad establishes ferry service to San Francisco; **1905** town incorporated; **1917** Richmond Inner Harbor built; **1931** Ford Assembly Plant built, closed 1952; **1957** Richmond-San Rafael Bridge completed across San Francisco Bay to San Rafael, replacing ferry; **1984** Standard Oil Refinery completed.

Ridgecrest *Kern County* *South central California, 118 mi/190 km north-northeast of Los Angeles*

1933 town founded; **1943** China Lake Naval Ordnance Test Station (NOTS) established in two large areas to north and east, becomes Naval Weaponry Center 1967, then Naval Air Warfare Center 1992; **1947** Inyokern Airport established; **1963** incorporated as a city; **1973** Cerro Coso Community College established.

Riverside *Riverside County* *Southwestern California, 52 mi/84 km east of Los Angeles*

1774 Capt. Juan de Anza builds bridge across Santa Ana River; **1862** flooding destroys herds of cattle; **1870** town founded by Southern California Colony Association; **1873** first navel orange trees planted, introduced by Eliza Tibbets, area becomes known for its citrus industry; **1883** incorporated as a city; **1893** Riverside County formed; town becomes county seat; **1903** county courthouse built; **1907** Mission Inn established by Capt. Christopher Columbus Miller; **1917** March Air Force Base established to southeast; **1922** La Sierra University established; **1924** Municipal Museum opened; Civic Center built; **1950** California Baptist College established; **1954** University of California at Riverside established; **1993** California Citrus State Historic Park established.

Rosamond *Kern County* *South central California, 60 mi/97 km north of Los Angeles*

1931 large-scale gold mining begins to west, suspended 1941; **1933** large Muroc Army Air Field established to east as bombing range; town founded at west entrance; **1949** air field becomes Edwards Air Force Base; **1951** Air Force Flight Test Center established; **Dec. 12, 1953** Chuck Yeager sets flight speed record at 1,650 mph/2,655 kph, pulls out of uncontrolled tumble, lands on Rogers Dry Lake bed; **Sept. 17, 1959** first powered flight of F-15 jet fighter.

Sacramento *Sacramento County* *North central California, 77 mi/124 km northeast of San Francisco*

1839 Capt. John Sutter Sr. arrives, swears allegiance to Mexico, receives grant, builds fort on Sacramento River, at confluence of American River, sole outpost in the California interior, run as a barony with Native Americans as subjects; **Jan. 24, 1848** James Marshall discovers gold at Sutter's Mill, on American River, 35 mi/56 km to southeast; **Jan. 1849** town of Sacramento founded on Sutter rancho; **1850** Sacramento County formed; town incorporated, becomes county seat; California Archives and State Library established; **Sept. 9, 1850** California admitted to Union as 31st state; **1852** fire destroys much of town; **1853** last in series of three disastrous floods occurs, first occurred 1849, periodic flooding continues; Tremont Hotel built; Sutterville Brewery built; **1854** state capital moved from Benicia; **Jan. 27, 1855** boilers explode on steamboat *Pearl* as it races the *Enterprise* on Sacramento River, 56 of 93 on board killed; **1856** Sacramento Valley Railroad, first in California, built to nearby Folsom by Theodore Judah; **Feb. 3, 1857** *Sacramento Bee* newspaper founded; **1859** California State Fair first held in Sacramento, held in various locations since 1854; **July 28, 1859** actress Mary Anderson born (died 1940); **1860–1861** Pony Express makes mail runs from St. Joseph, Missouri, office later serves as Pony Express Museum; **Sept. 2, 1866** U.S. Sen. Hiram Warren Johnson born (died 1945); **1869** Central Pacific Railroad completed to Promontory, Utah, joins Union Pacific Railroad as first transcontinental rail line; **1873** Sutter moves to Pennsylvania, dies 1880 at Washington, D.C., while seeking reinstatement of California properties lost to miners and squatters from Congress; **1874** state capitol completed, begun 1861; **1885** Crocker Art Museum established; **1916** Sacramento City College (2-year) established; **1918** city library completed; **Feb. 29, 1920** actor James Mitchell born; **1927** Memorial Auditorium completed; Sacramento Zoo established; **1928** twin state office building and state library/courts building completed; **1936** McClellan Army Air Field established, becomes Air Force Base 1948, closed 1995; **July 23, 1936** Supreme Court Justice Anthony McLeod Kennedy born; **1942** Sacramento Theatre Company established; **Aug. 9, 1944** actor Sam Elliott born; **1947** California State University, Sacramento established; Sacramento Opera founded; **Sept. 19, 1950** TV actress Joan Lunden born; **1955** American Valley College established; **1965** downtown county courthouse completed; North Sacramento annexed; **1967** Sacramento Metropolitan Airport established to north, renamed International Airport 1996; **1970** Cosumnes River College (2-year) established; **Sept. 24, 1972** rebuilt Korean War vintage Sabre jet slams into ice-cream parlor, 22 killed, 26 injured; **Sept. 5, 1975** Pres. Gerald Ford unharmed by pistol aimed at him by Lynette "Squeaky" Fromme, follower of Charles Manson as he enters state capitol; **1981** California State Railroad Museum opened; **Dec. 11, 1985** computer store operator Hugh Scrutton killed by package bomb, first death caused by unknown assailant the "Unabomber"; **Apr. 24, 1995** "Unabomber," identity unknown, kills Gilbert Murray of California Forestry Association with mailed package bomb, *New York Times* receives letter claiming responsibility; **June 23, 1996** Ted Kaczynski, the "Unabomber," pleads not guilty to mail bombings which killed three, injured 23 over 17-year period across U.S., sentenced to four life terms May 15; **Aug. 1997** Sacramento Philharmonic Orchestra established; **Aug. 20, 2001** Ukrainian immigrant kills wife, five relatives, later kills 3-year-old, captured Aug. 30; **Sept. 10, 2001** Joseph Ferguson, 20, after killing five people since Sept. 1 shoots self as police surround him; **Oct. 8, 2003** Gov. Gray Davis recalled in election, Austrian born actor Arnold Schwarzenegger sworn in as governor Nov. 18.

Salinas *Monterey County* *Western California, 50 mi/80 km south of San Jose, near Pacific Ocean*

1850 Monterey County formed; Monterey becomes county seat; **1856** Half-Way House inn built by Deacon Elias Howe; town founded near Monterey Bay; **1873** county seat moved to Salinas; **1874** incorporated as a city; **1920** Hartnell College (2-year) established; **Feb. 27, 1902** author John Steinbeck born (died 1968); **1926** guayule plantation established; **1931** American Rubber Producers Guayule Plant established; **1937** county courthouse built, addition built 1968; **1964** suburb Alisal (East Salinas) annexed by Salinas; **1998** National Steinbeck Center opened.

San Andreas *Calaveras County* *Central California, 52 mi/84 km southeast of Sacramento*

1849 town founded by Mexican miners; **1850** Calaveras County formed; Double Springs becomes county seat; Metropolitan Hotel built, immortalized in Mark Twain's short story "The Jumping Frog of Calaveras County," destroyed by fire 1926, same claim made of Hotel Angel at Angels Camp; **1851** county seat moved to Jackson; **1852** county seat moved to Mokelumne Hill; **1866** county seat moved to San Andreas; **1967** county courthouse built.

San Bernardino *San Bernardino County* *Southwestern California, 58 mi/93 km east of Los Angeles*

May 10, 1810 Padre Francisco Dumetz arrives on feast day of San Bernardino of Siena; **1851** town founded by 500 Mormons led by Capt. Jefferson Hunt; **1852** town platted by Hunt; **1853** San Bernardino County founded, largest county in U.S. (20,062 sq mi/51,961 sq km); town becomes county seat; **1854** incorporated as a city; **1857** Mormons called back to Utah by Brigham Young; **1885** Santa Fe Railroad reaches town; **1926** county courthouse built; **1927** San Bernardino College established; **Jan. 30, 1930** actor Gene Hackman born; **1940** McDonald brothers' restaurant established, replaced 1953 by familiar slope-roofed building with golden arches, sold to Ray Kroc 1961; **1942** Norton Army Air Field established, becomes Air Force Base after World War II, closed 1994; **June 19, 1962** singer Paula Abdul born; **1965** California State University, San Bernardino established; **1994** San Bernardino International Airport established at former air base; **Dec. 1998** McDonald's Museum established at original McDonald's Restaurant; **Dec. 25, 2003** mudslide kills 15 at church camp, triggered by heavy rains on slopes denuded by Oct. wildfires.

San Bruno   *San Mateo County*   *Western California, 12 mi/19 km south of San Francisco*

1862 San Bruno House roadhouse established by Richard Cunningham; **1863** San Francisco & San Jose Railroad reaches site; town founded on San Francisco Bay; **1884** Golden Gate National Cemetery established; **1899** Tanforan Race Track opened, closed 1912, reopened 1933 with legalized betting, closed again 1964; **1914** incorporated as a city; **Oct. 16, 1946** actress Suzanne Somers born; **1969** Skyline College (2-year) established.

San Buenaventura   *Ventura County*   *See* **Ventura**

San Clemente   *Orange County*   *Southwestern California, 53 mi/85 km southeast of Los Angeles*

1835 Richard Henry Dana, Jr. (1815–1882) anchors in ship *Pilgrim* at Dana Point to north, author of classic sea epic *Two Years Before the Mast* 1840; **1925** town founded on Pacific Ocean; **1927** mansion built by Hamilton Cotton, purchased 1969 by Pres. Richard M. Nixon for use as "Western White House"; **1928** town incorporated; **1942** large Camp Pendleton Marine Corps Base established to south; **Aug. 17, 1964** church bus accident leaves six dead, over 60 injured; **June 14, 1967** first phase of San Onofre Nuclear Power Plant begins production to southeast.

San Diego   *San Diego County*   *Southwestern California, 105 mi/169 km southeast of Los Angeles*

1539 site visited by Father Marcos de Niza; **Sept. 28, 1542** area explored by Portuguese explorer Juan Rodriguez Cabrillo; **1769** Mission San Diego de Alcalá founded on Pacific Ocean by Franciscan missionary Junipero Serra and Gov. Portolá; **1780** mission rebuilt following destructive 1775 Native American attack and death of Friar Luis Jaume; **1793** English research vessel *Discovery* visits harbor commanded by George Vancouver; **1803** American smuggling ship *Lelia Byrd* engages in battle with Spanish at Ballast Point; earthquake destroys mission, rebuilt by 1813; **1820** Casa de Carrillo built; **1829** Casa de Bandini built; **1834** San Diego pueblo organized; **Dec. 6, 1846** General Kearney retreats to San Diego following defeat by Mexicans; **1850** San Diego County formed; incorporated as a city, becomes county seat; **1856** Whaley House built by Thomas Whaley; **1867** Alonzo Erastus Horton arrives by boat, becomes "father of San Diego," credited with platting modern city; **1868** *San Diego Union* newspaper founded; **1872** fire destroys Old Town business center; businesses shift to New Town; **1881** *San Diego Evening Tribune* newspaper founded; **1885** Atchison, Topeka & Santa Fe Railroad reaches city; **1897** State Normal School established, becomes San Diego State University; **1902** Point Loma Nazarene College established; **1911** San Diego Symphony Orchestra founded; **1912** Museum of Natural History established; **Oct. 14, 1913** Cabrillo National Monument established at Point Loma; **1915–1916** Panama-Pacific Exposition held; **1918** influenza outbreak strikes city, 300 killed; **Aug.**

30, 1918 Boston Red Sox baseball star Ted Williams born (died 2002); **Nov. 9, 1918** professional swimmer Florence Chadwick born, first woman to swim English Channel 1950 (died 1995); **1919** San Diego & Arizona Eastern Railroad begins service to El Centro; **Oct. 27, 1920** actress Nanette Fabray born; **1922** San Diego Zoo established; **1926** San Diego Museum of Art opened; **1927** Charles Ryan builds *Spirit of St. Louis* airplane for aviator Charles Lindbergh; **1928** Lindbergh Field (San Diego International Airport) established through efforts of Charles Lindbergh; **June 5, 1928** actor Robert Lansing born; **1929** Fox Theatre built, converted to Copley Symphony Hall 1984; **1931** Mission San Diego Church rebuilt; **Jan. 5, 1931** actor Robert Duvall born; **June 24, 1931** golfer Billy Casper born; **Sept. 17, 1934** tennis player Margaret Connolly born (died 1969); **1936** County Administrative Center built; **1938** Civic Center built; **Dec. 30, 1942** actor Fred Ward born; **Feb. 29, 1947** TV actor Ted Danson born; **1949** University of San Diego established; **June 18, 1950** flying boat *Caroline Mars* arrives from Honolulu with 144 people, setting passenger record; **1952** U.S. International University established; **1957** annexation of San Ysidro to south takes city limits to Mexican border; **March 20, 1957** actress Theresa Russell born; **1960** Salk Institute for medical research established by Dr. Jonas Salk; San Diego Chargers NFL football team established; **1961** county courthouse built; **1964** San Diego Mesa College (2-year) established; SeaWorld marine park opened; **1965** San Diego Opera founded; **1967** Jack Murphy Stadium built; **Dec. 28, 1968** DC-3 airplane crashes into mountain to southeast killing all 12 on board; **1969** Coronado Bridge built across San Diego Bay; San Diego Miramar College (2-year) established; San Diego Padres National League baseball team established; **Dec. 22, 1969** Navy jet crashes into hanger at Miramar Naval Air Station killing 14, injuring 11; **Dec. 12, 1975** actress Mayim Bialik born; **Dec. 9, 1977** 61 Americans released from Mexican jails arrive at San Diego Airport, arrested for drug trafficking early 1970s; **Sept. 25, 1978** Pacific Southwest Boeing 727 is struck by Cessna aircraft, 137 in two planes killed, 13 killed on ground; **1980** San Diego Trolley light rail system dedicated; **1989** 34-story Symphony Tower built; **1991** 30-story Emerald-Shapery Center built; 34-story One American Plaza built; **1992** *Union* and *Evening Tribune* newspapers merge to become *Union-Tribune*; 41-story One Harbor Drive building built; 39-story Hyatt Regency Hotel built; **1997** QUALCOMM Stadium opened; Cox Arena opened; **Feb. 1, 2002** Danielle van Dam, 7, abducted, found slain, neighbor David Westerfield sentenced to death for her murder Jan. 3, 2003; **Oct. 2003** wildfires in county destroy hundreds of homes, at least 11 killed, also in San Bernardino area.

San Francisco   *San Francisco County*   *Western California, on San Francisco Bay, Pacific Ocean*

Nov. 2, 1769 Sgt. José Ortega, Spanish scout for Gaspar de Portolá discovers San Francisco Bay; **1776** Mission San Francisco de Asís founded by Father Junipero Serra, later renamed Mission Dolores; Presidio established by Col.

CALIFORNIA

Juan Bautista de Anza; **1834** Yerba Buena pueblo established; **1835** probable first house built by Englishman Capt. William A. Richardson; **1846** group of Mormons arrive led by Samuel Brannan; **1847** Russ House built by Christian Russ, destroyed by 1906 earthquake; pueblo renamed San Francisco; *California Star* newspaper founded by Brannan; **Jan. 1848** discovery of gold at Sutter's Mill in Sierra Nevada first depopulates town, later brings large influx of settlers and transients; **1850** San Francisco County formed; incorporated as a city, becomes county seat; first ferry begins operating across bay to Oakland; fire consumes 18 city blocks, one of six such fires in four-year period; **May 3–5, 1851** 2,500 buildings destroyed by fire, another 500 buildings in fire June 22; **June 1851** first vigilance committee formed to eradicate gangster activities from city politics; **1853** Golden Gate University established; California Academy of Science established; **1855** University of San Francisco established; **March 31, 1855** mining engineer John Hays Hammond born (died 1936); **Oct. 1855** U.S. Marshal George W. H. Richardson shot by powerful Italian mobster Charles Cora; *Bulletin* newspaper founded in response to shooting by James King, anticorruption advocate; **1856** San Mateo County separates from San Francisco County, leaving city of San Francisco coterminous with its county; **May 8, 1856** extralegal Vigilance Committee hangs four, exiles 70 in response to lawlessness; **May 14, 1856** James King gunned down at his *Bulletin* newspaper office by opponent James Casey; Casey and Charles Cora hanged May 22 by Vigilance Committee; **Sept. 17, 1857** artist Harry Wilson Watrous born (died 1940); **Oct. 30, 1857** author Gertrude Atherton born (died 1948); **1859** military prison established on Alcatraz Island; **Sept. 13, 1859** antislavery U.S. Sen. David Broderick duels with pro-slavery California Supreme Court Chief Justice David S. Terry at Merced Lake, in southwest part of city, Terry mortally wounded, dies three days later; **July 5, 1862** biologist George H. F. Nuttall born (died 1937); **Apr. 29, 1863** newspaper publisher William Randolph Hearst born (died 1951); **June 19, 1863** theatrical producer William Aloysius Brady born (died 1950); **1864** San Francisco & San Jose Railroad reaches city; **June 1, 1865** *San Francisco Daily Examiner* newspaper founded, William Randolph Hearst, 23, becomes editor 1887; **Apr. 6, 1866** journalist, author Lincoln Steffens born (died 1936); **Sept. 1, 1866** pro boxer John James Corbett born (died 1933); **Nov. 28, 1866** actor David Warfield born (died 1951); **1870** Golden Gate Park created in former sand dunes area; **Nov. 4, 1871** astronomer William Hammond Wright born (died 1959); **1873** Andrew Hallidie's cable cars introduced; tailor Jacob Davis invents first jeans, later joined by business partner Levi Strauss; **March 22, 1873** painter Ernest Lawson born (died 1939); **1874** Natural History Museum opened; California School of Fine Arts founded; **Jan. 5, 1874** physiologist Joseph Erlanger born, Nobel Prize 1944 (died 1965); **March 26, 1874** poet Robert Frost born (died 1963); **Jan. 12, 1876** author Jack London born (died 1916); **Apr. 30, 1877** author Alice B. Toklas born (died 1967); **May 8, 1878** sculptor Robert Ingersoll Aitken

born (died 1949); **May 27, 1878** dancer Isadora Duncan born, died Sept. 14, 1927, neckscarf entangled in wheel of moving sports car at Nice, France; **July 16, 1880** novelist Kathleen Thompson Norris born (died 1966); **1882** San Francisco Stock Exchange organized; **July 4, 1883** cartoonist Rube Goldberg born (died 1970); **Nov. 2, 1883** novelist Martin Flavin born (died 1967); **1884** Presidio National Cemetery established; **Jan. 19, 1888** World War II Gen. Millard Fillmore Harmon, Jr. born (died 1945); **Apr. 13, 1888** inventor John Hays Hammond, Jr. born, developed radio-control devices (died 1965); **1889** San Francisco Zoo established, opens in Golden Gate Park 1927; **1891** St. Mary's Catholic Cathedral built, narrowly escaped 1906 fire; **1893** De Young Art Museum opened, new museum scheduled to open 2005; **Jan. 8, 1893** architect Harvey Wiley Corbett born (died 1954); **1894** California Mid-Winter Exposition held in Golden Gate Park; **July 26, 1895** comedian Gracie Allen born (died 1964); **July 14, 1897** first gold shipment from Klondike Gold Rush arrives aboard the vessel *Excelsior*; **1899** State Normal School established, becomes San Francisco State University; **Feb. 20, 1902** landscape photographer Ansel Adams born (died 1984); **1903** 12-story Ferry Building completed, replaces 1877 structure; **May 27, 1903** Horatio Nelson Jackson begins first automobile journey across America, arrives New York July 26; **1904** St. Francis Hotel built, now Westin Hotel, narrowly missed destruction in 1906 earthquake; **1905** U.S. Post Office built, survived 1906 earthquake; **Apr. 21, 1905** Gov. Edmund Gerald "Pat" Brown born (died 1996); **Oct. 1905** Pacific Gas and Electric Company established; **Apr. 18, 1906** San Francisco Earthquake strikes San Andreas Fault at 5:16 A.M., 8.3 magnitude, leaves 503 dead, 700 dead with subsequent fire, thousands injured (coincided with earthquake in Chile on Apr. 16, 1,600 killed); **Oct. 12, 1906** baseball player, manager Joe Cronin born (died 1984); **1907** California College of Arts & Crafts established; Cliff House Restaurant built overlooking Pacific Ocean, successor to 1858 structure destroyed by fire 1894; **May 30, 1908** Mel Blanc born, voice of Looney Tunes cartoon characters (died 1989); **1909** Farallon National Wildlife Refuge established in Farallon Islands to west, part of city; **1910** Palace Hotel built; **1911** San Francisco Symphony Orchestra founded; **Jan. 27, 1911** actor Benay Vanuta born (died 1995); **June 13, 1911** physicist Luis Walter Alvarez born, Nobel Prize 1968 (died 1988); **1912** San Francisco Railroad Terminal opened; **Dec. 25, 1912** singer Tony Martin born; **1914** California State Building completed; **Aug. 15, 1914** Panama Canal opened, greatly increasing city's maritime activity; **1915** Panama-Pacific Exposition held in Marina District; Civic Auditorium and Palace of Fine Arts built for exposition; **Dec. 1915** city hall dedicated, damage by earthquake 1989, reopened Jan. 1999; **1916** Steinhart Aquarium opened; **June 9, 1916** Robert McNamara born, secretary of defense under Presidents Kennedy and Johnson; **July 22, 1916** explosion at Preparedness Day Parade kills ten, injures 40, five people charged; **1917** Barbary Coast district of bars and brothels closed; public library completed; **Aug. 18, 1917** Caspar W. Weinberger born, secretary of Health, Education, and Welfare under Presidents Nixon and Ford, secretary of defense under President Reagan; **Dec. 14, 1919** novelist Shirley Jackson born (died 1965); **Apr. 16, 1920** TV actor Barry Nelson born; **July 10, 1920** physicist Owen Chamberlain born, shared Nobel Prize 1959; **Aug. 2, 1923** Pres. Warren Harding dies after taking ill on return journey from Alaska; **1924** Sts. Peter and Paul Catholic Church built; Legion of Honor Museum opened, remodeled after 1989 earthquake; **1925** Temple Emmanuel built; Embarcadero Subway opened; **1927** San Francisco Municipal Airport (Mills Field) opened; **1928** 31-story Russ Building built on site of 1847 Russ House; **1929** Academy of Art College established; **Apr. 14, 1930** actor Bradford Dillman born; **May 31, 1930** actor Clint Eastwood born; **Sept. 24, 1930** astronaut John Young born; **1931** Seals Stadium opened, demolished 1959; **1932** Municipal Opera House and Veterans War Memorial twin buildings completed; **1933** Alcatraz Federal Prison established on island in San Francisco Bay; **1934** Hetch Hetchy Aqueduct completed, delivers water from reservoir in Yosemite National Park in Sierra Nevada; **Jan. 22, 1934** TV actor Bill Bixby born (died 1993); **1935** City College of San Francisco (2-year) established; Museum of Modern Art opened; **Sept. 30, 1935** singer Johnny Mathis born; **1936** San Francisco-Oakland Bay Bridge opened; federal office building built; **1937** U.S. Mint building completed; **July 20, 1938** actress Natalie Wood born (died 1981); **Apr. 7, 1938** Gov. Edmund Gerald "Jerry" Brown, Jr. born; **Aug. 15, 1938** Supreme Court Justice Stephen Gerald Breyer born; **1939** Golden Gate Exposition held on Treasure Island; San Francisco Terminal Building built; **1940** Cow Palace arena opened; **June 2, 1944** actor Charles Haid born; **Apr. 25, 1945** United Nations Conference opens, U.N. Charter adopted June 26; **June 6, 1945** actor David Dukes born; **Apr. 29, 1947** golfer Johnny Miller born; **July 9, 1947** football player O. J. (Orenthal James) Simpson born; **July 22, 1947** actor Danny Glover born; **Sept. 21, 1949** Iva D'Aquino (Tokyo Rose) gets 7–10 years in prison, broadcasted Japanese propaganda during World War II; **Sept. 4, 1951** address of President Truman at signing of Japanese Peace Treaty, first transcontinental television broadcast; **1952** Morrison Planetarium opened; **Feb. 12, 1953** actress Joanna Kerns born; **1954** San Francisco International Airport established to south; **1957** Bay Area Rapid Transit (BART) system established; **1960** Candlestick Park baseball stadium opened, renamed ThreeCom Park 1995; **Jan. 6, 1961** fire at Thomas Hotel kills 20; **Sept. 23, 1961** astronaut William C. McCool born, killed in breakup of space shuttle *Columbia* over eastern Texas Feb. 1, 2003; **1963** Alcatraz Prison closed; **May 26, 1964** church parish house fire kills six, injures 100; **May 27, 1965** actor Todd Bridges born; **Dec. 2, 1968** S. I. Hayakawa, president of San Francisco State College, reopens school, closed eight days during student strike followed by violence; **1969** 52-story Bank of America built; **Sept. 1, 1969** TWA Boeing 707 hijacked by AWOL Marine, flown to Rome, arrested after fleeing; **Nov. 15, 1969** "M-Day" demonstrations against Vietnam War by up to 175,000 protestors, coincides with large turnout in Washington, D.C.; **Nov. 20, 1969** group of 89 Native Americans occupies vacant Alcatraz prison claiming "right of discovery" to island; **1970** new 32-story St. Francis Hotel built; **1971** New College of California established; **June 11, 1971** U.S. marshals retake Alcatraz, occupied for 19 months by Native American group; **Aug. 29, 1971** Chinese stage sit-down protest in Chinatown, opposed to court-ordered busing, fearing change to tight knit community; **1972** 48-story Transamerica Pyramid building completed; **Oct. 27, 1972** Golden Gate National Recreation Area established, includes Alcatraz Island, Presidio of San Francisco, the Esplanade, and large natural area on Marin Peninsula; **1975** 39-story Standard Oil Building built; **Apr. 15, 1975** Patty Hearst, kidnapped Feb. 4, 1974 in Berkeley, participates in bank holdup with her captors; **Sept. 18, 1975** "Don't shoot. I'll go with you," are words of Patty Hearst as she is arrested along with William and Emily Harris for armed bank holdup; **Sept. 22, 1975** Sarah Jane Moore, 45, aims gun at Pres. Ford outside the St. Francis Hotel, deflected by Secret Service agent as it goes off, no one injured; **1976** 43-story One Market Plaza built; **Feb. 11, 1978** Native Americans leave Alcatraz Island on cross-country walk to Washington, protesting anti-Native American social sentiments; **1982** 45-story Embarcadero Center built; **1983** 43-story #5 Fremont Center built; **1989** 48-story California Center built; **Oct. 17, 1989** Loma Prieta Earthquake, 7.1 magnitude, collapses section of Bay Bridge, destroys city blocks in Marina District, collapses I-880 in Oakland, 62 killed, 370 injured; **1991** Museum of City of San Francisco opened; **Nov. 19, 1996** steel company owner Marshall Wais, 79, kidnapped, released after $500,000 is paid, two arrested; **2000** Pacific Bell Park baseball stadium opened.

San Gabriel   *Los Angeles County*   Southwestern
California, 10 mi/16 km east of Los Angeles

1768 Purcell Adobe built; **1771** Mission San Gabriel Arcangel founded by Father Junipero Serra; **1812** earthquake damages mission; **1851** May Place house built by J. R. Evertson; **1852** town founded; **Nov. 11, 1885** World War II Army Gen. George Smith Patton, Jr. born, died in auto accident in Germany Dec. 21, 1945; **1913** town incorporated.

San Jose   *Santa Clara County*   Western
California, 43 mi/69 km south-southeast of San Francisco

Nov. 1777 first Spanish settlers arrive from Mexico; Pueblo San Jose de Guadalupe founded at southern end of San Francisco Bay; **1795** San Jose Granary opened, first public school in California; **1797** Peralta Adobe built, oldest building in San Jose; **1821** Mexico gains independence from Spain; **May 1825** San Jose belatedly acknowledges Mexican rule; **1840s** large influx of American settlers arrive; **July 1846** San Jose taken for U.S. by Capt. Thomas Fallon; **1850** Santa Clara County formed; incorporated as a city, becomes county seat; **Sept. 9, 1850** California admitted to Union as 31st state; city becomes state capital;

1851 *San Jose Mercury* newspaper founded; state capital moved to Vallejo, to Benicia 1852, to Sacramento 1854; 1855 Fallon House built; 1857 San Jose State College (now University) established; 1864 Southern Pacific Railroad reaches city; boat service from San Francisco discontinued; 1868 county courthouse completed; 1875 San Jose Symphony Orchestra founded; 1880s 160-room Winchester Mystery House completed by Mrs. Sarah L. Winchester; 1883 *San Jose News* newspaper founded; 1888 Lick Observatory of University of California established at Mt. Hamilton to east; 1909 first ever radio broadcasting station established by Charles David Herrold, forerunner of KCBS; July 1, 1925 actor Farley Granger born; 1933 Spartan Arena opened; Nov. 26, 1933 Brooke Hart, 22, kidnapped, $40,000 ransom paid, body found in San Francisco Bay, kidnappers lynched; 1935 Southern Pacific Station built; 1936 Civic Auditorium built; 1972 Center for the Performing Arts opened; 1975 Evergreen Valley College (2-year) established; 1985 *Mercury* and *News* newspapers merge to form *San Jose Mercury News*; 1989 McEnery Convention Center opened; 1991 San Jose Sharks NHL hockey team established; Jan. 8, 2000 San Jose Symphony plays farewell concert following declaration of bankruptcy.

San Juan Capistrano   *Orange County*

Southwestern California, 52 mi/84 km southeast of Los Angeles

1776 Mission San Juan Capistrano founded near Pacific Ocean by Father Junipero Serra, named for St. John of Capistrano of the Crusades; town founded by Mexican settlers; c.1800 mission becomes known for swallows which return regularly on March 19, depart Oct. 23; Sept. 7, 1806 mission church completed, dedicated; Dec. 8, 1812 church destroyed by earthquake, 29 killed; 1820 Capistrano Mission Trading Post established; 1865 adobe church ruined by heavy rains; 1880 Atchison, Topeka & Santa Fe Railroad reaches town; 1936 first Festival de las Golondrinas held marking return of swallows; 1958 San Diego Freeway completed; 1961 incorporated as a city.

San Leandro   *Alameda County*   Western

California, 15 mi/24 km southeast of San Francisco

1837 Jose Joaquin Estudillo becomes first setter; c.1851 town founded on San Francisco Bay by Estudillo family; 1853 Alameda County formed; Alvarado becomes county seat; 1856 county seat moved to San Leandro; 1865 San Francisco, Alameda & Stockton Railroad reaches town; 1872 town incorporated; county courthouse destroyed by earthquake; county seat moved to Oakland; Jan. 15, 1913 TV actor Lloyd Bridges born (died 1998).

San Luis Obispo   *San Luis Obispo County*

Western California, 168 mi/270 km northwest of Los Angeles

1772 Mission San Luis Obispo de Tolosa established; 1793 mission church built; 1844 town founded; 1846

town taken for U.S. by John C. Fremont; 1850 San Luis Obispo County formed; town becomes county seat; 1856 incorporated as a city; 1894 Southern Pacific Railroad reaches city; 1901 California Polytechnic University established; 1907 pipeline built from Santa Maria oil fields to Port San Luis, extended to Taft-Coalinga Oil Field 1913; 1963 Mission Plaza cultural venue established; 1964 Cuesta College (2-year) established; Aug. 26, 1972 two firefighting helicopters crash in Los Padres National Forest, six killed; 1981 county government center completed, new center built 2004; Apr. 29, 1984 Diablo Canyon Nuclear Power Plant begins production to southwest.

San Mateo   *San Mateo County*   Western

California, suburb 12 mi/19 km south of San Francisco

Nov. 4-5, 1769 Portolá expedition passes through area on return journey south; 1776 area named for St. Matthew by Juan Bautista de Anza expedition; 1795 post established by mission fathers from San Francisco; 1822 Rancho San Mateo established on San Francisco Bay by Mexicans, remain through 1846; 1851 John B. Cooper, British navy deserter, becomes first settler; 1863 Southern Pacific Railroad built; town platted; 1888 Crystal Springs Reservoir formed to west on San Mateo Creek; 1894 incorporated as a city; 1922 College of San Mateo (2-year) established; July 6, 1925 TV personality Merv Griffin born; 1929 San Mateo Bridge (lift) built across San Francisco Bay to Hayward, rebuilt 1967 for freeway; 1934 Bay Meadows Race Track established; Feb. 24, 1946 actor Barry Bostwick born; Aug. 8, 1949 actor Keith Carradine born to actor John Carradine.

San Pedro   *Los Angeles County*   Southwestern

California, 22 mi/35 km south of Los Angeles

1805 U.S. ship *Lelia Byrd*, commanded by Capt. William Shaler, anchors in San Pedro Bay; 1826 port founded; 1852 harbor established as official port of call; 1869 Southern Pacific Railroad reaches port; 1876 Point Fermin Lighthouse built; 1877 harbor channel deepened; 1882 town platted; 1888 incorporated as a city; 1892 San Pedro wins over Santa Monica for federal funding for creation of expanded harbor for Los Angeles, construction begun 1899; July 15, 1906 author Richard Armour born (died 1989); 1909 city annexed by Los Angeles; 1910 breakwater completed in outer harbor; 1914 Fort MacArthur Military Reservation established, closed 1978.

San Rafael   *Marin County*   Western California,

14 mi/23 km north of San Francisco, near San Francisco Bay

1817 Mission San Rafael Arcangel established by Father Ventura Fortuni, moved north to Sonoma 1823; June 28, 1846 three Mexicans shot and killed by Kit Carson at San Pedro Point during Bear Flag Revolt; 1850 Marin County formed; town founded as county seat; 1852 San Quentin Prison founded at San Quentin Point to southeast; 1874 incorporated as a town; 1913 incorporated as a city; 1957

Richmond-San Rafael Bridge completed across northern part of San Francisco Bay replacing ferry; **May 2, 1960** Caryl Chessman executed at San Quentin Prison, convicted 1948 of robbery, kidnapping; **Aug. 21, 1971** attempted break at San Quentin leaves six "revolutionaries," five prison personnel dead; **1962** County Administration Building completed; **1970** County Hall of Justice completed.

San Simeon *San Luis Obispo County* *Western California, 130 mi/209 km south-southeast of San Jose*

1852 whaling station established; general store opened by John Wilson; town founded; **1865** Portuguese fishermen settle in area; **1874** Piedras Blancas Lighthouse built; **1878** Bay View Hotel built; **1922** construction begins to north on newspaper publisher William Randolph Hearst's "castle," completed 1947 with 165 rooms; **1958** Hearst San Simeon State Historical Monument established; **1990** new elephant seal colony established at Piedras Blancas.

Santa Ana *Orange County* *Southwestern California, 30 mi/48 km southeast of Los Angeles*

July 26, 1769 Spanish explorer Gaspar de Portolá visits area and makes first report of earthquake in California; **1869** town founded; **1878** Southern Pacific Railroad reaches town; **1886** incorporated as a city; **March 11, 1889** Orange County formed; city becomes county seat; **1905** *Orange County Register* newspaper founded; Pacific Electric (Red Car) Railway service established from Los Angeles, suspended 1950s; **Jan. 19, 1917** actor, baritone John Raitt born; **Oct. 1924** Toastmasters Club founded by Ralph C. Smedley, becomes Toastmasters International 1932; **March 10, 1933** Long Beach Earthquake damages business district, total 121 killed; **Sept. 1935** Howard Hughes breaks world speed record in 352 mph/566 kph airplane flight; **1942** Tustin Marine Corps Air Station established, becomes Santa Ana Marine Corps Helicopter Air Station 1985, closed 1996; **Jan. 5, 1946** actress Diane Keaton born; **1953** Santa Ana Freeway opened; **Apr. 29, 1957** actress Michelle Pfeiffer born; **Jan. 22, 1967** Marine Corps bomber crashes into house after colliding with another bomber, five killed, three injured; **1968** county courthouse built; **Dec. 5, 1994** Orange County files for Chapter 9 Bankruptcy, $1.5 billion in losses from failed investments.

Santa Barbara *Santa Barbara County* *Southwestern California, 90 mi/145 km northwest of Los Angeles*

1542 Juan Rodriguez Cabrillo lands here, encounters Canalinos in large canoes; Cabrillo fatally injured while landing, buried at undisclosed site in Channel Islands to south; **Dec. 4, 1603** site named Santa Barbara by Sebastian Vizcaino; **Apr. 1782** presidio established by Capt. José Francisco Ortega; **1850** Santa Barbara County formed; **1852** town founded as county seat on Pacific Ocean by Mormons; **1864** severe drought kills 97

percent of 200,000 head of cattle; **1872** shipping wharf built; **1887** Southern Pacific Railroad reaches town; **1894** *Santa Barbara Sun* newspaper founded; **1908** Santa Barbara City College (2-year) established; **1909** University of California at Santa Barbara established; **1924** Lobero Theatre built; **June 29, 1925** business district damaged by 6.2 magnitude earthquake, 13 killed; **1929** county courthouse completed; **1930** County Bowl amphitheater built; last survivor of Canalinos dies; **1937** Westmont College established; **Feb. 1942** Japanese submarines attack oil tanks; **Aug. 30, 1951** actor Timothy Bottoms born; **Apr. 22, 1954** actor Joseph Bottoms born; **Jan. 19, 1962** actor Anthony Edwards born; **Jan. 1969** oil leak from Dos Quadros offshore rig fouls harbor and beaches, leads to ban on California offshore drilling; **Feb. 25, 1970** anti-Vietnam rioting moves out of city, enters Isla Vista community, bank, other buildings burned, 26 injured, 36 arrested; **Oct. 7, 1971** brush fire east of city leaves four firefighters dead; **July 26, 1977** 185 homes destroyed by brush fire, started when box kite entangled in high-voltage wires; **1994** Opera Santa Barbara founded.

Santa Clara *Santa Clara County* *Western California, suburb 3 mi/4.8 km northwest of San Jose*

1777 Mission Santa Clara de Asís established; **1784** mission church built, destroyed twice by earthquake, 1812 and 1818, rebuilt 1822; **1844** town founded by immigrant squatters; town platted by Franciscan Father Real; **1850** Union Hotel built; **1851** Santa Clara University established; College of the Pacific established, destroyed by fire 1871, moved to Stockton, becomes University of the Pacific; **1852** incorporated as a city; **1977** Mission College (2-year) established; **1981** residents evacuate area as Mediterranean fruit fly invades Santa Clara Valley, threatening crops.

Santa Clarita *Los Angeles County* *Southwestern California, 33 mi/53 km north-northwest of Los Angeles*

1875 first oil well drilled in Newhall Potrero Oil Field to west; **1927** The Master's College and Seminary established; **March 13, 1928** collapse of St. Francis Dam on San Francisquito Creek at Saugus leaves 450 dead, destroys 700 houses as waters rush west down Santa Clara River; **1969** College of the Canyons (2-year) established; **1987** city of Santa Clarita incorporated through merger of Saugus, Valencia, Newhall, other communities.

Santa Cruz *Santa Cruz County* *Western California, 26 mi/42 km south-southwest of San Jose*

Oct. 17, 1769 Don Gaspar Portolá plants cross on San Lorenzo River, at its entrance to Pacific Ocean; **Sept. 1791** Mission Santa Cruz established at northern end of Monterey Bay; **1794** Santa Cruz Catholic Church built; **1797** Spanish immigrants arrive, found Villa de Branciforte pueblo; **Nov. 1818** pirate Bouchard attacks bay area, church damaged; **c.1840** town founded; **1848**

foundry established by Elihu Anthony; **1850** Santa Cruz County formed; town becomes county seat; **1858** Church of the Holy Cross (Catholic) built, rebuilt 1889; **1866** incorporated as a city; **1869** Santa Cruz Lighthouse built, demolished 1948, replica built 1968; **1879** stagecoach driver "Cockeyed Charley" Parkhurst dies, discovered "he" was a she, born Charlotte Parkhurst 1812 in New Hampshire, arrived in area 1851; **1906** Boardwalk built; **Oct. 17, 1926** actress Beverly Garland born; **1965** University of California at Santa Cruz established; **1966** sixth county courthouse built; **Oct. 17, 1989** Loma Prieta Earthquake damages city, six killed.

Santa Monica   *Los Angeles County*
Southwestern California, 14 mi/23 km west of Los Angeles

1874 town founded on Pacific Ocean by Col. R. S. Baker and Sen. John P. Jones; **1886** incorporated as a city; **1890s** Santa Monica Pier built by Southern Pacific Railroad; **1917** oceanfront acquired by city; **1920** Douglas-Davis Aircraft Company established by Donald Douglas and David Davis; **1926** city becomes western terminus of U.S. Highway 66 from Chicago; **Apr. 23, 1928** actress Shirley Temple born; **1929** Santa Monica College (2-year) established; **Aug. 16, 1930** sportscaster Frank Gifford born; **Aug. 18, 1937** actor Robert Redford born; **Sept. 12, 1940** actress Linda Gray born; **Jan. 19, 1942** actress Shelley Fabares born; **Jan. 6, 1944** TV actress Bonnie Franklin born; **Aug. 22, 1944** singer Kathy Lennon of the Lennon Sisters born; **July 31, 1944** actress Geraldine Chaplin born to actor Charlie Chaplin; **Jan. 20, 1958** TV actor Lorenzo Lamas born; **Feb. 1, 1967** actress Laura Dern born to actor Bruce Dern; **Oct. 25, 1963** actress Tracy Nelson born; **Feb. 5, 1997** O. J. Simpson found liable in wrongful deaths of wife Nicole Brown and Ron Goldman, Goldman family awarded $8.5 million, civil trial Feb. 10 awards $12.5 million to both families; **July 17, 2003** 86-year-old driver plows car through farmers market, ten killed.

Santa Paula   *Ventura County   Southwestern California, 54 mi/87 km northwest of Los Angeles*

1872 area's first communal orange groves established; **1875** town founded on Santa Clara River with discovery of oil at South Mtn.; **1890** Union Oil Company founded; **1902** incorporated as a city; **March 13, 1928** collapse of St. Francis Dam at Saugus at Santa Clara River headwaters to east floods valley, 450 killed.

Santa Rosa   *Sonoma County   Western California, 50 mi/80 km north of San Francisco*

1823 Mission San Rafael founded; **1829** Padre Juan Amarosa baptizes Native American girl on feast day of St. Rose of Lima, names her Rosa; **1850** Sonoma County formed; Sonoma becomes county seat; **1852** town founded; **1854** county seat moved to Santa Rosa; **1869** incorporated as a city; **1874** Church of One Tree built from single redwood tree; **1875** horticulturist Luther Burbank (1849–1926) arrives from Massachusetts to develop Burbank potato, thousands of other hybrids; Burbank House built, occupied by Burbank 1884–1906, built new house next door, lived there until his death; **1885** Fountain Grove utopian community established by Thomas Lee Harris, founds Fountain Grove Winery; **1926** Santa Rosa Symphony founded; **Sept. 26, 1926** singer Julie London born (died 2000); **1947** actress Karen Valentine born; **Jan. 29, 1961** actress Rebecca De Mornay born; **1965** County Hall of Justice (Courthouse) built.

Saratoga   *Santa Clara County   Western California, suburb 10 mi/16 km southwest of San Jose*

1848 sawmill built by William Campbell; **1852** toll road built by Martin McCarthy; town founded by McCarthy, originally named McCarthysville; **1865** town renamed for nearby springs, likened to Saratoga, New York; **1866** Congress Hall retreat opened at Congress Springs to west; **1901** California State Redwood Park established to southwest, becomes Big Basin Redwoods State Park; **1914** Villa Montalvo completed, home of Sen. James Duval Phelan; **1956** incorporated as a city; **1963** West Valley College (2-year) established; **1976** Saratoga Inn built.

Saugus   *Los Angeles County   See* **Santa Clarita (1928)**

Sausalito   *Marin County   Western California, suburb 6 mi/9.7 km north of San Francisco*

1838 Englishman Capt. William A. Richardson becomes first English-speaking settler, granted Rancho Sausalito by Mexican government; **1848** Richardson's holdings overrun by gold seekers; **1850** town founded on San Francisco Bay, north of Golden Gate (bay entrance); **1871** Pacific Coast Railroad reaches town; **1893** incorporated as a city; **1937** Golden Gate Bridge completed from San Francisco.

Searles   *Kern County   Southern California, 115 mi/185 km north-northeast of Los Angeles*

1862 borax discovered in dry Searles Lake by John W. Searles; **1876** Carson & Colorado Railroad built to town of Mojave; Searles uses 20-mule-team wagons for first time to haul borax to rail head, four day journey; **1914** Trona Railroad built 31 mi/50 km northeast from Carson & Colorado Railroad to company town of Trona at Searles Lake; town of Searles founded at junction; **1932** exploratory drilling reveals greater borax reserves.

Sequoia National Park   *Tulare County   See* **Three Rivers**

Soledad   *Monterey County   Western California, 73 mi/117 km south-southeast of San Jose*

1792 Mission Nuestra Senora de la Soledad established to west; **1874** town founded in Salinas Valley; **1886** town platted; **Jan. 16, 1908** Pinnacles National Monument proclaimed to east; **1921** incorporated as a city; **1940s** Salinas Valley (Soledad) State Prison established to northwest, expanded 1996; **1990** prison annexed by city.

Sonoma *Sonoma County Western California, 36 mi/58 km north of San Francisco*

1823 Mission San Francisco de Solano established, northernmost of Spanish missions; **1835** town founded by Gen. Mariano Vallejo, Native American term for "many moons"; **1836** adobe Sonoma Barracks built for Mexican troops; **c.1842** Blue Wing Inn built, California's first hotel north of San Francisco; **June 14, 1846** three American trappers dispatched by John C. Fremont arrive, raise bear flag of Republic of California for first time; town serves as "capital" of short-lived republic for 28 days; **1848** Hotel El Dorado opened; **1850** Sonoma County formed; town becomes county seat; **1851** Vallejo House built; **1854** county seat moved to Santa Rosa; **1856** Hungarian immigrant Col. Agaston Haraszthy, "father" of California's vast wine industry, establishes Buena Vista Vineyard east of town, expands to over 85,000 grape vines by 1858; **1876** Northwestern Pacific Railroad reaches town; **1881** incorporated as a city; **1895** Boyes Hot Springs Bath House established; **1908** city hall built; **1960** Sonoma State College, later University, established.

Sonora *Tuolumne County Central California, 75 mi/121 km southeast of Sacramento*

1848 town founded by Mexicans from Sonora state, originally named Sonoran Camp; **1850** Tuolumne County formed; town becomes county seat; Gunn Adobe built by Dr. Lewis C. Gunn; *Sonora Herald* newspaper founded; **1851** incorporated as a city; Big Bonanza gold mine discovered by Chilean prospectors; **Jan. 18, 1852** fire destroys Washington Street business district; **1860** St. James Catholic Church built; **1866** Bauman Brewery established, closed 1907; **1885** Opera Hall built; **1898** county courthouse built; **1899** Sierra Railroad reaches city; **1900** Sonora Inn built; **1968** Columbia College (2-year) established; **1970** second fire destroys part of business district; **1979** New Melones Lake formed by dam on Stanislaus River to northwest, replaces smaller Melones Lake formed 1926.

South Lake Tahoe *El Dorado County Eastern California, 90 mi/145 km east-northeast of Sacramento*

Feb. 14, 1844 John C. Fremont and Charles Preuss become first white men to see Lake Tahoe; **1864** log hotel built; resort town founded, originally named Lakeside; **Dec. 8, 1963** Frank Sinatra, Jr., 19, kidnapped, $280,000 ransom paid, released Dec. 11, three men later caught and sent to prison; **March 1, 1964** Paradise Air Constellation crashes in snowstorm killing all 85 on board; **1965** incorporated as a city; **1975** Lake Tahoe Community College established; **Jan. 1, 1998** Cong. Sonny Bono, former singer with Sonny & Cher, killed when he hits tree while downhill skiing.

Squaw Valley *Fresno County See* **Truckee**

Stanton *Orange County Southern California, 20 mi/32 km southeast of Los Angeles*

1906 Pacific Electric Railway reaches site; town founded, named Benedict; **1911** incorporated as a city; **1924** city disincorporates; **1956** city reincorporated, renamed for citizen Philip Stanton; **July 15, 2002** Samantha Runion, 5, abducted from home, found dead two days later, migrant Alejandro Avila, 27, charged with her murder July 19.

Stockton *San Joaquin County Central California, 64 mi/103 km east of San Francisco*

1844 Capt. Charles M. Weber arrives in San Joaquin Valley; **1847** town founded by Weber, named Tuleburg; **1849** town platted, renamed by Weber for Commodore Robert Stockton; gold rush overwhelms town with drifters; **1850** San Joaquin County formed; town becomes county seat, serves as shipping point for gold mines; incorporated as a city; E. S. Holden opens pharmacy, continues in business as Forty-Nine Drugstore; **1869** Southern Pacific Railroad reaches town; **1871** University of the Pacific moved from Santa Clara, established as College of the Pacific 1851, destroyed by fire 1871; **1895** *Stockton Record* newspaper founded; **1928** Deep Water Project inaugurated giving city port access to San Francisco Bay; **June 1934** William Campbell dies, last of Pony Express riders; **1935** San Joaquin Delta College (2-year) established; **1960** county courthouse built; **1964** Mokelumne Aqueduct built from Comanche Reservoir to northeast to deliver water to city; **Feb. 16, 1970** van stalled on tracks hit by freight train, eight boys killed, two injured; **Jan. 17, 1989** Patrick Purdy shoots and kills himself after killing 5 schoolchildren, wounding 29 others.

Sunnyvale *Santa Clara County Western California, suburb 7 mi/11.3 km west of San Jose*

1849 Martin Murphy, Jr. family become first settlers; Murphy House prefabricated in Boston, shipped around Cape Horn, South America; town founded on San Francisco Bay; **1912** incorporated as a city; **1929** Hangar One dirigible hangar built, second-largest freestanding structure in U.S.; **1930** Moffett Naval Air Station established, transferred to Army 1935, back to Navy 1941; **1939** Ames Research Center established at Moffett for aerospace research; **Apr. 12, 1973** NASA jet and Navy antisubmarine airplane collide, killing 16; **1994** Moffett Base turned over to NASA.

Susanville *Lassen County Northeastern California, 140 mi/225 km north-northeast of Sacramento*

1853 Isaac N. Roop becomes first settler; **June 1855** Peter Lassen, others arrive, strike gold; **Apr. 1856** Territory of Nataqua established in northeastern California; town founded on Susan River; **1859** locals rebel against Californian authority, with Roop as provisional governor; **Apr. 26, 1859** Lassen killed by natives, stone marker erected 1862; **1861** Nevada Territory created, area becomes Roop County; Roop cabin becomes Fort Defiance; Sagebrush War begins; **Feb. 15, 1863** Plumas County sheriff engages in shootout with Roop County faction at fort, compromise reached when sheriff threatens to burn town; **1864** Lassen County formed from Plumas County; town chosen county seat by one vote; **1900** incorporated as a town; **1917** county courthouse built; **1940** incorporated as a city.

Three Rivers   *Tulare County   South central California, 175 mi/282 km north of Los Angeles*

1873 Mineral King Lodge established 15 mi/24 km to east by group of spiritualists, destroyed by snow slide 1888; **Sept. 25, 1890** Sequoia National Park established to north; **Oct. 1, 1890** General Grant National Park established to north, small unit comprising Grant Grove (sequoias); **1891** Kaweah Cooperative Commonwealth Colony founded 2 mi/3.2 km to north by former members of socialist International Workingmen's Association, abandoned within few years; **March 4, 1940** Kings Canyon National Park established to north, north of Sequoia National Park, includes small unit formerly General Grant National Park; **1999** John Muir Lodge opened at Kings Canyon National Park.

Truckee   *Nevada County   Eastern California, 90 mi/145 km northeast of Sacramento*

1844 Paiute Chief Truckee leads wagon train headed by Elisha Stevens through Sierra Nevada mountain pass to west of here; **Oct. 1846–March 1847** snowbound Donner Party stranded at Donner Pass, named for them, 45 of 81 survive, many resort to devouring deceased, 12 called the "Forlorn Hope" walk west to seek help Dec. 21, seven reach Wheatland Jan. 22; **1848** gold discovered to southwest; **1863** town founded on Truckee River; cabin built by Joe Gray; **1867** Central Pacific Railroad completed through town and Donner Pass; **Dec. 2, 1902** TV actor Stuart Erwin born at Squaw Valley to south (died 1967); **1913** first ski club in California organized; **1918** pioneer monument erected; **Jan. 20, 1937** lowest temperature ever recorded in California reached, −45°F/−43°C, at Boca to northeast; **1960** Winter Olympics held at Squaw Valley to south; **1993** incorporated as a town.

Tulelake   *Siskiyou County   Northern California, 243 mi/391 km north of Sacramento*

Apr. 11, 1873 Gen. E. R. S. Canby meets with Kientpoos, nicknamed "Captain Jack," leader of Klamaths, at Lava Beds to discuss end to Modoc Wars; Canby and Dr. Eleazer Thomas killed during talks, perpetrators captured after bloody fight, Captain Jack hanged at Fort Klamath, Oregon, to north; **1908** Southern Pacific Railroad reaches site; **Nov. 21, 1925** Lava Beds National Monument established to south; **1931** town founded; **1937** incorporated as a city.

Twentynine Palms   *San Bernardino County   Southern California, 130 mi/209 km east of Los Angeles*

1855 area first explored; **1858** survey party reports 26, not 29, palms growing at site; **1910** Bill and Frances Keys among first settlers; **1918** World War I veterans suffering effects of mustard gas take refuge in clean desert air; **1927** first roads built; town founded; **Aug. 10, 1936** Joshua Tree National Monument proclaimed to south, reclassified as National Park 1994; **1952** large Twentynine Palms Marine Corps Base established to north; **1987** town incorporated.

Ukiah   *Mendocino County   Northwestern California, 106 mi/171 km north-northwest of San Francisco*

1850 Mendocino County formed; **1856** Samuel Lowry becomes first settler; town founded; **1859** county organized; town becomes county seat; **1860** county courthouse built; **1872** town incorporated; **1889** Northwestern Pacific Railroad reaches town; **1898** International Latitude Observatory established by International Geodetic Association; **1900** Charles Purdy promotes propagation of native flora; **1917** fire destroys west side of State Street; **1949** lumber rush begins in postwar building boom, redwoods called "red gold"; **1973** Mendocino College (2-year) established.

Vallejo   *Solano County   Western California, 24 mi/39 km north-northeast of San Francisco*

c.1838 Gen. Mariano G. Vallejo envisions important city bearing his name on his Rancho Soscol; **1850** site at north end of San Pablo Bay selected for state capital; **1851** state capital moved from San Jose; **1852** state capital moved to nearby Benicia to east; **1854** first shipyard established on West Coast; town founded by Adm. David Farragut; **1866** incorporated as a city; **1869** Mare Island Navy Yard established, closed 1996; **1927** Carquinez Bridge built across Carquinez Strait, estuary of Sacramento/San Joaquin rivers, parallel span built 1958, new span built 2003.

Van Nuys   *Los Angeles County   Southern California, 15 mi/24 km northwest of Los Angeles*

1911 town founded, named for pioneer Isaac Newton Van Nuys; **1914** flooding inundates town; **1915** annexed by Los Angeles; **1928** Los Angeles Metropolitan Airport established, becomes Van Nuys Airport 1957; **July 23, 1936** Dodgers baseball pitcher Don Drysdale born (died 1993); **Aug. 22, 1947** actress Cindy Williams born; **1949** Los Angeles Valley College (2-year) established.

Venice   *Los Angeles County   Southwestern California, 14 mi/23 km west-southwest of Los Angeles*

1904 town founded on Pacific Ocean by Abbott Kinney; **1905** canal system built in tidal flats by Kinney complete with gondolas, buildings styled after Venice, Italy; Kinney Pier built; **1907** Ocean Park Plunge indoor swimming center opened; **1909** Venice Aquarium opened; **1911** Ocean Park Pier built, burned 1924, rebuilt; **Sept. 3, 1912** fire destroys five blocks of Ocean Park business district; **1920** Kinney Pier destroyed by fire one month after Kinney's death, rebuilt; **1925** Venice annexed by Los Angeles; **1930** oil discovered; **1963** Marina del Ray harbor completed in former canal system; **1964** over 500 historic buildings razed by city of Los Angeles; **1967** Ocean Park Pier closed.

Ventura *Ventura County* *Southwestern California, 62 mi/100 km west-northwest of Los Angeles*

1782 Mission San Buenaventura founded by Father Junipero Serra; town founded on Pacific Ocean, full name San Buenaventura; **1866** incorporated as a city, name unofficially shortened to fit train schedules; oil discovered in Santa Clara Valley to east, first oil field in California; **1873** Ventura County formed; city becomes county seat; **1913** county courthouse built, used for city hall 1978; **1925** Ventura College (2-year) established; **Apr. 26, 1938** Channel Islands National Monument proclaimed to south, becomes National Park 1980; **1978** county government center completed.

Victorville *San Bernardino County* *Southwestern California, 67 mi/108 km northeast of Los Angeles*

1878 town founded on Mojave River, named Mormon Crossing; **1885** town becomes gold mining center, renamed Victor, later renamed Victorville; **1914** first motion picture filmed here, short feature, or "quickie," by William S. Hart; **1937** over 200 Western movies shot on location since 1916; **1961** Victor Valley College (2-year) established; **1962** incorporated as a city; **1976** Roy Rogers/Dale Evans Museum opened, moved to Branson, Missouri, Feb. 2003.

Visalia *Tulare County* *South central California, 175 mi/282 km north-northwest of Los Angeles*

1852 Tulare County formed; town founded as county seat by Nathaniel Vise, named by him, combination of his surname and wife's given name, Sallie; **1858** Butterfield Overland Stage route established from Missouri; **1862** Camp Babbitt established by Union Army to offset pro-South sentiment; **1874** incorporated as a city; **1892** warfare erupts between landowners and law enforcement over Southern Pacific Railroad's right to claim property along its route as granted by U.S. Congress; **1925** College of the Sequoias (2-year) established; **1926** county courthouse built; **1928** Visalia Municipal Airport established; **1962** Lake Kaweah formed by Terminus Dam to east on Kaweah River.

Watsonville *Santa Cruz County* *Western California, 30 mi/48 km south of San Jose, near Pacific Ocean*

1852 town founded by Judge John H. Watson and D. S. Gregory on Pajaro River, near its entrance to Monterey

Bay; **1853** area's first apple orchard planted by Jesse D. Carr; **1868** town incorporated; **1871** Southern Pacific Railroad reaches town; **Oct. 17, 1989** Loma Prieta Earthquake destroys 850 residences, 100 commercial buildings.

Weaverville *Trinity County* *Northwestern California, 213 mi/343 km north of San Francisco*

1850 Trinity County formed; town founded near Trinity River as county seat by John Weaver; **1852** Joss House Chinese temple built; Chinese Tong factions battle each other at Five-Cent Gulch while whites watch in amusement, two killed [see also Chinese Camp]; brewery established by Frederick Walter, becomes Pacific Brewery 1879, closed 1920; **1856** *Trinity Journal* newspaper founded; **1857** store built, used as county courthouse after 1865; **1873** Taoist Temple built; **1962** Clair Engle Lake reservoir formed by Trinity Dam on Trinity River to northeast.

Willows *Glenn County* *Northern California, 78 mi/126 km north-northwest of Sacramento*

1886 town founded; **1891** Glenn County formed, named for Dr. Hugh J. Glenn, leader in area's grain production; town incorporated, becomes county seat; **1894** county courthouse built; **1910** East Park Reservoir formed by dam to southwest on Stony Creek; **1911** Carnegie Library opened, replaced 1969; rice production in California introduced by W. K. Brown; **1928** Stony Gorge Reservoir formed on Stony Creek to west; **1935** incorporated as a city.

Wilmington *Los Angeles County* *Southwestern California, 18 mi/29 km south of Los Angeles*

1857 town founded by Phineas Banning on Inner San Pedro Harbor, Pacific Ocean, originally named New San Pedro; Banning's Wharf established; **1861** Drumm Barracks built as supply depot for U.S. Army; **1863** town renamed for Banning's home town of Wilmington, Delaware; **1864** post office established; **1869** Southern Pacific Railroad reaches town; **1871** jetty built; **1909** town annexed by Los Angeles; **1949** Los Angeles Harbor College (2-year) established.

Woodland *Yolo County* *North central California, 18 mi/29 km west-northwest of Sacramento*

1850 Yolo County formed, Patwin term for "abounding in rushes"; Broderick becomes county seat; **1853** first settlers arrive; **1855** blacksmith shop established; town founded near Cache Creek, named Yolo City; **1857** county seat moved to Cacheville (Yolo); **1859** post office opened; name changed to Woodland to avoid confusion with town of Yolo; **1862** county seat moved to Woodland from Yolo; **1871** incorporated as a city; **1892** Woodland Public Library established; **1918** county courthouse completed; **1984** County Administration Building completed.

Yorba Linda *Orange County* Southwestern California, 33 mi/53 km southeast of Los Angeles

1810 land grant made to José Antonio Yorba; **1834** hacienda built by Bernardo Yorba; **1907** town founded by Janss Corporation; **1912** Frank and Hannah Nixon settle here with son Harold; **Jan. 9, 1913** Richard Milhous Nixon, 37th U.S. President, born to Frank and Hannah Nixon (died Apr. 22, 1994); **1967** incorporated as a city; **July 1990** Nixon Library and Birthplaces opened.

Yosemite Village *Mariposa County* Eastern California, 160 mi/257 km east of San Francisco

June 30, 1864 Yosemite Valley and Mariposa Big Tree Grove granted to state of California; **1879** Wawona Hotel built at Mariposa Grove; **Oct. 1, 1890** Yosemite National Park established; **1904** Joseph Leconte Memorial Lodge built by Sierra Club; **1915** Yosemite Lodge built; **1923** Hetch Hetchy Reservoir formed by O'Shaughnessy Dam on Tuolumne River in western part of park, delivers water via Hetch Hetchy Aqueduct to San Francisco, lake enlarged 1938; **1927** Ahwahnee Hotel built at park headquarters; **1933** Wawona Tunnel completed on park road to west.

Yreka *Siskiyou County* Northern California, 235 mi/378 km north-northwest of Sacramento

1851 gold discovered; town founded as Shasta Butte City; **1852** Siskiyou County formed; town becomes county seat; town renamed (wy-REE-ka), corruption of Native American word "wairika" for "north mountain"; **1854** county courthouse built; **1857** incorporated as a city; **1950** Siskiyou County Museum built.

Yuba City *Sutter County* North central California, 41 mi/66 km north of Sacramento

1849 town founded on Feather River by Samuel Brannan, Pierson R. Reading, and Henry Cheever; **1850** Sutter County formed; **1856** town becomes permanent county seat after six county seat moves; **1873** William and George Thompson develop the Thompson Seedless Grape; **1899** county courthouse built; **1908** incorporated as a city; **July 12, 1971** Juan Corona indicted for murder of 25 farm workers found buried in fields, sentenced to 25 life terms.

Colorado

West central U.S. Capital and major city: Denver.

Colorado east of the Continental Divide became part of the U.S. with the Louisiana Purchase in 1803. The land west of the Divide was acquired in 1848 after the Mexican War. Colorado Territory was organized February 28, 1861. Colorado entered the Union as the 38th state August 1, 1876.

Colorado is divided into 64 counties. Denver County is unique in the U.S. in that it adjusts its boundaries every ten years to agree with the Denver city limits, absorbing annexations of the intervening years, reducing the land area of the three neighboring counties. In 2001, the City of Broomfield separated from Boulder and Jefferson counties to become Broomfield County, a city-county similar to Denver. Colorado municipalities are classified as towns and cities. There are no townships. See Introduction.

Akron   *Washington County*   *Northeastern Colorado, 95 mi/153 km east-northeast of Denver*

1882 Chicago, Burlington & Quincy Railroad built; town founded; **1887** Washington County formed; town incorporated, becomes county seat; **1909** county courthouse built.

Alamosa   *Alamosa County*   *Southern Colorado, 85 mi/137 km southwest of Pueblo, on Rio Grande*

1878 Denver & Rio Grande Western Railroad built; town founded, incorporated; **1913** Alamosa County formed from Conejos County; town becomes county seat; **1921** Adams State College established; **March 17, 1932** Great Sand Dunes National Monument proclaimed to northeast; **1938** county builds first county courthouse after eliminating its indebtedness to Conejos County.

Antonito   *Conejos County*   *Southern Colorado, 109 mi/175 km southwest of Pueblo*

1854 town founded; **1848** band of Utes and Apaches attacked by Maj. W. W. Reynolds' forces at Cumbres Pass to southwest, two soldiers killed, 36 natives killed; **1880** Denver & Rio Grande Railroad reaches town; **1889** town incorporated; **1974** Cumbres & Toltec Scenic Railway established to Chama, New Mexico.

Aspen   *Pitkin County*   *West central Colorado, 103 mi/166 km west-southwest of Denver*

1870s settlers agitate for removal of Ute people from area; silver prospecting begins; **1879** town founded, originally named Ute City; **1880** Ute people forced to relocate to Uintah Reservation, Utah; **1881** Pitkin County formed; town incorporated, becomes county seat, renamed Aspen; **1887** branch of Denver & Rio Grande Western Railroad reaches town; **1889** Wheeler Opera House built; **1891** county courthouse built, topped by controversial statue of Justice not blindfolded; **1893** Hotel Jerome built; **1936** Andre Roch established as Aspen's first ski run; **1941** Tenth Mountain Division of U.S. Army established, disbanded 1945; first National Downhill and Slalom Ski Championship held; **1950** Aspen Institute founded, dedicated to informed dialogue on issues of global concern; **1958** Buttermilk Ski Area opened; **1968** Snowmass Ski Area opened; **Jan. 22, 1970** plane crash kills eight; **Jan. 14, 1977** Claudine Longet, former wife of singer Andy Williams, found guilty of negligent homicide in shooting death of boyfriend Vladimir "Spider" Sabich, sentenced to 30 days jail; **Dec. 31, 1997** Michael Kennedy, son of late Robert F. Kennedy, killed when he hits tree while downhill skiing; **March 29, 2001** charter jet from Los Angeles crashes killing all 18 on board.

Aurora   *Arapahoe and Adams counties*   *Central Colorado, suburb 6 mi/9.7 km east of Denver*

1891 town founded, named Fletcher; **1903** incorporated as a town; **1908** town renamed; **1918** Fitzsimmons Army Medical Center established; **1928** incorporated as a city; **1929** Aurora Public Library founded; **1942** Buckley Air National Guard Base established; **1983** Community College of Aurora established.

Bennett *Adams County* *See* **Byers (1888)**

Black Hawk *Gilpin County* *Central Colorado, 22 mi/35 km west-northwest of Denver*

1859 first gold discovery in Colorado, gold rush begins; town founded, contiguous with Central City; **1864** incorporated as a town; **1868** Nathaniel P. Hill, future U.S. Senator, builds Colorado's first gold smelter; **1991** Black Hawk becomes one of three Colorado towns to offer limited legalized gambling, also Central City and Cripple Creek.

Boulder *Boulder County* *Northern Colorado, 24 mi/39 km northwest of Denver*

1858 settlers begin arriving; town founded; **1859** first irrigation ditches developed by Wellman brothers; **1861** Boulder County formed; town becomes county seat; **1865** martial law declared when South Platte Road blocked by Cheyennes and allies in aftermath of Sand Creek Massacre [see Eads]; **1867** toll road opened to Central City; **1871** town incorporated; **1874** Colorado Central and Denver & Boulder Valley railroads reach town; **1876** University of Colorado at Boulder established; **Dec. 14, 1909** geneticist Edward Lawrie Tatum born, Nobel Prize 1938 (died 1975); **May 1, 1925** astronaut M. Scott Carpenter born; **1934** county courthouse completed; **1952** Rocky Flats Plant established to south by U.S. Department of Energy for manufacture of plutonium triggers for nuclear weapons; Denver-Boulder Turnpike opened; **Dec. 26, 1996** body of JonBenet Ramsey, 6, found in basement of home, parents John and Pat Ramsey reported her missing 8 hours earlier, protracted scandal over police handling, unsolved case.

Breckenridge *Summit County* *Central Colorado, 58 mi/93 km west-southwest of Denver*

1859 first gold discovered in Blue River; town founded; **1861** Summit County formed; town becomes county seat; **1880** incorporated as a town; **1909** county courthouse built.

Brighton *Adams County* *North central Colorado, 19 mi/31 km north-northeast of Denver, on South Platte R.*

1869 Denver Pacific Railroad built; town founded, named Hughes Station; **1887** town incorporated; **1889** town platted by D. F. Carmichael, renamed for Brighton, Massachusetts, wife's birthplace; **1902** Adams County formed; town becomes county seat; **1906** county courthouse built; **1977** County Administration Building completed; **1995** Denver International Airport opened to south; **1998** County Justice Center opened; courthouse becomes city hall.

Broomfield *Broomfield County* *Northern Colorado, 13 mi/21 km north of Denver*

1877 town founded in southern Boulder County, named for broom corn grown in area; **1960** Jefferson County Airport established to south; **1961** incorporated as a city; **Nov. 2001** Broomfield County formed from parts of Boulder and Jefferson counties, coterminous with Broomfield city limits, similar to Denver city-county.

Burlington *Kit Carson County* *Eastern Colorado, 143 mi/230 km east-southeast of Denver*

1870s large herds of cattle introduced to area from Texas; **1887** town founded as grain shipping center; **1888** town incorporated; **1889** Kit Carson County formed; town becomes county seat; **1952** county courthouse built.

Byers *Arapahoe County* *East central Colorado, 40 mi/64 km east of Denver*

1868 livestock shipping center established by Oliver P. Wiggins; **1888** Union Pacific Railroad built; town platted by William N. Byers, editor of *Rocky Mountain News*, Denver; **July 11, 1888** highest temperature ever recorded in Colorado reached at Bennett to west, 118°F/48°C; **Jan. 27, 2001** crash in snowstorm of small aircraft kills 10, including two from Oklahoma State University basketball team, also staff and media, flight bound from Denver to Stillwater.

Cañon City *Fremont County* *Central Colorado, 35 mi/56 km west-northwest of Pueblo, on Arkansas River*

1806 Royal Gorge discovered to west by Lt. Zebulon M. Pike; **Jan. 1807** Lt. Pike builds blockhouse, arrested Feb. by Spanish, released; **1859** town founded ("CAN-yon") at entrance to Grand Canyon of the Arkansas River; **1860** Rudd House built; **1861** Fremont County formed; town becomes county seat; **1862** oil reserve discovered to north; **1870** Colorado State Penitentiary established; **1872** incorporated as a city; **1878** dinosaur fossil beds discovered to north; **1903** Skyline Drive built on mountain crest above city by prison inmates; **March 15, 1906** railroad accident at Florence to east, 35 killed; **Oct. 9–10, 1929** during prison riot, convict Danny Daniels executes guards and fellow convicts, 13 killed, ten injured; **Dec. 1929** Royal Gorge Suspension Bridge completed; **1959** county courthouse built.

Castle Rock *Douglas County* *Central Colorado, 25 mi/40 km south of Denver*

1861 Douglas County formed; **1870s** rhyolite quarrying becomes important, used as building material; **1874** town founded as county seat; **1881** town incorporated; **1890** county courthouse completed, destroyed by fire 1978; **June 1998** Christensen Justice Center completed.

Central City *Gilpin County* *Central Colorado,*
23 mi/37 km west-northwest of Denver

May 6, 1859 gold discovered by John H. Gregory at Gregory Gulch, named for him; town founded; **1861** Gilpin County formed; town becomes county seat; **1867** toll road opened from Boulder; **1872** Teller House hotel built; **1874** most of town destroyed by fire, rebuilt; **1878** Colorado Central Railroad extended from Golden; **1878** Central City Opera House built; **1886** town incorporated; **1900** county courthouse built; **1927** Moffat Tunnel completed to northwest, two parallel bores carrying diverted water in one, Denver & Rio Grande Western Railroad in other, at 9,094 ft/2,772 m elevation, highest main line railroad grade in U.S.; **1932** first Opera House Play Festival held; **1991** Central City becomes one of three Colorado towns allowing limited gambling, also at Black Hawk and Cripple Creek.

Cheyenne Wells *Cheyenne County* *Eastern Colorado, 150 mi/241 km southeast of Denver*

1865 town founded on Butterfield Overland Stage line; **1870** Kansas Pacific Railroad reaches site; town moved 6 mi/9.7 km south to railroad; **1889** Cheyenne County formed; town becomes county seat; **1890** town incorporated; **1894** County Jail built, used until 1961; **1908** county courthouse built; **1910** introduction of dry farming techniques leads to 635 percent increase in town's population since 1900; **1919** Plains Hotel built.

Colorado Springs *El Paso County* *Central Colorado, 60 mi/97 km south of Denver*

1859 town founded by gold miners, originally named El Dorado City; R. E. Cable suggests that rock formations to west look like "garden of the gods" after friend's joke that they would make ideal beer garden; **1860** town renamed Colorado City; **1861** El Paso County formed; town becomes county seat; Territorial Legislature meets here for four days; **1871** Denver & Rio Grande Western Railroad built; town of Colorado Springs founded by railroad promoter Gen. William Palmer; Colorado Springs Hotel built; **1872** incorporated as a town; **1873** county seat moved to Colorado Springs; **1874** Colorado College at Colorado Springs established; Colorado School for the Deaf founded; **1882** Antlers Hotel opened; **1883** Colorado School for the Blind founded; **Apr. 1, 1883** actor Alonso (Lon) Chaney born (died 1930); **1885** Colorado Midland Railroad reaches town; **1886** incorporated as a city; **1889** Chicago, Rock Island & Burlington Railroad reaches town; **1890** street car line built west to Manitou Springs; **Oct. 17, 1893** actress Spring Byington born (died 1971); **1899** Van Briggle Pottery Works founded by Artus Van Briggle; **Dec. 13, 1902** sociologist Talcott Parsons born (died 1979); **1903** county courthouse built; miners' strike at Colorado City turns town into armed camp; **1905** Public Library built; **1907** legislation allows city to create mountain parks beyond its city limits; **1909** Garden of the Gods park created; Modern Woodmen of America Sanitarium established for tuberculosis patients; **1912**

Golden Cycle Pulp Mill founded; **1917** Colorado City annexed by Colorado Springs, known as West Colorado Springs; **1918** Broadmoor Hotel opened at base of Cheyenne Mountain to south; **1921** Cheyenne Mountain Zoo established; **1924** Fort Carson Army Base founded to south; **1927** Colorado Springs Municipal Airport (Peterson Field) established to east; **1928** Colorado Springs Symphony Orchestra founded; **1929** Gen. William Palmer Statue unveiled; **1936** Fine Arts Center built, founded 1919; **1937** Will Rogers Shrine of the Sun Memorial dedicated on Cheyenne Mountain; **1954** U.S. Air Force Academy established to north; **1965** University of Colorado at Colorado Springs established; Colorado Technical University established; **1965** World Figure Skating Hall of Fame established; **Jan. 1965** cheating scandal jolts Air Force Academy affecting a dozen cadets; **1968** Pikes Peak Community College established; **1973** county courthouse built; old courthouse becomes Pioneers Museum; **1998** World Arena opened.

Como *Park County* *Central Colorado, 55 mi/89 km southwest of Denver*

1875 post office established; **1880** Colorado & Southern Railroad built to Leadville; town founded on railroad as mining shipping center; **1881** railroad shops and round-house built; **1909** railroad shops destroyed by fire; **Jan. 10, 1893** explosion and fire at King Cole Coal Mine kills 26; **1937** railroad abandoned; town rapidly declines.

Conejos *Conejos County* *Southern Colorado, 108 mi/174 km southwest of Pueblo*

1854 town founded by Maj. Lafayette Head and Selendonio Valdez; **1856** Church of Our Lady of Guadalupe built; **1861** Conejos County formed; town becomes county seat; **Jan. 24, 1895** boxer William Henry "Jack" Dempsey born at Manassa to northeast, heavyweight champion 1919–1926 (died 1983); **1981** county courthouse completed.

Cortez *Montezuma County* *Southwestern Colorado, 220 mi/354 km southwest of Pueblo*

1881 Ute tribes removed to reservations; **1887** town founded; **1889** Montezuma County formed; town becomes county seat; **1895** large Ute Mountain Indian Reservation established to south for Weeminuche band of Utes, Towaoc becomes administrative center; **1902** town incorporated; **June 29, 1906** Mesa Verde National Park established; **1909** highway bridge built across San Juan River in Four Corners area to southwest, eliminating centuries-old barrier to travelers; **Dec. 19, 1919** Yucca House National Monument proclaimed to south, remains of prehistoric village (park undeveloped); **March 2, 1923** Hovenweep National Monument proclaimed to west, extends into Utah, contains six groups of prehistoric structures; **1961** county courthouse built; **June 9, 2000** Canyons of the Ancients National Monument proclaimed in vast area to west and northwest, preserves Anasazi ruins.

Cotopaxi *Fremont County* *Central Colorado,*
55 mi/89 km southwest of Colorado Springs

1872 Denver & Rio Grande Railroad built; **1874** Henry "Gold Tom" Thomas files claim for Cotopaxi Lode, one of richest silver deposits in Fremont County; town founded, named by Thomas for Ecuadorian volcano where he once prospected; **c.1880** Russian Jewish farming colony established under leadership of Emanuel H. Saltiel.

Craig *Moffat County* *Northwestern Colorado,*
143 mi/230 km northwest of Denver, on Yampa River

Sept. 1879 cavalry under Maj. T. T. Thornburg ambushed by Utes to southeast while responding to deadly attack Sept. 20 on agent Meeker and men [see Meeker], 15 killed including Thornburg, 35 wounded; **1881** William Ross homesteads on Fortification Creek; **1888** town platted by W. H. Tucker; **1902** Denver, Pacific & Northwestern Railroad built by David H. Moffat; **1908** town incorporated; **1911** Moffat County formed; town becomes county seat; **1918** county courthouse built; **Feb. 1, 1985** lowest temperature ever recorded in Colorado reached, −61°F/−52°C.

Creede *Mineral County* *Southwestern Colorado,*
125 mi/201 km west-southwest of Pueblo

1840 first farmers settle at Wagon Wheel Gap; **1871** M. V. B. Warson becomes town's first homesteader; **1890** silver discovered at Willow Creek by Nicholas Creede; town founded; Ford's Saloon built by Bob Ford, reputed slayer of outlaw Jesse James; **1891** Denver & Rio Grande Railroad reaches town; **June 10, 1892** Bob Ford shot and killed by miner claiming he harassed his parents years earlier; **July 1892** incorporated as a city; **1893** Mineral County formed; town becomes county seat; economy suffers from fall in price of silver; **1908** Wheeler National Monument established to east, area of sandstone formations, closed 1950; **1950** county courthouse built; **1985** last silver mine closed.

Cripple Creek *Teller County* *Central Colorado,*
20 mi/32 km west-southwest of Colorado Springs

Oct. 1890 gold discovered on Poverty Gulch (Cripple Creek); town founded; **1892** town incorporated; **1893–1894** miners' strike marked by violence; **1899** Teller County formed; town becomes county seat; **1901** gold district's population peaks at c.50,000; **1904** county courthouse built; second miners' strike breaks union control of mines; **1906** overturned stove at hotel starts fire, most of town destroyed; **1941** mines drained, reactivated; **Aug. 20, 1969** Florissant Fossil Beds National Monument established to northwest; **1991** Cripple Creek becomes one of three Colorado towns to allow limited gambling, also in Central City and Black Hawk.

Del Norte *Rio Grande County* *Southern*
Colorado, 100 mi/161 km west-southwest of Pueblo

1860 town founded on Rio Grande as rendezvous for freight wagoners; **1874** Rio Grande County formed; town becomes county seat; **1882** Denver and Rio Grande Railroad reaches town; **1885** town incorporated; **1938** county courthouse built.

Delagua *Las Animas County* See **Trinidad (1910)**

Delta *Delta County* *Western Colorado, 285 mi/*
459 km west-northwest of Pueblo

1830 fort built by French trapper Antoine Robidoux, destroyed by Utes; **1881** town founded on Gunnison River; **1882** incorporated as a city; **1883** Delta County formed; town becomes county seat; **1938** Fruit Growers Dam built on Alfalfa Run to northeast, part of large irrigation project; **1958** county courthouse built.

Denver *Denver, Adams, Arapahoe, and Jefferson*
counties *Central Colorado, on South Platte River*

1858 gold discovered on South Platte River, at confluence of Cherry Creek; town founded by Gen. William Larimer, named Denver City for James W. Denver, Governor of Kansas Territory; Colorado's first saloon established by "Uncle Dick" Wootton; **Apr. 23, 1859** *Rocky Mountain News* newspaper founded; **1861** incorporated as a city; town of Auraria annexed; **1863** U.S Mint established; telegraph line reaches city; **1864** University of Denver established; **May 19, 1864** flash flood in Cherry Creek kills 20; **June 24, 1870** first train of Denver & Pacific Railroad arrives; **Aug. 1870** Kansas Pacific (Union Pacific) Railroad reaches city; **Aug. 1, 1876** Colorado enters Union as 38th state; **1877** Regis University established; **1879** State Historical Society of Colorado founded, later Colorado Historical Society; **1880** Windsor Hotel built; **1880s** silver mining boom triples population to over 100,000; **1881** Tabor Grand Opera House opened; **1883** University of Colorado Health Sciences Center established (main campus at Boulder); **May 23, 1885** actor Douglas Fairbanks born (died 1939); **1886** Denver Union Stockyards established; **1887** Regis College (Roman Catholic) established; **March 8, 1890** author Gene Fowler born (died 1960); **March 28, 1891** jazz musician, bandleader Paul Whiteman born (died 1967); **1892** Omaha-Grant Smelter (gold, silver) built, closed 1903; **1893** Chappell House built; Denver Art Museum founded; **1896** state capitol completed; Denver Zoo established; **1899** Temple Israel built; **1900** Colorado Museum of Natural History opened, renamed Denver Museum of Nature and Science 2000; **1901** Denver County formed; city becomes county seat; **1902** city and county become coterminous (county boundary adjusted every ten years to include city annexations, reducing size of neighboring counties); **Aug. 23, 1903** Charles Franklin Brannan born, secretary of Agriculture under Pres. Truman (died 1992); **1907** Denver Public Library built, established 1889; **Feb. 25, 1907** playwright Mary Chase born (died 1981); **1908**

Municipal Auditorium built; **1911** pioneer monument unveiled; **1912** University of Colorado at Denver established; Cathedral of Immaculate Conception (Catholic) completed; **1915** state museum built; **1916** post office built; **Jan. 10, 1917** William F. "Buffalo Bill" Cody dies, buried near Golden (born Le Claire, Iowa, 1846); **1920** civic center complex completed; **Dec. 18, 1922** robbers hold up Federal Reserve truck at U.S. Mint, get away with $200,000, one robber shot and killed, others never found; **1926** air mail service inaugurated to Cheyenne and Pueblo; **1927** Moffat Tunnel completed to west giving Denver direct rail link to Salt Lake City; **1929** Stapleton Airport opened in eastern part of city; **1930** U.S. Customs House built; **Jan. 4, 1930** actress Barbara Rush born; **Aug. 30, 1931** astronaut, U.S. Cong. John Swigert, Jr. born (died 1982); **1932** City and County Building completed after 26 years of construction; **1937** Lowry Field established by U.S. Army Air Corps, becomes Air Force Base after World War II, closed 1994; **1941** Denver Ordnance Plant established to west at Lakewood, converted to Denver Federal Center 1950; Red Rocks Amphitheater opened to west; **Dec. 11, 1943** Sen. John Kerry born, Democratic presidential candidate 2004; **July 15, 1944** actor Jan-Michael Vincent born; **1948** Mile High Stadium opened; **1951** Denver Botanical Gardens opened; **1952** Denver-Boulder Turnpike opened; Colorado Institute of Art established; Denver Coliseum opened; **June 13, 1953** actor Tim Allen born; **Sept. 24, 1955** President Eisenhower suffers heart attack while visiting here, later resumes duties at his Gettysburg farm; **1959** Denver Broncos NFL football team established; **1963** Metropolitan State College of Denver established; **1970** Community College of Denver established; Denver awarded 1976 Winter Olympics, rejected by voters 1972; **1971** Black American West Museum founded; new Denver Art Museum opened; **1972** Performing Arts Center founded, includes Auditorium Theatre built 1908; **1978** 40-story Qwest (Anaconda) Tower built; **1976** Denver Nuggets NBA basketball team begins first season; **1980** 36-story Amoco Building built; **1981** 41-story MCI (Arco) Tower built; **June 3, 1981** a dozen tornadoes hit city, 46 injured; **1982** 54-story US West Tower (Mountain Bell Center) built; **1983** 52-story Wells Fargo Bank built; **1985** 43-story 1999 Broadway building built; **1990** Colorado Convention Center opened; **1993** Colorado Rockies National League baseball team established; **Aug. 15, 1993** Pope John Paul II holds mass for 400,000, part of Youth Day festival; **1994** new Denver Public Library opened; Denver Light Rail System opened, extended south in 2000; **1995** Denver International Airport opened to northeast; Colorado Avalanche NHL hockey team begins first season; Coors Stadium opened; **Apr. 24, 1997** Oklahoma City bombing (Apr. 19, 1995) trial begins against Timothy McVeigh, conspirators Terry Nichols and Michael Fortier, Fortier sentenced May 27, 1998, to 12 years prison, $200,000 fine, Nichols sentenced June 4, 1998, to life, McVeigh executed at federal penitentiary, Terre Haute, Indiana, June 11, 2001; **1999** Pepsi Center arena opened; **Aug. 2001** Invesco Field opened, home of Denver Broncos football team.

Dinosaur *Moffat County* *Northwestern Colorado, 212 mi/341 km west-northwest of Denver*

Oct. 4, 1915 Dinosaur National Monument established to north in Yampa Valley, site of extensive dinosaur fossil finds, extends into Utah; **1945** town founded, named Artesia; **1947** town incorporated; **1965** town renamed Dinosaur.

Dolores *Montezuma County* *Southwestern Colorado, 213 mi/343 km west-southwest of Pueblo*

c.8000 BC earliest known human occupation of area by Anasazi people, predecessors of ancient Pueblo cultures; **Aug. 13, 1776** Fathers Dominguez and Escalante camp here on expedition to open new routes to Spanish missions; **1891** Rio Grande Southern Railroad reaches site; town founded; **1900** town incorporated; **1984** McPhee Reservoir formed by dam on Dolores River to north; **1988** Anasazi Heritage Center established.

Dove Creek *Dolores County* *Southwestern Colorado, 230 mi/370 km south-southwest of Pueblo*

1881 Dolores County formed; Rico becomes county seat; **1918** town founded; **1936** U.S. Highway 160 built, later redesignated U.S. Highway 666, renumbered 491 in 2003; **1939** town incorporated; **1946** county seat moved to Dove Creek; **1954** county courthouse completed.

Durango *La Plata County* *Southwestern Colorado, 185 mi/298 km southwest of Pueblo*

1874 La Plata County formed; **1880** Denver & Rio Grande Western Railroad built; town founded as county seat on Las Animas River; **1881** town incorporated; **1882** Fort Lewis moved from Pagosa Springs; **1892** *Durango Herald-Democrat* newspaper founded; **1907** Durango Public Library built; **1911** Fort Lewis Agricultural School established, becomes Fort Lewis College; **Aug. 16, 1933** astronaut Stuart Roosa born; **1959** county courthouse built.

Eads *Kiowa County* *Eastern Colorado, 110 mi/177 km east-southeast of Colorado Springs*

Nov. 28, 1864 in Sand Creek Massacre to northeast, up to 500 Cheyenne, mostly women, children, and elderly, killed in unprovoked attack by forces of Col. John Chivington, leads to Senate investigation Jan. 1865; **1887** Missouri Pacific Railroad reaches site; **1889** Kiowa County formed; Sheridan Lake becomes county seat; **1902** town founded as new county seat; **1916** town incorporated; **March 1931** school bus with 22 children caught in blizzard at Towner to east, driver, five children die of exposure; **1956** county courthouse built.

Eagle *Eagle County* *West central Colorado, 95 mi/153 km west of Denver, on Colorado River*

1883 Eagle County formed; **1884** Denver & Rio Grande Railroad reaches town; town founded as county seat; **1891**

White River National Forest established; **1905** town incorporated; **1985** county courthouse built.

Eden   *Pueblo County*   See **Pueblo (1904)**

Estes Park   *Larimer County*   *Northern Colorado, 50 mi/80 km north-northwest of Denver*

1859 Joel Estes builds first two log cabins; **1864** mountain valley named Estes Park by newspaperman William Byers; **1877** first hotel built by Irish Earl of Dunraven; **1905** town founded; **1909** Stanley Hotel opened; **1917** town incorporated; **Jan. 26, 1915** Rocky Mountain National Park established; **Sept. 1929** Trail Ridge Road completed west through national park; **June 30, 1951** United Airlines DC-6 airplane crashes in Rocky Mountain National Park killing 50; **1962** Estes Park Historical Museum founded; **July 31, 1976** Big Thompson River Flash Flood kills 139 from here east to Loveland; **July 15, 1982** Lawn Lake Flood occurs after collapse of dam on Roaring River, three killed.

Fairplay   *Park County*   *Central Colorado, 63 mi/ 101 km southwest of Denver, on South Platte River*

1859 town founded as gold prospecting camp; **1861** Park County formed; town becomes county seat; **1874** county courthouse built; **1880** town incorporated; **1930** monument erected in memory of Prunes, burro that worked in every mine in district in mid-1860s, owner Robert Sherwood, 82, buried next to burro 1931.

Florence   *Fremont County*   See **Cañon City (1906)**

Fort Collins   *Larimer County*   *Northern Colorado, 55 mi/89 km north of Denver*

1859 Antoine Janis builds cabin on Cache la Poudre River; **1860** Inverness Farm established by Philips Lariviere; **1861** Larimer County formed; Colona (La Porte) becomes county seat; **1864** Camp Collins military post established replacing post at Laporte, abandoned 1871; Eaton Irrigation Ditch built; **1868** county seat moved to Fort Collins; **1870** Colorado State University established; **1873** town founded by Gen. Robert A. Cameron; **1879** incorporated as a town; **1883** incorporated as a city; **1902** beet sugar refinery built; **1903** Carnegie Library opened; **June 8, 1917** Supreme Court Justice Byron White born (died 2002); **1919** red clover production begins after discovery of its resistance to alkaline soil; **1923** Fort Collins-Wellington Oil Field discovered; **1932** Roosevelt National Forest established; **1957** county courthouse built; **Sept. 2000** County Justice Center opened; old courthouse still in use.

Fort Morgan   *Morgan County*   *Northeastern Colorado, 70 mi/113 km northeast of Denver*

c.1858 Camp Tyler military post established on Overland Trail, on South Platte River; town founded; **1866** fort renamed for Col. C. E. Morgan; **1887** town incorporated; **1889** Morgan County formed; town becomes county seat; **1906** county courthouse built; **1967** Morgan Community College established; **1987** County Justice Center built.

Fountain   *El Paso County*   *Central Colorado, 12 mi/19 km south of Colorado Springs*

1859 town founded on Fountain Creek, one of oldest towns in Colorado; first meeting held here to discuss statehood of Colorado; **1888** town vies for state capital; **May 14, 1889** dynamite laden rail cars break loose, explode at depot, four killed, large part of town destroyed; accident ruins town's chance for state capital; **1903** town incorporated.

Georgetown   *Clear Creek County*   *Central Colorado, 38 mi/61 km west of Denver*

1859 placer gold discovered; town founded; **1861** Clear Creek County formed; town of Idaho becomes county seat; **1868** town incorporated; county seat moved to Georgetown; **1870** silver boom begins, continues until 1878; **1875** Hotel de Paris built by Louis du Puy; **1879** Colorado & Southern Railroad built from Denver, abandoned 1939; **1973** Eisenhower Memorial Tunnel built on I-70 to east, 8,941 ft/2,725 m long; **1978** county courthouse built.

Glenwood Springs   *Garfield County*   *Western Colorado, 121 mi/195 km west of Denver, on Colorado River*

1860 first white settlers arrive; **1882** Capt. Isaac Cooper of Glenwood, Iowa, arrives to establish spa; **1883** Garfield County formed; town founded as county seat and resort, named Defiance for nearby fort of same name; **1885** town incorporated, renamed Glenwood Springs; **1887** Denver & Rio Grande Western Railroad built; **May 1887** gunfighter Doc Holliday arrives for tuberculosis treatment, dies Nov. at age 35 with his boots on; **1893** Hotel Colorado opened; **1898** first Strawberry Day Festival held; **Sept. 17, 1925** Denver radio station KOA makes first broadcast from Hotel Colorado; **1929** county courthouse built; **1935** Dotsero Cutoff of Denver & Rio Grande Western Railroad completed providing link between Denver and Salt Lake City; **1982** oil companies discontinue oil shale exploration affecting economy; **July 6, 1994** 14 firefighters killed after being surrounded by forest fire.

Golden   *Jefferson County*   *Central Colorado, 12 mi/19 km west of Denver*

1859 town founded by Boston Company, named for early miner Tom Golden; **1860** provisional government of Territory of Jefferson meets here; **1861** Jefferson County formed; **1862** town becomes capital of Colorado Territory and county seat; **1867** territorial capital moved to Denver; Astor House Hotel built; **1873** Adolph Coors Brewery established by Adolph Coors and partner Jacob Schueler; **1874** Colorado School of Mines established; **1876** Calvary Episcopal Church built; **1881**

Colorado Industrial School for Boys established; **1886** town incorporated; **Jan. 1917** Buffalo Bill Cody buried south of town, died in Denver Jan. 10; **Dec. 1992** county government center completed.

Granada *Prowers County* See **Lamar (1942)**

Grand Junction *Mesa County* *Western Colorado, 190 mi/306 km west-southwest of Denver, on Colorado R.*

1881 Ute people expelled from area to Uintah Indian Reservation, Utah; town founded by George Crawford at confluence of Colorado and Gunnison rivers; **Dec. 1881** incorporated as a town; **1882** Grand Junction House hotel built; town platted; narrow gauge Denver & Rio Grande Western Railroad reaches town; **1883** Mesa County formed; town becomes county seat; **1886** Grand Junction Indian School (Teller Institute) founded, closed 1911; **1887** main line Denver & Rio Grande Western Railroad built; **1891** incorporated as a city; **1894** first orchards and vineyards established; **1899** Holly Beet Sugar Factory built; **1901** Carnegie Library opened; **May 24, 1911** Colorado National Monument established to west, preserves prehistoric cultural sites, fossil beds; **1924** county courthouse completed; **1925** Mesa State College established; Grand Valley Diversion Project completed, work begun 1913; **1930** Walker Field Airport established to northeast; **1961** uranium production reaches peak; **1966** Museum of Arts and Sciences opened, renamed Museum of Western Colorado 1977; **1980s** wine industry established in area.

Greeley *Weld County* *Northern Colorado, 47 mi/76 km north-northeast of Denver, on South Platte River*

1859 *New York Tribune* newspaper publisher Horace Greeley visits area, impressed by its potential for settlement; **1861** Weld County formed; **1862** Fort Lathan established on Overland Stage Line; **1868** town founded by Nathan C. Meeker, agent for Horace Greeley; **1869–1870** Union Pacific Railroad built from Denver to Cheyenne, first railroad in Colorado; **1870** *Greeley Tribune* newspaper founded by Meeker; **1877** incorporated as a town; town becomes county seat after five year dispute, moved from Fort Vasquez (Platteville); **1885** potato production becomes important; **1886** incorporated as a city; **1890** Colorado State College of Education established, becomes University of Northern Colorado; **1902** Great Western Beet Sugar Plant built; **1904** TV personality Ted Mack born (died 1976); **1907** Public Library built; **1915** Potato Experimental Station established; **1917** county courthouse built; **1922** Greeley West Rodeo established, renamed Greeley Independence Stampede 1970; **1967** Aims Community College established.

Gunnison *Gunnison County* *West central Colorado, 124 mi/200 km west-northwest of Pueblo*

1870 silver discovered, threat by Utes delays exploitation; **1874** town founded; **1877** Gunnison County formed; town becomes county seat; **1879** silver mining begins; county courthouse built; **1880** town incorporated; **1884** La Veta Hotel built; **1901** Western State College of Colorado established; **Feb. 11, 1965** Curecanti National Recreation Area established to west on Gunnison River; **1966** Blue Mesa Reservoir built on Gunnison River to west.

Hastings *Las Animas County* See **Trinidad (1917)**

Holyoke *Phillips County* *Northeastern Colorado, 150 mi/241 km northeast of Denver*

1886 Chicago, Burlington & Quincy Railroad built; town founded, named for Holyoke, Massachusetts; **1888** town incorporated; **1889** Phillips County formed; town becomes county seat; **1935** county courthouse built.

Hot Sulphur Springs *Grand County* *Northern Colorado, 63 mi/101 km northwest of Denver*

1862 Hot Sulphur Springs Resort and Spa established, renovated 1996; **1874** Grand County formed; town founded as county seat on Colorado River; **1903** town incorporated; **1937** county courthouse built, addition built 1970.

Hugo *Lincoln County* *Eastern Colorado, 90 mi/145 km southeast of Denver*

1880 trading post established; town founded; **1888** Union Pacific Railroad built; **1889** Lincoln County formed; town becomes county seat; **1909** incorporated as a town; **1992** county courthouse built.

Ignacio *La Plata County* *Southwestern Colorado, 180 mi/290 km southwest of Pueblo*

1868 treaty creates reservation for Ute people consisting of western one-third of Colorado; **1881** Denver & Rio Grande Railroad built; **1896** Southern Ute land allotments established; **1899** Southern Ute Reservation opened to white settlement; **1910** town platted on Los Piños River as Southern Ute headquarters; **1911** St. Ignatius Catholic Church built, rebuilt 1942 and 1980; **1913** town incorporated.

Julesburg *Sedgwick County* *Northeastern Colorado, 162 mi/261 km northeast of Denver, on South Platte R.*

1859 Frenchman Jules Beni establishes Julesburg trading post on Overland Trail; **Jan. 1865** Cheyenne, Sioux, and Arapaho attack town, damage buildings and possessions, return in Feb. to burn most buildings, retaliation for Sand Creek Massacre; **1881** Union Pacific Railroad cutoff projected; **1884** town platted on railroad; **1886** town incorporated; **1889** Sedgwick County formed; town becomes county seat; **1938** county courthouse completed.

Kiowa   *Elbert County   Central Colorado, 40 mi/ 64 km southeast of Denver*

1859 town founded; **1874** Elbert County formed; town becomes county seat; **1888** county subdivided into Lincoln, Kit Carson, Cheyenne, and Elbert counties; **1912** town incorporated; county courthouse built.

La Junta   *Otero County   Southeastern Colorado, 60 mi/97 km east-southeast of Pueblo, on Arkansas River*

1833 Bent's Fort built to east on Santa Fe Trail, abandoned 1849; **1875** town founded; **1881** incorporated as a city; **1889** Otero County formed, named for settler Miguel Otero; town becomes county seat; **1933** Koshare Indian Museum and Kiva established; **Sept. 15, 1935** author Ken Kesey born, wrote *One Flew Over the Cuckoo's Nest* (died 2001) **Dec. 1935** *Tyrannosaurus rex* dinosaur tracks discovered in bed of Purgatoire River c.20 mi/32 km to south; **1941** Otero Junior College established; **1957** county courthouse built, refaced 1993; **1960** Bent's Fort National Historic Site established; **1976** Bent's Fort reconstructed.

Lafayette   *Boulder County   Northern Colorado, 18 mi/29 km north of Denver*

1859 coal mining begins; **1874** Colorado & Southern Railroad built; **1888** town founded as coal mining center by Mary Miller, named for husband Lafayette Miller; **1890** town incorporated; **Nov. 2, 1927** police brought in to quell strike violence at Columbine Mine, fire into crowd killing six, injuring several; **1956** Black Diamond Mine becomes last coal mine to close; **1964** Lafayette Public Library founded.

Lake City   *Hinsdale County   Southwestern Colorado, 143 mi/230 km west of Pueblo*

1874 Hinsdale County formed; town founded as county seat by Enox Hotchkiss; **1875** town incorporated; **1877** county courthouse built; **Sept. 1877** Susan B. Anthony rides to town on horseback with her women's suffrage crusade; **1879** fire destroys 21 buildings; **1889** Denver & Rio Grande Railroad reaches town.

Lakewood   *Jefferson County   Central Colorado, 4 mi/6 km west of Denver*

1888 first four subdivisions platted; **1914** Colorado Christian University established; **1941** Denver Ordnance Plant established, closed 1945; **1950** Denver Federal Center established at former ordnance plant; **1969** incorporated as a city; Red Rocks Community College established.

Lamar   *Prowers County   Southeastern Colorado, 106 mi/171 km east of Pueblo, on Arkansas River*

1844 Big Timbers Trading Post established by William Bent; **1853** Bent builds second fort to west, abandons first fort, replaced 1866 by Fort Lyon, also to west; **1861** first cattle introduced to area by John W. Prowers; **1866** Atchison, Topeka & Santa Fe Railroad built; town of Grenada founded; **1873** railroad extended west; **1886** new town founded and incorporated, named for Lucius Q. C. Lamar, U.S. secretary of the interior; **1889** Prowers County formed; town becomes county seat; **1928** county courthouse built; **May 25, 1928** First National Bank robbed of $200,000 by Ralph and Jake Fleagle and two companions, kidnapped employee and abducted doctor murdered, three bandits hanged, fourth shot and killed; **1937** Lamar Community College established; **Aug. 1942** Camp Amache, Japanese-American internment camp, established at Granada to east, closed Oct. 1945.

Las Animas   *Bent County   Southeastern Colorado, 75 mi/121 km east-southeast of Pueblo, on Arkansas R.*

Nov. 15, 1806 Lt. Zebulon M. Pike makes first sighting of peak that bears his name; **1860** Fort Lyon established, abandoned 1868; **1866** first attempt to irrigate farmland in area made by Thomas O. Boggs; **1869** town founded at mouth of Las Animas (Purgatoire) River; **May 23, 1869** famed scout Kit Carson dies, born 1809 in Kentucky; **1870** Greenwood County formed, renamed Bent County 1874; town becomes county seat; **1873** Kansas Pacific Railroad built; town moved 6 mi/9.7 km west to railroad; **1874** area becomes known for its large cattle and buffalo roundups; **1880s** Prairie Cattle Company, owned by English interests, dominates local cattle industry; **1886** town incorporated; **1889** Bent County reformed, diminished in land area; town remains county seat; county courthouse completed; **1916** region's last great roundup held; **1926** Las Animas Public Library founded; **1934** Fort Lyon Veterans Administration Facility established to east; **1948** John Martin Reservoir formed to east on Arkansas River.

Leadville   *Lake County   Central Colorado, 75 mi/ 121 km southwest of Denver*

1845 John C. Fremont's party passes through on way to California; **1860** placer gold discovered at California Gulch; town founded near source of Arkansas River, named Oro City; **1861** Lake County formed; **1862** town nearly deserted with depletion of gold reserves; **1877** lead-silver deposits discovered; lead smelter built; **1878** town incorporated, renamed Leadville; **1878–1879** Starr Company's claim to entire town leads to confrontation between people and mine owners, vigilante group formed, notorious killer Mart Duggan appointed marshal; **1879** Robert E. Lee Silver Mine established; Tabor Opera House opened; Clarendon Hotel built, razed 1930s; **c.1880** Wyman Saloon built; Pioneer Club saloon opened; Healy House residence built; **1881** Matchless Silver Mine established by H. A. W. Tabor; **1885** Tabor Grand

Hotel opened, renamed Hotel Vendome 1894; **1893** drop in price of silver ruins miners; **Jan. 1896** Ice Palace built, world's largest palace of ice, closed May; **1955** county courthouse built; **1965** Colorado Mountain College, Timberline Campus, (2-year) established; **1987** National Mining Hall of Fame and Museum established.

Littleton   *Arapahoe County   Central Colorado, suburb 12 mi/19 km south of Denver*

1861 Arapahoe County formed; **1862** Richard and Angeline Little become first settlers; **1867** Rough and Ready Flour Mill established; **1871** Denver & Rio Grande Railroad built; **1872** town founded; **1887** Atchison, Topeka & Santa Fe Railroad reaches town; **1890** incorporated as a town; **1904** Arapahoe County divided into five counties; town becomes county seat of diminished county; **1917** Carnegie Library built, replaced by Bemis Library 1965; **1950** Centennial Race Track opened, closed 1984; **1955** Martin Defense Plant established; **1959** incorporated as a city; **1965** Arapahoe Community College established; **June 16, 1965** flash flood on South Platte River, 28 people killed, 100 horses killed at race track; **1972** Chatfield Reservoir built to south on South Platte River; **Apr. 20, 1999** students Eric Harris, 18, and Dylan Klebold, 17, kill 12 other students and one teacher, wound 30 others in shooting rampage at Columbine High School, before killing themselves; **July 2000** Denver Light Rail system reaches city.

Longmont   *Boulder County   Northern Colorado, 28 mi/45 km north of Denver*

1820 Maj. Stephen H. Long leads exploration team into St. Vrain Valley; **1859** first ore mill in Colorado established; **1871** town founded, name derived from Longs Peak to west; **1873** Colorado Central Railroad reaches town; incorporated as a town; **Aug. 19, 1873** actor Fred Stone born, scarecrow in *Wizard of Oz* (died 1959); **1882** Ryssby Lutheran Church built; **1902** Carnegie Library built; **1903** Great Western Beet Sugar factory established; **Nov. 1, 1955** bomb explodes on United Airlines DC-6B airplane in sky killing all 44 on board; **1961** incorporated as a city.

Louisville   *Boulder County   Northern Colorado, 18 mi/29 km north of Denver*

1873 Colorado Central Railroad built; **1877** Welch Coal Mine opened; **1878** town founded by Louis Nawatny; **1882** incorporated as a city; **1890** Alma Mine opened, operates beneath town through 1928; **1908** Denver & Interurban Railroad reaches town; **1936** explosion at Monarch Coal Mine kills 8; **1952** last coal mine closed.

Loveland   *Larimer County   Northern Colorado, 56 mi/90 km north of Denver*

1858 Fort Namaqua built by Mariano Medina, first settlement in area; **1862** stage station built along Overland Stage Line; town of St. Louis founded; **1877**

Colorado Central Railroad built by W. A. H. Loveland; new town founded on Big Thompson River; **1881** town incorporated; **1901** Great Western Beet Sugar refinery built; **1908** Loveland Carnegie Public Library built; **July 31, 1976** flash flood rushes down canyon of Big Thompson River from Estes Park killing 139, six missing; **Apr. 17, 1981** midair collision of commuter plane and private plane leaves 15 dead.

Ludlow   *Las Animas County   See* **Trinidad (1914)**

Manassa   *Conejos County   See* **Conejos (1895)**

Manitou Springs   *El Paso County   Central Colorado, suburb 5 mi/8 km west of Colorado Springs*

Nov. 1806 Zebulon Pike's men fail in attempt to climb peak that bears his name during blizzard, arrested by Spanish authorities, taken to Mexico; **1820** Dr. Edwin James of Maj. Stephen H. Long expedition makes first known ascent of Pikes Peak (14,110 ft/4,301 m) to west; **1833** Col. A. G. Boone, grandson of Daniel Boone, arrives as springs' first health seeker; **1843** explorer John C. Fremont visits springs; **1859** gold rush begins at Ute Pass, Pikes Peak; **1872** Denver & Rio Grande Western Railroad built to Pikes Peak; town founded by Dr. William A. Bell and Gen. William Palmer; **1876** incorporated as a town; **1882** Pikes Peak Summit House built; **1888** incorporated as a city; **1890** cog railway built to summit of Pikes Peak; streetcar line extended from Colorado Springs; **1915** toll road built to summit of Pikes Peak, becomes free road 1937; **1960s** U.S. Highway 24 bypass diverts traffic from heart of town.

Meeker   *Rio Blanco County   Northwestern Colorado, 153 mi/246 km west-northwest of Denver*

1868 Maj. John Wesley Powell winters here with 20 others; **1878** Nathan C. Meeker of White River Ute Agency arrives intent on changing Ute way of life; **Sept. 20, 1879** Meeker, ten others, killed on White River by Utes [see Craig]; **1880** treaty forces Utes to move to Uintah Reservation, Utah; **1883** town founded on White River; **1885** incorporated as a town; **1887** Second Ute War fought on White River to west, Utes return from Utah to reclaim lands, many slain by force from Fort Laramie, Wyoming; **1889** Rio Blanco County formed; town becomes county seat; **1896** Meeker Hotel built, favored by Theodore Roosevelt during hunting trips; **1935** county courthouse built.

Montrose   *Montrose County   Western Colorado, 173 mi/278 km west of Pueblo*

1880 Fort Crawford built to south, mostly abandoned 1884; **1881** area opened to white settlement; **1882** town founded on Umcompahgre River by Joseph Selig, name derived from Sir Walter Scott's "Legend of Montrose"; **1882** incorporated as a city; **1883** Montrose County formed; town becomes county seat; **1909** Gunnison

Diversion Tunnel opened to east, diverts water from Gunnison River to Uncompahgre Valley, 5.8 mi/9.3 km long; **1922** county courthouse built; **March 2, 1933** Black Canyon of the Gunnison National Monument established on Gunnison River to northeast; **1956** Ute Indian Museum built, expanded 1998; **Feb. 11, 1965** Curecanti National Recreation Area established on Gunnison River to east; **1968** Morrow Point Reservoir formed on Gunnison River to east.

Morrison   *Jefferson County*   *Central Colorado, suburb 12 mi/19 km west-southwest of Denver*

1870 George Morrison becomes first homesteader; **1872** narrow gauge Denver & South Park Railway built west to Mt. Morrison, used through 1925; **1874** town founded; **July 24, 1896** flash flooding rushes down from mountains, many killed; **1906** incorporated as a town; **1927** Denver Mayor Benjamin Stapleton acquires Red Rocks parcel, start of Denver Mountain Parks system; **1941** Red Rocks Amphitheatre opened; **1946** Morrison Library built.

Mount Harris   *Routt County*   See **Steamboat Springs (1942)**

New Castle   *Garfield County*   *Western Colorado, 130 mi/209 km west of Denver, on Colorado River*

1883 town founded as Chapman; **1886** coal discovered by Samuel Wraith; **1888** incorporated as a town; **Feb. 18, 1896** explosion at Vulcan Mine kills 49; **Dec. 16, 1913** second explosion at Vulcan Mine, 37 killed.

Ordway   *Crowley County*   *Southeastern Colorado, 46 mi/74 km east of Pueblo*

1887 Missouri Pacific Railroad built; town founded; **1900** town incorporated; Lake Meredith formed to southeast by dam on Bob Creek, linked to Arkansas River by Colorado Canal, both built for irrigation purposes; **1911** Crowley County formed; town becomes county seat; county courthouse built.

Ouray   *Ouray County*   *Southwestern Colorado, 162 mi/261 km west-southwest of Pueblo*

1875 rich silver lodes discovered; town founded on Uncompahgre River; **1876** incorporated as a town; **1883** Ouray County formed; town becomes county seat; **1884** incorporated as a city; **1886** Beaumont Hotel built; **1888** county courthouse completed; **1896** gold discovered at Camp Bird Mine by Thomas Walsh to southwest.

Pagosa Springs   *Archuleta County*   *Southwestern Colorado, 143 mi/230 km southwest of Pueblo*

1859 Pagosa Hot Springs discovered by surveyors under Capt. J. N. Macomb, Ute term for "healing waters"; **1878** Fort Lewis built, moved to Durango 1882; **1880** Denver & Rio Grande Western Railroad built; town founded; **1885** Archuleta County formed; town becomes county seat;

1891 incorporated as a town; **1928** county courthouse built.

Platteville   *Weld County*   *Northern Colorado, 32 mi/51 km north-northeast of Denver, on South Platte River*

1836 Fort Vasquez built by Louis Vasquez and Andrew Sublette for Rocky Mountain Fur Company, destroyed by natives 1842, rebuilt; **1861** Weld County formed; Fort Vasquez becomes county seat; **1869** Union Pacific Railroad built; **1871** town founded; **1876** incorporated as a town; **1877** county seat moved to Greeley.

Primero   *Las Animas County*   See **Trinidad (1907, 1910)**

Pueblo   *Pueblo County*   *Southern Colorado, 100 mi/161 km south of Denver, on Arkansas River*

1806 Lt. Zebulon Pike passes through area; **1842** El Pueblo Trading Post established; **1846–1847** Mormons settle here temporarily, move on to Utah; **1853** trader "Uncle Dick" Wootton arrives, builds fort; **1854** nearly all at Wootton's post killed by "friendly" Native Americans allowed into compound; **1858** prospectors arrive from St. Louis; Fountain City founded; **1860** town of Pueblo City founded, absorbs Fountain City; **1861** Pueblo County formed; town becomes county seat; **1863** post office established; **1868** *Weekly Chieftain* newspaper founded; **1870** town incorporated; **1870s** oil boom begins to west; **1871** first Colorado State Fair held; **1872** Denver & Rio Grande Railroad Western reaches town; **1873** incorporated as a city; **1879** Colorado State Hospital opened; **1881** Minnequa Steel Plant founded; **1888** Guggenheim Smelter opened using coal from Trinidad to south; **1891** Mineral Palace opened, showcase for area's mineral wealth; **1893** Rosemount House hotel built; **May 31, 1894** flash flood on Fountain Creek sweeps away train, many drowned; **1904** McClelland Public Library built; **Aug. 7, 1904** railroad bridge collapses into Hogan's Gulch at Eden to north, 96 killed; **1912** county courthouse completed; **July 3, 1921** city flooded by Arkansas River, about 100 killed; **1924** Arkansas River channelized to prevent flooding; **1933** University of Southern Colorado established; Southern Colorado Junior College established, becomes Pueblo Community College; **1942** Pueblo Ordnance Depot established to east; Pueblo Army Air Base established, deeded to city 1948, Municipal Airport opened 1953; **1971** High Speed Test Center established to northeast by U.S. Department of Transportation; **1972** Sangre de Cristo Arts and Conference Center opened; **1975** Pueblo Reservoir formed to west on Arkansas River.

Salida   *Chaffee County*   *Central Colorado, 65 mi/105 km west-southwest of Colorado Springs, on Arkansas River*

1879 Chaffee County formed; Buena Vista becomes county seat; **1880** Denver & Rio Grande Western

Railroad built; town founded; **1891** town incorporated; **1930** county seat moved to Salida; county courthouse completed; **Sept. 11, 1971** eight high school football players and coach killed, 10 injured, when bus crashes in Monarch Pass to west.

San Luis *Costilla County Southern Colorado, 83 mi/134 km south-southwest of Pueblo*

1851 town founded by six Mexican families at center of Sangre de Cristo Land Grant, first non-Native American settlement in Colorado; **1852** Fort Massachusetts established to north; **1857** general store established by Dario Gallegos, still open, oldest business in Colorado; **1858** Fort Garland built to replace Fort Massachusetts, abandoned 1883; **1861** Costilla County formed; San Miguel becomes county seat; Church of the Most Precious Blood (Catholic) built; **1863** county seat moved to San Luis; **1886** county courthouse built; **1968** incorporated as a town.

Silverton *San Juan County Southwestern Colorado, 165 mi/266 km west-southwest of Pueblo*

1861 Capt. Charles Baker leads prospectors into valley, later named Baker's Park; **1874** silver discovered; town founded on Animas River; **1876** San Juan County formed; town incorporated, becomes county seat; **1882** branch of Denver & Rio Grande Western extended from Durango with Silverton as terminus; **1908** county courthouse completed; **1952** last silver mine closed; railroad abandoned; **1959** mining activity resumes, again ceased 1999.

Springfield *Baca County Southeastern Colorado, 121 mi/195 km southeast of Pueblo*

1887 Atchison, Topeka & Santa Fe Railroad built; town founded, includes settlers from Springfield, Missouri; **1889** Baca County formed; town incorporated and becomes county seat; **1929** county courthouse built.

Steamboat Springs *Routt County Northwestern Colorado, 109 mi/175 km northwest of Denver*

1875 town founded by James H. Crawford; **1877** Routt County formed; Hayden becomes county seat; **1878** county seat moved to town of Hahns Peak; **1907** town incorporated; **1912** county seat moved to Steamboat Springs; **1919** first silver fox farm in Colorado established, pair brought from Prince Edward Island, Canada; **1923** county courthouse built; **Jan. 27, 1942** explosion at Wadge Coal Mine at town of Mount Harris to west, 34 killed; **1965** Colorado Mountain College, Alpine Campus, (2-year) established.

Sterling *Logan County Northeastern Colorado, 110 mi/177 km northeast of Denver*

July 11, 1869 in Battle of Summit Springs to southeast, 500 Cheyenne Dog Soldiers attacked by 250 U.S. soldiers and Pawnee allies, 52 Cheyenne killed, including Chief

Tall Bull; **1872** Daniel Leavitt begins ranching one year after surveying rail line; **1881** Union Pacific Railroad built; town founded; **1884** town incorporated; **1887** Logan County formed; town becomes county seat; **1910** county courthouse built; **1941** Northwestern Junior College established.

Telluride *San Miguel County Southwestern Colorado, 170 mi/274 km west-southwest of Pueblo*

1875 prospector John Fallon arrives; **1880** rich gold vein discovered at Smuggler Mine; town founded, named for tellurium content in rock; **1883** San Miguel County formed; town becomes county seat; **1887** town incorporated; county courthouse built; **1890** Rio Grande Southern Railroad reaches town; **1901** strike held over contract pay system led by Western Federation of Miners; **1978** Telluride Ski Area established.

Towner *Kiowa County See* **Eads** (1931)

Trinidad *Las Animas County Southern Colorado, 75 mi/121 km south of Pueblo*

1598 Spanish gold-seeking expedition enters area led by Juan de Oñate; **1821** Mexican Revolution allows open trade on Santa Fe Trail; **1846** Col. Stephen W. Kearney passes through on way to New Mexico; **1859** Gabriel Gutiérrez brings sheep to area; town founded on Santa Fe Trail, named for Trinidad Baca, daughter of early settler; **1861** town platted; **1866** Las Animas County formed; town becomes county seat; **1867** coal mining begun by Frank Bloom; **Dec. 25, 1867** evoking past tensions between U.S. and Mexico, "Battle of Trinidad" ("Christmas Day War") wrestling match held, Hispanic wrestler shot to death by his opponent; **1873** Denver & Rio Grande and Atchison, Topeka & Santa Fe railroads reach town; **1876** incorporated as a city; **1885** Holy Trinity Catholic Church built; **1904** Carnegie Public Library built; **Jan. 23, 1907** explosion at Primero Coal Mine, 24 killed; **Jan. 31, 1910** second explosion at Primero Coal Mine, 75 killed; **Nov. 3, 1910** coal mine explosion at Delagua to northwest, 79 killed; **Apr. 20, 1914** in Ludlow Massacre, amid coal strike violence at Ludlow to north, miners' tents burned, over 40 killed including two women, 11 children; **Apr. 27, 1917** coal explosion at Hastings Mine to north, 121 killed; **1918** county courthouse completed; **1925** Trinidad State Junior College established; **1955** Trinidad History Museum opened.

Twin Lakes *Lake County Central Colorado, 85 mi/137 km southwest of Denver*

1880 rich silver lodes discovered; town founded; **1939** Twin Lakes Diversion Tunnel completed sending water through 4 mi/6.4 km tunnel through Continental Divide to Arkansas River; **Oct. 2, 1970** chartered plane from Wichita, Kansas, to Logan, Utah, crashes, 30 killed, including 13 from Wichita State University football team.

Uravan   *Montrose County*   *Western Colorado,*
220 mi/354 km west of Pueblo

1881 carbonate ore deposits mined for gold near San
Miguel River; **1898** elements of uranium discovered in
gold deposits; **1912** uranium and vanadium mining begins;
over half of world's radium supply mined here; **1936**
company town named by U.S. Vanadium Corporation,
name combination of "uranium" and "vanadium."

Vail   *Eagle County*   *Central Colorado, 68 mi/109 km*
west of Denver

1939 U.S. Highway 6 built through Gore Valley; town
founded; **1961** Vail Ski Resort completed; **1962** incorporated as a town; **1976** Colorado Ski Museum established;
1977 Ski Hall of Fame established.

Walden   *Jackson County*   *Northern Colorado,*
94 mi/151 km northwest of Denver

1889 town founded on Illinois Creek, headstream of
North Platte River; **1890** incorporated as a town; **1909**
Jackson County formed; town becomes county seat; **1913**
county courthouse built.

Walsenburg   *Huerfano County*   *Southern*
Colorado, 43 mi/69 km south of Pueblo

1861 Huerfano County formed, Spanish for "orphan,"
reference to isolated mountain peaks in area; **1862** Spanish
village of La Plaza de los Leones founded; **1867** Bandito
becomes county seat; **1870** German merchant Fred
Walsen arrives; **1872** town founded by Walsen as new
county seat; **1873** town incorporated; **1876** first coal mine
established by Walsen; **1878** Denver & Rio Grande
Western Railroad reaches town; **1904** county courthouse
built.

Westcliffe   *Custer County*   *Southern Colorado,*
45 mi/72 km west-southwest of Pueblo

1870 silver lode discovered by Richard Irwin; **1872** Hope
Lutheran Church built by German immigrants; **1877**
Custer County formed; Rosita becomes county seat, later
moved to town of Silver Cliff to east; **c.1880** silver mining
reaches peak; **1881** Denver & Rio Grande Railroad
reaches town; **1885** town founded by Dr. J. W. Bell,
named for his home town of Westcliffe-by-the-Sea,
England; **1887** incorporated as a town; National Hotel
built; **1888** Westcliffe Calaboose built; **1890s** Silver Cliff
declines; Westcliffe becomes county seat; **1929** county
courthouse built.

Wray   *Yuma County*   *Northeastern Colorado,*
144 mi/232 km east-northeast of Denver

1868 in Battle of Beecher Island to south, 50 soldiers
under Col. George A. Forsyth and Lt. Fred Beecher
attacked by 1,000 Cheyenne, Beecher, several others killed
in 8-day siege in dry Arikaree River, relieved by African-
American Cavalry (Buffalo Soldiers); **1886** Chicago,
Burlington & Quincy Railroad built; town founded;
1889 Yuma County formed; **1905** Beecher Island
Battlefield Monument built; **1903** county courthouse
built; **1906** town incorporated.

Connecticut

Northeastern U.S. One of the six New England states. Capital: Hartford. Major cities: Hartford, New Haven.

Connecticut was one of the 13 colonies that adopted the U.S. Declaration of Independence July 4, 1776. It became the 5th state to ratify the U.S. Constitution January 9, 1788.

Connecticut is divided into eight counties. The counties are divided into townships, called towns, which have very strong governments. In 1955, all county governments were abolished in favor of the town governments. Scattered throughout most towns are villages which have no government of their own. Municipalities are classified as boroughs and cities. Boroughs remain part of their respective towns, or townships, while cities are formed from one or more former towns. See Introduction.

Ansonia *New Haven County* *Southern Connecticut, 8 mi/12.9 km west of New Haven*

1651 area settled; **1654** settler Edward Wooster begins hop production; **1686** Brownie Castle built; **1698** David Humphreys House built, rebuilt 1733; **1746** First Episcopal Church built; **1748** Richard Mansfield House built; **1760** Joseph Riggs House built; **1845** Anson G. Phelps establishes industrial tract; town founded; **1864** incorporated as a borough; **1889** town incorporated; **1893** incorporated as a city; **1896** Ansonia Public Library founded.

Avon *Hartford County* *North central Connecticut, 8 mi/12.9 km west-northwest of Hartford*

1728 Jonathan Humphreys House built; **1757** Old Farms Inn built; **c.1795** Phelps Tavern built; **March 1, 1807** Mormon leader Wilford Woodruff born (died 1898); **1818** Congregational Church built; **1828** Farmington Canal opened; **1830** town incorporated; **1865** Pine Grove School built, closed 1949; **1917** Heublein Tower (165 ft/ 50 m tall) completed, residence of Gilbert F. Heublein of noted Heublein family; **1890** Avon Free Library founded, built 1932, new facility opened 1982; **1918** Avon Old Farms established by Theodate Pope (Mrs. John Riddle) as school for boys in rural setting; **1972** Avon Valley Art Center founded.

Berlin *Hartford County* *Central Connecticut, 10 mi/16 km south-southwest of Hartford*

1686 town settled; **1740** Edward and William Pattison begin crafting tinware, sell door-to-door, first of so-called

Yankee Peddlers; **1769** Fuller Tavern built; **1785** town incorporated; **Feb. 23, 1787** educator Emma Willard born (died 1870); **1797** Elijah Loveland Tavern built; **1799** Simeon North contracts with U.S. government for manufacture of pistols; **1831** Worthington Academy founded; **1901** Berlin-Peck Memorial Library founded, new library opened 1989; **1920** World War (Veterans) Memorial erected; **1945** Hawthorne Inn established.

Bethel *Fairfield County* *Southwestern Connecticut, 25 mi/40 km west of New Haven*

c.1750 town settled; **1759** town named Bethel; **1760** Farnum Tavern built; **1793** hat manufacturing becomes main industry; **July 5, 1810** circus promoter Phineas T. Barnum born (died 1891); **1855** town incorporated, separates from Danbury; **1861** Bethel United Methodist Church built; **1867** Plumtrees Schoolhouse built.

Bethlehem *Litchfield County* *Eastern Connecticut, 29 mi/47 km west-southwest of Hartford*

1710 area purchased from Native Americans, called the North Purchase; **1734** area first settled by whites; **1740** Bird Tavern built by Samuel Church; **1754** Bellamy-Ferriday House built; **1759** Isaac Hill House built; **1787** town incorporated; **1829** church on the Green built, used as Town Hall from 1961; **1835** Christ Episcopal Church built; **1860** Bethlehem Methodist Church built; **1887** stone arch bridge built over Wood Creek; **1909** Bethlehem Public Library founded, new library opened 1969; **1929** Church of the Nativity (Catholic) completed; **1947** Abbey of Regina Laudis founded.

Bloomfield *Hartford County* *Northern Connecticut, 5 mi/8 km north-northwest of Hartford*

1640 town first settled; **1742** St. Andrew's Episcopal Church completed at North Bloomfield; **1746** Capt. Joseph Goodwin Tavern built; **Dec. 14, 1807** U.S. Sen. Francis Gillette born (died 1879); **Feb. 23, 1823** business executive James Goodwin Batterson born, founded Travelers Insurance Company 1863 (died 1901); **1830** Methodist Church built; **1835** town incorporated, separates from Windsor; **1856** Congregational Church built, replaces 1801 structure.

Bridgeport *Fairfield County* *Southwestern Connecticut, 16 mi/26 km southwest of New Haven*

1639 town settled on Long Island Sound; **1666** Fairfield County formed; **1700** Pixley Tavern built; **1759** Brothwell Beach House built; **c.1760** Capt. Abijah Sterling House built, boyhood home of Gen. Tom Thumb; **1776** fort built on Grovers Hill; **1800** incorporated as a borough, named for Pequonnock River drawbridge; **1809** lighthouse built on Fairweather Island, rebuilt 1823, discontinued 1933; **1821** incorporated as a town; **1825** Tongue Point Lighthouse built, automated 1954; **1836** incorporated as a city; **Jan. 4, 1838** entertainer Charles S. Stratton (Gen. Tom Thumb) born, member P. T. Barnum's Circus, married Lavinia Warren 1863 (died 1883); **1840** New York, New Haven & Hartford Railroad built; **1853** county seat moved from Fairfield; **1855** Tom Thumb House built by Sherwood S. Stratton, father of Charles S. Stratton (Tom Thumb); city hall completed; **1856** Singer Sewing Machine Company moves from Watertown, Connecticut, founded 1853; **1865** Bridgeport Brass Company founded; **1871** Harbor Lighthouse built, discontinued 1953; **c.1890** Barnum Institute of Science and History built by P. T. Barnum; **May 7, 1909** Polaroid camera inventor Edwin Herbert Land born (died 1991); **Feb. 17, 1917** biochemist Albert Lehninger born (died 1986); **1922** General Electric Plant established; **1926** United Congregational Church built; **1955** county governments abolished in Connecticut; **1965** Housatonic Community and Technical College (2-year) established.

Canaan *Litchfield County* *Northwestern Connecticut, 33 mi/53 km northwest of Hartford*

1738 town incorporated; **1751** Capt. Isaac Lawrence House built; **1762** Douglas Tavern built; **c.1770** Samuel Forbes House built; **1783** paper mill built at Falls Village; **1797** gun barrel factory built at Falls Village; **1800** fire destroys paper mill and gun factory; **1802** Congregational Church built at South Canaan; **1822** Congregational Church built at East Canaan; **1832** educator Prudence Crandall opens private school for African-American girls igniting social controversy, landmark event in civil rights struggle; **1837** Beckley Iron Furnace established at East Canaan, closed 1918; **Feb. 16, 1943** lowest temperature recorded in Connecticut reached at Falls Village to southwest, −32°F/−36°C.

Canterbury *Windham County* *Eastern Connecticut, 37 mi/60 km east of Hartford*

1675 town settled on land of Narragansett people; **1703** town incorporated; **Aug. 13, 1732** writer Jonathan Carver born, authored one of first tourist guides of North America (died 1780); **1738** Wright's Mill Farm established by Jedediah Benjamin; **Jan. 29, 1754** land speculator Moses Cleaveland born, founder of Cleveland, Ohio (died 1806); **1770** Westminster Congregational Church established, built 1805; **c.1849** Red Schoolhouse built.

Cheshire *New Haven County* *Central Connecticut, 13 mi/21 km north of New Haven*

1694 town settled; **1780** town incorporated; **1785** Col. Rufus Hitchcock House built; **1796** Cheshire Academy for boys established; **1814** Abijah Beach Tavern built; **March 22, 1818** artist John Frederick Kensett born (died 1872); **1827** Congregational Church built, replaces 1737 structure; **1892** Cheshire Library founded, built 1958; **1910** state reformatory established; **1951** Cheshire Historical Society founded; **1969** Cheshire Land Trust organized.

Clinton *Middlesex County* *Southern Connecticut, 21 mi/34 km east of New Haven, on Long Island Sound*

1663 town settled; **1675** Stevens Farm established, house built 1699, occupied by Stevens family for three centuries; **1700** Waterside Lane Bridge built, destroyed by 1938 hurricane; **c.1750** Elisha White House built; **1791** Adam Stanton House built; **1800** Farnham House built; **1807** Wright Homestead built; **1838** town incorporated, named for New York Gov. DeWitt Clinton; **1910** Henry Carter Hull Library founded, new library built 1998.

Colchester *New London County* *East central Connecticut, 22 mi/35 km southeast of Hartford*

1699 land purchased by Nathaniel Foote; town settled; **1702** Foote House built; **1706** town platted; **1776** Hayward House built; **1781** Rochambeau's Army camps here during Revolutionary War; **1803** Bacon Academy founded; **1824** town incorporated; **1847** Congregational Church built; Charles Goodyear establishes rubber vulcanizing plant, sold to United States Rubber Company 1893, destroyed by fire 1908; **1858** carriage factory opened; **1873** Lyman Viaduct built, trestle of Boston & New York Airline Railroad; **1905** Cragin Library founded, renovated 2002.

Cornwall *Litchfield County* *Western Connecticut, 34 mi/55 km west-northwest of Hartford*

1738 town settled; **1740** town incorporated; **May 1, 1751** political leader Ira Allen born, brother of Ethan Allen (died 1814); **Sept. 13, 1813** Union Gen. John Sedgwick born, killed at Spotsylvania, Virginia, May 9, 1864; **1817** Foreign Mission School founded to train Native Americans and foreigners to be missionaries; **1841** Congregational Church built; West Cornwall Covered

Bridge built on Housatonic River, rebuilt 1864; **1869** Cornwall Free Library founded.

Coventry *Tolland County* *East central Connecticut, 19 mi/31 km east of Hartford*

c.1700 town settled; **1711** town incorporated; **1728** two military companies and training ground established, active in Colonial wars through Civil War; **1736** Jesse Root House built; **June 6, 1755** patriot Nathan Hale born, executed by British Sept. 22, 1776; **1806** Pomeroy Tavern built; **1813** Coventry Glass Factory founded, closed c.1845; **1840** town becomes noted for development of medium-sized pacers (horses) capable of pulling rig round trip to Boston in two days; **1849** Congregational Church built, destroyed by fire 1897, rebuilt; **1912** Booth and Dimock Library established.

Danbury *Fairfield County* *Southwestern Connecticut, 28 mi/45 km west-northwest of New Haven*

1687 original eight families arrive from Norwalk; **1702** town incorporated; **1777** Gen. William Tryon's raid on military depot here repulsed, David Wooster killed; **1780** Zadoc Benedict establishes beaver hat factory; **1789** Taylor's Tavern built; **1792** horse breeding for harness racing begins; **c.1812** American Beauty House built, setting for Edna Ferber's 1931 novel *American Beauty*; **1822** incorporated as a borough; **1823** Mallory Hat Company established; **1852** railroad reaches town; **Jan. 31, 1869** Kohanza Reservoir dam breaks flooding town, 13 killed; **1865** *Danbury News* newspaper founded; **1869** Danbury Public Library founded, built 1970; **1871** Danbury Fair Grounds established; **Oct. 20, 1874** composer Charles Ives born (died 1954); **1889** incorporated as a city; **1902** Danbury Hatters' Case results in 1908 Supreme Court case prohibiting labor union boycotts; **1903** Western Connecticut State University established; **1935** Danbury Music Center founded; **1947** Danbury Museum and Historical Society founded; **1964** Aldrich Museum of Contemporary Art founded; **1965** town and city consolidated; **1967** Wooster Community Art Center founded; **1974** Ives Concert Park established; **1977** Union Carbide Corporation headquarters established; **1981** last Connecticut State Fair held; **1985** Military Museum of Southern New England founded; **1994** Danbury Railway Museum founded; **July 15, 1995** highest temperature ever recorded in Connecticut reached, 106°F/ 41°C.

Darien *Fairfield County* *Southwestern Connecticut, 32 mi/51 km southwest of New Haven*

1640 first Pilgrim settlers arrive on Long Island Sound; town founded; **1708** grist mill built; **c.1736** Bates-Scofield House built; **July 22, 1781** British raid town, take Rev. Dr. Mather, 50 others prisoner; **1820** town incorporated; **1848** New Haven Railroad reaches town; **1894** Darien Library founded, built 1957; **1897** trolley service begins, abandoned 1933; **1975** Darien Arts Center founded.

Deep River *Middlesex County* *Southern Connecticut, 25 mi/40 km east-northeast of New Haven*

1635 town founded; **c.1663** first wave of settlers arrives along lower Connecticut River; **c.1742** David Bushnell born, invented first submarine (died 1824); **1809** Phinehas Pratt begins manufacture of combs, becomes Pratt Read Company 1866; **1881** Spencer House built; **1899** Town of Saybrook incorporated; Deep River village serves as its administrative center; Deep River Public Library founded, opened 1900; **1947** town renamed Deep River.

Derby *New Haven County* *Southwestern Connecticut, 8 mi/12.9 km west of New Haven, on Housatonic R.*

1642 trading post founded by Capt. John Wakeman, land purchased from Paugacuks; **1652** David Humphreys House built; **c.1657** shipbuilding begins on river, until 1868 with construction of first dams; **1675** town incorporated; **1681** grist mill built; **1737** Immanuel St. James Episcopal Church built; **June 24, 1753** Gen. William Hull born, War of 1812 (died 1825); **1806** Derby Fishing Company founded, trades in Mediterranean; **1832** pin manufacturing begun by John Howe; **1836** copper mill established; **1848** Dr. Ireland Howe House built by father of Elias Howe; **1870** Housatonic Dam built; **1882** Osborne and Cheeseman Eyelet Factory established; **1888** Civil War monument dedicated; **1889** Sterling Opera House built; **1893** incorporated as a city; **1903** Derby Public Library opened.

Durham *Middlesex County* *Southern central Connecticut, 17 mi/27 km northeast of New Haven*

1698 town settled; **1708** town incorporated; **1755** Chauncey House built; **Oct. 4, 1761** Moses Austin born, local miner, established first lead mine west of Mississippi River in Missouri 1798, father of Stephen Austin, founder of Texas (died 1821); **1763** Rev. Elizur Goodrich House built; **1836** Methodist Church built; **1902** Durham Public Library dedicated; **1916** Durham Agricultural Fair founded.

East Granby *Hartford County* *Northern Connecticut, 11 mi/18 km north of Hartford*

1663 land granted to John Griffin; town founded; **1705** copper discovered at Copper Hill; **1773** old copper mine converted to Newgate State Prison, closed 1827; **Jan. 24, 1786** political leader Walter Forward born (died 1852); **1830** Congregational Church built; **1858** town incorporated; **1922** East Granby Library organized; **1942** Bradley Field airbase established, given to state of Connecticut, designated Bradley International Airport 1971.

CONNECTICUT

East Haddam   *Middlesex County*   *Southern Connecticut, 24 mi/39 km south-southeast of Hartford*

1685 town settled on Connecticut River; **1695** ferry service begins; **1734** town incorporated; **1736** Gelston House hotel built, originally Riverside Inn; **1763** Leesville Dam built on Connecticut River; **1769** Mumford House built; **1773–1774** Nathan Hale teaches school here; **1794** Congregational Church built; **c.1815** St. Stephen's Episcopal Church built; **1913** ferry service ends with construction of swing bridge; **1919** Gillette Castle built, home of actor William Hooker Gillette (1853–1937), played Sherlock Holmes; **1959** Goodspeed Musical Theatre established.

East Hartford   *Hartford County*   *Central Connecticut, 2 mi/3.2 km east of Hartford, on Connecticut River*

c.1640 town settled; **1693** Silas Eaton House built; **1711** Center Burying Ground founded; **1740** Elisha Pitkin House built; **1750** Abner Reed House built; **1765** James Forbes House built; **1776** Welles Tavern built at Welles Corner; **1782** Shem Stoughton House built; **1783** town incorporated; **1790** Thomas Spencer House built; **1800** Brewer House built; **1833** East Hartford Academy built, later used as Town Hall; **1836** Congregational Church built; **1880** Silver Lane Pickle Company founded.

East Haven   *New Haven County*   *Southern Connecticut, 3 mi/4.8 km southeast of New Haven*

1670 earliest section of Morris House built, majority built 1780; **1694** John Winthrop Forge founded, operated until 1920; **1750** Abraham Chidsey House built; **1760** Stephen Thompson House built; **1774** Congregational Church built; **c.1776** Fort Hale built, destroyed by British 1779, rebuilt 1809; **1785** town incorporated; **1810** Elnathan Street House built; **1847** Five Mile Point Lighthouse built, replaces 1804 light; **1900** Shore Line Trolley established; **1928** Hagaman Public Library founded; **1931** Tweed-New Haven Airport opened; **1945** Shore Line Trolley Museum founded.

East Windsor   *Hartford County*   *Northern Connecticut, 7 mi/11.3 km north-northeast of Hartford*

1630s area on Connecticut River first settled; **1636** warehouse built at portage around Enfield Falls; **Oct. 5, 1703** Congregationalist theologian Jonathan Edwards born (died 1758); **Jan. 21, 1743** steamboat inventor John Fitch born (died 1798); **1768** town incorporated, separates from Windsor; **1785** Watson-Bancroft House built; **Apr. 29, 1795** Congregationalist missionary Lorren Andrews born (died Honolulu 1868).

Enfield   *Hartford County*   *Northern Connecticut, 15 mi/24 km north-northeast of Hartford*

c.1680 town settled on Connecticut River; **1683** town incorporated by Massachusetts; **1749** town separates from Massachusetts, annexed by Connecticut Colony; **1775** Town Hall built; **1829** Enfield Canal opened; **1832** Orrin Thompson House built; **1848** Congregational Church built; **1874** Enfield Public Library founded; **1970** Enfield Hockey Association organized; **1972** Asnuntuck Community & Technical College (2-year) established.

Fairfield   *Fairfield County*   *Southwestern Connecticut, 20 mi/32 km southwest of New Haven*

July 1637 Great Swamp Fight, final battle in Pequot War; **1639** town settled on Long Island Sound by Roger Ludlow; **1643** town incorporated; **1661** land deeded to whites by Sascos; **1666** Fairfield County formed; town becomes county seat (shire town); **1750** Ogden House built; **1753** Benjamin Franklin places milestones along Post Road between Boston and New York; **1760** Augustus Jennings House built; **1765** William Bulkley House built; Justin Tucker House built; **1766** Isaac Tucker House built; **Apr. 20, 1777** British corvette *Cyrus* captured by U.S. ship *Defense* despite fact that the latter was taking on water and half of crew was sick with smallpox; **1779** Isaac Hull House built, completed 1790; **July 7, 1779** town burned by British; **1794** county courthouse built; **1804** Fairfield Academy founded; **1812** Stone Powder House built; **1813** Stratfield Baptist Church built; **1853** county seat moved to Bridgeport; **1876** Fairfield Library founded; **1942** Fairfield University established; **1947** incorporated as a city; **1963** Sacred Heart University established at Stratfield village; **Nov. 19, 1963** actress Meg Ryan born.

Falls Village   *Litchfield County*   See **Canaan (1943)**

Farmington   *Hartford County*   *Central Connecticut, 8 mi/12.9 km west of Hartford*

1640 town settled; **1645** town incorporated; **1665** Elm Tree Inn built; **1720** Stanley-Whitman House built by Rev. John Stanley; **1771** Congregational Church built; **1778** grist mill built by Cowles family; **1780** Samuel Cowles House built; **1781** Rochambeau camps here during Revolution; **1786** Whitman Tavern built by Capt. Judah Woodruff; **1802** linen products, hatmaking dominates town's economy; **1803** Gen. George Cowles House built; **1815** Maj. Timothy Cowles House built; **1828** Farmington Canal opens, closed 1848 due to landslides; **1844** Miss Porter's School founded by Sarah Porter; **1917** Farmington Public Library founded, new library opened 1983; **1947** Hillstead Museum opened, built c.1899; **1969** Tunxis Community and Technical College (2-year) established.

94

Glastonbury *Hartford County* *Central Connecticut, 5 mi/8 km southeast of Hartford, on Connecticut River*

1650 town settled; **1675** John Hollister House built; **1693** town incorporated; **1700** leather industry begins; **1720** first Daniel Wright House built; **1736** Welles House built at South Glastonbury; **1740** second Daniel Wright House built, both still standing; **July 1, 1802** political leader Gideon Welles born (died 1878); **1867** Congregational Church built; **1873** elderly sisters Julia and Abby Smith refuse to pay taxes while ineligible to vote because of their gender.

Goshen *Litchfield County* See **Torrington (1829)**

Greenwich *Fairfield County* *Southwestern Connecticut, 40 mi/64 km southwest of New Haven*

1640 town settled on Long Island Sound by Daniel Patrick and Robert Feaks; **1650** town ceded to Connecticut Colony by Dutch; **c.1700** Quintard House built, oldest in Greenwich; **1703** Peck Homestead built; **1705** Second Congregational Church organized; **1779** British raid town; **1805** Greenwich Public Library founded, built 1895; **1850** Bruce Mansion built, becomes Bruce Museum 1908; **1890s** town develops as artist colony and resort; **c.1890** First Congregational Church built; **1900** Rosemary Hall school for girls, established 1890, moved from Wallingford; **1905** Town Hall built, becomes Arts Center 1982; **1910** Christ Episcopal Church completed; **1947** town incorporated; **March 19, 1947** actress Glenn Close born; **1955** town incorporated; **1957** Greenwich Symphony Orchestra founded; **1973** Greenwich Arts Council founded; **1993** Bruce Museum of Arts and Sciences opened at new facility.

Groton *New London County* *Southeastern Connecticut, 43 mi/69 km southeast of Hartford*

1614 coastline explored by Adriaen Block; **1650** town settled on Thames River, at its entrance to Long Island Sound, opposite New London; **c.1700** Governor Winthrop House built at Poquonock Bridge; **1705** town incorporated; **1724** town's shipbuilding industry established; **Dec. 24, 1737** Revolutionary leader Silas Deane born (died 1789); **1775** Fort Griswold built; **Sept. 6, 1781** fort overtaken by British troops, Lt. Col. William Ledyard and most of his 150 militia killed; **1782** Mother Bailey House built, named for Anna Warner Bailey who contributed her flannel petticoat for gun wadding for Revolutionary cause; **March 14, 1797** merchant, railroad promoter Asa Whitney born at North Groton (died 1872); **1868** Navy Yard established on Thames River, re-established as New London Submarine Base 1916; **1890** Bill Memorial Library built; **1911** University of Connecticut, Avery Point Campus, established; **Jan. 21, 1954** USS Nautilus launched, first nuclear-powered submarine; **June 9, 1959** USS George Washington launched, first ballistic missile carrying submarine; **Nov. 22, 1960** USS Ethan Allen launched, first Polaris class nuclear submarine.

Guilford *New Haven County* *Southern Connecticut, 13 mi/21 km east of New Haven*

1639 town founded on Long Island Sound by Puritans; Whitfield House built; **1643** town incorporated; **c.1645** Comfort Starr House built; **1660** Hyland House built; **c.1670** Acadian House built by Joseph Clay, sheltered Acadian exiles; **Feb. 21, 1677** politician Samuel Hill born (died 1752), expression "Run like Sam Hill" attributed to his flamboyant style; **Oct. 14, 1696** Episcopalian clergyman, educator Samuel Johnson born (died 1772); **Jan. 6, 1730** Vermont Gov. Thomas Chittenden born (died 1797); **Nov. 22, 1754** patriot Abraham Baldwin born at North Guilford, member of Continental Congress (died 1807); **1761** Levi Hubbard House built; **1769** Governor William Leete House built; **July 8, 1790** poet Fitz-Greene Halleck born (died 1867); **1815** incorporated as a borough; **1829** Congregational Church built; **July 19, 1917** Pennsylvania Gov., Cong. William Warren Scranton born at Madison to east; **1926** Guilford Library founded, built 1933; **1939** town and borough consolidated.

Haddam *Middlesex County* *Central Connecticut, 21 mi/34 km south-southeast of Hartford*

1662 town settled on Connecticut River; **1668** town incorporated; **Feb. 13, 1805** lawyer, legal reformer David Dudley Field born (died 1894); **Nov. 4, 1816** Supreme Court Justice Stephen Johnson Field born (died 1899); **1839** Brainerd Academy founded, building later used for Town Hall; **1847** Congregational Church built; **1968** Connecticut Yankee Power Plant begins operation, closed 1996, decommissioning to be completed by 2004.

Hamden *New Haven County* *Southern Connecticut, 6 mi/9.7 km north of New Haven*

1664 first settlers arrive; **1770** Jonathan Dickerman House built; **1786** town incorporated, separates from New Haven; **1798** Eli Whitney invents technique for mass producing muskets to fulfill government contract for 10,000 firearms; **1819** Grace Episcopal Church built; **1840** Mount Carmel Congregational Church built; **Jan. 24, 1917** actor Ernest Borgnine born; **1929** Quinnipiac College established; **Sept. 1, 1956** Cynthia Ruotolo, six weeks old, kidnapped from her carriage at store, body found at lake; **1992** New England Academy of Theater founded.

Hartford *Hartford County* *Central Connecticut, 95 mi/153 km northeast of New York City*

1623 Dutch establish trading post on Connecticut River; **Oct. 1635** settled by John Steel, others, originally named Newtowne; **1636** Rev. Thomas Hooker and followers arrive, form colony; **1639** Hooker and other leaders adopt "Fundamental Orders," first written constitution in New World, for Hartford and neighboring towns of

Windsor and Wethersfield; **1654** trading post abandoned; **1657** John Eliot converts Podunk people to Christianity; **1666** Hartford County formed; town becomes county seat; **1701** becomes shared capital of colony with New Haven; **July 12, 1743** Revolutionary Gen. Jeremiah Wadsworth born (died 1804); **1764** Hartford *Courant* founded, oldest newspaper in U.S.; **1782** Butler McCook Homestead built; **1784** incorporated as a city; **Feb. 1, 1794** first insurance policy written by Hartford Fire Insurance Company; **1796** (Old) State House built, designed by Charles Bulfinch; **1807** First Church of Christ built; **July 19, 1814** gun maker Samuel Colt born (died 1862); **1814–1815** Hartford Convention held; **1817** *Hartford Times* newspaper founded; **Apr. 26, 1822** landscape architect, park designer Frederick Law Olmsted born (died 1903); **1823** Trinity College established; **1825** Connecticut Historical Society founded; **May 4, 1826** painter Frederick Edwin Church born (died 1900); **1827** South Congregational Church built; **1828** Christ Church Cathedral built; **Oct. 8, 1833** poet Edmund Stedman born (died 1908); **Apr. 17, 1837** J. P. Morgan the elder born, banker and financier (died 1913); **March 30, 1842** historian John Fiske born (died 1901); Wadsworth Atheneum built; **1848** slavery abolished in Connecticut; **July 24, 1853** actor, playwright William Hooker Gillette born (died 1937); **1855** Colt Firearms Factory established; **1860** Pratt and Whitney Company Plant built, maker of tools and gauges; **July 8, 1860** reformer, author Charlotte Gilman born, commits suicide 1935 during bout with cancer; **1865** Colt Armory built; **May 30, 1868** Broadway theatrical producer Charles Dillingham born (died 1934); **1870** Harriet Beecher Stowe House built; **1874** Mark Twain House built; **1875** joint state capital status withdrawn from New Haven, making Hartford sole capital; **1877** University of Hartford established at West Hartford; **1878** state capitol completed; Col. A. A. Pope builds first American-made bicycles; **1890** Hartford School of Music established; **March 25, 1901** actor Ed Begley born (died 1970); **June 16, 1902** geneticist Barbara McClintock born, Nobel Prize 1983 (died 1992); **1906** Charter Oak Memorial erected commemorating 1687 hiding place of Connecticut Charter, tree destroyed by wind 1856; Fuller Brush Company founded; **May 12, 1907** actress Katharine Hepburn born (died 2003); **1908** Royal Typewriter Company, founded 1906, moves from Brooklyn, New York; **1909** state armory built; **1910** state library and supreme court building built; **1911** Connecticut Institute for the Blind established; **1917** Phoenix Mutual Life Insurance Building built; **1919** Travelers Insurance Building completed; **1921** Hartford Fire Insurance Company Building built; **1926** Connecticut Mutual Life Insurance Building built; **1929** County Building completed; Aetna Insurance Company Building built; **1930** Bushnell Memorial Hall built; **1931** state office building built; federal building built; **1934** Avery Art Museum built; **1936** Caledonia Insurance Company Building built; Travelers Insurance Company's three-building complex completed; **Jan. 18, 1942** TV actress Linda Evans born; **July 6, 1944** fire in main tent at Ringling Brothers Circus leads to panic, 168 killed, 487 injured; **1946** Capital Community & Technical College (2-year) established; **June 4, 1952** actress Carlene Watkins born; **1955** county governments abolished in Connecticut; **Dec. 8, 1961** fire at Hartford Hospital kills 16; **1964** Hartford Plaza downtown commercial complex completed; **Jan. 18, 1978** Hartford Civic Center coliseum roof collapses under wet snow, no injuries, 5,000 attended basketball game 6 hours before; **1983** 38-story City Place Building completed; **Feb. 26, 2003** nursing home fire kills ten, injures 23.

Lebanon *New London County* *East central Connecticut, 25 mi/40 km east-southeast of Hartford*

1690s first settlers arrive; **1700** town incorporated; **1708** Clark Homestead built; **Oct. 12, 1710** Gov. Jonathan Trumbull, Sr. born (died 1785); **Nov. 24, 1726** economist Peletiah Webster born (died 1795); **Apr. 8, 1731** patriot William Williams born (died 1811); **1740** Governor Jonathan Trumbull, Sr. House built; **March 26, 1740** Gov., Cong. Jonathan Trumbull, Jr. born (died 1809); **1743** Nathan Tisdale Academy founded; **Jan. 28, 1754** educator John Wheelock born (died 1817); **June 6, 1756** painter John Trumbull born (died 1843); **1769** Jonathan Trumbull, Jr. House built; **Apr. 9, 1770** Lebanon freemen draft declaration of rights, precedent to Declaration of Independence; **Dec. 7, 1782** Cong. Joseph Trumbull the younger born (died 1861); **Nov. 21, 1785** physiologist Dr. William Beaumont born (died 1853); **1807** Congregational Church built; **1896** Trumbull Library founded.

Litchfield *Litchfield County* *Northwestern Connecticut, 26 mi/42 km west of Hartford*

1719 town incorporated; **1720** first settlers arrive; **Jan. 10, 1738** Ethan Allen born, leader of Green Mountain Boys militia in Vermont (died 1789); **1751** Litchfield County formed; town becomes county seat; **1760** Sheldon's Tavern built; **Jan. 17, 1760** Oliver Wolcott born, secretary of treasury under President Washington and Pres. John Adams (died 1833); **1774** Tapping Reeve Law School founded; **1775** Rev. Lyman Beecher Home built; **1780** Benjamin Hanks introduces clock making; **1782** Collins House built; **1787** Phelps Tavern built; **1792** Miss Sarah Pierce's Female Academy founded, closed 1863; **Aug. 27, 1792** revivalist Charles Grandison Finney born (died 1875); **1799** Elijah Wadsworth House built; **June 14, 1811** author Harriet Beecher Stowe born (died 1896); **June 24, 1813** clergyman Henry Ward Beecher born (died 1887); **Oct. 7, 1815** clergyman Charles Beecher born (died 1900); **1818** incorporated as a village; **1829** Congregational Church built; **1830** Asa Hopkins begins manufacture of flutes; **1879** incorporated as a borough; **1902** Oliver Wolcott Library opened; **1955** county governments abolished in Connecticut.

Madison *New Haven County* *See* **Guilford (1917)**

Meriden *New Haven County   Central Connecticut, 17 mi/27 km south-southwest of Hartford*

1661 land grant made to Jonathan Gilbert for farm, managed by Edward Higbee, town's first settler; **1760** Moses Andrews House built; **1794** Samuel Yale begins manufacture of pewter buttons; **1806** town incorporated; **1808** Ashbel Griswold begins manufacture of Britannia silverware, becomes International Silver Company; **1830** Eli Birdsey House built; **1831** Center Congregational Church built; **1847** Baptist Church built; **1856** St. Rose Catholic Church built, rebuilt 1926; **1867** incorporated as a city, separates from town; Methodist Church built; **1868** Main Street Baptist Church built; **1879** First Congregational Church built; **1888** St. Laurent Catholic Church completed; **1895** world's first mechanical piano, the Angelus, produced by H. K. Wilcox; **1922** town and city consolidate.

Middletown *Middlesex County   Central Connecticut, 14 mi/23 km south of Hartford, on Connecticut River*

1650 town settled by Puritans, originally named Mattabesett; **1651** town incorporated; **1653** town renamed Middletown; **1756** Benjamin Henshaw House built; **Jan. 23, 1761** poet Richard Alsop born (died 1816); **1765** Joseph Hall House built; **1784** incorporated as a city; **1785** Middlesex County formed; town becomes county seat; *Middlesex Gazette* newspaper founded; **1795** Benjamin Williams Mansion completed; **1799** Simeon North contracts with U.S. government, becoming first official pistol manufacturer; **1800s** pewter industry becomes important, maintained by descendants of Thomas Danforth; **1828** Russell House built; **1831** Wesleyan University established; **Oct. 1, 1832** songwriter Henry Clay Work born (died 1884); **1834** Female Anti-Slavery Society founded; **1851** Cromwell separates from Middletown; **Apr. 3, 1859** composer Reginald De Koven born (died 1971); **1868** state hospital opened; **Apr. 11, 1893** diplomat Dean Acheson born, secretary of state under President Truman (died 1971); **1923** city and town consolidate; **1927** flooding damages city, many killed, again 1936; **1931** St. Sebastian's Catholic Church completed; **1938** Arrigoni Bridge completed across Connecticut River; **July 6, 1946** actor James Naughton born; **1955** county governments abolished in Connecticut; **1966** Middlesex Community & Technical College (2-year) established.

Milford *New Haven County   Southwestern Connecticut, 9 mi/14.5 km southwest of New Haven*

1639 town founded on Long Island Sound by Rev. Peter Prudden; **1640** William Fowler builds mill on Wepawaug River; Thomas Buckingham House built; **1659** Stockade House built; **1660** Clark Tavern built, substantially altered 1815 through 1875; **1666** town annexed by Connecticut Colony; **1685** Robert Treat House built; **June 3, 1722** public official Jared Ingersoll the elder born (died 1781); **1823** First Congregational Church built; **1834** Plymouth Church built; **1845** cultivation of shellfish begins; **1851** St.

Peter's Episcopal Church built; **1854** Margaret Taylor Library built; **1889** Memorial Bridge built across Wepawaug River replacing Fowler's Bridge; **1894** Simon Lake invents the even-keeled submarine, makes trial run of the *Argonaut* 1897; **1947** town incorporated; **1959** incorporated as a city.

Mystic *New London County   Southeastern Connecticut, 47 mi/76 km southeast of New Haven*

May 15, 1637 Pequot fort destroyed by Colonials at West Mystic, 600 Native Americans killed; **1849** shipbuilding activity increases with California Gold Rush; **1860** the *Andrew Jackson* clipper ship built, held record 89 days, 4 hours for trip around Cape Horn to California; **1868** Morgan Point Lighthouse built, discontinued 1919; **1956** first Mystic Outdoor Festival held; **1974** Mystic Aquarium established.

Naugatuck *New Haven County   West central Connecticut, 14 mi/23 km north-northwest of New Haven*

1702 town settled; **1843** Charles and Henry Goodyear establish rubber mill here, becomes U.S. Rubber Company footwear plant; **1844** town incorporated; **1849** railroad reaches town; **1876** St. Michael's Catholic Church built, founded 1786; **1888** Harold Whittemore Memorial Library founded, built 1894; **1893** incorporated as a borough.

New Britain *Hartford County   Central Connecticut, 8 mi/12.9 km southwest of Hartford*

c.1686 town settled; **1746** Ezra Belden House built, oldest in city; **c.1754** Noah Stanley Tavern opened; **1780** Deacon John Osgood House built; **1790s** city's hardware industry has its beginnings; **Dec. 8, 1811** author, social reformer Elihu Burritt born (died 1879); **1842** South Congregational Church organized; **1849** Central Connecticut State University established; **1850** town incorporated; **Apr. 7, 1859** Walter Camp born, father of modern football (died 1925); **1871** incorporated as a city; **1884** city hall built; **1899** New Britain General Hospital opened; **1901** New Britain Public Library built; New Britain Institute Museum built; **1903** New Britain Museum of Art founded; **1905** town and city consolidate; **1916** Elihu Burritt Memorial erected in Franklin Square; **1972** Hole In the Wall Theater founded; **1994** New Britain Industrial Museum founded; **Feb. 1995** National Iwo Jima Monument dedicated.

New Haven *New Haven County   Southern Connecticut, 35 mi/56 km south-southwest of Hartford*

1638 town founded on Long Island Sound by Puritans, named Quinnipiac; **1639** town incorporated; **1664** New Haven Colony reluctantly unites with Connecticut Colony; **1666** New Haven County formed; town becomes county seat (shire town); **1701** town's joint status as colonial capital begins, shared with Hartford; **1718** Yale University, established 1701, moved from Saybrook; **1719**

first statehouse completed; **Oct. 27, 1749** Continental Congress member Jared Ingersoll the younger born (died 1822); **1764** second statehouse completed; **1767** Pierpont House built; **Oct. 12, 1775** Calvinist clergyman Lyman Beecher born (died 1863); **Jan. 14, 1780** Supreme Court Justice Henry Baldwin born (died 1844); **1783** steps of statehouse used for auctioning indigents as servants, through 1786; **1784** incorporated as a city; **1800** Bushnell House built; **Dec. 29, 1800** Charles Goodyear born, developed vulcanization process for production of synthetic rubber (died 1860); **Nov. 12, 1806** Union naval officer Andrew Hull Foote born (died 1863); **1812** harbor blockaded by British; *New Haven Register* newspaper founded; **1814** Trinity Episcopal Church built; Center Church completed; **1815** United Church completed; Elizabethan Club founded; **1826** New Haven Hospital organized, established first school of nursing in U.S. 1873; **1830** Governor Ingersoll House built; **1831** third statehouse completed; **Feb. 11, 1834** mathematical physicist Josiah Gibbs born, founded field of chemical thermodynamics (died 1903); **1835** Northampton-New Haven Canal completed from Northampton, Massachusetts, only used until 1847; **1845** New Haven Clock Company founded; **1854** First Methodist Church built; **Apr. 23, 1856** educator Arthur Twining Hadley born (died 1930); **Jan. 2, 1865** author, educator William Lyon Phelps born (died 1943); **Jan. 24, 1865** sculptor Paul Wayland Bartlett born (died 1925); **1866** Winchester Repeating Arms Company established; Peabody Museum of Natural History founded at Yale University; **1871** city hall built; **Dec. 8 1871** journalist Burton Jesse Hendrick born (died 1949); **1875** status as joint state capital dropped in favor of Hartford; **May 23, 1875** General Motors industrialist Alfred P. Sloan, Jr. born (died 1966); **1877** Connecticut Agricultural Experiment Station, founded 1875, moved from Middletown; **Jan. 28, 1878** first commercial telephone exchange begins operation; **1879** Walter Camp develops modern form of football; **Jan. 1, 1885** historian Charles Seymour born (died 1963); **Dec. 18, 1888** New York City public works official Robert Moses born, credited with building that city's modern infrastructure (died 1981); **Nov. 29, 1891** composer, conductor Richard Frank Donovan born (died 1970); **1893** Southern Connecticut State University established; New Haven Symphony Orchestra founded; **Feb. 7, 1897** composer Quincy Porter born (died 1966); **Apr. 6, 1897** author Robert Coates born (died 1973); **May 2, 1903** pediatrician, author Dr. Benjamin Spock born (died 1998); **Sept. 28, 1909** cartoonist Al Capp born, created "Li'l Abner" (died 1979); **1910** St. Paul's Catholic Church built; **1911** Ives Memorial Library opens; **1912** county courthouse built; **1914** Shubert Performing Arts Center opened; **Aug. 3, 1918** band leader Les Elgart born (died 1995); **1920** University of New Haven established at nearby West Haven; **Jan. 6, 1921** journalist, pollster Louis Harris born; **July 27, 1922** TV producer Norman Lear born; **1925** Albertus Magnus College established; **1928** Union and New Haven Trust Company Building completed; Gallery of Fine Arts opens at Yale University; **1931** Tweed New Haven Airport established; **1937** Southern New England

Telephone Company Building built; **Jan. 21, 1947** actress Jill Eikenberry born; **Feb. 26, 1953** singer Michael Bolton born; **1962** first antipoverty program in U.S. started; **1967** race riots cause serious damage; **June 7, 1971** Allegheny Airlines plane crashes into beach houses, 28 on board killed, three survive; **1972** Veterans Coliseum built; **1992** Gateway Community and Technical College (2-year) established; **1994** Audubon Arts Center Complex completed; **1996** first annual International Festival of Arts & Ideas held.

New London   *New London County   Southeastern Connecticut, 41 mi/66 km southeast of Hartford*

1646 New London County formed; town settled on Long Island Sound by John Winthrop, the younger, becomes county seat (shire town); **1650** grist mill built by Winthrop, rebuilt 1742; **1670** wharves designed by Joshua Raymond; **1678** original section of Hempstead House built; **1709** first printing press in Connecticut founded by Thomas Short; **1732** St. James Episcopal Church built, burned 1781, rebuilt 1787, rebuilt again 1850; **1756** Shaw Mansion built; **1760** New London Lighthouse built, replaced 1801; **1774** Nathan Hale School built; **Sept. 6, 1781** British led by Benedict Arnold, capture Fort Trumbull, partially burn town; **1784** town incorporated; town's whaling industry begins with sailing of *Rising Sun* to Brazil, returns 1785; county courthouse built; **May 1792** Norwich Turnpike chartered; **1838** third Fort Trumbull built, completed 1850; **1876** Whaling Museum founded; **1890** New London Public Library founded; **1895** incorporated as a city; **March 20, 1922** band leader Larry Elgart born; **1926** Lyman Allyn Museum of Art founded; **1955** county governments abolished in Connecticut; **1960s** U.S. Coast Guard Museum founded; **Oct. 26, 1970** first phase of Millstone Nuclear Power Plant completed on Thames River to north.

Norfolk   *Litchfield County   Northwestern Connecticut, 31 mi/50 km northwest of Hartford*

1755 town settled; **1758** town incorporated; **1794** Giles Pettibone, Jr. Tavern built; **1797** Ariel Lawrence Tavern built, used as tavern since 1820; **1800** Battell Homestead built; **1813** Congregational Church built; **Apr. 8, 1850** pathologist Dr. William Henry Welch born (died 1934); **1871** Connecticut Western Railroad reaches town; **1888** Norfolk Library founded; **1889** Litchfield County Choral Union established, first annual music festival held 1899, discontinued 1925 with death of founder Carl Stoeckel; **1941** first annual Norfolk Chamber Music Festival held.

North Haven   *New Haven County   Southern Connecticut, 7 mi/11.3 km north-northeast of New Haven*

1722 first meeting house built; **Nov. 29, 1727** clergyman Ezra Stiles born, president Yale College (died 1795); **1761** Trumbull Parsonage built, home of Rev. Benjamin Trumbull, historian; **1780** Timothy Andrews Tavern built; **1786** town incorporated; **1794** Doctor Foote House built; **1835** Church of St. John's built; **1838** New

Haven & Hartford Railroad reaches town; **1857** Martha Culver Memorial built; **1880s** Memorial Town Hall built.

Norwalk *Fairfield County* *Southwestern Connecticut, 28 mi/45 km west-southwest of New Haven*

1649 town settled on Long Island Sound by Roger Ludlow, others; **1651** town incorporated; **1688** Buttery Sawmill built on Silvermine Creek; **1700** Old Red School House built; **June 1700** colonial governor Thomas Fitch born (died 1774); **July 11, 1779** British landing force of 2,500 men in 26 ships overrun town, burn most of its structures; **1780** pottery making begins; **1835** Town House built; **July 13, 1863** educator Mary Emma Woolley born (died 1947); **1864** Lockwood-Matthews Estate built; **1868** Sheffield Island Lighthouse built; **1870** South Norwalk incorporated as a city; **1874** Capt. Peter Decker introduces steam-powered oyster dredging; **1879** Norwalk Library founded, joined by South Norwalk Library 1975; **March 8, 1886** biochemist Edward Calvin Kendall born, shared Nobel Prize 1850 (died 1972); **1893** incorporated as a city; **1913** South Norwalk merges with Norwalk; **1939** Norwalk Symphony Orchestra founded; **1961** Norwalk Community & Technical College (2-year) established; **1966** Lockwood Museum opened at Lockwood Mansion; **1977** first annual Oyster Festival held; **1988** Maritime Aquarium opened.

Norwich *New London County* *Southeastern Connecticut, 35 mi/56 km southeast of Hartford*

1647 Adams Tavern built; **1659** land on Thames River conveyed to Thomas Leffingwell, others; town founded by Maj. John Mason and Rev. James Fitch; **1660** first settlers arrive; **1666** New London County formed; Leffingwell Inn built; **Jan. 20, 1724** evangelist Isaac Bacchus born, led Great Awakening movement (died 1806); **1726** Long Society Congregational Church built; **July 1726** six Quakers arrested for traveling on Sunday; **1733** Thomas Danforth begins making pewter ware, later moves to Middletown; **Nov. 14, 1741** Gen. Benedict Arnold born, traitor to patriot cause (died 1801); **1744** Oldest Brick Building in Connecticut built at Long Society village; **1748** Glebe House built by Rev. John Tyler; **c.1760** Eleazar Lord Tavern built; **1784** incorporated as a city; **1801** Congregational Church built; **1832** Norwich & Worcester Railroad built; **1840** Adams Express Company package delivery founded by Alvin Adams; **1852** Christopher C. Brand patents whaling gun; **1853** pistol factory established by Smith and Wesson, later moved to New Haven; **1854** Norwich Free Academy founded; **Aug. 16, 1861** Edith Kermit Carow Roosevelt born, second wife of Pres. Theodore Roosevelt (married Dec. 2, 1886, died Sept. 30, 1948); **1865** Yantic Woolen Mill founded; **1886** Slater Memorial Museum founded; **May 15, 1907** Sen. Thomas Dodd born (died 1971); **May 30, 1919** author Margaret Louise Coit born (died 2003); **1955** county governments abolished in Connecticut; **1986** Mashantucket Pequot Tribe opens Foxwoods Resort and Casino on reservation to southeast.

Old Lyme *New London County* *Southern Connecticut, 31 mi/50 km east of New Haven*

1655 town settled on Long Island Sound, at mouth of Connecticut River; **1660** Thomas Lee House built; **1662** ferry service established on river; **1665** Town of Lyme incorporated, separates from Saybrook; **1675** Peck Tavern built; **1734** Little Boston Schoolhouse built; **Nov. 29, 1816** Chief Supreme Court Justice Morrison Remick White born (died 1888); Congregational Church built, burned 1907, restored 1910; **1818** Capt. John Sill House built; **1822** Col. Charles Griswold House built; **1848** Boxwood Manor built; **1855** Town of South Lyme incorporated, separates from Lyme; **1857** South Lyme renamed Old Lyme; **1911** highway bridge built across river, replacing ferry service.

Old Saybrook *Middlesex County* *Southern Connecticut, 28 mi/45 km east of New Haven*

1623 two Dutch families accompanied by six men from Manhattan Island become first whites to arrive in area; **1633** party finds no trace of settlers; **1635** town settled as Saybrook Colony; Fort Saybrook built; **1638** grist mill built, millstone brought from Holland; **1662** ferry begins on Connecticut River; **1701** Yale College established, moved to New Haven 1718; **c.1720** Black Horse Tavern built; **1750** William Tully House built; **1767** Gen. William Hart House built; **1785** Pratt Tavern built; **1800** Ye Old Saybrook Inn built; **1838** Lynde Point Lighthouse built, automated 1978; **1839** Congregational Church built; **1854** town incorporated as Saybrook; **1866** Saybrook Lighthouse built; **1886** Outer Lighthouse built, automated 1959; **1911** highway bridge replaces ferry; **1947** town renamed Old Saybrook.

Oxford *New Haven County* *Southwest central Connecticut, 13 mi/21 km northwest of New Haven*

c.1680 town settled; **1795** Congregational Church built; **1798** town incorporated; **1812** Episcopal Church built; **Nov. 21, 2001** 94-year-old Ottilie Lundgren dies of anthrax inhalation, origin undetermined, fifth anthrax death in Eastern U.S. since Sept. 11 terrorist attacks in New York and Washington.

Plainville *Hartford County* *Central Connecticut, 11 mi/18 km southwest of Hartford*

1657 town settled; **1774** Hooker House built; **1789** John Cook Tavern built; **1828** Farmington Canal opened, becomes part of New Haven-Northampton Canal in 1840s; **1829** Blossom's Tavern built; **1850** Stockinette Knitting Mill opened; **1869** town incorporated; **1890** Town Hall built.

Plymouth *Litchfield County* *See* **Terryville**

Portland *Middlesex County* *Central Connecticut, 13 mi/37 km south of Hartford, on Connecticut River*

c.1690 town settled; brownstone quarrying begun by James Stanclift, ends c.1935; **1741** town's boat building industry begins, continues through mid-1930s; **1790** original Episcopal Church built; **1830s** boat building reaches peak; Shaler and Hall Quarry begins operation; **1841** town incorporated; **1850** Congregational Church built; **1853** Episcopal Church built; **1879** Swedish Lutheran Church built; **1882** Trinity Church completed; **1891** Buck Library founded; **1894** new Town Hall built, used until 1999; **1938** Arrigoni Bridge built from Middletown.

Putnam *Windham County* *Northeastern Connecticut, 41 mi/66 km east-northeast of Hartford*

1693 town settled, named Pomfret Factory; **1726** Windham County formed; **1795** Armand Denys House built, home of African explorer; **1850s** Masonic Hall used as stop on Underground Railroad, which spirited slaves to freedom; **1855** town of Putnam incorporated, separates from Killingly; county seat moved from town of Windham; **1895** incorporated as a city; **1955** county governments abolished in Connecticut.

Redding *Fairfield County* *Southeastern Connecticut, 22 mi/35 km west of New Haven*

1711 town founded by Col. John Read; **c.1723** David Barlow House built; **1753** Aaron Sanford House built; Salt-Box House built by Rev. Nathaniel Bartlett; **March 24, 1754** poet, diplomat Joel Barlow born (died 1812); **1767** town incorporated; **1778–1779** General Putnam's troops winter over here; **1834** Town House built; **1852** Danbury & Norwalk Railroad completed; **1908** Stormfield House built by author Mark Twain; **1909** Mark Twain Library established by Mark Twain; **Apr. 21, 1910** Mark Twain dies at Stormfield (born 1835); **1923** Stormfield House destroyed by fire; **Nov. 28, 1931** actress Hope Lange born (died 2003); **1942** Saugatuck Reservoir completed on Saugatuck River.

Ridgefield *Fairfield County* *Southwestern Connecticut, 29 mi/47 km west of New Haven*

1708 land purchased from natives; **1709** town incorporated; **1760** Timothy Keeler Tavern built as dwelling, occupied by architect Cass Gilbert c.1915 until his death 1934; **Apr. 27, 1777** Battle of Ridgefield, effort made to prevent Tryon's British troops from retreating following raid on Danbury; **Aug. 17, 1793** publisher, writer Samuel Griswold Goodrich born (died 1862); **May 2, 1895** artist, author Peggy Bacon born (died 1987); **1968** Aldrich Museum of Contemporary Art founded by artist Larry Aldrich (1906–2001).

Rockville *Tolland County* *Northern Connecticut, 14 mi/23 km northeast of Hartford*

1785 Tolland County formed; village becomes county seat; **1802** carding mill established; **1808** Town of Vernon incorporated; **1856** paper mill opens, becomes U.S. Envelope Company; **1889** Rockville incorporated as a city; **1904** Rockville Public Library built; **1955** county governments abolished in Connecticut; **1965** town and city merge.

Roxbury *Litchfield County* *Western Connecticut, 26 mi/42 km northwest of New Haven*

1713 town settled; **1740** Episcopal Rectory built; **May 17, 1743** Revolutionary soldier Seth Warner born (died 1784); **1750** iron ore mining established at Mine Hill; **c.1784** General Hinman House built; Asahel Bacon House built; Phineas Smith House built; **1706** town incorporated; Records Building built; **1838** Congregational Church built.

Saybrook *Middlesex County* *See* **Deep River**

Shelton *Fairfield County* *Southwestern Connecticut, 8 mi/12.9 km west of New Haven, on Housatonic River*

1697 town settled; **1789** town incorporated, renamed Huntington, separates from Stratford; **1836** Shelton Tack Company founded by Edward N. Shelton, first tack factory in U.S.; **1870** dam built on Housatonic River, destroyed by flood 1891; **1882** incorporated as a borough; **1888** railroad reaches town from Derby; **1890** United Methodist Church completed; **1891** Plumb Memorial Library founded, built 1894; **1915** incorporated as a city; renamed.

Simsbury *Hartford County* *Northern Connecticut, 10 mi/16 km northwest of Hartford*

1643 trail blazed through area by John Griffin and Michael Humphrey of British Navy; **1670** town incorporated; **1676** Native American terror forces abandonment of settlement; **1705** copper discovered at East Granby, then part of Simsbury; **1728** first steel mill in U.S. begins operation; **1737** first copper coinage in colonies begun by John Higley; **1771** Capt. Elisha Phelps House built; **1801** Pettibone Tavern built; **1822** Englewood House built; **1828** Farmington Canal opened, closed 1847; **1830** Congregational Church built; **1840** Spoonville Bridge built on Farmington River; **Apr. 11, 1865** forester Gifford Pinchot born, governor of Pennsylvania, founder U.S. Forest Service (died 1946); **1892** Drake Hill Bridge built, replaced 1992, old bridge converted to Flower Bridge garden 1996; **1900** Westminster School for Boys, founded 1888, moved from Dobbs Ferry, New York; **1963** Emek Shalom Jewish Congregation organized.

Somers   *Tolland County*   *Northern Connecticut, 19 mi/31 km north-northeast of Hartford*

1706 Benjamin Jones becomes first settler; **1734** town incorporated by Massachusetts, named for Lord John Somers; **1749** town annexed by Connecticut; **1780** Shaker Settlement founded, later converted to Osborn State Prison Farm; **1804** Old Homestead Inn built; **1838** first Four-Town Fair held; **1839** Billings Satinette Mill opened on Scantic River, closed 1870; **1896** Somers Free Library built, new facility opened 1988; **1930s** Somers Mountain Museum founded.

Stamford   *Fairfield County*   *Southwestern Connecticut, 36 mi/58 km southwest of New Haven*

1641 town settled on Long Island Sound; **1721** Ingersoll (Black) House built; **1825** America's first wire factory established by Englishman William Lecon; **1834** St. Francis Episcopal Church built, rebuilt 2000; **1848** railroad built through town; **1893** incorporated as a city; **1938** Merritt Parkway opened, named for Cong. Schuyler Merritt of Stamford; **Oct. 22, 1938** actor Christopher Lloyd born; **1949** city and town consolidate; **May 28, 1957** actor Daniel Stern born; **1958** whale-shaped sanctuary of First Presbyterian Church built, designed by Wallace K. Harrison.

Stonington   *New London County*   *Southeastern Connecticut, 10 mi/16 km east of New London*

1649 town settled on Long Island Sound by group from Plymouth Colony; **1662** town incorporated as Southerton; **1665** town renamed Mystic; **1666** town renamed Stonington; **c.1711** patriot John Hart born (died 1779); **1765** Dudley Palmer House built; **July 16, 1769** explorer Edmund Fanning born (died 1841); **Aug. 30, 1775** H.M.S. *Rose* attacks town, repulsed by militia; **1798** Peleg Brown House built; **Aug. 8, 1799** Antarctic explorer Nathaniel Palmer born, Palmer (Antarctic) Peninsula named for him (died 1877); **May 1801** incorporated as a borough; **Aug. 9-12, 1814** British fleet bombards town during War of 1812; **1823** Customhouse built; **1829** Congregational Church built; **1840** Stonington Harbor Lighthouse built, discontinued 1889; **1888** Stonington Free Library founded, built 1900.

Storrs   *Tolland County*   *East central Connecticut, 22 mi/35 km east of Hartford*

1690s settlers arrive in town of Mansfield; **1775** Nathaniel Aspinwall introduces mulberry trees, establishes silkworm industry; **1810** Hanks Silk Company established; **1845** blight destroys mulberry trees and silk industry; **1881** Storrs Agricultural College established, becomes Connecticut State College, later University of Connecticut.

Stratford   *Fairfield County*   *Southwestern Connecticut, 13 mi/21 km southwest of New Haven*

1639 town settled; **1650** Moses Wheeler establishes ferry on Housatonic River; **March 2, 1711** Revolutionary officer David Wooster born (died 1777); **1723** David Judson House built; **Oct. 7, 1727** educator, Continental Congress member William Samuel Johnson born, signer of Declaration of Independence (died 1819); **1822** Stratford Point Lighthouse built; **1896** Stratford Library dedicated; **July 23, 1935** James M. and Amy Johnson Mollison of England crash land at Sikorsky Airport after successful flight across Atlantic; **1937** Bridgeport Airport established at Stratford Point, formerly Mollison Airport; **Sept. 14, 1939** Sikorsky Helicopter invented by Ivor Sikorsky, conducts first flight; **1955** American Shakespeare Festival Theater and Academy established; **1983** National Helicopter Museum founded.

Suffield   *Hartford County*   *Northern Connecticut, 15 mi/24 km north of Hartford, on Connecticut River*

1670 town settled by John Pynchon; land grant made by Massachusetts; **1676** settlement revives after King Philip's War; **1746** Alexander King House built; **1749** town annexed by Connecticut; **July 19, 1767** Madison Gideon Granger born, postmaster general under President Jefferson (died 1822); **Oct. 27, 1793** firearms manufacturer Eliphalet Remington born (died 1861); **1803** final state boundary determined; **1810** cigar-making industry founded by Simeon Viets; **1833** Second Baptist Church built; **1899** Sidney Kent Memorial Library founded, new library opened 1972.

Terryville   *Litchfield County*   *Central Connecticut, 18 mi/29 km west-southwest of Hartford*

1728 town settled by Henry Cook; **1793** Eli Terry establishes clock-making business; village of Terryville founded; **1795** Town of Plymouth incorporated; village serves as administrative center; **1817** blacksmith shop built, building later houses Blakeslee Ives Toy Factory; **1820** Plymouth Academy founded; **1838** Congregational Church built; **c.1895** Terryville Public Library founded, built 1922; **Dec. 7, 1923** TV actor Ted Knight born (died 1986).

Thomaston   *Litchfield County*   *West central Connecticut, 21 mi/34 km west-southwest of Hartford*

1728 town settled; **1775** Marsh House built; **1803** clock maker Eli Terry establishes factory here; **1812** Seth Thomas, former associate of Terry, opens clock shop, later becomes largest clock factory in world; **1814** Eli Terry markets his shelf clock; **1875** town incorporated; **1898** Thomaston Public Library founded, built 1906, new library opened 1971.

Torrington *Litchfield County* *West central Connecticut, 23 mi/37 km west of Hartford*

May 1738 town founded, originally named New Orleans Village for its swampy conditions, later renamed for town in England; **May 1740** town incorporated; **May 9, 1800** abolitionist John Brown born, died by hanging Dec. 2, 1859, for leading raid on arsenal at Harpers Ferry (then Virginia); **Oct. 15, 1829** astronomer Asaph Hall born at Goshen to west (died 1907); **1834** Israel Coe begins manufacture of brass kettles; **1857** first Borden's Condensed Milk factory opened at Burrville by Gail Borden for use by Union Army during Civil War.

Wallingford *New Haven County* *Southern Connecticut, 12 mi/19 km north-northeast of New Haven*

1670 town incorporated; **1672** Nehemiah Royce House built; **Apr. 12, 1724** patriot Lyman Hall born, signer of Declaration of Independence (died 1790); **1756** John Barker House built; **1759** Samuel Parsons House built; **1774** Caleb Atwater House built; **Jan. 15, 1800** newspaper publisher Moses Brach born (died 1868); **1835** Robert Wallace begins silverware manufacturing; **1853** borough incorporated within town; **Aug. 9, 1878** tornado damages town, 34 killed, 100 injured; **1881** Andrew Mellon Public Library founded, new library opened 1982; **1932** Winter Sports Building built; **1958** borough and town consolidate as City of Wallingford.

Waterbury *New Haven County* *West central Connecticut, 24 mi/39 km southwest of Hartford*

1674 town settled; **1686** town incorporated; **1741** Cooke Homestead built; **1807** clock works established by Eli Terry, Seth Thomas, Silas Hoadley; **1836** brass industry flourishes; **1853** incorporated as a city; **1868** Silas Bronson Library founded; **1870** St. John's Episcopal Church built; **1884** Civil War monument dedicated; **1890** Post College established, becomes Teikyo Post University; **July 14, 1896** actress Jean Dixon born (died 1981); **March 24, 1897** ballet dancer Lucia Chase born (died 1986); **1901** town and city merge; **1902** fire destroys business district; **March 19, 1904** D.C. district judge John Joseph Sirica born, presided over 1970s Watergate hearings (died 1992); **June 4, 1907** actress Rosalind Russell born (died 1976); **1986** Mattatuck Museum established for Connecticut artists; **1992** Naugatuck Valley Community & Technical College (2-year) established.

Watertown *Litchfield County* *Western Connecticut, 25 mi/40 km southwest of Hartford*

Apr. 24, 1750 poet, judge John Trumbull born (died 1831); **1780** town incorporated, separates from Waterbury; **1800** Bishop Tavern built; **1825** manufacture of palm-leaf hats begins; **Oct. 1, 1826** firearms inventor Benjamin Hotchkiss born (died 1885); **1840** Stephen Bucknall begins manufacture of locks; **1851** Wheeler and Wilson Sewing Machine company founded, later moves to Bridgeport; **1865** Watertown Library founded, library opened 1958.

West Hartford *Hartford County* *Central Connecticut, suburb 4 mi/6.4 km west of Hartford*

c.1679 town settled; **Oct. 16, 1758** lexicographer Noah Webster born (died 1843); **1777** Moses Goodman rides to Valley Forge, Pennsylvania, delivers $30,000 contribution from Hartford citizens to Continental Army; **1780** Quakers arrive in area of Quaker Lane, stay 50 years; **1854** town incorporated; **1877** University of Hartford established; **Feb. 10, 1897** virologist John Franklin Enders born, shared Nobel Prize 1954 (died 1985); **1932** St. Joseph College for women established; **1938** Noah Webster Memorial Library dedicated.

West Haven *New Haven County* *Southern Connecticut, 2 mi/3.2 km south-southwest of New Haven*

1648 town first settled; **1684** Ward Heitman House built; **1695** Peter Mallory House built; **July 5, 1779** town pillaged and burned by General Tryon's Redcoats; **1873** town incorporated, separates from New Haven; **1909** Christ Episcopal Church built; **1920** University of New Haven established; **1921** incorporated as a city.

Wethersfield *Hartford County* *Central Connecticut, 4 mi/6.4 km south of Hartford, on Connecticut River*

1634 town settled by John Oldham, others; **1637** town incorporated; **Apr. 1637** Wethersfield Massacre, six men, three women killed, two girls taken captive in Native American raid, precipitating Pequot War; **Apr. 11, 1640** citizens hold election in defiance of Royal Courts, are fined, refuse to pay; **1649** first Connecticut-built ship *Tryall* launched; **1680** fulling mill and carding mill established by Jacob Griswold, operated until c.1880; **1730** Michael Griswold House built; **1764** Silas Deane House built; **1774** Solomon Welles House built; **1820** plow factory established; **Feb. 22, 1863** educator Charles Andrews born (died 1943); **1893** Wethersfield Public Library founded, new library opened 1959.

Willimantic *Windham County* *East central Connecticut, 24 mi/39 km east-southeast of Hartford*

1680s area first settled; **1822** cotton mill opened; **1833** textiles become dominant industry; borough of Willimantic incorporated within Town of Windham, nicknamed "Thread City"; **1854** Willimantic Thread Company founded; Willimantic Library opened, replaced by new structure 1967; **1889** Eastern Connecticut State University established; **1893** Willimantic incorporated as a city, separates from Windham; **Feb. 13, 1920** soprano Eileen Farrell born; **1938** Willimantic disincorporated, reunites with Windham; **1991** Connecticut Eastern Railroad Museum opened.

Windham *Windham County* *East central Connecticut, 27 mi/43 km east-southeast of Hartford*

1686 town settled; **1692** town incorporated; **Apr. 22, 1711** clergyman Eleazar Wheelock born (died 1779); **1726** Windham County formed; town becomes county seat; **July 3, 1731** Cong. Samuel Huntington born (died 1796); **1773** Jedediah Elderkin plants mulberry grove for making silk products; **1783** Windham Inn built; **1829** Stafford and Phelps Company begins manufacture of first Fourdrinier paper-making machines in U.S.; **1833** textiles become dominant industry; Willimantic borough incorporated within town; **1855** county seat moved to Putnam; **1879** Loomer Opera House built, closed 1940; **1893** Willimantic incorporated as a city, separates from town; **1938** Willimantic city disincorporated, reunited with Windham; **1986** Windham Textile and History Museum founded.

Windsor *Hartford County* *Northern Connecticut, 6 mi/9.7 km north of Hartford, on Connecticut River*

1633 town settled by William Holmes and group from Plymouth Colony; stone fort erected, razed 1809; **1637** name Windsor adopted; town militia organized after Pequots attack town; **1640** Warham Grist Mill built; Lt. Walter Fyler House built; **1648** Bissell's Ferry established, ceased operations 1917; **1664** John Moore House built; **Jan. 4, 1679** colonial legislator Roger Wolcott born (died 1767); **Nov. 20, 1726** Oliver Wolcott born, signer of Declaration of Independence (died 1797); **1745** Dr. Alexander Wolcott House built; **Apr. 29, 1745** statesman Oliver Ellsworth born (died 1807); **1747** Thomas Hinsdale House built; **1763** Capt. Nathaniel Hayden House built; **1765** Dr. Hezekiah Chaffer House built; **1777** Oliver Mather House built; **1794** First Congregational Church built; **1822** James Loomis House built; **1895** Windsor Public Library founded; **1901** Huntington House built.

Windsor Locks *Hartford County* *Northern Connecticut, 12 mi/19 km north of Hartford, on Connecticut River*

1663 town settled, originally named Enfield Falls; **1691** Anthony Austin, Jr. House built; **1718** Mansion House built by Edmund Marshall; **1767** paper mill built; **1781** grist mill founded; **1783** cable ferry begins operating; **1794** Horace King House built; **1830** canal opens, circumventing falls; **1833** town renamed for canal locks; **May 1854** town incorporated; **May 10, 1919** Gov. Ella T. Grasso born (died 1981); **1941** Bradley Field airport established, named for Lt. Eugene M. Bradley, given to state 1946, renamed Bradley International Airport, flight center for Hartford area.

Winsted *Litchfield County* *Northwestern Connecticut, 22 mi/35 km northwest of Hartford*

1771 town incorporated; Old Mill House built; **1807** William L. Gilbert Clock Company established; **1813** Solomon Rockwell House built; **1833** Methodist Episcopal Church built; **1856** incorporated as a borough; **Feb. 2, 1898** historian Clarence Crane Brighton born (died 1968); **1915** incorporated as a city, separates from town; **Feb. 27, 1934** consumer advocate Ralph Nader born; **1939** Barkhamsted Reservoir formed to east on East Branch Farmington River by Saville Dam; **1965** Northwestern Community & Technical College (2-year) established.

Wolcott *New Haven County* *Central Connecticut, 19 mi/31 km southwest of Hartford*

1731 town settled by John Alcock; **Aug. 19, 1785** clock maker Seth Thomas born (died 1859); **1796** town incorporated; **Nov. 29, 1799** transcendental philosopher Amos Bronson Wolcott born (died 1888).

Woodstock *Windham County* *Northeastern Connecticut, 38 mi/61 km northeast of Hartford*

1674 John Eliot preaches to Wabbaquasetts; **1682** town settled; **1686** town founded; **1690** town incorporated by Massachusetts; **1749** town annexed by Connecticut; **Aug. 23, 1761** geographer Rev. Jedediah Morse born, father of inventor Samuel F. B. Morse (died 1826); **1780** Green's Tavern built; **1782** Bowen Tavern built; **1802** Woodstock Academy founded; **1820** Session's Tavern built; **1846** Roseland Cottage built by Henry Bowen.

Delaware

Eastern U.S. Capital: Dover. Largest city: Wilmington.

Delaware was one of the 13 colonies that adopted the U.S. Declaration of Independence July 4, 1776. It became the 1st state to ratify the U.S. Constitution December 7, 1787.

Delaware is divided into three counties. Municipalities are classified as villages, towns, and cities. There are no townships. See Introduction.

Arden *New Castle County   Northern Delaware, 5 mi/8 km north-northeast of Wilmington*

1682 town settled by John Grubb, known as Grubb's Landing, on South Branch Naaman's Creek; **c.1690** Old Lodge House built; **1746** Grubb descendant opens general store; **1900** (George) Frank Stephens purchases land on Grubb's Landing Road; town platted; **1909** The Homestead built by Stephens; **1911** Arden develops into society of liberal thinkers, living in cabins and tents, members include writer Upton Sinclair; one member arrested for explicit talks on sexual physiology; Upton Sinclair House built; **1918** Weavers Plant organized by Maude Rhodes; **1931** Robin Hood Theater founded by Edwin Ross; **1935** leader Frank Stephens dies, Arden society begins return to normalcy.

Bethany Beach *Sussex County   Southeastern Delaware, 48 mi/77 km south-southeast of Dover*

1898 Christian Church Disciples of Scranton, Pennsylvania, choose coastal site for summer camp; **1901** town founded and incorporated; octagonal Tabernacle built by Christian Missionary Society, uncompleted; **1902** developers assume control of project, includes Dr. T. E. Cramblet, president, Bethany College, West Virginia; **1903** boardwalk built; **1907** Bethany Beach Canal built; **1940** National Guard Camp established, used to house World War II prisoners; **March 1962** storm surge of 20–30 ft/ 6–9 m destroys older parts of town, rebuilt.

Centerville *New Castle County   Northern Delaware, 5 mi/8 km north-northwest of Wilmington*

1796 Friends Centre Meeting House built; log Centerville Schoolhouse built, replaced 1818; **1811** Kennett Pike toll road opens from Wilmington; **1859** Lower Brandywine Presbyterian Church built; **1885** Winterthur mansion built

by Col. Henry A. du Pont (1838–1906), later became home of son Henry F. du Pont, enlarged 1931, now historical site and museum; **1920** Vicmead Hunt Club organized; **1930** Camp Landis founded by Mrs. Irenee du Pont for blind children; **1933** Dauneport mansion built for Amy du Pont, modeled after Mount Vernon home.

Delaware City *New Castle County   Northern Delaware, 12 mi/19 km south of Wilmington, on Delaware River*

1814 small fort built on Pea Patch Island, Delaware River, claimed by New Jersey until 1843 suit settlement; **1826** town founded at eastern outlet of Chesapeake & Delaware Canal; **1828** Delaware City Hotel built; **1829** canal opened; **1832** practice of "budding" peach trees, grafting buds from mature trees to new trees producing superior fruit, introduced by Isaac Reeves; **1845** Lexington mansion built by peach grower Sen. John M. Clayton; **1846** tidal wave sweeps Pea Patch Island and its defenses; **1848** Fort Delaware built on Pea Patch Island; **1851** town incorporated; **1856** Delaware City Academy established; **1875** incorporated as a city; **1898** Fort Du Pont established south of canal entrance; **1957** Tidewater Oil Refinery opened; **1973** Delaware City Public Library founded.

Dover *Kent County   Central Delaware, 35 mi/56 km south of Wilmington*

1680 St. Jones County formed, renamed Kent County 1682; **1683** town site selected for county seat by order from William Penn; **1697** county seat moved from Town Point; **1718** town platted; **1728** Ridgely House built; **Oct. 7, 1728** patriot Rodney Caesar Rockne born (died 1784); **1734** Christ Church built; **1771** Little Creek Quaker Meeting House built; **May 12, 1777** state capital moved from New Castle; **Dec. 7, 1787** Delaware becomes first state to ratify

U.S. Constitution; **1792** (Old) State House completed; **1829** incorporated as a town; **1856** Delaware, Maryland & Virginia Railroad reaches town; Wesley Collegiate Institute founded; **1862** troops disarm secessionist minority; **Dec. 11, 1863** astronomer Annie Jump Cannon born, classified stars (died 1941); **1873** Wesley College established; **1874** county courthouse built; **1885** Dover Public Library founded; **1891** State College for Colored Students established, becomes Delaware State University; **1900** Rosedale Cheese Plant founded by Mennonites; **1904** Dover Opera House opened, becomes Capitol Theatre 1923; **1924** state-long divided highway built, named Coleman du Pont Boulevard, gift of Du Pont family; **1929** incorporated as a city; **1931** Delaware State Museum founded; **1933** Legislative Hall completed; **1941** Dover Army Air Field established to southeast, becomes Dover Air Force Base; **1968** Dover Downs International Speedway established; **1972** Delaware Technical and Community College, Terry Campus, established; **1974** Delaware Agricultural Museum founded; **2001** Schwartz Center for the Arts opened at Opera House.

Georgetown *Sussex County   Southern Delaware, 32 mi/51 km south of Dover*

1631 town site first settled by Dutch; **1683** Sussex County formed; **1717** official whipping post established, used into mid-1900s; **1775** boundary settlement with Maryland adds territory to county; **1791** James Pettyjohn purchases part of "Pettyjohn's oil field" for county seat; town founded, incorporated; **1792** county seat moved from Lewes; county courthouse built; **1836** Brick Hotel built, west wing added 1936; **1837** new county courthouse built on site of original structure; **1869** Junction & Breakwater Railroad built to Lewes, on Delaware Bay; **1917** U.S. Highway 113 extended south to Maryland; **1931** County Jail built; **1967** Delaware Technical and Community College, Jack F. Owens Campus, established; **Jan. 2, 2001** house fire at rural Oak Orchard to southeast kills all 11 family members.

Harrington *Kent County   Central Delaware, 16 mi/26 km south of Dover*

1855 Delaware, Maryland & Virginia Railroad reaches site; **1862** town founded at railroad junction, named for Chancellor Samuel M. Harrington; **1869** town incorporated; **1920** first Kent and Sussex Fair held, becomes Delaware State Fair 1962; **1945** Harrington Raceway established for harness racing.

Kenton *Kent County   North central Delaware, 12 mi/19 km northwest of Dover*

1771 Bryn Zion Baptist Church built; **1773** Downs House built; **c.1775** Prettyman House built; **c.1780** Cheney Clow's Fort built by Tory supporter arrested 1782 by County Sheriff, hanged 1788 for murder of posse member; **1809** Kenton Hotel built by Philip Lewis; **1869** Kenton Hundred formed by merger of western halves of Duck Creek and Little Creek Hundreds (hundreds: older form of county civil division still used in Delaware); **1880** original Downs Chapel built, new structure built 1927; **1887** incorporated as a town.

Laurel *Sussex County   Southwestern Delaware, 41 mi/66 km south of Dover*

1683 town founded; **1711** Bachelor's Delight land tract patented in area claimed by Maryland for use of Nanticokes; **c.1760** last of natives leave area; **1771** Christ Episcopal Church built to east, services held until 1850; **1768** survey marker erected 8 mi/12.9 km to southwest on Mason-Dixon Line, marking southwest corner of state of Delaware; **1802** town platted; **1883** town incorporated; **1936** Trappe Pond State Park established.

Lewes *Sussex County   Southeastern Delaware, 33 mi/53 km southeast of Dover, on Delaware Bay*

1609 Henry Hudson enters Delaware Bay; **1620** Capt. Cornelius Mey, or May, enters Delaware Bay, names north point Cape May, south point Cape Cornelius, renamed Cape Henlopen c.1800; **1631** Dutch establish settlement under direction of Peter Heyes and David Pietersen de Vries; town named Swanendael; **spring 1632** Native American attack on village leaves Thunis Willemsen as sole survivor; **1659** site fortified under orders of Peter Stuyvesant; **1660** trader Peter Alrichs arrives; **1663** utopian colony founded by Peter Cornelis Plockhoy; **1664** lands seized by Sir Robert Carr for Duke of York; **c.1665** Ryves Holt House built; **1671** land grants made, Herman Wiltbank among first settlers; town named Deale; **1680** Deal County formed; **1682** Lewes Commons granted by William Penn; **1683** Sussex County formed from former Deal County; town becomes county seat; **1707** Lewes Presbyterian Church built, replaced 1727, again in 1832; **1721** St. Peter's Episcopal Church built, replaced 1808, again in 1853; **1725** Fisher's Paradise residence built by Dr. Henry Fisher; **1767** Cape Henlopen Light built to replace 1725 lighthouse, abandoned 1924, destroyed by storm Apr. 13, 1926; **1791** county seat moved to Georgetown; **1795** Lewes Academy founded; **1835** Delaware Breakwater and Light completed, work begun 1818; **1853** St. Peter's Church built replacing church to southwest near Midway; **1857** incorporated as a town; **1869** Junction & Breakwater Railroad built; **1870** construction begins on Iron Pier, halted 1890, much of pier destroyed by storms; **1884** Lewes Coast Guard Station established; **1895** Queen Anne's Railroad built across Delmarva peninsula from Love Point, Maryland, ferry connection to Cape May, New Jersey, railroad abandoned 1924; **1913** Lewes & Rehoboth Canal opened paralleling Atlantic shore connecting Delaware Bay with Rehoboth Bay; **1930** Otis Smith turns port into important menhaden fishing center; **1931** Dutch-style Zwaanendael House built as town's tercentenary memorial; **1932** Lewes Public Library founded.

Marshallton *New Castle County* *Northern Delaware, 4 mi/6.4 km west of Wilmington*

Sept. 11, 1777 George Washington and Gen. Lafayette meet at Council Oak tree prior to Battle of Brandywine; **1790** Greenbank Mill built; **1827** Brandywine Springs Hotel resort opens, converted to military academy 1845, burned 1853; **1836** John Marshall establishes rolling mill on Red Clay Creek; town founded by Quakers; **1884** Ferris Industrial School for boys established; **1915** Edgewood Sanitarium established; **1920** State Industrial School for black girls opened; **June 26, 1937** Delaware Park Race Track opened for horse racing.

Middletown *New Castle County* *Northern Delaware, 22 mi/35 km south-southwest of Wilmington*

1675 land grants issued to Adam Peterson; **1678** town surveyed; **1762** Witherspoon's Tavern built, upper floor destroyed by fire 1946; **1761** Middletown Hotel built; **1768** St. Anne's Episcopal Church built; **1826** Middletown Academy founded, closed 1876; **1845** Cochran Grange built, home of Gov. John P. Cochran; **1850** peach orchard boom begins, ends with peach blight c.1880; **1861** incorporated as a town; **1929** St. Andrew's School established.

Milford *Kent and Sussex counties* *Central Delaware, 17 mi/27 km south of Dover*

1680 land purchased by Henry Bowman; **1707** St. Matthew's mission church (Church of England) built on Cedar Creek, rebuilt 1770, closed 1854; **1763** Causey Mansion built for Levin Crapper; **1770s** shipbuilding dominates economy; **1785** Parson Thorne House built; **1787** North Milford (Kent County) platted by Joseph Oliver; dam built on Mispillion River for sawmill and grist mill; **1791** Christ Episcopal Church built; **1807** incorporated as a town; **1819** South Milford (Sussex County) platted; **1850s** town serves as shipping port, last vessel launched 1917; **1882** Milford Public Library founded; **1918** Pearce Woolen Mill established, closed 1957; **1934** Sunnybrae house built.

Millsboro *Sussex County* *Southern Delaware, 40 mi/64 km south of Dover*

1792 Elisha Dickerson builds grist mill; town founded, named Rock Hole for rockfish found in Indian River; **1809** north side of river renamed Millsborough, south side named Washington; **1817** William D. Waples opens furnace for processing bog iron; **1830** Carey's Camp established, one of earliest resort camps in Delaware; **1833** iron industry flourishes, foundry makes railing for Independence Mall, Philadelphia, water pipes for Manhattan, New York; **1837** post office opened; both sides of river consolidated as Millsborough; **1893** incorporated as a town; **Jan. 17, 1893** lowest temperature ever recorded in Delaware reached, −17°F/−27°C; **July 21, 1930** highest temperature ever recorded in Delaware reached, 110°F/43°C; **1950s** manufacture of holiday holly wreaths begins.

Milton *Sussex County* *South central Delaware, 28 mi/45 km south-southeast of Dover*

1672 first settlers arrive; **1686** land patent awarded to James Gray; town develops at navigation head of Broadkill River, named Head of Broadkill; **c.1790** Governor Hazard House built; **1807** town renamed Milton for postmaster John Milton; **1809** shipyard established; **1822** Milton Academy established (closed 1880); **1835** Peter Parker House built; **1865** incorporated as a town; **1887** shipbuilding ceases; **1934** first annual Old Home Week celebration held.

New Castle *New Castle County* *Northern Delaware, 5 mi/8 km south of Wilmington, on Delaware River*

1651 Fort Casimir built by Dutch; site first settled by Finns and Swedes; **1655** Dutch organize village; **1657** Old Presbyterian Church built; **1664** village captured by British, retaken by Dutch 1673, restored to British 1674; **1672** New Castle County formed; town becomes county seat (shire town); **c.1680** original section of Courthouse built; **c.1690** ferry established to Pennsgrove, New Jersey; **1704** town becomes colonial capital of Delaware; **1710** Immanuel Anglican Church completed; **c.1728** Amstel House built; **May 10, 1730** George Ross born, signer of Declaration of Independence (died 1779); **1732** county courthouse built; Van Leuvenigh House built; **1774** town raises aid for destitute citizens of Boston; **Aug. 27, 1776** convention held to adopt constitution for new state of Delaware; town serves briefly as state capital; **1777** state capital moved to Dover; **1792** New Castle Common established; **1801** Read House completed; **1809** Old Arsenal built; **1823** Town Hall built; **1824** devastating town fire starts at Jefferson Hotel, hotel spared, citizens of Boston reciprocate by sending aid; **1832** New Castle & Frenchtown Railroad built; **1875** incorporated as a city; **1881** county seat moved to Wilmington; **1967** Wilmington College established; **1973** Delaware Memorial Bridge completed, replaces ferry.

Newark *New Castle County* *Northern Delaware, 12 mi/19 km west-southwest of Wilmington*

1661 iron mined at Iron Hill, until 1891; **1683** Valentine Hollingsworth obtains tract called New Wark; **1743** University of Delaware established; Newark Academy established, closed 1898; **1746** Welsh Tract Baptist Church built; **1747** England Manor House built; Old Red Mill built by John England, originally England's Mill; **1752** White Clay Creek Presbyterian Church built, rebuilt 1855; **1758** St. Patrick's Inn established; **1760** Cooch House built by John Cooch; **June 1764** surveyors Mason and Dixon establish post here in preparation for survey of Mason-Dixon Line; **Sept. 3, 1777** skirmish between Gen. Washington's troops and British under Gen. Howe at Cooch's Bridge, only Revolutionary War battle on

Delaware soil; **c.1780** Andrew Gray House built; **1798** Curtis Paper Plant started by Meteer family; **1849** Prismatic Stone erected on Maryland boundary by Col. J. D. Graham marking southern tip of The Wedge, 800 ac/ 324 ha, bounded by Maryland on west, Pennsylvania on north, continuation of arc of Delaware's northern boundary on east, awarded to Delaware 1893; **1852** incorporated as a city; **1912** Newark China Clay Company founded; **1968** Delaware Technical and Community College, Stanton-Wilmington Campus, established.

Newport   *New Castle County   Northern Delaware, 3 mi/4.8 km southwest of Wilmington, on Christina River*

c.1730 Galloway House built; **1735** town platted by John Justis, originally named Newport Ayre; **Sept. 13, 1755** Oliver Evans born, inventor of steam-powered dredges, other devices (died 1819); **1788** The Inn tavern opens; **1808** Newport and Gap Turnpike northwest to Pennsylvania authorized; **1817** Lancaster Pike opens from Wilmington; **1837** railroad extended through town; **1873** town incorporated.

Oak Orchard   *Sussex County   See **Georgetown** (2001)*

Odessa   *New Castle County   North central Delaware, 21 mi/34 km north-northwest of Dover*

1664 land titles awarded to settlers; **1721** Capt. Edmund Cantwell opens toll bridge over Appoquinimink Creek, locality named Cantwell's Bridge; **1767** Duncan Beard House built by Scottish clockmaker; **1769** David Wilson Mansion built; **1773** work begun on Drawyers Presbyterian Church at site of 1711 wooden church, completed c.1833; Castle William mansion built; Fairview House built; **1783** Comm. Thomas MacDonough born at MacDonough House to north, credited with capture of British fleet on Lake Champlain Sept. 1814 (died 1825); Friends Meeting House built; **1820s** town becomes important grain shipping point; **1822** Odessa Hotel built; **1854** Odessa Public School opens; **1855** grain trade collapses; **1856** Corbit Library founded.

Rehoboth Beach   *Sussex County   Southeastern Delaware, 38 mi/61 km southeast of Dover*

1609 Henry Hudson sails into Delaware Bay; **1610** Samuel Argyle names bay for Lord de la Warr; **1675** town's Biblical name applied by British settlers; **1742** The Homestead built by Peter Marsh; **1870** Louis Tredenick opens summer hotel and gun club camp at nearby Dewey Beach; **1872** Rehoboth Methodist Camp established, ends 1881; **1873** incorporated as a town; boardwalk built; **1874** two hotels, cottages built; **1878** railroad extended from Lewes; **1879** Henlopen Hotel built; **1897** incorporated as a city; **1914** storm washes away Horn's Pier, boardwalk, beachfront cottages; **1925** state-long Coleman du Pont Boulevard divided highway presented to state; **May 10,**

1960 nuclear submarine *Triton* surfaces after 84-day journey around world submerged.

Saint Georges   *New Castle County   Northern Delaware, 14 mi/23 km south-southwest of Wilmington*

1730 town founded at mill dam on St. Georges Creek; **c.1735** tavern established on King's Highway; **c.1790** Damascus House built; **1802** Sutton House built; **1829** Chesapeake & Delaware Canal opens, deepened to sea level 1930s; **1836** Linden Hill house built; **1861** canal provides vital link between Philadelphia and Washington during Civil War; **1940** town disincorporated; **1960** Summit Bridge, lift bridge, built across Chesapeake & Delaware Canal.

Seaford   *Sussex County   Southwestern Delaware, 35 mi/56 km south of Dover, on Nanticoke River*

1672 area first settled; **c.1701** Walnut Landing home built; **1726** town founded; **c.1793** Woodland Ferry established on Nanticoke River; **1799** town platted, named Hooper's Landing; Hooper House built; **c.1814** town renamed for Seaford, England, origin of its settlers; **1818** practice of "mercy killing" applied to Shadrach Cannon, who went mad days after being bitten by rabid dog, smothered between two mattresses by citizens; **Nov. 1831** panic ensues after false rumor that black slaves were in process of uprising following real uprising in Southampton County, Virginia; **c.1840** Lawrence mansion built; **1843** St. Luke's Episcopal Church built; **1849** Fairview House built by William W. Delaney; **1856** Delaware, Maryland & Virginia Railroad built through town; **1859** Ross Mansion completed; **Nov. 3, 1862** Federal troops arrive to police elections; **1865** incorporated as a city; **1902** Seaford Public Library founded; **1921** Frederick Douglass School for black children built; **1939** Du Pont Corporation builds nylon plant.

Smyrna   *Kent County   North central Delaware, 10 mi/16 km north-northwest of Dover*

1684 earliest section of Belmont Hall home built, expanded by Thomas Collins, High Sheriff, 1753; **1755** Clearfield house built to north by Capt. David Clark; **1761** (or 1767) Brick Hotel (Brick Store) built to north at Brick Store Landing on Duck Creek (Smyrna River); **1768** town founded as Duck Creek Cross Roads; **May 27, 1784** Cong. Louis McLane born, secretary of state under President Jackson (died 1857); **1791** Enoch Spruance House built; **1806** town renamed Smyrna; **1850s** shipbuilding becomes important; **1856** Delaware Railroad reaches town; **1859** town incorporated; **c.1860** Woodlawn House built; **1933** State Welfare Home opened.

Stanton   *New Castle County   Northern Delaware, 6 mi/9.7 km west-southwest of Wilmington*

1679 grist mill and sawmill established; town founded, one of Delaware's oldest settlements, originally named Cuckoldstown; **c.1740** Mermaid Tavern established;

1741 original section of Murray House built; **1742** Robinson's Mill built; **c.1750** Tatnall (Byrnes) House built; **1768** town renamed for landowner Stephen Stanton; **c.1774** Boyce House built; **Aug. 28–Sept. 8, 1777** George Washington camps here awaiting British, who detour through Newark; **1820** St. James' Episcopal Church built on original church site, earliest grave dates to 1726; **1839** Farmers Mutual Insurance Company organized; **1853** Red Clay Creek Presbyterian Church built; **1873** Stanton Meeting House built; **1874** Harmony Grange organized; **June 26, 1937** Legal Light wins first day opener at Delaware Park Race Track.

Town Point *Kent County Central Delaware, 7 mi/ 11.3 km southeast of Dover, on St. Jones Creek*

c.1679 Towne Point house built by Edward Pack; **1680** St. Jones County formed, renamed Kent County 1682; **1683** William Darvall buys Pack house, used as first county courthouse; Darvall establishes ferry on St. Jones Creek; **1690** court sessions moved to William Maxwell's tavern; **1697** county seat moved to Dover; **Oct. 7, 1728** patriot Caesar Rodney born (died 1784); **1734** Dickinson Mansion built to west; **July 1–2, 1776** Caesar Rodney makes 80-mi/129-km ride to Philadelphia to cast deciding vote allowing Delaware to become one of 13 original states.

Wilmington *New Castle County Northern Delaware, 24 mi/39 km southwest of Philadelphia*

1638 Peter Minuit arrives on Delaware River with two shiploads of Swedish and Finnish settlers, founds Fort Christina, named for Queen of Sweden; **1654** barley mill established; **1655** fort taken by Dutch Gov. Peter Stuyvesant; **1660** oldest section of Long Hook Farm house built; **1664** town taken by British; **1667** Crane Hook Church built, last service held after Easter, 1699; **1672** New Castle County formed; New Castle becomes county seat; **1698** Old Swedes Church built; **1730** land surveyed, platted by Andrew Justison, named Willingtown for Thomas Willing, who married Justison's daughter; **1731** incorporated as a borough; **1738** Ship Tavern built;

Friends Meeting House built, replaced 1748, again in 1816; **1739** town renamed Wilmington, for Earl of Wilmington; **Oct. 17, 1752** Jacob Broom born, signer of U.S. Constitution (died 1810); **1761** town's first printing press founded by James Adams; **1765** first bridge built at Brandywine Ford; **Aug. 25, 1777** Gen. Howe lands at Elk River in Maryland, Gen. Washington passes through town and camps near Newport; **Sept. 13, 1777** British capture John McKinly, President of the state of Delaware, held for full year, released through prisoner exchange; **c.1778** Perry's Tavern built; **1785** Alrich House built; **1788** Wilmington Public Library founded, built 1923; **1798** Brandywine Academy founded; **1802** Upper Hagley Powder Mill established; **1808** steamer service begins to Philadelphia; **July 1, 1810** banker, abolitionist James Sloan Gibbons born (died 1892); **1811** Kennett Pike toll road opened heading northwest; **1812** Father Kenny House built; **1816** Peter Bauduy establishes powder mill at Eden Park; Delaware Academy of Medicine built; original St. Peter's Catholic Church built; **1817** Lancaster Pike completed to Newport; **Oct. 29, 1828** Thomas Francis Bayard the elder born, secretary of state under President Cleveland (died 1898); **1832** incorporated as a city; **1837** Philadelphia, Wilmington & Baltimore Railroad reaches city; **1857** Cathedral Church of St. John (Episcopal) built; **1860s** port prospers during Civil War; **June 4, 1868** Sen. Thomas Francis Bayard the younger born (died 1942); **1881** county seat moved to Wilmington; **1886** Goldey-Beacom College established; **1892** St. Amour mansion built, home of Lammot du Pont; **1905** Brandywine Zoo founded; **1907** Emily P. Biswork originates Christmas Seals to finance three sanitariums; Du Pont Building completed; **1916** county courthouse built; **1923** marine terminal built; **1932** Art Center established; **1937** federal building completed; **1941** New Castle Army Air Base established, becomes New Castle County Airport 1947; **1951** Delaware Memorial Bridge completed across Delaware River, replacing New Castle ferry, second span built 1973; **Apr. 23, 1960** TV actress Valerie Bertinelli born; **1981** liberalization of state's banking laws enhances city's standing as financial center, furthered in 1986; **2002** new county courthouse built.

District of Columbia

Eastern U.S. Capital and major city: Washington.

The site for the nation's capital was selected by George Washington in October, 1790. In 1801, the District of Columbia was created by Congress from portions of Maryland and Virginia on both sides of the Potomac River. The city of Washington, on the eastern bank, was incorporated in 1802 as the capital city of the United States. In 1846, the Virginia portion of the District was returned to that state.

The District of Columbia originally had two counties in 1801, Arlington County on the western bank and Washington County on the eastern bank. Arlington County was returned to Virginia in 1846, at which time Washington County ceased to exist. The city of Washington is the only municipality and became coterminous with the District in 1874.

Washington
On east bank of Potomac River, 35 mi/ 56 km southwest of Baltimore, Maryland

1632 Henry Fleete visits fall line of Potomac River, establishes trade with natives; **1665** area first settled; **1703** land patent received by Ninian Bell; **c.1708** Inspection House for tobacco-rolling trade established by George Gordon; town founded at site of Georgetown, originally named Knave's Disappointment; wharves built for shipping tobacco; **1748** Mason's Ferry established to Virginia, operates only to Analostan Island (later Theodore Roosevelt Island), causeway built from island to Virginia mainland; **1751** George Town platted; original section of Beall Mansion built by George Beall; **1769** log Georgetown Lutheran Church built; **1782** Georgetown Presbyterian Church built, rebuilt 1821; **1783** Continental Congress hears first proposals for creation of a federal town; **1788** Maryland cedes land for District of Columbia; first bridge built across Rock Creek, collapses in storm 1814; **1789** Virginia cedes land for District of Columbia; Georgetown incorporated as a city; Georgetown University established; **1791** French landscape architect Pierre L'Enfant (1754–1825) designs city; **Oct. 1793** cornerstone laid for White House; **c.1793** Tunnicliff Tavern built, acquired by William Tunnicliff c.1796, demolished 1932; **Sept. 18, 1793** cornerstone laid for Capitol Building by President Washington in its North Wing; **1799** roof of Capitol completed over Senate Wing; **1799** Octagon House built, designed by William Thornton; Union Tavern opened at Georgetown; **June 3, 1800** Pres. John Adams (1735–1826) becomes first resident of the White House; **June 10, 1800** Congress meets in Washington for first time, Philadelphia ceases

role as temporary capital; **1800–1801** right of way cleared for Pennsylvania Avenue; **1801** District of Columbia formally created by Congress; **1802** Washington incorporated as a city; **1805** Francis Scott Key Mansion built at Georgetown; **Feb. 18, 1805** Union naval officer Louis M. Goldsborough born (died 1877); **c.1810** Blair House built by Surgeon General Joseph Lovell, third story later added by Preston Blair; **June 10, 1810** Confederate Gen. Benjamin Stoddert Ewell born at Georgetown (died 1894); **June 18, 1812** U.S. declares war on British over shipping blockade, lifted June 16, news not received in time; **Aug. 24, 1814** British Gen. Robert Ross burns Capitol, White House, city of Washington; **Feb. 17, 1815** U.S. ratifies Treaty of Ghent, signed by British Dec. 24, 1814, ending War of 1812; **1816** St. John's Episcopal Church built; **Feb. 8, 1817** Confederate Gen. Richard Stoddert Ewell born at Georgetown (died 1872); **Dec. 1817** rebuilding of White House completed; **1820** original section of District Court Building built, served as city hall until 1873, north extension completed 1881; **March 3, 1820** Missouri Compromise passed, allowing slavery in Missouri but no other state north of Missouri's southern boundary, repealed 1854; **1821** George Washington University established, originally Columbian College; **Dec. 2, 1823** Monroe Doctrine declared giving protection to Western Hemisphere against aggression from outside forces; **Feb. 4, 1826** surveyor, frontiersman Edward Beale born (died 1893); **1828** work begins on Chesapeake & Ohio Canal paralleling Potomac River; **1835** National Theater established; **Feb. 16, 1840** Kentucky Cong. Henry Watterson born (died 1921); **1842** Treasury Building completed, previous structure destroyed by fire 1833; **May 24, 1844** Samuel F. B. Morse sends first telegram message from U.S. Congress to Baltimore: "What hath God wrought?"; **1846** Virginia portion of District of Columbia (Arlington County) returned to that state; Smithsonian Institution established 17 years after death of donor, Englishman James Smithson, who had never been to U.S.; **May 13, 1846** Pres. James K. Polk declares war on Mexico over Texas boundary dispute, Mexico declares war May 23; **July 1, 1847** Franklin 5-cent, Washington 10-cent first adhesive stamps issued by U.S.; **Dec. 17, 1849** Richard Wainwright born, naval commander during Spanish American War (died 1926); **1850** original Willard Hotel built, site occupied by hotels since 1818; **1852** Smithsonian Institution building completed; **1861** old U.S. Naval Hospital built; New York Avenue Presbyterian Church built, established 1803; **Jan. 1, 1863** Lincoln's Emancipation Proclamation declares all slaves free in Southern states; **March 3, 1863** Congress approves military conscription, drafting men 20 to 45 years; **Apr. 16, 1863** slavery abolished in District of Columbia; **Aug. 1863** John T. Ford purchases abandoned First Baptist Church, establishes Ford's Theatre; **1864** Gallaudet University for the hearing impaired established, originally named National College for the Deaf and Dumb; **July 11, 1864** skirmishes by Confederate Gen. Jubal Early at Fort Stevens, in northern corner of D.C., observed by President Lincoln; **Jan. 31, 1865** House of Representatives proposes 13th Amendment abolishing slavery, ratified Dec. 6; **Apr. 14, 1865** John Wilkes Booth shoots Lincoln at Ford's Theatre, Lincoln dies Apr. 15 at Petersen House hotel, Booth shot to death Apr. 26 near Port Royal, Virginia; **1867** Howard University established; **Feb. 24, 1868** Pres. Andrew Johnson impeached by House of Representatives, acquitted by Senate May 1868; **1869** Corcoran Gallery of Art founded, opened 1897; **1871** municipal corporation established for District of Columbia, includes cities of Washington and Georgetown, and County of Washington; **May 1, 1872** first postcard issued by U.S. Post Office; **Feb. 27, 1873** in Credit Mobilier scandal, railroad construction company distributed shares to political figures, including Cong. James A. Garfield; **Apr. 13, 1876** historian Sidney Bradshaw Fay born (died 1967); **July 1, 1877** first black Army Gen. Benjamin Oliver Davis born (died 1970); **1878** U.S. Congress made governing body for District of Columbia; **July 2, 1881** Charles Guiteau shoots Pres. James A. Garfield at railroad station; dies Sept. 19; **June 20, 1883** Adm. Royal Eason Ingersoll born, commander Atlantic Fleet, World War II (died 1976); **1884** St. Patrick's Roman Catholic Cathedral completed, begun 1872; **1887** The Catholic University of America established; **1888** Washington Monument opened; State Department Building completed; **Feb. 25, 1888** diplomat John Foster Dulles born, secretary of state under President Eisenhower (died 1959); **1890** National Zoological Park opened under direction of Smithsonian Institution; **1893** American University chartered by act of Congress; Naval Observatory opened, established 1809, later used as U.S. vice-president's official residence; **June 9, 1893** Ford's Theatre building, used by U.S. Pension Bureau, collapses killing 22; **Apr. 29, 1894** 20,000 unemployed men descend on Washington led by Jacob S. Coxey, referred to as Coxey's Army, following Panic of 1893; **1895** city of Washington annexes Georgetown; **Jan. 1, 1895** J. Edgar Hoover born, director of Federal Bureau of Investigation 1924–1972 (died 1972); **Nov. 6, 1895** composer, band leader John Philip Sousa, "The March King," born (died 1932); **Aug. 8, 1896** author Marjorie Kinnan Rawlings born (died 1953); **1897** Trinity College established; **July 2, 1898** Army Gen. Anthony C. McAuliffe born, commander at Battle of the Bulge, World War II (died 1975); **1899** old U.S. Post Office built; **Feb. 11, 1899** lowest temperature ever recorded in D.C. reached, $-15°F/-26°C$; **Apr. 29, 1899** bandleader Edward Kennedy "Duke" Ellington born (died 1974); **Oct. 10, 1900** actress Helen Hayes born (died 1993); **Jan. 31, 1902** anthropologist Julian Hayes Stoddard born (died 1972); **1903** District Public Library opened; **1905** Department of Agriculture Administration Building completed; **Dec. 20, 1906** railroad accident, 53 killed; **Sept. 29, 1907** cornerstone laid for National Cathedral, final west tower section completed 1990; **Dec. 29, 1907** African-American economist Robert Clifton Weaver born (died 1997); **1908** Union Station completed; District Building completed, renamed John A. Wilson Municipal Building 1996; **1909** Senate Office Building completed; **1910** National Museum of Natural History completed; **1912** Anacostia Park system established; **Dec. 18, 1912** Benjamin Oliver Davis, Jr. born, appointed as first African-American Air Force general 1965; **Feb. 25, 1913** federal individual income tax started; **Dec. 23, 1913** Federal Reserve Bank System created; **1914** U.S. Post Office completed; Bureau of Engraving and Printing building completed; **1917** North Interior Department Building completed, South Building completed 1936; **1918** U.S. Naval Air Station established at Anacostia in southern part of D.C.; **Jan. 29, 1919** 18th Amendment prohibiting alcoholic beverages ratified, takes effect Jan. 16, 1920; **Oct. 26, 1919** African-American Massachusetts Sen. Edward William Brooke born; **1920** American Civil Liberties Union founded; **Nov. 8, 1921** *Washington Daily News* newspaper founded; **1922** Lincoln Memorial dedicated; **Jan. 28, 1922** Knickerbocker Movie Theatre roof collapse kills 98; **1924** National Academy of Sciences building completed; **Feb. 3, 1924** former Pres. Woodrow Wilson dies at age 67 after long illness; **Sept. 9, 1924** actress Jane Greer born; **1925** U.S. Chamber of Commerce Building completed; **1927** National Arboretum established; **June 11, 1927** aviator Charles Lindbergh honored by President Coolidge; **Feb. 9, 1928** newscaster Roger Mudd born; **March 12, 1928** writer Edward Albee born; **Nov. 1, 1929** in Teapot Dome Scandal, Secretary of Interior Albert Fall found guilty of accepting bribe by oil company for land lease in Wyoming; **Jan. 13, 1930** actress Frances Sternhagen born; **March 8, 1930** former Pres. William Howard Taft dies after month long illness; **July 20, 1930** highest temperature ever recorded in D.C. reached, $106°F/41°C$; **1932** Department of Commerce Building completed; Arlington Memorial Bridge completed across Potomac River to Arlington, Virginia; **Jan. 23, 1933** actress Chita Rivera born; **May 6, 1933** President Roosevelt orders closing of all U.S. banks for eight days; **June 13, 1933** Congress passes Pres. Franklin D. Roosevelt's National Recovery Act (NRA); **Dec. 5, 1933** Prohibition repealed in U.S. with ratification of 21st Amendment; **1934** Reflecting Basin built, designed by Bennett, Parsons, and Frost; Department of Justice Building completed; Post Office Department Building completed; **Jan. 30, 1934** actor Rip Taylor born; **Sept. 16, 1934** basketball player for Los Angeles Lakers Elgin Baylor born; **Oct. 3, 1934** actress Madlyn Rhue born; **1935** Supreme Court Building completed; National Archives Building completed; Internal Revenue Service Building completed; **May 27, 1935** NRA voided by Supreme Court; **1937** Federal Reserve Building completed; **Apr. 18, 1937** actor Robert Hooks born; **1939** Library of Congress opened; **Jan. 17, 1939** TV personality Maury Povich born; **Apr. 2, 1939** singer Marvin Gaye born (died 1984); **Apr. 9, 1939** TV actress Michael Learned born; **Apr. 23, 1939** TV actor David Birney born; **Sept. 8, 1939** limited national emergency proclaimed by Pres. Roosevelt in response to war in Europe; **1940** Social Security Administration Building completed; **1941** National Gallery of Art opened; War Department Building completed, incorporated later into State Department Building; Washington National Airport opened at Arlington; **Aug. 1, 1941** African-American official Ronald H. Brown born, secretary of commerce under President Clinton, killed in plane crash in Bosnia 1996; **May 27, 1941** President Roosevelt expands limited national emergency to full emergency; **1942** District National Guard Armory completed; **1943** Thomas Jefferson Memorial dedicated; **July 21, 1943** actor Edward Hermann born; **March 7, 1945** actor John Heard born; **Nov. 21, 1945** actress Goldie Hawn born; **Jan. 31, 1947** actor Jonathan Banks born; **1948** actress Blair Brown born; **March 31, 1948** Vice-Pres. Albert Arnold Gore, Jr. born, Democratic presidential candidate 2000; **Nov. 1, 1949** Eastern DC-4 rammed by Bolivian P-38 killing 55; **March 20, 1950** actor William Hurt born; **Nov. 1, 1950** assassination attempt on President Truman by two Puerto Rican nationalists, shootout at Blair House, guard killed, two wounded; **Nov. 21, 1951** TV personality Jayne Kennedy born; **Apr. 8, 1952** steel mills seized by President Truman, declared illegal by Court June 2, strike June 3, settled July 24; **Apr. 28, 1952** Truman lifts national emergency, in effect since 1941; **Dec. 22, 1953** Dr. J. Robert Oppenheimer's security clearance revoked, Communist dealings charged; **May 17, 1954** school segregation ruled unconstitutional in 21 states and D.C.; **Dec. 2, 1954** Sen. Joseph McCarthy of Wisconsin charged with contempt following investigation of committee on subversive activities; **1955** Washington Hebrew Congregation dedicated, founded 1856; **Jan. 27, 1957** TV personality Katie Couric born; **Nov. 25, 1957** President Eisenhower suffers mild stroke, recovers; **1958** American Association of Retired Persons (AARP) founded by Dr. Ethel Percy Andrus; **Apr. 15, 1959** Pres. Fidel Castro of Cuba begins 11-day goodwill tour of U.S.; **Sept. 15, 1959** Soviet Premier Nikita Khrushchev begins 13-day tour of U.S.; **Oct. 6, 1959** Congressional hearings open to investigate quiz show rigging, $64,000 Question,

others; **Feb. 6, 1960** House committee recommends penalties in broadcast payola scandal; **May 9, 1960** birth control pill Enovid, produced by Searle company, approved by FDA; **Oct. 20, 1960** U.S. places embargo on all exports to Cuba; **Oct. 1961** Washington ("D.C.") Stadium opened, renamed Robert F. Kennedy ("RFK") Stadium following his 1968 assassination; **1962** Dulles International Airport opened in Virginia; **Sept. 13, 1962** President Kennedy threatens military action against Cuba in response to weapons shipments from U.S.S.R.; **Oct. 22, 1962** President Kennedy announces discovery of Soviet missile sites in Cuba on TV, quarantines shipping; **Oct. 28, 1962** President Kennedy and Soviet Premier Khrushchev agree to dismantle missiles for lifting of quarantine; **May 15, 1963** Committee stresses caution in pesticide usage in reaction to Rachel Carson's book *Silent Spring*; **June 17, 1963** Supreme Court bans Lord's Prayer, Bible reading in public schools; **Aug. 28, 1963** Civil Rights demonstration draws 200,000 protestors; **Aug. 30, 1963** direct "Hot Line" to Moscow established to reduce risk of accidental war; **Dec. 5, 1963** Warren Commission opens investigation of Kennedy assassination; **1964** new headquarters of National Geographic Society opened; **Jan. 8, 1964** President Johnson announces his War on Poverty to Congress; **Apr. 28, 1964** Johnson asks Congress for $228 million for aid to Appalachia, 360 counties in 10 states; **Sept. 27, 1964** Warren Commission finds that Lee Harvey Oswald acted alone in Kennedy assassination; **Feb. 18, 1965** Secretary of Defense Robert McNamara proposes fallout shelter construction program; **June 30, 1965** Senate probe into Bobby Baker political payoffs ends with recommendation of indictment; **1967** 232-room Watergate Hotel opened near Potomac River; **Jan. 8, 1967** Naval training flight of twin-engine bomber ends in crash near D.C., killing nine reservists; **March 1, 1967** Congress votes to censure New York's Adam Clayton Powell for misuse of public funds, denying him his congressional seat; **June 23, 1967** Congress censures Connecticut Cong. Thomas Dodd for misuse of travel funds; **Oct. 21–22, 1967** 35,000 peace demonstrators march on Washington, most of c.650 arrests occur at Pentagon; **March 28, 1969** former President Eisenhower dies at Walter Reed Hospital at age 78; **May 14, 1969** Abe Fortas resigns from Supreme Court following reports of his accepting $20,000 from charitable organization; **Nov. 15, 1969** Veterans Day protests against Vietnam War attract 250,000, simultaneous demonstration in San Francisco; **Dec. 1, 1969** Selective Service draws Sept. 14 as first choice for draftees born on that date, first draft since 1942; **March 12, 1970** bomb scares force evacuation of eight federal office buildings, no bombs found; **Apr. 4, 1970** pro-Vietnam march for victory draws 50,000, many right-wing church groups; **Apr. 22, 1970** millions nation-wide observe first Earth Day; **July 2, 1970** embassies of Argentina, Haiti, Dominican Republic, and Uruguay firebombed day after firebombing of Inter-American Defense Building; **1971** John F. Kennedy Center for the Performing Arts opened; **March 1971** residents elect first nonvoting delegate from D.C. to House of Representatives; **March 1, 1971** Weather Underground claims responsibility for bombing of Capitol, $300,000 damage; **Apr. 19, 1971** Vietnam Veterans Against the War begins antiwar protests, swells to 200,000 by May 5; **May 1, 1971** Amtrak created by National Railroad Passenger Corporation, nationwide passenger service halved, originally named Railpax; **July 1, 1971** U.S. Postal Service replaces Post Office Department; **Aug. 12, 1971** tennis player Pete Sampras born; **Aug. 15, 1971** President Nixon imposes 90-day wage/price freeze to curb inflation; **Sept. 30, 1971** Washington Senators final baseball game held before becoming Texas Rangers (Dallas); **Dec. 28, 1971** 80 antiwar Vietnam veterans arrested for occupying Lincoln Memorial; **1972** Martin Luther King, Jr. Memorial Library opened in downtown Washington; **Jan. 3, 1972** columnist Jack Anderson releases secret government papers on India-Pakistan conflict; **Jan. 27, 1972** G. Gordon Liddy presents $1 million espionage plan against Democrats to John Mitchell, John Dean, and Jeb Magruder; **Apr. 16, 1972** Ling-ling and Hsing-hsing pandas arrive at National Zoo, gift from Chinese in exchange for musk ox; **May 28, 1972** Democratic National Committee's telephones bugged, documents photographed in first Watergate Hotel break-in; **June 6, 1972** John McCord, four others arrive with bugging equipment in second Watergate break-in, seize surveillance equipment, are arrested; **1973** home rule adopted by Congress for District of Columbia, granting its first elected government since 1834; **Jan. 5, 1973** Nixon orders installation of metal screening devices at all airports following average two hijackings per month; **Jan. 22, 1973** Supreme Court rules 7-2 in *Roe v. Wade* to legalize abortion; **Jan. 30, 1973** Mississippi Sen. John Stennis, 71, shot, wounded in robbery attempt in front of his D.C. home; **Apr. 30, 1973** Nixon accepts resignations of Haldeman, Ehrlichman, Dean, Att. Gen. Kliendienst; **May 1, 1973** federal investigators allege cover-up in Watergate break-in, obstruction of investigation; **July 17, 1973** Vice-Pres. Spiro T. Agnew casts tie-breaking vote, 49-48, approving controversial Alaska Pipeline; **Oct. 20, 1973** Vice-President Agnew resigns, convicted of tax evasion, gets three years probation, $10,000 fine; **Nov. 16, 1973** incriminating 18½-minute gap found in Nixon-Haldeman tape recorded June 20, 1972, three days after break-in disclosed by secretary Rose Mary Woods; **1974** Washington Capitals hockey team begins inaugural season; **Jan. 22, 1974** thousands protest against abortion in first annual March for Life; **July 24, 1974** Supreme Court rules against President Nixon, orders surrender of Watergate tapes and documents; **Aug. 9, 1974** Nixon resigns presidency; **Sept. 8, 1974** President Ford's unconditional pardon of Nixon receives widespread criticism; **Oct. 1, 1974** Watergate trial begins; **Nov. 20, 1974** AT&T sued by U.S. government, company divided into 23 regional firms ("Baby Bells"), for failure to allow other phone companies to interconnect with system; **Jan. 1, 1975** Ehrlichman, Mitchell, Haldeman, Robert Mardian found guilty of all Watergate charges; **1976** University of District of Columbia established; **June 25, 1976** Supreme Court rules that nonsectarian schools cannot exclude students on grounds of race; **Sept. 7, 1977** President

Carter, Panamanian President Torrijos sign agreement to transfer Canal Zone by year 2000; **May 15, 1978** Supreme Court lets stand North Carolina law restricting homosexual activities; **July 17, 1978** 1,000 Native Americans arrive at Capitol after 2,700 mi/4.345 km walk from Alcatraz Island to protest "Red backlash"; **March 30, 1981** Pres. Ronald Reagan, Press Secretary James Brady, two others wounded by gunshots fired by John Hinckley outside Washington Hilton, Reagan returns to White House Apr. 11; **Sept. 25, 1981** Sandra Day O'Connor becomes first woman to sit on Supreme Court; **Jan. 13, 1982** Air Florida Boeing 737 crashes into Potomac River after takeoff, killing 78; **Nov. 9, 1984** Vietnam Veterans Memorial unveiled, wall bearing names of 58,022 killed and missing; **Apr. 9, 1989** 300,000 march in support of abortion rights, organized by National Organization for Women (NOW); **May 26, 1989** Speaker James C. Wright, Jr. and Democratic majority leader Tony Coelho resign, used campaign funds to buy junk bonds; **Apr. 25, 1993** homosexual rights demonstration draws 300,000; **Sept. 12, 1994** Frank Corder flies Cessna from Aberdeen, Md., crash lands on South Lawn White House; **Oct. 29, 1994** gunman Francisco Duran shoots at White House, wrestled by bystander, President Clinton watching football; **1995** Korean War Memorial dedicated; **July 13, 1995** Clinton announces closing of 79 military bases, merger of 26 others, $1.6 billion savings, loss of 90,000 jobs; **Sept. 19, 1995** *Washington Post* prints "Unabomber's" 35,000-word manifesto stating that Industrial Revolution had damaged natural world, letter bomb suspect Theodore Kaczynski arrested in Montana Apr. 1996; **Nov. 16, 1995** Million Man March organized by Muslim leader Louis Farrakhan, c.827,000 attend, committed to responsible behavior; **July 4, 1998** gunman Russell E. Watson, Jr. of Illinois shoots and kills Officer Jacob Chestnus, wounds Special Agent John Gibson at Sen. Tom DeLay's office in Capitol; **Dec. 19, 1998** House of Representatives votes to impeach President Clinton; **Jan. 7, 1999** second impeachment trial in U.S. Senate history begins against Clinton for having lied under oath, acquitted Feb. 12; **July 29, 1999** Clinton fined $89,000 for lying in Monica Lewinsky affair; **Sept. 11, 2001** American Airlines Flight 77, Boeing 757, from Dulles Airport to Los Angeles, hijacked in suicide terrorist attack plane deliberately flown into side of Pentagon, Arlington, Virginia, all 64 on board plus four hijackers killed, 125 Pentagon workers killed, coordinated with World Trade Center attack in New York plus foiled airline suicide attack crashed in field near Shanksville, Pennsylvania, attacks linked to terrorist network of Osama bin Laden in Afghanistan; **Sept. 14, 2001** Pres. George W. Bush leads nation in Day of Prayer at National Cathedral three days after terrorist attacks on New York and Washington; **Oct. 7, 2001** U.S. begins air strikes on Taliban forces in Afghanistan for supporting Osama bin Laden's terrorist network, response to terrorist attacks on New York and Washington, fall of Kabul comes on Nov. 12; **Oct. 18, 2001** U.S. Capitol, five other government buildings evacuated after discovery of anthrax spores, Capitol reopens Oct. 23; **Oct. 22, 2001** two employees at Brentwood mail facility in Washington which handles

U.S. government mail die from inhaled anthrax; **Apr. 5, 2002** Pres. George W. Bush signs Born Alive Infants Protection Act stating that every child's life should be protected by law; **Oct. 3, 2002** sixth person killed by "D.C. Sniper," incidents started Montgomery County, Maryland, Sept. 3, two suspects captured Oct. 24 near Frederick, Maryland; **March 2003** Washington Convention Center completed; **March 19, 2003** President Bush authorizes war on Iraq, part of War on Terrorism, Baghdad and brutal regime of Saddam Hussein fall Apr. 9.

Florida

Southeastern U.S. Capital: Tallahassee. Major cities: Miami, Tampa, St. Petersburg, Orlando, and Jacksonville.

The U.S. seized Florida in 1811 and took formal control in 1821. Florida Territory was established March 30, 1822. Florida entered the Union as the 27th state March 3, 1845. It seceded as a Confederate state January 10, 1861, and was readmitted June 25, 1868.

Florida is divided into 67 counties. Municipalities are classified as villages, towns, and cities. In 1968, the city of Jacksonville consolidated with Duval County. Three municipalities opted not to participate in the merger. There are no townships. See Introduction.

Alachua *Alachua County* *Northern Florida, 13 mi/ 21 km northwest of Gainesville*

c.1620 mission village of Santa Fe de Toloca established; **spring 1702** mission church and village burned by Creeks from Georgia, residents escape; **1818** town of Newnansville founded near present town; **1824** Alachua County formed; **1826** town becomes county seat; **1884** Savannah, Florida & Western (Plant System) Railroad built; new town of Alachua founded on railroad as agricultural shipping point and county seat; **1854** county seat moved to Gainesville; **1905** incorporated as a city.

Apalachicola *Franklin County* *Northwestern Florida, 65 mi/105 km southwest of Tallahassee*

1528 Spanish explorer Narvaez camps on shores of Apalachicola Bay, Gulf of Mexico; **1799** English pirate William Bowles rejoins Creek allies here after escaping his Spanish captors at Pensacola; **1822** town founded, originally named West Point; **1829** incorporated as a city; **1831** town renamed for Apalachicola River and Bay; **1832** Franklin County formed; town becomes county seat; **1837** shipping channel dredged in bay; Orman House built; **1839** Lake Wimico & St. Joseph Railroad reaches town; third county courthouse built; Trinity Church built; **1843** nearby town of St. Joseph abandoned during yellow fever epidemic swelling local population with survivors; Raney House, built 1838, moved by barge from St. Joseph; **1848** Cape St. George Lighthouse built, automated 1949; **1850s** oyster industry becomes important; **June 1861** Union ships blockade harbor, land unopposed May 1862.

Arcadia *De Soto County* *South central Florida, 62 mi/100 km southeast of Tampa*

1878 railroad reaches site; town founded, named Tater Hill Bluff; **c.1881** phosphate mining begins; **1883** post office established; renamed for daughter of prominent resident; **1886** incorporated as a city; **1887** De Soto County formed from Manatee County; **1907** Florida Baptist Children's Home established; **1913** county courthouse built; **1916** Arcadia Municipal Tourist Camp organized; **1928** first annual Arcadia All-Florida Rodeo held. **Aug. 13–14, 2004** 1 killed, over 450 injured locally as Hurricane Charley damages nearly every home and business of this historic rural community.

Avon Park *Highlands County* *Central Florida, 65 mi/105 km south of Orlando*

1886 site purchased and developed by O. M. Crosby of Connecticut of Florida Development Company; town named by Crosby for Stratford-on-Avon, England; large citrus groves planted; **1888** Vernon Hotel built, becomes Avon Hotel 1906, destroyed by fire 1927; **1894–1895** hard freeze ruins citrus groves; **c.1910** citrus industry restarted; **1912** Atlantic Coast Line Railroad reaches site, revives town's economy; **1913** incorporated as a city; avocado production begun by Ward Nurseries; **1926** Jacaranda Hotel built; **1965** South Florida Community College established.

Bartow *Polk County* *Central Florida, 36 mi/58 km east of Tampa*

c.1835 Fort Blount built during Seminole Wars; **1851** area settled by farmers; **1861** Polk County formed; **1867** town founded as county seat, named for Confederate Gen. Francis Bartow; **1882** incorporated as a town; **1887** incorporated as a city; **1884** phosphate deposits discovered along Peace River; **1909** third county courthouse built.

Bascom *Jackson County* *See* **Marianna (1941)**

Belle Glade *Palm Beach County* *Southeastern Florida, 70 mi/113 km north-northwest of Miami*

1925 town founded at southeastern end of Lake Okeechobee; **1928** incorporated as a city; **Sept. 16, 1928** hurricane virtually destroys town, inundated by waters of Lake Okeechobee, 1,810 killed in region, town immediately rebuilt; **1929** flood control plan initiated by President Hoover's government; **1932** State Prison Farm No. 2 established.

Blountstown *Calhoun County* *Northwestern Florida, 50 mi/80 km west of Tallahassee*

1823 town founded, named for Seminole chief John Blount; **1824** small Seminole reservation granted to Blount; **1838** Calhoun County formed; town becomes county seat; **1903** incorporated as a city; **1973** county courthouse built.

Boca Raton *Palm Beach County* *Southeastern Florida, 40 mi/64 km north of Miami, on Atlantic Ocean*

1895 first house built by civil engineer Thomas Rickards; **1896** Florida East Coast Railway built by Henry Flagler; **c.1900** town originally founded as agricultural center; **1920s** Addison Mizner acquires 12,000 ac/6,885 ha of land, builds dream city called The Cloisters, opened 1926, later renamed Boca Raton Resort; **1923** first bridge built across Boca Raton Inlet; **1925** incorporated as a city; **1950** Boca Raton Museum of Art founded; **1961** Florida Atlantic University established; **1962** Lynn University established; **1996** International Museum of Cartoon Art opened, closed 2002; **Oct. 5, 2001** man from Lantana dies at home from inhaled anthrax, attack occurred at AMI tabloid offices at Boca Raton [see Lantana].

Bonifay *Holmes County* *Northwestern Florida, 90 mi/145 km west-northwest of Tallahassee*

1848 Holmes County formed; Cerro Gordo becomes county seat, later moved to Pittman's Ferry, later moved to Westville; **1870s** large number of Confederate soldiers settle on Holmes Creek; town founded; **1906** county seat moved from Westville; county courthouse built; **1907** incorporated as a city; **1963** new county courthouse built.

Bradenton *Manatee County* *West central Florida, 20 mi/32 km south of St. Petersburg*

June 1, 1539 De Soto's fleet lands at Shaw's Point with 600 soldiers, 215 cavalry, embarks on mission that would take them to Mississippi River where he would meet his death 1542; **c.1840** area first settled; **1854** Braden Castle plantation house built by Dr. Joseph Braden, estate burned 1903; **1855** Manatee County formed; Pine Level becomes county seat; **1878** town founded, named Bradentown; **1887** De Soto County separates from Manatee County; Manatee County seat moved to Bradentown; **1903** incorporated as a city; **1913** county courthouse built; **1924** city renamed Bradenton; **1957** Manatee Community College established.

Bristol *Liberty County* *Northwestern Florida, 45 mi/72 km west of Tallahassee*

c.1850 town founded as Riddeysville; **1855** Liberty County formed; **1858** town renamed; **Oct. 1865** steamboat *Alice* sinks in Apalachicola River taking with its casks filled with 15,000 gallons/58,781 liters of rum; **1940** county courthouse built; **1958** incorporated as a city.

Bronson *Levy County* *Northern Florida, 23 mi/37 km southwest of Gainesville*

1845 Levy County formed; **c.1850** town founded, originally named Chunky Pond; **1858** Levyville becomes first county seat; **1860** railroad reaches town; **1874** county seat moved from Levyville; **1884** incorporated as a town, renamed for early settler; **1937** fourth county courthouse built.

Brooksville *Hernando County* *West central Florida, 42 mi/68 km north of Tampa*

c.1842 Pierreville founded; **1843** Hernando County formed, named for Hernando de Soto; **1845** town of Melendez founded as county seat 3 mi/4.8 km to north; **1849** Robins House built, home of Col. Raymond Robins; **1856** two towns merge as county seat, renamed for U.S. Cong. Preston Brook of South Carolina; **1880** town incorporated; **1913** third county courthouse built; **1925** incorporated as a city; **1932** Chinsegut Hill Sanctuary established to north.

Bunnell *Flagler County* *Northeastern Florida, 65 mi/105 km south-southeast of Jacksonville*

1880 town founded by Ava A. Bunnell; **1911** incorporated as a city; **1917** Flagler County formed, named for Henry M. Flagler, builder of Florida East Coast Railroad; town becomes county seat; **1924** county courthouse built.

Bushnell *Sumter County* *Central Florida, 55 mi/89 km north-northeast of Tampa*

1539 Hernando de Soto passes through area, progress slowed by water, bogs; **Dec. 28, 1835** Maj. Francis L. Dade and his men slain by Seminoles under chiefs Micanope and Jumper in Dade Massacre, reported by severely wounded Private Ransom Clarke; **1853** Sumter County formed; Adamsville becomes county seat; **1870** town first settled; **1885** railroad built; town founded, named for railroad engineer J. W. Bushnell; county seat moved to Bushnell following several moves; **1913** incorporated as a city; **1914** second county courthouse built; **1935** Dade Memorial State Park established, later Dade Battlefield State Historic Site; **May 26, 1981** unrest at Sumter Correctional Institute, 40 prisoners transferred, eight prisoners, two guards injured; **Jan. 24, 1989** Ted Bundy given electric chair at Florida State Prison for killing three Florida girls, suspected of killing dozens of women 1974–1978 from Oregon to Florida.

Cape Canaveral   *Brevard County   Eastern Florida, 48 mi/77 km east of Orlando, on Atlantic Ocean*

1513 Cape Canaveral first sighted by Ponce de Leon, names it Cape of Currents; **1564** name Canaveral appears on map produced by LeMoyne; **July 1572** Pedro Menendez is shipwrecked here, walks to St. Augustine, reaches town in late fall; **1847** Cape Canaveral Lighthouse built, replaced 1868, moved back from encroaching shore line 1894; **1920s** first developers arrive in area; **1947** U.S. government establishes Cape Canaveral missile launching center; **1955** development of Port Canaveral bulk shipping facility begins, becomes busiest cruise port in Western Hemisphere by 1990s; **Dec. 17, 1957** first Atlas inter-continental ballistic missile successfully test fired; **1958** National Aeronautic and Space Administration (NASA) established; city of Cape Canaveral incorporated south of Space Center to avert annexation by Cocoa Beach; **Jan 31, 1958** Army launches *Explorer I* orbiting satellite; **Dec. 13, 1958** squirrel monkey shot 300 mi/483 km into space by Jupiter missile; **Aug. 12, 1960** *Echo I* communications satellite launched, forerunner of television and radio communications satellites; **May 5, 1961** Alan B. Shepard becomes first American in space, aboard Mercury space capsule; **Feb. 20, 1962** John Glenn orbits earth three times in capsule *Friendship 7*; **July 10, 1962** *Telstar* communications satellite launched into orbit, delivers first transatlantic television relay July 11; **Nov. 30, 1962** geodetic survey satellite launched to make precise measurements of earth's surface; **Dec. 1963** Cape Canaveral renamed Cape Kennedy following assassination of Pres. John F. Kennedy in Dallas; **July 31, 1964** *Ranger 7* yields first close-up photos of moon's surface; **Jan. 27, 1967** astronauts Virgil "Gus" Grissom, Edward White, and Roger Chaffee killed in fire inside space capsule on launch pad; **Aug. 3, 1970** nuclear submarine *James Madison* launches Poseidon missile 30 mi/48 km to east, trailed by Soviets; **Jan. 28, 1986** space shuttle *Challenger* explodes 73 seconds after launch killing all seven astronauts, Francis R. "Dick" Scobee, Michael J. Smith, Judith A. Resnick, Ellison S. Onizuka, Ronald E. McNair, Gregory B. Jarvis, and Christa McAuliffe; **Nov. 7, 1998** John Glenn, 77, completes his second trip into space, becomes oldest astronaut; **Nov. 23, 2002** Disney cruise ship disinfected after 275 passengers become ill with flu-like symptoms, 60 more become ill on following cruise Nov. 26, other cruise lines affected; **Feb. 1, 2003** space shuttle *Columbia* breaks apart over eastern Texas during reentry from space mission 16 minutes prior to scheduled 9:16 a.m. landing, killing all seven astronauts on board: Rick D. Husband, William C. McCool, Michael A. Anderson, David M.

Brown, Laurel Clark, first Indian-born woman in space Kalpana Chawla, and Israeli war hero Ilan Ramon [see also Nacogdoches, Texas].

Cedar Key   *Levy County   Northern Florida, 60 mi/97 km southwest of Gainesville, on Gulf of Mexico*

1500s Spanish establish town on Cedar Key; **1854** Cedar Keys Lighthouse built, discontinued 1915; **1860** Atlantic, Gulf & West Indies Railroad extended across Florida from Fernandina; **Jan. 1861** Union troops arrive on Sea Horse Island, to southwest, aboard gunboat *Hatteras*, destroy property, establish prison; **1869** incorporated as a city; **1880s** sawmills built to convert cedar wood into pencils; **1884** completion of railroad to Tampa diminishes town's role as seaport; **1920s** Cedar Key Museum founded by St. Clair Whitman, becomes state park 1962; **1929** Cedar Keys National Wildlife Refuge established; **1979** Lower Suwanee National Wildlife Refuge established to north.

Chipley   *Washington County   Northwestern Florida, 82 mi/132 km west-northwest of Tallahassee*

1843 Washington County formed, one of original counties at time of statehood 1845; **1882** Pensacola & Western Railroad built through area; town founded on railroad, originally named Orange, renamed for railroad official Col. William D. Chipley; **1885** incorporated as a city; **1927** county seat moved from Vernon; county courthouse built.

Clearwater   *Pinellas County   West central Florida, 18 mi/29 km north-northwest of St. Petersburg*

1835 Fort Harrison established on Gulf of Mexico during Seminole Wars, abandoned 1841; **1888** narrow-gauge railroad reaches site; town founded, named Clear Water Harbor; **1891** incorporated as a town; **1894** Orange Belt Railroad reaches town; **1896** railroad purchased by Henry Plant; Plant builds Belleview Biltmore Hotel; **1906** town renamed Clearwater; **1912** Pinellas County formed; town becomes county seat, builds courthouse in one day, beating St. Petersburg; **1914** Tampa & Gulf Coast Railroad reaches town; **1915** incorporated as a city; **1916** Clearwater (Carnegie) Public Library built; **1918** county courthouse built; **1923** Peace Memorial Church built to commemorate war dead; **1972** Marine Science Center established; **May 4, 1978** tornado hits elementary school, two killed, 96 injured.

Cocoa   *Brevard County   Eastern Florida, 40 mi/64 km east-southeast of Orlando, near Atlantic Ocean*

1868 area's first orange trees begin producing; **1882** town founded on Indian River, lagoon of Atlantic Ocean, named for abundant cocoa plum; **1895** incorporated as a city; **1950** population multiplies with advent of space industry; **1960** Brevard Community College (2-year) established; **March 28, 1981** collapse of condominium

119

under construction kills 11, injures 22 workers at Cocoa Beach.

Coral Gables   *Miami-Dade County*   *Southeastern Florida, suburb 3 mi/4.8 km southwest of Miami*

1925 town founded on Biscayne Bay by George Merrick; **1925** incorporated as a city; Miami-Biltmore Hotel built; University of Miami established; **1932** Tropical Park Race Track established; **1936** Parrot Jungle and Gardens founded by Frank Scherr; **1937** Coral Gables Library and Community House built; **1938** Fairchild Tropical Gardens established; **Jan. 27, 1956** actress Mimi Rogers born; **1996** Biltmore Hotel designated National Historic Landmark.

Crawfordville   *Wakulla County*   *Northwestern Florida, 18 mi/29 km south of Tallahassee*

c.1830 town founded, originally named Shell Point; **1831** post office established; **1843** Wakulla County formed; New Port (Newport) becomes first county seat; **1866** county seat moved from New Port (Newport); **Aug. 31, 1886** mysterious column of smoke dubbed the Wakulla Volcano which had appeared over swamps to the southeast for many years suddenly ends on day of great Charleston, South Carolina, earthquake; **1948** county courthouse built.

Crescent City   *Putnam County*   See **Palatka (2002)**

Crestview   *Okaloosa County*   *Northwestern Florida, 143 mi/230 km west-northwest of Tallahassee*

1870s turpentine industry established; **1883** town founded on Pensacola & Apalachicola Railroad; **1915** Okaloosa County formed; **1917** incorporated as a city, becomes county seat; **1918** county courthouse built, remodeled 1955; **1937** Maxwell Field established, becomes Eglin Air Force Base 1940, largest air force base in world.

Cross City   *Dixie County*   *Northern Florida, 123 mi/198 km north-northwest of Tampa*

1921 Dixie County formed; town founded as county seat; **1924** incorporated as a town; **1965** county courthouse built; **1972** Cross City Correctional Institution for men established, former air force base.

Dade City   *Pasco County*   *West central Florida, 33 mi/53 km northeast of Tampa*

1836 Maj. Francis Dade massacred near here by Seminoles; **1886** town platted by J. A. Hendley, originally named Hatton; **1887** Pasco County formed; town becomes county seat; **1889** incorporated as a city; **1908** Edwinola Hotel built; **1909** county courthouse built; **1961** Pioneer Florida Museum and Village founded; **1981** new county courthouse built; **Jan. 1996** first Kumquat Festival held.

Daytona Beach   *Volusia County*   *Northeastern Florida, 50 mi/80 km north-northeast of Orlando*

1587 Franciscan missionaries from Spain establish missions in area; **1702** the English and their Creek allies descend coast from Georgia, take land from Spanish, destroy missions, kill native Seminoles; **1765** English settlers arrive, establish plantations; **1783** Florida ceded back to Spain; **c.1820** land grants given to American settlers; **1870** resort town founded on Halifax River, tidewater lagoon of Atlantic Ocean, by Mathias Day of Mansfield, Ohio, names town Daytona; **1874** Palmetto House hotel built by Matthias Day; **1876** incorporated as a city; **1887** St. Johns & Halifax River Railroad extending to Daytona from north; **1887** Ponce de Leon Lighthouse built, automated 1953; **1888** Henry Flagler's East Coast Railroad reaches town from St. Augustine; **1902** city's first automobile race held on beach; **1904** Bethune-Cookman College established; **1905** Henry Ford uses long beach to test drive his automobile; **1914** sea wall and esplanade built along Beach Street by Charles C. Bourgoyne; **1924** city annexes part of sand barrier peninsula giving it ocean access; **1927** towns of Halifax River, Seabreeze and Daytona merge with Daytona Beach; St. Paul's Catholic Church built; **March 1935** Sir Malcolm Campbell drives his *Bluebird* car at record 276 mi/444 km per hour; **Feb. 15, 1947** National Association of Stock Car Auto Racing (NASCAR) established; **July 4, 1948** first NASCAR race held; **1958** Daytona Beach Community College established; **1959** Daytona International Speedway opened; **1992** Daytona Beach International Airport opened; **1995** Keiser College, Daytona Beach Campus, (2-year) established; **Feb. 18, 2001** race car driver Dale Earnhardt killed in final lap of Daytona 500 as car crashes into wall.

De Funiak Springs   *Walton County*   *Northwestern Florida, 115 mi/187 km west-northwest of Tallahassee*

1822 area first settled; **1824** Walton County formed; Alaqua becomes county seat, seat later moved to Euchee Anna; **1881** Louisville & Nashville Railroad built; town founded as county seat, named for railroad manager Col. Fred De Funiak; Confederate monument moved with county seat, erected 1871; **1884** Florida Chautauqua society organized; **1904** Carnegie Library built; **1920** Hotel De Funiak built; **1926** county courthouse built; **1921** incorporated as a city.

De Land   *Volusia County*   *Northeastern Florida, 32 mi/51 km north of Orlando*

c.1600 mission and village of Antonico established at Crows Bluff, on St. John's River to west; **1854** Volusia County formed; **1876** town founded by Henry A. DeLand, manufacturer of baking powder; **1882** incorporated as a city; **1886** Lue Gim Gong settles here from China, engages in citrus culture, introduces new orange variety 1886, new grapefruit 1892; **1885** De Land University established, became Stetson University 1889; **1888** county seat moved from Enterprise; **1929** county courthouse built; **Nov. 9, 2000** Volusia County named with Broward and Miami-Dade counties in Al Gore Democratic presidential campaign's request for manual recount of faulty punch card ballots in heavily Democratic counties in effort to overcome George W. Bush's 300-vote lead in Florida; **Dec. 9, 2000** Volusia County vote recount effort halted with U.S. Supreme Court ruling halting all Florida vote recounts.

Dunedin   *Pinellas County   West central Florida, 18 mi/29 km north-northwest of St. Petersburg*

1850s area on Gulf of Mexico first settled; town founded as Jonesboro; **1878** post office established, renamed for Dunedin, Scotland, by Scotsmen J. L. Douglas and James Somerville; **1888** Orange Belt Railroad reaches town; Duke of Sutherland married to Madame Carolina Blair of London in sensational wedding; **1898** incorporated as a town; **1925** incorporated as a city; **1972** A. C. Nielsen Company founded, developed Nielsen Rating System for television.

Eatonville   *Orange County   East central Florida, suburb 3 mi/4.8 km north of Orlando*

c.1880 freed blacks begin settling here; **1886** town founded by African-American orange grove workers persuaded to relocate from Maitland to east; town named for Capt. Josiah Eaton, one of founders of Maitland; Hungerford Normal and Industrial School for black students established; **1887** incorporated as a town; **Jan. 7, 1903** author Zora Neale Hurston born, wrote about black woman passing for a white woman (died 1960).

Fernandina Beach   *Nassau County   Northeastern Florida, 25 mi/40 km northeast of Jacksonville*

c.1000 AD Timucuan mound builders settle in area, name it Napoyca; **1562** French Huguenot Jean Ribault becomes first European visitor; **1573** Spanish Franciscans establish Santa Maria Mission, abandoned 1702; **c.1686** Spanish settlement founded on Santa Maria Island, on Atlantic Ocean, at mouth of St. Mary's River; **Sept. 1702** island and post captured for English by South Carolina Gov. James Moore; **1735** post reestablished by Gen. James Oglethorpe, later governor of Georgia; **1739** War of Jenkins Ear between English and Spanish relinquishes island to Spanish by 1748 treaty; **1775** British fort built at start of Revolutionary War; **1783** with return of Florida to Spain, large land grant made to Don Domingo Fernandez; village of Fernandina founded, named for Fernandez; **c.1785** Fort San Carlos built; **1807** island becomes refuge for pirates raiding U.S. coast; **March 1812** in Patriots' Rebellion, force of 200 men under U.S. Gen. George Matthews takes Spanish fort and settlement, establishes "Republic of Florida"; **Dec. 1817** following year of various rebellions and takeovers, U.S. Capt. J. E. Henry arrives in ship *John Adams*, assumes control of fort with no resistance; **1821** Florida ceded to U.S.; **1824** Nassau County formed; Nassauville becomes county seat; incorporated as a town; **1847** construction of Fort Clinch

begins; **1858** St. Peter's Mission established; **1861** Florida Railroad establishes eastern terminus here; county seat moved from Nassauville; Fort Clinch completed; fort seized by Confederates, abandoned March 1862 with approach of Union fleet; **1878** yellow fever epidemic takes numerous lives; **1888** yellow fever outbreak kills 52; **1891** county courthouse completed; **1898** Fort Clinch regarrisoned during Spanish-American War; **c.1905** shipping diverted to Jacksonville, other ports with building of railroad lines; **1921** incorporated as a city; **1913** shrimp fishing begun by Capt. Billy Corkum; **1938** pulp mills built.

Florida City   *Miami-Dade County   Southeastern Florida, 30 mi/48 km southwest of Miami*

1912 Florida East Coast Railroad to Key West opened; town founded near Atlantic Ocean as agricultural center, originally named Detroit; **1915** incorporated as a city, renamed Florida City; **1915** Royal Palm State Park established to west, forerunner of Everglades National Park; **1923** Dixie Highway reaches town; **May 30, 1934** Everglades National Park established to west; **Sept. 2, 1935** hurricane destroys sections of Florida East Coast Railroad and Overseas Highway under construction to Key West; **1938** Overseas Highway completed using abandoned railroad causeway; **1964** Florida City Speedway opened, closed 1976; **Aug. 24, 1992** Hurricane Andrew destroys city.

Fort Lauderdale   *Broward County   Southeastern Florida, 25 mi/40 km north of Miami, on Atlantic Ocean*

May 25-30, 1765 hurricane creates new inlet of New River on Atlantic Ocean; **1838** New River Fort (Fort Lauderdale) built during Seminole War by Maj. William Lauderdale; **1842** member of Mikasuki tribe who was friendly toward whites is bound to tree by tribesmen at Colee Hammock, forced to witness massacre of friends, parts of his ears cropped off; **1888** U.S. Coast Guard base established; **1893** Hotel Amphitrite built as part of federal government coastal defense monitoring system, later converted to floating night club; **1896** Florida East Coast Railroad built; **1911** incorporated as a city; **1915** Broward County formed; city becomes county seat; **1926** Port Everglades created as one of Florida's leading port facilities; **1928** county courthouse built, replaced 1960 by county government center; **1935** hurricane strikes area, forces *Amphitrite* floating night club onto beach, converted into hotel 1936; city becomes south terminus of Florida East Coast Railroad with washing away of link to Key West by hurricane; car ferry service begun to Havana, Cuba; **1950** War Memorial Auditorium opened; **Dec. 24, 1954** woman tennis player Chris Evert born; **1958** Museum of Art opened, replaced by new facility 1985; **1960** Broward Community College established; **1964** Nova Southeastern University established; **1965** Hall of Fame Aquatic Complex opened; **1968** Art Institute of Fort Lauderdale (2-year college) established; **1977** Keiser College, Fort Lauderdale Campus (2-year) established;

1998 Florida Panthers NHL hockey team moves from Miami to Sunrise, Fort Lauderdale suburb to west; Museum of Discovery and Science opened; **Nov. 13, 2000** Broward County joins Volusia and Miami-Dade counties in manual Presidential Election recount of faulty punch card ballots at request of Al Gore campaign in attempt to overcome 300-vote Florida lead of George W. Bush; **Dec. 9, 2000** Broward County vote recount stops with U.S. Supreme Court ruling halt to all Florida manual vote recounts.

Fort Myers *Lee County Southwestern Florida, 93 mi/150 km south-southeast of St. Petersburg*

1839 fort built here by Federal troops as defense against Seminoles, later named Fort Myers for Col. Abraham C. Myers, chief quartermaster in Florida; c.1840 town settled around fort; 1865 fort abandoned; c.1870 area begins to develop as sport fishing center; 1876 town platted; 1885 incorporated as a town; Thomas Edison's winter home built, considered first prefab home, pieces made in Fairfield, Maine, shipped to Fort Myers; 1887 Lee County formed; town becomes county seat; 1900 Fort Myers Public Library founded, opened 1906; 1904 Coast Railroad reaches town, terminus formed at dock facility; 1906 Cross-State Canal begun from West Palm Beach with Fort Myers as western terminus, halted 1974 by President Carter; 1907 city's royal palms transplanted from Royal Palm Park Hammock in Everglades; 1911 incorporated as a city; 1915 county courthouse built; 1927 Pleasure Pier built; 1931 Edison Memorial Bridge dedicated on Caloosahatchee River; 1937 Page Field airport opened; 1962 Edison Community College established; 1991 Florida Gulf Coast University established; **Jan. 1, 2001** ferry service begins to Key West. **Aug. 13–14, 2004** Hurricane Charley makes landfall at nearby Sanibel Island, packing winds of 145 mph/233 kph, with ocean storm surge of 13–15 ft/4–4.6 m, continues north toward Orlando, at least 19 killed.

Fort Pierce *Saint Lucie County Eastern Florida, 115 mi/185 km north of Miami, on Atlantic Ocean*

1838 Fort Pierce built as defense against Native Americans; 1860s town settled around fort on Indian River, lagoon of Atlantic Ocean, adjacent to Fort Pierce (St. Lucie) Inlet, entrance to lagoon; 1901 incorporated as a city; 1905 St. Lucie County formed; city becomes county seat; 1954 St. Lucie County Public Library founded; 1960 Indian River Community College established; 1962 second county courthouse built; 1968 St. Lucie Historical Museum opened.

Gainesville *Alachua County Northern Florida, 62 mi/100 km southwest of Jacksonville*

1539 Hernando De Soto visits area; 1824 Alachua County formed; 1826 Newnansville becomes county seat; 1830 village of Hog Town founded around trading post; 1853 town renamed for Gen. Edmund P. Gaines, Seminole War hero; 1854 county seat moved to Gainesville; Seaboard Air Line Railroad reaches town; 1867 state seminary established; 1869 incorporated as a city; 1903 Florida State Agricultural College moved from Lake City, closed 1905; 1906 University of Florida moved from Ocala, founded 1853 as East Florida Seminary; 1917 Florida State Museum founded, becomes Florida Museum of Natural History 1988; 1925 tung oil production begins with introduction of first tung tree groves from China; **Oct. 20, 1953** rock singer Tom Petty born; **March 3, 1964** South Central Airlines plane crashes on takeoff, killing ten; 1966 Santa Fe Community College established; 1975 county courthouse built.

Green Cove Springs *Clay County Northeastern Florida, 25 mi/40 km south of Jacksonville*

1737 Fort St. Francis de Pupa built by Spanish, destroyed 1740 by Georgia Gov. James Oglethorpe fighting for British; 1816 sawmill built; 1830 area on St. John's River first settled; 1854 town founded around mineral springs, originally named White Sulphur Springs; 1858 Clay County formed; 1866 town renamed Green Cove Springs; 1870s popular spa established, continues through 1880s; 1874 incorporated as a city; 1880s Magnolia Springs developed as spa, hotel destroyed by fire 1920; 1889 county courthouse built; 1895 hard freeze destroys citrus groves; 1927 merchant J. C. Penney founds Penney Farms Memorial Home Community for retired religious leaders; 1940 Benjamin Lee Field airport built by U.S. Navy, closed 1961; 1945 13 boat piers built for U.S. Navy's mothball fleet.

Hialeah *Miami-Dade County Southeastern Florida, suburb 5 mi/8 km northwest of Miami*

1921 town founded by Missouri rancher James H. Bright and aviator Glenn Curtiss; 1925 incorporated as a city; 1926 hurricane damages community; 1931 Hialeah Race Track built; **June 1. 1937** Amelia Earhart departs U.S from Miami Airport on her ill-fated flight around the world; 1982 Florida National College (2-year) established.

Hollywood *Broward County Southeastern Florida, 16 mi/26 km north of Miami, on Atlantic Ocean*

1921 resort city founded and platted by Joseph W. Young and his associates from California; 1925 incorporated as a city; 1926 Hollywood Beach Hotel opened; **Sept. 18, 1926** hurricane destroys city, 37 killed; population plummets to 2,500 from c.18,000 with evacuations; **Feb. 1928** Young builds deepwater Port Everglades for sailing ships; 1930 Hollywood Hills Inn built, converted to Riverside Military Academy 1932, founded 1907; 1935 first Fiesta Tropicale held; **July 25, 1981** Adam Walsh, 6, kidnapped, severed head found two weeks later, body never located, unsolved crime leads to creation of crime solving television show *America's Most Wanted* by boy's father John Walsh.

Homestead *Miami-Dade County* *Southeastern*
Florida, 28 mi/45 km southwest of Miami

1904 Florida East Coast Railroad reaches town; town founded near Atlantic Ocean as agricultural trading center; **1912** Johnston Palm Lodge estate built by Col. H. W. Johnston, merchant from Lebanon, Kentucky; **1913** incorporated as a city; **1923** Coral Castle begun by heartbroken Ed Leedskalnin whose 16-year-old fiancee left him on wedding day, took 20 years to complete; **1942** Homestead Air Force Base founded, closed 1993; **Dec. 6, 1947** Everglades National Park dedicated to west; **Oct. 18, 1968** Biscayne National Monument authorized in Biscayne Bay to east, redesignated Biscayne National Park June 28, 1980; **Aug. 24, 1992** Hurricane Andrew destroys entire city, total 14 killed, Homestead Air Force Base damaged beyond repair.

Inverness *Citrus County* *West central Florida,*
60 mi/97 km north of Tampa

1868 area first settled by A. D. Tompkins; **1887** Citrus County formed; Mannfield becomes first county seat; **c.1890** town founded on Lake Tsala Apopka; **1892** county seat moved to Inverness; **1912** second county courthouse built; **1907** Crown Hotel built; **1914** Public Library founded; **1919** incorporated as a city.

Islamorada *Monroe County* *Southern Florida,*
65 mi/105 km south-southwest of Miami, in Florida Keys

1835 Dr. Henry Perrine conducts experiments on subtropical vegetation at nearby Indian Key, chosen to avoid Native American threat of mainland Florida; **1840** Perrine, several neighbors killed in Native American raid, wife, daughter, and son escape; **1916** town founded on Upper Matecumbe Key as rail stop; **Sept. 2, 1935** hurricane strikes Florida Keys, relief train, backed into Islamorada to rescue World War I veterans hired to build final link in Overseas Highway, is swept away leaving only locomotive, c.800 killed, most of them workers at their camps; **1939** act passed prohibiting hunting of Key deer, estimated to number only 50; **1946** Theater of the Sea established; **1997** incorporated as a village.

Jacksonville *Duval County* *Northeastern Florida,*
on St. Johns River near its entrance to Atlantic Ocean

1564-1565 Fort Caroline built on St. Johns River to protect France's short-lived Huguenot colony; **1567** Spanish build blockhouse on Fort George Island; **1740** Spanish build Fort St. Nicholas; **1765** Kings Road built from Georgia to St. Augustine; **1790** settlement established at cow ford in road on St. Johns River, originally named Cowford; **1812** Patriots of Florida burn Fort St. Nicholas during actions against St. Augustine; **1816** Lewis Zachariah Hogans receives land grant from Spanish, builds cabin; **1817** land grant made to Zephaniah Kingsley, establishing Kingsley Plantation; **1818** rowboat ferry established on St. Johns River by John Brady; **1822** Duval County formed; town founded as county seat by

Isaiah Hart, named for Gen. Andrew Jackson; **1832** incorporated as a city, repealed 1840; **1835** Seminole War brings setback to city's development; short-lived *Courier* established as city's first newspaper; hard freeze kills citrus groves; **1840s** steamship service inaugurated to Charleston and Savannah; **1851** city reincorporated; **1863** after periodic occupation, Federal troops withdraw from city, leaving buildings, streets, dock facilities destroyed; **1869** St. James Hotel opens; **June 17, 1871** African-American author, poet James Weldon Johnson born (1938); **1883** *Union* newspaper (founded 1864) and *Times* (1881) merge to form *Florida Times-Union*; railroad extended south from city; **1887** *Jacksonville Journal* newspaper founded as the *Metropolis*; **1888** yellow fever epidemic devastates region; **1890** railroad bridge built on St. Johns River; **1892** Florida Baptist Academy founded, moves to St. Augustine 1917, becomes Florida Normal and Industrial Institute; **1898** harbor mined by U.S. troops to prevent arms smuggling by resident Cubans to homeland during Spanish-American War; **1901** city fire destroys over 2,300 buildings, over 10,000 left homeless, city rebuilds within decade; **1903** Bethel Baptist Church built; **1905** Jacksonville Public Library built; **July 9, 1911** theoretical physicist John Archibald Wheeler born; **1914** Jacksonville Zoological Gardens opened; **1915** Municipal Docks and Terminals established; **July 20, 1922** Alan S. Boyd born, secretary of transportation under President Eisenhower (died 1967); **1923** Paxon Air Field founded, becomes Jacksonville International Airport 1968; **1925** Riverside Baptist Church built; **1934** Jacksonville University established; **June 1, 1934** singer Pat Boone born; **1939** Jacksonville Naval Air Station established; **1946** Municipal Stadium built, renamed Alltell Stadium 1995; **1948** Jacksonville Museum of Modern Art founded; **Sept. 21, 1950** Fort Caroline National Memorial authorized, located to east; **1958** fourth county courthouse built; **June 8, 1959** 3,000 letters carried 100 miles by guided missile from submarine *Barbero* to auxiliary base in a type of experimental air mail; **1961** Cummer Gallery of Art opened; **1963** Florida Community College of Jacksonville established; **Dec. 29, 1963** fire at Roosevelt Hotel, 21 deaths; **Sept. 8-9, 1964** flooding and damage from Hurricane Dora in Jacksonville, St. Augustine, and Brunswick, Georgia; **1965** University of North Florida established; **Oct. 1, 1968** Jacksonville consolidates with Duval County, with three municipalities (Atlantic Beach, Jacksonville Beach, Neptune Beach) opting to remain separately incorporated; **1975** 37-story Independent Life Building (Modis Tower) built; **1990** 42-story Bank of America's Barnett Center built; **1995** Jacksonville Jaguars NFL football team launches first season.

Jasper *Hamilton County* *Northern Florida, 80 mi/*
129 km west-northwest of Jacksonville

1827 Hamilton County formed; Micco becomes first county seat, seat moved to Wallburg (site unknown) 1836; **1830** trading post established; town founded by settlers from South Carolina and Georgia; **1838** county seat moved to Jasper; **Dec. 12, 1897** writer, advocate of racial equality Lillian Smith born (died 1966); **1907** incorporated as a city; **1932** county courthouse built; **1936** Community Center built with WPA assistance.

Jay *Santa Rosa County* *See* **Milton (1967)**

Jupiter *Palm Beach County* *Southeastern Florida, 80 mi/129 km north of Miami, on Atlantic Ocean*

1763 English apply name Jupiter for Jobe Tribe, sounded like Roman god Jove (Jupiter); **1838** Fort Jupiter built by settlers on Jupiter Inlet, estuary of Atlantic Ocean, abandoned c.1842; town founded; **July 10, 1859** Jupiter Lighthouse first lighted, construction begun 1855, automated 1928; **c.1889** Celestial Railroad built, narrow-gauge 8-mi/12.9-km line named for its connection to settlements of Neptune, Mars, Venus, and Juno; **1925** incorporated as a city.

Key Biscayne *Miami-Dade County*
Southeastern Florida, 8 mi/12.9 km south-southeast of Miami

1513 island discovered by Ponce de Leon; **1825** Cape Florida Lighthouse built, deactivated 1836, reactivated 1978; **1839** town founded and platted; **1950s** Stiltsville established in shallow waters when squatters build dwellings using sunken barges as foundations, as many as 27 structures built; **1991** incorporated as a village; **Oct. 31, 2002** 187 Haitian refugees scramble to shore from small ship, some seek rides on Rickenbacker Causeway, most captured.

Key Largo *Monroe County* *Southern Florida, 50 mi/80 km south-southwest of Miami*

1718 pirates Black Caesar captured, Blackbeard (Edward Teach) shot and killed as their ship *Queen Anne's Revenge* is attacked by Lt. Robert Maynard on Key Largo island; **1912** Florida East Coast Railroad opened to Florida Keys; resort community founded; **1928** Dixie Highway extended to Key West; **Sept. 2, 1935** hurricane destroys railroad and highway extensions, killing hundreds; **1938** Overseas Highway opened to Key West on abandoned railroad causeway.

Key West *Monroe County* *Southern Florida, 135 mi/217 km southwest of Miami, in Gulf of Mexico*

1513 Key West island probably sighted by Ponce de Leon after his landing at St. Augustine; island originally called Cayo Hueso (Island of Bones) for human remains found here; **1750s** island occupied by bands of pirates, abandoned 1763 with British takeover; **1815** island granted to Juan Pablo Salas; **1823** island purchased from Salas by American John Simonton; U.S. government sends fleet to Key West under Commodore David Porter; **1824** Monroe County formed; town becomes county seat; **1825** Key West's first lighthouse built, washed away in 1846 storm, rebuilt; **1828** incorporated as a town; U.S. Superior Court established to oversee regulation of shipping; **1829** town

platted; **1832** incorporated as a city; **1844** construction begins on Fort Taylor, completed 1846; U.S. Naval Station established, closed 1865, reestablished 1944; **1846** U.S. Naval Hospital established; **1849** Confederate shipbuilder Asa Tift builds house, later occupied by author Ernest Hemingway (1899–1961); **1851** construction begins on Fort Jefferson in Dry Tortugas to west, completed 1866; **1860s** cigar factories established by Cubans; **1861** Fort Martello built by U.S. Army Coast Defense; **1865** Dr. Samuel Mudd imprisoned for life at Fort Jefferson for setting broken leg of Lincoln assassin John Wilkes Booth at his office in Beantown, Maryland, found guilty of complicity, pardoned by Pres. Andrew Johnson 1869; **1870** town becomes world's largest cigar manufacturer; **Apr. 1, 1886** fire destroys half of city; **1890** county courthouse built; **May 30, 1902** actor Stepin Fetchit (Lincoln Perry) born (died 1985); **1905** Henry M. Flagler begins extension of Florida East Coast Railroad through Florida Keys, first section opened Jan. 1912; **1915** car ferry service to Havana, Cuba, initiated as extension of railroad; **1916** Florida Keys railroad extension completed; **1924** San Carlos Institute established for Cuban community by Jose Marti, closed 1973; **1927** Pan American Airlines starts as mail route between Key West and Havana, Cuba; Key West Airport opened, became Key West International Airport 1957; **1928** Dixie Highway extended from Florida City parallel to railroad with exception of 40 mi/64 km gap served by ferry; **1933** World War I veterans employed to bridge water gap creating Overseas Highway; **1934** Key West Aquarium opened; **Jan. 4, 1935** Fort Jefferson National Monument proclaimed; **Sept. 2, 1935** as many as 800 veterans employed on Overseas Highway construction killed as hurricane sweeps through Florida Keys, work train had backed into work site from Miami, cars swept into sea, only engine remains on track; **July 1, 1938** Overseas Highway is opened connecting Florida Keys with mainland using former railroad causeway; **1954** Overseas Highway becomes toll free; **Feb. 21, 1963** Cuban MIGs fire on U.S. shrimp boat with engine trouble, no casualties; **Feb. 2, 1964** U.S. seizes 38 Cuban fishermen on four trawlers; **1965** Florida Keys Community College established; **Sept. 25, 1998** Hurricane Georges (HOR-hay) hits Florida Keys with 105 mi/169 km per hour winds, moves on to Biloxi; **Jan. 1, 2002** ferry service begins to Fort Myers and Naples.

Kissimmee *Osceola County* *East central Florida, 18 mi/29 km south of Orlando*

1813 first land grants made to settlers by Spanish for cattle raising; **1881** railroad extended from Orlando; town of Allendale founded; drainage and dredging projects built by Samuel Disston make sugar cane plantations possible; **1883** incorporated as a city, renamed Kissimmee (kis-SIM-mee); **1887** Osceola County formed; city becomes county seat; **1890** county courthouse built; **1940s** Kissimmee Airport established.

La Belle *Hendry County* *Southern Florida,
103 mi/166 km northwest of Miami*

1870 herds of cattle driven to area by Capt. Francis A.
Hendry; **1913** incorporated as a city; **1921** Hendry County
formed; town founded as county seat; **1926** county
courthouse built.

Lake Butler *Union County* *Northern Florida,
55 mi/89 km southwest of Jacksonville*

1832 Bradford County formed; town founded as county
seat, named for Col. Robert Butler, who received East
Florida on behalf of U.S. on its cession July 10, 1821; **1893**
incorporated as a city; **1902** county seat moved to Starke;
1921 Union County formed from Bradford County; town
becomes county seat; **1936** county courthouse built.

Lake City *Columbia County* *Northern Florida,
60 mi/97 km west of Jacksonville*

1832 Columbia County formed; town founded as county
seat, named Alligator for Seminole chief of that name;
Dec. 28, 1835 Dade Massacre led by Chief Halpatter
Tustenuggee (Alligator), only three of 108 soldiers under
Maj. Francis L. Dade survive; **1859** incorporated as a
town, renamed Lake City; **1888** Florida State Agricultural
College established, moved to Gainesville 1903, closed
1905; **1905** fifth county courthouse built; **1920** Veterans'
Home and Hospital established; **1921** incorporated as a
city; **1950** Stephen Foster State Folk Culture Center
established at White Springs to northwest, first Florida
Folk Festival held 1953; **1962** Lake City Community
College established.

Lakeland *Polk County* *Central Florida, 30 mi/
48 km east of Tampa*

1884 South Florida Railroad built; town founded on
railroad at center of Florida's lake district; town of Acton
founded 2 mi/3.2 km to east by group of Englishmen; **1885**
incorporated as a city; Florida Southern College established; **1894** hard freeze damages citrus crops; Acton
annexed by Lakeland; **Apr. 4, 1913** actress Frances
Langford born; **1935** Southeastern College of the
Assemblies of God established. **Aug. 14, 2004** *Florida
Citrus Mutual* reports about 35% of Florida's citrus
groves destroyed by Hurricane Charley, with most
damage in Hardee, De Soto and Lee counties to the south.

Lantana *Palm Beach County* *Southeastern
Florida, 58 mi/93 km north of Miami, near Atlantic Ocean*

1888 Morris B. Lyman becomes first settler, establishes
trading post on Lake Worth, lagoon of Atlantic Ocean;
1921 incorporated as a town; **Oct. 5, 2001** man, 63, dies of
inhaled anthrax, worked at tabloid press in Boca Raton,
one mile from flight school where suicide hijacker
Mohamed Atta trained in preparation for Sept. 11 suicide
attacks, followed by other anthrax attacks by delivered
mail in District of Columbia, Maryland, New Jersey, New
York, Connecticut.

Largo *Pinellas County* *West central Florida, 12 mi/
19 km northwest of St. Petersburg*

1823 Count Odet Phillippe becomes first settler on Pinellas
Peninsula; **1853** town founded on Gulf of Mexico; **1888**
Orange Belt Railroad reaches town; **1905** incorporated as
a city; **1930s** Lake Largo filled in for development; **March
29, 1953** nursing home fire kills 35.

Live Oak *Suwannee County* *Northern Florida,
80 mi/129 km east of Tallahassee*

c.1850 tobacco growing in northern Florida becomes
profitable; **1858** Suwannee County formed; **1860** railroad
reaches area; town founded; **1868** town becomes permanent county seat; **1873** Florida Memorial College established; **1878** incorporated as a city; **1885** forested lands
opened to homesteading; **1904** county courthouse built.

Macclenny *Baker County* *Northeastern Florida,
28 mi/45 km west of Jacksonville*

1861 Baker County formed, named for Judge James
McNair Baker; Sanderson becomes first county seat; **1829**
first settlers arrive; **1886** town founded as new county seat;
1890 post office established; **1903** incorporated as a city;
1911 County Jail built, converted to Historical Society
Museum 2002; **1948** county courthouse built.

Madison *Madison County* *Northern Florida,
52 mi/84 km east of Tallahassee*

1827 Madison County formed; San Pedro becomes county
seat; **1835** blockhouse built as defense against Seminoles;
1838 area first settled by cotton planters from South
Carolina; town founded as new county seat, named
Newton; **1843** Episcopal Church built; **1869** town incorporated; **1870s** cotton production begins in area; **1913**
county courthouse built; **1930s** Cherry Lake Farms
housing development built to north by U.S.
Resettlement Administration.

Maitland *Orange County* *East central Florida,
suburb 5 mi/8 km north of Orlando*

1838 Fort Maitland built, named for Capt. William S.
Maitland; **1873** area settled by group of Union veterans
led by George H. Packwood; **c.1875** first orange groves
begin production; **1885** incorporated as a city with aid of
African-American orange grove workers coerced to
register to vote specifically for this purpose, who then
settle here and run for office; **1886** black residents
persuaded to move to new town of Eatonville to west;
1895 hard freeze ruins local citrus industry; **1929–1930**
town becomes center of campaign aimed at ridding
Florida of destructive fruit fly.

Marianna *Jackson County* *Northwestern Florida,
65 mi/105 km west-northwest of Tallahassee*

1818 Andrew Jackson leads his troops across natural
bridge over Chipola River unaware of Native American

he was seeking hiding in caverns below ground; **1822** Jackson County formed; **1827** town founded on Chipola River by Robert Beveridge of Scotland, named Webbville; **1829** new town founded 9 mi/14.5 km to northeast as county seat, named for daughters Mary and Anna of local merchant; **1835** Nichols Inn built; **1851** incorporated as a city; **Sept. 27, 1864** Marianna Home Guards attacked by Union troops killing or wounding 60 guardsmen, 100 taken prisoner; **1866** Freedman's Bureau established to supervise contracted work among freed slaves; **1906** county courthouse built; **Jan. 14, 1941** actress Faye Dunaway born at rural Bascom to northeast; **Jan. 18, 1942** singer Bobby Goldsboro born; **1947** Chipola Junior College established; **1990** Apolachee Correctional Institute for men established to east.

Mayo *Lafayette County* *Northern Florida, 70 mi/ 113 km east-southeast of Tallahassee*

1856 Lafayette County formed; New Troy becomes first county seat; **1893** town founded as new county seat; **1903** incorporated as a town; **1908** county courthouse built.

Melbourne *Brevard County* *Eastern Florida, 57 mi/92 km southeast of Orlando, on Atlantic Ocean*

c.1880 resort town founded on Indian River, lagoon paralleling Atlantic Ocean; town named by prominent resident Cornthwaite John Hector from Melbourne, Australia; **1888** incorporated as a village; **1919** fire destroys downtown; **1921** Melbourne Causeway built to Melbourne Beach on barrier island, replacing ferry; **Nov. 1924** John Ashley and his gang members are killed in gun battle with sheriff's deputies at Sebastian River Bridge to south ending 14-year bank-robbing career; **1958** Florida Institute of Technology established; **1969** incorporated as a city; town of Eau Gallee annexed; **1989** Keiser College, Melbourne Campus (2-year) established.

Miami *Miami-Dade County* *Southeastern Florida, on Atlantic Ocean*

1836 Fort Dallas built as defense during Seminole War; Dade County formed; Indian Key becomes first county seat; **1844** county seat moved to Miami; **1870** William Brickell among first settlers; town founded, named Miami, Seminole word for "sweet water"; **1889** county seat moved from Miami to Juno; **c.1890** Bahamians settle in Coconut Grove district south of downtown; **1891** Coconut Grove Club founded by Flora McFarlane; **1895** settlement consists of three houses, including that of millionaire developer Henry M. Flagler, who, following two hard freezes in 1894 and 1895 that devastated citrus crop, went to site of downtown Miami to plant citrus trees on property owned by Julia Tuttle; **1896** incorporated as a city; Henry M. Flagler extends his East Coast Railroad to town, making it southern terminus; first hotel, the Royal Palm, built by Flagler; **1899** county seat moved back to Miami from Juno; **1900** First Presbyterian Church completed; **Dec. 1, 1910** *Miami Herald* newspaper founded; **1912** Miami Municipal Airport built; **1916**

James Deering Estate completed; Vizcaya Art Museum founded; **1920s** Florida land boom swells population; **1924** Bayfront Park created from reclaimed land; **Feb. 20, 1924** actor Sidney Poitier born here of Bahamian parentage; **July 19, 1924** actor Pat Hingle born; **1926** Seaboard Air Line railroad reaches Miami across state; old Danish barkentine *Prinz Valdemar* beached by hurricane, converted into 100-room hotel, refitted 1927 into Miami Aquarium; Coconut Grove Playhouse built, originally movie theater; **1929** 27-story county courthouse complex completed; **1928** Pan American Airways Base built on Dinner Key; **Feb. 15, 1933** president-elect Franklin D. Roosevelt shot at by Joseph Zangara, gun deflected by woman, killing Chicago Mayor Anton Cermak; **Oct. 12, 1935** singer Sam Moore of duo Sam and Dave born; **Dec. 1937** Orange Bowl stadium opened; **June 1, 1937** Amelia Earhart and Capt. Frederick Noonan depart from Miami Airport on round-the-world flight, become lost over Pacific Ocean following final radio message July 2; **July 16, 1938** Janet Reno born, Attorney General under President Clinton; **Dec. 22, 1944** National League baseball pitcher Steve Carlton born; **July 1, 1946** singer Debbie Harry born; **Oct. 10, 1946** comedian Ben Vereen born; **July 16, 1953** actor Mickey Rourke born; **Sept. 1955** Seaquarium opened; **1957** Flagler Dog Track opened; **1960** Miami-Dade Community College established; **1961** St. Thomas Aquinas University established; **Feb. 12, 1963** Chicago-bound Northwest Orient 720B airplane crashes in Everglades 45 mi. to west, killing all 43 on board; **Aug. 28, 1964** Hurricane Cleo causes $200 million in damage after striking Haiti, breaks apart Aug. 29 on Florida coast; **1965** Florida International University established; **1966** Miami Dolphins NFL football team begins inaugural season; **1968** Florida Memorial College moved from St. Augustine, established 1879; **June 23, 1969** DC-4 airplane crashes into street, four on board and six on ground killed; **Nov. 7, 1972** Meyer Lansky arraigned for gambling, tax evasion after seeking asylum in Israel, other countries; **Dec. 3, 1972** Eastern Airlines Lockheed Tristar airplane crashes into Everglades on approach to Miami International Airport killing 101; **June 7, 1977** antihomosexual campaign with Anita Bryant as spokesperson leads to defeat of rights law, protests against defeat follow June 26; **Nov. 19, 1980** first planeload of 120 refugees arrive from Havana, first of 600 left stranded since cease of Mariel boatlift by Fidel Castro in Sept.; **May 11, 1981** reggae icon Bob Marley dies of cancer; **June 5, 1981** deportation hearings on some 6,000 Haitian refugees ordered by U.S. Justice Department; **Aug. 17, 1981** hearings begin for 1,800 Cuban refugees from 1980 freedom flotillas considered unsuitable for granting asylum; **1983** 55-story First Union Financial Center completed; **1984** Metrorail light rail system opened; **1986** downtown Metromover pedestrian service opened; **1987** Joe Robbie Stadium opened, home of Miami Dolphins football team and later Florida Marlins baseball team, renamed Pro Player Stadium 1998; **1988** Miami Heat NBA basketball team begins inaugural season; **Aug. 24–25, 1992** Hurricane Andrew ravages south Miami and neighboring Homestead, 14 killed; **1993** Florida Panthers hockey team begins first season; Florida Marlins National League baseball team begins inaugural season; **Aug. 5, 1994** President Clinton begins intercepting boatloads of Cuban refugees, putting them in holding camps at Guantanamo Bay, other remote localities; **May 11, 1996** crash of 27-year-old ValuJet (now AirTran) DC-9 in Everglades, all 110 on board killed, airline accused of cost-cutting maintenance for lower fares, final blame leads to oxygen generators mislabeled empty; **1997** Dade County renamed Miami-Dade; 51-story Santa Maria Building completed; **1998** Florida Panthers NHL hockey team moves to Fort Lauderdale suburb of Sunrise; **Nov. 25, 1999** six-year-old Elian Gonzalez flees from Cuba, found by two fishermen floating off coast, mother drowned; **Apr. 22, 2000** INS agents raid home of Elian Gonzalez' relatives, Elian returned to father Juan Gonzalez waiting in Washington, 300 protestors in Miami arrested; **July 14, 2000** grand jury assesses fine of $145 billion against tobacco industry for misleading consumers on health risks of smoking, Philip Morris bears one-third of assessment, industry appeals decision; **Nov. 9, 2000** Vice Pres. Al Gore demands manual vote recount in Miami-Dade, Broward, and Volusia counties, all heavily Democratic, claiming faulty punch card voting system with dimpled or hanging chads, paper remnants in punch card supposedly showing voter's intent; **Nov. 14, 2000** Miami-Dade officials suspend manual vote recount, minor changes encountered in sample count; **2001** 46-story Three Tequesta Point building completed; **Sept. 7, 2001** 13 Miami police officers accused of cover-ups in three shootings by SWAT teams; **Dec. 12, 2001** Richard C. Reid (Tariq Raja) detained after attempt to blow up American Air Boeing 767 flight from Europe with 197 people on board by activating explosive device in his shoe, British subject linked to Al-Qaeda terrorist network; **2002** 64-story Four Seasons Hotel completed.

Miami Beach   *Miami-Dade County*
Southeastern Florida, 3 mi/4.8 km east of Miami, on Atlantic Ocean

1910s John S. Collins of New Jersey develops sand barrier between Biscayne Bay and Atlantic Ocean through loan from Indianapolis investor Carl F. Fisher; **1913** wooden bridge built to Miami Beach; **1915** incorporated as a city; **1928** gangster Al Capone purchases house, lives here until sentenced to prison for tax violations May 1932; **1957** Miami Beach Convention Center opened; **July 15, 1997** fashion designer Gianni Versace shot to death in front of home, intense search for suspect Andrew Cunanan ends with his suicide on houseboat which he broke into July 23; **2002** 48-story White Diamond Tower built, tallest unit in Diamond Tower complex.

Milton   *Santa Rosa County*   *Northwestern Florida, 170 mi/274 km west of Tallahassee*

1825 trading post established on Blackwater River; **1842** Santa Rosa County formed; town founded as county seat; **1844** incorporated as a city; **c.1882** Louisville & Nashville Railroad reaches town; **1885** fire destroys business district, again in 1892; **1909** third fire destroys almost entire town; **1920s** county courthouse built; **March 31, 1962** tornado kills 17, injures 80; **July 16, 1967** arson jail fire kills 38 inmates at rural town of Jay to north.

Monticello   *Jefferson County*   *Northern Florida, 25 mi/40 km east-northeast of Tallahassee*

1824 John Bellamy awarded contract to build road from Pensacola to St. Augustine; **1827** Jefferson County formed; town founded as county seat by planters from Georgia and Carolinas; **1831** incorporated as a city; **1850** Lynhurst Plantation House built by William J. Bailey; **1853** Silver Lake Plantation House built; **1882** watermelon production begun by William Cirardeau; **1890** Perkins Opera House built; **1906** tung oil production begins, peaks in 1950s; **1909** county courthouse built; **1920s** county produces 80 percent of world's watermelons; **June 29, 1931** highest temperature ever recorded in Florida reached, 109°F/43°C; **1950** first annual Watermelon Festival held.

Moore Haven   *Glades County*   *South central Florida, 92 mi/148 km northwest of Miami*

1915 town founded on southwestern shore of Lake Okeechobee by James A. Moore; **1917** incorporated as a city; Mrs. J. J. O'Brien elected mayor, first woman mayor in U.S.; **1921** Glades County formed; town becomes county seat; **1926** flooding destroys nearly all of town; town rebuilt; **1928** county courthouse built; **1995** Moore Haven Correctional Institution established.

Naples   *Collier County*   *Southwestern Florida, 123 mi/198 km south-southeast of St. Petersburg*

1887 resort town founded on Gulf of Mexico by group led by Walter N. Haldeman of Kentucky, named and planned after Naples, Italy, site originally accessible only by boat; T-shaped pier built; **1911** advertising executive Barron G. Collier acquires land for development; **1919** Caribbean Gardens founded, zoo added 1969; **1923** Collier County formed from Lee County; town becomes county seat; **1927** Atlantic Coast Line Railroad reaches town; incorporated as a city; **Apr. 25, 1928** Tamiami Trail highway opened to Miami, partially funded by contributions from Barron Collier; **1932** Naples Public Library founded; **1937** bus plunges into canal on Tamiami Trail to east killing driver, 12 passengers; **1962** county courthouse built; **Apr. 29, 1967** anesthesiologist Carl Coppolino gets life in prison for administering lethal dose of muscle relaxant to wife in 1965; **Jan. 1, 2001** ferry service begins to Key West.

New Smyrna Beach   *Volusia County*   *Northeastern Florida, 42 mi/68 km northeast of Orlando*

1564 coastal area visited by Spanish; Turtle Mound (Mount of Surruque) Native American burial site discovered on barrier island; **1696** Mission Atocuimi established, one of 44 Franciscan missions in Florida; Jororo

FLORIDA

people rebel against order's ban on tribal customs; **1767** Dr. Andrew Turnbull of Scotland leads 1,500 settlers to site, about 1,000 of them from island of Majorca, Spain; **1776** surviving settlers relocate to St. Augustine; **1803** Martin and Murray families given land grants by Spanish; **c.1835** all traces of white settlement destroyed during Seminole Wars; **1887** Blue Spring, Orange City & Atlantic Railroad reaches town; town founded; **1903** incorporated as a city.

North Miami *Miami-Dade County* *Southeastern Florida, suburb 8 mi/12.9 km north of Miami*

1896 Charles J. Ihle becomes first permanent resident; East Coast Railroad built to Miami by Henry Flagler; town founded near Atlantic Ocean; **1904** Arch Creek Railroad Depot established; **1924** Biscayne Bay Canal built; **1926** incorporated as a town, originally named Miami Shores; **Sept. 1926** devastating hurricane disrupts land boom; **1931** town renamed North Miami; **1953** incorporated as a city; **1992** Johnson & Wales University established.

Ocala *Marion County* *Northern Florida, 65 mi/ 105 km northwest of Orlando*

1531 Hernando de Soto passes through area; **1825** Indian trading post established; **1827** trading post fortified, named Fort King; **Apr. 3, 1835** Seminole chief Micanope refuses to sign treaty forcing them to emigrate to Indian Territory, Native American leader Osceola vows bloodshed; **Dec. 28, 1835** Osceola kills agent Wiley Thompson at Fort King, sparking Seminole War, lasting until Aug. 1842; **1844** Marion County formed; **1846** town founded as county seat; **1852** East Florida Seminary founded, later moved to Gainesville; **1869** incorporated as a city; **Sept. 26, 1927** actor Patrick O'Neal born; **1935** National Gulf-Atlantic Ship Canal begun shortening shipping route to Gulf of Mexico; **Jan. 16, 1935** fugitives Fred and Ma Barker, wanted for Bremer kidnapping in Milwaukee, are gunned down in shootout at house on Lake Weir to southeast; **Aug. 30, 1941** actress Elizabeth Ashley born; **1957** Central Florida Community College established; **1964** County Office Complex completed; East Ocala annexed; **1971** construction on Cross-Florida Canal, one-third completed, halted by President Carter over environmental concerns; **1975** West Ocala annexed.

Ocoee *Orange County* *East central Florida, 10 mi/ 16 km west of Orlando*

1859 Dr. J. S. Starke arrives at Lake Apopka, driven east by mosquitoes to smaller Lake Starke; resort town of Lake Starke founded; **c.1866** citrus orchard established by Confederate Capt. Buford M. Sims; **1880s** Florida Midland Railroad built; **1886** new town platted by Sims, named Ocoee, Native American word for "apricot vine place"; **1891** Ocoee Christian Church built; **Nov. 3, 1920** race riot follows disturbance at voting polls, accused leader July Perry hanged, black neighborhood burned by whites killing 35 black residents, week of unrest follows; **1925** incorporated as a city.

Okeechobee *Okeechobee County* *East central Florida, 110 mi/177 km north-northwest of Miami*

Dec. 25, 1837 fierce encounter between 1,000 troops of Col. Zachary Taylor and about 500 Seminoles under Billy Bowlegs leaves Americans with 138 casualties, Seminoles retreat with few casualties; **1914** branch of Florida East Coast Railroad reaches site near north end of Lake Okeechobee; town founded; **1915** incorporated as a city; **1917** Okeechobee County formed; town becomes county seat; **1926** county courthouse built; **Sept. 16, 1928** hurricane sweeps Florida, over 1,800 killed in Lake Okeechobee area, most by drowning.

Oldsmar *Pinellas County* *West central Florida, 16 mi/26 km north of St. Petersburg*

1913 automobile manufacturer Ransom E. Olds purchases land at head of Old Tampa Bay, founds and plats resort town of Oldsmar; **1921** Wayside Inn built; **1926** Tampa Bay Downs Race Track established for horse racing; St. Louis promoter Harry A. Prettyman caught selling bogus underwater lots; town moved, renamed Tampa Shores to avoid association with scandal; **1927** incorporated as a city; **1937** city reverts to original name.

Olustee *Baker County* *Northern Florida, 38 mi/ 61 km west of Jacksonville*

Feb. 6, 1864 in Battle of Olustee, to west, force of 5,000 Confederates under Gen. Joseph Finnegan repulse 12 regiments of Union troops under Gen. Truman Seymour, inflicting heavy casualties; **1909** Olustee Battlefield Historic State Park established; **1912** monument built by Daughters of the Confederacy; **1931** Osceola National Forest acquired by federal government; **1932** Olustee Experiment Station established by U.S. Department of Agriculture.

Orlando *Orange County* *East central Florida, 205 mi/330 km north-northwest of Miami*

1830s initial attempt to settle area interrupted by Seminole War; **1837** Fort Gatlin established, abandoned 1848; **1842** Aaron Jernigan becomes first permanent settler; **1845** Orange County formed; Mellonville (Sanford) becomes county seat; **1850** post office established; town named Jernigan; **1856** county seat moved to Jernigan; **1857** incorporated as a town, renamed for Orlando Reeves, soldier who died in Seminole War; **1865** first commercial orange grove planted by W. H. Holden; **1875** incorporated as a city; **1880** South Florida Railroad reaches city; **1895** hard freeze ruins citrus crops; **1905** city hall built; **1913** *Evening Star* merges with *Sentinel*, continue as two dailies; **1923** Albertson Public Library opens; Sanford Zoo established, later renamed Orlando Zoo; **1927** county courthouse built; **1928** Orlando Municipal Airport established; **Apr. 1929** Mediterranean fruit fly infestation quarantines citrus crops, lifted Nov. 1930; **1947** Tangerine Bowl football match first held, renamed Citrus Bowl 1983; **July 30, 1956** TV actress Delta Burke

128

born; **1960** Orlando Science Center and Planetarium opened, new facility completed 1997; **1963** University of Central Florida established; **July 31, 1963** actor Wesley Snipes born; **1967** Valencia Community College established; **1968** Orlando Naval Training Center established; **1969** Loch Haven Art Center opens; **Oct. 1971** Walt Disney World theme park opened to southwest, Epcot Center added 1982, MGM Studios added 1989; **1973** *Sentinel* becomes sole daily newspaper; **1982** Orlando International Airport opened to southeast; old airport becomes Orlando Executive Airport; **1983** Orange County Convention Center opened; **1988** 31-story Sun Bank Center Tower built; 28-story Du Pont Center building built; **Oct. 1988** Universal Studios theme park opened; **1989** Orlando Magic NBA basketball team established; **1997** 23-story county courthouse complex completed. **Aug. 14, 2004** Hurricane Charley crosses Florida Penninsula from the south with winds up to 145 mph/ 233 kph, at least 19 killed, as much as $10 billion in property damage.

Ormond Beach   *Volusia County   Northeastern Florida, 80 mi/129 km south-southeast of Jacksonville*

c.1500 Timucuan people settle in area, establish town of Nocoroco; **1815** Scottish Capt. James Ormond of Bahama Islands settles on Halifax River, lagoon on Atlantic Coast, establishes plantation on land grant; **1817** Ormond killed by runaway slave, family returns to Scotland; **1835** plantations destroyed in Seminole Wars; **1875** town of New Britain founded by Corbin Lock Company of New Britain, Connecticut, as retreat for company's tuberculosis victims; **1880** incorporated as a city, renamed Ormond; **1886** St. Johns & Halifax Railroad reaches town; **1888** Hotel Ormond opened by John Anderson; **1902** auto racing established by W. J. Morgan; **1904** The Casements built, winter home of industrialist John D. Rockefeller; **1950** town renamed Ormond Beach.

Palatka   *Putnam County   Northeastern Florida, 48 mi/77 km south of Jacksonville*

1655 area settled by Spanish; **1774** Native American village discovered by botanist William Bertram; **1821** trading post established on St. John's River by Belton A. Copp of Connecticut; **1822** ferry established; **1835** settlement burned by Seminoles; **c.1841** Fort Shannon built; **1849** Putnam County formed; town becomes county seat; **c.1850** St. Mark's Episcopal Church built; **1851** town platted as Pilatka, Native American term for "crossing over"; **1853** incorporated as a city; **March 10, 1864** town occupied by Union troops; **May 1864** Battle of Palatka, Confederates attack steamboat *Columbine*, just disembarked Union troops, killing 82, taking 65 prisoner; **1867** local council of Ku Klux Klan organized; **1870s** town becomes important timber shipping port; **1875** town renamed Palatka; **1880s** town becomes rail hub for citrus industry; **March 19, 1883** Army Gen. Joseph Warren Stillwell born, served in World Wars I and II (died 1946); **Nov. 1884** fire destroys business district; **1895** second year

of hard freeze ruins citrus; **1909** county courthouse built; **1958** St. Johns River Community College established; **1988** first Blue Crab Festival held; **Dec. 17, 1991** train derailment injures 55; **Apr. 14, 2002** Amtrak derailment at Crescent City to south, four killed, 160 injured.

Palm Beach   *Palm Beach County   Southeastern Florida, 65 mi/105 km north of Miami, on Atlantic Ocean*

1861 Confederate draft dodger named Lang builds first house, Lang disappears by 1865; **1872** Charlie Moore of Miami takes over Lang property; **1876** Capt. Elisha Dimick builds house, credited with founding of town; Colonel Bradley's Casino and Whitehall Hotel built on Dimick property; **1878** Spanish bark wrecks with cargo of coconuts, planted by residents; **1880** post office established, named Palm City; **1893** Henry M. Flagler establishes winter resort of Palm Beach on sand barrier island on Atlantic Ocean, separated from mainland by Lake Worth lagoon; Flagler's East Coast Railroad reaches west (mainland) side of Lake Worth; Flagler builds Royal Poinciana Hotel, used until 1930, demolished in phases until 1936; **1896** Palm Beach Inn established, renamed The Breakers 1901; **1898** Bradley's Beach Club founded by Col. Edward Bradley; **1911** incorporated as a city; **1925** Bethesda-by-the-Sea Episcopal Church built; **1926** Bath and Tennis Club built; **Sept. 16, 1928** hurricane causes $10 million in damage.

Panama City   *Bay County   Northwestern Florida, 88 mi/142 km west-southwest of Tallahassee*

c.1770s area on Gulf of Mexico settled during Revolutionary War; English establish indigo plantations; **1827** town of St. Andrews founded; **1862** salt works established by Confederates; **1908** town incorporated as Panama City; **1913** Bay County formed; town becomes county seat; **1915** county courthouse built, rebuilt after 1920 fire; **1925** incorporated as a city; **1927** St. Andrews and Millville merge with Panama City; **1931** paper mills established; **1934** City-County Airport established; **1936** Ritz Theatre built, closed 1978, reopened 1990 as the Martin Theatre; **1957** Gulf Coast Community College established; **1959** St. Andrews Marina built; **1988** Visual Arts Center established.

Pensacola   *Escambia County   Northwestern Florida, 180 mi/290 km west of Tallahassee*

1528 explorer Narvaez passes town site; **1559** Spanish fleet under Don Tristan de Luna reaches harbor, names it Santa Maria, fleet destroyed by storm 1561, settlement abandoned; **1698** fortifications built on Pensacola Bay by Don Andres d'Arriola to ward off French, name Pensacola gradually comes into use; **1719** fort captured by French, restored to Spain 1723; **c.1720** settlement founded on Santa Rosa Island; **1754** settlement destroyed by hurricane, rebuilt on north side of bay; **1763** British take over Florida, Pensacola made capital of West Florida; **1776** Scottish firm of Panton, Leslie, and Company operates trading interests as far as Tennessee with aid of Alexander McGillivray, chief of Creek Confederation; **1781** English pirate William Bowles, leading band of Creeks, lays siege on Spanish, is captured Feb. 1792, escapes to return to Apalachicola Bay 1799; **c.1785** Fort San Carlos built by Spanish; **Nov. 1814** Andrew Jackson captures British emplacements during War of 1812; **1818** Jackson returns, establishes military government; ferry established on Perdido River to west, remains in operation until 1919; **1821** Escambia County formed, one of two original Florida counties, the other St. Johns County (St. Augustine); town becomes county seat; *The Floridian* newspaper founded; First Methodist Church founded, Florida's oldest church; **1822** incorporated as a city; first legislative council of Territory of Florida convenes here; **1824** territorial capital moved to Tallahassee; **1825** Pensacola Navy Yard built; **1834** Fort Pickens completed on western tip of Santa Rosa Island to south; Christ Episcopal Church built; **1839** Fort Barrancas built, completed 1844, held by Confederates 1861–1862; **Feb. 1862** Confederates abandon town; **1880** business district destroyed by fire; **1886** Geronimo and his warriors imprisoned at Fort Pickens; **1888** St. Michael's Catholic Church built; **May 11, 1910** aviator Jacqueline Cochran born (died 1980); **1914** Pensacola Naval Air Station established; **Sept. 27, 1919** Illinois Gov., Sen. Charles Percy born; **1924** *The Journal* (founded 1898) and *News* (1899) newspapers merge to form *News-Journal*; **1933** Pensacola Regional Airport established; **June 30, 1936** actress Nancy Dussault born; **1948** Pensacola Junior College established; **1962** Pensacola Bay Bridge built to Santa Rosa Peninsula (Gulf Breeze); **1963** University of West Florida established; **Jan. 8, 1971** Gulf Islands National Seashore authorized, also in Mississippi; **1978** county courthouse built; **March 10, 1993** Michael Griffin surrenders after shooting death of Dr. David Gunn at abortion clinic amid demonstrations; **July 29, 1994** John Britton and escort shot to death at abortion clinic, Paul Hill arrested, executed Sept. 3, 2003.

Perry *Taylor County* Northern Florida, 47 mi/ 76 km southeast of Tallahassee

1856 Taylor County formed; town founded and incorporated as county seat, originally named Rosehead; **1869** post office established; **1879** town renamed Perrytown, later shortened; **1956** Pine Tree Festival established, renamed Florida Forest Festival 1966; **1969** county courthouse built; **1973** Forest Capital State Museum opened.

Plant City *Hillsborough County* West central Florida, 20 mi/32 km east of Tampa

1839 log blockhouse built; **1843** town platted by Irishman A. M. Randolph; **1849** post office established; **1884** extension of South Florida Railroad reaches town, promoted by Henry B. Plant; **1885** incorporated as a city, renamed for Henry B. Plant; **1887** yellow fever epidemic kills large number of town's citizens; **1908** southern half of town destroyed by fire; **1924** Primitive Baptist Church built; **1935** first Florida Strawberry Festival held.

Pompano Beach *Broward County* Southeastern Florida, 32 mi/51 km north of Miami, on Atlantic Ocean

1896 Florida East Coast Railroad reaches site; settled by rail employees George Butler and Frank Sheene; town founded, named for pompano, rare and choice edible fish, also known as butterfish; **1900** general store established by M. Z. Cavendish; **1907** Hillsboro Lighthouse completed; **1908** incorporated as a town; **1928** hurricane devastates town; **1929** town center moved inland to avoid storm surges; **Nov. 8, 1933** TV actress Esther Rolle born (died 1998).

Port Canaveral *Brevard County* See **Cape Canaveral (1955; 2002)**

Port Orange *Volusia County* Northeastern Florida, 47 mi/76 km north-northeast of Orlando

c.1725 Dunlawton Sugar Mill built; **1836** Battle of Dunlawton of Seminole War, mill and settlements destroyed by Seminoles led by King Philip, mill rebuilt, closed 1880; **1867** town founded by Civil War veterans on Halifax River, lagoon of Atlantic Ocean, as shrimp and oyster center; **1913** incorporated as a town; **1925** incorporated as a city.

Port Saint Joe *Gulf County* Northwestern Florida, 78 mi/126 km southwest of Tallahassee

1906 town founded on St. Joseph Bay, Gulf of Mexico; post office established; **1913** incorporated as a city; **1925** Gulf County formed; Wewahitchka becomes first county seat; **1938** Port St. Joe Paper Mill opens; **c.1940** Gulf County Shipbuilding Company established; **1964** county seat moved to Port St. Joe; county courthouse built.

Port Tampa City *Hillsborough County* West central Florida, 5 mi/8 km southwest of downtown Tampa

1853 Interbay Peninsula extending south into Tampa Bay used as cattle-shipping point; **1887** Florida Central Railroad built from Tampa by Henry B. Plant; town founded as ocean transfer point; Port Tampa Inn built; **1888** channel dredged directly to Tampa ruins town's hope of becoming major port; **1893** officials of closed Louisiana State Lottery arrive, open Honduras National Lottery with plans to build casino on Puerto Cortez Island, Honduras, with steamer *Breakwater* making trips from Port Tampa, tickets transmitted by Central American Express Company to circumvent postal laws, operation closed by U.S. authorities 1895; **1937** Ed's Rattlesnake Cannery and Reptilorium, founded 1931, moved from Arcadia, processor of rattlesnake meat and by-products; **1961** town annexed by Tampa.

Punta Gorda   *Charlotte County*   *Southwestern Florida, 70 mi/113 km south-southeast of St. Petersburg*

1870s town founded on Charlotte Harbor, Gulf of Mexico, by Isaac Trabue of Louisville, Kentucky, names it Trabue; **1897** Plant System Railroad reaches town; Trabue builds hotel; **1887** incorporated as a city, renamed Punta Gorda, Spanish for "flat point"; **1921** Charlotte County formed; town becomes county seat; **1926** county courthouse built. **Aug. 13–14, 2004** Hurricane Charley destroys much of city and nearby Port Charlotte as it makes landfall at Sanibel Island to south, continues northward toward Orlando, 25 Florida counties declared disaster areas; at least 19 killed.

Punta Rassa   *Lee County*   *Southwestern Florida, 100 mi/161 km south of St. Petersburg, on Gulf of Mexico*

1830s site used as cattle shipping point; **1837** military post established; **1860s** military post reactivated during Civil War; **1866** town platted by International Ocean Telegraph Company as terminus for line from Cuba; **1870** Jacob Summerlin builds 300 ft/91 m pier; **Feb. 15, 1898** initial transmission of news about sinking of *USS Maine* in Havana harbor arrives here; **1936** telegraph cable extended to Fort Myers ending town's role as receiving post.

Quincy   *Gadsden County*   *Northwestern Florida, 20 mi/32 km west-northwest of Tallahassee*

1823 Gadsden County formed; **c.1824** area settled along Apalachicola River; town founded as county seat; **1828** incorporated as a city; **1860** citizens raid U.S. arsenal days before Florida secession; **1893** fullers earth discovered, used for fulling process in making cotton cloth; **1913** third county courthouse built; **Aug. 18, 1962** Sunday school teacher, 17 students drown when boat sinks in lake; **1983** Quincy Music Theatre opened in 1940s movie theater.

Safety Harbor   *Pinellas County*   *West central Florida, 13 mi/21 km north of St. Petersburg*

1823 Odet Philippe, surgeon in Napoleon's army, arrives on west side of Tampa Bay, captured by pirates, presented with chest full of money for curing elder crew member; **1839** Philippe establishes fishery; orange groves planted by settlers; **1848** hurricane destroys Philippe home and orange groves; **1869** Philippe dies at age 100; **1917** incorporated as a city; **1930** Native American mounds excavated by Smithsonian Institute; **1938** Safety Harbor Public Library founded.

Saint Augustine   *Saint Johns County*   *Northeastern Florida, 35 mi/56 km southeast of Jacksonville*

March 27, 1513 Ponce de Leon lands at site of St. Augustine; **Sept. 8, 1565** town founded by Spaniard Don Pedro Menendez for its strategic location, surrounded on three sides by rivers, names it St. Augustine for Aug. 28, St. Augustine's Day, when he first sighted Florida; **1577** St. Francis Barracks built by Franciscans; **1580** coquina rock first quarried for building material; **1586** town sacked and burned by England's Sir Francis Drake; **1597** first hospital in U.S. built; **c.1600** Spanish Treasury building built; **1668** town attacked by pirate Capt. John Davis, 60 killed; **1672** Spanish begin building stone Fort San Marcos for defense against English, not completed until 1756; **1702** British launch attack from north, again in 1728; **1742** Fort Matanzas built by Spanish on coast to south as defense against British; **1745** wooden city gates built, replaced by permanent gates 1804; **1763** British take over town, Spanish flee to Cuba; **1767** large group of immigrants from Mediterranean island of Minorca brought here by Dr. Andrew Turnbull; **1777** British launch attack on Savannah from St. Augustine; **1797** Cathedral of St. Augustine completed, destroyed by fire 1887, rebuilt; **1783** British capture Bahamas in sea campaign based here; *East Florida Gazette* newspaper established; **c.1810** Fatio House built; **c.1815** Prince Murat House built; **1819** East Florida ceded to Spain, British abandon city; **1821** Spanish evacuate Florida, Americans take over; St. Johns County formed, one of two original Florida counties, the other Escambia County (Pensacola); town becomes county seat; yellow fever epidemic takes many lives; **1822** incorporated as a city; **May 16, 1824** Confederate Gen. Edmund Kirby-Smith born (died 1893); **1825** Fort San Carlos renamed Fort Marion by U.S.; construction begins on Trinity Episcopal Church, completed 1830; **1836** Fort Peyton built to south; **Oct. 20, 1837** Seminole Chief Osceola and party taken prisoner while approaching Fort Peyton under flag of truce, raising ire of public opinion; **1862** Union forces take city, stay through end of Civil War; **1871** mule-drawn railroad built from Tocoi; **1874** steam-driven railroad arrives; **1889** Ponce de Leon Hotel opens, rebuilt 1967 as county courthouse; **1890** Flagler Memorial Presbyterian Church built; **Oct. 15, 1924** Castillo de San Marcos National Monument established; Fort Matanzas National Monument established to south; **1927** Bridge of Lions built across Matanzas Bay to Anastasia Island; **Apr. 2, 1964** Mrs. Malcolm Peabody, 72, mother of Massachusetts Gov. Endicott Peabody, released after being jailed for participation in civil rights march; **June 25, 1964** mob of 800 whites attacks civil rights demonstrators, 33 injured; **1968** Flagler College established.

Saint Joseph   *Gulf County*   *Northwestern Florida, 80 mi/129 km southwest of Tallahassee*

1822 settlers arrive at St. Joseph's Bay from nearby Apalachicola following land dispute; **1838** town's population estimated at 6,000, largest town in Florida; **Feb. 1, 1838** first state constitutional convention called here with sessions held Dec. 3, 1838, through Jan. 11, 1839; **1841** ship from South America brings yellow fever epidemic killing three-fourths of population, survivors migrate to other towns; **1844** hurricane delivers final blow to deserted town.

Saint Marks *Wakulla County* *Northwestern Florida, 18 mi/29 km south-southeast of Tallahassee*

1677 fort built by Spanish on Gulf of Mexico at mouth of St. Marks River, burned by pirates 1682, rebuilt; **1739** Fort San Marcos built; **1763** fort captured by British, reoccupied by Spanish 1787; **1800** Creeks led by white pirate William Bowles takes fort, retaken by Spanish 1818; **1824** fort abandoned; **1831** St. Marks Lighthouse built; **1836** St. Marks Railroad reaches town; **July 1861** Union ships blockade St. Marks River; **1927** incorporated as a city.

Saint Petersburg *Pinellas County* *West central Florida, 210 mi/338 km northwest of Miami*

1528 Spanish explorer Narvaez lands here, crosses peninsula to Tampa Bay; **1843** Antonio Maximo becomes first white settler, establishes fish "rancho" at Maximo Point, destroyed by hurricane 1848; **1856** James K. Hay builds first house; **1861** bay blockaded by Union forces, most residents flee to Tampa; **1876** town founded by John C. Williams of Detroit; **1884** *Times* newspaper founded; **1888** Orange Belt Line railroad reaches town, built by Russian Peter Demens; town name chosen by drawing straws between Williams and Demens, won by Demens; **1892** incorporated as a city; Detroit Hotel built by Williams; **1904** *The Independent* newspaper founded; **1912** Pinellas County formed; Clearwater chosen as county seat; **1914** Tampa & Gulf Coast Railroad built; American Airline terminal built on bay front; **1917** federal building built; **1920** St. Petersburg Historical Museum founded; **1924** Coliseum built, renovated 1989; **1927** St. Petersburg Junior College established; **1935** Sunken Gardens established; **1938** large slum clearance project begins; **1941** St. Petersburg-Clearwater International Airport established; **1954** Sunshine Skyway Bridge opened across Tampa Bay entrance; **1958** Eckerd College established; **Jan. 28, 1980** Coast Guard cutter *Blackthorn* rammed by freighter *Capricorn*, 23 killed on cutter; **May 9, 1980** Skyway Bridge rammed by Liberian tanker, 35 motorists killed including 23 on Greyhound bus; **1982** Salvador Dali Museum opened; **1987** rebuilt Skyway Bridge opened to traffic; **1990** Tropicana Field opened, multi-sport venue; **1992** Tampa Bay Holocaust Museum opened, renamed Florida Holocaust Museum 1999; **1995** Devil Rays baseball team established.

Sanford *Seminole County* *East central Florida, 20 mi/32 km north-northeast of Orlando*

1837 town of Mellonville founded at Fort Mellon on Lake Monroe; **1845** Orange County formed; town becomes county seat; **1856** county seat moved to Orlando; **1871** land purchased by Gen. Henry R. Sanford, cleared for citrus with black labor, whites attack camp killing one; new town founded; **1877** incorporated as a city; **1883** Mellonville annexed by Sanford; **1894–1895** hard freeze forces change to truck farming; **1913** Seminole County formed; town becomes county seat; **1923** Sanford Zoo established, renamed Central Florida Zoo 1975; **1942**

Sanford Air Force Base established, closed 1995; **1966** Seminole Community College established; **1972** county courthouse built.

Sarasota *Sarasota County* *West central Florida, 30 mi/48 km south of St. Petersburg*

1768 site on Gulf of Mexico designated Port Sarasote by Elino de la Puente map; **1856** site homesteaded by William Whitaker of Tennessee; **1860s** Whitaker plants area's first orange grove; **1881** large land purchase made by Hamilton Disston, sells portion to Scottish syndicate 1884 for development; **1884** Scottish settlers arrive; town founded; **1902** Seaboard Air Line railroad reaches town; incorporated as a town; **1911** Mrs. Potter Palmer of Chicago purchases land, sells small farm lots; **1921** Sarasota County formed; incorporated as a city, becomes county seat; **1927** Mediterranean style county courthouse completed; **1929** John Ringling establishes winter headquarters for his circus here; **1935** dolomite mining begins for use as antacid fertilizer; **1937** Ringling Museum of Art willed to state by John and Mabel Ringling; **1938** Municipal Auditorium built; **1942** Sarasota-Bradenton International Airport opened; **1955** Mote Marine Laboratory founded on Lido Key; **1968** Van Wezel Performing Arts Center built; **1975** Marie Shelby Botanical Gardens opened; **1995** Keiser College, Sarasota Campus, established; **1989** Sarasota Bay National Estuary Program established; **May 19, 2000** 87-year-old nursing home patient dies, bitten 1,625 times by fire ants in her bed.

Sebring *Highlands County* *Central Florida, 70 mi/113 km south of Orlando*

1880s area first settled; citrus groves established; **1911** Atlantic Coastline Railroad reaches site; town founded on Lake Jackson by George Sebring of Ohio; **1913** incorporated as a city; **1917** hard freeze damages most citrus groves; **1921** Highlands County formed; town becomes county seat; **1924–1925** real estate boom brings new growth to area; **1925** Sebring Hotel built, razed 1985; **1925** Sebring International Airport opened; **1927** county courthouse built.

Starke *Bradford County* *Northern Florida, 38 mi/61 km southwest of Jacksonville*

1858 New River County formed; town of New River (now Lake Butler) becomes county seat; **1859** town of Starke founded, named for Gov. Starke Perry; **1861** county renamed for Confederate Capt. Richard Bradford; incorporated as a city; **1902** county seat moved to Starke; **1969** county courthouse built.

Stuart *Martin County* *Southeastern Florida, 98 mi/158 km north of Miami, near Atlantic Ocean*

1893 town founded by German brothers Otto and Ernest Stypman as fishing port on St. Lucie River estuary, named Potsdam; **1896** Florida East Coast

Railroad reaches town; town renamed for railroad officer Homer H. Stuart, Jr.; **1914** incorporated as a city; **1924** St. Lucie Canal completed to Lake Okeechobee for flood control; **1925** Martin County formed; town becomes county seat; **1937** high school converted to county courthouse, built 1915.

Tallahassee *Leon County Northwestern Florida, 205 mi/330 km north-northwest of Tampa*

1539 Hernando De Soto reaches site, departs following spring; **1633** Mission of San Luis de Talimali established by Franciscans friars; **1640** Fort San Luis built by Spanish; **1704** fort abandoned with British invasion; **1763** British establish dividing line here between East Florida and West Florida provinces; **1818** Andrew Jackson rides through area, burns 300 Native American dwellings to north; **1824** Leon County formed; town founded as territorial capital, moved from Pensacola, and as county seat, named Creek term for "deserted fields"; **1825** incorporated as a city; **1826** cornerstone laid for state capitol, only one wing completed; **1831** Williams House built; **1832** Presbyterian Church built; **1835** The Columns house built; **1845** state capitol completed; **March 3, 1845** Florida enters Union as 27th state; **1857** Florida State College for Women established, becomes Florida State University; **March 6, 1865** Battle at Natural Bridge fought to southeast, force of young Confederates from West Florida Seminary in Tallahassee stops advance of Union troops, making city only state capital not captured by Union; **1881** St. John's Episcopal Church built, replaces 1838 structure; **1887** Florida Agricultural and Mechanical University established; **Feb. 13, 1899** lowest temperature ever recorded in Florida reached, $-2°F/-19°C$; **1905** *The Democrat* newspaper founded; **1907** governor's mansion completed; **1908** governor's mansion built; **1927** Martin Building built; **1929** Tallahassee Regional Airport established, new airport built 1975; **1930** county courthouse built; **1957** Museum of History and Natural Science founded; **1966** Tallahassee Community College established; **1971** Museum of Florida History established; **1978** 22-story Capitol Complex completed; **1992** Keiser College, Tallahassee Campus, established; Civic Center opened; **Nov. 9, 2000** Democratic presidential candidate Vice Pres. Al Gore demands manual recount of heavily Democratic Volusia, Miami-Dade, and Broward counties (Palm Beach County added later) citing faulty punch card voting system, George W. Bush campaign opposes move fearing loss of slim 300-vote lead; **Nov. 14, 2000** Florida Secretary of State Katherine Harris certifies Bush's victory over Gore, rejected Nov. 17 by Florida Supreme Court; **Dec. 9, 2000** with manual vote recounts partially completed in several Florida counties, U.S. Supreme Court halts all manual recounts in 5-4 decision, effectively making Bush the decided winner of presidency.

Tampa *Hillsborough County West central Florida, 205 mi/330 km northwest of Miami, on Gulf of Mexico*

1528 Spanish explorer Panfilo de Narvaez reaches Tampa Bay; **1539** Hernando de Soto sails into Tampa Bay, takes control of Native American village; **1545** Spanish caravel becomes shipwrecked in Tampa Bay; **1823** Fort Brooke established at mouth of Hillsborough River during Seminole War; **Dec. 18, 1826** naval officer John Mercer Brooke born, designed Confederate ironclad ship *Virginia* (died 1906); **1834** Hillsborough County formed; town becomes county seat; **1843** Orange Grove Hotel built; **1855** incorporated as a town; **1863** town shelled by Union forces, later occupied; **1873** yellow fever epidemic kills hundreds; **1884** Henry Plant develops area as tourist center, terminus for his South Florida Railroad; **1885** incorporated as a city; **1886** city's first cigar factory established by Cuban Vicente Martinez Ybor; **1889** first bridge built across Hillsborough River; Seaboard Air Line railroad reaches city; Plant Park created by Henry Plant as setting for his new hotel; **1891** elaborate Tampa Bay Hotel built by Henry Plant; **1893** *Tampa Times* newspaper founded; **1895** *Tampa Tribune* newspaper founded; **1898** city becomes focal point of Cuban sympathy during Spanish-American War; typhoid epidemic kills hundreds of troops, hastens war's end; **1904** Florida State Fairgrounds established; **1905** Sacred Heart Catholic Church built; **Jan. 7, 1911** actress Butterfly McQueen born (died 1995); **1913** cigar manufacturing reaches peak; **1914** first scheduled airline service in world established by Percival Ellicott Fansler; **1915** Tampa Public Library built; **1925** Municipal Auditorium built; **1928** Tampa International Airport (Dow Field) established; **1931** University of Tampa established; **Aug. 8, 1932** country singer Mel Tillis born; **1933** Tampa Greyhound Race Track opened; **1934** Davis Causeway built across northern end of Tampa Bay; **1941** MacDill Air Force Base established on Interbay Peninsula; **1948** Tampa Technical Institute (2-year college) established; **1953** county courthouse built; **1956** University of South Florida established; **1959** Busch Gardens theme park established; **1961** Port Tampa City on Interbay Peninsula annexed by Tampa; **Nov. 18, 1963** President Kennedy makes speech at Florida Chamber of Commerce, denying his policies are antibusiness, final stop before proceeding to Dallas; **1968** Hillsborough Community College established; **1979** Tampa Museum of Art established; **1986** 42-story Bank of America Building completed; **1990** Tampa Convention Center opened; **1992** 42-story 100 North Tampa Building completed; Tampa Bay Lightning NHL hockey team begins inaugural season; **1998** Raymond James Stadium opened, home of Tampa Bay Buccaneers NFL football team; **Jan. 5, 2002** Charles Bishop, 15, flies small aircraft into high-rise Bank of America Building, apparent suicide.

Tarpon Springs *Pinellas County West central Florida, 25 mi/40 km north of St. Petersburg*

1873 sponge beds discovered by fishermen at mouth of Anclote River; **1876** town founded on Gulf of Mexico, named for mullet spawning in Spring Bayou mistaken for tarpon; **1877** George Inness, landscape painter, builds house and studio; **1881** town founded on Lake Butler by Philadelphia saw manufacturer Hamilton Disston; **1887** Anclote Key Lighthouse built, automated 1952; Atlantic Coastline Railroad reaches town; incorporated as a city; **1889** Duke of Sutherland builds manor house; **1905** Greek sponge divers migrate here from Key West, transform town into sponge capital of America beginning with John M. Cocoris and brothers; **1908** Sponge Cooperative Warehouse established.

Tavares *Lake County Central Florida, 28 mi/ 45 km northwest of Orlando*

1875 town founded between lakes Eustis and Dora by Maj. Alexander St. Clair Abrams, names it for one of his Spanish ancestors; **1887** Lake County formed; town becomes county seat; **1888** fire destroys large part of town; county courthouse built by Abrams, later serves as firehouse; **1894–1895** hard freeze ruins citrus crops, town nearly abandoned; **1880** incorporated as a city; **1924** county courthouse built; **1993** city hall completed.

Titusville *Brevard County Eastern Florida, 33 mi/ 53 km east of Orlando, near Atlantic Ocean*

1830s Dummitt Grove, area's first orange grove, planted by Douglas D. Dummitt; **1844** Brevard County formed; Susanna, near Fort Pierce, becomes county seat; **1867** town founded on Indian River, lagoon of Atlantic Ocean, named for settler Col. Henry T. Titus; **1880** county seat moved to Titusville; **1880s** town becomes shipping point for Indian River citrus products; **1887** incorporated as a city; **1890s** developer Henry M. Flagler offers to purchase Sand Point site, takes plans to Palm Beach when turned away by landowner's high asking price; **1912** county courthouse built; **1927** Arthur Dunn Airpark established; **Jan. 3, 1975** Canaveral National Seashore established.

Trenton *Gilchrist County Northern Florida, 117 mi/188 km north-northwest of Tampa*

1878 town founded; post office established; **1908** incorporated as a city; **1925** Gilchrist County formed; town becomes county seat; **1933** county courthouse built.

Vero Beach *Indian River County Eastern Florida, 130 mi/209 km north of Miami, near Atlantic Ocean*

c.1888 resort town founded on Indian River, lagoon paralleling Atlantic Ocean; **1916** "Vero Beach Man" discovered by Dr. E. H. Sellards, skeletal remains identified as Algonquin in origin; **1919** incorporated as City of Vero; **1925** Indian River County formed; city renamed Vero Beach; **1931** McKee Jungle Gardens founded by industrialist Arthur G. McKee, containing

large variety of introduced tropical flora from around world; **1937** county courthouse built.

Wauchula *Hardee County Central Florida, 48 mi/ 77 km southeast of Tampa*

c.1835 Fort Hartsuff built during Seminole Wars; town founded adjacent to fort; **1907** incorporated as a city; **1921** Hardee County formed; town becomes county seat; **1927** county courthouse built.

West Palm Beach *Palm Beach County Southeastern Florida, 65 mi/105 km north of Miami*

1880 site homesteaded by Irving R. Henry; **1893** Henry M. Flagler establishes resort of Palm Beach on sand barrier island on Atlantic Ocean to east; Flagler's East Coast Railroad reaches site on mainland side of Lake Worth, lagoon of Atlantic Ocean; town platted on Lake Worth; **1894** incorporated as a city; **1907** Flagler Park created from Flagler estate; **1909** Palm Beach County formed; city becomes county seat; **1916** county courthouse built; **1926** West Palm Beach Canal completed from Lake Okeechobee, for drainage, small craft; **1936** Palm Beach International Airport (Morrison Field) established; **1941** Norton Museum of Art founded; **1968** Palm Beach Atlantic College established; **1983** New England Institute of Technology at Palm Beach (2-year school) established; **1994** County Judicial Complex completed; **Nov. 14, 2000** Palm Beach County vote recount yields 98 additional votes for Vice Pres. Al Gore, Florida recount nullified by U.S. Supreme Court Dec. 9, ruling favors George W. Bush. **July 27, 2001** Nathaniel Brazill, 14, gets 28 years in prison for shooting death of teacher Barry Grunow in May 2000 at Lake Worth Middle School.

White Springs *Hamilton County See* **Lake City (1950)**

Winter Haven *Polk County Central Florida, 45 mi/72 km east of Tampa*

1860s first settlers arrive; **1883** lake resort town founded; **1884** town platted; **1911** incorporated as a city; **1915** Twenty Lakes Boat Course Club organized, course established on Chain of Lakes; **1924** first Florida Citrus Festival held; **1940** Cypress Gardens opened to southeast, Florida's first theme park.

Winter Park *Orange County East central Florida, suburb 3 mi/4.8 km northeast of Orlando*

1858 town founded, named Lakeview; **1870** town renamed Osceola; **1881** town platted by residents from New England, renamed Winter Park; **1885** Rollins College established; **1887** incorporated as a city; **May 9, 1981** sinkhole swallows house, cottage, six cars and camping vehicle, reaches 170 ft/52 m deep, extends over two blocks.

Georgia

Southeastern U.S. Capital and largest city: Atlanta.

Georgia was one of the 13 colonies that adopted the U.S. Declaration of Independence July 4, 1776. It became the 4th state to ratify the U.S. Constitution January 2, 1788. Georgia seceded from the Union January 19, 1861, as a Confederate state. It was readmitted to the Union July 15, 1870.

Georgia is divided into 159 counties, second in number to Texas' 254 counties. Its municipalities are classified as towns and cities. There are no townships. See Introduction.

Abbeville   *Wilcox County*   *South central Georgia, 138 mi/222 km south-southeast of Atlanta*

1857 Wilcox County formed, named for Gen. Mark Willcox [sp]; town founded as county seat on Ocmulgee River; **1858** first county courthouse built; **1883** incorporated as a town; **1903** present county courthouse built.

Adairsville   *Bartow County*   *Northwestern Georgia, 50 mi/80 km north-northwest of Atlanta*

c.1825 area first settled by Scotsman Walter S. Adair, marries into Choctaw nation; **1837** town founded as northern terminus of Western & Atlantic Railroad; **1848** economy declines with extension of railroad and transfer of shops to Chattanooga; **1854** incorporated as a town; **1859** Barnsley Gardens plantation built by Godfrey Barnsley; **Apr. 12, 1862** Great Locomotive Chase, 22 Union spies led by James Andrews (Andrews' Raiders) separate engine in high speed chase, pursued by Confederates, stopped at Ringgold, raiders captured; **1958** incorporated as a city.

Adel   *Cook County*   *Southern Georgia, 190 mi/ 306 km south-southeast of Atlanta*

1860s area first settled; **1873** post office established; **1880s** Georgia Southern & Florida Railroad reaches town; **1889** incorporated as a town; **1918** Cook County formed; town becomes county seat; **1919** incorporated as a city; **1939** county courthouse built.

Alamo   *Wheeler County*   *Central Georgia, 130 mi/ 209 km southeast of Atlanta*

1890 Seaboard Air Line Railroad built; town founded as depot, named for the Alamo in San Antonio, Texas; **1909**

incorporated as a town; **1912** Wheeler County formed; town becomes county seat; **1917** county courthouse built.

Albany   *Dougherty County*   *Southwestern Georgia, 152 mi/245 km south of Atlanta*

1836 land purchased on Flint River by Quaker Alexander Shotwell of New Jersey; Col. Nelson Tift becomes first settler; **1837** town platted; **1838** incorporated as a town; **1841** incorporated as a city; **1845** *Albany Patriot* newspaper founded, later becomes the *Albany News*; **1853** Dougherty County formed; town becomes county seat; **1857** first bridge over Flint River built by Colonel Tift; Bridge House built by Colonel Tift; **1881** first artesian well in state drilled here by John Porter Fort; **Apr. 29, 1885** avant-garde composer Wallingford Riegger born (died 1961); **Apr. 26, 1886** African-American Congressman from Illinois William Levi Dawson born (died 1970); **1901** Confederate Memorial erected; **1903** Albany State University established; **1915** Municipal Auditorium built; **May 15, 1916** band leader Harry James born (died 1983); **1925** resort developed by Barron Collier at Radium Springs to south; **Sept. 1926** Cudahy Packing Plant opens; **Sept. 23, 1930** singer Ray Charles born; (died 2004); **1940** Turner Field established by Army Air Corps; **1964** Albany Museum of Art opened; **1965** Darton College (2-year) established; **1968** third county courthouse built; **1973** Albany Civil Rights Movement Museum established; **1988** Miller Brewing Plant opened; **1993** Albany-Dougherty County Government Center completed; **1994** city heavily damaged by flooding of Flint River from Hurricane Camille.

Alma   *Bacon County*   *Southeastern Georgia, 88 mi/ 142 km southwest of Savannah*

1900 town founded as depot on Atlantic Coast Line Railroad; **1906** incorporated as a city; **1914** Bacon County formed; city becomes county seat; **1919** county courthouse built.

Alpharetta   *Fulton County   Northern Georgia, 22 mi/35 km north-northeast of Atlanta*

1857 Milton County formed; **1858** town founded as county seat; county courthouse built; **1900** incorporated as a town; **1932** Milton County absorbed by Fulton County, town's role as county seat ends; **1961** incorporated as a city.

Americus   *Sumter County   Western Georgia, 117 mi/188 km south of Atlanta*

1831 Sumter County formed, named for Gen. Thomas Sumter of Revolutionary War; **1832** town platted and incorporated as county seat; **1834** $980 raised to build courthouse, builder flees with money; **1855** Central of Georgia Railroad reaches town; incorporated as a town; **1882** incorporated as a city; **1906** Georgia Southwestern State University established; **1923** Charles A. Lindbergh purchases first airplane, makes first solo flight from Souther Field to east; **1959** fourth county courthouse built; **July 1994** 16 killed in tropical storm Alberto, 30 killed in statewide.

Andersonville   *Sumter and Macon counties   Western Georgia, 110 mi/177 km south of Atlanta*

1852 town founded; **1864** Andersonville Prison built to accommodate 10,000, as many as 33,000 held at one time; **1865** Andersonville National Cemetery established, over 16,000 Confederates buried here, 12,462 died in prison; **1881** incorporated as a town; **1941** incorporated as a city; **1970** Andersonville National Historic Site authorized.

Appling   *Columbia County   Eastern Georgia, 20 mi/32 km west-northwest of Augusta*

1772 Kiokee Anabaptist Church built; **1790** Columbia County formed; Cobbham becomes first county seat; **1792** county seat moved to Kiokee (Kioka); **1793** town founded as new county seat; **1816** incorporated as a village; **1856** third county courthouse built using shell of previous 1812 structure; **Sept. 5, 1856** author Thomas Edward Watson born in rural Columbia County (died 1922); **Jan. 18, 1892** Oliver Norville Hardy of comedy team Laurel and Hardy born at rural Harlem to south (died 1957), partner Stan Laurel (1895–1965) born in England; **1994** government center completed; **1995** village disincorporated; **2001** county courthouse annex completed at Evans to east.

Ashburn   *Turner County   Southern Georgia, 148 mi/238 km south-southeast of Atlanta*

1888 town founded, named Marion; **1890** incorporated as a town, renamed for timber man W. W. Ashburn; **1904** incorporated as a city; **1905** Turner County formed; town becomes county seat; **1907** county courthouse completed.

Athens   *Clarke County   Northeastern Georgia, 60 mi/97 km east-northeast of Atlanta*

1785 University of Georgia established; **1801** Clarke County formed; Watkinsville becomes first county seat; town founded around college; **1806** incorporated as a town; **1817** Camak House built by James Camak; **c.1845** Henry Grady House built; **c.1850** Howell Cobb House built; Lumpkin House built; **May 24, 1850** editor, publisher Henry Woodfin Grady born (died 1889); **1855** Benjamin H. Hill House built; **1872** incorporated as a city; county seat moved from Watkinsville with separation of Oconee County from Clarke County; **1895** State Normal School established, becomes Coordinate College; **1904** city hall completed; **1914** county courthouse built; **Dec. 8, 1953** actress Kim Basinger born; **1958** Athens Area Technical Institute (2-year) established; **1991** city and county governments merge.

Atlanta   *Fulton and De Kalb counties Northwestern Georgia, in Appalachian Mountains*

1736 delegation sent to investigate dispute between Cherokee and Creek peoples near Creek village of Standing Peachtree; **1837** first survey made establishing junction of Western & Atlantic and Georgia railroads; town founded, named Terminus; **1843** incorporated as at town, renamed Marthasville; **1844** Gen. William T. Sherman stationed here, gains valuable knowledge of area used in Civil War; **1845** town renamed Atlanta by railroad engineer, supposed feminine version of Atlantic; **1847** incorporated as a city; **1849** Cathedral of St. Philip (Episcopal) built; **1853** Fulton County formed; town becomes county seat; Angier Academy founded; **1855** Huff House built; **Apr. 1862** Atlanta placed under martial law by Confederates; **July 20, 1864** Confederate Gen. Hardee defeated at Battle of Peach Tree Creek (north Atlanta) by Union Gen. McPherson's forces; **July 22, 1864** Gen. Hardee defeated again at Battle of Atlanta by McPherson, who was killed; **July 28, 1864** Union Gen. Hood repulsed at Ezra's Church to west; **Sept. 2, 1864** Sherman occupies city; mayor surrenders; **Nov. 15, 1864** Sherman burns city before march to the sea with his 60,000 troops; **1865** Atlanta University established, merges with Clark College 1988 as Clark Atlanta University; **1866** city made headquarters of federal reconstruction; **1867** Morehouse College established; **1868** state capital moved from Milledgeville; *Constitution* newspaper founded; **1869** Church of the Immaculate Conception (Catholic) built; **1870** Kimball House hotel built, burned 1883, rebuilt; **1873** Atlanta & Charlotte Railroad reaches city; **1877** phoenix adopted as city's symbol; **1880** Atlanta Baptist Seminary founded, becomes Morris Brown College; **1880s** state library founded; **1881** Spelman College established for black women; **May 4, 1884** sociologist John Collier born (died 1968); **1885** Georgia Institute of Technology established; Fort McPherson Military Base established at its present site; **1886** Coca-Cola first made by druggist John S. Pemberton (1831–1888), company organized 1892 by Asa

G. Candler; **1889** state capitol completed; **July 1, 1893** African-American author Walter Francis White born (died 1955); **1895** Cotton States Exposition attracts 800,000 visitors; **Sept. 18, 1895** Booker T. Washington issues his "Atlanta Compromise," encourages blacks to emphasize education and skills over fighting against discrimination; **May 1, 1898** Eugene Robert Black born, president of World Bank 1949–1962 (died 1992); **Oct. 30, 1898** baseball player, manager of New York Giants Bill Terry born (died 1989); **Nov. 8, 1900** reporter, novelist Margaret Mitchell born, wrote *Gone With the Wind*, 1,000+ pages, her only book (died 1949); **1902** Carnegie Library built; federal penitentiary opened; **1906** Candler Building completed; **1909** Municipal Auditorium and Armory completed; **1911** Peace Monument erected, statue of kneeling Confederate soldier; **1913** Georgia Tech Evening School of Commerce established, becomes Georgia State University; **1914** Emory University established, founded as Emory College 1836 at Covington, later moved to Oxford, finally to Atlanta; Federal Reserve Bank established; Candler School of Theology founded; county courthouse built; **Oct. 1, 1914** historian Daniel J. Boorstin born (died 2004); **Dec. 30, 1914** TV personality Bert Parks born; **Sept. 30, 1915** segregationist cafe owner, Lester Maddox born, elected governor 1967–1971 (died 2003); **1916** Ebenezer Baptist Church built, founded 1886, Dr. M. L. King Jr. serves as pastor 1960; **1916** Oglethorpe University refounded, originally founded 1835 at Milledgeville, closed 1862; **May 21, 1917** over 2,000 homes and businesses destroyed by fire, 10,000 left homeless; **Jan. 20, 1920** TV actor De Forest Kelley born (died 1999); **1922** Big Bethel A.M.E. Church built, replacing previous structure destroyed by fire; **Oct. 13, 1924** comedian Nipsey Russell born; **1925** Candler Field established to south, later becomes Hartsfield-Atlanta International Airport; **1926** High Museum of Art built; **Apr. 12, 1926** actress Jane Withers born; **Oct. 25, 1927** actress Barbara Cook born; **1928** the *World* newspaper founded by African-American W. A. Scott; **June 25, 1929** civil rights leader Dr. Martin Luther King Jr. born, assassinated in Memphis Apr. 4, 1968; **1932** Campbell County to south and Milton County to north merge with Fulton County; **Aug. 15, 1935** civil rights leader Vernon Jordan born; **Feb. 3, 1936** state farmers' market opens; **March 20, 1937** country singer Jerry Reed born; **May 16, 1938** fire at Terminal Hotel, 35 killed; **1939** state office building built; **May 28, 1944** singer Gladys Knight born; **Dec. 11, 1944** singer Brenda Lee born; **Dec. 7, 1946** fire at Winecoff Hotel, 119 killed; **1949** Art Institute of Atlanta (2-year college) established; **March 20, 1957** actor, producer Spike Lee born; **1960** Interdenominational Theological Center formed by merger of three seminaries; **June 3, 1962** 121 members of Atlanta Art Association killed in crash of Boeing 707 in Paris, France, killing 130 of 132 on board, two stewardesses survive; **1965** Atlanta-Fulton County Stadium opened, demolished 1997; **Jan. 10, 1967** Lester Maddox elected governor, blocked effort in 1964 to desegregate his cafe with pistol in hand; **Dec. 17, 1968** Barbara Jane Mackle, 20, kidnapped, found alive three days later in coffin-box, $500,000 ransom, Gary

Krist gets life sentence; **Aug. 1, 1969** Gov. Lester Maddox outraged over U.S. lawsuit forcing Georgia schools to desegregate; **Oct. 7, 1969** Maynard Jackson, 31, elected vice mayor of Atlanta, first black elected in 122-year history of city; **Nov. 30, 1972** nursing home fire kills 9; **Oct. 16, 1973** Maynard Jackson elected first black mayor of Atlanta; **1974** Atlanta Metro College (2-year) established; **Feb. 20, 1974** J. Reginald Murphy, editor *Atlanta Constitution*, abducted, found alive, $700,000 ransom recovered, William A. H. Williams arrested; **June 30, 1974** Alberta Williams King, 69, mother of Dr. M. L. King Jr., shot to death while playing organ at Ebenezer Baptist Church, deacon killed, Marcus Chenault charged; **1976** Georgia World Congress Center opened; **Dec. 1979** West Line Rail opens of Metropolitan Rapid Transit Authority (MARTA); **1981** 51-story Georgia Pacific Tower building completed; **June 21, 1981** Wayne B. Williams, 23, arrested in slaying of Nathaniel Cater, suspected in killing 28 young black males since 1979; **1988** 52-story One Atlantic Center completed; **1989** county government center completed; **1990** 50-story Peachtree Center built; **1992** Georgia Dome stadium opened; 55-story Bank of America building completed; 60-story SunTrust Bank Tower completed; **1995** County Justice Center built; **July 19, 1996** opening ceremonies 26th Olympiad, games held through Aug. 4; **July 27, 1996** 1 person killed, over 100 injured at Centennial Olympic Park by pipe bomb hidden in abandoned knapsack; **Jan. 16, 1997** homosexual nightclub and abortion clinic bombed, Eric Rudolph apprehended June 2, 2003, Murphy, North Carolina, for these and Olympic Park incidents; **July 29, 1999** Mark Barton, loser in day trading, shoots and kills nine, wounds 13, takes own life, wife, two children found dead at home.

Augusta *Richmond County* Eastern Georgia, *145 mi/233 km east of Atlanta, on Savannah River*

1717 fort and trading post built; **1735** town platted by John Oglethorpe two years after his founding of Savannah; **1740** road built from Savannah; **1750** St. Paul's Church established; **1761** Old Kilpatrick House built; **1777** Richmond County formed; town becomes county seat; **1780** state capital of moved to Augusta from Savannah; incorporated as a town; British capture town; **May 1781** Fort Grierson captured by American forces led by Gen. Andrew Pickens; **1783** Academy of Richmond County founded, opens 1785; **1783** *Chronicle* newspaper founded; **1790** Government House built, later used as Dr. E. E. Murphey house; **1792** Campbell House built; **1796** state capital moved to Louisville; **1798** incorporated as a city; **c.1800** High Gate mansion built with slave labor; **1810** Bank of Augusta chartered; **1812** First Presbyterian Church built; **1814** Eve House built; **1818** De L'Aigle House built by Frenchman Nicholas de L'Aigle; **1819** U.S. Arsenal built; **1820** county courthouse built; **1828** Medical College of Georgia established; **Sept. 10, 1836** Confederate general, Mississippi Cong. Joseph Wheeler born (died 1906); **1837** Georgia Railroad built to Berzelia; **1841** Phinizy Place house built; **1844** Augusta Canal begun, completed 1846, 7 mi/ 11.3 km long, used to generate power for mills, lengthened to 9 mi/14.5 km, widened, deepened 1975; **1851** Clanton House built; **1854** Augusta & Savannah Railroad reaches city; **1859** Allen House built; **1861** Confederate Powder Works built here; **1862** St. Patrick's Catholic Church built; **Apr. 1865** city occupied by Federal forces with little warfare; **1867** Augusta Institute founded, moves to Atlanta 1879; **1869** iron works factory founded; **Feb. 1, 1882** African-American leader Channing Heggie Tobias born, headed YMCA (died 1961); **1883** Paine College for black students established; **June 25, 1900** classical scholar Moses Hadas born (died 1966); **1908** flooding destroys large areas; **1910** Springfield Baptist Church built; **1912** several killed in railroad strike rioting; **1916** fire destroys many businesses and historic homes; **1917** Camp Hancock established; **1918** St. Paul's Episcopal Church built; **1925** Augusta State University established; **1933** Augusta Museum established; **1934** Augusta National Golf Course opened, clubhouse built 1854 as Prosper Berckmans estate house; **Sept. 15, 1945** actress Jessye Norman born; **1950** Bush Field airport established, becomes Augusta Regional Airport 1999; **1957** Augusta-Richmond County Municipal Building completed; **Dec. 25, 1960** singer Amy Grant born; **1961** Augusta Technical Institute (2-year college) established; **July 30, 1961** actor Larry Fishburne born; **Nov. 9, 1965** President Eisenhower suffers second heart attack (first 1955); **May 12, 1970** rioting follows death of black youth held in jail, six killed, 60 injured, 50 buildings destroyed; **Sept. 30, 1974** banker E. B. Reville and wife kidnapped at Hephzibah to south, $30,000 ransom paid; he found alive, she found dead Nov. 2; **1997** National Science Center opened; **Apr. 24, 1997** Tiger Woods, 21, wins Masters Tournament at Augusta National Golf Club, record 270 strokes, youngest and first African-American winner.

Bainbridge   *Decatur County*   *Southwestern Georgia, 197 mi/317 km south of Atlanta*

c.1778 Indian trading post established by James Burgess; **1810** first settlers arrive on Flint River; town founded; **1817** Fort Hughes built, used by Gen. Andrew Jackson's troops during Indian wars; **1823** Decatur County formed; **1824** town becomes county seat, named for William Bainbridge, commander of *USS Constitution*; **1829** incorporated as a town; **1866** incorporated as a city; **1902** county courthouse built; **1972** Bainbridge College (2-year) established.

Barnesville   *Lamar County*   *Central Georgia, 50 mi/80 km south of Atlanta*

1823 Gachet House built by Charles Gachet; **1826** tavern opened by Gideon Barnes; town founded by Barnes; **1852** Barnesville Male and Female High School established, becomes Gordon Military College 1880, later Gordon College (2-year); **1854** incorporated as a town; **c.1890** town becomes South's main producer of buggies; **1899**

incorporated as a city; **1920** Lamar County formed; town becomes county seat; **1931** county courthouse built.

Baxley   *Appling County*   *Southeastern Georgia, 75 mi/121 km west-southwest of Savannah*

1814 David Summerall becomes first white man to enter area occupied by Creeks; **1818** Appling County formed; **1828** Holmesville becomes county seat; **1870** Macon & Brunswick Railroad built; town founded; **1873** county seat moved to Baxley; **1875** incorporated as a town; **1896** incorporated as a city; **1908** county courthouse completed.

Blackshear   *Pierce County*   *Southeastern Georgia, 85 mi/137 km southwest of Savannah*

1857 Pierce County formed; **1858** town founded as county seat; first county courthouse built, destroyed by fire 1875, rebuilt, survives as residence; **1859** incorporated as a town; **Nov. 1864–Jan. 1865** over 5,000 Union soldiers imprisoned here; **1902** third county courthouse built; **1911** incorporated as a city.

Blairsville   *Union County*   *Northern Georgia, 80 mi/ 129 km north-northeast of Atlanta*

1832 Union County formed; **1835** town founded and incorporated as county seat; **1838** town platted; **1830s** gold mining begins, continues until 1910; **1899** third county courthouse built; **1936** Chattahoochee National Forest created; **1941** incorporated as a city; **1976** County Office Building completed, Judicial Annex added 1978.

Blakely   *Early County*   *Southwestern Georgia, 170 mi/274 km south-southwest of Atlanta*

1818 Early County formed; **1825** town founded as county seat, named for Capt. Johnston Blakely, naval officer of War of 1812; **1870** incorporated as a town; **1891** Cohelee Covered Bridge built on Cohelee Creek; **1900** incorporated as a city; **1906** third county courthouse built; **1921** boll weevil cotton infestation leads to peanut production.

Blue Ridge   *Fannin County*   *Northern Georgia, 76 mi/122 km north of Atlanta*

1854 Fannin County formed; Morganton becomes county seat; **1879** Marietta & North Georgia Railroad built; town founded; **1887** incorporated as a town; **1895** Louisville & Nashville Railroad built; county seat moved to Blue Ridge; **1900** incorporated as a city; **1931** Blue Ridge Lake formed by dam on Toccoa River to east; **1937** county courthouse built; **1983** agents destroy moonshine operation; **1998** Blue Ridge Scenic Railway opens to McCoysville.

Brunswick   *Glynn County*   *Southeastern Georgia, 65 mi/105 km south of Savannah, on Atlantic Ocean*

1734 military outpost established by Capt. William Horton on Jekyll Island to southeast; **1742** plantation established by Mark Carr; **1771** town platted; **1777** Glynn

County formed; town becomes county seat; **1778** Glynn Academy founded; **1836** incorporated as a town; **1856** incorporated as a city; **Nov. 28, 1858** last slave ship, the *Wanderer*, seized by U.S. off Jekyll Island with over 300 Africans; **June 8, 1863** Confederate defenders repulse Federal gunboats and transports; **1885** Oglethorpe Hotel built; **1896** great hurricane damages coastal areas; **1907** county courthouse built; **1961** Coastal Georgia Community College established; **Nov. 7, 1972** Sidney Lanier Drawbridge rammed by freighter, ten killed as vehicles drop into channel; **2002** new Sidney Lanier Suspension Bridge completed.

Buchanan *Haralson County* *Northwestern Georgia, 47 mi/76 km west of Atlanta*

1856 Haralson County formed, named for Cong. Hugh A. Haralson; town founded as county seat, named for Pres. James Buchanan; **1857** incorporated as a town; **1892** county courthouse completed; **1902** incorporated as a city; **June 4, 1971** car collides with truck loaded with dynamite at Waco to south, explosions destroy vehicles, ambulance, fire truck, burns area size of three football fields, no deaths or injuries; **1972** new county courthouse built.

Buena Vista *Marion County* *Western Georgia, 105 mi/169 km south of Atlanta*

1827 Marion County formed; **1829** Horry (Marionville) becomes county seat; **1830** town founded; **1838** county seat moved to Tazewell; **1850** incorporated as a town; county seat moved to Buena Vista; county courthouse built; **Dec. 21, 1911** baseball player Josh Gibson born, greatest hitter of Negro Leagues (died 1947); **1920** incorporated as a city.

Butler *Taylor County* *Western Georgia, 85 mi/ 137 km south of Atlanta*

c.1850 Central of Georgia Railroad built; **1852** Taylor County formed, named for Pres. Zachary Taylor; town founded as county seat, named for Gen. William Butler, Democratic vice presidential nominee 1848; **1854** incorporated as a town; **1915** incorporated as a city; **1935** second county courthouse built.

Cairo *Grady County* *Southwestern Georgia, 200 mi/322 km south of Atlanta*

1835 town (KAY-ro) founded; **1844** Greenwood plantation home completed to east, begun by John Wood 1835; **1870** incorporated as a town; **1905** Grady County formed, named for Georgia orator, editor Henry Woodfin Grady; town becomes county seat; **1906** incorporated as a city; **1908** first tung trees planted, beginning of Georgia's tung oil industry; **1909** city becomes major center of Georgia's cane sugar industry; **Jan. 31, 1919** Jackie Robinson born, first African-American major league baseball player (died 1972); **1985** county courthouse completed.

Calhoun *Gordon County* *Northwestern Georgia, 60 mi/97 km north-northwest of Atlanta*

1821 Cherokee Sequoyah completes 85-character Cherokee alphabet, begun 1809; **1832** first settlers arrive; **1848** Western & Atlantic Railroad built; town founded, named Dawsonville; **1850** Gordon County formed; town becomes county seat, renamed for John Calhoun, secretary of state under President Tyler; **1852** incorporated as a town; **1864** town destroyed by Sherman's Union troops; **March 20, 1888** tornado destroys much of town; **Oct. 23, 1888** fire destroys remaining buildings; **1918** incorporated as a city; **1961** third county courthouse built.

Camilla *Mitchell County* *Southwestern Georgia, 175 mi/282 km south of Atlanta*

1818 Hawthorne Trail blazed by William Hawthorne; **1820** Hawthorne returns to settle here with his family; **1857** Mitchell County formed; **1858** town founded as county seat and incorporated; **1904** fourth county courthouse built; **1905** incorporated as a city; **Feb. 14, 2000** tornado damages town killing 12, total 19 killed in four counties.

Canton *Cherokee County* *Northwestern Georgia, 32 mi/51km north of Atlanta*

1831 Cherokee County formed; **1832** town founded as county seat, named Cherokee Court House; **1833** incorporated as a town, renamed Etowah; **1834** judge imports mulberry trees and silkworms from China, effort to establish silk industry; town renamed Canton; **1865** Union troops burn courthouse; **1879** Marietta & North Georgia Railroad reaches town; **1880** *Cherokee Advance* newspaper founded; **1899** textile mill established by R. T. Jones, grandfather of golfer Bobby Jones, closed 1981; **Feb. 9, 1909** Secretary of State Dean Rusk born, served under Presidents Kennedy and Lyndon Johnson (died 1994); **1941** incorporated as a city; **1994** county courthouse built.

Carnesville *Franklin County* *Northeastern Georgia, 80 mi/129 km northeast of Atlanta*

1784 Franklin County formed; **1805** town platted on Broad River as first permanent county seat, named for Thomas Carnes; **1819** incorporated as a town; **1901** incorporated as a city; **1906** third county courthouse built.

Carrollton *Carroll County* *Northwestern Georgia, 40 mi/64 km west-southwest of Atlanta*

1826 Carroll County formed; **1829** town founded as county seat; **1856** incorporated as a town; **1891** incorporated as a city; **1928** county courthouse built; **1933** West Georgia Junior College established, becomes State University of West Georgia; **1968** Carroll Technical Institute (2-year college) established.

Cartersville *Bartow County* *Northwestern Georgia, 35 mi/56 km northwest of Atlanta*

1830 cabin built by Pine Log, Cherokee chieftain; **1832** Cass County formed; **1835** Cassville becomes county seat; **1833** town founded on Western & Atlantic Railroad, named Birmingham; **1840** Valley View house built to southwest by Col. Robert Sproull; **1840s** Walnut Grove house built; **1845** Cooper Iron Works established to south by Mark Cooper; **1850** town moved north, incorporated as a town, renamed for landowner Farish Carter; **1861** county renamed Bartow County; **1864** town destroyed by Sherman's Union forces; **1867** county seat moved to Cartersville; **Sept. 17, 1869** author Corra Harris born (died 1931); **1872** incorporated as a city; **1882** Etowah Mounds explored by Bureau of American Ethnology; **1886** Sam Jones Tabernacle built by prominent evangelist, used until 1925; **1902** county courthouse built; **1917** barite mines opened to south; **1936** Corra Harris Memorial Chapel built by three nephews; **1950** Allatoona Lake formed by dam to east on Etowah River; **1992** County Judicial Center built.

CCC Camp F-16 *Walker County* See **La Fayette** (1940)

Cedartown *Polk County* *Northwestern Georgia, 53 mi/85 km west-northwest of Atlanta*

1832 blacksmith Asa Prior becomes first settler; **1851** Polk County formed; town founded as county seat; **1854** incorporated as a town; **1889** incorporated as a city; **1896** Cedartown Cotton Manufacturing Company established; **Jan. 5, 1905** actor Sterling Holloway born (died 1992); **1951** third county courthouse built.

Chatsworth *Murray County* *Northern Georgia, 72 mi/116 km north-northwest of Atlanta*

1804 Vann House built by Cherokee Chief James Vann; **1832** Murray County formed; **1905** Louisville & Nashville Railroad built; town founded; **1906** incorporated as a town; **1915** county seat moved from Spring Place; **1917** county courthouse built; **1923** incorporated as a city; **1977** Carters Lake formed by dam to southeast on Conasauga River.

Chickamauga *Walker County* *Northwestern Georgia, 11 mi/18 km south of Chattanooga, Tenn.*

1836 James Gordon settles near Crawfish Spring, builds mill on Chickamauga Creek; **1847** Gordon-Lee Mansion built by Gordon; **Sept. 8, 1863** Union General Rosecrans establishes headquarters at Gordon house; **Sept. 20, 1863** Battle of Chickamauga, Union troops under Gen. W. S. Rosecrans forced to retreat to Chattanooga after ambitious drive by Confederates under Gen. Braxton Bragg; **Aug. 19, 1890** Chickamauga and Chattanooga National Military Park established, extends into Tennessee; **1891** incorporated as a town; **1913** incorporated as a city.

Clarkesville *Habersham County* *Northeastern Georgia, 77 mi/124 km northeast of Atlanta*

1818 Habersham County formed; **1821** town founded as county seat, named for Gov. John C. Clarke, Revolutionary veteran; **1823** incorporated as a village; **1850** village disincorporated; **1870** incorporated as a town; **1882** Southern Railway reaches town; **1897** incorporated as a city; **1963** county courthouse built, bell tower added 1983.

Claxton *Evans County* *Southeastern Georgia, 48 mi/77 km west of Savannah*

c.1890 Seaboard Air Line Railroad; town founded; **1911** incorporated as a city; **1914** Evans County formed; town becomes county seat; **1923** county courthouse built.

Clayton *Rabun County* *Northeastern Georgia, 95 mi/153 km northeast of Atlanta*

1819 Rabun County formed; area settled by New Englanders; **1821** town founded as county seat, named Claytonsville; **1823** incorporated as a town, renamed Clayton; **1859** Dick's Creek Tunnel begun to west, planned for Black Diamond Railroad for hauling coal, work suspended during Civil War, abandoned, 80 percent completed; **1909** incorporated as a city; **c.1910** town becomes mountain resort; **1967** fourth county courthouse built.

Cleveland *White County* *Northern Georgia, 68 mi/109 km northeast of Atlanta*

1857 White County formed; town platted, becomes county seat; **1870** incorporated as a town; **1946** Truett-McConnell College (2-year) established; **1949** incorporated as a city; **1964** second county courthouse built; **Aug. 12, 1983** use of Paraquat herbicide to destroy marijuana crops denounced by Center for Disease Control, Atlanta.

Cochran *Bleckley County* *Central Georgia, 113 mi/182 km south-southeast of Atlanta*

1850s area first settled by B. B. Dykes; town founded, named Dykesboro; **1869** incorporated as a town, renamed for Arthur Cochran, responsible for building Macon & Brunswick Railroad through town; **1885** Middle Georgia College (2-year) established; **1904** incorporated as a city; **1912** Bleckley County formed, named for state Supreme Court Justice Logan Edwin Bleckley; town becomes county seat; **1914** county courthouse built.

College Park *Fulton and Clayton counties* *Northwestern Georgia, 10 mi/16 km south-southwest of Atlanta*

1890 Atlantic & West Point Railroad built; town founded as Atlantic City; **1891** incorporated as a city, renamed Manchester; **1892** Cox College established (closed 1938); **1896** city renamed College Park; **1900** Georgia Military

GEORGIA

Academy founded, renamed Woodward Academy 1964; **2002** Georgia International Convention Center built.

Colquitt *Miller County* *Southwestern Georgia, 180 mi/290 km south-southwest of Atlanta*

1856 Miller County formed; town founded as county seat, named for U.S. Sen. Walter T. Colquitt; **1860** incorporated as a town; **1905** incorporated as a city; **1977** fifth county courthouse built.

Columbus *Muscogee County* *Western Georgia, 95 mi/153 km south-southwest of Atlanta*

1825 lands ceded to state by Creek people; Muscogee County formed; **1828** town founded as county seat on Chattahoochee River; incorporated as a town; *Columbus Enquirer* newspaper founded; first steamboat reaches site; St. Luke's Methodist Church organized; **1829** First Baptist Church organized; **1832** St. Elmo house built by Seaborn Jones; **1835** incorporated as a city; **1838** Columbus Cotton Factory established; **c.1840** Lion House built, residence named for its Nubian lions guarding front portals; **1851** Mott House built; Eagle and Phoenix Textile Mills founded; **1853** Mobile & Girard Railroad reaches town from Alabama; Peabody House built; **1854** Pease House built; **Apr. 15, 1865** town attacked by Union forces one week after Lee's surrender, many businesses and public buildings destroyed; ironclad boat *Jackson* set ablaze; **1867** Georgia Home Bank Building completed; **1871** Lummus Cotton Gin Plant founded; Springer Opera House built; **1886** John S. Pemberton (1831–1888) develops formula for Coca-Cola, place of origin also claimed by Atlanta; *Columbus Ledger* newspaper founded; **1905** Chero-Cola soft drink developed by Claude A. Hatcher, becomes Nehi Company 1925; **1917** Fort Benning Military Reservation established; **Feb. 19, 1917** woman novelist Carson McCullers born (died 1967); **1921** Centennial Cotton Gin Plant moved from Fort Valley; **1925** Tom Huston Peanut and Candy Company founded, marketer of Tom's Toasted Peanuts; **1926** Bartlett's Ferry Dam built to north on Chattahoochee River forming Lake Harding; **1941** Columbus Museum of Arts and Crafts established; **July 8, 1942** Sen. Phil Gramm born at Fort Benning; **1950** Columbus Metropolitan Airport established; **1958** Columbus State University established; **1971** city and county governments consolidated; **March 29, 1971** Lt. William Calley convicted of My Lai massacre of 22 Vietnamese villagers March 16, 1968, overturned Sept. 25, 1974, due to pretrial publicity; **1973** 11-story county courthouse completed; **1996** Columbus Civic Center opened.

Conyers *Rockdale County* *North central Georgia, 25 mi/40 km east-southeast of Atlanta*

1845 Georgia Railroad built; town of Conyers Station founded; **1854** town incorporated as Conyers; **1870** Rockdale County formed; town becomes county seat; **1881** incorporated as a city; **1939** county courthouse built; **1944** Trappist (Cistercian) monastery established, closed 1960; **March 20, 1958** actress Holly Hunter born; **May 20, 1999** student wounds six with rifle at Heritage High School, copycat case to Columbine High shooting at Denver in April.

Cordele *Crisp County* *Central Georgia, 128 mi/206 km south-southeast of Atlanta*

1888 town founded at junction of three rail lines; **Dec. 1888** incorporated as a city; **1905** Crisp County formed, named for Judge Charles Crisp; town becomes county seat; **Dec. 12, 1918** blues singer Joe Williams born (died 1999); **1930** Lake Blackshear formed by dam to west on Flint River; **1950** second county courthouse built.

Covington *Newton County* *North central Georgia, 33 mi/53 km east-southeast of Atlanta*

1821 Newton County formed; **1822** town founded as county seat, named for Gen. Leonard Covington, Revolutionary War hero; **Dec. 1822** incorporated as a town; **c.1840** Usher House built; **1851** Southern Masonic Female College established; **1854** incorporated as a city; **1859** Dixie Manor house built; **1884** county courthouse built; **March 2, 1969** race car crashes into crowd at drag strip killing 11, injuring 50.

Crawfordville *Taliaferro County* *Eastern Georgia, 88 mi/142 km east of Atlanta*

Feb. 11, 1812 Gov. Alexander Hamilton Stephens born, Confederate vice president (died 1883); **1825** Taliaferro (TALL-a-ver) County formed, named for Revolutionary Gen. Benjamin Taliaferro; town founded as county seat; **1826** incorporated as a town; **c.1838** Georgia Railroad built; **1872** Stephens estate house built; **1902** county courthouse built; **1906** incorporated as a city; **May 5, 1938** blues singer Johnnie Taylor born (died 2000).

Cumming *Forsyth County* *Northern Georgia, 35 mi/56 km north-northeast of Atlanta*

1832 Forsyth County formed; **1833** town founded as county seat, named for Col. William Cumming of War of 1812; **1834** incorporated as a town; **1901** Poole's Mill Covered Bridge built; **1905** third county courthouse built, burned 1978; **1908** all black residents expelled following race riots; **1935** incorporated as a city; **1958** Buford Dam built on Chattahoochee River to east forming Lake Sidney Lanier; **1996** County Administration Building completed.

Cusseta *Chattahoochee County* *Western Georgia, 105 mi/167 km south-southwest of Atlanta*

1847 Sand Town founded; **1854** Chattahoochee County formed; town becomes county seat; **1855** incorporated as a town, renamed Cusseta (ku-SEE-tah) for former Muskogean town of Kasishta; county courthouse built, moved to Westville historic town 1974; **1963** incorporated as a city; **1975** new county courthouse completed.

Cuthbert *Randolph County* Southwestern Georgia, *140 mi/225 km south-southwest of Atlanta*

1828 Randolph County formed; **1831** town settled, founded as county seat; **1834** incorporated as a town; **c.1836** Toombs House built; **1850s** Central of Georgia Railroad built; **1854** Andrew College established; **1859** incorporated as a city; **1886** third county courthouse built; **Nov. 5, 1949** heavyweight boxer Larry Holmes born.

Dahlonega *Lumpkin County* Northern Georgia, *58 mi/93 km north-northeast of Atlanta*

1828 gold discovered by Benjamin Parks; **1829** gold and copper mining begins; state militia sent to protect Cherokee people from thousands of rowdy miners; **1830** land acquired from Cherokees; **1832** Lumpkin County formed; town founded as county seat, named Licklog; **1833** incorporated as a town, renamed Cherokee term for "golden color"; **1838** U.S. mint opens, closes 1861 with secession of Confederate states; **1873** North Georgia College and State University established; **c.1888** gold from old mint donated to sheath dome of state capitol; **1899** incorporated as a city; **1900** short-lived revival of gold mining activity occurs, continues into 1930s; **1965** county courthouse built.

Dallas *Paulding County* Northwestern Georgia, *27 mi/43 km west-northwest of Atlanta*

1832 Paulding County formed; Van Wert becomes county seat; **1851** Polk County separates from Paulding County taking Van Wert; **1852** town founded as new county seat; **1854** incorporated as a town; **May 27, 1864** Sherman's Union troops repulsed at Battle of Pickett's Mill to northeast; **1892** county courthouse built; **1927** incorporated as a city; **Apr. 4, 1977** Southern Airways DC-9 jet crashes during hailstorm at New Hope to northeast, killing 68.

Dalton *Whitfield County* Northwestern Georgia, *75 mi/121 km north-northwest of Atlanta*

1837 town founded, named Cross Plains; **1839** incorporated as a town; **1847** town renamed Dalton; **1850s** copper ore mined at Ducktown, Tennessee, shipped to Dalton by wagon; **1851** Whitfield County formed; town becomes county seat; **1853** incorporated as a city; **Nov. 1863** Confederate Gen. Braxton Bragg retreats after defeat at Missionary Ridge, resigns his command; **1864** first courthouse burned by Union forces; **1919** tufting handicrafts of Mrs. M. G. Cannon, Jr. mark beginning of town's major bedspread making industry; **1961** third county courthouse completed.

Danielsville *Madison County* Northeastern Georgia, *67 mi/108 km east-northeast of Atlanta*

1780s area settled by veterans of Revolution; **c.1790** town founded, named for Capt. Allen Daniel of Revolutionary War; **1811** Madison County formed; **1812** town becomes county seat; **Nov. 1, 1815** Dr. Crawford W. Long born, performed first operation using sulfuric anesthetic at Jefferson, Georgia (died 1878); **1817** incorporated as a town; **1901** third county courthouse built; **1908** incorporated as a city; **1997** fourth county courthouse built.

Darien *McIntosh County* Southeastern Georgia, *50 mi/80 km south of Savannah, near Atlantic Ocean*

1595 Tolomato Mission founded to north by Pedro Ruiz, remains until 1686; **1721** Fort King George built, destroyed by fire 1727, rebuilt to south; **Apr. 1736** settlers arrive by ship from Scotland; town founded near mouth of Altamaha River; **1760** The Thicket plantation established by Hugh Clark; **1793** McIntosh County formed; town becomes county seat; **c.1815** sawmills established in area; **1816** incorporated as a town; **1818** incorporated as a city; **1850s** rice growing reaches peak; **Jan. 11, 1863** town burned by Union force composed of freed black slaves; **1870** Presbyterian Church built; **1872** second county courthouse built; **1895** Darien Short Line Railroad reaches town; **1920s** timber industry declines; **1938** Fort King George State Historic Site established; **1969** R. J. Reynolds Wildlife Refuge established to northeast on Supelo Island; **1976** National Estuarine Research Reserve established on Supelo Island.

Dawson *Terrell County* Southwestern Georgia, *138 mi/222 km south of Atlanta*

1856 Terrell County formed; town founded as county seat, named for U.S. Sen. William C. Dawson; **1857** incorporated as a town; **1872** incorporated as a city; **1892** second county courthouse built; **1914** Dawson Carnegie Library; **Sept. 19, 1941** blues singer Otis Redding born, killed in plane crash Dec. 10, 1967, Madison, Wisconsin.

Dawsonville *Dawson County* Northern Georgia, *48 mi/77 km north-northeast of Atlanta*

1829 gold discovered in area; **1857** Dawson County formed; town founded as county seat, named for Sen. William C. Dawson; **1859** incorporated as a town; **1952** incorporated as a city; **1967** first annual Moonshine Festival held; **1978** second county courthouse built.

Decatur *De Kalb County* Northwestern Georgia, *5 mi/8 km east of Atlanta*

c.1820 town settled by English and Scots-Irish immigrants from Virginia and Carolinas; **1822** De Kalb (dee-KAB) County formed; town founded as county seat; **1823** incorporated as a town; **1828** Columbia Theological Seminary founded; **1830s** town rejects railroad, rerouted through Marthasville, now Atlanta; **June 19, 1835** writer Rebecca Latimer Felton born (died 1930); **July 22, 1864** Gen. James McPherson's Union troops attacked by Gen. Joseph Wheeler's Confederates, driven north; **1890** Agnes Scott College established; **1922** incorporated as a city; **Apr. 23, 1957** actress Jan Hooks born; **1964** Georgia Perimeter College (2-year) established; **1967** nine-story county courthouse built; Fernbank Science Center opened; **1992** Fernbank Museum of Natural History opened.

Donalsonville *Seminole County* *Southwestern Georgia, 190 mi/306 km south-southwest of Atlanta*

1816 Fort Scott built; **1818** Gen. Andrew Jackson embarks on campaign into Florida against Seminoles, expedition nearly caused war with Spain; **c.1890** Atlantic Coast Line Railroad built; town founded; **1897** incorporated as a town; **1920** Seminole County formed; town becomes county seat; **1922** incorporated as a city; county courthouse built; **1952** Jim Woodruff Lock and Dam built to south on Chattahoochee River forming Lake Seminole.

Douglas *Coffee County* *Southern Georgia, 110 mi/177 km southwest of Savannah*

1854 Coffee County formed; **1855** town founded as county seat, named for Illinois Sen. Stephen A. Douglas; **1895** incorporated as a town; **1906** South Georgia College (2-year) established; **1940**s county courthouse completed.

Douglasville *Douglas County* *Northwestern Georgia, 20 mi/32 km west of Atlanta*

1800 area settled by Creek and Cherokee people; **1829** gold discovered luring white squatters; **1830** Native Americans removed from region; **1870** Douglas County formed; **1874** Georgia & Western Railroad reaches site; town founded as county seat, named for Illinois Sen. Stephen A. Douglas, Abraham Lincoln's political opponent; **1875** incorporated as a town; **1951** incorporated as a city; **1997** county courthouse completed.

Dublin *Laurens County* *Central Georgia, 120 mi/193 km southeast of Atlanta*

1790 David Blackshear establishes ferry on Oconee River, later becomes U.S. Senator (1816–1825); **1807** Laurens County formed; **1809** Sumterville becomes county seat; **1811** town founded as new county seat, named by Irishman Peter (Jonathan) Sawyer, donated land for public buildings; **1812** incorporated as a town; **1893** incorporated as a city; **1908** Confederate monument erected; **1962** fourth county courthouse built; **1970** St. Patrick's Festival established.

Eastman *Dodge County* *Central Georgia, 130 mi/209 km southeast of Atlanta*

1870 Dodge County formed; **1871** town founded as county seat on Macon & Brunswick Railroad; **1873** incorporated as a town; **1905** incorporated as a city; **1908** county courthouse built.

Eatonton *Putnam County* *Central Georgia, 65 mi/105 km southeast of Atlanta*

1807 Putnam County formed; town founded as county seat, named for Revolutionary War officer William Eaton; **1809** incorporated as a town; **1824** original section of county courthouse built, remodeled 1906; **Sept. 17, 1825** Supreme Court Justice Lucius Lamar born in rural Putnam County (died 1893); **c.1830** Bronson House built; **c.1835** Slade House built; **c.1845** Panola Hall house built; **Dec. 9, 1848** writer Joel Chandler Harris born, created Uncle Remus character (died 1908); **1879** incorporated as a city; **Feb. 9, 1944** novelist, poet Alice Walker born.

Echota *Gordon County* *Northwestern Georgia, 60 mi/97 km north-northwest of Atlanta*

1819 site chosen for an assembly place by Cherokee people, name site New Echota; **Oct. 20, 1820** Cherokee adopt formal government, abiding by white men's rules, making New Echota their capital; **1821** Oothcaloga Mission founded by Moravian Church; **1825** town of Echota platted; businesses established; **1828** *Cherokee Phoenix* newspaper founded, first Native American newspaper in U.S.; **1833** all Indian missions ordered closed by state of Georgia; **1838** Cherokee among eastern nations ordered removed to Oklahoma; Gen. Winfield Scott's 20,000 troops headquartered here for Cherokee removal; **1962** New Echota State Historical Site established.

Elberton *Elbert County* *Northeastern Georgia, 92 mi/148 km east-northeast of Atlanta*

1780s town settled, named for Gen. Samuel Elbert of Revolutionary War; **1790** Elbert County formed; town becomes county seat; **1803** incorporated as a town; **c.1820** James House built; **1840** Oliver House built; **1853** Heard House built; **Oct. 14, 1857** Supreme Court Justice Joseph Rucker Lamar born in rural Elbert County (died 1916); **1878** Elberton (Seaboard) Air Line Railroad reaches town; **1882** first granite quarry opened by Nathaniel Long; **1893** county courthouse built; **1896** incorporated as a city; **Feb. 9, 1902** large section of town destroyed by fire; **1921** boll weevil infestation devastates cotton crops; **1926** silk mill established; **1981** Elberton Granite Museum opened; **1985** Richard B. Russell Lake formed by dam on Savannah River on South Carolina boundary.

Ellaville *Schley County* *Western Georgia, 107 mi/172 km south of Atlanta*

1857 Schley County formed; **1858** town founded as county seat on land owned by Richard Burton; first county courthouse built; **1859** incorporated as a town; **1899** second county courthouse built.

Ellijay *Gilmer County* *Northwestern Georgia, 65 mi/105 km north of Atlanta*

1832 Gilmer County formed; **1834** town founded as county seat, named for Elatseyi, Cherokee village formerly on this site; **1840** incorporated as a town; **1898** Hyatt Hotel built, converted to third county courthouse 1934, condemned 2003; **1909** incorporated as a city.

GEORGIA

Fayetteville *Fayette County   Western Georgia, 22 mi/35 km south of Atlanta*

1821 Fayette County formed, one of five counties created in Land Lottery Draw, land ceded by Creek people; **1822** town founded as county seat; **1823** incorporated as a town; **1825** county courthouse built, restored 1983 following arson fire; **1902** incorporated as a city; **1930s** author Margaret Mitchell spends time at rural home of her grandfather conducting research for her novel *Gone With the Wind*; **1985** Courthouse Annex completed, becomes new Courthouse; **1992** County Administration Complex completed.

Fitzgerald *Ben Hill County   Southern Georgia, 155 mi/249 km south-southeast of Atlanta*

1895 town founded by colony of c.2,700 of Union veterans, named for Indianapolis editor and colony leader Philander H. Fitzgerald; **1896** incorporated as a city; Lee-Grant Hotel established; **1906** Ben Hill County formed; town becomes county seat; **1909** county courthouse completed; **1961** Blue and Gray Museum founded.

Folkston *Charlton County   Southeastern Georgia, 100 mi/161 km south-southwest of Savannah*

1854 Charlton County formed; Traders Hill becomes first county seat; **1881** Savannah, Florida & Western Railroad reaches site; town founded on St. Mary's River (Florida state boundary); **1889** Suwannee Canal Company purchases area to southwest with intention of draining Okefenokee Swamp, project abandoned; **1894** cypress logging begins, ends 1901; **1895** incorporated as a town; **1901** county seat moved to Folkston; **1908** Hebard Lumber Company builds railroad into swamp, abandons timber cutting after cost overruns; **1911** incorporated as a city; **1914** Old McDonald Hotel built; **1928** county courthouse built; **1937** Okefenokee National Wildlife Refuge established.

Forsyth *Monroe County   Central Georgia, 58 mi/93 km south-southeast of Atlanta*

1821 Monroe County formed; Johnstonville becomes temporary county seat; **1822** Hill Ardin house built; **1823** town platted as new county seat on land owned by John T. Booth; incorporated as a town; **1847** Bessie Tift College founded, named 1907 for prominent benefactor; **Sept. 23, 1884** Gov. Eugene Talmadge born (died 1946); **1896** second county courthouse built; **1902** Georgia State Teachers' and Agricultural College for black students opens as Methodist school, becomes state institution 1922, merges 1939 to become part of Fort Valley State University.

Fort Gaines *Clay County   Southwestern Georgia, 155 mi/249 km south-southwest of Atlanta*

1814 Fort Gaines built on Chattahoochee River; **Apr. 1816** town founded adjacent to fort; **1830** incorporated as a town; **1854** Clay County formed; town becomes county seat; **1865** fort abandoned; **1873** county courthouse completed; **1907** incorporated as a city; **1962** Walter F. George Lock and Dam built upstream (north) on Chattahoochee River forming Lake Eufaula (Walter F. George Reservoir).

Fort Valley *Peach County   Central Georgia, 90 mi/145 km south-southeast of Atlanta*

1836 town settled, originally named Fox Valley; **1851** Central Railroad of Georgia reaches town; **1854** incorporated as a town, renamed for Revolutionary War hero Arthur Fort; **1876** Centennial Cotton Gin Company founded, moved 1921 to Columbus; **1887** Central of Georgia Railroad built from Atlanta; **1896** Fort Valley Normal and Industrial School, becomes Fort Valley State University; **1907** incorporated as a city; **1922** first Georgia Peach Festival held; **1924** Peach County formed as state's last (159th) county; town becomes county seat; **1936** county courthouse built.

Franklin *Heard County   Western Georgia, 50 mi/80 km southwest of Atlanta*

1770 village settled on Chattahoochee River; **1830** Heard County formed; **1831** incorporated as a town, becomes county seat; **1908** incorporated as a city; **1964** third county courthouse built.

Gainesville *Hall County   Northern Georgia, 50 mi/80 km northeast of Atlanta*

1818 Hall County formed, named for Lyman Hall, signer of Declaration of Independence; town founded, named for Gen. Edmund P. Gaines, served in War of 1812 and Black Hawk and Seminole wars; **1821** incorporated as a town; town becomes county seat; **1848** discovery of gold at nearby Dahlonega brings wave of new settlers; **1870** incorporated as a city; **1871** Charlotte & Atlanta Air Line Railroad built; **1874** Piedmont Hotel built; **1878** Brenau College established; **1901** cotton mill opens; **June 1, 1903** tornado strikes town, 98 killed; **1907** Riverside Military Academy founded; **1927** Chicopee Manufacturing Company plant, maker of surgical supplies for Johnson & Johnson, built to southwest; **1933** hosiery mill opens; **Apr. 5–6, 1936** tornado hits town, part of overnight series of tornadoes in Mississippi and Georgia, killing 170 locally, 203 in region, 950 injured; **Apr. 6, 1936** hardware store fire kills 57; **1937** sixth county courthouse built; **1958** Sidney Lanier Lake formed on upper reach of Chattahoochee River to northwest by Buford Dam; **1964** Gainesville College (2-year) established; **March 20, 1998** tornado strikes northern part of county and neighboring White County, 13 killed; **2002** multistory county government center completed.

Georgetown *Quitman County   Southwestern Georgia, 135 mi/217 km south-southwest of Atlanta*

c.1831 town founded on Chattahoochee River; **1858** Quitman County formed; town becomes county seat;

1859 incorporated as a town; **1939** second county courthouse built; **1970** incorporated as a city.

Gibson   *Glascock County*   *Eastern Georgia, 112 mi/ 180 km east-southeast of Atlanta*

1857 Glascock County formed; **1858** town founded as county seat; county courthouse built; **1913** incorporated as a town; **1919** second county courthouse built; **1943** incorporated as a city.

Gray   *Jones County*   *Central Georgia, 72 mi/116 km southeast of Atlanta*

1807 Jones County formed; Albany (Clinton) becomes county seat; **1850s** town founded, named for local citizen James M. Gray; **1860s** much of county destroyed during Civil War; **1905** county seat moved to Gray; **1906** county courthouse built; **1911** incorporated as a town; **1936** Jones County Library founded; **1961** incorporated as a city.

Greensboro   *Greene County*   *Northern Georgia, 72 mi/116 km east of Atlanta*

1773 Cherokee, Creek, and Chickasaw people grant lands to white settlers; **c.1780** town founded as intended site for University of Georgia, Athens chosen instead; **1786** Greene County formed; **1787** town becomes county seat; **1790s** land grants made to speculators exceeds amount of land granted to state by Native Americans; **June 30, 1802** Alabama Sen. Benjamin Fitzpatrick born in rural Greene County (died 1869); **Dec. 10, 1803** incorporated as a town; **1807** County Jail built, replaced 1895; **1810** Cobb-Dawson House built by Sen. Thomas W. Cobb, sold 1829 to his senatorial successor William C. Dawson; **1849** county courthouse completed; **1855** incorporated as a city.

Greenville   *Meriwether County*   *Western Georgia, 55 mi/89 km south-southwest of Atlanta*

1827 Meriwether County formed; town founded as county seat, named for Revolutionary War Gen. Nathanael Greene [sp]; **1828** town platted; incorporated as a town; **1832** first county courthouse built, repaired after tornado 1893; **1887** incorporated as a city; **1904** second county courthouse built.

Griffin   *Spalding County*   *Central Georgia, 35 mi/ 56 km south of Atlanta*

1812 Creek Chief William McIntosh blazes trail as he leads Creeks in attack against British; **1840** town platted on land owned by Col. Lewis Lawrence Griffin; **1842** Monroe Railroad reaches town, completed to Jonesboro 1845; **1843** incorporated as a city; **1851** Spalding County formed; town becomes county seat; **1855** fire destroys city block; **1860** First Baptist Church built; **1883** cotton textile mill built; **1889** Georgia Agricultural Experiment Station established; **1965** Griffin Technical Institute (2-year college) established; **1985** third county courthouse built.

Hamilton   *Harris County*   *Western Georgia, 75 mi/ 121 km south-southwest of Atlanta*

1827 Harris County formed; town founded as county seat; **1828** incorporated as a town; **1903** incorporated as a city; **1908** third county courthouse built; **1988** first annual Cattlemen's Rodeo held.

Hardwick   *Bryan County*   *Southeastern Georgia, 13 mi/21 km south-southwest of Savannah*

1754 town site selected on Ogeechee River, near entrance to Atlantic Ocean, by Royal Gov. John Reynolds; town platted by French engineer William De Brahm, named for Earl of Hardwicke; **1793** Bryan County formed; town becomes county seat; **1797** county seat moved to Cross Roads near Ogeechee River, to Clyde 1901, to Pembroke 1937; **1861** Fort McAllister built on Ogeechee River by Confederates; **Dec. 13, 1864** after withstanding attacks in 1862 and 1863, Fort McAllister is taken by Gen. William B. Hazen's Union forces; **1866** incorporated as a town.

Harlem   *Columbia County*   *See* **Appling (1892)**

Hartwell   *Hart County*   *Northeastern Georgia, 95 mi/153 km northeast of Atlanta*

1853 Hart County formed; **1854** town founded as county seat; town and county named for Revolutionary spy Nancy Morgan Hart; **1856** incorporated as a town; **1904** incorporated as a city; **1960** Hartwell Dam built on Savannah River on South Carolina state boundary forming Lake Hartwell; **1971** fourth county courthouse built.

Hawkinsville   *Pulaski County*   *Central Georgia, 117 mi/188 km south-southeast of Atlanta*

1808 Pulaski County formed; Hartford, on east bank of Ocmulgee River, becomes county seat; **1830** town founded on west bank of Ocmulgee River, named for Benjamin Hawkins of Continental Congress; county seat moved to Hawkinsville; **1836** incorporated as a town; **1874** second county courthouse built; **1892** incorporated as a city.

Hazlehurst   *Jeff Davis County*   *Southeastern Georgia, 165 mi/266 km southeast of Atlanta*

c.1880 town founded as station on Macon & Brunswick Railroad, named for railroad surveyor Col. George Hazlehurst; **1891** incorporated as a town; **1905** Jeff Davis County formed; town becomes county seat; **1907** incorporated as a city; county courthouse built.

Hiawassee   *Towns County*   *Northern Georgia, 90 mi/145 km north-northeast of Atlanta*

c.1820 first white settlers arrive; **1856** Towns County formed; town becomes county seat; **1864–1865** state of anarchy exists in county during Civil War; **1870** incorporated as a town; **1916** incorporated as a city; **1942** Chatuge Lake formed by dam on Hiwassee River, on North

Carolina state boundary; **1964** third county courthouse built.

Hinesville   *Liberty County   Southeastern Georgia, 32 mi/51 km southwest of Savannah*

1752 first settlers arrive; **1777** Liberty County formed; **1784** Sunbury becomes county seat; **1797** county seat moved to Riceborough (Riceboro); **1837** town founded as new county seat; **1916** incorporated as a city; **1926** county courthouse built; **1940** Fort Stewart Military Reservation established to north.

Homer   *Banks County   Northeastern Georgia, 65 mi/105 km northeast of Atlanta*

1793 Fort Hollingsworth built to north; **1858** Banks County formed, named for Dr. Richard Banks; town founded as county seat; **1859** incorporated as a town; **Dec. 18, 1886** baseball player Ty Cobb, the "Georgia Peach," born at rural Narrows to north (died 1961); **1911** Blind Suzy Covered Bridge built; **1987** second county courthouse built.

Homerville   *Clinch County   Southern Georgia, 210 mi/334 km south-southeast of Atlanta*

1850 Clinch County formed; Magnolia becomes first county seat; **1853** farm established on town site by John Homer Mattox; **1859** Atlantic & Gulf Railroad built, acreage donated by Mattox for station; town founded; **1860** county seat moved from Magnolia; **1869** incorporated as a town, name officially designated as Homerville; **1896** third county courthouse built; **Dec. 18, 1917** actor Ossie Davis born at rural Cogsdell to northeast; **1931** incorporated as a city.

Irwinton   *Wilkinson County   Central Georgia, 98 mi/158 km southeast of Atlanta*

1803 Wilkinson County formed; **1811** town founded as county seat; **1816** incorporated as a town; **1904** incorporated as a city; **1924** county courthouse built.

Irwinville   *Irwin County   Southern Georgia, 155 mi/ 249 km south-southeast of Atlanta*

1818 Irwin County formed; **1831** town founded as county seat after several site changes, named Irwinsville for Gov. Jared Irwin; **1857** incorporated as a town, renamed Irwinville; **May 10, 1865** Confederate Pres. Jefferson Davis, en route to southern port after holding final cabinet meeting at Washington, Georgia, overtaken by Union forces; **1907** county seat moved to Ocilla; **1934** Irwinville Farms organized to demonstrate farming methods.

Jackson   *Butts County   Central Georgia, 57 mi/ 92 km south-southeast of Atlanta*

1792 scout Douglas Watson discovers sulfuric Indian Springs to south; **1821** Varner House built, originally served as hotel; **Jan. 8, 1821** treaty signed at Indian Springs between U.S. government and Creek people yielding lands to white settlement; **1825** Butts County formed; town founded as county seat, named for Gov. James Jackson; **Feb. 12, 1825** second treaty signed at Indian Springs relinquishing all remaining Creek lands, sending them west of Mississippi River; **1826** incorporated as a town; **1873** Alberta Grist Mill built near springs; **1882** Macon & Brunswick Railroad reaches town; **1898** fourth county courthouse built; **1901** incorporated as a city; **1910** Lloyd Shoals Dame built on Ocmulgee River to east forming Jackson Lake; **1933** Indian Springs State Park established.

Jasper   *Pickens County   Northwestern Georgia, 48 mi/77 km north of Atlanta*

c.1825 area first settled; **1830s** marble quarries established; **1853** Pickens County formed; town founded as county seat, named for Revolutionary War Sgt. William Jasper; **1857** incorporated as a town; **1861** with lack of plantations, county remains pro-Union long after secession; **1949** third county courthouse built; **1957** incorporated as a city.

Jefferson   *Jackson County   Northern Georgia, 55 mi/89 km northeast of Atlanta*

1784 area settled by Revolutionary veterans; **1796** Jackson County formed; Clarkesboro becomes first county seat; **1800** town founded as new county seat; **1806** incorporated as a town; **1835** Harrison Hotel built; **March 30, 1842** Dr. Crawford Long of nearby Danielsville first to use sulfuric ether as anesthetic; **1879** third county courthouse built; **1883** Gainesville & Midland Railroad built; **1896** incorporated as a city.

Jeffersonville   *Twiggs County   Central Georgia, 100 mi/161 km south-southeast of Atlanta*

1809 Twiggs County formed; town site of Marion becomes first county seat; **1820s** town founded, named Rains Store; **1845** Richland Baptist Church built, founded as early as 1811; **1849** town renamed for founding Jefferson family; **1868** county seat moved to Jeffersonville; county courthouse physically moved 6 mi/ 9.7 km to new seat; **1901** incorporated as a town; **1903** second county courthouse built; **1905** incorporated as a city.

Jesup   *Wayne County   Southeastern Georgia, 55 mi/ 89 km southwest of Savannah*

1803 Wayne County formed; **1805** Tuckersville becomes county seat; **1843** county seat moved to Waynesville; **1856** Macon & Brunswick Railroad built, forms junction with Atlantic & Gulf Railroad; town founded; **1870** incorporated as a town; **1873** county seat moved to Jesup; **1903** county courthouse built; **1915** incorporated as a city.

Jonesboro   *Clayton County   Northwestern Georgia, 16 mi/26 km south of Atlanta*

1823 town founded, named Leaksville; **1846** Macon & Western Railroad built; town renamed to honor railroad engineer Samuel G. Jones; **1858** Clayton County formed; town becomes county seat; **1859** incorporated as a town; **Aug. 31–Sept. 1, 1864** in Battle of Jonesboro, Confederates fail to defend crucial Macon-to-Atlanta railroad besieged by Gen. Sherman's troops, forced to abandon Atlanta; **1898** third county courthouse built; **1904** incorporated as a city; **1939** town serves as setting for movie *Gone With the Wind*; **2000** County Office Complex completed.

Kennesaw   *Cobb County   Northwestern Georgia, 20 mi/32 km north-northwest of Atlanta*

1846 Western & Atlantic Railroad built from Atlanta; **1850s** Big Shanty Distillery Company established; town founded, named Big Shanty; **June 11, 1861** Camp McDonald established as training camp for Confederate soldiers; **June 20–July 2, 1864** Battle of Kennesaw Mountain, two major military engagements during Gen. Sherman's Atlanta Campaign, though losing 3,000 men to Gen. Johnston's loss of 800, Sherman outmaneuvers Confederates, forcing retreat to Atlanta; **Oct. 4, 1864** many Union troops taken prisoner in attack by Confederates; **Nov. 14, 1864** town burned by Sherman's Union forces; **1887** incorporated as a town; **Feb. 8, 1917** Kennesaw Mountain National Battlefield Park established to south; **1950** incorporated as a city; **1963** Kennesaw State University established.

Knoxville   *Crawford County   Central Georgia, 75 mi/121 km south-southeast of Atlanta*

1822 Crawford County formed; **1823** town founded as county seat; **1825** incorporated as a town; **1835** Joanna Troutman, 16, creates flag bearing single star, presents it to battalion of Georgia volunteers sent to help Texas win its independence, used as official flag of Republic of Texas; **c.1890** Southern Railway built; **1832** second county courthouse completed; **1995** municipal charter becomes inactive; **2002** new county courthouse completed.

La Fayette   *Walker County   Northwestern Georgia, 80 mi/128 km northwest of Atlanta*

1833 Walker County formed; **1835** town founded as county seat, incorporated as a town, named Chattooga; **1836** town renamed for General Lafayette; John B. Gordon Hall Academy built, used 1863 as headquarters for Gen. Braxton Bragg's Confederate army; **June 24, 1864** Confederates attack Union supply lines, defeated by Union reinforcements; **1888** Chattanooga, Rome & Columbus Railroad reaches town; **1903** incorporated as a city; **1918** county courthouse built; **Jan. 27, 1940** lowest temperature ever recorded in Georgia, −17°F/−27°C, at CCC Camp F-16.

La Grange   *Troup County   Western Georgia, 62 mi/100 km southwest of Atlanta*

1820s area first settled; Segrest House built; **1825** Marquis de Lafayette visits western Georgia, compares beauty to his La Grange estate in France; **1827** Ferrell Gardens planned by Mrs. Blount Ferrell; **1826** Troup County formed; **1828** town founded as county seat, named for Lafayette's estate; incorporated as a town; **Sept. 29, 1830** Texas Cong. David Browning Culberson born (died 1900); **1831** La Grange College established; **1853** Bellevue house built; **1856** incorporated as a city; **1865** town spared burning by Col. La Grange of Wilson's Raiders; **1900** Callaway Mill established by Fuller E. Callaway, Sr.; **1910** Dunson Mills established; **1939** third county courthouse built.

Lakeland   *Lanier County   Southern Georgia, 205 mi/330 km south-southeast of Atlanta*

c.1820 area first settled; **1901** town incorporated, originally named Milltown; **1919** Lanier County formed; town becomes county seat; **1921** first county courthouse built; **1925** town renamed Lakeland; incorporated as a city; **Aug. 4, 1944** railroad accident kills 47 at rural Stockton to southeast; **1973** second county courthouse built.

Lawrenceville   *Gwinnett County   Northern Georgia, 28 mi/45 km northeast of Atlanta*

1818 Gwinnett County formed; **1820** town founded as county seat, named for Capt. James Lawrence of War of 1812; **1821** incorporated as a town; **June 15, 1826** humorist Charles Henry Smith born, used pen name Bill Arp (died 1903); **Sept. 15, 1831** several missionaries from New England sentenced to prison for living with Cherokee people and encouraging them to hold their lands, reversed by U.S. Supreme Court 1832, remained in prison until 1833; **1837** Lawrenceville Female Seminary founded; **1884** fourth county courthouse built; **1897** incorporated as a city; **March 26, 1978** Larry Flynt, 35, editor of *Hustler* magazine, shot, paralyzed below waist, was in Georgia to face obscenity charges; **1984** Gwinnett Technical Institute (2-year college) established; **1988** county government center completed.

Leesburg   *Lee County   Southwestern Georgia, 131 mi/211 km south of Atlanta*

1826 Lee County formed, named for Col. Henry (Lighthorse Harry) Lee who took Augusta from British 1781; Starksville becomes first county seat; **c.1870** Central of Georgia Railroad built; town founded, originally named Wooten Station; **1872** county seat moved from Starksville; town renamed Wooten; **1874** incorporated as a town, renamed Leesburg; **1918** county courthouse built; **June 5, 1920** African-American football player Marion

Motley born, instrumental in desegregating professional football in 1940s (died 1999).

Lexington   *Oglethorpe County*   *Eastern Georgia,*
75 mi/121 km east of Atlanta

1793 Oglethorpe County formed; first county seat located at Philomath; **1800** town founded as new county seat, named for Lexington, Massachusetts; **c.1800** Gilmer House built; **1806** incorporated as a town; **1808** Meson Academy opened, became high school 1920; **1810** fire destroys 17 buildings; **1887** spur of Georgia Railroad reaches town from Crawford; third county courthouse built; **1896** Presbyterian Church built, organized 1785.

Lincolnton   *Lincoln County*   *Eastern Georgia,*
113 mi/182 km east of Atlanta, near Savannah River

1796 Lincoln County formed; **1798** town founded as county seat; **1817** incorporated as a town; **1915** third county courthouse built; **1953** incorporation as a city.

Louisville   *Jefferson County*   *Eastern Georgia,*
128 mi/206 km southeast of Atlanta

1758 slave market house built, still standing; **1764** Roger Lawson Estate house built by Lawson, originally called Mount Pleasant; **1786** town (LOO-is-vill) platted and incorporated; **1796** Jefferson County formed; town becomes county seat; statehouse completed; state capital moved from Augusta; **Feb. 15, 1796** ceremony held on statehouse grounds for burning of Yazoo Papers, records of speculative sale of millions of acres of land in present-day Alabama and Mississippi, rescinded by state legislature, declared unconstitutional by U.S. Supreme Court 1814; **1806** state capital moved to Milledgeville; former statehouse used as county courthouse; **Apr. 20, 1807** Florida politician John Milton born in rural Jefferson County, committed suicide Apr. 1, 1865, upon defeat of Confederacy; **Sept. 7, 1815** Cong. Howell Cobb born in rural Jefferson County, served as secretary of treasury under President Buchanan (died 1903); **1818** town reincorporated; **1848** new county courthouse built on site of statehouse, materials used from statehouse in its construction; **July 24, 1952** highest temperature ever recorded in Georgia reached, 112°F/44°C.

Ludowici   *Long County*   *Southeastern Georgia,*
45 mi/72 km southwest of Savannah

1840 Savannah, Florida & Western Railroad built; town founded, named for German immigrant Carl Ludowici, established red clay roofing tile business here; **1905** incorporated as a town; **1920** Long County formed; town becomes county seat; **1921** incorporated as a city; **1926** county courthouse built.

Lumpkin   *Stewart County*   *Western Georgia,*
120 mi/193 km south-southwest of Atlanta

1830 Stewart County formed; town founded as county seat, named for Gov. Wilson Lumpkin; **1831** incorporated as a town; **1923** fourth county courthouse built; **1960** incorporated as a city.

Lyons   *Toombs County*   *Eastern Georgia, 73 mi/*
117 km west of Savannah

c.1890 town founded on Central Georgia Railroad; **1897** incorporated as a town; **1905** Toombs County formed; town becomes county seat; **1907** incorporated as a city; **1964** fourth county courthouse built.

Macon   *Bibb County*   *Central Georgia, 80 mi/*
129 km south-southeast of Atlanta

8000 BC Paleo Ice Age cultures inhabit region; **c.900 AD** Mississippian ceremonial temples mounds built to east, remain in use through 1100 AD; **1690** trading post built by English, burned 1715 during Yamassee Wars; **1806** Fort Hawkins established by Americans at Ocmulgee Falls; lands ceded by Native Americans; **1818** first settlers arrive from North Carolina; **1821** village of Newtown founded on east bank of Ocmulgee River; **1822** Bibb County formed; town of Macon founded on west bank of Ocmulgee River as county seat, named for Nathaniel Macon, North Carolina statesman; **1823** incorporated as a town; **1824** Macon Hotel built; Macon Academy founded; **1825** *Georgia Messenger* newspaper moves to Macon from Newtown; Macon's first bank opens; **1834** incorporated as a city; **1836** Georgia Female College founded; **1838** Monroe Railroad built to Forsyth; **1839** Wesleyan College established; **Feb. 3, 1842** poet, musician Sidney Lanier born (died 1881); **1846** Ralph Small House built; **1851** first Georgia State Fair held; Christ Church built; **1855** P. L. Hay House built; **1858** First Presbyterian Church built, organized 1826; **July 30, 1864** Gen. George Stoneman's Union troops attack Macon, driven back to Clinton, defeated there, Stoneman and 500 others taken prisoner; **Apr. 20, 1865** Gen. James H. Wilson's Union troops, approaching from Columbus, met outside town by General Cobb's forces bearing message of armistice between Generals Johnston and Sherman; **1871** Mercer University, established 1833, moves from Penfield; Mount de Sales Academy founded by Catholic Church; **1874** Macon Public Library founded; **1876** Bibb Manufacturing Company, clothing factory, established; **Apr. 5, 1901** actor Melvyn Douglas born (died 1981); **1906** Georgia Academy for the Blind built; construction of river levee begun; Central of Georgia Railway establishes shops here; **1924** fourth county courthouse built; **1928** Wesleyan Conservatory built; **Dec. 5, 1932** singer Richard Wayne Penniman (Little Richard) born; **1933** Citizens and Southern National Bank completed; **June 14, 1934** Ocmulgee National Monument authorized to east, protects Mississippian cultural site; **1936** Training School for Negro Girls established; **1948** Middle Georgia Regional (Lewis B. Wilson) Airport opened to south; **1952** first

Cherry Blossom Festival held; **1956** Georgia Sports Hall of Fame founded; **1965** Macon Junior College established, becomes Macon State College 1997; **Oct. 29, 1971** singer/guitarist Duane Allman, 24, of Allman Brothers Band killed in motorcycle accident; **1976** Macon Symphony Orchestra established; **1996** Georgia Music Hall of Fame opened, collection started 1979; **1999** C. Jack Ellis becomes city's first black mayor.

Madison   *Morgan County*   *Central Georgia, 55 mi/ 89 km east of Atlanta*

1807 Morgan County formed; town founded as county seat, named for Pres. James Madison; **1809** incorporated as a town; **c.1810** Presbyterian Church built; **1817** will of Benjamin Braswell provides that sale of his 13 slaves provide for educations of indigent white children; **1832** Lancelot Johnson invents cottonseed crushing machine; **1835** Heritage Hall complex built by Dr. Elijah Evans Jones; **c.1835** Stokes-McHenry House built; **c.1845** Burney House built; Bonar Hall house built; **1945** Uncle Remus Regional Library founded; **c.1850** Travelers' Inn built; **1851** Kolb House built; **1865** incorporated as a city; **1905** county courthouse built; **1976** Madison-Morgan Cultural Center opened.

Marietta   *Cobb County*   *Northwestern Georgia, 15 mi/24 km north-northwest of Atlanta*

1832 Cobb County formed; town founded as county seat; **1834** incorporated as a town; **1842** St. James Episcopal Church built; **1850s** town develops as mountain resort; **1851** Georgia Military Institute established; **Oct. 31, 1863** William Gibbs McAdoo born, served as secretary of treasury under President Wilson (died 1941); **June 27, 1864** General Sherman's forces repulsed by General Johnston's Confederate troops in Battle of Kennesaw Mountain, 3,000 Union killed, 800 Confederates killed, Johnston forced to retreat to Atlanta; **Nov. 1864** General Sherman burns town on his march to the sea; **1873** fourth county courthouse built; **c.1890** Crosby House built; **Apr. 23, 1897** World War II Gen. Lucius Clay born (died 1978); **Feb. 8, 1917** Kennesaw Mountain National Battlefield Park authorized, located to west; **1948** incorporated as a city; Southern Polytechnic State University established; **1961** Chattahoochee Technical Institute (2-year college) established; **1966** County Office Building completed replacing courthouse.

Marshallville   *Macon County*   *Central Georgia, 95 mi/153 km south-southeast of Atlanta*

1820s town settled by Germans; Lewis Rumph House built; **c.1845** Frederick-Wade House built; **1854** incorporated as a town; **c.1855** McCaskill-Rumph House built; **1860s** Slappey House built; **1875** Samuel Rumph develops Elberta peach, named for his wife, at Willow Lake Farm, first commercial peach orchard in Georgia; **1953** incorporated as a city; **1968** American Camellia Society, founded 1945, establishes headquarters at Massee Lane Gardens.

McDonough   *Henry County*   *Central Georgia, 26 mi/42 km south-southeast of Atlanta*

1820s cotton becomes important crop, retains dominance until 1921 boll weevil infestation; **1821** Henry County formed, one of five original counties created from Land Lottery Draw; trading post established; town founded as county seat, named for naval officer Thomas MacDonough who defeated British on Lake Champlain Sept. 11, 1814; **1823** incorporated as a town; **1824** Henry Academy founded; **1828** the *Jacksonian* newspaper founded, first to support candidacy of Pres. Andrew Jackson; **July 22, 1864** General Sherman's army divides itself here on its march to the sea; **Aug. 30, 1864** 20,000 Confederate troops camp here, prepare for Union attack on Jonesboro; **1897** third county courthouse built; **1908** incorporated as a city; **1925** worst drought in county's history ruins crops.

McRae   *Telfair County*   *Central Georgia, 143 mi/ 230 km southeast of Atlanta*

1807 Telfair County formed; **c.1810** area settled by Scottish immigrants; **1870** Macon & Brunswick Railroad built; town founded on land owned by Daniel McRae; **1871** county seat moved from Jacksonville; **1874** incorporated as a town; **1902** incorporated as a city; **Aug. 9, 1913** Gov., Sen. Herman Talmadge born in rural Telfair County (died 2002); **Nov. 23, 1913** Kodak businessman Marion Bayard Folsom born, secretary of Health, Education, and Welfare under President Eisenhower (died 1976); **1934** county courthouse built.

Metter   *Candler County*   *Southeastern Georgia, 62 mi/100 km west-northwest of Savannah*

1889 town founded; post office established; **1901** Georgia Railroad built; **1903** incorporated as a town; **1914** Candler County formed; town becomes county seat; **1920** incorporated as a city; **1921** county courthouse built.

Milledgeville   *Baldwin County*   *Central Georgia, 83 mi/134 km southeast of Atlanta*

1540 explorer Hernando De Soto visits area via Oconee River; **1793** Fort Fidius established; **c.1800** Fort Wilkinson established to north, site of 1803 treaty with Creek people ceding lands to U.S.; **1803** Baldwin County formed; town founded as state capital and county seat; **1806** state capital moved from Louisville; incorporated as a town; **1807** old state capitol completed; **1808** Georgia State Prison founded; **1812** United States Hotel built; **1825** Sanford House built by Gen. John Sanford; *Federal Union* newspaper founded, becomes *Union Recorder* 1872; **March 1825** French General Lafayette visits town; **c.1830** Rockwell Mansion built by Col. W. S. Rockwell; **1832** Harris House built by Judge Iverson Louis Harris; **1836** incorporated as a city; Oglethorpe University established, closed 1862, refounded 1916 at Atlanta; **1838** Executive Mansion built; **1839** Lockerly House built; **1842** Georgia State Hospital opened; **1843** St.

Stephens Catholic Church built; **1864** on his march to the sea, General Sherman spares town, burns state penitentiary; **1868** state capital moved to Atlanta; **1879** Georgia Military College (2-year) established; **1887** third county courthouse completed; **1889** Georgia College and State University established; **1905** Georgia State Reformatory founded, becomes State Training School for Boys 1919; **1997** fourth county courthouse completed.

Millen *Jenkins County   Eastern Georgia, 70 mi/ 113 km northwest of Savannah*

1830s area settled; town founded, originally named Seventy-Nine for its road-distance from Savannah; **1836** town renamed for Capt. John Millen, engineer for Central of Georgia Railroad; **1881** incorporated as a town; **1905** Jenkins County formed; town becomes county seat; **1906** incorporated as a city; **1910** county courthouse built.

Monroe *Walton County   Northern Georgia, 40 mi/ 64 km east of Atlanta*

1818 Walton County formed; town founded as county seat; **c.1820** Selman House built by settler Walter Briscoe; **1821** incorporated as a town; **1884** third county courthouse built; **1887** McDaniel-Tichenor House built; **1896** incorporated as a city; **July 25, 1946** two black couples Roger and Dorothy Malcolm and George and Mae Murray Dorsey lynched by mob of whites, Roger Malcolm accused of stabbing white boss.

Monticello *Jasper County   Central Georgia, 53 mi/ 85 km southeast of Atlanta*

1807 Jasper County formed; **1808** town founded as county seat; **1810** incorporated as a town; **1901** incorporated as a city; **1908** third county courthouse built; **Sept. 19, 1964** country singer Trisha Yearwood born.

Morgan *Calhoun County   Southwestern Georgia, 155 mi/249 km south-southwest of Atlanta*

1854 Calhoun County formed; town founded as county seat; **1856** incorporated as a city; **1923** voters approve removal of county seat to Arlington, reverse decision 1929; **1935** third county courthouse built.

Morrow *Clayton County   Northwestern Georgia, 13 mi/21 km south of Atlanta*

1846 Monroe Railroad built; town founded; **1941** DC-3 twin-engine plane crashes in town, seven killed, flying ace Eddie Rickenbacker among survivors; **1943** incorporated as a city; **1969** Clayton College and State University established; **2003** Georgia Division of Archives and History completes new building, moves from downtown Atlanta.

Moultrie *Colquitt County   Southwestern Georgia, 180 mi/290 km south of Atlanta*

1850 town settled on Ocklockonee River; town named Ocklockonee; **1856** Colquitt County formed; town becomes county seat, **1857** town renamed for Gen. William Moultrie of Revolutionary War; **1859** incorporated as a town; **1890** incorporated as a city; **1902** third county courthouse built.

Mount Vernon *Montgomery County   South central Georgia, 88 mi/142 km west of Savannah*

1793 Montgomery County formed; **1797** town founded as county seat on plantation of Arthur Lott; **1813** first county courthouse built; **1872** incorporated as a town; **1904** Brewton-Parker College established; **1907** county courthouse built following several previous structures; **1960** incorporated as a city.

Nahunta *Brantley County   Southeastern Georgia, 78 mi/126 km southwest of Savannah*

c.1860 Brunswick & Western Railroad built east to west; **c.1870** town founded, originally named Victoria; **1899** town renamed to Nahunta for timber operator N. A. Hunter; **1902** Savannah, Florida & Western Railroad built north to south, forming junction 1.5 mi/2.4 km to east; town moved; **1920** Brantley County formed; Hoboken becomes first county seat; **1923** county seat moved to Nahunta; **1925** incorporated as a city; **1930** second county courthouse built.

Narrows *Banks County   See **Homer (1886)***

Nashville *Berrien County   Southern Georgia, 190 mi/306 km south-southeast of Atlanta*

c.1840 town founded; **1856** Berrien County formed; town becomes county seat; **1858** county courthouse built; **1892** incorporated as a town; **1898** second county courthouse built; **1900** incorporated as a city.

New Echota *Gordon County   See **Echota***

New Hope *Paulding County   See **Dallas (1968)***

Newnan *Coweta County   Western Georgia, 35 mi/ 56 km southwest of Atlanta*

1823 original section of Rosemary House built; **1825** Coweta (ky-EE-ta) County formed; **1827** town founded as Bullsboro; **1828** town moved 2.5 mi/4 km southwest; incorporated as a town; **1850** sawmill established, becomes R. D. Coyle Company, home manufacturer; **1850s** Calhoun House built; **1851** Atlanta & West Point Railroad reaches town; **1854** College Temple for women established, closed 1888; **July 1864** Union forces of Gen. E. M. McCook defeated by Confederates at Brown's Mill to south; **1866** incorporated as a city; **1904** county courthouse built.

Newton *Baker County Southwestern Georgia, 90 mi/145 km southeast of Columbus*

1825 Baker County formed; Byron becomes first county seat; **1837** town of Newton founded as new county seat; **1872** incorporated as a town; **1900** third county courthouse built; **1906** incorporated as a city; **1925** flooding Flint River damages town, again in 1929; **1994** worst of several floods damages town, courthouse; **2000** former school becomes new county courthouse; old Courthouse retained for public service agency offices.

Ocilla *Irwin County Southern Georgia, 163 mi/ 262 km south-southeast of Atlanta*

1818 Irwin County formed; **1831** Irwinville becomes county seat following several temporary county seat moves; **May 10, 1865** Confederate Pres. Jefferson Davis taken prisoner at dawn by Union forces; **c.1880** Ocilla founded 10 mi/16 km to southeast; **1897** incorporated as a town; **1902** incorporated as a city; **1907** county seat moved to Ocilla; **1910** fourth county courthouse built; **May 9, 1937** singer Dave Prater, Jr. of duo Sam and Dave born (died 1988).

Oglethorpe *Macon County Western Georgia, 105 mi/169 km south of Atlanta, on Flint River*

1837 Macon County formed; Lanier becomes first county seat; **1838** town founded; **1840s** Hansell-Keen House built; **1849** incorporated as a town; **c.1850** Colonel George Fish House built; **1851** Central of Georgia Railroad reaches town; **1852** incorporated as a city; **1857** county seat moved to Oglethorpe; **1894** third county courthouse built.

Oxford *Newton County North central Georgia, 33 mi/53 km east-southeast of Atlanta*

1836 Emory College established; **c.1836** Dixon House built; **1839** incorporated as a town; **1840** Branham Heights house built; **1841** Old Emory Church built, used as hospital during Civil War, completed 1876; **1914** incorporated as a city; **1915** Emory College becomes part of Atlanta's Emory University, becomes Emory Junior College 1928.

Pearson *Atkinson County Southern Georgia, 115 mi/185 km southwest of Savannah*

1875 Brunswick & Western (Atlantic Coastline) Railroad reaches site; town founded, named for county official Benejah Pearson; **1890** incorporated as a town; **1916** incorporated as a city; **1917** Atkinson County formed, named for Gov. William Yates Atkinson; town becomes county seat; **1920** county courthouse built.

Pembroke *Bryan County Southeastern Georgia, 30 mi/48 km west of Savannah*

1793 Bryan County formed; Hardwick becomes first county seat; **1797** county seat moved to Crossroads;

1854 county seat moved to Eden; **1883** county seat moved to Clyde; **1892** South & Western Railroad built; town founded; **1905** incorporated as a town; **1937** county seat moved to Pembroke, **1938** county courthouse built; **1940** Fort Stewart Military Reservation established to south, largest military base east of Mississippi River.

Perry *Houston County Central Georgia, 100 mi/ 161 km south-southeast of Atlanta*

1821 Houston (HOW-stun) County formed, one of five counties formed in Land Lottery Draw; town founded; **1823** town becomes county seat; **1824** incorporated as a town; **1827** First Methodist Church built; **1856** county courthouse built; **1849** Presbyterian Church built; **Jan. 5, 1887** World War II Gen. Courtney Hicks Hodges born (died 1966); **1905** incorporated as a city; **Sept. 8, 1938** U.S. Sen. Sam Nunn born; **1948** second county courthouse built; **May 19, 1970** 300 blacks begin 110 mi/177 km march across Georgia, ends with rally of 10,000 in Atlanta.

Plains *Sumter County Western Georgia, 120 mi/ 193 km south of Atlanta*

1885 town founded; **1896** incorporated as a town; **Oct. 1, 1924** Gov. James Earl "Jimmy" Carter, 39th President, born; **Aug. 18, 1927** Rosalynn Smith Carter born, wife of Pres. Jimmy Carter (married July 7, 1946); **1976** incorporated as a city; **Nov. 1976** President-elect Carter's church, Plains Baptist Church, lifts 11-year ban on black membership; **1987** Jimmy Carter National Historic Site established; **1997** first Plains Peanut Festival held.

Preston *Webster County Southwestern Georgia, 118 mi/190 km south-southwest of Atlanta*

1836 area first settled; **1853** Kinchafoonee County formed; McIntosh becomes first county seat; **1856** county renamed Webster County for Daniel Webster; town founded as new county seat; **1857** incorporated as a town; **Jan. 29, 1878** Sen. Walter F. George born, served 34 years, 1922–1957 (died 1957); **1915** second county courthouse built; **1977** incorporated as a city; **2000** new county jail built.

Quitman *Brooks County Southern Georgia, 212 mi/341 km south-southeast of Atlanta*

1858 Brooks County formed, named for South Carolina Cong. Preston Smith Brooks; town founded as county seat, named for Gen. John A. Quitman, played role in Texas' fight for independence from Mexico; **1859** incorporated as a town; **1864** county courthouse completed, delayed for years by death of contractor; **1904** incorporated as a city.

Reidsville *Tattnall County Southeastern Georgia, 60 mi/97 km west of Savannah*

1801 Tattnall County formed, named for Gen. Josiah Tattnall, Revolutionary hero and governor; **c.1828** town founded; **1832** post office established; town becomes county seat; **1838** incorporated as a town; **1902** county courthouse built; **1905** incorporated as a city; **1936** Reidsville State Penitentiary built, becomes Georgia State Prison.

Resaca *Gordon County* *Northwestern Georgia, 65 mi/105 km north-northwest of Atlanta*

1848 town founded with construction of Western & Atlantic Railroad by Irish laborers, originally named Dublin; **1854** incorporated as a town, renamed Resacca; **Apr. 12, 1862** Oostanaula River railroad bridge becomes intended target of James Andrews' Union Raiders, resulting in Great Locomotive Chase near Adairsville, raiders captured at Ringgold; **May 14-15, 1864** General Sherman's Illinois Mounted Infantry defeats Confederate Gen. Joseph Johnston's Georgia Military Institute Cadets in Battle of Resaca at Snake Creek Gap; **1871** town renamed Resaca.

Richmond Hill *Bryan County* *Southeastern Georgia, 14 mi/23 km southwest of Savannah*

Oct. 1, 1779 in King's Ferry engagement of Revolution, five British vessels are burned by Col. John White, captains George Melvin and A. G. Elholm, three soldiers, obtain British surrender by bluffing them at night into believing they had a larger force; **1925** automobile manufacturer Henry Ford builds winter home, develops model community similar to his community at Dearborn, Michigan, with emphasis on crafts and sciences; **1962** incorporated as a city.

Ringgold *Catoosa County* *Northwestern Georgia, 90 mi/145 km north-northwest of Atlanta*

1846 town founded, named for Mexican War hero Samuel Ringgold, Battle of Palo Alto 1846; **1847** incorporated as a town; **1853** Catoosa County formed; **1854** town becomes county seat; **1856** county courthouse built; **1864** courthouse set afire by Union forces, extinguished when General Sherman learns of its use as Masonic lodge; **1903** Fort Oglethorpe military reservation established to west; **1939** county courthouse built; **1951** incorporated as a city.

Rome *Floyd County* *Northwestern Georgia, 55 mi/ 89 km northwest of Atlanta*

1540 explorer Hernando De Soto thought to have camped here; **1792** Tennessee Gov. John Sevier raids Cherokees in retaliation for their raids; **1794** log cabin built by Major Ridge, Cherokee leader; **Dec. 12, 1806** Cherokee Confederate Gen. Stand Watie born (died 1871); **1832** Floyd County formed; Livingston becomes county seat; **1833** town founded; **1834** incorporated as a town; county seat moved to Rome; **1839** Rome Railroad built as branch from Kingston; **1847** incorporated as a city; **1853** Rome Female College founded; **1855** iron works established by Noble family; **May 1863** Union forces under Col. Abel D. Streight captured by Confederates under Gen. Nathan B.

Forrest as they prepare to attack Rome; **May 1864** General Sherman captures and occupies Rome, establishes headquarters, remains six months; **Oct. 7, 1866** philanthropist, educator Martha McChesney Berry born (died 1942); **1870s** cotton becomes important industry; **1872** Clock Tower built for water storage, becomes city's most prominent landmark; **1873** Shorter College established; **1886** steamboat reported to have traveled up Broad Street during flooding of Coosa River; **1905** Darlington School for boys founded; **1921** Rome Symphony Orchestra established; **Sept. 1926** Berry College founded for indigent students by Martha Berry; **1929** Italian leader Benito Mussolini visits area, presents city with sculpture of Capitoline Wolf with Romulus and Remus; **1970** Floyd College (2-year) established; **1993** sixth county courthouse built; **1994** Forum Civic Center opened; **1995** Rome Area History Museum founded.

Roswell *Fulton County* *Northwestern Georgia, 18 mi/29 km north of Atlanta*

1837 Roswell King becomes first settler; Roswell Mills established; **c.1840** Presbyterian Church built, used as Union hospital during Civil War; **1840s** Archibald Smith Plantation House built with 12 outbuildings; town founded as Hammond; **1842** Barrington Hall house built; Bulloch Hall house built; **c.1842** Mimosa Hall house built by John Dunwody, one of original settlers; **Dec. 22, 1853** future Pres. Theodore Roosevelt marries Martha Bulloch at Bulloch Hall; **1854** incorporated as a town; **c.1857** Colonial Place house built by Rev. Francis R. Goulding; **1864** town destroyed by General Sherman's troops during his Atlanta Campaign; **1950** incorporated as a city.

Saint Marys *Camden County* *Southeastern Georgia, 95 mi/153 km south of Savannah, near Atlantic Ocean*

1562 Jean Ribault arrives by sea with French Huguenot settlers; **1568** Spanish mission Santa Maria de Guadaloupe founded by Pedro Menendez de Avilé; **1736** Fort St. Andrew built by Gov. James Ogelthorpe at north end of Cumberland Island, on Atlantic Coast; **1763** St. Marys Parish founded, becomes Camden County 1777; **c.1785** Dungeness house built at south end of Cumberland Island by Gen. Nathanael Greene; **1788** town of St. Patrick platted; **1792** town renamed St Marys; **1802** incorporated as a town, becomes important ship building center; Archibald Clark House built; **1808** Presbyterian Church built; **1812** Christ Episcopal Church founded; **1837** Orange Hall house completed; **1858** incorporated as a city; **Oct. 23, 1972** Cumberland Island National Seashore established to north, declared Biosphere Reserve 1986; **Sept. 21, 1996** John F. Kennedy, Jr. weds Carolyn Bessette in private party at Cumberland Island; **1978** Kings Bay Naval Submarine Support Base established.

Saint Simons Island *Glynn County*
Southeastern Georgia, 65 mi/105 km south of Savannah

1575 Spanish Franciscan priests establish missions among Georgia's Sea Islands, introduce orange and olive trees; **1736** Capt. James Oglethorpe, after delivering two shiploads of English settlers at Savannah, arrives in man-of-war *Hawk* at Gascoigne Bluff; construction of Fort Frederica begun on landward side of island by Oglethorpe as protection against Spanish, completed 1748; **July 7, 1742** defeat of Spanish in Battle of Bloody Marsh assures Britain of supremacy over area; **1797** timber cut on island used in construction of U.S. Navy's first warship, the frigate *Constitution*; **1804** first St. Simon Lighthouse built at south end of island, destroyed by Confederates during Civil War, rebuilt 1871; **1808** Christ Church founded; **1875** Christ Episcopal Church built at center of island; **1880** Hamilton Plantation house built as winter home of Eugene W. Lewis of Detroit; **1888** Hotel St. Simons built, burned 1898, rebuilt 1910; **1935** Battle of Bloody Marsh monument erected; **Feb. 17, 1936** actor, football player Jim Brown born; **May 26, 1936** Fort Frederica National Monument authorized; **1965** National Guard Armory established.

Sandersville *Washington County* *Central Georgia, 108 mi/174 km southeast of Atlanta*

1783 Creek people cede lands to white settlers; **1784** Washington County formed; **1796** town founded as county seat on land owned by M. Saunders; town named Saundersville, later renamed Sandersville; **1812** incorporated as a town; **1869** county courthouse built; **1872** incorporated as a city; **1893** Sandersville Railroad established; **Oct. 8, 1897** Black Muslim leader Elijah Muhammed (Elijah Poole) born (died 1975).

Savannah *Chatham County* *Southeastern Georgia, 225 mi/362 km southeast of Atlanta, near Atlantic Ocean*

1562 Frenchman Jean Ribault sails Georgian coast; **Feb. 12, 1733** Gen. James Oglethorpe lands first settlers here, plats town on Savannah River, both named for Sawana (Shawnee) peoples; **1736** Oglethorpe delivers two shiploads of settlers from England, continues on to St. Simons Island; **1744** town's first commercial enterprise founded; **1749** first eight bags of cotton shipped from town; **1750** Silk Hope Plantation established to south with land grant made to James Habersham, begins cultivation of mulberry trees; **1751** silk filature built for training apprentice silk weavers; **March 25, 1751** patriot, political leader Joseph Habersham born (died 1815); **1753** Trustees' Garden established by Oglethorpe; Herb House built at Garden, oldest house in Georgia; **1754** provincial capital established, town called "mother city of Georgia"; **1756** Wild Hern Plantation granted to Francis Harris, remains in family until 1935; **c.1764** McIntosh House built, oldest brick house in Georgia; **1771** Pink House built for James Habersham, Jr.; **1777** Chatham County formed; town becomes state capital and county seat; **Dec. 27, 1778** 2,000 British troops led by Col. Sir Archibald Campbell attack

town, defeat Gen. Robert Howe, who loses half of his 600 men, capture town; **Oct. 9, 1779** British repulse Continental forces under Gen. Benjamin Lincoln and French fleet; **1780** state capital moved to Augusta; **1782** British forced out of Savannah by Gen. Anthony Wayne's forces; state capital moved here temporarily from Augusta; **1785** state capital moved back to Augusta; First Bryan Baptist Church founded; **1789** incorporated as a city; **c.1790** Supreme Court Justice James Moore Wayne born (died 1867); **1793** Eli Whitney develops cotton gin at Mulberry Grove Plantation to west, estate of Gen. Nathanael Greene; **c.1795** city becomes cotton center with invention of Eli Whitney's cotton gin; **1796** great fire destroys much of town; **c.1800** Dennis House built; Woodbridge House built; **1812** Davenport House built; **May 1814** British ship *Epervier* captured by U.S. sloop *Peacock*, brought into harbor; **1816** steamboat *Enterprise* sails up Savannah River to Augusta; **1818** Savannah Theater opens; **May 22, 1819** steamer *City of Savannah* sets sail for Liverpool, England, first steamer to cross Atlantic; **c.1825** Lebanon plantation house built; **1829** W. W. Gordon House built; **1830** rice mill built on Savannah River; **1832** Georgia Infirmary opens, first hospital for blacks in U.S.; **1837** *Chatham* and *Lamar* built, first U.S.-built vessels, of iron imported from England; **1838** Christ Episcopal Church built, organized 1733; **1840** Roberts House built; **1843** Lutheran Church of the Ascension built, replaces 1756 structure; **c.1847** Low House built for cotton merchant Andrew Low; **1850** U.S. Customhouse built; **May 15, 1860** Ellen Louise Axson Wilson born, first wife of Pres. Woodrow Wilson (married June 28,1885, died Aug. 6, 1914); **Oct. 31, 1860** Juliette Gordon Low born, organized Girl Scouts, married Boy Scouts founder Sir Robert Baden-Powell (died 1927); **1862** Fort Pulaski to east falls to Union forces; **Dec. 21, 1864** after burning Atlanta, General Sherman ends his march to the sea, occupies city; **1870** City Market built, replaces 1763 structure; **c.1875** African-American cult leader Father Divine (George Baker) born (died 1965); **1876** devastating yellow fever epidemic strikes city; Cathedral of St. John the Baptist completed; **1877** Chandler Hospital built, founded 1819; **1882** Naval Stores Exchange established; **1889** Telfair Academy of Arts and Sciences founded; **Aug. 5, 1889** poet Conrad Potts Aiken born (died 1973); **1890** Savannah State University established to southeast; **1893** Independent Presbyterian Church built, replaces 1819 structure; **1905** city hall built, replacing 1799 structure; **Nov. 18, 1909** lyricist Johnny Mercer born (died 1976); **1916** Savannah Public Library built, organized 1809; **1921** boll weevil infestation destroys cotton market, regained 1926; **March 25, 1925** essayist Flannery O'Connor born (died 1964); **1927** Savannah National Wildlife Refuge established to north, mostly in South Carolina; **1929** Savannah Technical Institute (2-year college) established; Savannah Municipal Airport opened, becomes Hunter Army Air Field 1942; **1935** Armstrong Atlantic State University established; **June 2, 1941** TV actor Stacy Keach born; **Sept. 15, 1945** African-American soprano Jessye Norman born; **June 23, 1948** Supreme Court Justice Clarence Thomas born; **June 28,**

1959 two rail tank cars explode on trestle near Bloomingdale to west, 25 killed, including 22 swimmers and picnickers below on Ogeechee River; **1950** airport established at Travis Field, becomes Savannah International Airport 1983; **1978** Savannah College of Art and Design established; six-story county courthouse completed; **Feb. 2000** Savannah Convention Center opened on Hutchinson Island, Savannah River.

Smyrna *Cobb County* *Northwestern Georgia, 10 mi/16 km north-northwest of Atlanta*

1832 religious camp founded on former Cherokee lands; **1838** Methodist Church organized; **1870** town founded; **1872** incorporated as a city; **1934** Smyrna Public Library founded, new facility opened 1990; **1943** Dobbins Air Force Base established to north, becomes Air Reserve Base 1992; **Oct. 28, 1967** actress Julia Roberts born.

Soperton *Treutlen County* *Eastern Georgia, 143 mi/230 km southeast of Atlanta*

1784 area first settled; **c.1850** pine resin industry surpasses cotton and tobacco in importance; **1901** Macon, Dublin & Savannah Railroad built; town founded, named for railroad construction manager Henry Soper; **1902** incorporated as a town; **1917** Treutlen County formed, named for first Georgia governor John A. Treutlen; town becomes county seat; **1920** incorporated as a city; county courthouse built; **1972** Million Pines Arts and Crafts Festival founded.

Sparta *Hancock County* *Central Georgia, 90 mi/ 145 km east-southeast of Atlanta*

Nov. 3, 1786 treaty signed between Creek people and state of Georgia meant to end Oconee War, rejected by half-breed chief Alexander McGillivray; **1793** Hancock County formed; **1795** town founded as county seat by Maj. Charles Abercrombie; **1805** incorporated as a town; **c.1811** Judge Little House built by Timothy Rosseter, Revolutionary army surgeon; **1832** Sparta Female Academy founded; **c.1850** Mount Zion Methodist Church built to north, originally Presbyterian church; **1851** Edwards House hotel built, later used as residence; **1881** Harris Mill built on Shoulder Bone Creek to west; **1883** second county courthouse completed; **1893** incorporated as a city.

Springfield *Effingham County* *Southeastern Georgia, 25 mi/40 km north-northwest of Savannah*

1777 Effingham County formed; **1784** Tuckasee King becomes first county seat; **1787** county seat moved to Elberton; **1797** county seat moved to Ebenezer; **1799** town founded near Savannah River; county seat moved to Springfield; **1838** incorporated as a town; **1907** incorporated as a city; Brinson (Savannah & Atlanta) Railroad reaches town; **1908** county courthouse built.

Statenville *Echols County* *Southern Georgia, 150 mi/240 km southwest of Savannah*

1858 Echols County formed; town founded as county seat, named for store owner Henry Staten; **1859** incorporated as a town; **1899** third county courthouse built; **1956** fourth county courthouse built; **1995** town's charter revoked.

Statesboro *Bulloch County* *Southeastern Georgia, 45 mi/72 km northwest of Savannah*

c.1779 local Whig settlers kill most of Daniel McGirth's Tory-sympathetic raiders; **1796** Bulloch County formed; **1803** town platted as county seat; **1864** town destroyed during Gen. Sherman's March to the Sea; **1866** incorporated as a town; **1894** fourth county courthouse built, restoration completed 2000; **1902** incorporated as a city; **1906** Georgia Normal College established, becomes Georgia Southern University.

Stone Mountain *De Kalb County* *Northern Georgia, 14 mi/23 km east of Atlanta*

1790 half-breed Creek chief Alexander McGillivray meets with other tribesmen at Stone Mountain, traditional signaling site for the Creek people, prior to journey to New York to meet with government officials; **1825** hotel built at stagecoach terminus at base of mountain; **1839** town incorporated as New Gibraltar; **1842** Cloud's Tower, 165-ft/50-m observation tower, built at summit; **1847** town renamed Stone Mountain; **1880** Samuel Hoyt Venerable acquires mountain, begins quarrying granite; **1912** incorporated as a city; **1915** Daughters of the Confederacy invite sculptor Gutzon Borglum to carve figure of Robert E. Lee on mountain face; **1920s** summit used as meeting place for Ku Klux Klan; **Jan. 19, 1924** sculpted head of Robert E. Lee unveiled; **1925** Borglum abandons project in dispute with management, departs for South Dakota to work on Mt. Rushmore; work assumed by Augustus Lukeman, suspended 1930; **1963** sculpture work resumes; **1972** Confederate Memorial Carving completed by Walter Hahock.

Summerville *Chattooga County* *Northwestern Georgia, 72 mi/116 km northwest of Atlanta*

1832 first settlers arrive on Cherokee lands; **1838** Chattooga County formed; town founded as county seat; **1839** incorporated as a town; **Sept. 1863** heavy fighting occurs here during Chickamauga campaign of Civil War; **Oct. 18, 1909** incorporated as a city; second county courthouse built.

Sunbury *Liberty County* *Southeastern Georgia, 22 mi/35 km south of Savannah*

1566 Spanish explorer Pedro Menendez de Aviles sails into area; Jesuit priests establish missions in vicinity of St. Catharines Island, to east abandoned by 1570; **1573** missions reestablished, continue into 1600s; **1597** many priests killed in French-incited Native American uprising; **1715** estuaries used as refuge by pirate Blackbeard

(Edward Teach); **1733** Ossabaw, St. Catherines, and Sapelo coastal marsh islands purchased from Native Americans for hunting preserve by James Oglethorpe; **1734** one of earliest Masonic lodge meetings in U.S. held here by Oglethorpe; **1758** land grant on Sunbury River conveyed to Mark Carr; town platted by Carr and Oglethorpe; **1776** Fort Morris built to defend town, town ultimately destroyed during Revolution; **1777** Liberty County formed; town becomes first county seat; **1788** Sunbury Academy founded; **1790s** town declines with growth of nearby Savannah; **1791** incorporated as a town; **1797** county seat moved to Riceborough, to Hinesville 1837; **1864** Union army destroys remaining buildings.

Swainsboro *Emanuel County Eastern Georgia, 145 mi/233 km southeast of Atlanta*

1812 Emanuel County formed, named for Revolutionary veteran Gov. David Emanuel; **1814** town founded as county seat, named Swainsborough; **1818** Canoochee Baptist Church built to east; **1854** incorporated as a town, renamed Paris; **1857** town renamed Swainsboro; **1899** incorporated as a city; **1936** post office built, converted 1938 to sixth county courthouse; **1973** East Georgia College (2-year) established; **2002** seventh county courthouse completed.

Sylvania *Screven County Eastern Georgia, 55 mi/ 89 km north-northwest of Savannah, near Savannah River*

1793 Screven County formed; **1797** Jacksborough becomes first county seat; **1847** town founded as new county seat; **1854** incorporated as a town; **1902** incorporated as a city; **1964** fourth county courthouse built.

Sylvester *Worth County Southern Georgia, 158 mi/254 km south-southeast of Atlanta*

1853 Worth County formed; San Bernard (Isabella) becomes county seat; **1872** Brunswick & Albany Railroad built; town founded as Isabella Station; **c.1893** town renamed Sylvester; **1898** incorporated as a town; **1904** incorporated as a city; county seat moved to Sylvester; **1905** county courthouse completed, rebuilt after Jan. 1982 fire.

Talbotton *Talbot County Western Georgia, 75 mi/ 121 km south of Atlanta*

1827 Talbot County formed; town site chosen as county seat; **1828** town platted; **1848** Episcopal Church built; **1852** Lazarus Straus arrives from Bavaria, opens store, later goes to New York City, becomes sole owner of R. H. Macy & Company 1896; **1859** Le Vert College established; **1892** county courthouse built; **1952** incorporated as a city.

Tallapoosa *Haralson County Northwestern Georgia, 50 mi/80 km west of Atlanta*

1839 post office established; **1860** incorporated as a town; **1882** Southern Railway reaches town; Lithium Springs Hotel completed, razed 1943; **1884** gold, silver, copper discovered in area; **1887** Tallapoosa Mining & Manufacturing Company founded; **1888** incorporated as a city; Tallapoosa Glass Works established; **1891** mining reaches peak.

Tallulah Falls *Habersham County Northeastern Georgia, 88 mi/142 km northeast of Atlanta*

1882 Tallulah Gorge Railroad reaches site, discontinued 1961; **1885** incorporated as a town; **1908** Georgia Power Company begins acquisition of land along Tallulah River for development of hydroelectric power, through 1920; **1909** Tallulah Falls Industrial School founded; **1913** Tallulah Falls Lake formed by dam, greatly reducing volume of falls; **1921** fire destroys town; **1971** movie *Deliverance* filmed here; **1993** Tallulah Gorge State Park established.

Thomaston *Upson County Western Georgia, 62 mi/100 km south of Atlanta*

1824 Upson County formed; **1825** town founded and incorporated as county seat, named for Gen. Jett Thomas of War of 1812; **July 6, 1832** Confederate army commander John Brown Gordon born in rural Upson County (died 1904); **1833** Franklin Factory, cotton goods manufacturer, founded; **1875** Robert E. Lee Institute founded; **1897** incorporated as a city; **1908** third county courthouse built; **1940s** Thomaston annexes Silvertown and its cotton mill.

Thomasville *Thomas County Southern Georgia, 205 mi/330 km south of Atlanta*

1825 Thomas County formed; **1826** town founded as county seat; town and county named for Gen. Jett Thomas of War of 1812; **c.1830** Boxhall house built by McIntyre family to west; **1831** incorporated as a town; **1855** Pebble Hill estate built; **1861** Atlantic & Gulf Railroad reaches town; **c.1865** resort town begins attracting northern visitors; **1875** Piney Woods Hotel established, burned 1900; **1877** Mark Hanna House built; **1889** incorporated as a city; **1903** Vashti Industrial School for women founded by Mrs. Vashti Blassingame; **1922** first Thomasville Rose Show held; **Feb. 27, 1930** actress Joanne Woodward born; **c.1939** packing plant established; **1958** county courthouse built.

Thomson *McDuffie County Eastern Georgia, 113 mi/182 km east-southeast of Atlanta*

1785 Rock House built by Thomas Ansley; **1823** gold discovered to northwest, Columbia Gold Mines established; **1837** Georgia Railroad completed; town founded, named the Slashes; **1833** Georgia's first gold stamp mill founded by Jeremiah Griffin; **1853** town renamed for

GEORGIA

155

railroad surveyor J. Edgar Thomson; **1854** incorporated as a town; **Sept. 5, 1856** U.S. Sen. Tom Watson born (died 1922); **1860** granite railroad depot built; **1870** McDuffie County formed; town becomes county seat; **1872** county courthouse built; **1920** incorporated as a city.

Tifton   *Tift County*   *Southern Georgia, 148 mi/ 238 km south-southeast of Atlanta*

1872 sawmill established by Henry H. Tift at junction of Brunswick & Western and Georgia Southern & Florida railroads; town founded; **1890** incorporated as a city; **1905** Tift County formed; town becomes county seat; **1913** county courthouse completed; **1933** Abraham Baldwin Agricultural College (2-year) established; **March 3, 1959** school bus with 80 on board crashes into pond, nine killed; **1976** Georgia Agrirama opened, living history museum.

Toccoa   *Stephens County*   *Northeastern Georgia, 85 mi/137 km northeast of Atlanta*

1775 Jarrett Manor house built to east by Jesse Walton; **1874** town founded on Atlanta & Charlotte (Seaboard Air Line) Railroad; **1875** incorporated as a town; **1897** incorporated as a city; **1905** Stephens County formed; town becomes county seat; **1907** Toccoa Falls College established; **1908** county courthouse built; **1911** Toccoa Orphanage founded; **Nov. 6, 1977** dam collapses sending 35-ft/11-m surge of water through trailer park at Toccoa Falls College, 37 killed, 45 injured; **2000** second county courthouse completed.

Trenton   *Dade County*   *Northwestern Georgia, 100 mi/161 km northwest Atlanta*

1830 first settlers arrive; town founded, originally named Salem; **1837** Dade County formed, named for Maj. Francis Langhorne Dade, killed 1835 in Seminole War, Florida; **1839** incorporated as a town, becomes county seat; **1841** town renamed Trenton; **1850s** coal mining begins, mostly discontinued 1908; **1926** fourth county courthouse built; **1935** incorporated as a city; **2001** County Administration Building completed.

Tybee Island   *Chatham County*   *Southeastern Georgia, 15 mi/24 km east of Savannah, on Atlantic Ocean*

1520 Spanish slave hunter Francisco Gordillo lands here, leaves knife and rosary; **1540** Gordillo items discovered by Hernando De Soto's party; **1736** Tybee Light erected by Noble Jones; **1741** Fort Wimberley built; **1761** Fort George built by British on Cockspur Island in Savannah River, replaced 1794 by Fort Greene, destroyed by 1804 hurricane; **1812** Fort Pulaski built on Cockspur Island; **1840** summer colony of Parkersburg founded; **1862** Fort Pulaski shelled by Union forces; **1867** Tybee Lighthouse built, fourth light at site, automated 1933; **1887** incorporated as a city, originally named Savannah Beach; **1893** Diamondback Terrapin Farm established for experimental breeding of terrapins for commercial use; **1898** colony

renamed Isle of Hope; Fort Screven army camp established; **Apr. 15, 1924** Fort Pulaski National Monument proclaimed; **1978** city renamed Tybee Island.

Unadilla   *Dooly County*   See **Vienna (2001)**

Valdosta   *Lowndes County*   *Southern Georgia, 215 mi/346 km south-southeast of Atlanta*

1825 Lowndes County formed; **1827** village of Lowndes Court House becomes first county seat; **1833** county seat moved to Lowndesville, renamed Troupville 1837; **1860** railroad built 4 mi/6.4 km to east; town moved to railroad and incorporated as a town, renamed Valdosta; **1901** incorporated as a city; **1905** county courthouse completed; **1906** Georgia State Woman's College established, becomes Valdosta State University; **1928** Emory Junior College established as 2-year branch of Emory University, Atlanta; **Oct. 13, 1946** TV actor Demond Wilson born.

Vidalia   *Toombs County*   *Eastern Georgia, 78 mi/ 126 km west of Savannah*

1850 Savannah, Americus & Montgomery Railroad built; town founded; **1892** incorporated as a town; **1902** incorporated as a city; **1931** sweet tasting Vidalia onion discovered by accident by farmer Mose Coleman; **1977** first Onion Festival held; **1990** Vidalia onion named official state vegetable.

Vienna   *Dooly County*   *Central Georgia, 120 mi/ 193 km south-southeast of Atlanta*

1821 Dooly County formed, one of five original counties created in Georgia Land Lottery Draw, named for Col. John Dooly, killed 1780 at Augusta by Tories; **1827** town of Berrien founded as county seat, renamed Drayton 1833; **1836** new town founded as county seat, also named Drayton; **1841** county seat moved back to Berrien, renamed Vienna; **1854** incorporated as a town; **1892** fourth county courthouse built; **1901** incorporated as a city; **June 20, 1969** ten women and children killed when freight train hits their car; **March 3, 2001** C-23 Sherpa National Guard military transport crashes killing all 21 near Unadilla to north.

Villa Rica   *Carroll County*   *Northwestern Georgia, 30 mi/42 km west of Atlanta*

1826 gold discovered; town founded, named Hixtown for innkeeper William Hix; **1830** incorporated as a town; **1842** town renamed; **Dec. 20, 1851** Coca Cola founder Asa Candler born, established soft drink company in Atlanta 1887 (died 1929); **June 1882** Georgia Pacific Railroad built through town; town name changed; **1912** incorporated as a city; **Dec. 5, 1957** explosion in natural gas line kills 17; **1973** Villa Rica Library founded.

Warm Springs *Meriwether County* *Western Georgia, 63 mi/101 km south-southwest of Atlanta*

1832 resort established by David Rose at spring known for its constant 88°F/31°C temperature; **1893** resort town of Bullochville founded and incorporated on railroad; Meriwether Inn built by Charles Davis; **1899** Warm Springs National Fish Hatchery established; **1924** Bullochville reincorporated as city of Warm Springs; **1927** Warm Springs Foundation established by Pres. Franklin D. Roosevelt, treatment center for poliomyelitis patients; **1932** President Roosevelt's Little White House built on grounds of Foundation; **1938** Pine Mountain Park established by National Park Service, becomes F. D. Roosevelt State Park 1945; **Apr. 12, 1945** President Roosevelt dies of cerebral hemorrhage age 63 at his retreat; **1990** Warm Springs Regional Fisheries Center and Aquarium established.

Warner Robins *Houston County* *Central Georgia, 93 mi/150 km south-southeast of Atlanta*

c.1890 Georgia Southern & Florida Railroad built; Wellston station founded; **1942** Wellston Army Air Depot established at Robins Field; town founded, named for Gen. Augustin Warner Robins, considered father of modern U.S. Air Force; **1943** incorporated as a town; **1950** depot becomes Robins Air Force Base; **1956** incorporated as a city; **1973** Houston Vocational Center established, becomes Middle Georgia Technical College 2000; **1981** Museum of History founded, displays include over 90 aircraft and missiles; **2003** Georgia Military College established.

Warrenton *Warren County* *Eastern Georgia, 105 mi/169 km east-southeast of Atlanta*

1793 Warren County formed; **1797** town founded as county seat; town and county named for Revolutionary War Gen. Joseph Warren; **c.1800** County Jail built; **1810** incorporated as a town; **1820** Walker House built; **c.1820** Pilcher House built, site of 1825 masked ball attended by French General Lafayette; **1868** Macon branch of Georgia Railroad reaches town; **1908** incorporated as a city; **1910** third county courthouse built, expanded to triple its size 2000.

Washington *Wilkes County* *Eastern Georgia, 97 mi/156 km east of Atlanta*

1773 area first settled; **1777** Wilkes County formed, considered Georgia's first county, named for Parliamentarian John Wilkes; **Feb. 14, 1779** Patriots gain victory over Tories in Battle of Kettle Creek to west, saving Georgia from total British control; **1780** town platted, first town in U.S. named for George Washington; **c.1790** Mount Pleasant plantation house built; **1793** Eli Whitney improves his cotton gin with financial support from plantation owner Catharine Greene, widow of Revolutionary War Gen. Nathanael Greene; **c.1795** Robert Toombs House built; **1796** Phineas Miller marries

Catharine Greene, forms partnership with Eli Whitney, provides Whitney secluded workshop for perfecting his cotton gin; **1804** Alexander House built; **1805** incorporated as a town; **Oct. 18, 1809** poet Thomas Holley Chivers born (died 1858); **1811** Wilkes Cotton Cloth Factory established on Miller-Whitney Plantation; **June 24, 1811** Supreme Court Justice John Archibald Campbell born in rural Wilkes County (died 1887); **1820** Samuel Barnett House built; **1826** Presbyterian Church built; **1830** St. Patrick's Catholic Church built, organized 1790; **c.1840** Franklin House built; **May 5, 1865** Confederate Pres. Jefferson Davis holds final cabinet meeting at Heard House; **1887** Mary Willis Library built; **1899** incorporated as a city; **1904** second county courthouse built.

Watkinsville *Oconee County* *Northern Georgia, 56 mi/90 km east of Atlanta*

c.1789 blockhouse named Fort Edwards built as protection against Cherokees; **1801** Clarke County formed; Eagle Tavern opened at converted blockhouse, later becomes Eagle Hotel; **1802** town becomes county seat; **1806** incorporated as a town; **1872** Clarke County seat moved to Athens; **1875** Oconee County formed from Clarke County; town becomes county seat; **1939** county courthouse built; **1983** incorporated as a city.

Waycross *Ware County* *Southeastern Georgia, 95 mi/153 km southwest of Savannah*

1818 first settlers arrive; **1824** Ware County formed; Waresborough becomes county seat; **c.1855** town founded at railroad junction, named Number Nine; **1857** town renamed Tebeauville; **1873** county seat moved to Tebeauville; **1874** incorporated as a town, renamed Waycross; **1889** incorporated as a city; **May 18, 1930** TV actor Pernell Roberts born; **Feb. 11, 1936** actor Burt Reynolds born; **1957** county courthouse built.

Waynesboro *Burke County* *Eastern Georgia, 148 mi/238 km east-southeast of Atlanta*

c.1768 Belleview Plantation house built by Samuel Eastlake; **1777** Burke County formed; **1798** town founded, named for Gen. "Mad" Anthony Wayne; **c.1800** Buckhead Baptist Church built; **1812** incorporated as a town; **1857** county courthouse built; **1883** incorporated as a city; **March 1987** first phase of Alima Vogtle Nuclear Power Plant opened.

West Point *Troup County* *Western Georgia, 75 mi/121 km southwest of Atlanta*

c.1825 Franklin trading post established on Chattahoochee River; **1831** incorporated as a town; **1832** town renamed West Point; **1851** Montgomery & West Point Railroad completed; **1853** incorporated as a city; **1854** Atlanta & West Point Railroad reaches town; **1857** Griggs House built; **Apr. 16, 1865** Gen. Robert Tyler's Confederates hold Fort Tyler against assault by Union Col. O. H. La Grange, Tyler killed in action; **1866**

West Point Manufacturing Company textile mill founded; **1933** flood control project begun by Civil Works Administration (CWA); **1974** West Point Lake formed by dam of same name on Chattahoochee River, on Alabama state boundary.

White Oak   *Camden County*   *See* **Woodbine (1903)**

Winder   *Barrow County*   *Northern Georgia, 45 mi/ 72 km east-northeast of Atlanta*

1790s town founded, named Jug Tavern for popular wayside; **Aug. 3, 1864** skirmish occurs here between Confederate cavalry and 14th Illinois cavalry; **1884** Seaboard Air Line Railroad built; town incorporated as Jug Tavern; **1893** incorporated as a city, renamed Winder; **Nov. 2, 1897** Sen. Richard B. Russell born (died 1971); **1914** Barrow County formed; town becomes county seat; **1920** county courthouse built.

Woodbine   *Camden County*   *Southeastern Georgia, 84 mi/135 km south-southwest of Savannah*

1755 trading post established on Satilla River by Edmund Gray; **1763** first settlers arrive; town founded; **1777** Camden County formed; town becomes county seat; **1798** Refuge Plantation house built; **1800** Jeffersonton becomes first county seat; **Oct. 12, 1815** Confederate Gen. William Joseph Hardee born (died 1873); **1869** county seat moved to St. Marys; **Dec. 17, 1903** Erskine Caldwell born at White Oak to north, wrote *Tobacco Road* (died 1987); **1908** incorporated as a town; **1923** county seat moved to Woodbine; **1928** county courthouse built; **1953** incorporated as a city; **c.1970** Thiokol Chemical Plant established; **Feb. 3, 1971** chemical plant explosion kills 25, injures 33.

Wrightsville   *Johnson County*   *Central Georgia, 123 mi/198 km southeast of Atlanta*

1858 Johnson County formed; **1859** town founded as county seat on land owned by William Hicks; **1866** incorporated as a town; **1895** second county courthouse built; **1899** incorporated as a city.

Zebulon   *Pike County*   *Western Georgia, 45 mi/ 72 km south of Atlanta*

1822 Pike County formed; Newnan, near county center, becomes first county seat; town of Zebulon founded; town and county named for Gen. Zebulon Pike; **1823** incorporated as a town; **1825** county seat moved to Zebulon; **1850** town's incorporation reaffirmed; **1895** county courthouse built; **1909** incorporated as a city.

Hawaii

North central Pacific Ocean, detached from contiguous U.S. Capital and major city: Honolulu.

The islands were annexed by the U.S. July 7, 1898, as the Territory of Hawaii. Hawaii was admitted as the 50th state August 21, 1959.

Hawaii has four counties. A fifth county, Kalawao, on the northern shore of Molokai, was created to serve the leper colony on Kalaupapa peninsula now closed. The county is no longer functioning. The City and County of Honolulu are coterminous, otherwise there are no municipalities in Hawaii. All four counties have mayors and councils similar to municipal governments. There are no townships. See Introduction.

Captain Cook   *Hawaii County Hawaii island*
Southeastern Hawaii, 55 mi/89 km west-southwest of Hilo

Jan. 17, 1779 Capt. James Cook's two ships *Resolution* and *Discovery* drop anchor in Kealakakua Bay, greeted by 10,000 Hawaiians, hailed as return of god Lono; **Feb. 4, 1779** Capt. Cook departs, *Resolution* mast damaged in storm, returns; **Feb. 14, 1779** Capt. Cook lands intending to take Chief Kalaniopau hostage in dispute over stolen boat and tools, Cook and four men killed, six Hawaiian chiefs killed; **1850** Captain Cook Memorial School founded; **July 24, 1946** astronaut Ellison S. Onizuka born at Kealakekua, killed Jan. 28, 1986, in *Challenger* space shuttle disaster.

Hana   *Maui County Maui island*   *Central Hawaii, 125 mi/201 km east-southeast of Honolulu*

c.1400 Pi'i-lani Heiau Temple built, largest prehistoric temple in Hawaii; **1777** Queen Ka'ahumanu born in birthing cave (died 1832); **1849** sugar mill established by George Wilfong; **c.1900** modern town founded; **1927** north coastal road reaches town; **1944** Hana Cattle Ranch established by Paul Fagan; **1946** area's largest sugar mill closed; first hotel opened; **Apr. 1, 1946** tsunami strikes town, 12 killed; **1974** aviator Charles A. Lindbergh lives out final days, dies Aug. 26.

Hanalei   *Kauai County Kauai island*
Northwestern Hawaii, 120 mi/193 km northwest of Honolulu

1837 mission home built by Rev. William P. Alexander; Wananalua Congregational Church built; **1841** Waioli Mission built, later used as community center; **1853** Princeville Ranch established to east; **1913** Kilauea Point Lighthouse built to east, automated 1976; **1940s** ranching replaces sugar production as main industry; **1941** Christ Memorial Episcopal Church built; **1951** St. William's Catholic Church built; **Jan. 1956** 45 in/114 cm of rain falls in 36 hours at Kilauea to east causing road and property damage; **1957** movie *South Pacific* shot at Hanalei Bay.

Hilo   *Hawaii County Hawaii island*   *Southeastern Hawaii, 210 mi/338 km southeast of Honolulu*

1791 King Kamehameha gains control of island of Hawaii after nine year struggle; **c.1822** settled by missionaries; **1839** Lyman Mission House built; **1859** Haili Church built; **1905** Hawaii County formed; town becomes county seat; **Jan. 1907** Mauna Loa volcano becomes active; **1911** incorporated as a city; **1934** Cape Kumukahi Light Tower erected to southeast, automated 1960; **1928** Hilo Airport established, becomes General Lyman Field 1943; **Feb. 1, 1934** singer Bob Shane born, founding member of Kingston Trio; **Apr. 1, 1946** tsunami devastates community; **c.1950** breeding program of the nene (Hawaiian goose) resleases hundreds of nearly extinct bird into wilderness of Mauna Loa, also on Haleakala, Maui; **1954** Hawaii Community College, University of Hawaii, established; **May 22, 1960** second tsunami destroys much of city, 61 killed; **1970** University of Hawaii at Hilo established; **1975** Mauna Loa volcano erupts after 25 years of dormancy; **1977** Hilo city merges with Hawaii County; Pana'ewa Rainforest Zoo established; **May 17, 1979** lowest temperature recorded in Hawaii reached, 12°F/−11°C, at Mauna Kea Observatory to northwest; **1989** Hilo International Airport established at Lyman Field; **1994** Pacific Tsunami Museum established.

Honaunau *Hawaii County Hawaii island*

Southeastern Hawaii, 57 mi/92 km west-southwest of Hilo

1500s Great Wall built at Honaunau (City of Refuge), vanquished warriors, violators of kapu system of law allowed to flee here, until 1819; **July 1, 1961** Pu'uhonua o Honaunau (City of Refuge) National Historical Park established.

Honolulu *Honolulu County Oahu island* *Central Hawaii, on Mamala Bay, Pacific Ocean*

c.500 first migrations of Polynesians arrive from Marquesas Islands; **c.1100** greater numbers of Tahitians arrive in double-hulled canoes bringing many food staples; **Jan. 18, 1778** James Cook discovers Hawaiian Islands beginning with Kauai; **1786** two British ships led by Capt. William Brown visit village of Waikiki; **1820** town of Honolulu settled by missionaries; royal capital removed from Kailua on Big Island's Kona Coast; **Sept. 2, 1838** monarch Lydia Kamakaeha Liliuokalani born (died 1917); **1842** Kawaiahao Church built, funerals of Hawaiian monarchs held here; **June 1843** Hawaii seized by British Lord George Paulet, disavowed by British government; **1852** first Chinese laborers brought to Hawaii; whaling reaches peak, declines after 1859 with discovery of oil in Pennsylvania; **July 2, 1856** *Honolulu Advertiser* newspaper founded; **1865** Royal Mausoleum built, burial place of Hawaii's royalty; **Dec. 4, 1865** physical education pioneer Luther Halsey Gulick born (died 1918); **1868** first Japanese immigrants arrive; **Dec. 10, 1872** reign of the Kamehamehas ends with death of Kamehameha V on 43rd birthday; **1874** Judiciary Building completed; **Nov. 19, 1875** explorer Hiram Bingham born (died 1956); **1882** Iolani Palace completed by David Kalakaua, Hawaii's last king; **1889** Bishop Museum of Hawaiian Natural History established by Charles Reed Bishop; **1892** Hawaiian Historical Society founded; **1893** monarchy under Queen Liliuokalani deposed; **July 4, 1894** Republic of Hawaii established under leadership of Sanford B. Dole; **1896** Honolulu Zoo established, modern zoo reestablished 1974; **Aug. 12, 1898** Hawaii annexed by U.S.; **1899** Diamond Head Lighthouse built, automated 1924; **1901** Hawaiian Pineapple Company established by James D. Dole; U.S. Navy builds base at Pearl Harbor; **1904** Waikiki Aquarium founded, part of University of Hawaii; **1905** Honolulu County formed; town becomes county seat; **1907** City and County of Honolulu incorporated as single unit; University of Hawaii, Manoa Campus, established; Tripler Army Medical Center established, named 1920 for Brig. Gen. Charles Tripler; **1911** Fort De Russy established, closed after World War II; **1912** Ginaca machine invented by Henry Ginaca, pineapple corer revolutionized pineapple industry, improved model developed 1925; **1919** first unsuccessful statehood bills introduced; **1920** Territorial Trade School established, becomes Honolulu Community College, University of Hawaii 1965; **Sept. 7, 1924** U.S. Cong. Daniel Inouye born; **1926** Royal Hawaiian Hotel built; **1927** John Rodgers

Field airport established to west, renamed Honolulu International Airport 1951; Honolulu Academy of Contemporary Arts founded; **1929** city hall dedicated; **1930** Foster Botanical Gardens founded; **Aug. 13, 1930** entertainer Don Ho born in suburban Kakaako; **1935** Hickam Army Air Field established to west, becomes Air Force Base 1957; **Dec. 7, 1941** 7:55 a.m., Japanese launch surprise attack on Pacific fleet at Pearl Harbor, 2,300 killed; **Oct. 19, 1934** singer Dave Guard born, founding member of Kingston Trio (died 1991); **1936** first Pro Bowl annual football all-star classic held; **1940** first Hula Bowl all-star football game held, moved to Wailuku, Maui, 1997; **1955** Chaminade University of Honolulu established; **March 22, 1955** Navy DC-6 plane crashes into cliff, killing 66; **1957** Kapiolani Community College, University of Hawaii, established; **Aug. 21, 1959** Hawaii enters Union as 50th state; **July 23, 1962** Canadian Pacific turboprop airplane crashes upon landing, 27 killed; **1965** Hawaii Pacific University established; **1967** Hawaii Loa College established; **Jan. 14, 1969** blast on USS *Enterprise* during bombing practice near Hawaii kills 27, injures 80; **1975** Aloha Stadium built; **Sept. 9, 1980** USS *Arizona* Memorial established in Pearl Harbor by National Park Service; **1988** Contemporary Museum opened at Spalding House, built 1925; **1990** 46-story Waterfront Towers built; **1991** 45-story Nauru Tower built; **1992** 40-story Imperial Plaza built; **1998** Hawaii Convention Center opened; **Jan 29, 1999** Battleship *Missouri* permanently docked at Pearl Harbor as memorial, launched 1944, retired after Persian Gulf War 1991; **Feb. 9, 2001** surfacing U.S. Navy submarine strikes Japanese trawler, sinking it, nine of 35 on board killed.

Kahoolawe *Maui County Kahoolawe island*

Central Hawaii, 95 mi/153 km southeast of Honolulu

1910 Angus McPhee becomes first white settler on Kahoolawe island, leases entire island as cattle ranch; **1941** island seized by U.S. Navy for use as bombing and gunnery range; **1970s** Hawaiians protest military presence on island; **1994** island turned over to state; **Nov. 2003** U.S. Navy completes environmental cleanup of island.

Kailua *Honolulu County Oahu island* *Central Hawaii, 10 mi/16 km northeast of Honolulu*

1500s Hawaiian royalty attracted to site, origin of many legends; **1795** Kamehameha I conquers Oahu, grants village and surrounding lands to chiefs and warriors for their assistance; **1909** Makapuu Lighthouse built to southeast, automated 1974; **1918** Bellows Army Air Base established to south near Makapuu Point, becomes Air Force Base after World War II; **1942** Kaneohe Ranch donated to community by Harold K. L. Castle.

Kailua-Kona *Hawaii County Hawaii island*

Southeastern Hawaii, 58 mi/93 km west of Hilo

1820 group of missionaries arrive from New England after journey at sea around Cape Horn; royal capital moved to Honolulu; **1828** first coffee trees planted at Kona by missionary Samuel Ruggles; **1837** Moku'aikaua Church completed; **1838** Hulihee Palace completed as retreat for Hawaiian royalty; **c.1840** area becomes known for its Kona coffee; **1875** Greenwell's General Store built, later houses Kona Historical Society Museum.

Kakaako *Honolulu County Oahu island* See **Honolulu (1930)**

Kalaupapa *Maui County Molokai island* See **Kalawao**

Kalawao *Kalawao County Molokai island*
Central Hawaii, 58 mi/93 km east-southeast of Honolulu

1865 Hawaiians forcibly removed from site on small peninsula on northern coast of Molokai isolated by high cliffs; **1866** leper colony established; first group of nine men, three women arrive Jan. 3; **1872** St. Philomena Catholic Church built; **1873** Belgian Father Damien (Joseph De Veuster) arrives to minister to colony; **1885** Father Damien contracts leprosy, dies Apr. 15, 1889, buried in Belgium; **1905** Kalawao County formed to further isolate leper colony from remainder of island; **1906** Kalaupapa Lighthouse completed at Kahiu Point; **1946** leper colony disbanded with development of sulfone drugs; **1969** colony closed; **Dec. 22, 1980** Kalaupapa National Historical Park authorized.

Kamuela (Waimea) *Hawaii County Hawaii island Southeastern Hawaii, 42 mi/68 km northwest of Hilo*

1794 Capt. George Vancouver presents five head of cattle as gift to Kamehameha I; **1809** sailor John Parker jumps ship, given task of shooting maverick cattle by Kamehameha I, legacy of Capt. Vancouver, develops into Parker Ranch; **1819** system of stone walls built by Kamehameha I to protect people from longhorn cattle roaming area; **1857** Imola Church built by missionary Lorenzo Lyons; **1941** Kamuela Bordelon Airfield built by U.S. Marine Corps.

Kaneohe *Honolulu County Oahu island Central Hawaii, 10 mi/16 km north-northeast of Honolulu*

1939 Navy seaplane base established at Kaneohe Bay; **Dec. 7, 1941** Japanese attack Kaneohe Bay ahead of attack on Pearl Harbor; **1952** Kaneohe Bay Marine Corps Base established on Mokapu Peninsula; **1960s** two highway tunnels built through Koolau Range from Honolulu; **1998** Interstate Highway H-3 tunnel built through Koolau Range.

Kealakekua *Hawaii County Hawaii island* See **Captain Cook**

Kohala *Hawaii County Hawaii island*
Southeastern Hawaii, 60 mi/97 km northwest of Hilo

c.1758 King Kamehameha born (died 1819); **1797** King Kamehameha II born to Kamehameha I, reigned 1819–1824 (died of measles 1824); **Aug. 11, 1813** King Kamehameha III born, also to Kamehameha I, reigned 1825–1854 (died 1863); **Dec. 11, 1830** King Kamehameha V born, brother of Kamehameha IV, reigned 1863–1872 (died 1872); **Feb. 6, 1834** King Kamehameha IV born, nephew of Kamehameha III, reigned 1854–1863 (died 1863).

Koloa *Kauai County Kauai island Northwestern Hawaii, 110 mi/177 km northwest of Honolulu*

1835 Koloa Mill established, Hawaii's first sugarcane plantation; town founded; **1837** Koloa Church (the White Church) built by Assemblies of God; **1841** Roman Catholic mission built; **1856** St. Raphael's Catholic Church built by Father Robert Walsh; **March 26, 1871** Prince Jonah Kuhio born, delegate to U.S. Congress 1903–1921 (died 1922).

Kona *Hawaii County Hawaii island* See **Kailua-Kona**

Lahaina *Maui County Maui island Central Hawaii, 82 mi/132 km east-southeast of Honolulu*

1823 first missionaries arrive from Boston; **1831** Lahainaluna School built; **1840** town becomes important whaling center, through 1865; **1851** Hale Paahao prison built; **1857** courthouse built; **1865** whale oil industry collapses with development of petroleum reserves in continental U.S.; **1890** Lahaina, Kaanapali & Pacific Railroad built to haul sugarcane; **1901** Pioneer Inn built; **1910** rail line ceases commercial hauling; **1917** fire destroys Front Street, rebuilt by 1920; **1947** rail passenger service suspended; **1966** Holy Innocents Episcopal Church built, replaces 1927 structure.

Laie *Honolulu County Oahu island Central Hawaii, 23 mi/37 km north of Honolulu*

1864 sugarcane production begun by Mormons; town founded; **1919** Laie Mormon Temple built under direction of Samuel Wooley; **1955** Brigham Young University, Hawaii Campus, established; **May 9, 1999** rock fall pummels visitors with boulders in Kaluanui Canyon at Sacred Falls State Park to south, eight killed, 35 injured, park closed.

Lanai City *Maui County Lanai island Central Hawaii, 70 mi/113 km southeast of Honolulu*

1835 first Protestant missionaries arrive; **1854** Mormons attempt to colonize island led by Walter Murray Gibson, later excommunicated for refusing to turn his personal land holdings over to Mormon church; **1922** Hawaiian

Pineapple Company, established 1901, acquires island for pineapple plantation; town founded at center of island.

Lihue   *Kauai County Kauai island*   *Northwestern Hawaii, 108 mi/174 km northwest of Honolulu*

c.500 AD Polynesians first land on Kauai at mouth of Wailua River to north; **Jan. 18, 1778** Capt. James Cook discovers Hawaii starting with Kauai, drops anchor at mouth of Wailua River; **c.1820** Congregationalist mission established; **1824** Kingdom of Kauai and Niihau absorbed by Kingdom of Hawaii; **1825** first sugarcane planted in area; **1849** Lihue Sugar Plantation established; **1883** Lihue Lutheran Church built; **1905** Kauai County formed; town becomes county seat; **1906** Ninini Point Lighthouse built near Nawiliwili Harbor, automated 1953; **Dec. 31, 1941** Japanese submarine scores direct hit on gasoline storage tank at Nawiliwili Harbor, fails to detonate; **Dec. 15, 1991** flash flooding destroys 50 homes; **2001** county courthouse completed, replaces structure built early 1980s.

Pearl City   *Honolulu County Oahu island*
Central Hawaii, 10 mi/16 km northwest of Honolulu

1840 Navy Lt. Charles Wilkes surveys Pearl Harbor, determines narrow entrance could be dredged to allow passage of ships; **1873** work begins on blasting channel, completed 1898; **1908** Pearl Harbor Naval Base established; **1913** dry dock collapses as it nears completion, many killed; **Dec. 7, 1941** Japanese launch surprise attack at 7:55 a.m. on U.S. Pacific fleet in Pearl Harbor, 2,300 killed; **1968** Leeward Community College, University of Hawaii, established.

Puuwai   *Kauai County Niihau island*
Northwestern Hawaii, 155 mi/249 km west-northwest of Honolulu

1863 Mrs. Elizabeth Sinclair arrives from Scotland by way of New Zealand, purchases island for $10,000, offered by Kamehameha IV (died 1863), sold by Kamehameha V; **1900s** Robinson family, descendants of Mrs. Sinclair, retain sole ownership of Niihau, small native population maintains traditional way of life; **Dec. 7, 1941** Japanese pilot crash lands on island after running out of fuel, islanders build large bonfire to warn island of Kauai of impending attack.

Wahiawa   *Honolulu County Oahu island*   *Central Hawaii, 18 mi/29 km north-northwest of Honolulu*

1700s Leilehua Plateau in Oahu interior used by Oahu chiefs as military training ground for their armies prior to

Kamehameha's conquest in 1795; **1800s** cattle production becomes important; **1895** cattle leases withdrawn in favor of diversified farming; **1902** pineapple cannery established, later taken over by Del Monte Company; town founded; **1904** town becomes center of Hawaiian pineapple industry; **1909** Schofield Barracks Military Reservation established to west; **1920s** Wahiawa Botanical Gardens established to east; **Dec. 7, 1941** Schofield Barracks attacked by Japanese during assault on nearby Pearl Harbor to south; **1977** Interstate Highway H-2 completed from Honolulu.

Wailuku   *Maui County Maui island*   *Central Hawaii, 90 mi/149 km east-southeast of Honolulu*

c.500 AD Polynesians migrate to Hawaiian Islands; **mid-1700s** King Kamehameha I conquers Maui after bloody battle; **Nov. 26, 1778** Capt. James Cook discovers Maui; **1790** Haleakala Crater last erupts to southeast; **1837** missionaries arrive from New England; town founded; **Jan. 30, 1839** educator Samuel Chapman Armstrong born (died 1893); **1873** Kaahumanu Congregational Church built; **1905** Maui County formed; town becomes county seat; **Dec. 6, 1927** U.S. Cong. Patsy Mink born at Paia to east (died 2002); **1967** Maui Community College, University of Hawaii, established at Kahului to east; **1968** War Memorial Stadium built; **1972** County Administration Building built; **1986** county courthouse built; **1997** annual Hula Bowl NFL all-star football classic moved from Honolulu.

Waimea   *Hawaii County Hawaii island*   See **Kamuela**

Waimea   *Kauai County Kauai island*
Northwestern Hawaii, 125 mi/201 km northwest of Honolulu

Jan. 18, 1778 Capt. James Cook drops anchor in Waimea Bay, Kauai, his first island of discovery in Hawaii; **1816** Fort Elisabeth built by Russians on Waimea River, expelled by king of Kauai under orders of Kamehameha, fort completed by Hawaiians; **1821** Kamehameha V invites King Kaumualii of Kauai aboard his boat, kidnaps him to Honolulu, assumes control of Kauai; **1846** Waimea Foreign Church founded by Rev. George R. Rowell; **1890** lepers Koolau, 28, wife and son resist transfer to leper colony on Molokai, take refuge among razor-sharp ridges to north, Koolau shoots at anyone that approaches, six killed, one wounded, he and son die of leprosy within two years at hideout.

Idaho

Northwestern U.S. Capital and largest city: Boise.

Idaho entered the U.S. as part of Oregon Territory in 1848. Idaho Territory was established March 3, 1863. Idaho became the 43rd state July 3, 1890.

Idaho is divided into 44 counties. Municipalities are classified as villages and cities. There are no townships. See Introduction.

American Falls *Power County Southeastern Idaho, 22 mi/35 km west-southwest of Pocatello, on Snake River*

1843 explorer John C. Fremont camps near here; **1863** 11 covered wagons on Oregon Trail attacked by Native Americans at Massacre Rocks to southwest, nine killed; **1883** Union Pacific Railroad reaches site; **1888** town founded; **1904** bridge built on Snake River, later flooded by dam; **1906** incorporated as a city; **1913** Power County formed; town becomes county seat; **1927** American Falls Reservoir formed on Snake River; town relocated; county courthouse built.

Arco *Butte County South central Idaho, 70 mi/ 113 km west of Idaho Falls*

1879 Union Pacific Railroad built; town founded on Big Lost River, named Root Hog Junction, later renamed for settler Arco Smith; **1909** incorporated as a city; **1917** Butte County formed; town becomes county seat; **May 2, 1924** Crater of the Moon National Monument established to southwest; **1934** county courthouse built; **1945** National Reactor Testing Station established to east; **1949** EBR-1 experimental breeder reactor built to southeast; **July 17, 1955** town becomes first to be lighted by nuclear power; **1979** EBR-1 National Historic Landmark established.

Blackfoot *Bingham County Southeastern Idaho, 22 mi/35 km north of Pocatello, on Snake River*

1867 Fort Hall Indian Reservation established to south; **1878** town founded, named for Blackfeet peoples; **1885** Bingham County formed; town becomes county seat; **1901** town incorporated; **1902** first annual Eastern Idaho State Fair held; **1987** county courthouse built.

Boise *Ada County Southwestern Idaho, on Boise River*

early 1800s French fur trappers refer to area as *les bois*, "the trees"; **1863** I. N. Coston and Ira B. Pearce build cabins; freighting station established by Jesus "Kossuth" Urquides of San Francisco; town founded; **1864** Ada County formed, named for Ada Riggs, first white child born in Idaho; town incorporated, becomes county seat; territorial capital moved from Lewiston; *The Idaho Statesman* newspaper founded; **1866** Christ Episcopal Church built; **1869** blockhouse built; **1870** Idaho Penitentiary established to east, closed 1973; **1871** U.S. Assay Office built; **1886** territorial capitol completed; Idaho Central Railroad reaches town; **July 3, 1890** Idaho enters Union as 43rd state; **1892** De Lamar House built, originally built by C. W. Moore c.1875; **1896** Ahaveth Beth Israel synagogue built; **1897** first Western Idaho State Fair held; **1902** St. Michael's Episcopal Cathedral built; **1906** St John's Roman Catholic Cathedral built; **1912** state capitol built, completed 1920; **1916** Zoo Boise established in Julia Davis Park after resident captures monkey in nearby desert, apparently escaped from traveling circus; **1926** Boise Airport established; **1932** Boise Junior College established, becomes Boise State University 1974; **2001** county courthouse completed.

Bonners Ferry *Boundary County Northern Idaho, 90 mi/145 km north-northeast of Spokane, Washington*

1883 ferry *Midge* launched on Kootenai River, remains in service 25 years; town founded; **1884** Boundary County formed; town becomes county seat; **1892** Great Northern Railroad reaches town; **1899** incorporated as a village; **1938** county courthouse completed; **May 1948** flooding causes serious damage; **1962** incorporated as a city; **Aug. 22, 1992** shootout at Ruby Ridge in Selkirk Mountains to southwest between alleged white supremacist Randy Weaver, family, neighbor, and Federal agents follows murder of Weaver's son, agent William Degan killed, mother Vicki, son Samuel Weaver, Labrador retriever killed.

Burley   *Cassia County*   *Southern Idaho, 75 mi/ 121 km west-southwest of Pocatello, on Snake River*

1879 Cassia County formed; Albion becomes county seat; **1905** town founded as new county seat; **1906** town incorporated; **1911** Oakley (Lower Goose Creek) Reservoir formed to south; **1939** county courthouse built; **June 20, 1971** powerboat sinks in Oakley Reservoir, eight killed; **1988** City of Rocks National Reserve established to south.

Caldwell   *Canyon County*   *Southwestern Idaho, 23 mi/37 km west of Boise, on Boise River*

1834 Fort Boise established; **1854** Native American attack on 23-unit wagon train leaves few survivors; **1883** Union Pacific Railroad built; town founded; **1890** incorporated as a city; **1891** Canyon County formed; town becomes county seat; College of Idaho established, renamed Albertson College 1991; **Dec. 30, 1905** former Gov. Frank Steunenberg killed by bomb at gate to his property, stems from miners' union violence; **1973** county courthouse built.

Cascade   *Valley County*   *Western Idaho, 48 mi/ 77 km north of Boise*

1912-1913 town founded on North Fork Payette River through merger of Van Wyck, Crawford, and Thunder City; **1917** Valley County formed; town incorporated, becomes county seat; **1920** county courthouse built; **1948** Cascade Dam completed on Payette River forming Cascade Reservoir, built for Boise Irrigation Project.

Cataldo   *Kootenai County*   *Northern Idaho, 52 mi/ 84 km east of Spokane, Washington*

1846 Mission of Sacred Heart built, moved from St. Maries; **July 4, 1861** Capt. John Mullan and men camp in canyon while building Mullan Road, named Fourth of July Canyon; **1878** mission named for Father Cataldo, leader of Rocky Mountain missions; **1887** mission relocated to De Smet; **1973** Old Mission State Park established.

Challis   *Custer County*   *Central Idaho, 120 mi/ 193 km northeast of Boise*

1873 gold discovered in area; **1878** town founded near East Fork Salmon River; **1881** Custer County formed; town becomes county seat; **1907** town incorporated; **1934** Public Library founded; **1952** county courthouse built.

Coeur d'Alene   *Kootenai County*   *Northern Idaho, 28 mi/45 km east of Spokane, Washington*

1864 Kootenai County formed; **1873** Coeur d'Alene Indian Reservation established to south; **1876** Fort Coeur d'Alene established on Spokane River, renamed Fort Sherman 1878; town founded as county seat; **1883** silver lode discovered to east; **1901** fort abandoned; **1907** town incorporated; **1933** North Idaho College (2-year) established; **1991** Veterans Memorial Centennial Bridge built across Spokane River; **1997** County Administration Building built.

Council   *Adams County*   *Western Idaho, 80 mi/ 129 km north of Boise*

1876 George and Elizabeth Moses become first settlers in Council Valley; town founded on Weiser River; **1903** town incorporated; **1911** Adams County formed; town becomes county seat; **1915** county courthouse built.

Driggs   *Teton County*   *Eastern Idaho, 90 mi/145 km northeast of Pocatello, near Teton River*

1812 trapper Pierre Trevanitagon discovers valley ("hole") west of Teton Range; **1832** in Battle of Pierre's Hole, 42 fur trappers encounter Gros Ventre tribe after traders' rendezvous, many killed; **1888** town founded by Mormons; **1910** incorporated as a city; **1915** Teton County formed; town becomes county seat; **1924** county courthouse built.

Dubois   *Clark County*   *Eastern Idaho, 50 mi/80 km north of Idaho Falls*

1914 Union Pacific Railroad reaches site; town founded as cattle and sheep ranching center, named for U.S. Senator Fred Dubois; **1916** town incorporated; **1919** Clark County formed, named for settler, state Sen. Sam K. Clark; town becomes county seat; county courthouse built; **1960** Hoggan Rodeo established by Hoggan family.

Emmett   *Gem County*   *Southwestern Idaho, 22 mi/ 35 km northwest of Boise*

1864 trading post established on Payette River; town founded; **1900** incorporated as a village; **1909** incorporated as a city; **1915** Gem County formed; town becomes county seat; **1924** Black Canyon Dam built to east on Payette River, part of Boise Irrigation Project; **1935** county courthouse built.

Fairfield   *Camas County*   *South central Idaho, 75 mi/121 km east-southeast of Boise*

1911 town founded; **1912** incorporated as a city; **1917** Camas County formed, named for type of lily commonly found in area, food source for Shoshoni; town becomes county seat; bank converted into county courthouse, built 1912.

Franklin *Franklin County* *Southeastern Idaho, 70 mi/113 km south-southeast of Pocatello*

Apr. 1860 town founded by Mormons who thought they were in Utah, oldest town in Idaho, named for Apostle Franklin D. Richards; **Jan. 29, 1863** in Battle River Massacre to north, troops under Col. Patrick Connor kill 250 Shoshoni men, women, and children following incidents with whites, 14 soldiers killed; **1869** town incorporated.

Gooding *Gooding County* *Southern Idaho, 92 mi/ 148 km southeast of Boise*

1883 town founded on Little Wood River, named Toponis; **1896** town renamed for U.S. Sen. Frank R. Gooding; **1908** town incorporated; **1913** Gooding County formed; town becomes county seat; **1971** county courthouse built.

Grangeville *Idaho County* *Northern Idaho, 165 mi/266 km north of Boise*

1861 Idaho County formed; Florence becomes county seat; **1869** county seat moved to Warrens; **1875** county seat moved to Mount Idaho; **1876** town founded as agricultural center; **1897** town incorporated; **1898** gold discovered in Buffalo Hump Mountains to south; **1899** Centennial Library founded, new library opened 1964; **1902** county seat moved to Grangeville; **1908** Northern Pacific Railroad reaches town; **1954** county courthouse completed.

Hailey *Blaine County* *South central Idaho, 100 mi/ 161 km east of Boise*

1895 Blaine County formed; **1881** town founded on Big Wood River as mining center and county seat, named for John Hailey; **1883** county courthouse built; **Oct. 30, 1885** poet Ezra Pound born (died 1972); **1903** incorporated as a village; **1909** incorporated as a city.

Idaho City *Boise County* *Southwestern Idaho, 25 mi/40 km northeast of Boise*

1862 gold discovered; town founded, population jumps to c.30,000; **1864** Boise County formed; town becomes county seat; **1865** fire destroys most of town; **1871** county courthouse built; **1962** incorporated as a city.

Idaho Falls *Bonneville County* *Eastern Idaho, 215 mi/346 km east of Boise, on Snake River*

1867 Taylor Toll Bridge built on Snake River; town founded as Taylor's Crossing; **1879** town renamed Eagle Rock; **1891** town renamed Idaho Falls; **1900** incorporated as a city; **1911** Bonneville County formed; city becomes county seat; **1916** Carnegie Library built, new library opened 1977; **1920** county courthouse built; **1929** Idaho Falls Airport (Fanning Field) established; **1934** Tautphaus Park Zoo established; **1941** Latter-day Saints Temple completed.

Island Park *Fremont County* See **Saint Anthony** (1943)

Jerome *Jerome County* *Southern Idaho, 110 mi/ 177 km southeast of Boise, near Snake River*

1907 town founded as center for Twin Falls North Side Irrigation Project; **1909** incorporated as a village; **1919** Jerome County formed; town becomes county seat; incorporated as a city; **1927** Twin Falls-Jerome Bridge built across Snake River; **1932** county courthouse built; **1967** new U.S. Highway 93 bridge built across Snake River.

Kellogg *Shoshone County* *Northern Idaho, 63 mi/ 101 km east of Spokane, Washington*

1893 Noah Kellogg discovers lead-bearing galena; town founded, named Milo; **1894** Kellogg establishes Bunker Hill Lead Mine; town renamed; **1923** town incorporated; **May 2, 1972** 91 miners killed in fire at Sunshine Silver Mine.

Ketchum *Blaine County* *South central Idaho, 95 mi/153 km east of Boise*

1880 lead and silver discovered by trapper David Ketchum; town founded as Leadville; **1883** Union Pacific Railroad completed; town renamed; **1920** town becomes largest sheep shipping point in U.S.; **1936** Sun Valley Resort built to northeast; **1937** gambling flourishes through 1947, banned 1954; **1947** town incorporated; **1937** Sawtooth National Recreation Area established to north; **July 2, 1961** author Ernest Hemingway, 61, commits suicide with shotgun.

Lapwai *Nez Perce County* *Northern Idaho, 10 mi/ 16 east of Lewiston*

1836 Presbyterian Mission founded among Nez Perce peoples by Rev. Henry Harmon Spalding, becomes known for first irrigation, first potatoes, first printing press in Idaho; **1855** Nez Perce Indian Reservation established; **1862** Fort Lapwai built to protect mining interests, first military fortification in Idaho; **1874** St. Joseph's Catholic Mission established by Father Joseph Cataldo; **May 15, 1965** Nez Perce National Historical Park (Spalding Unit) established.

Lewiston *Nez Perce County* *Northern Idaho, 200 mi/322 km north-northwest of Boise, on Snake River*

1805 Lewis and Clark Expedition stops here, trades with Nez Perce; **1861** Nez Perce County formed; town founded as county seat; **1862** *Golden Age* newspaper founded, first in Idaho; **1863** town becomes first capital of Idaho Territory, moved to Boise 1864; William Craig establishes ferry on Snake River; town incorporated; **1890** county courthouse built; **1893** Lewis-Clark State College established; **1897** bridge built across Snake River to Clarkston,

Washington; **1905** Public Library founded; **1944** Lewiston-Nez Perce County Airport established.

Malad City *Oneida County Southeastern Idaho, 50 mi/80 km south of Pocatello*

Aug. 29, 1843 explorer John C. Fremont camps in Standing Rock Pass to southeast; **1864** Oneida County formed; Soda Springs becomes county seat; town founded near Malad River by Mormons from Oneida, New York; **1866** county seat moved to Malad City; **1870s** hordes of Mormon crickets ruin crops; **1888** LDS tabernacle begun, completed 1900, rebuilt 1928; **1906** Union Pacific Railroad reaches town; **June 19, 1910** Deep Creek Dam collapse inundates town; **1939** county courthouse built; **1977** Oneida County Public Library opened.

Montpelier *Bear Lake County Southeastern Idaho, 73 mi/117 km southeast of Pocatello*

1863 Mormon settlers arrive in Bear Valley; **1864** town founded on Bear River, originally named Clover Creek, later Belmont; **1865** town renamed by Brigham Young for Montpelier, Vermont, capital of his native state; **1891** incorporated as a city; **Aug. 13, 1896** Montpelier Bank robbed by Butch Cassidy, Elza Lay, and Bob Meeks.

Moscow *Latah County Northern Idaho, 225 mi/ 362 km north-northwest of Boise*

1871 area opened to white settlement; town founded; **1877** Fort Russell built; **1887** town incorporated; **1888** Latah County formed; town becomes county seat; **1889** University of Idaho established; **1958** county courthouse built.

Mountain Home *Elmore County Southwestern Idaho, 33 mi/53 km southeast of Boise*

1889 Elmore County formed; town founded as county seat; **1896** incorporated as a village; **1903** incorporated as a city; **1915** county courthouse built; **1942** Mountain Home Army Air Field established, closed 1945, becomes Air Force Base 1948, **1950** Anderson Ranch Reservoir formed to northeast on South Fork Boise River; **1952** C. J. Strike Dam completed on Snake River to southwest.

Murphy *Owyhee County Southwestern Idaho, 32 mi/51 km south-southwest of Boise, near Snake River*

1819 fur trappers arrive including three Hawaiians; **1863** Owyhee County formed, variation of "Hawaii"; Ruby City becomes county seat; gold mining begins in Owyhee Mountains; **1867** county seat moved to Silver City; **1899** Union Pacific Railroad built; town founded, named for railroad boss Cornelius "Con" Murphy; **1934** county seat moved to Murphy, one of smallest county seats in U.S. (pop. c.50); **1963** county courthouse converted from old school.

Nampa *Canyon County Southwestern Idaho, 18 mi/29 km west of Boise*

1885 town founded by Alexander Duffes, named for Shoshoni Chief Nampuh; **1886** town incorporated; **1887** Idaho Central Railroad reaches town; **1908** Lake Lowell (Deer Flat Reservoir) formed by dam to west for irrigation; Nampa Public Library opened; **1913** Northwest Nazarene College (University) established.

Nezperce *Lewis County Northern Idaho, 40 mi/ 64 km east-southeast of Lewiston*

1855 Nez Perce Indian Reservation established; **1895** town founded on Nez Perce Indian Reservation; **1911** Lewis County formed; town becomes county seat; **May 15, 1965** Nez Perce National Historical Park (East Kamiah Unit) established to east; **1974** county courthouse built [incorporation date not available]

Orofino *Clearwater County Northern Idaho, 38 mi/61 km east of Lewiston*

1855 Nez Perce Indian Reservation established; **1860** gold discovered on Orofino Creek by E. D. Pierce c.25 mi/ 40 km to east; town of Oro Fino City founded; **1895** part of Nez Perce Indian Reservation opened to white settlement; **1898** new town founded near Clearwater River; **1900** Camas Prairie Railroad arrives; **1904** Idaho State Hospital established; **1905** town incorporated; **1911** Clearwater County formed; town becomes county seat; **1928** county courthouse completed; **July 28, 1934** highest temperature ever recorded in Idaho reached, 118°F/48°C; **1947** first annual Lumberjack Days held; **1972** Dworshak Reservoir formed on North Fork Clearwater River.

Paris *Bear Lake County Southeastern Idaho, 53 mi/85 km southeast of Pocatello*

1863 town founded by Mormons near Bear River, north of Bear Lake; **1875** Bear Lake County formed; **1885** county courthouse built; **1889** LDS Tabernacle built; **1897** town incorporated.

Payette *Payette County Southwestern Idaho, 48 mi/77 km northwest of Boise, on Snake River*

1883 Union Pacific Railroad built; town founded, named Boomerang; **1901** town incorporated, renamed Payette for Francois Payette; **1917** Payette County formed; town becomes county seat; **1972** county courthouse built.

Pierce *Clearwater County Northern Idaho, 60 mi/ 97 km east of Lewiston*

1858 Shoshone County formed; **1860** gold discovered by E. D. Pierce, first in Idaho; town founded, second oldest town in Idaho; **1864** town becomes county seat; **1878** artist Elling William "Bill" Gollings born (died 1932); **1885** county seat moved to Murray; **1911** Clearwater County formed from Shoshone County; **1935** incorporated as a city.

Pocatello *Bannock County* *Southeastern Idaho, 200 mi/322 km east-southeast of Boise*

1834 Fort Hall built to north, abandoned 1855; **1879** Utah Northern Railroad reaches site; **1882** town founded on Pocatello River, in Snake River Valley; **1889** incorporated as a village; **1893** Bannock County formed; town becomes county seat; incorporated as a city; **1901** Academy of Idaho founded, becomes Idaho State College 1947, University 1963; **1908** county courthouse built; **1934** Idaho Museum of Natural History established.

Preston *Franklin County* *Southeastern Idaho, 63 mi/101 km south-southeast of Pocatello*

Jan. 29, 1863 Col. Patrick E. Connor attacks Shoshonis to east, 250 Native Americans killed; **1866** town founded near Bear River; **Aug. 4, 1899** Ezra Taft Benson born, secretary of agriculture under President Eisenhower (died 1994); **1913** Franklin County formed; town becomes county seat; incorporated as a city; **1939** county courthouse built.

Rexburg *Madison County* *Eastern Idaho, 25 mi/ 40 km north-northeast of Idaho Falls*

1883 town founded near Snake River by Mormons led by Thomas E. Ricks; **1884** irrigation projects inaugurated; **1888** Ricks College established, becomes Brigham Young University-Idaho 2001; **1899** Utah Northern Railroad reaches town; **1903** town incorporated; **1911** Fremont Stake Tabernacle built; **1913** Madison County formed; town becomes county seat; **1917** county courthouse built; **June 5, 1976** collapse of Teton Dam on Teton River at town of Teton to northeast causes flash flood, 11 killed; **1981** Teton Flood Museum established in former 1911 tabernacle.

Rigby *Jefferson County* *Eastern Idaho, 15 mi/ 24 km north-northeast of Idaho Falls, near Snake River*

1884 town founded by Mormons; first irrigation canals built; **1903** incorporated as a village; **1913** Jefferson County formed; city becomes county seat; **1915** incorporated as a city; **1939** county courthouse built.

Rupert *Minidoka County* *Southern Idaho, 65 mi/ 105 km west-southwest of Pocatello, near Snake River*

1905 town founded near Snake River as planned city by engineers of U.S. Reclamation Service, named for chief engineer; **1906** incorporated as a village; **1913** Minidoka County formed; town becomes county seat; Lake Walcott formed on Snake River by Minidoka Dam to east; **1917** incorporated as a city; county courthouse built.

Saint Anthony *Fremont County* *Eastern Idaho, 40 mi/64 km north-northeast of Idaho Falls*

1810 Fort Henry established on Snake River by Andrew Henry of Missouri Fur Company, first fort in Snake River

basin; **1887** bridge built across Snake River; **1890** town founded, named for St. Anthony Falls, Minnesota; **1893** Fremont County formed; town becomes county seat; **1905** incorporated as a city; **1909** county courthouse built; **Jan. 18, 1943** lowest temperature ever recorded in Idaho reached at Island Park to north, −60°F/−51°C.

Saint Maries *Benewah County* *Northern Idaho, 47 mi/76 km southeast of Spokane, Washington*

1842 Mission of Sacred Heart established, moved to Cataldo 1846; **1888** town founded on St. Maries River; **1902** town incorporated; **1908** Chicago, Milwaukee, St. Paul & Pacific Railroad builds St. Paul Pass Tunnel from Montana through Bitterroot Mountains to east; **Aug. 1910** forest fires destroy large areas of Northern Idaho and Western Montana, 85 killed; **1915** Benewah County formed; town becomes county seat; **1924** county courthouse built.

Salmon *Lemhi County* *Northeastern Idaho, 160 mi/257 km northeast of Boise*

c.1786 Shoshoni guide Sacajawea born in Lemhi Valley, died Dec. 20, 1812, at Fort Manuel, South Dakota, guided Lewis and Clark through mountains; **Aug. 12, 1805** Lewis and Clark cross Continental Divide from Montana, enter Lemhi Valley; **1855** Mormons establish Lemhi Mission; **1866** gold discovered; **1867** town founded on Salmon River, at mouth of Lemhi River, named Salmon City; **1869** Lemhi County formed, named for character in *Book of Mormon*; town becomes county seat, renamed Salmon; **1892** town incorporated; **1910** county courthouse built.

Sandpoint *Bonner County* *Northern Idaho, 60 mi/ 97 km northeast of Spokane, Washington*

1898 town founded on Pend Oreille River, at its exit from Lake Pend Oreille; **1900** town incorporated; **1907** Bonner County formed; town becomes county seat; county courthouse built; **May 29, 2001** standoff begins with six children bearing weapons whose white supremacist mother with multiple sclerosis died at their home May 12, ends June 2.

Shoshone *Lincoln County* *South central Idaho, 110 mi/177 km southeast of Boise*

1882 Union Pacific Railroad built; town founded on Little Wood River, originally named Naples, later renamed Shoshone; **1895** Lincoln County formed; town becomes county seat; **1902** incorporated as a city; **1907** county courthouse built; **1909** Magic Reservoir built on Big Wood River to north as part of Minidoka Irrigation Project.

Soda Springs *Caribou County* *Southeastern Idaho, 35 mi/56 km east-southeast of Pocatello*

1840s bubbling spring on Oregon Trail named Soda Springs; **1863** Fort Connor established by anti-Mormon

IDAHO

Morrisites, 160 of the group escorted out of Salt Lake City by Col. Patrick E. Connor; **1870** town platted on Bear River by Brigham Young; **1896** town incorporated; **1911** Blackfoot Reservoir formed to north on Blackfoot River; **1919** Caribou County formed; town becomes county seat; county courthouse built.

Sun Valley   *Blaine County*   *South central Idaho, 96 mi/155 km east of Boise*

1880 Union Pacific Railroad built to nearby Ketchum; **1936** town founded as ski resort by W. Averell Harriman, railroad chairman; **Dec. 1936** Sun Valley Lodge opened; **1937** Challenger Inn built; **July 2, 1961** author Ernest Hemingway commits suicide with shotgun at neighboring Ketchum (born 1899); **1964** resort sold to former Olympic skier Bill Janss, resold 1977; **1966** Hemingway Memorial dedicated; **1967** town incorporated.

Teton   *Madison and Fremont counties*   See **Rexburg (1976)**

Twin Falls   *Twin Falls County*   *Southern Idaho, 120 mi/193 km southeast of Boise, near Snake River*

1811 Astoria expedition led by William Price Hunt passes down Snake River on way to Oregon, first whites to discover Shoshone and Pillar falls; **1904** town founded as center for Twin Falls South Side irrigation project; **1905** incorporated as a village; **1907** Twin Falls County formed; town becomes county seat; incorporated as a city; **1909** Twin Falls Public Library opened; **1911** county courthouse built; **1927** Twin Falls-Jerome Bridge built across Snake River; **1965** College of Southern Idaho (2-year) established; **1976** new highway bridge built across Snake River.

Wallace   *Shoshone County*   *Northern Idaho, 75 mi/121 km east of Spokane, Washington*

1858 Shoshone County formed; **1864** county organized; Pierce becomes county seat; **1884** William R. Wallace builds first cabin; town founded as mining center, named Placer Center; **1885** county seat moved to Murray; **1888** town incorporated, renamed Wallace; **1890** county seat moved to Osborn; **1893** county seat moved to Wallace; **1905** county courthouse built; **1910** forest fires destroy part of town; **Feb. 8, 1920** actress Lana Turner born (died 1995).

Weiser   *Washington County*   *Southwestern Idaho, 58 mi/93 km northwest of Boise, on Snake River*

1877 town founded at former ford on Oregon Trail, named Weiser Bridge for trapper Jacob Weiser (WEE-ser); **1879** Washington County formed; town becomes county seat; **1887** town incorporated; **1890** town destroyed by fire; first fiddling contest held; **1944** county courthouse completed; **1953** National Oldtime Fiddlers' Contest first held.

168

Illinois

Central U.S. Capital: Springfield. Major city: Chicago.

The region joined the U.S. in 1787 as part of the Northwest Territory. Indiana Territory, which included Illinois, was established May 7, 1800. Illinois Territory was established February 2, 1809. Illinois entered the Union as the 21st state December 3, 1818.

Illinois is divided into 102 counties. 88 counties are divided into townships with governments having broad powers. 14 counties are divided into precincts with no governments. Municipalities are classified as villages, towns, and cities. See Introduction.

Addison *Du Page County* *Northeastern Illinois, 21 mi/34 km west of Chicago*

1832 soldiers of Gen. Scott's army killed during Black Hawk War; **1840s** town settled by German Lutherans, named for writer Joseph Addison; **1852** post office established; **1867** Heideman Mill built, used until 1929; **1873** Evangelical Lutheran Home orphanage founded; **1884** incorporated as a village; **1893** Century House built; **1902** Kinderheim school for wayward children founded by Rev. Augustus Schlechte; **1962** Addison Public Library founded.

Albion *Edwards County* *Southeastern Illinois, 115 mi/185 km east-southeast of St. Louis*

1818 Edwards County formed; town founded by Englishmen Morris Birkbeck and George Flower; **1826** Harris House built; **1841** George French House built; **1850** county courthouse built; **1869** incorporated as a city.

Aledo *Mercer County* *Northwestern Illinois, 24 mi/ 39 km south-southwest of Rock Island*

1825 Mercer County formed; **1855** town founded as county seat; **1885** incorporated as a city; **1894** county courthouse built; **1924** Roosevelt Military Academy founded.

Alton *Madison County* *Southwestern Illinois, 18 mi/29 km north of St. Louis, on Mississippi River*

1673 Father Marquette expedition observes Piasa (PEI-a-saw) Bird image, part man, part beast, painted on bluffs by Native Americans; **1818** town platted by Col. Rufus Easton; **1821** incorporated as a town, **1831** Rock Spring Seminary moved from Lebanon, Illinois, becomes

Shurtleff College; **1833** Illinois' first state prison opened; **1837** incorporated as a city; **Nov. 7, 1837** abolitionist newspaper publisher Elijah P. Lovejoy murdered by angry proslavery mob; **1863** smallpox epidemic rages through Illinois State Prison, several thousand die through 1864; **1865** prison evacuated and razed; **1870** quarrying destroys Piasa Bird; **1891** Haynee Library opened, becomes Public Library 1952; **1897** Lovejoy monument erected; **Feb. 22, 1918** "Alton Giant" Robert Wadlow born, grows to be 8 ft 11½ in/2.73 m (died 1940); **May 26, 1926** jazz trumpeter Miles Davis born (died 1991); **June 10, 1933** August Luer kidnapped, released, three men, one woman sentenced to life in prison; **1934** new Piasa Bird painted on bluff; **1993** Melvin Price Lock & Dam (Lock & Dam No. 26) completed 2 mi/3.2 km south of old dam built 1930s; **Aug. 2, 1993** flooding inundates downtown, overwhelms water treatment plant, drinking water halted for 60,000; **1994** new Clark Bridge (cable-stayed) opens to Missouri, old bridge demolished by explosives.

Arcola *Douglas County* *Eastern Illinois, 30 mi/ 48 km south of Champaign*

1855 town platted on Illinois Central Railroad, named for town in Italy; **1865** incorporated as a city; **Dec. 24, 1880** John Barton Gruelle born, creator of Raggedy Ann doll (died 1938); **1940** Rockome Gardens established in Amish area to west, rock and floral displays; **May 1999** Raggedy Ann Museum opened.

Aurora *Kane and Du Page counties* *Northeastern Illinois, 37 mi/60 km west-southwest of Chicago, on Fox River*

1834 Joseph McCarty of Elmira, New York, becomes first white settler, trades with Potawatomi community; **1835**

McCarty builds mill; **1836** town platted; **1837** incorporated as separate towns, East Aurora and West Aurora; **1848** Chicago, Burlington & Quincy Railroad reaches town; **1853** two Auroras merge, incorporated as a city; **1860** Peck Merino Sheep Farm established; **1881** city among first to be lighted by electricity; **1893** Aurora University established; **1919** Col. George Fabyn founds Riverbank Laboratories to test acoustical equipment; **1931** Memorial Bridge opens on Fox River; **Jan. 2, 1942** U.S. Cong. J. Dennis Hastert born, House Speaker from 1999; **1966** Waubonsee Community College established at Sugar Grove to west; **1967** Fermi National Acceleration Laboratory established to northeast; **1983** Tevatron Energy Doubler particle accelerator completed at Fermi Lab, 4 mi/6.4 km in circumference; **1986** Illinois Mathematics and Science Academy opened; **1989** Sci-Tech Museum opened.

Batavia   *Kane County*   *Northeastern Illinois, 37 mi/ 60 km west of Chicago, on Fox River*

1833 area settled following Black Hawk War (1832); town founded **1837** flour mill established; **1850** limestone quarrying industry established; **1856** incorporated as a village; Bellevue Place sanitarium founded; **1864** Batavia Creamery built; **1870** Chicago, Aurora & Elgin Railroad reaches town; Van Nortwick Paper Mill established; **May 20, 1875** President Lincoln's widow Mary Todd Lincoln admitted at Bellevue Place for insanity, legally declared sane, released Sept. 11; **1891** incorporated as a city; **1950** Chicago, Burlington & Quincy commuter rail line established.

Beardstown   *Cass County*   *Western Illinois, 45 mi/ 72 km west-northwest of Springfield, on Illinois River*

1819 Thomas Beard begins operating ferry; **1837** Cass County formed; town becomes county seat; incorporated as a city, **1845** county courthouse built; **1858** Abraham Lincoln succeeds in defending Duff Armstrong against murder charges in dramatic trial; **1872** after several moves between Beardstown and Virginia, county seat permanently moved to Virginia; **1922** entire town inundated with 23 ft/7 m of flood water; **1923** 29-ft/8.8-m flood wall constructed.

Belleville   *Saint Clair County*   *Southwestern Illinois, 15 mi/24 km southeast of St. Louis*

1790 St. Clair County formed; **1814** town established; county seat moved from Cahokia; **1818** Gov. Ninian Edwards creates inducements to area settlers; **1819** incorporated as a city; **1820** Gov. John Reynolds mansion built; **1825** first commercial coal mine opened; **1828** coal mining expanded to south and east; German immigrants drawn by mining activities; **1851** Western Brewery established, maker of Stag beer, closed Sept. 1988; **1873** German *Liederkranz* singing society established; **March 5, 1938** tornado hits East St. Louis and Belleville, eight killed, many injured; **1946** Belleville Area College (2-year) established; **Apr. 2, 1908** TV actor Buddy Ebsen born

(died 2003); **1917** Scott Field established to east, becomes Scott Air Force Base 1948; **1937** Belleville Fountain erected at center of town square, renovated 1985; **Sept. 2, 1952** tennis player Jimmy Connors born; **1975** county courthouse built.

Belvidere   *Boone County*   *Northern Illinois, 13 mi/ 21 km east of Rockford*

1836 town founded on Kishwaukee River; **1837** Boone County formed; **1847** incorporated as a village; **1849** Galena & Chicago Union Railroad arrives; **1854** county courthouse built; **1879** National Sewing Machine Plant opens; **1882** incorporated as a city; **1913** Ida Public Library opened with grant from Andrew Carnegie.

Benton   *Franklin County*   *Southern Illinois, 83 mi/ 134 km southeast of St. Louis*

1818 Franklin County formed; Frankfort becomes first county seat; **1839** town founded as new county seat with formation of Williamson County from Franklin to south; **1841** incorporated as a city; county seat moved to Benton; **1874** third county courthouse completed.

Berwyn   *Cook County*   *Northeastern Illinois, 9 mi/ 14.5 km west of downtown Chicago*

1862 Chicago, Burlington & Quincy Railroad built; **1870s** town founded, originally named La Vergne Station; **1889** Swedish immigrants arrive; **1890** section secedes from Cicero, becomes Berwyn; **1902** incorporated as a village; **1908** incorporated as city; **July 24, 1915** Western Electric company excursion boat *Eastland* overturns on Chicago River in Chicago killing 844, mostly residents of Berwyn.

Bloomington   *McLean County*   *Central Illinois, 115 mi/185 km southwest of Chicago*

1822 first settlers, mainly British, name site Keg Grove, soon changed to Blooming Grove; **1830** McLean County formed; James Allin purchases quarter-section of land north of village; **1831** town of Bloomington platted on Allin's land, becomes county seat; **1837** *The Daily Pantagraph* newspaper founded; **1839** incorporated as a city; **1850** Illinois Wesleyan University established; **1852** elder Adlai E. Stevenson of Kentucky arrives here to practice law, becomes U.S. Congressman, later vice-president 1893–1897 (died 1914); **1854** Illinois Central and Chicago & Mississippi railroads reach town; **May 29, 1856** Abraham Lincoln denounces slavery in speech delivered here; **June 19, 1856** author, publisher Elbert Hubbard born, died May 7, 1915, aboard *Lusitania*; **Oct. 20, 1856** Cong. James Robert Mann born in rural McLean County, sponsored 1910 Elkins-Mann Act making it illegal to transport women across state lines for prostitution (died 1922); **1900** business district destroyed by fire; **1976** county courthouse built; **Jan. 5, 1999** lowest temperature ever recorded in Illinois reached at Congerville to northwest, −36°F/−38°C.

Bourbonnais *Kankakee County* Northeastern
Illinois, 53 mi/85 km south of Chicago

1832 Frenchman Noel La Vasseur founds trading post;
town founded, named for courier Francois Bourbonnais;
1847 Trinity Catholic Church built; **1855** Illinois Central
Railroad bypasses town to south; city of Kankakee
founded on railroad; **1865** St. Viator College (Catholic)
established; **1875** incorporated as a village (BUR-bo-
NAIZ), **1907** Olivet Nazarene University established;
March 15, 1999 Amtrak passenger train hits trailer
truck, derails, 11 killed.

Braidwood *Will County* Northeastern Illinois,
50 mi/80 km southwest of Chicago

1865 William Henneberry digs well, finds coal; **Feb. 4,
1870** mine labor leader John Mitchell born (died 1919);
1873 incorporated as a city amid booming coal mining
district; boasts 117 saloons; **1877** black laborers brought
in to break 9-month mining strike, unrest follows; **Feb. 16,
1883** Diamond Coal Mine floods, 69 miners drown.

Brookfield *Cook County* Northeastern Illinois,
11 mi/18 km west of downtown Chicago

c.1890 prominent families, including Rockefellers,
Armours, and McCormicks, purchase large tracts; **1893**
incorporated as a village, named Grossdale; **1905** village
renamed Brookfield; **1913** Brookfield Public Library
founded; **1934** Chicago Zoological Park (Brookfield
Zoo) established; **Aug. 16, 1996** 3-year-old boy falls into
gorilla pit at Brookfield Zoo, 8-year-old gorilla Binti Jua,
with baby on its back, carries boy safely to door of
compound.

Byron *Ogle County* Northern Illinois, 12 mi/19 km
southwest of Rockford, on Rock River

May 14, 1832 Battle of Stillman's Run, 12 soldiers killed in
encounter with Native Americans in Black Hawk War, to
east; **1835** town founded by settlers from New England,
named for poet Lord Byron; **Sept. 2, 1850** Albert Spalding
born, organized National Baseball League, established
sporting goods business (died 1915); **1866** soldiers monument erected; **1878** incorporated as a village; **1904**
incorporated as a city, **1985** Byron Nuclear Power Plant
opened.

Cahokia *Saint Clair County* Southwestern
*Illinois, 4 mi/6.4 km south of St. Louis, on Mississippi
River*

1698 site of Tamaroa Native American camp visited by
Fathers Joliet, Davion, and Buisson St. Cosme, guided by
native guide Tonti, called Iron Hand for his artificial
hand; **May 1699** house and Church of the Holy Family,
first church in Illinois, built by St. Cosme, considered
"Birthplace of Midwest"; **June 7, 1701** decree grants
missionaries sole governing authority; **1737** log cabin
built, used as courthouse until 1814; **1765** British assume
control; **1778** George Rogers Clark takes Kaskaskia and
Cahokia from British for U.S., removes his troops 1880;
1795 two large counties composing present state of Illinois
formed, Randolph to south, St. Clair to north; **1799** Jarrot
House built; **1809** town becomes county seat of extensive
St. Clair County, includes 80 modern day counties; **1814**
county seat moved to Belleville; **1833** Parish House built
by Father Loisel; **1904** old courthouse moved to St. Louis
World's Fair, returned to original site 1939; **1927**
incorporated as a village. [Cahokia Mounds archaeological site, see Collinsville.]

Cairo *Alexander County* Southern Illinois, 30 mi/
*48 km west of Paducah, Kentucky, on Mississippi and
Ohio rivers*

1818 St. Louis merchant John G. Comegys settles here,
names town for city in Egypt; **1819** Alexander County
formed; **1837** town incorporated; **Apr. 9, 1842** Charles
Dickens visits town, appalled by its raw character, uses it
as setting for nightmarish City of Eden in *Martin
Chuzzlewit*, 1843; **1851** county seat moved from Thebes;
1855 Illinois Central Railroad reaches town; **1857** incorporated as a city; **1859** Halliday Hotel opens; **Sept. 1861**
Union establishes major base of operations; **Oct. 27, 1869**
steamboat *Stonewall* burns in Mississippi River below
Cairo, killing 200; **1883** Cairo Public Library built; **1921**
county courthouse built; **1929** Mississippi River Bridge
opens to Missouri; **1937** flooding rivers come within 4
inches/10 cm of topping levees; **1938** Ohio River Bridge
opens to Kentucky.

Cambridge *Henry County* Northwestern Illinois,
25 mi/40 km southeast of Rock Island

1825 Henry County formed; **1839** Richmond becomes
county seat; **1843** town founded as new county seat;
county courthouse physically moved, completed 1845;
1853 incorporated as a village; **1880** new county courthouse built.

Canton *Fulton County* West central Illinois, 25 mi/
40 km southwest of Peoria

1824 New Yorker Isaac Swan arrives; **1825** town platted
by Swan, named in belief that it was antipodal to Canton,
China; **1835** tornado damages town, several killed; **1837**
incorporated as a village; **1846** Maple & Parlin Company
begins manufacture of steel moldboard plows, becomes
Parlin and Orendorff Company 1852; **1849** incorporated
as a city; **Dec. 15, 1861** automobile manufacturer Charles
A. Duryea born (died 1938), brother James born at
Washburn Oct. 8, 1869 (died 1967); **1892** Parlin-Ingersoll
Library founded; **1919** International Harvester takes over
P & O Plow Works, becomes largest farm implement
manufacturer in world; **1959** Spoon River College (2-year)
established.

ILLINOIS

Carbondale   *Jackson County*   *Southern Illinois,*
80 mi/129 km southeast of St. Louis

July 4, 1854 first train of Illinois Central Railroad arrives
from Cairo; **1856** incorporated as a town; **1858** Dixon
House built; **Feb. 22, 1862** Albert S. Thompson, body-
guard for Confederate Pres. Jefferson Davis, chisels name
on face of Giant City rock formations; **Apr. 29, 1866**
Memorial Day holiday established by Gen. John Logan;
1869 incorporated as a city; **1874** Southern Illinois
University established; **1927** Giant City State Park
established to south; **1939** Crab Orchard Lake formed
by dam on Crab Orchard Creek to east; **June 16, 1955**
actress Laurie Metcalf born.

Carlinville   *Macoupin County*   *Central Illinois,*
37 mi/60 km south-southwest of Springfield

1829 Macoupin County formed; town site founded as
county seat; **1837** incorporated as a city; **1857** Blackburn
College established; **Aug. 31, 1858** Abraham Lincoln
delivers speech to pro-Douglas audience; **1870** second
county courthouse completed; **1929** Lincoln Memorial
boulder erected.

Carlyle   *Clinton County*   *South central Illinois,*
45 mi/72 km east of St. Louis, on Kaskaskia River

1812 Fort Hill established; **1818** town platted at ford on
Kaskaskia River; **1837** incorporated as a village; **1849**
county courthouse built; **1855** Clinton County formed;
town becomes county seat; **1857** Ohio & Mississippi
Railroad reaches town; **1858** Truesdale Hotel built; **1860**
General Dean Suspension Bridge built across Kaskaskia
River on St. Louis-Vincennes Trail; **1884** incorporated as
a city; **1911** oil discovered in area; **1938** Case-Holstead
Library opened; **1967** large Lake Carlyle reservoir built on
Kaskaskia River; **1996** Veterans' Memorial dedicated.

Carmi   *White County*   *Southeastern Illinois, 115 mi/*
185 km east-southeast of St. Louis

1809 first settlers arrive; **1815** John M. Robinson Home
built, U.S. Senator 1835–1843 (1794–1843); **1816** town
platted (CAR-mei); **1819** incorporated as a village; **1820s**
John Craw House built; **1824** White County formed; town
becomes county seat; **1873** incorporated as a city; **1883**
county courthouse built.

Carrollton   *Greene County*   *Western Illinois, 45 mi/*
72 km north-northwest of St. Louis

1818 area settled; town founded; **1821** Greene County
formed; town becomes county seat; **1833** incorporated as
a town; **1861** incorporated as a city; **1868** Walnut Hall
mansion built, home of Cong. Henry T. Rainey; **1891**
second county courthouse built; **1902** Carrollton Carnegie
Library built; **Oct. 5, 1951** actress Karen Allen born.

Carterville   *Williamson County*   *Southern Illinois,*
92 mi/148 km southeast of St. Louis, Missouri

1869 coal mining begins in area; **1872** Carbondale &
Shawneetown Railroad reaches site; town founded; **1892**
incorporated as a city; **Jan. 10, 1962** coal mine explosion
kills 11; **1967** John A. Logan College (2-year) established.

Carthage   *Hancock County*   *Western Illinois,*
14 mi/23 km east of Keokuk, Iowa

1825 Hancock County formed; town founded as county
seat; **1837** incorporated as a city; **June 27, 1844** Mormon
leader Joseph Smith and brother Hyrum Smith, both
jailed for destroying opposition press in Nauvoo, killed by
mob; **Oct. 22, 1858** Abraham Lincoln delivers speech
during senatorial campaign against Stephen A. Douglas;
1870 Carthage College established; **1893** Carthage Public
Library founded; **1908** third county courthouse built.

Cave in Rock   *Hardin County*   *Southern Illinois,*
135 mi/217 km southeast of St. Louis, on Ohio River

1729 Frenchman Martin Chartier discovers cave in river
bluff; **1797** Samuel Mason establishes "Liquor Vault and
House of Entertainment" in cave, plundering victims as
they arrive; **1807** Solomon Perkins becomes first permanent settler; **1839** town platted; **1901** incorporated as a
village; **1929** Cave-in-Rock State Park established.

Cedarville   *Stephenson County*   *See* **Freeport**
(1860)

Centralia   *Marion and Clinton counties*   *South*
central Illinois, 58 mi/93 km east-southeast of St. Louis

1853 area settled by German immigrants; town platted on
Illinois Central Railroad; **1855** railroad establishes shops
here, experiments conducted in conversion of locomotives
from wood-burning to coal-burning machines; **1859**
incorporated as a city; **1868** coal-burning train engines
become standard equipment; first refrigerated car, the
Thunderbolt Express, put into service for Southern
Illinois' fruit-growing industry; **1874** coal mining begins
in area; **March 25, 1947** coal mine explosion, 111 killed;
1966 Kaskaskia College (2-year) established.

Champaign   *Champaign County*   *East central*
Illinois, 125 mi/201 km south-southwest of Chicago

1822 town of Urbana settled; **1833** Champaign County
formed; Urbana becomes county seat; **1854** Illinois
Central Railroad bypasses Urbana to west; new town of
West Urbana founded; **1855** Urbana attempts to annex
West Urbana; **1861** incorporated as a city, renamed
Champaign; **1867** University of Illinois established;
1870s attempts to wrest county seat from Urbana by
Champaign fail; **1937** City Building built; **1967** Parkland
College (2-year) established.

Charleston *Coles County* *Eastern Illinois, 43 mi/ 69 km south of Champaign*

1830 Coles County formed; town founded as county seat; **1831** Lincoln family moves into cabin from their first Illinois home in Macon County, near Decatur; **1834** Lincolns move into third Illinois home; **1835** incorporated as a village; first county courthouse built; **1837** Thomas Lincoln purchases farm 5 mi/8km to south, purchased in turn by son Abraham 1841; **1839** incorporated as a city, **Jan. 17, 1851** Thomas Lincoln, father of Abraham Lincoln, dies (born Jan. 6, 1778); **Sept. 8, 1858** fourth Lincoln-Douglas debate held at county fairgrounds; **Jan. 31, 1861** Abraham Lincoln visits father's grave with Sarah Lincoln prior to his inauguration as president; **March 28 1864** rioting breaks out between local pro-Union factions and proslavery "Copperheads," nine killed over several days; **Apr. 10, 1869** stepmother Sarah Bush Lincoln dies (born Dec. 13, 1788); **1895** Eastern Illinois University established; **1898** county courthouse built; **1902** Carnegie Library built; **May 26, 1917** tornadoes hit Charleston and Mattoon, 101 killed.

Chester *Randolph County* *Southwestern Illinois, 55 mi/89 km south-southeast of St. Louis, on Mississippi River*

1733 Fort Kaskaskia built on Mississippi River to northwest; **1755** French abandon fort in favor of Fort de Chartres; **1795** Randolph County formed; **1802** Pierre Menard House built; **1819** town founded as county seat; **1835** incorporated as a city; **1836** fort rebuilt; **1878** Menard State Prison established; **Dec. 8, 1894** Elzie C. Segar born, creator of Popeye, character based upon true life local scrapper (died 1938); **1924** Chester Public Library established; **1974** county courthouse built; **1977** bronze Popeye Statue erected in Segar Memorial Park near Chester Bridge.

Chicago *Cook and Du Page counties* *Northeastern Illinois, on Lake Michigan*

Sept. 1673 Father Marquette, Louis Joliet, and their five canoeists visit site after ascending Illinois River, continue to Mackinac; **1696** Father Pinet establishes Jesuit Mission of the Guardian Angel, learn of name Checagou applied to area by Native Americans, term for strong-odored wild onions growing along streams; **1803** Ft. Dearborn built by U.S.; **1812** Ft. Dearborn seized by British in War of 1812; **1816** Fort Dearborn rebuilt; **early 1830s** settlement founded south of Fort Dearborn; **1831** Cook County formed; **1832** Harbor Lighthouse built at mouth of Chicago River, moved to end of breakwater 1919; **1833** incorporated as a town, becomes county seat; 20,000 immigrants arrive from Buffalo in one year; **1837** incorporated as a city; **1847** St. Xavier University established; **June 10, 1847** *Chicago Tribune* newspaper founded; **1855** massive undertaking begins to raise city streets 12 ft/3.6 m, clearing swampy water table; **1856** Marshall Field begins career as store clerk; St. Patrick's Catholic Church built; Chicago Historical Society

founded; **Jan. 9, 1857** novelist Henry Blake Fuller born (died 1929); **1864** George Pullman builds The Pioneer sleeping car; **1865** Chicago Clearing House established to handle large volume of business transactions; **1866** School of the Art Institute of Chicago established; Union Stock Yards open, closed 1970s; **1867** Chicago State University established; **1868** Lincoln Park Zoo established, oldest zoo in U.S.; **June 29, 1868** astronomer George Emery Hale born (died 1938); **1869** system of forest reserves established surrounding city; Water Tower built on North Michigan Avenue, survived Chicago Fire; **March 21, 1869** theatrical producer Florenz Ziegfeld born, produced Ziegfeld Follies (died 1932); **1870** Loyola University Chicago established; **March 5, 1870** novelist Frank Norris born (died 1902); **Apr. 30, 1870** Homer S. Cummings born, Attorney General under Pres. Franklin D. Roosevelt (died 1956); **1871** flow of Chicago River reversed, sending raw sewage into Mississippi River system via Des Plaines and Illinois rivers; **Oct. 8–11, 1871** in Great Chicago Fire, Mrs. Patrick O'Leary's cow knocks over lantern about 8:30 p.m. at 558 De Koven Street, destroys barn and total 17,400 buildings, $200 million in property loss, 250–300 killed, 100,000 left homeless, O'Leary house spared (same night as disastrous fire at Peshtigo, Wisconsin), Chicago Fire Department Training Academy established later at same address; **1874** Chicago Harbor built; **Sept. 1, 1875** novelist Edgar Rice Burroughs born, creator of Tarzan (died 1950); **July 30, 1880** *Tribune* publisher Robert R. McCormick born (died 1955); **1881** Marshall Field and Company department store established; **Nov. 15, 1881** journalist, humorist Franklin Peirce Adams born (died 1960); **Apr. 3, 1884** cartoonist Bud Fisher born, creator of Mutt and Jeff (died 1954); **1886** Moody Bible Institute established; **May 4, 1886** Haymarket Riots sparked by police action against strikers from Eight-Hour Day Movement, bomb kills seven policemen, wounds 66, eight hanged Nov. 11, 1887; **1889** Jane Addams founds Hull House, residence for indigent women in city's worst slum; **1890** Illinois Institute of Technology established; Columbia College established; **1891** University of Chicago established; North Park University established; **1893** Columbian Exposition held in Jackson Park; Congress Hotel opens; Field Museum established; Chicago Art Institute built, founded 1879; **Oct. 28, 1893** Mayor Carl H. Harrison, Sr. assassinated; **1894** John Crerar Scientific Library established, housed in Marshall Field store until 1920; **June 1894** Pullman strike led by Eugene Debs, President Cleveland calls out troops, ends Aug. 7; **1897** Chicago Loop comes into existence, downtown loop connecting urban rail system; Chicago Library completed, founded 1871; **1898** De Paul University established; **1899** Carson, Pirie, Scott department store built; **March 27, 1899** actress Gloria Swanson born (died 1983); **May 20, 1899** Supreme Court Justice John Marshall Harlan the younger born (died 1971) [see Danville, Kentucky]; **1900** Chicago Drainage Canal, now Sanitary and Ship Canal, opens, linking Chicago River with Des Plaines River (Mississippi River system); **1901** Charles R. Wahlgreen (1873–1939) opens his first drug store, "h"

ILLINOIS

dropped from name; **Dec. 5, 1901** movie producer Walt Disney born (died 1966); **May 4, 1902** insurance magnate W. Clement Stone born, died age 100 Sept. 2, 2002; **May 15, 1902** Mayor Richard Joseph Daley born (died 1976); **Feb. 16, 1903** ventriloquist Edgar Bergen born (died 1978); **Aug. 19, 1903** writer James Cozzens born (died 1978); **Dec. 30, 1903** Iroquois Theater fire, 602 deaths; **1904** Orchestra Hall built; **Feb. 23, 1904** correspondent William Lawrence Shirer born (died 1993); **Feb. 27, 1904** author James T. Farrell born (died 1979); **June 17, 1904** actor Ralph Bellamy born (died 1991); **Feb. 22, 1907** TV actor Robert Young born (died 1998); **Aug. 8, 1908** Supreme Court Justice Arthur J. Goldberg born (died 1990); **1909** Chicago Plan Commission formed; **Jan. 15, 1909** jazz drummer Gene Krupa born (died 1973); **May 30, 1909** jazz clarinetist, band leader Benny Goodman born (died 1986); **Oct. 13, 1909** political cartoonist Herbert Block (Herblock) born (died 2001); **1910** Comiskey Park stadium built, home of White Sox baseball team; **Feb. 27, 1910** author Peter De Vries born (died 1993); **1911** Chicago City Junior College established, now Malcolm X College (2-year), first of seven junior colleges in Chicago system; **March 23, 1912** TV actor Karl Malden born; **July 4, 1912** actress Virginia Graham born (died 1998); **1913** Robert Morris College established; **March 30, 1913** singer Frankie Laine born; **July 13, 1913** TV personality Dorothy Kilgallen born (died 1965); **Sept. 4, 1913** biochemist Stanford Moore born, won shared Nobel Prize 1972 (died 1982); **1914** Wrigley Field opened, home of Chicago Cubs baseball team; **Sept. 14, 1914** TV actor Clayton Moore born (died 1999); **Dec. 14, 1914** TV actor Morey Amsterdam born (died 1996); **July 24, 1915** excursion steamboat *Eastland* capsizes in Chicago River killing 844; **1916** Navy Pier built; **Feb. 11, 1917** writer Sidney Sheldon born; **Apr. 8, 1918** Betty Ford born, wife of Pres. Gerald R. Ford; **May 20, 1919** comedian George Gobel born (died 1991); **June 14, 1919** movie producer Sam Wanamaker born (died 1993); **July 1919** at least 38 killed, 500 injured in clash between new black arrivals from South and established white residents; **1920** John Crerar Library built; **Apr. 20, 1920** Supreme Court Justice John Paul Stevens born; **Jan. 31, 1921** actor John Agar born (died 2002); **March 31, 1921** actor Richard Kiley born (died 1999); **1922** Soldier Field stadium built; Meigs Field airport established on Northerly Island, Lake Michigan; Chicago Bears football team established; **July 26, 1922** actor Jason Robards, Jr. born (died 2000); **1923** runway built in western part of city, becomes Midway (Chicago Municipal) Airport 1927; **Oct. 16, 1923** pianist Leonid Hambro born (died 1995); **May 22, 1924** Robert Franks, 13, kidnapped by Richard Loeb and Nathan Leopold, boy killed, ransom ignored; **1925** Palmer House Hotel built; **Jan. 30, 1925** actress Dorothy Malone born; **Aug. 11, 1925** newscaster Mike Douglas born; **Aug. 28, 1925** entertainer Donald O'Connor born (died 2003); **Sept. 13, 1925** singer Mel Torme born (died 1999); **1926** Union Station built; **Feb. 3, 1926** comedian Shelley Berman born; **Apr. 8, 1926** comedian Shecky Green born; **Apr. 9, 1926** publisher Hugh Hefner born; **1927** Buckingham Fountain dedicated in Grant Park; **Sept.**

15, 1927 TV actor Harvey Korman born; **June 23, 1927** choreographer Bob Fosse born (died 1987); **July 14, 1927** newscaster John Chancellor born (died 1996); **Oct. 1, 1927** TV actor Tom Bosley born; **1928** Chicago Stadium built; **Apr. 6, 1928** biochemist James Dewey Watson born, won 1962 Nobel Prize; **Feb. 14, 1929** Valentines Day Massacre, seven rival gangsters shot dead; **June 10, 1929** astronaut James McDivitt born; **1930** Merchandise Mart completed; Adler Planetarium opens; Chicago Board of Trade built; **May 19, 1930** African-American playwright Lorraine Hansberry born, wrote *Raisin In the Sun* (died 1965); **Sept. 4, 1930** entertainer Mitzi Gaynor born; **1931** Shedd Aquarium opens; **June 14, 1931** actress Marla Gibbs born; **Sept. 13, 1931** TV actress Barbara Bain born; **1933** Century of Progress Exposition opens at Burnham Park, continues into 1934; **1933** Museum of Science and Industry opens; **Feb. 13, 1933** actress Kim Novak born; **Feb. 15, 1933** Mayor Anton Cermak shot by would-be assassin of Pres. Franklin D. Roosevelt in Miami, died March 6; **1934** New Post Office completed; **March 14, 1934** astronaut Eugene A. Cernan born; **July 22, 1934** John Dillinger shot to death in front of Biograph Theater by Federal agents; **March 1, 1935** TV actor Robert Conrad born; **March 17, 1936** astronaut Thomas Mattingly born; **June 5, 1936** actor Bruce Dern born; **Dec. 1, 1936** singer Lou Rawls born; **Sept. 25, 1937** Charles Ross kidnapped, found dead, kidnapper John Seadlund put to death; **1938** control lock built at mouth of Chicago River on Lake Michigan; construction begins on first subway line; **Jan. 19, 1938** singer Phil Everly of the Everly Brothers born; **Oct. 30, 1939** rock singer Grace Slick born; **Apr. 12, 1940** jazz musician Herbie Hancock born; **Sept. 5, 1940** actress Raquel Welch born; **Apr. 24, 1942** Mayor Richard M. Daley born; **June 3, 1942** singer Curtis Mayfield born; **July 13, 1942** actor Harrison Ford born; **Oct. 23, 1942** writer Michael Crichton born; **Dec. 2, 1942** University of Chicago physicists Enrico Fermi, Arthur Compton, others, develop first nuclear reaction; **Dec. 9, 1942** football player, announcer Dick Butkus born; **Dec. 11, 1942** actress Donna Mills born; **Jan. 28, 1943** actor John Beck born; **March 9, 1943** champion chess player Bobby Fischer born; **Aug. 18, 1943** TV actor Martin Mull born; **Aug. 28, 1943** TV actor David Soul born; **1945** Roosevelt University established; **June 5, 1945** fire at La Salle Hotel, 61 killed; **Oct. 4, 1945** actor Clifton David born; **1946** University of Illinois at Chicago established; **Jan. 26, 1946** movie critic Gene Siskel born (died 1999); **June 21, 1946** actor Michael Gross born; **Oct. 26, 1947** TV personality Pat Sajak born; **Nov. 13, 1947** actor Joe Montegna born; **Nov. 26, 1947** first lady, Sen. Hillary Rodham Clinton born; **Oct. 17, 1948** actor George Wendt born; **Jan. 24, 1949** comedian John Belushi born (died 1982); **Oct. 10, 1949** actress Jessica Harper born; **May 31, 1950** actor Tom Berenger born; **Aug. 3, 1950** TV actor John Landis born; **Apr. 6, 1952** actress Marilou Henner born; **May 21, 1952** TV actor Lawrence Taro (Mr. T) born; **July 21, 1952** comedian, actor Robin Williams born; **Nov. 30, 1952** actress Mandy Patinkin born; **Apr. 16, 1953** metalworking plant fire, 35 killed; **June 15, 1954** comedian Jim Belushi born; **Oct. 1955**

174

O'Hare International Airport established; **Feb. 14, 1956** actor Ken Wahl born; **Feb. 6, 1957** actor Robert Townsend born; **Dec. 1, 1958** fire in Catholic grade school kills 95, injures 73; **March 8, 1959** actor Aidan Quinn born; **Nov. 24, 1959** cargo plane crashes in residential area killing three crew, eight on ground; **Dec. 16, 1959** gangster Roger Touhy, 61, killed in gangland-style shooting; **July 27, 1960** Sikorsky-58 crashes, killing 13, first crash of a commercial helicopter; **Dec. 3, 1960** actress Daryl Hannah born; **1961** Northeastern Illinois University established; **June 4, 1963** Jimmy Hoffa indicted on loan fraud, diverting $1 million in Teamster funds to himself; **1964** 61-story twin corncob-shaped Marina City apartment towers built; **July 24–26, 1965** series of civil rights demonstrations by Marin Luther King target de facto school segregation; **Aug. 16, 1965** all 30 on board killed when United Boeing 707 crashes into Lake Michigan; **Apr. 21, 1967** series of tornadoes centered on Chicago, 52 killed in eight states; **1968** 100-story John Hancock Building completed; **Aug. 9, 1968** TV actress Gillian Anderson born; **Dec. 27, 1968** turboprop plane crashes into hangar at fog-bound O'Hare Airport killing all 27 on board; **Sept. 18, 1969** collision of two elevated trains injures 249; **Sept. 24, 1969** large printing press explodes killing four, injuring 46; **Oct. 9, 1969** demonstration by Weathermen militant faction at trial of eight protestors turns violent, 60 arrested, three shot by National Guard; **Dec. 4, 1969** two Black Panther leaders killed in shootout with police at their apartment headquarters; **Feb. 18, 1970** guilty verdicts for five of "Chicago 7" for crossing state lines to incite riots at 1968 Chicago Democratic Convention, include Abbie Hoffman, Jerry Rubin, Tom Hayden; **May 11, 1970** apartment fire kills ten; **July 17, 1970** rooftop sniper on high rise North Side apartment kills two policemen; **Oct. 5, 1970** bombing in Haymarket Square damages police statue, Weathermen faction blamed; **Nov. 25, 1970** fire sweeps apartment building, nine killed, nine injured; **Dec. 15, 1971** Judge Otto Kerner, former Illinois governor, indicted for illegal racetrack activity; **Oct. 30, 1972** commuter train crashes into back of double-decker train car, 45 killed, 230 injured, worst commuter rail accident in 14 years; **Nov. 21, 1972** "Chicago 7" convictions of Feb. 18, 1970 overturned; **Dec. 8, 1972** United Air passenger jet crashes in neighborhood near Midway Airport, killing 43 on board and two on ground; **Dec. 20, 1972** North Central Airlines plane crashes at O'Hare Airport killing nine; **1973** 83-story Amoco Building (later Aon Center) completed; **Aug. 1, 1973** actress Tempestt Bledsoe born; **Feb. 19, 1973** former Gov. Otto Kerner indicted on conspiracy, bribery, tax evasion, other counts; **1974** 110-story Sears Tower completed, tallest building in world at the time; **1976** 74-story Water Tower Place building completed; **Dec. 20, 1976** Mayor Richard Daley dies of heart attack, age 74, had been elected to six 4-year terms, leader of Chicago and Cook County Democratic Machine; **Feb. 4, 1977** elevated train crash, 11 killed; **July 9, 1978** Nazi (National Socialist Party) rally turns violent, 72 arrested; **May 25, 1979** American Airlines DC-10 crashes after takeoff from O'Hare Airport killing 275; **1980** St. Augustine College (2-year) established; **1980s** work begins on 130-mi/209-km "Deep Tunnel" sewer project; **March 14, 1981** fire at residential hotel kills 19; **Oct. 1982** seven die from Tylenol cold tablets laced with cyanide, copycat incidents sweep country, leads to tamper-proof packaging; **Apr. 29, 1983** Harold Washington sworn in as city's first black mayor, succeeds Jane Byrne who narrowly lost Democratic Primary; **1991** new Comiskey Park stadium opens for White Sox baseball team; **July 13, 1995** temperatures reach record 106°F/41°C, 536 die from heat; **2000** 67-story Park Tower building completed; **May 17, 2000** Sue unveiled at Field Museum, largest complete fossilized skeleton of a *Tyrannosaurus rex*, discovered in South Dakota 1990; **Feb. 17, 2003** pepper spray used to quell fight in South Side night club creates panic, 21 killed, 38 injured; **June 29, 2003** third-floor porch collapse kills 12, injures 45.

Chicago Heights   *Cook County*   Northeastern Illinois, 25 mi/40 km south of downtown Chicago

1830s settlement of Thorn Grove established at junction of Hubbard and Sauk trails; **1849** town renamed Bloom by German settlers for Robert Bluehm, compatriot executed in Vienna 1848; **1890** Chicago Heights Land Association attracts industrial enterprises to area; **1901** incorporated as a city; Chicago Heights Public Library established; **Sept. 11, 1929** columnist David Broder born; **1958** Prairie State College (2-year) established.

Cicero   *Cook County*   Northeastern Illinois, 7 mi/11.3 km west of downtown Chicago

1857 town founded; **1867** incorporated as a city; **1891** Hawthorne Race Course opened; **1892** two sections of city secede, annexed by Chicago; **c.1900** Portus Weire establishes "Ranch 47," 20-room house surrounded by rows of cabins, built to draw new residents; **1901** two more sections secede, become Berwyn and Oak Park; **1902** Western Electric Plant opens; **1920** Cicero Public Library founded; **1920s** gangster Al Capone establishes headquarters here, indicted for tax evasion 1931; **1924** Morton College (2-year) established; **1967** Dr. Martin Luther King Jr. leads massive civil rights rally through blue-collar neighborhoods; **1932** Sportsman's Park Race Track built.

Clinton   *De Witt County*   Central Illinois, 22 mi/35 km south of Bloomington

1835 town founded; Gray House built, home of Postmaster Miles Gray; **1839** De Witt County formed; town becomes county seat; **1854** Illinois Central Railroad reaches town; **1855** town incorporated; **Sept. 1858** Abraham Lincoln utters famous words during speech, "You can fool all the people some of the time and some of the people all the time, but you cannot fool all the people all the time," disputed by historians; **1901** Vespasian Warner Public Library established, built 1906; **1986** county courthouse built; **1987** Clinton Nuclear Power Plant begins production.

Collinsville   *Madison and Saint Clair counties*
Southwestern Illinois, 12 mi/19 km east of St. Louis

900–1500 A.D. Cahokia Mounds built to west, center of Mississippian mound-building culture of c.20,000 people; **1809** Trappist Monks establish monastery at Monks Mound; **1810** John Cook of Virginia becomes first settler; **1813** monks beset by epidemic, return to France; **1817** five Collins brothers arrive from Connecticut; town founded; **1855** incorporated as village; **1869** first railroad built through town; **1870** coal mining begins; **1872** incorporated as a city; **1885** city hall built; **1921** Professor W. K. Moorehead excavates mounds; **1925** Fairmount Race Track opened.

Congerville   *Woodford County*   See **Mount Carroll** (1930)

Danville   *Vermilion County*   *Eastern Illinois, 125 mi/201 km south of Chicago, on Vermilion River*

June 1765 trader Col. George Croghan visits Kickapoo village at site; **1801** Joseph Barron, interpreter for William H. Harrison, reports salt licks in area; **1819** Kickapoo cede large area to U.S.; **Oct. 1819** Truman Blackman, one of Barron's men, claim-jumps salt deposits; **1824** Maj. John W. Vance breaks legal dispute, obtains lease, begins salt manufacturing; **1826** Vermilion County formed; **1827** Gurdon S. Hubbard makes famous ride from Chicago to gather support against impending raid by Winnebagos on Chicago, attack never occurred; town platted as county seat, incorporated as a village; **1828** post office established; Hubbard establishes trading post, returns to Chicago 1833; **1830** Fithian House built, south balcony site of Abraham Lincoln speech, Sept. 21, 1858; **1839** incorporated as a city; **1850s** Col. Harmon Mansion built; **1876** Cannon House built, home of Cong. Joseph Cannon (1836–1929); **Sept. 10, 1885** novelist, editor Carl Van Doren born at Hope to west (died 1950); **1890s** Victorian structures of business district built; **June 13, 1894** poet, editor Mark Van Doren born at Hope (died 1972); **1896** Stony Creek Bridge, stone bridge, built on East Main Street; **1897** Veterans Administration Facility built; **1914** second county courthouse built; **1922** victory monument erected; Memorial Bridge built across Vermilion River; **Sept. 15, 1924** actor Bobby Short born; **July 27, 1931** TV actor Jerry Van Dyke born; **1967** Danville Area Community College established; **1985** Danville Correctional Center established.

De Kalb   *De Kalb County*   *Northern Illinois, 30 mi/48 km southeast of Rockford*

1837 De Kalb County formed; Coltonville, now part of city of De Kalb, founded as county seat; **1839** county seat moved to Sycamore; **1854** Galena & Chicago Union Railroad reaches town; **1856** incorporated as a village; **1861** incorporated as a city; **1874** Joseph E. Glidden patents improved barbed wire fencing; **1895** Northern Illinois University established; **Apr. 18, 1922** TV actress Barbara Hale born; **Feb. 20, 1966** model Cindy Crawford born.

De Soto   *Jackson County*   *Southern Illinois, 7 mi/11.3 km north of Carbondale*

1855 town founded; **1895** incorporated as a village; **March 18, 1925** one-third of town destroyed by Tri-State Tornado (Mo., Ill., Ind.), locally 80 killed, including 38 schoolchildren, total 695 killed.

Decatur   *Macon County*   *Central Illinois, 37 mi/60 km east of Springfield*

1829 Macon County formed; James Renshaw builds first log cabin and store; **1830** town founded as county seat; Thomas and Sarah Lincoln arrive from Spencer County, Indiana, build cabin to southwest, move to second Illinois home near Charleston 1831; **1836** incorporated as a town; **1839** incorporated as a city; **1854** first railroad reaches town; **1874** coal mining begins in region; **1875** Decatur Public Library founded; **1901** Milikin University established; **1902** major food processor Archer Daniels Midland Company established; **1904** M. L. Harry Fountain erected; **1923** Lake Decatur formed by dam on Sangamon River; Staley Manufacturing established, corn refiners; **1939** county courthouse built; **1971** Richland Community College established; **Aug. 14, 2000** many of 6.4 million Firestone tires recalled because of tread separation made during 1994 strike at Decatur plant, causing 46 traffic deaths nationwide.

Des Plaines   *Cook County*   *Northeastern Illinois, 18 mi/29 km northwest of Chicago, on Des Plaines River*

1835 town founded, originally named Rand for first settler Socrates Rand; **1853** first railroad reaches town; **1860** Methodist retreat established; **1869** incorporated as a city, renamed for Des Plaines (des-PLAINZ) River; **1925** neighboring town of Riverview annexed; **1969** Oakton Community College established.

Dixon   *Lee County*   *Northern Illinois, 36 mi/58 km southwest of Rockford, on Rock River*

1830 tavern and trading post opened by settler John Dixon; town founded; **1832** Abraham Lincoln serves in military here during Black Hawk War; **1839** Lee County formed; town becomes county seat; **1843** incorporated as a village; **1857** incorporated as a city; **1869** plow factory, founded by John Deere in 1841, moves from Grand Detour; **1901** county courthouse built; **1913** chronic hospital opens, becomes Dixon State Hospital 1931; **1965** Sauk Valley Community College established to west; **1982** Dixon Correctional Center opened, formerly Dixon State School.

Downers Grove *Du Page County* *Northeastern Illinois, 20 mi/32 km west-southwest of Chicago*

1832 first settled by Pierce Downer of Rutland, Vermont; town founded; **1836** Israel Blodgett House built; **1845** Rogers Homestead built; **1873** incorporated as a village; **1900** Avery Coonley Experimental School opens with pre-, lower, and middle divisions; **1921** Morton Arboretum established; **Jan. 10, 1935** baritone singer Sherrill Milnes born.

Du Quoin *Perry County* *Southern Illinois, 67 mi/108 km southeast of St. Louis*

1802 encounter between Kaskaskia and Shawnee people leaves nearly all killed on both sides; **1803** Jarrold Jackson becomes first white settler; **1808** store established by Chester A. Keyes; **1819** area settled; **1846** town (du-COIN) founded, named for Jean Baptiste Du Quoigne (1750–1811), part-French chief of Kaskaskias; **1853** Illinois Central Railroad built to west; new town platted by Isaac C. Metcalf; **1855** coal mining begins; **1861** incorporated as a city; **1923** first Du Quoin State Fair held by local interests, taken over by state 1985; **1935** 13 coal mines in operation.

East Moline *Rock Island County* *Northwestern Illinois, 7 mi/11.3 km east of Rock Island, on Mississippi River*

July 19, 1814 Battle of Campbell's Island, Lt. John Campbell attacked by band of Native Americans under Chief Black Hawk during War of 1812, 16 Americans killed, now Campbell's Island State Memorial; **1899** town founded; **1902** incorporated as a village; **1907** incorporated as a city; **1980** East Moline Correctional Center opened.

East Peoria *Tazewell County* *Central Illinois, on Illinois River, opposite Peoria*

Jan. 15, 1680 La Salle establishes Fort Creve Coeur; abandoned late 1680; **1832** David Schertz family become first settlers; **1840** grist mill built by Schertz; **1864** town of Bluetown platted; **1884** Bluetown merges with Fond Du Lac, incorporated as a village of Hilton; **1889** village renamed East Peoria; Hilton Coal and Iron Mining Company established; **1919** Banjamin Holt begins manufacture of farm equipment, becomes Caterpillar Tractor Company 1945; **1938** Peoria Lock & Dam completed on Illinois River; **1967** Illinois Central College (2-year) established.

East Saint Louis *Saint Clair County* *Southwestern Illinois, on Mississippi River, opposite St. Louis, Missouri*

1795 ferry service established to St. Louis; **1816** Illinoistown platted by firm McKnight and Brady; **Sept. 27, 1817** political feud between Col. Thomas Hart Benton and Charles Lucas of Missouri leads to duel at Bloody Island, Lucas killed; **Aug. 27, 1830** Missouri Cong. Spencer Pettis and Maj. Thomas Biddle both lose duel on Bloody Island, now at foot of Eads Bridge; **July 1855** Ohio & Mississippi Railroad extended to town; **1859** Illinoistown incorporated; new town of East St. Louis platted; **1861** East St. Louis incorporated as a town, annexes Illinoistown; **1865** incorporated as a city; **1873** National Stockyards established in neighboring village of National City; **1874** Eads Bridge completed to St. Louis; **May 27, 1896** tornado destroys business district, 100 killed; **June 1903** flood waters top levee, one-fourth of city inundated; **1917** Municipal Bridge built to St. Louis, later renamed Veterans Bridge, now M. L. King Bridge; **May 28 and July 2, 1917** more than 100 blacks killed in race riots; **1954** Cahokia Downs Race Track opened, closed 1979; **July 14, 1954** highest temperature ever recorded in Illinois reached, 117°F/47°C.

Edwardsville *Madison County* *Southwestern Illinois, 18 mi/29 km northeast of St. Louis*

1800 James Gillham becomes first settler; **1812** Madison County formed; **1813** town founded as county seat; named for Ninian Edwards, governor of Illinois Territory; **1819** incorporated as a city **July 30, 1819** Treaty of Edwardsville moves Kickapoo peoples to southwestern Missouri; **1850** coal discovered by Henry Ritter; **1879** Edwardsville Public Library founded; **1914** county courthouse built; **1957** Southern Illinois University at Edwardsville established; **Aug. 13, 1982** Dr. Hector Zevalloses, wife, kidnapped by Army of God antiabortionists, released unharmed.

Effingham *Effingham County* *South central Illinois, 77 mi/124 km southeast of Springfield*

1831 Effingham County formed; town of Ewington, to south, becomes county seat; **1852** Illinois Central Railroad bypasses Ewington; **1853** town founded on railroad; **1855** incorporated as a village; **1859** county seat moved to Effingham; **1861** incorporated as a city; **1872** county courthouse built; **Apr. 5, 1949** hospital fire results in 77 killed.

Elgin *Kane and Cook counties* *Northeastern Illinois, 35 mi/56 km west-northwest of Chicago, on Fox River*

1835 settlers James and Hezekiah Gifford arrive from New York; **1837** Fox River dammed, sawmill built; **1838** town founded by B. W. Raymond of Chicago; **1847** incorporated as a village; **1848** Chicago & Galena Railroad reaches town; **c.1850** area becomes dairying center for Chicago; Gail Borden embarks on his condensed milk business; **1854** incorporated as a city; **1856** Elgin Academy founded; **1864** Elgin Watch Company founded; **1872** Northern Illinois State Hospital opens; **1909** Elgin Observatory founded; **1911** Borden condensed milk plant built; **1935** reproduction of Gifford cabin built; **1949** Elgin Community College established; **May 12, 1950** actor Bruce Boxleitner born.

Elizabethtown *Hardin County* *Southern Illinois,*
130 mi/209 km southeast of St. Louis, Missouri

1812 area first settled; **1839** Hardin County formed; town
founded on Ohio River as county seat; **1857** incorporated
as a village; **1926** county courthouse built.

Elmhurst *Du Page County* *Northeastern Illinois,*
18 mi/29 km west of Chicago

1836 first settlers arrive; **1843** town founded; Hill Cottage
built by J. L. Hovey; **1849** Galena & Chicago Union
Railroad reaches town; **1850** Ahler's Grist Mill built; **1868**
Seth Wadham house built, later becomes Elmhurst Public
Library; **1869** town renamed Elmhurst; **1871** Elmhurst
Seminary founded, later becomes Elmhurst College; **1882**
incorporated as a village; **1910** incorporated as city.

Eureka *Woodford County* *Central Illinois, 17 mi/*
27 km east of Peoria

1830s town founded; **1841** Woodford County formed;
Versailles becomes county seat; **1843** county seat moved to
Hanover (Metamora); **1855** Eureka College established;
1859 incorporated as a city; **1894** county seat moved to
Eureka; **1897** county courthouse built; **1928–1932** future
Pres. Ronald Reagan attends Eureka College.

Evanston *Cook County* *Northeastern Illinois,*
12 mi/19 km north of Chicago, on Lake Michigan

1674 Father Marquette enters natural harbor; **1826** first
cabin built; **1851** Northwestern University established;
1854 town platted; **1857** incorporated as a city; **1865** Rest
Cottage built, home of temperance leader Frances
Willard; **1873** Grosse Point Lighthouse built, retired
1935; **Jan. 11, 1895** electric organ inventor Laurens
Hammond born (died 1973); **Dec. 13, 1897** journalist
Drew Pearson born (died 1969); **1904** Public Library built;
Oct. 4, 1924 actor Charlton Heston born; **Feb. 24, 1929**
actor Richard B. Shull born; **Oct. 20, 1932** actor William
Christopher born; **July 25, 1935** actress Barbara Harris
born; **Sept. 21, 1950** comedian Bill Murray born; **July 18,
1961** actress Elizabeth McGovern born; **Oct. 11, 1962**
actress Joan Cusack born; **June 28, 1966** actor John
Cusack born.

Fairfield *Wayne County* *Southeastern Illinois,*
100 mi/161 km east-southeast of St. Louis

1819 Wayne County formed; town founded as county
seat; **1840** incorporated as a city; **1891** county courthouse
built; **1922** Fairfield Public Library founded, built 1955;
1976 Frontier Community College established.

Forest Park *Cook County* *Northeastern Illinois,*
10 mi/16 km west of downtown Chicago, on Des Plaines
River

1856 town founded by John Henry Quick of Harlem, New
York; **1884** incorporated as a village, named Harlem; **1907**
village renamed Forest Park; **June 1918** 68 circus crew

killed in train wreck at Gary, Indiana, buried at
Woodlawn Cemetery, monument has five granite ele-
phants; **1920** Hines Memorial Hospital established for
World War I veterans.

Freeport *Stephenson County* *Northern Illinois,*
27 mi/43 km west of Rockford, on Pecatonica River

June 25, 1832 Battle of Kellogg's Grove to northwest, 25
soldiers of Gen. John Dement killed fighting Chief Black
Hawk's forces; **1835** first settled, town founded by William
"Tutty" Baker, named "free port" in apparent reference
to Baker's free generosity to travelers; **1837** Stephenson
County formed; town becomes county seat; **1853** Galena
& Chicago Union Railroad arrives; **1855** incorporated as
a city; **Aug. 27, 1858** second Lincoln-Douglas Debate held;
Sept. 6, 1860 Jane Addams born at Cedarville to north,
established Hull House for destitute women in Chicago
1889 (died 1935); **1869** Civil War monument erected; **1908**
Lincoln-Douglas Debate monument dedicated; **1962**
Highland Community College established; **Nov. 11, 1964**
TV actress Calista Flockhart born; **1975** county court-
house built.

Galena *Jo Daviess County* *Northwestern Illinois,*
15 mi/24 km southeast of Dubuque, Iowa

1690 French explorer Nicholas Perrot visits Indian lead
mines; **Aug. 1700** French explorer Le Sueur discovers
Galena River, names it River of Mines; **1717** area included
in John Law's "Mississippi Bubble" scheme, promoting
worthless mining speculation; **1826** town platted and
named; post office opened; **1827** Jo Daviess County
formed, named for Col. Joseph Daviess, killed at Battle
of Tippecanoe, Indiana, 1811; town becomes county seat;
1828 Dowling House built; **1828–1829** galena mining
peaks; **1835** incorporated as a city; **1838** county courthouse built; **1845** Market House built, later used as city
hall; **1846** General Smith House built; **1855** Chicago &
Galena Railroad completed; 200-room De Soto House
hotel built; **1860** Grant House originally built for City
Clerk; Ulysses S. Grant arrives from St. Louis to assist
father's leather works, leaves to join Illinois Volunteers
1861; **1865** U. S. Grant purchases Grant House, lives here
until 1867, returns 1879–1881; **1907** Galena Public Library
built; **1938** Galena Museum opened.

Galesburg *Knox County* *Northwestern Illinois,*
45 mi/72 km northwest of Peoria

1825 Knox County formed; **1836** settlers arrive led by
Presbyterian Rev. George Washington Gale; **1837** town
founded, county seat moved from Knoxville; Knox
College established; **1841** incorporated as a village; **1856**
Chicago, Burlington & Quincy Railroad built; **Oct. 7,
1858** Lincoln and Douglas hold fifth debate in campaign
for Senate; **1876** incorporated as a city; **Jan. 6, 1878** poet
Carl Sandburg born (died 1967); **1886** county courthouse
built; **Jan. 6, 1967** Carl Sandburg College (2-year)
established.

Geneva *Kane County* *Northeastern Illinois, 37 mi/ 60 km west of Chicago, on Fox River*

1832 returnees from Black Hawk War settle in area; **1836** Kane County formed; town founded as county seat; **1858** incorporated as a village; **1865** Bennett Grist Mill established; **1867** incorporated as a city, **1905** Riverbank Estate established by George and Nelle Fabyan; **1988** county courthouse built.

Golconda *Pope County* *Southern Illinois, 128 mi/ 206 km southeast of St. Louis, Missouri*

1797 ferry to Kentucky established on Ohio River by Maj. James Lusk; **1798** town founded as county seat, named Sarahsville; **1803** Lusk dies, wife Sarah assumes control of ferry; **1816** Pope County formed; incorporated as a town; **1817** renamed Golconda; **1845** incorporated as a city; **1873** county courthouse completed; **1937** flooding inundates town; **Apr. 12, 1971** explosion at fluorspar mine, six killed; **1980** Smithland Lock & Dam built on Ohio River to south.

Gorham *Jackson County* *Southern Illinois, 75 mi/ 121 km south-southeast of St. Louis, Missouri*

1912 town founded on Mississippi River; **1906** incorporated as a village; **March 18, 1925** entire town destroyed by Tri-State Tornado (Mo., Ill., Ind.), 34 killed locally, total 695 killed.

Grand Detour *Ogle County* *Northern Illinois, 30 mi/48 km south-southwest of Rockford, on Rock River*

1835 Maj. Leonard Andrus brings settlers from Vermont; power dam, sawmill, and grist mills built; **1837** John Deere of Vermont settles in town, opens blacksmith shop; Deere invents steel plow; **1841** Deere and Andrus form partnership; **1842** Deere manufactures 100 of his plows; **1847** Deere breaks partnership, opens plow factory in Moline; **1850** St. Peter's Episcopal Church built; **1855** Illinois Central Railroad bypasses town in favor of Dixon.

Granite City *Madison County* *Southwestern Illinois, 6 mi/9.7 km north-northeast of St. Louis*

1815 area near Mississippi River settled; **1857** Frederick and William Niedringhaus of St. Louis begin manufacture of kitchen utensils from sheet metal; **1874** William Niedringhaus patents "graniteware," kitchenware coated with ground granite compound; **1891** Niedringhaus purchases site for his National Enameling and Stamping plant; town founded; **1893** American Steel Foundry established, becomes Granite City Steel; **1896** incorporated as a city.

Greenville *Bond County* *South central Illinois, 45 mi/72 km northeast of St. Louis*

1815 town settled; **1817** Bond County formed; town becomes county seat; **c.1838** Hotel Eureka established, razed 1890; **1855** incorporated as a village; Almira College

established; **1872** incorporated as a city; **1884** county courthouse built; **1892** Greenville College established at former Almira College; **1905** Public Library built.

Hardin *Calhoun County* *Southwestern Illinois, 40 mi/64 km northwest of St. Louis, on Illinois River*

1825 Calhoun County formed; town founded as county seat; **1837** Illinois Assembly narrowly defeats bill to abolish Calhoun County; **1848** county courthouse built; **1880** incorporated as a village; **1993** town damaged by flooding.

Harrisburg *Saline County* *Southern Illinois, 117 mi/188 km southeast of St. Louis*

1847 Saline County formed; Raleigh becomes first county seat; **1852** town founded; **1859** county seat moved to Harrisburg; **1861** incorporated as a city; **1923** Dorrisville annexed by Harrisburg; **1885** coal mining begins to south along Big Four Railroad; **1905** coal boom begins with opening of 13 new mines; **1960** Southeastern Illinois College (2-year) established; **1968** third county courthouse completed.

Havana *Mason County* *West central Illinois, 37 mi/60 km southwest of Peoria, on Illinois River*

1824 ferry service established by Maj. Ossian M. Ross; **1827** town founded by Ross; **1828** first steamboat arrives; **1841** Mason County formed; **1848** incorporated as a village; **1851** county seat moved from Bath; **1853** incorporated as a city; Chicago & Illinois Midland Railroad arrives; **1939** county courthouse built.

Hennepin *Putnam County* *North central Illinois, 98 mi/158 km southwest of Chicago, on Illinois River*

1817 site first visited by Father Hennepin; trading post established; **1825** Putnam County formed; **1831** county organized; town founded as ferry landing and as county seat; **1838** county courthouse built, renovated 1964; **1839** incorporated as a village; **1933** Illinois Waterway completed on Illinois River.

Herrin *Williamson County* *Southern Illinois, 84 mi/135 km southeast of St. Louis*

1816 town founded as Herrin's Prairie; **1895** first coal mine established; **1898** incorporated as a village; **1900** incorporated as a city; **June 21-22, 1922** Herrin Massacre, clash during lengthy strike protesting nonunion hiring, 24 killed; **Jan. 10, 1962** explosion at Blue Blaze Coal Mine, 11 killed.

Highland *Madison County* *Southwestern Illinois, 30 mi/48 km east-northeast of St. Louis*

1804 area settled by families from Kentucky and North Carolina; **1831** Dr. Caspar Koepfli of Switzerland brings settlers to area; **1836** town platted by Gen. Joseph Semple; **1863** incorporated as a city; **1884** John Mayenard invents nonfat dry milk process, opens factory; **1908** Wicks Organ Company founded by John Wicks; **1909** Swiss Society monument erected; **1920** strike leads Mayenard to close plant, moves business (Pet Milk Company) to St. Louis.

Highland Park   *Lake and Cook counties*
Northeastern Illinois, 25 mi/40 km north of Chicago

1834 Green Bay House tavern built on Chicago-Milwaukee post road; **1850** town founded on Lake Michigan as Port Clinton; **1854** Milwaukee & Chicago Railroad built; town renamed; **1867** incorporated as a village; **1869** incorporated as a city; **March 24, 1886** photographer Edward Weston born (died 1958); **July 9, 1976** actor Fred Savage born.

Hinsdale   *Du Page and Cook counties*
Northeastern Illinois, 17 mi/27 km west-southwest of Chicago

1835 settled by Jacob Fuller family, called Fullersburg; **1836** Fullersburg Inn built by Fuller; **1850** plank road built to Chicago; **1852** Graue Grist Mill built by Fred Graue; **1862** Chicago, Burlington & Quincy Railroad built; town founded, named for railroad director H. W. Hinsdale; **1873** incorporated as a village; **1892** Hinsdale Public Library founded; **1923** Fullersburg annexed by Hinsdale; **Sept. 1, 1961** TWA Constellation airplane crashes killing 78.

Jacksonville   *Morgan County*   *Western Illinois, 30 mi/48 km west of Springfield*

1812 Charles Collins establishes camp with Kickapoo family; **1823** Morgan County formed; **1825** town founded as county seat by Johnston Shelton, named for Andrew Jackson; **1829** Illinois College established; **1830s** settlers arrive from New England; **1835** Duncan Park mansion built; **1840** incorporated as a town; elm tree planting program initiated by John Lathrop, town referred to as "Elm City"; **1843** State School for the Deaf opens; **1847** State School for the Blind opens; **1846** Illinois Conference Female Academy founded, becomes MacMurray College; **1852** Jacksonville State Hospital opened; **1867** incorporated as a city; **1869** county courthouse built; **1883** William Jennings Bryan begins law practice; **1889** Public Library founded, Carnegie library opened 1903; **1903** Jacksonville Female Academy established; **1946** Municipal Airport established; **1984** Jacksonville Correctional Center opened.

Jerseyville   *Jersey County*   *Southwestern Illinois, 32 mi/51 km north-northwest of St. Louis*

1834 town platted; post office established; **1839** Jersey County formed; town becomes county seat; **1855** incorporated as a city; **1894** county courthouse built.

Joliet   *Will County*   *Northeastern Illinois, 35 mi/56 km southwest of Chicago, on Des Plaines River*

1831 Charles Reed becomes first settler; **1832** Black Hawk War causes settlers to temporarily flee area; **1834** town platted; **1836** Will County formed; town becomes county seat; **1837** incorporated as a village, repealed 1841; **1845** incorporated as a city; **Apr. 11, 1848** first boat arrives on Illinois & Michigan Canal; **1852** Rock Island Railroad arrives; **1858** Joliet State Prison replaces disease-stricken prison at Alton; **1894** city among first to require above-grade railroad crossings in built-up areas; **1901** Joliet Junior College established; **June 22, 1910** choreographer Katherine Dunham born; **March 17, 1918** actress Mercedes McCambridge born (died 2004); **1920** University of St. Francis established; **1925** Stateville Correctional Center opened; **1941** Joliet Army Ammunition Plant completed; **June 5, 1942** explosion at Joliet Army Ammunition Plant, 49 killed; **1968** county courthouse built; **May 10, 1994** John Wayne Gacy executed at Stateville Correctional Center, serial killer of 33 young men and boys 1972–78; **Jan. 26, 2001** Salvation Army van carrying prison visitors crushed by tractor-trailer truck on I-55, 10 killed, 1 survives.

Jonesboro   *Union County*   *Southern Illinois, 95 mi/153 km south-southeast of St. Louis*

1816 town platted, named for early settler and physician; **1818** Union County formed; town becomes county seat; **1857** incorporated as a city; county courthouse built; **Sept. 15, 1858** Third Lincoln-Douglas Debate held at county fairgrounds; **Oct. 1937** county courthouse destroyed by fire, rebuilt.

Kankakee   *Kankakee County*   *Northeastern Illinois, 55 mi/89 km south of Chicago, on Kankakee River*

1820s Gurdon S. Hubbard drives semi-wild hogs over large area from Danville to Crete; **1832** first settlers arrive; town of Bourbonnais founded; **1853** Kankakee County formed; **1855** Illinois Central Railroad built through southern part of town; city of Kankakee incorporated on railroad as county seat; **1878** Kankakee State Hospital established; **1907** Olivet Nazarene University established (at Bourbonnais); **Aug. 30, 1908** TV actor Fred MacMurray born (died 1991); **1912** county courthouse built; **1966** Kankakee Community College established.

Kaskaskia   *Randolph County*   *Southwestern Illinois, 53 mi/85 km south-southeast of St. Louis*

1703 area on Mississippi River settled by Jesuit missionaries; **1721** Fort Kaskaskia built on bluff to north by French; **1741** Liberty Bell of the West cast in France, gift of King Louis XV to new colony; **1762** fort destroyed by British; **1778** George Rogers Clark takes Cahokia and Kaskaskia from British; Forts Clark and Gage built by Clark; **1809** made capital of Illinois Territory; **1818** incorporated as a village; becomes first state capital of Illinois; **1820** state capital moved to Vandalia; **Apr. 3, 1838**

John Willis Menard born, first African-American elected to Congress (Louisiana) 1868, seat given to opponent because Menard was black (died 1893); **1844** flooding devastates town, again 1881; **1910** flood creates Kaskaskia Island from large bend in river; town site becomes part of new river channel; new town site established at center of island, road access from Missouri; **1993** island inundated by great flood.

Kewanee *Henry County* Northwestern Illinois, 40 mi/64 km southeast of Rock Island

1836 John Kilverton builds log cabin; town of Wethersfield founded; **1839** first school built; **1854** Military Tract Railroad, later Chicago, Burlington & Quincy, built to north; new town platted; **1855** incorporated as a city; **1856** Fred Francis born, inventor for Elgin Watch Company (died 1926); **1924** Kewanee annexes Wethersfield.

La Salle *La Salle County* Northern Illinois, 65 mi/105 km south of Rockford, on Illinois River

1673 Louis Joliet ascends Illinois River with Father Marquette, becomes first European to discover coal in Illinois, to east; **1679** French explorer La Salle descends Illinois River; **1827** town founded on proposed Illinois & Michigan Canal; **June 16, 1832** Abraham Lincoln enlists as private at Fort Wilbourn; **May 27, 1837** James Butler "Wild Bill" Hickok born at Troy Grove to north, murdered by Jack McCall, Deadwood, South Dakota, 1876; **1848** I & M Canal opened; **1852** incorporated as a city; **1858** Matthiesen & Hegeler Zinc Company plant established; **1874** Hegeler Home built; **1907** La Salle Carnegie Public Library built; **1924** La Salle-Peru-Oglesby Junior College established, now Illinois Community College at Oglesby; **1982** first phase of La Salle Nuclear Power Plant completed.

Lacon *Marshall County* North central Illinois, 26 mi/42 km north-northeast of Peoria, on Illinois River

1826 town founded, originally named Columbia; **1839** Marshall County formed; town becomes county seat; incorporated as a city, renamed; Lacon Library founded, new library built 1991; **1853** county courthouse built.

Lake Forest *Lake County* Northeastern Illinois, 27 mi/43 km north of Chicago, on Lake Michigan

1835 area first settled at portage between Lake Michigan and Des Plaines River; **1854** first railroad arrives; **1856** site platted by St. Louis architect David Hotchkiss; **1857** Lake Forest Academy for boys founded, becomes Lake Forest College; **1861** incorporated as a city; **1877** Fort Sheridan army base established following Chicago's Haymarket Riots; **Nov. 11, 1915** Wisconsin Sen. William Proxmire born; **Nov. 5, 1943** actor Sam Shepard born at Fort Sheridan.

Lawrenceville *Lawrence County* Southeastern Illinois, 133 mi/214 km east of St. Louis

1780 Capt. Toussaint Dubois settles near Wabash River; **1821** Lawrence County formed; town founded as county seat, named for Capt. James Lawrence of War of 1812 ("Don't give up the ship!"); **1835** incorporated as a city; **1845** Elizabeth Reed hanged for poisoning husband, first woman executed in state; **1889** county courthouse built; **1906** county's first oil well begins production; **1931** Lincoln Memorial Bridge built across Wabash River to Vincennes.

Lebanon *Saint Clair County* Southwestern Illinois, 20 mi/32 km east of St. Louis

1804 town founded; **1827** Rock Spring Seminary established, moved to Alton 1831, renamed Shurtleff College; **1828** McKendree College established; **1830** Mermaid Inn built on St. Louis-Vincennes Trail; **1842** English author Charles Dickens visits town, area named Looking Glass Township; **1857** incorporated as a city; **1889** flour mill established.

Lewistown *Fulton County* Western Illinois, 35 mi/56 km southwest of Peoria

1816 Military Tract set aside for veterans of War of 1812; **1821** town founded by Maj. Ossian M. Ross, named for son Lewis Ross; **1823** Fulton County formed through Ross' efforts; town becomes county seat; **1825** Fulton County greatly reduced, had extended to Lake Michigan; Judge Stephen Phelps builds Phelps Store; **1833** Walker House built; **1857** incorporated as a town; **1861** Church of St. James built; **1882** incorporated as a city; **1895** courthouse destroyed by arson during county seat dispute with Canton; **1898** fourth county courthouse built.

Libertyville *Lake County* Northeastern Illinois, 34 mi/55 km north-northwest of Chicago

c.1835 area settled, named Independence Grove; **1837** post office established, present name adopted; **1839** Lake County formed; town becomes county seat; **1841** county seat moved to Little Fort (Waukegan); **1882** incorporated as a village; **1923** St. Sava Serbian Orthodox Monastery established; **1968** Cook Memorial Library built.

Lincoln *Logan County* Central Illinois, 30 mi/48 km northeast of Springfield

1790 Mrs. James Gillham and three children, captured by Kickapoos in Kentucky, brought here, first white people in county; **1819** James Latham among first settlers; **1839** Logan County formed; Postville to west becomes county seat; Isaac and Joseph Loose arrive from Pennsylvania, acquire land; **1847** county seat moved to Mount Pulaski; **1853** Loose tract purchased for town site; town founded as new county seat, named for attorney Abraham Lincoln; **1854** Chicago & Mississippi Railroad built; **1857** incorporated as a city; **1865** Lincoln College established; **1902** first annual Lincoln Chautauqua held; Lincoln Carnegie Public Library built; **1905** county courthouse built.

Lisle   *Du Page County   Northeastern Illinois, 25 mi/ 40 km west-southwest of Chicago*

1832 town founded; **1833** First Congregational Church built; **1834** post office established; **1864** Chicago, Burlington & Quincy Railroad reaches town; **1890** St. Procopius College established, becomes Benedictine University; **1895** Lisle Creamery established; **1956** incorporated as a village.

Lockport   *Will County   Northeastern Illinois, 25 mi/40 km southwest of Chicago*

1837 town founded on Des Plaines River; **1838** Gaylord Building built; **1840** Congregational Church built; **1848** Illinois & Michigan Canal built; **1853** incorporated as a city; **1869** city hall built on Central Square; **1900** Lockport Lock and Dam built, link between Chicago River and Illinois River, controls water taken from Lake Michigan.

Louisville   *Clay County   South central Illinois, 92 mi/148 km east of St. Louis, Missouri*

1820 area first settled; **1824** Clay County formed; Maysville becomes county seat; **1838** town (LOO-is-vill) founded; **1841** county seat moved to Louisville; **1867** incorporated as a village; **1913** county courthouse built.

Macomb   *McDonough County   Western Illinois, 60 mi/97 km west-southwest of Peoria*

1823 McDonough County formed, named for Commodore Thomas Macdonough of Battle of Lake Champlain, 1814; town founded as county seat, named Washington; **1841** incorporated as a village; renamed for Alexander Macomb (1782–1841), U.S. Army Commander; **1856** incorporated as a city; **1872** third county courthouse completed; **1899** Western Illinois University established; **1969** Macomb Municipal Airport established; **June 2002** city hall dedicated.

Marion   *Williamson County   Southern Illinois, 92 mi/148 km southeast of St. Louis*

1839 Williamson County formed; **1840** town founded as county seat; post office established; **1841** incorporated as a city, becomes county seat; **1939** Crab Orchard Lake reservoir built to west; **1967** Marion Federal Prison established to southwest; **1971** county courthouse built; **May 29, 1982** tornado hits city and county, ten killed, 200 injured

Marshall   *Clark County   Eastern Illinois, 140 mi/ 225 km east-northeast of St. Louis*

1819 Clark County formed; **1837** town founded as county seat by William B. Archer; town named for Chief Justice John Marshall; Stone Arch Bridge built; **1853** incorporated as a city; **1904** county courthouse built.

Mascoutah   *Saint Clair County   Southwestern Illinois, 25 mi/40 km southeast of St. Louis*

1837 town founded, named Mechanicsburgh; **1839** incorporated as a town, renamed Mascoutah; **1883** incorporated as a city; **1917** Scott Air Force Base established to northwest; **1938** town incorporated; **1998** MidAmerica Airport opened adjoining Scott Air Force Base on east, intended second air facility for St. Louis; **June 2, 2000** farmer Harvey Culli, 80, sentenced to six months jail, fined $20,000 for lacing corn with pesticide in field killing 26,000 migratory birds; **2000** MidAmerica Airport lands first passenger carrier, the reorganized Pan Am, service suspended 2002.

Mattoon   *Coles County   Eastern Illinois, 110 mi/ 177 km northeast of St. Louis*

Sept. 25, 1843 glacial geologist Thomas Chamberlain born (died 1928); **1854** Terre Haute & Alton Railroad reaches town, forming junction with Big Four Railroad; town founded, named for William Mattoon (mat-TOON), TH & A Railroad official; **1861** incorporated as a city; **June 1861** Illinois 21st Infantry mustered by Gen. Ulysses S. Grant; **1903** Carnegie Library opened; **May 26, 1917** series of tornadoes hit Mattoon and nearby Charleston, 101 killed; **May 31, 1924** Patricia Harris born, secretary of Health, Education, and Welfare under President Carter (died 1985); **1940** oil discovered; **1966** Lake Land College (2-year) established.

McLeansboro   *Hamilton County   Southern Illinois, 98 mi/158 km southeast of St. Louis*

1821 Hamilton County formed; town founded as county seat; **1840** incorporated as a city; **1874** Hamilton College established, closed 1880; fire destroys Goudy House hotel, other structures; **1884** McCoy Memorial Library built; **Dec. 19, 1907** newspaper publisher, humorist H. Allen Smith born (died 1976); **1937** county courthouse built.

Metropolis   *Massac County   Southern Illinois, 8 mi/12.9 km northwest of Paducah, Kentucky, on Ohio River*

1757 French establish Fort Massac at start of French and Indian War; **1763** fort abandoned following Treaty of Paris; **1778** Gen. George Rogers Clark stops here on way to capture of Kaskaskia; **1794** Gen. Anthony Wayne ordered by President Washington to regarrison the fort during troubles with Spain; **1796** village settled just west of fort; **1815** fort abandoned again after War of 1812; **1839** town of Massac platted; William A. McBane and James Wilcox also plat Metropolis City at site of Ohio River railroad bridge; **Apr. 1839** incorporated as a village; **1843** Massac County formed; Metropolis becomes county seat; **1892** two towns merge; **1859** incorporated as a city; **Jan. 1884** African-American film director Oscar Micheaux born (died 1951); **1908** Fort Massac State Park established; **1917** railroad bridge built across Ohio River; **1942**

county courthouse built; **1981** first annual Superman Celebration held.

Moline   *Rock Island County   Northwestern Illinois, 6 mi/9.7 km east of Davenport, Iowa, on Mississippi River*

1820s area settled; **1836** David B. Spears arrives at hamlet of Rock Island Mills, builds brush dam at edge of river; **1843** town platted; **1847** John Deere moves from Grand Detour, Illinois, opens plow factory; **1848** incorporated as a town; **1854** first railroad arrives; **1855** railroad bridge built, first bridge over Mississippi River; **1872** incorporated as a city; **Aug. 12, 1882** engineer Vincent Bendix born, founded Bendix Aviation (died 1929); **1922** Moline Airport established; **1929** Scottish Rite Cathedral built; **Nov. 1, 1933** TV actor Ken Berry born; **1935** Iowa-Illinois Bridge built to Bettendorf, Iowa, second span built 1959 for I-74; **1946** Black Hawk College (2-year) established.

Monmouth   *Warren County   Northwestern Illinois, 55 mi/89 km west-northwest of Peoria*

1825 Warren County formed; **1827** Allen Andrews settles on land won in New Orleans poker game; **1831** town founded as county seat; **1836** incorporated as a village; **March 19, 1848** lawman Wyatt Earp born, participated in shootout at OK Corral, Tombstone, Arizona, 1881 (died 1929); **1852** incorporated as a city; **1853** Chicago, Burlington & Quincy Railroad reaches city; Monmouth College established; **1893** county paves its roads, early leader in county road systems; **1894** county courthouse built; **1897** Illinois Bankers Life Assurance Company organized.

Monticello   *Piatt County   Eastern Illinois, 23 mi/ 37 km northeast of Decatur*

1829 James A. Piatt becomes first settler; **1837** town founded; **1839** inn built by Nicholas De Vore; **1841** Piatt County formed; town becomes county seat; incorporated as a village; **1853** Galena & Chicago Union Railroad built 2 mi/3.2 km south of town; **1872** incorporated as a city; **1893** William Caldwell begins marketing Caldwell's Syrup Pepsin remedy, plant closed 1984; **1903** second county courthouse built.

Morris   *Grundy County   Northern Illinois, 55 mi/ 89 km southwest of Chicago, on Illinois River*

1841 Grundy County formed; **1842** town founded as county seat, named for Isaac N. Morris, commissioner of Illinois & Michigan Canal; **1848** I & M Canal completed; **1853** incorporated as a city; **1912** county courthouse built; **1935** Gebhard Woods State Park established, land donated by Fred Gebhard; **1970** Dresden Nuclear Power Plant opened.

Morrison   *Whiteside County   Northwestern Illinois, 55 mi/89 km southwest of Rockford*

1836 Whiteside County formed; Sterling becomes county seat; **1855** town founded; county seat moved to Morrison; **1858** Unionville Mill built on Rock Creek; **1866** county courthouse built; **1867** incorporated as a city; **March 22, 1868** physicist Robert Anderson Millikan born, 1923 Nobel Prize (died 1953); **May 1874** inventor James Sargent demonstrates new vault time lock at First National Bank, used for forty years; **1879** Odell Public Library opened.

Mound City   *Pulaski County   Southern Illinois, 118 mi/190 km south-southeast of St. Louis, near Ohio River*

1843 Pulaski County formed; town founded as county seat; **1857** incorporated as a city; **1861–1864** Union base for ironclad vessels established; **1864** Mound City National Cemetery established; **1912** county courthouse built; **Jan. 1937** flooding from Ohio River destroys entire town, immediately rebuilt.

Mount Carmel   *Wabash County   Southeastern Illinois, 130 mi/209 km east of St. Louis, on Wabash River*

1818 town platted by Rev. Thomas S. Hinde of Ohio as ideal religious community; **1824** Wabash County formed; town becomes county seat; **1825** incorporated as a city; **1831** county courthouse built; **1900** mussel industry developed, continues into 1930s; **1911** Carnegie Library opened; **1960** Wabash Valley College (2-year) established.

Mount Carroll   *Carroll County   Northwestern Illinois, 45 mi/72 km southwest of Rockford*

1843 town founded; **1853** Frances Shimer Junior College for girls established, later Shimer College (4-year; closed c.1970); **1867** incorporated as a city; **1912** county courthouse built; **Jan. 22, 1930** lowest temperature ever recorded in Illinois reached, −35°F/−37°C, long-held record broken at Congerville 1999.

Mount Olive   *Macoupin County   South central Illinois, 38 mi/61 km northeast of St. Louis*

1835 Mary Harris (1830–1930) brought from Cork, Ireland, at age 5, becomes known as Mother Jones, played major role in American mineworkers' labor movement; **1840s** German settlers arrive; **1870** Wabash Railroad reaches site; town founded; **1917** incorporated as a city; **1936** monument built to Mary Mother Jones at Union Miners Cemetery.

Mount Sterling   *Brown County   Western Illinois, 60 mi/97 km west-northwest of Springfield*

1830 area settled by Robert Curry, who builds house atop highest elevation; names site for "sterling" quality of the soil; town founded; **1837** incorporated as a city; **1839** Brown County formed; town becomes county seat; **1868**

county courthouse built; **1989** Western Illinois Correctional Center to south.

Mount Vernon *Jefferson County Southern Illinois, 75 mi/121 km east-southeast of St. Louis*

1819 Jefferson County formed; town founded as county seat; **1837** incorporated as a city; **1854** Appellate Court Building built, originally Illinois Supreme Court; **1872** railroad reaches town; **1888** tornado destroys 500 buildings, 30 killed; **1893** Opera House built; **1914** railroad car shops established, closed 1950s; **1939** county courthouse built.

Murphysboro *Jackson County Southern Illinois, 76 mi/122 km southeast of St. Louis*

1816 Jackson County formed; Brownsville becomes county seat; **Feb. 9, 1826** U.S. Sen. John A. Logan born (died 1886); **1843** town founded as county seat, named for county commissioner William C. Murphy by hat draw; **1867** incorporated as a city; **March 18, 1925** 40 percent of town destroyed by Tri-State Tornado (Missouri, Illinois, Indiana), 234 killed in town, greatest tornado loss ever for one locality, 695 killed in three states; **1928** third county courthouse built; **1938** Sallee Logan Public Library opened, new facility opened 1975.

Naperville *Du Page and Will counties Northeastern Illinois, 28 mi/45 km west-southwest of Chicago*

1830 Bailey Hobson first settler; **1831** Black Hawk War forces settlers to evacuate region; **1832** Fort Payne built; Joseph Naper builds sawmill; town platted; **1834** Greek Revival Preemption House built; **1839** Du Page County formed; town becomes county seat; **1857** incorporated as a village; **1859** attempt to move county seat to Wheaton fails; **July 1868** group forcibly moves county seat to Wheaton by raiding courthouse in Naperville; **1870** North Central College moved from Plainfield; **1887** Naperville Lounge Factory established, later Kroehler Furniture Company; **1890** incorporated as a city; **Apr. 25, 1946** train rammed from behind by another, 47 killed.

Nashville *Washington County South central Illinois, 50 mi/80 km east-southeast of St. Louis*

1818 Washington County formed; Covington becomes county seat; **1830** town founded; **1831** county seat moved to Nashville; **1853** incorporated as a city; **1884** county courthouse built; **Nov. 12, 1908** Supreme Court Justice Harry A. Blackmun born (died 1999); **1920** Nashville Public Library founded.

Nauvoo *Hancock County Western Illinois, 10 mi/16 km north of Keokuk, Iowa, on Mississippi River*

1823 Joseph Smith Homestead built; **1830** town settled, first named Commerce; **1839** Mormons led by Joseph Smith arrive following eviction from western Missouri, take over and rename town; **1841** incorporated as a city; population reaches 20,000, briefly the largest city in Illinois; Nauvoo House built; **1842** Red Brick Store built; Mansion House built; **1843** Wilford Woodruff House built; **1844** Seventies Hall built; **June 27, 1844** Joseph and Hyrum Smith gunned down by mob at jail in Carthage, to east; **1846** clashes continue between Mormons and local residents over Mormon polygamy, other practices, Mormons head for Utah; **1848** unfinished Mormon temple burned by vandals; **1849** French Icarian sect under Etienne Cabet establishes colony in vacant community; **1856** Icarians abandon town, sect dissolved two years later; **1857** winery established by Cecil J. Baxter; **1928** after lengthy search, bodies of Joseph and Hyrum Smith are located, reinterred at Smith Homestead; **c.1938** Nauvoo Bleu Cheese industry begins; **1950** Nauvoo State Park established; **1993** flooding inundates historic town; **2002** Nauvoo Temple completed atop bluff.

New Salem *Menard County Central Illinois, 18 mi/29 km northwest of Springfield*

1828 town first settled; **1829** post office established; **1831** Abraham Lincoln arrives, obtains job at Denton Offut's grocery store; meets Ann Rutledge, with whom he falls in love, takes up residence with her family; **1832** Offut's store closed; Lincoln enlists in Black Hawk War, announces candidacy for state legislature before leaving, fails election; **1834** Lincoln succeeds in second bid for state legislature, reelected 1836; **1835** Lincoln's girlfriend Ann Rutledge dies of sudden illness; **1836** post office closed; **Apr. 1837** Lincoln moves to Springfield; **1839** Menard County organized; Petersburg beats New Salem for county seat; **1906** publisher William Randolph Hearst purchases town site, conveys it to state; New Salem State Park established, becomes Lincoln's New Salem State Historic Site.

Newton *Jasper County Eastern Illinois, 113 mi/182 km east-northeast of St. Louis*

1828 town founded; **1831** Jasper County formed; town becomes county seat; incorporated as a city; **1876** county courthouse built; **June 14, 1909** singer Burl Ives born in rural Jasper County (died 1995).

Normal *McLean County Central Illinois, 2 mi/3.2 km north of Bloomington*

1820s first settlers arrive, form village of Keg Grove, later Blooming Grove, then Bloomington, to south; **1857** Illinois State Normal University established, becomes Illinois State University **1867** incorporated as a town; **Nov. 14, 1929** TV actor McLean Stevenson born (died 1996).

North Chicago *Lake County Northeastern Illinois, 34 mi/55 km north of Chicago, on Lake Michigan*

1895 town founded; **1909** incorporated as a city; **1912** Finch University Health Sciences and Chicago Medical School established; **1914** Great Lakes Naval Training

Center opens, closed 1918; **1937** sit-down strike by workers at Fansteel Metallurgical Plant dispersed with tear gas, leads to U.S. Supreme Court ruling March 1939 declaring sit-down strikes illegal; **July 1937** Great Lakes Training Base reopens; **March 23, 1953** actress Chaka Khan born.

Norway *La Salle County* *Northern Illinois, 60 mi/ 97 km southwest of Chicago*

1825 Cleng Peerson brings group of Norwegian settlers by boat from Orleans County, New York; **1834** town founded, first of over 30 Norwegian settlements established by Peerson from Wisconsin to Texas (died at Norse, Texas, Dec. 16, 1865, age 83); **1934** Cleng Peerson Memorial unveiled at town's centennial celebration, epitaph reads "Good humored and quiet, of a roving nature, he was welcomed wherever he went. Rarely did he work for pay, and whenever a few odd dollars came his way they were spent in founding new settlements."

Oak Park *Cook County* *Northeastern Illinois, 7 mi/11.3 km west of downtown Chicago*

1833 area first settled by Joseph Kettlestrings of Baltimore, Maryland; **1837** town founded; **1849** Galena & Chicago Union Railroad built; **1890s** community called Saints' Rest for its large number of churches; **1891** Frank Lloyd Wright House built, architect's own residence in area where most of his Prairie Style residential designs were built, 1889–1909 (born 1867, died 1959); **July 21, 1899** author Ernest Hemingway born, died July 2, 1961, at Ketchum, Idaho, of self-inflicted gunshot; **1902** town secedes from Cicero, incorporated as a village; **1905** Wright's Unity Temple built; **1907** a de facto "dry community," act passed excludes taverns within village; **Jan. 17, 1922** TV actress Betty White born; **Sept. 29, 1929** comedian Bob Newhart born; **Feb. 19, 1932** astronaut Joseph Kirwin born.

O'Fallon *Saint Clair County* *Southwestern Illinois, 15 mi/24 km east of St. Louis*

1854 Baltimore & Ohio Railroad reaches site; town founded; **1865** incorporated as a village; **1905** incorporated as a city; **1917** Scott Field established to south, becomes Scott Air Force Base 1948; **Apr. 17, 1918** actor William Holden born (died 1981).

Olney *Richland County* *Southeastern Illinois, 112 mi/180 km east of St. Louis*

c.1840 town founded; **1841** Richland County formed; incorporated as a city, becomes county seat, named for Civil War Lt John Olney; **early 1900s** white squirrels discovered on Lawrence County farm to east, trapped and set loose in center of Olney; **1916** county courthouse built; **1936** major oil lease established; **1941** estimated number of white squirrels peaks at 800, reduced to 100 by 1990s, reasons unknown; **1962** Olney Central College (2-year) established.

Oquawka *Henderson County* *Northwestern Illinois, 30 mi/48 km west of Galesburg, on Mississippi River*

1827 trading post established by Phelps brothers; **1830s** Radmacher Mill built to east; **1841** Henderson County formed; town becomes county seat; Stephen A. Douglas serves as first circuit court judge (until 1843); **1842** county courthouse built; **1846** covered bridge built at Radmacher Mill, later demolished; **1857** incorporated as a village.

Oregon *Ogle County* *Northern Illinois, 22 mi/ 35 km southwest of Rockford, on Rock River*

1836 Ogle County formed; town founded as county seat; **1843** incorporated as a city; **July 4, 1843** writer Margaret Fuller (1810–1850) finds inspiration at Ganymede Spring, at bluff called Eagle's Nest, both named by her; **1891** county courthouse built; **1898** Eagle's Nest Art Colony founded by Wallace Heckman, inspired by Margaret Fuller's soliloquy; **1911** Black Hawk monument erected atop Eagle's Nest bluff, created by colony member Lorado Taft; **1916** soldiers monument erected at courthouse; **1978** Castle Rock State Park established.

Ottawa *La Salle County* *Northern Illinois, 73 mi/ 117 km southwest of Chicago, on Illinois River*

1679 La Salle and Henri de Tonti visit Starved Rock; **1682** Fort St. Louis de Rocher established; **1769** band of Illinois tribe killed by rival Pottawatomis and Ottawas at Starved Rock; **1830** town platted on new Illinois & Michigan Canal; **1831** La Salle County formed; town becomes county seat; **1832** Fort Johnson established; settlers arrive in larger numbers following Black Hawk War; **1837** incorporated as a village; **1848** I & M Canal opened; **1853** incorporated as a city; **1855** Little Red Schoolhouse built, closed 1932; **1856** Reddick Mansion built by William Reddick; **Aug. 21, 1858** first Lincoln-Douglas debate held in race for Senate; **1860** The Oaks stone house built for Gen. W. H. L. Wallace, killed Battle of Shiloh, Apr. 1862; **1883** county courthouse completed; **1885** Reddick Public Library established; **1912** Starved Rock State Park established; **1933** Illinois Waterway completed on Illinois River.

Paris *Edgar County* *Eastern Illinois, 147 mi/ 237 km northeast of St. Louis*

1823 Edgar County formed; town founded as county seat; **1849** incorporated as a village; **Oct. 21, 1892** Dennis Hanks, 93-year-old cousin of Abraham Lincoln's, dies month after being run over by team of horses at county fair; **1853** town platted; **1856** Lincoln campaigns on behalf of presidential candidate John C. Fremont; **Sep. 17, 1858** Lincoln makes Senate campaign speech; **Feb. 1864** several hundred Copperheads, pro-Confederate political group, conspire to attack town, thwarted by Union troops; **1869** incorporated as a city; **1892** county courthouse built; **1904** Paris Carnegie Library built; **Aug. 27, 1927** actor Carl

Switzer born, "Alfalfa" of "Our Gang" film series (died 1959).

Park Ridge   *Cook County   Northeastern Illinois, 15 mi/24 km northwest of Chicago*

1853 George Penny arrives, opens brickyard and lumberyard; town founded, originally named Brickton; **1854** Penny House built, now Park Ridge Masonic Temple; **1873** incorporated as a village; **1876** Park Ridge School for Girls opens; **1910** incorporated as a city; **July 1, 1942** actress Karen Black born; **1948** George B. Carpenter becomes prominent in village affairs, serves at village hall through 1962; **Sept. 20, 1957** actor Gary Cole born.

Paxton   *Ford County   Eastern Illinois, 97 mi/156 km south-southwest of Chicago*

1850s area settled by Swedish immigrants; **1850** Illinois Central Railroad reaches site; town founded, named Paxton City; **1863** Augustana College (Lutheran) moved from Chicago, established 1853, closed 1875; **1859** Ford County formed, remnant of larger county diminished by creation of other new counties; town becomes county seat; **1865** incorporated as a city; **1900** city hall built; **1903** Paxton Carnegie Library built; **1908** county courthouse built.

Pekin   *Tazewell County   Central Illinois, 9 mi/ 14.5 km south of Peoria, on Illinois River*

1824 town founded; **1827** Tazewell County formed (TAZwell); **1830** incorporated as a village; **1832** Fort Doolittle established during Black Hawk War; **1839** county seat moved from Mackinaw; incorporated as a city; **1850** county courthouse built; **Jan. 1, 1896** Sen. Everett McKinley Dirkson born (died 1969); **Jan. 3, 1924** food processing plant explosion, 42 killed; **Dec. 10, 1952** actress Susan Dey born; **1994** federal penitentiary established.

Peoria   *Peoria County   Central Illinois, 130 mi/ 209 km southwest of Chicago, on Illinois River*

1673 Marquette and Joliet ascend Illinois River; **1680** Sieur de La Salle builds Fort Creve Coeur on east site of river; **1790** French refer to site with variation of present name; **1813** Americans establish Fort Clark; **1819** first American settlers arrive; town founded; **1825** Peoria County formed; town becomes county seat; **1828** first steamboat arrives; **1835** incorporated as a town; **1839** incorporated as a city; **1844** farm machinery industry begins; **1847** Jubilee College established to northwest (closed 1883); **1849** first bridge built across river; **Oct. 16, 1854** Abraham Lincoln delivers rebuttal speech to one given earlier in day by Stephen Douglas, his first public opposition to slavery; **1876** county courthouse built; **1885** Peoria State Hospital established; **Feb. 2, 1890** radio personality C. J. Correll (Andy of Amos & Andy) born (died 1972); **Nov. 6, 1896** radio personality Jim Jordan (Fibber McGee) born (died 1988); **1897** Bradley University established; **Feb. 4, 1921** women's rights activist Betty Friedan born, organized National Organization for Women (NOW); **1933** Cedar Street Bridge built across river; **1934** Jubilee College State Park established; **Dec. 1, 1940** comedian Richard Pryor born; **Oct. 31, 1942** TV actor David Ogden Stiers born; **Aug. 13, 1951** singer Dan Fogelberg born; **Oct. 21, 1971** commuter plane crashes on approach to airport killing all 16 on board.

Peru   *La Salle County   Northern Illinois, 65 mi/ 105 km south of Rockford, on Illinois River*

1835 town founded as terminus of Illinois & Michigan Canal, head of navigation of Illinois River; **1845** incorporated as a city; Star Union Brewery opens; **1848** I & M Canal completed; **1869** Illinois River Bridge built; **1885** Westclox clock factory established; **1910** Peru Carnegie Library built, new library opened 1986.

Petersburg   *Menard County   Central Illinois, 18 mi/29 km northwest of Springfield*

1835 town founded; **1839** Menard County formed; town becomes county seat; **1841** incorporated as a village; **1882** incorporated as a city; **1897** county courthouse built.

Pinckneyville   *Perry County   Southern Illinois, 60 mi/97 km southeast of St. Louis*

1827 Perry County formed; town founded as county seat; **1850** fourth county courthouse built; **1857** incorporated as a village; **1861** incorporated as a city.

Pittsfield   *Pike County   Western Illinois, 73 mi/ 117 km north-northwest of St. Louis*

1821 Pike County formed; Coles Grove becomes first county seat; **1823** county seat moved to Atlas; **c.1830** town founded as new county seat by settlers from Pittsfield, Massachusetts; **1833** town platted; **1834** incorporated as a village; **1838** John Shastid House built; **1839** Abraham Lincoln brings his law practice here, tries 54 legal cases through 1852; **Oct. 1, 1858** Abraham Lincoln delivers campaign speech at Central Park; **1869** incorporated as a city; **1894** county courthouse built; **1907** Pittsfield Carnegie Library opened; **1972** Penstone Airport established.

Pontiac   *Livingston County   North central Illinois, 35 mi/56 km northeast of Bloomington*

1833 area first settled; **1837** Livingston County formed; town founded as county seat, named by developer Jesse W. Fell; **1854** Chicago & Mississippi Railroad built; **1857** incorporated as a city; **1871** Pontiac Correctional Institute opened; **1875** county courthouse built; **1902** soldiers and sailors monument erected.

Prairie du Rocher   *Randolph County*
Southwestern Illinois, 38 mi/61 km south of St. Louis, Missouri

1718 French build earthen Fort de Chartres near Mississippi River; settlement develops adjacent to fort; **1720** John Law's "Mississippi Bubble" scheme promoting exploitation of nonexistent precious gems and metals collapses after attracting prospectors to area; **1722** town founded near Mississippi River by settlers left stranded by scheme; **1756** timber fort completed by French; **1765** French surrender fort to British; **1772** British withdraw from fort, destroying it as they depart; **1873** incorporated as a village; **1915** Fort de Chartres State Park established.

Princeton   *Bureau County*   *Northern Illinois, 50 mi/80 km north of Peoria*

1832 Lovejoy House built by abolitionist Owen Lovejoy, station on Underground Railroad from 1838; **1833** town platted by settlers from Northampton, Massachusetts; **1837** Bureau County formed; town becomes county seat; **1844** Cyrus Bryant House built; **1849** incorporated as a city; **1937** county courthouse built.

Quincy   *Adams County*   *Western Illinois, 75 mi/121 km west of Springfield, on Mississippi River*

1822 John Wood and Willard Keyes stake first land claims; **1825** Adams County formed; town founded as county seat through efforts of Keyes, named for Pres. John Quincy Adams; **1831** first church built, called the Lord's Barn for its awkward design; **1832** cholera epidemic decimates population; **1834** incorporated as a town; **1835** John Wood House built; **1836** Mission Institute founded by abolitionist Rev. David Nelson, scene of disputes between proslavery and antislavery groups; **1839** incorporated as a city; **c.1845** city develops sizable hog market; **1847** St. Boniface Church completed; **c.1855** White House Inn built; **Oct. 13, 1858** sixth Lincoln-Douglas debate held; **1860** Quincy College established; **1870** Gem City College (2-year) established; **1887** Illinois Soldiers and Sailors Home established; **May 3, 1906** actress Mary Astor born (died 1987); **1915** county courthouse built; **1930** Quincy Memorial Bridge built across Mississippi River; **1946** Quincy Regional Airport established to east; **1974** John Wood Community College established; **1987** Bayview Bridge (cable-stayed) built across Mississippi River adjacent to Memorial Bridge; **July 17, 1993** flooding forces closing of Bayview Bridge, only remaining bridge open between Davenport and St. Louis.

Rantoul   *Champaign County*   *Eastern Illinois, 15 mi/24 km north-northeast of Champaign*

1868 Illinois Central Railroad reaches town; **1856** town platted; depot built; **1869** incorporated as a village; **1917** Chanute Field established by Army Air Corps, closed 1993; **1935** Rantoul Public Library established; **1937** fire at Chanute Field destroys firehouse, other buildings.

River Forest   *Cook County*   *Northeastern Illinois, 10 mi/16 km west of downtown Chicago*

1833 sawmill built on east side of Des Plaines River; **1836** Ashbel Steele and family become first settlers; **1849** Galena & Chicago Union Railroad built through area; **1854** Thatcher House built by Chicago businessman Daniel Cunningham Thatcher; **1862** Thatcher establishes station on Chicago & North Western Railroad, named for him; **1864** Concordia University, originally Concordia Teachers College, established; **1872** community renamed River Forest; **1880** incorporated as a village; **1906** Frank Lloyd Wright's Winslow House, Bock Studio, and River Forest Tennis Club built; **1913** River Forest Women's Clubhouse built; **1922** Rosary College established, originally St. Clara College at Fairplay, Wisconsin, becomes Dominican University 1997.

Robinson   *Crawford County*   *Southeastern Illinois, 136 mi/219 km east-northeast of St. Louis*

1816 Crawford County formed; Palestine becomes first county seat; **1843** town founded as new county seat; **1866** incorporated as a village; **1875** incorporated as a city; **1897** second county courthouse built; **1906** Robinson Public Library founded; **Nov. 6, 1921** novelist James Jones born, wrote *From Here to Eternity* (died 1977); **1969** Lincoln Trail College (2-year) established.

Rock Island   *Rock Island County*   *Northwestern Illinois, on Mississippi River, opposite Davenport, Iowa*

c.1783 Chief Keokuk born of Sauk tribe, died Apr. 1848 at Sauk and Fox Reservation, Kansas; **1828** area settled; **1833** Rock Island County formed; Farhamsburg, one of several towns located here, becomes county seat; **1841** towns consolidate, incorporate as city of Rock Island as new county seat; **1855** River Bend Public Library founded; **Apr. 21, 1856** Chicago & Rock Island Railroad bridge across Mississippi River opened to Davenport, Iowa; **1860** Augustana College established; **1862** U.S. Arsenal established on Rock Island in Mississippi; **1863** Rock Island National Cemetery established; **1897** county courthouse built; **Apr. 22, 1908** TV actor Eddie Albert born; **1934** Lock & Dam No. 15 completed; government bridge built to Davenport; **June 10, 1926** actress June Haver born.

Rockford   *Winnebago County*   *Northern Illinois, 80 mi/129 km northwest of Chicago, on Rock River*

1834 town of Rockford founded by Germanicus Kent and Thatcher Blake; Kent builds sawmill; **1835** Daniel Haight founds second town on opposite side of Rock River; **1836** Winnebago County formed; Rockford becomes county seat; **1839** two towns merge, incorporated as a town; rivalry continues; **1853** J. L. Manny, inventor of combination reaper/mower, brings farm implement business to Rockford; **1852** incorporated as a city; **1855** Chicago & Galena Railroad completed; **June 29, 1858** social worker Julia Clifford Lathrop born, joined Jane Addams' Hull House in Chicago 1890 (died 1932); **1860s** furniture industry established; **May 11, 1877** cupola of courthouse collapses while under construction, nine killed; **1878** county courthouse completed; **Feb. 15, 1922** Cong. John Anderson born; **1933** federal building completed; **1964** Rock Valley College (2-year) established; **1865** Tinker Swiss Cottage mansion built by Robert Tinker; **1917** Camp Grant National Guard training base established, becomes Greater Rockford Airport 1946; **1928** J. L. Case Company takes over Manny Company; **1973** county courthouse built; **1978** federal courthouse moved from Freeport; **1985** Klehm Arboretum and Botanic Garden established, completed 1998.

Rushville   *Schuyler County*   *Western Illinois, 53 mi/ 85 km west-northwest of Springfield*

1825 Schuyler County formed; **1826** town founded as county seat, named Rushton for Dr. William Rush; **1831** incorporated as a village; **1839** incorporated as a city; **Oct. 20, 1858** Abraham Lincoln gives speech in town square; **1878** Rushville Public Library founded, building opened 1913; **1881** third county courthouse built.

Saint Charles   *Kane and Du Page counties* *Northeastern Illinois, 37 mi/60 km west of Chicago, on Fox River*

1833 area resettled by Shelby and William Franklin following end of Black Hawk War; **1834** town founded, originally named Charleston; **1839** incorporated as a village, renamed St. Charles; **1842** Franklin Medical School established; **Apr. 19, 1849** in Richards' Riot, irate townspeople react to medical school students stealing cadaver of prominent family member to dissect, one person killed, school's Dr. George Richards fatally wounded; **1874** iron bridge built across Fox River; **1889** St. Charles Public Library founded; **1928** Du Page Airport established to east.

Salem   *Marion County*   *South central Illinois, 70 mi/ 113 km east of St. Louis*

1818 town founded on Vincennes-St. Louis Road; **1823** Marion County formed; town becomes county seat, incorporated as a village; **1837** incorporated as a town; **March 19, 1860** William Jennings Bryan born, Democratic Presidential candidate 1896, 1900, "The Great Commoner" (died 1925); **1865** incorporated as a city; **1912** county courthouse built; **1931** Kraft Miracle Whip invented by Max Crossett, originally Max's X-tra Fine Salad Dressing; **1934** William Jennings Bryan statue erected, sculpted by Gutzon Borglum, creator of Mount Rushmore Memorial; **1939** oil boom benefits economy; **June 10, 1971** City of New Orleans passenger train derails, 11 killed, 94 injured.

Savanna   *Carroll County*   *Northwestern Illinois, 45 mi/72 km north-northeast of Rock Island, on Mississippi River*

1828 town founded; **1835** town platted by Luther Bowen; **1838** John Smith arrives with family, establishes brick kiln; **1850** Chicago, Burlington & Quincy Railroad built through town; **1862** grain elevator built; **1874** incorporated as a city; **1917** Savanna Army Ordnance Depot established, large tract on Mississippi River, closed March 2000; **1929** Mississippi Palisades State Park established; **1932** bridge built across Mississippi to Sabula, Iowa.

Shawneetown   *Gallatin County*   *Southern Illinois, 125 mi/201 km southeast of St. Louis, on Ohio River*

c.1800 Michael Sprinkle becomes first settler; **1809** town platted; **1812** Gallatin County formed; town becomes county seat; cottage built, used as bank 1816–1839, oldest bank building in Illinois; **1814** incorporated as a town; **1834** Cranshaw (Old Slave) House built, antislavery laws allow their use at salt works; **Sept. 2, 1837** Spanish American War Gen. James Harrison Wilson born (died 1925); **1839** New First National Bank built; **1860** incorporated as a city; **1870** Dockers Riverside Hotel built; **1884** severe flooding inundates town; **1898** flooding reoccurs, many killed; **1913** flooding on Ohio occurs again after levee break; **1932** levee raised 5 ft/1.5 m above 1913 high level; **Jan. 24, 1937** citizens rescued just as river inundates town and two-thirds of county, rising 6 ft/1.8 m above levee; **1939** town relocated 4 mi/6.4 km to west of river, Old Shawneetown included in corporate limits; county courthouse built.

Shelbyville   *Shelby County*   *Central Illinois, 92 mi/ 148 km northeast of St. Louisi*

1827 Shelby County formed; town founded as county seat on Kaskaskia River; **1839** incorporated as a village; **1863** incorporated as a city; **1883** county courthouse built; **1970** Lake Shelbyville formed by dam on Kaskaskia River.

Skokie   *Cook County*   *Northwestern Illinois, suburb 13 mi/21 km north-northwest of Chicago*

1840s town founded by German immigrants; **1888** incorporated as a village, named Niles Centre; **1910** name altered to Niles Center; **1930** Skokie Public Library founded; **1940** renamed Skokie; **1952** Rand McNally Map Company moved from Chicago, established 1856; **1958** Hebrew Theological College moved from Chicago, founded 1922.

Spring Valley   *Bureau County*   *Northern Illinois, 90 mi/145 km southwest of Chicago, on Illinois River*

1884 town founded on Illinois River; **1886** incorporated as a city; **1888** Chicago and Northwestern Railroad reaches town; **Nov. 13, 1909** in Illinois' worst coal mining accident, fire kills 259 miners at Cherry Mine to north.

Springfield *Sangamon County* *Central Illinois, 85 mi/137 km north-northeast of St. Louis*

1818 area first settled; **Dec. 3, 1818** Illinois becomes 21st state; **1821** Sangamon County formed; Sangamon Town on Sangamon River becomes county seat; town of Springfield founded; **1824** *The Republican* newspaper founded; **1825** Springfield becomes new county seat; **1832** first steamboat, *Talisman*, arrives on Sangamon River; **1837** (old) state capitol built, scene of Lincoln's "House Divided" speech 1858; **1839** state capital moved from Vandalia; Lincoln Home built, occupied by Abraham Lincoln 1844–1861; **1840** incorporated as a city; **1853** first Illinois State Fair held; **1857** governor's mansion completed; **Feb. 11, 1861** Abraham Lincoln leaves Springfield for Washington, D.C., to assume presidency; **1862** Camp Butler National Cemetery established; **Oct. 15, 1874** Lincoln Tomb monument dedicated in Oak Ridge Cemetery; **1877** statehouse completed; old capitol sold to county as courthouse; **Nov. 10, 1879** woman poet Vachel Lindsay born (died 1931); **1880** *Daily News* newspaper founded; **1889** state historical library founded; **1923** Centennial Building completed; **1935** Spaulding Dam built on Sugar Creek forming Lake Springfield; **1938** state library organized; **1947** Capital Airport opened; **1969** Sangamon State University established, later becomes University of Illinois at Springfield; **May 6, 1972** nursing home fire kills nine, injures 32; **1991** new county courthouse completed; **Nov. 18, 2002** Lincoln Presidential Library dedicated.

Sterling *Whiteside County* *Northern Illinois, 45 mi/72 km southwest of Rockford, on Rock River*

1834 Hazelwood Brink builds first cabin; **1836** Whiteside County formed; Capt. Daniel Harris arrives from Galena with provisions for local settlers, exchanges goods for half-interest in new town, named Harrisburg; **1838** Harrisburg merges with town of Chatham as Sterling, becomes county seat; incorporated as a town; **1841** incorporated as a village; **1855** county seat moved to Morrison; **July 18, 1856** Abraham Lincoln delivers speech at Central School; **1857** incorporated as a city; dam built on Rock River; **1879** Northwestern Steel and Wire Company founded, files for bankruptcy 2000; **1907** branch of Illinois-Mississippi Canal (Hennepin Feeder Canal) extended from south.

Streator *La Salle County* *North central Illinois, 78 mi/126 km southwest of Chicago*

1868 town founded; **1872** coal mining begins in area; **1870** George "Honey Boy" Evans born, composer of "The Good Old Summer Time" (died 1915); **1873** bottle works established, beginning of town's glass manufacturing industry; **1882** incorporated as a city.

Sullivan *Moultrie County* *Central Illinois, 25 mi/40 km southeast of Decatur*

1843 Moultrie County formed; **1845** town founded as county seat; **1850** incorporated as a village; **1872** incorporated as a city; **1871** Opera House built, burned 1910; **1873** iron railroad bridge built over Illinois River, still in use; **1906** county courthouse completed; **1957** Little Theatre on the Square established.

Sycamore *De Kalb County* *Northern Illinois, 28 mi/45 km southeast of Rockford*

1836 town founded; county seat moved from Coultonville (De Kalb); **1837** De Kalb County formed; **1858** incorporated as a village; **1869** incorporated as a city; spur of Galena & Chicago Railroad reaches city from Cortland; **1903** county courthouse built.

Tampico *Whiteside County* *Northwestern Illinois, 32 mi/51 km east-northeast of Rock Island*

c.1869 town founded; **1870** post office established; **1875** incorporated as a village; **Feb. 6, 1911** actor, 40th U.S. Pres. Ronald Wilson Reagan born, served 1981–1989 (died June 5, 2004).

Taylorville *Christian County* *Central Illinois, 25 mi/40 km southeast of Springfield*

1839 Dane County formed; town founded as county seat; incorporated as a town; **1840** county renamed Christian County; **1881** incorporated as a city; **1902** county courthouse built; **Aug. 30, 1912** physicist Edward Mills Purcell born, won 1952 Nobel Prize (died 1997); **1965** County Historical Museum opened.

Toledo *Cumberland County* *Eastern Illinois, 110 mi/177 km east-northeast of St. Louis*

1843 Cumberland County formed; Greenup becomes first county seat; **1854** town founded, originally named Prairie City; **1857** incorporated as a village; county seat moved from Greenup; **1866** incorporated as a city; **1881** city renamed Toledo; **1887** county courthouse built.

Toulon *Stark County* *North central Illinois, 32 mi/51 km north-northwest of Peoria*

1829 first white settlers arrive; **1839** Stark County formed; **1841** town founded as county seat by Carson Berfield; **1856** second county courthouse completed; **1859** incorporated as a town; **1909** incorporated as a city.

Troy Grove *La Salle County* See **La Salle (1837)**

Tuscola *Douglas County* *Eastern Illinois, 22 mi/35 km south of Champaign*

1855 Illinois Central Railroad extended through town; **1857** town platted; **1859** Douglas County formed; town becomes county seat; **1859** incorporated as a village; **1861**

incorporated as a city; **1868** county courthouse completed; **1903** Tuscola Carnegie Public Library built.

Urbana   *Champaign County   East central Illinois, 125 mi/201 km south-southwest of Chicago*

1822 site first settled by Willard Tompkins; **1833** Champaign County formed; town founded as county seat; **1854** Illinois Central Railroad bypasses town to west; West Urbana founded around depot; Abraham Lincoln makes speech opposing slavery; **1855** Urbana incorporated as a city, attempts unsuccessfully to annex West Urbana; **1860** West Urbana incorporated as city of Champaign; **1863** street car line built linking Urbana to rail line; **1867** University of Illinois established; **1870s** attempts to move county seat to Champaign fail; **Oct. 9, 1871** fire destroys downtown, same day as major fires in Chicago and Peshtigo, Wisconsin; **1901** fourth county courthouse completed; **1918** Urbana Free Library opened; **Jan. 28, 1922** biochemist Robert William Holley born (died 1993); **June 18, 1942** movie critic Roger Ebert born; **1950** Willard Airport established; **1965** city hall built.

Vandalia   *Fayette County   South central Illinois, 65 mi/105 km east-northeast of St. Louis*

1819 town platted at western end of National Road; state capital moved from Kaskaskia; **1821** Fayette County formed; town becomes county seat, incorporated as a city; **1823** log statehouse destroyed by fire, replaced with brick structure; **1836** fourth statehouse built; **1837** delegation led by Abraham Lincoln, called the "Long Nine" for the tall stature of all of them, succeed in having Springfield named new capital; **1839** state capital moved to Springfield; capitol building becomes county courthouse; **1921** Vandalia Public Library opened, renamed Evans Library 1960; **1928** Madonna of the Trail Monument erected by Daughters of the American Revolution; **1933** new county courthouse completed; former state capitol becomes Vandalia Statehouse State Historical Site.

Vienna   *Johnson County   Southern Illinois, 108 mi/ 174 km southeast of St. Louis*

1812 Johnson County formed; **1818** town founded as county seat; **1837** incorporated as a city; **1870** county courthouse built; **1965** Vienna Correctional Center to east; **1984** Shawnee Correctional Center opened to east.

Virginia   *Cass County   Western Illinois, 30 mi/ 48 km west-northwest of Springfield*

1836 town platted by Dr. Henry A. Hall, who served in British Navy; **1837** Cass County formed; **1842** incorporated as a village; **1857** incorporated as a city; **1872** town becomes permanent county seat following several moves to and from Beardstown; county courthouse built.

Waterloo   *Monroe County   Southwestern Illinois, 20 mi/32 km south of St. Louis*

1816 Monroe County formed; area first settled; **1818** town platted; **1825** town becomes county seat; **1849** incorporated as a town; **1888** incorporated as a city; **1900** county courthouse built.

Watseka   *Iroquois County   Northeastern Illinois, 75 mi/121 km south of Chicago*

1818 Gurdon Hubbard sent to area by American Fur Company to establish trade with Potawatomis, marries Watch-e-kee, niece of Chief Tamin; **1820** Hubbard divests of Watch-e-kee, gives her to partner La Vasseur; **1821** Hubbard cabin built; **1833** Iroquois County formed; **Nov. 24, 1853** frontiersman Bat Masterson born in rural Iroquois County (died 1921); **1860** town platted as South Middleport; **1865** town renamed Watseka; county seat moved from Bunkum (town of Iroquois); **1866** county courthouse built; **Nov. 28, 1866** architect Henry Bacon born, designed Lincoln Memorial (died 1924); **1867** incorporated as a city; **1898** Watseka Public Library founded, built 1904.

Waukegan   *Lake County   Northeastern Illinois, 35 mi/56 km north of Chicago, on Lake Michigan*

1760 French abandon Little Fort; **1835** first settlers arrive; town founded, originally named Little Fort; **Aug. 1836** Potawatomis vacate region under treaty; **1839** Lake County formed; Libertyville becomes county seat; **1845** county courthouse completed, burned 1875, rebuilt, demolished 1967; **1849** incorporated as a village, renamed; **1852** incorporated as a city; **Apr. 2, 1860** speech by Abraham Lincoln at Dickinson Hall interrupted by fire alarm; **Feb. 14, 1894** comedian Jack Benny born (died 1974); **Aug. 22, 1920** fiction writer Ray Bradbury born; **Dec. 6, 1921** football player Otto Graham born; **1948** Illinois Beach State Park established to north; **1954** Conference Center opened at Illinois Beach; **1970** County Administration Building completed; **1989** County Judicial Center completed.

West Dundee   *Kane County   Northeastern Illinois, 38 mi/61 km northwest of Chicago, on Fox River*

1830s area on west side of Fox River settled by Scottish and English, named for Dundee, Scotland, remains separate from German community of East Dundee; **1843** Allan Pinkerton establishes cooperage; **1850** Pinkerton discovers counterfeiting operation on island in Fox River, becomes Chicago's first detective, appointed by Abraham Lincoln to head Secret Service 1861 after uncovering plot to assassinate president; **1887** incorporated as a village.

West Frankfort   *Franklin County   Southern Illinois, 87 mi/140 km southeast of St. Louis, Missouri*

1818 Franklin County formed; town of Frankfort founded as county seat; **1839** county seat moved to

Benton with separation of Williamson County from Franklin; Chicago, Paducah & Memphis Railroad built to west; West Frankfort founded; **1901** incorporated as a city; **March 18, 1925** Tri-State Tornado (Mo., Ill., Ind.) damages 20 percent of town, 95 killed locally, total 695 killed; **Dec. 21, 1951** explosion at Orient No. 2 Coal Mine, 119 killed.

Wheaton *Du Page County* *Northeastern Illinois, 25 mi/40 km west of Chicago*

1832 Erastus Gary settles in area; **1838** Warren and Jesse Wheaton acquire land; **1839** Du Page County formed; **Oct. 8, 1846** Judge Elbert Gary born, industrialist, major figure in steel industry, namesake of Gary, Indiana (died 1927); **1848** land donated for town by Elbert Gary and Wheaton brothers; **1853** town platted; Illinois Institute established by Methodists, renamed Wheaton College 1860; **1857** Wheaton makes unsuccessful attempt to wrest county seat from Naperville; **1859** incorporated as a village; **July 1868** group raids courthouse, forcibly move county seat to Wheaton; **1890** incorporated as a city; **1938** county courthouse completed; **1992** County Judicial Office Building opened.

Wilmette *Cook County* *Northeastern Illinois, 15 mi/24 km north of Chicago, on Lake Michigan*

1829 French-Canadian Antoine Ouilmette becomes first settler; **Sept. 8, 1860** cruise ship *Lady Elgin* collides with lumber schooner on Lake Michigan, 293 killed; **1869** town founded; **1872** incorporated as a village; **1874** village of Grosse Point incorporated; **1910** North Shore Channel and Wilmette Harbor completed; **1920** Baha'i House of Worship begun, completed 1953; **1924** Grosse Point annexed by Wilmette.

Winchester *Scott County* *Western Illinois, 45 mi/ 72 km west-southwest of Springfield*

1824 grist mill built; **1830** town platted; **1833** Stephen A. Douglas begins legal career here; **1839** Scott County formed; Winchester becomes county seat; **1843** incorporated as a city; **1885** county courthouse built.

Winnetka *Cook County* *Northeastern Illinois, 17 mi/27 km north of Chicago, on Lake Michigan*

1854 town founded on proposed route of Chicago & Milwaukee Railroad; **1869** incorporated as a village; **June 10, 1907** painter Fairfield Porter born (died 1975); **Nov. 17,**

1925 actor Rock Hudson born (died 1985); **July 25, 1965** up to 15,000 hear Dr. Martin L. King at school desegregation rally; **June 26, 1970** actor Chris O'Donnell born.

Woodstock *McHenry County* *Northeastern Illinois, 53 mi/85 km northwest of Chicago*

1830s first settlers arrive; **1836** McHenry County formed; McHenry becomes first county seat; **1843** town founded, named Centerville; county seat moved from McHenry; **1845** town renamed Woodstock; **1848** Todd School for Boys established, alumni include Orson Welles; **1852** incorporated as a village; **1856** Chicago & North Western Railroad built; **1857** county courthouse built; **1873** incorporated as a city; **1890** Opera House built; **1896** Olivetti Typewriter Company factory established, closed 1928; **1909** Woodstock Typewriter Plant established, closed 1971; **1972** county government center built; **1974** Woodstock Musical Theater Company founded; **1987** Mozart Festival founded.

Yorkville *Kendall County* *Northeastern Illinois, 45 mi/72 km west-southwest of Chicago*

1829 first settlers arrive; **1832** settlers return after end of Black Hawk War; **1836** town platted on Fox River by Rulief Duryea; **1841** Kendall County formed; town becomes county seat; **1845** county seat moved to Oswego; **1864** county seat moved back to Yorkville; county courthouse built, rebuilt after 1887 fire; **1870** Chicago, Burlington & Quincy Railroad reaches town; **1873** incorporated as a village; **1928** Yorkville Airport established; **1975** County Office Building completed; **1997** new county courthouse built.

Zion *Lake County* *Northeastern Illinois, 40 mi/ 64 km north of Chicago, on Lake Michigan*

1899 Scottish faith-healer John Alexander Dowie announces creation of community governed by his Christian Catholic Apostolic Church, founded 1885; **1901** town founded by Dowie; **1902** incorporated as a city; Zion Hotel built; Shiloh House built; **1907** Dowie dies; Wilbur Glenn Voliva succeeds him, leads community through prosperity in 1920s and two bankruptcies 1910, 1933, is succeeded 1939; **1904** Zion Home built, domicile for divine healing; **Feb. 8, 1968** TV actor Gary Coleman born; **1973** Zion Nuclear Plant begins operations, closed 1997.

Indiana

East central U.S. Capital and major city: Indianapolis.

The region became part of the U.S. with creation of the Northwest Territory in 1787. Indiana Territory, including Illinois, was established July 4, 1800. Michigan Territory separated from Indiana January 11, 1805, and Illinois Territory separated February 2, 1809. Indiana became the 19th state December 11, 1816.

Indiana is divided into 92 counties. The counties are divided into townships with limited governments. Municipalities are classified as towns and cities. In January 1970, the city of Indianapolis consolidated with Marion County. Several smaller municipalities opted not to participate in the merger. See Introduction.

Albion *Noble County* *Northeastern Indiana, 25 mi/ 40 km northwest of Fort Wayne*

1836 Noble County formed; Augusta becomes first county seat, site 2 mi/3.2 km to west; **1843** county seat moved to Port Mitchell; **1847** town founded as new county seat; **1850s** town plays role in Underground Railroad, providing safe haven for runaway slaves on way to Canada; **1874** town incorporated; **1889** second county courthouse built; **1949** Camp Lutherhaven founded; **1994** Black Pine Animal Park established, haven for domestic and exotic animals.

Anderson *Madison County* *Central Indiana, 31 mi/50 km northeast of Indianapolis*

1801 Moravian mission established for Native Americans, closed 1806 after several converts killed by other Delawares, including Chief Ta-ta-pach-sit, burned at stake; **1821** Government Road built from Muncie; **1823** Madison County formed; town founded on White River by John Berry, named Andersontown for Captain Anderson, English name for Delaware Chief Kikthawenund; **1827** county seat moved from Pendleton; **1838** incorporated as a town; **1853** Indianapolis & Bellefontaine Railroad reaches town; town name shortened to Anderson; **1865** incorporated as a city; **1874** Indiana Central Canal opened, branch of Wabash & Erie Canal, planned 1837, not started until 1868; **1882** county courthouse built; **March 1887** natural gas discovered in area leads to industrial boom, reserves depleted 1912; **1895** Remy Electric Company founded, acquired by General Motors 1920, becomes Delco-Remy, manufacturer of automobile electrical equipment; **1905** publishing house of *Gospel Trumpet* religious publication moved from Moundsville, West Virginia, by Noah

Byrum, ceased publication 1998; **1917** Anderson University established; **Feb. 2, 1924** two streetcars collide, 21 killed; **1930** Mounds State Park established.

Angola *Steuben County* *Northeastern Indiana, 37 mi/60 km north of Fort Wayne*

1835 Steuben County formed; **1838** town founded as county seat, platted by Thomas Gale and Cornelius Gilmore; **1866** town incorporated; **1868** second county courthouse built; **1884** Tri-State University established; **1915** Carnegie Library dedicated.

Auburn *De Kalb County* *Northeastern Indiana, 20 mi/32 km north of Fort Wayne*

1836 town settled; **1837** De Kalb County formed; town founded as county seat; **1849** incorporated as a town; **1874** Eckart Carriage Company established, closed 1918; **1900** incorporated as a city; Auburn Automobile Company established (closed 1937); **1911** county courthouse completed; Eckart Public Library founded; Warner Automotive Parts (Borg-Warner) established, distributor of Auburn, Cord, and Duesenberg auto parts; **1973** Auburn-Cord-Duesenberg Museum opened; **2000** Hoosier Air Museum opened.

Aurora *Dearborn County* *Southeastern Indiana, 77 mi/124 km southeast of Indianapolis, on Ohio River*

1819 town founded; **1822** incorporated as a town; **1848** incorporated as a city; **1854** Ohio & Mississippi Railroad reaches town; **1855** Hillforest Mansion built by financier Thomas Gaff; **July 13, 1863** Confederate Gen. John Morgan's Raiders pass through county plundering residents; **1888** salt lick discovered near Hogan Creek; **Jan.**

13, 1890 writer Elmer Davis born (died 1958); **1937** town inundated by Great Ohio Flood.

Battle Ground   *Tippecanoe County   Western Indiana, 58 mi/93 km northwest of Indianapolis*

Nov. 7, 1811 Battle of Tippecanoe, Gen. William Henry Harrison leads 900 army troops, defeat Native Americans led by Chief Tecumseh's brother, The Prophet, 61 of Harrison's men killed, 127 wounded, Native American village of Prophet's Town burned; **1867** town incorporated; **1908** Battle of Tippecanoe monument erected.

Bedford   *Lawrence County   Southern Indiana, 60 mi/97 km south-southwest of Indianapolis*

1818 Lawrence County formed; Palatine becomes first county seat; **1825** town founded as new county seat; **1834** county courthouse built; **1864** incorporated as a town; **1889** incorporated as a city; **1915** Moses Fell Experimental Farm of Purdue University founded; **1930** county courthouse built; Indiana Limestone Corporation founded, provided stone for Empire State Building, The Pentagon, Nebraska State Capitol; **1930–1931** Empire Hole formed, site of limestone used in construction of Empire State Building, New York.

Bloomfield   *Greene County   Southwestern Indiana, 37 mi/60 km southeast of Terre Haute*

1821 Greene County formed; **1824** town founded and platted as county seat; **1850** town incorporated; **1886** county courthouse completed.

Bloomington   *Monroe County   South central Indiana, 43 mi/69 km south-southwest of Indianapolis*

1815 town settled; **1818** Monroe County formed; town founded; **1820** Indiana University established; **1849** incorporated as a town; **1878** incorporated as a city; **Nov. 22, 1899** pianist, actor Hoagy Carmichael born (died 1981); **1908** county courthouse built; **Oct. 10, 1955** singer David Lee Roth born.

Bluffton   *Wells County   Eastern Indiana, 22 mi/35 km south of Fort Wayne*

1835 Wells County formed; **1838** town founded on Wabash River as county seat; **1858** town incorporated; **Aug. 30, 1865** botanist Charles C. Deam born (died 1953); **1891** county courthouse completed.

Boonville   *Warrick County   Southwestern Indiana, 125 mi/201 km southwest of Indianapolis*

1813 Warrick County formed; town founded, named for Jesse Boon, son Ratliff Boon instrumental in choosing site for county seat; **1814** county seat moved from McGary's Ferry (now Evansville, then part of Warrick County); **1818** town platted; **1858** town incorporated; **1880** railroad reaches town; **1904** county courthouse built; **1914** as many as 17 coal mines in operation in county.

Brazil   *Clay County   Western Indiana, 50 mi/80 km west-southwest of Indianapolis*

1825 Clay County formed; Bowling Green becomes first county seat; **1844** town founded by Owen Thorpe; **1866** town incorporated; **1873** incorporated as a city; **1877** county seat moved to Brazil; county courthouse built; **1893** electric rail line built to Harmony, one of first interurban lines, 3 mi/4.8 km long; **Feb. 14, 1913** Teamsters union leader James Hoffa born, disappeared in Detroit suburbs July 30, 1975, presumed dead.

Brookville   *Franklin County   Eastern Indiana, 62 mi/100 km east-southeast of Indianapolis*

1808 town founded by Amos Butler and Jesse Brooks Thomas, originally spelled Brooksville; **1811** Franklin County formed; town becomes county seat, renamed Brookville; **1812** Little Cedar Baptist Church built to south; **1817** The Hermitage house built by Amos Butler, later owned by painter J. Ottis Adams (1851–1927); **1818** Hanna House built; **c.1823** Pioneer Hardware Store built; **Apr. 10, 1827** Union Maj. Gen. Lew Wallace born, lived in Crawfordsville (died 1905); **1839** town incorporated; **1843** Whitewater Canal completed; **1852** third county courthouse built; **1865** Whitewater Valley Railroad built parallel to canal; **1912** Carnegie Library opened; **1913** flooding destroys town's industries, 13 killed; **1974** Brookville Lake formed by dam on East Fork Whitewater River to north.

Brownstown   *Jackson County   Southern Indiana, 57 mi/92 km south of Indianapolis*

1816 Jackson County formed; town founded as county seat; **1857** Ohio & Mississippi Railroad reaches neighboring Ewing, later annexed by Brownstown; **1870** town incorporated; third county courthouse built.

Cannelton   *Perry County   Southern Indiana, 125 mi/201 km south-southwest of Indianapolis*

1814 Perry County formed; Troy becomes first county seat; **1816** Thomas and Nancy Hanks Lincoln ferry across Ohio River with children Abraham and Sarah from Cloverport, Kentucky, on way to Spencer County, Indiana [see Lincoln City]; **1818** county seat moved to Rome; **1837** town founded on Ohio River as coal mining center, named for cannel coal deposits in area; American Cannel Coal Company established; **1859** town incorporated; county seat moved to Cannelton; **1897** county courthouse completed.

Charlestown   *Clark County   Southern Indiana, 13 mi/21 km north-northeast of Louisville, Kentucky*

1801 Clark County formed; Jeffersonville becomes first county seat; **1807** Bethel Meeting House built, first Methodist church in Indiana; **1808** town founded near Ohio River; **1811** county seat moved to Charlestown; **1820** Tunnel Mill and Dam built on Fourteen Mile Creek to south by John Wade, mill burned 1927; **1814** town incorporated; **1878** county seat moved back to Jeffersonville; **1940** E. I. du Pont establishes Indiana Army Ammunition Plant for production of smokeless gunpowder; **1941** Goodyear Tire and Rubber Company plant built; **1998** ammunition plant site conveyed to state of Indiana for creation of state park.

Chesterton *Porter County* *Northwestern Indiana, 14 mi/23 km east of Gary, near Lake Michigan*

1852 town founded, named Calumet; **1869** town incorporated, renamed; **1880** C. O. Hillstrom organ factory moves from Chicago; **1902** business district destroyed by fire; **Feb. 27, 1921** railroad accident, 37 killed; **1925** Indiana Dunes State Park established to north; **1966** Indiana Dunes National Lakeshore established.

Clarksville *Clark County* *Southern Indiana, 2 mi/ 3.2 km north of Louisville, Kentucky, on Ohio River*

1783 town founded on Ohio River, opposite Louisville, by George Rogers Clark; chartered by state of Virginia; **Dec. 1808** quarrel between Henry Clay and Humphrey Marshall settled by duel, both walk away with flesh wounds, honor intact; **1929** Municipal Bridge (U.S. Highway 31) built from Louisville.

Columbia City *Whitley County* *Northeastern Indiana, 18 mi/29 km west of Fort Wayne*

Nov. 5, 1780 in La Balme Massacre, Miami Chief Little Turtle destroys French force of 100 men under Col. Auguste de La Balme near Miamis' Eel River Post; **Sept. 12, 1812** Gen. William Henry Harrison defeats Miamis at Paige's Crossing, retaliation for attacks on Fort Wayne and Fort Harrison; **1835** Whitley County formed; **1839** town founded as Columbia; **1854** town renamed Columbia City; **March 14, 1854** Thomas Riley Marshall born, vice-president under Woodrow Wilson (died 1925); **Aug. 27, 1877** author Lloyd Cassel Douglas born (died 1951); **1888** town incorporated; **1890** county courthouse completed.

Columbus *Bartholomew County* *South central Indiana, 38 mi/61 km south-southeast of Indianapolis*

1819 Cox family become first settlers; **1820** town settled by Gen. John Tipton, John Lindsay, and Luke Bonesteel; **1821** Bartholomew County formed; town founded as county seat on land donated by Gen. Tipton, originally named Tiptonia, immediately renamed Columbus to chagrin of Tipton; **1864** incorporated as a town; **1874** third county courthouse built; **1921** incorporated as a city.

Connersville *Fayette County* *Eastern Indiana, 52 mi/84 km east-southeast of Indianapolis*

1808 trading post established by John Conner; **1813** town founded by Conner; **1819** Fayette County formed; town becomes county seat; **1841** incorporated as a town; **1845** Whitewater Canal built from southeast; **1865** Whitewater Valley Railroad reaches town; **1870** incorporated as a city; **1891** county courthouse completed.

Corydon *Harrison County* *Southern Indiana, 19 mi/31 km west of Louisville, Kentucky*

1800 Indiana Territory created from Northwest Territory; **1808** Harrison County formed; town founded as county seat by Gen. William Henry Harrison, named for shepherd in song "Pastoral Elegy" from songbook *Missouri Harmony*; **1811** Posey Mansion built; **1812** county courthouse built, used as state capitol; **1813** capital of Indiana Territory moved from Vincennes; **1816** Indiana becomes a state; town becomes state capital; **1817** state treasury built; incorporated as a town; **1825** state capital moved to Indianapolis; **March 17, 1832** Walter Quinton Gresham born at Lanesville to east, secretary of state under President Cleveland (died 1895); **1849** incorporated as a city; **July 8, 1863** Confederate Gen. John Morgan's Raiders cross into Indiana from Kentucky, attack town July 9, three defenders killed, eight raiders killed, enter Ohio July 13; **1894** W. H. Keller Wagon Works founded; **1929** county courthouse built.

Covington *Fountain County* *Western Indiana, 66 mi/106 km west-northwest of Indianapolis*

1826 Fountain County formed; **1826** town founded on Wabash River as county seat; **1851** town incorporated; **1937** county courthouse completed.

Crawfordsville *Montgomery County* *Western Indiana, 41 mi/66 km west-northwest of Indianapolis*

1822 Montgomery County formed; **1823** town founded as county seat by Maj. Ambrose Whitlock, named for Indian fighter Col. William Crawford; **1831** incorporated as a town; **1833** Wabash College established; **Aug. 17, 1859** in earliest air mail delivery, balloon sent aloft carrying 123 letters from Lafayette intended for New York, ends here, continued by train; **1866** incorporated as a city; **1876** county courthouse completed; **1898** Gen. Lew Wallace builds study, becomes Ben-Hur Museum 1941, named for his best-selling 1880 novel *Ben Hur: A Tale of Christ*.

Crown Point *Lake County* *Northwestern Indiana, 10 mi/16 km south of Gary*

1834 town founded by Solon Robinson of Connecticut; **1836** Lake County formed; town becomes county seat; **1868** town incorporated; **1909** county courthouse built; **June 19, 1909** Cobe Cup Race held near courthouse, first major auto race in U.S.; **March 3, 1934** gunman John Dillinger and inmate Robert Youngblood escape from County Jail, Dillinger shot to death in Chicago July 22, Youngblood captured March 16 at Port Huron, Michigan, near Canada.

Dale *Spencer County* *See* **Jasper (1934)**

Danville *Hendricks County* *Central Indiana, 19 mi/31 km west of Indianapolis*

1823 Hendricks County formed; **1824** Daniel Clark builds first log cabin; town founded as county seat; **1829** Danville Academy founded; **1839** incorporated as a town; **1859** incorporated as a city; **1878** Central Normal College moved from Ladoga, buildings of Danville Academy used; **1915** third county courthouse built.

Decatur *Adams County* *Northeastern Indiana, 19 mi/31 km south-southeast of Fort Wayne*

1835 Adams County formed; **1836** town founded as county seat, named for U.S. naval hero Steven Decatur; **1853** town incorporated; **1871** railroad reaches town; **1873** county courthouse built; **1905** Decatur Public Library built.

Delphi *Carroll County* *Northern Indiana, 58 mi/93 km northwest of Indianapolis*

1828 Carroll County formed; town founded as county seat, near Wabash River; **1835** town incorporated; **1852** incorporated as a city; **1917** third county courthouse completed.

Dugger *Sullivan County* *See Sullivan (1931)*

East Chicago *Lake County* *Northwestern Indiana, 6 mi/9.7 km west-northwest of Gary*

1889 Standard Oil Refinery built on Lake Michigan at Whiting, extends into East Chicago; town incorporated; **1893** steel mill built, becomes Inland Steel Company; incorporated as a city; **1903** Indiana Harbor and Ship Canal built; **1907** Harrison-Walker Refractories plant opened; **1916** Youngstown Sheet and Tube Company plant built; **1917** Sinclair Oil Refinery established; **Nov. 1, 1929** actress Betsy Palmer born.

Elkhart *Elkhart County* *Northern Indiana, 14 mi/23 km east of South Bend*

1830 Elkhart County formed; **1832** town founded as county seat by Dr. Havilah Beardsley on St. Joseph River, at mouth of Elkhart River, named for river island shaped like elk's heart; **1850** shops of Michigan Southern Railroad established; **1858** town incorporated; **1875** incorporated as a city; Charles G. Conn begins manufacture of band instruments; **1884** Dr. Franklin Miles establishes Dr. Miles Medical Company, maker of pharmaceuticals, later became Miles Laboratories; **1894** Elkhart Institute founded, moved to Goshen 1903, renamed Goshen College; **1903** Elkhart Carnegie Public Library built; **1908** Rathmere House built; **1943** Elkhart Municipal Airport established.

Elwood *Madison County* *Central Indiana, 36 mi/58 km north-northeast of Indianapolis*

1852 general store established by William Barton, originally named Quincy; **1853** town founded; **1869** town renamed for son of town founder J. B. Frazier; **1887** natural gas discovered; **1891** town incorporated; **Feb. 18, 1892** Wendell L. Willkie born, Republican Presidential candidate 1940 (died 1944).

English *Crawford County* *Southern Indiana, 95 mi/153 km south-southwest of Indianapolis*

1818 Crawford County formed; **1839** town founded, originally named Hartford; **1884** town incorporated, renamed for Cong. William Hayden English; **1893** county seat moved from Leavenworth; county courthouse built; **1954** Crawford County Library established.

Evansville *Vanderburgh County* *Southwestern Indiana, 135 mi/217 km southwest of Indianapolis*

c.1400 Native Americans establish village of about 800 people, build Angel Mounds to southeast on Ohio River over 200-year period; **1809** steamboat *Robert Fulton* arrives, first to ply Ohio River; **1812** Col. Hugh McGary becomes first settler, begins ferry service; **1813** Warrick County formed; **1814** McGary's Ferry becomes county seat; **1817** town platted, renamed for surveyor Col. Robert Evans; **1818** Vanderburgh County formed from Warrick County; town becomes seat of new county; **1819** incorporated as a town; **1820s** financial depression and epidemic of "milch sickness" devastates town; **1831–1832** Ohio River freezes solid, halting river commerce; **1832** settler Col. McGary charged with horse stealing, forced to leave town; town inundated by flooding; cholera epidemic kills 391; **1834** town selected as south terminus for Wabash & Erie Canal; **1840** influx of German immigrants arrive over next 30 years; **1848** incorporated as a city; Willard Carpenter House built; **1852** Mozart Hall theater opens; **1853** Wabash & Erie Canal completed, first canal boat arrives from Petersburg; **1854** University of Evansville established; **1861** canal abandoned; **1884** city inundated again by flooding Ohio River; **1890** county courthouse completed; **1904** Museum of Arts and Sciences established; **July 2, 1906** *Evansville Press* newspaper founded; **1922** Dade Park Race Track built by James Ellis in enclave of Kentucky north of Ohio River cut off by changing river course, later renamed Ellis Park; **1928** Evansville Regional Airport established; **1929** Mesker Park Zoo established; **1932** Ohio River Bridge (U.S. 41) built to Henderson, Kentucky, second span added 1962; **Jan. 1937** Great Ohio Flood reaches record level 53.74 ft/16.4 m, covers half of city; **Oct. 2, 1948** actor Avery Brooks born; **1965** Indiana State University, Evansville Campus, established, becomes University of Southern Indiana 1985; **Dec. 13, 1977** U.S. Airlines DC-3 crashes after takeoff in fog and rain killing 29 of 31, including University of Evansville basketball team.

Fairmount *Grant County* *North central Indiana, 50 mi/80 km northeast of Indianapolis*

1871 town incorporated; **1887** natural gas discovered in area; **Feb. 8, 1931** movie icon James Dean born, killed in automobile crash in Paso Robles, California, Sept. 30, 1955, funeral held at Fairmount Friends Church Oct. 8; **July 28, 1945** cartoonist Jim Davis born, creator of Garfield the Cat.

Fort Wayne *Allen County* *Northeastern Indiana, 100 mi/161 km northeast of Indianapolis*

c.1686 Fort Miami built, origin obscure; **1697** French rebuild fort; first white settlement in Indiana founded; **1748** Fort Miami burned by Native Americans, rebuilt, abandoned 1750; **1760** fort transferred to British; **1790** Gen. Josiah Harmar sent to establish trading post at Miami Town, forced out by Chief Little Turtle four days later, Oct. 19; **1795** Gen. Anthony Wayne builds Fort Wayne after Battle of Fallen Timbers [see Maumee, Ohio]; town of Fort Wayne founded; Treaty of Greenville opens parts of Ohio and Indiana to white settlement; **1809** treaty with Miami and Delaware peoples establishes Ten O'Clock Line, line running parallel to shadow cast by sun at 10 o'clock, Sept. 30, as northern limit of Native American occupation; **Sept. 5, 1812** Fort Wayne besieged by Potawatomi, lifted Sept. 12 by General Harrison; **1813** several of Maj. Joseph Jenkinson's men massacred in final Native American action at fort; **1815** Maj. John Whistler builds final Fort Wayne, torn down 1857; **Apr. 1819** Judge Samuel Hanna builds trading post; **1823** Allen County formed; **1824** town becomes county seat; **1829** incorporated as a town; **1832** construction of Wabash & Erie Canal from Toledo, Ohio, begins, completed 1843 to Lafayette, Indiana; **1838** McCulloch House built; **1839** Concordia College (2-year) established; **1840** incorporated as a city; **1846** many Miami peoples removed to Kansas; **1853** Brass Foundry and Machine Company founded, maker of railroad car wheels; **1854** Ohio & Indiana Railroad built; Ewing House built by Judge William G. Ewing; **1856** Fort Wayne & Chicago Railroad reaches town; **1869** remainder of Miamis removed to Oklahoma; **1871** Horton Manufacturing Company founded, early manufacturer of washing machines; **July 12, 1881** physician George F. Dick born, developed tests for scarlet fever (died 1967); **Feb. 14, 1882** author George Nathan born (died 1958); **June 2, 1883** first baseball night game played at League Park; **1888** Fort Wayne Art School and Museum founded; **1890** University of St. Francis established; **1899** *Journal-Gazette* newspaper formed by merger of *Journal* and *Daily Gazette*; **1902** county courthouse completed; **1913** flooding inundates city; **1917** Indiana University-Purdue University Fort Wayne Campus established; **1918** Anthony Wayne monument dedicated; **June 22, 1922** fashion designer Bill Blass born (died 2002); **1930** Indiana Institute of Technology established; **1941** Baer Field military base established, becomes Fort Wayne Airport 1946; **1944** Fort Wayne Philharmonic Orchestra

founded; **Aug. 23, 1949** TV actress Shelley Long born; **1965** Children's Zoo founded; **1977** Museum of Art founded; **May 29, 1980** civil rights leader Vernon Jordan shot, wounded; **1982** flooding reoccurs; **1989** Memorial Coliseum opened.

Fowler *Benton County* *Western Indiana, 80 mi/129 km northwest of Indianapolis*

1840 Benton County formed; Oxford becomes first county seat; **1872** Central Indiana, St. Louis & Cincinnati Railroad reaches site; town founded on land of Moses Fowler; **1875** county seat moved from Oxford; town incorporated; county courthouse built; **Jan. 19, 1907** railroad accident, 29 killed.

Frankfort *Clinton County* *Central Indiana, 37 mi/60 km northwest of Indianapolis*

1830 Clinton County formed, named for Gov. DeWitt Clinton of New York, responsible for construction of Erie Canal; town founded as county seat on land owned by Pence brothers, named for their ancestral hometown of Frankfurt, Germany; **1855** town incorporated; **1882** third county courthouse completed.

Franklin *Johnson County* *Central Indiana, 20 mi/32 km south of Indianapolis*

1822 Johnson County formed; **1823** town founded as county seat; **1834** Franklin College of Indiana established; **1861** incorporated as a city; **1882** fourth county courthouse completed; **Jan. 19, 1994** lowest temperature ever recorded in Indiana reached at rural New Whiteland to north, −36°F/−38°C.

French Lick *Orange County* *Southern Indiana, 82 mi/132 km south-southwest of Indianapolis*

1811 trading post established by French near salt lick; **1811** town founded; **1840** French Lick Springs Hotel built by Dr. William A. Bowles, among several convicted of treason 1864 for involvement in Knights of Golden Circle pro-Confederate group, death sentence commuted; **1857** town platted; **1886** Sam Bunch shot to death in Outlaw Cave by members of Archer clan, three lynched, fourth hanged legally; **1891** hotel purchased by Thomas Taggart, controlling force in state Democratic party; **1897** hotel destroyed by fire, rebuilt; **1904** gambling introduced, abolished 1949; **Dec. 7, 1956** basketball star Larry Bird born at West Baden Springs to north.

Gary *Lake County* *Northwestern Indiana, 25 mi/40 km southeast of Chicago, on Lake Michigan*

1673 Father Jacques Marquette visits site; **1896** Octave Chanute completes successful glider flight on lake dunes; **1905** land purchased on Lake Michigan by United States Steel Corporation; **1906** town founded; **1909** incorporated as a city; **1910** first steel mill opened; **May 15, 1915** economist Paul Anthony Samuelson born, Nobel Prize

1970; **June 22, 1918** circus train rear ended by empty troop train at Ivanhoe, 68 killed, buried at Woodlawn Cemetery, Forest Park, Illinois; **Aug. 1919** U.S. Army under Gen. Leonard Wood quells steel strike unrest, settled Oct. 1919; **Sept. 28, 1919** football player Tom Harmon born (died 1990); **March 14, 1928** astronaut Frank Borman born; **July 15, 1935** football player, actor Alex Karras born; **1949** Gary Regional Airport established, renamed Gary Chicago Airport 1995; **Dec. 11, 1954** singer Jermaine Jackson born; **May 29, 1956** singer LaToya Jackson born; **Aug. 29, 1958** singer Michael Jackson born; **1959** Indiana University Northwest Campus established; **May 16, 1966** singer Janet Jackson born.

Goshen *Elkhart County* *Northern Indiana, 21 mi/ 34 km east-southeast of South Bend*

1830s Fort Beane built during Native American troubles; **1830** Elkhart County formed; **1831** town founded; **1854** incorporated as a town; **1868** incorporated as a city; **1869** county courthouse completed; **May 30, 1896** movie director Howard Hawks born (died 1977); **1901** Goshen Public Library founded; **1903** Goshen College moved from Elkhart, founded 1894 as Elkhart Institute.

Gosport *Owen County* See **Spencer (1957)**

Greencastle *Putnam County* *Western Indiana, 35 mi/56 km west-southwest of Indianapolis*

1821 Putnam County formed; **1822** town founded as county seat; **1823** incorporated as a town; **1837** De Pauw University established; **1861** incorporated as a city; **1903** county courthouse built.

Greenfield *Hancock County* *Central Indiana, 29 mi/47 km east of Indianapolis*

1827 Hancock County formed; **1828** town founded as county seat; **c.1833** National Road reaches town; **Oct. 7, 1849** poet James Whitcomb Riley born (died 1914); **1850** incorporated as a town; Riley House built around poet's cabin birthplace; **1853** Indiana Central Railroad reaches town; **1876** incorporated as a city; **1898** county courthouse completed; **1914** Eli Lilly Biological Laboratories established for pharmaceutical research; **1918** Riley Statue erected.

Greensburg *Decatur County* *Southeastern Indiana, 43 mi/69 km southeast of Indianapolis*

1821 Decatur County formed; **1822** town founded as county seat; **1837** incorporated as a town; **1859** incorporated as a city; **1860** second county courthouse completed.

Hammond *Lake County* *Northwestern Indiana, 8 mi/14.5 km west of Gary, on Lake Michigan*

1850 Gibson Inn established on Michigan Central Railroad; **1851** area settled by Ernest and Caroline Holman; **1869** State Line Slaughterhouse built by George H. Hammond; **1875** town founded; **1881** Hohman Opera House built; **1882** Nickel Plate Railroad reaches town; **1883** incorporated as a town; **1884** incorporated as a city; **1901** Hammond Packing House destroyed by fire; **1905** Carnegie Library built; **1935** city hall built; **1951** Purdue University Calumet Campus established; **1996** Empress Casino opened; **2000** federal courthouse completed.

Hartford City *Blackford County* *Eastern Indiana, 60 mi/97 km northeast of Indianapolis*

1832 area first settled; **1838** Blackford County formed; **1839** town platted, founded as county seat, originally named Hartford; **1840s** town renamed Hartford City; **1867** incorporated as a town; **1890s** natural gas discovery brings prosperity to area; **1893** incorporated as a city; **1895** county courthouse completed.

Huntington *Huntington County* *Northeastern Indiana, 22 mi/35 km southwest of Fort Wayne*

1831 town founded; **1832** Huntington County formed; town becomes county seat, named for Samuel Huntington, member of First Continental Congress; **c.1835** La Fontaine Homestead built; **1846** Miami Native Americans removed from area; **1848** incorporated as a town; **1873** incorporated as a city; **1898** Huntington College established; **1906** county courthouse completed; **1912** Sunday Visitor Publishing House founded; **1925** Victory Noll Missionary School founded; **1968** Huntington Lake formed by dam on Wabash River to southeast; **March 1, 1968** town becomes first in Bell Telephone System to adopt 9-1-1 emergency phone number, home of Ed Roush, "Father of 9-1-1" (born 1920).

Indianapolis *Marion County* *Central Indiana, 155 mi/249 km south-southeast of Chicago*

Dec. 11, 1816 Indiana becomes 19th state; **1819** George Pogue becomes first settler; **1820** town founded by Pogue, John McCormick, others, many from Connersville, Indiana; settlement called Fall Creek by travelers; **1821** new site selected as state capital at center of state, named Indianapolis; Marion County formed; town becomes county seat; **1822** *Gazette* newspaper founded; **1824** first county courthouse built, used later as state capitol; **1825** state capital moved from Corydon; **1830** National Road built east-west through town; **1836** incorporated as a town; **1839** Central Canal completed, branch of Wabash & Erie Canal; **1843** Indiana School for the Deaf founded; **1846** Indiana School for the Blind founded; **1847** Madison Railroad arrives; incorporated as a city; **1851** Marian College established; **1852** first annual Indiana State Fair held; **1853** first Union Station built, rebuilt 1888; **1854** Mannerchor concert group founded by German immigrants; **1855** Butler University established; **1857** Christ Episcopal Church built; **1864** military court held for leaders of Knights of the Golden Circle, Indiana group, some of them prominent citizens, that aided Confederate cause, several sentenced to death for treason, commuted by U.S. Supreme Court; **1865** post-Civil War economic boom begins; **1869** *Indianapolis Star* newspaper founded; **July 29, 1869** novelist, playwright Booth Tarkington born (died 1946); **1872** Benjamin Harrison Home built by Gen. Harrison 18 years after coming to city, lived here until his death 1901; **Jan. 14, 1871** Louis McHenry Howe born, confidant of Pres. Franklin D. Roosevelt (died 1936); **1877** Indianapolis Stockyards opened; nation's first Belt Railroad built around city; **1888** state capitol building completed; **1891** John Herron Art Institute opened; **Oct. 5, 1895** World War II Gen. Walter Bedell Smith born (died 1961); **March 13, 1901** Pres. Benjamin Harrison dies at age 67; **1902** Indiana Central College established, later becomes University of Indianapolis; soldiers and sailors monument completed; **1903** *Indianapolis Star* newspaper founded; Fort Benjamin Harrison Army Base established to northeast; Columbia Conserve Plant, maker of canned soups, founded by Hapgood family; **June 22, 1903** notorious criminal John Dillinger born, shot and killed July 22, 1934, at Biograph Theatre, Chicago; **Oct. 7, 1905** Phillies baseball player Chuck Klein born (died 1958); **1907** Indiana Girls' School established out of Indiana Reformatory Institution for Women and Girls; **1911** first Indianapolis 500 auto race held at suburb of Speedway to west; **1915** Civic Theater organized; **1917** Public Library built; **Nov. 11, 1922** author Kurt Vonnegut, Jr. born; **July 4, 1927** cornerstone of Memorial Hall laid by Gen. John J. Pershing in World War Memorial Plaza; **1929** Scottish Rite Cathedral built; **1930** Indianapolis Symphony Orchestra founded; **1931** Weir Cook Field airport established; Veterans' Hospital built; **1934** state library built; **1937** Lockefield Gardens Apartments slum clearance project completed; **Feb. 4, 1947** Vice-Pres. Dan Quayle born; **Apr. 12, 1948** talk show host David Lettermen born; **Oct. 31, 1950** newscaster Jane Pauley born; **Oct. 31, 1963** gas explosion at State Fair Coliseum during ice show kills 73, injures 335; **1964** Indianapolis Zoo opened, reopened 1988 at White River Park; **1967** Indiana Pacers basketball team established; **1969** Indiana University-Purdue University Indianapolis Campus established; **Jan. 1970** City of Indianapolis and Marion County consolidate, several municipalities remain separately incorporated; **1972** expansion of Weir Cook Airport completed, becomes Indianapolis International Airport; Indiana Convention Center opened; **1974** Market Square Arena opened; **1981** 38-story American United Life Center building completed; **1983** Hoosier Dome football stadium completed, added to Convention Center, later renamed RCA Dome; **1984** Colts football team moves here from Baltimore; **1989** Eiteljorg Museum of American Indian and Western Art opened; **1990** 51-story Bank One Tower completed; **July 7, 2001** Market Square Arena imploded.

Jasper *Dubois County* Southwestern Indiana, *97 mi/156 km south-southwest of Indianapolis*

1817 Dubois County formed; **1818** town founded by Germans; **1830** town platted; **1866** Enlow's Mill built;

incorporated as a town; **1868** St. Joseph's Catholic Church built, completed c.1872; **1910** county courthouse built; **1915** incorporated as a city; **Feb. 14, 1934** actress Florence Henderson born at Dale to south.

Jeffersonville *Clark County* Southern Indiana, *2 mi/3.2 km northeast of Louisville, Kentucky, on Ohio River*

1786 Fort Finney established, later renamed Fort Steuben; **1801** Clark County formed; **1802** town founded as county seat by William Henry Harrison and other members of George Rogers Clark's Northwest Expedition; town plan suggested by Pres. Thomas Jefferson; **1807** incorporated as a town; **1811** county seat moved to Charlestown; **1817** incorporated as a city; **1821** Indiana State Prison established, site used 1923 by Colgate-Palmolive Company; **1834** Howard Shipyards established, closed 1931; **1837** Grisamore House built; **1874** U.S. Quartermaster Depot built; **1876** Ford Plate Glass Company established; **1878** county seat moved back to Jeffersonville; **1929** Municipal Bridge built across Ohio River to Louisville, renamed George Rogers Clark Bridge 1949; **1937** city inundated by Great Ohio Flood; **Dec. 1963** John F. Kennedy Memorial Bridge (I-65) completed; **1971** county courthouse built.

Kendallville *Noble County* Northeastern Indiana, *25 mi/40 km north-northwest of Fort Wayne*

1833 David Bundle becomes first settler, converts his log cabin into the Bundle Tavern; **1839** town founded; **1856** foundry established; **1857** New York Central Railroad reaches town; **1863** incorporated as a town; **1865** Flint and Walling Manufacturing Company founded, maker of windmills and pumps; **1866** incorporated as a city; **1907** interurban train reaches city from Fort Wayne.

Kentland *Newton County* Northwestern Indiana, *53 mi/85 km south-southwest of Gary*

1859 Newton County formed, last county formed in Indiana; **1860** town founded as county seat by Alexander Kent; **Feb. 9, 1866** author George Ade born (died 1944); **1868** town incorporated; **1870** fire destroys 15 businesses; **1906** county courthouse built.

Knox *Starke County* Northern Indiana, *40 mi/64 km southeast of Gary*

1850 Starke County formed; **1851** town founded; **1871** incorporated as a town; **1882** Nickel Plate Railroad reaches town; **1897** county courthouse built; **1956** incorporated as a city; **1967** city hall built.

Kokomo *Howard County* North central Indiana, *46 mi/74 km north of Indianapolis*

1844 Howard County formed; town founded as county seat; **1853** Peru & Indianapolis Railroad reaches town; **1865** incorporated as a city; **1886** natural gas discovered;

1894 Elwood Haynes invents clutch-operated automobile; **1932** Kokomo Junior College established, becomes Indiana University at Kokomo 1945; **1937** county courthouse built.

La Porte *La Porte County* *Northern Indiana, 30 mi/48 km east of Gary*

1830 site on Michigan Road first settled; **1832** La Porte County formed; town founded as county seat; **1835** incorporated as a town; **1852** incorporated as a city; **1863** La Porte-Daniels Woolen Mills founded; Camp Anderson established as Union training camp; **1892** county courthouse built; **1907** Interlaken Experimental School opened, moved to Silver Lake 1911; **1913** Rumely Hotel opened; **1978** County Complex opened.

Lafayette *Tippecanoe County* *Western Indiana, 55 mi/89 km northwest of Indianapolis*

Nov. 7, 1811 Gen. William Henry Harrison defeats Native Americans in Battle of Tippecanoe to north, Col. Jo Daviess killed; **1825** town founded on Wabash River by river pilot William Digby, named for General Lafayette; **1826** Tippecanoe County formed; town becomes county seat; **1832** Lake Hotel opened; **1837** incorporated as a town; **1843** Wabash & Erie Canal reaches town; **1853** incorporated as a city; **1860s** four railroad lines begin serving city; **1884** county courthouse completed; **July 1, 1934** movie producer Sidney Pollack born.

Lagrange *Lagrange County* *Northeastern Indiana, 40 mi/64 km north-northwest of Fort Wayne*

1832 Lagrange County formed; Howe (Lima) becomes first county seat; **1836** town founded, named for General Lafayette's French estate; **1838** ague epidemic empties region to west; **1844** county seat moved to Lagrange; **1855** town incorporated; **1879** third county courthouse completed; **1926** Wainwright Band and Orchestra Camp founded at Oliver Lake to south, later renamed Limberlost Camps.

Lanesville *Harrison County* *See* **Corydon (1832)**

Lawrenceburg *Dearborn County* *Southeastern Indiana, 78 mi/126 km southeast of Indianapolis*

1801 town founded on Ohio River by Capt. Samuel C. Vance; **1803** Dearborn County formed; town becomes county seat; **1815** town incorporated; **1818** Vance-Tousey House built; **1819** three-story Grand Hotel built, considered Indiana's first "skyscraper"; **May 23, 1820** civil engineer James Buchanan Eads born (died 1887); **1836** county seat moved to Wilmington, returned to Lawrenceburg 1844; **1851** Joseph E. Seagram and Sons establish one of several distilleries in town, becomes world's largest; **July 13, 1863** Gen. John Morgan's Confederate Raiders ride into Ohio to north after storming through Indiana for five days; **1870** county courthouse built; **1937** floods inundate town.

Leavenworth *Crawford County* *Southern Indiana, 102 mi/102 km south of Indianapolis*

1818 Crawford County formed; town founded on Ohio River as county seat; **1824** David Lyon establishes wood yard to provide fuel for boats, begins shipbuilding 1830; **1843** town incorporated; **July 8, 1863** Gen. John Morgan's Confederate Raiders cross Ohio River from Kentucky, attack Corydon, Morgan captured in eastern Ohio July 26; **1893** county seat moved to English; **1937** Great Ohio Flood destroys town, town relocated to higher ground 1938.

Lebanon *Boone County* *Central Indiana, 23 mi/37 km northwest of Indianapolis*

1830 Boone County formed; town founded; **1832** town becomes county seat; **1853** incorporated as a town; **1871** incorporated as a city; **1905** Lebanon Public Library established; **1911** county courthouse completed.

Liberty *Union County* *Eastern Indiana, 63 mi/101 km east-southeast of Indianapolis*

1821 Union County formed; **1822** town founded; **1823** county seat moved from Brownsville; **May 23, 1824** Union Gen., Rhode Island Sen. Ambrose Burnside born (died 1881); **Sept. 1836** town incorporated; **March 10, 1841** poet Joaquin Miller born, moved to Oregon 1854 (died 1913); **1891** county courthouse built.

Lincoln City *Spencer County* *Southwestern Indiana, 114 mi/183 km south-southwest of Indianapolis*

1816 Thomas Lincoln moves here from Hodgenville, Kentucky, with wife Nancy Hanks and young Abraham and Sarah, builds cabin; **Oct. 1818** Nancy Hanks Lincoln dies of "milch sickness" fever, epidemic affecting people and milch cows; **1819** Thomas Lincoln returns to Kentucky with children, marries Sarah Johnston at Elizabethtown, returns; **1830** Lincolns move to farm near Decatur, Illinois; **1872** town founded.

Logansport *Cass County* *Northern Indiana, 64 mi/103 km north of Indianapolis*

1826 area first settled; **1828** Cass County formed; town founded on Wabash River as county seat; Pioneer Inn built by Alexander Chamberlain; **1831** town incorporated; **1837** Wabash & Erie Canal reaches town; **1838** incorporated as a city; **1844** county courthouse built, renovated 1888, razed 1979; **1855** first railroad arrives; **1861** Camp Logan occupied by army of Col. G. M. Fitch; **May 21, 1872** actor Richard Bennett born in rural Cass County (died 1944); **1888** Logansport State Hospital opened; **1979** county courthouse built.

Madison *Jefferson County* *Southeastern Indiana, 76 mi/122 km south-southeast of Indianapolis*

1805 first settlers arrive; **1809** town founded by Revolutionary War veteran Col. John Paul, named for

Pres. James Madison; **1811** Jefferson County formed; town becomes county seat; Madison Library established; **1817** Schofield Mansion built by Maj. Alexander Lanier; **1818** Sullivan House built; **1824** incorporated as a town; **1830s** riverboat building becomes major industry; **1838** incorporated as a city; **1844** James Lanier Mansion built; **1846** Shrewsbury House built; **1850s** tobacco becomes main agricultural commodity; **1855** third county courthouse built.

Marion *Grant County* *North central Indiana, 56 mi/90 km north-northeast of Indianapolis*

1826 first settled by Martin Boots, John Ballinger, and David Branson; **1831** Grant County formed; town founded as county seat, land donated by Martin Boots and David Branson; **Apr. 17, 1859** Supreme Court Justice Willis Van Devanter born (died 1948); **1867** first railroad reaches town; **1880** county courthouse built; **Jan. 1887** natural gas discovered leading to economic boom; **1889** incorporated as a city; **1890** Marion College established, becomes Indiana Wesleyan University 1920; **1902** Carnegie Library opened.

Martinsville *Morgan County* *Central Indiana, 26 mi/42 km southwest of Indianapolis*

1819 area first settled; **1821** Morgan County formed; **1822** town founded as county seat; **1859** county courthouse built; **1863** town incorporated; **1908** Morgan County Public Library opened; **Oct. 14, 1910** UCLA basketball coach John Wooden born; **Aug. 15, 1933** songwriter Bobby Helms born, wrote "Jingle Bell Rock" (died 1997).

Michigan City *La Porte County* *Northwestern Indiana, 23 mi/37 km east-northeast of Gary*

1832 resort town founded on Lake Michigan, northern terminus of Michigan Road; **1836** incorporated as a city; **1840s** town serves as lake port; **1852** railroad freight car manufacturing begins; **1856** Michigan City Lighthouse built; **1880s** town becomes major lumber distribution center; **1883** Barker Mansion built; **1904** New Lighthouse built, only operating lighthouse in Indiana, automated 1933; **May 7, 1923** actress Anne Baxter born; **1926** World War Memorial dedicated; **July 10, 1933** Gary, Indiana, Mayor Richard Hatcher born; **Sept. 26, 1933** ten escapees from Indiana State Prison raid county jail, kill sheriff, free villain John Dillinger, captured in Arizona.

Mishawaka *Saint Joseph County* *Northern Indiana, 4 mi/6.4 km east of South Bend*

c.1830 town settled; bog iron discovered in area; **1831** town founded, originally named St. Joseph Iron Works; **1835** two adjacent communities merge with original town, incorporated as Mishawaka; **June 27, 1852** 32 killed in Great Mishawaka Train Wreck; **Sept. 5, 1872** fire destroys business district; **1899** incorporated as a city; **1919–1920**

wave of Belgian immigrants arrive; **1947** Bethel College established.

Mitchell *Lawrence County* *South central Indiana, 69 mi/111 km south-southwest of Indianapolis*

1813 first settlers arrive; **1853** Louisville, New Albany & Salem (Monon) Railroad reaches site; town founded; **1856** Ohio & Mississippi Railroad (Baltimore & Ohio) Railroad reaches town forming junction; town named for railroad engineer O. M. Mitchell; **1864** incorporated as a town; **1907** incorporated as a city; **1917** Mitchell Public Library founded; **Apr. 3, 1926** astronaut Virgil "Gus" Grissom born, killed Jan. 27, 1967, in Apollo fire on launch pad.

Monticello *White County* *Northern Indiana, 70 mi/113 km north-northwest of Indianapolis*

1829 first settlers arrive; **1834** White County formed; town founded on Tippecanoe River as county seat; **1853** town incorporated; **1854** Louisville, New Albany & Chicago Railroad built; **1894** third county courthouse built; **1923** Shafer Lake formed on Tippecanoe River by Norway Dam to north; **1925** Freeman Lake formed on Tippecanoe River by Oakdale Dam to south; **Apr. 3, 1974** tornado destroys large part of town, including courthouse; **1975** new government building built, replaces courthouse.

Mount Vernon *Posey County* *Southwestern Indiana, 148 mi/238 km southwest of Indianapolis*

1805 town founded on Ohio River, east of Wabash River, by Andrew McFadden, named McFadden's Bluff; **1814** Posey County formed; Blackford becomes first county seat, seat moved to Springfield 1817; **1816** town renamed; **1825** county seat moved to Mount Vernon; **1832** incorporated as a town; **1865** incorporated as a city; **1869** county courthouse built; **1938** oil discovered in Wabash River valley to west.

Muncie *Delaware County* *Eastern Indiana, 46 mi/74 km northeast of Indianapolis*

1818 Native Americans removed by Treaty of St. Mary's; first white settlers arrive; **1827** Delaware County formed; town founded as county seat, named Munseytown for Munsee peoples; **1845** town renamed Muncie; **1854** incorporated as a town; **1865** incorporated as a city; **1876** natural gas deposit discovered in area, depleted early 1900s; **1886** Ball Brothers Glass Company, maker of canning jars, moves from Buffalo, New York; **1894** glass factory founded, taken over by Owens-Illinois Glass Company 1933; **1901** Indiana Steel and Wire Mill founded; **1918** Ball State University established; **1924** sociologists Robert and Helen Merrell Lynd publish book *Middletown*, synopsis of life in Muncie, Depression-era follow-up study published as *Middletown in Transition* 1937; **1969** county courthouse completed.

Nashville *Brown County* *South central Indiana, 36 mi/58 km south of Indianapolis*

1836 Brown County formed; town founded as county seat; **1837** log jail built; **1872** town incorporated; **1874** county courthouse built; **1898** Country Doctor's Office built.

New Albany *Floyd County* *Southern Indiana, 3 mi/4.8 km northwest of Louisville, Kentucky*

Dec. 1806 two boats built by Maj. Davis Floyd depart from mouth of Silver Creek under command of Aaron Burr and Harman Blennerhassett, Floyd believing they were invading Mexico, unaware of plot to establish empire on lower Mississippi River; **1808** land grant made to Col. John Paul of Madison, seeking to use Falls of the Ohio for water power; **1813** town founded on Ohio River by Joel, Nathaniel, and Abner Scribner of New York, named for Albany, New York; **1814** Scribner House built by Joel Scribner; **1819** Floyd County formed; incorporated as a town; **1827** Black Horse Tavern established by Darius Genung, also called Hole in the Wall for discreet entranceway in basement back wall; **1839** incorporated as a city; **1841** Anderson Female Seminary founded; **1853** Sloan House built by Dr. John Sloan; **1862** National Soldiers' Cemetery established, later becomes New Albany National Cemetery; **July 1863** townspeople gather on bluffs to defend town against Confederate Gen. John Morgan's Raiders; **1866** steamboat *Robert E. Lee* built by Hill and Company shipbuilders; **1869** Culbertson Mansion built by philanthropist William S. Culbertson; **Oct. 20, 1890** Indiana Sen., Supreme Court Justice Sherman Minton born at Georgetown to west (died 1965); **Sept. 26, 1892** sociologist Robert Stoughton Lynd born, observed life in Midwest town using Muncie as subject (died 1970); **1912** Kentucky and Indiana Bridge completed; **March 23, 1917** tornado ravages town, 45 killed; **Jan. 1937** record flooding of Ohio River inundates half of city; **1941** Indiana University Southeast Campus established; **1960** county courthouse built; **1964** Sherman Milton Bridge (I-64) completed.

New Carlisle *Saint Joseph County* *Northern Indiana, 12 mi/19 km west-northwest of South Bend*

1835 town platted by Richard R. Carlisle; **1839** incorporated as a town; **1852** Lake Shore Railroad reaches town; **1866** incorporated as a city; **Apr. 16, 1867** airplane inventor Wilbur Wright born (died 1912), family moved to Dayton, Ohio, before birth of Orville.

New Castle *Henry County* *Eastern Indiana, 40 mi/64 km east-northeast of Indianapolis*

1821 Henry County formed; **1823** town founded as county seat; **1839** incorporated as a town; **1869** county courthouse completed, begun 1865.

New Harmony *Posey County* *Southwestern Indiana, 140 mi/225 km southwest of Indianapolis*

1814 New Harmony Colony founded on Wabash River by Harmony Society led by George Rapp (1770–1847); town named Harmonie; Rapp-Maclure House built; **summer 1815** colony members arrive from Pennsylvania; Fauntleroy House built; **c.1820** Rappites develop extensive vineyards, flocks of sheep, cattle herds; **1825** following discord within colony, Rappites sell land to Robert Owen of England, return to Pennsylvania; **Dec. 1825** 1,000 new settlers arrive at Owen's New Harmony; *New Harmony Gazette* newspaper founded; **Jan. 26, 1826** efforts of William Maclure to transform Owen's ideal social order into educational laboratory leads to arrival of "Boatload of Knowledge" with group of well-known educators; **1827** social experiment declared failure by Owen, returns to England; **1829** *Gazette* newspaper moved to New York, becomes *Free Enquirer*; **Apr. 1838** Workingmen's Institute founded by William Maclure; **1839** town develops into major scientific center; U.S. Geological Survey headquarters established; **1850** town incorporated; **1856** Geological Survey moved to Washington, D.C.; **1859** Minerva Club founded by Constance Fauntleroy, first women's club in U.S.; Owen House built by David Dale Owen; **1874** Economy Society, followers of late George Rapp, builds new quarters for Workingmen's Institute and its library; **1938** New Harmony Memorial Commission organized by Indiana legislature for restoration of historic structures.

New Whiteland *Johnson County* *See* **Franklin (1994)**

Newburgh *Warrick County* *Southwestern Indiana, 9 mi/14.5 km east of Evansville, on Ohio River*

1803 town settled by John Sprinkle; **1818** town founded; **1832** town incorporated; **c.1840** Wies House built; **1850** coal mining begins; **July 17, 1862** town raided, captured for five hours by Confederate forces under Gen. Adam R. Johnson; **1939** excavations of Angel Mounds yield prehistoric village of c.5,000 people.

Noblesville *Hamilton County* *Central Indiana, 18 mi/29 km north-northeast of Indianapolis*

1818 William Conner opens trading post to south; **1823** Hamilton County formed; town founded by Indian trader William Conner; **1824** town becomes county seat; **1851** incorporated as town; **1879** county courthouse built; **1887** incorporated as a city; **1960** Indiana Transportation Museum founded; **1992** Judicial Center built.

North Manchester *Wabash County* *Northern Indiana, 31 mi/50 km west of Fort Wayne*

1837 town founded by members of German Dunkers religious sect; **1846** Zion Lutheran Church founded; **March 14, 1854** Vice-Pres. Thomas Riley Marshall born, served under President Wilson (died 1975); **1874** town incorporated; **1889** Manchester College established; **1930** Estelle Peabody Memorial Home founded.

Ogden Dunes *Porter County* *Northwestern Indiana, 7 mi/11.3 km east of Gary, on Lake Michigan*

1909 South Shore Railroad reaches site; town founded, originally named Wickliffe; **1916** fishermen discover hermit Alice Gray living in driftwood hut, called "Diana of the Dunes," wide publicity leads to her marriage to Texan 1922 who lives with her, but she dies of illness 1925 before leaving her lakeside home; **1925** town incorporated; **1927** highest ski jump in U.S., 590 ft/180 m high, built on Sky Hill, dismantled 1932.

Oxford *Benton County* *Western Indiana, 73 mi/ 117 km northwest of Indianapolis*

1840 Benton County formed; town founded as county seat; **1855** county courthouse built; **1865** Oxford Academy founded; **1869** town incorporated; **1875** county seat moved to Fowler; **Dec. 1896** racehorse Dan Patch born, broke mile record 1907 at one minute, 55 seconds, Minnesota State Fair, record held until 1938.

Paoli *Orange County* *Southern Indiana, 80 mi/ 129 km south-southwest of Indianapolis*

1805 Pivot Point established 7 mi/11.3 km to south, point from which all Indiana boundaries are measured; **1807** town settled; **1815** Lick Creek Friends Church built; **1816** Orange County formed; town founded as county seat; **1825** William Bowles House built; **1850** county courthouse built; **1869** town incorporated.

Peru *Miami County* *Northern Indiana, 63 mi/ 101 km north of Indianapolis*

May 15, 1812 Osage Chief Tecumseh calls final Great Council of the Mississinewa to unite native peoples against Americans, failing to do so, Tecumseh moves to Canada; **Dec. 18, 1812** Miamis under Francis Godfroy make final stand against white settlers in Battle of Mississinewa, 30 Native Americans killed, eight whites killed; **1832** Miami County formed; **1834** town founded as county seat; **1837** Western Hotel built, becomes Bearss Hotel; **1848** incorporated as a city; **1883** Ben Wallace and James Anderson establish staged exhibition, becomes Hagenbeck-Wallace Circus; **June 9, 1893** composer Cole Porter born (died 1964); **1910** third county courthouse built; **1967** Mississinewa Lake formed by dam on Mississinewa River to east.

Petersburg *Pike County* *Southwestern Indiana, 100 mi/161 km southwest of Indianapolis*

1817 Pike County formed; town founded as county seat, named for landowner Peter Brenton; **1860s** coal discovered in county; **1885** town incorporated; **1921** county courthouse built.

Plainfield *Hendricks County* *Central Indiana, 11 mi/18 km west-southwest of Indianapolis*

1839 town platted by Levi Jessup and Elias Hadley; incorporated as a town; **Dec. 1, 1854** zoologist William Temple Hornaday born (died 1937); **1867** Indiana Boys' School founded; **1907** incorporated as a city; **Feb. 12, 1919** actor Forrest Tucker born (died 1986).

Plymouth *Marshall County* *Northern Indiana, 22 mi/35 km south of South Bend*

1834 town founded; **1835** Marshall County formed; town becomes county seat; **1838** last Potawatomi Chief Menominee and 859 of his people allowed final visit to grave sites before making trek to Kansas; **1851** incorporated as a town; **1872** second county courthouse built; **1873** incorporated as a city; **1879** County Jail built; **Sept. 4, 1909** Chief Menominee monument erected, dedicated to removal of Native Americans.

Portland *Jay County* *Eastern Indiana, 72 mi/ 116 km northeast of Indianapolis*

1836 Jay County formed, named for Chief Justice John Jay; **1837** town founded; **1843** town incorporated; **Oct. 14, 1857** Elwood Haynes born, invented automobile clutch (died 1925); **1883** incorporated as a city; **Jan. 20, 1903** actor Leon Ames born (died 1993); **1919** county courthouse completed; **July 1, 1941** choreographer Twyla Tharp born.

Princeton *Gibson County* *Southwestern Indiana, 116 mi/187 km southwest of Indianapolis*

1812 area first settled; **1813** Gibson County formed; **1814** town founded as county seat by Capt. William Prince; **1818** incorporated as a town; **1827** young Abraham Lincoln brings wool to Evens Mill; **1884** incorporated as a city; **July 12, 1893** fire destroys part of business district; **March 18, 1925** Tri-State Tornado (Mo., Ill., Ind.) damages 25 percent of town near end of 220-mi/354-km path, 20 killed locally, total 695 killed; **1884** third county courthouse built.

Rensselaer *Jasper County* *Northwestern Indiana, 43 mi/69 km south-southeast of Gary*

1835 Jasper County formed; **1836** first settlers arrive; **1837** town founded as county seat by James Van Rensselaer of Utica, New York; Van Rensselaer builds grist mill; **1858** incorporated as a town; **1897** incorporated as a city; **1898** county courthouse completed; **July 14, 1936** highest temperature ever recorded in Indiana reached, 116°F/ 47°C; **Oct. 31, 1994** American Airlines Eagle commuter plane crashes in soybean field at Roselawn to northwest killing 68.

Richmond *Wayne County   Eastern Indiana, 63 mi/ 101 km east of Indianapolis*

1805 town founded by veterans of George Rogers Clark capture of Fort Sackville, Vincennes, Indiana; **1810** Wayne County formed; Centerville becomes first county seat; **1812** Pioneer Schoolhouse built; **1816** town platted; **1818** incorporated as a town; **1822** Gray Gables house built as tavern; **1840** incorporated as a city; **1847** Earlham College established; **1873** county seat moved from Centerville; **1893** county courthouse built; **1964** motor home production begun by Tom Raper; **Apr. 6, 1968** sports store explosion kills 43; **1971** Indiana University East Campus established.

Rising Sun *Ohio County   Southeastern Indiana, 82 mi/132 km southeast of Indianapolis, on Ohio River*

1798 area first settled by whites; **1814** town founded on Ohio River, named for grand sunrises afforded this eastward-facing river town; **1827** Presbyterian seminary founded; **1844** Ohio County formed; town becomes county seat; **1845** county courthouse built; **1849** town incorporated.

Roanoke *Huntington County   Northeastern Indiana, 14 mi/23 km southwest of Fort Wayne*

1810 Kilsoquah born, granddaughter of Miami Chief Little Turtle, died Sept. 1915 at 105 years of age; **July 4, 1835** Wabash & Erie Canal opened from Fort Wayne to nearby Dickey Lock; **1837** town platted by James Darrow; **1850** town incorporated; **1856** Wabash Railroad reaches town; **1861** Roanoke Classical Seminary founded.

Rochester *Fulton County   Northern Indiana, 84 mi/ 135 km north of Indianapolis*

1831 town founded on Lake Manitou; **1835** Fulton County formed; **1836** town becomes county seat; **1853** incorporated as a town; **1896** third county courthouse built; **1910** incorporated as a city.

Rockport *Spencer County   Southwestern Indiana, 130 mi/209 km south-southwest of Indianapolis*

1806 first settled by Daniel Grass; **1808** James Lankford arrives, lives in cave with wife and daughter; **1818** Spencer County formed; town founded on Ohio River as county seat; **1828** Abraham Lincoln, living 16 mi/26 km to north with father and stepmother, hired by James Gentry to accompany son on flatboat with produce to New Orleans; **1838** town incorporated; **1921** fifth county courthouse completed; **1928** Lock & Dam No. 47 built on Ohio River.

Rockville *Parke County   Western Indiana, 55 mi/ 89 km west of Indianapolis*

Sept. 30, 1809 Ten O'Clock Line established in treaty with Miami and Delaware peoples at Fort Wayne, Native Americans moved south of line running parallel to shadow cast at 10 o'clock on this date, **1821** Parke County formed; **1823** town founded as county seat; **1854** town incorporated; **1882** county courthouse completed; **1883** Railroad Depot built; **1957** first Covered Bridge festival held, celebrating county's 32 covered bridges.

Roselawn *Newton County   See* **Rensselaer (1994)**

Rushville *Rush County   Eastern Indiana, 37 mi/ 60 km east-southeast of Indianapolis*

1821 Rush County formed; **1822** town founded, named for Benjamin F. Rush, signer of Declaration of Independence; **1828** Laughlin Academy founded; **c.1842** incorporated as a town; **1883** incorporated as a city; **1896** county courthouse built.

Salem *Washington County   Southern Indiana, 75 mi/121 km south of Indianapolis*

1808 Beck's Mill built to south on Blue River; **1813** Washington County formed; **1814** town founded as county seat by settlers of German origin; **1814** incorporated as a town; **1816** Hucksite Quaker Meeting House built to northeast; **1833** town's growth slowed by cholera epidemic; county overrun with countless squirrels, plague ends abruptly one day for reasons unknown; **Oct. 8, 1838** Secretary of State John Hay born, served under Presidents McKinley and Theodore Roosevelt (died 1905); **June 10, 1863** Confederate Gen. John Morgan's Raiders burn bridges, depot, loot stores, pursued by Federal cavalry, abandon plans to attack Indianapolis as they ride north, turn eastward; **1887** county courthouse built; **1936** incorporated as a city.

Santa Claus *Spencer County   Southwestern Indiana, 113 mi/182 km south-southwest of Indianapolis*

Dec. 1846 town founded, name suggestion made in jest during Christmas season; **1852** name formally adopted by post office after Santa Fe is ruled out; **1935** beloved postmaster Jim Martin dies, acted as Santa Claus to entire nation by applying postmark to holiday mail since 1914; **1967** town incorporated.

Scottsburg *Scott County   Southern Indiana, 71 mi/ 114 km south-southeast of Indianapolis*

Sept. 3, 1812 band of Shawnee and Delaware attack village of Pigeon Roost (founded 1809), kill 24, including 16 children; **1820** Scott County formed; Lexington becomes first county seat; **1871** town founded; county seat moved to Scottsburg; **1874** second county courthouse built; **1884** town incorporated.

Seymour *Jackson County   Southern Indiana, 54 mi/87 km south-southeast of Indianapolis*

1816 James Shields becomes first settler; **1852** Baltimore & Ohio Railroad built; town founded; **1864** incorporated as a city; **1928** Swope Memorial Art Gallery founded through bequest of H. Vance Swope; **Oct. 7, 1951** singer John Cougar Mellencamp born.

Shelbyville   *Shelby County*   *Central Indiana, 25 mi/ 40 km southeast of Indianapolis*

1821 Shelby County formed; **1822** town founded as county seat, named for Isaac Shelby, first governor of Kentucky; **1834** first railroad in Indiana built, 1.5 mi/ 2.4 km line owned by Judge W. J. Peasley; **1860** town incorporated; **1937** county courthouse completed; **Dec. 18, 1964** nursing home fire at Fountaintown to north, 30 killed; **Sept. 9, 1969** Allegheny jet collides with plane flown by student pilot, all 82 killed.

Shoals   *Martin County*   *Southwestern Indiana, 78 mi/126 km south-southwest of Indianapolis*

1816 town founded at shallow ford on East Fork White River; **1820** Martin County formed; Hindostan becomes first county seat; **1867** town incorporated as Memphis; **1872** reincorporated as Shoals; **1876** county seat moved from West Shoals, sixth county seat move; **1877** county courthouse built.

South Bend   *Saint Joseph County*   *Northern Indiana, 53 mi/85 km east of Gary*

Dec. 5, 1679 La Salle makes portage between St. Joseph and Kankakee Rivers; **May 1681** on second journey, La Salle makes peace treaty with Miami and Illinois peoples under Council Oak; **1805** boundary dispute between Michigan on north and Indiana and Ohio on south resolved by U.S. Congress, ruled against Michigan, originated with surveying error; **1820** Pierre Navarre establishes trading post; **1827** Col. Lathrop Taylor opens trading post, founds town of St. Joseph's; **1829** town name changed to Southold; **1830** St. Joseph County formed; town founded, renamed South Bend; **1831** town becomes county seat; **1835** incorporated as a town; **1838** Potawatomis removed to Kansas; **1842** University of Notre Dame established; **1844** St. Mary's College established; **1852** Henry and Clement Studebaker arrive, establish wagon and blacksmith shop; **1856** James Oliver and T. M. Bissel establish Oliver Farm Equipment Company, maker of plows; **1864** James Oliver invents process for making plow moldboards of hardened steel; **1865** incorporated as a city; **1898** third county courthouse built; **1899** Studebaker begins manufacture of automobiles; **1922** Indiana University at South Bend established; **1931** Bendix Airport built to west, becomes Michiana Regional Transportation Center 1974; **March 31, 1931** famed Notre Dame football coach Knute Rockne killed in airplane crash; **June 11, 1936** actor Chad Everett born; **1963** Studebaker plant closed; **1982** Studebaker National Museum established; **Aug. 1995** National College Football Hall of Fame opened.

Speedway   *Marion County*   *Central Indiana, suburb 4 mi/6.4 km west-northwest of Indianapolis*

1911 first Indianapolis 500 auto race held; **1912** town platted around 500 Speedway by Carl Fisher, James T. Allison, and Frank H. Wheeler; town founding clause forbids sale of any property to African-Americans; **1926** town incorporated; **May 30, 1960** two killed, more than 70 injured when spectator scaffold collapses at Indianapolis Speedway; **Jan. 1970** municipality rejects participation in Indianapolis-Marion County merger.

Spencer   *Owen County*   *Southwest central Indiana, 42 mi/68 km southwest of Indianapolis*

1815 town settled; **1818** Owen County formed; town founded on White River as county seat, named for Capt. Spencer of Kentucky killed in Battle of Tippecanoe; **1866** town incorporated; **July 8, 1869** poet, dramatist William Vaughn Moody born (died 1910); **1911** county courthouse built; **1957** Ten O'Clock Line marker erected near Gosport to northeast commemorating 1809 treaty between Native Americans and William Henry Harrison, north-south demarcation line determined by 10 o'clock shadow of Miami Chief Little Turtle's spear stuck in ground.

Sullivan   *Sullivan County*   *Western Indiana, 76 mi/ 122 km southwest of Indianapolis*

1816 Sullivan County formed; **1842** town founded; county seat moved from Merom; **1853** town incorporated; **Aug. 27, 1871** novelist Theodore Dreiser born (died 1945); **Nov. 5, 1879** movie producer William H. Hays born (died 1954); **Feb. 21, 1925** gas explosion at City Coal Mine kills 51, only four rescued; **1927** county courthouse built; **Jan. 28, 1931** coal mine accident at Dugger to east, 28 killed.

Tell City   *Perry County*   *Southern Indiana, 122 mi/ 196 km south-southwest of Indianapolis, on Ohio River*

1857 town founded by Swiss immigrants, named for legendary William Tell; **1858** town incorporated; **1888** Southern Railway reaches town; **1889** steamboat *Tell City* begins service between Louisville and Evansville until 1916; **March 17, 1960** Northwest Electra airplane explodes over town killing all 63 on board.

Terre Haute   *Vigo County*   *Western Indiana, 65 mi/105 km west-southwest of Indianapolis*

1720 French establish settlement on Wabash River, abandoned 1763; **1811** Fort Harrison built on Wabash River to north; first American settlers arrive; **1816** town founded by Indiana and Kentucky business interests; **1818** Vigo County formed, named for Col. Francis Vigo, financial supporter of Gen. George Rogers Clark's conquest of Northwest Territory; town becomes county seat; **1822** steamboat *Florence* arrives, first to ply Wabash River; **1830** Preston House built; **1832** incorporated as a town; **1838** National Road built through town; **1840** St. Mary-of-the-Woods College established at West Terre

Haute; **1849** Wabash & Erie Canal completed to Terre Haute; **1852** Terre Haute, Indianapolis & Richmond Railroad reaches town; **1853** incorporated as a city; **Nov. 5, 1855** labor leader Eugene V. Debs born, organizer of Social Democratic party, ran for president as Socialist (died 1926); **1858** Chicago & Eastern Illinois Railroad built from Evansville; **Apr. 22, 1859** songwriter Paul Dresser born, wrote Indiana State Song (died 1906); **1865** Indiana State University established; **1874** Rose-Hulman Institute of Technology established; **c.1875** coal mining begins; **1888** second county courthouse built; **1906** Emeline Fairbanks Public Library opened; **May 23, 1910** entertainer Scatman Crothers born (died 1986); **1935** Temple Israel established; **July 23, 1935** National Guardsmen use tear gas on 1,800 coal strikers, strike called off; **1940** Terre Haute Federal Penitentiary completed; **March 2, 1961** explosion at Vining Coal Mine, 22 killed; **Oct. 3, 1962** packing plant explosion kills 16; **Jan. 2, 1963** second packing plant explosion kills 16, injures 52; **June 11, 2001** Timothy McVeigh executed by lethal injection for bombing of Murrah Federal Office Building in Oklahoma City Apr. 19, 1995, killing 168.

Tipton *Tipton County* *Central Indiana, 33 mi/ 53 km north of Indianapolis*

1839 town founded; **1844** Tipton County formed; town becomes county seat; **1894** third county courthouse built; **1902** Tipton County Library founded; **1953** town incorporated.

Troy *Perry County* *Southern Indiana, 120 mi/ 193 km south-southwest of Indianapolis, on Ohio River*

1814 Perry County formed; **1815** town founded as county seat; **1818** county seat moved to Rome; **1825** young Abraham Lincoln operates small scow ferry, taking passengers to midstream to board boats, taken to court in Kentucky for operating without license, ruled not guilty since he was not ferrying across entire river, enters law as result of experience; **1837** town incorporated; **1838** Indiana Pottery Company established.

Valparaiso *Porter County* *Northwestern Indiana, 15 mi/24 km southeast of Gary*

1832 land transferred from Potawatomi people; **1835** Porter County formed; **1836** town founded as county seat, named Portersville; **1837** town renamed Valparaiso; **1850** incorporated as a town; **1859** Valparaiso Male and Female College established by Methodists, renamed Valparaiso College 1900, Valparaiso University 1906, acquired by Lutheran Church 1925; **1865** incorporated as a city; **1883** county courthouse built, rebuilt after 1934 fire.

Vernon *Jennings County* *Southeastern Indiana, 58 mi/93 km south-southeast of Indianapolis*

1815 town founded; **1816** Jennings County formed; town becomes county seat; **1817** town incorporated; **1837**

Semon Mill built; **1861** county courthouse completed; **July 11, 1863** Confederate Gen. John Morgan's Raiders overwhelmed by town militia, first offers truce, rejected, withdraws after small skirmish.

Versailles *Ripley County* *Southeastern Indiana, 63 mi/101 km southeast of Indianapolis*

1816 Ripley County formed; **1819** town founded as county seat; **1845** town incorporated; **1852** county courthouse built; **July 12, 1863** Confederate Gen. John Morgan passes through town with his Morgan's Raiders, county treasurer's office looted, Morgan captured near Lisbon, northeastern Ohio, July 26.

Vevay *Switzerland County* *Southeastern Indiana, 85 mi/137 km southeast of Indianapolis, on Ohio River*

1801 town settled by Swiss immigrants, name variation of Swiss town of Vevey; **1813** town founded; **1814** Switzerland County formed; town becomes county seat; **1823** Swiss Inn opened; **c.1835** Morerod House built; **1836** town incorporated; **1837** Hoosier Theater built; **Dec. 10, 1837** writer Edward Eggleston born (died 1902); **1864** second county courthouse completed; **1917** Carnegie Library opened.

Vincennes *Knox County* *Southwestern Indiana, 50 mi/80 km north of Evansville, on Wabash River*

c.1683 French trading post established on Wabash River; **1727** first settlers arrive; **1732** fort built by French, named Fort Vincennes 1736 for Francois Vincennes, burned at stake by Chickasaws; **1763** fort ceded to British, renamed Fort Sackville; **Feb. 1779** George Rogers Clark takes fort; **1787** Northwest Territory created; **1788** Fort Knox built; **1790** Knox County formed; town becomes county seat; **1800** Indiana Territory created from Northwest Territory; Vincennes becomes capital; Legislative Hall built; **1804** William Henry Harrison Mansion built; **1813** capital moved to Corydon; **1814** incorporated as a town; **1822** Bonner-Allen Mansion built by David Bonner; **1826** St. Francis Xavier Catholic Church dedicated; **1836** Ellis Mansion built by Judge Abner T. Ellis; **1843** St. Rose Academy founded; **1852** incorporated as a city; St. John the Baptist Catholic Church completed by Germans; **1857** Ohio & Mississippi Railroad reaches town; **1867** Indianapolis & Vincennes Railroad completed; **1874** county courthouse completed; **1875** coal fields begin production; **1887** city hall built; **1888** Germans organize *Harmonie Verein* singing society; **July 18, 1913** comedian, actor Red Skelton born (died 1997); **1931** Lincoln Memorial Bridge built across Wabash River; **1932** Old Post Museum founded; **June 14, 1936** George Rogers Clark Memorial Building dedicated by Pres. Franklin D. Roosevelt; **July 23, 1966** George Rogers Clark National Historical Park authorized.

Wabash *Wabash County* *Northern Indiana, 68 mi/ 109 km north-northeast of Indianapolis*

Oct. 1826 Treaty of Paradise Springs opens large area to white settlement; **1834** Wabash County formed; town founded on Wabash River as county seat; **1835** Wabash & Erie Canal begun, completed 1853; **1849** incorporated as a town; **1866** incorporated as a city; **1879** county courthouse completed; **1903** Wabash Carnegie Library opened; **1966** Salamonie Lake formed by dam on Salamonie River to east.

Warsaw *Kosciusko County* *Northern Indiana, 34 mi/55 km southeast of South Bend*

1835 Kosciusko County formed, named for Polish hero Thaddeus Kosciusko who aided General Washington during Revolution; **1836** town founded, platted by W. H. Knott; **1848** county courthouse built; **1854** Pittsburgh, Fort Wayne & Chicago Railroad reaches town; incorporated as a town; **1875** incorporated as a city; **1885** Hotel Hays opened; Warsaw Public Library founded; **1947** Warsaw Airport established.

Washington *Daviess County* *Southwestern Indiana, 90 mi/145 km southwest of Indianapolis*

1805 Fort Flora built; town settled; **1815** town platted; **1817** Daviess County formed; town founded as county seat; **1829** incorporated as a town; county courthouse completed; **1843** Van Trees Mansion built by Col. John Van Trees; **1857** Ohio & Mississippi Railroad reaches town; **1871** incorporated as a city.

West Baden Springs *Orange County* See **French Lick (1956)**

West Lafayette *Tippecanoe County* *Western Indiana, 56 mi/90 km northwest of Indianapolis*

1720 Fort Ouiatenon built by French; **1836** town of West Lafayette platted by August Wylie on Wabash River, opposite Lafayette, plan fails: **1855** town of Kingston platted; **1860** town of Chauncey platted; **1867** Kingston merges with Chauncey, incorporated as a town; **1869** Purdue University established; **1886** Indiana State Soldiers Home established; **1888** town renamed West Lafayette; **1924** incorporated as a city.

Williamsport *Warren County* *Western Indiana, 65 mi/105 km northwest of Indianapolis*

1827 Warren County formed; **1828** town founded on Wabash River as county seat, named for Gen. William Henry Harrison; **1853** tavern built on Old Town Hill; **1854** town incorporated; **1856** Wabash Railroad reaches town; town moved from river; **1908** county courthouse completed; **1916** Carnegie Library built.

Winamac *Pulaski County* *Northern Indiana, 86 mi/138 km north-northwest of Indianapolis*

1832 Potawatomi lands ceded to U.S.; **1835** Pulaski County formed; town founded as county seat, named for Potawatomi Chief Winamac; **1868** town incorporated; **1895** county courthouse completed.

Winchester *Randolph County* *Eastern Indiana, 64 mi/103 km east-northeast of Indianapolis*

1812 area first settled by whites; **1818** Randolph County formed; town founded as county seat; incorporated as a town; **1877** county courthouse built; **1888** James A. Moorman Orphans Home founded; **1893** incorporated as a city; **1916** Winchester Speedway established; **1931** nearby Fudge Mounds excavated.

Iowa

North central U.S. Capital and largest city: Des Moines.

The region became part of the U.S. with the Louisiana Purchase 1803. Iowa Territory was established in July 4, 1838. Iowa was admitted to the U.S. as the 29th state December 28, 1846.

Iowa is divided into 99 counties. The counties are divided into townships, which have very limited governments. The municipalities are classified as cities. See Introduction.

Adair *Adair and Guthrie counties* *West central Iowa, 55 mi/89 km west of Des Moines*

1869 Rock Island Railroad reaches site; **1872** town founded; county and town named for Gen. John Adair of War of 1812; **July 21, 1873** Jesse James Gang creates train derailment, take $75,000 in gold, rob passengers, engineer killed; **1884** town incorporated; **May 26, 1909** Eugenie Anderson born, Ambassador to Denmark 1949–1953 (died 1997).

Adel *Dallas County* *Central Iowa, 21 mi/34 km west of Des Moines*

1846 Dallas County formed, named for U.S. Vice Pres. George M. Dallas; **1847** town founded on North Raccoon River, originally named Penoach; **1849** county organized; town becomes county seat; town renamed Adel; **1877** town incorporated; **1902** county courthouse built.

Afton *Union County* *Southwestern Iowa, 50 mi/80 km southwest of Des Moines*

1851 Union County formed; **1855** town founded as county seat, named for river in Scotland; **1857** county courthouse built; **1868** town incorporated; **1869** Chicago, Burlington & Quincy Railroad built; county seat moved to Creston; **1931** Afton Overhead Cantilever Arch Bridge (U.S. Highway 169) built at public square.

Albia *Monroe County* *Southern Iowa, 58 mi/93 km southeast of Des Moines*

1843 Kishkekosh County formed, named for Mesquakie (Fox) chief; **1845** town founded as county seat, named Princeton; **1846** county renamed Monroe; **1848** town renamed Albia; **1857** town incorporated; **1883** poet Badger Clark born, family moved to South Dakota 1884 (died 1957); **1903** county courthouse built.

Algona *Kossuth County* *Northern Iowa, 110 mi/177 km north-northwest of Des Moines*

1851 Kossuth County formed, named for Hungarian patriot Louis Kossuth; **1854** town first settled by Asa C. and Ambrose A. Call; town founded as county seat on East Fork Des Moines River, named Call's Grove; **1857** two forts built following Spirit Lake Massacre; **1872** incorporated as a city; **1899** Algona Public Library opened; **Jan. 31, 1903** magazine publisher Gardner Cowles born, published *Look* magazine (died 1985); **1955** county courthouse built.

Allison *Butler County* *North central Iowa, 30 mi/48 km northwest of Waterloo*

1851 Butler County formed; **1854** county organized; Clarksville becomes first county seat; **1879** town founded as county seat; **1881** town incorporated; county courthouse built; **1975** new county courthouse built.

Amana *Iowa County* *East central Iowa, 16 mi/26 km southwest of Cedar Rapids*

1855 village founded near Iowa River by members of Amana Society religious sect arriving from colony near Buffalo, New York, originally left Germany 1843 to escape religious persecution, splinter group of Lutheran Church called Community of True Inspiration led by Christian Metz, Amana oldest of seven villages in colony (West Amana and South Amana founded 1856; High Amana, 1857; East Amana, 1859; Homestead; 1860; Middle Amana, 1862); **1860** Mississippi & Missouri Railroad reaches Homestead village; **1867** commune leader Christian Metz dies; **1932** Amana Church Society organized to collectively manage affairs of colony, ends communal system; **1968** Amana Heritage Society founded. [see also Homestead]

Ames *Story County* *Central Iowa, 32 mi/51 km north of Des Moines*

1858 Iowa State University of Science and Technology established, originally Iowa State College; **Nov. 15, 1862** White Sox baseball player turned evangelist William Ashley "Billy" Sunday born (died 1935); **1864** town founded on South Skunk River by John I. Blair; town originally named College Farm; Noah Webster House built; **1866** town renamed for railroad proprietor Oakes Ames; **1869** incorporated as a village; **c.1870** Octagonal House built; **1874** narrow gauge Cedar Rapids & Missouri Railroad reaches town from Des Moines; **1887** fire destroys most of business section, rebuilt by 1891; **1891** the "dinky" railroad built from town to campus; **1893** incorporated as a city; **1903** public library built; **March 10, 1961** astronaut Laurel Clark born, moved during college years to Racine, Wisconsin, killed with six other astronauts in *Columbia* space shuttle disaster over eastern Texas Feb. 1, 2003.

Anamosa *Jones County* *Eastern Iowa, 43 mi/69 km southwest of Dubuque*

1837 Jones County formed; Edinburgh becomes first county seat, moved to Newport 1846; **1847** town founded as new county seat on Wapsipinicon River; town named Lexington; **1854** Riverside Cemetery established, later planned by Chicago landscape artist Ossian Simonds (1855–1931); **1856** incorporated as a town, name changed to Anamosa, for daughter of Winnebago Chief Nasinus, means "white fawn"; **1867** incorporated as a city; **1872** Anamosa State Penitentiary established; **Feb. 13, 1891** artist Grant Wood born at rural Stone City to northwest (died 1942); **1932-1933** artist colony established at Stone City by Grant Wood; **1937** county courthouse built.

Ankeny *Polk County* *Central Iowa, 11 mi/18 km north of Des Moines*

1875 town founded by landowners Col. John and Sarah Ankeny; **1879** Chicago & Northwestern Railroad reaches town; **1903** incorporated as a town; **1940** U.S. Ordnance Plant established, sold to John Deere Tractor Company 1947; **1961** incorporated as a city; Kirkendall Public Library opened; **1966** Des Moines Area Community College established; **1967** Faith Baptist College established; **1976** Saylorville Reservoir formed on Des Moines River to west.

Arnolds Park *Dickinson County* *Northwestern Iowa, 148 mi/238 km northwest of Des Moines*

1856 resort town founded between southern ends of East and West Okoboji lakes by Red Wing Land Site Company of Minnesota; **March 7, 1857** Spirit Lake Massacre led by Dakota warrior Inkpadutah begins with slaying of Mr. and Mrs. Rowland Gardner and four of their children, total 37 settlers killed [see Spirit Lake]; **1897** incorporated as a city; **c.1900** Arnolds Park amusement park established, Ferris wheel erected 1927.

Atlantic *Cass County* *Western Iowa, 75 mi/121 km west-southwest of Des Moines*

1851 Cass County formed; **1853** county organized; Lewis becomes county seat; **1868** town founded on East Nishnabotna River; **1869** county seat moved to Atlantic; town incorporated; **1907** community-owned Atlantic Northern Railroad completed to Kimballtown, abandoned 1936; **Aug. 13, 1921** country singer Neville Brand born (died 1992); **1934** third county courthouse built.

Audubon *Audubon County* *Western Iowa, 70 mi/113 km west of Des Moines*

1851 Audubon County formed, named for naturalist John J. Audubon; Hamlin's Grove (Hamlin) becomes county seat; **1874** county seat moved to Exira; **1878** Chicago, Rock Island & Pacific Railroad built; town founded; **1879** county seat moved to Audubon; **1880** town incorporated; **1974** county courthouse built.

Bedford *Taylor County* *Southwestern Iowa, 87 mi/140 km southwest of Des Moines*

1847 Taylor County formed; town founded as county seat; **1866** town incorporated; **1893** county courthouse completed; **1934** Bedford State Park established to north, later becomes Lake of Three Fires State Park.

Bettendorf *Scott County* *Eastern Iowa, 3 mi/4.8 km east of Davenport, on Mississippi River*

c.1840 area first settled on Mississippi River; **1858** town founded, originally named Gilbert Town; **1895** town incorporated; **1901** Joseph and William Bettendorf move their iron wagon factory here, establish Bettendorf Company railroad equipment factory; **1903** incorporated as a city, renamed Bettendorf; **1935** Iowa-Illinois Bridge built to Moline, second span added 1959 to accommodate Highway I-74; **1966** Scott Community College established.

Bloomfield *Davis County* *Southern Iowa, 85 mi/137 km southeast of Des Moines*

1843 Davis County formed; **1844** county organized; town founded as county seat on Fox River; Dr. William Findley House built; **c.1850** town becomes important wool-producing center; **1855** incorporated as a town; **1863** incorporated as a city; **1877** county courthouse completed; **1950** Davis County Hospital opened.

Boone *Boone County* *Central Iowa, 37 mi/60 km north-northwest of Des Moines*

1846 Boone County formed; **1851** town of Boonesboro founded as county seat 1.5 mi/2.4 km to west on Des

Moines River; **July 9, 1852** lawyer Richard A. Ballinger born, served as secretary of interior under President Taft (died 1922); **1854** first steam mill built on Polecat Slough; **1865** Chicago & Northwestern Railroad bypasses original town over right-of-way costs; town of Boone founded; **May 10, 1867** U.S. Supreme Court Justice Curtis Dwight Wilbur born (died 1954); **1876** town incorporated, annexes Boonesboro, becomes county seat; **July 6, 1881** railroad bridge over Honey Creek washed out by storm plunging west bound train engine into stream, two of four-man crew killed, local resident Kate Shelley, 15, crawls across Des Moines River bridge to inform station master, saving passengers of oncoming eastbound train; **Nov. 14, 1896** Mamie Geneva Doud Eisenhower born, wife of Pres. Dwight D. Eisenhower (married July 19, 1916, died 1979); **1900** Ericson Public Library built; **1901** Kate Shelley Memorial Railroad Bridge built across Des Moines River; **1912** Kate Shelley dies while serving as agent at rail station (born 1866); county courthouse built; **1926** Boone Biblical College (2-year) established.

Burlington   *Des Moines County*   Southeastern *Iowa, 145 mi/233 km southeast of Des Moines*

1805 Lt. Zebulon Pike raises U.S. flag for first time on Iowa soil, near Crapo Park; **1820** Native American village of Shokolon established on Mississippi River by Sac Chief Taimah (Tama), area known for its valued flint deposits; **1833** first white settlers arrive; store built by Dr. William R. Ross; Jeremiah Smith, Jr. Cabin built; **1834** Des Moines County formed; town founded by John Gray of Burlington, Vermont; **1836** town incorporated; town serves as temporary capital of Wisconsin Territory; *Hawkeye Gazette* newspaper founded; **1837** Territorial Assembly Hall built, destroyed by fire Dec. 13 of same year; assembly moved to Old Zion Church; **1838** town becomes capital of Iowa Territory; incorporated as a city; **Oct. 3, 1838** Chief Black Hawk dies, remains placed in museum July 3, 1839, lost in fire 1855; **1841** territorial capital moved to Iowa City; **1843** county organized; city becomes county seat; **1844** Silas Hudson House built; **1845** murder of John Miller leads to hangings of William and Stephen Hodges attracting thousands of onlookers; **1855** Chicago, Burlington & Quincy Railroad completed to opposite side of river from Chicago; **1856** construction on Burlington & Missouri Railroad begins; **1868** railroad bridge opened on Mississippi River, replaced 1892; **1870s** large stockyards established on east side of river; **1871** lumber industry reaches its peak; **1873** fire destroys five blocks in downtown; **1874** horse-drawn streetcars introduced; **1875** incorporated as a city under new state laws; **Feb. 26, 1887** TV actor William Frawley born (died 1966); **1892** St. Paul Roman Catholic Church built; **Apr. 27, 1896** chemist Wallace Hume Carothers born, developed synthetic fibers (died 1937); **1898** Burlington Free Library built; **1917** MacArthur Bridge opened on Mississippi River; **1920s** city experiences surge in industrial development; **May 1922** flash flooding inundates downtown; **1927** U.S. Naval Barracks established; **Oct. 1928** Municipal Docks dedicated; **1929** Burlington Municipal Airport

established; **1940** county courthouse built; **June 22, 1967** Army ordnance plant explosion kills four, injures three; **1993** Burlington Bridge (cable-stayed) built.

Carroll   *Carroll County*   Western Iowa, 75 mi/ *121 km northwest of Des Moines*

1851 Carroll County formed; **1855** county organized; Carrollton becomes county seat; **1868** Chicago & Northwestern Railroad built; town of Carroll platted by railroad as new county seat, named for Charles Carroll, signer of Declaration of Independence; **1869** town incorporated; **Sept. 23, 1959** Russian Premier Nikita Khrushchev, on U.S. tour, visits farm of Roswell Garst near Coon Rapids to southeast; **1966** county courthouse built.

Carter Lake   *Pottawattamie County*   Western *Iowa, 3 mi/4.8 km northeast of Omaha, Nebraska*

1853 Edmond Jeffries becomes first settler; **July 1877** shifting Missouri River leaves 2,000 ac/810 ha pocket of land belonging to Iowa on Nebraska side of river; **1888** additional flooding creates oxbow lake in former river channel on north boundary of enclave; **1892** U.S. Supreme Court rules that Carter Lake enclave belongs to Iowa; residential community of Carter Lake begins to develop; **1930** incorporated as a city.

Cedar Falls   *Black Hawk County*   Northeast *central Iowa, 5 mi/8 km west of Waterloo*

1843 Black Hawk County formed; **1845** William Sturgis family becomes first settlers; **1851** town founded on Cedar River; **1853** county organized; town becomes county seat; **1854** incorporated as a town; **1855** county seat moved to Waterloo; **1858** incorporated as a city; **1861** Waterloo, Cedar Falls & Northern Railroad (Illinois Central) reaches town; **1869** railroad extended west, delayed by Civil War; **Feb. 17, 1881** author Bess Streeter Aldrich born (died 1954); **1890** University of Northern Iowa established; **May 17, 1919** author Ronald Verlin Cassill born.

Cedar Rapids   *Linn County*   Eastern Iowa, 105 mi/ *169 km east-northeast of Des Moines*

1837 Linn County formed, named for Missouri Sen. Lewis Fields Linn; Marion becomes county seat; **1838** first settler Osgood Shepherd builds cabin; **1841** town platted on Cedar River, originally named Rapids City; dam built on Cedar River to provide power for grist mills and sawmills; **1844** Masonic Library established; **1849** town incorporated; **1851** Coe College established; squatters establish themselves on Municipal Island; **1852** Czech immigrants arrive to work in meatpacking plants; **1856** incorporated as a city; **June 1858** railroad reaches town; **1870** town of Kingston annexed; **1870s** Stuart and Douglas oatmeal mills established; **1872** Douglas Estate built by meatpacking heir Mrs. T. M. Sinclair; **1873** Quaker Oats Plant founded; **June 17, 1880** writer, photographer Carl Van Vechten born (died 1964); **Dec. 27, 1880** Greene's Opera

House opened; **1890** First Presbyterian Church completed; **1906** Public Library built; **1911** Peoples' Savings Bank built; **1913** St. Paul's Methodist Church built, designed by Louis Sullivan; **Nov. 5, 1913** economist Beardsley Ruml born (died 1960); **Aug. 25, 1917** actor Don Defore born; **May 22, 1919** explosion at food processing plant damages neighborhood, 44 killed; **1922** Cedar Rapids Symphony founded; **1926** county seat moved to Cedar Rapids; county courthouse built on Mays Island, Cedar River; **1928** Mount Mercy College established; seven-story Memorial Building civic center built on Municipal (Mays) Island; **1933** federal building completed; **1947** Cedar Rapids Regional Airport established to south, renamed Eastern Iowa Airport 1997; **1966** Kirkwood Community College established; **Nov. 1989** Museum of Art opened.

Centerville   *Appanoose County   Southern Iowa, 72 mi/116 km south-southeast of Des Moines*

1843 Appanoose County formed; **1846** town founded as county seat by J. F. Stratton, originally named Sentersville for Gov. Senter of Tennessee; **1847** name change result of submission error to Iowa General Assembly; **1857** town incorporated; **1896** Drake Public Library built; **1904** county courthouse built; **1930** Centerville Junior College established, becomes branch of Indian Hills Community College 1967; **May 22, 1962** Continental Airlines Boeing 707 explodes in midair killing all 45 on board; **1972** Rathbun Lake formed by dam on Chariton River to north.

Chariton   *Lucas County   Southern Iowa, 44 mi/ 71 km south-southeast of Des Moines*

1846 Lucas County formed, named for first Territorial Gov. Robert Lucas (1838–1841); **1850** town founded as county seat on Chariton River; **1857** town incorporated; **1874** incorporated as a city; **Feb. 12, 1880** United Mine Workers labor leader John L. Lewis born at rural town of Lucas to west (died 1969); **1885** county courthouse built; **1904** Chariton Carnegie Library built; **March 17, 1913** archaeologist Gordon Randolph Willey born (died 2002).

Charles City   *Floyd County   Northern Iowa, 44 mi/ 71 km north-northwest of Waterloo*

1850 first settler Joseph Kelly arrives; town founded on Cedar River, named The Ford; **1851** Floyd County formed; **1854** county organized; town becomes county seat; **1857** county seat moved temporarily to town of Floyd, returned to The Ford; **1869** town incorporated, renamed for Kelly's son Charles; **1884** Sherman Nursery founded by Erwin Milo Sherman; **1896** Charles Hart and Charles Parr begin building engines for use in farming equipment, first to use the term "tractor," establish Hart-Parr Tractor Works, becomes Oliver Farm Equipment Company; **1906** suspension bridge built on Cedar River; **1941** county courthouse built; **May 15, 1968** tornado heavily damages town, 13 killed.

Cherokee   *Cherokee County   Northwestern Iowa, 47 mi/76 km northeast of Sioux City*

1851 Cherokee County formed; **1856** original town of Cherokee founded as county seat north of present site by settlers from Milford, Massachusetts; **Feb. 1857** band of Dakota responsible for Spirit Lake Massacre terrorizes settlement for three days; small stockade built [see Arnolds Park, Spirit Lake]; **1869** separate town of Blair City founded to southeast; **1870** Illinois Central Railroad built between two towns; new town of Cherokee founded on railroad; two original town sites abandoned; **1873** town incorporated; **c.1880** coal prospectors discover water at 200 ft/61 m containing highly magnetic properties, considered wonder cure for ailments; **1902** state hospital for mentally handicapped opened; **Jan. 12, 1912** lowest temperature ever recorded in Iowa reached at Washta to southeast, −47°F/−44°C, record matched at Elkader 1996; **1956** Cherokee Symphony founded; **1966** county courthouse built.

Clarinda   *Page County   Southwestern Iowa, 95 mi/ 153 km southwest of Des Moines*

1847 Page County formed; **1853** county organized; town founded as county seat; **1856** first post office established in dugout, hollowed out from an embankment; **1861** town serves as stop on Underground Railroad; **1866** town incorporated; **1885** county courthouse built, remodeled 1991; **1888** Clarinda State Hospital established; **March 1, 1904** band leader, trombonist Glenn Miller born, airplane disappeared over English Channel Dec. 16, 1944.

Clarion   *Wright County   Northern Iowa, 82 mi/ 132 km north of Des Moines*

1851 Wright County formed; **1856** county organized; Liberty becomes county seat; **1866** town founded as new county seat, named for Clarion, Pennsylvania; **1881** town incorporated; **1893** county courthouse built; **Feb. 3, 1973** 13 killed in explosion and fire at restaurant and neighboring hardware store at Eagle Grove to southwest; **1990** first Teddy Bear Reunion held, becomes world's largest teddy bear convention.

Clinton   *Clinton County   Eastern Iowa, 30 mi/48 km northeast of Davenport, on Mississippi River*

1835 Elijah Buell becomes first settler; ferry established by Buell; **1836** town platted by Joseph M. Bartlett, originally named New York; **1837** Old Stone House built; **1840** Clinton County formed; Camanche becomes county seat, moved to town of De Witt 1861; **1850s** town serves as stop on Underground Railroad; **1855** town replatted by Chicago, Iowa & Nebraska (Chicago & Northwestern) Railroad, renamed for Gov. DeWitt Clinton of New York, responsible for construction of Erie Canal; **1856** Randall Hotel built, complete with five-story outhouse; **1857** Elijah Buell House built; **1859** incorporated as a city; **Dec. 4, 1861** actress Lillian Russell born (died 1922); **1865** county seat moved to Clinton; **1878** town of Ringwood annexed; **1880s** town becomes major lumber milling center; **1882** Clinton Theater built; **1890s** towns of Chancy and Lyons annexed; **1897** county courthouse built; **March 17, 1903** journalist Marquis Childs born (died 1990); **1904** Public Library built; **1909** Chicago & Northwestern Railroad bridge built, third bridge at site, first built 1859, second 1865; **1939** Lock & Dam No. 13 built on Mississippi River **1946** Clinton Community College established; **1957** Gateway Bridge (Hwy. 30) built across Mississippi at South Clinton, replaces 1892 structure; **1981** Lyons-Fulton Bridge (Hwy. 136) built, previous structure built 1891, demolished 1975.

Colfax   *Jasper County*   See **Newton (1857)**

Coon Rapids   *Carroll County*   See **Carroll (1959)**

Coralville   *Johnson County*   *Eastern Iowa, 3 mi/ 4.8 km northwest of Iowa City*

1856 2,200 European Mormon converts arrive by train, build hand carts for journey west to Utah, known as Mormon Hand Cart Expedition; **1866** town founded on Iowa River, named for coral rock formations; **1873** town incorporated; **1958** Coralville Reservoir formed by dam to northeast on Iowa River; **1965** Coralville Public Library founded; **1967** Iowa Medical Classification Center (Security Medical Facility) established.

Corning   *Adams County*   *Southwestern Iowa, 73 mi/ 117 km southwest of Des Moines*

1851 Adams County formed; Quincy becomes first county seat; **1853** colony of the Icarians utopian society established here; **1855** town founded by D. M. Smith, named for Erastus Corning of New York; **1871** town incorporated; **1872** county seat moved to Corning; **1883** Icarians migrate west to Cloverdale, California; **1890** county courthouse built; **Oct. 23, 1925** TV talk show host Johnny Carson born; **1955** new county courthouse built.

Corydon   *Wayne County*   *Southern Iowa, 60 mi/ 97 km south-southeast of Des Moines*

1846 Wayne County formed; **1851** county organized; town founded as county seat, named Springfield; **1862** town incorporated, renamed for Corydon, Indiana, decision made over poker game; **1964** county courthouse built.

Council Bluffs   *Pottawattamie County*   *Western Iowa, on Missouri River, opposite Omaha, Nebraska*

1804 Lewis and Clark Expedition passes site on its ascent of Missouri River; **c.1820** Hart's Bluff trading post established on Missouri River; **1827** Francis Guittar becomes first permanent settler, appointed trading post agent; **1837** Potawatomis arrive in forced move from Ohio and Indiana, temporary camp established to protect them from native tribes; **1838** Father Pierre Jean De Smet arrives to teach Native Americans, mission abandoned 1841; **June 14, 1846** Mormons arrive, name settlement

Miller's Hollow, later renamed Kanesville for officer Thomas L. Kane; **1847** Pottawattamie County formed; **1849** town becomes important embarkation point during California Gold Rush; **1851** county organized; Kanesville becomes county seat; **1852** Brigham Young leads Mormons west to Utah; first surveys made by Grenville Dodge for Rock Island Railroad; **1853** incorporated as a city, renamed Council Bluffs; **Aug. 12–14, 1859** lawyer Abraham Lincoln visits city to discuss railroad construction; **1863** town becomes Missouri Pacific Railroad terminus; **1867** Wilcox Greenhouses established by J. F. Wilcox; **1870** Grenville Dodge House built; Iowa School for the Deaf established; **1873** Union Pacific railroad bridge completed across Missouri River, rebuilt 1887, again 1914; **Aug. 26, 1873** inventor Lee DeForest born, developed vacuum tube used in radios and televisions (died 1961); **June 15, 1884** silent film producer Harry Langdon born (died 1944); **1886** Avoca becomes shared county seat; **1889** Douglas Street Bridge built across Missouri River from Omaha, widened 1924; **Nov. 22, 1889** writer Thomas Beer born (died 1940); **1893** Cooperative Farmers' Market organized; **1894** train carrying Charles T. Kelly's army of the unemployed arrives from Utah adding men from Omaha and Council Bluffs to its march on Washington, D.C.; **1904** Public Library built; **1911** Lincoln Memorial erected; **1922** Grenville Dodge Memorial erected; **1932** strike by Farm Holiday Association of farmers blocks all roads to city; **1935** Lewis and Clark monument erected; **1936** South Omaha Bridge built across Missouri River; **1966** Iowa Western Community College established; **1977** county courthouse built; **1992** Avoca loses shared county seat status, Council Bluffs becomes sole county seat.

Cresco   *Howard County*   *Northeastern Iowa, 97 mi/ 156 km northwest of Dubuque*

1851 Howard County formed; **1855** county organized; **1859** town of Pikes Peak becomes first permanent county seat; **1866** town founded as new county seat by Augustus Beadle; **1868** town incorporated; **1879** county courthouse built, addition built 1964; **1880** Kellow House built; **1914** Opera House built.

Creston   *Union County*   *Southwestern Iowa, 55 mi/ 89 km southwest of Des Moines*

1851 Union County formed; **1855** county organized; Afton becomes county seat; **1869** Chicago, Burlington & Quincy Railroad built; town founded as new county seat, located on crest between Missouri and Mississippi rivers; **1871** town incorporated; **March 16, 1932** astronaut Walter Cunningham born; **1934** severe drought requires town to ship water by train; **1952** county courthouse built; **1966** Southwestern Community College established.

Dakota City   *Humboldt County*   *Northern Iowa, 86 mi/138 km north-northwest of Des Moines*

1851 Humboldt County formed; **1857** county organized; town founded as county seat on East Branch Des Moines

River; **1878** town incorporated; **1939** county courthouse built.

Davenport *Scott County* *Eastern Iowa, 160 mi/ 257 km east of Des Moines, on Mississippi River*

1814 Zachary Taylor's forces defeated by British at Credit Island during War of 1812; **1816** Fort Armstrong built on Rock Island (Illinois); **1832** Gen. Winfield Scott and John Reynolds negotiate treaty with chiefs Keokuk and Wapello for evacuation of Sac people with Antoine Le Claire acting as interpreter; **c.1832** Claim House built; **1833** Col. George Davenport House built; **1836** town founded on land owned by Le Claire; fugitive slave Dred Scott takes up residence here with Dr. John Emerson, bases defense on residency here in trial of May 15, 1854, St. Louis; **1837** Scott County formed, named for Gen. Winfield Scott; town becomes county seat; **1838** St. Anthony's Catholic Church completed; **1839** incorporated as a town; **Feb. 26, 1846** frontiersman William F. "Buffalo Bill" Cody born at rural McCausland to northeast (died 1917); **1851** incorporated as a city; German citizens organized their first *turnverein* societies, emphasizing physical and mental fitness; **Dec. 15, 1851** economist Henry C. Adams born (died 1921); **Jan. 1856** railroad to Iowa City completed; **Apr. 21, 1856** first railroad bridge across Mississippi opened, from Rock Island, Illinois; **July 4, 1857** abolitionist John Brown gathers support at Independence Day celebrations, buys supplies for journey to Kansas; **Sept. 25, 1860** journalist Charles Edward Russell born (died 1946); **1861** Camp McClellan established as Civil War base of operations; **1862** Sioux held prisoner at Camp McClellan following battle in Minnesota; **1865** Iowa Soldiers' Orphans Home established; **1873** Trinity Episcopal Cathedral completed; **Oct. 7, 1873** writer George Cram Cook born, founded Provincetown Players, Massachusetts (died 1924); **July 1, 1876** novelist Susan Glaspell born (died 1948); **1877** Davenport Public Museum built; **1880s** limestone quarrying begins; **1881** soldier's monument dedicated; **1882** St. Ambrose College established, became University 1987; **1888** county courthouse built; **1895** D. D. Palmer discovers science of chiropractic, founds Palmer School of Chiropractic 1920s; original government bridge built to Rock Island, Illinois; **1896** city hall built; **1897** Palmer College of Chiropractic established; **1901** Crescent Railroad Bridge built; **March 10, 1903** bandleader Bix Beiderbecke born (died 1931); **1902** Carnegie Library opened; **1915** Quad City Symphony organized; **1921** Municipal Natatorium (swimming pool) built; **1925** Municipal Art Gallery opened; **1928** 19-story Davenport Bank and Trust Building completed; **1933** federal building built; **1934** Lock & Dam No. 15 completed; government bridge built to Rock Island (city), Illinois, crosses tip of Rock Island (island); **Jan. 7, 1950** fire at Mercy Hospital, 41 killed; **1955** county courthouse built.

De Witt *Clinton County* *Eastern Iowa, 22 mi/ 35 km north of Davenport*

1837 town settled; **1840** Clinton County formed; Camanche becomes first county seat; **1841** town founded as new county seat, originally named Vanderburg; **1854** town renamed for Gov. DeWitt Clinton of New York, responsible for building of Erie Canal; county courthouse built; **1858** town incorporated; **1869** county seat moved to Clinton.

Decorah *Winneshiek County* *Northeastern Iowa, 81 mi/130 km northwest of Dubuque*

1847 Winneshiek County formed, named for Winnebago chief; **1849** first settled by William Day; **1853** town founded as county seat on Upper Iowa River, named for Chief Decorah, aided white men during Black Hawk War; **1857** town incorporated; **1861** Luther College established; **1902** county courthouse built; **1933** Norwegian Museum opened.

Denison *Crawford County* *Western Iowa, 63 mi/ 101 km southeast of Sioux City*

1851 Crawford County formed; **1855** town founded as county seat on Boyer River by Rev. J. W. Denison, Baptist minister, agent of Providence Western Land Company; **May 1856** Fort Purdy built during Native American troubles; **1857** Sanlandes Bell builds log cabin near Dow City to southwest, moved to Washington Park as historic site 1926; **1875** town incorporated; **Nov. 11, 1893** transatlantic aviator Clarence Chamberlin born (died 1976); **1904** county courthouse built; **1914** Germania Opera House built; **Jan. 27, 1921** TV actress Donna Reed born (died 1986); **Apr. 28, 1933** Gov. Clyde Herring declares martial law as 800 farmers riot over foreclosure of John Shield farm, 64 arrested; **1995** Donna Reed Center for the Arts established at former Opera House; **June 22, 2002** 11 Mexican stowaways discovered dead inside sealed grain hopper rail car, trapped since leaving Texas four months earlier.

Des Moines *Polk County* *Central Iowa, on Des Moines River*

1834 John Dougherty explores area searching for sites for military posts; **1843** Fort Des Moines military post established on Des Moines River, at mouth of Raccoon River; **1845** Sac and Fox lands opened to white settlement; **1846** Polk County formed; town becomes county seat; **Dec. 28, 1846** Iowa enters Union as 29th state; **1847** fort abandoned; town platted; **July 26, 1849** *Register* and *Tribune* newspapers founded; **1851** incorporated as town of Fort Des Moines; **1857** incorporated as a city, renamed Des Moines; state capital moved from Iowa City; **May 1861** 100 Capital Guard volunteers depart for Keokuk on way to Civil War front lines; **1866** Des Moines Valley Railroad reaches city; **1867** Equitable Life Insurance

Company founded, oldest west of Mississippi River; **1877** Hoyt Sherman Place mansion built; **1878** first Iowa State Fair held in Des Moines; **1881** Drake University established; **1884** state capitol completed; **1894** Des Moines Hosiery Mill founded, becomes Rollins Hosiery Mills 1922; **May 1894** train carrying Charles T. Kelly's Army of the Unemployed arrives, headed to march on Washington, D.C., Kelly persuaded to take 150 flatboats down river on next leg of journey; **1896** Grand View College established; **1897** soldiers and sailors monument erected; **1898** University of Osteopathic Medicine and Health Sciences established; **1900** State Historical, Memorial, and Art Building completed; **1902** new Fort Des Moines established as Army cavalry post; **1904** Public Library completed; **1906** county courthouse built; **1907** Camp Dodge National Guard base founded to northwest; **Dec. 21, 1909** diplomat George W. Ball born (died 1994); **1910** city hall built; **1912** City Market House built; **July 18, 1914** TV actress Harriet Hilliard Nelson born (died 1994); **1922** St. Gabriel's Monastery built; **1924** 19-story Equitable Building completed; **1926** Polk County War Memorial built; **Apr. 4, 1926** TV actress Cloris Leachman born; **Sept. 27, 1929** actress Sada Thompson born; **1930** federal building completed; **1933** Des Moines Municipal Airport established, became International Airport 1986; **Sept. 1936** President Roosevelt visits city to discuss drought situation in West; **1937** Des Moines Symphony established; **1948** Des Moines Art Center opened; **1970** Science Center of Iowa opened; **1973** Saylorville Dam completed on Des Moines River north of city; **1974** 35-story Ruan Center built; **1979** Civic Center opened; **1981** 33-story Marriott Hotel built; **July 7, 1993** flooding overwhelms water treatment plant, depriving tap water to 250,000 people, restored July 22.

Dubuque   *Dubuque County*   *Eastern Iowa, 168 mi/ 270 km northeast of Des Moines, on Mississippi River*

1785 Julien Dubuque founds settlement in lead mining district; **1788** lead mining begins on Catfish Creek; **1833** treaty with Native Americans opens region to white settlement; **1834** Dubuque County formed; town becomes county seat; first church in Iowa (Methodist) built; **June 1834** Patrick O'Connor murders fellow miner George O'Keaf, tried and hanged by vigilantes; **1836** Miners' Bank chartered, first bank in Iowa; **1837** town incorporated; **1839** Loras College established, originally Columbia College; **1843** incorporated as a city; Clarke College established; **1847** Edward Langworthy House built; **1852** University of Dubuque established; **1854** Wartburg Seminary established; **1855** Illinois Central Railroad reaches east side of river opposite city; shot tower built for molding lead shot; **1857** Dubuque & Pacific Railroad founded, begins building line across Iowa; St. Raphael's Catholic Cathedral built; **1859** Clarke College established; **1868** city's first railroad bridge built across Mississippi River; **1876** flash flood kills 30 along Catfish Creek; **1887** city's first road bridge built across

Mississippi; **1889** Grand Opera House built; **1894** lumber district destroyed by fire, followed by larger lumber fire 1911, industry closes for good 1915; **1891** county courthouse built; **1897** memorial erected at bluff-top grave of Julien Dubuque; **1902** Carnegie-Stout Library opened; **1919** flooding of Mississippi River inundates city, seven killed; **1928** Federal Barge Line terminal completed; Dubuque Municipal Airport opened; **1934** federal building built; **1937** Lock & Dam No. 11 completed on Mississippi River; **Apr. 29, 1955** actress Kate Mulgrew born; **1958** Dubuque Symphony Orchestra organized; **1975** Dubuque Museum of Art opened.

Eagle Grove   *Wright County*   See **Clarion (1973)**

Eldora   *Hardin County*   *Central Iowa, 60 mi/97 km north-northeast of Des Moines*

1851 Hardin County formed; **1853** county organized; town founded as county seat on Iowa River; John Ellsworth discovers flecks of gold glittering in soil sparking flurry of gold rush activity, no vein found; town originally named Eldorado, later shortened; **1868** State Training School for Boys founded; **1892** county courthouse built; **1895** town incorporated; **1932** first meeting of United Farmers organization held at tourist camp to west.

Elkader   *Clayton County*   *Northeastern Iowa, 46 mi/74 km northwest of Dubuque*

1836 first settlers arrive; **1837** Clayton County formed; **1840** county organized; Prairie La Porte becomes first county seat, seat moved to Jacksonville 1843 (renamed Garnavillo), to Guttenberg 1845; **1845** town founded on Turkey River, named for Abd-el-Kader, who was fighting the French in Algeria, a popular world figure; **1849** stone mill built; **1853** county seat moved to Elkader; **1868** town incorporated; **1876** county courthouse built; **1891** incorporated as a city; **1903** Opera House built; **1919** Civil War monument erected; **1936** schoolhouse built entirely of glass blocks; **Feb. 3, 1996** lowest temperature ever recorded in Iowa reached, −47°F/−44°C, matches record set in 1912 at Washta.

Emmetsburg   *Palo Alto County*   *Northern Iowa, 120 mi/193 km northwest of Des Moines*

1851 Palo Alto County formed; **1858** county organized; Paoli becomes county seat; **1874** town founded as new county seat by Irish immigrants; **1877** town incorporated; **1880** county courthouse built.

Estherville   *Emmet County*   *Northern Iowa, 144 mi/ 232 km north-northwest of Des Moines*

1851 Emmet County formed, named for Irish patriot Robert Emmet; **1857** town site settled; **1858** county organized; town founded as county seat, named for wife of Robert Ridley, one of men who platted town; **1862** Fort Defiance built; **1876** town incorporated; **1879** county seat moved to Swan Lake, returned to Estherville 1882; **May 10, 1879** meteorite descends upon area, sending three large pieces to ground with three loud explosions 2 mi/3.2 km to north, largest piece weighs 437 pd/198 kg; **1881** incorporated as a town; **1894** incorporated as a city; **1904** Carnegie Library built, addition built 1995; **1927** Iowa Lakes Community College established; **1958** county courthouse built.

Fairfield   *Jefferson County   Southeastern Iowa, 96 mi/155 km southeast of Des Moines*

1836 Bonifield Cabin built, later moved to Old Settlers' Park as historical site; **1839** Jefferson County formed; town founded as county seat; first county courthouse in Iowa built; **1847** incorporated as a city; **1854** first annual Iowa State Fair held; **1875** incorporated as a city; Parsons College established, closed 1973; **1893** county courthouse built; **1973** Maharishi University of Management established on former Parsons College campus.

Forest City   *Winnebago County   Northern Iowa, 120 mi/193 km north of Des Moines*

1851 Winnebago County formed; **1856** town founded as county seat, named by Judge Robert Clark for region's stands of fine timber; **1868** Ida Fuller born, popular dancer of 1890s (died 1922); **1878** town incorporated; **May 2, 1890** meteorite explodes in midair 11 mi/18 km to northwest at 5:15 P.M. making trail of smoke and loud rushing sound; **c.1891** Flax Palace built to promote area's primary crop; **1896** county courthouse built; **1903** Waldorf Junior College established; **Feb. 18, 1909** author Wallace Earle Stegner born at Lake Mills to northeast (died 1993); **1930s** stone observation tower built at Pilot Knob State Park to east; **1958** John K. Hanson establishes travel trailer company, becomes Winnebago Industries 1960; **1966** first Winnebago motor home rolls off assembly line.

Fort Dodge   *Webster County   Northwest central Iowa, 72 mi/116 km north-northwest of Des Moines*

1846 town founded on Des Moines River; **1850** Fort Clarke built, renamed Fort Dodge 1851, abandoned 1853; **1851** Webster County formed; Homer becomes county seat; **1856** county seat moved from Homer (abandoned); **1858** Henry A. Flatt begins town's clay-products industry; **July 1868** George Hull of Binghamton, New York, and H. B. Martin of Marshalltown, Iowa, meet here to create the Cardiff Giant hoax, large gypsum slab made to appear like petrified prehistoric man, shipped to Cardiff, New York, where it was "discovered" and presented to gullible public; **1869** incorporated as a city; two gypsum quarries opened; **1890** four gypsum mills founded to east; **1892** Tobin College established, burned 1929; **1902** county courthouse built; Public Library built; **1920** King Music House founded by composer Karl King; **1933** Blanden Memorial Art Museum opened; **1934** Tobin Packing Plant opened.

Fort Madison   *Lee County   Southeastern Iowa, 16 mi/26 km southwest of Burlington, on Mississippi River*

1808 trading post established on Mississippi River; **Aug. 1813** post attacked by Chief Black Hawk; **Sept. 1, 1813** evacuating troops burn post as Black Hawk's band mounts second attack; **1833** John H. Knapp builds log cabin; **1836** Lee County formed; town founded as county seat; **1837** Atlee Lumber Company founded; **1838** incorporated as a town; **1839** Iowa State Penitentiary established; **1847** S. D. Morrison begins manufacturing plows; **1849** Lost Creek Church of Christ built to northwest; **1851** incorporated as a city; **1876** third county courthouse built, rebuilt after 1911 fire; **1879** Santa Fe Railroad establishes division point here; paper mills established; **1913** Sheaffer Pen Company founded; **1927** railroad swing bridge built across Mississippi River; **1948** first annual Tri-State Rodeo held.

Garner   *Hancock County   Northern Iowa, 108 mi/174 km north of Des Moines*

1851 Hancock County formed; **1858** county organized; Amsterdam becomes county seat; **1865** county seat moved to Concord; **1869** Chicago, Milwaukee, St. Paul & Pacific Railroad built 1 mi/1.6 km south of Concord; new town of Garner founded on railroad, named for Gen. Winfield Scott Garner; **1881** town incorporated; **1898** Concord annexed by Garner, making Garner the new county seat; **1899** county courthouse built.

Glenwood   *Mills County   Southwestern Iowa, 18 mi/29 km southeast of Omaha, Nebraska*

1851 Mills County formed; town settled by Mormons on Keg Creek, named Rushville; **1852** town renamed Coonsville for Dr. Libeud Coons after Mormon residents leave for Utah; **1853** town founded as county seat, renamed Glenwood; **1857** town incorporated; **1876** Glenwood State Hospital established; **1959** county courthouse built.

Green Mountain   *Marshall County   See* **Marshalltown (1910)**

Greenfield   *Adair County   Southwest central Iowa, 48 mi/77 km west-southwest of Des Moines*

1851 Adair County formed; **1856** Fontanelle becomes county seat; town of Greenfield founded; **1874** county seat moved to Greenfield; **1876** town incorporated; **Oct. 7, 1888** Henry A. Wallace born, vice president under Pres. Franklin D. Roosevelt (died 1965); **1891** county courthouse built.

Grinnell   *Poweshiek County   Central Iowa, 47 mi/76 km east of Des Moines*

1853 town founded by Congregationalist Rev. Josiah Bushnell Grinnell of New York City and Dr. Thomas Holyoke of Maine; **Dec. 1855** Grinnell College established; **1865** town incorporated; **June 17, 1882** college and large part of town destroyed by tornado, 40 killed.

Grundy Center   *Grundy County   Central Iowa, 70 mi/113 km northeast of Des Moines*

1841 Grundy County formed; **1853** town founded as county seat; **Oct. 23, 1861** writer Herbert Quick born in rural Grundy County, near Steamboat Rock (died 1925); **1877** town incorporated; **1891** county courthouse built.

Guthrie Center   *Guthrie County   West central Iowa, 47 mi/76 km west of Des Moines*

1851 Guthrie County formed; Panora becomes county seat; **1859** town founded on South Raccoon River; **1876** county seat moved to Guthrie Center; **1880** town incorporated; **1964** county courthouse built.

Guttenberg   *Clayton County   Northeastern Iowa, 30 mi/48 km northwest of Dubuque, on Mississippi River*

1834 town founded, originally named Prairie la Porte; **1837** Clayton County formed; **1845** German immigrants begin arriving under auspices of Western Settlement Society of Cincinnati; town renamed for Johan Gutenberg (spelling variation), inventor of printing press; county seat moved from Jacksonville (Garnavillo); **1851** town incorporated; **1853** county seat moved to Elkader; **1871** last known great flock of passenger pigeons passes north through White Pine Hollow, become extinct by 1876; **1937** Lock & Dam No. 10 (Guttenberg Dam) completed on Mississippi River.

Hampton   *Franklin County   Northern Iowa, 84 mi/135 km north-northeast of Des Moines*

1852 first settlers arrive; **1855** Franklin County formed; **1856** town founded as county seat by Job Garner and George Ryan; **1856** Maysville Schoolhouse built to southeast; **1857** Beeds Lake formed by dam to west, built by F. K. Hansberry, also builds mill at dam, ceased operation 1904; **1870** town incorporated; **May 6, 1875** World War I Adm. William Daniel Leahy born (died 1959); **1881** Ellis Ferris Nursery established; **1891** county courthouse built; **1905** Hampton Public Library built; **1913** Windsor Theater built; **1915** Lutheran Hospital established.

Harlan   *Shelby County   Western Iowa, 43 mi/69 km northeast of Omaha, Nebraska*

1851 Shelby County formed; Shelbyville becomes county seat; **1858** town founded on West Nishnabotna River, named for James Harlan; **1859** Harlan becomes new county seat following bitter dispute; **1879** town incorporated; **1893** county courthouse built.

Harpers Ferry   *Allamakee County   Northeastern Iowa, 56 mi/90 km north-northwest of Dubuque*

1852 town platted, originally named Winfield; **1860** David Harper begins operating ferry on Mississippi River; town renamed Harpers Ferry; **1860s** freshwater mussel fishing becomes important, used for decorative articles; **1892** over 900 effigy Native American mounds located to date on high bluffs near town; **1901** town incorporated; **1938** Lock & Dam No. 9 (Harpers Ferry Dam) built on Mississippi; **Oct. 25, 1949** Effigy Mounds National Monument established to south.

Homestead   *Iowa County   East central Iowa, 18 mi/29 km southwest of Cedar Rapids*

1855 members of religious sect led by Christian Metz begin arriving, escaping dogma of Lutheran church in Germany and negative influences of city life in Buffalo, New York; **1861** Mississippi & Missouri Railroad reaches site; town founded, part of Amana Colony; **1932** Amana Church Society established to govern affairs of seven villages (Homestead, Amana, East Amana, Middle Amana, High Amana, West Amana, South Amana). [see also Amana]

Ida Grove   *Ida County   Western Iowa, 48 mi/77 km east-southeast of Sioux City*

1851 Ida County formed; **1856** town founded as county seat near Maple River by settlers of Dutch and Scottish origin; **1878** town incorporated; **1880** county courthouse built, annex build 1982; **1902** arrangement of boulders discovered buried in earth by well digger, apparent prehistoric fortification; **1970** private lake and first of castle-like structures built by boat manufacturer Byron Godbersen as product research site, built through 1980s.

Independence   *Buchanan County   East central Iowa, 64 mi/103 km west of Dubuque*

1837 Buchanan County formed; **1842** Rufus B. Clark becomes first settler; **July 4, 1847** town founded as county seat on Wapsipinicon River; **1864** town incorporated; **1873** state hospital opened; **Jan. 22, 1874** mathematician Leonard Eugene Dickson born (died 1951); **Oct. 18, 1875** World War I naval commander Henry Ervin Yarnell born (died 1959); **1889** Charles W. Williams builds kite-shaped horse race track, closed 1892; **1939** county courthouse built.

Indianola   *Warren County   Southern Iowa, 15 mi/24 km south of Des Moines*

1846 Warren County formed; **1849** county organized; town founded as county seat, named by surveyor for town in Texas mentioned in newspaper that his lunch was wrapped in; **1860** Simpson College established; **1863** town incorporated; **June 12, 1917** actress Priscilla Lane born (died 1995); **1939** third county courthouse completed.

Iowa City   *Johnson County   Eastern Iowa, 108 mi/ 174 km east of Des Moines*

1836 Iowa Territory established; **1839** Johnson County formed; Napoleon becomes first county seat; town founded on Iowa River; road surveyed from Dubuque by Lyman Dillon, later becomes Old Military Road; **1841** territorial capital moved from Burlington; Territorial Capitol building completed, donated to University of Iowa 1857; county seat moved to Iowa City; **1844** Robert Lucas House built; **Dec. 28, 1846** Iowa enters Union as 29th state; **1847** University of Iowa established; **1853** town incorporated; **1856** Mormon handcart expedition camps here during spring and summer, European converts built makeshift handcarts for journey to Utah; **Jan. 1, 1856** railroad from Davenport reaches town through valorous efforts of townspeople working in zero weather as deadline approached; **1857** state capital moved to Des Moines; **1899** county courthouse built; **1908** Oakdale Sanitarium established, closed 1981, later used for Iowa Hygienic Laboratory; **1958** Coralville Reservoir formed by dam to north on Iowa River.

Iowa Falls   *Hardin County   Central Iowa, 68 mi/ 109 km north-northeast of Des Moines*

1853 town founded on Iowa River, originally named Rocksylvania, later changed to White's Mills; **1856** incorporated as a town; town renamed Iowa Falls; **1889** incorporated as a city; **1929** Ellsworth Community College established.

Jefferson   *Greene County   Central Iowa, 50 mi/ 80 km northwest of Des Moines*

1851 Greene County formed; **1854** town founded as county seat near North Raccoon River, originally named New Jefferson; **1871** town incorporated; **Nov. 18, 1901** pollster, opinion analyst George Horace Gallup born (died 1984); **1903** Jefferson Carnegie Library built, addition built 1968; **1918** third county courthouse built; **1966** Mahanay Memorial Carillon Tower dedicated, donated by local resident, 14 bells rung every quarter hour during daytime.

Keokuk   *Lee County   Southeastern Iowa, 33 mi/ 53 km south-southwest of Burlington, on Mississippi River*

1820 Samuel C. Muir builds log cabin here; **1829** American Fur Company trading post established at mouth of Keokuk River by Moses Stillwell and Mark Aldrich; town founded, named for Sac Chief Keokuk; **1836** Lee County formed; **1837** town platted by Isaac Galland of New York Land Company; **1847** incorporated as a city; *Daily Gate City* newspaper founded; **1850** Ivins House built; **1853** Lee County Home for the Poor established; **1855** Iowa State Insurance Building built, includes Mark Twain Memorial Room where Mark Twain did job printing in 1856; **1856** first rail line built 12 mi/19 km north around Des Moines Rapids; **1857** Estes House hotel built, converted into hospital 1862; **1861** city serves as embarkation point for Iowan troops during Civil War; Keokuk National Cemetery established; **1871** railroad bridge built across Mississippi River, rebuilt 1916 and 1985; **1877** Des Moines Rapids Canal, 9 mi/14.5 km long, built north around rapids, construction begun 1866; **1881** Public Library built, new facility opened 1962; **1889** federal building built; **1890** Du Pont de Nemours Plant built at Mooar to north for manufacture of gunpowder; **March 14, 1903** explosion at Du Pont mill kills two, injures three; **1913** Lock & Dam No. 19 (Keokuk Dam) completed on Mississippi, flooding rapids and canal; Chief Keokuk Statue erected; **July 20, 1934** highest temperature ever recorded in Iowa reached, 118°F/48°C; **Nov. 24, 1965** gas explosion at National Guard Armory disrupts square dance, 11 killed, 50 injured; **1993** extensive flooding damages low-lying areas of three-state region.

Keosauqua   *Van Buren County   Southeastern Iowa, 46 mi/74 km west of Burlington*

1836 Van Buren County formed; Rochester becomes county seat; **1837** town founded on Des Moines River; **1839** Bonneyview House built; Missouri-Iowa boundary dispute leads to Honey War, conflict over cutting down of honey trees in disputed jurisdictions; **1842** county seat moved to Keosauqua; **1843** county courthouse completed, oldest in Iowa; **1847** Pearson House built; **1851** town incorporated.

Knoxville   *Marion County   Southern Iowa, 32 mi/ 51 km southeast of Des Moines*

May 1843 Red Rock Line established by treaty halting advance of settlers until midnight, Oct. 11, 1845, violated by many claim jumpers; **1845** Marion County formed; town founded as county seat, named for Revolutionary War Gen. Henry Knox; **1855** town incorporated; **1896** county courthouse built; **1921** local resident Dixie Cornell Gebhardt's design adopted for state flag; **1968** Lake Red Rock formed by dam on Des Moines River to northeast.

Ladora   *Iowa County   See **Marengo** (1905)*

Lake Mills   *Winnebago County   See **Forest City** (1909)*

Lamoni   *Decatur County   Southern Iowa, 70 mi/ 113 km south-southwest of Des Moines*

1879 town founded by members of Reorganized Church of Jesus Christ of Latter-day Saints; **1885** town incorporated; **1895** Graceland College, now University, established.

Le Claire   *Scott County   Eastern Iowa, 13 mi/ 21 km east-northeast of Davenport, on Mississippi River*

1829 first three white families arrive; **1832** land granted to Antoine Le Claire; town founded; **Feb. 26, 1846** frontier scout, showman William F. "Buffalo Bill" Cody born (died 1917); **1855** town incorporated; **1939** Lock & Dam No. 14 built; **1993** widespread flooding occurs in area.

Le Mars *Plymouth County* *Northwestern Iowa, 24 mi/39 km north-northeast of Sioux City*

1851 Plymouth County formed; **1853** county organized; Melbourne becomes county seat; **1856** first settlers arrive at town site; **1869** town founded; town name derived from combination of initials of six young women who were visiting at time—Lucy Underhill, Elizabeth Parsons, Mary Weare, Anna Blair, Rebecca Smith, and Sarah Reynolds; **1872** county seat moved to Le Mars; **1881** town incorporated; **1900** Western Union College established, becomes Westmar College; **Jan. 11, 1905** anthropologist Clyde Kluckhohn born (died 1960); **1998** county courthouse built.

Leon *Decatur County* *Southern Iowa, 60 mi/97 km south of Des Moines*

1840 town founded, originally named South Independence because there was another Independence in state; **1846** Decatur County formed; Decatur City becomes county seat; **1853** county seat moved to South Independence; **1855** town renamed Leon; **1867** town incorporated; **1908** county courthouse completed.

Logan *Harrison County* *Western Iowa, 29 mi/ 47 km north-northeast of Omaha, Nebraska*

1851 Harrison County formed; Magnolia becomes first county seat; **1864** town founded on Boyer River, originally named Boyer Falls; Henry Reed builds dam, sawmill; **1867** town renamed for Civil War Gen. John A. Logan; **1876** town incorporated; county seat moved to Logan; **1911** county courthouse built.

Lucas *Lucas County* See **Chariton (1880)**

Manchester *Delaware County* *Eastern Iowa, 41 mi/66 km west of Dubuque*

1837 Delaware County formed; Delhi becomes first county seat; **1850** Norwegian Steiner Eiverson builds first cabin; town founded on South Fork Maquoketa River, originally named Burrington; **1856** name changed for its similarity to "Burlington," new name probable rearrangement of settler's name Chesterman; **1859** Dubuque & Pacific Railroad reaches town; **1864** town incorporated; **1880** county seat moved to Manchester; **1894** county courthouse built.

Maquoketa *Jackson County* *Eastern Iowa, 48 mi/ 77 km north of Davenport*

1837 Jackson County formed; Bellevue becomes county seat; **1840** town founded on Maquoketa River, originally named Springfield; **1841** county seat moved to Andrew; **1844** town renamed; **1857** town incorporated; **1873** county seat moved to Maquoketa; **1903** Maquoketa Public Library built; **1958** county courthouse built.

Marengo *Iowa County* *East central Iowa, 24 mi/ 39 km southwest of Cedar Rapids*

1843 Iowa County formed; **1845** town founded as county seat on Iowa River; **1859** town incorporated; **Nov. 5, 1871** opera singer Clarence Eugene Whitehill born (died 1932); **1893** county courthouse built; **July 10, 1905** author Mildred Benson (Carolyn Keene) born at rural Ladora to southwest, wrote Nancy Drew mysteries (died 2002).

Marion *Linn County* *Eastern Iowa, 5 mi/8 km northeast of Cedar Rapids*

1837 Linn County formed; **1839** town founded as county seat, named for Revolutionary War Gen. Francis Marion; **1855** second county courthouse built; **1863** East Star Mill built on Indian Creek; First National Bank established; **1865** town incorporated; **1872** Chicago, Milwaukee, St. Paul & Pacific Railroad reaches town; **1905** Marion Carnegie Library opened, new facility opened 1996; **1926** county seat moved to Cedar Rapids.

Marquette *Clayton County* *Northeastern Iowa, 47 mi/76 km north-northwest of Dubuque, on Mississippi River*

1673 Father Marquette and Louis Joliet land on Wisconsin side of Mississippi River, become first white men to view Iowa territory; **1799** Frenchman Basil Giard believed to have settled here; **1857** town founded as North McGregor; **1874** town incorporated; **1896** flooding damages town, again in 1916; **1920** town renamed Marquette; **1932** highway bridge built to Prairie du Chien, Wisconsin, replaced 1974 by Marquette-Joliet Bridge; **1938** Lock & Dam No. 9 completed to north on Mississippi River; **Oct. 25, 1949** Effigy Mounds National Monument established to north.

Marshalltown *Marshall County* *Central Iowa, 50 mi/80 km northeast of Des Moines*

1846 Marshall County formed; Marietta becomes county seat; **1851** Henry Anson arrives from Marshall, Michigan, becomes first settler; town founded as county seat on Iowa River; **Apr. 11, 1851** baseball player Cap Anson born, played for Chicago White Sox (died 1922); **1859** court rules in favor of Marshalltown in county seat dispute with Marietta; **1863** incorporated as a town; Cedar Rapids & Missouri River Railroad reaches town; **May 2, 1872** fire destroys part of town; **Apr. 6, 1876** second fire destroys warehouse and lumber yard district; **Aug. 29, 1885** World War II naval commander Frank Jack Fletcher born (died 1973); **1886** county courthouse built; **1887** Iowa Soldiers' Home established; **1903** Public Library built; **March 21, 1910** railroad accident at Green Mountain to northeast, 55 killed; **1923** incorporated as a city; **1927** Marshalltown Community College established; **1929** Memorial Coliseum completed; **Nov. 13, 1938** actress Jean Seberg born (died 1979); **Sept. 26, 1946** actress Mary Beth Hurt born.

IOWA

Mason City *Cerro Gordo County* *Northern Iowa, 104 mi/167 km north-northeast of Des Moines*

1851 Cerro Gordo County formed, named for Mexican War battlefield; **1853** John B. Long and John L. McMillan become first settlers; **1854** town founded as county seat on Winnebago River; **1855** Elisha Randall builds mill on Lime Creek; town platted; **1858** dispute with town of Clear Lake over location of county seat settled by popular vote; **1869** Chicago, Milwaukee, St. Paul & Pacific Railroad (Milwaukee Road) reaches town, extended to Austin, Minnesota, 1870; town incorporated; **1872** Randall invents and patents his perpetual lime kiln, process adopted throughout country; **1881** incorporated as a city; **1886** clay tile and brick industry established; **1889** Chicago & Northwestern Railroad reaches town; **1899** county courthouse built, addition built 1960; **May 18, 1902** composer Meredith Willson born (died 1984); **1903** Carnegie Public Library built, new library built 1940; **1908** Stockman House built, designed by Frank Lloyd Wright; **1910** Park Inn hotel completed, designed by Frank Lloyd Wright; **1918** North Iowa Community College established; **1927** Mason City Airport established to west; **1933** John Dillinger's gang robs First National Bank, gets away with $52,000; **Feb. 3, 1959** rock and roll stars Buddy Holly, Richie Valens, and The Big Bopper (J. P. Richardson) die in plane crash after takeoff from Mason City Airport on concert tour.

McCausland *Scott County* See **Davenport (1846)**

Montezuma *Poweshiek County* *Central Iowa, 57 mi/92 km east of Des Moines*

1843 Poweshiek County formed; **1848** town founded as county seat, named for last Aztec emperor; **1859** county courthouse built, renovated 1933; **1868** town incorporated.

Montrose *Lee County* *Southeastern Iowa, 25 mi/ 40 km southwest of Burlington, on Mississippi River*

1799 trading post established on Mississippi River by French-Canadian Louis Tesson; **1832** Capt. James White becomes first settler; **1834** Fort Des Moines built, abandoned 1836; **Feb. 1846** 2,000 Mormons cross frozen Mississippi River in −20°F/−29°C weather fleeing Nauvoo, Illinois, led by Brigham Young following shooting death of leader Joseph Smith, Jr.; **1854** town founded by David W. Kilbourne; **1857** town incorporated.

Mount Ayr *Ringgold County* *Southwestern Iowa, 69 mi/111 km south-southwest of Des Moines*

1847 Ringgold County formed, named for Samuel B. Ringgold, hero wounded in Battle of Palo Alto, Texas; town founded as county seat; **1855** county organized; **1875** town incorporated; **1926** fourth county courthouse built.

Mount Pisgah *Union County* *Southern Iowa, 45 mi/72 km south-southwest of Des Moines*

June 1846 Mormons stop on bluff above Thomson River after leaving Nauvoo, Illinois, following death of leader Joseph Smith; town founded; mill and tabernacle built; **1850** post office established; **1852** Mormons head west after about 800 members die of natural causes; **1888** monument erected as memorial to Mormons who perished.

Mount Pleasant *Henry County* *Southeastern Iowa, 65 mi/105 km southwest of Davenport*

1836 Henry County formed; **1839** county organized; town founded near Skunk River as county seat; first county courthouse in Iowa built; **1842** incorporated as a town; **1844** Iowa Wesleyan College established; **1851** plank road from Burlington completed; **c.1855** Chicago, Burlington & Quincy Railroad reaches town; **1856** incorporated as a city; **1861** Iowa State Hospital opened; **1914** county courthouse built; **Sept. 7, 1914** physicist James Alfred Van Allen born, discovered earth's Van Allen radiation belts; **1921** Soldiers' and Sailors' Memorial Hospital founded.

Muscatine *Muscatine County* *Eastern Iowa, 25 mi/40 km west of Davenport, on Mississippi River*

1833 trading post established; **1835** James W. Casey begins cutting timber for steamboats, site called Casey's Landing; **1836** Muscatine County formed; town founded as county seat by John Vanatta, named Bloomington; **1837** post office established; German immigrants begin arriving; **Aug. 22, 1837** steamboat *Dubuque* explodes, 22 killed; **1838** incorporated as a city; **1842** St. Matthias Catholic Church built; **1843** sawmill built by Cornelius Cadle; **1851** town renamed Muscatine; **1852** Trinity Episcopal Church built; **1853-1854** Mark Twain lives here briefly with his widowed mother and brothers Orion and Henry; **1855** Mississippi & Missouri Railroad reaches town; **Dec. 5, 1869** writer Ellis Parker Butler born (1973); **1875** Civil War Veterans' Memorial dedicated; **1891** High Bridge built across Mississippi River, last ferry, the *Ida May*, retired; German immigrant J. F. Boepple begins manufacture of pearl buttons from river mussels; **1901** Musser Public Library founded; **1909** third county courthouse completed; **1929** Muscatine Community College established; **1937** Lock & Dam No. 16 built on Mississippi River.

Nevada *Story County* *Central Iowa, 32 mi/51 km north-northeast of Des Moines*

1846 Story County formed; **1853** county organized; town founded as county seat by settler named Thrift, named for Thrift's daughter Sierra Nevada, named for California mountain range; **1864** Cedar Rapids & Missouri River Railroad reaches town; **1869** town incorporated; **1899** Iowa Sanitarium established; **1968** county courthouse built.

New Hampton *Chickasaw County* *Northeastern Iowa, 40 mi/64 km north of Waterloo*

1851 Chickasaw County formed; town founded as intended county seat, named Chickasaw Center; **1854** Bradford becomes county seat; **1856** county seat moved to Forest City, later renamed Williamstown, amid bitter dispute; **1873** town incorporated; **1880** New Hampton (Chickasaw Center) makes financial offer to build county courthouse; county seat returned from Williamstown; **1930** new county courthouse completed.

Newton *Jasper County* *Central Iowa, 30 mi/48 km east of Des Moines*

1846 Jasper County formed; **1847** town founded as county seat; county and town named for Revolutionary War generals; **1848** Thomas Reese log house built, moved to Maytag Park 1936; **1855** Hough House built; **1857** town incorporated; **June 28, 1857** novelist Emerson Hough born at rural Colfax to west (died 1923); **1898** Newton's washing machine industry begins with manufacture of ratchet-slat washers; **1902** Public Library built; **1907** Fred L. Maytag buys interest in Parsons Band Cutter and Self-Feeder Company, introduces hand-powered washer invented by Howard Snyder; **1911** county courthouse completed; Snyder's electric washing machine introduced by Maytag, followed by cylinder washer 1911 and most successful "gyrafoam" washer 1917; **1935** Fred Maytag Park established.

Northwood *Worth County* *Northern Iowa, 135 mi/217 km north-northeast of Des Moines*

1851 Worth County formed; Bristol becomes first county seat; **1853** Gilbrand Nellum becomes first settler, soon followed by other Norwegian immigrants; town founded on Shell Rock River; **1863** county seat moved to Northwood; **1875** town incorporated; **1893** county courthouse built.

Onawa *Monona County* *Western Iowa, 36 mi/58 km south-southeast of Sioux City*

1851 Monona County formed, possibly Native American term for "beautiful valley"; **1854** county organized; Ashton (Bloomfield) becomes county seat; **1857** town founded near Missouri River; ferry established; **1859** town incorporated; county seat moved to Onawa; **1892** county courthouse built; **1920** Eskimo Pie ice cream confection invented by Christian K. Nelson, later sold to Russell Stover candy maker.

Orange City *Sioux County* *Northwestern Iowa, 40 mi/64 km north-northeast of Sioux City*

1851 Sioux County formed; **1860** county organized; Calliope becomes first county seat; **1869** town settled by Dutch immigrants, led by Henrik Hospers, named for Prince William of Orange; **1870** county seat moved to Sioux Center; **Jan. 1872** county seat moved to Orange City by force on 80 bobsleds; **1882** Northwestern College established; **1884** town incorporated; **1904** county courthouse built; **1940** first annual Tulip Festival held.

Osage *Mitchell County* *Northern Iowa, 61 mi/98 km north-northwest of Waterloo*

1851 Mitchell County formed; **1853** Hiram Hart becomes first settler; **1854** town founded as county seat near Cedar River by Dr. A. H. Moore; town originally named Coral for Dr. Moore's daughter; **1858** banker Orrin Sage of Massachusetts replats town, renamed for him (O. Sage); county courthouse built; **1871** town incorporated.

Osceola *Clarke County* *Southern Iowa, 40 mi/64 km south of Des Moines*

1846 Clarke County formed; **1851** county organized; town founded as county seat by settlers from Ohio; **1859** town incorporated; **1866** incorporated as a city; **1953** Clarke County Hospital opened; **1956** county courthouse built.

Oskaloosa *Mahaska County* *Southern Iowa, 55 mi/89 km southeast of Des Moines*

1843 Mahaska County formed, named for Chief Mahaska; Quakers settle in county; Iowa Phalanx colony founded to south by members of Fourierist cooperative society, disbanded 1845; **1844** town founded by Quakers, becomes county seat; **1850** *Oskaloosa Weekly Herald* newspaper founded; **1853** incorporated as a town; **Nov. 23, 1855** World War I naval commander Frank Friday Fletcher born (died 1928); **1870** first coal mines developed attracting large group of Welsh miners; **Nov. 15, 1871** composer Frederick Knight Logan born, published "Missouri Waltz" 1912 (died 1928); **1873** William Penn College established; **1875** incorporated as a city; **1886** county courthouse built; **1910** coal veins depleted; miners turn to business and agriculture; **1913** Friends' Meeting House dedicated.

Ottumwa *Wapello County* *Southern Iowa, 75 mi/121 km southeast of Des Moines*

1843 Wapello County formed; territory opened to settlement; **1844** town founded as county seat on Des Moines River by Appanoose Rapids and Milling Company; town originally named Louisville; first hotel built; **1845** town renamed Ottumwa, Native American term for "rippling waters"; **1851** incorporated as a town; **1857** incorporated as a city; **1860** hastily assembled bridge created across Des Moines River by placing wagons end-to-end to provide access to political rally held on south side of river during Lincoln-Douglas campaign; **1870** wooden toll bridge built across river, later destroyed by floods; **1880** discovery of gold leads to short-lived rush, hoax uncovered; **1890** Coal Palace built to promote city's bituminous coal industry, demolished 1892; **1894** county courthouse built; **1902** Ottumwa Public Library built; **1930** St. Mary's Catholic Church built; **1966** Indian Hills Community College established.

Pella *Marion County   Southern Iowa, 38 mi/61 km southeast of Des Moines*

1847 town founded by Dutch immigrants led by Henry Peter Scholte; **1853** Central College established; **1868** town incorporated; **1869** 14-room John Smith House built; **1871** sizable John Voorhees House built to upstage neighbor John Smith; **1925** Pella Window Company established by Peter and Lucille Kuyper, originally manufactured window screens; **1935** first annual Tulip Time celebration held; **1948** Vermeer Manufacturing Company, maker of hay baling equipment, established by Gary Vermeer; **1968** Lake Red Rock formed by dam on Des Moines River to west.

Pocahontas *Pocahontas County   Northern Iowa, 98 mi/158 km northwest of Des Moines*

1851 Pocahontas County formed; **1859** county organized; Old Rolfe (Parvin) becomes county seat; **1875** county seat moved to Pocahontas; **1892** town incorporated; **1923** county courthouse built.

Primghar *O'Brien County   Northwestern Iowa, 57 mi/92 km northeast of Sioux City*

1851 O'Brien County formed; **1862** county organized; cabin of Archibald Murray on Little Sioux River serves as first county seat; **1873** town founded as county seat by German immigrants; town name combines last name initials of eight original town proprietors: Pumphrey, Roberts, Inman, McCormick, Green, Hayes, Albright, Rereick; **1888** town incorporated; **1915** fourth county courthouse built.

Red Oak *Montgomery County   Southwestern Iowa, 42 mi/68 km southeast of Omaha, Nebraska*

1851 Montgomery County formed; **1853** county organized; Frankfort becomes county seat; **1865** town founded on East Nishnabotna River by Alfred Hobard, named Red Oak Junction; **1865** county seat moved to Red Oak Junction; **1869** town incorporated; **1873** mill built on river; **1890** county courthouse built; **1901** name shortened to Red Oak; **Nov. 5, 1906** astronomer Fred Lawrence Whipple born.

Rock Rapids *Lyon County   Northwestern Iowa, 67 mi/108 km north of Sioux City*

1851 Buncombe County formed, named for Edmund Buncombe of North Carolina, **1862** county renamed for Union Gen. Nathaniel Lyon; **1873** town founded as county seat on Rock River, county court previously held at various homes throughout county; **1885** town incorporated; **1916** second county courthouse built.

Rockwell City *Calhoun County   West central Iowa, 80 mi/129 km northwest of Des Moines*

1851 Calhoun County formed, named for South Carolina patriot John C. Calhoun; **1856** county organized; Lake City becomes county seat; **1876** town founded, named for settler J. M. Rockwell; **1877** county seat moved to Rockwell City; **1882** town incorporated; **1914** county courthouse built; **1918** Iowa State Reformatory for Women established.

Sabula *Jackson County   Eastern Iowa, 40 mi/64 km southeast of Dubuque, on Mississippi River*

1836 E. A. Wood becomes first settler; **1837** town founded, originally named Carrolport, later Charlestown; **1846** town renamed for Mrs. Sabula Wood; **1864** town incorporated; **1875** pearl button factory opened; **1876** first Old Settlers' Picnic held, suspended 1918; **1933** bridge to Savanna, Illinois, completed; **1939** town becomes an island linked by causeways with completion of Lock & Dam No. 13 downstream at Clinton.

Sac City *Sac County   Western central Iowa, 93 mi/ 150 km northwest of Des Moines*

1851 Sac County formed; **1855** town platted on North Raccoon River; **1856** county organized; town becomes county seat; **1856** town incorporated; **1874** incorporated as a city; **1879** railroad reaches town; **1883** Opera House built; **1890** county courthouse completed; **1899** creamery opened, closed 1971; **1904** Sac City Chautauqua organized.

Sergeant Bluff *Woodbury County   Western Iowa, 6 mi/9.7 km south-southeast of Sioux City*

Aug. 20, 1804 Sgt. Charles Floyd of Lewis and Clark Expedition dies, possibly of ruptured appendix, expedition's only fatality, buried atop bluff above Missouri River; **1851** Woodbury County formed; town founded as county seat; **1854** town platted; **1856** county seat moved to Sioux City; **1857** flooding erodes bluff, undermines Floyd's grave, remains reburied at Sioux City; **1901** Floyd monument dedicated atop Floyd's Bluff honoring Sgt. Charles Floyd; **1904** incorporated as a town; **1972** incorporated as a city.

Sibley *Osceola County   Northwestern Iowa, 73 mi/ 117 km north-northeast of Sioux City*

1851 Osceola County formed; **1871** county organized; town founded as county seat, named for Gen. G. H. Sibley of Minnesota; **1876** town incorporated; **1902** county courthouse built; **1923** Osceola County Creamery Co-op founded.

Sidney   *Fremont County*   *Southwestern Iowa, 39 mi/ 63 km south-southeast of Omaha, Nebraska*

1847 Fremont County formed; **1849** county organized; Austin becomes county seat; **1851** town founded as new county seat by Milton Richard, named for Richard's home town of Sidney, Ohio; **1858** county courthouse built, dynamited 1863 by suspected Confederate guerillas; **1868** Sidney Library founded, facility built 1956; **1870** town incorporated; **1889** new county courthouse built; **1924** rodeo founded as part of American Legion Veterans' event, later becomes Iowa Championship Rodeo; **1978** Nebraska City-Sidney Bridge built across Missouri River.

Sigourney   *Keokuk County*   *Southeastern Iowa, 77 mi/124 km east-southeast of Des Moines*

1837 Keokuk County formed; **1844** town founded as county seat near North Skunk River, named for Connecticut author Lydia Huntley Sigourney (1791–1865), in turn presented town with 50-volume library; **1848** county seat moved to Lancaster, moved back to Sigourney 1856; **1858** town incorporated; **Aug. 1, 1863** in Skunk River War, or Tally War, "Copperhead" Rev. Cyphert Tally, Baptist preacher from Tennessee opposed to war with secessionists, is "accidentally" shot to death by armed residents, state militia called out; **1910** fourth county courthouse built.

Sioux Center   *Sioux County*   *Northwestern Iowa, 43 mi/69 km north-northeast of Sioux City*

1851 Sioux County formed; **1860** county organized; Calliope becomes county seat; **1870** town founded; county seat moved to Sioux Center; **1872** county seat moved to Orange City; **1891** town incorporated; **1927** Sioux Center Public Library founded; **1955** Dordt College established.

Sioux City   *Woodbury County*   *Western Iowa, 160 mi/257 km northwest of Des Moines, on Missouri River*

1804 Lewis and Clark Expedition passes mouth of Big Sioux River on their ascent of Missouri River; **1839** explorer J. N. Nicollet visits site; **Sept. 1848** town founded by William Thompson of Illinois, named Thomsonville; **1849** French-Canadian trader Theophile Bruguier settles here with his Sioux wives and their father Chief War Eagle; **1851** Woodbury County formed, originally named Wahkaw, renamed 1853; Sergeant's Bluff becomes county seat; **1852** trapper Joe Leonais purchases Bruguier's claim; **1854** Dr. John K. Cook buys Leonais' farm, founds town of Sioux City; **1856** steamboat *Omaha* arrives; town becomes new county seat; **1857** town incorporated; *Sioux City Eagle* newspaper founded; **1860s** first African-American residents arrive as boat deck hands; **1868** Chicago, Rock Island & Pacific Railroad reaches city; **1870** Illinois Central Railroad arrives; **Oct. 1885** Rev. George Channing Haddock wages crusade against saloons, gambling, bawdy houses; **1887** Live Stock Exchange

organized, built 1892; grandiose Corn Palace built for festival, replaced four times, final palace resembled Russian Orthodox church; **Aug. 17, 1890** New York Gov. Harry Lloyd Hopkins born, headed Pres. Franklin D. Roosevelt's New Deal program (died 1946); **1891** city hall built; Combination Bridge, pivot-span, completed across Missouri River to South Sioux City, Nebraska; **1894** Morningside College established; **1907** First Presbyterian Church built; **1913** Public Library built; **March 15, 1913** actor Macdonald Carey born (died 1994); **1918** county courthouse built, includes eight-story office tower of Prairie School architectural style; **July 4, 1918** columnist Ann Landers born (died 2002); columnist Abigail Van Buren ("Dear Abby") born, twin of Ann Landers; **1930** Briar Cliff College established; **1933** federal building completed; **1937** Civic Art Center organized; **June 8, 1953** heavy rains to north send wall of water down Floyd River inundating city, 14 killed; **1966** Western Iowa Technical Community College established; **July 19, 1989** United Airlines DC-10 Flight 232 makes fiery landing at Sioux City Airport, 111 killed, 185 survive.

Spencer   *Clay County*   *Northwestern Iowa, 136 mi/ 219 km northwest of Des Moines*

1851 Clay County formed; Peterson becomes first county seat; **1859** town founded as county seat, named for U.S. Senator George E. Spencer; **1871** county seat moved to Spencer; **1880** town incorporated; **1900** county courthouse built; **July 4, 1931** fireworks set off blaze, destroys most of business section.

Spirit Lake   *Dickinson County*   *Northwestern Iowa, 152 mi/245 km northwest of Des Moines*

1838 surveyor J. N. Nicollet explores area for U.S. War Department; **1851** Dickinson County formed; **1856** first settlers arrive; town founded as county seat at southern end of Big Spirit Lake; **March 13, 1857** William Marble killed, his wife taken hostage at Marble Lake to northwest during Spirit Lake Massacre led by Dakota warrior Inkpadutah, perpetrators flee before volunteer forces reach site from Fort Dodge, total 37 settlers killed [see Arnolds Park]; **1858** post office established; **1878** town incorporated; **1890** county courthouse built.

Storm Lake   *Buena Vista County*   *Northwestern Iowa, 112 mi/180 km northwest of Des Moines*

1851 Buena Vista County formed; **1870** Sioux Rapids becomes first county seat; town founded as county seat on north shore of Storm Lake; **1873** town incorporated; **1878** county seat moved to Storm Lake; **1891** Buena Vista University established; **1972** county courthouse built; **2002** dredging program begun in effort to save lake.

Tabor *Fremont and Mills counties* *Southwestern Iowa, 28 mi/45 km southeast of Omaha, Nebraska*

1852 town founded by Congregationalists led by Rev. John Todd; **1853** Todd House built, established as stop on Underground Railroad, giving safe haven to runaway slaves on way to Canada; **1858–1859** abolitionist John Brown camps here while staging his activities; **1866** Tabor College established; **1868** town incorporated.

Tama *Tama County* *Central Iowa, 60 mi/97 km east-northeast of Des Moines*

1845 small groups of Mesquakie (Fox) return from Kansas to join members who had remained in Iowa after forced removal; **July 1857** Mesquakie Indian Settlement (reservation) established to west; **1862** town founded on Iowa River, named for Sac Chief Taimah; **1869** incorporated as a town; **1887** incorporated as a city.

Tipton *Cedar County* *Eastern Iowa, 34 mi/55 km northwest of Davenport*

1837 Cedar County formed; Rochester becomes county seat; **1840** town founded; county seat moved to Tipton; **1857** town incorporated; **Sept. 22, 1931** Gov. Turner puts county under military rule during "Cow War" resulting from dairy farmers refusing to submit cows to testing for bovine tuberculosis, several farmers jailed, released by mob, protests suppressed by troops; **1968** fourth county courthouse built.

Toledo *Tama County* *Central Iowa, 60 mi/97 km east-northeast of Des Moines*

1843 Tama County formed, named for Chief Taimah; **1853** town founded as county seat near Iowa River; **1866** town incorporated; county courthouse built; **1881** Western College moved from Linn County, renamed Leander Clark College, merges with Coe College, Cedar Rapids 1919; **1912** sanatorium opened for Native American tuberculosis patients.

Vinton *Benton County* *East central Iowa, 30 mi/ 48 km southeast of Waterloo*

1837 Benton County formed; **1839** Reuben Daskirk becomes first settler; town founded near Cedar River, originally named Northport, later changed to Fremont; **1846** post office established; town becomes county seat, renamed in honor of Ohio Cong. Plym Vinton who paid $50 for the distinction; **1858** Iowa State School for the Blind established, later renamed Iowa Braille and Sight Saving School; **1869** town incorporated; **1906** fourth county courthouse built.

Wapello *Louisa County* *Southeastern Iowa, 50 mi/ 80 km southwest of Davenport*

1836 Louisa County formed, named for pioneer woman Louisa Massey who shot and wounded her brother's murderer; **1837** town (WAH-pel-lo) founded on Iowa River in strip of land called the Black Hawk Purchase; town named for Chief Wapello; **1838** Lower Wapello becomes county seat; **1839** county seat moved to Wapello; **1856** town incorporated; **1928** second county courthouse built; **1993** widespread flooding occurs on county's rivers.

Washington *Washington County* *Southeastern Iowa, 60 mi/97 km west-southwest of Davenport*

1838 Washington County formed; Astoria becomes first county seat; **1839** town founded as new county seat; **1864** town incorporated; **1887** third county courthouse built.

Washta *Cherokee County* *See* **Cherokee (1912)**

Waterloo *Black Hawk County* *Northeast central Iowa, 90 mi/145 km northeast of Des Moines*

1843 Black Hawk County formed; **1845** George W. Hanna settles on Cedar River; **1848** town founded, named Prairie Rapids; **1851** post office established; town renamed Waterloo; **1853** county organized; Cedar Falls becomes county seat; **1855** county seat moved to Waterloo; **1857** Dubuque & Pacific Railroad reaches town; **1858** town inundated by flooding, only year when steamboats made regular trips this far on Cedar River; *Waterloo Daily Courier* newspaper founded; **1868** incorporated as a city; South Waterloo Church built; **1870s** Illinois Central Railroad reaches city; **1875** horse racing begins, ends 1895; **March 29, 1875** Lou Henry Hoover, wife of Pres. Herbert Hoover, born (married 1899, died Jan. 7, 1944); **1891** Boulder Presbyterian Church built from granite boulders found on farm; **1896** Waterloo Library founded, Carnegie Library built 1906; **1905** Waterloo Gasoline Traction Engine Company founded by John Froelich for manufacture of his gasoline engine invented 1892, becomes John Deere Tractor plant; **1910** Dairy Cattle Congress founded; **1922** First Presbyterian Church completed, replaces Boulder Church; **1927** Rath Packing Plant built; **Oct. 17, 1928** actress Julie Adams born; **1964** county courthouse built; **1967** Hawkeye Community College established; **1975** Conway Civic Center opened, renamed Five Sullivan Brothers Convention Center for five brothers killed in sinking of USS *Juneau* Nov. 13, 1942; **1985** Waterloo Museum of Art founded.

Waukon *Allamakee County* *Northeastern Iowa, 69 mi/111 km north-northwest of Dubuque*

1847 Allamakee County formed; Rossville becomes county seat; **1849** G. C. Shattuck becomes first settler; town founded on Shattuck's land on condition it be made county seat, named for Winnebago chief; **1852** county seat moved to Waukon; **1861** county seat moved to Lansing; **1866** sheriff and posse return county records to Waukon; **1867** Supreme Court rules in favor of Waukon as seat; **1883** town incorporated; **1939** county courthouse built.

Iowa

Waverly *Bremer County* Northeast central Iowa, 17 mi/27 km north-northwest of Waterloo

1851 Bremer County formed, named for Swedish novelist Fredrika Bremer; town founded by W. P. Harmon as county seat on Cedar River, named for popular Waverly novels that town chairman was in process of reading; **1852** Wartburg College established; **1857** Waverly Public Library founded; **1859** town incorporated; **1864** Cedar Falls & Minnesota Railroad reaches town; **1894** Waverly Museum founded; **1937** fourth county courthouse built.

Webster City *Hamilton County* Central Iowa, 64 mi/103 km north-northwest of Des Moines

1850 town site on Beaver River first settled by Wilson C. Brewer; **1854** town platted by Brewer, named Newcastle; **1856** Hamilton County formed; town founded as county seat, named for stagecoach operator named Webster; **1874** town incorporated; **Feb. 4, 1904** author MacKinlay Kantor born (died 1977); **1976** county courthouse built.

West Branch *Cedar County* Eastern Iowa, 42 mi/68 km west-northwest of Davenport

1850 David Tatum becomes first settler; **1853** town founded; **1869** Burlington, Cedar Rapids & Great Northern Railroad reaches town; town platted; **Aug. 10, 1874** Herbert Clark Hoover, 31st U.S. President, born (died Oct. 20, 1964); **1875** town incorporated; **Aug. 12, 1965** Herbert Hoover National Historic Site authorized.

West Union *Fayette County* Northeastern Iowa, 68 mi/109 km northwest of Dubuque

1837 Fayette County formed; **1849** county organized; town founded as county seat, originally named Knob Prairie; Dutton's Cave discovered; **1857** town incorporated; **May 9, 1862** historian George Willis Botsford born (died 1917); **1879** incorporated as a city; **1923** county courthouse built.

Williams *Hamilton County* Central Iowa, 64 mi/103 km north of Des Moines

1868 Peter Laforge becomes first settler; **1869** town founded, named for Maj. William Williams of Fort Dodge who aided settlers following Spirit Lake Massacre of 1857; **1883** town incorporated; **1911** wooden water tower collapses sending surge of water across street against house of 90-year-old Thomas Duffy, breaking out all the windows, sending him hurtling across the room, walks away with broken collar bone.

Winterset *Madison County* Southern Iowa, 25 mi/40 km southwest of Des Moines

1846 Madison County formed; **1849** county organized; town founded as county seat near Middle Raccoon River; **1872** original Delicious apple tree propagated by Jess Hiatt, rights sold to Stark Brothers Orchards [see Stark, Missouri]; **1876** town incorporated; county courthouse built; **1883** Cedar Covered Bridge built, featured in novel by Robert James Waller, basis for 1995 movie *Bridges of Madison County*; **May 26, 1907** actor John Wayne born Marion Morrison (died 1979); **1970** first annual Covered Bridge Festival held; **Sept. 2002** Cedar Covered Bridge destroyed by vandals.

225

Kansas

Central U.S. Capital: Topeka. Largest city: Wichita.

The territory was acquired by the U.S. with the Louisiana Purchase in 1803. Kansas Territory was created May 30, 1854. Kansas was admitted to the U.S. as the 34th state January 29, 1861.

Kansas is divided into 105 counties. The counties are divided into townships (civil divisions with limited governmental functions). Municipalities are classified as cities, of which there are three classes. See Introduction.

Abilene   *Dickinson County*   *Central Kansas, 83 mi/ 134 km west of Topeka, on Smoky Hill River*

1857 Dickinson County formed; town founded as county seat; **1867** Kansas Pacific Railroad reaches town, serves as railhead for Chisholm Trail, cattle-driving route from Texas; Joseph G. McCoy builds stockyards; **1869** incorporated as a city; **1871** Old Gulf House hotel opens, becomes National Hotel; **Apr.–Dec. 1871** James "Wild Bill" Hickock arrives from Hays, Kansas, serves as town marshal, rids town of prostitutes, gambling; **1883** Eisenhower Home built, purchased by Eisenhower family 1898; **1898** Cleyson L. Brown establishes first telephone exchange in U.S.; **Sept. 15, 1899** educator Milton Stover Eisenhower born (died 1985); **1947** Eisenhower Visitor's Center opened; **1968** Eisenhower Presidential Library dedicated; **1978** Museum of Independent Telephony established.

Alma   *Wabaunsee County*   *East central Kansas, 32 mi/51 km west of Topeka*

1857 town founded, named for settlers' home city in Germany; **1859** Wabaunsee County formed; town becomes county seat; **1866** incorporated as a city; **1931** county courthouse built; **Jan. 2, 1907** railroad accident at Voland to southwest, 33 killed; **1963** Alma Public Library founded.

Alton   *Osborne County*   *North central Kansas, 175 mi/282 km west-northwest of Topeka*

1870 town founded, named Bull City for Gen. H. C. Bull, won coin toss with Lyman T. Earl; **Oct. 12, 1879** pet elk kills Gen. Bull, three others as they attempt to rescue it, antlers end up in museum; **1888** incorporated as a city; **1885** renamed for Alton, Illinois, origin of most settlers; **1888** candy manufacturer Russell Stover born (died 1954); **1930** General Bull monument dedicated; **July 24, 1936** highest temperature ever recorded in Kansas reached, 121°F/49°C.

Anthony   *Harper County*   *Southern Kansas, 54 mi/ 87 km southwest of Wichita*

1873 Harper County formed, named for Civil War Sgt. Marion Harper; area settled; town of Harper becomes county seat; **1878** town founded, named for Gov. George T. Anthony, 1877–1879; **1879** incorporated as a city; county seat moved to Anthony; **1904** Anthony Downs Race Track established; **1908** county courthouse built.

Arkansas City   *Cowley County*   *Southern Kansas, 45 mi/72 km south-southeast of Wichita*

Jan. 1870 town founders arrive at site; **July 1870** town platted, originally named Walnut City; **1872** incorporated as a town; present name adopted; **1880** Santa Fe Railroad reaches town; **1884** incorporated as a city; **Sept. 1893** as many as 60,000 people congregate in town for Sept. 16, 1893 land rush into Cherokee Strip of Oklahoma; **1914** oil discovered; **1922** Cowley County Community College established; **1960** Cherokee Strip Land Rush Museum opened.

Asherville *Mitchell County* *See* **Beloit (1868)**

Ashland *Clark County* *Southwestern Kansas, 137 mi/220 km southwest of Wichita*

1868 Mt. Jesus named by Gen. George C. Custer 7 mi/11.3 km to northeast; **1884** town platted by settlers from Kentucky; incorporated as a city; **1885** Clark County formed; town becomes county seat; **1920** Ashland Public Library founded; **1935** first oil wells begin production; **1951** county courthouse built.

Atchison *Atchison County* *Northeastern Kansas, 40 mi/64 km northwest of Kansas City, Kansas*

1724 French explorer M. de Bourgmont crosses area to negotiate with Native Americans; **July 4, 1804** members of Lewis and Clark expedition celebrate Independence Day here, first such observance on Kansas soil; **1818–1819** military post founded on Cow Island, in Missouri River by Maj. Stephen Long's Yellowstone expedition; **1850** California Gold Rush brings fortune seekers through river landing point; **1854** town founded on Missouri River; **1855** Atchison County formed; incorporated as a town, becomes county seat; **1857** incorporated as a city; **1859** Benedictine College established; Atchison, Topeka & Santa Fe Railroad chartered by Cyrus K. Holliday; **Dec. 2, 1859** Abraham Lincoln makes campaign speech here; **1871** foundry established by John Seaton, maker of locomotive parts; **1868** Trinity Episcopal Church built; **1875** toll bridge built across Missouri River; **1877** *Atchison Globe* newspaper founded by Ed Howe; **1883** Midland Lutheran College established, moved to Beatrice, Nebraska, 1919; **1885** Kansas State Orphans' Home established; **1897** county courthouse built; **July 24, 1897** aviator Amelia Earhart born, presumed dead on world-circling flight over Pacific Ocean July 1 or 2, 1937; **1938** toll-free bridge built over Missouri River.

Atwood *Rawlins County* *Northwestern Kansas, 330 mi/531 km west of St. Joseph, Missouri*

1875 area first settled by T. A. Andrews and O. M. Matheny; **1878** town founded, named Attwood for Attwood Matheny, son of town founder; **1880** Chicago, Burlington & Quincy Railroad built; town site moved 1.5 mi/2.4 km; **1881** Rawlins County organized; town becomes county seat following rivalry with Blakeman to west; **1882** town named altered to Atwood; **1885** incorporated as a city; **1906** county courthouse built.

Baxter Springs *Cherokee County* *Southeastern Kansas, 12 mi/19 km west-southwest of Joplin, Missouri*

1849 area first settled by John Baxter; sawmill and tavern built by Baxter; **1860s** cattle drives from Texas arrive in search of pasture; **Oct. 6, 1863** in Baxter Springs Massacre, members of pro-South Quantrill gang kill 106 Union soldiers under Gen. James Blunt, only Blunt and few survivors return to Fort Scott; **1869** incorporated as a city; **1870** soldiers monument erected; **1872** intended county courthouse built, never used; Columbus remains county seat; **1888** first railroad arrives; **1903** lead and zinc discovered to south; **1905** Baxter Springs Public Library founded; **1914** town's last Old Civil War Soldiers and Sailors Reunion held; **1920** Johnson House built by star Washington Senators pitcher Walter Perry "Big Train" Johnson (1887–1946), born in Humboldt, Kansas.

Bazaar *Chase County* *See* **Cottonwood Falls (1931)**

Belleville *Republic County* *Northern Kansas, 150 mi/241 km west of St. Joseph, Missouri*

1866 Republic County formed; **1869** town founded as county seat; **1878** incorporated as a city; **1884** Union Pacific Railroad reaches town; **1927** Belleville Public Library founded; **1939** second county courthouse completed.

Beloit *Mitchell County* *North central Kansas, 133 mi/214 km west-northwest of Topeka*

1868 A. A. Bell builds log cabin, becomes first settler; settlement named Willow Springs; **Apr. 12, 1868** in Bell-Bogardus Massacre at Asherville to east, more than a dozen settlers killed, including members of Bell and Bogardus families, by 200 Cheyenne dissatisfied with terms of Medicine Lodge Treaty; **1870** Mitchell County formed; town becomes county seat; **1872** town platted, incorporated as a city, renamed for Beloit, Wisconsin, home of town promoter T. F. Hersey; **1888** State Industrial School for Girls established, later becomes Beloit Juvenile Correctional Facility; **1901** county courthouse built, Seth Thomas clock tower added 1904; **1916** Beloit Public Library built.

Burlington *Coffey County* *East central Kansas, 60 mi/97 km south of Topeka*

1859 Coffey County formed; town founded as county seat, named for Burlington, Vermont; **1870** incorporated as a city; **1875** Burlington Public Library founded, became Coffey County Library 1988; **1922** flooding on Rock Creek, tributary of Neosho River, inundates town; **1964** third county courthouse built; John Redmond Reservoir built on Neosho River to north; **1985** Wolf Creek Nuclear Power Plant begins operation northeast of town.

Caney *Montgomery County* *Southeastern Kansas, 78 mi/126 km west of Joplin, Missouri*

1869 first white settlers arrive on Little Caney River; **1871** town founded; **Aug. 2, 1879** four members of Barker Gang raid town, one killed; **1887** incorporated as a city; **1890s** oil boom begins; **1906** natural gas well catches fire, burns for six weeks; special train excursions added for spectators wishing to see fire; **1910s** oil production declines.

Cawker City *Mitchell County* *North central Kansas, 148 mi/238 km west-northwest of Topeka*

1872 town named for Col. E. H. Cawker, winner of founders' poker game; **1874** incorporated as a city; Cawker City Public Library founded; **1878** Levi Aldrich founds *Cawker City Free Press* newspaper, later becomes *Public Record*; **1880s** Aldrich Home built; **1881** Missouri Pacific Railroad reaches town; **1953** farmer Frank Storber begins creating his Ball of Twine, by 1957 reaches 17,000 pd/7,710 kg, 40 ft/12 m in circumference, donated to city 1961, dies 1974.

Chanute *Neosho County* *Southeastern Kansas, 65 mi/105 km northwest of Joplin, Missouri*

1824 Mission Neosho founded by Rev. Benton Pixley, abandoned 1829; **1840s** Canvill Trading Post established; town founded; **1865** treaty with Osage Tribe clears way for white settlers; **1872** Leavenworth, Lawrence & Galveston Railroad built; incorporated as a city with merger of four adjoining towns, suggestion of Octave Chanute, railroad engineer, named for him; **1936** Neosho County Community College established.

Cherryvale *Montgomery County* *Southeastern Kansas, 58 mi/93 km west-northwest of Joplin, Missouri*

1871 Kansas City, Lawrence & Southern Kansas Railroad reaches site; town founded by railroad as temporary terminus; **1880** incorporated as a city; **1889** while prospecting for coal, natural gas field discovered; **1898** zinc mining begins to northwest; **1912** natural gas reserve depleted; **July 26, 1912** TV actress Vivian Vance born (died 1979).

Cimarron *Gray County* *Western Kansas, 165 mi/266 km west of Wichita*

1878 town founded; **1885** incorporated as a city; **1887** Gray County formed; Ingalls becomes county seat; **Jan. 1889** legal fight with Montezuma over county seat leads to violence, one killed, one wounded; **1893** county seat moved to Cimarron; **1929** county courthouse built.

Clay Center *Clay County* *North central Kansas, 80 mi/129 km west-northwest of Topeka*

1862 town founded by John and Alonzo Dexter; **Nov. 1866** Clay County formed; town becomes county seat; **1873** Junction City & Fort Kearney Railroad reaches town; **1875** incorporated as a city; **1901** second county courthouse completed; **1903** flooding of Republican River devastates area; **1911** Civil War monument erected at courthouse; **1912** Carnegie Library built; **1915** Republican River floods again, repeated 1925, major flooding 1935.

Coffeyville *Montgomery County* *Southeastern Kansas, 60 mi/97 km west of Joplin, Missouri*

July 1869 James A. Coffey builds house and trading post; **1871** Missouri, Kansas & Texas Railroad reaches site, winning competition with two other railroads; town platted by engineer Octave Chanute; **1872** incorporated as a city; **1882** Dalton family settles here; **1890s** town boasts several brick factories; **Oct. 5, 1892** famous shoot-out at 9:30 A.M. between Dalton boys and law authorities in attempted robbery of Condon Bank, four bandits, four citizens killed; **1909** Natatorium built, includes mineral baths, dance hall; **1923** Coffeyville Community College established.

Colby *Thomas County* *Northwestern Kansas, 287 mi/462 km west-northwest of Topeka*

1885 Thomas County formed, named for Union Gen. George H. Thomas; town founded as county seat, named for settler J. R. Colby; **1886** incorporated as a city; **1906** county courthouse built; **1926** Pioneer Memorial Library established; **March 27, 1942** opera singer, actor Samuel Ramey born; **1964** Colby Community College established; **1976** Prairie Museum of Art and History opened, new building opened 1988, renamed Prairie Museum.

Coldwater *Comanche County* *Southern Kansas, 112 mi/180 km west-southwest of Wichita*

1884 Santa Fe Railroad built; town founded; incorporated as a city; **1885** Comanche County formed; town becomes county seat; **1928** county courthouse completed.

Columbus *Cherokee County* *Southeastern Kansas 18 mi/29 km west-northwest of Joplin, Missouri*

1866 Cherokee County formed; Pleasant View becomes county seat; **1868** L. N. Lee opens general store near center of county called "the Center"; **1870** Kansas City, Fort Scott & Gulf Railroad reaches site; **1871** town platted as new county seat, named for Columbus, Ohio, by settler A. V. Peters; incorporated as a city; **1889** county courthouse built; **c.1900** extensive coal fields discovered; **March 30, 1938** tornado destroys 200 houses, 12 killed, 200 injured.

Concordia *Cloud County* *North central Kansas, 110 mi/177 km west of St. Joseph, Missouri*

1860 Shirley County formed; **1864** J. M. Hageman builds road from Junction City to site; **1866** county organized; Clyde becomes county seat; **1867** county renamed Cloud County; Hageman builds town's first house; **1869** town founded; **1870** county seat moved to Concordia; **1870s** Boston Corbett, apparent killer of Lincoln assassin John Wilkes Booth, hides from enemies by living in dugout (dwelling dug into hillside), is rarely seen; **1872** incorporated as a city; **1892** Frank Carlson Public Library founded; **1907** Grand Opera House built; **1958** county courthouse built.

Cottonwood Falls   *Chase County   Eastern central Kansas, 65 mi/105 km southwest of Topeka*

1856 first settlers arrive; **1858** town founded by Free Staters; **1859** Chase County formed; town becomes county seat; **c.1867** Nelson Ranch established to east by Samuel N. Wood, prominent figure in Stevens County Seat War late 1880s, shot and killed at Hugoton 1891; **1872** incorporated as a city; **1873** county courthouse completed, oldest courthouse in use in Kansas; **1886** Clements Stone Arch Bridge built to south; **Mar. 31, 1931** Notre Dame football coach Knute Rockne, seven others die in airplane crash near town of Bazaar to south.

Council Grove   *Morris County   East central Kansas, 50 mi/80 km southwest of Topeka*

Aug. 10, 1825 Treaty of Council Grove signed with Osage allowing establishment of Santa Fe Trail; Post Office Oak Tree used as letter depository for passing travelers, used through 1847; **1826** Josiah Gregg leads first caravan across Neosho River ford on Santa Fe Trail; **1847** town founded; Hays Tavern built; Kaw Indian Reservation established, dissolved 1873; **1849** Methodist mission founded; **1857** Last Chance Store built; Hays House Restaurant established by Seth Hays, still in business; **1858** incorporated as a city; **1859** Morris County formed; **1868** Missouri, Kansas & Texas Railroad reaches town; **1871** town becomes permanent county seat; **1883** Missouri Pacific Railroad reaches town; **1903** flooding inundates town; **1964** Council Grove Reservoir built; **1969** county courthouse built.

Dexter   *Cowley County   Southern Kansas, 50 mi/80 km southeast of Wichita*

1870 area first settled; **1874** grasshopper plague devastates area; **1875** town platted, named for Dexter, famed New York trotting horse; **1881** incorporated as a city; **1886** Missouri Pacific Railroad reaches town; **1903** oil drillers strike nonflammable gas; **1905** analysis reveals gas contains helium, first known helium gas deposit in U.S.; **1927** helium processing plant established; **1938** U.S. government purchases helium plant, dismantled 1942.

Dodge City   *Ford County   Western Kansas, 148 mi/238 km west of Wichita*

1821 William Becknell opens Santa Fe Trail from Franklin, Missouri, to Santa Fe, New Mexico, used until 1880; **1835** Army outpost established; **1864** Fort Dodge built to protect freight haulers; **1865** town founded; **1871** H. L. Sitler builds sod house, town's first house; **1872** Atchison, Topeka & Santa Fe Railroad reaches town; two cowboys have shootout, loser buried with boots on where he fell, beginning of Boot Hill Cemetery, used until 1878; c.850,000 buffalo hides shipped from town through 1874; **1873** Ford County formed; town becomes county seat; **1875** town becomes major cattle shipping center; incorporated as a city; **1877** Bat Masterson elected sheriff; **1882** Fort Dodge closed; **1886** blizzard destroys large numbers

of cattle; **1910** City Library built; **1913** county courthouse built; **1915** Sacred Heart Catholic Church built; **1925** First Presbyterian Church built; **1929** Cowboy Statue erected on Boot Hill; **1935** Dodge City Community College established; **May 17, 1936** movie director, actor Dennis Hopper born.

El Dorado   *Butler County   East central Kansas, 27 mi/43 km east-northeast of Wichita*

1855 Butler County formed; **1857** town founded as county seat; **1871** incorporated as a city; **1895** Bradford Memorial Library founded, Carnegie Library built 1912; **1908** county courthouse built; **1915** oil discovered to west; **1927** Butler County Community College established; **1957** Kansas Oil Museum and Hall of Fame established; **1970** Coutts Memorial Museum of Art established, named for attorney Bud Coutts, killed in plane crash 1965; **1981** El Dorado Lake reservoir built to northeast on Walnut River; **2003** new county courthouse completed.

Elk City   *Montgomery County   See* **Independence (1887)**

Elkhart   *Morton County   Southwestern Kansas, 250 mi/402 km west-southwest of Wichita*

1886 Morton County formed; Richfield becomes county seat; **1912** Santa Fe Railroad built to Oklahoma state line; town founded at railhead; **1913** town platted; incorporated as a city; **1922** Morton County Library founded; **1926** railroad extended into Oklahoma; **1965** county seat moved to Elkhart; county courthouse completed.

Ellsworth   *Ellsworth County   Central Kansas, 138 mi/222 km west-southwest of Topeka*

1864 Fort Ellsworth established to east, relocated and renamed Fort Harker 1866, abandoned 1872; **1867** Ellsworth County formed; town founded as county seat, named for Lt. Allen Ellsworth; incorporated as a city; Kansas Pacific Railroad reaches site; **1872** Grand Central Hotel built; **c.1885** cholera outbreak leads to mass burials; **1890s** Mother Bickerdyke Home founded for Civil War widows, mothers, daughters, nurses; **1913** J. H. Robbins Memorial Library opened; **1948** Kanopolis Reservoir built on Smoky Hill River to southeast; **1950** county courthouse built.

Elwood   *Doniphan County   Northeastern Kansas, 2 mi/3.2 km west of St. Joseph, Missouri, on Missouri River*

1856 town founded by George (?) Rose, named Roseport; **1857** Rose found to be ex-convict, driven out of town; John B. Elwood takes charge; **1859** town renamed; Abraham Lincoln stops here prior to presidential campaign, gives his first speech in Kansas Territory; **1860** river sweeps away part of town, many citizens move to St. Joseph; **Apr. 3, 1860** William H. Russell establishes Pony Express in St. Joseph with

Elwood as way station, service ends 1861 with westward extension of telegraph; **Apr. 23, 1860** first railroad in Kansas, 5 mi/8 km Elwood & Marysville Railroad, built to Wathena, abandoned after a few years; **1878** incorporated as a city; **1952** river changes course separating enclave with St. Joseph's Rosecrans Airport from remainder of state of Missouri; **1993** flooding damages town.

Emporia *Lyon County*   *East central Kansas, 50 mi/ 80 km southwest of Topeka*

1857 town founded; **1859** Second Presbyterian Church built; **1860** Lyon County organized; town becomes county seat; **1863** Kansas State Normal School established, becomes Kansas State Teachers College 1923, Emporia State College 1974, University 1977; **Feb. 10, 1868** newspaper editor, author William Allen White born (died 1944); **1869** Missouri, Kansas & Texas Railroad reaches town; **1870** Santa Fe Railroad reaches town; incorporated as a city; **1882** College of Emporia established by Presbyterians; **1887** Santa Fe stockyard built; **1902** county courthouse built; **1906** Emporia Library built; **1938** Kahola Valley irrigation project completed; **2002** new county courthouse completed.

Erie *Neosho County*   *Southeastern Kansas, 50 mi/ 80 km northwest of Joplin, Missouri*

1864 Neosho County formed; Osage Mission becomes county seat; **1866** town founded; **1869** incorporated as a city; **1874** county seat moved to Erie; **1932** Erie Public Library founded, library built 1975; **1963** county courthouse built.

Eureka *Greenwood County*   *East central Kansas, 57 mi/92 km east-northeast of Wichita*

1862 Greenwood County formed; Janesville becomes county seat; **1867** town platted; **1870** incorporated as a city; **1872** county seat moved to Eureka; **1914** Carnegie Library built; **1917** oil discovered; **1957** county courthouse built.

Florence *Marion County*   See **Marion (1876)**

Fort Scott *Bourbon County*   *Eastern Kansas, 90 mi/145 km south of Kansas City, Kansas*

1842 Fort Scott established along "permanent frontier" of Indian Territory; **1853** fort abandoned; **1855** Bourbon County formed; Henry S. Cobb establishes short-lived Kansas Vegetarian Society to west, fails due to poor management, lack of farming skills; **1860** incorporated as a city; **1861** fort reactivated; **1862** Fort Scott National Cemetery established; **c.1868** Wilder House hotel opened; **1893** Congregational Church built; **1903** Goodlander Children's Home founded; **Dec. 25, 1906** Clark M. Clifford born, secretary of defense under Pres. Lyndon Johnson (died 1998); **1918** Borden Company plant established; **1919** Fort Scott Community College estab-

lished; **1931** county courthouse built; **May 7, 1979** Fort Scott National Historic Site established.

Fredonia *Wilson County*   *Southeastern Kansas, 78 mi/126 km west-northwest of Joplin, Missouri*

1865 Wilson County formed; **1868** town founded as county seat; named Twin Mounds, later renamed for Fredonia, New York; **1871** incorporated as a city; **1914** Fredonia Public Library opened; **1960** county courthouse built.

Frontenac *Crawford County*   See **Pittsburg (1888)**

Garden City *Finney County*   *Western Kansas, 195 mi/314 km west of Wichita, on Arkansas River*

1878 town founded by brothers James R. and William D. Fulton; **1884** Finney County formed; **1886** farmers obtain single great year of corn production, followed by enduring drought; **1887** incorporated as a city; **1907** Garden City Experiment Station established for agricultural research; **1910s** sugar beet production begins; **1919** Garden City Community College established; **1929** county courthouse completed; **Nov. 15, 1959** Clutter family of four shot to death in their home at Holcomb to west by Richard Hickock and Perry Smith, both executed Apr. 15, 1965, murders covered in Truman Capote's 1966 novel *In Cold Blood*; **1980** IBP Incorporated beef packing plant opened.

Garnett *Anderson County*   *Eastern Kansas, 65 mi/ 105 km south-southwest of Kansas City, Kansas*

1855 Anderson County formed; **1856** town founded as county seat; **1861** incorporated as a town; **1864** County Jail built; **July 14, 1865** U.S. Sen. Arthur Capper born (died 1951); **Aug. 23, 1869** poet, author Edgar Lee Masters born (died 1950); **1870** incorporated as a city; **1897** Harry Houdini, stranded with wife Beatrice while traveling, gives free show by breaking out of jail cell claimed to be inescapable; **1902** county courthouse built.

Girard *Crawford County*   *Southeastern Kansas, 35 mi/56 km north-northwest of Joplin, Missouri*

1867 Crawford County formed; **1868** town founded by as county seat; named for pre-Civil War Philadelphia merchant Stephen Girard; **1869** incorporated as a city; **1890s** Socialist J. A. Wayland founds newspaper *Appeal to Reason*, reaches over half-million subscribers, ceased publication 1922; **1906** Carnegie Library built, smallest city to receive a Carnegie grant through efforts of Jane Addams, founder of Chicago's Hull House for homeless women, who had family here and ties to the *Appeal*; **1922** third county courthouse built; **1995** Veterans' Memorial dedicated.

Goodland   *Sherman County*   *Northwestern Kansas, 323 mi/520 km west of Topeka*

1881 town founded; post office established; **1886** Sherman County formed; town becomes county seat; **1887** incorporated as a city; **1930** county courthouse built.

Great Bend   *Barton County*   *Central Kansas, 90 mi/145 km northwest of Wichita*

1864 Fort Zarah Military Reservation established as protection against Native American raids, dismantled 1869; **1872** Barton County formed; town founded as county seat; incorporated as a city; **1874** town becomes Santa Fe railhead on Chisholm Cattle Trail; **1876** in response to rowdiness of cowhands, law passed limiting driven cattle to within 30 mi/48 km west of town; **1915** Union soldier statue erected; **1911** county courthouse built; **1930s** oil boom boosts economy; **1969** Barton County Community College established.

Greensburg   *Kiowa County*   *South central Kansas, 105 mi/169 km west of Wichita*

1885 world's largest hand-dug well built, 109 ft/33 m deep, 32 ft/10 m wide, completed 1887; **1886** Kiowa County formed; incorporated as a city, becomes county seat; **Jan. 1886** extremely cold blizzard kills many cowboys and ranchers and nearly all cattle; **Feb. 1886** 1,000 pd/454 kg meteorite discovered on Frank Kimberly farm, largest of twenty pieces found near Brenham to east; **1913** county courthouse built.

Hays   *Ellis County*   *West central Kansas, 195 mi/ 314 km west of Topeka*

1865 Fort Hays established; "Buffalo Bill" Cody credited with killing over 4,000 buffalo in 18 months; **1867** Ellis County formed; town founded as county seat; **1869** James "Wild Bill" Hickok appointed county sheriff for few months, loses November election after altercation with army troops, moves to Abilene; **1885** incorporated as a city; **1886** St. Joseph's Catholic Church built, replaced 1904; **1889** fort abandoned; **1902** West Branch Kansas Normal School of Emporia established, becomes Fort Hays State College 1931, University 1977; **1914** Sternberg Museum of Natural History founded, new facility opened 1999; **1936** oil boom begins; **1942** county courthouse built.

Hiawatha   *Brown County*   *Northeastern Kansas, 37 mi/60 km west of St. Joseph, Missouri*

1832 Kickapoo peoples from Wisconsin and Illinois relocated to Kickapoo Indian Reservation to southwest, originally over 76,000 ac/30,780 ha, reduced to 6,500 ac/ 2,633 ha; **1855** Brown County formed; **1857** town founded, named for Longfellow's poem; **1858** town becomes county seat; **1870** incorporated as a city; **1925** county courthouse built.

Highland   *Doniphan County*   *Northeastern Kansas, 25 mi/40 km west-northwest of St. Joseph, Missouri*

1837 Presbyterian mission established by Rev. S. M. Irvin ("Father Irvin") for Iowa, Sac, and Fox peoples; **1854** town founded near Missouri River by Gen. John Bayless and J. P. Johnson; **1856** Highland Presbyterian Academy established, becomes Highland University 1857, later Highland Community College; **1857** incorporated as a city; **1914** Highland Presbyterian Church built on site of original 1880s structure.

Hill City   *Graham County*   *Northwestern Kansas, 220 mi/354 km west-northwest of Topeka*

1877 first settler John Stanley arrives; **1880** Graham County formed; town platted for county seat; **1882** incorporated as a city, named for Mayor W. R. Hill; **1925** replica sod house built as example of pioneer architecture; **1958** county courthouse built; **1971** Graham County Library established.

Holcomb   *Finney County*   See **Garden City (1959)**

Holton   *Jackson County*   *Northeastern Kansas, 30 mi/48 km north of Topeka*

1837 tribes from Indiana and other eastern states moved to Potawatomi Indian Reservation to southwest; **1857** Jackson County formed; town founded as county seat by Free Staters from Milwaukee; serves as station on Underground Railroad, movement to help fugitive slaves to freedom; **1862** occupants of Potawatomi Reservation refuse to be relocated, reservation allowed to remain; **1870** incorporated as a city; **c.1881** Campbell University established, merged with Lane University at Lecompton, moved to Kansas City 1913; **1921** county courthouse completed.

Howard   *Elk County*   *Southeastern Kansas, 60 mi/ 97 km east-southeast of Wichita*

1870 Howard County formed; town founded; Elk Falls becomes county seat; **1875** Chautauqua and Elk counties formed from Howard County; Howard becomes Elk County seat; **1887** incorporated as a city; **1908** county courthouse completed.

Hoxie   *Sheridan County*   *Northwestern Kansas, 255 mi/410 km west-northwest of Topeka*

1880 Sheridan County formed; town of Kenneth founded as county seat 3 mi/4.8 km to north; **1886** Union Pacific Railroad built; town relocated to railroad, renamed for railroad vice president H. M. Hoxie; incorporated as a city; **1917** county courthouse built.

Hugoton   *Stevens County*   *Southwestern Kansas, 220 mi/354 km west-southwest of Wichita*

1885 town founded, named for French novelist Victor Hugo (1801–1885); **1886** Stevens County formed; town becomes county seat over rival town of Woodsdale to east; **July 25, 1888** Sheriff John Cross and three deputies, Woodsdale men, shot to death by Hugoton forces; **1890** arrests of Hugoton men responsible for deaths leads to killing of Col. S. N. Wood 1891, founder of Woodsdale; **1910** incorporated as a city; **1912** Santa Fe Railroad reaches town; **1914** Stevens County Library founded, built 1934; **1927** first natural gas well begins production, leading to natural gas boom; **1933** Northern Natural Gas Company Absorption Plant built; **1952** county courthouse built.

Humboldt *Allen County East central Kansas, 100 mi/161 km south-southwest of Kansas City, Kansas*

spring 1856 vegetarian colony established to south; **1857** area settled by German immigrants; town platted; **1861** town sacked and burned by proslavery rebels; **1870** incorporated as a city; **Nov. 6, 1887** Walter Perry "Big Train" Johnson born, star pitcher for Washington Senators (died 1946).

Hutchinson *Reno County Central Kansas, 40 mi/ 64 km northwest of Wichita, on Arkansas River*

1871 town platted by C. C. Hutchinson; **1872** Reno County formed; incorporated as a city, becomes county seat; Santa Fe Railroad reaches town; **1887** natural gas deposit discovered in large salt reserve; **1888** dozen salt processing plants in operation; **Sept. 1913** first official Kansas State Fair held [see Leavenworth]; **1919** soldiers' monument dedicated; **1928** Hutchinson Community College established; **1930** county courthouse completed; **1962** Hutchinson Planetarium established at old State Fair Poultry Building, becomes Kansas Cosmosphere and Space Center 1980.

Independence *Montgomery County Southeastern Kansas, 65 mi/105 km west-northwest of Joplin, Missouri*

1869 Montgomery County formed; **1870** town founded as county seat; **1871** incorporated as a city; **1872** Kansas City, Lawrence & Southern Railroad reaches town; **1881** natural gas field discovered; **1886** county courthouse built; **May 30, 1887** Gov. Henry Hines Woodring born at Elk City to west, secretary of war under Pres. Franklin D. Roosevelt (died 1967); **1903** first oil reserves discovered; **May 3, 1913** playwright William Inge born (died 1973); **1925** Independence Community College established; **1976** Elk City Lake reservoir built to west on Elk River.

Iola *Allen County Eastern Kansas, 92 mi/148 km south-southwest of Kansas City, Kansas*

1855 Allen County organized; **1859** town founded as county seat; **1870** incorporated as a city; **1898** natural gas deposits discovered; **1906** prohibitionist steals dynamite from cement factory, five saloons destroyed by blasts, two fail to explode; Carnegie Library built, demolished 1965, new library built 1967; **c.1920** last of gas wells closed; **1923** Allen County Community College established; **1924**

dairying reaches peak; **1958** county courthouse completed.

Jetmore *Hodgeman County Western Kansas, 142 mi/229 km west-northwest of Wichita*

1879 Hodgeman County formed; town founded as county seat, originally named Buckner; **1882** town platted, renamed for railroad lawyer influential in making town the county seat; **1887** incorporated as a city; **1888** National Bank built; **1929** county courthouse built; **1989** King Community Center and Library built.

Johnson (Johnson City) *Stanton County Southwestern Kansas, 245 mi/394 km west of Wichita*

1885 Atchison, Topeka & Santa Fe Railroad built; town founded by Civil War veterans, originally named Veteran; **1887** Stanton County organized; **1888** town moved 7 mi/ 11.3 km to present site, becomes county seat; incorporated as a city, renamed for Union Civil War veteran Col. A. S. Johnson; **1925** county courthouse built.

Junction City *Geary County East central Kansas, 60 mi/97 km west of Topeka, on Kansas River*

1855 Davis County formed, named for Jefferson Davis; **1858** town founded as county seat at joining of Smoky Hill and Republican rivers, form Kansas (Kaw) River; **1859** incorporated as a city; **1866** Bartell House hotel built; **1882** Opera House built; **1889** county renamed for John W. Geary, territorial governor; **1898** Civil War Memorial Arch dedicated; **1900** county courthouse completed.

Kansas City *Wyandotte County Eastern Kansas, 2 mi/3.2 km west of Kansas City, Missouri*

June 26, 1804 Lewis and Clark expedition camps for two days at mouth of Kaw (Kansas) River on their ascent of Missouri River; **1832** Delaware Methodist mission founded at White Church, former village in west part of city; **1843** land purchased from Delaware peoples by the Wyandot Tribe, just moved from Ohio, for town site, named Wyandot City; **1844** log White Church destroyed by fire, new church built; **1849** California Gold Rush brings influx of white transients and settlers; **1850** neighboring Kansas City, Missouri, incorporated as a city; **Jan. 1852** Quindaro Cemetery founded; **1853** Territorial Convention organizes provisional government for Kansas and Nebraska; **1854** Kansas Territory organized; **1855** Wyandotte County formed; **1857** town passes into white ownership, renamed Wyandotte; **1859** incorporated as a city; **1860** first slaughterhouse established; **1862** Freedman's School established for black students, becomes Western University 1891, closed 1948; **1871** suburb of Armstrong established; Anthony Sauer Castle built on estate of pioneer freight magnate; **1872** town of Old Kansas City incorporated adjacent to Missouri state line; Armourdale founded around Armour packing plant, incorporated 1882; **1879** suburb of Riverview incorporated; **c.1880** influx of freed slaves leads to construction of river shanty towns, including Rattlesnake Hollow and Mississippi Town; **1880** Riverview annexed by Wyandotte; **1886** Old Kansas City, Armourdale, and Armstrong annexed by Wyandotte, renamed Kansas City; **Aug. 29, 1893** jazz saxophonist Charlie Parker born (died 1973); **1895** St. Augustin Seminary established; **1903** St. Mary's Catholic Church dedicated; parts of city damaged by flooding, including St. Mary's Church; Kansas River bridge destroyed; **1905** University of Kansas Hospitals founded; **1911** John Brown statue dedicated at Western University; **1920** Victory monument, bronze statue of soldier, dedicated at Victory Junction (U.S. Highways 40 & 73), to west; **1923** Kansas City Community College established; **1924** Mississippi Town demolished for industrial development; Carnegie Library completed; **1927** county courthouse built; **1929** Fairfax Airport opened on Missouri River, closed 1985; **1955** Lakeside Speedway established, moved to new location 1989; **1989** Woodlands Race Track (horse racing) established at former speedway.

Kingman *Kingman County* *South central Kansas, 44 mi/71 km west of Wichita*

1872 Norman Ingraham becomes first settler; **1874** Kingman County formed; town founded as county seat by J. H. Fical; **1883** Atchison, Topeka & Santa Fe Railroad arrives; incorporated as a city; **1887** area's first salt works established; **1907** county courthouse built; **1911** Clyde Cessna flies his first airplane; **1914** Carnegie Library built.

Kinsley *Edwards County* *Central Kansas, 115 mi/ 185 km west-northwest of Wichita*

June 5, 1848 in Battle of Coon Creek, army uses new breech-loading rifles in defeating Comanche Native American attack; **1873** town founded by group from Massachusetts; **1874** Edwards County formed; **1878** incorporated as a city, becomes county seat; **1884** influx of immigrants arrive from Eastern states; **1928** county courthouse built.

Kirwin *Phillips County* See **Phillipsburg (1889)**

La Crosse *Rush County* *West central Kansas, 195 mi/314 km west-southwest of Topeka*

1874 Rush County formed; Rush Center becomes county seat; **1876** county boundary change puts Rush Center off center; town founded at new county center crossroads, named La Crosse; **1886** incorporated as a city; **1888** county seat moved to La Crosse; county courthouse built; **1931** St. Joseph's College and Military Academy established; **1937** Barnard Library built; **1968** Kansas Barbed Wire Museum opens with 500 examples of barbed wire on display.

Lakin *Kearny County* *Western Kansas, 135 mi/ 217 km west of Wichita*

1873 Atchison, Topeka & Santa Fe Railroad built; town founded as county seat by John O'Laughlin; incorporated as a city; **1876** second Harvey House restaurant opened by Fred Harvey, first opened same year at Florence, Kansas; **1888** Kearny County formed; **1939** county courthouse built; Kearny County Public Library founded.

Lansing *Leavenworth County* *Northeastern Kansas, 36 mi/58 km northwest of Kansas City, Kansas*

1868 Kansas State Penitentiary built with convict labor, prisoners mine coal beneath prison foundation; **1878** town founded by "Doc" James William Lansing; **1959** incorporated as a city; **1985** Lansing Medium Security Prison built.

Larned *Pawnee County* *Central Kansas, 100 mi/ 161 km northwest of Wichita*

Aug. 31, 1825 survey team under John C. Sibley camps here while surveying Santa Fe Trail; **1859** Fort Larned established on trail, sold by U.S. 1884; **1872** Pawnee County formed; **1873** town founded as county seat; **1886** incorporated as a city; **1919** county courthouse built; **Oct. 14, 1966** Fort Larned National Historic Site established.

Lawrence *Douglas County* *Eastern Kansas, 35 mi/ 56 km west-southwest of Kansas City, on Kansas River*

1854 town founded by New England Emigrant Aid Company; named for Amos A. Lawrence of Boston; Plymouth Congregational Church founded; **1855** Douglas County formed; town becomes county seat; **Nov. 1855** in Wakarusa War, Free State sympathizer Charles Dow shot by proslavery man Franklin Coleman, violence leads to surrender of Free State forces to proslavery force largely comprising Missourians; **1856** Fort Titus built to west by Col. H. T. Titus, leader of Southern battalion; **May 21, 1856** posse led by Sheriff Sam Jones enters town, destroys printing press and Free State hotel, robs citizens, arrests Free State leaders; **May 24, 1856** John Brown's forces kill five proslavery men; **Aug. 1856** 600 Free-Staters destroy Fort Titus, wound Colonel Titus; **Sept. 15, 1856** 2,700 proslavery Missouri forces persuaded to return by Territorial Gov. John W. Geary; **1857** First Methodist Church built; **1858** incorporated as a city; Trinity Episcopal Church built; **Aug. 21, 1863** pro-South William Quantrill gang comprising 450 "Bushwhackers" sack town; **1864** Union Pacific Railroad reaches town; **1866** University of Kansas established; **July 2, 1878** city planner Henry Wright born (died 1936); **Feb. 17, 1879** author Dorothy Canfield Fisher born (died 1958) **1884** Haskell Institute founded for Native Americans; **1905** county courthouse completed; **1917** Reuter Organ Factory established; **1926** Eldridge Hotel opened; **1937** Carnegie Library built; **1977** Spencer Art Museum opened.

Leavenworth *Leavenworth County* *Northeastern Kansas, 20 mi/32 km northwest of Kansas City, Kansas*

1827 Fort Leavenworth Military Reservation established on Missouri River by Col. Henry Leavenworth to protect commercial traffic on Santa Fe Trail; **1828** ferry service established by Zadoc Martin; **1854** town settled by proslavery sympathizers from Missouri; **1855** Leavenworth County formed; incorporated as a city, becomes county seat; Union Pacific Railroad reaches town; **1856** Abernathy Furniture Plant opens; Planters' House hotel opens; **July 15, 1858** fire destroys business district; **1860** pro-Union factions become dominant; St. Mary's College established; **Oct. 1863** first annual Kansas State Fair held, moved to Hutchinson 1913; **1868** Immaculate Conception Cathedral completed; **c.1872** J. C. Lysle flour mill built; **1874** Leavenworth U.S. military prison founded; **1885** National Hotel built, burned 1963; **1886** Leavenworth National Cemetery established; **Nov. 7, 1901** 26 prison inmates escape under hail of bullets; **1902** Public Library opened; **Apr. 20, 1910** six inmates escape by forcing locomotive engineer to crash through prison barrier; **1912** county courthouse built; **Dec. 11, 1931** seven inmates are smuggled out of prison in barrels; **1934** Leavenworth Veterans Hospital established; **1993** widespread flooding occurs along Missouri River.

Lebanon *Smith County* See **Smith Center (1905)**

Lecompton *Douglas County* *Eastern Kansas, 16 mi/26 km east of Topeka, on Kansas River*

1850s ferry established by first white settler William K. Simmons; **1854** town founded, named for Samuel D. Lecompte, first Chief Justice of Kansas Territory; **1855** incorporated as a city; **Aug. 1855** territorial legislature moves seat of government to Lecompton; **1857** Stanton Home built; **Sept. 1857** proslavery Lecompton Constitution drawn; **1858** Kansas voters reject Constitution; **Jan. 29, 1861** Kansas admitted to Union as 34th state and as a free state, legislature was meeting at Lawrence at the time; Topeka chosen as state capital; **1865** Lane University established.

Leoti *Wichita County* *Western Kansas, 305 mi/491 km west-southwest of Topeka*

1885 town platted at center of proposed county; rival town of Coronado founded 3 mi/4.8 km to east; **1887** Wichita County formed; Leoti incorporated as a city; two towns engage in violent dispute over county seat; Leoti handily wins county seat election; Missouri Pacific Railroad wins county-induced race by reaching Leoti while Santa Fe Railroad barely reaches county line; **1916** county courthouse built; **May 1982** Museum of the Great Plains opened.

Liberal *Seward County* *Southwestern Kansas, 195 mi/314 km west-southwest of Wichita*

1886 Seward County formed; town founded as county seat; **1888** Chicago, Rock Island & Pacific Railroad reaches town; **1915** Public Library built; **1920** natural gas field discovered to west; **1945** incorporated as a city; **1947** county courthouse built; **1951** oil discovered to southwest; **1969** Seward County Community College established.

Lincoln *Lincoln County* *Central Kansas, 135 mi/217 km west of Topeka*

1864 four white buffalo hunters killed by band of 100 Cheyenne; **1870** Lincoln County formed; town platted as county seat by George Green, named Lincoln Center; **1878** town renamed Lincoln; **1879** incorporated as a city; **1886** Salina, Lincoln & Northwestern Railroad reaches town; **1900** county courthouse built; **1913** Carnegie Library built.

Lindsborg *McPherson County* *Central Kansas, 110 mi/177 km southwest of Topeka*

1869 Swedes settle in Smoky Hill River valley; town founded by Chicago Swedish Company; **1870** McPherson County formed; town serves as temporary county seat; **1873** county seat moved to town of McPherson; **1879** incorporated as a city; **1881** Bethany College established by Lutheran Church under efforts of Dr. Carl Swensson.

Lyndon *Osage County* *Eastern Kansas, 30 mi/48 km south of Topeka*

1859 Sac and Fox peoples removed to Oklahoma; Osage County formed; Burlingame becomes county seat; **1869** town founded as new county seat; **1870** incorporated as a city; **1923** county courthouse built; **1963** Pomona Lake formed by dam on Dragoon Creek to north; **1972** Melvern Reservoir formed on Marais des Cygnes River to south.

Lyons *Rice County* *Central Kansas, 65 mi/105 km northwest of Wichita*

1871 Rice County formed; towns of Atlanta and Peace (Sterling) vie over county seat; **1876** Lyons platted at county center as county seat; **1880** Santa Fe Railroad reaches town; incorporated as a city; **1890** first salt mine shaft sunk in area; **1910** county courthouse built; **1911** Carnegie Library built; **1918** city hall built; **1920s** oil production begins.

Manhattan *Riley County* *East central Kansas, 48 mi/77 km west-northwest of Topeka, on Kansas River*

1853 Fort Riley established to west by Maj. E. A. Ogden to protect emigrants and traders on Santa Fe Trail; **1854** town of Paleska platted by Col. George S. Park of Parkville, Missouri; second town of Canton founded nearby by New England Emigrant Aid Company; **1855** Riley County formed; Paleska and Canton merge to

KANSAS

become Boston, soon renamed Manhattan; Fort Riley National Cemetery established; **July 2, 1855** first territorial legislature convenes at town of Pawnee adjacent to Fort Riley, moved to Shawnee Mission July 16; **1857** incorporated as a city; **1859** Belmont College founded, becomes Kansas State University 1863; **1865** St. Paul's Episcopal Church built; **Oct. 4, 1884** writer Damon Runyon born (died 1946); **1904** Carnegie Library built; **1906** County Office Building built; **1917** Camp Funston established as World War I training camp; **Jan. 12, 1918** robbery of Camp Funston Bank leaves four dead, one wounded, $62,000 taken, robber commits suicide; **1927** Manhattan Christian College established; **1933** Sunset Zoo opened; **1939** Municipal Airport established to west; **1994** Kansas State Campus annexed by city.

Mankato   *Jewell County   Northern Kansas, 180 mi/ 290 km west of St. Joseph, Missouri*

1870 Jewell County formed; **1872** town founded as Jewell Center, becomes county seat; **1880** incorporated as a city, renamed Mankato averting confusion with Jewell City, in same county; **1930s** Limestone Valley Soil Erosion Project implemented to reverse effects of Depression era Dust Bowl; **1938** county courthouse built.

Marion   *Marion County   Central Kansas, 48 mi/ 77 km north-northeast of Wichita*

1860 area settled by Free Staters; Marion County formed; **1866** town founded as county seat; **1874** Presbyterian church completed; **1875** incorporated as a city; **1876** Fred Harvey opens first of his Harvey House restaurants at Florence to south, known for Harvey Girls waitresses, site closed 1900; **1909** county courthouse built; **July 1951** flooding of Cottonwood River damages area; **1967** Marion Lake formed by dam to northwest on Cottonwood River.

Marysville   *Marshall County   Northeastern Kansas, 97 mi/156 km west of St. Joseph, Missouri*

1842 region explored by John C. Fremont; **May 1846** Sarah "Grandma" Keyes buried here, member of ill-fated Donner Party, many of whom died in Sierra Nevada during following winter; **1851** Francis J. Marshall begins ferry service on Big Blue River, on Oregon Trail; town founded; **1855** Marshall County formed; town becomes county seat; **1860-1861** incorporated as a city; **1938** Marysville Public Library founded; **1979** county courthouse built.

McPherson   *McPherson County   Central Kansas, 50 mi/80 km north-northwest of Wichita*

1870 McPherson County formed, named for Union Gen. James McPherson; Lindsborg becomes county seat; **1872** town founded as new county seat; **1874** incorporated as a city; **1879** Missouri Pacific and Rock Island railroads reach town; **1887** McPherson College established; **1894** county courthouse built; **1914** Central College and

Academy established; **July 4, 1917** statue of General McPherson mounted on his horse dedicated.

Meade   *Meade County   Southwestern Kansas, 165 mi/266 km west-southwest of Wichita*

1874 O. E. Short and survey party killed by Native Americans; **1885** Meade County formed; town incorporated, becomes county seat; **1887** home of Eva Dalton Whipple used as hideout by Dalton Gang; **1888** Rock Island Railroad built through town; **1895** incorporated as a city; Meade Public Library founded; **1917** natural gas deposit discovered, developed by Skelly Oil 1959; **1928** second county courthouse built.

Medicine Lodge   *Barber County   Southern Kansas, 75 mi/121 km southwest of Wichita*

Oct. 1867 Medicine Lodge Peace Treaty signed by federal government and representatives of numerous Native American nations; **1873** Barber County formed; town platted as county seat; first log houses built; **1879** incorporated as a city; **May 1, 1884** Medicine Valley Bank held up, bank president and cashier killed, four bandits surrender, two of them killed in jail by lynch mob, including Henry Newton Brown, sheriff of Caldwell, Kansas, past associate of Billy the Kid; **1899** prohibitionist Carrie Nation, who arrived here 1890 from Texas with second husband David Nation, begins her temperance movement, preaching evils of liquor consumption, begins destroying saloons with her axe 1900; **1927** annual Peace Treaty Pageant begun; **1929** Peace Treaty monument erected; **1956** county courthouse built.

Merriam   *Johnson County   Eastern Kansas, 7 mi/ 11 km southwest of Kansas City, Missouri*

1812 Shawnee people forced to migrate from Ohio, settle at Gum Springs; **1825** Shawnee Indian Reservation established; **1836** Shawnee Mission established by Quakers; **1854** most Shawnee lands ceded to U.S.; **1864** town founded by David Campbell of Tennessee, named Campbell Town; **1890s** Kansas City, Fort Scott & Gulf Railroad arrives; town renamed for railroad man Charles Merriam; **1950** incorporated as a city.

Minneapolis   *Ottawa County   North central Kansas, 108 mi/174 km west of Topeka, on Solomon River*

1860 Ottawa County formed; **1866** county organized; town founded as county seat; **1871** incorporated as a city; **1878** Solomon Valley Railroad reaches town; **1880** African-American scientist George Washington Carver (1861–1943) spends youth here, through 1885; Minneapolis Opera House built; **1956** county courthouse built.

Montezuma *Gray County* *Southwestern Kansas, 170 mi/274 km west of Wichita*

1887 town promoted by Asa Soule; **1912** incorporated as a city; second land boom attracts new arrivals; **1913** prairie fire from south narrowly misses town; **1931–1937** area experiences seven consecutive years of crop failures; **2001** Gray County Wind Farm completed with 170 wind turbines, landowner's income $2,000 per year for each turbine.

Mound City *Linn County* *Eastern Kansas, 70 mi/113 km south of Kansas City, Kansas*

1855 Linn County formed; Paris becomes county seat; **1857** town founded as new county seat, named for nearby Sugar Mound; county records taken by force from Paris (abandoned); **1871** incorporated as a city; **1876** Mary Somerville Library founded; **1886** county courthouse built.

Ness City *Ness County* *Western Kansas, 150 mi/241 km northwest of Wichita*

1878 town founded; **1880** Ness County formed; town becomes county seat, named for Union Cpl. Noah V. Ness; **1886** incorporated as a city; **1887** Santa Fe Railroad reaches town; Ness City Public Library founded; **1888** African-American scientist George Washington Carver (1861–1943) moves here, conducts geological research involving oil-rich strata, through 1891; **1917** county courthouse built.

Newton *Harvey County* *Central Kansas, 25 mi/40 km north of Wichita*

1870s German Mennonites settle in area; **1871** Santa Fe Railroad built; town founded; **Aug. 9, 1871** Tuttle Dance Hall Massacre gunfight leaves three dead, three wounded; **1872** Harvey County formed; town becomes county seat; incorporated as a city; **1886** Bernhard Warkentin mills Turkey Red winter wheat, credited with making Kansas "world's breadbasket"; **1887** Bethel College established; **1903** Carnegie Library built; **1964** county courthouse built.

Nicodemus *Graham County* *North central Kansas, 210 mi/338 km west-northwest of Topeka*

1877 group of African-Americans from South arrives at town site, often considered part of larger early 1870s exodus organized by Benjamin "Pap" Singleton, others; **1880** St. Francis Hotel built; **1880s** Priscilla Art Club Building built; **1882** Nicodemus School built; **1910** population dwindles to 200; **1974** town designated National Historic Landmark.

Norton *Norton County* *Northwestern Kansas, 267 mi/430 km west of St. Joseph, Missouri*

1872 Norton County formed; town founded as county seat by N. H. Billings, named Billingsville; **1873** Robinson House built of stone; **1885** incorporated as a city; **1888** Chicago, Rock Island & Pacific Railroad reaches town; **1909** Norton Public Library founded; **1913** state tuberculosis sanitarium opened; **1929** county courthouse completed.

Oakley *Logan County* *Western Kansas, 280 mi/451 km west of Topeka*

1865 army post and station established on Butterfield Overland stagecoach route at Monument Rocks; **1870** Kansas Pacific Railroad built; **1884** town founded; **1887** Logan County formed; Russell Springs becomes county seat; incorporated as a city; **Sept. 23, 1904** business district destroyed by fire; **1923** Oakley Public Library founded; **1963** county seat moved to Oakley; **1965** county courthouse built; **1975** Fick Fossil and History Museum established.

Oberlin *Decatur County* *Northwestern Kansas, 302 mi/486 km west of St. Joseph, Missouri*

1872 town founded, originally named Westfield; **Sept. 27–28, 1878** last Native American massacre in Kansas, many settlers killed, including six-member Laing family; **1879** Decatur County formed; town founded as county seat; **1885** town incorporated, renamed for Oberlin, Ohio, origin of settlers; **1926** county courthouse built.

Olathe *Johnson County* *Eastern Kansas, 20 mi/32 km southwest of Kansas City, Kansas*

1855 Johnson County formed; Shawnee becomes county seat; **1857** town founded; **1858** incorporated as a city; county seat moved to Olathe; **Sept. 6, 1862** town raided by pro-South Quantrill gang led by William Clarke Quantrill, prisoners are marched into Missouri; **c.1880** Charles H. Hyer begins making cowboy boots, becomes one of world's largest boot manufacturers by 1920s; **1871** Atchison, Topeka, & Santa Fe Railroad reaches town; **Aug. 13, 1904** actor Charles Buddy Rogers born (died 1999); **1907** interurban rail line reaches town from Kansas City, abandoned 1940; **1942** Olathe Naval Air Station established to southwest, closed 1970; **May 1943** tornado destroys over 100 airplanes at Olathe Air Station; **1951** county courthouse built; **1966** MidAmerica Nazarene University established.

Osawatomie *Miami County* *Eastern Kansas, 45 mi/72 km south-southwest of Kansas City, Kansas*

1827 Potawatomi people forced to move here from Missouri; **1837** Methodist mission established, closed 1848; **1854** town founded, name combination of Osage and Potawatomi; **Aug. 30, 1856** in Battle of Osawatomie, about 40 of John Brown's Free State forces attacked by 400 proslavery Missouri troops under Gen. John W. Reid, Brown's son Frederick killed, five of Reid's men killed; **1861** Old Stone Church built; **1864** state hospital founded; **Aug. 30, 1877** John Brown Memorial (soldiers monument) dedicated; **1883**

incorporated as a city; **1910** President Roosevelt dedicates John Brown Battlefield Memorial Park; **1987** Osawatomie Correctional Facility established at former state hospital.

Osborne   *Osborne County   North central Kansas, 160 mi/257 km west-northwest of Topeka*

1871 Osborne County formed; town founded as county seat; both named for Kansas cavalry Sgt Vincent B. Osborne; area settled by Dutch immigrants from Pennsylvania; **1879** incorporated as a city; **1891** North American Geodetic Center determined to south, point of origin for all surveying in U.S.; **1908** county courthouse built.

Oskaloosa   *Jefferson County   Northeastern Kansas, 37 mi/60 km west-northwest of Kansas City, Kansas*

1855 Jefferson County formed; area first settled; **1857** town platted; **1858** town wins dispute with Valley Falls over county seat; **1860** *Oskaloosa Independent* newspaper founded by Free Stater John Wesley Roberts; **1869** incorporated as a city; **1897** artist John Stuart Curry born at Winchester to north (died 1946); **1962** third county courthouse completed; **1969** Perry Lake reservoir built on Delaware River to west.

Oswego   *Labette County   Southeastern Kansas, 32 mi/51 km west-northwest of Joplin, Missouri*

1841 John Matthews establishes trading post; town of Little Town founded; **1861** post and town abandoned; **1865** new settlers arrive; town founded, renamed Oswego; D. M. Clover establishes ferry on Neosho River; **1867** Labette County formed; town becomes county seat; **1870** incorporated as a city; **1948** county courthouse built.

Ottawa   *Franklin County   Eastern Kansas, 25 mi/40 km south of Lawrence*

1832 land ceded by Ottawa peoples; **1837** Ottawa Baptist Mission established by Jotham Meeker; **1855** Franklin County formed; **1857** hotel owned by Free State sympathizer Tauy Jones burned by proslavery group; **1860s** Tauy Jones House built, home of part-Native American born in Canada, founded Ottawa University; **1864** town platted on Marais des Cygnes River; tornado damages town; **1865** Ottawa University founded; **1867** incorporated as a city; Ottawa peoples moved to Indian Territory; **1868** Missouri Pacific Railroad reaches town; **1883** Chautauqua assembly established; **1893** county courthouse built; **1900** natural gas discovered; **Nov. 28, 1937** Colorado Sen. Gary Hart born.

Overland Park   *Johnson County   Eastern Kansas, 10 mi/16 km south of Kansas City, Kansas*

1834 Quaker mission established for Shawnee people by Rev. Thomas Johnson; **1838** Shawnee Mission established by Methodist Episcopal Church; **1845** boarding school built; **1855** proslavery legislature meets at Gov. Andrew Reeder's office at boarding school; **Jan. 2, 1865** Johnson shot and killed by Quantrill gang at Westport (Kansas City), Missouri; **1960** incorporated as a city; **1967** Johnson County Community College established.

Paola   *Miami County   Eastern Kansas, 40 mi/64 km south-southwest of Kansas City, Kansas*

1848 Baptist Indian school established to east; **1855** town platted, named Peoria Village; **1856** current name adopted, variation of original name; **1859** incorporated as a city; **1860** oil discovered; first oil well west of Mississippi River dug; **1861** Miami County formed; town becomes county seat; **1872** Paola Free Library founded; **1884** natural gas discovered; **1894** Ursuline Academy founded; **1998** county courthouse built, replaces 1898 structure.

Parsons   *Labette County   Southeastern Kansas, 43 mi/69 km northwest of Joplin, Missouri*

1870 Missouri, Kansas & Texas Railroad built; town founded, named for railroad president Levi Parsons; **1871** incorporated as a city; **March 1873** three years of disappearances of individuals traced to William Bender, son John, and daughter Kate, killed and robbed their dinner guests, disappeared without a trace; **June 3, 1898** actress ZaSu Pitts born (died 1965); **1903** Kansas State Hospital founded; **1909** Carnegie Library built, replaced 1977, converted to Carnegie Art Center 1996; **1923** Labette Community College established; **1941** Kansas Ordnance Plant established.

Phillipsburg   *Phillips County   Northern Kansas, 237 mi/381 km west of St. Joseph, Missouri*

1872 Phillips County formed; town platted as county seat, named for Union Col. William A. Phillips; **1873** Fort Bissell built; **1880** incorporated as a city; **Nov. 27, 1889** New Mexico Sen. Carl Atwood Hatch born at Kirwin to southeast, authored Hatch Act limiting political activities of Federal employees (died 1963); **1912** county courthouse built; **1939** oil discovered in county; **1955** Kirwin Reservoir built to southeast on North Fork Solomon River.

Piqua   *Woodson County   See **Yates Center** (1895)*

Pittsburg   *Crawford County   Southeastern Kansas, 23 mi/37 km north-northwest of Joplin, Missouri*

1808 Osage people of Missouri forced to settle along Neosho River; **1865** Osage forced again to move south into Indian Territory; **1876** town founded as coal mining camp, named for Pittsburgh, Pennsylvania; **1878** zinc smelter established by Robert Lanyon; **1880** incorporated as a city; **1888** zinc transported from other mining sites for smelting utilizing Pittsburg's coal; **Nov. 1888** defective dynamite charge causes coal mine explosion at Frontenac to north, nearly 50 killed; **1923** Manual Training School established, branch of State Normal School at Emporia, later Kansas State Teachers College, becomes Pittsburg State University 1978; **1925** Memorial Auditorium opened.

Pratt *Pratt County* *South central Kansas, 78 mi/ 126 km west of Wichita*

1879 last buffalo in region killed, had numbered up to 40,000 in a single view; Pratt County formed; **1884** town founded, named for Civil War veteran Caleb Pratt; town engages in bitter struggle with Saratoga for county seat; **1884** town becomes county seat during "Indian scare" causing Saratoga residents to flee, Pratt accused of creating false incident; incorporated as a city; **1910** county courthouse built; **1938** Pratt Community College established.

Reserve *Brown County* *Northeastern Kansas, 40 mi/64 km west-northwest of St. Joseph, Missouri*

1837 Sac and Fox peoples are moved from Iowa to northeastern Kansas; **1856** Thomas Hart builds log cabin, Hart and wife serve meals to freight wagons operating between St. Joseph and Nebraska City; **1867** Sac and Fox are moved to Indian Territory, remainder retreat to small reservation to east; **1881** Missouri Pacific Railroad reaches site; town founded; **1896** tornado destroys town, five killed; **1913** incorporated as a city.

Russell *Russell County* *Central Kansas, 170 mi/ 274 km west of Topeka*

Apr. 1871 Kansas Pacific Railroad built; 60 families arrive from Ripon, Wisconsin; **1872** Russell County formed; town founded as county seat; incorporated as a city; **1903** county courthouse completed, tower added 1908; **July 22, 1923** U.S. Sen. Robert Joseph Dole born, Republican presidential nominee 1996.

Saint Francis *Cheyenne County* *Northwestern Kansas, 370 mi/595 km west of St. Joseph, Missouri*

Sept. 1868 57 scouts under Col. George A. Forsyth attacked by 750 Cheyenne and Sioux on Arikaree River, west of Colorado state boundary, four scouts killed, many Native Americans killed, scouts relieved by African-American Cavalry; **1885** town founded, named Waco; **1886** Cheyenne County formed; Chicago, Burlington & Quincy Railroad built, town renamed for settler A. L. Emerson's wife; **1888** town becomes county seat; **1903** incorporated as a city; **1924** county courthouse built; **Nov. 20, 1930** astronaut Ronald Evans born; **May 31, 1935** Republican River floods, 19 killed.

Saint John *Stafford County* *Central Kansas, 80 mi/129 km northwest of Wichita*

1875 area settled by Mormons; **1879** Stafford County formed; town platted, originally named Zion Valley, **1882**

town becomes county seat; **1885** incorporated as a city, renamed St. John; **1886** Atchison, Topeka & Santa Fe Railroad reaches town; **1929** county courthouse built.

Salina *Saline County* *Central Kansas, 105 mi/ 169 km west of Topeka, on Smoky Hill River*

1858 town founded by Free Staters led by William A. Phillips; **1859** Saline County formed; town becomes county seat; **1860** town thrives as embarkation point for Pike's Peak gold rush; **1867** Union Pacific Railroad reaches town; **1870** incorporated as a city; **1874** alfalfa production begun by Dr. W. R. Switzer; **1886** Kansas Wesleyan University established; **1903** Salina Public Library built; **1907** Christ Episcopal Cathedral completed; **1922** Marymount College established; **June 1938** Smoky Hill River floods town; **1942** Smoky Hill Army Air Field established, closed 1948, becomes Schilling Air Force Base 1951, becomes Salina Airport 1967; **1969** county courthouse built; **1973** Smoky Hill Air National Guard base established to southwest at former Schilling Bombing Range.

Scott City *Scott County* *Western Kansas, 280 mi/ 451 km west-southwest of Topeka*

Sept. 27, 1878 encounter of Cheyenne Chief Dull Knife and Little Wolf with U.S. Cavalry in Battle of Squaw's Den, last battle with Native Americans in Kansas, Col. William H. Lewis mortally wounded; **1879** town platted, originally named Nixon; **1885** incorporated as a city; **1886** Scott County formed; **1887** town becomes county seat; **1888** Santa Fe Railroad reaches town; **1913** town renamed Scott City; **1924** county courthouse built, remodeled 2002.

Sedan *Chautauqua County* *Southeastern Kansas, 75 mi/121 km southeast of Wichita*

1875 Chautauqua County formed; town founded as county seat; **1876** incorporated as a city; **1886** Missouri Pacific Railroad reaches town; **1896** Opera House built, later becomes Emmett Kelly Museum; **June 19, 1898** world's most famous clown Emmett Kelly born (died 1979); **1904** oil discovered in county; **1918** county courthouse built.

Sedgwick *Harvey and Sedgwick counties* *Central Kansas, 15 mi/24 km north-northwest of Wichita*

1601 Spanish explorer Juan de Oñate finds native village with over 1,200 lodges; **1865** Little Arkansas River Peace Treaty reached granting lands to Arapaho and Cheyenne people in reparation for Sand Creek Massacre Nov. 1864 [see Eads, Colorado]; **1870** town founded; **1872** incorporated as a city; **1929** Lillian Tear Public Library founded.

Seneca *Nemaha County* *Northeastern Kansas, 65 mi/105 km west of St. Joseph, Missouri*

1855 Nemaha County formed; **1857** town founded on branch of Oregon Trail; **1860–1861** Pony Express station established; **1867** Unitarian Church built, converted to Free Library 1931; **1870** Union Pacific Railroad reaches town; **1870** incorporated as a city; **1873** county organized; town becomes county seat; **1955** county courthouse built.

Sharon Springs   *Wallace County   Western Kansas, 325 mi/523 km west of Topeka*

1886 town founded; **1887** Wallace County formed; town of Wallace made temporary county seat; **1889** Sharon Springs becomes permanent county seat; **1890** incorporated as a city; **1914** county courthouse built.

Shawnee   *Johnson County   Eastern Kansas, 8 mi/ 12.9 km southwest of Kansas City, Kansas*

1830 Frederick Chouteau Home built by relative of Auguste Chouteau, founder of St. Louis; **1830s** Bluejacket Home built by Shawnee chief and Methodist minister Charles Bluejacket; **1834** Quakers establish mission for Shawnee people; **1838** Shawnee Mission established by Methodist Episcopal church; **1855** Johnson County formed; town founded as county seat; **1858** county seat moved to Olathe; **1922** incorporated as a city.

Smith Center   *Smith County   Northern Kansas, 208 mi/335 km west of St. Joseph, Missouri*

1871 town founded; **1872** Smith County formed; town becomes county seat; William A. Plaster homesteads Sitting Bull Fort tract, builds Plaster's Castle, never completed; **1873** homesteader Dr. Brewster Higley pens words to "Home on the Range," published 1910, recorded hit 1934; **1886** incorporated as a city; **Feb. 13, 1905** lowest temperature ever recorded in Kansas reached at Lebanon to east, −40°F/−40°C; **1919** county courthouse completed.

Stockton   *Rooks County   North central Kansas, 190 mi/306 km west-northwest of Topeka*

1872 Rooks County formed; Missouri Pacific Railroad reaches site; town founded as county seat; **1880** incorporated as a city; **1921** county courthouse built; **1939** Rooks County State Lake reservoir completed to south; **1956** Webster Reservoir built on South Solomon River to west.

Sublette   *Haskell County   Southwestern Kansas, 193 mi/311 km west of Wichita*

1887 Haskell County formed; Santa Fe at county center becomes county seat; **1912** Santa Fe Railroad built through southern part of county, bypassing Santa Fe; town of Sublette founded on railroad, named for fur trader William Sublette; **1920** county seat moved to Sublette; **1923** incorporated as a city; **1978** county courthouse built.

Syracuse   *Hamilton County   Western Kansas, 240 mi/386 km west of Wichita*

1885 town founded; **1886** Hamilton County formed; **1887** incorporated as a city; **1888** Syracuse becomes county seat after legal battle with Kendall, both towns having county offices for three years; **1937** county courthouse built.

Topeka   *Shawnee County   Eastern Kansas, 60 mi/ 97 km west of Kansas City, Missouri, on Kansas River*

1842 ferry established on Kansas (Kaw) River; **1848** Baptist Mission built, closed 1859; Abram Burnett (1811–1870), Potawatomi subchief, arrives from Michigan, signer of treaties affecting Kansas (chief weighed 450 lb/ 208 kg); **1854** town founded by Cyrus K. Holliday of Pennsylvania, becomes Free State town; **1855** Shawnee County formed; town becomes county seat; **1857** incorporated as a city; **1858** bridge replaces ferry; **Jan. 25, 1860** U.S. Sen. Charles Curtis born at North Topeka, vice president under Herbert Hoover (died 1936); **Jan. 29, 1861** Kansas admitted to Union as 34th state; capital moved from Lecompton; **1865** Washburn College established; **1866** construction of state capitol begins, east wing completed 1873, west wing 1881, central section and cupola 1906; **Aug. 6, 1879** journalist Frank Irving Cobb born, worked for *Detroit Evening News* (died 1923); **1878** Kansas State Hospital established; **1884** First Presbyterian Church built, stained glass windows by Louis C. Tiffany installed 1911; **1889** Executive Mansion built; **July 22, 1893** psychiatrist Dr. Karl A. Menninger born (died 1990); **1895** Kansas Vocational School founded for black students; **Oct. 14, 1899** psychiatrist Dr. William C. Menninger born (died 1966); **1903** flooding inundates North Topeka, 29 killed, levee system later built; **1912** Capper Mansion built; **July 17, 1917** poet, novelist Gwendolyn Brooks born; **1919** Grace Episcopal Cathedral completed; **1937** Gov. Alf M. Landon mansion completed; **1938** Topeka Boulevard Bridge across Kansas River dedicated; **1940** Phillip Billard Airport established to east; **1941** Menninger Foundation established for treatment of mental illnesses; **1942** Forbes Army Air Base established to south, becomes Air Force Base after World War II, becomes Forbes Field Airport 1974; **1944** Goodyear Tire Plant opened; **1965** county courthouse built; **June 8, 1966** tornado strikes city, 17 killed, narrowly misses state capitol; **1984** Kansas Museum of History built; **1991** performing arts center opened.

Trading Post   *Linn County   Eastern Kansas, 60 mi/97 km south of Kansas City, Kansas*

1842 Gen. Winfield Scott builds fort; town founded; **May 19, 1858** Marais des Cygnes Massacre, 30 proslavery men from Missouri under Capt. Charles Hamelton seize Free State men on Marais des Cygnes River, five wounded, five killed; **Nov. 12, 1860** Free Staters hang Russell Hinds for returning slave to his owner; **Oct. 25, 1864** in Battle of Mine Creek, Confederate Gen. Sterling Price is soundly defeated by forces of Union Generals Samuel R. Curtis,

Alfred Pleasonton, and James Blunt; Price retreats to Arkansas.

Tribune *Greeley County* *Western Kansas, 330 mi/ 531 km west-southwest of Topeka*

1885 town founded; originally named Chappaqua; **1887** incorporated as a city, renamed; **1888** Greeley County formed, named for New York *Tribune* founder Horace Greeley; town becomes county seat; Missouri Pacific Railroad built; **1890** county courthouse built, becomes Horace Greeley Museum 1975; **1912** State Agricultural Experiment Station established by Kansas State College of Agriculture and Applied Science; **1975** county courthouse completed.

Troy *Doniphan County* *Northeastern Kansas, 15 mi/24 km west of St. Joseph, Missouri*

1855 Doniphan County formed; town founded as county seat; **Dec. 2, 1859** Abraham Lincoln makes campaign speech here during five-day visit to Kansas; **1860** incorporated as a city; **Feb. 22, 1901** Supreme Court Justice Charles Evans Whittaker born (died 1973); **1906** county courthouse built.

Ulysses *Grant County* *Southwestern Kansas, 220 mi/354 km west of Wichita*

1831 Jedediah Smith, first white man to cross Sierra Nevada into California, killed and scalped by Native Americans while quenching his thirst at Cimarron River 12 mi/19 km to south; **1885** town founded, named for Ulysses S. Grant; **1888** Grant County formed; town becomes county seat; **1921** incorporated as a city; **1929** county courthouse built; **1936** north extension Hugoton natural gas field discovered in Grant County; **1937** Jedediah Smith monument erected.

Valley Falls *Jefferson County* *Northeastern Kansas, 24 mi/39 km north-northeast of Topeka*

1854 Henry Zen becomes first settler; **1855** Jefferson County formed; town founded by Free Staters with hope of making it the county seat, named Grasshopper Falls; **1856** town sacked, burned by proslavery guerillas; **1858** town loses county seat bid to Oskaloosa after bitter dispute; **1869** incorporated as a city; **1874** grasshopper plague destroys crops; **1875** town renamed Valley Falls; **1878** Piazzek Mill built; **1913** fire destroys New Century Hotel block.

Volland *Wabaunsee County* *See* **Alma (1907)**

Wabaunsee *Wabaunsee County* *East central Kansas, 35 mi/56 km west of Topeka, on Kansas River*

1856 abolitionist members of Beecher Bible and Rifle Colony arrive from Connecticut, found town; station established on Underground Railroad for freed slaves; **1857** Capt. William Mitchell log cabin built; **1862** Beecher

Church completed; **June 1907** colony dwindles following 50th anniversary; **1920** church services discontinued.

WaKeeney *Trego County* *West central Kansas, 225 mi/362 km west of Topeka*

1878 Union Pacific Railroad reaches site; town founded, named for Chicago businessmen Warren and Keeney; **1879** Trego County formed; **1880** incorporated as a city; **1889** county courthouse completed; **1902** Emanuel Lutheran Church built; **1952** Cedar Bluff Reservoir built on Smoky Hill River to south.

Wallace *Wallace County* *Western Kansas, 320 mi/515 km west of Topeka*

c.1865 Fort Wallace military outpost established; **Sept. 1868** detachment of African-American Cavalry (Buffalo Soldiers) heads out from Fort Wallace to aid George Forsyth's scouts trapped by 750 Cheyenne at Beecher Island, Arikaree River, Colorado; **1870** Kansas Pacific Railroad reaches site; Peter Robideaux opens store; town becomes major shipping point for central plains; **1881** fort abandoned; **1887** Wallace County formed; town becomes county seat; **1889** county seat moved to Sharon Springs; railroad extended into Colorado; **1895** Robideaux's Store closed.

Wamego *Pottawatomie County* *East central Kansas, 35 mi/56 km west-northwest of Topeka, on Kansas River*

1856 area settled by Beecher Bible and Rifle Colony, abolitionists based in Connecticut under Henry Ward Beecher; **1869** incorporated as a city; **Apr. 2, 1875** automobile manufacturer Walter Percy Chrysler born, established Chrysler Corporation 1925 (died 1940); **1879** stone Dutch Windmill built in rural part of county, moved to City Park 1923.

Washington *Washington County* *Northern Kansas, 120 mi/193 km west of St. Joseph, Missouri*

1820 region explored by S. H. Long expedition; **1860** Washington County formed; town founded, as county seat; **1875** incorporated as a city; **1877** Union Pacific Railroad reaches town; **1884** Chicago, Burlington & Quincy Railroad reaches town; **1934** county courthouse built, addition built 2000, previous courthouse destroyed by tornado 1932.

Wellington *Sumner County* *Southern Kansas, 30 mi/48 km south of Wichita*

1870s large cattle drives move north from Texas on Chisholm Trail; **1871** Sumner County formed; town platted, becomes county seat; **1872** incorporated as a city; **May 27, 1892** tornado seriously damages town, 17 killed; **1916** Carnegie Library built; **1930s** oil fields developed, production reaches peak 1936; **1952** county courthouse built.

Westmoreland *Pottawatomie County* *East central Kansas, 45 mi/72 km northwest of Topeka*

1856 Pottawatomie County formed; St. George becomes county seat; **1858** town founded as new county seat; post office established; **1883** incorporated as a city; **1884** county courthouse built.

Wichita *Sedgwick County* *Southern Kansas, 175 mi/282 km southwest of Kansas City, Missouri*

1864 trading post established; **1865** Wichita peoples removed to Oklahoma; **1868** town founded on Arkansas River; **1870** Sedgwick County formed; incorporated as a city, becomes county seat; **1872** railroad reaches town from Newton, establishing market for cattle driven on Chisholm Trail from Texas; *Eagle* and *Beacon* newspapers founded, merge 1961; **May 20, 1891** American Communist Earl Russell Browder born (died 1973); **1892** Fairmount College established, becomes Wichita Municipal University, later Wichita State University; **1898** Garfield University established, becomes Friends University; **1900** temperance leader Carrie Nation destroys Hotel Carey bar; **1912** Cathedral of the Immaculate Conception built; **1915** oil discovered to east; **1918** postwar airplane industry begins; Carrie A. Nation Memorial Fountain dedicated by Woman's Christian Temperance Union; **1928** Wichita Mid-Continent Airport established to west; **1929** stock market crash ruins all but four Wichita aircraft manufacturers; **1930** major oil reserve discovered; **1932** U.S. Post Office and Courthouse built; **1933** Newman College established; **May 19, 1934** news analyst Jim Lehrer born; **1935** Wichita Art Museum completed; **1942** McConnell Army Air Field established to southeast, becomes Air Force Base 1954; **Apr. 29, 1947** Olympic track star, U.S. Cong. Jim Ryan born; **Jan. 12, 1955** TV actress Kirstie Alley born; **1958** county courthouse built; **Jan. 16, 1965** Air Force tanker plane crashes, 7 crew and 23 on ground killed; **1971** Sedgwick County Zoo established to west.

Winchester *Jefferson County* *See* **Oskaloosa** **(1897)**

Winfield *Cowley County* *Southern Kansas, 35 mi/56 km southeast of Wichita*

1541 Coronado's expedition believed to have camped on Walnut River; **1870** Cowley County formed; town founded as county seat, named for Winfield Scott, Baptist missionary who built town's first church; **1872** incorporated as a city; **1883** state training school moved from Lawrence, founded 1881; **1911** Carnegie Library built, new library opened 1962; **1962** county courthouse built; **Sept. 12, 1966** actor Darren E. Burrows born.

Yates Center *Woodson County* *Eastern Kansas, 195 mi/314 km southwest of Kansas City, Kansas*

1855 Woodson County formed; **1875** county organized; town founded as county seat by Abner Yates; **1884** incorporated as a city; **Oct. 4, 1895** comedian, actor Buster Keaton born at Piqua to east (died 1966); **1900** county courthouse completed.

Kentucky

East central U.S. Capital: Frankfort. Major cities: Louisville, Lexington.

In 1584, the Virginia charter included areas now part of Kentucky. It was ceded by Virginia and entered the U.S. as the 15th state June 1, 1792. The Jackson Purchase of 1818 extended the state west from the Tennessee River to the Mississippi River. Kentucky remained in the Union during the Civil War although sentiments were deeply divided.

Kentucky is divided into 120 counties. All municipalities are classified as cities, for which there are six classes based on population. There are no townships. See Introduction.

Albany *Clinton County* *Southern Kentucky, 98 mi/ 158 km south-southwest of Lexington*

c.1790 area first settled; **1836** Clinton County formed; Paoli, 2 mi/3.2 km to south, becomes first county seat; first county courthouse built, burned by Confederates 1864; **1837** town founded as county seat, named for New York's state capital; **1838** town incorporated; **1981** fourth county courthouse built.

Alexandria *Campbell County* *Northern Kentucky, 12 mi/19 km south-southeast of Cincinnati, Ohio*

1794 Campbell County formed; **1834** town founded; **1840** county seat moved from Visalia when Kenton County separates from Campbell County; county seat shared with Newport; **1842** county courthouse built; **1856** town incorporated; **c.1965** Alexandria becomes sole county seat when Newport relinquishes shared status.

Ashland *Boyd and Greenup counties* *Northeastern Kentucky, 103 mi/166 km east-northeast of Lexington*

1815 George, Robert (Sr.), and Robert (Jr.) Poage settle on Ohio River; **1824** Williams' Halfway Inn built to southwest; **1826** Bellefonte Iron Furnace opened; **1850** town platted, named for Henry Clay's home in Lexington; **1857** first railroad reaches Ashland; **1858** incorporated as a village; **1868** Star Iron Works built; **1870** incorporated as a city; **1873** Norton Iron and Nail Works established; **Nov. 14, 1881** Jean Thomas born, founder of American Folk Song Festival in 1932 (died 1982) [see Catlettsburg]; **1886** North American Refractories plant built; **1891** Ashland Steel opens its Bessemer mill; **1920** American Rolling Mill (Armco) plant built; **1924** Ashland Oil Company founded;

1937 City Library opens; Ashland Community College established; **Jan. 11, 1946** country singer Naomi Judd born; **Feb. 14, 1959** fire in theater converted to apartments kills 10; **May 3, 1964** country singer Wynonna Judd born; **1984** Thirteenth Street Bridge built across Ohio River to Coal Grove, Ohio.

Barbourville *Knox County* *Southeastern Kentucky, 85 mi/137 km south-southeast of Lexington*

1750 Dr. Thomas Walker, surveyor from Virginia, builds first log cabin to south; **1799** Knox County formed; **1800** town founded as county seat on land donated by James Barbour; **1846** small building built, housed law offices of Samuel F. Miller, U.S. Supreme Court Justice 1862–1890, and Silas Woodson, governor of Missouri 1873–1875; **1854** town incorporated; **Sept. 16, 1861** Confederates under Col. Joel A. Battle destroy Union training camp; **1879** Union College established; **1964** county courthouse built.

Bardstown *Nelson County* *Central Kentucky, 33 mi/53 km south-southeast of Louisville*

1775 town founded near Beech Fork river; **1784** Nelson County formed; town becomes county seat; **Dec. 5, 1792** Louisville & Nashville Railroad promoter James Guthrie born (died 1869); **1795** Jacob Beam develops recipe for Jim Beam bourbon whiskey, establishes distillery at Clermont, to northwest; **c.1795** Beal House built; **1798** steamboat inventor John Fitch takes own life with poison, arrived here 1796 seeking seclusion after storm destroyed his boat on Ohio River prior to its going into regular service; **c.1800** Talbott Hotel built; **1814** Nazareth Junior College and Academy established; **1818** Federal Hill mansion built to east by Judge John Rowan; **1819** Cathedral of St. Joseph completed; Ben Hardin House built; **1838** town incorporated; **1844** first commercial whiskey production begins; **1848** Our Lady of Gethsemane Trappist monastery established; **1852** Stephen Foster composes "My Old Kentucky Home" at cousin John Rowan's Federal Hill home, first performed a few months later by Christy's Minstrels; **1892** county courthouse built; **1983** Oscar Getz Museum of Whiskey History opened; **1992** first Kentucky Bourbon Festival held.

Bardwell   *Carlisle County*   *Western Kentucky,*
26 mi/42 km southwest of Paducah

1874 town founded near Mississippi River; **1879** town incorporated; **1886** Carlisle County formed; town becomes county seat; **1887** county courthouse built; **July 1982** second county courthouse completed.

Beattyville   *Lee County*   *East central Kentucky,*
53 mi/85 km southeast of Lexington

1842 town founded on Kentucky River, at joining of Middle and South forks, originally named Taylor's Landing; **1850** town renamed for landowner Samuel Beatty; **1870** Lee County formed; town becomes county seat; **1872** town incorporated; **1977** county courthouse built.

Bedford   *Trimble County*   *Northern Kentucky,*
33 mi/53 km northeast of Louisville

1805 town first settled; **1816** town incorporated; **1818** post office established; **1837** Trimble County formed; town becomes county seat; **1838** county courthouse built; **1890** second county courthouse built, remodeled 1952.

Benton   *Marshall County*   *Western Kentucky,*
20 mi/32 km southeast of Paducah

1842 Marshall County formed; town founded, named for Missouri U.S. Sen. Thomas Hart Benton; **1845** town incorporated; **1884** first annual Southern Harmony Singing Festival held, established by J. R. Lemon; **1915** county courthouse built; **1944** Kentucky Dam built by TVA on Tennessee River 10 mi/16 km to northeast forming large Kentucky Lake, extends into Tennessee; **1966** Barkley Dam completed by TVA on Cumberland River 12 mi/19 km to northeast, only 2 mi/3.2 km east of Kentucky Dam, forming large Lake Barkley, paralleling Kentucky Lake.

Berea   *Madison County*   *Central Kentucky, 34 mi/*
55 km south-southeast of Lexington

1854 town founded by abolitionist Rev. John Gregg Fee; **1855** Berea College established; **1890** town incorporated; **1909** Boone Tavern Hotel built; **1922** Churchill Weavers, institute of folk art cloth weaving, founded by D. C. Churchill of Massachusetts using traditional Kentucky mountaineer designs.

Blue Lick Spring   *Nicholas County*   *Northeastern Kentucky, 37 mi/60 km northeast of Lexington*

Aug. 19, 1782 British and Native American allies, retreating from defeat at Bryan Station, northeast of Lexington, under Capt. William Caldwell, overwhelm Kentucky volunteers while crossing Licking River, 60 killed, 7 taken prisoner; **1814** Forest Retreat built, home of Thomas Metcalfe, governor 1829–1833; **1845** Blue Lick Springs Tavern built by John and L. P. Holladay, holds up to 600 guests, destroyed by fire Apr. 7, 1862; **1864** Blue Lick Church built; **1880s** William Bartlett begins bottling spring water, sells it as a medicinal; **Aug. 1882** Battle of Blue Licks monument dedicated; **1896** spring ceases flow, resort closes by early 1900s; **1928** Blue Licks Battlefield State Park established.

Boonesboro   *Clark County*   *Central Kentucky,*
15 mi/24 km southeast of Lexington

1775 Daniel Boone builds Fort Boonesborough on south side of Kentucky River (Madison County), sponsored by Col. Richard Henderson of North Carolina; town founded; **Aug. 7, 1776** Samuel Henderson, brother of Richard, marries Elizabeth Callaway under the "divine elm," officiated by Squire Boone, Daniel's brother; **1778** Boone and 15 companions captured by Shawnee, later escape, warn town of impending Native American attack; **Sept. 8, 1778** attack by 400 Shawnee and 40 French-Canadians held off by mere 60 fort defenders; **1779** town incorporated, later renamed Boonesboro, moved to north side of river; **1965** Fort Boonesborough State Park dedicated.

Booneville   *Owsley County*   *East central Kentucky,*
58 mi/93 km southeast of Lexington

1843 Owsley County formed; town founded as county seat on South Fork Kentucky River on property of Elias Moore; **1844** post office established; **1846** town incorporated; **1967** county courthouse built.

Bowling Green   *Warren County*   *Southern Kentucky, 92 mi/148 km south-southwest of Louisville*

1778 settlement of McFadden's Station established on north side of Barren River; **1790** new town of Bowling Green established on south side of river by Robert and George Moore of Virginia; **1796** Warren County formed; town becomes county seat; **1812** town incorporated; **1857** Riverview Mansion begun, completed 1872; **Nov. 1861** Gen. Simon Buckner's Kentuckians capture town in advance of arrival of Gen. Albert Johnston; **1862** Confederates abandon town after fall of forts Donelson and Henry in Tennessee; **1868** county courthouse built; **1906** Western Kentucky University established; **1938** Bowling Green Public Library founded; **1939** Kentucky Museum opened; **1942** Bowling Green-Warren County Airport established; **1995** Convention Center opened.

Brandenburg *Meade County* *Northwestern Kentucky, 27 mi/43 km southwest of Louisville*

1804 Col. Solomon Brandenburg settles on Ohio River; Walnut Tavern built; **1821** Doe Run Hotel built; **1823** Meade County formed, named for Col. James Meade; Claysville becomes county seat; **1824** town founded as new county seat; **1825** incorporated as a town; **1838** Methodist Church built; **1855** Buckner Home built; **July 7, 1863** Confederate Gen. John Morgan's Cavalry (Morgan's Raiders) cross Ohio River to begin raids in Indiana and Ohio; **1872** incorporated as a city; **Apr. 3, 1974** tornado strikes county, 31 killed; **1976** fourth county courthouse built.

Brooksville *Bracken County* *Northern Kentucky, 49 mi/79 km north-northeast of Lexington*

1796 Bracken County formed; Augusta becomes first county seat; town founded, originally named Woodward's Crossing; **1839** town incorporated, renamed Brooksville; county seat moved from Augusta; **1881** Walcott Covered Bridge built to east, replaces 1824 structure; **1905** county courthouse completed.

Brownie *Muhlenberg County* See **Central City (1937)**

Brownsville *Edmonson County* *Southern Kentucky, 75 mi/121 km south-southwest of Louisville*

1825 Edmonson County formed; **1826** town founded as county seat; **1828** town incorporated; **1874** county courthouse built; **1926** Mammoth Cave National Park authorized to east, fully established 1941; **1954** Edmonson County Public Library founded.

Bryantsville *Garrard County* *Central Kentucky, 25 mi/40 km south-southwest of Lexington*

1779 town founded as Smith's Station; **1782** Fork Baptist Church built to south; **May 20, 1788** Henry Smith born, provisional governor of Texas 1824 and 1837–1838 (died 1851); **c.1835** Burnt Tavern built as stagecoach stop by Edward Smith of Virginia, father of Henry Smith, destroyed by fire twice, rebuilt; **1836** town incorporated, renamed; **Nov. 25, 1846** temperance leader Carrie Amelia Moore Nation born, noted for her axe-wielding attacks on saloons (died 1911); **1861** Camp Dick Robinson established as first Federal recruiting station south of Ohio River.

Burkesville *Cumberland County* *Southern Kentucky, 100 mi/161 km south-southeast of Louisville*

1768 first settlers arrive; **1798** Cumberland County formed; town founded on Cumberland River as county seat, named for settler Samuel Burke; **1810** incorporated as a town; **March 12, 1829** one of earliest oil discoveries in U.S. made by John Croghan drilling for salt, ignites into raging treetop inferno; **1926** incorporated as a city; **1934** county courthouse built.

Burlington *Boone County* *Northern Kentucky, 12 mi/19 km west-southwest of Cincinnati, Ohio*

1798 Boone County formed; **1799** town founded near Ohio River as county seat, originally named Wilmington; **1816** town renamed Burlington; **1824** town incorporated; **1842** Dinsmore Homestead built; **1889** third county courthouse built; **1946** Cincinnati-Northern Kentucky International Airport established to northeast; **Nov. 20, 1967** TWA Convair 880 airplane crashes into orchard at Hebron to north killing 70 of 82 on board.

Cadiz *Trigg County* *Western Kentucky, 145 mi/233 km southwest of Louisville*

1820 Trigg County formed, named for Indian fighter Col. Stephen Trigg of Virginia; town founded as county seat; **1821** post office established; first county courthouse built; **1822** incorporated as a town; **1901** Cadiz Railroad built; **1920** incorporated as a city; **1922** sixth county courthouse built.

Calhoun *McLean County* *Western Kentucky, 94 mi/151 km southwest of Louisville*

1785 town platted by Henry Rhoades, named Rhoadesville; **1787** Fort Vienna built by Solomon Rhoades, town renamed Fort Vienna; **1849** town renamed for Circuit Judge John Calhoun; **1852** town incorporated; **1854** McLean County formed, named for Judge Alney McLean; town becomes county seat; **1908** third county courthouse built; **1966** large Lake Barkley reservoir to west formed by Barkley Dam on Cumberland River.

Campbellsville *Taylor County* *Central Kentucky, 65 mi/105 km south-southeast of Louisville*

1791 Baptist Church organized; **1808** area first settled; **1817** town founded, named for landowner Andrew Campbell; **1823** Jacob Hiestand House built to northwest; **1848** Taylor County formed; town becomes county seat; **1851** town incorporated; **1879** Cumberland & Ohio Railroad reaches town; **1906** Campbellsville University established; **1966** county courthouse completed; **1969** Green River Lake formed by dam on Green River to south.

Campton *Wolfe County* *East central Kentucky, 55 mi/89 km east-southeast of Lexington*

1850s town founded, originally named Camp Town; **1860** Wolfe County formed; town becomes county seat; **1870** town incorporated, renamed Campton; **1903** first oil well drilled to west; **1907** narrow gauge Mountain Central Railway reaches town; **1917** county courthouse completed.

Carlisle *Nicholas County* *Northeastern Kentucky, 31 mi/50 km northeast of Lexington*

1799 Nicholas County formed; **1816** town founded as county seat; **1817** post office established; **1880** town incorporated; **1893** county courthouse built; **1947** Nicholas County Public Library founded.

Carrollton *Carroll County* *Northern Kentucky, 43 mi/69 km northeast of Louisville*

Apr. 19, 1791 U.S. Sen. William O. Butler born, served in Battle of New Orleans (died 1808); **1794** town founded on Ohio River, originally named Port William; **1805** Riverview House built; **1825** Butler House built, home of William O. Butler; **1838** Carroll County formed; town becomes county seat; town incorporated and renamed; **c.1845** Darling House built; **1884** county courthouse built; **1934** General Butler State Park established.

Catlettsburg *Boyd County* *Northeastern Kentucky, 104 mi/167 km east-northeast of Lexington*

1772 Rev. David Jones leads expedition to site on Ohio River, at mouth of Big Sandy River, party includes young George Rogers Clark, first known white visitors; **1808** trading post established by Sawney Catlett of Virginia, remains in business until 1857; **c.1840** Traipsin' Woman's Cabin built 10 mi/16 km to south, owned by Jean Thomas, founder of American Folk Song Festival, Ashland; **1849** town founded, originally named Mouth of Sandy; **1858** town incorporated; **1860** Boyd County formed; town becomes county seat; **1912** second county courthouse built.

Cave City *Barren County* *Southern Kentucky, 75 mi/121 km south of Louisville*

1853 town founded; **1866** town incorporated; **Jan. 30, 1925** farmer Floyd Collins becomes wedged vertically 300 ft/91 m deep in Sand Cave, kept alive with food and water, dies of exposure about two weeks later still in cave; **July 1, 1941** Mammoth Cave National Park established to west; **1980** Cave City Convention Center opened.

Cayce *Fulton County* *See* **Hickman (1864)**

Central City *Muhlenberg County* *Western Kentucky, 96 mi/154 km southwest of Louisville*

1826 Charles S. Morehead builds horse powered grist mill; town founded, named Morehead's Horse Mill; **1870** Illinois Central Railroad built; town renamed Stroud City; **1873** incorporated as a town; **1882** town renamed for Central City Coal and Iron Company; **1902** incorporated as a city; **Feb. 1, 1937** singer Don Everly born at Brownie to east.

Clay City *Powell County* *Central Kentucky, 33 mi/53 km east-southeast of Lexington*

1769 Daniel Boone camps to northwest on Lulbegrud Creek with John Finley, others, creek name derived by them from mythical Lorbrulgrud in *Gulliver's Travels*; **1786** iron ore discovered, one of first forges west of Alleghenies; **1805** Red River Iron Works established, made cannon balls during War of 1812; town founded on Red River; **1890** town incorporated.

Clinton *Hickman County* *Western Kentucky, 35 mi/56 km south-southwest of Paducah*

1821 Hickman County formed; **1826** town founded, platted by James Gibson; **1829** county seat moved from Columbus; county courthouse built; **1831** town incorporated; **c.1846** Clinton Academy, burned 1854, rebuilt as seminary, closed 1912.

Cloverport *Breckinridge County* *Northwestern Kentucky, 53 mi/85 km southwest of Louisville*

1798 Joe Huston becomes first settler; **1808** town founded as port on Ohio River, originally named Joe's Landing; **1816** Thomas Lincoln family ferries here on way to new home in Spencer County, Indiana; **1828** town renamed Cloverport; **1860** town incorporated; **1888** Louisville & Nashville Railroad beaches town; **July 20, 1894** Supreme Court Justice Wiley B. Rutledge, Jr. born (died 1949).

Columbia *Adair County* *Southern Kentucky, 80 mi/129 km south-southeast of Louisville*

1793 town first settled by William Hurt, Revolutionary soldier; Hurt House built; **1801** Adair County formed; **1803** town founded as county seat; **1884** second county courthouse built; **1893** town incorporated; **1903** Lindsey Wilson College established; **1920s** Columbia Public Library founded, became County Library 1970.

Columbus *Hickman County* *Western Kentucky, 35 mi/56 southwest of Paducah*

1730s French explorers discover iron deposits on cliffs overlooking Mississippi River, name site Iron Banks; **1784** Revolutionary War soldiers granted land in area as payment for their services; **1804** military post established during Aaron Burr's scheme to establish republic; **1814** burning of Capitol at Washington inspires effort to have nation's capital moved here; **1820** town founded on Mississippi River; **1821** Hickman County formed; town becomes county seat; **1829** county seat moved to Clinton; **1860** town incorporated; **1861** Confederate fortifications built here and at Belmont, Missouri, across Mississippi, heavy chain laid across river to snag Union gunboats; **Nov. 1861** General Grant arrives, overwhelms Confederates on both sides of river, burns camp on Missouri side, Union forces driven out by counterattack by General Polk's Confederate army; **1862** Grant gains surrender of Columbus by round-about strategy of capturing forts Henry and Donelson and bitterly fought battle at Shiloh, all in Tennessee; **1927** flooding Mississippi, overwhelms town, new town built on higher ground; **1934** Columbus-Belmont Battlefield State Park established.

Corbin   *Whitley and Knox counties   Southern Kentucky, 77 mi/124 km south-southeast of Lexington*

1775 Daniel Boone blazes Wilderness Road through area; **1798** Boone associate Alex McClardy receives land grant; **1883** Louisville & Nashville Railroad built; **1884** town founded on railroad near Laurel River by James Eaton and David T. Chestnut; **1894** town incorporated; **1902** incorporated as a city; **1937** Harland T. Sanders establishes Sanders Cafe, markets secret fried chicken recipe, later becomes Kentucky Fried Chicken, one of world's largest fast-food enterprises; **1974** Laurel River Lake formed by dam to west by Corps of Engineers.

Covington   *Kenton County   Northern Kentucky, 1 mi/1.6 km south of Cincinnati, Ohio, on Ohio River*

Feb. 14, 1780 George Muse swaps keg of whiskey for 200 ac/81 ha of land on Ohio River; **1801** after several changes of ownership, Thomas Kennedy buys land, builds first house, opens tavern, establishes Ohio River ferry to Cincinnati; **1814** Kennedy sells land to John and Richard Gano and Thomas Carneal, who plat town 1815, name it for Gen. Leonard Covington, War of 1812 hero; **1815** Carneal House built; **c.1820** Stevenson House built; **1832** Ohio River flooding damages much of town; **1834** town incorporated; **1839** Clayton House built by John W. Clayton; **1840** Kenton County formed; Independence becomes county seat; **c.1843** Covington becomes shared county seat with Independence; **Oct. 9, 1848** artist Frank Duveneck born (died 1919); **c.1850** Monte Casino Benedictine Abbey built; **1850s** Kentucky Central Railroad built to Lexington; **1857** Odd Fellows Hall built, destroyed by fire 2002; **1860** St. Elizabeth's Hospital established; **1866** John A. Roebling Suspension Bridge completed to Cincinnati; **1883** Ohio River floods ruin city, again 1884; Latonia Race Track opens; **1888** second bridge built across Ohio River; **Jan. 30, 1900** William Goebel mortally wounded by assassin while contesting race for governor that he lost by 2,000 votes, immediately declared governor by legislature, dies Feb. 3; **1900** St. Mary's Catholic Cathedral completed; **1901** Public Library built; **1902** county courthouse built; **1903** Kelley-Koett Manufacturing Plant established, maker of X-ray equipment; **1910** Roman Catholic Basilica of the Assumption completed; **Aug. 24, 1912** TV personality Durwood Kirby born (died 2000); **1931** Williams Natural History Museum founded; **Jan. 22, 1937** Ohio River floods two-thirds of city's businesses; **May 1, 1960** jockey Steve Cauthen born; **1970** 10-story City-County Building completed.

Crestwood   *Oldham County   See La Grange*

Cynthiana   *Harrison County   Northern Kentucky, 25 mi/40 km north-northeast of Lexington*

c.1775 Robert Harrison becomes first settler; **1793** Harrison County formed; town founded as county seat, named for Harrison's daughters Cynthia and Anna; **1801** statesman Henry Clay admitted to bar here; **1802** town incorporated; **Feb. 10, 1806** Illinois Sen. Orville Hickman Browning born in rural Harrison County (died 1881); **1807** Judge Boyd Place mansion built; **1837** Main Street Covered Bridge built on South Fork Licking River; **1853** county courthouse completed, addition built 1916; **July 17, 1862** town captured by Confederate forces of Gen. John H. Morgan from Union Col. John J. Landrum; **June 12, 1864** General Morgan's forces are overwhelmed by Gen. Stephen Burbridge's Union troops, heavy losses on both sides; **c.1865** Lewis Hunter Distillery established to south at Lair; **Jan. 28, 1963** lowest temperature ever recorded in Kentucky reached, −34°F/−37°C, record broken 1994 at Shelbyville.

Danville   *Boyle County   Central Kentucky, 30 mi/48 km south-southwest of Lexington*

1775 town founded; **1780** Transylvania Seminary founded, moved to Lexington 1787, later becomes Transylvania University; **1785** town made regional capital of part of Virginia west of the Allegheny Mountains; first county courthouse in Kentucky built; **1792** Kentucky becomes state, Frankfort chosen as state capital; **Feb. 4, 1792** antislavery social reformer James Gillespie Birney born (died 1857); **1798** post office established, Kentucky's first; **1804** Phillip Yeiser House built; **Dec. 25, 1809** Dr. Samuel McDowell performs successful ovariotomy on Mrs. Jane Crawford without use of anesthesia; **1836** town incorporated; **1819** Centre College established; **1823** Kentucky School for the Deaf founded; **June 1, 1833** Supreme Court Justice John Marshall Harlan the elder born (died 1911) [see Chicago, 1899]; **1842** Boyle County formed; town becomes county seat; **1862** county courthouse built.

Dixon   *Webster County   Western Kentucky, 115 mi/185 km southwest of Louisville*

1794 Halfway House inn built by William Jenkins, captured shortly afterward by Native Americans; **1816** liked by his captors, Jenkins is released, enlarges inn, later builds cotton gin; **1860** Webster County formed; town founded as county seat, named for U.S. Sen. Archibald Dixon; **1861** town incorporated; **Aug. 4, 1917** coal mine explosion at Clay No. 7 Mine to southwest, 62 killed; **1939** county courthouse built.

Eddyville   *Lyon County   Western Kentucky, 147 mi/237 km southwest of Louisville*

1798 Livingston County formed; town founded on Cumberland River as county seat; **1809** Caldwell County formed; town becomes county seat; Livingston County seat moved to Salem; **1812** town incorporated;

1817 Caldwell County seat moved to Princeton; 1854 Lyon County formed; town becomes county seat; 1885 state penitentiary built; 1960 town relocated away from new Lake Barkley reservoir; 1961 county courthouse built; 1966 Lake Barkley Dam completed on Cumberland River.

Edmonton   *Metcalfe County   Southern Kentucky, 85 mi/137 km south of Louisville*

1800 town founded, named for Revolutionary War soldier Edmond P. Rogers, first settler; 1818 town platted; 1826 post office established; 1860 Metcalfe County formed; town becomes county seat; town incorporated; 1868 county courthouse built; 1871 incorporated as a city; 1907 Lower Hotel established by Ben Shirley.

Elizabethtown   *Hardin County   Central Kentucky, 38 mi/61 km south of Louisville*

1780 three stockades built by Capt. Thomas Helm, Col. Andrew Hynes and Col. Samuel Haycraft of Virginia; 1793 Hardin County formed; 1795 town platted as county seat by Col. Hynes, named for his wife; 1797 town incorporated; 1818 Brown-Pusey Community House built; Dec. 2, 1819 after 1818 death of Nancy Hanks, Thomas Lincoln marries widowed Sarah Johnston; 1847 incorporated as a city; 1854 Louisville & Nashville Railroad reaches town; Dec. 26–27, 1862 town shelled by Confederates under Gen. John Morgan; 1932 county courthouse partially destroyed by fire, rebuilt 1936 with WPA assistance; 1964 Elizabethtown Community College established.

Elkton   *Todd County   Western Kentucky, 122 mi/ 196 km southwest of Louisville*

1817 town founded; 1819 Todd County formed; 1820 town becomes county seat; 1835 county courthouse built; 1843 town incorporated; Feb. 3, 1862 Supreme Court Justice James Clark McReynolds born (died 1946); Apr. 24, 1905 novelist Robert Penn Warren born at Guthrie to south (died 1989); Oct. 23, 1918 architect Paul Rudolph born (died 1997).

Fairview   *Todd and Christian counties   Western Kentucky, 125 mi/201 km southwest of Louisville*

1793 town founded by Samuel Davis; 1802 post office established as Davistown; June 3, 1808 Confederate Pres. Jefferson Davis born (died in New Orleans 1889); 1846 post office renamed Fairview; 1929 Jefferson Davis monument erected by Daughters of the Confederacy, designated state historic site; 1957 town incorporated.

Falmouth   *Pendleton County   Northern Kentucky, 30 mi/48 km south-southeast of Cincinnati, Ohio*

c.1776 area settled; Aug. 19, 1782 in Battle of Blue Licks on Licking River, Kentuckians ambushed by Native American allies of British retreating from Bryan Station (near Lexington), 60 killed within 15 minutes; 1793 one of earliest sawmills in state established; town founded as Fallsmouth; 1798 Pendleton County formed; 1799 town becomes county seat; 1848 county courthouse built; 1854 Louisville & Nashville Railroad reaches town; 1856 town incorporated; c.1870 Butler Covered Bridge built to north on Licking River, 456 ft/139 km long, destroyed by flood 1937.

Flemingsburg   *Fleming County   Northeastern Kentucky, 48 mi/77 km northeast of Lexington*

1787 John Fleming and George Stockton of Virginia arrive in area, both build blockhouses, Stockton here, Fleming 5 mi/8 km to west; 1790 Stockton killed by Native Americans while hunting; 1794 Fleming dies of wounds suffered in attack by Native Americans at Battle Run; 1796 town founded by George P. Stockton; 1798 Fleming County formed; town becomes county seat; 1912 town incorporated; 1952 county courthouse built.

Fort Knox   *Bullitt, Hardin, and Meade counties*
See Radcliff

Fort Mitchell   *Kenton County   Northern Kentucky, 4 mi/6.4 km southwest of Cincinnati, Ohio*

1836; town founded near Ohio River; Institute of Science and Language established by Ormsby M. Mitchell, also founded Cincinnati Observatory 1843; 1862 Union Gen. Lew Wallace leads 15,000 men across Ohio River from Cincinnati on bridge made of coal barges, builds several fortifications, including Fort Mitchell, to eliminate threat of Confederate invasion of Ohio; 1910 town incorporated; 1967 South Fort Mitchell merges with Fort Mitchell.

Frankfort   *Franklin County   North central Kentucky, 27 mi/43 km east of Louisville*

1751 Christopher Gist probably first white man to view area; 1773 survey party led by Robert McAfee arrives at site, sent by Gov. Dunmore of Virginia; 1774 Native Americans attack settlers requiring militia; 1786 town founded on Kentucky River by Gen. James Wilkinson; 1792 town selected for state capital; June 1, 1792 Kentucky enters Union as 15th state; 1794 Franklin County formed; town becomes county seat; 1796 town incorporated; Liberty Hall built; May 10, 1813 Montgomery Blair born, Postmaster General under President Lincoln (died 1883); 1830 statehouse completed; 1835 Lexington & Ohio Railroad reaches town; incorporated as a city; 1850 state arsenal built; Nov. 26, 1861 New Mexico Sen. Albert Bacon Fall born, secretary of interior under President Harding (died 1944); 1862 General Bragg's Confederate troops invade town, establish state government for Confederacy, driven out by Union forces; 1886 State Industrial Institute (Kentucky Negro College) established, becomes Kentucky State University; 1910 new state capitol completed; Ziegler House built, designed by Frank Lloyd Wright; 1935 county courthouse built;

1937 great Ohio River flood forces Kentucky River over its banks, inundating city; 1955 Capitol City Airport established.

Franklin *Simpson County* *Southern Kentucky, 112 mi/180 km south-southwest of Louisville*

1819 Simpson County formed, named for Capt. John Simpson, War of 1812 hero; Duncan Inn established as stagecoach stop; 1820 town founded as county seat, named for Benjamin Franklin; Nov. 1820 town incorporated; 1883 county courthouse built.

Frenchburg *Menifee County* *East central Kentucky, 47 mi/76 km east of Lexington*

1869 Menifee County formed; town founded as county seat, named for Judge Richard French; 1871 town incorporated; post office established; 1928 county courthouse built.

Georgetown *Scott County* *Central Kentucky, 12 mi/19 km north of Lexington*

1776 first settled by John McClelland family of Pittsburgh; town of McClelland's Station founded; 1784 Johnson's Fort built to west by Robert Johnson; 1785 Crossings Baptist Church organized to west; 1790 town incorporated, renamed for George Washington; 1792 Scott County formed; town becomes county seat; 1821 Cardome house built by Maj. Benjamin Chambers; 1829 Georgetown College established; 1877 fourth county courthouse built.

Glasgow *Barren County* *Southern Kentucky, 85 mi/137 km south of Louisville*

c.1795 area settled by pioneers from Virginia; 1798 Barren County formed; 1799 town founded as county seat on land owned by John Gorin, named for Glasgow, Virginia; 1809 town incorporated; 1813 gunpowder mill built to supply War of 1812; c.1815 Spottswood House built by Alexander Spottswood, grandson of Gov. Spottswood of Colonial Virginia; Dec. 22, 1945 newscaster Diane Sawyer born; 1965 county courthouse completed.

Grayson *Carter County* *Northeastern Kentucky, 85 mi/137 km east-northeast of Lexington*

1811 Little Sandy Salt Works established; 1838 Carter County formed; 1844 town founded as county seat, named for Col. Robert Grayson; 1860 town incorporated; May 13, 1905 explosion at coal mine at Mt. Savage to south, 300 miners killed; 1907 county courthouse built, additions built 1950 and 1964.

Greensburg *Green County* *Southern Kentucky, 68 mi/109 km south of Louisville*

1777 area first settled; town of Glovers Station founded; 1792 Green County formed; 1794 town incorporated and renamed, becomes county seat; town and county named

for Revolutionary Gen. Nathanael Green; July 28, 1930 highest temperature ever recorded in Kentucky reached, 114°F/46°C; 1931 third county courthouse built.

Greenup *Greenup County* *Northeastern Kentucky, 95 mi/153 km northeast of Lexington*

1803 Greenup County formed; town founded as county seat, originally named Greenupsburg; town and county named for Christopher Greenup, governor 1804–1808; 1811 county courthouse built; 1848 town incorporated; 1872 town renamed Greenup to avoid confusion with Greensburg; 1937 town devastated by flood, residents marooned as they attempt to save town; 1940 county courthouse built; 1962 Greenup Lock & Dam built on Ohio River.

Greenville *Muhlenberg County* *Western Kentucky, 103 mi/166 km southwest of Louisville*

1798 Muhlenberg County formed, named for Gen. John P. G. Muhlenberg, Lutheran pastor from Virginia; 1799 town founded as county seat; 1837 Buckner Furnace built by Aylette H. Buckner, father of Gen. Simon B. Buckner; 1849 town incorporated; 1852 Presbyterian Academy founded, closed 1873; 1907 county courthouse built.

Guthrie *Todd County* *See Elkton (1905)*

Hardinsburg *Breckinridge County* *Northwestern Kentucky, 48 mi/77 km southwest of Louisville*

1780 fort built by Capt. William Hardin, named Hardin's Station; 1799 Breckinridge County formed, named for U.S. Sen. John Breckinridge; 1800 town founded as county seat; 1890 town incorporated; 1959 Rough River Lake formed by dam to south; 1960 county courthouse built.

Harlan *Harlan County* *Southeastern Kentucky, 102 mi/164 km south-southeast of Lexington*

1796 town settled and founded, originally named Mount Pleasant; 1819 Harlan County formed; town becomes county seat, renamed Harlan; county and town named for Maj. Silas Harlan, died in Battle of Blue Licks, Kentucky; 1865 town renamed Harlan; 1884 town incorporated; 1911 thick seams of bituminous coal discovered in Harlan County, start of large-scale coal mining; Louisville & Nashville Railroad reaches town; 1913 Pine Mountain Settlement School founded by William Creech to northeast; 1916 first widespread strike instills bitter rapport between coal company employees and management; 1922 county courthouse built; 1931 several miners killed during strike violence at Evarts Coal Company; Dec. 9, 1932 coal mine explosion at Zero Mine, at rural Yancey to southeast, 23 killed.

Harrodsburg *Mercer County* *Central Kentucky, 27 mi/43 km southwest of Lexington*

1774 town founded by James Harrod, named Harrodstown, most settlers driven out by Native Americans, return 1775; **1776** Kentucky County formed as part of Virginia; town becomes county seat; **1780** Lincoln County formed; town remains county seat; **1785** Mercer County formed; town becomes county seat; Lincoln County seat moved to Stanford; **1800** Mud Meeting House (Dutch Reformed) built to west; **1812** Clay Hill house built; **1836** town incorporated; **1839** Bacon College moves from Georgetown, destroyed by fire 1864, merged with Transylvania College, Lexington; **1840** Greenville Female College established; Beaumont Inn built; **c.1845** Fair Oaks house built by Dr. Guilford D. Runyon; **1913** county courthouse built; **1934** Pioneer Memorial State Park dedicated by Pres. Franklin D. Roosevelt.

Hartford *Ohio County* *Western Kentucky, 80 mi/129 km southwest of Louisville*

1782 town founded, named Deer Crossing; **1797** Lyon Inn built, later becomes Commercial Hotel; **1799** Ohio County formed; town becomes county seat, renamed Hartford ("hart ford" synonymous with "deer crossing"); **1808** town incorporated; **Sept. 13, 1911** singer Bill Monroe born at Rosine to east, "Father of Bluegrass Music" (died 1996); **Aug. 19, 1835** Missouri Cong. Richard Parks Bland born (died 1899); **1943** county courthouse completed.

Hawesville *Hancock County* *Northwestern Kentucky, 58 mi/93 km west-southwest of Louisville*

1829 Hancock County formed; town founded on Ohio River as county seat, named for landowner Richard Hawes; **1831** ferry established to Cannellton, Ohio, suspended 1966; **1836** town incorporated; **1867** county courthouse built.

Hazard *Perry County* *Southeastern Kentucky, 88 mi/142 km southeast of Lexington*

1821 Perry County formed; town founded as county seat; town and county named for Adm. Oliver Hazard Perry; **c.1866** natural gas deposit discovered; **1884** town incorporated; **1888** French-Eversole feud, started 1882, reaches climax when factions do battle at courthouse, 12 killed, several wounded; **1912** Louisville & Nashville Railroad extended from Jackson to serve coal and timber industries; **1917** oil discovered; **Jan. 1937** town destroyed by worst flooding in its history, five killed; **1966** sixth county courthouse built; **1968** Hazard Community College established.

Hebron *Boone County* See **Burlington (1967)**

Henderson *Henderson County* *Northwestern Kentucky, 100 mi/161 km west-southwest of Louisville*

1797 town founded by Transylvania Company, later renamed Richard Henderson Company, on large land grant awarded to it on Ohio River; **1798** Henderson County formed; town becomes county seat; **1810** incorporated as a town; ornithologist John James Audubon arrives, lives here until 1819; **1818** Lazarus Powell House built by father of U.S. Sen. Lazarus W. Powell; **c.1830** P. J. Lambert House built; **1840** Indian Valley Farm established to west by Haywood Alves on Ohio River; **1856** Lockett House built for Judge Paschal Hickman Lockett; **1866** third county courthouse built; **1867** incorporated as a city; **Jan. 22, 1886** composer John Joseph Becker born (died 1961); **July 14, 1898** Sen. Commissioner of Baseball Albert B. "Happy" Chandler born (died 1982); **1922** Dade Park horse race track established in enclave of Kentucky on north side of Ohio River adjacent to Evansville, Indiana, cut off by change in river's course, track renamed Ellis Park 1924; **1932** Audubon Highway Bridge (U.S. 41) built across Ohio River to Evansville to north, second span added 1962; **1963** Henderson Community College established.

Hickman *Fulton County* *Western Kentucky, 47 mi/76 km southwest of Paducah*

1812 persistent tremors of New Madrid Earthquake create large Reelfoot Lake to southwest, mainly in Tennessee, from former channel of Mississippi River; **1819** area settled by James Mills; Mills' cabin becomes shipping point on Mississippi; town founded as Mills Point; **1834** town incorporated; **1845** Fulton County formed; **March 14, 1864** James Luther Jones, later known as Cayce (Casey) Jones, born at Jordan to southeast near town of Cayce, sacrificed his own life to save 12 carloads of passengers in head-on collision with freight train near Vaughan, Mississippi, Apr. 30, 1900, buried at Jackson, Tennessee; **1903** county courthouse built; **1934** flood wall built on Mississippi River.

High Bridge *Jessamine County* *Central Kentucky, 19 mi/31 km south-southwest of Lexington*

1805 area on Kentucky River settled by Shakers religious sect; town founded, named Pleasant Hill, referred to as Shakertown; **1809** Farm Manager's House built; **1812** Shaker colony initiates farm building program; **1817** East Family House built, later serves as Shakertown Inn; **1831** North Family House built; **1839** Guest House built; **1850s** suspension bridge designed by John A. Roebling begun, never completed; **1877** Cincinnati Southern Railroad built; cantilever High Bridge on Kentucky River completed, 317 ft/97 m high; post office opened, named North Tower; **1887** post office renamed High Bridge; **1911** new bridge built, second track added 1929; **1925** Herrington Lake formed on Dix River to southeast by Dix Dam; Sister Mary Settles dies at age 87, last Kentucky Shaker; **1929** remnant suspension cable towers from abandoned Roebling bridge dismantled; **1976** post office closed.

Hindman *Knott County* *Eastern Kentucky, 94 mi/ 151 km southeast of Lexington*

1884 Knott County formed; town founded as county seat; **1886** town incorporated; **1902** Hindman Settlement School founded by May Stone and Katherine Pettit under auspices of Woman's Christian Temperance Union; **1936** county courthouse completed.

Hodgenville *Larue County* *Central Kentucky, 45 mi/72 km south of Louisville*

1789 Robert Hodgen builds mill and tavern on Nolin River; **Dec. 1808** Thomas Lincoln and wife Nancy (Hanks) purchase Sinking Spring Farm 3 mi/4.8 km to south, then part of Hardin County; **Feb. 12, 1809** Abraham Lincoln, 16th President, born (died April 15, 1865); **1810** Robert Hodgen dies; **1818** town founded, named Hodgensville; **1813** Lincoln family moves to Knob Creek, to east, **1816** the Lincolns move to Spencer County, Indiana; **1839** town incorporated; **1843** Larue County formed; town becomes county seat; **1904** town renamed Hodgenville; **1909** Abraham Lincoln Statue erected in town square; **July 17, 1916** Abraham Lincoln National Park established, redesignated Abraham Lincoln Birthplace National Historic Site 1959; **1967** county courthouse built.

Hopkinsville *Christian County* *Western Kentucky, 132 mi/212 km southwest of Louisville*

1796 Christian County formed; **1797** Bartholomew Wood donates part of his land for county seat; town founded as county seat; town originally named Elizabeth; **1804** incorporated as a town, renamed for Gen. Samuel Hopkins, hero of War of 1812; **c.1832** Knight House built; **Oct. 23, 1835** Illinois Cong. Adlai Ewing Stevenson the elder born (died 1914) [see Los Angeles, 1900]; **1840s** Walter Downes House built; **c.1850** Stites House built; **1854** Bethel Women's Junior College established; **1856** Ross Dillard House built; **1869** county courthouse built; **1897** incorporated as a city; **1965** Hopkinsville Community College (2-year) established.

Hyden *Leslie County* *Southeastern Kentucky, 85 mi/137 km southeast of Lexington*

1817 John Sizemore and wife Nancy become first white settlers; **1878** Leslie County formed, named for Preston H. Leslie, governor 1871–1875; **1879** town founded as county seat on Middle Fork Kentucky River; **March 1882** town incorporated; **1894** *Thousand Sticks* newspaper founded, named for highest hill in area; **1954** county courthouse completed; **Dec. 30, 1970** coal mine accident kills 38 miners.

Independence *Kenton County* *Northern Kentucky, 10 mi/16 km south of Cincinnati, Ohio*

1840 Kenton County formed; town founded as county seat (shared with Covington); **1842** town incorporated; **c.1843** Covington becomes shared county seat with Independence; **1912** second county courthouse completed.

Inez *Martin County* *Eastern Kentucky, 105 mi/ 169 km east of Lexington*

1810 area settled; **1838** town founded, named Eden; **1870** Martin County formed; town becomes county seat; **1874** post office established; **1941** county courthouse built; **1942** town incorporated, renamed for postmaster's daughter.

Irvine *Estill County* *Central Kentucky, 36 mi/58 km southeast of Lexington*

1808 Estill County formed; **1812** town founded as county seat; **1849** town incorporated; **1941** county courthouse built; **1959** Marcum and Wallace Memorial Hospital founded, becomes Estill County Hospital 1980.

Jackson *Breathitt County* *East central Kentucky, 68 mi/109 km southeast of Lexington*

1839 Breathitt County formed; town founded as county seat, named Breathitt Town; **1845** town incorporated, renamed Jackson; **1864** Lee's Junior College established; **1890** Louisville & Nashville Railroad reaches town from Lexington, extended to Hazard 1912; **1914** incorporated as a city; **1963** county courthouse built.

Jamestown *Russell County* *Southern Kentucky, 78 mi/126 km south-southwest of Lexington*

1825 Russell County formed; James Wooldridge donates land for town site; town founded as county seat, originally named Jacksonville in honor of Andrew Jackson; **1826** town incorporated, renamed Jamestown; **1950** large Lake Cumberland formed to southeast on Cumberland River by Wolf Creek Dam; **1978** county courthouse completed.

Junction City *Boyle County* *Central Kentucky, 35 mi/56 km south-southwest of Lexington*

1786 Traveler's Rest house built to east by Thomas Metcalf, home of Gov. Isaac Shelby, first Governor of Kentucky 1792–1796 and 1812–1816, destroyed by fire c.1930; **c.1847** Warrenwood mansion built by Capt. William Warren; **1880** town founded, named Gore; **1882** Cincinnati Southern Railroad reaches town; town incorporated, renamed.

Kuttawa *Lyon County* *Western Kentucky, 150 mi/ 241 km southwest of Louisville*

1846 William Kelly of Pennsylvania settles here, becomes engaged in iron-founding business, builds experimental converters during 1850s, invents pneumatic conversion process, fails to patent process for fear of publicizing it; **1857** Kelly belatedly receives patent, declared original inventor of conversion process only after it is lifted by associates of Henry Bessemer and patented to Bessemer 1856, becomes known as the Bessemer Process; **1872** town incorporated; **c.1960** town relocated to make way for

KENTUCKY

Lake Barkley, completed 1966, formed by Barkley Dam to west.

La Grange *Oldham County   Northern Kentucky, 23 mi/37 km northeast of Louisville*

1824 Oldham County formed; Westport becomes first county seat; **July 25, 1824** Union Gen., Illinois Sen. Richard James Oglesby born in rural Oldham County (died 1899); **1827** town founded at major crossroads as new county seat, named for Gen. Lafayette's French estate; **1830** Robert Morris House built; **1840** town incorporated; **1875** county courthouse built; **Jan. 23, 1875** movie producer D. W. (David Wark) Griffith born at rural Crestwood to south (died 1948); **1939** Medium Security Prison built to replace prison at Frankfort.

Lancaster *Garrard County   Central Kentucky, 28 mi/45 km south of Lexington*

1789 Letcher House built by John Boyle; **1796** Garrard County formed; **1797** town founded as county seat by pioneers from Lancaster, Pennsylvania; first county courthouse built; **1813** William Ownsley House built; **1837** town incorporated; **1850** Bradley House built, home of Gov. William O. Bradley; **1868** second county courthouse built.

Lawrenceburg *Anderson County   Central Kentucky, 24 mi/39 km west of Lexington*

1776 Dutchman named Coffman becomes first setter; town founded near Kentucky River, named for settler William Lawrence; **1820** town incorporated; **1827** Anderson County formed; town becomes county seat; **March 7, 1850** Missouri Cong., Speaker of the House James Beauchamp "Champ" Clark born (died 1921); **1915** county courthouse built; **1932** Joe Blackburn Bridge built across Kentucky River to east.

Lebanon *Marion County   Central Kentucky, 53 mi/ 85 km southeast of Louisville*

1795 area settled by pioneers from Maryland; **1814** town founded; **1815** town incorporated; **1816** post office established; **1834** Marion County formed; town becomes county seat; **1935** county courthouse built.

Leitchfield *Grayson County   West central Kentucky, 60 mi/97 km south-southwest of Louisville*

1810 Grayson County formed; town founded as county seat on land donated by Maj. David Leitch; **1813** post office established as Litchfield (actual pronunciation of current name); **1815** Jack Thomas Home built, oldest house in county; **1825** health spa established by Joe Clarkson at Grayson Spring to east, damaged by fire 1909, closed 1920s; **1866** town incorporated; **1877** spelling of town name altered to present form; **1937** county courthouse built.

Lexington *Fayette County   Central Kentucky, 70 mi/113 km east of Louisville*

June 1775 Robert Patteson, Simon Kenton, others camp here while en route to build fort on Kentucky River; **1779** town founded, named for Battle of Lexington; blockhouse built to protect settlement from Native American raids; **1780** Fayette County formed, one of three original Kentucky counties (with Jefferson, Lincoln); town becomes county seat; **May 1781** town incorporated; **Aug. 15, 1782** British with native allies under Capt. William Caldwell and renegade Simon Girty surround Bryan Station fort 6 mi/9.7 km to northeast, defeated by defenders with aid of reinforcements, retreat to Blue Licks to north where they ambush Kentucky volunteers; **1783** South Elkhorn Baptist Church founded to southwest; **1787** Transylvania University, then Transylvania Seminary, moved from Danville, established 1780; *Kentucky Gazette* newspaper founded; first impromptu horse races held among settlers who had ridden their best horses across Alleghenies from Virginia; **c.1790** Old Keene Place mansion built to west on land grant made to Francis Keene of Virginia; **1792** Mount Brilliant mansion built to north; **1794** post office established; original section of Ewalt House built to north; **1797** Bryan Station House residence built to northeast; first jockey club organized; Postlethwait's Tavern built by Revolutionary Capt. John Postlethwait; **1798** Eothan house built by Rev. James Moore; **early 1800s** breeding stallions imported from England and Arabia; **1806** original Ashland mansion built by Henry Clay; Gratz mansion built; Castleton mansion built to north; **1811** Hopemont mansion built by John Wesley Hunt; **c.1816** Senator Pope House built for U.S. Sen. John Pope; **Dec. 13, 1818** Mary Todd Lincoln, wife of Pres. Abraham Lincoln, born (married Nov. 4, 1842, died 1882); **Jan. 15, 1821** Confederate Gen. John Cabell Breckinridge born, served as U.S. vice president 1857–1861 (died 1875); **Feb. 19, 1821** Union Gen., Missouri Sen. Francis Preston Blair, Jr. born (died 1875); **c.1825** Patchen Wilkes Horse Stock Farm founded to east; **1830s** Leafland mansion built by Jacob Hughes to east; **1831** incorporated as a city; **1832** Lexington & Ohio Railroad completed; **1833** cholera epidemic sweeps through region killing 300 in Lexington; **1840s** David Prewitt Place estate house built by J. Howard Sheffer to east; **1847** Christ Episcopal Church built; **1850** horse named Lexington born at The Meadows estate, progenitor of famed race horses Man o' War, Fair Play, War Admiral, others; **1850s** Botherum house built for Maj. Madison C. Johnson; **1854** Sayre College for women established; **Nov. 13, 1856** educator, Supreme Court Justice Louis Dembitz Brandeis born, Brandeis University, Waltham, Massachusetts, named for him (died 1941); **1857** new Ashland mansion built by architect Maj. T. Lewinski replacing original 1806 structure; **c.1860** Alleghan Hall mansion built by William Pettit; **1865** University of Kentucky established; **Sept. 25, 1866** biologist Thomas Hart Morgan born, Nobel Prize 1933 (died 1945); **1870s** first trackside horse race betting begins; **1872** First Presbyterian Church completed; **1873** Trotting Track built at Tattersall's

Sales Stables on Broadway; **1879** Phoenix Hotel built on site of Postlethwaite's Tavern, hotel named for three tavern fires which occurred during its years of operation, the first two of which it survived; **1886** Opera House opened, renovated 1976; **1892** Walnut Hall Horse Stock Farm established to north; **1897** Hamburg Place horse estate founded to east; **1898** county courthouse built; **Nov. 22, 1898** educator Sarah Gibson Blanding born (died 1985); **1900** elegant Elmendorf mansion built to northeast, razed 1929 to avoid payment of taxes; **1903** Lexington Public Library built, gift of Andrew Carnegie; **1915** Coldstream Stud Farm established to north; **1926** Episcopal Church of the Good Shepherd completed; **1928** Macedonian Christian Church built to east; **1936** Keeneland Race Course built to west; Spindletop mansion built to north; **1937** Bluegrass Field airport opened to west; **1965** Lexington Community College of University of Kentucky established; **1974** city and county governments merge; **1976** Rupp Arena (Lexington Center) opened; **1978** International Museum of the Horse opened at Kentucky Horse Park to north; **1980** 22-story Kincaid Tower built; **1986** 30-story Lexington Financial Center completed; **1995** Heritage Exposition Hall opened; **2002** new county courthouse completed.

Liberty *Casey County* *Central Kentucky, 55 mi/ 89 km south-southwest of Lexington*

1791 town settled and named by Revolutionary War veterans from Virginia; Col. William Casey establishes defense station against Native Americans; **1806** Casey County formed; **1808** town becomes county seat; **1830** town incorporated; **1889** county courthouse built.

London *Laurel County* *Southern Kentucky, 65 mi/ 105 km south-southeast of Lexington*

1815 first permanent settlers arrive; **1825** Laurel County formed; **1826** town founded as county seat; **1836** town incorporated; **1866** incorporated as a city; **1897** Sue Bennett College established; **1961** county courthouse built.

Louisa *Lawrence County* *Northeastern Kentucky, 100 mi/161 km east of Lexington*

1789 settlement founded by Charles Vancouver of London, England, at joining of Tug Fork and Levisa Fork rivers to form Big Sandy River; **1815** town platted; **1821** Lawrence County formed; **1822** town becomes county seat; **c.1840** Freese House built; **1869** town incorporated; **Jan. 22, 1890** Supreme Court Chief Justice Frederick Moore Vinson born, served 1946–1953 (died 1953); **1896** Big Sandy Dam built on Big Sandy River; **1906** Fort Gay Bridge built across Big Sandy River to Fort Gay, West Virginia, rebuilt 1971; **1964** county courthouse completed; **1988** Yatesville Lake formed by dam to west on Blaine Creek.

Louisville *Jefferson County* *Northern Kentucky, 90 mi/145 km southwest of Cincinnati, Ohio*

1778–1779 explorer George Rogers Clark's men build fort at Falls of the Ohio following capture of British forts farther west at Kaskaskia, Cahokia, and Vincennes; settlement founded as exploration base; **1780** Jefferson County formed, one of three original counties in Kentucky District, Virginia (with Fayette, Lincoln counties); 300 settlers arrive; **May 1780** town incorporated, named for King Louis XVI of France; **1781** Native Americans attack settlement, bluff their escape across river, ambush pursuers in their canoes, nine whites killed; **Oct. 17, 1781** Vice Pres. Richard Mentor Johnson born, served under President Van Buren (died 1850); **1782** Fort Nelson completed, named for Governor Nelson of Virginia; **1795** post office established; **1798** University of Louisville established; **1801** *Farmer's Library* becomes town's first newspaper; **June 14, 1805** Union army officer Robert Anderson born, defended Fort Sumter Apr. 1861 (died 1871); **1808** naturalist John James Audubon arrives, lives here until 1810, moves downriver to Henderson; **c.1808** Grayson House built by John Gwathmey; **1810** Farmington mansion built to east by John Speed; **Oct. 1811** steamboat *New Orleans* docks at Louisville on way to Natchez, first steamboat to visit city; **Dec. 16, 1811** first shocks of New Madrid Earthquake strike town at 2 P.M., followed by 87 aftershocks during 1812; **1814** Spalding University established; **1822** Christ Church Cathedral (Episcopal) built; **March 16, 1822** Union Gen. John Pope born (died 1892); **c.1825** Thomas Crowe establishes livery business; **1827** Benjamin Smith House built; **1828** incorporated as a city; **1830** *Louisville Journal* newspaper founded; **Dec. 1830** Louisville & Portland Canal completed on Ohio River around south side of 27-ft/8.2-m Falls of the Ohio, built with slave labor; **1831** opening of canal brings economic depression on city due to loss in portaging business; **1832** Louisville Hotel built; Bank of the United States built; **c.1835** the Galt House hotel opens, razed 1920; **1837** Bank of Louisville built; **March 27, 1840** fire destroys much of business district; **1840s** large surge of German immigrants arrives; **1844** *Morning Courier* newspaper founded; **1850** Pres. Zachary Taylor buried east of city, near Ohio River, in Zachary Taylor National Cemetery; **1851** Louisville, Frankfort & Lexington Railroad completed; **1852** Cathedral of the Assumption (Catholic) completed; **1855** Kentucky School for the Blind established; **Aug. 6, 1855** known as Black Monday, several people killed in rioting touched off by Know Nothing Party anti-Catholic movement; **1858** Courier-Journal Building built; American Printing House for the Blind established; **1859** Louisville & Nashville Railroad completed to Nashville; Southern Baptist Theological Seminary founded, reopens 1865 following Civil War; **1860** county courthouse completed, begun 1836; **1860s** city serves as military headquarters for Union forces through course of Civil War; **1864** Sullivan College established; **1868** *Louisville Courier-Journal* newspaper founded with merger of two dailies; **1869** Bourbon Stockyards established; **1870** Louisville Free Library founded; **1875** Churchill Downs Race Track opened; **c.1875** railroad bridge built across Ohio River; **May 17, 1875** first Kentucky Derby held, won by Aristides; **1884** *Louisville Times* newspaper founded, folded 1987; Louisville Slugger baseball bat developed by Hillerich & Bradsby Company; **June 4, 1884** cartoonist Fontaine Talbot Fox, Jr. born, drew "Toonerville Trolley" series (died 1964); **March 27, 1890** wind storm hits city's west side, 106 killed, moves into Indiana; **Apr. 28, 1892** folksinger John Niles born (died 1980); **1893** Louisville Presbyterian Theological Seminary founded; **1895** Confederate Memorial erected; **1904** Seabach Hotel built; **Dec. 20, 1904** actress Irene Dunne born (died 1990); **1905** Falls City Brewery opened, closed 1978; **1908** Louisville Public Library opened; Kentucky State Fairgrounds opened, first year of regular exhibitions; **1912** Fort Nelson monument erected; **Apr. 1913** jazz vibraphone player Lionel Hampton born (died 2002); **Jan. 29, 1916** actor Victor Mature born (died 1999); **Dec. 20, 1917** railroad accident, 41 killed; **1919** Bowman Field airport established; **Sept. 27, 1920** TV actor William Conrad born (died 1994); **1925** Falls of Ohio harnessed for electricity production; **1927** Louisville & Portland Canal rebuilt; Southern Baptist Theological Seminary founded; **1929** Louisville Memorial Auditorium opens; **Oct. 10, 1934** Alice Speed Stoll kidnapped, released, Thomas Robinson sentenced to life in prison; **Dec. 23, 1935** football player Paul Hornung born; **Nov. 9, 1936** singer Mary Travers (Peter, Paul, and Mary) born; **Jan.–Feb. 1937** worst flooding in Ohio River's history; **July 6, 1937** actor Ned Beatty born; **1941** Standiford Field established as military base, becomes Municipal Airport 1947, renamed Louisville International Airport 1995; **Jan. 17, 1942** heavyweight boxer Muhammad Ali (Cassius Clay, Jr.) born; **Oct. 28, 1948** actress Telma Hopkins born; **1950** Bellarmine Collage established; **1954** General Electric Appliance Park established; **1970** Louisville Zoo established; **Sept. 8, 1970** DC-9 airplane splits in two on landing at Standiford Airport, 14 of 39 on board injured (similar occurrence at JFK Airport, New York, July 15); **1971** 30-story Citizen's Plaza building completed; **1972** 40-story First National Building completed, later renamed National City Tower; **Sept. 5, 1975** antibusing riots break out, 50 injured, 500 arrested; **Nov. 25, 1984** William Schroeder of Jasper, Indiana, becomes second person to receive artificial heart, at Humana Hospital (first was Barney Clark, Salt Lake City, 1983); **Feb. 17, 1985** Murray Hayden becomes third person to receive artificial heart, also at Humana Heart Institute; **Sept. 14, 1989** Joseph Wesbecker shoots print shop employees, killing 7, wounding 13, then kills himself; **2000** city and county governments merge; **July 22, 2001** Robert Tools, 59, receives artificial heart at Jewish Hospital, dies Nov. 30 after surviving 151 days.

Madisonville   *Hopkins County*   Western Kentucky, *112 mi/180 km southwest of Louisville*

1806 Hopkins County formed; town founded as county seat; **1807** town incorporated; **1817** Daniel McGary House built; **1853** incorporated as a city; **1937** county courthouse built; **1968** Madisonville Community College established.

Manchester   *Clay County*   Southeastern Kentucky, *72 mi/116 km south-southeast of Lexington*

c.1785 salt works established at spring by James White of Virginia; **1798** town founded, originally named Grenville; **1806** Clay County formed; town becomes county seat; **1807** named for English manufacturing center of Manchester; **1808** first salt wells drilled; **1844** town incorporated; **1932** incorporated as a city; **1939** county courthouse built.

Marion   *Crittenden County*   Western Kentucky, *138 mi/222 km southwest of Louisville*

1815 first galena mine shaft dug by company headed by Andrew Jackson in search of silver, finds little silver content, abandons enterprise; **1824** Crittenden County formed; town founded as county seat, named for Revolutionary War hero Gen. Francis Marion; **1844** town incorporated; **1961** county courthouse built; **1977** Amish colony founded.

Mayfield   *Graves County*   Western Kentucky, *23 mi/37 km south of Paducah*

1817 settler named Mayfield arrives from Mississippi, captured by bandits, shot while attempting to escape across creek that now bears his name; **1821** Graves County formed; **1823** town founded as county seat; **c.1840** Woolridge monuments erected over grave of horse trader Henry Woolridge at Maplewood Cemetery, 18 statues of himself mounted on horse, his mother, brothers, girlfriends, dogs, wild animals, all facing east; **1846** town incorporated; **Nov. 24, 1877** Vice Pres. Alben William Barkley born in rural Graves County, served under President Truman (died 1956); **1889** county courthouse built; **1891** extraction of clay deposits begins.

Maysville   *Mason County*   Northeastern Kentucky, *55 mi/89 km northeast of Lexington*

1782 Simon Kenton, others become first settlers at site on Ohio River, site named Limestone; **c.1786** Daniel Boone and wife Rebecca open tavern; **1787** town founded; **1788** Mason County formed; **c.1790** town becomes leading port of entry for Kentucky; shipbuilding becomes important; **1833** town incorporated; **1838** city hall built; Cochran House built; **1848** county seat moved from Washington; city hall converted to county courthouse, clock tower added 1850; **Dec. 31, 1884** Supreme Court Justice Stanley Forman born at rural Minerva to west (died 1980); **May 23, 1928** singer Rosemary Clooney born (died 2002); **1931** Simon Kenton Memorial Bridge built across Ohio River to Aberdeen, Ohio; **1967** Maysville Community College established; **1990** town of Washington merges with Maysville; **Oct. 2000** William H. Harsha Bridge (cable-stayed suspension) completed on Ohio River east of town.

McKee *Jackson County*   *Central Kentucky, 50 mi/ 80 km south-southeast of Lexington*

1858 Jackson County formed; settlers arrive from Virginia and the Carolinas; town founded as county seat; **1882** town incorporated; **1951** fourth county courthouse built.

Middlesboro *Bell County*   *Southeastern Kentucky, 105 mi/169 km south-southeast of Lexington*

1750 Dr. Thomas Walker passes through Cumberland Gap from Virginia; **1775** Wilderness Road built through Gap by Daniel Boone; **1769** U.S. government makes improvements on road; **1885** Scottish-Canadian mining engineer Col. Alexander Arthur surveys region, discovers commercial potential of its coal, limestone, and iron deposits; **1889** town founded, promoted by British investors; **1890** Louisville & Nashville and Southern railroads reach town; town incorporated; **1893** collapse of London bank Baring Brothers and Company brings economic collapse to town; **June 11, 1940** Cumberland Gap National Historical Park authorized to east, extends into Virginia and Tennessee; **1996** Cumberland Tunnel completed at Cumberland Gap to Virginia eliminating hazardous road section.

Minerva *Mason County*   See **Maysville (1884)**

Monticello *Wayne County*   *Southern Kentucky, 83 mi/134 km south-southwest of Lexington*

c.1795 town founded; **1800** Wayne County formed; town becomes county seat; **1810** town incorporated; **summer 1863** in Battle of Rocky Gap, Union troops advance on Confederates under General Morgan, 20 Confederates killed, 4 Union killed; **1901** Sunnybrook Oil Field discovered; **1912** last stagecoach run in Kentucky completes journey from Burnside; **1950** county courthouse built; large Lake Cumberland formed by Wolf Creek Dam on Cumberland River.

Morehead *Rowan County*   *Northeastern Kentucky, 57 mi/92 km east of Lexington*

1856 Rowan County formed; town founded as county seat; **1869** town incorporated; **1899** county courthouse built; **1922** Morehead State University established; **1974** Cave Run Lake formed by dam on Licking River to southwest.

Morganfield *Union County*   *Western Kentucky, 120 mi/193 km west-southwest of Louisville*

1811 Union County formed; **1812** town founded as county seat; **1820** St. Vincent's Academy founded to east; **1870** town incorporated; **1872** county courthouse built.

Morgantown *Butler County*   *West central Kentucky, 85 mi/137 km southeast of Louisville*

1810 Butler County formed; **1811** town founded on Green River as county seat; **1813** town incorporated; post office established; **1975** county courthouse built.

Mount Olivet *Robertson County*   *Northern Kentucky, 41 mi/66 km northeast of Lexington*

1820 town founded; **1867** Robertson County formed; town becomes county seat; **1851** town incorporated; **1873** county courthouse built.

Mount Sterling *Montgomery County*   *East central Kentucky, 30 mi/48 km east of Lexington*

c.800 BC Gaitskill Mounds to north built by Adena people; **1782** Capt. James Estill killed in combat with Native Americans during Battle of Little Mountain; **1793** town platted by Enoch Smith, named Little Mountain, renamed shortly after; **1796** Montgomery County formed; town becomes county seat; **1851** town incorporated; **1855** Peter Lee Hensley born, African-American horse breeder whose racers Temple Bar and Alcyo won multiple events (died 1926); **Dec. 1863** town captured by Confederates; **1878** Ascension Church built; **1960** county courthouse built.

Mount Vernon *Rockcastle County*   *Central Kentucky, 47 mi/76 km south of Lexington*

1790 blockhouse built as defense against Native Americans, later converted to Langford House; **1810** Rockcastle County formed; town founded as county seat; **1818** town incorporated; **1953** Rockcastle County Public Library founded; **1964** third county courthouse built; **1992** Judicial Complex completed.

Munfordville *Hart County*   *Central Kentucky, 67 mi/108 km south of Louisville*

1801 town first settled; **1806** frame structure built, becomes Munford Inn; **1816** town site donated by Richard Jones Munford; **1819** Hart County formed; town becomes county seat; **Apr. 1, 1823** Confederate Gen. Simon Bolivar Buckner born (died 1914); **Sept. 25, 1823** Union Gen. John Wood born (died 1906); **1858** town incorporated; **Sept. 17, 1863** Confederates under General Bragg capture town from Union Col. John T. Wilder; **July 18, 1886** World War II Gen. Simon Bolivar Buckner, Jr. born, killed June 18, 1945, invasion of Okinawa; **1928** county courthouse built.

Murray *Calloway County*   *Western Kentucky, 35 mi/56 km south-southeast of Paducah*

1821 Calloway County formed; Wadesboro becomes first county seat; **1822** town founded, originally named Williston; **1843** town renamed for Cong. John L. Murray; county seat moved to Murray; **1844** town incorporated; **1902** Nathan B. Stubblefield transmits human voice across site of present-day university, device becomes known as radio, patented invention 1908; **1913** county courthouse built; **1922** Murray State University established.

New Haven   *Larue County*   *Central Kentucky, 40 mi/64 km south of Louisville*

1781 James Harrod establishes shipping station on Rolling Fork river; Col. Samuel Pottinger builds warehouse and landing; originally called Pottinger's Landing, Pottinger renames settlement for New Haven, Connecticut; **1820** town founded; **1839** town incorporated; **Feb. 26, 1844** Supreme Court Justice Horace Harmon Lurton born (died 1914); **1848** Our Lady of Gethsemane Trappist monastery founded to east; **Dec. 31, 1860** inventor John Taliaferro Thompson born, developed submachine gun (Tommy gun) (died 1940); **1964** county courthouse built.

Newport   *Campbell County*   *Northern Kentucky, 1 mi/1.6 km southeast of Cincinnati, Ohio*

1790 Hubbard Taylor arrives at site on Ohio River with Kentucky troops, acquires land for town; Taylor roughly plans town, names it for Christopher Newport, commander of first ships to arrive in Jamestown, Virginia, 1607; **1792** James Taylor arrives to check on welfare of his brother, finds no trace of him, returns here 1793 with family; **1794** Campbell County formed; **1795** incorporated as a village; **1796** town becomes county seat, shared with Visalia; **1798** Newport Academy founded; **1806** Newport Barracks established at mouth of Licking River by U.S. government; **1812** James Taylor House built; **1821** Southgate House built by Col. Wright Southgate; **1831** Taylor Methodist Episcopal Church built; **1835** incorporated as a city; **1840** Kenton County separates from Campbell County, shared county seat moved to Alexandria; **1856** offices of *True South*, Kentucky's only antislavery newspaper, destroyed by mob of Southern sympathizers; **1858** Newport Iron and Steel founded, becomes Andrews Steel 1891; **1880s** large number of German immigrants arrive; **1884** flooding inundates Newport Barracks, post moved to Fort Thomas 1888; county courthouse built; **1896** Newport Bridge built across Ohio River to Cincinnati; **1921** steel workers strike, lasts seven years; **1999** World Peace Bell installed at Millennium Monument; **May 1999** Newport Aquarium opened.

Nicholasville   *Jessamine County*   *Central Kentucky, 11 mi/18 km south of Lexington*

c.1775 Joseph Drake House built to west, home of apparent descendant of Sir Francis Drake; **1782** grist mill built; **1798** Jessamine County formed; town founded as county seat, named for Col. George Nicholas of Virginia, one of framers of Kentucky state constitution; **1800** La Chaumiere du Prairie house built to north by Col. Davis Meade; **1806** post office established; **1837** town incorporated; **1863** Camp Nelson established to south by Federals, used as prison camp, enlistment base for black recruits, closed 1865; **1878** county courthouse built.

Owensboro   *Daviess County*   *Northwestern Kentucky, 80 mi/129 km west-southwest of Louisville*

1780 first white settlers arrive; **1798** town founded on Ohio River, originally named Yellow Banks; **1815** Daviess County formed, named for Col. Joseph Daviess, killed in Battle of Tippecanoe; town becomes county seat, renamed Rossborough for landowner David Ross; **1828** Griffith House built; **1846** Planter's Hotel built; **1850** incorporated as a town; **1866** incorporated as a city, renamed for Col. Abraham Owen of Virginia; **Apr. 29, 1909** actor Tom Ewell born (died 1994); **1948** Owensboro Airport established; **June 9, 1963** actor Johnny Depp born; **1964** county courthouse built; **1986** Owensboro Community College established.

Owenton   *Owen County*   *Northern Kentucky, 38 mi/61 km north-northwest of Lexington*

1819 Owen County formed; **1822** town founded as county seat; town and county named for Col. Abraham Owen, early settler and prominent figure in War of 1812; **1828** town incorporated **1858** third county courthouse built; **1953** Owen County Public Library founded.

Owingsville   *Bath County*   *Northeastern Kentucky, 40 mi/64 km east of Lexington*

1790 Slate Creek Iron Furnace established to east; **1791** resort established at Olympia Springs to southeast; **1811** Bath County formed; town founded as county seat on land owned by Richard Menifee and Col. Thomas Owings; **1814** post office opened; **June 1, 1831** Confederate Gen. John Bell Hood born (died 1879); **1868** county courthouse built, extensively remodeled 1904; **1912** Owings House completed.

Packard   *Whitley County*   See **Williamsburg (1946)**

Paducah   *McCracken County*   *Western Kentucky, 170 mi/274 km southwest of Louisville*

1775 George Rogers Clark establishes base on Ohio River, at mouth of Tennessee River, before launching raids on British posts at Kaskaskia, Cahokia, and Vincennes; **1817** first arrival of white settlers in advance of Jackson Purchase agreement; James and William Pore build first cabin; settlement named Pekin; **1818** Jackson Purchase cedes Chickasaw land between Tennessee and Mississippi rivers to Kentucky; **1824** McCracken County formed; **1826** first store built; **1827** town founded as county seat by explorer William Clark, brother of George Rogers Clark, names town for legendary Chickasaw Chief Paduke; **1830** town chartered; Floydsburg and Brownsboro merge with Paducah; inn built by John Field; **1833** Oaklands mansion built; **1838** incorporated as a town; **1850s** Southern Hotel built on site of John Field's inn; **1854** Marine Ways barge manufacturer established, later becomes Ingram Barge Lines; **1856** incorporated as a city; **1857** county courthouse built; Whitfield House built; **1858** Hazelton House built; **Sept. 1861** General Grant takes possession of city for Union, builds Fort Anderson, serves as Union supply base for duration of Civil War; **1864** Confederate Gen. Nathan B. Forrest's forces destroy Union supply base, withdraws with impending smallpox epidemic; **1866** Whitehaven mansion built to west; **June, 23, 1876** humorist Ervin S. Cobb born (died 1944); **Oct. 30, 1886** author Elizabeth Madox Roberts born (died 1941); **1909** Tilghman Statue erected in honor of Confederate Gen. Lloyd Tilghman; Chief Paduke Statue erected; **1917** railroad bridge built across Ohio River from Metropolis, Illinois; **1920** U.S. government barge-building plant established; **1928** highway bridge built across Ohio River; **1929** Irvin Cobb Hotel built; Irvin S. Cobb Bridge built across Ohio River; **1931** George Rogers Clark Memorial Bridge (U.S. Hwy. 60) across Tennessee River; **1932** Paducah Community College established; **Jan. 1937** great Ohio River flood inundates city; **1942** county courthouse built; **Dec. 1, 1997** Michael Carneal, 14, shoots and kills three students, injures five others attending prayer meeting at Heath High School, West Paducah.

Paintsville *Johnson County Eastern Kentucky, 92 mi/148 km east-southeast of Lexington*

1826 town founded, originally named Paint Creek; **1834** town chartered, renamed Paintsville; **1843** Johnson County formed; town becomes county seat; **1846** coal mining begins in county; **1872** town incorporated; **1892** second county courthouse built; **1904** Chesapeake & Ohio Railroad reaches town; **Apr. 14, 1934** country singer Loretta Lynn born at Butcher Hollow to south; **Jan. 9, 1951** country singer Crystal Gayle born, sister of Loretta Lynn.

Paris *Bourbon County Central Kentucky, 17 mi/27 km northeast of Lexington*

c.**1775** popular Johnson's Inn built to west, later became Rosedale residence; **1785** Bourbon County formed; **1786** Mount Lebanon house built, damaged by New Madrid Earthquake Dec. 1811; **1788** Duncan Tavern built; **1789** town founded as county seat on Stoner River, named Hopewell; **1790** town renamed for Paris, France, in appreciation of French assistance in Revolutionary War; **1790** one of Kentucky's first distilleries established by Jacob Spears of Pennsylvania; **1791** Cane Ridge Meeting House built by Presbyterians from North Carolina; **July 29, 1794** Ohio Cong. Thomas Corwin born in rural Bourbon County, secretary of treasury under President Fillmore (died 1865); **1795** first bridge over Stoner Creek built; **1804** Disciples of Christ denomination established; Indian Queen Hotel built, later assimilated into larger Windsor Hotel; c.**1810** Brest Tavern built on Cane Ridge Pike; **1839** town incorporated; **Dec. 16, 1863** author John Fox, Jr. born (died 1919); **1893** incorporated as a city; **1905** county courthouse built.

Park City *Barren County Southern Kentucky, 80 mi/129 km south-southwest of Louisville*

1790s bear hunter discovers entrance of Mammoth Cave to north; **1820s** Bell's Tavern established by Col. William Bell; town of Bell Tavern founded; **1858** tavern destroyed by fire; **1871** town incorporated, renamed Glasgow Junction; **1886** Mammoth Cave Railroad built, abandoned 1929; **1921** oil driller George Morrison creates new entrance through ceiling of Mammoth Cave; **July 1, 1841** Mammoth Cave National Park established; **1938** town renamed Park City.

Perryville *Boyle County Central Kentucky, 36 mi/58 km southwest of Lexington*

1792 Halfway Inn built to south at halfway point between Louisville and Boonesboro; **1817** town founded on Chaplin River; **1856** post office established; **Oct. 8, 1862** in Battle of Perryville, Union Gen. Don Carlos Buell faces Confederate Gen. Braxton Bragg, though not clear victory, General Bragg retreats into Tennessee after battle, ending attempts to bring Kentucky into Confederacy; **1969** town incorporated.

Pewee Valley *Oldham County Northern Kentucky, 15 mi/24 km east-northeast of Louisville*

1852 town founded on Louisville & Lexington Railroad, named Smith's Station; **1870** town incorporated, renamed for large flocks of Eastern phoebes (flycatchers, also called pewees) in area; c.**1890** Villa Ridge Resort built, converted to Confederate Home 1902, closed 1934, razed; **1897** Jennie Casseday Rest Cottage established, retreat for young working women, former home (1860s) of author Catherine Warfield; **1901** The Beeches house built.

Pikeville *Pike County Eastern Kentucky, 112 mi/180 km southeast of Lexington*

1821 Pike County formed; **1824** town founded as county seat; town and county named for explorer Zebulun Pike; **1848** town incorporated; **1889** Pikeville College established; **1931** Hotel James Hatcher built; **1893** incorporated as a city; **1932** county courthouse built; **Oct. 23, 1956** country singer Dwight Yoakam born; **Jan. 4, 1957** country singer Patty Loveless born; **1985** Pikeville Cut-Thru Project built, diversion of Levisa Fork river through deep cut, natural channel filled, ending perpetual flood threat, initiated by Dr. William C. Hambley, Jr., dubbed Hambley's Dream; **June 14, 2003** perennially feuding Hatfield and McCoy families of Kentucky and West Virginia sign peace pact.

Pineville *Bell County Southeastern Kentucky, 98 mi/158 km south-southeast of Lexington*

1775 Wilderness Road built by Daniel Boone; **1781** area settled; **1792** tollgate established, road improvements made; town founded, named Cumberland Fort; **1818** post office established; **1830** tollgate abandoned; **1867** Bell County formed; town platted as county seat, renamed

Pineville; **1873** town incorporated; **1919** county courthouse built.

Prestonsburg *Floyd County* *Eastern Kentucky, 95 mi/153 km east-southeast of Lexington*

1791 area first settled; **1797** town founded; **1799** Floyd County formed; **1817** May House built, oldest house in Big Sandy Valley; **1818** county organized; town becomes county seat; **Jan. 10, 1862** Battle of Middle Creek, Union troops under future president Col. James A. Garfield defeat Brig. Gen. Humphrey Marshall, ending Confederate dominance in region; **1867** town incorporated; **1946** Dewey Lake formed by dam on Johns Creek to north; **1964** county courthouse built; Prestonsburg Community College established.

Princeton *Caldwell County* *Western Kentucky, 137 mi/220 km southwest of Louisville*

1809 Caldwell County formed; Eddyville becomes first county seat; **1817** town founded; county seat moved to Princeton; **1854** incorporated as a town; **1930** incorporated as a city; **1941** county courthouse built.

Radcliff *Hardin County* *Northern Kentucky, 30 mi/48 km south-southwest of Louisville*

1917 Fort Knox established as U.S. Army World War training camp, becomes permanent military post 1932; **1919** town founded as service center for Fort Knox, named for Maj. William Radcliffe [sp]; **1936** U.S. Bullion Depository established at Fort Knox by U.S. Treasury Department; **1956** incorporated as a city; **May 12, 1973** Huey helicopter crashes at Fort Knox Army Base, killing six Army officers, one civilian.

Richmond *Madison County* *Central Kentucky, 23 mi/37 km south-southeast of Lexington*

1784 Col. John Miller, veteran of Battle of Yorktown, becomes first settler; **1785** Madison County formed; Milford becomes county seat; **1787** Whitehall mansion built to north by Gen. Green Clay, rebuilt by T. Lewinski 1864; **1798** town founded by Col. Miller as new county seat; **1809** town incorporated; **Oct. 19, 1810** abolitionist Cassius Marcellus Clay born in rural Madison County (died 1903); **Apr. 5, 1816** Supreme Court Justice Samuel Freeman Miller born (died 1890); **1822** Woodlawn mansion built by Gen. Green Clay; **May 7, 1848** Missouri Gov., Cong. William Joel Stone born (died 1918) **1849** county courthouse built; **1852** Mount Zion Church built to south; **spring 1861** in Battle of Richmond, Union forces take control of Madison County; **Aug. 29–31, 1862** Gen. Kirby Smith's Confederate forces engage Union Gen. William Nelson's troops; **1906** Eastern Kentucky University established.

Rosine *Ohio County* See **Hartford (1911)**

Russellville *Logan County* *Southern Kentucky, 112 mi/180 km southwest of Louisville*

c.1790 town founded, named Big Boiling Spring; **1792** Logan County formed; town becomes county seat; **1796** frontiersman James Bowie born, killed defending the Alamo March 6, 1836; **1798** incorporated as a town, renamed in honor Revolutionary War Gen. William Russell; **1840** incorporated as a city; **1861** Kentucky secessionists meet at Coke House, unofficially declare state part of Confederacy with Bowling Green as capital; **March 20, 1868** Jesse James, four gang members rob Southern Bank of $9,000, wound bank president, gang member George Shepherd captured in Tennessee two weeks later; **1904** county courthouse built.

Salyersville *Magofin County* *Eastern Kentucky, 78 mi/126 km east-southeast of Lexington*

1800 blacksmith shop established by pioneer Billy Adams; town founded on Licking River, named Adamsville; **1860** Magofin County formed, named for Gov. Beriah Magoffin (1859–1862); town becomes county seat, renamed for Cong. Sam Salyers; **1867** town incorporated; **1959** county courthouse built.

Sandy Hook *Elliott County* *Eastern Kentucky, 73 mi/117 km east of Lexington*

1850 town founded on Little Sandy River; **1869** Elliott County formed; town becomes county seat; **1872** town renamed Martinsburg, reverts to Sandy Hook 1874; **1888** town incorporated; **1968** county courthouse built.

Scottsville *Allen County* *Southern Kentucky, 103 mi/166 km south-southwest of Louisville*

1797 first white settlers arrive; **1815** Allen County formed; town founded as county seat; town incorporated; **1965** county courthouse completed.

Shelbyville *Shelby County* *Northern Kentucky, 30 mi/48 km east of Louisville*

1779 Squire Boone, brother of Daniel Boone, builds fort at nearby Painted Rock; **1781** group of settlers heads for stronger fort at Louisville on warning of impending Native American attack, are ambushed, c.50 killed; **1792** Shelby County formed; town founded as county seat; **1800** Watkins House built; **1825** Science Hill School for girls established, closed 1939; **1846** town incorporated; **1867** Stanley-Casey House built; **1914** county courthouse built; **Jan. 19, 1994** lowest temperature ever recorded in Kentucky reached, −37°F/−38°C, breaking record set at Cynthiana 1963.

Shepherdsville *Bullitt County* *Northern Kentucky, 16 mi/26 km south of Louisville*

1793 town founded and incorporated on Salt River; **1796** Bullitt County formed; town becomes county seat; **1901**

county courthouse built; **Dec. 20, 1917** collision of passenger and mail trains, 51 killed.

Simpsonville *Shelby County* *Northern Kentucky, 22 mi/35 km east of Louisville*

1782 Abraham Lincoln, grandfather of Pres. Abraham Lincoln, builds log cabin, killed by Native Americans 1786, Mordecai Lincoln saves remainder of family, including brother Thomas, president's father; **c.1794** Old Stone Inn built; **1816** town founded, named for Capt. John Simpson, killed in Battle of River Raisin, Michigan, 1813; **1833** town incorporated; **1904** Lincoln Institute established for black students after passage of law prohibiting blacks from attending schools with whites.

Smithland *Livingston County* *Western Kentucky, 11 mi/18 km east-northeast of Paducah*

1780 original Smithland established downstream on Ohio River from current site; **1798** Livingston County formed; Eddysville becomes first county seat; **c.1800** Smithland relocated to mouth of Cumberland River; **1805** town incorporated; **1809** county seat moved to Salem; **1843** county seat moved to Smithland; **1845** county courthouse built; **1980** Smithland Lock & Dam built on Ohio River.

Somerset *Pulaski County* *Southern Kentucky, 65 mi/105 km south of Lexington*

1799 Pulaski County formed; **1801** town founded as county seat; **1810** incorporated as a town; **Jan. 19, 1862** in Battle of Mill Springs, Confederate Gen. Felix K. Zollicoffer killed, his troops defeated by Union regiment led by Gen. George Thomas; **1874** third county courthouse built; **1883** incorporated as a city; **Aug. 23, 1901** Sen. John Sherman Cooper born (died 1991); **1904** Carnegie Library built; **1965** Somerset Community College established.

Southgate *Campbell County* *Northern Kentucky, 3 mi/4.8 km south-southeast of Cincinnati, Ohio*

c.1795 area settled by William Southgate, others; town founded near Ohio River; **1907** incorporated as a city; **May 28, 1977** electrical fire at Beverly Hills Supper Club spreads quickly, 165 killed, over 100 injured.

Springfield *Washington County* *Central Kentucky, 47 mi/76 km southeast of Louisville*

1782 Thomas Lincoln homesteads to north; **1783** ferry established on Beech Fork River; **1792** Washington County formed; **1793** town founded as county seat; **c.1795** John Pope House built by Gen. Matthew Walton, later home of U.S. Sen. John Pope; **1796** town incorporated; **June 12, 1806** Thomas Lincoln marries Nancy Hanks, move to Hodgenville Dec. 1808; **1816** county courthouse built, still in use; **1851** Maple Hill Manor house built.

Stanford *Lincoln County* *Central Kentucky, 35 mi/56 km south-southwest of Lexington*

1775 Logan's Fort established by Col. Benjamin Logan; **May 20, 1777** under attack by Native American allies of British, Logan slips through enemy lines, returns with ammunition and reinforcements; **1780** Lincoln County formed, one of three original Kentucky counties (with Jefferson, Fayette counties); Harrodsburg becomes county seat; **1786** town founded as new county seat; **c.1799** fur trader William Lewis Sublette born (died 1845); **1816** Bright's Inn built by Capt. John Bright; **1861** town incorporated; **1909** third county courthouse built.

Stanton *Powell County* *Central Kentucky, 37 mi/60 km east-southeast of Lexington*

1805 Red River Iron Works established to west, closed 1869; **1825** oil discovered, production continues until 1920; **1849** town founded on Red River; town named Beaver Pond; **1845** Louisville & Nashville Railroad reaches town; **1852** Powell County formed; town becomes county seat, renamed for Cong. Richard H. Stanton; **1854** town incorporated; **1926** Natural Bridge State Park established; **1977** county courthouse built.

Taylorsville *Spencer County* *North central Kentucky, 28 mi/45 km southeast of Louisville*

1799 town founded on Salt River, named for landowner Richard Taylor; **1824** Spencer County formed; town becomes county seat; **1829** town incorporated; **1915** county courthouse built; **1983** Taylorsville Lake formed by dam to east on Salt River.

Tompkinsville *Monroe County* *Southern Kentucky, 105 mi/169 km south of Louisville*

1773 Old Mulkey Meeting House built by Baptists from North and South Carolina, rebuilt 1798; **1819** town founded; **1820** Monroe County formed; town becomes county seat; **1856** town incorporated; **1976** county courthouse built.

Vanceburg *Lewis County* *Northeastern Kentucky, 73 mi/117 km northeast of Lexington, on Ohio River*

1791 salt works established; **1796** area first settled; **1797** town founded by Joseph Vance; **c.1805** log hunter house built by W. B. Parker for hunting expeditions; **1807** Lewis County formed; Poplar Flat becomes first county seat, seat moved to Clarksburg 1810; **1827** town incorporated; **June 2, 1832** steamboat *Hornet* capsizes in gale force winds, 20 killed; **1863** county seat moved to Vanceburg; **1940** county courthouse completed.

Versailles *Woodford County* *Central Kentucky, 12 mi/19 km west of Lexington*

1784 Pisgah Presbyterian Church organized; Buck Pond estate house built to east by Col. Thomas Marshall, father of U.S. Chief Justice John Marshall; **Sept. 10, 1787** Sen. John Jordan Crittenden born (died 1863); **1788** Woodford County formed; **1792** town founded as county seat, named by settler Gen. Marquis Calmes of France; **1793** town platted; **1797** Labrot and Graham Distillery established, oldest in Kentucky; **1812** Pisgah Presbyterian Church built to east; **1820s** Watkins Tavern opened by Henry Watkins, stepfather of Henry Clay, destroyed by fire 1932; **March 4, 1826** Union Gen. John Buford born in rural Woodford County (died 1863); **1837** town incorporated; **1863** Stone Wall Farm house built to north; **1970** third county courthouse completed.

Warsaw   *Gallatin County   Northern Kentucky, 30 mi/48 km southwest of Cincinnati, Ohio*

1798 Gallatin County formed; Port William becomes first county seat; **c.1800** town site first settled; **1814** town founded on Ohio River, originally named Fredericksburg; **Jan. 18, 1815** Illinois Cong. Richard Yates born (died 1873); **1831** town renamed Warsaw; **1833** town incorporated; **1838** county seat moved to Warsaw; county courthouse built, remodeled 1940; **1850** Payne Manor house built by Gen. John Payne of Revolutionary War; **1963** Markland Lock & Dam built to west on Ohio River; **2002** Kentucky Speedway opened to south.

Washington   *Mason County   Northeastern Kentucky, 53 mi/85 km northeast of Lexington*

1786 town founded at day's-journey stopping point from Ohio River port of Maysville, uphill climb of 4 mi/6.4 km; **1788** Mason County formed; town becomes first county seat; **1794** county courthouse built, used as courthouse until 1848, destroyed by fire 1909; **1797** *Washington Mirror* newspaper founded; **1800** The Hill mansion built by Thomas Marshall, Jr., brother of Chief Justice John Marshall; **Feb. 2, 1803** Confederate Gen. Albert Sidney Johnston born, killed Feb. 1862; **1848** county seat moved to Maysville; Marshall Key House built, later becomes Slavery to Freedom Museum; **1874** Dover Covered Bridge built; **1962** town incorporated; **1990** town merges with Maysville.

Water Valley   *Graves and Hickman counties Western Kentucky, 36 mi/58 km south-southwest of Paducah*

1858 town founded on New Orleans & Ohio Railroad, originally named Morse Station; **Aug. 1861** Confederate Camp Beauregard established as training base, named for Gen. P. G. T. Beauregard; **Nov. 1861** following arrival of 6,000 soldiers from six Southern states, combined epidemic breaks out including measles, meningitis, typhoid, and pneumonia, 1,500 killed in one month; **1872** town renamed Water Valley; **1884** town incorporated.

West Liberty   *Morgan County   Eastern Kentucky, 67 mi/108 km east of Lexington*

1822 Morgan County formed, named for Revolutionary War hero Gen. Daniel Morgan; **1823** town founded on Licking River as county seat; **1840** town incorporated; **1907** county courthouse built.

Whitesburg   *Letcher County   Southeastern Kentucky, 110 mi/177 km southeast of Lexington*

1840 town founded as lumber center on North Fork Kentucky River, named for legislator C. White; **1842** Letcher County formed; town becomes county seat; **1872** town incorporated; **1912** Louisville & Nashville Railroad reaches town; **1965** county courthouse built; **March 9–11, 1976** coal mine disaster at Oven Fork Mine to south, 26 killed.

Whitley City   *McCreary County   Southern Kentucky, 90 mi/145 km south of Lexington*

1912 McCreary County formed; **1913** town founded; county seat moved from Pine Knot; **1914** county courthouse built; **March 7, 1974** Big South Fork National River and Recreation Area established, extends into Tennessee.

Wickliffe   *Ballard County   Western Kentucky, 27 mi/43 km west of Paducah*

1780 Fort Jefferson built by Gen. George Rogers Clark under orders from Thomas Jefferson, then governor of Virginia; **1842** Ballard County formed; Blandville becomes first county seat; **1880** town founded on Mississippi River, near mouth of Ohio River; **1882** town incorporated; county seat moved to Wickliffe; county courthouse built; **1905** new county courthouse completed; **1938** railroad and highway bridges built across Ohio River to Cairo, Illinois.

Williamsburg   *Whitley County   Southern Kentucky, 90 mi/145 km south-southeast of Lexington*

1817 Whitley County formed; **1819** town founded on Cumberland River as county seat; town and county named for William Whitley; **1851** town incorporated; **1889** Cumberland College established; **Jan. 20, 1926** actress Patricia Neal born at rural Packard to northeast; **1970s** county courthouse built.

Williamstown   *Grant County   Northern Kentucky, 30 mi/48 km south of Cincinnati, Ohio*

1790 area first settled; **1820** Grant County formed; town founded as county seat; William Arnold donates land for public buildings; **1825** town incorporated; **1877** Texas Pacific Railroad (Southern Railway) reaches town; **1939** county courthouse built.

Winchester *Clark County* *Central Kentucky,*
17 mi/27 km east of Lexington

1779 town founded by John Baker of Winchester, Virginia; **1792** Clark County formed; town becomes county seat; **1793** town incorporated; **Feb. 10, 1810** sculptor Joel Tanner Hart born (died 1877); **1814** Hickman House built by William Hickman; **1824** John Strode Cabin built to west; **1855** county courthouse built; **1866** Kentucky Wesleyan College established; **1878** John Winn Place house built to west; **Nov. 19, 1899** poet Allen Tate born (died 1979).

Yancey *Harlan County* *See* **Harlan** (1932)

Louisiana

Southern U.S. Capital: Baton Rouge. Major city: New Orleans.

Louisiana was admitted to the U.S. as the Louisiana Purchase October 19, 1803, which included all of the Mississippi Basin west of the river. The Florida Parishes, that part of Louisiana east of the Mississippi River once part of Spanish West Florida, were annexed in 1810. Louisiana was admitted to the Union as the 18th state April 30, 1812. It seceded as one of the Confederate states January 26, 1861, and was readmitted January 25, 1868.

Louisiana is divided into 64 parishes. Originally called counties, they were renamed parishes to retain the state's Catholic tradition. The parishes have the same function as counties. Municipalities are classified as villages, towns, and cities. The City of New Orleans is coterminous with Orleans Parish. There are no townships. See Introduction.

Abbeville   *Vermilion Parish*   *Southern Louisiana, 80 mi/129 km west-southwest of Baton Rouge*

1843 Capuchin Abbe A. D. Megret arrives by pirogue, builds St. Marie Madeleine's Chapel, founds town; **1844** Vermilion Parish formed; town becomes parish seat; **1845** Colomb Bakery established by Jean Boyance; **1850** incorporated as a city; **1850s** vigilance committees organized to rid region of cattle thieves; **1852** parish seat moved from Perry's Bridge (Perry) following bitter dispute; **1854** chapel destroyed by fire; **1880s** Edwards House built; **1901** Edward's Bamboo Grove planted at Mt. Carmel Academy; **1910** new St. Marie Madeleine's Church dedicated; Steen's Syrup Company established; **1953** parish courthouse built.

Alexandria   *Rapides Parish*   *Central Louisiana, 103 mi/166 km northwest of Baton Rouge*

1763 St. Louis des Appalages Chapel built at rapids in Red River by Capuchin fathers for Appalache Native Americans just arrived from Mobile, Alabama, area; **c.1765** first Acadian exiles arrive; **1785** town founded; **1796** Kent Plantation House built; **1807** Rapides Parish formed; **1810** town founded as parish seat by Alexander Fulton; **1819** town incorporated; **1819** College of Rapides established; **1837** Ralph Smith-Smith Railroad built to Cheneyville, one of first railroads west of Mississippi River; **1854** river channel deepened through rapids; **1858** St. Francis Xavier Academy founded, closed during Civil War, reopened 1872; **1864** Forts Buhlow and Randolph built by Confederates, neither saw action; **May 13, 1864** much of Alexandria burned as Union forces retreat from

Natchitoches and Mansfield; **1869** Harris Plantation house built to south; **1898** St. Francis Xavier Cathedral built; **1907** Alexandria Public Library built **1908** Hotel Bentley built; **1909** city hall built; **1917** Esler Field established for artillery training, becomes Esler Airport 1930s; **1925** Masonic Home for Indigent Children founded; **1926** St. James Episcopal Church built; **1932** city charter adopted; **1939** parish courthouse built, addition built 1976; **1942** England Air Force Base established, closed 1992; **1960** Louisiana State University at Alexandria (2-year) established; **1966** Rapides Symphony Orchestra founded; **June 11, 1972** 11 children, woman in pickup truck killed in collision with trailer truck; **1977** Alexandria Museum of Art founded; **1996** England International Airport opened; Riverfront Center exhibition facility opened.

Amite   *Tangipahoa Parish*   *Southeastern Louisiana, 60 mi/97 km north-northwest of New Orleans*

1836 town founded on Tangipahoa River; **1845** New Orleans, Jackson & Northern Railroad extended through town; **1861** incorporated as a city; **May 1861** Camp Moore established by Confederates; **1869** Tangipahoa Parish formed; town becomes parish seat; **Apr. 24, 1908** tornado damages town, also Purvis, Mississippi, to northeast, total 143 killed; **1949** first annual Oyster Festival held; **1969** parish courthouse built.

Arcadia   *Bienville Parish*   *Northern Louisiana, 52 mi/84 km east of Shreveport*

1848 Bienville Parish formed; Sparta becomes parish seat; **1850** town founded; **1855** incorporated as a town; **1893**

parish seat moved to Arcadia; **1903** incorporated as a city; **1940s** natural gas discovered to south; **May 21, 1934** outlaws Clyde Barrow and Bonnie Parker killed in shootout with Texas Rangers and Sheriff's men at hideout at Black Lake (Ambrose Mountain) to west; **1953** parish courthouse built.

Avery Island   *Iberia Parish   Southern Louisiana, 65 mi/105 km southwest of Baton Rouge*

1791 salt dome island settled by John Hays; **c.1799** John C. Marsh of New Jersey acquires island, establishes sugar cane plantation, begins drawing salt from springs for War of 1812; **1830s** Avery family arrives; **1862** J. M. Avery begins mining salt for Confederates; **1863** Union Gen. Nathaniel Banks destroys salt mines; **1868** Tabasco hot pepper sauce first marketed by McIlhenny Company by Edmund McIllhenny, peppers brought from Tabasco, Mexico, later grown on island; **1893** Edward Avery McIlhenny establishes egret colony and sanctuary, part of his Jungle Gardens attraction; **1899** salt mining resumes; **1942** oil discovered, strict environmental standards set by island owners.

Bastrop   *Morehouse Parish   Northeastern Louisiana, 175 mi/282 km north-northwest of Baton Rouge*

1844 Morehouse Parish formed; **1845** town founded near Bayou Bartholomew as parish seat, platted 1846; **1852** town incorporated; **1900** Missouri Pacific Railroad reaches town; **June 6, 1907** Yankees baseball player Bill Dickey born (died 1993); **1915** parish courthouse built; **1916** natural gas discovered in area.

Baton Rouge   *East Baton Rouge Parish   Southeastern Louisiana, 70 mi/113 km northwest of New Orleans*

1699–1700 French explorer Pierre Le Moyne d'Iberville mentions site in his writings, site named for red posts (*baton rouge*, "red stick") used by Native Americans to mark boundary of Houma and Bayou Goula nations; **1719** possible French fort built here; **Dec. 31, 1721** Father François Xavier de Charlevoix lands here, celebrates mass following day; **1763** town ceded to Britain as part of West Florida; **Sept. 21, 1779** British garrison overwhelmed by Spanish in First Battle of Baton Rouge; **1781** all of West Florida ruled by Spain; **1805** Spanish Town becomes city's first subdivision; **1806** Elias Beauregard plats elaborate city on his plantation, fails to attract settlers; **Sept. 23, 1810** revolt against Spanish by Americans in Second Battle of Baton Rouge; West Florida Republic declared; **Dec. 1810** republic annexed by Louisiana Gov. Claiborne; Parish of Feliciana formed; **Apr. 1811** East Baton Rouge Parish formed from Feliciana Parish; town becomes parish seat; **Apr. 30, 1812** Louisiana enters Union as 18th state; **1817** town incorporated; **1824** The Cottage plantation built to south by Col. Abner Duncan; **c.1829** Pentagon

Barracks completed, built to house U.S. troops, used until 1877, Zachary Taylor was post commander when elected president 1849; **1835** Louisiana State Penitentiary built, moved to Angola (Tunica) 1890; **1840** Dougherty-Prescott House built; **1840s** Louisian Hotel built; **1842** *State-Times and Morning Advocate* newspaper founded as the *Democratic Advocate*; **1849** state capital moved here from New Orleans; state capitol built, restored as historical site 1993; **1852** Louisiana State School for the Deaf founded; Louisiana State School for the Blind founded; **1853** construction of St. Joseph's Catholic Church begun; **1856** Goodwood plantation house built by Dr. S. G. Laycock; **1859** Old City Market built, abandoned 1925; **May 1862** Union forces capture city after fall of New Orleans; ceases function as state capital; **Aug. 5, 1862** in Third Battle of Baton Rouge, attempt to retake city by Confederate General Breckinridge fails, withdraws to Port Hudson; **July 8, 1863** General Banks takes Port Hudson to north from Confederates following siege May 21–July 8, giving U.S. control of Mississippi River; **1869** Louisiana Seminary of Learning moved from Pineville, becomes Louisiana State University 1870; **June 20, 1870** steamboat *Princess*, loaded with viewers of race between *Robert E. Lee* and *Natchez*, catches fire, 70 killed; **1880** Southern University established; **1880s** William Garig House built; **1882** reestablished as state capital; old state capitol building rebuilt, burned during Civil War occupation; **1886** Confederate monument erected; **1909** Standard Oil of Louisiana organized; **1930** governor's mansion built, reopened as historical site 1998; **1932** new 34-story state capitol completed, tallest in U.S.; **Sept. 8, 1935** Sen. Huey P. Long shot by Dr. Carl Austin Weiss, in turn slain by bodyguards, Long dies Sept. 10; **1939** The Louisiana Scandals send Gov. Richard Leche and LSU Pres. James Monroe to jail on corruption charges; **1940** Huey P. Long Statue erected; railroad bridge built across Mississippi River; **1947** Baton Rouge Symphony Orchestra founded; **1948** Baton Rouge Metro Airport (Ryan Field) established; **1963** new governor's mansion built; Foundation for Historical Louisiana chartered; **1965** Louisiana State Fair moved to Baton Rouge, previously held in Shreveport for over 75 years; **1968** Airline Highway (I-10) Bridge built across Mississippi River; **Apr. 26, 1970** state capitol heavily damaged by bomb blast; **Jan. 10, 1972** shootout leaves two policemen, two black militants dead, eight wounded; **1974** 24-story Hancock Bank Building built; **1977** Riverside Centroplex Governmental Complex opened; **1982** World War II USS *Kidd* permanently docked, opened as Louisiana Maritime Museum 1983; **2000** former Gov. Edwin Edwards, son Stephen, five others indicted on racketeering and fraud charges, later convicted; **2003** Pennington Planetarium opened.

Benton   *Bossier Parish   Northwestern Louisiana, 13 mi/21 km north of Shreveport*

1843 Bossier Parish formed, named for Louisiana Creole militia Gen. Pierre Evariste Jean Baptiste Bossier;

Bellevue becomes parish seat; **1888** town founded on Cotton Belt Railroad as new parish seat; **1890** parish records removed by force from Bellevue by citizens of Benton; **1902** town incorporated; **Aug. 10, 1936** highest temperature ever recorded in Louisiana reached at Plain Dealing to north, 114°F/46°C; **1972** parish courthouse completed.

Bogalusa *Washington Parish* *Southeastern Louisiana, 60 mi/97 km north-northeast of New Orleans*

1905 Great Southern Lumber Mill established; **1906** town founded on Bogalusa Creek, near Pearl River; **1914** incorporated as a city; **1938** Great Southern Mill closes; reforestation program initiated by Gaylord Paper Company; **May 23, 1965** Mayor Cutrere calls for repeal of all segregation ordinances amid civil rights demonstrations; **1967** black Civil Rights protesters march from Bogalusa to Baton Rouge under protection of National Guardsmen.

Bossier City *Bossier Parish* *Northwestern Louisiana, 1 mi/1.6 km east of Shreveport*

c.1850 first settlers arrive; **1862** Fort Smith built by Confederates; **1883** town founded on Red River, opposite Shreveport, named for Pierre Evariste Bossier (BOHS-yer); **1884** Vicksburg, Shreveport & Pacific Railroad completed; **1907** incorporated as a village; **1908** north-south Shreveport & Arkansas Railroad completed; **1918** oil discovered; **1923** incorporated as a town; **1925** fire destroys large part of town; **1933** Barksdale Army Air Base established, becomes Air Force Base after World War II; **1951** incorporated as a city; **1967** Bossier Parish Community College established; **1980** I-20 bridge built across Red River; **1988** Bossier Central Library built.

Breaux Bridge *Saint Martin Parish* *Southern Louisiana, 50 mi/80 km west of Baton Rouge*

1771 Acadian settler Firmin Breaux acquires land; **1799** Breaux builds first bridge across Bayou Teche; **1817** son Agricole Breaux builds first vehicular bridge; **1829** town founded by Scholastique Picou Breaux, 33-year-old widow of Agricole; **1871** town incorporated; **1950** fourth successor bridge to 1817 structure built; **1959** first Crawfish Festival held; **1972** Henderson (I-10) Bridge built east across Atchafalaya Basin to Baton Rouge, 18 mi/29 km long.

Cameron *Cameron Parish* *Southwestern Louisiana, 35 mi/56 km south of Lake Charles*

1840 first settlers arrive; town founded at mouth of Calcasieu River on Gulf of Mexico; **1870** Cameron Parish formed; town becomes parish seat; **1902** Gulf Biological Station established for study of marine life, abandoned by 1940; **1932** road built to Cameron from Sulphur, previously accessible only by boat; **1937** parish courthouse built; **June 27, 1957** area devastated by Hurricane Audrey, hundreds killed in Cameron Parish.

Carville *Iberville Parish* See **Plaquemine (1894)**

Chalmette *Saint Bernard Parish* *Southeastern Louisiana, suburb 10 mi/16 km east of New Orleans*

1805 Versailles plantation house built by Pierre Denis Delaronde, destroyed by fire 1876; **1807** St. Bernard Parish formed; St. Bernard becomes parish seat; town founded on Mississippi River; **Dec. 23, 1814** in Battle of New Orleans, British forces advance capturing Louisiana militia, are fired upon by gunboat *Carolina*; **Jan. 8, 1815** British attack American fortifications, soundly defeated by group of Creoles, Native Americans, and pirates led by Andrew Jackson, 13 of Jackson's men killed, 30 wounded, 700 British killed, 1,400 wounded; **1840** Beauregard House built; **1864** Chalmette National Cemetery established, burial site of 14,000 Union soldiers; **1939** parish courthouse built; **Aug. 10, 1939** Chalmette National Monument established at site of Chalmette Battlefield, Battle of New Orleans, absorbed by Jean Lafitte National Historical Park Nov. 10, 1978; **1992** Elaine P. Nunez Community College established.

Clinton *East Feliciana Parish* *Southeastern Louisiana, 30 mi/48 km north-northeast of Baton Rouge*

1806 stone house built by Judge Lafayette Saunders; **1824** East Feliciana Parish formed from Feliciana Parish; town founded; **1825** parish seat moved from Jackson; **c.1825** William Bennett House built; **1825–1829** Lawyers' Row buildings built; **1830** incorporated as a town; **c.1830** Chase House built; **1836** Hardcastle house built; **1837** Marston House built; **1841** parish courthouse built, restored 1936; **1852** incorporated as a city; Silliman College established, closed 1931; **1855** Woodward Plantation House completed, built with slave labor.

Cloutierville *Natchitoches Parish* See **Natchitoches (1886)**

Colfax *Grant Parish* *Central Louisiana, 125 mi/201 km northwest of Baton Rouge*

1869 Grant Parish formed; **1870** town founded on Red River as parish seat, named by carpetbag legislature for Schuyler Colfax, vice president under Ulysses S. Grant; **Apr. 13, 1873** rioting begins Easter Sunday when freed blacks evict white municipal administration, overrun days later by the White League, 3 whites, c.120 blacks killed; **1878** town incorporated; **1955** parish courthouse built.

Convent *Saint James Parish* *Southeastern Louisiana, 46 mi/74 km west of New Orleans*

1807 St. James Parish formed; St. James becomes parish seat; **1825** St. Michael's Convent established on Mississippi River, closed 1926; **c.1825** Zenon Trudeau House built; **1831** Joseph College established, closed 1855; **1835** Welham plantation house built; **1838** Jefferson College established, closed 1927; **1841** Uncle Sam plantation house built by Judge Dominique Tureaud, destroyed by fire, rebuilt 1849 by Samuel Fagot, demolished 1940; **1869** town founded as parish seat; **Sept. 29, 1838** architect Henry Hobson Richardson born (died 1886); **1971** parish courthouse built.

Coushatta   *Red River Parish   Northwestern Louisiana, 178 mi/286 km northwest of Baton Rouge*

1865 Paul Lisso builds store near Red River; town founded, named for Coushatta Tribe; **1871** Red River Parish formed; town becomes parish seat; **1872** town incorporated; **1874** in Coushatta Massacre, carpetbagger Marshall Harvey Twitchell loses both arms in assassination attempt, brother, two brothers-in-law, three others killed at hands of White League; **1929** parish courthouse built.

Covington   *Saint Tammany Parish   Southeastern Louisiana, 35 mi/56 km north of New Orleans*

1769 area near north shore of Lake Pontchartrain first settled; **1810** St. Tammany Parish formed, named for chief of Delaware peoples, dubbed "saint" for his friendliness toward white people; Enon becomes parish seat; **1813** town founded, originally named Wharton; **1816** town incorporated, renamed for War of 1812 Gen. Leonard Covington; **1828** parish seat moved to Covington; **1877** Mount Carmel Monastery founded; **1959** parish courthouse built.

Crowley   *Acadia Parish   Southern Louisiana, 80 mi/ 129 km west-southwest of Baton Rouge*

1884 Southern Pacific Railroad built through town; **1886** Acadia Parish formed; town founded as parish seat; **1887** town incorporated, named for railroad foreman Patrick Crowley, becomes rice capital of Louisiana; **1909** first rice experimental station established by Louisiana State University; **1951** parish courthouse built.

Delta   *Madison Parish   Northeastern Louisiana, 130 mi/209 km north of Baton Rouge, opposite Vicksburg*

1838 Madison Parish formed; Richmond becomes parish seat; **1863** parish seat moved to Tallulah; General Grant attempts unsuccessfully to cut new channel in river during siege of Vicksburg, trench called Grant's Canal; **Dec. 23, 1867** Mrs. C. J. Walker (Sarah Breedlove) born, first African-American woman millionaire, made fortune in lotions, hair care products (died 1919); **1868** town founded; parish seat moved to Delta; **1869** town incorporated; **1883** parish seat moved back to Tallulah; **1940** highway bridge built across Mississippi River from Vicksburg, replaced 1972.

De Ridder   *Beauregard Parish   Southwestern Louisiana, 140 mi/225 km west-northwest of Baton Rouge*

1897 town founded; **1903** town incorporated; **1912** Beauregard Parish formed; town becomes parish seat;

1914 parish courthouse built; **1941** De Ridder Army Air Base established, closed 1946.

Donaldsonville   *Ascension Parish   Southeastern Louisiana, 57 mi/92 km west of New Orleans*

1750 trading post established on Mississippi River; **1760s** Acadian exiles arrive; **1781** church built by Father Revillagodos; **1806** town founded by William Donaldson; **1830** state capital moved to Donaldsonville, moved back to New Orleans 1831; **June 1863** Union fort taken by Confederates, retaken by Union gunboats, find bodies of own Union soldiers; **1889** parish courthouse built; **1920** incorporated as a city; **1963** Sunshine Bridge built across river.

Edgard   *Saint John the Baptist Parish Southeastern Louisiana, 30 mi/48 km west of New Orleans*

1720s area settled by Germans, becomes known as Cote des Allemands (German Coast); **1768** exiled Acadians begin arriving from Nova Scotia; **1807** St. John the Baptist Parish formed; Lucy becomes parish seat; **1840** Evergreen plantation house built; **1848** town founded on Mississippi River as new parish seat; **1968** parish courthouse built.

Eunice   *Saint Landry Parish   Southern Louisiana, 80 mi/129 km west of Baton Rouge*

1894 town founded by C. C. Duson, named for his wife; **1895** incorporated as a city; **1967** Louisiana State University at Eunice (2-year) established; **1987** Liberty Center for the Performing Arts opened, vintage theater built 1924; **1997** Cajun Music Hall of Fame opened; **May 27, 2000** 2,000 residents evacuated after freight train derails, hazardous chemicals catch fire, explosions cause large mushroom cloud.

Farmerville   *Union Parish   Northern Louisiana, 185 mi/298 km northwest of Baton Rouge*

c.1790 town founded near Bayou D'Arbonne by John Honeycutt; **1839** Union Parish formed; town becomes parish seat; **1842** town incorporated; **1961** Bayou D'Arbonne Reservoir formed to west; parish courthouse completed.

Ferriday   *Concordia Parish   Eastern Louisiana, 90 mi/145 km north-northwest of Baton Rouge*

1803 notorious criminal Samuel Mason beheaded by fellow criminals John Setton and James Mays who turn in head for reward, in turn are tried and beheaded by authorities for their crimes; **1903** town founded on Cocodrie Bayou, named for plantation owner John C. Ferriday; **May 12, 1914** newsman Howard K. Smith born (died 2002); **1927** town incorporated; **March 15, 1935** evangelist Jimmy Swaggart born; **Sept. 29, 1935** singer Jerry Lee Lewis born.

Fort Jesup *Sabine Parish* *Western Louisiana, 165 mi/266 km northwest of Baton Rouge*

1822 frontier fort established by Zachary Taylor; **1844** Brig. Gen. Zachary Taylor placed in command of fort during Mexican War; **July 1845** General Taylor ordered to move against Mexicans following annexation of Texas; **1846** fort abandoned save for caretaker regiment; **1960** Fort Jesup State Park established, becomes state historic site 1999.

Franklin *Saint Mary Parish* *Southern Louisiana, 90 mi/145 km west of New Orleans*

1800 town founded on Bayou Teche by Guinea Lewis of Pennsylvania, names it for Benjamin Franklin; **1804** Haifleigh (Sterling) Plantation House built, destroyed by fire 1938; **1812** St. Mary Parish formed; town becomes parish seat; **1820** town incorporated; **1829** Oaklawn Manor built, destroyed by fire during restoration 1926, rebuilt; **c.1830** town becomes important shipping port; **1850** Dixie home built by Wilkes family; **c.1850** Gates House built; **1850s** Arlington house (Old Baker Place) built; **1853** Grevemberg House built; **1862** Union gunboats patrol Bayou Teche, assume control of sugar cane operations through end of war; **1907** parish courthouse built.

Franklinton *Washington Parish* *Southeastern Louisiana, 65 mi/105 km north of New Orleans*

1819 Washington Parish formed; town founded as parish seat near Bogue Chitto River; **1821** town founded; **1861** town incorporated; **1960** parish courthouse built.

Gonzales *Ascension Parish* *Southeastern Louisiana, 20 mi/32 km south-southeast of Baton Rouge*

c.1845 area first settled near Mississippi River; **1887** post office established; town named for Sheriff Joseph Gonzales; **1906** town platted by son Joseph "Tee-Joe" Gonzales; **1908** Louisiana Railroad & Navigation Company builds railroad, names station Edenborn for company president William Edenborn, concedes to original name following public opposition; **1922** incorporated as a village; **1952** incorporated as a town; **1977** incorporated as a city.

Grambling *Lincoln Parish* *Northern Louisiana, 60 mi/97 km east of Shreveport*

1900 sawmill established; town founded on Shreveport & Pacific Railroad by Judd Grambling; **1901** Colored Industrial and Agricultural School established, renamed Grambling College 1946, becomes Grambling State University 1970s; **1962** incorporated as a city.

Grand Isle *Jefferson Parish* *Southeastern Louisiana, 55 mi/89 km south of New Orleans*

1811 Jean Lafitte organizes band of pirates and smugglers on islands of Barataria Bay, Gulf of Mexico; **1814** Lafitte feigns acceptance of British proposal to support them in attack on New Orleans, turns information over to U.S., receives pardon from President Madison 1815 for past crimes, resumes pirating from Galveston Island; **1835** Fort Livingston built at site of Jean Lafitte's hideout; **Oct. 26, 1863** Federal troops take fort from Confederates; **1893** island settlement destroyed by hurricane; fort abandoned; **1897** Barataria Lighthouse built; **1959** town incorporated.

Greensburg *Saint Helena Parish* *Southeastern Louisiana, 70 mi/113 km north-northwest of New Orleans*

1810 St. Helena Parish formed; **1812** Montpelier becomes parish seat; **1832** town founded near Tickfaw River as new parish seat; **1860** town incorporated; **1938** parish courthouse built.

Gretna *Jefferson Parish* *Southeastern Louisiana, suburb 1 mi/1.6 km south of New Orleans*

1825 Jefferson Parish formed; Lafayette becomes parish seat; **c.1830** town founded on west side of Mississippi River by Nicholas Destrehan, named Mechanicsham; **1839** town platted as Gretna; **1852** parish seat moved to Carrollton; **c.1874** Carrollton annexed by New Orleans; parish seat moved to Gretna; **March 2, 1909** New York Yankees baseball player Mel Ott born (died 1958); **1913** incorporated as a city; **1958** parish courthouse built; **1967** parish divided into two districts; auxiliary parish courthouse built on east side of river.

Hahnville *Saint Charles Parish* *Southeastern Louisiana, 20 mi/32 km west of New Orleans*

1719 area first settled by Germans from Alsace-Lorraine; **1766** over 200 Acadian exiles arrive from Nova Scotia; **1807** St. Charles Parish formed; St. Charles becomes parish seat; **1840** Keller House built; **1872** town founded on Mississippi River by Louisiana Gov. Michael Hahn; **1880** town becomes new parish seat; post office established; **1977** parish courthouse built; **March 4, 1985** first phase of Waterford Nuclear Power Plant opened.

Hammond *Tangipahoa Parish* *Southeastern Louisiana, 50 mi/80 km north-northwest of New Orleans*

c.1810 Peter Hammond becomes first settler; **1859** Charles Emery Cate family arrives; **1860** town founded by Cate; **1885** settlement program by Illinois Central Railroad lures residents from northern states; **1888** incorporated as a city; **Feb. 3, 1907** newspaper publisher Hodding Carter born (died 1972); **1925** Southeastern Louisiana College (now University) established; **1943** Hammond Municipal Airport established by military, becomes civilian facility 1949.

Harrisonburg   *Catahoula Parish   Eastern*
Louisiana, 105 mi/169 km north-northwest of Baton Rouge

1808 Catahoula Parish formed; **c.1810** town founded on Ouachita River as parish seat; **1863** Fort Beauregard built by Confederates, shelled by Union May 4, destroyed Sept. 4 by Confederates as they abandon it; **1928** town incorporated; **1931** parish courthouse completed.

Homer   *Claiborne Parish   Northern Louisiana,*
47 mi/76 km northeast of Shreveport

1828 Claiborne Parish formed; Russellville becomes parish seat; **1830** town founded; **1836** parish seat moved to Overton; **1846** parish seat moved to Athens; **1849** parish seat moved to Homer; **1850** town incorporated; **1860** parish courthouse built; **1919** Homer Oil Field discovered west of town; **1920** Haynesville Oil Field discovered to north; **1966** Lake Claiborne formed by dam to southeast on Bayou D'Arbonne.

Houma   *Terrebonne Parish   Southeastern*
Louisiana, 50 mi/80 km southwest of New Orleans

1822 Terrebonne Parish formed; Williamsburg becomes parish seat; **1827** Crescent Farms established by William Shaffer; **1828** Southdown Plantation founded for indigo production, later converts to sugar cane, plantation house built 1858; **1834** town founded as new parish seat on Bayou Terrebonne; **1848** town incorporated; **1850** Belle Grove plantation house begun, completed 1881; **Aug. 10, 1856** Montegut resort on Isle Deniere to southeast on Terrebonne Bay destroyed by hurricane, over 200 killed; **1925** U.S. Sugar Cane Experimental Station established; **1929** offshore oil and natural gas production begins; **1938** parish courthouse built; **May 1943** Lighter Than Air Blimp Naval Air Station established, closed Sept. 1944; **1961** Houma Navigational Channel completed to Gulf of Mexico.

Jackson   *East Feliciana Parish   Southeastern*
Louisiana, 27 mi/43 km north of Baton Rouge

1808 The Shades house built on land grant made to Alexander Scott; **c.1810** Hickory Hill plantation house built by David McCants of South Carolina; **1814** Andrew Jackson's forces camp on Thompson's Creek during War of 1812; **1815** town platted on Thompson's Creek by John Horton; **1816** Feliciana Parish formed; town becomes parish seat; parish courthouse built; **1824** parish divided into East and West Feliciana parishes; town becomes East Feliciana Parish seat; **1825** parish seat moved to Clinton; Centenary College established, moved to Shreveport 1908; **1832** town incorporated; **1840** Henry Johnson House built; **1847** East Louisiana State Hospital founded.

Jefferson Island   *Iberia Parish   Southern*
Louisiana, 65 mi/105 km southwest of Baton Rouge

1870s salt dome island purchased by actor Joseph Jefferson (1829–1905), builds Bob Acres residence, named for a favorite role; **1895** salt discovered by Jefferson; **1917** Lawrence Jones and J. L. Bayless organize Jefferson Island Salt Company organized; **1923** Spanish gold coins unearthed by salt mine employee; **Nov. 21, 1980** oil drilling team punctures hole in salt dome, draining Lake Peigneur, swallows tugboat, 11 barges, drilling platform, ruins botanical gardens, 50-ft/15-m waterfall (highest ever in state) formed where canal from Gulf enters lake.

Jena   *La Salle Parish   Central Louisiana, 110 mi/*
177 km northwest of Baton Rouge

1860s first settlers arrive from Georgia and South Carolina; **1871** town founded; **1872** Jena Academy founded; **1892** Jena Seminary founded, burned 1911; **1903** Louisiana & Arkansas Railroad reaches town; **1906** town incorporated; **1908** La Salle Parish formed; town becomes parish seat; **1968** parish courthouse completed.

Jennings   *Jefferson Davis Parish   Southwestern*
Louisiana, 98 mi/158 km west of Baton Rouge

1884 Southern Pacific Railroad built; town founded on Bayou Nezpique, named for railroad construction engineer Jennings McComb; **1888** incorporated as a city; **1901** first discovery of oil in Louisiana made in Jennings Oil Field; **1910** Jefferson Davis Parish formed; **1912** town becomes parish seat; **1966** parish courthouse built.

Jonesboro   *Jackson Parish   Northern Louisiana,*
162 mi/261 km northwest of Baton Rouge

1845 Jackson Parish formed; Vernon becomes parish seat; **c.1860** town founded as lumber center; **1901** town incorporated; **1908** parish seat moved to Jonesboro; **1938** parish courthouse built.

Kenner   *Jefferson Parish   Southeastern Louisiana,*
suburb 10 mi/16 km west of New Orleans

1830s Belle Grove Plantation established by Philip Minor Kenner; **1820** Soniat house built on Tchoupitoulas Plantation; **1855** New Orleans & Jackson Railroad reaches site; town founded on Mississippi River; iron foundry established; **1873** incorporated as a town; **1899** ferry established; **1915** interurban rail line built from New Orleans; **1934** Wendell Williams Airport established; **1946** Moisant Field established, becomes New Orleans International Airport 1960, renamed Louis Armstrong New Orleans International 2001; **1950** Hale Boggs Bridge (I-310) built to Luling, second span completed 1983; **1952** incorporated as a city; **Oct. 26, 1976** ferry *George Prince* and Norwegian tanker *Frosta* collide in river, killing 77; **July 9, 1982** Pan Am Boeing 727 crashes after takeoff killing 153, including 8 on ground; **1983** railroad bridge built to Luling; **March 1991** Pontchartrain Centre convention hall opened.

Lafayette   *Lafayette Parish   Southern Louisiana, 60 mi/129 km west-southwest of Baton Rouge*

1770 Acadian exile Andrew Martin becomes first settler; **1811** Myrtle Plantation House built; **1823** Lafayette Parish formed; **1824** founded on Vermilion River by Jean Mouton, named Vermilionville; **1825** Petit Manchac becomes parish seat; **1826** parish seat moved to Vermilionville; **1836** town incorporated; **1842** Vermilionville Academy founded, closed 1872; **1848** Charles Mouton House built; **1859** 4,000 vigilantes organized to accomplish what law enforcement failed to, capture of c.200 cattle rustlers, their leaders hanged; **Nov. 1863** Union Gen. Nathaniel Banks loses battle with Confederate forces of Gen. Dick Taylor; **1878** New Orleans, Opelousas & Great Western Railroad reaches town, completed to Houston 1881; First Presbyterian Church built; **1884** town renamed Lafayette; **1898** University of Southwestern Louisiana established; **1916** St. John's Cathedral built; **1930** Association of Louisiana Acadians founded for perpetuation of Acadian traditions; Lafayette Regional Airport established; **1940** oil and natural gas industry established; **1948** Blackman Coliseum built; **1964** parish courthouse built; **1969** Natural History and Science Museum opened; **1984** Cajun Dome opened; **1992** parish and city governments consolidated.

Lake Charles   *Calcasieu Parish   Southwestern Louisiana, 133 mi/214 km west of Baton Rouge*

1781 Martin Le Bleu becomes first settler; **c.1782** Spaniard Carlos Salia arrives, changes name to Charles Sallier; **1830** Cantonment Atkinson established by U.S. as frontier defense; **1840** Calcasieu Parish formed; **1842** settlers take claims in disputed territory between Calcasieu and Sabine rivers; **c.1850** Barbe House built; **1852** town founded as parish seat on Calcasieu River at widening named Lake Charles, named Charlestown; **1861** incorporated as a town; **1867** incorporated as a city, renamed Lake Charles; **1887** Capt. J. B. Watkins of New York brings his *American Press* newspaper to city, begins campaign boosting city; **1890** Southern Pacific Railroad completed; **1910** fire destroys most of city including courthouse, built 1890; **1912** parish courthouse completed; **1926** deepwater channel opened to Gulf of Mexico; **1939** Lake Charles Junior College established, becomes McNeese State University; **Aug. 8, 1967** oil refinery explosion kills six; **Dec. 23, 1971** chemical plant explosion leaves five killed, three injured.

Lake Providence   *East Carroll Parish Northeastern Louisiana, 168 mi/270 km north of Baton Rouge*

c.1800 area serves as a base for river pirates; **c.1812** town founded as port on Mississippi River; **1832** Carroll Parish formed; **1841** Arlington plantation house built; **1863**

General Grant's forces abort attempt to cut canal between river and lake, intended to changing river's course; **1876** town incorporated; **1877** East Carroll Parish formed from Carroll Parish; town becomes parish seat; **1901** parish courthouse built, second building completed 1937.

La Place   *Saint John the Baptist Parish Southeastern Louisiana, 25 mi/40 km west of New Orleans*

1850 break in levee system cause flooding Mississippi River to flow into Lake Pontchartrain at Bonnet Carre; **1874** during another levee break, river flows for months into Lake Pontchartrain, **1892** town founded as sugar refining center; **1913** *L'Observateur* newspaper founded; **Dec. 1935** Bonnet Carre Spillway completed, allowing river to overflow deliberately into lake, preventing flooding downstream; highway bridge built across spillway.

Leesville   *Vernon Parish   Western Louisiana, 143 mi/230 km west-northwest of Baton Rouge*

1871 Vernon Parish formed, named for popular horse racing track; town founded as parish seat; **1899** incorporated as a city; **1910** parish courthouse built.

Livingston   *Livingston Parish   Southeastern Louisiana, 25 mi/40 km east of Baton Rouge*

1832 Livingston Parish formed; Springfield becomes parish seat; **1869** parish seat moved to Centerville; **c.1915** cypress timber cutting begins, ceases by 1930; **1918** town founded as lumber milling center, named for statesman Edward Livingston; **1941** parish seat moved to Livingston; **1955** town incorporated; **1970** parish courthouse built.

Mandeville   *Saint Tammany Parish   Southeastern Louisiana, 27 mi/43 km north of New Orleans*

1717 Moore House built; **1834** town founded on Lake Pontchartrain by Bernard Xavier de Marigny de Mandeville; ferry established to New Orleans, discontinued 1936; **1840** incorporated as a town; **1956** Lake Pontchartrain Causeway completed to New Orleans, 24 mi/39 km long, parallel span completed 1969; **1985** incorporated as a city.

Mansfield   *De Soto Parish   Northwestern Louisiana, 35 mi/56 km south of Shreveport*

1843 De Soto Parish formed; **1844** town founded as parish seat; **1847** town incorporated; **1855** Mansfield Female College established, closed 1929, served as Confederate hospital and barracks during Civil War; **Apr. 8, 1864** Confederates under generals Edmund Kirby-Smith and Dick Taylor numbering 12,000 defeats Union force of 25,000 under Gen. Nathaniel Banks in Battle of Sabine Crossroads, marking collapse of Union's Red River Campaign, 1,800 Confederate killed or wounded, 1,900 Union killed or wounded; **1911** parish courthouse built.

Many *Sabine Parish* *Western Louisiana, 168 mi/270 km northwest of Baton Rouge*

1806 Gen. James Wilkinson establishes Camp Sabine near Sabine River to west; **1836** blockhouse built at site by Gen. Edmund P. Gaines; **1837** town founded by Belgian immigrants, named for Col. John B. Many of Mexican War; **1843** Sabine Parish formed; town becomes parish seat; **1853** town incorporated; **1956** parish courthouse built.

Marksville *Avoyelles Parish* *Central Louisiana, 77 mi/124 km northwest of Baton Rouge*

140 BC Avoyel people build mounds in area; **1807** Avoyelles Parish formed, becomes known as Free State of Avoyelles for its seclusion and independent nature of its people; **1809** town founded as parish seat; **1843** town incorporated; **1927** parish courthouse built.

Minden *Webster Parish* *Northwestern Louisiana, 30 mi/48 km east of Shreveport*

1836 town founded by German Charles Hance Veeder, named for German town; **1838** Minden Academy founded, splits into Minden Male Academy and Minden Female Seminary 1850, closed 1895; **1851** town incorporated; **1871** Webster Parish formed; town becomes parish seat; **Feb. 13, 1899** lowest temperature ever recorded in Louisiana reached, $-16°F/-27°C$; **1926** Minden Sanitarium established; **1933** fire destroys business district; **May 1, 1933** tornado strikes town, 28 killed, 400 injured; **1934** oil discovered in area; **May 1953** parish courthouse completed.

Monroe *Ouachita Parish* *Northeastern Louisiana, 160 mi/257 km north-northwest of Baton Rouge*

1542 Hernando de Soto believed to have passed mouth of Tensas River while descending Ouachita River; **1700** site visited by Bienville and St. Denis; **1785** Ouachita Post founded on Ouachita River by Don Juan Filhiol; **1790** Filhiol builds Fort Miro; **1795–1796** land grants made to Marquis de Maison Rouge and Baron de Bastrop; **1807** Ouachita Parish formed; town founded as parish seat; **c.1810** Layton Castle house built; **1819** first steamboat *James Monroe* reaches town; town renamed Monroe; **1820** incorporated as a town; **1855** Filhiol plantation house built to south by John B. Filhiol; **1860** Vicksburg, Shreveport & Pacific Railroad built to Shreveport; **July 1863** town shelled by Union gunboats; **1900** incorporated as a city; **1912** St. Francis Sanitarium built; **1916** natural gas discovered; **1924** Delta Airlines founded; **1926** parish courthouse completed; Cooley House built, designed by Walter Burley Griffin; **1927** Monroe Regional Airport established; **1931** Northeast Louisiana State University established; **Feb. 12, 1934** Boston Celtics basketball player Bill Russell born; **1936** ring levee completed; **1963** Masur Museum of Art founded.

Mooringsport *Caddo Parish* *Northwestern Louisiana, 16 mi/26 km northwest of Shreveport*

1836 settlers arrive from Alabama; **1837** ferry established by John and Timothy Mooring; **1876** cotton gin established; **1887** Kansas City Southern Railroad reaches site; **Jan. 20, 1889** blues singer Huddie William Ledbetter (Lead Belly) born (died 1949); **1896** town founded on Cypress Bayou; **1907** gas and oil drilling begins in Caddo Lake; **1909** mussel pearl harvesting begins, ends with building of dam 1911; **1914** dam completed on Cypress Bayou enlarging natural Caddo Lake; Caddo Lake Drawbridge built, declared historic landmark 1996; **1927** town incorporated.

Morgan City *Saint Mary Parish* *Southeastern Louisiana, 73 mi/117 km west-southwest of New Orleans*

1850 New Orleans, Opelousas & Great Western Railroad built; town founded on Atchafalaya River as western rail terminus, named Brashear City for Brashear plantation; **1860** incorporated as a city, renamed for railroad president Charles Morgan; **1870** colony of Russian Jews settles here; **1909** Port Allen Canal built from Port Allen, opposite Baton Rouge, as alternate shipping route to Gulf of Mexico; **1933** Long-Allen Bridge built across Atchafalaya River to Berwick, replaced 1978; **1947** area's first successful offshore oil well established; **March 6, 1968** salt mine accident at Calumet to west, 21 killed; **1995** International Petroleum Museum and Exposition opened.

Napoleonville *Assumption Parish* *Southeastern Louisiana, 60 mi/97 km west of New Orleans*

1750 area first settled; **1807** Assumption Parish formed; **1818** town founded as parish seat on Bayou Lafourche; **1835** Woodlawn plantation house built by W. W. Pugh; **1836** Wildwood plantation house built by James Beasley; **1848** Madewood plantation house built for Col. Thomas Pugh; **1853** Christ Episcopal Church built; **1878** incorporated as a village; **1890** Southern Pacific Railroad built; **1896** parish courthouse built; **1909** St. Ann's Catholic Church built.

Natchitoches *Natchitoches Parish* *Central Louisiana, 155 mi/249 km northwest of Baton Rouge*

1687 area explored by La Salle; **1691** region settled by Canary Islanders, brought here through Mexico by Bernardo de Gálvez; **1713** trading and military post established by French Governor Cadillac on Red River; **1732** Natchez people lay siege on fort 22 days, broken after St. Denis launches attack killing 92 Native Americans; **1742** Melrose Plantation built; **1759** inn built by Jean Baptiste Prudhomme; **1776** Tauzin-Wells House built; **1807** Natchitoches ("NAK-ki-tush") Parish formed; town founded as parish seat near Red River; **1819** town incorporated; **1821** Phanor Prudhomme Plantation house built to south; **c.1830** Lemee House built; **1832** Cane River Lake formed by changing course of Red River; **1838** Church of the Immaculate Conception (Catholic) built;

c.1840 Narcisse Prudhomme House built to south; 1844 Gen. Zachary Taylor's army stationed at Camp Salubrity to north while waiting to move west against Mexico; c.1850 Serdot Prudhomme House built; 1850s Sompayrac Plantation house built to south; 1852 Lacoste Building built; 1858 Trinity Episcopal Church built; 1864 Union forces under General Banks burn every building in town while retreating from Mansfield; 1884 State Normal School established, becomes Northwestern State University; 1886 African-American folk artist Clementine Hunter born near Cloutierville to southeast (died 1988); 1912 First Methodist Church built; Northwest Louisiana Game and Fish Preserve established; 1915 U.S. Fish Hatchery founded at Cane River Lake; 1940 fifth parish courthouse built; March 4, 1965 natural gas pipeline explodes, 17 killed.

New Iberia *Iberia Parish* *Southern Louisiana, 53 mi/85 km southwest of Baton Rouge*

1690s Canary Islanders brought here by Bernardo de Gálvez; 1779 colony of Iberia founded by Spaniards on Bayou Teche; 1814 post office established; c.1820 Darby Place house built; 1830 The Shadows house built by David Weeks; 1839 town incorporated as Iberia; yellow fever epidemic affects every family; slave woman Felicite cares for many fever sufferers both black and white; 1847 town renamed New Iberia; 1852 Felicite dies, lies in state at master's house; 1857 Episcopal Church of the Epiphany built; Oct. 1863 town taken by Union during Gen. Banks' Red River Campaign; 1868 Iberia Parish formed; town becomes parish seat; 1880 Texas & New Orleans Railroad reaches town; 1917 oil production begins in Little Bayou Oil Field; 1940 parish courthouse built.

New Llano *Vernon Parish* *Western Louisiana, 142 mi/229 km west-northwest of Baton Rouge*

1917 150 members of Llano del Rio Cooperative Colony move from Antelope Valley, California, founded 1914 by Job Harriman; 1922 rice mill established; 1931 Christian Commonwealth Colony established by Samuel W. Irwin; 1937 colony enters into receivership; May 1, 1994 80th anniversary reunion of Llano del Rio Colony held.

New Orleans *Orleans Parish* *Southeastern Louisiana, on Mississippi River, near Gulf of Mexico*

1699–1700 lower Mississippi River explored by Iberville; 1718 town founded as port by Jean Baptiste Le Moyne, Sieur de la Bienville; 1722 town becomes capital of Louisiana (New France); 1727 Ursuline College for women established; 1756 first wave of French Acadians (Cajuns) arrive after their eviction from Nova Scotia; 1763 town becomes capital of Spanish Louisiana; 1764 Sarpy House built; Oct. 27, 1768 Acadians and Germans revolt against government of Antonio de Ulloa, is sent packing for Cuba; 1784 Schertz plantation house built; 1788 fire destroys more than 800 buildings; 1791 French Market established; 1793 Fort Pike built at Rigolets Pass, rebuilt by U.S. 1818, occupied by Confederates 1861, taken without bloodshed by Union 1862, fort abandoned 1865; 1794 second city fire destroys more than 200 buildings; St. Louis Cathedral completed; 1795 The Cabildo built, seat of Spanish rule, replacing structure destroyed by 1794 fire; first granulated sugar developed at De Bore estate, now Audubon Park; 1797 New Orleans Opera established; 1798 Walter Parker House built; Nov. 30, 1803 Louisiana reverts to French rule; Dec. 20, 1803 Louisiana Purchase agreement signed, doubling land area of U.S.; 1805 Orleans Parish formed; incorporated as a city, becomes parish seat; March 17, 1806 African-American inventor Norbert Rillieux born, developed sugar refining process (died 1894); c.1807 Absinthe House built; 1811 College of Orleans established; Le Monier Residence built, first building in city over two stories; Apr. 30, 1812 Louisiana admitted as 18th state; New Orleans becomes first state capital; Dec. 12, 1814 Andrew Jackson attacks British in Battle of New Orleans, soundly defeats them Jan. 8, 1815; 1815 Fort Chef Menteur built by Andrew Jackson at Chef Menteur Pass to east, rebuilt by U.S. as Fort McComb 1820–1828; Jan. 18, 1815 British withdraw by sea following Battle of New Orleans; 1820s Grima House built; 1821 Old Bank of Louisiana built; 1826 Mortgage Office built, later becomes American Legion Home; May 8, 1829 pianist, composer Louis Gottschalk born (died 1869); 1830–1831 state capital moved briefly to Donaldsonville; 1834 Tulane University (University of Louisiana) established; 1835 construction begins on St. Louis Hotel, damaged by storm 1917, later torn down; U.S. Mint built, operated 1838–1862 and 1879–1910; Oct. 12, 1844 author George Washington Cable born, shared billing with Mark Twain as The Twins of Genius (died 1925); 1847 public school system established; 1849 state capital moved to Baton Rouge; 1850 Felicity Street Methodist Church built, rebuilt 1888; 1851 Trinity Episcopal Church built; Feb. 21, 1852 drama critic Brander Matthews born (died 1929); 1853 city hall dedicated; Apr. 25, 1862 New Orleans surrenders to U.S. General Farragut after destruction of forts Jackson and St. Philip downriver; 1865 Luling Mansion built; Dec. 19, 1865 actress Minnie Fiske born (died 1932); 1869 Dillard University established; 1870 Algiers section annexed by New Orleans, absorbed by Orleans Parish 1803; 1870s Reconstruction Era brings political strife to city; engineer Capt. James B. Eads reconstructs levee system to mouth of Mississippi River ensuring uninterrupted passage of oceangoing ships to New Orleans and Baton Rouge; Sept. 14, 1874 Crescent White League forms own government after defeating Police Department; military rule established; 1877 home rule restored; Jan. 3, 1880 *States-Item* newspaper founded; 1882 electric lights installed on Canal Street; c.1883 city becomes major railroad hub; Sept. 20, 1885 jazz musician Jelly Roll Morton born (died 1941); 1884 World Exposition held; Audubon New Orleans Zoo established; 1887 Christ Church Cathedral (Episcopal) built; 1892 St. Joseph's Catholic Church completed, construction begun 1869; May 1, 1896 World War II Gen. J. Lawton Collins born (died 1987); May 14, 1897 jazz clarinetist Sidney Bechet born (died 1959); Aug. 4, 1900 jazz trumpeter Louis Armstrong born (died 1971); June 20, 1905 playwright

Lillian Hellman born (died 1984); **1909** Touro Synagogue dedicated; **1910** New Orleans Courthouse built; **1911** New Orleans Museum of Art opened; **Oct. 16, 1911** gospel singer Mahalia Jackson born (died 1972); **1912** Loyola University established; **Dec. 12, 1912** entertainer Louis Prima born (died 1978); **Dec. 10, 1914** actress Dorothy Lamour born (died 1996); **1915** Xavier University established; **Sept. 3, 1915** actress Kitty Carlisle born; **1916** Our Lady of Holy Cross College established; Little Theater built; **1917** New Orleans Baptist Theological Seminary established; **1921** Delgado Community College established; **Jan. 17, 1922** musician Al Hirt born (died 1999); **1923** Notre Dame Seminary founded; **Sept. 30, 1924** author Truman Capote born (died 1984); **1925** Xavier University of Louisiana established; **1927** Saenger Theater for the Performing Arts opened; **Feb. 5, 1927** actor Val Dufour born (died 2000); **Feb. 26, 1928** singer Fats Domino born; **Dec. 21, 1928** actor Ed Nelson born; **July 8, 1929** author Shirley Ann Grau born; **1930** Rigolets Pass Bridge (swing bridge) built to east at entrance to Lake Pontchartrain; St. Charles Avenue Presbyterian Church built; **1931** District Court and Parish Jail built; **May 31, 1931** actress Shirley Verett born; **March 12, 1932** civil rights leader, U.S. Congressman from Georgia Andrew Young born; **1934** New Orleans Lakefront Airport opened; **1935** Huey P. Long Bridge built across Mississippi River; **1939** Charity Hospital built; **Oct. 18, 1939** Lee Harvey Oswald born, assassinated Pres. John F. Kennedy in Dallas Nov. 22, 1963, shot and killed by Jack Ruby Nov. 24, 1963; **Oct. 14, 1941** writer Anne Rice born; **1946** Moisant Field established to west at Kenner, becomes New Orleans International Airport 1960, renamed Louis Armstrong New Orleans International Aug. 2001; **May 3, 1946** announcer Greg Gumbel born; **Nov. 25, 1947** TV actor John Larroquette born; **July 12, 1948** fitness expert Richard Simmons born; **July 12, 1948** actor Jay Thomas born; **Sept. 29, 1948** TV personality Bryant Gumbel born; **1954** Orleans Parish Civil District Courthouse built; **1956** Lake Pontchartrain Causeway completed to Mandeville, 24 mi/39 km to north, longest bridge in world at the time, parallel span completed 1969; **1958** University of New Orleans established; bridge built over Mississippi River to Algiers; **1959** Southern University at New Orleans established; **Nov. 16, 1959** National Airlines DC-7B from Miami crashes 107 mi/172 km to southeast in Gulf, killing all 42 on board **Aug. 26, 1960** musician Branford Marsalis born; **Nov. 16, 1960** violent demonstrations held in response to admission of four black school girls; **Oct. 18, 1961** African-American jazz musician Wynton Marsalis born; **Apr. 16, 1962** Rev. Joseph Rummel, Archbishop of New Orleans, excommunicates three segregationists; **Apr. 21, 1962** segregationists provide bus transport to North for blacks who wish to leave South; **1963** I-10 highway bridge built across Rigolets Pass to Slidell to east; **June 16, 1964** two barges ram Lake Pontchartrain causeway, bus plunges through 264-foot gap, six killed; **July 9, 1964** New Orleans Cotton Exchange closes after 93 years, New York Cotton Exchange only remaining major exchange; **Oct. 2–3, 1964** 36 killed as Hurricane Hilda hits Louisiana, moves on to Carolinas and Georgia; **1967** Saints football team join NFL; **March 30, 1967** Delta Airlines DC-8 strikes motel on landing approach killing 18, injuring 40; **Sept. 11, 1967** singer Harry Connick, Jr. born; **1969** 45-story Plaza Tower built; **Jan. 21, 1969** Clay Shaw acquitted of plot to assassinate President Kennedy, arrested two years earlier by District Attorney Jim Garrison, accused of seeking publicity; **March 20, 1969** 16 of 24 hunters from Memphis on way to British Honduras (Belize) killed as plane crashes at New Orleans airport; **Apr. 6, 1969** fire follows collision of Nationalist Chinese freighter and oil barge under Mississippi River Bridge, 25 killed; **Aug. 17–18, 1969** Hurricane Camille hits Louisiana and Mississippi, total 256 killed; **May 5, 1970** Chevron fined $1 million for environmental damage caused by eight wells that caught fire in Gulf in Feb., causing largest oil spill on record; **1972** 51-story One Shell Square built; 42-story Marriott Hotel built; **Jan. 17, 1973** sniper atop Howard Johnson Hotel kills 6, injures 12, is shot and killed from Marine helicopter; **June 24, 1973** arson fire in barroom kills 32, injures 17; **1975** Louisiana Superdome stadium built; **1980** *States-Item* newspaper merges with the *Times-Picayune*; **1984** 39-story Energy Center office building built; **Nov. 6, 1984** Louisiana World Exposition files for bankruptcy, closes Nov. 11 after six months; **1985** Morial Convention Center opened; 47-story Sheraton Hotel built; 53-story Place St. Charles built; **1986** Riverwalk Shopping and Pedestrian area built at edge of Mississippi River; **1988** Hornets basketball team joins NBA; Greater New Orleans Bridge built across Mississippi River; **Jan. 1992** Louisiana Symphony Orchestra holds first concert; **Dec. 14, 1996** freighter *Bright Field* crashes into Riverwalk complex on Mississippi River, no injuries; **2002** Hornets NBA basketball team moves from Charlotte; **2003** Ogden Museum of Southern Art opened.

New Roads   *Pointe Coupee Parish*   *Southeastern Louisiana, 25 mi/40 km north-northwest of Baton Rouge*

1719 Pointe Coupee military and trading post established; **1750** Parlange plantation house built to south on Spanish land grant; **1789** Alma Plantation house built to south, scene of racial riots 1795, 25 black slaves killed; **1812** Pointe Coupee Parish formed; Pointe Coupee Fort becomes parish seat; **1822** Chemin Neuf (New Road) built at portage between Mississippi River and False River; **1823** St. Mary's Catholic Church built; **1832** Austerlitz plantation house built to south; **1858** town founded on Mississippi River as new parish seat, named St. Mary's; **1875** incorporated as a town, renamed; **Jan. 1886** steamboat *J. M. White* destroyed by fire upstream killing 80; **1894** incorporated as a city; **1902** parish courthouse built, annex built 1939; **1975** extensive Tuscaloosa Trend natural gas field discovered.

Oak Grove   *West Carroll Parish*   *Northeastern Louisiana, 175 mi/282 km north of Baton Rouge*

1832 Carroll Parish formed; Floyd becomes parish seat; **1877** West Carroll Parish formed by splitting Carroll

Parish; Floyd becomes parish seat; **1906** Missouri Pacific Railroad reaches site; town platted; **1909** incorporated as a village, renamed; **1917** parish seat moved to Oak Grove; **1918** parish courthouse built; **1928** incorporated as a town; **1988** Poverty Point National Monument established to south, prehistoric earth works date to second millennium BC.

Oberlin   *Allen Parish*   *Southern Louisiana, 103 mi/ 166 km west of Baton Rouge*

1885 "old town" founded near Calcasieu River by settlers from Oberlin, Ohio; **1890** Kansas City, Watkins & Gulf (Missouri Pacific) Railroad built; **1893** new town founded on railroad; **1900** town incorporated; **1912** Allen Parish formed; town becomes parish seat; parish courthouse built.

Opelousas   *Saint Landry Parish*   *Southern Louisiana, 60 mi/97 km west of Baton Rouge*

c.1750 French trading post established near Bayou Teche; **1769** settlement becomes seat of Opelousas District, becomes County 1805; **1807** Opelousas County becomes St. Landry Parish; **1821** town incorporated; Academy of the Sacred Heart established; **1828** St. Landry's Catholic Church built, rebuilt 1909; **c.1830** Hebrard House built; **c.1840** Halfway House residence built by Clement Hollier; **1863** state government moves here during occupation of Baton Rouge by Union forces, state supreme court remains until 1898; **1868** racial rioting plagues town during Reconstruction Era; **1882** Louisiana & Texas Railroad reaches town; **1940** parish courthouse built.

Patterson   *Saint Mary Parish*   *Southeastern Louisiana, 80 mi/129 km west-southwest of New Orleans*

c.1798 Captain Patterson becomes first settler; **c.1835** Fairfax house built, home of Thomas Bisland, demolished c.1940; **1855** All Saints Episcopal Church built, moved to present site 1942; **1861** novelist Elizabeth Bisland (Wetmore) born at Fairfax House (died 1929); **1887** town founded on Bayou Teche, named Pattersonville; **1890s** Shadyside house built to west; **1907** town incorporated, renamed Patterson; **1929** Wedell-Williams Airport founded.

Pineville   *Rapides Parish*   *Central Louisiana, 125 mi/201 km northwest of Baton Rouge, north of Alexandria*

1760s area at rapids in Red River settled by Appalache peoples removed from area of Mobile, Alabama; town founded; **1854** river channel deepened through rapids; **1857** Mount Olive Episcopal Chapel built; **1860** Louisiana Seminary of Learning established, moved to Baton Rouge 1869, becomes Louisiana State University 1870; William Tecumseh Sherman appointed seminary's first superintendent, resigns position with Louisiana's secession from Union Jan. 1861; **1867** Pineville National Cemetery established; **1878** town incorporated; **1902** Central

Louisiana State Hospital organized; **1906** Louisiana College established; **1923** tornado destroys much of town.

Plain Dealing   *Bossier Parish*   *See* **Benton (1936)**

Plaquemine   *Iberville Parish*   *Southeastern Louisiana, 13 mi/21 km south-southwest of Baton Rouge*

1807 Iberville Parish formed; Point Pleasant becomes parish seat; **1822** town founded on Mississippi River, at outflow of Plaquemine Bayou; **c.1835** Middleton House built; **1838** town incorporated; **1842** parish seat moved to Plaquemine; **1894** National Leprosarium founded to south at Carville; **1906** parish courthouse built; **1909** Plaquemine Locks built on Port Allen-Morgan City Canal; distinctive Canal House built in Dutch style; **1927** St. John the Evangelist Catholic Church built.

Pointe a la Hache   *Plaquemines Parish*   *Southeastern Louisiana, 30 mi/48 km southeast of New Orleans*

1700 Fort Iberville built to north by Sieur de Bienville for his brother Sieur d'Iberville, maintained until 1811; **1807** Plaquemines Parish formed; **1820** St. Thomas' Catholic Church built; town founded; **1846** town becomes parish seat on Mississippi River; **1857** botanist Father A. B. Langlois arrives, spends 30 years collecting plant specimens; **1892** parish courthouse completed, destroyed by fire Jan. 2002, nine months after proposal for new courthouse was rejected; **1927** prow of tanker rams levee to north, break inundates marsh and truck farms at West Pointe a la Hache.

Port Allen   *West Baton Rouge Parish*   *Southeastern Louisiana, 1 mi/1.6 km west of Baton Rouge*

1765 Acadian exiles begin arriving from Nova Scotia; **1807** West Baton Rouge Parish formed; St. Michel becomes parish seat; **1850s** Monte Vista house built to north by Louis Favrot; **1854** town platted on Mississippi River as new parish seat, named for Brig. Gen. Henry W. Allen; **1884** Poplar Grove plantation house moved to site to north, pagoda-style building featured at New Orleans Cotton Centennial Exposition, shipped by steamboat; **1909** Port Allen Canal built to Morgan City as alternate route to Gulf of Mexico; **1916** Hill Place house built on Homestead Plantation; **1923** incorporated as a city; **1940** highway and railroad bridge built across Mississippi River to Baton Rouge; **1957** parish courthouse built; **1968** Airline Highway (I-10) Bridge built across Mississippi River.

Port Hudson   *East Baton Rouge Parish*   *Southeastern Louisiana, 20 mi/32 km north of Baton Rouge*

c.1820 James Hudson acquires land on Mississippi River; **1829** Plains Presbyterian Church built; **1832** Port Hudson trading post established; **1833** Asphodel plantation house built to north; **1840** Linwood plantation house completed;

1862 town moved away from river after repeated flooding; **May–July, 1863** Confederate fortifications besieged by Union Gen. N. P. Banks' forces for 48 days, surrendered after fall of Vicksburg, first use of black troops in U.S.

Rayville *Richland Parish*   *Northeastern Louisiana, 152 mi/245 km north-northwest of Baton Rouge*

1867 town founded, named for landowner John Ray; **1868** Richland Parish formed; town becomes parish seat; **1901** town incorporated; **1890** town damaged by fire, again 1891; **1951** parish courthouse built.

Reserve *Saint John the Baptist Parish*
Southeastern Louisiana, 30 mi/48 km west of New Orleans

c.1785 Voisin plantation house built; **1860** centralized sugar processing methods developed by Leon Godchaux, owner of Reserve Plantation; sugar factory established; **1886** St. Peter's Catholic Church built, completed 1897; town founded on Mississippi River; **1917** Godchaux Sugar Refinery established; **1931** Maurin's Theater opened, closed 1979, reopened 1981 as St. John Theatre; **1965** St. Peter's Church destroyed by Hurricane Betsy.

Robeline *Natchitoches Parish*   *Western Louisiana, 163 mi/262 km northwest of Baton Rouge*

1717 Mission of San Miguel de los Adais established; **1721** Presidio de Nuestra Señora del Pilar de los Adais (Our Lady of the Pillar) established by the Marques de Aguayo to defend Spanish sovereignty over Texas, serves as Texas capital until 1773; **1881** New Orleans & Pacific Railroad built; town founded; **1914** incorporated as a village.

Ruston *Lincoln Parish*   *Northern Louisiana, 70 mi/ 113 km east of Shreveport*

1825 stagecoach stop established; **1873** Lincoln Parish formed by carpetbag administration, named for President Lincoln; Vienna becomes parish seat; **1884** Vicksburg, Shreveport & Pacific Railroad built; town founded as new parish seat on land owned by Robert E. Russ; incorporated as a city; **1891** Chautauqua Society establishes retreat at Chautauqua Springs; **1894** Louisiana Technical University established; **1930s** commercial peach growing begins; **1935** natural gas deposit discovered; **1951** parish courthouse completed; first Louisiana Peach Festival held.

Saint Bernard *Saint Bernard Parish*
Southeastern Louisiana, 20 mi/32 km east-southeast of New Orleans

1759 blockhouse built, second floor added 1800 creating Kenilworth house; **1778** land grant made by French to Marigny de Mandeville; over 1,500 Canary Islanders brought to settle the Terre aux Boeufs by Gov. Don Bernardo de Gálvez; St. Bernard Catholic Church built, destroyed by fire 1917, rebuilt; **1807** St. Bernard Parish formed; town founded as parish seat; **May 28, 1818** Confederate Gen. Pierre G. T. Beauregard born, ordered first shot at Fort Sumter (died 1893); **1853** Turner House built, destroyed by vandals c.1935; **1939** parish seat moved to Chalmette.

Saint Francisville *West Feliciana Parish*
Southeastern Louisiana, 28 mi/45 km northwest of Baton Rouge

early 1700s French build Fort St. Reine, abandoned 1736; **1765** first settlers arrive; **c.1785** St. Francis Monastery built by Capuchin friars, destroyed by fire soon afterward; **1790** town founded on Mississippi River by John H. Mills and Christopher Stewart; **1807** town incorporated; **c.1810** Oakley plantation house built; **1819** Audubon Hall built as public market; **1824** West Feliciana Parish formed from Feliciana Parish (formed 1816); town becomes parish seat; **1835** Rosedawn plantation house built; **1841** Yazoo & Mississippi Valley Railroad reaches town; **1845** Fairview plantation house built; **1858** Grace Episcopal Church built, organized 1826; **1903** parish courthouse built.

Saint Joseph *Tensas Parish*   *Eastern Louisiana, 105 mi/169 km north of Baton Rouge*

c.1810 trading post established by John Densmore, site named Densmore's Landing; **1843** Tensas Parish formed; town becomes parish seat (year of town's founding uncertain); **1852** Bondurant House built; **1854** Lakewood house built at Lake Bruin to north; **1874** post office established; **1901** town incorporated; **1906** parish courthouse built.

Saint Martinville *Saint Martin Parish*
Southern Louisiana, 50 mi/80 km southwest of Baton Rouge

c.1760 area settled by Acadian exiles, first apparent settler being Gabriel Fuselier de la Claire; **1765** St. Martinville Catholic Chapel built, replaced by church 1832; **c.1770** Poste des Attakapa military post founded on Bayou Teche; town founded, named for 4th-century French Bishop Martin; **c.1800** Lake Plantation house built to south; **1803** County of Attakapas formed, becomes Parish 1807; **1805** town becomes county seat; **1811** St. Martin Parish formed from Attakapas Parish; town retained as parish seat; **1813** town incorporated; **1828** St. John plantation house built; **1829** Pine Alley, avenue lined with oaks and pines, planted with slave labor; **c.1855** yellow fever decimates population; **1859** parish courthouse built; **1870s** railroads bypass town, steamboat trade declines; **1934** Longfellow-Evangeline Memorial Park established to commemorate Henry Longfellow's poem "Evangeline."

Shreveport *Caddo Parish*   *Northwestern Louisiana, 220 mi/354 km northwest of Baton Rouge*

1803 Larkin Edwards of Tennessee settles near Caddo village, acts as interpreter with Native Americans; **late**

1820s Military Road built as freight route; 1834 after a year of work, Henry Miller Shreve reaches site from Campti in effort to free Red River of "Great Raft" log jam for navigation, spends another five years reaching Fort Towson, Oklahoma; 1835 land awarded to Edwards by Native Americans for his years of service to them; July 1, 1835 treaty with Caddo people turns Northwestern Louisiana over to U.S.; 1836 Texas independence increases trade; settlers from Southeastern states arrive, starting point of Texas Trail; 1837 Larkin Edwards sells land interest to Henry Shreve, others; town platted, named Shreve Town; 1838 Caddo Parish formed; town becomes parish seat; 1839 incorporated as town of Shreveport; 1855 town defeats Greenwood by one vote to retain parish seat; 1860 Vicksburg, Shreveport & Pacific Railroad reaches town; 1863 town becomes temporary capital of state during occupation of Baton Rouge by Union forces; 1866 St. Vincent's College and Academy established; 1871 incorporated as a city; Crisp's Gaiety Theater built; 1886 Grand Opera House built; 1873 Texas & Pacific Railroad extended west to Dallas; 1895 Shreveport Journal newspaper founded as The Judge, renamed 1897; 1896 Holy Trinity Catholic Church built; 1905 St. Mark's Episcopal Church built, replacing 1867 structure destroyed by fire; 1906 oil discovered at Caddo Lake to northwest; 1908 Centenary College, founded 1825, moved from Jackson, Louisiana; 1912 federal building built; 1914 B'Nai Zion Temple built; 1915 El Karubah Shriners' Temple built; 1923 Shreve Memorial Library built; 1925 First Presbyterian Church built; 1927 Dodd College established; May 5, 1927 actor Pat Carroll born; 1928 parish courthouse completed; St. John's Catholic Church built; 1929 Municipal Auditorium built; 1931 Shreveport Downtown Airport established; 1933 Barksdale Army Air Field established to east, becomes Air Force Base after World War II; 1934 Long-Allen Bridge completed across Red River; July 12, 1934 pianist Van Cliburn born; 1935 Rodessa Oil Field discovered to northwest; 1946 Norton Art Gallery opened; May 26, 1949 country singer Hank Williams, Jr. born; 1952 Shreveport Regional Airport established to west; 1964 Southern University at Shreveport (2-year) established; 1965 Louisiana State University at Shreveport established; Civic Theatre built; 1980 I-20 bridge built across Red River to Bossier City; 1981 Expo Hall opened; 2004 Shreveport Convention Center completed.

Slidell *Saint Tammany Parish* *Southeastern Louisiana, 28 mi/45 km northeast of New Orleans*

1699 Rigolets (RIG-o-lees) Pass, entrance to Lake Pontchartrain, discovered by Iberville; c.1870 settlers arrive at eastern end of Lake Pontchartrain; 1883 New Orleans & Northeastern Railroad reaches site; town founded, named for statesman John Slidell; 1888 town incorporated; 1930 Rigolets Pass Bridge (swing bridge) built across Rigolets Pass; 1951 Grantham College of Engineering established; 1963 I-10 highway bridge built across Rigolets Pass.

Sulphur *Calcasieu Parish* *Southwestern Louisiana, 5 mi/8 km west of Lake Charles*

1865 sulfur dome discovered by oil prospectors; 1893 Union Sulphur Company acquires lands, commercial production begins 1905; 1914 town incorporated; 1924 oil discovered; 1926 sulfur mines abandoned.

Tallulah *Madison Parish* *Northeastern Louisiana, 142 mi/229 km north of Baton Rouge*

1830s first settlers arrive; 1832 Crescent Plantation House built; 1838 Madison Parish formed; Richmond becomes parish seat; 1850s Vicksburg, Shreveport & Mississippi Railroad built; town founded, named for engineer's girlfriend; 1858 Adams House built; 1863 parish seat temporarily moved to Tallulah, moved to Delta 1868; 1870 north-south Iron Mountain Railroad built, forming junction; 1883 parish seat moved back to Tallulah; 1887 parish courthouse built; 1902 incorporated as a city; Oct. 1907 Pres. Theodore Roosevelt stops at hunting lodge on Tensas Bayou with hunter Ben Lilley, who trees bear cub by propping it up with his feet against bear's posterior until Roosevelt bags it, spares its life, story inspires popular "teddy bear" toy; 1909 Tallulah Laboratory established by U.S. Department of Agriculture for study of cotton boll weevil infestation, airplane dusting methods; Feb. 1927 great flood keeps region under water through July; Oct. 13, 2003 tour bus rear ends parked semi trailer truck, 8 of 15 passengers killed.

Thibodaux *Lafourche Parish* *Southeastern Louisiana, 50 mi/80 km west-southwest of New Orleans*

1807 Interior Parish formed; town founded on Bayou Lafourche as parish seat, named Thibodauxville for landowner Henry Schuyler Thibodaux; 1822 Lafourche Parish formed from Interior Parish; town retained as parish seat 1838 town incorporated; name shortened to Thibodaux; 1844 St. John's Episcopal Church built; Nov. 3, 1845 Chief Supreme Court Justice Edward Douglas White born (died 1921); 1847 St. Joseph's Catholic Church built, replacing 1803 structure; 1856 parish courthouse built; 1863 Confederate Colonel Pyron attacks Union stockade at railroad bridge in Battle of Lafourche Crossing to east, repulsed, 53 killed, 150 wounded; 1948 Nichols State University established.

Tunica *West Feliciana Parish* *Southeastern Louisiana, 45 mi/72 km north-northwest of Baton Rouge*

1699 Sieur d'Iberville erects cross at Lake Angola, on Mississippi River; 1700 Catholic church built by Jesuit Father Du Ru; c.1790 Rosebank plantation house built; 1802 Weyanoke plantation established by Capt. Robert Percy; c.1830 Greenwood plantation house built by William Ruffin; 1833 town founded on Mississippi River; 1835 Ellerslie plantation house built by Judge W. C. Wade; c.1851 Retreat plantation house built by Capt. Clive Mulford; 1857 St. Mary's Episcopal Church built;

1890 Louisiana State Penitentiary moved from Baton Rouge to Angola to west.

Vidalia   *Concordia Parish*   *Eastern Louisiana, 83 mi/134 km north-northwest of Baton Rouge*

1798 Post of Concord founded by Spanish on Mississippi River opposite Natchez to counteract British presence, soon abandoned; **1801** town founded by Don José Vidal; **1805** Concordia Parish formed; town becomes parish seat; **1811** town renamed Vidalia; **Sept. 19, 1827** James Bowie stabs Major Wright to death in duel on sandbar with Bowie knife designed by brother Resin Bowie; **1863** town taken by Union forces, held through end of Civil War; **1877** town incorporated; **1939** town moved away from river to allow for levee construction; **1940** bridge built across Mississippi River; **1976** parish courthouse built; **1988** new bridge built to Natchez; **1989** first annual Jim Bowie Festival held.

Ville Platte   *Evangeline Parish*   *Central Louisiana, 75 mi/121 km west-northwest of Baton Rouge*

c.1780 area settled by French Acadians; **1824** town founded; **1842** post office established; **1858** incorporated as a city; **1910** Evangeline Parish formed; town becomes parish seat; **1977** parish courthouse built.

White Castle   *Iberville Parish*   *Southeastern Louisiana, 21 mi/34 km south of Baton Rouge*

1817 Cora Plantation established; **c.1820** White Castle plantation house built by Thomas Vaughan, moved four times with changing channel of Mississippi River; **1857** Belle Grove plantation house built; **1859** Nottoway Plantation built by John H. Randolph, one of largest plantations in South; **1887** town founded; **1907** town incorporated; **Dec. 7, 1968** Nationalist Chinese freighter and Coast Guard buoy tender collide in river, killing 17 Coast Guard crewmen.

Winnfield   *Winn Parish*   *Central Louisiana, 140 mi/225 km northwest of Baton Rouge*

c.1840 area first settled; **1852** Winn Parish formed from Natchitoches Parish; town founded on Dugdemona River as parish seat, named for legislator Walter O. Winn; **1855** town incorporated; **Aug. 30, 1893** politically powerful Gov. Huey Pierce Long born, assassinated at state capitol, Baton Rouge, Sept. 8, 1935; **Aug. 28, 1895** Gov. Earl Kemp Long born (died 1960); **1901** Chicago, Rock Island & Pacific Railroad reaches town; **1922** parish courthouse built.

Winnsboro   *Franklin Parish*   *Northwestern Louisiana, 130 mi/209 km north-northwest of Baton Rouge*

1843 Franklin Parish formed; **1844** town founded as parish seat on plantation owned by J. W. Willis; **1902** incorporated as a village; **1977** parish courthouse built.

Maine

Northeastern U.S. One of the six New England states. Capital: Augusta. Major city: Portland.

Maine entered the U.S. as a detached part of Massachusetts, one of 13 colonies which adopted the Declaration of Independence July 4, 1776. Maine separated from Massachusetts to become the 23rd state on May 15, 1820.

Maine is divided into 16 counties which have weak governments. The counties are divided into townships, called towns, which have strong governments, except in northern parts of the state where towns have not been formed. Within the towns are villages which have no government of their own. Municipalities are classified as cities, which are formed from one or more towns. See Introduction.

Acton *York County* *Southwestern Maine, 33 mi/ 53 km west-southwest of Portland*

1661 land purchased from Newichawannock peoples; **1771** Hubbardstown Plantation incorporated; **1776** town settled by Benjamin Kines, Clement Steele, and John York, all of York, Maine; **1779** grist mill built; **1790** sawmill established; **1830** plantation divided between new towns of Acton and Shapleigh; town incorporated; **1866** Acton Agricultural Society founded; **1877** silver discovered, mining peaks 1880s; **1889** town's first agricultural fair held.

Albion *Kennebec County* *Southern Maine, 73 mi/ 117 km northeast of Portland*

Nov. 9, 1802 Elijah P. Lovejoy born, abolitionist editor killed by proslavery mob in Alton, Illinois, Nov. 7, 1837; **1804** town incorporated; **Jan. 1811** abolitionist clergyman Owen Lovejoy born, brother of Elijah (died 1864); **1845** Rum and Water Elms planted on opposite sides of road in competition between temperance group (south side) and antiprohibition group (north side) to find out whose side God was on; the north elms far outgrew the south elms.

Alfred *York County* *Southwestern Maine, 25 mi/ 40 km southwest of Portland*

1658 York County formed as Maine's first county; **c.1661** land acquired by Maj. William Phillips; **1764** town first settled; **1794** incorporated as a district; **1800** floggings carried forth at Whipping Tree, through 1830; **1802** Alfred shares county seat (half-shire) status with York; Holmes House built; **1806** county courthouse built, destroyed by fire 1933, rebuilt 1934; **1808** incorporated as a town; **1832** Alfred becomes sole county seat.

Ashland *Aroostook County* *Northern Maine, 130 mi/209 km north of Bangor*

1837 town settled by William Dalton; **1840** area organized as a plantation; **1862** town incorporated as Ashland; **1869** town renamed Dalton; **1876** town name reverts to Ashland; **1915** lumber industry reaches its peak; **1964** Ashland Logging Museum established; **Sept. 12, 2002** van carrying 15 Hispanic migrant workers plunges off bridge over Allagash River waterway c.50 mi/80 km to southwest killing 14, deadliest vehicular accident in Maine's history.

Atlantic *Hancock County* *Southern Maine, 100 mi/161 km east-northeast of Portland, on Atlantic Ocean*

1604 Samuel de Champlain sails past Swans Island; **Sept. 8, 1750** displaced Native Americans return to island, kidnap family members of Capt. James Whidden, taken to Canada and sold into slavery to French; **1765** Col. James Swan of Scotland settles Burntcoat island group; **1808** Swan arrested by French, confined to debtors' prison, remained until 1830, refusing to pay debt he did not owe, released on ascent to throne by Louis Philippe, Swan died three days after release; **1897** Town of Swans Island incorporated, includes village of Atlantic.

Auburn *Androscoggin County* *Southwestern Maine, 30 mi/48 km north of Portland, on Androscoggin River*

1690 Native American village on Laurel Hill attacked by force of 60 English under Maj. Benjamin Church; **1768** first land grant given along Androscoggin River; **1786** town settled; **1835** shoe industry established with opening of Minot Shoe Company; **1836** dam built on

MAINE

Androscoggin River; **1842** town incorporated; **1854** Androscoggin County formed; town, becomes county seat (shire town); **1857** county courthouse completed; **1867** Auburn annexes Danville; **1869** incorporated as a city; **1890s** Lake Grove resort flourishes on eastern shore of Lake Auburn; **1923** Androscoggin Historical Society Museum founded; **1933** mill workers' district south of Little Androscoggin River swept by fire, over 250 buildings destroyed; **March 1936** flooding damages Auburn and Lewiston, South Bridge destroyed, North Bridge impassable; **1964** Central Maine Technical College (2-year) established.

Augusta *Kennebec County* *Southern Maine, 50 mi/ 80 km north-northeast of Portland, on Kennebec River*

1628 land grant received as part of Kennebec Patent; men from Plymouth colony, Massachusetts, establish trading post; **1754** Fort Western, named for Thomas Western of England, built on east bank of Kennebec River, one of three built on river same year; **1762** settlement of Hallowell founded south of fort; **1771** Town of Hallowell incorporated, includes fort; **Sept. 1775** Benedict Arnold's military expedition to Quebec gathers here; **Feb. 1797** second settlement at fort separates from Hallowell as Town of Harrington after rivalry, renamed Augusta in June; **1799** Kennebec County formed; town becomes first county seat (shire town); **1809** in the Malta War, dispute between settlers and land owners leads to murder of surveyor Paul Chadwick at nearby Malta (Windsor), sporadic rioting and jailings; **1826** steamboat service to Bath and Boston inaugurated; **1827** town designated state capital; **1828** U.S. Arsenal established; **1829** statehouse built; **1830** county courthouse built, housed Maine Supreme Court until 1969; **1831** Blaine House (Executive Mansion) built; **1832** state capital moved from Portland; state capitol completed; **Feb. 11, 1833** Chief Supreme Court Justice Melville Weston Fuller born (died 1910); **1837** Maine State Museum founded; cotton mill and sawmills established; first Kennebec Dam built, rebuilt 1870; **1845** Edwards Manufacturing Company cotton mill established; **1849** incorporated as a city; **1851** first railroad reaches city; **1861** Augusta Lumber Mill founded; **1865** fire destroys business district; **1866** South Congregational Church built; Kennebec Veterans' Medical Center established; **1895** Lithgow Library built; **1896** Maine State Hospital established; **March 30, 1929** actor Richard Dysart born; **1965** University of Maine at Augusta established.

Bangor *Penobscot County* *Central Maine, 110 mi/ 122 km northeast of Portland, on Penobscot River*

Sept. 1604 Samuel de Champlain explores Penobscot River to waterfall; **1769** town first settled by trader Jacob Buswell of Salisbury, Massachusetts; settlement named Kenduskeag; **1787** town renamed Sunbury; **1791** town incorporated, renamed Bangor after old hymn title; shipbuilding industry begins; **1804** Bangor Theological Seminary founded, built 1830s; **1812** old city hall built; **Sept. 1814** town surrenders to British fleet and army; **1816**

Penobscot County formed; **1830** lumber boom begins, lasts until 1870s; Garland House built; **1832** town's first bridge across Penobscot River built; **1834** incorporated as a city; two-year land speculation boom begins; **1836** Symphony House completed; Richard Upjohn House completed, used later as Bangor Historical Society museum; **1846** Isaac Farrar Mansion completed; **1850s** Bangor becomes world's leading lumber port; **1856** St. John's Catholic Church built; **1864** Bangor Historical Society Museum established; **1874** Bangor House hotel built, replaces structure built 1840s; **1898** Husson College established; **1903** third county courthouse built; **1911** fire destroys much of business district; new public library built following fire; **1912** Bangor Savings Bank built; Beth Israel Synagogue completed; **1915** city hall completed; **1922** "Remember the *Maine*" Memorial erected in honor of battleship *Maine* blown up at Havana 1898; **1933** Norumbega Parkway created as memorial to Norwegian settlers; **1941** Dow Army Air Field established to west, becomes Air Force Base 1946; **1954** bridge built across Penobscot River; civic auditorium built; **1966** Eastern Maine Technical College (2-year) established; **1968** Dow Air Force Base closed, becomes Bangor International Airport; **1990** Cole Land Transportation Museum established.

Bar Harbor *Hancock County* *Southern Maine, 40 mi/64 km southeast of Bangor, on Atlantic Ocean*

1604 Samuel de Champlain visits area; **1763** town settled; **1796** town incorporated, named Eden; **1855** Agamant House hotel built; **1868** town's first summer cottage built by Alpheus Hardy; **1870s** Birch Point develops into favored retreat for such notables as Vanderbilts and Pulitzers; **Sept. 17, 1902** actress Esther Ralston born (died 1994); **1903** county courthouse built; **July 8, 1908** Nelson Rockefeller born, governor of New York, Vice Pres. under Gerald Ford (died 1979); **1916** St. Edward's Convent built, used later as historical society museum; **July 8, 1916** Sieur de Monts National Monument proclaimed; **1918** town renamed Bar Harbor; **Feb. 26, 1919** Lafayette National Park established, absorbing Sieur de Monts National Monument; **1928** Abbe Museum founded; **1929** Jackson Laboratory founded for genetic and human health research; **Jan. 19, 1929** national park renamed Acadia; **Oct. 1947** forest fire destroys large part of town including 237 houses; **1969** College of the Atlantic established.

Bath *Sagadahoc County* *Southern Maine, 28 mi/ 45 km northeast of Portland, on Kennebec River*

1605 Kennebec River explored by Samuel de Champlain and Capt. George Waymouth; **c.1670** area first settled; **1734** Fort Noble built at Fiddlers Beach; **1738** Town of Georgetown incorporated, includes Arrowsic and Long Reach (Bath); **1781** town of Bath incorporated by Massachusetts; **Aug 24, 1846** geographer Henry Gannett born, helped found National Geographic Society (died 1914); **1847** incorporated as a city; **1854** Sagadahoc

278

County formed; city becomes county seat; **1862** Bath becomes largest seaport in U.S., through 1902; **1866** Bath Iron Works, shipbuilding firm, established by Gen. Thomas Hyde following his return from Civil War; **1869** county courthouse built; **1905** Hill House built by Gov. John F. Hill, converted to government center 1995; **1963** Maine Maritime Museum founded.

Belfast *Waldo County* *Southern Maine, 82 mi/ 132 km northeast of Portland, on Atlantic Ocean*

1765 area settled by John Mitchell and 35 Scottish-Irish immigrants from New Hampshire; **1773** town incorporated; **1779** town sacked by British during Revolutionary War; **1800** Otis House built; **1807** Ben Field House built; **1812** Old Johnson House built; **1814** British sack town again during War of 1812; **1825** Clay House built; **1827** Waldo County formed; town becomes county seat; **1839** county courthouse built; **1853** incorporated as a city; **1887** Belfast Free Library established; **1940s** shoe and poultry industries become important.

Bethel *Oxford County* *Western Maine, 105 mi/ 169 km west-southwest of Bangor, on Androscoggin River*

1774 town settled; village of Bethel Hill founded; **1796** town incorporated, renamed Bethel; **Apr. 22, 1781** Native American raid takes possessions, two captives taken to Canada; **1813** Dr. Moses Mason House built; **1821** O'Neal Robinson House built; **1836** Gould Academy established; **1851** Atlantic & St. Lawrence Railroad reaches town from Portland; **1897** Maine Music Festivals established, held through 1926; **c.1900** Bethel Inn established by Dr. John G. Gehring; **1947** National Training Laboratory established by Dr. Gehring for treatment of nervous disorders.

Biddeford *York County* *Southwestern Maine, 15 mi/24 km southwest of Portland, on Atlantic Ocean*

1616 thatch-roofed Richard Vines House built; **1630** first settled; **1654** Henry Waddock opens Maine's first hotel; **c.1670** town becomes exporter of lumber and fish; **1688** Fort Hill built at Hills Beach; **1717** Goldthwaite House built; **1718** town incorporated; **1730** Haley House built by Benjamin Haley; **1831** University of New England established; **1840** first cotton mill built; **1845** Pepperell Manufacturing Company plant established; **1855** incorporated as a city; **1870** French Canadians arrive to work in the mills; **1896** City Theater opened; **1910** first French-speaking mayor elected, French-speaking mayors continue as a tradition through 20th century.

Blue Hill *Hancock County* *Southern Maine, 28 mi/45 km south of Bangor, on Atlantic Ocean*

1762 area first settled by Joseph Wood and John Roundy of Andover, Massachusetts; **1789** town incorporated; **1792** town's shipbuilding industry begins, continues through 1882; **1796** Blue Hill Public Library founded;

c.1800 cotton milling and shipbuilding become established industries; **1803** George Stevens Academy established; **1814** Fisher House built by Rev. Jonathan Fisher; **1825** Holt House built; **1879** copper mining begins; **Feb. 24, 1887** author Mary Ellen Chase born (died 1973); **c.1910** Kneisel Quartet founded by Dr. Franz Kneisel (1865–1926) of Boston Symphony, part of summer colony of musicians, authors, and artists established here; **1917** American Smelting and Refining Company begins copper mining operations; **1922** Kneisel Chamber Music Festival inaugurated by Kneisel.

Boothbay Harbor *Lincoln County* *Southern Maine, 35 mi/56 km east-northeast of Portland, on Atlantic Ocean*

1630s area first settled, arrivals driven away by Native American attacks; **1729** first permanent settlers arrive; **1880s** area developed as summer resort; **1885** Luther Maddocks captures whale using scow weighted down on rock reef, bailed out at low tide, refloated at high tide, exhibited at Portland, its remains foul bay and shoreline for months; **1889** town incorporated, separates from Boothbay; **1903** U.S. Fish Hatchery established at McKown's Point; **1964** Boothbay Region Art Foundation established; **1974** Bigelow Laboratory for Ocean Sciences established.

Brewer *Penobscot County* *Southern Maine, opposite Bangor, on Penobscot River*

1770 town settled; early settler Col. John Brewer serves as first postmaster; **1812** town incorporated, separates from Orrington; **Sept. 8, 1828** Union Civil War general Joshua Lawrence Chamberlain born (died 1914); **1832** bridge built across Penobscot River to Bangor, destroyed by flood 1846, rebuilt, again 1906; **1889** incorporated as a city.

Bristol *Lincoln County* *See* **Pemaquid**

Brownville *Piscataquis County* *Central Maine, 37 mi/60 km north of Bangor*

1819 town originally organized as a plantation; **1824** town incorporated; **1843** Katahdin Iron Works established with discovery of bog iron ore at foot of Ore Mountain, closed March 1890; **1880s** Silver Lake Hotel built, destroyed by fire 1913; **1965** Katahdin Iron Works State Memorial established.

Brunswick *Cumberland County* *Southwestern Maine, 23 mi/37 km northeast of Portland, near Atlantic Ocean*

1628 town first settled by trader named Thomas Purchase; trading post established; **1688** Fort Andros built by English as defense against allied French and Native Americans; **1700** settlement develops around post; trading post abandoned; Fort Andros established; **1702** fort and village destroyed by Native Americans; **1715** British build

MAINE

Fort George at old fort site; **1717** town name chosen in honor of duchy of Brunswick, Germany; first sawmill established; **1722** fort and town again destroyed by Native Americans in Lovewell's War; **1737** town experiences several years of uninterrupted growth; fort dismantled; **1739** town incorporated; **1753** first dam built on Androscoggin River; **1789** first sailing vessels built, industry continues until 1807; **1794** Bowdoin College established; **1799** Gilman Mansion built; **1806** Harriet Beecher Stowe House built, where author wrote *Uncle Tom's Cabin*; Chandler House built; **1809** Brunswick Cotton Mill established; **1814** Emmons House built; **1836** bridge built across Androscoggin River, destroyed by floods 1896, never rebuilt; **1843** Aaron Dennison begins manufacture of paper boxes; **1846** First Congregational Church built; **1880** pulp and textile milling industries begin; **1888** Pejepscot Historical Society established; **March 18, 1892** poet Robert Coffin born (died 1955); **1894** Dennison Manufacturing Company moves to Roxbury, Massachusetts; **March 1943** Brunswick Naval Air Station established; **1998** new Androscoggin River Bridge built (Interstate 95).

Bucksport *Hancock County* *Southern Maine, 95 mi/153 km northeast of Portland, on Penobscot River*

1762 town settled by 352 people from Massachusetts and New Hampshire; **c.1783** inn built by Asa Peabody, becomes Jed Prouty Tavern 1804; **1792** town incorporated; **1799** Dr. Moulton House built, occupied by British during War of 1812; **1839** Fort Knox built to protect river shipping from British, fort reused 1863–1866 and 1898; **1851** Eastern Maine Conference Seminary established, closed 1934; **1876** actors William and Dustin Farnum born (Dustin died 1929, William died 1953); **1930** Marine Seaboard Paper Mill built; **1931** Waldo-Hancock Suspension Bridge built to Verona; **1964** Bucksport Historical Society museum founded; **1992** Northeast Historic Film Archives moved to Bucksport at Alamo Theatre, built 1916, archives established 1986 at University of Maine.

Calais *Washington County* *Eastern Maine, 78 mi/126 km east-northeast of Bangor, on St. Croix River*

June 26, 1604 Samuel de Champlain lands on Dochet Island in St. Croix River with 80 colonists, move on to what is now Annapolis Royal, Nova Scotia, in 1605 following harsh winter on island; **1779** town first settled by Daniel Hill of Jonesport; **1801** town's shipbuilding industry begins with launch of the *Liberty*; **1804** Holmes Cottage built, oldest building in Calais; **1807** West Quoddy Head Lighthouse built, rebuilt 1858; **1809** town incorporated, named for French city; **1851** incorporated as a city; **1853** St. Anne's Episcopal Church built; **Apr. 27 1860** educator Charles Townsend Copeland born (died 1952); **1870** great fire destroys downtown and shipping piers; **1892** Whitlock Mill Lighthouse built, rebuilt 1910; Calais Free Library established; **1935** French ship

Normandie makes voyage from Calais, France; **1937** Moosehorn National Wildlife Refuge established.

Camden *Knox County* *Southern Maine, 72 mi/116 km northeast of Portland, on Atlantic Ocean*

1605 Samuel de Champlain visits site on Penobscot Bay; **1769** town settled; **1791** town incorporated as Cambden; **1893** town renamed Camden; town of Rockport formed from Camden; **1896** Curtis Island Lighthouse built, automated 1972; **1912** Camden Yacht Club clubhouse built by John Calvin Stevens for publisher Cyrus Curtis; **1947** Camden Hill State Park established; **July 2, 1967** amphibious plane crashes into Penobscot Bay, killing five.

Caribou *Aroostook County* *Northeastern Maine, 145 mi/233 km north-northeast of Bangor*

1807 area surveyed by Charles Turner; **1808** land granted to Capt. William Easton; **1824** settlers arrive from New Brunswick, Canada; **1852** first school built; **1859** town incorporated, originally named Lyndon; **1877** town renamed; **1921** Nylander Museum established; **1930s** Caribou Municipal Airport established; **1938** Aroostook State Park established; **1952** Loring Air Force Base established to northeast, closed 1994; **1968** incorporated as a city; **Sept. 16, 1986** balloonist Joe W. Kittinger launches from here on first solo transatlantic balloon flight.

Castine *Hancock County* *Southern Maine, 29 mi/47 km south of Bangor, on Atlantic Ocean*

1626 trading post established by Edward Ashley, a Pilgrim; site named Pentagoat; **1631** trading post destroyed by La Tour, French governor of Acadia; **c.1640** Capuchin mission established by French; **1648** Our Lady of Hope chapel built; **c.1655** British take post; **1667** area settled; **1670** settlement retaken by French; **1673** Jean-Vincent d'Abbadie, Baron de St. Castin assumes control of village; **1675** village attacked by Dutch; **1676** British plunder village; **1693** Castin makes arrangement with British to be allowed to continue on in his position, is ordered back to France 1701; **1765** Parson-Mason House built; **1779** British take town during Revolutionary War; Fort George built; **1783** Americans retake town and fort; **1787** Hancock County formed; town of Penobscot becomes county seat; **1790** Old Meeting House built, later used by Castine Unitarian Church; **1796** town incorporated; county seat moved to Castine; **1803** Bartlett House built; **1805** Johnston House built; **1810** Wheeler House built; **1811** Fort Madison built, rebuilt during Civil War; **1812** Whiting House built; **1814** British take town for eight months during War of 1812; **1829** Dice Head Lighthouse built, discontinued 1935; **1838** county seat moved to Ellsworth; **1921** Wilson Museum (Castine Historical Society) founded; **1941** Maine Maritime Academy established.

China *Kennebec County* *Southern Maine, 68 mi/ 109 km northeast of Portland*

1774 area settled; **1796** town founded as Harlem; **1818** town incorporated, renamed China for line in favorite old hymn; **1836** inventor Leroy S. Starrett born at South China village, invented various hand tools and gadgets which he also manufactured (died 1922); **1961** China Lake Spiritual Conference Center founded; **1989** China Lake Center for Spiritual Growth founded.

Dover-Foxcroft *Piscataquis County* *Central Maine, 35 mi/56 km northwest of Bangor*

1791 area first explored by Samuel Weston; **1794** land grant made to Chandler Robbins, Jr.; **1803** town of Dover settled; **1806** town of Foxcroft settled; **1812** Town of Foxcroft incorporated; **1821** Town of Dover incorporated; **March 1, 1844** Lillian Stevens born at Dover, president of Women's Temperance Union (died 1914); **1886** county courthouse completed; **1898** Piscataquis County formed; Dover becomes county seat; **Dec. 19, 1919** accident on Canadian Pacific Railroad at village of Onawa to north, 23 killed; **1922** towns merge as Town of Dover-Foxcroft.

Dresden *Lincoln County* *Southern Maine, 40 mi/ 64 km northeast of Portland, on Kennebec River*

1718 Scotch-Irish immigrants settle here, abandon area 1722; **1752** permanently settled by German immigrants; **1765** Maj. Reuben Colburn House built; **Sept. 21–23, 1775** Col. Benedict Arnold and men entertained at Major Colburn house; **1794** town incorporated; **1798** bridge built across Kennebec River; **1870** ice cutting becomes important industry, through 1920; **1890** Bridge Academy founded.

Durham *Androscoggin County* *Southwestern Maine, 23 mi/37 km north-northeast of Portland*

1761 land grant made to David Dunning, originally named Royalsborough for British Gen. Isaac Royal; **c.1770** area first settled; **1781** town founded, renamed Durham; **1789** town incorporated; **1818** two bridges built on Androscoggin River, last of two destroyed by flood 1936; **1835** Union Baptist Church built; **1897** Shiloh Temple built by Sanfordite religious movement; **1906** Grange Hall built; **1951** Congregational Church built.

Eastport *Washington County* *Eastern Maine, 90 mi/145 km east of Bangor, on Atlantic Ocean*

c.1675 European traders visit area; **1780** town settled; **1795** General Brewer House built; **1798** town incorporated; **1808** Fort Sullivan founded; **July 1814** British capture town during War of 1812, remain through 1818; **1828** Pembroke Iron Works established, closed 1886; **1852** Grace Episcopal Church built; **c.1875** first sardine factory in U.S. established; **1893** incorporated as a city; **1992** construction begins on new breakwater.

Ellsworth *Hancock County* *Southern Maine, 25 mi/40 km southeast of Bangor, near Atlantic Ocean*

1763 town settled by the English; Benjamin Milliken builds two sawmills on Union River; **1787** Hancock County formed; **1800** town incorporated; **1802** Black Mansion built by Col. John Black; **1805** first bridge built across Union River; **1818** Congregational Church built; **c.1819** Tisdale House built, later becomes Ellsworth Library; **1838** county seat moved from Castine; **1868** incorporated as a city; **1907** dam built on Union River for generating electricity, **1923** flooding destroys Highway 1 bridge; **1931** county courthouse built; **May 1933** fire destroys city's business district.

Falmouth *Cumberland County* *Southwestern Maine, 5 mi/8 km northeast of Portland, on Atlantic Ocean*

1632 area first settled; **1688** town founded; **1698** Fort New Casco built as defense and trading post, abandoned 1716; **1718** town incorporated by Massachusetts; **1785** *Falmouth Gazette* founded, Maine's first newspaper; **1786** Portland separates from Falmouth; **1899** town hall built; **1952** Falmouth Memorial Library established.

Farmington *Franklin County* *West central Maine, 70 mi/113 km west of Bangor*

1754 land grant made by Massachusetts; town incorporated; **1776** exploration party of six led by hunter Thomas Wilson in search of town site, discover Native American village named Pierpole, **1782** first settlers pass through rough winter in crude cabins; **1788** first school opens; **1820** town reincorporated by Maine; **1838** Franklin County formed; town becomes county seat; **1857** vocalist Lillian Nordica born (died 1914); **1864** University of Maine at Farmington established as Farmington State Normal School; **1886** county courthouse built, annex built 1917.

Fort Kent *Aroostook County* *Northern Maine, 170 mi/274 km north of Bangor, on St. John River*

1829 area settled by Acadians; **1839** Fort Kent built as defense during Aroostook War, border dispute with Canada, named for Gov. Edward Kent of Maine; **1860s** Bradbury Lumber Company builds mill to southwest at Fort Kent Mills; **1869** town incorporated; **1916** mill ceases operations; **1967** Fort Kent Campus University of Maine established.

Foxcroft *Piscataquis County* See **Dover-Foxcroft**

Freeport *Cumberland County* *Southwestern Maine, 15 mi/24 km northeast of Portland, on Atlantic Ocean*

c.1700 area first settled; town founded, named for Sir Andrew Freeport; **1756** Thomas Means scalped in bed, wife and son killed by Native Americans in home at Flying Point, two children escape, wife's sister kidnapped, carried to Canada; **1779** Jameson's Tavern built; **1789** town incorporated; **1820** documents officially making Maine a state signed here by commissioners from state of Massachusetts and Province of Maine; town founded; **1830** Harrington House built; **1903** Casco Castle hotel built by Amos Gerald, all but tower burned 1904; **1912** L. L. Bean Company founded, becomes well known nationwide catalog retailer; **1969** Freeport Historical Society founded.

Fryeburg *Oxford County* *Southwestern Maine, 42 mi/68 km northwest of Portland*

1614 Native American settlement of Pequawket visited by Capt. John Smith; **May 8, 1725** 33 men of Massachusetts Rangers under Capt. John Lovewell do combat with 80 Pequawkets under Paugus, both the chief and the captain are killed, Pequawkets flee to Canada; **1762** land grant made to Gen. Joseph Frye; **1763** town settled; **1777** town incorporated; **1792** Fryeburg Academy founded; **1802** Daniel Webster employed as Recorder of Deeds, taught school at Fryeburg Academy Jan.–Oct.; **1817** Saco Canal built, 3-mi/4.8-km bypass of old river channel; **1850** First Congregational Church built; **1851** West Oxford Agricultural Society established; **1857** Hemlock Covered Bridge built on old channel of Saco River; **1883** Meridian Stones placed here by Arctic explorer and former resident Robert E. Peary.

Gardiner *Kennebec County* *Southern Maine, 48 mi/77 km north-northeast of Portland, on Kennebec River*

1760 town settled, named for landowner Dr. Sylvester Gardiner; **1803** town incorporated; **1814** Yellow House built, family residence of author Laura E. Richards (1850–1943); **1850** incorporated as a city; **1865** poet Edwin A. Robinson born (died 1935); **1881** Gardiner Public Library built; **1896** flooding destroys Gardiner-Randolph Bridge.

Gorham *Cumberland County* *Southwestern Maine, 7 mi/11.3 km west of Portland*

1728 town settled on land granted to veterans and their heirs of Narragansett War of 1675; **1736** town founded; **1745** Fort Gorhamton built; **1764** town incorporated; **1765** Smith House built; Crockett-Jewett-Broad House built; **1773** Old Brick House built by Hugh McLellan; **c.1776** Prentiss House built by Samuel Prentiss; **1805** Western State Normal School established; **1808** Baxter Museum built as residence, was home of Gov. Percival Baxter (1921–1924); **1908** Baxter Memorial Library founded; **1969** University of Maine at Portland-Gorham Campus established, renamed University of Southern Maine 1978; **1998** Gorham Industrial Park created.

Gray *Cumberland County* *Southwestern Maine, 15 mi/24 km north of Portland*

1762 town first settled, originally named New Boston; **1770** woolen mill built in North Gray by Samuel Mayhall; **1778** town incorporated, renamed; **1862** body of unknown Confederate soldier mistakenly shipped here buried at Gray Cemetery, belated tribute performed Aug. 6, 2000; **1879** Pennell Institute founded; **1912** Opportunity Farm established as home and school for boys; **1962** Gray Historical Society founded.

Hallowell *Kennebec County* *Southern Maine, 50 mi/80 km north-northeast of Portland, on Kennebec River*

c1754 town settled; named for landowner Benjamin Hallowell; **1771** town incorporated, includes present day city of Augusta; **1791** Old Hallowell Academy founded; **1830** Hubbard House built, home of Dr. John Hubbard, Maine governor; **1832** Worster House built; **1850** incorporated as a city; **1963** Harlow Art Gallery founded.

Hampden *Penobscot County* *Southern Maine, 5 mi/8 km southwest of Bangor, on Penobscot River*

1767 town settled; **1794** town incorporated, named for English parliamentarian John Hampden; **Apr. 4, 1802** prison and asylum reformer Dorothea Dix born (died 1887); **1814** town occupied by British during War of 1812; **1833** Sen. Hannibal Hamlin begins law practice here, law office razed 1988; **1970** Hampden Historical Society museum founded.

Harpswell *Cumberland County* *Southern Maine, 18 mi/29 km northeast of Portland, on Atlantic Ocean*

1659 land purchased from Native Americans; **1714** area first settled; **1757** Congregational Church built, rebuilt 1843; **1758** town incorporated; **1759** Old Meeting House completed; **Sept. 24, 1774** earliest known burial at old cemetery at Cundy's Harbor; **1871** Halfway Rock Lighthouse built; **1928** humpbacked Cobwork Bridge built between Bailey and Orrs islands, designed to clear tides; **1958** Cundys Harbor Library established; **1979** Harpswell Historical Society founded.

Houlton *Aroostook County* *Northeastern Maine, 100 mi/161 km north-northeast of Bangor*

1799 land granted to citizens of New Salem, Massachusetts; **1805** settled by Joseph Houlton and Aaron and Joseph Putnam; **1813** Black Hawk Tavern built; **1822** William H. Cary of New Salem builds large house on hill above town; **1826** Peabody House built by Amos Pearce; **1828** garrison formed by U.S. Infantry; **1831** town incorporated; **1832** Aroostook War border dispute fought during bitterly cold winter by 12 militia companies; **1839** Aroostook County formed; town becomes county seat; **1847** Ricker Classical Institute founded; **1862** New Brunswick Railway (later Canadian Pacific) extended from St. Andrews, New Brunswick, eventually built across Maine as short-cut to Maritime Provinces; **1863** European & North American (Maine Central) Railroad reaches town; **1885** county courthouse built, annex built 1917; **1894** Bangor & Aroostook Railroad reaches town; **late 1800s** summer camp meetings held as form of social life; **1904** Cary Library built, founded by Dr. George Cary; **Jan. 7, 1927** Trans-Atlantic Receiving Station begins oceanic service, part of world communications network; **1940** Houlton Army Air Base established, later becomes Houlton International Airport; **1984** Greater Houlton Christian Academy founded.

Islesboro *Waldo County Southern Maine, 82 mi/ 132 km northeast of Portland, on Atlantic Ocean*

1692 Isleborough Island visited by Church Expedition; **1769** island settled by British; **1789** town incorporated; **1814** British take nearby Castine during War of 1812; **1874** Grindle Point Lighthouse built, discontinued 1934, reactivated 1987; **c.1880** summer tourists begin arriving; **1892** Christ Church established at Dark Harbor village; **1902** Alice L. Pendleton Library opened; **1936** Sailors' Memorial Museum established; **1964** Isleboro Historical Society founded.

Kennebunk *York County Southwestern Maine, 15 mi/24 km southwest of Portland, on Atlantic Ocean*

1603 Martin Pring explores Kennebunk River; **1620s** area first settled; **1650** town founded, remains under threat of Native American attack for almost a century; **1681** sawmill built; **1720** Larrabee Garrison House built; **1730** shipbuilding industry begins, continues through 1918; **1774** First Parish Unitarian Church built; **1797** Taylor House completed; **1803** Robert Lund House completed; **1815** Bourne Mansion built; **1820** town incorporated; **1825** French military hero Lafayette honored in person under Lafayette Elm; **1872** Boston & Maine Railroad reaches town; **1899** Atlantic Shore Line Railway trolley begins service, discontinued 1927; **1936** Brick Store Museum founded, built 1825 by William Lord; **1947** Maine Turnpike opened; **1982** Astronomical Society of Northern New England organized.

Kennebunkport *York County Southwestern Maine, 23 mi/37 km south of Portland, on Atlantic Ocean*

1629 town settled; **1653** Town of Cape Porpoise incorporated by Massachusetts; **1689** town depopulated by Native American threat; **1719** town renamed Arundel; **1749** Perkins Mill (grain) established; **1764** First Congregational Church built; **1785** town becomes shipbuilding center; **1821** town renamed Kennebunkport; **c.1880** Goat Island Lighthouse built, automated 1990; **1880s** summer colony established at Goose Rocks (Beachwood), destroyed by forest fire 1947; **1900**

Atlantic Shore Line Railway reaches town, discontinued 1927; New Belvidere Hotel built; **1952** Kennebunkport Historical Society founded; **1989–1993** residence of Pres. George Bush serves as "summer white house."

Kittery *York County Southwestern Maine, 2 mi/ 3.2 km north of Portsmouth, New Hampshire, on Atlantic Ocean*

c.1623 town first settled; oldest town in Maine founded; **1647** town incorporated by Massachusetts, Maine's oldest town; **1682** Pepperell House built at Kittery Point by William Pepperell, father of Sir William Pepperell; **1690** Fort McClary built; **Jan. 14, 1730** William Whipple born, signer of Declaration of Independence (died 1785); First Congregational Church built; **1742** Sparhawk House built; **1757** Sewall Bridge built; **1765** Lady Pepperell House built by Sir William Pepperell; **1777** John Paul Jones' *Ranger* built; **1800** the *Falkland*, first U.S. warship, is launched; **1806** Portsmouth Navy Yard established on several islands in Piscataqua River; **1815** gunship *Washington* launched; **1861** *Kearsarge* launched during Civil War; **1923** Memorial Bridge built across Piscataqua River to Portsmouth, New Hampshire; **1976** Kittery Historical and Naval Museum founded.

Lewiston *Androscoggin County Southwestern Maine, 30 mi/48 km north of Portland, on Androscoggin River*

1768 land grant given to Jonathan Bagley and Moses Little of Newbury, Massachusetts; **1770** Paul Hildreth of Dracut, Massachusetts, becomes first settler; **1795** town incorporated; **1809** first dam built on Androscoggin River; sawmill built by Michael Little, burned 1814; **1819** first woolen mill opens; **1823** first bridge built; **1836** second dam built on Androscoggin River; **1844** first cotton mill built; **1845** construction begins on canal for supplying water to mills, completed 1864; **1848** Lewiston Water Power Company established; **1855** Bates College established; **1861** incorporated as a city; **1864** Maine State Seminary founded; **1873** city hall built; **1877** Music Hall built; **Jan. 8, 1877** painter Marsden Hartley born (died 1943); **1889** St. Mary's Hospital established; **1891** Central Maine Hospital established; **1906** work begins on building Sts. Peter and Paul Catholic Church, completed 1938; **March 1936** flooding destroys South Bridge, inundates North Bridge, damages areas in Lewiston and Auburn; **1937** shoe industry strike cripples economy in both cities, testing National Labor Relations Act.

Lincoln *Penobscot County Central Maine, 40 mi/ 64 km north of Bangor, on Penobscot River*

1825 settled by Ira Fish; town founded, named for Maine Gov. Enoch Lincoln; sawmill built; **1826** second mill built; **1827** first school built, used after 1830 as Town Hall; **1829** town incorporated; **1830** Chesley Hayes hotel built; **1831** Congregational Church built; **1869** spool mill built by John MacGregor, burned 1885, rebuilt; **1879** Lincoln

Memorial Library founded; **c.1880** granite quarrying begins; **1882** Lincoln Pulp and Paper Mill established; **1902** Catholic Church built; **1935** Lincoln Historical Society organized; **Jan. 2002** part of business district destroyed by fire.

Livermore *Androscoggin County* *West central Maine, 50 mi/80 km north of Portland*

c.1760 town founded; **1795** town incorporated; **1813** Israel Washburn, Jr. born, governor of Maine 1851–1861 (died 1883); **Sept. 23, 1816** U.S. Congressman from Wisconsin, Elihu Washburn born, secretary of state under President Grant (died 1887); **Apr. 22, 1818** U.S. Congressman from Wisconsin Cadwallader Washburn born (died 1882); **Jan. 14, 1831** U.S. Senator from Minnesota William Drew Washburn born (died 1912); **1870** Washburn Mansion completed; **Aug. 11, 1897** poet Louise Bogan born (died 1970); **1974** Washburn Mansion opened as a museum.

Lubec *Washington County* *Southeastern Maine, 87 mi/140 km east of Bangor, on Atlantic Ocean*

c.1780 area settled; **1804** Chaloner Tavern opens; **1811** town incorporated; **1890** Lubec Channel Lighthouse built, discontinued 1939; **1896–1898** minister named Jernegan claims invention of method for extracting gold from seawater by electrolysis, includes plant, imported workers, disappears with investors' money before hoax is discovered; **1939–1945** Pres. Franklin D. Roosevelt establishes summer home on Campobello Island, Canada, accessible by small bridge from Lubec; **1964** Roosevelt Campobello International Park established, also in New Brunswick, Canada.

Machias *Washington County* *Eastern Maine, 65 mi/105 km east of Bangor, near Atlantic Ocean*

1633 trading post established by British under Richard Vines, almost immediately destroyed by French; **1675** site used as base by Rhodes the pirate; **1763** town settled by British; **1770** Burnham Tavern built by Joe Burnham; **1784** town incorporated; **1789** Washington County formed; town becomes county seat; **1841** Machias & Whitneyville Railroad built for hauling lumber; **1853** county courthouse built; **1875** Avery Rock Lighthouse built, destroyed by storm 1946; **1909** Washington State Normal School established, later becomes University of Maine at Machias.

Millinocket *Penobscot County* *North central Maine, 60 mi/97 km north of Bangor, on Penobscot River*

1804 Boston surveyor Charles Potter becomes first known white man to climb Mt. Katahdin, Maine's highest point (5,267 ft/1,605 m); **1899** St. Martin's Catholic Church built; **1900** Great Northern Paper Company newsprint plant and dam built; Great Northern Hotel built, "Palace of the Woods," razed 1961; **1901** town incorporated; **1902** Millinocket School built, burned 1921; **1917** Ripogenus

Dam completed on West Branch Penobscot River, 30 mi/48 km to northwest; **1931–1933** Baxter State Park, initially containing 9 sq mi/23.3 sq km of wilderness, set aside by former Gov. Percival Baxter, additional acreage added 1962, total over 204,733 ac/82,917 ha.

Monhegan *Lincoln County* *Southern Maine, 50 mi/80 km east of Portland, Monhegan Island, Atlantic Ocean*

1000 AD Norsemen thought to have reached New England coast; **1498** explorers John and Sebastian Cabot sail around island; **1569** explorer David Ingram describes island from mainland; **1605** Capt. George Waymouth visits island, names it St. George's Island; Samuel de Champlain views island; **1614** Capt. John Smith lands here; **1625** temporary first settlement established on island; **1654** island resettled by English; **1689** settlement destroyed by French under Baron de Castin; **1720** island reoccupied by English fishermen; **1717** pirate Paulsgrave builds prison and dwellings for his base; **Sept. 5, 1813** privateer USS *Enterprise* defeats brigantine HMS *Boxer* southeast of island during War of 1812; **1824** first Monhegan Lighthouse built, rebuilt 1850; **1968** Monhegan Museum founded.

Monson *Piscataquis County* *Central Maine, 50 mi/80 km northwest of Bangor*

1816 Joseph Bearce builds first house; **1820** dam built on outlet of Lake Hebron; **1821** sawmill and grist mill built; **1822** town incorporated; **1845** Baptist Church built; **1847** Monson Academy founded; **May 1860** fire destroys entire town; **1870** slate deposits discovered, quarrying begins 1872, slate used in Kennedy Memorial, Arlington National Cemetery, 1964; **1917** Sheldon Slate Products Company established; **1969** Monson Library built, organized 1909.

Naples *Cumberland County* *Southwestern Maine, 25 mi/40 km north-northwest of Portland*

1799 The Manor inn built by first settler George Pierce; **1834** town incorporated; **1900s** rift between Republican and Democratic families runs so deep that the children sit on opposite sides of the one-room school; **1904** excursion boat *Columbia*, originally a masted vessel, makes its last trip on Long Lake; **July 10, 1911** highest temperature ever recorded in Maine reached at village of North Bridgton to north, 105°F/41°C.

New Gloucester *Cumberland County* *Southwestern Maine, 20 mi/32 km north of Portland*

1736 land grant given to 60 residents of Gloucester, Massachusetts, settled by them 1739; **1744** Capt. Isaac Eveleth makes financial offers to permanent settlers; **1753–1754** garrison built to protect settlement; **1783** Sabbathday Lake Shaker Community founded; **1894** Town of New Gloucester incorporated; **1931** Sabbathday Lake Village becomes last surviving Shaker community in U.S., joined by Shakers from town of Alfred; **1931** Shaker Museum founded.

New Sweden *Aroostook County* *Northeastern Maine, 153 mi/246 km north-northeast of Bangor*

1870 town settled as immigration experiment offering free farms to Swedish immigrants; **July 1870** town incorporated; Capitolium public building built on Capitol Hill; **1870s** Larson-Ostlund log house built; **1880** Gustaf Adolph Evangelical Lutheran Church built; **1891** Evangelical Covenant Church built; **1892** First Baptist Church built; **1900** Noak Blacksmith Shop established; **Apr. 28, 2003** Walter Morrill, 78, dies from poisoned pot of coffee at Lutheran Church social, others sickened, suspect Daniel Bondeson commits suicide by gunshot May 2.

Norridgewock *Somerset County* *Central Maine, 50 mi/80 km west of Bangor*

1636 Somerset County formed; **1646** mission established at Old Point by Jesuits and Abnaki peoples from Quebec; **1691** French missionary Father Sebastian Rasle takes charge of mission; **1724** Rasle and Native Americans killed by English; **1775** Benedict Arnold's expedition camps at Old Point on way to Quebec; **1788** town incorporated; **1806** county organized; town becomes county seat; **1872** county seat moved to Skowhegan; **1833** Father Rasle Memorial obelisk erected; **1845** Sophie May House built by U.S. Cong. Cullen Sawtelle.

North Bridgton *Cumberland County* *See* **Naples** (1911)

Ogunquit *York County* *Southwestern Maine, 33 mi/53 km southwest of Portland, on Atlantic Ocean*

Apr. 1682 wrecked crew of the *Increase* reach unnamed island, rescued by Native Americans, converts of Aspinquid, disciple of John Eliot's Praying Indians; crew names island Boon in honor of being saved; **1710** shipwrecked survivors of *Nottingham Galley* marooned on Boon Island 25 days prior to rescue; **1811** Boon Island Lighthouse built, automated 1980; **1888** Ogunquit village founded within Town of Wells; **1913** village incorporated; **1928** Ogunquit Art Association founded; **1933** Ogunquit Playhouse established, new theater built 1937; **1952** Ogunquit Museum of American Art founded by Henry Slater; **1980** Town of Ogunquit incorporated, separates from Wells.

Old Orchard Beach *York County* *Southwestern Maine, 10 mi/16 km south of Portland, on Atlantic Ocean*

c.1628 trading post established; **1630** area settled; **1730** Staples Inn built; **1883** town incorporated; **Dec. 1883** town heavily damaged by storm, rebuilt; **July 1889** Old Orchard Beach Pier completed, includes The Casino dance hall,

venue for big name entertainers like Louis Armstrong and Benny Goodman; **1957** Libby Memorial Library built.

Old Town *Penobscot County* *Central Maine, 8 mi/12.9 km north-northeast of Bangor, on Penobscot River*

1774 first settled by Joseph Marshon on Marsh Island in Penobscot River; **1798** sawmill built by Richard Winslow; **1818** Penobscot Indian Reservation established on islands in Penobscot River, only Old Town Island inhabited; **1836** Bangor, Milford & Old Town Railroad, Maine's first railroad, reaches town; **1840** town incorporated, separates from Town of Orono; **c.1860** town becomes largest lumber supplier in U.S.; **1878** fire destroys sawmills; **1888** Ounegan Woolen Mill established, town's first; **1891** incorporated as a city; **1892** Old Town Library founded; **1958** Municipal Building completed; **1960s** last of town's woolen mills closes; **1976** Old Town Museum founded.

Onawa *Piscataquis County* *See* **Dover-Foxcroft** (1919)

Orland *Hancock County* *Southern Maine, 100 mi/161 km northeast of Portland, near Penobscot River*

1764 town settled by Joseph Gross; **1770s** more settlers arrive; **1800** town incorporated; **1838** Boston publisher Edwin Ginn born, founded World Peace Foundation 1910 (died 1914); **Aug. 3, 1909** writer Walter Van Talburg Clark born at East Orland (died 1971); **1966** Orland Historical Society founded.

Orono *Penobscot County* *Central Maine, 10 mi/16 km north-northeast of Bangor, on Penobscot River*

c.1775 area settled; originally named Stillwater; **1806** town incorporated; name changed; **1836** Maine's first railroad, the narrow gauge Bangor, Milford & Old Town Railroad, built through town; **1840** Old Town separates from Orono; **1865** University of Maine established; **1966** Hudson Museum of Anthropology founded by Dr. Richard G. Emerick; **1986** Maine Center for the Arts established.

Paris *Oxford County* *See* **South Paris**

Pemaquid *Lincoln County* *Southern Maine, 40 mi/64 km east-northeast of Portland, on Atlantic Ocean*

1569 explorer David Ingram visits site; **1602** Capt. Bartholomew Gosnold enters Pemaquid port; **1607** Sir Francis Popham arrives with his people, remain for several years; **1630** Shurt's Fort built, settlement then called Jamestown; **1677** Fort Charles built; **1689** Shurt's Fort destroyed by Native Americans or pirates; **1692** Fort William Henry built, destroyed 1696 by French; **1729** Fort House residence built by Col. David Dunbar; **1765** Town of Bristol incorporated; **1827** Pemaquid

MAINE

Lighthouse and residence built at Pemaquid Point, automated 1934; **1972** Fishermen's Museum founded.

Phippsburg *Sagadahoc County* *Southern Maine, 25 mi/40 km east-northeast of Portland, on Atlantic Ocean*

1609 George Popham establishes short-lived Popham Colony at Popham Beach to south, first English colony in New England; colonists build Fort St. George; **1645** first permanent settlers arrive in area; **1716** Augusta fishing village established on Casco Bay by Dr. Oliver Noyes, abandoned c.1821; **1774** James McCobb House built; **1816** town incorporated, separates from Bristol; **1855** Pond Island Lighthouse built, automated 1963; **1857** Seguin Island Lighthouse built, replaces light built in 1795; **1861** construction on Fort Popham begun, never completed; **1890** Sugar Loaves summer resort colony established; **1905** Fort Baldwin built, completed 1912, purchased by state 1924.

Pittsfield *Somerset County* *Central Maine, 30 mi/48 km west of Bangor*

1795 area settled by Moses Martin; town founded, named Warsaw; **1816** Sepasticook Plantation organized; **1819** town incorporated; **1824** town renamed Pittsfield; **1866** Central Maine Institute established; **1867** Lancey House hotel built, destroyed by fire 1906; **1869** woolen mill established; Maine Central Institute established; **Aug. 28, 1875** poet Hugh Pendexter born, creator of Wizard of Oz (died 1940); **1881** fire destroys downtown; **1892** Waverly Mill built.

Portland *Cumberland County* *Southwestern Maine, 102 mi/164 km north of Boston, on Atlantic Ocean*

c.1600 first European explorers enter Casco Bay; **1623–1624** Christopher Levett winters on Hog (House) Island in Casco Bay, returns to England to engender support for colony leaving behind ten men, never returns, fate of men unknown; **1628** Walter Bagnall occupies town site, killed by natives 1631; **1631** permanent settlement founded by Richard Tucker and George Cleeve, named Casco; **1643–1644** Cleeve summons first court; **1658** Massachusetts Bay Colony assumes control of area, town renamed Falmouth; Cleeve's authority over town ends; **1676** town destroyed by Native Americans, again in 1690 by French and natives; **1716** town resettled; **1755** Tate House built by George Tate, mast agent for British Navy; **1760** Cumberland County formed; **1775** post office established by Benjamin Franklin; **Oct. 18, 1775** British begin bombarding town at 9:30 A.M., over 400 buildings burned, no deaths; **1785** *Falmouth Gazette* founded, Maine's first newspaper; **July 4, 1786** Town of Portland incorporated, separates from Falmouth; **1790** Portland Head Lighthouse built, automated 1958; **1800** Sweat Mansion built; **1801** Dole (Churchill) House built; **1804** Deering Mansion built; **March 20, 1804** temperance leader Neal Dow born (died 1897); **Jan. 20, 1806** essayist Nathaniel P. Willis born (died 1867); **1807** Portland Observatory built

for observing ships in distress, closed 1923; **Feb. 27, 1807** poet Henry Wadsworth Longfellow born (died 1882); **1820** Maine becomes state, Portland serves as first capital, former courthouse serves as state capitol; **1822** Maine Historical Society founded; **1825** First Parish (Unitarian) Church built; **1832** state capital moved to Augusta; Portland incorporated as a city; **1834** State Street Hospital built; **Jan. 9, 1839** organist, composer John Knowles Paine born (died 1906); **Oct. 18, 1839** Cong. Thomas B. Reed born (died 1902); **1842** first railroad reaches Portland from Portsmouth, New Hampshire; **1845** Casco Bay Lines ferry system begins serving islands in Casco Bay; **June 18, 1850** publisher Cyrus H. K. Curtis born, founded Curtis Publishing (died 1933); **1852** Portland Breakwater built; **1853** steamer *Sarah Sands* becomes first transatlantic run to dock in Portland; **1855** St. Luke's Cathedral built; Breakwater Lighthouse built; **1863** Confederates enter harbor, commandeer gunboat *Caleb Cushing*, setting it ablaze, rebels captured in lifeboats; **July 4–5, 1866** Independence Day celebration sparks disaster, over 1,500 buildings destroyed in city fire; **1869** Cathedral of the Immaculate Conception completed, construction delayed by 1866 fire; **1871** old post office built; **Jan. 29, 1874** essayist Owen Davis born (died 1956); **1876** Williston Congregational Church built; Edwards and Walker Hardware Company established; **1878** University of Southern Maine established; **1881** St. Joseph's Academy established; **1882** Portland Museum of Art established; **1903** Grand Trunk Station built; **1907** county courthouse completed, annex built 1991; **1912** city hall completed; **Oct. 15, 1937** TV actress Linda Lavin born; **Sept. 9, 1947** author Stephen King born; **1916** "Million Dollar" Bridge built across Casco Bay at cost of $970,000; **Nov. 28, 1959** actor Judd Nelson born; **1977** Cumberland County Civic Center opened, home of Portland Pirates hockey team; Children's Museum founded; **1993** Maine Narrow Gauge Railroad established, touring train on shore of Casco Bay; **1997** Casco Bay Bridge opened, replaces "Million Dollar" Bridge; **1998** Museum of African Tribal Art founded.

Presque Isle *Aroostook County* *Northeastern Maine, 135 mi/217 km north-northeast of Bangor*

1820 first settlers arrive in area; **1860** town incorporated; **1874** town's first potato starch mill built; **1881** New Brunswick reaches town from Canada; **1895** Bangor & Aroostook Railroad built from Bangor; **1903** University of Maine at Presque Isle established; **1940** incorporated as a city; **1941** Presque Isle Army Air Force Base established, closed 1961; **Aug. 11, 1978** balloon *Double Eagle II* departs on voyage across Atlantic carrying three Americans, arrives outside Paris Aug. 17, first successful transatlantic balloon crossing.

Rangeley *Franklin County* *Western Maine, 92 mi/148 km west of Bangor*

1796 land purchased by James Rangeley, Sr., three others from Philadelphia; **1817** Luther Hore family become town's first settlers; **c.1825** Squire Rangeley of Yorkshire, England, establishes large estate here; Rangeley gives away sections of his property to settlers; **1855** town incorporated; **1877** village rebuilt after fire; Rangeley Lake Hotel built by John A. Burke, building moved quarter-mile to lake shore 1895, razed 1958; **1909** Rangeley Public Library built; **1920s** town becomes popular resort; **Nov. 3, 1957** controversial Freudian analyst Wilhelm Reich dies, founder of science of cosmic life energy, born Austria 1892; **1960** Wilhelm Reich Museum founded.

Raymond *Cumberland County* *Southwestern Maine, 18 mi/29 km north of Portland*

1770 first settlers arrive; **1841** town incorporated, separates from Casco; **1765** Morton Homestead built; **1786** Hayden House built; **1812** Hawthorne House built by Richard Manning for Nathaniel Hawthorne, occupied by Hawthorne as summer retreat while attending Bowdoin College, Boston, through 1825.

Readfield *Kennebec County* *Southern Maine, 52 mi/84 km north-northeast of Portland*

c.1775 town settled; **1791** town incorporated; **1787** Kennebec Agricultural Society founded, active until 1818; **1792** Baptist church built; **1824** Maine Wesleyan Seminary founded, later becomes Kents Hill School; **Nov. 8, 1836** game manufacturer Milton Bradley born at rural Vienna to north (died 1911); **1856** first annual Kennebec County Fair held.

Rockland *Knox County* *Southern Maine, 65 mi/105 km northeast of Portland, on Atlantic Ocean*

1605 Samuel de Champlain visits nearby Owl's Head promontory; **c.1770** town settled; **1826** Owl's Head Light erected; **1848** town incorporated, separates from Thomaston as East Thomaston, renamed Rockland 1850; **1854** incorporated as a city; **1860** Knox County formed; town becomes county seat; **1875** county courthouse built, addition built 1979; **Feb. 22, 1892** poet Edna St. Vincent Millay born (died 1950); **1895** Rockland Public Library founded; **1902** Rockland Breakwater Lighthouse built, automated 1964; **1948** The Farnsworth Library and Art Museum founded; **1977** Shore Village Museum founded; **1987** Rockland Harbor Southwest Lighthouse built.

Rockport *Knox County* *Southern Maine, 70 mi/113 km northeast of Portland, on Atlantic Ocean*

1769 town settled; **1850** Indian Head Lighthouse built, discontinued 1934; **1891** town incorporated, separates from Camden; **1925** Spite House, built 1806, moved from 85 mi/137 km by road from Phippsburg; **1952** Maine Coast Artists Museum founded; **1999** Aldermere Farm natural area established, bequeathed by farmer Albert Chatfield, Jr.

Rumford *Oxford County* *Western Maine, 90 mi/145 km west of Bangor*

1774 town settled; **1800** town incorporated; **c.1890** Dr. Dexter Abbott begins bottling healthful spring water found at Mt. Zircon, establishes Mount Zircon Bottling Company 1915, closed 1935; **1892** Rumford Falls & Rangeley Lakes Railroad built; **1893** Rumford Paper Mill begins operation, becomes Oxford Mill 1899; **1903** Rumford Carnegie Public Library built; **March 28, 1914** Sen. Edmund Muskie born (died 1996); **1976** Lufkin School Museum founded.

Saco *York County* *Southwestern Maine, 12 mi/19 km southwest of Portland, on Atlantic Ocean*

1631 town settled; **1762** town incorporated as Pepperellborough; **1800** 17 sawmills in operation on Saco Island, called Factory Island; **1803** First Congregational Church built, rebuilt after 1860 fire; **1805** town renamed Saco; **1807** Cyrus King House built; **1811** Thornton Academy founded; nail factory established; **March 2, 1819** Mormon publisher Samuel Brannan born, publicized 1848 gold strike at Sutter's Mill, California (died 1898); **1825** first cotton mill built, becomes York Mills following 1830 fire, closed 1958; **1827** Trinity Episcopal Church built; **1828** Joseph Hobson House built; James Curtis House built; **1834** J. P. Mellen House built; **1842** Portland, Saco & Portsmouth Railroad reaches town; **1856** Town Hall completed; **1866** incorporated as a city; York Institute museum founded, built 1928; Saco Museum founded; **1872** Boston & Maine Railroad arrives; **1893** public library built, replaced 1955.

Saint George *Knox County* *Southern Maine, 60 mi/97 km northeast of Portland, on Atlantic Ocean*

1605 George Waymouth visits area; **c.1630** trading post established by English, abandoned 1675 during Indian War; **1803** town incorporated; **1809** Fort St. George built; **1814** British capture Fort St. George during War of 1812; **1852** Whitehead Lighthouse built, automated 1982.

Sanford *York County* *Southwestern Maine, 30 mi/48 km southwest of Portland*

1661 land purchased by Maj. William Phillips of Boston from Chief Fluellin, originally named Phillipstown; **1730** grist mill built; **1768** town incorporated, renamed for Peleg Sanford, Governor of Rhode Island; **1867** Goodall Mills established by Thomas Goodall, maker of carriage robes and kersey blankets, closed 1954; **1871** Goodall Mansion built; **1912** Nasson College for Women established as vocational school, closed 1983.

Sangerville *Piscataquis County* *Central Maine, 38 mi/61 km northwest of Bangor*

1801 town settled; **1814** town incorporated; **Feb. 5, 1840** Hiram Maxim born, inventor of machine gun (died 1916); **1857** Low's Covered Bridge built over Piscataquis River.

Scarborough *Cumberland County* *Southwestern Maine, 6 mi/9.7 km south of Portland, on Atlantic Ocean*

1651 area first settled; **1658** town incorporated; first Anglican church in Maine built; **1684** Hunnewell House (Old Red House) built; **1703** Capt. John Larrabee and eight men withstand siege for several days by 500 French and Native American forces; **1728** First Parish Congregational Church built; **1766** Parson Lancaster House built; **Feb. 9, 1768** William King born, first governor of Maine 1820–1821 (died 1852); **1899** Scarborough Public Library established.

Sebago *Cumberland County* *Southwestern Maine, 23 mi/37 km northwest of Portland*

1774 land grant made to Captain Flint of Concord, Massachusetts, named Flintstown; **1790** Joseph Lakin and Jacob House become first settlers; **1826** Town of Sebago incorporated, separates from Baldwin; **1830** Fitch's Store built by Luther Fitch, destroyed by lightning 1864, rebuilt, destroyed by lightning 1919, again rebuilt; **1847** steamboats begin service on Sebago Lakes with maiden voyage of the *Fawn*; **1932** steamboat era closes with demise of the *Goodridge*.

Skowhegan *Somerset County* *Central Maine, 47 mi/76 km west of Bangor*

1636 Somerset County formed; **1724** Father Sebastian Rasles massacred by Abenaki peoples; **1771** area settled; **Sept. 29, 1775** Benedict Arnold's army encamps here en route to Quebec; **1806** Somerset County organized; **1823** Town of Milburn incorporated, separates from Canaan; **1863** town renamed Skowhegan, Abenaki term for "place for watching salmon"; **1872** county seat moved from Norridgewock; **1873** county courthouse built, addition built 1904; **Dec. 14, 1897** U.S. Sen. Margaret Chase Smith born (died 1995); **1900** summer theater opens at Lake Wesserunsett; **1916** State Reformatory for Women opens; **1937** Skowhegan History House founded, house built 1839 by blacksmith Aaron Spear; **1969** Skowhegan Indian Monument erected; **1982** Margaret Chase Smith Library built.

South Berwick *York County* *Southwestern Maine, 40 mi/64 km southwest of Portland*

1631 town first settled by Ambrose Gibbons; **Sept. 24, 1674** defenders of Tozier Garrison massacred by Native Americans; **1728** first known interments at Old Cemetery; **1744** Jonathan Hamilton House built; **1774** Sarah Orne Jewett House built by John Haggins; **1785** Hamilton House built by shipbuilder Capt. John Hamilton; **1791** Berwick Academy founded; **1814** town incorporated, separates from Berwick; **Sept. 3, 1849** author Sarah Orne Jewett born (1909).

South Paris *Oxford County* *Southwestern Maine, 40 mi/64 km north of Portland*

1779 town settled; **1793** Town of Paris incorporated; **1803** Baptist church built; **1805** Oxford County formed; village of South Paris becomes county seat; **1806** Hubbard House built; **1808** Lyonsden house built by Rear Adm. Henry W. Lyon; **Aug. 27, 1809** Hannibal Hamlin born, Maine governor, vice pres. under President Madison (died 1891); **1828** Old Stone Jail built; **1896** county courthouse built.

South Portland *Cumberland County* *Southwestern Maine, 1 mi/1.6 km south of Portland, on Atlantic Ocean*

c.1633 town settled; **1791** Portland Head Light erected; **c.1810** Fort Preble built on Portland Harbor, named for Commodore Edward Preble; **1852** Portland Breakwater built; **1855** Breakwater Lighthouse built; **1861** Fort Preble enlarged during Civil War; construction of Fort Gorges begins on harbor, completed 1865; **1887** Coast Guard station established; **1897** Spring Point Lighthouse built, automated 1934; **1898** town incorporated; **1922** Fort Williams Army Base established to south; **1948** Southern Maine Technical College (2-year) established; **1967** incorporated as a city.

South Windham *Cumberland County* *Southwestern Maine, 8 mi/12.9 km northwest of Portland*

1737 town settled; **1740** mill built on Presumpscot River at South Windham; **1744** Fort Old Province Fort built, used through 1751; **1762** Town of Windham incorporated; **1843** Babb's Covered Bridge built across Presumpscot River to Gorham, burned 1973, rebuilt; **1919** Maine Correctional Center established.

Standish *Cumberland County* *Southwestern Maine, 14 mi/23 km west of Portland*

1745 land granted to Moses Pearson; **1752** town surveyed; fort built at crossroads; **1756** town founded, named for Miles Standish; **1785** town incorporated by Massachusetts; **1789** Marrett House built, coin supply from Boston banks secretly stored here during War of 1812; **1804** Unitarian (Old Red) Church built, used until 1859; **1848** Standish Academy founded, closed 1852; **1912** St. Joseph's College established.

Swans Island *Hancock County* *See* **Atlantic**

Thomaston *Knox County* *Southern Maine, 62 mi/100 km northeast of Portland, on Atlantic Ocean*

1630 trading post established; **1719** fort built; **1777** town incorporated; **1793** Montpelier house built by Gen. Henry Knox; **1800** Thompson House built; **1820** General Veazie House built; **1824** Maine State Prison opened, rebuilt 1924, closed 2002, new prison opened at Warren; **1828** Dr. McKeen House built; **1835** Baptist Church built.

Topsham *Sagadahoc County* *Southwestern Maine, 1 mi/1.6 km north of Brunswick, on Androscoggin River*

1684 land grant made to Richard Wharton; **1716** first sawmill built on Cathance River; **1717** town founded; **c.1720** town settled; **1750** lumber industry begins; **1764** town incorporated; **c.1800** Aldrich House built; **1868** Pejepscot Paper Mill established; **c.1868** Whitten House built, later used as library.

Union *Knox County* *Southern Maine, 64 mi/103 km northeast of Portland*

1772 town settled by Scottish immigrants; **1786** town incorporated; **c.1809** Cobb Tavern opened; **1840** old Town House built; **1849** Robbins House built; **1876** popular Moxie nerve tonic developed by Augustin Thompson, born here 1835; **1897** bandstand built in Town Common; **1907** large Moxie tonic bottle built as tourist attraction with door at base; **1965** Matthews Museum of Maine Heritage founded.

Van Buren *Aroostook County* *Northeastern Maine, 170 mi/274 km north-northeast of Bangor*

late 1700s exiled French Acadians arrive from Nova Scotia, original town named Violette Brook for settler Francois Violette; **1839** town founded on St. John River at end of bloodless Aroostook War boundary dispute, named for Pres. Martin Van Buren; **1881** town incorporated; **Nov. 1899** Bangor & Aroostook Railroad reaches town; **Jan. 19, 1925** lowest temperature ever recorded in Maine reached, −48°F/−44°C.

Warren *Knox County* *Southern Maine, 60 mi/97 km northeast of Portland, near Atlantic Ocean*

1736 town settled; **1776** town incorporated, originally named Meduncook; **1807** town renamed Warren; **1864** Mary Baker Grover Eddy begins work in promulgation of her Christian Science faith; **2002** new Maine State Correctional Center opened, formerly located at Thomaston.

Waterboro *York County* *Southwestern Maine, 23 mi/37 km west-southwest of Portland*

1768 settled by Capt. John Smith; **1787** town incorporated; **1806** Elder Grey Meeting House built; **1834** Town House built, originally used as a church; **1863** Boston & Maine Railroad reaches town, discontinued 1961; **1880** Taylor Hall built; **1918** Ossipee Mtn. Fire Tower built, rebuilt 1954; **1947** forest fire destroys 58 homes at South Waterboro.

Waterford *Oxford County* *Southwestern Maine, 42 mi/68 km north-northwest of Portland*

1775 town first settled by David McWain; **1797** town incorporated; **Apr. 26, 1834** humorist Artemus Ward born, son of Revolutionary War hero of same name (died 1867); **1899** Waterford Library opened, new library completed 1994.

Waterville *Kennebec County* *Central Maine, 70 mi/113 km north-northeast of Portland, on Kennebec River*

1754 Fort Halifax built at Ticonic Falls, dismantled 1763; settlement founded; **1792** sawmill built; **1794** shipbuilding industry begins; **1802** town incorporated; **1813** Colby College established; **1814** Asa Remington House built; **1816** tannery established; **1832** steamship *Ticonic* begins passenger service on river; **1837** Hathaway Shirt manufacturer established by Charles F. Hathaway; **1849** Androscoggin & Kennebec Railroad reaches town; fire destroys downtown area; **1852** St. John's Catholic Church built; **1855** Penobscot & Kennebec Railroad reaches town; **1866** Unitarian Church built; **1868** dam built at falls as power source for manufacturing; **1869** Methodist Church built; **1888** incorporated as a city; **1894** Thomas College established; **1901** city hall built; **1903** Pennington Museum of Waterville Historical Society opened; **1905** six Native American skeletons unearthed during construction of Crescent Hotel; **1927** Redington Museum founded; **Aug. 20, 1933** U.S. Sen. George Mitchell born.

Wells *York County* *Southwestern Maine, 28 mi/45 km southwest of Portland, on Atlantic Ocean*

1622 land grant made to Sir Ferdinand Gorges; **c.1640** area settled by English, originally part of Kennebunk; **1643** town founded; First Congregational Church built; **1650** series of Indian wars begin, continue through 1730; **1653** town incorporated; **1692** French and Native Americans burn Congregational Church, lay two-day siege on town; **1799** Lindsey Tavern built.

Westbrook *Cumberland County* *Southwestern Maine, suburb 3 mi/5 km west of Portland*

1657 town settled; **1814** town incorporated, separates from Falmouth; **1805** Bean House built; **1852** S. D. Warren Paper Mills established at Cumberland Mills village; **1866** Dana Warp Mills established; **1891** incorporated as a city.

Windham *Cumberland County* See **South Windham**

Wiscasset *Lincoln County* *Southern Maine, 38 mi/61 km northeast of Portland, near Atlantic Ocean*

1663 town settled; originally named Pownalborough for Royal Gov. Thomas Pownal; **1754** Fort Frankfort built, later renamed Fort Shirley; **1760** Lincoln County formed; town becomes county seat; town incorporated, renamed, Native American term meaning "three rivers"; **1761** Pownalborough Courthouse built, oldest surviving judicial building in Maine; **1789** Alna Meeting House built; **1802** town incorporated; **1807** Castle Tucker mansion built, copy of Scottish castle; **1808** Nickels-Sortwell House built; **1809** Lincoln County Jail built; **1812** Powder House built; Abiel Wood House built; **1824** second county courthouse built; **1958** Maine Art Gallery opened; **1972** Maine Yankee Nuclear Power Plant established, deactivated 1997.

Woolwich   *Sagadahoc County*   *Southern Maine, 30 mi/48 km northeast of Portland, on Kennebec River*

1638 town settled; **Feb. 2, 1651** Sir William Phips born, first American-born governor-general of Massachusetts (died 1695); **1658** sawmill established; **1675** settlement destroyed during King Philip Indian War; **c.1683** Phipps Point estate built by Sir William Phipps; **1718** Mayne's Ferry established, later becomes Day's Ferry; **1734** town resettled; **1740** town platted by Ben Johnson; **1757** Nequasset Meeting House built; **1759** town incorporated; **1777** Appleton Day House built; **1781** Tallman Academy founded; **1803** shipbuilding begins with launching of the *United States*; **1841** First Baptist Church built; **1927**

Carlton Bridge built, replaced by Sagadahoc Bridge in 2000.

York   *York County*   *Southwestern Maine, 40 mi/ 64 km southwest of Portland, on Atlantic Ocean*

1624 town founded by Plymouth Company, originally named Agamenticus; **1630** first settlers arrive; **1642** town chartered as Gorgeana in honor Sir Ferdinando Gorges, first English town chartered in America; **c.1645** McIntire Garrison House built by Alexander Maxwell, restored 1909 by John R. McIntire; **1652** town incorporated; **1658** York County (Shire) formed, Maine's first county; **1716** York becomes county seat; **1719** Old Jail built; **c.1740** John Hancock Warehouse built; **1745** Schull House built; **1747** Town Hall built; **1754** Jefferds' Tavern built; **1802** town of Alfred becomes shared county seat with York; **1811** York Cotton Factory established, Maine's first cotton mill; **Oct. 6, 1816** editor, hymn writer William Bradbury born (died 1868); **1832** Alfred becomes sole county seat.

Maryland

Eastern U.S. Capital: Annapolis. Major city: Baltimore.

Maryland was one of the 13 colonies which adopted the U.S. Declaration of Independence July 4, 1776. It became the 7th state to ratify the U.S. Constitution April 28, 1788. Maryland remained in the Union, although it was a slave state and its citizens had strong sentiments toward the Confederacy. The District of Columbia separated from Maryland and Virginia in 1801 and the city of Washington was established to become the national capital. The Virginia portion was returned in 1846.

Maryland is divided into 23 counties. Municipalities are classified as villages, towns, and cities. In 1851, the city of Baltimore separated from Baltimore County to become an independent city. There are no townships in Maryland. See Introduction.

Aberdeen   *Harford County*   *Northeastern Maryland, 28 mi/45 km northeast of Baltimore, near Chesapeake Bay*

1750 Bush Tavern built; **c.1800** town site first settled; **1810** Oakington built, home of U.S. senators Millard D. Tydings (1890–1961) and son Joseph Tydings (born 1928); **1822** Tudor Hall residence built by actor Junius Brutus Booth, father of actors Edwin and John Wilkes Booth, latter assassin of President Lincoln; **1826** Wesleyan Chapel built; **1892** incorporated as a city; **1917** Aberdeen Proving Ground established by U.S. Army for testing of ordnance materials; **Aug. 24, 1960** Cal Ripken, Jr. born, baseball shortstop for Baltimore Orioles.

Annapolis   *Anne Arundel County*   *Central Maryland, 23 mi/37 km south of Baltimore*

1649 Puritans arrive as first settlers; town of Providence founded; **1650** Anne Arundel County formed; **1655** Puritans raise ire of other Maryland inhabitants after they attempt to seize provincial government; **March 15, 1655** Gov. William Stone attempts to restore order, defeated at Herring Bay at hands of Puritans, afterward Puritans' power dwindles; **c.1660** town renamed Anne Arundel Town; becomes county seat; **1683** attempt to move provincial offices here from St. Mary's City fails due to lack of accommodations; **Dec. 1694** town renamed Annapolis; **1695** town becomes Maryland capital; **Feb. 28, 1695** first meeting of government held at home of Edward Dorsey; **1696** King William's School established; **1697** first statehouse completed, replaced 1706; **1708** incorporated as a city; **1735** Old Treasury Building built; **1737** Public Library built; **March 17, 1764** Sen. William Pinkney born, Attorney General under Pres. James Madison (died 1822); **1765** William Paca House mansion completed; **1766** city hall built; **1772** construction on third statehouse begun, completed 1795; **June 19, 1774** First Provincial Convention meets at Annapolis, sends delegates to First Continental Congress; **Oct. 19, 1774** British cargo ship *Peggy Stewart* burned in harbor, prelude to Boston Tea Party; **June 26, 1776** Provincial Gov. Robert Eden departs peacefully, returns 1783 as a visitor; **Feb. 5, 1777** First General Assembly elected under State Constitution of 1776 meets at Annapolis; **Nov. 26, 1783–June 3, 1784** Continental Congress meets at Annapolis; **Dec. 23, 1783** Gen. George Washington resigns as commander in chief of Continental army; **1784** St. John's College established; **1808** Fort Severn built after HMS *Leopard* attacks USS *Chesapeake*, with war imminent; **Aug. 16, 1817** pro-Union Cong. Henry Winter Davis born (died 1865); **Oct. 9, 1833** army officer, polar explorer James Booth Lockwood born (died 1876); **1845** U.S. Naval Academy established at Fort Severn; **1859** St. Anne's Church built; **1860** St. Mary's Roman Catholic Church completed; **Apr. 22, 1861** Federal troops occupy city; **1866** Executive Mansion completed; **July 1, 1892** crime novelist James M. Cain born (died 1977); **1899** Carvel Hall Hotel built around William Paca House, built 1763; **1903** Court of Appeals building completed; **1939** state office building built; **1952** William Preston Lane Memorial Bridge (Bay Bridge) completed across Chesapeake Bay, parallel span built 1973; **Apr. 28, 1994** 24 midshipmen expelled in cheating scandal at U.S. Naval Academy, 134 men involved; **2000** county government center completed.

Baltimore *Baltimore City* Central Maryland, 35 mi/56 km northeast of Washington, on Chesapeake Bay

1659 Baltimore County formed; **1661** site for town surveyed; **1691** first settlement occurs; **c.1706** frontiersman Christopher Gist born (died 1759); **1712** Joppatowne becomes first county seat; **1726** grist mill built at Jones Falls; **1729** town founded by enactment of Maryland Provincial Assembly, named Baltimore Town; **1745** town incorporated; **Jan. 8, 1748** Georgia Sen. William Few born (died 1828); **July 6, 1759** Revolutionary War naval officer Joshua Barney born (died 1818); **1762** Zion Lutheran Church built, rebuilt after 1840 fire; **1768** county seat moved to Baltimore Town; **Aug. 20, 1773** *Maryland Journal and Baltimore Advertiser* newspaper founded; **Dec. 1776–Feb. 1777** third location of Continental Congress during British occupation of Philadelphia; **1796** City of Baltimore incorporated; **Sept. 7, 1797** U.S. military frigate *Constellation* launched; **Sept. 17, 1800** naval officer Franklin Buchanan born, established U.S. Naval Academy (died 1874); **1811** Maryland Penitentiary established, becomes Metropolitan Transition Center 1998; **Sept. 12, 1814** British Gen. Robert Ross, after burning Washington, is killed by Maryland militia; **Sept. 13–14, 1814** while British bombard Fort McHenry for 25 hours, Francis Scott Key pens the *Star Spangled Banner*; **1818** National Road opens from Cumberland, Maryland, across Appalachians to Wheeling, (West) Virginia, boosting Baltimore's status as a port of entry; **1817** First Unitarian Church built; **1821** Basilica of the Assumption dedicated; **Nov. 16, 1823** West Virginia Sen. Henry Gassaway Davis born (died 1916); **1825** Barnum's City Hotel built, replaced by Equitable Building 1894; **1826** Maryland Institute, College of Art, established; **1827** local businessmen charter the Baltimore & Ohio Railroad to compete with the new Erie Canal in New York; **1829** Washington monument completed; **July 23, 1834** Catholic cardinal James Gibbons born (died 1921); **Jan. 3, 1840** publisher, writer Henry Holt born (died 1926); **1845** Lloyd Street Synagogue built; **1851** Baltimore City separates from Baltimore County; **1852** Loyola College in Maryland established; Camden Station of B & O Railroad built; **1854** county seat moved to Towson; Emmanuel Episcopal Church built; **Apr. 19, 1861** Massachusetts Regiment attacked by pro-Southern mob; **1867** Morgan State University established; **1868** Peabody Institute conservatory opens; **1873** College of Notre Dame of Maryland established; first Preakness Horse Race held at Pimlico Race Course; **Oct. 3, 1873** writer, etiquette expert Emily Post born (died 1960); **1874** First Presbyterian Church completed; **1875** playwright Rida Young born (died 1926); **1876** Johns Hopkins University established; B'Nai Israel Synagogue built; Baltimore Zoo founded; **Sept. 20, 1878** author Upton Sinclair born (died 1968); **Sept. 12, 1880** journalist H. L. Mencken born (died 1956); **Feb. 7, 1883** ragtime music composer Eubie Blake born (died 1983); **1885** Goucher College established, makes gradual move to Towson 1948–1954; **Aug. 10, 1885** first electric streetcar in U.S. begins service; **1886** Enoch Pratt Free Library opened; **July 3, 1886** World War II Adm. Raymond Spruance born (died 1969); **1888** Johns Hopkins Hospital opened; **1892** Strayer University established; **March 2, 1892** *Baltimore News* newspaper begins publication; **Feb. 6, 1895** baseball great George Herman "Babe" Ruth born (died 1948); **1899** Baltimore City Courthouse completed; **1900** Coppin State College established; **Feb. 7, 1904** warehouse fire spreads to more than a thousand buildings in water front and most of original 1730s town; **Nov. 11, 1904** public official Alger Hiss born, convicted spy 1950 (died 1996); **June 19, 1908** actress Mildred Natwick born (died 1994); **July 2, 1908** African-American Supreme Court Justice Thurgood Marshall born (died 1993); **1909** Walters Art Gallery opened by Henry Walters (1848–1931); **March 7, 1913** dynamite explosion in harbor, 55 killed; **Nov. 10, 1913** poet Karl Jay Shapiro born (died 2000); **Feb. 10, 1914** harmonica player Larry Adler born (died 2001); **Jan. 31, 1915** TV personality Garry Moore born (died 1993); **1922** Municipal Stadium built; **1923** Baltimore Museum of Art founded, opened 1929; **1925** University of Baltimore established; War Memorial completed; **March 30, 1930** TV actor John Astin born; **June 2, 1932** TV personality Barry Levinson born; **1933** new Enoch Pratt Library built; **Dec. 19, 1934** baseball player Al Kaline born; **Aug. 16, 1936** actress Anita Gillette born; **Dec. 30, 1937** singer Paul Stookey of Peter, Paul, and Mary born; **Dec. 21, 1940** singer Frank Zappa born (died 1993); **Feb. 6, 1944** actor Michael Tucker born; **July 4, 1944** fire destroys Oriole Park baseball stadium, team out of town; **1947** Baltimore City Community College established; **Apr. 12, 1947** author Tom Clancy born; **Nov. 18, 1947** actor Jameson Parker born; **1950** Memorial Stadium completed; Friendship International Airport completed (later renamed Baltimore-Washington International); **Oct. 17, 1950** actor Howard Rollins born; **Jan. 30, 1951** actor Charles S. Dutton born; **July 17, 1952** TV actor David Hasselhoff born; **1954** St Louis Browns baseball team moves to Baltimore, becomes Baltimore Orioles; **1957** Harbor Tunnel opened; **1958** downtown renewal project started; **May 12, 1959** Capital Airlines Viscount turbo-prop explodes killing all 32 on board; **1962** Baltimore Arena opened; **Jan. 13, 1964** *Baltimore American* and *Baltimore News-Post* merge to form *News American*; **June 3, 1965** strike at *Baltimore Sun* ends after 47 days; **May 10, 1969** Anne K. Jenkins, 22, kidnapped, released three days later after $10,000 ransom is paid; **Feb. 22, 1974** airplane hijacking attempt at Baltimore Washington Airport by Samuel Byck, kills copilot, policeman, shoots and kills himself; **1976** Maryland Science Center opened; **1979** Convention Center opened; **1980** Baltimore Blast Soccer Team established; **1981** Museum of Industry founded; **Apr. 27, 1981** former Vice Pres. Spiro Agnew ordered to repay state of Maryland $248,000 for bribes; **1983** rapid transit system opened; **1984** Colts football team moves to Indianapolis; **Nov. 24, 1985** Fort McHenry Tunnel (I-95) opened in Baltimore Harbor; **1986** National Association of Advancement of Colored People (NAACP) moves headquarters from New York; **1992** Oriole Park at

Camden Yards baseball stadium opens near harbor; **Oct. 8, 1995** Pope John Paul holds mass for 50,000 in Camden Yards Stadium; **1996** Cleveland Browns football team relocates to Baltimore, becomes Baltimore Ravens; **Apr. 15, 2001** explosives used to demolish Memorial Stadium.

Barton *Allegany County* Western Maryland, *16 mi/26 km southwest of Cumberland*

1810 coal seam exposed by heavy downpour in Potomac Hollow; **1845** coal mining begins; **1853** John and Anna Maria Creutzburg become first settlers; **1869** general store established by Henry Creutzburg, operated until 1917; **1870** Lutheran Church built, closed 1920; **1900** town incorporated; E. Frederick Creutzburg becomes first mayor; **1901** post office established; **1919** town fire destroys 20 buildings; Presbyterian Church built, replaces 1858 church destroyed in fire; **1922** Methodist Church completed, previous structure destroyed in 1919 fire.

Beantown *Charles County* Southern Maryland, *22 mi/35 km south-southeast of Washington, D.C.*

c.1830 Mudd House built; **1859** Dr. Samuel Mudd and wife move into Mudd House; **Apr. 15, 1865** Dr. Mudd sets John Wilkes Booth's broken leg morning following Booth's fatal wounding of President Lincoln at Ford's Theatre, Washington, Mudd later sentenced to life in prison at Fort Jefferson, Florida Keys, for complicity, pardoned Feb. 8, 1869.

Bel Air *Harford County* Northeastern Maryland, *22 mi/35 km northeast of Baltimore*

1634 first white settlers arrive on lands of Susquehanna peoples; **1718** Eagle Hotel built, later becomes Country Club Inn; **1731** land patent granted to Daniel Scott; **1773** Harford County formed; **1780** town platted; **1782** town becomes county seat; **Jan. 9, 1806** Gov. Augustus Bradford born, abolished slavery in Maryland (died 1881); **Nov. 18, 1833** Edwin Booth born, greatest American actor of 19th century (died 1893); **Aug. 26, 1838** actor John Wilkes Booth born, assassinated President Lincoln Apr. 14, 1865, Booth shot to death Apr. 26, 1865 [see Bel Alton]; **1859** county courthouse built; **1874** incorporated as a town; first Harford County Fair held, last held Aug. 1982; **1945** Harford County Public Library founded; **1957** Harford Community College established; **March 9, 1970** two black militants killed when dynamite explodes in their car, retaliation for H. Rap Brown trial in Bel Air, case moved to Cambridge.

Bel Alton *Charles County* Southern Maryland, *31 mi/50 km south of Washington, D.C., near Potomac River*

1662 Catholic chapel built; **1741** Father George Hunter builds St. Thomas Manor House; **1789** St. Ignatius Catholic Church built on site of chapel; **Apr. 14-22, 1865** John Wilkes Booth and accomplice hide in woods here after shooting President Lincoln, Booth shot to death Apr. 26 in Virginia; **1923** first Charles County Fair held.

Berlin *Worcester County* Southeastern Maryland, *82 mi/132 km southeast of Annapolis*

1677 land grant made creating Burleith Plantation; **1683** Buckingham Presbyterian Church organized; **Jan. 5, 1779** Commodore Stephen Decatur born (died 1820); **1790** town founded; **1814** Hammond House built; **1832** Calvin R. Taylor House built, becomes museum 1981; **1834** Burleigh Cottage built; **c.1855** Henry's Lime Kiln established; **1868** incorporated as a town; **1869** Wicomico & Pocomoke Railroad extended from Salisbury; **1895** Atlantic Hotel built; **1939** most wood pilings used to support New York World's Fair buildings shipped from Worcester County.

Bethesda *Montgomery County* Central Maryland, *5 mi/8 km northwest of Washington, D.C.*

c.1700 original Bethesda Presbyterian Church built, destroyed by fire 1847; town founded, named for church; **1848** Bethesda Church rebuilt; **1887** National Institutes of Health (N.I.H.) established; **1919** Georgetown Preparatory School moves from Georgetown, D.C., founded 1789; **1942** National Naval Medical Center dedicated, founded in Washington, D.C., 1812; **July 24, 1947** actor Robert Hays born; **Oct. 8, 1965** Pres. Lyndon B. Johnson has gall bladder removed at Bethesda Naval Hospital; **Sept. 25, 1971** Supreme Court Justice Hugo Black, 85, dies from stroke at Bethesda Hospital eight days after retiring; **1986** Museum of Medical Research founded at N.I.H.

Bladensburg *Prince George's County* Central Maryland, *5 mi/8 km northeast of Washington, D.C.*

1677 indentured servant Ninian Beall granted freedom and parcel of land in Terrapin Thicket; **1717** Beall dies at age 92, leaves holdings of thousands of acres; **1718** Presbyterian Church built; **1732** Indian Maid Tavern built, later renamed the George Washington Tavern; **1742** town chartered as Garrison's Landing, renamed later in year for Thomas Bladen, provincial governor (1742–1747); **1746** Bostwick House built; **c.1750** Ship Ballast House built of stone from ship's ballast; **Nov. 8, 1772** William Wirt born, Attorney General under President Monroe (died 1834); **1776** tobacco production reaches peak; **1795** Beall's Pleasure, residence, built by Benjamin Stoddert, first U.S. secretary of Navy; **c.1800** silting of Anacostia River caused by clear-cutting land ends town's role as river port; **Aug. 24–25, 1814** in Battle of Bladensburg, British Gen. Robert Ross defeats 5,000 U.S. troops, moves on to burn Washington; **c.1834** Baltimore & Ohio Railroad reaches town; **1854** town incorporated; **1894** 20,000 unemployed workers led by Jacob Coxey camp here on way to march on Capitol; **1925** Peace Cross erected to honor dead of World War I.

Boonsboro   *Washington County*   *Northwestern Maryland, 18 mi/29 km northwest of Frederick*

1788 settled by George and William Boone; **1792** town founded, platted by the Boones; **1810** Trinity Reformed Church built; **1811** United States Hotel opened; **July 4, 1827** citizens build Washington monument in one day; **1830s** town serves as supply point on National Road; **1831** incorporated as a town; **Sept. 11, 1862** Stonewall Jackson narrowly eludes capture on outskirts of town; **Sept. 14, 1862** Battle of South Mountain, Fitzhugh Lee's Confederate troops forced to retreat to Antietam by Union Gen. James Longstreet and Gen. Harvey Hill, 2,900 Confederate casualties, 2,340 Union casualties; **Sept. 18, 1862** Fitzhugh Lee's Confederates skirmish with Federal troops; **July 8, 1863** General Stuart's forces battle Federal troops holding town; **1868** Mount Nebo United Brethren Church built; **1935** William Boone monument erected; **1959** Mason-Dixon Dragway opened.

Bowie   *Prince George's County*   *Central Maryland, 13 mi/21 km west of Annapolis*

1708 chapel of St. Barnabas Episcopal Church built, rebuilt 1774; **1740s** original section of Belair Mansion built by Benjamin Tasker for son-in-law Gov. Samuel Ogle; **1742** Whitemarsh Catholic Church built to east, rebuilt 1856 after fire; **c.1743** Woodward Mansion built, served later as city hall; **c.1785** Fairview House built to west; **1836** Holy Trinity Church built, replacing early 1700's chapel built by Huguenots; **1870** town founded, originally named Huntington; **1872** Baltimore & Ohio Railroad reaches town; **1874** town incorporated; **1882** town renamed for Gov. Oden Bowie; **1908** Maryland Normal and Industrial School moves here from Baltimore, established 1865, later renamed Bowie State University; **1914** Bowie Race Track established, closed 1985; **1957** developer Levitt and Sons acquires Belair Estate plantations, build residential community; **1963** incorporated as a city; **1994** Railroad Station Museum opened; **1999** Radio and Television Museum opened; **Oct. 7, 2002** 13-year-old boy shot, wounded by "D.C. sniper," series of random shootings in Maryland, Virginia, D.C. Oct 3–24 [see Rockville and Frederick, Maryland].

Cambridge   *Dorchester County*   *Eastern Maryland, 36 mi/58 km southeast of Annapolis, on Chesapeake Bay*

1669 Dorchester County formed; **1684** town founded on Daniel Jones' Plantation; **1686** county seat moved from Madison; **1695** original Christ Episcopal Church built; **1750** Shoal Creek House built; **1760** Glasgow Mansion built; Meredith House built; **1760s** La Grange (Muse House) residence built; **1793** incorporated as a city; **c.1823** Harriet Tubman born in rural Dorchester County, "conductor" on Underground Railroad (died 1913); **1853** third county courthouse built; **1902** Phillips Packing Company plant founded; **May 27, 1930** writer John Barth born; **1933** Blackwater National Wildlife Refuge established to south; **1935** Harrington Bridge built

across Choptank River; **July 11, 1963** National Guard called out to calm racial unrest; accord reached July 23; **July 1967** black business district destroyed by fire during racial unrest, militant leader H. Rap Brown arrested for inciting violence; **March 11, 1970** county courthouse damaged by dynamite blast, H. Rap Brown case had been moved from Bel Air after bomb threat.

Catonsville   *Baltimore County*   *Central Maryland, 7 mi/11.3 km west of downtown Baltimore*

1720s area first settled; **1787** land developed by Richard Caton, named Catonville; Castle Thunder house built by Caton family; **1830s** town renamed Catonsville; **1844** St. Timothy's Episcopal Church built; **1845** Catonsville Military Academy established, attended by Lincoln assassin John Wilkes Booth, 1851–1852, destroyed by fire 1861; **1852** Mount de Sales Academy founded; **1884** Short Line Railroad reaches town; **1889** St. Timothy's School for girls opens; **1911** St. Charles College moved from Howard County, founded 1830; **1957** Baltimore County Community College, Catonsville Campus, established; **May 1968** "Catonsville Nine" anti-Vietnam War protests held, Daniel and Phillip Berrigan among notable participants, Selective Service records burned leading to highly publicized trial 1970.

Centreville   *Queen Anne's County*   *Eastern Maryland, 34 mi/55 km southeast of Baltimore*

1706 Queen Anne's County formed; **Apr. 15, 1741** painter, naturalist Charles Willson Peale born in rural Queen Anne's County (died 1827); **c.1744** Wright's Chance plantation home moved from original location, built 1681; **1792** town platted as Chester Mills; county seat moved from Queenstown; county courthouse completed, oldest courthouse in Maryland; **1794** incorporated as a town; **c.1794** Tucker House built; **1797** town renamed Centreville; **1835** St. Paul's Episcopal Church completed, founded 1692; **1933** Mother of Sorrows Catholic Church built.

Chaptico   *Saint Mary's County*   *Southern Maryland, 40 mi/64 km south-southeast of Washington, D.C.*

1651 tract surveyed on Wicomico River; town founded as Maryland's oldest town, named Calverton, later renamed for friendly Chaptico peoples; **1683** Chaptico Hundred (district) established; town becomes port of entry; **1692** King and Queen Episcopalian Parish (Christ Church) established; **1737** Christ Church built, used for stable during War of 1812; **1745** Capt. Gilbert Ireland, County High Sheriff, dies, buried in upright position at Christ Church graveyard.

Chesapeake City   *Cecil County*   *Northeastern Maryland, 45 mi/72 km east-northeast of Baltimore*

1661 Augustine Herman predicts canal between Delaware and Chesapeake bays; **1801** construction on Chesapeake

& Delaware Canal begins; **1813** Brantwood Mansion built; **1829** canal completed; **1837** government pumphouse built; **1849** incorporated as a town; **1919** U.S. takes jurisdiction over canal; **1927** canal deepened to sea level; lift bridge built; **July 28, 1942** tanker *Franz Klasen* collides with lift bridge, destroying bridge; **1949** suspension bridge built.

Chestertown   *Kent County   Eastern Maryland, 30 mi/48 km east-southeast of Baltimore*

1642 Kent County formed; **1696** site selected for new county seat, moved from New Yarmouth; named New Town; **1706** town platted; **1735** The Abbey (Hynson-Ringgold House) built; **c.1750** White Swan Tavern built; **1768** Emmanuel Episcopal Church built; **May 13, 1774** "tea party" held, tea thrown overboard from ship *Geddes* in protest of British tea levies; **1780** town renamed; **1782** Washington College established; **1805** incorporated as a town; **Aug. 31, 1814** in Battle of Caulk's Field to west, British forces under Sir Peter Parker repulsed twice by Americans, 14 British killed, including Parker, 28 wounded, Americans suffer only 3 wounded; **1860** county courthouse built; **1907** Chestertown Library opened; **Sept. 25, 1910** fire destroys 20 stores, 6 houses; **1917** Civil War monument erected.

Chevy Chase   *Montgomery County   Central Maryland, 6 mi/9.7 km north of Washington, D.C.*

1890s town founded by Sen. Francis Newlands; **1897** Audubon Naturalist Society founded; **1918** incorporated as a town; **July 1, 1973** Israeli Col. Yosef Alon shot to death at home, apparent retaliation for Arab slain in Paris.

Clinton   *Prince George's County   Southern Maryland, 12 mi/19 km south-southeast of Washington, D.C.*

1852 Surratt Tavern opened by Mary Surratt; town originally named Surrattsville; **Apr. 14, 1865** John Wilkes Booth believed to have stopped here for gun and ammunition after fatally wounding President Lincoln in Washington; **July 7, 1865** Mary Surratt, tavern owner, hanged for her complicity in assassination of Lincoln; town later renamed.

College Park   *Prince George's County   Central Maryland, 8 mi/12.9 km northeast of Washington, D.C.*

1745 area first settled; **1798** Rossborough Inn built, rebuilt 1888; **1856** University of Maryland established; **1888** Maryland Agricultural Research Station established; **1945** incorporated as a city; **Sept. 24, 2001** one of two tornadoes strikes University of Maryland campus, two women students killed.

Columbia   *Howard County   Central Maryland, 15 mi/24 km southwest of Baltimore*

1729 Christ Church (Episcopal) built, rebuilt 1809 after being destroyed by fire; **c.1811** Oakland mansion built; **Oct. 1963** Rouse Company announces plan to build new city midway between Baltimore and Washington comprising nine planned villages; **1966** construction begins on new city; Howard Community College established; **1967** first residents move in; **1980** unincorporated city exceeds 50,000 people, over 75,000 by year 2000.

Crisfield   *Somerset County   Southeastern Maryland, 30 mi/48 km south-southwest of Salisbury*

1640s first settlers arrive in area; **1663** first tracts surveyed for John Roach and Benjamin Summer (Somers); town of Somers Cove founded on Chesapeake Bay; **c.1800** Makepeace estate built; **1867** Somers Cove Lighthouse built, dismantled 1932; **1868** Eastern Shore Railroad reaches town; town renamed for railroad promoter John W. Crisfield; **1872** incorporated as a city; **1880s** town becomes leading oystering port; **1883** fire destroys many waterfront buildings; **1910** town among largest sailing registries in U.S.; **1928** second fire destroys part of town; **March 6–7, 1962** Ash Wednesday wind storm pushes continuous waves ashore flooding city.

Crofton   *Anne Arundel County   Central Maryland, 20 mi/32 km northeast of Washington, D.C.*

1761 Whites Hall (Whitehall) built, birthplace of Johns Hopkins; **May 19, 1795** banker, philanthropist Johns Hopkins born, founder of Johns Hopkins University and Johns Hopkins Hospital, Baltimore (died 1873); **1842** St. Stephen's Catholic Church built to east; **1893** Mount Tabor Methodist Church built to east.

Cumberland   *Allegany County   Western Maryland, 115 mi/185 km west-northwest of Baltimore*

1750 the Ohio Company establishes trading post and storehouse on North Branch Potomac River; **Nov. 1753** George Washington arrives on his westward military expedition, returns to build Fort Necessity 1754; **1786** town platted; **1789** Allegany County formed; town becomes county seat; **1811** work begins on National Road, town serves as eastern terminus; **1815** incorporated as a city; **1818** first section of National Road opens across Appalachians to Wheeling, (West) Virginia; Sts. Peter and Paul Catholic Church built; **Apr. 14, 1833** 75 buildings in business district destroyed by fire; **1842** Baltimore & Ohio Railroad reaches town; coal production begins, peaks by 1872; **1850** western section of Chesapeake & Ohio Canal opens; Emmanuel Episcopal Church built; **1872** First Presbyterian Church built; **1877** rail strike broken with arrival of Federal troops; **1879** Warren Glass Works makes first glass milk containers for New York's Echo Dairy; **May 30–31, 1889** flooding sets record of 29.2 ft/8.9 m, coincides with flood at Johnstown, Pennsylvania; **1897** First Methodist Church built; **1920** Kelly Springfield Tire plant built; **March 17, 1936** flooding inundates downtown; **July 10, 1936** highest temperature ever recorded in Maryland reached, 109°F/43°C, shared with Frederick; **1961** Allegany College of Maryland (2-year) established; **May 6, 1981** jet explodes over farm killing all 27 military crewmen; **1991** Kelly-Springfield Tire Company headquarters building converted to county government complex, built 1987; **1996** Western Correctional Institution opened.

Denton *Caroline County* *Eastern Maryland, 50 mi/ 80 km southeast of Baltimore, near Chesapeake Bay*

1730 Potter Mansion built; **c.1765** area settled, town founded on Choptank River, named Eden-Town for Sir Robert Eden, last colonial governor of Maryland; **1773** Caroline County formed, named for Eden's wife; **c.1783** town platted, renamed Denton; town of Melvill's Warehouse on Choptank River becomes county seat; **1791** county seat moved to Denton; ferry established; **1798** county courthouse completed; **1802** incorporated as a town; **1811** first bridge built across river, replaced 1875, 1913, 1981; **Feb. 7, 1817** African-American leader Frederick Douglass born at Tuckahoe Creek to west (died 1895); **c.1830** Brick Hotel built, burned 1863, rebuilt; **1850** first steamboat arrives; **1865** Freedman's Bureau built by federal government for care of emancipated slaves, used after 1870 as school for African-American boys; **Aug. 23, 1880** artist Sophie Kerr born (died 1965); **c.1895** county courthouse built.

Easton *Talbot County* *Eastern Maryland, 27 mi/ 43 km southeast of Annapolis, on Chesapeake Bay*

c.1661 Talbot County formed; **1676** Troth's Fortune residence built by William Troth; **1684** Third Haven Friends Meeting House (Quaker) completed; **1710** town of Talbot Court House founded; county courthouse completed, expanded 1794; **1749** Ratcliffe Manor house built to west; **1789** town renamed Easton; **1790** incorporated as a town; **1791** Old Market House built; **1794** Foxley Hall residence built; **1833** Fayette Gibson exhibits his reaping machine at Easton Fairgrounds, examined by Obed Hussey whose own reaper is considered the earlier invention; **1876** Trinity Cathedral built, replaced 1894; **1881** hexagonal Methodist church built, leaving "no corner for the devil"; **1884** Peachblossom Church built; **1890** Little Red Schoolhouse built.

Elkton *Cecil County* *Northeastern Maryland, 46 mi/74 km northeast of Baltimore*

1674 Cecil County formed; **1679** county court held at Ordinary Point; **1680s** George Talbot establishes system of warning signals against Native American attacks from Beacon Hill; **1681** town founded as Friendship, later renamed Head of Elk (head of Elk River navigation); **1717** court moved to Courthouse Point; **c.1750** Hollingsworth Tavern built; **1760** Gilpin Manor built; **1761** Elk Forge established; **Aug. 1777** General Howe's troops land here on way to occupation of Philadelphia; **Sept. 1777**

Washington passes through on way to Yorktown, Virginia; **1778** county seat moved to Head of Elk; **1787** incorporated as a town, renamed Elkton; **1807** area becomes major wheat market; **Apr. 1813** town attacked by British fleet under Admiral Cockburn; **1820** Holly Hall mansion built; **1834** Turkey Point Lighthouse built at Elk Neck; **1837** railroad reaches town; **1840** Creswell Hall built by A. J. Creswell, Postmaster General under President Grant; **1939** county courthouse built, addition built 1967; **1938** easy no-wait marriages abolished, was haven for couples from across Mason-Dixon Line; **Dec. 8, 1963** Pan Am 707 crashes during storm, all 82 on board killed.

Ellicott City *Howard County* *Central Maryland, 10 mi/16 km west of Baltimore*

1735 Doughoregan Manor built, completed 1745, home of Charles Carroll (1737–1832), signer of Declaration of Independence; **1772** town founded; John Ellicott House built; **c.1774** flour and grist mills built by John, Joseph, and Andrew Ellicott; settlement founded as Ellicott Mills; **1782** Jonathan Ellicott House built; **1789** George Ellicott House built; **c.1790** John Ellicott Store built; **1829** Patapsco Female Institute established on land donated by Ellicott family, opened 1837; **1830** Baltimore & Ohio Railroad reaches town; **1831** Angelo Cottage built by French artist Samuel Vaughn; **1843** county courthouse completed, originally district courthouse; **1851** Howard County formed; town becomes county seat; **1857** incorporated as a city, renamed; **1935** city incorporation reverted; **Nov. 23, 1962** crash of United Viscount turboprop kills all 17 on board; **1968** county adopts home rule.

Frederick *Frederick County* *Northwestern Maryland, 44 mi/71 km west-northwest of Baltimore*

1725 land surveyed by Benjamin Tasker, named tract Tasker's Chance; **1744** Daniel Dulany purchases part of Tasker tract; **1745** town platted by Dulany; first house built by John Thomas Schley; **1746** Evangelical Lutheran Church built, rebuilt 1762; **1748** Frederick County formed; town becomes county seat; **1764** Trinity Chapel (German Reformed) built; **Nov. 1765** county declares Stamp Act not applicable; **1775** men from county march to Boston to fight British; **1777** Hessian Barracks built; **1807** Jug Bridge built across Monocacy River, named for large stone jug built into eastern end; **1808** road improvements made in link to Cumberland (National) Road; **1815** Taney House built, home of U.S. Supreme Court Justice Roger Brooke Taney (1777–1864), authored Dred Scott decision 1857, lived in Frederick until 1823; **1817** incorporated as a town; **1828** cornerstone laid for St. John's Catholic Church; **1832** Baltimore & Ohio Railroad arrives; B & O Iron Bridge built to south; **1848** Evangelical Reformed Church built; **1862** third county courthouse built; **Sept. 4, 1862** General Lee crosses Potomac into Maryland with 50,000 troops, occupies town; **July 9, 1864** Battle of Monocacy, Confederate Gen. Jubal Early defeats Union Brig. Gen. Lew Wallace, action delays

Early's advance on Washington, allowing Union to build defenses; **1870** Maryland School for the Deaf built; **1893** Women's College of Frederick established, renamed Hood College 1912; **1934** Monocacy National Military Park established, becomes National Battlefield 1976; **1936** Artz Library opened; **July 10, 1936** highest temperature ever recorded in Maryland reached, 110°F/43°C, shared with Cumberland; **1943** Biological Warfare Laboratory established by U.S. Army Chemical Corps; **1951** incorporated as a city; **1957** Frederick Community College established; **Oct. 24, 2002** clues from shooting death in Montgomery, Alabama, leads to capture of "D.C. sniper" suspects John Allen Mohammed, 41, and John Lee Malvo, 17, at rest stop on I-70, random shooting spree began Oct. 3 in Montgomery County (Rockville), Maryland, continued at sites in Maryland, Virginia and D.C.

Frenchtown *Cecil County* *Northeastern Maryland, 45 mi/72 km northeast of Baltimore*

1806 freight line operates across land bridge of 16.5 mi/ 26.5 km from New Castle, Delaware, shortening journey to this port at head of Chesapeake Bay; **Apr. 29, 1813** port bombarded by British, destroying fishing and warehouse facilities; **June 21, 1813** the *Chesapeake*, first steamboat to ply Chesapeake Bay, docks here on maiden voyage from Baltimore; **1815** toll road opened from New Castle; **1818** stagecoach line established; **1829** Chesapeake & Delaware Canal opens; **July 4, 1831** first horse-drawn locomotive of New Castle & Frenchtown Railroad makes initial journey, line completed from New Castle 1832; **1837** new rail line built through Elkton; **1854** service suspended on NC & F Railroad; **1858** line dismantled; port facilities close; **1964** tavern burns, making old dock the sole remnant of town.

Frostburg *Allegany County* *Western Maryland, 9 mi/14.5 km west of Cumberland*

1811 National Road surveyed; **1812** Meshach Frost becomes first settler, builds tavern; town founded, named Mount Pleasant; **1820** post office established; town renamed Frostburg; coal mining begins; **1839** incorporated as a town; **1842** Baltimore & Ohio Railroad reaches town; **1846** Frost Mansion built; **1852** Cumberland & Pennsylvania Railroad arrives; **1864** brick manufacturing begins; **1870** incorporated as a city; **1898** Maryland Normal School No. 2 established, becomes Frostburg State University; **1913** Miner's Hospital founded.

Gaithersburg *Montgomery County* *Central Maryland, 17 mi/27 km northwest of Washington, D.C.*

1722 tract surveyed; **1765** Log Town founded; **1802** Benjamin Gaither settles in area; **1858** town renamed Forest Oak; **1873** Baltimore & Ohio Railroad reaches town; **1878** incorporated as a city, renamed Gaithersburg; **1884** railroad station built, used until 1982; **1889** U.S. Coast and Geodetic Survey observatory established at Observatory Hill; **1899** Gaithersburg Latitude

Observatory established to gauge earth's wobble; **1913** Edward P. Schwartz establishes peony garden of 40 varieties adjacent to train station; **1961** National Institute of Standards & Technology established; **1997** historic Forest Oak, planted 1802 on Gaither's property, knocked down in wind storm.

Germantown *Montgomery County* *Central Maryland, 23 mi/37 km northwest of Washington, D.C.*

1845 log church built at crossroads; town founded; **1864** Baptist Church built; **1883** St. Rose of Lima Catholic Church built; **1885** Methodist Episcopal Church built; **1888** Liberty Mill established by Bowman brothers, rebuilt 1914 after fire, destroyed by arson 1971; **1975** Montgomery College, Germantown Campus, (2-year) established.

Glen Echo *Montgomery County* *Central Maryland, 6 mi/9.7 km northwest of Washington, on Potomac R.*

c.1860 Cabin John Bridge built; **1889** town founded by brothers Edwin and Edward Baltzley from earnings from eggbeater factory established to market their invention; **1891** Chautauqua Assembly opens Glen Echo Park retreat; **1897** Clara Barton House built by City of Johnstown, Pennsylvania, in appreciation of Red Cross founder's assistance during 1889 Johnstown Flood, becomes headquarters of American Red Cross; **1899** Glen Echo Amusement Park opened, closed 1968; **1904** town incorporated; **1971** National Park Service Glen Echo Park reopens as arts center.

Greenbelt *Prince George's County* *Central Maryland, 10 mi/16 km northeast of Washington, D.C.*

1935 town founded by Resettlement Administration as model community for lower income households, coincides with establishment of Greendale, Wisconsin, near Milwaukee, and Greenhills, Ohio, near Cincinnati; **1937** incorporated as a city; **1939** first public swimming pool in D.C. area opened; **1964** Greenbelt Regional Park opened.

Hagerstown *Washington County* *Northwestern Maryland, 65 mi/106 km northwest of Baltimore*

1739 German immigrant Jonathan Hager arrives, receives land patent called Hager's Fancy; **1762** town platted as Elizabeth Town, named for Hager's wife, also called Hager's Town; **1774** Zion Reformed Church built; **1776** Washington County formed; Hager rides to Annapolis to persuade state to designate town as county seat; **1791** incorporated as a town; Hager Mill built; **1813** incorporated as a city; **1823** macadam road section completed on National Road from Boonsboro, initial use of new road building technique; **1829** city renamed Hagerstown; **1832** Asiatic cholera spreads through region; Dr. William D. Bell makes connection between cholera and filthy living conditions, initiates cleanup effort; **Sept. 14, 1862** General Lee's Confederate troops fight General McClellan's

Union forces, Lee drops back to Antietam Creek; **1867** Baltimore & Ohio Railroad reaches town; **1873** county courthouse completed; **1880** Mathias P. Moller opens pipe organ factory; **1901** Washington County Library founded; **1929** Maryland Correctional Institution built; **1931** Washington County Museum of Fine Arts opened; **1934** Fairchild Aircraft Company plant opened; **1935** Hagerstown Symphony Orchestra organized; **1938** city hall built; Hagerstown Airport dedicated; **1946** Hagerstown Community College established; **1980** Roxbury Correctional Institution opened.

Hancock   *Washington County   Western Maryland, 25 mi/40 km west of Hagerstown, on Potomac River*

1749 town founded, probably named for settler Joseph Hancock; **1755** Fort Tonoloway built on Potomac River following Braddock's defeat; **1762** Old Mr. Flint's Home built by Indian trader; **1835** St. Thomas Episcopal Church built, used to shelter wounded Federal soldiers 1861–1862; **1839** Chesapeake & Ohio Canal completed; **1853** town incorporated; **Aug. 1984** Sideling Hill Cut, dramatic manmade pass through ridge on Interstate 68 to west, completed after 16 months of blasting, highway itself completed Aug. 1985.

Havre de Grace   *Harford County   Northeastern Maryland, 33 mi/53 km northeast of Baltimore*

1658 site on Chesapeake Bay developed as stage stop on old Post Road, named Lower Susquehanna Ferry; **c.1760** Ferry House built; **1785** town incorporated, renamed Havre de Grace; **Oct. 1790** site narrowly defeated in consideration for nation's capital city in favor of present-day Washington; **May 3, 1813** after siege on Washington, British sack and burn town; **1827** Concord Point Lighthouse built, decommissioned 1975; **1832** St. John's Episcopal Church built, replaces earlier structure; **1840** Lock House built, later becomes Susquehanna Museum; **1912** Havre de Grace (The Grace) Race Track opened, closed 1950; **1940** highway bridge built near mouth of Susquehanna River.

La Plata   *Charles County   Southern Maryland, 26 mi/42 km south of Washington, D.C., near Potomac River*

1658 Charles County formed; Port Tobacco becomes county seat; **Aug. 6, 1866** African-American explorer Matthew Alexander Henson born, accompanied Robert E. Peary to North Pole (died 1955); **1868** Pope's Creek Railroad reaches site; town founded; **1888** town incorporated; **1895** county seat moved to La Plata; county courthouse built; **Nov. 9, 1926** tornado destroys school, 15 children killed, many injured; **1943** U.S. Army Radio Receiving Station established; **1958** Charles County Community College established; **Apr. 28, 2002** tornado strikes downtown, five killed.

Laurel   *Prince George's County   Central Maryland, 17 mi/27 km northeast of Washington, D.C.*

c.1658 land patented to Quaker Richard Snowden; **1736** Patuxent Iron Ore Company founded by heirs of Snowden; **1783** Montpelier Mansion completed by Thomas Snowden; **c.1800** town founded, named Laurel Factory; **1811** grist mill built; **1824** cotton mill established by Nicholas Snowden; **1870** incorporated as a city; **1875** town renamed Laurel; **1884** Railroad Station built; **1887** David J. Weems offers express service between Baltimore and Washington using electric trains; **1911** last of cotton mills abandoned; Laurel Race Track established; **May 15, 1972** Alabama Gov. George Wallace, on presidential campaign tour, shot four times by Arthur Bremer, paralyzed from waist down.

Leonardtown   *Saint Mary's County   Southern Maryland, 48 mi/77 km southeast of Washington, D.C.*

1637 St. Mary's County formed; **1654** county seat moved from St. Mary's City to Newton, site near present day Leonardtown; **1708** town platted on Potomac River as Seymour Town; **1710** county seat moved from Newton; **1728** town renamed in honor of Leonard Calvert, fourth Lord Baltimore; **c.1765** Mulberry Fields manor built by William Somerville, burned 1831; **1780** Tudor Hall residence built; **1858** incorporated as a town; **1876** Town Jail built, later becomes County Historical Society Museum; **1885** St. Mary's Academy established; **1930** county courthouse built.

Lewistown   *Frederick County   Northwestern Maryland, 8 mi/12.9 km north of Frederick*

c.1745 area first settled; **c.1775** Richfield house built by Thomas Johnson; **1780s** Hessian soldiers, captured during Revolutionary War, settle in area; **1800** ministers meet at Peter Kemp House to organize United Brethren in Christ denomination; **1815** town platted by Daniel Fundenburg; **Oct. 9, 1839** Winfield Scott Schley born in Richfield House, Navy commander during Spanish-American War (died 1909); **1848** Cog's Covered Bridge built, restored 1994; **c.1856** Roddy Covered Bridge built on Ownes Creek; **1930s** state fish hatchery established.

Lexington Park   *Saint Mary's County   Southern Maryland, 55 mi/89 km southeast of Washington, D.C.*

1634 mission established by Jesuit priests; **1641** mission reclaimed by Lord Baltimore; **1648** Long Lane Farm house built; **1654** Susquehanna House built; **1894** Cedar Point Lighthouse built; **1942** Patuxent River Naval Air Station established; **1950** town renamed Lexington Park, originally Jarboesville, named for French pioneer John Jarboe.

Lusby   *Calvert County   See **Prince Frederick** (1975)

Marshall Hall *Charles County* *Southern Maryland, 15 mi/24 km south of Washington, D.C.*

1690 land grant on Potomac River given to William Marshall; **c.1730** Marshall Hall house built by Thomas Marshall, historic structure destroyed by arsonists Oct. 17, 1981; **1931** Marshall Hall historical marker erected; **1949** slot machines authorized by county; Pot of Gold Casino opened; **1968** slot machines abolished; casino closed.

Middletown *Frederick County* *West central Maryland, 7 mi/11.3 km west of Frederick*

1767 town founded; **1782** Fox's Tavern built; **1783** Zion Lutheran Church built, new structure built 1860; **1819** Christ Reformed Church built; **1833** incorporated as a town; **1844** *Valley Register* newspaper founded; **Sept. 14, 1862** Battle of South Mountain fought on General Lee's invasion of Maryland, forced to retreat by McClellan's Union troops, 1,831 killed on Federal side, similar loss for Confederates; **1881** Little Stone Church built at South Mountain.

Morningside *Prince George's County* *Central Maryland, 10 mi/16 km southeast of Washington, D.C.*

c.1800 Forest Grove Methodist Church built; **1938** town founded by developers Morgan Wayson and Randolph Hopkins; **1941** Camp Springs Army Airfield established to south; **1945** base becomes Andrews Air Force Base; **1949** incorporated as a town; **Apr. 9, 1951** pilotless B-25 bomber crashes into house, three killed on ground.

Mount Savage *Allegany County* *Western Maryland, 7 mi/11.3 km northwest of Cumberland*

c.1835 coal and iron deposits discovered nearby; **1839** Irish laborers arrive to work in iron rolling mill; **1841** fire brick plant of Union Mining Company established, headed in 1880s by James Roosevelt, father of Franklin D. Roosevelt; **1844** first solid-track rails in America produced here; **c.1848** ironworks closed.

New Carrollton *Prince George's County* *Central Maryland, 9 mi/14.5 km northeast of Washington, D.C.*

1927 land purchased by Edward L. Mahoney; **1939** Mahoney converts horse track into midget car racing circuit; **1953** incorporated as a city; **1957** Mahoney dies, estate purchased by developer Albert Turner, named Carrollton for Charles Carroll, signer of Declaration of Independence; **1966** post office established; city renamed New Carrollton to overcome confusion with town of same name in Carroll County.

North East *Cecil County* *Northeastern Maryland, 42 mi/68 km northeast of Baltimore*

c.1700 area first settled; **1711** Mill House built; **1742** St. Anne's Episcopal Church built; **1780** Green Hill house built by Thomas Russell of Principio Company; **1850** incorporated as a town; **1860** Gilpin's Falls Covered Bridge built; **1876** Day Basket Company established by the Day brothers; **1938** Sandy Cove Yacht Club founded; **1968** Cecil Community College established; **1986** North East State Park established.

North Point *Baltimore County* *Northeastern Maryland, 8 mi/14.9 km southeast of Baltimore*

1664 first property deed in Baltimore County granted for Todd's Inheritance; **Sept. 12, 1814** in Battle of North Point, Maryland militia under Gen. John Stricker attack British, thwarting their intention to take Baltimore, British Gen. Robert Ross is killed, British retreat; **1896** Fort Howard military base established, named for Col. John Howard, Revolutionary hero; **1906** Bay Shore Amusement Park established, closed 1947; **1940** Fort Howard converted to Veterans Hospital; **1986** North Point State Park established at former amusement park site.

Oakland *Garrett County* *Western Maryland, 35 mi/56 km southwest of Cumberland*

1755 Braddock's Trail built; **1806** William Armstrong becomes first settler, builds cabin at ford in Youghiogheny River; **1847** Baltimore & Ohio Railroad built; **1849** town platted; **1862** incorporated as a town; **1868** St. Matthew's Episcopal Church built; **1872** Garrett County formed; town becomes county seat; **1906** county courthouse built; **Jan. 13, 1912** lowest temperature ever recorded in Maryland reached, −40°F/−40°C.

Ocean City *Worcester County* *Southeastern Maryland, 88 mi/142 km southeast of Annapolis*

1790 U.S. Coast Guard Station established; **c.1870** first railroad arrives; **1872** town platted on Atlantic sand barrier; **1875** Atlantic Hotel built; town founded; **1876** Wicomico & Pocomoke Railroad reaches town; **1880** incorporated as a town; **1891** Ocean Life Saving Station built; **1933** storm destroys railroad bridge ending direct rail service to resort town; **1970** Ocean City Convention Center opened, renamed Roland E. Powell Convention Center 1997.

Oldtown *Allegany County* *Western Maryland, 12 mi/19 km southeast of Cumberland*

1729 Englishman Thomas Cresap applies for land Maryland patent in what is now York County, Pennsylvania, leading to 24-year boundary conflict; **1736** Cresap is captured, his house burned by Pennsylvanians, released year later; **1741** Cresap's Fort built on North Branch Potomac River; town founded; **1750** courts resolve boundary dispute in Pennsylvania's favor; **1765** Michael Cresap House built; **1832** Chesapeake & Ohio Canal opened, includes Paw Paw Tunnel, 3,118 ft/950 m long, under Anthony Ridge, bypassing 6-mile/9.7-km river section; **Aug. 1864** Confederate forces repulse

Federal forces on approach to Potomac Ford, clearing escape route into Virginia.

Perryville   Cecil County   Northeastern Maryland, 34 mi/55 km northeast of Baltimore, on Chesapeake Bay

1608 Capt. John Smith explores Susquehanna River; **1622** Edward Palmer establishes trading post on Garrett Island in Susquehanna River; **1658** John Bateman becomes first permanent settler; **c.1695** town founded, originally named Lower Ferry; **1779** Rodgers Tavern established by Capt. John Rodgers; **1882** incorporated as a town, renamed for Mary Perry, wife of John Bateman; **1919** Perry Point Hospital (Veterans Administration) opened; **1940** highway bridge built across Susquehanna, near its mouth; **2001** Town Museum founded through efforts of Barbara Brown.

Pikesville   Baltimore County   Northern Maryland, 8 mi/12.9 km northwest of downtown Baltimore

1698 Garrison Fort built; **1700** Grey Rock house built, birthplace (1752) of John Eager Howard, governor, U.S. senator (died 1827); **c.1770** area settled; **1815** town named for Brig. Gen. Zebulon Pike of New Jersey, killed in Battle of York, Canada; **1819** U.S. Arsenal established; **1835** Mettam Memorial Baptist Church built, dedicated by Rev. Joseph Mettam; **1853** Dumbarton house built by merchant Noah Walker; **1888** Maryland Line Confederate Soldiers' Home founded at arsenal site, remaining veterans removed to private homes 1932, buildings sold to county; **1903** Queen Victoria monument erected in Druid Ridge Cemetery, only monument to her in U.S.

Piney Point   Saint Mary's County   Southern Maryland, 60 mi/97 km southeast of Washington, D.C.

1642 Poplar Hill Anglican Church built; **1730** St. George's Church built near site of old Poplar Hill Church; **1740** Porto Bello house built by William Hebb; **1835** town becomes favored summer resort for Washington dignitaries, through c.1853; Piney Point Lighthouse built, deactivated 1964; **1933** hurricane destroys landmarks, including cabin used as Pres. James Monroe's summer White House; **Sept. 19, 1949** test explosion on U-1105 captured German submarine in Potomac River estuary, wreck rediscovered June 29, 1985, designated state historic shipwreck 1994.

Port Deposit   Cecil County   Northeastern Maryland, 34 mi/55 km northeast of Baltimore, on Susquehanna River

1606 Capt. John Smith reaches falls, later named Smith's Falls; **1700** Creswell family acquires tract named Anchor and Hope Farm; **1729** Col. Thomas Cresap establishes Creswell's Ferry; **1808** Susquehanna Canal completed (closed 1890s); town founded, named for its role as commerce transfer point; **1812** Physick House built;

1824 incorporated as a town; **1849** iron foundry established; **1894** Washington Hall, Tome Institute, built (closed 1941); **1928** Conowingo Dam completed to north on Susquehanna River; **1942** Bainbridge Naval Training Center established (closed 1976); **May 30, 1947** Eastern Airlines DC-4 crashes killing 53.

Port Tobacco   Charles County   Southern Maryland, 27 mi/43 km south of Washington, D.C., on Potomac River

1606 Capt. John Smith visits Native American village of Potopaco; **c.1650** John Chandler becomes first settler; village founded, originally named Chandler's Town, later renamed Charlestown; **1658** Charles County formed; town becomes county seat; **1660s** St. Ignatius Catholic Church founded by Jesuit Father Andrew White, present church built 1798; **1758** La Grange house built by Scottish Dr. James Craik (1730–1814); **1771** Habre de Venture mansion built by Thomas Stone, signer of Declaration of Independence; **1775** Dr. Craik establishes smallpox hospital, inoculates many of town's residents; **1888** incorporated as a village; **1892** town renamed Port Tobacco; courthouse destroyed by fire; **1895** county seat moved to La Plata; **Nov. 10, 1978** Thomas Stone National Historic Site authorized.

Prince Frederick   Calvert County   Southern Maryland, 30 mi/48 km south of Annapolis

1654 Calvert County formed; Lusby becomes first county seat; **1722** town founded, originally named Williams Oil Fields; county seat moved from Lusby; **1725** town renamed; **Nov. 4, 1732** Supreme Court Justice Thomas Johnson born in rural Calvert County, first governor of Maryland (died 1819); **March 17, 1777** Chief Supreme Court Justice Roger Brooke Taney born in rural Calvert County (died 1864); **1788** Margaret Mackall Smith Taylor born in rural Calvert County, wife of Pres. Zachary Taylor, married 1810, died 1852; **1814** town burned by British forces during War of 1812; **1882** fire sweeps through entire town; **1915** county courthouse built, remodeled 1948; **1975** Calvert Cliffs Nuclear Power Plant opened near Lusby to southeast.

Princess Anne   Somerset County   Southeastern Maryland, 12 mi/19 km south-southwest of Salisbury

1666 Somerset County organized; **1733** town platted, named Princess Anne Town for daughter of King George II; **1742** town becomes first permanent county seat; **1744** Washington Hotel built; **1765** Manokin Presbyterian Church built; **1767** Washington Academy founded, closed 1865; **1801** original section of Teackle Mansion built; **1838** Washington Hotel built; **1842** Boxwood Gardens founded; **1867** town incorporated; **1886** Princess Anne College established, becomes University of Maryland Eastern Shore; Metropolitan United Methodist Church built, replaces 1756 structure; **1896** St. Andrew's Episcopal Church built, replaces 1767 structure; **1904**

third county courthouse built; **1910** Princess Anne Public Library opened; **1987** Eastern Correctional Institution (Westover) opened to south.

Reisterstown *Baltimore County* *Northern Maryland, 17 mi/27 km northwest of Baltimore*

1758 German immigrant John Reister acquires property here, names tract Reister's Desire; settlement develops mainly of Reister extended family members; **1765** log cabin built, used for Lutheran services; **1768** German immigrant Daniel Bower and family joins Reisters; **1770** Bower Inn built; Chatsworth House built by Daniel Bower; **1779** Polly Reister House built; **1804** Yellow Tavern built; **1820** Franklin Academy established; **1831** Maryland House of Refuge founded, became Montrose School for Girls 1918; **1832** Hannah Moore Academy opens.

Rockville *Montgomery County* *Central Maryland, 13 mi/21 km northwest of Washington, D.C.*

1700 trading post established; **c.1700** settlement founded around Hungerford's Tavern, town's original name; **c.1770** Tusculum Academy established (closed 1781); **1774** citizens meet at tavern to pass resolutions against continued trade with British; **1776** Montgomery County formed, named for Gen. Richard Montgomery, killed in battle at Quebec; **1777** town becomes county seat, renamed Montgomery Court House, later renamed Williamsburg; **1803** town resurveyed, renamed Rockville; **1808** Loughborough Place house built; **1860** incorporated as a city; **July 1864** Confederate Gen. Jubal Early's forces pass through on way to attack on Washington; **1965** Montgomery College, Rockville Campus, (2-year) established; **1982** County Judicial Center built; **Oct 3, 2002** "D.C. sniper" series of random shootings in Maryland, Virginia and D.C. begins with 6 shootings in Montgomery County, 5 killed, 1 injured same day, 7th shooting in D.C., total 13 shot, 10 killed before suspects apprehended at Frederick Oct. 24.

Saint Mary's City *Saint Mary's County* *Southern Maryland, 60 mi/97 km southeast of Washington, D.C.*

March 25, 1634 after stopping at St. Clements Island Nov. 22, 1633, English ships *Ark* and *Dove* sail up St. Mary's River (then St. George's River), purchase village from Piscataways; **1637** St. Mary's County formed; town becomes county seat; **1647** Smith's Town House built, site of 1662 provincial legislative meetings; **1654** county seat moved to Newton; **1667** town incorporated; **1676** town becomes Maryland's first colonial capital; first statehouse built; **1694** capital moved to Ann Arundel Town (Annapolis); **1708** county seat moved to Leonardtown; **1829** Trinity Episcopal Church built using bricks from first statehouse; **1840** St. Mary's College of Maryland established as St. Mary's Seminary; **1934** replica of St. Mary's Statehouse built.

Saint Michaels *Talbot County* *Eastern Maryland, 20 mi/32 km southeast of Annapolis, on Chesapeake Bay*

c.1637 town founded; **1677** Christ Episcopal Church of St. Michael's founded; **1778** town platted by James Braddock; **1781** armed barge *Experiment* refitted to protect bay against British; **1804** incorporated as a town; **Aug. 10, 1813** British bombard town, damage averted with lights-out measure, lit lanterns hung in trees lead adversary to overshoot town; **Feb. 3, 1819** poet Amelia Ball Coppuck born (died 1852); **1820s** seafood replaces shipbuilding as chief industry; **1878** St. Michael's Church built on original site; **1879** Hooper Strait Lighthouse built, decommissioned 1966; **1963** Chesapeake Bay Maritime Museum founded at lighthouse.

Salisbury *Wicomico County* *Southeastern Maryland, 65 mi/105 km southeast of Annapolis*

1732 land patent awarded to William Winder, a minor; town platted; **1741** Col. Isaac Handy of Maryland militia builds Pemberton Hall residence, served as rendezvous for Confederate troops during Civil War; **1795** Poplar Hill Mansion built by Maj. Levin Landy; **1854** incorporated as a city; **1860** Pennsylvania Railroad reaches town; fire devastates town; **1861–1865** Federal troops stationed here during Civil War; **1867** Wicomico County formed; town becomes county seat; **1868** Wicomico & Pocomoke Railroad built eastward to Berlin; **1878** county courthouse completed, addition built 1981; **1886** fire again sweeps through town; **1923** Bethesda Methodist Church built; **1925** State Normal School established, becomes Salisbury University; **1953** Art Institute and Gallery established; **Sept. 26, 1956** actress Linda Hamilton born; **1976** Wor-Wic (Worcester-Wicomico) Community College established.

Sharpsburg *Washington County* *Northwestern Maryland, 13 mi/21 km south of Hagerstown*

1730–1736 Catawbas slaughter Delawares near mouth of Antietam Creek; **1763** town founded by Joseph Chapline, named for Gov. Horatio Sharpe; **1765** Antietam Iron Works founded by Chapline; **1800** Mount Airy mansion built; **1813** Ferry Hill house built by Col. John Blackford; **1832** Chesapeake & Ohio Canal opened; town incorporated; **Sept. 17, 1862** Battle of Antietam, General Lee's Confederates invade Maryland, Federal troops under General McClellan attack Lee's forces at Antietam Creek, forcing Lee to withdraw across Potomac, bloodiest day in U.S. history with 12,410 Federals, 10,700 Confederates casualties; Antietam National Cemetery established; **1880** ironworks closed; **Aug. 30, 1890** Antietam National Battlefield established.

Snow Hill *Worcester County* *Southeastern Maryland, 17 mi/27 km southeast of Salisbury*

1666 Somerset County formed; **1686** town founded as county seat; **1742** Worcester County separates from

MARYLAND

Somerset County; town becomes county seat; Somerset County seat moved to Princess Anne; **1755** All Hallows Episcopal Church built; **1812** incorporated as a town; **1832** Nassawango Iron Furnace established to northwest, abandoned 1847; **1834** fire destroys part of town; Union Academy opened; **1869** *Democratic Messenger* newspaper founded; **1890** new Makemie Memorial Presbyterian church built; **1892** Catholic church built; **1893** fire damages town; **1894** county courthouse built; **Oct. 27, 1933** black man Euel Lee hanged for murder of white family of four Oct. 1931.

Suitland   *Prince George's County*   *Central Maryland, 6 mi/9.7 km southeast of Washington, D.C.*

1867 land purchased by Samuel Taylor Suit; **1880s** distillery established by Suit; town founded; **1941** Suitland Federal Complex established; **1956** National Weather Bureau located here; **1962** U.S. Naval Oceanographic Office founded, moved to Stennis Space Center, Mississippi, 1976; **May 4, 1972** bus rolls over on rain slick highway killing 5, injuring 37; **1976** National Ice Center formed by NOAA and U.S. Navy for study of world ice cap and ocean levels.

Takoma Park   *Montgomery County*   *Central Maryland, 6 mi/9.7 km north of Washington, D.C.*

1873 trolley service begins, abandoned 1922; **1883** town founded on Baltimore & Ohio Railroad by Benjamin Franklin Gilbert, originally named Brightwood; **1890** incorporated as a city, renamed Takoma Park; **1890s** Seventh Day Adventist church establishes headquarters here; **1892** Watkins Hotel opened; **Dec. 1893** fire destroys business district, including Watkins Hotel; **1898** Washington Sanitarium built; **1904** Columbia Union College established; **1939** Gilbert Memorial dedicated; **1946** Montgomery College, Takoma Park Campus, (2-year) established; **July 1, 1997** boundary with Prince George's County adjusted to allow town to be entirely within Montgomery County.

Thurmont   *Frederick County*   *Northwestern Maryland, 15 mi/24 km north of Frederick*

1751 Jacob Weller becomes first settler; town of Mechanicstown founded; **1831** incorporated as a town; **1850** Utica Covered Bridge built, moved 1889; **c.1855** Loy's Station Covered Bridge built; **1856** Roddy Road Covered Bridge built; **1857** Eyler Valley Chapel built; **1894** town renamed Thurmont; **1942** Camp David, U.S. presidential retreat, established in Catoctin Mountain Park to west, originally called Shangri-La; **Sept. 5–17,**

1978 Camp David Accord reached between Israel's Menachem Begin and Egypt's Anwar Sadat, host and mediator Pres. Jimmy Carter.

Towson   *Baltimore County*   *Northern Maryland, 7 mi/11.3 km north of downtown Baltimore*

1659 Baltimore County formed; **1712** Joppatowne becomes first county seat; **1750** William and Thomas Towson arrive from Pennsylvania; **1768** town founded by Ezekiel Towson; county seat moved to Baltimore; **1839** Epsom Chapel built; **1851** Baltimore City separates from Baltimore County; **1854** county seat moved to Towson; **1860** Trinity Episcopal Church dedicated; **1864** Jericho Covered Bridge built; **1866** Maryland State Teachers' College established, becomes Towson University; **1891** Sheppard Asylum opened, becomes Sheppard-Pratt Hospital; **1899** Eudowood Sanatorium moved from Baltimore; **1909** St. Vincent's Orphanage built, founded in Baltimore 1840; **1948** Goucher College, founded 1885, begins gradual move from Baltimore to new campus through 1954; **1956** county adopts home rule; **Aug. 1–2, 1971** flash flooding in Baltimore County leaves 13 dead; **1974** county courthouse built.

Upper Marlboro   *Prince George's County*   *Central Maryland, 17 mi/27 km east-southeast of Washington*

1695 Prince George's County formed; Charlestown (Croom) becomes first county seat; **1706** town platted; **1721** county seat moved to Upper Marlboro; **July 22, 1730** Continental Congress member Daniel Carroll born, signer of U.S. Constitution (died 1796); Old Marlboro House built; **Jan. 8, 1735** John Carroll born, first Catholic bishop and archbishop in U.S. (died 1815); **1870** incorporated as a town; **1881** county courthouse built.

Westminster   *Carroll County*   *Northern Maryland, 28 mi/45 km northwest of Baltimore*

1755 Old Meeting House (Quaker) built; **1764** town platted, named Winchester for founder William Winchester; **1768** town renamed Westminster to avoid confusion with nearby Winchester, Virginia; **1795** Shriver Mill opens; **1818** incorporated as a city; **1837** Carroll County formed; town becomes county seat; county courthouse built; **1844** Church of the Ascension built; **1861** Western Maryland Railroad arrives; **1867** Western Maryland College established; **1882** Westminster Theological Seminary established; **Nov. 9, 1915** public official R. (Robert) Sargent Shriver born, first Peace Corps director; **1976** Carroll Community College established, campus built 1993.

Massachusetts

Northeastern U.S. One of the six New England states. Capital and largest city: Boston.

Massachusetts was one of the 13 colonies which adopted the U.S. Declaration of Independence July 4, 1776. It became the 6th state to ratify the U.S. Constitution February 6, 1788. In 1820, the state of Maine separated from Massachusetts.

Massachusetts is divided into 14 counties. The counties are divided into townships, called towns, which have very strong governments. Within the towns are villages which have no government of their own. The governments of Massachusetts' counties are in the process of being abolished in favor of the town, or township, governments. The municipalities are classified as cities, which are formed from one or more former towns. See Introduction.

Abington *Plymouth County   Southeastern Massachusetts, 18 mi/29 km south-southeast of Boston*

1668 town settled; **c.1695** Shedd House built; **1712** town incorporated; **c.1815** James Reed invents machine capable of making up to 250,000 tacks per day; **1846** meetings held at Island Grove promoting abolition of slavery, continue through 1865; **1909** Memorial Boulder placed in Island Grove Park commemorating efforts of local abolitionists; **June 10, 1912** Memorial Arch dedicated, honors war dead; **1932** Abington Public Library founded.

Adams *Berkshire County   Western Massachusetts, 42 mi/68 km northwest of Springfield*

1762 town first settled by Quakers; **1778** town incorporated, named for Samuel Adams; Old Brown House built by Eleazar Brown; **1786** Friends' Meeting House built, served Quakers until 1850; **1790** Samuel Jenks House built; **Apr. 12, 1796** Gov., U.S. Cong. George D. Briggs born (died 1861); **1817** birthplace home of Susan B. Anthony built; **Feb. 15, 1820** suffragette Susan B. Anthony born (died 1906); **1822** lumber mill built; **1868** First Congregational Church built; **1887** Notre Dame Catholic Church built; **1897** St. Thomas Aquinas Catholic Church built; **1897** Adams Free Library built; **1903** McKinley Statue erected; **1930** Miss Adams' Diner established, prefab diner erected 1949.

Amesbury *Essex County   Northeastern Massachusetts, 35 mi/56 km north-northeast of Boston*

1654 town settled; Macy-Colby House built, Thomas Macy exiled 1655 for offering shelter to Quakers during rain storm; **c.1660** Challis Hill Farmhouse built; **1668** town incorporated; **1693** Susanna (Goody) Martin convicted of witchcraft, hanged at Salem; **Nov. 21, 1729** patriot Josiah Bartlett born (died 1795); **c.1775** shipbuilding begins; **1777** John Paul Jones' ship *Alliance* built; **1785** Rocky Hill Meeting House built; **1792** Essex-Merrimack Covered Bridge built, demolished 1882; **1812** first mill built at Powow River falls; **1838** Isaac Martin begins hat manufacturing; **1841** William Osgood Sawmill built at falls; **1850** shipbuilding ends with advent of steamships; **1852** Amesbury Public Library founded, built 1900; **1856** carriage manufacturing begins; **1869** Christian Science founder Mary Baker Eddy writes "Comments on the Scriptures" here; **1880** Hamilton Woolen Company founded.

Amherst *Hampshire County   West central Massachusetts, 18 mi/29 km north of Springfield*

1703 town settled; **1744** Strong House built; **1767** Captain Lombard House built; **1775** town incorporated; **May 24, 1795** New York Sen. Silas Wright born (died 1847); **1813** Dickinson Homestead built; **1814** Amherst Academy founded, closed 1868; **1821** Amherst College established; **Oct. 15, 1830** author Helen Hunt Jackson born (died 1885); **Dec. 10, 1830** poet Emily Dickinson born (died 1886); **1834** improved wool-milling process applied to two local mills; **1835** First Baptist Church built, used as town and county building after 1957; **1839** Eugene Field House built, poet's boyhood home; **1853** Amherst & Belchertown Railroad arrives, station completed; **1857** Amherst Ornamental Tree Association founded; **1863** University of Massachusetts, Amherst Campus, established as Massachusetts

Agricultural College; **1866** Grace Episcopal Church built; **1867** First Congregational Church built; **July 27, 1870** chemist Bertram Boltwood born (died 1927); **1875** Robert Frost House built, poet lived here 1931–1938; **1890** town hall completed; **1894** Unitarian Church built; **1899** Amherst History Museum founded at historic Strong House; **June 26, 1901** Missouri Sen. Stuart Symington born (died 1988); **Jan 17, 1904** sculptor Sidney Waugh born (died 1963); **1907** Hope A.M.E. Church built; **1919** Jones Public Library founded, built 1928; **1924** St. Brigid's Catholic Church completed; **1926** Post Office built; **1965** Hampshire College established.

Andover   *Essex County*   *Northeastern Massachusetts, 21 mi/34 km north of Boston*

1642 first white settlers arrive; **1643** John Woodbridge purchases land from Native Americans for £6 and a coat; **1646** town incorporated; **1652** most of town's citizens become involved in witch hunt; **1680** Isaac Abbot Tavern built; **1685** Benjamin Abbott Homestead built; **1778** Phillips Andover Academy for boys, oldest incorporated school in U.S., established by Samuel Phillips; **1819** Amos Blanchard House built; **1828** Stowe House built; **1829** Abbott Academy founded; **1852** author Harriet Beecher Stowe arrives, remains until 1863, becomes central to abolitionist movement; **Jan. 6, 1853** Benjamin Pierce, 11, youngest son and only surviving child of three of President-elect Franklin Pierce, killed in train accident days before inauguration; **1872** Memorial Hall Library founded; **1907** John Esther Art Gallery established; **1917** Sts. Constantine and Helen Greek Orthodox Church founded; **1931** Addison Gallery of American Art established; **1957** Temple Emanuel built; **1961** St. Robert Bellarmine Catholic Church completed.

Aquinnah   *Dukes County*   *Southeastern Massachusetts, 21 mi/34 km south-southeast of New Bedford*

1004 visit to Martha's Vineyard island by Viking explorer Leif Ericson supported by date found on rock; **1669** area settled; **1711** Society for Propagating the Gospel purchases Gay Head lands for use of its native peoples; **1799** Gay Head Light built, rebuilt 1856, automated 1960; **1870** Town of Gay Head incorporated; **1998** town renamed Aquinnah, only remaining town in Massachusetts with substantial Native American population.

Arlington   *Middlesex County*   *Eastern Massachusetts, 6 mi/9.7 km northwest of Boston*

1630 town settled; **1652** John Adams House built; **1693** Abraham Hill House built, all five of Zachariah Hill's sons born here, joined Minutemen's cause at Concord on Apr. 19, 1775; **1740** Jason Russell House built; **Apr. 18, 1775** Safety and Supply Committee of Continental Congress meets at Black Horse Tavern; **Apr. 19, 1775** Mother Batherick captures six British grenadiers during bloody day of fighting, marches them to prison; **Sept. 13, 1766** merchant Samuel Wilson born, the original "Uncle Sam"

(died 1854); **1799** town's industrial development begins with establishment of Whittemore and Company, manufacturer of cotton and wool cards; **1800** Whittemore-Robbins Mansion completed; **1807** Arlington Historical Society founded; **1846** railroad built from Cambridge; **1850** Wood Ice Tool Company established, manufactures tools for cutting and export of natural ice; **1862** Whittemore factory destroyed by fire; **1864** Old Schwab Mill built; **1867** town incorporated; **1892** Arlington Library opens; **1914** town hall built; **1916** St. Ann's Chapel completed; **1931** Addison Gallery of American Art opened.

Ashfield   *Franklin County*   *Western Massachusetts, 31 mi/50 km north-northwest of Springfield*

1743 F. G. Howes becomes first settler; grist mill built; **1755** area abandoned during Native American hostilities; **1761** Baptist Church founded; **1763** Congregational Church established; **1765** town incorporated; **1814** town hall built; post office established; **1816** Sanderson Academy established, building built 1888; **1829** Episcopal Church built; **1835** Northampton Silk Company founded; **1846** Connecticut Railroad reaches town; **1879** first annual Ashfield Dinner held, continued until 1903; **Apr. 12, 1881** movie producer Cecil B. De Mille born (died 1959).

Attleboro   *Bristol County*   *Southeastern Massachusetts, 30 mi/48 km south-southwest of Boston*

1634 town settled by reclusive Englishman William Blackstone; **1694** town incorporated; **1706** Peck Homestead built; **1780** jewelry manufacturing begins; **1865** Attleboro Library founded, built 1907; **1914** incorporated as a city; **Nov. 6, 1916** chorus director Ray Conniff born (died 2002); **1929** Center for the Arts founded, new facility opened 1994.

Barnstable   *Barnstable County*   *Southeastern Massachusetts, 55 mi/89 km southeast of Boston*

1637 town settled; **1639** town incorporated; **1640** Coach House built; **1645** Sturgis Library founded; **1685** Barnstable County formed; town becomes county seat; **1700** codfish trading station founded; **Feb. 2, 1725** political leader James Otis born (died 1783); **Sept. 25, 1728** author Mercy Otis born (died 1814); **1832** county courthouse built.

Bedford   *Middlesex County*   *Eastern Massachusetts, 15 mi/24 km northwest of Boston*

1639 at Twin Brothers Boulders on Concord River, Governor Winthrop and Assistant Governor Dudley meet to settle local boundary disputes; **1640** Shawseen House established as trading post; town settled; **1660** Lane House built; **1664** Old Garrison House built, used as stronghold in 1775; **1687** Page House built; **1729** town incorporated; **1790** Stearns House built, home of author William Stearns Davis; **1846** Lexington & West

Cambridge Railroad reaches town; **1856** Dr. William R. Hayden builds hotel, patent medicine factory at Bedford Springs; **1876** Bedford Free Library founded, built 1952, new library opened 1967; **1929** U.S. Veterans Hospital opens; St. Therese de Lisieux Convent and Maryvale Seminary opened; **July 13, 1970** race riots leave three dead, three injured.

Beverly *Essex County* *Northeastern Massachusetts, 16 mi/26 km northeast of Boston, on Atlantic Ocean*

c.1626 town settled; **1656** First Church built; **1668** town incorporated; **1690** Old Woodbury Tavern built; **1693** Mistress Hale, wife of respectable minister, accused of witchcraft, case later dismissed; **1775–1776** site used as naval base by George Washington, considered birthplace of U.S. Navy; **1855** Beverly Public Library founded, built 1913; **May 12, 1855** poet George Edward Woodberry born (died 1930); **1894** incorporated as a city; **1903** United Shoe factory ("The Shoe") established; **1939** Endicott College established.

Boston *Suffolk County* *Eastern Massachusetts, on Massachusetts Bay, Atlantic Ocean*

1625 first settlers arrive; **1630** town founded by John Winthrop's Puritans; **Sept. 30, 1631** judge William Stoughton born, oversaw Salem witchcraft trials (died 1701); **1634** Boston Commons created, first public park in Colonies; **Sept. 16, 1637** colonial leader Elisha Cooke born (died 1715); **June 21, 1631** Presbyterian leader Increase Mather born in Dorchester (died 1723); **1643** Suffolk County formed; town becomes county seat; **Apr. 5, 1649** philanthropist Elihu Yale born (died 1721); **1653** first library in Colonies opened; **Feb. 12, 1663** theologian Cotton Mather born (died 1728); **Dec. 10, 1664** clergyman John Williams born in Roxbury (died 1729); **Apr. 19, 1666** diarist Sarah Kemble Knight born (died 1727); **1704** first newspaper in Colonies, the *Boston News Letter*, started by postmaster John Campbell; **Jan. 17, 1706** inventor, statesman Benjamin Franklin born (died 1790); **1713** old statehouse built; **1716** Boston Light, oldest lighthouse in U.S., built at entrance to Boston Harbor; **Sept. 27, 1722** patriot Samuel Adams born (died 1803); **1723** Old North Church built; **Aug. 7, 1726** patriot James Bowdoin born (died 1790); **March 11, 1731** signer of Declaration of Independence Robert Trout Paine born (died 1814); **Jan. 1, 1735** patriot Paul Revere born (died 1818); **May 27, 1738** Continental Congress president, signer of Constitution Nathaniel Gorham born at Charlestown (died 1796); **June 11, 1741** Revolutionary officer Joseph Warren born in Roxbury, died June 17, 1775 at Battle of Bunker Hill, Charlestown; **1742** Faneuil Hall, "Cradle of Liberty," completed, destroyed by fire 1762, rebuilt; **June 17, 1742** patriot, signer of Declaration of Independence William Hooper born (died 1790); **Feb. 23, 1744** patriot Josiah Quincy the elder born (died 1775); **July 25, 1750** Revolutionary War general Henry Knox born (died 1806); **1759** novelist Hannah Foster born (died 1840);

Aug. 8, 1763 architect Charles Bulfinch born (died 1844); **Oct. 8, 1765** Sen. Harrison Gray Otis born (died 1848); **March 5, 1770** in Boston Massacre, British troops kill three, wound eight near old statehouse when they fire on angry mob protesting taxes; **Feb. 4, 1772** political leader Josiah Quincy the younger born (died 1864); **Dec. 16, 1773** in Boston Tea Party, protestors throw crates of tea over side of ship into Boston Harbor, British government closes harbor in lieu of repayment; **June 17, 1775** colonials retreat after Battle of Bunker Hill, Charlestown, over 1,000 British killed; **March 1776** British lift siege, withdraw from Boston; **1783** Massachusetts Supreme Court outlaws slavery; **Jan. 19, 1785** publisher Isaiah Thomas born (died 1831); **1791** Massachusetts Historical Society founded; **Apr. 27, 1791** telegraph inventor Samuel Finley Bresse Morse born at Charlestown (died 1872); **1795** statehouse built; **Jan. 4, 1796** portrait painter John Nangle born (died 1865); **Sept. 20, 1797** U.S. military frigate *Constitution* ("Old Ironsides") launched; **1800** Boston Naval Shipyard established; **March 12, 1801** lifeboat inventor Joseph Francis born (died 1893); **May 24, 1803** poet, essayist Ralph Waldo Emerson born (died 1882); **Sept. 6, 1805** sculptor Horatio Greenough born (died 1852); **1807** Boston Atheneum founded; **Nov. 30, 1810** arms manufacturer Oliver Winchester born (died 1880); **1811** Massachusetts General Hospital founded; **Jan. 6, 1811** Sen. Charles Sumner born (died 1874); **Nov. 29, 1811** orator Wendell Phillips born (died 1884); **1812–1815** Jefferson Embargo cripples city's economy during War of 1812; **July 23, 1816** actress Charlotte Cushman born (died 1876); **Feb. 6, 1818** political leader William Maxwell Evans born (died 1901); **Jan. 2, 1819** sculptor Charles Ball born at Charlestown (died 1911); **1820** St. Paul's Cathedral completed; **Feb. 23, 1822** incorporated as a city; **Apr. 31, 1822** author, Unitarian clergyman Edward Everett Hale born (died 1909); **1823** Massachusetts College of Pharmacy and Health Sciences established; **1824** filling of Back Bay begins, continues through 1858 using material taken from city's hills, more than doubling area of Boston peninsula; **1825** *Boston Traveler* newspaper founded; **May 20, 1825** astronomer George Phillips Bond born in Dorchester (died 1865); **1830** Museum of Science founded, built 1864, rebuilt 1948; **1832** old statehouse damaged by fire; **1834** astrophysicist Samuel Pierpont Langley born (died 1906); **1835** Boston & Providence Railroad established; **Feb. 24, 1836** painter Winslow Homer born (died 1910); **1839** Boston College established; **March 8, 1841** Supreme Court Justice Oliver Wendell Holmes, Jr. born (died 1935); **1842** Bunker Hill monument completed; **1846** *Boston Herald* newspaper founded; **July 19, 1846** astronomer Charles Pickering born (died 1919); **Sept. 30, 1846** Dr. William Morton uses ether for tooth extraction, in tumor operation Oct. 16; **May 12, 1850** Sen. Henry Cabot Lodge born (died 1924); **May 4, 1851** painter Thomas Wilmer Dewing born (died 1938); **March 13, 1855** astronomer Percival Lowell born (died 1916); **July 2, 1855** *Wall Street Journal* publisher Clarence Walker Barron born (died 1928); **Sept. 3, 1856** architect Louis Henry Sullivan born (died 1924); **March 23, 1857** cooking instructor Fanny Farmer born (died 1915); **July 15, 1857** actor Nat

Goodwin born (died 1919); **Oct. 15, 1858** bare knuckle boxer John L. Sullivan born in Roxbury (died 1918); **July 5, 1860** banker, diplomat Robert Bacon born (died 1919); **1861** Alice Hathaway Lee Roosevelt born, first wife of Pres. Theodore Roosevelt (married Oct. 27, 1880, died Feb. 14, 1884); **Dec. 8, 1861** automobile manufacturer William Durant born, founded Buick 1905, General Motors 1908 (died 1947); **1863** Boston College established; **July 13–16, 1863** riots in Boston and New York against military conscription, total 1,000 killed; **Jan. 8, 1863** pacifist leader Emily Greene Balch born at Jamaica Plain, 1946 Nobel Prize for founding International League of Peace and Freedom (died 1961); **1866** Mary Baker Eddy founds Christian Science Church; **Sept. 14, 1867** illustrator Charles Dana Gibson born in Roxbury, creator of "Gibson Girl" fashion look (died 1944); **1868** town of Roxbury annexed; **March 9, 1868** lawyer, historian Charles Warren born (died 1954); **May 14, 1869** Chicago mayor William "Big Bill" Thompson born (died 1944); **Nov. 9–10, 1872** city fire destroys 800 buildings; **1873** Massachusetts College of Art established; **1874** towns of Dorchester, Charlestown and Brighton annexed; **Nov. 20, 1874** Democratic boss, Cong. James Michael Curley born (died 1958); **1876** School of the Museum of Fine Arts established; **July 4, 1876** actor William Farnum born (died 1953); **1877** Trinity Episcopal Church built on Copley Square; **1880** Emerson College established; **1881** Boston Symphony founded; Boston Historical Society founded; **Dec. 14, 1884** stage actress Jane Cowl born (died 1950); **Dec. 2, 1885** physician George Minot born, shared Nobel Prize 1934 for research in anemia (died 1950); **June 6, 1886** physician Paul Dudley White born in Roxbury, authority on heart disease (died 1973); **May 2, 1887** banker, diplomat Stanton Griffis born (died 1974); **1888** Wheelock College established; **June 22, 1888** Supreme Court Justice Harold Hitz Burton born at Jamaica Plain (died 1964); **Sept. 6, 1888** financier Joseph Patrick Kennedy born (died 1969); **Dec. 21, 1891** Speaker of the House John McCormick born (died 1980); **March 26, 1893** James Bryant Conant born in Dorchester, president of Harvard University 1933–1953 (died 1978); **1894** Christian Science Church (The Mother Church) built; **Dec. 17, 1894** Boston Pops Orchestra leader Arthur Fiedler born (died 1979); **1895** Boston Public Library completed; **July 12, 1895** mathematician R. (Richard) Buckminster Fuller born, developed geodesic dome (died 1983); **Aug. 24, 1895** Archbishop Richard J. Cushing born (died 1970); **Apr. 19, 1897** first Boston Marathon begins at 12:15 P.M. at Metcalf's Mill, Ashland; **Sept. 1, 1897** Boston subway, first in U.S., begins operating between Public Gardens and Park Street; **1898** Northeastern University established; **Aug. 10, 1898** actor Jack Haley born (died 1979); **1899** Simmons College established; Boston School for the Deaf founded; **1900** Symphony Hall built; **1904** Wentworth Institute of Technology established; **Jan. 10, 1904** actor Ray Bolger born in Dorchester (died 1987); **Jan. 23, 1904** African-American educator Benjamin Arthur Quarles born (died 1996); **1906** Suffolk University established; Boston Opera House built; **Oct. 30, 1906** chemist Max Tishler born (died 1989); **May 6,**

1908 writer Nancy Hale born (died 1988); **Oct. 20, 1908** TV personality Arlene Francis born (died 2001); **1912** Fenway Park (Red Sox) baseball stadium built; **May 6, 1915** author Theodore H. White born (died 1986); **June 24, 1916** poet John Ciardi born (died 1986); **1919** Emmanuel College established; **July 20, 1920** Elliott Richardson, secretary of defense under President Nixon, born (died 1999) **March 26, 1923** actor Bob Elliott born; **Sept. 23, 1923** Logan International Airport established; **May 21, 1924** TV actress Peggy Cass born (died 1999); **Dec. 23, 1924** actress Ruth Roman born (died 1999); **July 9, 1927** singer Ed Ames born; **Sept. 22, 1928** actor Eugene Roche born; **March 26, 1931** actor Leonard Nimoy born; **Sept. 25, 1931** news journalist Barbara Walters born; **Sept. 17, 1933** actress Dorothy Loudoun born; **Dec. 14, 1935** actress Lee Remick born (died 1991); **Oct. 18, 1939** actress Jane Alexander born; **Sept. 29, 1942** actress Madeline Kahn born (died 1999); **Nov. 28, 1942** fire at Cocoanut Grove night club kills 491; **1945** Berklee College of Music established; **March 12, 1948** singer James Taylor born; **Dec. 31, 1948** singer Donna Summer born; **Jan. 17, 1950** over $2.7 million taken from Brink's Inc. express office by masked bandits; **Apr. 24, 1953** actor Eric Bogosian born; **Jan. 12, 1956** eight men arrested by FBI for 1950 Brink's express office holdup, sentenced to life in prison Nov. 6; **Feb. 7, 1960** actor James Spader born; **Oct. 4, 1960** Eastern Airlines Electra crashes on takeoff from Logan Airport, killing 61 of 72 on board; **March 29, 1963** fire at Sherry Biltmore Hotel kills 4, injures 26; **Aug. 9, 1963** Patrick Bouvier Kennedy dies, born prematurely to Pres. and Mrs. John F. Kennedy Aug. 7; **1964** University of Massachusetts at Boston established; 52-story Prudential Center completed; **March 10, 1964** actress Jasmine Guy born; **July 8, 1965** Air Force patrol plane crashes off Massachusetts coast, 16 of 19 on board killed; **July 10, 1967** *Traveler* and *Herald* newspapers merge to become *Herald-Traveler*, later changed to the *Herald*; **1970** Suffolk County Building completed; **March 17, 1970** wounded pilot lands Newark-to-Boston plane after hijacking attempt, copilot shot and killed, hijacker injured; **1973** Naval Shipyard closes, part of nationwide cutback; **June 28, 1971** Daniel Ellsberg, former Pentagon aide, surrenders to Federal officials, wanted for Pentagon Papers leak, charged with illegal possession of classified documents; **June 17, 1972** burning hotel collapses killing nine firemen; **July 31, 1973** Delta Airlines passenger jet crashes in fog on approach to Logan Airport, killing 89; **1976** 60-story John Hancock Tower completed; **Feb. 6-7, 1978** city hit with 27 in/69 cm of snow, about 50 killed in Northeast; **Apr. 23, 1981** researchers at General Hospital announce creation of artificial skin for grafts; **1983** Federal Reserve Building completed; **1987** 46-story One International Place building completed; **1995** Fleet Center opens, new home of Boston Celtics basketball team; Ted Williams Tunnel completed under Boston Harbor, first facet of Big Dig project replacing downtown elevated Central Artery system with sublevel highway; **1996** Boston Harbor Islands National Recreation Area established on Long, Moon, Rainsford, and Spectacle islands, formerly a state park; **March 18, 1996** John Salvi guilty of murder, assault, gets two life terms for shootings at abortion clinics in Brookline Dec. 1994; **1999** county government abolished; **Dec. 12, 2002** Cardinal Bernard Law resigns after conferring with Pope John Paul II for failure to protect children from sexually abusive Catholic priests; **Dec. 2003** Big Dig completed, massive downtown highway and infrastructure relocation project, demolition remains.

Braintree   *Norfolk County*   *Eastern Massachusetts, 10 mi/16 km south of Boston*

1634 town settled by English colonists; **1640** town incorporated, separates from Quincy and Randolph; **1665** title to land purchased by town from chief Wampatuck; **Oct. 30, 1735** John Adams, 2nd President, born in what is now part of Quincy (died July 4, 1826, same day as Pres. Thomas Jefferson); **Jan 23, 1737** first signer of Declaration of Independence John Hancock born (died 1793); **July 11, 1767** John Quincy Adams, 6th President, born, site now part of Quincy (died Feb. 23, 1848); **1803** Thayer House built; **Apr. 16, 1920** Bartolomeo Venzetti and Nicola Sacco hold up payroll office, both executed Aug. 22, 1927 though evidence of guilt lacking.

Bridgewater   *Plymouth County*   *Southeastern Massachusetts, 25 mi/40 km south of Boston*

1650 town settled; **1656** town incorporated; **1700** Washburn House built; Joseph Alden House built; **July 22, 1708** almanac creator Nathaniel Ames born (died 1764); **1840** Bridgewater State College established as Bridgewater Teachers' College; **1845** Unitarian Church built; **Apr. 6, 1903** baseball player Mickey Cochrane born (died 1962).

Brockton   *Plymouth County*   *Southeastern Massachusetts, 18 mi/29 km south of Boston*

1649 Miles Standish and John Alden purchase land from Native Americans for $30; **1700** town settled; **1821** town incorporated as North Bridgewater, separates from Bridgewater; **1861-1865** production of shoes for government orders makes town largest shoe maker in America at time; **1874** town renamed Brockton; **Sept. 1874** Brockton Fair first held; **1876** W. L. Douglas Shoe Factory opens; **1881** incorporated as a city; **March 20, 1905** fire at shoe factory, 50 killed; **Sept. 2, 1923** boxer Rocky Marciano born (died 1969; **1929** city has over 60 shoe factories, declines 1930s.

Brookfield   *Worcester County*   *Central Massachusetts, 15 mi/24 km west of Worcester*

1660 first white settlers arrive on land of Quabaug peoples; **1662** Quabaug leader Massasoit dies; **1664** town settled; **1675** town attacked by Narragansett leader King Philip's forces, evacuated; **1687** town resettled; **1717** Meeting House built, burned 1902; **1718** town incorporated; **1756** Third Church of Christ founded; **1771** Brookfield Inn established; **March 1, 1778** Joshua Spooner murdered by his wife, Bathsheba, and three Revolutionary soldiers, all four hanged; **1797** Chapin House built; **1812** North Brookfield separates from Brookfield; **Aug. 13, 1818** women's rights pioneer, activist Lucy Blackwell Stone born (died 1893); **Apr. 5, 1825** author Mary Jane Holmes born (died 1907); **Dec. 22, 1862** baseball player Connie Mack born at North Brookfield, manager Philadelphia Athletics (died 1956); **1869** Unitarian Church built, destroyed by fire 1911; **1979** first Apple Country Fair held.

Brookline   *Norfolk County*   *Eastern Massachusetts, 3 mi/4.8 km southwest of downtown Boston*

1630 wealthy John Cotton receives land grant; **1638** town settled; **1662** area known for its truck farms; **1680** Edward Devotion House built by constable of same name; **1705** town incorporated; **1721** physician Dr. Zabdiel Adams, uncle of John Adams, introduces smallpox inoculation; **1806** Boston-Worcester Turnpike built; **1870** attempt by Boston to annex town blocked by citizens; **1873** incorporated as a city; **Feb. 9, 1874** poet Amy Lowell born (died 1925); **1882** The Country Club established; **1910** Brookline Library built; **May 29, 1917** John Fitzgerald Kennedy born, 35th President, assassinated Dallas, Texas, Nov. 11, 1963; **May 9, 1918** TV journalist Mike Wallace born; **Nov. 20, 1925** Sen. Robert Francis Kennedy born, Attorney General under Presidents Kennedy and Lyndon Johnson, shot June 5, 1968, Los Angeles, died June 6; **1926** All Saints' Church completed; **Feb. 22, 1932** Sen. Edward M. Kennedy born; **Apr. 4, 1932** actor Anthony Perkins born (died 1992); **Nov. 3, 1933** Gov. Michael Dukakis born, 1988 Democratic presidential candidate; **Apr. 18, 1963** TV talk show host Conan O'Brien born; **1969** John F. Kennedy National Historic Site established; **Feb. 1994** two killed, five wounded in shootings at two abortion clinics.

Cambridge   *Middlesex County*   *Eastern Massachusetts, 2 mi/3.2 km west-northwest of downtown Boston*

1630 Gov. John Winthrop arrives from London with Company of Massachusetts Bay; from its start as Newtowne, town inhabited by wealthy individuals; **c.1635** Belcher House built; **1636** town incorporated; Harvard University established; designated a court town; **1638** town platted, renamed Cambridge; **1643** Middlesex County formed; town becomes county seat; **Oct. 12, 1666** printer, publisher Bartholomew Green born (died 1732); **June 10, 1753** Cong. William Eustis born (died 1825); **1759** Longfellow House built by Maj. John Vassall, occupied by Henry Wadsworth Longfellow 1837 until his death 1882; **1761** Christ Church completed; **Sept. 2, 1774** thousands of patriots assemble at Cambridge Common to volunteer to fight British; **July 3, 1775** George Washington takes Cambridge during Revolutionary War; **1793** West Boston Bridge built across Charles River; **1809** East Cambridge Canal built; **Aug. 29, 1809** writer Oliver Wendell Holmes born (died 1894); **May 23, 1810** feminist, author Margaret Fuller born (died 1850); **1811** Cock Horse Tavern built; **Aug. 1, 1815** lawyer, writer Richard

Henry Dana, Jr. born (died 1882); **Feb. 22, 1819** poet, essayist James Russell Lowell born (died 1891); **Dec. 22, 1823** abolitionist clergyman Thomas Wentworth Higginson born (died 1911); **Nov. 26, 1827** scholar, educator Charles Eliot Norton born (died 1908); **1833** First Parish Church built, established 1633; **1835** county seat shared with Lowell; **Sept. 10, 1839** philosopher Charles Sanders Peirce born (died 1914); **Apr. 6, 1843** U.S. senator from New Hampshire Isaac Hill born (died 1851); **1846** incorporated as a city; **1861** Massachusetts Institute of Technology (MIT) established; **Apr. 26, 1868** educator, author Robert Welch Herrick born (died 1938); **June 28, 1875** actor, producer Otis Skinner born (died 1942); **Apr. 12, 1882** Nobel physicist Percy Williams Bridgman born (died 1961); **1889** Cambridge Library founded; **Jan. 1, 1891** actor Charles Bickford born (died 1967); **May 31 1894** comedian Fred Allen born (died 1956); **Oct. 14, 1894** poet E. E. Cummings born (died 1962); **June 29, 1908** composer, conductor Leroy Anderson born (died 1975); **1909** Lesley College established; **Dec. 9, 1912** Speaker of the House Thomas P. "Tip" O'Neill born (died 1994); **Nov. 15, 1940** TV actor Sam Waterston born; **March 25, 1942** actor Paul Michael Glaser born; **Sept. 6, 1947** TV actress Jane Curtin born; **Jan. 29, 1950** TV actress Ann Jillian born; **Jan. 18, 1967** Albert De Salvo, the "Boston Strangler," gets life in prison for strangling 13 women 1962–1964; **Apr. 10, 1969** 37 injured, 200 arrested in violent demonstrations against Harvard's ROTC program; **Dec. 10, 1969** 75 black students suspended by Harvard for occupying campus in protest over hiring practices; **1971** Cambridge College established; **1997** county government abolished.

Canton   *Norfolk County*   *Eastern Massachusetts, 14 mi/23 km south of Boston*

1630 town settled; **1704** John Fenno House built; **c.1740** May's Tavern built by Samuel May; **1797** town incorporated; named for city in China thought to be exactly opposite on globe; **1804** copper rolling mill built by Paul Revere, established in Boston 1801; **1806** Baptist Church formed; **1807** Swan's Tavern built as stagecoach stop; **1812-1815** town manufactures muskets for War of 1812; **1820** Universalist Church built; **1828** Orthodox Church established; **c.1833** Canton Lyceum organized; **1836** William Otis invents steam shovel; **1858** Rising Sun Stove Factory opened; **Nov. 19, 1887** biochemist James Batcheller Sumner born, Nobel Prize 1946 (died 1955).

Charlton   *Worcester County*   *South central Massachusetts, 12 mi/19 km southwest of Worcester*

1735 town settled; **1750** Burying Ground established; **1755** town incorporated, named for Sir Francis Charlton, Privy Councilor of England; **Oct. 12, 1812** mountain man John "Grizzly" Adams born, heads for Rockies 1852 (died 1860); **Aug. 19, 1819** Dr. William T. G. Morton born (died 1868); **Sept. 30, 1846** Dr. Morton performs first tooth extraction using ether as anesthetic, later demonstrates procedure at Boston's Massachusetts General Hospital.

Chatham   *Barnstable County*   *Southeastern Massachusetts, 75 mi/121 km southeast of Boston, on Cape Cod*

1664 town settled by William Nickerson; **1712** town incorporated; **1750** shifting sands of Cape Cod force closing of town's harbor; **1760** smallpox epidemic greatly reduces town's population; **1792** Old Atwood House built; **1797** Old Windmill built, ceased operation 1907; **1830** Congregational Church built; salt works established; **1877** Chatham Lighthouse built, automated 1982; **1887** railroad reaches town; **1896** Chatham Public Library opened.

Chelmsford   *Middlesex County*   *Northeastern Massachusetts, 22 mi/35 km northwest of Boston*

1633 settlers arrive from Concord and Woburn; **1655** town incorporated; **c.1663** Barrett-Ryan Homestead built by James Parker; **1775** Spaulding House built by Col. Simeon Spaulding of Provincial Congress; **1790** Fiske House built; **Aug. 11, 1814** anatomist Jeffries Wyman born (died 1874); **1835** Ezekial Byam begins manufacture of lucifer matches at South Chelmsford; **1840** Unitarian Church built, organized 1644; **1866** Deacon Otis Adams House built.

Chelsea   *Suffolk County*   *Eastern Massachusetts, 2 mi/3.2 km northeast of downtown Boston*

1624 town first settled by Samuel Maverick and followers; **1629** Bellingham-Cary House built; **1634** Maverick sells land to Gov. Richard Bellingham; **1662** Thomas Pratt House built; **1739** town incorporated; **Sept. 4, 1841** Lewis Howard Latimer born, invented incandescent lamp (died 1928); **1857** incorporated as a city; **Apr. 12, 1908** Palm Sunday, town destroyed by fire fanned by heavy gale, $6,000,000 in property loss, 450 left homeless; **1931** Pulaski monument dedicated; **June 12, 1941** jazz musician Chick Corea born; **1995** incorporated as a city.

Chester   *Hampden County*   *Western Massachusetts, 24 mi/39 km northwest of Springfield*

1760 town settled; **1765** town originally incorporated as Murrayfield, after treasurer John Murray; **1770** De Wolf House built; **1775** town renamed because of Murray's Tory sympathies; **1778** Murray banished from U.S.; **Aug. 2, 1975** highest temperature ever recorded in Massachusetts reached, 107°F/49°C, record shared with New Bedford; **Jan. 12, 1981** lowest temperature ever recorded in Massachusetts reached, −35°F/−37°C.

Chicopee   *Hampden County*   *West central Massachusetts, 2 mi/3.2 km north of downtown Springfield*

Apr. 20, 1641 Native American leader Nippumsuit deeds land to William Pynchon; **1652** town settled; **1805** mining of bog iron begins; iron foundry established by Benjamin Belcher; **1822** Edmund Dwight establishes textile mill for Boston and Springfield Manufacturing Company, becomes Dwight Mills 1830; **1829** Nathan Ames begins manufacture of cutting tools; **1844** Ames Mansion built; **1848** town incorporated; **March 26, 1850** author Edward Bellamy born (died 1898); **1871** town hall built; **1890** incorporated as a city; **1928** College of Our Lady of the Elms established.

Clinton   *Worcester County   East central Massachusetts, 32 mi/51 km west of Boston*

1654 area first settled; **1844** Lancaster Mills established, producer of gingham cloth; **1845** Erastus Bigelow obtains land patent for new town, establishes carpet mill; **1850** town incorporated, separates from Lancaster; **1860s** fire station built; **1904** Holder Memorial Building completed; **1905** Wachusett Reservoir formed by dam on Nashua River; **1930** Lancaster Cotton Mills closed; **1933** Bigelow Sandford Carpet Company closed.

Cohasset   *Norfolk County   Southeastern Massachusetts, 15 mi/24 km southeast of Boston, on Atlantic Ocean*

1614 Capt. John Smith lands here; **1647** town settled; **1708** building of small ships becomes important industry, through 1880; **1737** fishing gains importance, through c.1885; **1770** town incorporated; **1783** Danish ship *Maria* wrecks offshore; **1824** Congregational Church built with 56-bell carillon, gives weekly Sunday concerts; **Oct. 7, 1849** brigantine *Saint John* wrecks on Grampus Rocks, many Irish immigrants lost; **1850** Minot's Light erected, storm takes out light 1851, killing two light keepers; **1860** new lighthouse built; **1900** St. Stephen's Episcopal Church built.

Concord   *Middlesex County   Eastern Massachusetts, 16 mi/26 km northwest of Boston*

1635 town settled by fur trader Simon Willard, Rev. Peter Bulkeley, others, purchase land from natives; town incorporated; **1644** Bullet Hole House built, oldest house in Concord, bullet hole from British firing left of front door; **1716** Concord Inn built; **1747** Wright Tavern built; **Aug. 19, 1751** patriot Samuel Prescott born, died in New Jersey prison c.1777; **1765** Old Manse built by Rev. William Emerson, grandfather of Ralph Waldo Emerson; **1770** Colonial Inn built; **Aug. 1774** first county convention held to protest Acts of Parliament; **Apr. 18, 1775** Paul Revere makes famous night horseback ride from Boston to Concord to warn of advancing British troops; **Apr. 19, 1775** Battle at Concord Bridge, Minutemen advance on British Redcoats, fire "shot heard round the world"; **July 12, 1817** author Henry David Thoreau born (died 1862); **1820** Emerson House built by Ralph Waldo Emerson, resided here 1835 until his death in 1882; **Aug. 29, 1826** Sen. George Frisbee Hoar born (died 1904); **July 26, 1840** artist Mary Alcott born, sister of writer Louisa May Alcott (died 1879); **1845** Henry David Thoreau builds cabin at Walden Pond, lives there for two years; **Apr. 20, 1850** sculptor Daniel French born (died 1931); **May 2, 1868** physicist Robert Williams Wood born (died 1955);

1901 Middlesex School for Boys established; trolley service begins, ends 1923.

Conway   *Franklin County   West central Massachusetts, 28 mi/45 km north-northwest of Springfield*

1762 town settled; **1767** town incorporated; **Sept. 1, 1792** portrait artist Chester Harding born (died 1866); **Feb. 9, 1827** philologist William Dwight Whitney born (died 1894); **Aug. 18, 1834** retail magnate Marshall Field born, enters retail trade in Chicago 1856 (died 1906); **July 5, 1841** financier William Collins Whitney born (died 1904); **1870** Burkeville Covered Bridge built on South River; **1885** Marshall Field Memorial Library built, gift of Marshall Field.

Cuttyhunk   *Dukes County   Southeastern Massachusetts, 15 mi/24 km south of New Bedford*

1602 Bartholomew Gosnold settles temporarily on Cuttyhunk Island; **1641** Thomas Mayhew permitted to settle in islands; village of Gosnold founded on Cutthyhunk, accessible only by boat; **1759** lighthouse built at Tarpaulin Cove; **Jan. 17, 1759** African-American ship owner, philanthropist Paul Cuffe born, secured freedom for black slaves (died 1817); **1864** Town of Gosnold incorporated; **1873** Penikese Island to north given to Louis Agassiz for establishment of game sanctuary, natural history school; **1907** state establishes leper colony on Penikese Island, abandoned 1921.

Danvers   *Essex County   Northeastern Massachusetts, 16 mi/26 km north-northeast of Boston*

c.1630 area first settled; **1636** town founded; **1656** Anne Hibbins hanged, accused of being a witch; **Jan. 7, 1718** Gen. Israel Putnam born, gave command at Bunker Hill, "Don't fire until you see the whites of their eyes" (died 1790); **1757** town incorporated; **1787** covered wagon of emigrants departs for Marietta, Ohio (Northwest Territory); Zerubbabel Porter establishes shoe factory; **1830s** town's carpet weaving industry begins; **Apr. 12, 1831** Union Gen. Grenville Dodge born (died 1916); **1833** Samuel Nathan Reed develops nail-cutting machine; **1840s** known for its vegetable production, the Danvers carrot and onion become popular; **1843** Gilbert Tapley establishes carpet factory; **1874** state hospital built; **1876** poet John Greenleaf Whittier resides at Oak Knoll house until his death in 1892.

Dartmouth   *Bristol County   Southeastern Massachusetts, 55 mi/89 km south of Boston*

1652 land sold to Plymouth Colony by Massasoit, Chief Sacham of Wampanoag Federation; **Nov. 1652** town settled; **1664** town incorporated; **1676–1677** town virtually destroyed during King Philip's War; **Aug. 1699** town's first Society of Friends (Quaker) meetings held; **1790** Friends' Meeting House built; **1870** Portuguese arrive in whaling ship, establish colony; **1895** University of Massachusetts at Dartmouth established.

Dedham   *Norfolk County   Eastern Massachusetts, 9 mi/14.5 km southwest of Boston*

1635 town settled; **1636** town incorporated; Fairbanks House built; **1640** Mother Brook canal built connecting Neponset River in east with Charles River to provide water for mills; **1737** Fairbanks House built; **Apr. 9, 1758** U.S. Cong. Fisher Ames born (died 1808); **1768** First Unitarian Church built; **1774** convention held at Woodward Tavern to protest Coercive Acts; **1793** Norfolk County formed; town becomes county seat; **1827** second county courthouse built; **1828** educator Horace Mann establishes law office here, through 1835; **c.1830** town's industries include two cotton mills, two woolen mills; **1835** Boston & Providence Railroad reaches town; **1854** New York Central Railroad arrives; **1886** Noble and Greenough School for boys established; **2000** county government abolished.

Deerfield   *Franklin County   West central Massachusetts, 30 mi/48 km north of Springfield*

1663 land grant awarded to citizens from Dedham; **1665** town platted; **1673** town settled by Samson Frary, others; **Sept. 18, 1675** Bloody Brook Massacre during King Philip's War, Captain Lathrop and 63 of his 84 men killed by Native Americans while fording stream; beginning of thirty years of terror; **1673** town incorporated; **1689** Frary House built; **c.1695** Bloody Brook Tavern established; **Feb. 28–29, 1704** town attacked by Native Americans, 47 killed, 112 captured; **1797** Deerfield Academy for boys established; **July 17, 1822** painter George Fuller born (died 1884); **1824** Unitarian Meeting House built; **1880** Memorial Hall opened; **1936** flooding Connecticut River washes away highway bridge.

Dracut   *Middlesex County   Northeastern Massachusetts, 25 mi/40 km north-northwest of Boston*

1664 Charles Varnum becomes first white settler, site of administrative center of Pawtucket peoples; **1675–1676** King Philip's War takes heavy toll on town with several attacks; **c.1700** Coburn-Cutter House built; **1702** town incorporated; **March 20, 1914** actor Wendell Corey born (died 1968).

Duxbury   *Plymouth County   Southeastern Massachusetts, 30 mi/48 km southeast of Boston, on Atlantic Ocean*

1624 Miles Standish, John Alden, other Pilgrims enter area seeking land for settlement; **1633–1636** short canal cut through Gurnet Headland, Plymouth Bay, shortening transit to Boston; **1637** town incorporated; **1639** grist mill and fulling mill established; **1656** Miles Standish dies (born 1584), buried in Old Burying Ground at Hall's Corner village; **1666** Alexander Standish House built by Miles' son; **May 6, 1748** Revolutionary soldier Peleg

Wadsworth born, captain of Minutemen patriot militia (died 1829); **early 1800s** shipbuilding and fishing become major industries.

Eastham   *Barnstable County   Southeastern Massachusetts, 67 mi/108 km southeast of Boston, on Cape Cod*

1606 coastline first explored by Samuel de Champlain, prevented from settling due to hostility of Native Americans; **1620** natives prevent Pilgrims from landing, move on to Plymouth; **1644** town settled by Pilgrims returning from Plymouth on *Mayflower*; **1651** town incorporated; **1662** proceeds from stranded whales given to clergy as pay; **1667** ordinance demands every homeowner to kill 12 blackbirds to rid area of the pests, becomes requirement for marriage license by 1695; **1750** Tom Crosby's Tavern established; **1793** Old Windmill built, restored 1936; **1870** railroad reaches town.

Easthampton   *Hampshire County   West central Massachusetts, 12 mi/19 km north-northwest of Springfield*

1664 town settled; **1704** Native American massacre takes place; **1780** town's industrial development begins; **1785** town incorporated; **1822** Samuel Williston and wife begin making wooden button molds, later invent button-making machine; **1841** Williston Seminary founded, becomes Williston Academy; **1861** Nashawannock Company begins production of vulcanized rubber woven goods; **1869** Emily Williston Library founded, building completed 1881.

Easton   *Bristol County   Southeastern Massachusetts, 22 mi/35 km south of Boston*

1668 land purchased by Thomas Leonard; **1694** Clement Briggs becomes first settler; **1717** Josiah Keith House built; **1725** town incorporated; **Jan. 10, 1804** industrialist Oakes Ames born, built Union Pacific Railroad (died 1873); **1837** cannon foundry established; **c.1880** Oakes Ames Memorial Hall built; **1883** Ames Free Library opened; **1902** production of Morse automobile begins, ends 1914; **1948** Stonehill College established.

Edgartown   *Dukes County   Southeastern Massachusetts, 28 mi/45 km southeast of New Bedford*

1602 Bartholomew Gosnold visits island of Martha's Vineyard; **1642** island settled; **1660** island becomes part of Province of New York; **1671** town incorporated, named for Edgar, son of King James II; **1672** Vincent House built; **1692** New York grant cedes island to Massachusetts; **1695** Dukes County formed; town becomes county seat; **1700s** town becomes center for Arctic whaling; **1766** Thomas Cooke House built; **July 18, 1969** Mary Jo Kopechne, 28, drowns when car driven by Edward M. Kennedy plunges off bridge to Chappaquiddick Island; **July 16, 1999** John F. Kennedy, Jr., wife, and sister-in-law killed in small plane crash to south off Martha's Vineyard.

Everett *Middlesex County* *Eastern Massachusetts, 4 mi/6.4 km north of downtown Boston*

1629 first whites visit area; **1640** ferry established on Mystic River; **1649** town settled as South Malden; **1792** Malden Bridge replaces ferry; **1858** Cochrane Chemical Company established, later Merrimac Chemical Company; **1870** town incorporated; **March 11, 1890** Vannevar Bush born, invented the differential analyzer, forerunner of computer (died 1974); **1892** incorporated as a city; **1926** Mystic Iron Works built; **Dec. 28, 1966** railroad accident, 12 killed.

Fairhaven *Bristol County* *Southeastern Massachusetts, 2 mi/3.2 km east of New Bedford*

1670 town settled; **1798** Fairhaven Academy established; **1812** town incorporated; **1823** marine artist William Bradford born (died 1892); **Sept. 25, 1832** architect William Le Baron Jenney born (died 1907); **1893** Millicent Library founded; **1894** town hall built; **Nov. 11, 1898** Manjiro Nakahama (1827–1898) shipwrecked here, arrested upon his return to Japan under act prohibiting leaving and returning to Japan, was instrumental in 1854 Treaty of Friendship between Japanese and Commodore Matthew Perry; **1903** American Tack Company mill built; **1904** Unitarian Memorial Church built; **1916** Coggeshall Memorial Building built; **1994** first annual Manjiro Festival held.

Fall River *Bristol County* *Southeastern Massachusetts, 45 mi/72 km south of Boston*

1656 town settled, part of land grant called Freeman's Purchase; town named Pocasset; **1685** Bristol County formed; Fall River becomes county seat; **1690** sawmill built by Benjamin Church; **1777** home guard organized by Col. Joseph Durfee; **May 25, 1778** Battle of Fall River, town fires upon flotilla of British boats, in turn burn several buildings; **c.1780** Joseph Durfee opens first cotton mill; **1803** town incorporated, renamed Troy; **1834** town renamed Fall River; first textile mills established; **1843** Brayton House mansion built; **1854** incorporated as a city; **July 19, 1860** Sunday school teacher Lizzie Borden born (died 1927); **1871** cotton mill boom begins, continues until 1929; **1875** Fall River Academy built; **1881** Border Flats Lighthouse built, automated 1963; **Aug. 4, 1892** Andrew Jackson Borden and wife Abby Durfee (Gray) Borden brutally axed to death, Lizzie A. Borden accused of murdering father and stepmother, found not guilty June 1893; **1899** Fall River Public Library opened, founded 1861; **1916** Lafayette monument dedicated; **1920s** textile manufacturers move to the South; **1930** city declares bankruptcy, begins industrial diversification plan; **1966** Braga Bridge built; **1968** Marine Museum founded; **1987** Railroad Museum opened.

Falmouth *Barnstable County* *Southeastern Massachusetts, 60 mi/97 km south-southeast of Boston*

1660 town settled by Quakers led by Isaac Robinson; **1686** town incorporated; **1779** British ships attack town; **1812–1815** town attacked by British during War of 1812; **1828** Nobska Lighthouse built, rebuilt 1876, automated 1985; **Aug. 12, 1859** author, educator Katharine Lee Bates born, wrote "America the Beautiful" 1911 (died 1929).

Fitchburg *Worcester County* *East central Massachusetts, 41 mi/66 km west-northwest of Boston*

c.1730 town settled; **1764** town incorporated; **1805** Gen. Leonard Burbank establishes paper mill at falls of Nashua River; **Aug. 25, 1837** educator Calvin Milton Woodward born (died 1914); **May 5, 1838** railroad shipping merchant George Hammond born (died 1886); **1845** Boston & Fitchburg Railroad reaches town; **1848** Vermont & Massachusetts Railroad built; **1860** French-Canadians arrive to work in the mills; **1868** Cushing Flour and Grain Company established; **1870** Heywood Chair factory built, becomes Iver Johnson Armchair and Cedar Works 1894, closed 1973; **1872** incorporated as a city; **1890** Swedish immigrants arrive, led by Iver Johnson; **1894** Fitchburg State College established; **1911** Fitchburg Plan created allowing boys to work three days a week, attend high school three days, includes engineering courses; **2000** Fitchburg Conservatory Orchestra moves from Lancaster, established 1974.

Foxboro *Norfolk County* *Southeastern Massachusetts, 22 mi/35 km south-southwest of Boston*

1704 town settled; **1778** town incorporated, originally spelled Foxborough, named for Charles James Fox, British advocate of Colonial rights; **1781** Foxborough Foundry established; **Nov. 18, 1788** inventor Seth Boyden born (died 1870); **1798** town legislates pioneering 8-hour work day; **1868** Memorial Hall built; Public Library founded at hall; **1967** Boyden Library opened; **1972** Foxboro Stadium opens, home of New England (formerly Boston) Patriots National Football team; **2002** Gillette Stadium completed, replaces Foxboro Stadium.

Framingham *Middlesex County* *East central Massachusetts, 20 mi/32 km west-southwest of Boston*

1640 Natick tribe member Tantamous, also called Old Jethro, settles here; **1650** first whites settlers arrive; **1675** Tantamous allies himself with Eliot's Praying Indians against King Philip's forces; **1676** Tantamous shuns Christianity, English deprive him of his lands, allies himself with King Philip's bands; **1693** Pike-Haven Homestead built by Jeremiah Pike; **1700** town incorporated; **1837** New England Worsted Company moves its factory from Lowell; Old Stone Academy established; **1853** Framingham State College locates here, established 1839 in Lexington; **1872** diversion of Sudbury River by city of Boston brings decline in town's mill industry; **1873** Framingham Library completed.

Franklin *Norfolk County* *East central Massachusetts, 25 mi/40 km southwest of Boston*

1660 land purchased from Wampanoag peoples; **1676** first permanent settlers arrive after King Philip's War; **1713** sawmill established at falls of Mine Brook; **1778** town incorporated, named for Benjamin Franklin; **May 4, 1796** educator Horace Mann born, father of American education system (died 1859); **1799** manufacture of straw bonnets begins; **1865** hat making dominates town's industries; **1904** Ray Memorial Library opened.

Gardner *Worcester County* *Central Massachusetts, 24 mi/39 km north-northwest of Worcester*

1764 town settled; **1785** town incorporated; **1805** James M. Comee establishes chair factory, start of town's designation as "Chair City of the World"; **1832** Elijah Putnam begins manufacture of cane seats; **1844** Philander Derby invents the Boston rocker; **1884** Mount Gardner Seminary for women founded; **1886** Gardner Library founded; **1904** Gardner State Colony for the Insane built; **1923** incorporated as a city.

Gay Head *Dukes County* *See* **Aquinnah**

Gloucester *Essex County* *Northeastern Massachusetts, 27 mi/43 km northeast of Boston*

1623 Dorchester Adventurers' colony established; **1642** town incorporated; **May 1, 1753** Sargent Winthrop born, served as governor of Northwest Territory (died 1820); **1830** Gloucester Lyceum established; **1854** Sawyer Free Library founded; **1868** Universalist Church built; **1771** twin harbor lights erected on Thatcher's Island; **1873** incorporated as a city; **July 6, 1875** statistician Roger Ward Babson born (died 1967).

Gosnold *Dukes County* *See* **Cuttyhunk**

Great Barrington *Berkshire County* *Western Massachusetts, 40 mi/64 km west of Springfield*

1676 Major Talcott overtakes band of Narragansetts, final Native American encounter in area; **1724** Chief Konkapot cedes first land grants; **1726** town settled; **1739** William Cullen Bryant House built; **1761** town incorporated; **Jan. 20, 1798** Anson Jones born, last president of Texas 1844–1846, committed suicide Jan. 9, 1858, despondent over lack of recognition; **Feb. 23, 1868** African-American educator William E. B. Du Bois born (died 1963).

Greenfield *Franklin County* *West central Massachusetts, 33 mi/53 km north of Springfield*

1686 town settled; **1704** raid on town by 240 Native Americans, 112 prisoners taken to Vermont; **1753** town incorporated; **June 15, 1773** architect Asher Benjamin born (died 1845); **1797** Leavitt-Hovey House built; **Oct. 3, 1802** religious reformer George Ripley born (died 1880); **1811** Franklin County formed; town becomes county seat; **1847** St. James' Episcopal Church built; **1932** county courthouse built; **1998** county government abolished.

Groton *Middlesex County* *Northeastern Massachusetts, 32 mi/51 km northwest of Boston*

1655 town settled; town incorporated; **1675** Native Americans destroy town during King Philip's War, rebuilt; **1707** several residents killed, children carried away in Native American raid; **Feb. 20, 1726** Col. William Prescott born, commander of American forces at Battle of Bunker Hill (died 1795); **1755** First Parish Meeting House built; **1767** Dix House built; **Apr. 19, 1775** Minutemen assemble in Town Common to march against British at Concord; **1776** Groton Inn built, later used as clubhouse of Groton Golf Club; **1841** paper mills established; **1851** Boutwell House built, home of Gov. George S. Boutwell (1818–1905); **1854** Groton Public Library founded, building opened 1893; **1884** Groton School established, alumni includes Franklin D. Roosevelt; **1987** first annual National Shepley Hill Horse Trials held.

Hadley *Hampshire County* *West central Massachusetts, 15 mi/24 north of Springfield, on Connecticut River*

1659 town first settled by John Webster and Rev. John Russell; **1661** town incorporated; **1664** Edmund Whalley and William Goffe of England's High Court of Justice flee to Colonies, arrive in Hadley, hidden for 15 years by Rev. Russell; **1675** fortification built around town during King Philip's War; **1683** Mary Webster, accused of witchcraft, survives hanging and burial in snow, dies of natural causes several years later; **c.1750** Allen Tavern built; **1752** Porter Phelps-Huntington House built; **1753** Bishop Huntington House built, home of Frederick Huntington (1819–1904), Episcopal bishop of Central New York; **1797** town becomes first broom manufacturing center in U.S.; **1808** First Congregational Church built; **Nov. 13, 1814** Union Gen. Joseph Hooker born, defeated at Charlottesville 1863 (died 1879); **1817** Hopkins Academy founded; **c.1840** tobacco production begins; **Feb. 27, 1863** philosopher George Herbert Mead born (died 1931); **1930** Hadley Farm Museum established; **1936** flooding damages town.

Hatfield *Hampshire County* *West central Massachusetts, 18 mi/29 km north of Springfield*

1659 first land grants made; **1661** town settled on Connecticut River; **1662** grist mill built by Thomas Merkins; **1670** town incorporated; **1675** high casualties suffered by attack of 800 natives; **1677** Native American attack leaves 12 residents dead, many captured; **1677-1678** Stephen Jennings and Benjamin White paddle north on Connecticut River to Quebec, pay ransom of £200 for release of wives and children; **March 7, 1714** Col. Ephraim Williams born, founded Williams College, Williamstown (died 1755); **1737** linseed oil mill established; **1790** Sophia Smith Homestead built, born 1796, founded Smith College, Northampton (died 1870); **1905** tobacco, onions become area's leading crops.

Haverhill *Essex County* *Northeastern Massachusetts, 30 mi/48 km north of Boston, on Merrimack River*

1640 Rev. John Ward and followers land here, found town, name it for their home of Haverhill, England; **1643** first pelt tanneries established; **1645** town incorporated; **1697** Haverhill shipyard launches first vessel; **March 15, 1697** Hannah Dustin abducted by Native Americans, becomes hero when she escapes with scalps of ten of her captors (died 1737); **1747** town's hat industry begins; **Dec. 10, 1785** publisher David Appleton born (died 1849); **c.1800** shoe making begins, continues into early 1900s; **1803** Bradford Junior College established; **Dec. 17, 1807** poet John Greenleaf Whittier born in what is now town of Merrimac to east (died 1892); **1811** Chain Bridge built across Merrimack; **1848** First Church of Christ built; **1851** retailer Rowland Macy opens store here; **1870** incorporated as a city; **1873** Winnikenni Castle built, center for popular recreation area of same name; **1879** Hannah Dustin Statue erected.

Hingham *Plymouth County* *Eastern Massachusetts, 12 mi/19 km southeast of Boston*

1633 town settled, originally named Bare Cove; **1635** town incorporated, renamed; **1665** lands conveyed by Algonquins to English; **1667** Samuel Lincoln House built; **1680** Old Ordinary (tavern) built; **1681** Old Ship Church built, oldest continuously used church in U.S.; **1733** Revolutionary War officer Benjamin Lincoln born (died 1810); **May 15, 1749** Cong. Levi Lincoln born, Attorney General under President Jefferson (died 1820); **1784** Derby Academy founded, built 1819, first coed school in U.S., purchased by historical society 1966; **1807** New North Church built; **Sept. 12, 1811** geologist James Hall born, founded field of stratigraphy (died 1898); **July 2, 1825** poet Richard Stoddard born (died 1903); **1852** Loring Hall built as social venue; **1869** Hingham Public Library founded, built 1966.

Holyoke *Hampden County* *West central Massachusetts, 6 mi/9.7 km north of downtown Springfield*

1633 area explored by Elizur Holyoke; **1745** town settled; **1828** dam built on Connecticut River; several mills established; **1848** new dam built, collapses on day of its completion, rebuilt; **1850** town incorporated; **1870** Holyoke Public Library founded; **1873** incorporated as a city; **1880s** city's paper milling industry established, reaches peak c.1920; **1895** game of volleyball invented here by William G. Morgan at YMCA; **1900** the "Million Dollar Dam" built, withstands floods of 1936; **Aug. 21, 1924** Cardinals baseball announcer Jack Buck born (died 2002).

Hopkinton *Middlesex County* *East central Massachusetts, 15 mi/24 km west-southwest of Boston*

1715 town settled; **1744** town incorporated; **c.1747** Daniel Shays born, leader of Shays' Rebellion (died 1825); **c.1750**

Valentine Tavern opened; **Nov. 19, 1791** Lee Claflin born, a founder of Boston University, founder of Claflin College, South Carolina (died 1871); **1818** Joseph Walker begins manufacture of pegged shoes; **Dec. 4, 1903** World War II (Burma) Army Gen. Frank Dow Merrill born (died 1955).

Hudson *Middlesex County* *East central Massachusetts, 26 mi/42 km west of Boston*

1662 Williams Tavern built; **1699** town settled; **1702** Goodale House built, becomes stop on Underground Railway during pre-Civil War era; **Aug. 18, 1707** Mary Goodnow and friend ambushed, scalped by natives while gathering herbs by Stirrup Brook; **1776** Williams Inn burned by Native Americans, rebuilt 1777; **1861** Unitarian Church built; **1866** town incorporated; **1867** Hudson Library founded, built 1905; **Oct. 23, 1873** physical chemist William Coolidge born (died 1975); **Feb. 27, 1882** senator from Montana Burton Kendall Wheeler born (died 1975); **1894** fire destroys many downtown buildings; **1901** Mossman House built by Col. Adelbert Mossman; trolley service begins, abandoned 1923.

Ipswich *Essex County* *Northeastern Massachusetts, 25 mi/40 km northeast of Boston, near Atlantic Ocean*

1614 Capt. John Smith observes Ipswich harbor; **1633** town settled; **1634** town incorporated; **1635** First Parish Church built; **March 14, 1638** colonial governor John Winthrop born (died 1707); **1687** angry mob gathers to protest oppression by Governor Andros, very early prelude to Revolutionary War; **1748** South Church built; **1764** bridge built across Ipswich River; **Sept. 27, 1786** bibliographer Joseph Cogswell born (died 1871); **1847** Congregational Church built on site of First Parish Church; **1868** Ipswich Mills opened by Amos A. Lawrence, closed 1927.

Lancaster *Worcester County* *East central Massachusetts, 32 mi/51 km west-northwest of Boston*

1643 town settled; **1653** town incorporated; **1675-1676** town destroyed during King Philip's War; **1704** final episode of Native American attacks; **1816** Old Meeting House (Lancaster Church) built, designed by Charles Bulfinch; **March 7, 1849** plant breeder, geneticist Luther Burbank born (died 1926); **July 4, 1868** astronomer Henrietta Swan Leavitt born (died 1921); **1974** Thayer Conservatory Orchestra founded, moved to Fitchburg in 2000.

Lawrence *Essex County* *Northeastern Massachusetts, 24 mi/39 km north of Boston, on Merrimack River*

1655 area first settled; **1840s** Lawrence built as America's first planned industrial city; **1845** Essex Company organizes to harness water power from Bodwell's Falls on Merrimack; **1846** Amos Pillsbury opens first store;

Merrimac Courier newspaper founded; **1847** town incorporated; **1853** incorporated as a city; **1860** roof of Pemberton Mill collapses, followed by fire, 525 workers either killed or injured; **1865** Arlington Mills established; **1868** *Eagle Tribune* newspaper founded by Alexander H. Rogers; **1887** Lawrence Experimental Station established to conduct sewage disposal research; **1890** tornado strikes south end of city, many killed; **1905** Wood Mill built by American Woolen Company; **1906** Malden Mills founded by Henry Fouerstein; **Aug. 25, 1918** conductor Leonard Bernstein born (died 1990); **Nov. 26, 1933** singer Robert Goulet born; **1934** Lawrence Municipal Airport established.

Lee *Berkshire County* *Western Massachusetts, 37 mi/60 km west-northwest of Springfield*

1760 town settled; **1777** town incorporated; **1787** Peter Wilson, condemned to die for his part in Shays' Rebellion, captured in cave, pardoned; **1808** Lee Paper Mills established; **March 2, 1836** Supreme Court Justice Henry Billings Brown born at South Lee (died 1913); **1852** marble quarrying begins; **1857** Congregational Church built; **Aug. 11, 1919** industrialist Andrew Carnegie dies at villa on Lake Mahkeenac (born 1835).

Lenox *Berkshire County* *Western Massachusetts, 40 mi/64 km west-northwest of Springfield*

c.1750 town settled; **1761** Berkshire County formed; **1767** town founded as county seat; **1775** town incorporated, name for Charles Lenox, Duke of Richmond, defender of Colonial causes; **c.1785** Shaker Colony established; **1805** Congregational Church built, designed by Peter Bulfinch; **1816** county courthouse built, later used as Lenox Library; **1868** county seat moved to Pittsfield; **June 19, 1886** photographer James Van der Zee born (died 1983); **1890** Nathaniel Hawthorne's cottage destroyed by fire, rebuilt 1948; **1937** first annual Tanglewood Music Festival held; **1993** National Music Center established at former Bible camp.

Leominster *Worcester County* *North central Massachusetts, 18 mi/29 km north of Worcester*

1643 land grant made; **1653** town settled; **1740** town incorporated; **1770** manufacture of combs begins; **Sept. 26, 1774** arborist, folk hero John Chapman "Johnny Appleseed" born (died 1845); **1845** first railroad reaches town; 24 comb factories in existence at industry's peak; *Enterprise* newspaper founded, merges with *Fitchburg Sentinel* 1973, retains *Sentinel* name; **1873** fire destroys business district; **Dec. 6, 1891** Columbia University football coach Lou Little born (died 1979); **1915** incorporated as a city; **1925** manufacture of celluloid products becomes major industry; **Sept. 21, 1938** great hurricane destroys 2,500 homes.

Lexington *Middlesex County* *Eastern Massachusetts, 9 mi/14.5 km northwest of Boston*

1642 town settled, named Cambridge Farms; **1680** Mason House built; Buckman Tavern built; **1695** Munroe Tavern

built; **1698** Hancock-Clarke House built by Rev. John Hancock, father of Gov. John Hancock; **1713** town incorporated; **1729** Munroe House built on Town Green; **Apr. 19, 1775** in Battle of Lexington, Revolutionary War, 8 Minutemen killed, 10 wounded, British lose 273 men; **1789** George Washington attends testimonial dinner at Munroe Tavern; **1839** Framingham State Teachers' College established as State Normal School, moved to Framingham 1853; **1868** Lexington Library founded; **1930** Botanic Garden established.

Lowell *Middlesex County* *Northeastern Massachusetts, 24 mi/39 km northwest of Boston, on Merrimack River*

1643 Middlesex County formed; county seat (shire town) established at Cambridge, then called Newtowne; **1653** town settled as part of Chelmsford; **1760** Spalding House built, originally served as tavern; **1822** Merrimack Manufacturing Company formed by associates of Francis Cabot Lowell, father of American cotton manufacturing; **1824** Whistler's birthplace built; **1826** town incorporated, separates from Chelmsford; First Congregational Church built; **1827** Lowell Textile Institute trade school established; **July 10, 1834** painter James Whistler born (died 1903); **1835** town becomes shared county seat with Cambridge; Boston & Lowell Railroad reaches city, New England's first steam railroad; **1836** incorporated as a city; **1844** Pollard Memorial Library founded; **1848** county courthouse built; **Nov. 13, 1854** composer George Whitefield Chadwick born (died 1931); **1866** Music Hall opened; **1868** St. Joseph's Catholic Church built; **1894** Lowell State Teachers' College established, becomes University of Massachusetts Lowell Campus; **1902** Lowell Historical Society founded; **1908** Holy Trinity Greek Orthodox Church opened, demolished 1996; **Apr. 5, 1908** actress Bette Davis born (died 1989); **1910** Notre Dame of Lourdes Catholic Church built; **March 12, 1922** novelist, poet Jack Kerouac born, beat generation icon (died 1969); **1927** Temple Beth-El founded; **June 20, 1931** actress Olympia Dukakis born; **1949** Temple Emmanuel built; **Aug. 30, 1963** actor Michael Chiklis born; **1978** Lowell National Historical Park established; **1982** Brush Art Gallery opened; **1986** first Lowell Folk Festival held; **1987** New England Quilt Museum founded; **1997** county government abolished.

Lynn *Essex County* *Eastern Massachusetts, 10 mi/16 km northeast of Boston, on Atlantic Ocean*

1629 town settled; **1631** town incorporated; **1635** Philip Kirtland and Edmund Bridges begin manufacture of shoes adjacent to town tannery; **1638** earthquake collapses entrance of cave at Dungeon Rock, supposedly trapping hidden pirate treasure; **1643** ironworks established; **1666** Molly Pitcher House built; **1750** Welshman John Dagyr begins manufacture of shoes, reaches one million pairs by 1810; **Feb. 9, 1819** feminist Lydia Pinkham born, manufactured patent medicines (died 1883); **1850** incorporated as a city; **1858–1860** shoemakers' strike becomes longest, largest in history; **July 14, 1864** painter Charles

Woodbury born (died 1940); **1867** strike shuts down shoe industry for seven weeks; **1881** Lynn Woods Reservation established; **July 24, 1892** historian Lynn Thorndike born (died 1965); **Nov. 1889** fire destroys 375 buildings in city's business area; **Nov. 20, 1927** actress Estelle Parsons born; **Jan. 30, 1934** actress Tammy Grimes born; **Nov. 28, 1981** fire destroys Benson Shoe Company, 17 other buildings.

Malden *Middlesex County* *Eastern Massachusetts, 5 mi/8 km north of downtown Boston*

1622 Robert Gorges receives land grant by Northern Virginia Company, nullified by Council at Plymouth 1628; **1640** first settlers move north from Charlestown, new town founded; **1648** Greene House built on Greene Hill; **1649** town incorporated; **1724** Judson Parsonage House built; **Jan. 22, 1747** eccentric merchant "Lord" Timothy Dexter born (died 1806); **Sept. 23, 1774** resolution drawn by citizens protests acts of British Parliament, spawns Revolutionary War; **1832** First Congregational Church built; **1882** incorporated as a city; **1885** Malden Public Library completed, founded 1879; **July 17, 1889** Erle Stanley Gardiner born, author of Perry Mason novels (died 1970); **1891** First Baptist Church built; **1892** Spanish-American War monument erected; Sacred Heart Catholic Church built; **1907** Malden Armory built; **May 12, 1932** painter Frank Stella born; **1975** government center completed.

Marblehead *Essex County* *Northeastern Massachusetts, 15 mi/24 km northeast of Boston, on Atlantic Ocean*

1629 town settled by fishermen from Cornwall and Channel Islands, England; **1649** town incorporated; **1680** Old Tavern built; **1714** St. Michael's Church completed; **1720** Old Brig built; **1727** Old Town House built; **1742** Fort Sewall built, used against British during Revolution; **July 17, 1744** Cong., Gov. Elbridge Gerry born, signer of Declaration of Independence (died 1814); **1745** King Hooper House built by Robert Hooper, nicknamed for his wealth; **1768** Colonel Jeremiah Lee Mansion built by Revolutionary War officer; **1774** town replaces Boston as port of entry following passage of Boston Port Bill by patriots; **Sept. 18, 1779** Supreme Court Justice Joseph Story born (died 1845); **1824** Old North Church built; **1846** great gale severely damages town's merchant fleet; **1877** Abbot Hall Library opened, new building opened 1954; **1962** Marblehead Festival of Arts established.

Marion *Plymouth County* *Southeastern Massachusetts, 46 mi/74 km south-southeast of Boston*

1679 town settled, originally named Sippicon; **1812** Handy's Tavern built; **1833** Universalist Church built; **1834** Dr. Walter Ellis House built; **1841** Congregational Church built; **1852** town incorporated, separates from Rochester, named for Revolutionary War hero Gen. Francis Marion; shipbuilding becomes important, ends 1878; **1872** Elizabeth Taber Library founded through donation from childless widow; **1876** Tabor Academy

established; **March 11, 1876** composer Charles Ruggles born (died 1971); **1953** Marion Art Center opened at former Universalist Church.

Marlborough *Middlesex County* *East central Massachusetts, 25 mi/40 km west of Boston*

1657 town settled; **1660** town incorporated, separates from Sudbury; **1662** Williams Tavern built by Lt. Abraham Williams; **March 20, 1676** congregation of John Eliot's Praying Indians attacked by King Philip's forces, only one injured; **1772** stagecoach service inaugurated; **1775** dysentery epidemic takes many lives; **1799** post office established; **1837** shoe manufacturing reaches peak; **1840** town hall built; **1852** Marlborough Branch Railroad reaches town; **1866** Church of the Immaculate Conception (Catholic) built; **1869** soldiers monument erected; **1889** trolley service begins, ends 1928; **1890** incorporated as a city; **1914** Marlborough Theater built; **1922** Lyonhurst Ballroom opened, destroyed by fire 1963; **1925** Dennison Paper Box Factory opened.

Mattapoisett *Plymouth County* *Southeastern Massachusetts, 50 mi/80 km south-southeast of Boston*

c.1740 shipbuilding industry begins; **1750** town founded; named for Native American word for "place of rest"; **c.1755** Nye Homestead built; **1821** Meeting House built; **Nov. 3, 1846** author Francis Davis Millet born, died April 15, 1912, with sinking of the *Titanic*; **1857** town incorporated; town becomes whaling and shipbuilding center; **1878** the last whaler, the *Wanderer*, built at Mattapoisett Shipyard; **1882** Mattapoisett Library founded, built 1904.

Medfield *Norfolk County* *Eastern Massachusetts, 17 mi/27 km southwest of Boston*

1651 town settled and incorporated, separates from Dedham; **1660** town platted; **1680** Peak House built by Seth Clark, received indemnity for original house burned by King Philip in 1676; **1705** grist mill built; **Oct. 2, 1755** Hannah Adams born, one of first women authors in America (died 1831); **1800** straw hat manufacturing begins, reaches peak c.1875; **1806** Clark's Tavern established; **1931** Westinghouse Radio Station established.

Medford *Middlesex County* *Eastern Massachusetts, 5 mi/8 km north-northwest of downtown Boston*

1630 town settled; **1678** Peter Tufts House built; **1684** town incorporated; **1689** Jonathan Wade House built; **c.1697** Usher Royall House built; **1732** Isaac Royall House built; **May 1, 1752** last Federalist governor of Massachusetts John Brooks born (died 1825); **c.1795** poet Marin Gowen Brooks born (died 1845); **1802** shipbuilding begins, ends 1872; **Feb. 11, 1802** abolitionist, author Lydia Maria Francis Child born (died 1880); **1835** Medford Library built; **1852** Tufts University established; **1892**

incorporated as a city; **1896** Medford State Hospital established; **Apr. 10, 1941** economist Paul Theroux born.

Melrose   *Middlesex County*   *Eastern Massachusetts, 7 mi/11.3 km north of Boston, near Atlantic Ocean*

1629 town settled; **1845** Boston & Maine Railroad built through town; **1850** town incorporated; **1871** Melrose Public Library founded, built with Carnegie grant 1900; **Feb. 28, 1883** soprano Geraldine Farrar born (died 1967); **Nov. 28, 1894** New York theater critic Brooks Atkinson born (died 1984); **1900** incorporated as a city; **1918** Melrose Symphony Orchestra founded; **Sept. 17, 1939** Supreme Court Justice David Souter born.

Merrimac   *Essex County*   *Northeastern Massachusetts, 33 mi/53 km north of Boston, on Merrimack River*

1638 town settled; **1688** Whittier birthplace built; **1700** Merrimacport conducts coastal and West Indies trade; **1726** Pilgrim Congregational Church organized; **c.1750** Sawyer Home built; **Dec. 17, 1807** Quaker poet, abolitionist John Greenleaf Whittier born (died 1892); **1876** town incorporated, separates from Haverhill.

Methuen   *Essex County*   *Northeastern Massachusetts, 26 mi/42 km north of Boston, near New Hampshire*

1642 town settled; **1726** town incorporated, separates from Haverhill; **Nov. 7, 1731** frontiersman Robert Rogers born, led Rogers Rangers during French and Indian War (died 1795); **1807** Exchange Hotel built; **1825** Waldo House built; **1853** town hall built; **c.1880** Searles Estate built; **1888** Nevins Memorial Hall and Library opens; **1892** Methuen Organ Company established, closed 1942; **1896** St. Monica's Catholic Church built.

Middleborough   *Plymouth County*   *Southeastern Massachusetts, 33 mi/53 km south-southeast of Boston*

1660 town settled by descendants of Pilgrims; **1669** town incorporated; **1744** Muttock (Oliver) Herring Slitting Mill built; **1762** dam built on Nemasket River at Upper Factory; **1813** cotton factory built; **1863** Star Cotton Mill established at Lower Factory village; **1888** Clark and Cole Sawmill established, closed 1909; **1898** Church of Our Savior (Catholic) built; **1974** Nemasket River Environmental Corridor implemented; **1996** fish ladder built at dam.

Milford   *Worcester County*   *East central Massachusetts, 16 mi/26 km southwest of Boston*

1662 town settled; **1741** Easterly Precinct incorporated; **1780** town incorporated; **1819** boot manufacturing begins; **1848** Milford Branch Boston & Albany Railroad completed; **c.1850** pink granite discovered by Rev. Patrick Cudahy, first quarry opens; **1858** Milford Town Library founded; **1870** town's industries include two largest boot factories in U.S.; **1900** town's footwear industry declines.

Milton   *Norfolk County*   *Eastern Massachusetts, 7 mi/11.3 km south of Boston*

1636 town settled; Barnard Capen House built; **1662** town incorporated; **1707** Manassah Tucker House built; **1764** first chocolate factory in New England established; **1800** Martin Crahore begins manufacture of pianos; **1801** G. H. Bent's Water Cracker Factory first to produce water crackers; **1807** Milton Academy established, closed 1866, reopens 1885; **1826** Granite Railway Company, first chartered railroad in America, lays track for horse-drawn transfer of granite blocks from Quincy to Neponset River for building of Bunker Hill monument; **1870** Milton Library founded, building opened 1904; **May 21, 1870** businessman, diplomat William Cameron Forbes born (died 1959); **1879** Curry College established; **June 12, 1924** George Herbert Walker Bush, 41st U.S. President, born.

Nahant   *Essex County*   *Eastern Massachusetts, 9 mi/14.5 km east-northeast of Boston, on Atlantic Ocean*

1630 town settled; **1657** town platted; **1730** island of Nahant sold to Thomas Dexter by Chief Poquanum; **1802** The Castle tavern built by Joseph Johnson; **1817** steamer service established from Boston; **1823** hotel built by Thomas Perkins; **1825** Avenue of Elms planted by Frederic Tudor along Nahant Road; **1853** town incorporated; **1872** Nahant Public Library founded, built 1895; **July 5, 1902** Sen. Henry Cabot Lodge, Jr. born (died 1985).

Nantucket   *Nantucket County*   *Southeastern Massachusetts, 50 mi/80 km southeast of New Bedford*

1621 Nantucket Island included in Plymouth Company royal land grant; **1641** island purchased by Thomas Mayhew; **1659** Mayhew sells nine-tenths of island to nine settlers; **1660** island becomes part of New York; **June 1661** Peter Folger leads settlers from Salisbury and Amesbury to Nantucket to escape harsh Puritan ways; **1668** Oldest House built; **1671** town incorporated; **1692** island granted to Massachusetts; **1695** Nantucket County formed from Dukes County (Martha's Vineyard); town becomes county seat; **1696** Indian Meeting House built; **1746** Old Mill built, milled corn meal; **1765** First Congregational Church built; **1790** Maria Mitchell House built; **Jan. 3, 1793** abolitionist, women's rights activist Lucretia Mott born (died 1880); **1797** shipbuilding becomes major industry; **1812** British take 11 ships during War of 1812; **Aug. 1, 1818** Maria Mitchell born, first woman astronomy professor (died 1889); **1840** Grove Street Evangelical Church dedicated; **July 13, 1846** fire destroys town center; **1847** Whaling Museum built; **1850** Sankaty Head Light built at east end of island; St. Paul's Episcopal Church built; **July 26, 1956** Italian ocean liner *Andrea Doria* collides with Swedish liner *Stockholm*, sinks, killing 51; **1965** county courthouse/town building built;

May 28, 1971 during "lobster wars," Russian trawlers cut through U.S. fishing nets twice in 24 hours; Dec. 22, 1976 tanker *Argo Merchant* splits in half after grounding, worst oil spill on record, 7.5 million gallons oil, fouling beaches, fishing banks; 1984 Nantucket Land Bank founded, first local land trust in U.S.; Oct. 31, 1999 Egyptair flight 990 plunges into Atlantic killing all 217 on board, suicidal copilot blamed.

Natick *Middlesex County* East central *Massachusetts, 16 mi/26 km west-southwest of Boston*

1650 land granted to John Eliot as plantation for his Praying Indians that he converted to Christianity; 1651 John Eliot's House built, used as Native American meeting house; 1718 town settled; 1762 Morrill's Tavern established, destroyed by fire 1872; 1781 town incorporated; 1816 Stowe House built, boyhood home of Prof. Calvin Stowe, husband of author Harriet Beecher Stowe; 1828 Eliot Church built; 1836 Boston & Albany Railroad reaches town; 1857 Sen. Henry Wilson plants long-standing Henry Wilson Tree on Town Common; 1858 Natick Baseball Park established; 1874 fire destroys business district; 1880 town boasts 23 shoe factories; 1971 town's last shoe factory closed.

Needham *Norfolk County* Eastern Massachusetts, *10 mi/16 km southwest of Boston*

Apr. 16, 1680 Native Americans sell tract of land to Dedham Company of Watertown, part of which becomes Needham; 1711 town incorporated; 1714 sawmills and grist mills established; 1754 Fuller House built; Oct. 22, 1882 painter Newell Convers Wyeth born (died 1945); 1930s area's skiing industry developed; 1961 Needham Free Public Library built.

New Bedford *Bristol County* Southeastern *Massachusetts, 50 mi/80 km south of Boston, on Atlantic Ocean*

May 15, 1602 Capt. Bartholomew Gosnold lands here, first European to arrive in New England; 1640 area settled by Quakers; 1760 named Bedford Village by whaler Joseph Russell, "Father of New Bedford"; 1767 *Dartmouth* becomes first ship launched from New Bedford; May 14-15, 1775 25 men rescue two sloops captured by British for use as decoys; Sept. 5, 1778 British ravage town following years of harassment at sea by town's patriots; 1787 town incorporated; Feb. 13, 1799 shipping merchant Henry Grinnell born, patron of Arctic expeditions (died 1874); 1826 notorious district referred to as Hard Dig set ablaze by angry citizens; 1832 Seaman's Bethel church dedicated, has ship's-prow pulpit; Nov. 21, 1835 publishing heir Hetty Green born (died 1916); 1846 Wamsutta Mills established; 1847 incorporated as a city; March 19, 1847 painter Albert Pinkham Ryder born (died 1917); 1856 New Bedford Library opened; 1860 city serves as stop on Underground Railway, freed slaves sent to safety of Canada; 1881–1883 cotton mill boom shared with all of New England; 1907 New Bedford Whaling

Museum opened; 1912 city hall built; Aug. 2, 1975 highest temperature ever recorded in Massachusetts reached, 107°F/42°C, shared with Chester; 1987 New Bedford Art Museum opened; 2003 New Bedford Oceanarium established at former power plant built 1915.

Newbury *Essex County* Northeastern *Massachusetts, 33 mi/53 km north-northeast of Boston*

1635 town incorporated; settlers survive harsh winter by building dugouts, dwellings dug into base of Oldtown Hill, sapling branches used as windbreaks; 1636 Dummer-Spencer Mill built; Sept. 14, 1645 silversmith Jeremiah Dummer born (died 1718); 1646 Noyes House built by teacher James Noyes; 1653 Coffin House built; 1670 Swett-Ilsley House built, later becomes Blue Anchor Tavern; 1697 limestone quarrying begins; 1708 Cart Creek Sawmill built; 1735 Wheeler-Tenney Snuff Mill built; 1794 Byfield Woolen Factory established; 1845 shoe industry becomes well established; Dec. 23, 1853 Supreme Court Justice William Henry Moody born (died 1917); 1857 railroad reaches town; 1869 Newbury Congregational Church built, fifth structure since 1630; c.1900 dairying becomes important.

Newburyport *Essex County* Northeastern *Massachusetts, 33 mi/53 km north-northeast of Boston*

1635 town settled; 1642 port established at entrance to Merrimack River; 1681 first ships launched; 1711 St. Paul's Church built; 1744 county jail built; 1764 town incorporated; 1771 Tracy House built, later used as public library; 1790 Jefferson Embargo Act devastates town's shipping industry; 1801 Unitarian Church built; Dec. 12, 1805 abolitionist William Lloyd Garrison born (died 1879); 1807 Wolfe Tavern built; 1808 Caleb Cushing House built; John Cushing House built; 1810 Chain Bridge built across Merrimack; 1811 fire destroys city center; c.1815 general development of cotton mills ruins import trade; 1851 incorporated as a city; 1859 clipper ship *Dreadnought* launched, later makes record Atlantic crossing to Liverpool in 9 days, 13 hours; 1866 Newburyport Public Library founded.

Newton *Middlesex County* Eastern *Massachusetts, 6 mi/9.7 km west of downtown Boston*

1630s town settled; 1646 John Eliot begins preaching to Native Americans, establishes Praying Indians of Massachusetts and Rhode Island; 1681 Woodward Farmhouse built; 1691 town incorporated; Apr. 19, 1721 Connecticut Cong., Sen. Roger Sherman born, signer of Declaration of Independence (died 1793); July 15, 1796 author Thomas Bulfinch born, son of Charles Bulfinch (died 1867); 1809 Jackson Homestead built; 1825 Andover Newton Theological School founded; 1834 Boston & Worcester Railroad reaches town; 1873 incorporated as a city; 1875 Newton Free Library founded, new library opened 1991; 1906 First Unitarian Church built; June 8, 1918 actor Robert Preston born (died 1987); Feb. 8,

1925 actor Jack Lemmon born (died 2001); **May 18, 1931** actor Robert Morse born.

Norfolk   *Norfolk County   Eastern Massachusetts, 21 mi/34 km southwest of Boston*

1637 Pequoits destroyed by Puritans during Pequoit War; **1691** sawmill built on Stop River; **1795** town settled by whites, originally named North Wrentham; **1796** first Meeting House built; **1812** first cotton mill established at Stony Brook; **1823** Pond House built by Gen. Lucas Pond; **1853** Medway Branch Railroad reaches town, abandoned 1864; **1870** town incorporated; **1879** Public Library founded; **1927** Norfolk State Prison Colony established.

North Adams   *Berkshire County   Western Massachusetts, 50 mi/80 km northwest of Springfield*

1745 Fort Massachusetts built, westernmost of four forts built by Massachusetts Bay Colony, burned by 900 French and Native Americans 1746; **1765** Congregationalists from Connecticut attempt to settle here, effort short-lived; **1778** second settlement attempt by Rhode Islanders succeeds; **1846** railroad reaches town from Pittsfield; first cotton textile mill established; **1875** Hoosac Tunnel completed to east for Boston & Maine Railroad, 25,081 ft/7,645 m long, begun 1851, cost of $20 million, 195 lives; **1878** town incorporated; **Nov. 5, 1885** historian Will Durant born (died 1981); **1894** Massachusetts College of Liberal Arts established; **1895** incorporated as a city; **1923** Robert C. Sprague invents radio condenser (capacitor); **Aug. 1937** road opened to top of Mt. Greylock; **1957** first Fall Foliage Festival held.

North Andover   *Essex County   Northeastern Massachusetts, 25 mi/40 km north of Boston, on Merrimack River*

c.1640 town settled; **1667** Bradstreet House built by Gov. Bradstreet; **1690s** witchcraft hysteria affects town, 41 indicted, 8 condemned, 3 executed at Salem; **1752** Samuel Phillips, a founder of Phillips Andover Academy, builds Phillips Mansion; **1784** Kittredge Mansion built by Thomas Kittredge, Revolutionary War surgeon; **1855** town incorporated; **1875** Stevens Memorial Library founded, built 1907; **1947** Merrimack College established.

North Attleboro   *Bristol County   Southeastern Massachusetts, 30 mi/48 km south-southwest of Boston*

1669 John Woodcock becomes first settler, originally named North Purchase; **1670** Woodcock establishes tavern; **1780** Frenchman opens brass forge and jewelry shop; **1807** town's first major jewelry manufacturer established; **1830s** town becomes important button manufacturing center; **1840** Woodcock Tavern closes after 170 years, with George Washington, Lafayette, and Daniel Webster counted among its distinguished guests; **1887** town incorporated.

North Brookfield   *Worcester County   See Brookfield (1862)*

Northampton   *Hampshire County   West central Massachusetts, 14 mi/23 km north of Springfield*

1654 town settled; **c.1655** Bliss House built; **1656** town incorporated; **1662** Hampshire County formed; Springfield becomes county seat; **1740** Puritan Jonathan Edwards' "Great Awakening" revival movement leads many to experience visions and trances; **May 26, 1745** Congregational minister Jonathan Edwards, Jr. born (died 1801); **1786** Wiggins Tavern built; William Butler founds *Hampshire Gazette* newspaper; **May 22, 1786** abolitionist Arthur Tappan born (died 1865); **May 23, 1788** abolitionist Lewis Tappan born (died 1873); **1812** Hampden County separates from Hampshire County; Hampshire County seat moved to Northampton; Springfield becomes Hampden County seat; **Nov. 23, 1819** geologist Josiah Dwight Whitney born (died 1896); **1835** Northampton-New Haven Canal completed, used until 1847; **Aug. 16, 1868** composer Charles Skilton born (died 1941); **1871** Smith College established; **1883** incorporated as a city; **1887** county courthouse built; **1888** Lilly Library founded; **Jan. 5, 1933** Pres. Calvin Coolidge dies of heart attack at his home The Beeches; **1998** county government abolished.

Northfield   *Franklin County   North central Massachusetts, 41 mi/66 km north-northeast of Springfield*

1673 town settled; **1714** town founded; **1723** town incorporated; **1771** sheep raising begins with "merino craze"; **1784** Samuel Field House built; **Feb. 5, 1837** evangelist Dwight Lyman Moody born (died 1899); **1878** Dickinson Memorial Library founded, named for patron Elijah Dickinson; **1879** Northfield Seminary for women founded by Moody; **1881** Mount Hermon School for Boys established by Moody; **1886** Moody founds Student Volunteer Movement in collaboration with YMCA; **1890** Schell Chateau built; **1934** first American Youth Hostel established.

Norton   *Bristol County   Southeastern Massachusetts, 28 mi/45 km south-southwest of Boston*

1669 town settled; **1709** incorporated as a precinct; **1711** town incorporated; **May 18, 1740** judge, Revolutionary loyalist Daniel Leonard born (died 1829); **1834** Wheaton Female Seminary established, becomes Wheaton College; **1871** jewelry first manufactured by W. A. Sturdy; **1879** Norton Public Library founded, new library opened 1991.

Oak Bluffs   *Dukes County   Southeastern Massachusetts, 23 mi/37 km southeast of New Bedford*

1642 area on northern shore of Martha's Vineyard island first settled; **1646** Thomas Mayhew names locality Easternmost Chop of Howe's Hole; **1752** Norton House built; **1835** Methodist Tabernacle and summer camp established; **1850s** Gothic cottages built to replace camp tents, called Cottage City; **1860s** first hotel built; **1878** East Chop Lighthouse built, automated 1933; **1880** Town of Cottage City incorporated; **1907** town renamed Oak Bluffs.

Orleans   *Barnstable County   Southeastern Massachusetts, 68 mi/109 km southeast of Boston, on Cape Cod*

1693 town settled; **1717** original Cape Cod Canal opens to Cape Cod Bay, used until 1914; **1792** Kenrick House built by Jonathan Kenrick; **1797** town incorporated; named for Louis Philippe, Duke of Orleans, visited Massachusetts same year; **Dec. 1814** in Battle of Orleans, War of 1812, British forces repulsed by local militia; **1829** Higgins Tavern founded as stagecoach stop; **1855** Linnell House built by Capt. Eben Linnell, tea trader; **1877** Snow Library founded, named for patron David Snow; **1915** town develops into popular summer resort; **July 1918** tugboat, three barges bombed by German submarine near Nauset Beach, U.S. planes drop monkey wrenches on spot where sub surfaced.

Oxford   *Worcester County   South central Massachusetts, 10 mi/16 km south of Worcester*

1681 land purchased from Nipmucks; **1687** town first settled, abandoned because of Native American attacks; **1693** incorporated as a district; **1713** town incorporated; Huguenots immigrants become first permanent settlers; **1792** church built by Universalists; **Dec. 25, 1821** nurse Clara Barton born, organizer of Red Cross (died 1812); **Sept. 15, 1835** lawyer Richard Olney born (died 1917); **1904** Larned Memorial Library founded.

Peabody   *Essex County   Northeastern Massachusetts, 14 mi/23 km northeast of Boston*

c.1626 town settled; **1638** Ananias Conklin opens lamp and bottle factory, start of city's glass making industry; **1668** first tannery established; **Feb. 15, 1795** financier, banker George Peabody born (died 1869); **1800** St. Joseph's Juniorate founded, preparatory school for boys; **1852** Peabody Institute founded with donation from financier George Peabody; **1855** town incorporated, originally named South Danvers; leather products becomes primary industry, town nicknamed "Tanner City"; **1868** town renamed Peabody; **1916** incorporated as a city.

Pelham   *Hampshire County   West central Massachusetts, 21mi/34 km north-northeast of Springfield*

1738 town first settled by Colonel Stoddard of Northampton, originally named Lisburn; **1743** town incorporated; renamed for Lord Pelham, who was touring the Bay Colony at the time; **1786** resident Daniel Shays (1747–1825) leads rebellion in response to hard economic times, fails to capture arsenal at Springfield, retreats to Pelham; **Jan. 10, 1815** social reformer Abigail Kelley Foster born (died 1887); **c.1873** asbestos mining becomes chief industry.

Pepperell   *Middlesex County   Northeastern Massachusetts, 35 mi/56 km northwest of Boston*

1720 town settled, named for Sir William Pepperell, hero of Battle of Louisbourg, Nova Scotia; **1769** Congregational Church built, destroyed by fire 1917; **1770** Meeting House built, replaces 1745 structure; **1775** town incorporated; **1776** Mrs. Prudence Wright with several other women guarding covered bridge, capture Leonard Whiting of New Hampshire, preventing him from reaching Boston with traitorous message concealed in his boot; **1777** British prisoners of war quartered here, allowed liberal use of town's amenities; **1830s** shoe manufacturing begins; **1834** Pepperell Academy founded; **c.1834** paper mill established by Andrew Emerson; **1848** Worcester & Nashua Railroad reaches town, abandoned 1981; **1851** bridge built across Nashua River, replaced c.1890, destroyed by flood 1936; **1860** community church built; **1874** town hall built; **1875** Prescott Grange organized; **c.1891** Hotel Prescott built, destroyed by fire c.1970; **1897** Lawrence Library built; **1938** Methodist Church built, replaces 1873 structure.

Peru   *Berkshire County   See **Pittsfield** (1942)*

Pittsfield   *Berkshire County   Western Massachusetts, 40 mi/64 km northwest of Springfield*

1752 state boundary dispute with New York ends; Solomon and Sarah Deming become first settlers; **1754** Brattle Homestead built on Court Hill; **1761** Berkshire County formed; Lenox becomes county seat; town incorporated; **1762** Brattle House built; **1773** Williams-Newton House built; **1776** Peace Party House built, scene of celebration of Treaty of Paris, 1783; **Feb. 15, 1782** revivalist William Miller born (died 1849); **1801** Arthur Schofield invents wool-carding machine, opens factory; **1810** America's first cattle show held in City Hall Park; **1812** clothing manufacturing begins; **1818** Agricultural Bank founded; **1825** Marquis de Lafayette is guest at Peace Party House; **1850** author Herman Melville purchases Arrowhead Farm, writes *Moby Dick*, other works; **1868** county seat moved to Pittsfield; **1871** county courthouse built; **1872** Pittsfield Library founded, built 1975; **1876** Berkshire Athenaeum built; **1891** incorporated as a city; **1903** Colonial Theater opened; **1907** Stanley Electrical Company factory established, plant built 1912, bought by General Electric 1930; **1918** concert hall built at South Mountain Music Camp; **1929** Walton Sanctuary established by Izaak Walton League; **Aug. 15, 1942** plane crash on Garnet Mtn. at Peru to east kills 15 soldiers, monument erected 1946; **1960** Berkshire Community College established; **Oct. 2, 1968** Appalachian National Trail established, runs north-south to east; **2000** county government abolished.

Plymouth   *Plymouth County   Southeastern Massachusetts, 35 mi/56 km southeast of Boston*

Dec. 21, 1620 first settlement with arrival of Puritans aboard *Mayflower*, enters harbor after month moored off

Cape Cod; town incorporated; date "1620" carved on Plymouth Rock; **Feb. 27, 1621** Miles Standish elected captain by popular vote; **March 1621** Pilgrims winter aboard *Mayflower*, half perish before coming ashore; **Apr. 21, 1621** *Mayflower* sets sail for return trip to England; **1639** colonial soldier Benjamin Church born (died 1718); **1664** William Crowe House built; **1666** Kendall House built; **1677** Harlow House built; **1685** Plymouth County formed, town becomes county seat; **1690** whaling activities begin, abandoned by 1840; **1722** Tabitha Plaskett House built; **June 10, 1762** lawyer, state legislator Joseph Bartlett born (died 1827); **June 21, 1805** chemist, geologist Charles Thomas Jackson born (died 1880); **June 14, 1820** author, publisher John Bartlett born (died 1905); **1824** Pilgrim Hall memorial built; **1916** Miles Standish State Forest established; **Aug. 14, 1962** $1.5 million taken from U.S. mail truck, largest heist in U.S. history; **June 1972** Pilgrim Nuclear Power Plant begins production to southeast.

Provincetown *Barnstable County* *Southeastern Massachusetts, 50 mi/80 km east-southeast of Boston*

c.1000 Norsemen believed to have sailed as far south as Cape Cod; **1602** Bartholomew Gosnold rounds tip of peninsula, names it Cape Cod; **Nov. 11, 1620** Pilgrims arrive aboard *Mayflower*, spend month moored at tip of Cape Cod, blown off course with Virginia their intended destination, move across Cape Cod Bay to settle at Plymouth; **Nov. 20, 1620** Peregrine White born aboard *Mayflower*, becomes military and civil figure (died 1704); **c.1699** town settled; **1727** town incorporated; **1800** collection of sea salt begins; **1853** Francis Paine excavates stone wall, fireplace believed to be Viking dwelling; **1873** Provincetown Extension Railroad built, abandoned 1959; **1874** Provincetown Library opened; **Nov. 10, 1874** Arctic explorer Donald MacMillan born (died 1970); **1898** gale destroys town's wharves; **Nov. 26, 1898** U.S. steamship *Portland* wrecks off Cape Cod killing 157; **1901** artist colony begins with arrival of painter Charles W. Hawthorne, founds Cape Cod School of Art (died 1930); **1910** Pilgrim monument erected; **1915** Provincetown Players theater group established in old fish house on town wharf, move to New York City 1916, disband 1922; **Nov. 15, 1969** hull failure of tanker *Keo* spills 8.8 million gallons of oil onto beaches; **Jan. 11, 1977** Panamanian-registered tanker *Grand Zenith* sinks off Cape Cod killing 38 Taiwanese crewmen.

Quincy *Norfolk County* *Eastern Massachusetts, 7 mi/11.3 km south-southeast of Boston, on Atlantic Ocean*

1625 first settled by Thomas Morton; **1640** town (QUIN-zee) founded; **1666** earliest interments at Old Cemetery; **1681** John Adams birthplace built; **1731** Vassal-Adams Mansion built; **Oct. 30, 1735** John Adams, 2nd President, born, then part of Braintree (died July 4, 1826, same day as Pres. Thomas Jefferson); **July 11, 1767** John Quincy Adams, 6th President, born, then part of Braintree (died Feb. 23, 1848); **1770** Josiah Quincy House built; **1792** town incorporated; **1825** Quincy granite used in Bunker

Hill monument, Boston; **1828** Unitarian Chapel built, burial place of John Adams and his wives; **June 24, 1848** historian Brooks Adams born (died 1927); **1880** Crane Memorial Library established, built 1939; **1883** shop established for development of marine engines, taken over by Bethlehem Steel 1913; **1888** incorporated as a city; **Oct. 30, 1896** actress Ruth Gordon born at Wollaston, now part of Quincy (died 1985); **May 27, 1912** comic writer John Cheever born (died 1982); **1918** Eastern Nazarene College established.

Randolph *Norfolk County* *Eastern Massachusetts, 13 mi/21 km south of Boston*

c.1710 town settled, originally named Cochato; **1793** town incorporated, renamed for Peyton Randolph, first president of the Continental Congress; **early 1800s** town becomes known for its shoe production, reaches peak c.1850; **1806** Jonathan B. Hall House built; **Oct. 31, 1832** author Mary E. Wilkins Freeman born (died 1930); **July 15, 1854** educator, scholar Benjamin Ide Wheeler born (died 1927); **1895** after long decline, shoe production ceases.

Rehoboth *Bristol County* *Southeastern Massachusetts, 37 mi/60 km south-southwest of Boston*

1636 Plymouth Congregationalists become first settlers; **1645** town incorporated; **1663** Baptist Church founded, fourth congregation in America, moved soon after to Swansea; **1675-1676** town is scene of bloody fighting during King Philip's War; **1680** Kingsley House built; **1720** iron mine established at Anawan Rock; **1747** first sawmills established; Palmer River Iron Works established, maker of cast iron plows, other implements; **1802** two cotton mills established; **1826** Orleans Manufacturing Company established, maker of cotton yarn; **c.1850** bobbin factory opened.

Revere *Suffolk County* *Eastern Massachusetts, 5 mi/8 km northeast of Boston, on Atlantic Ocean*

1624 area first settled near Rumney Marsh; **1630** Winthrop House built by Capt. William Pearce, *Mayflower* skipper, bought by Deane Winthrop 1647; **1710** Church of Christ built; **1739** Chelsea separates from Boston, includes Revere; **1775** first naval battle of Revolution fought at Rumney Marsh; **1782** Hastings House built; **Jan. 13, 1832** author Horatio Alger born (died 1899); **1838** Eastern (Boston & Maine) Railroad reaches town; **1852** Winthrop, separates from Chelsea; **1871** town of Revere incorporated, separates from Chelsea; **1881** Grand Ocean Pier and Pines Hotel built; **1900** first of several ballrooms built at Revere Beach; **1906** Wonderland Theme Park opened, closed 1911; **1896** Revere Beach opened as first public beach in U.S.; **1914** incorporated as a city; **May 18, 1922** actor Bill Macy born; **1927** Lightning Roller Coaster built at beach, includes inverted loop; **1935** Wonderland Dog Track opened.

Rockland   *Plymouth County*   *Southeastern Massachusetts, 17 mi/27 km south-southeast of Boston*

1647 land grant made to Timothy Hatherly; **c.1670** site may have been headquarters for Narragansett leader King Philip; **1673** town settled; **1703** sawmill, first frame house built by Thaxter family; **c.1835** shoe manufacturing becomes important; **1874** town incorporated; **c.1881** iron pyrite mine opened by H. J. Davil, closed 1911; **1961** Yankee Nuclear Power Plant begins production, closed 1991.

Rockport   *Essex County*   *Northeastern Massachusetts, 30 mi/48 km northeast of Boston, on Cape Ann*

c.1650 Dogtown established, fishing community known for its ferocious watchdogs, diminished by war and shipwrecks, 40 house cellars remain; **1670** Garrison Witch House built, used as refuge by Elizabeth Proctor, husband, four others found guilty of witchcraft; **1690** town settled; **1770** Old Tavern built; **1803** First Congregational Church built; **1805** Ebenezer Pool Mansion built; **1812** fort built during War of 1812; **1840** town incorporated.

Rutland   *Worcester County*   *Central Massachusetts, 11 mi/18 km north-northwest of Worcester*

1713 town founded; **1714** town platted; **1719** first settlers arrive; grist mill built; **1722** town incorporated; **1765** dysentery epidemic kills 60 children; **1778** barracks built during Revolutionary War to house Hessian prisoners; **1786** town's citizens, many faced with bankruptcy, join Daniel Shays' rebellion, stage march on Worcester; **1893** Massachusetts Hospital for Consumptive and Tubercular Patients established; **1923** Veterans Hospital built.

Salem   *Essex County*   *Eastern Massachusetts, 15 mi/24 km northeast of Boston, on Atlantic Ocean*

1626 town first settled by Robert Conant with immigrants from Cape Ann; **1628** autocratic Governor Endicott arrives with group of followers resulting in land dispute; **1630** the two groups settle differences, name Salem selected in reference to peace agreement; town incorporated; **1635–1636** persecution of Quakers causes Roger Williams and followers to flee to Rhode Island; **1643** Essex County formed; town becomes county seat; **1668** House of Seven Gables built, setting for Hawthorne's novel; **1688** Cotton Mather travels to Salem, leads witchcraft purge; **1692** West Indian woman named Tituba sentenced to death for telling witchcraft tales, 19 others hanged on Gallows Hill of 200 arrested for witchcraft that year; **July 17, 1745** Sen. Timothy Pickering born (died 1829); **Jan. 16, 1752** Sen. George Cabot born (died 1823); **1785** vessel *Grand Turk* sails out of harbor for China; **June 24, 1788** machine tools inventor Thomas Blanchard born (died 1864); **May 4, 1796** historian William Hocking Prescott born (died 1859); **July 4, 1804** author Nathaniel Hawthorne born (died 1864); **Oct. 30, 1829** sculptor

John Rogers born (died 1904); **1836** incorporated as a city; **1841** county courthouse built; **1848** Essex Institute founded; **March 5, 1853** composer Arthur Foote born (died 1937); **1854** Salem State College established; **Sept. 3, 1860** retailer Edward Albert Filene born (died 1937); **March 24, 1862** painter Frank Watson Benson born (died 1951); **1868** Peabody Essex Museum founded; **1889** Salem Public Library founded; **March 26, 1892** Illinois Sen. Paul Howard Douglas born (died 1976); **June 25, 1914** fire destroys large part of Salem, 15,000 left homeless; **1999** county government abolished.

Salisbury   *Essex County*   *Northeastern Massachusetts, 35 mi/56 km north of Boston, near Atlantic Ocean*

1638 town settled; **1640** town incorporated; Saltbox House built; **1752** Quaker Meeting House built, front step later used as whipping stone; **1687** John March establishes ferry on Merrimack River to Newbury; **1690** March opens March's Tavern; **1715** Governor Dummer Mansion built, kitchen haunted by ghost of a child peering through a doorway until her bones were discovered in a box in cellar and properly buried; **1762** Dummer Academy established; **Jan. 17, 1800** diplomat, Cong. Caleb Cushing born (died 1879); **1834** Methodist Church built; **1891** town hall built.

Sandwich   *Barnstable County*   *Southeastern Massachusetts, 52 mi/84 km south-southeast of Boston*

1627 trading post established at village of Sagamore; **1637** town settled; Hoxie House built; **1639** town incorporated; **1697** Massachusetts General Court orders feasibility study of canal across base of Cape Cod; **1825** town becomes known for its trademark glass, secret formula lost after 1888; **June 24, 1839** meat packer Gustavus Franklin Swift born, founded Swift & Company, Chicago, 1875 (died 1903); **Jan. 4, 1874** writer Thornton Waldo Burgess born, wrote children's books (died 1965); **1909** Boston, Cape Cod & New York Canal Company begins work on Cape Cod Canal; **1914** Cape Cod Canal opens; **1927** federal government assumes ownership of canal.

Saugus   *Essex County*   *Northeastern Massachusetts, 7 mi/11.3 km northeast of Boston, near Atlantic Ocean*

1629 first white men, William, Richard, and Ralph Sprague, pass through area on Old Indian Trail; **1630** town settled; **1643** John Winthrop, Jr. sails from England, establishes iron works; Thomas Dexter, one of original iron works owners, builds Old Ironworks House; **1654** iron works fail following worker unrest and lack of cooperation among Scottish prisoners employed in the operation; **1815** town incorporated.

Scituate   *Plymouth County*   *Eastern Massachusetts, 20 mi/32 km southeast of Boston, on Atlantic Ocean*

1630 town settled; **1636** town incorporated; town suffers from long series of Native American attacks; **1650**

Stockbridge Mill built by John Stockbridge; **c.1655** Stockbridge Mansion built; **1723** Cudworth Cottage built; **March 1, 1732** first Supreme Court appointee William Cushing born (died 1810); **1739** Capt. Benjamin James House built, later used as historical museum; **1812–1815** town strongly opposes British in War of 1812, many of its vessels are burned in harbor; **1825** Grand Army of the Republic Hall built; **1893** Little Red School House built.

Shelburne   *Franklin County*   *West central Massachusetts, 34 mi/55 km north-northwest of Springfield*

1756 town first settled by several families who arrive at Shelburne Falls, leave soon after during French and Indian War; **1760** new settlers arrive; town founded, named for second Earl of Shelburne; **1768** town incorporated; **1851** Linus Yale begins manufacture of Yale Locks here; **1856** Mayhew Tack Factory established; **1896** trolley line reaches town, abandoned 1926; **1908** trolley bridge built over Deerfield River, converted 1929 to "Bridge of Flowers."

Shirley   *Middlesex County*   *East central Massachusetts, 33 mi/53 km northwest of Boston*

1720 town settled; **c.1740** fulling mills established; **c.1746** Revolutionary Tavern built by Obadiah Sawtell; **Sept. 18, 1765** hymn writer Oliver Holden born (died 1844); **1786** town incorporated; **1789** Bull Run Tavern built; **c.1790** paper mill established; **c.1810** ironworks and nail factory founded; **March 17, 1819** author Sarah Edgerton Mayo born (died 1848); **1845** railroad reaches town from Boston; **1871** Shaker community established at Shirley village.

Shrewsbury   *Worcester County*   *East central Massachusetts, 5 mi/8 km east-northeast of Worcester*

1664 first land grants made; **1722** Gersham Wheelock becomes first settler; **1727** town incorporated, named for Charles Talbot, Duke of Shrewsbury; **Nov. 26, 1727** Revolutionary Gen. Artemus Ward born (died 1800); **1797** gunsmithy established; **1809** Baptist minister Luther Goddard becomes possibly America's first watchmaker; **1872** Shrewsbury Public Library opened, new library opened 1981; **1898** Shrewsbury Historical Society founded.

Shutesbury   *Franklin County*   *West central Massachusetts, 25 mi/40 km north-northeast of Springfield*

1686 Granther Pratt born, became known as Methuselah of Shutesbury, tombstone reads "1686–1800," died at 113 years of age; **1735** town settled in part of Roadtown grant; **1761** town incorporated; named for Bay Colony Gov. Samuel Shute; **May 5, 1815** hymn writer Ithamar Conkey born (died 1867); **1827** Federated Church built; **1829** town hall built; **1836** Congregational Church built; **1894** M. N. Spear Public Library founded, built 1902.

Somerset   *Bristol County*   *Southeastern Massachusetts, 40 mi/64 km south of Boston, on Taunton River*

1677 area first settled; **c.1710** shipyard established by Samuel Lee; **1779** Jarathmeal Bowers House built by town founder; **1779** Jemima Wilkinson arrives claiming she had died three years earlier, returned to life through soul of Christ, chooses 12 disciples, gains following; **1790** town incorporated; **1795** slave of Henry Bowers, son of town founder, sent to sea for his wild behavior, escapes at Haiti, leads rebellion against French under name Toussaint L'Ouverture, declares himself emperor 1801, overthrown 1804; **1872** Somerset & Dighton Railroad reaches town.

Somerville   *Middlesex County*   *Eastern Massachusetts, 4 mi/6.4 km northwest of downtown Boston*

1630 town settled; **Sept. 1, 1774** 250 half-barrels of gunpowder seized by British General Gage at Old Powder House; **1777–1778** British soldiers captured at Saratoga, New York, held at fortress on Prospect Hill; **1803** Middlesex Canal completed; **1834** anti-Catholic mob burns Ursuline Convent; **1835** Boston & Lowell Railroad built; **1842** town incorporated; **Sept. 19, 1859** historian John Franklin Jameson born (died 1937); **1871** incorporated as a city; Somerville Public Library founded, built 1914; **Dec. 26, 1871** composer Henry Kimball Hadley born (died 1937); **1892** St. Catherine's Catholic Church completed; **1926** Ford Motor Plant built, closed 1958.

South Hadley   *Hampshire County*   *West central Massachusetts, 10 mi/16 km north of Springfield*

1659 town settled; **1737** first meeting house completed; **1775** town incorporated; **1795** South Hadley Canal opened at Falls Village; **1837** Mount Holyoke Seminary founded, becomes Mount Holyoke College; **1840s** large influx of Irish immigrants arrives; **1897** South Hadley Public Library founded, opened 1907; **1908** town hall built.

Southampton   *Hampshire County*   *West central Massachusetts, 11 mi/18 km northwest of Springfield*

1704 Native American raid on Northampton, Mrs. Benjamin Janes kidnapped, found alive on Mt. Pomeroy; **1732** town settled; **1775** town incorporated; **1917** 104th Infantry of 26th Yankee Division recruited here, monument erected later; **June 19, 1964** Sen. Edward Kennedy injured in private plane crash, two killed, Indiana Sen. Birch Bayh and wife survive.

Southbridge   *Worcester County*   *South central Massachusetts, 18 mi/29 km southwest of Worcester*

1633 John Oldham and Samuel Hall of Plymouth enter area on scouting expedition, encounter Native American party with graphite rubbed on their faces; **1638** John Winthrop, Jr. purchases tract 4 mi/6.4 km square, graphite vein unprofitable for its perpendicular angle to surface;

1730 town settled; **Dec. 12, 1786** New York Sen. William Leonard Marcy born, secretary of war under President Polk (died 1857); **1816** town incorporated; **1915** Jacob Edmunds Library opened.

Spencer *Worcester County* *Central Massachusetts, 10 mi/16 km west of Worcester*

1717 town settled by Nathaniel Wood; **1753** town incorporated; **1811** Josiah and Nathaniel Green begin manufacture of shoes sewn with thread; **1812** wire drawing mill established by Elliot Prouty, merged 1916 with Wickwire Steel Company; **July 9, 1819** Elias Howe born, invented lock-stitch sewing machine 1846 (died 1867); **1874** Richard Sugden Public Library founded; **1899** Sibley Mansion completed; **May 29, 1910** Howe monument dedicated.

Springfield *Hampden County* *Western Massachusetts, 100 mi/161 km west of Boston, on Connecticut River*

1636 town founded by William Pynchon and Puritans; **1641** town incorporated; **1662** Hampshire County formed; town becomes county seat; **1675** town burned during King Philip's War; **1777** federal arsenal built; **1786–1787** thousands of town's citizens support Shays' Rebellion; **1794** U.S. Armory established, first muskets manufactured in U.S. 1795; **Oct. 27, 1800** Ohio Sen. Benjamin Franklin Wade born (died 1878); **1805** bridge built across Connecticut River; **1812** Hampden County formed from Hampshire County; Springfield becomes Hampden County seat; Hampshire County seat moved to Northampton; **1819** First Church of Christ built; **1824** the *Springfield Republican* newspaper founded; **1828** Noah Webster publishes his *American Dictionary of the English Language*; **June 17, 1828** economist David Ames Wells born (died 1898); **1839** Western Railroad reaches city from Boston; **1845** John Brown arrives from Akron, opens wool warehouse, promotes abolition; **June 2, 1845** military governor of Philippines Gen. Arthur MacArthur born, father of Gen. Douglas MacArthur (died 1912); **1851** Massachusetts Mutual Life Insurance Company founded; **1852** incorporated as a city; **1864** the *Union* newspaper founded; **Apr. 14, 1866** Anne Mansfield Sullivan Macy born, teacher, companion to blind student Helen Keller (died 1936); **1871** county courthouse built; **1876** Christ Church Cathedral (Episcopal) built; **1880** *Daily News* newspaper founded; **1883** Forest Park Zoo established; **1885** Springfield College established; American International College established; **1891** game of basketball developed by Dr. James Naismith; **Apr. 19, 1893** Charles and Frank Duryea test drive their gasoline powered buggy, establish first automobile company 1896; **1895** Smith Art Museum built; **1899** Museum of Natural History founded, becomes Springfield Science Museum; **Apr. 5, 1901** diplomat, Connecticut Cong. Chester Bowles born (died 1986); **1902** first motorcycles in U.S. manufactured; **1903** Springfield rifle developed; **Jan. 2, 1904** poet Richard Palmer Blackmur born (died 1965); **March 2, 1904** Theodor Seuss Geisel (Dr. Seuss) born, author, illustrator of children's books (died 1991); **Sept. 1, 1908** *Scientific American* publisher Alfred Ely Beach born (died 1896); **1912** city library founded; **Nov. 21, 1912** actress Eleanor Powell born (died 1982); **1919** Western New England College established; **Nov. 1, 1922** actor George Irving born; **1933** Museum of Fine Arts opened; **1936** worst flooding in New England history, many lives lost; **1944** Springfield Symphony Orchestra founded; **March 17, 1951** actor Kurt Russell born; **1968** Naismith Memorial Basketball Hall of Fame established; **1974** county Hall of Justice opened; **1998** county government abolished; **2002** Dr. Seuss National Memorial established.

Stockbridge *Berkshire County* *Western Massachusetts, 40 mi/64 km west-northwest of Springfield*

1734 area first settled with land grant establishing Indian mission; **1737** town incorporated; Stockbridge Mission House built by Calvinist Jonathan Edwards; **1745** grist mill built; **1755** tranquility between whites and Native Americans ends with hostilities; **1785** local Native Americans removed to New York State; **Feb. 4, 1802** educator Mark Hopkins born (died 1887); **Nov. 30, 1819** merchant Cyrus West Field born, promoted first transatlantic telegraph cable (died 1892).

Sudbury *Middlesex County* *Eastern Massachusetts, 18 mi/29 km west of Boston*

March 1626 Lieutenant Curtis responds to Native American attack on Marlborough to west by mustering attack party, kills leader Metus; **Apr. 1626** natives attack Sudbury, Captain Wadsworth of Milton comes to village's defense, he and 28 men killed; **1638** town settled; **1639** town incorporated; **1654** town platted; **1686** Wayside Inn built by Samuel Howe, subject of Longfellow's "Tales of a Wayside Inn" 1862; **1690** Goulding House built; **1725** Israel Brown House built, served as Underground Railroad station for black slaves escaping to Canada; **1852** Wadsworth monument erected; **1862** Goodnow Public Library built; **1923** automobile inventor Henry Ford purchases Wayside Inn, burned 1955.

Swampscott *Essex County* *Eastern Massachusetts, 11 mi/18 km northeast of Boston, on Atlantic Ocean*

1629 town settled by Francis Ingalls; **1632** Ingalls builds tannery; **c.1640** Humphrey House built by lawyer John Humphrey; **1808** lobster pot invented by Ebenezer Thorndike; **1835** Ocean House built, town's first resort, rebuilt 1884, destroyed by fire 1969; **1840** the Swampscott dory invented by Theophilus Brackett; **1852** town incorporated; **1853** Swampscott Public Library founded, built 1917; **1865** Lincoln House hotel opened; **1866** Mary Baker Eddy, founder of Christian Science, begins her demonstrations of faith healing; **1872** Hotel Preston opened; **July 25,**

1894 actor Walter Brennan born (died 1974); **1905** Hotel Bellevue opened; **Feb. 28, 1956** railroad accident, 13 killed.

Swansea   *Bristol County   Southeastern Massachusetts, 43 mi/69 km south of Boston*

1632 area first settled, part of Rehoboth; **1649** Obadiah Holmes leads group of Baptist settlers to Rehoboth; **1663** First Baptist Church established by John Myles; **1667** Holmes founds town within Rehoboth; town incorporation applied for, not completed until 1785; **1675** earliest outbreak during King Philip's War takes place here, assemblage point for Massachusetts troops; entire town destroyed in fighting; **c.1685** Cape Codder House built; **1785** town incorporated; **1883** Swansea Public Library founded, opened 1900; **1891** town hall dedicated.

Taunton   *Bristol County   Southeastern Massachusetts, 31 mi/50 km south of Boston*

1638 town settled; **1639** town incorporated; **1652** iron bloomery established, first successful foundry in America; **1685** Bristol County formed; Bristol (now Rhode Island) becomes county seat; **1699** shipyard established; **May 22, 1703** pewterer Thomas Danforth born (died 1786); **1746** western part of county annexed by Rhode Island; county seat moved to Taunton; **Oct. 1774** Union Jack bearing words "Liberty and Union; Union and Liberty" raised on Town Green, declaration of rights placed at base of flagpole; **July 26, 1799** inventor Isaac Babbitt born, developed antifriction metal alloys (died 1862); **1823** Taunton Manufacturing Company textile firm established; **1824** Reed and Barton begin manufacture of silverware and plateware; **1846** Taunton Locomotive becomes first locomotive maker in New England; **1860** Taunton Public Library founded, built 1904; **1864** incorporated as a city; **Feb. 25, 1881** Communist party leader William Zebulun Foster born (died 1961); **1883** Rogers Silverware Company incorporated; **1898** Providence & Taunton Railroad reaches town; **1919** Taunton Municipal Airport established.

Townsend   *Middlesex County   North central Massachusetts, 40 mi/64 km northwest of Boston*

1676 town settled; **1732** town incorporated, named for Viscount Townshend [sp]; first Meeting House built; **1733** first grist mills and sawmills built; **1734** Harbor Dam built; **1744** Conant House built on Spannacook River; **1774** The Tavern at West Townsend opened; **Dec. 1, 1791** Asa Whitney born, inventor of railroad car wheels (died 1857); **1835** Female Academy founded, closed 1860; **1894** Memorial Hall built; **1936** floods destroy Townsend Harbor bridge.

Tyringham   *Berkshire County   Western Massachusetts, 33 mi/53 km west-northwest of Springfield*

1735 town first settled, land purchased from Stockbridge Native Americans; **1762** town incorporated; **1784** Shakers hold first meeting in area; **1787** region witnesses two skirmishes during Shay's Rebellion; **1792** Shakers establish colony of Fernside on slopes of Mt. Horeb; **c.1825** manufacture of hand rakes begins; **1832** paper mill built; **1903** Mark Twain spends summer here, donates entire set of his books to library.

Wakefield   *Middlesex County   Eastern Massachusetts, 10 mi/16 km north of Boston*

1638 town settled; **c.1681** Hartshorne House built; **1812** town incorporated; **1845** Boston & Maine Railroad reaches town; **1856** Wakefield Public Library founded, becomes Beebe Memorial Library 1923; **1851** foundry, cotton factory established by Cyrus Wakefield; **1868** town renamed Wakefield; town hall built with donation by Wakefield; **1889** Moller Piano Factory established; **June 23, 1904** anthropologist Carleton Stevens Coon born (died 1981); **Dec. 26, 2000** Michael McDermott, 42, shoots fellow workers at internet consulting firm, killing 7, disgruntled over tax audit.

Waltham   *Middlesex County   Eastern Massachusetts, 9 mi/14.5 km west of downtown Boston*

1634 town settled; **1738** town incorporated; **1806** Governor Gore House mansion built; **1813** Boston Manufacturing Company founded by Francis Cabot Lowell, builds cotton cloth finishing plant; **Jan. 30, 1816** Cong. Nathaniel Prentiss Banks born (died 1894); **1848** Massachusetts School for the Feeble-Minded established; **1854** American Waltham Watch Company founded; **1866** Robert Treat Paine Estate (Stonehurst) built; **1884** incorporated as a city; **1915** Waltham Library built; **1917** Bentley College established; **1925** city hall built; **1948** Brandeis University established; **1972** Waltham Museum founded; **1985** Waltham Philharmonic Orchestra founded.

Watertown   *Middlesex County   Eastern Massachusetts, 6 mi/9.7 km west of downtown Boston*

1630 Governor Winthrop's party arrives in Boston Harbor, 100 families of group move inland to present town site; town incorporated; **1631** dam built at falls of Charles River to power mills and factories; **1663** Capt. Abraham Browne House built; **1700** James Otis builds summer residence, becomes part of Oakley Country Club; **c.1750** Fowle House built; **Nov. 4, 1809** Supreme Court Justice Benjamin Robbins Curtis born, dissented in 1857 Dred Scott Case (died 1874); **Sept. 2, 1821** sculptor Anne Whitney born (died 1915); **1830** shoe industry founded by Bent family, declines by 1910; **1912** Perkins Institution and Massachusetts School for the Blind, founded 1829, moves from Boston.

Wellesley   *Norfolk County   Eastern Massachusetts, 12 mi/19 km west-southwest of downtown Boston*

1660 town settled; **1704** sawmill established; **1763** Harvard graduate Samuel Welles arrives; **1870** Female Seminary established, renamed Wellesley College 1875; **1881** town incorporated; **Jan. 21, 1884** reformer Roger Nash Baldwin born, founding director of American Civil Liberties Union (died 1981); **1885** town hall completed; **1911** Pine Manor Junior College established; **1914** fire destroys Wellesley College Hall, auditorium, dormitories; **1919** Babson Institute of business founded, becomes Babson College.

Wellfleet   *Barnstable County*   *Southeastern Massachusetts, 61 mi/98 km southeast of Boston, on Cape Cod*

Dec. 6–7, 1620 Pilgrims explore coast in *Mayflower's* shallop, move on to Plymouth; **Apr. 1717** pirate Black Sam Bellamy drowns when his ship founders in Cape Cod Bay; **c.1720** town settled; **1763** town incorporated; **1830** town enjoys monopoly on oystering, through 1870; **1850** port ranks second to Gloucester as cod and mackerel fishery; **1899** Capt. Lorenzo Dow Baker founds United Fruit Company, imports bananas from West Indies; **Jan. 19, 1901** Marconi's Transatlantic Wireless Station begins operating; **June 1, 1966** Cape Cod National Seashore established.

Wenham   *Essex County*   *Northeastern Massachusetts, 19 mi/31 km northeast of Boston*

1635 town settled; **1643** town incorporated; **1644** John Fiske begins serving as pastor of First Church parish, arrived from England after hiding in cellar for six months fearing reprisal for his religious dissent; **1664** Claflin-Richards House built, served as Tabby-Cat Tea House in 1930s; **1747** Henry Hobbs House built; **1843** First Church built on Town Green; **1889** Gordon College established; **2001** Hamilton-Wenham Public Library formed through merger.

West Boylston   *Worcester County*   *Central Massachusetts, 7 mi/11.3 km north of Worcester*

1642 town settled; **Apr. 24, 1766** Robert Bailey Thomas born, original creator of *Old Farmer's Almanac* (died 1846); **1808** town incorporated; **Apr. 2, 1814** Erastus Bigelow born, invented power carpet loom (died 1879); **1895** land purchased for Wachusett Reservoir, lake completed 1905 on South Branch Nashua River.

West Springfield   *Hampden County*   *West central Massachusetts, 2 mi/3.2 km west of Springfield*

1636 land purchased from Algonquins by William Pynchon, others; **c.1665** town settled on Connecticut River; **1754** Day House built; **1774** town incorporated; **1789** Figure born, horse owned by Justin Morgan, progenitor of Morgan horse, America's first horse breed; **1800** First Congregational Church built; **Apr. 10, 1810** journalist Benjamin Henry Day born, founded *New York Sun* (died 1889); **1841** Boston & Albany Railroad reaches town; **1854** West Springfield Public Library founded; **July 27, 1906** baseball player, manager Leo Ernest Durocher born (died 1991); **1921** Eastern States Agricultural and Industrial Exposition Grounds established; **1992** statue of horse Figure created by John Dann.

Westborough   *Worcester County*   *East central Massachusetts, 10 mi/16 km east of Worcester*

1675 town settled; **1717** town incorporated; **Dec. 8, 1765** cotton gin inventor Eli Whitney born (died 1825); **1835** Boston & Albany Railroad reaches town; **June 28, 1891** writer, editor Esther Forbes born (died 1967).

Westfield   *Hampden County*   *West central Massachusetts, 9 mi/14.5 km west of Springfield*

c.1660 area first settled; **1669** town incorporated; **1672** Capt. Aaron Cook builds tavern; **1801** Joseph Jokes opens town's first buggy whip factory; **1838** Westfield State College established, originally State Teachers College; **1839** town hall built; **1855** town boasts 30 buggy whip factories, produces 90 percent of world's buggy whips, becomes known as "Whip City"; **1860s** H. B. Smith Boiler Company established, beginning of town's boiler industry; **1920** incorporated as a city; **1923** Barnes Airport established; **1958** city hall built; **1998** Amelia Park Ice Arena built.

Weston   *Middlesex County*   *Eastern Massachusetts, 12 mi/19 km west of Boston*

1642 town settled; **1712** town incorporated; **1751** Elisha Jones House built, also known as Golden Ball Tavern; **1775** British spy John How discovered at Golden Ball Tavern, escapes, ire of citizens is so great that British alter plans, move on to Lexington; **1785** Artemus Ward House built; **1870s** estates built in area by wealthy Bostonians; **1888** organ factory established; **1903** Weston Aqueduct built to deliver water to Boston; **1927** Regis College established.

Weymouth   *Norfolk County*   *Eastern Massachusetts, 11 mi/18 km south-southeast of downtown Boston*

1622 ships *Charity* and *Swan* enter King's Cove with first settlers; town founded, originally named Wessagassett; **1635** town incorporated, renamed; **Nov. 23, 1744** Abigail Smith Adams, wife of Pres. John Adams, born (married 1764, died Oct. 28, 1818); **1771** bog iron mining and manufacture of nails begins; **1800** Old Toll House built; **1803** Samuel Arnold House built; **1853** Clapp Shoe Company founded; **1898** Fogg Public Library dedicated; **1930** toll house chocolate chip cookie developed by Ruth Wakefield at Toll House Restaurant.

Williamstown   *Berkshire County*   *Western Massachusetts, 57 mi/92 km northwest of Springfield*

1749 town settled; **1750** River Bend Tavern built; **1755** town platted; Col. Ephraim Williams bequeaths money for school conditional on town being named for him, killed six weeks later while fighting French and natives;

MASSACHUSETTS

1756 Fort Hoosac built; 1765 town incorporated; 1772 Green River Mansion built by Colonel Smedley; May 6, 1775 Col. Benedict Arnold stops at Smedley mansion, pays wife to make bread for troops; 1793 Williams College chartered; 1826 Walley Textile Mill opened; July 14, 1862 geologist Florence Bascom born (died 1945); 1863 Alpine Club founded by Prof. Albert Hopkins; 1865 Station Textile Mill established; 1873 Water Street Twine Mill built; 1874 Williamstown Public Library founded; c.1893 Sand Springs Sanitarium opened; 1955 Clark Art Institute opened.

Wilmington *Middlesex County* *Northeastern Massachusetts, 15 mi/24 km north-northwest of Boston*

1639 town settled; 1682 Bacon House built; c.1700 Capt. William Kidd rumored to have buried treasure at mouth of Devil's Den cave; 1720 Ford-Blanchard House built by Capt. Cadwalader Ford; 1730 town incorporated; Pearson Tavern built; 1790s Baldwin apple developed at Butter's Farm; 1806 Hop Brokerage House built by Caleb S. Harriman; 1835 Boston & Lowell Railroad reaches town; town becomes largest hop producer in state.

Winchester *Middlesex County* *Eastern Massachusetts, 8 mi/12.9 km northwest of Boston*

1640 town settled; c.1725 Black Horse Tavern opened, demolished 1892; 1803 Middlesex Canal opened, closed 1852; 1835 Boston & Lowell Railroad reaches town; 1839 Joel Whitney and Amos Whittemore build factory, various products include shoe-making machinery; 1850 town incorporated; 1859 Winchester Public Library founded, built 1930; 1860 tanning industry reaches peak; 1887 town hall built; 1893 Mackey Metallic Fastener Corporation founded; 1929 United Shoe Machinery Corporation acquires factory.

Woburn *Middlesex County* *Eastern Massachusetts, 10 mi/16 km north-northwest of downtown Boston*

1640 town settled; 1642 town incorporated; 1661 Baldwin Mansion built; 1714 Count Rumford's birthplace built; March 26, 1753 physicist, expatriate Sir Benjamin Thompson born, self-titled Count Rumford (died 1814); 1803 Middlesex Canal completed; Nov. 27, 1827 inventor of textile machinery Horace Wylie born (died 1915); 1835 Woburn Public Library founded; Boston & Lowell Railroad reaches town; 1855 shoe manufacturing begins, shifts to leather tanning by 1865, peaks 1880s; 1889 incorporated as a city; 1917 Woburn Armory built.

Wollaston *Norfolk County* *See **Quincy** (1896)*

Worcester *Worcester County* *East central Massachusetts, 39 mi/63 km west-southwest of Boston*

1674 Daniel Gookin accompanies Rev. John Eliot on visit with Nipmucks; 1682 Gookin returns with group of settlers; 1702 Queen Anne's War disrupts settlement;

1713 original settler Jonas Rice returns, builds first house; 1722 town incorporated; 1731 Worcester County formed; town becomes county seat; May 11, 1751 painter Ralph Earle born (died 1801); 1784 Becker College established; 1786 courthouse raided during Shays' Rebellion; 1789 textile industry begins with Worcester Cotton Manufactory; 1791 lower court applies "all men are born free and equal" in case of black slave; 1812 American Antiquarian Society established by Isaiah Thomas; Oct. 3, 1800 historian George Bancroft born (died 1891); 1818 Columbus, first elephant ever seen in America, displayed to public; Oct. 6, 1820 urban planner Andrew Haswell Green born (died 1903); 1825 Worcester Lyceum of Natural History founded, renamed Eco Tarium 1998 after several name changes; May 18, 1825 firearms inventor Daniel Baird West born (died 1906); 1828 Blackstone Canal completed to Woonsocket, Rhode Island; 1833 Pullman-Standard Car Company produces first railroad coach; Feb. 20, 1837 librarian Samuel Swett Green born, founded American Library Association (died 1918); 1843 College of the Holy Cross established; 1848 incorporated as a city; Whig Party dissolved at convention, Free Soil Party established as successor; 1850 Suffrage Movement launched at Women's Rights Convention; Sept. 25, 1856 archaeologist Edward Herbert Thompson born, authority on Yucatan Maya (died 1955); 1859 Henry David Thoreau eulogizes John Brown following abolitionist's hanging; Worcester Library founded; Jan. 8, 1859 explorer Fanny Bullock Workman born (died 1925); 1865 Worcester Polytechnic Institute established; 1874 Worcester State College established; 1887 Clark University established; Oct. 20, 1891 historian Samuel Bemis born (died 1973); 1896 Worcester Art Museum founded; 1898 city hall built; 1904 Assumption University established; July 29, 1905 poet Stanley Kunitz born; 1909 Union Station built, reopened 1999; Feb. 8, 1911 poet Elizabeth Bishop born (died 1979); Feb. 17, 1914 actor Arthur Kennedy born (died 1990); 1931 Higgins Armory Museum opened; 1946 Worcester Municipal Airport established, renamed Regional Airport 1996; June 9, 1953 tornado strikes city, 90 killed; March 14, 1971 fire at residential, commercial building, 7 killed, 20 injured; 1998 county government abolished; Dec. 4, 1999 fire in vacant warehouse, six firefighters killed.

Yarmouth *Barnstable County* *Southeastern Massachusetts, 62 mi/100 km southeast of Boston, on Cape Cod*

1639 town settled, incorporated; 1680 Thatcher House built; 1690 Old Yarmouth Inn built, probably oldest inn on Cape Cod; 1710 Baxter Mill built; 1780 Nantucket House relocated from Nantucket island, floated to Yarmouth; 1791 Judith Baker Windmill erected; 1809 Quaker Meeting House built; 1815 period of sea-based prosperity begins, through 1855; 1852 South Yarmouth Methodist Church built; 1826 Bass River Baptist Church built; 1870 First Congregational Church built; 1872 Kelley Chapel built; 1899 Sacred Heart Catholic Church built.

Michigan

Northern U.S. Capital: Lansing. Major city: Detroit.

The region became part of the U.S. as the Northwest Territory in 1787. It became part of Indiana Territory January 4, 1805. Michigan Territory was established January 11, 1805, and included present-day Wisconsin. Michigan entered the Union as the 26th state on January 26, 1837, the same date that Wisconsin became a territory.

Michigan is divided into 83 counties. The counties are divided into townships with limited government functions. Many urban townships have become charter townships, giving them stronger governmental powers, while others have incorporated as cities. Municipalities are classified as villages and cities. See Introduction.

Adrian *Lenawee County* *Southern Michigan, 60 mi/97 km southwest of Detroit*

1826 Lenawee County formed; Tecumseh becomes first county seat; town founded near River Raisin by Addison J. Comstock, name is variation of Roman Emperor Hadrian, Comstock's wife's hero; **1836** incorporated as a village; Erie & Kalamazoo Railroad reaches town from Toledo, Ohio; **1837** county seat moved to Adrian; **1853** incorporated as a city; **1859** Adrian College established; **1866** Croswell Opera House opened, becomes movie theater 1921, saved from demolition 1970s as live theater; **1870** Adrian Soldiers Monument dedicated; **1886** county courthouse built; **Apr. 27, 1893** stage designer Norman Bel Geddes born (died 1958); **1919** Siena Heights University established.

Albion *Calhoun County* *Southern Michigan, 88 mi/142 km west of Detroit*

1836 town founded; **1838** incorporated as a village; **1861** Albion College established, formerly Wesleyan Seminary, moved from Spring Arbor 1843; **1877** Mothers Day celebrated here 37 years before national observance; **1885** incorporated as a city; **1896** reinforced Cass Street Bridge built, called Dickie's Folly for Mayor Samuel Dickie; **Feb. 1903** heat wave follows 60 in/152 cm snowfall leads to record flooding; Cass Street Bridge only bridge to survive torrents, remains in use until 1993; **1913** Starr Commonwealth, home for delinquent boys, founded by Floyd Starr.

Algonac *Saint Clair County* *Southeastern Michigan, 34 mi/55 km northeast of Detroit, on St. Clair River*

1805 area first settled; **1826** town founded as Plainfield; **1843** town renamed Algonac; **1867** incorporated as a village; **1900** ferry established to Wallaceburg, Ontario, via Walpole Island; **1920s** ferry established to Harsens Island, Lake St. Clair; **1922** Chris Craft boat factory founded by Christopher Columbus Smith; **1967** incorporated as a city.

Allegan *Allegan County* *Southwestern Michigan, 32 mi/51 km south-southwest of Grand Rapids*

1834 town founded on Kalamazoo River by Elisha Gray; **1835** Allegan County formed; town becomes county seat; **1838** incorporated as a village; **1847** Pine Grove Seminary founded; **1868** first railroad reaches town; **1880** Second Street Bridge built on Kalamazoo River; **1884** fire destroys business district; **1907** incorporated as a city; **1914** Carnegie Library built; **1929** Griswold Auditorium built; **1961** county courthouse built.

Alma *Gratiot County* *Central Michigan, 58 mi/93 km northeast of Grand Rapids*

1853 town founded by Ralph Ely; **1854** sawmill built by Ely; **1872** incorporated as a village; **1883** Wright Hotel opened; **1887** Alma College established; **1894** Toledo & Ann Arbor Railroad begins service; **1899** Alma Sugar Company established, closed 1952; **1905** incorporated as a city; **1910** Libby canning plant opened; **1916** St. Mary's

MICHIGAN

Church built; **1931** Michigan Masonic Home built; **1943** Alma Airport established.

Alpena *Alpena County* *Northeastern Michigan, 183 mi/295 km northeast of Grand Rapids, on Lake Huron*

1856 town platted by George N. Fletcher; Daniel and Sarah Cook become first settlers at town site; **1857** Alpena County formed; town becomes county seat; **1857** incorporated as a village; **1859** town renamed Alpena; sawmill established; **1871** incorporated as a city; **1903** limestone quarrying begins; **1935** county courthouse built; **1952** Alpena Community College established; **1967** Alpena County Library established.

Ann Arbor *Washtenaw County* *Southeastern Michigan, 36 mi/58 km west of Detroit*

1824 John and Ann Allen of Virginia and Walker and Ann Rumsey of New York become first settlers; town founded, named for two Anns; **May 1824** town platted; **1826** Washtenaw County formed; town becomes county seat; **1833** incorporated as a village; **1836** Michigan Anti-Slavery Society organized; **1837** University of Michigan established, chartered 1817 in Detroit; **1847** town makes unsuccessful bid for state capital; **1851** incorporated as a city; **1855** Astronomical Observatory opened; **Aug. 17, 1864** sociologist Charles Horton Cooley born (died 1929); **1878** Toledo, Ann Arbor & Northern Railroad reaches city; **1890** interurban rail line established from Detroit, abandoned 1929; **July 20, 1907** railroad accident at rural Salem to northeast, 33 killed; **June 15, 1915** bacteriologist Thomas H. Weller born; **1955** county courthouse built; **1965** Washtenaw Community College established.

Arcadia *Manistee County* *Western Michigan, 110 mi/177 km north-northwest of Grand Rapids, on Lake Michigan*

1865 area first settled; **1880** sawmill founded by Henry Starke; **1881** town platted; **1888** steamer *Arcadia* launched to haul lumber, sinks 1907, all hands lost; **1895** Arcadia & Betsey River Railway established, abandoned 1936; **1906** Arcadia Furniture Factory established, closed 1953; **1922** Camp Arcadia established by Lutheran Church.

Atlanta *Montmorency County* *Northern Michigan, 160 mi/257 km north-northeast of Grand Rapids*

1840 Montmorency County formed; **1881** county organized; Hillman becomes first county seat; town of Atlanta founded by Alfred J. West; **1891** incorporated as a village; **1893** county seat moved to Atlanta; **1894** county courthouse completed; **1939** forest fires plague region.

Bad Axe *Huron County* *Eastern Michigan, 103 mi/166 km north of Detroit*

1859 Huron County formed; Harbor Beach becomes first county seat; **1861** town founded as road surveyors' camp by Rudolph Papst; **1864** Port Austin becomes second county seat; **1874** county seat moved to Bad Axe; **1876** county courthouse completed; **1881** land cleared for agriculture following great forest fire; county becomes producer of most of world's navy beans; fire reveals extensive Native American petroglyphs dating 300 to 1,000 years to south, later designated Sanilac Petroglyphs State Historic Park; **1885** incorporated as a village; **1905** incorporated as a city.

Baldwin *Lake County* *Western Michigan, 65 mi/105 km north of Grand Rapids*

1870 Flint & Pere Marquette Railroad built; town founded on railroad; **1871** Lake County formed; **1872** first store built; **1874** town becomes county seat; **1884** first known introduction of European brown trout in U.S. made in Pere Marquette River; **1885** county courthouse built, rebuilt 1927 following fire; **1887** incorporated as a village.

Bath *Clinton County* See **Lansing (1927)**

Battle Creek *Calhoun County* *Southern Michigan, 100 mi/161 km west of Detroit*

1825 tributary of Kalamazoo River named Battle Creek for skirmish between Native Americans and land surveyors; **1831** land purchased by J. J. Garnsey; **1832** post office established, originally named Garnsey; **1834** town renamed for Battle Creek; **1846** town platted; **1850** incorporated as a village; **1855** headquarters and printing house of Seventh-Day Adventist Church moved here from New Hampshire; **Oct. 1856** human rights reformer Sojourner Truth (Isabella Baumfree) arrives on speaking engagement, resides here until her death 1893 (born c.1797); **1859** incorporated as a city; **1866** Western Health Reform Institute built by Adventists, becomes Battle Creek Sanitarium 1876; **1874** Battle Creek College, later Emmanuel Missionary College, established by Adventists; **1877** Dr. John Harvey Kellogg of Battle Creek Sanitarium invents Granola; **1891** Adventist C. W. Post spends time in Battle Creek Sanitarium, establishes La Vita Inn after his release, caters to clients with ill health; **1894** C. W. Post develops healthful cereal drink Postum; Dr. John Kellogg and brother Will invent corn flakes, introduced 1898; **1895** Post Products factory built; **1903** Adventist Conference headquarters moved to Washington, D.C.; **1906** Will Kellogg splits with brother, founds Kellogg Toasted Corn Flake Company; **Feb. 26, 1921** actress Betty Hutton born; **1927** new sanitarium built; **1929** Kellogg Foundation health organization founded; **1956** Kellogg Community College established; **1977** Binder Park Zoo established; **1981** Kellogg Arena opened; **1995** Sojourner Truth Institute organized.

328

Bay City   *Bay County*   *Eastern Michigan, 98 mi/ 158 km north-northwest of Detroit, on Lake Huron*

1831 first white settlers arrive; **1835** trading post established; **1837** brothers James and Mader Tromble build first house on east side of river; **c.1838** more settlers arrive; town founded on west side of Saginaw River near its entrance to Saginaw Bay, Lake Huron; town named Lower Saginaw; **1858** Bay County formed; town becomes county seat; **1859** incorporated as a village with consolidation of Lower Saginaw and east shore settlements; renamed Bay City; **1860s** lumber industry becomes important; **1865** incorporated as a city; **1872** town boasts 36 lumber mills; Polish immigrants begin arriving; **1877** western shore settlements of Wenona, Salzburg, and Banks merge to form West Bay City; **1883** Sage Library opened; **1898** Michigan Sugar Company established, first viable beet sugar factory in Michigan; **1903** West Bay City annexed by Bay City; **1922** Bay City Public Library built; **1928** James Clement Airport (Tri-City Airport) opened, later becomes MBS International Airport; **1934** second county courthouse built; **Aug. 16, 1958** singer Madonna (Ciccone) born; **1961** Delta College (2-year) established to west at University Center.

Bay Mills   *Chippewa County*   *Northern Michigan, 12 mi/19 km west-southwest of Sault Ste. Marie*

1850s Bay Mills Indian Mission established by Methodists, school turned over to community 1971; **1875** James Norris Lumber Company established; **1882** town founded on Whitefish Bay, Lake Superior, at mouth of St. Marys River; **1885** Gillingham Fish Company established; town becomes important fishing port; **1890** sash and door factory established, destroyed by fire 1904; **1909** sawmilling ceases with depletion of forests; **1934** Bay Mills Indian Reservation established, called "The Farms," government attempt to turn Ojibwa people into farmers; **1984** Bay Mills Community College established; Bay Mills Casino opened; **Nov. 1995** Bay Mills Resort (Big Casino) opened.

Bellaire   *Antrim County*   *Northern Michigan, 142 mi/229 km north-northeast of Grand Rapids*

1840 Meguzee County formed; **1843** county renamed Antrim; Elk Rapids becomes first county seat; **1859** town founded by Ambrose E. Palmer between Lake Bellaire and Intermediate Lake, originally named Keno; **1879** incorporated as a village; county seat moved from Elk Rapids; **1880** village renamed Bellaire; **July 14, 1921** windstorm causes power lines to break, resulting fire destroys 12 buildings; **1978** county courthouse built.

Benton Harbor   *Berrien County*   *Southwestern Michigan, 175 mi/282 km west of Detroit, on Lake Michigan*

1669 Father Marquette enters St. Joseph River; **1679** Fort Miami built at mouth of river by La Salle; **1700** Jesuit mission founded; new fort built; **1763** fort destroyed by Chief Pontiac; **1783** area's first apple and cherry orchards planted by William Barnett of New Jersey; **1862** mile-long canal completed at mouth of St. Joseph River creating harbor; **1863** town founded, named Brunson Harbor, twin town to St. Joseph; **1866** incorporated as a village, renamed Benton Harbor for Missouri Sen. Thomas Hart Benton; **1891** incorporated as a city; **1899** Benton Harbor Library founded; **1903** Benjamin Franklin Purnell (King Ben) establishes Israelite House of David cult [see St. James]; **Jan. 20, 1929** comedian Arte Johnson born; **Jan. 17, 1942** boxer Muhammad Ali (Cassius Clay) born; **1946** Lake Michigan College (2-year) established; **Apr. 1968** race riots follow assassination of Dr. Martin Luther King.

Berrien Springs   *Berrien County*   *Southwestern Michigan, 172 mi/277 km west-southwest of Detroit*

1829 first settlers arrive; **1830** Berrien County formed; town founded as county seat on Lake Chapin, at outflow of Dowagiac River; **1839** county courthouse built; **1863** incorporated as a village; **1894** county seat moved to St. Joseph; **1901** Battle Creek College moved from Battle Creek, established 1874, becomes Emmanuel Missionary College 1901, renamed Andrews University 1960.

Bessemer   *Gogebic County*   *Northwestern Michigan, 285 mi/459 km west of Sault Ste. Marie*

1880 iron ore deposits discovered; **1883** first iron mine established; **1884** Milwaukee, Lake Shore & Western Railroad built; town founded; **1886** Gogebic (go-GEE-bik) County formed; town becomes county seat; Wakefield Iron Mine founded to east; **March 1887** incorporated as a village; **1888** county courthouse built, enlarged 1915; **1889** incorporated as a city; **1890s** railroad reaches town; iron ore mining flourishes; **1966** last iron mine closed.

Beulah   *Benzie County*   *Western Michigan, 118 mi/ 190 km north-northwest of Grand Rapids*

1869 Benzie County formed; Frankfort becomes first county seat; **1872** county seat moved to Benzonia, moved to town of Honor 1908; **1880** town founded by Rev. Charles E. Bailey at eastern end of Crystal Lake, near Lake Michigan; **1916** county seat moved to Beulah; Community Center, built 1912, converted to county courthouse; **1925** first Smelt Run Festival held; **1932** incorporated as a village; **1976** new county courthouse completed.

Big Rapids   *Mecosta County*   *Central Michigan, 52 mi/84 km north of Grand Rapids*

1851 John Parish becomes first settler; **1855** town founded on Muskegon River, originally named Leonard for land owner Dr. F. B. Leonard; Ferris Institute founded by Woodbridge N. Ferris; **1859** Mecosta County formed; town becomes county seat, renamed Big Rapids; **1860**

town platted; **1869** incorporated as a city; **1870** Grand Rapids & Indiana Railroad completed; **1884** Ferris State University established, originally named Big Rapids Industrial School; **1905** Rogers Dam Pond built to south on Muskegon River; **1970** second county courthouse built.

Bloomfield Hills   *Oakland County   Southeastern Michigan, suburb 20 mi/32 km north-northwest of Detroit*

1819 area first by Col. Benjamin H. Pierce, brother of Pres. Franklin Pierce; **1904** Ellen Scripps Booth and George G. Booth of *Detroit News* establish 300 ac/122 ha Cranbrook Estate; **1922** Brookside School opened at Cranbrook Estate; **1927** incorporated as a village, Christ Church (Episcopal) and Cranbrook School completed at Cranbrook; **1931** Kingswood School opened at Cranbrook; **1932** incorporated as a city; **1936** Cranbrook Academy of Art established; **1938** Cranbrook Institute of Science established, part of Cranbrook Educational Community, many buildings designed by Eliel Saarinen; **1964** Oakland Community College established.

Bridgman   *Berrien County   Southwestern Michigan, 182 mi/293 km west-southwest of Detroit*

1834 John Harner becomes first settler; **1856** Charlottesville Lumber Company founded; **1860** town founded on Lake Michigan; **1870** town platted by George W. Bridgman, renamed; **1918** Warren Dunes used as secret meeting place for illegal Workers' Party; **1927** incorporated as a village; **1949** incorporated as a city; **Aug. 1975** Cook Nuclear Power Plant begins production; **July 4, 2003** seven drownings reported in section of beach, possible strong undertow.

Cadillac   *Wexford County   North central Michigan, 90 mi/145 km north of Grand Rapids*

1840 Wexford County formed; **1869** county organized; **1870** Grand Rapids & Indiana Railroad reaches town; **1871** town founded as county seat on Lake Cadillac; pine lumber milling begins; **1873** Clam Lake Canal built, connects lakes Cadillac (Little Clam) and Mitchell (Big Clam); **1875** incorporated as a village; **1877** incorporated as a city; **1908** Carnegie Library completed; **1910** county courthouse built; **1935** first annual Winter Sports Festival held.

Calumet   *Houghton County   Northwestern Michigan, 210 mi/338 km west-northwest of Sault Ste. Marie*

1864 Calumet Mining Company organized; **1866** Hecla Mining Company organized; post office established; **1871** Calumet and Hecla Consolidated Copper Mining Company established; town founded; **1875** incorporated as a village; **1890** Finnish Evangelical Lutheran Church, Suomi Synod, organized; **1900** Calumet Theater opened; **Dec. 24, 1913** during gathering at Italian Hall, someone cries "Fire!" 72 women and children trampled to death by false alarm.

Caro   *Tuscola County   Eastern Michigan, 83 mi/134 km north of Detroit*

1850 Tuscola County formed; **1852** town first settled; **1853** Vassar becomes first county seat; **1866** town founded, originally named Centerville; county seat moved from Vassar; **1869** town renamed, variation of Cairo; **1871** incorporated as a village; **1899** large sugar beet mill built; **1933** county courthouse built.

Centreville   *Saint Joseph County   Southern Michigan, 130 mi/209 km west-southwest of Detroit*

1826 area settled; **1829** St. Joseph County formed; **1831** Thomas W. Langley becomes town's first settler, builds tavern; town founded as county seat; **1837** incorporated as a village; **1878** Doctor Denton Sleeping Garment Mills founded, maker of underwear; **1887** Langley Covered Bridge built to north on St. Joseph River; **1900** county courthouse built; **1965** Glen Oaks Community College established.

Charlevoix   *Charlevoix County   Northern Michigan, 165 mi/266 km north of Grand Rapids, on Lake Michigan*

1840 Charlevoix County formed, named for Jesuit missionary Pierre F. X. Charlevoix; **1852** first settlers arrive; town founded as fishing colony, originally named Pine River; **1853** skirmish takes place between Mormons living on Beaver Island to northwest and mainlanders, one killed, several wounded [see St. James]; **1864** large dock built; **1869** county organized; town becomes county seat, renamed; **1876** short Pine River dredged to Lake Charlevoix creating harbor; **1878** town platted; **1879** incorporated as a village; **1885** Charlevoix Lighthouse erected; **1905** incorporated as a city; **1958** second county courthouse completed; **Sept. 27, 1962** Big Rock Point Nuclear Power plant begins operation.

Charlotte   *Eaton County   South central Michigan, 20 mi/32 km southwest of Lansing*

1837 Easton County formed; Bellevue becomes first county seat; **1840** town founded as new county seat; **1863** incorporated as a village; **1871** incorporated as a city; **1894** county courthouse built.

Cheboygan   *Cheboygan County   Northern Michigan, 200 mi/322 km north-northeast of Grand Rapids*

1855 Cheboygan County formed; **1857** town founded as county seat on Lake Huron, named Duncan; **1859** Cheboygan Lighthouse erected; **1867** Inland Waterway built connecting Lake Huron with smaller lakes to south, alternate route to Lake Michigan for small craft; **1870** town renamed Cheboygan; **1871** incorporated as a village;

1877 Opera House built, closed 1950s, reopened 1984; **1880s** town becomes important lumbering center; **1889** incorporated as a city; **1913** Carnegie Library opened; **1969** county courthouse built.

Coldwater *Branch County Southern Michigan, 103 mi/166 km west-southwest of Detroit*

1829 Branch County formed; Masonville becomes county seat; **1830** first cabin built on Coldwater River, at crossing of Chicago Turnpike; **1831** county seat moved to town of Branch, near Bronson; **1832** town platted; **1837** incorporated as a village; malaria epidemic kills 32 of town's 140 people; **1842** county seat moved to Coldwater; **1850** Michigan Southern & Northern Indiana Railroad reaches town; **1861** incorporated as a city; **1871** Coldwater Regional Center for Developmental Disabilities founded; **1882** Coldwater Opera House built; **1884** public library established from private library of H. C. Lewis; **1887** county courthouse built, destroyed by fire 1972; **1934** Legg Airport established; **1976** new county courthouse completed; **March 19, 2002** Maud Farris-Luse dies at age 115 and 56 days, oldest person in world according to Guinness' Book of Records, born Jan. 21, 1887.

Copper Harbor *Keweenaw County Northwestern Michigan, 188 mi/303 km northwest of Sault Ste. Marie*

1843 town founded at north end of Keweenaw Peninsula as chief port for Copper Country mining district; **1844** Fort Wilkins built to east on Lake Superior, abandoned 1870; **1866** Copper Harbor Lighthouse erected; **1890s** logging briefly replaces town's loss as copper shipping port caused by construction of railroads; **1921** Fort Wilkins State Park established; **1936** Keweenaw Park Cottages, Golf Course built by WPA overlooking Lake Superior, nucleus of Keweenaw Mountain Lodge; **c.1938** passenger ferry service on *Isle Royale Queen* begins to Isle Royale to northwest.

Corunna *Shiawassee County Central Michigan, 71 mi/114 km northwest of Detroit*

1836 town founded; **1837** Shiawassee County formed; **1840** town becomes county seat; **1843** flour mill built on Shiawassee River; **1858** incorporated as a village; **1869** incorporated as a city; **1904** county courthouse built.

Cross Village *Emmet County Northern Michigan, 190 mi/306 km north-northeast of Grand Rapids*

1671 Father Marquette (1637–1675) plants cross on shore of Lake Michigan; **c.1850** log Catholic church built; **1855** Society of St. Francis Convent established by Father Weikamp, abandoned 1896, buildings destroyed by lightning 1906; **1875** town founded, given present name; **1898** Holy Cross Catholic Church built; **1913** present cross erected.

Croswell *Sanilac County Eastern Michigan, 70 mi/113 km north-northeast of Detroit*

1845 first settlers arrive; town founded on Black River; **1881** incorporated as a village; Great Fire destroys one million acres in Huron and Sanilac counties, 125 killed; **1902** Pioneer Sugar Company founded; **1905** incorporated as a city; 139 ft/42 m swinging foot bridge built across river; **1912** William H. Aitkin Public Library opened.

Crystal Falls *Iron County Northwestern Michigan, 200 mi/322 km west-southwest of Sault Ste. Marie*

1881 Chicago & Northwestern Railroad reaches site; town founded on Paint River as mining and timber center; **1882** Bristol Iron Mine opens; **1885** Iron County formed; **1889** incorporated as a village; **1890** county courthouse built; **1899** incorporated as a city.

Dearborn *Wayne County Southeastern Michigan, suburb 9 mi/14.5 km west of Detroit*

1763 French establish farms in area outside Detroit following defeat of Pontiac; **1796** A. J. Bucklin and Thomas brothers of Ohio become first American settlers; **1804** Methodist Episcopal Church holds first meetings; **1818** Protestant church and schoolhouse built (school burned 1830); **1832** U.S arsenal moved from Detroit, abandoned 1875, becomes City Historical Museum 1950; **1833** Haigh House built by Col. Joshua Howard; **1835** Great Sauk Trail completed between Detroit and Chicago; **1837** Michigan Central Railroad reaches town; town of Dearbornville founded short distance east of present Dearborn; **1838** Dearbornville incorporated as a village, disincorporated 1846; **1842** Holy Cross Catholic Church built; **1860** Christ Church (Episcopal) built; **July 30, 1863** automobile inventor Henry Ford born (died 1947); **1871** St. Paul's Lutheran Church built; **1893** Dearborn incorporated as a village; **1900** *Dearborn Independent* newspaper founded, purchased by Henry Ford 1918; **1917** Henry Ford establishes factory on River Rouge for manufacture of "Eagle Boats" used by U.S. Navy against submarines; **1920s** Ford Industries develops its River Rouge Plant for making Model T cars and Fordson tractors; **1921** Dearbornville reincorporated as a village, renamed Springwells; **1923** Springwells incorporated as a city; **1927** Dearborn incorporated as a city; dirigible mooring tower erected at Ford Airport 210 ft/64 m tall; Springwells renamed Fordson; **1927** Ford's Model A car introduced; **1928** Dearborn annexes Fordson; **1931** Cosmopolitan Club of Dearborn organized; Henry Ford Museum and Greenfield Village historical attraction established; **Oct. 23, 1934** Jean and wife Jeannette Piccard ascend in stratospheric balloon, rises to 57,579 ft/17,550 m, descend at Cadiz, Ohio, three hours later; **1938** Henry Ford Community College established; first units of large Ford Foundation housing project built; **Apr. 7, 1947** Henry Ford dies at age 83, leaves estate of up to $700 million; **1959** University of Michigan at Dearborn established.

Deerfield   *Lenawee County*   Southeastern
Michigan, 48 mi/77 km southwest of Detroit

1824 William Kedzie becomes first settler; **1828** town founded on River Raisin, named Kedzie's Grove; **1837** town renamed Deerfield; **1873** incorporated as a village; **Jan. 6, 1914** TV actor Danny Thomas born (died 1991).

Detroit   *Wayne County*   Southeastern Michigan, on
Detroit River, opposite Windsor, Ontario, Canada

1701 Frenchman Antoine de la Mothe Cadillac establishes Fort Pontchartrain du Detroit; St. Anne's Roman Catholic Church founded; **1760** British seize fort during French and Indian War; **1783** Northwest Territory ceded to U.S. under Treaty of Paris, remains under British occupation; **1796** U.S. takes possession of town with signing of Jay's Treaty; Wayne County formed, named for Gen. Anthony Wayne; town becomes county seat; **1802** town incorporated; **1805** fire destroys entire town; Michigan Territory created; new town platted, becomes territorial capital; **1806** town rebuilt, plan based upon design by Pierre l'Enfant's design of Washington, D.C.; **Aug. 16, 1812** British Gen. Isaac Brock captures Detroit from American Gen. William Hull, War of 1812; **1813** Detroit retaken by Gen. William Henry Harrison; **1815** incorporated as a city; **1818** first Great Lakes steamboat *Walk-on-the-Water* arrives; **Sept. 14, 1819** Union Gen. Henry Jackson Hunt born (died 1889); **1822** first stagecoach service inaugurated; **1825** opening of Erie Canal in New York brings commerce and people to city; **1828** first Michigan capitol built; **1831** *Detroit Free Press* and *Michigan Intelligencer* newspapers founded; **1833** rioting follows arrest of fugitive slaves; **1835** old city hall built; **1837** Michigan becomes 26th state; Detroit becomes first state capital; Detroit Anti-Slavery Society organized; **1838** first section of Detroit & Pontiac Railroad completed; **1839** abolitionist John Brown brings 14 fugitive slaves from Missouri, meets with Frederick Douglass, others; **1844** Sts. Peter and Paul's Roman Catholic Church completed; **1847** state capital moved to Lansing; **July 4, 1847** James Anthony McGinnis born, changes last name to Bailey upon joining a circus at age 14, became partner with P. T. Barnum 1881 (died 1906); **1848** first Michigan State Fair held; **1849** Fort Wayne completed on Detroit River; Mariners' Church holds first services; **1850** Temple Beth El Jewish congregation formed; **1852** railroad completed Chicago; **1854** railroad opened from New York through Canada; **1855** Fort Street Presbyterian Church built; **1856** railroad opened to Toledo, Ohio; **1859** railroad opened to Port Huron; **1863** proslavery factions riot against blacks; 895 blacks join Union army; **c.1863** city's industrial development begins; **1867** Central Methodist Church completed; **1868** Wayne State University established, originally Detroit Medical College; **1870** R. L. Polk publishes his first city directories; **1871** city hall dedicated; railroad completed to Lansing; **1873** final stagecoach service ends; Leon Czolgosz born, assassinated President McKinley Sept. 6, 1901, in Buffalo, New York, executed at Auburn, New York, Oct. 29, 1901;

1874 Parke-Davis Laboratories established on Detroit River, company pioneers standardized pharmaceutical manufacturing; **1876** *Detroit News* newspaper founded; **1877** University of Detroit established; **1879** Belle Isle Park established; **1882** Belle Isle Lighthouse built, only light on Belle Isle until 1930; **1883** Detroit Zoo established; **1888** Detroit Institute of Arts opened, new building completed 1927; **1889** Belle Isle Bridge built, destroyed by fire 1915, rebuilt 1923, later renamed Douglas MacArthur Bridge; **1891** Detroit Institute of Technology organized; **1896** Henry Ford hand-builds his first car; **1899** R. E. Olds builds Detroit's first automobile factory; **early 1900s** succession of reform mayors—Hazen Pingree (1890–1901), James Couzens (1919–1923), and Frank Murphy (1930–1933)—succeed in eliminating corruption, transform city into major industrial entity; **1902** Wayne County Building completed; fire destroys Olds Motor Works plant; **Feb. 4, 1902** aviator Charles A. Lindbergh born (died 1974); **1903** Henry Ford organizes Ford Motor Company; **Aug. 7, 1904** African-American political scientist Ralph Bunche born, Nobel Peace Prize (died 1971); **1905** Marygrove College established; U.S. Rubber Company plant opened; **1906** Packard Motor Car Plant built on Grand Avenue; first Shriners' Circus held; **1907** Jefferson Avenue Chrysler Plant opened, closed 1990, new plant opened 1992 at same site; **1909** Hudson Motor Car Plant opened, closed 1954; **March 28, 1909** novelist Nelson Algren born (died 1981); **1911** St. Paul's Episcopal Cathedral completed; Continental Motors Company plant opened, closed 1939; **Feb. 23, 1911** Gov. G. (Garland) Mennen Williams born (died 1988); **1912** Tiger Stadium built in Corktown district; **Sept. 5, 1913** Attorney General John Newton Mitchell born, served under President Nixon (died 1988); **1914** Detroit Symphony Orchestra organized; **Apr. 10, 1915** TV actor Harry Morgan born; **May 3, 1920** heavyweight boxer Walker Smith "Sugar Ray" Robinson born (died 1989); **1921** Detroit Public Library completed; sea lamprey becomes known to have invaded waters of Lake Erie and Lake St. Clair; Cosmopolitan Women's Club of Detroit organized; Cadillac Plant built on Jefferson Avenue; **Nov. 14, 1921** singer Johnny Desmond born (died 1985); **Nov. 12, 1922** actress Kim Hunter born (died 2002); **Jan. 30, 1923** comedian Dick Martin (of Rowan & Martin) born; **March 6, 1923** TV personality Ed McMahon born; **July 22, 1924** singer Margaret Whiting born; **Dec. 6, 1924** TV actor Wally Cox born (died 1973); **1925** Scott Memorial Fountain erected in Belle Isle Park, designed by Cass Gilbert; 35-story Book Tower Building completed; Chrysler Kercheval Plant purchased from American Body Corporation; **Jan. 26, 1925** actress Joan Leslie born; **Feb. 22, 1925** singer Guy Mitchell born (died 1984); **Oct. 21, 1925** actress Joyce Randolph born; **1926** Center for Creative Studies–College of Art and Design established; **Feb. 2, 1926** actress Elaine Stritch born; **1927** Detroit Institute of Arts completed; **Dec. 28, 1927** TV actor Martin Milner born; **1928** 47-story Penobscot Building completed; 28-story Fisher Building completed; 38-story David Stott Building completed; 40-story Guardian Building completed; 40-story Cadillac Tower

Building completed; **Oct. 1, 1928** actor George Peppard born (died 1994); **1929** Detroit Zoological Gardens reestablished at suburban Huntington Woods to north; Edison Fountain erected in Grand Circus Park; U.S. Marine Hospital completed on Lake St. Clair; Chrysler Plymouth Plant opened on Lynch Road; Ambassador Bridge opened across Detroit River to Windsor, Ontario; **1930** Detroit-Windsor Fleetway Tunnel completed under Detroit River; St. Aloysius Roman Catholic Church completed; Livingstone Memorial Lighthouse completed at eastern end of Belle Isle, old Belle Isle Light retained as supplemental signal; **1930** Wayne County Airport established, renamed Detroit Metropolitan-Wayne County Airport 1958; **Feb. 10, 1930** actor Robert Wagner born; **July 6, 1931** singer/actress Della Reese born; **1932** Downtown Library opened; **Jan. 1, 1932** actress Piper Laurie born; **Jan. 4, 1932** actor Richard Stahl born; **Dec. 7, 1932** actress Ellen Burstyn born; **1933** Windmill Point Lighthouse built on Lake St. Clair at Detroit River entrance; **Apr. 27, 1933** TV, radio personality Casey Kasem born; **Aug. 25, 1933** actor Tom Skerritt born; **1936** Chrysler De Soto Plant opened, closed 1958; **Nov. 20, 1937** actress Ruth Laredo born; **1938** Parkside Housing Project completed on east side; Dodge Truck Plant completed; **Apr. 7, 1939** movie director Francis Ford Coppola born; **Sept. 1, 1939** comedian Lily Tomlin born; **Feb. 19, 1940** singer Smokey Robinson born; **Apr. 5, 1941** actor Michael Moriarty born; **Apr. 5, 1943** actor Max Gail born; **June 21, 1943** 34 killed, 700 injured in race rioting, also in Harlem, New York; **Nov. 21, 1943** TV actress Marlo Thomas, daughter of Danny Thomas, born; **March 26, 1944** singer Diana Ross born; **July 12, 1944** actress Denise Nicholas born; **Aug. 24, 1944** astronaut Gregory B. Jarvis born, killed Jan. 28, 1986, in *Challenger* disaster; **Jan. 29, 1945** actor Tom Selleck born; **June 28, 1946** comedian Gilda Radner born (died 1989); **Apr. 5, 1950** actress Christine Lahti born; **1951** Detroit Historical Museum dedicated; **July 7, 1951** actress Roz Ryan born; **June 30, 1955** actor David Alan Grier born; **1960** Cobo Hall convention center opened, expanded 1989; Motown Records company established; **March 2, 1962** singer, U.S. Cong. Sonny Bono born, formerly of singing team Sonny & Cher (died 1998); **Nov. 21, 1964** Detroit *News* and *Free Press* strike settled after 132 days, longest newspaper strike in U.S. history; **1965** Museum of African-American History established by Dr. Charles Wright; **Nov. 16, 1965** Alice Hertz, 81, immolates herself on busy street to protest Vietnam War, dies several days later; **1967** Wayne County Community College established; **July 1967** racial rioting causes $150 million in damage, 43 killed; **Oct. 25, 1967** 49-day walkout at Ford Motor Company ends with 3-year contract; **1970** Detroit Science Center established; **Feb. 19, 1970** baseball commissioner Bowie Kuhn suspends pitcher Denny McLain for 1967 bookmaking operations, reinstated July 1; **Aug. 1, 1972** Miami-bound plane hijacked by five armed men, lands in Algiers, hijackers given asylum, ransom returned; **Jan. 7, 1975** Chrysler announces first car rebate offer, $200–400 cash back, others follow suit; **1977** Renaissance Center completed on river front, complex of 39-story four

office towers connected to 73-story hotel at core; **Jan. 26, 1978** snowstorm hits Michigan and Indiana, 70 killed, thousands stranded in their cars; **Nov. 1, 1979** Chrysler Corporation receives $1.5 billion in government loans; **Dec. 1979** Joe Louis Arena opened; **1984** Holocaust Memorial Center dedicated; **1987** *Detroit Free Press* and *Detroit News* merge operations; **July 1987** Detroit People Mover mini-rail system opened in downtown; **1991** 45-story Comerica Tower building completed; **Jan. 6, 1994** figure skater Nancy Kerrigan clubbed during practice, rival Tanya Harding wins competition, Harding's bodyguard arrested in Portland, Oregon, Harding pleads guilty to hindering prosecution; **1996** Detroit Opera House opened; **1998** 15 die, c.100 become ill nationwide from contaminated meat produced here at Sara Lee Company; **Apr. 11, 2000** first game held in $300 million Comerica Stadium, replacing Tiger Stadium; **Aug. 13–14, 2003** massive power outage affects 50 million people from Michigan to New England.

Dowagiac *Cass County* *Southwestern Michigan, 160 mi/257 km west-southwest of Detroit*

1831 carding mill established by William Renesten; **1848** Michigan Central railroad built; town settled; **1854** Round Oak Stove Company established by Philo D. Beckwith; **1863** incorporated as a village; **1866** Beckwith Memorial Theatre built, razed 1966; **1877** incorporated as a city; **1964** Southwestern Michigan College (2-year) established.

Eagle River *Keweenaw County* *Northwestern Michigan, 205 mi/330 km northwest of Sault Ste. Marie*

1845 Douglass Houghton, first state geologist, drowns in Lake Superior off Eagle River; **1846** Houghton County formed; Phoenix becomes first county seat; **1853** town founded on Lake Superior; Houghton County seat moved to Eagle River; **1861** Keweenaw County formed from Houghton County; Eagle River becomes Keweenaw County seat; Houghton County seat moved to Houghton; **1862** Eagle River Fuse Company plant founded, maker of blasting fuses for mining; county courthouse built, remodeled 1927; **1871** Eagle River Lighthouse erected, discontinued 1908.

East Lansing *Ingham County* *South central Michigan, 3 mi/4.8 km east of Lansing*

1849 D. Robert Burcham becomes first settler; town founded on Red Cedar River, named Okemos; **1850** Grand Rapids plank road built; **1855** Michigan Agricultural College established, becomes Michigan State University; **1890s** temperance movement succeeds in restricting alcohol sales; **1907** incorporated as a city, renamed East Lansing; **1923** People's Church (interdenominational) built, founded 1920; **1932** Michigan State Police Headquarters built.

Eaton Rapids *Eaton County* *South central Michigan, 16 mi/26 km south-southwest of Lansing*

1838 town founded on Grand River by Amos and Pierpont Spicer, originally named Spicerville; **Aug. 2, 1846** law educator Melville M. Bigelow born (died 1921); **1859** incorporated as a village; **1881** incorporated as a city; **1921** Davidson Woolen Mill established, provides material for 95 percent of major league baseball uniforms, burned 1969.

Elberta *Benzie County* *Western Michigan, 118 mi/ 190 km north-northwest of Grand Rapids, on Lake Michigan*

1866 town founded, named South Frankfort; **1867** Frankfort Iron Works established, closed 1883; **1872** Toledo, Ann Arbor & Northern Michigan Railroad reaches town; **1892** car ferry service to Kewaunee, Wisconsin, begins, ended 1982; **1894** incorporated as a village; **1896** car ferry service to Manitowoc, Wisconsin, begins, ended 1973; **1899** car ferry service to Menominee, Upper Peninsula, Michigan, begins, ended 1970; **1902** car ferry service to Manistique, Upper Peninsula, Michigan, begins, ended 1968; **1911** town renamed for Elberta peaches grown in area.

Escanaba *Delta County* *Northwestern Michigan, 145 mi/233 km southwest of Sault Ste. Marie*

1852 town founded at entrance to Little Bay de Noc, Lake Michigan; **1861** Delta County formed; Masonville becomes county seat; **1863** county seat moved to Escanaba; shipping dock built; **1864** first shipment of iron ore exits harbor; **1866** incorporated as a village; **1870s** commercial fishing established; **1871** Chicago & Northwestern Railroad reaches town from south; **1883** incorporated as a city; **1887** Minneapolis, St. Paul & Sault Ste. Marie (Soo Line) Railroad built; **1963** Bay de Noc Community College established; **1961** county courthouse built.

Essexville *Bay County* *Eastern Michigan, 58 mi/ 93 km north-northwest of Detroit, on Lake Huron*

1819 Nobobish Indian Reservation established, named for Chippewa chief; **1837** reservation abandoned; **1850** brothers John T., Jr. and Ransom P. Essex become first white settlers; **1852** town founded on Saginaw River, at its entrance to Saginaw Bay, Lake Huron; **1867** Carriere Sawmill established; **1871** post office established; **1883** incorporated as a village; **1898** first sugar beet refinery in state opens; **1934** incorporated as a city.

Farmington Hills *Oakland County* *Southeastern Michigan, 20 mi/32 km northwest of Detroit*

1827 Farmington Township formed; **1836** Botsford Tavern built as residence, becomes tavern 1842, restored 1924 by Henry Ford; **1907** Ford Republic, training school for delinquent boys, founded; **Oct. 18, 1951** actress Pam Dawber born; **1973** township incorporated as city of Farmington Hills, surrounds city of Farmington.

Flint *Genessee County* *Eastern Michigan, 58 mi/ 93 km northwest of Detroit*

1819 fur trader Jacob Smith persuades Chippewa and Potawatomi to align themselves against French and British, granting land along Flint River for settlement by Americans; Smith becomes first settler; **1830** settler John Todd builds tavern, establishes ferry; town founded; **1833** road built linking town with Detroit and Saginaw; **1835** incorporated as a village; **1836** Genessee County formed; town becomes county seat; **1854** Michigan School for the Deaf founded; **1855** incorporated as a city; **1872** McCreery Mansion built by Maj. Fenton R. McCreery; **1890s** manufacture of road carts and carriages begins; **1904** Buick Motor Company organized; **1905** Flint Public Library built; **1903** Buick automobile factory opened; **1908** General Motors organized by William C. Durant; A.C. Spark Plugs plant opened; **1911** Baker College of Flint established; **1919** Kettering University established; General Motors Institute established for technical training; **1923** Flint Junior College established, becomes Charles Stewart Mott Community College; **1926** county courthouse built; **1929** Industrial Mutual Association Auditorium built; **Dec. 30, 1936** first organized strike against Flint auto industry occurs at Fisher Body Plant, factory occupied by workers, violence Jan. 11, 1937, brings out National Guard, 27 injured, strike ends Feb. 11; **June 8, 1953** tornado damages city, kills 115 in Flint and Lakeport to east, series of 12 tornadoes, 142 total killed in Michigan and Ohio June 7-9; **June 6, 1955** actress Sandra Bernhard born; **1956** University of Michigan, Flint Campus, established.

Frankenmuth *Saginaw County* *Eastern Michigan, 78 mi/126 km north-northwest of Detroit*

1845 town founded on Cass River by Bavarian Lutherans led by Rev. Friedrich Auguste Craemer; **1847** flour mill built; **1848** refugees from German revolution arrive; **1888** Union House hotel opened, becomes Bavarian Inn 1959; **1904** incorporated as a village; **1959** incorporated as a city; first Bavarian Festival held.

Frankfort *Benzie County* *Western Michigan, 120 mi/193 km north-northwest of Grand Rapids, on Lake Michigan*

1869 Benzie County formed; **1870** town founded as first county seat; **1872** county seat moved to Benzonia; Toledo, Ann Arbor & Northern Michigan Railroad reaches town; **1874** incorporated as a village; **1876** Point Betsie Lighthouse built, replaces 1858 structure, automated 1983; **1903** Congregational Assembly Grounds retreat founded to north on Crystal Lake; **1935** incorporated as a city; **1892** first car ferry service across Lake Michigan begins, operated by Ann Arbor Railroad, last of four routes suspended 1982 [see Elberta].

Fremont *Newaygo County   Western Michigan,*
38 mi/61 km north of Grand Rapids

1854 town settled by Daniel R. Joslin; **1855** town founded; post office established, named Weaversville for first postmaster Daniel Weaver; **1862** town renamed for Union Gen. John C. Fremont; **1875** incorporated as a village; **1911** incorporated as a city; **1928** Gerber Products Company baby food manufacturer founded by Dorothy Gerber.

Gaylord *Otsego County   Northern Michigan,*
153 mi/246 km north-northeast of Grand Rapids

1874 town founded; **1875** Otsego County formed; Otsego Lake becomes first county seat; **1877** county seat moved to Gaylord; **1881** incorporated as a village; **1891** county courthouse built; **Apr. 30, 1916** mathematician Claude E. Shannon born (died 2001); **1922** incorporated as a city; **1932** Dearborn Colony established by six families from Dearborn attempting to return to land to escape Depression hardships; **1967** City-County Building completed.

Gladwin *Gladwin County   Central Michigan,*
92 mi/148 km northeast of Grand Rapids

1865 area first settled; **1873** town founded by lumbermen as logging center; **1875** Gladwin County formed; **1885** incorporated as a village; **1893** incorporated as a city; **1939** county courthouse built.

Grand Haven *Ottawa County   Western Michigan,*
29 mi/47 km west of Grand Rapids

1833 trading post built by Rix Robinson; **1835** town founded on Spring Lake, natural harbor on Lake Michigan formed by Grand River; **1837** Ottawa County formed; town becomes county seat; **1867** incorporated as a city; **1881** beacon erected on South Pier, lighthouse added 1907; **1903** car ferry service begun to Milwaukee by Grand Trunk Railroad, suspended 1982; **1965** county courthouse built.

Grand Marais *Alger County   Northern Michigan,*
81 mi/130 km west of Sault Ste. Marie, on Lake Superior

1650 harbor visited by Pierre Esprit Raddison; **1830** town founded as fishing center, trading post; **1852** town platted; **1870s** lumber industry becomes important, ends c.1910; **1899** Grand Marais Lighthouse established; **1942** first defense radar station in Michigan built; **Oct. 15, 1966** Pictured Rocks National Lakeshore authorized to west.

Grand Rapids *Kent County   Western Michigan,*
142 mi/229 km west-northwest of Detroit

1825 Baptist Mission established on Grand River; **1826** Louis Campau becomes first settler, establishes trading post 1827; **1831** Campau plats town; rival Lucius Lyon plats competing town immediately to north, retaliating for having been beaten for best site by platting his tract with odd-angled streets, evident in city's downtown street pattern; Lyon wins over Campau by having town named Kent instead of Grand Rapids; **1836** Kent County formed; town becomes county seat; **1837** first steamboats arrive from Grand Haven, on Lake Michigan; William Haldane establishes cabinetmaking business, beginning of city's status as furniture capital of U.S.; **1838** incorporated as a village; ice jam on Grand River causes serious flooding; **1842** Campau succeeds in having town renamed Grand Rapids; **1850** incorporated as a city; **1852** city again inundated by flooding; **1854** logging becomes important; **1858** first railroad reaches town; Leavitt House built; **1860** Gunnison Octagonal House built by Ira Jones; **c.1870** thousands of families immigrate from Norway and Sweden at invitation of Grand Rapids & Indiana Railroad; **March 12, 1873** author Stewart Edward White born (died 1946); **1876** Calvin College established; **1883** millions of feet of logs break loose from upstream booms destroying three railroad bridges, damaging large part of city; **1886** Aquinas College established; **1889** county courthouse built; **1891** Grand Rapids Zoo opened; **1893** St. Cecilia Society Building recital hall built; **May 1, 1895** organist, composer Leo Sowerby born (died 1968) **1904** flooding inundates 1,500 homes, leaves city without electrical power for several nights; **1910** Art Museum opened; **1914** Grand Rapids Community College established; **1919** Kent County Airport established to southeast, renamed Gerald R. Ford International Airport 1999; **1925** catalog-printing industry begins; **Apr. 4, 1925** actress Elizabeth Wilson born; **1935** Municipal Wholesale Market built; **Feb. 15, 1935** astronaut Roger B. Chaffee born, killed Jan. 27, 1967, in *Apollo I* fire on launch pad; **Feb. 29, 1936** astronaut Jack Lousma born; **1941** Cornerstone University established; **Apr. 1981** Gerald R. Ford Presidential Library dedicated; **1991** Fred Meijer Gardens and Sculpture Park opened.

Grayling *Crawford County   Northern Michigan,*
127 mi/204 km north-northeast of Grand Rapids

1874 town platted by Saginaw & Jackson Railroad; **1879** Crawford County formed; **1901** county courthouse built; **1903** incorporated as a village; **1914** Grayling State Fish Hatchery established; **1935** incorporated as a city.

Grosse Ile *Wayne County   Southeastern Michigan, 14 mi/23 km south of Detroit, on Grosse Ile, Detroit River*

1679 Father Hennepin mentions large island while passing from Lake Erie to Lake Huron; **1707** Cadillac deeds island to daughter Magdalene; **1740** mission established by Father de la Richardie; **1763** Native Americans under Pontiac use island as base during their siege of Detroit; **July 1776** natives transfer title of island to Alexander and William Macomb; **1856** Little Cote house built on island's east side; **1873** Chicago & Canadian Southern Railroad completed between Detroit and Buffalo, New York, crossing Trenton Channel from Michigan mainland across island to Stony Island, rail ferry across main channel to Canada; **1909** Great Flowing Well discovered at South Pointe by oil drillers; **1913** Grosse Ile Toll Bridge opened; **1927** Navy seaplane base established, becomes Grosse Ile Naval Air Station 1942, closed 1969.

Grosse Pointe   *Wayne County*   *Southeastern Michigan, suburb 10 mi/16 km east-northeast of Detroit*

1712 Fox and Sauk peoples from Wisconsin besiege French Fort Pontchartrain at urging of British, c.1,200 die at hands of Huron and Ottawa tribes, allies of French, who launch surprise attack, c.60 French die at fort on Lake St. Clair; **1870** post office established on Lake St. Clair; **1880** incorporated as a village; **1888** post office established; **1893** village of Grosse Pointe Farms separates from Grosse Pointe over liquor sales issue; **Dec. 2, 1925** actress Julie Harris born; **1934** incorporated as a city.

Hamtramck   *Wayne County*   *Southeastern Michigan, suburb 4 mi/6.4 km north of Detroit*

1818 area settled by French farmers; **1857** town founded (ham-TRA-meck) by German immigrants, named for Col. John F. Hamtramck; **1901** incorporated as a village; **1910s** Polish immigrants flock to community's industrial jobs; **1910** automobile parts factory built by Dodge Brothers Company; **1914** Dodge begins manufacturing automobiles, acquired by Chrysler 1928; **1921** incorporated as a city, surrounded by city of Detroit; **1928** Tau Beta Community House built as settlement house for industrial workers; St. Florian's Roman Catholic Church built.

Hancock   *Houghton County*   *Northwestern Michigan, 215 mi/346 km west-northwest of Sault Ste. Marie*

1848 Quincy Copper Mine established; **1852** Christopher C. Douglas becomes first settler; **1859** town founded on Portage Lake, Lake Superior, on Keweenaw Peninsula, opposite Houghton, named for patriot John Hancock; **1860** post office established; **1875** incorporated as a village; **1880s** Finnish immigrants arrive; **1896** Suomi College (2-year) established; **1903** incorporated as a city; **1954** Houghton-Hancock Lift Bridge built across Portage Ship Canal.

Harbor Beach   *Huron County*   *Eastern Michigan, 108 mi/174 km north-northeast of Detroit, on Lake Huron*

1837 town founded; **1840** Huron County formed; town becomes county seat; county courthouse built; **1856** post office established; **1865** courthouse destroyed by fire; county seat moved to Port Austin; **1871** forest fires devastate region, again in 1881; **1873** Harbor of Refuge built; **1882** incorporated as a village; **Apr. 13, 1890** Supreme Court Justice Frank Murphy born (died 1949); **1909** incorporated as a city.

Harrison   *Clare County*   *North central Michigan, 85 mi/137 km northeast of Grand Rapids*

1840 Clare County formed; **1871** county organized; Farwell becomes county seat; **1878** town founded as new county seat after Farwell courthouse burns 1877; **1879** Flint & Pere Marquette Railroad reaches town; Hatfield Hotel built by John Hatfield; **1885** incorporated as a village; **1891** incorporated as a city; **1965** Mid Michigan Community College established; **1966** county courthouse built.

Harrisville   *Alcona County*   *Northeastern Michigan, 177 mi/285 km northeast of Grand Rapids, on Lake Huron*

1854 Davison's Mill established by Simeon Holden and Crosier Davison; town founded; **1868** Sturgeon Point Lighthouse built; **1869** Alcona County formed; town becomes county seat; U.S. Coast Guard Station established at Sturgeon Point to north; **1887** incorporated as a village; **1905** incorporated as a city; **1956** county courthouse built.

Hart   *Oceana County*   *Western Michigan, 62 mi/100 km northwest of Grand Rapids, near Lake Michigan*

1855 Oceana County formed; **1856** settlers arrive at Hart Lake; **1862** sawmill built; **1864** town platted; **1865** town becomes county seat; **1885** incorporated as a village; **1946** incorporated as a city; **1958** county courthouse built.

Hastings   *Barry County*   *South central Michigan, 116 mi/187 km west-northwest of Detroit*

1836 area settled by Eurotus P. Hastings; **1839** Barry County formed; **1841** town founded as county seat; sawmill and grist mill built; **1855** incorporated as a village; **1871** incorporated as a city; **1893** county courthouse completed.

Highland Park   *Wayne County*   *Southeastern Michigan, suburb 5 mi/8 km north of Detroit*

1818 Judge Augustus B. Woodward purchases land; **1825** town of Woodwardville founded; **1887** investors promote new town of Highland Park; **1889** incorporated as a village; **1910** Henry Ford begins manufacture of Model T cars; **1913** Maxwell Company establishes automobile factory; **1916** Henry Ford Trade School founded; **1917** incorporated as a city; Ford automobile manufacturing moved to River Rouge Plant, Dearborn, decreasing city's economic base; **1922** Islamic Mosque built; **1925** Maxwell Company reorganized to form Chrysler Corporation; Chrysler Highland Park Plant established; **1926** McGregor Public Library built; **1932** Lawrence Institute of Technology founded.

Hillsdale *Hillsdale County* *Southern Michigan, 85 mi/137 km west-southwest of Detroit*

1834 town site on St. Joseph River first settled; **1835** Hillsdale County formed; town becomes county seat; **1843** railroad completed from Monroe, later becomes part of New York Central Railroad; **1847** incorporated as a village; **1851** county courthouse completed; **1853** Hillsdale College moved from Spring Arbor, established 1847; **1869** incorporated as a city; **1898** Hillsdale County Building built.

Holland *Ottawa and Allegan counties* *Western Michigan, 25 mi/40 km southwest of Grand Rapids*

Feb. 1847 town founded on Black Lake (Lake Macatawa), arm of Lake Michigan, by Dutch immigrants led by pastor Dr. A. C. Van Raalte; log Dutch Reformed church built, rebuilt 1856; **1848** town platted; **1857** Holland Academy founded; **1862** Western Theological Seminary established; **1866** Hope College established; **1867** incorporated as a city; **Oct. 1871** fire destroys business district, over 200 homes; **1926** Holland State Park established on Lake Michigan; **1929** annual *Tulpen Feest* (Tulip Festival) organized; **1937** Netherlands Museum opened.

Houghton *Houghton County* *Northwestern Michigan, 215 mi/346 km west-northwest of Sault Ste. Marie*

1846 Houghton County formed; **1852** town founded on Portage Lake, arm of Lake Superior, on Keweenaw Peninsula; **1855** copper prospecting begins south of Portage Lake; **1861** county seat moved from Eagle River with separation of Keweenaw County from Houghton County; **1867** incorporated as a village; **1870s** copper boom begins, continues into 1910s; **1873** Portage Lake Ship Canal completed across base of Keweenaw Peninsula; **1875** wooden highway bridge built across canal; **1885** Michigan College of Mining and Technology established, becomes Michigan Technological University; **1887** county courthouse built; **1901** steel bridge built across canal, closed 1905 after being struck by steamer; **1959** Houghton-Hancock Lift Bridge built across canal; **1970** incorporated as a city.

Howell *Livingston County* *South central Michigan, 49 mi/79 km northwest of Detroit*

1834 town settled on Thompson Lake; **1835** town platted; **1836** Livingston County formed; town becomes county seat; **1855** Samuel Balcom's saloon destroyed by women's temperance movement; **1863** incorporated as a village; **1890** county courthouse completed; **1906** Howell Carnegie Library completed; **1914** incorporated as a city.

Inkster *Wayne County* *Southeastern Michigan, suburb 13 mi/21 km west of Detroit*

1825 town founded, named Moulin Rouge; **1857** post office established; **1863** town renamed; **1926** incorporated as a village; **1926-1927** African-Americans arrive during industrial expansion; **1964** incorporated as a city.

Interlochen *Grand Traverse County* *See* **Traverse City (1928)**

Ionia *Ionia County* *Central Michigan, 30 mi/48 km east of Grand Rapids, on Grand River*

1831 first settlers arrive; **1833** town founded; **1837** Ionia County formed; town becomes county seat; **1841** town platted; **1865** incorporated as a village; **1873** incorporated as a city; **1880** Michigan Reformatory built; **1886** county courthouse completed; **May 22, 1981** riot at Michigan Reformatory leaves 42 prisoners and 4 guards injured.

Iron Mountain *Dickinson County* *Northwestern Michigan 190 mi/306 km west-southwest of Sault Ste. Marie*

1878 iron ore deposits discovered; **1879** town founded near Menominee River; **1887** incorporated as a village; **1888** incorporated as a city; **1889** Milwaukee investor Ferdinand Schlesinger monopolizes iron mines; **1891** Dickinson County formed; town becomes county seat; **1896** county courthouse built; **1930s** iron ore veins exhausted.

Ironwood *Gogebic County* *Northwestern Michigan, 290 mi/467 km west of Sault Ste. Marie*

1870 hundreds of Cornish miners transported to region; **1884** iron ore deposits discovered in area by J. L. Norrie; **1885** town founded on Montreal River, named for businessman James R. Wood, nicknamed "Iron" Wood for his mining deals; iron ore mining begins; Milwaukee, Lake Shore & Western (Chicago & Northwestern) Railroad built; **1887** incorporated as a village; **1889** incorporated as a city; **1932** Gogebic Community College established.

Ishpeming *Marquette County* *Northwestern Michigan, 163 mi/262 km west of Sault Ste. Marie*

1844 large iron ore deposit discovered, prelude to large scale mining in Marquette Iron Range; **1854** town first settled; **1857** Iron Mountain Railroad built to Marquette; **1862** town founded, Chippewa term for "high place" or "heaven"; **1871** incorporated as a village; **1873** incorporated as a city; **1883** Ropes Gold Mine opened at Deer Lake, continues production through 1897; **1887** organized skiing in America begins when three Norwegians establish Ishpeming Ski Club, first jumping contests held Feb. 1888, national association formed 1904; **1888** Michigan Gold Mine opened to west, remains active into 1900s; **1911** explosion at National Iron Mine kills 11 workers; **Apr. 12, 1912** nuclear chemist Glenn T. Seaborg born, shared Nobel Prize 1951 (died 1999); **Nov. 3, 1926** 52 workers left to die in Barnes-Hecker Iron Mine to west at 1,000 ft/305 m below surface with no hope of rescue; **1953**

MICHIGAN

National Ski Hall of Fame founded, new building opened 1992; **1973** Tilden Open Pit Iron Mine begins operations.

Ithaca *Gratiot County* *Central Michigan, 104 mi/ 167 km northwest of Detroit*

1855 Gratiot (GRAT-ee-oh) County formed; town founded as county seat; **1869** incorporated as a village; **1871** county courthouse built; **1961** incorporated as a city.

Jackson *Jackson County* *Southern Michigan, 70 mi/113 km west of Detroit*

1829 Indian trail crossing of Grand River selected for town site; **1830** town founded; **1832** Jackson County formed; town becomes county seat; **1838** Michigan State Prison established; **1841** Michigan Central Railroad reaches town; **1854** incorporated as a village; **July 6, 1854** first Republican Party convention held here; **1857** incorporated as a city; **1871** county courthouse built; **1903** The Military Group erected, Civil War memorial; **1910** memorial tablet honoring Republican Party founding dedicated by Pres. William Howard Taft; **Jan. 13, 1915** Supreme Court Justice Potter Stewart born (died 1978); **1928** Jackson Community College established; **1930** Michigan State Prison closed, replaced by Southern Michigan State Prison at Leslie to north; Illuminated Cascades established, attraction includes 16 waterfalls, 6 fountains; **Feb. 7, 1932** astronaut Alfred Worden born; **1994** Baker College of Jackson established.

Kalamazoo *Kalamazoo County* *Southwestern Michigan, 130 mi/209 km west of Detroit*

1823 trading post established, takes name Kee-Kalamazoo, Native American term for "Where water boils in the pot"; **1828** Titus Bronson becomes first settler; town founded on Kalamazoo River, originally named Bronson; **1830** Kalamazoo County formed; town becomes county seat; **1833** *Gazette* newspaper founded; Kalamazoo College established; town of College Park founded, annexed 1861; **1836** town renamed Kalamazoo; **1843** incorporated as a village; **1847** group of Dutch immigrants arrive; **1856** Scottish immigrant James Taylor introduces celery as new vegetable, first cultivated 1866 by Dutchman Marinus De Bruin; **Aug. 27, 1856** Abraham Lincoln delivers his only speech in Michigan; **1859** Kalamazoo State Hospital opened; **1874** Michigan Supreme Court rules in favor of Kalamazoo high school offer of free education setting national precedent; **1884** incorporated as a city; **Aug. 15, 1887** novelist Edna Ferber born (died 1968); **1893** Public Library established; **1897** Nazareth College established; **1904** Western Michigan University established, originally Western State Normal School; **Dec. 1921** Kalamazoo Symphony Orchestra debuts; **1924** Kalamazoo Institute of Arts founded; **1929** Kalamazoo Civic Theatre established; **1931** city hall built; civic auditorium built; **1937** third county courthouse built; **1966** Kalamazoo Valley Community College established; **1979** Kalamazoo Aviation History Museum (Air Zoo)

opened; **May 13, 1980** tornado strikes city, 5 killed, 79 injured.

Kalkaska *Kalkaska County* *Northern Michigan, 125 mi/201 km north-northeast of Grand Rapids*

1837 trading post established; **1871** Kalkaska County formed; **1873** tannery and sawmill established; town founded as county seat; **1883** county courthouse completed; **1887** incorporated as a village; **c.1900** economic base begins shift to agriculture with depletion of forest reserves.

Kingsford *Dickinson County* *Northwestern Michigan, 190 mi/306 km west-southwest of Sault Ste. Marie*

1920 E. G. Kingsford acquires land on behalf of Ford Motor Company as source for wooden materials used in automobile detailing; **1924** incorporated as a village; **1924** Ford Motor Company builds plant to supply cars with wooden parts; town founded on Menominee River; **1947** incorporated as a city; **1951** Kingsford Chemical Company founded, maker of charcoal for barbecuing; **1961** Kingsford Charcoal Company moves to Louisville, Kentucky.

L'Anse *Baraga County* *Northwestern Michigan, 203 mi/327 km west of Sault Ste. Marie*

1660 French Jesuit Rene Menard winters here; **1830** Father Frederick Baraga, the Snowshoe Priest, immigrates from Slovenia to minister among native people of Lake Superior south shore; **1837** trading post established by Peter Crebassa; town founded on Keweenaw Bay; **1843** Father Baraga arrives in L'Anse, consecrated as bishop of Upper Michigan 1853; **1866** post office established; **1867** Marquette, Houghton & Ontonagon Railroad built; **1873** incorporated as a village; **1875** Baraga (BEAR-a-ga) County formed; town becomes county seat; **1884** county courthouse completed; **1960s** Bishop Frederick Baraga Shrine (statue) erected on bluff to west.

Lake City *Missaukee County* *North central Michigan, 98 mi/158 km north-northeast of Grand Rapids*

1868 Daniel Reeder build first cabin; **1869** Missaukee County formed; Falmouth becomes first county seat; **1872** town founded on Lake Missaukee; **1873** county seat moved to Lake City; **1877** Grand Rapids & Indiana Railroad reaches town; **1889** incorporated as a village; **1932** incorporated as a city; **1956** county courthouse built.

Lansing *Ingham, Eaton, and Clinton counties* *South central Michigan, 82 mi/132 km northeast of Detroit*

1837 Jacob F. Cooley builds first dwelling; **Jan. 26, 1837** Michigan admitted as 26th state; **1847** town founded on Grand River; state capital moved from Detroit; **1848** *Lansing Free Press* newspaper founded; **1854** state capitol built; **1855** *Lansing State Republican* newspaper founded;

1859 incorporated as a city; 1871 first railroad reaches city; 1874 State Pioneer Museum founded; 1879 new state capitol completed; 1880 Michigan School for the Blind founded; 1887 Ransom Olds develops three-wheeled horseless carriage; 1894 Michigan Avenue Bridge built over Grand River; 1902 Olds Motor Works Plant built after fire destroys Detroit plant; c.1904 city becomes important automobile manufacturing center; 1911 city's two newspapers merge as *Lansing State Journal*; 1922 state office building completed; May 18, 1927 explosion at Bath School to northeast, 38 killed, mostly students; 1929 Capital City Airport established; 1931 25-story Olds Tower building completed; Dec. 11, 1934 fire destroys Hotel Kerns, 34 killed; Apr. 10, 1951 actor Steven Seagal born; 1957 Lansing Community College established; June 12, 1957 actor Timothy Busfield born; Aug. 14, 1959 Los Angeles Lakers basketball player Earvin "Magic" Johnson born.

Lapeer *Lapeer County   Eastern Michigan, 52 mi/ 84 km north of Detroit*

1831 Alvin N. Hart becomes first settler; 1833 Lapeer County formed; town founded as county seat; 1839 county courthouse built; 1858 incorporated as a village; 1869 incorporated as a city; 1895 Lapeer State Home established.

Laurium *Houghton County   Northwestern Michigan, 208 mi/335 km west-northwest of Sault Ste. Marie*

1889 incorporated as a village, originally named Calumet; c.1890 Laurium Mining Company established; 1895 renamed Laurium; Feb. 18, 1895 Notre Dame football player George Gipp born, origin of saying "Win one for the Gipper," died Dec. 13, 1920 of pneumonia at end of football season.

Leland *Leelanau County   Northern Michigan, 145 mi/233 km north of Grand Rapids, on Lake Michigan*

1838 lighthouse built on South Manitou Island; 1852 Coast Guard station established on North Manitou Island; 1853 first sawmill built on Carp River, near Lake Michigan; town founded; 1863 Leelanau County formed on Leelanau Peninsula, Lake Michigan; Northport becomes first county seat; 1870 iron ore smelting begins, discontinued 1884; 1882 county seat moved to Leland; 1966 county courthouse built; Oct. 21, 1977 Sleeping Bear Dunes National Lakeshore established, includes mainland section to south and South Manitou and North Manitou islands to west.

Livonia *Wayne County   Southeastern Michigan, suburb 15 mi/24 km west-northwest of Detroit*

1818 Dennison Palmer and William Woodridge, later governor of Michigan and U.S. Senator, among first settlers; 1835 Livonia Township formed; 1947 Madonna College, later University, established; 1948 General Motors automatic transmission plant built; 1949 Ladbroke Harness Racing Course established; 1950 township incorporated as city of Livonia; 1961 Schoolcraft College (2-year) established.

Ludington *Mason County   Western Michigan, 80 mi/129 km northwest of Grand Rapids, on Lake Michigan*

1675 Father Jacques Marquette dies, buried here, reinterred at St. Ignace 1677; 1855 Mason County formed; 1857 Flint & Pere Marquette Railroad reaches town; 1863 James Ludington establishes lumber mill; town founded as county seat; 1867 Big Sable Point Lighthouse built to north, rebuilt 1900, automated 1949; 1873 incorporated as a city; 1876 car ferry service begins to Milwaukee, suspended 1980; 1890 car ferry begins to Manitowoc, Wisconsin; 1893 county courthouse built; Sept. 9, 1910 *Pere Marquette* car ferry sinks, 28 killed; 1924 lighthouse built at end of North Breakwater, automated 1972; Sept. 6, 1952 SS *Badger* ferry steamer launched providing daily service to Manitowoc, suspended Nov. 1990, resumed May 1992 through efforts of local businessman Charles Conrad.

Mackinac Island *Mackinac County   Northern Michigan, 208 mi/335 km north-northeast of Grand Rapids*

1634 explorer Jean Nicolet canoes through Straits of Mackinac (MAC-ki-naw), observes island at Lake Huron end of channel; 1671 Father Marquette visits island from mission at St. Ignace; 1780–1781 British build Fort Mackinac; 1796 British evacuate fort following signing of Jay Treaty; 1812 British retake island at start of War of 1812; U.S. Fort Holmes built, renamed Fort George by occupying British; 1814 U.S. Maj. Andrew Hunter Holmes killed Aug. 14 in unsuccessful attempt to retake fort; U.S. warship *Tigress* captured, *Scorpion* destroyed by British in occupied vessel; 1815 British withdraw from area after Treaty of Ghent; 1817 American Fur Company owned by John Jacob Astor begins operations on island; Astor House built; 1822 Dr. William Beaumont investigates human digestive processes through observations made on young Alexis St. Martin (1804–1880) who survived gunshot through stomach, work interrupted 1825 when subject vanishes, reunited 1829 at Prairie du Chien, Wisconsin; 1825 Old Mission House built as Indian school, refurbished as a hotel 1838; 1830 Astor closes fur trading company office; Old Mission Church built; 1860s resort town founded at south end of island; 1875 Fort Mackinac designated a military reservation; 1881 first passenger ferry service to mainland begins; 1887 Grand Hotel built; 1894 remaining military garrison removed from Fort Mackinac, becomes state historic site; 1895 95 percent of island established as Mackinac Island State Park; 1915 Cass monument erected in honor of Lewis Cass, governor 1813–1831; U.S. Coast Guard Station established; 1917 incorporated as a village; 1931 Marquette monument erected; 1936 Mackinac Island Public Library founded.

Mackinaw City *Cheboygan County* *Northern Michigan, 202 mi/325 km north-northeast of Grand Rapids*

1634 Jean Nicolet explores region, sent to area by Samuel de Champlain; **1681** French build Fort Michilimackinac on north side of Straits of Mackinac (pronounced MAC-ki-naw) [see St. Ignace]; **1715** fort reestablished on south side of straits; **1760** French abandon fort, seized by British 1761; **June 2, 1763** massacre of 21 men in garrison, capture of 27 by Native Americans as part of Pontiac's Conspiracy leaves fort unoccupied; **1764** British reoccupy fort; **1780–1781** British establish Fort Mackinac on Mackinac Island; **1812** Fort Michilimackinac seized by British during War of 1812; **1857** town founded; **1881** railroad ferry service begins to St. Ignace; passenger ferry service to Mackinac Island begins; **1882** incorporated as a village; **1957** Mackinac Bridge built across straits to St. Ignace.

Manistee *Manistee County* *Western Michigan, 95 mi/153 km north-northwest of Grand Rapids*

1820s trading post established on Lake Michigan by American Fur Company; **1840** Manistee County formed; **1841** mill established; town founded on harbor formed by mouth of Manistee River; **1855** county organized; town becomes county seat; **1869** incorporated as a city; **1871** forest fires destroy much of city; **1878** county courthouse built; **1879** Charles Rietz drills first salt well; **1883** Pere Marquette Railroad reaches town; **1885** over 40 sawmills in operation in area; **1888** Fire Hall built; **1920** Manistee Lighthouse erected.

Manistique *Schoolcraft County* *Northwestern Michigan, 100 mi/161 km southwest of Sault Ste. Marie*

1832 church established by Bishop Frederic Baraga; **1860** town founded on Lake Michigan as lumber milling center; **1871** Schoolcraft County formed; town becomes county seat; **1885** incorporated as a village; **1893** Hiawatha colony established to west by socialist Thomas Mills, abandoned 1896; **1901** incorporated as a city; **1902** car ferry begins on Lake Michigan to Frankfort (Elberta), Michigan, operated by Ann Arbor Railroad, suspended 1968; **1903** car ferry established to Northport, Lower Michigan, suspended 1906; **1976** county courthouse built.

Marquette *Marquette County* *Northwestern Michigan, 150 mi/241 km west of Sault Ste. Marie*

1841 state geologist Dr. Douglass Houghton verifies existence of large iron ore deposits; **1844** William A. Burt finds large iron lode to west; Jackson Mine opened at Negaunee; first settlers arrive from Mackinac Island led by Robert Graveraet; **1849** town founded as iron ore shipping point on Marquette Bay, Lake Superior, named Worcester for Worcester, Massachusetts, home of Amos R. Harlow, leader of second group of settlers; **1850** town renamed to honor Father Marquette; **1851** Marquette County formed; **1854** town platted by Peter White; **1855** tramway built from Negaunee for transfer of iron ore;

1857 Iron Mountain Railroad built from Negaunee and Ishpeming; **1859** incorporated as a village; **1864** St. Peter's Roman Catholic Cathedral built; **1868** fire destroys business area, some residential parts of town; **1871** incorporated as a city; **1880s** lumber milling, brownstone quarrying established; **1885** Marquette State Prison established; **Oct. 29, 1885** archaeologist Alfred Vincent Kidd born (died 1963); **1894** city hall built; **1897** Father Marquette monument dedicated; **1899** Northern Michigan University established; **early 1900s** Huron Mountain Club established to north at Big Bay, secluded colony of summer residences owned by such leading business families as the Fords and Armours; **1904** county courthouse completed; Peter White Public Library built; **1929** iron ore mining in immediate vicinity of Marquette ends; **1933** Presbyterian Church completed; **Nov. 1935** St. Peter's Cathedral destroyed by fire, rebuilt 1936–1937; **1936** Marquette County Airport opened; **1955** K. I. Sawyer Air Force Base to south, closed 1995; **1998** new Sawyer International Airport opened to south at former air base.

Marshall *Calhoun County* *Southern Michigan, 98 mi/158 km west of Detroit*

1831 town settled; Halfway House roadhouse built; **1833** Calhoun County formed; town becomes county seat; **1835** John D. Pierce and Isaac E. Cary establish state-controlled education system in Michigan; town vies for designation as state capital; **1836** incorporated as a village; **1839** state senate approves Marshall as state capital, defeated in house in favor of Lansing 1847; **1840s** town becomes active stop on Underground Railroad; **1846** town rescues runaway Kentucky slave Adam Crosswhite seized by slave hunters, freed, sent to safety of Canada; **1848** abolitionist townspeople sued, fined in federal court, case leads to passage of New Fugitive Slave Bill 1850; **1859** incorporated as a city; **1885** old Back Road planked, tollgate erected, operated until 1893; **1954** third county courthouse built.

Marysville *Saint Clair County* *Eastern Michigan, 52 mi/84 km northeast of Detroit, near St. Clair River*

c.1780 sawmill established near St. Clair River; **1805** four sawmills built to supply wood to Detroit following disastrous city fire; **1821** road built parallel to St. Clair River, becomes State Highway 29; **1855** post office established; **1910** Morton Salt Works established; **1920** Wills-St. Clair Company builds automobile plant; **1921** incorporated as a village; **1924** incorporated as a city; **1930** Gar Wood Boat Works established by speedboat champ Garfield Arthur Wood; **1935** Chrysler Corporation acquires Wills-St. Clair plant for its Marysville Parts Plant.

Mason *Ingham County* *South central Michigan, 14 mi/23 km south-southeast of Lansing*

1836 sawmill built by Lewis Lacey; **1838** Ingham County formed; **1840** town founded as county seat;

1865 incorporated as a village; 1875 incorporated as a city; 1905 county courthouse built; 1994 Hilliard Building completed, houses county offices.

Menominee   *Menominee County   Northwestern Michigan, 187 mi/301 km southwest of Sault Ste. Marie*

1796 fur trader Louis Chappee builds fort at mouth of Menominee River, Green Bay, Lake Michigan; 1836 sawmill and dam built; 1863 Menominee County formed; town founded as county seat and timber and fishing center, opposite Marinette, Wisconsin; 1871 Chicago & Northwestern Railroad reaches town; 1883 incorporated as a city; 1884 county courthouse built; 1899 ferry begins service on Lake Michigan to Frankfort (Elberta), Michigan, suspended 1970; 1910 timber reserves depleted; 1929 Interstate Bridge built to Marinette; 1934 Jordan College established.

Midland   *Midland County   Eastern Michigan, 108 mi/174 km north-northwest of Detroit*

1830 last of great Native American battles in Michigan fought on Tittabawassee River between Sauk and Chippewas; 1850 Midland County formed; 1855 county organized; 1856 town founded as county seat; 1869 incorporated as a village; 1887 incorporated as a city; 1890 Dr. Herbert H. Dow organizes Midland Chemical Company, later becomes Dow Chemical Company; 1899 Dow Gardens designed by Herbert Dow and wife; Dow Memorial Library founded; 1919 county courthouse built; 1928 first oil produced in area; 1934 Dow Housing Project begun to provide low-cost housing for Dow employees; Apr. 6, 1958 Capital Airlines Viscount airplane crashes killing 47; 1959 Northwood University established; 1961 Great Lakes College (2-year) established.

Mio   *Oscoda County   Northern Michigan, 142 mi/ 229 km northeast of Grand Rapids*

1881 town founded; 1882 post office established; 1886 Oscoda County formed; town becomes county seat; 1888 county courthouse built; July 13, 1936 highest temperature ever recorded in Michigan reached, 112°F/44°C.

Monroe   *Monroe County   Southeastern Michigan, 34 mi/55 km south-southwest of Detroit, on Lake Erie*

1778 first settlers arrive at western end of Lake Erie; blockhouse built; 1780 town founded as Frenchtown by Francis Navarre; 1796 American flag raised over blockhouse; Jan. 22, 1813 River Raisin Massacre (Battle of Frenchtown), forces under William Henry Harrison defeated by British forces under Col. Henry Proctor, in addition to battle casualties, 30–60 prisoners held by British executed at the site; 1817 Monroe County formed; town of Monroe founded as county seat; 1827 incorporated as a village; 1835 town becomes center of "Toledo War," boundary dispute between Michigan versus Ohio and Indiana, resolved by act of Congress 1836 against Michigan's favor; 1836 glass factory opened by entrepre-

neurs Hall and Grover; 1837 incorporated as a city; 1843 railroad completed west to Hillsdale, later extended to Chicago as part of New York Central system; 1879 county courthouse built; 1932 St. Mary's Academy built; Feb. 2, 1953 model Christie Brinkley born; 1964 Monroe County Community College established; June 21, 1985 Fermi 2 Nuclear Power Plant begins production, located to south on Lake Erie.

Mount Clemens   *Macomb County   Southeastern Michigan, suburb 20 mi/32 km north-northeast of Detroit*

1781 town of Gnadenhutten founded by Moravians, abandoned 1786 [see Gnadenhutten, Ohio]; 1796 area surveyed by Christian Clemens; 1798 town settled near Lake St. Clair; 1818 Macomb County formed; town becomes county seat, renamed Mount Clemens; 1837 construction of Clinton-Kalamazoo Canal begins; 1851 incorporated as a village; 1870 mineral wells discovered by Dorr Kellogg; 1879 incorporated as a city; 1920s bath houses flourish; 1934 Selfridge U.S. Army Base established to east on Lake St. Clair, becomes Michigan Air National Guard base July 1971; 1970 county courthouse built; 1974 last public bath house closed.

Mount Pleasant   *Isabella County   Central Michigan, 64 mi/103 km northwest of Grand Rapids*

1855 Isabella Indian Reservation established; 1859 Isabella County formed; 1860 town founded as county seat; 1864 first railroad reaches town; 1872 reservation disbanded; 1875 incorporated as a village; 1889 incorporated as a city; 1891 Mount Pleasant Indian School opened, becomes Michigan State Home and Training School 1934; 1892 Central State Teachers College established, becomes Central Michigan University; 1928 first producing oil well dug; 1930s Isabella Indian Reservation reestablished; 1972 county courthouse built; 1996 Soaring Eagle Casino opened.

Munising   *Alger County   Northern Michigan, 113 mi/182 km west of Sault Ste. Marie, on Lake Superior*

1665 Pierre Radisson expedition passes shoreline, first white men to see colorful lakeside cliffs known later as Pictured Rocks; 1850 vessel *Superior* smashed against lake cliffs, 243 of 250 passengers and crew killed; 1855 town platted for Munising Iron Company; 1870s after delay brought on by Civil War, iron furnaces begin operation, ceased work 1877; town founded, name taken from Gitchi-Menesing, Ojibwe name for nearby Grand Island; 1885 Alger County formed; town becomes county seat; 1895 tannery, sawmills established starting second economic boom; 1897 incorporated as a village; 1901 county courthouse built, burned 1978, rebuilt; 1904 paper mill established, purchased by Kimberley Clark 1954; 1915 incorporated as a city; 1920 Hanley Airport established; Oct. 15, 1966 Pictured Rocks National Lakeshore, on Lake Superior, authorized to east of town, includes former Pictured Rocks State Park.

Muskegon *Muskegon County* *Western Michigan, 35 mi/56 km northwest of Grand Rapids, on Lake Michigan*

1634 explorer Jean Nicolet visits area; **1812** trading post established on Bear Lake by Baptiste Ricollet; **1837** first sawmill built; town founded on Muskegon Lake, lake formed behind dunes of Lake Michigan at mouth of Muskegon River; **1859** Muskegon County formed; town becomes county seat; **1861** incorporated as a village; **1869** incorporated as a city; county courthouse built; **1870s** city becomes major lumber milling center; **1874** Sherman House hotel built, beginning of city's role as lake resort; **1888** Baker College of Muskegon established; **1890** Hackley Public Library built, gift of lumberman C. H. Hackley; **1892** St. Paul's Episcopal Church built; **c.1900** timber industry declines; **1903** Grand Trunk Railroad begins car ferry service to Milwaukee, abandoned 1978; **1912** Hackley Art Gallery opened; **1926** Muskegon Community College established; **May 25, 1929** Hackley Memorial dedicated on Hackley Day.

Negaunee *Marquette County* *Northwestern Michigan, 160 mi/257 km west of Sault Ste. Marie*

1845 large iron ore deposit discovered at Jackson Hill; **1846** town founded in Marquette Iron Range; **1848** first iron forges erected; **1855** tramway built to Marquette for hauling ore to Lake Superior; **1857** Iron Mountain Railroad built to Marquette; **1865** town platted; incorporated as a village; **1873** incorporated as a city; **1904** Jackson monument erected by Jackson Iron Company to commemorate discovery of iron ore.

Newberry *Luce County* *Northern Michigan, 59 mi/95 km west-southwest of Sault Ste. Marie*

1882 town founded on Tahquamenon River; Newberry Lumber and Chemical Company mill established; **1885** incorporated as a village; **1887** Luce County formed; town becomes county seat; **1890** county courthouse built.

Niles *Berrien County* *Southwestern Michigan, 168 mi/270 km west-southwest of Detroit*

1690 Indian mission established by French Jesuit Claude Aveneau; **1697** Fort St. Joseph established by French, taken by British 1761, briefly held during Pontiac's uprising 1763, briefly by Spanish 1781; **1822** Carey Mission founded on St. Joseph River by Protestant missionary Rev. Isaac McCoy; **1827** first white settlers arrive; **1828** site permanently settled; **1830s** town becomes stagecoach stop on run between Detroit and Chicago; **1835** incorporated as a village; **1859** incorporated as a city; **March 6, 1885** writer Ring (Ringgold Wilmer) Lardner born (died 1933).

Ontonagon *Ontonagon County* *Northwestern Michigan, 248 mi/399 km west of Sault Ste. Marie*

1667 French missionary Father Dablon confirms reports of massive copper boulder (Ontonagon Boulder) on shore of Lake Superior; **1771** first mining expedition led by Alexander Henry, abandons efforts after steady rains cause mine cave-in; **1843** treaty with Chippewas allows white men to remove metals from region; Ontonagon Boulder removed, acquired by Smithsonian Institution, Washington, 1846; **1848** Ontonagon (AHN-tah-nah-gon) County formed; **c.1865** town founded on Lake Superior as county seat and lumber milling center; **1885** incorporated as a village; **Aug. 25, 1896** fire destroys town and mills; **1904** Ontonagon Township Library established; **1965** county courthouse built.

Owosso *Shiawassee County* *Central Michigan, 74 mi/119 km northwest of Detroit*

1833 town founded on Shiawassee River, originally named Big Rapids; **1838** town renamed; **1859** incorporated as a city; **June 12, 1878** writer James Oliver Curwood born (died 1927); **March 24, 1902** Thomas E. Dewey born, prosecuted hoodlums in 1930s, governor of New York, 1948 Republican Presidential candidate, narrowly defeated by Truman (died 1971); **1984** Baker College of Owosso established.

Paw Paw *Van Buren County* *Southwestern Michigan, 145 mi/233 km west of Detroit*

1832 town settled; **1837** Van Buren County formed; **1838** town becomes county seat; **1859** incorporated as a village; **1901** county courthouse built; **1908** Maple Lake formed by dam on Paw Paw River.

Petoskey *Emmet County* *Northern Michigan, 172 mi/277 km north-northeast of Grand Rapids, on Lake Michigan*

1852 Presbyterian mission founded by Rev. Andrew Porter; **1853** Emmet County formed; **1857** Little Traverse becomes first county seat; post office established, named Bear River; **1865** Hazen Ingalls becomes first permanent settler; **1869** county seat moved to Harbor Springs; **1873** Pennsylvania Railroad reaches town; town renamed Petoskey, for Chippewa Chief Petosega; **1879** incorporated as a village; **1896** incorporated as a city; **Oct. 9, 1899** Civil War historian Bruce Catton born (died 1978); **1902** county seat moved to Petoskey; **1958** North Central Michigan College (2-year) established; **1965** county courthouse built; **1971** Crooked Tree Arts Center founded.

Phoenix *Keweenaw County* *Northwestern Michigan, 203 mi/327 km west-northwest of Sault Ste. Marie*

1845 Phoenix Copper Mine opened; town founded; **1846** Houghton County formed; Phoenix Mine serves as first county seat; **1853** county seat moved to nearby Eagle River; **1861** Keweenaw County separates from Houghton County; **1905** Phoenix Mine closed; **1928** Calumet and Hecla Mining Company purchases and drains mine, explores mine for possible further exploitation; **1936** Phoenix Mine exploration suspended, closed permanently.

Pontiac *Oakland County* *Southeastern Michigan, 24 mi/39 km north-northwest of Detroit*

1818 town founded on the Saginaw Trail by the Pontiac Company, land promoters from Detroit; town named for Ottawa Chief Pontiac; **1820** Oakland County formed; town becomes county seat; **1821** Baptist Church built; **1837** incorporated as a village; town's industrial base includes woolen mills, foundries, sawmills; **1840** Hodges House hotel, (Hotel Milner) built; **1843** Detroit & Pontiac Railroad built; **1861** incorporated as a city; **1878** Eastern Michigan Hospital for the Insane opened, becomes Pontiac State Hospital; **c.1885** Pontiac Spring Wagon Works established; **1898** Pontiac Public Library built; **1905** Rapid Motor Truck Company organized; **1907** Oakland Motor Car Company founded by W. C. Durant; **1909** General Motors becomes established by Durant with acquisition of several factories; **Nov. 16, 1942** actress Donna McKechnie born; **1959** county courthouse built; **1965** Creative Arts Center opened in former library building; **Aug. 30, 1971** 10 empty school buses blown up days before start of court-ordered desegregation program; **Aug. 1975** Metropolitan Stadium opened, home of Detroit Lions football team, later renamed Silverdome; **1979** Pontiac Motor Division factory built; **Oct. 22, 1993** Merian Frederick, woman with Lou Gehrig's disease, becomes Dr. Jack Kevorkian's 19th assisted suicide, administered carbon monoxide; **Nov. 25, 1998** Dr. Kevorkian charged with first-degree murder for assisted suicide televised on CBS' "60 Minutes" Nov. 20, lethal injection administered to woman with Lou Gehrig's disease, over 130 assisted suicides, found guilty March 26, 1999.

Port Huron *Saint Clair County* *Eastern Michigan, 55 mi/89 km northeast of Detroit, on St. Clair River*

1686 Fort St. Joseph built on St. Clair River by French as defense against English, burned 1688; **1782** French settlers arrive from Detroit; **1790** settlement founded by Anselm Petit; **1814** Fort Gratiot built; town of Gratiot founded; **1821** St. Clair County formed; **1829** Fort Gratiot Lighthouse built; **1836** John Miller Homestead built; **1849** Gratiot incorporated as a village; **1857** towns of Peru, Desmond, Huron, and Gratiot merge, incorporated as city of Port Huron; **1858** Jenks House built; **1862** young Thomas Edison (born Milan, Ohio, 1847) saves son of stationmaster by pulling him off tracks ahead of oncoming train, out of gratitude is taught telegraphy, given boxcar as laboratory; **1871** county seat moved from town of St. Clair; **1881** Fort Gratiot monument erected; **1908** Port

Huron-Sarnia Railroad Tunnel completed under St. Clair River to Sarnia, Ontario; **1917** Public Library built; Mueller Brass Company plant opened; **1923** Port Huron Junior College established, becomes St. Clair County Community College; **March 16, 1934** Herbert Youngblood shot to death, escaped from Crown Point, Indiana, jail March 3 with bank robber John Dillinger, Dillinger shot July 22 in Chicago; **1938** Blue Water International Bridge built to Sarnia; **1945** county courthouse built; **1990** Baker College of Port Huron established.

Reed City *Osceola County* *Central Michigan, 65 mi/105 km north of Grand Rapids*

1840 Osceola County formed; **1848** town settled by German immigrants; **1869** county organized; Hersey becomes first county seat; **1871** Grand Rapids & Indiana Railroad reaches town; **1872** incorporated as a village; **1927** county seat moved to Reed City; county courthouse built; **1932** incorporated as a city.

River Rouge *Wayne County* *Southeastern Michigan, suburb 4 mi/6.4 km south of Detroit*

Late 1700s French families from Detroit settle in area; **1891** town founded on Detroit River, at mouth of River Rouge; **1899** incorporated as a village; **1903** Great Lakes Engineering builds large shipbuilding facility; **1920s** area grows with expansion of Ford Motor Company; **1922** incorporated as a city; **Apr. 27, 1970** rioting between whites and blacks ends with police intervention, includes fire bombings, looting.

Rochester *Oakland County* *Southeastern Michigan, 26 mi/42 km north of Detroit*

1817 town founded on Clinton River; **1837–1838** construction of Clinton-Kalamazoo Canal from Lake St. Clair to Lake Michigan reaches Rochester, work suspended; **1869** incorporated as a village; **1908** Parke Davis Biological Farm established; **1957** Oakland University established; **1967** incorporated as a city.

Rock Harbor *Keweenaw County* *Northwestern Michigan, 220 mi/354 km northwest of Sault Ste. Marie*

1634 Jean Nicolet reports gold, precious gems on Isle Royale (ROY-al), near north shore of Lake Superior; **1783** Isle Royale recognized as U.S. possession at Treaty of Paris; **1842** Webster-Ashburton Treaty sets U.S.-Canada border north of island; Ojibwe people cede island to U.S.; **1846** copper mining begins; **1858** Rock Harbor Lighthouse built, deactivated 1879; **1883** copper mines closed; **1912** moose arrive from Canada during channel freeze-over; **March 3, 1931** Isle Royale National Park authorized; **1936** forest fire burns nearly one-third of island; **1938** all but 3 percent of private land claims yielded to government; passenger ferry *Isle Royale Queen* begins service from Copper Harbor, Michigan; **1948–1949**

wolves arrive by crossing ice from mainland; **1956** Rock Harbor Lodge built.

Rogers City *Presque Isle County* *Northeastern Michigan, 195 mi/314 km north-northeast of Grand Rapids*

1869 town founded on Lake Huron; **1875** Presque Isle County formed; town becomes county seat; **1877** incorporated as a village; **1888** county courthouse built; **1944** incorporated as a city.

Romulus *Wayne County* *Southeastern Michigan, suburb 17 mi/27 km southwest of Detroit*

1826 area first settled; **1832** Romulus Township formed; **1930** Wayne County Airport established, becomes Detroit-Wayne County International Airport 1958; **1965** incorporated as a city; **1970** township merges with city of Romulus; **Aug. 16, 1987** Northwest MD-82 airplane crashes after takeoff from Detroit's Wayne County Airport killing 156; **Jan. 9, 1997** Comair Embraer 120 aircraft crashes on approach to Wayne County Airport killing 29.

Roscommon *Roscommon County* *North central Michigan, 120 mi/193 km north-northeast of Grand Rapids*

1873 town founded; **1875** Roscommon County formed; town becomes county seat; **1882** incorporated as a village; **1964** county courthouse built; **1966** Kirtland Community College established.

Saginaw *Saginaw County* *Eastern Michigan, 88 mi/142 km north-northwest of Detroit, near Lake Huron*

1816 Louis Campau builds fur trading post on Saginaw River, 15 mi/24 km south of its entrance to Saginaw Bay; **1818** council house built at request of Gov. Lewis Cass; **1819** treaty reached with Ojibwe people granting settlement rights to whites; Fort Saginaw built; **1822** troops stationed here following Native American unrest; **1835** Saginaw County formed; town becomes county seat; **1837** incorporated as a village; **1850s** lumber milling reaches peak; **1857** incorporated as a city; **1868** Schuch Hotel built; **1873** East Saginaw merges with South Saginaw; **1889** South Saginaw annexed by Saginaw; **c.1890** area becomes state's primary coal mining district; **1893** Baker-Perkins Company founded, maker of cooking equipment; **Nov. 20, 1896** actor Robert Armstrong born (died 1973); **1898** federal building dedicated; **1907** iron foundry established; **1915** Saginaw Public Library built; **May 13, 1950** singer, musician Stevie Wonder born; **1963** Saginaw Valley State University established; **1968** county courthouse built.

Saint Ignace *Mackinac County* *Northern Michigan, 210 mi/338 km north-northeast of Grand Rapids*

1634 Jean Nicolet visits region while searching for Northwest Passage; **1671** Father Marquette builds mission; town founded on Lake Huron, north side of Straits of Mackinac; **1679** La Salle party's vessel *Griffon* visits site, disappears after departure without La Salle on board; Fort de Buade built by French, renamed Fort Michilimackinac 1681; **1706** mission's last priest burns chapel to prevent desecration; **1715** fort reestablished on south side of Straits (Mackinaw City), abandoned to British 1760; **1780–1781** British build Fort Mackinac on Mackinac Island to east; **1818** Mackinac County formed; town becomes county seat; **1834** church built by Jesuit missionaries; **1839** county courthouse built, rebuilt 1936; **1874** post office established; **1881** railroad ferry service inaugurated across Straits from Mackinaw City; passenger ferry service to Mackinac Island begins; **1882** incorporated as a village; **1883** incorporated as a city; **1904** St. Ignatius Roman Catholic Church built, organized 1837; **1926** Native American village built by Chippewas, make articles for sale to tourists; **1957** Mackinac Bridge built across Straits of Mackinac to Mackinaw City.

Saint James *Charlevoix County* *Northern Michigan, 196 mi/315 km north of Grand Rapids*

1832 Father Baraga visits (Big) Beaver Island, Lake Michigan; **1847** Mormons from Voree, Wisconsin, settle on island led by James Jesse Strang; **1849** town founded by Strang at north end of Beaver Island; Mormon tabernacle built; **July 8, 1850** Strang declares island chain a kingdom, crowned king; **1851** Iron Ore Bay Lighthouse built at south end of island, rebuilt 1891; **1855** Strang arrested for mail tampering, counterfeiting, stealing, acquitted for lack of witnesses; **June 16, 1856** Strang shot by rebellious colony members, dies July 1 at Voree; **July 1856** mainlanders outraged by Mormons capture town, force all 2,600 Mormons to leave for Chicago aboard boat *Keystone State*; **1863** Holy Cross Roman Catholic Church founded; **1875** U.S. Coast Guard Station established; **1892** Protar Place house built by Russian exile Fedor Protar (1838–1925); **1912** Benjamin Franklin Purnell (King Ben) establishes penal colony on High Island to west for his Israelite House of David cult based in Benton Harbor; **1923** in trial against House of David, King Ben's immoral practices corroborated; **1927** King Ben dies, 500 "sinners" released from High Island.

Saint Johns *Clinton County* *Central Michigan, 90 mi/145 km northwest of Detroit*

1839 Clinton County formed; De Witt becomes first county seat; **1853** Detroit & Milwaukee Railroad built; town founded; **1856** county seat moved to St. Johns; **1857** incorporated as a village; **1904** incorporated as a city; **2000** county courthouse completed.

Saint Joseph *Berrien County* *Southwestern Michigan, 175 mi/282 km west of Detroit, on Lake Michigan*

1669 Father Marquette sails into Benton Harbor and St. Joseph River; **1679** La Salle builds Fort Miami; **1700** new fort built; Jesuit mission founded; **1763** fort destroyed by Chief Pontiac; **1783** William Barnett of New Jersey plants area's first apple and cherry orchards; **1831** Berrien County formed; Berrien Springs becomes first county seat; town founded, named Newburyport; **1834** incorporated as a village, renamed St. Joseph; **1836** town site inundated by shifting sands, moved to higher ground; **1859** St. Joseph Lighthouse built, operated until 1924; **1891** incorporated as a city; **1894** county seat moved to St. Joseph; **1898** North Pier Lighthouse built, replaces 1831 structure; **Oct. 10, 1898** Augustus Moore Herring flies airplane of his own invention on beach; **1968** county courthouse built.

Sandusky *Sanilac County* *Eastern Michigan, 78 mi/126 km north-northeast of Detroit*

1849 Sanilac County formed; **1870** town founded as county seat, originally named Sandusky; **1885** incorporated as a village; **1889** town renamed Sanilac Center; **1905** incorporated as a city; city name reverts to Sandusky; **1916** county courthouse completed.

Sault Sainte Marie *Chippewa County* *Northern Michigan, 300 mi/483km north-northwest of Detroit*

1618 Etienne Brule visits site while searching for Northwest Passage; **1634** Jean Nicolet arrives, also in search of elusive passage to Pacific Ocean; **1668** Father Jacques Marquette establishes Jesuit mission here; **1751** Fort Repentigny built by French to defend fur trade; **1762** fort destroyed; British take control; **1783** area ceded to U.S.; **1795** Johnstone House built; **1823** Fort Brady built; **1826** Chippewa County formed; **1827** Schoolcraft House built by Indian agent Henry R. Schoolcraft; **c.1845** town founded on St. Mary's River, opposite Sault Ste. Marie, Ontario, Canada; town becomes county seat; **1849** incorporated as village of St. Mary, disincorporated 1851; **1855** Sault Ste. Marie (Soo) Canal completed on U.S. side of St. Mary's River after two years construction; first locks built; **1870** Weitzel Lock built, completed 1881, major improvement on Soo Canal; **1877** county courthouse built, restored 1989; **1879** incorporated as a village, renamed Sault Ste. Marie; **1887** incorporated as a city; International Bridge (bascule) built for Canadian Pacific Railway; Poe Lock built, completed 1896; **1904** Davis Lock built, completed 1914; **1905** Bayliss (Carnegie) Public Library built; **1907** construction begins on St. Mary's Locks, completed 1919; **1911** Sabin Lock built, completed 1919; **1943** MacArthur Lock completed, replaces Weitzel Lock; **1946** Michigan College of Mining and Technology established, becomes Lake Superior State University; **1962** Soo Bridge built to Sault Ste. Marie, Ontario; **1968** New Poe Lock completed; **Nov. 10, 1975** laker *Edmund Fitzgerald* sinks in Lake Superior during fierce storm c.150 mi/c.240 km to northwest, near Ontario shore, killing all 29 crew.

Shelby *Oceana County* *Western Michigan, 58 mi/93 km northwest of Grand Rapids, near Lake Michigan*

1866 town founded, originally named Churchill's Corners; **1874–1876** massive flock of now extinct passenger pigeons extending 3 mi/4.8 km in width, 11 mi/18 km in length plague region to southeast, 700,000 birds systematically killed by hunters; **1885** incorporated as a village, renamed Shelby.

South Haven *Van Buren County* *Southwestern Michigan, 50 mi/80 km southwest of Grand Rapids*

1831 Jay R. Monroe becomes first settler; **1836** settlers begin area's first peach plantings, by 1839 learn of less harsh growing conditions nearer to Lake Michigan; **1839** town founded; **1850** sawmill established; **1869** incorporated as a village; **1902** incorporated as a city; **May 24, 1971** Palisades Nuclear Power Plant begins operation.

Standish *Arenac County* *Eastern Michigan, 112 mi/180 km northeast of Grand Rapids, near Lake Huron*

1831 Arenac County formed; **1871** town founded near Saginaw Bay; **1883** county organized; town becomes county seat; **1893** incorporated as a village; **1903** incorporated as a city; **1965** county courthouse completed.

Stanton *Montcalm County* *Central Michigan, 38 mi/61 km northeast of Grand Rapids*

1831 Montcalm County formed; **1850** county organized; Greenville becomes first county seat; **1860** town founded as new county seat, originally named Hall for landowner Fred Hall; **1863** town renamed Stanton; **1869** incorporated as a village; **1881** incorporated as a city; **1910** county courthouse built.

Sterling Heights *Macomb County* *Southeastern Michigan, 16 mi/26 km north of Detroit*

1820s first white settlers arrive on Clinton River; **1867** Upton House built; **1950s** major manufacturers begin entering the "Golden Corridor" of Sterling Township; **1968** township incorporated as city of Sterling Heights.

Tawas City *Iosco County* *Eastern Michigan, 133 mi/214 km northeast of Grand Rapids, on Lake Huron*

1853 town founded on Saginaw Bay by Gideon O. Whittemore; **1857** Iosco County formed; town becomes county seat; **1872** Tawas Point Lighthouse built, sand bar builds southward rendering lighthouse useless; **1885** incorporated as a village; **1895** incorporated as a city; **1936** first annual Perch Festival held; **1954** county courthouse built.

Traverse City   *Grand Traverse County*   *Northern Michigan, 125 mi/201 km north of Grand Rapids*

1847 town founded on Grand Traverse Bay, Lake Michigan, by first settlers William Boardman and son Horace; sawmill built; **1851** Grand Traverse County formed; town becomes county seat; docking facilities built; **1870s** apple orchards become major industry; **1880s** cherry production becomes important; **1881** incorporated as a village; **1891** opera house built; **1895** incorporated as a city; **1900** county courthouse completed; **Jan. 30, 1914** actor David Wayne born (died 1995); **1920** Traverse City State Park created; **1927** first National Cherry Festival held; **1928** National Music Camp founded at Interlochen to south by Joseph E. Maddy and Thaddeus P. Giddings; **1951** Northwestern Michigan College (2-year) established; Traverse Symphony Orchestra founded.

Vanderbilt   *Otsego County*   *Northern Michigan, 160 mi/257 km north-northeast of Grand Rapids*

1870 town founded, named for the prominent Vanderbilt family of New York; **1901** incorporated as a village; **Feb. 9, 1934** lowest temperature ever recorded in Michigan reached, −51°F/−46°C.

Warren   *Macomb County*   *Southeastern Michigan, suburb 11 mi/18 km north of Detroit*

1835 area first settled; **1837** town founded; **1909** incorporated as a village; **1940** Detroit Arsenal established, begins manufacture of tanks; **1954** Macomb Community College established; **1957** incorporated as a city.

West Branch   *Ogemaw County*   *North central Michigan, 117 mi/188 km northeast of Grand Rapids*

1872 Jackson, Lansing & Saginaw Railroad built; town founded on West Branch Rifle River; **1873** post office established; **1875** Ogemaw County formed; town becomes county seat; **1885** incorporated as a village; **1905** incorporated as a city; **1931** first annual Trout Festival held; **1976** county courthouse built.

White Cloud   *Newaygo County*   *Western Michigan, 42 mi/68 km north of Grand Rapids*

1851 Newaygo County formed; town of Newaygo becomes county seat; **1873** town founded, named Morgan; **1877** town renamed White Cloud; **1878** incorporated as a village; **1908** city hall built; **1910** county seat move to White Cloud; city hall converted to county courthouse; **1950** incorporated as a city; **1990s** new county courthouse built.

Wyandotte   *Wayne County*   *Southeastern Michigan, 10 mi/16 km south of Detroit, on Detroit River*

1818 Maj. John Biddle becomes first settler; **1853** Eureka Iron and Steel Company established on former Biddle estate; **1854** town platted, incorporated as a village; **1864** Eureka Steel becomes first to adopt Bessemer steelmaking process; **1867** incorporated as a city; **1891** saltworks established; **Apr. 23, 1940** TV actor Lee Majors born.

Ypsilanti   *Washtenaw County*   *Southeastern Michigan, 28 mi/45 km west of Detroit*

1809 trading post established; **1823** first settlers arrive; town founded, named by Chief Justice Augustus Woodward for Greek military hero Gen. Demetrios Ypsilanti; **1830** Ballard House built; **1832** incorporated as a village; **1835** Breakey Mansion built; **1838** first railroad reaches town; **1842** Ladies' Literary Clubhouse built; **1849** Michigan State Normal School established, becomes Eastern Michigan University; **1858** incorporated as a city; **1883** Cleary College established; **1899** Ypsilanti Watertower erected; **1900** Hutchinson House built; **1922** first Bach Music Festival held.

Minnesota

Northern U.S. Capital: St. Paul. Major cities: Minneapolis, St. Paul (Twin Cities).

The area west of the Mississippi River became part of the U.S. with the Louisiana Purchase in 1803. The area east of the Mississippi was added to Minnesota in 1846. Minnesota Territory was established March 3, 1849. Minnesota entered the Union as the 32nd state May 11, 1858.

Minnesota is divided into 87 counties. The counties are divided into townships which have governments with limited powers. Municipalities had been classified as villages and cities until 1974, when a state statute declared all villages to be cities, eliminating any classification. See Introduction.

Ada *Norman County* *Northwestern Minnesota, 32 mi/51 km north-northeast of Fargo, North Dakota*

1876 William Shields becomes first settler; town founded on Wild Rice River, named for Ada Fisher, daughter of St. Paul & Pacific Railroad official who died 1880 at age six; **1877** Hotel Ada built; **1881** Norman County formed; incorporated as a village, becomes county seat; **1897** large sawmill established; **1903** county courthouse built; **1904** Village Hall built; **July 27, 1918** bandleader Skitch Henderson born at Halstad to west; **1924** logging suspended with depletion of forest reserves; **1975** County Office Building completed.

Aitkin *Aitkin County* *Central Minnesota, 108 mi/174 km north-northwest of Minneapolis, on Mississippi River*

c.1850 trading post established on nearby Mad River by William Aitkin; **1857** Aitkin County formed; **1871** Northern Pacific Railroad built; town founded; **1881** large sawmill established by J. D. Knox; **1883** incorporated as a city; **1903** opera house built; **1929** county courthouse built; **1938** flooding inundates large area; **1950** severe flooding leads to building of Mississippi diversion channel.

Albert Lea *Freeborn County* *Southern Minnesota, 92 mi/148 km south of Minneapolis*

1835 Col. Albert Lea surveys area; **1855** Freeborn County formed; **1856** town founded as county seat by Joseph N. Nicollet; **1878** incorporated as a city; **1888** county courthouse built; **1897** Albert Lea Public Library founded; **Oct. 25, 1928** actress Marion Ross born.

Alexandria *Douglas County* *Central Minnesota, 118 mi/190 km northwest of Minneapolis*

1857 Douglas County formed; **1858** Alexander and William Kincaid build cabin and hotel; town founded as county seat, named for Alexander Kincaid; **1862** region abandoned during Dakota Conflict; Fort Alexandria built; **1866** treaties with Dakota Sioux end conflict; Douglas County organized; town becomes county seat; **1873** St. Paul & Pacific Railroad built, succeeded by St. Paul, Minneapolis & Manitoba Railroad; **1876** incorporated as a village; **1895** county courthouse built; **1898** Kensington Runestone discovered by Olof Ohman at Kensington to southwest with runic writing bearing date 1362, weighing 200 lb/91 kg; **1909** incorporated as a city; **1956** Runestone Museum founded to house inscribed Kensington Runestone; **1961** Alexandria Technical College (2-year) established; **Dec. 1965** Big Ole the Viking statue, 28 ft/8.5 m tall, erected at end of Broadway, created for New York World's Fair.

Angle Inlet *Lake of the Woods County* *Northern Minnesota, 225 mi/362 km northwest of Duluth*

1731 Fort St. Charles built on south shore of Angle Inlet; **1736** Sioux massacre 21 Frenchmen on Massacre Island, in Canadian territory; **1783** geographical error made in setting of boundary in Treaty of Paris creates Northwest Angle, protrusion of U.S. territory into Canada, northernmost point in contiguous U.S.; **1895** lake commercial fishing and sturgeon roe production reaches peak; **1934** feldspar mining begins on south shore of Northwest Angle.

Anoka *Anoka County* *Eastern Minnesota, 15 mi/ 24 km north of Minneapolis, on Mississippi River*

1680 area visited by Father Lewis Hennepin; **1844** first settlers arrive; Joseph Belanger founds town; **1854** first sawmill built; Woodbury House built by Dr. Edward P. Shaw, used as refuge during 1862 Sioux conflict; **1857** Anoka County formed; town becomes county seat; **1878** incorporated as a city; county courthouse built; **1884** steel bridge built across Mississippi; fire destroys 86 downtown businesses; **1886** potato starch factory established; **1898** Anoka State Hospital established; **1915** Municipal Stadium built; **Aug. 7, 1942** radio personality Garrison Keillor born.

Austin *Mower County* *Southeastern Minnesota, 90 mi/145 km south of St. Paul*

1855 Mower County formed; Frankfort becomes county seat; **1856** Austin R. Nicholas becomes first settler; town founded; **1857** county seat moved to Austin; **1868** incorporated as a village; **1869** Austin Public Library founded; **1887** waterworks opened; **1891** incorporated as a city; Hormel Packing Company established; **Apr. 5, 1904** poet Richard Eberhart born; **Apr. 10, 1936** football coach, announcer John Madden born; **1940** Riverland Community College established; **1959** former Horace Austin State Park deeded to city; **1966** county courthouse built.

Bagley *Clearwater County* *Northwestern Minnesota, 80 mi/129 km northeast of Fargo, North Dakota*

1898 town founded, incorporated as a village; **1902** Clearwater County formed; town becomes county seat; **1938** county courthouse built by Works Progress Administration (WPA); **1974** incorporated as statutory city.

Barnesville *Clay County* *Western Minnesota, 24 mi/39 km southeast of Fargo, North Dakota*

1877 Great Northern Railroad built by George I. Barnes; town founded; **1880** wheat growing becomes primary industry, through c.1910; **1881** incorporated as a village; **1882** town platted; **1889** incorporated as a city; **1891** Opera House built; **1901** first municipal telephone system in Minnesota installed; **1907** railroad shops moved to North Dakota; **c.1908** area's first seed potatoes grown; **1938** first Potato Day Festival held.

Baudette *Lake of the Woods County* *Northern Minnesota, 177 mi/285 km northwest of Duluth*

1891 Thomas Cathcart becomes first settler; town founded on Rainy River at mouth of Baudette River; **1906** incorporated as a village; **1910** forest fire destroys town, 43 killed; **1922** Lake of the Woods County formed; town becomes county seat; **1938** resettlement program completed for depression-era homeless families; **1954** Spooner annexed by Baudette; Spooner School converted to county courthouse; **1974** incorporated as statutory city.

Bemidji *Beltrami County* *Northern Minnesota, 137 mi/220 km west-northwest of Duluth*

1803 William Morrison becomes first white man to discover Lake Itasca to southwest, source of Mississippi River; **1866** Beltrami County formed; **1891** Itasca State Park established at source of Mississippi River; **1894** first homesteaders arrive; town founded on Lake Bemidji, Mississippi River, named for Chippewa Chief Bemidji; **1896** incorporated as a village; **1897** county organized; town becomes county seat; **1898** Chief Bemidji Statue erected; **1901** county courthouse built; **1905** incorporated as a city; **1919** Bemidji State University established; **June 21, 1921** actress Jane Russell born; **1938** Paul Bunyan Statue erected, Mayor Earl Bucklin used as model.

Benson *Swift County* *Western Minnesota, 115 mi/185 km west-northwest of Minneapolis*

1866 Norwegian Ole Corneiliusen becomes first settler; **1869** store established; **1870** Swift County formed; Great Northern Railroad built; town founded as county seat on Chippewa River; **1870s** town becomes important wheat-shipping center; **1876** Pacific House Hotel built; **1877** incorporated as a village; **1880** fire destroys 20 downtown businesses; **1897** county courthouse built; **1908** incorporated as a city; **1911** Benson Carnegie Library built.

Bloomington *Hennepin County* *Eastern Minnesota, 10 mi/16 km south of Minneapolis, on Minnesota River*

1855 Gideon Pond House built by missionary Gideon Pond; **1935** Bush Lake Ski Slide opened to west; **1953** incorporated as a city; **1956** Metropolitan Stadium built, home of Minnesota Twins baseball team and Vikings football team; **1963** Normandale Community College established; **1982** Twins move into Minneapolis' Metrodome; Metropolitan Stadium demolished 1985; **1992** Mall of America, largest shopping mall in world, built on stadium site.

Blue Earth *Faribault County* *Southern Minnesota, 101 mi/163 km south-southwest of Minneapolis*

1855 Faribault County formed; first white settlers arrive; **1856** town founded as county seat on Blue Earth River; **1863** Capt. P. B. Davy organizes Dakota Sioux, whose 1862 uprising had just been suppressed, into Blue Earth Wild West Show; **1874** incorporated as a village; **1891** county courthouse built; **1899** incorporated as a city.

Brainerd *Crow Wing County* *Central Minnesota, 104 mi/167 km north-northwest of Minneapolis*

1857 Crow Wing County formed; **1870** Northern Pacific Railroad built; town founded as county seat on

Mississippi River, named for railroad president's wife, Ann Eliza Brainerd Smith; **May 5, 1886** baseball player Chief Bender born, played for Philadelphia A's (died 1954); **1896** incorporated as a village; **1905** incorporated as a city; **1920** county courthouse built; **1938** Central Lakes College (2-year) established.

Breckenridge *Wilkin County* *Western Minnesota, 44 mi/71 km south of Fargo, North Dakota*

1857 town founded on Bois de Sioux River, opposite Wahpeton, North Dakota, named for Vice Pres. John C. Breckinridge [sp]; **1858** Wilkin County formed, named for Col. Alexander Wilkin; town becomes county seat; **Aug. 23, 1862** with Civil War recruits away, only three men remain, all three killed in Dakota Conflict, mail driver also killed; **1871** Great Northern Railroad reaches town; **1907** incorporated as a city; **1928** county courthouse built.

Buffalo *Wright County* *Central Minnesota, 32 mi/ 51 km northwest of Minneapolis*

1855 Wright County formed; Monticello becomes county seat; **1856** town founded on north shore of Buffalo Lake; **1873** county seat moved to Buffalo; **1877** county courthouse built; **1887** railroad reaches town; incorporated as a village; **c.1890** commercial fishing reaches peak; **March 18, 1891** writer Margaret Culkin Banning born (died 1982); **1959** county government center built, annex built 1980; **1974** incorporated as statutory city.

Caledonia *Houston County* *Southeastern Minnesota, 120 mi/193 km southeast of St. Paul*

1852 town founded on Root River by Sam McPhail; **1854** Houston County formed; town platted; Jacob Webster arrives from New England, sows dandelion seeds brought from that area to provide greens to eat, becomes prolific weed; **1855** town becomes county seat; **1870** incorporated as a village; **1875** County Jail built, still in use; **1883** county courthouse built; **1974** incorporated as a city.

Cambridge *Isanti County* *Eastern Minnesota, 41 mi/66 km north of Minneapolis*

1849 Isanti County formed, named for Sioux Chief Isanti; **1860** town founded as county seat by Swedish immigrants on Rum River; **1886** incorporated as a village; **1887** county courthouse built; **1893** Matthias Smith House built; **1974** incorporated as a statutory city; **1994** new county courthouse built.

Carlton *Carlton County* *Northeastern Minnesota, 15 mi/24 km southwest of Duluth*

1857 Carlton County formed; **1870** county organized; Thomson becomes county seat; Northern Pacific Railroad built; town founded on St. Louis River; **1881** incorporated as a village, named Northern Pacific Junction; **1889** town becomes new county seat; **1891** town renamed Carlton; **1915** Jay Cooke State Park established to east; **1917** Carlton Public Library founded; **1923** county courthouse completed; **1974** incorporated as statutory city.

Center City *Chisago County* *Eastern Minnesota, 31 mi/50 km north-northeast of St. Paul*

1850 first settlers arrive; **1851** Chisago County formed; **1903** incorporated as a village; **1972** county government center built, addition built 1990; **1974** incorporated as statutory city.

Ceylon *Martin County* *See* **Fairmont (1928)**

Chaska *Carver County* *Eastern Minnesota, 21 mi/ 34 km southwest of Minneapolis, on Minnesota River*

1853 area first settled; town founded; **1855** Carver County formed; **1856** town becomes county seat; **1860s** German and Swedish immigrants arrive; brick making begins with discovery of clay deposits, last factory closed 1950s; **1871** incorporated as a village; **1891** incorporated as a city; **1910** alfalfa become important crop; **1964** county courthouse built; **1973** County Administration Building completed; **1994** County Justice Center completed.

Cloquet *Carlton County* *Northeastern Minnesota, 15 mi/24 km west of Duluth*

1880 town founded on St. Louis River, originally named Knife Falls; first sawmills built; **1884** incorporated as a village, renamed Cloquet; **1904** incorporated as a city; **Oct. 12, 1918** great forest fire sweeps widespread area west of Duluth, over 400 killed, 2,000 injured, 13,000 left homeless; **Apr. 20, 1949** actress Jessica Lange born.

Crookston *Polk County* *Northwestern Minnesota, 63 mi/101 km north-northeast of Fargo, North Dakota*

1858 Polk County formed; Douglas becomes first county seat (trading post on Pembina Trail, Red River); **1872** Great Northern Railroad reaches site; town founded on Red Lake River, named for railroad chief engineer Col. William Crooks; **1879** incorporated as a city; county seat moved to Crookston; **1908** Crookston Carnegie Public Library built, new library opened 1984; **1966** University of Minnesota at Crookston established; **1969** county courthouse built.

Detroit Lakes *Becker County* *Western Minnesota, 45 mi/72 km east of Fargo, North Dakota*

1858 Becker County formed; town founded as county seat on northern shore of Detroit Lake; **1871** Northern Pacific Railroad reaches town; **1881** incorporated as a village; **1892** Church of the Holy Rosary (Catholic) built; **1900** incorporated as a city; **1913** Carnegie Library built, new facility opened 1984; **1926** town renamed Detroit Lakes; **1930** Soo Line Railroad built through town; **1941** county courthouse built.

Duluth *Saint Louis County* *Northeastern Minnesota, 135 mi/217 km north-northeast of Minneapolis*

1622 Pierre Radisson and Medard Chouart, Sieur de Groseiliers, explore southern shore of Lake Superior; Fond du Lac used to describe western end of lake; **1632** Father Allouez visits mouth of St. Louis River; **1679** Daniel Greysolon, Sieur du Luth, visits site; **1794** Northwest Trading Company builds large trading post; **1826** Treaty of Fond du Lac negotiated with Ojibwe allowing white settlement of area; **1847** area's fur trading ends; **1855** St. Louis County formed; Robert E. Jefferson builds first house; **1856** town founded, becomes county seat; **1857** incorporated as a town; **1858** Minnesota Point Lighthouse built; **1859** scarlet fever epidemic sweeps town, emptying nearly entire town through death or evacuation; **1860s** lumber men from Maine arrive to work the mills; **1865** first reports of iron-bearing ranges emerge from interior; **1870** incorporated as a city; Lake Superior and Mississippi (Northern Pacific) Railroad reaches city through efforts of financier Jay Cooke; Immigrant House established for transient settlers; **1871** channel cut through Minnesota Point allowing easier access to Duluth-Superior Harbor; **1874** St. Paul's Evangelical Church built; **1877** city reverts to town status following failure of Jay Cooke's ventures; **1878** economy rebounds with increased logging activity; **1887** reincorporated as a city; **1891** incline railway built on slopes of lake escarpment; **1905** large-scale shipping of iron ore from Mesabi Iron Range through Lake Superior begins; first Aerial Lift Bridge built across Duluth Ship Canal; **1895** Duluth Normal School established, becomes State Teachers College 1921, University of Minnesota at Duluth 1947; **1901** South Breakwater Lights (inner and outer) built; **1908** Glensheen Mansion completed; **1909** county courthouse built; **1910** Civic Center built; Duluth-Oliver Bridge built across St. Louis River to Oliver, Wisconsin; North Breakwater Lighthouse built; **1912** College of St. Scholastica established; **1914** Little Theater established; **1915** United States Steel Company plant built; Jay Cooke State Park established to southwest from estate of financier Jay Cooke (1821–1905); **1916** American Steel Company plant opened; Duluth Armory built; **1923** St. George's Serbian Orthodox Church founded; Lake Superior (Duluth) Zoo established by Bert Onsgard; **1926** Arrowhead Bridge built to Superior, Wisconsin; **1930** new Aerial Lift Bridge built across Ship Canal; Williamson-Johnson Airport established, becomes Duluth International Airport 1962; **1937** Duluth Homesteads Project completed by WPA with 84 houses for homeless; **1941** Wade Auditorium built; **May 24, 1941** singer, songwriter Bob Dylan born; **Aug. 2, 1956** Albert Woolson, last survivor of Civil War's Union Army, dies at age 109.

East Grand Forks *Polk County* *Northwestern Minnesota, on Red River, opposite Grand Forks, North Dakota*

1800 trading post established on Red River; **1870** first settlers arrive; **1871** store established by James Deering; **1873** town founded by W. C. Nash; post office established, named Nashville; **1879** Great Northern Railroad reaches town; **1882** incorporated as a village, renamed East Grand Forks; **1887** incorporated as a city; **1890s** city benefits from neighboring North Dakota's early prohibition laws; **1915** prohibition comes to Polk County, lifted 1947; **1929** Sorlie Memorial Bridge built across Red River; **Apr. 19, 1997** extensive flooding inundates town and most of its larger neighbor of Grand Forks, North Dakota, 8,500 left homeless in East Grand Forks, 50,000 homeless in Grand Forks.

Elbow Lake *Grant County* *Western Minnesota, 148 mi/238 km northwest of Minneapolis*

1868 Grant County formed; **1870** town founded as county seat; **1887** incorporated as a village; **1905** county courthouse built; **1934** Municipal Auditorium and Library built; **1974** incorporated as a statutory city.

Elk River *Sherburne County* *Eastern Minnesota, 25 mi/40 km north-northwest of Minneapolis*

1846 trading post built by David Faribault on Mississippi River, at mouth of Elk River; **1848** post sold to Pierre Bottineau; **1850** hotel built by Bottineau; **1851** dam, sawmill built on Elk River; **1855** town of Orono (Upper Town) platted; **1856** Sherburne County formed; **1865** town founded as county seat; **1868** town replatted; **1872** county organized; town becomes county seat; **1881** incorporated as a village; Orono annexed; **c.1900** lumber milling declines; **1960** Elk River Nuclear Plant begins operations; **1978** incorporated as a city; **1980** construction begins on county government center, completed in stages until 2002; **1988** nuclear plant converted to refuse burning plant.

Ely *Saint Louis County* *Northeastern Minnesota, 80 mi/129 km north of Duluth*

1883 high-grade iron ore discovered at western edge of nearby Miner's Lake in Mesabi Iron Range; **1887** town founded on southern shore of Lake Shagawa, town originally named Florence; **1888** incorporated as a village; renamed Ely (EE-lee) for Michigan miner Samuel B. Ely, who never visited town; **1891** incorporated as a city; **1892** Zenith Iron Mine opens to south; **1967** Pioneer Mine becomes last of four mines to close.

Eveleth *Saint Louis County* *Northeastern Minnesota, 50 mi/80 km north-northwest of Duluth*

Aug. 1891 tornado passes through woods uprooting trees, exposing iron deposits; **1892** town founded as lumber milling center in Mesabi Iron Range; **1893** town platted, named for timber owner Erwin Eveleth; incorporated as a village; **1895** town moved after ore is depleted at old site; **c.1900** iron mining begins, transforming town's economy; **1902** incorporated as a city; **Oct. 25, 2002** Democratic U.S. Sen. Paul Wellstone, 58, daughter, five others killed in crash of small airplane 11 days prior to midterm elections, a key factor in Republican Congressional sweep.

Fairmont   *Martin County*   *Southern Minnesota, 108 mi/174 km southwest of Minneapolis*

1857 Martin County formed; town founded as county seat; **1862** Fort Fairmont established during Dakota Conflict; **1866** Livingston Log Cabin (Tall Oak) built by William Robert Livingston; **1873–1877** grasshopper plague devastates agriculture in area; English immigrants arrive, bring fox hunting and lavish life styles with them; **1878** first railroad arrives; incorporated as a village; **1899** Wohlheter Mansion built; **1901** Opera House built; **1902** incorporated as a city; **1907** county courthouse built; **Jan. 5, 1928** U.S. Sen. Walter Mondale born at rural Ceylon to southwest, vice president under Pres. Jimmy Carter, Democratic presidential candidate 1984.

Faribault   *Rice County*   *Southeastern Minnesota, 47 mi/76 km south of Minneapolis*

1852 trading post founded by Alexander Faribault on Cannon River, at mouth of Straight River; **1855** town platted; Faribault House built; **1858** Rice County formed; town becomes county seat; State School for Deaf established; **1860** Episcopal Bishop Henry Whipple establishes mission church here; **1864** State School for the Blind established; **1872** incorporated as a city; Whipple House built, later demolished; **1879** State School for Retarded established; **1897** Buckham Memorial Library founded, built 1930; **1901** St. James Military Academy founded, became Shattucks-St. Mary's School 1972; **1934** county courthouse built; **1989** Faribault Correctional Facility established.

Fergus Falls   *Otter Tail County*   *Western Minnesota, 160 mi/257 km northwest of Minneapolis*

1857 town site selected on Otter Tail River by Joseph Whitford hired by land speculator James B. Fergus; **1858** Otter Tail County formed; Ottertail (Otter Tail City) becomes county seat; **1862** Whitford killed during Dakota Conflict; Fergus joins Montana gold rush; **1865** Ernest Buse becomes first settler; **1870** town platted; **1872** incorporated as a city; county seat moved to Fergus Falls; **1879** railroad reaches town; **June 22, 1919** tornado destroys town, 59 killed; **1920** county courthouse built; **1960** Fergus Falls Community College established.

Foley   *Benton County*   *Central Minnesota, 56 mi/ 90 km northwest of Minneapolis*

1849 Benton County formed, named for T. Hunt Benton of Massachusetts; Sauk Rapids becomes first county seat; **1856** county seat moved to Watab, then

back to Sauk Rapids 1859; **1883** town founded; **1897** county seat moved to Foley; **1901** incorporated as a village; **1903** county courthouse built; **1974** incorporated as a statutory city.

Frontenac   *Goodhue County*   *Southeastern Minnesota, 47 mi/76 km southeast of St. Paul, on Mississippi River*

1839 trading post established; **1855** St. Hubert's Lodge house built by Gen. Israel Garrard of Kentucky; town founded on shore of natural Lake Pepin, named for Louis de Buade, Comte de Frontenac; **1856** Villa Maria established by Catholic nuns from St. Louis; **1867** Little Grey Episcopal Church built; **1871** Frontenac Inn (Lakeside Hotel) built as steamboat hostelry.

Gaylord   *Sibley County*   *Southern Minnesota, 55 mi/89 km southwest of Minneapolis*

1853 Sibley County formed; **1879** county organized; Henderson becomes county seat; **1881** town founded, platted; **1883** incorporated as a village; **1915** county seat moved to Gaylord; **1916** county courthouse built; **1950** incorporated as a city.

Glencoe   *McLeod County*   *Central Minnesota, 45 mi/72 km west-southwest of Minneapolis*

1855 town founded; **1856** McLeod County formed (mac-CLOUD); town becomes county seat; **1873** incorporated as a village; **1876** county courthouse built, remodeled 2001; **1909** incorporated as a city.

Glenwood   *Pope County*   *Central Minnesota, 112 mi/180 km northwest of Minneapolis*

1862 Pope County formed, named for surveyor Capt. John Pope; **1866** Stockholm becomes first county seat; town founded on northeast end of Lake Minnewaska; county seat moved to Glenwood later in year; **1881** incorporated as a village; **1912** incorporated as a city; **1930** county courthouse built.

Grand Marais   *Cook County*   *Northeastern Minnesota, 108 mi/174 km northeast of Duluth, on Lake Superior*

1850 first discovery of iron ore in Minnesota reported in Gunflint Range to north by geologist J. G. Norwood; **1874** Cook County formed; town founded as county seat; **1885** North Superior Coast Guard Station established; Grand Marais Lighthouse erected, rebuilt 1922; **1889** county courthouse built; **1899** Grand Marais Library founded; **1903** incorporated as a village; **1974** incorporated as a statutory city.

Grand Portage   *Cook County*   *Northeastern Minnesota, 142 mi/229 km northeast of Duluth, on Lake Superior*

1792 Northwest Company establishes trading post near mouth of Pigeon River; site named for 9 mi/14.5 km canoe portage west from Lake Superior paralleling rapids of Pigeon River, important route to Western Canada; **1838** Catholic mission school established; **1854** Grand Portage (Ojibwe) Indian Reservation established; **1948** passenger ferry established to Isle Royale, Michigan; **Sept. 15, 1951** Grand Portage National Historic Site established, becomes National Monument Sept. 2, 1958; **1975** Grand Portage Lodge opened; **1990** Grand Portage Casino established.

Grand Rapids   *Itasca County*   *Northern Minnesota, 73 mi/117 km northwest of Duluth*

1849 Itasca County formed; **1877** town founded on Mississippi River, near western end of Mesabi Iron Range; **1881** incorporated as a village; **1891** county organized; town becomes county seat; **1910** paper mill established by newspaper man Charles K. Blandin, sold 1977; **1922** Itasca Community College established; **June 10, 1922** singer, actress Judy Garland born, died of sleeping pill overdose July 22, 1969, in London; **1954** county courthouse built; **1957** incorporated as a city; **1981** Myles Reif Performing Arts Center opened.

Granite Falls   *Yellow Medicine County*   *Southwestern Minnesota, 110 mi/177 km west of Minneapolis*

1854 Upper Sioux Indian Agency established, abandoned 1862 at outbreak of Dakota Conflict, its occupants escorted to safety by friendly Native Americans; Riggs and Williamson missions founded, moved to South Dakota 1863; **1871** Yellow Medicine County formed; Yellow Medicine City becomes county seat; **1872** town founded on Minnesota River; **1874** county seat moved to Granite Falls; **1879** incorporated as a village; **1889** incorporated as a city; **1893** county courthouse built; **1920** Granite Falls Library founded; **1938** Upper Sioux Indian Reservation established.

Hallock   *Kittson County*   *Northwestern Minnesota, 133 mi/214 km north of Fargo, North Dakota*

c.1850 fur trader Norman Kittson begins oxcart hauling service for trappers, taking loads of furs to St. Paul; **1878** Kittson County formed; **1879** town founded as county seat near Red River, named for editor Charles W. Hallock (1834–1917), founder of sportsman's magazine *Field and Stream*; **1887** incorporated as a village; **1912** Florence Farm House built to north by Walter Hill; **1965** county courthouse built; **1974** incorporated as a statutory city.

Halstad   *Norman County*   *See **Ada** (1918)*

Hastings   *Dakota County*   *Southeastern Minnesota, 19 mi/31 km southeast of St. Paul*

1819 Lt. William G. Oliver's troops camp near Mississippi River here; **1833** Joseph R. Brown becomes first settler, establishes trading post; town founded at mouth of Vermillion River, named Oliver's Grove; **1840** St. Croix County, Wisconsin, formed; town becomes first county seat; **1846** area becomes part of Minnesota; county seat moved to Stillwater, also later part of Minnesota; **1853** town platted; grist mill built by Harrison Graham, family credited with inventing the graham cracker; **1855** Ramsey Mill built by Gov. Alexander Ramsey; **1857** incorporated as a city; Nininger House built by Ignatius Nininger; **1859** Dakota County formed; town becomes county seat; **1860** mansion of Gen. William Gates Le Duc built; **March 17, 1866** Supreme Court Justice Pierce Butler born in rural Dakota County (died 1939); **1870s** town becomes important lumber milling center; **1871** county courthouse built; **1895** Spiral Bridge built across Mississippi River, spiral ramp on Minnesota end delivers traffic to street level in alley near American Legion Hall, replaced 1951; **1927** Lock & Dam No. 2 (Hastings Dam) built; **1987** Hastings Hydro Dam completed, replaces old dam; **1974** new county courthouse completed; old courthouse converted to city hall.

Hibbing   *Saint Louis County*   *Northeastern Minnesota, 58 mi/93 km northwest of Duluth*

1893 town founded as lumber milling center in Mesabi Iron Range; incorporated as a village, named for Capt. Frank Hibbing, built town's infrastructure; **1900** first Hibbing Fair held, predecessor of St. Louis County Fair; **1908** Carnegie Library opened; **1912** interurban Mesabi Electric Railroad established to Gilbert, abandoned 1927; **1914** Greyhound Bus Company established; **1916** Hibbing Community College established; **1919** town moved 2 mi/3.2 km south to allow for expansion of open-pit iron mine; **1921** Androy Hotel completed; **Sept. 10, 1934** baseball player Roger Maris born, outfielder for New York Yankees (died 1985); **1935** Hibbing Memorial hockey arena built.

Hinckley   *Pine County*   *Eastern Minnesota, 72 mi/116 km north-northeast of Minneapolis*

1854 first white settlers arrive; **1869** Lake Superior & Mississippi Railroad built; first sawmill built; town founded; **1885** incorporated as a village; **Sept. 1, 1894** Great Forest Fire sweeps large area, destroying most of town, total 432 killed; hero Jim Root backs his Northern Pacific train engine into town from Duluth, saves 350 people, his hands are burned fast to throttle; **Sept. 1, 1900** monument to fire victims dedicated, now Hinckley State Monument; **1974** incorporated as a statutory city; **1976** Hinckley Fire Museum opened; **1992** Grand Casino established by the Ojibwe.

Hutchinson *McLeod County* *Central Minnesota, 53 mi/85 km west of Minneapolis*

1855 town founded on South Fork Crow River by Asa, Judson and John Hutchinson, family of touring singers known for abolitionist songs; **1862** town partly destroyed by fire during Dakota Conflict; Dakota leader Little Crow and 16-year-old son killed by Nathan Lamson and son Chauncey; **1881** incorporated as a village; **1904** incorporated as a city.

International Falls *Koochiching County*
Northern Minnesota, 140 mi/225 km north-northwest of Duluth

1732 French explorer La Verendrye passes through Rainy Lake; **c.1890** town founded at falls of Rainy River, opposite Fort Frances, Ontario, Canada; town named Koochiching; **1901** incorporated as a village; **1903** town renamed International Falls; **1904** Minnesota and Ontario Paper Company Mill built on river, later becomes Boise Cascade; **1906** Koochiching County formed; town becomes county seat; **1909** county courthouse built; **1911** Public Library established; **1912** International Bridge built to Fort Frances; **1913** Insulite Mill opened by E. W. Backus to process waste from paper industry; Kettle Falls Hotel built to east, now part of Voyageurs National Park; **Oct. 1954** Smokey the Bear Statue dedicated; **1965** Boise Cascade acquires Backus mill; **Apr. 8, 1975** Voyageurs National Park established on Rainy Lake (U.S.-Canada border), to east; **Jan. 1980** first annual Icebox Days celebration held; **Jan. 1988** Giant Thermometer dedicated in Smokey Bear Park; **1974** incorporated as a statutory city.

Ivanhoe *Lincoln County* *Southwestern Minnesota, 150 mi/241 km west-southwest of Minneapolis*

1873 Lincoln County formed; Marshfield becomes county seat; **1880** wave of Polish immigrants arrives; **1883** county seat moved to Lake Benton; **1900** town founded; **1901** incorporated as a village; **1904** county seat moved to Ivanhoe; **1920** county courthouse completed; **Aug. 1972** first annual Polska Kielbasa Days celebration held.

Jackson *Jackson County* *Southwestern Minnesota, 126 mi/203 km southwest of Minneapolis*

1856 Fort Belmont built; trading post established; **1857** Jackson County formed; town founded as county seat on Des Moines River; **March 1857** renegade Dakotas under Inkpadutah plunder area and Spirit Lake, Iowa, to south, c.40 settlers killed; **1861** tow mill opened for processing flax; **1862** incorporated as a village; **1873** grasshoppers devastate crops; **1881** incorporated as a city; **1908** county courthouse built; **1948** Jackson Municipal Airport established.

Kasson *Dodge County* *Southeastern Minnesota, 65 mi/105 km south of St. Paul*

1865 Chicago & Northwestern Railroad built, passes to south of county seat of Mantorville; town founded; **1870** incorporated as a village; **1899** Kasson Public Library founded; **1974** incorporated as a statutory city.

Keewatin *Itasca County* *Northeastern Minnesota, 62 mi/100 km northwest of Duluth*

1904 iron ore discovered, part of Mesabi Iron Range; **1905** Mississippi and St. Paul iron mines opened; **1909** Great Northern Railroad arrives; town founded with activation of more mines; incorporated as a village; **1927** Mesabi Chief Iron Mine established; **1974** incorporated as a statutory city; National Steel Pellet Taconite plant established.

Kensington *Douglas County* *See **Alexandria** (1898)*

Lake City *Wabasha County* *Southeastern Minnesota, 52 mi/84 km southeast of St. Paul, on Mississippi River*

1853 Jacob Boody becomes first white settler; **1855** town founded on Lake Pepin, natural lake formed on Mississippi River by sediment from Wisconsin's Chippewa River; **1864** town designated as grain shipping port; **c.1870** town's nursery industry established; **1872** incorporated as a village; **1880s** freshwater clam industry gains importance, used in making pearl buttons, declines after 1920; **July 13, 1890** steamboat *Seawing* capsizes upstream in storm, 98 killed.

Le Center *Le Sueur County* *Southern Minnesota, 47 mi/76 km southwest of Minneapolis*

1853 Le Sueur County formed; **1864** town founded as county seat; town originally named Le Sueur Center; **1876** town platted; **1877** post office established; **1890** incorporated as a village; **1931** town name changed to Le Center to avoid confusion with town of Le Sueur; **1897** county courthouse built; **1974** incorporated as a statutory city.

Le Sueur *Le Sueur County* *Southern Minnesota, 47 mi/76 km southwest of Minneapolis, on Minnesota River*

1852 town founded, named for explorer Pierre Le Sueur; **1858** Mayo House built by Dr. W. W. Mayo, founder of Rochester's Mayo Clinic; **1858** Le Sueur City incorporated as a city; **1867** Le Sueur City renamed Le Sueur; **1903** Minnesota Valley Canning Company established, later renamed Green Giant Corporation.

Litchfield *Meeker County* *Central Minnesota, 62 mi/100 km west of Minneapolis*

1856 Meeker County formed; first settlers arrive; **Aug. 17, 1862** band of Dakota kill three white men, two white women in area to southwest, prelude to Dakota Conflict; **1869** St. Paul & Pacific Railroad built; town platted as county seat, named for three Litchfield brothers, railroad financiers; **1872** incorporated as a village; **March 29, 1916** U.S. Sen. Eugene McCarthy born at Watkins to north; **1974** incorporated as a statutory city; **1976** county courthouse built.

Little Falls   *Morrison County   Central Minnesota, 86 mi/138 km northwest of Minneapolis*

1805 Zebulon M. Pike explores area; **1855** Morrison County formed; town founded as county seat; **1879** incorporated as a village; **1889** incorporated as a city; **1890** dam built on Mississippi River; county courthouse built; **1899** Weyerhauser House built by timber magnate Charles Weyerhauser; **1903** Musser House built by bank president Richard Musser; **1906** Lindbergh House built, aviator Charles A. Lindbergh, Jr. spends boyhood here until his admission to University of Wisconsin 1920; **1973** Lindbergh History Center opened; **1995** Linden Hill Conference and Retreat Center established at historic Weyerhauser and Musser houses.

Long Prairie   *Todd County   Central Minnesota, 103 mi/166 km northwest of Minneapolis*

1848 Indian agency founded by U.S. government; group of Winnebago moved from Iowa to act as buffer between feuding Sioux and Ojibwe; **1851** mission school built by Italian Francis Vivaldi; **1855** Todd County formed; Indian agency abandoned; Winnebago group moved to Mankato area; **1857** town founded; **1867** county organized; town platted as county seat; **1883** incorporated as a village; county courthouse built; **1974** incorporated as a statutory city.

Luverne   *Rock County   Southwestern Minnesota, 171 mi/275 km southwest of Minneapolis*

1839 Joseph N. Nicollet explores area; **1857** Rock County formed; **1867** town settled, founded as county seat; **1870** town platted; **1877** incorporated as a village; **1888** county courthouse built; **1904** incorporated as a city.

Madison   *Lac Qui Parle County   Western Minnesota, 142 mi/229 km west of Minneapolis*

1871 Lac Qui Parle County formed, French for "talking lake"; **1875** settlers arrive from Iowa led by Jacob F. Jacobson; town founded as county seat; **1885** town platted; **1886** incorporated as a village; **1899** county courthouse built; **1902** incorporated as a city; **1982** city declared Lutefisk Capital of U.S. for its high per capita consumption of lutefisk, Scandinavian fish delicacy cured in salt brine.

Mahnomen   *Mahnomen County   Western Minnesota, 50 mi/80 km northeast of Fargo, North Dakota*

1867 White Earth Indian Reservation established; **June 14, 1868** first displaced Ojibwe people arrive, date celebrated annually; **1904** town founded on Wild Rice River; **1906** Mahnomen County formed; town becomes county seat; **1905** incorporated as a village; **1906** county courthouse built; **1974** incorporated as a statutory city.

Maine Prairie   *Stearns County   See* **Saint Cloud** (1898)

Mankato   *Blue Earth County   Southern Minnesota, 65 mi/105 km southwest of Minneapolis, on Minnesota River*

1852 Henry Jackson, Parsons K. Johnson, and Daniel Williams become first settlers, offer Chief Sleepy Eye barrel of pork to ignore treaty banning white settlement; town founded, name derived from Dakota term for blue earth; **1853** Blue Earth County formed; town becomes county seat; **1862** stonemason Louis Sheppman begins building windmill at Minneopa Falls, interrupted by Dakota Conflict, completed 1864; conflict disrupts settlement; **Sept. 1862** 303 of 400 Dakota people held at Camp Lincoln condemned to death for part in uprising, all pardoned by President Lincoln except for 38 executed by hanging Dec. 26; **1864** Sheppman Grist Mill completed; **1868** incorporated as a city; Mankato Normal School established, becomes Mankato State Teachers College 1921, Minnesota State University 1975; **1880** first bridge built to North Mankato; **1901** county courthouse built; **1911** Bethany Lutheran College established; **1931** Minneopa State Park established; **1951** flooding inundates North Mankato.

Mantorville   *Dodge County   Southeastern Minnesota, 62 mi/100 km south of St. Paul*

1853 town founded by brothers Peter and Riley Mantor; **1854** incorporated as a village; **1855** Dodge County formed, named for Gov. Henry Dodge of Wisconsin Territory; town becomes county seat; limestone quarrying begins; **1856** Hubble House built of limestone; **1858** tavern built; **1861** Peter Mantor organizes Minnesota Regiment's Company C for duty in Civil War, nearly all killed, leaving town full of widows and orphans; **1865** Chicago & Northwestern Railroad misses town to south, built through nearby Kasson; **1869** St. John's Episcopal Church built; **1871** county courthouse built, oldest courthouse in use in Minnesota, annex built 1990; **1974** incorporated as a statutory city.

Marshall   *Lyon County   Southwestern Minnesota, 128 mi/206 km west-southwest of Minneapolis*

1868 Lyon County formed; **1871** county organized; town founded as county seat on Redwood River; **1872** town platted; incorporated as a village; **1901** incorporated as a city; **1963** Southwest State University established; **1994** county courthouse built.

Mendota   *Dakota County   Eastern Minnesota, suburb 5 mi/8 km southwest of St. Paul, on Mississippi River*

c.1819 site at confluence of Minnesota River serves as rendezvous for French fur trappers; settlement named St. Peter; **1834** first permanent settlers arrive; town founded; **1835** Henry Hastings Sibley House built, becomes Sibley House Museum 1910; **1837** town renamed; **1837** Jean Baptiste Faribault House built; **1854** Hypolite Du Puis House built; **1887** incorporated as a city; **1926** Mendota Bridge built across Minnesota River, comprises 13 arches.

Milaca   *Mille Lacs County   Eastern Minnesota, 55 mi/89 km north-northwest of Minneapolis*

1857 Mille Lacs County formed; **1860** county organized; Princeton becomes first county seat; **1888** town founded on Rum River; **1897** incorporated as a village; **1920** county seat moved to Milaca; county courthouse built; **1937** Milaca Community Library opened; **1974** incorporated as a statutory city.

Minneapolis   *Hennepin County   Eastern Minnesota, 10 mi/16 km west of St. Paul, on Mississippi River*

1683 site visited by Father Louis Hennepin; **1805–1806** Sioux relinquish land in treaty promulgated by Lt. Zebulun Pike; **1819** Fort Snelling established on Mississippi River, at confluence of Minnesota River, by Lt. Col. Henry Leavenworth; **1823** lumber mill and grist mill built by Colonel Snelling on west side of St. Anthony Falls; **May 10, 1823** steamboat *Virginia* arrives at Fort Snelling, first steamboat to ascend Mississippi River; **1838** Franklin Steele builds cabin on east side of falls; **1847** Steele builds sawmill on east side of falls; **1848** Coultier House built by Alex Coultier; Godfrey House built by Ard Godfrey; **1849** Stevens House built at Minnehaha Creek; **1851** University of Minnesota (Twin Cities Campus) established; shoemaker Nils Nyberg becomes first Scandinavian to settle in city; **1852** Hennepin County formed; town becomes county seat; **1855** St. Anthony incorporated as a city; city's first bridge across Mississippi River built, replaced 1878 by Tenth Avenue Bridge; **1856** Minneapolis incorporated as a village; **1857** Notre Dame of Lourdes Catholic Church built; Nicollet House built; **1861** St. Anthony Padua Catholic Church built; **1866** Minneapolis incorporated as a city; **1869** Augsburg College established; two tunnels being built below falls, one for water, the other for transportation, discovered threatening to stability of falls, work halted, reinforcement walls built; **1872** city of St. Anthony annexed by Minneapolis; **1878** explosion of flour-dust destroys Washburn "A" Mill, 18 workers killed; **1879** hydroelectric project at St. Anthony Falls completed; **1880** Pillsbury "A" Mill built; **1881** Great Northern Stone Arch Bridge built below St. Anthony Falls; **1882** West Hotel built; **1883** Minnesota General Hospital founded; **1889** Minneapolis Public Library opened; **1903** Minneapolis Symphony founded; **June 14, 1906** actor Gil Lamb born (died 1995); **Dec. 28, 1908** actor Lew Ayres born (died 1996); **1911** St. Marks Episcopal Church completed; **1915** Minneapolis Art Institute completed, founded 1883; **1915** Catholic Basilica of St. Mary dedicated; **1917** Laverne Andrews (Andrews Sisters) born (died 1967); **Jan. 3, 1918** singer Maxine Andrews (Andrews Sisters) born (died 1995); **Feb. 13, 1918** golf pro Patty Berg born; **May 9, 1918** Gov. Orville L. Freeman born, secretary of Agriculture under President Kennedy (died 2003); **Feb. 16, 1920** singer Patty Andrews (Andrews Sisters) born; **Sept. 24, 1922** actor Cornell MacNeil born; **Nov. 26, 1922** cartoonist Charles Schulz born, creator of Peanuts comic strip (died 2000); **Dec. 20, 1922** movie director George Roy Hill born (died 2002); **1923** Wold-Chamberlain Field airport established at former speedway built 1914, becomes Minneapolis-St. Paul International Airport 1948; **May 26, 1923** TV actor James Arness born; **1925** Institute of Child Welfare established; **March 18, 1926** actor Peter Graves born; **1927** Highland-Ford Parkway (Intercity) Bridge built across Mississippi to St. Paul; Municipal Auditorium built; **Aug. 11, 1928** actress Arlene Dahl born; **1929** 32-story Foshay Tower office building completed; 26-story Rand Tower building completed; American Institute of Swedish Art, Literature, and Sciences founded; **1930** Father Hennepin Statue erected in front of St. Mary Basilica; **1932** 26-story Northwestern Bell Telephone Building completed; **Dec. 29, 1934** actor Ed Flanders born; **1935** National Guard Armory built; main post office completed; **1936** federal housing project begun, designed to rid city of substandard housing; **1937** Fort Snelling conveyed to state historical society; **Jan. 23, 1950** actor Richard Dean Anderson born; **June 27, 1951** actress Julia Duffy born; **June 7, 1958** singer Prince (Prince Rogers Nelson) born; **1961** Central Branch Public Library completed; **1964** College of St. Catherine (2-year) established; **1965** Minneapolis Community and Technical College established; **1966** North Hennepin Community College established; **July 27, 1972** Virginia Piper, 40, kidnapped, $2 million ransom paid, released unharmed; **1973** 51-story IDS Center built; **1974** 24-story Hennepin County Government Center completed; **1982** Hubert Humphrey Metrodome stadium completed, home of Minnesota Twins baseball team, replacing Metropolitan Stadium in suburban Bloomington; **1983** 53-story Multifoods Tower office building built; **1984** 42-story Piper Jaffray Tower built; **1988** 57-story Wells Fargo Center built; **Dec. 1990** Minneapolis Convention Center opened, expansion completed Apr. 2002; **1992** 53-story US Bank Place built.

Minnetonka   *Hennepin County   Eastern Minnesota, suburb 12 mi/19 km west of Minneapolis*

1852 Col. John H. Stevens explores Minnehaha Creek; **1853** first settlers arrive, build sawmill; town founded, name derived from Dakota term for "place covered by water"; **1860** steamboat *Governor Ramsey* first to ply waters of Lake Minnetonka to west; **1876** Minnetonka Milling Company established by Charles H. Burwell; **1882** steamboat *Phil Sheridan*, veteran of Ohio and Mississippi rivers since 1866, dismantled, rebuilt on Lake Minnetonka, renamed *Belle of Minnetonka*, plies lake waters through 1926; **1883** Burwell House built; **1916** Glen Lake Tuberculosis Sanatorium opened; **1956** incorporated as a village; **1969** incorporated as a city.

Montevideo *Chippewa County* *Western Minnesota, 120 mi/193 km west of Minneapolis, on Minnesota River*

1862 Chippewa County formed; **Sept. 26, 1862** Sioux release 269 prisoners, mostly women and children, taken during Dakota Conflict; **1870** town founded as county seat; **1879** incorporated as a village; **1894** Camp Release State Monument dedicated; **1908** incorporated as a city; **1949** bronze statue of Uruguayan champion of independence José Artigas presented to city by people of Montevideo, Uruguay; **1957** county courthouse built.

Monticello *Wright County* *Central Minnesota, 33 mi/53 km northwest of Minneapolis, on Mississippi River*

1852 first white settlers arrive; **1854** town platted; **1855** Wright County formed; town becomes county seat; **1856** town incorporated; **1859** Oscar F. Johnson accused of killing neighbor H. A. Wallace, acquitted, lynched, all lynchers eventually arrested; **1861** reincorporated as a village; **1873** county seat moved to Buffalo; **Dec. 10, 1970** Monticello Nuclear Power Plant begins production; **1974** incorporated as a statutory city.

Moorhead *Clay County* *Western Minnesota, 210 mi/338 km northwest of Minneapolis, on Red River*

1862 Clay County formed; **1871** Northern Pacific Railroad built; town founded as county seat on Red River, opposite Fargo, North Dakota; town named in honor of Dr. William G. Moorhead, railroad director; **1881** incorporated as a city; 140-room Grand Pacific Hotel built, demolished 1996; **1885** Moorhead State University established, originally Moorhead State Teachers' College; **1891** Concordia College established; **July 6, 1936** highest temperature ever recorded in Minnesota reached, 114°F/46°C; **1959** county courthouse built; **1994** Plains Art Museum opened in old Post Office, built 1904; **Apr. 1997** severe flooding inundates broad area of flat prairie bounding Red River.

Mora *Kanabec County* *Eastern Minnesota, 62 mi/ 100 km north of Minneapolis*

1858 Kanabec County formed; **1881** town founded on Snake River by Swedish immigrants, named for Mora, Sweden; **1882** county organized; town becomes county seat; incorporated as a village; **1894** county courthouse

built; **1930** Izaak Walton League Museum opened; **1974** incorporated as a statutory city.

Morris *Stevens County* *Western Minnesota, 135 mi/217 km west-northwest of Minneapolis*

1862 Stevens County formed; **1871** county organized; St. Paul & Pacific Railroad built; town founded as county seat on Pomme de Terre River; town named for chief railroad engineer Charles F. Morris; **1878** incorporated as a village; **1903** incorporated as a city; **1922** county courthouse built; **1959** University of Minnesota at Morris established.

Morton *Renville County* *Southern Minnesota, 88 mi/142 km west-southwest of Minneapolis, on Minnesota River*

1852 first white settlers arrive following ratification of treaties not to liking of either whites or Native Americans; **Aug. 18, 1862** Dakota Conflict (Sioux uprising) begins at Lower Agency, spreads over several weeks through 23 counties, c.500 whites killed, c.60 Native Americans killed; **Sept. 2, 1862** force of 160 U.S. troops attacked by Dakota at Birch Coulee, about one-third of soldiers killed; **May 1863** U.S. government fines Dakotas their reservations, transports all but 25 Dakota families out of state; **1895** Birch Coulee State Park established, later becomes state historical site.

New Ulm *Brown County* *Southern Minnesota, 75 mi/121 km southwest of Minneapolis, on Minnesota River*

1854 town founded by German immigrants led by Frederick Beinhorn, many from city of New Ulm, Germany; **1855** Brown County formed; town becomes county seat; **1857** incorporated as a village; **Aug. 19-23, 1862** Dakotas attack town, defeated after second battle against Col. Flandrau's forces, 26 soldiers killed; **1876** incorporated as a city; **1889** county courthouse built; **1936** New Ulm Library and Museum built.

Northfield *Rice County* *Southeastern Minnesota, 35 mi/56 km south of Minneapolis*

1855 town founded on Cannon River; **1866** Carleton College established; **1871** incorporated as a village; **1874** St. Olaf College established; **1875** incorporated as a city; **Sept. 7, 1876** Jesse and Frank James attempt holdup of First National Bank, two citizens killed, one wounded, two of James' gang killed, one wounded, remainder captured in Watonwan County Sept. 21, one killed, James brothers escape; **1910** Northfield Carnegie Public Library opened.

Olivia *Renville County* *Southern Minnesota, 85 mi/ 137 km west of Minneapolis*

1855 Renville County formed, named for pioneer Joseph Renville; **1862** Dakota Conflict disrupts county affairs;

1866 county organized; Beaver Falls becomes county seat; **1878** Milwaukee Road railroad built; town founded, named for first station master; **1881** town incorporated; **1901** county seat moved to Olivia; **1902** county courthouse built.

Ortonville   *Big Stone County   Western Minnesota, 155 mi/249 km west-northwest of Minneapolis*

1862 Big Stone County formed; **1872** C. K. Orton becomes first settler; trading post established; **1873** town founded by Orton as county seat on Minnesota River; **1875** post office established; **Apr. 20, 1879** fire destroys half of town; **1881** incorporated as a village; **1892** Columbian Hotel built; **1902** county courthouse built; **1937** diversion channel completed from South Dakota's Whetstone River to dry Big Stone Lake, forming large lake on South Dakota state line; **1915** Carnegie Library opened; **1931** first annual Corn Festival held; **1974** incorporated as a statutory city.

Owatonna   *Steele County   Southeastern Minnesota, 62 mi/100 km south of Minneapolis*

1854 town founded as mineral springs health resort; incorporated as a village; **1855** Steele County formed; **1877** Minnesota Academy founded, becomes Pillsbury Military Academy 1886; **1891** county courthouse built; **1900** Owatonna Public Library founded; **1908** National Farmers' Bank Building built, designed by Louis Sullivan; **June 18, 1920** actor E. G. Marshall born (died 1998); **1974** incorporated as a statutory city.

Park Rapids   *Hubbard County   Northern Minnesota, 140 mi/225 km west of Duluth*

1880 town founded as wheat farming center; **1882** town platted by Joseph Sombs; **1883** Hubbard County formed; town becomes county seat; **1890** incorporated as a city; **1890s** falling wheat prices force farmers to turn to dairying; **1975** county courthouse completed.

Pelican Rapids   *Otter Tail County   Western Minnesota, 40 mi/64 km east-southeast of Fargo, North Dakota*

1868 area first settled by Canadian fur trappers; **1882** Great Northern Railroad reaches site; town founded on Pelican River; **1883** incorporated as a village; **1931** prehistoric skeleton dubbed "Minnesota Woman" discovered to north during construction of U.S. Highway 59, estimated to be 10,000 years old; **1974** incorporated as a statutory city.

Pine City   *Pine County   Eastern Minnesota, 59 mi/ 95 km north of St. Paul*

1856 Pine County formed; **1869** town founded as county seat on Snake River; **1881** incorporated as a village; **1920** Pine City Public Library founded, built 1978; **1939** county courthouse built; **1965** Pine Technical College (2-year)

established; **1968** incorporated as a city; **Oct, 2, 1968** St. Croix National Scenic Riverway established to east.

Pipestone   *Pipestone County   Southwestern Minnesota, 163 mi/262 km southwest of Minneapolis*

1836 painter George Catlin visits Sioux pipestone quarries, sends samples home to Pennsylvania; **1838** Joseph Nicollet explores area, names of party inscribed in rock at Winnewissa Falls; **1857** Pipestone County formed; **1873** Charles H. Bennett becomes first settler; **1874** town founded as county seat by Bennett; **1881** incorporated as a village; **1901** incorporated as a city; **July 4, 1901** county courthouse dedicated; **Aug. 25, 1937** Pipestone National Monument established; **1949** Song of Hiawatha Pageant first held; **1994** Pipestone Performing Arts Center opened.

Preston   *Fillmore County   Southeastern Minnesota, 100 mi/161 km south-southeast of St. Paul*

1853 Fillmore County formed; Chatfield becomes county seat, later moved to Carimona; **1855** store established by Tom Meighen, closed c.1908; town founded; **1856** county seat moved to Preston; **1871** incorporated as a village; **1912** town hall and library completed; **1958** county courthouse built; **1974** incorporated as a statutory city.

Red Lake Falls   *Red Lake County   Northwestern Minnesota, 75 mi/121 km north-northeast of Fargo, North Dakota*

1798 Northwest Company fur trading post established on Red Lake River under Jean Baptiste Cadotte; **1863** treaty with Ojibwe cedes lands to U.S.; **1876** white settlers arrive; town founded; **1881** incorporated as a village; **1896** Red Lake County formed; town becomes county seat; **1897** incorporated as a city; **1911** county courthouse built.

Red Wing   *Goodhue County   Southeastern Minnesota, 38 mi/61 km southeast of St. Paul, on Mississippi River*

1805 Zebulon Pike visits site, finds Dakota village; **1836** Swiss Protestant mission established, abandoned 1840, reopened 1846 by American Foreign Missions Board; **1853** Goodhue County formed, named for Minneapolis newspaper editor James Madison Goodhue; town founded as county seat; **1854** Hamline University established, moved to St. Paul 1869; **1857** incorporated as a city; **1860** U.S. Cong. Andrew J. Volstead born in rural Goodhue County (died 1947); **1893** Red Wing Library founded, Carnegie building opened 1903; **1932** county courthouse built; **Dec. 1, 1973** Prairie Island Nuclear Power Plant begins operations to northwest on Mississippi River.

Redwood Falls   *Redwood County   Southern Minnesota, 95 mi/153 km west-southwest of Minneapolis*

1858 Wahpeton Sioux physician, writer Charles Alexander Eastman born (died 1939); **1862** Redwood

County formed; **1864** area settled at end of Dakota Conflict; Col. Sam McPhail builds stockade; **1865** town founded as county seat on Redwood River, near its mouth on Minnesota River; **1875** incorporated as a village; **1878** Minnesota Valley Railroad reaches town; **1884** Minneapolis & St. Louis Railroad reaches town; Richard W. Sears becomes first depot agent, later founds Sears & Roebuck Company; **1891** incorporated as a city; county courthouse built.

Rochester   *Olmsted County*   *Southeastern Minnesota, 77 mi/124 km south-southeast of Minneapolis*

1854 crossroads wagon train camp established at town site; town founded by George Head of Rochester, New York; **1855** Olmsted County formed; town becomes county seat; **1858** incorporated as a city; **Aug. 21, 1883** tornado heavily damages city, 31 killed; **1889** St. Mary's Hospital founded, nucleus of city's hospital group; **1892** Mayo Clinic founded by Dr. William Worrall Mayo and sons William James and Charles Horace Mayo; **1919** Rochester Orchestra and Chorale founded; **1928** Lobb Field airport established, dedicated as Rochester International Airport 1960; **1946** Rochester Art Center founded; **May 1956** ground broken for International Business Machines (IBM) complex; **May 31, 1961** actress Lea Thompson born; **1993** county courthouse completed.

Roseau   *Roseau County*   *Northwestern Minnesota, 145 mi/233 km north-northeast of Fargo, North Dakota*

1822 trading post established; **1885** town founded on Roseau River; **1894** Roseau County formed; town becomes county seat; **1895** incorporated as a village; **1936** Roseau Public Library established; **1974** incorporated as a statutory city; **1995** county courthouse built; **June 2002** heavy flooding inundates 95 percent of town and hundreds of farmsteads.

Rush City   *Chisago County*   *Eastern Minnesota, 50 mi/80 km north of St. Paul, near St. Croix River*

1873 town founded; incorporated as a village; **Feb. 16, 1903** previous lowest temperature ever recorded in Minnesota reached at Pokegama Dam, –59°F/–51°C, record broken 1996 at village of Tower, St. Louis County; **1974** incorporated as a statutory city; **Feb. 2000** Rush City Correctional Facility established.

Saint Cloud   *Stearns, Sherburne, and Benton counties*   *Central Minnesota, 66 mi/106 km northwest of St. Paul*

1853 Norwegian Ole Bergeson becomes first white settler at site on Mississippi River; **1854** town founded by John L. Wilson on land bought from Bergeson; **1855** Stearns County formed; town becomes county seat; **1856** incorporated as a city; St. Mary's Catholic Church founded; St. Cloud Presbyterian Church founded; **1858** land office moved from Sauk Rapids, ceased operating 1906; group supporting southerner Gen. Sylvanus B. Lowry, a town

proprietor, breaks into office of antislavery editor Jane Gray Swisshelm, throw printing press parts into Mississippi River; **Aug. 1862** fort built to protect town from attack during Dakota Sioux conflict; **1868** incorporated as a city; granite quarrying begins; **1869** St. Cloud State University established, originally St. Cloud State Teachers' College; **Apr. 14, 1886** deadliest tornado in Minnesota history strikes St. Cloud and nearby Sauk Rapids, total 72 killed, 213 injured; **1887** Minnesota State Reformatory established; **1889** East St. Cloud, on east side of Mississippi River, annexed by St. Cloud; **Oct. 16, 1898** U.S. Supreme Court Justice William Orville Douglas born at rural Maine Prairie to south (died 1980); **1902** Public Library built; **Nov. 14, 1917** actor Gig Young born (died 1978); **1922** Stearns County courthouse completed; **1924** U.S. Veterans Hospital opened; **1928** St. Cloud Hospital built; **1948** St. Cloud Technical College (2-year) established; **May 1986** Stearns County Law Enforcement Center opened.

Saint James   *Watonwan County*   *Southern Minnesota, 95 mi/153 km southwest of Minneapolis*

1860 Watonwan County formed; **1870** town founded as county seat; **1871** incorporated as a village; **1895** county courthouse built; **1899** incorporated as a city; **1911** St. James Public Library founded, becomes County Library 1943.

Saint Paul   *Ramsey County*   *Eastern Minnesota, 10 mi/16 km east of Minneapolis, on Mississippi River*

1680 area visited by Father Louis Hennepin; **1805–1806** Dakotas surrender land by treaty; **1819** Fort Snelling built at confluence of Mississippi and Minnesota rivers; **1823** steamboat *Virginia* reaches Fort Snelling, first steamboat to ascend Mississippi; **1838** trader Pierre "Pig's Eye" Parrant moves from fort, first to settle on site of present city, names site Pig's Eye; **Oct. 1841** chapel built by Father Lucian Galtier to serve squatters, renames community St. Paul; **1844** half-breed guide Pierre Bottineau makes land claim; **1846** town platted as north terminus for steamboat commerce; **1849** Ramsey County formed; incorporated as a village; becomes territorial capital and county seat; *Pioneer Press* newspaper founded as *Minnesota Pioneer*; state historical society established; **1850** First Presbyterian Church built; **1853** Territorial Capitol built; **1854** incorporated as a city; **May 11, 1858** Minnesota enters Union as 32nd state; city becomes state capital; Wabasha Street Bridge built across Mississippi River; **1862** first railroad reaches city; **1863** St. Joseph's Academy founded; **1867** Old Customs House built; **1868** *St. Paul Dispatch* newspaper founded; **1869** Hamline University moved from Red Wing, established 1854; **1871** Bethel College established; Catholic Church of the Assumption built; **1874** Macalester College established; **March 1, 1881** state capitol destroyed by fire; **1883** second state capitol built; **1885** University of St. Thomas established; **Dec. 25, 1885** sculptor Paul Manship born, created Prometheus figure at Rockefeller Plaza, New York (died 1966); **1886**

Armstrong-Quinlan House built, moved from downtown area Oct. 2001; **1887** James J. Hill House built; **1889** High Bridge completed over Mississippi River; **Nov. 12, 1889** publisher De Witt Wallace born (died 1981); **Sept. 24 1896** novelist F. Scott Fitzgerald born (died 1940); **1897** Como Park Zoo established; **June 6, 1898** actor Walter Abel born (died 1987); **1893** Concordia University at St. Paul established, originally St. Paul Seminary; **1900** Post Office and federal courts building completed; **1902** Northwestern College established; **Feb. 19, 1902** short story writer Kay Boyle born (died 1992); **1904** third state capitol completed, begun 1893, designed by Cass Gilbert after St. Peter's in Rome; **1905** College of St. Catherine established; **1907** St. Paul Institute of Science and Letters founded, becomes Science Museum of Minnesota 1970; Municipal Auditorium built; **Apr. 13, 1907** Gov. Harold Stassen born at West St. Paul to south, perennial presidential candidate (died 2001); **Nov. 23, 1907** biographer William A. Swanberg born (died 1992); **1911** first Minnesota State Fair held; Gillette State Hospital for Crippled Children opened; **1913** St. Paul Public Library built; **1915** Cathedral of St. Paul (Catholic) built; Como Park Conservatory opened; **1919** St. Paul Technical College (2-year) established; **1920** Union Depot completed; **1921** Hill Reference Library opened; **1923** Ford Motor Plant founded; **1926** Robert Street Bridge built across Mississippi River; **1927** Highland-Ford Parkway (Intercity) Bridge built across Mississippi to Minneapolis; **1932** city hall and county courthouse completed; Roy Wilkins Auditorium opened; **1932** state office building completed; **June 15, 1933** William Hamm, 39, kidnapped, $100,000 ransom paid, Alvin Karpis gets life in prison, paroled 1969; **Jan. 17, 1934** Edward Bremer kidnapped, released three weeks later, two men sentenced to life; **Sept. 14, 1934** author Kate Millett born; **Feb. 6, 1939** TV actor Mike Farrell born; **Aug. 5, 1946** actress Loni Anderson born; **1963** Minnesota Opera founded, Opera Center opened 1990; **1972** Metropolitan State University established; Como Zoo visitor falls into bear pit, officials shoot Whitey the polar bear; **March 15, 1974** wife of banker Gunnar Kronholm abducted, found alive after $200,000 ransom paid, local contractor arrested; **1976** St. Paul Downtown Airport (Holman Field) opened; **1977** Civic Center opened; **1986** 46-story Jackson Tower, Galtier Plaza, built; **1987** 36-story Minnesota World Trade Center built; **1998** RiverCentre exhibition complex opened; **2000** Xcel Energy Center (The Arena) opened.

Saint Peter *Nicollet County Southern Minnesota, 56 mi/90 km southwest of Minneapolis, on Minnesota River*

1853 Nicollet County formed; town founded by Capt. William B. Dodd (1811–1862), killed in battle with Dakotas at New Ulm; **1857** attempt by legislature to move territorial capital from St. Paul fails; **1865** incorporated as a village; **1868** St. Peter State Hospital established; **1873** incorporated as a city; **1876** Gustavus Adolphus College established; **1881** county courthouse built, remodeled 1998 following tornado.

Sartell *Stearns County Central Minnesota, 63 mi/ 101 km northwest of Minneapolis, on Mississippi River*

1854 Joseph B. Sartell becomes first settler; town founded; **1884** Sartell Lumber Company established; **1905** Watab Paper Mill established, becomes St. Regis Paper Mill 1946; **1907** incorporated as a village; dam built on Mississippi River, seven killed in its two-year construction; **1973** village council void of Sartell family members first time since village's incorporation; **1974** incorporated as a statutory city.

Sauk Centre *Stearns County Central Minnesota, 95 mi/153 km northwest of Minneapolis*

1856 area first settled; **1857** dam built on Sauk River; **1863** town platted; **1876** incorporated as a village; **Feb. 7, 1885** novelist Sinclair Lewis born (died 1951); **1889** incorporated as a city; **1975** Sinclair Lewis Museum opened.

Sauk Rapids *Benton County Central Minnesota, 2 mi/3.2 km north of St. Cloud, on Mississippi River*

1849 Benton County formed; **1851** Lynden Terrace mansion built by W. H. Wood; town founded as county seat; **1856** county seat moved to Watab, returned to Sauk Rapids 1859; **1881** incorporated as a village; **Apr. 14, 1886** tornado hits St. Cloud and Sauk Rapids, 72 killed, 213 injured, 45 killed locally; **1897** county seat moved to Foley.

Savage *Scott County Eastern Minnesota, 15 mi/ 24 km south of Minneapolis, on Minnesota River*

1852 trading post established on Minnesota River, at mouth of Credit River; town founded, named Hamilton; **1865** railroad reaches town; **1892** incorporated as a village; **1902** M. W. Savage purchases race horse Dan Patch, builds covered half-mile racetrack; **1904** town renamed Savage; **1906** Dan Patch breaks mile record at 1 minute 55 seconds, record stands until 1960; **July 4, 1916** horse and owner become ill same day, Dan Patch dies July 11, Savage dies July 12 upon hearing sad news; **1922** track destroyed by fire; **1941** Camp Savage Military Intelligence Service Language School established, moved to Fort Snelling, Minneapolis, 1944; **1974** incorporated as a statutory city.

Shakopee *Scott County Eastern Minnesota, 18 mi/ 29 km southwest of Minneapolis, on Minnesota River*

1844 Tamarack Log Cabin built by Oliver Faribault; **1851** town founded; **1853** Scott County formed; town becomes county seat; **1854** town platted; **1857** incorporated as a village; **1870** incorporated as a city; **March 22, 1908** philanthropist Maurice Stans born (died 1998); **1915** State Reformatory for Women established, new facility opened 1986; **1974** county courthouse built; **1994** Stans Historical Museum established; **1999** County Justice Center built.

Silver Bay *Lake County* *Northeastern Minnesota, 57 mi/92 km northeast of Duluth, on Lake Superior*

1951 Silver Bay Mining Company builds taconite processing plant for ore transported by rail from Mesabi Iron Range, completed 1955; town founded; **1956** incorporated as a village; **1956** first shipment of iron pellets made by laker *C. L. Austin*; **1974** incorporated as a statutory city; **1980** water and air pollution cleanup program mandated by federal government; **1910** Split Rock Lighthouse built to southwest, deactivated 1969; **1986** Reserve Taconite closes with decline in steel market, later reopened as Northshore Mining.

Slayton *Murray County* *Southwestern Minnesota, 140 mi/225 km southwest of Minneapolis*

1857 Murray County formed; **Aug. 1862** attack at Shetek Lake to north during Dakota Conflict, two women, seven children taken hostage, taken to present day Mobridge, South Dakota, released Nov.; **1872** county organized; Currie becomes county seat; **1881** town founded; **1886** county seat moved to Slayton, returned to Currie 1888; **1887** incorporated as a village; **1889** county seat moved permanently to Slayton; **1892** county courthouse built; **1940** Slayton Public Library founded; **1974** incorporated as a statutory city; **1981** county government center completed.

Stillwater *Washington County* *Southeastern Minnesota, 13 mi/21 km northeast of St. Paul*

1839 Joseph Renshaw Brown becomes first settler; **1840** St. Croix County, Wisconsin, formed; town founded on St. Croix River, originally part of Wisconsin; **1843** first raft of logs taken down river by Capt. Stephen B. Hanks, cousin of Abraham Lincoln; **1844** incorporated as a town; **1848** Minnesota Territorial Convention held here; **1849** Washington County formed; **1853** Stillwater becomes part of Minnesota, becomes Washington County seat; St. Croix County seat moved to Hudson, Wisconsin; **1854** incorporated as a city; **1867** county courthouse built; **1902** Carnegie Library built; **1914** Stillwater Correctional Facility established; **1931** lift bridge built across St. Croix River; **Oct. 25, 1972** Lower St. Croix National Scenic Riverway established; **1974** new county courthouse built, addition built 1990.

Thief River Falls *Pennington County* *Northwestern Minnesota, 91 mi/146 km north-northeast of Fargo*

1879 Frank Russell becomes first settler; **1883** town founded on Red Lake River, at mouth of Thief River; **1890** incorporated as a village; **1892** Great Northern Railroad reaches town; **1896** incorporate as a city; **1901** Thief River Falls Public Library founded; **1905** Soo Line railroad reaches town; **1910** Pennington County formed; town becomes county seat; **1955** county courthouse built; **1965** Northland Community and Technical College established.

Tower *Saint Louis County* *Northeastern Minnesota, 71 mi/114 km north of Duluth*

1865–1866 Minnesota's first gold rush draws prospectors to Vermilion Lake; **1882** iron mining begins; town founded on southern shore of Lake Vermilion; **1884** incorporated as a village; **1974** incorporated as a statutory city; **Feb. 2, 1996** lowest temperature ever recorded in Minnesota reached, −60°F/−51°C, breaking record set 1903 at Rush City.

Tracy *Lyon County* *Southwestern Minnesota, 125 mi/201 km west-southwest of Minneapolis*

1872 town founded, named for Chicago & Northwestern Railroad official; **1874** town platted; **1881** incorporated as a village; **1893** incorporated as a city; **1927** first annual Box Car Day attracts 30,000 hoboes and hobo aspirants.

Two Harbors *Lake County* *Northeastern Minnesota, 28 mi/45 km northeast of Duluth, on Lake Superior*

1866 Lake County formed; Beaver Bay becomes county seat; **1882** town founded on Burlington Bay, originally named Burlington; **1884** iron ore dock built; Duluth, Missabe & Northern (Duluth, Missabe & Iron Range) Railroad reaches town and ore docks; first load of iron ore shipped from here; **1886** county seat moved to Two Harbors; **1888** incorporated as a village; **1906** county courthouse built; **1907** incorporated as a city.

Tyler *Lincoln County* *Southwestern Minnesota, 148 mi/238 km west-southwest of Minneapolis*

1879 town founded by Danish immigrants, named for agent C. B. Tyler; **1884** Danish settlement organization, the Grundtvigians, makes land parcels available exclusively to Danes; **1887** incorporated as a village; **1888** Danebod Folk School founded; **Aug. 21, 1918** tornado destroys large part of town, 36 killed; **1974** incorporated as a statutory city.

Virginia *Saint Louis County* *Northeastern Minnesota, 45 mi/72 km north-northwest of Duluth*

1890 first settlers arrive; **1892** town founded in Mesabi Iron Range; iron mining begins; **1892** incorporated as a village; **1893** fire destroys village; **1895** incorporated as a city; **1900** second fire destroys entire city except for two hotels; **1918** Mesabi Range Community and Technical College established; **1982** mining declines.

Wabasha *Wabasha County* *Southeastern Minnesota, 65 mi/105 km southeast of St. Paul, on Mississippi River*

c.1778 British trading post established by Augustin Rocque; **1834** Alexis Bailly opens trading post; **1838** Oliver Cratte builds blacksmith shop atop levee; **1840** Joseph La Bathe becomes first permanent settler; **1843** town founded; **1849** Wabasha County formed, named for

Dakota Chief Wabasha; town becomes county seat; **1858** incorporated as a village; **1889** county courthouse built; **1974** incorporated as a statutory city.

Wadena *Wadena County* *Central Minnesota, 135 mi/217 km northwest of Minneapolis*

1858 Wadena County formed; **1871** town founded; **1873** county organized; **1879** fight between Wadena and Verndale intensifies over selection of county seat; **1881** incorporated as a village; **1887** both towns build courthouses, courts select Wadena as county seat; **1974** incorporated as a statutory city; **1978** county courthouse built.

Walker *Cass County* *Northern Minnesota, 117 mi/ 188 km west of Duluth*

1851 Cass County formed; **1862** Thomas Barlow Walker surveys right-of-way for St. Paul & Duluth Railroad, purchases vast amounts of timber land; **1872** county partially organized, attached to Crow Wing County; **1879** county fully organized; town founded as county seat at western end of Leech Lake; **1896** incorporated as a village; **1898** battle between Ojibwes and Federal troops on eastern shore of Leech Lake over illicit liquor sales, six soldiers killed, no Ojibwes killed; **1905** county courthouse built, addition built 1973; state nursery established to south at Badoura.

Warren *Marshall County* *Northwestern Minnesota, 92 mi/148 km north of Fargo, North Dakota*

1878 town founded; **1879** Marshall County formed; town becomes county seat; **1881** factions from towns of Argyle and Stephen to north attempt to move county seat to Argyle, election in blinding snowstorm retains Warren as seat; **1891** incorporated as a village; **1909** county courthouse built; **1974** incorporated as a statutory city.

Waseca *Waseca County* *Southern Minnesota, 63 mi/101 km south-southwest of Minneapolis*

1854 town founded; **1857** Waseca County formed; town becomes county seat; **1864** Waseca County Anti-Horse Theft Detective Society organized; **1867** Chicago & Northwestern Railroad built; **1868** incorporated as a village; **1870** two accused horse thieves narrowly avoid being lynched by Anti-Horse Theft Society; **1881** incorporated as a city; **1897** county courthouse built; **1911** state experimental farm established.

Watkins *Meeker County* See **Litchfield (1916)**

West Saint Paul *Dakota County* See **Saint Paul (1907)**

Wheaton *Traverse County* *Western Minnesota, 71 mi/114 km south of Fargo, North Dakota*

1862 Traverse County formed; **Apr. 19, 1866** during one of many threats by Dakotas, Sam Brown rides his horse 120 mi/193 km from Fort Wadsworth, Dakota Territory, through night storm to warn settlers of impending attack; **1884** town founded on Mustinka River; **1886** county organized; town becomes county seat; **1887** incorporated as a village; **1892** county courthouse built; **1974** incorporated as a statutory city.

Willmar *Kandiyohi County* *Central Minnesota, 86 mi/138 km west of Minneapolis*

1856 Elijah Woodcock becomes area's first settler; **1858** Kandiyohi County formed, name is Sioux term for "where buffalo fish come"; **1862** Dakota Conflict leads settlers to evacuate area; **1869** St. Paul & Pacific Railroad completed; town founded on railroad, named for railroad agent Leon Willmar; **1871** town becomes county seat; grain elevator built; **1874** incorporated as a village; **1901** incorporated as a city; **1904** Willmar Public Library founded; **1961** Ridgewater Community College established; **1964** county courthouse built.

Windom *Cottonwood County* *Southern Minnesota, 120 mi/193 km southwest of Minneapolis*

1857 Cottonwood County formed; **1870** county organized; town founded as county seat on Des Moines River; **1875** incorporated as a village; **1904** county courthouse built; **1920** incorporated as a city.

Winona *Winona County* *Southeastern Minnesota, 93 mi/150 km southeast of St. Paul, on Mississippi River*

1820s fur traders settle in area; **Oct. 1851** Capt. Smith of steamboat *Nominee* establishes cordwood supply point for steamboat fuel; **1852** settlers arrive; town founded, briefly named Montezuma, renamed Winona, derived from Dakota name given to every first-born daughter; **1854** Winona County formed; town becomes county seat; first sawmill established; **1856** first flour mill built; **1857** incorporated as a city; Mississippi River cuts new channel depriving city of boat landing, channel blocked by townspeople by sinking load of building stone; **1858** State Normal School established, becomes Winona State University 1975; **1868** J. R. Watkins Medical Plant founded, maker of patent liniment; **1874** Bay State Flour Milling plant founded; **Nov. 4, 1876** sculptor James Earle Fraser born (died 1953); **1889** county courthouse built; **1899** Winona Public Library founded; **1907** St. Teresa College established; **1912** St. Mary's University of Minnesota established; **1915** last raft of logs passes city on way to timber mills; **Oct. 29, 1971** actress Winona Ryder born; **1992** Minnesota State College Southeast (2-year) established.

Worthington   *Nobles County*   *Southwestern Minnesota, 148 mi/238 km southwest of Minneapolis*

1857 Nobles County formed; **1870** county organized; **1871** railroad reaches site from Mankato; town founded as county seat on Lake Okabena, town originally named Okabena, Native American term for "heron gathering place"; **1871** town incorporated; **1873** grasshopper plague devastates crops; **1894** county courthouse built.

Mississippi

Southern U.S. Capital and largest city: Jackson.

Mississippi Territory, including Alabama, was established April 7, 1798. The portion of Mississippi extending to the Gulf known as West Florida was annexed by the U.S. in 1811. Alabama Territory separated from Mississippi August 15, 1817, and Mississippi entered the Union as the 20th state December 10 the same year. Mississippi seceded from the Union as a Confederate state January 9, 1861, and was readmitted February 23, 1870.

Mississippi is divided into 82 counties. Ten counties have shared (two) county seats, a vestige of the past when a natural feature such as a river made travel to a central location difficult; also, the arrangement often settled rivalries between competing sites for the county seat. Municipalities are classified as towns and cites. There are no townships. See Introduction.

Aberdeen *Monroe County* *Northeastern Mississippi, 136 mi/219 km northeast of Jackson*

1821 Monroe County formed; Hamilton becomes first county seat; **1830** county seat moved to Athens; **1835** town founded on Tombigbee River by Scottish immigrant Robert Gordon, names it for city in Scotland, rejecting Dundee because townspeople could not pronounce it correctly; **1837** town incorporated; **1847** Reuben Davis House built; **1849** county seat moved to Aberdeen; **c.1850** cotton becomes primary industry; **1857** county courthouse built.

Ackerman *Choctaw County* *Central Mississippi, 87 mi/140 km northeast of Jackson*

1833 Choctaw County formed; **1834** Greensboro becomes first county seat; **1881** county seat moved to Chester; **1883** town founded; **1884** town incorporated; **1896** town becomes shared county seat with Chester; **1922** Ackerman becomes sole county seat; **1942** county courthouse built with Works Progress Administration (WPA) funding.

Alcorn *Claiborne County* *See* **Port Gibson (1871)**

Ashland *Benton County* *Northern Mississippi, 54 mi/87 km east-southeast of Memphis, Tennessee*

1870 Benton County formed; town founded as county seat; **1871** town incorporated; **1873** county courthouse built.

Baldwyn *Prentiss and Lee counties* *Northeastern Mississippi, 170 mi/274 km northeast of Jackson*

1859 town founded; **June 10, 1864** Union forces soundly defeated in Battle of Brice's Crossroads by clever tactics of Confederate Cavalry of General Forrest; **1871** town incorporated; **Feb. 21, 1929** Brice's Crossroads National Battlefield Site established to southwest.

Batesville *Panola County* *Northwestern Mississippi, 55 mi/89 km south of Memphis*

1836 Panola County formed; town of Panola becomes first county seat; **1855** town founded on proposed railroad line; **1858** Mississippi & Tennessee Railroad completed through town; residents of Panola abandon town; county seat moved to Batesville; **1860** town incorporated; **1866** Sardis becomes shared county seat with Batesville; **1952** Enid Lake formed by dam on Yocona River to southeast; **1968** county courthouse built.

Bay Saint Louis *Hancock County* *Southeastern Mississippi, 25 mi/40 km west of Biloxi, on Gulf of Mexico*

1699 bay explored by Bienville, names it for late King Louis IX of France; **1720** deed of land given to Madame de Mezieres by John Law during Mississippi Bubble land scheme, no settlement; **1720s** Acadians arrive from Nova Scotia; **c.1810** town of Shieldsborough founded as retreat for planters; **1812** Hancock County formed; **1817** Center (Caesar) becomes county seat; **1837** county seat moved to Gainesville; **1854** town incorporated as Shieldsboro; St.

Stanislaus College founded; **1869** New Orleans, Mobile & Chattanooga Railroad reaches town; **1875** town renamed Bay Saint Louis; **1882** incorporated as a city; **1911** county courthouse built; **1922** St. Augustine Seminary established; **1926** Church of Our Lady of the Gulf completed, begun 1908; **1961** Mississippi Test Operations Center established to west by NASA, renamed John C. Stennis Space Center 1988; **1992** Casino Magic established.

Bay Springs *Jasper County* *Eastern Mississippi, 55 mi/89 km southeast of Jackson*

1833 Jasper County formed; **1896** town founded as yellow pine lumber center by L. L. Denson; **1901** town platted; **1904** town incorporated; **1905** becomes shared county seat with Paulding; **1908** Mobile, Jackson & Kansas City Railroad reaches town; **c.1925** lumber industry fails with depletion of Piney Woods; **1975** county courthouse built.

Belzoni *Humphreys County* *Western Mississippi, 60 mi/97 km north-northwest of Jackson*

1827 Alvarez Fisk purchases land, founds town on Yazoo River, named Fisk's Landing; **c.1860** town renamed to honor Egyptologist Giovanni Belzoni (1778–1823); **1895** town incorporated; **1918** Humphreys County formed; town becomes county seat; **1922** county courthouse built; **c.1951** Native American artifacts discovered at Jaketown archaeological site; **1976** first annual World Catfish Festival held.

Biloxi *Harrison County* *Southeastern Mississippi, 150 mi/241 km south-southeast of Jackson*

1699 Pierre le Moyne, Sieur d'Iberville lands at Ship Island offshore; Fort Maurepas built on east shore of Biloxi Bay; original town of Biloxi (Old Biloxi) founded; town becomes capital of Louisiana; **1702** Louisiana capital moved to Mobile; **1719** capital returned to Old Biloxi; **1721** capital moved again to Fort Louis at New Biloxi; **1723** Louisiana capital moved to New Orleans; **c.1780** area comes under Spanish rule; **c.1790** Spanish House built; **1812** U.S. assumes control of Gulf Coast section of Mississippi; **1838** town incorporated; **1841** Harrison County formed; **1846** Magnolia Hotel built; **1848** Biloxi Lighthouse built; **1853** yellow fever epidemic strikes town, reoccurs 1878 and 1897; **1857** construction of Fort Massachusetts begins on Ship Island in Gulf; **1861** Union forces occupying Ship Island, destroy fort in May to prevent its use by Confederates, occupied by Confederates July–Sept., retaken by Union Dec.; **1869** New Orleans & Mobile Railroad reaches town; **1871** Seashore Methodist Camp established; **1872** first oyster packing plant opens; **1875** Federal troops abandon Fort Massachusetts; **1877** Confederate Pres. Jefferson Davis rents Pavilion cottage from Mrs. Dorsey, owner of Beauvoir plantation house, his last place of residence (died 1889); **1878** Quarantine Station established on Ship Island; **1879** Ship Island Lighthouse built; **1883** shrimp canning industry established; **1888** first schooner races held, continued until 1933; **1890** Church of the Redeemer (Episcopal) built; **c.1890** Montross Hotel built, becomes Riviera Hotel; **1896** incorporated as a city; **1908** first Biloxi Mardi Gras Parade held; **1914** Mother of Sorrows Catholic Church built for black parishioners; **1925** large influx of immigrants from Eastern Europe build numerous shanties, many close to water's edge; **1926** Iberville Bridge built north across Back Bay; Edgewater Park development begun by Chicago business interests; **1930** War Memorial Bridge built across Biloxi Bay from Ocean Springs; **1933** U.S. Veterans Hospital opens; **Nov. 14, 1933** astronaut Fred Haise, Jr. born; **1941** Keesler Air Force Base established; **Apr. 18, 1956** actor Eric Roberts born; **1968** Biloxi becomes shared county seat with Gulfport; county courthouse built; **Aug. 17, 1969** Hurricane Camille devastates Gulf Coast; **Nov. 8, 1982** fire in Harrison County jail kills 29 inmates, caused by cigarette; **1986** Seafood Industry Museum opened; **1992** dockside gambling legalized, city has nine casinos by 2003; **1994** Ohr-O'Keefe Museum of Art opened.

Booneville *Prentiss County* *Northeastern Mississippi, 180 mi/290 km northeast of Jackson*

1859 town founded; **1861** town incorporated; **July 1, 1862** Union General Sheridan's troops engage Confederate General Hardy's cavalry in daylong battle; **1870** Prentiss County formed; town becomes county seat; **1925** county courthouse built; **1948** Northeast Mississippi Community College established.

Brandon *Rankin County* *Central Mississippi, 13 mi/21 km east of Jackson*

1828 Rankin County formed; town founded, named for Gerard Brandon, governor 1825–1831; **1830** McCaskill House built by Capt. James L. McCaskill; **1831** town incorporated, becomes county seat; **1834** McLaurin House (Ben Venue) built, home of governors Robert Lowry, 1882–1890, and A. J. McLaurin, 1896–1900, demolished 1950s; **1860s** town destroyed during Civil War; **1924** fourth county courthouse built.

Brookhaven *Lincoln County* *Southern Mississippi, 50 mi/80 km south-southwest of Jackson*

1818 Samuel Jayne arrives from New York, builds grist mill; **c.1820** Jayne founds town; **1857** New Orleans, Jackson & Great Northern Railroad built 1.5 mi/2.4 km from town; town moved; **1858** Whitworth College established; **1858** town incorporated; **1870** Lincoln County formed; town becomes county seat; **1978** county courthouse built.

Canton *Madison County* *Central Mississippi, 20 mi/32 km north-northeast of Jackson*

1822 Marie Rucker House built by original settler Col. D. M. Fulton; **1828** Madison County formed; **1834** town founded as county seat; **1836** town incorporated; **1836** George Harvey plantation house built to west; **1852** county courthouse built; **1856** Mosby House built by

Col. William Lyons; **1878** county courthouse built; yellow fever epidemic decimates town; **Apr. 30, 1900** legendary railroad engineer Casey Jones stays in cab, faces head-on collision with freight train, credited with keeping train on track, saves lives of 12 carloads of passengers at Vaughan to north, Jones is killed.

Carrollton *Carroll County* *Central Mississippi, 80 mi/129 km north of Jackson*

1833 Carroll County formed; **1834** town founded as county seat; **1836** town incorporated; **1854** Malmaison mansion built by Greenwood Leflore, last Choctaw chief before forced migration to Indian Territory; **1874** Vaiden becomes shared county seat with Carrollton; **1878** second county courthouse built.

Carthage *Leake County* *Central Mississippi, 46 mi/74 km northeast of Jackson*

1833 Leake County formed; **1834** town founded as county seat on Pearl River; **1837** town incorporated; **1910** county courthouse built.

Charleston *Tallahatchie County* *Northwestern Mississippi, 113 mi/182 km north of Jackson*

1833 Tallahatchie County formed; **1837** town founded as county seat; **1848** incorporated as a city; **1900** county courthouse built; **1902** Sumner becomes shared county seat with Charleston; **1974** new county courthouse built.

Clarksdale *Coahoma County* *Northwestern Mississippi, 128 mi/206 km north-northwest of Jackson*

1836 Coahoma County formed; **1848** John Clark purchases land from government; other settlers arrive; **1858** Hopedale plantation house built by Clark; **1868** Clark builds store, plats town; **1882** town incorporated; **1914** Carnegie Library built; **Aug. 22, 1917** blues artist John Lee Hooker born (died 2001); **1930** county seat moved from Friars Point; **Nov. 5, 1931** singer, guitarist Ike Turner, of Ike & Tina Turner, born; **1949** Coahoma Community College established; **1955** county courthouse built; **1979** Delta Blues Museum opened by Clarksdale Public Library.

Cleveland *Bolivar County* *Western Mississippi, 100 mi/161 km north-northwest of Jackson*

1836 Bolivar County formed; **c.1868** town founded; **1886** incorporated as a town; **1900** Rosedale becomes shared county seat with Cleveland; **1924** Delta State College, now University established; second county courthouse built; **1930** incorporated as a city.

Clinton *Hinds County* *Central Mississippi, suburb 9 mi/14.5 km west of Jackson*

c.1810 Moss Home built, visited by Andrew Jackson 1818; **c.1824** Mount Salus House built by Gov. Walter Leake; town of Mount Salus founded around residence; **1826**

Mississippi College established; **1828** town renamed in honor of Gov. De Witt Clinton of New York; **1829** duel between Judge Isaac Caldwell and Maj. John R. Peyton over Peyton's deciding vote on establishing Jackson over Clinton as state capital, both uninjured; **1830** town incorporated; **c.1830** town's springs turn area into health resort; **1835** Isaac Caldwell and Samuel Gwin duel over Gwin's hissing during speech by George Poindexter, both injured, Caldwell dies next day, Gwin survives one year; **1853** Central Female Institute founded, becomes Hillman College; **1875** one of worst race riots of Reconstruction days, c.50 killed; **1942** Camp Clinton prisoner of war camp established for German, Italian, and Japanese prisoners, closed 1946.

Coffeeville *Yalobusha County* *Northern Mississippi, 115 mi/185 km north-northeast of Jackson*

1833 Yalobusha County formed; Hendersonville becomes first county seat; **1834** town founded as new county seat; **1836** town incorporated; **1858** Mississippi Central Railroad reaches town; **Dec. 5, 1862** Battle of Coffeeville, Union Lt. Col. William McCollough killed in skirmish with 14th Mississippi regiment; **1873** town of Water Valley becomes shared county seat with Coffeeville; **1891** second county courthouse built, restored after 1941 fire.

Collins *Covington County* *South central Mississippi, 58 mi/93 km southeast of Jackson*

1819 Covington County formed; Williamsburg becomes first county seat; **1899** town founded as new county seat; **1902** Gulf & Ship Island Railroad built; **1906** town incorporated; **1907** county courthouse built; **Jan. 1, 1909** actor Dana Andrews born (died 1992); **1912** tornado destroys town; **Aug. 19, 1948** actor Gerald McRaney born.

Columbia *Marion County* *Southern Mississippi, 75 mi/121 km south-southeast of Jackson*

c.1800 town founded on Pearl River; **1811** Marion County formed; town becomes county seat; **1812** town incorporated; **Nov. 1821** state legislature convenes here for three months between former capital at Washington and new capital at Jackson; **1905** county courthouse built; **1920s** Hugh White House built by future governor.

Columbus *Lowndes County* *Eastern Mississippi, 127 mi/204 km northeast of Jackson*

1540 Hernando De Soto enters state 8 mi/12.9 km north of here; **1736** Jean Baptiste le Moyne, Sieur de Bienville, passes site; **1817** Thomas Thomas becomes first white settler, builds store; Spirus Roach builds tavern; town founded, originally named Possum Town; **1821** town incorporated, renamed Columbus; Franklin Academy founded; **c.1824** Belmont House built to east by Capt. William Neilson; **1830** Lowndes County formed; town becomes county seat; **1844** Stephen D. Lee House built;

1847 county courthouse built; Columbus Female Academy founded; c.1852 Jesse Woodrow House built; c.1854 Billups House built; Alexander Meek House built; 1855 Rosedale House built; 1861 Mobile & Ohio Railroad built through town; 1863 town becomes one of several temporary sites of state government after fall of Jackson; 1884 Mississippi University for Women established, originally Mississippi Industrial Institute and College; Feb. 17, 1908 baseball announcer Red Barber born (died 1992); March 26, 1911 playwright Tennessee (Thomas Lanier) Williams born (died 1983); Dec. 12, 1912 boxer Henry "Perpetual Motion" Armstrong born (died 1988); 1941 Army Air Corps training facility established, closed 1945; 1951 Columbus Air Force Base established.

Corinth   *Alcorn County   Northeastern Mississippi, 200 mi/322 km northeast of Jackson*

1853 site chosen for junction of Memphis & Charleston and Mobile & Ohio railroads; town founded at junction, named Cross City; 1856 town incorporated; 1857 town renamed for Greek crossroads town of Corinth; Curlee House built; 1861 Mobile & Ohio Railroad completed; Apr. 1862 Confederate General Beauregard retreats to Corinth from loss at Shiloh, Tennessee; Union General Halleck takes town; Oct. 1862 Union General Rosecrans' forces begin to leave, attacked by Col. William P. Rogers' Confederates, Rosecrans' men retreat into town until reinforcements arrive, defeat Rogers' troops, Rogers killed; 1866 Corinth National Cemetery established, 6,000 Union soldiers interred here; 1870 Alcorn County formed; town becomes county seat; 1919 county courthouse built; Jan. 30, 1966 lowest temperature ever recorded in Mississippi reached, −19°F/−28°C; Apr. 19, 1970 tornado kills 5, injures 70.

Cotton Gin Port   *Monroe County   Northeastern Mississippi, 145 mi/233 km northeast of Jackson*

1736 Bienville erects fort on Tombigbee River seeking revenge against Chickasaw people for massacre of French at Fort Rosalie, near Natchez; 1800 cotton gin established by George Washington to encourage cotton production among the Chickasaws; 1816 town founded after treaty with the Chickasaws as trading post at terminus of Gaines Trace; 1838 transfer of Chickasaws west to Indian Territory deprives town of source of income; c.1850 town reaches peak of prosperity, begins decline; 1887 town's buildings rolled on logs to railroad, shipped to Amory.

Crystal Springs   *Copiah County   South central Mississippi, 22 mi/35 km south-southwest of Jackson*

1858 New Orleans, Jackson & Northern Railroad built; town founded as cotton shipping center; 1859 town incorporated; Oct. 6, 1863 Sen. Joseph Weldon Bailey born (died 1929); 1870 James Sturgis establishes peach growing industry; 1878 German immigrant Augustus Lotterhos founds successful tomato and vegetable growing business; Aug. 29, 1881 Cong., Sen. Byron Harrison

born (died 1941); 1903 Mississippi Chautauqua Society establishes summer community on Lake Chautauqua, to west, closed 1915.

De Kalb   *Kemper County   Eastern Mississippi, 93 mi/150 km east-northeast of Jackson*

1790 Sciples Mill built; 1833 Kemper County formed; town founded as county seat; 1839 town incorporated; 1868 bloody dispute begins between carpetbag judge William Chisholm and Ku Klux Klan, continues through 1876; Aug. 3, 1901 Sen. John Cornelius Stennis born (died 1995); 1911 county courthouse built.

Decatur   *Newton County   Eastern Mississippi, 60 mi/97 km east of Jackson*

1836 Newton County formed; town founded as county seat; 1840 town incorporated; Sept 13, 1922 civil rights leader Charles Evers born; July 2, 1925 civil rights leader Medgar Evers born, shot to death at Jackson, Mississippi, June 12, 1963; 1928 East Central Community College established; 1974 sixth county courthouse built.

Doddsville   *Sunflower County   See Indianola (1904)*

Edwards   *Hinds County   Central Mississippi, 15 mi/24 km west of Jackson*

1827 town founded; May 16, 1863 General Grant, on drive toward Vicksburg from taking Jackson, confronts three divisions of General Pemberton's Confederates, arrival of Union reinforcements leads to decisive rout, 324 Confederate killed, 410 Federals killed; 1871 town incorporated 1875 Southern Christian Institute for black students founded.

Ellisville   *Jones County   Southeastern Mississippi, 74 mi/119 km southeast of Jackson*

1826 Jones County formed; 1861 county residents opposed to secession, local woodsmen refer to confrontation as planters' war; antisecessionist guerilla movement led by Newt Knight; 1884 town incorporated; 1906 Laurel becomes shared county seat with Ellisville; 1909 county courthouse built; 1920 Ellisville State Training School founded; 1928 Jones County Junior College established.

Fayette   *Jefferson County   Southwestern Mississippi, 64 mi/103 km southwest of Jackson*

1786 Springfield plantation house built to west, completed 1791; 1791 Andrew Jackson marries Rachel Robards at Springfield Plantation, unaware that her divorce had not become official, remarries her 1794; 1799 Pickering County formed, one of two territorial counties (the other Adams County, Natchez); 1802 Jefferson County formed from Pickering County; 1805 Old Greenville becomes first county seat; 1807 Aaron Burr taken to Calverton plantation house southwest after his arrest for plotting to establish a southwestern empire; 1825 town founded; county seat moved to Fayette; **1830** town incorporated; **1840s** Richland plantation house built to southwest; **1969** Charles Evers, brother of slain civil rights leader Medgar Evers, elected mayor; **1987** county courthouse built.

Forest *Scott County* *Central Mississippi, 40 mi/ 64 km east of Jackson*

1833 Scott County formed; Berryville becomes county seat; **1835** county seat moved to Hillsboro; **1858** Mississippi & Alabama Railroad completed; town founded; **1860** incorporated as a town; **1866** county seat move from Hillsboro delayed by destruction of courthouse foundation at Forest on three occasions by angry Hillsboro citizens; **1873** state legislature reaffirms Forest as new county seat; **1930** incorporated as a city; **1934** Bienville National Forest established; **1955** fifth county courthouse built; **1962** major flooding leads to construction of levee system; **Apr. 1979** worst flooding ever occurs in spite of levees, part of statewide flooding.

Fulton *Itawamba County* *Northeastern Mississippi, 165 mi/266 km northeast of Jackson*

1836 Itawamba County formed; **1837** town founded as county seat; town incorporated; **c.1853** county courthouse built; **1948** Itawamba Community College established.

Grand Gulf *Claiborne County* *Western Mississippi, 52 mi/84 km west-southwest of Jackson*

1828 town platted on Mississippi River, founded as cotton shipping center; **1833** town incorporated; **1835** town ranks third in state in cotton shipments; **1850s** shifting river erodes river bank and parts of town; **1862** Union gunboats shell town, remainder of town destroyed by fire; **1863** General Grant takes town in advance of his siege of Vicksburg; **1962** Grand Gulf Military Park opened; **1985** Grand Gulf Nuclear Power Plant begins operation.

Greenville *Washington County* *Western Mississippi, 87 mi/140 km northwest of Jackson, on Mississippi River*

1827 Washington County formed; Princeton becomes county seat, located on Mississippi River near Issaquena County line; **1828** site of (Old) Greenville settled by Col. W. W. Blanton; **1840s** Swiftwater mansion built to south; **1841** Loughborough House built to north; **1846** county seat moved to (Old) Greenville; **1855** Belmont Mansion completed to south; **1865** Mississippi Levee Board established; **1866** new town founded on plantation of Mrs. Harriet B. Theobald away from river channel; **1870** incorporated as a town; **1886** incorporated as a city; **1891** county courthouse built; **1927** flooding inundates city for 70 days; **1930** U.S. Gypsum Plant established; Chicago Mill and Lumber Plant founded; **1935** Lake Katherine formed by shifting river channel, renamed Lake Ferguson 1937; **Sept. 24, 1936** puppeteer Jim Henson born (died 1990); **1942** Greenville Air Force Base established,

becomes Mid-Delta Regional Airport 1965; **Jan. 18, 1969** nursing home fire kills seven, injures five; **1973** devastating floods inundate city.

Greenwood *Leflore County* *Central Mississippi, 80 mi/129 km north of Jackson*

1834 John Williams settles at confluence of Yazoo and Yalobusha rivers; **1844** town founded, named Williams Landing; town incorporated; Malmaison built, home of Greenwood Leflore, last Choctaw chief before forced removal of Choctaws to Indian Territory; **March 11, 1863** Union gunship *Star of the West* scuttled at Fort Pemberton by General Van Dorn's Confederates while Union troops are ashore; **1871** Leflore County formed; town becomes county seat; **1880s** Yazoo & Mississippi Valley and Columbus & Greenville railroads reach town; **1906** county courthouse built.

Grenada *Grenada County* *North central Mississippi, 100 mi/161 km north of Jackson*

1833 rival towns develop on Yalobusha River, Pittsburg founded on west by Franklin Plummer, Tulahoma founded on east by Hiram Runnels; **1835** towns attempt to annex each other; **July 4, 1836** towns merge to form Grenada; incorporated as a town; **1839** Glenwild mansion built to south by Col. A. M. Payne; **1842** Ike Cohen House built from materials taken from stranded steamboat; **1846** tornado destroys 112 homes; **1851** Yalobusha Female Institute founded, becomes Grenada College 1882; **1855** fire destroys business district; **1860** Mississippi Central Railroad reaches town; **1862** town serves as headquarters for Confederate Gen. John Pemberton during General Grant's second campaign on Vicksburg; **1870** Grenada County formed; town becomes county seat; **1878** yellow fever epidemic affects half of population, kills 326; **1884** second fire destroys business district; **Oct. 9, 1941** U.S. Cong. Trent Lott born; **1942** Camp McCain Army Base established, closed 1944, became National Guard Base 1947; **1954** Lake Grenada formed by dam to east on Yalobusha River; **1962** county courthouse built; **Feb. 4, 1971** tornado kills 7.

Gulfport *Harrison County* *Southeastern Mississippi, 10 mi/16 km west of Biloxi*

1841 Harrison County formed; Mississippi City becomes first county seat; **1855** St. Mark's Episcopal Chapel built; **1887** site selected by Gulf & Ship Island Railroad as rail terminus and ship transfer point for yellow pine harvesting in Piney Woods area; **c.1891** town founded, platted by Judge W. H. Hardy; railroad completed to Saucier, 20 mi/ 32 km to north, work halted due to legal difficulties; **1898** incorporated as a city; county seat moved to Gulfport; **1901** Capt. J. T. Jones of New York purchases Gulf & Ship Island's stock, completes project 1902; **1902** plan to extend railroad 12 mi/19 km out to Ship Island abandoned, city's manmade harbor improved; **1903** county courthouse built, destroyed by fire 1975; **1906** hurricane destroys Piney Woods timber stock; economy turns to tourism; **1917** city hosts Mississippi Centennial Exposition; **1925–1926** Illinois Central Railroad acquires the Gulf & Ship Island line, second building boom begins; **1928** cotton spinning mill built; **1930** Gulfport Air Field opened, closed 1946; **1965** Mississippi City and Handsboro annexed by Gulfport; **1968** Biloxi becomes shared county seat with Gulfport; **Aug. 17, 1969** Hurricane Camille damages area 200 mph/322 kph winds; **1977** new county courthouse built; **1993** city's first two casinos opened; **Dec. 1993** city annexes 33 sq mi/85 sq km to north; **2003** federal courthouse completed.

Hattiesburg *Forrest and Lamar counties*
Southeastern Mississippi, 83 mi/134 km southeast of Jackson

1880 town founded by lumberman Capt. William H. Hardy, also founded Gulfport; **1883** Southern Railway reaches town; **1884** incorporated as a city; **1889** John L. Sullivan declared winner in bare knuckle boxing match against Jake Kilrain after 75 rounds, all participants arrested after illegal match; **1902** Gulf & Ship Island Railroad built to haul Piney Woods timber to Gulfport; **1906** William Carey College established; **1908** Forrest County formed; city becomes county seat; county courthouse built; **1910** Mississippi Normal College established, becomes University of Southern Mississippi; **1912** Mississippi Women's College founded; **1935** pine felt factory opened; **Apr. 6, 1983** 14 in/35.6 cm rain causes flash flooding, total 15 killed; **March 1999** County Multi-Purpose Center opened.

Hazlehurst *Copiah County* *South central Mississippi, 32 mi/51 km south-southwest of Jackson*

1819 original town of Gallatin founded 4 mi/6.4 km from present site; **1823** Copiah County formed; **1829** Gallatin becomes first county seat; **1857** New Orleans, Jackson & Northern Railroad built; town founded as rail depot; **1865** town incorporated; **1872** county seat moved to Hazlehurst; **1902** county courthouse built.

Hermanville *Claiborne County* *See* **Port Gibson** **(1893)**

Hernando *De Soto County* *Northwestern Mississippi, 20 mi/32 km south of Memphis*

1836 De Soto County formed; town founded as county seat; town and county named for Hernando de Soto; **1837** town incorporated; Hernando Academy founded; **1860** Farrington House built; **1941** fourth county courthouse built.

Holly Springs *Marshall County* *Northern Mississippi, 42 mi/68 km southeast of Memphis*

1828 William Strickland Place built; **1830** Gray Gables House built; Crump House built; **1832** lands of Chickasaw Nation opened to white settlement; **1835** town founded by John Randolph; **1836** Marshall County formed; town becomes county seat; **1837** town incorporated; **1849** Methodist Church built; **1857** Rufus Jones House built; **1858** Christ Church (Episcopal) built; Presbyterian Church built; Bonner-Belk House built; **1862** Confederate General Van Dorn's forces take town from General Grant's army, delaying a full year the fall of Vicksburg; **July 16, 1862** journalist, civil rights leader Ida Bell Wells-Barnet born (died 1931); **1866** Rust College established; **1872** second county courthouse built; **Oct. 2, 1874** Tennessee Cong. Edward Hull Crump born, Memphis political boss (died 1954); **1878** yellow fever epidemic claims 2,000 victims, many residents flee town; **1883** Maury Institute founded; **July 29, 1930** highest temperature ever recorded in Mississippi reached, 115°F/46°C.

Houston *Chickasaw County* *Northeastern Mississippi, 125 mi/201 km north-northeast of Jackson*

1836 Chickasaw County formed; town founded as county seat; **1837** town incorporated; post office established; **1845** Bates Tabb House built; **c.1855** J. M. Griffin House built; **1886** Okolona becomes shared county seat with Houston; **1905** Gulf, Mobile & Northern Railroad built; **1909** Houston Carnegie Library built, first Carnegie library in state; **1911** county courthouse built; **July 27, 1944** female country singer Bobbie Gentry born in rural Chickasaw County.

Indianola *Sunflower County* *Western Mississippi, 80 mi/129 km north-northwest of Jackson*

1844 Sunflower County formed; McNutt becomes county seat; **1871** Leflore County separates from Sunflower County; county seat moved to Johnsonville; **1882** town founded as new county seat, named Indian Bayou; **1886** town incorporated, renamed Indianola; **Nov. 28, 1904** Sen. James Oliver Eastland born at rural Doddsville to northeast (died 1986); **1966** county courthouse built.

Iuka *Tishomingo County* *Northeastern Mississippi, 200 mi/322 km northeast of Jackson*

1836 Tishomingo County formed; Jacinto becomes first county seat; **1857** Memphis & Charleston Railroad completed; town founded and incorporated; Methodist Church built; Matthews House built; **Sept. 19, 1862** up to 1,500 killed in Battle of Iuka, Confederates defeated by General Rosecrans' forces, Iuka taken; **1870** county seat moved to Iuka; **1937** Pickwick Lake formed on Alabama boundary on Tennessee River to northeast by Pickwick Dam located in Tennessee, part of Tennessee Valley Authority hydroelectric project; **1971** county courthouse built.

Jackson *Hinds and Madison counties* *Central Mississippi, 155 mi/249 km north of New Orleans*

Dec. 10, 1817 Mississippi admitted to Union as 20th state; Washington becomes first state capital; **1821** Hinds County formed; town of Doak's Stand becomes first county seat, later moved to Clinton; town platted on Pearl River by Peter Van Dorn; **1822** state capital moved to Jackson; town incorporated; **1829** town of Raymond becomes new county seat; **1830s** Judge Brame House built; **1837** Jackson & Natchez Railroad begun; **1842** state capitol completed; governor's mansion built; **1847** Mississippi Institute for the Blind founded; **1857** Charles Manship House built; **c.1860** New Orleans, Jackson & Great Northern Railroad built through town; **Jan. 1861** secession convention held at Capitol; **July 1863** town captured by Union forces shortly after fall of Vicksburg; state capital moved temporarily to Enterprise, then to Meridian, later to Columbus and Macon; **1865** state government returned to Jackson; **1869** first state fair held, permanent fairgrounds established 1928; **1882** Natchez Seminary moved to Jackson, renamed Jackson College 1899, becomes Jackson State University 1974; **1884** Jefferson Davis makes final public appearance at speech before state legislature; **1890** convention held to establish new state constitution; Millsaps College established; **1894** Belhaven College established; **1898** Campbell College for black students moved from Vicksburg; **1900** city becomes shared county seat with town of Raymond; **1902** Gulf & Ship Island railroad completed to Gulfport; Department of Archives and History and State Museum established; **1903** new state capitol completed; **1904** Deaf and Dumb Institute built, now Mississippi School for the Deaf; **Apr. 13, 1909** Pulitzer Prize winning writer Eudora Welty born (died 2001); **1930** county courthouse built; **Feb. 1930** first well opens in Rankin County Natural Gas Field to east; **1936** Filtrol Corporation Plant opened to south, maker of bentonite clay filtering agents; **1955** University of Mississippi Medical Center established; **1965** Ross Barnett Reservoir formed to northeast by dam on Pearl River; **June 12, 1963** NAACP's Medgar Evers shot to death outside home, Byron de la Beckwith charged with murder, two trials deadlocked 1964; **March 3, 1966** tornado destroys shopping center, kills 57; **May 11, 1967** locals blame outsiders in two days of racial and antiwar violence, one killed, two wounded; **Oct. 20, 1967** federal court convicts seven in Ku Klux Klan of conspiracy in murder of three civil rights workers in 1964 in Philadelphia, Mississippi; **May 14, 1970** 2 students killed, 10 wounded by state and city police in racial rioting at predominantly black Jackson State College; **Aug. 19, 1971** one policeman killed, one policeman and FBI agent wounded in shootout; 11 black separatists charged with treason; **1978** Mississippi Museum of Art opened; **Apr. 15, 1979** Easter floods worst on record; **1994** Byron de la Beckwith convicted in 1963 murder of Medgar Evers, Beckwith dies 2001.

Kosciusko *Attala County* *Central Mississippi, 60 mi/97 km northeast of Jackson*

1800 Natchez Trace post road built; **1811** Red Bud Springs created by New Madrid, Missouri, earthquake; **1833** Attala County formed; **1834** town founded as county seat on Natchez Trace, originally named Peking, later renamed Paris; **1836** town incorporated, renamed for

Thaddeus Kosciusko, Polish hero of American Revolution; **1845** Beechwood Seminary for women founded; **1874** New Orleans, St. Louis & Chicago Railroad reaches town; **1897** county courthouse built; **1920** dairying begins to replace clear-cut timber industry; **1929** Pet Milk Company plant opened; **1931** Attala County Library founded; **1934** Kosciusko Mound built by 3,000 school children bearing cupfuls of earth as memorial to Kosciusko; **Jan. 29, 1954** TV personality Oprah Winfrey born.

Laurel *Jones County* *Southeastern Mississippi, 72 mi/116 km southeast of Jackson*

1826 Jones county formed; **c.1850** Rushton brothers build pottery kiln, B. J. Rushton becomes well-known potter prior to Civil War, shot dead Feb. 2, 1864 by Newt Knight's antisecessionist gang; **1882** New Orleans & Northeastern Railroad built; town founded; **1886** town incorporated; **1897** *The Leader* newspaper founded; **1902** Gulf & Ship Island Railroad completed to Gulfport; **1906** Laurel becomes shared county seat with Ellisville; **1909** county courthouse built; **1920s** collapse of timber industry, economy sustained by agriculture; **1920** Masonite Corporation, maker of wood derivative products, founded by William H. Mason, associate of Thomas Edison; **Dec. 2, 1924** actor Ray Walston born (died 2001); **Feb. 10, 1927** opera singer Leontyne Price born; **1934** sweet potato starch plant established; **May 9, 1939** long jump athlete Ralph Harold Boston born; **1942** oil discovered in area.

Leakesville *Greene County* *Southeastern Mississippi, 55 mi/89 km north-northeast of Biloxi*

1811 Greene County formed; **1812** town founded as county seat, named for Gov. Walter Leake; **1904** town incorporated; **May 2, 1925** Sheriff MacIntosh shot to death by outlaw Kinnie Wagner, captured in Texarkana, sentenced to Parchman Penal Farm near Tutwiler; **1939** county courthouse built.

Lexington *Holmes County* *Central Mississippi, 55 mi/89 km north of Jackson*

c.1815 first settlers arrive on Black Creek; **1817** Rogers House built by J. H. Rogers; **1820** town founded as trading post; **1833** Holmes County formed; town becomes county seat; **1836** town incorporated; **1894** county courthouse built; **1906** incorporated as a city.

Liberty *Amite County* *Southwestern Mississippi, 85 mi/137 km south-southwest of Jackson*

1809 Amite County formed; town founded and incorporated as county seat; **1824** Skinner House built; **1840** second county courthouse built; Opera House built; **1853** Presbyterian Church built; Amite Female Academy founded; Thomas Talbert House completed; **1856** Gail Borden condenses first can of milk, patented 1883; **1863** all but one building destroyed by Federal troops; **1871**

Confederate monument erected; **1872** incorporated as a city.

Louisville   *Winston County*   *Eastern Mississippi, 83 mi/134 km northeast of Jackson*

1828 store, blacksmith shop established; **1833** Winston County formed; town founded as county seat on land donated by Jesse Dodson; town and county named for Col. Louis Winston; **1836** town incorporated; **1905** Gulf, Mobile & Nashville Railroad reaches town; **1964** county courthouse built.

Lucedale   *George County*   *Southeastern Mississippi, 40 mi/64 km north-northeast of Biloxi*

1898 town founded as timber center; **1901** town incorporated; **1910** George County formed; town becomes county seat; **1911** county courthouse built; **1914** Luce Farms established by Luce Products, vegetable processing company; **1920s** timber industry declines; **1958** Palestinian Gardens opened to northwest, replica of Holy Land.

Macon   *Noxubee County*   *Eastern Mississippi, 107 mi/172 km northeast of Jackson*

Sept. 1830 Dancing Rabbit Treaty accepted by deeply divided Choctaws at conference site to west, relinquishing lands of northern Mississippi to white control; **1833** Noxubee County formed; **1834** town founded on Noxubee River as county seat; **1836** town incorporated; **1856** Calhoun Institute for girls founded; **c.1858** Bankhead House built to east by William Bankhead; **Aug. 1864** state government meets here temporarily after Union forces burn Jackson; **March 7, 1889** writer Ben Ames Williams born (died 1953); **1952** county courthouse built.

Magnolia   *Pike County*   *Southern Mississippi, 80 mi/129 km south-southwest of Jackson*

1815 Pike County formed; **1856** New Orleans, Jackson & Northern Railroad built; town founded on railroad; **1859** town incorporated; **1872** county seat moved from Holmesville; **1878** yellow fever epidemic strikes area; **c.1879** St. Mary of the Pines Catholic school for girls founded; **1918** county courthouse built.

Marks   *Quitman County*   *Northwestern Mississippi, 130 mi/209 km north of Jackson*

1877 Quitman County formed; Belen becomes first county seat, town site 4 mi/6.4 km to west; **1881** town moved 5 mi/8 km to north, renamed Riverside; **1890** railroad built; new town founded at present site by Marks Townsite Company; **1907** town incorporated; **1911** county seat moved to Marks; county courthouse built.

Mayersville   *Issaquena County*   *Western Mississippi, 62 mi/100 km northwest of Jackson*

1830 Ambrose Gipson becomes first settler; town founded on Mississippi River, originally named Gipson's Landing; **1844** Issaquena County formed; Skipwith becomes first county seat, later moved to Duncansby, both sites fell into river by 1890; **1848** county seat moved to Tallula; **1870** town site purchased by David Mayer, renamed Mayersville; **1871** county seat moved to Mayersville; **1872** town incorporated; **1927** levee built; **1958** county courthouse built.

McComb   *Pike County*   *Southern Mississippi, 73 mi/117 km south-southwest of Jackson*

1812 Sabine House built to west; **1857** New Orleans, Jackson & Northern Railroad built; town founded by Col. H. S. McComb; railroad shops located here; **1872** town incorporated; **Dec. 30, 1928** guitarist, singer Bo Diddley born.

Meadville   *Franklin County*   *Southwestern Mississippi, 70 mi/113 km southwest of Jackson*

1797 Traveler's Rest plantation house built; **1809** Franklin County formed; town founded as county seat, originally named Franklin; **1816** town site moved, renamed; **1906** town incorporated; **1913** county courthouse built.

Mendenhall   *Simpson County*   *South Central Mississippi, 30 mi/48 km southeast of Jackson*

1824 Simpson County formed; Westville becomes first county seat; **c.1870** town founded near Strong River as county seat; **1902** Gulf & Ship Island Railroad reaches town; **1905** town incorporated; **1907** county seat moved to Mendenhall; county courthouse completed; **1978** Ida Thompson Museum opened by county historical society.

Meridian   *Lauderdale County*   *Eastern Mississippi, 85 mi/137 km east of Jackson*

1831 Richard McLemore of South Carolina becomes first settler; **1833** Lauderdale County formed; **1837** McLemore House built; **1854** depot built at junction of proposed railroads, the Mobile & Ohio and Alabama & Vicksburg; **1860** town incorporated; **1861** Vicksburg & Montgomery Railroad completed; **1863** exiled state legislature arrives from Enterprise, meets for one month before returning to Jackson, moves again to Meridian, then to Columbus; **Feb. 1864** General Sherman's army destroys town and railroads; **1866** foundry established; **1870** county seat moved from Marion; **1878** yellow fever epidemic depopulates town; **1882** fire destroys several city blocks; East Mississippi Insane Hospital built; **1890** cotton mill established; Mississippi Grand Opera House opened; **1893** Soule Steam Feed Works established; **1903** county courthouse built, remodeled 1939; **March 3, 1906** tornado extensively damages town, 50 killed; **1913** incorporated as a city; **1917** Hamm Lumber Mill established; **Nov. 29, 1932** actress Diane Ladd born; **1935** Meridian Union

MISSISSIPPI

Stockyards established; **1937** Meridian Community College established; **July 8, 2003** employee at Lockheed Martin aircraft factory shoots and kills five workers, injures nine, turns gun on himself.

Monticello *Lawrence County Southern Mississippi, 50 mi/80 km south of Jackson*

1798 town founded on Pearl River; **1814** Lawrence County formed; **1815** town becomes county seat; **1904** town incorporated; **1911** third county courthouse built.

Natchez *Adams County Southwestern Mississippi, 85 mi/137 km southwest of Jackson, on Mississippi River*

1702 first land grants made; **1716** Bienville builds Fort Rosalie; town founded around fort; **1718** area's first plantation established on St. Catherine's Creek; **Nov. 1729** Natchez attack fort, massacre its defenders and occupants; **1730** French retaliate by exterminating Natchez peoples; French defeated by Chickasaws; **1763** area ceded to England; **1779** Galvez takes Natchez for Spain, Spanish occupy town until 1798; **c.1783** Don Estevan Minor house built; **1785** The Elms mansion built by Spanish government; **1786** original section of Richmond house built; **c.1787** Conti House built; **1788** Spanish House built; **1789** Linden plantation house built, wings added 1825; **1793** cotton production begins with use of slave labor; **1795** Connelly's Tavern built; **c.1795** Spanish House built; **1799** Adams County formed, one of two territorial counties created (the other Pickering County, Fayette); **1801** town grows rapidly following Treaty of Chickasaw Bluffs, allowing free migration of whites across Native American lands; **1802** *Mississippi Herald* newspaper founded; **1803** incorporated as a city; Natchez Trace post road established to Nashville, Tennessee; **1809** Old Commercial Bank built; Banker's House built; **1810** Elmscourt mansion built by Lewis Evans; **1812** Auburn house built by Judge Lyman G. Harding; **1812–1815** city subject to the constant threat of Native American attacks during War of 1812; **1818** Mercer House built; **c.1819** county courthouse built; **1820** Monmouth mansion built; Protestant orphanage built; **1822** Trinity Episcopal Church built; **1829** First Presbyterian Church built; **1830** Oakland mansion built; **1831** Magnolia Vale house built; **1832** Ingleside plantation house built; **c.1835** Glenwood mansion built; **c.1837** Elgin House built; **1840** D'Evereux mansion completed for William St. John Elliott; **May 6–7, 1840** deadliest pre-Civil War tornado destroys city, 317 killed; **1841** St. Mary's Cathedral completed; **1847** Dunleith mansion built; **1852** Memorial Hall built; **1853** Lansdowne House built; **1854** Melmont mansion built; **1855** Monteigne plantation house built; **1857** Stanton Hall mansion completed; **July 1863** town shelled by USS *Essex*, occupied by Union Ransom's Brigade; **Nov. 1863** civil government suspended through Aug. 1865; **1865** Homewood mansion completed; **1867** St. Joseph's Academy founded; **Sept. 4, 1908** author Richard

Nathaniel Wright born (died 1960); **March 9, 1936** country singer Mickey Gilley born; **May 18, 1938** Natchez Trace Parkway, Natchez to Nashville, established by National Park Service; **Apr. 23, 1940** fire at Rhythm Night Club, 209 killed.

New Albany *Union County Northern Mississippi, 75 mi/121 km southeast of Memphis*

1840 grist mill and sawmill built by Moses Collins; town founded; **1841** post office established; **1870** Union County formed; town becomes county seat; **1871** town incorporated; **1887** Gulf, Mobile & Northern Railroad reaches town; **Sept. 25, 1897** author William Faulkner born (died 1962); **1909** third county courthouse completed.

New Augusta *Perry County Southeastern Mississippi, 55 mi/89 km north of Biloxi*

1820 Perry County formed; **1822** town of Augusta (Old Augusta) founded on Leaf River as county seat; **c.1840** town declines; **1857** outlaw James Copeland hanged for murder, robbery; **1903** Mobile, Jackson & Kansas City Railroad built; town moved south 2 mi/3.2 km from river to railroad, renamed New Augusta; **1904** town becomes county seat; county courthouse built, burned 1990; **1953** town incorporated; **1990** new county courthouse built.

Ocean Springs *Jackson County Southeastern Mississippi, 4 mi/6.4 km east of Biloxi, on Gulf of Mexico*

1699 Fort Maurepas built; original town of Biloxi founded on east side of Biloxi Bay, Gulf of Mexico, by Iberville; town becomes capital of Louisiana; **1702** capital of Louisiana moved to Mobile; **1835** first hotel built; **1852** post office established; **1854** incorporated as town of Ocean Springs; **1870** Louisville & Nashville Railroad reaches town; **1880s** summer tourists begin arriving; **1928** Shearwater Pottery founded; **1930** War Memorial Bridge built across Biloxi Bay to Biloxi; **1947** incorporated as a city; **Jan. 8, 1971** Gulf Islands National Seashore established, partly in Florida (Alabama excluded).

Okolona *Chickasaw County Northeastern Mississippi, 140 mi/225 km northeast of Jackson*

1836 Chickasaw County formed; **1845** town founded, named Rose Hill; **1848** town moved 6 mi/9.7 km south to proposed Mobile & Ohio Railroad; town renamed Okolona; **1850** town incorporated; **1859** railroad completed; **Feb. 22, 1864** hospital and depot destroyed by Union forces; **1865** Union troops burn entire town; **1886** town becomes shared county seat with Houston; **1902** Okolona College established, closed 1965; **1915** Carnegie Library built; **1925** county courthouse built.

Oxford *Lafayette County Northern Mississippi, 140 mi/225 km north-northeast of Jackson*

1835 log store built by new arrivals John Chisholm, John J. Craig, and John D. Martin; **1836** Lafayette County formed; town founded as county seat; **c.1836** Isom House built; **1837** town incorporated; **1844** University of Mississippi (Ole Miss) established; **1848** Rowan Oak house built; **1855** Neilson House built; **Dec. 1862** town occupied by General Grant's Union forces; **Aug. 1864** entire town burned by Union; **1883** county courthouse built; **1898** yellow fever outbreak leads to region wide quarantine; **1930** William Faulkner purchases Rowan Oak house, lives here until his death 1962; **Sept. 10, 1962** Gov. Ross Barnett defies integration ruling, prevents admission of James Meredith as first black student at University of Mississippi; **Sept. 30, 1962** several hundred marshals escort Meredith to university, rioting by segregationists quelled after 15 hours, 2 killed, 375 injured, including 166 marshals.

Pascagoula   *Jackson County*   *Southeastern Mississippi, 20 mi/32 km east of Biloxi, on Gulf of Mexico*

1718 fort built by Frenchman Simon de la Pointe; **1763** British assume control of territory; **1779** territory ceded to Spanish; settlers arrive from Ohio Valley; **1810** region becomes part of territory of West Florida; **1811** territory taken by U.S. as Orleans Territory; **1812** Jackson County formed in Mississippi Territory; **1826** Americus becomes first permanent county seat; **1838** town founded and incorporated; **1858** *Handsboro Democrat* and *Star of Pascagoula* newspapers founded, merge 1878 to become *Pascagoula Democrat Star*; **1870s** timber becomes important regional industry; **1871** county seat moved to Scranton; **1890s** shipbuilding becomes important, ends with close of World War I; **1892** incorporated as a village; **1904** incorporated as a city; **1912** Pascagoula annexes Scranton, becomes new county seat; **1920s** commercial fishing, pecan growing gain importance; **1950** county courthouse built.

Pass Christian   *Harrison County*   *Southeastern Mississippi, 20 mi/32 km west of Biloxi, on Gulf of Mexico*

1699 Christian L'Adnier discovers channel later named Christian's Pass; **c.1800** trading center established with opening of Mississippi Territory to settlement; **1811** U.S. stations garrison here; **1814** Battle of Pass Christian fought at nearby town of Bay St. Louis, final naval engagement of War of 1812; **c.1830** town founded; **1838** town incorporated; **1840s** town becomes popular resort; **1848** Ossian Hall house built, scene of motion picture *Come Out of the Kitchen* (1919) starring Marguerite Clark; **1849** Trinity Episcopal Church built; first yacht club in South opens; **1854** Dixie White House built; **1880s** tourists from Northern states begin arriving on Gulf Coast.

Paulding   *Jasper County*   *Eastern Mississippi, 70 mi/113 km east-southeast of Jackson*

c.1815 English settlers arrive after War of 1812; **1833** Jasper County formed; town founded; town becomes county seat; **c.1840** Deavours House built; Catholic

Church built; **1905** Bay Springs becomes shared county seat with Paulding; **1972** county courthouse built.

Philadelphia   *Neshoba County*   *Eastern Mississippi, 70 mi/113 km northeast of Jackson*

1833 Neshoba County formed; **c.1838** town founded as county seat; **1904** town incorporated; **1918** Choctaw Indian Agency established; **1928** county courthouse built; **1934** Choctaws granted self-rule through Indian Reorganization Act; **June 23, 1964** burned car of three Freedom Riders found after their release from jail, bodies found Aug. 4 at dam to southwest; **Oct. 2, 1964** four police officers, former sheriff indicted for beating seven civil rights demonstrators.

Picayune   *Pearl River County*   *Southeastern Mississippi, 45 mi/72 km west-northwest of Biloxi*

1832 post office established, named Hobolochitto; **1883** New Orleans & Northeastern Railroad built; town platted, renamed Bailey Switch; **1904** incorporated as a town, renamed Picayune; **1916** *Picayune Item* newspaper founded; **1920s** lumber boom begins; **1922** incorporated as a city; **1930s** Col. L. O. Crosby establishes largest tung tree orchard in state; town's economy centers on Crosby Tung Oil Mill; **1980** Crosby Arboretum founded, opened 1990.

Pittsboro   *Calhoun County*   *Northern Mississippi, 120 mi/193 km north-northeast of Jackson*

1830s first settlers arrive; **1852** Calhoun County formed; Hartford becomes county seat for several months; town founded and incorporated as new county seat, originally named Orrsville; **1856** town renamed Pittsboro; county courthouse built, burned 1922, store converted to courthouse; **1972** new county courthouse built.

Pontotoc   *Pontotoc County*   *Northern Mississippi, 145 mi/233 km north-northeast of Jackson*

May 20, 1736 French Commander Pierre D'Artaguiette defeated in battle by Chickasaws, he and 20 others burned alive at the stake; **1821** Monroe Mission established by Presbyterian Rev. Thomas C. Stewart; **c.1835** John Pearson House built; **1836** Pontotoc County formed; town founded as county seat; Pontotoc Female Academy founded; **1837** town incorporated; **1849** Stony Lonesome house built by Judge Joel Pinson; **1850** grist mill built on Rosalba Lake to west; **1852** Chickasaw College established on site of academy; **1918** county courthouse built; **1934** D'Artaguiette Marker erected by Children of the American Revolution; **Feb. 24, 2001** tornado strikes area, killing eight.

Poplarville   *Pearl River County*   *Southeastern Mississippi, 50 mi/80 km northwest of Biloxi*

1872 Pearl County formed; town founded as county seat; **1878** Pearl County abolished; **1884** town incorporated; **1890** Pearl River County formed; town becomes county seat; **1920** county courthouse completed; **1922** Pearl River Community College established; **c.1928** Lamont Rowlands begins tung nut production; **1935** Dream House of U.S. Sen. Theodore G. Bilbo built; Juniper Grove Baptist Church built by Senator Bilbo.

Port Gibson   *Claiborne County   Western Mississippi, 50 mi/80 km southwest of Jackson*

1788 Samuel Gibson establishes plantation near Bayou Pierre; town founded by Gibson; **1802** Claiborne County formed; **1803** town incorporated, becomes county seat; **1810** Harman Blennerhassett of West Virginia arrives with his wife, establishes La Cache ("Hiding Place") Plantation after his involvement with Aaron Burr's collapsed scheme to establish a southwestern empire at Natchez, moves to Montreal 1818; **1829** Presbyterian church built; **1830** Oakland College for black students established; **1831** Port Gibson Female College established, closed 1928; **1845** county courthouse built; **1861** Windsor plantation house built to west by S. C. Daniel, used as hospital by Union troops during Civil War, destroyed by fire 1890; **May 1, 1863** General Grant transports 24,000 Union troops across Bayou Pierre to west, overwhelms 5,000 Confederates defending town; **1871** Alcorn Agricultural and Mechanical College for black students established at site of Oakland College, becomes Alcorn State University; **May 26, 1893** poet, writer Maxwell Bodenheim born at Hermanville to east, murdered in New York Feb. 6, 1954.

Prentiss   *Jefferson Davis County   Southern Mississippi, 50 mi/80 km south-southeast of Jackson*

c.1877 town of Blountsville founded, later absorbed by Prentiss; **1903** town of Prentiss founded and incorporated; **1906** Jefferson Davis County formed; town becomes county seat; **1907** county courthouse built; **1935** bank held up by notorious criminal Raymond Hamilton, later holds up vigilantes chasing him, flees to Memphis.

Purvis   *Lamar County   Southeastern Mississippi, 60 mi/97 km northwest of Biloxi*

1888 town incorporated; **1904** Lamar County formed; town becomes county seat; **1905** county courthouse built, damaged by storm 1908, by fire 1930; **Apr. 24, 1908** tornado damages town and county, also Wayne County to northeast, seven killed, hundreds injured; **1999** South Mississippi State Hospital opened.

Quitman   *Clarke County   Eastern Mississippi, 85 mi/137 km east-southeast of Jackson*

1833 Clarke County formed; **c.1836** town founded as county seat; **1839** town incorporated; **Feb. 17, 1864** town totally destroyed by General Sherman's army; **1913** second county courthouse built.

Raleigh   *Smith County   Central Mississippi, 43 mi/69 km east-southeast of Jackson*

1833 Smith County formed; Fairfield becomes first county seat, site 4 mi/6.4 km to south; **1835** town founded as county seat; **1912** county courthouse built; **1935** town incorporated.

Raymond   *Hinds County   Central Mississippi, 13 mi/21 km west of Jackson*

1809 town founded; **1821** Hinds County formed; Clinton becomes county seat; **1829** town founded as new county seat; **1830** town incorporated; **c.1832** Major Peyton House built; **c.1835** Raymond Railroad established; **1837** Rev. Preston Cooper purchases mineral springs to east, named Cooper's Wells, hotel built, burned during Civil War; **1845** *Raymond Gazette* newspaper founded; **1853** Ratliff House built; **1854** St. Mark's Episcopal Church built; **1859** county courthouse built; **May 12, 1863** Battle of Raymond, 4,000 Confederates under Gen. John Gregg face 12,000 troops under Union Gen. James McPherson on march to Jackson, 514 Confederates killed, 442 Federals killed; **1880** second hotel built at springs, remains popular into 1900s; **1900** city of Jackson becomes shared county seat; **1917** Hinds Community College established; **1935** Mississippi Hospital for the Insane opened.

Ripley   *Tippah County   Northern Mississippi, 175 mi/282 km north-northeast of Jackson*

c.1835 town founded; **1836** Tippah County formed; town becomes county seat; **1837** town incorporated; **1842** Thomas Hindman House built; **1899** Col. William C. Falkner [sp], grandfather of novelist William Faulkner and novelist in his own right, shot to death on night of his election to state legislature by political rival Col. R. J. Thurmond; **1928** county courthouse built.

Rolling Fork   *Sharkey County   Western Mississippi, 55 mi/89 km northwest of Jackson*

1826 Rolling Fork Plantation established; town founded on plantation; **1876** Sharkey County formed; town becomes county seat; **1880** town incorporated; **1902** county courthouse built; **Apr. 14, 1915** blues singer, guitarist Muddy Waters (McKinley Morganfield) born (died 1983); **July 30, 1973** head-on collision of two automobiles, 10 killed.

Rosedale   *Bolivar County   Western Mississippi, 112 mi/180 km north-northwest of Jackson*

1836 Bolivar County formed; **c.1838** town founded on Rosedale Plantation on Mississippi River, opposite mouth of Arkansas River; **1872** town becomes county seat following several county seat moves; **1882** town incorporated; **1900** Cleveland becomes shared county seat with Rosedale; **1923** county courthouse built; **1930** incorporated as a city.

MISSISSIPPI

Sardis *Panola County Northwestern Mississippi, 46 mi/74 km south of Memphis*

1836 Panola County formed; town of Panola becomes county seat; **c.1846** Laird House built, used as Ku Klux Klan rendezvous after Civil War; **1856** town founded; **1858** county seat moved to Batesville; **1866** town incorporated, becomes shared county seat with Batesville; **1873** county courthouse built; **1940** Sardis Lake formed by dam on Little Tallahatchie River to east.

Senatobia *Tate County Northwestern Mississippi, 35 mi/56 km south of Memphis*

1856 Tennessee & Mississippi Railroad (Illinois Central) built; town founded on railroad, named for Senatobia Creek, Native American term for white sycamore; McGehee's Gate antebellum mansion built by Col. Abner McGehee as gift for his bride; **1860** town incorporated; **1873** Tate County formed; town becomes county seat; **1875** county courthouse built; **1891** *The Democrat* newspaper founded; **1904** Spahn House mansion built; **1927** Northwest Mississippi Community College established; **Jan. 17, 1931** actor James Earl Jones born in rural Tate County.

Starkville *Oktibbeha County Eastern Mississippi, 110 mi/177 km northeast of Jackson*

1818 Mayhew Mission established on Ash Creek; **Sept. 27, 1830** Treaty of Dancing Rabbit Creek removes remaining Choctaw people to Oklahoma; **1833** Oktibbeha County formed; **1834** town founded as county seat; **1835** Outlaw House built by Dorsey Outlaw; **1837** town incorporated; **1839** Montgomery House built; **1850** Gillespie House built; **1874** Gulf, Mobile & Northern Railroad reaches town; **Apr. 25, 1875** fire destroys 52 business district buildings; **1878** Mississippi A & M College established, becomes Mississippi State University; **Apr. 20, 1920** 87 killed in series of six tornadoes in Oktibbeha and Franklin counties, other areas; **1963** county courthouse built.

Sumner *Tallahatchie County Northwestern Mississippi, 110 mi/177 km north of Jackson*

1833 Tallahatchie County formed; **1873** town founded; **1885** post office established; **1900** town incorporated; **1902** town becomes shared county seat with Charleston; county courthouse built; **1909** fire destroys business district; **1913** Southern Soldiers monument erected.

Tunica *Tunica County Northwestern Mississippi, 35 mi/56 km south-southwest of Memphis*

1541 Hernando de Soto makes first observance of Mississippi River in area; **1836** Tunica County formed; Commerce becomes first county seat, seat moved to Austin 1848; **Aug. 12, 1874** racial riots at rural Austin to west suppressed by military, 12 killed; **1884** town platted near Mississippi River; **1888** town incorporated; county seat moved from Austin; **1922** county courthouse built;

1974 St. Anthony of Padua Mission of Sacred Heart founded; **1990s** establishment of large Las Vegas style casinos transforms impoverished area into major tourist attraction.

Tupelo *Lee County Northeastern Mississippi, 155 mi/249 km northeast of Jackson*

1540 Hernando De Soto passes through region; **1736** Bienville attacks Chickasaw Fort Ackia, is defeated, ruining French scheme to create barrier against English settlement; **1832** settlers arrive following Treaty of Pontotoc with Chickasaws; **1840** Walker House built to west by William H. Thompson; **1848** town of Harrisburg founded, named for Judge W. R. Harris; **1859** Mobile & Ohio Railroad built 2 mi/3.2 km to east; new town founded, named for tupelo gum trees; **July 13–15, 1864** Confederate Gen. Nathan B. Forrest's cavalry fights 14,000 Union troops in attempt to cut railroad supply line for General Sherman's march on Atlanta; **1866** Lee County formed; town becomes county seat; **1870** incorporated as a town; **1887** Kansas City, Memphis & Birmingham Railroad built, forms junction; **1891** incorporated as a city; **1905** county courthouse built; **Feb. 21, 1929** Tupelo National Battlefield established; **Oct. 1933** town purchases power from TVA project; **Jan. 8, 1935** singer Elvis Presley born, King of Rock n' Roll (died 1977); **Aug. 27, 1935** Ackia National Monument established to west, merged with Natchez Trace Parkway 1961, site named Chickasaw Village; **Apr. 5, 1936** tornado devastates town, 216 killed locally, one of 22 tornadoes affecting Mississippi and Georgia, 455 killed; **Apr. 8, 1937** cotton mill workers strike, mill closed; **1971** Tupelo Symphony Orchestra founded; **1982** Tupelo Ballet organized; **1992** Pied Piper Playhouse founded; **July 6, 2001** Sheriff Harold Ray Presley, 53, cousin of Elvis Presley, killed in shootout with Billy Ray Stone, suspect also killed.

Tylertown *Walthall County Southern Mississippi, 80 mi/129 km south of Jackson*

c.1805 mills built on Dry Creek; town founded, named for first settler William G. Tyler; **1822** Collins House built; **1907** town incorporated; **1910** Walthall County formed; town becomes county seat; county courthouse built.

Vaiden *Carroll County Central Mississippi, 72 mi/116 km north-northeast of Jackson*

1820s town founded, originally named Shongola; **1833** Carroll County formed; **1859** Mississippi Central (later Illinois Central) Railroad reaches town; town moved 1 mi/1.6 km to east, renamed; **1860** town incorporated; **1874** Vaiden becomes shared county seat with Carrollton; **1905** county courthouse built.

Vaughan *Yazoo County See* **Canton (1900)**

Vicksburg *Warren County* *Western Mississippi, 40 mi/64 km west of Jackson, on Mississippi River*

1719 Fort St. Peter built by French on Yazoo River to northeast, renamed Fort Snyder during General Grant's siege of Vicksburg 1863; **1791** Fort Nogales built by Spanish; **1798** U.S. assumes control of Mississippi Territory; **1809** Warren County formed; **1811** town founded; first steamboat *New Orleans* arrives; **1814** Rev. Newitt Vick establishes mission, involved with development of cotton industry; **1822** McNutt House begun, home of Gov. Alexander McNutt (1838–1842); **1825** town incorporated; *The Republican* newspaper founded; **1830** Luckett House built; **1835** Plain Gables house built; **July 5, 1835** Dr. Hugh Bodley murdered by drunken rowdies, five lynched; **1836** county seat moved from Warrenton, town site to south; **1840** Vicksburg & Clinton Railroad built; **c.1840** Willis-Cowan House built; **c.1845** Christ Church (Episcopal) completed; **1861** county courthouse completed; **May-June 1862** town shelled by Union Admiral Farragut's gunboats; **Dec. 1862** General Sherman's Union troops defeated in Battle of Chickasaw Bayou attempt to take Vicksburg, 1,776 Federals killed, 207 Confederates killed; **July 4, 1863** 47-day siege ends with surrender of city by Confederate Gen. John Pemberton to Gen. Ulysses S. Grant; **1866** Vicksburg National Cemetery established, 17,000 Union soldiers interred here; **Dec. 7, 1874** carpetbag sheriff attempts reinstatement, 75 blacks killed in rioting; **1876** Mississippi River alters course, leaving town without a port; **Feb. 21, 1899** Vicksburg National Military Park established; **1902** Yazoo River diverted past Vicksburg, to its original confluence with the Mississippi, reestablishing city's port; **1927** flooding devastates area; **1929** U.S. Waterways Experiment Station established; **1930** toll bridge built across Mississippi River; Mississippi River Commission, founded 1879, moved from St. Louis; **1939** county courthouse built; **Dec. 5, 1953** tornado strikes city, 38 killed.

Walthall *Webster County* *Central Mississippi, 100 mi/161 km north-northeast of Jackson*

1833 William Castle House built; **1874** Sumner County formed; Old Greensboro becomes county seat; **1876** town founded as new county seat; **1877** town incorporated; **1882** county renamed Webster; **1915** county courthouse built.

Washington *Adams County* *Southwestern Mississippi, 80 mi/129 km southwest of Jackson*

1700s town founded; Spanish House built; **c.1781** Selma Plantation established by Gerard Brandon I; **c.1795** Foster House built; **c.1800** Mead House built by Cowles Mead, who ordered Aaron Burr's arrest for treason; **1802** territorial capital moved from Natchez; Fort Dearborn built to protect Washington; Jefferson College established; **1810** Propinquity house built; **1817** town becomes first state capital; **1818** Elizabeth Female Academy founded; **1822** state capital moved to Jackson; **1824** Mount Repose plantation house built; **1825** Methodist Church built; **1830** Peachland plantation house built; **1850s** Inglewood House built; **1857** Christ Episcopal Church built to northeast.

Water Valley *Yalobusha County* *Northern Mississippi, 128 mi/206 km north of Jackson*

Sept. 1830 Treaty of Dancing Rabbit Creek removes Choctaw people to Oklahoma; **1833** Yalobusha County formed; **1843** town founded on Town Creek; **1858** town incorporated; **1860** Mississippi Central Railroad reaches town; **1863** The Cedars house built; **1873** town becomes shared county seat with Coffeeville; yellow fever epidemic strikes town; **1896** county courthouse built; **1931** first annual Watermelon Carnival held; **1985** Casey Jones Museum founded.

Waynesboro *Wayne County* *Southeastern Mississippi, 98 mi/158 km southeast of Jackson*

1809 Wayne County formed; Winchester becomes first county seat; **1850s** town founded on Chickasawhay River; **1870** county seat moved to Waynesboro; **1876** town incorporated; **1935** county courthouse built; **Oct. 12, 1981** 3 students killed, 24 injured when log protruding from passing truck crashes through school bus windshield.

West Point *Clay County* *Eastern Mississippi, 122 mi/196 km northeast of Jackson*

1844 land sold to James Robertson by natives; **1846** town founded; **1852** Waverly Mansion completed to east; **1857** Mobile & Ohio Railroad built; town moved to railroad; **1858** town incorporated; **1871** Clay County formed; town becomes county seat; **1892** Mary Holmes Presbyterian Seminary established, becomes Mary Holmes College; **1957** county courthouse built.

Wiggins *Stone County* *Southeastern Mississippi, 35 mi/56 km north-northwest of Biloxi*

c.1830 area first settled by whites; **1890s** Gulf & Ship Island Railroad completed; town founded on railroad; large timber mill established; **1904** town incorporated; **1912** pickle factory established; **1916** Stone County formed; town becomes county seat; **1918** county courthouse completed.

Winona *Montgomery County* *Central Mississippi, 82 mi/132 km north-northeast of Jackson*

c.1830 Moore House built by Col. O. J. Moore, oldest house in county; **1837** C. G. Pace House built; **1850s** town founded; **1861** town incorporated; **1871** Montgomery County formed; town becomes county seat; **1883** *Winona Advance* newspaper founded, later renamed *Winona Democrat*; **1976** third county courthouse built.

Woodville *Wilkinson County* *Southwestern Mississippi, 102 mi/164 km southwest of Jackson*

1802 Wilkinson County formed; **1808** Lewis House (Oldfields) built by Col. John S. Lewis; **1809** Baptist Church built, oldest standing church in Mississippi; **c.1810** Rosemont Plantation House built by Samuel and Jane Davis, boyhood home of Confederate Pres. Jefferson Davis; **1811** town incorporated; county seat moved from Pinckneyville; **1812** *Woodville Republican* newspaper founded, oldest in Mississippi; **1824** St. Paul's Episcopal Church built; Methodist Episcopal Church South built; **1832** Hampton Hall mansion built; **May 11, 1895** African-American composer William Grant Still born (died 1978); **1903** county courthouse built.

Yazoo City *Yazoo County* *Western Mississippi, 38 mi/61 km north-northwest of Jackson*

1823 Yazoo County formed; Beatties Bluff becomes first county seat, moved to Benton 1828; **1824** town founded on Yazoo River, named Hanan's Bluff; **1830** Treaty of Dancing Rabbit Creek forces removal of Choctaw people to Oklahoma; town incorporated, renamed Manchester; **1838** Cedar Grove Plantation built to east; **1839** town renamed Yazoo City; **1849** county seat moved to Yazoo City; **1862** ironclad gunboat CSS *Arkansas* built here; **July 12, 1863** Union ironclad USS *Baron De Kalb* sunk by underwater mine, one of earliest uses of device; **May 1864** Union troops burn town; **1870** county courthouse built; **1884** Yazoo & Mississippi Valley Railroad completed; **1900** Ricks Memorial Library founded; **1904** fire destroys 32 buildings, many from antebellum era; **1927** flooding devastates town; **Oct. 1, 1936** actress Stella Stevens born; **1939** Tinsley Oil Fields discovered; **1948** Mississippi Chemical Corporation founded; **1980** Triangle Cultural Center opened; **1995** Oakes African-American Cultural Center opened.

Missouri

Central U.S. Capital: Jefferson City. Major cities: St. Louis, Kansas City.

The area became part of the U.S. with the Louisiana Purchase 1803. Missouri Territory was established June 4, 1812. Missouri was admitted as the 24th state August 10, 1821. In 1837, the Platte Purchase was added to the northwestern corner of Missouri. The government of Gov. Claiborne Jackson was exiled by the pro-Union legislature July, 1861. The act of secession passed by the "Rebel Legislature" October 28, 1861, was ineffective.

Missouri is divided into 114 counties and one independent city. The city of St. Louis separated from St. Louis County in 1876. The counties are divided into townships, which have limited governments. The municipalities are classified as villages, towns, and cities, the latter of which has five classes. See Introduction.

Albany *Gentry County* *Northwestern Missouri, 43mi/69 km northeast of St. Joseph*

1841 Gentry County formed; **1845** county organized; town platted as county seat, named Ashton; town incorporated; **1857** town renamed Albany; **1859** Irish immigrants led by Father John Hogan settle in wilderness to northeast; **1885** county courthouse built; **1906** Carnegie Library completed; **1984** Irish Wilderness natural area designated.

Altenburg *Perry County* *Eastern Missouri, 75 mi/ 121 km south-southeast of St. Louis, near Mississippi River*

1839 town founded by over 600 Saxon German immigrants led by Martin Stephen of Dresden, Dresden later "deported" to Illinois for "voluptuous conduct"; **1839** Concordia Lutheran Seminary founded, moved to St. Louis 1849; **1854** post office established; **1867** Trinity Lutheran Church built; **1870** town incorporated.

Alton *Oregon County* *Southern Missouri, 110 mi/ 177 km east-southeast of Springfield*

1815 Thomas Hatcher becomes first settler; **1845** Oregon county formed; Thomasville becomes county seat; **1852** Greer Spring Mill built; **1859** town platted as new county seat; **1862–1865** Maj. M. G. Norman hides county records in cave during Civil War, much of town destroyed; **1929** town incorporated; **1942** county courthouse completed.

Annapolis *Iron County* *Southeast central Missouri, 63 mi/101 km west of Cape Girardeau*

1871 post office established; **1876** town founded; **March 18, 1925** 90 percent of town destroyed by Tri-State Tornado (Missouri, Illinois, Indiana), near its start, killing 4 locally, 695 total; **1961** town incorporated.

Arnold *Jefferson County* *Eastern Missouri, 17 mi/ 27 km south-southwest of St. Louis, on Meramec River*

1774 John Hildebrand becomes first settler; **1776** Jean Beptiste Gomache establishes ferry on Meramec River near confluence with Mississippi River; Camino Real built to New Madrid; **1858** Iron Mountain Railroad built; **1873** post office established; **1874** village of Maxville incorporated; **1915** town of Arnold incorporated; **1967** Interstate 55 completed; **1972** Arnold incorporated as a city, annexes Maxville; **1993** parts of city damaged by flooding.

Arrow Rock *Saline County* *Central Missouri, 32 mi/51 km west-northwest of Columbia, near Missouri River*

May 1804 Lewis and Clark expedition passes site; **1811** ferry established; **1813–1814** trading post established with abandonment of Fort Osage near Independence; **1820** Saline County formed; **1821** post office established; **1829** town platted, incorporated as New Philadelphia; **1833** town renamed; **1834** Old Tavern built; **1837** painter George Caleb Bingham builds house, resides here until 1845; **1839** county seat moved from Jonesboro; county courthouse built; **1840** county seat moved to Marshall;

MISSOURI

1842 Arrow Rock Academy for girls established; 1844 Sappington House built to west by William B. Sappington; 1871 jail built; 1872 Baptist church built, becomes Lyceum Theatre 1961; 1926 Arrow Rock State Park established, becomes State Historic Site 1972; 1993 flooding damages town.

Augusta *Saint Charles County* *Eastern Missouri, 35 mi/56 km west of St. Louis, near Missouri River*

1830s German immigrants begin arriving; 1836 town platted by Leonard Harold who followed Daniel Boone to area, named Mount Pleasant, later renamed for his wife; 1855 town incorporated; 1856 *Harmonieverein* German vocalist group established; 1860 Mount Pleasant Winery established; 1892 Missouri, Kansas & Eastern (& Texas) Railroad reaches town; 1970 Montelle Winery established; 1979 Blumenhof Winery established; 1987 Katy Trail State Park established, bike trail from St. Charles to Sedalia on MKT Railroad right-of-way.

Ava *Douglas County* *Southern Missouri, 39 mi/63 km southeast of Springfield*

1830s area settled; 1857 Douglas County formed; Vera Cruz becomes county seat; 1864 town founded, named Militia Springs; 1866 county seat moved to Arno; 1870 town becomes new county seat; 1871 town platted; 1881 town renamed Ava; 1886 second county courthouse burned, county assessor suspected of arson in attempt to cover up embezzlement activities; 1908 town incorporated; 1937 fourth county courthouse built.

Belton *Cass County* *Western Missouri, 20 mi/32 km south of Kansas City, Missouri*

1868 Carrie Moore marries Dr. W. P. Gloyd, alcoholic husband who dies within year, inspiration for her temperance movement, later marries David Nation; 1871 town platted; 1872 post office established; town incorporated; June 9, 1911 Carrie Nation dies (born 1846), buried at Belton Cemetery; 1955 author, lecturer Dale Carnegie dies (born 1888), also buried at Belton Cemetery.

Benton *Scott County* *Southeastern Missouri, 14 mi/23 km south of Cape Girardeau*

1821 Scott County formed; 1822 town founded as county seat, named for Senator Thomas Hart Benton; 1861 St. Lawrence Church completed; 1863 county seat moved to Commerce to avoid Confederate raids, returned to Benton 1878; 1913 county courthouse built; 1953 incorporated as a city; 1968 Benton Memorial Airport established.

Bethany *Harrison County* *Northwestern Missouri, 55 mi/89 km northeast of St. Joseph*

1840 John Seehorn Allen becomes first settler; 1845 Harrison County formed, named for Missouri publisher Albert C. Harrison; town founded as county seat; 1860

incorporated as a city; 1890 Chicago, Burlington & Quincy Railroad reaches town; 1904 statue "Two Children Under an Umbrella" erected at town square; 1916 first Northwest Missouri State Fair held; 1920 U.S. Highway 69 built; 1940 county courthouse built; 1984 three-story Geodesic House built.

Bloomfield *Stoddard County* *Southeastern Missouri, 35 mi/56 km southwest of Cape Girardeau*

1824 town settled at site of Shawnee village, its Chief Wapepilese served under Gen. Henry Dodge during War of 1812 (nearby Lake Wappapello derivation of chief's name); 1835 Stoddard County formed; town platted and incorporated as county seat; 1836 post office established; Bloomfield Seminary founded; 1850 Evans Pottery works established; 1861–1865 town destroyed by Civil War activity; Nov. 9, 1861 *Star & Stripes* newspaper first published, becomes service-wide paper of Department of Defense; c.1890 first railroad arrives; 1895 Dexter becomes shared county seat, later repealed; 1909 county courthouse built; 1997 Stars and Stripes Museum established.

Bolivar *Polk County* *Southwestern Missouri, 29 mi/47 km north of Springfield*

1835 county formed; town platted as county seat; 1878 Southwest Baptist University established; 1879 jail built, closed 1978, now museum; 1881 incorporated as a city; 1884 St. Louis & San Francisco Railroad reaches town; 1906 county courthouse completed; 1948 statue of Simon Bolivar dedicated by president of Venezuela.

Bonne Terre *Saint Francois County* *Eastern Missouri, 50 mi/80 km south of St. Louis*

c. 1825 French begin lead mining; 1864 town platted and incorporated, named St. Joe Mines; 1865 St. Joseph Lead Company begins mining; 1868 town renamed; 1890 Mississippi River & Bonne Terre Railroad built to Herculaneum; 1917 incorporated as a city; 1983 flooded Bonne Terre Mine explored by Jacques Cousteau's crew.

Boonville *Cooper County* *Central Missouri, 23 mi/37 km west of Columbia, on Missouri River*

1810 widow Hannah Cole builds cabin for her and nine children; 1812 Fort Cole built, used until 1816; 1817 town platted; 1818 Cooper County formed; town becomes county seat; 1832 Cobblestone Road built, considered oldest pavement west of St. Louis; 1839 incorporated as a city; 1840s German immigrants arrive; 1844 Kemper Military College (2-year) established; 1848 jail built, used until 1978; 1850s first Boonville Agricultural Fair held, serves as State Fair 1853–1855; c.1856 Senator George G. Vest House built; 1857 Lyric Theater (Thespian Hall) completed; June 17, 1861 in First Battle of Boonville, U.S. Gen. Nathaniel Lyon defeats State forces under Col. John S. Marmaduke, keeping Missouri in Union; Sept. 13, 1861 Second Battle of Boonville, Missouri Home Guard made up of German immigrants attacked by Confederates under Colonel Brown, rebels retreat; **1874** Missouri, Kansas & Texas Railroad reaches town, railroad bridge built across Missouri River, replaced 1930; **1889** Missouri Training School for Boys founded; **1913** county courthouse completed; **1924** Boonville Bridge completed.

Bowling Green *Pike County* *Eastern Missouri, 26 mi/42 km south-southeast of Hannibal*

1808 area first settled; **1818** Pike County formed, named for Gen. Zebulun Pike; town of Louisiana becomes county seat; **1823** town platted as new county seat; **1826** town incorporated; **1829** original section of Basye House built; **1870s** Chicago & Alton and Hannibal & Keokuk railroads reach town forming junction; **1873** incorporated as a city; **1919** sixth county courthouse completed; **1934** Federal Nursery and Experiment Station established.

Branson *Taney County* *Southwestern Missouri, 40 mi/64 km south of Springfield, on White River*

1880 Reuben S. Branson becomes first settler; **1881** town platted; **1882** post office established; **1906** White River Railroad reaches town; **1907** Harold Bell Wright's book *Shepherd of the Hills* draws attention to region; Shepherd of the Hills Farm established as tourist attraction; **1912** incorporated as a city; **1913** Powersite Dam completed, forms Lake Taneycomo; **1915** fire at School of the Ozarks at Forsyth, college moved to Point Lookout to west; **1960** Silver Dollar City theme park opened; **1980s** Branson becomes major entertainment center, includes 50 music theaters; **1993** Branson Scenic Railway established; **2003** Roy Rogers-Dale Evans Museum moved from Victorville, California.

Brunswick *Chariton County* *North central Missouri, 52 mi/84 km northwest of Columbia, near Grand River*

1723 Fort d'Orleans established by French on Missouri River, west of Grand River; **1728** fort abandoned; **c.1800** Osage villages occupy Missouri River at mouth of Grand River; **1817** Fox and Sauk (Sac) village at mouth of Grand River abandoned, forced to move again to Nebraska and Kansas; **1836** town platted by James Keyte (also founded Keytesville) on Missouri River, at mouth of Grand River, named for Keyte's home in England; town incorporated; **1867** Wabash Railroad reaches town; **1875** Missouri River channel shifts to south, leaving town on Grand River; **March 1914** Missouri Farmers Association (MFA) founded; **1981** first annual Pecan Festival held.

Buffalo *Dallas County* *Southern Missouri, 32 mi/55 km north-northeast of Springfield, near Niangua River*

1839 town settled; **1841** Niangua County formed; town platted as county seat; **1844** county renamed Dallas County due to difficulty in spelling Niangua; **1854** incorporated as a town; **1892** incorporated as a city; first

annual Red Top All Day Sing held, last Sunday in June; **1958** third county courthouse completed.

Butler *Bates County* *Western Missouri, 58 mi/93 km south of Kansas City*

1821 Protestant mission established among Osage peoples; **1841** Bates County formed; Harmony Mission becomes county seat; **1847** county seat moved to Papinville; **1854** town platted, named for William O. Butler, officer in Mexican War; **1856** county seat moved to Butler; **1858** incorporated as a town; **Dec. 1858** John Brown's forces raid farm to west, freeing slaves; **1861** most of town burned under orders from Union Col. James Montgomery; **Aug. 1863** Union Gen. Thomas Ewing releases Federal Order No. 11 ordering evacuation of Jackson, Cass, Bates, and Vernon counties; **1873** incorporated as a city; **1901** county courthouse built; **July 7, 1907** author Robert A. Heinlein born, wrote *Stranger in a Strange Land* (died 1988).

California *Moniteau County* *Central Missouri, 21 mi/34 km west of Jefferson City*

1845 Moniteau County formed; town founded as county seat, named Boonesborough; **1847** town renamed for "California" Wilson who bribed lawmaker with demijohn of liquor; **1857** town incorporated; **1859** Missouri Pacific Railroad reaches town; first Moniteau County Fair held, oldest county fair west of the Mississippi; **1867** county courthouse built; **Dec. 9, 1991** man shoots, kills county sheriff, sheriff's wife, two other law enforcement officials.

Camdenton *Camden County* *Central Missouri, 50 mi/80 km southwest of Jefferson City*

1827 Reuben Berry and William Payne settle in county; **1841** Kinderhook County formed; Oregon (Erie) becomes county seat; **1843** county renamed for Charles Pratt, Earl of Camden, for his sympathies against taxation without representation; **1855** county seat moved to town of Linn Creek on Osage River; **1905** Kansas City millionaire R. M. Snyder begins building Hahatonka Castle to southwest, dies 1906, completed 1922 by son LeRoy; **1931** town of Linn Creek flooded by Lake of the Ozarks, formed by Bagnell Dam to north; Camdenton platted to south, incorporated as new county seat; **1932** county courthouse completed; **1936** Hurricane Deck Bridge built to north across Lake of the Ozarks (toll until 1953); **1942** Hahatonka Castle destroyed by fire; **1979** Ha Ha Tonka State Park established.

Canton *Lewis County* *Northeastern Missouri, 30 mi/48 km north of Hannibal, on Mississippi River*

c.1821 trading post established on Cottonwood Prairie; **1827** town settled; **1830** town platted, named for Canton, Ohio, settlers' hometown; **1853** Christian University established, renamed Culver-Stockton College 1917; ferry across Mississippi River established, still in use; **1862** *Canton Press* newspaper founded by Jesse W.

Bennett, cofounder of Missouri Press Association (1867); **1867** town incorporated; **1868** library established.

Cape Girardeau   *Cape Girardeau County*
Southeastern Missouri, 100 mi/161 km south of St. Louis

1699 Fathers Montigny, Davion, and St. Cosme erect crosses at Cape de la Croix (Gray's Point) on Mississippi River; **1734** French ensign named Girardot settles at "the cape"; **1786** Louis Lorimier arrives with Shawnee and Delaware peoples on their move west; **1790s** German immigrants arrive; **1793** town founded; Red House built by Lorimier, damaged by 1850 tornado; **1808** incorporated as a city; **1812** Cape Girardeau County formed; town becomes county seat; **1815** county seat moved to Jackson; **1836** *Cape Girardeau Patriot* newspaper founded; **1838–1839** Cherokee people forced to migrate from Southeastern U.S. to Oklahoma on Trail of Tears; **1843** incorporated as a city; St. Vincent's College (Catholic) established; **Feb. 4, 1849** gunpowder shipment on steamboat *Seabird* explodes, damages St. Vincent's College; **1850** tornado damages college; **July 1861** Union troops occupy town, erect forts at four approaches; **Apr. 17, 1863** Confederates attack town, are defeated; **1873** Southeast Missouri State Normal School established, becomes Southeast Missouri State University; St. Louis & Iron Mountain Railroad bypasses town; **1881** Cape Girardeau Railroad built to main line; **1912** first Missouri Farm Bureau established; **1922** public library founded, new library built 1980; **1928** highway bridge built across Mississippi River; **Jan. 12, 1941** talk show host Rush Limbaugh born; **1942** Cape Girardeau Regional Airport established to south; **1957** Trail of Tears State Park established to north; **2003** Bill E. Emerson Suspension Bridge completed on Mississippi River.

Carrollton   *Carroll County*   *West central Missouri, 58 mi/93 km northeast of Kansas City, near Missouri River*

1819 first settled by John Stadley; **1833** Carroll County formed; town incorporated on Stadley's land, becomes county seat; county and town named for Charles Carroll, signer of Declaration of Independence; **1867** Wabash, St. Louis & Pacific Railroad reaches town; **1904** county courthouse completed; **1921** State Children's Home founded.

Carthage   *Jasper County*   *Southwestern Missouri, 12 mi/19 km northeast of Joplin, on Spring River*

1841 Jasper County formed; first house built by Henry Piercey; **1842** town platted as county seat; **Feb. 5, 1848** Belle Starr (Myra Belle Shirley) born, the "Bandit Queen," moved to Texas 1866, shot dead at Eufaula, Indian Territory, Feb. 3, 1889; **July 5, 1861** in Battle of Dry Fork Creek (Battle of Carthage), 6,000 Missouri Guardsmen led by deposed Gov. Claiborne F. Jackson force Union Col. Franz Siegel's 1,100 troops into retreat; **1868** incorporated as a city; **1880** C. W. Fisher corners national building material market with Carthage white

marble; **1895** county courthouse built; **June 22, 1903** New York Giants baseball pitcher Carl Hubbell born (died 1988); **1905** public library opened; **1916** Missouri Dairy Club organized as area becomes important dairying center.

Caruthersville   *Pemiscot County*   *Southeastern Missouri, 75 mi/121 km south of Cape Girardeau*

1794 site on Mississippi River first settled by fur trader François Le Sieur; **1810** settler John Hardeman Walker arrives from Tennessee; **1811-1812** town devastated by New Madrid earthquake; **1818** John Walker successfully lobbies to keep his land within Missouri to 36° north latitude, creating the Missouri "Boot Heel"; **1851** Pemiscot County formed; Gayoso becomes county seat; **1857** town platted, incorporated as a town, named for Judge Samuel Caruthers; **1874** incorporated as a city; **1890s** city serves as terminus of St. Louis, Kennett & Southern Railroad; **1899** county seat moved to Caruthersville; **1902** water tower built, one of first standard water towers common throughout U.S.; **1925** county courthouse completed; **1976** I-155 Bridge completed across Mississippi River.

Cassville   *Barry County*   *Southwestern Missouri, 45 mi/72 km southwest of Springfield*

1835 Barry County formed; Mount Pleasant becomes county seat; **1840** county seat moved to McDowell (McDonald); **1845** town platted as new county seat; **1846** incorporated as a city; **Oct. 31–Nov. 7, 1861** pro-Southern state government-in-exile holds session after being forced from temporary capital of Neosho; **1862** courthouse and much of town destroyed following Battle of Pea Ridge, Arkansas, March 6–8, to southwest; **1913** third county courthouse built; **1919** Cassville & Exeter Railroad established, at 4.8 mi/7.7 km the shortest broad-gauged railroad in U.S. at time; **Dec. 15, 1949** actor Don Johnson born at Flat Creek Township, rural Cassville.

Centerville   *Reynolds County*   *Southeastern Missouri, 90 mi/145 km south-southwest of St. Louis*

1845 Reynolds County formed; Lesterville becomes county seat; **1847** town platted; **1865** county seat moved to Centerville following Civil War destruction of Lesterville; **1871** county courthouse built; **1872** jail built; **1885** lumber boom begins in county, lasts into early 1900s; **1955** Johnson Shut-Ins State Park established to northeast, "shut-ins" local term for granite rock formations and rapids formed in enclosed valley; **1976** incorporated as a city.

Centralia   *Boone County*   *Central Missouri, 20 mi/32 km north-northeast of Columbia*

1819 Bonne Femme Church built, replaced 1843; **1829** Bonne Femme Academy established; **1857** North Missouri Railroad built; town platted, named for location between St. Louis and Ottumwa; **Sept. 27, 1864** Centralia Massacre, Bill Anderson and 80 Confederates raid town, hold up train, execute 22 Union soldiers riding train on furlough, raids kill 150 Unionists; **1867** incorporated as a city; **1904** A. B. Chance Home built; **1935** Chance Gardens established.

Charleston *Mississippi County* *Southeastern Missouri, 27 mi/43 km south-southeast of Cape Girardeau*

1801 first settlers arrive; **May 1837** town platted by John Rodney; **1845** Mississippi County formed; town becomes county seat; **1847** post office opened; **Nov. 6, 1861** Battle of Belmont to southeast, on Mississippi River, ends in Federal victory for Gen. U. S. Grant; **1872** incorporated as a city; **1901** county courthouse completed.

Chillicothe *Livingston County* *North central Missouri, 70 mi/113 km northeast of Kansas City*

1837 Livingston County formed; town platted as county seat, named for Chillicothe, Ohio; **1855** incorporated as a city; **1859** Hannibal & St. Joseph Railroad reaches town; **1866** Graham Mill built on Grand River to west; Graham Covered Bridge built at mill, replaces bridge burned by Confederates; **1869** Grace Episcopal Church built; **1888** State Industrial Home for Girls opened, now Chillicothe Correctional Center for Women; **1890** Chillicothe Business College established; **Apr. 9, 1905** U.S. Sen. from Arkansas J. (James) William Fulbright born at Sumner to southeast (died 1995); **1914** county courthouse completed; **Aug. 3, 1976** U.S. Cong. Jerry Litton, wife Sharon, daughter Linda killed in plane crash during takeoff on election night to claim Democratic nomination to U.S. Senate.

Clark *Randolph County* *See* **Moberly (1893)**

Clayton *Saint Louis County* *Eastern Missouri, 7 mi/11.3 km west of downtown St. Louis*

1812 St. Louis County formed; St. Louis becomes county seat; **1830s** settlers Ralph Clayton and Marion Hanley arrive from Virginia; **1855** Hanley House built; **1876** St. Louis City secedes from St. Louis County; **1877** Clayton and Hanley donate land for new county seat; **1913** incorporated as a city; **1917** Fontbonne College established, now University; **1926** Concordia Lutheran Seminary established, founded 1839 at Altenburg; **1960s** building boom transforms Clayton into St. Louis' "second downtown"; **Jan. 31, 1934** TV actor James Franciscus born (died 1991); **1949** county courthouse built; **1971** County Government Center completed.

Clinton *Henry County* *West central Missouri, 65 mi/105 km southeast of Kansas City*

1834 Henry County formed; **1836** town platted as county seat; **1837** incorporated as a town; **1870** Missouri, Kansas & Texas Railroad reaches town; **1870s** coal mining begins; dairying becomes important; **1886** incorporated as a city; **1893** county courthouse completed; **Dec. 25, 1904** mezzo soprano Gladys Swarthout born at Deepwater to south

(died 1969); **1939** Lawrence Brown develops Chinese checkers derived from Chinese chess, becomes national rage.

Columbia *Boone County* *Central Missouri, 125 mi/201 km west of St. Louis*

1819 town platted, named Smithton; **1820** Boone County formed; Smithton becomes county seat; **c.1820** Van Horn Tavern built to west by Ishmael Van Horn; **1821** town moved 1 mi/1.6 km east, renamed Columbia; **1822** Boone's Lick Trail reaches Columbia; **1823** Gordon Manor house built, burned 1998; **1826** incorporated as a city; **1830** *Columbia Intelligencer* newspaper founded; **1833** Columbia Female Academy founded; **1839** University of Missouri established, construction completed 1841; **1851** Columbia College established; Christian College established; **1856** Stephens College established; **1859** African-American horse trainer Tom Bass born, cofounder of Royal American Horse Show, Kansas City (died 1934); **1867** North Missouri Railroad reaches city; **Nov. 26, 1894** mathematician Norbert Wiener born (died 1964); **1898** State Historical Society of Missouri established; **c.1900** first garment and shoe factories founded; **1909** county courthouse completed; **1941** Ellis Fischel State Cancer Hospital established.

Conception *Nodaway County* *Northwestern Missouri, 35 mi/56 km north-northeast of St. Joseph*

1858 first settlers arrive; **1860** town founded on Platte River by Irish Catholics from Pennsylvania; **1864** post office established; **1873** Conception Abbey established; **1882** Benedictine Monastery established at nearby village of Clyde; **1883** Conception Seminary College established; **1888** Abbey Church completed; **June 10, 2002** 71-year-old man from Kearney, Missouri, enters Abbey Church, shoots and kills two clerics, wounds two others, then kills himself.

Concordia *Lafayette County* *West central Missouri, 80 mi/129 km east of Kansas City*

1839 German immigrant Heinrich Dierking becomes first settler; **1850s** area settled by Germans; **1862–1864** town subjected to pro-South Bushwhacker raids killing dozens; **1868** town platted; **1871** Lexington & St. Louis Railroad reaches town; **1877** town incorporated; **1884** St. Paul's Lutheran College established, becomes junior college 1905, high school c.1980; **May 9, 1910** Baptist evangelist Kathryn Kuhlman born (died 1976).

Crystal City *Jefferson County* *Eastern Missouri, 30 mi/48 km south of St. Louis, on Mississippi River*

1803 area first settled; **1843** mineral surveys begin in region; **1854** Selma Hall antebellum house built; **1868** white silica discovered by geologist Forrest Shepherd; **1871** American Plate Glass Company established by Capt. Ebenezer B. Ward, becomes Crystal Plate Glass 1877; **1878** spur of Iron Mountain Railroad reaches town; **1887** incorporated as a town; **1911** incorporated as a city; **July 28, 1943** basketball player, New Jersey Sen. Bill Bradley born.

Danville   *Montgomery County   East central Missouri 40 mi/64 km northwest of Jefferson City*

7800–6000 BC evidence of early civilizations at Graham Cave to west on Loutre River; **1818** Montgomery County formed; Pinckney becomes county seat, moved to Lewiston 1834; **1828** Davault Tavern wayside stop opened to east; **1834** town founded as new county seat; **1855** Sylvester Marion Baker House built; **1856** Danville Female Academy founded; **Oct. 14, 1864** Bloody Bill Anderson and 80 pro-South Bushwhackers attack town, kill 2, burn 18 buildings; **1924** county seat moved to Montgomery City; **1964** Graham Cave State Park established to west.

De Soto   *Jefferson County   Eastern Missouri, 35 mi/56 km south-southwest of St. Louis*

1000–1600 AD ceremonial sites of Mississippian cultures established; **1803** Isaac van Metre builds first house; **1857** St. Louis & Iron Mountain Railroad built; town platted, nicknamed "Fountain City" for its artesian wells; **1869** town incorporated; **1932** Washington State Park established to south, known for its Native American rock paintings (petroglyphs).

Defiance   *Saint Charles County   Eastern Missouri, 22 mi/35 km southwest of St. Charles, near Missouri River*

1796 Daniel Morgan Boone, Daniel Boone's son, builds home; **1799** Daniel Boone, 65, arrives from Kentucky, builds cabin; **c.1810** son Nathan Boone builds house; **March 18, 1813** Rebecca Boone, wife of Daniel, dies (born c.1738); **Sept. 26, 1820** Daniel Boone dies at Nathan's home, buried in Frankfort, Kentucky; **1840** Abraham Matson builds farmhouse; **1893** town platted on Missouri, Kansas & Texas Railroad; **2000** Boone House becomes centerpiece of Lindenwood University's (St. Charles) Boonesfield Village, pioneer folklife complex.

Diamond   *Newton County   Southwestern Missouri, 12 mi/19 km southeast of Joplin*

c.1864 African-American scientist George Washington Carver born, discovered new uses for peanuts, sweet potatoes (died 1943); **c.1880** town founded as Diamond Grove; **1883** post office established; town renamed Diamond; **July 14, 1943** George Washington Carver National Monument established; **1950** town incorporated.

Doniphan   *Ripley County   Southern Missouri, 85 mi/137 km west-southwest of Cape Girardeau*

1819 Lionel Kittrell builds house and grist mill on Current River; **1833** Ripley County formed; Van Buren becomes county seat; **1847** town founded, named for Col. Alexander Doniphan of Mexican War; **1859** county seat moved to Doniphan; **Sept. 19, 1864** town burned by

Federal troops, mill spared; **1890** jail built, used until 1960; **1891** town incorporated; **1895** mill abandoned; **1899** county courthouse completed; **1922** Current River Bridge opened.

Edina   *Knox County   Northeastern Missouri, 83 mi/134 km north of Columbia*

1839 town platted on South Fabius River by William J. Smallwood; **1845** Knox County formed; town becomes county seat; **1851** incorporated as a town; **July 1861** town occupied by Confederate militia for several days; **1875** St. Joseph Catholic Church built; **1879** incorporated as a city; **1935** new county courthouse built.

El Dorado Springs   *Cedar County   Western Missouri, 60 mi/97 km northwest of Springfield*

1881 town founded; Mrs. Joshua Hightower, en route to Hot Springs, Arkansas, stops for water, stays two weeks, word of restorative properties spreads; hotel built; town incorporated; **1886** town becomes important health resort; **1887** nearby Nine Wonders Spa established, becomes town's rival; **1996** monument dedicated to nearly 200 alumni of Bureau of Land Management (BLM) Cadastral Survey Organization from area, began with the Bandy family c.1900.

Elkton   *Hickory County   See **Hermitage (1904)***

Elsberry   *Lincoln County   See **Troy (1879)***

Eminence   *Shannon County   Southern Missouri, 105 mi/169 km east of Springfield*

1837 copper mining begins; **1841** Shannon County formed, named for Judge George G. "Pegleg" Shannon, veteran of Lewis and Clark expedition; town of Round Spring becomes county seat; **1843** town founded as new county seat on Current River; **1863** town burned by Federal troops, moved to Jacks Fork River; **1924** Alley Spring State Park established to west; Round Spring State Park established to north; **1939** county courthouse completed; **1948** town incorporated; **1949** proposed dam on Current and Jacks Fork rivers defeated; **1972** Ozark National Scenic Riverways established on Current and Jacks Fork rivers, absorbs Round Spring, Alley Spring, and Big Spring state parks.

Excelsior Springs   *Clay and Ray counties   Western Missouri, 25 mi/40 km northeast of Kansas City*

June 1880 Negro man suffering from scrofula (tuberculosis) cured after drinking from waters of Fishing River, now Old Siloam Spring; **1880** town founded at spring by V. B. Flack; **1881** town incorporated; **1887** Chicago, Missouri & St. Paul Railroad built through town; **1912** Elms Hotel opened, restored 1998; **1915** Excelsior Springs Golf Club open; **1938** Siloam Park established; Hall of Water built in park, Art Deco pool and bath; **1986** incorporated as a city.

MISSOURI

Farmington *Saint Francois County Eastern Missouri, 58 mi/93 km south of St. Louis*

1799 Baptist minister William Murphy arrives with family and friends; **1801** Tom V. Brown House built; **1821** St. Francois County formed; town becomes county seat; **1823** town platted; **1858** St. Louis & Iron Mountain Railroad reaches town; **1879** incorporated as a city; **1904** State Hospital No. 4 opened; **1927** fourth county courthouse built.

Far (Farr) West *Caldwell County Northwestern Missouri, 43 mi/69 km north-northeast of Kansas City*

1836 Caldwell County formed as refuge for Mormons; **1837** town founded as county seat; **Sept. 1838** Mormon War begins, ends with Mormon surrender Oct. 31; **Nov. 13, 1838** Latter-day Saints Church president Joseph Fielding Smith born (died 1918); **1839** Mormons evicted from county; **1843** county seat moved to Kingston.

Fayette *Howard County Central Missouri, 23 mi/ 37 km northwest of Columbia, near Missouri River*

1805 Boone's Lick salt works opened to southwest by Nathan and Morgan Boone; **1816** Howard County formed, the Mother of Counties, 36 Missouri counties and 10 Iowa counties spawned from it over time; Franklin becomes county seat; **1823** town incorporated; **1827** county seat moved to Fayette; **1832** Lilac Hill house built; **c.1835** Judge Abiel Leonard House built; **1848** Central College established, becomes Central Methodist College 1854; **1855** incorporated as a city; **1887** county courthouse built; **1935** Morrison Observatory moved from Glasgow, established 1874.

Flat River *Saint Francois County See* **Park Hills**

Florida *Monroe County Northeastern Missouri, 28 mi/45 km southwest of Hannibal*

1831 town founded; **1832** post office established; **1835** John Clemens family moves from Tennessee; **Nov. 30, 1835** author Samuel L. Clemens (Mark Twain) born (died 1910); **1837** Florida Academy opened; **1839** Clemens family moves to Hannibal; **1924** Mark Twain State Park established; **1930** Mark Twain cabin birthplace moved to park; **1968** post office closed; **1984** Clarence Cannon Dam built on Salt River, forming Mark Twain Lake.

Florissant *Saint Louis County Eastern Missouri, 17 mi/27 km northwest of St. Louis, near Missouri River*

1769 settled by French; **1785** town of St. Ferdinand de Florissant founded; **1788** log St. Ferdinand Catholic Church built, rebuilt 1821 with brick; **1790** Casa Alvarez log home built by Eugene Alvarez; Taille de Noyer plantation house built by John Mullanphy; **1793** natives kill wife and sons of Antoine Riviere; **1800s** German immigrants arrive; **1803** Native American attack leaves five dead; **1823** St. Regis Seminary for Indian boys established; **1824** St. Stanislaus Seminary founded; **1829** incorporated as a town; **1857** incorporated as a city; **1939** city renamed Florissant; **Nov. 2, 2000** James Eagan, 74, dies after serving as mayor since 1963; **Apr. 3, 2001** hail storm damages at least 40,000 structures.

Forsyth *Taney County Southern Missouri, 35 mi/ 56 km south-southeast of Springfield, on White River*

1837 Taney County formed; town founded as county seat; **Apr. 22, 1863** Union troops burn town; **Oct. 1884** Bald Knobbers vigilante group organized atop Bald Jess, hill with rock outcrop, group degenerates into band of terrorists; **1885** courthouse burned by arsonist; **1886** Bald Knobbers disband, feuds continue until 1888; **1890** incorporated as a village; **1907** College of the Ozarks established, destroyed by fire Jan. 12, 1915, moved to nearby Point Lookout; **1913** Powersite Dam completed on White River, forms Lake Taneycomo; **1928** incorporated as a city; **1950–1952** rising Bull Shoals Reservoir necessitates removal of part of town; **1951** fourth county courthouse built.

Franklin *Howard County Central Missouri, 2 mi/ 3.2 km north of Boonville, near Missouri River*

1810 family of Kit Carson (born 1809) settles here from Kentucky; **1812** Cooper's Fort built on Boone's Lick Trail; **1816** Howard County formed; town founded as county seat; **1819** *Missouri Intelligencer* newspaper founded; **1821** town serves as head of Santa Fe Trail; **1826** Kit Carson leaves for Santa Fe; flooding destroys much of town, town gradually moves north to New Franklin; **1827** county seat moved to Fayette; **1835** Scott-Kingsbury House built; **1869** Rivercene house built by Capt. Joseph Kinney; **1894** town incorporated.

Fredericktown *Madison County Southeastern Missouri, 75 mi/121 km south of St. Louis*

1719 first lead mine in North America opened by French at Mine la Motte to north; first slaves introduced to Missouri; **1799** Creole French settlement of St. Michel established; **1814** flooding on Saline Creek forces town to relocate; **1818** Madison County formed; **1819** Fredericktown founded as county seat, later absorbs St. Michel; **1827** town incorporated; **Oct. 15, 1861** in Battle of Fredericktown, Confederates under Col. W. P. Corlin forced to retreat by Col. J. B. Plummer's Union forces, 7 Union killed, 25 Confederates killed, 40 wounded; **1872** St. Louis, Iron Mountain & Southern Railroad reaches town; **1877** Silver Mines established on St. Francis River to west; **1899** second county courthouse built; **1918** wolframite (tungsten-bearing ore) mining becomes viable; **1927** St. Michael's Catholic Church built; **1972** first lead mine in North America ceases production.

383

Fulton *Callaway County* *Central Missouri, 22 mi/ 35 km northeast of Jefferson City*

1820 Callaway County formed; Elizabeth becomes county seat; **1824** George Nichols becomes first settler; **1825** town founded as new county seat; **1849** State Lunatic Asylum opened, becomes State Hospital No. 1; Westminster College established; **1851** Missouri School for Deaf founded; **1859** incorporated as a city; **1870** William Woods College, now University, established; **1938** county courthouse built; **March 5, 1946** Winston Churchill delivers Iron Curtain speech at Westminster College, "An iron curtain has descended across the Continent"; **1964** Church of St. Mary Aldermanbury dismantled at London, England, rebuilt at Westminster College; **1984** Callaway Nuclear Power Plant begins operating near Missouri River to southeast; **May 6, 1992** former Soviet Pres. Mikhail Gorbachev delivers speech on Westminster campus on the lifting of Iron Curtain, segment of Berlin Wall as backdrop.

Gainesville *Ozark County* *Southern Missouri, 63 mi/101 km south-southeast of Springfield*

1841 Ozark County formed; Rockbridge becomes county seat; **1857** county land area reduced by creation of new counties; **1860** town platted as new county seat; **1896** town incorporated; **1837** Hodgson Mill built by Ava Hodgson; **1939** county courthouse built; **1961** first annual Hootin' and Hollarin' Festival held.

Galena *Stone County* *Southwestern Missouri, 30 mi/48 km south-southwest of Springfield, on James River*

1851 Stone County formed; town founded as county seat, named James Town; **1853** post office established; town renamed for area's abundance of lead ore; **1903** town incorporated; **1904** White River Railroad arrives; **1920** county courthouse built; **1928** Y Bridge built on Fourth Street across James River.

Gallatin *Daviess County* *Northwestern Missouri, 47 mi/76 km east-northeast of St. Joseph, on Grand River*

1831 William Peniston becomes first settler; **1832** town of Mill Port platted; **1836** Daviess County formed, named for Joseph H. Daviess, soldier from Kentucky in War of 1812; **1834** Mormons arrive, found nearby town of Adam-ondi-Ahman, Egyptian for "Adam's Consecrated Land"; **1837** new town platted as county seat, named for Albert Gallatin, secretary of U.S. Treasury; Mormon Lyman Wright establishes ferry on Grand River; **Aug. 6, 1838** Mormon-Gentile Riot, brawl breaks out when Mormons come to town to vote; **Sept. 1838** Mormon War requires call-out of state militia; **Oct. 11, 1838** Mormons capture town, destroy businesses; **Nov. 8, 1838** inquiry held at Adam-ondi-Ahman by Brig. Gen. Robert Wilson, Mormons acquitted, ordered to leave state; **1856** town incorporated; **1871** Chicago, Rock Island & Pacific Railroad built; **1888** Octagon Rotary Jail built, pie-

wedge cells rotated by steel crank to single doorway, abandoned 1975; **1908** county courthouse completed; **1931** McDonald's Tea Room opened, closed 1998.

Gasconade *Gasconade County* *See* **Hermann (1855)**

Grant City *Worth County* *Northwestern Missouri, 55 mi/89 km north-northeast of St. Joseph*

1861 Worth County formed, last county in Missouri to organize; Smithton (Worthville) becomes county seat; **1863** town platted as new county seat; incorporated as a city; **1898** county courthouse built; **1989** Glenn Miller marker erected, commemorates musician's time here as shoe shine boy, received trombone lessons from local band master.

Greenfield *Dade County* *Southwestern Missouri, 33 mi/53 km northwest of Springfield*

1841 Dade County formed; town platted as county seat; **1867** Washington Hotel opened; **1876** town incorporated; **1880** Hulston Mill built; **1881** Kansas City, St. Joseph & Gulf Railroad bypasses town to south; **1886** short spur Greenfield & Northern Railroad built; **1888** Greenfield Opera House opened; **1935** county courthouse built.

Greenville *Wayne County* *Southeastern Missouri, 105 mi/169 km south of St. Louis, on St. Francis River*

1818 Wayne County formed; **1819** town platted as county seat, named Bettis Ferry, later renamed for Gen. Anthony Wayne's Treaty of Greenville (Ohio), 1794; town incorporated; **1892** Williamsville, Greenville & St. Louis Railroad reaches town, abandoned 1915; **1903** Shook General Store opened; **1941** Wappapello Dam built to southeast on St. Francis River, town moved to north 1942 from lake basin; **1943** county courthouse built.

Hamilton *Caldwell County* *Northwestern Missouri, 45 mi/72 km east of St. Joseph*

1855 town founded, platted on Hannibal & St. Joseph Railroad right-of-way; **1859** railroad reaches town; **1868** town incorporated; **Sept. 16, 1875** department store founder James Cash (J.C.) Penney born on farm to east, first store opened at Kemmerer, Wyoming, 1902 (died 1971).

Hannibal *Marion and Ralls counties* *Northeastern Missouri, 96 mi/154 km north-northwest of St. Louis*

1818 Abraham Bird receives land grant in exchange for land destroyed in New Madrid Earthquake 1811–1812; **1819** town platted on Mississippi River by Moses Bates; **1820** cave discovered by Jack Sims south of town, named Big Saltpetre Cave, later renamed Mark Twain Cave; **Nov. 30, 1835** author Samuel Langhorne Clemens (Mark Twain) born at town of Florida to southwest; **1837**

Commercial Advertiser newspaper founded; **1838** town incorporated; **1839** Clemens family moves to Hannibal; **1844** John Clemens builds house, becomes "Mark Twain Home"; **1845** incorporated as a city; Hatch Dairy Farm established by William Henry Hatch, born in Kentucky, future secretary of Agriculture; **1859** Hannibal & St. Joseph Railroad completed across state; **March 1865** the *General Grant* completed, first locomotive built west of Mississippi; **July 18, 1867** feminist, activist Margaret Tobin Brown born, *Titanic* survivor became subject of *Unsinkable Molly Brown*, never called "Molly" in real life (died 1932); **June 14, 1895** Cliff Edwards (Ukelele Ike) born, voice of Jiminy Cricket in Walt Disney's *Pinocchio* (died 1971); **1926** Tom and Huck Statue erected on "Cardiff Hill" in Riverview Park; **1929** Hannibal-La Grange College, established in 1857, moves from La Grange, Missouri; **1935** highway bridge completed across Mississippi River; Mark Twain Museum and House opened; Mark Twain Memorial Lighthouse dedicated; **July 4, 1956** first annual Tom Sawyer Days held; **1993** city spared flooding by flood wall; **Sept. 2000** new bridge opened, old bridge dynamited Jan. 8, 2001.

Harrisonville   *Cass County*   *Western Missouri, 32 mi/51 km south-southeast of Kansas City, Missouri*

1835 Samuel Sharp builds cabin; **1835** Van Buren County formed; **1837** town platted as county seat, named for Cong. Albert G. Harrison; **1845** county renamed Cass County; **1851** incorporated as a city; **1858** pro-Union Col. William H. Younger buys land for farm; **July 20, 1862** Younger robbed, shot dead en route from Kansas City; **Aug. 1863** Union Order No. 11 calls for evacuation of county, crackdown on Confederate guerilla raids; **1865** Missouri Pacific Railroad reaches town; James Gang organized, outlaws Cole Younger and Frank and Jesse James members; **1867** hexagonal Deane House built; **1885** brick and tile manufacturing begins; **1897** third county courthouse built.

Hartville   *Wright County*   *South central Missouri, 43 mi/69 km east of Springfield, on Gasconade River*

1832 settled by Isaac Hart, who donates land for town site; **1841** Wright County formed; town becomes county seat; **Jan. 9–11, 1863** in Battle of Hartville, Confederates under Gen. John S. Marmaduke assault Union posts, capture garrison and town, forced back by Union; **1905** incorporated as a city; **1965** county courthouse built.

Herculaneum   *Jefferson County*   *Eastern Missouri, 25 mi/40 km south of St. Louis, on Mississippi River*

1808 town platted by Moses Austin as shipping point for lead mines to west; **1809** largest lead smelter in U.S., with notable shot tower, built by John N. Maclot; **1818** Jefferson County formed; town becomes county seat; **1819** two more shot towers built; **1839** county seat moved to Hillsboro; **1972** incorporated as a city.

Hermann   *Gasconade County*   *East central Missouri 65 mi/105 km west of St. Louis, on Missouri River*

1820 Gasconade County formed; Gasconade City becomes county seat; **1825** county seat moved to Bartonville, to Mount Sterling 1832; **1837** town settled by members of the German Society; town platted; **1839** incorporated as a city; **1840** Pommer-Gentner House built, nearby Strehly House built 1842, both part of Deutschheim State Historic Site; **1842** county seat moved to Hermann; **1844** wine grape industry introduced; **1847** Stone Hill Winery established; **1852** Musik Halle built; Hermannhoff Winery established; **1854** *Volksblatt* newspaper founded; **Nov. 1, 1855** railroad bridge at town of Gasconade to west, at mouth of Gasconade River, collapses on Pacific (Missouri Pacific) Railroad's first passenger run, eight cars plunge into water, engine rolls backward on top of them, 28 killed, 30 injured, train service to St. Louis delayed until 1856; **1858** Adam Puchta Winery built; **1870s** town's first Maifest held; **1878** concert hall built; **1898** county courthouse built; **1947** Stone Hill Winery established; **1993** parts of town damaged by flooding.

Hermitage   *Hickory County*   *Central Missouri, 50 mi/80 km north of Springfield, on Pomme de Terre River*

c.1843 Thomas Davis becomes first settler; **1845** Hickory County formed; town founded as county seat; **1847** town platted; **1871** county jail built, used until 1974; **1891** Pomme de Terre Bridge built, new bridge built 1961; **1896** county courthouse built; **Jan. 2, 1904** actress Sally Rand (Helen Gould Beck) born at Elkton to southwest (died 1979); **1957** town incorporated; **1961** Pomme de Terre Lake formed by dam to south on Pomme de Terre River.

Higginsville   *Lafayette County*   *West central Missouri, 43 mi/69 km east of Kansas City*

1869 town platted by Harvey Higgins; **1872** Chicago & Alton Railroad reaches town; **1880** town incorporated; **1888** C & A Depot built; **1891** Confederate Home for the Aged established, transferred to state 1897, becomes State Historic Site 1949; **1892** Confederate Chapel built; **May 9, 1950** last Civil War veteran resident John Graves dies at age 107; Confederate Home closed; **1956** Confederate Home razed, State School for Retarded Children built at site.

Hillsboro   *Jefferson County*   *Eastern Missouri, 35 mi/56 km south-southwest of St. Louis*

1818 Jefferson County formed; Herculaneum becomes county seat; **1839** town platted as new county seat; incorporated as a city, originally named Hillsborough; **1872** Sandy Creek Covered Bridge built to north, rebuilt 1886; **1892** town name shortened; **1957** county courthouse built, addition built 1976; **1963** Jefferson College (2-year) established; **Oct. 14, 2000** Gov. Mel Carnahan,

---

Democratic candidate for U.S. Senate, son Randy, campaign aide killed in crash of small aircraft to north en route from St. Louis Bi-State Airport, Cahokia, Illinois, to New Madrid.

Houston   *Texas County*   *South central Missouri, 73 mi/117 km east pf Springfield*

1845 Texas County formed; **1846** town platted as county seat, named for Sam Houston, President of Republic of Texas; **1861–1865** town destroyed twice during Civil War, temporarily abandoned; **1872** incorporated as a town; **1893** incorporated as a city; **1904** Emmett Kelly (1898–1979), world's most famous clown, born Sedan, Kansas, spends boyhood here until 1917; **1932** eighth county courthouse built; **1988** first annual Clown Festival held.

Huntsville   *Randolph County*   *North central Missouri, 35 mi/56 km north-northwest of Columbia*

1829 Randolph County formed; town founded as county seat, named for settler Daniel Hunt, donated town site; **1831** town platted and incorporated; **1858** north-south route of North Missouri Railroad bypasses town to east; **1868** North Missouri Railroad west line reaches town; **1884** county courthouse built.

Independence   *Jackson County*   *Western Missouri, 7 mi/11.3 km east of Kansas City, near Missouri River*

1808 Fort Osage built to east; **1825** town settled with opening of Native American lands in Kansas Territory; **Dec. 1826** Jackson County formed; **1827** town platted as county seat; **1830** Samuel Weston establishes blacksmith shop and wagon works; **1831** Mormons arrive from Kirtland, Ohio, area called "The Centerplace," original Garden of Eden, site of Zion by leader Joseph Smith; **1834** Mormons expelled north to Clay County, 300 Mormon houses burned by mobs; **Apr. 1834** Nathaniel J. Wyeth and Rev. Jason Lee leave for Oregon, among first pioneers to blaze Oregon Trail; **1839** evicted from Missouri following Mormon War, Mormons move to Nauvoo, Illinois; **May 1, 1841** first wagon train departs for California carrying 47 pioneers, arrives San Francisco Nov. 4; **1849** incorporated as a city; California Gold Rush brings stream of emigrants through town; **May 1846** Butterfield Mail stage line established to Santa Fe; **1857** Chrisman-Sawyer Bank built, used 1862 as Union fort; **Aug. 11, 1862** Confederate Col. John T. Hughes killed in battle, town surrendered to Lt. Col. James T. Buell; **Oct. 20, 1864** town occupied for one day by Confederate Gen. Sterling Price, moves on to defeat at Westport (Kansas City); **1881** Vaille Mansion built; **Feb. 13, 1885** Elizabeth Virginia Wallace Truman, wife of Pres. Harry Truman, born (married June 28, 1919, died Oct. 18, 1982); **July 16, 1911** dancer, actress Ginger Rogers born (died 1995); **1926** War Memorial Building built; Latter-day Saints Auditorium built; **1934** 28-story county courthouse dedicated, Sen. Harry Truman presiding; **July 6, 1957** Truman Presidential Library dedicated; **Dec. 26, 1972** Harry S. Truman, 33rd President, dies at age 88.

Ironton   *Iron County*   *Eastern Missouri, 130 mi/209 km south-southwest of St. Louis*

1815 first iron furnaces built near Stout's Creek; **1830s** area settled; **1857** Iron County formed; town platted as county seat; **1859** town incorporated; **1860** county courthouse completed, addition built 1964; **Aug. 8, 1861** Ulysses S. Grant arrives to assume command as Brigadier General in Federal army; **Sept. 27, 1864** Battle of Pilot Knob fought to north; courthouse used as refuge for Union troops in retreat from Sterling Price's forces; **1870** St. Paul's Episcopal Church built; **1880s** Arcadia Valley becomes popular resort area, through 1960s; **1886** county jail built.

Jackson   *Cape Girardeau County*   *Southeastern Missouri, 10 mi/16 km northwest of Cape Girardeau*

1794 Spanish establish Cape Girardeau district; **1800** German immigrants arrive led by George F. Bollinger; **1812** Cape Girardeau County formed; Bethel Baptist Church built, first Baptist church west of Mississippi River; **1814** town founded as county seat; **1819** *Missouri Herald* newspaper founded by Tubal E. Strange; McKendree Chapel built, oldest existing Protestant church west of Mississippi; **1849** cholera epidemic takes many lives; **1880s** St. Louis, Iron Mountain & Southern Railroad reaches town; **1885** incorporated as a city; **1908** county courthouse built.

Jefferson City   *Cole and Callaway counties*   *Central Missouri, 108 mi/174 km west of St. Louis*

1820 Cole County formed; **Aug. 10, 1821** Missouri enters Union as 24th state; St. Charles becomes state capital; **1822** site platted as state capital and county seat by Maj. Elias Bancroft; **1823** brick building built, becomes first state capitol 1826; **1825** *Jeffersonian* newspaper founded; incorporated as a town; **1826** state capital moved to Jefferson City; **1836** Missouri State Penitentiary completed; **Nov. 17, 1837** fire destroys state capitol; **1839** incorporated as a city; **1840** new State Capitol completed; **1849** Mormon steamboat *Monroe* discharges cholera victims, 63 die initially, plague lasts two years; **1855** Pacific Railroad completed from St. Louis; **Feb.–March 1861** state convention meets in unsuccessful attempt to bring opposing anti- and proslavery sides to compromise; **July 30, 1861** state convention reconvenes, pro-Confederate Gov. Claiborne Jackson deposed, forced into exile at Neosho; provisional state government established; **July 2–14, 1862** state convention requires oath of loyalty to Union for all voters, office seekers, lawyers, juries; **1864** city shelled by Confederate Gen. Sterling Price, continues west toward Westport (Kansas City); **Jan. 11, 1865** slavery abolished in Missouri; **Sept. 17, 1866** Lincoln University established; **1867** National Cemetery established; **June 3, 1875** official day of prayer called for deliverance from statewide grasshopper plague; **1881** shoe industry established, expands to three plants; **1895** drawbridge built across river; **1896** county courthouse built, damaged by fire 1913; **1907** Supreme Court

Building completed; **July 29, 1909** African-American novelist Chester Romar Himes born (died 1984); **1911** fire destroys second state capitol; **1917** present state capitol completed; **1932** Algoa Farms Reformatory built to east; **1935** artist Thomas Hart Benton paints murals of Missouri life on walls of State Capitol; **1938** State Office Building completed; **1948** Memorial Airport established north of river; **1952** Jefferson Building completed; **1953** J. E. Frazier creates Missouri Bear Sculpture from Carthage marble for front of Jefferson Building; **1983** Truman Building completed; **1993** parts of city and airport damaged by flooding.

Joplin *Jasper and Newton counties* *Southwestern Missouri, 65 mi/105 km west-southwest of Springfield*

1838 town site first settled by John C. Cox of Tennessee; **c.1840** cabin built by Rev. Harris G. Joplin near spring; **1841** Cox opens store; town founded as Blytheville for Billy Blythe, popular Cherokee living near Shoal Creek; **1849** David Campbell discovers galena in Linville Hollow while visiting friend William Tingle; **1850** Tingle & McKee Mining Company builds furnace; **1865** lead mining boom begins; **1871** Murphysboro platted west of Joplin Creek by Patrick Murphy; Joplin City platted east of Joplin Creek by Judge Cox; **1872** first zinc mining begins; **March 19, 1872** bitter rivalry between two towns ends with merger, named Union City; **1873** incorporated as city of Joplin; **1877** Joplin Railroad built to Girard, Kansas; **1880** zinc production eclipses lead in importance; **1882** Missouri Pacific Railroad reaches Joplin; **Feb. 1, 1902** African-American writer Langston Hughes born (died 1967); **Aug. 13, 1909** actor John Beal born (died 1994); **June 9, 1910** TV actor Robert Cummings born (died 1990); **1912** Municipal Market built; **June 4, 1924** actor Dennis Weaver born; **1930** Tristate Mining Museum opened; **1931** stockyards established; **1935** mining strike halts lead and zinc production, unresolved until Oct. 1939; **1937** Missouri Southern State College established; **1944** Ozark Christian College moved from Bartonville, Arkansas, established 1942.

Kahoka *Clark County* *Northeastern Missouri, 50 mi/80 km north-northwest of Hannibal*

1818 Clark County formed, named for explorer William Clark; **1836** county organized; Waterloo becomes county seat; **1847** county seat moved to Alexandria, returned to Waterloo 1854; **1854** Anti-Horse Thief Association established by Maj. David McKee, organization expands to eleven states; **1858** town platted; **Aug. 5, 1861** in Battle of Athens to north, northernmost battle of Civil War, Federal Col. David Moore defeats State Guard Col. Martin Green; Federals 3 killed, 8 wounded; Confederates 14 killed, 14 wounded; **1865** county seat moved to Kahoka; **1869** town incorporated; **1871** county courthouse built; Missouri, Iowa & Nebraska Railroad reaches town; **1992** Illiniwek Village State Park established, only known site of Illinois tribal habitation west of Mississippi.

Kansas City *Jackson, Clay and Platte counties* *Western Missouri, on Missouri River*

1821 French fur trading outpost established by François Chouteau on Missouri River, at confluence of Kansas (Kaw) River; **1827** founding of Independence to east precedes founding of Kansas City; **1833** town of Westport founded by John C. McCoy south of present-day downtown; **c.1845** Westport replaces Independence as embarkation point to West; **1850** town of Westport incorporated; **1853** incorporated as city of Kansas; **1859** adjoining Wyandotte, Kansas, incorporated as a city, later renamed Kansas City; **Aug. 14, 1863** collapse of jail kills female relative of pro-South Quantrill raiders, retaliatory raid Aug. 21 at Lawrence, Kansas, kills 100; **Oct. 21-23, 1864** Confederate Gen. Sterling Price defeated in Battle of Westport; **1865** Pacific Railroad reaches city from St. Louis; **1869** Hannibal Bridge completed, first bridge across Missouri River, carries tracks of Hannibal & St. Joseph Railroad; **1870** Kansas City Stockyards established, most buildings built 1925; **1878** Union Station built; first American Royal Horse and Livestock Show held; **1880** *Kansas City Star* newspaper founded by William Rockhill Nelson; **1881** Pendergast political machine begins with election of James Pendergast as alderman, continues into 1940s; **Apr. 1, 1885** actor Wallace Beery born (died 1949); **1886** first Priest of Pallas festival held; **1887** Chouteau Bridge built across Missouri River; **1889** city renamed Kansas City; **1890** New York Life Building completed; **June 30, 1890** baseball player, manager Casey Stengel born (died 1975); **Oct. 21, 1891** choreographer Ted Shawn born (died 1972); **1896** Swope Park created, land donated by Thomas Hunt Swope; Convention Hall built, destroyed by fire Apr. 4, 1900, months before Democratic Convention, rebuilt in time; **1900** Democratic Convention nominates William Jennings Bryan for president; **1910** Rockhurst College (now University) established; **1911** Kansas City Symphony Orchestra founded; **March 3, 1911** actress Jean Harlow born (died 1937); **1914** new Union Station built; **Nov. 23, 1915** actress Ellen Drew born (died 2003); **1916** Avila College established; **1917** Missouri born actress Sally Rand makes stage debut at Empress Theatre at age 13; **1922** Country Club Plaza, with its Spanish architecture and outdoor fountains, opens as first shopping center in America; American Royal Building completed for horse shows, new structure built 1992; **Feb. 20, 1925** actor Robert Altman born; **1926** Liberty Memorial (217 ft/66 m high) dedicated by President Coolidge; **1927** Kansas City Municipal Airport established, becomes Downtown Airport 1977; **1929** University of Kansas City established, becomes University of Missouri at Kansas City; **May 12, 1929** songwriter Burt Bacharach born; **Nov. 15, 1929** TV actor Edward Asner born; **1930s** African-American musicians create the unique Kansas City sound of jazz music; **1931** 32-story Kansas City Power and Light Building completed; **1932** Kansas City Philharmonic Orchestra founded; **1933** William Rockhill Nelson Art Gallery opens; **May 27, 1933** Mary McElroy kidnapped, released next day, Walter McGee sentenced to life; **1936**

Municipal Auditorium built; **1937** 29-story city hall completed; **March 28, 1948** actress Dianne Wiest born; **Sept. 4, 1949** golfer Tom Watson born; **July 23, 1951** actress Edie McClurg born; **Sept. 28, 1953** Robert Greenlease, 6, kidnapped, found dead Oct. 7, Bonnie Healy and Carl Hall convicted, executed; **1955** Seneca (Wyandotte) Indian cemetery in Huron Park returned to tribe following protests of 900 tribal members; **1962** 35-story Federal Office Building completed; **c.1965** city's annexations extend into three counties totaling 316 sq mi/916 sq km; **1969** Maple Woods (Clay County) and Penn Valley (south of downtown) community colleges established; **1972** Arrowhead Stadium completed, home of Chiefs football team; **1973** Kauffman (Royals) Stadium completed near Arrowhead Stadium, home of Royals baseball team; **June 3, 1969** apartment building fire kills 12; **1972** Kansas City International Airport completed to northwest in Platte County; **1973** Crown Center complex opened; **1974** Kemper Arena opened; **1976** Bartle Exposition Hall built; **Sept. 12, 1977** flash flood hits Brush Creek and Country Club Plaza, 26 killed; **Jan. 28, 1978** fire at Coates House Hotel kills 16; **1980** 40-story Hyatt Regency Hotel completed; **July 17, 1981** suspended walkway in atrium of Hyatt Regency Hotel collapses, 43 killed, 150 injured; **1986** 38-story AT&T Town Pavilion office building built; **1988** 42-story One Kansas City Place building completed; **Dec. 8, 2001** 114-year old Chouteau Bridge demolished by explosives.

Kearney   *Clay County*   *Western Missouri, 24 mi/39 km northeast of Kansas City*

1839 Waltus Watkins purchases land; **1842** Robert and Zerelda James move to area, buy farm 1845; **Sept. 5, 1845** outlaw Jesse James born, died Apr. 3, 1882, at St. Joseph, buried at Kearney; **1849** Watkins Mill, flour and woolen mill, built by Watkins, used until 1886; **1867** town platted; **1869** incorporated as a village; **1871** Mount Vernon Baptist Church built; **1883** incorporated as a city; **1964** Watkins Mill State Park established.

Kennett   *Dunklin County*   *Southeastern Missouri, 77 mi/124 km south-southwest of Cape Girardeau*

1845 Dunklin County formed; **1846** town founded as county seat, named Chilletecaux for Delaware tribe member living in area; **1849** town renamed Butler; **1852** town renamed for St. Louis Mayor Dr. Luther M. Kennett, made unsuccessful bid to win rail line; **1862** county declares itself State of Dunklin, secedes from Union, never recognized; **1873** town incorporated; **1890s** St. Louis, Kennett & Southern Railroad reaches town; **1940** fourth county courthouse built.

Keytesville   *Chariton County*   *North central Missouri, 45 mi/72 km northwest of Columbia*

1820 Chariton County formed; Old Chariton becomes county seat; **1833** town platted as new county seat on land donated by Rev. James Keyte; **1854** Corinth Presbyterian Church built; **Sept. 20, 1864** Confederates burn court-house; **1868** town incorporated; **Aug. 26, 1901** World War II Gen. Maxwell D. Taylor born (died 1987); **1915** Sterling Price statue erected; **1964** Sterling Price Museum established; **1975** third county courthouse built.

Kimmswick   *Jefferson County*   *Eastern Missouri, 18 mi/29 km south of St. Louis, near Mississippi River*

1789 El Camino Real wagon road built from St. Louis; **1839** mastodon skeletons discovered to west; **1857** town platted by Theodore Kimm; **1858** post office established; **1859** Franz Hermann House begun, completed after Civil War; **1871** town incorporated; St. Louis & Iron Mountain Railroad reaches town; **1917** El Camino Real marker erected; **Aug. 5, 1922** railroad accident to north, 43 killed; **1930** wrought iron Windsor Harbor Bridge transferred from Carondelet (now part of St. Louis City), built 1874; **1976** Mastodon State Park established, redesignated Historic Site 1996; **1993** flooding damages historic town; **2002** town defeats proposal for casino riverboat.

Kingston   *Caldwell County*   *Northwestern Missouri, 40 mi/64 km east-southeast of St. Joseph*

1836 Caldwell County formed; **1837** town of Far West, established by Mormons, becomes county seat; **Sept. 1838** Mormon War; **Oct. 30, 1838** in Mormon Massacre, 17 Mormons killed, 14 wounded at Haun's Mill to east by 240 militia from Livingston County; **1843** town founded as new county seat; **1857** town incorporated; **1865** Christian Church built; **1867** county jail built, still in use; **c.1895** Hannibal & St. Joseph Railroad reaches town; **1898** county courthouse built; **1925** Haun's Mill Memorial marker erected using millstone found in Shoal Creek, replaced by new marker 2001; **1990s** significant Mormon migration returns to county.

Kirksville   *Adair County*   *Northern Missouri, 130 mi/209 km northeast of Kansas City*

1841 Adair County formed; town founded as county seat; Mr. and Mrs. Jesse Kirk serve county commissioners sumptuous turkey dinner in exchange for honor of having town named for them; **1857** incorporated as a city; **1861** Cumberland Academy founded, burned 1872; **Aug. 6, 1862** in Battle of Kirksville, 1,000 Federal troops rout 2,000 Confederates, ending Confederate recruiting in northern Missouri; **1867** Missouri Normal School established, becomes Northeast Missouri State Teachers College 1919, renamed Truman State University 1996; **1892** American School of Osteopathy founded by Dr. Andrew Still, becomes Kirksville College of Osteopathic Medicine; **1898** county courthouse built; **Nov. 22, 1924** actress Geraldine Page born (died 1987).

Kirkwood   *Saint Louis County*   *Eastern Missouri, 15 mi/24 km southwest of St. Louis, near Meramec River*

1853 Missouri Pacific Railroad built; town platted, named for engineer James P. Kirkwood; **1865** incorporated as a city; **Nov. 15, 1887** poet Marianne Craig Moore born (died

1972); **1893** train depot built; **1944** Museum of Transport established, becomes county park 1980s; **1963** Meramec Campus, St. Louis Community College, established.

Laclede   *Linn County*   *North central Missouri, 75 mi/121 km north-northwest of Columbia*

1853 town platted; **1859** Hannibal & St. Joseph Railroad reaches town; **Sept. 13, 1860** Gen. John J. Pershing born, served in Spanish-American War 1898 (died 1948); **1864** Union Soldiers Memorial erected; **1866** town incorporated; Pershing Home built; **1868** Locust Creek Covered Bridge built to northwest; **1930** Pershing State Park established.

Lamar   *Barton County*   *Southwestern Missouri, 32 mi/51 km north-northeast of Joplin*

1852 grist mill and sawmill built by George E. Ward; **1853** town founded, named for Mirabeau B. Lamar, second President of Texas 1838–1841; *Lamar Democrat* newspaper founded; **1855** Barton County formed; **1862** bitterly divided town damaged, courthouse burned during Civil War; **1867** incorporated as a town; **1880** incorporated as a city; **1881** Missouri Pacific Railroad reaches town; **May 8, 1884** Harry S. Truman, 33rd U.S. President, born, died Dec. 26, 1972, house built 1881; **1888** fourth county courthouse built; **1910** Civil War reconciliation meeting held in town square with mass public handshake; **1980** Prairie State Park established to west, bison reintroduced 1985.

Lancaster   *Schuyler County*   *Northern Missouri, 82 mi/132 km northwest of Hannibal*

1845 Schuyler County formed; town founded as county seat; **1846** Bryant James builds log tavern; **1856** incorporated as a village; **1868** North Missouri Railroad reaches town; **1872** Missouri, Iowa & Nebraska Railroad reaches town; **1889** incorporated as a city; **1961** third county courthouse built.

Lebanon   *Laclede County*   *South central Missouri, 47 mi/76 km northeast of Springfield*

1820 Jesse Ballew becomes area's first settler; **1849** Laclede County formed; town founded as county seat, originally named Wyota; **1869** Missouri Pacific Railroad bypasses town site; town moved, renamed Lebanon; **1876** jail built, used until 1955; **1877** incorporated as a city; **1890** Gasconade Hotel built at magnetic spring; **Sept. 15, 1914** track washed out causing train wreck, 28 killed; **1925** third county courthouse built; **1927** U.S. Highway 66 completed.

Lees Summit   *Jackson and Cass counties*   *Western Missouri, 16 mi/26 km south-southeast of Kansas City*

1858 Josiah N. Hargis becomes first settler; **1865** town platted by William B. Howard on Missouri Pacific Railroad, named Strother, maiden name of Howard's wife; **1868** incorporated as a town, renamed for Dr. Pleasant Lea [sp], resident shot during Civil War; **1877** incorporated as a city; **Jan. 15, 1844** outlaw Cole Younger born (died 1916); **1885** fire destroys downtown; **1899** Unity School of Christianity founded; **1912–1916** Longview Farm built by lumber magnate P. A. Long; **1969** Longview Community College established.

Lexington   *Lafayette County*   *West central Missouri, 35 mi/56 km east of Kansas City, on Missouri River*

1815 Gilead Rupe becomes first settler; **1819** William Jack establishes ferry; **1820** Lillard County formed; **1822** John Hall opens store; **1822** town platted, named for Lexington, Kentucky, origin of its settlers; **1823** town becomes county seat; **1825** county renamed Lafayette County; **1840** Cumberland Presbyterian Church built; **1845** town incorporated; **1846** Masonic College moved from Philadelphia, Missouri (closed 1859); **1849** county courthouse completed; **1850** Christ Episcopal Church completed; **Apr. 9, 1852** sidewheeler *Salada*, with 250 Mormons on way to Utah runs into heavy ice, next day boilers explode on third attempt to run jam killing all on board; **1853** Anderson House built by Col. Oliver Anderson, later used as Union hospital; **Sept. 18–21, 1861** Battle of Lexington ends in victory for Gen. Sterling Price and the Confederates over Union Col. James A. Mulligan, 3,000 prisoners for Price, cannonball left embedded in courthouse column; **1869** Lexington & St. Joseph Railroad reaches town; **1871** Central College established; **1880** Wentworth Military Academy founded; **1889** pontoon bridge built across Missouri River; **1925** World War Memorial erected; highway bridge built; **1928** Lexington Battlefield State Historic Site established; Pioneer Mother Monument (Madonna of the Trail) dedicated; **1932** fire destroys Central College, forces its closing.

Liberty   *Clay County*   *Western Missouri, 13 mi/21 km northeast of Kansas City*

1820 first settlers arrive; **1822** Clay County formed; town platted as county seat; **1823** Big Shoal Baptist Church founded; **1827** monthly Bonnet Sunday started, begins 80-year tradition; **1829** incorporated as a town; **1833** Mormons driven north from Independence; **1836** U.S. Arsenal established, used until 1869, razed 1900; **1849** William Jewell College established; **1851** incorporated as a city; **1852** Lightburne Hall mansion built; **1854** Multnomah house built by fur trader Maj. John Dougherty; **July 24, 1854** proslavery convention represented by 25 Missouri counties adopts proposals to prevent Kansas from becoming a free state; **Dec. 4, 1855** arsenal raid by 100 citizens led by Maj. Luther Leonard to aid arrested proslavery Kansans, first hostile act by Missourians; **Apr. 20, 1861** arsenal captured by pro-Southerners; **Apr. 22, 1861** town meeting advocates secession from Union; **Apr. 23, 1861** pro-Union Home Guard organized; **Sept. 16, 1861** 500 Federal troops of Lt.

MISSOURI

Col. John Scott ambushed by 700 pro-Southern State Guardsmen at Blue Mills to southeast, 17 Union killed, 80 wounded, 5 Guard killed, 18 wounded; **July 20, 1864** guerillas condemned at public meeting; **Feb. 14, 1866** James gang suspected of $72,000 Clay County Bank heist, 12-year-old George Wymore shot to death when told to run for help; **July 8, 1918** TV actor Craig Stevens born (died 2000); **1936** county courthouse completed; **1963** Latter-day Saints Visitor's Center opened.

Linn *Osage County* *Central Missouri, 19 mi/31 mi east of Jefferson City*

1841 Osage County formed; **1842** town founded as county seat, originally named Linnville for U.S. Sen. Lewis F. Linn; **1844** post office established; town name shortened; **1866** newspaper *The Unterrified Democrat* founded; **1911** town incorporated; **1925** county courthouse built.

Linneus *Linn County* *North central Missouri, 78 mi/126 km north-northwest of Columbia*

1837 Linn County formed; **1839** town platted as county seat; **1840** post office established; **Dec. 30, 1858** Kansas Jayhawkers antislavery group launch raids into Linn County; **1859** town incorporated; **1869** jail built, addition 1935; **1872** Burlington & Southwestern Railroad reaches town; **1914** third county courthouse built.

Louisiana *Pike County* *Eastern Missouri, 70 mi/113 km north of St. Louis, on Mississippi River*

1811-1812 Buffalo Fort established; **1816** town settled; James Stark establishes Stark Brothers Nursery to south, Stark Delicious apple developed later; **1818** Pike County formed; town platted as county seat; **1823** county seat moved to Bowling Green; **1848** town incorporated; **1866** Dove Baptist Church built; **1871** Clarksville & Western Railroad reaches town; **1880s–1890s** town's Victorian homes built on river bluff, many home to steamboat captains; **1928** highway bridge built across Mississippi; **1950** Stark Cabin moved from village of Stark, built 1841.

Macon *Macon County* *North central Missouri, 52 mi/84 km north of Columbia*

1827 area first settled; **1837** Macon County formed; Bloomington, to northwest, becomes county seat; **1856** town founded; **1857** rival town of Hudson founded to west; **1858** Hannibal & St. Joseph Railroad reaches both towns; **1859** town annexes Hudson; incorporated as a city; **1863** county seat moved to Macon; **1865** county courthouse built; **1875** St. James Military Academy established, closed 1897; **1914** Still-Hildreth Sanatorium established.

Marble Hill *Bollinger County* *Southeastern Missouri, 24 mi/39 km west of Cape Girardeau*

1851 Bollinger County formed; town platted as county seat, originally named Dallas; **1865** town renamed Marble Hill; **1867** St. Louis, Iron Mountain & Southern Railroad bypasses town to south; neighboring Lutesville founded on railroad; **1868** post office established; **1885** second county courthouse built; **1942** Glenallen dinosaur fossil site discovered to northwest; **1947** incorporated as a city; **1986** Marble Hill annexes Lutesville.

Marshall *Saline County* *North central Missouri, 47 mi/76 km west-northwest of Columbia*

1820 Saline County formed; Jefferson (Cambridge) becomes county seat; town founded, named Elk's Hill; **1831** county seat moved to Jonesboro, moved to Arrow Rock 1839; **1839** town incorporated, renamed for Supreme Court Justice John Marshall; **1840** county seat moved to Marshall; **1862** town occupied by Federal troops, **Oct. 13, 1863** Gen. Joseph Shelby's Confederate forces defeated in raid by Union forces under Gen. E. B. Brown and Col. John F. Phillips; **1866** reincorporated as a town; **1874** Chicago & Alton Railroad reaches town; **1878** incorporated as a city; **1882** county courthouse built; **1889** Missouri Valley College established; **1899** State School for Feeble-Minded and Epileptic founded, later renamed Missouri State School; **1963** Marshall Philharmonic Orchestra founded.

Marshfield *Webster County* *South central Missouri, 22 mi/35 km east-northeast of Springfield*

c.1830 area first settled by Flannagan family; **1855** Webster County formed; **1856** town platted as county seat; first county courthouse built, destroyed 1861 during Civil War; **1869** town incorporated; **1872** Atlantic & Pacific Railroad reaches town; **1878, 1880** pair of tornadoes in successive years, total 87 killed, 200 injured; **Nov. 20, 1889** astronomer Edwin Powell Hubble born (died 1953); **1939** third county courthouse built.

Maryville *Nodaway County* *Northwestern Missouri, 40 mi/64 km north of St. Joseph*

1836 Platte Purchase added to northwestern Missouri; **1845** Nodaway County formed; town founded as county seat, named for Mrs. Mary Graham, town's first woman resident; **1854** town incorporated; **1869** *Nodaway Democrat* newspaper founded; **1875** Benedictine Convent established; **1882** county courthouse built; **Nov. 24, 1888** motivational lecturer, writer Dale Carnegie born (died 1955); **1889** Kansas City, St. Joseph & Council Bluff Railroad reaches town; **1905** Northwest Missouri State College (now University) established; **March 6, 1924** opera singer Sarah Caldwell born; **1937** The Big Pump built, Art Deco gas station designed in shape of giant gas pump.

Maysville *De Kalb County* *Northwestern Missouri, 26 mi/42 km northeast of St. Joseph*

1845 De Kalb County formed; town founded as county seat; town incorporated; **1885** Chicago, Rock Island & Pacific Railroad reaches town; **1939** third county courthouse built.

Memphis *Scotland County* *Northeastern Missouri, 65 mi/105 km northwest of Hannibal*

1838 area settled; **1841** Scotland County formed; town platted, **1843** town becomes county seat; **1871** Missouri, Iowa & Nebraska Railroad reaches town; **1883** town incorporated; **1908** third county courthouse built.

Mexico *Audrain County* *Northeast central Missouri, 28 mi/45 km northeast of Columbia*

1836 Audrain County formed, named for legislator Col. James H. Audrain; **1837** town platted as county seat; Doan's Race Track built; **1857** town incorporated; **1858** Northern Missouri Railroad reaches town; Audrain Female Academy established, renamed Hardin College 1873 (closed 1930); **c.1870** African-American Tom Bass moves from Columbia, hired as stable boy, moves to Kansas City 1893 to become cofounder of American Royal Horse Show; **1886** King's Daughters Home for aged established; **1889** Missouri Military Academy established; **1893** horse stables established by Lee Brothers, horse and mule raising becomes major industry; **1900** fire clay discovered in area, brick refractories established; **1910** A. P. Green Fire Brick Company founded, closed 2002; **1951** county courthouse built.

Milan *Sullivan County* *Northern Missouri, 94 mi/151 km north-northwest of Columbia*

1845 Sullivan County formed; town (MY-lan) platted as county seat; **1847** post office established; **1872** Burlington & Southwestern Railroad reaches town; **1877** town incorporated; **1879** Quincy, Missouri & Pacific Railroad reaches town creating junction; **1939** fourth county courthouse built.

Moberly *Randolph County* *North central Missouri, 32 mi/51 km north of Columbia*

1823 salt extraction begun at Randolph Springs to south; **1850s** coal mining begins; **1858** North Missouri Railroad built north-to-south; **1859** Chariton & Randolph County Railroad built east-to-west; town founded, named for railroad president William Moberly; **1866** town platted; **1868** incorporated as a town; **1873** Wabash Railroad shops established; **1889** incorporated as a city; **Feb. 12, 1893** U.S. Army Gen. Omar Bradley born at Clark to south (died 1981); **Dec. 5, 1898** author Jack Conroy born (died 1990); **1927** Moberly Area Community College established.

Montgomery City *Montgomery County* *East central Missouri, 45 mi/72 km northeast of Jefferson City*

March 7, 1815 Capt. James Callaway, four others attacked by natives on Loutre River; **1818** Montgomery County formed; Pinckney becomes county seat; **1824** county seat moved to Lewiston, to Danville 1834; **1853** town platted; **1857** North Missouri Railroad built; **1859** town incorporated; **1889** in perennial bid to win county seat, town builds courthouse to house some county records; **1924** county seat moved from Danville; **1955** county courthouse built.

Monticello *Lewis County* *Northeastern Missouri, 33 mi/53 km north-northwest of Hannibal*

1833 Lewis County formed; town platted as county seat; incorporated as a village; **1834** post office established; **1875** county courthouse built.

Mount Vernon *Lawrence County* *Southwestern Missouri, 30 mi/48 km west-southwest of Springfield*

1845 Lawrence County formed; town platted as county seat; **1848** town incorporated; **1874** county jail built; **1891** Greenville & Northern Railroad reaches town; **1902** county courthouse built; **1907** State Sanatorium founded, now Missouri Rehabilitation Center; **1926** Chesapeake Fish Hatchery established; **1966** first Apple Butter Days held.

Neosho *Newton County* *Southwest Missouri, 16 mi/26 km south-southeast of Joplin*

1838 Newton County formed; **1839** town platted as county seat by James Wilson; **July 1850** three lead mines in operation; **1855** incorporated as a village; **Oct. 28, 1861** exiled pro-Confederate state legislature votes to secede from Union, an ineffective measure; **1863** Federal troops take control of town, downtown burned; **Oct. 4, 1863** Union Captain McAfee surrenders to Confederate Gen. Joseph Shelby; **1870** Atlantic & Pacific Railroad reaches town; **1879** incorporated as a city; **1887** Federal Fish Hatchery established, oldest in U.S.; **Apr. 16, 1889** painter Thomas Hart Benton born, grandnephew of Missouri Sen. Thomas Hart Benton (died 1975); **1936** county courthouse built; **1942** Camp Crowder military training base established, closed 1958; **1963** Crowder College (2-year) established.

Nevada *Vernon County* *Western Missouri, 52 mi/84 km north of Joplin*

1700 Osage people establish village after eviction from other parts of Missouri, move farther west 1775; **1855** Vernon County formed; town (ne-VAI-da) platted, incorporated as county seat; **Dec. 19, 1858** John Brown's forces raid county, free 11 slaves; **1861** town declared Bushwhacker Capital, base for Confederate guerilla group; **May 26, 1863** Union forces burn town; **Aug. 1863** Union Gen. Thomas Ewing releases Federal Order No. 11 ordering evacuation of Jackson, Cass, Bates, and Vernon counties, retaliation for Confederate raids; **1870** town made division point for Missouri, Kansas & Texas Railroad; **1880** incorporated as a city; **1884** Cottey College established; **Aug. 5, 1906** movie director John Huston born (died 1987); **1908** county courthouse built; **1965** Bushwhacker Museum opened.

New London *Ralls County* *Northeaster Missouri, 8 mi/12.9 km south of Hannibal*

1819 town founded by William Jamieson; **1820** Ralls County formed; **1821** town becomes county seat; **1829** Purdom Tavern built; **1858** county courthouse completed, outside balcony used by orators like Sen. Thomas Hart Benton; **1869** jail built, used into 1980s; **1870** town incorporated; Hannibal & St. Joseph Railroad built through town.

New Madrid *New Madrid County* *Southeastern Missouri, 145 mi/233 km south of St. Louis*

1776 earthquake hits area, centered on New Madrid (MAdrid) Fault; **1783** trading post established on Mississippi River by François and Joseph Le Sieur; **1789** El Camino Real (King's Highway) built from St. Louis by Spanish; Spanish post established; town platted by Col. George Morgan; **c.1792** second known earthquake affects area; **1795** third earthquake hits area; **1803** incorporated as a city; **1804** Louisiana transferred to U.S.; **Dec. 16, 1811** 2 A.M., residents awaken to first earth tremors, 8.7 magnitude among strongest in U.S. history, continues through 1812, forms nearby Reelfoot Lake, Tennessee, causes Mississippi River to reverse flow, low death toll due to sparse population; **1812** New Madrid County formed; town becomes county seat; **1815** certificates issued for land destroyed by 1811 quake, redeemed for property elsewhere in Missouri; **1860** Hunter Dawson Mansion built; **March 14, 1862** town captured by Union Gen. Albert Pope, Confederates flee to Island No. 10 in riverbend to east; **Apr. 7, 1862** island captured by Union; **1878** Little River Valley & Arkansas Railroad reaches city; **1886** Kendall Saloon opened; **1919** county courthouse built.

O'Fallon *St. Charles County* *Eastern Missouri, 30 mi/48 km west-northwest of St. Louis, near Mississippi River*

1798 Jacob Zumwalt builds cabin; **1812** Fort Zumwalt built around cabin; **1817** cabin bought by Nathan Heald, wife captured by Native Americans near Fort Dearborn (Chicago), brought here, pursued by Heald, got her back for a mule and a bottle of whiskey; **1856** Northern Missouri Railroad reaches town; town founded, named for Maj. John O'Fallon, railroad director; **1912** incorporated as a city; **1940** Fort Zumwalt State Park established, becomes city park 1978.

Old Mines *Washington County* *Eastern Missouri, 50 mi/80 km south-southwest of St. Louis*

1720 Philippe François Renault establishes lead mining, remains active industry until 1744; **1773** discovery of richer lead deposits 5 mi/8 km to south leads to abandonment of mines; **1802** town settled by 15 French Creole families; log St. Joachim Catholic Church built; **1818** Etienne Lamarque House built; **1827** post office established, closed 1969; **1830** new Catholic church completed, addition built 1868; **1940s** local dialect of French still spoken in town.

Oregon *Holt County* *Northwestern Missouri, 22 mi/35 km northwest of St. Joseph*

Apr. 17, 1811 English botanist John Bradbury joins Wilson Hunt party camped at mouth of Nodaway River for journey up Missouri River; **1836** Platte Purchase added to northwestern Missouri; **1841** Holt County formed; town platted and incorporated as county seat; **July 8, 1851** lightning strikes hotel, six killed; **1935** Squaw Creek National Wildlife Refuge established to northwest; **1966** third county courthouse built.

Osceola *Saint Clair County* *Western Missouri, 60 mi/97 km north-northwest of Springfield, on Osage River*

1835 Sanders Nance builds first cabin; **1837** town platted; **1841** St. Clair County formed; town becomes county seat; **1844** first steamboat arrives on Osage River; **Sept. 23, 1861** town sacked and burned by Kansas Jayhawkers, militant antislavery group led by Jim Lane; **1883** St. Louis & San Francisco Railroad reaches town; incorporated as a city; **1923** county courthouse completed, work begun 1916, delayed by unrelated lawsuit by railroad against county.

Ozark *Christian County* *Southwestern Missouri, 14 mi/23 km south of Springfield*

1818 Smallin's Cave discovered by Henry R. Schoolcraft, later renamed Civil War Cave; **1833** Joseph Kimberling builds mill; **1843** town platted; **1859** Christian County formed; town becomes county seat; **1865** courthouse burned by arsonist; **1882** incorporated as a village; **1887** manhunt organized by citizens against Bald Knobbers terrorist group, 30 arrested; **1888** incorporated as a city; **May 10, 1889** three Bald Knobbers hanged for harassment of local people; **1892** Old Spanish Cave discovered; **1920** third county courthouse built.

Palmyra *Marion County* *Northeastern Missouri, 10 mi/16 km northwest of Hannibal*

1819 first settlers arrive; town founded; **c.1821** First Methodist Church built; **1826** Marion County formed; town becomes county seat; **1839** *Palmyra Spectator* newspaper founded; **1855** incorporated as a city; **1857** Hannibal & St. Joseph Railroad reaches town; **1860** Palmyra & Quincy Railroad reaches town; **Sept. 12, 1862** town attacked by Confederate forces under Joseph C. Porter, capture Union spy Andrew Allsman; **Oct. 18, 1862** Union forces retaliate with brutal execution of 10 prisoners, called the Palmyra Massacre, referred to as darkest crime of Civil War by both presidents Lincoln and Davis; **1901** third county courthouse completed; **1907** Palmyra Massacre monument erected.

Paris *Monroe County* *Northeastern Missouri, 38 mi/61 km southwest of Hannibal*

1831 Monroe County formed; town platted as county seat; settlers from Kentucky and Tennessee arrive; Broughton House built; **1837** *Missouri Sentinel* newspaper founded by Gen. Lucian J. Eastin, becomes the *Mercury* 1843; **1838** Potawatomis camp here on forced move to Kansas; **1842** town incorporated; **1850** Paris Male Academy established; **1857** Union Covered Bridge built on Elk (South) Fork Salt River by Robert Elliott; **1870** columnist Tom Bodine born (died 1937); **1872** Hannibal & Central Railroad reaches town; **1912** county courthouse built.

Park Hills *Saint Francois County* *Eastern Missouri, 55 mi/89 km southwest of St. Louis*

1890 lead mining boom begins; town of Flat River founded; **May 1891** first lead mine dug; several boom towns established in close proximity at each mine site; **1895** incorporated as a town; **1907** Federal Lead Mill established; **1922** Flat River Junior College established, later renamed Mineral Area College; **1934** incorporated as a city; **Oct. 1972** last lead mine closed; **1976** St. Joe State Park established; Missouri Mines State Historic Site established; **Jan. 1, 1994** towns of Rivermines, Elvins, and Esther merge with city of Flat River to form city of Park Hills.

Parkville *Platte County* *Northwestern Missouri, 10 mi/16 km northwest of Kansas City, on Missouri River*

1840 Park House built by Col. George S. Park; **1844** town founded by Park; **1853** *Industrial Luminary* newspaper founded by Park; **Apr. 14, 1855** abolitionists W. J. Patterson and Colonel Park expelled by proslavery Platte County Self-Defensive League, Park's printing press thrown into river; Patterson and Park flee, Park returns at invitation of pro-Union citizens; **1858** town incorporated; **1875** Park College established; **1993** town suffers heavy flood damage.

Perryville *Perry County* *Eastern Missouri, 65 mi/105 km south of St. Louis*

1789 El Camino Real (King's Highway) built by Spanish from St. Louis to New Madrid; **1801** Isadore Moore establishes farm on Saline Creek; **1818** St. Mary's-of-the-Barrens Seminary founded, first Missouri college, built 1848; **1820** Perry County formed; **1822** town founded, platted; **1827** Church of the Assumption built; **1831** incorporated as a town; **1839** Saxon Lutherans arrive in Perry County; **1856** incorporated as a city; **1890s** Chester, Perryville, Ste. Genevieve & Farmington Railroad reaches town; **1904** county courthouse built.

Pilot Knob *Iron County* *Southeast central Missouri, 128 mi/206 km south-southwest of St. Louis*

1834 town settled; **1836** Missouri Iron Company begins working deposits here and at nearby Iron Mountain; **1858** St. Louis & Iron Mountain Railroad completed; town founded; **1861** Fort Davidson built by Union troops; **Sept. 27, 1864** Confederate Gen. Sterling Price assaults Fort Davidson in Battle of Pilot Knob at loss of 1,500 men, Union Gen. Thomas Ewing retreats north leaving three men behind to blow up powder magazine; **1946** town incorporated.

Pineville *McDonald County* *Southwestern Missouri, 34 mi/55 km south-southeast of Joplin*

1818 town founded as Cumberland Ford; **1849** McDonald County formed; town renamed Maryville, becomes shared county seat with Rutledge to end rivalry; **1857** town, now Pineville, becomes sole county seat; **1863** courthouse burned during Civil War, rebuilt 1870; **1919** incorporated as a village; **1978** fourth county courthouse built.

Platte City *Platte County* *Western Missouri, 22 mi/35 km north-northwest of Kansas City*

c.1830 flour mill built; **1836** Platte Purchase added to northwestern Missouri; **1838** Platte County formed; **1839** town platted as county seat; **1843** incorporated as a village; **June 29, 1854** Platte County Self-Defensive Association sends proslavery settlers into Kansas to help prevent its becoming a free state; **Dec. 16, 1861** town burned by Union forces under Colonel Morgan; **July 15, 1864** partially rebuilt town again burned by Union forces; **1867** county courthouse built; **1870** Chicago & Southwestern Railroad reaches town; **1882** incorporated as a city.

Plattsburg *Clinton County* *Northwestern Missouri, 24 mi/39 km southeast of St. Joseph*

1826 first settlers arrive; **1833** Clinton County formed; town founded as county seat; **1835** incorporated as a village; **1843** U.S. Land Office established, closed 1859; **1861** incorporated as a city; **1871** Hannibal & St. Joseph and St. Louis, Kansas City & Northern railroads reach town; **Dec. 30, 1900** lexicographer Clarence Lewis Barnhart born (died 1993); **Feb. 18, 1884** O. O. McIntyre born, New York newspaper writer (died 1938); **1975** county courthouse built.

Poplar Bluff *Butler County* *Southeastern Missouri, 130 mi/209 km south of St. Louis*

1800 last of Native American mounds built in area; **1819** Solomon Kittrell becomes first settler; **1830s** Scotch-Irish families arrive from Kentucky; **1849** Butler County formed; **1850** town founded as county seat; **1870** incorporated as a city; **1873** Iron Mountain Railroad built, giving increase to lumber industry; **1874** Cairo, Arkansas & Texas Railroad reaches town; **1899** ceramic clay deposits discovered; **1917** Hargrove Bridge built across Black River, only pivotal bridge in Missouri; **May 8–9, 1927** tornado strikes city, 93 killed; **1929** county courthouse completed; **1949** Rodgers Theatre opened; **1966** Three Rivers Community College established; **1981** Margaret Harwell Art Museum opened.

Potosi *Washington County* *Southeast central Missouri, 55 mi/89 km southwest of St. Louis*

1773 lead discovered by François Azor dit Breton, establishes Mine au Breton; **1795** Valle-Perry House built; **Jan. 1797** Moses Austin arrives from Virginia, builds reverberating lead furnace; **1813** Washington County formed; town founded as county seat; **1816** town renamed for Mexican mining city San Luis Potosí; **Jan. 10, 1821** Moses Austin dies, born Durham, Connecticut, 1761; **1823** Springfield Iron Furnace established to south; **1826** town incorporated; **1838** Cresswell lead furnace built; **1880s** lead mining declines; **1908** county courthouse completed; **Apr. 1938** Texas attempts to have Austin's remains moved to Austin for burial beside son Stephen F. Austin, town blocks move.

Princeton *Mercer County* *Northern Missouri, 105 mi/169 km northeast of Kansas City*

1845 Mercer County formed, named for Gen. Hugh Mercer, Battle of Princeton, 1777; **1846** town platted, becomes county seat; **May 1, 1852** Martha Canary (Calamity Jane) born, earned nickname while serving as scout in Black Hills (died 1903) [see Deadwood, South Dakota]; **1853** incorporated as a village; **1872** Chicago, Rock Island & Pacific Railroad reaches town; **1891** incorporated as a city; **1913** third county courthouse built.

Richmond *Ray County* *West central Missouri, 35 mi/56 km east-northeast of Kansas City*

1820 Ray County formed, named for John Ray, who died earlier in year attending state constitutional convention; Bluffton becomes county seat; **1827** town platted and incorporated, named for Richmond, Virginia, origin of many of its settlers; **1829** county seat moved to Richmond; **1871** St. Louis, Kansas City & Northern Railroad reaches town; **1915** county courthouse completed; **1981** first annual Mushroom Festival held.

Rock Port *Atchison County* *Northwestern Missouri, 55 mi/89 km northwest of St. Joseph*

1836 Platte Purchase added to northwestern Missouri; **1843** grist mill established; **1845** Atchison County formed; Linden becomes county seat; German immigrants arrive led by Herman Schubert, establish socialist colony, destroyed by flood in first year; **1851** town platted by Meeks; **1855** incorporated as a village; **1856** county seat moved to Rock Port; **1878** incorporated as a city; **1882** county seat challenge by Tarkio fails; **1883** county courthouse completed.

Rolla *Phelps County* *Central Missouri, 100 mi/161 km southwest of St. Louis*

1818 first settlers arrive; **1844** John Webber builds town's first house; **1853** town founded by Webber on route of St. Louis-San Francisco Railroad, named Raleigh at suggestion of North Carolinian George Coppedge, spelled as it sounded (RAH-lah); **1857** Phelps County formed; town becomes county seat; **1861** incorporated as a city; Union forces build defenses; **Jan. 1, 1861** first train arrives; **1862** county courthouse completed, used as Union hospital; **1870** Missouri School of Mines established, becomes University of Missouri at Rolla; **1904** Mineral Museum founded; **1932** U.S. Geological Survey Mid-Continent Mapping Center established; **1939** Missouri Trachoma Hospital established to treat eye disease common among Ozark families; **1993** new county courthouse built.

Saint Charles *St. Charles County* *Eastern Missouri, 18 mi/29 km northwest of St. Louis, on Missouri River*

1769 area settled by French fur traders; Louis Blanchette builds cabin and mill near Missouri River; **1781** settlement established as Les Petites Cotes; **1787** Auguste Chouteau plats town, named for King Charles V of France; **1791** San Carlos Borromeo Church built; **1799** Daniel Boone arrives from Kentucky at Defiance to southwest; **1805** Aaron Burr arrives seeking to organize a Western Empire; **1809** incorporated as a village; **1812** St. Charles County formed; town becomes county seat; **1819** the *Independence* becomes first steamboat to ascend Missouri River; **1820** *Missourian* newspaper founded; **Sept. 26, 1820** Daniel Boone, 86, dies near Defiance; **Aug. 10, 1821** Missouri admitted to Union as 24th state; city becomes state capital; **1826** capital moved to Jefferson City; **1827** Lindenwood College established, now University; **1832** German immigrants begin arriving; **1849** incorporated as a city; **1851** woolen mill built on Blanchette Creek, damaged by fire 1966; **1859** North Missouri Railroad built from Macon; **1867** Friedens Church built, founded 1834; **1871** railroad bridge built across river, trains crash through deck 1879, 1881; **1903** county courthouse completed; **1904** highway bridge built across Missouri River; **1935** St. Charles College established; **1959** I-70 (Blanchette Memorial) Bridge opened on Missouri River; **1992** Discovery Bridge opened on Missouri River; Family Arena opened; **2003** Page Avenue Bridge completed over Missouri River.

Saint James *Phelps County* *Central Missouri, 88 mi/142 km southwest of St. Louis*

1826 iron works established at Maramec [sp] Spring to east near Meramec River by Thomas James and Samuel Massey; **c.1857** town founded, named Scioto; **1859** town platted by John Wood on St. Louis-San Francisco Railroad as shipping point for Maramec Iron Works; **1860** town renamed; **1861–1865** Germans arrive as Union volunteers; **1867** Missouri Veterans Home established; **1870** incorporated as a village; **1891** iron works closed;

1892 incorporated as a city; **1896** State Soldiers' Home founded; **1938** privately owned Maramec Spring Park established; **1948** Missouri Boys Town founded by Bill James; **1970** St. James Winery established.

Saint Joseph *Buchanan County* *Northwest Missouri, 48 mi/77 km north-northwest of Kansas City*

1799 town site visited by Joseph Robidoux; **1826** Blacksnake Hills Trading Post founded on Missouri River by Robidoux; **1836** Platte Purchase added to northwestern Missouri; **1838** Buchanan County formed; **1840** Sparta, near center of county, becomes county seat; **c.1840** last herds of antelope and elk seen in Missouri; **1843** town platted by Robidoux; **1844** first wave of 800 emigrants crosses river heading west led by Gen. Cornelius Gallatin, including James W. Marshall, discovered gold at Sutter's Mill 1848; **1845** incorporated as a city; **1846** county seat moved to St. Joseph; **1849** thousands of prospectors pass through on way to California gold fields; **1858** Colorado gold rush creates new wave of migration;**1859** Hannibal & St. Joseph Railroad completed; M. K. Goetz Brewery opened; **Apr. 3, 1860** Pony Express service to Sacramento begins, ends Oct. 1861; **1865** Stetson Hat Company founded by John B. Stetson; **July 22, 1872** Kansas City political boss Thomas Pendergast born (died 1945); **1873** railroad and toll highway bridges built across river; **1876** county courthouse completed, burned 1884, rebuilt; **1878** Lake Contrary Amusement Park opened to southwest, closed 1964 after tornado; **Apr. 5, 1882** Jesse James shot by own gang members Charles and Robert Ford following reward offer of $10,000; **1887** stockyards established; **1902** Carnegie Library built; **Nov. 21, 1904** jazz saxophonist Coleman Hawkins born (died 1969); **Jan. 2, 1914** actress Jane Wyman born; **1915** Missouri Western College established; **June 29, 1915** actress Ruth Warrick born; **Nov. 4, 1916** newsman Walter Cronkite born; **May 23, 1919** actress Betty Garrett born; **1922** Rosecrans Airport built at Lake Contrary, moved to French Bottoms 1939; **1952** change in river course leaves airport in Missouri enclave on Kansas side.

Saint Louis *Saint Louis City* *Eastern Missouri, on Mississippi River, 12 mi/19 km south of Missouri River*

July 1673 Fathers Marquette and Joliette descend Mississippi River past mouth of Missouri River; **Feb. 14, 1682** Robert Cavalier, Sieur de la Salle descends Mississippi River, claims entire valley for France Apr. 9 upon reaching Gulf of Mexico; **1700** Kaskaskia settlement established on Mississippi at mouth of River Des Peres; Mission of St. Francis Xavier established, abandoned 1703; **Dec. 1763** trading post established by Pierre Laclede Ligueste; **1764** Church of St. Louis of France founded; town founded by 13-year-old Auguste Chouteau; **1765** capital of Upper Louisiana moved to St. Louis from Fort Chartres, Illinois, surrendered to British; **1770** Upper Louisiana transferred to Spanish; first Cathedral of St. Louis built; **May 26, 1780** force of British and Native

Americans attacks town, repulsed; **1798** ferry service across Mississippi begun by Capt. James Piggott; **1800** Louisiana reverts to French; **March 9, 1804** Louisiana becomes part of U.S. in Treaty of Cession for $15 million; **May 14, 1804** Lewis and Clark Expedition begins opposite confluence of Missouri River, to north, returns 1806; **July 4, 1804** first post office in Missouri established; **1806** Fort Bellefontaine established on Missouri River to north, embarkation point of Zebulon Pike expedition July 16; **1808** incorporated as a town; *Missouri Gazette* begins publication, first newspaper in Missouri; **May 23, 1809** fur trader William Bent born (died 1869); **1812** St. Louis County formed; town becomes county seat; **Oct. 1, 1812** Missouri Territory created from Louisiana Territory; town becomes capital; **1816** Bank of St. Louis chartered; **Aug. 9, 1817** first steamboat, the *Zebulon M. Pike*, arrives; **Aug. 23, 1817** Charles Lucas killed in duel by Thomas Hart Benton, one of first two U.S. senators from Missouri; **1818** St. Louis University established; fur trader Manuel Lisa builds warehouse on Wharf Street (Old Rock House dismantled 1959 for Gateway Arch, reassembly plan lost); **1820** Missouri Constitutional Convention held at Mansion House Hotel, adopted July 19; first assembly held Sept. 18; **Aug. 10, 1821** Missouri admitted to Union as 24th state; capital moved to St. Charles; **1823** incorporated as a city; **Jan. 26, 1826** Julia Dent Grant born, wife of Pres. Ulysses S. Grant (married Aug. 1848, died 1902); Jefferson Barracks military post established to south, replaces Fort Bellefontaine; **1834** *St. Louis Herald* founded, Missouri's first daily newspaper; **1835** Cathedral of St. Louis of France (Old Cathedral) built, oldest standing Catholic church west of Mississippi; **Jan. 1, 1836** first meeting of a Jewish congregation in Missouri; **Sept. 1, 1838** explorer Gen. William Clark dies at age 68; **1839** county (old) courthouse built; **June 1840** McDowell Medical College established, first medical school west of Mississippi, served as Gratiot Prison during Civil War; **June 7, 1843** teacher Susan E. Blow born, started one of first kindergartens in U.S. 1873 (died 1916); **1844** flooding occurs on Mississippi and Missouri rivers; **1846** Mercantile Library (private) established, oldest library west of Mississippi; **Dec. 20, 1847** first telegraph message sent to eastern cities; **1849** cholera epidemic kills thousands; **May 17–18, 1849** Great St. Louis Fire begins on steamboat *White Cloud*, burns 15 city blocks, 24 steamboats; **Sept. 3, 1850** poet Eugene Field born (died 1895); **1851** Missouri State School for Blind established; **Feb. 8, 1851** author Kate O'Flaherty Chapin born (died 1904); **1853** Washington University established; **1857** Harris-Stowe State College established; **March 6, 1857** Dred Scott court case at (old) courthouse leads to Supreme Court ruling that slaves were property even in free states; **1858** Shaw's Garden (Missouri Botanical Garden) established by Henry Shaw; **May 10, 1861** Camp Jackson captured by Federal troops; **June 12, 1861** Planters' House (Hotel) Conference held, last attempt to avert conflict between state forces and Federal troops ends in war declaration by U.S. Gen. Lyon; **March 19, 1864** western painter, sculptor Charles M. Russell born, lived in Great Falls, Montana (died 1926); **1866** Missouri Historical Society founded; **Dec. 22,**

1869 Wilson Bainbridge Cody born, secretary of state under President Wilson (died 1950); **Feb. 22, 1872** actress Fannie Ward born (died 1952); **Dec. 25, 1867** Christ Church Episcopal Cathedral completed; **Nov. 10, 1871** novelist Winston Churchill born (died 1947); **July 4, 1874** Eads Bridge, first steel arch bridge, completed across Mississippi, designed by James Eads; **1875** Forest Park created; **1876** City of St. Louis separates from St. Louis County, becoming one of few independent cities in U.S., later becomes limiting factor in city's growth; **1878** first Veiled Prophet Ball held; **Dec. 12, 1878** *St. Louis Post-Dispatch* newspaper founded by Joseph Pulitzer, Jr.; **July 5, 1879** philanthropist Dwight Davis born, donor of Davis Cup in tennis (died 1945); **1880** St. Louis Symphony founded; *St. Louis Advocate* African-American American newspaper founded; **Aug. 8, 1884** poet Sara Teasdale born, committed suicide 1933; **1889** Tower Grove Park created from Shaw estate; **1890** Wainwright Building built, designed by Louis Sullivan; **1892** Barnes Medical College founded; Anheuser-Busch Brewery built; **1896** Union Station opened; **May 27, 1896** tornado passes south of downtown, into East St. Louis, Illinois, total 255 killed; **June 16, 1899** opera singer Helen Traubel born (died 1972); **Aug. 30, 1901** civil rights leader Roy Wilkins born (died 1981); **Jan. 2, 1903** actress Sally Rand born (died 1979); **Spring 1903** heavy flooding occurs on Mississippi and Missouri rivers; **Nov. 3, 1903** photographer Walker Evans born (died 1975); **1904** Olympic Games held at Washington University; Louisiana Purchase Exposition (World's Fair) held in Forest Park; **1906** St. Louis Art Museum built, funded by proceeds from World's Fair; Ranken Technical College (2-year) established; **June 3, 1906** actress Josephine Baker born (died 1975); **1907** Cathedral of St. Louis begun, completed 1912, mosaics completed 1988; **Dec. 24, 1907** Archbishop of Chicago John Patrick Cody born (died 1982); **1911** city hall completed; **May 27, 1911** actor Vincent Price born (died 1993); **1912** Public Library built; **1913** St. Louis Zoo established; **Feb. 5, 1914** novelist William Burroughs born (died 1997); **March 9, 1914** fire at Missouri Athletic Club building kills 37; **1915** Webster University established at Webster Groves to southwest; **1919** Municipal (Muny) Opera opened in Forest Park; **1920** Lambert Field airport established to northwest, becomes St. Louis International Airport 1970s; **Nov. 30, 1920** actress Virginia Mayo born; **1921** WEW begins broadcasting, first radio station in Missouri; **Aug. 18, 1922** actress Shelley Winters born; **May 12, 1925** baseball player, manager Yogi Berra born; **Feb. 12, 1926** baseball player, announcer Joe Garagiola born; **July 29, 1926** champion bowler Don Carter born; **Oct. 18, 1926** singer Chuck Berry born; **1927** United Hebrew Temple completed, now Missouri Historical Society library; **Jan. 17, 1927** humanitarian Southeast Asia Dr. Thomas A. Dooley III born (died 1961); **June 17, 1927** furniture designer Charles Eames born (died 1978); **Sept. 29, 1927** tornado destroys city center, 90 killed; **1929** St. Louis Arena built; **Nov. 4, 1929** actress Doris Roberts born; **1930** Civil Courts Building completed; **Oct. 12, 1932** comedian Dick Gregory born; **Sept. 27, 1933** actress Kathy Nolan born; **1935** large tract of river front ware-houses cleared for creation of Jefferson National Expansion Memorial 1939, site of future Gateway Arch; U.S. Courthouse completed; **Oct. 13, 1936** African-American diplomat Donald F. McHenry born, Ambassador to U.N.; **Jan. 4, 1937** opera singer Grace Bumbry born; **Nov. 30, 1937** TV actor Robert Guillaume born; **1938** KSD begins experimental TV broadcasts of newspaper editions; **June 23, 1939** TV actor Burt Convy born; **Jan. 31, 1941** U.S. Cong. Richard Gephardt born; **Apr. 3, 1942** actress Marsha Mason born; **Feb. 27, 1943** TV actress Mary Frann born (died 1998); **Feb. 18, 1945** golfer Judy Rankin born; **Oct. 24, 1947** actor Kevin Kline born; **1951** *St. Louis Star-Times* newspaper folds, purchased by *Post-Dispatch*; **June 17, 1953** actor Mark Linn-Baker born; **June 20, 1953** actor John Goodman born; **July 11, 1953** 1978 heavyweight boxing champion Leon Spinks born; **Oct. 9, 1955** actor Scott Bakula born; **1959** Mill Creek Valley urban renewal project begun west of downtown; **Jan. 13, 1959** NASA places space capsule order with McDonnell Aircraft Corporation; **Jan. 22, 1959** actress Linda Blair born; **Feb. 10, 1959** tornado hits city center, 22 killed, 5,000 homeless; **1960** NFL's St. Louis Cardinals move from Chicago; **1962** Forest Park Campus, St. Louis Community College, established; **1963** University of Missouri at St. Louis established to northwest; **1965** Gateway Arch, 630 ft/192 m wide at base, 630 ft/192 m high, completed on river front at Jefferson National Expansion Memorial, opened 1967; **1966** Busch Stadium completed downtown, home of Cardinals baseball team; **Apr. 25, 1973** 43.3 ft/13.2 m river crest highest in 100 years, 11 dead, 35,000 homeless in nine states; **July 23, 1973** Ozark Airlines flight crashes near University of Missouri campus, killing 39; **1973** 37-story Mercantile Center (now US Bank) built; **1984** 44-story One Bell Center built; **1985** Union Station reopened as hotel and shopping complex; **1986** St. Louis Centre shopping complex opened downtown; **Oct. 29, 1986** *St. Louis Globe-Democrat* newspaper folds; **1988** 42-story Metropolitan Square Tower built; football Cardinals move to Phoenix; **1989** St. Louis Walk of Fame established in University City; **1993** MetroLink light rail system completed from airport to East St. Louis; **Aug. 1, 1993** Mississippi River crests at 49.4 ft/15.1 m, 2.5 ft/0.8 m below top of flood wall; **1995** Trans World (TWA) Dome stadium completed, home of Rams football team, renamed Edward Jones Dome 2002; **Jan. 13, 1997** Steve Fossett ascends in balloon from Busch Stadium, lands in Northern India Jan. 20, failed attempt to circle the earth; **Jan. 27, 1999** Pope John Paul II holds mass at TWA Dome for 130,000; **Feb. 27, 1999** St. Louis Arena demolished with explosives; **2000** 29-story Thomas Eagleton Federal Building dedicated, begun 1990; **June 18, 2002** Cardinals announcer Jack Buck, 77, dies; **2004** construction begins downtown on new Cardinals baseball stadium.

Sainte Genevieve   *Sainte Genevieve County*
Eastern Missouri, 45 mi/72 km south of St. Louis

1703 salt works established by Native Americans and French; **1715** lead mining begins to southwest; **1749** town founded on Mississippi River; **1752** first Catholic church in Missouri established; **1770** Bolduc House built; **1785** town inundated by flooding, moved to higher ground; Jean Baptiste Valle House built; **1787** Memorial Cemetery established, oldest in Missouri; **1789** El Camino Real road built from St. Louis to New Madrid; **1791** Green Tree Tavern built; **1792** Amoureaux House built; **1793** Nouvelle Bourbon village established on bluffs by Baron de Carondelet, governor of Louisiana, as refuge for French loyalists; **1805** incorporated as a city; **1807** Louisiana Academy established; **1812** Ste. Genevieve County formed; town becomes county seat; **1851–1853** Iron Mountain & Ste. Genevieve Plank Road built; **1880** Ste. Genevieve Catholic Church built; **1886** county courthouse built; **1899** St. Louis & San Francisco Railroad built; **1935** City Museum established; **1993** historic district spared flooding by intense sandbagging.

Salem *Dent County* *Southeast central Missouri, 100 mi/161 km southwest of St. Louis*

1835 Lewis Dent arrives from Tennessee, promotes iron mining; **1851** Dent County formed; **1853** town founded as county seat by Joseph Milsaps; **1860** town incorporated; **1870** third county courthouse built; **1872** iron mining begins at Simmons Mountain; St. Louis-San Francisco Railroad reaches town; **1938** Indian Trail Fish Hatchery built.

Savannah *Andrew County* *Northwestern Missouri, 12 mi/19 km north of St. Joseph*

1836 Platte Purchase added to northwestern Missouri; **1837** Samuel Crowley arrives from Savannah, Georgia; **1841** Andrew County formed; **1842** town platted as county seat; **1853** incorporated as a city; **1861** *Northwest Democrat* newspaper destroyed by Federals, rival *Plain Dealer* destroyed by Confederates; **1900** county courthouse built.

Sedalia *Pettis County* *West central Missouri, 73 mi/117 km east-southeast of Kansas City*

1833 Pettis County formed; Point St. Helena becomes county seat; **1837** Georgetown founded as new county seat by George R. Smith; **1857** new town platted by Smith on Pacific Railroad, named Sedville; **1860** town renamed Sedalia; **1864** incorporated as a city; county seat moved to Sedalia; **1872** stockyards established; **1894** composer Scott Joplin arrives to play at the Maple Leaf Club, publishes first hit "Maple Leaf Rag"; **1898** Bothwell Lodge, 29-room retreat, built to north by attorney John R. Bothwell; **1901** first Missouri State Fair held; **Nov. 12, 1903** actor Jack Oakie born (died 1978); **1920s** Lona Theatre opened, now Liberty Center; **1925** county courthouse completed; **1966** State Fair Community College established; **1974** Bothwell State Park established to north; **1991** first Scott Joplin Festival held.

Shelbyville *Shelby County* *Northeastern Missouri, 36 mi/58 km west-northwest of Hannibal*

1835 peaceable Sac and Fox peoples continue to live in area; town platted; **1835** Shelby County formed; town becomes county seat; **1836** town platted; **1838** Looney Creek Primitive Baptist Church built; **1857** Hannibal & St. Joseph Railroad reaches town; **1867** town incorporated; **1893** county courthouse completed.

Sikeston *Scott and New Madrid counties* *Southeastern Missouri, 30 mi/48 km south of Cape Girardeau*

c.1802 area settled; **1860** town platted on Cairo & Fulton Railroad by John Sikes; **1875** incorporated as a city; **1906** St. Louis & San Francisco Railroad reaches city; **c.1910** cotton production begins; **Jan. 1939** 1,700 sharecroppers camp along U.S. Highway 61 to demonstrate against harsh working and living conditions; **1942** Lambert's Cafe established by Earl and Agnes Lambert, known for "throwed rolls," dinner rolls tossed through air to customers.

Springfield *Greene County* *Southwestern Missouri, 145 mi/233 km south-southeast of Kansas City*

1815 bands of Delaware tribe arrive; **1821** Thomas Patterson becomes first white settler; **1829** town founded; Native Americans moved to Indian Territory; **1833** Greene County formed; town becomes county seat; **1838** incorporated as a town; **1839** Butterfield Stage Line begins service to Southwest; **1846** incorporated as a city; **Aug. 10, 1861** Battle of Wilson's Creek fought to southwest, Confederate victory leaves Union Gen. Nathaniel Lyon dead, c.200 killed on each side; **Jan. 8, 1863** in Battle of Springfield, Confederate Gen. John Marmaduke fails to take Union fort, retreats to Arkansas, 100 killed; **July 21, 1865** Wild Bill Hickok, who served as Union spy during Civil War, shoots former Confederate Dave Tutt in duel; **1869** Springfield National Cemetery established; **1870** St. Louis-San Francisco Railroad reaches town; **1873** Drury College established; **1881** Kansas City, Fort Scott & Memphis Railroad arrives; city of North Springfield, nearly equaling Springfield in size, merges with Springfield; **Aug. 29, 1891** journalist Marquis James born (died 1955); **1905** Southwest Missouri State Teachers College established, becomes Southwest Missouri State University; **1915** county courthouse completed; **1923** Shriners Mosque built; **Feb. 11, 1925** sexual behavior researcher Virginia E. Johnson born, teamed with husband Dr. William H. Masters; **1928** Springfield Art Museum founded; **1933** U.S. Hospital for Criminally Insane opened, now Department of Justice Medical Center; **1945** airfield built to west, becomes Springfield-Branson Regional Airport; **June 19, 1954** actress Kathleen Turner born; **1955** Evangel College established; **Jan. 30, 1957** golfer Payne Stewart born, died 1999 in plane crash; **Apr. 10, 1960** Wilson's Creek National Battlefield Park established; **1990** Ozarks Technical Community College established.

Stark *Pike County*   See **Louisiana (1816)**

Steelville *Crawford County*   *East central Missouri, 77 mi/124 km southwest of St. Louis, on Meramec River*

1829 Crawford County formed; Arlington becomes county seat; **1831** James Steel settles in area; **1835** town founded; **1836** county seat moved to Steelville; iron mining begins; **1850** town incorporated; **1862** publisher William Randolph Hearst marries Phoebe Apperson; **1870** Cherry Valley Mine opened to east by Sligo Iron Company; **1872** St. Louis, Salem & Little Rock Railroad reaches town; **1886** county courthouse built; **1900** Dillard Mill built, closed 1956.

Stockton *Cedar County*   *Western Missouri, 42 mi/ 68 km northwest of Springfield*

1845 Cedar County formed; **1846** town founded as county seat on Cedar River, originally named Lancaster, renamed Fremont 1847; town incorporated; **1859** town renamed Stockton; **1940** third county courthouse built; **1974** Stockton Lake formed by dam on Sac River; **May 4, 2003** tornado destroys downtown area, three killed.

Sullivan *Franklin and Crawford counties*   *East central Missouri, 55 mi/69 km southwest of St. Louis*

c.1800 Stephen Sullivan arrives from Kentucky, makes fortune from tobacco and mining; **Sept. 3, 1820** U.S. Sen. George Hearst born, California mining engineer, father of newspaper publisher William Randolph Hearst (died 1891); **1856** town founded, named Mount Helicon; **1858** St. Louis-San Francisco Railroad reaches town; town renamed Sullivan; **1861** Confederates manufacture gunpowder, expelled by Union forces; **1873** Harney Mansion built; **1883** town incorporated; **1921** International Shoe factory opened; **1927** Meramec State Park established to east; **1936** Meramec Caverns opened to public; **1950s** Pea Ridge Iron Mine opened to southeast.

Sumner *Chariton County*   See **Chillicothe (1905)**

Times Beach *Saint Louis County*   *Western Missouri, 23 mi/37 km southwest of St. Louis, on Meramec River*

1925 town platted in small parcels in unprotected flood plain by *St. Louis Times* newspaper, free lots given with subscription; **1926** town incorporated; **1927** U.S. Highway 66 built; **1930s** Depression forces owners to live in flood prone town; **Dec. 1982** town evacuated during flooding; **Jan. 1983** streets found to be tainted with hazardous waste dioxin applied by road contractor Russell Bliss also under contract to Northeastern Pharmaceutical and Chemical Company to dispose of toxic waste; **1985** town disincorporated; **1991** town razed; incinerator built to burn dioxin-tainted topsoil; **1999** vacant site developed as Route 66 State Park.

Trenton *Grundy County*   *Northern Missouri, 83 mi/134 km northeast of Kansas City*

1834 town settled around Lomaz's General Store, named Bluff Grove; **1841** Grundy County formed; town platted as county seat; **1842** town renamed Trenton; **1850** Grand River College established, closed 1893; **1857** incorporated as a city; **1869** Chicago & Southwestern Railroad reaches town; **1891** Ruskin College established as by socialist Walter Vrooman, closed 1905; **1905** county courthouse completed; **1925** North Central College (2-year) established.

Troy *Lincoln County*   *Eastern Missouri, 45 mi/ 72 km northwest of St. Louis*

1801 first settlers arrive; **1812** Fort Woods built on Cuivre River, War of 1812; **May 24, 1815** in Battle of Sink Hole, War of 1812, Missouri Rangers attacked by Native American allies of British; **1818** Lincoln County formed; (Old) Monroe becomes county seat; **1819** town platted, incorporated; **1823** county seat moved to Troy; **1841** "slickers" vigilantes organize to control horse rustling and petty lawlessness, leads to Slicker War; **1870** county courthouse built; **1884** incorporated as a city; **Apr. 11, 1879** U.S. Cong. Clarence Cannon born at Elsberry to northeast (died 1964).

Tuscumbia *Miller County*   *Central Missouri, 27 mi/43 km south-southwest of Jefferson City, on Osage River*

1822 settler John Wilson arrives from Ireland (died 1855, age 100); **1837** Miller County formed; town platted as county seat; post office established; **1857** incorporated as a village; town becomes main shipping point on Osage River; **1859** second county courthouse built; **1929** jail built; **1933** truss bridge built across Osage River.

Union *Franklin County*   *East central Missouri, 45 mi/72 km west-southwest of St. Louis, on Bourbeuse River*

1818 Franklin County formed; Newport becomes county seat; **1826** town platted as new county seat; **1848** incorporated as a town; **1854** Missouri Pacific Railroad reaches town; **1887** St. Louis, Kansas City & Colorado Railroad built through town; **1888** incorporated as a city; **1923** county courthouse built; **1968** East Central College (2-year) established; **May 7, 2000** 14 in/36 cm of rain falls in 12 hours, flash flood kills two.

Unionville *Putnam County*   *Northern Missouri, 125 mi/201 km northeast of Kansas City*

1845 Putnam County formed; Putnamville becomes county seat; **1847** county seat move to Calhoun (Winchester); **1853** town platted as new county seat, named Harmony; **1854** post office established; town renamed Unionville; **1857** town incorporated; **1872**

Burlington & Southwestern Railroad built; **1924** sixth county courthouse built.

Van Buren   *Carter County   Southern Missouri, 120 mi/193 km south-southwest of St. Louis*

1812 Zimri Carter builds log cabin; **1830** town founded; **1833** Ripley County formed; town becomes county seat; **1859** Carter County formed from Ripley County; town continues as Carter County seat; Ripley County seat moved to Doniphan; **1871** county courthouse built; **1924** Big Spring State Park established; **1927** town incorporated; **1972** Ozark National Scenic Riverways established on Current and Jacks Fork rivers, absorbs Big Spring State Park.

Versailles   *Morgan County   Central Missouri, 37 mi/60 km west-southwest of Jefferson City*

1820 mills built by settlers from Tennessee, Kentucky, and Virginia; **1833** Morgan County formed, named for Revolutionary War Gen. Daniel Morgan; Millville becomes county seat; **1834** town (ver-SALES) founded as new county seat; **1851** log tavern built; **1853** log hotel opened by Martin family; **1858** Pacific Railroad reaches town; **1878** town incorporated; **1879** Samuel Martin builds new Martin Hotel; **1889** county courthouse built; **1906** Grandma Martin operates hotel, until her death at age 103 in 1926; **1972** Martin Hotel closed; **1980** first Apple Festival held.

Vienna   *Maries County   Central Missouri, 28 mi/ 45 km south-southeast of Jefferson City*

1855 Maries (MAY-reez) County formed; town (vei-EN-na) founded as county seat by German and Irish immigrants; **1930** Swinging Bridge built over Maries River; **1942** third county courthouse built; **1953** town incorporated.

Warrensburg   *Johnson County   Western Missouri, 45 mi/72 km southeast of Kansas City*

1833 Martin Warren becomes first settler; **1834** Johnson County formed; **Oct. 1, 1834** Francis M. Cockrell born, led Cockrell's Brigade for Confederates (died 1915); **1836** town founded as county seat; **1841** old county courthouse completed; **1855** incorporated as a city; **1864** Missouri Pacific Railroad reaches town; **Oct. 28, 1869** Charles Burden's hound Old Drum shot by Leonidas Hornsby, accused of killing his sheep; **Sept. 23, 1870** attorney George Graham Vest delivers "Eulogy of the Dog" in defense of Old Drum, Burden wins $50 lawsuit; **1871** Central Missouri State Teachers College established, becomes Central Missouri State University; Francis Cockrell House built; **1877** abolitionist Carrie Moore marries David Nation, first husband Charles Gloyd died of alcoholism 1868; **1898** county courthouse built; **1942** Whiteman Air Force Base established to east; **Sept. 1958** Old Drum Dog Statue erected at county courthouse.

Warrenton   *Warren County   East central Missouri 50 mi/80 km west-northwest of St. Louis*

1814 Mordecai Morgan becomes first settler; **1833** Warren County formed; **1835** town founded as county seat, named for Gen. Joseph Warren, Revolutionary War hero killed at Bunker Hill, Massachusetts; **1852** Central Wesleyan College established, closed 1941; **1857** North Missouri Railroad reaches town; **1864** incorporated as a city; **1871** county courthouse built; **1908** County Jail built; **Feb. 17, 1957** Sunday afternoon fire destroys Katie Jane Home for aged, 72 of 151 patients killed, many rescued by Rev. Walter Schwane; **1997** new county courthouse completed.

Warsaw   *Benton County   West central Missouri, 85 mi/137 km southeast of Kansas City, on Osage River*

1835 Benton Country formed; **1837** town founded as county seat; **1840** Disciples of Christ Church built; **1841** vigilantes called "slickers" organize to curb horse theft, other lawlessness, Slicker War continues through 1845; **1861** incorporated as a city; **1879** Sedalia, Warsaw & Southern Railroad built; **1887** third county courthouse built; **Feb. 13, 1905** lowest temperature ever recorded in Missouri reached, −40°F/−40°C; **July 14, 1954** highest temperature ever recorded in Missouri reached, 118°F/ 48°C; **1978** Harry S. Truman Reservoir formed by dam on Osage River.

Washington   *Franklin County   East central Missouri, 45 mi/72 km west of St. Louis, on Missouri River*

c.1818 area settled by German immigrants; **1828** town founded by William G. Owens; **1830** Elijah McLean Mansion built; **1837** post office established; **1839** incorporated as a town; **1841** incorporated as a city; **1850s** surge of German immigrants arrive; **1854** Missouri Pacific Railroad reaches town; **1859** *Turnverein* German athletic society organized, enlist in Union army 1861; **c.1860** Washington Hotel built; **1865** Franz Schwarzer Zither Factory established; **1869** Henry Tibbe founds Missouri Meerschaum Pipe Company; St. Francis Borgia Catholic Church built; **1923** railroad depot built; **1936** Missouri River bridge built; **Oct. 3, 1959** TV actor Jack Wagner born.

Waynesville   *Pulaski County   Central Missouri, 120 mi/193 km southwest of St. Louis*

1831 G. W. Gibson becomes first settler; **1833** Pulaski County formed; **1839** town platted as county seat; **c.1857** Old Stagecoach Stop hotel built; **June 1862** Federal troops build fort after overrunning pro-Confederate county; **1901** incorporated as a town; **1904** third county courthouse built; **1931** incorporated as a city; **1940** Fort Leonard Wood Army training base established to south; **1990** fourth county courthouse built.

Webster Groves   *Saint Louis County*   *Eastern Missouri, 10 mi/16 km southwest of St. Louis*

1853 Missouri Pacific Railroad built; town of Webster founded; **c.1860** abolitionist Artemus Bullard founds Webster College, boarding school for boys, later closed; **1884** town renamed Webster Groves; **1896** incorporated as a village; **1914** incorporated as a city; **1916** Loretto College established, renamed Webster College 1924, Webster University 1983; **1924** Eden Theological Seminary moved from Marthasville, Missouri, established 1850.

West Plains   *Howell County*   *Southern Missouri, 90 mi/145 km east-southeast of Springfield*

1840 Josiah Howell becomes first settler; **1848** post office established; **1857** Howell County formed; **1858** town platted as county seat; **1865** only 50 families remain after town is ravaged by Civil War; **1873** Cornelius Bolin ships piano from Rolla, backwoods oddity becomes major local attraction; **1883** Kansas City, Springfield & Memphis Railroad reaches town; incorporated as a city; **Dec. 13, 1925** TV actor Dick Van Dyke born; **Aug. 12, 1927** country singer Porter Wagoner born (died 1999); **Apr. 13, 1928** explosion at Bond Dance Hall kills 40, injures 25, destroys three other buildings, damages courthouse beyond repair; **1937** new county courthouse built.

Weston   *Platte County*   *Western Missouri, 30 mi/48 km northwest of Kansas City, near Missouri River*

1837 Joseph Moore becomes first settler; town founded; **1842** town incorporated; **1849** Ben Holladay House built; **1856** Maj. David Holladay, brother of Ben, discovers four springs, quality ideal for making whiskey, opens distillery, becomes McCormick Distillery; **1857** river channel shifts 2 mi/3.2 km away from town; **1861** St. Joseph & Council Bluffs Railroad reaches town; **May 4, 1875** African-American sociologist George Washington Ellis born (died 1919); **1910** first tobacco warehouse established by J. B. Doran, county becomes important tobacco producer.

Montana

Northwestern U.S. Capital: Helena. Largest city: Great Falls.

The region east of the Continental Divide became part of the U.S. with the Louisiana Purchase in 1803. The part western of the Divide became part of Oregon Territory in 1848. Montana Territory was established May 26, 1864. Montana entered the Union as the 41st state November 8, 1889.

Montana is divided into 56 counties. Municipalities are classified as towns and cities. There are no townships. See Introduction.

Anaconda *Deer Lodge County* *Southwestern Montana, 30 mi/48 km west-northwest of Butte*

1860 Evans House built by Mrs. Gwenellen Evans, first woman landowner in Montana; **1865** Deer Lodge County formed; **1867** Atlantic Cable Gold Mine discovered to northwest; **1882** copper smelter built by "Copper King" Marcus Daly; town founded as county seat, named for Anaconda Copper Mine at Butte; **1888** town incorporated; **1888** Montana Hotel built; **1894** Butte, Anaconda & Pacific Railroad built from Butte; **1895** city hall built, becomes museum 1982; **1898** county courthouse built; Hearst Library established, donated by Phoebe Hearst, mother of newspaper baron William Randolph Hearst; **1977** city and county governments merge; **1980** copper smelter closed.

Bainville *Roosevelt County* *Northeastern Montana, 330 mi/531 km east-northeast of Great Falls*

1828 Fort Floyd built to southeast on Missouri River at boundary of Dakota Territory by John Jacob Astor's American Fur Company, renamed Fort Union 1830, dismantled 1868; **1926** Great Northern Railroad extended to northwest; **June 17, 1832** steamboat *Yellowstone* arrives; **1906** town founded; **1929** incorporated as a town; **June 20, 1966** Fort Union Trading Post National Historic Site established, extends into North Dakota.

Baker *Fallon County* *Eastern Montana, 207 mi/ 333 km east-northeast of Billings*

1888 101 Ranch established to north near Cannonball Butte; **1905** town founded on Custer Trail, named Lorraine; **1907** Chicago, Milwaukee, St. Paul & Pacific Railroad built; **1908** town renamed Baker for railroad construction superintendent A. G. Baker; **1911** town incorporated; **1913** Fallon County formed; Baker Lake formed by dam on Coral Creek in town; **1914** town becomes county seat; **Aug. 29, 1915** natural gas deposit discovered to north in Baker Gas Field; **1919** final county boundaries defined; **1920** oil production begins; **1974** county courthouse built.

Bannack *Beaverhead County* *Southwestern Montana, 60 mi/97 km south-southwest of Butte*

1862 gold discovered on Grasshopper Creek; town founded; **1863** renegade sheriff Henry Plummer and men murder and rob over 100 people, he and two deputies hanged Jan. 10, 1864; **Sept. 1863** Ohio attorney Sidney Edgerton arrives en route to Idaho Territory to assume role of Chief Justice, winters over here, succeeds in creating Montana Territory, named first Governor; **1864** town becomes first territorial capital; **1865** Beaverhead County formed; town becomes county seat; territorial capital moved to Virginia City; county courthouse built; **1881** county seat moved to Dillon; courthouse converted to Hotel Meade; **Jan. 1938** post office closed; **1954** Bannack State Park established.

Big Timber *Sweet Grass County* *Southern Montana, 66 mi/106 km west of Billings, on Yellowstone River*

1882 Northern Pacific Railroad built; town founded; **1890s** wool production becomes important; **1895** Sweet Grass County formed; town becomes county seat; **1897** county courthouse built; **1901** state's first woolen mill established; **1902** town incorporated; **1911** first dude ranch in Montana founded in Crazy Mountains to northwest.

Billings   *Yellowstone County   Southern Montana, 193 mi/311 km east of Butte*

c,1835 Crow victims of smallpox hurl themselves over 200-ft/61-m Sacrifice Cliff to appease their gods; **1879** first irrigation ditch dug in Yellowstone Valley; **1882** Northern Pacific Railroad built; town founded on Yellowstone River, named for Frederic Billings, railroad president; **1883** Yellowstone County formed; town becomes county seat; **1885** town incorporated; *Billings Gazette* newspaper founded; three large fires destroy many of town's wooden buildings; **1886–1887** hard winter forces many residents to leave, halving population; **1901** Parmly Billings Memorial Library founded; **1903** Moss Mansion built by Preston Boyd Moss; **1906** sugar beet refinery built, result of successful irrigation programs; **1908** Billings Polytechnic Institute founded; **1927** Eastern Montana Normal School established, becomes Montana State University-Billings Campus; **1928** Billings Logan Airport established; **1930s** crop irrigation dominates landscape; **1958** county courthouse built; **1993** Zoo Montana opened.

Boulder   *Jefferson County   Western Montana, 25 mi/40 km northeast of Butte*

1865 Jefferson County formed; town founded as county seat on Boulder River; Radersburg becomes county seat; **1872** Elkhorn Mining Camp (gold, silver) established to east; **1883** Radersburg annexed by Broadwater County; county seat moved to Boulder; **1889** county courthouse completed; **1911** incorporated as a town.

Bozeman   *Gallatin County   Southwestern Montana, 75 mi/121 km east-southeast of Butte*

July 14, 1806 Lt. William Clark's party camps here; **1864** trail blazer John M. Bozeman guides first white settlers to area; town founded; **1865** Gallatin County formed; town becomes county seat; **Aug. 1867** Fort Ellis built; **Aug. 1870** Washburn-Langford expedition to Yellowstone region outfitted at Fort Ellis, leads to creation of Yellowstone National Park; **1883** incorporated as a city; **1890** Opera House opened, later used as city hall; **1893** Bozeman State College established, becomes Montana State University-Bozeman Campus; **1935** county courthouse built.

Broadus   *Powder River County   Southeastern Montana, 152 mi/245 km east-southeast of Billings*

1919 Powder River County formed; town founded on Powder River as county seat; **1945** incorporated as a town; **1980** county courthouse built.

Browning   *Glacier County   Northwestern Montana, 117 mi/188 km northwest of Great Falls*

1855 Blackfeet Indian Reservation established; **1883–1884** buffalo leave area during harsh winter, most destroyed by white buffalo hunters, 600 Blackfeet starve to death; **1893** Great Northern Railroad built; town founded as trading post on reservation; **1919** part of reservation sold to U.S., added to Glacier National Park; **1929** incorporated as a

town; **1934** Blackfeet adopt self-governing constitution; **1941** Museum of the Plains Indians opened.

Butte   *Silver Bow County   Southwestern Montana, 48 mi/77 km south-southwest of Helena*

1864 placer gold discovered in Silver Bow Creek by G. O Humphrey and William Allison; **1866** first house built; **1874** William L. Farlin returns from Idaho to work silver claims, beginning of silver mining boom; Marcus Daly, searching for silver, uncovers rich copper deposits; **1876** town founded; **1879** incorporated as a city; **1881** Silver Bow County formed; town becomes county seat; Utah & Northern Railroad reaches town; **1885** Maguire's Opera House opened, closed 1902; **1889** Great Northern Railroad reaches town; **1894** Butte, Anaconda & Pacific Railroad built to copper smelter at Anaconda to northwest; **1895** Montana Technical School of the University of Montana established; **1897** St. Lawrence O'Toole Church built; **1898** Columbia Gardens created, transforming barren mining area into landscaped park; **1899** Amalgamated Copper Mining Company established by Marcus Daly, renamed Anaconda Mining 1910; **1906** Marcus Daly statue erected; **Dec. 10, 1911** newscaster Chet (Chester Robert) Huntley born at Cardwell to east (died 1974); **1912** county courthouse completed; **Aug. 27, 1916** actress Martha Raye born (died 1994); **June 8, 1917** copper mine accident kills 168, among worst U.S. mining disasters; **1938** Butte Art Center founded; **1977** city of Butte merges with Silver Bow County, Walkerville remains separate municipality.

Cardwell   *Jefferson County   See* **Butte (1911)**

Chester   *Liberty County   Northern Montana, 70 mi/113 km north-northeast of Great Falls*

1891 Great Northern Railroad built; town founded; **1895** post office established; **1910** town incorporated; **1920** Liberty County formed; town becomes county seat; county courthouse completed; **1956** Lake Elwell formed by Tiber Dam on Willow Creek to south.

Chinook   *Blaine County   Northern Montana, 120 mi/193 km northeast of Great Falls, on Milk River*

Oct. 5, 1877 Chief Joseph of the Nez Perce surrenders to Col. Nelson A. Miles following Battle of Bear's Paw to south, ending last of major Indian wars in U. S.; **1887** Great Northern Railroad built; town founded; **1901** town incorporated; **1912** Blaine County formed; town becomes county seat; **1914** county courthouse completed; **1925** Chinook Sugar Refinery established; **1991** Blaine County Wildlife Museum opened.

Choteau   *Teton County   Northwestern Montana, 46 mi/74 km northwest of Great Falls*

1859 St. Peter's Mission established to south by Father Hoecken, moved to Sun River 1861; **1879** town founded, named for fur trader Pierre Chouteau, Jr., first "u" deliberately omitted; **1893** Teton County formed; town becomes county seat; **1906** county courthouse built; **1913** incorporated as a city.

Circle *McCone County* *Eastern Montana, 266 mi/ 428 km east of Great Falls*

1905 Circle Home Ranch established by Pete Rorvik; town founded; **1919** McCone County formed; town becomes county seat; **1928** Northern Pacific Railroad built; **1929** incorporated as a town; **1949** county courthouse built.

Columbus *Stillwater County* *Southern Montana, 37 mi/60 km west-southwest of Billings*

1875 trading post established by Horace Countryman; **1880** hotel built by Countryman; **1882** Northern Pacific Railroad reaches site; town founded on Yellowstone River, originally named Eagle's Nest, later renamed Stillwater; **1884** town renamed Columbus; **1907** town incorporated; **1913** Stillwater County formed; town becomes county seat; **1914** county courthouse built, completed 1917.

Conrad *Pondera County* *Northern Montana, 55 mi/89 km north-northwest of Great Falls*

1901 Great Northern Railroad built; town founded; **1903** post office established; **1909** short line Montana Western Railroad built to Valier to northwest; town incorporated; **1916** public library built; **1919** Pondera County formed; town becomes county seat; **1922** Kevin-Sunburst Oil Field discovered to north; **1938** county courthouse built.

Crow Agency *Big Horn County* *Southern Montana, 52 mi/84 km east-southeast of Billings*

1851 Crow Indian Reservation established; **June 25, 1876** Gen. George Custer and 276 men killed at Battle of Little Big Horn, overwhelmed by Sioux (Oglala and Hunkpapa bands) and Cheyenne warriors led by Sitting Bull; **1879** Little Bighorn National Cemetery established; **March 22, 1946** Custer Battlefield National Monument established, absorbs national cemetery, later renamed Little Bighorn Battlefield National Monument.

Cut Bank *Glacier County* *Northwestern Montana, 90 mi/145 km north-northwest of Great Falls*

July 21, 1806 Meriwether Lewis' party camps on Cut Bank River; **1889** Great Northern Railroad built; town founded; railroad work halted during construction of trestle across deep coulee; **c.1900** steel bridge replaces wooden trestle; **1911** town incorporated; **1919** Glacier County formed; town becomes county seat; **1925** oil and natural gas boom brings prosperity to region; **1936** county courthouse built.

Deer Lodge *Powell County* *Western Montana, 30 mi/48 km north-northwest of Butte*

1855 log Grant House built to north by rancher John F. Grant; **1862** first important gold strike occurs; town founded on Clark Fork river, Deer Lodge Valley, named Cottonwood, renamed La Barge City same year; **1864** town renamed Deer Lodge City; **1871** state penitentiary established; **1880s** area becomes major copper producer; **1883** Northern Pacific Railroad reaches town; **1889** town incorporated; **1896** town renamed Deer Lodge; **1901** Powell County formed; town becomes county seat; **Aug. 11, 1915** actress Jean Parker born; **1921** county courthouse built; **Aug. 25, 1972** Grant-Kohrs Ranch National Historic Site established to north; **1979** state penitentiary closed.

Dillon *Beaverhead County* *Southwestern Montana, 55 mi/89 km south of Butte, on Beaverhead River*

1865 Beaverhead County formed; **1880** Utah & Northern Railroad built; town founded, named for railroad president Sidney Dillon; **1881** county seat moved from Bannack; **1885** town incorporated; **1889** county courthouse built, Seth Thomas clock tower built 1906; **1893** Montana State Normal College established, becomes Western Montana College of University of Montana; **1964** Clark Canyon Lake formed by dam on Red Rock River to south.

Ekalaka *Carter County* *Southeastern Montana, 192 mi/309 km east of Billings*

1875 first homesteader David H. Russell marries Sioux woman Ijkalaka, niece of Sitting Bull; **1885** town founded by Claude Carter, builds Old Stand Saloon where his draft animals bogged down in the mud; **1901** Ijkalaka dies; **1914** incorporated as a city; **1917** Carter County formed; town becomes county seat; **1920** county courthouse completed.

Forsyth *Rosebud County* *Southeastern Montana, 95 mi/153 km east-northeast of Billings*

1882 Northern Pacific Railroad arrives; town founded on Yellowstone River, named for Gen. James Forsyth; **1901** Rosebud County formed; town becomes county seat; **1908** town incorporated; **1914** county courthouse completed.

Fort Benton *Chouteau County* *Northern Montana, 36 mi/58 km northeast of Great Falls*

1846 Fort Lewis fur trading post established on Missouri River by American Fur Company, renamed Fort Benton 1850; **1865** Chouteau County formed; town founded as county seat, considered birthplace of Montana; **1870** fort leased to U.S. Government; **1883** town incorporated; **1887** fort abandoned; county courthouse completed.

Fort Shaw *Cascade County* *West central Montana, 25 mi/40 km west of Great Falls*

1867 Fort Shaw military post built on Mullan Road to provide refuge to settlers from Blackfeet raids; town founded; **June 1876** Gen. John Gibbon departs from Fort Shaw to join generals Terry and Custer in Battle of Little Bighorn, Terry and Gibbon were executing encircling maneuver when Custer's forces were decimated June 25; **1891** fort abandoned, converted to Indian school; **1910** Indian school abandoned.

Frenchtown *Missoula County* *See* **Missoula** (1960)

Gardiner *Park County* *Southern Montana, 110 mi/177 km southeast of Butte, on Yellowstone River*

1830s trapper John Gardiner works his trade in area; **March 1, 1872** Yellowstone National Park established to south, mainly in Wyoming, extends into Montana and Idaho; **1880** town founded; **1883** Northern Pacific Railroad extended south from Livingston stopping at Cinnabar, 4 mi/6.4 km short of town, finally reaches Gardiner 1902; **1903** Pres. Theodore Roosevelt lays foundation to entrance arch named for him at boundary of Yellowstone National Park.

Glasgow *Valley County* *Northeastern Montana, 220 mi/354 km east-northeast of Great Falls*

1887 Great Northern Railroad built; town founded on Milk River; **1888** incorporated as a town; **1893** Valley County formed; town becomes county seat; **1902** incorporated as a city; **1908** Glasgow Carnegie Public Library built; **1920** final county boundaries adopted; **1932** Montana aviator John W. Schnitzler killed when his plane strikes nearby butte; **1940** Fort Peck Lake formed on Missouri River by Fort Peck Dam, begun 1933; **1973** county courthouse built.

Glendive *Dawson County* *Eastern Montana, 205 mi/330 km northeast of Billings*

1869 Dawson County formed; **1880** town founded on Yellowstone River, becomes county seat; town name a corruption of nearby Glendale Creek; **1881** Northern Pacific Railroad reaches town; **1902** town incorporated; **1919** final county boundaries established; **1962** county courthouse built.

Great Falls *Cascade County* *West central Montana, 72 mi/116 km north-northeast of Helena*

June 13, 1805 Capt. Meriwether Lewis discovers Great Falls, head of navigation on Missouri River, party spends month portaging around falls; **July 11, 1806** Capt. Lewis camps here on return from Oregon; **1822** trapper Jim Bridger passes through area; **1849** Charles M. Russell, 16, arrives from St. Louis to work as a cowboy, becomes renowned Western artist; **Apr. 1849** Bridger and 83

trappers attacked by Blackfeet, three killed; **1883** town founded by Paris Gibson; **1887** Cascade County formed; town becomes county seat; Great Northern Railroad reaches town; **1888** incorporated as a city; silver smelter built at Giant Springs; **1892** copper reduction plant opened, closed 1916; **1903** county courthouse built; **1906** St. Anne's Catholic Cathedral built; **1911** Ursuline Academy built; **June 6, 1892** painter, novelist Will James born (died 1942); **1926** Paris Gibson Statue dedicated; **1930** Charles M. Russell Memorial Museum opened; **1931** North Montana Fair organized; oil refinery established; **1932** University of Great Falls established; **1942** Malmstrom Army Air Base established to east, becomes Air Force Base 1954, closed 1997; **1969** Montana State University College of Technology (2-year) established.

Hamilton *Ravalli County* *Western Montana, 43 mi/69 km south of Missoula*

1887 Bitterroot Stock Farm established by Marcus Daly; town founded on Bitterroot River; **1890** Northern Pacific Railroad arrives; town platted; 42-room Daly Mansion built by "Copper King" Marcus Daly; **1893** Ravalli County formed; town becomes county seat; **1894** town incorporated; **1900** county courthouse built; **1907** irrigation brings "apple boom" to Bitterroot Valley; **1979** new county courthouse built; old courthouse becomes museum.

Hardin *Big Horn County* *Southern Montana, 44 mi/71 km east of Billings*

1877 Fort Custer built on Bighorn River at mouth of Little Bighorn River; **1906** town founded on Bighorn River; **1911** town incorporated; **1913** Big Horn County formed; town becomes county seat; **1936** county courthouse built; **1966** Bighorn Lake formed by Yellowtail Dam on Bighorn River to southwest, in recreation area; **Oct. 15, 1966** Bighorn Canyon National Recreation Area established to southwest, extends into Wyoming.

Harlowton *Wheatland County* *Central Montana, 82 mi/132 km northwest of Billings, on Musselshell River*

1902 Devil's Pocket fossil bed discovered to east; **1908** Chicago, Milwaukee, St. Paul & Pacific Railroad built; town founded, named for railroad builder Richard Harlow; **1909** Graves Hotel built; **1917** Wheatland County formed; town incorporated, becomes county seat; county courthouse converted from school, built 1910.

Havre *Hill County* *Northern Montana, 101 mi/163 km northeast of Great Falls, on Milk River*

1879 Fort Assiniboine built; **1887** Great Northern Railroad built; town founded, named for James J. Havre, railroad construction camp foreman; **1893** town incorporated; fire destroys part of town; **c.1910** farming takes precedence over ranching; **1912** Hill County formed; town becomes county seat; **1915** county courthouse built; **1929** Northern Montana College established, becomes Montana State University-Northern Campus; **1939** Fresno Reservoir formed by dam to west on Milk River.

Helena   *Lewis and Clark County   Western Montana, 48 mi/77 km north-northeast of Butte*

July 19, 1805 Lewis and Clark Expedition camps on island at Gates of the Mountains, gorge of Missouri River to northeast; **1862** immigrant train pauses here, temporary settlement established; **1864** gold discovered at Last Chance Gulch; town founded, named Helena (hel-LEE-nah) by John Somerville for his home town in Minnesota; miners, who liked to say the word "hell," alter pronunciation to HEL-e-nah; **1865** Edgerton County formed; town becomes county seat; Montana Historical Society founded; **1867** county renamed Lewis and Clarke, spelling changed to Clark 1905; incorporated as a town; Helena Public Library founded, opened 1933; **1870s** gold mining boosts local economy; **1875** territorial capital moved from Virginia City; **1881** incorporated as a city; **1883** Great Northern Railroad reaches city; **1887** county courthouse completed; **1888** smelter built at East Helena; **1889** Broadwater Resort built to north by Col. C. A. Broadwater; **Nov. 8, 1889** Montana enters Union as 41st state; city becomes state capital; **1898** Canyon Ferry Dam built on Missouri River to east, rebuilt 1952; **1892** Fort Harrison army base established to west, many buildings damaged in 1935 earthquake; **May 7, 1901** actor Gary Cooper born (died 1961); **1904** federal building built, later converted to city-county building; **Aug. 2, 1905** actress Myrna Loy born (died 1993); **1909** Carroll College established; **1911** state capitol completed; Placer Hotel built, enough gold found in excavation to pay for its construction; Hauser Dam built on Missouri River to northeast; **1920** Algeria Shrine Temple built, Muslim mosque; **1924** St. Helena Roman Catholic Cathedral completed, begun 1908; **1930** Helena Regional Airport established; **1931** natural gas pipeline built from Cut Bank; **1935** earthquake causes $4 million in damage, four killed, state capitol, other public buildings damaged; **March 1, 1945** actor Dirk Benedict born; **Jan. 20, 1954** lowest temperature ever recorded in Montana reached, −70°F/−57°C recorded at Rogers Pass to northwest; **Apr. 3, 1996** Theodore Kaczynski arrested at cabin hideaway near Lincoln to northwest, identified as the "Unabomber" by brother David from his writing style in Manifesto published in *Washington Post*, wanted for sending letter bombs to professors and others since 1978.

Hysham   *Treasure County   Southern Montana, 70 mi/113 km northeast of Billings*

1907 town founded on Yellowstone River, named for Charles Hysham, owner of Flying E cattle brand, whose herd extended for 70 mi/113 km across country; **1916** incorporated as a town; **1919** Treasure County formed; town becomes county seat; **1960** county courthouse built.

Jordan   *Garfield County   East central Montana, 204 mi/328 km east of Great Falls*

1901 town founded by Arthur Jordan; **1902** paleontologist Barnum Brown discovers first full *Tyrannosaurus rex* skeleton at Hell Creek; **1919** Garfield County formed; town becomes county seat; **1951** town incorporated; **1953** hospital built, converted 1998 into county courthouse; **June 13, 1996** 81-day standoff with Montana Freemen paramilitary group ends, wanted for writing $15.5 billion in bogus checks to finance their antitax objectives.

Kalispell   *Flathead County   Northwestern Montana, 150 mi/241 km west-northwest of Great Falls*

1809 David Thompson of North West Company explores area; **1881** trading post established on Flathead River by Angus McDonald of Hudson's Bay Company; **1891** Great Northern Railroad built; town founded; **1892** town incorporated; **1893** Flathead County formed; town becomes county seat; **1895** Conrad Mansion built; **1903** county courthouse completed; Carnegie Library built; **1942** Flathead County Airport established, renamed Glacier Park International Airport 1970; **1943** Flathead County Library established, merges with Carnegie Library 1967; **June 8–10, 1964** regional flooding kills over 30, destroys 400 homes; **1967** Flathead Valley Community College established.

Lake McDonald   *Flathead County   Northwestern Montana, 142 mi/229 km northwest of Great Falls*

1815 trapper Hugh Monroe of Hudson's Bay Company becomes first white man to enter area; **1846** Father De Smet visits area; **Oct. 1889** Marias Pass, on southern edge of Glacier Park, discovered by Maj. Marcus D. Baldwin; **1892** Great Northern Railway completed through Marias Pass; **1895** trail built from Belton (West Glacier); hotel built by George Snyder; **1900** forest preserve established through efforts of George Bird Grinnell; **May 11, 1910** Glacier National Park established; **1913** Lake McDonald Lodge built; Glacier Park Hotel completed; **1915** Many Glacier Hotel completed in eastern part of park; **June 30, 1932** Waterton-Glacier International Peace Park proclaimed, includes Waterton Lakes National Park, Alberta, Canada; **1933** tunnel built near Logan Pass completing Going-to-the-Sun Road; **July 4, 1970** bodies of six climbers removed from Mt. Cleveland to north, died six months earlier.

Lewistown   *Fergus County   Central Montana, 92 mi/148 km east-southeast of Great Falls*

1874 Fort Lewis established to south by Maj. William H. Lewis; **1881** Maj. A. S. Reed opens post office; town founded, named Reed's Fort; **July 4, 1884** shootout at town center kills cattle rustlers Edward "Longhair" Owen and Charles "Rattlesnake Jake" Fallon; **1886** Fergus County formed; town becomes county seat; **1899** town incorporated, renamed Lewistown; **1903** Central Montana Railroad reaches town; **1908** county courthouse built.

Libby *Lincoln County* *Northwestern Montana,*
206 mi/332 km west-northwest of Great Falls

1864 gold discovered on Libby Creek; town founded; **1892** Northern Pacific Railroad built on Kootenai River; town moved 20 mi/32 km north to railroad; **1909** Lincoln County formed; town becomes county seat; town incorporated; **1936** county courthouse built; **1972** Libby Dam completed on Kootenai River to east forming Lake Koocanusa.

Lincoln *Lewis and Clark County* *See* **Helena** (1996)

Livingston *Park County* *Southern Montana,*
98 mi/158 km east-southeast of Butte, on Yellowstone River

July 1806 William Clark party descends Billman Creek to Yellowstone River; **1873** area first settled; **1882** Northern Pacific Railroad built; town founded, named Clark City; **1883** town renamed for railroad director Crawford Livingston; **1887** Park County formed; town becomes county seat; **1889** town incorporated; **1894** railroad strike turns violent, martial law declared by President Cleveland; **1904** Carnegie Library built; **1976** county courthouse built.

Malta *Phillips County* *Northern Montana, 170 mi/ 274 km northeast of Great Falls*

1870 town founded on Milk River; **1887** Great Northern Railroad built; **1890s** artist Charles M. Russell paints many of his Western-themed paintings in area; **1909** town incorporated; **1915** Phillips County formed; town becomes county seat; **1920** county courthouse completed; **1936** Lake Bowdoin National Wildlife Refuge established to east.

Medicine Lake *Sheridan County* *See* **Plentywood** (1937)

Miles City *Custer County* *Southeastern Montana, 135 mi/217 km northeast of Billings*

1876 Fort Keogh built; **1877** Custer County formed; town founded as county seat, named Milestown for Gen. Nelson A. Miles; **1878** town incorporated, renamed Miles City; county courthouse completed; **1881** Northern Pacific Railroad reaches town; **1902** Public Library built; **1908** fort abandoned; **June 19, 1938** railroad accident, 46 killed.

Missoula *Missoula County* *Western Montana, 90 mi/145 km northwest of Butte*

July 4, 1806 party of Meriwether Lewis camps here before proceeding up Hell Gate Canyon; **1812** David Thompson maps area; **1853** railroad survey team enters area led by Gov. Isaac I. Stevens; **1855** area opened to white settlement; **1860** Frank L. Worden and Christopher P.

Higgins arrive, open Hell Gate store to west; William Hamilton builds first cabin; town founded, named Hell Gate; **1862** Mullan Road completed to Idaho; **1864** town renamed Missoula, Flathead Native American term for "place of fear by the waters"; **Jan. 27, 1864** 21-man posse rounds up six members of Henry Plummer gang, tried and hanged; **1865** Missoula County formed; town becomes county seat; sawmill built; **1873** Sacred Heart Academy founded; **1877** Fort Missoula established on Bitterroot River in face of threat by Nez Perce under Chief Joseph; **June 11, 1880** suffragist, U.S. Cong. Jeannette Rankin born (died 1973); **1880s** Rankin House built; **1883** Northern Pacific Railroad built; incorporated as a town; **1889** Missoula County formed; town becomes county seat; incorporated as a city; **1891** St. Xavier Catholic Church built; **1892** white laborers attack Chinese immigrants, four killed; **1893** University of Montana established; **1903** Chicago, Milwaukee, St. Paul & Pacific Railroad reaches town; **1908** Chicago, Milwaukee, St. Paul & Pacific Railroad reaches city; county courthouse built; **1910** county courthouse completed; **1928** beet sugar factory established; **Jan. 20, 1946** movie director David Lynch born; **June 6, 1955** comedian Dana Carvey born; **Oct. 28, 1960** Northwest Airlines DC-4 crashes at Frenchtown to northwest killing all 12 on board; **June 10, 1962** passenger train plunges down embankment, 1 killed, 243 injured.

Philipsburg *Granite County* *Western Montana, 43 mi/69 km northwest of Butte*

1866 silver mining begins; town founded, named for mine superintendent Philip Deidesheimer; Hope Silver Mill built; **1890** town incorporated; **1893** Granite County formed; town becomes county seat; **1912** county courthouse built.

Plentywood *Sheridan County* *Northeastern Montana, 325 mi/523 km northeast of Great Falls*

1910 town founded; **1912** town incorporated; **1913** Sheridan County formed; town becomes county seat; **1920s** town becomes center of Communist Party activity; **July 15, 1937** highest temperature recorded in Montana reached at Medicine Lake to south, 117°F/47°C; **1938** county courthouse completed; **1970s–1980s** oil boom affects area.

Polson *Lake County* *Northwestern Montana, 135 mi/217 km west of Great Falls*

1855 Flathead Indian Reservation established; **1880** Harry Lambert becomes first white settler; **1889** town founded at southern end of Flathead Lake; **1899** University of Montana Biological Experiment Station established on eastern shore of Flathead Lake; **1910** town incorporated; **1923** Lake County formed; town becomes county seat; **1935** county courthouse completed; **1938** Flathead (Kerr) Dam on Flathead River to south completed for irrigation.

Poplar   *Roosevelt County   Northeastern Montana, 285 mi/459 km east-northeast of Great Falls*

1867 Fort Peck established on Missouri River by Comdr. E. H. Durfee and Col. Campbell K. Peck; **1872** Fort Peck Indian Reservation established, occupied by Assiniboine people; town founded on Poplar River, near its mouth on Missouri River; **1879** fort abandoned; **1886** Yankton Sioux moved from Dakota Territory, become target of Assiniboine hostilities; **1887** Great Northern Railroad reaches town; **1916** town incorporated.

Red Lodge   *Carbon County   Southern Montana, 53 mi/85 km southwest of Billings*

1887 Northern Pacific Railroad reaches site; town founded on railroad; **1892** town incorporated; **1895** Carbon County formed; town becomes county seat; county courthouse built; coal mining becomes major industry; **1906** town's first mining accident kills eight; **Feb. 27, 1943** coal mine accident at Washoe Mine to southeast, 75 killed.

Roundup   *Musselshell County   Central Montana, 46 mi/74 km north of Billings*

1903 settlers arrive; town founded on Musselshell River; **1907** Chicago, Milwaukee, St. Paul & Pacific Railroad reaches town; **1909** town incorporated; **1911** Musselshell County formed; town becomes county seat; **1939** county courthouse built; **1989** Montana Centennial Cattle Drive held, reenacts six-day journey to Billings.

Ryegate   *Golden Valley County   Central Montana, 50 mi/80 km northwest of Billings*

1879 Seventynine Ranch established at Sweetgrass Creek by John T. Murphy; **1908** Chicago, Milwaukee, St. Paul & Pacific Railroad built; town founded on Musselshell River; **1917** incorporated as a town; **1920** Golden Valley County formed; town becomes county seat; **1921** county courthouse completed; **Apr. 10, 1938** rancher W. L. Lee Simpson murders ranch hands Robert and Gerald MacDonald and Deputy Sheriff Buzz Burford, executed Dec. 30, 1939.

Saugus   *Prairie County   See* **Terry (1910)**

Scobey   *Daniels County   Northeastern Montana, 285 mi/459 km northeast of Great Falls*

1900 town founded on Poplar River by Mansfield Daniels, named for Indian agent Charles R. A. Scobey; **1913** Great Northern Railroad built; town moved 2 mi/3.2 km to northeast; Commercial Hotel opened as house of pleasure by "One-Eyed" Molly, converted to county courthouse 1920; **1915** town incorporated; **1920** Daniels County formed; town becomes county seat; **1920s** ranchland converted to dry-land wheat farming.

Shelby   *Toole County   Northern Montana, 72 mi/116 km north-northwest of Great Falls*

1806 Meriwether Lewis ascends Marias River as far as Cut Bank thinking it might be Missouri River; **1831** James Kipp builds small fort; **1891** Great Northern Railroad built; town founded; **1910** town incorporated; **1914** Toole ("tool") County formed; town becomes county seat; **1921** oil discovered by Gordon Campbell; **July 4, 1923** fight between Jack Dempsey and Tommy Gibbons, Gibbons beaten before crowd of 7,000; **1934** county courthouse built.

Sidney   *Richland County   Eastern Montana, 332 mi/534 km east of Great Falls*

1888 town founded near Yellowstone River; **1911** town incorporated; **1914** Richland County formed; town becomes county seat; **1919** final county boundaries defined; **1928** county courthouse completed.

Stanford   *Judith Basin County   Central Montana, 55 mi/89 km east-southeast of Great Falls*

1882 town founded; **1911** incorporated as a town; **1920** Judith Basin County formed; town becomes county seat; **Oct. 1922** wolf named Old Snowdrift trapped with his mate Lady Snowdrift and shot by U.S. government hunter Don Stevens, wanted for killing cattle, as many as 21 in one year; **1925** county courthouse built.

Superior   *Mineral County   Western Montana, 48 mi/77 km west-northwest of Missoula*

1859 John Mullan party builds road from Fort Benton, Montana, to Walla Walla, Oregon Territory; **1869** gold discovered at Cedar Creek by L. A. Barrette; town founded on Clark Fork river by settler from Superior, Wisconsin; **1886** gold and silver deposits found to north; Iron Mountain Mine opened; **1891** Northern Pacific Railroad built; **Aug. 19, 1910** forest fires spread through Western Montana and Northern Idaho, 85 killed; **1914** Mineral County formed; town becomes county seat; **1920** county courthouse built; **1948** incorporated as a town.

Terry   *Prairie County   Eastern Montana, 170 mi/274 km northeast of Billings*

Oct. 1876 Gen. Nelson A. Miles' troops encounter Sitting Bull's warriors to north, defeat them at Cedar Creek; **1882** town founded on Yellowstone River, named for Gen. Alfred H. Terry, led expedition against Sioux and Cheyenne in 1876; **1910** town incorporated; **1915** Prairie County formed; town becomes county seat; **June 19, 1938** railroad accident at Saugus to southwest, 47 killed; **1998** county courthouse built.

Thompson Falls   *Sanders County   Western Montana, 80 mi/129 km northwest of Missoula*

1809 Salish House built by David Thompson, one of first white habitations in Montana; **1883** Northern Pacific

Railroad built; town founded; **1883-1884** over 10,000 spend winter here on way to gold fields of Idaho; **1906** Sanders County formed; town becomes county seat; **1930** incorporated as a city; **1950** county courthouse completed.

Three Forks   *Gallatin County   Southwestern Montana, 48 mi/77 km east of Butte*

July 25, 1805 site visited by Lewis and Clark Expedition, three forks of Missouri River–Gallatin, Madison, and Jefferson—named by them; **1810** trading post established by Missouri Fur Company, driven out by Blackfeet with heavy casualties; **1840** Father De Smet spends time in region; **1864** town founded, named Gallatin City, soon abandoned when determined that Great Falls was head of navigation; **1902** Lewis and Clark Caverns discovered to southwest by Daniel Morrison, originally named Morrison Cave; **1908** Northern Pacific Railroad built; town of Three Forks founded; Lewis and Clark National Monument established, becomes state park 1937; **1909** town incorporated.

Townsend   *Broadwater County   West central Montana, 40 mi/64 km southeast of Helena, on Missouri River*

1883 town founded; **1895** town incorporated; **1897** Broadwater County formed; town becomes county seat; **1935** county courthouse built; **March 17, 1949** actor Patrick Duffy born; **1954** Canyon Ferry Lake formed by dam on Missouri River to north.

Virginia City   *Madison County   Southwestern Montana, 55 mi/89 km southeast of Butte*

1863 gold discovered by six Southern prospectors; town founded; **1864** town incorporated; **Jan. 14, 1864** four road agents hanged by secessionist vigilantes; **1865** Madison County formed; town becomes county seat; territorial capital moved from Bannack; **1875** territorial capital moved to Helena; **1876** county courthouse completed.

West Yellowstone   *Gallatin County   Southwestern Montana, 115 mi/185 km southeast of Butte*

1907 Oregon Shortline (Union Pacific) Railroad extended north from Idaho; **1908** town founded at west entrance to Yellowstone National Park, named Riverside; Hebgen Lake formed by dam to northwest on Madison River; **1909** town renamed Yellowstone; **1920** town renamed West Yellowstone; **Aug. 17-20, 1959** earthquake kills 28, injures 60; Earthquake (Quake) Lake formed by landslide on Madison River below Hebgen Lake; **1966** town incorporated.

White Sulphur Springs   *Meagher County   Central Montana, 68 mi/109 km south-southeast of Great Falls*

1866 town founded by James Brewer, named Brewer Springs; **1867** Meagher County formed (pronounced "mar"), named for Gen. Thomas Francis Meagher, federal official who disappeared from Fort Benton without trace July 1, 1867; town becomes county seat; **1869** Fort Logan built to west; **1870** town renamed for popular resort in West Virginia; **1888** incorporated as a city; **1891** stone house built by Byron Sherman, later becomes Castle Museum; **1910** White Sulphur Springs & Yellowstone Park Railroad built from Ringling; **1953** county courthouse built.

Wibaux   *Wibaux County   Eastern Montana, 222 mi/357 km northeast of Billings*

1883 Pierre Wibaux (WEE-bo) becomes first settler; **1886** Northern Pacific Railroad built; town founded on Beaver Creek, named Mingusville; **1886–1887** harsh winter devastates cattle industry; **1895** town renamed Wibaux; **1911** incorporated as a town; **1914** Wibaux County formed; town becomes county seat; **1953** county courthouse built.

Winnett   *Petroleum County   Central Montana, 142 mi/229 km east-southeast of Great Falls*

1879 Walter Winnett establishes ranch near McDonald Creek; **1910** town founded; **1916** incorporated as a town; **1917** Chicago, Milwaukee, St. Paul & Pacific Railroad reaches town; **1919** oil discovered; **1925** Petroleum County formed; town becomes county seat; **1929** First State Bank building converted to county courthouse, built 1917.

Wisdom   *Beaverhead County   Southwestern Montana, 50 mi/80 km southwest of Butte*

July 1806 William Clark party crosses east from Bitterroot River through Gibbon's Pass to Big Hole Valley while Meriwether Lewis heads north along the Bitterroot; **Aug. 9, 1877** Nez Perce led by Chief Joseph attacked by troops of Gen. John Gibbon in Battle of Big Hole, Nez Perce use fire against troops, wind shift spares Gibbon's men; **June 23, 1910** Big Hole Battlefield National Monument established, redesignated Big Hole National Battlefield 1963.

Wolf Point   *Roosevelt County   Northeastern Montana, 265 mi/426 km east-northeast of Great Falls*

1872 Fort Peck Indian Reservation established; **1878** town founded in reservation near Missouri River; **1887** Great Northern Railroad reaches town; **1915** incorporated as a city; **1919** Roosevelt County formed, most of county within reservation; **1924** first annual Wolf Point Stampede rodeo held; **1940** county courthouse built.

Nebraska

North central U.S. Capital: Lincoln. Major city: Omaha.

The region was acquired by the U.S. with the Louisiana Purchase of December 30, 1803. Nebraska Territory was established May 30, 1854. Nebraska was admitted to the U.S. as the 37th state March 1, 1867.

Nebraska is divided into 93 counties. Most counties are divided into townships which have limited governments. Other counties have precincts. Municipalities are classified as villages and cities. There are two classes of cities. See Introduction.

Ainsworth *Brown County* *Northern Nebraska, 232 mi/373 km northwest of Omaha*

1883 Brown County formed; Sioux City & Pacific Railroad built; town founded as county seat, named for Capt. James E. Ainsworth of Missouri Valley, Iowa, railroad construction engineer; incorporated as a city; **1912** Ainsworth Public Library founded; **1959** county courthouse built.

Albion *Boone County* *East central Nebraska, 115 mi/185 km west-northwest of Omaha*

1871 area first settled; **1872** town founded; **1873** incorporated as a village; Frontier Hotel opened; **1875** Boone County formed; town becomes county seat; **1881** Chicago, Niobrara & Black Hills Railroad reaches town; **1882** incorporated as a city; **1908** Albion City Library built; **1976** county courthouse built.

Alliance *Box Butte County* *Northwestern Nebraska, 375 mi/604 km west-northwest of Omaha*

1886 Box Butte County formed; Nonpareil becomes county seat; **1888** town founded by Chicago, Burlington & Quincy Railroad; **1891** county seat moved to Hemingford; **1899** county seat moved to Alliance; **1913** county courthouse built; **1921** incorporated as a city.

Alma *Harlan County* *Southern Nebraska, 152 mi/245 km southwest of Lincoln*

1871 Harlan County formed; town founded as county seat on Republican River; **1880** Burlington & Missouri River Railroad reaches town; **1881** incorporated as a city; **1887** Kansas City & Omaha Railroad built; **1952** Harlan County Lake formed by dam on Republican River to southeast; **1965** county courthouse built.

Ansley *Custer County* See **Broken Bow (1910)**

Arthur *Arthur County* *West central Nebraska, 310 mi/499 km west of Omaha*

1888 Arthur County formed; **1911** Arthur *Enterprise* newspaper founded; **1913** county organized; **1914** town founded as county seat; **1944** incorporated as a village; **1962** county courthouse built.

Auburn *Nemaha County* *Southeastern Nebraska, 62 mi/100 km south of Omaha*

1854 Nemaha County formed; **1857** county organized; Brownville becomes county seat; **1868** town of Sheridan founded; **1881** Missouri Pacific Railroad built; neighboring town of Calvert founded on railroad; **1882** two towns merge, incorporated as a city, renamed Auburn; **1889** county seat moved to Auburn; **1900** county courthouse built.

Aurora *Hamilton County* *Eastern Nebraska, 95 mi/153 km west-southwest of Omaha*

1870 Hamilton County formed; **1871** town founded as county seat by David Stone of Chariton, Iowa, acting for seven investors from Aurora, Illinois; **1877** incorporated as a city; **1895** county courthouse built.

Bartlett *Wheeler County* *Central Nebraska, 148 mi/238 km northwest of Omaha*

1877 Wheeler County formed; **1884** Ezra Bartlett Mitchell becomes first settler; county organized; town founded as county seat; incorporated as a village; **1982** third county courthouse built.

Bassett   *Rock County   Northern Nebraska, 215 mi/ 346 km northwest of Omaha*

1871 rancher J. W. Bassett drives first herd of cattle into region; **1883** Sioux City & Pacific Railroad built; town founded; **1884** cattle rustler Kid Wade, member of Pony Boys' gang, captured east of town and hanged; **1887** incorporated as a city; **1888** Rock County formed; town becomes county seat; **1940** county courthouse built.

Beatrice   *Gage County   Southeastern Nebraska, 38 mi/61 km south of Lincoln*

1857 Gage County formed; town (bee-AT-triss) founded as county seat, named for daughter of founder Judge John Kinney; **July 1861** J. W. "Doc" Brink, Horace Wellman, and James "Wild Bill" Hickok tried, acquitted for killing three men over lease payments owed to owner of Rock Creek Station near Endicott; **Jan. 1, 1863** National Homestead Act takes effect; claim filed by Daniel Freeman regarded as first in U.S.; **1868** U.S. Land Office established; **1871** Chicago, Burlington & Quincy Railroad reaches town; incorporated as a town; **1873** incorporated as a city; **1874** Keyes Factory founded by German immigrant Frederick Keyes, maker of metal hardware; **1875** Sonderegger Nursery Farm established by Swiss immigrant Carl Sonderegger; **1878** Dempster Mill Factory founded, maker of farm implements; **1879** Black Brothers Flour Mill built, destroyed by fire 1937; **1885** Beatrice State Hospital founded; **1892** county courthouse completed; **1893** Beatrice Public Library founded, new library built 1991; **1920** Store-Kraft Company organized, maker of showcases; **1930** Methodist Episcopal Church completed; **March 19, 1936** Homestead National Monument established to west, preserves 1865 farm of Daniel and Agnes Freeman.

Beaver City   *Furnas County   Southern Nebraska, 175 mi/282 km west-southwest of Lincoln*

1873 Furnas County formed; town founded as county seat; **1880** branch of Burlington & Missouri River Railroad reaches town; **1887** incorporated as a village; **1938** incorporated as a city; **1951** county courthouse built.

Bellevue   *Sarpy County   Eastern Nebraska, 7 mi/ 11.3 km south of Omaha, on Missouri River*

1807 fur trader Manuel Lisa visits site, credited with its naming; **1814** Fort Lisa established by Manuel Lisa, for many years most important trading post on Missouri River; **1833** Merrill Baptist Mission established to southwest by Moses Merrill and wife Eliza Wilcox; **1847** Presbyterian mission founded, moved to Macy, Omaha Indian Reservation, 1857; **1855** town incorporated; **1856** Presbyterian mission house built, later converted into Bellevue House hotel; **1857** Sarpy County formed; town becomes county seat; **1858** Presbyterian Church com-

pleted, steeple toppled by tornado 1908; **1875** county seat moved to Papillion; **1896** Fort Crook Army Base established to south, becomes Offutt Army Air Field 1924, Offutt Air Force Base 1948, center of Strategic Air Command; **1965** Bellevue University established.

Benkelman   *Dundy County   Southwestern Nebraska, 316 mi/509 km west-southwest of Omaha*

1873 Dundy County formed; **Oct. 1–2, 1878** band of Sioux led by Chief Dull Knife camp here, having escaped their assigned lands in Indian Territory, on way to Canada intending to join forces with Sitting Bull; **1880** county organized; town founded as county seat on Republican River, named for cattleman J. G. Benkelman; **1887** incorporated as city; **1921** county courthouse built; **May 1935** town damaged by flooding on Republican River.

Blair   *Washington County   Eastern Nebraska, 23 mi/37 km north-northwest of Omaha, on Missouri River*

1854 Washington County formed; **1864** construction of Sioux City & Pacific Railroad begins; **1869** town founded on completed railroad, named for railroad builder John I. Blair; county seat moved from Fort Calhoun; **Aug. 1869** incorporated as a city; **1884** Dana College established; **1891** county courthouse built.

Boys Town   *Douglas County   Eastern Nebraska, suburb 9 mi/14.5 km west of Omaha*

1917 refuge established for homeless boys by Father Edward J. Flanagan (1886–1948) in Omaha; **1921** Flanagan purchases Overlook Farm, builds wooden shelters for increasing number of boys; **1936** incorporated as a village, with youths taking responsibility for municipal affairs; Dan Kampan, 17, becomes first mayor; **1977** Father Flanagan Statue dedicated; **1979** foundation admits girls, renamed Girls and Boys Town; municipality name remains unchanged.

Brewster   *Blaine County   Central Nebraska, 215 mi/346 km west northwest of Omaha*

1884 town founded; **1885** Blaine County formed; **1886** Ladora becomes county seat; **1887** county seat moved to Brewster; **1908** second county courthouse built; **1947** incorporated as a village.

Bridgeport   *Morrill County   Western Nebraska, 385 mi/620 km west of Omaha, on North Platte River*

1812 pointed rock shaft named Chimney Rock by emigrants, landmark for pioneers; **1813** Astor trading party camps here in late winter during futile attempt to canoe down North Platte River; **1876** first bridge over North Platte built at Camp Clarke to west by Henry T. Clarke, used until 1900; **1887** Union Pacific Railroad built; town founded; **1901** incorporated as a city; **Feb. 13, 1905** lowest temperature ever recorded in Nebraska reached, −47°F/−44°C, at Camp Clarke; **1909** Morrill

County formed; town becomes county seat; **1909** county courthouse dedicated; **1910** prairie fire destroys buildings at Camp Clarke; **Aug. 2, 1956** Chimney Rock National Historic Site established to west.

Broken Bow   *Custer County*   *Central Nebraska, 202 mi/325 km west of Omaha*

1877 Custer County formed; **1879** Wilson Hewitt builds dugout dwelling on bank of Muddy Creek, discovers fragments of Pawnee bow and arrows; town founded as county seat; **1880** post office established; **1882** town platted; **1886** Grand Island & Wyoming Railroad reaches town; **1888** incorporated as a city; **Sept. 1, 1910** biologist James Frederick Bonner born at Ansley to southeast (died 1996); **1911** county courthouse built.

Brownville   *Nemaha County*   *Southeastern Nebraska, 63 mi/101 km south-southeast of Omaha*

1854 Otoe peoples surrender lands to white settlement; Nemaha County formed; town founded as county seat on Missouri River by Richard Brown of Missouri; **1855** flatboat ferry established by Brown; Christian Church built, replaced 1901; **1856** Fairbanks Hotel built; **1867** schoolhouse built, still in use 1930s; **1885** county seat moved to Auburn; **Feb. 21, 1974** Cooper Station Nuclear Power plant begins production on Missouri River to north.

Burchard   *Pawnee County*   See **Pawnee City (1893)**

Burwell   *Garfield County*   *Central Nebraska, 175 mi/282 km west-northwest of Omaha*

1874 Fort Hartsuff established to southeast; **1883** Chicago, Burlington & Quincy Railroad built; town founded on North Loup River by Frank Webster, named for brother's fiance Ada Burwell; **1884** Garfield County formed; town becomes county seat; **1889** incorporated as a city; **1922** first Nebraska's Big Rodeo held; **1963** county courthouse built; **1986** Calamus Reservoir formed on Calamus River to northwest; **1991** Calamus Fish Hatchery opened.

Butte   *Boyd County*   *Northern Nebraska, 197 mi/317 km northwest of Omaha*

1870 town founded near Niobrara River by John Gormley; **1891** Boyd County formed, named for Gov. James E. Boyd; town becomes county seat; **1966** county courthouse built.

Camp Clarke   *Morrill County*   See **Bridgeport (1905)**

Center   *Knox County*   *Northeastern Nebraska, 140 mi/225 km northwest of Omaha*

1857 L'Eau Qui Court County formed, French for "running water" (Omaha-Ponca translation of

Niobrara); **1873** county organized, renamed Knox County; Niobrara becomes county seat; **1901** town founded by James Lovell at center of county; **1902** county seat moved to Center; **1904** incorporated as a village; **1934** county courthouse built.

Central City   *Merrick County*   *Eastern Nebraska, 112 mi/180 km west of Omaha, on Platte River*

1858 Merrick County formed; Lone Tree Ranch established; **1866** Union Pacific Railroad built; town founded as county seat, originally named Lone Tree; **1875** incorporated as a city, renamed Central City; **Jan. 6, 1910** author Wright Morris born (died 1998); **1912** county courthouse built; **1924** county's first irrigation system established.

Chadron   *Dawes County*   *Northwestern Nebraska, 395 mi/636 km northwest of Omaha*

Oct. 22, 1876 two encampments of Chief Red Cloud's Sioux to south are surprised by Major Mackenzie's Fifth Cavalry, forced to surrender; **1884–1885** temporary town of O'Linn built while Chadron is platted; Fremont, Elkhorn & Missouri Valley Railroad built; **1885** Dawes County formed; town founded as county seat, name corruption of a local French-Native American named Chardon; incorporated as a city; **1902** Niobrara Division of Nebraska National Forest established, seedlings from Halsey Division in Sand Hills used to create planted forest; **1911** Chadron State College established, originally Nebraska State Teachers' College; **1921** Chadron State Park established to south; **1927** county courthouse built; **1949** trading post opened to east by James Bordeaux, becomes Museum of the Fur Trade 1955.

Chappell   *Deuel County*   *Western Nebraska, 355 mi/571 km west of Omaha*

1884 Union Pacific Railroad built; town founded on Lodgepole Creek, named for railroad official John Chappell; **1888** Deuel County formed; town becomes county seat; **1907** incorporated as a city; **1915** county courthouse built.

Clay Center   *Clay County*   *Southeastern Nebraska, 75 mi/121 km west-southwest of Lincoln*

1871 Clay County formed; **1879** town founded as county seat; county seat moved from Sutton, ending feud over county seat among county's towns; **1887** incorporated as a city; **1918** second county courthouse built.

Columbus   *Platte County*   *Eastern Nebraska, 80 mi/129 km west of Omaha*

1855 Platte County formed; **1856** town founded as county seat on Loup River, near mouth on Platte River; **1866** Union Pacific Railroad reaches town; **1877** incorporated as a city; **March 3, 1899** World War II Gen. Alfred M. Gruenther born at Platte Center to northwest (died 1983);

1917 county courthouse built; **1968** Central Community College, Platte Campus, established; **May 4, 2002** pipe bombs found in mailboxes in western Illinois, eastern Iowa, eastern Nebraska, Luke Helder, 21, arrested May 20 in Nevada, intended to create "smiley face" pattern across U.S.

Crawford   *Dawes County*   *Northwestern Nebraska, 412 mi/663 km northwest of Omaha*

1874 Camp Robinson established near Red Cloud Indian Agency, becomes Fort Robinson 1879; **Apr. 1877** Crazy Horse and his band of Sioux camp at Cottonwood Creek prior to surrendering; **1886** Fremont, Elkhorn & Missouri Valley Railroad built; town founded, named for Lt. Emmet Crawford; incorporated as a city; **1889** Chicago, Burlington & Quincy Railroad reaches town; **1948** Fort Robinson closed, becomes Fort Robinson State Park.

Crete   *Saline County*   *Southeastern Nebraska, 19 mi/31 km southwest of Lincoln*

1870 town founded on Big Blue River; **1871** Burlington & Missouri River Railroad reaches town; **1872** Nebraska University, established 1855, moved from Fontanelle, reorganized as Doane College; **1873** town incorporated.

Dakota City   *Dakota County*   *Northeastern Nebraska, 87 mi/140 km north-northwest of Omaha*

Aug 16, 1804 Lewis and Clark reach mouth of Omaha Creek to south; **1855** Dakota County formed; town founded as county seat on Missouri River; **1858** incorporated as a city; **1860** Emanuel Lutheran Church built, first Lutheran church in Nebraska, now historic landmark; **1940** county courthouse built, annex built 1975.

David City   *Butler County*   *Eastern Nebraska, 65 mi/105 km west of Omaha*

1868 Butler County formed; Savannah becomes county seat; **1873** town founded as new county seat, named for Welsh immigrant William David; **1874** incorporated as a village; **1886** incorporated as a city; **1964** third county courthouse built.

Elba   *Howard County*   See **Saint Paul (1887)**

Elwood   *Gosper County*   *Southern Nebraska, 172 mi/277 km west of Lincoln*

1873 Gosper County formed; Homerville becomes county seat; **1883** town founded; county seat moved to Elwood; **1885** incorporated as a village; **1939** county courthouse built.

Fairbury   *Jefferson County*   *Southeastern Nebraska, 53 mi/85 km south-southwest of Lincoln*

1840s emigrant traffic increases on Oregon Trail; **1857** Rock Creek Station established to southwest as trail wayside; **July 12, 1861** James Butler "Wild Bill" Hickok kills outlaw David McCanles at Rock Creek Station; **1868** sawmill built; **1869** town founded on Little Blue River by Woodford G. McDowell and James B. Mattingly, named for Mattingly's hometown of Fairbury, Illinois; **1871** Jefferson County formed; town becomes county seat; incorporated as a city; **1872** Burlington & Missouri River and St. Joseph & Denver railroads reach town; **1874** colony of Russian immigrants arrives; **1887** Chicago, Rock Island & Pacific Railroad reaches town; **1891** county courthouse built.

Falls City   *Richardson County*   *Southeastern Nebraska, 86 mi/138 km south-southeast of Omaha*

1854 Richardson County formed; **1855** James L. Stumbo builds mill on Big (Great) Nemaha River; **1857** town founded by John A. Burbank, others; Salem becomes county seat; **1858** incorporated as a city; **1860** county seat moved to Falls City; **1865** Union House built; **1870** Atchison & Nebraska (Missouri Pacific) Railroad reaches town from Missouri; **1877** fire destroys seven prominent buildings; **1900** poultry and dairying become important; **1901** Lydia Braun Library opened; **1925** county courthouse built; **1939** state's first oil well drilled to west.

Fort Calhoun   *Washington County*   *Eastern Nebraska, 16 mi/26 km north of Omaha*

Aug. 3, 1804 Lewis and Clark Expedition camps on Missouri River bluffs, holds council with Otoes; **1812** Fort Lisa founded to south by trader Manuel Lisa, died at post 1820; **1819** Fort Atkinson, first military fort west of Missouri River, established to enforce treaties, protect fur trade, counteract British influence; **1824** soldiers plant locust trees brought from Kentucky; **1825** J. B. Cabanne establishes post for American Fur Company near site of Fort Lisa, abandoned by 1840; **1827** fort abandoned; **1854** Washington County formed; **1855** town founded as county seat, named for statesman John C. Calhoun; **1858** incorporated as a city; county seat moved to De Soto; **1866** county seat moved back to Fort Calhoun; **1869** county seat moved to Blair; **1904** monument erected on 100th anniversary of Lewis and Clark Expedition; **1927** Fort Atkinson monument erected, becomes Fort Atkinson State Historical Park.

Franklin   *Franklin County*   *Southern Nebraska, 133 mi/214 km southwest of Lincoln*

1871 Franklin County formed; town founded as county seat on Republican River; county and town named for Benjamin Franklin, town originally named Franklin City; **1874** county seat moved to Bloomington after bitter struggle; **1879** incorporated as a city; **1881** Franklin Academy founded, closed 1922; **1920** county seat returned to Franklin; **1926** county courthouse built; **March 27, 1930** actor David Jannsen born at Naponee to west (died 1980).

Fremont *Dodge County Eastern Nebraska, 34 mi/ 55 km west-northwest of Omaha, near Platte River*

1854 Dodge County formed; Fontanelle becomes county seat; **1855** Gen. John M. Thayer holds council with Pawnee Chief Pita Lesharu, receives pledge of peace, denial that Pawnee had been stealing cattle; **1856** town founded, named for John C. Fremont; **1860** county seat moved to Fremont; **1861** incorporated as a city; **1866** Union Pacific Railroad reaches town; *Fremont Tribune* newspaper founded; **1869** Sioux City & Pacific Railroad built forming junction; **1885** First Congregational Church built; **1892** Lutheran Orphans' Home established; **1901** Carnegie Library built; **1918** county courthouse completed; **1919** Midland Lutheran College moved from Atchison, Kansas, established 1883; **1937** Fremont Auditorium completed; **1949** Western Theological Seminary established, closed 1967.

Geneva *Fillmore County Southeastern Nebraska, 52 mi/84 km southwest of Lincoln*

1871 town founded; **1872** incorporated as a city; **1891** Girls' Industrial School for juvenile delinquents built; **1893** county courthouse completed; **1942** Fairmont Army Air Base established to north, closed 1946.

Gering *Scotts Bluff County Western Nebraska, 420 mi/676 km west of Omaha, on North Platte River*

1887 town founded on south side of North Platte River, named for Martin Gering, one of founders; **1888** Scotts Bluff County formed; town becomes county seat; **1890** incorporated as a city; **1902** irrigation projects lead to sugar beet production; **1910** Union Pacific Railroad finally builds line on south side of river; **Dec. 12, 1919** Scotts Bluff National Monument established to south; **1921** county courthouse built; **1938** packing plant and stockyards opened.

Gibbon *Buffalo County See* **Kearney (1936)**

Grand Island *Hall County Central Nebraska, 133 mi/214 km west-southwest of Omaha, near Platte River*

1857 town founded by German immigrants opposite long island in Platte River; **1859** Hall County formed; town becomes county seat; gold prospector who hated Germans sets fire to prairie, burns town; **1860** George Stolley plants 6,000 trees along river; **1864** Fort Independence built; **1866** Union Pacific Railroad built; **1873** incorporated as a city; **1879** St. Joseph & Western Railroad reaches town; **1887** first sugar beets grown with introduction of irrigation; **1904** county courthouse built; **Aug. 15, 1904** puppeteer Bill Baird born (died 1987); **May 16, 1905** actor Henry Fonda born (died 1982); **1927** Stolley State Park established, becomes Mormon Island State Recreation Area; **1930** Central Monitoring Station established by Federal Communications Commission to maintain assigned radio frequencies; **1936** town becomes first in U.S. to install

mercury vapor street lighting; **1967** part of city flooded; **1976** Central Community College, Grand Island Campus, established; **June 3, 1980** tornado hits town, four killed.

Grant *Perkins County Southwestern Nebraska, 315 mi/507 km west-southwest of Omaha*

1886 Chicago, Burlington & Quincy Railroad built; town founded, named for Pres. Ulysses S. Grant; incorporated as a city; **1887** Perkins County formed, named for railroad president Charles E. Perkins; town becomes county seat; **1926** county courthouse built.

Greeley *Greeley County Central Nebraska, 142 mi/229 km west-northwest of Omaha*

1872 Greeley County formed; Scotia becomes county seat; **1885** town founded as county seat by Thomas Fox, named for newspaper publisher Horace Greeley; **1886** incorporated as a village; **1887** Burlington & Missouri River Railroad reaches town; **1890** county seat moved to Greeley; **1914** county courthouse built.

Harrisburg *Banner County Western Nebraska, 420 mi/676 km west of Omaha*

1888 Banner County formed; town becomes county seat; **1889** town founded as county seat by settler Charles A. Schooley from Harrisburg, Pennsylvania; **1958** county courthouse built.

Harrison *Sioux County Northwestern Nebraska, 440 mi/708 km northwest of Omaha*

1877 Sioux County formed; **1878** area's first ranch established; **1886** Chicago & Northwestern Railroad built; town founded as county seat, named for Pres. Benjamin Harrison; **1887** Capt. James H. Cook establishes Agate Springs Ranch to south, had discovered fossilized bones there 1878; **1888** incorporated as a village; **1904** settlers flock to county with passage of Kinkaid Land Law; **1930** county courthouse built; **June 5, 1965** Agate Fossil Beds National Monument established to south, site of Miocene epoch mammal fossils.

Hartington *Cedar County Northeastern Nebraska, 120 mi/193 km north-northwest of Omaha*

1857 Cedar County formed; St. James becomes county seat; **1869** county seat moved to St. Helena; **1883** town founded; incorporated as a city; **1885** county seat moved to Hartington; **1892** county courthouse built; **1914** Carnegie Library built; **Aug. 31, 1928** actor James Coburn born at rural Laurel to southeast (died 2002).

Hastings *Adams County Southern Nebraska, 141 mi/227 km west-southwest of Omaha*

1871 group of English emigrants become first settlers; Adams County formed; Juniata becomes county seat; **1872** St. Joseph & Denver Railroad built; town founded; **1873** *Hastings Journal* newspaper founded; **1874** incorporated as a city; **1877** county seat moved to Hastings; **1878** farm machinery manufacturing begins; **1879** fire sweeps through town; **1882** Hastings College established; **1908** Carnegie Library built; **1912** St. Cecilia's Roman Catholic Church dedicated; **1929** St. Mark's Episcopal Cathedral completed; **Apr. 26, 1937** actress Sandy Dennis born (died 1992); **1964** county courthouse dedicated; **1966** Central Community College, Hastings Campus, established.

Hayes Center   *Hayes County*   *Southwestern Nebraska, 282 mi/454 km west-southwest of Omaha*

1872 William F. "Buffalo Bill" Cody leads Russian Grand Duke Alexis on buffalo hunt on Red Willow Creek to east; **1877** Hayes County formed; **1885** county organized; town founded as county seat; **1906** county courthouse built.

Hebron   *Thayer County*   *Southeastern Nebraska, 65 mi/105 km southwest of Lincoln, on Little Blue River*

1869 town founded; **1871** Thayer County formed; town becomes county seat; **1872** incorporated as a city; **1873** Premium Mill built; **1902** county courthouse built; **1911** Hebron Academy founded; **May 9, 1953** tornado destroys large part of town, 5 killed.

Holdrege   *Phelps County*   *Southern Nebraska, 148 mi/238 km west-southwest of Lincoln*

1873 Phelps County formed; Williamsburg becomes county seat, soon moved to Phelps Central; **1883** town founded by Scandinavian immigrants; Orphans' Home founded; **1884** incorporated as a city; county seat moved to Holdrege; **1886** Burlington & Missouri River Railroad reaches town; **1911** second county courthouse built.

Hyannis   *Grant County*   *West Central Nebraska, 318 mi/512 km west-northwest of Omaha*

1887 Grand Island & Wyoming Railroad built; Grant County formed; town founded as county seat, named for Hyannis, Massachusetts, by engineer Anselmo B. Smith; incorporated as a village; **1957** county courthouse built.

Imperial   *Chase County*   *Southwestern Nebraska, 313 mi/504 km west-southwest of Omaha*

1885 Thomas Mercier becomes first settler; town founded; incorporated as a city; **1886** Chase County formed; town becomes county seat; **1888** Chicago, Burlington & Quincy Railroad built; **1910** county courthouse completed.

Kearney   *Buffalo County*   *Southern Nebraska, 175 mi/282 km west-southwest of Omaha, on Platte River*

1848 Fort Kearny [sp] built, replaces Fort Kearny, Nebraska City; **1866** Union Pacific Railroad reaches site; **1870** Buffalo County formed; Wood River Centre becomes county seat, seat moved to Gibbon 1871; **1871** Burlington & Missouri River Railroad forms junction; town founded; **1872** county seat moved to Kearney; **1873**

incorporated as a city; **1886** Kearney Irrigation Canal built; **1903** Kearney State Teachers College established, becomes University of Nebraska at Kearney; **1911** Kearney State Hospital established, closed 1972; **Nov. 19, 1936** TV personality Dick Cavett born at Gibbon to east; **1942** Kearney Army Air Field established, closed 1949; **1974** county courthouse built; **2000** Great Platte River Road Archway Monument built across I-80.

Kimball   *Kimball County*   *Western Nebraska, 418 mi/673 km west of Omaha*

1867 Union Pacific Railroad built; town founded; **1885** incorporated as a city; **1888** Kimball County formed; town becomes county seat; **1911** Oliver Reservoir formed for irrigation, rebuilt 1980; **1928** second county courthouse built; **1951** oil discovered in county, production reaches peak 1960; highest point in Nebraska determined to be at the southwest corner of county, in corner of state, at 5,424 ft/1,653 m above sea level, unnamed, marker erected 1971.

Laurel   *Cedar County*   *See* **Hartington (1928)**

Lewellen   *Garden County*   *Western Nebraska, 332 mi/534 km west of Omaha, on North Platte River*

1840s Ash Hollow becomes favored stop for Oregon Trail emigrants; **1849** Rachael Patterson shot by natives while fetching water at spring, buried with other settlers Joe Clary and W. H. Gilliard; **1854** Lt. John L. Grattan and 28 men killed after firing upon Sioux near Fort Laramie, Wyoming, in misunderstanding over butchered cow; **1855** Gen. W. S. Harney attacks Sioux at Blue Water Creek in retaliation for Grattan killings, over 100 men, women, and children killed; **1886** ferry established by Frank Lewellen; town founded; **1907** Union Pacific Railroad reaches town.

Lexington   *Dawson County*   *Southern Nebraska, 210 mi/338 km west-southwest of Omaha, on Platte River*

1860 trading post established on Oregon Trail; **Aug. 7, 1864** in Plum Creek Massacre, Frank Morton, 11 others, killed by Native Americans while traveling the Oregon Trail from Iowa, Morton's wife taken prisoner; **1866** Union Pacific Railroad built; **1867** Cheyenne led by Chief Turkey Leg derail train, scalp crew, make off with contents of boxcars; **1871** Dawson County formed; **1872** town founded as county seat, originally named Plum Creek; **1889** incorporated as a city, renamed Lexington; **1914** second county courthouse built; **1919** Lexington Public (Carnegie) Library opened; **1936** work begins to south on Middle Diversion Dam, part of Tri-County Irrigation Canal.

Lincoln   *Lancaster County*   *Eastern Nebraska, 52 mi/84 km southwest of Omaha*

1859 Lancaster County formed; **1861** Capt. W. T. Donovan files county's first homestead, begins extracting salt; **1864** town founded as county seat, originally named Lancaster; **1867** town renamed for Pres. Abraham Lincoln; Nebraska State Penitentiary built; **March 1, 1867** Nebraska admitted to Union as 37th state; town becomes state capital; **1869** state capitol completed; incorporated as a town; University of Nebraska established; **1870** Burlington & Missouri River Railroad reaches town; state hospital built, destroyed by fire 1871, rebuilt; **1871** Midland Pacific Railroad reaches town; **1873** three-year grasshopper plague begins; **1883** St. Paul Methodist Church built, destroyed by fire 1899, rebuilt 1901; **1887** incorporated as a city; Nebraska Wesleyan University established; **1888** Holy Trinity Episcopal Church built; William Jennings Bryan elected as delegate to Democratic state convention; **1889** Cotner University established, closed 1933; University Place incorporated, annexed by Lincoln 1926; **1891** Union College established; **1892** Western Normal College established, reopened 1908 as Nebraska Military Academy; College View incorporated, annexed by Lincoln 1929; **1900** state fairgrounds established; **1902** city library built; Fairview mansion built by William Jennings Bryan; **1906** federal building and post office built; **Sept. 3, 1907** anthropologist Loren C. Eiseley born (died 1977); **1909** College of Agriculture established, becomes East Campus, University of Nebraska; **1912** Lincoln monument completed; **Jan. 26, 1919** Nebraska becomes 36th state to ratify Prohibition (18th) Amendment, final state needed for passage; **1921** State Reformatory for Men opened at former military academy; **1925** First Presbyterian Church built; **1926** Westminster Presbyterian Church completed; **1930** veterans' hospital opened; Lindbergh Field airport established, becomes Lincoln Army Air Field 1942, Air Force Base 1952, Lincoln Municipal Airport 1966; **1931** First Plymouth Congregational Church completed; **1934** 14-story state capitol built, designed by Bertram Goodhue; **1935** Nebraska State Library established; **1937** state's first unicameral legislature meets, halving legislative budget; **Jan. 30, 1941** Vice Pres. Richard Cheney born; **Dec. 1, 1957** Charles Starkweather, 19, kills gas station attendant, first of 11 murders in five states; **Dec. 6, 1962** actress Janine Turner born; **1968** county courthouse built; **1973** Southeast Community College, Lincoln Campus, established.

Loup City *Sherman County* *Central Nebraska, 165 mi/266 km west of Omaha*

1873 Sherman County formed; town founded as county seat on Middle Loup River, Loup being French for Skidi (Wolf) band of Pawnee; 28 horses die in blizzard in Deadhorse Canyon; **1881** incorporated as a city; **1886** Union Pacific Railroad reaches town; **1887** Chicago, Burlington & Quincy Railroad reaches town; **1900** Jenner's Zoological and Amusement Park established, closed 1940; **1921** county courthouse built; **1966** first Polish Days held.

Macy *Thurston County* *Northeastern Nebraska, 65 mi/105 km north-northwest of Omaha, near Missouri River*

c.1800 the Omaha people, originally from Ohio River valley, forced by whites to abandon their homes, arrive after wandering through Minnesota, Missouri, and South Dakota; **Aug. 11, 1804** Lewis and Clark climb observation point on Missouri River called Blackbird Hill, burial place in 1800 of Chief Blackbird; **1832** artist George Catlin unearths skull of Blackbird, sent to Smithsonian Institution; **1854** Omaha Indian Reservation created; town founded, name Macy combination of letters from Omaha Agency; **1857** Presbyterian mission, founded 1847, moved from Bellevue.

Madison *Madison County* *Eastern Nebraska, 92 mi/148 km northwest of Omaha*

1866 town founded by Germans from Wisconsin; **1867** Madison County formed; town becomes county seat; **1873** incorporated as a city; **1879** Union Pacific Railroad reaches town; **1881** 200 mi/322 km of tree shelterbelts for wind protection and 1.5 million trees planted throughout county; **1977** county courthouse built.

McCook *Red Willow County* *Southwestern Nebraska, 268 mi/431 km west-southwest of Omaha*

1873 Red Willow County formed; Indianola becomes county seat; **1881** town founded; **1882** Burlington & Missouri River Railroad reaches town; over 100 buildings built within one month; town renamed for Gen. McDowell McCook; **1883** incorporated as a village; **1886** incorporated as a city; **1892** county seat moved to McCook; **1926** McCook Junior College established; **1927** county courthouse built; **1928** tornado strikes city, 1,000 left homeless; **May 1935** flooding damages city, c.100 killed; **1942** McCook Army Air Base established, closed 1945; **1956** oil boom begins.

Milford *Seward County* *Eastern Nebraska, 18 mi/29 km west of Lincoln*

1864 town founded; **1865** Seward County formed; town becomes county seat; **1871** county seat moved to Seward; **1874** grasshopper plague devastates area; **1879** Atchison & Nebraska Railroad reaches town; **1882** incorporated as a village; **1895** Soldiers' and Sailors' Home established, closed 1937; **1941** Nebraska State Industrial Home for Women established, destroyed by tornado Apr. 1957; **1964** incorporated as a city.

Minden *Kearney County* *Southern Nebraska, 172 mi/277 km west-southwest of Omaha*

1873 Kearney County formed; Lowell becomes county seat; **1876** town founded; **1878** county seat moved to Minden; **1883** Burlington & Missouri River Railroad reaches town; incorporated as a village; **1887** Kansas City

& Omaha Railroad built; **1888** incorporated as a city; **1889** first phase of county irrigation system built, completed 1941; **1915** county courthouse built; **July 24, 1936** highest temperature ever recorded in Nebraska reached, 118°F/ 48°C.

Morrill   *Scotts Bluff County   Western Nebraska, 430 mi/692 km west of Omaha, on North Platte River*

1851 Native American tribes gather to negotiate Horse Creek Treaty, determine reservation boundaries, rules; **1889** town founded; **1907** incorporated as a village; **1929** Horse Creek Treaty monument dedicated.

Mullen   *Hooker County   Central Nebraska, 280 mi/ 451 km west-northwest of Omaha*

1877 North and Cody Ranch founded to southwest by Frank and Luther North and William F. Cody; **1887** Grand Island & Wyoming Railroad builds line; trading post established; **1888** town founded as county seat; **1889** Hooker County formed; town becomes county seat; **1907** incorporated as a village; **1912** county courthouse built.

Naponee   *Franklin County   See* **Franklin (1930)**

Nebraska City   *Otoe County   Southeastern Nebraska, 42 mi/68 km south of Omaha, on Missouri River*

1847 Fort Kearny founded, abandoned 1848; **1853** trading post founded on Missouri River; **1855** Otoe County formed; town founded as county seat by Stephen F. Nuckolls; J. Sterling Morton and wife Caroline Joy arrive, build house overlooking river, plant abundance of shade trees, evergreens, orchards on treeless site; **1856** incorporated as a city; **1865** county courthouse built, oldest public building in use in Nebraska; **1871** Midland Pacific Railroad built; **Apr. 10, 1874** first Arbor Day declared in honor of Morton, Apr. 22 declared holiday 1885; **1875** Nebraska State School for the Blind established; **1888** Burlington & Missouri River Railroad built; **1893** Morton becomes secretary of Agriculture under President Cleveland; **1896** public library founded; **1923** Morton estate deeded to state by family; **1933** Nebraska City-Sidney Bridge built; **1993** conference center opened at Morton Memorial Orchard.

Neligh   *Antelope County   Northeastern Nebraska, 128 mi/206 km northwest of Omaha*

1872 Antelope County formed; Oakdale becomes county seat; Omaha & Northwestern Railroad built; town founded (NEE-lee); **1873** incorporated as a city; **1884** county seat moved to Neligh; **1894** county courthouse built, annex built 1966; **1911** Neligh Public Library built, new structure completed 1989.

Nelson   *Nuckolls County   Southern Nebraska, 85 mi/137 km southwest of Lincoln*

1860 Nuckolls County formed, named for legislator Stephen F. Nuckolls; **1870** town founded; **1871** county organized; Elkton becomes county seat; **1873** county seat moved to Nelson; **1883** incorporated as a city; **1880** county courthouse built.

Niobrara   *Knox County   Northeastern Nebraska, 154 mi/248 km northwest of Omaha, on Missouri River*

1856 town founded at mouth of Niobrara River by B. Y. Shelley, Omaha-Ponca term for "running water" (French: L'Eau Qui Court); Old Cabin garrison built; **1857** L'Eau Qui Court County formed; steamboat *Omaha* arrives with load of lumber for building construction; Bruns House built; **1877** county organized, renamed Knox County; town becomes county seat; **1878** incorporated as a village; **1885** 24-piece musical band organized among Santees, gives concerts around state through 1897; **1902** Chicago & Northwestern Railroad reaches town; county seat moved to town of Center; **1930** Niobrara State Park established; **1974** town relocated away from Missouri River flood plain.

Norfolk   *Madison County   Northeastern Nebraska, 97 mi/148 km northwest of Omaha*

July 12, 1859 troops under Gen. John M. Thayer charge at group of Pawnee migrating up Elkhorn River, Pawnee surrender six men accused of robbing settlers; **1866** town founded on Elkhorn River; **c.1868** Dederman log house built; **1869** Col. Charles Mathewson opens store, builds grist mill, becomes Norfolk Cereal and Flour Mill Company; **1874** area hit hard by grasshopper plague; **1879** Fremont, Elkhorn & Missouri Valley Railroad reaches town; **1881** incorporated as a village; **1887** Norfolk State Hospital founded; **1891** beet sugar refinery established, closed 1904; **1896** Norfolk Public Library built; **1909** incorporated as a city; **1945** Nebraska Christian College established; **1973** Northeast Community College established; **Sept. 26, 2002** robbers shoot, kill four bank employees, one customer, later captured, state trooper commits suicide next day, despondent over release of one suspect in routine traffic stop.

North Platte   *Lincoln County   West central Nebraska, 262 mi/422 km west of Omaha*

1860 Shorter County formed; **1866** county organized, renamed Lincoln County; town founded as county seat by Gen. G. M. Dodge of Union Pacific Railroad where North Platte and South Platte rivers form Platte River; *Pioneer Wheels* newspaper founded; **1871** incorporated as a village; **1875** incorporated as a city; **1887** "Buffalo Bill" Cody acquires Scouts Rest Ranch with partners Frank and Luther North; **July 4, 1882** Cody stages Old Glory Blowout, considered first rodeo in U.S.; **Apr. 7, 1893** prairie fire sweeps city's outskirts, 35 houses destroyed;

1912 Carnegie Library opened, new library opened 1967, old library becomes Children's Museum; **1920** Lee Bird Field airport built; **1923** work begins on county courthouse, completed until 1932; **1965** Mid-Plains Community College established.

O'Neill *Holt County* *Northern Nebraska, 168 mi/ 270 km northwest of Omaha*

1873 J. T. Prouty becomes first settler; **1874** town founded, named for Gen. John J. O'Neill; **1876** Holt County formed; Paddock becomes county seat; **1879** county seat moved to O'Neill; **1882** incorporated as a city; **1892** county treasurer Barrett Scott accused of embezzlement, flees to Mexico, returned, kidnapped while out on bail, body found with rope around neck; **Aug. 27, 1908** football player Frank Leahy born (died 1973); **1936** county courthouse built.

Ogallala *Keith County* *Western Nebraska, 305 mi/ 491 km west of Omaha, on South Platte River*

1869 Ogallala Trail established, extension of Chisholm Trail used to drive cattle from Texas to northern rail heads; **1873** Keith County formed; **1874** Union Pacific Railroad built; town founded as county seat; **1930** incorporated as a city; **1941** Lake C. W. McConaughy formed by dam on North Platte River to north; **1963** county courthouse built.

Omaha *Douglas and Sarpy counties* *Eastern Nebraska, on Missouri River*

1804 explorers Meriwether Lewis and William Clark ascend Missouri River on way to Oregon, return 1806; **1810** Hunt-Astor party passes site on way to Oregon; **1825** trading post established, just north of Platte River; **1846** Mormons stop here, name it Winter Quarters; **1854** Douglas County formed; Weber Mill built to north; **1855** town founded as capital of Nebraska Territory and as county seat; **1857** incorporated as a town; **1858** territorial capitol building completed; **1863** Union Pacific Railroad arrives; *Daily Herald* newspaper founded; **March 1, 1867** Nebraska enters Union as 37th state; Lincoln becomes state capital; **1868** Sherman Barracks built, later renamed Fort Omaha; **1869** University of Nebraska Medical Center established; Nebraska School for the Deaf built; **1870** Omaha Smelting Company founded, becomes American Smelting 1889; **1871** city's first meatpacking plant opened; **1873** Union Pacific railroad bridge built across Missouri River from Council Bluffs, replaced 1887, again 1914; **1875** incorporated as a city; **1877** Omaha Public Library founded, built 1893; **1878** Creighton University established; **1881** Missouri River flooding creates land boom on higher ground; **1884** Union Stockyards established; **1885** *World-Herald* newspaper founded; Cudahy Packing Plant founded; **1887** Diamond Gambling House established, closed by officials 1893, torn down 1936; Swift Packing Plant opened; **1889** Douglas Street Bridge completed across Missouri River, widened 1924; **1891** Presbyterian Theological Seminary

established; **1894** Omaha Zoo opened; **1895** Armour Meat Packing Plant built; Knights of Ak-Sar-Ben businessmen's organization formed, influenced by New Orleans' Mardi Gras; **1896** Fort Crook army base established to south; **1898** Trans-Mississippi and International Exposition held; **July 9, 1897** World War II Gen. Albert Wedemeyer born (died 1989); **May 10, 1899** dancer, actor Fred Astaire born (died 1987); **Dec. 18, 1900** Edward Cudahy, Jr., 16, kidnapped, $25,000 ransom paid, released Dec. 20, Pat Crowe convicted; **1904** Municipal Auditorium completed; **1908** University of Nebraska at Omaha established; **Feb. 11, 1909** prizefighter Max Baer born (died 1959); **1912** county courthouse built; **March 23, 1913** Easter tornado ravages city, 97 killed; **July 14, 1913** Gerald Rudolph Ford born, 38th U.S. President; **June 14, 1919** actress Dorothy McGuire born (died 2001); **1921** Omaha Symphony founded; **1923** College of St. Mary established; **Apr. 3, 1924** actor Marlon Brando born (died 2004); **Jan. 1, 1925** pianist Roger Williams (Louis Weertz) born; **1926** Livestock Exchange built; **1928** Omaha Community Playhouse built; Ak-Sar-Ben Field coliseum opened; **1929** Eppley Airfield established to north, named 1960; **1931** Joslyn Memorial Art Museum opened; Union Station completed; **1933** Federal Building completed; **1934** gambler Tom Dennison dies, city's political boss early 1900s; **May 19, 1935** civil rights leader Malcolm X (Malcolm Little) born, assassinated in Chicago Feb. 21, 1965; **Nov. 9, 1935** St. Louis Cardinals baseball pitcher Bob Gibson born; **1936** South Omaha Bridge built across Missouri River; **Feb. 8, 1940** actor Nick Nolte born; **Sept. 19, 1940** musician Paul Williams born; **Sept. 6, 1944** actress Swoosie Kurtz born; **1969** 30-story Woodmen Tower built; **1974** Metropolitan Community College established; **1979** Ak-Sar-Ben Aquarium opened; **1986** Lauritzen Gardens established, Omaha Botanical Center opened 2001; **1988** Kountze Planetarium opened; **1993** widespread area along Missouri River affected by flooding; **2002** 40-story First National Building built.

Ord *Valley County* *Central Nebraska, 164 mi/ 264 km west-northwest of Omaha*

1873 Valley County formed; **1874** Fort Hartsuff built to northwest; Burlington & Missouri River Railroad reaches site; town founded as county seat on North Loup River; grasshopper plague devastates region; **1876** county courthouse built; **1881** incorporated as a city; fort closed; **1939** Ord Township Public Library founded.

Osceola *Polk County* *Eastern Nebraska, 87 mi/ 140 km west of Omaha*

1868 area first settled; **1870** Polk County formed; **1871** town founded as county seat, named for Seminole chief; **1874** grasshoppers plague region; **1879** Omaha & Republican Valley Railroad built; **1881** incorporated as a city; **1916** retains Osceola retained as county seat after bitter fight with Stromsburg; **1922** county courthouse built.

Oshkosh *Garden County* *Western Nebraska, 345 mi/555 km west of Omaha, on North Platte River*

1889 town founded; post office established; **1908** Union Pacific Railroad reaches town; **1910** Garden County formed; town becomes county seat; county courthouse built; **1912** incorporated as a city.

Papillion *Sarpy County* *Eastern Nebraska, 8 mi/ 12.9 km southwest of Omaha*

1847 Omahas build village on Papillion Creek; **1849** Omahas moved to reservation to north; **1857** Sarpy County formed; Bellevue becomes county seat; **1866** Union Pacific Railroad reaches site; **1870** town founded; Peter Sarpy builds mill; **1875** county seat moved to Papillion; **1883** incorporated as a city; **1972** county courthouse built.

Pawnee City *Pawnee County* *Southeastern Nebraska, 82 mi/132 km south-southwest of Omaha*

1855 town founded on North Fork Big Nemaha River; **1857** Pawnee County formed; town becomes county seat; **1858** incorporated as a city; **1881** Burlington & Missouri River Railroad completed; **Aug. 9, 1881** 26 buildings of business district destroyed by fire; **Apr. 20, 1893** comedian Harold Lloyd born at Burchard to west (died 1971); **1911** county courthouse built; **Dec. 25, 1929** actress Irish McCalla born (died 2002).

Pender *Thurston County* *Northeastern Nebraska, 70 mi/113 km north-northwest of Omaha*

1854 Omaha Indian Reservation established; **1865** northern portion of reservation granted to Winnebagos removed from Wisconsin; **1884** Native American land opened to white settlers; Chicago, St. Paul & Minneapolis Railroad built; town founded, named for railroad director John Pender; **1886** incorporated as a village; **1889** Thurston County formed; town becomes county seat; **1895** Pender School built, converted to county courthouse 1924.

Peru *Nemaha County* *Southeastern Nebraska, 56 mi/90 km south of Omaha, on Missouri River*

1853 settlers arrive from Peru, Illinois; **1857** town founded; **1860** incorporated as a city; **1867** Nebraska State Normal School established, becomes Peru State College; **1875** Burlington & Missouri River Railroad reaches town; **Feb. 20, 1904** Herbert Brownell, Jr. born, Attorney General under President Eisenhower (died 1996); **1910s** southeastern Nebraska fruit industry developed; **Nov. 11, 1940** hard freeze ruins fruit industry.

Pierce *Pierce County* *Northeastern Nebraska, 108 mi/174 km northwest of Omaha*

1856 Pierce County formed; **1869** town founded as county seat; J. H. Brown builds first house, serves as hotel, post office, and first county courthouse; **1883** incorporated as a city; **1975** third county courthouse completed; **1993** Gilman Park Arboretum established; **Dec. 1994** Cuthills Vineyards established, Nebraska's first commercial winery.

Platte Center *Platte County* *See Columbus (1899)*

Plattsmouth *Cass County* *Eastern Nebraska, 41 mi/66 km south of Omaha, on Missouri River*

1853 Claim Club courts held to protect land against claim jumpers, those caught sent to Iowa, through 1856; **1854** town founded south of Platte River mouth; **1855** incorporated as a city; **1868** Cass County formed; town becomes county seat; **1869** Chicago, Burlington & Quincy Railroad built; **1880** railroad bridge built across Missouri River; **1892** county courthouse built; **1915** Carnegie Library built; **1931** first annual Kass Kounty King Korn Karnival held.

Ponca *Dixon County* *Northeastern Nebraska, 102 mi/164 km north-northwest of Omaha, near Missouri River*

1856 town founded by Frank West; **1858** Dixon County formed; town becomes county seat; **1871** incorporated as a village; **1874** grasshopper plague devastates area; **1876** Covington, Columbus & Black Hills Railroad reaches town; **1883** county courthouse built, addition built 1939; **1886** incorporated as a city; **1933** railroad line abandoned.

Red Cloud *Webster County* *Southern Nebraska, 163 mi/262 km southwest of Omaha*

Sept. 29, 1806 council held between Pawnees and Lt. Zebulon M. Pike, Pawnees lower Spanish flag, hoist U.S. flag; **1871** Webster County formed; town founded as county seat on Republican River, named for Oglala Chief Red Cloud; **1878** incorporated as a city; **1885** author Willa Cather brought here at age nine from Virginia; **1914** county courthouse built; **1935** flooding devastates towns along Republican River; **1955** Willa Cather Historical Center established.

Rushville *Sheridan County* *Northwestern Nebraska, 365 mi/587 km northwest of Omaha*

1885 Sheridan County formed; Chicago & Northwestern Railroad built; town founded as county seat; incorporated as a village; **May 11, 1896** historian, novelist Mari Sandoz born near Hay Springs to west (died 1966); **1904** county courthouse built; **1932** incorporated as a city.

Saint Paul *Howard County* *Central Nebraska, 136 mi/219 km west of Omaha*

1871 Howard County formed; town founded on South Loup River as county seat by surveyor James N. Paul and 31 other Danish settlers; **1872** post office established; **1873** grasshopper plague ravages area; **1874** Fort Hartsuff built; **1881** Chicago, Burlington & Quincy Railroad reaches town; **1886** incorporated as a city; **Feb. 26, 1887** baseball pitcher Grover Cleveland "Pete" Alexander born at Elba to northwest (died 1950); **1913** county courthouse built.

Santee *Knox County* *Northeastern Nebraska, 152 mi/245 km north-northwest of Omaha, on Missouri River*

1862 Santee Sioux moved here from Minnesota and Dakota Territory following Dakota Conflict (Sioux Uprising); **1864** Sioux attack settlements and stagecoach stations; **1869** Santee Indian Reservation established; **1870** Santee Normal Training School established, closed 1936; **1871** Santee Agency established; **1974** incorporated as a village.

Schuyler *Colfax County* *Eastern Nebraska, 63 mi/ 101 km west of Omaha, on Platte River*

1866 Union Pacific Railroad built; **1868** Commercial Hotel built; **1869** Colfax County formed; town founded as county seat, named for U.S. Vice Pres. Schuyler Colfax; **1870** incorporated as a village; **1887** incorporated as a city; **1922** county courthouse completed; **1968** Spencer Foods beef packing plant opened, closed 1984.

Scottsbluff *Scotts Bluff County* *Western Nebraska, 420 mi/676 km west of Omaha, on North Platte River*

1843 great migration on Oregon Trail begins, continues into late 1860s; **1864** Fort Mitchell established; **1899** town founded in irrigated farming region opposite Gering; **1900** incorporated as a city; **1910** Great Western Sugar Company beet sugar processing plant established; **Dec. 12, 1919** Scotts Bluff National Monument established to south, landmark on Mormon and Oregon trails; **1926** Western Nebraska Community College established; **1951** Platte Valley Bible College established; **June 5, 1965** Agate Fossil Beds National Monument established to north.

Seward *Seward County* *Eastern Nebraska, 68 mi/ 109 km southwest of Omaha*

1865 Seward County formed; **1867** town founded as county seat on Big Blue River, named for Secretary of State William H. Seward; **1870** incorporated as a village; **1873** Midland Pacific (Chicago, Burlington & Quincy) Railroad reaches town; **1874** incorporated as a city; **1894** Concordia Teachers' College established, now Concordia University; **May 14, 1913** tornado damages 16 city blocks, 13 killed; **1957** county courthouse completed.

Sidney *Cheyenne County* *Western Nebraska, 380 mi/612 km west of Omaha*

1867 Union Pacific Railroad built; Fort Sidney built, named for railroad solicitor Sidney Dillon; town founded; **1870** Cheyenne County formed; town becomes county seat; incorporated as a city; **1894** fort closed; **1914**

Carnegie Library built, replaced by new library 1965; **1968** county courthouse completed.

South Sioux City *Dakota County* *Northeastern Nebraska, 90 mi/145 km north-northwest of Omaha*

Aug. 1804 Lewis and Clark Expedition pauses at town site on way up Missouri River; **1858** town of Pacific City founded on Missouri River, opposite Sioux City, Iowa; **1887** incorporated as a city, renamed South Sioux City; **1889** pontoon bridge built from Sioux City; **1893** Covington, known for its saloons and rowdy characters, annexed; **1896** Combination Bridge, pivot-span, built from Sioux City; **1976** Sergeant Floyd Memorial Bridge built.

Springview *Keya Paha County* *Northern Nebraska, 232 mi/373 km northwest of Omaha*

1884 Keya Paha County formed, Sioux term for "turtle hill"; town founded at Seeping Spring; **1885** post office established; incorporated as a village; **1914** county courthouse built.

Stanton *Stanton County* *Eastern Nebraska, 92 mi/ 148 km northwest of Omaha*

1865 settlers arrive from Indiana and Wisconsin; **1867** Stanton County formed; **1869** town founded as county seat; **1870** town platted; **1879** Chicago & Northwestern Railroad reaches town; **1881** incorporated as a village; **1893** incorporated as a city; **1914** Carnegie Library built; **1976** county courthouse built.

Stapleton *Logan County* *Central Nebraska, 247 mi/398 km west of Omaha*

1885 Logan County formed; Gandy becomes county seat; **1912** Union Pacific Railroad reaches town; town founded; **1913** incorporated as a village; **1930** county seat moved to Stapleton; **1964** second county courthouse built.

Stockville *Frontier County* *Southwestern Nebraska, 247 mi/398 km west-southwest of Omaha*

1871 town founded by W. L. McCleary; **1872** Frontier County formed; town becomes county seat; incorporated as a village; **1889** county courthouse built; **1949** Harry Strunk Lake formed by Medicine Creek Dam to southeast; **1962** Hugh Butler Lake formed by Red Willow Dam on Red Willow Creek to southwest.

Taylor *Loup County* *Central Nebraska, 190 mi/ 306 km west-northwest of Omaha*

1881 town founded on North Loup River, named for pioneer Ed Taylor; **1883** Loup County formed; county seat located briefly at Kent before being moved to Taylor; **1887** Pavillion Hotel built; **1911** incorporated as a village; **1957** county courthouse built; **1986** Calamus Reservoir formed by dam to northwest on Calamus River.

Tecumseh *Johnson County* Southeastern
Nebraska, 65 mi/105 km south-southwest of Omaha

1856 Johnson County formed; town founded as county seat, named for Shawnee Chief Tecumseh; post office established; **1857** incorporated as a city; **Jan. 19, 1869** author Eugene Manlove Rhodes born (died 1934); **1872** Atchison & Nebraska Railroad reaches town; **1917** county courthouse built.

Tekamah *Burt County* Eastern Nebraska, 40 mi/
64 km north-northwest of Omaha, near Missouri River

Dec. 12, 1846 Omaha village attacked by Yankton and Santee Sioux, 80 killed; **1854** Burt County formed; town founded as county seat by Col. Benjamin R. Folsom and eight others from Utica, New York; **1855** incorporated as a city; **1876** Chicago & Northwestern Railroad reaches town; **1916** county courthouse built.

Thedford *Thomas County* Central Nebraska,
255 mi/410 km west-northwest of Omaha

1825 Thomas County formed; **1887** Grand Island & Wyoming Railroad reaches site; county organized; town founded as county seat; **1904** Kinkaid Act permits homesteaders in 37 Nebraska counties to claim up to 640 ac/259 ha; **1914** incorporated as a village; **1902** Halsey Division of Nebraska National Forest established to southeast, 100,000 pine seedlings planted 1903 creating man-made forest; **1920** county courthouse built.

Trenton *Hitchcock County* Southwestern
Nebraska, 288 mi/463 km west-southwest of Omaha

1866 Texas-Ogallala Cattle Trail established for driving cattle from Texas to northern railheads; **1873** Hitchcock County formed; **1882** Chicago, Burlington & Quincy Railroad built; town founded on railroad and on Republican River, named Trail City; **1885** town renamed Trenton; **1887** incorporated as a city; **1923** Pow-Wow Grounds established for Native American dance demonstrations, ended 1956; **1935** flash flood devastates towns on Republican River; **1953** Swanson Reservoir formed by Trenton Dam on Republican River to west; **1969** third county courthouse built.

Tryon *McPherson County* West central Nebraska,
272 mi/438 km west of Omaha

1887 McPherson County formed; **1890** county organized; town founded as county seat, originally named McPherson; **1892** post office established; town renamed Tryon; **1927** county courthouse built; **March 31, 1933** over 5,000 head of cattle lost in blizzard; **May 22, 1933** tornado strikes county in circular path, 12 killed.

Valentine *Cherry County* Northern Nebraska,
270 mi/435 km northwest of Omaha, on Niobrara River

1877 Cherry County formed; **1879** Fort Niobrara established; rivalry between ranchers and open-range cowboys

leads to violence; **1882** town founded as county seat; **1883** Sioux City & Pacific Railroad reaches town; **1884** incorporated as a city; **1901** county courthouse built; **1964** Merritt Reservoir formed on Snake Creek to southwest.

Wahoo *Saunders County* Eastern Nebraska, 37 mi/
60 km west of Omaha

1865 town founded; **1867** Saunders County formed; town becomes county seat; **1874** incorporated as a city; **1876** Union Pacific Railroad reaches town; **Apr. 18, 1880** Cincinnati Reds baseball player "Wahoo" Sam Crawford born (died 1968); **1883** Luther College (2-year) established (closed 1961); **1886** Chicago & Northwestern Railroad reaches town; **Oct. 28, 1896** musician, composer Howard Hanson born (died 1981); **Sept. 5, 1902** movie producer Daryl F. Zanuck born (died 1979); **1950** county courthouse completed.

Wayne *Wayne County* Northeastern Nebraska,
91 mi/146 km north-northwest of Omaha

1870 Wayne County formed; La Porte becomes county seat; **1881** Chicago & Northwestern Railroad built; town founded, named for Gen. "Mad" Anthony Wayne; **1882** county seat moved to Wayne; **1884** incorporated as a city; **1891** Wayne Normal School established, becomes Wayne State Teachers College 1910, later Wayne State College; **1899** county courthouse built; **1912** Carnegie Library built.

West Point *Cuming County* Eastern Nebraska,
60 mi/97 km northwest of Omaha

1855 Cuming County formed; **1857** town founded as county seat on Elkhorn River by John D. Neligh; **1858** incorporated as a city; **1870** Fremont, Elkhorn & Missouri Valley Railroad built; **1955** county courthouse built.

Wilber *Saline County* Southeastern Nebraska,
27 mi/43 km south-southwest of Lincoln

1862 first settlers arrive on Big Blue River; **1867** Saline County formed; Pleasant Hill becomes county seat; **1873** town founded; Wilber Mill built, rebuilt 1913; **1877** county seat moved to Wilber; **1879** incorporated as a city; **1928** county courthouse built; **1961** first annual Nebraska Czech Festival held; **1968** Dvoracek Memorial Library opened.

Winnebago *Thurston County* Northeastern
Nebraska, 75 mi/121 km north-northwest of Omaha

1854 Omaha Indian Reservation established; **Aug. 1862** Winnebago people, originally from Wisconsin, driven from Minnesota during Sioux uprising; **1865** Winnebago Indian Reservation created from Omaha Indian Reservation; **1907** incorporated as a village; **1910** Catholic mission and school founded; **1914** Missouri River forms Flower's Island forcing redefinition of reservation boundaries; Wilbur Flower, others build squatter shanties; **1935** hospital built.

York   *York County*   *Eastern Nebraska, 48 mi/77 km west of Lincoln*

1869 town founded; **1870** York County formed; town becomes county seat; **1874** grasshopper plague ravages area; **1875** Midland Pacific Railroad built; incorporated as a village; **1877** Burlington & Missouri River Railroad reaches town; incorporated as a city; **1880** adjoining town of New York annexed; **1890** York College established by United Brethren in Christ; **1920** State Reformatory for Women opened; **1981** county courthouse built.

Nevada

Western U.S. Capital: Carson City. Major cities: Las Vegas, Reno.

The area was acquired by the U.S. in 1848 as a result of the Mexican War. Utah Territory, which included Nevada, was created on September 9, 1850. Nevada Territory separated from Utah on March 2, 1861. Nevada entered the U.S. as the 36th state October 31, 1864.

Nevada is divided into 16 counties. There is one independent city, Carson City. In 1969, Ormsby County went out of existence when Carson City annexed the county and eliminated the county government. Municipalities are classified as cities. Many Nevada towns are unincorporated. See Introduction.

Austin *Lander County Central Nevada, 160 mi/ 257 km east of Reno*

1862 William Talcott discovers silver deposit; Lander County formed; Jacobsville becomes county seat; **1863** county seat moved to Austin; International Hotel opens; *Reese River Reveille* newspaper founded; **1864** incorporated as a city; **1868** flash flooding damages town; **1869** county courthouse built; **1874** flooding occurs again; **1880** Nevada Central Railroad built north to town of Battle Mountain, replaced by highway 1938; **1887** most silver mining ceases; **1897** Stokes Castle built, home of millionaire Anson Phelps Stokes; **1982** county seat moved to Battle Mountain.

Battle Mountain *Lander County North central Nevada, 185 mi/298 km east-northeast of Reno*

1845 trail established along Humboldt River, used by pioneers; **1862** Lander County formed; **1866** Battle Mountain Mining District established; **1867** Little Giant silver mine opened; **1868** town founded on Humboldt River to serve Battle Mountain Mining District; **1872** town boasts 32 gold mines; **late 1870s** copper mined by English company at Copper Canyon to southwest; **1880** Nevada Central Railroad completed from Austin; Betty O'Neal Mining Camp established to south around gold and silver deposits, shut down 1882 by boiler explosion, reopened; **1916** school built, used as county courthouse 1982; **1918** manager at Betty O'Neal Camp dies, mine shut down, reopened 1920; **1938** hauling activity on railroad replaced by highway transport; **1982** county seat moved from Austin.

Boulder City *Clark County Southeastern Nevada, 20 mi/32 km southeast of Las Vegas, near Colorado River*

1857 Lt. J. C. Ives ascends Colorado River in steamboat, foundering on rocks in Black Canyon, site of dam; **1859** Mormons of Moapa Valley establish boat landing above Black Canyon under direction of Anson Call; **1869** Maj. John Wesley Powell descends Grand Canyon with party of five; **1931** city built by federal government as construction camp for Boulder Dam project; Boulder City Municipal Airport established, new airport built 1992; **1933** Boulder Dam Hotel built for project managers; **May 1935** Boulder Dam completed; **1936** Boulder Dam Recreational Area established around reservoir; **1947** dam renamed Hoover Dam; recreational area renamed Lake Mead National Recreation Area; **1958** incorporated as a city, only municipality in Nevada to outlaw gambling.

Caliente *Lincoln County Southeastern Nevada, 115 mi/185 km north-northeast of Las Vegas*

1849 Manly party of emigrants breaks away from experienced leadership of Jefferson Hunt, trek into Death Valley, most of party die; **1895** gold discovered at Delamar to west, operations continue until 1909; **1901** town founded; **1905** San Pedro, Los Angeles & Salt Lake Railroad reaches town; **Jan. 1910** rainstorm washes out 110 mi/177 km of railroad track south to Las Vegas interrupting service for five months; **1943** incorporated as a city.

Candelaria *Mineral County* *Southwestern Nevada, 140 mi/225 km southeast of Reno*

1863 Mexicans discover silver ore followed by larger discovery 1864; Columbus Marsh borax field discovered to south; **1867** salt works established at Teel's Marsh to northwest; **1871** borax field discovered by William Troop; **1873** large borax plant built at Teel's Marsh; **1875** borax mining moves to Fox Lake Valley to northeast; **1876** Northern Belle silver mine begins operation; town founded.

Carlin *Elko County* *North central Nevada, 225 mi/362 km east-northeast of Reno, on Humboldt River*

1867 Central Pacific Railroad built; **1868** town founded at site of large springs; railroad shops established; **1907** Western Pacific Railroad built parallel to Central Pacific; **1925** incorporated as a town; **Aug. 12, 1939** Southern Pacific Streamliner *City of San Francisco* wrecks on dislodged track at Palisade to southwest, 24 killed; **1960s** gold mining becomes important; **1971** incorporated as a city; **1980s** gold mining expanded significantly.

Carson City *Independent city* *Western Nevada, 25 mi/40 km south of Reno*

1844 John C. Fremont becomes first white man to view Lake Tahoe, to west, names it Mountain Lake, renamed Lake Bigler 1853, popularly called Lake Tahoe from 1863; **1851** gold prospectors cross Sierra Nevada from California; trading post established on Overland Stage Route; **1857** Mormon members of population ordered back to Utah by Brigham Young; **1858** town platted by Abraham V. Z. Curry, named for scout Kit Carson; **1859** discovery of Comstock Lode brings prosperity to area; telegraph line extended from San Francisco; **1860–1861** station established on Pony Express; **1861** Nevada Territory separates from Utah; Ormsby County formed, named for Maj. William Ormsby, killed in Paiute conflict in 1860; town becomes territorial capital and county seat; Opera House built; **Oct. 31, 1864** Nevada joins Union as 36th state; town becomes state capital; **1865** *Daily Appeal* newspaper founded; **1869** U.S. Mint building completed, closed 1893, later becomes Nevada State Museum; **1871** state capitol completed, additions completed 1915; **1872** 52-mi/84-km Virginia & Truckee Railroad completed to Virginia City, tracks removed 1950; **1875** incorporated as a city; **1878** larger Carson Opera House built, destroyed by fire 1931; **1888** Post Office and Federal Building built; **May 17, 1897** Bob Fitzsimmons wins world championship heavyweight fight over Gentleman Jim Corbett; **1905** Virginia & Truckee Railroad built to Minden; governor's mansion built; **1920** Heroes Memorial Building built; Ormsby County courthouse built; **Sept. 1926** fire rages down King Canyon burning ranch homes, five killed; **1966** Carson City Public Library founded; **1969** Carson City merges with Ormsby County to form independent city, Ormsby County ceases to exist; **1971** Western Nevada Community College established.

Charleston *Elko County* *See* Wells (1916)

Elko *Elko County* *Northeastern Nevada, 250 mi/402 km east-northeast of Reno, on Humboldt River*

1841 pioneers follow Humboldt River on westward migration to California; **1846** ill-fated Donner Party passes site; **1868** construction camp of Central Pacific Railroad established; advance settlers arrive; **1869** Elko County formed; railroad completed with driving of Golden Spike at Promontory, Utah; town founded as county seat; Bullion gold mining camp established to north, ceases operation 1884, revived 1905 and 1916; **1873** University of Nevada established, moved to Reno 1885; **1879** opera hall built; **1880–1891** succession of blizzards ruins cattle industry; **1911** county courthouse completed; **1917** town incorporated; **1919** Elko Regional Airport established; **1967** Northern Nevada Community College (2-year) established, becomes Great Basin College (4-year) 1999.

Ely *White Pine County* *Eastern Nevada, 285 mi/459 km east of Reno*

1869 White Pine County formed; large blast furnace built to serve Robinson Mining District; **1870** town founded as gold mining camp (pronounced EE-lee); **1878** Lehman Caves discovered by local citizen Abe Lincoln near Wheeler Peak to southeast; **1887** county seat moved from Hamilton; **1888** incorporated as a village; county courthouse completed; **1891** incorporated as a city; **1900** prospectors Dave Bartley and Edwin Gray discover copper at Ruth claim to west; **1902** Mark Requa buys Ruth copper mine site, organizes White Pine Copper Company; **1904** copper company merger forms Nevada Consolidated; **1906** Nevada Northern Railroad completed for hauling copper ore; **1907** copper smelter begins operating; **1912** eight large steam shovels in operation at Ruth copper mine; **March 6, 1912** Thelma Catherine Patricia Ryan (Pat) Nixon, wife of President Nixon, born (married 1940; died June 22, 1993); **Jan. 24, 1922** Lehman Caves National Monument established to southeast; **1926** profits of Nevada Copper reach $47 million; **Oct. 27, 1986** Great Basin National Park created to southeast, absorbs Lehman Caves National Monument.

Eureka *Eureka County* *Central Nevada, 220 mi/354 km east of Reno*

Sept. 1864 rich silver deposit discovered; town founded; **1869** first smelter built; **1873** Eureka County formed; town becomes county seat; **1875** Central Pacific Railroad completed from Palisade; **Apr. 19, 1879** fire sweeps town, only *Sentinel* newspaper and Paxton Bank spared; **Aug. 18, 1879** in Charcoal War, militia quells dispute between Charcoal Burners' Association and smelter, miners attack charcoal ranch killing five, wounding six; **1880** county courthouse completed; opera house built; **1883** silver production declines; **1891** last smelter closed; **1905** first of periodic revivals in mining activity; **1910** early spring thaw cause 30 mi/48 km of railroad track to wash out.

Fallon   *Churchill County*   *West central Nevada, 60 mi/97 km east of Reno*

1861 Churchill County formed; Buckland's Station becomes county seat; **1868** county seat moved to Stillwater; **1896** post office established on Mike Fallon's ranch; **1904** county seat moved to Fallon; **1903** Truckee-Carson Irrigation Project begun by Federal government, completed 1908; county courthouse built; **1905** town becomes supply point for silver rush towns of Fairview and Wonder; **1908** town incorporated; **1942** Fallon Naval Air Station established.

Genoa   *Douglas County*   *Western Nevada, 35 mi/ 56 km south of Reno, near Lake Tahoe*

1850 first structure built by Hampden S. Beattie, oldest settlement in Nevada, named Mormon Station; **1851** trading post founded by John Reese and Stephen A. Kinsey; **1854** Carson County, Utah Territory, formed; town becomes county seat; **1855** town renamed; **1858** *Territorial Enterprise* newspaper founded, moved to Carson City 1859, moved to Virginia City later same year; **1861** Douglas County formed, town remains county seat; Carson (Ormsby) County seat moved to Carson City; **1916** Douglas County seat moved to Minden.

Goldfield   *Esmeralda County*   *Southwestern Nevada, 170 mi/274 km northwest of Las Vegas*

1861 Esmeralda County formed; Aurora becomes county seat; **1882** county seat moved to Hawthorne; **1902** gold discovered; **1903** gold boom leads to development of city of 20,000; **1904** Tonopah & Goldfield Railroad reaches town; **1906** boxing match between Gans and Nelson staged by Tex Rickard draws national attention; **1907** county seat moved to Goldfield; miners' strike requires call-out of Federal troops; **1908** county courthouse completed; **1910** gold production reaches peak; **1919** gold mining dwindles; **1923** fire destroys 52 blocks in lower part of city.

Hamilton   *White Pine County*   *East central Nevada, 250 mi/402 km east of Reno*

1865 A. J. Leathers discovers silver at White Pine Mountain, forms Monte Christo Mining Company; **1867** mill begins operation; **1868** local Native American presents large chunk of silver to Leathers, beginning great silver rush; town founded, named for promoter W. H. Hamilton; **1869** White Pine County formed; town becomes county seat; **1873** silver production declines; fire damages mine site; **1885** second fire ends operation; **1887** county seat moved to Ely.

Hawthorne   *Mineral County*   *Western Nevada, 100 mi/161 km southeast of Reno*

Nov. 1845 John Fremont camps on eastern shore of Walker Lake to north, named for guide Joseph Walker; **1861** Esmeralda County formed; Aurora becomes county seat to southwest; **1864** gold reserve discovered at Aurora;

1881 Carson & Colorado Railroad built; town founded, named for Judge W. A. Hawthorne; **1883** county seat moved to Hawthorne; **1907** county seat moved to Goldfield; **1911** Mineral County formed from Esmeralda County; town becomes county seat; **1941** U.S. Naval Ammunition Depot established; **1944** town mushrooms into tent city of 14,000; **1970** county courthouse built; **1980** depot becomes privately owned Hawthorne Ammunition Plant.

Henderson   *Clark County*   *Southeastern Nevada, 10 mi/16 km southeast of Las Vegas*

1942 Basic Magnesium Plant established by U.S. War Department with 14,000 employees; town founded; **1943** Henderson Public Library founded; **1947** plant closed; town offered for sale; **1948** plant acquired by state as industrial site, conveyed to private interests; **1953** incorporated as a city; **1986** first Shakespeare in the Park festival held.

Jackpot   *Elko County*   *Northeastern Nevada, 345 mi/555 km northeast of Reno*

1859 first mining camps established along Salmon Falls Creek; **1954** town founded at remote point on Idaho state line; **1959** first gaming tables make their debut at this remote outpost on Idaho state line; town officially named; **1980s** town develops into major gambling port-of-entry.

Las Vegas   *Clark County*   *Southeastern Nevada, near Colorado River*

1776 Old Spanish Trail established by Escalante party; **1829** traders traveling on trail stop at springs of Las Vegas Valley; **1844** John C. Fremont camps here during his Colorado River expedition; **1847** Jefferson Hunt, a Mormon returning to Utah following trip to California for supplies, speaks favorably of Las Vegas site; **1855** 30 Mormon men from Salt Lake City, led by William Bringhurst, establish fort; **1856** post office and mission established; lead mining begins to southwest; **1857** "lead" deposit turns out to be silver-laced galena, mining abandoned; Mormons abandon mission; **1861** Federal troops occupy Mormon fort to protect route to California during Civil War; **1878** O. D. Gass acquires land for ranch; **1881** Gass Ranch acquired by Archibald Stewart; **1905** San Pedro, Los Angeles & Salt Lake Railroad built from Salt Lake City; town founded; **1906** Las Vegas & Tonopah Railroad completed from California; **1909** Clark County formed; town becomes county seat; **Jan. 10, 1910** flash flooding washes out 110 mi/177 km of railroad north to Caliente interrupting service for five months; **1911** incorporated as a city; **Aug. 1, 1921** tennis player Jack Kramer born; **1925** need for water exceeds supply from springs, artesian well dug; **1931** construction begins on Boulder (Hoover) Dam on Colorado River to east, completed 1937; **March 19, 1931** gambling legalized in Nevada; development of famous Las Vegas Strip begins in unincorporated area south of Sahara Avenue; **Aug. 15, 1935** actress Abby Dalton born; **1940** Union Pacific

Railroad Station completed; **1941** Nellis Army Air Base established to northeast, becomes Air Force Base after World War II; **1948** Clark County Public Airport established, becomes McCarran International Airport; **1952** Sahara Club opened; Sands Hotel opened; **1955** Dunes Hotel opened, closed 1993, imploded Nov. 27, 1993; Riviera Club opened; **1957** University of Nevada at Las Vegas established; **Apr. 21, 1958** United DC-7 airline collides with Air Force jet, killing 49; **Nov. 15, 1964** Bonanza Airlines twin-prop plane crashes, all 29 on board killed; **Jan. 7, 1967** suicide at motel sets off bomb, 6 killed, 12 injured; **1968** Circus Circus casino opened; **Jan. 20, 1972** plane hijacked on takeoff, man parachutes into Colorado wheat field; **1974** county courthouse completed; **1979** Liberace Museum founded; **Nov. 21, 1980** fire at MGM Grand Hotel, 84 killed, over 500 injured; **Feb. 10, 1981** fire at Las Vegas Hilton Hotel, eight killed; **1982** Nevada State Museum and Historical Society opened, new facility at Las Vegas Springs Preserve to open 2005; **1990** Excalibur casino opened; **1993** new MGM Grand casino opened, monorail added 1995; **1996** Orleans casino opened; Stratosphere Tower built; **1997** 48-story New York New York casino opened; **June 26, 1997** boxer Mike Tyson bites off piece of Evander Holyfield's right ear in third round, $30 million purse denied, fined $3 million; **1999** 34-story Paris Las Vegas casino opened; 43-story Mandalay Resort and Casino built; 35-story Venetian Resort and Casino built.

Laughlin *Clark County* *Southeastern Nevada, 80 mi/129 km south-southeast of Las Vegas, on Colorado River*

1949 Davis Dam completed on Colorado River; **1964** site below dam acquired by Don Laughlin; town founded; **1968** town boasts three casinos; **1980s** town experiences casino boom; **1987** Laughlin Bridge built to Bullhead City, Arizona; **June 26, 1990** highest temperature ever recorded in Nevada reached, 125°F/52°C.

Lovelock *Pershing County* *Northwestern Nevada, 90 mi/149 km northeast of Reno, on Humboldt River*

1840s pioneers follow Humboldt River to California; **1861** George Lovelock establishes stagecoach station; town founded; **1868** Central Pacific Railroad reaches town; **1911** guano mine established at Lovelock Cave; **1912** researchers retrieve artifacts from 2,000 years of habitation in Lovelock Cave, ending c.1300 AD; **1919** Pershing County formed; incorporated as a city, becomes county seat; **1921** county courthouse completed; **1936** Rye Patch Dam built on Humboldt River to north, ensures water supply from river which disappears into Carson Sink to south.

Mesquite *Clark County* *Southeastern Nevada, 80 mi/129 km northeast of Las Vegas, on Virgin River*

1880 area settled by Mormons; **1882** heavy flooding destroys irrigation canals; site abandoned; **1887** Leavitt family returns, repairs canals; **1895** resettled by Mormons;

1970s town develops as entry-point gambling resort at Arizona state line; **1980s** Peppermill Resort built by Si Redd, later renamed Oasis Resort.

Minden *Douglas County* *Western Nevada, 40 mi/64 km south of Reno*

1857 German immigrant Henry Dangberg settles in Carson Valley to take up ranching, ignores silver mining activity of area, adopts Mormon irrigation methods; **1861** Douglas County formed; **1864** Dangberg grows first alfalfa in state, brought from Chile; **1905** Dangberg founds town; Virginia & Truckee Railroad reaches town from Carson City; **1916** county seat moved from Genoa; county courthouse completed; **1942** Minden-Tahoe Airport established.

Moapa *Clark County* *Southeastern Nevada, 50 mi/80 km northeast of Las Vegas*

1860s Moapa Valley settled by Mormons, build extensive irrigation projects; **1859** boat landing established above Black Canyon on Colorado River under leader Anson Call; **1867** Federal survey assigns strip of Arizona to Nevada; **1871** Nevada assesses retroactive taxes against valley residents to be paid in gold; Mormons ordered back to Utah by Brigham Young; **1873** Mormon exodus and drop in silver prices hurts economy of southern Nevada.

Palisade *Eureka County* See **Carlin (1939)**

Pioche *Lincoln County* *Southeastern Nevada, 140 mi/225 km north-northeast of Las Vegas*

1863 William Hamblin arrives in Pioche (pee-oache) district; **1864** Hamblin discovers silver and gold; Meadow Valley Mining District organized; **1866** Lincoln County formed; Crystal Springs becomes county seat; **1870** post office established; **1871** county seat moved to Pioche; **1872** construction begins on county courthouse, completed 1876; **1937** courthouse paid off at cost of over $800,000, nicknamed Million Dollar Courthouse.

Reno *Washoe County* *Western Nevada, 375 mi/604 km northwest of Las Vegas, on Truckee River*

1859 Charles W. Fuller becomes first settler; **1861** Fuller builds toll bridge across Truckee River; **1861** Washoe County formed; **1863** Myron C. Lake establishes trading post, names site Lake's Crossing; **1868** town founded on land auctioned by Central Pacific Railroad, renamed for Union Gen. Jesse Reno; **1869** Lake builds hotel; **1870** *Nevada State Journal* newspaper founded; **1871** county seat moved from Washoe City; **1876** *Gazette* newspaper founded; **1879** incorporated as a town; **1885** University of Nevada, established 1873, moved from Elko; **1889** Newlands Residence built by Sen. Francis Newlands; **1900** Newlands Reclamation Project begun to divert water from Truckee River to dry lands east of Reno, named for Sen. Newlands; **1903** incorporated as a city; **1907** St. Thomas Aquinas Cathedral dedicated; **1910** boxing match gives Jack Johnson victory over the Great Jeffries; **1927** California Building built for Transcontinental Highway Exposition; **1928** Hubbard Field airport established, becomes new Reno Cannon International Airport 1960, renamed Reno-Tahoe International 1998; **1931** gambling legalized in Nevada; liberalized divorce laws attract divorce-seekers; **1934** post office and federal building completed; **1947** Mapes Hotel built, city's first high-rise casino hotel; **1959** Desert Research Institute established to north; **1971** Truckee Meadows Community College established; **Jan. 21, 1985** Galaxy Airlines Lockheed Electra crashes after takeoff, 68 of 71 on board killed; **1989** County Administration Complex completed; **1991** Reno Livestock Events Center established; **Nov. 1994** National Bowling Stadium completed; **2000** Latter-day Saints Temple dedicated, replaces 1940s structure.

Ruby Valley *Elko County* *Northeastern Nevada, 260 mi/418 km east-northeast of Reno*

1859 trading post established by old scout "Uncle Billy Rogers"; **1862** Fort Ruby established along Overland Stage route; **1863** Goshute War, involving united Goshute and Paiute people against white rivals, draws military troops into skirmishes, many soldiers and Native Americans killed; **1865** Overland Stage Line Company establishes Overland Ranch in Ruby Valley to circumvent paying high prices for grain and farm produce for its operations.

Ruth *White Pine County* *See* **Ely**

San Jacinto *Elko County* *See* **Wells (1937)**

Searchlight *Clark County* *Southeastern Nevada, 50 mi/80 km south of Las Vegas*

1897 gold discovered in area; **1898** camp established, name apparently taken from brand of matches used to start initial camp fire, name source of dispute; Duplex Mine begins gold production; **1906** gold production reaches peak with over $590,000 in gold produced; town boasts nine saloons; **1920** gold production dwindles.

Silver Peak *Esmeralda County* *Southwestern Nevada, 180 mi/290 km southeast of Reno*

1864 silver discovered; three-stamp mill built; **1867** 30-stamp silver mill built; **1870** mining camp abandoned; **1906** Pittsburgh Silver Peak Gold Mining Company purchases properties, builds branch of Tonopah & Goldfield Railroad, also 100-stamp mill; **1915** operations cease; **1926** mining revival begins; **1948** fire destroys part of town.

Silver Springs *Lyon County* *Western Nevada, 35 mi/56 km east-southeast of Reno*

spring 1860 Native Americans raid Williams Station trading post, three defenders shot to death, two burned to death; **July 1860** Fort Churchill established to south on Overland Trail; **1869** fort abandoned; **1902** Newlands Project converts desert into farmland by diverting waters from Truckee River; **1915** Lahontan Reservoir completed to east on Carson River; **1957** Fort Churchill State Park established.

Sparks *Washoe County* *Western Nevada, 2 mi/3.2 km east of Reno, on Truckee River*

1903 town founded by Southern Pacific Railroad, named for Gov. John Sparks; large rail switching yard established; **Feb. 28, 1905** incorporated as a town; **March 15, 1905** incorporated as a city.

Tonopah *Nye County* *Southwestern Nevada, 185 mi/298 km southeast of Reno*

1864 Nye County formed; **1899** large gold deposit discovered at Klondyke to south; **1900** town founded, **1902** miners develop "Tonopah sickness" from high silicate content of mines; **1903** opera house built; **1904** Tonopah & Goldfield Railroad reaches town; **1905** county seat moved from Belmont; county courthouse built; **1942** Tonopah Army Air Field established, becomes Tonopah Airport.

Unionville *Pershing County* *Northwestern Nevada, 120 mi/193 km northeast of Reno*

1861 Humboldt County formed; town founded as county seat, briefly named Dixie, renamed Unionville with outbreak of Civil War; **1863** local stagecoach service begins within two-mile-long town; Samuel Clemens tries his luck at gold mining here for a few weeks, decides instead to seek his fortune with the Virginia City *Enterprise* under pen name Mark Twain; **c.1870** silver production begins in Buena Vista Valley, ceases by 1880; **1871** Methodists build town's first church; **1873** county seat moved to Winnemucca; **1919** Pershing County formed from Humboldt county.

Virginia City *Storey County* *Western Nevada, 15 mi/24 km south-southeast of Reno*

May 15, 1850 sizable gold strike made in Gold Canyon; **1851** prospectors begin mining canyon; silver ore discovered by Brazilian prospector; **1855** Chinese laborers begin placer gold mining, site called Johntown; **1859** Peter O'Riley and Patrick McLaughlin discover deposit in Six Mile Canyon, fail to identify "black stuff" found with the gold; Henry Comstock takes up claim, assay reveals "black stuff" is silver mixed with gold, named Comstock Lode; *Territorial Enterprise* newspaper moves from Genoa; **Nov. 1859** James Fennimore, Six Mile Canyon claim worker, spills liquor on ground, christens site Virginia for his home state, "City" added later; **1860** George Hearst arrives to amass his personal fortune; Comstock sells interests for meager $11,000, claim yields $80 million; St. Mary's in the Mountains Church built, first Catholic church in Nevada; **1861** Storey County formed; town becomes county seat; **1862** incorporated as a city; **1863** Samuel Clemens gives up mining at Unionville, takes first writing assignment for *Territorial Enterprise* under pen name Mark Twain; **1865** county courthouse built; **Apr. 1869** mine shaft fire, 49 killed; **1872** Virginia & Truckee Railroad completed from Carson City; town damaged by fire; **1873** Big Bonanza becomes one of largest gold/silver ore strikes; **1878** dramatic drop in silver production leads to virtual halt by 1886.

Wells *Elko County* *Northeastern Nevada, 300 mi/ 482 km east-northeast of Reno*

1869 Central Pacific Railroad built; town established on railroad; named for Humboldt Wells, source of Humboldt River; **1889** harsh winter leaves hundreds of cattle dead; **Dec. 4, 1916** last stagecoach hold-up in Nevada takes place near Charleston to north, lone bandit stops stage from Jarbridge, wounds driver, takes loot; **1927** incorporated as a town; **Jan. 8, 1937** lowest temperature ever recorded in Nevada reached at San Jacinto to north, −50°F/−46°C.

Winnemucca *Humboldt County* *North central Nevada, 160 mi/257 km northeast of Reno*

1850 French Ford trading post established at trail crossing of Humboldt River; **1861** Humboldt County formed; **1862** Joseph Ginacca builds canal connecting site with Golconda to east and Mill City to southwest, completed 1865, fails to supply ditch with adequate water; **1863** Winnemucca Hotel opens; **1865** bridge built; post renamed French Bridge; **1868** Central Pacific Railroad reaches town; town renamed for Paiute Chief Winnemucca; **1872** Ginacca builds stamping mill next to canal; **1873** after hard-fought campaign, county seat moved from Unionville; **1874** teamsters hold successful strike for 5-cent increase in hauling fees to Silver City, Idaho; **Sept. 19, 1900** Butch Cassidy's Wild Bunch gang take $32,640 in bank hold-up, Cassidy not among them; **1902** josshouse built, temple used by Chinese workers; **1917** incorporated as a city; **1921** county courthouse completed; **1924** St. Paul's Catholic Church built.

Yerington *Lyon County* *Western Nevada, 55 mi/ 89 km southeast of Reno*

1845 John C. Fremont surveys Wilson Canyon of West Walker River to southwest; **1860** town settled during Aurora gold rush, originally named Pizen Switch; **1861** Lyon County formed; Dayton becomes county seat; town renamed Greenfield; **1879** effort taken to rename town for Henry M. Yerington, official of Carson & Colorado Railroad, until railroad bypasses town to north; **1894** town renamed for son James A. Yerington, instrumental in promoting state of Nevada; **1907** town incorporated; **1911** county seat moved to Yerington; county courthouse built; **1920s** copper mining becomes active, dwindles by 1930s; short line Nevada Copper Belt Railroad built from Wabuska to north.

New Hampshire

Northeastern U.S. One of the six New England states. Capital: Concord. Major cities: Manchester, Portsmouth.

New Hampshire was one of the 13 colonies which adopted the U.S. Declaration of Independence July 4, 1776. It became the 9th state to ratify the U.S. Constitution June 21, 1788.

New Hampshire is divided into 10 counties which have weak governments. The counties are divided into townships, called towns, which have very strong governments. Within the towns are villages which have no government of their own. Municipalities are classified as cities, which are formed from one or more former towns. See Introduction.

Alstead *Cheshire County* *Southwestern New Hampshire, 47 mi/76 km west-northwest of Manchester*

1752 land grant made for town, originally named Newton; first settlers arrive on Cold River; **1763** town incorporated, renamed Alstead; **1781** town's allegiance shifts to Vermont, conducts business under authority of Vermont, reverts to New Hampshire 1782; **1793** paper founded by Ephraim and Elisha Kingsbury; **1799** Bill Blake opens second paper mill, moves it to Bellows Falls, Vermont, 1802; **1910** Shedd-Porter Memorial built, building donated by John Graves Shedd, Alstead native associated with Marshall Field's department store, Chicago's Shedd Aquarium named for him.

Amherst *Hillsborough County* *Southern New Hampshire, 13 mi/21 km south-southwest of Manchester*

1733 town settled, named Narragansett No. 3; **1751** first Meeting House completed; **1760** town incorporated, named for Lord Jeffrey Amherst, General in French and Indian War; **1769** Hillsborough County formed; town becomes county seat; **1785** Robert Means House built, site of 1834 wedding of Pres. Franklin Pierce and Jane Means Appleton, granddaughter of Robert Means; **July 4, 1804** Cong. Charles Atherton born (died 1853); **Feb. 3, 1811** New York newspaper publisher Horace Greeley born (died 1872); **1825** third county courthouse built, later used as town hall; **1859** Amherst Library organized, built 1892; **1864** county seat moved to Nashua.

Ashland *Grafton County* *Central New Hampshire, 35 mi/56 km north of Concord*

c.1770 first grist mills and sawmills begin operation; **1818** First Universalist Society of Ashland established, dis-

banded 1937; **1868** town incorporated, separated from Holderness; **Aug. 28, 1878** pathologist George Hoyt Whipple born, shared Nobel Prize 1934 (died 1976).

Bath *Grafton County* *Northwestern New Hampshire, 70 mi/113 km north-northwest of Concord*

1761 first land grant made to Andrew Gardner, others; **1765** John Herriman becomes first settler; **1769** town incorporated as Bath; **1804** old brick store built across from town common, later used as post office; **1810** Moses P. Payson Mansion built; **1832** Bath Covered Bridge built, 392 ft/199 m long; **1836** William L. Hutchins House built.

Bedford *Hillsborough County* *Southern New Hampshire, 4 mi/6.4 km south-southwest of Manchester*

1733 land for town granted to veterans of Narragansett War; **1737** town first settled; **1750** town incorporated; **Dec. 10, 1813** Zachariah Chandler born, congressman from Michigan, secretary of interior under President Grant (died 1870); **1832** Presbyterian Church built; **Oct. 9, 1837** educator Francis Wayland Parker born (died 1902).

Berlin *Coos County* *Northern New Hampshire, 90 mi/145 km north-northeast of Concord*

Dec. 31, 1771 land granted to Sir William Mayne, others, for town, named Maynesborough; **1802** two surveyors sent by Massachusetts proprietors to survey town; **1821** first settlers arrive; **1825** first logging camp established; **1829** town incorporated, renamed Berlin (BER-lin); **1837** Berlin Ski Jump built; **1852** Brown Paper Company established; **1859** Jasper Cave discovered by William Sanborn; **1894** St. Kieran's Catholic Church built; **1897**

incorporated as a city; **1906** district courthouse built; **1914** city hall completed; **1926** Berlin Symphony Orchestra established; **1966** New Hampshire Technical Community College, Berlin-Laconia Campus, (2-year) established.

Bethlehem *Grafton County* *Northwestern New Hampshire, 76 mi/122 km north of Concord*

1774 petition for incorporation made under name of Lloyd Hills, named for Byfield Lloyd, friend of Gov. Benning Wentworth, settlers fail to materialize; **1787** first settlers arrive, often calling village Lord's Hill; **Dec. 25, 1799** town incorporated on Christmas Day, named Bethlehem; **1857** Sinclair Hotel built, closed 1978; **1863** Henry Howard of Rhode Island involved in rollover of coach while descending Mount Agassiz, taken by beauty of area during recuperation, establishes American Hay Fever Association retreat; **1870** Maplewood Hotel built, closed 1963; **1871** Isaac Cruft of Boston builds hotel; **1887** first annual Coaching Parade held; **1908** Milburn Inn built; **1914** Colonial Theater built; **1929** Christ the King Roman Catholic Church built; **1931** Ivie Memorial Episcopalian Church built; **1936** St. Mary's of the Mountains Episcopal school for girls founded.

Boscawen *Merrimack County* *Central New Hampshire, 9 mi/14.5 km north-northwest of Concord*

1733 land grant made by Massachusetts Bay Colony to John Coffin, others; **1734** town settled on Merrimack River; **1739** fort and first meeting house (church) built; **1760** town incorporated, named for British commander at siege of Louisbourg, Nova Scotia; **July 24, 1798** John Adams Dix born, senator from New York (died 1879); **Apr. 1805** Daniel Webster opens law office; **Oct. 1, 1806** William Pitt Fessenden born, senator from Maine (died 1869).

Bow *Merrimack County* *South central New Hampshire, 5 mi/8 km south of Concord*

May 1727 town granted on Merrimack River, original settlers include Timothy Dix; **1759** town incorporated; **July 16, 1821** Mary Baker Eddy born, founder of Christian Science Church, resides here until 1836 (died 1910); **1835** Bow Bog Meeting House built; **1842** railroad reaches town; **1866** Cornish-Windsor Covered Bridge built.

Campton *Grafton County* *Central New Hampshire, 47 mi/76 km north of Concord, on Pemigewasset River*

1761 land granted to Capt. Jarvis Spencer; **1765** town settled; **1767** town incorporated, possibly named for Spencer Compton, Earl of Wilmington (spelling variation); **1869** Blair Covered Bridge built across Pemigewasset River; **1877** Bump Covered Bridge built across Beebe River; **1874** Turkey Jim Covered Bridge built; **Sept. 15, 1907** accident on Boston & Maine Railroad at Campton Hollow, 24 killed.

Candia *Rockingham County* *Southeastern New Hampshire, 12 mi/19 km northeast of Manchester*

1743 town settled by David McCluer, others, originally named Charmingfare; **1763** town incorporated as Candia; **Jan. 19, 1858** poet Sam Walter Foss born (died 1911), birthplace renamed for his popular poem "House on the Side of the Road"; **1885** Fitts Museum founded, displays wooden miniatures of historical sites.

Canterbury *Merrimack County* *Central New Hampshire, 10 mi/16 km north of Concord*

1727 land grant made for town near Merrimack River; **1741** Town of Canterbury incorporated; **1792** Shaker Village established by Elder Clough; Shaker Meeting House built; **Nov. 17, 1809** abolitionist Stephen Symonds Foster born (died 1881); **1839** Worsted Church built.

Claremont *Sullivan County* *Southwestern New Hampshire, 42 mi/68 km west-northwest of Concord*

1762 Moses Spafford and David Lynde become first settlers; **1764** town incorporated; **1767** Col. Benjamin Tyler builds dam on Sugar River, builds grist mill and sawmill at dam; **1770** John Tyler Place built, town's oldest house; **1773** Union Episcopal Church built; **1780** Swasey House built by John Swasey; **1800** Colonel Tyler builds flax mill; old Tremont Hotel built by Josiah Stevens, destroyed by fire 1879; **1810** Dexter House built; paper making begins at West Claremont; **1813** Asa Meacham builds woolen mill; **1825** St. Mary's Catholic Church completed; **1831** Sugar River Manufacturing Company founded, maker of cotton and woolen goods, becomes Monadnock Mill 1846; **March 3, 1840** author Constance Fenimore Woolson born (died 1894); **1846** Stevens House built by Paran Stevens; **1891** Diamond Prospecting Company of Chicago establishes diamond drill factory; **1896** town hall built; **1903** Fiske Free Library built, founded 1873; **1921** New Hampshire Tuberculosis Association founded; **1948** incorporated as a city.

Concord *Merrimack County* *South central New Hampshire, 15 mi/24 km north of Manchester*

1659 land grant made on Merrimack River to Richard Waldron by Massachusetts Bay Colony for Plantation of Penny Cook (Penacook); trading post established; **1725** grant reissued to Ebenezer Eastman, others; **1727** New Hampshire makes conflicting grant for town of Bow, dispute continues until 1762; **1733** town incorporated as Rumford by Massachusetts; **1734** Timothy Walker House built; **Aug. 11, 1746** in Bradley Massacre, Samuel and Jonathan Bradley, three others killed by Native Americans; **1765** town reincorporated as Concord by New Hampshire; **June 21, 1788** New Hampshire becomes ninth of original 13 states to join Union; **1803** Middlesex Canal completed; **1808** state capital moved from Portsmouth; **1812** first state prison built; **1813** Lewis Downing begins manufacture of wagons, hires Stephen Abbot 1826, becomes Abbot-Downing Company; **1819**

statehouse completed; **1842** Boston & Maine Railroad reaches town; **1823** Merrimack County formed; town becomes county seat; New Hampshire Historical Society founded; **Dec. 28, 1835** Sen. William Eaton Chandler born (died 1917); **1852** Eagle Hotel built after Eagle Coffee House is destroyed by fire, hotel rebuilt 1890, closed 1960s; **1853** incorporated as a city; **1855** Concord Public Library opened, new library opened 1888, again 1939; **1856** St. Paul's School founded; **1857** county courthouse built, addition built 1989; **1880** new state prison built; Women's Prison founded, closed 1941; **Aug. 7, 1890** American communist leader Elizabeth Gurley Flynn born (died 1964); **1895** state library built, oldest state library in U.S.; **1905** First Church of Christ Scientists built; **1909** Rumford Press founded, printed *Reader's Digest*, other magazines for many years; **1927** city damaged by flooding; Pleasant View Home for aged opened by Christian Scientists; **1936** one-third of city inundated by flooding Merrimack; **1964** New Hampshire Technical Institute (2-year college) established; **1992** Museum of New Hampshire opened by New Hampshire Historical Society.

Conway *Carroll County* *Eastern New Hampshire, 59 mi/95 km north-northeast of Concord*

1764 town first settled, originally named Pigwackett; **1765** town incorporated as Conway; **1773** grist mills and sawmills built around Walker's Pond at Center Conway village; **1795** iron works begun at Coffin farm, cease operations 1838; **1851** Bartlett Covered Bridge built over Saco River to north; **1870** Swift River Covered Bridge built; **1886** quarrying of red granite begins at Redstone Ledge; **1936** flooding threatens historical sites on Saco River.

Cornish *Sullivan County* *Western New Hampshire, 44 mi/71 km west-northwest of Concord*

1763 land grant patented; town incorporated; **c.1769** Wellman House built, oldest house in Cornish; **June 5, 1775** physician Lyman Spalding born (died 1821); **Dec. 14, 1775** Episcopalian bishop Philander Chase born, president of Dartmouth College (died 1852); **1796** first bridge built across Connecticut River; **1808** Trinity Episcopal Church built; **Jan. 13, 1808** U.S. Supreme Court Chief Justice Salmon P. Chase born (died 1873); **1825** Godfrey Cooke House built; **1866** floods destroy Connecticut River bridge, replaced by covered bridge, oldest covered bridge in New Hampshire; **1877** Blow-Me-Down Covered Bridge built; **1883** Beaman House built; **1885** Augustus Saint-Gaudens settles here, born in France March 1, 1848, becomes one of America's foremost sculptors, died here 1907; **1891** Blow-Me-Down Grist Mill built; **1898** Harlakenden House built by New Hampshire's own Winston Churchill, state legislator; **1949** first annual Cornish Fair held; **May 30, 1977** Saint-Gaudens National Historic Site established.

Deerfield *Rockingham County* *Southeastern New Hampshire, 16 mi/26 km east of Concord*

1756 town first settled; **1765** town incorporated, named for plentiful deer stock in area; **Nov. 5, 1818** Union Civil War Gen. Benjamin F. Butler born (died 1897); **1876** first Deerfield Fair held; **1994** first annual New Hampshire Shakespearean Festival held, becomes New England Shakespearean Festival 2002.

Derry *Rockingham County* *Southern New Hampshire, 10 mi/16 km south-southeast of Manchester*

1719 area first settled by Sottish and Irish immigrants; **1748** town becomes known for its linen industry; **1804** Londonderry Turnpike built through East Derry, making that part of town its business center; **1814** Pinkerton Academy founded; **1823** Adams Female Academy founded at East Derry; **1827** town incorporated, separates from Londonderry; **1849** Manchester & Lawrence Railroad reaches town; **1993** Derry Arts Council founded.

Dixville *Coos County* *Northern New Hampshire, 118 mi/190 km north of Concord*

1805 land granted to Col. Timothy Dix; **1812** John Whittemore, wife Betsey become town's only settlers until 1865; **Dec. 1815** Betsey Whittemore dies, husband keeps body frozen until spring for burial, moves to Colebrook, dies 1846, buried in Dixville with wife; **1865** new settlers arrive; **1866** Dix House hotel built, later becomes The Balsams resort; **1964** Neil Tillotson begins tradition of being first person to cast a ballot in statewide and nationwide elections, dies 2001 at age 101; **1968** tradition begins of town being first to cast ballots just after midnight in presidential primary and every state and national election thereafter, considered a bellwether district.

Dover *Strafford County* *Southeastern New Hampshire, 33 mi/53 km northeast of Manchester*

1603 Martin Pring perhaps first white visitor to area; **1614** area visited by Capt. John Smith; **1620** plantation granted by Plymouth Council; **1623** the *Providence* delivers merchant families from England; town founded; **1633** Capt. Thomas Wiggin purchases property, founds settlement; First Orthodox Congregational Meeting House built, Second Meeting House built 1654; **1634** town incorporated; **1652** original section of Wentworth Manor house built; **1675** Damme Garrison fortifications built in response to Native American threat; **1680** sawmills and grist mills built at Cocheco Falls; Quaker Meeting House built; **1689** village of Cocheco destroyed by Native American attack; **1768** Friends Meeting House built; **1769** Strafford County formed; **1771** town becomes county seat; **c.1778** Tebbet House built; **1787** Parson Grey House built; **1790** post office established; **1794** bridge built across Piscataqua River; **1812** Dover Cotton Factory founded; **1813** Hale House built; **1818** Woodman House built; **c.1820** first cotton mill built; **1824** Sawyer Woolen Mills established; **1831** Lincoln House built, President Lincoln spends night here in 1860; **1841** Boston & Maine Railroad reaches town; **1847** shoe manufacturing begins; **1855** incorporated as a city; **1884** Dover Public Library opened, new library built 1905; **March 6, 1896** flooding of Piscataqua River devastates city; **1913** First Church of Christ Scientist built; **1935** Municipal Building built; **1973** county courthouse completed.

Dublin *Cheshire County* Southern New *Hampshire, 32 mi/51 km west-southwest of Manchester*

1749 town granted by Masonian Proprietors to Matthew Thornton, others; **1752** William Thornton becomes first settler; **1753** other setters follow, only to return to Peterborough by c.1757; **1758** Alexander Scott Tavern built; **1763** wave of settlers arrive from Massachusetts and eastern New Hampshire; **1771** town incorporated; **1822** Dublin Free Library founded; **1840** Solomon Piper establishes town's first summer boarding house, beginning of tourism industry; **1879** town boasts ten summer houses; **1964** Dublin Christian Academy founded.

Durham *Strafford County* Southeastern New *Hampshire, 30 mi/48 km east-northeast of Manchester*

1635 first settlers ascend Piscataqua River from Dover Point; **1649** Judge Frost House built by Valentine Hill; Three Chimneys Inn built, originally a residence; **1655** first meeting house built; **1675** area ravaged by Native American attacks during King Philip's War; **1694** over 100 settlers killed or captured in Native American attack; **1704** in resurgence of attacks, more than 50 whites killed; **1716** Gen. John Sullivan House built; **1732** town incorporated; **c.1735** Valentine Smith House built; **1792** town incorporated; **1866** University of New Hampshire established.

Effingham *Carroll County* Eastern New *Hampshire, 48 mi/77 km northeast of Concord*

1749 land granted for town, originally called Leavitt's Town; **1778** town incorporated, renamed Effingham; **1798** Congregational Church built at Effingham Falls; **1820** Wakefield Gore and Ossipee Gore annexed by town; Effingham Academy founded; **1822** Lord Mansion built by Isaac Lord; Dearborn House built by Jacob Dearborn; **c.1825** Jameson House built; Thomas Drake House built; **1859** town hall built.

Enfield *Grafton County* Western New Hampshire, *43 mi/69 km northwest of Concord*

1761 town settled; charter applied for, named for Enfield, Connecticut; town incorporated; **1768** land regranted to new proprietors; **1782** Shaker religious sect settles here; **1840** large stone building erected by Shakers; **1841** Shaker Inn built, originally residence; **1849** Shaker Bridge built; **1986** Shaker Museum opened.

Exeter *Rockingham County* Southeastern New *Hampshire, 27 mi/43 km east of Manchester*

Apr. 1638 land grant made to John Wheelwright and Augustine Storr; town settled; **1639** town incorporated; **1650s** Garrison House built, one of oldest buildings in New Hampshire; **c.1721** Ladd-Gilman House built by Capt. Nathaniel Ladd; **1724** Giddinge's Tavern built; **1734** Mast Tree Riot breaks out in protest of Royal Navy's marking of best trees for shipbuilding; **1740** Nathaniel Gilman House built; Leavitt House built; **1750** Jeremiah Smith House built; **Aug. 3, 1755** Cong. Nicholas Gilman born (died 1814); **1769** Rockingham County formed; town becomes county seat; **1770** The Raleigh Tavern built, later becomes Folsom Tavern; **1771** Powder House built at Duck Point; **1774** town becomes provincial capital of New Hampshire, capital moved to Portsmouth 1775; **Oct. 9, 1782** Lewis Cass born, Governor of Michigan Territory, later secretary of war (died 1866); **1783** Phillips Exeter Academy founded; **1798** Congregational Church built; Tenney House built; **1826** Gardner House built; **Apr. 20, 1850** sculptor Daniel French born, created Lincoln Memorial statue, also Minuteman statue at Concord, Massachusetts (died 1931); **1867** Robinson Seminary for women founded; **1892** Town Office Building built; **1893** Exeter Library built, new library opened 1987; **1916** bandstand built on Front Street; **March 2, 1942** author John Irving born; **1974** monument to war dead dedicated; **1991** American Independence Museum founded; **1995** county courthouse completed.

Farmington *Strafford County* Southeastern New *Hampshire, 28 mi/45 km east-northeast of Concord*

1798 town incorporated, separates from Rochester; **Feb. 16, 1812** Jeremiah James Colbath born, changes name to Henry Wilson at age 21, vice president under President Grant, 1873–1875 (died 1875); **1929** Goodwin Library opened.

Francestown *Hillsborough County* Southern New *Hampshire, 18 mi/29 km west of Manchester*

1752 land granted for town; **1772** town incorporated; **1787** Woodbury House built by Peter Woodbury; **1788** Lolly House built by Dr. Samuel Lolly; **Dec. 22, 1789** Supreme Court Justice Levi Woodbury born (died 1851); **c.1791** Willard House built; **c.1800** soapstone quarry established, closed 1891.

Franconia *Grafton County* Northwestern New *Hampshire, 73 mi/117 km north of Concord*

1764 town receives land grant as Franconia, lapses; Franconia Road blazed through Franconia Notch to south; **1772** town regranted as Morristown; **1774** Capt. Artemas Knight, others, become first settlers; **1782** town incorporated as Franconia; **1808** iron ore industry begins, flourishes until c.1865; **1863** Franconia Inn built; **1884** Dow Academy built; **1982** New England Ski Museum opened.

Franklin *Merrimack County* *Central New Hampshire, 18 mi/29 km north of Concord, on Merrimack River*

c.1762 Capt. Ebenezer Webster builds log cabin to southwest on land allotted him for his military service; **1764** town settled; **Jan. 18, 1782** statesman Daniel Webster born (originally part of Salisbury), spends first year of his life here (died 1852); **1802** first Congregational Church built, damaged by fire 1902, restored; **1808** Sulloway Mills textile factory founded; **1828** town incorporated; **1840** Acme Needle Company founded by Walter Aiken; **1895** incorporated as a city; **1907** Franklin Library built; **1931** Daniel Webster Bridge built across Pemigewasset River.

Goffstown *Hillsborough County* *Southern New Hampshire, 8 mi/12.9 km west-northwest of Manchester*

1733 town originally granted by Massachusetts as Narragansett No. 4; **1748** land regranted for town by New Hampshire, named for settler Col. John Goffe; **1761** town incorporated; **1845** Congregational Church built, founded 1650; **1859** St. Matthew's Episcopal Church built; **1989** New Hampshire State Prison for Women opened.

Gorham *Coos County* *Northern New Hampshire, 85 mi/137 km north-northeast of Concord*

1770 land grant made called Shelburne Addition; **1803** first road built from Connecticut River to site; **c.1805** Stephen Messer of Andover, Massachusetts, becomes first settler; **c.1820** lead discovered at Lead Mine Brook; **1836** town incorporated; **1852** Atlantic & St. Lawrence Railroad reaches town; **1881** silver discovered, processing plant built.

Hampton *Rockingham County* *Southeastern New Hampshire, 32 mi/51 km east of Manchester*

1635 blockhouse built near Atlantic Ocean, maintained by Massachusetts Bay Colony; **1638** town settled by Englishmen led by Rev. Stephen Bachiler, one of four original New England settlements; **1639** town incorporated; **1791** town hall built; **1797** fourth meeting house built; **March 12, 1806** Jane Means Appleton Pierce, wife of Pres. Franklin Pierce, born (married 1834, died 1863); **1820** first hotel opened at Great Boar's Head; **1826** Boar's Head Hotel built; **1843** First Congregational Church built on site of Fourth Meeting House; **1844** Ocean House Hotel built, destroyed by fire 1885; **May 27, 1874** actor Dustin Farnum born at Hampton Beach (died 1929); **1881** Lane Memorial Library founded, built 1910, new library built 1983; **1897** Exeter, Hampton & Amesbury Street Railway built, abandoned 1926; **1902** wooden Mile Bridge built across entrance to Hampton Harbor to Seabrook Beach to south; Hampton Beach Casino built; **Sept. 23, 1915** great fire sweeps through resort town of Hampton Beach.

Hampton Falls *Rockingham County* *Southeastern New Hampshire, 31 mi/50 km east of Manchester*

1638 area settled near Atlantic Ocean; **1650s** dreaded witch Goody Cole becomes local scourge, imprisoned and persecuted by town; **1681** tidal mill built here for grinding corn, remains in operation until 1879; **1703** Garrison House built by Col. Joshua Wingate; **1726** town incorporated, separates from Hampton; first annual horse show held; **Aug. 10, 1737** assembly held here between New Hampshire and Massachusetts to determine common boundary line; **1748** Meshech Weare House built; **1769** house built by Gen. Jonathan Moulton, Revolutionary War veteran, later called the Haunted House; **1825** ban on Sunday travel lifted; **Dec. 15, 1831** journalist Franklin B. Sanborn born, aided John Brown's Harpers Ferry raid 1859 (died 1917); **Dec. 16, 1863** architect George Cram born (died 1942); **Sept. 2, 1895** poet John Greenleaf Whittier dies at Elmfield house (born 1807).

Hanover *Grafton County* *Western New Hampshire, 51 mi/82 km northwest of Concord, on Connecticut River*

1761 town incorporated; **1765** first settlers arrive; **1769** Dartmouth College established; **Apr. 4, 1810** Unitarian clergyman James Freeman Clarke born (died 1888); **Nov. 8, 1821** petroleum industry pioneer George Henry Bissell born, founded Pennsylvania Rock Oil Company (died 1884); **1859** covered Ledyard Bridge built across Connecticut River, replaces 1796 structure; **Apr. 3, 1888** World War II naval officer Thomas Casson Kinkaid born (died 1972).

Haverhill *Grafton County* *Western New Hampshire, 64 mi/103 km north-northwest of Concord*

c.1760 Capt. John Hazen, others from Haverhill, Massachusetts, become first settlers; **1763** town incorporated; **1765** Captain Hazen builds house; **1769** Grafton County formed; town becomes **1770** Col. Charles Johnston House built; **1772** town becomes shared county seat with Plymouth; **c.1790** Montgomery House built by Gen. John Montgomery; **1794** Haverhill Academy chartered; **1802** covered bridge built by Moody Bedel on Connecticut River; **1829** Bath-Haverhill Covered Bridge built across Ammonoosuc River; **1853** village of Woodsville to north becomes commercial center of Haverhill with arrival of Boston, Concord & Montreal Railroad; **1889** fifth county courthouse built at Woodsville; **1969** town becomes sole county seat; sixth county courthouse built at village of North Haverhill.

Henniker *Merrimack County* *Central New Hampshire, 14 mi/23 km west of Concord*

1761 first settlers arrive; **1763** first house built; **1768** land granted for town to John Henniker, friend of Gov. Benning Wentworth; town incorporated; **1780** bridge built over Contoocook River, replaced 1835 by double-arched stone bridge; **1790** Friends Meeting House built; **c.1791** Henniker Academy founded; **1796** National Hotel built, later used for New England College administration building; **Sept. 5, 1867** pianist Amy Mary Brach born (died 1944); **1904** Tucker Free Library built; **1946** New England College established; **1963** Pat's Peak Ski Area established; **1971** Henniker Historical Society founded; **1972** Henniker Covered Bridge built at college.

Hillsborough *Hillsborough County* *Southern New Hampshire, 19 mi/31 km west-southwest of Concord*

1730s area first settled; **1740** Arthur Dowlin House built; **1772** town incorporated; **1774** Barns House built; **1794** Friends Meeting House built; **1799** bridge built across Contoocook River, later replaced the Great Bridge; **1804** Franklin Pierce Homestead built by Gov. Benjamin Pierce; **Nov. 23, 1804** Franklin Pierce, 14th President, born in log cabin, family moved to homestead six months later (died Oct. 8, 1869); **Aug. 12, 1815** Benjamin Pierce Cheney born, builder of Atchison, Topeka & Santa Fe Railroad (died 1895); **1825** Hillsborough Instrumental Band organized; **1877** Fuller Public Library founded through bequest of Mark W. Fuller; **1880** identical Twin Houses built, originally called the Dutton Houses; **1894** Community House built by John B. Smith as residence; **1900** Beards Brook Stone Arch Bridge built; **c.1918** Henry Iram Camp established as health retreat, intellectual forum.

Hinsdale *Cheshire County* *Southwestern New Hampshire, 55 mi/89 km west-southwest of Manchester*

1687 land grant made on Connecticut River, at mouth of Ashuelot River, by Nawellet, chief of Squakeag tribe; **1742** Col. Ebenezer Hinsdale builds fort, grist mill; **July 14, 1748** attack by French and Native Amercans, four killed, five captured, second attack July 16, four killed; **1753** town incorporated; **1756** Hinsdale House built by Colonel Hinsdale; **Aug. 8, 1819** editor Charles Anderson Dana born (died 1897); **Jan. 10, 1844** educator Elisha Andrews born (died 1917).

Holderness *Grafton County* *Central New Hampshire, 37 mi/60 km north of Concord, on Squam Lake*

1751 original land grant on Pemigewasset River patented by Gov. Benning Wentworth; **1752** town site platted, settlers fail to materialize; **1761** land grant reissued following defeat of French at Quebec, eliminating Native American threat; Town of New Holderness incorporated; **1816** town renamed Holderness; **1870** Squam Lake begins to attract tourists; **1966** Squam Lakes Natural Science Center founded; **1980** movie *On Golden Pond* filmed at Squam Lake.

Hopkinton *Merrimack County* *Central New Hampshire, 6 mi/9.7 km west of Concord*

1735 land granted for town to settlers from Hopkinton, Massachusetts; **1763** development of town begins follow-ing French and Indian War; **1765** town incorporated; **1766** First Congregational Church built, burned 1789, rebuilt; **Jan. 18, 1782** Grace Fletcher born, wife of statesman Daniel Webster (died 1827); **1786** Wiggins Tavern built by Benjamin Wiggins; **c.1816** Burns House built; **1825** General Lafayette is entertained at Wiggins Tavern; **1828** St. Andrew's Church built; **1850** Railroad Covered Bridge built across Contoocook River, rebuilt 1889; **1853** Rowell's Covered Bridge built across Contoocook River; **1890** Long Memorial Library established; **1915** first annual state fair held.

Jackson *Carroll County* *Eastern New Hampshire, 70 mi/113 km north-northeast of Concord*

1642 Darby Field makes first known ascent of Mount Washington (6,288 ft/1,917 m) to north, highest point in Northeastern U.S.; **1774** mountain pass discovered to north by road builders, later named Pinkham Notch; **1778** Benjamin Copp and wife settle here, lone settlers for 12 years; **1790** five families join Copp family, including Joseph Pinkham; **1800** town incorporated, originally named Adams for Pres. John Adams; **July 4, 1829** town renamed for Pres. Andrew Jackson; **1852** original Summit House built on Mount Washington; **July 1869** road and cog railway completed to summit of Mount Washington by Sylvester Marsh; **1873** second Summit House built on Mount Washington, destroyed by fire 1908; **1876** Honeymoon Covered Bridge built across Ellis River; **July 1902** Mount Washington Hotel opened by Joseph Stickney; **1915** third Summit House built; **1932** Mt. Washington Observatory established at summit for meteorological research; **Sept. 17, 1967** cog railway to summit of Mount Washington derails, 8 killed, 73 injured; **1973** Summit Museum opened; **1979** Sherman Adams Summit Visitors Center built.

Jaffrey *Cheshire County* *Southwestern New Hampshire, 31 mi/50 km southwest of Manchester*

1725 Capt. Samuel Willard and his 14 rangers make first known ascent of Monadnock Mountain (3,165 ft/965 m) while tracking Native Americans; **1749** town surveyed, bounties offered to prospective settlers; **c.1758** town first settled; **1773** town incorporated; **1775** town meeting house built; **1787** textile mill built in East Jaffrey village, industrial center of town; **1801** Amos Fortune dies, ex-slave who became prosperous enough to purchase free-dom for himself and wife and to bequeath money for the town's school district; **1802** Third New Hampshire Turnpike opened; **1808** farmhouse built by Joseph Cutter, Jr., later becomes The Ark inn; **1823** Grand Monadnock Hotel built at summit of Monadnock Mountain, destroyed by fire 1866, rebuilt; **c.1825** Friends Meeting House built, later used as town hall; **1832** Melville Academy founded; **1896** Clay Memorial Library built; **1931** granite World War Memorial dedi-cated.

Keene *Cheshire County* *Southwestern New Hampshire, 43 mi/69 km west of Manchester*

1733 grant made for town by Massachusetts Colony, named Upper Ashuelot; **1736** Nathan Blake builds first log cabin; **1737** town platted; First Meeting House (Quaker) built; **1746** settlement comes under full Native American attack, Nathan Blake captured, entire village burned; **1750** town resettled; **1753** town incorporated as Keene, named for Sir Benjamin Keene, friend of Governor Wentworth; **1762** Wyman Tavern built; **1769** Cheshire County formed; town becomes county seat; **1795** Daniel Adams House built; pottery making begins, led by Hampshire Pottery, ceased operation 1926; **1799** *New Hampshire Weekly Sentinel* newspaper founded; **1809** bottle making begun by Henry Schoolcraft, until 1845; **1815** Faulkner and Colony Company woolen mill founded; **Jan. 4, 1831** publisher Edward Payson Dutton born (died 1923); **1840s** large group of Irish immigrants arrive; **1849** Boston & Maine Railroad built; **1858** county courthouse built; **1859** Thayer Public Library established; **1873** incorporated as a city; **1909** Keene Normal School established, becomes Keene State College; **1943** Keene Dillant-Hopkins Airport established.

Kingston *Rockingham County* *Southeastern New Hampshire, 21 mi/34 km east-southeast of Manchester*

1694 town granted to James Prescott, others; originally named Kingstown; **1738** East Kingston separates from Kingstown; **1750** Josiah Bartlett (1729–1795) arrives from Amesbury, Massachusetts, opens medical practice, becomes signer of Declaration of Independence, governor 1790–1794, first president of New Hampshire Medical Society 1793; **1774** original Josiah Bartlett House burns, rebuilt; **1800** spelling changed to Kingston.

Laconia *Belknap County* *Central New Hampshire, 23 mi/37 km north of Concord, on Winnipesaukee River*

1652 region surveyed; **1727** land granted to extended Gilman family, others; **1736** two blockhouses built; **1777** first log cabin built at town site by Samuel Jewett; **1780** Jewett House built by Jacob Jewett; **1824** Congregational Church organized; **1840** Belknap County formed; town becomes county seat; **1848** Boston, Concord & Montreal Railroad reaches town, car shops established 1850; **1855** town incorporated; **1893** incorporated as a city; **1894** county courthouse built, addition built 1975; **1898** Gale Memorial Library built; **1929** St. Joseph's Catholic Church built.

Lancaster *Coos County* *Northern New Hampshire, 90 mi/145 km north of Concord, on Connecticut River*

1762 land grant made to David Page, others; **July 1763** area chartered as Lancaster plantation; **1764** town incorporated; **1780** Holton House built; **1803** Coos County formed; **1805** town becomes county seat; **1837** Stone House built; **July 25, 1840** author Flora Adams born (died 1910); **Apr. 11, 1860** financier John W. Weeks born,

secretary of war under Presidents Harding and Coolidge (died 1926); **1862** Mechanic Street Covered Bridge built across Israels River; **1870** Boston & Maine Railroad reaches town; **1997** county courthouse completed.

Lisbon *Grafton County* *Northwestern New Hampshire, 73 mi/117 km north-northwest of Concord*

1753 first settlers arrive; **1763** land grant made; town incorporated as Concord, renamed Chiswick 1764; **1768** town reincorporated as Gunthwaite, renamed Concord soon after; **1778** town among several in western New Hampshire to join independent Vermont; **c.1779** Cobleigh Tavern built, used for first Lisbon town meeting 1790; **1781** Travena House built; **1792** association of New Hampshire towns with Vermont dissolved; **1805** iron ore discovered in Sugar Hill section of town, mined until 1850; **1824** town renamed Lisbon; **1864** gold discovered, proves unprofitable.

Londonderry *Rockingham County* *Southern New Hampshire, 11 mi/18 km south-southeast of Manchester*

1719 Scotch Irish immigrants settle here; town of Nutfield founded; **July 28, 1720** "Ocean Born Mary" Wilson born at sea to immigrants, captured by pirates off Boston, life spared, brought here, becomes focus of future civic celebrations; **1722** land granted for town to John Moor, renamed Londonderry; **Aug. 28, 1728** Gen. John Stark born, hero at battles of Bunker Hill (Boston) and Bennington, Vermont (died 1822); **1810** White's Tavern built; **1837** Presbyterian Church built; **1880** Leach Library founded, new building opened 1973; **1884** Soldiers' Memorial erected; **1909** Grange Hall built; **1934** New Hampshire Egg Auction opened; **1976** Revolutionary War monument dedicated.

Manchester *Hillsborough County* *Southern New Hampshire, 48 mi/77 km north-northwest of Boston*

1636 first white men explore Merrimack Valley; **1650** John Eliot conducts school for natives who become known as the Praying Indians; **1722** John Goffe, Jr., Edward Lingfield, and Benjamin Kidder become first settlers; **1735** Massachusetts Colony grants town to Capt. William Tyng, named Tyngstown; **1751** town incorporated, renamed Derryfield; **1769** Hillsborough County formed; town becomes county seat; **1792** toll bridge built across river; **1805** Benjamin Prichard founds cotton mill, becomes Amoskeag Cotton and Woolen Factory 1874, world's largest cotton miller at the time; **1807** canal built by Samuel Blodgett; **1810** town renamed for Manchester, England; **1831** Isaac Huse House built; **1845** Irish immigrants arrive during Irish potato famine; **1846** incorporated as a city; **1854** Carpenter Memorial Library founded, built 1913; **1889** St. Anselm College established; **1900** Hesser College (2-year) established; **1922** J. F. McElwain Shoe Company founded; **1927** Manchester Airport established, new terminal built 1994; Currier Art Gallery founded; **1932** New Hampshire College established; **1945** New Hampshire

Community Technical College, Manchester-Stratham Campus, (2-year) established; **1950** Notre Dame College established; **1985** University of New Hampshire at Manchester established; **Nov. 2001** Verizon Wireless Arena opened.

Mason *Hillsborough County* *Southern New Hampshire, 23 mi/37 km south-southwest of Manchester*

1629 land granted by Plymouth Council to Capt. John Mason (1586–1635), founder of New Hampshire; **1768** town incorporated; **1780** young Samuel Wilson, born Sept. 1766 at West Cambridge (Arlington), Massachusetts, arrives here with family, becomes known as original "Uncle Sam" for "U.S." marked on his arriving provisions at docks in Troy, New York (died July 31, 1854); **1788** dam built on Souhegan River to harness water power for textile mills.

Milford *Hillsborough County* *Southern New Hampshire, 15 mi/24 km south-southwest of Manchester*

1738 Thomas Nevins builds first house; **1741** Shepard Mill built by John Shepard; **1745** Benjamin Hopkins builds bullet-proof cabin as protection against Native Americans during King George's War; **1793** sawmill and grist mill built by William and John Crosby, grist mill operates until 1938; **1794** town incorporated; White Meeting House built; **c.1803** Buxton Tavern (Milford Inn) established by Jonathan Buxton, destroyed by fire 1959; **1810** textile milling industry begins; **1816** United Methodist Church built; **1837** Old Fire Station built, replaced 1974; **1842** Livermore Mansion built; Community House built by Squire Solomon R. Livermore; **1845** stone bridge built across Skouhegan River; **1850** Swinging Footbridge built, replaced by iron bridge 1889; **1850s** granite quarrying begins; **1852** Boston & Maine Railroad reaches town; **1870** town hall built; **1888** Unitarian Church completed; **1891** *Milford Cabinet* newspaper moved from Amherst, founded 1802; **1895** Milford Historical Society founded; **1950** Wadleigh Library built.

Mount Washington *Coos County* *See* **Jackson**

Nashua *Hillsborough County* *Southern New Hampshire, 15 mi/24 km south of Manchester, on Merrimack River*

1652 area surveyed; **1656** man named Cromwell becomes first settler; **1667** forge established by Lieutenant Robbins; **1678** first log meeting house built, replaced 1684; **1695** Daniel Waldo builds grist mill; **1701** Native American attacks force some settlers to leave; **1746** originally incorporated as part of Town of Dunstable; **1769** Hillsborough County formed; town becomes county seat; **1803** Colonial House built; **1804** Marsh Tavern built; **1822** Nashua Manufacturing Company founded; **1825** city plan designed by Asher Benjamin; **1826** canal completed opening navigation on Merrimack River; **1832** *Nashua Telegraph* newspaper founded; **1842** city hall built;

1853 incorporated as a city; **1860** Nashua Watch Factory established; **1864** county seat moved from Amherst; **1865** American Shearer Company founded, maker of shearing equipment; **July 4, 1911** highest temperature ever recorded in New Hampshire reached, 106°F/41°C; **1922** McElwain Shoe Factory founded; **1923** Nashua Symphony Orchestra founded, Choral Society added 1988; **May 4, 1930** Allds Street district destroyed by fire, 411 families left homeless; **1931** *Monitor* Marker erected commemorating Civil War gunboat; **1933** Rivier College established; **1965** Daniel Webster College established; **1967** New Hampshire Community Technical College, Nashua-Claremont Campus, (2-year) established.

New Boston *Hillsborough County* *Southern New Hampshire, 12 mi/19 km west of Manchester*

1735 town granted by Massachusetts to survivors of ill-fated military expedition to Canada, 1690, under Sir William Phipps, named Lane's Town; **1751** town regranted by New Hampshire; **1763** town incorporated; **Aug. 16, 1777** Molly Stark Cannon, cast 1743, captured from British at Bennington, Vermont, by John Stark, brought here as memorial; **1822** Meeting House built; **May 22, 1826** Harvard legal scholar Christopher Columbus Langdell born (died 1906); **1893** Maine & Central Railroad reaches town; **1913** Whipple Free Library founded.

New Castle *Rockingham County* *Southeastern New Hampshire, 2 mi/3.2 km east of Portsmouth*

1682-1683 Provincial Assembly meets at Jaffrey Cottage; **1690** Wendell Farmhouse built; **1693** town incorporated, founded at entrance to Piscataqua River, Atlantic Ocean; **1695** original wing of Benning Wentworth Mansion built, expanded to 32 rooms by 1930s; **1730** Seavey Homestead built; **1771** original Fort Point Lighthouse built; **1774** Fort William and Mary seized by colonists, renamed Fort Constitution; **1828** Quaker Meeting House built; **1783** town charter and records dating 1693–1726 discovered in Hertfordshire, England, returned; **1905** delegates to Russo-Japanese peace conference are entertained at Hotel Wentworth during signing of Treaty of Portsmouth.

New London *Merrimack County* *West central New Hampshire, 27 mi/43 km northwest of Concord*

1753 town granted land as Heidelberg; **1779** town incorporated, renamed New London; **c.1790** barn built, later becomes Barn Playhouse; **1823** Capt. Jonathan Everett House built, used as library 1926; **1836** Colby Junior College established, later becomes Colby-Sawyer College; **1897** Tracy Memorial Library founded.

Newbury *Merrimack County* *West central New Hampshire, 26 mi/42 km west-northwest of Concord*

1762 Zephaniah Clark becomes first settler; settlement originally named Danzick; **1772** Town of Fishersfield incorporated, named for John Fisher, an original grantee;

1837 town renamed Newbury; 1849 Concord & Claremont Railroad extended to town; 1855 Sunapee House built by C. Y. and N. S. Gardner; 1875 Lake View House hotel built on Lake Sunapee; 1876 Nathan Young's *Mountain Maid* begins excursion service on Lake Sunapee; 1877 Runnals House built; 1884 steamer *Edmund Burke* begins service, capacity 800 passengers.

Newington   *Rockingham County*   *Southeastern New Hampshire, 3 mi/4.8 km west of Portsmouth*

1656 Newington Shipyards established at Bloody Point by Thomas Trickery, built ships in 1940s for World War II; 1670 town settled near Piscataqua River; 1690 Native American raid at Fox Point destroys several houses, 14 settlers killed, 6 taken captive, some rescued; 1697 Old Parsonage built; 1699 Congregational "Little White" Church built by John Quint, said to be oldest continuously used church in U.S.; 1712 Quaker Meeting House built; 1713 parish established, named for Newington, England; 1764 town incorporated, separates from Dover; 1821 part of town annexed by Portsmouth; Aug. 1934 Gen. John Sullivan Bridge dedicated, crosses entrance to Great Bay to Dover.

Newport   *Sullivan County*   *Southwestern New Hampshire, 34 mi/55 km west-northwest of Concord*

1754 land granted to trapper named Eastman, returns to settle, skeleton found later apparently his; 1761 town incorporated; 1762 David Lyne and Moses Spafford become first permanent settlers; 1768 Benjamin Giles builds dam on Sugar River, builds grist mills and sawmills; 1773 Congregational Church built, rebuilt 1822; 1814 Newport House hotel built, rebuilt 1860 after fire, destroyed by fire Dec. 25, 1965; 1819 Newport Academy founded; 1826 Sullivan County formed from Cheshire County; 1827 town becomes county seat; 1835 Corbin Covered Bridge built; 1872 county courthouse built, burned 1885, rebuilt; 1949 Parlin Field airport opened.

North Hampton   *Rockingham County* *Southeastern New Hampshire, 32 mi/51 km east of Manchester*

1690 area on Atlantic Ocean first settled; June 26, 1696 many Native Americans captured and killed by Captain Shackford following massacre of settlers at Portsmouth Plains; 1742 town incorporated, separates from Hampton; Feb. 23, 1751 Henry Dearborn born, secretary of war under President Jefferson (died 1829).

North Woodstock   *Grafton County*   *Central New Hampshire, 58 mi/93 km north of Concord*

1803 The Flume discovered, large fissure formed in granite; 1805 road builders in Franconia Notch to north discover mountainside rock formation Old Man of the Mountain; 1835 Lafayette Place tavern built; 1840 Town of Woodstock incorporated; 1847 geologist Louis Agassiz studies rock formations of Agassiz Basin, named for him,

returns in 1870; 1848 Flume Tea House built, destroyed by fire 1871, rebuilt, again destroyed by fire 1918, rebuilt; 1853 Profile House hotel built at Old Man rock formation, replaced 1906, burned 1922; c.1858 Mount Lafayette House built, burned 1861; 1881 narrow gauge railroad built to Profile House from Bethlehem, widened to standard gauge 1897; June 1883 large boulder lodged for centuries in The Flume dislodged by flood creating two new waterfalls; May 2–3, 2003 Old Man of the Mountain rock formation, state symbol, collapses during the night.

Northumberland   *Coos County*   *Northern New Hampshire, 96 mi/154 km north of Concord*

1761 land grant made, town named Stonington; 1767 first settlers arrive; 1771 town renamed Northumberland; 1775 Fort Wentworth built by British on Connecticut River, at mouth of Ammonoosuc River; 1778 fort occupied by American Colonel Bedell during Revolutionary War, abandoned 1782; 1779 town incorporated; 1784 first road reaches town; 1786 ferry established on Connecticut River; 1791 bridge built across Connecticut River; 1852 Groveton Covered Bridge built across Ammonoosuc River.

Orford   *Grafton County*   *Western New Hampshire, 58 mi/93 km northwest of Concord*

1761 land grant made; town incorporated; 1765 first claims made by settlers; 1770 Congregational Meeting House built; 1793 Samuel Morey builds small steamboat in advance of Robert Fulton's invention; 1799 beaver hat factory built by William Howard; 1802 Orford Hotel built, burned 1875; 1807 Wheeler Store built; 1816 General Wheeler House built; 1824 John Mann store established; 1831 Britton House built; 1840 Universalist Church built; milliner's shop built, becomes Orford Social Library 1902; 1847 Thomas Mann House built; 1851 Orford Academy founded.

Ossipee   *Carroll County*   *Eastern New Hampshire, 41 mi/66 km north-northeast of Concord*

1650s English contingent sent to assist Ossipees in fighting Mohawks; timber fort built, later taken by Ossipees in change of loyalty; 1676 fort destroyed by English; 1725 Captain Lovewell builds stockade, used for attacks on Native Americans; 1785 town incorporated; 1794 Amos Garland and brother build sawmill and grist mill on Birch River; 1840 Carroll County formed; town becomes county seat; 1899 Ossipee Library founded; 1916 county courthouse built.

Pelham   *Hillsborough County*   *Southern New Hampshire, 8 mi/12.9 km east-southeast of Nashua*

1719 first settlers arrive; blockhouses built as defense against Native Americans; 1721 John Butler and David Humboldt become first permanent settlers; c.1735 town founded; 1746 town incorporated; First Congregationalist Church built; town meeting house built, rebuilt 1785; 1820

Methodist Church organized; **1837** first of three stone bridges built across Beaver Brook by Jonathan Atwood, others built 1839, 1840; **1913** St. Patrick Roman Catholic Church built, rebuilt 1946 and 1969.

Pembroke *Merrimack County* South central New Hampshire, 10 mi/16 km north of Manchester

1727 survivors of 1725 expedition to Maine to eliminate Native American threat granted land; town founded on Merrimack River, at mouth of Suncook River; **1738** sawmill and grist mill built; **1748** garrison fights off major Native American attack; **1759** town incorporated; **c.1764** Thompson House built; **1773** fulling mill established; **1780** Kimball Tavern built; **1812** cotton mill opened on Suncook River by Maj. Caleb Stark; **1818** Pembroke Academy founded, damaged by fire in 1936, rebuilt; **1836** Congregational Church built; **1839** Chelmsford Glass Company established; **1852** Portsmouth & Concord Railroad built; **1869** Suncook Valley Railroad built; **1902** trolley service to Concord begins, ends 1927.

Peterborough *Hillsborough County* Southern New Hampshire, 27 mi/43 km southwest of Manchester

1738 town granted to citizens from Concord, Massachusetts; **1749** first settlers arrive; **1760** town incorporated; **1796** Samuel Eliot Morison House built, also called Bleak House; **1797** Wilson Tavern built; **1818** Old Bell cotton linen factory founded; **1824** Unitarian Church built; **1828** The Lyceum established; **1831** Joseph Noone's Sons Company established, was sole source of felt for Bureau of Printing and Engraving for printing currency; **1833** Public Library founded, one of first free public libraries in nation; **1854** Frederick Douglass addresses speech, helps establish Underground Railroad station; **1877** American Guernsey Club established by William H. Caldwell; **1907** MacDowell Artist Colony founded by composer Edward MacDowell (1861–1908); **1912** Sargent Camp for girls established; **1914** Outdoor Players founded by Marie Ware Laughton; **1918** Town House built; **1923** All Saints' Episcopal Church built; **Sept. 21, 1938** heavy flooding caused by New England Hurricane, fire follows, half of downtown destroyed.

Pittsburg *Coos County* Northern New Hampshire, 131 mi/243 km north of Concord

1829 first settlers arrive, area becomes Indian Stream Territory; **1832** Republic of Indian Stream organized, complete with constitution and government; **1835** republic dissolved by New Hampshire militia after short dispute with Canada; **1840** town incorporated; **1842** Ashburton Treaty awards town to New Hampshire; **1876** Pittsburg-Clarksville Covered Bridge built across Connecticut River; **1930** dam built on Connecticut River forming First Connecticut Lake; **1934** dam built creating Second Connecticut Lake; **1939** dam built creating Third Connecticut Lake.

Pittsfield *Merrimack County* Southeastern New Hampshire, 14 mi/23 km northeast of Concord

1768 town first settled by John Cram; **1777** Fort Ichord built; **1782** town incorporated; **1789** first town meeting house built; **c.1792** sawmills and grist mills begin operation; **Oct. 11, 1798** historian Samuel G. Drake born (died 1875); **1820** Washington House inn built; **c.1820** scythe factory built by James Joy; **1826** cotton mill built; **1869** Suncook Valley Railroad reaches town, becomes Boston & Maine Railroad 1924, service ended 1950; **1870** shoe factory built; **1901** Carpenter Library founded; first annual Old Home Week celebrated; **Jan. 28, 1925** lowest temperature recorded in New Hampshire reached, −46°F/ −43°C; **2000** Frank Lyman Park and Historic Trail opened.

Plymouth *Grafton County* Central New Hampshire, 40 mi/64 km north of Concord, on Pemigewasset River

1712 expedition led by Capt. Thomas Baker passes through area; **July 1763** town incorporated; **1765** town's first industries develop, including sawmill, mattress factory; **1769** Grafton County formed; **1773** town becomes shared county seat with Haverhill; **1790** Smith Millennium Covered Bridge built, rebuilt 1825 and 1850, destroyed by arsonist 1993, rebuilt 1999; **1805** Daniel Webster makes first court appearance as defense attorney; **1808** Plymouth Academy founded; **1823** Holmes Academy built; **1836** Congregational Church built, destroyed by fire 1985, rebuilt; **1863** Pemigewasset House built by John E. Lyon, president of Boston, Concord & Montreal Railroad, later burned, rebuilt next to railroad station, burns again 1909; **May 18, 1864** novelist Nathaniel Hawthorne dies, a frequent visitor to area (born 1804); **1871** Plymouth State College established as Plymouth Normal School; **1879** Holderness School built; **1890** third county courthouse built; **1896** Pense Public Library founded, new structure built 1991; **1969** Haverhill becomes sole county seat; courthouse becomes town hall.

Portsmouth *Rockingham County* Southeastern New Hampshire, 37 mi/60 km east of Manchester

1603 Martin Pring sails into Piscataqua River estuary; **1614** Capt. John Smith discovers entrance to Piscataqua River; **1621** land grant made to Capt. John Mason; **1623** first settlers arrive at Odiorne's Point; **1653** town incorporated by Massachusetts; **1664** Richard Jackson House built; **July 24, 1696** provincial governor Benning Wentworth born (died 1770); **1705** Deer Tavern built; **1712** first North Church built; **1718** Warner House built; **June 26, 1741** Sen. John Langdon born (died 1819); **1758** old statehouse built; John Paul Jones House built by Captain Purcell, Jones stayed here during building of his ship *Ranger*, 1777; **1760** Wentworth Gardiner House built; **1766** William Pitt Tavern built by John Stavers; **1775** New Hampshire capital moved from Exeter; **1784** Governor Langdon House built; **1789** Jacob Wendell House built by Jeremiah Hill; **1800** Rollins House built; **1803** Athenaeum built; **1806** Portsmouth Naval Yard established on several islands in Piscataqua River in neighboring Kittery, Maine; **1807** St. John's Church built, replaces 1732 chapel; **1808** state capital moved to Concord; **1810** Edward Cutt House built; **Jan. 11, 1813** Union naval officer Tunis Craven born, died at Battle of Mobile Bay Aug. 5, 1864; **July 13, 1817** publisher James Thomas Fields born (died 1881); **Aug. 3, 1822** Union Gen. Fitz-John Porter born (died 1901); **1826** South Parish Church built; **June 29, 1835** author Celia Leighton Thaxter born (died 1894); **Nov. 11, 1836** writer, editor Thomas B. Aldrich born (died 1907); **1849** incorporated as a city; **1896** public library established; **1923** Memorial Bridge built across Piscataqua River to Kittery, Maine; **June 7, 1939** submarine *Thetis* sinks in Atlantic killing all 26 on board.

Rindge   *Cheshire County   Southern New Hampshire, 33 mi/53 km southwest of Manchester*

1738 town surveyed; named Rowley-Canada by people from Rowley, Massachusetts, returned from ill-fated 1690 military expedition to Canada; **1742** Abel Platts attempts to settle here, driven out by Native Americans; **1752** Ezekiel Jewett becomes first permanent settler; **1760** sawmill established; **1768** town incorporated, named for Daniel Rindge, Provincial Council member; **1797** Congregational Church built; **1962** Franklin Pierce College established.

Rochester   *Strafford County   Southeastern New Hampshire, 33 mi/53 km northeast of Manchester*

1656 first land grants made; **1722** town incorporated as Norway Plains; **1737** town renamed Rochester; **1728** Capt. Timothy Roberts family become first settlers, settlement delayed by Native American threat; **1731** Congregational Church built; Quaker Meeting House built; **1738** 60 more families arrive; **June 27, 1746** 5-man garrison ambushed by natives, four killed, one injured, taken to Quebec; **1758** Dame House built by Jabez Dame; **1771** General Wolfe Tavern built; **1785** bridge built on Cocheco River; **Aug. 16, 1802** inventor Isaac Adams born, improved printing press (died 1883); **March 31, 1806** Cong., reformer John Parker Hale born (died 1873); **1811** Gonic Woolen Mills founded; **1834** Dodge's Hotel established, rebuilt after 1896 fire; **1843** shoe manufacturing begins; **1849** Great Falls & Conway Railroad reaches town; **1871** Portsmouth & Rochester Railroad built; **1874** first annual Rochester Fair held; **1891** incorporated as a city; **1896** Parson Main monument erected; **1901** electric railroad connects city with Somersworth and Dover; **1905** Rochester Public Library built; **1908** Rochester Opera House opened, closed 1973, restored 2001.

Rumney   *Grafton County   Central New Hampshire, 44 mi/71 km north-northwest of Concord*

Apr. 1752 David Stinson and Gen. John Stark become first white men to visit area, attacked by band of ten Native Americans along Stinson Brook, Stinson killed, Stark taken captive, ransomed; **1765** town settled; **1767** town

incorporated; **Aug. 18, 1803** Supreme Court Justice Nathan Clifford born (died 1881); **1922** Polar Caves opened to tourists.

Rye   *Rockingham County   Southeastern New Hampshire, 35 mi/56 km east of Manchester, on Atlantic Ocean*

1603 Martin Pring party lands at Oriorne's Point in vessels *Speedwell* and *Discoverer*; **1605** Samuel de Champlain reaches Point, followed by Capt. John Smith 1614; **1623** Scotsman David Thompson lands here with group of Englishmen, found first town in New Hampshire; **1726** town incorporated, separated from New Castle; **c.1738** Rand Store opened, owned by Rand family for over 200 years; **1747** Garland Tavern built; **1810** Parsons House built; **1837** First Congregational Church built; **1874** first transatlantic cable laid here; **1911** Rye Public Library opened.

Salem   *Rockingham County   Southern New Hampshire, 20 mi/32 km southeast of Manchester*

1725 town separates from Haverhill, Massachusetts, named Methuen; **1741** new state boundary divides Methuen, New Hampshire portion becomes Town of Salem; **1750** town incorporated; **1860s** town becomes major shoe manufacturer; **1894** Salem Free Library founded, new Kelley Library opened 1966; **1932** Rockingham Park racetrack converted to horse racing with legalization of parimutuel betting, former car and motorcycle course.

Salisbury   *Merrimack County   See* **Franklin (1782)**

Seabrook   *Rockingham County   Southeastern New Hampshire, 32 mi/51 km east-southeast of Manchester*

1638 town settled near Atlantic Ocean; **1764** Old South Meeting House built; **1768** town incorporated; **1830s** whaling becomes chief industry; **1840** Eastern Railroad reaches town; **1893** Brown Memorial Library opened; **1902** trolley bridge built across harbor; **May 1, 1977** over 1,400 demonstrators arrested in protest against proposed Seabrook Nuclear Power Plant, another 500 arrested May 13; **Aug. 4, 1978** Environmental Protection Agency approves construction of first nuclear power plant; **June 13, 1989** Seabrook Nuclear Power Plant begins production.

Somersworth   *Strafford County   Southeastern New Hampshire, 14 mi/23 km north-northwest of Portsmouth*

1750 Joseph Wentworth House built; **1754** town of Great Falls incorporated; **1822** first cotton mills established; **1823** Great Falls Manufacturing Company cotton mill founded by Isaac Wendell; **March 8, 1888** economist Stuart Chase born (died 1985); **1889** Somersworth Library founded; **1893** incorporated as a city; renamed Somersworth.

Stratham *Rockingham County* *Southwestern New Hampshire, 28 mi/45 km east of Manchester*

1629 part of Squamscott Patent granted to Edward Hilton of England; **1631** town founded; **1673** first settlers arrive; **1690s** 30 more families settle in area; **1715** town incorporated, named for Lady Stratham of England; **1766** Kenniston Tavern built; **1911** Wiggin Memorial Library built; **1950s** Timberland Shoe Company founded by Nathan Swartz.

Sutton *Merrimack County* *Southern New Hampshire, 22 mi/35 km west-northwest of Concord*

1749 town charter granted to Obadiah Perry, others, originally named Perrytown; **1784** town incorporated; renamed, possibly for town of same name in Massachusetts; **July 29, 1828** John Pillsbury born, went to Minnesota 1855 founded Pillsbury Company with brother George (died 1901); **Dec. 5, 1829** educator John Eaton born (died 1906).

Swanzey *Cheshire County* *Southwestern New Hampshire, 43 mi/69 km west-southwest of Manchester*

1733 land grants made along Ashuelot River, including Lower Ashuelot (Swanzey); **1738** three forts built on land granted to Capt. Nathaniel Hammond; **1747** warned of Native American attack, settlers bury belongings, flee area before houses are burned; **1752** settlers return following 1749 peace treaty; **1753** town incorporated; **1755** natives resume attacks, suppressed by militia; **1800** Slate Covered Bridge built on Ashuelot River, rebuilt 1842, again 1862; **1832** Swanzey Covered Bridge built by Zadoc Taft on Ashuelot River; **March 8, 1993** Slate Covered Bridge burned by arsonists.

Troy *Cheshire County* *Southwestern New Hampshire, 39 mi/63 km southwest of Manchester*

1764 William Barker of Massachusetts becomes first settler; **1768** grist mill built by Thomas Tollman; **1779** tannery established by David Cutting; **1786** store, tavern built by Jonas Warren; **1812** Morse Tavern built by Josiah Morse; **1814** town hall completed, building turned to face common 1856; **1815** town incorporated; **1818** Dr. Whitney House built; **1828** Old Academy opened, closed 1838; **1835** Trinitarian Church built; **1837** town's woolen and quarrying industries founded; **1840** Cheshire Railroad reaches town, station built 1843; **1848** David W. Farrar House built; **1849** First Baptist Church built; **1857** Troy Blanket Mills opened by Thomas Goodall; **1870s** Kimball House hotel opened; **1903** Immaculate Conception Catholic Church completed; **1953** Gay-Kimball Library built.

Wakefield *Carroll County* *Eastern New Hampshire, 37 mi/60 km northeast of Concord*

1723 skirmish between Capt. John Lovewell's forces and Native Americans, 10 natives killed; **1749** land grant made to John Horne, others; **1770** Samuel Haines builds sawmill and grist mills at Union village, first settlement in Town of Wakefield; **1774** town incorporated; town pound built; **1804** Wakefield Inn built; **c.1852** Old Union Hotel built; **1871** Boston & Maine Railroad reaches town; **2001** public safety building opened.

Walpole *Cheshire County* *Southwestern New Hampshire, 51 mi/82 km west of Manchester*

1736 land grant made by Massachusetts Colony; **1749** John Kilburn becomes first settler; **1752** town incorporated in New Hampshire by Col. Benjamin Bellows; **1762** Walpole Inn built; **c.1770** Col. John Bellows House built; **Apr. 22, 1771** editor, satirist Thomas Green Fessenden born (died 1837); **1785** first bridge across Connecticut River built to Bellows Falls, Vermont, by Col. Enoch Hale; **1792** Amasa Allen House built; Josiah Bellows House built; **1812** Knapp House built; **1815** Old Colony Inn completed; **1905** steel bridge built across river.

Warner *Merrimack County* *Central New Hampshire, 15 mi/24 km northwest of Concord*

1735 land granted for town by Massachusetts Colony, originally named New Amesbury; **1749** town regranted, fails to attract settlers; **1762** Daniel Annis becomes first settler; **1765** grist mill and sawmill built; **1769** town regranted again by Masonian proprietors; **1774** town incorporated as Warner, named for Col. Jonathan Warner; first bridge built; **1810** post office established; **Jan. 19, 1810** tornado strikes followed by drop in temperature to −25°F/−32°C, called "Cold Friday"; **Sept. 1821** tornado damages area, lends name to Hurricane Corner crossroads; **1833** Gen. Aquilla Davis House built; **1849** Concord & Claremont Railroad extended to town; **1871** first annual local fair held.

Washington *Sullivan County* *Southwestern New Hampshire, 28 mi/45 km west of Concord*

1762 town charter granted; **1768** first settlers arrive, originating from Massachusetts; **1776** town incorporated, first town in U.S. to be named for George Washington; **1787** town hall built; **1840** Congregational Church built; **1842** Christian Brethren Church built; **1859** Grange Hall built at East Washington; **1869** Shedd Free Library established, built 1881; **1877** East Washington Baptist Church built; **1883** Center School built, later used as police station.

Weare *Hillsborough County* *Southern New Hampshire, 15 mi/24 km northwest of Manchester*

1735 land grant made to Robert Hale by Massachusetts Colony, originally named Beverly-Canada; **1749** regranted to Ichabod Robie, renamed Robie's Town; **1764** town incorporated; renamed for Meschech Weare, first President (governor) of New Hampshire, 1776–1785; first settlers arrive; **1770** Quakers settle at Weare Center; **Apr. 13, 1772** in Pine Tree Riot, crowd attacks Sheriff Whiting, string him up, crop ears of his horse in dispute over ownership of log harvest, eight arrested; **1799** Friends

Meeting House built; **1938** flooding destroys town's toy manufacturing industry.

Willey House   *Carroll County*   *North central New Hampshire, 68 mi/109 km north of Concord*

1771 Timothy Nash discovers Crawford Notch mountain pass; **1800** tavern built at Crawford Notch by Abel Crawford; **Aug. 29, 1826** Willey family killed by avalanche, ran from house into path of slide, house spared; **1828** Notch House Hotel built by Abel Crawford and son Ethan Allen Crawford, burned 1853, rebuilt as Crawford House; **c.1840** Gray Stone Inn built, managed by Dr. Samuel A. Bemis until his death 1882; **1875** Portland & Ogdensburg (Maine Central) Railroad builds 500 ft/152 m trestle at Frankenstein Cliffs, rebuilt 1905.

Winchester   *Cheshire County*   *Southwestern New Hampshire, 50 mi/80 km southwest of Manchester*

1732 town first settled, originally named Earlington, later Arlington; mill built at mouth of Roaring Brook; **1739** town renamed Winchester; **1744** new provincial boundary puts most of town in New Hampshire, portion in Warwick, Massachusetts; garrisons built around homes as defense against Native Americans under command of French; **1753** town incorporated; displaced settlers return, Native American attacks continue; **1828** local artist Cordelia Hinds Wheeler born (died 1918); **1837** Coombs

Covered Bridge built across Ashuelot River; **Oct. 9, 1860** World War I Gen. Leonard Wood born, U.S. Army training facility in Missouri named for him (died 1927); **1864** Ashuelot Covered Bridge built.

Wolfeboro   *Carroll County*   *Eastern New Hampshire, 32 mi/51 km northeast of Concord*

1759 land granted for town, named Wolfeborough for Gen. James Wolfe, fought in Battle of Plains of Abraham, Quebec City; **1768** Wentworth Mansion begun by Gov. John Wentworth, occupied 1770, never completed, he died 1820; **1770** town incorporated; **1778** Clark House built; **1792** Town House built; **1838** steamship *Belknap* launched on Lake Winnipesaukee, wrecked in storm 1841, site named Steamboat Island; **1849** Pavilion Inn built, razed 1899; **1872** Boston & Maine Railroad arrives, abandoned 1915; hotel built, becomes Hobbs-is-Inn 1899, Glendon House 1909, razed 1935; sidewheeler *Mount Washington* launched by railroad, destroyed by fire 1939, replaced 1940; **1881** Brewster Academy chartered, built 1905; **1883** shoe factory built; **1889** town's first summer home built on Wolfeboro Bay; **1890** Brewster Library opened, renamed Wolfeboro Library 1979; **1895** town name shortened to Wolfeboro.

Woodsville   *Grafton County*   See **Haverhill (1853, 1889)**

New Jersey

Northeastern U.S. Capital: Trenton. Major cities: Atlantic City, Newark.

New Jersey was one of the 13 colonies which adopted the U.S. Declaration of Independence July 4, 1776. It became the 3rd state to ratify the U.S. Constitution December 18, 1787.

New Jersey is divided into 21 counties. The counties are divided into civil divisions called townships, all of which are incorporated with strong municipal-like governments. Municipalities are classified as villages, towns, cities, and boroughs. See Introduction.

Asbury Park   *Monmouth County*   *Eastern New Jersey, 37 mi/60 km south-southeast of Newark*

1871 town founded on Atlantic Ocean as religious retreat, named for Methodist Bishop Francis Asbury; **March 14, 1877** *Vogue* editor Edna Chase born (died 1957); **Oct. 2, 1895** comedian Bud Abbott born (died 1974); **1897** incorporated as a city; **1912** Steinbach Department Store opened, closed 1990s; **1917** fire destroys four blocks of hotels; **Sept. 8, 1934** steamer *Morro Castle* on way to New York from Havana burns, killing 134, its smoking hull stranded on beach near boardwalk; **June 20, 1956** Venezuelan aircraft plunges into Atlantic killing 74; **July 5, 1970** four days of racial rioting leaves 165 injured; **1980s** several projects left incomplete as city falls into decay.

Atlantic City   *Atlantic County*   *Southeastern New Jersey, 57 mi/92 km southeast of Philadelphia*

c.1790 area first settled; **1852** beach resort town founded on Absecon Island on Atlantic Ocean; **1854** Absecon Lighthouse built, used until 1932; incorporated as a city; Camden & Atlantic Railroad reaches city; **1869** first Ferris wheel built; **1870** boardwalk and amusement pier built, first in world, idea of hotelier Jacob Keim; **1884** M. D. Shill invents rolling chair, predecessor to the baby carriage, which he rents to tourists; **1895** first picture postcard developed by Carl M. Voelker and wife, inspired by German picture cards; **July 30, 1896** railroad accident, 60 killed; **1898** Heinz Pier built as promotional display for Heinz Foods; **1902** Atlantic City Free Library founded, new library opened 1985; **1906** 1,700-ft/518-m Million Dollar Pier completed, name adopted 1938; **Oct. 28, 1906** railroad accident, 40 killed; **1913** Garden Pier built; **Sept. 7, 1917** African-American painter Jacob Lawrence born (died 2000); **Sept. 1921** first Miss America pageant held to attract late season visitors, winner Margaret Gorman,

Washington, D.C.; **1922** Masonic Temple established; **1924** bridge built north across Absecon Channel to Brigantine; **1930** board game *Monopoly* invented here, produced 1935 by Parker Brothers, "property" names taken from Atlantic City street names; **1932** convention hall and auditorium completed, site of 1964 Democratic Convention; **1937** Stanley S. Holmes Village housing project opened; **1941** Pitney Village built, intended model residential village between Texas and Bellevue avenues; **Jan. 7, 1952** $4 million in property loss in boardwalk fire; **Nov. 18, 1963** 25 killed as fire sweeps through Surfside Hotel convalescent home; **1965** Atlantic City Expressway opened; **March 28, 1973** second Norwegian freighter, *Anita,* sinks with 32 on board, first on March 22 off Cape May; **May 26, 1978** gambling legalized in Atlantic City, Resorts International Hotel Casino opens June 5, first casino outside Nevada; **1985** Atlantic City Historical Museum opened; **2001** city boasts at least twelve major casino-hotels; **1997** Atlantic City Convention Center built; **July 2001** highway tunnel opened under Absecon Channel north to Brigantine.

Barnegat Light   *Ocean County*   *Eastern New Jersey, 33 mi/53 km north of Atlantic City, on Atlantic Ocean*

1609 area sighted by explorer Henry Hudson; **1855** Barnegat Lighthouse ("Old Barney") built, replaces 1824 light, decommissioned 1927; village originally named Barnegat City; **c.1900** Oceanic Hotel built, washed away 1929; Sunset Hotel built, destroyed by fire 1932; **1904** incorporated as a borough; **1930** lighthouse abandoned after repeated storms erode its base, replaced by light ship stationed offshore; **1948** borough renamed Barnegat Light.

Batsto *Burlington County* *Southeastern New Jersey, 23 mi/37 km northwest of Atlantic City*

1697 area along Mullica River settled by Swedes; **1765** Batsto Iron Works established by Charles Read, munitions made here during Revolutionary War and War of 1812; **1766** town founded; **1784** Richards Mansion built, home of iron works manager Col. William Richards, remains in Richards family until 1876; **1876** industrialist Joseph Wharton restores village, contributes to its Victorian appearance; **1954** state acquires town as historic site.

Bayonne *Hudson County* *Northeastern New Jersey, 5 mi/8 km southeast of Newark, on Hudson River*

1609 Henry Hudson stops here on his exploration of Hudson River; **1646** Jacob Jacobsen Roy receives land patent; **1654** settled by Dutch traders, soon driven out by Native Americans, resettled 1658 after treaty; **1664** British gain possession of area; **c.1861** rail trestle built across Newark Bay from Elizabethport; **1869** incorporated as a city; **1875** Prentice Refinery built, city's first oil refinery; **1881** Trinity Episcopal Church built; **1892** Elco Iron Works organized, builder of ocean cruisers; **1900** oil refinery fire burns three days; **1915–1916** Standard Oil of New Jersey beset by major labor dispute; **Nov. 14, 1921** TV actor Brian Keith born (died 1997); **Feb. 15, 1921** physicist Herman Kahn born (died 1983); **1928** Bayonne Bridge built across Kill van Kull strait to Staten Island, New York; **1930** spectacular blaze destroys Gulf Oil Refinery; **Jan. 1, 1940** actor Frank Langella born; **Apr. 23, 1942** actress Sandra Dee born.

Belleville *Essex County* *Northeastern New Jersey, 4 mi/6.4 km north of Newark, on Passaic River*

c.1680 town settled, originally named Second River; **1710** Spear Mansion built; **1725** Dutch Reformed Church built; **1777** Newark's Second River section scene of rearguard fighting during Revolution; **1797** town renamed; **1798** John Stevens manufactures steam engine, first made in America, installs engine in steamboat, makes runs to New York; **1897** trolley service begins, abandoned 1937; **1900** Wesley Methodist Church built, replaces 1803 structure; **1910** incorporated as a town; **1956** Congregation Ahavath Achim synagogue built, replaces 1924 structure.

Belvidere *Warren County* *Northwestern New Jersey, 48 mi/77 km west of Newark, on Delaware River*

c.1690 area first settled by Dutch; **c.1770** Robert Patterson becomes first permanent settler; town founded as Greenwich-on-the-Delaware; **1775** town renamed by Maj. Robert Hoops, purchased land from Patterson; **1824** Warren County formed; town becomes county seat; **c.1825** county courthouse built; **1845** incorporated as a town; **1986** Wayne Dumont, Jr. County Administration Building opened; **1998** war memorial dedicated.

Bloomfield *Essex County* *Northeastern New Jersey, 5 mi/8 km north-northwest of Newark*

1666 area settled by Dutch; town founded as Wardsesson; **1758** first school built; **c.1765** sandstone quarrying begins, used in New York City's brownstone buildings; **1796** First Presbyterian Church built; town renamed for Joseph Bloomfield, Revolutionary War general; **1806** construction of Newark & Pompton Turnpike begins; **1812** incorporated as a town, separates from Newark; **1830** woolen mill founded, used through 1940s; **1837** musical instrument company established by Luis Peloubet; **Apr. 12, 1840** publisher Frank Howard Dodd born (died 1916); **1856** first railroad reaches town; **1868** Bloomfield College established; **1872** *Bloomfield Gazette* newspaper founded, becomes *Independent Press* 1883; **1900** incorporated as a city; **1952** Garden State Parkway completed.

Boonton *Morris County* *Northeastern New Jersey, 17 mi/27 km northwest of Newark*

1760 town settled as Boone Town, named for Colonial Gov. Thomas Boone (1760–1761); **1747** Obadiah Baldwin establishes iron furnace; **1775** town becomes important producer of iron war implements; **1830** New Jersey Iron Company founded; **1852** iron industry collapses with opening of Great Lakes iron reserves; **1867** incorporated as a town; **1875** Lackawanna Railroad reaches town; **1890** Boonton-Holmes Public Library founded; **1903** Boonton Dam built on Passaic River, forms Parsippany (Jersey City) Reservoir, town moved to north.

Bordentown *Burlington County* *Western New Jersey, 6 mi/9.7 km south of Trenton, on Delaware River*

1682 town founded by Quaker Thomas Farnsworth, called Farnsworth's Landing; **1725** Patience Lovell born, popular wax figure artist (died 1785); **1740** Friends Meeting House built; **1750** Hopkinson House built; **Jan. 1778** "mechanical kegs," explosive marine mines produced here by Col. Joseph Borden, kill four British in Delaware River, British respond May 1778, townspeople destroy their own 20-boat fleet in advance; **1816** mansion of ex-king of France Joseph Bonaparte built, now Bonaparte Park; **1825** incorporated as a borough; **1831** Camden & Amboy Railroad built; **1834** Delaware & Raritan Canal completed; **Feb. 8, 1844** editor, poet Richard Gilder born (died 1909); **1852** Clara Barton establishes Bordentown School for boys, becomes state-supported school for African-Americans; **1867** incorporated as a city; **1870** Bordentown Military School established.

Bridgeton *Cumberland County* *Southern New Jersey, 37 mi/60 km south of Camden, near Delaware River*

1686 settled by Richard Hancock, others; **1716** bridge built across Cohansey Creek, town named Cohansey Bridge; **1748** Cumberland County formed; **1749** town becomes county seat, renamed Bridge Town; **1752** county courthouse built; **1776** Potters Tavern opened; **1792** Broad

Street Presbyterian Church built; Gen. Giles Manor House built; **1797** Masonic Hall built; **1814** dam built for mill, later becomes Tumbling Dam Park; Cumberland Nail and Iron Works established; **1816** new bank incorrectly uses "Bridgeton" in its name; town renamed to agree with bank; **1834** glass making industry begins; Dr. William J. Elmer House built; **1864** incorporated as a city; **1934** Cohanzick Zoo opened.

Burlington   *Burlington County   West central New Jersey, 16 mi/26 km northeast of Camden, on Delaware River*

1677 town founded by Quakers; **c.1678** Henry Carey House built; **1681** Burlington County formed; town becomes capital of West Jersey colony; **1683** Friends Meeting House built, replaced 1784; **1693** incorporated as a borough; **1694** county organized; town becomes first county seat; **1698** shipyard established at Barbarroux Wharf; **1702** following merger of East and West Jersey, colonial capital alternates between Burlington and Perth Amboy until 1790; **1703** St. Mary's Catholic Church built, replaced 1854; **1733** incorporated as a city; **1750** Blue Anchor Tavern built; **c.1750** Birch-Bloomfield Mansion built; **1751** Metropolitan Inn built; **1776** Provincial Congress meets, adopts state constitution; **Dec. 1776** town attacked by British; **1778** town bombarded by British ships; **Oct. 1, 1781** Capt. James Lawrence born, quoted as saying "Don't give up the ship," died in action off Boston June 5, 1813; **Sept 15, 1789** novelist James Fenimore Cooper born (died 1851); **1796** county seat moved to Mount Holly; **1798** Bradford Mansion built; **1801** Temple B'nai Israel built as residence, purchased 1916; **1808** Steamboat Hotel established; **1834** first tracks laid by Camden & Amboy Railroad; **1839** Lyceum Hall built; **1847** Broad Street Methodist Church built; **1864** city library built; **1877** Birch Opera House built, closed 1927; **1931** Burlington-Bristol Bridge built to Bristol, Pennsylvania; **Aug. 9, 2000** two small Piper aircraft collide, killing all, nine in one, two on training flight in other.

Caldwell   *Essex County   Northeastern New Jersey, 9 mi/14.5 km northwest of Newark*

1785 town settled; **March 18, 1837** Grover (Stephen) Cleveland, 22nd and 24th President, born (died June 24, 1908); **1892** incorporated as a borough; **1901** Monomonock Inn opened; **1934** Cleveland House becomes state historic site; **1939** Caldwell College established; **1981** town officially becomes Township of the Borough of Caldwell; **1994** advertising executive Thomas Mosser killed at North Caldwell by mail bomb sent by "Unabomber," 14th bomb since 1978 from unknown origin, 3 killed, 23 injured, traced to Ted Kaczynski living in shack in Montana.

Camden   *Camden County   Southwestern New Jersey, on Delaware River, opposite Philadelphia*

1623 Fort Nassau built by Dutch Capt. Cornelius Jacobsen Mey, rebuilt 1651; **1681** William Cooper becomes first settler, establishes ferry on Delaware River; settlement called Cooper's Ferry; **1726** Charles S. Boyer Hall built by Joseph Cooper, Jr., used as Historical Museum; **1734** Benjamin Cooper House built; **1773** town renamed for Earl of Camden, opponent of Stamp Act; **1794** Friends School built; Ferry House built; **1801** Newton Friends Meeting House built; **1809** steamboat ferry begins operation; **1828** incorporated as a city; **1834** town becomes terminus of Camden & Amboy Railroad; **1844** Camden County formed; city becomes county seat; **1848** Walt Whitman Home built, occupied by poet from 1884 until his death in 1892; **May 15, 1856** steam ferry *New Jersey* burns, sinks in river, 61 killed; **1858** Esterbrook Steel Pen Company begins manufacture of fountain pens; **Dec. 19, 1858** author Horace L. Traubel born (died 1919); **1869** Campbell Soup Company plant begun by Joseph Campbell and Abraham Anderson; **1894** Radio Corporation of America (RCA) begins with production of Victor talking machine; **1904** county courthouse built; **1926** Delaware River Bridge completed to Philadelphia, later renamed Ben Franklin Bridge; **1927** Rutgers University Camden Campus established; **1929** Central Airport opens; **1957** Walt Whitman Bridge completed across Delaware River to Philadelphia; **July 21, 1959** first atomic powered merchant ship, the *Savannah*, launched.

Cape May   *Cape May County   Southeastern New Jersey, 40 mi/64 km south of Atlantic City*

1623 Cornelius Jacobsen Mey sails past cape, later named for him; **1631** land purchased by Samuel Godyn and Samuel Blommaert; **1699** pirate Captain Kidd pursued to Cape May by Col. William Quary, Kidd eludes capture; **1801** first rooming house begins town's role as resort; **1848** incorporated as a borough, named Cape Island; **1857** incorporated as a city; **1859** Cape May Lighthouse built; **1863** Southern Mansion built by industrialist George Allen of Philadelphia; **1867** Church of the Advent built; **1869** city renamed Cape May; **1876** Chalfonte Hotel built; **1878** fire destroys Congress Hall hotel, rebuilt; **1879** Franklin Street Methodist Church built; **1903** first Ford dealer receives its first car from Henry Ford; **March 22, 1973** 29 of 30 on board Norwegian freighter *Norse Variant* lost as it sinks off cape (second Norwegian freighter sinks March 28 off Atlantic City).

Cape May Court House   *Cape May County Southeastern New Jersey, 28 mi/45 km south of Atlantic City*

1630s area near Great Sound, Atlantic Ocean, first settled; **1692** Cape May County formed; original county seat located at Town Bank; **1703** village of Cape May Courthouse platted; **1745** village becomes county seat;

1848 county courthouse built; 1923 Cape May County Library founded.

East Brunswick Middlesex County Northeastern New Jersey, 23 mi/37 km south-southwest of Newark

1660s first permanent settlers arrive; c.1685 town of Old Bridge founded; 1820s town becomes important river port; 1833 Camden & Amboy Railroad reaches town; 1850 brick manufacturing begins, continues through 1878; 1860 East Brunswick Township formed; July 10, 1936 highest temperature ever recorded in New Jersey reached at Runyon to southeast, 110°F/43°C; 1952 New Jersey Turnpike completed; 1967 East Brunswick Library founded.

East Orange Essex County Northeastern New Jersey, 3 mi/4.8 km west-northwest of Newark

1678 area settled, named for England's William, Prince of Orange; 1720 copper mining begins; 1813 Second Presbyterian Church built, burned 1927, rebuilt; Nov. 11, 1899 poet, writer Thomas Chubb born (died 1972); 1909 incorporated as a city; Apr. 11, 1910 educator Margaret Clapp born (died 1974); March 12, 1921 singer Gordon MacRae born (died 1986); 1923 Upsala College moved here from Kenilworth, established 1893, closed 1995; 1929 municipal center built; Dec. 12, 1941 singer Dionne Warwick born; Aug. 9, 1963 singer Whitney Houston born.

East Rutherford Bergen County Northeastern New Jersey, 7 mi/11.3 km north-northeast of Newark

1894 incorporated as a borough; June 9, 1940 sports announcer Dick Vitale born; 1976 Giants Stadium built, home of New York Jets and Giants football teams; Meadowlands Racetrack opened; 1981 Brendon Byrne Arena opened, renamed Continental Airlines Arena 1996; Oct. 5, 1995 Pope John Paul II delivers homily to 83,000 at Giants Stadium.

Elizabeth Union County Northeastern New Jersey, 5 mi/8 km south of Newark, on Atlantic Ocean

1664 land purchased from Staten Island Native Americans; first settled by people from Long Island, named Elizabethtown; 1668 town becomes capital of East Jersey Province; 1669 mill built by John Ogden; 1686 capital moved to Perth Amboy; 1687 town becomes important leather goods producer; c.1700 original section of Belcher Mansion built; 1740 incorporated as a borough; 1746 College of New Jersey established, moved to Newark 1740, to Princeton 1756 to become Princeton University; 1779 Elizabeth Daily Journal newspaper founded; 1789 First Presbyterian Church completed, original church built 1665; 1855 incorporated as a city; renamed Elizabeth; 1857 Union County formed; city becomes county seat; 1860 St. John's Episcopal Church built; 1861 town of Linden separates from Elizabeth; 1865 city hall built; 1873 manufacture of Singer sewing machines begins; Oct. 30, 1882 Adm. William Frederick Halsey, Jr. born (died 1959); 1887 St. Patrick's Cathedral built; 1903 county courthouse built; 1910 Sts. Peter and Paul Catholic Church built; 1912 Public Library built, founded 1755; 1931 Goethals Bridge built across Arthur Kill estuary to Staten Island, New York; 17-story office tower added to county courthouse complex; Dec. 16, 1951 Miami Airlines C-46 plunges into Elizabeth River killing 56; Jan. 22, 1952 American Airlines Convair crashes killing 30; Feb. 11, 1952 National Airlines DC-6 crashes killing 33; Sept. 15, 1958 commuter train accident, 48 killed.

Englewood Bergen County Northeastern New Jersey, 15 mi/24 km north-northeast of Newark

1632 village established by Lenape tribe members; 1703 Lydecker House built; 1776 Liberty Pole Tavern built, rendezvous for Revolutionary activists; 1780 Gen. George Washington establishes headquarters here; 1858 railroad reaches site; 1859 town founded; 1860 First Presbyterian Church built; Englewood House hotel opened, demolished 1902; June 12, 1864 ornithologist Frank Chapman born (died 1945); 1866 St. Cecelia's Catholic Church built; 1890 The Lyceum opened; Englewood Public Library founded; 1896 incorporated as a village; trolley service established, abandoned 1937; 1899 incorporated as a city; June 22, 1906 writer Anne Morrow Lindbergh born, wife of Charles Lindbergh (died 2001); 1928 Actor's Fund Home for retired actors and entertainers moved from Staten Island; July 18, 1929 Olympic skater Dick Button born; Nov. 28, 1950 actor Ed Harris born; Feb. 18, 1954 actor John Travolta born.

Flemington Hunterdon County Northwestern New Jersey, 20 mi/32 km north of Trenton

1712 land acquired by William Penn and Daniel Coxe; 1714 Hunterdon County formed; c.1730 area settled; 1746 Samuel Fleming arrives, opens tavern; town founded; 1768 Jasper Smith House built; 1780 Flemington Vigilante Society organized for detection of horse thieves; 1785 county seat moved to Flemington after being held alternately between Hopewell and Maidenhead since 1714; 1814 Union Hotel built by Neal Hart; 1828 second county courthouse built; 1910 incorporated as a borough; 1930 Flemington Egg, Poultry, and Livestock Auction established; 1937 Standard Oil of New Jersey establishes headquarters here; Aug. 4, 1958 Olympic runner Mary Decker born.

Fort Lee Bergen County Northeastern New Jersey, 14 mi/23 km north-northeast of Newark, on Hudson River

1756 Stephen Bourdette builds first house, used in 1776 as headquarters of George Washington; July 1776 Fort Constitution built, later renamed Fort Lee; Nov. 18, 1776 Hessians capture Fort Lee as George Washington abandons fort; 1898 Palisades Park established to south as picnic grove, developed as amusement park by 1908;

c.1900–1915 serves as movie industry center; 1904 incorporated as a borough; 1919 Fort Lee Public Library founded, new library opened 1972; 1922 Judge Moore House built; Oct. 25, 1931 George Washington Bridge opened to upper Manhattan, second deck opened 1962; Sept. 12, 1971 Palisades Park closed, later demolished for condominiums.

Freehold   *Monmouth County*   *East central New Jersey, 33 mi/53 km south of Newark*

1650s first settlers arrive; 1665 Monmouth County formed; 1670 county court alternates between Middletown and Shrewsbury; c.1692 Old Scots Meeting House built; 1715 town founded as county seat, named Monmouth Court House; 1731 Old Tennent Church built on site of meeting house, rebuilt 1751; 1755 Hankinson Mansion built; June 28, 1778 in Battle of Monmouth, British repulsed by Washington's forces in 96-degree heat, Molly Pitcher takes her wounded husband's place in front lines, estimated 250 British and 70 Americans killed, largest land battle of Revolution; 1795 post office established; 1834 *Democrat* newspaper founded; 1853 Freehold & Jamesburg Agricultural Railroad reaches town; Freehold Race Track founded, reopened 1937 after years of neglect; 1869 town renamed Freehold; 1874 county courthouse built; 1878 Monmouth Battle monument built; 1919 incorporated as a borough; Sept. 23, 1949 singer Bruce Springsteen born; 1977 National Broadcasters Hall of Fame founded.

Glassboro   *Gloucester County*   *Southwestern New Jersey, 17 mi/27 km south of Camden*

1775 area first settled; 1779 land acquired by German immigrant Solomon Stanger; 1780 Stanger's widow Catherine opens glass factory; town founded; c.1785 Heston Tavern established; 1840 glass bottle shaped like log cabin produced here for William Henry Harrison's presidential campaign, promoting his grassroots origins, bottles filled by Philadelphia distillery of E. C. Booz, origin of term "booze"; 1842 Glassboro Academy founded; 1849 Holly Bush Mansion built; 1920 incorporated as a borough; 1923 Glassboro State College established as Glassboro State Normal School, renamed Rowan University 1992; 1936 Glassboro Public Library opened, joined county system 1996; June 23–25, 1967 Soviet Premier Alexei Kosygin and Pres. Lyndon Johnson meet for ten hours at the Glassboro Summit, Glassboro State College, considered first sign of thaw in Cold War; 1979 Heritage Glass Museum founded.

Hackensack   *Bergen County*   *Northeastern New Jersey, 13 mi/21 km north-northeast of Newark*

1577 Chief Oratam of the Lenapes born, "Sagamore of the Hacquinsacq"; 1647 Dutch establish trading post, named New Barbados; 1670 Terhune House built by John Terhune; 1664 land deeded to Dutch by Chief Oratam; 1682 Bergen County formed; 1710 town becomes county seat; 1696 Church on the Green (First Dutch Reformed)

built; 1751 Mansion House built, used by George Washington as headquarters 1776; 1776-1780 frequent skirmishes occur during Revolution, raided 1780 by Hessians and British; June 12, 1798 Confederate Gen. Samuel Cooper born (died 1876); c.1816 Hopper House built; 1868 incorporated as a town; 1901 Johnson Free Library opened; 1912 county courthouse built; 1921 incorporated as a city, renamed; March 12, 1923 astronaut Walter Shirra, Jr. born; 1933 county administrative building built; Sept. 22, 1956 singer Debby Boone born to singer Pat Boone.

Haddonfield   *Camden County*   *Southwestern New Jersey, 5 mi/8 km east-southeast of Camden*

1711 town founded by Quaker Elizabeth Haddon on property purchased by her father, who remained in England; 1712 original Haddon House built, burned 1742, brick house built on site in 1845; 1750 town becomes favored destination for well-to-do vacationers; Indian King Tavern built; c.1775 Old Guardhouse built; 1777 state legislature first meets at Indian King Tavern; 1858 "Haddonfield Hadrosaur" discovered, first complete dinosaur fossil ever found; 1875 incorporated as a borough; 1993 dinosaur excavation designated a national historic site.

Highland Park   *Middlesex County*   *Northeastern New Jersey, 21 mi/34 km south-southwest of Newark*

1667 area first settled by dissident Baptist group; 1675 town of Raritan Falls established on Raritan River; 1695 extensive land grant awarded to John Field; 1741 Low House built by Cornelius Low; 1743 Field Homestead overlooking Raritan River built by grandson of John Field; 1744 Mercer House built by Dr. William Mercer; 1793 Ross Hall residence built by Edward Antill; 1830s Delaware & Raritan Canal built; 1835 New Jersey Railroad reaches town; 1844 bridge built across Raritan River replacing ferry; 1905 incorporated as borough of Highland Park.

Highlands   *Monmouth County*   *Northeastern New Jersey, 25 mi/40 km southeast of Newark, on Atlantic Ocean*

1762 Water Witch House built, setting for James Fenimore Cooper's novel of same name; 1763 Sandy Hook Lighthouse built on tip of Sandy Hook peninsula; 1776 Fort Hancock built by Americans at tip of Sandy Hook point; June 28, 1778 Sir Henry Clinton's army arrives at Fort Hancock following Battle of Monmouth; 1828 Navesink Lighthouse built; 1856 Chapel Hill Lighthouse built, discontinued 1957; 1862 Twin Lights replace 1828 light, decommissioned 1949; 1900 incorporated as a borough; 1903 U.S. Navy erects first wireless station at Monmouth Hills; Oct. 27, 1972 Gateway National Recreation Area established, includes Sandy Hook, extends into New York.

Hoboken   *Hudson County   Northeastern New Jersey, 7 mi/11.3 km east of Newark, on Hudson River*

1640 Dutch settle on land occupied by Lenape peoples; **1642** first brewery in America established by Aert T. van Putten; **1804** Col. John Stevens operates experimental steamboat with twin-screw propellers, makes 9-mi/14.5-km demonstration trip on Hudson River; **1808** Colonel Stevens establishes steam ferry service on *Phoenix;* **1811** Stevens' *Juliana* begins service, first regularly scheduled steam ferry in world; **1816** Paterson Plank Road built; **1846** organized baseball makes its debut with Hoboken Knickerbocker Giants; **1855** incorporated as a city, separates from North Bergen; **Jan. 1, 1864** photographer Alfred Stieglitz born (died 1946); **May 27, 1867** chemist Julius Oscar Stieglitz born (died 1937); **1868** Morris & Essex Railroad reaches town; **1870** Stevens Institute of Technology established; **June 11, 1876** anthropologist Alfred Louis Kroeber born (died 1960); **1894** Hoboken Public Library founded; **May 26, 1895** photographer Dorothea Lange born (died 1965); **March 9, 1900** mathematician Howard H. Aiken born, designed programmable computer (died 1973); **June 30, 1900** fire at shipping docks, 326 killed; **Dec. 12, 1915** singer, actor Frank Sinatra born (died 1998); **Sept. 29, 1973** fire in four tenement buildings, 10 killed, 6 injured.

Hopewell   *Mercer County   North central New Jersey, 11 mi/18 km north of Trenton*

c.1695 area settled; **1714** Hunterdon County formed; town becomes county seat, alternates with Maidenhead (now Lawrenceville); **1748** Old School Baptist Church built; **1756** Arthur King House built; **c.1782** explorer, fur trader William Price Hunt born (died 1842); **1785** county seat moved to Flemington; **1812** Mercer County formed, includes Hopewell; **1891** incorporated as a borough; **March 1, 1932** Charles Lindbergh, Jr., 20 months old, kidnapped from Lindbergh home; **May 12, 1932** body of Charles Lindbergh, Jr. found on road to Princeton by truck driver 5 mi/9 km from home, Bruno Hauptmann charged, executed Apr. 3, 1936; **1941** Lindbergh estate becomes state historic site.

Jersey City   *Hudson County   Northeastern New Jersey, 3 mi/4.8 km west of New York City, on Hudson River*

1630 first settlement begins with purchase of tract by Michael Pauw; **1633** Dutch establish trading post for interior Native Americans; **1661** New Jersey's first court, school, and church established; **1668** town incorporated; **1680** Old Bergen Church built, rebuilt 1773; **1764** ferry service established; **c.1770** Paulus Hook Race Track established; **1775-1781** British build fortifications at Paulus Hook; **Aug. 19, 1779** British defenses successfully stormed by "Light Horse" Harry Lee and his 300 men; **1804** incorporated as a city; **1808** Jersey City Medical Center founded; **1827** Joseph Dixon Crucible Plant opens; **1834** New Jersey Railroad establishes terminus at waterfront; **1840** Hudson County formed; city becomes county

seat; **1847** Colgate-Palmolive Plant moved from New York City; **1872** St. Peter's College established; **1901** public library opened; **1916** Black Tom munitions dock explosion kills two, German sabotage suspected; **Aug. 24, 1917** TV personality Dennis James born (died 1997); **1927** Jersey City University established; **Sept. 26, 1930** actor Philip Bosco born; **Dec. 8, 1933** comedian Flip Wilson born (died 1998); **March 19, 1935** actress Phyllis Newman born; **June 8, 1940** singer Nancy Sinatra born, daughter of Frank Sinatra; **Nov. 24, 1940** baseball commissioner Paul Tagliabue born; **Sept. 30, 1943** singer Marilyn McCoo, of Fifth Dimension singing group, born; **July 3, 1962** $2.5 million found in domestic garage by workers, another $168,000 found in second garage, investigation leads to gambler Joseph Moriarty serving time in prison; **March 6, 1969** tenement fire kills nine, including eight children; **July 5, 1971** Mayor Thomas Whelan, seven city officials, indicted for extortion; **1974** Hudson County Community College established; **1975** county courthouse built; **March 4, 1993** FBI arrests Mohammed Salameh, Islamic militant leader, four others, for conspiring to blow up World Trade Center in Feb. 1993.

Keansburg   *Monmouth County   Northeastern New Jersey, 20 mi/32 km south-southeast of Newark*

1620s area on Lower New York Bay first settled by Dutch; **1884** town named for Sen. John Kean of Elizabeth; **1903** Keansburg Amusement Park established; **1917** incorporated as a borough; **May 22, 1958** Nike missiles explode in their silos at Leonardo to east, 10 killed; **Jan. 9, 1981** fire at boarding home for elderly, 30 killed.

Kenvil   *Morris County   Northern New Jersey, 26 mi/42 km west-northwest of Newark*

1870 hotel established by McCain family; town founded as McCainville; **1871** Hercules Powder Company plant opens; **1889** town renamed Kenvil; **March 8, 1934** explosion at powder plant packing house, four killed; **Sept. 11–12, 1940** two explosions at Hercules Powder plant, 51 killed and 49 killed on respective days.

Lakehurst   *Ocean County   East central New Jersey, 47 mi/76 km north of Atlantic City*

1789 cannonball forge established for Continental Army; **c.1850** town settled, named Manchester; **1860** New Jersey Central Railroad shops established, closed 1932; **1874** St. John's Roman Catholic Church built; **1884** Rogers Hotel built; **1897** post office established; **1898** Pine Tree Inn opened, razed 1940; **1919** Lakehurst Naval Air Station established; **1921** incorporated as a borough; **1923** first U.S. airship *Shenandoah* makes initial departure; **1924** transatlantic airship terminus established; **1936** German zeppelin/airship *Hindenburg* makes ten Atlantic flights during year; **May 6, 1937** German airship *Hindenburg* burns while docking at mooring tower, 36 killed.

Lakewood *Ocean County* *Eastern New Jersey, 45 mi/72 km south of Newark*

1800 area settled; **1814** iron smelter established by Jesse Richards; **1863** New Jersey Southern Railroad reaches town; **1865** Bricksburg House built by Riley A. Brick; **1879** Laurel House residence built by two New York stock brokers, Rudyard Kipling, Mark Twain, Oliver Wendell Holmes entertained here; **1890s** prominent New Yorkers build mansions on Lake Carasaljo, including the Rockefellers, Tilfords, Vanderbilts, Astors; **1891** Laurel-in-the-Pines Hotel opened; Lakewood Hotel opened; **1893** Lakewood Township formed; **1908** Georgian Court College established.

Lawrenceville *Mercer County* *Central New Jersey, 5 mi/8 km north of Trenton*

1697 town founded as Maidenhead; **1761** Beardsley House built; **1764** Lawrenceville Presbyterian Church built; **Dec. 1776** Cherry Grove residence of Capt. George Green used by British troops; **1816** town renamed Lawrenceville in honor of Capt. James Lawrence, famous for quote, "Don't give up the ship!"; **1830** Port Mercer Canal House built; **1834** Lawrenceville Female Seminary founded, closed 1883; **1865** Rider University established.

Long Branch *Monmouth County* *Eastern New Jersey, 32 mi/51 km southeast of Newark, on Atlantic Ocean*

1788 summer resort community established; **1819** ocean bathing becomes popular, genders segregated during specific hours; **c.1840** New Yorkers begin building second homes here; **June 3, 1844** Garret A. Hobart born, vice president under President McKinley (died 1899); **1852** National House hotel opened; **1859** Congress Hall hotel opened, merged with National House in 1866 by joining two buildings, renamed Continental Hotel; **1866** Ulysses S. Grant house built, lived here 1869–1871; **1867** incorporated as a borough; **1870** Monmouth Park Race Track opens; **1874** railroad extended from New York; **1878** Long Branch Public Library founded; **Sept. 19, 1881** President Garfield dies at nearby Elberon from gunshot wound received July 2 at train station in Washington, D.C.; **Aug. 25, 1889** novelist Frank Waldo born (died 1967); **1904** incorporated as a city; **1916** Woodrow Wilson's Shadow Long House built; **1918** President Garfield statue dedicated; **1925** San Alfonso Retreat House built; **Jan. 31, 1923** novelist Norman Mailer born; **Aug. 8, 1926** actor Richard Anderson born; **1933** Monmouth University established at West Long Branch; **1935** Greyhound Race Track opened, permanently opened 1937; **Oct. 20, 1940** poet Robert Pinsky born.

Madison *Morris County* *Northeastern New Jersey, 12 mi/19 km west of Newark*

1685 area settled; **c.1745** Sayre House built, served as headquarters of Gen. "Mad" Anthony Wayne 1781; **1812** Bottle Hill Tavern built; settlement of Bottle Hill founded around tavern; **1834** town renamed; **1867** Drew University established; **1889** incorporated as a borough; **1899** College of St. Elizabeth established; **1900** Madison Public Library founded, new library opened 1969; **1942** Fairleigh Dickinson University, Florham-Madison Campus, established.

Mays Landing *Atlantic County* *Southeastern New Jersey, 17 mi/27 km west-northwest of Atlantic City*

c.1710 area settled; **1760** town founded by Philadelphian George May; **1837** Atlantic County formed; town becomes county seat; **1838** county courthouse built; **Aug. 11, 1880** railroad accident, 40 killed; **1926** Atlantic County Library founded; **1930s** Sunshine Nudist Camp established; **1966** Atlantic Cape Community College established.

Menlo Park *Middlesex County* *See **Metuchen** (1879)*

Metuchen *Middlesex County* *Northeastern New Jersey, 15 mi/24 km south-southwest of Newark*

c.1689 town founded by Dutch and English settlers, named for Native American Chief Metaching; **1705** town platted; **1756** Presbyterian Church organized; **1740** Alan (Ayres) House built; **June 1777** British under Gen. William Howe engage in brief but bloody skirmish with Americans under William Alexander; **1793** First Presbyterian Church built; **1836** New Jersey Railroad reaches town; **1870** Metuchen Public Library founded; **Oct. 21, 1879** Edison demonstrates his incandescent lamp at his Menlo Park laboratory; **1880** Thomas A. Edison begins production of incandescent lamps at his Edison Lamp Works; **May 13, 1880** Edison operates first electric railroad in U.S.; **1900** incorporated as a borough; **1937** Edison Memorial Tower erected; **Sept. 16, 1956** magician David Copperfield born.

Montclair *Essex County* *Northeastern New Jersey, 6 mi/9.7 km north-northwest of Newark*

c.1666 settlers arrive from Connecticut; **1694** Azariah Crane builds first house; **1786** Egbert House built; **1831** Morris Canal completed; **1856** Newark & Bloomfield Railroad reaches town; **1887** Montclair Academy established; **1894** incorporated as a town; **1908** Montclair State University established; **March 26, 1916** actor Sterling Hayden born (died 1986); **1918** Montclair Art Museum opened; **May 23, 1925** geneticist Joshua Lederberg born, Nobel Prize 1958; **Jan. 20, 1930** astronaut Edwin "Buzz" Aldrin born, second man to walk on moon July 20, 1969.

Moorestown *Burlington County* *Southwestern New Jersey, 10 mi/16 km east of Camden*

1682 area settled by Quakers; **1721** Zelley House built; **1722** town platted by Thomas Moore; **1738** Smith Mansion built; **1778** General Knyphausen and Hessian troops spend night here on their retreat from Philadelphia;

c.1785 Friends Meeting House and Academy founded, built 1878, razed 1927; **1790** town named Moorestown; **1853** Moorestown Library founded; **Jan. 21, 1885** women's rights activist Alice Paul born (died 1977); **1922** township incorporated.

Morgan *Middlesex County* See **South Amboy** (1918)

Morris Plains *Morris County* *Northeastern New Jersey, 17 mi/27 km west-northwest of Newark*

1837 Samuel F. B. Morse wraps Alfred Vail House with three miles of magnetic cable to record Morse' first telegraph message; **1871** New Jersey State Mental Hospital established in Greystone Park; **1926** incorporated as a borough; **June 9, 1976** Karen Ann Quinlan, 22, moved to nursing home from Denville hospital, removed from life support system May 22 at family request following long legal fight, survives on her own until 1985.

Morristown *Morris County* *Northeastern New Jersey, 17 mi/27 km west of Newark*

c.1710 magnetite iron deposits discovered; area settled; **1728** First Presbyterian Church built; **1739** Morris County formed from Hunterdon County; town becomes county seat; town and county named for Lewis Morris, first governor of New Jersey; **1750** Kemble House built; **1760** Jabez Campfield House built; **c.1763** Arnold's Tavern built, burned 1918; **1774** Ford House built by Col. Jacob Ford, Jr.; **July 25, 1775** Anna Tuthill Symmes Harrison born, wife of Pres. Benjamin Harrison (married 1795, died 1864); **Jan. 1777** Washington's troops camp at Jockey Hollow, again in winter of 1779–1780, use Ford House as headquarters; **1807** Sansay Mansion built; **Sept. 25, 1807** inventor Alfred Lewis Vail born, partner of Samuel F. B. Morse (died 1859); **Oct. 21, 1813** Caroline Carmichael Fillmore born, second wife of Pres. Millard Fillmore (married 1858, died 1889); **1818** SS *Savannah* built, first steam-powered transatlantic vessel; **1827** county courthouse built; **Jan. 1838** Morris & Essex Railroad reaches town; **1853** Speedwell Iron Works established by Stephen Vail, closed 1873; **Feb. 5, 1858** Supreme Court Justice Mahlon Pitney born (died 1924); **1865** incorporated as a town; **1894** First Presbyterian Church founded; **1870** United Methodist Church built; **1886** Christ the Redeemer Church built, destroyed by fire 1917, rebuilt; **1899** College of St. Elizabeth established; **Mar. 2, 1933** Morristown National Historical Park authorized; **Apr. 2, 1945** actress Linda Hunt born.

Mount Holly *Burlington County* *West central New Jersey, 18 mi/29 km east-northeast of Camden*

1676 settled by Quakers John Ridges and Thomas Rudyard; **1681** Burlington County formed; **1694** county organized; **1720** Mill Street Hotel built; **1723** dam and sawmill built on Rancocas Creek; **1730** iron works established, destroyed by British during Revolution; **1759** Brainerd School built; **1775** Friends Meeting House built; **1796** county seat moved from Burlington; county courthouse built; **Dec. 3, 1807** abolitionist Gamaliel Bailey born (died 1859).

New Brunswick *Middlesex County* *Northeastern New Jersey, 22 mi/35 km south-southwest of Newark*

1681 settlement founded by John Inian and others on Raritan River on land occupied by Lenape tribe; **1683** Middlesex County formed; **1686** Inian establishes ferry; **1713** town named Inian's Ferry; **1717** Dutch Reformed Church established; **1724** town renamed Brunswick in honor of King George I, Duke of Brunswick; **1730** town incorporated; **1739** Buccleuch Mansion built; **1743** Christ Episcopal Church built, replaced in 1852; **1759** barracks built, occupied by British 1767; **1760** Guest House built by Henry Guest; **1766** Rutgers University (State University of New Jersey) established, originally Queen's College; New Jersey Medical Association formed; **1776** Provincial Congress meets at White Hart Tavern; **Nov. 28, 1776** retreating George Washington's army passes through town; **June 29, 1778** Washington returns after Battle of Monmouth; **1784** incorporated as a city; New Brunswick Theological Seminary founded; **1793** county seat moved from Perth Amboy; **1812** First Reformed Church built; **1834** Delaware & Raritan Canal opened, used until 1933; **1838** construction of bridge brings New Jersey Railroad to town; **1886** Johnson & Johnson pharmaceutical manufacturer established by Johnson brothers; **Dec. 6, 1886** poet Joyce Kilmer (male) born (died 1918); **1916** E. R. Squibb and Sons pharmaceutical company, founded 1858, moves here; **1922** Rev. Edward Hall found shot to death, body of choir director Eleanor Mills beside him; **1923** Congregation Poile Zedeksyn synagogue built; **1926** Hall-Mills murder trial creates sensation, reverend's wife, her two brothers acquitted; **Sept. 25, 1944** actor Michael Douglas born, son of Kirk Douglas; **Nov. 9, 1959** 10 Trenton State College coeds, teacher killed when bus is rammed by tank truck; **1960** county courthouse completed.

Newark *Essex County* *Northeastern New Jersey, 9 mi/14.5 km east of New York City*

1666 town founded by settlers from New Haven, Connecticut, led by Robert Treat; **1682** Essex County formed; town becomes county seat; **c.1710** John Plume House built; **1713** incorporated as a town; **1747** College of New Jersey moves from Elizabeth, moves 1756 to Princeton to become Princeton University; **Feb. 6, 1756** Aaron Burr born, vice president under President Jefferson (died 1836); **Jan 11, 1757** statesman Alexander Hamilton born, died in duel with Aaron Burr July 11, 1804, at Weehawken; **1774** Newark Academy founded; **Apr. 4, 1788** David G. Barnet born, president Republic of Texas (died 1870); **1790s** Moses Combs establishes town's shoe industry; **1791** First Presbyterian Church completed; **1801**

jewelry manufacturing begun by Epaphras Hinsdale; **c.1830** hatmaking and brewing industries established; **1832** Morris Canal opens; **1833** poet Edmund Stedman born (died 1908); **1834** New Jersey Railroad extended from Jersey City; **1836** incorporated as a city; **Aug. 13, 1839** Catholic archbishop Michael Augustine Corrigan (died 1902); **1855** Kean College established, moved to Union 1958; **Aug. 4, 1865** sculptor John Flanagan born (died 1952); **1869** John Wesley Hyatt invents celluloid, used by Rev. Hannibal Goodwin 1887 in development of photographic film; **Nov. 1, 1871** novelist Stephen Crane born (died 1900); **Dec. 21, 1872** author Albert Terhune born, wrote dog stories (died 1942); **1878** Ballantine House built by brewing family; **1889** Newark Public Library founded, opened 1901; **Nov. 10, 1895** aircraft designer John Northrop born (died 1981); **1898** construction begins on Sacred Heart Cathedral, completed 1954; **1906** county courthouse built; city hall built; **Apr. 25, 1906** Supreme Court Justice William Joseph Brennan, Jr. born (died 1997); **Dec. 1915** Temple B'nai Jeshurun dedicated; **Sept. 18, 1920** actor Jack Warden born; **Nov. 21, 1921** actress Vivian Blaine born (died 1995); **July 4, 1924** actress Eva Marie Saint born; **1926** Newark Museum established; **March 16, 1926** comedian, actor Jerry Lewis born; **1927** County Hall of Records built; **Oct. 1928** Newark Airport opened, renamed Newark Liberty International 2002; **1931** National Newark Building built, tallest building in New Jersey at time (472 ft/760 m); **1934** Rutgers University, University College at Newark, established; **May 3, 1937** singer Frankie Vallie born; **Dec. 12, 1938** singer Connie Francis born; **Sept. 11, 1940** movie director Brian de Palma born; **Oct. 13, 1941** singer, songwriter Paul Simon born; **Dec. 27, 1942** actor John Amos born; **Feb. 9, 1943** actor Joe Pesci born; **1946** Rutgers University, Newark College, established; **Dec. 18, 1955** actor Ray Liotta born; **Sept. 23, 1959** actor Jason Alexander born; **Nov. 26, 1964** Norwegian tanker *Stolt Dagali* cut in two by Israeli liner *Shalom*, 19 of 43 crew killed; **1966** Essex County Community College established; **July 1, 1970** Kenneth Gibson becomes first black mayor of major eastern U.S. city.

Newton   *Sussex County   Northwestern New Jersey, 38 mi/61 km northwest of Newark*

1715 land surveyed; **1753** Sussex County formed; Johnsonburg becomes first county seat; Henry Harelocker opens tavern, becomes town's first settler; **1760** county seat moved to Newton; **1769** Christ Church built; **July 27, 1782** Washington and his men stop at tavern on way to Newburgh, New York; **1847** county courthouse built after fire destroys earlier structure; **1854** Sussex Railroad built; **1864** town incorporated; **1873** Merriam Shoe Factory established; **1928** Don Bosco College established; **1937** Camp Nordland opened to south by Nazi group supporting Hitler over condemnation of media, confiscated several years later; **1981** Sussex Community College established.

Orange   *Essex County   Northeastern New Jersey, 4 mi/6.4 km west-northwest of Newark*

1664 land conveyed to Sir John Berkeley and Sir George Carteret; **1666** settled by families from Connecticut; **1678** town founded, named for William, Prince of Orange; **1776** townspeople give heavy resistance to British; **1792** hat making industry begins; **1793** Orange Public Library founded; **1806** Orange Township incorporated, separates from city of Newark; **1836** Morris & Essex Railroad built; **Sept. 14, 1857** women's rights activist Alice Stone Blackwell born (died 1950); **1860** incorporated as a city; **c.1890** hat making reaches peak with 20 firms; **1901** Orange Brewery built, becomes Rheingold 1950, closed 1977; **Nov. 10, 1932** actor Roy Scheider born; **1982** city reverts to township.

Paramus   *Bergen County   Northeastern New Jersey, 16 mi/26 km north of Newark*

1666 settled by Dutch, nicknamed Celery Town, black muck ideal for growing celery; **1701** Van Emburgh House built; **1708** earliest known use of Paramus (Parames) as town name; **c.1800** Old Paramus Church built; **Jan. 5, 1904** lowest temperature ever recorded in New Jersey reached at River Vale to north, −34°F/−37°C; **1922** incorporated as a borough; **1952** Jewish Community Center established; **1965** Bergen Community College established.

Passaic   *Passaic County   Northeastern New Jersey, 9 mi/14.9 km north of Newark, on Passaic River*

1685 settled by Dutch traders; town founded by Hartman Michielson, originally named Acquakanonk; **1830s** first railroads arrive; **1854** town renamed Passaic; **1873** incorporated as a city; **1890** Botany Worsted Mills established; **1891** city hall completed; **1911** Sts. Peter and Paul Orthodox Church built; **Nov. 4, 1937** TV actress Loretta Swit born; **June 11, 1940** singer Joey Dee born; **June 17, 1951** actor Joe Piscopo born.

Paterson   *Passaic County   Northeastern New Jersey, 13 mi/21 km north of Newark, on Passaic River*

1679 town settled by Dutch; **1791** Alexander Hamilton founds Society for Establishing Useful Manufactures (S.U.M.) for establishment of water power at falls on Passaic River; town founded, named for Gov. William Paterson; **1794** America's first labor strike organized by calico printers, results in mill closing; **1816** Paterson Plank Road extended from Jersey City; **1825** strike halts work at Bull House cotton mill; **1831** Morris Canal completed; **1836** Samuel Colt builds gun mill for manufacture of first successful revolver; **1837** Passaic County formed; Paterson becomes county seat; John Clark begins manufacture of locomotives; **Apr. 4, 1838** Shakespearean actor Lawrence Barrett born (died 1891); **1840** John Ryle founds silk factory at Old Gun Mill, surpasses cotton milling by 1850, peaks 1910; **1851** incorporated as a city;

1867 St. Joseph's Hospital founded; 1891 Lambert Castle built on Garret Mountain by Catholina Lambert; 1893 city hall built; 1898 county administration building built, served as post office until 1932; 1908 Barnert Hospital founded; 1913 landmark strike by Industrial Workers of the World leads to unrest; Jan. 1926 textile workers' strike at Botany Mills followed by year of strife leads to union recognition, right to arbitrate; 1920 Wright Aeronautical Plant (Curtiss-Wright Corporation) founded; 1925 Paterson Museum founded; June 3, 1926 beat generation poet Allen Ginsberg born (died 1997); Oct. 1933 500 textile dyers cross Passaic River bridge to support striking East Paterson dyers, settled 1934; Dec. 1, 1945 actress Bette Midler born; Aug. 14, 1964 calm restored after three days of racial rioting, total 36 injured; 1968 Passaic County Community College established; Dec. 21, 1976 Rubin "Hurricane" Carter and John Artis found guilty of three murders committed 10 years earlier, overturned 1985.

Pennsville   *Salem County*   *Southwestern New Jersey, 29 mi/47 km southwest of Camden, on Delaware River*

early 1700s William Mecum House built; c.1780 Pennsville Ferry established to New Castle, Delaware (near Wilmington); 1859 Fort Delaware established on Pea Patch Island in Delaware River; 1861 Fort Mott established to south on Delaware River during Civil War; Fort Mott National Cemetery established, later renamed Finn's Point National Cemetery; 1877 Finn's Point Range Lighthouse built, automated 1939, discontinued 1957; 1951 Delaware Memorial Bridge built across Delaware River from Wilmington, Delaware, replacing ferry, new span built 1968.

Perth Amboy   *Middlesex County*   *Northeastern New Jersey, 16 mi/26 km south of Newark, on Arthur Kill*

1651 tract purchased from Native Americans by Augustine Herman of Staten Island; 1682 area first settled; 1683 Middlesex County formed; town becomes county seat (shire town); 1684 200 Scots emigrate here by permission of Earl of Perth; 1686 capital transferred from Elizabeth; name Perth Amboy adopted, derivation of Native American word "ompoge," meaning "level ground"; 1718 incorporated as a city; 1722 St. Peter's Episcopal Church built; 1723 William Bradford, State Printer, prints Session Laws, first printing job in New Jersey; Parker Castle built; 1766 Proprietary House built, governor's residence; c.1770 Westminster house built, rebuilt as Brighton House 1815; 1776 Benjamin Franklin, Edward Rutledge, and John Adams stop at Perth Amboy Inn as they travel together to conference at Staten Island; June 1776 Colonialists arrest Gov. William Franklin, occupy governor's house, inspiring Royalists to flee; Dec. 1776 General Howe occupies town after General Mercer joins George Washington in retreat from New York; 1780 Kearny House built; 1790 state capital moved to Trenton; 1793 county seat moved to New Brunswick;

1852 St. Peter's Episcopal Church built; 1854 Atlantic Terra Cotta Plant founded by A. Hall; 1859 Lehigh Valley Railroad reaches city; 1866 Simpson Methodist Church built; 1896 city hall built; June 15, 1921 nine firemen killed in collision of fire truck with train; 1928 Outerbridge Crossing bridge built across Arthur Kill estuary from Staten Island, New York; 1963 ferry service to Staten Island (Tottenville) suspended, begun in 1700s.

Plainfield   *Union County*   *Northeastern New Jersey, 15 mi/24 km southwest of Newark*

1684 area settled by Quakers; c.1705 town founded; 1717 Martine House built; 1746 Drake House built, used as Washington's headquarters 1777; 1760 grist mill built; May–June 1777 Gen. George Washington observes British military movements on plain below from Washington Rock; 1788 Quaker Meeting House built; 1800 post office established; 1838 railroad reaches town; 1869 incorporated as a city; 1886 Plainfield Public Library founded.

Princeton   *Mercer County*   *Central New Jersey, 10 mi/16 km northeast of Trenton*

1681 Capt. Henry Greenland settles here; 1696 six Quaker families arrive; Thomas Olden House built; town founded as Stony Brook; 1713 incorporated as a borough; 1724 town renamed Prince's Town, later shortened to Princeton; 1756 Princeton University, founded 1746 at Elizabeth, is moved here from Newark; May 7, 1774 naval commander William Bainbridge born (died 1833); 1776 state government organized here; Jan. 3, 1777 George Washington defeats British General Cornwallis; summer 1777 first state legislature convenes; June 20, 1778–Nov. 4, 1783 Continental Congress held in its eighth location; Aug. 20, 1795 naval officer Robert Field Stockton born (died 1866); 1812 Princeton Theological Seminary established; 1813 borough reincorporated; 1832 Drumthwacket estate built by Moses Taylor Pyne; 1835 First Presbyterian Church built; Apr. 9, 1898 singer Paul Robeson born (died 1976); 1901 Rockefeller Institute for Medical Research founded; June 24, 1908 former Pres. Grover Cleveland dies of cancer.

Rahway   *Union County*   *Northeastern New Jersey, 10 mi/16 km south of Newark, on Rahway River*

1680 first settlers arrive; 1720 town founded; originally named Spanktown; Jan.-June 1777 skirmishes with British fought here during Revolutionary War, British troops defeated by George Washington's forces aided by New Jersey militia; 1858 incorporated as a city; Rahway Public Library founded, destroyed by Tropical Storm Floyd Sept. 1999, new library opened 2002; 1895 New Jersey Reformatory established; 1901 Rahway State Prison established.

Ringwood   *Passaic County   Northern New Jersey, 28 mi/45 km north-northwest of Newark*

1730 iron discovered in area; **1740** town founded by Ogden family; **1742** iron blast furnace established by Ogden; **1763** iron deposits first worked by Peter Hasenclever; **c.1765** original section of 78-room Ringwood Manor estate built, completed 1878; **Jan. 20, 1781** George Washington stays at Ringwood estate during mutiny of his New Jersey units at Pompton; **1875** Montclair Railroad reaches town; **c.1880** iron mining declines with competition of Minnesota iron ranges, ceases 1931; **1918** incorporated as a borough; **1924** Skylands Manor mansion built by Clarence Lewis.

River Vale   *Bergen County   See* **Paramus (1904)**

Runyon   *Bergen County   See* **East Brunswick (1936)**

Salem   *Salem County   Southwestern New Jersey, 32 mi/51 km south-southwest of Camden, on Delaware River*

1623 Dutch settlers arrive in area; **1643** English and Swedish settlers arrive; **1675** town founded by Quakers led by John Fenwick; **1682** town designated a port of entry; **1691** Bradway House built; **Feb. 23, 1691** slave Thomas Lutherland hanged, found guilty of murder through Law of the Bier in which corpse spouted blood when accused hand extended toward it; **1694** Salem County formed; town becomes county seat; **1695** incorporated as a village; **1717** black woman named Hager found guilty of hatchet murder of her master Sheriff James Sherron, sentenced by popular vote of courtroom, burned at stake; **1721** Alexander Grant House built; **1772** Friends Meeting House built; **1775** county jail built, rebuilt 1866; **Feb. 1778** General Washington sends Anthony Wayne to area for supplies for forces at Valley Forge, Pennsylvania, British fail to stop Wayne's return with 150 head of cattle; **1799** Green's Hotel built; **1817** county courthouse built, rebuilt 1908; **1858** incorporated as a city; **1863** first railroad reaches city.

Somerville   *Somerset County   North central New Jersey, 25 mi/40 km southwest of Newark*

1683 area settled; **1688** Somerset County organized; **1751** Dutch Reformed Parsonage built by Rev. Jacob Hardenbergh, considered as cradle of Rutgers University, founded by Hardenbergh at New Brunswick as Queen's College 1766; **1771** Tunison's Tavern established, becomes Somerville Hotel; **1778–1779** Wallace House used as headquarters by General Washington; **1782** county seat moved from Millstone; **1871** Somerville Library founded; **Sept. 7, 1885** poet, novelist Eleanor Morton Wylie born (died 1928); **1909** incorporated as a borough; county courthouse built; **June 1, 1945** opera singer Frederica Von Stade born; **1965** Raritan Valley Community College established.

South Amboy   *Middlesex County   Northeastern New Jersey, 13 mi/21 km south of Newark*

1652 area settled by Dutch; **1807** clay pits dug in area, runoff leads to silting of Arthur Kill estuary and Raritan Bay; **1832** town serves as terminus of Camden & Amboy Railroad, New Jersey's first railroad; **1888** incorporated as a borough; **1908** incorporated as a city; **Oct. 4, 1918** Shell Oil munitions plant explosion at nearby Morgan kills 64; **May 19, 1950** munitions barges explode, 30 killed.

South Orange   *Essex County   Northeastern New Jersey, 4 mi/6.4 km west of Newark*

1678 settlers arrive on land purchased from Lenapes; **c.1680** Stone House built, oldest in town; **1836** Morris & Essex Railroad reaches town; **1841** post office established; **1856** Seton Hall University established; **1869** incorporated as a village, separates from Orange; **1894** Village Hall built; **July 26, 1959** actor Kevin Spacey born.

Teaneck   *Bergen County   Northeastern New Jersey, 13 mi/21 km north-northeast of Newark*

early 1600s area settled; **c.1728** Brinkerhoff-Demarest House built; **Nov. 1776** George Washington makes tactical withdrawal his troops as 6,000 British enter Hudson River by boat; **1865** William Phelps Mansion built; **1895** township incorporated; **1927** Phelps Estate housing development opened; **May 8, 1940** TV actor, singer Eric (Rick) Nelson born (died 1985); **1942** Fairleigh-Dickinson University, Teaneck-Hackensack Campus, established; **Aug. 23, 1942** actress Patricia McBride born; **1965** Teaneck becomes first predominantly white community to vote for school desegregation.

Toms River   *Ocean County   Eastern New Jersey, 44 mi/71 km north of Atlantic City, near Atlantic Ocean*

1673 river discovered by Capt. William Tom; **1767** town founded; **1778** British raid town; **March 24, 1782** town burned by Tories; **1787** Ocean House tavern built; **1837** Mormons establish colony at South Toms River, move to Salt Lake City 1852; **1850** Ocean County formed; town becomes county seat; county courthouse built; **1964** Ocean County Community College established; **May 1969** Oyster Creek Nuclear Power Plant begins operation on Forked River to south; **1976** Toms River Maritime Museum founded.

Trenton   *Mercer County   West central New Jersey, 30 mi/48 km northeast of Philadelphia, on Delaware River*

1679 settled by English Quaker Mahlon Stacy; **1714** site purchased by William Trent, named Trent Town; **1719** Trent House built by William Trent, oldest building in city; **1739** Friends Meeting House built; **1750** first public library in New Jersey established, discontinued 1855; **1770** South Street Ferry begins service to Morrisville, Pennsylvania; **1772** fire destroys most of town; **1775** Boxwood Manor built; **Dec. 25, 1776** Washington crosses Delaware River, defeats Hessian troops in Battle of

Trenton Dec. 26, one of most decisive battles of Revolution; **Jan. 5, 1779** explorer Zebulon M. Pike born, killed Apr. 27, 1813, at Toronto (York) in War of 1812; **Nov. 1–Dec. 24, 1784** Continental Congress held in its tenth location; **1790** state capital moved from Perth Amboy; **1792** incorporated as a city; first statehouse built, destroyed by fire 1885; **1793** Masonic Lodge built; **1798** New Jersey State Prison opened; **c.1798** Hotel Sterling built, originally served as governor's mansion; **1806** covered bridge built across Delaware River; **1819** Mercer County formed; city becomes county seat; St. Michael's Episcopal Church built; **1837** Philadelphia & Trenton Railroad reaches town; **1841** First Presbyterian Church built, replaces 1712 structure; **1846** slavery abolished in New Jersey; **1848** bridge builder John Roebling moves his cable works from Pennsylvania; Ellerslie Villa built as summer retreat of Henry McCall, Sr., used as city museum from 1889; **1850** pottery making industry thrives; **1851** South Trenton annexed; **1856** Lamberton annexed; **1871** St. Mary's Cathedral completed; **1873** first porcelain sanitary ware manufactured; **Aug. 26, 1874** 16 blacks, accused of killing 2 white men, abducted and killed by lynch mob; **1888** state fairgrounds established, final fair held 1980; **1889** new statehouse built; **1893** battle monument dedicated; **1895** New Jersey State Museum founded; **1902** county courthouse built, addition built 1938; **1914** Old Barracks Museum founded; **1927** Mercer County Airport established; **1932** deepening of Delaware River transforms city into ocean port; war memorial building completed; **Aug. 22, 1934** Gen. Norman H. Schwarzkopf born, commanded forces in Operation Desert Storm, Kuwait, 1990; **spring 1936** sit-down strike in statehouse by unemployed protesting termination of aid lasts nine days; **March 11, 1936** Supreme Court Justice Antonin Scalia born; **Apr. 3, 1936** Bruno Hauptmann, convicted Lindbergh child kidnaper and murderer, electrocuted at state prison; **Feb. 9, 1949** actress Judith Light born; **1966** Mercer County Community College established.

Union   *Union County*   *Northeastern New Jersey, 5 mi/8 km southwest of Newark*

1749 first settlers arrive from Connecticut, originally named Connecticut Farms; **June 23, 1780** Rhode Island infantry fight British at Rahway River bridge in Battle of Springfield; **1908** Self-Masters' Colony established by Andress S. Floyd to help 40 "hoboes, drunks, and dope fiends do better for themselves"; **1925** incorporated as a city; **1958** Kean College moves from Newark, established 1855, becomes Kean University 1997.

Weehawken   *Hudson County*   *Northeastern New Jersey, 8 mi/12.9 km northeast of Newark, on Hudson River*

July 11, 1804 Alexander Hamilton shot dead by Vice Pres. Aaron Burr in gun duel at base of Hudson River cliff, Hamilton deliberately shot into the air; **1859** Weehawken Township incorporated; **1887** St. Lawrence Catholic Church dedicated; **Dec. 22, 1937** Lincoln Tunnel opened to Manhattan, New York City, second tube opened 1940.

West Orange   *Essex County*   *Northeastern New Jersey, 5 mi/8km west-northwest of Newark*

Aug. 16, 1862 football coach Amos Alonzo Stagg born (died 1965); **1880** Glenmount house built for eccentric Henry C. Peddler; **1883** West Orange Public Library founded; **1887** Thomas Edison purchases Glenmount, establishes plant and laboratory, remains until his death 1931; **1900** incorporated as a town; **1912** Edison invents his talking machine; **Oct. 18, 1931** Thomas A. Edison dies at age 84 at Glenmount; **1960** Edison National Historic Site established.

Woodbury   *Gloucester County*   *Southwestern New Jersey, 7 mi/11.3 km south of Camden*

1681 settled by Quakers; **1694** Gloucester County formed; **1716** Quaker Meeting House built; **1720** Paul Hotel built; **1777** John Cooper House used as Cornwallis' headquarters; **1765** Lawrence House built by Rev. Andrew Turner; **1786** county seat moved from Gloucester City; **1787** county courthouse built; **Jan. 9, 1793** first manned balloon ascent in U.S., observed by Pres. George Washington; **1854** incorporated as a borough; **1871** incorporated as a city; **1897** Woodbury Free Library founded; **May 2, 1925** actor Roscoe Lee Browne born; **1926** County Hall of Records built; **Feb. 6, 1951** railroad accident, 84 killed; **Nov. 29, 1969** 18-car pileup on New Jersey Turnpike, 18 killed.

Wrightstown   *Burlington County*   *Central New Jersey, 16 mi/26 km south-southeast of Trenton*

1917 Camp Dix military base established to south; **1937** base renamed Fort Dix; Rudd Field air base established at Fort Dix, becomes Fort Dix Army Airfield 1942; **1948** McGuire Air Force Base established at former airfield; **July 13, 1956** Military Air Transport C-118 crashes in storm at Fort Dix killing 46; **1992** Fort Dix becomes training base.

New Mexico

Southwestern U.S. Capital: Santa Fe. Largest city: Albuquerque.

The area was acquired by the U.S. in 1848 as a result of the Mexican War. The Territory of New Mexico was established in December 1850. The Gadsden Purchase added Mexican land to the southern part of the territory in 1853. Arizona Territory separated from New Mexico in 1863. New Mexico was admitted to the U.S. as the 47th state January 6, 1912.

New Mexico is divided into 33 counties. The municipalities are classified as villages, towns, and cities. There are no townships. See Introduction.

Abiquiu   *Rio Arriba County*   *Northern New Mexico, 42 mi/68 km north-northwest of Santa Fe*

c.1300 AD Anasazi people leave after occupying Chama Valley since as early as 10,000 BC; Tewa Pueblos become established in valley; **c.1600** Navajo Apaches occupy area; **1734** town founded by Spanish; **1747** town abandoned following Ute-Comanche raid; resettled by genizaros, Hispanicized Native Americans once bound as servants in New Mexican households; **1778** stage stop established here on old Spanish Trail; town founded on Rio Chama, serves as major trade center through 1800; **1963** Abiquiu Dam built on Chama River.

Abo   *Torrance County*   *Central New Mexico, 48 mi/ 77 km south-southeast of Albuquerque*

1598 Abo Pueblo established by Piro Native Americans; **1629** pueblo becomes seat of San Gregorio Mission, founded by Father Francisco de Acevedo, dedicated to San Gregario, patron saint of ancient city of Abo, Finland; **1646** Abo Mission built at Abo Pueblo; **1680** village abandoned; **Aug. 1939** site declared a state monument; **Nov. 1981** site absorbed by Salinas Pueblo Missions National Monument.

Acoma   *Cibola County*   *Western New Mexico, 55 mi/89 km west-southwest of Albuquerque*

1540 Acoma Pueblo, situated atop 357-ft/109-m Acoma Mesa, visited by Capt. Hernando de Alvarado of Coronado's army, oldest continually occupied village in U.S.; **1598** pueblo occupants submit to Spanish authority as lure to trick Spanish into ambush atop mesa; troops of Don Juan de Zaldivar attacked as they visit Acoma Native Americans, four killed as they leap from mesa; **Jan. 22–24,** **1599** Spanish retaliate with attack, forcing pueblo into submission after bitter struggle; **1629** Father Ramirez makes ascent on ladder trail to Acoma Pueblo, Native Americans hurl rocks and arrows at him, Ramirez rescues Acoma girl who fell from rock amid melee, is accepted by pueblo occupants; San Esteban Rey Mission church built, destroyed 1680 with murder of Father Lucas Maldonado; **1699** mission church rebuilt.

Alamogordo   *Otero County*   *Southern New Mexico, 160 mi/257 km south-southeast of Albuquerque*

1848 Fort Bliss Military Reservation established to south, extends north from El Paso, Texas; **1898** Southern Pacific Railroad built; mining activities begin; town founded; Alameda Park Zoo established; **1899** Otero County formed; town becomes county seat; **1900** Alamogordo Public Library founded; **1912** town incorporated; **Oct. 29,** **1921** political cartoonist Bill Mauldin born at Mountain Park to east (died 2003); **1925** New Mexico School for the Blind established, renamed School for Visually Handicapped 1953; **Jan. 18, 1933** White Sands National Monument proclaimed to southwest; **1942** Holloman Army Air Field established, becomes Air Force Base 1947; **1945** White Sands Proving Ground established to west, renamed White Sands Missile Range 1958; **July 16,** **1945** first atomic bomb exploded at Trinity Site to northwest; **1956** county courthouse completed; **1958** New Mexico State University, Alamogordo, (2-year) established; **1959** Alamogordo White Sands Regional Airport established; **Nov. 16, 1959** Capt. Joseph Kittinger parachutes 14 mi/23 km from balloon under conditions of −104°F and 450 mph winds at White Sands; **1976** International Space Hall of Fame (The Space Centre) opened; **1996** Tays Event Center opened.

Albuquerque *Bernalillo County* *Central New Mexico, on Rio Grande*

1541 Spanish explorer Coronado's troops camp at site to north; **1600s** first haciendas built by Spanish in area along Rio Grande; **1680** Spanish routed by Native Americans; **1706** town founded by 35 families led by Don Francisco Cuervo y Valdes, named for Duke of Alburquerque, Viceroy of New Spain, first "r" later dropped; Church of San Felipe de Neri built; **1846** Americans occupy town; **1852** Bernalillo County formed; town becomes county seat; **1862** Union Captain Enos evacuates citizens to Santa Fe as Confederate Gen. Hopkins Sibley advances, captures town without resistance, evacuates two months later with approach of Union force under Col. R. S. Canby; **1875** first telegraph service begins; **1881** Atchison, Topeka & Santa Fe Railroad arrives; new town established 2 mi/3.2 km to east; **1882** Vincent Wallace House built; **1884** incorporated as a town; **1889** University of New Mexico established; **1890** incorporated as a city; **June 22, 1922** *Albuquerque Tribune* newspaper founded; **1942** Sandia Army Base established to southeast; Kirtland Army Air Base opened at Sandia Base, becomes Kirtland Air Force Base 1947; **1965** Albuquerque Technical Vocational Institute (2-year) established; **1967** Albuquerque Museum established at old airport, new buildings opened 1979; **March 9, 1970** police defuse bomb 15 minutes before set to go off at Reserve Training building, part of 7-day Weathermen militant bombing campaign; **Nov. 27, 1971** 3 fugitives accused of murdering patrol officer hijack TWA jet, 43 passengers left in Tampa, hijackers fly to Cuba; **1971** Albuquerque Convention Center opened; **May 19, 1972** plane crashes on takeoff from Kirtland Air Force Base killing nine; **June 15, 1973** actor Neil Patrick Harris born; **1976** Indian Pueblo Cultural Center opened; **1986** New Mexico Museum of Natural History and Science opened; **June 1990** Petroglyph National Monument established to west; **1997** Rio Grande Botanic Garden Biological Park opened; Albuquerque Aquarium opened; **March 18, 2000** transformer fire causes nearly statewide power outage for up to three hours; **2001** 8-story Bernalillo County Courthouse opened.

Aztec *San Juan County* *Northwestern New Mexico, 142 mi/229 km northwest of Santa Fe*

1887 San Juan County formed; **1890** town founded as county seat on Animas River, tributary of San Juan River; **1911** Aztec Public Library founded; **1905** incorporated as a city; **1950** oil and natural gas production begins; San Juan Valley Irrigation Project begun, delivering water to fruit growers; **Jan. 24, 1923** Aztec Ruins National Monument proclaimed; **1997** county courthouse built.

Bayard *Grant County* *Southwestern New Mexico, 187 mi/301 km south-southwest of Albuquerque*

1866 Fort Bayard built to protect gold and silver mining activities; town founded; **July 1877** 9th Cavalry of Buffalo Soldiers under Corp. Clinton Greaves force their way out of encirclement by Chiricahuas; **1899** fort closed; Fort Bayard U.S. Veterans' Hospital established, turned over to state 1966; **1938** incorporated as a city; **July 1992** Buffalo Soldier Memorial dedicated to African-American cavalry.

Bernalillo *Sandoval County* *North central New Mexico, 15 mi/24 km north of Albuquerque*

1540 Francisco Vasquez de Coronado believed to have camped here; **c.1600** Church of Santa Ana de Alamillo built at Santa Ana Pueblo to northwest, burned 1687, rebuilt 1692; **1696** Real de Bernalillo first appears on maps; **1698** town founded on Rio Grande by Spanish; **1858** Spanish land grant for Sandia Pueblo reestablished by U.S.; **1903** Sandoval County formed; town becomes county seat; **1927** county courthouse built; **1948** incorporated as a city.

Bloomfield *San Juan County* *Northwestern New Mexico, 135 mi/217 km northwest of Santa Fe*

1876 Englishman William B. Haines becomes first settler; town founded on San Juan River; **1906** Citizens' Ditch and Irrigating Company organized, begins delivering water to San Juan Valley crops; **March 11, 1907** Chaco Canyon National Monument proclaimed to north, becomes Chaco Culture National Historical Park 1980, preserves 13 major Pueblo Native American ruins dating from c.900 A.D.; **1911** Bloomfield Irrigation District formed; **1950** San Juan Irrigation Project initiated; **1953** incorporated as a city; **1963** Navajo Dam and Reservoir completed to east on San Juan River.

Carlsbad *Eddy County* *Southeastern New Mexico, 238 mi/383 km southeast of Albuquerque*

1884 cattlemen Charles B. and John Eddy establish ranch; **1889** Eddy County formed; town of Eddy founded as county seat on Pecos River; **Sept. 1889** town incorporated; **1891** Atchison, Topeka & Santa Fe Railroad reaches town; county courthouse completed; **1899** town renamed Carlsbad for Czech resort; **1901** cowboy James Larkin White becomes first known individual to explore Carlsbad Cave to southwest, **1902** flooded Pecos River destroys irrigation systems; **1906** Carlsbad Reclamation Project begun for irrigation of farmland; Lake Avalon formed by dam on Pecos River; **1918** incorporated as a city; **c.1918** cotton becomes important crop; **Oct. 25, 1923** Carlsbad Cave National Monument established, becomes Carlsbad Caverns National Park 1930; **1931** potash mining begins to east, town becomes potash capital of U.S.; **1988** Brantley Reservoir formed to north on Pecos River; **June 27, 1994** highest temperature ever recorded in New Mexico reached at Waste Isolation Pilot Plant to north, 122°F/50°C; **Aug. 19, 2000** 11 campers, including 5 children, killed by gas pipeline explosion 20 mi/32 km to south on Pecos River.

Carrizozo *Lincoln County* *South central New Mexico, 112 mi/180 km south-southeast of Albuquerque*

1869 Lincoln County formed, named for President Lincoln; town of Lincoln becomes county seat; **1880** gold discovered to northeast; **1899** El Paso & Northeastern (Southern Pacific) Railroad built; town founded and incorporated; **1906** town platted; **1909** county seat moved to Carrizozo following four-year court battle; **July 16, 1945** first nuclear test explosion conducted at Trinity Site to west, in White Sands Missile Range; **1964** county courthouse built.

Chama *Rio Arriba County* *Northern New Mexico, 93 mi/150 km north-northwest of Santa Fe*

1848 large band of Utes and Apaches attacked by forces of Maj. W. W. Reynolds at Cumbres Pass to north, 2 soldiers killed, 36 Native Americans killed; **1850** town founded on Chama River; **1879** jail built, used until 1967; **1880** Denver & Rio Grande Railroad reaches site in Chama Valley; **1937** oil discovered in Chromo Valley to north, inside Colorado; **1961** incorporated as a village; **1974** Cumbres & Toltec Scenic Railway established to Antonito, Colorado.

Chimayo *Santa Fe and Rio Arriba counties* *Northern New Mexico, 23 mi/37 km north of Santa Fe*

1598 trading post established by Spanish in Chimayo Valley, name derived from Tsimayo, settlement of a Tewa Native American Pueblo; **1695** trading post abandoned; **1696** Jacona Pueblo abandoned to south, inhabitants join other Tewa pueblos; **1740** Plaza San Buenaventura (Plaza del Cerro) built; **c.1813** adobe El Santuario de Chimayo Church built, masterpiece of colonial architecture and artwork; **c.1900** communal loom industry begins, produces woven goods.

Cimarron *Colfax County* *Northeastern New Mexico, 85 mi/137 km northeast of Santa Fe*

1844 first settled by Cornelio Vigil of Taos; **1848** Agency Warehouse built; **1849** town founded on Cimarron River by Lucien B. Maxwell of Kaskaskia, Illinois; **1849** Rayado Ranch established to south by famed scout Kit Carson; adobe Carson House built on ranch; **1854** Swink's Gambling Hall built; **1858** National Hotel built; **1864** Maxwell House built; **1865** Maxwell and wife become sole owners of land grant, vast holding three times size of Rhode Island, extends into Colorado; **1869** Colfax County formed; **1872** town becomes county seat; St. James Hotel built; **1875** Maxwell dies penniless from bad railroad investment; **c.1875** Don Diego Tavern built by Henry Lambert, former personal chef to General Grant and President Lincoln; **1882** county seat moved to Springer; **1906** St. Louis, Rocky Mountain & Pacific Railroad reaches town; new town section platted; two hotels built; **1910** town incorporated; **1941** Philmont Ranch, formerly Kit Carson's Rayado Ranch, donated by Waite Philips to Boy Scouts.

Clayton *Union County* *Northeastern New Mexico, 168 mi/270 km northeast of Santa Fe*

1717 several hundred Comanche killed by force of 500 Spaniards at Rabbit Ear Mtn. to north; **1880** camp established by cattle drivers; **1887** Denver & Fort Worth Railroad built; town founded as rail division point; **1888** post office established; **Oct.–Nov. 1889** severe blizzard cuts off town for weeks, seven killed, two passenger trains snowbound; **1893** Union County formed; town becomes county seat; **1895** county courthouse built; **Apr. 26, 1901** train robber Black Jack Ketchum hanged, special stockade built to prevent any rescue attempt; **1908** town incorporated; winds remove roof from courthouse, several killed; **1909** new county courthouse built.

Clovis *Curry County* *Eastern New Mexico, 218 mi/351 km east-southeast of Albuquerque*

1907 Atchison, Topeka & Santa Fe Railroad built; town founded, named Riley Switch; **1909** Curry County formed; town becomes county seat; town incorporated, renamed for King Clovis, founder of French monarchy (466–511 AD); **1911** county courthouse built; **1929** Clovis Man archaeological site discovered at Blackwater Draw to southwest, human evidence dating to 10,500 BC; **1942** Cannon Army Air Field established to southwest, becomes Air Force Base after World War II; **1943** public library founded; **1957** Clovis Music Company established, makes recording history with legends Buddy Holly, Roy Orbison, Waylon Jennings; **1971** Clovis Community College established.

Columbus *Luna County* *Southwestern New Mexico, 72 mi/116 km west of El Paso, Texas*

1891 town founded adjacent to Palomas, Chihuahua, Mexico; **1903** El Paso & Southwestern Railroad reaches town; **March 9, 1916** Mexican Gen. Pancho Villa raids town, killing 17, U.S. General Pershing enters Mexico in pursuit March 15, clashes with Mexican troops Apr. 12 at Parral, Mexico, retreats across border, over 100 of Villa's men killed.

Dawson *Colfax County* *Northeastern New Mexico, 98 mi/158 km northeast of Santa Fe*

c.1868 brothers J. B. and L. S. Dawson begin ranching along Vermejo River; **1895** coal discovered on Dawson Ranch; town founded; **1900** Chicago millionaire W. H. Bartlett builds retreat in mountains to northwest for health reasons, developed into private club after his death 1918, members included Will Rogers, Andrew Mellon, Cecil B. De Mille; **1906** Phelps Dodge Company acquires mining operations; **Oct. 22, 1913** explosion at No. 2 Coal Mine, 263 killed; **Feb. 8, 1923** second coal mine explosion, 120 killed; **Apr. 1950** last of coal veins depleted; coal mining ceases; townspeople given 30 days to abandon homes, town razed, Dawson Cemetery remains.

Deming *Luna County* *Southwestern New Mexico, 210 mi/338 km south-southwest of Albuquerque*

1881 Atchison, Topeka & Santa Fe and Southern Pacific railroads meet, giving New Mexico access to both coasts; town founded, named New Chicago, renamed Nov. for Mary Deming Crocker, wife of SP Railroad magnate; **1901** Luna County formed; town becomes county seat; **1902** town incorporated; **1910** county courthouse completed; **1917** Marsh Memorial Library built; **1965** incorporated as a city; **Jan. 19, 1973** head-on car crash kills nine, injures three.

Estancia *Torrance County* *Central New Mexico, 43 mi/69 km southeast of Albuquerque*

1900 first homesteaders arrive; **1901** branch of New Mexico Central Railroad reaches town; town founded; **1903** Torrance County formed; post office established; **1905** Central Hotel opened; **1909** town incorporated, becomes county seat; **1967** county courthouse built.

Farmington *San Juan County* *Northwestern New Mexico, 150 mi/241 km northwest of Santa Fe*

1879 William Locke arrives from Florence, Colorado, plants fruit and nut trees; town founded on San Juan River, at mouth of La Plata River; **1880s** apple growing industry led by orchardist W. C. McHenry; **1901** town incorporated; **1950** oil and natural gas discovered; simultaneous discovery of uranium creates mining boom; San Juan Irrigation Project begins; **1958** San Juan College (2-year) established.

Folsom *Union County* *Northeastern New Mexico, 143 mi/230 km northeast of Santa Fe*

1862 Madison Emery settles here; **1865** town of Madison founded by Emery; **1888** Colorado & Southern Railroad reaches area, missing Madison; town of Folsom founded, named for President Cleveland's wife, Frances Folsom; **1895** large stockyards built; **1906** town platted; **Aug. 1908** flash flooding destroys most of town, 17 killed, including telephone operator Sarah J. Rooke, used switchboard to warn town; **1909** incorporated as a village; **1926** fossil bones with stone darts in them found by George McJunkin, evidence of paleolithic Native American culture 10,000 years prior.

Fort Sumner *De Baca County* *Eastern New Mexico, 148 mi/238 km east-southeast of Albuquerque*

1851 trading post established on Pecos River; town founded around; **1862** Fort Sumner built, named for Gen. E. V. Sumner, head of U.S. military in New Mexico; **1864** c.10,000 Navajos and 400 Apaches subjected to the Long Walk, 350 mi/563 km from northeastern Arizona, held prisoner until 1868; **1875** fort acquired by Lucien Maxwell as a home; **July 14, 1881** Billy the Kid shot, killed by Sheriff Pat F. Garrett in bedroom of Maxwell house; **1906** Atchison, Topeka & Santa Fe Railroad built; town moved north to railroad; Sumner Lake formed by dam to

northwest on Pecos River; **1916** town incorporated; **1917** De Baca County formed; town becomes county seat; county courthouse built; **Dec. 26, 1972** church bus carrying youth group collides with cattle truck to east, 19 killed, 16 injured.

Fort Wingate *McKinley County* *Western New Mexico, 112 mi/180 km west-northwest of Albuquerque*

1882 Fort Wingate Military Reservation established, unrelated to previous Forts Wingate at Cebolleta and Grants; town founded; **1914** Mexican troops housed here during uprising of Pancho Villa; **1918** Fort Wingate Army Depot established; **1936** Southwestern Range and Sheep Breeding Laboratory established to reestablish Navajo and Hispanic breeds decimated during years of conflict, program continues through 1966; **1993** Army Depot closed.

Gallup *McKinley County* *Western New Mexico, 125 mi/201 km west-northwest of Albuquerque*

1879 large coal deposits discovered by railroad surveyors; town founded, named for railroad paymaster David Gallup; **1881** Atchison, Topeka & Santa Fe Railroad reaches town; **1891** town incorporated; **1899** McKinley County formed; **1901** town becomes county seat; **1922** Gallup Indian Ceremonial organized; **1926** U.S. Highway 66 built; **1937** county courthouse built; **1968** University of New Mexico, Gallup Campus, (2-year) established.

Gavilan *Rio Arriba County* *See* **Tierra Amarilla** **(1951)**

Grants *Cibola County* *Western New Mexico, 70 mi/113 km west of Albuquerque*

1862 Fort Wingate moved from Cebellota to 5 mi/8 km south of town site; **1868** Fort Lyon built in place of Fort Wingate; **1872** Don Jesus Blea settles here, site named Los Alamitos; **1881** Atchison, Topeka & Santa Fe Railroad reaches site; town founded, named for Grant brothers, railroad builders; **Dec. 8, 1906** El Morro National Monument proclaimed to southwest, includes Inscription Rocks, bears names of explorers, settlers; **1941** incorporated as a town; **1966** incorporated as a city; **1981** Cibola County formed from Valencia County; town becomes county seat; **1985** county courthouse built; **Dec. 31, 1987** El Malpais National Monument established to south in Malpais lava fields.

Hobbs *Lea County* *Southeastern New Mexico, 267 mi/430 km southeast of Albuquerque*

1907 town founded by Texan James Hobbs; **1927** oil and natural gas discovered in area; **1928** Midwest Refinery established; **1929** town incorporated; **1930** Texas & New Mexico Railroad reaches town from Texas; **June 1930** Humble Oil Company strikes largest producing oil well in area; **1965** New Mexico Junior College established.

Hot Springs *Sierra County* *See* **Truth or Consequences**

Jal *Lea County* *Southeastern New Mexico, 296 mi/ 476 km southeast of Albuquerque*

1886 JAL Ranch established by brothers James, Amos, and Liddon Cowden, bears their initials; **1910** post office established at ranch; **1916** post office moved to watering place on Muleshoe Ranch; town founded; **1927** oil and natural gas discovered to southeast; **1928** incorporated as a town; **1930** Texas & New Mexico Railroad reaches town; **1973** lake formed in shape of "JAL" at town park, footbridge to island at center of "A" only bridge in dry county.

Jemez Springs *Sandoval County* *North central New Mexico, 47 mi/76 km north of Albuquerque*

1541 Spanish arrive in area, find village of Guisewa inhabited by ancestors of Jemez Pueblo Native Americans; **1622** Mission of San José de Guisewa established; **c.1697** Jemez Pueblo founded; **1935** Jemez State Monument established; **1937** Chapel of San Diego built at Jemez Pueblo; **1954** incorporated as a village.

La Mesilla *Doña Ana County* *Southern New Mexico, 40 mi/64 km north-northwest of El Paso, Texas*

1848 Spanish and Mexican settlers arrive on Rio Grande; **1851** Fort Fillmore established by U.S. as protection against Apaches; **1852** Doña Ana County formed; **1853** town founded; **Nov. 16, 1854** flag-raising ceremony transfers Gadsden Purchase from Mexico to U.S.; **1855** town becomes county seat; **1857** town becomes important stop on Butterfield Overland Route; **1860** *Mesilla Times* newspaper founded; **1861** town incorporated; **July 25, 1861** Lieutenant Colonel Baylor's Confederates take Fort Fillmore, use town as headquarters; **Aug. 1862** Confederates driven back to Texas by California Column under Gen. James H. Carleton; **1863** Rio Grande changes course leaving town on island with mosquito-borne diseases, c.50 die; **1881** Atchison, Topeka & Santa Fe Railroad bypasses town; county seat moved to Las Cruces; **1885** river again changes course, town restored to dry ground; **1958** incorporated as a city.

Laguna *Cibola County* *Western New Mexico, 40 mi/64 km west of Albuquerque*

1697 settled by Pueblo Native American refugees from Cochiti and Santo Domingo; **1699** Laguna Pueblo established; San Jose de Laguna Catholic Church built; **1936** mission church restored; **1952** Anaconda Corporation begins uranium strip mining; **1970s** Pueblo Native American pottery-making tradition revived for tourist trade; **1981** uranium mining ceases.

Las Cruces *Doña Ana County* *Southern New Mexico, 45 mi/72 km north-northwest of El Paso, Texas*

1830 40 travelers from Chihuahua massacred by Apaches; site named Las Cruces for crosses over graves; **1848** town founded on Rio Grande; **1851** Fort Fillmore built to south; **1852** Doña Ana County formed; Loretto Academy for girls founded, razed 1959; **1853** Amador Hotel built by Don Martin Amador; **1855** La Mesilla becomes county seat; **1865** Fort Seldon built to north as defense against Gila Apaches; **1881** Atchison, Topeka & Santa Fe Railroad reaches town; county seat moved to Las Cruces; **1888** New Mexico State University established; **1907** incorporated as a town; **1937** county courthouse built; **1945** White Sands Proving Grounds established to east; **1973** Doña Ana Branch Community College established; **1999** Museum of Fine Arts opened, founded late 1960s.

Las Vegas *San Miguel County* *North central New Mexico, 40 mi/64 km east of Santa Fe*

1823 land grant made to Luis Maria C. de Baca by Mexican government; **1833** town founded by Spanish on Santa Fe Trail; **1836** Our Lady of Sorrows Catholic Church built; **1862** San Miguel County formed; **1864** town becomes county seat; **1879** Atchison, Topeka & Santa Fe Railroad reaches town; **1880** Montezuma Hotel built at Montezuma Hot Springs to west, destroyed by fire 1881, rebuilt, destroyed again by fire 1885, rebuilt, closed 1903; **1888** incorporated as a city; **1893** New Mexico Highlands University established; **1906** race track established in Gallinas Park, abandoned 1911; **1912** county courthouse built; **1921** Baptist college established at old Montezuma Hotel, closed 1932; **1982** millionaire Armand Hammer purchases old Montezuma Hotel, donates it to United World College.

Lincoln *Lincoln County* *Southern New Mexico, 135 mi/217 km southeast of Albuquerque*

1852 Torreon fortification built as defense against Native Americans; **1855** Fort Stanton built to west; town founded, named Las Placitas del Rio Benito; **1861** fort destroyed by Confederates, captured by U.S. 1863, rebuilt 1868, abandoned 1896; **1869** Lincoln County formed; town becomes county seat; **Feb. 18, 1878** in Lincoln County War, English cattleman John H. Tunstall with ruffian group The Regulators including outlaw Billy the Kid feud with rival cattlemen; Tunstall gunned down by sheriff William Brady posse July 19, ends Oct. with appointment of Gen. Lew Wallace as Territorial Governor, federal troops called out; **1887** San Juan Catholic Church dedicated; **1899** State Tuberculosis Sanitarium established at fort site; **1913** county seat moved to Carrizozo; **1979** Lincoln State Monument established; **Oct. 6, 2000** actor Richard Farnsworth, 80, dies of self-inflicted gunshot wound, same year became oldest Oscar nominee.

NEW MEXICO

Lordsburg *Hidalgo County* *Southwestern New Mexico, 227 mi/365 km southwest of Albuquerque*

1853 Gadsden Purchase annexed by U.S.; **1880** Southern Pacific Railroad built; town founded; **1919** Hidalgo County formed; town incorporated, becomes county seat; **1920** county courthouse built; **1927** Lordsburg Airport dedicated by Charles A. Lindbergh.

Los Alamos *Los Alamos County* *North central New Mexico, 24 mi/39 km northwest of Santa Fe*

c.1880 Hispanic settlement of Los Alamos established; **Feb. 11, 1916** Bandelier National Monument proclaimed to south and east, protects 13th century Pueblo cliff dwellings; **1918** Los Alamos School for Boys founded; **1942** Los Alamos Scientific Laboratory established at boys' school site by University of California for nuclear fission research; town founded; **1943** Manhattan Project initiated by U.S. Army for nuclear bomb development; **1946** Mesa Public Library founded; **1947** Manhattan Project completed; U.S. Atomic Energy Commission takes control of laboratory; **1949** Los Alamos County formed from parts of Santa Fe and Sandoval counties; town becomes county seat; **1962** U.S. control of town ends; **1969** incorporated as a city, coterminous with county; **1976** Municipal Building completed, functions as county courthouse; **1980** University of New Mexico, Los Alamos Campus, (2-year) established; **1988** nuclear weapons research ended; **May 2000** controlled burn in Santa Fe National Forest spreads through Bandelier National Monument to city, 25,000 evacuated, over 230 structures destroyed, brought under control July.

Los Lunas *Valencia County* *Central New Mexico, 20 mi/32 km south of Albuquerque, on Rio Grande*

1613 St. Anthony Mission Church established; **1716** Spanish land grant made to Don Felix Candelaria; town founded; church rebuilt, renamed St. Augustine; **1852** Valencia County formed; **1875** town becomes county seat; **1880** Atchison, Topeka & Santa Fe Railroad built on property of Luna-Otero dynasty; hacienda built by railroad for Luna family in exchange for right-of-way, mansion completed 1920s; **1899** Luna grant renewed; **1914** county courthouse built; **1928** incorporated as a village; **1981** University of New Mexico, Valencia Campus, (2-year) established.

Lovington *Lea County* *Southeastern New Mexico, 245 mi/394 km southeast of Albuquerque*

1908 town founded on land homesteaded by brothers Robert F. and James B. Love; **1917** Lea County formed; town becomes county seat; incorporated as a village; **1920s** drought nearly ruins economy; **1928** oil discovered; **1930** Texas & New Mexico Railroad extended north from Monahans, Texas, with Lovington as terminus; incorporated as a town; **1936** county courthouse built; **1950** Denton Oil Pool discovered to northeast; **1955** incorporated as a city.

Madrid *Santa Fe County* *North central New Mexico, 38 mi/61 km northeast of Albuquerque*

1835 coal discovered; **1869** first commercial coal mining begins; town founded; **1892** narrow gauge railroad built to mines; **1899** mining operations consolidated; **1920** Madrid becomes company town of Albuquerque & Cerrillos Coal Company, through 1940; **1921** with unlimited supply of electricity, tradition of Christmas Lights begun, final year held in 1941 with advent of World War II; **1930s** last coal mines closed; **1960** limited mining resumed.

Mora *Mora County* *Northern New Mexico, 42 mi/68 km northeast of Santa Fe*

1816 Hispanic settlers move into Mora Valley; settlement of San Antonio do lo de Mora established; **1833** settlers driven out by Plains tribes; **1835** Mora Land Grant given to 76 individuals; town founded by Mexicans; **1843** Texas forces under Col. Charles A. Warfield conduct unsuccessful raid on town; **Jan. 20, 1847** day after assassination of Governor Bent at Taos, prominent St. Louis trader Lawrence L. Waldo shot and killed by raiders led by Manuel Cortes; **1860** Mora County formed; town becomes county seat; **1939** county courthouse built, addition built 1978.

Mosquero *Harding County* *Northeastern New Mexico, 117 mi/188 km east of Santa Fe*

1839 cattle introduced to region by Hispanic settlers; **1880s** Melvin Mills plants 14,000 fruit trees in Mosquero Valley; **1906** El Paso & Northeastern Railroad reaches site; **1908** town platted; **1921** Harding County formed; town becomes county seat; existing building built 1905 remodeled as county courthouse; **1922** incorporated as a village.

Mountainair *Torrance County* *Central New Mexico, 48 mi/77 km south-southeast of Albuquerque*

1629 Immaculate Conception Monastery and Church built to north at Quarai pueblo; **c.1674** Quarai pueblo abandoned under pressure from Apaches and epidemics brought by Spanish; **1900** Atchison, Topeka & Santa Fe Railroad built; town founded; **1901** incorporated as a town; **Nov. 1, 1909** Gran Quivira National Monument proclaimed, protects ruins of Humanas Mission (built c.1627) and San Buenaventura Mission (built c.1642), renamed Salinas Pueblo National Monument 1980, absorbs Abo and Gran Quivira state monuments.

Pecos *San Miguel County* *North central New Mexico, 18 mi/29 km southeast of Santa Fe*

c.1350 Pecos Pueblo established containing large communal dwellings; **1540** pueblo conquered by Francisco Vasquez Coronado; **1598** Catholic Franciscan mission established; **1617** Our Lady of Los Angeles Church built, destroyed in Pueblo Revolt 1680; **1716** new church built by Fray José de Arrangui; **1720s** population declines with raids by Apache and Comanche, continues until c.1750; **1768** only 180 survivors remain following smallpox epidemic; **1805** population reduced to just over 100 by typhoid epidemic; **1838** pueblo abandoned; **1953** incorporated as a village; **June 28, 1965** Pecos National Monument established, becomes Pecos National Historical Park 1990.

Portales *Roosevelt County Eastern New Mexico, 215 mi/346 km east-southeast of Albuquerque*

c.1880 cattleman Doak Good becomes first settler, introduces cattle to area; **1898** Atchison, Topeka & Santa Fe Railroad built; town founded; **1890** subsurface water supply lures cattlemen into region; **1903** Roosevelt County formed; town becomes county seat; **1909** town incorporated; irrigation system built by Portales Irrigation Company, continued 1918 by private efforts after company fails; **1934** Eastern New Mexico University established; **1938** county courthouse built; **1942** Cannon Army Air Base established to north, becomes Air Force Base after World War II.

Questa *Taos County Northern New Mexico, 75 mi/ 121 km north-northeast of Santa Fe, near Rio Grande*

1822 Fowler expedition finds abandoned site of Spanish village; **1829** Don Francisco Laforet builds home on Red River, forced to higher ground by threat from Apache and Ute peoples; town founded, named San Antonio del Rio Colorado; **1842** land grant made to 35 families; **1854** defensive wall built around town during Native American attack; **1873** Catholic church built; **1884** post office established; town renamed Questa; **1964** incorporated as a village; **1968** Rio Grande Wild and Scenic River established by Bureau of Land Management.

Raton *Colfax County Northeastern New Mexico, 122 mi/196 km northeast of Santa Fe*

1822 Santa Fe Trail built from Franklin, Missouri, crossed by William Becknell; **1860s** U.S. Government foraging station established at Willow Springs Ranch on Raton Creek; **1867** Clifton House built to south by Tom Stockton; **1869** Colfax County formed; **1871** Charles B. Thacker family become first settlers; **1872** Cimarron becomes first county seat; **1879** Atchison, Topeka & Santa Fe Railroad built; first coal mine opened; **1880** town founded near Canadian River; **1882** county seat moved to Springer; **1891** town incorporated; **1897** county seat moved to Raton after lengthy dispute; **Aug. 9, 1916** Capulin National Monument proclaimed to east, later renamed Capulin Volcano National Monument; **1934** Ice Caves discovered to east by Eli and Fred Gutiérrez; **1936** county courthouse built.

Reserve *Catron County Western New Mexico, 155 mi/249 km southwest of Albuquerque*

1860s town founded as gold mining center on San Francisco River, named Upper Frisco Plaza; **1870s** town

of Milligan's Plaza founded to north; **1921** Catron County formed; Milligan's Plaza becomes county seat; **1924** Milligan's Plaza renamed Reserve; **1968** county courthouse built; **1974** incorporated as a village.

Roswell *Chaves County Southeastern New Mexico, 175 mi/282 km southeast of Albuquerque*

1869 store, post office established by Van C. Smith, professional gambler from Omaha, and Aaron O. Wilburn; town founded near Pecos River, named Rio Hondo; **c.1870** Chisum Ranch established by John Chisum, extends 200 mi/322 km from Fort Sumner south to Texas boundary; **1873** town renamed for Smith's father; **1889** Chaves County formed; town becomes county seat; **1891** artesian water discovered; New Mexico Military Institute built; **1894** Atchison, Topeka & Santa Fe Railroad reaches town; **1903** incorporated as a city; **Feb. 22, 1904** painter, illustrator Peter Hurd born (died 1984); **1906** Public Library founded; **1911** county courthouse completed; **1937** Roswell Museum and Art Center established; **1941** Walker Army Air Field established to south, becomes Air Force Base 1948, site of Strategic Air Command; **Nov. 11, 1942** actress Demi Moore born; **Dec. 31, 1943** singer John Denver born (died 1997); **1945** oil speculator Robert O. Anderson arrives, oversees oil production for next 20 years; **July 1947** many claim witness to crash of unidentified flying object (UFO) in desert, never verified; **1958** Eastern New Mexico University, Roswell Campus, (2-year) established; **1959** Roswell Symphony Orchestra founded; **1962** Walker Air Force Base closed, later converted into Roswell Industrial Air Center; U.S. builds 12 missile silos within 12 mi/17 km radius, discontinued 1967; **1967** oil production reaches peak, ends 1970s; **1997** first annual UFO Festival held.

San Juan Pueblo *Rio Arriba County Northern New Mexico, 25 mi/40 km north of Santa Fe*

July 12, 1598 Don Juan de Oñate takes possession of ancient Tewa village of O'ke, christens it San Juan de los Caballeros; **1599** Spanish settle on west side of Rio Grande at Tewa village of Yungueingge, name it San Gabriel; **1680** Pueblo Revolt begins here, led by Popay of San Juan Pueblo.

Santa Clara Pueblo *Rio Arriba County Northern New Mexico, 18 mi/29 km north-northwest of Santa Fe*

c.1550 Pueblo Santa Clara established, ancestors migrated during drought to Rio Grande Valley from Puye Cliff Dwellings of Santa Clara Canyon; **1622** Spanish Mission church, monastery established by Fray Alonso de Benavides.

Santa Fe *Santa Fe County* *North central New Mexico, 57 mi/92 km northeast of Albuquerque*

1540 Tesuque Pueblo visited to north by Coronado, southernmost Tewa village; **early 1600s** San Lorenzo de Tesuque Mission established; **1609** town founded on Santa Fe River by Spaniard Don Pedro de Peralta, named La Villa Real de Santa Fe; Palace of the Governors built by Spanish; **1610** town becomes capital of province of New Mexico; **1636** San Miguel Church built, one of oldest churches in U.S.; **1680** Pueblos revolt following persecution by Spanish and church officials; **1692** Gen. Don Diego de Vargas subdues Pueblos; original part of Church of Santo Rosario built, renamed Nuestro Padre San Francisco 1717; **1761** Cristo Rey Church built; **1821** Mexico gains independence from Spain; **1822** William Becknell arrives with wagon load of goods from Missouri, opening Santa Fe Trail for trade with Mexico; **1846** Gen. Stephen W. Kearney rides into Santa Fe to assume control of New Mexico Territory (includes Arizona) for U.S.; Fort Marcy built; La Fonda hotel built, refurbished 1929; **1851** incorporated as a city; **1852** Santa Fe County formed; town becomes county seat; **1853** Loretto Academy built; **1859** St. Michael's College (Catholic) founded; **1869** Cathedral of St. Francis begun, completed 1884; **1879** Atchison, Topeka & Santa Fe Railroad arrives; **1884** Territorial Capitol built, destroyed by fire 1892; New Mexico Penitentiary built; **1887** New Mexico School for the Deaf founded; **1899** U.S. Indian School established; **1900** new capitol built, later used as state capitol; **Jan. 6, 1912** New Mexico enters Union as 47th state; city becomes state capital; **1907** public library built; **1909** Museum of New Mexico opened; **1912** Old Santa Fe Association established to preserve city's historical integrity; **1917** New Mexico Museum of Fine Arts built; **1921** post office built; **1931** Laboratory of Anthropology built; **1937** city hall built; state supreme court building built; Wheelwright Museum of Indian Art founded; **1940** county courthouse built; **1947** College of Santa Fe established; **1956** new state penitentiary completed; **1983** Santa Fe Community College established; **July 1997** Georgia O'Keeffe Museum opened.

Santa Rita *Grant County* *Southwestern New Mexico, 180 mi/290 km south-southwest of Albuquerque*

1800 Santa Rita Mine discovered by Spanish Lt. Col. Manuel Carrisco on land opened by Don Francisco Manuel Elguea; mine worked by convicts; town founded, named Santa Rita del Cobre; **1837** Spanish call "peace conference" with Apaches, kill 300 Apaches gathered for meeting, Apaches retaliate by killing 200 settlers; **1862** all mining ceases; **1873** Santa Rita Copper Camp established by Americans; **1899** interest sold to Amalgamated Copper Company; **1902** Chino Copper Mining Company begins open pit mining; **Oct. 27, 1922** Pittsburgh Pirates baseball player Ralph Kiner born; **1934** Santa Rita Copper Mine closed, later reopened by Kennecott Copper Company; **July 3, 1935** astronaut Harrison Schmitt born; **2002** Phelps Dodge Mining Company suspends mining at Chino open pit mine.

Santa Rosa *Guadalupe County* *East central New Mexico, 115 mi/185 km east of Albuquerque*

c.1865 town founded on Pecos River, originally named Agua Negra Chiquita; **1891** Guadalupe County formed; Puerto de Luna becomes county seat; **1899** Southern Pacific Railroad reaches town; county seat moved to Santa Rosa; **c.1900** cattlemen move herds eastward leaving range to sheep herders; **1914** incorporated as a city; **1946** county courthouse built; **1956** Joseph's Restaurant opened on U.S. Highway 66.

Shiprock *San Juan County* *Northwestern New Mexico, 175 mi/282 km northwest of Santa Fe*

1903 town founded on San Juan River in Navajo Indian Reservation, named for Ship Rock to southwest, 7,178 ft/2,188 m above sea level, 1,400 ft/2,253 m above valley, known as "Rock with wings" by Navajos; San Juan School and Northern Navajo Indian Agency established by U.S.; **1939** Ship Rock first climbed, later placed off limits to climbers for its sacred status among Navajo; **1955** five subagencies established; town becomes headquarters of Shiprock Subagency; **1957** discovery of Four Corners Oil Field produces royalties to residents of reservation.

Silver City *Grant County* *Southwestern New Mexico, 190 mi/306 km south-southwest of Albuquerque*

1868 Grant County formed; **1870** town founded, originally named San Vicente de la Cienega; **1871** town becomes county seat; **1878** town incorporated; **c.1880** gold and silver mining begins; town renamed; **1881** Atchison, Topeka & Santa Fe Railroad reaches town, serves as terminus; **1893** Western New Mexico University established; **Nov. 16, 1907** Gila Cliffs Dwellings National Monument proclaimed to north; **1930** county courthouse built.

Socorro *Socorro County* *Central New Mexico, 75 mi/121 km south of Albuquerque, on Rio Grande*

1598 first Church of San Miguel mission built, rebuilt 1615; Juan de Oñate applies Spanish name Socorro to Piro pueblo of Teypana; **1626** Franciscan mission of Nuestra Señora de Socorro built at Piro pueblo of Pilabo; **1680** Piro pueblos take no part in Pueblo Revolt against Spanish; Pilabo residents follow Governor Otermin south to El Paso, establish Socorro del Sur; **1817** settlers arrive, receive Spanish land grant; town founded; **1836** Park Hotel built; **1852** Socorro County formed; town becomes county seat; **1861–1862** Union officers use town as rendezvous; **Feb. 16–21, 1862** first Civil War engagement in New Mexico occurs at Fort Craig to south between Texas Confederates under Gen. H. H. Sibley and Union cavalry garrisoned at fort, Federals hold fort, Sibley moves on to capture Santa Fe and Albuquerque; **1867** silver discovered, boom continues into 1890s; **1880**

Atchison, Topeka & Santa Fe Railroad reaches town; **1886** town incorporated; **Dec. 25, 1887** hotel entrepreneur Conrad Nicholson Hilton born at San Antonio to southeast (died 1989); **1889** New Mexico Institute of Mining and Technology established; **1925** Socorro Public Library founded; **1940** county courthouse completed; **July 16, 1945** first nuclear explosion made at Trinity test site, White Sands Missile Range, 40 mi/64 km to southeast, 21 days before Aug. 6 nuclear bombing of Hiroshima; **1973** construction begins on National Radio Astronomy Observatory to west, dominated by track-mounted VLA (Very Large Array) Telescope, 22 mi/36 km in diameter, completed 1980.

Taos   *Taos County   Northern New Mexico, 55 mi/ 89 km north-northeast of Santa Fe*

1541 Francisco de Varronuevo visits Tewa pueblo of Tua-Tah; **1617** church built by Fray Pedro de Miranda, killed 1631; **1680** Pueblos rebel against Spanish and church authorities; church destroyed; **1692** town founded south of pueblo by De Vargas, town's full name Don Fernando de Taos; **1704** San Geronimo de Taos mission built at Taos Pueblo; **1710** Cristobal de la Serna petitions for land grant; **c.1730** St. Francis of Assisi Mission founded to south; **1760** large band of Ute, Apache, Navajo, and Comanche attack town, carry away some 50 women and children, never seen again; **1826** Padre Antonio José Martinez credited with bringing education and religion to the people; **1832** La Fonda hotel established; **Jan. 19, 1847** Gov. Charles Bent, other officials assassinated by Taos that revolt; **1852** Taos County formed; town becomes county seat; **1856** Trujillo House built; **1858** scout Kit Carson establishes headquarters at his house, through 1866; **1866** gold discovered in mountains to north; **1884** town name shortened to Taos; **1923** Harwood Foundation artists colony established; **July 3, 1929** decapitated body of eccentric A. R. Manby discovered at home, case unsolved; **1932** incorporated as a village; fire damages many historic buildings; **1933** third county courthouse built; **Dec. 15, 1932** Don Fernando Hotel destroyed by fire; **1934** incorporated as a town.

Tierra Amarilla   *Rio Arriba County   Northern New Mexico, 77 mi/124 km north-northwest of Santa Fe*

1822 Tierra Amarilla land grant made to Manuel Martinez, others; settlement hindered by raids; **1852** Rio Arriba County formed, one of seven original New Mexico counties; San Pedro de Chamita becomes county seat; **1855** county seat moved to Los Luceros; **1860** county seat moved to Alacalde; **1880** county seat moved to Tierra Amarilla; **1918** county courthouse completed; **1934** El Vado Reservoir formed by dam on Rio Chama to west; **Feb. 1, 1951** lowest temperature ever reached in New Mexico, at Gavilan to southwest, $-50°F/-46°C$; **June 5, 1967** Mexican-American Land Grant activists seize county courthouse, claiming territory of northern New Mexico, wound 2 policemen, 11 workers freed; **1982** gruesome discovery of two glass jars unearthed beneath courthouse

containing embalmed heads of two men murdered in 1922, had been used as evidence in sensational trial.

Truth or Consequences   *Sierra County   Southern New Mexico, 142 mi/229 km south of Albuquerque*

1685 first gold claim in New Mexico registered by Pedro de Abalos; **1846–1847** battalion of 400 Mormon infantry under Lt. Col. Philip St. George Cooke march down Rio Grande before turning west to San Diego in show of support for U.S. in its military effort against Mexico; **1853** Fort Thorn established to south, abandoned 1859, reused by Confederate General Sibley 1862 to assemble his forces for march north; **c.1910** town founded on Rio Grande, originally named Hot Springs; **1879** silver discovered at Chloride to northwest by Harry Pye; **1884** Sierra County formed; Hillsboro becomes county seat; **1890** first bathhouse built, used by local cowboys; **1916** town incorporated; county seat moved to Hot Springs from Hillsboro; Elephant Butte Reservoir formed by dam on Rio Grande, begun 1912; **1938** county courthouse built; Caballo Reservoir formed on Rio Grande to south; **1950** town renamed by popular vote in honor of television and radio game show "Truth or Consequences" hosted by Ralph Edwards.

Tucumcari   *Quay County   Eastern New Mexico, 170 mi/274 km east of Albuquerque, near Canadian River*

1901 Chicago, Rock Island & Pacific Railroad built; town founded; **1903** Quay County formed; town becomes county seat; **1908** town incorporated; **1926** U.S. Highway 66 extended through town; **1927** Tucumcari Public Library founded; **1939** county courthouse built; **1940** Conchas Reservoir formed by dam on Canadian River to northwest.

Waste Isolation Pilot Plant   *Eddy County   See* **Carlsbad (1994)**

Watrous   *Mora County   North central New Mexico, 56 mi/90 km east of Santa Fe*

1843 land grant petition made, site named La Junta; **1848** trading station founded by Samuel B. Watrous; **1851** Fort Union built to north at base of Turkey Mountains to protect Santa Fe Trail; **1879** Atchison, Topeka & Santa Fe Railroad built, right-of-way donated by landowner Samuel B. Watrous; town founded near Mora River; **1891** Fort Union abandoned; **June 28, 1954** Fort Union National Monument established.

Zuñi   *McKinley County   Western New Mexico, 127 mi/204 km west of Albuquerque*

1539 Fray Marcos de Niza encounters people of Hawikuh (Ahacus), largest of seven Zuñi villages in area called Cibola, descendents of ancient A'shiwi people; **1540** Coronado expedition descends upon Cibola, **1583**

Espejo visits Cibola, finds Hawikuh abandoned; **1598** visit by Oñate reveals all remaining six villages abandoned; **1629** mission established at Hawikuh; **Feb. 22, 1632** Fray Francisco Letrado murdered by Zuñi, Fray Martin de Arvide murdered five days later; **1705** Zuñi Mission Church built; town founded around mission.

New York

Northeastern U.S. Capital: Albany. Major cities: New York (5 boroughs: Bronx, Brooklyn, New York, Queens, Staten Island), Buffalo.

New York became the 11th of the original 13 states to ratify the U.S. Constitution on July 26, 1788.

New York was one of the 13 colonies that adopted the U.S. Declaration of Independence July 4, 1776. It became the 11th state to ratify the U.S. Constitution July 26, 1788. In 1794, the state of Vermont separated from New York.

New York is divided into 62 counties. Five counties are coterminous with the 5 boroughs of New York City. The remaining 57 counties are divided into townships, called towns, that are incorporated with governments having broad powers. Two counties have shared (two) county seats, Oneida County (Rome and Utica) and Seneca County (Ovid and Waterloo. Municipalities are classified as villages and cities. Villages remain part of their respective towns, or townships, while cities separate from them. See Introduction.

Adams *Jefferson County* *Northern New York, 55 mi/89 km north of Syracuse*

1800 area first settled; **1802** incorporated as a village; **1841** Mormons arrive, gather converts, move to Ohio 1842; **Dec. 10, 1851** librarian Melvil Dewey born, developed Dewey Decimal System for filing library books (died 1931).

Albany *Albany County* *Eastern New York, 135 mi/ 217 km north of New York City, on Hudson River*

Sept. 1609 Henry Hudson reaches navigable limit of Hudson River aboard the *Half Moon*; **1624** Dutch post Fort Orange established by 18 Walloon families; **1660** Peter Stuyvesant proclaims Fort Orange as village of Beverwyck; **1664** British capture fort, rename it Albany; **1683** Albany County formed; **1686** incorporated as a village; becomes county seat; **Nov. 30, 1723** Revolutionary leader, New Jersey Gov. William Livingston born (died 1790); **Nov. 20, 1733** Revolutionary soldier, Sen. Philip Schuyler born (died 1804); **1754** Benjamin Franklin presents his Plan of Union, forerunner of U.S. Constitution, to the Albany Congress, giving Albany distinction of Cradle of the Union; **1797** state capital moved here from New York; construction begins on First Dutch Reformed Church; **June 3, 1811** theologian Henry James born (died 1882); **1822** Champlain Canal opens; **1825** Erie Canal opens, with Albany at its eastern terminus, increasing its role as a river port; **July 4, 1827** state of New York abolishes slavery; **Oct. 30, 1829** Cong. Roscoe Conkling born (died 1888); **March 6, 1831** Union Gen. Philip Sheridan born, moved with parents 1832 to Somerset, Ohio (died 1888); **Sept. 24, 1831** first steam locomotive in U.S., the *De Witt Clinton*, makes 15-mile journey on Mohawk & Hudson Railroad from Albany to Schenectady; **Feb. 8, 1836** engineer John Bogart born, developed Niagara Falls hydro system (died 1920); **Aug. 25, 1836** author Bret Harte born (died 1902); **Nov. 8, 1838** Supreme Court Justice Rufus Peckham born (died 1909); **1841** incorporated as a city; **Sept. 25, 1841** humorist James Bailey born (died 1894); **1842** state court of appeals building completed; **1843** *Knickerbocker News* newspaper founded; **1844** State University of New York at Albany established; **1855** *Union-Star* newspaper founded; **1856** *Times-Union* newspaper founded; **1859** St. Peter's Episcopal Church built; **1860** St. Joseph's Catholic Church built; **Jan. 27, 1872** judge, opinion writer Learned Hand born (died 1961); **1882** city hall built; **Nov. 18, 1886** Pres. Chester A. Arthur dies of apoplexy; **1901** John Pruyn Library built; **1904** Cathedral of All Saints completed after 20 years of construction; **1908** Albany Airport founded, "America's oldest airport"; **1912** state education building completed; **1916** county courthouse built; **1918** Delaware & Hudson Building built; **Jan. 14, 1919** news commentator Andy Rooney born; **1920** College of St. Rose established; **1927** city's Democratic political machine begins with election of

William S. Hackett over William Van Rensselaer; New York State Bank Building built; **Jan. 16, 1928** writer William Kennedy born; **1930** state office building completed; **1933** Parker Dunn Bridge built across Hudson River; **Sept. 5, 1937** TV actor William Devane born; **May 11, 1959** actress Martha Quinn born; **July 6, 1959** Gov. Nelson Rockefeller proposes compulsory fallout shelters for all citizens; **July 1, 1970** most liberal abortion law in nation goes into effect, up to 2,000 abortions per week in New York City; **March 3, 1972** plane crashes into house killing all 16 on board, 1 in house; **1978** The Egg performing arts center opened at Empire State Plaza, named for building's shape; **1981** Repertory Theater opened; **1990** Knickerbocker Arena opened, renamed Pepsi Arena 1997.

Albion *Orleans County Western New York, 25 mi/ 40 km west of Rochester*

1824 Orleans County organized; town founded as county seat, originally named Newport; **1828** incorporated as a village, renamed Albion; **1858** county courthouse built; **1895** Pullman Memorial Universalist Church dedicated on site of George Pullman home, 1848–1855 (lived 1831–1897); **1900** Swan Library opened.

Alexandria Bay *Jefferson County Northern New York, 22 mi/35 km north of Watertown, on St. Lawrence R.*

1829 Cornwall Brothers Store built; **1847** Sunken Rock Lighthouse built; **1851** Reformed Church of the Islands completed; **1875** United Methodist Church completed; **1878** incorporated as a village; **1890** Church of the St. Lawrence built; **1900** Boldt Caste begun on Heart Island, estate of George C. Boldt (1851–1916), left uncompleted after death of wife Louise, finished and restored 1977; **1922** Monticello Hotel opened; St. Cyril's Catholic Church built; **Aug. 13, 1938** Thousand Islands International Bridge dedicated by President Franklin D. Roosevelt.

Amsterdam *Montgomery County East central New York, 16 mi/26 km northwest of Schenectady*

Aug. 1669 last great battle fought between Mohawks and Mohicans at Toureuna Mountain; **1711** Fort Hunter established by British Governor Robert Hunter; **1712** Queen Anne's Parsonage built; **1783** area first settled by Albert Veeder; **1804** town founded; **1825** town begins to grow with opening of Erie Canal; **Nov. 21, 1832** poet, mystic Benjamin Blood born (died 1919); **1841** Schoharie Creek Aqueduct built as branch of Erie Canal; **1836** Utica & Schenectady Railroad extended through town; **1856** William E. Greene establishes town's knitting industry, forerunner of Bigelow Sanford mills; **c.1862** William Greene Mansion built; **1885** incorporated as a city; city hall built; **1904** St. Casimir's Catholic Church founded by Lithuanians; **Feb. 9, 1918** actor Kirk Douglas born.

Attica *Wyoming and Genesee counties West central New York, 30 mi/48 km east of Buffalo*

1804 area settled; **1837** incorporated as a village; **1931** Attica State Prison completed; **1893** Stevens Memorial Library founded; **Sept. 13, 1971** four day prison rebellion ends when state troopers storm Attica Prison, total 43 killed, worst prison death toll in 20th century.

Auburn *Cayuga County Central New York, 23 mi/ 37 km west-southwest of Syracuse*

1793 first cabin built by surveyor Col. John Hardenburgh, named Hardenburgh Corners; **1794** Hardenburgh builds grist mill; **1799** Cayuga County formed; **Jan. 7, 1800** Millard Fillmore, 13th President, born at rural Genoa, to south (died 1874); **1804** county seat moved from Cayuga; **1805** town renamed; **1816** Seward Mansion built, home of William H. Seward; **1817** Auburn State Prison opened; **1836** Cayuga Museum of History and Art built; **1840s– 1850s** Harriet Tubman frees over 300 black slaves at her home on Underground Railway; **1848** incorporated as a city; **1855** county courthouse built, addition built 1929; **Sept. 23, 1859** prison reformer Thomas Osborne born (died 1926); **Feb. 2, 1873** historian Harry Barnes born (died 1968); **1876** Seymour Library founded, facility opened 1903; **Aug. 6, 1890** William Kemmler becomes first person to be executed by electric chair at Auburn Prison for murder; **1913** Harriet Tubman dies, memorial plaque dedicated 1914; **1930** city hall built; **1938** Auburn Schine Theater opened; **1953** Cayuga County Community College established; **1981** Schweinfurth Memorial Art Center opened; **1997** Ward W. O'Hara Agricultural Museum founded.

Ballston Spa *Saratoga County Eastern New York, 25 mi/40 km north-northwest of Albany*

1771 area first settled; **1791** Saratoga County formed; town becomes county seat; **1807** incorporated as a village; **1817** county courthouse built; **June 26, 1819** Union Gen. Abner Doubleday born, inventor of baseball (died 1907).

Batavia *Genesee County Western New York, 35 mi/56 km east-northeast of Buffalo*

1802 Joseph Ellicott establishes land office, headquarters for Holland Land Purchase, on old Genesee Road at its crossing of Tonawanda Creek; site named for Dutch republic, original home of company's proprietors; **1802** Genesee County formed; town becomes county seat; **1804** Holland Land Office built, rebuilt 1815; **1817** Cary Mansion built; incorporated as a village; **1826** William Morgan, a Mason, publishes secrets of Freemasonry, is arrested, kidnapped, never seen again; **1837** railroad reaches town; **1841** county courthouse built; **1865** State School for the Blind opens; **1872** Richmond Memorial Library founded, built 1889; **1876** Thomas Wiard's plow factory moved from East Avon; **1879** natural gas boom begins; **1915** incorporated as a city; **1964** Genesee County Airport built near original 1930 airfield; **1966** Genesee

Community College established; **1997** county court facility completed.

Bath *Steuben County* *Central New York, 30 mi/ 48 km northwest of Elmira*

1793 area first settled by Col. Charles Williamson; **1796** Steuben County formed; town becomes county seat; **1816** incorporated as a village; **1860** county courthouse built; **1878** U.S. Veterans' Hospital opened.

Beacon *Dutchess County* *Southeastern New York, 52 mi/84 km north of New York City, on Hudson River*

1663 land purchased from Native Americans by Francis Rombout for himself and friend Gulian Verplanck; **1709** Brett-Teller House built; **1743** Beacon-Newburgh Ferry established; **1815** John Jacob Astor, others, build cotton mill and foundry; **1872** Howland Library built; **Feb. 15, 1892** Secretary of Navy, Defense James Forrestal born (died 1949); **1913** Matteawan and Fishkill Landing merge with Beacon; incorporated as a city; **1963** Newburgh-Beacon Bridge opened across Hudson River, ending ferry service, second span opened 1980.

Belmont *Allegany County* *Western New York, 63 mi/101 km southeast of Buffalo, on Genesee River*

1806 Allegany County formed; Angelica becomes county seat; **1808** grist mill built by Roger Mills; **1857** county courts, located at Angelica, begin alternating between Angelica and Belmont creating shared county seats; **1871** incorporated as a village; **1892** Belmont becomes sole county seat; **1938** county courthouse built.

Bemis Heights *Saratoga County* *Eastern New York, 25 mi/40 km north of Albany, on Hudson River*

Sept. 19, 1777 in Revolutionary War, British Gen. Burgoyne attacks American forces led by Maj. Gen. Horatio Gates; Benedict Arnold and Col. Daniel Morgan inflict heavy losses on British forces at Freeman's Farm; **Oct. 7, 1777** Burgoyne beaten back by American forces, British escape route blocked; **1883** Saratoga monument built, 155 ft/47 m high; **1940** Saratoga National Historical Park established.

Binghamton *Broome County* *Southern New York, 143 mi/230 km northwest of New York City*

1779 Revolutionary Forces of Gen. James Clinton battle with Native Americans along Susquehanna River; **1787** first settlers move into region; **1800** village of Chenango founded by William Binghamton at confluence of Susquehanna and Chenango rivers; **1806** Broome County organized; village becomes county seat; **Sept. 20, 1833** journalist, humorist David Ross Locke born (died 1888); **1834** incorporated as a village, renamed Binghamton; **1837** Chenango Canal from Utica opened, closed 1874; **1848** Erie Railroad arrives; **1854** manufacture of shoes begun by Lester brothers; Binghamton State

Hospital founded; **1855** Christ Church built; **1867** incorporated as a city; **1869** first railroad reaches city; **1870** cigar making becomes major industry; **1881** George F. Johnson of Massachusetts takes job at shoe factory here, persuades company to build new plant outside edge of city, now called Johnson City, beginnings of Endicott-Johnson shoe manufacturer; **1898** county courthouse built; **1904** Binghamton Public Library opened, becomes Broom County Library 1985; **Apr. 11, 1904** *Evening/Sunday Press* newspaper founded; **July 22, 1913** factory fire, 35 killed; **1946** State University of New York at Binghamton established.

Brewster *Putnam County* *Southeastern New York, 50 mi/80 km north-northeast of New York City*

July 31, 1763 judge, legal scholar James Kent born nearby (died 1847); **1792** Old Southeast Church built; **1849** village founded, platted by Walter Brewster; **c.1850** Brewster House built; **1853** Tilly Foster Iron Mine established, closed 1895 following mine collapse; **1864** Borden Condensed Milk factory established by Gail Borden, milk shipped to Union troops, destroyed by fire 1935; **1891** Sodus Dam built creating East Branch Reservoir, provides water for New York City; **1894** incorporated as a village; **1901** St. Andrew's Cathedral completed, begun 1881; **1931** Railroad Station opened; **1963** Southeast Museum founded.

Bronx (The Bronx) *Bronx County* *Borough of New York City*

1639 area first settled by Swede Jonas Bronck; **1748** Van Cortlandt House built, later becomes Bronx County Historical Museum; **Oct. 18, 1776** heavy fighting in Battle of Pell's Point on Long Island Sound, George Washington retreats after Battle of Long Island; **1797** Harlem Bridge built across Harlem River; **1833** construction of Fort Schuyler begins at Throg's Neck, completed 1845; **1841** Fordham University established; **1847** State University of New York Maritime College established; **Jan. 16, 1878** actor Harry Carey born (died 1947); **July 19, 1879** reform mayor of New York John Mitchel born (died 1918); **1891** New York Botanical Garden opened; **Sept. 22, 1891** Democratic political leader Edward Joseph Flynn born (died 1953); **1895** Westchester, Wakefield, other communities to east of Harlem River annexed by New York City; **1898** New York City consolidates; Bronx Borough created; **1899** Bronx Zoo opened; **1904** first subway reaches the Bronx from Manhattan; **1911** College of Mount St. Vincent established; **Dec. 23, 1911** actor James Gregory born (died 2002); **1914** Bronx County formed, last county formed in New York State, coterminous with Bronx Borough; **Dec. 2, 1915** actor Adolph Green born (died 2002); **Apr. 30, 1917** singer Bea Wain born; **Oct. 7, 1917** singer June Allyson born; **Feb. 3, 1918** comedian Joey Bishop born; **March 20, 1922** TV actor Carl Reiner born; **Apr. 18, 1923** Yankee Stadium opened; **Aug. 17, 1923** pop painter Larry Rivers born (died 2002); **1924** TV personality Bess Myerson born; **July 4, 1927**

playwright Neil Simon born; **July 26, 1928** movie director Stanley Kubrick born (died 1999); **1931** Lehman College (City University) established; **Aug. 16, 1932** singer Edie Gorme born; **Sept. 10, 1934** illegal German immigrant Bruno Hauptmann arrested for kidnap and murder of Lindbergh baby; **July 17, 1935** TV actress Diahann Carroll born; **1933** Monroe College (2-year) established; **1936** Triborough Bridge completed to Queens and Manhattan; **1939** Bronx-Whitestone Bridge built to Queens; **Jan. 10, 1939** actor Sal Mineo born (died 1976); **Oct. 14, 1939** fashion designer Ralph Lauren born; **1942** Parkchester Housing Development completed; **March 6, 1945** TV actor, producer Rob Reiner born, son of Carl Reiner; **May 9, 1949** singer Billy Joel born; **Feb. 15, 1951** singer Melissa Manchester born; **1959** Bronx Community College (City University) established; **1961** Throg's Neck Bridge completed to Queens; **1968** Eugenio Maria de Hostos Community College (City University) established; **1968** Bronx History Museum opened; **1972** Bronx Museum of the Arts opened; **Oct. 24, 1976** fire at Club Puerto Rico social club kills 25; **1982** Judaica Museum opened; **1986** Maritime Industry Museum opened; **March 25, 1990** fire at Happy Land Social Club kills 87.

Brooklyn *Kings County Borough of New York City*

c.1645 village of Breuckelen founded; **1683** Kings County formed; village becomes county seat; **Aug. 27, 1776** British defeat Gen. George Washington's forces in Battle of Long Island; Washington escapes to Manhattan; **May 11, 1799** poet Robert Sands born at Flatbush (died 1832); **1801** Brooklyn Naval Shipyard established, closed late 1960s; **March 10, 1810** Catholic prelate Father John McCloskey born (died 1885); **1816** incorporated as a village; ferry established to New York (Manhattan); **1834** chartered as a city; **Oct. 19, 1834** Union Gen. Francis Barlow born (died 1896); **Nov. 11, 1846** detective story writer Anna Green born (died 1935); **Sept. 20, 1849** naturalist, explorer George Grinnell born (died 1938); **Jan. 18, 1850** educator Sarah Low born (died 1916); **June 29, 1852** historian John McMaster born (died 1932); **1853** Manhattan College established; **1854** Polytechnic University Brooklyn Campus established; **1855** Williamsburg and Bushwick annexed; incorporated as a city; **1860s** Prospect Park created; **Jan. 8, 1862** book publisher Frank Doubleday born (died 1934); **1863** Brooklyn Historical Society founded; **Dec. 5, 1876** theater fire, 295 killed; **1877** Manhattan Hotel opened at eastern end of Coney Island; **Sept. 6, 1877** painter Paul Dougherty born (died 1947); **Oct. 27, 1877** painter Walt Kuhn born (died 1949); **June 30, 1879** actor Walter Hampden born (died 1955); **Jan. 31, 1881** Nobel chemist Irving Langmuir born (died 1957); **1883** Brooklyn Bridge completed across East River from Manhattan; **1884** St. Francis College established (Brooklyn Heights); world's first roller coaster built at Coney Island; **Feb. 2, 1886** poet William Benet born (died 1950); **1887** Pratt Institute established; **1890** Coney Island (Norton Point) Lighthouse built; **Aug. 17, 1892** actress Mae West born (died 1979); **1896** city boundaries become coextensive with Kings County; **Dec. 28, 1896** composer Roger Sessions born (died 1985); **1897** Steeplechase Amusement Park opened at Coney Island, closed 1964; **1898** New York City consolidates; Brooklyn Borough created, coextensive with Kings County; **Sept. 26, 1898** pianist, composer George Gershwin born (died 1937); **Jan. 17, 1899** educator Robert Hutchins born (died 1977); **1900** composer Aaron Copland born (died 1990); **June 11, 1900** newscaster Lawrence Spivak born (died 1994); **Sept. 5, 1901** actress Florence Eldridge born (died 1988); **Feb. 1, 1904** humorist, writer S. J. Perelman born (died 1979); **Aug. 6, 1905** actress Clara Bow born (died 1965); **July 16, 1907** actress Barbara Stanwyck born (died 1990); **1910** Brooklyn Botanic Garden founded; **1911** College of Mount St. Vincent established; **Jan. 1, 1911** comedian Joey Adams born (died 1999); **May 11, 1912** comedian Phil Silvers born (died 1985); **July 31, 1912** economist Milton Friedman born; **1913** Ebbets Field Stadium opened (baseball Dodgers), demolished 1960 after team's 1958 move to California; **Jan. 18, 1913** actor Danny Kaye born (died 1987); **June 11, 1913** Green Bay Packers football coach Vince Lombardi born (died 1970); **March 29, 1914** comedian Phil Foster born (died 1985); **Aug. 26, 1914** novelist Bernard Malamud born (died 1986); **Aug. 28, 1914** tenor Richard Tucker born (died 1975); **Dec. 2, 1914** playwright Adolph Green born (died 2002); **Feb. 28, 1915** entertainer Zero Mostel born (died 1977); **June 15, 1915** writer Alfred Kazin born (died 1998); **Sept. 29, 1915** historian Oscar Handlin born; **Dec. 7, 1915** actor Eli Wallach born; **1916** St. Joseph's College established; **Feb. 26, 1916** entertainer Jackie Gleason born (died 1987); **1917** actress Susan Hayward born (died 1975); **June 30, 1917** singer Lena Horne born; **March 9, 1918** writer Mickey Spillane born; **May 3, 1918** biochemist Arthur Kornberg born; **Nov. 2, 1918** Malbone Street subway crashes, 97 killed, 100 injured; **March 15, 1919** actor Lawrence Tierney born (died 2002); **May 3, 1919** screenwriter Betty Comden born; **June 4, 1919** tenor Robert Merrill born; **Sept. 23, 1920** actor Mickey Rooney born; **Nov. 20, 1920** actor Gene Tierney born (died 1991); **June 22, 1921** theatrical producer Joseph Papp born (died 1991); **May 1, 1923** writer Joseph Heller born; **Aug. 17, 1923** pop artist Larry Rivers (Irving Grossberg) born (died 2002); **Aug. 31, 1924** comedian Buddy Hackett born (died 2003); **Nov. 30, 1924** Cong. Shirley Chisholm born (died 1996); **1927** Long Island University Brooklyn Campus established; Cyclone roller coaster ride opened at Astroland Amusement Park, Coney Island; **Dec. 26, 1927** comedian Alan King born (died 2004); **June 10, 1928** writer Maurice Sendak born; **June 12, 1928** singer Vic Damone born; **May 25, 1929** opera singer Beverly Sills born; **1930** Brooklyn College of New York established; **Apr. 25, 1930** actor Paul Mazursky born; **1932** fire destroys Coney Island Amusement Park; **1932** actress Abbe Lane born; **March 15, 1933** Supreme Court Justice Ruth Bader Ginsburg born; **Aug. 1, 1933** comedian Dom Deluise born; **Nov. 5, 1933** actor Herb Edelman born; **Nov. 19, 1934** talk show host Larry King born; **July 8, 1935** singer Steve Lawrence born; **Dec. 1, 1935** actor Woody Allen born; **Dec. 30, 1935** baseball player Sandy Koufax born; **May 27, 1936** actor Louis

Gossett, Jr. born; **June 8, 1937** TV personality Joan Rivers born; **Dec. 29, 1937** TV actress Mary Tyler Moore born; **Feb. 24, 1938** TV actor James Farentino born; **Aug. 8, 1938** actress Connie Stevens born; **Aug. 29, 1938** actor Elliott Gould born; **Nov. 18, 1939** TV actress Brenda Vaccaro born; **Jan. 24, 1941** singer Neil Diamond born; **Nov. 27, 1941** country singer Eddie Rabbitt born (died 1998); **Feb. 9, 1942** singer, songwriter Carole King born; **Apr. 24, 1942** singer, actress Barbra Streisand born; **May 28, 1944** Rudolph Giuliani born, New York mayor 1994–2001, became heroic figure for his leadership after Sept. 11, 2001, terrorist attacks on World Trade Center, called "Mayor of America"; **1946** New York City Technical College (City University) established; **Oct. 29, 1947** actor Richard Dreyfuss born; **March 31, 1948** actress Rhea Perlman born; **May 25, 1950** Brooklyn-Battery Tunnel opened under East River; **Jan. 10, 1953** singer Pat Benatar born; **1957** Brooklyn (New York) Aquarium opened; **1958** Brooklyn Dodgers baseball team moves to Los Angeles; **Dec. 19, 1960** USS *Constellation* aircraft carrier burns in Brooklyn Naval Yard killing 49; **Apr. 3, 1961** actor, comedian Eddie Murphy born; **1963** Kingsborough Community College (City University) established; **Feb. 17, 1963** basketball player Michael Jordan born; **1969** Medgar Evers College of City University of New York established; **March 6, 1970** building fire kills seven children, injures three; **May 30, 1970** truck loaded with liquid oxygen explodes at hospital, two killed, 40 injured; **July 17, 1970** collision of two subway trains injures 37; **Jan. 22, 1973** hostage siege at sporting goods store by four militant Muslims, one policeman killed, two wounded; **1986** Waterfront Museum founded.

Buffalo *Erie County* *Western New York, 300 mi/ 483 km northwest of New York City, on Lake Erie*

Aug. 7, 1679 first vessel built by white men on upper Great Lakes, La Salle's *Griffon*, sets sail from Squaw Island; **1758** French establish settlement at mouth of Buffalo Creek, destroyed by English 1759; **1780** Buffalo Creek Indian Reserve established for Senecas; **1800** Niagara County formed; **1803** town platted by Joseph Ellicott of Holland Land Company; town becomes county seat; **Dec. 1813** town burned by British during War of 1812; **1816** incorporated as a village; **1821** Erie County formed from Niagara County; village becomes Erie County seat; Niagara County seat moved to Lockport; **Oct. 26, 1825** Erie Canal opens, first boat departs for New York City, arrives there Nov. 4; **1832** incorporated as a city; **May 5, 1832** publisher Hubert Howe Bancroft born (died 1918); **1840s** city's initial period of industrial growth; **1843** Amana Society religious sect, escaping dogma of official Lutheran church, arrive from Germany led by Christian Metz, establish colony of Ebenezer outside Buffalo, move on to establish Amana colony of east central Iowa 1855–1861; **1846** State University of New York at Buffalo established; **1850** St. Mary's Catholic Church consecrated; **1856** Chippewa Market opens; **Feb. 29, 1860** Herman Hollerith born, invented tabulating machine (died 1929); **1861** Buffalo Museum of Science founded, building

completed 1929; **1862** Buffalo and Erie County Historical Society founded; **July 21, 1864** Frances Folsom Cleveland, wife of Pres. Grover Cleveland, born (married June 2, 1886, died Oct. 29, 1947); **May 31, 1866** Irish Fenian zealots invade Canada from Buffalo, driven back by British forces; **1867** State University of New York College at Buffalo established; **1870** Canisius College established; **1870s** further growth spawned by Pennsylvania coal fields and Lake Superior iron ranges; **1872** old city hall built, later used as county courthouse; **July 21, 1873** singer Harry Witherspoon born (died 1935); **Oct. 31, 1873** International Bridge opened across Niagara River to Fort Erie, Ontario; **March 8, 1874** Pres. Millard Fillmore dies, lived here since retiring from presidency in 1858; **1875** Buffalo Zoo established, third oldest in U.S. after Philadelphia and Central Park; Medaille College established; **1880** Ball Brothers Company founded, maker of canning jars, moved to Muncie, Indiana, 1886; **1881** Buffalo State Hospital built; **1882** Grover Cleveland becomes mayor; **Jan. 1, 1883** diplomat William J. Donovan born (died 1959); **1884** soldiers' and sailors' monument completed; **1886** Buffalo Public Library founded; **1890** Temple Beth Zion dedicated; **Apr. 9, 1893** painter Charles Burchfield born (died 1967); **July 9, 1894** journalist Dorothy Thompson born at suburban Lancaster to east (died 1961); **1896** Prudential Building built, designed by Louis Sullivan; **1898** Roswell Park Cancer Institute founded; **1901** Historical Society Museum opened; **1901** Pan-American Exposition held; **Sept. 6, 1901** Pres. William McKinley shot by anarchist Leon Czolgosz at Exposition, dies Sept. 14; **1902** Lackawanna Iron and Steel Company moves from Scranton, Pennsylvania; **1905** Albright-Knox Art Gallery opened at Delaware Park; Frank Lloyd Wright's Darwin-Martin House completed; **1907** McKinley monument dedicated; **1908** D'Youville College established; **1914** St. Joseph's Cathedral completed; **Aug. 6, 1916** historian Richard Hofstadter born (died 1970); **Nov. 27, 1917** TV personality Buffalo Bob Smith born (died 1998); **Jan. 3, 1919** actor Jesse White born (died 1997); **Apr. 23, 1921** baseball pitcher Warren Spann born; **1926** Buffalo-Niagara International Airport established; **June 14, 1926** *Courier-Express* newspaper founded; **1927** Peace Bridge to Fort Erie, Ontario, completed; **June 19, 1928** actress Nancy Marchand born; **1929** New York Central Terminal completed; **Jan. 4, 1930** actor Sorrell Booke born (died 1994); **1931** New York State Building completed; **Feb. 20, 1931** TV actress Amanda Blake born (died 1989); **1932** 32-story city hall completed; **Aug. 23, 1932** comedian Mark Russell born; **1933** Sts. Peter and Paul Russian Orthodox Church built; **1934** U.S. courthouse dedicated; **1935** Buffalo Philharmonic Orchestra founded; **1959** St. Lawrence Seaway opens; **1971** Erie Community College, City Campus, established; **1973** football Buffalo Bills' Rich Stadium opened, renamed Ralph Wilson Stadium 1998; **1975** Hallwalls Contemporary Art Center founded; **Dec. 28, 1993** four of six letter bombs explode at western New York destinations killing five, injuring two; **2001** Buffalo Transportation Pierce-Arrow Museum opened; **Dec. 27,**

2001 city shovels out from 7 ft/2.1 m of snow accumulated over three days.

Canandaigua   *Ontario County*   *West central New York, 25 mi/40 km southeast of Rochester*

1783 town settled; **1789** Ontario County formed; town platted, becomes county seat; **Dec. 1, 1792** Francis Granger born, served as Postmaster General under Jefferson and Madison (died 1868); **1802** Oliver Phelps (1749–1809) shows up after being involved in Mississippi Bubble land scheme which collapsed in 1796, serves in Congress 1803–1805; **1812** First Congregational Church built; **1815** incorporated as a village; **1816** Granger Homestead built; **1858** county courthouse built; old courthouse becomes city hall; **1873** trial of Susan B. Anthony for voting, refuses to pay fine or go to jail, sentence never carried out; **Aug. 2, 1880** painter Arthur Dove born (died 1907); **Jan. 4, 1853** writer Max Eastman born (died 1969); **1913** incorporated as a city; **1965** Finger Lakes Community College established; **1971** Finger Lakes Symphony Orchestra founded; **March 29, 1971** 117-year-old inn destroyed by fire, seven killed.

Canton   *Saint Lawrence County*   *Northern New York, 60 mi/97 km northeast of Watertown*

1799 area settled by Vermonters; **1801** Stillman Foote becomes town's first settler; **1802** St. Lawrence County formed; **1828** county seat moved from Ogdensburg; **1847** incorporated as a village; **1856** St. Lawrence University established; **Sept. 26, 1859** writer Irving Bacheller born at Pierrepont, to southeast (died 1950); **Oct. 4, 1861** painter, sculptor Frederic Remington born (died 1909); **1890s** J. Henry Rushton becomes known for his canoe manufacturing; **1893** county courthouse built, addition built 1957; **1906** State University of New York College of Technology established; **1978** Silas Wright Museum opened, named for Senator from New York.

Cardiff   *Onondaga County*   *Central New York, 12 mi/19 km south of Syracuse*

1868 stone workers ship large carved figure made of Iowa gypsum to Binghamton, taken during night to rural site of Cardiff, buried; **Oct. 1869** well diggers on William Newell's farm unearth figure, thought to be prehistoric, dubbed "Cardiff Giant," sensational hoax later revealed, chiseled gypsum figure devised by George Hull of Binghamton and H. B. Martin of Marshalltown, Iowa [see Fort Dodge, Iowa]; **1934** "Giant" returned to Iowa for permanent display.

Carmel   *Putnam County*   *Southeastern New York, 50 mi/80 km north-northeast of New York City*

July 29, 1797 speculator, capitalist Daniel Drew born (died 1879); **1812** Putnam County formed from Dutchess County; village becomes county seat; **1814** county courthouse built, oldest continuously used courthouse in state.

Catskill   *Greene County*   *Eastern New York, 32 mi/51 km south of Albany, on Hudson River*

1600s settled by Dutch, named Kaatskill, for wildcats seen there; **Aug. 6, 1792** *Catskill Packet* newspaper founded, becomes *Greene County News*; **1800** Greene County organized; town becomes county seat; **March 14, 1800** James Bogardus born, invented postage stamp engraving machine (died 1874); **1806** incorporated as a village; **1814** Thomas Cole House built; **1836** artist Thomas Cole forms Hudson River School, first American artists' movement; **1910** county courthouse completed; **1937** Rip Van Winkle Bridge built across Hudson River from town of Hudson.

Chautauqua   *Chautauqua County*   *Southwestern New York, 55 mi/89 km southwest of Buffalo*

Aug. 5, 1819 pioneer, California Cong. John Bidwell born in rural Chautauqua County (died 1900); **1874** John Heyl Vincent, Methodist clergyman, establishes Chautauqua Institute, training school for Sunday school teachers, name of gathering becomes synonymous with town; **1890** nationwide association of "Chautauquas" established, featuring lectures, orations, concerts, and readings in alcohol free environment, attracts large numbers of followers, other "Chautauquas" eventually established throughout country; **1931** Smith Memorial Library founded.

Cherry Valley   *Otsego County*   *East central New York, 54 mi/87 km west of Albany*

1740 Rev. Samuel Dunlop settles here, builds log church; **Nov. 11, 1778** Cherry Valley Massacre, village destroyed by 700 Native Americans and Tories under Walter Butler and Joseph Brant, 32 residents and 16 soldiers killed; **1799** Cherry Valley Turnpike built; **1810** Dr. Delos White House built; **1850** village hall built; **1878** Cherry Valley monument erected; **1924** Memorial Library built; **1957** Cherry Valley Museum founded.

Clinton   *Oneida County*   *Central New York, 8 mi/12.9 km southwest of Utica*

1787 first settlers arrive; **1797** hematite discovered, beginning of area's iron ore industry; **1812** Hamilton College established; **1843** incorporated as a village; **Feb. 14, 1854** Elihu Root born, secretary of state under Theodore Roosevelt (died 1937); **1887** William Bristol and John Myers establish pharmaceutical maker Bristol-Myers Company; **1890s** lithia water from Franklin Springs bottled, used in Split Rock brand soft drinks through 1970s; **1948** Clinton Arena built, destroyed by fire 1953, rebuilt; **1963** iron ore mining ceases.

Cobleskill   *Schoharie County*   *East central New York, 30 mi/48 km west-southwest of Schenectady*

1752 area first settled; **May 30, 1778** American Capt. Samuel Patrick ambushed by Native Americans and Tories led by Joseph Brant, retreat ordered with Patrick's death; **1800** Borst and Burnhans feed, flour and grist mill founded, begins manufacture of pancake flour in 1890; **1859** threshing machine manufacturing plant opens; **1860s** railroad reaches village; **1868** incorporated as a village; **1898** George Harder invents continuous opening stave silo, standard feature on dairy farms; **1916** State University of New York at Cobleskill established.

Cohoes   *Albany County*   *Eastern New York, 9 mi/ 14.5 km north of Albany, on Hudson River*

1665 area settled by Dutchman Gassen Gerritse Van Schaick at mouth of Mohawk River; **1755** Anthony Van Schaick Mansion built; **1795** one of first canals in country, "Schuyler's Ditch," opened; **Aug.–Sept. 1777** Kosciuszko's forces hold Burgoyne's invasion in check at Peebles Island in Mohawk River; **1832** knitting mill established; **1836** excavation for Harmony Mill yields mastodon remains; **1869** incorporated as a city; **1880** Cohoes Library founded.

Cooperstown   *Otsego County*   *Central New York, 62 mi/100 km west of Albany, on Otsego Lake*

July 1779 Gen. James Clinton dams Otsego Lake to float supplies down Susquehanna River, dam breaks Aug. 8, sending 208 boats down river; **1787** town founded by Judge William Cooper; **Aug. 6, 1789** author James Fenimore Cooper born to William Cooper (died 1851); **1791** Otsego County formed; town becomes county seat; **1807** incorporated as a village; **1813** farm established by James F. Cooper; **1839** Abner Doubleday invents baseball; **1890** county courthouse built; **1938** State Historical Society moves to Cooperstown; **June 12, 1939** centennial celebration of founding of baseball held at Doubleday Field; National Baseball Hall of Fame dedicated; **1944** Farmers' Museum founded at Cooper Farm; **1975** Glimmerglass Opera founded, becomes Alice Busch Opera Theater 1987.

Corning   *Steuben County*   *Southern New York, 13 mi/21 km west-northwest of Elmira*

1788 area settled; **1833** Erastus Corning plats village on new Chemung Canal, named Painted Post; **1852** village renamed Corning; **1868** Flint Glass Company of Brooklyn reestablished as Corning Glass Works at invitation of village; **Sept. 14, 1883** birth control advocate Margaret Sanger born (died 1966); **1890** incorporated as a city; **1910** Corning Glass establishes research laboratory, leads to invention of Pyrex; **July 4, 1912** railroad accident at East Corning, 39 killed; **1934** lens cast at Corning Glass for Mount Palomar Observatory, California; **1939** Observatory Museum established to display Mount Palomar lens after second lens cast; **1951** Corning Museum of Glass founded; **1956** Corning Community College established; **1972** flooding from Hurricane Agnes causes widespread damage.

Cortland   *Cortland County*   *Central New York, 35 mi/56 km south of Syracuse*

1791 town settled; **1808** Cortland County formed, named for Pierre Van Cortlandt [sp], first lieutenant governor of New York; village becomes county seat; **1854** railroad reaches town; **Oct. 12, 1860** inventor Elmer A. Sperry born, created gyrocompasses and ship stabilizers (died 1930); **1868** State University of New York College at Cortland established; **Oct. 16, 1893** folklore writer Carl Lamson Carmer born (died 1976); **1900** incorporated as a city.

Dansville   *Livingston County*   *Central New York, 40 mi/64 km south of Rochester*

1795 area settled; **1808** Old South Church built; **c.1825** Hartman's Tavern built; **1845** incorporated as a village; **1851** Eagle Hotel built; **1858** McFadden-Dansville Health Resort established; Dansville Water Cure hydrotherapy developed by Dr. James Caleb Jackson; **1860s** Foster Wheeler factory established, maker of boilers, generators for ships; **Aug. 22, 1881** Clara Barton organizes first unit of Red Cross at Jackson Sanitarium; **1887** Blum Shoe factory built; **1893** Shepard Memorial Library founded; **1927** Dansville Municipal Airport established.

Delhi   *Delaware County*   *East central New York, 68 mi/109 km west-southwest of Albany*

c.1785 town settled by Abel and John Kidder; indirectly named for Ebenezer Foote, area's "Great Mogul," refers to Delhi, India, home of authentic Great Mogul; **1797** Delaware County formed; village becomes county seat; **1820** county courthouse built; **1821** incorporated as a village; **1843** in Cat Hollow, strong woman cook at lumber camp punches bully who killed her cat, serves cat's remains in meat pie unbeknownst to crew; **1913** State University of New York College of Technology at Delhi established.

Dobbs Ferry   *Westchester County*   *Southeastern New York, 20 mi/32 km north of New York City*

1698 Jeremiah Dobbs establishes ferry across Hudson River initially using hollowed out log, through 1759; village founded at landing; **c.1700** Philip Livingston House built; **1820** Anthony Inn built, demolished 1933; **1834** Zion Episcopal Church built; **1868** South Presbyterian Church built; **1873** incorporated as a village, named Greenborough; **1882** village renamed Dobbs Ferry; **1896** Sacred Heart Catholic Church built; **1901** The Children's Village asylum, established 1851, moves from New York City; **1933** Mayflower Diner established; **1951** Mercy College established.

East Hampton *Suffolk County* *Southeastern New York, 95 mi/153 km east of New York City, on Long Island*

1648 area settled by English from Kent, originally named Maidstone; **1650** Home, Sweet Home built, birthplace of John Howard Payne; **1784** Clinton Academy established; **June 9, 1791** author John Howard Payne born, wrote *Home, Sweet Home* (died 1852); **1799** Lyman Beecher becomes pastor of Presbyterian Church, through 1810; **Sept. 6, 1800** educator Catherine Esther Beecher born (died 1870); **Aug. 27, 1803** clergyman Edward Beecher born (died 1895); **1892** Long Island Railroad reaches town; **1897** East Hampton Library founded, opened 1912; **1920** incorporated as a village; **1932** Guild Hall art museum opened; **Sept. 21, 1938** hurricane causes widespread damage.

Elizabethtown *Essex County* *Northeastern New York, 35 mi/56 km south of Plattsburgh*

c.1790 town founded; **1798** Town of Elizabethtown formed; **1799** Essex County formed; town becomes county seat; **1811** county courthouse built, destroyed by fire 1823, rebuilt, addition built 1843; **1818** Hale House built.

Elmira *Chemung County* *Southern New York, 185 mi/298 km northwest of New York City*

Aug. 29, 1779 Sullivan-Clinton Expedition enters area, destroys Seneca village of Kanaweola in Battle of Newtown; **1788** settled by Pennsylvanians; **1792** Newtown incorporated as a village; **1828** village renamed Elmira; **1836** Chemung County formed; town becomes county seat; **1849** Erie Railroad reaches town; **1855** Elmira College established; **1860** Elmira Rolling Mills founded; **1861** county courthouse built; **1864** incorporated as a city; **May 2, 1865** playwright Clyde Fitch born (died 1909); **1869** Elmira Reformatory established, renamed Elmira Correctional Facility 1970; **Feb. 2, 1870** author Mark Twain weds Olivia Langdon; **Sept. 27, 1884** composer Charles Griffes born (died 1920); **1893** Steele Memorial Library founded; **1910** Mark Twain buried in Langdon plot, Woodlawn Cemetery; **1913** Arnot Art Gallery opens; **1930** first U.S. National Soaring (glider) Competition held; **1935** Remington Rand Corporation established, maker of business machines; **May 28, 1946** city flooded by Chemung River; **1969** National Soaring Museum founded; **June 22-23, 1972** city's worst flooding caused by Tropical Storm Agnes, 23 killed; **1975** Clemens Center for Performing Arts founded; **1983** National Warplane Museum founded.

Endicott *Broome County* *Southern New York, 8 mi/12.9 km west of Binghamton*

Aug. 1779 Gen. James Sullivan and Gen. James Clinton meet here to begin the Sullivan-Clinton Campaign against Tories and Native Americans in Battle of Newtown; **c.1795** area first settled; **1900** Endicott-Johnson Corporation, shoe manufacturer, establishes headquarters here; town founded around factory, named for Henry B. Endicott; **1906** incorporated as a village; International Business Machines (IBM) established, originally International Time Recording Company; **1915** George F. Johnson Memorial Library founded; **1917** Lyric Theater built; **1921** villages of Union and West Endicott merge with Endicott; **1998** Endicott Performing Arts Center founded at Lyric Theater.

Farmingdale *Nassau County* *Southeastern New York, 29 mi/47 km east of New York City, on Long Island*

1695 area settled; **1841** general store opened by Ambrose George; village of Hardscrabble founded around store; **1845** village renamed Farmingdale; platted by George; **1854** Polytechnic University Farmingdale Campus established; **1904** incorporated as a village; **1912** State Institute of Applied Agriculture established, becomes State University of New York at Farmingdale; **1927** Republic Airport founded by Fairchild Manufacturing, becomes public field 1969.

Fonda *Montgomery County* *East central New York, 25 mi/40 km west-northwest of Schenectady*

c.1720s area settled by Dutch, town originally named Caughnawaga; **1742** Butler House built by "Old" Walter Butler of disliked Tory family, allies of Sir William Johnson; **1772** Tryon County formed; **1779** Sullivan-Clinton Campaign sent to disarm Butlers; **May 21, 1780** village burned by Johnson's raiders; **Oct. 30, 1781** young Walter Butler shot, scalped by Oneidas; **1784** county renamed for Gen. Richard Montgomery; **1791** Jellis Fonda House built; **1836** county seat moved from Johnstown; county courthouse built; Utica & Schenectady Railroad reaches town; **1850** incorporated as a village, present name adopted; **1854** 35 counties created from Montgomery County since 1789.

Fredonia *Chautauqua County* *Western New York, 38 mi/61 km southwest of Buffalo, near Lake Erie*

1798 area surveyed by Holland Land Company; **c.1800** town founded, originally named Canadaway; **1820** town renamed Fredonia; **1826** Fredonia Normal School established, becomes State University of New York College at Fredonia; **1829** incorporated as a village; **1868** White Inn established, replaces 1811 wooden structure destroyed by fire; **1873** Mrs. Esther McNeil organizes one of first units of Women's Christian Temperance Union, meeting held at First Baptist Church; **July 24, 1876** writer Jean Webster born (died 1916); **1891** Fredonia Opera House built.

Garden City *Nassau County* *Southeastern New York, 20 mi/32 km east of New York City, on Long Island*

1869 town founded and planned by Alexander Stewart; **1885** Cathedral of the Incarnation built; **1896** Adelphi University established; **1916** First Aero Company of New York National Guard organized at Garden City Aerodrome, first aviation company in U.S.; Salisbury

Golf Club established; **1919** incorporated as a village; **1923** first nonstop transcontinental flight departs Mitchell Field for San Diego, 26 hours, 50 minutes; **Jan. 21, 1924** TV actor Telly Savalas born (died 1994); **1959** Nassau Community College established; **Dec. 7, 1993** gunman Colin Ferguson shoots passengers on Long Island Railroad train, 6 killed, 17 wounded, sentenced to 200 years to life 1995.

Geneseo   *Livingston County*   *West central New York, 25 mi/40 km south-southwest of Rochester*

c.1790 settled by William and James Wadsworth, family of wealthy squires from Connecticut; **1793** Inn established by Richard Steele; **1797** Wadsworth cabin used for signing Big Tree Treaty with Senecas; **Oct. 30, 1807** Union Gen. Samuel James Wadsworth born, died May 8, 1864 in Battle of the Wilderness, Virginia; **1821** Livingston County formed; town becomes county seat; **1826** Geneseo Academy founded on Temple Hill; **1832** incorporated as a village; **1871** State University of New York College at Geneseo established; **1876** first Genesee Valley Fox Hunt held; **Aug. 12, 1877** Sen. James Wolcott Wadworth, Jr. born (died 1952); **1898** county courthouse built.

Geneva   *Ontario County*   *Central New York, 36 mi/ 58 km southeast of Rochester*

1779 Sullivan-Clinton Campaign destroys Kanadesaga village; **1788** area settled; town platted on Seneca Lake; **1816** incorporated as a village; **1822** Hobart College established; **1840s** railroad reaches town; **1841** Trinity Episcopal Church built; **1891** Belhurst Castle mansion built for Carrie Harron Collins, used as speakeasy and casino 1933–1952; **1897** incorporated as a city; **1906** William Smith College for women established; **1995** Geneva Free Library founded.

Genoa   *Cayuga County*   See **Auburn (1800)**

Glens Falls   *Warren County*   *Northeastern New York, 43 mi/69 km north of Albany, on Hudson River*

1759 land granted to 23 grantees; **1762** area settled; **1788** land purchased by Col. John Glen of Schenectady, builds mills here; **1839** incorporated as a village; **1860s** paper production begins, reaches peak 1896; **Apr. 11, 1862** Chief Supreme Court Justice Charles Evans Hughes born (died 1948); **1868** Zopher DeLong House built, becomes Chapman Historical Museum 1968; **1893** Crandall Public Library founded, building opened 1931; **1895** Glens Falls Armory built; **1908** incorporated as a city; **1912** Mary and Nell Pruyn homes built, heiresses of Pruyn Paper Mill owner Samuel Pruyn; **1960** Adirondack Community College established; **1963** The Hyde Collection Art Museum opened; **1979** Glens Falls Civic Center opened; **1995** World Awareness Children's Museum founded.

Gloversville   *Fulton County*   *East central New York, 27 mi/43 km northwest of Schenectady*

1760s settlers arrive from Scotland with Sir William Johnson, include glove makers from Perthshire; **1762** Johnson Hall house built; **1810** James Burr establishes first glove factory; **1851** incorporated as a village; **1890** incorporated as a city; **c.1910** 95 percent of leather gloves in U.S. manufactured here; **1990s** glove industry ends with foreign competition.

Goshen   *Orange County*   *Southeastern New York, 50 mi/80 km northwest of New York City*

1683 Orange County formed; Orangetown (Tappan) and Goshen become shared county seats, necessitated by large mountain dividing county east to west; **1730s** Isaac Joynter House built; **1770s** Benjamin Tustin House built; **1798** Rockland County separates from Orange County; Newburgh becomes shared Orange County seat with Goshen; **1809** incorporated as a village; **c.1840** Harriman Harness Racing Track established; **1845** county courthouse built; **1855** St. James Episcopal Church built; **1894** Goshen Public Library founded, opened 1918; **1951** Hall of Fame of the Trotter founded, renamed Harness Racing Museum and Hall of Fame 1999; **1970s** Goshen becomes sole county seat.

Grand Island   *Erie County*   *Western New York, 10 mi/16 km north-northwest of Buffalo, on Niagara River*

1651 Senecas destroy Neutre Nation, survivors adopted by captors; **1697** Father Louis Hennepin arrives aboard ship *Griffin* on Niagara River; **1796** British expelled from area; **1815** New York assumes control of island; **1817** first settlers arrive; **1824** island surveyed; **1825** first ferry established; **1873** Oakfield Club founded boasting 400 exclusive members at height of island's Golden Era, destroyed by fire 1890s; **1876** Bedell House hotel built, destroyed by fire Jan. 1, 1887, rebuilt, destroyed by fire 1935, annex burned 1988; **1887** McComb House hotel built; **c.1900** cinder cycle paths built around perimeter of island; **June 23, 1912** dock collapses, 37 killed attending river party; **1935** north and south bridges opened on Niagara River east channel.

Greenport   *Suffolk County*   *Southeastern New York, 90 mi/145 km east of New York City, on Long Island*

1640 area settled by English Puritans; **1682** land acquired by Youngs family; **1812** Clark House built; **1831** town named Greenport; **1835** Cogswell House built by George Cogswell, becomes Townsend Manor Inn 1926; **1838** incorporated as a village; **1840** whaling becomes town's main industry; **1844** Long Island Railroad reaches town; **Nov. 1846** steamer *Atlantic* sinks off Race Rock, 45 killed; **1878** Race Rock Lighthouse built; **1899** Orient Point Lighthouse (the Coffee Pot) built to east, automated 1960s; **Sept. 21, 1938** area devastated by Great New England Hurricane; **1990** *Glory* excursion boat built, reproduction of 1893 boat; Railroad Museum of Long Island founded.

Hammondsport *Steuben County* *Central New York, 30 mi/48 km northwest of Elmira, on Keuka Lake*

1860 C. B. Champlin organizes Pleasant Valley Winery, one of earliest wineries in U.S.; **1871** incorporated as a village; **May 21, 1878** aviation pioneer Glenn Hammond Curtiss born (died 1930); **July 4, 1908** Curtiss flies *June Bug* 6,000 ft/1,829 m at Stony Brook Farm; **1961** Glenn H. Curtiss Museum founded, present site opened 1992.

Hempstead *Nassau County* *Southeastern New York, 16 mi/26 km east of New York City, on Long Island*

1644 settled by English; **1688** Joseph Haviland builds tidewater powered grist mill; **March 19, 1748** Quaker preacher Elias Hicks born (died 1830); **1822** St. George's Episcopal Church built; **1846** Presbyterian Church built; **Feb. 20, 1848** railroad financier Edward Henry Harriman born, financed Illinois Central Railroad (died 1909); **1853** incorporated as a village; **May 5, 1905** Belmont Race Track opened, closed 1963, new park opened 1968; **1935** Hofstra University established; **1962** Haviland Mill purchased by citizens for historical museum.

Herkimer *Herkimer County* *East central New York, 15 mi/24 km east-southeast of Utica*

1725 town settled by Palatines, named German Flats; **1728** Revolutionary Gen. Nicholas Herkimer born, died Aug. 16, 1777, from wounds suffered at Fort Stanwix Aug. 6; **1754-1763** town subject to raids during French and Indian War; **1776** Fort Dayton built; **Aug. 4, 1777** Gen. Nicholas Herkimer marches off to Battle of Oriskany from Fort Dayton; **1778** town attacked by Native Americans led by Joseph Brant, evacuated under warning from Adam Helmer; **1791** Herkimer County formed; town becomes county seat; **1807** incorporated as a village; **1834** Dutch Reformed Church built; **1866** Warner Miller acquires mill, begins manufacture of paper, becomes International Paper; **1875** county courthouse built; **1966** Herkimer County Community College established.

Hudson *Columbia County* *Eastern New York, 30 mi/48 km south of Albany, on Hudson River*

1662 Jan Frans Van Hoesen buys land from Native Americans; **1783** settled by whalers, most from Nantucket; **1786** Columbia County formed; **March 1, 1794** Army Gen. William Jenkins Worth born, fought in Seminole War (died 1849); **1796** The Hill manor built; **1836** Christ Episcopal Church built; **1845** county seat moved from Clavarack; **Apr. 7, 1845** the *Swallow* hits rocks in Hudson racing the *Express* and *Rochester*, 15 killed, boat salvaged by Ira Buchman, builds Swallow House; **1872** Olana Mansion built by painter Frederic Edwin Church; **1874** Hudson-Athens Lighthouse built in center of Hudson River, automated 1954; **1908** county

courthouse built; **1937** Rip Van Winkle Bridge built across Hudson River to Catskill; **1969** Columbia-Greene College (2-year) established.

Hudson Falls *Washington County* *Eastern New York, 50 mi/80 km north of Albany, on Hudson River*

1761 first settlers arrive; sawmills and grist mills built; **1772** Washington County formed; town becomes county seat; **1780** Sir Guy Carleton burns town; **1810** incorporated as a village; **1872** county courthouse built; **1910** Hudson Falls Free Library founded; **1995** new county courthouse built.

Hyde Park *Dutchess County* *Southeastern New York, 75 mi/121 km north of New York City, on Hudson River*

1705 Peter Fauconier obtains land patent; **1772** Dr. John Bard builds first Hyde Park home on land inherited through wife; **1826** Holbrock House built by Ephraim Holbrock; **c.1835** James Roosevelt Estate built by Joseph Giraud; **1844** St. James Episcopal Church built on site of 1811 church; **1866** James Roosevelt, Franklin D. Roosevelt's father, acquires Holbrock house; **1871** Hudson River State Hospital opened; **Jan. 30, 1882** Franklin Delano Roosevelt born, 32nd President (died Apr. 12, 1945); **1895** Hyde Park home bought by Vanderbilts, demolished for The Breakers mansion designed by Stanford White, completed 1898; **1938** Franklin D. Roosevelt's self-designed "Dream Cottage" built; **1941** Franklin D. Roosevelt Library opens; **1946** The Culinary Institute of America established.

Irvington *Westchester County* *Southeastern New York, 22 mi/35 km north of New York City, on Hudson River*

c.1655 area settled; settlement originally called Dearman; **1693** Odell Inn built; **1723** Albany Post Road opens; **1835** Nevis mansion built by James Alexander Hamilton, third son of Alexander Hamilton; **1857** village renamed for Washington Irving; **Sept. 7, 1867** financier John Pierpont Morgan, Jr. born (died 1943); **1872** incorporated as a village; **1891** Bennett School and Junior College founded, moved to Millbrook 1907; **1895** Ardsley Club, exclusive golf course, organized; **1918** mansion built by African-American businesswoman Mrs. C. J. Walker of St. Louis (1867–1919), made fortune in cosmetics industry.

Ithaca *Tompkins County* *Central New York, 50 mi/80 km south-southwest of Syracuse, on Cayuga Lake*

June 1779 John Sullivan expedition burns Native American crops; **1788** first white settlers begin arriving; **1817** Tompkins County formed; town becomes county seat; **1821** incorporated as a village; **Jan. 22, 1832** Western Union official Alonzo Cornell born (died 1904); **1864** Cornell Public Library founded; **1865** Cornell University established; **1888** incorporated as a city; **1892** Ithaca

College established; **Aug. 11, 1921** author Alex Haley born (died 1992); **1931** county courthouse built; **Apr. 5, 1967** dormitory fire at Cornell University kills eight students, professor.

Jamaica   *Queens County*   *See* **Queens**

Jamestown   *Chautauqua County*   *Southwestern New York, 56 mi/90 km south-southwest of Buffalo*

c.1805 land purchased by Prendergast brothers; town founded by James Prendergast; **July 4, 1819** Cong. Reuben E. Fenton born (died 1885); **1828** 30-mi/48-km mail route established to Wattsburg, Pennsylvania, carrier walked both directions for years; **1849** Swedish immigrants arrive; **1886** incorporated as a city; **1888** manufacture of furniture begins; **Aug. 6, 1911** comedienne Lucille Ball born (died 1989).

Johnstown   *Fulton County*   *East central New York, 26 mi/42 km northwest of Schenectady*

1762 Sir William Johnson settles here; **1763** Drumm House built by Johnson; **1771** Fort Johnstown built; **1772** Tryon County formed; town becomes county seat; county courthouse and jail built by Johnson, still in use; **Oct. 25, 1781** Battle of Johnstown, last Revolutionary War battle in New York State, fought here, victory sends Royalists into flight; **1784** county renamed Montgomery County; **1793** Jimmy Burke's Inn built; **1798** Union Hall Inn built by De Fon Claire; **1808** incorporated as a village; **Nov. 12, 1815** Elizabeth Cady Stanton born, women's suffrage leader (died 1902); **1836** Montgomery County seat moved to Fonda; **1838** Fulton County formed from Montgomery County; Johnstown becomes county seat; **1890** Knox Gelatin Company founded by Charles Knox; **1895** incorporated as a city; **1898** Rose Hill House built by Charles Knox; **1964** Fulton-Montgomery Community College established.

Kinderhook   *Columbia County*   *Eastern New York, 20 mi/32 km south of Albany, on Hudson River*

1614 town name first appears on Dutch maps; **1736** Beekman House built; **Dec. 5, 1782** Martin Van Buren born, 8th President of U.S., first president born in independent U.S. (died July 24, 1862); **March 8, 1783** Hannah Hoes Van Buren, wife Pres. Martin Van Buren, born (married 1807, died 1819); **Dec. 14, 1795** Benjamin Franklin Butler born, Attorney General under Presidents Jackson and Van Buren (died 1858); **1797** Lindenwald home built; **1814** Dutch Reformed Church built; **1825** *Kinderhook Herald* newspaper founded; **1838** incorporated as a village; **1840** Van Buren retires to Lindenwald, purchased 1839, remains here until his death; **1851** St. Paul's Episcopal Church built; **1880** fire destroys part of business district; **Oct. 26, 1974** Martin Van Buren National Historic Site authorized.

Kingston   *Ulster County*   *Southeastern New York, 85 mi/137 km north of New York City, on Hudson River*

c.1614 trading post established, named Wiltwyck; **1652** settlement founded by Dutch; **1658** Peter Stuyvesant builds stockade; **June 1660** 45 white women and children taken hostage by Esopus peoples, held in exchange for Native American captives sent to Caribbean as slaves; **Sept. 1660** rescue party frees hostages, some of rescuers settle in area; **1661** village chartered as Wiltwyck; **1664** village renamed Kingston; **1676** Senate House built; **1683** Ulster County formed; village becomes county seat; **Oct. 15, 1775** painter John Vanderlyn (died 1852); **Sept. 1777** first state senate meets here; **Oct. 16, 1777** state legislature forced to move to Poughkeepsie as British troops advance, burn town; **1805** incorporated as a village; **1818** county courthouse built; **1828** Delaware & Hudson Canal opened to Delaware River; **1838** Kingston-Roundout Lighthouse built, razed 1953; **1852** Dutch Reformed Church built; **1861** passenger boat *Mary Powell*, "Queen of the Hudson," begins service, ended 1918, junked 1920; **1866** West Shore Railroad arrives; **1872** incorporated as a city; **1899** Kingston Public Library founded; **1917** Ashokan Reservoir and Catskill Aqueduct completed for New York City water supply; **July 30, 1929** actor Peter Bogdanovich born; **1955** Trolley Museum of New York founded; **1957** Kingston-Rhinecliff Bridge built across Hudson River; **1977** Ulster Bullet Company founded, maker of ordnance; **1980** Maritime Museum founded.

Lackawanna   *Erie County*   *Western New York, 3 mi/4.8 km south of Buffalo, on Lake Erie*

c.1655 Seneca people eliminate other native tribes from area; **1780** Native American log villages built with aid of British; **1842** Native American lands sold to Odgen Land Company; first whites soon move into area; **1901** Lackawanna Iron and Steel Company plant completed on Lake Erie; town founded adjacent to plant; **1909** incorporated as a city; **1922** plant acquired by Bethlehem Steel Corporation; **1926** Basilica of Our Lady of Victory (Catholic) completed, replaces 1876 structure; **1970s** local steel industry experiences total decline; **Sept. 13, 2002** six Muslims from Middle Eastern countries arrested, suspected of having ties with al-Qaida Islamic terrorist group, formally charged Oct. 4.

Lake George   *Warren County*   *Northeastern New York, 58 mi/93 km north of Albany, on Lake George*

Aug. 1642 area visited by Jesuit Father Isaac Joques to serve among Iroquois, killed by Mohawks 1646; **Sept. 8, 1755** Gen. Sir William Johnson defeats French and Native Americans at Lake George; **1756** British Fort William Henry built by Sir William Johnson; **Aug. 1757** British at Fort William Henry surrender to French General Montcalm, many massacred by natives in spite of French promise of safe conduct; **1759** Fort George built, never completed; **1813** Warren County formed; town founded as county seat, originally named Caldwell; **c.1822** Civil War photographer Matthew B. Brady born in rural

Warren County (died 1896); **1903** incorporated as a village; **1908** steamer *Mohican* launched on Lake George; **1939** Father Isaac Joques monument erected; **1962** village renamed Lake George; county courthouse built.

Lake Placid   *Essex County*   *Northeastern New York, 120 mi/193 km north of Albany*

1850 area first settled; **Dec. 1859** body of abolitionist John Brown buried at his farm here, born 1800, hanged Dec. 2 for raid on Harpers Ferry, (West) Virginia; **1882** Henry Van Hoevenberg builds Adirondack Lodge as memorial to his intended bride Josephine Schofield who died 1881; **1895** Lake Placid Club established by Melvil Dewey, inventor of Dewey Decimal System for libraries; **1900** incorporated as a village; **1903** forest fire destroys Adirondack Lodge; **1909** three years of tree plantings completes Pettis Memorial Forest; **Nov. 14, 1919** actress Veronica Lake born (died 1973); **1920** Intervales (Olympic) Ski Jump built; **1924** Mirror Lake Inn established; **1932** Olympic Arena built for Winter Olympics; **c.1936** Adirondack Lodge rebuilt; **1969** World Bobsled Championship held; **1980** Winter Olympics held, one of three locations in world chosen twice for Olympics (also Innsbruck and St. Moritz).

Lake Pleasant   *Hamilton County*   *North central New York, 70 mi/113 km northwest of Albany*

1806 inn established by George Wright; **1816** Hamilton County formed; **1817** first store opened by William B. Peck; **1838** county organized; town becomes county seat; **1929** county courthouse completed.

Lancaster   *Erie County*   See **Buffalo (1894)**

Levittown   *Nassau County*   *Southeastern New York, 27 mi/43 km east of New York City, on Long Island*

1947 planned community founded on Ernie Knoell's potato farm by developer William Levitt and architect brother Abraham Levitt, considered first modern American suburb, two other developments of same name built north of Philadelphia and in Burlington County, New Jersey, early 1950s; **1951** complex totals 17,447 simple two-bedroom ranch homes sprawled across Long Island farmland.

Lewiston   *Niagara County*   *Western New York, 20 mi/32 km north-northwest of Buffalo, on Niagara River*

1626 Franciscan mission founded; **1678** Robert de La Salle builds storehouse and portage trail to upper Niagara River; **1796** first settlers arrive; **1817** First Presbyterian Church built; **1822** incorporated as a village; **1824** Frontier House inn built; **Sept. 13, 1826** William Morgan publishes secrets of Masonic Order, disappears mysteriously; **1851** suspension bridge built across Niagara River to Queen's Town, Ontario; **c.1890** shipping terminal built by Canada Steamship Lines, Ltd, closed 1938; **1966**

first Fine Arts Festival held; **1969** Lewiston Council of the Arts founded.

Little Falls   *Herkimer County*   *East central New York, 20 mi/32 km east of Utica*

1723 log Dutch Reformed Church built; **1730** construction begins on new Dutch Reformed Church, enlarged to serve as Fort Herkimer during French and Indian War; **1764** Herkimer Estate built by Gen. Nicholas Herkimer; **Aug. 1, 1778** patriot Adam Helmer runs ahead of advancing Tory-native allied raiders warning residents to evacuate; **1792** Western Inland Canal built; **1811** incorporated as a village; **1825** Erie Canal opens; **1836** Utica & Schenectady Railroad built; **1850s** large numbers of Irish immigrants arrive; **1853** town becomes prominent cheese producer; cheese exchange organized, closed 1875; **1870** cheese factory built; **1871** New York Dairymen's Association and Board of Trade founded; **1895** incorporated as a city; **Apr. 19, 1940** railroad accident, 31 killed.

Little Valley   *Cattaraugus County*   *Western New York, 43 mi/69 km south of Buffalo*

1808 Cattaraugus County formed; **1817** county organized; Ellicottville becomes county seat; **1851** New York & Erie Railroad completed; town founded; **1866** county seat moved to Little Valley; **1876** incorporated as a village; **1966** county courthouse completed.

Locke   *Cayuga County*   *Central New York, 31 mi/50 km southwest of Syracuse*

1790 town founded, named Milan; **Jan. 7, 1800** Millard Fillmore born to west, 13th President of U.S. 1850–1853 (died March 8, 1874); **1802** town renamed Locke; **1849** Methodist Church built, destroyed by fire 1912, rebuilt, demolished 1979; **Apr. 26, 1912** town fire destroys 30 buildings; **Apr. 10, 1975** second fire destroys 11 buildings.

Lockport   *Niagara County*   *Western New York, 18 mi/29 km/north-northeast of Buffalo*

1808 Niagara County formed; Buffalo becomes county seat; **1816** town settled; **1821** Erie County separates from Niagara County; county seat moved to Lockport; Buffalo becomes Erie County seat; **1825** Erie Canal completed; **1865** incorporated as a city; **1914** county courthouse built; **June 16, 1938** writer Joyce Carol Oates born.

Long Beach   *Nassau County*   *Southeastern New York, 20 mi/32 km east-southeast of New York City*

Jan. 1, 1837 barque *Mexico* carrying Irish immigrants runs aground, 62 killed as ship breaks apart; **1849** lifesaving station established; **1880** Long Island Railroad reaches site; Long Beach Hotel built by railroad, largest hotel in world; **1894** railroad line abandoned due to coastal washouts; **1907** community and boardwalk developed by William Reynolds; **1922** incorporated as a city; **Oct. 10, 1926** actor Richard Jaeckel born (died 1997); **1928**

Long Beach Library opened; **1939** Mayor Louis Edwards fatally shot by patrolman Alvin Dooley, latter gets 15 years in prison; **Oct. 30, 1940** actor Ed Lauter born; **March 14, 1947** comedian Billy Crystal born.

Lowville *Lewis County* *Northern New York, 50 mi/ 80 km north-northwest of Utica*

1798 area settled; **1805** Lewis County formed; Martinsburg becomes county seat; **1820** first annual Lewis County Fair held; **1850s** Hough Residence built for Franklin B. Hough; **1854** incorporated as a village; **1855** town hall completed, used as county courthouse 1865, addition built 1948; **1863** county seat moved to Lowville.

Lynbrook *Nassau County* See **Rockville Centre** (1927)

Lyons *Wayne County* *North central New York, 32 mi/51 km east of Rochester*

1789 town settled; **1811** Town of Lyons formed; **1821** Erie Canal built; **1823** Wayne County formed; town becomes county seat; **Aug. 9, 1827** Nevada Sen. William Morris Stewart born (died 1909); **1831** incorporated as a village; **1840** Grace Episcopal Church built; **1854** county courthouse built; **June 13, 1854** naval officer Bradley Allen Fiske born (died 1942); **Jan. 18, 1874** industrialist Myron Charles Taylor born (died 1959).

Malone *Franklin County* *Northeastern New York, 45 mi/72 km west-northwest of Plattsburgh*

1802 area settled by Vermonters; named by William Constable for friend Edmund Malone; **1808** Franklin County formed; town becomes county seat; Embargo Act leads to smuggling of potash to Canada; **June 13, 1819** William Almon Wheeler born, vice president under President Hayes, 1877–1881 (died 1887); **1853** incorporated as a village; **1857** Wheeler House built; **1866** staging point for 2,000 Irish Fenians for invasion of Canada, in hope of capturing Canada as leverage in securing Ireland's independence from Britain; **June 2, 1866** Fenians cross border in feeble attack on Canada, disband; **1880** Wead Public Library founded; **1930** county courthouse built, addition built 1988.

Manchester *Ontario County* *North central New York, 22 mi/35 km southeast of Rochester*

May 14, 1814 beekeeper Timothy Ryan stung to death by his own bees; **Apr. 1820** Joseph Smith visited in woods by two personages revealed to be God the Father and Jesus Christ, is advised not to join any existing church; **1823** Smith visited by Angel Moroni, retrieves golden inscribed plates 1827, translates them 1830; **Apr. 6, 1830** Joseph Smith of makes known his spiritual revelations to his father, Joseph Smith, Sr., and others, beginnings of Church of Latter-day Saints (Mormon); **1892** incorpo-

rated as a village; **Aug. 25, 1911** railroad accident, 29 killed.

Manhattan *New York County* See **New York**

Massena *Saint Lawrence County* *Northern New York, 87 mi/140 km northeast of Watertown*

1792 Anable Fancher builds sawmill on Grass River; names settlement for Marshall Andre Massena, veteran of Napoleonic wars; **1822** mineral springs become popular, through 1900; **1886** incorporated as a city; **1900** Henry H. Warren begins work on canal between Grass River and St. Lawrence for hydro power; **1902** Aluminum Company of America plant established; **1934** Roosevelt International Peace Bridge opens to east, crosses St. Lawrence River to Cornwall, Ontario; **Sept. 1944** earthquake causes $1 million in damage; **1959** President Eisenhower officially opens St. Lawrence Seaway; **May 4, 1972** explosions rock oil tanker *Venus* between Wilson Head and Ault islands in St. Lawrence River to west, Capt. Charles Stanley killed, four injured; **1996** St. Lawrence Aquarium and Ecological Center founded, to open 2005; **Jan. 1998** ice storm devastates region and neighboring Quebec and Ontario.

Mayville *Chautauqua County* *Southwestern New York, 53 mi/85 km southwest of Buffalo*

1804 town first settled by Dr. Alexander McIntyre; **1808** Chautauqua County formed; town becomes county seat; **1830** incorporated as a village; **1872** St. Mark Lutheran Church completed; **1876** First Baptist Church built; **1895** Mayville Library founded, new library opened 1960; **1908** county courthouse built; **1925** Dart Airport established, named for owner Bob Dart; **1935** railroad depot completed, replaces wooden depot destroyed by fire 1923.

Mineola *Nassau County* *Southeastern New York, 18 mi/29 km east of New York City, on Long Island*

1872 town founded; **1896** Winthrop-University Hospital founded, originally Nassau Hospital; **1899** Nassau County formed from Queens County; town becomes county seat; **1906** incorporated as a village; **May 20, 1927** Charles Lindbergh departs from Roosevelt Field at 7:52 A.M. in the *Spirit of St. Louis* on his trans-Atlantic solo flight, arrives in Paris, France, in 33 hours, 29 minutes, 30 seconds; **1937** county courthouse built.

Montauk *Suffolk County* *Southeastern New York, 110 mi/177 km east of New York City, on Long Island*

1604 Montauk Point discovered by Adrian Block; **1687** land at Montauk Point purchased from Montauks for settlement; **1696** Capt. William Kidd, hired to fight pirates, becomes pirate himself, buries loot on Gardiners Island to north; **Apr. 1776** area plundered by 12 British warships; **1796** Montauk Point Lighthouse built, automated 1987; **July 28, 1820** Julia Gardiner Tyler, second wife of Pres. John Tyler, born on Gardiners Island (married June 16, 1844, died 1889); **1895** Long Island Railroad reaches town; **1898** U.S. force of 25,000 men arrive under quarantine from Cuba during Spanish-American War; **1926** Carl Graham Fisher attempts to create "Miami of the North," builds luxury hotel at Fort Pond Bay, endeavor fails; **Sept. 21, 1938** New England Hurricane causes extensive damage.

Monticello *Sullivan County Southeastern New York, 65 mi/105 km northwest of New York City*

1804 sawmill established; town founded; **1809** Sullivan County formed; town becomes county seat; **1830** incorporated as a village; **1845** county courthouse completed, previous structure destroyed by fire; **1909** third county courthouse built.

Mount Vernon *Westchester County Southeastern New York, 12 mi/19 km north-northeast of New York City*

1664 area settled; **1733** editor John Peter Zenger arrested for libel for story on election of assemblyman, released months later, establishing right to free press; **1761** St. Paul's Episcopal Church built; **1850** Home Industrial Association establishes planned community; **1852** town platted; first 300 homes sold to members, becomes stop on New York, New Haven & Hartford Railroad; **1853** incorporated as a village; **1892** incorporated as a city; **July 11, 1899** author E. B. White born (died 1985); **Nov. 4, 1918** actor Art Carney born (died 2003); **Oct. 20, 1925** humorist Art Buchwald born; **Nov. 30, 1929** TV personality Dick Clark born; **Dec. 28, 1954** actor Denzel Washington born.

New City *Rockland County Southeastern New York, 27 mi/43 km north of New York City*

1735 Maj. John Smith House built; **1798** Rockland County formed from Orange County; town founded as county seat; **1875** New York & New Jersey Railroad reaches town; **1928** county jail built; **1929** Christie Airport opened, closed 1969; **1933** New City Library founded, new library opened 1980; **1956** Lake De Forest formed by dam on Hackensack River by Hackensack Water Company; **Jan. 2002** third county courthouse completed.

New Paltz *Ulster County Southeastern New York, 72 mi/116 km north of New York City*

1677 French Huguenot Louis DuBois, 11 others purchase land from Esopus peoples; **1678** town founded, named for town in Germany; **1700** first stone dwellings replace cabins; **1705** Daniel DuBois House built; **1712** Hasbrouck House built; **1828** State University of New York at New Paltz established; **1833** New Paltz Academy founded, destroyed by fire 1884; **1839** Dutch Reformed Church built; **1870** Mohawk Mountain House hotel opened; Walkill Valley Railroad reaches town; **1887** incorporated as a village; **1909** New Paltz Free Library founded, Etling Memorial Library opened 1920; **1921** New Paltz Turnpike built, first concrete highway in New York; **1927** opera house built.

New Rochelle *Westchester County Southeastern New York, 15 mi/24 km north-northeast of New York City*

1654 Thomas Pell purchases land from Siwanoys; **1688** village on Long Island Sound settled by French Huguenots; **1689** Huguenots purchase land from agent Jacob Leisler, name settlement La Rochelle; **June 10, 1700** architect Peter Faneuil born, designed Boston's Faneuil Hall (died 1743); **1710** Dutch Reformed Church built; **Oct. 1776** British occupy town prior to defeat at Battle of White Plains Oct. 21–23; **1801** Premium Flour Mill built by Mott family; **1824** Town House built; **1857** incorporated as a village; **1892** New Church of the Blessed Sacrament (Catholic) built; New Rochelle Public Library founded; **Oct. 1, 1893** novelist Faith Baldwin born (died 1978); **Apr. 4, 1896** playwright, journalist Robert E. Sherwood born (died 1955); **1899** incorporated as a city; **1904** College of New Rochelle established; **Feb. 4, 1905** actor Eddie Foy, Jr., son of actor Eddie Foy, born (died 1983); **1917** Huguenot Memorial Bridge dedicated, constructed of stones from Reformed Church (1710); **1928** First Presbyterian Church built; **Jan. 9, 1935** TV actor Bob Denver born; **Feb. 24, 1938** Peter Levine, 12, kidnapped, $30,000 ransom not paid, dismembered body found May 29; **1940** Iona College established; **July 9, 1942** actor Richard Roundtree born; **1945** Municipal Marina built at Echo Bay; **Oct. 2, 1945** singer Don McLean born; **Apr. 28, 1950** talk show host Jay Leno born; **Sept. 21, 1962** actor Rob Morrow born; **Feb. 28, 1964** actor Matt Dillon born; **Feb. 14, 1977** gunman kills five, wounds five, then kills himself at moving company warehouse; **1987** East Coast Arts Theater opened.

New Windsor *Orange County Southeastern New York, 53 mi/85 km north of New York City, on Hudson River*

1694 land patented to John Evans; **1762** town of New Windsor formed; **1740** Rock Tavern built; **March 2, 1769** De Witt Clinton, governor of New York, born (died 1828); **1779** George Washington establishes headquarters here June 24 until July 21, again from Dec. 6, 1780 until June 25, 1781; **July 4, 1779** at Independence Day celebration, Washington pardons all war prisoners; **Oct. 1782** encampment established for housing 6,000 to 8,000 war refugees from five states; **1807** Vails Gate Methodist Church built; **1847** St. Thomas Episcopal Church built; **1939** Stewart Air Force Base established; **Jan. 25, 1981** 52 of 63 hostages held in Iran 444 days (Nov. 3, 1979–Jan. 20, 1981) land at Stewart Air Base; **1990** Stewart Airport opened to commercial flights.

New York   *New York County, Manhattan*
Borough   *Southeastern New York, at mouth of Hudson River*

See also **Bronx, Brooklyn, Queens, and Staten Island Boroughs**

1524 Giovanni da Verrazano discovers New York Harbor; **Sept. 1609** Manhattan Island and New York Harbor explored by Henry Hudson in sloop *Half Moon*, enters Hudson River; **1613** Adriaen Block builds first houses in lower Manhattan; **May 1624** Dutch arrive in larger numbers; **May 6, 1626** Manhattan purchased from Native Americans by Peter Minuit for $24 worth of trinkets; **1633** first church built; **1642** first public meeting house built on site of 73 Pearl Street; **1653** wall erected near present-day Wall Street; **Feb. 2, 1653** incorporated as town of New Amsterdam; **Sept. 8, 1664** Peter Stuyvesant yields to English; town renamed New York; **1665** Thomas Willett becomes first English mayor; **1668** severe yellow fever outbreak, first epidemic in New World, also affects Philadelphia; **Aug. 9, 1673** town recaptured by Dutch; **Nov. 10, 1674** town reverts to English rule; **1683** New York County formed; town becomes county seat; **Apr. 27, 1686** city charter written; **1698** Trinity Church (Anglican) erected; **1700** first city hall built at northeast corner of Broad and Wall streets; **1701** pirate Capt. William Kidd captured, sent to England for trial, is hanged; **Apr. 6, 1712** slave rebellion, 27 dead (6 by suicide, 21 by execution); **Oct. 16, 1725** city's first newspaper goes to print; **1726** Revolutionary War Gen. William Alexander born (died 1783); **1741** second slave uprising, 26 executed, 71 deported; **May 1741** plan by black slaves to set New York ablaze uncovered, 33 executed, 71 deported; **Jan. 14, 1745** patriot, rabbi Gershom Mendes Seixas born (died 1816); **1749** steamboat inventor John Stevens born (died 1838); **1754** King's College established, reopened after Revolution as Columbia University 1784; **1756** stagecoach service begins to Philadelphia; **Nov. 25, 1757** Supreme Court Justice Henry B. Livingston born (died 1836); **Oct. 7-25, 1765** Declaration of Rights adopted by nine colonies in response to 1764 Stamp and Sugar Acts; **June 30, 1768** Elizabeth Kortright Monroe, wife of Pres. James Monroe, born (married 1786, died 1830); **Aug. 28, 1774** Elizabeth Ann Seton born, first American canonized by Catholic Church (died 1821); **July 9, 1776** Gen. George Washington reads Declaration of Independence to his troops near site of present city hall; **Sept. 16, 1776** General Washington repulses British General Howe at Harlem Heights, Howe retreats to White Plains; **Sept. 21, 1776** over 500 houses destroyed by fire; **Nov. 16, 1776** Hessian forces capture Manhattan and Fort Washington for British; **Aug. 27, 1776** U.S. forces lose Battle of Long Island and evacuate New York; **July 17, 1779** scholar, poet Clement Moore born (died 1863); **Oct. 25, 1780** businessman Philip Hone born, promoted construction of Delaware & Hudson Canal (died 1851); **Nov. 25, 1782** British abandon New York; **Dec. 4, 1782** George Washington bids farewell to his troops at Fraunce's Tavern; **Apr. 3, 1783** author Washington Irving born (died 1859); **Nov. 28, 1783** first U.S. post office established; **Jan. 11, 1785–March 2, 1789** Continental Congress held in eleventh and final location; **1789** state capital moved from Poughkeepsie; Federal Hall used for state offices; **Feb. 1789** George Washington elected first U.S. President by Electoral College; **March 4, 1789** first U.S. Congress called into assembly at Federal Hall; **Apr. 30, 1789** President Washington inaugurated at Federal Hall; **Sept. 24, 1789** Supreme Court created by Federal Judiciary Act; **Sept. 19, 1792** William B. Astor born to John Jacob Astor, as "Landlord of New York," disregarded tenement conditions (died 1875); **c.1793** Louisiana Cong., Sen. John Slidell born (died 1871); **Aug. 7, 1795** poet Joseph Rodman Drake born (died 1820); **Aug. 15, 1796** botanist John Torrey born (died 1873); **Sept. 19, 1796** President Washington gives Farewell Address; **1797** state capital moved to Albany; **1805** Shakespearean actor Ira F. Aldrich born (died 1867); **Aug. 17, 1805** Robert Fulton's steamboat *Clermont* leaves on first journey, ascends Hudson River, reaches Albany in 32 hours; **Aug. 3, 1808** Hamilton Fish born, secretary of state under President Grant (died 1893); **June 8, 1809** John Stevens' *Phoenix* steamboat, departs for Philadelphia; **1811** city hall built; **March 22, 1813** sculptor Thomas Crawford born (died 1857); **June 19, 1816** shipbuilder William Henry Webb born (died 1899); **May 27, 1819** social reformer Julia Ward Howe born (died 1910); **Aug. 1, 1819** author Herman Melville born (died 1891); **Apr. 17, 1820** baseball pioneer Alexander Cartwright, Jr. born, organized New York Knickerbockers, standardized the game (died 1892); **Feb. 21, 1821** publisher Charles Scribner born (died 1871); **March 23, 1823** Indiana Cong. Schuyler Colfax born, Speaker of House (died 1885); **1831** New York University established; **June 19, 1832** mayor Jimmy Walker born (died 1946); **June 24, 1834** poet George Arnold born (died 1865); **Dec. 16-17, 1835** fire begins at store at Pearl and Merchant streets, destroys 674 buildings in 17 block area; **Feb. 26, 1836** painter Elihu Vedder born (died 1923); **May 28, 1837** vaudeville entertainer Tony Pastor born (died 1908); **Apr. 22, 1838** steamship *Sirius* arrives, departed Liverpool March 28 and Queenstown Apr. 4; **Apr. 23, 1838** steamship *Great Western* arrives, departed Bristol, England, Apr. 8; **Apr. 15, 1843** novelist Henry James born (died 1916); **1846** Trinity Episcopal Church built at west end of Wall Street; **1847** City College of the City of New York established; **Feb. 18, 1848** glass maker Louis Comfort Tiffany born (died 1933); **March 29, 1848** fur trader, agent John Jacob Astor dies, born Waldorf, Germany, 1763, entered U.S. 1783, helped found Oregon Territory; **May 10, 1849** 34 killed in Astor Place riots in feud over English actor Macready, retaliation for rude treatment of American actor in 1845; **July 22, 1849** poet Emma Lazarus born (died 1887); **Sept. 11, 1850** Jenny Lind's debut concert held at Castle Garden, P. T. Barnum manager; **1852** dance sensation Lola Montez performs at Castle Garden in honor of 100th anniversary of New York stage; **July 14, 1853** Crystal Palace opens as part of World's Fair; **Nov. 9, 1853** architect Sanford White born (died 1906); **1856** land acquired by city for Central Park; **March 9, 1856** actor Eddie Foy born (died 1928); **Aug. 12, 1856** financier, bon vivant James Buchanan "Diamond Jim" Brady born (died 1917); **1858** Know

Nothing political faction formed, opposed to Roman Catholics, disbands 1860; **March 30, 1858** actor De Wolfe Hopper born (died 1935); **Aug. 5, 1858** first cable message service to Europe started; **Oct. 5, 1858** Crystal Palace burns; **Oct. 27, 1858** Theodore Roosevelt, 26th President, born (died Jan. 6, 1919); **March 11, 1860** architect Thomas Hastings born (died 1929); **Dec. 18, 1860** composer, pianist Edward MacDowell born (died 1908); **Apr. 26, 1861** economist Edwin Seligman born (died 1939); **Sept. 20, 1861** librarian Herbert Putnam born, headed Library of Congress 1899–1939 (died 1955); **Jan. 24, 1862** novelist Edith Wharton born (died 1937); **March 2, 1862** essayist, poet John Jay Chapman born (died 1933); **July 13–16, 1863** riots in New York and Boston against military conscription, over 1,000 killed; **Jan. 1, 1867** Lew Fields born, of comedy team Weber and Fields (died 1941); **Aug. 11, 1867** Joseph M. Weber born, of comedy team Weber and Fields (died 1942); **Sept. 21, 1867** statesman Henry Lewis Stimson born (died 1950); **Nov. 27, 1867** Catholic cardinal Patrick Joseph Hayes born (died 1938); **Sept. 24, 1869** "Black Friday" crash caused by attempt to corner gold market; **1870** Hunter College of City of New York established; **Jan. 6, 1872** Edward Stokes shoots Col. James Fisk, Jr., the "King of Wall Street," dies Jan. 8, Stokes gets four years in prison; **July 12, 1872** Orange riots, 52 killed, 178 injured; **July 30, 1872** boiler explodes on Staten Island ferry *Westfield*, over 100 killed; **Sept. 20, 1873** panic hits financial industry causing numerous bank failures; **Dec. 30, 1873** Gov. Alfred E. Smith born, Democratic presidential candidate 1928 (died 1944); **Jan. 1, 1874** Kingsbridge, West Farms and Morrisania west of Harlem River annexed by New York; **Apr. 24, 1874** architect John Russell Pope born (died 1937); **Nov. 18, 1874** author, illustrator Clarence Shepard Day, Jr. born (died 1935); **Nov. 19, 1874** "Boss" W. M. Tweed convicted of fraud, gets 12 years in prison; **March 16, 1875** playwright, poet Wallace MacKage born (died 1956); **May 17, 1875** African-American educator Joel Elias Spingarn born (died 1939); **June 1875** "Boss" Tweed released from Blackwell's Island (later Welfare Island, now Roosevelt Island) prison, in East River, served 7 months of 12 year sentence for fraud; **Nov. 27, 1875** anthropologist Elsie Clews Parsons born, worked with Pueblo peoples (died 1941); **Dec. 4, 1875** jailed in a civil case, "Boss" Tweed escapes, flees to Cuba, then to Spain, returned to New York Nov. 1876; **Apr. 12, 1878** "Boss" Tweed dies in jail; **1879** St. Patrick's Cathedral completed; **Feb. 12, 1879** first indoor ice rink in U.S. opens at Madison Square Garden; **Oct. 5, 1879** author, musician John Erskine born (died 1951); **Apr. 10, 1882** Jumbo the elephant makes debut at Madison Square Garden, presented by P. T. Barnum; **Oct. 14, 1882** Irish Nationalist leader Eamon De Valera born (died 1973); **Dec. 11, 1882** Fiorello La Guardia born, three-term mayor, 1934–1945 (died 1947); **March 30, 1883** sculptor Joseph Davidson born (died 1952); **May 24, 1883** Brooklyn Bridge opens, designed by John Roebling, completed by son Washington Roebling; **May 30, 1883** 12 trampled to death on Brooklyn Bridge, panicked by bridge's motion; **Apr. 1, 1884** actress Laurette Taylor born (died 1946); **May 5–7, 1884** another panic on Wall Street,

Ulysses S. Grant financially ruined, failure of his Grant & Ward business venture; **Oct. 11, 1884** Anna Eleanor Roosevelt born, wife of Pres. Franklin D. Roosevelt (married March 17, 1905; died 1962); **Jan. 27, 1885** composer Jerome Kern born (died 1945); **Aug. 19, 1885** actress Elsie Ferguson born (died 1961); **Dec. 22, 1885** composer Brook Taylor born (died 1966); **1886** Yeshiva University established; **Oct. 28, 1886** Statue of Liberty unveiled on Bedlow's Island to a million onlookers; **1888** Interboro Institute (2-year college) established; **March 22, 1887** comedian, actor Chico Marx born (died 1961); **March 11–14, 1888** Great Blizzard of '88 centers on New York City, total 400 dead; **June 22, 1888** poet Alan Seeger born (died 1916); **Oct. 16, 1888** playwright Eugene O'Neill born (died 1953); **Nov. 23, 1888** comedian, actor Arthur Harpo Marx born (died 1964); **1889** Barnard College established; **Sept. 9, 1889** painter Preston Dickinson born (died 1930); **Sept. 23, 1889** journalist Walter Lippmann born (died 1974); **June 1, 1890** actor Frank Morgan born (died 1949); **Oct. 2, 1890** comedian, actor Julius Groucho Marx born (died 1977); **Oct. 16, 1890** photographer Paul Strand born (died 1976); **Oct. 31, 1890** Ellis Island opens as U.S. immigration depot, replacing Castle Garden; **Dec. 18, 1890** Edwin Armstrong born, inventor of radio technology (died 1954); **Dec. 21, 1890** biologist Hermann Muller born, Nobel Prize 1946 (died 1966); **March 10, 1891** actor Sam Jaffe born (died 1984); **May 11, 1891** Henry Morgenthau, Jr. born, secretary of treasury under Pres. Franklin D. Roosevelt (died 1967); **Aug. 22, 1891** upper floor collapses at Park Place killing 64; **Oct. 29, 1891** singer, comedienne Fanny Brice born (died 1951); **Nov. 15, 1891** diplomat W. Averell Harriman born (died 1986); **Dec. 26, 1891** author Henry Miller born (died 1980); **1892** Washington Square Monument erected; **Jan. 31, 1892** singer, comedian Eddie Cantor born (died 1964); **Feb. 6, 1892** Hotel Royal destroyed by fire, 28 killed; **June 28, 1892** actor Max Gordon born (died 1978); **Sept. 12, 1892** publisher Alfred Abraham Knopf born (died 1984); **1893** comedian, actor Milton Gummo Marx born (died 1977); **Feb. 10, 1893** comedian, actor Jimmy Durante born (died 1980); **1894** Eastchester and Pelham Manor annexed by popular vote; Westchester annexed by legislative act; **Feb. 28, 1894** writer Ben Hecht born (died 1964); **Apr. 14, 1894** Thomas Edison opens first kinetoscope parlor at 1155 Broadway; **Dec. 26, 1894** poet, writer Jean Toomer born (died 1967); **May 22, 1895** lyricist Lorenz Hart born (died 1943); **May 24, 1895** publisher Samuel Newhouse born (died 1979); **July 12, 1895** lyricist Oscar Hammerstein II born (died 1960); **Aug. 13, 1895** actor Bert Lahr born (died 1967); dancer Arthur Murray born (died 1991); actor George Raft born (died 1980); **1896** Parsons School of Design, New School University, established; **Jan. 20, 1896** comedian George Burns born (died 1996); **Dec. 6, 1896** lyricist Ira Gershwin born (died 1983); **1897** Grant's Tomb built overlooking Hudson River; **May 25, 1897** boxer Gene Tunney born (died 1978); **Apr. 7, 1897** newscaster Walter Winchell born (died 1972); **1898** humorist, columnist Bennett Cerf born (died 1971); **Jan. 1, 1898** five boroughs consolidate to form New York City; **Apr. 3, 1898** actor George Jessel born (died 1981); **Sept. 9, 1898** baseball player, manager Frank Frisch born (died 1973); **Jan. 23, 1899** actor Humphrey Bogart born (died 1957); **March 3 1899** fire at the Windsor Hotel, 45 killed; **July 17, 1899** actor James Cagney born (died 1986); **Sept. 9, 1899** songwriter, producer Billy Rose born (died 1966); **Oct. 3, 1899** actress Gertrude Berg born (died 1966); **Feb. 10, 1901** actress Stella Adler born (died 1992); **Feb. 25, 1901** comedian, actor Herbert Zeppo Marx born (died 1979); **Feb. 2, 1902** Park Avenue Hotel burns, 21 killed; **July 25, 1902** longshoreman, author, philosopher Eric Hoffer born (died 1983); **Sept. 28, 1902** TV personality Ed Sullivan born (died 1974); **Oct. 17, 1902** novelist Nathanael West born (died 1940); **Dec. 28, 1902** Jewish educator Mortimer Adler born (died 2001); **May 4, 1903** actor Luther Adler born (died 1984); **March 14, 1903** abstract painter Adolph Gottlieb born (died 1974); **March 16, 1903** Montana Cong. Mike Mansfield born (died 2001); **Apr. 10, 1903** playwright Clare Boothe Luce born (died 1987); **July 26, 1903** Horatio Nelson Jackson completes first automobile journey across America, begun at San Francisco May 27; **June 19, 1903** baseball player Lou Gehrig born, died 1941 of Lou Gehrig's Disease; **Jan. 3, 1904** tenor Jan Peerce born (died 1984); **Jan. 8, 1904** cartoonist Peter Arno born (died 1968); **Apr. 22, 1904** physicist J. Robert Oppenheimer born, developed atomic bomb (died 1967); **May 18, 1904** Sen. Jacob Javitts born (died 1986); **June 15, 1904** excursion steamship *General Slocum* burns at Hell Gate, north entrance to East River, killing 1,030; **Oct. 22, 1904** actress Constance Bennett born (died 1965); **Oct. 27, 1904** New York subway opened; **Dec. 17, 1904** painter Paul Cadmus born (died 1999); **1905** The Juilliard School established; **March 15, 1905** actress Margaret Webster born (died 1972); **Sept. 3, 1905** Nobel physicist Carl David Anderson born (died 1991); **Sept. 18, 1905** ballerina, choreographer Agnes De Mille born (died 1993); **1906** Pace University established; **Jan. 4, 1906** actor William Bendix born (died 1964); **Feb. 2, 1906** TV actor Gale Gordon born (died 1995); **June 24, 1906** actor John Carradine born (died 1988); **June 25, 1906** millionaire Henry Thaw shot at Roof Garden of old Madison Square Garden by architect Stanford White for seducing his wife, sensational trial ends in hung jury; **1907** The Plaza Hotel opened; **Feb. 3, 1907** author James Michener born (died 1997); **Feb. 15, 1907** actor Cesar Romero born (died 1994); **Feb. 16, 1907** railroad accident, 22 killed; **Feb. 22, 1907** actor Sheldon Leonard born (died 1997); **July 25, 1907** actor Jack Gilford born (died 1990); **Jan. 11, 1908** actor Lionel Stander born (died 1994); **June 18, 1908** TV personality Bud Collyer born (died 1969); **July 12, 1908** comedian Milton Berle born (died 2002); **Aug. 13, 1908** actor Gene Raymond born (died 1998); **Sept. 1, 1908** cosmetics designer Estee Lauder born (died 2004); **Oct. 17, 1908** actress Jean Arthur born (died 1991); **Feb. 26, 1909** actor James Mason born (died 1984); **March 8, 1909** actress Claire Trevor born (died 2000); **Aug. 30, 1909** actress Shirley Booth born (died 1992); actress Joan Blondell born (died 1979); **Dec. 9, 1909** actor Douglas Fairbanks, Jr. born (died 2000); **1910** Pennsylvania Station opened, demolished 1963; **Apr. 20, 1910** mayor Robert Ferdinand Wagner, Jr. born (died 1991); **May 23, 1910** clarinetist, band leader Artie Shaw born; **May 26, 1910** businessman Laurence Rockefeller born; **Aug. 6, 1910** Mayor William J. Gaynor shot and wounded by fired city employee; **May 29, 1910** Glenn Curtiss completes first continuous airplane flight, from Albany; **Aug. 4, 1910** composer William Schuman born (died 1992); **Aug. 8, 1910** actress Sylvia Sidney born (died 1999); **1911** New York Public Library built; **March 25, 1911** fire at Triangle Shirtwaist factory, 146 killed, tragedy leads to new building codes; **Sept. 9, 1911** writer Paul Goodman born (died 1972); **Sept. 17, 1911** C. P. Rogers begins transcontinental flight with stops, lands in Pasadena, California, Nov. 5; **Oct. 20, 1911** actor Will Rogers, Jr., son of humorist Will Rogers, born (died 1993); **Dec. 8, 1911** actor Lee J. Cobb born (died 1976); **May 5, 1912** actress Alice Faye born (died 1998); **July 16, 1912** gambler Herman Rosenthal shot to death, Police Lt. Charles Becker, four others charged, executed at Sing Sing Prison, Ossining, New York; **Aug. 29, 1912** TV actor Barry Sullivan born (died 1994); **1913** Grand Central Station completed; **Feb. 27, 1913** playwright Irwin Shaw born (died 1984); **June 11, 1913** actress, opera singer Rise Stevens born; **June 18, 1913** lyricist Sammy Cahn born (died 1993); **Aug. 10, 1913** actor Noah Beery, Jr. born (died 1994); **Sept. 29, 1913** movie director Stanley Kramer born (died 2001); **Nov. 2, 1913** actor Burt Lancaster born (died 1994); **Dec. 15, 1913** poet Muriel Rukeyser born (died 1980); **Feb. 26, 1914** actor Robert Alda born (died 1986); **Aug. 10, 1914** actor Jeff Corey born (died 2002); **Sept. 16, 1914** TV personality Allen Funt born (1999); **Oct. 28, 1914** scientist Jonas Edward Salk born, developed Salk vaccine for polio (died 1995); **Feb. 5, 1915** Nobel physicist Robert Hofstadter born (died 1990); **March 31, 1915** actor Henry Morgan born (died 1994); **May 27, 1915** author Herman Wouk born; **June 1, 1915** actor John Randolph born; **Sept. 10, 1915** actor Edmond O'Brien born (died 1985); **Oct. 17, 1915** playwright Arthur Miller born; **1916** actor Keenan Wynn, son of Ed Wynn, born (died 1986); **Jan. 13, 1916** TV personality Betty Furness born (died 1994); **Apr. 22, 1916** musician Yehudi Menuhin (died 1999); **May 21, 1917** actor Dennis Day born (died 1988); **June 16, 1917** *Washington Post* publisher Katharine Graham born (died 2001); **Aug. 29, 1917** actress Isabel Sanford born (died 2004); **Feb. 12, 1918** physicist Julian Schwinger born, Nobel 1965 (died 1994); **May 11, 1918** physicist Richard Feynman born, 1965 shared Nobel Prize (died 1988); **Oct. 11, 1918** actor Jerome Robbins born (died 1998); **Oct. 17, 1918** actress Rita Hayworth born (died 1987); **Oct. 27, 1918** actress Teresa Wright born; **1919** New School University established; Baruch College of the City of New York established; **Jan. 1, 1919** author J. D. Salinger born; **Feb. 5, 1919** comedian Red Buttons born; **Apr. 29, 1919** actress Celeste Holm born; **June 4, 1919** singer Robert Merrill born; **June 14, 1919** TV actor Gene Barry born; **Aug. 15, 1919** actor Huntz Hall of the Dead End Kids born (died 1999); **Nov. 4, 1919** actor Martin Balsam born (died 1996); **Sept. 16, 1920** bomb explosion outside Stock Exchange on Wall Street, 30 killed, 100 injured, $2,000,000 damage; **Oct. 1, 1920** actor Walter Matthau born (died 2000); **Dec. 13, 1920** economist George Shultz born, secretary of Labor under President Nixon; **Dec. 19, 1920** commentator David Susskind born (died 1987); **March 21, 1921** poet Richard Purdy Wilbur born; **Apr. 6, 1921** composer Andrew Imbrie born; **May 21, 1921** Catholic archbishop Terrence James Cooke born (died 1983); **July 6, 1921** Anne Francis "Nancy" Reagan born, wife of Pres. Ronald Reagan (married 1952); **Nov. 8, 1921** director Gene Saks born; **Nov. 24, 1921** John Vliet Lindsay born, mayor 1965–1972; **Dec. 26, 1921** comedian Steve Allen born (died 2000); **1922** actress Judy Holiday born (died 1965); **June 7, 1922** actor Rocky Graziano born (died 1990); **Aug. 30, 1922** soprano Regina Resnik born; **Oct. 31, 1922** actress Barbara Bel Geddes born; **Dec. 22, 1922** TV personality Paul Winchell born; **Dec. 30, 1922** TV actor Jack Lord born (died 1998); **1923** actor Herschel Bernardi born (died 1986); **Jan. 19, 1923** actress Jean Stapleton born; **March 14, 1923** photographer Diane Arbus born, committed suicide July 26, 1971; **Apr. 1923** Lee de Forest's vaudeville films shown at Rivoli Theater, first "talkies"; **Apr. 12, 1923** entertainer Tiny Tim (Herbert Khaury) born (died 1996); **June 24, 1923** actor Jack Carter born; **June 29, 1923** playwright Paddy Chayefsky born (died 1981); **July 25, 1923** actress Estelle Getty born; **Sept. 28, 1923** actor William Windom born; **Oct. 27, 1923** modern painter, sculptor Roy Lichtenstein born (died 1997); **Nov. 30, 1923** actor Efrem Zimbalist, Jr. born; **Feb. 19, 1924** actor Lee Marvin born (died 1987); **March 26, 1924** poet Erica Jong born; **Aug. 2, 1924** TV actor Carroll O'Connor born (died 2001); writer James Baldwin born (died 1987); **Sept. 16, 1924** actress Lauren Bacall born; **Nov. 26, 1924** sculptor George Segal born; **1925** Madison Square Garden arena opens; **Feb. 18, 1925** TV actor George Kennedy born; **June 3, 1925** actor Tony Curtis born; **June 25, 1925** TV actress June Lockhart born; **Aug. 15, 1925** TV actress Rose Marie born; **Nov. 24, 1925** writer, editor, commentator William F. Buckley, Jr. born; **Dec. 8, 1925** entertainer Sammy Davis, Jr. born (died 1990); **Dec. 9, 1925** actress Dina Merrill born (died 1995); **Dec. 23, 1925** actor Harry Guardino born (died 1995); **Apr. 19, 1926** TV actor Don Adams born; **May 8, 1926** comedian Don Rickles born; **May 13, 1926** actress Beatrice Arthur born; **June 28, 1926** comedian Mel Brooks born; **Aug. 3, 1926** singer Tony Bennett born; **1927** Holland Tunnel opened under Hudson River; **March 1, 1927** singer Harry Belafonte born; **March 20, 1927** art editor Albert Snyder killed by wife Ruth and lover Henry Judd Gray; both executed at Sing Sing Prison, Ossining; **June 13, 1927** Charles Lindbergh honored for trans-Atlantic flight with tickertape parade; **July 2, 1927** actor Brock Peters born; **July 4, 1927** playwright Neil Simon born; **Sept. 16, 1927** TV actor Peter Falk born; **Oct. 6, 1927** *The Jazz Singer* debuts, feature film with partial sound track starring Al Jolson; **Nov. 21, 1927** actor Joseph Campanella born; **Nov. 29, 1927** announcer Vin Scully born; **March 19, 1928** actor Patrick McGoohan born; **July 6, 1928** *The Lights of New York*, first all-sound feature movie, debuts at Strand Theatre; **Aug. 9, 1928** basketball player Bob Cousy born; **Aug. 24, 1928** subway collision beneath Times Square, 18 killed, 97 injured; **Sept. 20, 1928** columnist, TV personality Dr. Joyce Brothers born; **Oct.**

21, 1928 baseball pitcher Whitey Ford born; **Oct. 25, 1928** TV actor Tony Franciosa born; **Dec. 9, 1928** TV actor Dick Van Patten born; **Feb. 15, 1929** James Schlesinger born, secretary of defense under Presidents Nixon and Ford ; **June 8, 1929** comedian Jerry Stiller born; **Aug. 13, 1929** actor Pat Harrington, Jr. born; **Sept. 20, 1929** comedienne Anne Meara born; **Oct. 31, 1929** actress Lee Grant born; **Nov. 29, 1929** stock market crashes, beginning of Great Depression, 16 million shares change hands; **Dec. 9, 1929** actor John Cassavetes born (died 1989); **Apr. 16, 1930** jazz musician Herbie Mann born (died 2003); **May 4, 1930** actress Roberta Peters born; **June 11, 1930** Cong. Charles Rangel born; **Aug. 6, 1930** New York State Supreme Court Justice Joseph Crater disappears without trace, never found; **Aug. 28, 1930** TV actor Ben Gazzara born; **Sept. 7, 1930** saxophonist Sonny Rollins born; **1931** Empire State Building completed; Waldorf-Astoria Hotel opened; George Washington Bridge completed to Fort Lee, New Jersey; **Jan. 13, 1931** TV actor Charles Nelson Reilly born; **March 20, 1931** TV actor Hal Linden born; **July 11, 1931** actor Tab Hunter born; **Aug. 3, 1931** actor Alex Cord born; **July 8, 1931** singer Jerry Vale born; **Sept. 17, 1931** actress Anne Bancroft born; **Sept. 1, 1932** Mayor James Walker resigns amid corruption scandal; **Nov. 13, 1932** actor Richard Mulligan born (died 2000); **Nov. 22, 1932** actor Robert Vaughn born; **Jan. 8, 1933** newscaster Charles Osgood born; **Jan. 28, 1933** writer Susan Sontag born; **Jan. 30, 1933** economist, talk show host Louis Rukeyser born; **June 20, 1933** actor Danny Aiello born; **June 21, 1933** actor Bernie Kopell born; **Nov. 19, 1933** talk show host Larry King born; **Dec. 19, 1933** actress Cicely Tyson born; **1934** TV actress Tina Louise born; **Jan. 17, 1934** puppeteer Shari Lewis born (died 1998); **March 26, 1934** actor Alan Arkin born; **May 22, 1934** pianist Peter Nero born; **June 20, 1934** TV actor Martin Landau born; **Aug. 25, 1934** TV personality Regis Philbin born; **Nov. 9, 1934** astronomer, author Carl Sagan born (died 1996); **1935** Hayden Planetarium opens; **March 15, 1935** actor Judd Hirsch born; **Oct. 20, 1935** actor Jerry Orbach born; **1936** Marymount Manhattan College established; Berkeley College (2-year) established; Triborough Bridge opens; **Jan. 27, 1936** actor Troy Donahue born (died 2001); **Jan. 28, 1936** TV actor Alan Alda born; **Oct. 24, 1936** TV actor David Nelson born; **Jan. 3, 1937** actress Suzanne Pleshette born; **Feb. 2, 1937** comedian Tom Smothers born; **Apr. 5, 1937** Colin Powell born, secretary of state under Pres. George W. Bush; **Apr. 6, 1937** actor Billy Dee Williams born; **May 12, 1937** comedian George Carlin born; **June 18, 1937** West Virginia Sen. John D. "Jay" Rockefeller born; **July 28, 1937** pianist Peter Duchin born; **Oct. 11, 1937** actor Ron Leibman born; **Nov. 15, 1937** TV actor Yophet Kotto born; **Dec. 21, 1937** actress Jane Fonda, daughter of Henry Fonda, born; **Nov. 22, 1937** Lincoln Tunnel opened under Hudson River to Weehawken, New Jersey; **May 22, 1938** actor Richard Benjamin born; actress Susan Strasberg born (died 1999); **May 31, 1938** singer Peter Yarrow of Peter, Paul, and Mary born; **Sept. 12, 1938** soprano Tatiana Troyanos born (died 1993); **1939** New York World's Fair held; Rockefeller Center completed; **Feb. 23, 1939** actor Peter

Fonda, son of Henry Fonda, born; **March 13, 1939** singer Neil Sedaka born; **March 26, 1939** actor James Caan born; **Apr. 11, 1939** actress Louise Lasser born; **Oct. 22, 1939** actor Tony Roberts born; **Nov. 20, 1939** comedian Dick Smothers born; **1940** Queens Midtown Tunnel opens under East River; **Apr. 25, 1940** actor Al Pacino born; **Apr. 30, 1940** actor Burt Young born; **June 1, 1940** actress Rene Auberjonois born; **June 21, 1940** actress Mariette Hartley born; **Nov. 5, 1941** singer Art Garfunkel born; **Feb. 13, 1942** actress Carol Lynley born; **Feb. 28, 1942** actor Robert Klein born; **May 15, 1942** entertainer Lainie Kazan born; **Nov. 17, 1942** movie director Martin Scorsese born; **Nov. 19, 1942** fashion designer Calvin Klein born; **Dec. 7, 1942** singer Harry Chapin born, killed in auto accident July 16, 1981, at Jericho, Long Island; **May 25, 1943** female singer Leslie Uggams born; **June 12, 1943** announcer Marv Albert born; **June 16, 1943** actress Joan Van Ark born; **June 21, 1943** six killed in Harlem race riots, complementing extensive riots in Detroit same day; **July 4, 1943** TV personality Geraldo Rivera born; **Aug. 17, 1943** actor Robert De Niro born; **Aug. 27, 1943** actress Tuesday Weld born; **Oct. 8, 1943** comedian Chevy Chase born; **Dec. 15, 1943** actress Penny Marshall born; **1944** Fashion Institute of Technology established; **Feb. 13, 1944** actress Stockard Channing born; **March 18, 1944** actor Kevin Dobson born; **Apr. 3, 1944** singer Tony Orlando born; **Apr. 30, 1944** actress Jill Clayburgh born; **Nov. 8, 1944** TV actress Susan Sullivan born; **Nov. 12, 1944** announcer Al Michaels born; **June 25, 1945** singer, songwriter Carly Simon born; **July 28, 1945** U.S. Army B-52 aircraft crashes into Empire State Building, killing 14; **June 14, 1946** real estate tycoon Donald Trump born; **Aug. 16, 1946** actress Lesley Ann Warren born; **Sept. 15, 1946** movie director Oliver Stone born; **Oct. 10, 1946** TV actor Henry Winkler born; **Feb. 14, 1946** entertainer Gregory Hines born (died 2003); **May 24, 1946** actress Priscilla Presley, daughter of Elvis Presley, born; **June 17, 1946** singer Barry Manilow born; **July 6, 1946** actor Sylvester Stallone born; **Sept. 2, 1946** actor Ron Silver born; **Oct. 4, 1946** actress Susan Sarandon born; **Dec. 12, 1946** fire at ice plant and tenement kills 37; **Dec. 14, 1946** actress Patty Duke born; **1947** School of Visual Arts established; **Feb. 20, 1947** actor Peter Strauss born; **June 29, 1947** actor Richard Lewis born; **July 10, 1947** singer Arlo Guthrie, son of Woody Guthrie, born; **Aug. 14, 1947** author Danielle Steel born; **Feb. 28, 1948** actress Bernadette Peters born; **Aug. 10, 1948** singer Patti Austin born; **March 10, 1949** Mildred Gillars (Axis Sally) receives 10–30 years in prison for broadcasting Nazi propaganda; **March 16, 1949** TV actor Erik Estrada born; **Oct. 8, 1949** actress Sigourney Weaver born; **Nov. 17, 1949** Alger Hiss sentenced to five years prison for passing documents to Communists; **March 11, 1950** singer Bobby McFerrin born; **Apr. 12, 1950** TV actor David Cassidy born; **Apr. 13, 1950** actor Ron Perlman born; **Apr. 21, 1950** TV actor Tony Danza born; **Nov. 13, 1950** actress Whoopi Goldberg born; **March 23, 1951** Julius and Ethel Rosenberg and Morton Sobell convicted of sabotage, Rosenbergs executed at Sing Sing Prison at Ossining, Sobell receives 30 years; **Apr. 7, 1951** singer Janis Ian born;

Apr. 20, 1951 singer Luther Vandross born; **June 13, 1951** TV actor Richard Thomas born; **July 5, 1951** singer Huey Lewis born; **March 22, 1952** announcer Bob Costas born; **Sept. 25, 1952** actor Christopher Reeve born; **June 20, 1953** singer Cyndi Lauper born; **1954** Ellis Island immigration depot closes; **Jan. 12, 1954** radio talk show host Howard Stern born; **Apr. 29, 1954** TV actor Jerry Seinfeld born; **July 6, 1954** actress Allyce Beasley born; **Apr. 16, 1955** actress Ellen Barkin born; **May 25, 1955** actress Connie Sellecca born; **June 8, 1955** actor Griffin Dunne born; **Dec. 3, 1956** explosion at shipping pier kills 10; **Apr. 5, 1956** assailant blinds labor columnist Victor Riesel by throwing acid in his face; **March 23, 1957** actress Amanda Plummer born; **March 30, 1957** TV actor Paul Reiser born; **Sept. 9, 1957** actress Melanie Griffith born; **Jan. 25, 1958** actress Dinah Manoff born; **March 19, 1958** fire in loft building, 24 killed; **June 8, 1958** TV actor Keenan Ivory Wayans born; **Dec. 10, 1958** first jet airline passenger service begins, New York to Miami; **Dec. 11–28, 1958** strike halts production on all nine major New York newspapers; **Feb. 3, 1959** American Airlines Lockheed Electra crashes into East River killing 65, five rescued; **March 18, 1959** actress Irene Cara born; **May 20, 1959** actor Bronson Pinchot born; **March 22, 1960** actress Jennifer Grey born; **June 2–12, 1960** actors' strike shuts down Broadway's theater district for first time in 41 years;. **Aug. 7, 1960** actor David Duchovny born; **Aug. 16, 1960** New York Mercantile Exchange established, third New York stock exchange; **Sept. 4, 1960** TV actor Damon Wayans born; **Dec. 16, 1960** TWA Super-Constellation and United DC-8 aircraft collide killing 134, including six on ground; **Jan. 12, 1962** Pennsylvania Railroad and New York Central announce merger, eleventh-largest corporation in U.S.; **Jan. 13, 1962** TV actress Julia Louis-Dreyfus born; **March 15, 1962** Gus Hall, Benjamin Davis indicted for failure to register the Communist Party as a subversive organization; singer Terence Trent D'Arby born; **March 21, 1962** actor Matthew Broderick born; **May 11, 1962** Dow Jones average declines to 640.03 in five months from all time high of 734.91; **May 12, 1962** TV actor Emilio Estevez born to actor Martin Sheen; **Oct. 3, 1962** New York Telephone Company building boiler explosion kills 23, injures 94; **Oct. 26, 1962** six firemen die when wall collapses on them during five-alarm blaze at soap factory; **Nov. 7, 1962** Eleanor Roosevelt dies of anemia and lung infection, age 78; **Nov. 19, 1962** actress Jodie Foster born; **Dec. 8, 1962** Typographical Union strikes four of nine New York daily newspapers, lasts 117 days; **March 4, 1963** hospital bus plunges into East River on Welfare (Roosevelt) Island, seven killed, four survive; **March 18, 1963** actress Vanessa Williams born; **Aug. 23, 1963** Yeoman Nelson Drummond, 34, given life for passing documents to Soviets; **Oct. 16, 1963** final issue of tabloid *The Mirror* published, leaving New York with six daily newspapers; **Nov. 3, 1963** automobile speeds through dead end street barrier, plunges into Harlem River, 11 of 12 occupants killed; **1964** John Jay College of Criminal Justice, City University of New York, established; Audrey Cohen College established; New York World's Fair held, continued 1965; **July 18, 1964** several days of rioting in

Harlem follow shooting of a 15-year-old by policeman; **Oct. 20, 1964** Pres. Herbert Hoover dies at age 90 after long illness; **Oct. 29, 1964** $410,000 gem theft at Natural History Museum, including the Star of India and the DeLong ruby, planted and unwittingly carried to Miami in woman's travel bags; **Nov. 19, 1964** Brooklyn Navy Yard, Brooklyn Army Terminal, and Fort Jay (New York) among 95 bases scheduled to close nationwide; **Dec. 22, 1964** bazooka fired at United Nations from Queens by anti-Castro group during Ernesto "Che" Guevara speech; **Feb. 21, 1965** Malcolm X, black nationalist leader, assassinated at rally on upper West Side by three black Muslims; **Apr. 4, 1965** actor Robert Downey, Jr. born; **Apr. 6, 1965** three men get three years in prison for theft of Star of India gem (returned) and the DeLong ruby (never recovered); **May 31, 1965** actress Brooke Shields born; **Sept. 3, 1965** actor Charlie Sheen born, son of Martin Sheen; **Sept. 12, 1966** *Herald Tribune*, *World-Telegraph & Sun*, and *Journal America* merge to form the *World Journal Tribune* following a 140-day newspaper strike; **Oct. 17, 1966** building fire takes the lives of 12 firefighters; **Apr. 21, 1967** Stalin's daughter, Svetlana Aliluyeva, 42, arrives from Soviet Union via India seeking asylum; **May 5, 1967** the *World Journal Tribune* ceases publication after less than eight months; **May 13, 1967** 70,000 marchers participate in eight-hour parade in support of men fighting in Vietnam; **Feb. 22, 1969** *Saturday Evening Post* publishes last issue, started in 1821; **Feb. 25, 1969** Fifth Avenue office building fire kills 11, injures five; **March 3, 1969** learner's permit driver runs off Williamsburg Bridge, hits car below, six in his car killed, 13 injured; **June 28, 1969** actress Danielle Brisebois born; **Aug. 19, 1969** actor Christian Slater born; **Nov. 12, 1969** SS *Manhattan* oil tanker arrives, completing transit through Northwest Passage; **Dec. 9, 1969** actress Allison Smith born; **March 6, 1970** Greenwich Village four-story townhouse leveled by Weathermen faction explosion in seven-day nationwide bombing campaign, three killed; **March 12, 1970** Socony Oil, IBM, GTE buildings hit by terrorist bombs, bomb threats to 12 others; **March 18, 1970** first large-scale postal strike, spreads nationwide except South, pay hike settles strike by March 25; **Aug. 31, 1970** singer Debbie Gibson born; **Oct. 13, 1970** Angela Davis, wanted for two months for killing California judge, apprehended in midtown motel; **Dec. 11, 1970** gas explosion levels three-story building, 12 killed; **1971** Touro College established; **June 15, 1971** Justice Department issues injunction against *New York Times*, published Pentagon Papers leaked by Daniel Ellsberg June 13, raising security versus free press argument; **Aug. 11, 1971** Mayor John Lindsay abandons Republican Party, registers as Democrat; **Aug. 27, 1971** after nine weeks at sea, Dane Hans Tholstrup completes first ever Atlantic crossing in 20-foot speedboat; **Dec. 28, 1971** antiwar Vietnam veterans end two-day occupation of Statue of Liberty on court order; **March 13, 1972** Clifford Irving admits to fraud in hoax biography of Howard Hughes; **Apr. 8, 1972** crime figure Crazy Joe Gallo shot at Manhattan restaurant as he celebrates 43rd birthday; **Aug. 11, 1972** two killed, two injured at restaurant in mobster error killing; **Nov. 14, 1972** Dow Jones average tops 1,000

points for first time in 88-year history; 1,013.16; **March 29, 1973** H. Rap Brown, two others convicted of robbery, assault at New York City bar, gets 5–10 years prison; **July 13, 1977** power outage in city and Westchester County caused by lightning strikes, lasts 4½–25 hours, 2,700 arrested for looting, 100 police injured; **June 2, 1973** Belgian oil tanker, U.S. cargo ship collide in Narrows of New York Harbor, explosion kills 16; **1974** Boricua College established; **Apr. 4, 1976** Operation Sail in New York Harbor tops bicentennial celebration with six million spectators, involves hundreds of boats and tall-masted ships; **May 16, 1977** helicopter falls on its side while landing atop Pan Am Building, rotor slashes and kills four, blade falls 59 stories killing one on street, five injured; **Apr. 13, 1978** Radio City Music Hall spared closing, plan to provide funds from rents from addition of new 20-story office building; **June 13, 1978** "Son of Sam" David Berkowitz sentenced for six murders, eligible for parole in 2007, also liable for 2,000 set fires; **Nov. 20, 1978** market closes worst week in history, fall of 59.08 points to 838.01 due to rising interest rates; **Aug. 26, 1980** actor Macaulay Culkin born; **Dec. 8, 1980** former Beatle John Lennon shot, killed outside his apartment by Mark David Chapman; **Nov. 3, 1982** Dow Jones hits all time high 1,965.49 points, rose record 43.41 points, 300 since August; **Dec. 22, 1984** Bernhard Goetz shoots four teenage panhandlers on subway, public sentiment in his favor, surrenders to police Dec. 31, charged with attempted murder; **1986** Jacob Javits Convention Center opened; **March 29, 1989** junk-bond king Michael Milken indicted for high-risk securities investments used for takeovers, levied buyouts worth $330 million; **Feb. 26, 1993** terrorist bomb leaves 200 ft/61 m crater in sublevel parking garage at World Trade Center, eight killed, over 1,000 suffer from smoke inhalation, other injuries; **May 24, 1994** four Islamic men get 240 years each for 1993 World Trade Center bombing; **May 29, 1994** Jackie Kennedy Onassis, 64, dies of non-Hodgkins lymphoma; **Nov. 17, 1994** Pres. Richard M. Nixon dies at age 81; **Feb. 9, 1995** Ramzi Ahmed Yousef indicted for masterminding 1993 World Trade Center bombing, arrested in Islamabad, Pakistan Feb. 7; **Oct. 1, 1995** 10 convicted of "day of terror" plan to bomb UN, other sites, leader Abdel Rahman also accused of plot to assassinate Egyptian President Mubarak; **Jan. 7–8, 1996** up to 3 ft/1 m of snow falls in blizzard in Middle Atlantic, New England, 27.5 in/67 cm in New York City, total 100 dead, $1.5 billion damage; **Apr. 23–26, 1996** 5,900 items of Jackie Onassis' (died 1994) nets $34 million at Sotheby's; **Oct. 6, 1995** Pope John Paul holds morning mass for 75,000 Aqueduct Race Track, for 120,000 at Central Park Oct. 7; **Sept. 5, 1996** three Muslims convicted of plot to bomb 12 U.S. planes bound from East Asia, Ahmed Yousef leader; **Feb. 23, 1997** one killed, six injured, shot by anti-Zionist Ali Abu Kamal on observation deck of Empire State Building; **Nov. 12, 1997** Muslim militants Ramzi Ahmed Yousef and Eyad Ismoil receive 240-year sentences for 1993 World Trade Center bombing; **March 29, 1999** Dow Jones closes at 10,006.78, first time over 10,000; **Apr. 14, 2000** Dow Jones falls record 617 points (7.3 percent for week), Nasdaq 356 points (25.3 percent for week); **Aug. 23, 2001** French parachutist dangles from torch of Statue of Liberty for 30 minutes after stunt goes awry; **Sept. 11, 2001** two passenger airliners commandeered by suicide hijackers, associated with Osama bin Laden's Al-Qaeda terrorist network in Afghanistan, American Airlines Boeing 767, Flight 11, Boston to Los Angeles, with 92 on board deliberately flown into World Trade Center North Tower in lower Manhattan, and American Airlines Boeing 767, Flight 175, Boston to Los Angeles, with 65 on board flown into World Trade Center South Tower, all 110 stories of both towers collapse with floors pancaking as burning jet fuel weakens structural supports, North Tower, struck first, collapses in 1 hour 44 minutes, South Tower collapses in only 47 minutes, 2,380 killed out of c.30,000 in buildings at the time plus 330 emergency workers, mostly firefighters, coordinated with suicide-hijacking attack on Pentagon and fourth hijacking foiled by passengers, crashed in woods near Shanksville, Pennsylvania, total 19 hijackers on four flights, 20th hijacker failed to enter U.S., worst attack on U.S. in history, pretext to Pres. George W. Bush's War on Terrorism initially launched against Afghanistan Oct. 7; **Oct. 31, 2001** 61-year old woman dies of inhaled anthrax, 4th anthrax death in eastern U.S. since Sept. 11; **Aug. 13–14, 2003** power blackout affects 50 million people from Great Lakes to New England and southern Canada, New York streets clogged with stranded cars and pedestrians.

Newburgh   *Orange County*   *Southeastern New York, 55 mi/89 km north of New York City, on Hudson River*

1683 Orange County formed; **1709** site settled by 50 Germans led by Lutheran pastor Joshua Kocherthal, named Quassaick; **1723** Burger Mynders builds house; **1734** John Ellison builds hunting lodge; **1743** ferry established on Hudson River to Beacon; **1762** town renamed Newburgh after arrival of Scottish and English immigrants; **1781** Last Cantonment of British troops centers on John Ellison's lodge from surrender of Cornwallis to signing of peace treaty 1783; **Apr. 1, 1782** George Washington establishes headquarters here, through Aug. 18, 1783; **1793** *Newburgh Packet* newspaper founded; **1798** Newburgh becomes shared Orange County seat with Goshen; **1799** Associated Reformed Church built; **1800** incorporated as a village; **1819** St. George Episcopal Church built; **May 1, 1825** painter George Inness born (died 1894); **1834** Danskammer Lighthouse built to north, razed 1928; **1850** Lehigh & Hudson River Railway extended from Chester; **1852** Newburgh Free Library founded, new library opened 1977; **Jan. 14, 1854** Cong. Benjamin Odell, Jr. born (died 1926); **1865** incorporated as a city; **1867** Montgomery & Erie Railroad reaches town; **1868** Dutchess & Columbia Railroad arrives; **Dec. 6, 1870** actor William S. Hart born (died 1946); **1883** West Shore Railroad begins service to New York City; **1902** Congregation B'Nai Israel founded; **May 31, 1923** modern painter Ellsworth Kelley born; **Aug. 26, 1935** Cong. Geraldine Ferraro born, Democratic vice presidential candidate 1984; **1939**

Stewart Airfield built, later becomes Stewart International Airport; **1960** Mount St. Mary College established; **1963** Newburgh-Beacon Bridge completed on Hudson River, second span built 1980; **1970s** Goshen becomes sole county seat; **Nov. 16, 1989** tornado strikes city, nine killed.

Niagara Falls   *Niagara County*   *Western New York, 15 mi/24 km northwest of Buffalo, on Niagara River*

1000 AD Iroquois tribe the Neutrals settle in region; **1651** Senecas move into region as the Neutrals disappear; **Dec. 6, 1678** Father Louis Hennepin visits falls, makes sketch published later; **1745** French build fort at falls, second fort in 1750; **1759** French burn forts as site is taken by British; **Sept. 14, 1763** portage keeper John Stedman and 24 men ambushed by Senecas, Stedman, 2 others escape; **c.1805** Augustus Porter settles near falls, founds settlement of Manchester; **1813** settlement burned by British; **1814** American forces advance against British in Battle of Lundy's Lane, one of bloodiest conflicts of War of 1812, losing battle and territory, regained in Treaty of Ghent Dec. 1814; **1827** old schooner *Michigan*, with a load of wild animals, sent over falls for bit of bizarre entertainment; **1846** first *Maid of the Mist* excursion boat sails to base of Horseshoe Falls; **March 29, 1848** ice jam at Lake Erie effluent dries up falls for first time in recorded history; **1855** Niagara Falls suspension bridge opened; **1856** Our Lady of Angels Seminary established, becomes Niagara University; **1881** water power from falls first used to generate electricity; **1885** Niagara Reserve State Park established; **1887** Whirlpool Rapids Bridge built; **1892** incorporated as a city; **1898** Falls View Bridge (Honeymoon Bridge) completed: **Oct. 24, 1901** Annie Taylor becomes first daredevil to survive plunge over falls; **May 25, 1931** actor John Gabriel born; **Jan. 27, 1938** ice jam destroys Honeymoon Bridge; **1941** Rainbow Bridge opened; **1965** Aquarium of Niagara opened; **1969** water diverted from American Falls to allow concrete reinforcement of escarpment; **Oct. 1, 1995** Robert Overacker killed when he rides jet ski over falls.

Norwich   *Chenango County*   *Central New York, 45 mi/72 km south-southwest of Utica*

1788 area settled; **1790** Col. William Monroe, "drummer boy of Revolution," builds town's first log cabin; **1798** Chenango County organized; town becomes county seat; **Nov. 9, 1801** Gail Borden born, developer of nonfat dried milk (died 1874); **1833** Chenango Canal opened from Utica to Binghamton; **1837** county courthouse built; **1885** manufacture of pharmaceuticals begins; **1915** incorporated as a city.

Ogdensburg   *Saint Lawrence County*   *Northern New York, 55 mi/89 km north-northeast of Watertown*

1749 Fort La Presentation built by Abbe François Picquet; **1755** French and Native Americans, based at fort, defeat General Braddock; **1760** British take fort; **1792**

Col. Samuel Ogden purchases town site; **1796** British evacuate fort; **1802** St. Lawrence County formed; town becomes county seat; **1809** mansion built by David Parish, later used as Remington Art Memorial, devoted to work of painter Frederic Remington; **Nov. 1813** U.S. General Wilkinson defeated by British in War of 1812; **1817** incorporated as a village; **1828** county seat moved to Canton; **1832** Van Rensselaer Mansion built; **1837** town used as staging area for Patriots' War, failed effort to take Canada from British; **1868** incorporated as a city; **1870** Fenian Irish plan major thrust into Canada to wrest control of Canada from British, thwarted by U.S.; **1893** Ogdensburg Public Library founded; **1923** Frederic Remington Museum founded by wife Eva Remington.

Old Forge   *Herkimer County   Northern New York, 45 mi/72 km north-northeast of Utica*

1811 Charles F. Herreshoff settles here with his Merino sheep; **c.1815** Herreshoff opens iron ore mine, shoots himself after mine's failure 1819; **1892** Mohawk & Malone Railroad built through area by Dr. William Webb; **1897** First Presbyterian Church dedicated; **1899** Holy Rosary Catholic Church built; **Feb. 9, 1934** lowest temperature ever recorded in New York reached, −52°F/−47°C, at Stillwater Reservoir to north.

Oneida   *Madison County   Central New York, 27 mi/43 km east of Syracuse*

c.1533 Oneidas build village on southern shore of Lake Oneida; **1790** first permanent white settlers arrive; **1834** Sands Higinbotham becomes town's first settler; **1839** New York Central Railroad reaches town; **1841** post office established; **1842** Adam Storey opens first store; **1843** St. John's Episcopal Church organized; Catholic Church organized, new church built 1881; **Oct. 1847** John Humphrey Noyes and his communal followers flee from Putney, Vermont, jumping bond for arrest for liberal sexual practice called Complex Marriage; **1848** incorporated as a village; **March 11, 1876** painter Kenneth Hayes Miller born (died 1952); **Jan 1881** Noyes reorganizes town, eliminates communal marriage practice; Oneida Ltd. silverware company founded; **1901** incorporated as a city.

Oneonta   *Otsego County   Central New York, 52 mi/84 km northeast of Binghamton*

c.1780 area settled; **1797** Hartwick College established by Lutheran Church; **1863** Albany & Susquehanna Railroad extended to town, builds railroad shops here; **1880** Solon Huntington House built, donated 1920 for Huntington Memorial Public Library; **1889** Oneonta State Normal School established, becomes State University of New York College at Oneonta; **1908** incorporated as a city; **1935** Homer Folks State Hospital established, later used as Job Corps Center; **1979** National Soccer Hall of Fame founded, new museum opened 1999.

Oriskany   *Oneida County   Central New York, 8 mi/14.9 km northwest of Utica, on Mohawk River*

Aug. 6, 1777 in Battle of Oriskany, Gen. Nicholas Herkimer's forces rout Mohawks, continue on to Fort Stanwix (Rome); **1819** first boat, the *Chief Engineer*, passes through Utica-Rome section of Erie Canal; **1914** incorporated as a village; **Aug. 6, 1933** "Second Battle of Oriskany," 150 farmers, angry over low milk prices, wage rock-throwing battle with 24 state troopers; **1997** Oriskany Village Museum dedicated, includes carrier USS *Oriskany*.

Ossining   *Westchester County   Southeastern New York, 30 mi/48 km north of New York City, on Hudson River*

1655 land purchased from Sint Sinck peoples by Frederick Philipse; **1781** Hunter's Landing founded; **1813** village of Sing Sing incorporated; **May 1828** first block of 800 cells completed in Sing Sing Prison; **1842** Croton Aqueduct completed to New York City from Croton Reservoir; **1865** fire consumes businesses and upper-class residences; **1901** village renamed Ossining to end name association with prison; **Apr. 13, 1914** "Lefty" Rosenberg, "Whitey Lewis" Seidenschner, "Gyp the Blood" Horowitz, and "Dago Frank" Cirofici executed for murder of Herman Rosenthal July 16, 1912, in New York City, Police Lt. Charles Becker executed July 30, 1915; **Sept. 16, 1930** actress Anne Francis born; **June 19, 1953** Julius and Ethel Rosenberg executed for spying.

Oswego   *Oswego County   North central New York, 35 mi/56 km northwest of Syracuse, on Lake Ontario*

1722 trading post established; **1727** Fort Oswego founded by British; **1755** Fort Ontario built by British; **1756** forts taken by Montcalm for French; **July 3, 1758** Col. John Bradstreet repels attack by French and Native Americans at Battle Island; **1759** forts retaken by British under Sir William Johnson; **1766** Johnson confers with Chief Pontiac, gaining control of Great Lakes for Britain; **1796** British surrender forts to U.S.; **1816** Oswego County formed; town becomes county seat, shared with Pulaski; **1828** incorporated as a village; **1829** Oswego Branch of Erie Canal opened; **Nov. 26, 1832** physician, women's rights activist Mary Edwards Walker born (died 1919); **1848** incorporated as a city; **1852** Oswego becomes sole county seat; **1860** county courthouse built; **1861** State University of New York at Oswego established as Oswego State Normal School; **1870** city hall built; **Aug. 3, 1855** fiction writer Henry Bunner born (died 1896); **1897** Mary Edwards Walker establishes colony for women called "Adamless Eden."

Ovid   *Seneca County   Central New York, 43 mi/69 km north of Elmira*

1789 Andrew Dunlap becomes first settler; **1804** Seneca County formed; town becomes county seat; **1819** county seat moved to Waterloo; **1823** Ovid becomes shared county seat with Waterloo; **Jan. 1, 1838** scholar, literary critic Thomas Lounsbury born (died 1915); **1845** county courthouse, jail, sheriff's office built, three nearly identical Colonial buildings referred to as "Three Bears" for their descending size.

Owego *Tioga County* *Southern New York, 18 mi/ 29 km west of Binghamton*

1779 Sullivan-Clinton military campaign destroys Native American village of Ah-wah-ga; **1787** area settled; **1791** Owego County formed; town becomes county seat; **1827** incorporated as a village; **July 15, 1833** Thomas Platt born, Republican who broke Horace Greeley political machine (died 1910); **July 8, 1839** industrialist John D. Rockefeller born at Richford to north (died 1937); **1872** county courthouse completed; **1893** Diamond Match Company moves from Frankfort, New York; **1915** Theodore Dreiser drives to Indiana in his 60-hp Pathfinder automobile.

Oyster Bay *Nassau County* *Southeastern New York, 25 mi/40 km northeast of New York City, on Long Island*

1653 area settled by Dutch; **1740** Raynham Hall built, headquarters of Col. John Simcoe's Queens Rangers during Revolutionary War; **Oct. 25, 1877** astrophysicist Charles Marion Russell born (died 1957); **1884** Sagamore Hill home built by Pres. Theodore Roosevelt; **1889** Long Island Railroad reaches town; **Jan. 6, 1919** President Roosevelt dies in his sleep at Sagamore Hill; **July 25, 1962** Sagamore Hill National Historic Site authorized.

Palatine Bridge *Montgomery County* *East central New York, 34 mi/55 km west of Schenectady*

1668 Jesuit mission established at Tionondogue to west, until 1684; **1689** Hendrick Frey builds log cabin, among earliest settlers of middle Mohawk Valley; **1720** settled by 60 families of Palatines from Schoharie Valley under leadership of John Christopher Gerlach; **1739** Fort Frey built on site of Frey cabin, served through Queen Anne's War (1702–1713) and French and Indian War (1755–1763); **1795** Union Academy founded, burned c.1806; **c.1798** bridge built on Mohawk River; **1877** Wagner House built by freight agent Webster Wagner (1817-1882); **Nov. 30, 1881** U.S. Cong. from Alaska Territory Anthony J. Dimond born, championed Alaska statehood (died 1953).

Palmyra *Wayne County* *North central New York, 24 mi/39 km east-southeast of Rochester, on Erie Canal*

1788 land purchase made by Oliver Phelps and Nathaniel Gorham; **1789** first settlers arrive; **1792-1793** settlers arrive from Rhode Island and Long Island; **1815** family of Joseph Smith, 10 years old, founder of Mormon Church, arrives from Vermont; **Nov. 26, 1817** *Palmyra Register* newspaper founded; **1823** Angel Moroni, son of Mormon, appears in vision before Joseph Smith; **1822** Erie Canal reaches town, completed 1825; **1828** incorporated as a village; Rifenburg Hotel built; **1830** Joseph Smith publishes Book of Mormon; **1832** Western Presbyterian Church built; **Feb. 9, 1840** William T. Sampson born, Rear Admiral of American fleet during Spanish-American War (died 1902); **1855** printing press factory established by John M. Jones; **1872** Episcopal Church built, completing unique occurrence of four corner churches at Main and Church streets intersection; **1899** Palmyra Free Library founded; **March 2, 1902** fire destroys city block, including *Journal* newspaper; **1906** Syracuse & Eastern trolley begins service, abandoned 1931; **1935** Mormon monument dedicated at Hill Cumorah; **1936** Moroni Headquarters Building dedicated.

Peekskill *Westchester County* *Southeastern New York, 40 mi/64 km north of New York City, on Hudson River*

1665 Dutch trader Jan Peek settles at mouth of creek later named Peek's Kill; **1767** St. Peter's Church built; **1777** supply base and barracks established by Continental Army; Gen. Israel Putnam orders Tory spy Edward Palmer hanged at Gallows Hill; barracks burned by British; **1781** site resettled; **1816** incorporated as a village; **1833** Peekskill Academy established; **Apr. 23, 1834** Sen. Chauncey M. Depew born (died 1928); **1846** First Presbyterian Church built; **Nov. 1924** Bear Mountain Bridge across Hudson River opened; **1940** incorporated as a city; **Jan. 24, 1945** Gov. George E. Pataki born; **Aug. 27, 1952** personality Pee Wee Herman (Paul Reubens) born; **Jan. 3, 1956** actor Mel Gibson born.

Pelham Manor *Westchester County* *Southeastern New York, 13 mi/21 km north of New York City*

1642 Anne Hutchinson rebels against Massachusetts Puritanism, settles here, murdered 1643 by Native Americans at Throgg's Neck; **1654** Thomas Pell acquires land from Siwanoys; **1664** Pell persuades British to accept surrender of Dutch; **1680** John Pell sells acreage; **Oct. 18, 1776** Battle of Pelham, 600 Boston seamen stop Sir William Howe's plan to attack George Washington's supply route, saving Revolution for American side; **June 18, 1887** illustrator James Flagg born, created Uncle Sam "I want you" recruiting poster (died 1960); **1891** incorporated as a village.

Penn Yan *Yates County* *Central New York, 43 mi/69 km southeast of Rochester, on Keuka Lake*

1789 settled by Jacob Fredenburgh, others from Pennsylvania and New England "Yankees," origin of name "Penn" and "Yan"; **1823** Yates County formed, named for Gov. Joseph C. Yates; town becomes county seat; **1824** county courthouse built, burned 1835, rebuilt; **1833** incorporated as a village; **1891** Abraham Wagener arrives, "father of Penn Yan"; **1895** Penn Yan Library founded, built 1905; **2002** County Government Center completed.

Plattsburgh   *Clinton County   Northeastern New York, 138 mi/222 km north of Albany, on Lake Champlain*

1609 Samuel de Champlain travels through lake named for him; **1767** area settled; **Oct. 1776** Colonial Lake Champlain fleet involved in first naval encounter, intercept British fleet of 29 vessels; **c.1784** town founded by Zephaniah Platt; **1788** Clinton County formed; town becomes county seat; **1879** Kent-Delord House built; **Sept. 11, 1814** British defeated in Battle of Plattsburgh at Cumberland Beach, retreat to Canada; **1816** incorporated as a village; **1838** Plattsburgh Military Reservation established, later becomes Plattsburgh Air Force Base (closed 1995); **1844** Dannemora Prison established; Lozier Manufacturing Company founded, maker of bicycles, developed Lozier automobile 1904, moved to Detroit 1910, closed 1918; **1889** Plattsburgh State Normal School established, becomes Plattsburgh State University of New York; county courthouse built; **1890** Champlain Hotel completed, burned 1910, rebuilt, closed 1950s; **1902** incorporated as a city; **Dec. 25, 1959** astronaut Michael A. Anderson born, killed Feb.1, 2003, in *Columbia* space shuttle breakup over eastern Texas; **1969** Clinton County Community College established.

Pocantico Hills   *Westchester County Southeastern New York, 25 mi/40 km north-northeast of New York City*

1893 financier John D. Rockefeller (1839–1937), one of wealthiest men in world, establishes his 4,000 ac/1,620 ha Kykuit estate (name Dutch for "high place"), completed 1908; **Jan. 29, 1874** John D. Rockefeller, Jr. born (died 1960); **July 10, 1978** John D. Rockefeller III, 72, dies in auto accident; **1994** Kykuit Museum opened.

Pompey   *Onondaga County   Central New York, 12 mi/19 km south-southeast of Syracuse*

1797 Handy's Tavern built; **1806** village serves as western terminus of Great Western Turnpike through c.1815; **May 31, 1810** Horatio Seymour born, Democratic presidential candidate against Grant 1868 (died 1886); **May 20, 1818** William George Fargo born, co-founder of Wells, Fargo & Company express agents (died 1881); **1819** Presbyterian Church completed, originally Congregationalist; **1836** general store built.

Port Chester   *Westchester County   Southeastern New York, 25 mi/40 km north-northeast of New York City*

1650 town on Long Island Sound first settled, first called Saw Log Swamp, or Saw Pit; **1660** earliest burials at Brown Graveyard, continuous Brown family interments to 1900; **1774** Samuel Brown House built; **1837** town renamed; **1868** incorporated as a village; **June 30, 1974** arson fire at Gulliver's Discotheque, 24 killed.

Port Jervis   *Orange County   Southeastern New York, 60 mi/97 km northwest of New York City, on Delaware River*

1698 settled by Dutch and French Huguenots; **1760** Fort Decker House built; **July 20, 1779** village destroyed by British and natives; **1793** fort built by Martinus Decker; **1826** construction of Delaware & Hudson Canal begins, completed 1828, abandoned 1899; town named for canal engineer John B. Jervis; **1848** first railroad reaches town; **1853** incorporated as a village; **1898** trolley system established, abandoned 1924; **1899** Deerpark Sanitarium opened, closed 1920s; **1903** Port Jervis Free Library built; **1907** incorporated as a city; **1924** Hotel Minisink built; **1939** bridge built across Delaware River to Matamoras, Pennsylvania, previous three structures each destroyed by river.

Potsdam   *Saint Lawrence County   Northern New York, 70 mi/113 km northeast of Watertown*

1802 land purchased from St. Regis peoples by David Clarkson; **1804** William Bullard arrives with communal sect from Massachusetts called The Union, dissolved by internal dissent by 1810; **1816** St. Lawrence Academy established, evolves to become State University of New York College at Potsdam 1948; **1831** incorporated as a village; **Dec. 22, 1856** Minnesota Sen. Frank Billings Kellogg born, secretary of state under President Coolidge (died 1937); **1887** Potsdam Public Library founded; **Aug. 22, 1889** Barnum & Bailey circus train wrecks at Clark's Crossing killing many prized animals; **1895** Clarkson University established; **1917** sandstone quarried here used in construction of Canadian Parliament Building, Ottawa; **1935** civic center completed.

Poughkeepsie   *Dutchess County   Southeastern New York, 68 mi/109 km north of New York City*

1683 first settled on Hudson River by two Dutchmen; Dutchess County formed; town becomes county seat; **1735** Zephaniah Platt House built; **1759** Abraham Fort Homestead built by Johannes A. Fort; **Oct. 1777** state capital moved from Kingston; **July 26, 1788** New York ratifies U.S. Constitution; **1789** state capital moved to New York City; **1798** Sleight House built; **1853** St. Peter's Catholic Church built; **1854** incorporated as a city; **1861** Vassar College established; **1869** Bardavon Opera House opened; **1887** Vassar Brothers Hospital founded; **1888** Christ Church (Episcopal) built; **1904** county courthouse completed; **1914** Smith Brothers Plant built, maker of cough drops; **1929** Marist College established; **1930s** Dutchess County Airport opened; **1957** Dutchess Community College established; **Oct. 30, 1969** 35 black Vassar coeds seize administration building demanding black studies, separate dorms; **Jan. 27, 1972** hijacker of Mohawk Airlines plane shot while running to getaway car with stewardess hostage.

Queens *Queens County* *Borough of New York City*

1635 settled by Dutch; **1670** Onderdonk House built; **1683** Queens County formed; county seat originally at North Hempstead; **1852** Rosemont House built in Astoria; **Oct. 22, 1854** minstrel performer, songwriter James A. Bland born (died 1911); **1870** St. John's University (Jamaica) established; **Oct. 19, 1895** sociologist, writer Lewis Mumford born (died 1990); **1898** Queens County joins New York City consolidation, county coterminous with Queens Borough; **1899** towns of Hempstead, North Hempstead and Oyster Bay join Nassau County; Queens County seat moved to Jamaica; **Jan. 16, 1909** actress Ethel Merman born in Astoria (died 1984); **Dec. 10, 1913** actor Morton Gould born (died 1996); **Feb. 7, 1920** actor Eddie Bracken born (died 2002); **1932** College of Aeronautics established; **June 15, 1932** Gov. Mario Cuomo born; **Jan. 9, 1936** TV actor Michael Landon born (died 1991); **1937** Queens College of City University of New York established; **1939** Queens Midtown Tunnel completed under East River; La Guardia Airport dedicated; **1942** Idlewild Airport built, renamed John F. Kennedy Airport 1963; **Nov. 17, 1942** movie director Martin Scorsese born; **Nov. 22, 1950** train collision at Richmond Hill kills 78; **March 1, 1962** American Airlines Boeing 707 crashes after takeoff, killing 95; **Nov. 30, 1962** Eastern DC-7B airplane crashes in fog at Idlewild (JFK) Airport, killing 25 of 32 on board; **March 1, 1962** American Airlines 707 crashes into Jamaica Bay after takeoff from Idlewild Airport, 95 killed; **Feb. 8, 1965** all 84 killed as Eastern DC-7B airplane from Kennedy International Airport crashes into Atlantic Ocean; **Oct. 17, 1965** World's Fair at Flushing Meadows closes after two years, 51.6 million visitors; **1967** York College of City University of New York (Jamaica) established; **1970** La Guardia Community College (City University) established; **Sept. 8, 1970** crash of DC-8 on takeoff from JFK kills all 11 crew; **1972** Queens Museum of Art founded at Flushing Meadows; **1975** Queens County Farm Museum founded; **June 24, 1975** Eastern Airlines Boeing 727 crashes in storm at Kennedy International Airport, 113 killed, 11 injured; **Dec. 29, 1975** bomb placed in locker at La Guardia Airport explodes, killing 11, injuring 70; **1998** civil courthouse completed; **May 24, 2000** gunmen shoot, kill five Wendy's restaurant employees, two injured; **Nov. 12, 2001** American Airlines Airbus Flight 387 crashes into residential Rockaway Beach area after takeoff from John F. Kennedy Airport, all 260 on board, 5 on ground killed.

Red Hook *Dutchess County* *Southeastern New York, 55 mi/89 km south of Albany, near Hudson River*

1650s Dutch settlers arrive; site named Roode Hoeck for profusion of red berries on peninsula; **1688** land acquired from Native Americans by Col. Peter Schuyler; **1720** Redder Homestead built; **1730** St. Peter Lutheran Church built; **1777** town's mills burned by British; **c.1790** The Pynes mansion built; **1790s** Maiceland mansion built by Gen. David Van Ness; **1820** Edgewater mansion built; **1851** Hudson River Railroad reaches town; **1860** St.

Stephen's Episcopal Seminary founded, later renamed Bard College; **1920s** Village Diner established.

Rensselaer *Rensselaer County* *Eastern New York, 1 mi/1.6 km east of Albany, on Hudson River*

1630 area settled by Dutch; **1704** Fort Crailo built by Henry Van Rensselaer; **1723** Jan Bries House built; **1742** Van Rensselaer-Genet House built; **1758** British surgeon Dr. Richard Shuckburgh pens words to "Yankee Doodle Dandee" while watching Colonial troops marching at fort; **c.1842** Beverwyck manor house built by William Van Rensselaer, becomes Order of St. Francis monastery 1912; **1897** villages of East Albany, Greenbush, and Bath-on-Hudson merge, incorporated as city of Rensselaer.

Richford *Tioga County* *See* **Owego** (1839)

Rifton *Ulster County* *Southeastern New York, 77 mi/124 km north of New York City*

1690 Hendrick Smit becomes first settler; **c.1797** orator Sojourner Truth (Isabella Baumfree) born into slavery, instrumental in release of herself, other slaves (died 1883); **c.1820** Perrines Hotel built; **c.1827** grist mill built by Ebenezer Rider; **c.1846** Perrine's Covered Bridge built; **1863** Rifton Hotel built; **1891** Upper (New) Canton Mill built at Buttermilk Falls; **1892** Methodist Church built; **Jan. 6, 1894** explosion at Rifton Powder Mill, four killed; **1898** St. Thomas Chapel completed; **1901** incorporated as a village; **1919** village disincorporated.

Riverhead *Suffolk County* *Southeastern New York, 70 mi/113 km east of New York City, on Long Island*

1683 Suffolk County formed; town founded as county seat on Great Peconic Bay; **1792** Town of Riverhead formed; **1822** Fresh Pond Schoolhouse built; **1929** county courthouse built; **1933** Suffolk Theater built.

Rochester *Monroe County* *North central New York, 37 mi/60 km east-northeast of Buffalo, on Lake Ontario*

1789 Ebenezer Allen builds grist mill on Genesee River; **1812** town founded by Nathaniel Rochester, William Fitzhugh and Charles Carroll of Maryland; **1812** bridge built across Genessee River; Isaac Stone's Tavern opened; **1815** Abelard Reynolds opens tavern; **1817** incorporated as a village, named Rochesterville; **1818** paper mill built; **1821** Monroe County formed; town becomes county seat; Arctic explorer Charles Francis Hall born, died 1871 in Greenland; **1822** village renamed Rochester; Old Charlotte Lighthouse built; **1824** St. Luke's Episcopal Church built; **1825** Erie Canal opens to south, connector built to Lake Ontario; **1826** Charlotte-Genesee Lighthouse built; **1829** Rochester Institute of Technology established; **1834** incorporated as a city; presence of flour mills leads to nickname "Flour City"; **Nov. 3, 1841** Isabella M. Alden born, wrote 60 "Pansy

Books" Sunday school series (died 1930); **Aug. 7, 1843** author Charles Stoddard born (died 1909); **1849** county courthouse built; **1850** University of Rochester established; **Oct. 28, 1855** William Burroughs born, invented adding machine (died 1898); **c.1858** Bausch and Lomb Optical Plant established; **July 21, 1860** Catholic archbishop Edward Joseph Hanna born (died 1944); **1866** Roberts Wesleyan College established; **1875** city hall built; **1880** Eastman Kodak Company founded by George Eastman; **Dec. 12, 1881** civil rights leader Arthur Garfield Hays born (died 1954); **1892** landscape architect Frederick Law Olmsted endows city with large lilac collection for Highland Park; **Dec. 21, 1892** golfer Walter Hagen born (died 1969); **1896** county courthouse built; **June 18, 1896** author Philip Barre born (died 1949); **1898** first Lilac Festival held; **1899** Frederick Douglass monument dedicated; **Dec. 25, 1907** entertainer Cab Calloway born (died 1994); **1911** Rochester Public Library founded; **July 4, 1911** musical director Mitch Miller born; **1913** Kodak Tower office building built; Memorial Art Gallery founded; **1914** New York Central Railroad Station built; Rochester Museum and Science Center founded, built 1942; **1924** Nazareth College of Rochester established; **Apr. 19, 1925** actor Hugh O'Brian born; **c.1937** Greater Rochester International Airport established; **Nov. 29, 1940** musician Chuck Mangione born; **Oct. 19, 1945** actor John Lithgow born; **1948** St. John Fisher College established; **1949** International Museum of Photography and Film opened; **1961** Monroe Community College established; **1982** Strong Museum founded.

Rockville Centre *Nassau County Southeastern New York, 19 mi/31 km east-southeast of New York City*

1850 first settlers arrive; **1854** town founded; **1869** Coney Island Railroad reaches town; **1792** original Methodist Church organized; **1890** Rockville Centre Public Library opened; **1893** incorporated as a village; **1894** St. Agnes Parish established, cathedral dedicated 1935; **1900** St. Mark's Methodist Episcopal Church organized; **June 27, 1927** TV personality Bob Keeshan (Captain Kangaroo) born at Lynbrook to west (died 2004); **Sept. 14, 1944** singer Joey Heatherton born; **Feb. 17, 1950** railroad accident, 31 killed; **1955** Molloy College established.

Rome *Oneida County Central New York, 14 mi/23 km northwest of Utica*

1725 first British fortifications built; **1756** Fort Ball destroyed by Oneidas, occupants massacred; **1758** Fort Stanwix established by Brig. Gen. John Stanwix against French and Native Americans; **Aug. 6, 1777** Benedict Arnold raises St. Leger's siege at Fort Stanwix; **1786** town platted by Irishman Dominick Lynch, named Lynchville; **1798** Oneida County formed; town becomes county seat; **1801** Whitestown becomes shared county seat with Lynchville; **1819** incorporated as a village, renamed Rome; **1825** Erie Canal completed; **1839** railroad reaches village; **1851** Jesse Williams founds cheese factory; **1863**

Rome Iron Works founded, becomes Rome Brass and Copper 1891; **1870** incorporated as a city; **1871** shared county seat moved from Whitestown to Utica; **May 4, 1872** novelist Harold Bell Wright born (died 1944); **1895** Jervis Public Library founded; **1906** Rome Fish Hatchery established, taken over by state 1932; **1942** Rome Air Depot established, becomes Griffis Air Force Base 1948, closed 1995; **1973** Fort Stanwix National Monument established; **1997** Air Force Research Laboratory founded.

Rye *Westchester County Southeastern New York, 23 mi/37 km north-northeast of New York City*

1660 area first settled; **1730** Hayland Inn built; **1847** railroad reaches town; **1884** Rye Free Reading Room founded; **Aug. 19, 1902** poet Ogden Nash born (died 1971); **1904** incorporated as a village; **June 8, 1925** Barbara Bush born, wife of Pres. George H. W. Bush (married 1945); **1928** Playland Amusement Park opened; **1942** incorporated as a city.

Sackets Harbor *Jefferson County Northern New York, 11 mi/18 km southwest of Watertown*

1801 town founded on Lake Ontario by Augustus Sacket; **1812** town becomes leading U.S. shipbuilding center of War of 1812; **July 19, 1812** U.S. ship *Oneida* drives off five British warships, first shot of War of 1812; **May 29, 1813** in Battle of Sackets Harbor, British assault narrowly defeated by Americans, military stores destroyed; **1814** incorporated as a village; **1815** Union Library founded; **1817** Old Union Hotel built; **1843** cinders from steamboat set warehouses, 40 buildings ablaze; **1853** Sackets Harbor & Ellisburg Railroad built, abandoned 1862; **1875** Utica & Black River Railroad reaches town, abandoned 1949.

Saint Johnsville *Montgomery County East central New York, 30 mi/48 km east-southeast of Utica*

1722 Jacob Zimmerman becomes first settler; **1750** Johannes Klock builds stone house called Fort Klock; **1757** town founded by Zimmerman; **1770** Palatine Lutheran Church built to east; **Oct. 19, 1780** Battle of Klock's Field, 700 of Johnson's raiders clash with 1,500 of Gen. Van Rensselaer's militia; **1800** Mohawk Turnpike completed; **1803** town boasts 52 taverns and inns; **1830** Mohawk & Hudson Railroad built; **1852** St. Johnsville Covered Bridge built; **1857** incorporated as a village; **1865** cigar manufacturing begins; **1888** Mohawk Condensed Milk factory established; **1892** knitting mill established; **1902** Opera House built; **1909** Margaret Reaney Memorial Library founded.

Salamanca *Cattaraugus County Southwestern New York, 50 mi/80 km south of Buffalo*

1862 Atlantic & Great Western Railroad reaches site; town founded, named for prominent railroad stockholder; **1912** railroad station built; **1913** incorporated as a city; **1920** Carnegie Library opened, replaced 1976; **1921**

Allegany State Park established (65,000 ac/26,325 ha); **1995** Allegany State Park Historical Society founded.

Saranac Lake   *Essex and Franklin counties*
Northeastern New York, 145 mi/233 km north of Albany

1819 town founded by Jacob Moody; **1827** sawmill built by Capt. Pliny Miller; **1858** William J. Stillman establishes Adirondack Club at Lake Ampersand, members include Ralph Waldo Emerson, James Russell Lowell, Louis Agassiz; **1884** Dr. Edward Trudeau founds tuberculosis sanatorium, closed 1954; **1887–1888** Robert Louis Stevenson resides under Trudeau's care; **1892** incorporated as a village; Adirondack Park established, includes all or part of ten counties; **1897** first annual Winter Carnival held; **1907** Society for Control of Tuberculosis founded; **1927** Hotel Saranac opened, acquired by Paul Smith's College c.1960; **1930** Will Rogers Memorial Sanatorium built for tubercular members of radio and movie industry; **1967** North Country Community College established.

Saratoga Springs   *Saratoga County   Eastern New York, 32 mi/51 km north of Albany*

1642 Jesuit Father Isaac Jogues visits springs; **1767** Sir William Johnson brought to High Rock Springs by Mohawks for their healing properties; **1775** Dirck Schouten builds log cabin; **Oct. 17, 1777** British General Burgoyne's 5,000 men surrender to Americans; **1811** Congress Hotel built by Gideon Putnam, died 1812 before completion, later renamed Union Hall hotel, becomes Grand Union Hotel 1872; **1826** incorporated as a village; **1832** Schenectady & Saratoga Railroad reaches town; **1863** thoroughbred horse racing begins; **1865** opera house opens; **1869** Saratoga Race Track begins annual August horse racing event; **1881** White Sulphur Spring Hotel built by Boston & Maine Railroad; **Sept. 22, 1892** columnist, humorist Frank Sullivan born (died 1976); **1903** Skidmore College established; **1915** incorporated as a city; **June 1, 1938** Saratoga National Historical Park authorized; **1950** Saratoga Springs Public Library opens, new library completed 1995; **1971** State University of New York Empire State College established.

Saugerties   *Ulster County   Southeastern New York, 43 mi/69 km south of Albany, on Hudson River*

1812 Rev. Henry Ostrander arrives to serve Katsburg Reformed Church, brings 700-volume book collection; **1831** incorporated as a village; **1867** Saugerties Lighthouse built, automated 1914; **Feb. 27, 1867** economist Irving Fisher born (died 1947); **1872** Saugerties Public Library founded, Carnegie library opened 1905 houses Ostrander collection; **Aug. 12–14, 1994** 25th Anniversary Woodstock concert held, 350,000 attend; **1998** ferry service begins to Tivoli.

Schenectady   *Schenectady County   Eastern New York, 13 mi/21 km northwest of Albany, on Mohawk River*

1661 town founded by Dutchman Arant van Curler; **1664** English gain control of colony; **1690** town destroyed by natives; **1705** Queen's Fort built; **1759** St. George's Episcopal Church built; **1765** incorporated as a borough; **1795** Union College established; **1798** incorporated as a city; **1809** Schenectady County formed; town becomes county seat; **1825** Erie Canal opens; **1831** county courthouse built; **Sept. 24, 1831** steam locomotive, the *De Witt Clinton*, makes initial run from Albany on Mohawk & Hudson Railroad; **1848** locomotive manufacturing begins; **1862** Dutch Reformed Church built; **1886** General Electric Corporation establishes headquarters; **1894** Schenectady Public Library built; **Dec. 10, 1923** actor Harold Gould born; **May 5, 1926** actress Ann B. Davis born; **1931** city hall built; **Sept. 28, 1950** movie director John Sayles born; **1968** Schenectady County Community College established.

Schoharie   *Schoharie County   East central New York, 29 mi/47 km west of Albany*

1772 settlement founded; Dutch Reformed Church built; **1775** Stone House built by Jost Becker; **1777** stockade built; **Oct. 17, 1780** attack by Joseph Brant and Sir John Johnson repulsed by defenders of stockade; **1795** Schoharie County formed; town becomes county seat; Johannes Ingold House built; **1867** incorporated as a village; **1870** county courthouse built; **1973** Blenheim Lower Dam and Gilboa Upper Dam built on Schoharie Creek to south.

Seneca Falls   *Seneca County   Central New York, 35 mi/56 km west-southwest of Syracuse*

1750 Red Jacket born to east of here, grand sachem and diplomat for Iroquois (died 1830); **1787** area first settled by Job Smith; **1831** incorporated as a village; **July 1848** first Women's Rights convention called by Cady Stanton; **Jan. 20, 1856** suffragist Harriet Stanton Blatch born (died 1940); **Oct. 11, 1891** painter Edwin Dickinson born (died 1978); **Dec. 21, 1898** physicist, astronomer Ira Sprague Bowen born (died 1973); **1979** National Women's Hall of Fame founded; **Dec. 8, 1980** Women's Rights National Historical Park authorized.

Southampton   *Suffolk County   Southeastern New York, 85 mi/137 km east of New York City, on Long Island*

1640 town founded; **1662** Old Hollyhocks Church built; **1845** 8-year voyage to Japan by Commodore Matthew Perry ends here; **1870** Long Island Railroad reaches town; **1879** St. Andrews-Dunes Church built; **1887** The Meadow Club founded; **1891** Shinnecock Golf Club founded, first private 18-hole club in U.S.; **1894** incorporated as a village; **1897** Parrish Memorial Art Museum founded; **July 28, 1929** first lady Jacqueline Bouvier Kennedy

Onassis born (married John F. Kennedy Sept. 12, 1953, died May 19, 1994); **Sept. 21, 1938** hurricane destroys many seaside mansions; **Aug. 22, 1939** baseball player Carl Yastrzemski born; **1963** Long Island University Southampton College established.

Staten Island   *Richmond County*   *Borough of New York City*

1609 island visited by Henry Hudson; **1661** first Dutch settlers arrive; **1683** Richmond County formed; St. George, in northeastern corner of island, becomes county seat; **1799** Quarantine Station established at Duxbury, deliberately burned 1858; **June 15, 1859** botanist Nathaniel Lord Britton born (died 1934); **July 8, 1862** socialist leader Ella Reeve Bloor born (died 1951); **1869** lighthouse completed at Marine Hospital Grounds, Castleton, replaced 1883, abandoned 1968; **1883** Wagner College established; **1898** Richmond County joins consolidated New York City as Staten Island Borough, county coterminous with borough; **1912** Staten Island Lighthouse built at The Narrows (Ambrose Channel); **1928** Bayonne Bridge built across Kill van Kull strait from Bayonne, New Jersey; **1928** Outerbridge Crossing bridge built across Arthur Kill to Perth Amboy, New Jersey, named for Eugenius H. Outerbridge, chairman of New York Port Authority; **1931** Goethals Bridge built across Arthur Kill estuary from Elizabeth and Linden, New Jersey; **c.1934** Staten Island Zoo established; **Jan. 9, 1941** folk singer Joan Baez born; **1955** College of Staten Island of City University of New York established; **1964** Verrazano Narrows Bridge completed across entrance to New York Harbor from Brooklyn; **Feb. 10, 1973** gas storage tank explodes, 40 killed; **2002** National Lighthouse Museum opened; **Oct. 15, 2003** Staten Island ferry crashes into dock, 10 killed, 65 injured.

Syracuse   *Onondaga County*   *West central New York, 205 mi/330 km northwest of New York City*

1615 area explored by Samuel de Champlain; **1654** Jesuit Father Simon LeMoyne discovers salt in water supply, town becomes known as "Salt City"; **1786** Ephraim Webster establishes trading post; **1794** Onondaga County formed; town becomes county seat; **1825** incorporated as a village; Erie Canal opens, passes north of town; **1838** Auburn & Syracuse Railroad reaches town; **1841** first New York State Fair held; **Sept. 26, 1846** novelist Edward Westcott born (died 1898); **1848** incorporated as a city; **1852** Syracuse Public Library founded, building opened 1902; **1858** county courthouse built; **1870** Syracuse University established; **March 15, 1875** theatrical producer Lee Shubert born (died 1953); **Jan. 15, 1877** *Herald-Journal* newspaper founded; **1884** St. Paul's Episcopal Church built; **1904** Cathedral of Immaculate Conception completed; **1905** Continental Can Plant opened; **1911** State University of New York College of Environmental Science and Forestry established; **1912** Rosamond Gifford Zoo established; **1924** Hotel Syracuse opened; **1927** Syracuse-Hancock International Airport

established; **1928** State Tower Building built; **1946** Le Moyne College established; **1950** State University of New York Health Sciences Center established; **1962** Erie Canal Museum founded; Onondaga Community College established; **July 3, 1962** actor Tom Cruise born; **1968** Everson Museum of Art opened, designed by I. M. Pei; **1997** P & C Stadium opened.

Tappan   *Rockland County*   *Southeastern New York, 20 mi/32 km north of New York City, near Hudson River*

1683 Orange County formed; town founded as shared county seat with Goshen; **1700** De Wint House built; **1755** Seventy-Six House built, used as prison for spy John Andre 1780; **1780** De Wint House used as George Washington's headquarters; **Oct. 2, 1780** British Maj. John Andre hanged as spy, held documents implicating traitor Benedict Arnold; **1798** Rockland County formed from Orange County; New City becomes county seat; **1835** Dutch Reformed Church built; **1900** Palisades Interstate Park created in New Jersey and New York; **1955** Tappan Zee Bridge completed across Hudson River to Tarrytown.

Tarrytown   *Westchester County*   *Southeastern New York, 25 mi/40 km north of New York City, on Hudson River*

1683 Frederick Philipse of Dutch West India Company builds Castle Philipse; **1699** Sleepy Hollow Dutch Reformed Church built; **Sept. 23, 1780** papers implicating Benedict Arnold as traitor found in socks of British spy Maj. John Andre, Andre hanged Oct. 2 at Tappan; **1870** incorporated as a village; **1840** Lyndhurst mansion built for Philip R. Paulding; **June 21, 1882** artist Rockwell Kent born (died 1971); **1883** Tarrytown Lighthouse built on Hudson River, discontinued 1965; **1907** Marymount College established; **1910** Castle on the Hudson built for Col. Howard Carroll.

Ticonderoga   *Essex County*   *Northeastern New York, 90 mi/145 km north of Albany, on Lake Champlain*

1755 French build Fort Carillon and military road across isthmus between Lake Champlain and Lake George; **July 8, 1758** Montcalm successfully fends off British attack on fort; **1759** French surrender to British Gen. Jeffrey Amherst; fort renamed Ticonderoga; **May 10, 1775** Vermont's Col. Ethan Allen, with Benedict Arnold and Green Mountain Boys, capture Fort Ticonderoga; **July 6, 1777** British Gen. John Burgoyne retakes fort; **1815** graphite mining begins; **1830** pencil factory built; **1889** incorporated as a village; **1906** Black Watch Memorial (Carnegie) Library opened.

Tivoli   *Dutchess County*   *Eastern New York, 95 mi/153 km north of New York City, on Hudson River*

1794 Callander House built by Henry Gilbert Livingston; **1795** Blithewood Estate established by Gen. John

Armstrong; **1802** Peter de Labigarre completes construction of Chateau de Tivoli, first unit of model community; **1805** Montgomery Place built by widow of Gen. Richard Montgomery, killed in battle at Quebec 1775; **1807** Labigarre dies, his plans die with him; **1857** Church of the Holy Innocents built, burned 1858, rebuilt; **1860** St. Stephens College established, becomes Bard College, unit of Columbia University 1928; **1868** St. Paul's Episcopal Church built; **1872** incorporated as a village; **Oct. 11, 1884** Anna Eleanor Roosevelt, wife of President Franklin D. Roosevelt, born (married March 17, 1905, died Nov. 7, 1962); **1998** ferry service begins to Saugerties.

Tonawanda *Erie County Western New York, 8 mi/12.9 km north of Buffalo, on Niagara River*

1805 first settlers arrive; **1825** Erie Canal completed; **1835** canal outlet opened to Gateway Point, Niagara River; town becomes major lumber port; **1836** Buffalo & Niagara Falls Railroad reaches town; **1854** incorporated as a village; **1861** J. S. Noyes creates first lake-going barge by demasting old schooner; **1867** shingle mill established; **Aug. 30, 1902** Kenilworth Race Track opened; **1903** incorporated as a city; **1944** art-deco Calvin Theater opened.

Troy *Rensselaer County Eastern New York, 10 mi/ 16 km north of Albany, on Hudson River*

1609 Henry Hudson explores river; **1786** town platted; **1791** Rensselaer County formed; Troy becomes county seat; **1798** incorporated as a village; **1802** toll road built to Schenectady; **1809** iron mill established; **1812** shirt industry develops, town nicknamed "Collar City"; Samuel Wilson becomes main beef supplier for army during War of 1812, the original "Uncle Sam"; **1816** incorporated as a city; **Sept. 16, 1822** railroad promoter Charles Crocker born (died 1888); **1824** Rensselaer Polytechnic Institute established; **1825** Erie Canal opens; **1827** St. Paul's Episcopal Church built; Hart-Cluett Mansion built; **1836** First Presbyterian Church built; **1856** St. Joseph's Seminary built; **1861** foundries produce metal plates for ironclad ship *Monitor*; **1898** county courthouse completed; **1916** Russell Sage College established; **June 21, 1925** actress Maureen Stapleton born; **July 22, 1926** highest temperature recorded in New York reached, 108°F/42°C; **1953** Hudson Valley Community College established; **1954** Junior Museum opened.

Tuxedo Park *Orange County Southeastern New York, 33 mi/53 km north-northeast of New York City*

1880s large tract owned by tobacco millionaire Pierre Lorillard IV subdivided, sold to upper-income buyers; Tuxedo Park colony founded; **1885** Lorillard builds first 19 houses, called "Versailles of U.S."; **1886** incorporated as a village; **1901** Tuxedo Park Library built; **2002** King's College moved from Briarcliff Manor, New York, established 1938.

Utica *Oneida County East central New York, 90 mi/145 km west-northwest of Albany, on Mohawk River*

1734 land grant made to William Cosby; **1758** Fort Schuyler built by British, abandoned 1760s; **1772** Cosby Tract subdivided, town founded; **1776** town destroyed by Tories and Native Americans; **March 6, 1797** abolitionist Gerrit Smith born, founded Liberty Party (died 1874); **1798** Oneida County formed; Rome becomes county seat; **1801** Whitestown becomes shared county seat with Rome; **Feb. 12, 1813** naturalist James Dwight Dana born (died 1895); **1825** Erie Canal opened; **Oct. 31, 1831** Union Gen. Daniel Butterfield born, composer of "Taps" (died 1901); **1832** incorporated as a city; **1836** Utica & Schenectady Railroad reaches town; Chenango Canal opens; **1843** Utica State Hospital opened; **1853** city hall completed; **1860** Grace Church (Episcopal) completed; **Sept. 26, 1862** painter Arthur Davies born (died 1928); **1871** shared county seat moved from Whitestown to Utica; **Feb. 22, 1879** Frank W. Woolworth opens his first five-and-ten cent store, ends in failure; **1909** Utica Zoo founded; county courthouse completed; **1919** Munson-Williams-Proctor Art Institute established; **1922** First Presbyterian Church built; **Oct. 22, 1942** TV personality Annette Funicello born; **1946** Utica College of Syracuse University established; Mohawk Valley Community College established; **1966** State University of New York Institute of Technology established.

Walloomsac *Rensselaer County Eastern New York, 30 mi/48 km northeast of Albany*

Aug. 16, 1777 Battle of Bennington (Battle of Walloomsac), British Col. Frederick Baum dispatched to capture stores at Bennington, Vermont, arms citizens as Tory sympathizers who then turn on him, backed by New Hampshire troops under John Stark and Vermont Militia under Seth Warner, loss leads to Burgoyne's surrender at Saratoga; **1784** State Line House built on state boundary; **1927** Bennington Battlefield State Historical Site established.

Wampsville *Madison County Central New York, 23 mi/37 km east of Syracuse*

c.1790 tavern established by blacksmith Myndert Wemple; town of Wemplesville founded; **1806** Madison County formed; Cazenovia becomes county seat; **1817** county seat moved to Morrisville; **1907** town renamed Wampsville; county seat moved to Wampsville; **1910** incorporated as a village; county courthouse built.

Warsaw *Wyoming County West central New York, 38 mi/61 km southwest of Rochester*

1803 town settled; **1824** Gates House built, acquired by abolitionist Seth M. Gates 1843, becomes station on Underground Railway; **1841** Wyoming County formed; town becomes county seat; **1842** county courthouse completed; **1843** incorporated as a village.

Waterford *Saratoga County* *Eastern New York, 10 mi/16 km north of Albany, on Hudson River*

1607 Henry Hudson lands here at mouth of Mohawk River; **1620s** area settled by Dutch; **1777** Americans use Eagle Tavern as rendezvous for anti-British activities, use ford in Mohawk River; **1794** incorporated as a village; **1823** Champlain Canal completed from northeast, begun 1819; **1825** Erie Canal completed; **1875** Waterford Public Library founded; **March 29, 1889** actor, playwright Howard Lindsay born (died 1968); **1964** Waterford Museum founded.

Waterloo *Seneca County* *Central New York, 40 mi/64 km west-southwest of Syracuse*

1792 Samuel Bear becomes first settler; **1793** store established by Bear; grist mill built on Seneca River; **1804** Seneca County formed; Ovid becomes county seat; **1819** county seat moved to Waterloo; **1823** Ovid becomes shared county seat with Waterloo; **1824** incorporated as a village; **May 5, 1866** first official Memorial Day celebration in U.S. held; **1880** Waterloo Library founded; **1914** county courthouse built; **1930** stallion Brooklyn Supreme born, "world's largest horse" at 3,000 lb/1,361 kg, died 1933 just prior to showing at Chicago World's Fair; **1966** Memorial Day Museum opened.

Watertown *Jefferson County* *Northern New York, 70 mi/113 km north of Syracuse, near Lake Ontario*

1800 site at Black River Falls first settled by five people from New England; **1805** Jefferson County formed; town founded as county seat; **1809** rag mill built, begins town's paper making industry; **1816** incorporated as a village; **1823** Stephen Blanchard builds inn, becomes Blanchard Library 1913; **July 12, 1854** inventor, businessman George Eastman born (died 1932); **Oct. 17, 1864** Robert Lansing born, secretary of state under President Wilson (died 1928); **1869** incorporated as a city; **1878** Frank W. Woolworth offers pile of odds and ends for 5¢ each while clerking at county fair, takes idea to Utica, opens first five-and-ten store 1879; **1879** Babcock Wagon Factory established; **Apr. 7, 1893** government official Allen Dulles born (died 1969); **1903** Pine Army Camp opened to northeast, renamed Camp Drum 1951, Fort Drum 1974; **1909** Flower Memorial Library established; **1961** Jefferson Community College established; **1962** county courthouse built; **March 14, 2003** Black Hawk helicopter crashes at Fort Drum, 11 killed.

Watervliet *Albany County* *Eastern New York, 6 mi/9.7 km north of Albany, on Hudson River*

1609 Henry Hudson explores river; **1643** Dutch settlers arrive; **1666** Philip Schuyler builds homestead; **1735** town founded; **1774** Shaker founder Mother Ann Lee leads eight converts from England, establishes colony at New Lebanon 1785; **March 28, 1793** explorer Henry Rowe Schoolcraft born (died 1864); **1813** U.S. Arsenal established; **March 9, 1824** railroad man, California Sen.

Leland Stanford born (died 1893); **1825** Erie Canal opened; **1836** incorporated as a village; **1896** incorporated as a city; **March 1913** major flooding damages city.

Watkins Glen *Schuyler County* *Central New York, 20 mi/32 km north of Elmira, on Seneca Lake*

1794 town founded by John W. Watkins and Royal Flint, originally named Catlin; **1842** incorporated as village of Jefferson; **1852** village renamed Watkins Glen for Dr. Samuel Watkins; **1854** Schuyler County formed; village becomes county seat; **1870** Watkins Glen Public Library founded, new library opened 1987; **1898** county courthouse built, addition built 1957; **1948** Grand Prix auto race begins with street racing, becomes permanent event 1956; **July 28, 1973** 12-hour rock concert at Grand Prix race track attracts 600,000, more than Woodstock four years earlier.

West Point *Orange County* *Southeastern New York, 45 mi/72 km north of New York City, on Hudson River*

1776 Fort Montgomery and Fort Clinton built to south; **Oct. 7, 1777** British overwhelm Gen. George Clinton's forces defending both forts; **1778** Fort Putnam built, partial restoration completed 1910; **March 16, 1802** U.S. Military Academy established; **July 4, 1802** first 10 cadets admitted; **1841** library built; **1900** Chapel of the Most Holy Trinity consecrated; **1904** administration building built; **Oct. 3, 1925** writer Gore Vidal born.

Westfield *Chautauqua County* *Western New York, 52 mi/84 km southwest of Buffalo, on Lake Erie*

1800 area settled; **1802** town founded; **c.1815** Eber Stone House built; **1820** McClurg Mansion completed; **1831** St. John's Episcopal Church completed; **1833** incorporated as a village; **1859** grape growing begins; **1879** Presbyterian Church completed; **1893** Dr. Thomas Branwell Welch arrives from New Jersey with method for producing unfermented grape juice, response to temperance movement; **1896** Welch establishes Welch's Grape Juice Company, largest grape juice producer in world; Patterson Library founded; **1910** Welch's plant built.

Westhampton *Suffolk County* *Southeastern New York, 70 mi/113 km east of New York City, on Long Island*

1666 area becomes part of Quogue purchase; **1879** Gen. John A. Dix builds area's first summer home; **1920s** region becomes haven for rich and famous; **Apr. 14, 1925** actor Rod Steiger born (died 2002); **1928** incorporated as a village; **Sept. 21, 1938** area battered by hurricane, 40 killed; **1945** Suffolk County (Gabreski) Airport established; **July 17, 1998** TWA Flight 800 breaks apart in midair offshore, plunges into Atlantic Ocean, 230 killed.

White Plains *Westchester County* *Southeastern New York, 25 mi/40 km north-northeast of New York City*

1683 Westchester County formed; village of Westchester designated first county seat; **c.1721** Jacob Purdy House built; **1735** town established as iron production center; **1759** county seat moved to White Plains; **July 9, 1776** Provincial congress moves from New York City due to military activity, ratifies Declaration of Independence, first read publicly July 11; **Oct. 21, 1776** Britain's Lord Howe fails to advance on George Washington's troops, retreats Oct. 28; **1812** White Plains Public Library founded; **1844** railroad reaches town; **1866** incorporated as a village; **1916** incorporated as a city; **1930** Westchester County Convention Center built; **1973** county courthouse completed.

Woodstock *Ulster County* *Southeastern New York, 50 mi/80 km south-southwest of Albany*

1902 artists' colony formed by Ralph Whitehead, home to over 140 artists by 1940; **1906** Arts Student League of New York opens summer school; **1921** communist factions meet at Overlook Mountain Hotel to form Communist Party of America; **Aug. 15–17, 1969** Woodstock Music Festival draws up to 500,000 spectators. [see Saugerties].

Yonkers *Westchester County* *Southeastern New York, 15 mi/24 km north of New York City, on Hudson River*

1646 Dutch make land grant to Adriaen Van der Donck; **1664** grant subdivided by British; **1693** Philipse Manor Hall estate established by Frederick Philipse, confiscated 1779; **1752** St. John's Episcopal Church built; **1805** cotton mill built, used until 1852; **1849** Hudson River Railroad reaches site; **1854** Otis Elevator Works established; **1855** incorporated as a village; **1872** incorporated as a city; **1873** Abram Gould begins rowboat ferry to Alpine, New Jersey; **Nov. 14, 1888** St. Andrews, first golf club in U.S., opens to north in former apple orchard; **July 5, 1891** biochemist John Howard Northrop born, Nobel Prize 1946 (died 1987); **1893** Yonkers Public Library founded, Carnegie Library built 1903; **May 11, 1894** diplomat Ellsworth Bunker born (died 1984); **1899** Empire City Race Track built, becomes Yonkers Raceway; **Sept. 8, 1922** comedian Sid Caesar born; **1923** Yonkers-Alpine Ferry established on site of Gould's Ferry, ends 1956; **1924** Museum of Science and Arts founded, becomes Hudson River Museum 1939; **1926** Sarah Lawrence College established; **Dec. 29, 1938** actor Jon Voight born.

North Carolina

Eastern U.S. Capital: Raleigh. Major cities: Charlotte, Winston-Salem, Raleigh.

North Carolina was one of the 13 colonies which adopted the U.S. Declaration of Independence July 4, 1776. It became the 12th state to ratify the U.S. Constitution November 21, 1789. It seceded from the Union as a Confederate state May 20, 1861, and was readmitted July 4, 1868.

North Carolina is divided into 100 counties. The counties are divided into townships which have no government. Municipalities are classified as villages, towns, and cities. See Introduction.

Albemarle *Stanly County* *Central North Carolina, 37 mi/60 km east-northeast of Charlotte*

1770 region first settled by German immigrants; **1820s** gold mining begins in area, continues today; **1826** post office established, originally named Smith's Store; **1841** Stanly County formed; town founded as county seat, renamed Albemarle; **1842** first county courthouse built; **1843** town platted; **1857** incorporated as a city; **1858** county poorhouse established; **1891** Yadkin Railroad reaches town; **1899** Wiscasset (Cannon) Mills established; **1904** Lillian Knitting Mills established; **1916** Stanly County Library founded; **1928** Lake Tillery formed by dam to southeast on Pee Dee River; **1962** Lake Tuckertown formed by dam on Pee Dee River to northeast; **1971** Stanly Community College established; **1972** new county courthouse completed; **1976** Stanly County Museum founded.

Asheboro *Randolph County* *Central North Carolina, 25 mi/40 km south of Greensboro*

c.1740 first white settlers arrive in region; **1779** Randolph County formed; **1793** town founded as county seat, originally named Randolph Court House; Jesse Hendley conveys property for county courthouse; **1796** town incorporated, renamed Asheborough; **1837** John Wesley Stand Church built; **c.1850** name altered to Asheboro; **1909** county courthouse built; **1962** Randolph Community College established.

Asheville *Buncombe County* *Western North Carolina, 100 mi/161 km west-northwest of Charlotte*

1673 James Needham and Gabriel Arthur begin trading with Native Americans; **1776** Gen. Griffith Rutherford leads force through region on way to defeat of Cherokees;

c.1786 Vance House built by Col. David Vance, birthplace of Zebulon B. Vance, governor and U.S. Senator (1830–1894); **1792** Buncombe County formed, named for Revolutionary Col. Edward Buncombe; **1794** town platted as county seat by John Burton, named Morristown; **1797** town incorporated; renamed for Gov. Samuel Ashe; **1827** Buncombe Turnpike completed; **1879** Swannanoa Tunnel completed to east on Southern Railroad, 1,800-ft/549-m long, built at cost of $600,000 and 120 lives; Asheville Library founded; **1883** incorporated as a city; **1895** Biltmore House completed by George Vanderbilt; **1900** Tuberculosis Sanitarium founded by Sisters of Mercy, burned 1938; **Oct. 3, 1900** novelist Thomas Wolfe born (died 1938); **1909** St. Lawrence Catholic Church completed; **1912** Grove Park Inn built; **Apr. 10, 1924** painter Kenneth Clifton Noland born; **1925** Pack Memorial Library built; **1927** University of North Carolina at Asheville established, originally Buncombe County Junior College; city hall built; county courthouse completed; First Baptist Church completed; **1928** Southern Highland Craft Guild formed, becomes Folk Art Center 1980; **1929** American Enka Corporation Plant founded to west, maker of rayon thread from spruce pulp; **Feb. 20, 1939** singer Roberta Flack born at Black Mountain to east; **1949** Thomas Wolfe Memorial Museum opened, house damaged by fire 1998; **1959** Asheville Industrial Education Center established, becomes Asheville-Buncombe Community College; **1986** North Carolina Arboretum established.

Atlantic Beach *Carteret County* *Eastern North Carolina, 137 mi/220 km southeast of Raleigh*

1826 Fort Macon built, abandoned 1835; **1861** fort reused by Confederates; **1862** fort taken by Union forces; **1880** Atlantic & North Carolina Railroad reaches site; town founded as resort; **c.1910** Money Island Beach developed, includes pagoda-style pavilion, declines c.1927; **1928** Atlantic Beach Hotel built; **1930** The Casino dance hall built; **1935** Fort Macon restored; **1937** town incorporated; **1940** boardwalk built, replaces earlier structure.

Bakersville *Mitchell County Western North Carolina, 93 mi/150 km northwest of Charlotte*

1783 general assembly opens region for settlement; **1797** David Baker becomes town site's first settler; **c.1850** town founded; **1861** Mitchell County formed; Calhoun becomes first county seat; **1863** county seat moved to Davis; **1866** town platted; **1868** county seat moved to Bakersville; county courthouse built; **1870** town incorporated; **1870s** mining of mica begins; **1947** first Rhododendron Festival held; **1955** Spruce Pine Community Hospital founded; **2002** new county courthouse completed, replaces 1907 structure; **May 4, 2002** fire in county jail, 8 killed, 13 injured.

Bath *Beaufort County Eastern North Carolina, 107 mi/172 km east of Raleigh, on Pamlico River*

c1690 area settled; **1696** Bath County formed; town becomes county seat; **1701** first public library in North Carolina founded; **1705** town incorporated, oldest town in North Carolina; **1711** Cary's Rebellion erupts when Edward Hyde arrives from Britain, claims governorship from Thomas Cary; **1712** Beaufort County formed; town remains county seat; **1723** county courthouse built; **1734** St. Thomas Episcopal Church built; **1743** Bonner House built; **1748** Williams House built; **1751** Palmer-Marsh House built; **1785** county seat moved to Washington.

Bayboro *Pamlico County Eastern North Carolina, 116 mi/187 km east-southeast of Raleigh*

1872 Pamlico County formed; Vandemere becomes first county seat; **1876** town founded near Pamlico Sound, Atlantic Ocean; county seat moved from Vandemere; **1881** town incorporated; **1938** county courthouse built.

Beaufort *Carteret County Eastern North Carolina, 137 mi/220 km southeast of Raleigh, on Atlantic Ocean*

1709 first settlers arrive; **1711** settlers fight the Tuscarora people, build fort 1712; **1713** town platted; **June 1718** Blackbeard's ship *Queen Anne's Revenge* (captured as the *Concorde* in Bahamas 1717) sinks in Beaufort Inlet, wreckage discovered Nov. 1996; **1719** town founded, originally named Fish Town; **1722** Carteret County formed from Bath County; town becomes county seat; **1723** town incorporated; **1747** town captured by Spanish pirates, driven out within a few days; **c.1830** Odd Fellows Building built; **1859** Cape Lookout Lighthouse built, replaces 1812 structure; **1907** fourth county courthouse built; **Apr. 30, 1945** astronaut Michael J. Smith born, killed with six others in *Challenger* disaster Jan. 28, 1986;

March 10, 1966 Cape Lookout National Seashore authorized to east.

Belmont *Gaston County Southern North Carolina, 10 mi/16 km west of Charlotte, on Catawba River*

1839 Goshen Presbyterian Church built; **1865** Rev. Jeremiah O'Connell acquires Caldwell plantation, property given to Catholic Church 1876; **1871** Atlanta & Charlotte Railroad reaches site, named Garibaldi Station; **1876** Maryhelp Abbey established by Benedictines, Mary Help of Christians Chapel dedicated 1877; **1883** town renamed; **1884** St. Mary's College established, later renamed Belmont Abbey College; **1895** town incorporated; **1899** Sacred Heart Academy founded, later becomes Sacred Heart College, closed 1984; **1910s** cotton milling industry established.

Bentonville *Sampson County See Newton Grove (1865)*

Bethabara *Forsyth County See Winston-Salem*

Black Mountain *Buncombe County See Ashville (1939)*

Bolivia *Brunswick County Southeastern North Carolina, 15 mi/24 km southwest of Wilmington*

1764 Brunswick County formed; **1892** town founded; post office established; **1911** town incorporated; **Jan. 6, 1960** bomb carried on board airplane by passenger explodes, killing himself, 33 others; **1977** county seat moved from Southport; **May 2002** county courthouse completed.

Boone *Watauga County Northwestern North Carolina, 80 mi/129 km west of Winston-Salem*

1760 Daniel Boone passes through Deep Gap to Watauga River, builds home, remains through 1769; **1776** settlers organize the Watauga Association, small republic with own constitution; **1778** North Carolina exerts authority over area; **1800** Councill Store established by Jordan Councill; **1849** Watauga County formed; town becomes county seat; **1872** town incorporated; **1886** East Tennessee & Western North Carolina Railroad built, narrow gauge logging line; **1899** Appalachian State University established, originally Appalachian State Teachers College.

Brevard *Transylvania County Western North Carolina, 27 mi/43 km south-southwest of Asheville*

1861 Transylvania County formed; town founded as county seat near French Broad River, named for Revolutionary Col. Dr. Ephraim Brevard; **1866** county courthouse built; **1867** town incorporated; **1912** Transylvania County Library founded; **1934** Brevard College (2-year) established.

Bryson City *Swain County* *Western North Carolina, 55 mi/89 km west of Asheville*

1871 Swain County formed; named for David L. Swain, governor 1832–1835; town becomes county seat, originally named Charleston; **1887** town incorporated; **1889** town renamed Bryson City; **1910** county courthouse built; **June 15, 1934** Great Smoky Mountains National Park established to northwest, extends into Tennessee.

Buies Creek *Harnett County* See **Lillington** (1887)

Burgaw *Pender County* *Southeastern North Carolina, 95 mi/153 km south-southeast of Raleigh*

1875 Pender County formed, named for Confederate Gen. William Dorsey Pender; town founded as county seat; **1879** town incorporated; **1936** county courthouse built.

Burlington *Alamance County* *Central North Carolina, 22 mi/35 km east of Greensboro*

c.1700 area settled; **May 16–17, 1771** band of farmers called the Regulators, opposed to tax laws and provincial rule, do battle with forces of Governor Tryon, are defeated while inflicting heavy casualties on troops; **1837** Alamance Cotton Mill established by Edwin M. Holt; **1855** North Carolina Railroad reaches site; railroad shops built; town founded, originally named Company Shops; **1866** incorporated as a town; **1886** railroad shops closed; **1887** town renamed Burlington; **1889** Elon College established, later becomes Elon University; **1893** incorporated as a city; **1896** first hosiery mill opened; **1920s** Burlington Mills established boosting local economy; **1960s** racial unrest plagues town.

Burnsville *Yancey County* *Western North Carolina, 95 mi/153 km northwest of Charlotte*

1833 Yancey County formed, named for educator Bartlett Yancey; town founded as county seat, named for Capt. Otway Burns; **1871** town incorporated; **1915** Mount Mitchell State Park established to south, highest point in Eastern U.S. (6,684 ft/2,037 m), North Carolina's first state park; **1970s** county courthouse built; **Jan. 21, 1985** lowest temperature ever recorded in North Carolina reached, −34°F/−37°C, at Mt. Mitchell.

Buxton *Dare County* *Eastern North Carolina, 180 mi/290 km east-southeast of Raleigh*

1798 first Cape Hatteras Lighthouse established, built 1803, damaged during Civil War; **Aug. 27, 1861** Fort Hatteras attacked by Federal fleet, surrenders Aug. 29; **March 10, 1862** ironclad battleship *Monitor* sinks in rough seas while being towed by ship *Rhode Island*, 16 killed, 49 rescued; **1870** second Cape Hatteras Lighthouse built, tallest in U.S. (208 ft/63 m), abandoned 1936; **1873** The Cape post office established; **1882** post office renamed Buxton; **Apr. 16, 1891** British ship *St. Catharis* wrecks, 90 killed; **1918** Diamond Shoals Lightship established, sunk Aug. 8, 1918 by German submarine, crew reached shore, ship replaced; **Apr. 10, 1963** U.S. submarine *Thresher* sinks off Cape Hatteras killing all 129 on board; **March 27, 1971** 31 of 44 crewmen lost when oil tanker *Texaco Oklahoma* splits in two, 100-million gallons (378.5 million liters) of oil spilled; **May 26, 2000** Cape Hatteras Lighthouse reopened, moved in 1999 1,600 ft/488 m from eroding shoreline.

Camden *Camden County* *Northeastern North Carolina, 145 mi/233 km east-northeast of Raleigh*

1650 area first settled; **1740** first settlers arrive, site named Plank Bridge; **1746** Sawyer House built to north; **1777** Camden County formed from Pasquotank County; **1792** town founded, named Jonesborough; **1840** town renamed Camden; **1910** county courthouse built; **1911** bridge built across Pasquotank River to Elizabeth City.

Carthage *Moore County* *Central North Carolina, 53 mi/85 km southwest of Raleigh*

c.1750 area settled; **1770s** Scottish immigrants begin to arrive; **1784** Moore County formed; first county courthouse built on Killetts Creek; **1796** town incorporated; **1803** town platted; **1804** town becomes county seat; **1806** town renamed Fagansville, reverts to Carthage 1818; **1856** buggy factory established, final unit produced 1929; **1904** Elise Academy founded to west; **1923** county courthouse completed.

Cary *Wake County* *Central North Carolina, 7 mi/11.3 km west of Raleigh*

1805 Nancy Jones House built; **1852** town site established as railroad stop for A. Frank Page's lumber business (also founded Aberdeen), named Page's Siding; **Aug. 15, 1855** diarist and ambassador to England Walter Hines Page born to A. Frank Page (died 1918); **1868** Seaboard Railroad reaches town, forms junction; Page-Walker Hotel built by Page, closed 1916; **1871** town incorporated, renamed Cary.

Chapel Hill *Orange County* *Central North Carolina, 23 mi/37 km west-northwest of Raleigh*

1789 University of North Carolina established, opened 1795; **1795** town platted; **1819** town incorporated; **1851** incorporated as a city; **1950s** Research Triangle Park established to east to advance state's standing in technological development.

Charlotte *Mecklenburg County* *Southern North Carolina, 130 mi/209 km southwest of Raleigh*

1748 Scotch-Irish and German immigrants arrive in area; **1755** Thomas Spratt family become first settlers; **1761** Catawba people withdraw from area; **1762** Mecklenburg County formed from Anson County; **1765** town site chosen for county seat, named for Queen Charlotte, wife of King George III of England; **1768** town incorporated;

log county courthouse built; **1770** Queen's College founded, becomes Liberty Hall Academy 1776; **1778** Wallis Rock House built to east; **Sept.-Oct. 1780** Gen. Charles Cornwallis occupies town, refers to it as a "hornet's nest of rebellion"; **Oct. 3, 1780** Battle of the Bees skirmish at McIntyres Branch to north, British under Major Doyle routed when patriots under Capt. James Thompson and Capt. George Graham overturn beehive causing mass confusion; **1795** post office established; **Nov. 2, 1795** James K. Polk, 11th President of U.S., born at Pineville, in rural Mecklenburg County (died June 15, 1849); **early 1800s** county becomes major gold producer; **1815** First Presbyterian Church built, rebuilt 1894; **1831** Cedar Grove estate built by James G. Torrance; **1836** U.S. mint established, closed Oct. 1861; **1857** Queens College established, becomes Queens University 2002; **Apr. 1865** Confederate Pres. Jefferson Davis spends nine days here as he flees southward; **1867** Johnson C. Smith University established; **1880** first cotton mill established; **1886** *Charlotte Chronicle* newspaper founded, becomes *The Observer* March, 1892; **July 10, 1892** bacteriologist William Smith Tillett born (died 1974); **1903** Carnegie Free Library established; **Sept. 2, 1911** artist Romare Bearden born (died 1988); **1914** Horner Military School, established 1851, moves to Charlotte; **1917** Camp Greene established, WWI training camp, closed 1919; **Nov. 7, 1918** Baptist evangelist Billy Graham born; **1922** Dilworth Methodist Church built; **1926** Wayside Cottage, refuge for handicapped, founded by Harold C. "Old Wayside" Brown; **Oct. 3, 1935** astronaut Charles Duke, Jr. born; **1937** Charlotte-Douglas Airport opened, named 1954, became International Airport 1982; **1936** Mint Museum of Art opened; **1940** Carolinas Medical Center established; **1946** University of North Carolina at Charlotte established; **Apr. 30, 1946** Olympic swimmer Donald Schollander born; **1955** Charlotte Coliseum built, renamed Cricket Arena 1993; **1960** Charlotte Motor Speedway opens to northeast, near Concord; **1963** Central Piedmont Community College established; **1974** 40-story NationsBank Plaza building completed; **Sept. 11, 1974** Eastern DC-9 crashes into woods killing 69 of 82 on board; **1988** Independence Arena opened, later renamed Charlotte Coliseum, home of Hornets basketball team; 42-story First Union Center completed; **Oct. 5, 1989** evangelist Jim Bakker convicted of fraud and conspiracy, spent $3.5 million in donations from PTL evangelism program; **1992** 60-story NationsBank Corporate Center completed; **July 1994** USAir jet flight 1016 crashes, 37 of 57 on board killed; **1995** Charlotte Convention Center opened; **1996** Ericsson Stadium opened, home of football's Carolina Panthers; **2002** 50-story Hearst Tower building built; Hornets NBA basketball team moves to New Orleans; **Jan. 8, 2003** commuter jet crashes into hangar on takeoff, killing all 21 on board, exceeded weight limit.

Clinton *Sampson County* East central North Carolina, 58 mi/93 km south-southeast of Raleigh

1740 first settlers arrive; **1784** Sampson County formed; **Apr 7, 1786** William Rufus King born, vice president

under Franklin Pierce (died 1853); **1810** Daniel Joyner House built, used in Sept. 1831 as refuge for white women and children during threatened insurrection of black slaves; **1818** Richard Clinton donates land for county seat; town platted; **1822** town incorporated; **1904** county courthouse built; **1965** Sampson Community College established.

Columbia *Tyrrell County* Eastern North Carolina, 137 mi/220 km east of Raleigh

1680 area explored by Capt. Thomas Miller and Col. Joshua Tarkenton; **1729** Tyrrell County formed; **1748** first county courthouse built on Kendricks (now Mackeys) Creek; **1793** town incorporated as Elizabeth Town; **1810** town renamed Columbia; **1903** new county courthouse built.

Columbus *Polk County* Western North Carolina, 30 mi/48 km southeast of Asheville

1855 Polk County formed; town founded as county seat, named for Dr. Columbus Mills; **1857** town incorporated; **1859** county courthouse completed; **1892** Columbus Public Library founded, becomes Polk County Library 1950; **1922** Stearns Institute established; **Feb. 21, 1933** singer Nina Simone born at Tryon to south (died 2003).

Concord *Cabarrus County* South central North Carolina, 20 mi/32 km northeast of Charlotte

1745 Buffalo Creek Lutheran Church built by Dutch, later becomes St. John's Lutheran Church, one of first Lutheran meeting houses in state, new church built 1845; **May 9, 1777** Cabarrus Black Boys Action, wagon train loaded with supplies for Governor Tryon's forces raided by members of Regulators band disguised with blackened faces, participants flee state after informants are bribed; **1792** Cabarrus County formed; **1796** town founded as county seat; **1799** first gold discovery in U.S. made here; **1837** town incorporated; **1867** Barber-Scotia College established; **1876** county courthouse built; **1907** Stonewall Jackson Training School for boys established; **1924** First Baptist Church built, became Old Courthouse Theater 1976; **1928** Charles A. Cannon House completed, home of founder of Cannon Mills [see Kannapolis]; **1960** Charlotte Motor Speedway opens; **1979** county governmental center opened; **May 20, 2000** pedestrian walkway over U.S. Highway 29 crowded with NASCAR race fans collapses, injuring more than 100.

Currituck *Currituck County* Northeastern North Carolina, 155 mi/249 km east-northeast of Raleigh

1672 Currituck County formed, Algonquin term for "land of wild goose"; **1720** Timothy Hanson introduces grass *Phleum pratense* to area, becomes known as Timothy Grass; **1723** first county courthouse built; **1728** settlement of boundary dispute with Virginia puts county in North Carolina; **1776** county jail built; **1875** Currituck Beach Lighthouse built on Atlantic Ocean to east; **1876** third county courthouse built; **July 31, 1878** ship *Metropolis* wrecks on Outer Banks to southeast, more than 100 killed; **July 23, 1965** explosion on fishing trawler 45 mi/72 km to east kills eight; **1998** county government center completed.

Danbury *Stokes County* *Northern North Carolina, 20 mi/32 km north of Winston-Salem, on Dan River*

1789 Stokes County formed, named for Revolutionary officer Col. John Stokes; **1790s** trading post established, named Crawford; **1841** Moody Tavern built; **1849** Forsyth County separates from Stokes County; **1852** county officials stop at Moody Tavern while on county seat search, decide to move county seat here from Germantown; town renamed Danbury; **c.1860** iron mining begins; **1904** county courthouse built; **1957** town incorporated.

Dobson *Surry County* *Northwestern North Carolina, 33 mi/53 km northwest of Winston-Salem*

1770 Surry County formed; first county courthouse built at old Richmond, in northwest part of present-day Forsyth County; **1790** county seat moved to Rockford; **1850** town founded; county subdivided, county seat moved to Dobson; **1891** town incorporated; **1918** fourth county courthouse built; **1965** Surry Community College established.

Dunn *Harnett County* *East central North Carolina, 35 mi/56 km south of Raleigh*

1886 Wilmington & Weldon Railroad completed from Fayetteville; town founded by Henry Pope, named for railroad engineer Bennett R. Dunn; **1887** town incorporated; **March 16, 1865** Gen. William J. Hardee's 6,000 Confederate troops launch unsuccessful attack on General Sherman's Union forces in Battle of Averasboro; **March 12, 1895** World War II Gen. William Carey born, father of the Army Airborne Division (died 1948).

Durham *Durham County* *North central North Carolina, 20 mi/32 km northwest of Raleigh*

c.1750 area first settled; **1802** Duke Homestead built by Duncan Cameron to north; **1850s** town of Durhamsville founded; **1853** post office established; **1855** town renamed Durham; **1856** North Carolina Railroad completed, land for station right-of-way refused by landowner William Pratt, donated instead by Dr. Bartlett Durham; **1858** Robert F. Morris begins manufacture of tobacco products; Bull Durham blend originated at Bennett Farmhouse; **Apr. 26, 1865** Confederate Gen. Joseph E. Johnston surrenders to General Sherman at Durham Station; **1869** incorporated as a city; **c.1880** James B. "Buck" Duke begins manufacturing cigarettes; **1881** Durham County formed; town becomes county seat; **1884** Durham Cotton Manufacturing Plant established; **1898** Durham Public Library opened; **1890** American Tobacco Company founded by James B. Duke; **1892** Trinity College moves from Randolph County, estab-lished 1859, becomes Duke University 1924; Erwin Cotton Mills established; **1900** Durham Hosiery Mill built by Julian Carr; **1910** North Carolina Central University established; **1911** American Tobacco subdivided into smaller companies by order of U.S. Supreme Court; **1913** Public Library for Negroes established; **May 9, 1942** journalist David Gergen born; **1946** Museum of Life and Science founded; **1950s** Research Triangle Park established to southeast to advance state's standing in technological development; **1961** Durham Technical Community College established.

Edenton *Chowan County* *Northeastern North Carolina, 118 mi/190 km east-northeast of Raleigh*

1622 John Pory explores Chowan River region; **1653** possible early settlement occurs on land granted to Roger Green by Virginia Assembly; **1672** Chowan County formed; **1714** town platted as county seat, originally named Queen Anne's Towne; **1722** town incorporated, renamed for Gov. Charles Eden; **1729** King's Arms Tavern built, later named Horniblow's Tavern; **1758** Cupola House built; **1760** Richard Brownrigg pioneers local fishing industry; St. Paul's Church completed, begun 1736, replaces original 1702 structure; **1767** county courthouse built; **1769** seine fishing begins yielding larger catches; **1773** Iredell House built; **1810** Beverly Hall house built; **Feb. 1862** Federal troops occupy town, remain to end of Civil War; **1863** Union fort on Chowan River to north destroyed by Confederates; **May 5, 1864** ironclad vessel *Albermarle* does battle with Federal fleet off nearby Sandy Point.

Elizabeth City *Pasquotank County* *Northeastern North Carolina, 142 mi/229 km east-northeast of Raleigh*

1666 area on Pasquotank River first settled by Bermudians; **1672** Pasquotank County formed; Broomfield becomes county seat, seat moved to Belfe's Point 1758; **1706** Quaker meeting house built; **1709** brick house built to north on Pasquotank River by Edward Teach, also known as Blackbeard the pirate who made river one of his haunts; **1722** naval inspection station established; **1740** Fearing House built; **1793** town incorporated as Reading, renamed Elizabeth Town 1794; **1785** county seat moved to Nixonton; **1800** county seat moved to Elizabeth Town; **early 1800s** shipyards built; **1801** town renamed Elizabeth City; **1805** Dismal Swamp Canal completed to Virginia; **1819** City Hotel built; **1826** Christ Episcopal Church completed; **Feb. 8, 1862** Federal forces of Admiral Goldsborough's fleet occupy town; **1882** county courthouse built; **1891** Elizabeth City State University established; **1908** federal building built; **1911** bridge built across Pasquotank River replacing ferry established in 1700s; **1915** first domestic production of soybeans in U.S. begins; **1921** Elizabeth City & Norfolk Railroad reaches town, becomes Norfolk & Southern 1891; **1926** Chowan River Bridge built; **1960** College of the Albemarle (2-year) established.

Elizabethtown *Bladen County* Southeastern
North Carolina, 81 mi/130 km south of Raleigh

1734 Bladen County formed; **c.1738** town site settled by Scotch, English, and Irish immigrants, becomes county seat, named Bladen Court House; **1773** town founded, named for Queen Elizabeth; **1781** in Battle of Elizabethtown, Tory troops are attacked by band of Whig patriots along Cape Fear River, British forced to retreat into ravine named Tory Hole; **1895** town incorporated; **1965** county courthouse built.

Fayetteville *Cumberland County* South central
North Carolina, 53 mi/85 km south-southwest of Raleigh

1736 area settled by Scottish immigrants led by Colonel McAllister; town of Campbelltown founded; **1747** grist mill established at Cross Creek; village of Cross Creek founded; **1754** Cumberland County formed; town becomes county seat; **1762** Campbelltown incorporated; **1764** McNeill's Grist Mill built; **1765** Cross Creek incorporated; **June 20, 1775** group of Whigs meets at Liberty Point, resolve to resist Tory forces; **1778** two towns merge, incorporated as Upper and Lower Campbelltown; McKeithan House built; **1781** town occupied by Cornwallis' forces; **1783** Cross Creek and Campbelltown merge, incorporated as Fayetteville; **Nov. 21, 1789** convention held to ratify U.S. Constitution; **1792** state capital moved to Raleigh; **1800** First Presbyterian Church built, destroyed by fire 1831; **c.1807** Sanford House built; **1827** first African-American senator from Mississippi Hiram Revels born (died 1901); **May 29, 1831** fire destroys 600 homes, 125 businesses; **1838** Market House built on site of Convention Hall destroyed by 1831 fire; **1847** Long Street Church completed, organized 1758; **March 10, 1865** in Battle of Monroe's Crossroads, Confederate forces of Lt. Gen. Wade Hampton sent into retreat by Maj. Gen. Judson Kirkpatrick's Union forces; arsenal burned; **1867** Fayetteville State University established; **1885** railroad reaches town; **Oct. 14, 1886** U.S. Sen. Frank Porter Graham born (died 1972); **1897** St. John's Episcopal Church consecrated, previous structures built 1817 and 1832; **1908** Wesley Memorial Methodist Church built; **1918** Camp Bragg established to west, becomes Fort Bragg Military Reservation in 1922; **1956** Methodist College established; **1967** County Arena and Auditorium opened, renamed Crown Coliseum 1997; **1969** Fayetteville Technical Community College established; **Aug. 21, 1983** highest temperature ever recorded in North Carolina reached, 110°F/43°C.

Franklin *Macon County* Western North Carolina,
55 mi/89 km southwest of Asheville

1819 land sold to whites by Cherokees, site of native settlement of Nikwasi; **1828** Macon County formed, named for Sen. Nathaniel Macon; town founded as county seat, named for Jesse Franklin, governor 1820–1821; **1855** town incorporated; **1972** county courthouse built; **1994** Scottish Tartan Museum moved from Highlands, founded 1938.

Gastonia *Gaston County* Southwestern North
Carolina, 20 mi/32 km west of Charlotte

1846 Gaston County formed; **1877** town incorporated; **1888** Lincoln Academy for black children founded to west; **1909** county seat moved from Dallas; county courthouse built; **1929** police chief killed in strike violence at Loray Mills, largest textile mill in Southeast, followed by sensational trial; **1961** Schiele Museum of Natural History opened.

Gatesville *Gates County* Northeastern North
Carolina, 115 mi/185 km northeast of Raleigh

c.1660 first white settlers arrive; **1775** Dr. Smith House built at Buckland, to north; **1779** Gates County formed; town becomes county seat, named Gates Court House, named for Revolutionary Gen. Horatio Gates; **1831** town renamed Gatesville; **1836** county courthouse built; **1891** town incorporated; **1915** Confederate monument erected.

Goldsboro *Wayne County* East central North
Carolina, 46 mi/74 km southeast of Raleigh

1779 Wayne County formed; Waynesboro (2 mi/3.2 km to south) becomes county seat; **1840** Wilmington & Raleigh Railroad built; town founded as Goldsborough; **1847** town incorporated; county seat moved from Waynesboro; **Dec. 14, 1862** Confederate troops under General Evans repulse Union forces under General Foster; **1869** town renamed Goldsboro; **1913** county courthouse built; **Jan. 26, 1923** actress Anne Jeffreys born; **1942** Seymour Johnson Army Air Field established, closed 1946, reopened as Air Force Base 1956; **1957** Wayne Community College established.

Graham *Alamance County* Central North
Carolina, 45 mi/72 km west-northwest of Raleigh

1849 Alamance County formed; town founded as county seat, named for William A. Graham, governor, secretary of Navy; **1851** town incorporated; **1923** county courthouse built; **1959** Alamance Community College established.

Greensboro *Guilford County* Central North
Carolina, 65 mi/105 km west-northwest of Raleigh

1749 area first settled by Scottish and Irish immigrants; **1761** McNairy House built to northwest; **1762** log Alamance Presbyterian Church built to southeast, new structure built 1875; **1767** Dr. David Caldwell establishes his Log College, forerunner of town's educational institutions; **May 12, 1768** Dorothea (Dolly) Payne Madison, wife of Pres. James Madison, born in rural Guilford County (married Sept. 15, 1794, died July 12, 1849); **1771** Guilford County formed; Guilford Court House (Martinsville) becomes first county seat, 4 mi/6.4 km to northwest; **March 15, 1781** American forces under Gen. Nathanael Greene suffer defeat by British under Cornwallis at Battle of Guilford Court House; **1808** town founded as new county seat; **1825** Blandwood Mansion built; **1827** Buffalo Presbyterian Church built;

1829 town incorporated; **1837** Guilford College established by Quakers; **1861** in spite of county's opposition to secession, city serves as Confederate supply depot; **Sept. 11, 1862** writer O. Henry (William Sydney Porter) born (died 1910); **1891** University of North Carolina at Greensboro established; North Carolina Agricultural and Technical State University established; **1895** Cone Textile Mills established; **Apr. 25, 1908** newscaster Edward R. Murrow born (died 1965); **March 2, 1917** Guilford Courthouse National Military Park established; **1923** Jefferson Standard Life Insurance Building built; **1926** World War Memorial Stadium completed; **1927** Tri City Airport established, becomes Piedmont Triad International Airport 1988; **June 16, 1940** singer Billy "Crash" Craddock born; **1959** Greensboro Coliseum opened; **Feb. 1, 1960** black sit-down demonstration at lunch counter, inspires similar actions in other cities.

Greenville *Pitt County* *Eastern North Carolina, 72 mi/116 km east of Raleigh*

1760 Pitt County formed; **1771** town founded, originally named Martinsboro; **1774** town incorporated; town becomes county seat; **1787** town renamed Greenesville for Gen. Nathanael Greene, later shortened to Greenville; **1907** East Carolina University established; **1910** county courthouse built; **1961** Pitt Community College established.

Halifax *Halifax County* *Northeastern North Carolina, 70 mi/113 km northeast of Raleigh*

c.1750 town settled; **1757** Halifax County formed; **1758** town platted; county seat moved from Enfield; **1760** town incorporated; **1769** Masonic Temple built; **1776** North Carolina Fourth and Fifth Provincial Congresses meet at Constitution House, through 1781; **Apr. 12, 1776** Halifax Resolves adopted delineating colonial grievances, leading to passage of resolution for independence one month later; **Aug. 1, 1776** Cornelius Harnett reads Declaration of Independence from courthouse steps, is carried through streets on shoulders of celebrating citizens; **March 4, 1781** Generals Cornwallis and Tarleton lodge at Eagle Hotel; **June 18, 1790** Tennessee Sen. John Henry Eaton born (died 1856); **c.1790** Eagle Hotel built; **1830** St. Mark's Episcopal Church built; **1910** third county courthouse built.

Hamlet *Richmond County* *Southern North Carolina, 70 mi/113 km east-southeast of Charlotte*

c.1875 town founded; **1877** Raleigh & Augusta Air Line Railroad reaches town, becomes important rail center; **1897** town incorporated; **c.1912** Hamlet Opera House built; **Sept. 23, 1926** jazz saxophonist John Coltrane born (died 1967); **1935** Hamlet Public Library opened; **1964** Richmond Community College established; **1982** first Seaboard Festival held; **Sept. 3, 1991** fire at meat processing plant, 25 killed.

Hayesville *Clay County* *Western North Carolina, 82 mi/132 km southwest of Asheville*

1838 Fort Hembree built during Cherokee removal campaign; **1855** Hicksville Academy founded by John O. Hicks, later becomes Hayesville High School; **1861** Clay County formed; **1868** town founded as county seat, named for representative George W. Hayes; **1889** county courthouse built; **1891** town incorporated.

Henderson *Vance County* *Northern North Carolina, 40 mi/64 km north of Raleigh*

c.1811 area settled; **1840** town platted, named for state Chief Justice Leonard Henderson (1772–1833); **1841** town incorporated; **1881** Vance County formed; town becomes county seat; **1883** county courthouse built; **1969** Vance-Granville Community College established.

Hendersonville *Henderson County* *Western North Carolina, 20 mi/32 km south of Asheville*

1838 Henderson County formed; **1841** town founded as county seat; **1847** town incorporated; **c.1858** Dixon's Sanatorium built; **1904** county courthouse built; **1914** Henderson County Library founded, new library opened 1970; **July 19, 1967** Piedmont Airlines Boeing 727 and Cessna 310 collide in midair killing 82.

Hertford *Perquimans County* *Northeastern North Carolina, 126 mi/203 km east-northeast of Raleigh*

1672 Perquimans County formed; Quaker William Edmundson, follower of George Fox, preaches one of first religious sermons in North Carolina; **1701** town founded as port of entry and county seat; **c.1730** Newbold-White House built; **1731** county courthouse built, second floor added 1818, restored 1932; **c.1754** Old Eagle Tavern built, razed 1929; **1758** town incorporated; **1775** Ashland Mansion built to south on Harvey's Neck; **1849** Church of the Holy Trinity (Catholic) built; **1929** Edmundson-Fox Memorial erected.

Hickory *Catawba County* *Western North Carolina, 43 mi/69 km northwest of Charlotte*

1784 Hickory Tavern established; **1860** Western Railroad built; town of Hickory Tavern founded; **1870** town incorporated; **1873** town renamed Hickory; **1880** manufacture of wagons begins; **July 20, 1890** historian Ellis M. Coulter born (died 1981); **1891** Lenoir-Rhyne College established; **1901** first large furniture factory established; **c.1960** city boasts 40 furniture factories, 90 hosiery mills; **May 1974** Catawba River Science Center established.

High Point *Guilford County* *Central North Carolina, 15 mi/24 km southwest of Greensboro*

1750 area settled by Quakers; **1773** Springfield Friends Meeting House organized, fourth structure built 1926, connected to 1858 church; **1778** Deep River Quaker Meeting House built, founded 1758, rebuilt 1875; **1786**

Welch's Inn built; **1798** Blair Family log house built; **c.1830** Hunt's Tavern built; **1853** town platted on North Carolina & Midland Railroad at highest point on line; **1859** town incorporated; **1888** furniture manufacturing begins; **1891** school for black children founded by Quakers; **Apr. 2, 1907** baseball player for Chicago White Sox Lucius Appling born (died 1991); **1921** Southern Furniture Exposition Building built; **1924** High Point University established; **1925** the Giant Bureau built, giant chest of drawers housed Chamber of Commerce; **1926** High Point Public Library founded.

Hillsborough   *Orange County   Central North Carolina, 30 mi/48 km northwest of Raleigh*

1700 area first settled; **1754** Orange County formed; town founded as county seat, named Orange, later renamed Corbinton for Francis Corbin; **1759** town incorporated as Childsboro; **1766** town renamed for Earl of Hillsborough; **Sept. 24, 1768** the Regulators plunder and burn homes of officials, defeated May 16, 1771, at Battle of Alamance; **1769** Nash House built by Isaac Edwards; **June 19, 1771** Regulators Benjamin Merrill, Captain Messer, four others hanged; **1775** Third Provincial Congress meets here; **1778** Constitutional Convention held; **Feb. 20–25, 1781** town occupied by Cornwallis' forces; **Sept. 13, 1781** town raided by Tories under Col. David Fanning and Col. Hector McNeill seizing Governor Burke and his officials; **March 14, 1782** Missouri Sen. Thomas Hart Benton born (died 1858); **1788** anti-Federalist convention held rejecting U.S. Constitution, delaying state's entry into Union until Nov. 1789; **1826** St. Matthew's Episcopal Church completed; **1825** Eagle Lodge residence completed; **1845** county courthouse built; **1859** Hillsborough Military Academy established; **1934** Confederate Memorial Library built.

Jackson   *Northampton County   Northeastern North Carolina, 80 mi/129 km northeast of Raleigh*

1741 Northampton County formed; **1742** town founded, named Northampton Court House; **1823** town incorporated; **1826** town renamed Jackson, for Pres. Andrew Jackson; **1835** Bragg House built by Thomas Bragg, governor, U.S. Senator, Attorney General of Confederate States; **1857** Ransom House built; **1859** county courthouse built.

Jacksonville   *Onslow County   Southeastern North Carolina, 100 mi/161 km southeast of Raleigh*

1734 Onslow County formed from Great County of Bath; **1757** town founded as county seat, originally named Wantland's Ferry; **1842** incorporated as a city; **1904** county courthouse built; **1936** Onslow County Library founded; **1941** Camp Lejeune Marine Corps Base established; **June 23, 1967** two helicopters collide at Camp Lejeune, killing 22 Marines, injuring 13 others; **1964** Coastal Carolina Community College established; **June 8, 1970** seven Green Berets killed by TNT explosion during training exercise; **1971** Albert J. Ellis Airport established to west.

Jamestown   *Guilford County   Central North Carolina, 10 mi/16 km southwest of Greensboro*

1757 town settled by Quakers; **1759** town named for settler James Mendenhall; **1811** Steele House built; **1815** gold and copper discovered along Deep River to south, cost of production unprofitable; **1819** Quaker Meeting House built; **c.1819** Coffin House built by Dr. S. G. Coffin; **1820** Telmont Law School founded by George C. Mendenhall; **1881** town incorporated, reincorporated 1947; **1958** Guilford Technical Community College established.

Jefferson   *Ashe County   Northwestern North Carolina, 72 mi/116 km west-northwest of Winston-Salem*

1799 Ashe County formed, named for Gov. Samuel Ashe (1795–1798); **1803** town platted as county seat; county courthouse built; **1903** town incorporated.

Kannapolis   *Cabarrus and Rowan counties Central North Carolina, 21 mi/34 km northeast of Charlotte*

1877 first cotton mills begin production; **1898** towel manufacturing begins; **c.1905** town founded; **1906** Cannon Mills Company founded by James W. Cannon, Sr.; town founded around towel mill; **1984** incorporated as a city.

Kenansville   *Duplin County   East central North Carolina, 70 mi/113 km southeast of Raleigh*

1736 Golden Grove Church built; **1750** Duplin County formed; **1765** Col. James Kenan leads local militia to Brunswick to show opposition to Stamp Act; **1784** county seat moved from Goshen; **March 15, 1787** two black slaves sentenced for murder of their owner, one burned to death, other's ears cut off, branded on cheeks; **c.1830** Liberty Hall built by Owen Kenan; **1831** Dave Morisy, other black slaves accused of fomenting insurgency, he and one other hanged, beheaded; **1838** Wilmington & Raleigh Railroad reaches town; **1852** town incorporated; **1919** county courthouse built; **1964** James Sprunt Community College established.

Kings Mountain   *Cleveland County Southwestern North Carolina, 30 mi/48 km west of Charlotte*

Oct. 7, 1780 British Col. Patrick Ferguson threatens to destroy mountain region, mountain men launch offensive employing Native American tactics, killing Ferguson, 206 others, injuring or capturing remaining 728, Battle of Kings Mountain, fought short distance to south in South Carolina; **July 15, 1815** Dr. William McLean visits battlefield to properly inter remains of fallen soldiers; **1874** incorporated as a city; **1909** granite marker erected at battleground.

Kinston   *Lenoir County*   *Eastern North Carolina, 70 mi/113 km southeast of Raleigh, on Neuse River*

1729 Richard Caswell born, first governor of state of North Carolina (died 1789); **1762** town of King's Town founded; **1784** town renamed Kinston; **1791** Lenoir County formed; town becomes county seat; **1824** Peebles House built; **1849** town incorporated; **c.1855** buggy factory established by Dibble family; **Dec. 13-14, 1862** Union troops quartered in town's factory section, giving it the name Yankee Row; **March 8, 1865** Union forces under Gen. Jacob Cox repulsed by Gen. Braxton Bragg's Confederates, many taken prisoner; **1901** St. Mary's Episcopal Church built; **1929** Women's Industrial Farm Colony established, part of state prison system; **1940** fourth county courthouse built; **1960** Lenoir Community College established; **Jan. 29, 2003** fire at pharmaceutical supply factory, 4 killed, 36 injured.

Kitty Hawk   *Dare County*   *Eastern North Carolina, 165 mi/266 km east-northeast of Raleigh*

1738 early map refers to point on Atlantic Ocean coastal barrier island as Chickahauk; **c.1790** area first settled; **Dec. 30, 1812** ship *Patriot* drifts ashore, its passengers victims of pirates, some forced to walk the plank, pirates caught and executed; **1838** post office established; **1900** Orville and Wilbur Wright arrive to conduct aviation experiments on sand barrier island; **Dec. 17, 1903** Orville Wright makes historic 4 mi/6.4 km first flight at Kill Devil Hill; **Dec. 17, 1928** Wright memorial marker erected by National Aeronautic Association; **1932** Wright Brothers Memorial Pylon, 60 ft/97 m high, built by federal government; **1981** town incorporated.

Laurinburg   *Scotland County*   *Southern North Carolina, 85 mi/137 km south-southwest of Raleigh*

1857 St. Andrew's Presbyterian College established; **c.1865** town of Laurenburg founded by Scottish settlers; **1877** town incorporated; **1883** town name spelling changed to Laurinburg; **1899** Scotland County formed; town becomes county seat; **1902** county courthouse built; **March 18, 1996** Scotch Meadows Retirement Home fire kills eight.

Lenoir   *Caldwell County*   *Western North Carolina, 61 mi/98 km northwest of Charlotte*

1841 Caldwell County formed; town becomes county seat; **1851** town incorporated; **1884** Chester & Lenoir Railroad reaches town; **1889** first furniture factories established; **c.1910** county courthouse built.

Lexington   *Davidson County*   *Central North Carolina, 20 mi/32 km south of Winston-Salem*

1755 area first settled; **1822** Davidson County formed; **1824** town becomes county seat; first county courthouse built; **1827** town incorporated; **1870** county courthouse built; **1879** Grimes Brothers Mill established; **1927** High

Rock Lake reservoir built on Yadkin (Pee Dee) River; **1958** Davidson County Community College established.

Lillington   *Harnett County*   *Central North Carolina, 30 mi/48 km south-southwest of Raleigh*

1720s area first settled; town founded, named Long Creek; **1855** Harnett County formed; Summerville becomes county seat 3 mi/4.8 km to west; **1858** county seat moved to Long Creek; **1859** town incorporated, renamed for Col. Alexander Lillington; **1887** Campbell University established at Buies Creek to east; **March 17, 1894** dramatist Mark Green born (died 1981); **1898** county courthouse built, addition built 1959; **2002** new county courthouse opened.

Lincolnton   *Lincoln County*   *Western North Carolina, 28 mi/45 km northwest of Charlotte*

1779 Lincoln County formed; town founded as county seat, named for Col. Benjamin Lincoln of Rhode Island; **June 20, 1780** victory for patriots at Battle of Ramsour's Mill precedes decisive Battle of Kings Mountain; **1785** town incorporated; **Sept. 5, 1804** Gov. Sen. William Alexander Graham born in rural Lincoln County (died 1875); **March 31, 1808** James Pinckney Henderson born, first governor of Texas 1846–1847 (died 1858); **1813** Pleasant Retreat Academy opened, closed 1878; **1833** Michael Hoke House built; **1923** county courthouse completed.

Louisburg   *Franklin County*   *North central North Carolina, 30 mi/48 km northeast of Raleigh*

1758 area along Tar River first settled; **1779** Franklin County formed; town founded as county seat; **1787** Franklin Academy established, becomes Louisburg College; **1779** town incorporated; **1818** John Allen house built; **1850** county courthouse built.

Lumberton   *Robeson County*   *Southeastern North Carolina, 84 mi/135 km south-southwest of Raleigh*

1725 first settlers arrive, area occupied by Croatan peoples; **1787** Robeson County formed; named for Col. Thomas Robeson, veteran of Battle of Elizabethtown, opposed creation of county until offered to name it for him; **1787** town founded as county seat; **1788** town incorporated; **1851** incorporated as a city; **1886** county becomes first in state to prohibit sale of alcoholic beverages; **1908** county courthouse built; **Dec. 16, 1943** two trains collide, 73 killed.

Maiden   *Catawba County*   See **Newton (1780)**

Manteo   *Dare County*   *Eastern North Carolina, 170 mi/274 km east of Raleigh, on Roanoke Island*

July 1584 Amadas and Barlow reach North Carolina coast, claim continent for England, return with two natives Manteo and Wanchese; **1585** colonial expedition of 108 people arrives under Sir Richard Grenville; Fort Raleigh built; **1586** colonists depart with Sir Francis Drake following Native American troubles and near-starvation; **July 22, 1587** John White arrives at Roanoke Island with 117 English immigrants, establish first permanent European settlement in the Americas; **Aug. 18, 1587** Virginia Dare born to Eleanor and Ananias Dare, first European child born in America; **Aug. 16, 1590** John White returns to island, finds no trace of settlers; **1848** Bodie Lighthouse built on Bodie Island, on Outer Banks, to east, rebuilt 1859, destroyed during Civil War, rebuilt again 1872; **1863** Outer Banks seized by Union during Civil War, became refuge for freed slaves; **1870** Dare County formed; town becomes county seat; **1896** stone monument erected to honor lost colony; **1899** town incorporated; **1902** Reginald A. Fessenden of U.S. Weather Service builds experimental wireless station, maintains contact with ship similarly equipped; **1937** outdoor drama "The Lost Colony" by Paul Green opens; **Aug. 17, 1937** Cape Hatteras National Seashore established; **Apr. 5, 1941** Fort Raleigh National Historic Site designated; **1951** Elizabethan Gardens created.

Marion *McDowell County* *Western North Carolina, 72 mi/116 km west-northwest of Charlotte*

1842 McDowell County formed; town founded as county seat; **1844** county courthouse built; town incorporated; **1964** McDowell Community College established.

Marshall *Madison County* *Western North Carolina, 15 mi/24 km north-northwest of Asheville*

1780s first settlers arrive at town site; **1816** area settled; **1851** Madison County formed; town of Jewel Hill, now Walnut, becomes county seat; **1855** county seat moved to Marshall, county seat dispute continues until 1859; **1863** town incorporated; **1907** county courthouse built.

Mebane *Alamance and Orange counties* *Central North Carolina, 40 mi/64 km northwest of Raleigh*

c.1812 Bingham School military academy founded, moved to Hillsborough 1826, to Asheville 1889; **1854** town founded by Frank Mebane, named Mebanesville; **1881** incorporated as a town; White Furniture Company established; **1883** town renamed Mebane; **1904** Mebane Bedding Company established, later becomes Kingsdowne Company; **1987** incorporated as a city.

Mocksville *Davie County* *Central North Carolina, 23 mi/37 km southwest of Winston-Salem*

c.1745 area settled by Scotch, Irish, and English immigrants; **1810** post office established as Mock's Old Field; **c.1824** town renamed Mocksville; **1836** Davie County formed; **1837** town becomes county seat; **1839** town incorporated; **1909** county courthouse built; **1995** archaeological site yields burials dating to 900–1500 AD.

Monroe *Union County* *Southern North Carolina, 25 mi/40 km southeast of Charlotte*

1751 town first settled; **1842** Union County formed; town becomes county seat; **1843** town incorporated; **1848** town hall completed; **Feb. 17, 1866** David F. Houston born, secretary of Agriculture under President Wilson (died 1940); **1874** railroad reaches town; **1886** county courthouse built; **1888** William Henry Belk opens his first department store; **1894** *Monroe Enquirer* newspaper founded; **Oct. 18, 1921** U.S. Sen. Jesse Helms born.

Morehead City *Carteret County* *Eastern North Carolina, 135 mi/217 km southeast of Raleigh*

1740s fort built as protection against Spaniards; **1835** Fort Macon completed on Beaufort Inlet; **1857** town founded by John Motley Morehead; **1858** North Carolina Railroad reaches town; **1861** town incorporated; **Apr. 24, 1862** Fort Macon taken from Confederates by Gen. Ambrose E. Burnside's forces; **1899** hurricane survivors from whaling towns settle here; **1937** Ocean Shipping Port Terminal completed; **1963** Carteret Community College established.

Morganton *Burke County* *Western North Carolina, 60 mi/97 km northwest of Charlotte*

1777 Burke County formed; county named for Gov. Thomas Burke; **1784** town founded as county seat; **Feb. 1865** Union General Stoneman's forces burn county records in street; **1883** Murray Mill built, closed 1965; **1885** town incorporated; **1886** state hospital opened; **1891** School for the Deaf established; **1895** Bunker Hill Covered Bridge built; **Sept. 27, 1896** U.S. Sen. Samuel James Ervin born, chaired Watergate Committee hearings 1970s (died 1985); **1903** Drexel Heritage furniture company established at Drexel to east; **1929** Alva Theatre built; **1964** Western Piedmont Community College established; **1974** Waldensian Museum opened; **1976** county courthouse built.

Mount Airy *Surry County* *Northwestern North Carolina, 33 mi/53 km northwest of Winston-Salem*

c.1850 area first settled; **1885** town incorporated; **June 1, 1926** TV actor Andy Grffith born; **Nov. 10, 1945** country singer Donna Fargo born; **1971** first annual Bluegrass and Old Time Fiddlers Convention held; **1972** Andy Griffith Playhouse opened; **1980** Blue Ridge Jamboree established; **1990** first annual Mayberry Days celebration held.

Mount Olive *Wayne County* *East central North Carolina, 53 mi/85 km southeast of Raleigh*

1839 Wilmington & Weldon Railroad built; **1853** post office established; **1854** town founded; **March 1865** Union troops encamp here prior to Battle of Bentonville; **1870** town incorporated; **1951** Mount Olive College established.

Murfreesboro *Hertford County* *Northeastern North Carolina, 98 mi/158 km northeast of Raleigh*

c.1707 first settlers arrive; **1787** William Murfree donates land for town at Murfree's Landing on Meherrin River; town incorporated; **1790** store built, possibly oldest commercial structure in North Carolina, later becomes William Rea Museum; **1810** John Wheeler House built; **Sept. 12, 1818** Richard Jordan Gatling born at nearby Maney's Neck, invented multibarrel Gatling gun (died 1903); **1848** Chowan College established.

Murphy *Cherokee County* *Western North Carolina, 96 mi/155 km west-southwest of Asheville*

1830 town founded on Hiwassee River, named Huntersville for founder Col. A. R. S. Hunter; **1838** Fort Butler built as part of Cherokee removal; **1839** Cherokee County formed; town becomes county seat; **1851** town incorporated, renamed for statesman Archibald D. Murphey, spelling variation from typographical error; **1926** county courthouse built; **1940** Hiwassee Lake reservoir built on Hiwassee River to west; **1964** Tri-County Community College established; **June 2, 2003** Eric Rudolph, 36, captured, wanted in pipe bombing at Atlanta Summer Olympics 1996, also 1997 Atlanta abortion clinic and night club bombings and 1998 Birmingham abortion clinic bombing.

Nashville *Nash County* *East central North Carolina, 40 mi/64 km east-northeast of Raleigh*

1743 first land grants patented; **1777** Nash County formed; **1780** town settled, founded as county seat; town and county named for Brig. Gen. Francis Nash of Revolutionary War; **1792** Rose Hill mansion built by George Boddie; **1815** town incorporated; **1883** county courthouse built, cornerstone laid containing quart of Nash County brandy.

New Bern *Craven County* *Eastern North Carolina, 103 mi/166 km southeast of Raleigh, on Neuse River*

Sept. 1710 band of Swiss and Palatine immigrants led by Baron Christopher de Graffenried settles on lands purchased from the Lord Proprietors; fort built; town platted by John Lawson; **Sept. 1711** town destroyed by Tuscaroras, 80 settlers killed, Lawson tortured to death, de Graffenried held prisoner for six months; **1712** Craven County formed; town becomes county seat; **1723** town incorporated; **1745** Colonial assembly meets here, through 1761; **1749** James Davis establishes *North Carolina Gazette*, colony's first newspaper; **1750** original Christ Church (Episcopal) built, present structure built 1875; **1766** New Bern Academy founded, built 1810; **1770** Tryon Palace completed for royal Gov. William Tryon, restored 1959; **1776** Louisiana House built; **1808** Masonic Temple built; **1810** Oaksmith House built; **March 14, 1862** Union forces defeat Confederate Gen. L. O'Bryan Branch, occupy town; **1863** Fort Totten built by Union troops,

restored 1939; county courthouse built; **1890s** hardwood lumber industry begins; **1910s** seafood industry developed; **1941** Cherry Point Marine Corps Station established to southeast; **1965** Craven Community College established; **Aug. 2000** New Bern Riverfront Convention Center opened.

Newland *Avery County* *Western North Carolina, 85 mi/137 km northwest of Charlotte*

1911 Avery County formed, last of state's 100 counties; county named for Col. Waightstill Avery of Revolutionary War; town founded as county seat; **1912** post office established; **1913** town incorporated; county courthouse built.

Newton *Catawba County* *Western North Carolina, 35 mi/56 km northwest of Charlotte*

1748 Adam Sherrill receives area's first land grant; **1762** Barringer House built; **June 20, 1780** 1,300 Tory troops surprised and routed by 400 patriots under Francis Locke at village of Maiden to south; **1790** Grace Lutheran Church founded; **c.1800** region becomes leading gold producer, eclipsed 1848 by California Gold Rush; **1842** Catawba County formed; **1843** town founded as county seat; **1855** town incorporated; **1924** county courthouse built.

Newton Grove *Sampson County* *East central North Carolina, 41 mi/66 km south-southeast of Raleigh*

1825 Coxe's Store opened; post office established; **March 19–21, 1865** Confederates under Gen. Joseph E. Johnston suffer 2,606 casualties compared to 1,646 Union casualties under General Sherman in Battle of Bentonville to north, Confederate defeat last major battle of Civil War; **1879** town incorporated; **1927** Bentonville Battle monument built.

North Wilkesboro *Wilkes County* *See* **Wilkesboro (1917)**

Ocracoke *Hyde County* *Eastern North Carolina, 160 mi/257 km east-southeast of Raleigh*

1680s town founded on Ocracoke Island, in Outer Banks at site of Native American community of Wococon; **1700s** large shipping storage warehouses maintained here; **1718** Blackbeard the Pirate killed in battle; **1803** Ocracoke Lighthouse built, destroyed by lightning 1818, rebuilt 1823; **1904** Coast Guard Station established; **1933** town inundated by hurricane; **Aug. 17, 1937** Cape Hatteras National Seashore authorized, includes Ocracoke Island.

Oxford   *Granville County*   *Northern North Carolina, 35 mi/56 km north of Raleigh*

c.1711 first settlers arrive from Virginia; 1746 Granville County formed; village of Granville Court House becomes county seat; 1760 area settled; 1764 former Bute County separates from Granville County, becomes Warren and Franklin counties; 1811 town founded as county seat; 1816 town incorporated; 1817 Oxford Academy established, closed 1880; 1838 county courthouse built; 1851 Horner Military School established, moved to Charlotte 1914; 1860s tobacco production begins; 1866 North Carolina's first warehouse devoted to curing tobacco built.

Pineville   *Mecklenburg County*   *Southern North Carolina, 12 mi/19 km south of Charlotte*

1761 Thomas Spratt family become first settlers; Nov. 2, 1795 James Knox Polk, 11th President, born (died June 15, 1849); 1852 Charlotte, Columbia & Augusta Railway reaches town; town founded; post office established; 1873 town incorporated; 1892 Dover Yarn Mill established.

Pittsboro   *Chatham County*   *Central North Carolina, 30 mi/48 km west of Raleigh*

1770 Chatham County formed; 1771 town founded by settlers from Cape Fear, named Chatham Courthouse; July 16, 1781 town raided by party of Tories led by David Fleming, 44 Whig leaders captured; 1787 Pittsborough Scientific Academy established, built 1886; town incorporated, name eventually altered to become Pittsboro; 1790 Aspen Hall built, home of Joseph "Chatham Jack" Alston; c.1810 Alston-Degraffenried House built by Joseph Alston for son John; July 13, 1824 Confederate naval commander James Iredell Waddell born (died 1886); 1833 St. Bartholomew's Episcopal Church built; 1882 fourth county courthouse built; 1907 Confederate statue erected.

Plymouth   *Washington County*   *Eastern North Carolina, 107 mi/172 km east of Raleigh*

1745 town site first settled; 1780 Arthur Rhodes of Plymouth, Massachusetts, donates land for town site; town founded; 1799 Washington County formed; Lee's Mill becomes first county seat; 1807 town incorporated; 1823 county seat moved to Plymouth; July 30, 1838 theatrical producer Agustin Daly born (died 1899); 1842 Grace Episcopal Church organized, built c.1860; c.1860 twelve sycamore trees planted on grounds of Grace Church, individually named for the Apostles, Judas tree later struck by lightning; 1864 town captured by Gen. R. F. Hoke's Confederate forces; 1980s last of the Apostle Trees removed for safety concerns.

Princeville   *Edgecombe County*   *Eastern North Carolina, 63 mi/101 km east of Raleigh*

1861 Powell House mansion built; 1865 town founded by ex-slaves, originally named Freedom Hill; 1885 town incorporated; Sept. 1999 Hurricane Floyd destroys most of town, total 49 killed in region over two week period.

Raeford   *Hoke County*   *Southern North Carolina, 65 mi/105 km south-southwest of Raleigh*

Sept. 1, 1781 Tories under Col. David Fanning kill 19 Whig patriots under Col. Daniel Wade, capture 54 in Battle of McFall's Mill to south; 1855 Bethel Presbyterian Church built to southwest, organized c.1780; 1867 town site settled; 1899 Aberdeen & Rockfish Railroad reaches site; town founded; 1901 town incorporated; 1907 North Carolina Sanatorium established; 1911 Hoke County formed, named for Confederate Gen. Robert F. Hoke; town becomes county seat; county courthouse built; 1934 Hoke County Library founded.

Raleigh   *Wake County*   *East central North Carolina, near Neuse River*

1771 Wake County formed from parts of Cumberland, Johnson, and Orange counties; town founded as county seat, named Wake Courthouse; 1788 site chosen for state capital; 1792 town platted by state Sen. William Christmas, becomes state capital; 1792 town incorporated as Raleigh; 1799 Haywood Hall house built; 1801 Raleigh Academy founded; 1803 incorporated as a city; c.1803 Indian Tree Tavern opens; 1804 Casso's Inn opens; Apr. 10, 1806 Confederate Gen. Leonidas Polk born, died June 14, 1864, at Pine Mountain, Georgia; Dec. 29, 1808 Andrew Johnson, 17th President, born (died July 15, 1875); 1816 First Presbyterian Church organized, used as interim state capitol 1831–1840; 1831 third town fire destroys statehouse (also 1818, 1821); 1840 state capitol completed; 1846 Raleigh Guards organized, serve in Mexican War; 1853 Christ Episcopal Church built; 1854 Richard B. Haywood House built; 1865 Shaw University established; Apr. 14, 1865 Union General Sherman's forces occupy city; 1867 St. Augustine's College established; 1872 Peace Junior College for Women established; 1884 St. Paul African Methodist Episcopal Church built; 1887 North Carolina State University established; 1891 Meredith College established; c.1900 cotton and knitting mills established; 1913 state supreme court building completed; 1923 state agricultural building built; 1924 Sacred Heart Cathedral built; 1931 North Carolina School for Negro Deaf and Blind Children founded; 1932 Memorial Auditorium built; 1935 Richard B. Harrison Library founded; 1937 William B. Umstead State Park established to west; 1938 state office building built; 1943 Raleigh-Durham International Airport established; 1950s Research Triangle Park established to northeast to advance state's technological development; 1956 North Carolina Museum of Art opened; 1958 Wake Technical Community College established; 1977 Raleigh Convention Center opened; Nov. 2, 1984 Velma Barfield executed by lethal injection, first woman executed in U.S. in 22 years; **1991** 24-story First Union Capital Square building completed; **1999** Exploris Museum opened.

Roanoke Rapids   *Halifax County   Northeastern North Carolina, 72 mi/116 km northeast of Raleigh*

1893 town founded on Roanoke River by industrialists John Armstrong Chaloner and John Emry as site for cotton mills; **1897** town incorporated; **1900** Rosemary textile mill established outside of town; **Apr. 1, 1928** actor George Grizzard born; **1931** incorporated as a city; Rosemary annexed; **1962** Lake Gaston formed by dam on Roanoke River.

Robbinsville   *Graham County   Western North Carolina, 73 mi/117 km west-southwest of Asheville*

March 29, 1814 in Battle of Horseshoe Bend between Creeks and U.S. troops, Chief Junalaska spares life of Andrew Jackson, later regrets move when forced to live in Oklahoma 1838; **1843** post office established, originally named Cheoah Valley; **1858** Chief Junalaska dies at nearly 100 years of age, buried here; **1872** Graham County formed, named for U.S. Sen. William A. Graham; town becomes county seat; **1893** town incorporated as Robinsville, altered as Robbinsville 1897; **1942** county courthouse built; **Jan. 16, 1944** country singer Ronnie Milsap born.

Rockingham   *Richmond County   Southern North Carolina, 93 mi/150 km southwest of Raleigh*

1779 Richmond County formed; Zion becomes county seat; **1784** new town founded at Zion town site; **1833** cotton mill established; **1865** mill burned by Union forces, rebuilt 1869, burned 1972; **1887** town incorporated; **1923** county courthouse built; **1965** Richmond Technical Institute established; **Oct. 1965** North Carolina Speedway opened.

Rocky Mount   *Nash and Edgecombe counties   Eastern North Carolina, 48 mi/77 km east of Raleigh*

1818 Rocky Mount Cotton Mills founded at the Falls of the Tar River by Joel Battle; town founded; **1839** Lewis Home built; **1845** Wilmington & Weldon Railroad reaches town; **1863** cotton mills burned by Union troops, rebuilt 1871; **1867** town incorporated; **1880s** tobacco industry introduced; **Oct. 10, 1917** jazz pianist Theolonius Monk born (died 1982): **1923** Braswell Memorial Library founded; **Oct. 11, 1926** actor Earle Hyman born; **1956** North Carolina Wesleyan University established; **1967** Nash Community College (2-year) established.

Roxboro   *Person County   Northern North Carolina, 45 mi/72 km north-northwest of Raleigh*

1791 Person County formed, named for Revolutionary Gen. Thomas Person; **1793** town founded as county seat; **1855** town incorporated; **1880s** tobacco industry moves into area; **1899** Roxboro Cotton Mill established; **1930** county courthouse built; **1970** Piedmont Community College established.

Rutherfordton   *Rutherford County   Western North Carolina, 65 mi/105 km west of Charlotte*

1768 Brittain Presbyterian Church organized; **1779** Rutherford County formed; **1787** town founded as county seat, named for Revolutionary Gen. Griffith Rutherford; **1790** gold discovered, mining subsides 1848 with California gold rush; **1793** town incorporated; **1831** Bechtler's Mint established, closed 1849; **1926** county courthouse built.

Salisbury   *Rowan County   Central North Carolina, 35 mi/56 km northeast of Charlotte*

1740s settlers of German descent arrive from Pennsylvania; **c.1760** St. John's Lutheran Church organized, built c.1768; **1753** Rowan County formed; town founded as county seat; **1755** town incorporated; **Nov. 6, 1787** Andrew Jackson admitted to bar; **July 5, 1846** writer Frances Fisher Tiernan, pen name Christian Reid, born (died 1920) **1851** Catawba College established; **1861** Salisbury Prison established for Confederate deserters and Union prisoners, up to 10,000 by 1864; **1875** old courthouse built; **1909** Confederate monument erected; **1925** Catawba College moved from Newton, founded 1852; **1926** county courthouse built; **July 29, 1936** Sen. Elizabeth Dole born, wife of Kansas Sen. Robert Dole; **1963** Rowan-Cabarrus Community College established.

Sanford   *Lee County   Central North Carolina, 36 mi/58 km southwest of Raleigh*

1760 Pine Knots house built, home of Isaac Brooks; **c.1820** Shallow Well Christian Church built; **1872** Raleigh & Augusta Air Line Railroad built; town founded, named for railroad engineer Col. Charles O. Sanford; **1874** town incorporated; **1908** Lee County formed; town becomes county seat; county courthouse built; **1913** Central Carolina Hospital founded, new facility built 1981; **1962** Central Carolina Community College established.

Shelby   *Cleveland County   Southern North Carolina, 40 mi/64 km west of Charlotte*

c.1720s first settlers arrive; **1841** Cleveland County formed; town founded as county seat, named for Col. Isaac Shelby; **1843** town incorporated; **Jan. 11, 1864** minister, author Thomas Dixon born, wrote book *The Klansmen* on which movie *Birth of a Nation* based (died 1946); **1880s** Cleveland Springs, originally Sulphur Springs, becomes popular resort, to east; **1907** county courthouse built; **Jan. 4, 1935** heavyweight boxer Floyd Patterson born at rural Waco to northeast; **1965** Cleveland Community College established; **1974** new county courthouse built.

Smithfield *Johnston County* *East central North Carolina, 26 mi/42 km southeast of Raleigh*

c.1740 area first settled by Col. John Smith of Virginia; **1746** Johnston County formed, named for Gabriel Johnston, colonial governor; Clayton becomes county seat; **1759** ferry established by Smith; **1770** town founded at head of navigation on Neuse River; **1771** county seat moved from Clayton; **1774** meetings held at courthouse condemning British tyranny; **1777** town incorporated; **1921** county courthouse built; **Dec. 24, 1922** actress Ava Gardner born (died 1990); **1941** Smithfield Library founded; **1969** Johnston Community College established.

Snow Hill *Greene County* *Eastern North Carolina, 60 mi/97 km southeast of Raleigh*

1711 John Lawson, surveyor general responsible for taking lands from Native Americans for North Carolina, is brought to Native American town of Catechna, tortured and killed; **March 20–23, 1713** in battle with Tuscaroras at Contentnea Creek, Col. Maurice Moore deprives Native Americans of power, are later sent to New York to join the Five Nations; **1791** Glasgow County formed; **1799** county renamed for Revolutionary Gen. Nathanael Greene; **1811** town founded as county seat; **1828** town incorporated; **1935** third county courthouse built.

South Mills *Camden County* *Northeastern North Carolina, 138 mi/224 km east-northeast of Raleigh*

c.1800 town founded as New Lebanon; **c.1800** Halfway House stage stop, built on North Carolina-Virginia boundary; **1820** Dismal Swamp Canal built parallel to coast connecting Albermarle Sound with Chesapeake Bay; **1839** town renamed South Mills; **1840s** Abbott plantation house built by William Riley Abbott; **Apr. 19, 1862** in Battle of South Mills (Sawyers' Lane), Union troops prevented from blowing up locks of Dismal Swamp Canal; **1883** town incorporated; **Apr. 1989** Dismal Swamp Visitor Center opened, new building completed 1996.

Southport *Brunswick County* *Southeastern North Carolina, 135 mi/217 km south-southeast of Raleigh*

1764 Brunswick County formed; town of Brunswick becomes county seat; **1792** town founded on Atlantic Ocean, originally named Smithville; **1764** Fort Johnston built, burned 1775, rebuilt; **1779** county seat moved to John Brill Plantation; **1796** Bald Head Lighthouse built, present structure built 1817, decommissioned 1935; **1808** county seat moved to Smithville; **1821** Fort Caswell built to south, seized by Confederates 1861, abandoned 1865; **1861** Fort Johnston seized by Confederates; **1887** town renamed Southport; **1977** county seat moved to Bolivia.

Sparta *Alleghany County* *Northwestern North Carolina, 55 mi/89 km northwest of Winston-Salem*

1825 post office established as Bower's Store, renamed Gap Civil 1846; **1859** Alleghany County formed from Ashe County; town founded as county seat; **1879** town incorporated, renamed Sparta; **1910** county courthouse built, burned 1933, rebuilt same year; **1992** first Mountain Heritage Festival held.

Statesville *Iredell County* *West central North Carolina, 42 mi/68 km southwest of Winston-Salem*

1750 Fourth Creek Presbyterian Meeting House established; **1788** Iredell County formed; **1789** town founded as county seat; **1795** Fort Dobbs built; **1822** Ebenezer Academy founded, closed 1856, remains public school until 1903, oldest schoolhouse in North Carolina; **1847** town incorporated; **1855** Bethany Presbyterian Church built to north, organized 1775; **1856** Mitchell College for Women established, renamed Mitchell Community College 1973; **1899** county courthouse built; **1930** Central Piedmont Soil Erosion Experimental Farm established.

Swan Quarter *Hyde County* *Eastern North Carolina, 135 mi/217 km east of Raleigh, on Pamlico Sound*

1705 Hyde precinct incorporated in Bath County; **1739** Hyde County formed; Woodstock becomes county seat (seat moved to Germantown 1790, to Lake Landing 1820); **c.1812** town founded; **1836** town becomes county seat; **1850** county courthouse built; **Aug. 1876** storm surge sweeps through town after completion of Methodist Church, church only building moved off its foundation, renamed Providence Church; **1903** town incorporated, repealed 1929; **1915** pumping station built to drain Lake Mattamuskeet for farmland, converted to hunting lodge 1930s.

Sylva *Jackson County* *Western North Carolina, 43 mi/69 km west-southwest of Asheville*

1851 Jackson County formed; Webster becomes first county seat; **1899** town incorporated, named for William Sylva, Danish settler; **1913** county seat moved to Sylva; **1914** county courthouse built; **1964** Southwestern Community College established; **1994** county administration building completed.

Tarboro *Edgecombe County* *Eastern North Carolina, 62 mi/100 km east of Raleigh, on Tar River*

1735 Edgecombe County formed; **1741** county organized; **1745** Enfield becomes first county seat; **1757** Halifax County separates from Edgecombe County, includes Enfield; **1760** town platted and incorporated as new county seat; **1787** state legislature meets here, one of several towns to host early legislative sessions; **1867** Calvary Episcopal Church completed, begun 1860, delayed by Civil War; **1964** county courthouse built; **1968** Edgecombe Community College established; **Sept. 1999** Hurricane Floyd devastates region with heavy rains, high winds, flooding.

Taylorsville *Alexander County* *West central North Carolina, 50 mi/80 km north-northwest of Charlotte*

c. 1745 area first settled; **1847** Alexander County formed, named for Gov. Nathaniel Alexander (1805–1807); town founded as county seat; **1879** town incorporated; **c.1900** Lucas Mansion built; **1902** county courthouse built; **1970** new county courthouse built, previous structure destroyed by fire.

Thomasville *Davidson County* *Central North Carolina, 16 mi/26 km south-southeast of Winston-Salem*

1852 town founded; **1855** North Carolina Railroad reaches town; **1856** Thomasville Female College established, closed 1888; **1857** town incorporated; **1870s** manufacture of furniture begins, grows to at least seven factories by 1905; **1895** Heidelburg Reformed Church built; **c.1920** cotton, rayon, and silk mills established; **1922** Big Chair monument erected honoring furniture industry.

Trenton *Jones County* *Southeastern North Carolina, 90 mi/145 km southeast of Raleigh*

1779 Jones County formed; town founded as county seat, originally named Trent; **1784** town renamed Trenton; **1790** Lees United Methodist Chapel organized; **1791** George Washington's Southern Tour brings him to Shine's Tavern 7 mi/11.3 km to southwest; **1874** town incorporated; **1939** county courthouse built.

Troy *Montgomery County* *Central North Carolina, 55 mi/89 km east of Charlotte*

1778 Montgomery County formed, separates from Anson County; **1816** Laurenceville becomes first permanent county seat; **1843** Troy founded as new county seat; **1852** town incorporated; **1921** county courthouse built.

Tryon *Polk County* See **Columbus (1933)**

Waco *Cleveland County* See **Shelby (1935)**

Wadesboro *Anson County* *Southern North Carolina, 47 mi/76 km east-southeast of Charlotte*

1748 Anson County formed; **1755** Mount Pleasant becomes county seat, site to northeast; **1783** town founded, named New Town; **1785** town incorporated; **1787** town becomes county seat, renamed for Col. Thomas Wade of Revolutionary War; **1900** scientists converge on town to observe solar eclipse; **1914** county courthouse built.

Wake Forest *Wake County* *North central North Carolina, 15 mi/24 km north-northeast of Raleigh*

c.1788 Isaac Hunter's Tavern opened; **1833** Wake Forest College, now University, established; town founded around college; **1880** town incorporated; **1950** Southeastern Baptist Theological Seminary established.

Warrenton *Warren County* *Northeastern North Carolina, 53 mi/85 km north-northeast of Raleigh*

1779 Warren County formed; town founded and incorporated as county seat; county and town named for Gen. Joseph Warren of Massachusetts, killed in Battle of Bunker Hill; **1783** first county courthouse built; **c.1800** Bragg House built by Thomas Bragg; **March 22, 1817** Confederate Gen. Braxton Bragg born (died 1876); **1824** Emmanuel Episcopal Church completed; **July 5, 1836** newspaper publisher Horace Greeley marries Mary Cheney at Emmanuel Church; **1843** Eaton Place mansion built by William Eaton, Sr.; **1906** current county courthouse built.

Washington *Beaufort County* *Eastern North Carolina, 90 mi/145 km east of Raleigh*

1705 Pamtecough Precinct (County) formed; **1712** county renamed Beaufort; **1771** town founded, named Forks of Tar River by James Bonner; **c.1776** town renamed, first town in U.S. to be named for George Washington; **1782** town incorporated; **1785** county seat moved from Bath; **1864** town nearly destroyed by two fires set during Civil War action; **1868** St. Peter's Episcopal Church built; **1923** Washington Field Museum founded; **1967** Beaufort County Community College established; **1972** county courthouse built.

Waxhaw *Union County* *Southern North Carolina, 23 mi/37 km south of Charlotte*

March 15, 1767 Pres. Andrew Jackson born to southwest on South Carolina border, probably in South Carolina (died June 8, 1845); **1888** railroad reaches site; town founded; **1889** town incorporated; **1963** Jungle Aviation and Radio Service incorporated, missionary service to Central America, for Wyckliffe Bible Institute, Dallas.

Waynesville *Haywood County* *Western North Carolina, 26 mi/42 km west of Asheville*

1800 area settled, originally named Mount Prospect; **1808** Haywood County formed, named for State Treasurer John Haywood; **1809** town founded as county seat; **May 8, 1865** Gen. James G. Martin surrenders the army of western North Carolina, last organized Confederate force in state; **1871** town incorporated; **1879** White Sulphur Springs Hotel built by William W. Stringfield; **1932** county courthouse built; **1995** Hazelwood annexed by Waynesville.

Wentworth   *Rockingham County*   *Northern North Carolina, 22 mi/35 km north of Greensboro*

1770 Speedwell Iron Works open; **1785** Rockingham County formed; **1787** town founded as county seat on land owned by Charles Mitchell, originally named Rockingham Court House; **1798** town incorporated as Wentworth; **1799** town platted; **1816** Cunningham (Patrick) Mill built, later served as haven for Ku Klux Klan activities; Wright Tavern built; **1907** county courthouse built; **1964** Rockingham Community College established.

Whiteville   *Columbus County*   *Southeastern North Carolina, 100 mi/161 km south of Raleigh*

1781 Truce Land set aside near South Carolina boundary as refuge for noncombatants during Revolutionary War; **1808** Columbus County formed; **1810** town founded as county seat on land owned by James B. White, named White's Crossing; **1833** town incorporated, renamed Whiteville; **1868** the Memory grape introduced by horticulturist Col. T. S. Memory; **1915** third county courthouse completed; **1964** Southeastern Community College established.

Wilkesboro   *Wilkes County*   *West central North Carolina, 50 mi/64 km west of Winston-Salem*

c.1754 area settled by Moravian immigrants; **1778** Wilkes County formed; town founded as county seat; **1801** town platted; **1803** Cowles House built; **1847** town incorporated; **1849** St. Paul's Episcopal Church built; **1902** county courthouse built; **Nov. 20, 1917** U.S. Sen. Robert Carlyle Byrd of West Virginia born at North Wilkesboro; **1965** Wilkes Community College established; **1998** new county courthouse built.

Williamston   *Martin County*   *Eastern North Carolina, 90 mi/145 km east of Raleigh*

c.1730 town settled, originally named Skewarky; **1774** Martin County formed, named for Lt. Gov. Josiah Martin; town becomes county seat; **1779** town incorporated; town named Williamstown for Col. William Williams of Martin County militia, name evolves to become Williamston; **1780** Skewarky Baptist Church organized; **1835** Asa Biggs House built; **1882** Coastline Railroad reaches town; **1922** highway bridge built across Roanoke River; **Sept. 15, 1938** San Francisco Giants baseball player Gaylord Perry born; **1983** county courthouse built.

Wilmington   *New Hanover County*   *Southeastern North Carolina, 117 mi/188 km south-southeast of Raleigh*

1665 settlers arrive from Barbados; **1725** first plantations established; **1729** New Hanover County formed; Brunswick becomes first county seat, site on west side of Cape Fear River; **1733** town founded on east side of river, named Newton; **1739** county seat moved to Newton; **1745** Fort Johnston built as defense against pirates, completed 1764; **1747** town renamed Wilmington; **1751** St. James Episcopal Church established; **1770s** Cornwallis House built for British Gen. Charles Cornwallis; **Feb. 27, 1776** patriots defeat regiment of Scottish Highlanders at Moores Creek to northwest, first American victory on North Carolina soil; **June 29, 1781** town occupied by Cornwallis, used as staging point for raids; **Sept. 28, 1785** African-American abolitionist David Walker born (died 1830); **Nov. 19, 1811** Confederate naval officer John Ancrum Winslow born (died 1873); **1834** Wilmington & Weldon Railroad chartered; **1835** Dudley Mansion completed; **1845** St. Thomas Catholic Church built **1852** Light Infantry Armory built; **1859** Bellamy Mansion built by James F. Post; **1862** blockade runners bring yellow fever from Nassau killing hundreds; **1865** Fort Fisher captured by Union forces, had protected blockade runners; **Sept. 23, 1867** *Wilmington Star*, North Carolina's oldest newspaper, founded; **1876** Temple Israel built, first Jewish synagogue in North Carolina; **1892** county courthouse built; **1895** Red Shirts clan formed to overthrow carpetbagger government; **Nov. 10, 1898** black-owned newspaper *Daily Record* burned following shooting of white man; **1913** St. Mary's Cathedral completed; **July 10, 1920** newscaster David Brinkley born (died 2003); **June 2, 1926** Moores Creek National Battlefield established to northwest; **Sept. 10, 1934** TV journalist Charles Kuralt born (died 1997); **Oct. 28, 1936** singer Charlie Daniels born; **1947** University of North Carolina at Wilmington established; **1959** Cape Fear Community College established; **Sept. 6, 1996** Hurricane Fran hits Cape Fear with 115 mph/185 kph winds, tornadoes to north, 28 killed, $1 billion damage; **Sept. 16, 1999** Hurricane Floyd causes widespread flooding in eastern third of state, 40 killed.

Wilson   *Wilson County*   *Eastern North Carolina, 42 mi/68 km east of Raleigh*

1765 Toignot Baptist Church established; town of Hickory Grove develops around church; **1849** town incorporated as Wilson; **1855** Wilson County formed; town becomes county seat; **Sept. 26, 1878** Robert Digges Wimberly Connor born, first U.S. Archivist (died 1950); **1902** Barton College established, originally named Atlantic Christian College; **1924** second county courthouse built; **1958** Wilson Technical Community College established.

Windsor   *Bertie County*   *Northeastern North Carolina, 97 mi/156 km east of Raleigh*

1722 Bertie County formed; Hoggard's Mill becomes county seat; **1750s** tobacco production becomes important; Gray's Landing established; **1768** town founded at landing; **1774** county seat moved to Windsor; **c.1800** Oak Grove Academy founded; **1847** town incorporated; **1858** Windsor Castle built by Patrick Henry Winston on site of eight-room log cabin; **1856** Rosefield Homestead built; **1887** county courthouse built, cupola added 1899.

Winston-Salem *Forsyth County* *Central North Carolina, 92 mi/145 km west-northwest of Raleigh*

Nov. 1753 town of Bethabara founded in what is now northwest part of city, first Moravian settlement in North Carolina; **Jan. 1766** town of Salem established by Moravian settlers (first house stood until 1907); **1768** original section of Brothers House built; **1772** Salem College established, originally Salem Academy; **1773** Matthew Micksch becomes town's first tobacconist; **1781–1782** Continental Army troops continually raid area for supplies; **1784** Salem Tavern built; **1787** Nissen Wagon Plant established; **1788** Bethabara Church built; **1797** Salem Land Office Building built; **1800** Home Moravian Church dedicated; **1836** first cotton mill established; **1849** Forsyth County formed; **1851** town north of Salem platted for county seat, named Winston; **1856** *Twin City Sentinel* newspaper founded as the *Western Sentinel*; **1856** town of Salem incorporated; giant Coffee Pot erected by Julius Mickey as advertisement for his tin shop; **1859** town of Winston incorporated; **1872** Winston-Salem Tobacco Market opens; **1875** R. J. Reynolds builds area's first tobacco factory; Western North Carolina Railroad reaches town; **1882** Dixie Classic Fair first held, new fairgrounds opened 1952; **1892** Winston-Salem State University established; **1897** county courthouse built; *Winston-Salem Journal* newspaper founded; **1913** cities of Salem and Winston merge; **1919** Maynard Field airport established; **March 25, 1920** sports announcer Howard Cosell born (died 1995); **March 27, 1921** actor Harold Nicholas born (died 2000); **Feb. 9, 1922** actress Kathryn Grayson born; **1924** R. J. Reynolds Memorial Auditorium built; **1927** 18-story Nissen Building built; **1933** Miller Municipal Airport established; **1956** Wake Forest College moved from Wake County near Raleigh, established 1834, becomes University 1961; Southeastern Center for Contemporary Art opened; **1962** Sci-Works environmental park founded; **1964** Forsyth Technical Community College established; North Carolina School of the Arts established; **1965** 30-story Wachovia Bank building completed; **1989** Lawrence Joel Veterans Memorial Coliseum opened.

Winton *Hertford County* *Northeastern North Carolina, 105 mi/169 km northeast of Raleigh*

c.1685 Meherrin peoples inhabit area, through 1727; **1710** first white settlers arrive; **1729** Meherrin Baptist Church organized; **1754** town founded, named for landowner Benjamin Wynns; **1759** Hertford County formed, named for Marquis of Hertford; **1766** town incorporated, becomes county seat; **1956** county courthouse completed.

Yadkinville *Yadkin County* *Central North Carolina, 25 mi/40 km west of Winston-Salem*

1850 Yadkin County formed, separates from Surry County; town founded on Yadkin River as county seat, originally named Wilson; **1852** town renamed; **1857** town incorporated; **1862** courthouse and most of town burned by Federal troops, first town in North Carolina to be burned during Civil War; **1959** second county courthouse built.

Yanceyville *Caswell County* *Northern North Carolina, 56 mi/90 km northwest of Raleigh*

1777 Caswell County formed; Leasburg becomes first county seat; **1791** town founded as new county seat, named Caswell Court House; **c.1822** Gatewood House built; **1833** town renamed for Cong. Bartlett Yancey; **1861** county courthouse built; **1870** carpetbagger John W. Stephens slain in basement of courthouse by Ku Klux Klan amid reign of terror by Klan, leads to Kirk-Holden War, impeachment of Gov. William Holden 1871; **1906** town incorporated.

North Dakota

Northern U.S. Capital: Bismarck. Largest city: Fargo.

The region entered the U.S. as part of the Louisiana Purchase December 30, 1803. Dakota Territory was established March 2, 1861. Both North Dakota and South Dakota entered the U.S. jointly as the 39th and 40th states November 2, 1889.

North Dakota is divided into 53 counties. The counties are divided into townships which do not have governments. The municipalities had been classified as villages, towns, and cities until 1969, when a state statute declared all villages and towns as cities, eliminating any classification. See Introduction.

Abercrombie *Richland County* *Southeastern North Dakota, 31 mi/50 km south of Fargo, near Red River*

1858 Fort Abercrombie built on Red River; **1859** *Anson Northrup* reaches fort from Fort Garry, Manitoba, first steamboat to ply waters of Red River; **Sept. 1862** fort besieged for five weeks during Dakota Conflict; **1878** fort closed; **1884** town founded; **1904** incorporated as a village; **1967** incorporated as a statutory city.

Amidon *Slope County* *Southwestern North Dakota, 128 mi/206 km west-southwest of Bismarck*

c.1900 burning coal vein to north encountered by white settlers, integrated into Native American legend, original cause probably lightning strike; **1910** town founded, named for Judge Charles F. Amidon; **1915** Slope County formed; town becomes county seat, **1917** county courthouse built; **1918** incorporated as a village; **1967** incorporated as a statutory city.

Ashley *McIntosh County* *Southern North Dakota, 143 mi/230 km southwest of Fargo*

1883 McIntosh County formed; town of Hoskins founded as county seat on Lake Hoskins; **1888** Minneapolis, St. Paul & Sault Ste. Marie Railroad built to east; new town founded on railroad, named for railroad official Ashley E. Morrow; **1903** incorporated as a village; **1920** incorporated as a city; **1921** county courthouse completed.

Beach *Golden Valley County* *Western North Dakota, 160 mi/257 km west of Bismarck*

1880 Northern Pacific Railroad built; town founded, named for Capt. Warren Beach, railroad surveyor; **1907** incorporated as a village; **1912** Golden Valley County formed; town becomes county seat; incorporated as a city; **1923** county courthouse built.

Belcourt *Rolette County* *Northern North Dakota, 146 mi/235 km northwest of Grand Forks*

1882 Turtle Mountain Indian Reservation established for Chippewa peoples; **1883** town founded in reservation, named Turtle Mountain; **1888** town renamed for founder, Catholic priest Rev. George Antoine Belcourt; **1980s** Turtle Mountain Casino opened; **1988** Turtle Mountain Heritage Center founded; **1997** Sky Dancer Casino opened.

Bismarck *Burleigh County* *Central North Dakota, 190 mi/306 km west of Fargo, on Missouri River*

1863 Gen. Henry Sibley fights Dakotas at Sibley Island, Missouri River; **1872** Camp Hancock established to protect railroad workers; town founded, named Edwinton for engineer Edwin F. Johnson; **1873** Burleigh County formed, named for railroad official Dr. Walter Burleigh; town becomes county seat, renamed Bismarck; *Bismarck Tribune* newspaper founded; Northern Pacific Railroad completed; **1875** incorporated as a city; **Dec. 1875** Ben Ash blazes Bismarck Trail to Black Hills, timber supply route to plains towns; **1879** Northern Pacific Railroad extended to west; **1882** railroad bridge built across river; **1883** territorial capital moved from Yankton (South Dakota); **1884** Asa Fisher House built, becomes governor's mansion 1893, new mansion built 1960; **1889** North Dakota State Penitentiary completed; **Nov. 2, 1889** North Dakota enters Union as 39th state; city becomes state capital; **1896** Fort Lincoln military reservation established, served as German and Japanese internment camp 1941–1946; **1922** Memorial Bridge built across Missouri River, first highway span across river in North Dakota; **1924** Liberty Memorial Building opened; **1931** county courthouse built; Bismarck Airport (Straus Field) established; **1932** 19-story State Capitol built; **1939** Bismarck Community College established; **1959** University of Mary established; **1965** Bismarck Civic Center built; **1969** United Tribes Technical College established; **1981** North Dakota Heritage Center opened.

Bottineau *Bottineau County* *Northern North Dakota, 148 mi/238 km north of Bismarck*

1873 Bottineau County formed; **1884** county organized; town founded as county seat, named for Pierre Bottineau; **1885** Great Northern Railroad built 1 mi/1.6 km from town site; town moved; **1886** prairie fire sweeps large area to north destroying fields and buildings; **1888** incorporated as a village; **1904** incorporated as a city; **1968** State School of Forestry established, becomes North Dakota State University-Bottineau 1987; **1976** county courthouse built.

Bowbells *Burke County* *Northern North Dakota, 163 mi/262 km north-northwest of Bismarck*

1896 Minneapolis, St. Paul & Sault Ste. Marie Railroad built; town founded, named by English stockholders for the Bow Bells in St. Mary-le-Bow Church, London; **1906** incorporated as a city; **1910** Burke County formed; town becomes county seat; **1927** county courthouse built.

Bowman *Bowman County* *Southwestern North Dakota, 140 mi/225 km southwest of Bismarck*

1883 Bowman County formed; **1907** county organized; town founded as county seat following bitter dispute with Atkinson (Griffin); town originally named Lowden, later Twin Buttes; **1908** incorporated as a village, renamed Bowman for legislator E. W. Bowman; **1966** Bowman Haley Lake formed by dam to southeast on North Fork Grand River; **1967** incorporated as a statutory city; **1972** county courthouse built; **1992** Pioneer Trails Museum established.

Cando *Towner County* *Northeastern North Dakota, 145 mi/233 km northeast of Bismarck*

1883 Towner County formed; **1884** town founded as county seat, named by County Chairman P. P. Parker; **1888** Great Northern Railroad reaches town; **1894** Dunkard Colony founded to east by members of German sect Baptist Brethren; **1898** county courthouse built; **1901** incorporated as a town; **1967** incorporated as a statutory city.

Carrington *Foster County* *East central North Dakota, 95 mi/153 km northeast of Bismarck*

1873 Foster County formed; **1882** town founded by M. D. Carrington; **1883** county organized; town becomes county

seat; **1900** incorporated as a town; **1909** county courthouse built; **1967** incorporated as a statutory city.

Carson *Grant County* *Southern North Dakota, 47 mi/76 km southwest of Bismarck*

1910 Great Northern Railroad built; town founded, named for settlers Frank Carter and Simon Pederson; **1916** Grant County formed; town becomes county seat; **1917** incorporated as a village; **1967** incorporated as a statutory city; **1981** county courthouse built.

Cavalier *Pembina County* *Northeastern North Dakota, 70 mi/113 km north-northwest of Grand Forks*

1867 Pembina County formed; Pembina becomes first county seat; **1875** town founded on Tongue River by settlers from Missouri, named for Rene Robert Cavalier, Sieur de la Salle; **1885** incorporated as a village; **1890** incorporated as a town; **1902** incorporated as a city; **1964** Icelandic State Park established to west; **1979** county courthouse built.

Center *Oliver County* *Central North Dakota, 34 mi/55 km northwest of Bismarck*

1829 Fort Clark trading post established to north on Missouri River; **1885** Oliver County formed; Sanger (Raymond) becomes county seat; **1902** town founded as new county seat; **1920** Hazel Miner, 16, caught in blizzard with younger brother and sister, Hazel's body found next morning shielding siblings, their lives saved by her; **1928** incorporated as a village; **1937** Log Cabin Museum built; **1967** incorporated as a statutory city; **1978** county courthouse built.

Cooperstown *Griggs County* *Eastern North Dakota, 77 mi/124 km northwest of Fargo*

1879 first cabin in county built by Omund Nels Opheim; **1880** brothers T. J. and Rollin C. Cooper arrive from goldfields of Colorado, begin farming; **1881** Griggs County formed; **1882** town founded as county seat by Cooper brothers; **1884** county courthouse built; **1892** incorporated as a village; **1906** incorporated as a city.

Crosby *Divide County* *Northwestern North Dakota, 198 mi/319 km northwest of Bismarck*

1904 town founded at junction of Great Northern Railroad and Soo Line; **1907** incorporated as a village; **1910** Divide County formed; town becomes county seat; **1917** county courthouse built; **1967** incorporated as a statutory city.

Devils Lake *Ramsey County* *East central North Dakota, 90 mi/145 km west of Grand Forks*

1867 Fort Totten Indian Agency established on southern shore of Devils Lake; **1873** Ramsey County formed; **1882** white settlers allowed to move into region held by Chippewas and Dakotas; town founded on lake as county seat, named Creelsburgh; **1883** Great Northern Railroad reaches town; **1884** town renamed Devils Lake; **1887** incorporated as a city; **1890** fort decommissioned; State School for the Deaf established; **1941** University of North Dakota, Lake Region Campus, (2-year) established; **1959** county courthouse built.

Dickinson *Stark County* *Western North Dakota, 100 mi/161 km west of Bismarck*

1879 Stark County formed; **1880** Northern Pacific Railroad built; **1882** town founded, named Pleasant Valley Siding; **1883** town renamed for merchant H. L. Dickinson; **1884** town becomes county seat; **1899** incorporated as a village; **1900** incorporated as a city; **June 21, 1900** actress Dorothy Stickney born (died 1998); **1905** North Dakota Agricultural Experiment Station established; **1908** Carnegie Library built; **1918** Dickinson State University established; **1937** county courthouse completed; **1943** Dickinson Airport established to south.

Edgeley *La Moure County* *Southeastern North Dakota, 110 mi/177 km southeast of Bismarck*

Sept. 3, 1863 in response to 1862 Dakota Conflict in Minnesota, Gen. Alfred Sully attacks band of Dakota in Battle of Whitstone Hill, 19 soldiers killed, 34 wounded, c.150 Dakota killed, Dakota band later found innocent in conflict; **1883** town founded; **1886** Chicago, Milwaukee, St. Paul & Pacific Railroad reaches town; **1906** Midland Continental Railroad reaches town; **1911** incorporated as a village; **Sept. 30, 1931** actress Angie Dickinson born at Kulm to southwest; **1967** incorporated as a statutory city.

Ellendale *Dickey County* *Southeastern North Dakota, 127 mi/204 km southeast of Bismarck*

1881 Dickey County formed; **1882** Chicago, Milwaukee, St. Paul & Pacific Railroad built; town founded as county seat; **1883** incorporated as a village; **1887** Northern Pacific Railroad reaches town; **1889** incorporated as a city; State Normal and Industrial School established, becomes University of North Dakota-Ellendale 1965, closed 1972; **1910** county courthouse built; **1973** Trinity Bible College established at former state university.

Fargo *Cass County* *Eastern North Dakota, 210 mi/338 km northwest of Minneapolis, on Red River*

1866 Father Genin Mission House founded on Red River to south; **1871** town founded by Northern Pacific Railroad at best crossing point of Red River, named for railroad director William G. Fargo; **1872** Headquarters Hotel built, destroyed by fire 1874, rebuilt; **June 8, 1872** first train crosses river into Fargo; **1873** Cass County formed; town becomes county seat; **1874** *Fargo Express* newspaper founded, becomes the *Forum*; **1875** incorporated as a city; **1887** Fargo College established, closed 1919; **1890** North Dakota State University established; **1893** opera house built; **June 1893** fire sweeps business area and northeast part of city; **Apr. 7, 1895** sculptor John

Bernard Flannagan born (died 1942); **spring 1897** flooding inundates city as ice blocks river; **1899** St. Mary's Cathedral completed; Headquarters Hotel destroyed by fire; **1903** First Lutheran Church built; **1906** county courthouse built; **1912** Gange Rolf monument erected in honor of Norse hero; **1917** Armour packing plant built at West Fargo; **1929** veterans' hospital built; **1930** county courthouse built; **1931** Hector Airport established; Fargo-Moorhead Symphony established; **1933** Good Samaritan School for Crippled Children founded; **Dec. 1992** Fargo Dome stadium opened.

Fessenden *Wells County* *Central North Dakota, 85 mi/137 km northeast of Bismarck*

1873 Wells County formed; **1884** Sykestown becomes county seat; **1893** Minneapolis, St. Paul & Sault Ste. Marie Railroad built; town founded, named for Cortez Fessenden, surveyor general of Dakota Territory; **1894** county seat moved to Fessenden; **1895** county courthouse built; **1904** incorporated as a village; **1905** incorporated as a city.

Finley *Steele County* *Eastern North Dakota, 69 mi/111 km northwest of Fargo*

1883 Steele County formed; Hope becomes county seat; **1885** county seat moved to Sherbrooke; **1897** town founded; **1903** incorporated as a village; **1919** county seat moved to Finley; **1926** incorporated as a city; county courthouse completed; **1950** Finley Air Force Base established, closed 1980.

Forman *Sargent County* *Southeastern North Dakota, 70 mi/113 km southwest of Fargo*

1883 Sargent County formed; Milnor becomes county seat; town founded by Cornelius Forman; **1886** county seat moved to Forman; **1889** incorporated as a village; **1910** county courthouse built; **1954** incorporated as a city.

Fort Totten *Benson County* *East central North Dakota, 95 mi/153 km west of Grand Forks*

1867 Fort Totten Indian Reservation established by treaty, later becomes Devils Lake Reservation; Fort Totten military post built, named for Gen. Gilbert Totten of U.S. Army Engineer Corps; town founded; **1874** St. Michael's Mission founded to east; **1890** fort decommissioned; **c.1998** reservation renamed Spirit Lake Indian Reservation.

Fort Yates *Sioux County* *Southern North Dakota, 52 mi/84 km south of Bismarck, on Missouri River*

1877 Fort Yates built on Missouri River; **1878** Standing Rock Indian Reservation established comprising Sioux County and neighboring Corson County, South Dakota; **Dec. 17, 1890** Sitting Bull buried here, killed by Native American police led by James McLaughlin, later reburied near Missouri River opposite Mobridge, South Dakota;

1914 Sioux County formed; 1915 town becomes county seat; 1981 county courthouse built; 1964 incorporated as a city.

Garrison *McLean County* *Central North Dakota, 69 mi/111 km north-northwest of Bismarck*

1844 Fort Berthold Trading Post built on Missouri River c.35 mi/56 km to west by Bartholomew Berthold; 1867 Fort Stevenson military post built to south on Missouri River; 1870 Fort Berthold Indian Reservation established to west for Arikara, Hidatsa, and Mandan people; 1905 town founded; 1907 incorporated as a village; 1916 incorporated as a city; 1956 Lake Sakakawea formed to south on Missouri River by Garrison Dam, extends west to Montana.

Grafton *Walsh County* *Northeastern North Dakota, 40 mi/64 km north-northwest of Grand Forks*

1879 post office established; 1881 Walsh County formed; town becomes county seat on Park River by settlers from Grafton County, New Hampshire; 1883 incorporated as a city; 1897 first public library in North Dakota established; 1903 Grafton State School founded; 1940 county courthouse built; 1997 Marvin Window and Door factory opened.

Grand Forks *Grand Forks County* *Eastern North Dakota, 203 mi/327 km east-northeast of Bismarck*

1801 fur trading depot founded on Red River by Alexander Henry, Jr.; 1868 Nicholas Hoffman and August Loon build cabin as overnight shelter; 1871 Capt. Alexander Griggs builds first permanent house, establishes sawmill; post office established; telegraph station established; 1873 Grand Forks County formed; Arlington House Hotel built by Hudson's Bay Company; 1875 town platted as county seat by Griggs; 1877 flour mill founded by Frank Viets; 1879 incorporated as a village; *Herald* newspaper founded by George Winship; 1881 incorporated as a city; 1883 University of North Dakota established; June 1887 tornado destroys many buildings, two killed; 1892 Wesley College established; 1897 flooding Red River inundates city; c.1900 Cream of Wheat hot cereal first manufactured; 1913 county courthouse built; 1906 Arlington-Park Hotel opened; 1910 Greater Grand Forks Symphony founded; 1919 Northern Packing Company established; 1922 North Dakota State Mill and Elevator opened; 1929 Sorlie Memorial Bridge built to East Grand Forks, Minnesota; 1935 large potato warehouse built; Sept. 26, 1947 country singer Lynn Anderson born; 1964 Grand Forks International Airport established to west; 1989 North Dakota Museum of Art opened; Apr. 19, 1997 Red River floods vast area, 50,000 evacuate Grand Forks, 8,500 in East Grand Forks; fire destroys flooded city block, including *Herald* newspaper building; 1999 six-story county office building completed.

Hettinger *Adams County* *Southwestern North Dakota, 110 mi/177 km southwest of Bismarck*

1907 Adams County formed from Hettinger County; Chicago, Milwaukee, St. Paul & Pacific Railroad built; town founded as county seat; 1916 incorporated as a town; 1929 county courthouse built; 1967 incorporated as a city.

Hillsboro *Traill County* *Eastern North Dakota, 40 mi/64 km north of Fargo, near Red River*

1870 Norwegian settlers arrive; 1875 Traill County formed; Caledonia becomes county seat; 1880 Great Northern Railroad built; town founded railroad, on Goose River; 1883 incorporated as a city; 1891 county seat moved to Hillsboro; 1907 county courthouse completed.

Jamestown *Stutsman County* *East central North Dakota, 105 mi/169 km east of Bismarck*

1871 Fort Seward built to protect railroad workers; town founded on James River; 1872 Northern Pacific Railroad reaches town; 1873 Stutsman County formed; town becomes county seat; 1877 fort abandoned; 1879 flour mill built by Anton Klaus; 1881 incorporated as a village; Presbyterian church built; 1883 incorporated as a city; Jamestown College established; old county courthouse built, oldest standing courthouse in state; 1885 North Dakota State Hospital established; Sept. 25, 1888 prairie fire devastates large area to south; 1901 Alfred Dickey Public Library founded, opened 1919; March 22, 1908 Western writer Louis L'Amour born (died 1988); 1918 county courthouse built; May 26, 1920 singer Peggy Lee born (died 2002); 1936 Park Auditorium built; 1945 Jamestown Airport established; 1953 Jamestown Reservoir (Jim Lake) formed by dam to north on James River; 1982 new county courthouse built.

Killdeer *Dunn County* *Western North Dakota, 105 mi/169 km northwest of Bismarck*

July 28, 1862 Gen. Alfred H. Sully's troops attack Dakotas, 5 soldiers killed, c.27 Dakota killed; 1914 Northern Pacific Railroad built; town founded; 1915 incorporated as a village; 1919 incorporated as a city; 1924 first annual Killdeer Mountain Roundup held, oldest rodeo in North Dakota.

Kulm *La Moure County* See **Edgeley (1931)**

La Moure *La Moure County* *Southeastern North Dakota, 130 mi/209 km east-southeast of Bismarck*

1873 La Moure County formed; 1881 county organized; Grand Rapids becomes county seat; Sept. 1881 prairie fire sweeps wide area to north; 1882 town platted on James River; 1883 railroad reaches site; incorporated as a town; 1886 county seat moved to La Moure; 1909 county courthouse built; 1967 incorporated as a statutory city.

Lakota   *Nelson County*   *Eastern North Dakota,*
63 mi/101 km west of Grand Forks

1880s Wamduska Hotel built on Lake Wamduska, now
Stump Lake, to south; **1883** Nelson County formed; town
founded as county seat; **1885** incorporated as a village;
1889 incorporated as a city; **1927** Tofthagen Library and
Museum built; **Aug. 9, 1945** railroad accident at town of
Michigan to east, 34 killed; **1951** county courthouse built.

Langdon   *Cavalier County*   *Northeastern North*
Dakota, 90 mi/145 km northwest of Grand Forks

1879 Cavalier County formed; **1884** county organized;
town founded as county seat; **1888** incorporated as a
town; **1957** county courthouse built; **1967** incorporated as
a statutory city.

Linton   *Emmons County*   *Southern North Dakota,*
47 mi/76 km southeast of Bismarck

1879 Emmons County formed; **1883** Williamsport
becomes county seat; town founded, named for settler
George W. Lynn; **1899** incorporated as a town; county
seat moved to Linton; **March 11, 1903** bandleader
Lawrence Welk born at Strasburg to south (died 1992);
1933 county courthouse built; **1967** incorporated as a
statutory city.

Lisbon   *Ransom County*   *Southeastern North*
Dakota, 54 mi/87 km southwest of Fargo

1873 Ransom County formed; **1878** first settlers arrive;
1880 town founded on Sheyenne River; **1881** county
organized; town becomes county seat; **1882** railroad
reaches town; **1883** incorporated as a town; **1938** county
courthouse built; **1967** incorporated as a statutory city.

Mandan   *Morton County*   *Central North Dakota,*
3 mi/4.8 km west of Bismarck, on Missouri River

1864 Fort Rice established to south on Missouri River by
Gen. Alfred H. Sully, closed 1877; **1872** Fort Abraham
Lincoln established, abandoned 1891; **May 17, 1876** Gen.
George A. Custer departs for Little Big Horn, Montana;
1873 Morton County formed; **1879** Northern Pacific
Railroad reaches site, trains ferried across river; town
founded as county seat; **1881** incorporated as a village;
1882 railroad bridge built; **1883** incorporated as a city;
1922 Memorial Bridge built, first highway bridge across
Missouri River in North Dakota; **1955** county courthouse
built.

Manning   *Dunn County*   *West central North*
Dakota, 103 mi/166 km west-northwest of Bismarck

1883 Dunn County formed, named for pioneer John P.
Dunn; **1908** county organized; town founded as county
seat on Knife River; **1995** county courthouse built.

Mayville   *Traill County*   *Eastern North Dakota,*
52 mi/84 km north-northwest of Fargo

1875 Traill County formed; **1881** town founded; incorporated as a village; **1883** Great Northern Railroad reaches
town; town becomes county seat; **1890** Mayville State
University established; **1967** incorporated as a statutory
city.

McClusky   *Sheridan County*   *Central North*
Dakota, 50 mi/80 km north-northeast of Bismarck

1905 town founded; **1907** incorporated as a village; **1908**
Sheridan County formed, named for Union Gen. Philip
Sheridan; town becomes county seat; **1911** incorporated
as a city; **1939** county courthouse built.

Medora   *Billings County*   *Western North Dakota,*
137 mi/220 km west of Bismarck, on Little Missouri River

1879 Billings County formed; **1880** Northern Pacific
Railroad built; **1883** packing plant established by
Marquis de Mores, closed 1886; town founded, named
for de Mores' wife; Chateau de Mores built; Theodore
Roosevelt, 25, establishes Elkhorn Ranch to north for
hunting trips; **1884** Rough Riders Hotel built; **1886** county
organized; town becomes county seat; **Apr. 25, 1947**
Theodore Roosevelt National Memorial Park established
to north, "Memorial" dropped 1978; **1954** incorporated as
a village; **1967** incorporated as a statutory city; **1982**
county courthouse built.

Michigan   *Nelson County*   See **Lakota** (1945)

Minnewaukan   *Benson County*   *North central*
North Dakota, 120 mi/193 km northeast of Bismarck

1879 Benson County formed; **1884** county organized;
town founded as county seat, originally located at western
end of Devils Lake; **1898** incorporated as a city; **1901**
county courthouse completed.

Minot   *Ward County*   *Northern North Dakota,*
107 mi/172 km north-northwest of Bismarck

1885 Ward County formed; Erik Ramstad becomes first
settler; **1886** town founded on Souris River, named for
Henry G. Minot (MY-not); **1887** Great Northern
Railroad reaches town; town becomes county seat;
incorporated as a city; **1893** Chicago, Milwaukee &
Sault Ste. Marie Railroad reaches city; **1896** county
opened to homesteaders, known as "Imperial Ward"
County for its size 5,000 sq mi/8,045 sq km; **1904** flooding
inundates city; **1910** county divided into Renville, Burke,
Mountrail and Ward counties; **1912** Carnegie Library
built, new library opened 1966; **1913** Minot State
University established; **1928** Minot International Airport
established; **1930** county courthouse completed; **1954**
Minot Air Force Base established; **1966** permanent site
of North Dakota State Fair established.

Mohall   *Renville County   Northern North Dakota, 147 mi/237 km north-northwest of Bismarck*

1901 Great Northern Railroad built to site; town founded as railroad terminus near Canadian border; *Tribune* newspaper founded by M. O. Hall, for whom town is named; **1908** incorporated as a city; **1910** Renville County formed from Ward County; town becomes county seat; **1937** county courthouse built.

Mott   *Hettinger County   Southwestern North Dakota, 132 mi/103 km southwest of Bismarck*

1883 Hettinger County formed; **1903** town founded; **1905** town platted; **1907** county organized; town becomes county seat; **1910** incorporated as a village; **1911** Chicago, Milwaukee, St. Paul & Pacific Railroad built; **1916** Great Northern Railroad reaches town; **1934** county courthouse built; **1967** incorporated as a statutory city.

Napoleon   *Logan County   Southern North Dakota, 150 mi/241 km west-southwest of Fargo*

1873 Logan County formed; **1884** county organized; town founded as county seat by Napoleon Goodsill; **Jan. 1899** county seat moved to King, returned to Napoleon Sept.; **1921** county courthouse built; **1947** incorporated as a city.

New Rockford   *Eddy County   East central North Dakota, 105 mi/169 km northeast of Bismarck*

1883 Great Northern Railroad built; town founded on James River; **1885** Eddy County formed; town becomes county seat; **1899** county courthouse built; **1912** incorporated as a city.

New Town   *Mountrail County   West central North Dakota, 90 mi/145 km northwest of Bismarck*

Apr. 7, 1805 Lewis and Clark Expedition resumes up Missouri River after wintering at Fort Mandan; **1845** Fort Berthold trading post built on Missouri River 25 mi/40 km to southeast by Bartholomew Berthold; **1867** Fort Stevenson military post built east of old fort; **1870** Fort Berthold Indian Reservation established to west for Arikara, Hidatsa, and Mandan peoples; **1889** Sacred Heart Mission established to southeast; **Feb. 15, 1936** lowest temperature ever recorded in North Dakota reached at Parshall to east, −60°F/−51°C; **1950** town platted to replace villages of Sanish, Van Hook, and Elbowoods inundated by Lake Sakakawea reservoir; **1952** incorporated as a city.

Parshall   *Mountrail County   See New Town (1936)*

Pembina   *Pembina County   Northeastern North Dakota, 87 mi/140 km north of Grand Forks, on Red River*

1797 trading post established by North West Company, rebuilt 1801; **1812** first settlers arrive; **1843** town founded; **1870** Fort Pembina built, abandoned 1895; **1873** Fort Pembina Military Reservation established; **1885** incorporated as a town; **1965** Pembina State Museum opened, new facility opened 1996; **1967** incorporated as a statutory city.

Rhame   *Bowman County   Southwestern North Dakota, 150 mi/241 km west-southwest of Bismarck*

Sept. 1864 80-unit wagon train attacked by Dakotas, nine emigrants killed, scout Jefferson Dilts, returning from Badlands, killed as he confronts fleeing Dakotas; Fort Dilts built; **1907** Chicago, Milwaukee, St. Paul & Pacific Railroad built; town founded, named for M. D. Rhame, railroad engineer; **1913** incorporated as a village; **1967** incorporated as a statutory city.

Rolla   *Rolette County   Northern North Dakota, 142 mi/229 km northwest of Grand Forks*

1873 Rolette County formed; town founded; **1884** county organized; Dunseith becomes county seat; **1885** county seat moved to St. John; **1889** county seat moved to Rolla; Rolla University established, later closed for lack of funding; **1907** incorporated as a city; **1931** International Peace Garden on Manitoba, Canada, border to north established by State of North Dakota; **1960** county courthouse built.

Rugby   *Pierce County   Northern North Dakota, 120 mi/193 km north-northeast of Bismarck*

1885 town founded on Great Northern Railroad as Rugby Junction; **1887** Pierce County formed; **1889** county organized; town becomes county seat; **1897** incorporated as a village, renamed Rugby; **1905** incorporated as a city; **1911** Rugby Public Library founded; **1912** county courthouse completed; **1931** Geographical Center of North America determined to be at Rugby; **1999** 88 ft/27 m Northern Lights Tower erected, dedicated to Aurora Borealis.

Stanley   *Mountrail County   Northwestern North Dakota, 135 mi/217 km northwest of Bismarck*

1886 Great Northern Railroad built; town founded; **1909** Mountrail County formed from Ward County; incorporated as a village, becomes county seat; **1914** county courthouse built; **1967** incorporated as a statutory city.

Stanton   *Mercer County   Central North Dakota, 47 mi/76 km northwest of Bismarck, on Missouri River*

1805 Frenchman Charbonneau and Hidatsa wife Sakakawea (born Shoshone) join Lewis and Clark Expedition as guides, ensuring expedition's success; **1845** area last occupied by Hidatsa and Mandan people; **1883** town founded; **1884** Mercer County formed; town becomes county seat; **1909** incorporated as a village; **1947** incorporated as a city; **1973** county courthouse completed; **Oct. 26, 1974** Knife River Villages National Historic Site established.

Steele *Kidder County* Central North Dakota, *44 mi/71 km east of Bismarck*

1873 Kidder County formed; Northern Pacific Railroad built; 1878 town founded, named for land owner Col. Wilbur P. Steele; 1881 county organized; town becomes county seat; 1883 incorporated as a city; hotel built by Steele, later used as county courthouse; July 6, 1936 highest temperature ever recorded in North Dakota reached, 121°F/49°C.

Strasburg *Emmons County* See **Linton (1903)**

Towner *McHenry County* Northern North Dakota, *115 mi/185 km north of Bismarck*

1873 McHenry County formed; 1884 county organized; Villard becomes county seat; 1885 county seat moved to Scriptown; 1886 Great Northern Railroad built; town founded as new county seat on Souris River, named for rancher Col. O. M. Towner; 1892 incorporated as a village; 1904 incorporated as a city; 1905 county courthouse built.

Valley City *Barnes County* Eastern North Dakota, *58 mi/93 km west of Fargo*

1872 Northern Pacific Railroad built; town founded on Sheyenne River, named Worthington; 1873 Barnes County formed; 1878 incorporated as a village, renamed Valley City; 1879 town becomes county seat; 1881 All Saints Episcopal Church built; 1883 incorporated as a city; 1890 Valley City State Teachers College (now University) established; 1901 Carnegie Library built; 1908 Hi-Line Railroad Bridge completed across Sheyenne River Valley; Jan. 22, 1909 TV actress Ann Sothern born (died 2001); 1926 county courthouse completed; 1938 Federal Fish Hatchery established; 1951 Lake Ashtabula formed to north on Sheyenne River by Baldhill Dam.

Velva *McHenry County* Central North Dakota, *90 mi/145 km north of Bismarck*

1883 Swede August Peterson becomes first settler; 1886 Minnesota, St. Paul & Sault Ste. Marie Railroad built; town founded; 1893 Muus Brothers General Store opened; 1905 incorporated as a town; Nov. 26, 1912 TV correspondent Eric Sevareid born (died 1992); 1967 incorporated as a statutory city.

Wahpeton *Richland County* Southeastern North Dakota, *45 mi/72 km south of Fargo, on Red River*

1869 town founded by Morgan T. Rich at joining of Otter Tail and Bois de Sioux rivers forming Red River, named Richville; 1871 St. Paul, & Pacific Railroad built; town renamed Chahinkapa, Dakota for "tops of trees"; 1873 Richland County formed; town becomes county seat; 1881 incorporated as a town; 1885 incorporated as a city; 1893 town renamed Wahpeton, Dakota for "village of leaves"; 1903 North Dakota State College of Science (2-year) established; 1914 second county courthouse completed; 1923 Leach Public Library founded.

Walhalla *Pembina County* Northeastern North Dakota, *85 mi/137 km north-northwest of Grand Forks*

1801 temporary trading post established by Alexander Henry, Jr.; 1843 permanent post built by Norman Kittson of American Fur Company; 1845 St. Joseph's Mission founded for Chippewa people by Father G. A. Belcourt; 1877 town platted, renamed for palace in Norse mythology; 1898 Great Northern Railroad reaches town; incorporated as a village; 1915 Kittson building moved, becomes Walhalla State Historic Site; 1918 incorporated as a city.

Washburn *McLean County* Central North Dakota, *33 mi/53 km north-northwest of Bismarck, on Missouri River*

Oct. 1804 Fort Mandan built by Lewis and Clark to winter over on their journey to Oregon; Apr. 7, 1805 Lewis and Clark continue their journey; fort later destroyed by Sioux; May 22, 1869 battle fought between Dakota and Arikara (Ree) people, Ree Chief Swift Runner killed; 1870s cabin built by Joseph Henry Taylor; 1882 town founded; 1883 McLean County formed; town becomes county seat; 1901 incorporated as a city; 1917 county courthouse built.

Watford City *McKenzie County* Western North Dakota, *144 mi/232 km northwest of Bismarck*

1883 McKenzie County formed; town founded as terminus of branch of Great Northern Railroad; 1891 county eliminated; 1905 county reestablished; Alexander becomes county seat; 1907 county seat moved to Schafer; 1934 incorporated as a city; 1941 county seat moved to Watford City; Apr. 25, 1947 Theodore Roosevelt Memorial National Park established to south, "Memorial" dropped from name 1978; 1974 county courthouse built.

Williston *Williams County* Northwestern North Dakota, *170 mi/274 km northwest of Bismarck*

Apr. 1805 Lewis and Clark pass site on Missouri River after wintering at Fort Mandan; 1828 Fort Union built 25 mi/40 km to southwest on Missouri River by John Jacob Astor's American Fur Company; 1832 the *Yellowstone* becomes first steamboat to pass site; July 7, 1863 steamboat *Robert Campbell* attacked by Dakotas to east, followed boat 600 mi/966 km from Fort Pierre, South Dakota, seeking goods owed them, 3 crewmen killed, 18 Dakota killed; 1866 Fort Buford built to replace Fort Union; 1870s Robert Matthews becomes first white settler; **1886** Great Northern Railroad built; town founded on Missouri River, at mouth of Muddy River, named for D. Willis James, friend of railroad builder James J. Hill; **1891** Williams County formed; town becomes county seat; **1904** town incorporated; **1927** Lewis and Clark Bridge built across Missouri River; **Jan. 4, 1951** oil discovered in Williston Basin; **1952** Standard Oil Refinery built; **1953** county courthouse built; **1954** Great Northern Refinery built; **1956** Lake Sakakawea formed on Missouri River by Garrison Dam 120 mi/193 km to southeast; new highway bridge built across river to southwest; **June 20, 1966** Fort Union National Historic Site established, extends into Montana.

Ohio

East central U.S. Capital: Columbus. Major cities: Cleveland, Cincinnati, Columbus.

Ohio became part of the U.S. with creation of the Northwest Territory in 1787. Indiana Territory, which included Indiana, Illinois, Michigan, and Wisconsin, was created July 4, 1800. Ohio was admitted to the U.S. as the 17th state March 1, 1803.

Ohio is divided into 88 counties. The counties are divided into townships having limited government functions. The municipalities are classified as villages and townships. A state statute allows a village to automatically become a city when it reaches a population of 5,000. See Introduction.

Akron *Summit County* *Northeastern Ohio, 29 mi/ 47 km south-southeast of Cleveland*

1799 first settlers arrive in region; **1804** town of Middlebury founded 2 mi/3.2 km east of Little Cuyahoga River by Capt. Joseph Hart, area now called East Akron; **1811** Paul Williams builds cabin in what is now downtown Akron; settlement of Spicertown develops; **1825-1840** series of dams create East, West, and New reservoirs on Tuscarawas River add to glacially formed Long, Nesmith, and Turkeyfoot lakes, creating Portage Lakes District; **1825** town incorporated; construction begins on Ohio & Erie Canal, with 17 locks in two-mile section; **Dec. 1825** town platted by Simon Perkins; **1827** Ohio & Erie Canal begun, completed 1832 linking Ohio and Cuyahoga rivers; **1836** incorporated as a city; adjacent town of Cascade to north annexed by Akron; **1839** *Akron Beacon Journal* newspaper founded; **1840** Summit County formed; town becomes county seat; Ohio & Pennsylvania Canal opens to Beaver, Pennsylvania; **1844** abolitionist John Brown moves here from nearby Hudson, moves on to Kansas 1855 after short stay in upstate New York; **1848** state adopts Akron Plan of graded schools; **1851** Sojourner Truth gives her "Ain't I a Woman" speech at women's rights convention; **1852** Cleveland, Akron & Zanesville Railroad reaches town; **1870** Buchtel College established, becomes University of Akron 1913; **Nov. 1870** Dr. Benjamin F. Goodrich opens small factory to make fire hoses and beer tubing, start of city's role as the "Rubber Capital of the World"; **1874** Akron Public Library founded; **1891** American Cereal Company founded through merger of smaller companies, including Quaker Oats Mills of Ravenna, retains Quaker Oats trademark; **1898** Goodyear Tire and Rubber Company founded by C. W. and F. A. Seiberling; **1900** Firestone Tire and Rubber Company founded by Harvey Firestone;

Sept. 24, 1902 theatrical producer Cheryl Crawford born (died 1986); **1908** county courthouse built; **1910s** rubber tire industry greatly expanded; **Oct. 7, 1911** singer Vaughn Monroe born (died 1973); **1912** Portage Hotel built on site of old Empire Hotel; **1915** High Level Bridge built over Cuyahoga River gorge to north; **1919** Fritz Pollard joins Akron Pros, first African-American to play pro football; **Feb. 14, 1921** TV personality Hugh Downs born; **1922** Akron Art Museum founded; North Main Street Viaduct built; **July 20, 1924** actress Lola Albright born; **1929** Akron Civic Theatre built; **1931** 28-story Central Trust Tower Building completed; **1935** Dr. Bob Smith and Bill Wilson form Alcoholics Anonymous; **Nov. 26, 1935** actress Marian Mercer born; **Oct. 14, 1938** John Wesley Dean III born, counsel to President Nixon, Watergate scandal figure; **1946** Akron Fulton International Airport established; **Apr. 5, 1949** astronaut Judith A. Resnick born, killed Jan. 28, 1986, in *Challenger* disaster; **1953** Akron Children's Zoo established; **Feb. 16, 1956** singer James Ingram born; **Dec. 27, 1974** Cuyahoga Valley National Recreation Area established to north; **1982** All American Y Bridge built, replaces North Main viaduct; **mid 1980s** last of Akron's tire factories closes, remains headquarters of four of five largest U.S. tire companies, Goodrich, Goodyear, Firestone, and General; **1991** Goodyear Polymer Science Center opened; **1994** John S. Knight Convention Center opened.

Alliance *Stark County* *Northeastern Ohio, 48 mi/ 77 km south-southeast of Cleveland*

c.1805 town founded on Mahoning River by Quakers from Virginia, named Lexington; **1846** Mount Union College established; **1854** Freedom, Williamsport, and Liberty merge with Lexington, incorporated as village of

Alliance; **1867** Mabel Hartzell House built; **1886** Scarlet Carnation, Ohio's state flower, developed by Levi Lamborn; **1889** becomes a statutory city; **1909** Morgan Mansion completed; **June 20, 1935** football player Len Dawson born; **1945** Alliance Art Center established; **Apr. 3, 1948** actor Perry King born; **1989** Alliance Symphony Orchestra founded.

Ashland   *Ashland County   North central Ohio, 52 mi/84 km southwest of Cleveland*

1786 area settled; **1815** town platted by William Montgomery, named Uniontown; **1822** town renamed Ashland; **1836** John Studebaker builds house and blacksmith shop, sons Henry and Clement later establish wagon factory at South Bend, Indiana; **1844** incorporated as a village; **1846** Ashland County formed; town becomes county seat; **1878** Ashland University established; **May 16, 1884** 12,000 spectators overwhelm National Guardsmen at hanging of murderers George Andrew Horn and William Henry Gribben, leads to passage of state law ending public executions; **1915** Johnny Appleseed monument erected; **1916** becomes a statutory city; **1928** county courthouse built.

Ashtabula   *Ashtabula County   Northeastern Ohio, 52 mi/84 km northeast of Cleveland, on Lake Erie*

1796 surveyor Moses Cleaveland stops here with group of New Englanders; two of party remain in area; **1801** Thomas Hamilton becomes town's first settler; **1816** town founded; **1831** incorporated as a borough; **1853** incorporated as a village; **1870s** immigrants from Finland and Sweden arrive; **Dec. 29, 1876** railroad bridge collapses, 92 killed; **1880s** Italian immigrants arrive; hothouse cultivation of vegetables begins; **1891** becomes a statutory city.

Athens   *Athens County   Southeastern Ohio, 62 mi/100 km southeast of Columbus*

1787 Ohio Company of Associates purchases land for establishing university; **1797** first settlers arrive; **1800** town platted on Hocking River by Gen. Rufus Putnam; **1804** Ohio University established; **1805** Athens County formed; town becomes county seat; **1811** incorporated as a village; **1843** Hocking Canal opened; **1867** Athens State Hospital established; **1870** Baltimore & Ohio Railroad reaches town; **1880** third county courthouse built; **1912** becomes a statutory city; **Nov. 5, 1930** explosion at Millfield Mine No. 6 to north, 83 coal miners killed; **1971** Hocking River channelization effort completed eliminating threat of flooding; **1975** Athens County Historical Museum opened.

Ava   *Noble County   East central Ohio, 74 mi/119 km east-southeast of Columbus*

1873 town founded; **1876** post office established; **Sept. 3, 1925** dirigible *Shenandoah* splits into two during storm on its way from Lakehurst, New Jersey, to Kansas City, 14 killed in larger section, occupants of smaller section saved by tree; **1937** Mrs. Faye Larson discovers class ring of *Shenandoah* Capt. Zachary Lansdowne while gardening.

Barberton   *Summit County   Northeastern Ohio, suburb 7 mi/11.3 km southwest of Akron*

1764 Chief Hopocan becomes well-known regional figure, signs 1795 Greenville Treaty while remaining engaged in warfare against whites, disappears 1812; **1881** Diamond Match Company founded by Ohio Columbus Barber; **1891** town founded by Barber; **1891** incorporated as a city; **1905** Barber develops extravagant Anna Dean Farm, dies 1920.

Batavia   *Clermont County   Southwestern Ohio, 17 mi/27 km east of Cincinnati*

1797 area first settled by Ezekiel Dimmitt; **1800** Clermont County formed; Williamsburg becomes county seat; **1814** town founded on East Fork Little Miami River, named for Batavia, New York; **1815** Old Parrott House built; **1823** county seat moved to New Richmond; **1824** county seat moved to Batavia; **1842** incorporated as a village; **July 14, 1863** Confederate Gen. John Morgan (Morgan's Raiders) rides through town stealing horses, food; **1903** Cincinnati, Georgetown & Portsmouth Railroad reaches town, discontinued 1934; **1936** second county courthouse built.

Bellaire   *Belmont County   Eastern Ohio, 110 mi/177 km south-southeast of Cleveland, on Ohio River*

1802 town founded, named for Bellaire, Maryland, by settler from there; **1849** bridge built across Ohio River from Wheeling, West Virginia; **1860** incorporated as a village; **1870** Jacob Heatherington builds House-That-Jack-Built, named for Jack his mule; **1873** becomes a statutory city; **July 6, 1944** fire in Powhatan Coal Mine, 66 killed.

Bellefontaine   *Logan County   West central Ohio, 48 mi/77 km northwest of Columbus*

1806 area first settled; **1818** Logan County formed; town founded; **1820** town becomes county seat; **1835** incorporated as a city; **1850s** natural Indian Lake enlarged for Miami & Erie Canal; **Sept. 1, 1868** cartoonist Kin Hubbard, born, creator of rural philosophical character Abe Martin (died 1930); **1871** county courthouse built; **1875** mob lynches James Schell, accused of murdering 16-year-old girl, hanging tree at courthouse reduced to chips by souvenir hunters; **1891** first concrete pavement in America completed on Main Street at Courthouse Square.

Berea   *Cuyahoga County   Northeastern Ohio, suburb 11 mi/18 km southwest of Cleveland*

1809 land purchased by Gideon Granger of Connecticut Land Company; town site named by coin toss; **1827** town platted by John Baldwin; **1845** Baldwin College established, merges with Wallace College 1913 as Baldwin-

Wallace College; **1850** incorporated as a village; **1930** becomes a statutory city.

Blooming Grove *Morrow County* *North central Ohio, 52 mi/84 km north-northeast of Columbus*

1821 Ebenezer Harding settles here with sons George T. and Salmon E. Harding; **1822** town founded as Corsica by Salmon E. Harding; **Nov. 2, 1865** Warren G. Harding, 29th president of U.S., born (died Aug. 2, 1923); **1835** town renamed Blooming Grove.

Bowling Green *Wood County* *Northwestern Ohio, 7 mi/11.3 km south-southwest of Toledo*

1820 Wood County formed; **1835** town founded on Maumee River by Joseph Gordon, named for his hometown of Bowling Green, Kentucky; **1855** incorporated as a city; **1866** county seat moved from Perrysburg; **1886** oil discovered, oil boom follows; **1896** county courthouse completed; **1914** State Normal School established, becomes Bowling Green State University; H. J. Heinz opens tomato products plant; **1977** county office building completed.

Bryan *Williams County* *Northwestern Ohio, 52 mi/84 km west-southwest of Toledo*

1820 Williams County formed; Defiance becomes first county seat; **1841** town founded as new county seat; **1849** incorporated as a village; **1882** Bryan Library organized, built 1903 with Carnegie endowment; **1889** county courthouse completed; **1941** becomes a statutory city.

Bucyrus *Crawford County* *North central Ohio, 57 mi/92 km north of Columbus*

1819 Samuel Norton, 17 others arrive from Pennsylvania; **1820** Crawford County formed; **1822** town founded by Norton and Col. James Kilbourne; **1826** county organized; town becomes county seat; **1830** incorporated as a village; **1855** W. A. Riddell Company founded, maker of sawmill equipment; **1874** D. Picking and Company copper works founded, now only copper kettle factory in U.S.; **1885** becomes a statutory city; **1908** county courthouse built.

Cadiz *Harrison County* *Eastern Ohio, 90 mi/145 km south-southeast of Cleveland*

1804 town founded at joining of Mingo and Moravian trails; **1814** Harrison County formed; town becomes county seat; **1818** incorporated as a village; **Dec. 5, 1839** Gen. George Armstrong Custer born at New Rumley to north, killed in Battle of Little Bighorn, Montana, June 22, 1876; **1895** county courthouse completed; **Feb. 1, 1901** actor Clark Gable born (died 1960); **Oct. 23, 1934** Jean and Jeannette Piccard's stratosphere balloon, launched from Detroit, rising to 57,579 ft/17,550 m, descends into tree with the Piccards in it, safely drops to ground; **1936** Tappan Lake formed to northwest by dam on Little Stillwater Creek; **Nov. 29, 1940** explosion in Nelms Coal Mine, 31 killed.

Caldwell *Noble County* *East central Ohio, 78 mi/126 km east-southeast of Columbus*

1814 Joseph Caldwell drills Ohio's first oil well 2 mi/3.2 km to west; **1851** Noble County formed; Sarahville becomes first county seat; **1857** town founded as new county seat; **March 29, 1868** John Gray, last survivor of Revolutionary War, dies at age 104 at Hiramsburg to northwest, born 1764 at Mount Vernon, Virginia; **1870** incorporated as a village; **1870s** Pennsylvania Railroad reaches town; **1880** large-scale coal production begins; **1934** county courthouse; **June 27, 1998** flooding in county kills six, Wood-Hoffman Covered Bridge destroyed, built 1914.

Cambridge *Guernsey County* *East central Ohio, 73 mi/117 km east of Columbus*

1798 first settlers arrive from Cambridge, Maryland; **1806** town founded; **1810** Guernsey County formed; town becomes county seat; **1826** National Road reaches town; **1837** incorporated as a city; **1880s** oil and natural gas discovered; coal mining becomes important; **1883** second county courthouse built; **1901** Cambridge Glass Company plant built; **July 18, 1921** astronaut, U.S. Sen. John Glenn born; **1973** Cambridge Glass Museum established.

Canton *Stark County* *Eastern Ohio, 50 mi/80 km south-southeast of Cleveland*

1784 land deeded to white traders by Delaware Chief Turtle Heart; **1793** area viewed by five government scouts, impressed by its fertility; **1805** town founded by Bezaleel Wells and James Leonard; **1808** Stark County formed; **1809** town becomes county seat; **1815** incorporated as a village; *Canton Repository* newspaper founded by John Saxton, grandfather of Mrs. William McKinley; **1817** county courthouse completed; **1827** Ohio & Erie Canal reaches town; **1834** incorporated as a town; **1836** Joshua Gibbs develops bar share plow, becomes major plow manufacturer; **June 8, 1847** Ida Saxton McKinley, wife of Pres. William McKinley, born (married 1871, died 1907); **1851** Ball and Aultman Company founded, maker of reapers; **1852** Ohio & Pennsylvania Railroad reaches town; **1854** becomes a statutory city; **1884** Canton Public Library established, built 1905; **1892** Cleveland Bible College established, becomes Malone College; **1907** McKinley Memorial Tomb dedicated, remains brought to Canton shortly after his assassination in Buffalo Sept. 1901; **May 1, 1918** TV personality Jack Paar born (died 2004); **1926** *Daily News* editor Don Mellett murdered by racketeers for articles written exposing their underworld activities; **Oct. 15, 1926** actress Jean Peters born; **1934** Canton Museum of Art (Art Institute) opened; **1936** Canton Symphony Orchestra founded; **1946** Akron-Canton Regional Airport established to north; **1963** Pro Football Hall of Fame opened; **1965** Canton Ballet

OHIO

founded; **1970** Cultural Center for the Arts opened; **1998** National First Ladies Library dedicated.

Carrollton   *Carroll County*   *Eastern Ohio, 21 mi/ 34 km southeast of Canton*

1815 town founded, originally named Centreville; **1833** Carroll County formed; town becomes county seat; **1833** town renamed; **1837** McCook House completed; **1876** incorporated as a village; **1885** county courthouse built; **1936** Leesville Lake formed by dam on Conotton River, dam rebuilt 1963.

Celina   *Mercer County*   *Western Ohio, 91 mi/ 146 km west-northwest of Columbus*

1820 Mercer County formed; **1824** county organized; St. Marys becomes first county seat; **1834** area settled; town founded as new county seat; **1840** county seat moved to Celina; **1860** incorporated as a village; **1923** fourth county courthouse completed; **1952** becomes a statutory city.

Chardon   *Geauga County*   *Northeastern Ohio, 25 mi/40 km east-northeast of Cleveland*

1806 Geauga (jee-AW-gah) County formed; **1808** town founded as county seat, named for landowner Peter Chardon Brooks; **1851** incorporated as a village; **1869** fourth county courthouse built.

Chillicothe   *Ross County*   *Southern Ohio, 42 mi/ 68 km south of Columbus*

200 BC–500 AD Hopewell people build 23 ceremonial mounds; **1796** town founded on Scioto River by Nathaniel Massie; **1797** Cross Keys Tavern built by John Robinson, closed 1860; **1798** Ross County formed; town becomes county seat; **1800** town becomes capital of Northwest Territory; **1802** incorporated as a city; **May 1, 1803** Ohio becomes 17th state; town becomes first state capital; **1805** Felix Renick establishes overland livestock route for driving herds to Eastern cities; **1807** Adena Mansion built to west by Gov. Thomas Worthington; **1810** state capital moved to Zanesville, reinstated at Chillicothe 1812; **1812** Camp Bull established by military, reactivated as Camp Sherman 1917; **1816** state capital moved to Columbus; **Sept. 6, 1819** Union Gen. William Starke Rosecrans born at Kingston to north (died 1898); **Aug. 29, 1831** Lucy Webb Hayes, wife of Pres. Rutherford B. Hayes, born (married Dec. 30, 1852, died June 1889); **1832** Ohio & Erie Canal completed; **1846** archaeologists Squier and Davis excavate Hopewell Mounds, named for land owner Capt. M. C. Hopewell; **1850** Mountain House residence built; **1852** Marietta & Cincinnati Railroad reaches town; **1855** county courthouse built; **1859** Chillicothe Public Library founded, built 1907; **Sept.–Oct. 1917** influenza epidemic at Camp Sherman kills 1,177 soldiers; **March 2, 1923** Mound City National Monument proclaimed to northwest, redesignated Hopewell Culture National Historical Park 1992; **1924** U.S. Veterans' Hospital opens; **1928** U. S. Industrial Reformatory for men established; **Feb. 20, 1937** singer Nancy Wilson born; **1946** Ohio University–Chillicothe established.

Cincinnati   *Hamilton County*   *Southwestern Ohio, on Ohio River*

1679 French explorer La Salle visits region; **Nov. 18, 1788** town founded on Ohio River, at mouth of Little Miami River, by 23 settlers led by Benjamin Stites of Pennsylvania, originally named Columbia; **Dec. 28, 1788** another group founds Losantiville 6 mi/9.7 km downstream from Columbia; **1789** Fort Washington built, serves as Indian defense through 1795; **1790** Hamilton County formed; town becomes county seat; Losantiville renamed Cincinnati by Arthur St. Clair, first governor of Northwest Territory, in honor of Society of Cincinnati, Revolutionary War veterans' group; first church (Presbyterian) organized; **1793** Gen. Anthony Wayne takes his army north, defeats Native Americans of Western Ohio; **1802** incorporated as a village; **Oct. 1811** first steamboat *New Orleans* arrives on its maiden journey; **1819** incorporated as a city; University of Cincinnati established; **1821** first Catholic church built; **July 21, 1924** Supreme Court Justice Stanley Matthews born (died 1889); **1825** work begins on Miami & Erie Canal, opened 1832; **July 19, 1825** Cong., Sen. George Pendleton born (died 1889); **1829** Ohio Mechanics Institute founded; **1830s** large wave of German immigrants arrives; **1831** Xavier University established; **1832** first cholera epidemic takes many lives; **1835** first Jewish synagogue built; **1836** abolitionist newspaper *The Philanthropist* published by James G. Birney, forced to flee city; **1840** Irish immigrants begin arriving with start of Potato Famine; **1845** St. Peter in Chains Catholic Church completed; **1846** Little Miami Railroad reaches city; **1849** second cholera epidemic kills over 4,000; **1850s** city becomes world's leading pork producer; **1856** public library founded, built 1870; **Sept. 15, 1857** William Howard Taft, 27th President, born (died March 8, 1930); **1860s** city becomes center of Peace Democrat movement, referred to by opposition as Copperheads for advocating negotiation with Confederacy, riots and bombings of Federal gunboats becomes common; **June 2, 1861** Helen Herron Taft, wife of President Taft, born (married 1886, died 1943); **1862** martial law declared with threat from Kirby Smith's band of Confederate raiders from Kentucky; **1867** John A. Roebling builds bridge across Ohio River to Covington, Kentucky; Cincinnati Conservatory of Music founded; **1869** Cleveland Abbe establishes first weather forecasting service, reorganized 1891 as U.S. Weather Bureau; **Nov. 5, 1869** Cong. Nicholas Longworth born (died 1931); **c.1870** city greatly expands its boundaries; **1873** Mount Adams Incline built to pull streetcars on Zoo-Eden line up bluff; **1875** Hebrew Union College established; Cincinnati Zoo opened, Botanical Gardens added 1987; **1878** Cincinnati

Music Hall and Exposition Building built; **Dec. 1879** St. Francis de Sales Catholic Church completed; **1880** Art Museum founded at Eden Park; *Cincinnati Times-Star* newspaper founded; **1881** Cincinnati Southern Railroad reaches city from south, reviving trade lost by sagging river commerce; *Cincinnati Post* newspaper founded; **1884** floods damage city; **March 1884** rioting occurs over corrupt city hall and police force; **1886** Cincinnati Art Museum built; **1887** Coney Island Amusement Park developed 10 mi/16 km to east at former picnic grounds on Ohio River established 1870; **Sept. 8, 1889** Sen. Robert Alphonso Taft born, son of President Taft (died 1953); **1893** city hall built; **1895** Cincinnati Symphony Orchestra founded; **June 14, 1895** rabbi, Jewish theologian Louis Finkelstein born (died 1991); **June 4, 1900** archaeologist, rabbi Nelson Glueck born (died 1971); **Aug. 30, 1907** inventor John William Mauchley born, instrumental in development of the computer (died 1980); **1908** Hamilton County Memorial Building built, honoring pioneers, war veterans; **Nov. 5, 1912** actor, singer Roy Rogers born (died 1998); **May 5, 1914** actor Tyrone Power born (died 1958); **Sept. 4, 1918** tennis player Billy Talbert born (died 1999); **1919** sixth county courthouse built; **1920** College of St. Joseph established; **1920s** river trade revived with construction of locks and dams; **Apr. 3, 1924** singer, actress Doris Day born; **Aug. 16, 1930** tennis player Tony Trabert born; **1930** Cincinnati Municipal Airport (Lunken Field) dedicated to east; **1931** 49-story Carew Tower building completed; **1933** Union Station completed; **Jan. 1937** Ohio River floods again, heavy losses in neighboring Kentucky, 225 killed; **1938** Laurel Homes slum clearance project completed; **Nov. 19, 1938** businessman Ted Turner born; **Feb. 5, 1942** Dallas Cowboys football player Roger Staubach born; **Apr. 14, 1942** Reds baseball player Pete Rose born; **June 23, 1943** actor James Levine born; **Dec. 18, 1947** movie producer Steven Spielberg born; **1958** *Post* and *Times-Star* newspapers merge; **Nov. 8, 1965** American Airlines 727 crashes in storm, 58 of 62 on board killed; **1969** The Union Institute established **Aug. 9, 1969** tornado kills 4, injures 243; **1970** Riverfront Stadium built, home of Reds baseball and Bengals football teams, renamed Cinergy Field 1997, demolished 2002; **Apr. 1, 1973** explosion in 3-story building kills 7, injures 25; **Feb. 8, 1977** Larry Flynt, publisher of *Hustler* magazine, found guilty of obscenity and organized crime, gets 7–25 years in prison, $10,000 fine; **June 2, 1983** fire aboard Dallas-Toronto Air Canada flight, forced to land, 23 killed, 23 survive; **1986** Proctor & Gamble Performance Pavilion opened; **Aug. 24, 1989** Commissioner Bart Giamatti bans Pete Rose from baseball for betting on games (Giamatti dies of heart attack Sept. 1); **1990** 26-story Scripps Center building completed; **1991** 32-story Chemed Center building completed; **Feb. 3, 1993** Cincinnati Reds owner Marge Schott suspended from participating in baseball, fined $25,000 for making racial and anti-Semitic slurs; **2000** Paul Brown Stadium opened, home of Bengals football team; **Apr. 7–10, 2001** shooting death of black youth by white police officer followed by three days of rioting, 700

arrested; **2004** National Underground Railroad Freedom Center opened. **March 2, 2004** Marge Schott dies, controversial principal owner of Cincinnati Reds baseball team (born 1928).

Circleville *Pickaway County* *Central Ohio, 24 mi/ 39 km south of Columbus*

1774 relatives of Mingo Chief Logan murdered by Americans at Logan Elm to south, avenged by Logan with wave of murders; **Oct. 1774** Colonial Governor of Virginia Lord Dunmore arrives at Camp Charlotte to remove Shawnee from area, heavy losses on both sides; **1810** Pickaway County formed; town founded as county seat, named for two streets that completely encircle town; **1814** incorporated as a village; **1832** Ohio & Erie Canal opened; **1853** becomes a statutory city; **1856** railroad reaches town; circular streets "squared off"; **1888** third county courthouse built.

Cleveland *Cuyahoga County* *Northeastern Ohio, on Lake Erie, at mouth of Cuyahoga River*

July 22, 1796 group of settlers headed by Gen. Moses Cleaveland sent by Connecticut Land Company, founds town of Cleaveland; **1799** Lorenzo Carter and wife remain in swampy area at mouth of Cuyahoga River, other settlers disperse to higher ground; **1807** Cuyahoga County formed; town becomes county seat; **1818** *Cleveland Gazette and Commercial Register* founded as first newspaper; **1827** Ohio & Erie Canal opens to Akron; **June 6, 1831** *Cleveland Advertiser* drops "a" in town name for sake of space, inspiring town name change; **1832** Dunham Tavern built; **1836** incorporated as a city; Lake Shore & Michigan Railroad built along shore of Lake Erie; **1847** Weddell House built by Peter Weddell; **1848** David N. Myers College established; **1854** city annexes Ohio City on west side of Cuyahoga following violent feud between two cities over location of river bridge; **1855** Old Stone Presbyterian Church built; first iron ore shipment arrives from iron ranges of Michigan's Upper Peninsula; Cleveland Iron Mining Company founded; Stadium Hotel opened; **May 19, 1857** chemist John Jacob Abel born, isolated insulin (died 1938); **Nov. 25, 1865** chemist, industrialist William Meriam Burton born, developed method for converting petroleum to gasoline (died 1954); **1867** Western Reserve Historical Society founded; **Oct. 31, 1867** baseball player Ed Delahanty born (died 1903); **Apr. 8, 1869** founder of neurosurgery Dr. Harvey Williams Cushing born (died 1939); **1870** Standard Oil Company organized; Sherwin Williams Paint Company established; **Aug. 10, 1873** philosopher William Ernest Hocking born (died 1966); **1875** Euclid Avenue Opera House built; **Nov. 2, 1878** *Cleveland Press* newspaper founded; **1882** Western Reserve College, founded 1826, moved from Hudson, becomes Case Western Reserve University 1967; **1886** St. Ignatius College established; **1888** Moses Cleaveland Statue erected in public square; Central Viaduct built across Cuyahoga River; **1894**

OHIO

Soldiers' and Sailors' monument erected; **Sept. 12, 1902** actress Margaret Hamilton born (died 1985); **1907** Trinity Cathedral (Episcopal) completed; **March 4, 1908** Lake View School fire in suburban Collinwood, 174 students, 2 teachers killed; **Nov. 16, 1908** actor Burgess Meredith born (died 1997); **May 4, 1909** actor Howard DaSilva born (died 1986); **1910** federal building built; **Feb. 25, 1913** actor Jim Backus born (died 1989); **1915** Cleveland Play House Company founded; **Dec. 27, 1915** sexual behavior researcher William H. Masters born, teamed with wife Virginia Johnson (died 2000); **1916** city hall built; Cleveland Museum of Art completed; **1917** Detroit-Superior High Level Bridge built across Cuyahoga River; **1918** Cleveland Symphony Orchestra organized; **1919** county courthouse completed; **1920** Museum of Natural History founded; **May 6, 1921** actor Ross Hunter born (died 1986); **1922** Municipal Auditorium completed; **1923** Federal Reserve Bank built; **Apr. 16, 1924** orchestra leader Henry Mancini born (died 1994); **Aug. 21, 1924** actor Jack Weston (Weinstein) born (died 1996); **Oct. 27, 1924** actress Ruby Dee born; **1925** Cleveland Municipal Airport opened, becomes Cleveland-Hopkins International Airport 1964; public library built; **Jan. 26, 1925** actor Paul Newman born; **Feb. 17, 1925** actor Hal Holbrook born; **Sept. 21, 1926** physicist Donald A. Glaser born, 1960 Nobel Prize; **Nov. 20, 1926** actress Kaye Ballard born; **June 21, 1927** African American Mayor Carl Burton Stokes born (died 1996); **March 25, 1928** astronaut James Lovell, Jr. born; **May 15, 1929** fire at Crile Hospital leaves 125 dead; **1930** era of late-1920s corruption ends with ouster of city manager William R. Hopkins; 52-story Terminal Tower building completed; **1931** Cleveland Municipal Stadium opens, home of Indians baseball team; **1932** Lorain-Carnegie Bridge built over Cuyahoga River; **Apr. 11, 1932** actor Joel Grey born; **Jan. 29, 1935** writer Sarah Chauncey Woolsey born (died 1905); **Dec. 21, 1935** TV personality Phil Donahue born; **May 30, 1936** actor Keir Dullea born; **1939** Main Street High Level Bridge built across Cuyahoga River at Lake Erie; **Oct. 20, 1944** liquid gas tank explosion, 135 killed; **Aug. 11, 1947** Burke Lakefront Airport opened; **Aug. 11, 1949** singer Eric Carmen born; **1952** disc jockey Alan Freed coins term "rock n' roll"; **June 18, 1952** actress Carol Kane born; **Dec. 21, 1954** Dr. Sam Sheppard convicted of murdering wife in sensational case, receives life sentence; **Feb. 12, 1955** TV personality Arsenio Hall born; **May 16, 1955** actress Debra Winger born; **Nov. 29, 1962** strike of two daily newspapers lasts 127 days; **1964** Cleveland State University established; **March 30, 1964** actress Tracy Chapman born; **July 23, 1968** racial rioting leaves four dead, including three policemen; **Aug. 14, 1968** actress Halle Berry born; **Nov. 1968** light rail system opened to Hopkins Airport; **May 12, 1969** Black Nationalist Ahmed Evans sentenced to death for four deaths in 1968 riots; **July 4, 1969** storms pound Lake Erie shore, 41 killed; **Jan. 28, 1970** commuter plane crashes into Lake Erie killing all 9; **Apr. 13, 1971** fire at Pick Carter Hotel kills seven, injures eight; **Dec. 27, 1974** Cuyahoga Valley National Recreation Area established to south; **1978** Cleveland Lakefront State Park established; city defaults on $15.5 million municipal

loan payment; **1981** Children's Museum founded, opened 1986; **1985** 45-story Sohio (BP) Building completed; **1992** 57-story Key Tower (Society Center) completed; **1994** Jacobs Field, home of Indians baseball team, and Grand Arena opened, part of Gateway Sports Complex; **1995** Rock n' Roll Hall of Fame opened; **1996** Cleveland Browns football team moves to Baltimore; **1999** new Cleveland Browns Stadium completed; new Cleveland Browns NFL football franchise established; **2001** 24-story Federal Court Building completed; **2003** Crawford Auto-Aviation Museum opened; **Aug. 13–14, 2003** massive power outage affects 50 million people from Michigan to New England, city's hydraulic system fails.

Clifton   *Greene County*   *See* **Yellow Springs (1839)**

Columbiana   *Columbiana County*   *See* **Salem (1868)**

Columbus   *Franklin County*   *Central Ohio, 120 mi/ 193 km southeast of Cleveland*

1797 town of Franklinton founded on west side of Scioto River by Lucas Sullivant, surveyor from Virginia; **1803** Franklin County formed; town becomes county seat; **1812** town of Columbus founded on east side of Scioto River, chosen for state capital; **1816** state capital moved from Chillicothe; Columbus incorporated as a borough; **Oct. 15, 1818** Union Gen. Irvin McDowell born (died 1885); **1821** incorporated as a village; **1824** Columbus annexes Franklinton, becomes new county seat; **1829** Ohio State School for the Deaf established; **1830** Capital University established; **1831** branch of Ohio & Erie Canal opened from east; **1833** National Road completed from Wheeling, (West) Virginia; **1834** incorporated as a city; Ohio State Penitentiary opened; **1837** Ohio State School for the Blind established; **1839** cornerstone laid for state capitol, completed 1861; **1850** Columbus & Xenia Railroad reaches city; **1854** first Ohio State Fair held; **1861** city serves as military staging center for Union Civil War effort; **1863** U.S. Fort Hayes established; Camp Chase Confederate Cemetery established; **1868** St. Mary's of the Springs Academy for women founded; **1873** Ohio State University established; **1877** Columbus State Hospital built; **1878** Columbus Museum of Art founded; **1879** Columbus School of Art and Design established; **Aug. 12, 1882** painter George Wesley Bellows born (died 1925); **1887** county courthouse built; **Oct. 8, 1890** aviator Eddie Rickenbacher born (died 1973); **Dec. 8, 1894** author James Thurber born (died 1964); **1899** *The Citizen* newspaper founded; **1902** Franklin University established; **1905** Griggs Dam built on Scioto River; **1906** Columbus Public Library completed; **Sept. 1906** McKinley Memorial dedicated; **Nov. 15, 1906** World War II Air Force Gen. Curtis Emerson "Bombs Away" LeMay born (died 1990); **1910** streetcar strike leads to violence, bombings, one death; **1911** Ohio Dominican College established; **March 1913** extensive flooding in western and central Ohio leaves 467 dead; **1917** Columbus Zoo founded to north; **Oct. 15, 1917** author, historian Arthur

Schlesinger, Jr. born; **1919** governor's mansion purchased; **March 29, 1919** actress Eileen Heckart born (died 2002); **1927** 47-story Lincoln-Leveque Tower (American Insurance Union Citadel) completed; **Oct. 17, 1927** TV personality Tom Poston born; **1928** city hall completed; Ohio Theatre built, becomes permanent symphony venue 1970; **1929** Port Columbus International Airport established to east; **July 8, 1929** world's first airmail service inaugurated; **Apr. 21, 1930** fire at Ohio State Penitentiary kills 322 inmates, followed by weeks of rioting; **June 23, 1930** astronaut Donn Eisele born; **1932** Columbus Gallery of Fine Arts completed; **Apr. 14, 1932** gas explosion at state office building under construction kills 11, injures over 50; **1933** state office building completed; **1934** U.S. Post Office and courthouse built; **Dec. 14, 1938** actor Hal Williams born; **Jan. 21, 1940** golfer Jack Nicklaus born; **Oct. 12, 1942** Ruby Cremeans kidnaps 8-month-old Daniel Scanlon from St Ann's Hospital, apprehended with baby Dec. 5 at hotel in Portsmouth, Ohio; **1951** Columbus Symphony Orchestra established; **Sept. 7, 1956** actor Michael Feinstein born; **1964** Center of Science and Industry opened; **1970** Bolton Field Airport built to southwest; **1974** 41-story James A. Rhodes State Office Building completed; **1988** 33-story Verne-Riffe State Office Building completed; **1989** Wexner Center for the Arts opened; **1991** 27-story county courthouse completed.

Conneaut *Ashtabula County* *Northeastern Ohio, 65 mi/105 km northeast of Cleveland, on Lake Erie*

July 4, 1796 surveyor Moses Cleaveland of Connecticut Land Company stops here with 50 settlers from New England, moves on; **1799** Thomas Montgomery and Aaron Wright become first settlers at mouth of Conneaut (KAH-nee-aht) Creek; town founded; **1834** incorporated as a city; **March 27, 1953** railroad accident, 21 killed.

Coshocton *Coshocton County* *East central Ohio, 65 mi/105 km east-northeast of Columbus*

1730s Mary Harris of New England brought to area as Native American captive, possibly first white woman in Ohio; **1776** Moravian mission of Lichtenau established, abandoned 1780; **1802** town founded on Muskingum River, named Tuscarawas; **1811** Coshocton County formed; town becomes county seat, renamed Coshocton; **1830** Ohio & Erie Canal completed; **1833** incorporated as a city; **1840** Price House inn built, later called Stagecoach Tavern; **1865** Pennsylvania Railroad reaches town; coal fields exploited; **March 3, 1873** AFL labor leader William Green born (died 1952); **1875** county courthouse built; **1913** flooding seriously damages town; **1935** flooding occurs again, leads to construction of flood control dams; **Sept. 11, 1950** troop train carrying 700 soldiers rear-ended to east, 33 killed.

Cuyahoga Falls *Summit County* *Northeastern Ohio, 4 mi/6.4 km north-northeast of Akron*

1812 town founded on Cuyahoga River by William Wetmore, originally named Manchester; **1825** town platted, renamed Cuyahoga Falls; **1836** incorporated as a city; **c.1840** city becomes important industrial center; **July 31, 1940** Doodlebug shuttle bus struck at railroad crossing, 43 killed; **June 26, 1975** Cuyahoga Valley National Recreation Area established to south; **1986** Northampton Township merges with city.

Dayton *Montgomery County* *Western Ohio, 47 mi/76 km north-northeast of Cincinnati*

c.1200 village built to southwest by early Native American cultures; **c.1768** Shawnee Chief Tecumseh born near Mad River, killed in Battle of the Thames, Upper Canada (Ontario) Oct. 5, 1813; **1795** town platted by Col. Israel Ludlow; **Apr. 1796** settlers led by Samuel Thompson arrive on Great Miami River from Cincinnati; **1798** Necom Tavern built by Col. George Newcom; **1803** Montgomery County formed; town becomes county seat; **1805** incorporated as a village; first public library in state established; **1808** *The Journal Herald* newspaper founded; **Jan. 1829** Miami & Erie Canal opened from Cincinnati; **June 12, 1833** Iowa Cong. James Baird Weaver born (died 1912); **1841** becomes a statutory city; **1845** Miami & Erie Canal opened to Lake Erie; **1850** University of Dayton established; **1851** Mad River & Lake Erie Railroad reaches city; **1856** Pierce and Stanley gypsy clans arrive, remain for several years; **Nov. 1, 1862** J. F. Bollmeyer, editor at pro-states' rights newspaper *Empire*, shot to death amid turmoil between Unionists and Peace Democrats (Copperheads); **May 1863** Copperheads destroy *Journal* newspaper office, leader Clement Vallandigham arrested, banished from Union; **1866** Turner Opera House opened; **1867** first soldiers' home in America founded, becomes Veterans' Administration Facility 1930; **June 5, 1869** Turner Opera House destroyed by fire, many killed, inspires establishment of municipal water works system, rebuilt as Victory Theatre; **Aug. 19, 1871** airplane inventor Orville Wright born (died 1948); **June, 27, 1872** African-American poet Paul Laurence Dunbar born (died 1906); **1883** flooding tops existing levees, prompting construction of higher embankments; **1886** National Cash Register factory founded by John Patterson, built 80 percent of glass for better working environment; **1888** Dayton Public Library built, new library opened 1962; **1889** counterfeiting Driggs Gang broken up by U.S. Secret Service, agent Donello killed, gang leader Nelson Driggs acquitted; **1898** Wright brothers begin developing their heavier-than-air flying machine; **1899** Dr. L. E. Custer develops electric buggy; Barney Oldfield begins winning local races in his Olds 999 racing car; **1903** Main Street Bridge built across Great Miami River, one of first concrete bridges; **1904** Wright Brothers' Hangar, world's second, built year after initial flight at Kitty Hawk, North Carolina; **1909** Charles F. Kettering invents automobile self-starter, sells gadget to Cadillac Motor Company 1910, establishes Dayton

Engineering Laboratories Company (Delco); **1911** Wright brothers establish experimental aircraft factory; **March 1913** Great Miami River inundates city, many fires burn out of control, 361 killed, $100 million in damage; **1917** Wright Air Field established, renamed Patterson Field 1924, becomes Wright-Patterson Air Force Base 1948; **1919** Frigidaire "electric ice box" introduced by General Motors; Dayton Art Institute founded, built 1930; **1921** Grace Methodist Church completed; **1922** Huffman Dam built on Great Miami River; **1924** airfield built to north, becomes James M. Cox-Dayton International Airport 1952; **Nov. 11, 1925** comedian Jonathan Winters born; **1926** Westminster Presbyterian Church built; **Feb. 21, 1927** columnist Erma Bombeck born; **Apr. 1, 1932** actor Gordon Jump born (died 2003); **1938** Dunbar House Museum opened; **Aug. 3, 1940** actor Martin Sheen born; **Aug. 6, 1951** actor Dorian Haywood born; **1964** Wright State University established; **1970** 30-story Kettering Tower building completed; **1978** county courthouse built; **1981** Sunwatch Archaeological Park established at Native American village site to southwest; **1998** National Aviation Hall of Fame opened at Wright-Patterson Air Force Base; **2003** Schuster Center for the Performing Arts opened.

Defiance   *Defiance County*   *Northwestern Ohio, 48 mi/77 km southwest of Toledo, on Maumee River*

c.1720 Pontiac born, great chief over Ottawa, Potawatomi, and Ojibwa peoples, assassinated 1769; **1760** French traders pass through area; **1790** area first settled; **1794** Gen. Anthony Wayne establishes Fort Defiance at mouth of Auglaize River; **1813** Gen. William Henry Harrison arrives, finds fort in ruins, builds Fort Winchester; **1823** town founded; **1836** incorporated as a city; **1843** Wabash & Erie Canal opened from Indiana; **1845** Defiance County formed; town becomes county seat; Miami & Erie Canal opened from Ohio River; **1850** Defiance Female Seminary founded, becomes Defiance College 1902; **1873** county courthouse completed; **1904** Carnegie Library built; **1936** Fort Winchester Bridge built across Auglaize River; **1966** AuGlaize Village established to depict area's early history.

Delaware   *Delaware County*   *Central Ohio, 23 mi/ 37 km north of Columbus*

1804 town founded by Moses Byxbe, soon abandoned; **1807** Joseph Barber builds house and tavern; town founded; **1808** Delaware County formed; town becomes county seat; **1816** incorporated as a village; **Oct. 4, 1822** Rutherford Birchard Hayes born, 19th U.S. President (died Jan. 17, 1893); **1834** Mansion House hotel built at mineral springs; **1842** Ohio Wesleyan University established; **1869** Ohio State Girls' Industrial School established; **1870** second county courthouse built; **1903** becomes a statutory city; **1935** Olentangy Caverns opened to public, earliest graffiti date 1821; **1936** city hall built; **1989** Delaware County Cultural Art Center opened.

East Liverpool   *Columbiana County*   *Eastern Ohio, 80 mi/129 km southeast of Cleveland, on Ohio River*

1800 area settled by Thomas Fawcett; town founded, named St. Clair, or Fawcett's Town; **c.1816** town renamed Liverpool; **1834** incorporated as a city, renamed East Liverpool; **1839** pottery and ceramics industry established by James Bennett of England; **1840** Etruria Pottery Works founded by Benjamin Harker; **1852** flooding damages city; **1876** Thompson House completed; **1903** Hall China Company founded; **Oct. 22, 1934** bank robber Pretty Boy Floyd captured and killed; **1976** U.S. Highway 30 bridge built on Ohio River to Chester, West Virginia, east of old bridge.

Eaton   *Preble County*   *Western Ohio, 43 mi/69 km north of Cincinnati*

Jan. 1792 Fort St. Clair built, one of series built to defend western frontier; **Nov. 6, 1792** fort attacked by 250 Native Americans under Chief Little Turtle, natives defeated, six defenders killed; **1806** town founded, named for Gen. William Eaton of Tripolitan War; **1808** Preble County formed; town becomes county seat; **1826** incorporated as a village; **1836** becomes a statutory city; **1918** third county courthouse built.

Elyria   *Lorain County*   *Northern Ohio, 22 mi/35 km west-southwest of Cleveland*

1755 Col. James Smith brought here by Native Americans, first known white man; **1817** town founded at falls of Black River by Heman Ely; **1822** Lorain County formed; town becomes county seat; **1833** incorporated as a town; **1864** Octagonal House built; **1870** Elyria Public Library opened; **1881** third county courthouse built; **1892** incorporated as a city.

Findlay   *Hancock County*   *Northwestern Ohio, 41 mi/66 km south of Toledo*

1769 Jean Jacques Blanchard arrives among Shawnee people; **1812** Fort Findlay built by Col. James Findlay; **1820** Hancock County formed; **1821** town founded by Joseph Vance and Elnathan Cory, incorrectly spelled Findley; **1828** county organized; town becomes county seat; **1836** natural gas field discovered by Richard Wade; **1838** incorporated as a village; **c.1866** Dr. Charles Osterlin organizes Findlay Natural Gas Company; **1870** name officially corrected to Findlay; **1882** University of Findlay established; **Jan. 1886** Karg natural gas well lights night sky with 100-ft/30.5-m column of flame; **1887** incorporated as a city; **1888** county courthouse completed, topped with figure of John Hancock; **1890s** Lima Oil Field yields abundance of oil, natural gas; **1968** Flag Day first observed here.

Franklin   *Warren County*   *Southwestern Ohio, 33 mi/53 km north-northeast of Cincinnati*

1795 town founded on Great Miami River by William Schenck, officer in William Henry Harrison's Army during War of 1812; **Oct. 4, 1809** Cong. Robert Cumming Schenck born (died 1890); **1814** incorporated as a city; **1829** Miami & Erie Canal completed; **1850** Franklin Hydraulic Canal built, completed c.1870, ancient stone dam unearthed.

Fremont   *Sandusky County   Northern Ohio, 30 mi/ 48 km southeast of Toledo*

c.1650 Wyandot people establish two villages on Sandusky River, later destroyed by British; **1757** James Smith passes through area with his Native American captors; **1780** under orders from George Washington, Samuel Brady explores area to assess military strength of Native Americans; **1782** British establish outpost; **1795** land set aside for town in Greenville Treaty; **1812** Fort Stephenson built; **Aug. 2, 1813** Maj. George Croghan and 160 men defend fort against large British force by shifting position of fort's sole cannon; **1816** Chroghansville founded; **1817** town of Lower Sandusky founded; **1820** Sandusky County formed; Lower Sandusky becomes county seat; **1822** two towns merge as Lower Sandusky; **1829** incorporated as a city; **1849** city renamed for explorer John C. Fremont; **1863** Hayes House (Spiegel Grove) built, estate of Pres. Rutherford B. Hayes 1873 until his death in 1893; **1885** oil discovered to west; **1916** Rutherford B. Hayes Presidential Center (Hayes Memorial) opened, first presidential library and museum in U.S.; **1937** county courthouse built completed, rebuilt existing 1840 structure.

Gallipolis   *Gallia County   Southern Ohio, 88 mi/ 142 km south-southeast of Columbus, on Ohio River*

1788 Scioto Company agent John Barlow sent to Paris, France, to sell town parcels, referred to "City of the Gauls"; **Oct. 1790** French arrive to claim land, find 80 crude log cabins, gradually abandon town; **1794** post office built; **1803** Gallia County formed; town becomes county seat; **1819** Our House tavern built by Henry Cushing, hosted Lafayette 1825, Jenny Lind 1851; **1842** incorporated as a village; **1865** becomes a statutory city; **1879** second county courthouse built; **1880** coal mining begins; **1928** Silver Bridge built across Ohio River to Point Pleasant, West Virginia; **July 21, 1934** highest temperature ever recorded in Ohio reached, 113°F/45°C; **1938** Gallipolis Lock & Dam built on Ohio River to south, originally named Eureka Lock & Dam; **Dec. 15, 1967** Silver Bridge collapses due to metal fatigue, 46 motorists killed; **1969** new Silver Memorial Bridge completed.

Gambier   *Knox County   See **Mount Vernon (1824)***

Garrettsville   *Portage County   Northeastern Ohio, 35 mi/56 km southeast of Cleveland*

1804 town founded by John Garrett III; **Apr. 19, 1832** Lucretia Rudolph Garfield, wife of President Garfield, born (married Nov. 11, 1858, died March 13, 1918); **1864**

incorporated as a village; **1899** town becomes largest maple syrup producing center in the world.

Georgetown   *Brown County   Southwestern Ohio, 36 mi/58 km east-southeast of Cincinnati*

1817 Brown County formed; Ripley becomes county seat; **1819** town founded; **1821** county seat moved to Georgetown; **1823** Grant House built, boyhood home of Ulysses S. Grant, brought here from Point Pleasant, Ohio (born Apr. 1822); **1829** Grant Schoolhouse built, converted to museum 1899; **1832** incorporated as a village; **1851** county courthouse built, destroyed by fire 1977, rebuilt 1986; **1870s** town becomes tobacco distribution center.

Gilmore   *Tuscarawas County   See **Uhrichsville (1867)***

Gnadenhutten   *Tuscarawas County   East central Ohio, 78 mi/126 km south of Cleveland*

1772 David Zeisberger founds Moravian mission for Christian Indians at nearby Schoenbrunn; **1772** Moravian Mohican elder named Joshua founds town; **1781** Christian Indians forced to move to Sandusky plains near Lake Erie by white renegade named Elliott and Delaware chiefs Captain Pipe and Half-King where they proceed to starve to death; **Feb. 1782** Christian Indians return to site to reclaim what they can of crops; **March 8, 1782** Capt. David Williamson arrives from Pennsylvania, imprisons Christian Indians in their church while town votes on their fate, 96 massacred following morning, town burned; **1885** incorporated as a village. [see Mount Clemens, Michigan]

Granville   *Licking County   Central Ohio, 25 mi/ 40 km east-northeast of Columbus*

1805 first settlers arrive from Granville, Massachusetts; **1806** town founded; **1812** Buxton Inn built; **c.1830** National Road built through town; **1831** Granville Literary and Theological Institute established, becomes Denison University 1854; **1832** incorporated as a village; **c.1842** Avery-Hunter House built.

Greenville   *Darke County   Western Ohio, 86 mi/ 138 km west-northwest of Columbus*

Oct. 1791 Fort Jefferson built to south by Arthur St. Clair; **Nov. 4, 1791** St. Clair's forces defeated by Chief Little Turtle on Wabash River with 900 casualties, biggest loss of Revolution; **1793–1794** Gen. Anthony Wayne establishes Fort Greeneville; **1796** General Wayne signs Greenville Treaty with Shawnee, Wyandot, Delaware, Miami, Ottawa, Chippewa, Pottawatomi, Wea, Kickapoo, Piankashaw, and Kaskaskia tribes; **1808** town platted; **1809** Darke County formed; **1816** county organized; town becomes county seat; **1838** incorporated as a town; **Aug. 13, 1860** Western heroine Annie Oakley born at North Star to north (died 1926); **1874** third county courthouse built; **1887** becomes a statutory city; **Apr. 6, 1892** radio personality, explorer Lowell Thomas born at Woodington to north (died 1981).

Hamilton   *Butler County   Southwestern Ohio, 20 mi/32 km north of Cincinnati*

1791 Fort Hamilton built on Great Miami River by Gen. St. Clair; **1794** Hamilton platted on east side of river by Col. Israel Ludlow; **1803** Butler County formed; town becomes county seat; **1804** Rossville founded on west side of river; **1810** incorporated as a village; **1814** *Miami Intelligencer* newspaper founded; **1827** Miami & Erie Canal reaches town; **1842** Estate Stove Company founded; **1845** water-power plant, the Hydraulic, built; **1851** Cincinnati, Hamilton & Dayton Railroad reaches town; **1854** Rossville annexed by Hamilton; **1857** becomes a statutory city; **1889** county courthouse built; **Oct. 18, 1889** author Fannie Hurst born (died 1968); **1913** flooding causes extensive damage; **March 31, 1975** James Ruppart arrested for slaying 11 family members Easter Sunday, March 30.

Hillsboro   *Highland County   Southern Ohio, 47 mi/ 76 km east of Cincinnati*

1805 Highland County formed; **1807** town founded as county seat, named Hillsborough; **1814** incorporated as a village; **1808** settlers arrive from Maryland, Virginia, New Jersey, Pennsylvania; **1834** county courthouse built; **1860s** tobacco boom started by Gen. James Loudoun; **Oct. 6, 1862** Indiana Sen. Albert Beveridge born (died 1927); **Dec. 1873** Women's Temperance Crusade launched by Eliza Jane Thompson; **1894** town renamed Hillsboro; **Feb. 28, 1907** Milton Caniff born, created Steve Canyon comic strip (died 1988); **1951** becomes a statutory city.

Hiramsburg   *Noble County   See* Caldwell (1868)

Hudson   *Summit County   Northeastern Ohio, 21 mi/ 34 km south-southeast of Cleveland*

1799 David Hudson and party arrive from Connecticut; town founded; **1805** abolitionist John Brown (1800–1859) brought here from Torrington, Connecticut, moves to Akron 1844; **1826** Western Reserve College established, moves to Cleveland 1882; **1837** incorporated as a village; **1850s** Cleveland & Pittsburgh Railroad reaches town; **c.1900** town enters period of decline; **1904** Produce Exchange Bank closes following embezzlement case; **1912** James W. Ellsworth erects Clock Tower on the Green as symbol of town's economic recovery; **1916** Western Reserve Academy founded by Ellsworth; **1991** becomes a statutory city; **1994** Hudson Township merges with city of Hudson.

Huron   *Erie County   Northern Ohio, 44 mi/71 km west of Cleveland, on Lake Erie*

c.1749 French trading post established at mouth of Huron River; **1805** B. F. Flemond establishes trading post; town

founded; **1809** incorporated as a village; **1820s** town prospers as shipbuilding center; **1834** cholera epidemic kills many; **1835** Huron Lighthouse built, replaced 1936; **1839** Huron-Milan Canal opened; **1878** Wheeling & Lake Erie Railroad Docks established; **1937** large one-man coal dumper built at docks, able to unload 50 rail cars in one hour; **1961** becomes a statutory city; **Aug. 27, 1967** 16 of 18 sky divers killed when they miss target, land in Lake Erie.

Ironton   *Lawrence County   Southern Ohio, 104 mi/ 167 km east-southeast of Cincinnati, on Ohio River*

1815 Lawrence County formed; Burlington becomes first county seat; **1826** iron ore deposits discovered at Hecla Mine, near Ohio River; **1834** Mount Vernon Furnace built by John Campbell; **1849** town founded; **1849** incorporated as a village; **1852** county seat moved to Ironton; **1865** becomes a statutory city; **1908** third county courthouse built.

Jackson   *Jackson County   Southern Ohio, 63 mi/ 101 km south-southeast of Columbus*

1798 salt production begins at Salt Springs; **1804** state saltworks established; **1816** Jackson County formed; Purgatory becomes county seat; **1817** town founded as new county seat; **1847** incorporated as a village; **1850s** Welsh immigrants arrive to serve as ironworkers; **1853** Baltimore & Ohio Railroad reaches town; **1868** county courthouse built, rebuilt 1951 following fire; **1893** becomes a statutory city; **1922** first Jackson Eisteddfod, Welsh songfest, held; **1934** John Wesley Powell Memorial erected, explorer spent childhood here; **1971** Welsh History Museum founded.

Jefferson   *Ashtabula County   Northeastern Ohio, 50 mi/80 km east-northeast of Cleveland*

1804 area settled; **1811** Ashtabula County formed; town becomes county seat; **1823** Giddings Law Office built, headquarters of attorney Joshua Giddings; **1836** incorporated as a village; **1837** second county courthouse built, rebuilt 1850, expanded 1919; **1851** Congregational Church built; **Dec. 20, 1851** Sen. Theodore Elijah Burton born (died 1929); **1868** South Denmark Road Covered Bridge built to southeast on Mill Creek; **1876** Doyle Road Covered Bridge built to west on Mill Creek; **1984** first Covered Bridge Festival held recognizing county's 16 covered bridges.

Kelleys Island   *Erie County   Northern Ohio, 52 mi/ 84 km west-northwest of Cleveland, on Lake Erie*

c.1200 first known habitation of Lake Erie islands; **1656** French cartographer Nicholas Sanson names islands Isles of the Apostles; **1679** French explorer La Salle passes islands; **1763** islands ceded to Britain; **1783** islands ceded to U.S.; **1800** trader named Cunningham settles here, named Cunningham's Island; **1833** Inscription Rock bearing Native American pictographs discovered; **1833** Irad and Datus Kelley acquire island, island renamed;

OHIO

1840 town founded; **1846** first vineyards planted; **1850** wine production begins; **1867** Addison Kelley House built; **1888** incorporated as a village.

Kent *Portage County* *Northeastern Ohio, 29 mi/ 47 km southeast of Cleveland*

1805 town founded, named Franklin Mills; **1863** Atlantic & Great Western Railroad built through efforts of Marvin Kent; Carthage merges with Franklin Mills, renamed Kent; **1867** incorporated as a village; **1910** Kent State University established; **1915** Lake Rockwell formed to northeast by dam on Cuyahoga River; **1920** becomes a statutory city; **May 4, 1970** 100 National Guardsmen suppress 600 students protesting U.S. involvement in Cambodia, 4 killed, 9 wounded; **Oct. 16, 1970** Grand Jury indicts 25 participants in Kent State incident, National Guardsmen cleared.

Kenton *Hardin County* *West central Ohio, 55 mi/ 89 km northwest of Columbus*

1833 Hardin County formed; town founded as county seat, named for Indian fighter Simon Kenton; **1845** incorporated as a city; **1914** third county courthouse built; **Nov. 9, 1941** passenger train derails into oncoming train at rural Dunkirk to north, 13 killed; **March 5, 1967** 38 killed in crash of Lake Airlines prop-jet during snowstorm.

Kingston *Ross County* See **Chillicothe (1819)**

Kinsman *Trumbull County* See **Warren (1857)**

Kirtland *Lake County* *Northeastern Ohio, 19 mi/ 31 km northeast of Cleveland*

Oct. 1830 four Mormon disciples stop at nearby Mentor, Ohio, on way to Missouri, convert minister Sidney Rigdon to their new faith, 127 other converts added within weeks; **Feb. 1831** Mormon leader Joseph Smith arrives from Western New York with followers, over 1,000 more arrive in coming months; **summer 1831** Smith and others return from Missouri, determine it unfit for settlement and Stake of Zion; **1832** town platted; **Nov. 6, 1832** Mormon leader Joseph Smith the younger born to Mormon founder Joseph Smith (died 1914); **1836** Kirtland Temple completed, begun 1833; **1837** Mormon followers increase to 4,000; **Jan. 12, 1838** Smith and Rigdon flee to Missouri, wanted in Ohio for violating banking laws stemming from colony's operations, Kirtland colony collapses; **1913** Holden Arboretum founded; **1968** incorporated as a village to avert annexation by Mentor; **1971** becomes a statutory city.

Lakewood *Cuyahoga County* *Northeastern Ohio, suburb 4 mi/6.4 km west of Cleveland*

1888 town founded on Lake Erie, originally named East Rockport; **1889** town renamed Lakewood; **1903** incorporated as a village; **1911** becomes a statutory city; **March**

13, 1910 bandleader Sammy Kaye born (died 1987); **Dec. 11, 1945** actress Teri Garr born.

Lancaster *Fairfield County* *Central Ohio, 26 mi/ 42 km southeast of Columbus, on Hocking River*

1797 settlers arrive on Zane's Trace; **1800** Fairfield County formed; town founded as county seat by Ebenezer Zane, named New Lancaster; **1805** town name shortened to Lancaster; **1811** Sherman birthplace built; **Feb. 8, 1820** Union Gen. William Tecumseh Sherman born (died 1891); **May 10, 1823** U.S. Sen. John Sherman born (died 1900); **1831** incorporated as a village; **Oct. 26, 1831** John Willock Noble born, secretary of interior under Pres. Benjamin Harrison (died 1912); **1834** Lancaster Lateral Canal opens; **1835** Reese Peters House built; **1851** becomes a statutory city; **Jan. 14, 1863** cartoonist Richard Felton Outcault born (died 1928); **1872** county courthouse built; **1887** natural gas discovered; **1905** Anchor-Hocking Glass Company founded.

Lebanon *Warren County* *Southwestern Ohio, 28 mi/45 km northeast of Cincinnati*

1796 area first settled; **1802** town founded; **1803** Warren County formed; town becomes county seat; **1807** *Western Star* newspaper founded; **1810** incorporated as a village; **1835** county courthouse built; **1855** Southwestern Normal School established, became National Normal University 1881, closed 1917; **1962** becomes a statutory city.

Lima *Allen County* *Western Ohio, 68 mi/109 km south-southwest of Toledo*

1831 Allen County formed; **1831** town founded as county seat, name Lima (LEI-ma) drawn from hat; **1842** incorporated as a city; **1845** Miami & Erie Canal completed to west; **1854** Ohio & Lima Railroad reaches town; **1884** county courthouse completed; **1885** Benjamin C. Faurot discovers oil, oil boom declines after 1900; **1891** Deisel and Wemmer Cigar Factory established; **1900** interurban electric rail line built from Piqua; **1901** Lima Locomotive Works plant opened at South Lima; **1915** Lima State Hospital built; Garford Truck Company moves from Elyria, becomes Superior Coach Company 1925; **July 17, 1917** comedian Phyllis Diller born; **1918** Liberty Motor Truck plant built for U.S. Army; **May 23, 1921** actress Helen O'Connell born (died 1993); **Oct. 1933** John Dillinger gang murder Sheriff Jesse Sarber, results in nationwide manhunt and Dillinger's death; **1936** Lima Municipal Stadium completed.

Lisbon *Columbiana County* *Eastern Ohio, 66 mi/ 106 km southeast of Cleveland*

1803 town founded, originally named New Lisbon; **1803** Columbiana County formed; town becomes county seat; **July 20, 1820** Cong. Clement L. Vallandigham born, leader of Peace Democrats (Copperheads) during Civil War (died 1871); **1825** incorporated as a village; **Sept. 24, 1837** U.S. Sen. Marcus A. Hanna born (died 1904); **Sept.**

18, 1857 Supreme Court Justice John Hessin Clarke born (died 1945); **July 26, 1863** Confederate Gen. John Morgan of Morgan's Raiders surrenders to Union Maj. George W. Rue at West Point to southeast, ending band's reign of terror in Indiana and Ohio [see Long Bottom]; **1885** county courthouse built.

Logan   *Hocking County   Central Ohio, 41 mi/66 km southeast of Columbus*

1816 town founded on Hocking River; **1818** Hocking County formed; town becomes county seat; **1839** incorporated as a city; **1840** Hocking Canal opens; **1869** Hocking Valley Railroad reaches town; **1925** county courthouse built.

London   *Madison County   Central Ohio, 23 mi/ 37 km west-southwest of Columbus*

1810 Madison County founded; **1811** town founded as county seat on property of John Murfin; **1831** incorporated as a city; **1856** town's livestock industry begins; **1892** county courthouse built; **1925** London State Prison Farm built.

Long Bottom   *Meigs County   Southeastern Ohio, 85 mi/137 km southeast of Columbus, on Ohio River*

Oct. 28, 1770 George Washington and men camp here during tour of Ohio Valley; **July 19, 1863** Battle of Buffinton Island, only significant Civil War engagement in Ohio, Gen. John Morgan's 700 Confederates blocked by small Union force on west, gunboats on east, Morgan and others escape, captured at West Point, Ohio, July 26 [see Lisbon].

Lorain   *Lorain County   Northern Ohio, 24 mi/39 km west of Cleveland, on Lake Erie*

1787 Moravian missionaries camp with Native American converts on Lake Erie, ordered to move by Delaware peoples; **1807** trading post established by Nathan Perry and Azariah Beebe; town founded, named Charleston; **1819** shipbuilding begins; **1834** incorporated as a village; **1872** Cleveland, Lorain & Wheeling Railroad reaches town; **1874** becomes statutory city, renamed Lorain; **Nov. 23, 1878** World War I naval officer Ernest Joseph King born (died 1956); **1880s** Nickel Plate Railroad reaches town; **1894** steel mill established; **1898** American Shipbuilding Plant established; **1911** U.S. Coast Guard Station established; **June 28, 1924** four tornadoes destroy town, 79 killed locally, also Sandusky, Ohio, total 85 killed; **Feb. 18, 1931** African-American author Toni Morrison born, Nobel Prize 1993.

Loudonville   *Ashland County   North central Ohio, 65 mi/105 km south-southwest of Cleveland*

1814 town founded; **1850** incorporated as a village; **Aug. 29, 1876** inventor Charles Kettering born, developer of automobile ignition system, Freon refrigeration systems, leaded gasoline, electric cash register (died 1958); **1909** Ohio Theatre built; **1937** Pleasant Hill Lake formed by dam to west on Clear Fork Mohican River.

Mansfield   *Richland County   North central Ohio, 65 mi/105 km southwest of Cleveland*

1800 area first settled; **1808** Richland County formed; town platted by Jared Mansfield, U.S. Surveyor General; **1809** first cabin built; **1812** John Chapman (Johnny Appleseed) runs 30 mi/48 km to Mount Vernon, returns with troops to repel attack by British and Native American allies; **1813** county organized; town becomes county seat; **1814** two blockhouses built to protect against Native American raids; **1818** town's first newspaper *The Olive* founded; **1828** incorporated as a village; **1846** Mansfield & Sandusky Railroad reaches town; **1850** Pittsburgh, Fort Wayne & Chicago Railroad built; **1857** becomes a statutory city; **1858** Richland County Lincoln Society makes first group endorsement of Abraham Lincoln for presidency; **Nov. 9, 1861** Missouri Sen. James Alexander Reed born (died 1944); **1885** Ohio State Reformatory built; **1888** Ohio Brass Company founded; **Dec. 27, 1896** author Louis Bromfield born (died 1906); **1912** Mansfield Tire Company organized; **1918** Westinghouse Electric plant opens; **1925** Lahm Airport established; **1934** first all-electric home built with assistance of Westinghouse Company; **1969** fourth county courthouse built.

Marblehead   *Ottawa County   Northern Ohio, 5 mi/ 8 km north of Sandusky, on Lake Erie*

1809 Benajah Wolcott family arrives, first settlers at end of peninsula north side of Sandusky Bay, Lake Erie, discover orchards planted by French; **1821** Marblehead Lighthouse built; **1834** limestone quarrying begun by John Clemens, relative of Samuel Clemens (Mark Twain); **1861** prison camp built on Johnson Island to south, at entrance to Sandusky Bay, housed 15,000 Confederate prisoners during course of Civil War; **1891** incorporated as a village.

Marietta   *Washington County   Southeastern Ohio, 88 mi/142 km east-southeast of Columbus, on Ohio River*

1785 Fort Harmar built at mouth of Muskingum River; **1788** Washington County formed; first settlers arrive led by Rufus Putnam; town founded, named for Marie Antoinette of France; Campus Martius fort built; **1797** Marietta College established; **1803** Meigs Mansion built by Gov. Return Jonathan Meigs, Jr.; **1810s** town becomes active in Underground Railroad, harboring runaway slaves en route to freedom in Canada; **March 22, 1818** Union Gen. Don Carlos Buell born (died 1898); **1825** incorporated as a village; **1851** becomes a statutory city; **1931** Campus Martius State Memorial Museum built; **1967** I-77 Bridge built across Ohio River to Williamstown, West Virginia; **Jan. 9, 1970** nursing home fire, 27 killed; **1972** Ohio River Museum established.

Marion *Marion County* *Central Ohio, 43 mi/69 km north of Columbus*

c.1819 Jacob Foos arrives, digs well; town of Jacob's Well founded; **1822** town platted, renamed for Revolutionary War Gen. Francis Marion; **1823** Marion County formed; **1824** town becomes county seat; **1830** incorporated as a village; **Aug. 15, 1860** Florence Kling De Wolfe Harding, wife of President Harding, born (married 1891, died Nov. 21, 1924); **1865** Edward Huber arrives, begins building tractors, farm machines; **1875** Huber Manufacturing Company established; **1884** Marion Steam Shovel Company founded; **Nov. 20, 1884** Socialist leader Norman Thomas born (died 1968); **1885** county courthouse completed; **1890** becomes a statutory city; **1891** Harding House built; **1926** Harding Memorial built, dedicated 1931; **July 1, 1959** plane crash kills eight Continental Can executives, two pilots.

Martins Ferry *Belmont County* *Eastern Ohio, 106 mi/171 km south-southeast of Cleveland, on Ohio River*

1785 town of Norristown founded by squatters; ferry established; **1795** Absalom Martin plats town of Jefferson; **1801** Martin cancels plat after St. Clairsville is chosen county seat; **1835** town replatted by son Ebenezer Martin, renamed Martinsville; **March 1, 1837** writer William Dean Howells born (died 1920); **1849** glass industry established; **1865** incorporated as a village, renamed Martins Ferry; **1885** becomes a statutory city; **Dec. 13, 1927** poet James Arlington Wright born (died 1980); **1928** Betty Zane monument erected, brought gunpowder to defenders of Fort Henry at site of Wheeling while under attack Sept. 11, 1782; **Apr. 8, 1940** Celtics basketball player John Havlicek born.

Marysville *Union County* *Central Ohio, 27 mi/43 km northwest of Columbus*

1809 town platted by Samuel Culbertson, named for landowner's wife; **1816** Jonathan Summers becomes first settler; **1820** Union County formed; **1821** town becomes county seat; **1838** incorporated as a village; **1840** symbols of William Henry Harrison's presidential campaign against Martin Van Buren have origins here, the log cabin logo and "Log Cabin Song," written by Otway Curry; **1883** fourth county courthouse completed; **1909** Marysville Public Library opened, replaced 1988; **1916** Ohio State Reformatory for Women established; **1971** becomes a statutory city.

Massillon *Stark County* *Eastern Ohio, 48 mi/77 km south of Cleveland, on Tuscarawas River*

1810 Massum Metcalf becomes first settler; **1812** town of Kendal founded by Thomas Rotch; **1826** new town founded by James Duncan and Ferdinand Huxthal, named for Jean Baptiste Massillon, Mrs. Duncan's favorite writer; **1828** first coal shipment made from Bridgeport mine; **Aug. 25, 1828** arrival of steamboat Allen Trimble signals opening of Ohio & Erie Canal; **1833** Massillon Iron Company established; **1835** Duncan House built by James Duncan; **1842** Russell and Company begins manufacture of farm implements; **1852** coming of railroad renders canal obsolete; **1853** incorporated as a village; **1898** Massillon State Hospital established; **March 11, 1898** actress Dorothy Gish born (died 1968); **1915** Central Steel Company built; **1916** National Pressed Steel Company plant built; **1921** Central and National Pressed steel companies merge, acquired 1930 by Republic Steel.

Maumee *Lucas County* *Northwestern Ohio, suburb 8 mi/12.9 km south-southwest of Toledo*

1680 trading post established by French-Canadians, destroyed by natives, rebuilt 1693, abandoned; **1764** Fort Miami built by English; **Aug. 20, 1794** Gen. Anthony Wayne defeats group of Shawnee, Iroquois, Ottawa, and Miami at Battle of Fallen Timbers to south; **1813** in Dudley Massacre, force of 800 Kentuckians led by Col. Dudley ambushed by English, all but 140 killed; **1817** town founded; **1824** work begins on Miami & Erie Canal, completed to Cincinnati 1845; **1825** Knaggs House built; **1828** Hoffman's Inn built; **1835** Lucas County formed; **1838** incorporated as a city; **1840** city becomes county seat; **1852** county seat moved to Toledo; **1880s** natural gas deposits discovered.

McArthur *Vinton County* *Southern Ohio, 54 mi/87 km south-southeast of Columbus*

1815 town founded at road junction, named McArthurstown, for Ohio Gov. Duncan McArthur; **1850** Vinton County formed; town becomes county seat; **1851** incorporated as a village, name shortened; **1938** county courthouse built.

McConnelsville *Morgan County* *Southeastern Ohio, 63 mi/101 km east-southeast of Columbus*

Jan. 6, 1791 Native Americans attack group of settlers at Big Bottom to south, 12 settlers killed; **1817** town founded on Muskingum River by Robert McConnel; **1818** Morgan County formed; town becomes county seat; **1827** salt production becomes important; **1836** incorporated as a village; **Feb. 13, 1853** Frederick Dellenbaugh born, illustrator, cartographer for John Wesley Powell expedition (died 1935); **1858** county courthouse built; **1905** Big Bottom State Park established, later becomes state monument; **1934** Morgan County Library founded, new facility opened 1997.

Medina *Medina County* *Northern Ohio, 25 mi/40 km south-southwest of Cleveland*

1812 Medina County formed; **1818** county organized; Captain Badger builds cabin; town founded as county seat; **1835** incorporated as a village; **1841** county courthouse built; **1869** jewelry manufacturer A. I. Root purchases swarm of bees, founds A. I. Root Company, maker of honey and beekeeping accessories; **1950** becomes a statutory city.

Mentor   *Lake County   Northeastern Ohio, 22 mi/ 35 km northeast of Cleveland, near Lake Erie*

1797 Charles Parker becomes first settler; **1799** town founded; **1832** Pres. James A. Garfield House built, acquired by Garfield 1876, enlarged 1880, inaugurated March 4, 1881, died Sept. 19, 1881; **1855** incorporated as a village; **Nov. 3, 1858** explorer, aeronaut Walter Wellman born (died 1934); **1894** memorial stone, windmill built by President Garfield's wife Lucretia; **1963** becomes a statutory city; **Dec. 28, 1980** James A. Garfield National Historic Site authorized.

Miamisburg   *Montgomery County   Southwestern Ohio, 38 mi/61 km north-northeast of Cincinnati*

1800 Zachariah Hole builds blockhouse on Great Miami River; **1818** town founded by Pennsylvanian Germans, originally named Hole's Station; **1829** Miami & Erie Canal completed; **1832** incorporated as a village; **1840** Hoover and Company begins manufacture of reapers; **1932** incorporated as a city; **1954** Mound Advanced Technology Center founded by U.S. Government for nuclear defense research, passes to private sector 1993 for general research.

Middletown   *Butler County   Southwestern Ohio, 29 mi/47 km north of Cincinnati*

1802 town founded on Great Miami River by Stephen Vail and James Sutton, named for its location between Dayton and Cincinnati; **1829** Miami & Erie Canal completed; **1833** incorporated as a village; **1859** first tobacco processing plant established; **1899** American Steel and Roofing Company established, became American Rolling Mill Company 1901; **1913** becomes a statutory city; **July 30, 1929** singer Christine McGuire (McGuire Sisters) born; **Feb. 13, 1930** singer Dorothy McGuire born; **Feb. 14, 1931** singer Phyllis McGuire born.

Milan   *Erie County   Northern Ohio, 47 mi/76 km west-southwest of Cleveland*

1787 David Zeisberger's Christian Indians forced to relocate here from Gnadenhutten; **1804** town of Pequotting founded by Moravian missionary; **c.1806** white settlers from Connecticut begin arriving; **1816** town of Milan platted; **1824** construction started on canal to Lake Erie, completed 1839; **1833** incorporated as a village; **1841** Edison birthplace built; **1847** Mitchell-Turner House built; **Feb. 11, 1847** inventor Thomas Alva Edison born (died 1931); **1852** town refuses right-of-way to Lake Shore & Michigan Southern Railroad, route diverted to Norwalk.

Millersburg   *Holmes County   Central Ohio, 67 mi/ 108 km northeast of Columbus*

1815 town founded Andrew Johnston and Charles Miller; **1824** Holmes County formed; town becomes county seat; **1835** incorporated as a village; **1886** third county courthouse built; **1905** Carnegie grant for new library goes unclaimed by village; **1928** Holmes County Public Library opened.

Millfield   *Athens County   See* **Athens (1930)**

Milligan   *Perry County   See* **New Lexington (1899)**

Mount Gilead   *Morrow County   Central Ohio, 41 mi/66 km north-northeast of Columbus*

1817 area settled by Lewis and Ralph Hardenbrook, originally named Whetstone; **1824** town founded by James Young, renamed Youngstown; **1832** town renamed Mount Gilead; **1839** incorporated as a village; **1848** Morrow County formed; town becomes county seat; **1852** county courthouse completed, addition built 1890; **1883** hydraulic press manufacturing plant founded; **1919** victory monument dedicated on town square to World War I fallen.

Mount Vernon   *Knox County   Central Ohio, 39 mi/63 km northeast of Columbus*

1805 town founded and platted by Benjamin Butler, Thomas Patterson, and Joseph Walker; **1808** Knox County formed; town becomes county seat; **Oct. 29, 1815** songwriter Daniel Decatur Emmett born, wrote "Dixie" (died 1904); **1824** Kenyon College established at Gambier to southeast; **1828** John Chapman (Johnny Appleseed) acquires property here; **1830** incorporated as a village; **1856** second county courthouse built; **1880** becomes a statutory city; **1897** Jacob Coxey builds steel plant; **1968** Mount Vernon Nazarene College established, now University.

Napoleon   *Henry County   Northwestern Ohio, 34 mi/55 km southwest of Toledo*

1820 Henry County formed; **1834** county organized; town founded as county seat on Maumee River; **1843** Miami & Erie Canal opened; **1863** incorporated as a city; **1882** third county courthouse built.

New Concord   *Muskingum County   East central Ohio, 66 mi/106 km east of Columbus*

1828 National Road reaches site; town platted; **1837** Muskingum College established; **1838** incorporated as a village; **July 24, 1856** educator William Rainey Harper born (died 1906).

New Lexington *Perry County* *Central Ohio, 44 mi/71 km east-southeast of Columbus*

1800 first white settlers arrive; **1805** town platted; **1817** Perry County formed; Somerset becomes first county seat; incorporated as a village; **1830** area's first coal mine opened; **1840** incorporated as a city; **June 12, 1844** J. A. MacGahan born, newspaper reporter turned international soldier, rode with Russian army, liberator of Bulgaria (died 1878); **1857** county seat moved to New Lexington; **1886** third county courthouse built; **Feb. 10, 1899** lowest temperature ever recorded in Ohio reached at Milligan to east, −39°F/−39.4°C.

New Philadelphia *Tuscarawas County* *East central Ohio, 69 mi/111 km south of Cleveland*

1804 town founded; **1808** Tuscarawas County formed; town becomes county seat; **1833** incorporated as a village; **1854** Cleveland & Pittsburgh Railroad reaches town; **1882** county courthouse built; **1895** becomes a statutory city.

New Rumley *Harrison County* See **Cadiz (1839)**

Newark *Licking County* *Central Ohio, 31 mi/50 km east-northeast of Columbus, on Licking River*

1755 Christopher Gist becomes first white man to enter region; **1800** town founded by Gen. William Schenck of Newark, New Jersey; Black's Tavern opened by James Black; **1801** John Chapman (Johnny Appleseed, 1774–1845) arrives from Massachusetts, plants orchard, first appearance west of Ohio River, next seen 1806 floating down Ohio River; **1808** Licking County formed; town becomes county seat; **1816** Mary Ann Iron Foundry established, named for Mary Ann Township, source of iron ore; **Aug. 3, 1824** Supreme Court Justice William Burnham Woods born (died 1887); **1826** incorporated as a town; **Oct. 19, 1828** Iowa Cong., Sen. James Falconer Wilson born (died 1895); **1832** Ohio & Erie Canal completed; **c.1835** Buckingham House built; **1853** Sandusky, Mansfield & Newark Railroad reaches town; **1854** cholera epidemic strikes town; **1855** Steubenville & Indiana Railroad built; **1860** becomes a statutory city; **1865** Warden Hotel built on site of Black's Tavern, closed 1959; **1878** third county courthouse built; **1883** Newark Stove Company founded; **1896** A. H. Heisey Company founded, makers of fine glassware; **1900** Holophane Glass Company moves from New York; **1908** Newark Public Library opened; **1910** Pharis Rubber Company opens plant; **July 10, 1910** 23 "dry detectives" search for illegal saloons, Last Chance Saloon proprietor killed by detective Carl Etherington, arrested and jailed, lynched by mob, upset because Prohibition closed bottle factory; **1929** Dawes Arboretum established by oil executive B. G. Dawes; **1933** Owens-Corning Fiberglass Company opens experimental plant for making insulating wool and textiles; **1954** Newark Air Force Base established, closed 1996.

Niles *Trumbull County* *Northeastern Ohio, 8 mi/12.9 km northwest of Youngstown*

1806 settler James Heaton builds grist mill, first blast furnace; town founded, named Heaton's Furnace; **1834** town renamed Nilestown for Baltimore newspaper editor admired by Heaton; **Jan. 29, 1843** William F. McKinley, 25th President, born (shot Sept. 6, 1901, died Sept. 14); **1865** incorporated as a village; **1897** becomes a statutory city; **1917** McKinley Memorial Library opened; **Oct. 5, 1917** McKinley Birthplace Memorial dedicated.

North Bend *Hamilton County* *Southwestern Ohio, 12 mi/19 km west of Cincinnati, on Ohio River*

1789 area first settled; town founded; **1829** Benjamin Harrison birthplace built, burned 1845; **Aug. 20, 1833** Benjamin Harrison, 23rd President, born, grandson of Pres. William Henry Harrison (died March 13, 1901); **Apr. 1841** Pres. William Henry Harrison buried here, died Apr. 4, one month after assuming office (born 1773); **1845** incorporated as a village.

North Star *Darke County* See **Greenville (1860)**

Norwalk *Huron County* *Northern Ohio, 49 mi/79 km west-southwest of Cleveland*

1792 Connecticut dedicates 500,000 ac/202,500 ha in Western Reserve (Ohio) called the Firelands, land available to citizens who lost property during Revolution; **1809** Huron County formed; **1815** county organized; Avery becomes county seat; **1817** town founded by Platt Benedict; **1818** county seat moved to Norwalk; **1828** incorporated as a village; **1852** Toledo, Norwalk & Cleveland (Lake Shore & Michigan) Railroad reaches town; **1881** becomes a statutory city; third county courthouse built, rebuilt after 1913 fire; **1907** Firelands Museum opened; **Sept. 7, 1908** Cleveland Browns football coach Paul Brown born (died 1991).

Oberlin *Lorain County* *Northern Ohio, 29 mi/47 km west-southwest of Cleveland*

1832 town founded by Phillip Steward and Rev. John Shipward; **1833** Oberlin College established; **1846** incorporated as a city; **Feb. 23, 1886** Charles Martin Hall develops electrolytic process for making aluminum one year after his graduation from Oberlin College; **1871** Civil War memorial built; **1943** soldiers memorial built at Wright Park.

Oldtown *Greene County* *West central Ohio, 51 mi/82 km west-southwest of Columbus*

1773 Captain Bullitt arrives at Shawnee village of Old Chillicothe to negotiate peaceful settlement of Kentucky by settlers from Virginia; **1778** Daniel Boone brought here as captive of Shawnees, forced to run the gauntlet to Ohio River; **Aug. 1780** George Rogers Clark stops here en route to Piqua, destroys crops and Native American village, natives flee to Piqua; **1786** following Shawnee violation of peace settlement agreement, Colonel Logan destroys Shawnee villages.

Orange *Cuyahoga County Northeastern Ohio, 12 mi/19 km east-southeast of Cleveland*

1815 Serenus Burnett becomes first settler; **Nov. 19, 1831** James Abram Garfield, 20th President, born (died Sept. 19, 1881); **1928** incorporated as a village.

Ottawa *Putnam County Northwestern Ohio, 50 mi/80 km southwest of Toledo*

1820 Putnam County formed; Kalida becomes county seat; **1833** town founded soon after removal of Ottawa people to western areas, named Tawa Town; **1834** town platted; incorporated as a village; **1837** post office established; **1866** county seat moved to Ottawa; **1913** third county courthouse built; **1917** Ohio Sugar Company established.

Oxford *Butler County Southwestern Ohio, 30 mi/ 48 km north-northwest of Cincinnati*

1809 Miami University established, opened 1824; **1810** town founded; **1830** incorporated as a village; Mansion House residence built; **c.1830** Spinning Wheel Tavern built; **Oct. 1, 1832** Caroline Lavinia Scott Harrison, first wife of Pres. Benjamin Harrison, born (married Oct. 29, 1853, died 1892); **1833** McGuffey House built; **1855** Western College for Women established; **1872** town's saloons closed by university; **1971** becomes a statutory city.

Painesville *Lake County Northeastern Ohio, 28 mi/45 km northeast of Cleveland, near Lake Erie*

1805 town founded by settlers from Connecticut, named Champion; **1811** Jonathan Goldsmith arrives from New England, serves as Western Reserve's primary architect and builder; **1818** Rider Tavern built, designed by Goldsmith; **1832** incorporated as a village; **1840** Lake County formed; town becomes county seat; **1852** city hall built; **1857** Lake Erie College established; **1902** becomes a statutory city; **1907** county courthouse completed.

Paulding *Paulding County Northwestern Ohio, 63 mi/101 km southwest of Toledo*

1820 Paulding County formed; **1839** county organized; Rochester becomes first county seat; **1841** county seat moved to Charloe; **1850** town founded; **1851** county seat moved to Paulding; **1872** first Paulding County Fair held; **1874** incorporated as a village; **1887** third county courthouse built; **1916** Paulding County Carnegie Library opened.

Perrysburg *Wood County Northwestern Ohio, 7 mi/11.3 km south-southwest of Toledo*

Feb. 1813 Fort Meigs built on Maumee River by Gen. Benjamin Harrison; **spring 1813** British besiege fort, fail to seize it; **1816** town founded at Maumee Rapids, named for Adm. Oliver Hazard Perry; **1820** Wood County formed; **1822** town becomes county seat; **1830s** town becomes important Lake Erie port; **1833** incorporated as a village; Hollister House built, completed 1838; **1866** county seat moved to Bowling Green; **1960** becomes a statutory city.

Piqua *Miami County Western Ohio, 66 mi/106 km west-northwest of Columbus*

1749 Fort Piqua built to north by French, destroyed 1752; **1763** Shawnee establish headquarters adjacent to fort, through 1780; **1793** Gen. Anthony Wayne rebuilds Fort Piqua; **1797** town founded on Great Miami River, named Washington; **1807** town platted; **1814** Johnston House built by Col. John Johnston; **1816** town renamed Piqua; **1823** incorporated as a village; **1824** linseed oil becomes important industry; **1845** Miami & Erie Canal completed from Cincinnati, remains in use until 1912; **1891** Fort Piqua Hotel built; **Oct. 19, 1910** singer John Mills, Jr. (Mills Brothers) born (died 1936); **Apr. 12, 1912** singer Herbert Mills born (died 1989); **Aug. 19, 1913** singer Harry F. Mills born (died 1982); **Apr. 29, 1915** singer Donald Mills born (died 1999); **1929** becomes a statutory city.

Point Pleasant *Clermont County Southwestern Ohio, 20 mi/32 km southeast of Cincinnati, on Ohio River*

1813 town founded; **1817** Grant Homestead built; **Apr. 27, 1822** Ulysses Simpson Grant, 18th President, born (died July 23, 1885); **1927** Grant Memorial Bridge completed, crosses Big Indian Creek, replaced 1990s; **Oct. 4, 1936** Grant cabin birthplace dedicated as state memorial; **1937** town damaged by Great Ohio Flood.

Pomeroy *Meigs County Southeastern Ohio, 80 mi/129 km southeast of Columbus, on Ohio River*

1770 coal discovered in area; **1804** Samuel Pomeroy of Boston purchases land here; town founded; **1809** Nicholas Roosevelt opens first coal mine to fuel steamboats; **1819** Meigs County formed; **1825** salt making begins, industry surges after 1850; **1832** coal mining, develops into major operation; **1840** incorporated as a village; **1841** county seat moved from Chester; **June 24, 1842** satirist Ambrose Bierce born in rural Meigs County (died 1914); **1846** county courthouse completed; **1928** Pomeroy-Mason Bridge, built on Ohio River.

Port Clinton *Ottawa County Northern Ohio, 32 mi/51 km east-southeast of Toledo, on Lake Erie*

1754 French engineer De Lery passes through en route from Quebec to Mississippi River; **1764** Colonel Bradstreet's forces encamp at town site; **1828** Scottish immigrants bound for Chicago shipwreck here, decide to stay; town founded, named for Gov. DeWitt Clinton of New York, builder of Erie Canal; **1840** Ottawa County formed; town becomes county seat; **1871** incorporated as a village; **1874** Port Clinton Lighthouse built, replaces 1833 light; **1886** Island House Hotel built; **1901** county courthouse completed; **1933** Portage River Bridge (bascule), the "Whistling Bridge," built; **1950** becomes a statutory city; **Aug. 28, 1977** Davis-Besse Nuclear Power Plant begins operation.

Portsmouth *Scioto County* *Southern Ohio, 83 mi/ 134 km east-southeast of Cincinnati, on Ohio River*

1803 Scioto County formed; town founded as county seat by Maj. Henry Massie of Virginia; **1811** first steamboat *New Orleans* travels past town; **1814** incorporated as a city; **Dec. 1832** Ohio & Erie Canal opened to Portsmouth; **1852** Scioto Valley Railroad reaches town from Cincinnati; **1865** fire brick industry established; **1890s** Norfolk & Western Railroad reaches town; **1908** flood wall built, raised to 62 ft/19 m 1933; **1927** county courthouse completed; suspension bridge built across Ohio River to South Portsmouth; **1937** town loses battle with Great Ohio Flood as it reaches 71 ft/22 m; **Aug. 13, 1948** actress Kathleen Battle born; **1986** Shawnee State University established.

Put-in-Bay *Ottawa County* *Northern Ohio, 58 mi/ 93 km west-northwest of Cleveland, on Lake Erie*

1679 explorer La Salle passes Lake Erie islands; **1765** islands ceded to Britain by France; **1783** islands ceded to U.S.; **Sept. 10, 1813** Admiral Perry defeats British in naval battle aboard his ship *Niagara*; **1854** town founded on South Bass Island; **1858** wine production begins; **1864** mansion built on Gibraltar Island by financier Jay Cooke; **1866** Perry's Victory memorial erected by Cooke; **1877** incorporated as a village; **1890s** village becomes millionaires' playground; **1897** South Bass Island Lighthouse built; **Sept. 10, 1913** Perry Memorial dedicated; **June 2, 1936** Perry's Victory National Monument established, redesignated Perry's Victory and International Peace Memorial 1972.

Ravenna *Portage County* *Northeastern Ohio, 32 mi/51 km southeast of Cleveland*

1799 town founded by Benjamin Tappan, Jr., named for Italian city; **1807** Portage County formed; town becomes county seat; **1808** town platted; **1840** Pennsylvania & Ohio Canal, branch of Ohio & Erie Canal, completed; **Apr. 17, 1849** Supreme Court Justice William Rufus Day born (died 1923); **1851** Cleveland & Pittsburgh Railroad reaches town; **1852** incorporated as a village; Pennsylvania Railroad reaches town; **1877** Quaker Oats Company founded; **1960** third county courthouse built; **Sept. 4, 1962** Lockheed Lodestar airplane crashes, 2 crewmen, 11 Ashland Oil executives killed; **1965** Michael J. Kirwan Reservoir formed by dam to east on West Branch Mahoning River.

Ripley *Brown County* *Southern Ohio, 43 mi/69 km southeast of Cincinnati, on Ohio River*

1812 area settled by Col. James Poage of Virginia; **1818** Brown County formed; town becomes county seat; **1821** county seat moved to Georgetown; **1822** Rankin House built by Rev. John Rankin, station on Underground Railroad; **1826** incorporated as a village; **1830s** steamboat building becomes important industry; **1865** freed black slaves begin settling here; **1901** Rosa Washington Riles (Aunt Jemima) born in Red Oak Township to southeast, cook employed by Quaker Oats Company used in pancake mix demonstrations, Mrs. Riles' picture becomes product trademark (died 1969); **1937** Great Ohio Flood severely damages town; **1976** Ripley Museum founded.

Saint Clairsville *Belmont County* *Eastern Ohio, 109 mi/175 km east of Columbus*

1801 Belmont County formed; Putney becomes first county seat; **1805** town founded as county seat, named for Arthur St. Clair, first governor of Northwest Territory; **1807** chartered as a city; **1815** abolitionist group Union Humane Society founded by Quaker Benjamin Lundy; **1838** St. Clairsville Collegiate Female Seminary founded; **1886** fourth county courthouse completed; **March 16, 1940** coal mine accident, 73 killed.

Saint Marys *Auglaize County* *Western Ohio, 82 mi/132 km northwest of Columbus*

Sept. 17, 1818 treaty signed between Wyandot people and U.S. agents Lewis Cass and Duncan McArthur opening large areas to white settlement; **1820** Mercer County formed; **1823** town founded, named Girty's Town, for James Girty, brother of renegade Simon Girty; **1824** county organized; town becomes county seat; **1834** incorporated as a village; **1840** Mercer County seat moved to Celina; **1845** Grand Lake St. Marys formed by dam on Wabash River, providing 60 mi/97 km link for Miami & Erie Canal; **1848** Auglaize County formed from Mercer County; **1904** becomes a statutory city; **1921** St. Marys Public Library founded; **1939** Goodyear Tire Company plant opened.

Salem *Columbiana County* *Northeastern Ohio, 58 mi/93 km southeast of Cleveland*

1801 Quaker settlers arrive from Salem, New Jersey; **1803** town founded; more Quakers arrive from Virginia and Pennsylvania; **June 30, 1835** abolitionist Edwin Coppock born, hanged with John Brown 1859 for raid on Harpers Ferry; **1845** *Anti-Slavery Bugle* newspaper published, folded 1861; **1852** incorporated as a village; **Dec. 20, 1868** tire manufacturer Harvey S. Firestone born at Columbiana to east (died 1938), founded Firestone Tire and Rubber Company at Akron 1900; **1887** becomes a statutory city; **May 4, 1944** government official William Bennett born.

Sandusky *Erie County* *Northern Ohio, 51 mi/ 82 km west of Cleveland, on Lake Erie*

1760 English trader Charles Groghan lands here, finds Ottawa and Wyandotte camp; **1816** first settlers arrive;

town founded by Zalmon Wildman of Danbury, Connecticut; **1818** town platted, named Sandusky City; **Aug. 10, 1821** financier Jay Cooke born (died 1905); **1824** incorporated as a city; **1835** Cleveland chosen over Sandusky as terminus for Ohio & Erie Canal; construction of Mad River & Lake Erie Railroad begins, reaches Bellevue 1839, Dayton 1851; **1837** Oran Follett House built; **1838** Erie County formed; town becomes county seat; **1845** city renamed Sandusky; **1849** cholera epidemic strikes town, 400 die within two months; **July 11, 1861** Nebraska Cong., Sen. George William Norris born, sponsor of Tennessee Valley Authority hydroelectric project (died 1944); **1869** John G. Dorn Winery founded; **1870** Cedar Point Amusement Park established; **1874** county courthouse built, remodeled 1936; **1878** Engels and Krudwig Wine Company founded; Hommel Wine Company founded; **1886** Ohio State Soldiers and Sailors Home established; **1906** coal docking facilities established on Lake Erie by Pennsylvania Railroad; **June 28, 1924** tornadoes centered on Lorain strike city, total 85 killed; **1929** Sandusky Bay Bridge built to west, parallel span built 1965; **1939** fire destroys eight downtown blocks.

Sidney *Shelby County* *Western Ohio, 65 mi/105 km west-northwest of Columbus, on Great Miami River*

1769 Peter Loramie establishes trading post, destroyed 1782 by George Rogers Clark; **1794** fort rebuilt by Gen. Anthony Wayne; **1805** first settlers arrive; **1819** Shelby County formed; **1820** town founded as county seat, named for English poet Sir Philip Sidney; **1834** incorporated as a village; **1845** Miami & Erie Canal completed; **1850** Baltimore & Ohio Railroad reaches town; **1883** county courthouse completed; **1897** becomes a statutory city; **1918** Peoples' Savings and Loan Building built, designed by Louis Sullivan; **1923** Big Four Railroad Bridge built across river.

Springfield *Clark County* *West central Ohio, 42 mi/68 km west of Columbus*

Aug. 1780 George Rogers Clark destroys Shawnee town of Piqua to west; **1799** James Demint of Kentucky builds cabin; **1801** town founded by surveyor John Daugherty; Griffith Foos arrives with settlers from Kentucky; tavern founded by Foos; **1803** manor house built to north by Simon Kenton; town named Springfield at suggestion of Mrs. Kenton; Kenton builds sawmill, grist mill; **1810** incorporated as a town; **1818** Clark County formed; town becomes county seat; **1829** Jacob Huffman House built to southwest; **1830** Hunt Tavern built by Maj. William Hunt on site of Kenton's log house; **1839** National Road reaches town; **1845** Wittenberg University established; **1846** Little Miami Railroad arrives; **1850** incorporated as a city; St. Raphael Catholic Church dedicated; **1856** Champion Binder Company founded by William Whiteley, maker of farm machinery; **1877** Crowell-Collier Publishing Company founded; **1880s** Champion reaper developed; **1890** city hall opened; Warder Public

Library built; **Oct. 14, 1893** actress Lillian Gish born (died 1993); **Nov. 25, 1899** writer William Riley Burnett born (died 1982); **1902** McCormick Company buys Champion Binder following its 1886 collapse and 1902 fire, becomes International Harvester; **1905** Westcott House built by Frank Lloyd Wright; **1913** Great Miami River inundates city; **1918** third county courthouse built; **1927** Covenant Presbyterian Church built; **1943** Springfield Symphony Orchestra founded; **1946** Springfield Municipal Airport opened; **1979** new city hall opened; **1993** Clark Performing Arts Center opened.

Steubenville *Jefferson County* *Eastern Ohio, 94 mi/151 km southeast of Cleveland, on Ohio River*

1775 first settler Jacob Walker claims land; **1786** Fort Steuben built by Major Hamtramck, named for Prussian Baron von Steuben, aided Revolutionary War; **1790** fort burned; **1797** Jefferson County formed; town of Steubenville founded as county seat; **1802** grist mill and sawmill founded; **1805** incorporated as a village; **1806** pottery works founded; **1810** first coal mine established; **1811** first steamboat *Orleans* arrives; **1814** town becomes known for its wool and cotton industries; **Dec. 19, 1814** Supreme Court Justice Edwin M. Stanton born, served as attorney general under President Buchanan (died 1869); **1851** incorporated as a city; **1854** Pittsburgh & Steubenville Railroad arrives; **1856** Jefferson Iron Works rolling mill established; **1857** Steubenville Coal and Mining Company sinks its first shaft on Liberty Street; **1874** county courthouse completed; **1879** Steubenville Pottery founded; **1910** steel milling becomes leading industry; **June 17, 1917** singer, actor Dean Martin born (died 1995); **1926** Pennsylvania Railroad bridge built; **1928** Fort Steuben Suspension Bridge built; **1946** Franciscan University of Steubenville established; **1990** Veterans Memorial Bridge built across Ohio River to Weirton, West Virginia.

Tiffin *Seneca County* *Northern Ohio, 40 mi/64 km south-southeast of Toledo*

c.1690 French missionary Father Rasles passes through area; **1813** Fort Ball established during War of 1812; **1817** Erastus Bowe builds Pan Yan Tavern on north side of Sandusky River; **1819** town of Oakley founded around tavern; **1820** Seneca County formed; Oakley renamed Fort Ball; **1821** Josiah Hedges founds town of Tiffin as county seat on south side of river, named for Edward Tiffin, Ohio's first governor; **1835** incorporated as a city; **1841** Mad River Railroad spur reaches town; **1846** Baldwin House built; **1850** Fort Ball annexed by Tiffin; Heidelberg College established; **1883** flooding destroys four bridges; **1884** county courthouse built; **1888** Tiffin University established; natural gas field discovered; **1913** flooding destroys six bridges, 19 killed; **1944** Tiffin State Hospital founded.

Toledo   *Lucas County   Northwestern Ohio, 94 mi/ 151 km west-northwest of Cleveland, on Lake Erie*

1615 Etienne Brule, guide for French Canadian Samuel de Champlain, visits site at mouth of Maumee River, finds Erie peoples living here; **1794** Fort Industry established by Gen. Anthony Wayne; **Aug. 20, 1794** Wayne defeats Native Americans in Battle of Fallen Timbers [see Maumee]; **1817** town settled following War of 1812, originally named Port Lawrence; **1832-1833** cholera epidemic ravages town; **1833** Port Lawrence merges with Vistula to north, renamed Toledo; **1835** Lucas County formed to assert Ohio's sovereignty against Michigan's claims; town becomes county seat; **1835-1836** "Toledo War" boundary dispute between Michigan and Ohio resolved by U.S. Congress in Ohio's favor, narrowly averting armed conflict between two states; **1836** *Toledo Blade* newspaper founded; **1836** Erie & Kalamazoo Railroad reaches town from Michigan, first railroad in Ohio; **1837** incorporated as a city; **1843** Wabash & Erie Canal opened to Fort Wayne, Indiana; **1845** Miami & Erie Canal opened from Cincinnati and Ohio River; **1853** Oliver House built by J. C. Hall; **1862** St. Francis de Sales Catholic Church built; **1865** first bridge built across Maumee River; **1869** Wheeling & Lake Erie and Toledo, Ann Arbor & Northern railroads reach city; **1872** University of Toledo established; **1873** Toledo & Woodville Railroad arrives; Toledo Public Library built; **1876** Toledo, Columbus & Hocking Railroad built; **1880s** Presque Isle on Maumee Bay becomes popular resort, replaced during World War I by nitrate plant; **1888** Maumee natural gas field discovered to southeast; Libbey Glass Company moved from Cambridge, Massachusetts, hires glass blower Michael Owens; **1895** Valentine Theater opened; **1896** Edward Ford establishes plate glass factory; **1897** county courthouse built; Samuel M. Jones becomes "Golden Rule" Mayor for his reform efforts, died 1904; **1898** St. John's College established; **1899** Toledo Zoo founded; **1901** Toledo Scale Company founded; **1903** Michael Owens invents mass-production bottle making machine, forms Owens Bottle Machine Company 1905; **Dec. 28, 1905** TV actor Cliff Arquette (Charley Weaver) born (died 1974); **1908** John Willys moves his Overland Automobile Company from Indianapolis, reorganized as Willys-Overland Company 1936; **Oct. 13, 1910** jazz pianist Art Tatum born (died 1956); **1912** Toledo Museum of Art opened, founded 1901 by Edward Libbey; **1914** Cherry Street Bridge built across Maumee River; **1919** Dempsey-Willard prize fight held in Bay View Park, Dempsey wins; **Feb. 17, 1921** post office hit with million-dollar robbery; **1929** convention hall completed; **1930** 25-story Ohio Savings Bank & Trust Building completed; **May 7, 1931** singer Teresa Brewer born; **Oct. 1931** Anthony Wayne High Level Bridge opened on Maumee River; **1933** Museum of Natural History built; Rosary Cathedral completed; **March 25, 1934** women's rights activist Gloria Steinem born; **July 1, 1934** TV actor Jamie Farr born; **1951** Toledo Symphony Orchestra founded; **Jan. 26, 1958** singer Anita Baker born; **Oct. 29, 1960** crash of C-46 aircraft kills 22 of 48 on board;

1969 Medical College of Toledo established; **1982** 32-story Owens-Illinois Building completed; **1997** Center of Science and Technology opened.

Toronto   *Jefferson County   Eastern Ohio, 30 mi/ 48 km southeast of Cleveland, on Ohio River*

1818 town founded by John Depuy; **1856** Cleveland & Pittsburgh Railroad reaches town; **1881** town renamed by prominent citizen from Toronto; **1887** incorporated as a village; **Dec. 19, 1946** TV actor Robert Urich born (died 2002); **1961** New Cumberland Lock & Dam completed on Ohio River eliminating Dams 7, 8, and 9 built 1914.

Troy   *Miami County   Western Ohio, 63 mi/101 km west of Columbus, on Great Miami River*

1798 Michael Garver builds first cabin; **1807** Miami County formed; Staunton becomes county seat; Troy founded; **1808** county seat moved to Troy; **1814** incorporated as a city; **1837** Miami & Erie Canal completed; **1850** Dayton & Michigan Railroad reaches town; **1885** county courthouse built; **1913** flooding inundates town.

Uhrichsville   *Tuscarawas County   Eastern Ohio, 76 mi/122 km south-southeast of Cleveland*

1798 David Zeisberger establishes Moravian mission named Goshen for Christian Indians, homeless survivors of 1782 massacre at nearby Gnadenhutten; **1804** area first settled by Michael Uhrich of Pennsylvania; **1806** Uhrich builds flour mill; **1822** town platted; **1823** Goshen mission abandoned; **1833** Ohio & Erie Canal opened; decade of prosperity follows; **1855** Steubenville & Indiana Railroad reaches town; **1866** incorporated as a village; **May 29, 1867** baseball player Cy Young (Denton True Young) born at Gilmore to southwest (died 1955); **1890** becomes a statutory city.

Upper Sandusky   *Wyandot County   North central Ohio, 60 mi/156 km north-northwest of Columbus*

June 4, 1782 Col. William Crawford is separated from his men while pursuing Wyandot peoples, captured, tortured to death June 11; **1812** William Henry Harrison establishes Fort Ferree; **1818** Wyandot people move here following treaty, forced to move west of Mississippi River 1843; **1823** Wyandot Mission built; **1843** town founded; **1845** Wyandot County formed; town becomes county seat; **1848** incorporated as a city; **1900** county courthouse built.

Urbana   *Champaign County   West central Ohio, 41 mi/66 km west-northwest of Columbus*

1805 Champaign County formed; Springfield becomes county seat; **1807** county seat moved to Urbana; **1812** Col. William Hull uses town square for training camp; **1816** incorporated as a village; **June 29, 1830** sculptor John Quincy Adams Ward born (died 1910); **1839** painter Edgar Melville Ward born (died 1915); **1848** Mad River &

Lake Erie Railroad reaches town; **1850** Urbana University established; **1868** becomes a statutory city; **1956** county courthouse completed; **March 9, 1967** TWA DC-9 airliner collides with private plane, 26 killed.

Van Wert   *Van Wert County*   *Northwestern Ohio, 75 mi/121 km southwest of Toledo*

1820 Van Wert County formed; **1835** county organized; Willshire becomes first county seat; Capt. James Watson Riley becomes first settler of Van Wert; **1838** county seat moved to Van Wert; **1848** incorporated as a city; **1876** county courthouse completed; **1901** Brumback Public Library dedicated, first county library in U.S.

Wapakoneta   *Auglaize County*   *Western Ohio, 75 mi/121 km northwest of Columbus*

1812 Fort Amanda built to northwest by Col. Thomas Poague, named for his wife; **1833** town founded on Auglaize River, named for Native American chief Wapaugh and his squaw Konetta; **1841** incorporated as a city; **1848** Auglaize County formed; town becomes county seat; **1880** town becomes known for its wood products; **1894** second county courthouse built; **Aug. 5, 1930** astronaut Neil Armstrong born.

Warren   *Trumbull County*   *Northeastern Ohio, 47 mi/76 km east-southeast of Cleveland*

1798 Ephraim Quinby and Richard Storr of Connecticut Land Company arrive; **1800** Trumbull County formed; town founded as county seat and seat of Western Reserve; **1807** Edwards House built; **1811** first bank in Western Reserve established; **1812** first newspaper in Western Reserve founded; **1832** Kinsman House built; **1834** incorporated as a village; **1839** Pennsylvania & Ohio Canal opened; **1850s** flaxseed oil and linseed oil become important commodities; **Apr. 18, 1857** lawyer Clarence Darrow born at Kinsman to northeast, defense attorney in 1925 Scopes trial, Dayton, Tennessee (died 1938); **1862** Packard and Barnum iron forge built; **1869** incorporated as a city; Dana Musical Institute founded; **1890** electrical products factory founded by Packard brothers; **1897** third county courthouse completed; **1899** J. Ward Packard manufactures first Packard automobiles, brother William goes to Detroit to begin full production; **1910** Warren becomes first city to illuminate its streets with Mazda tungsten lights; **1912** Trumbull Steel Mill built, merges with Republic Steel 1928; **1937** lengthy steel strike broken by National Guard; **1944** Mosquito Creek Lake formed by dam to northeast; **March 1, 1954** actress Catherine Bach born.

Washington Court House   *Fayette County*   *South-central Ohio, 36 mi/58 km southwest of Columbus*

1807 Thomas Hinde becomes first settler; **1810** Fayette County formed; Bloomingburg becomes county seat; **1812** town founded as new county seat; **1831** incorporated as a

city; **Jan. 26, 1860** Henry M. Daugherty born, attorney general under President Harding, center of 1920s Teapot Dome Scandal (died 1941); **1885** county courthouse built.

Wauseon   *Fulton County*   *Northwestern Ohio, 31 mi/50 km west-southwest of Toledo*

1839 area first settled; **1850** Fulton County formed; Ottokee becomes first county seat; **1854** town founded; **1859** incorporated as a village; **1871** county seat moved to Wauseon; **1872** county courthouse built; **1875** Wauseon Public Library founded; **Jan. 29, 1878** race car driver Barney Oldfield born (died 1946); **1982** becomes a statutory city.

Waverly   *Pike County*   *Southern Ohio, 80 mi/129 km east of Cincinnati*

1815 Pike County formed; **1829** town founded by James Emmitt, originally named Uniontown; **1830** town renamed for Sir Walter Scott's Waverly novels favored by Capt. Francis Cleveland, engineer on Ohio & Erie Canal; **1842** incorporated as a village; **1861** county seat moved from Piketon; **1866** county courthouse built; **1935** Lake White formed by dam to south on Pee Pee Creek; **1939** Garnet A. Wilson Public Library founded; **1949** Lake White State Park established; **1956** gaseous diffusion plant built by Atomic Energy Commission; **1970** incorporated as a city.

Wellington   *Lorain County*   *Northern Ohio, 34 mi/55 km southwest of Cleveland*

1818 town founded; **1855** incorporated as a village; **Sept. 1858** U.S. marshal stops with captured runaway black slave in this strongly abolitionist town, people rescue slave, 37 arrested, released after sensational courtroom drama involving Gov. Salmon P. Chase and Joshua R. Giddings; **1868** town becomes important cheese producer.

West Union   *Adams County*   *Southern Ohio, 55 mi/89 km east-southeast of Cincinnati*

1797 Adams County formed; Manchester becomes first county seat; **1804** town founded as new county seat; **1855** Harshaville Covered Bridge built to north; **1859** incorporated as a village; **1890** Kirker Covered Bridge built to west; **1911** county courthouse built.

Willoughby   *Lake County*   *Northeastern Ohio, 18 mi/29 km northeast of Cleveland, near Lake Erie*

1798 grist mill established by David Abbott; **1800** town founded, originally named Chagrin; **1834** Willoughby Medical College established; town renamed; **1848** medical college closed; **1853** incorporated as a village; **Dec. 15, 1933** TV actor Tim Conway born; **1951** becomes a statutory city.

Wilmington *Clinton County* *Southwestern Ohio,*
42 mi/68 km northeast of Cincinnati

1810 Clinton County formed; town founded as county
seat, originally named Clinton; **1811** town renamed
Wilmington; **1820** roadside inn built, later used as clubhouse for Snow Hill Country Club; **1828** incorporated as a
village; **1870** Wilmington College established; **1922**
becomes a statutory city; **1919** third county courthouse
built.

Woodington *Darke County* *See* **Greenville (1892)**

Woodsfield *Monroe County* *Eastern Ohio, 48 mi/*
77 km east-southeast of Zanesville

1813 Monroe County formed; area first settled; town
founded as county seat; **1835** incorporated as a village;
1908 fourth county courthouse built.

Wooster *Wayne County* *North central Ohio,*
48 mi/77 km south-southwest of Cleveland

1807 brothers William, Joseph and John Larwill become
first settlers; **1808** Wayne County formed; town founded,
named for Revolutionary War Gen. David Wooster; **1812**
county organized; town becomes county seat; **1817**
incorporated as a village; *Ohio Spectator* newspaper
founded; **1866** The College of Wooster established; **1869**
becomes a statutory city; **1879** third county courthouse
completed; **Sept. 14, 1887** physicist Karl Taylor Compton
born (died 1954); **1892** Ohio Agricultural Experimental
Station moved from Columbus; **Sept. 10, 1892** physicist
Arthur Holly Compton born, Nobel Prize 1927 (died
1962).

Worthington *Franklin County* *Central Ohio,*
suburb 8 mi/12.9 km north of Columbus

1803 100 settlers led by Col. James Kilbourne arrive from
Worthington, Connecticut; town founded; **1804** Griswold
Inn built by Capt. Ezra Griswold, completed 1811; **1807**
Worthington Academy founded; **1830** Worthington
Medical College established, closed 1840 following grave
robberies attributed to college's need for cadavers; **1831**
St. John's Episcopal Church completed; **1835** incorpo-
rated as a village; **1956** becomes a statutory city.

Xenia *Greene County* *West central Ohio, 52 mi/*
84 km west-southwest of Columbus

1786 Judge John Symmes of New Jersey purchases land;
1803 Greene County formed; Beavercreek becomes
county seat; **1804** town founded as new county seat;
1817 incorporated as a village; **1834** incorporated as a city;
1869 Ohio Soldiers' and Sailors' Home established for
Civil War orphans; **Feb. 27, 1888** historian Arthur M.
Schlesinger born (died 1965); **1899** Xenia Public Library
opened; **1902** third county courthouse completed; **Apr. 3,
1974** half of city destroyed by tornado, 32 killed, series of
tornadoes from Michigan to Georgia, total 315 killed, $1
billion damage.

Yellow Springs *Greene County* *West central*
Ohio, 47 mi/76 km west-southwest of Columbus

1804 town founded; **Sept. 10, 1839** lexicographer, publisher Isaac Kaufman Funk born at Clifton to east,
formed partnership in 1881 with college classmate Adam
Willis Wagnalls, founded *Literary Digest*, edited *Standard
Dictionary of the English Language* (died 1912); **1846** Little
Miami Railroad reaches town; **1853** Antioch College
established, now Antioch University; **1856** incorporated
as a village.

Youngstown *Mahoning and Trumbull counties*
Northeastern Ohio, 60 mi/97 km southeast of Cleveland

1797 settlers arrive on Mahoning River led by John
Young of Whitestown, New York; town founded; **1802**
incorporated as a town; iron smelter established; **1820**
Pennsylvania & Ohio Canal opened; **1826** first coal mine
opens; **1839** Pennsylvania & Ohio Canal completed; **1846**
Mahoning County formed; **1848** Canfield becomes county
seat; **1853** first railroad reaches town; **1867** becomes a
statutory city; **1869** *The Vindicator* newspaper founded;
1870 soldiers monument erected; **1876** county seat moved
to Youngstown; **1888** Youngstown College established;
1892 Union Iron and Steel Company founded; **1900**
Youngstown Sheet and Tube Company plant founded,
closed 1977; **1908** Youngstown State University established; **1910** Reuben McMillan Public Library built;
county courthouse built; **1919** Butler Art Institute built;
1925 Stambaugh Auditorium built; **1932** Meander Creek
Reservoir formed by dam to west; **Apr. 12, 1946** actor Ed
O'Neill born; **July 27, 1949** actress Maureen McGovern
born.

Zanesville *Muskingum County* *East central Ohio,*
51 mi/82 km east of Columbus

1797 Ebenezer Zane claims tract on Muskingum River, at
mouth of Licking River, sells interest to brother Jonathan
Zane; **1800** town founded; **1801** John and Increase
Matthews open first store; **1802** Headly Inn built to
west; **1804** Muskingum County formed; town becomes
county seat; Matthews House built by Increase Matthews;
dishware and stoneware making begins with discovery of
clay deposits; **1809** Taylor House built, meeting place for
Ohio Anti-Slavery Society, station on Underground
Railroad; **1810** state capital moved from Chillicothe,
moved back to Chillicothe 1812, moved to Columbus
1816; **1814** incorporated as a city; first Y-bridge built by
Moses Dillon at confluence of Licking and Muskingum
rivers connecting three shores, sections joined at center of
river, rebuilt 1819, 1832, 1900, and 1984; Blue Lion inn
built to west; **1815** first glass plant in Ohio opened; **Sept. 7,
1819** Indiana Cong. Thomas Andrews Hendricks born,
vice president under President Cleveland for five months
1885 (died 1885); **1830** National Road reaches city from

OHIO

Wheeling; **1834** Buckingham House built; Dr. William G. Thompson develops lucifer matches, founds first lucifer match factory in U.S.; **1841** dams and dredging improve transportation on Muskingum River; **Nov. 24, 1859** architect Cass Gilbert born (died 1934); **1875** American Encaustic Tiling Company founded; **Jan. 31, 1875** Western novelist Zane Grey born (died 1939); **1877** third county courthouse built; **1887** Burton-Townsend Brick Company founded; **1888** S. A. Weller Pottery founded;

1890 Roseville Pottery founded; **1894** Mosaic Tile Company founded; **1913** flood brings $3 million in damage; **Aug. 31, 1919** actor Richard Basehart born (died 1984); **1935** flooding causes much property damage, again in 1937; **1936** Zanesville Art Institute established, renamed Zanesville Art Center 1977; **1946** Ohio University-Zanesville established; **1961** Dillon Lake formed by dam to northwest on Licking River; **1969** Muskingum Area Technical College established.

Oklahoma

South central U.S. Capital: Oklahoma City. Major cities: Oklahoma City, Tulsa.

The area became part of the U.S. with the Louisiana Purchase of 1803. Beginning in the 1820s, Oklahoma became a destination for native American tribes removed from eastern states and became known as Indian Territory, which had no formal government. Most notable of the removals were the Five Civilized Tribes of the Southeastern states, the Cherokee, Choctaw, Chickasaw, Creek, and Seminole people, whose harsh journey west is referred to as the Trail of Tears. Comanche, Osage, Plains peoples, and other groups were also sent to the area. On April 22, 1889, the Cherokee Outlet, or Cherokee Strip, was formed in the northwest, opening the area to white settlers, resulting in a "land run." Another "land run" occurred with the formation of Oklahoma Territory in the central part May 2, 1890. Oklahoma was admitted as the 46th state November 16, 1907.

Oklahoma has 77 counties. The counties are divided into townships which have no governments. The municipalities are classified as towns and cities. See Introduction.

Ada *Pontotoc County* *South Central Oklahoma, 67 mi/108 km southeast of Oklahoma City*

1890 William Jeffrey Reed becomes first white settler, builds log store and dwelling; **1891** post office established, Reed becomes first postmaster, named for daughter Ada Reed; **1893** town founded; **Sept. 11, 1896** U.S. Sen. Robert S. Kerr born (died 1963); **1900** St. Louis & San Francisco Railroad reaches town; *Ada Evening News* newspaper founded; **1901** incorporated as a town; **1907** Pontotoc County formed; town becomes county seat; **1909** East Central State Normal School established, becomes East Central State University 1985; **Apr. 19, 1909** slaying of respected citizen by "Killin' Jim" Miller, involved earlier in killing of Pat Garrett (slayer of Billy the Kid), results in lynching; **July 14, 1917** newscaster Douglas Edwards born (died 1990); **Jan. 24, 1918** evangelist Oral Roberts born; **1919** incorporated as a city; **1926** county courthouse built; **1933** oil field discovered; **1936** Ada Public Library founded.

Altus *Jackson County* *Southwestern Oklahoma, 120 mi/193 km southwest of Oklahoma City*

1891 town founded as Fraiser; flooding forces town to move to higher ground, renamed; **1897** cotton production has its beginnings; **1907** Jackson County formed; town incorporated, becomes county seat; county courthouse built; **1926** Western Oklahoma State College (2-year) established; **1941** Altus Lake formed by dam to north on North Fork Red River; **1942** Altus Army Air Field established to east, becomes Air Force Base 1953.

Alva *Woods County* *Northwestern Oklahoma, 110 mi/177 km northwest of Oklahoma City*

1886 Atchison, Topeka & Santa Fe Railroad built; **1893** Woods County formed; Cherokee Strip (Outlet) opened to white settlers; town founded as county seat; land office opened; town named for Santa Fe Railroad official Alva B. Adams; **1901** incorporated as a city; **1897** Northwestern Oklahoma State Normal School established, becomes Northwestern Oklahoma State University 1974; **1905** Alva Public Library founded; **Nov. 30, 1931** actor Jack L. Ging born; **1945** Alva Regional Airport established; **1955** county courthouse built.

Anadarko *Caddo County* *South central Oklahoma, 52 mi/84 km southwest of Oklahoma City*

1861 Camp McIntosh established to east by Confederates, abandoned 1865; **Oct. 23, 1862** Osage, Shawnee, and Delaware peoples move down from Kansas, attack Fort Cobb to west, kill Confederates occupying fort, nearly annihilate Tonkawas, Confederate allies; **1892** St. Patrick's Mission School established by Father Isidore Ricklin, closed 1966; **1901** Caddo County formed; town founded as county seat, named for Nadarko tribe of Caddoans; incorporated as a town; **1920s** oil fields developed; **1947** incorporated as a city; **June 1955** Indian

City U.S.A. tourist attraction established; **1958** Fort Cobb Lake formed by dam on Pond Creek to northwest; **1959** county courthouse built; American Indian Hall of Fame established.

Antlers *Pushmataha County Southeastern Oklahoma, 140 mi/225 km southeast of Oklahoma City*

1886 St. Louis-San Francisco Railroad reaches site; town founded near Kiamachi River; town originally named Antlers Spring; **1892–1893** Locke War political insurrection between opposing factions, instigated by Victor M. Locke, suppressed by tribal militia, federal troops called out to restore order; **1903** incorporated as a town, renamed Antlers; **1907** Pushmataha County formed; town becomes county seat; **1935** county courthouse built.

Arapaho *Custer County Western Oklahoma, 83 mi/134 km west of Oklahoma City*

1892 Custer County formed; town founded as county seat; post office established; *Arapaho Arrow* newspaper established; **Feb. 1902** incorporated as a town; **1935** county courthouse built.

Arcadia *Oklahoma County Central Oklahoma, 15 mi/24 km north-northeast of Oklahoma City*

1832 Washington Irving leads party of wild horse hunters; **1883** Camp Alice established to south by David L. Payne and other land boomers, driven into Kansas by U.S. troops; **Apr. 22, 1889** Great Land Run of '89 begins at noon at demarcation line 5 mi/8 km to east; **1890** post office established; **1903** town platted; **c.1917** incorporated as a town (records destroyed 1924); **1924** fire destroys all businesses on east side of Main Street; **1928** U.S. Highway 66 built through town; **1987** Arcadia declared a "legal town" for lack of records.

Ardmore *Carter County Southern Oklahoma, 75 mi/121 km south of Oklahoma City*

1887 Atchison, Topeka & Santa Fe Railroad built; town founded, named for Ardmore, Pennsylvania, home town of railroad official; **1888** *Alliance Courier* newspaper founded; **1893** *Daily Ardmoreite* newspaper founded; **June 6, 1894** outlaw Bill Dalton killed in shootout with posse and lawmen near his home; **1896** fire destroys most of downtown area; **1898** incorporated as a city; **1905** first oil discovered in area; **1906** Carnegie Library built; **1907** Carter County formed from Pickens County of Cherokee Nation; town becomes county seat; **1910** county courthouse built, renovated 1970s; **1910s** town becomes important agricultural center; **1913** Healdton Oil Bed discovered to west; **1914** Carter Seminary, founded 1852, moved from Durant after being destroyed by fire; **Sept. 27, 1915** gasoline railroad car tank explodes leveling downtown, 43 killed; **1927** St. Philip's Episcopal Church built, replaces 1897 structure; **1970** Charles A. Goddard Center for the Visual and Performing Arts founded.

Arnett *Ellis County Northwestern Oklahoma, 135 mi/217 km northwest of Oklahoma City*

1858 battle takes place between Texas Rangers and Comanches at Little Robe Creek to southwest, Comanches defeated after death of leader Chief Pohebits Quasho (Iron Jacket); **1900** grist mill built to southwest on Little Robe Creek by W. F. Burnett, abandoned 1925; **1902** post office established; **1907** Ellis County formed; **1908** town becomes county seat; incorporated as a town; **1912** county courthouse built; **1930** Packsaddle Bridge built to south on Canadian River, new bridge opened 1985.

Atoka *Atoka County Southeastern Oklahoma, 110 mi/177 km southeast of Oklahoma City*

1857 stage stop established on Butterfield Overland Route; **1867** town founded by Baptist missionary Rev. J. S. Murrow, named for Choctaw subchief; **1887** Atoka Baptist Academy founded; **1897** Atoka Agreement signed allotting lands to Choctaws and Chickasaws; **1901** incorporated as a city; **1907** Atoka County formed; **1908** town becomes county seat; **1962** county courthouse built; **1964** Atoka Reservoir formed by dam on North Boggy Creek.

Bartlesville *Washington and Osage counties Northeastern Oklahoma, 41 mi/66 km north of Tulsa*

1868 grist mill built on Caney River by Nelson Carr, first white settler; **1873** Carr's Mill bought by Native American trader Jacob Bartles; store and trading post established by Bartles; **1876** Bartles hauls dynamo to town, produces first electricity in Oklahoma; **1879** town founded on Caney River; **1893** Cherokee Strip (Outlet) opened to white settlement; **1897** incorporated as a town; oil discovered near old mill; **1898** Atchison, Topeka & Santa Fe Railroad reaches town; **1903** Missouri-Kansas-Texas Railroad arrives; **1904** glass factory established; **1906** zinc processing plant founded; **1907** Washington County formed; town becomes county seat; incorporated as a city; **1914** county courthouse built; **Jan. 1917** Iowa brothers Frank and L. E. Phillips establish Phillips Petroleum Company; **1921** Washington County Memorial Hospital built; **1922** civic center built; **1925** Phillips Ranch established by Frank Phillips, president of Phillips Petroleum Company, lodge completed 1927; **1928** Cities Service Oil Company established; **1930** municipal stadium built; **Feb. 1950** African-American librarian Ruth Brown fired from job for attempting to be served at segregated lunch counter, remains defiant until her death in 1975; **1956** 19-story Price Tower office building dedicated, designed by Frank Lloyd Wright; **1959** Bartlesville Wesleyan College established, now Oklahoma Wesleyan University; **1971** Woolaroc ("wood, lake, rock") Museum and Preserve established to southwest in Osage Indian Reservation, on Phillips Ranch; **1986** flooding damages city; **1972** federal building converted to new county courthouse, built 1933.

Beaver *Beaver County* *Northwestern Oklahoma, 195 mi/314 km northwest of Oklahoma City*

1879 area first settled by squatters; cattleman's store built of sod; **1883** town founded on Beaver River, originally named Beaver City; **1886** *Beaver City Pioneer* newspaper founded; **1887** town becomes capital of short-lived Territory of Cimarron, attempt by citizens of No Man's Land to bring law and order to isolated region, dissolved 1890; incorporated as a city; **1890** Beaver County formed; town becomes county seat; **1910** Wichita Falls & Northwestern Railroad reaches town; **1912** county courthouse built.

Bethany *Oklahoma County* *Central Oklahoma, suburb 8 mi/12.9 km west of Oklahoma City*

Oct. 1884 group of land boomers led by David L. Payne camps to south; plats town, destroyed Nov. by U.S. troops eradicating land jumpers (Payne died Nov. 28 in Kansas); **1909** Bethany Nazarene College, moves from Oklahoma City, becomes Southern Nazarene University 1986; town founded; **1910** incorporated as a town; **1930** incorporated as a city.

Blackwell *Kay County* *Northern Oklahoma, 91 mi/146 km north of Oklahoma City*

1884 colony of white trespassers from Kansas called "Payne's boomers" established, later forced out by U.S. troops; **1893** town founded and incorporated on Chikaskia River with opening of Cherokee Strip (Outlet) to white settlers; town named for founder A. J. Blackwell, Baptist preacher adopted by Cherokee people; **1926** Blackwell Zinc Company moves from Bartlesville, zinc imported from Mexico; **1931** Blackwell Public Library built.

Boggy Depot *Atoka County* *Southern Oklahoma, 105 mi/169 km southeast of Oklahoma City*

1837 first Native American log cabin built; **1840** town church built by Rev. Cyrus Kingsbury; **1849** town founded on Texas Road on Clear Boggy Creek, named Boggy Depot; post office established; **1855** treaty places town in Choctaw Nation; **1860** Chief Wright House built by Choctaw Chief Allen Wright, destroyed by fire March 1952; **1866** Wright suggests Oklahoma as name for territory, Choctaw term for "red man"; **1872** Missouri, Kansas & Texas Railroad bypasses town; **1957** Boggy Depot State Park established, donated by Wright family.

Boise City *Cimarron County* *Northwestern Oklahoma, 295 mi/475 km northwest of Oklahoma City*

1822 Santa Fe Trail blazed across western end of Oklahoma Panhandle; **1907** Cimarron County formed; **1908** town founded (pronounced "boice") as county seat; **1925** Atchison, Topeka & Santa Fe Railroad reaches town; town incorporated; **1927** oil discovered; **1928** county courthouse built; **Aug. 23, 1929** actress Vera Miles born in rural Cimarron County; **1930s** Rita Blanca National Grassland established; **1943** town accidentally bombed by contingent from Dalhart Army Base, Texas; **c.1950** area's first full commercial oil production begins.

Bokchito *Bryan County* *See* **Durant (1863)**

Boley *Okfuskee County* *Central Oklahoma, 57 mi/92 km east of Oklahoma City*

1903 Fort Smith & Western Railroad built; town founded by African-Americans led by T. M. Hayes, named for railroad official W. H. Boley; **Sept. 22, 1904** official town dedication attended by Booker T. Washington; **1905** incorporated as a town; first Boley Rodeo held; **Nov. 22, 1932** Pretty Boy Floyd's gang makes robbery attempt at Farmer's State Bank, three robbers, bank president killed.

Boswell *Choctaw County* *See* **Hugo (1959)**

Buffalo *Harper County* *Northwestern Oklahoma, 150 mi/241 km northwest of Oklahoma City*

1886 branch of Atchison, Topeka & Santa Fe Railroad reaches site, serves as its permanent terminus; **1907** Harper County formed; town founded as county seat; **1908** incorporated as a town; **1927** county courthouse built.

Cache *Comanche County* *Southwestern Oklahoma, 88 mi/142 km southwest of Oklahoma City*

1884 Star House built, home of Quanah Parker, last chief of Comanches, born c.1845 to Cynthia Ann Parker, kidnapped from her Texas home, and Chief Peta Nokomi [see Groesbeck, Texas]; **1901** town founded; **1905** incorporated as a town; **1910** body of Cynthia Anne Parker, originally buried at Stevens, Texas, reburied at Indiahoma to west; **Feb. 23, 1911** Quanah Parker dies, buried next to his mother; **1956** remains of Quanah and Cynthia Parker removed to Fort Sill Cemetery to allow for expansion of army base.

Caddo *Bryan County* *See* **Durant (1978)**

Canton *Blaine County* *See* **Watonga**

Chandler *Lincoln County* *Central Oklahoma, 36 mi/58 km east-northeast of Oklahoma City*

1891 Lincoln County formed; town founded as county seat, named for George Chandler of Kansas, assistant secretary of interior under Pres. Benjamin Harrison; **1897** tornado destroys every building except for Presbyterian Church, 14 killed; **Feb. 12, 1898** composer Roy Harris born in rural Lincoln County (died 1979); **1901** incorporated as a city; **1969** county courthouse built.

Cherokee *Alfalfa County* *Northern Oklahoma, 100 mi/161 km north-northwest of Oklahoma City*

1811 Indian agent Maj. George C. Sibley probable first white man to view Great Salt Plains; **1845** war council called by Plains peoples against newly arrived Cherokees from eastern states via Trail of Tears on reservation to east, resolved peacefully; **1874** "U" Ranch established to north by Maj. Andrew Drumm (1828–1919), one of region's first cattlemen; **1893** Cherokee Strip (Outlet) opened to white settlement; **1901** town founded and incorporated; **1903** Atchison, Topeka & Santa Fe Railroad reaches town; **1905** Denver, Enid & Gulf Railroad arrives; **1907** Alfalfa County formed; town becomes county seat; **1921** county courthouse built; **1941** Great Salt Plains Lake formed by dam to east on Salt Fork Arkansas River.

Cheyenne *Roger Mills County* *Western Oklahoma, 125 mi/201 km west of Oklahoma City*

Nov. 27, 1868 in Battle of Washita to west, encampment of Cheyenne attacked by Gen. George A. Custer's troops, 200 men, women, children killed or wounded including respected Chief Black Kettle (Custer killed in battle with Sioux at Little Big Horn, Montana, June 25, 1876); **1892** Roger Mills County formed; town founded as county seat; **1908** incorporated as a town; **1960** Black Kettle National Grassland designated; **1970s** Anadarko Oil Pool discovered, boom lasts through 1980s; **1986** third county courthouse built; **1996** Washita National Battlefield Site established.

Chickasha *Grady County* *South central Oklahoma, 40 mi/64 km southwest of Oklahoma City*

1892 Chicago, Rock Island & Pacific Railroad built; town founded; **1898** town incorporated; **1907** Grady County formed; town becomes county seat; **1908** Industrial Institute for Girls established, becomes Oklahoma College for Women 1916, then University of Science and Arts of Oklahoma 1974; **1920** large Golden Trend Oil Field discovered to southeast; **1934** county courthouse built; **1941** Chickasha Natural Gas Field developed.

Claremore *Rogers County* *Northeastern Oklahoma, 23 mi/37 km northeast of Tulsa*

1817 battle takes place between Cherokee and Osage people at Clermont (now Claremore) Mound; **Nov. 4, 1879** humorist Will Rogers born at Oologah to northwest, killed in plane crash with aviator Wiley Post Aug. 15, 1935, Barrow, Alaska; **1896** incorporated as a town; **1903** artesian mineral springs discovered; **1907** Rogers County formed, named for Cherokee Chief Clem Rogers; town becomes county seat; **1908** incorporated as a city; **1909** Rogers State University established; **May 2, 1920** tornadoes strike Rogers, Mayes, and Cherokee counties, 64 killed; **Nov. 8, 1927** singer Patti Page born; **1928** U.S. Indian Hospital built; **1937** county courthouse built, renovated 1981; **Nov. 4, 1938** Will Rogers Memorial

dedicated; **Apr. 27, 1942** tornadoes kill 32 in Rogers and Mayes counties; **1957** Will Rogers Turnpike (toll) completed; **1963** Oologah Lake formed by dam to north on Verdigris River.

Clinton *Custer County* *Western Oklahoma, 84 mi/135 km west of Oklahoma City*

1892 area opened to white settlement; **1903** St. Louis & San Francisco Railroad built; town founded on Washita River, named for Federal Judge Clinton F. Irwin; **1904** incorporated as a town; **1909** incorporated as a city; **1917** Western Oklahoma Tuberculosis Sanatorium established at Supply, moved to Clinton 1919; **1941** Mohawk Lodge moves from Seger Colony (The Colony), successful experiment established 1898 to employ Native Americans in creation of salable arts and crafts.

Coalgate *Coal County* *Southern Oklahoma, 98 mi/158 km southeast of Oklahoma City*

1882 first coal mine opened; **1890** town founded; **1898** town incorporated; **c.1900** full-scale coal mining begins; **1907** Coal County formed; Lehigh becomes county seat; **1908** county seat moved to Coalgate; **1911** county courthouse completed; **Aug. 14, 1958** county's last coal mine closes; **1969** new county courthouse built.

Colbert *Bryan County* *Southern Oklahoma, 127 mi/204 km south-southeast of Oklahoma City*

1846 Chickasaw Benjamin F. Colbert arrives from Mississippi on Trail of Tears, builds sawmill, grist mill and cotton gin on his plantation on Red River; town founded; **1853** incorporated as a town; Colbert begins operating ferry on Red River to Denison, Texas; **1875** Colbert builds wagon toll bridge, replacing ferry; **1929** in Red River Bridge War, Texas and Oklahoma embark on joint effort to build toll-free bridge across Red River, stockholders of toll bridge sue to stop construction, bridge prevails after series of court maneuvers, bridge opened 1931; **1944** Denison Dam built to west on Red River forming large Lake Texoma; **Dec. 1995** Red River Bridge dynamited, new bridge built 1996.

Collinsville *Tulsa County* *Northeastern Oklahoma, 17 mi/27 km north-northeast of Tulsa*

1884 Hillside Mission founded by Quaker John Murdock of Philadelphia; **1897** town founded, named for landowner who donated site on proposed railroad right-of-way; **1899** incorporated as a town; **1900** Atchison, Topeka & Santa Fe Railroad built; **1908** brick manufacturing begins; **1911** zinc smelter established; **1917** Carnegie Library built.

Cordell *Washita County* *Western Oklahoma, 85 mi/137 km west-southwest of Oklahoma City*

1892 Washita County formed; Cloud Chief becomes county seat; **1892** Cheyenne and Arapaho reservation opened to white settlers; town founded; **1897** incorporated as a town; **1900** county seat moved to Cordell; **1902** St. Louis-San Francisco Railroad reaches town; **1911** county courthouse completed; Carnegie Library built; **1918** first annual Pumpkin Festival held.

Cushing *Payne County* *Central Oklahoma, 52 mi/ 84 km northeast of Oklahoma City*

1892 town founded near Cimarron River, named for Marshall Cushing, secretary to Postmaster General John Wanamaker; **1894** incorporated as a town; **Apr. 11, 1912** Cushing Oil Field discovered at Wheeler No. 1 well to northeast; **1913** incorporated as a city; **1915** town surrounded by forest of oil derricks as production peaks.

Duncan *Stephens County* *Southern Oklahoma, 73 mi/117 km south-southwest of Oklahoma City*

1872 William Duncan becomes first white settler after marrying Chickasaw woman; **1890** Chicago, Rock Island & Pacific Railroad built; town founded; **1892** incorporated as a city; **1901** Kiowa-Comanche reservation opened to white settlers; **1907** Stephens County formed; town becomes county seat; **1921** oil discovered; Erle P. Halliburton develops oil well cementing technique; **Nov. 19, 1926** diplomat, U.N. Ambassador Jeanne Kirkpatrick born; **March 25, 1938** country singer Hoyt Axton born (died 1999); **March 1, 1954** actor, director Ron Howard born; **1956** town has four large refineries in operation; **1967** county courthouse built; **1998** Chisholm Trail Museum established.

Durant *Bryan County* *Southern Oklahoma, 122 mi/196 km south-southeast of Oklahoma City*

1830 Choctaw people begin forced removal to Oklahoma from Mississippi and Alabama on Trail of Tears, only 7,000 of 20,000 survive; **1842** Fort Washita established to northwest by Gen. Zachary Taylor, abandoned 1861; **1852** Carter Methodist Seminary founded, destroyed by fire 1914, moved to Ardmore; **1862** Fort McCulloch established to north by Confederates under Gen. Albert Pike; **1863** Choctaw capital established at Bokchito to east, moved to nearby Tuskahoma 1883; **1870** site first settled by Dixon Durant family; **1872** Missouri-Kansas-Texas Railroad built; town of Durant Junction founded; **1873** incorporated as a city; **1882** town name shortened; **1907** Bryan County formed; **1908** town becomes county seat; **1909** Southeastern State Normal School established, becomes Southeastern Oklahoma State University 1974; **1917** county courthouse built; **1945** Denison Dam built on Red River to southwest forming Lake Texoma, on Texas boundary; **1975** Choctaw Nation establishes headquarters here; **May 26, 1978** three state troopers slain by prison escapee at Caddo to northeast, captured ending month-long killing spree.

Eagletown *McCurtain County* *Southeastern Oklahoma, 195 mi/314 km southeast of Oklahoma City*

c.1820 first settlers arrive; **June 1832** Beth-a-tiara Mission established for Choctaws; **1834** Eagle Town founded; **1837** Stockbridge Mission established by Rev. Cyrus Byington; **c.1840** Byington produces *Dictionary of the Choctaw Language*; **1842** Iyanubbee Seminary for Girls founded by Choctaw General Council; **1850** log courthouse built by Choctaws, used until 1907, destroyed by storm c.1925; **1884** Chief Jefferson Gardner House built by Choctaw Chief.

Earlsboro *Pottawatomie County* See **Shawnee (1941)**

Edmond *Oklahoma County* *Central Oklahoma, 10 mi/16 km north of Oklahoma City*

1887 Santa Fe Railroad built; **1889** first white settlers arrive; town founded; **1890** Central State Teachers College established, becomes University of Central Oklahoma 1991; **1925** incorporated as a city; **1943** West Edmond Oil Field discovered; **1947** East Edmond Oil Field begins production; Edmond Regional Medical Center established.

El Reno *Canadian County* *Central Oklahoma, 27 mi/43 km west of Oklahoma City*

1874 Fort Reno established during Cheyenne uprising, built 1875, abandoned 1908, reopened for World War I, used as German prisoner camp during World War II, closed 1948; **1879** *Cheyenne Transporter* newspaper founded, first newspaper in western Oklahoma; **1889** Chicago, Rock Island & Quincy Railroad built; town founded; **1890** Canadian County formed; town becomes county seat; incorporated as a town; **1901** Kiowa-Apache-Comanche reservation opened to white settlement; **1910** incorporated as a city; **Sept. 13, 1929** Cheyenne artist Jerome Bushyhead born (died 2000); **1934** U.S. Southwestern Reformatory built; **1938** Redlands Community College established; **1949** Fort Reno abandoned; Fort Reno Livestock Research Farm founded at site; **1964** county courthouse completed.

Enid *Garfield County* *Northern Oklahoma, 65 mi/ 105 km north-northwest of Oklahoma City*

1835 Cherokee Outlet created, 57 mi/92 km wide strip between 96th and 100th meridians, for resettlement of Cherokee people from Georgia, also called Cherokee Strip; **1893** Cherokee Strip land run begins at noon, Sept. 16, opening area to white settlers; Garfield County formed; town founded as county seat; Rock Island Railroad arrives; **1894** incorporated as a city; **July 13, 1894** derailment at bridge in South Enid blamed on tampering of bridge supports; railroad gives in to establishing ticket office in South Enid, officially named Enid; **1897** first successful wheat harvest occurs; Atchison, Topeka & Santa Fe Railroad reaches town; **1903** St. Louis

& San Francisco Railroad reaches town; **1905** county courthouse built; **1906** Oklahoma Christian University established, becomes Phillips University 1913, closed 1998; **1909** Enid State School founded; **1910** town becomes important regional flour milling center; Carnegie Library built; **1921** oil discovered in Tonkawa area to northeast; **1926** Crescent Oil Pool discovered to southeast; **1928** Pillsbury Mill built; **Nov. 22, 1930** astronaut Owen Garriott born; **1932** Woodring Regional Airport established; **1941** Vance Air Force Base established; Federal Building and Post Office completed.

Eufaula *McIntosh County* *Eastern Oklahoma, 65 mi/105 km south-southeast of Tulsa*

1836 Creeks arrive after forced migration from Southeast; **1849** Asbury Mission boarding school founded by Methodist Episcopal church, destroyed by fire 1889; **1861** Creeks, Choctaws, and Chickasaws sign treaty of cooperation with Confederates; **1872** Missouri-Kansas-Texas Railroad built; town founded on Canadian River; **Aug. 3, 1873** popular Creek writer Alexander Lawrence Posey born, drowned in Canadian River May 27, 1908; **1876** *Indian Journal* newspaper founded; **1892** Eufaula Boarding School for girls opened; **1907** McIntosh County formed; town becomes county seat; **1912** incorporated as a city; **1926** county courthouse built; **1957** large Eufaula Lake formed by Eufaula Dam on Canadian River, town occupies peninsula with North Fork Arm to north.

Fairview *Major County* *Northern Oklahoma, 78 mi/126 km northwest of Oklahoma City*

Sept. 16, 1893 Cherokee Outlet opened to white settlement; **1894** town founded; **1901** incorporated as a town; **1907** Major County formed; **1908** town becomes county seat; **1909** incorporated as a city; **1920** county courthouse built.

Foraker *Osage County* *See* **Pawhuska** (1918)

Fort Gibson *Muskogee County* *Eastern Oklahoma, 49 mi/79 km southeast of Tulsa*

1824 Fort Gibson built on Grand (Neosho) River, near its mouth on Arkansas River, serves as chief military post for Indian Territory; town founded; **1857** fort abandoned; **1861** fort occupied by Confederates, reoccupied by Union forces, renamed Fort Blunt; **1868** Fort Gibson National Cemetery established; **1873** incorporated as a town; **1890** fort again abandoned; **1953** Fort Gibson Lake formed by dam to north on Grand (Neosho) River.

Fort Supply *Woodward County* *Northwestern Oklahoma, 140 mi/225 km northwest of Oklahoma City*

1837 Cheyennes and Arapahos wage battle against united Kiowas, Comanches, and Apaches; **1839** warring Native American tribes make peace accord; **Nov. 1868** Fort Supply army post established on North Canadian River; town founded around post; **1893** post abandoned; **1903** Western State Correctional Center and Hospital built; post office established; **1906** incorporated as a town; **1942** Fort Supply Lake formed to south by dam on Wolf Creek.

Fort Towson *Choctaw County* *Southeastern Oklahoma, 163 mi/262 km southeast of Oklahoma City*

1821 town of Doaksville founded near Red River by Doaks brothers; **1824** Fort Towson established; **1837** treaty signed by Choctaws allows sharing of their land with Chickasaws; **1850** town becomes Choctaw capital, until 1863; **1900** Arkansas & Choctaw Railroad built; **1903** town renamed Fort Towson; **1904** incorporated as a town.

Frederick *Tillman County* *Southwestern Oklahoma, 115 mi/185 km southwest of Oklahoma City*

1901 Kiowa-Comanche reservation opened to white settlers; town founded; **1902** incorporated as a city; **1903** Blackwell, Enid & Southwestern Railroad built; **1907** Tillman County formed; town becomes county seat; **1921** county courthouse completed; **1937** West Frederick Oil Field discovered; **1945** South Frederick Oil Field discovered; **June 27, 1994** highest temperature ever recorded in Oklahoma reached at Tipton to northwest, 120°F/49°C, matches record at Tishomingo 1943.

Geary *Blaine County* *Central Oklahoma, 48 mi/77 km west of Oklahoma City*

March 4, 1868 legendary cattleman Jesse Chisholm dies from eating tainted bear meat at Left Hand Spring, his last camp, salt manufacturer turned pathfinder, blazed Chisholm Trail from Texas to Kansas, used by cattlemen to drive herds to rail heads, born in Tennessee 1805; **1892** Ed Guerrier becomes first settler; **1898** Choctaw, Oklahoma & Gulf Railroad reaches site; town founded, town name variation of Guerrier; **1904** incorporated as a city.

Guthrie *Logan County* *Central Oklahoma, 27 mi/43 km north of Oklahoma City, near Cimarron River*

1887 St. Louis & San Francisco Railroad built; town founded; **Apr. 22, 1889** Great Land Run begins at noon, opens Native American lands to white settlement, land offices established at Guthrie and Kingfisher; **1890** Oklahoma Territory created; Logan County formed; incorporated as a city, becomes capital and county seat; **1892** Catholic College of Oklahoma established, closed 1955; **1902** Carnegie Library built; **1905** prohibitionist Carrie Nation begins publishing *The Hatchet* newspaper after divorcing husband David Nation; **Nov. 1906** state constitutional convention held; **1907** Oklahoma admitted to Union as 46th state; city becomes first state capital; **1908** county courthouse built; **1910** state capital moved to Oklahoma City; **1922** State Masonic Home for Children founded, closed 1978.

Guymon *Texas County* *Northwestern Oklahoma, 236 mi/380 km northwest of Oklahoma City*

1890 Panhandle made part of Oklahoma Territory through Organic Act; **1901** town founded; **1905** town incorporated; **1907** Texas County formed; town becomes county seat; **1926** county courthouse built.

Harrah *Oklahoma County* *Central Oklahoma, suburb 18 mi/29 km east of Oklahoma City*

1896 Choctaw, Oklahoma & Gulf Railroad reaches site; town founded, originally named Sweeney; **1899** town renamed for merchant Frank Harrah; **Apr. 16, 1905** Pittsburgh Pirates baseball hitter Paul Waner born (died 1965); **1908** incorporated as a town; **July 14, 1923** actor Dale Robertson born.

Hobart *Kiowa County* *Western Oklahoma, 96 mi/155 km southwest of Oklahoma City*

1901 Kiowa Indian Reservation opened to white settlers; Kiowa County formed; town founded as county seat, named for U.S. Vice Pres. Garrett A. Hobart; town incorporated; **1902** county courthouse built; **Dec. 24, 1924** Babbs Switch School destroyed by fire, 36 killed, replaced by brick Babbs Memorial School; **1939** Hobart Oil Field opened.

Holdenville *Hughes County* *Central Oklahoma, 68 mi/109 km southeast of Oklahoma City*

1834 Fort Holmes established to south on Little River; **c.1890** post office established; town named Fentress; **1895** Choctaw, Oklahoma, & Gulf and St. Louis & San Francisco railroads built; new town platted at railroad junction 2 mi/3.2 km south of original town, renamed Holdenville; **1898** town incorporated; **1907** Hughes County formed; town becomes county seat; **May 22, 1928** oil magnate T. Boone Pickens born; **1964** county courthouse built.

Hollis *Harmon County* *Southwestern Oklahoma, 148 mi/238 km southwest of Oklahoma City*

1901 town founded by George Washington Hollis; **1905** incorporated as a town; **1909** Harmon County formed from Greer County, named for U.S. Secretary of State Judson Harmon; town becomes county seat; **1926** county courthouse built; **1929** incorporated as a city.

Hugo *Choctaw County* *Southeastern Oklahoma, 153 mi/246 km southeast of Oklahoma City*

1900 Arkansas & Choctaw (St. Louis & San Francisco) Railroad built; town founded near Red River, named for author Victor Hugo, favorite of town surveyor's wife; **1901** incorporated as a town; **1907** Choctaw County formed; town becomes county seat; **1909** incorporated as a city; **1912** county courthouse built; **June 5, 1934** TV journalist Bill Moyers born; **Jan. 10, 1959** house fire at Boswell to west kills mother, her 10 children, 5 cousins;

1974 Hugo Lake formed by dam on Kiamichi River to east; **1992** Hugo Heritage Railroad established.

Idabel *McCurtain County* *Southeastern Oklahoma, 188 mi/303 km southeast of Oklahoma City*

1902 town founded near Red River; **1904** post office established; **1906** town incorporated; **1907** McCurtain County formed; town becomes county seat; **1964** county courthouse built.

Indiahoma *Comanche County* See **Cache (1910)**

Ingalls *Payne County* *Central Oklahoma, 53 mi/85 km north-northeast of Oklahoma City*

1890 town founded, named for U.S. Senator from Kansas John J. Ingalls; post office opened; **1892** following bank robbery at Coffeyville, Kansas, in which three gang members were killed, Bill Doolin and Bill Dalton reorganize gang at cave on Cimarron River; **Sept. 1, 1893** U.S. marshals "Dynamite" Dick Speed, Tom Houston, and Lafe Shadley gunned down by Doolin-Dalton gang; **1907** post office closed; **1956** monument erected in memory of slain marshals.

Jay *Delaware County* *Northeastern Oklahoma, 70 mi/113 km east-northeast of Tulsa*

1832 Fort Wayne built to south by Capt. Nathan Boone, son of Daniel Boone, as border outpost; **1861** Fort Wayne used as Confederate recruiting station by Cherokee Stand Watie; **1907** Delaware County formed; Grove becomes county seat; **1908** town founded, named for Claude Jay Washburn, nephew Stand Watie; county seat moved to Jay by popular vote, feud follows; **1911** incorporated as a city; **1913** county courthouse built, remodeled after 1941 fire.

Kellyville *Creek County* See **Tulsa (1917)**

Kingfisher *Kingfisher County* *Central Oklahoma, 35 mi/56 km northwest of Oklahoma City*

Apr. 22, 1889 Great Land Run begins at noon, opens large area of Native American lands to white settlement, land offices established at Kingfisher and Guthrie; town founded and incorporated; **1890** Kingfisher County formed; town becomes county seat; **1892** Chicago, Rock Island & Pacific Railroad completed; **1960** county courthouse built.

Krebs *Pittsburg County* See **McAlester (1892)**

Langston *Logan County* *Central Oklahoma, 34 mi/102 km north-northeast of Oklahoma City*

1890 primarily African-American town founded by E. P. McCabe, named for black educator, Cong. John M. Langston; **1891** incorporated as a town; **1897** Langston University established.

OKLAHOMA

Lawton   *Comanche County   Southwestern Oklahoma, 80 mi/129 km southwest of Oklahoma City*

1869 Fort Sill established to north by Gen. Philip Sheridan, named for Civil War Gen. Joshua W. Sill; **1871** Fort Sill Indian School established; **1901** Kiowa-Comanche Indian Reservation opened to white settlers; town founded and incorporated; Wichita Mountains forest reserve established to northwest, becomes National Wildlife Refuge 1935; town boasts 86 saloons; **1904** Fort Sill abandoned; **1907** Comanche County formed; town becomes county seat; **1908** Cameron State Agricultural College established, becomes Cameron University; **1911** Fort Sill reestablished as army training base; **1921** Carnegie Library built; **1955** McMahon Auditorium built; **1977** county courthouse built.

Madill   *Marshall County   Southern Oklahoma, 105 mi/169 km south-southeast of Oklahoma City*

July 21, 1834 Gen. Henry Leavenworth dies at Camp Leavenworth to southeast, expedition continues under Col. Henry Dodge, includes Jefferson Davis and George Catlin; **1900** St. Louis-San Francisco Railroad built; town founded, named for railroad attorney George A. Madill; **1905** town incorporated; **1907** Marshall County formed; town becomes county seat; **1914** county courthouse built; **1945** Lake Texoma formed to south by Denison Dam on Red River (Texas boundary), large Washita River Arm to east.

Mangum   *Greer County   Southwestern Oklahoma, 122 mi/196 km southwest of Oklahoma City*

July 21, 1834 Plains peoples and representatives of U.S. meet to discuss peace at Devil's Canyon to east near Quartz Mountain; **1860** Greer County (Texas) formed, named for Texas Lt. Gov. John Alexander Greer; **1883** town founded on Salt Fork Red River; **1885** ten families arrive with 60,000 head of cattle; **1886** county organized; town becomes county seat; **1889** Oklahoma Organic Act claims Greer County; **1896** U.S. Supreme Court defines Greer County as part of Indian Territory; county subdivided into Greer, Jackson, and part of Harmon counties; **1900** incorporated as a city; **1906** county courthouse built; **1927** dam built to east on North Fork Red River forming Lake Altus; **1936** Margaret Carder Public Library opened; **1958** Quartz Mountain Lodge built to east, rebuilt after 1995 fire, burned again before opening, rebuilt 2001; **1978** Oklahoma Summer Arts Institute established at Quartz Mountain.

Marietta   *Love County   Southern Oklahoma, 110 mi/177 km south-southeast of Oklahoma City*

1887 Atchison, Topeka & Santa Fe Railroad built through area; town founded on railroad near Red River; **1898** incorporated as a city; **1907** Love County formed from Pickens County of Chickasaw Nation; town becomes county seat; **1910** county courthouse built.

McAlester   *Pittsburg County   Eastern Oklahoma, 85 mi/137 km south of Tulsa*

1828 White Chimney log house built; **1870** town founded around James J. McAlester's tent store on California Trail, junction of Texas Road; **1872** Missouri-Kansas-Texas Railroad reaches town; **Jan. 7, 1892** explosion at Osage Coal Mine at Krebs to east, 100 killed; **1899** incorporated as a city; **1907** Pittsburg County formed; town becomes county seat; **1908** Oklahoma State Penitentiary established; **May 10, 1908** Cong., Speaker of the House Carl Albert born (died 2000); **Oct. 25, 1918** poet John Berryman born (died 1972); **1927** county courthouse built; **Dec. 27, 1929** explosion at Old Town coal mine, 61 killed; **Oct. 27, 1930** explosion at Westley No. 4 coal mine, 30 killed; **1942** McAlester Army Ammunition Plant established to southwest; **March 28, 1954** country singer Reba McEntire born.

Medford   *Grant County   Northern Oklahoma, 92 mi/148 km north of Oklahoma City*

1892 Chicago, Rock Island & Pacific Railroad completed to Texas; **1893** Grant County formed; Cherokee Strip (Outlet) opened to white settlers; Pond Creek becomes first county seat; town founded on railroad, incorporated; **1908** county seat moved to Medford; county courthouse built.

Miami   *Ottawa County   Northeastern Oklahoma, 80 mi/129 km northeast of Tulsa*

1891 trading post established to southeast; town founded and incorporated on Grand (Neosho) River; **1897** lead and zinc mining begins in Tri-State Mining Area; **1905** mining boom begins; **1907** Ottawa County formed; town becomes county seat; **1919** Northeastern Oklahoma Agricultural and Mechanical College (2-year) established; **1921** Carnegie Library built, replaced 1962; **1953** county courthouse built; **1957** Will Rogers Turnpike (toll) completed to Tulsa.

Midwest City   *Oklahoma County   Central Oklahoma, 6 mi/9.7 km southeast of Oklahoma City*

1941 town founded by William "Bill" Atkinson in anticipation of airfield being built; **1941** Tinker Air Force Base established; **1943** incorporated as a town; **1948** incorporated as a city; **1968** Rose State College (2-year) established.

Muskogee   *Muskogee County   Eastern Oklahoma, 45 mi/72 km southeast of Tulsa, on Arkansas River*

Jan. 1807 battle between French trader Joseph Bogy and his men and Chief Pushmataha's Choctaws ends in rout of Bogy's tradesmen; **1824** Fort Gibson built to east; **1828** Creeks arrive in forced move from Alabama over Trail of Tears; **1850** Tullahassee School founded to north, part of Presbyterian mission for Creek nation, destroyed by fire 1880; **1861** Fort Davis established by Confederates, abandoned 1863; **1871** Missouri, Kansas & Texas

Railroad built; town founded on railroad opposite confluences of Grand (Neosho) and Verdigris rivers; **1874** Union Agency for Five Civilized Tribes established here; **1875** International Indian Fair organized; **1876** *Indian Journal* newspaper founded; **1880** Bacone College (2-year) established; **1888** *Phoenix* newspaper founded; **1889** federal court established; **1896** *Morning Times* founded; **1898** incorporated as a town; **1904** oil discovered in area; **1907** Muskogee County formed; town becomes county seat; **1909** public library built; **1910** incorporated as a city; **Jan. 2, 1915** African-American educator John Hope Franklin born at Rentiesville to south; **1917** iron works founded for building oil derricks; **1920** Muskogee Municipal Junior College established; **1923** U.S. Veterans' Hospital built; **1928** county courthouse built; **1971** Port of Muskogee built on Arkansas River, part of Kerr-McClellan Waterway Project; Chouteau Lock & Dam built to north on Verdigris River, also part of Waterway; Muskogee (Creek) people elect first Principal Chief without Presidential approval; **1966** Five Civilized Tribes Museum established at Indian Agency Building built 1875; **May 27, 2002** barge operator passes out at helm, barges collide with Interstate 40 bridge on Arkansas River near Webbers Falls to southeast, collapsing eastbound span, plunging vehicles into river, 14 killed, 4 horses in trailer killed.

Newkirk *Kay County* *Northern Oklahoma, 100 mi/161 km north-northeast of Oklahoma City*

1740 French trading post established to east, abandoned c.1750, first white settlement in Oklahoma; **1893** Cherokee Strip opened to white settlement; Kay County formed; town founded; **1900** incorporated as a city; **1919** area's first oil fields discovered; **1926** county courthouse built; **1976** Kaw Lake formed by dam to east on Arkansas River.

Norman *Cleveland County* *Central Oklahoma, 20 mi/32 km south of Oklahoma City, on Canadian River*

1870s Topeka & Santa Fe Railroad built; **1889** town founded, named for railroad survey engineer; **1890** Cleveland County formed; town becomes county seat; University of Oklahoma established; **1891** incorporated as a city; **1893** Griffin Memorial State Hospital founded; **1899** Sam Noble Museum of Natural History established at University of Oklahoma; **Oct. 22, 1905** radio engineer Karl Jansky born, first to detect radio waves in space (died 1950); **Apr. 13, 1918** fire at State Hospital, 38 killed; **Apr. 7, 1928** TV actor James Garner born; **1939** county courthouse built.

Nowata *Nowata County* *Northeastern Oklahoma, 43 mi/69 km north-northeast of Tulsa*

1888 town founded near Verdigris River; **1889** St. Louis & Iron Mountain Railroad reaches town; **1895** incorporated as a town; **1904** oil discovered in county; **1907** Nowata County formed; town becomes county seat; **1912** county courthouse built; **1913** incorporated as a city; **1963**

Oologah Lake formed by dam on Verdigris River to south.

Okay *Wagoner County* *Northeastern Oklahoma, 40 mi/64 km southeast of Tulsa*

c.1805 trading post established on Verdigris River; **1822** post sold to Col. Auguste Chouteau; **Feb. 1828** first Creek peoples arrive from Alabama and Georgia; **1830** Wigwam Neosho cabin built by Sam Houston, where he lived until 1832 with Cherokee wife Diana Rogers; **1871** Kansas & Texas Railroad built; town founded; **1911** tornado destroys town; **1919** incorporated as a town; **1953** Fort Gibson Dam built on Grand (Neosho) River to east.

Okemah *Okfuskee County* *Central Oklahoma, 67 mi/108 km east of Oklahoma City*

1902 town founded; named for Creek Chief Okemah; **1903** Fort Smith & Western Railroad reaches town; town incorporated; **1907** Okfuskee County formed; **1908** town becomes county seat; **July 14, 1912** folksinger Woody Guthrie born (died 1967); **1927** county courthouse built.

Oklahoma City *Oklahoma, Canadian, Cleveland, and Pottawatomie counties* *Central Oklahoma*

1872 Missouri, Kansas & Texas Railroad built, first railroad completed across Indian Territory, site established as railroad stop; **1889** *Oklahoma Times* newspaper founded; **Apr. 22, 1889** with the Land Run, quiet railroad stop transformed into city of 10,000 in only 12 hours; **1890** Oklahoma County formed; incorporated as a city, becomes county seat; **1892** Atchison, Topeka & Santa Fe Railroad reaches city from north; **1893** Oklahoma Historical Society founded; **1894** *The Oklahoman* newspaper founded; **1899** Bethany Nazarene College established, moves to nearby Bethany 1906, becomes Southern Nazarene University; **1904** Oklahoma City University established; Oklahoma Zoo established at Wheeler Park, destroyed by flood 1923, reestablished at Lincoln Park 1924; **Feb. 10, 1906** actor Lon Chaney, Jr. born (died 1973); **1907** first Oklahoma State Fair held, present Fairgrounds opened 1954; **Nov. 16, 1907** Oklahoma admitted to Union as 46th state; **1910** state capital moved from Guthrie; **1916** Lake Overholser formed by dam to west on North Canadian River, named for Mayor Ed Overholser; **1917** state capitol completed; **1926** Oklahoma City Oil Field discovered, opened to drilling at city center Dec. 1928; Oklahoma City Philharmonic Orchestra founded; **1927** Will Rogers World Airport established to southwest; **1928** governor's mansion built; **March 1930** Mary Sudik oil well blows out of control spewing spray as far as Norman, fire hazard forces closing of other wells; **July 22, 1933** Charles Urschel kidnapped, $200,000 ransom paid, gangster Machine Gun Kelly, five others charged, given life sentences; **1936** Oklahoma City Symphony Orchestra founded; **1937** civic center completed; **1941** Tinker Air Force Base established to east; **June 23, 1946** actor Ted Shackelford born; **1950** Oklahoma Christian University of Science and Arts established; **1953** Turner Turnpike (toll) opened to Tulsa; medical center completed; **1958** Oklahoma Art Center opened; **1960** Oklahoma Museum of Art founded, merged with Art Center 1989; **1961** Oklahoma State University, Oklahoma City Campus (2-year) established; **1963** Civic Ballet founded, renamed Metropolitan Ballet 1971, Ballet Oklahoma 1980; **1965** National Cowboy Hall of Fame opened; **1967** six-story County Building built; **1968** Oklahoma Firefighters Museum established; **1969** Oklahoma City Community College established; **1971** 36-story Liberty Tower building built; **1973** 30-story Kerr-McGee Center built; **1974** 33-story First National Center built; **March 1977** nine-story Murrah Federal Building completed; **1981** 19-story Mid America Tower built; **1982** 31-story First Oklahoma Tower built; **1985** 32-story City Place office building built; **1988** Oklahoma City Philharmonic Orchestra founded, replaces Symphony; Myriad Botanical Garden established downtown; Remington Park Race Track opened; **Apr. 19, 1995** truck loaded with 2,000 pd/907 kg of ammonium nitrate explodes at 9:02 A.M., destroying front half of Alfred P. Murrah Federal Building, killing 169, including 19 children and 1 rescue worker, Timothy McVeigh arraigned Apr. 21, executed June 11, 2001, Terre Haute, Indiana; **May 3, 1999** tornado leaves 30-mi/48-km swath through suburbs, one of 40 tornadoes in central Oklahoma, 44 killed; **2000** Oklahoma City National Memorial established; **2002** Oklahoma City Art Museum opened; Ford Center Sports Arena opened.

Okmulgee   *Okmulgee County   East central Oklahoma, 36 mi/58 km south of Tulsa*

1828 Muskogee (Creek) people forced to migrate on Trail of Tears from Southeastern states, first capital established at High Springs; **1868** town founded, Creek term for "bubbling water," becomes capital of Creek Nation; **1878** Creek Council House built; **1884** Nuyaka Mission founded to west by Presbyterians, closed 1898; **1900** incorporated as a town; St. Louis & San Francisco Railroad built; *Record* newspaper founded; **1904** oil discovered near old Creek Council House; **1907** Okmulgee County formed; town becomes county seat; **1908** incorporated as a city; **1910s** oil production peaks; **1911** glass manufacturing begins; **1916** county courthouse completed; *Times* newspaper founded.

Oktaha   *Muskogee County   Eastern Oklahoma, 48 mi/77km southeast of Tulsa*

July 17, 1863 Union forces from Fort Gibson under Maj. Gen. James G. Blunt advance on Confederates under Gen. Douglas H. Cooper at Honey Springs, leaving 200 Confederates dead or wounded, securing Indian Territory for Union; **1872** Missouri-Kansas-Texas Railroad built; town founded; **1876** incorporated as a town.

Oologah   *Rogers County   See* **Claremore (1879)**

Pauls Valley   *Garvin County   Southern Oklahoma, 55 mi/89 km south-southeast of Oklahoma City*

1847 Smith Paul becomes first settler; **1887** Atchison, Topeka & Santa Fe Railroad built north-to-south; Gulf, Colorado & Santa Fe Railroad extended west; town founded on Washita River, named Pauls Valley; **1899** town incorporated; **1907** Garvin County formed; **1908** town becomes county seat; **1915** boys' reformatory established; **1918** county courthouse built, annex built 1974; **1953** Pauls Valley State Hospital established at reformatory site.

Pawhuska   *Osage County   Northern Oklahoma, 40 mi/64 km north-northwest of Tulsa*

1872 Osage people moved from Kansas to reservation purchased from Cherokees; **Oct. 1897** oil and natural gas discovered in eastern part of reservation; town founded on Bird River, named for Osage Chief Paw-Hu-Scah (White Hair); **1906** town incorporated; **1907** Osage County formed, coterminous with reservation; town becomes county seat; **1908** Cathedral of the Osage built; **1909** first boy scout troop in America organized by Rev. John Mitchell; **1914** county courthouse built; **June 13, 1918** actor Ben Johnson born at Foraker to northwest (died 1996); **1921** Chapman-Barnard Ranch built to north by James A. Chapman, subdivided 1966; **1938** Osage Tribal Museum built.

Pawnee   *Pawnee County   Northern Oklahoma, 70 mi/113 km north-northeast of Oklahoma City*

1876 Pawnee people moved from Nebraska; Pawnee Agency trading post established; **1892** Pawnee County formed; town founded as county seat; **1894** incorporated as a city; **Nov. 20, 1900** cartoonist Chester Gould born, creator of *Dick Tracy* (died 1985); **1908** ranch house built by Gordon W. "Pawnee Bill" Lillie, becomes Pawnee Bill Museum 1962; **1932** county courthouse built.

Perry   *Noble County   Northern Oklahoma, 56 mi/90 km north of Oklahoma City*

1835 Cherokee Outlet created for Cherokee people relocated from Georgia; **1893** Noble County formed; area opened to white settlement, part of Cherokee Strip (Outlet) Land Run; Atchison, Topeka & Santa Fe Railroad built; town founded as county seat; **1894** town incorporated; **1910** Carnegie Library built; **1916** county courthouse built; **1947** incorporated as a city; **1968** Cherokee Strip Museum opened; **1982** Stagecoach Community Theatre established.

Perryville   *Pittsburg County   Eastern Oklahoma, 7 mi/11.3 km south-southwest of McAlester*

1838 town founded as stop on Butterfield Overland Mail route; **1841** post office opened; **1852** Colbert Institute, school for Chickasaw children, opened by Methodist church; **1861** supply depot established by Confederates; **Aug. 26, 1863** in Battle of Perryville, Confederates under

Gen. Douglas H. Cooper retreat at Honey Creek [see Oktaha], greeted by reinforcements, overwhelmed by Union forces under Maj. Gen. James G. Blunt; town destroyed.

Picher   *Ottawa County*   *Northeastern Oklahoma,*
87 mi/140 km northeast of Tulsa

1897 zinc and lead mining begins in area; town founded; **1918** incorporated as a city; **1932** Eagle-Picher Central Mill built for processing lead-zinc ore, replaces less efficient mill; **1950** two support columns in underground mine threaten to collapse, forcing evacuation of four-block area around Main and Second streets; **1965** mining activity ceases.

Ponca City   *Kay County*   *Northern Oklahoma,*
87 mi/140 km north-northeast of Oklahoma City

1893 Cherokee Strip (Outlet) opened to white settlement; town of New Ponca founded on Arkansas River by B. S. Barnes, at edge of Ponca Indian Reservation; **1893** town incorporated; **1899** incorporated as a city, renamed Ponca City; **1928** Marland Mansion completed, home of Gov. Ernest Wentworth; **1929** Conoco Oil Refinery established; **Apr. 22, 1930** Pioneer Woman Statue dedicated; **1935** Ponca City Library built; **1958** Pioneer Woman Museum opened; **1976** Kaw Lake formed by dam to east on Arkansas River.

Poteau   *Le Flore County*   *Eastern Oklahoma,*
108 mi/174 km southeast of Tulsa

1898 town founded, incorporated near Poteau River; **1907** Le Flore County formed; town becomes county seat; **1927** county courthouse built; **1934** Carl Albert State College (2-year) established; **1960** Kerr Country Mansion built.

Pryor   *Mayes County*   *Northeastern Oklahoma,*
39 mi/63 km east-northeast of Tulsa

1820 trading post established by Nathaniel Pryor, scout for Lewis and Clark Expedition; **1872** town founded, named Pryor's Creek; **1897** Whitaker Orphans' Home founded; **1898** incorporated as a town; **1907** Mayes County formed; town becomes county seat; **1951** incorporated as a city; **1957** Lake Hudson formed on Grand (Neosho) River by Markham Ferry Dam to southeast; **1958** nitroguanadine plant built by U.S. Government at Pryor Ordnance Works; **1959** county courthouse built; **1963** town renamed Pryor.

Purcell   *McClain County*   *Central Oklahoma,*
35 mi/56 km south of Oklahoma City

1887 Atchison, Topeka & Santa Fe Railroad arrives; town founded on Canadian River, named for railroad engineer; **1898** incorporated as a city; **1907** McClain County formed; town becomes county seat; **1910** toll bridge built across river to Lexington, replaced by free bridge 1938; **1928** county courthouse completed.

Rentiesville   *McIntosh County*   See **Muskogee** (1915)

Salina   *Mayes County*   *Northeastern Oklahoma,*
48 mi/77 km east-northeast of Tulsa

1804 Maj. Jean Pierre Chouteau of St. Louis persuades 3,000 Osage peoples to move from Missouri to Grand (Neosho) River area; **c.1817** trading post established by Chouteau; **1822** son Auguste Chouteau moves post south to mouth of Grand River on Arkansas River; **1849** post office established with traffic headed for California gold mines; **1872** Cherokee Orphans' Home founded, destroyed by fire 1903, moved to Tahlequah 1904, becomes Sequoyah Vocational School; **1912** incorporated as a town.

Sallisaw   *Sequoyah County*   *Eastern Oklahoma,*
84 mi/135 km southeast of Tulsa, near Arkansas River

1829 Dwight Presbyterian Mission established, Indian school maintained until 1930s; Cherokee Chief Sequoyah's Cabin built to northeast; **1886** town founded as trading post; **1898** incorporated as a city; **1907** Sequoyah County formed; town becomes county seat; **1913** county courthouse built, remodeled 1961; **1963** Blue Ribbon Downs race track established; **1971** Robert S. Kerr Lake formed by dam on Arkansas River to south.

Sapulpa   *Creek County*   *Northeastern Oklahoma,*
13 mi/21 km southwest of Tulsa

c.1850 Jim Sapulpa begins farming near Rock Creek, operates store out of his home; **1886** Atlantic & Pacific (St. Louis & San Francisco) Railroad reaches site; town founded; **1896** Euchee Boarding School for Creeks opened, closed 1947; **1898** town incorporated; **1901** Carnegie Library built; **1905** large Glenn Oil Pool discovered to south by Ida E. Glenn; **1907** Creek County formed; town becomes county seat; **1914** county courthouse completed.

Sayre   *Beckham County*   *Western Oklahoma,*
123 mi/198 km west of Oklahoma City

1896 U.S. Supreme Court rules Texas-Oklahoma boundary should follow South Fork Red River to 100th meridian; **1901** Chicago, Rock Island & Pacific Railroad built; town founded on North Fork Red River, named for railroad stockholder Robert H. Sayre; **1903** incorporated as a town; **1907** Beckham County formed; town becomes county seat; **1910** incorporated as a city; **1911** county courthouse built.

Seminole   *Seminole County*   *Central Oklahoma,*
50 mi/80 km east-southeast of Oklahoma City

1890 town founded, originally named Tidmore; Mekasukey Mission built to southwest; **1891** Mekasukey Academy for Seminole boys opened, closed 1930; **1906** post office opened; town renamed Seminole;

1908 incorporated as a town; **1922** Bowlegs Oil Field discovered to south; **1926** incorporated as a city; **July 1926** Greater Seminole Oil Field discovered; population jumps from 1,000 to 35,000; **1931** Seminole State College (2-year) established.

Shawnee *Pottawatomie County* *Central Oklahoma, 35 mi/56 km east-southeast of Oklahoma City*

1891 area opened to white settlement; Pottawatomie County formed; town founded as county seat on North Canadian River; **1894** incorporated as a town; **1895** Choctaw, Oklahoma & Gulf (Rock Island) Railroad arrives; **1902** Atchison, Topeka & Santa Fe Railroad reaches town; **1910** Oklahoma Baptist University established; **1915** St. Gregory's College established; **March 28, 1924** tornado flattens 28 city blocks, eight killed; **1926** Greater Seminole Oil Pool discovered to east; **March 6, 1927** astronaut Leroy Gordon Cooper born; **Apr. 4, 1928** flash flooding destroys hundreds of houses, six killed; **1934** county courthouse built; **March 6, 1941** Pittsburgh Pirates baseball player Willie Stargill born at Earlsboro to southeast; **1950** Sylvania Electric Products plant established; **1957** incorporated as a city; **Dec. 18, 1963** actor Brad Pitt born; **Oct. 5, 1970** tornado damages six downtown blocks, 4 killed, 40 injured.

Spavinaw *Mayes County* *Northeastern Oklahoma, 55 mi/89 km east-northeast of Tulsa*

1922 original town site purchased by City of Tulsa for creation of Lake Spavinaw reservoir on Spavinaw Creek; **1923** lake completed; **1930** incorporated as a town; **Oct. 20, 1931** New York Yankees baseball player Mickey Mantle born (died 1995); **1952** Upper Spavinaw Lake formed by dam on Spavinaw Creek, later renamed Lake Eucha.

Spiro *Le Flore County* *Eastern Oklahoma, 15 mi/24 km southwest of Fort Smith, Ark., near Arkansas River*

600–1400 AD prehistoric mound culture flourishes in area; **1539** Spanish explorer Hernando De Soto visits mounds; **June 1834** Fort Coffee established, abandoned 1838; **1842** Choctaw people establish Fort Coffee Academy for boys; **1895** Kansas City Southern Railroad built; town founded; **1899** incorporated as a town.

Stigler *Haskell County* *Eastern Oklahoma, 80 mi/129 km southeast of Tulsa*

1889 Joseph S. Stigler builds first house; **1894** Missouri Pacific Railroad built; **1895** cotton gin established; town founded; **1905** town incorporated; **1907** Haskell County formed; **1908** town becomes county seat; **March 20, 1912** explosion at San Bois No. 2 coal mine to southeast, 73 killed; **1931** county courthouse built.

Stillwater *Payne County* *North Central Oklahoma, 50 mi/80 km north-northeast of Oklahoma City*

May 1872 Ezekiel Proctor stands trial in Cherokee court held at Goingsnake Schoolhouse to northwest for murder of Polly Chesterton, U.S. marshals arrive from Fort Smith, leads to Goingsnake Massacre, eight killed, including seven officers and prisoner, judge wounded; **Dec. 1884** about 200 boomers settle on Stillwater Creek led by William L. Couch, Federal troops starve them out; **1889** town founded; **1890** Payne County formed; town becomes county seat; Oklahoma Agricultural and Mechanical College established, becomes Oklahoma State University; **1891** incorporated as a city; **1900** Eastern Oklahoma Railroad reaches town; **1917** county courthouse built; **1922** Stillwater Public Library founded, new library opened 1994; **Sept. 1976** National Wrestling Hall of Fame opened.

Stilwell *Adair County* *Eastern Oklahoma, 80 mi/129 east-southeast of Tulsa*

1833 area settled by relocated Cherokees; **c.1838** Bitting Water Mill built to west; **1897** Kansas City Southern Railroad built; town founded, named for railroad magnate Arthur Stilwell; incorporated as a town; **1907** Adair County formed; **1910** town becomes county seat; **Jan. 18, 1930** lowest temperature ever recorded in Oklahoma reached at Watts to north, −27°F/−33°C; **1931** county courthouse built; **1946** incorporated as a city.

Sulphur *Murray County* *Southern Oklahoma, 75 mi/121 km south-southeast of Oklahoma City*

1895 town founded; **July 1, 1902** Sulphur Springs Reservation recreation area established; **June 29, 1906** Platt National Park established, replaces recreation area, named for Sen. Orville Hitchcock Platt of Connecticut, of Committee for Indian Affairs; **1907** Murray County formed; town becomes county seat; **1908** incorporated as a city; Oklahoma School for the Deaf moved from Guthrie, founded 1898; **1922** tornado destroys 60 buildings, 2 killed, 20 injured; state veterans hospital established; **1923** county courthouse completed; **March 17, 1976** Chickasaw National Recreation Area established, absorbs Platt National Park; **1977** Mary E. Parker Library dedicated.

Tahlequah *Cherokee County* *Northeastern Oklahoma, 60 mi/97 km east-southeast of Tulsa*

1836 Park Hill Mission established to south by Presbyterians; **1839** area on Illinois River settled by Cherokee people forcibly removed on Trail of Tears from Southeastern states; town becomes capital of Cherokee Nation; **1843** town platted; **1845** Cherokee Supreme Court built, rebuilt after 1874 fire; **c.1845** Murrell House built by George Murrell; **1846** Cherokee Female Seminary founded, becomes Northeastern State University; **1848** National Hotel built; **1869** Cherokee capitol built; **1874** Cherokee National Prison built; **1889** incorporated as a city; **1903** Cherokee Orphans' Home moved from Salina; **1904** Sequoyah Vocational School moved from Salina; **1907** Cherokee County formed; town becomes county seat; Capitol becomes county courthouse; **1963** Cherokee Heritage Center founded, includes ancient village of Tsa-La-Gi; **1979** new county courthouse built; capitol returned to Cherokee Nation.

Taloga *Dewey County* *Western Oklahoma, 90 mi/ 145 km northwest of Oklahoma City*

1892 Dewey County formed, named for Adm. George Dewey, hero of Battle of Manila; town founded as county seat on Canadian River; Cheyenne and Arapaho lands opened to white settlement; **1906** incorporated as a city; **1926** county courthouse built.

Tipton *Tillman County* See **Frederick (1994)**

Tishomingo *Johnston County* *Southern Oklahoma, 100 mi/161 km south-southeast of Oklahoma City*

1837 forced removal of Chickasaw people from mid-Southern states begins on Trail of Tears; **1850** town founded near Washita River, named Good Springs; **1856** town made capital of Chickasaw Nation, renamed Tishomingo; **1857** post office opened; **1898** Chickasaw Capitol Building completed; **1901** incorporated as a city; **1907** Johnston County formed; town becomes county seat; **1908** capitol becomes county courthouse; Murray State College (2-year) established; **July 26, 1943** highest temperature recorded in Oklahoma reached, 120°F/49°C, matched at Tipton 1994.

Tulsa *Tulsa and Osage counties* *Northeastern Oklahoma, 95 mi/153 km northeast of Oklahoma City*

1848 trading post established by Lewis Perryman, named Tulsa, Creek term for "village," derived from Tallassee, Alabama, origin of Creeks; **1879** first post office established; **1882** Atlantic & Pacific (St. Louis & San Francisco) Railroad reaches town; guerilla activity among Creeks ruins town's businesses; **1884** mission school built; **1894** University of Tulsa established; **1898** incorporated as a city; **June 25, 1901** oil discovered at Red Fork; **1905** real estate boom follows discovery of Glenn Oil Pool; **1904** *Tulsa Tribune* newspaper founded; **1907** Tulsa County formed; city becomes county seat; **1911** county courthouse completed; **1913** DX Sunray Oil Refinery opened; **1915** federal building built; **Sept. 28, 1917** railroad accident at Kellyville to southwest, 23 killed; **1918** 24-story National Bank of Tulsa built; **Sept. 4, 1918** radio commentator Paul Harvey born; **March 2, 1919** actress Jennifer Jones born; **Feb. 26, 1920** actor Tony Randall born (died 2004); **June 1, 1921** incident between white and black laborers develops into racial rioting, black Greenwood neighborhood burned, 36 killed; after riot, other whites aid burned-out black residents; **July 26, 1922** movie director Blake

Edwards born; **March 16, 1927** New York Sen. Daniel Patrick Moynihan born (died 2003); **1928** Tulsa International Airport established; Tulsa Zoo opened; **1929** Boston Avenue Methodist Church completed; **1931** Union Depot built; **1939** Philbrook Art Center opened; **1943** Gilcrease Museum founded by oilman Thomas Gilcrease, a Creek, opened to public at his estate 1949; **1950** Tulsa Garden Center founded; **1951** Jaycee War Memorial Building dedicated; **1953** Turner Turnpike opened to Oklahoma City; **Nov. 2, 1953** actor Alfre Woodard born; **1955** county courthouse built; **1956** Tulsa Ballet founded; **1957** Will Rogers Turnpike completed; **Feb. 7, 1962** country singer Garth Brooks born; **1963** Oral Roberts University established; **1964** Tulsa Convention Center opened; **1966** 33-story Fourth National Bank built; **1968** Tulsa Community College established; **Nov. 11, 1970** explosives truck blows up killing seven oil surveyors; **1971** Kerr-McClellan Waterway opens Arkansas River to barge traffic with Port of Tulsa (Port Catoosa), on Verdigris River, as terminus; **1973** 41-story First National Bank built; **1975** 52-story Williams Center built; **1981** 60-story Cityplex Central Tower built; **1984** 36-story Mid-Continent Tower built; **May 27, 1984** flash flooding kills 13; **May 3, 1999** $1 billion damage, 44 killed in series of tornadoes in central Oklahoma.

Vinita *Craig County* *Northeastern Oklahoma, 58 mi/93 km northeast of Tulsa*

1838–1839 Cherokee people arrive in forced migration from Southeastern U.S. on Trail of Tears; **1871** Missouri-Kansas-Texas and Atlantic & Pacific (later Frisco) railroads reach site; town founded by Col. Elias C. Boudinot, a Cherokee, named for woman sculptor Vinnie Ream; town incorporated; **1907** Craig County formed; town becomes county seat; **1913** Eastern State Hospital established; **1920** county courthouse built; **1941** Lake of the Cherokees formed by Pensacola Dam on Grand (Neosho) River to southeast; **1957** section of Will Rogers Turnpike completed.

Wagoner *Wagoner County* *Northeastern Oklahoma, 37 mi/60 km east-southeast of Tulsa*

1886 Arkansas Valley & Kansas Railroad built; **1887** Missouri-Kansas-Texas Railroad reaches site; town founded at junction, named for train dispatcher Big Foot Wagoner; **1896** incorporated as a town; **1898** incorporated as a city; **1907** Wagoner County formed; **1908** town becomes county seat; **1913** Carnegie Library built; **1940** county courthouse built; **1946** Fort Gibson Lake formed by dam on Grand (Neosho) River to east.

Walters *Cotton County* *Southern Oklahoma, 92 mi/148 km south-southwest of Oklahoma City*

1901 Apache land opened to homesteaders; town founded, originally named Walter; **1902** incorporated as a town; **1912** Cotton County formed; town becomes county seat; **1917** town renamed Walters;

1919 incorporated as a city; **1927** county courthouse built; **Nov. 13, 1930** U.S. Sen. Fred Roy Harris born.

Watonga *Blaine County* *Central Oklahoma,*
58 mi/93 km northwest of Oklahoma City

1891 Blaine County formed; **1892** town founded as county seat on North Canadian River; **1894** Watonga Public Library established; **1903** town incorporated; **1906** county courthouse built; **1917** Henry Roman Nose dies, last of Cheyenne warrior chiefs; **1948** Canton Lake formed to northwest by dam on North Canadian River; **Aug. 14, 1964** gas well explosion near Canton to northwest creates large crater, flame visible of miles, capped June 11, 1965.

Watts *Adair County* *See* **Stilwell (1930)**

Waurika *Jefferson County* *Southern Oklahoma,*
97 mi/156 km south-southwest of Oklahoma City

1886 Henry Price Ranch settled to northeast on Chisholm Trail by J. C. Price; **1890** area first settled; **1892** Chicago, Rock Island & Pacific Railroad reaches site; town platted near Red River, named Monika; **1893** stone monument erected atop Monument Hill on Chisholm Trail, one rock added at a time over the years by campers; **1903** town incorporated; **1907** Jefferson County formed; **1908** town becomes county seat after dispute with town of Ryan; **1931** county courthouse built; **1977** Waurika Lake formed by dam on Beaver Creek to north.

Weatherford *Custer County* *Western Oklahoma,*
70 mi/113 km west of Oklahoma City

1893 town founded, named for U.S. Marshal William J. Weatherford; post office established; **1898** Choctaw, Oklahoma & Gulf Railroad reaches town; town platted and incorporated; **1901** Southwestern State Normal School established, becomes Southwestern Oklahoma State University; **Sept. 17, 1930** astronaut Thomas Stafford born.

Webbers Falls *Muskogee County* *See* **Muskogee (2002)**

Wewoka *Seminole County* *Central Oklahoma,*
61 mi/98 km southeast of Oklahoma City

1845 Seminoles arrive in forced move on Trail of Tears from Florida, settle peacefully among Creeks, tension arises over Seminoles' lenient treatment of their black slaves; **June 1849** Creeks threaten armed action against blacks after passing ordinance prohibiting black communities on their land, troops from Fort Smith, Arkansas, intervene; **1866** town founded by Seminoles; **1868** town designated capital of Seminole Nation; **1907** Seminole County formed; town becomes county seat; incorporated as a town; Seminoles suspend use of Whipping Tree at Courthouse, 25 lashes issued for minor crime; **1925** incorporated as a city; **1926** oil boom begins; **1927** county courthouse built.

Wilburton *Latimer County* *Eastern Oklahoma,*
93 mi/150 km south-southeast of Tulsa

1887 town founded, named for railroad contractor Will Burton; **1890** Choctaw, Oklahoma & Gulf (later Rock Island) Railroad reaches town; **1902** town incorporated; **1907** Latimer County formed; town becomes county seat; **1908** Oklahoma Eastern Agricultural and Mechanical College established, becomes Eastern Oklahoma State College (2-year); **Jan. 13, 1926** coal mine accident, 91 killed; **1938** county courthouse built; **May 5-6, 1960** 13 killed by tornado, part of series of tornadoes in Oklahoma and Arkansas, total of 30 killed.

Woodward *Woodward County* *Northwestern Oklahoma, 125 mi/201 km northwest of Oklahoma City*

Sept. 16, 1893 Cherokee Strip (Outlet) land run begins noon for white settlers; Woodward County formed; town founded as county seat; **1906** incorporated as a city; **1936** county courthouse built; **Apr. 9, 1947** tornado 2 mi/3.2 km wide destroys 100 blocks, 83 killed, 500 injured, tornado series also in Texas and Kansas [see Higgins, Texas].

Yale *Payne County* *Central Oklahoma, 40 mi/64 km west of Tulsa, near Cimarron River*

Nov. 19, 1861 2,000 pro-Union Creeks led by Opothle Yahola surrounded by 1,400 Confederate troops, Yahola escapes to Kansas, many starve or freeze to death before reaching Kansas Jan. 1862; **1895** town founded; **1903** town incorporated; **1917** 1912 Olympic champion Jim Thorpe (1888–1953) moves here, stays through 1923.

Oregon

Northwestern U.S. Capital: Salem. Major city: Portland.

Oregon became part of the U.S. in 1843 and was organized as Oregon Territory on August 14, 1848. Oregon was admitted to the Union as the 33rd state February 14, 1859.

Oregon is divided into 36 counties. The municipalities are classified as towns and cities. There are no townships. See Introduction.

Albany *Linn and Benton counties* *Western Oregon, 63 mi/101 km south-southwest of Portland*

1847 Linn County formed; Calapooia (Brownsville) becomes county seat; **1849** town founded on Willamette River by Walter and Thomas Monteith, named for home town of Albany, New York; Monteith Cabin built; **1851** county seat moved to Albany; grist mill built; **1852** steamboat *Multnomah* arrives; Steamboat Inn built; **1859** *Oregon Democrat* newspaper founded; **1865** incorporated as a city; **1867** Albany College established, becomes Lewis and Clark College 1941; **1870** Oregon & California (Southern Pacific) Railroad reaches city; **1893** first bridge built across Willamette River; **1940** third county courthouse built; **1966** Linn-Benton Community College established.

Ashland *Jackson County* *Southwestern Oregon, 227 mi/365 km south of Portland*

1852 grist mill established; town founded by Abel D. Hillman, named Ashland Mills; **1865** marble quarry established; **1871** town renamed Ashland; **1874** incorporated as a city; **1887** Southern Pacific Railroad reaches city; **Oct. 11, 1923** in train holdup at Siskiyou Pass to south, Hugh, Roy, and Ray D'Autremont shoot and kill three trainmen, fail to take loot, given life sentences; **1925** nine-story Ashland Springs Hotel opened; Southern Oregon State Normal School established, becomes Southern Oregon University 1997.

Astoria *Clatsop County* *Northeastern Oregon, 73 mi/117 km northwest of Portland, on Columbia River*

May 1792 Capt. Robert Gray visits site in ship *Columbia Rediviva*; **Nov. 7, 1805** Lewis & Clark Expedition arrives on Pacific Ocean at mouth of Columbia River, spend winter at makeshift Fort Clatsop; **March 1806** Lewis and Clark begin return journey, having rained all but 12 days during their stay; **Apr. 1811** trading post established by John Jacob Astor's Pacific Fur Company; town of Astoria founded; **1813** Astor's post sold to North West Company, renamed Fort George; **1818** U.S. gains sovereignty over Oregon Territory; post remains under British control; **1821** Hudson's Bay Company assumes control of post; **1825** trading operations shift to Fort Vancouver on Columbia River to southeast; **1844** Clatsop County formed; town becomes county seat; **1847** first post office in Oregon established; **1856** incorporated as a town; **1860** Fort Vancouver abandoned; **1866** town's first salmon cannery founded; **1873** incorporated as a city; **1885** Flavel Mansion built; **1898** Spokane, Portland & Seattle Railroad reaches city; **1904** city hall built; **1908** county courthouse completed; **Dec. 9, 1922** waterfront fire destroys 32 city blocks; **1925** Liberty Theater opened; **1926** Astoria Column dedicated on Coxcomb Hill, 125-ft/ 38-m Roman column commemorates discovery of Columbia River by Robert Gray; **1936** Port of Astoria Airport established; **1958** Clatsop Community College established; **1966** Astoria Bridge built across Columbia River to Chinook, Washington, 4-mi/6.4-km long.

Baker City *Baker County* *Northeastern Oregon, 240 mi/386 km east-southeast of Portland*

1811 William Price Hunt of John Jacob Astor expedition passes through Baker Valley; **1841** settlers begin arriving on Oregon Trail, continues through 1869; **1861** gold discovered; **1862** Baker County formed; Auburn becomes county seat; **1863** first house built; **1864** quartz mill built by Col. J. S. Ruckels; Arlington Hotel opened; **1865** gold mining begins; town founded on Powder River, named for Union Col. E. D. Baker killed at Battle of Ball's Bluff, Virginia; **1868** county seat moved to Baker; **1870** *Bedrock Democrat* newspaper founded, becomes *Baker Democrat-*

Herald 1929; **1874** incorporated as Baker City; **1884** Oregon Short Line railroad reaches city; **1886** Eagle Sawmill Company opened; **1888** Triangle Planing company opened; **1892** Baker City Iron Works established; **1900** opera house built; **1905** St. Francis Cathedral built; **1909** county courthouse built; Carnegie Library built; **1911** city renamed Baker; **1990** city renamed Baker City; **1992** National Historic Oregon Trail Interpretive Center opened.

Beaverton *Washington County* *Northwestern Oregon, 8 mi/12.9 km west of Portland*

1845 Philip Harris among first settlers, establishes Harris-Landess Ferry on Tualatin River to southwest, Harris Bridge named for him; **1848** Cedar Mill sawmill founded on Cedar Creek to northwest by Elam Young; **1849** sawmill established at town site by Thomas Denney; **1865** Wesley Methodist Church built at Cedar Mill, rebuilt 1891; **1868** Oregon Central Railroad built; town founded; **1893** incorporated as a city; **1912** Jenkins Estate built by Ralph Jenkins; **1920** Beaverton Airport established; **1925** Beaverton Library established, new facility opened 2000.

Bend *Deschutes County* *Central Oregon, 117 mi/188 km southeast of Portland*

1900 A. M. Drake and wife settle on Deschutes River for health benefits of dry climate; **1904** town founded, incorporated; **1911** Great Northern Railroad reaches town; **1915** Shevlin-Hixon Sawmill established; **1916** Deschutes County formed; town becomes county seat; Brooks-Scanlon Sawmill built; **1940** county courthouse built; **1949** Central Oregon Community College established; **1990** Newberry National Volcanic Monument established to south.

Burns *Harney County* *East central Oregon, 218 mi/351 km southeast of Portland*

1867 Fort Harney established to northeast; **1884** town founded; **1889** Harney County formed; Harney City becomes county seat; **1890** county seat moved by force to Burns; **1891** town incorporated; **1908** Malheur Migratory Bird Refuge established to south, becomes Malheur National Wildlife Refuge; **1942** second county courthouse built.

Canyon City *Grant County* *East central Oregon, 195 mi/314 km southeast of Portland*

1862 gold discovered at Whiskey Flat; town founded; **July 4, 1863** Oregon men storm Rebel Hill, remove Confederate flag flown by California gold miners; **1864** Grant County formed; town becomes county seat; Joaquin Miller House built; **1870** fire destroys much of town, again 1937; **1891** town incorporated; **Feb. 10, 1933** lowest temperature ever recorded in Oregon reached at Seneca to south, −54°F/−48°C; **1953** county courthouse completed.

Cascade Locks *Hood River County* *Northwestern Oregon, 40 mi/64 km east of Portland, on Columbia River*

1856 portage road built past cascades of Columbia River; **1864** *Oregon Pony* steam engine used to transport freight and passengers past rapids; **1872** first road built through Columbia Gorge; **1896** locks and canals completed at cascades, begun 1878; town founded; **1926** Bridge of the Gods built across river to Stevenson, Washington, named for stone bridge of Native American legend, subject of novel *Bridge of the Gods* by Frederic Homer Balch; **1935** town incorporated; **1940** deck of Bridge of the Gods raised to allow for rising waters of Bonneville Dam.

Champoeg *Marion County* *Northwestern Oregon, 21 mi/34 km south-southwest of Portland*

1811 trading post established on Willamette River by William Wallace and J. C. Halsey; **c.1830** town founded, named for Native American village Cham-poo-ick; **1834** first cattle brought to area from California by Ewing Young; **May 2, 1843** 52 delegates convene establishing Oregon provisional government, result of efforts by Joseph Meek (1810–1875); capital established at Oregon City; **Dec. 2, 1861** flooding destroys town; **1901** Champoeg State Park established.

Chiloquin *Klamath County* *Southern Oregon, 202 mi/325 km south-southeast of Portland*

1826 party of trappers led by Peter Skeen Ogden camp here; **1864** Klamath Indian Reservation established to north; **1910** Southern Pacific Railroad built; town founded on Williamson River, near Agency Lake; **1912** post office established; **1916** Knapp Lumber Mill built, destroyed by fire 1939; **1918** Chiloquin Lumber Company established; town platted; **1926** incorporated as a city; **1947** Collier Logging Museum and Pioneer Village opened to north; **1954** Klamath Indian Reservation terminated against continuing opposition; **1988** Chiloquin Lumber Company closed.

Condon *Gilliam County* *Northern Oregon, 120 mi/193 km east of Portland*

1879 first home built by William F. Potter; **1880** town founded, originally named Summit City; **1884** post office established; town renamed for Dr. Thomas Condon, geologist credited with discovery of fossils in area; **1885** Gilliam County formed; Alkali (Arlington) becomes county seat; **1890** county seat moved to Condon; **1893** town incorporated; **1899** city hall built; **1905** Union Pacific Railroad reaches town; **1955** county courthouse built.

Coos Bay *Coos County* *Southwestern Oregon, 165 mi/266 km south-southwest of Portland, on Pacific Ocean*

1853 first cabin built by trapper J. C. Tolman; **1854** town founded on Coos Bay, named Marshfield; **1855** first coal mine opens to south; **c.1858** John and George Pershbaker establish shipyards; **1874** town incorporated; **1908** Coos Bay Lumber Mill built; **1909** Chandler Hotel opened; **1916** Southern Pacific Railroad reaches town; **1922** fire sweeps business area; **1936** Coos Bay (McCullough) Bridge completed; **1944** town renamed Coos Bay; **1961** Southwestern Oregon Community College established; **1972** Oregon Dunes National Recreation Area established to north.

Coquille   *Coos County   Southwestern Oregon, 175 mi/282 km south-southwest of Portland*

1853 Coos County formed; Empire City becomes county seat; **1854** town founded on Coquille River; **1870** post office established; **1885** town incorporated; **1896** county seat moved to Coquille; **1916** county courthouse built.

Corvallis   *Benton County   Western Oregon, 70 mi/ 113 km south-southwest of Portland*

1845 first settlers arrive; **1846** Joseph C. Avery establishes ferry on Willamette River; town platted by Avery, named Marysville; **1847** Benton County formed; **1851** town becomes county seat; **1852** Haman Lewis House built; **1853** town renamed Corvallis, Latin variation for "heart of the valley"; **1855** state capital moved to Corvallis, returned to Salem 1856; **1857** town incorporated; **1858** Corvallis College established, becomes Oregon State University 1868; **1859** *Corvallis Union* newspaper founded; **1878** Oregon Central Railroad built; **1889** county courthouse completed.

Crater Lake   *Klamath County   Southern Oregon, 180 mi/290 km south-southeast of Portland*

June 1853 Crater Lake discovered by gold miner John Wesley Hillman, names it Deep Blue Lake; **1869** lake renamed Crater Lake by James M. Simon and David Linn while visiting Wizard Island; **1896** Mt. Mazama, volcano containing Crater Lake caldera, named for local mountain climbing organization; **May 22, 1902** Crater Lake National Park established; **1915** Crater Lake Lodge opened; **1994** Crater Lake Lodge rehabilitation completed.

Dallas   *Polk County   Northwestern Oregon, 50 mi/ 80 km south-southwest of Portland*

1840s area settled; town founded, named Cynthia Ann, wife of trailblazer Jesse Applegate; **1845** Polk County formed; **1852** town platted, becomes county seat, renamed for Vice Pres. George Mifflin Dallas; **1856** woolen mill built; town moved 1 mi/1.6 km to south; **1858** John E. Lyle House built; **1874** town incorporated; **1880** narrow gauge railroad reaches town; **1880s** county becomes leading hops producing area; **1900** county courthouse completed.

Enterprise   *Wallowa County   Northeastern Oregon, 258 mi/415 km east of Portland*

c.1840 Nez Perce Chief Joseph born in Wallowa Valley, died Sept. 21, 1904, at Colville, Washington; **1886** town founded on Wallowa River, named Franklin; **1887** Wallowa County formed; Joseph becomes county seat; Franklin renamed Enterprise; **1888** county seat moved to Enterprise; murder of 31 Chinese gold miners occurs to northeast at mouth of Imnaha River, on Snake River; **1889** town incorporated; **1909** county courthouse built.

Eugene   *Lane County   Western Oregon, 102 mi/ 164 km south of Portland, on Willamette River*

1846 log cabin built by Eugene F. Skinner; town founded, named Skinner's; **1851** Lane County formed; ferry established by Skinner; **1852** town platted, renamed Eugene City; **1853** town becomes county seat; **March 1857** steamboat *James Clinton* arrives; **1862** incorporated as a town; *State-Republican* newspaper founded; **1864** incorporated as a city; **1871** Oregon & California Railroad reaches town; **1876** University of Oregon established; **1895** Northwest Christian College established; **1901** Spanish-American War memorial erected; **1904** Eugene Public Library established, Carnegie library opened 1906, new library opened 1959, again 2003; **1941** Mahlon Sweet Army Air Field established to northwest, becomes airport after World War II; Fern Ridge Reservoir formed on Long Tom River to west; **1959** county courthouse built; **1964** Lane Community College established.

Florence   *Lane County   Western Oregon, 125 mi/ 201 km south-southwest of Portland, on Pacific Ocean*

1876 first white settlers arrive; first fish cannery established; **1877** town founded at mouth of Siuslaw River; **1893** incorporated as a city; **1894** Heceta Head Lighthouse built to north; **1972** Oregon Dunes National Recreation Area established to south; **1996** Florence Convention and Performing Arts Center built.

Fossil   *Wheeler County   Northern Oregon, 123 mi/ 198 km east-southeast of Portland*

1876 town founded, named for fossils discovered in area; **1891** town incorporated; **1899** Wheeler County formed; town becomes county seat; **1902** county courthouse built; **Oct. 26, 1974** John Day Fossil Beds National Monument established, Clarno Unit to southwest, Painted Hills Unit to south, Sheep Rock Unit to southeast.

Gold Beach   *Curry County   Southwestern Oregon, 228 mi/367 km south-southwest of Portland, on Pacific Ocean*

1852 gold discovered in Rogue River region; town founded at mouth of river, named Ellensburg; **1855** Curry County formed; Port Orford becomes county seat; **1859** county seat moved to Ellensburg; **1861** flooding destroys most mining operations; **1891** Ellensburg renamed Gold Beach; **1945** town incorporated; **1958** county courthouse built.

Grants Pass   *Josephine County   Southwestern Oregon, 210 mi/338 km south of Portland*

1856 Josephine County formed, named for Josephine Rollins, county's first white woman 1851; Sailor Diggings (Waldo) becomes first county seat; **1857** county seat moved to Kerbyville (Kerby); **1865** town founded on Rogue River; **1874** Oregon Caves discovered to south by Elijah Davidson when dog chases bear into cave; **1886** county seat moved to Grants Pass; **1887** town incorporated; **1917** county courthouse built; **July 12, 1909** Oregon Caves National Monument proclaimed; **1970** Rogue Community College established.

Heppner   *Morrow County   Northern Oregon, 150 mi/241 km east of Portland*

1858 first cattlemen arrive with their herds; **1869** George W. Standsbury becomes first settler; **1872** town founded, named Standsbury Flat; **1872** store established by Henry Heppner and J. D. Morrow; **1873** town renamed Heppner; **1883** Union Pacific Railroad reaches town; **1885** Morrow County formed; town becomes county seat; **1887** town incorporated; **1903** county courthouse completed; **June 14, 1903** flash flooding of Willow Creek leaves 325 dead.

Hillsboro   *Washington County   Northwestern Oregon, 17 mi/27 km west of Portland*

1842 David Hill settles in area; town founded by Hill, named Columbia; **1843** Tuality County formed; **1850** county organized, renamed Washington County; town becomes county seat, renamed Hillsboro; **1876** town incorporated; **1928** county courthouse built; **1972** justice services building completed; **1990** public services building completed.

Hood River   *Hood River County   Northwestern Oregon, 55 mi/89 km east of Portland, on Columbia River*

1792 snowcapped volcano Mt. Hood (11,239 ft/3,426 m) to south sighted by British Lt. William Broughton; **Oct. 1805** Lewis and Clark Expedition reaches area; **1852** W. C. Laughlin and Dr. Farnsworth drive in herds of cattle, leave after hard winter destroys stock; **1854** Nathaniel Coe family become first settlers; **1857** H. L. Pittock, L. Chittenden, W. Cornell, Rev. T. A. Wood become first white men to reach summit of Mt. Hood; **1881** town founded; **1883** Oregon Short Line Railroad reaches town; **1884** train stranded in snow drifts to west at Starvation Creek, named for incident, food delivered to passengers with great difficulty; **1895** town incorporated; **1900** apple industry established; **1908** Hood River County formed; town becomes county seat; **1912** Columbia Gorge Hotel completed; **1919** hard freeze destroys apple crops, replaced by heartier pear orchards; **1954** county courthouse built.

Klamath Falls   *Klamath County   Southern Oregon, 227 mi/365 km south-southeast of Portland*

May 5, 1846 Klamaths attack camp of Capt. John C. Fremont on Howard Bay, Upper Klamath Lake, 3 of Fremont's party killed, 14 Klamaths killed; **1850** emigrant train attacked by natives, nearly all members killed; **1858** Wendolen Nus builds first cabin; **1867** town founded by George Nurse near southern end of Upper Klamath Lake, named Linkville; **1872** Modoc troubles bring months of terror; **1878** town platted; **1882** Klamath County formed; town becomes county seat; **1889** incorporated as a town; **1893** town renamed Klamath Falls; **1899** Union Pacific Railroad magnate Edward H. Harriman (1848–1909) builds Harriman Lodge on Pelican Bay, Upper Klamath Lake, destroyed by fire 1929; **1900** Klamath Irrigation Project begun; **1905** incorporated as a city; **1908** Klamath Lake Bird Reserve established to south, becomes Lower Klamath National Wildlife Refuge; **1909** Southern Pacific Railroad reaches town; **1918** county courthouse built; **1926** city library built; **1947** Oregon Institute of Technology established; **Sept. 20, 1993** county courthouse damaged by earthquake; **1999** new county courthouse completed.

La Grande   *Union County   Northeastern Oregon, 220 mi/354 km east of Portland*

1861 Ben Brown becomes first settler; town founded on Grande Ronde River, named Brown Town or Brownsville; **1863** post office established; town renamed La Grande; **1864** Union County formed; **1865** town incorporated, becomes county seat; **1874** county seat moved to town of Union by popular vote; county records removed by force from La Grande; **1875** Blue Mountain University established, closed 1884; **1884** second vote reverses previous decision, county seat moved back to La Grande; Oregon Railroad reaches town; **1885** incorporated as a city; **1905** county courthouse built; **1929** Eastern Oregon University established; **1997** new county courthouse completed.

Lakeview   *Lake County   Southern Oregon, 252 mi/406 km southeast of Portland*

1876 U.S. government land office established; town founded, named for its proximity to Goose Lake to south, lake extends into California; **1874** Lake County formed; town becomes county seat; **1889** town incorporated; **1900** most of town destroyed by fire, leaving only the courthouse and Methodist church; **1954** county courthouse built.

Lebanon   *Linn County   Western Oregon, 67 mi/108 km south of Portland, on South Santiam River*

1847 settler Jeremiah Ralston arrives from Lebanon, Tennessee; **1852** town founded; **1854** Santiam Academy founded, closed 1907; **Dec. 14, 1861** author Frederic Homer Balch born at Tallman to west (died 1891); **1878** incorporated as a city; **1888** Southern Pacific Railroad reaches town; **Feb. 27, 1940** actor Howard Hesseman born.

Madras *Jefferson County Central Oregon, 95 mi/ 153 km southeast of Portland*

1910 Oregon Trunk Railroad built; town founded; **1911** incorporated as a city; **1914** Jefferson County formed; Culver becomes county seat; **1916** county seat moved to Madras; **1961** county courthouse built; **1964** Lake Billy Chinook formed on Deschutes River to west by Round Butte Dam; **Aug. 23, 1970** actor River Phoenix born (died 1993).

McMinnville *Yamhill County Northwestern Oregon, 33 mi/53 km southwest of Portland*

1843 Yamhill County formed; Lafayette becomes county seat; William T. Newby arrives with first wagon train on Oregon Trail from McMinnville, Tennessee; **1849** Linfield College established; **1853** Newby builds grist mill on South Yamhill River; town founded; **1876** incorporated as a town; **1880** Oregon Central Railroad reaches town; **1882** incorporated as a city; **1889** county seat moved to McMinnville; **1964** county courthouse built.

Medford *Jackson County Southwestern Oregon, 218 mi/351 km south of Portland*

1851 gold discovered in area; **1856** Rogue River peoples moved to reservation; **1854** Jackson County formed; Jacksonville becomes county seat; **1883** Oregon & California Railroad (Southern Pacific) built; town founded by railroad, named for engineer David Loring's hometown of Medford, Massachusetts; **1885** incorporated as a town; **1905** incorporated as a city; **1927** county seat moved to Medford; **1932** county courthouse completed.

Milton-Freewater *Umatilla County Northeastern Oregon, 207 mi/333 km east of Portland*

1872 town of Milton founded by William Samuel Frazier as alcohol-free community; **1886** city of Milton City incorporated; **1889** neighboring town of Freewater founded north of Milton, liquor sold by the gallon; **1892** Freewater incorporated as a city; Frazier Home built; **1950** two cities consolidate as Milton-Freewater.

Moro *Sherman County Northern Oregon, 92 mi/ 148 km east of Portland*

1889 Sherman County formed; Wasco becomes county seat; **1892** town founded as new county seat; **1898** Columbia Southern (Union Pacific) Railroad reaches town; **1899** town incorporated; county courthouse built.

Newberg *Yamhill County Northwestern Oregon, 20 mi/32 km southwest of Portland*

1834 Ewing Young takes first land claim; mission established to south on Willamette River by Jason Lee;

1869 town founded by Sebastian Brutscher, named for Newburgh, Germany; **1884** Pacific Academy founded by Quakers; **1888** Herbert Hoover graduates from academy; **1889** incorporated as a town; **1891** Friends Pacific College established by Quakers at academy site, becomes George Fox College 1949, University 1996; **1893** incorporated as a city.

Newport *Lincoln County Western Oregon, 90 mi/ 145 km southwest of Portland, on Pacific Ocean*

1855 town founded on Yaquina Bay, estuary of Yaquina River; **1856** blockhouse built by Lt. Philip Sheridan; **1866** Ocean House resort built; **1871** Abbey House and Fountain House hotels opened; **1871** Yaquina Bay (Yaquina Head) Lighthouse built; **1882** incorporated as a town **1891** incorporated as a city; **1893** Lincoln County formed; Toledo becomes county seat; **1936** Yaquina Bay Bridge built; **1954** county seat moved to Newport; county courthouse built; **1965** Marine Science Center built by Oregon State University, reopened 1997 as Mark O. Hatfield Marine Science Center; **1988** Newport Performing Arts Center opened; **1992** Oregon Coast Aquarium opened.

Oregon City *Clackamus County Northwestern Oregon, 10 mi/16 km south of Portland*

1812 first white trappers arrive led by Donald McKenzie of John Jacob Astor's Pacific Fur Company; **1829** mill built by John McLoughlin; **1832** flour mill built; **1841** sawmill built below falls by Methodist missionaries; **1842** town founded on Willamette River by John McLoughlin at western end of Oregon Trail; town platted by Sidney Walter Moss; **1843** Oregon Territory created through efforts of Joseph Meek; Clackamas County formed; town becomes county seat; **1844** incorporated as a town; **1846** *Oregon Spectator* newspaper founded; McLoughlin Mansion built by John McLoughlin, resides here until his death 1857; Barclay House built; **1847** survivors of Whitman Massacre arrive [see Walla Walla, Washington], perpetrators hanged; **1848** woolen mill founded by Jacobs brothers; **1849** town becomes territorial capital; **Feb.-Sept. 1849** mint operated to eliminate coin shortage; **1852** territorial capital moved to Salem; Albion Post House built; **Apr. 23, 1852** poet Edwin Markham born (died 1940); **Apr. 8, 1854** steamer *Gazelle* explodes at Conemah, now part of Oregon City, 24 killed; **1861** first Oregon State Fair held, moved to Salem 1862; **Jan. 1, 1873** Willamette Falls Locks opened; **1908** Hawley Pulp and Paper Mill opened; **1912** Carnegie Library built, replaced 1995; **1925** incorporated as a city; **1937** county courthouse built; **June 27, 1941** McLoughlin House National Historic Site established; **Sept. 16, 1950** actress Susan Ruttan born; **1955** Municipal Elevator built to top of bluff, replaces tower built 1915; **1968** Museum of the Oregon Territory opened, new facility opened 1990.

Pendleton   *Umatilla County   Northeastern Oregon, 185 mi/298 km east of Portland, on Umatilla River*

1855 Umatilla Indian Reservation established to east; **1862** Umatilla County formed; Marshall Station becomes county seat; **1865** county seat moved to Umatilla; **1868** town founded by Moses Goodwin and G. W. Bailey; named for George Pendleton, Democratic candidate for president 1868; **1869** county seat moved to Pendleton; **1875** *East Oregonian* newspaper founded; **1877** Nez Perce Indian War puts town on full alert; **1880** incorporated as a city; city inundated by flooding, again 1882; **1889** Oregon Railroad reaches town; **1893** fire destroys many buildings, again 1895; **Aug. 10, 1898** highest temperature ever recorded in Oregon reached, 119°F/48°C; **1905** Hamley and Company saddlery established; **1909** Pendleton Woolen Mills built, established 1889 at Salem; **1910** first Round-Up rodeo held; **1913** Eastern Oregon State Hospital established; **1932** Pendleton Airport established, renamed Eastern Oregon Regional Airport 1990; **1956** county courthouse built; **1962** Blue Mountain Community College established.

Portland   *Multnomah County   Northwestern Oregon, on Willamette River, near its mouth on Columbia River*

1792 American Robert Gray sails up Columbia River, claims territory for U.S.; **1805** Lewis and Clark Expedition descends Columbia River to Pacific Ocean; **1829** French-Canadian Etienne Lucier builds first cabin; **1845** town founded on Willamette River by group from New England led by Francis W. Pettygrove and A. L. Lovejoy, named for Portland, Maine, chosen by coin toss instead of Boston; first store built; **1848** canoe ferry established by Stephen Coffin; sawmill opened by John Waymire; **1850** steam sawmill established by W. P. Abrams and Cyrus A. Reed; *Weekly Oregonian* newspaper founded; **1851** incorporated as a city; **1853** W. S. Ladd builds first brick building; **1854** Multnomah County formed; city becomes county seat; **1865** salmon industry established; **1867** Lewis and Clark College established; **1871** St. Charles Hotel completed; **1872** fire destroys three city blocks; **1873** second fire destroys 22 city blocks; **1875** New Market Theater opened; **1881** Esmond Hotel built; **1883** Oregon Railroad reaches Portland from east; **May 27, 1885** World War II naval officer Adm. Richmond Kelly Turner born (died 1961); **1887** Morrison Street Bridge built, replaces ferry; Oregon Zoo established, present site opened 1959; **Oct. 22, 1887** journalist, poet John Reed born (died 1920); **1888** Skidmore Fountain erected; **1889** Hotel Portland completed; **1890** Union Depot built; **1891** East Portland and Albina annexed by Portland; **1895** city hall built; **1896** Portland Symphony Orchestra founded; **1898** Oregon Historical Society established; **1901** University of Portland established; U.S. Customhouse built; **Feb. 28, 1901** chemist Linus C. Pauling born, Nobel Prize 1954 and 1962 (died 1994); **1902** railroad bridge built across Columbia River to Vancouver; **Apr. 1902** *Oregon Journal* newspaper

founded; **1905** Lewis and Clark Exposition held; **1908** Reed College established; first annual Rose Festival and Parade held; **1913** county courthouse built; Multnomah Public Library built; **1917** Interstate Bridge built across Columbia River to Vancouver, Washington; civic auditorium built; **1919** first unit Portland Medical Center built; **1922** Theodore Roosevelt Rough Rider statue unveiled; Shriners' Hospital for Children built; **1926** Burnside Bridge built across Willamette River; civic stadium opened; **1927** George Washington statue dedicated; **1927** Portland Airport established on Columbia River, becomes International Airport 1959, referred to as "PDX" Airport; **1928** Lincoln statue dedicated; Hoyt Arboretum founded; **Apr. 1, 1928** actress Jane Powell born; **1931** Leach Botanical Gardens established; St. John's Suspension Bridge completed across Willamette River; **1932** Portland Art Museum built; **Sept. 11, 1932** Sen. Bob Packwood born; **1939** Trinity Episcopal Church built; **May 26, 1939** announcer Brent Musburger born; **July 30, 1940** Cong. Patricia Schroeder of Colorado born; **1944** Oregon Museum of Science and Industry founded, opened 1949; **1946** Portland State University established; **July 28, 1948** TV actress Sally Struthers born; **Feb. 19, 1955** actress Margaux Hemingway born (died 1996); **1961** Portland Community College established; Portland International Raceway established; **1970** Portland Trailblazers NBA basketball team established; **1973** 41-story Wells Fargo Tower built; **1983** 39-story US Bancorp Tower built; **1984** 31-story Pacwest Center built; 35-story Koin Tower Plaza built; Arlene Schnitzer Concert Hall opened; **1986** MAX Light Rail system Blue Line opened to Gersham, Red Line opened to Airport 2001; **1989** Oregon Ballet Theatre established; **1990** Oregon Convention Center opened, expanded 2003.

Prineville   *Crook County   Central Oregon, 118 mi/ 190 km southeast of Portland*

1868 Barney Prine becomes first settler; town founded on Crooked River; **1870** town platted; **1880** incorporated as a city; **1882** Crook County formed; town becomes county seat; **1909** county courthouse built; **1918** Prineville Short Line Railroad built from west; **1961** Prineville Reservoir formed on Crooked River to south.

Rainier   *Columbia County   See Saint Helens (1974)*

Roseburg   *Douglas County   Southwestern Oregon, 160 mi/257 km south of Portland*

1851 Aaron Rose becomes first settler; town founded on Umpqua River, originally named Deer Creek; **1852** Douglas County formed; **1854** town platted, renamed Roseburg; county seat moved from Winchester; **1867** Umpqua County (formed 1851) absorbed by Douglas County; **1872** town incorporated; **1929** county courthouse built; **Aug. 7, 1959** dynamite truck explodes at warehouse, 13 killed, 100 injured; **1964** Umpqua Community College established.

Saint Helens *Columbia County* *Northwestern Oregon, 25 mi/40 km north-northwest of Portland*

1834 trading post established by Nathaniel Wyeth; **1848** town founded on Columbia River, in view of Mt. St. Helens, Washington; Knighton House built; **1854** Columbia County formed; Milton becomes county seat; **1857** county seat moved to Saint Helens; **1889** incorporated as a city; **1907** county courthouse built, annex built 1968; **March 1974** Trojan Nuclear Power Plant opened to north at Rainier on Columbia River, decommissioned June 1993.

Salem *Marion and Polk counties* *Northwestern Oregon, 42 mi/68 km south of Portland*

1840 Methodist mission founded by Jason Lee; **1842** Oregon Institute founded, becomes Willamette University 1853; **1844** town founded; **1845** Champoeg County formed; town becomes county seat; **1849** county renamed Marion County; **1852** territorial capital moved from Oregon City; **1855** capital moved to Corvallis, returned to Salem same year; **Dec. 31, 1855** capitol destroyed by fire; **1857** incorporated as a town; **Feb. 14, 1859** Oregon enters Union as 33rd state; **1860** incorporated as a city; **Dec. 1861** flooding destroys business district; **1862** second State Fair held, moved from Oregon City; **1866** State Penitentiary established; **1870** State School for the Deaf established, built 1910; **1871** Oregon Central Railroad reaches city; **1872** State School for the Blind established, built 1892; **1876** state capitol completed; **1883** state hospital built; **1914** supreme court building completed; state office building built; **1928** McNary Airport established; **1929** First Presbyterian Church completed; **Apr. 25, 1935** state capitol destroyed by fire; **1938** new State Capitol completed; **1949** West Salem in Polk County annexed; **1954** county courthouse built; **1955** Chemeketa Community College established; **1984** Salem Chamber Orchestra founded.

Seaside *Clatsop County* *Northwestern Oregon, 70 mi/113 km northwest of Portland, on Pacific Ocean*

Nov. 7, 1805 Lewis and Clark reach Pacific Ocean 15 mi/24 km to north, establish Fort Clatsop, winter over until March 23, 1806; salt making camp established here by expedition, abandoned Feb. 21, 1806; **1871** Holladay House hotel built by Ben Holladay, owner of Overland Stage route; **1881** Tillamook Lighthouse ("Terrible Tilly") erected on rocky islet; **1882** town founded; **1899** town incorporated; **1971** Seaside Civic and Convention Center completed; **1990** End of the Trail Monument erected commemorating end of Lewis and Clark journey.

Seneca *Grant County* See **Canyon City (1933)**

Silverton *Marion County* *Northwestern Oregon, 35 mi/56 km south of Portland*

1846 sawmill built on Silver Creek; town of Milford founded; **1854** town moved downstream, renamed

Silverton; **1859** incorporated as a town; **March 8, 1867** cartoonist Homer Calvin Davenport born (died 1912); **1891** incorporated as a city.

Springfield *Lane County* *Eastern Oregon, 100 mi/161 km south of Portland*

1849 town founded by Elias Briggs on Willamette River; **1885** incorporated as a city; **1908** Springfield Public Library founded; **1949** Weyerhaeuser Mill built for timber processing; **May 21, 1998** Kipland Kinkel, 15, shoots and kills parents, then shoots, kills 2, injures 22 at high school.

The Dalles *Wasco County* *Northern Oregon, 70 mi/113 km east of Portland, on Columbia River*

1805 Lewis and Clark Expedition camp here on descent of Columbia River; **1806** Lewis and Clark Expedition bargains with Native Americans for horses on return journey; **1830s** site used as French traders' rendezvous point, rapids referred to as the "grand dalles"; **1838** Methodist mission established at Amaton Spring; **1841** Catholic mission established; **1847** missions abandoned following Whitman Massacre near Walla Walla, Washington; **1849** Fort Lee built; **1851** town founded, named Dalles City; **1853** town renamed Wascopum; **1854** Wasco County formed; town becomes county seat; **1857** incorporated as a town; **1859** *Journal* newspaper founded, renamed *Mountaineer* 1860; **1860** town renamed The Dalles; **1863** St. Mary's Academy founded; portage railroad built to east paralleling rapids; **1868** The Dalles Mint established during gold rush, mines depleted before coins are minted; **1884** Oregon Short Line railroad reaches town; **1898** St. Peter's Landmark Roman Catholic Church completed, cornerstone used as surveyor's benchmark; **1899** incorporated as a city; **1914** county courthouse built; **1915** Celilo Portage Canal built replacing portage railroad; **July 12, 1922** U.S. Sen. Mark Odem Hatfield born; **Jan. 10, 1927** singer Johnnie Ray born (died 1990); **1929** Granada Theater built; **1957** The Dalles Dam completed to east on Columbia River forming Lake Celilo.

Tillamook *Tillamook County* *Northwestern Oregon, 58 mi/93 km west of Portland, near Pacific Ocean*

1853 Tillamook County formed; town founded on Trask River, near its mouth on Tillamook Bay, originally named Lincoln; **1866** town renamed Tillamook; **1873** town becomes first permanent county seat; **1881** Tillamook Rock Lighthouse built; **1891** incorporated as a city; **1933** county courthouse built.

Umatilla *Umatilla County* *Northern Oregon, 162 mi/261 km east of Portland, on Columbia River*

Apr. 27, 1806 site visited by Lewis and Clark on return journey; **1862** Umatilla County formed; Marshall Station, east of Pendleton, becomes county seat; **1863** town founded at mouth of Umatilla River; **1864** incorporated as a town; **1865** county seat moved to Umatilla; **1868** county seat moved to Pendleton; **1906** incorporated as a city; **1941** Umatilla Army Depot established to southwest; **1955** highway bridge built across Columbia River, replaced 1987 by I-82 Bridge; **1956** McNary Dam completed on Columbia River, forms Lake Wallula; **1976** town of McNary annexed.

Vale *Malheur County* *Eastern Oregon, 283 mi/ 455 km southeast of Portland*

1864 Jonathan Keeney becomes first settler; town founded on Malheur River; **1872** Old Stone House built; **1887** Malheur County formed; town becomes county seat; **1889** town incorporated; **c.1930** Vale Irrigation Project estab-

lished; **1955** attempt by other communities to move county seat fails; **1958** third county courthouse built.

West Linn *Clackamus County* *Northwestern Oregon, suburb 8 mi/12.9 km south of Portland*

1840 town founded on Willamette River by Robert Moore, originally named Robin's Nest (Robin nickname for Robert); **1844** ferry from Oregon City established by Moore; **1845** town renamed Linn City for U.S. Sen. Lewis F. Linn of Missouri, advocate of annexation of Oregon by U.S.; **1861** flood destroys town; new town built to west, renamed West Linn; **1893** Maryhurst University established; **1913** incorporated as a city.

Pennsylvania

Northeastern U.S. Capital: Harrisburg. Major cities: Philadelphia, Pittsburgh.

Pennsylvania was one of the 13 colonies which adopted the U.S. Declaration of Independence July 4, 1776. It became the 2nd state to ratify the U.S. Constitution December 12, 1787.

Pennsylvania is divided into 67 counties. The counties are divided into civil divisions called townships which are incorporated with limited governments. Municipalities are classified as boroughs, towns (1), and cities. The city of Philadelphia is coterminous with Philadelphia County. See Introduction.

Allegheny *Allegheny County* See **Pittsburgh** (1907)

Allentown *Lehigh County* *Eastern Pennsylvania, 48 mi/77 km north-northeast of Philadelphia*

1723 area settled by Germans; **1735** tract of land acquired by William Allen; **1747** hunting lodge built by Lynford Lardner; **1762** town platted; originally named Northampton, or Northamptontown; **1770** Trout Hall built by James Allen; **1773** original Zion's Reformed Church built, rebuilt 1888; **Sept. 18, 1777** Liberty Bell moved by baggage car from Philadelphia under threat by advancing British forces, hidden in Zion's Church; **June 27, 1778** Liberty Bell returned to Philadelphia; **1794** Spring House built; **1803** post office established; **1811** incorporated as a borough; **1812** Lehigh County formed; town becomes county seat; bridge built across Lehigh River; **1819** county courthouse built; **1829** Lehigh Canal completed; **1838** town name changed to Allentown; **1841** bridge swept away by floods; much of town destroyed by fire; **1847** iron industry has its beginnings; **1848** Muhlenberg College established; **1852** corporate limits extended east to Lehigh River; **1850** cement industry established; **1867** incorporated as a city; Cedar Crest College established; **1869** Allentown Business School (2-year) established; **1882** silk mill opens; **1883** *Morning Call* newspaper founded; **1884** Dorney Amusement Park established; **1890s** Allentown Symphony Hall built, originally Lyric Theater; cotton milling becomes important; **1899** state hospital founded; **1902** First Presbyterian Church built, later used as art museum; **1906** Flag Day originates here, founded by G.A.R. (Grand Army of the Revolution); **1912** Allentown Public Library opened; Lehigh Valley College established, campus of Pennsylvania State University; **Oct. 15, 1924** businessman Lee Iacocca born, former chairman of Chrysler Corporation; **1927** Americus Hotel opened, becomes Americus Centre Hotel 2000; **1929** Allentown Airport established, became Allentown-Bethlehem Airport 1938, renamed Lehigh Valley International Airport 1994; **1939** Allentown Art Museum founded; **1962** Queen City Airport completed; **1964** city hall built; **1965** new county courthouse completed; **1970** tour bus from Long Island runs off U.S. Highway 22, 7 children killed, 32 injured; **1995** federal courthouse opened.

Altoona *Blair County* *Central Pennsylvania, 84 mi/135 km east of Pittsburgh*

c.1769 area settled; **1840** Baker Mansion built by Belgian Elias Baker; **1849** town platted by Pennsylvania Railroad; **1854** Horseshoe Curve built on Pennsylvania Railroad, engineering feat making rail travel west possible; **1855** Logan House built; **May 6, 1856** North Pole explorer Adm. Robert E. Peary born at Loretto to west (died 1920); **1868** incorporated as a city; **Apr. 23, 1921** actress Janet Blair born; **1927** Altoona Area Public Library founded; **1931** railroad station built on site of Logan House; **1939** Pennsylvania State University Altoona College established.

Ambler *Montgomery County* *Southeastern Pennsylvania, 14 mi/23 km north of Philadelphia*

1723 Joseph Ambler settles in area; Ambler Homestead built; **1728** William Harmer establishes mill; **Oct.-30–Dec. 11, 1777** George Washington camps here following retreat from Germantown before moving to Valley Forge; **July 17, 1856** collision of two trains, 60 killed, over 100 injured, worst train disaster to date; **1888** incorporated as a borough.

PENNSYLVANIA

Ambridge *Beaver County* *Western Pennsylvania, 16 mi/16 km northwest of Pittsburgh, on Ohio River*

1825 third Harmony Society communal group established, second splinter group from town of Economy founded 1805 by Father George Rapp and Frederick Reichert; **1832** two houses built 1825 by Society joined to form the Great House; **1901** American Bridge Company establishes structural steel plant on land purchased from dwindling Society; **1905** incorporated as a borough; Harmony Society dissolved; **1917** Sts. Peter and Paul Ukrainian Catholic Church established in former Methodist Church; **1929** Laughlin Memorial Free Library founded; **1940** St. Mary's Byzantine Catholic Church established; **1983** American Bridge Company closed.

Beaver *Beaver County* *Western Pennsylvania, 24 mi/39 km northwest of Pittsburgh, on Ohio River*

1778 town founded on Ohio River, at mouth of Beaver River; **1791** town platted; **1800** Beaver County formed; town becomes county seat; **1802** incorporated as a borough; **1845** Quay House built by Samuel French for Sen. Matthew S. Quay; **1933** county courthouse built; **1936** Montgomery Island Lock & Dam completed on Ohio River; **1948** Beaver Area Memorial Library founded; **2002** county government center completed, courthouse razed.

Beaver Falls *Beaver County* *Western Pennsylvania, 28 mi/45 km north-northwest of Pittsburgh*

1793 area opened to settlement, delayed by Native American troubles; **1806** town platted, named Brighton; **c.1810** town renamed Beaver Falls with founding of nearby New Brighton; **1853** Beaver College for women established, moved to Jenkintown, suburb of Philadelphia, 1933; **1868** incorporated as a borough; **1880** Geneva College moved here from Northwood, Ohio, founded 1848; **1902** Carnegie Free Library founded, later houses county museum; **1930** incorporated as a city; **May 31, 1943** football player Joe Namath born; **Apr. 28, 2000** Richard Baumhammer, 34, arrested after ethnic shooting rampage in suburban Pittsburgh, five killed, one injured, all Asians, Jews, other minorities.

Bedford *Bedford County* *Southern Pennsylvania, 34 mi/55 km south of Altoona*

1750 area first settled by John Fraser and wife Jean; Scottish trader Robert Ray establishes trading post; town founded, originally named Raystown; **1758** 7,500 soldiers under Brig. Gen. John Forbes and 1,000 wagoners arrive, build Forbes Road west, becomes important route for westbound pioneers; Fort Raystown built, later renamed Fort Bedford 1759; **1766** town platted by John Lukens; **1769** Capt. James Smith's men launch attack on fort defeating British, first British fort taken by rebels; **1771** Bedford County formed; town becomes county seat; **1795** incorporated as a borough; **1815** Anderson House built;

1828 county courthouse built; **1944** Bedford County Library founded.

Bellefonte *Centre County* *Central Pennsylvania, 44 mi/71 km northeast of Altoona*

1769 area first settled; town platted; **1785** William Lamb establishes flour mill on Spring Creek, named Lamb's Crossing; **1794** iron works established at mill site by James Dunlap; **1795** town renamed for admiring comment made about area by exiled statesman Talleyrand of France; James Harris House built; **1800** Centre County formed; town becomes county seat; **1806** incorporated as a borough; county courthouse built, enlarged 1911; **1810** Linn House built; **1813** Brockerhoff House built; **1886** Buffalo Run, Bellefonte & Bald Eagle Railroad built, becomes Bellefonte Central 1892; **May 24, 1863** sculptor George Grey Barnard born (died 1938); **1938** Centre County Library founded.

Berwick *Columbia County* *East central Pennsylvania, 39 mi/63 km southwest of Scranton*

1777 Fort Jenkins built 5 mi/8 km downstream (west) of town site; **1783** town settled on Susquehanna River; **1786** town founded by Quaker Evan Owen; **1818** incorporated as a borough; **May 1826** steamboat *Susquehanna* founders on rapids, explosion kills passengers and crew; **1840** foundry established, forerunner of American Car Company; **1904** first all-steel railroad passenger car built at American Car; **1916** Berwick Public Library founded; **1982** Susquehanna Nuclear Power Plant opened to east in Luzerne County.

Bethlehem *Northampton and Lehigh counties* *Southeastern Pennsylvania, 48 mi/77 km north of Philadelphia*

1740 Moravian Church members from Savannah, Georgia, arrive to join their Pennsylvanian members; **1741** Bishop David Nitschmann buys land on Lehigh River at mouth of Monocacy Creek; town founded; **1742** Moravian College established; **1748** Burnside Plantation House built; **1749** Schnitz House built; **1758** Sun Inn built; **1769** Widows' House built; **Dec. 1776** hospital established for Revolutionary War wounded; **1806** Central Moravian Church completed; **1820** Philharmonic Society organized; **1829** Lehigh Canal completed; **1845** incorporated as a borough; **1855** Lehigh Valley Railroad reaches town; **1857** iron mill established; **1861** Saucona Iron Company begins making steel rails for Lehigh Valley Railroad; **1865** South Bethlehem incorporated as a borough; Lehigh University established; **Sept. 10, 1896** poet H. D. (Hilda) Doolittle born (died 1961); **July 22, 1898** poet, author Stephen Benet born (died 1943); **1901** Bethlehem Public Library founded, built 1931, new library opened 1964; **1904** Bethlehem Steel incorporated with Charles M. Schwab as chairman; **1917** incorporated as a city; South Bethlehem annexed by Bethlehem; **1920** Northampton Heights annexed; **1924** Hill-to-Hill Bridge built across Lehigh River; **1929** Allentown Airport established, renamed Allentown-Bethlehem Airport 1938, renamed Lehigh Valley International 1994; **Dec. 29, 1952** ballerina Gelsey Kirkland born; **1967** Northampton County Area Community College established.

Birdsboro *Berks County* *Southeastern Pennsylvania, 40 mi/64 km northwest of Philadelphia*

1720 George Boone, grandfather of Daniel Boone, builds cabin to north; **1730** Exeter Friends Meeting House built, burial place of Abraham Lincoln and Daniel Boone ancestors; **c.1732** Daniel Boone Birthplace built by his father Squire Boone; **1733** Mordecai Lincoln Homestead built to west by great-great-grandfather of Abraham Lincoln, arrived in area 1720; **Oct. 22 or Nov. 2, 1734** frontiersman Daniel Boone born (died 1820), family moved to North Carolina 1750; **1740** town founded; **1744** Hopewell Forge built to south by William Bird; **1751** Bird Mansion built; **1872** incorporated as a borough; **1888** Brooke Mansion built by industrialist Edward Brooke II; **Aug. 3, 1938** Hopewell Village National Historic Site established, renamed Hopewell Furnace National Historic Site 1985.

Bloomsburg *Columbia County* *East Central Pennsylvania, 50 mi/80 km southwest of Scranton*

1772 first settled on Susquehanna River by James McClure; **1802** town platted; **1813** Columbia County formed; **1839** Bloomsburg University of Pennsylvania established; **1846** county seat moved from Danville; **1847** county courthouse built; Rupert Covered Bridge built, one of 23 covered bridges in county; **1870** incorporated as a town, only municipality in state with this classification; **1889** Bloomsburg Public Library founded; **Dec. 22, 1903** physiologist Haldan Hartline born, shared Nobel Prize 1983 (died 1967); **1978** Bloomsburg Theatre Ensemble founded.

Blossburg *Tioga County* *Northern Pennsylvania, 30 mi/48 km north of Williamsport, on Tioga River*

1792 coal discovered by the Patterson brothers; site originally named Peter's Camp; **1802** Aaron Bloss establishes tavern; town renamed; **c.1810** coal mining begins; **1826** iron smelter built by Judge John H. Knapp; **July 1840** railroad reaches town from Corning, New York; **1871** incorporated as a borough; **1939** Blossburg Library founded; **June, 23, 1967** Mohawk Airlines airplane crashes in thunderstorm, 34 killed; **1993** first annual Coal Festival held.

Bradford *McKean County* *Northern Pennsylvania, 100 mi/161 km north of Altoona*

1823 area settled; **1879** Bradford oil fields opened; incorporated as a city; **1901** Bradford Area Public Library founded; **Jan. 16, 1943** opera singer Marilyn Horne born; **1963** Bradford Campus of University of Pittsburgh established; **Jan. 6, 1969** Allegheny Airlines passenger jet crashes in light snowstorm killing 11 of 29 on board.

Bristol *Bucks County* *Southeastern Pennsylvania, 19 mi/31 km northeast of Philadelphia, on Delaware River*

1681 town founded; **1682** Bucks County formed; **1687** Bolton Mansion built; **1697** area first settled; **1705** county seat moved from Falls Township; Ferry House hotel established; **c.1710** Friends Meeting House built; **1720** incorporated as a borough; **1725** county seat moved to Newtown; **1765** Ferry House hotel destroyed by fire, replaced by Delaware House, renamed George II Hotel before Revolution; **1834** Lehigh Canal completed to Easton; **1931** Burlington-Bristol Bridge built from Burlington, New Jersey.

Brookville *Jefferson County* *Central Pennsylvania, 58 mi/93 km northwest of Altoona*

1797 sawmill established by Samuel Scott and Joseph Barnett; town founded as Port Barnett; **1804** Jefferson County formed; town becomes county seat; **1830** town platted, renamed Brookville; **c.1840** Craig Brady House built; **1843** incorporated as a borough; **1850s** lumber industry reaches its peak, stripping forests; **1867** county courthouse built; **1907** Brookville Hospital founded; **1958** Rebecca M. Arthurs Memorial Library founded.

Brownsville *Fayette County* *Southwestern Pennsylvania, 30 mi/48 km south of Pittsburgh*

May 28, 1754 in George Washington's first battle, he and Virginia militia defeat French; **1758** Redstone Old Fort built for Col. James Burd; **1785** town founded by Thomas and Basil Brown; **1789** trading post established by Jacob Bowman; **July 21, 1791** beginning of Whiskey Rebellion, protest against Federal four pence whiskey tax; **1794** Krepp's Ferry established, service ends 1845; **fall 1794** troops under Gen. Daniel Morgan sent to quell rebellion, collect whiskey tax; **1797** Brashear Inn built; **c.1800** Nemacolin Castle built by Jacob Bowman at his trading post; **1811** Brownsville Academy founded; **1813** the *Comet* built, first steamboat to ply Monongahela River; **1815** incorporated as a borough; **1839** Brownsville Iron Bridge completed; **1845** St. Peter's Roman Catholic Church built; **May 6, 1853** Sen. Philander Chase Knox born, Attorney General under President McKinley, secretary of state under President Taft (died 1921); **1859** Christ Episcopal Church built; **1903** Wayside Manor restaurant built; **1927** Brownsville Free Public Library founded; **1928** Union Station completed; **1933** South Brownsville merges with Brownsville.

Bryn Athyn *Montgomery County* *Southeastern Pennsylvania, 14 mi/23 km north-northeast of Philadelphia*

1877 Academy of the New Church founded, becomes Bryn Athyn College; **1895** chapel of New Church Society built, 50-year building program begun; **1916** incorporated as a borough; **1919** Bryn Athyn Cathedral built, completed 1945; **Dec. 5, 1921** railroad accident at Woodmont to north, 27 killed; **1981** Bryn Athyn Community Theater founded.

Bryn Mawr *Montgomery County Southeastern Pennsylvania, 10 mi/16 km northwest of Philadelphia*

1680s area settled by Welsh immigrants; **1885** Bryn Mawr College established; **1893** Bryn Mawr Hospital founded; **1907** M. Carey Thomas Library built, named for Bryn Mawr president Martha Carey Thomas; **Dec. 10, 1912** Michigan Sen. Philip Hart born (died 1976); **1916** Ludington Public Library founded.

Butler *Butler County Western Pennsylvania, 29 mi/47 km north of Pittsburgh*

Dec. 27, 1753 George Washington has close scrape with death in area to southwest when lone Native American fires gun point blank but misses him, Washington forgives him of the incident; **1796** first white settlers arrive; **1800** Butler County formed; **1803** town platted as county seat, named for Richard Butler, Indian agent in Ohio killed 1791 in St. Clair expedition; **1811** Butler Academy founded; **1817** incorporated as a borough; **1870s** Western Pennsylvania Railroad reaches town; **1885** county courthouse built; **1894** Butler Public Library founded; **1902** Standard Steel Car Company established, maker of railroad cars; **1913** natural gas deposit discovered to east; **1917** incorporated as a city; **1965** Butler County Community College established.

Cambridge Springs *Crawford County Northwestern Pennsylvania, 22 mi/35 km south of Erie*

c.1800 first settled by German and Irish immigrants; **1815** bridge built across Furnace Creek; **1826** John Brown builds tannery here; **1835** Brown leaves area to begin abolitionist activities; **1860** mineral waters discovered by Dr. John H. Gray while searching for oil; **1862** Atlantic & Great Western Railroad reaches town; **1866** incorporated as a borough, originally named Cambridgeboro; **1884** springhouse built by Dr. Gray; **1886** Riverside Hotel built, still in business 2003; **1897** borough renamed Cambridge Springs; **1902** trolley service established from Erie, abandoned 1928; **1912** Alliance College established, closed 1987; **1928** Cambridge Springs Public Library founded.

Canonsburg *Washington County Southwestern Pennsylvania, 16 mi/26 km southwest of Pittsburgh*

1773 Col. John Canon settles on Chartiers Creek; **1780** Log Cabin School built, founded 1777, oldest school west of Alleghenies; **1787** town platted; log tavern built by Andrew Munroe; **1791** Canonsburg Academy founded; **1802** incorporated as a borough; **1804** Roberts House built; **1879** Canonsburg Public Library founded; **May 18, 1912** singer Perry Como born (died 2001); **Apr. 16, 1935** singer Bobby Vinton born.

Carlisle *Cumberland County South central Pennsylvania, 17 mi/27 km west of Harrisburg*

c.1718 trading post established; **1750** Cumberland County formed; **1751** town platted by Nicholas Scull; county seat moved from Shippensburg; **1756** Col. John Armstrong destroys Native American town of Kittanning; **1757** First Presbyterian Church built; **1760s** first iron furnaces established; **1773** Dickinson College established; **1782** incorporated as a borough; **1794** Blaine House built; **1825** St. John's Episcopal Church built; **1837** Cumberland Valley Railroad arrives; **1846** county courthouse completed; **July 1, 1863** town shelled, Union barracks burned by troops of Confederate Gen. Fitzhugh Lee; **1878** Market House built; **1879** Carlisle Indian School founded, closed 1918; **1899** Bosler Memorial Library built; **1940** first section of Pennsylvania Turnpike opened, 160 mi/257 km from nearby Middlesex west to Irwin, near Pittsburgh; **1989** Carlisle Area Performing Arts Center founded at Comerford Theater, built 1939.

Carmichaels *Greene County See Waynesburg (1962)*

Carnegie *Allegheny County Western Pennsylvania, suburb 5 mi/8 km west-southwest of Pittsburgh*

1768 first settlers John and James Bell arrive; **1853** post office established; First Presbyterian Church built; **1859** Methodist Church built; **1858** Baptist Church organized; **1872** Mansfield and Chartiers boroughs incorporated; **Feb. 24, 1874** baseball player Honus Wagner born, the "Flying Dutchman" (died 1955); **1880** St. Luke's Catholic Church built; **1883** J. C. Kirkpatrick Steel Mill established; **1894** Carnegie incorporated as a borough, formed by merger of Mansfield and Chartiers, named for steel magnate Andrew Carnegie; **1899** Carnegie Free Library and Music Hall founded, gift of Andrew Carnegie, opened 1901; **1962** steel mill closed.

Cashtown *Adams County Southern Pennsylvania, 36 mi/58 km southwest of Harrisburg*

1750s Mary Jemison, her parents, and several neighbors taken captive by Delawares, married Chief Hiokatoo, granted land after Revolution, accepted Christianity in her 91st and final year; **1797** Cashtown Tavern established, all patrons required to pay in cash; **1817** Conewago Mission established to north, one of first Jesuit missions in Eastern Pennsylvania; **1837** abolitionist Thaddeus Stevens builds Caledonia Furnace to west; **June 28, 1863** Caledonia Furnace destroyed by forces of Confederate Gen. Jubal Early.

Centralia *Columbia County East central Pennsylvania, 41 mi/66 km northeast of Harrisburg*

1826 town founded; **1866** incorporated as a borough; **May 1962** anthracite coal seam begins burning slowly, possibly ignited by garbage dump lying over seam; **1992** slow-burning coal vein deemed environmentally unsafe, town condemned; **1995** most residents evacuate town through government buyout, less than 40 remain of 1,100 in 1980.

Chadds Ford *Delaware County* *Southeastern Pennsylvania, 23 mi/37 km west-southwest of Philadelphia*

1722 first Birmingham Friends Meeting House built, replaced 1763; **1737** Chadds Ford Inn built by John Chadd; **1753** octagonal schoolhouse built; **1776** Percy Chandler Estate built; **Sept. 11, 1777** George Washington's 12,000 troops defeated by 18,000 British and Hessian troops under Generals Howe and Knyphausen in the Battle of Brandywine Creek, followed by occupation of Philadelphia; **1864** grist mill built, **July 12, 1917** painter Andrew Wyeth born; **1967** Brandywine River Museum founded, opened 1971, at grist mill; **1969** Chadds Ford Art Gallery established at mill.

Chalkhill *Fayette County* See **Farmington (1953)**

Chambersburg *Franklin County* *Southern Pennsylvania, 47 mi/76 km southwest of Harrisburg*

1730 area settled by Benjamin Chambers; **1764** town platted by Chambers; **1784** Franklin County formed; town becomes county seat; **1803** incorporated as a borough; **June 1859** abolitionist John Brown establishes headquarters here in attempt to create free state out of Maryland or Virginia, hanged for treason Dec. 2, 1859, after Oct. 16 raid on U.S. Arsenal at Harpers Ferry; **Oct. 10, 1862** Confederate Gen. J. E. B. Stuart launches raid on town; **July 30, 1864** town sacked and burned by Confederate Generals McCausland and Johnson in retaliation for Union march through Virginia's Shenandoah Valley; **1865** county courthouse rebuilt; **1869** Wilson College for women established; **1924** Coyle Free Library founded; **1925** cabin birthplace (1791) of Pres. James Buchanan moved from Mercersburg.

Chester *Delaware County* *Southeastern Pennsylvania, 12 mi/17 km southwest of Philadelphia*

1642 town on Delaware River settled by Swedes following land grant to Joran Kyn, oldest city in Pennsylvania; **1655** area captured by Dutch under Peter Stuyvesant; **1664** English take control; **1682** Chester County formed; town becomes county seat; **Oct. 1682** William Penn comes ashore here, his first arrival in colony; **Dec. 1682** first general assembly of Pennsylvania convenes here; **1683** Caleb Pusey House built; **1700** Black Bear Inn built; **1701** incorporated as a borough; **1724** Colonial county courthouse built; **1736** Friends Meeting House built; **1747** Washington House built, used as refuge by George Washington following Battle of Brandywine Sept. 1777; **1760s** warehouses and piers built by Francis Richardson; **1765** Steamboat Hotel built; **Feb. 1776** Gen. Anthony Wayne establishes his headquarters here; **Sept. 1777** Lafayette retreats to town following Battle of Brandywine for treatment of wounds; **1789** Delaware

County formed from Chester County; Chester becomes Delaware County seat, Chester County seat moved to West Chester; **1821** Widener University established as Pennsylvania Military College; **1850** St. Paul's Church built; **1851** county seat moved to Media; **1866** incorporated as a city; **1876** Chester Free Library founded, named J. Lewis Crozer Library 1897; **Oct. 31, 1896** gospel singer Ethel Waters born (died 1977); **1914** munitions industry established with World War; Deshong Art Gallery established; **1917** city hall built; **1974** Chester (Commodore Barry) Bridge built across Delaware River to Bridgeport, New Jersey, replacing ferry.

Clairton *Allegheny County* *Western Pennsylvania, 10 mi/16 km south of Pittsburgh*

1770 town settled on Monongahela River; **1892** glass plant and brick factory established; **c.1896** steel mills begin operations; **c.1900** largest coke plant in country built; **1903** incorporated as a borough; **1920** Clairton Public Library founded; **1922** incorporated as a city; **1935** St. Paulinus Catholic Church built primarily with volunteer labor; **1938** Irvin Plant of Carnegie-Illinois Steel Corporation opens; **1988** city declared economically distressed municipality.

Clarion *Clarion County* *West central Pennsylvania, 63 mi/101 km north-northeast of Pittsburgh*

1839 Clarion County formed; **1840** town platted as county seat; **1841** incorporated as a borough; **1867** Clarion University of Pennsylvania established; **1885** county courthouse completed; **1914** Clarion Free Library founded.

Clarksville *Greene County* See **Waynesburg (1970)**

Clearfield *Clearfield County* *Central Pennsylvania, 37 mi/60 km north of Altoona, near Clearfield River*

1783 Capt. Edward Ricketts becomes county's first settler; **1804** Clearfield County formed; **1805** town platted by Abraham Witmer; **1812** county organized; town becomes county seat; **1840** incorporated as a borough; **1862** county courthouse built; **1872** county jail built, replaced 1981; **1940** Joseph & Elizabeth Shaw Public Library founded.

Columbia *Lancaster County* *Southeastern Pennsylvania, 10 mi/16 km west of Lancaster*

1726 Quaker John Wright arrives from Chester to preach to Native Americans; Wright establishes ferry on Susquehanna River; settlement named Wright's Ferry; **1738** Wright's Ferry Mansion built by John Wright; **1788** town platted by grandson Samuel Wright, renamed Columbia; **1803** Lutheran Church founded, built 1850, later used as history museum; **1812** bridge built to Wrightsville, second span built 1834; **1814** incorporated as a borough; **1833** Susquehanna-Tidewater Canal opened, closed 1901; **1863** bridge deliberately burned to stop advancing Confederate troops; **1887** first blast furnace established; **1901** railroad reaches town; **1956** Columbia Public Library founded.

Conestoga   *Lancaster County*   *See* Lancaster (1750)

Connellsville   *Fayette County*   *Southwestern Pennsylvania, 37 mi/60 km south-southeast of Pittsburgh*

1770 area on Youghiogheny River first settled by Zachariah Connell and others; coal discovered in region; **1788** boat building industry begins; **1793** town platted by Connell; **1806** incorporated as a borough; **Jan. 8, 1839** Montana Sen. William Anderson Clark born (died 1925); **1903** Carnegie Free Library founded; **1911** incorporated as a city; **1939** Frank Lloyd Wright's Fallingwater home completed at Mill Run to southeast, Kaufmann family home until 1963; **2001** Mill Run Wind Farm established, ten wind turbines provide power to 5,700 homes [see also Somerset].

Coudersport   *Potter County*   *Northern Pennsylvania, 109 mi/174 km east-southeast of Erie, on Allegheny River*

1767 Moravian missionary David Zeisberger ministers to Native American tribes; **1804** Potter County formed; **1807** town platted, becomes county seat; **1843** Ives House built; **1834** Coudersport-Jersey Shore Turnpike completed; **1848** incorporated as a borough; **1850** Underground Railroad operated by John Mann; Coudersport Public Library founded; **1853** county courthouse built, rebuilt 1889; **1872** first railroad reaches town; **1880s** timber industry established, continues through 1920; **1899** glass production begins.

Cresson   *Cambria County*   *Central Pennsylvania, 9 mi/14.5 km west-southwest of Altoona*

c.1800 area first settled; **1816** first coal mining begins; **1834** Allegheny Portage Railroad built across mountains as portage for Pennsylvania Canal system; **1854** Pennsylvania Railroad replaces canal; **May 6, 1856** explorer Robert E. Peary born at rural Loretto to north, discovered the North Pole (died 1920); **c.1900** Cresson Tuberculosis Sanitarium founded; **1906** incorporated as a borough; **1939** Mount Aloysius College established.

Danville   *Montour County*   *East central Pennsylvania, 59 mi/95 km southwest of Scranton*

1774 John Simpson sells land on Susquehanna River to Col. William Montgomery; **1792** town platted; Montgomery House built by Col. Montgomery; **1813** Columbia County formed; town becomes county seat; **1840** Montour Iron Works established, forerunner of Reading Iron Company; **Oct. 8, 1845** first iron railroad track made here; **1846** Columbia County seat moved to Bloomsburg; **1849** incorporated as a borough; **1850** Montour County formed from Columbia County; town becomes county seat; **1871** county courthouse built; **1886**

Thomas Beaver Free Library founded; **1915** Greisinger Medical Center established; **1931** Slovak Girls' Academy built.

Dingmans Ferry   *Pike County*   *Northeastern Pennsylvania, 54 mi/87 km northeast of Allentown*

1735 Andrew Dingman settles on Delaware River, at mouth of creek named for him, founds town; **1750** Dingman establishes ferry to Layton, New Jersey; **1850** Dutch Reformed Church built; **1900** iron bridge built to New Jersey, replacing two previous structures destroyed by the elements; **1892** George W. Childs State Forest Park established with land donation by publisher of *Philadelphia Public Ledger*; **Sept. 1, 1965** Delaware Water Gap National Recreation Area authorized, absorbs Childs State Park; **Nov. 10, 1978** Delaware National Scenic River established.

Doylestown   *Bucks County*   *Southeastern Pennsylvania, 25 mi/40 km north of Philadelphia*

1682 Bucks County formed; **1714** Water Wheel Tavern built; **1735** town first settled by William Doyle; **1748** Fountain House built; **1758** Cross Keys Inn built; **1778** town platted; **1813** county seat moved from Newtown; **1838** incorporated as a borough; **1856** North Pennsylvania Railroad reaches town; **1896** Delaware Valley College established; **1910** surrealistic Fonthill mansion built by Dr. Henry Chapman Mercer, donated 1916 for historical museum; **1916** Melinda Cox Free Library founded; **1927** Aldie Mansion built by William Mercer, Henry Mercer's brother; **1960** county courthouse built; **1988** James A. Michener Art Museum dedicated.

Duquesne   *Allegheny County*   *Western Pennsylvania, 9 mi/14.5 km southeast of Pittsburgh*

1789 area along Monongahela River settled by farmers; **1885** Duquesne Steel Company builds mill here; town platted; **1889** strike halts operations at steel mill; **1890** Andrew Carnegie acquires steel mill, becomes Carnegie-Illinois Steel Company; **1891** incorporated as a city; **1916** Carnegie Library and Gymnasium built, razed 1968.

Easton   *Northampton County*   *Eastern Pennsylvania, 15 mi/24 km east-northeast of Bethlehem*

1751 town founded on Delaware River by Thomas Penn, son of William Penn; **1752** Northampton County formed; town platted as county seat by William Parsons and Nicholas Scull; **1756** peace conferences with Native Americans held here, through 1761; **1757** Taylor House built, home of George Taylor, signer of Declaration of Independence; William Parsons House built; **1776** First United Church of Christ built; **1789** incorporated as a borough; **1794** first of several grist mills built on Bushkill Creek; **c.1807** Easton Area Public Library founded; **1826** Lafayette College established; **1832** Lafayette College established; **1833** Mixsell House built; **1834** Lehigh Canal completed from Bristol; **1836** St. Bernard's

Catholic Church dedicated; **1861** county courthouse completed; **Dec. 27, 1864** World War I Army Chief of Staff Peyton Conway March born (died 1955); **1887** incorporated as a city; South Easton merges with Easton; **1903** Crayola Factory established, popular crayon manufacturer; **1996** Crayola Museum founded.

Ebensburg *Cambria County* *West central Pennsylvania, 16 mi/26 km west of Altoona*

1796 area settled; **1797** town founded by Rev. Rees Lloyd, leader of Welsh immigrants; **1804** Cambria County formed; **1805** town becomes county seat; **1806** town platted; **1825** incorporated as a borough; **1882** third county courthouse completed; **Nov. 3, 1922** actor Charles Bronson born at Ehrenfeld to south, near South Fork (died 2003); **1923** Ebensburg Free Public Library founded.

Eddystone *Delaware County* *Southeastern Pennsylvania, 9 mi/14.5 km southwest of Philadelphia*

1828 Baldwin Locomotive Works founded as steam engine plant, first locomotive *Old Ironsides* built 1832; **1888** incorporated as a borough; **1915** Eddystone Ammunition Plant established by Remington Arms; **Apr. 10, 1917** series of explosions at Eddystone Plant, 139 killed; **1940** Platt-Le Page Aircraft Company begins development of Tandem Rotor Helicopters, U.S. contract canceled 1944 due to control problems; **1999** operations at arms plant cease.

Ehrenfeld *Cambria County* *See* **Ebensburg (1922)**

Elizabethtown *Lancaster County* *Southeastern Pennsylvania, 17 mi/27 km southeast of Harrisburg*

1730 trading post established by Capt. Thomas Harris, brother of founder of Harrisburg; **1735** Black Bear Tavern established by Harris, **1751** town platted by Hughes, names it for his wife; **1827** incorporated as a borough; **1799** St. Peter's Catholic Church built; **1899** Elizabethtown College established; **1925** Elizabethtown Public Library founded.

Emporium *Cameron County* *Northern Pennsylvania, 70 mi/113 km north of Altoona*

1810 town settled; **1860** Cameron County formed; **1861** town platted, becomes county seat; **1864** incorporated as a borough; **1890** county courthouse built; **March 1936** Sinnemahoning Creek isolates entire communities in worst state-wide flooding in history; **1940** Cameron County Public Library founded, new library completed 2001.

Ephrata *Lancaster County* *Southeast central Pennsylvania, 12 mi/19 km north-northeast of Lancaster*

1732 Johann Beissel settles here by moving into hut with hermit Emanuel Eckerlin; **1735** Society of the Solitary Brethren founded by Beissel and followers; **1738** religious community of Ephrata founded; **1741** the Cloisters buildings, community focal point, built by the Solitary Brethren; **1745** grist mill built; **1777** tavern built by Solomon Gorgas; **1848** Mountain Spring Hotel built; **1891** incorporated as a borough; **1962** Ephrata Public Library founded.

Erie *Erie County* *Northwestern Pennsylvania, 117 mi/188 km north of Pittsburgh, on Lake Erie*

1654 Eriez peoples eliminated by Seneca, region comes under control of Iroquois Confederacy; **1753** Fort Presque Isle built by French on Presque Isle Peninsula; **1760** fort occupied by British, rebuilt; **1763** fort destroyed during Pontiac's Rebellion; **1784** Erie Triangle sold to Pennsylvania for $151,640, extending state's territory to Lake Erie; **1795** town platted by Maj. Andrew Ellicott and Gen. William Irvine; **1800** Erie County formed; town becomes county seat; **1805** incorporated as a borough; **1812** ship *Niagara* built, used by Oliver Perry in Battle of Lake Erie, 1813; **1818** Presque Isle Lighthouse built, rebuilt in 1840 and 1872, decommissioned 1885; **1833** Erie Iron Mill established; **1839** Old Customshouse built; **1844** Erie & Pittsburgh Canal completed; **1846** steamboat service established to Buffalo; **1850s** railroads arrive; **1851** incorporated as a city; **1888** *Daily Times* newspaper founded; **1893** St. Peter's Cathedral dedicated; **1899** Erie Public Library built, new library opened 1996; **1921** Presque Isle State Park established; **1925** Gannon University established, originally Villa Maria College; **1926** Mercyhurst College established; first of Erie's numerous plastics factories opened; **July 25, 1932** astronaut Paul Weitz born; **1943** county courthouse built; **1948** Pennsylvania State University at Erie (Behrend College) established; Perry monument erected in Crystal Point Park; **Sept. 6, 1973** former UMW president Tony Boyle arrested for 1969 murder of opposition candidate Joseph Yablonski, gets life in prison [see Waynesburg]; **1997** Family First Sports Park opened.

Essington *Delaware County* *Southeastern Pennsylvania, 7 mi/11.3 km southwest of Philadelphia*

Feb. 1643 first settlement in Pennsylvania founded on Tinicum Island, Delaware River, by Swedes led by Col. Johann Printz; **Nov. 25, 1645** explosion of powder magazine destroys entire colony; **1654** first log section of Morton House built; **1655** Swedish settlement seized by Dutch; **c.1724** John Morton, signer of Declaration of Independence, born at Morton House (died 1777); **1799** first quarantine station in U.S. opens, sold in 1937; **1805** fire again destroys town.

Farmington *Fayette County* *Southwestern Pennsylvania, 50 mi/80 km south-southeast of Pittsburgh*

Apr. 1754 Fort Necessity built; **May 28, 1754** first skirmish of French and Indian War fought at nearby Brownsville; **July 3, 1754** Col. George Washington, 22 years old, withdraws from Fort Necessity; **c.1818** Mount

Washington Tavern built, converted to museum 1932; **March 4, 1931** Fort Necessity National Battlefield Site established, redesignated National Battlefield 1961; **1953** I. N. Hagan House built at rural Chalkhill to northwest, designed by Frank Lloyd Wright, house later renamed Kentuck Knob; **1987** Nemacolin Woods Resort and Spa established.

Finleyville *Washington County* See **Washington (1913)**

Franklin *Venango County* *Northwestern Pennsylvania, 66 mi/106 km north of Pittsburgh, on Allegheny R.*

1753 Fort Machault built by French, abandoned 1759; **Dec., 1753** George Washington passes through area carrying orders to evacuate in face of advancing British; **1760** British build Fort Venango, taken by Native Americans 1763 in Pontiac's War; **1787** Fort Franklin built by U.S., abandoned 1796; **1795** town platted; **1800** Venango County formed; **1808** county organized; town becomes county seat; **1828** incorporated as a borough; **1860** oil discovered by James Evans; **1868** incorporated as a city; **1869** county courthouse built; **1884** Franklin Library founded; **1870** Galena Oil Company established, acquired by Standard Oil 1878; **1886** Franklin Opera House built; **1954** Chess-Lamberton Airport established, became Venango Regional Airport 1994; **1982** first annual Applefest held.

Gallitzin *Cambria County* *Central Pennsylvania, 8 mi/12.9 km west of Altoona*

c.1796 town settled named for missionary Demetrius Gallitzin; **1803** Gallitzin Tunnel completed, east end of town, through Atlantic-Mississippi divide, length 2,120-ft/649-m long eastbound, 3,612-ft/1,101-m westbound; **1886** incorporated as a borough; **Feb. 18, 1947** railroad accident, 24 killed; **1957** Gallitzin Public Library founded.

Germantown *Philadelphia County* See **Philadelphia**

Gettysburg *Adams County* *Southern Pennsylvania, 35 mi/56 km south-southwest of Harrisburg*

c.1780 area settled; town platted by James Gettys, named Marsh Creek Settlement; **1800** Adams County formed; town becomes county seat with Gettys as first presiding judge; town renamed Gettysburg; **1806** incorporated as a borough; **1826** Lutheran Theological Seminary founded; **March 12, 1831** blacksmith, wagon maker Clement Studebaker born (died 1901); **1832** Gettysburg College established, originally named Pennsylvania College; **July 1–3, 1863** in Battle of Gettysburg, General Lee's Virginia Army attacks Pennsylvania Army, Lee retreats back into Virginia, over 51,000 soldiers killed, bloodiest battle of Civil War; **Nov. 19, 1863** Lincoln delivers his Gettysburg Address at the dedication of the Gettysburg National

Cemetery; **1859** county courthouse completed; **Feb. 11, 1895** Gettysburg National Military Park established; **July 3, 1938** Eternal Light Peace Memorial dedicated by President Franklin D. Roosevelt; **Apr. 8, 1939** Maj. Calvin Gilbert, town's last Civil War veteran, celebrates his 100th birthday, dies Sept. 13 of same year; **1945** Adams County Library founded; **July 4, 2000** 393 ft/120 m observation tower demolished with explosives, controversial since it was built in 1974 due to its incompatibility with the national park setting.

Greensburg *Westmoreland County* *Southwestern Pennsylvania, 25 mi/40 km east-southeast of Pittsburgh*

c.1770 town settled, originally called New Town; **1773** Westmoreland County formed; nearby Hannastown becomes first county seat; **1785** town founded; county seat moved to Greensburg; **1850** county courthouse built; **1883** Seton Hall College established, became Seton Hall University 2002; **1926** Palace Theatre opened, originally the Manos Theatre; **1928** incorporated as a city; **1936** Greensburg Public Library founded; **1950** Westmoreland County Community College established at Youngwood to south; **1963** University of Pittsburgh at Greensburg established.

Hanover *York County* *Southern Pennsylvania, 17 mi/27 km southwest of York*

1736 town founded; **1750s** tavern established by Adam Forney; **1763** incorporated as a borough; **Jan. 1, 1861** author John Luther Long born, wrote *Madame Butterfly* (died 1927); **June 30, 1863** in first Civil War battle fought north of Mason-Dixon Line, Confederate Gen. James E. B. Stuart's forces engage Union forces of Generals Custer and Kilpatrick, 100 Southern casualties, 200 Northern casualties, battle delayed Stuart from joining Lee until day after July 3 Battle of Gettysburg; **1926** Hanover Shoe Farms founded, producer of renowned trotting horses.

Harmony *Butler County* *Western Pennsylvania, 25 mi/40 km north of Pittsburgh*

1805 Harmony Society organized by George Rapp, town founded as idealistic colony; **1810** woolen factory established; **1814** Harmonists sell their properties; **1818** Rapp Granary built; Rapp Mansion built, destroyed by fire 1844; **1822** Community House Number Two built; **1824** Thrall's Opera House built; **1838** incorporated as a borough; **1979** The Atheneum and Visitors Center opened.

Harrisburg *Dauphin County* *South central Pennsylvania, 95 mi/153 km west-northwest of Philadelphia*

1712 John Harris establishes ferry and trading post on Susquehanna River; **1733** town founded as Harris' Ferry; **1766** Harris Mansion built; **1785** Dauphin County formed; town platted by John Harris, Jr. as county seat; **Dec. 12, 1787** Pennsylvania becomes second state to ratify

U.S. Constitution; **1791** incorporated as a borough; Maclay Mansion built; **1812** state capital moved from Lancaster; **1816** Pennsylvania State Library founded; **1829** Pennsylvania Canal built; **1834** first railroad arrives; **1845** Pennsylvania's first telegraph line completed to Lancaster; **1860** incorporated as a city; **1863** General Lee's advance guard reaches west side of Susquehanna, opposite Harrisburg, repulsed by Union forces; **1889** Harrisburg Public Library founded; **1897** fire destroys state capitol; **1906** new state capitol built; **1916** capitol buildings complex started on Capitol Hill, last structure, the finance building, completed 1939; **1930** Soldiers' and Sailors' Memorial Bridge built across Paxson Creek to Capitol Hill; **1943** county courthouse completed; **1964** Harrisburg Area Community College established; **Apr. 16, 1972** bus runs off road, 4 killed, 43 injured; **June 22, 1972** region worst hit by Hurricane Agnes, city isolated by flooding.

Hazleton *Luzerne County* *Eastern Pennsylvania, 36 mi/58 km south-southwest of Scranton*

1818 legend has it that anthracite coal seam discovered by deer pawing the ground; **1827** railroad built from coal mines to Lehigh Railway, link to Pennsylvania Canal system; **1837** town platted on Buck Mountain Plateau; **1856** incorporated as a borough; **c.1865** full-scale coal mining develops at end of Civil War; **Dec. 1891** incorporated as a city; **1898** Duplun Silk Mill established by J. L. Duplun, closed 1923; **1907** Hazleton Area Public Library founded; **1934** Pennsylvania State University Hazleton Campus, Commonwealth College (2-year), established.

Hershey *Dauphin County* *South central Pennsylvania, 12 mi/19 km east of Harrisburg*

1724 log Derry Presbyterian Church built, replaced 1884; **1732** Old Session House of Derry Presbyterian Church built; **1903** Lancaster caramel manufacturer Milton S. Hershey (1857–1945) purchases cornfield, builds chocolate factory; planned community founded near Spring Creek; **1909** Milton S. Hershey School founded; **1913** Hershey Public Library founded, new library opened 1997; **1933** Hotel Hershey completed; **Apr. 1937** sitdown strike disrupts chocolate production for week, strikers ejected, CIO leaders defeated in labor election; **1963** Penn State Hershey Medical Center founded through donation by Milton S. Hershey School Trust Fund.

Hollidaysburg *Blair County* *Central Pennsylvania, 5 mi/8 km south of Altoona*

1768 town founded by Irish immigrants Adam and William Holliday; **1820** incorporated as a borough; **1840** Portage Railroad completed from Johnstown as link between Pennsylvania's eastern and western canal systems, answer to New York's Erie Canal; **1846** Blair County formed; town becomes county seat; **1877** county courthouse built; **June 2, 1890** actress Hedda Hopper born (died 1966); **1943** Hollidaysburg Free Public Library founded.

Homestead *Allegheny County* *Western Pennsylvania, suburb 5 mi/8 km southeast of Pittsburgh*

1770s squatter Sebastian Frederick becomes first settler; town founded on Monongahela River, named Amity Homestead; **1786** John McClure acquires property; **1871** town platted on McClure tract; **1880** incorporated as a borough; **1881** Andrew Carnegie opens Pittsburgh-Bessemer Steel Company, later becomes part of United States Steel; **July 6, 1892** Carnegie steel mill struck by labor dispute, 300 Pinkerton guards brought by barge to dislodge strikers, 7 guards and 11 strikers killed in clashes July 10, 8,000 National Guardsmen sent to stabilize situation.

Honesdale *Wayne County* *Northeastern Pennsylvania, 23 mi/37 km northeast of Scranton*

1798 Wayne County formed; **1803** area first settled; **1808** transfer point established for anthracite coal mines; **1826** construction of Delaware & Hudson Canal begins under direction of Philip Hone, former mayor of New York City; town founded; **Aug. 8, 1829** the *Sturbridge Lion* becomes first locomotive to run on American track, built by Horatio Allen to transfer coal to canal; **1831** incorporated as a borough; **1841** county seat moved from Bethany; **1842** Hotel Allen built; **Nov. 27, 1848** physicist Henry Augustus Rowland born (died 1901); **Apr. 8, 1858** Mary Scott Lord Dimmick Harrison born, second wife of Pres. Benjamin Harrison (married 1896, died 1948); **1880** county courthouse completed; **1889** *Sturbridge Lion* locomotive sent to Smithsonian Institute in Washington; **1892** Wayne Hotel built; **Aug. 29, 1899** World War II Army Gen. Lyman L. Lemnitzer born (died 1988); **1926** Revolutionary War memorial erected; **1938** Wayne County Public Library founded; **Oct. 19, 1971** nursing home fire kills 15 residents.

Huntingdon *Huntingdon County* *Central Pennsylvania, 20 mi/32 km east of Altoona, on Juniata River*

c.1755 town settled; **1767** town platted by Dr. William Smith; **1787** Huntingdon County formed; town becomes county seat; **1796** incorporated as a borough; **1829** Pennsylvania Canal opens; **1862** county courthouse built; **1876** Juniata College established; **1878** Pennsylvania Industrial School established; **May 1930** crew building U.S. Highway 22 discover Lincoln Caverns to west, opened to public June, 1931; **1935** Huntingdon County Public Library opened; **1973** Raystown Reservoir formed by dam to south on Raystown Branch Juniata River.

Indiana *Indiana County* *West central Pennsylvania, 46 mi/74 km east-northeast of Pittsburgh*

1772 Fergus Moorhead settles here with family and friends; **1777** Moorhead and friend named Simpson attacked by Native Americans, Simpson is scalped, Moorhead taken prisoner, escapes; **1781** fort built by

Moorhead to protect settlement; **1803** Indiana County formed; **1804** land donated for county seat by George Clymer, signer of Declaration of Independence; county and town named for Indiana Territory, formed 1800; **1805** town platted; **1810** post office established; **1816** incorporated as a borough; **1850s** town becomes important station on Underground Railroad, haven for runaway slaves; **1875** Indiana University of Pennsylvania established as Indiana State Teachers College; **1876** Clark House built; **1908** Indiana Free Library founded; **May 20, 1908** actor Jimmy Stewart born (died 1997); **1971** county courthouse completed; **1995** Jimmy Stewart Museum opened.

Jacobs Creek   *Westmoreland County*
Southwestern Pennsylvania, 25 mi/40 km south-southeast of Pittsburgh

1870s coal mining begins at Eureka Mine; town founded; **1900** Pittsburgh Coal acquires mine; **c.1903** Darr Coal Mine opened; **Dec. 19, 1907** coal mine accident at Darr Mine, 239 killed; **1910** Darr Mine reopened as Banning Mine; **1919** Banning Mine closed; **1961** Eureka Mine closed.

Jeannette   *Westmoreland County   Southwestern Pennsylvania, 22 mi/35 km east-southeast of Pittsburgh*

Aug. 5-6, 1763 Ottawa Chief Pontiac's forces attack horse team loaded with flour, overwhelmed by flank attack by Col. Henry Bouquet, wounded kept behind makeshift "Flourbag Fort"; **1888** town platted, named for wife of glass manufacturer Hiram Sellers McKee; first glass plant established; **1932** Jeannette Public Library founded; **1937** incorporated as a borough; **1938** incorporated as a city.

Jim Thorpe   *Carbon County   Eastern Pennsylvania, 23 mi/37 km north-northwest of Allentown*

1791 anthracite coal discovered in area; **1816** town founded on Lehigh River, originally named Mauch Chunk, Native American term for "sleeping bear"; **1818** road built to Summit Hill coal mines from newly completed Lehigh Canal; **1824** East Mauch Chunk founded, incorporated as a borough 1854; **1827** first gravity-powered switchback railroad in U.S. laid to mines; **1833** Asa Parker establishes coal barge business, builds mansions for himself and son Henry; **1843** Carbon County formed; town becomes county seat; **1859** flooding devastates valley, again in 1862; **1870** railroad abandoned, converted to scenic railway, discontinued 1930s; **1870s** Hotel Switzerland built; **Oct. 10, 1888** railroad accident at Mud Run to north, 55 killed; **1890** Dimmick Memorial Library founded; **1894** county courthouse built; **1954** Mauch Chunk and East Mauch Chunk merge, renamed Jim Thorpe in honor of football legend (1888–1953); **1955** severe flooding of Lehigh River leads to building of Mauch Chunk Dam upstream 1965.

Johnstown   *Cambria County   West central Pennsylvania, 57 mi/92 km east of Pittsburgh, on Conemaugh River*

1769 area settled following Treaty of Fort Stanwix with Iroquois Nov. 1768; **1800** town platted by Joseph Johns; **1808** iron forge built by John Holliday; flooding occurs on Conemaugh River; **1831** incorporated as a borough; **1840** Portage Railroad completed from Hollidaysburg, final link in Pennsylvania Canal, built in response to New York's Erie Canal; South Fork Dam built as part of canal basin; **1851** seven-arch Stone Bridge built for Pennsylvania Railroad, saved lives in great 1889 flood; **1853** Bethlehem Steel Cambria Plant opened, formerly Cambria Iron Foundry; **1861** first Kelly pneumatic converter built at Bethlehem Steel for converting iron to steel; **1870** Johnstown Public Library founded; **Dec. 24, 1881** composer Charles Wakefield Cadman born (died 1946); **May 31, 1889** South Fork Dam collapses after week of heavy rains, massive flash flood of Conemaugh River inundates town, 2,209 killed; **Dec. 1889** incorporated as a city; **1891** Inclined Plane built to lift iron workers to top of Yoder Hill, used later to save flood victims, rebuilt 1984; **July 10, 1902** coal mine accident, 112 deaths; **June 2, 1903** actor Johnny Weissmueller (Tarzan) born at Windber to southeast, Olympic swimmer 1924 and 1928 (died 1984); **1927** University of Pittsburgh at Johnstown established; **1929** Johnstown Symphony Orchestra founded; **May 28, 1931** actress Carroll Baker born; **March 17, 1936** flooding Conemaugh River kills 25; **1937** strike at Cambria Plant leads to martial law; **1943** river channelized to alleviate flooding; **Aug. 31, 1964** Johnstown Flood National Memorial authorized; **July 19–20, 1977** flash flood occurs again on Conemaugh River following 7 in/18 cm of rain, 68 killed, 31 missing, 2,000 homeless.

Kennett Square   *Chester County   Southeastern Pennsylvania, 30 mi/48 km west-southwest of Philadelphia*

1705 town settled; **c.1825** Kennett Square Inn built; **Jan. 11, 1825** travel writer Bayard Taylor born (died 1878); **1850s** region serves Underground Railroad network, giving runaway slaves safe haven; **1855** incorporated as a borough; **1870** Kennett Square Academy built, closed 1882; **1884** Chalfont Mansion built; **1895** Bethel African Methodist Episcopal Church built; Bayard Taylor Memorial Library founded; **1911** New Garden Church dedicated; **1940** Kennett Symphony founded; **1998** Kennett Area Underground Railroad Center founded.

King of Prussia   *Montgomery County*
Southeastern Pennsylvania, 15 mi/24 km northwest of Philadelphia

1709 King of Prussia Inn built, its first proprietor a native of Prussia; village develops around inn; **1758** building built, served as Washington's headquarters during Valley Forge campaign 1777–1778; **1763** house built on Valley Creek, becomes Lafayette's headquarters winter of 1777–1778; **1767** Washington Inn built; **Dec. 19, 1777** Washington's army camps here, degraded by illness and shortage of supplies; **1926** carillon erected at Washington Chapel.

Kittanning *Armstrong County* *West central Pennsylvania, 35 mi/56 km northeast of Pittsburgh*

Sept. 8, 1756 Col. John Armstrong destroys Native American town of Kittanning, on Allegheny River, killing Chief Jacob and his warriors; **1791** first settlers arrive; **1797** town founded by German and Scotch-Irish immigrants; **1800** Armstrong County formed; **1804** town platted as county seat; **1821** incorporated as a borough; **1827** steamboat *Albion* (a "water-walker") makes debut run from Pittsburgh; **1860** county courthouse built; **1922** Kittanning Free Library founded; **1930** Lock and Dam No. 7 built on Allegheny River.

Lackawaxen *Pike County* *Northeastern Pennsylvania, 35 mi/56 km east of Scranton, on Delaware River*

1770 village founded at mouth of Lackawaxen Creek by Jonathan Conkling and John Barnes; **July 22, 1779** Battle of Minisink occurs nearby, 300 Tories and natives led by Chief Joseph Brant kill most of 175 settlers; **July 14, 1869** passenger trains collide, nine killed; **1905** author Zane Grey arrives, resides here until 1918.

Lancaster *Lancaster County* *Southeastern Pennsylvania, 60 mi/97 km west of Philadelphia*

1709 German squatters occupy site; **1721** Englishman George Gibson becomes first known settler; Gibson builds inn and brewery; village named Gibson's Pasture; **1729** Lancaster County formed; **1730** town platted by James Hamilton as county seat; **1736** First Reformed Church dedicated; **1742** incorporated as a borough; **c.1750** Conestoga wagon developed by Pennsylvania German settlers to transport produce to market in Conestoga Valley to south, wagon becomes vehicle of choice for westward migration for more than a century; **1751** making of firearms becomes early industry, origin of "Kentucky rifle"; **1759** Lancaster Area Library founded, becomes Lancaster County Library System 1969; **Dec. 27, 1763** Paxton Boys raid jail, murder 14 Conestogas as revenge for earlier killing of whites; **Nov. 14, 1765** steamboat inventor Robert Fulton born at rural Wakefield to south (died 1815); **1774** citizens show early resistance to British oppression; **Sept. 27, 1777** displaced Continental Congress convenes here for one day, its fifth location, moves to York; **Feb. 6, 1778** French sign treaty with U.S. recognizing the 13 colonies, send naval fleet to assist in Revolutionary War; **1779** George Washington first referred to as "Father of his Country" by Francis Bailey in pamphlet printed in German; **1780s** iron industry gains importance; **1787** Franklin and Marshall College established; **1794** Philadelphia and Lancaster Pike completed; Holy Trinity Lutheran Church completed, cornerstone laid 1760s; Edward Hand Mansion built; **1795** old city hall built; **1796** Central Market built, rebuilt 1889; **1799** state capital moved from Philadelphia; **Feb. 24, 1808** aeronaut

John Wise born (died 1879); **1812** state capital moved to Harrisburg; **1818** incorporated as a city; **1820** St. James Episcopal Church built; **1829** Wheatland built, home of Pres. James Buchanan (1791–1868) from 1849 until his death; **March 1834** Lancaster & Columbia Railroad extended to city; **1845** first telegraph line in Pennsylvania completed to Harrisburg; **1852** Fulton Opera House opened; **1853** county courthouse built; **1871** Seminary of the Reformed Church founded; **1879** Frank W. Woolworth opens his first "5 and 10 cent" store; **Nov. 8, 1883** painter Charles Demuth born (died 1935); **1906** Thaddeus Stevens Industrial School established; **1953** North Museum of History and Science built, founded mid-1800s; **Dec. 14, 1969** bus overturns on Christmas delivery mission for Masonic home, 7 killed, 30 injured; **1979** Lancaster Museum of Art opened at Grubb Mansion, built 1845.

Laporte *Sullivan County* *North central Pennsylvania, 43 mi/69 km west of Scranton*

1847 Sullivan County formed; **1850** town founded as county seat by Michael Mylert, town named for John Laporte, Surveyor General of Pennsylvania, becomes lumber and leather tanning center; **1853** incorporated as a borough; Celestia Community of Adventists founded by Peter Armstrong, dissolved after his death 1887; **1888** Lake Mokoma formed by dam on Mill Creek, on east side of town; **1889** St. John's Episcopal Church built; **1895** Sacred Heart Catholic Church dedicated; **1894** third county courthouse built; **1897** United Methodist Church built.

Latrobe *Westmoreland County* *Southwestern Pennsylvania, 34 mi/55 km east-southeast of Pittsburgh*

1851 town platted on Loyalhanna Creek by Oliver Barnes, named for Benjamin Latrobe, Jr.; **1854** incorporated as a borough; **1870** St Vincent College established; **1909** Latrobe Area Hospital opened; **1927** Adams Memorial Library founded; **March 20, 1928** TV personality Fred Rogers (Mr. Rogers) born (died 2003); **Sept. 10, 1929** golfer Arnold Palmer born; **1951** Tri-City Municipal Airport established, renamed Arnold Palmer Regional Airport 1970.

Laurel Run *Luzerne County* *See* **Wilkes-Barre (1903)**

Lebanon *Lebanon County* *Southeastern Pennsylvania, 25 mi/40 km east of Harrisburg*

1756 town platted by George Steitz, originally named Steitztown; **1794** construction begun on Lebanon Canal, branch of Union Canal, completed 1827; **1813** Lebanon County formed; town becomes county seat; **1821** incorporated as a borough; **1823** Lebanon Canal Tunnel built, first of its kind in America; **1868** incorporated as a city; **1925** Lebanon Library System founded; **1963** county courthouse/Municipal Building built.

Levittown *Bucks County* *Southeastern Pennsylvania, 22 mi/35 km northeast of Philadelphia*

1951 land purchased by William Levitt of Levitt and Sons developers; **1952** town founded, considered one of first planned subdivisions with nearly identical small ranch houses, serpentine streets, follows 1947 development of Levittown, Long Island, New York; **1958** total 17,311 houses built since 1952. [see also Levittown, New York]

Lewisburg *Union County* *Central Pennsylvania, 48 mi/77 km north of Harrisburg*

1785 town platted on West Branch Susquehanna River, named for settler Ludwig (Lewis) Doerr; **1813** Union County formed; town becomes county seat; incorporated as a borough; **Sept. 23, 1823** prohibitionist James Black born (died 1893); **1846** Bucknell University established; **1855** county courthouse built, annex built 1973; **1894** Union County Public Library founded; **1930** Northeastern Federal Penitentiary built; **Jan. 14, 1969** Morton Sobell released from prison after 17 years, 9 months of 30-year sentence for espionage with Rosenbergs (executed 1953); **Dec. 23, 1971** Teamsters boss Jimmy Hoffa released after 4 years, 9 months of 13-year sentence for fraud, jury tampering.

Lewistown *Mifflin County* *Central Pennsylvania, 43 mi/69 km northwest of Harrisburg, on Juniata River*

1710 fur trappers John Le Tort and Jonah Davenport discover Shawnee village of Ohesson; **1789** Mifflin County formed; **1790** town platted; **1791** town becomes county seat; **1795** incorporated as a borough; **1829** Pennsylvania Canal opens; **1841** McCoy House built; **1842** Lewistown Public Library founded, becomes Mifflin County Library 1942; **c.1850** railroad reaches town; **1908** Lewistown Hospital opened; **1981** county courthouse completed.

Lititz *Lancaster County* *Southeastern Pennsylvania, 8 mi/12.9 km north of Lancaster*

1722 Christian Bomberger becomes first settler, lives in dugout (hole dug in embankment); **c.1740** settled by Moravian immigrants; **1757** town platted by Moravian missionaries, named for Moravian barony; **1787** Moravian Church dedicated; **1794** Linden Hall Junior College established; **1861** hard pretzel bakery founded, one of first in U.S.; **1863** first railroad reaches town; **1871** John A. Sutter moves here, ruined mill operator on whose property California Gold Rush began, overrun by gold miners, died 1880; **1888** incorporated as a borough; **1935** Lititz Public Library founded.

Lock Haven *Clinton County* *North central Pennsylvania, 95 mi/153 km west-southwest of Scranton*

1769 area settled on West Branch Susquehanna River; **1832** Bald Eagle Canal completed; **1833** town founded; **1839** Clinton County formed; town becomes county seat; **1840** incorporated as a borough; **1842** county courthouse built; **1870** incorporated as a city; Lock Haven University

of Pennsylvania established; **Aug. 2, 1872** painter John Sloan born (died 1951); **1910** Annie Halenbake Ross Library founded; **1937** Piper Aircraft Corporation established by William T. Piper; **1984** Lock Haven Piper Factory closed; **1995** Piper Aviation Museum founded.

Loretto *Cambria County* See **Altoona (1856)**

Manheim *Lancaster County* *Southeastern Pennsylvania, 10 mi/16 km north-northwest of Lancaster*

1762 town founded by Heinrich Wilhelm Stiegel; **1764** Manheim glassworks established by Stiegel, becomes American Flint Glass Manufactory; **1766** Trinity Lutheran Church built, called Red Rose Church for Stiegel's charge of five shillings and one red rose as church property rent; **1770** all of town owned by Stiegel; **1778** Stiegel Mansion completed; **1847** Shearer's Covered Bridge built on Chickies Creek, rebuilt 1856; **1862** Columbia & Reading Railroad reaches town; **1967** Manheim Library founded; **1987** Railroad Station Museum founded.

Marianna *Washington County* See **Washington (1908)**

Mather *Greene County* See **Waynesburg (1928)**

Mauch Chunk *Carbon County* See **Jim Thorpe**

McConnellsburg *Fulton County* *Southern Pennsylvania, 45 mi/72 km south-southeast of Altoona*

c.1730 first settlers arrive; **1749** first land grants awarded; **1755** half of original 93 settler families are either killed or taken prisoner by this date; **1757** Native Aemricans destroy Colonial militia; **Nov. 14, 1765** steamboat inventor Robert Fulton born in rural part of county later named for him (died 1815); **1782** George Diven born, invented friction brake for Conestoga wagons (died 1858); **1786** town platted by Daniel and William McConnell; **1814** incorporated as a borough; **1850** Fulton County formed; town becomes county seat; **1852** county courthouse built.

McKeesport *Allegheny County* *Western Pennsylvania, 9 mi/14.5 km southeast of Pittsburgh*

1768 settled by David McKee; **1775** McKee establishes ferry on Monongahela River; town founded; **1794** town plays role in Whiskey Rebellion; **1795** town platted; **1830** coal mining begins; **1842** incorporated as a borough; **1870** National Tube Company founded by John H. and Harvey K. Flagler, town nicknamed "Tube City"; **1891** incorporated as a city; **1898** American Sheet and Tin Plate Company established; **1902** Carnegie Free Library opened.

Meadville *Crawford County* *Northwestern*
Pennsylvania, 33 mi/53 km south of Erie

1788 area first settled by David Mead; **1797** David Mead House built; **1800** Crawford County formed; town becomes county seat; **1815** Allegheny College established; **1823** incorporated as a borough; **1866** incorporated as a city; **Nov. 21, 1867** social reformer Frederic Clemson Howe born (died 1947); **1879** Meadville Library founded; **1897** county courthouse built; **1913** Col. Lewis Walker moves his slide fastener (zipper) factory here from Hoboken, New Jersey, established 1893; **March 10, 1958** actress Sharon Stone born.

Media *Delaware County* *Southeastern*
Pennsylvania, 11 mi/18 km west of Philadelphia

1682 area settled by Quakers; **1684** Providence Friends Meeting House built; **1739** Black Horse Tavern built, used until 1939; **1789** Delaware County formed; **1848** town platted; **1850** incorporated as a borough; county courthouse built; **1851** county seat moved to Media; **1853** post office established; **1901** Media Library founded; **1967** Delaware County Community College (2-year) of Pennsylvania State University established, moved from Chester 1970.

Mercer *Mercer County* *Northwestern*
Pennsylvania, 63 mi/101 km south of Erie

1795 town founded on Neshannock River; **1800** Mercer County formed; town becomes county seat; county and town named for Brig. Gen. Hugh Mercer; **1803** town platted; **1810** Old Stone Jail built, used until 1868; **1814** incorporated as a borough; **1911** county courthouse built; **1915** Mercer Library founded; **1952** Mercer Raceway Park established.

Mercersburg *Franklin County* *Southern*
Pennsylvania, 62 mi/100 km southwest of Harrisburg

c.1730 town settled, originally named Blacks Town; **1759** town site purchased by William Smith, Sr., renamed for Revolutionary soldier and physician Gen. Hugh Mercer; **1780** town platted; **Apr. 23, 1791** James Buchanan, 15th U.S. President, born (died June 1, 1868); **1792** Creigh House built; **1796** James Buchanan Hotel built; **1831** incorporated as a borough; **1836** Mercersburg Academy established; **1840s** relatively close to slave states, region becomes center for abolitionist activities on Underground Railroad; **1893** Mercersburg Academy founded; **1904** Star Theater built.

Middleburg *Snyder County* *Central Pennsylvania,*
36 mi/58 km north-northwest of Harrisburg

c.1756 area first settled by whites; **1800** town platted by John Swineford; **1855** Snyder County formed; town becomes county seat; county courthouse built, annex built 1970s; **1860** incorporated as a borough.

Middletown *Dauphin County* *Southern*
Pennsylvania, 9 mi/14.5 km southeast of Harrisburg

1755 town founded on Susquehanna River; **1828** incorporated as a borough; **1829** Union and Pennsylvania canals joined here; **1888** Middletown & Hummelstown Railroad established, becomes Reading Railroad 1890, reverts to M & H Railroad 1976; **1917** Middletown Air Depot established; **1926** Middletown Public Library founded; **1939** Trafficscope installed at crest of hill to east on U.S. Highway 230, giant glass lens mounted on steel scaffold affording motorists view of oncoming traffic on far side of hill; **1966** Pennsylvania State University, Harrisburg Campus, established; **1910** fire in business district destroys several blocks; **1911** Elks Theater opened, longest operating theater in U.S.; **1974** Three Mile Island Nuclear Plant begins operation; **March 28, 1979** core meltdown caused by equipment malfunction and human error at Three Mile Island Nuclear Plant, most serious nuclear accident to date.

Mifflintown *Juniata County* *Central*
Pennsylvania, 34 mi/55 km northwest of Harrisburg

1789 Mifflin County formed; **1791** town platted by John Harris, Jr., named for Thomas Mifflin, Pennsylvania's first post-Revolutionary governor; intended for county seat, Lewistown chosen in its stead; **1831** Juniata County formed out of Mifflin County; town becomes county seat; **1833** incorporated as a borough; **1873** county courthouse built.

Milford *Pike County* *Northeastern Pennsylvania,*
45 mi/72 km east of Scranton, on Delaware River

1733 Tom Quick becomes first settler, killed 1755 by Native Americans as son watched; **1773** Tom Quick's son dies, having carried out vendetta by killing 99 natives in retaliation for father's killing, 100th killed at his death bed; **1798** Wayne County formed; town becomes county seat, moved to Wilsonville 1799–1802, returned to Milford; **1814** Pike County formed from Wayne County; town becomes county seat; Wayne County seat moved to Bethany; **1874** incorporated as a borough; county courthouse built; **1886** Grey Towers estate built by Gov. Gifford Pinchot; **1901** Pike County Public Library founded; **1985** county administration building completed.

Mill Run *Fayette County* See **Connellsville** (1939, 2001)

Montrose *Susquehanna County* *Northeastern*
Pennsylvania, 30 mi/48 km north-northwest of Scranton

1799 town settled; **1800** town founded; **1810** Susquehanna County formed; town becomes county seat; **1824** incorporated as a borough; **1855** county courthouse completed; **1907** Susquehanna County Free Library founded.

Morrisville *Bucks County   Southeastern Pennsylvania, 27 mi/43 km northeast of Philadelphia*

1624 trading post established on Delaware River by Dutch West India Company, until 1627; **c.1649** ferry established; **1770** South Street Ferry begins service from Trenton, New Jersey; **1770s** Summerseat mansion built, served as Washington's headquarters in 1776 prior to Battle of Trenton; **Oct. 7, 1783** resolution introduced in U.S. Congress setting aside both sides of Delaware River for federal town, defeated by two votes, favoring site on Potomac River in Maryland; **1804** incorporated as a borough; **1904** Morrisville Free Library founded; **1925** Langhorne Speedway built.

Muncy *Lycoming County   North central Pennsylvania, 60 mi/97 km west-southwest of Scranton*

fall 1777 Capt. John Brady builds Fort Brady, is killed two years later when ambushed by Native Americans, after which British and natives overrun region in so-called Big Runaway; **1797** town platted on West Branch Susquehanna River, at mouth of Muncy Creek, named Pennsborough; **1826** incorporated as a borough; **1827** borough renamed Muncy; **1938** the Last Raft, launched on West Branch to commemorate logging on river, departs McGees Mills carrying 48 passengers, 6 crew, crashes into railroad bridge at Muncy killing 10; **1965** Muncy Public Library founded.

Murrysville *Westmoreland County   West central Pennsylvania, 15 mi/24 km east of Pittsburgh*

1769 land purchased by Robert Hays; **1781** grist mill and store established by Jeremiah Murry; **1788** first wave of settlers arrives; **1819** Northern Turnpike built; **1820** town platted by Murry; Emmanuel Reformed Church organized; **1866** Pennsylvania Railroad reaches town; **1868** Methodist Church built, rebuilt 1913; **1878** first natural gas well bored by Michael and Obadiah Haymaker; speculation conflicts lead to deadly Haymaker Riots; **1880** United Presbyterian Church built; **1922** Murrysville Library founded; **1976** incorporated as a city.

New Bloomfield *Perry County   Central Pennsylvania, 19 mi/31 km northwest of Harrisburg*

1820 Perry County formed; Landisburg becomes first county seat; **1825** town platted; **1826** county seat moved to New Bloomfield; county courthouse built; **1931** incorporated as a borough; **1837** New Bloomfield Academy established, becomes Carson Long Institute military academy 1917; **1986** New Bloomfield Public Library founded.

New Castle *Lawrence County   Western Pennsylvania, 43 mi/69 km north-northwest of Pittsburgh*

1756 site becomes chief town of Delaware peoples following destruction of Kittanning Native American community by Col. John Armstrong; **1798** site surveyed by John Stewart as free land for Revolutionary War veterans; Stewart builds iron furnace, names site for Newcastle, England; **1825** incorporated as a borough; becomes important iron production center; **1833** Erie Extension Canal is completed, stimulating economic growth; **1840** White Homestead built; **1849** Lawrence County formed; town becomes county seat; **1852** county courthouse built; **1859** incorporated as a city; **1863** brick Ten-Sided House built by Frank Phillis on theory that the devil could never corner him there; **1911** New Castle Public Library founded; **1925** Scottish Rite Cathedral completed; **1929** Italian immigrants brought in as strikebreakers; **1931** Carnegie Steel Plant shut down, followed by 1937 and 1941 closings of two other Carnegie plants; **1958** New Castle Playhouse established; **July 7, 1963** Marine Fury jet crashes into Willow Grove camp to southwest, killing seven on ground, pilot bails out; **1965** Hoyt Institute of Fine Arts founded; **1987** Parou Ballet Company founded.

New Cumberland *Cumberland County   Southern Pennsylvania, 2 mi/3.2 km south of Harrisburg*

1725 Peter Chartier becomes first settler; **1738** Shawnees abandon village here on Susquehanna River, opposite Harrisburg; **1801** Jacob Haldeman settles here; **1811** town platted by Haldeman; **1819** Benjamin House built, used as Public Library from 1976; **1831** incorporated as a borough; **1888** New Cumberland Army Base established, becomes New Cumberland Army Depot 1918, Defense Distribution Center 1991; **1936** Harrisburg Airport established, later renamed Capital City Airport; **1941** New Cumberland Public Library founded; **1986** first annual Apple Festival held.

New Kensington *Westmoreland County   Western Pennsylvania, 14 mi/23 km northeast Pittsburgh*

1778 Fort Crawford built on Allegheny River; **1888** discovery of aluminum processing method by Charles M. Hall leads to founding of Aluminum Corporation of America 1892; **1891** town platted on site of fort; **1928** Peoples Library founded; **1934** incorporated as a city; **March 21, 1929** explosion at Kinlock Coal Mines, 46 killed.

Newtown *Bucks County   Southeastern Pennsylvania, 22 mi/35 km north-northeast of Philadelphia*

1682 Bucks County formed; **1684** area settled; town founded; **1725** county seat moved from Bristol; county courthouse built; **1813** county seat moved to Doylestown; **1838** incorporated as a borough; **1964** Bucks County Community College established; **1974** Newtown Public Library founded.

Norristown *Montgomery County   Southeastern Pennsylvania, 14 mi/23 km northwest of Philadelphia*

1704 Isaac Norris and William Trent purchase tract of land on north bank of Schuylkill River from William

Penn, Jr.; site named Williamstown; **1712** Norris buys Trent's land interest, builds grist mill; town founded around mill, renamed Norris; **Dec. 13, 1777** Washington's troops cross Schuylkill River here on way to Valley Forge; **1784** Montgomery County formed; town becomes county seat; **1794** Norristown Public Library founded; **1799** *Gazette* newspaper founded, one of oldest in U.S.; **1803** Norris Academy founded; **1812** incorporated as a borough, renamed Norristown; **1883** Borough Hall built; **1894** Borough Market built; **1904** county courthouse built, annex built 1930.

North East *Erie County Northwestern Pennsylvania, 14 mi/23 km east-northeast of Erie, on Lake Erie*

1778 land purchased from Iroquois; **1801** area settled; **1809** two taverns established to cater to land travelers; **1833** Brawley House hotel built; **1834** incorporated as a borough; **1850** area's first vineyard planted by vintners Hammond and Griffith; **1869** South Shore Wine Company established, first of several in region; **1899** McCord Memorial Library founded; **1911** Welch's Grape Juice Company plant established; **1984** first Wine Country Festival held.

Northampton *Northampton County Eastern Pennsylvania, 6 mi/9.7 km north of Allentown*

1739 Old Log Fort built on Hokendauqua Creek; **1756** blockhouse built by Hugh Wilson; **c.1760** area settled; **1895** Atlas Cement Plant established by Jose Navarro, region designated as "cement belt," plant closed 1912; **1902** incorporated as a borough, originally named Alliance; **1908** region provides cement for Panama Canal; **1909** borough renamed Northampton; **1921** Lyric Theatre opened, renamed Roxy 1933; **1997** Memorial Museum founded.

Oil City *Venango County Northwestern Pennsylvania, 50 mi/80 km south-southeast of Erie*

Aug. 27, 1859 Edwin L. Drake strikes oil at nearby Titusville; town founded at mouth of Oil Creek, on Allegheny River; **1862** Andrew Carnegie buys farm for $40,000, value rises to $5 million with oil production; **1871** incorporated as a city; **1885** world price of oil controlled by Oil City; **June 5, 1892** collapse of Spartansburg Dam on Oil Creek floods town, mixes with naphtha gas resulting in series of explosions, 72 killed, over 500 left homeless.

Paoli *Chester County Southeastern Pennsylvania, 17 mi/27 km west-northwest of Philadelphia*

c.1685 area settled by Welsh; **1710** Great Valley Mill built by Thomas Jarman; **c.1795** Paoli Tavern built by Corsican Gen. Pasquale Paoli, destroyed by fire 1906; town founded around tavern; **Sept. 20, 1777** General Wayne soundly defeated by British, referred to as Paoli Massacre, 300

Americans killed; **1855** Goshen Friends Meeting House built.

Pen Argyl *Northampton County Eastern Pennsylvania, 22 mi/35 km northeast of Allentown*

1757 Native Americans make last raid in area, four settlers killed, two kidnapped, taken to Canada; **1854** first slate quarry opened; **1868** town founded, settled by Welsh slate miners; **1880** Delaware, Lackawanna & Western Railroad; **1882** incorporated as a borough; **1884** Correll's Opera House built; **1899** trolley service begins, abandoned 1920 shortly after trolley shed fire; **1907** Realty Building built; **1909** town hall completed; **1920s** quarrying activity slows.

Philadelphia *Philadelphia County Southeastern Pennsylvania, on Delaware River*

1643 Tinicum becomes first European settlement in Pennsylvania; **1682** Philadelphia County formed; town founded by William Penn as refuge for Society of Friends (Quakers), source of nickname "Quaker City," adopts pattern of streets and squares already drawn by Thomas Holme, chooses name meaning "City of Brotherly Love"; town becomes county seat; **1688** Quakers hold first ever antislavery protest at Friends' Yearly Meeting; **1700** Betsy Ross House built; Old Swedes (Gloria Dei) Church built; **1701** incorporated as a city; **1721** Cedar Grove Mansion built; **1728** Samuel Keimer founds the *Philadelphia Gazette* newspaper; **1731** Bartram's Gardens established; **1732** Benjamin Franklin publishes *Poor Richard's Almanac*, through 1757; Philadelphia General Hospital has its beginnings as an almshouse; **Sept. 21, 1737** author Francis Hopkinson born, signer of Declaration of Independence (died 1791); **March 16, 1739** merchant George Clymer born, signer of Declaration of Independence (died 1813); **1740** University of Pennsylvania established; **1741** Independence Hall completed; **1743** Philosophical Hall built, housed Benjamin Franklin's American Philosophical Society founded same year; Mary Jemison born at sea on approach to Philadelphia from Belfast, later captured, adopted by Shawnee, marries two Seneca husbands (died 1833); **Jan. 4, 1746** physician Dr. Benjamin Rush born (died 1813); **1751** Pennsylvania Hospital founded; **Jan. 2, 1752** seamstress Betsy Ross (Elizabeth Griscom) born, designed U.S. flag (died 1836); **June 15, 1752** Benjamin Franklin flies kite during thunderstorm, captures electrical charge in jar; **1754** Christ Church completed; **1760** Germantown Academy established; **1761** St. Peter's Episcopal Church completed; St. Paul's Episcopal Church built; **1763** St. Mary's Catholic Church built; **Sept. 2, 1766** African-American abolitionist, philanthropist James Forten born (died 1842); **1770** First Church of the Brethren completed; **1771** Fort Mifflin established; *Philadelphia Inquirer* newspaper founded; **Sept. 5-Oct. 26, 1774** First Continental Congress held at Carpenters' Hall (built 1774); **Nov. 1774** Thomas Paine arrives from England, becomes first advocate for colonial independence (born Jan. 29, 1737, died 1809); **1775** city becomes Nation's Capital; **March 10, 1775–Dec. 12, 1776** Second Continental Congress held; **June 14, 1775** George Washington named commander in chief by Continental Congress; **July 2, 1776** Continental Congress adopts resolutions leading to independence; **July 4, 1776** Declaration of Independence adopted; **June 4, 1777** Fourth Continental Congress convenes; **June 14, 1777** Continental Congress adopts Stars and Stripes flag; **Sept. 18, 1777** Congress evacuates to Lancaster as British occupy city; **Oct. 4, 1777** George Washington's attack on British in Battle of Germantown ends inconclusively; **June 18, 1778** British evacuate Philadelphia after arrival of French fleet under Adm. d'Estaing; **July 2, 1778-June 21, 1783** Seventh Continental Congress convenes; **Aug. 29, 1780** Richard Rush born, Attorney General under President Madison, secretary of state under President Monroe (died 1859); **March 1782** U.S. independence recognized in London by new British government; **Oct. 3, 1782** Cong. Charles Ingersoll born (died 1862); **Sept. 21, 1784** *Pennsylvania Packet and General Advertiser* established, first profitable daily newspaper in U.S.; **May 14, 1787** Constitutional Convention opens with George Washington presiding; **Aug. 22, 1787** John Fitch demonstrates his steamboat on Delaware River; **Sept. 18, 1787** U.S. Constitution adopted by Congress, sent to individual states for ratification; **Dec. 10, 1787** educator of the deaf Thomas Hopkins Gallaudet born, Gallaudet University, Washington, D.C., named for him (died 1851); **June 21, 1788** U.S. Constitution officially adopted with ratification by New Hampshire, 9th state to adopt it; **1789** Nation's Capital moved to New York; **1790** John Fitch operates first steamboat service between Philadelphia and Trenton, New Jersey; Penitentiary House built; **July 10, 1791** old city hall built; U.S. military frigate *United States* launched; **1792** Carpenters' Hall completed; **Apr. 2, 1792** first U.S. Mint established; **July 10, 1792** Sen. George Mifflin Dallas born, vice president under Polk (died 1864); **1792–1793** yellow fever epidemic takes 5,000 lives; **1793** U.S. Mint established, building built 1833; **July 19, 1793** painter Thomas Doughty born, founded Hudson River School of painting (died 1856); **1794** turnpike completed to Lancaster; **1797** First Bank built, perhaps oldest bank building in U.S.; **Dec. 12, 1797** Pennsylvania becomes second state to ratify U.S. Constitution; **1799** state capital moved to Lancaster; **1800** Schuylkill Arsenal built; **1801** Navy Ship Yard opened, first ship houses built 1821; **Dec. 7, 1801** abolitionist Abigail Hopper Gibbons born (died 1893); **1804** Arch Street Friends Meeting House built; **1805** Academy of Fine Arts founded; **March 9, 1806** actor Edwin Forrest born (died 1872); **July 19, 1806** physicist Alexander Bache born (died 1867); **Nov. 13, 1809** naval officer John A. B. Dahlgren born, invented Dahlgren gun used in Civil War (died 1870); **June 14, 1812** New York Cong., New York City Mayor Fernando Wood born (died 1881); **1821** University of the Sciences established; **1824** Thomas Jefferson University established; Science Museum of the Franklin Institute founded, building opened 1934; **May 29, 1825** Union Gen. David Birney born (died 1864); **Sept. 13, 1826** banker, philanthropist Anthony Drexel born (died 1893); **Dec. 3, 1826** Union

Gen. George McClellan born (died 1885); **May 11, 1827** songwriter Septimus Winner born, wrote "Listen to the Mockingbird," "Where Oh Where Has My Little Dog Gone?" (died 1903); **1829** Eastern State Penitentiary opened, closed 1970, reopened 1994 as historic site; **Nov. 8, 1831** Minnesota Cong. Ignatius Donnelly born (died 1901); **1832** cholera epidemic claims 800 lives; St. John the Evangelist Church built; **Nov. 29, 1832** author Louisa May Alcott born (died 1888); **1835** Liberty Bell cracks while tolling for death of Chief Justice John Marshall; **July 11, 1838** merchant John Wanamaker born (died 1922); **1840** log-cabin-shaped glass bottles made in Glassboro, New Jersey, for William Henry Harrison's presidential campaign filled here by distiller E. C. Booz, origin of term "booze," first coined 1812 by evangelist Parson Weems; **Aug. 10, 1843** Supreme Court Justice Joseph McKenna born (died 1926); **1847** St. Augustine's Catholic Church built; **1848** Hahnemann University established; **Feb. 12, 1850** geographer William Morris Davis born (died 1916); **1851** St. Joseph's University established; **1854** Philadelphia County formed; Consolidation Act extends city limits to county line, becoming largest Pennsylvania city in land area (153.1 sq mi/217.4 sq km); **July 9, 1856** mining, smelting industrialist Daniel Guggenheim born (died 1930); **Sept. 28, 1856** writer Kate D. Wiggins born (died 1923); **1857** Academy of Music opened; **Jan. 5, 1857** baritone David Bispham born (died 1921); **Nov. 26, 1858** Katherine Drexel born, founder of Sisters of Blessed Sacrament for Indians and Colored People (died 1953); **Sept. 12, 1859** social activist Florence Kelley born, spoke against exploitation of child and women laborers (died 1932); **1861** Jay Cooke establishes banking firm Jay Cooke & Company; **1863** La Salle University established; painter Cecilia Beaux born (died 1942); **June 15, 1863** general call for 100,000 militia, all business suspended with news of General Lee's march across Maryland; **1865** Peirce College established; **1870** University of the Arts established; **March 13, 1870** painter William Glackens born (died 1938); **1874** Philadelphia Zoological Gardens opens; **July 1, 1874** Charles B. Ross, four years old, is kidnapped in Germantown and never found, $20,000 ransom not paid, abductors later shot in robbery; **May 2, 1875** Supreme Court Justice Owen J. Roberts born (died 1955); **1877** Philadelphia Museum of Art (Memorial Hall) opened; **Apr. 28, 1878** actor Lionel Barrymore born (died 1954); **Apr. 9, 1879** comic actor W. C. Fields born (died 1946); **Aug. 15, 1879** actress Ethel Barrymore born (died 1959); **Sept. 30, 1882** actor George Bancroft born (died 1956); **July 31, 1882** physicist Herbert Eugene Ives born, developed television (died 1953); **1884** Temple University established; Philadelphia College of Textiles and Science established; **Apr. 12, 1887** baseball manager Joe McCarthy born (died 1978); **Jan. 24, 1895** artist George Biddle born (died 1973); **Nov. 9, 1886** actor Ed Wynn born (died 1966); **1891** Drexel University established; **1892** city's first trolley car installed; Philadelphia Free Library founded; **1893** Reading Railroad terminal built; **1894** basic construction of city hall completed with hoisting in place of William Penn statue atop building;

Feb. 24, 1894 football commissioner Bert Bell born (died 1959); Dec. 7, 1894 abstract painter Stuart Davis born (died 1964); Feb. 27, 1897 African-American opera singer Marian Anderson born (died 1993); Apr. 19, 1897 actress Vivienne Segal born (died 1992); July 22, 1898 sculptor Alexander Calder born (died 1971); 1900 Philadelphia Symphony Orchestra founded at Academy of Music; Apr. 1, 1901 editor, author Whittaker Chambers born, convicted of being Communist spy 1950 (died 1961); Dec. 16, 1901 anthropologist Margaret Mead born (died 1978); 1902 Philadelphia Rapid Transit Company chartered; 1903 actress Jeannette MacDonald born (died 1965); Sept. 15, 1908 actress Penny Singleton born (died 2003); Nov. 6, 1906 actress Janet Gaynor born (died 1986); 1908 Metropolitan Opera House built for Oscar Hammerstein; Nov. 18, 1908 actress, comedian Imogene Coca born (died 2001); Apr. 25, 1910 painter Joseph Hirsch born (died 1981); Dec. 9, 1911 actor Broderick Crawford (died 1986); Aug. 1, 1912 actor Henry Jones born (died 1999); Apr. 7, 1915 jazz singer Billie Holiday (Eleanora Hagan) born (died 1959); Apr. 10. 1917 explosion at Eddystone Ammunition Works kills over 100 employees; Jan. 15, 1920 Catholic cardinal John Joseph O'Connor born (died 2000); May 10, 1921 TV actress Nancy Walker born (died 1992); Nov. 19, 1921 baseball player Roy Campanella born, paralyzed waist down in car accident Jan. 1958 (died 1993); 1922 Samuel Fleischer Art Memorial school and gallery established; June 27, 1922 actor Jack Klugman born; Sept. 27, 1922 movie director Arthur Penn born; 1924 Chestnut Hill College established; March 24, 1924 TV actor Norman Fell born (died 1999); June 25, 1924 movie director Sidney Lumet born; Dec. 2, 1924 army Gen. Alexander Haig, Jr. born; 1926 Delaware River Bridge completed to Camden, New Jersey, later renamed Ben Franklin Bridge; 1925 Philadelphia Municipal Airport established at Hog Island to south, opening delayed until 1940, becomes International Airport 1945; 1926 American Swedish Historical Museum opened; Aug. 14, 1926 singer Buddy Greco born; 1927 Philadelphia Free Library completed; Oct. 7, 1927 singer Al Martino born; 1928 Philadelphia Museum of Art opens, founded 1876; Aug. 10, 1928 singer Eddie Fisher born; 1929 Rodin Museum opened; Tacony-Palmyra Bridge built across Delaware River to Palmyra, New Jersey; Nov. 12, 1929 actress, Princess of Monaco Grace Kelly born, killed in auto crash in France Sept. 14, 1982; June 6, 1930 astronaut Charles Conrad born; Dec. 13, 1930 actor Robert Prosky born; 1931 convention hall opens; Apr. 21, 1932 comedian Elaine May born; Oct. 18, 1933 actor Peter Boyle born; Sept. 2, 1935 actor Henry Gibson born in Germantown; June 8, 1936 actor James Darren born; Aug. 21, 1936 basketball player Wilt Chamberlain born (died 1999); July 12, 1937 comedian Bill Cosby born; Feb. 1, 1938 TV actor Sherman Hemsley born; 1939 federal building built; Sept. 18, 1939 singer Frankie Avalon born; June 22, 1941 newscaster Ed Bradley born; Oct. 3, 1941 singer Chubby Checker born; Apr. 26, 1942 singer Bobby Rydell born; Feb. 6, 1943 singer Fabian (Fabian Forte) born; Sept. 6, 1943 railroad accident in North Philadelphia kills 79; Nov. 20, 1943 actress Veronica Hamel born; Feb. 3, 1944 actress Blythe Danner born; Oct. 4, 1944 singer Patti LaBelle born; Feb. 4, 1945 comedian David Brenner born; Sept. 11, 1946 actress Lola Falana born; June 28, 1948 Independence National Historical Park established, includes Independence Hall, Liberty Bell Pavilion, other sites; Aug. 31, 1949 actor Richard Gere born; March 26, 1950 singer Teddy Pendergrass born; June 4, 1952 actor Parker Stevenson born; 1954 Holy Family College established; 1955 Historical Commission established; May 17, 1956 actor Bob Saget born; 1957 Walt Whitman Bridge completed to Camden, New Jersey; July 8, 1958 actor Kevin Bacon born; Nov. 5, 1963 actress Andrea McArdle born; Jan. 15, 1963 transit strike halts bus, streetcar, subway service, resumes Feb. 3; 1945 Northeast Philadelphia Airport established; 1964 Community College of Philadelphia established; Aug. 28–30, 1964 riots in North Philadelphia result of false report of police killing, 500 injured; 1966 Art Institute of Philadelphia (2-year college) established; 1967 Spectrum Sports Arena opened; June 5, 1967 40 million people left without power for 10 hours in Eastern Pennsylvania, New Jersey, Delaware, and Maryland after three generators fail; Sept. 22, 1969 singer Joan Jett born; Sept. 25, 1969 singer, actor Will Smith born; 1970 Parker Avenue Marine Terminal established; May 11, 1970 oil refinery explosion kills 7, injures 42; 1971 Franklin Park renewal project begun; Veterans Stadium opened, home of Phillies baseball team; Sept. 14, 1971 flash flooding from heavy rains, 12 killed; Oct. 21, 1972 Thaddeus Kosciuszko National Memorial established; Sept. 13, 1973 nursing home fire kills 11, injures 3; 1976 Betsy Ross Bridge completed to New Jersey; National Museum of Jewish History established; July 21–24, 1976 American Legion convention at Bellevue Stratford Motel hit with 179 cases of previously unknown Legionnaires Disease, blamed on bacteria in air cooling system, 28 die; Feb. 11–12, 1983 21 in/53 cm of snow, falls, Philadelphia's worst blizzard since 1947, 11 dead; May 13, 1985 standoff with MOVE black radical group ends in fire started by incendiary device dropped on house by police, 60 other houses in two block area destroyed, 11 group members killed; July 13, 1985 Live Aid concert co-broadcast from Philadelphia and London, raises $70 million for African famine victims; 1990 city narrowly averts bankruptcy; 1991 U.S. Navy Shipyard closes; 2001 Regional Performing Arts Center established at Academy of Music; Dec. 2001 Kimmel Center opened, home of Philadelphia Symphony; Aug. 2003 Lincoln Financial Field stadium opened, home of Phillies baseball team.

Phoenixville *Chester County Southeastern Pennsylvania, 22 mi/35 km northwest of Philadelphia*

1720 area first settled by German Rev. Francis Buckwalter; 1849 incorporated as a borough; c.1855 town becomes iron manufacturing center; 1886 manufacture of steel begins; July 10, 1936 highest temperature ever recorded in Pennsylvania reached, 111°F/44°C; 1958 iron industry ends; 1987 steel industries close.

Pittsburgh   *Allegheny County*   Western
Pennsylvania, where Allegheny and Monongahela rivers join to form Ohio River

1714 first European hunters and trappers enter region; **1748** land granted by George II of England to Ohio Land Company; **1754** French and Indian War begins, French capture British outpost, name it Fort Duquesne; **July 9, 1755** Gen. Edward Braddock ambushed by French and Native Americans to southeast, most of his troops slaughtered; **Nov. 25, 1758** French burn Fort Duquesne as they surrender to British Brig. Gen. John Forbes; British establish Fort Pitt; **1759** trading post and village established at Fort Pitt; **1763** villagers destroy own homes, take refuge in fort under threat during Pontiac's War; **1764** town platted by Col. John Campbell; **1783** first stone house built; **July 29, 1786** *Gazette* becomes first newspaper published west of Alleghenies; Pittsburgh Academy founded; **1787** Allegheny Town platted north of Allegheny River; University of Pittsburgh established; **1788** Allegheny County formed; town becomes county seat; **1789** First Presbyterian Church built; **1794** incorporated as a borough; **1809** Oliver Evans employs steam engine to operate grist mill; **1811** the *New Orleans* built, first steamboat to ply western rivers; **Aug. 22, 1811** blast furnace process inventor William Kelly born, lost patent to Henry Bessemer (died 1888); **1816** incorporated as a city; **1817** Pittsburgh-Harrisburg Turnpike opens; **July 4, 1826** Stephen Foster born at Lawrenceville, now part of Pittsburgh, America's first popular song writer (died 1864); **July 8, 1826** Union Gen. Benjamin Henry Grierson born (died 1911); **1839** the *Valley Forge* launched, first iron-hulled vessel built in U.S. of iron mined in U.S.; **Dec. 8, 1839** Pennsylvania Railroad executive Alexander Johnston Cassatt born (died 1906); **May 22, 1844** artist Mary Cassatt born at Allegheny (died 1926); **March 24, 1855** industrialist Andrew William Mellon born, secretary of treasury under Presidents Harding and Coolidge (died 1937); **1858** United Sons of Vulcan organized, parent to United Steelworkers' Union; **Sept. 19, 1858** George Wickersham born, Attorney General under President Taft (died 1936); **1865** Pennsylvania Railroad Terminal built; **1872** Trinity Episcopal Cathedral completed; **Feb. 3, 1874** author Gertrude Stein born at Allegheny (died 1946); **Aug. 12, 1876** mystery writer Mary Roberts Rinehart born (died 1958); **July 29, 1877** railroad strike turns violent, militia called out, 50 killed or injured; **1878** Duquesne University established; **1881** meeting held by Samuel Gompers combining eight trade unions into Federation of Organized Trades and Labor Unions; **June 23, 1884** *The Pittsburgh Press* newspaper founded; **Jan. 10, 1887** poet Robinson Jeffers born (died 1962); **1888** county courthouse completed; **Nov. 16, 1889** playwright George S. Kaufman born (died 1961); **Dec. 8, 1889** poet, novelist Harvey Allen born (died 1949); **1892** actor William Powell born (died 1984); **July 23, 1892** Henry Frick, chairman of Carnegie Steel, shot and wounded by business associate Alexander Berkman; **May 11, 1894** dancer, choreographer Martha Graham born (died 1992); **June 6, 1894** boxer Harry Greb born (died 1926); **1895** Pittsburgh Symphony Orchestra founded; Carnegie Library founded; **1900** Carnegie Mellon University established; **May 10, 1902** movie producer David O. Selznick born (died 1965); **1904** Frick Building built by Henry Frick; **1907** Allegheny, third-largest city in Pennsylvania, annexed by Pittsburgh; **1912** Allegheny Observatory built in Riverview Park; **Aug. 23, 1912** entertainer Gene Kelly born (died 1996); **July 8, 1914** entertainer Billy Eckstine born (died 1993); **Apr. 13, 1919** atheist leader Madelyn Murray O'Hair born, disappeared 1995, feared murdered; **1920** National Museum of Broadcasting founded; **Feb. 18, 1920** TV personality Bill Cullen born (died 1990); **1921** Art Institute of Pittsburgh (2-year college) established; Robert Morris College established, becomes University 2002; **Sept. 3, 1925** actress Anne Jackson born at Allegheny, now part of Pittsburgh; **Jan. 19, 1926** actor Fritz Weaver born; **Oct. 13, 1926** actor Ray Brown born (died 1995); **1927** German Protestant Church built; **Aug. 6, 1928** pop artist Andy Warhol born (died 1987); **1929** Carlow College established; **March 17, 1930** astronaut James Irwin born; **1931** Federal Reserve Bank built; **July 24, 1931** fire at home for aged kills 48; **1932** Gulf Oil Building built; **May 7, 1933** Johnny Unitas born, star quarterback for Baltimore Colts football team (died 2002); **Apr. 5, 1934** actor Frank Gorshin born; **Apr. 21, 1935** actor Charles Grodin born; **1936** St. Patrick's Day flood inundates The Triangle city center; **1937** Mellon Institute for industrial research dedicated; **Oct. 24, 1939** actor F. Murray Abraham born; **Feb. 12, 1941** TV actress Barbara Feldon born; **Dec. 13, 1941** singer John Davidson born; **Jan. 26, 1942** actor Scott Glenn born; **March 22, 1943** singer George Benson born; **1946** Pittsburgh Technical Institute (2-year) established; **Sept. 8, 1951** actor Michael Keaton born; **Oct. 22, 1952** actor Jeff Goldblum born; **Nov. 3, 1953** comedian Dennis Miller born; **Nov. 7, 1959** 80-day injunction halts longest steel strike in history on 116th day; **1960** Point Park College established; **1963** La Roche College established; **1966** Community College of Allegheny County established; **1970** Three Rivers Stadium opened, home of Pirates baseball and Steelers football teams; **1971** Heinz Hall for the Performing Arts dedicated, originally Loew's Penn Theater built 1927; **March 12, 1970** bomb blast damages 23 stores, part of nationwide rash of bombings; **1994** Andy Warhol Museum founded; **Sept. 8, 1994** US Air Boeing 737 crashes near Pittsburgh Airport killing 132; **2001** PNC Park stadium opened, home of Pirates baseball team; **2002** Heinz Field stadium opened, home of Steelers football team.

Plymouth   *Luzerne County*   Northeastern
Pennsylvania, 20 mi/32 km southwest of Scranton

1742 Moravian missionary Nicholas Louis Zinzendorf arrives, preaches to Shawnee and Delaware; **1769** town founded on Susquehanna River, settled by Welsh and Polish immigrants; **1806** Abijah Smith becomes first to exploit anthracite coal deposits; **1866** incorporated as a borough; **Sept. 6, 1869** fire at Avondale Anthracite Coal

Mine, 110 killed; **1938** Plymouth Public Library founded, new library opened 1968; **1940** flooding inundates town.

Portage *Cambria County Central Pennsylvania, 14 mi/23 km west-southwest of Altoona*

1794 land grant made to Arent Sonman; **1826** Washington House hotel built; **1834** railroad portage completed across Allegheny Mountain ridge, final link in Allegheny Canal; **1874** Sonman Coal Mine opened; **1890** incorporated as a borough; **1927** Portage Public Library founded; **July 15, 1940** fire at Sonman Mine, 63 killed.

Pottstown *Montgomery County Southeastern Pennsylvania, 33 mi/53 km northwest of Philadelphia*

c.1700 area first settled; town founded by Samuel Potts; **1716** Pennsylvania's first iron works established by Thomas Rutter; **1752** Mill Park Hotel built; **1754** Pottsgrove Manor built by ironmaster John Potts; **1796** Union Church built, used jointly by Lutheran and Reformed congregations; **1815** incorporated as a borough; **1838** Shenkel Reformed Church built; **1920** Pottstown Public Library founded; **Oct. 11, 1948** singer Daryl Hall of duo Hall and Oates born.

Pottsville *Schuylkill County East central Pennsylvania, 47 mi/76 km northeast of Harrisburg*

1780 family of first settler Henry Neyman killed by Native Americans; **1806** John Pott buys land on West Branch Schuylkill River, founds town; **1811** Schuylkill County formed; Orwigsburg becomes county seat; **1816** town platted; **c.1820** Benjamin Pott House built; **1824** coal boom begins, through 1829; **1847** incorporated as a borough; **1851** county seat moved to Pottsville; county courthouse completed; **July 1877** Molly Maguires, Irish miners' group, hold rallies protesting absentee landlords and unscrupulous mining agents, six Mollies hanged for murder; **Jan. 31, 1905** author John O'Hara born (died 1970); **1911** Pottsville Free Public Library founded; **1913** incorporated as a city.

Punxsutawney *Jefferson County West central Pennsylvania, 64 mi/103 km northeast of Pittsburgh*

1772 town settled by Moravian Rev. John Ettwein with 241 Christianized Delawares; **c.1818** town platted; **1850** incorporated as a borough; **1886** first local observance of Ground Hog Day based on German custom, with the perennial groundhog Punxsutawney Phil's shadow serving as indicator of late spring.

Reading *Berks County Southeastern Pennsylvania, 48 mi/77 km northwest of Philadelphia*

1733 William Penn sends two relatives to acquire tract from Lenape peoples; **1748** town platted by Nicholas Scull and William; **1750s** Germans settle here in large numbers; **1752** Berks County formed; Reading becomes county seat; **Apr. 1775** town sends two regiments to fight at Cambridge, Massachusetts; **Nov. 25, 1777** meeting takes place at home of Thomas Mifflin of those involved in the Conway Cabal, plan to ouster George Washington as Commander of Revolution in favor of Gen. Horatio Gates following defeats at Brandywine and Germantown; **1783** incorporated as a borough; **1793** Holy Trinity Lutheran Church completed; **c.1805** hat manufacturing begins, one of town's dominant industries; **1816–1817** Berks and Dauphin Turnpike built; **Feb. 3, 1823** zoologist Spencer F. Baird born (died 1887); **1829** Pennsylvania Canal system completed; **1831** bridge built across Schuylkill River; **1838** Philadelphia & Reading Railroad completed; **1847** incorporated as a city; **1850** town becomes leading iron industry center; **1856** Albright College established; **1857** Skew Arch railroad bridge built over Sixth Street; **1867** Reading Hospital founded at West Reading; Wertz's (Red) Covered Bridge built; **1873** J. T. Adams Pretzel Bakery founded; **July 1877** militia quells railroad strike unrest, 10 killed; **Oct. 2, 1879** poet Wallace Stevens born (died 1955); **1882** Gruber Wagon Works established; **1884** Pennsylvania Railroad opens division headquarters; **1898** Reading Public Library founded; **1904** Reading Museum and Art Gallery founded at West Reading; **1908** The Pagoda built as hotel, later donated to city as observation tower; **1924** Pennsylvania State University Berks Campus–Lehigh Valley College established; **May 22, 1927** actor Michael Constantine born; **1932** 19-story county courthouse built; **1936** Reading Regional Airport established; **Feb. 4, 1952** actress Lisa Eichhorn born; **1958** Alvernia College established; **1966** presidential commission probes police corruption, many police and city officials jailed; **1971** Reading Area Community College established; **1973** extensive flooding occurs from Hurricane Agnes; **1986** Hiester Canal Museum opened.

Ridgway *Elk County Northern Pennsylvania, 67 mi/108 km north-northwest of Altoona*

1817 Jacob Ridgway purchases land on Clarion River; **1822** first settlers arrive; **1826** town founded; **1833** town platted; **1843** Elk County formed; town becomes county seat; **Sept. 11, 1853** Populist Movement leader Mary Elizabeth Lease born (died 1933); **1880** county courthouse built; **1881** incorporated as a borough; **1904** Ridgway Public Library founded, building opened 1922.

Saint Marys *Elk County Northern Pennsylvania, 65 mi/105 km north of Altoona*

1842 settled by German Catholics from Baltimore and Philadelphia; **1844** town platted; **1848** incorporated as a borough; **1860s** Irish Catholics arrive with building of railroads; **1921** Saint Marys Public Library founded; **1994** Benzinger Township merges with Borough of St. Marys, reincorporated as City of St. Marys, at 99.3 sq mi/159.8 sq km, second largest city in land area in Pennsylvania after Philadelphia.

Schuylkill Haven   *Schuylkill County*   *East central Pennsylvania, 45 mi/72 km northeast of Harrisburg*

1748 area first settled by John Fincher, Quaker from Chester; **1755** log Zion Lutheran Church built, replaced 1884 by frame structure (Old Red Church); **1825** Schuylkill Canal completed; **1829** town platted; **1841** incorporated as a borough; **1934** Pennsylvania State University Schuylkill Campus established; Schuylkill Haven Free Public Library founded; **June 3, 1959** 10 killed as propane gas truck explodes 30 minutes after collision with tractor trailer.

Scranton   *Lackawanna County*   *Northeastern Pennsylvania, 105 mi/169 km north-northwest of Philadelphia*

1798 Ebenezer and Benjamin Slocum found town of Unionville; **1800** Slocums build forge and distillery; **1816** town renamed Slocum Hollow; **1840** George and Selden Scranton arrive from New Jersey, build iron forge for making railroad track, becomes Lackawanna Iron & Steel Company; **1845** town renamed Scranton; **1850** Pennsylvania Gravity Railroad reaches town, abandoned 1885; **1856** incorporated as a borough; **c.1860** five blast furnaces in operation; **1866** incorporated as a city; **1877** martial law declared to quell miners' strike unrest; **1878** Lackawanna County formed; city becomes county seat; **1883** Scranton Steel Company founded; **1884** county courthouse completed; **1887** University of Scranton established; **1893** Scranton Public Library built; **1894** Lackawanna Junior College established; **1902** Lackawanna Iron & Steel moves to Buffalo, blow to economy; **1908** Everhart Museum founded; **Apr. 7, 1911** fire at Price-Pancoast coal mine at Throop to northeast, 73 killed; **1915** Marywood University established; **Sept. 29, 1922** actress Lizabeth Scott born; **1925–1926** miners' strike lasts 170 days; **Nov. 20, 1942** Delaware Sen. Joseph Biden born; **1950** Memorial Stadium opened; **Oct. 18, 1986** Steamtown National Historic Site authorized; **1989** Lackawanna Stadium opened; **1994** Holocaust Museum founded; **1996** Houdini Museum founded.

Shamokin   *Northumberland County*   *Central Pennsylvania, 40 mi/64 km north-northeast of Harrisburg*

1835 town platted; **1840** coal mining begins; **1864** incorporated as a borough; **1873** St. Edward's Catholic Church built; **1884** Shamokin State Hospital founded, becomes Shamokin Area Community Hospital 1992; **1941** Shamokin and Coal Township Library founded; **1947** Palmer's Diner established; **1993** Shamokin Correctional Institute opened.

Shanksville   *Somerset County*   See **Somerset (2001)**

Shenandoah   *Schuylkill County*   *East central Pennsylvania, 52 mi/84 km northeast of Harrisburg*

1835 town settled; **1862** town platted; first large-scale coal mining begins attracting Welsh, Irish, and English immigrants; **1866** incorporated as a borough; **1883** fire destroys town; **1887** St. Michael's Greek Catholic Church built; **May 7, 1894** Catholic cardinal Francis Brennan born (died 1968); **Feb. 29, 1904** band leader, clarinetist James Francis "Jimmy" Dorsey born (died 1956); **Nov. 19, 1905** band leader, trombonist Thomas Francis "Tommy" Dorsey born (died 1957); **March 4, 1940** massive mine collapse involves 16 city blocks, affects 4,000 residents.

Shippensburg   *Cumberland County*   *Southern Pennsylvania, 37 mi/60 km west-southwest of Harrisburg*

1730 town founded by Edward Shippen; **1735** Widow Piper's Tavern built by Samuel Perry; **1750** Cumberland County formed; Piper's Tavern converted to county courthouse; **1751** county seat moved to Carlisle; **1853** incorporated as a borough; **1871** Shippensburg University of Pennsylvania established.

Smethport   *McKean County*   *Northern Pennsylvania, 87 mi/140 km east-southeast of Erie*

1804 McKean County formed; **1808** town platted, becomes county seat; named for Dutch agents Raymond and Theodore de Smeth; **1853** incorporated as a borough; **1860s** oil speculation boom goes bust after "bubble" bursts, area later becomes oil and natural gas producer; **1882** iron Kinzua Bridge (Erie Railroad) built across Kinzua Creek to southwest, replaced by steel bridge 1900; **1890** Hamlin Memorial Library founded; **Jan. 5, 1904** lowest temperature ever recorded in Pennsylvania reached, $-42°F/-41°C$; **1940** fourth county courthouse built.

Somerset   *Somerset County*   *South central Pennsylvania, 57 mi/92 km southeast of Pittsburgh*

1771 area first settled; **1787** Ulrich Bruner arrives, founds Brunerstown; **1795** Somerset County formed; town becomes county seat, renamed; **1804** incorporated as a borough; **1833** large part of town destroyed by fire; **1872** second fire destroys 150 buildings; **1907** third county courthouse built; **1941** Mary S. Biesecker Public Library founded, became Somerset County Library 1995; **2001** Somerset Wind Farm established, six wind turbines erected near Pennsylvania Turnpike providing power for 3,400 homes [see also Mill Run]; **Sept. 11, 2001** all 45 people on board United Airlines Boeing 757, Flight 93, from Newark, New Jersey, to Los Angeles, killed in suicide hijacking by terrorists linked to Al-Qaeda network operated from Afghanistan by Osama Bin Laden, possibly meant for attack on Washington, D.C., after making radical U-turn near Cleveland, crashes into wooded area near Shanksville, east of Somerset, plan foiled by passengers, coordinated with attacks on World Trade Center, New York, and Pentagon near Washington, three hijackers killed on this flight; **July 27–28, 2002** nine coal miners rescued after spending 77 hours in small air pocket at flooded Quecreek Mine to north, only 10 mi/16 km northwest of Flight 93 crash site of Sept. 11, 2001.

State College *Centre County* *Central Pennsylvania, 35 mi/56 km northeast of Altoona*

1855 Pennsylvania State University, University Park Campus, established as small farm school, present designation adopted 1874; **1859** first classes held at partially completed campus; town founded around new campus; **1896** incorporated as a borough; **1957** Schlow Memorial Library founded.

Stroudsburg *Monroe County* *Eastern Pennsylvania, 30 mi/48 km north-northeast of Allentown*

1738 area first settled; **1739** Daniel Brodhead establishes Moravian mission on creek named for him; **1750** wooden bridge built across Brodhead Creek; **1776** Col. Jacob Stroud, French and Indian War veteran, builds Fort Penn; **1778** survivors of Wyoming (Pennsylvania) Massacre take refuge at fort; **1795** Stroud Mansion built by Daniel Stroud; **1815** incorporated as a borough; **1836** Monroe County formed; town becomes county seat; **1856** Delaware & Cobb Railroad reaches town; **1882** freight station built for New York, Susquehanna & Western Railroad; **1890** county courthouse built; **1916** Stroudsburg Public Library founded; **1976** Monroe County Museum founded.

Sunbury *Northumberland County* *Central Pennsylvania, 42 mi/68 km north of Harrisburg*

1755 Fort Augusta built on Susquehanna River as protection against French and natives; **1772** Northumberland County formed; town platted by William Maclay; town becomes county seat; **1797** incorporated as a borough; **1866** county courthouse built; **July 4, 1883** Thomas Edison builds three-wire station extended to City Hotel to create first electrical power system in U.S.; **1921** incorporated as a city; **1937** John R. Kauffman, Jr. Public Library founded.

Swarthmore *Delaware County* *Southeastern Pennsylvania, 10 mi/16 km west-southwest of Philadelphia*

c.1650 Swarthmore Hall residence built by George Fox, founder of Society of Friends (Quakers); **1724** Benjamin West House built; **1807** snuff mill built in Possum Hollow; **1864** Swarthmore University established; **1893** incorporated as a borough; **1929** Swarthmore Public Library founded.

Throop *Lackawanna County* *See* **Scranton (1911)**

Tionesta *Forest County* *Northwestern Pennsylvania, 55 mi/89 km southeast of Erie, on Allegheny River*

1767 David Zeisberger establishes short-lived Moravian mission here; **c.1788** settlement begins on Allegheny River, at mouth of Tionesta Creek; originally named Goshgoning, later renamed Saqualinguent; **1830s** oil boom occurs with discovery of Bradford Oil Field; **1848**

Forest County formed; **1852** incorporated as a borough; **1868** county seat moved from Marienville; county courthouse built; **1969** Sarah Stewart Bovard Memorial Library opened.

Titusville *Crawford County* *Northwestern Pennsylvania, 40 mi/64 km southeast of Erie, on Oil Creek*

1796 area settled by Jonathan Titus and Samuel Kerr; **1809** town platted; **1847** incorporated as a borough; **1857** Edwin L. Drake arrives to search for oil under employ of Pennsylvania Rock Oil Company; **Aug. 27, 1859** Drake's first oil well starts regional boom, continues into 1860s; **1865** Samuel Van Syckel builds 4 mi/6.4 km oil pipeline, sparking violence between oil workers and teamsters; **1866** incorporated as a city; **Dec. 28, 1873** chemist William Draper Harkins born (died 1951); **1880** fire destroys part of town; **1891** oil production peaks; **1892** second town fire destroys remainder of boom era structures; **1901** Drake Memorial erected; **1904** Benson Memorial Library founded; **1963** Titusville Campus, University of Pittsburgh, established; **1950** last oil refinery closes.

Towanda *Bradford County* *Northeastern Pennsylvania, 47 mi/76 km northwest of Scranton*

1794 area first settled; **1812** Bradford County formed; town platted by William Means as county seat, originally named Meansville; **1828** incorporated as a borough, renamed Towanda (locally pronounced "town-day"); **March 12, 1847** fire destroys business district; **1850** county courthouse built; **1870** Troy becomes shared county seat with Towanda; carriage factory established; iron works established; **1873** Eureka Mower Company organized; **1880** Towanda Public Library founded; **1923** shared county seat status ends; Towanda remains sole county seat.

Tunkhannock *Wyoming County* *Northeastern Pennsylvania, 13 mi/21 km northwest of Scranton*

1775 first permanent settler Jeremiah Osterhout of Holland builds cabin on Susquehanna River, at mouth of Tunkhannock Creek; **1841** incorporated as a borough; **1842** Wyoming County formed; town becomes county seat; **1845** county courthouse built, additions made 1938, 1992; **1890** Tunkhannock Public Library founded.

Uniontown *Fayette County* *Southwestern Pennsylvania, 40 mi/64 km south-southeast of Pittsburgh*

1769 town founded Henry Beeson; **1783** Fayette County formed; town becomes county seat; **1796** incorporated as a borough; **Dec. 31, 1880** Gen. George C. Marshall born, U.S. Chief of Staff (died 1959); **Nov. 30, 1906** mystery writer John Dickson Carr born (died 1977); **1916** incorporated as a city; **1919** county courthouse built; **1944** Youghiogheny River Lake formed by dam to southeast inundating Great Crossings Stone Bridge built 1818.

PENNSYLVANIA

Valley Forge *Chester County* *Southeastern Pennsylvania, 17 mi/27 km west-northwest of Philadelphia*

1705 Old Camp Schoolhouse built; **c.1718** bloomery forge established on Valley Creek; **c.1742** first iron works established by Stephen Evans, Joseph Williams, and Daniel Walker, becomes Mount Joy Forge 1751; **1777–1778** George Washington and his troops winter here, 2,000 troops lost to elements, greater death toll than battles of Germantown and Brandywine combined; **July 4, 1976** Valley Forge National Historical Park authorized, formerly Valley Forge State Park; **1985** Freedoms Foundation at Valley Forge founded.

Wakefield *Lancaster County* See **Lancaster (1765)**

Warren *Warren County* *Northwestern Pennsylvania, 52 mi/84 km east-southeast of Erie*

1795 town platted on Allegheny River; **1784** Cornplanter Indian Settlement established on tract obtained through treaty by Chief Cornplanter (1750–1836), only Native American reserve in Pennsylvania; **1800** Warren County formed; **1819** county organized; town becomes county seat; **1831** Warren Public Library founded, first building opened 1884, second opened 1915; **1832** incorporated as a borough; **1860** oil boom occurs; **1877** county courthouse completed; **1965** Kinzua Dam built to east on Allegheny River forming large Allegheny Reservoir, extends into New York.

Washington *Washington County* *Southwestern Pennsylvania, 23 mi/37 km southwest of Pittsburgh*

1769 area settled; **1781** Washington County formed; town founded, becomes county seat; Washington and Jefferson College established; **1788** David Bradford House built; **1812** Le Moyne House built by abolitionist Dr. Francis J. Le Moyne; **1819** incorporated as a borough; **1870** Citizens Library founded; **1900** county courthouse built; **Nov. 28, 1908** explosion at Marianna Coal Mine to southeast, 154 killed; **Apr. 23, 1913** coal mine accident at Finleyville to northeast, 96 killed; **1924** incorporated as a city; **1963** Arden Trolley Museum opened, founded 1953.

Washington Crossing *Bucks County* *Southeastern Pennsylvania, 28 mi/45 km northeast of Philadelphia*

1702 Thompson-Neely House built by John Pidcock; Neely grist mill built on Pidcock Creek; **1757** Old Ferry House built; **1776** observation tower erected on Bowman's Hill to guard Delaware River ferries; **Dec. 25, 1776** Gen. George Washington crosses Delaware River with 2,400 men en route to Battle of Trenton; **1917** Washington Crossing State Park established; **c.1817** McConkey's Ferry Inn built, renamed Washington Crossing Inn 1877.

Wayne *Delaware County* *Southeastern Pennsylvania, 13 mi/21 km west-northwest of Philadelphia*

c.1685 settled by Welsh immigrants; **1724** Waynesborough home built by grandfather of Gen. Anthony Wayne; **Jan. 1, 1745** Gen. Anthony Wayne born, died at Erie 1796 fighting Native Americans, entombed at nearby St. David's Church 1809; **1880** town founded; **June 27, 1927** actress Anna Moffo born.

Waynesboro *Franklin County* *Southern Pennsylvania, 51 mi/82 km southwest of Harrisburg*

1797 town platted by John Wallace, originally named Waynesburg; **c.1810** Renfrew House built, becomes Renfrew Museum 1977; **1818** incorporated as a borough; **1831** borough renamed Waynesboro to overcome naming conflict; **July 23, 1863** Confederate Gen. Jubal Early's army of 75,000 enters town, forces housewives to bake bread for troops, remain for 15 days; **1921** Alexander Hamilton Memorial Free Library founded.

Waynesburg *Greene County* *Southwestern Pennsylvania, 40 mi/64 km south-southwest of Pittsburgh*

1796 Greene County formed; town platted, becomes county seat; town named for Gen. Anthony Wayne; **1797** first county courthouse built of logs, rebuilt 1800; **1816** incorporated as a borough; **1849** Waynesburg College established; **1851** third county courthouse built, original log courthouse still stands; **May 19, 1928** coal mine explosion at Mather Mine to northeast, 195 killed; **1944** Eva K. Bowlby Public Library founded; **Dec. 6, 1962** coal mine explosion kills 37 miners at Carmichaels to east; **Jan. 5, 1970** United Mine Workers' Union officer Joseph Yablonski, wife and 25-year-old daughter found shot to death at home in rural Clarksville to northeast [see Erie].

Wellsboro *Tioga County* *Northern Pennsylvania, 37 mi/60 km north-northwest of Williamsport*

1799 first settled by Benjamin W. Morris; town founded, named for Morris' wife's maiden name; **1804** Tioga County formed from Lycoming County; **1806** town platted by Morris; **1813** county organized; town becomes county seat; **1830** incorporated as a borough; **1835** county courthouse built; **1911** Green Free Library founded.

West Chester *Chester County* *Southeastern Pennsylvania, 23 mi/37 km west of Philadelphia*

1682 Chester County formed; Chester, on Delaware River, becomes county seat; **1789** Delaware County formed from Chester County; West Chester founded as new seat of Chester County; **1799** incorporated as a borough; **1812** West Chester Academy established; **1842** the *Jeffersonian* newspaper first published, one of few pro-Southern publications in Northern states; **1847** county courthouse built; **1871** West Chester University of Pennsylvania established; **1872** West Chester Public Library founded; **March 9, 1910** composer Samuel Barber born (died 1981); **March 17, 1912** civil rights

588

activist Bayard Rustin born (died 1987); **1996** American Helicopter Museum opened.

Wilkes-Barre   *Luzerne County   Northeastern Pennsylvania, 16 mi/26 km southwest of Scranton*

early 1760s anthracite coal discovered in area; **1769** John Durkee leads group of Connecticut settlers to Wyoming Valley of Susquehanna River, builds Fort Durkee to promote Connecticut's claims to region; town platted by Durkee, named for John Wilkes and Col. Isaac Barre of British Parliament; **1771** first phase of Pennamite-Yankee War ends with Connecticut settlers in control; **1775** Continental Congress calls end to hostilities between feuding provinces; **July 1778** town destroyed by allied British and Native Americans; **1782** second phase of Pennamite-Yankee War follows awarding of area to Pennsylvania with Decree of Trenton; town burned by Connecticut settlers; **1786** Luzerne County formed; town becomes county seat; **1787** Fell Tavern built; **July 26, 1796** painter George Catlin born (died 1872); **1800** Connecticut relinquishes claims to area; **1806** incorporated as a borough, becomes county seat; **1830s** area becomes important coal mining center; **1871** incorporated as a city; **1885** lace-making industry begins; **1889** Osterhout Free Library founded; **1891** Wilkes-Barre Conservatory organized; **Dec. 23, 1903** railroad accident at nearby Laurel Run, 53 killed; **1909** county courthouse built; **May 23, 1910** abstract artist Franz Kline born (died 1962); **June 5, 1919** coal mine disaster, 92 killed; **1922** anthracite coal mining reaches peak; **1933** Wilkes University established; **1946** King's College established; **Apr. 28, 1952** actress Mary McDonnell born; **1986** Kirby Center for the Performing Arts opened; **1999** First Union Arena opened; **May 21, 2000** commuter plane crashes, 19 killed.

Williamsport   *Lycoming County   North central Pennsylvania, 71 mi/114 km west-southwest of Scranton*

1772 area settled; boat landing established on Susquehanna River by William Russell; **June 10, 1778** wagon train attacked by natives, four killed, two children found later at Niagara, New York; **1795** Lycoming County formed; **1796** town platted as county seat by Michael Ross; **1806** incorporated as a borough; **1812** Dickinson Seminary founded; **1832** Bald Eagle Canal completed; **1833** Susquehanna Canal opened to west; **1840s** lumber industry becomes important, reserves depleted by 1890; **1865** trolley service begins, ends 1933;

1866 incorporated as a city; **1889** flooding destroys primarily black riverside neighborhoods; **1907** James V. Brown Library built; **Dec. 1, 1959** Allegheny Airlines Executive airplane crashes into mountain to east in snowstorm, 25 killed, one survives; **1965** Pennsylvania College of Technology (2-year) established; **1971** county courthouse completed.

Windber   *Somerset County   See* **Johnstown (1903)**

Wyoming   *Luzerne County   Northeastern Pennsylvania, 11 mi/18 km southwest of Scranton*

July 3, 1778 in Battle of Wyoming, 300 men, women and children massacred by Tory group Butler's Raiders aided by Iroquois allies totaling 1,000 men; **1843** Wyoming monument erected commemorating battle; **1885** incorporated as a borough; **1927** Wyoming Public Library founded.

York   *York County   Southern Pennsylvania, 22 mi/35 km south-southeast of Harrisburg*

1737 Old Valley Inn built to east; **1741** town platted by Thomas Cookson; **1749** York County formed; town becomes county seat; **1750s** German immigrants outnumber Scotch-Irish settlers; **1765** Friends Meeting House built; **1766** St. John's Episcopal Church built; **1774** first military resistance to British organized; **Sept. 30, 1777–June 27, 1778** sixth Continental Congress held here; **Nov. 15, 1777** Articles of Confederation adopted; **1787** incorporated as a borough; York College of Pennsylvania established; **1789** First Presbyterian Church built, rebuilt 1860; **1820** iron foundry established; **Feb. 27, 1823** Union Gen. William Buel Franklin born (died 1903); **1825** John Elgar builds first iron-clad steamboat, the *Codorus*; **1831** Phineas Davis builds the *York* locomotive for Baltimore & Ohio Railroad; **1841** county courthouse built; **June 28, 1863** town invaded by Confederate Gen. Jubal Early three days before Battle of Gettysburg; **1864** Glatfelter Paper Mill established at Spring Grove to southwest; **1887** incorporated as a city; **1912** York Reservoir built on East Branch Codorus Creek to south; **1916** Martin Memorial Library founded; **Nov. 26, 1925** TV actress Lois Hunt born; **1926** Pennsylvania State University York Campus, Commonwealth College (2-year) established; **1973** Peach Blossom Nuclear Power Plant opened on Susquehanna River to northeast.

Rhode Island

Northeastern U.S. One of the six New England states. Capital and largest city: Providence.

Rhode Island was one of the 13 colonies which adopted the U.S. Declaration of Independence July 4, 1776. It became the 13th state to ratify the U.S. Constitution May 29, 1790.

Rhode Island is divided into five counties. The counties are divided into townships, called towns, which have very strong governments. Within the towns are villages, which have no government of their own. The county governments serve judicial functions only, in favor of town governments. Municipalities are classified as cities, which are formed from one or more towns. See Introduction.

Anthony   *Kent County   Central Rhode Island, 11 mi/18 km southwest of Providence*

1743 Town of Coventry incorporated, separates from Warwick; **1770** Nathanael Greene House built, served as general in Battle of Valley Forge, second in command to George Washington; **1805** William and Richard Anthony settle here, build cotton mill; village founded within town of Coventry; **1811** competing cotton mill built; **1818** Coventry Library chartered; **1874** Coventry Manufacturing Company builds third, larger cotton goods plant; **Feb. 5, 1996** lowest temperature ever recorded in Rhode Island reached at village of Greene to west, −25°F/−32°C.

Barrington   *Bristol County   Eastern Rhode Island, 7 mi/11.3 km southeast of Providence*

1632 trading post established on west shore of Barrington River; **1633** Plymouth Colony distributes lands of Wampanoag peoples; **1649** first Baptist church in Massachusetts founded; **1667** town settled by John Myles and his Baptist followers; **1678** ferry established on Warren River; **1701** ferry established on Barrington River; **1717** town incorporated by Massachusetts; **1720** Matthew Watson establishes brick factory; **1737** Congregational Church built; **1746** town annexed by Rhode Island; **1770** town reincorporated by Rhode Island; **May 25, 1778** British forces burn town; **1794** bridge built across Warren River; **1848** Nayatt Brick Company founded by Nathaniel Potter; **1855** railroad reaches town; **1859** St. John's Episcopal Church built; **1880** Barrington Public Library founded; **1887** town hall built; **1897** cotton mill established; **1898** trolley service begins, abandoned 1938; **1904** Rhode Island Laceworks established, closed 1990; **1908** Barrington Yacht Club established; **1913** Holy Angels Catholic Church founded; **1914** Barrington and Palmer river bridges built; **1930** America's Cup yacht race to Bermuda brought here; **Sept. 21, 1938** surge from New England hurricane lifts yachts onto highway, three killed; **1995** America's Cup Hall of Fame opened.

Block Island   *Newport County   Southern Rhode Island, 45 mi/72 km south of Providence, in Atlantic Ocean*

c.1000 possibly the southernmost extent of Viking exploration, though no evidence exists of their presence; **1524** Italian explorer Verrazano discovers island, called Manisses, or Manitou's Little Island, by Narragansetts; **1614** coastal areas explored by Adrian Block; **1658** island granted to Governor Endicott and other officials by General Court of Massachusetts; **1660** island grantees sell island to 16 others; **Apr. 1661** island surveyed, village of Block Island founded on eastern shore; **1672** Town of New Shoreham incorporated, coextensive with Block Island; **July 1689** fleet of French privateers, under English pirate William Trimming, gain confidence of island residents, then occupy and plunder island, later captured and killed on Fishers Island to east; **1812** town hall originally built on Cemetery Hill as Baptist Church, moved to present site in 1875; **1850** life-saving station established for sea rescues, incorporated into Coast Guard station 1915; **1875** Southeast Point Lighthouse built; **1876** library founded; **Nov. 1878** construction of Old Harbor completed at village; **1880** communication cable laid from Point Judith; **1896** New Harbor completed; **1900** passageway to Great Salt Pond completed, New Harbor built on village side of pond; **1936** Tercentenary Monument erected to commemorate 300th anniversary of founding of Rhode Island; **Aug. 11, 1970** FBI apprehends Father

Daniel Berrigan, wanted for destroying draft records, one of "Cantonville 9."

Bristol *Bristol County* *Eastern Rhode Island, 12 mi/19 km southeast of Providence*

c.1590 Massasoit born, Chief of Wampanoag peoples (died 1661); **1669** area first settled by John Gorham; **June 1675** in first battler of King Philip's War, Gorham's house destroyed by Wampanoags, settlers at Pokanoket Neck plundered; **1680** town incorporated by Plymouth Colony; Bristol Ferry established linking mainland with island of Rhode Island and Newport; North Burial Ground platted; **1685** Bristol County, Plymouth Colony (Massachusetts) formed; town becomes county seat; **1746** town annexed, reincorporated by Rhode Island; seat of Bristol County, Massachusetts, moved to Taunton; **1747** Bristol County, Rhode Island, formed from Bristol County, Massachusetts; town becomes county seat; **Oct. 7, 1775** British bombard town, withdraw after levy of 40 sheep is paid; **1825** town's extensive whaling industry begins, continues until 1846; **1835** Bristol Steam Mill built, town's first cotton mill; **1861** St. Michael's Church completed; **1863** Herreshoff boat manufacturing company established; **Aug. 28, 1864** editor, author Mark Antony De Wolfe Howe born (died 1960); **1865** railroad linking Newport to Providence renders ferry useless; **1877** Rogers Free Library founded; **1878** Trinity Church built, razed 1937; **1885** first torpedo built in U.S. at Bristol boat yards; **1898** electric trolley service begins from Providence, ends 1938 with hurricane damage; **1904** King Philip Museum opens; **1905** ferry service begins, part of new electric rail line to Newport; **1929** Mount Hope Bridge opens, replacing Bristol Ferry; **1934** St. Columban's Seminary founded; **1956** Roger Williams University established.

Central Falls *Providence County* *Northeastern Rhode Island, 4 mi/6.4 km north of Providence*

March 26, 1676 in Captain Pierce's Fight, Michael Pierce's Plymouth forces are decimated by attacking Narragansetts; **1730** Town of Smithfield separates from Providence; **1790** village founded, originally named Chocolate Mill for chocolate factory established by a man named Wheat; **1847** Central Falls Fire District established, creating new name for village; **1871** town of Lincoln separates from Smithfield; **1895** Central Falls incorporated as a city; **May 1900** Adams Memorial Library opens; **1927** Notre Dame Catholic Church built; **1928** St. Mathieu's Church built.

Charlestown *Washington County* *Southern Rhode Island, 18 mi/29 km southwest of Newport*

c.1630 Fort Ninigret probably built by Dutch, originally thought to be Niantic fortification; **1637** Capt. John Mason of Connecticut camps here, persuades Ninigret, Niantic chief, to join forces with white settlers in fighting the Pequots; **1669** town founded; **1730** Old Wilcox Tavern built, also called Monument House; **1738** town of Charlestown incorporated, created from Westerly,

named for King Charles II, who granted Rhode Island's charter in 1663; **1739** Joseph Stanton, Jr. born at Monument House, served as general in French and Indian War (died 1807); **1750** wooden Narragansett Indian Church built; **c.1750** King Tom Farm house built by Thomas Ninigret; **1755** General Stanton Inn established, center of Rhode Island state political functions during mid-1800s; **1770** Narragansetts induct final leader at Coronation Rock; **1859** granite Narragansett Indian Church built to northwest; **1925** Kimball Bird Sanctuary established; **1927** Burlingame State Park established; **Sept. 21, 1938** extensive damage, many killed by Great New England Hurricane; **1983** Narragansett Indian Reservation created to northwest.

Coventry *Kent County* *See* **Anthony**

Cranston *Providence County* *Northeastern Rhode Island, 3 mi/4.8 km southwest of Providence*

1638 area settled by associates of Roger Williams, including William Harris, Zachariah Rhodes, and William Arnold, first governor of state, father of Benedict Arnold; **1677** Thomas Fenner House built; **1754** town incorporated, named for Gov. Samuel Cranston; **1720** Friends Meeting House built; **c.1760** Caleb Arnold Tavern built; **1790** Governor Sprague Mansion built; **1824** Cranston Print Works clothing mill established, city's first factory; **1890** Narragansett Brewing Company established during dry era, expanded with repeal of prohibition 1933 (closed 1975); **1901** Possner Castle mansion built for Hermann G. Possner, president Sure-Lock Paper Clip Company; **1910** incorporated as a city; **1920** WPRO established at The Castle mansion, Rhode Island's first radio station; **1937** city hall built.

Cumberland Hill *Providence County* *Northeastern Rhode Island, 10 mi/16 km north of Providence*

1740 Elder Ballou Meeting House built; **Nov. 29, 1752** religious leader Jemima Wilkinson born (died 1819); **c.1820** Amos Cook House built, serves as Cumberland Bank building from 1823; **1746** area annexed by Rhode Island; **1747** Town of Cumberland incorporated with Cumberland Hill as seat of government; **1868** town government moved to Valley Falls; **1976** Cumberland Library opened, new facility completed 2000.

Davisville *Washington County* *Central Rhode Island, 14 mi/23 km south of Providence, on Narragansett Bay*

1637 Roger Williams Trading Post established; **1639** Richard Smith builds trading post; **1651** Smith purchases Williams' trading post; **1675** 40 men killed in Swamp Fight engagement with Narragansetts; **1676** Native Americans burn Smith's house, rebuilt 1680 by Richard Smith, Jr.; **1707** Narragansett Church built, oldest church north of Philadelphia; **1941** Davisville Naval

Construction Battalion Center (Quonset Point) established (closed 1996).

East Greenwich   Kent County   Central Rhode Island, 11 mi/18 km south of Providence, on Narragansett Bay

1676 area settled by veterans of King Philip's War; **1677** town incorporated; **1680** Governor William Greene Homestead built, Gen. Nathanael Greene married here 1774, Governor Greene lived here 1778–1786; **1711** Capt. John Cogdon House built; **1750** Kent County formed; town becomes county seat; county courthouse built, figures of white man and black man chained together over doorway symbolizing equality of justice; **1767** the Brick House built, town's first brick house; **1770** Col. William Arnold Tavern built, later the Updike Tavern; **1774** Kentish Guards, also called Kentish Light Infantry, organized; **1802** East Greenwich Academy established, sold to Episcopal church 1841; **1804** Kent County jail built; Friends Meeting House built; **1805** second county courthouse built, serves as seat of state government; **1818** Windmill Cottage built, purchased 1866 by poet Henry Wadsworth Longfellow for friend George Washington Greene; **1833** Methodist Church built; **Nov. 5, 1842** Constitution of Rhode Island and Providence Plantations adopted, Methodist Church used as meeting site; **1850** Methodist Church, requiring more space, is cut into two and separated, new section added in middle; **1854** state government moved to Providence; **1860** Abraham Lincoln stops at Updike Tavern; **1896** Greenwich Inn built on site of Updike Tavern; **1914** Varnum Memorial Armory built; **2003** new county courthouse built, to be completed 2005.

East Providence   Providence County   Eastern Rhode Island, 2 mi/3.2 km east of Providence, on Seekonk River

March 1623 John Hampden and Edward Winslow visit Massasoit, leader of Wampanoags, to negotiate trade for Plymouth Governor Bradford; **1636** Roger Williams, founder of Rhode Island, builds his first dwelling here following his banishment from Massachusetts, location marked by Roger Williams Tree; **c.1660** first burials at Little Neck Cemetery; **c.1699** first school established; **1750** Bishop House built; **1805** Old Stone House built; White Congregational Church built, originally Baptist church founded by Rev. John Myles, 1663; **1810** Newman Church built near site of original 1643 structure; **1862** Town of East Providence incorporated; **1870** Squantum Club business men's retreat established; **1871** Pomham Lighthouse built on Narragansett Bay; **1872** St. Mary's Seminary established; **1889** town hall built; **1893** Rumford Baking Powder marketed by Rumford Chemical Works; St. Andrew's School established, private school for boys; **1906** Belton Court estate built by prominent politician; **1930** Washington Bridge opens to Providence; **1938** Weaver Memorial Public Library built with donation by Susan B. Anthony; **Sept. 21, 1938** hurricane washes away

railroad tracks, sets oil tanker on shore; **1958** incorporated as a city.

Greene   Kent County   See Anthony (1996)

Hamilton   Washington County   Southern Rhode Island, 18 mi/29 km south of Providence, on Narragansett Bay

1700 Franklin Ferry begins operating to Newport; **c.1710** Hannah Robinson House built, story of Hannah's life subject of Alice Morse Earle's story "Old Narragansett"; **1725** Casey House built, Casey Farm site of Revolutionary War encounters; **1751** Gilbert Stuart House built, used as grist mill during 1800s, restored 1930s; **Dec. 3, 1755** portrait painter Gilbert Stuart born (died 1828); **1940** Jamestown Bridge built to Conanicut (Jamestown) Island.

Hopkinton   Washington County   Southwestern Rhode Island, 30 mi/48 km southwest of Providence

1669 town founded; **1680** Seventh Day Adventist Meeting House built; **1757** town incorporated, formed from Westerly; **1762** Thurston Mansion built; **1789** Union Meeting House built, used as town hall until 1860, later used as Second Hopkinton Seventh Day Baptist Church; **1792** Joseph Spicer, saddlemaker, builds shop, converts it to Spicer Tavern 1806; **Sept. 3, 1803** educator, abolitionist Prudance Crandall born (died 1889); **1815** turnpike extended through Hopkinton village (Hopkinton City) from Providence to New London; **1846** Hopkinton City becomes center for manufacture of carriages and sleighs; **1860** town hall built; **1888** Spicer Tavern destroyed by fire.

Jamestown   Newport County   Southern Rhode Island, 22 mi/35 km south of Providence, on Narragansett Bay

1616 Dutch visit small island in West Channel of Narragansett Bay; **1639** town founded; **1656** Benedict Arnold (great-grandfather of Revolutionary War traitor), William Coddington and other Rhode Island founders purchase Conanicut Island from Narragansett peoples; artillery lot and town cemetery set aside as military training ground and burial site; **1678** town incorporated, includes Conanicut Island and lesser Gould and Dutch islands; **1680** Capt. Thomas Paine settles on Conanicut, builds house called Cajacet, was friend of pirate Captain Kidd; **1693** Gov. Benedict Arnold builds house; **1709** first Friends' Meeting House built, moved 1734; **1749** makeshift lighthouse constructed at Beaver Tail Point, on Conanicut's southern tip; **1765** Friends' Meeting House built in Jamestown; **Dec. 10, 1775** British military expedition under Capt. James Wallace marches across Conanicut Island leaving path of destruction, burns village of Jamestown, leaves in Spring, 1776; **June 1776** Americans build Beaver Head Fort on west side of Conanicut, Beaver Tail Fort at southern end, and Fort Dumplings on southeast end; **Dec. 1776** American fortifications abandoned as British take island, remain until Oct. 1778; **1787** The Windmill built as part of grist milling operation; **1803** Old Schoolhouse built; **1857** Dutch Island Lighthouse built, replaces 1827 structure; **1863** Fort Greble built on Dutch Island, enlarged 1902, abandoned by 1930s; **1865** granite Beaver Tail Lighthouse built at Beaver Tail Point; **1873** East Ferry village platted; **May 1873** first ferry to Newport established; **1880s** several hotels built at East Ferry; **1883** town hall built at Jamestown village; **1896** Fort Wetherell built, site of Fort Dumplings, named 1900 for Capt. James Wetherell, died in Spanish-American War; **1900** Fort Getty established on west side of Conanicut, built by 1909, abandoned by 1930s; **1940** Jamestown Bridge built from mainland to west; **1969** Newport (Pell) Bridge built east to Newport; **1992** Jamestown-Verrazano Bridge built, replacing Jamestown Bridge.

Johnston *Providence County* *North central Rhode Island, 4 mi/6.4 km west of Providence*

1650 Thomas Clarence becomes one of town's first settlers; **1768** town incorporated, named for Augustus Johnston, Rhode Island Attorney General; **1775** general assembly establishes powder mill during Revolutionary War; explosion at mill kills founder James Goff and one employee; **1835** James Simmons builds cotton mill, destroyed by flash flood 1840; **1870** dyestuffs factory established; **1884** British Hosiery Company founded by R. W. Cooper; **1944** Johnston Memorial Park created to honor World War soldiers; **1960** Marian J. Mohr Memorial Public Library founded.

Kingston *Washington County* *Southern Rhode Island, 10 mi/16 km west of Newport*

1670 first farm properties platted in area; **Dec. 1675** Colonial troops rest here on way to Great Swamp Fight to southwest, in which Narragansetts were defeated by Colonials; **1700** village platted, originally named Little Rest; **1723** Town of South Kingstown incorporated; **1729** Kings County formed; county seat established at Tower Hill, near Point Judith; **1750** Elisha Reynolds House built; **1752** county seat moved to Little Rest; Old Tavern built; **1757** Kingston Inn built; **1759** post office built; **1775** county courthouse built, becomes Kingston Library 1900; **1781** county renamed Washington County; **1809** Potter House built by Cong. Elisha R. Potter, Jr.; **1856** Eldred House built, served as county jail into mid-1900s; **1885** village renamed Kingston; **1892** Rhode Island State College established, becomes University of Rhode Island; **1900** county seat moved to West Kingston.

Lincoln *Providence County* *See* **Lonsdale**

Lonsdale *Providence County* *Northeastern Rhode Island, 5 mi/8 km north of Providence*

1650 town of Lincoln founded; **1700** original section of Israel Arnold House built; **1703** Friends Meeting House built; **1811** Stephen H. Smith builds Hearthside house from money received in Louisiana Lottery; **c.1812** Moffett Mill built on Moshassuck River, acquired by Moffett family 1853; **1829** first textile manufacturing begun by Lonsdale Company; **1871** town of Lincoln incorporated; Lonsdale village becomes seat of government; **1884** textile dyeing and bleaching industry begins; **1909** Lincoln Woods State Park established.

Middletown *Newport County* *Southeastern Rhode Island, 2 mi/3.2 km northeast of Newport*

1731 town founded; **1743** town of Middletown incorporated, separates from Newport; **1760** Bannister House built, occupied by British during Revolution; **1765** Jonathan Anthony builds house, operates tannery; **Aug. 28–19, 1778** in Battle of Rhode Island, fort built on Narragansett Bay by British (Old Fort Farm); **Dec. 8, 1776** British troops under Sir Peter Parker land in 11 ships, ravage town before marching to Newport, occupying island for three years; **c.1790** Taggart's Ferry begins operating from Little Compton, through 1870; **1794** Peabody School built; **May 1814** Swedish cargo ship loaded with molasses chased by British man-of-war *Nimrod* from West Indies into Narragansett Bay, cargo ship grounded, crew saved at Third Beach; **c.1935** Newport State Airport developed.

Narragansett *Washington County* *Southern Rhode Island, 8 mi/12.9 km southwest of Newport*

1675–1676 Narragansett peoples driven from area in King Philip's War; **1777** fort at Bonnet Point to north built during Revolutionary War, rebuilt for War of 1812, briefly reactivated during Civil War after Confederate cruiser *Alabama* sighted off shore; **1846** Hazard Castle begun by Joseph Peace Hazard, referred to as Haunted Castle until completed 1883 by nephew; **1872** Whale Rock Light built between mainland and Conanicut Island; **1883** The Casino and Pier resort built, designed by Stanford White, destroyed by fire 1900 leaving only The Towers section; **1887** Coast Guard station built; **1901** town incorporated; **1905** Fort Philip Kearney established to north.

New Shoreham *Washington County* *See* **Block Island**

Newport *Newport County* *Southern Rhode Island, 22 mi/35 km south of Providence, on Narragansett Bay*

1639 first white settlers arrive at south end of island of Rhode Island; **1641** town of Newport incorporated; **1657** Quakers (Friends) arrive in Newport Harbor aboard small vessel *Woodhouse*; **1658** first Jewish families arrive from Holland; **1685** Long Wharf erected; **1700** Franklin Ferry begins operating to Hamilton, on west side of Narragansett Bay; **1700** Friends' Meeting House built; **1703** Newport County formed; town becomes county seat; **1725** Samuel Ward the Elder born, governor of Rhode Island Colony (died 1776); Trinity Church built; **Dec. 22,**

1727 patriot William Ellery born, signer of Declaration of Independence (died 1820); **1730** Literary and Philosophical Society founded; **Aug. 25, 1734** physician Benjamin Church born, traitor to patriot cause, lost at sea 1778; **1747** Redwood Library and Atheneum founded by Abraham Redwood, building completed 1750, designed by Peter Harrison; **1755** Jewish immigrants arrive from Portugal following earthquakes in that country; Oliver Hazard Perry House built; **1756** first black slaves brought to city; **1763** Touro Synagogue completed; **1764** British schooner *St. John* seizes sugar cargo at Howland's Ferry; **July 1769** townspeople burn British Ship *Liberty*; **Dec. 9, 1776** British troops march on town from north, occupy island for three years, nearly 500 buildings destroyed; **Oct. 1779** as British depart, town records and books taken from Redwood Library; **July 1780** French assume friendly occupation of Newport under Count de Rochambeau; **1784** incorporated as a city; **1787** city reverts to town government; **Dec. 12, 1790** educator Tyrrell Channing born (died 1856); **1830** town gains status as summer resort with visitors from Southern states and Cuba; **1835** Coddington Mill built; **1852** addition of 12 large residences expands resort section south of Touro Street; **1853** reincorporated as a city; **Jan. 5, 1862** architect Christopher Grant La Farge born (died 1938); **Feb. 1864** first train arrives on Old Colony & Fall River Railroad; **1870** People's Library founded; **1877** Naval War College established; **1880** Newport Casino established; **1894** frigate *Constellation* arrives in Newport 100 years after it was built; **Sept. 30, 1895** first National Open Golf Tournament held, Horace Rawlins of England winner; **1900** city hall built; **1902** Newport Historical Society Museum established; **1907** Navy torpedo factory built at Goat Island; **1913** U.S. Naval Hospital opens; **Aug. 25, 1916** actor Van Johnson born; **1918** expansion of U.S. Navy presence begins; **1925** De La Salle Academy established; **1933** county courthouse built; **1934** Salve Regina University established; Rochambeau monument dedicated; **Oct. 14, 1949** actor Harry Anderson born; **May 26, 1954** steamship *Pennington* sinks off Rhode Island killing 103; **1969** Newport Bridge built to Jamestown, later renamed Pell Bridge.

North Smithfield *Providence County* See **Slatersville**

Pawtucket *Providence County* *Northeastern Rhode Island, 3 mi/4.8 km north of Providence*

1638 area deeded to Rhode Island founder Roger Williams; **1640** Old Pidge Tavern built; **1671** town founded; **1790** dam built on Blackstone River, later provides electrical power to town; **1793** Slater Mill built by Samuel Slater, first water-powered cotton mill; **1815** Colonel Slack Mansion built; **1828** town incorporated by Massachusetts; **1829** Congregational Church built, destroyed by fire 1864; Immaculate Conception Catholic Church built; **1842** First Baptist Church built; **1862** town reincorporated by Rhode Island; **1886** incorporated as a city; **1899** boundary settled with Massachusetts; **Dec. 29,**

1900 New Deal attorney Thomas Gardiner Corcoran born (died 1981); **1902** St. Paul's Episcopal Church built; **Mary 19, 1935** actor David Hartman born; **1936** city hall built.

Portsmouth *Newport County* *Southeastern Rhode Island, 7 mi/11.3 km north-northeast of Newport*

1638 town founded by settlers from Massachusetts Bay Colony led by John Clarke and William Coddington at north end of island of Rhode Island at Founder's Brook; **1641** town of Newport incorporated coextensive with all of island; **1644** town of Pocasset incorporated, separates from Newport; **1649** town renamed Portsmouth; **1702** Quaker Meeting House built; **1707** ferry established on Sakonnet River estuary to Tiverton; **1742** Honyman House built by James Honyman; **Feb. 1776** Bristol Ferry Fort built; **July 9, 1777** Col. William Barton captures British Gen. Richard Prescott; **Aug. 29, 1778** about 30 Hessians buried in mass grave following fierce Battle of Rhode Island, site called Hessian Hole, Americans retreat by way of Tiverton; **Oct. 1779** British evacuate island; **1800** coal mining begins, abandoned 1911; **1807** Portsmouth Free Library founded, building opened 1893; **1821** Rhode Island Union Society founded seeking to eliminate sectarianism among local Christian churches; **1865** Union Meeting House built; **1896** St. George's School founded; **1929** Old Grist Mill moved here, third move since its construction at Warren in 1812.

Providence *Providence County* *Northeastern Rhode Island, at north end of Narragansett Bay*

1635 Roger Williams and followers flee Massachusetts Bay Colony in search of site for new colony based on religious freedom; **1636** Williams' group arrives at head of bay 25 mi/40 km inland from Atlantic Ocean, purchase site from Narragansett peoples, establish Rhode Island Colony; **1638** First Baptist Meeting House founded, oldest Baptist Church in U.S.; **1644** incorporated as Providence Plantations; **1663** new colony's charter includes religious freedom clause; **1675–1676** much of town destroyed in King Philip's War; **Aug. 12, 1676** New England Indian war ends; **1680** Pardon Tillinghast builds first wharf on Providence River; **1703** Providence County formed; town becomes county seat; **1717** *Firefly* becomes first steamboat to ply waters between Providence and Newport; **Sept. 26, 1733** Revolutionary naval officer Abraham Whipple born (died 1819); **1753** Providence Library founded; **1762** *Providence Gazette and Country Journal* established, town's first newspaper; Old State House built; **Apr. 4, 1769** philanthropist Nicholas Brown born (died 1841); **1770** Brown University moved from Warren, established 1764; **1775** First Baptist Church built, one of few Baptist churches having steeple and bells, survived gale of 1815; **May 4, 1776** Rhode Island Colony declares itself a republic two months before the other colonies; city shares role of capital with Newport; **1782** Hoyle Tavern built; **1784** Golden Ball Inn built; **Nov. 27, 1785** jurist, diplomat Henry Wheaton born (died 1848);

May 29, 1790 Rhode Island becomes last state of 13 colonies to ratify U.S. Constitution; Jan. 19, 1803 poet Sarah Whitman born (died 1878); 1805 state government moved to East Greenwich; Oct. 23, 1805 historian John Russell Bartlett born (died 1886); 1812 forts at Robin Hill and Sassafras Point strengthened, Fort William Henry built on Providence River during War of 1812; Sept. 1815 town devastated by Great Gale, destroying buildings and 35 ships with 12-ft/3.7-m tidal surge; Apr. 12, 1821 historian Sam Arnold born (died 1880); 1822 Rhode Island Historical Society founded; 1824 Dexter Asylum established by Ebenezer Dexter; Apr. 4, 1824 essayist, journalist George William Curtis born (died 1892); 1828 The Arcade business center built, possibly oldest indoor shopping mall in U.S.; 1829 *Providence Journal* newspaper founded; 1831 Providence Athenaeum established; Gorham Manufacturing Company established, maker of silverware; Nov. 1831 incorporated as a city; 1833 Talma Theatre built, served as Civil War morgue; 1835 Boston & Providence Railroad established; 1837 architect Josiah Cleveland Cady born (died 1919); 1842 followers of Thomas Dorr, former governor, raid arsenal, Dorr sentenced to life in prison in 1844, released 1847; 1854 state government moved back from East Greenwich; Rhode Island College established; 1856 Cullen Whipple obtains patent for machine for manufacture of pointed screws; 1863 *Providence Bulletin* newspaper founded; Apr. 4, 1866 educator George Pierce Baker born (died 1935); Oct. 2, 1867 Sen. Theodore Francis Green born (died 1966); 1875 Providence Public Library founded; 1877 Rhode Island School of Design established; 1878 Cathedral of Sts. Peter and Paul built; July 3, 1878 actor, playwright George M. Cohan born (died 1942); Nov. 2, 1885 banker, diplomat Winthrop Aldrich born (died 1974); Aug. 20, 1890 horror writer H. P. (Howard Phillips) Lovecraft born (died 1937); 1891 Roger Williams Park donated by descendant Betsey Williams; 1892 Pembroke College for women founded, associated with Brown University; 1898 Union Station completed; 1900 Newport ceases role with Providence as joint capital of Rhode Island; Providence Public Library completed; June 29, 1901 actor Nelson Eddy born (died 1967); March 25, 1903 actor Frankie Carle born (died 2001); 1904 state-house completed, modeled after U.S. Capitol, one of largest freestanding marble domes in world; 1908 federal building built; 1909 Pleasant Valley Parkway built; 1914 Johnson and Wales University established; Providence Grays baseball team wins International League title with aid of Babe Ruth; Oct. 30, 1914 actress Ruth Hussey born; 1917 Providence College established; July 29, 1917 novelist Edwin O'Connor born (died 1968); 1925 Rhode Island Auditorium built; 1927 Fleet National Bank building completed; 1928 Kent Dam built on North Branch Pawtuxet River to west, Scituate Reservoir provides water for half of Rhode Island; Industrial Trust Building completed; 1930 Washington Bridge built to East Providence; 1931 T. F. Green International Airport established to southwest, originally Hills Grove Airport; 1933 county courthouse completed; 1934 Narragansett Race Track holds inaugural meet; 1938 Great New England Hurricane damages city, 7 ft/2.1 m of water inundates downtown, 600 killed in Northeast, 311 in Rhode Island; 1949 Veterans Hospital opened; 1954 Hurricane Carol damages city; 1966 hurricane barrier completed along harbor; 1973 Bank of Boston Tower built; Aug. 2, 1975 highest temperature ever recorded in Rhode Island reached, 104°F/40°C; c.1990 *Journal* and *Bulletin* newspapers merge to form *Providence News*; 1991 bank assets frozen statewide with collapse of State Deposit Insurance Corporation; 1999 Providence Place Mall opens downtown.

Richmond *Washington County* See Usquepaug

Slatersville *Providence County* *Northern Rhode Island, 4 mi/6.4 km west of Woonsocket*

1794 Elisha Bartlett builds First Scythe Factory; 1796 cotton mill built by John Slater; 1804 Slatersville Finishing Company established, stone mill built 1826; 1810 Slater House built; Congregational Church built; Old Schoolhouse built; 1871 town of North Smithfield incorporated; village becomes town administrative center; Samuel Slater begins manufacture of cotton goods; 1921 town hall built; 1966 North Smithfield Library founded.

South Kingstown *Washington County* See Wakefield (1723)

Tiverton *Newport County* *Southeastern Rhode Island, 10 mi/16 km northeast of Newport*

1629 land purchased from Pocasset peoples, part of Massachusetts; 1640 ferry established to island of Rhode Island, first regular ferry in Rhode Island; 1692 town incorporated; 1707 ferry established to Portsmouth by Capt. Thomas Townsend; 1735 Lafayette House built, Lafayette's headquarters during Revolution; 1746 town annexed by Rhode Island; Aug. 1778 at Fort Barton, Americans make tactful retreat from British in Battle of Rhode Island; Oct. 1778 British galley *Pigot* blockades Sakonnet River, Maj. Silas Talbot descends river in sloop at night, captures ship; 1794 wooden bridge built across Sakonnet River; 1827 woolen and cotton mills established; 1862 part of town annexed back by Massachusetts as part of city of Fall River; 1878 menhaden oil becomes important commodity, through 1909; 1909 steel bridge built across Sakonnet River; 1917 Holy Trinity Church built.

Valley Falls *Providence County* *Northeastern Rhode Island, 5 mi/8 km north of Providence*

1635 William Blackstone becomes first white settler in Rhode Island; 1746 area annexed by Rhode Island; 1747 town of Cumberland incorporated; 1807 cotton spinning industry begins; 1810 William Harris builds cotton mill; 1848 coal discovered; Blackstone Mining Company founded; 1868 town government seat moved from Cumberland Hill; 1886 Ann and Hope Mill built by

Lonsdale Company; **1889** William Blackstone monument erected in front of mill near his grave, died here May, 1675; **1936** Blackstone River floods, coal mines cave in.

Wakefield *Washington County* *Southern Rhode Island, 25 mi/40 km south of Providence*

1658 at Pettaquamscutt Rock, or Treaty Rock, white settlers acquire Pettaquamscutt Purchase from Native Americans; **1674** town of Kingstown incorporated; **1675–1676** area cleared for white settlement with defeat of Narragansetts in King Philip's War; **1702** Perry House built by Benjamin Perry, birthplace of Oliver and Matthew Perry, "the house that launched a thousand ships"; **1723** town splits into North and South Kingstown, with Wakefield administrative center for South; **1725** Dockray House built; **1729** Kings County formed, renamed Washington County 1781; **Aug. 20, 1785** Oliver Hazard Perry born, Commodore in Battle of Lake Erie, War of 1812 (died 1819); **Apr. 10, 1794** explorer Matthew Perry born (died 1858); **1800** Narragansett Woolen Mills established; **1989** county seat moved from West Kingston; J. Howard McGrath County Judicial Center opened.

Warren *Bristol County* *Eastern Rhode Island, 9 mi/14.5 km southeast of Providence, on Warren River*

1632 trading post established at Massasoit's Spring by settlers from Plymouth, first in present-day Rhode Island, founds town; **1678** ferry established on Warren River to Barrington; **1746** town annexed from Massachusetts by Rhode Island; town incorporated; **1764** Rhode Island College established, becomes Brown University, moved to Providence 1770; **Jan. 13, 1776** citizens join forces with Bristol in routing British Captain Wallace's troops from Prudence Island; **May 25, 1778** town ravaged by 500 British troops, several buildings burned, many boats destroyed; **Aug. 1778** Lafayette takes command of U.S. forces, makes Warren his headquarters; **1779** whaling industry revived; **March 13, 1781** George Washington spends night at Burr's Tavern; **1784** Warren Baptist Church built on site of meeting house destroyed 1778; **1794** bridge on Warren River replaces ferry; **1850** textile industry becomes important; **1851** St. Mary's Catholic Church built, destroyed by fire 1882, rebuilt; **1884** new Baptist church built.

Warwick *Kent County* *Central Rhode Island, 7 mi/ 11.3 km south of Providence, on Narragansett Bay*

1636 Samuel Gorton of Boston purchases land; **1643** town settled; **1647** town incorporated; **1675–1676** King Philip's War delays town's growth; **1676** town hall built; **Aug. 7, 1707** Revolutionary War Gen. Nathanael Greene born (died 1786); **1716** Proprietors' School established; **1774** Kentish Guards founded, becomes Kentish Artillery 1804; **1794** textile mill opened, eight more built 1803–1834; **1913** town of West Warwick separates from Warwick; **1931** incorporated as a city; Hills Grove Airport established, later renamed T. F. Green International Airport; **1964** Warwick Public Library founded, new facility opened

1998; **Feb. 20, 2003** fire destroys The Station night club at West Warwick, caused by sparks from pyrotechnics during rock concert by Great White, 99 killed, 50 injured.

Watch Hill *Washington County* *Southwestern Rhode Island, 30 mi/48 km southwest of Newport*

c.1755 watch tower built to send smoke signals during French and Indian War, used again in Revolutionary War; **1808** wooden Watch Hill Lighthouse built; Jonathan Nash serves as first light keeper until 1835; **Sept. 1815** gale damages area, washes away sole house on sand spit Napatree Point (the Naps), Rhode Island's most southwesterly point; **1858** brick Watch Hill Lighthouse built; **1872** steamer *Metis* founders off coast, 33 rescued by volunteer rescue crew; **1908** Coast Guard Station completed; **1898** Fort Mansfield built by U.S. on Napatree Point, sold 1927; **c.1930** imposing Holiday House residence built by Mrs. George G. Snowden; **1937** Watch Hill Beach Club opens.

West Kingston *Washington County* *Southern Rhode Island, 12 mi/19 km west of Newport*

Dec. 19, 1675 Great Swamp Fight to southwest, major engagement involving forces from all colonies in defeat of Narragansetts; **1729** Kings County formed, renamed Washington County 1781; **1837** Providence & Stonington Railroad reaches village; **1874** Washington County Fairgrounds established; **1900** county seat moved from Kingston village to West Kingston village; county courthouse completed; **1989** county seat moved to Wakefield; South County Center for the Arts established in former county courthouse.

West Warwick *Kent County* *See* **Warwick (2003)**

Westerly *Washington County* *Southwestern Rhode Island, 27 mi/43 km west-southwest of Newport*

1614 Capt. Adriaen Block explores coastal Rhode Island; **1620s** Dutch explorers reach as far east as Pawcatuck River; **1649** trading post established by a Thomas Stanton; **1660** land deed secured from Pequot and Niantic peoples; **1664–1665** Niantic sachem (ruler) Ninigret repulses other Native American groups and white Connecticut invaders; **1669** town incorporated; **1712** bridge built to Connecticut, replaced 1735; **March 10, 1742** snow accumulation measures 3 ft/1 m, Long Island Sound iced over; **1814** Old Stone Mill built, start of town's cotton milling industry, razed 1935; **Aug. 1814** in War of 1812, British shell nearby Stonington, Connecticut, Rhode Island militia put on alert; **Apr. 1826** during town meeting at Gavitt House (Whipping Post Farm), floor gives way, sending participants into cellar, no injuries; **1830** buttonwood tree used for final time at Whipping Post Farm, sheep rustler receives 19 lashes; **1847** Smith Granite Quarry established; **1876** Friends Meeting House built; **1893** *Daily Sun* newspaper founded; **1894** Westerly Library built; **1902** Art Gallery opens; **1912** Westerly Rail Station built; **1928** Westerly Yacht Club formed; **1932** Pawcatuck River Bridge built to Connecticut; **July 24, 1936** TV comic Ruth Buzzi born.

Wickford *Washington County* *Southern Rhode Island, 17 mi/27 km south of Providence, on Narragansett Bay*

c.1650 area settled; **1674** town of King's Towne incorporated; **1709** Lodowick Updike begins selling lots at town site; **1711** first house built; **1723** North Kingstown incorporated; village becomes town government seat; **1728** Stephen Cooper House built; **1745** John Updike House built; **1777** Americans force barge load of British soldiers to land at Poplar Point, capturing them; **1786** Immanuel Case House built; **1800** Washington Academy founded, first academy in Rhode Island; **1807** Old Town House built; **1831** Poplar Point Lighthouse built, discontinued 1882.

Woonsocket *Providence County* *Northeastern Rhode Island, 13 mi/21 km north-northwest of Providence*

1662 lands deeded by Nipmuck peoples; **1666** Richard Arnold builds sawmill on Blackstone River; **1695** John Arnold builds cabin; **1712** John Arnold builds first house; **1720** forge established by Quakers at falls; **1810** city's textile industry begins with establishment of the Social Manufacturing Company; **1826** Blackstone Canal opened; **1833** First Baptist Church built; **1840** woolen industry started by Edward Harris; **1844** St. Charles Catholic Church built, destroyed by fire 1868, rebuilt; **1847** Providence & Woonsocket Railroad reaches town; **1856** Harris Institute Library founded; **1858** town hall built; **1867** town incorporated; **1870** soldiers' monument erected to honor Civil War dead; **Sept. 5, 1874** baseball player Nap Lajoie born (died 1959); **1880** Church of Precious Blood built; **1888** incorporated as a city; **Dec. 9, 1894** song and dance man Eddie Dowling born (died 1976); **1920s** cotton milling industry declines; **1927** Stadium Theater built; **1974** Woonsocket Public Library built; **1997** Museum of Work and Culture founded.

South Carolina

Southeastern U.S. Capital: Columbia. Major cities: Columbia, Charleston.

South Carolina was one of the 13 colonies which adopted the U.S. Declaration of Independence July 4, 1776. It became the 8th state to ratify the U.S. Constitution May 23, 1788. It became the first state to secede from the Union as a Confederate state December 20, 1860. It was readmitted to the Union June 25, 1868.

South Carolina is divided into 46 counties, which at varying times were formerly referred to as districts. The counties are divided into townships which have no government. Municipalities have no official classifications, but are classified informally as villages, towns, or cities. See Introduction.

Abbeville *Abbeville County* *Western South Carolina, 70 mi/113 km west of Columbia*

c.1750 area settled by French Huguenots; **1756** town founded; **March 18, 1782** Vice Pres. John Caldwell Calhoun born (died 1850); **1784** Upper Long Cane Presbyterian Church built, founded 1756; **1785** Abbeville County formed from Ninety-Six District; town becomes county seat; **1830s** Burt-Stark Mansion built; **1832** town incorporated; **Nov. 22, 1860** secessionist meeting held, designated Birthplace of the Confederacy; **May 2, 1865** Jefferson Davis holds last cabinet meeting at Burt Mansion; **1860** Trinity Episcopal Church completed, founded 1842; **1902** Eureka Hotel opened, closed 1932, reopened 1984; **1908** Opera House opened; county courthouse built, rebuilt 2002.

Aiken *Aiken County* *Southwestern South Carolina, 45 mi/72 km southwest of Columbia*

1833 Charleston & Hamburg Railroad built by William Aiken; **1834** town platted; **1835** town incorporated; **1845** cotton mill founded by William Gregg; **1856** Southern Porcelain Company established, advent of local kaolin industry; **1871** Aiken County formed; town becomes county seat; county courthouse built; **1876** town becomes focal point of radical political activity as Democrats gain dominance; **1882** Aiken Polo Club organized; **1961** University of South Carolina at Aiken established; **1972** Aiken Technical College (2-year) established.

Allendale *Allendale County* *Southern South Carolina, 65 mi/105 km south-southwest of Columbia*

c.1750s German and Swiss pioneers arrive; **1849** town founded; **1873** town incorporated; Port Royal Railroad

completed; **1901** town hall built; **1919** Allendale County formed; town becomes county seat; **1922** county courthouse completed; **1929** Allendale County Training School for black students founded.

Anderson *Anderson County* *Western South Carolina, 90 mi/145 km west-northwest of Columbia*

1826 Anderson County formed; town becomes county seat; **1833** town incorporated; **1853** First Baptist Church built; **1898** second county courthouse completed; **1911** Anderson College established, originally junior college; **1991** Anderson Civic Center opened; **1999** Anderson Sports Center and William A. Floyd Amphitheater opened.

Bamberg *Bamberg County* *South central South Carolina, 45 mi/72 km south of Columbia*

1832 Charleston & Hamburg (South Carolina) Railroad built; town founded, originally named Lowery's; **1852** town platted; **1855** town incorporated; **1882** bridge built across Edisto River, site of Highway 301; **1890s** community developed through efforts of Gen. Francis M. Bamberg; **1893** Carlisle Fitting School, military academy, founded; **1897** Bamberg County formed; town becomes county seat; county courthouse; **1918** flu epidemic takes heavy toll.

Barnwell *Barnwell County* *Southwestern South Carolina, 50 mi/80 km south-southwest of Columbia*

1785 Winton County formed; **1798** town founded as county seat; **1800** county renamed Barnwell; **1829** town incorporated; **1832** Charleston & Hamburg Railroad built; **1879** county courthouse built; **1897** Voorhees

Industrial and Normal School for black students founded; **1951** large reservation of Savannah River Nuclear Power Plant established to west by U.S. Government, completed 1956; **1983** Defense Waste Processing Facility established.

Beaufort *Beaufort County* *Southern South Carolina, 100 mi/161 km south of Columbia, near Atlantic Ocean*

1710 town founded; **1715** Yamasees nearly destroy town; **1722** town platted; **1724** St. Helena Episcopal Church built; **1769** Beaufort District formed; town becomes district seat; **1795** Gold Eagle Tavern built; Beaufort Arsenal built, rebuilt 1852; Beaufort College established, later becomes University of South Carolina, Beaufort; **c.1800** Beaufort District becomes Beaufort County; **Dec. 21, 1800** Cong. Robert Barnwell Rhett born (died 1876); **1803** town incorporated; **1820** Tabby Mansion built, destroyed by fire 1907; **c.1820** Sea Island Hotel built by George Stoney; **1839** Robert Smalls born, African-American slave piloted Confederate ship *Planter* into Union lines 1861 (died 1937); **1844** Baptist Church built, organized 1804; **1856** The Oaks house built; **Nov. 7, 1861** town falls to Federal forces; **1865** National Cemetery founded, contains 12,000 Union soldiers; **1868** Mather School for female black students founded, now Technical College of the Lowcountry; **1893** hurricane heavily damages town; **1918** Beaufort Library built, organized 1802; **1940** town again damaged by hurricane; **Jan. 12, 1944** heavyweight boxer Joe Frazier born; **1959** University of South Carolina, Beaufort Campus, (2-year) established; **1972** Technical College of the Low Country (2-year) established; **1980s** county government complex built.

Bennettsville *Marlboro County* *Northeastern South Carolina, 80 mi/129 km northeast of Columbia*

1737 first settlers arrive at Welsh Neck from Delaware; **1785** Marlboro County formed; Carlisle becomes first county seat; **1791** Argyle Plantation house built, burned 1969; **1818** town platted, named for Gov. Thomas Bennett; **1819** town becomes new county seat; **1866** town incorporated; **1884** second county courthouse built.

Bishopville *Lee County* *Northeast central South Carolina, 43 mi/69 km east-northeast of Columbia*

1825 town founded; **c.1840** cotton gin established; **1888** town incorporated; **1902** Lee County formed; town becomes county seat; **1908** county courthouse built; **1930s** Ashwood Plantation Resettlement Project builds new homes for Depression era victims; **1977** first Lee County Cotton Festival held; **1994** Southern Cotton Museum opened.

Camden *Kershaw County* *Central South Carolina, 25 mi/40 km northeast of Columbia*

1733–1734 area settled by English; **1750** Irish Quakers arrive; **1760** grist mill built by Joseph Kershaw; **June 1, 1780** Cornwallis enters Camden, establishes town as principal British garrison; **Aug. 16, 1780** Baron Johann DeKalb, champion of American independence, killed in Battle of Camden; **May 1781** town burned, evacuated by British under Lord Rawdon; **1791** Kershaw County formed; town incorporated, becomes county seat; **1803** Greenleaf Villa built by Samuel Flake; **1826** old county courthouse built; **1830** Court Inn built, closed 1962; **Aug. 19, 1870** Bernard Baruch born, economic advisor to Presidents Wilson through Truman (died 1965); **c.1886** opera house built; **March 12, 1922** AFL-CIO labor leader Lane Kirkland born; **May 17, 1923** school fire kills 76; **Dec. 23, 1923** baseball player Larry Doby born, first African-American to play in American League, Cleveland Indians 1947 (died 2003); **1930** Springdale Race Course (horse racing) established; **June 28, 1954** highest temperature ever recorded in South Carolina reached, 111°F/44°C; **1968** county courthouse built; **1974** Fine Arts Center founded.

Charleston *Charleston County* *Southeastern South Carolina, 90 mi/145 km southeast of Columbia, on Atlantic Ocean*

1670 English found Charles Town at Albermarle Point; **1680** present town established at Oyster Point; Huguenot Church founded and built, burned 1797, rebuilt; **1698** first public library in colonies established; **1731** *South Carolina Weekly Journal* newspaper founded; Heyward-Washington House built; **1736** Dock Street Theatre opens; **June 26, 1742** signer of Declaration of Independence Arthur Middleton born (died 1787); **1748** Charleston Library Society organized; **Nov. 23, 1749** signer of Declaration of Independence Edward Rutledge born (died 1800); **Oct. 23, 1750** Gov., Cong. Thomas Pinckney born (died 1828); **1753** colonial Government House built, burned 1788; **Oct. 26, 1757** Sen. Charles Pinckney born (died 1824); **1769** Charleston District formed; town becomes district seat; **1770** College of Charleston established; **1771** Old Exchange customhouse built; **Dec. 17, 1771** Supreme Court Justice William Johnson born (died 1834); **1773** Charleston Museum opened, one of first museums in U.S.; **June 28, 1776** British sea attack repulsed by Col. William Moultrie's defenses; **May 12, 1780** British defeat American forces and capture Charleston; **Aug. 12, 1781** architect Robert Mills born (died 1855); **1783** town incorporated; **1786** capital moved to Columbia; **May 8, 1786** Cong., Gov. James Hamilton born (died 1857); **1787** Congregationalist Church built, becomes Unitarian Church 1817; **1788** Government House rebuilt as district courthouse; **May 15, 1788** minister to Mexico James Gadsden born, acquired Gadsden Purchase in Southwest (died 1858); **Nov. 26, 1792** Sarah Moore Grimke born, she and sister Angelina critics of Episcopal Church and slavery (died 1873); **1800** Charleston District becomes Charleston County; **1801** city hall built; **1804** South Carolina Society Hall built; **Feb. 20, 1805** Angelina Emily Grimke born, with sister Sarah, critic of slavery (died 1879); **1809** Planters Hotel opens; **1814** First Scotch Presbyterian Church built, founded 1731; **1815** St. John's Lutheran Church built, founded 1752; **March 22, 1818** Confederate Gen. Wade Hampton born (died 1902); **c.1820** seawall built to protect The Battery, district of fashionable homes; **1822** First Baptist Church completed, founded 1682; **1824** Medical College (University) of South Carolina founded; **1827** Fireproof Building completed, served as Charleston District Records Office, now South Carolina Historical Society; **1829** construction of Fort Sumter begins in Charleston Harbor, unfinished when South Carolina seceded in 1860; **1830** Chisholm Rice Mill built; **Jan. 1, 1830** poet Paul Hamilton Hayne born (died 1886); **1833** South Carolina Railroad completed to Hamburg; **1838** St. Philip's Episcopal Church completed; St. Mary's Catholic Church built; **1839** Charleston Hotel built; **1840** Beth Elohim Synagogue built; Hibernian Hall built; **1841** Market Hall built, became Confederate museum 1903; **Jan. 1, 1842** African-American Protestant Episcopal bishop Samuel Ferguson born (died 1916); **Dec. 1842** The Citadel (The Military College of South Carolina) established; **1855** South Carolina Historical Society founded; **Feb. 22, 1857** journalist, poet Frank Stanton born (died 1927); **Dec. 28-30, 1860** South Carolina troops seize Castle Pinckney, island fortress in Charleston Harbor, cutter ship *Aiken*, and Charleston Arsenal; **Apr. 12, 1861** Civil War begins with Confederate General Beauregard shelling U.S. Fort Sumter, fort surrenders Apr. 14; **Feb. 17, 1865** Confederates evacuate city after 567 continuous days of military operations; **May 2, 1879** James Francis Byrnes born, secretary of state under President Truman (died 1972); **Aug. 31, 1885** poet, novelist DuBose Heyward born, wrote *Porgy,* basis for musical *Porgy and Bess* (died 1940); **Aug. 31, 1886** earthquake estimated at 6.6 magnitude, 60 killed, rings church bells in St. Augustine, Florida; **1890** Cathedral of St. John (Catholic) begun, consecrated 1907; **1891** Circular Congregational Church completed; **1899** Thompson Auditorium built, occupied 1907 by Charleston Museum; **1901** U.S. Navy Shipyard established; **Jan. 1, 1922** Sen. Ernest "Fritz" Hollings born; **1926** Ashley River Bridge (bascule) built; **1929** Copper River Bridge completed; **1930** Cypress Gardens opened to north; **1938** Intracoastal Waterway completed, inland canal paralleling Atlantic and Gulf shores accommodating barge traffic; **Sept. 20, 1938** two tornadoes strike city killing 32; **Nov. 17, 1944** actress Lauren Hutton born; **1964** Charleston Southern University established; Trident Technical College (2-year) established; **1973** Patriots Point Naval and Maritime Museum founded, USS *Yorktown* aircraft carrier added 1976; **1984** Johnson and Wales University, Charleston Campus, established; **Sept. 21–22, 1989** state hit hard by Hurricane Hugo, 24 killed in U.S.; **July 22, 1994** court orders The Citadel to admit women, breaking tradition since 1842, first women admitted 1996; **Apr. 1996** Navy Shipyard closed, loss of over 8,000 military jobs and over 6,000 civilian jobs; **Aug. 8, 2000** Confederate submarine *H. L. Hunley* raised by salvagers, sunk Feb. 17, 1864, with nine on board.

Cheraw   *Chesterfield County*   *Northeastern South Carolina, 72 mi/116 km northeast of Columbia*

c.1752 area first settled; **1773** St. David's Episcopal Church completed; **c.1820** Pee Dee River opened to

traffic; **1820** McKay House built; **Dec. 1820** town incorporated; **1836** Old Market Hall built; **Oct. 21, 1917** jazz trumpeter Dizzy Gillespie born (died 1993); **1967** Chesterfield-Marlboro Technical College (2-year) established.

Chester   *Chester County*   *Northern South Carolina, 45 mi/72 km north of Columbia*

1755 settlers arrive from Chester, Pennsylvania; town founded; **1770** Purity Presbyterian Church founded to east, burned 1904, rebuilt in town; **1785** Chester County formed; town founded as county seat; **1840** town incorporated; **1850** second county courthouse built; **1851** Columbia & Chester Railroad reaches town; **1893** incorporated as a city.

Chesterfield   *Chesterfield County*   *Northern South Carolina, 67 mi/108 km northeast of Columbia*

1785 Chesterfield County formed; town founded as county seat; Craig House built; **1821** first library opened at Cheraw Lyceum; **1872** town incorporated; **1977** county courthouse built.

Clemson   *Pickens County*   *Northwestern South Carolina, 102 mi/164 km west-northwest of Columbia*

1776 military post built; **1803** Fort Hill residence built by Rev. James McElhenny, becomes estate of John C. Calhoun; **1872** town of Calhoun founded on Air Line (Southern) Railroad; **1889** Clemson Agricultural College established, becomes Clemson University; **1892** town incorporated; **1901** incorporated as a city; **1943** town renamed Clemson; **1957** South Carolina Botanical Garden established at Clemson University.

Clover   *York County*   *Northern South Carolina, 70 mi/113 km north of Columbia*

Oct. 7, 1780 Battle of Kings Mountain to west, detachment of militia under Col. William Campbell defeats British under Col. Patrick Ferguson, wresting South Carolina from British hands; **c.1875** town founded on Chester & Lenoir narrow gauge railroad; **1881** Clover Presbyterian Church organized; **1887** town incorporated; **March 3, 1931** Kings Mountain National Military Park established.

Columbia   *Richland County*   *Central South Carolina, on Congaree River*

1718 fort and trading post founded; **1785** Richland County formed; **1786** town founded as capital and county seat; capital moved from Charleston; **May 23, 1788** South Carolina becomes 8th state to ratify U.S. Constitution; **1790** horse racing established; **1797** city platted; **1801** University of South Carolina established; **1805** town incorporated; **c.1812** first cotton factory built with slave labor; **1814** First Presbyterian Church built; **1822** Boylston House built; **1824** Columbia Canal completed allowing water access from the "upcountry"; **1828** South Carolina State Hospital built; **1829** Columbia Theological Seminary (Presbyterian) established; **1854** incorporated as a city; Columbia College established; **1855** governor's mansion built; **Dec. 20, 1860** South Carolina secedes from Union; **Feb. 16, 1865** General Sherman's troops shell city, burn 84 blocks; *The Phoenix* newspaper established amid ashes by William Simms; **1870** Benedict College established for black students; **1880** Allen University for black students moved from Cokesbury; **1886** Winthrop College established, moves to Rock Hill 1895; **1907** statehouse construction halted for lack of funds, foundation laid 1851, completed 1998; **1911** Lutheran Theological Southern Seminary established, founded 1830 at Lexington; **1915** Chicora College moved from Greenville; **1917** Camp Jackson military base established to east, became Fort Jackson 1940; **1932** U.S. Veterans' Hospital established; **1936** county courthouse built; **1938** Women's Unit of State Penitentiary established at Irmo to northwest; **1941** Columbia Metro Airport established; **1974** Midlands Technical College (2-year) established; Riverbanks Zoological Garden established; **May 23, 2000** Confederate flag removed from state capitol after 38 years under pressure of African-American boycott.

Conway   *Horry County*   *Eastern South Carolina, 105 mi/169 km east of Columbia*

1732 town platted, named Kingston; **1801** Horry County formed from Georgetown District, named for Brig. Gen. Peter Horry; town becomes county seat, renamed Conwayborough; **1854** extensive logging operations begin; **1855** town incorporated, renamed Conwayboro; **1858** Kingston Presbyterian Church built, replaces 1795 structure; **1883** town renamed Conway; **Oct. 13, 1893** tidal wave damages town; **1898** incorporated as a city; **1900** Seashore & Conway Railroad built; **1908** third county courthouse built; **1954** Coastal Carolina University established; **1965** Horry-Georgetown Technical College (2-year) established.

Cowpens   *Spartanburg County*   *Northwestern South Carolina, 75 mi/121 km northwest of Columbia*

Jan. 17, 1781 decisive victory won by Brig. Gen. Daniel Morgan over British Lt. Col. Banastre Tarleton in Battle of Cowpens, to north; **1856** monument erected at battle site by Washington Light Infantry of Charleston; **Apr. 29, 1929** Cowpens National Battlefield established.

Darlington   *Darlington County*   *Northeastern South Carolina, 63 mi/101 km east-northeast of Columbia*

1785 Darlington County formed; town settled, founded as county seat; **1835** town incorporated; **1894** Gov. B. R. Tillman's liquor regulations, including unwarranted search of homes, leads to Darlington War riot, three killed, several wounded; **1949** Darlington International Raceway established; **1965** county courthouse completed.

Dillon   *Dillon County*   *Western South Carolina, 90 mi/145 km east-northeast of Columbia*

1887 Atlantic Coast Line Railroad reaches site; town founded, named for railroad promoter J. W. Dillon; **1888** town incorporated; **1910** Dillon County formed from Marion County; town becomes county seat; county courthouse built; **1950** Alan Schafer founds South of the Border tourist attraction to north on North Carolina boundary.

Edgefield   *Edgefield County*   *Southwestern South Carolina, 50 mi/80 km west-southwest of Columbia*

1775 Blocker House built by John Blocker; **1785** Edgefield County formed; town founded as county seat; **1790** Cedar Grove house built by James Blocker; **Nov. 18, 1796** Sen. Andrew Pickens Butler born (died 1857); **c.1810** Halcyon House built by Andrew Pickens; **c.1818** Mims-Norris House built by Col. Robert Norris; **Aug. 4, 1819** U.S. Cong. Preston S. Brooks born (died 1857), noted for his caning of Massachusetts Sen. Charles Sumner in 1856 for accusing him of fathering illegitimate children; **1826** Furman University established, moved to Greenville 1851; **1830** town incorporated; **1839** county courthouse built, renovated 1998; **Aug. 11, 1847** Gov., Sen. Benjamin R. Tillman born in rural Edgefield County (died 1918); **Dec. 5, 1902** Sen. Strom Thurmond born (died 2003, age 100).

Florence   *Florence County*   *Eastern South Carolina, 67 mi/108 km east of Columbia*

1732 area settled by Scotch-Irish Presbyterians; **1736** Welsh Baptists settle in area; **1853** Wilmington & Manchester and Northwestern railroads form junction; town founded, named Wilds for its forested location; **1859** Cheraw & Darlington Railroad reaches town, establishes shops; town renamed Florence for daughter of Gen. William Harllee, president of Wilmington & Manchester Railroad; **1871** town chartered; **1888** Florence County formed; town becomes county seat; **Dec. 1890** incorporated as a city; **March 18, 1901** African-American painter William H. Johnson born (died 1970); **1908** South Carolina Industrial School founded; **1963** Florence-Darlington Technical College (2-year) established; **1970** Francis Marion University established; **1972** city-county government complex opened.

Gaffney   *Cherokee County*   *Northern South Carolina, 73 mi/117 km north-northwest of Columbia*

1804 Irishman Michael Gaffney settles here, opens store; town founded at mineral springs; **1835** hotel built at springs, waters used as therapy for malaria, called "country fever"; **1845** Limestone College for women established; **1857** town incorporated; **1873** railroad reaches town; **1887** cotton textile industry established; **1897** Cherokee County formed; town becomes county seat; **May 2, 1901** writer Wilbur Joseph Cash born (died 1941); **1914** Carnegie Library built; **1930** county courthouse built; **Apr. 21, 1958** actress Andie MacDowell born.

Georgetown   *Georgetown County*   *Southeastern South Carolina, 100 mi/161 km southeast of Columbia*

c.1725 area first settled; **1732** site designated a seaport by King George II; **1734** town founded on Waccamaw River, near Atlantic Ocean; **c.1735** Hampton Plantation House built; **1746** Episcopal Church completed; **1769** Georgetown District formed; town becomes district seat; **Nov. 5, 1779** poet, author Washington Allston born (died 1843); **1785** Winyah County formed from Georgetown District; **1800s** rice production becomes major industry, ends by 1920; **1800** county renamed Georgetown County; **1805** town incorporated; **1824** county courthouse built; **June 21, 1832** African-American Cong. Joseph Hayne Rainey born (died 1887); **1857** Winyah Indigo Society Hall built.

Great Falls   *Chester County*   *Northern South Carolina, 35 mi/56 km north of Columbia*

Aug. 18, 1780 Battle of Fishing Creek, British Lt. Col. Banastre Tarleton's forces surprise Gen. Thomas Sumter's men, Sumter narrowly escapes capture; **1803** arsenal built on river island to east, becomes Fort Dearborn military post 1812; town founded on Catawba River; **1823** Landsford Canal completed permitting commerce on Catawba River; **1849** cotton mill built; **1865** Camp Welfare organized by African Episcopal Church; **1968** town incorporated.

Greenville   *Greenville County*   *Northwestern South Carolina, 88 mi/142 km northwest of Columbia*

1765 trader Richard Pearis becomes area's first settler; Pearis builds mill; **1777** land granted by Cherokees who leave area; **1786** Greenville County formed; **1797** town platted as Pleasantburg, becomes county seat; **1816** Vardry McBee acquires Alston's holdings, develops town as resort; cotton mill built by George Putnam; **c.1825** county courthouse built; **1831** town incorporated, renamed Greenville; **1851** Furman University moved from Edgefield, established 1826; **1852** Christ Episcopal Church built; **1853** Columbia & Greenville Railroad arrives; **1860** First Baptist Church built; **1874** Charlotte & Atlanta Air Railroad (Southern Railway) reaches city; **Jan. 9, 1878** psychologist John Broadus Watson born (died 1958); **Feb. 11, 1908** blues singer Josh White born (died 1969); **July 28, 1915** physicist Charles Townes born, invented the laser 1958; **1927** Shriners Hospital opened; **1936** municipal stadium built; **Oct. 8, 1941** civil rights leader Jesse Jackson born; **1947** Bob Jones University moved from Cleveland, Tennessee, established 1927 at College Point, Florida; **1950** county courthouse built; **1962** Greenville Technical College (2-year) established.

Greenwood   *Greenwood County*   *Western South Carolina, 60 mi/97 km west of Columbia*

1824 area first settled; **1833** general store opens; settlement named Green Wood; **1837** first post office established, named Woodville; **1850** post office renamed Greenwood; **1852** Greenville & Columbia Railroad arrives; **1857** town incorporated; **1897** Greenwood County formed; town becomes county seat; **1898** county courthouse built; **Nov. 8, 1898** in Phoenix Riot at Kirksey to south, investigation into Republican ballot box discrepancies draws hundreds of white protesters, seven blacks, one white Republican killed; **1904** Lander College moves from Williamston, founded 1872; **1911** town served by five railroads; **1914** Bailey Military Academy moves from Edgefield, destroyed by fire 1936; **1917** Carnegie Library founded; **1927** incorporated as a city; **1966** Piedmont Technical College (2-year) established.

Greer   *Greenville County*   *Northwestern South Carolina, 85 mi/137 km northwest of Columbia*

1820 Cedar Hill Cotton Mill built; **1873** town founded on Richmond & Danville Air Line Railroad (Southern Railway) on property owned by Manning Greer, originally named Greer's Depot; **1876** town incorporated; **1896** Victor Cotton Mill established; **1900** Franklin Mill established; **1901** town renamed; **1908** Greer Mill established.

Hampton   *Hampton County*   *Southern South Carolina, 72 mi/116 km south of Columbia*

1878 Hampton County formed; town founded as county seat; construction of county courthouse begins with parade, includes Red Shirts white supremacist group; **1879** town incorporated; **1942** first Watermelon Festival held.

Irmo   *Lexington County*   See **Columbia (1938)**

Kingstree   *Williamsburg County*   *Southeastern South Carolina, 67 mi/108 km east-southeast of Columbia*

1732 area first settled by Scotch-Irish who build homes around white birch called Kings's Tree; **Aug. 27, 1780** Williamsburg Battalion surprised by British force in Battle of King's Tree, 30 killed; **1785** Williamsburg County formed; town becomes county seat; **1823** county courthouse built; **1866** town incorporated; **1890** Williamsburg Presbyterian Church moved from rural part of county, first built 1736; **1939** market building built.

Lancaster   *Lancaster County*   *Northern South Carolina, 46 mi/74 km north-northeast of Columbia*

Feb. 12, 1767 Andrew Jackson, 7th President, born on North Carolina border (died June 18, 1845) [see Waxhaw, North Carolina]; **May 29, 1780** Virginia patriots under Col. Abraham Buford massacred by Col. Tarleton's British troops after their surrender; **1785** Lancaster County formed; town founded as county seat; **1823** county courthouse built; **1830** town incorporated; **1959** University of South Carolina, Lancaster Campus, (2-year) established.

Laurens   *Laurens County*   *Northwestern South Carolina, 60 mi/97 km northwest of Columbia*

1754 John Duncan becomes first settler; **1785** Laurens County formed; town founded as county seat; **c.1820** cotton clothing production becomes important, flourishes by 1840; **1840** second county courthouse completed; **1850** Church of the Epiphany dedicated; **1870** riot at National Guard Armory, eight blacks, one white Republican killed; **1873** town incorporated; **1895** Laurens Cotton Mill established; **1917** incorporated as a city.

Lexington   *Lexington County*   *Central South Carolina, 10 mi/16 km west of Columbia*

1735 town site first settled, originally named Saxe Gatha; **1785** Lexington County formed; Granby becomes first county seat; **1820** town of Lexington platted; county seat moved from Granby; **1861** town incorporated; **Feb. 1865** Federal troops burn town; **1890** textile mill built; **1894** fire destroys many of town's buildings, again 1916; **1940** county courthouse built; **2003** new county courthouse completed.

Manning   *Clarendon County*   *Southeast central South Carolina, 47 mi/76 km southeast of Columbia*

1785 Clarendon County formed; **1800** county merges with Sumter District; **1813** Brewington Presbyterian Church built; **1855** town founded; Wolfe House built; **1857** Clarendon County reformed; town becomes county seat; **1861** town incorporated; **1908** Manning Library built; **1909** county courthouse completed; **Sept. 25, 1927** African-American tennis star Althea Gibson born at rural Silver to west (died 2003); **1938** large Lake Marion formed by dam on Santee River to south; **1941** Santee National Wildlife Refuge established to south.

Marion   *Marion County*   *Eastern South Carolina, 86 mi/138 km east of Columbia*

1769 land granted to James Godbold; **June 8, 1782** Battle of Bowling Green, British Maj. Gainey defeated by Gen. Francis "Swamp Fox" Marion in brief skirmish; **1800** Marion County formed; town founded as county seat, named Gilesboro for Col. Hugh Giles; **1804** Durham House built by Thomas Godbold; **1830s** town renamed Marion; **1847** town incorporated; **1854** county courthouse completed; **1886** Marion Academy built; **1892** Little Pee Dee Causeway built to southeast; Marion Public Library founded; **Sept. 16, 1903** novelist Gwen Bristow born (died 1980).

McCormick   *McCormick County*   *Southwestern South Carolina, 66 mi/106 km west of Columbia*

1852 rich gold vein discovered, first mined by William F. Dorn; **late 1850s** labyrinth of gold mine tunnels underlie town; **1882** town incorporated, named for Cyrus McCormick, inventor of the reaper; **1884** fire destroys two city blocks; McCormick Hotel built, becomes Fannie Kate's Inn 1995; **c.1900** Keturah Hotel built, becomes

Carolina Hotel 1985; **1916** McCormick County formed; town becomes county seat; **1923** county courthouse built.

Moncks Corner   *Berkeley County*   *Southeastern South Carolina, 74 mi/119 km southeast of Columbia*

1712 Biggin Church built to east, rebuilt 1756; **1714** Mulberry Castle house built to south by Thomas Broughton; **1726** Exeter plantation house built to south; **1732** Revolutionary leader Francis "Swamp Fox" Marion born in rural Berkeley County (died 1795); **1735** town founded by Thomas Monck; **1762** Mepkin estate built to east by Henry Laurens; **1774** Lewisfield plantation built by Keating Simons; **1800** Santee Canal completed, begun 1792; **1863** Confederate torpedo boat *David* built at Stony Landing Plantation, 37 killed later aboard *David* at Charleston Harbor; **1882** Berkeley County formed; town becomes county seat; **1885** town incorporated; **1897** county courthouse built; **1942** Pinopolis Dam built on West Branch Cooper River forming Lake Moultrie.

Myrtle Beach   *Horry County*   *Eastern South Carolina, 115 mi/185 km east of Columbia*

1900 Seashore & Conway Railroad completed to Atlantic Ocean; resort town founded; **1938** incorporated as a city; **1941** Myrtle Beach Air Force Base established, closed 1993; **1954** first Sun Fun Festival held; **Feb. 18, 1957** TV personality Vanna White born at North Myrtle Beach; **May 13, 1959** three Air Force F-100 jet airplanes crash into ocean, killing all three pilots; **1984** Honey Creek Railroad established to continue rail service to city.

New Ellenton   *Aiken County*   *Southwestern South Carolina, 50 mi/80 km southwest of Columbia*

c.1870 town of Ellenton founded; **May 15, 1876** two days of rioting over arrest of black men for beating white woman leaves 15 blacks, 2 whites dead, quelled by state militia; **1951** Savannah River Nuclear Facility established to south; town moved north 3 mi/4.8 km, renamed New Ellenton; **1952** town reincorporated.

Newberry   *Newberry County*   *Central South Carolina, 35 mi/56 km northwest of Columbia*

1785 Newberry County formed; town founded as county seat; **1852** county courthouse completed; **1855** St. Luke's Episcopal Church built; **1856** Newberry College established; **1882** opera house built, closed 1952, reopened as live theater 1998; **1894** town incorporated; **1926** experiment conducted on section of U.S. Highway 76 incorporating cotton fabric into surfacing material to minimize wear, project suspended; **1936** Art Deco Ritz Theatre built.

Ninety Six   *Greenwood County*   *Western South Carolina, 52 mi/84 km west of Columbia*

c.1730 trading post established by Capt. John Francis; town founded; named for estimated mileage from Keowee; **Nov. 1775** Revolutionaries under Col. Andrew

Williamson, outnumbered two to one, defeat British Colonel Robinson's forces; **May 12, 1781** Gen. Nathanael Greene's forces camp here, begin 37-day siege of Star Fort, rid town of British; **1855** railroad reaches site; town relocated; **1872** town incorporated; **1940** Buzzard Roost Dam built on Saluda River to east, forms Lake Greenwood; **Aug. 19, 1976** Ninety-Six National Historic Site established to south.

North Augusta   *Aiken County   Southwestern South Carolina, on Savannah River, adjacent to Augusta, Ga.*

1821 land grant made to Henry Schultz; town of Hamburg founded; **1833** Charleston-Hamburg (South Carolina) Railroad completed to divert commerce from Savannah, Georgia; **1876** the Hamburg Riot sparked by a white supremacist gang; **1902** new town platted by James U. Jackson; **1906** city of North Augusta incorporated.

Orangeburg   *Orangeburg County   Central South Carolina, 33 mi/53 km south of Columbia*

1704 trader George Sterling settles here; **1730s** Swiss, German and Dutch immigrants arrive; **1769** Orangeburg District formed; town becomes district seat; **1785** Orangeburg County formed; **1791** Orangeburg District reestablished; **1800** Orangeburg County reformed; **1831** town incorporated; **1858** Presbyterian Church built; **1869** Claflin College (University) established for black students; **1883** incorporated as a city; **1896** State Agricultural and Mechanical College established for black students, becomes South Carolina State University; **1927** fifth county courthouse built; **1968** Orangeburg-Calhoun Technical College (2-year) established.

Pendleton   *Anderson County   Northwestern South Carolina, 100 mi/161 km west-northwest of Columbia*

1790 town founded as seat of Pendleton District; **1802** Hopewell Presbyterian Church built, organized 1789; **1807** *Pendleton Messenger* newspaper founded; **c.1810** Woodburn house (Smythe Place) built; **1822** St. Paul's Episcopal Church built; **1826** Anderson County formed; construction begins on county courthouse, Anderson chosen as county seat, building used for Farmers' Society Hall; **1832** town incorporated; **1845** Montpelier house built.

Pickens   *Pickens County   Northwestern South Carolina, 102 mi/164 km northwest of Columbia*

1717 Keowee Path used as early transportation route; **1753** Fort Prince George built by British; **1756** fort becomes central to Cherokee War; **1761** Cherokee War ends, Native American settlements destroyed; **1826** Pickens County formed; Pickens Court House becomes county seat; **1868** Oconee County separates from Pickens County; town founded as new county seat; **July 11, 1888** Chicago White Sox baseball player "Shoeless" Joe

Jackson born in rural Pickens County (died 1951); **1908** town incorporated; **1960** county courthouse built.

Port Royal   *Beaufort County   Southern South Carolina, 103 mi/166 km south of Columbia, on Atlantic Ocean*

1562 French explorer Jean Ribaut visits harbor, builds fort at Parris Island; **1565** Spanish arrive, destroy French settlement; **1663** English Capt. William Hilton arrives, claims land; **1670** site considered for settlement by English, Charles Town chosen instead; **1732** Fort Frederick built; **Feb. 12, 1779** British attack repulsed by forces of Col. Barnwell in Battle of Port Royal; **Aug. 29, 1861** town seized by Union troops; **1870s** railroad coaches built here; **1874** town incorporated; **1876** U.S. Naval Station established at Parris Island, becomes Marine Corps base 1915; **Aug. 30, 1935** singer John Phillips of Mamas & Papas born at Parris Island (died 2001); **1959** port terminal built.

Ridgeland   *Jasper County   Southern South Carolina, 96 mi/155 km south of Columbia*

c.1850 Charleston & Savannah Railroad built; town founded, named Gopher Hill; **1884** town renamed Ridgeland; **1894** town incorporated; **1912** Jasper County formed; town becomes county seat; **1915** county courthouse built; **1927** Savannah National Wildlife Refuge established to south on Savannah River.

Rock Hill   *York County   Northern South Carolina, 58 mi/93 km north of Columbia*

1831 White Homestead plantation house built; **1852** Charlotte & Columbia Railroad built; town founded; **1870** town incorporated; town becomes center of intense Ku Klux Klan activity; **1880** Rock Hill Cotton Factory opens; **1892** incorporated as a city; **1895** Winthrop College (University) moved from Columbia, established 1886; **1934** The Oratory founded, Catholic school for underprivileged boys; **1961** York Technical College (2-year) established.

Saint George   *Dorchester County   Southeastern South Carolina, 57 mi/92 km south-southeast of Columbia*

1697 area settled by Congregationalists from Dorchester, Massachusetts, return by 1707; **1788** town founded; **Jan. 1875** town incorporated; **1889** incorporated as a city; **1897** Dorchester County formed; **1898** town becomes county seat; **1964** county courthouse built.

Saint Matthews   *Calhoun County   Central South Carolina, 25 mi/40 km southeast of Columbia*

1730s area settled by Palatine Germans; trading post established; **1775** Fort Motte built to north; **1833** South Carolina Railroad built; **1841** town founded; **1872** town incorporated; **1908** Calhoun County formed; town becomes county seat; **1913** county courthouse built; **1938** in reforestation program, 200,000 pine trees planted in Congaree Swamp; **Oct. 18, 1976** Congaree Swamp National Monument authorized to north.

Saluda   *Saluda County*   *Central South Carolina,*
38 mi/61 km west of Columbia

1895 Saluda County formed from Edgefield County; town founded as county seat; **1897** town incorporated; **1913** brick Red Bank Baptist Church built, log structure built 1784, frame structure 1855; **1917** county courthouse built.

Silver   *Clarendon County*   *See* **Manning (1927)**

Spartanburg   *Spartanburg County*   *Northwestern South Carolina, 75 mi/121 km northwest of Columbia*

1761 area first settled; **1773** Wofford's Iron Works established to east; **1785** Spartanburg County formed; site selected for county seat; **1801** Foster's Tavern built by Anthony Foster; **1816** two cotton mills opened in area; **1824** Word Academy founded; **1830** cotton mill built near iron works; **1831** town incorporated; **1854** Wofford College established; **1855** South Carolina School for the Deaf and Blind founded; **1873** Charlotte & Atlanta Air Line railroad reaches town; **1885** Kennedy Free Library built; **1889** Converse College established; **1911** Textile Industrial Institute founded, becomes Spartanburg Methodist College; **1917** Camp Wadsworth military base founded, closed 1919; **1958** county courthouse completed; **1967** University of South Carolina at Spartanburg established.

Sumter   *Sumter County*   *Central South Carolina, 36 mi/58 km east of Columbia*

c.1740 area first settled; **1785** town founded as Sumterville, named for Revolutionary War Gen. Thomas Sumter; **1800** Sumter District formed; town becomes district seat; **1800** town platted; **1806** district (county) courthouse built; **1843** South Carolina Railroad reaches town; **1845** town incorporated; **1855** town renamed Sumter; **1862** St. Joseph's Academy founded; **1868** Sumter District becomes Sumter County; **1908** Morris College established for black students; **1939** South Carolina Home for Crippled Children established; Sears, Roebuck establishes furniture factory; **1941** Shaw Army Air Field established, becomes Shaw Air Force Base 1947; **1963** Central Carolina Technical College (2-year) established; **1965** University of South Carolina, Sumter Campus, (2-year) established.

Union   *Union County*   *Northern South Carolina, 50 mi/80 km northwest of Columbia*

Nov. 20, 1780 200 British killed or wounded, Americans under General Sumter suffer three casualties in Battle of Blackstock to southwest; **1785** Union County formed as part of Ninety-Six District; town founded, named Unionville; **1791** Union County absorbed by Pinckney District; **1800** Union County reformed; county seat moved from Pinckneyville; **1832** Gist Mansion built by Gov. William H. Gist; **1837** town incorporated as Union; **1913** county courthouse completed; **1965** Union Campus of University of South Carolina established; **Oct. 25, 1994** Susan Smith, drives vehicle into lake drowning sons Michael, 3, and Alexander, 14 months, claims African-American carjacker took them, charged with murder, sentenced to life.

Walhalla   *Oconee County*   *Northwestern South Carolina, 105 mi/169 km northwest of Columbia*

1849 town founded by John A. Wagener of German Colonization Society; **1853** construction begins on Stump House Mountain Tunnel on Blue Ridge Railroad to west, abandoned 1859; **1855** town incorporated; **1868** Oconee County formed; town becomes county seat; **1869** county courthouse built; **1973** Oconee Nuclear Power Plant opened.

Walterboro   *Colleton County*   *Southern South Carolina, 72 mi/116 km south-southeast of Columbia*

1784 area settled by rice planters; town founded; **1800** Colleton District formed; town becomes district seat; **1820** Walterboro Library built; **1822** district (county) courthouse built; **1826** incorporated as a city; **1845** Klein's Drug Store opens, still in business; **1868** Colleton District becomes Colleton County; **1965** University of South Carolina, Salkehatchie Campus, established.

Winnsboro   *Fairfield County*   *North central South Carolina, 22 mi/35 km north of Columbia*

1755 area first settled; **1777** Mount Zion Institute founded; **1780** town occupied by British troops; **1785** Fairfield County formed; town chartered as Winnsborough, becomes county seat; public market established; **1823** county courthouse built; **1832** town incorporated, renamed Winnsboro.

York   *York County*   *Northern South Carolina, 62 mi/100 km north of Columbia*

1757 area settled by Scotch-Irish from Pennsylvania; town founded at Fergus Crossroads Tavern, named Yorkville; **1785** York County formed; **1786** town becomes county seat; **1819** York Female Academy, later College, founded, closed 1875; **July 12, 1821** Confederate Gen. Daniel Harvey Hill born (died 1889); **1841** town incorporated; **1855** Kings Mountain Academy founded, closed 1909; **1868** South Carolina's first Ku Klux Klan organized here; town becomes center of Klan activity; **1914** county courthouse built; **1915** town renamed York.

South Dakota

North central U.S. Capital: Pierre. Largest city: Sioux Falls.

The region entered the U.S. with the Louisiana Purchase December 30, 1803. Dakota Territory was formed March 2, 1861. South Dakota and North Dakota entered the U.S. jointly as the 39th and 40th states November 2, 1889.

South Dakota is divided into 66 counties. The counties are divided into townships which have limited governments. Municipalities are classified as towns and cities. See Introduction.

Aberdeen *Brown County* *Northeastern South Dakota, 160 mi/257 km northwest of Sioux Falls*

1879 Brown County formed, organized 1880; **1880** party of 12 led by the Rice brothers and Charles Boyden arrives; town founded on right of way of Chicago, Milwaukee, St. Paul & Pacific Railroad at junction with Chicago & Northwestern Railroad; town named Grand Crossing; post office established; Rice Brothers and Boyden Store founded; **1881** second town of Aberdeen founded 2 mi/3.2 km north of junction, named for Scottish birthplace of Milwaukee Railroad president Alexander Mitchell; stockyards founded; store moved to Aberdeen; **1882** incorporated as a city; **1886** Great Northern Railroad reaches town; **1887** county seat moved from Columbia; **1888** L. (Lyman) Frank Baum (1856–1919), author of *Wizard of Oz*, arrives, operates Baum's Bazaar novelty shop, later works for Aberdeen *Saturday Pioneer* newspaper, leaves Aberdeen 1891; **1900** Carnegie Library built; **1901** Northern State University established; **1905** county courthouse completed; **1916** Industrial Workers of the World (IWW) establishes headquarters here, five murders, several fires occur within weeks, businessmen organize Home Guard, evict union members from city, attempted boycott of South Dakota by IWW fails; **1921** Aberdeen Regional Airport established to south; **Jan. 13, 1931** the Schense quadruplets born to Mr. and Mrs. Fred Schense of rural Hecla to northeast, at hospital in Aberdeen; **1950** Alexander Mitchell Library established in temporary quarters, replaces Carnegie Library, new library opened 1963; **1961** South Dakota School for the Blind moved from Gary, established 1895; **Sept. 14, 1963** Mr. and Mrs. Andrew Fisher become parents of quintuplets, added to their five other children.

Alexandria *Hanson County* *Southeastern South Dakota, 52 mi/84 km west of Sioux Falls*

1871 Hanson County formed; town founded as county seat by German immigrants; **1895** Rockport Mennonite Colony founded on James River to west; **1905** incorporated as a city; **1930s** small Lake Hanson formed to south by dam built with WPA assistance; **1963** county courthouse built.

Armour *Douglas County* *Southeastern South Dakota, 82 mi/132 km west-southwest of Sioux Falls*

1883 Douglas County formed; Grand View becomes county seat; **1886** town founded as new county seat, named for Philip D. Armour, railroad director and meat-packing entrepreneur, who in turn provided new bell for the town church; *Armour Chronicle* newspaper founded; **Jan. 1891** fire destroys 18 businesses on Main Street; **1904** incorporated as a city; **1915** Carnegie Library built; **1927** county courthouse built.

Avon *Bon Homme County* *Southeastern South Dakota, 77 mi/124 km southwest of Sioux Falls*

1879 town founded; post office established; named by postmaster George Phoenix for hometown in New York; **1903** incorporated as a city; **July 19, 1922** U.S. Sen. George McGovern born, 1972 Democratic nominee for president.

Belle Fourche *Butte County* *Western South Dakota, 52 mi/84 km northwest of Rapid City*

1878 sheep ranching introduced, becomes important regional industry; **1881** Butte County formed; **1890** town founded as county seat by Powersite Land Company; Chicago & Northwestern Railroad reaches town; **1894** 4,700 train carloads of cattle shipped out, evidence of town's importance as cattle center; **1903** town incorporated; **1905** construction begins on Orman Dam, on Owl Creek, part of Belle Fourche Reclamation Project, dam completed 1908, project completed 1917; **1908** land opened for settlement; **1910** temperance crusader Carrie Nation arrives from Texas, dies 1911; **1911** county courthouse built; **1912** experimental sugar beet production begins, through 1917; **1918** first annual Black Hills Round Up rodeo held; **1927** Black Hills Sugar Company plant built (closed 1965).

Big Stone City *Grant County Northeastern South Dakota, 122 mi/196 km north-northeast of Sioux Falls*

1818 trading post established on south shore of Big Stone Lake (Minnesota border) by Hazen P. Moers; **July 22, 1823** Maj. Stephen H. Long expedition camps here while surveying Red River; **1857** Dakota Chief Inkpaduta brings seven captive white women here following Spirit Lake, Iowa, massacre; **1865** trading post established by Moses Moreau and Soloman Robar; **1873** Grant County formed; **1878** John Marten establishes ferry at point where lake exits through Minnesota River; settlement named Inkpa City, after Chief Inkpaduta; **1880** town becomes county seat; **1883** county seat moved to Milbank; **1885** incorporated as a city, renamed Big Stone City; **1890s** Chautauqua societies attracted to lake's surroundings; **1937** water diversion project completed, started 1934, sending waters of Whetstone River into nearly dry Big Stone Lake, source of Minnesota River.

Bison *Perkins County Northwestern South Dakota, 130 mi/209 km northwest of Pierre*

1907 town founded; **1908** Perkins County formed, named for Sturgis official Henry E. Perkins; town becomes county seat; **1940** incorporated as a town; **1968** county courthouse built.

Blunt *Hughes County Central South Dakota, 20 mi/32 km east-northeast of Pierre*

1881 Chicago & Northwestern Railroad built; town founded; **1883** school teacher Mentor Graham arrives from Sangamon County, Illinois, retires to his son's homestead, taught Abraham Lincoln, considered foremost influence on Lincoln's thinking, guest of honor on platform at Lincoln's inauguration, died here 1886; **1884** incorporated as a city; **c.1900** new line of Chicago & Northwestern Railroad joins existing line from northeast.

Britton *Marshall County Northeastern South Dakota, 163 mi/262 km north-northwest of Sioux Falls*

1884 Chicago, Milwaukee, St. Paul & Pacific Railroad built; town founded, named for founder and railroad promoter Col. Isaac Britton; **1885** Marshall County formed; town becomes county seat; **1906** incorporated as a city; **1908** county courthouse completed.

Brookings *Brookings County Eastern South Dakota, 53 mi/85 km north of Sioux Falls*

1857 town of Medary founded to south, first town site in Dakota Territory; **1862** Brookings County formed; soldiers deployed to prevent Dakota Sioux incursions; **1873** county organized; Medary becomes county seat; **1880** Chicago & Northwestern Railroad built; town founded as county seat, absorbs Medary; town and county named for Wilmot W. Brookings, Sioux Falls legislator who had both legs amputated because of frostbite suffered upon his arrival in winter 1857; **1881** South Dakota State University established; **1883** town incorporated; **1912** county courthouse built; **1950** Municipal Airport built; **1986** Dakota, Minnesota & Eastern Railroad headquarters established.

Buffalo *Harding County Northwestern South Dakota, 178 mi/286 km northwest of Pierre*

Sept. 9, 1876 Battle of Slim Buttes waged to east between Gen. George Crook's troops and Sioux, revenge for Custer's defeat at Little Bighorn, four Sioux, three of Crook's men killed; **1908** Harding County formed; **1909** town founded as county seat; **1911** county courthouse built; **1949** incorporated as a town; **1953** Antelope Range Livestock Research Station established to south.

Burke *Gregory County Southern South Dakota, 130 mi/209 km west-southwest of Sioux Falls*

1862 Gregory County formed; **1898** county organized; **1904** large part of Rosebud Indian Reservation opened to white settlement, including Gregory County; town founded as county seat, named for U.S. Cong. Charles Burke; **1905** African-American Oscar Micheaux (1884–1951) homesteads in area on money earned as a porter, writes novels, becomes film producer 1919, his over 40 films include *The Homesteader* namesake of Black Filmmakers Hall of Fame annual Oscar Micheaux Awards; **1906** incorporated as a city; **1934** county courthouse built.

Canton *Lincoln County Southeastern South Dakota, 18 mi/29 km south-southeast of Sioux Falls*

1860 town founded on Big Sioux River (Iowa state boundary); **1862** Lincoln County formed; **1866** L. P. Hyde and son Henry become first settlers; **1867** town becomes county seat; **Dec. 1867** town renamed for Canton, China, thought to be opposite the town on the globe; **1868** blockhouse and general store built; **1871** town's first newspaper published; **1872** Chicago, Milwaukee, St. Paul & Pacific Railroad reaches town; **1875** county courthouse built; **1880–1881** blizzard, heavy snows lead to extensive spring flooding; **1881** incorporated as a city; **1884** Augustana College moved from Beloit, Iowa, merges with Lutheran Normal School, Sioux Falls, 1918; **June 27, 1901** Merle Tuve born, inventor of radio proximity fuse in World War II to guide bombs to targets (died 1982); **Aug. 8, 1901** physicist E. O. Lawrence born, inventor of the cyclotron (died 1958); **1913** Canton Public Library opened.

Chamberlain *Brule County* *Central South Dakota, 130 mi/209 km west of Sioux Falls, on Missouri River*

Sept. 16–17, 1804 Lewis and Clark camp across river, near present-day Oacoma; **Aug. 28, 1806** Lewis and Clark revisit campsite on return journey; **1809** trading post established on American Island; **1822** Fort Recovery built after fire destroys American Island post; **Nov. 1868** Samuel H. Morrow surveys area; **1875** Brule County formed; **1879** Brule City founded as county seat south of Chamberlain town site at narrowest point on Missouri River, assumed future railroad crossing; **1880** town platted at actual crossing point of Chicago, Milwaukee, St. Paul & Pacific Railroad; town becomes county seat, named for railroad official Selah Chamberlain; **1881** heavy snows bring spring flooding, destroys much of new town; **1882** railroad reaches town; town incorporated; **1893** pontoon bridge built across river, replaces ferry service; **July 4, 1905** railroad bridge completed; **1925** highway bridge built across Missouri River; **early 1950s** railroad and highway bridges rebuilt to allow for rising waters of Fort Randall Dam; **1953** waters from dam cover historic American Island; **1958** county courthouse built; **2000** incorporated as a city.

Clark *Clark County* *Eastern South Dakota, 105 mi/169 km north-northwest of Sioux Falls*

1873 Clark County formed; **1882** town founded, named for legislator Newton Clark; area becomes known for potato production; **1883** incorporated as a city; **1935** county courthouse built; **1991** first annual Potato Day held.

Clear Lake *Deuel County* *Eastern South Dakota, 85 mi/137 km north of Sioux Falls*

1833 explorers Fremont and Nicollet visit region; **1840** Rev. Stephen R. Riggs visits with Native Americans; **1862** Deuel County formed; **1871** town founded; **1878** county organized; town designated county seat; **1879** last buffalo hunt in county takes place, part of effort to exterminate Native Americans' primary means of existence; **1884** town incorporated; **1890** bitter county seat feud settled with Gary losing contest to Clear Lake; **1917** county courthouse built.

Custer *Custer County* *Southwestern South Dakota, 30 mi/48 km southwest of Rapid City*

1874 Lt. Col. George Custer's thousand-man military expedition to Black Hills confirms existence of gold in hills, comes away with wagonloads of it; **July 27, 1874** Horatio N. Ross becomes first real discoverer of gold in region, found on French Creek; **1875** Custer County formed; town founded as county seat, named Stonewall for Gen. Stonewall Jackson; Jenney-Newton Expedition conducts geological survey of Black Hills; Dr. Valentine T. McGillycuddy becomes first white man to climb to summit of Harney Peak (7,242 ft/2,207 m), South Dakota's highest point; **1876** town renamed Custer; **1879** first narrow gauge railroads begin hauling ore out of hills; **1880** incorporated as a city; **1881** county courthouse built, becomes museum after 1973; **1890** Chicago, Burlington & Quincy Railroad reaches town from south; **1890s** town becomes center of Black Hills lumber industry; **1897** Black Hills Forest Reserve (now National Forest) created by Pres. Grover Cleveland; **Feb. 7, 1908** Jewel Cave National Monument established to west; **1909** Custer State Sanitarium founded; **1913** 60,000 ac/24,300 ha set aside for game preserve through efforts of Gov. Peter Norbeck, additional 30,000 ac/12,150 ha added to preserve in 1920, becomes Custer State Park; **1921** Ross Monument erected honoring gold discoverer Horatio N. Ross; **1925** Blue Bell Lodge built in Custer State Park; **1927** "Summer White House" established by Pres. and Mrs. Calvin Coolidge at State Game Lodge, Custer State Park; **1937** new Sylvan Lake Hotel completed to northeast, in extension of Custer State Park, replaces lodge destroyed by fire 1936; **1939** ashes of Valentine McGillycuddy scattered on Harney Peak; **1946** Black Hills Playhouse built in Custer State Park; **1947** sculptor Korczak Ziolkowski arrives at invitation of Sioux leader Henry Standing Bear to begin work on mountain sculpture of Crazy Horse; **Oct. 20, 1982** Ziolkowski dies, wife Ruth continues work on Crazy Horse sculpture (born Boston, Sept. 6, 1908); **1989** Centennial Trail opens, winds 111 mi/179 km from Wind Cave National Park north to Bear Butte State Park; **1992** county courthouse built.

De Smet *Kingsbury County* *Eastern South Dakota, 70 mi/113 km northwest of Sioux Falls*

1857 party of Santees overtake Dakota Chief Inkpaduta, wanted for massacres in Iowa and Minnesota, bones found later possibly those of Inkpaduta and followers; **1873** Kingsbury County formed, named for Yankton editor George W. Kingsbury; **1879** town founded as county seat, named for Father Pierre De Smet, who ascended Missouri River through the Dakotas 1839; author Laura Ingalls Wilder and husband Almanzo Wilder arrive from Burr Oak, Iowa; **1880** Chicago & Northwestern Railroad built; town incorporated; **March 8, 1884** artist Harvey Dunn born near rural Manchester to west (died 1952); **Dec. 5, 1886** writer Rose Wilder Lane born to Laura and Almanzo Wilder (died 1968); **1887**

house built by Charles Ingalls; **1891** Wilders move to Minnesota briefly, then to Florida, among thousands who head south during Great Panic, move to Mansfield, Missouri, 1894; **1898** county courthouse built.

Deadwood   *Lawrence County   Western South Dakota, 32 mi/51 km northwest of Rapid City*

1875 Lawrence County formed; **Aug. 1875** gold discovered at Deadwood Gulch by John B. Pearson; gold seekers move north from Custer; **1876** town founded; Frawley Ranch established, Centennial Park Hotel built on ranch; **Aug. 2, 1876** Wild Bill (James Butler) Hickok shot in back, killed by desperado Jack McCall; **1876–1879** lawlessness leads to 97 murders in three years; **1877** Lawrence County formed; town becomes county seat; **1878** placer gold reserves dwindle; **1879** fire destroys business district; **1882** incorporated as a city; **1883** Centennial Park Hotel burns, new hotel built 1888; heavy snows combined with heavy spring rains bring flooding, city heavily damaged; **1887** silver boom begins, declines 1894; **1890** Fremont, Elkhorn & Missouri Valley Railroad reaches town; **Aug. 7, 1903** Calamity Jane dies in hotel room in nearby town of Terry, buried in Mount Moriah Cemetery next to Wild Bill Hickok at her request; **1908** county courthouse built; **1914** Preacher Smith Monument unveiled; **1930** Adams Memorial Hall Museum opened; **1930s** Deadwood Amusement Park built; **Jan. 20, 1937** actress Dorothy Provine born; **1989** legalized gambling begins, other Main Street businesses forced to close within months in favor of casinos.

Dupree   *Ziebach County   West central South Dakota, 80 mi/129 km northwest of Pierre*

1910 Chicago, Milwaukee, St. Paul & Pacific Railroad built; town founded in Cheyenne River Indian Reservation by Frank Barnes, named for early French fur trapper Frank Dupris; **1911** Ziebach County formed, with Dewey County comprises Cheyenne River Reservation; town becomes county seat; **1931** county courthouse built.

Edgemont   *Fall River County   Southwestern South Dakota, 60 mi/97 km south-southwest of Rapid City*

1878 E. W. Whitcomb begins ranching in area; **1891** town founded with arrival of Chicago, Burlington & Missouri Railroad from Nebraska; **1895** town incorporated; **1896** over 200 farmers settle along new Edgemont Irrigation Canal; **1922** Fossil Cycad National Monument established to northeast, preserves elaborate plant fossils, transferred to Bureau of Land Management 1956; **1955** uranium mining brings economic boom, mine closed 1980s.

Elk Point   *Union County   Southeastern South Dakota, 60 mi/97 km south of Sioux City, on Big Sioux River*

Aug. 22, 1804 Lewis & Clark Expedition ascends Missouri River southwest of here, report large herds of elk; **1859** first settlers arrive; **1860** town founded; **1862** Cole County formed; town incorporated; fortifications built following killing of Judge Amidon and son near Sioux Falls; 25 French-Canadian families arrive led by Father Pierre Boucher; **1863** Civil War veterans begin arriving; **1864** county renamed Union County; **1865** town becomes county seat; **1872** Southern Dakota Railroad reaches town; **1873** flour mill established; **1874–1875** grasshopper plague ravages area; **May 1876** Father Bouchard plants three crosses to mark deliverance from plague; **1978** county courthouse built.

Faulkton   *Faulk County   Central South Dakota, 157 mi/253 km northwest of Sioux Falls*

1873 Faulk County formed; **1882** town founded, incorporated as a city; **1883** county organized; town becomes county seat; town and county named for Andrew Jackson Faulk, third governor of Dakota Territory; **1886** Chicago & Northwestern Railroad built; town platted by Western Town Lot Company at junction with Chicago, Milwaukee & St. Paul Railway; **1905** county courthouse built; **1970** Faulk County Library opened.

Flandreau   *Moody County   Eastern South Dakota, 35 mi/56 km north-northeast of Sioux Falls*

1822 trading post built by Joseph La Framboise, closed 1840; **1853** Charles E. Flandreau arrives in area to fight Native Americans on behalf of fur traders; **1857** town founded; settlers soon driven away by Dakota Indians; **1859** town resettled by Santee Sioux desiring to homestead like the white men; **1873** Moody County formed; **1878** white settlers make their return; town becomes county seat; **1879** town incorporated; **1880** Chicago, Milwaukee, St. Paul & Pacific Railroad reaches town; **1892** U.S. Indian Industrial School (later Riggs Institute) opened; **1913** Central Theater built; **1914** second county courthouse built; **1939** rural electric lighting introduced to region.

Fort Pierre   *Stanley County   Central South Dakota, on Missouri River, opposite Pierre*

March 30, 1743 brothers Joseph and François Verendrye bury lead tablet claiming region for France; **1813** St. Louis merchant Manuel Lisa settles in area; **1817** settlement founded as trading post; Fort Tecumseh established; **1827** Fort Teton replaces original fort; **1831** steamboat *Yellow Stone* reaches site, continues to mouth of Yellowstone River, Montana; **1832** Fort Teton rebuilt by Pierre Chouteau, Jr., renamed in full for himself, surname later dropped; **1873** Stanley County formed; town becomes county seat; **1890** town incorporated; **1907** Chicago & Northwestern Railroad reaches town; **1911** James "Scotty" Philip dies, leaving herd of 1,000 buffalo developed from small herd, species nearly exterminated by whites 1890s; **Feb. 16, 1913** Verendrye tablet discovered near mouth of Bad River by three teenagers, rewarded $700 by State Historical Society; **March 5, 1929** champion cowboy Casey Tibbs born on Cheyenne River; **1933** historical marker erected commemorating Verendrye tablet; **1971** county courthouse built.

Fort Thompson *Buffalo County* Central South Dakota, 50 mi/80 km east-southeast of Pierre

c.1325 archaeological evidence at site on Missouri River indicates a mass grave from one-day massacre of some 500 people; **c.1782** Registre Loisel establishes trading post on Cedar Island in Missouri River; **Sept. 22, 1804** Lewis and Clark camp at Loisel's post; **July 4, 1839** Nicollet and Fremont hold fireworks display on Medicine Creek, to west, 12 mi/19 km south of Missouri River; **1842** Fort Defiance established on Medicine Creek; **1859** Yankton Sioux peoples moved by steamboat from Yankton to Crow Creek Indian Reservation; **1863** town of Fort Thompson founded at mouth of Crow Creek as trading post; **May 15, 1915** Oscar Howe born, pioneer of Native American art, Artist Laureate of South Dakota (died 1983); **1930s** Bedashosha Lake formed by dam on Crow Creek to south; **Sept. 1933** flash flood on Soldier Creek kills eight; **1966** Big Bend Dam completed on Missouri River forming Lake Sharpe.

Gannvalley *Buffalo County* Central South Dakota, 120 mi/193 km west-northwest of Sioux Falls

1885 town founded (also spelled Gann Valley); post office established; **July 5, 1936** highest temperature ever recorded in South Dakota reached, 120°F/49°C; **1979** county courthouse completed.

Gettysburg *Potter County* Central South Dakota, 190 mi/306 km northwest of Sioux Falls

1825 Atkinson-O'Fallon Peace Treaty Expedition observes Medicine Rock in Missouri River, 15 mi/24 km to west, site sacred to Sioux peoples; **1863** Capt. John Fielner of Gen. Alfred Sully Expedition makes lone journey to observe Medicine Rock, killed in ambush by Native Americans, attackers pursued and killed by Sully; **1873** Potter County formed; Forest City on Missouri River becomes county seat; **1881** town founded by Union Civil War veterans, named for Gettysburg, Pennsylvania; **1885** in feud with Forest City over county seat, armed veterans bring county records to Gettysburg, Forest City abandoned; **Aug. 17, 1889** casts made of handprints and footprints carved on Medicine Rock, put on display at Pierre; **1907** town incorporated; **1910** county courthouse built; **1924** bridge built across Missouri River to west; **1954** with waters of Oahe Dam encroaching on sacred Medicine Rock, rock is removed to Gettysburg; **1958** new bridge built across Missouri River (Lake Oahe); **1997** Civil War monument dedicated.

Hayti *Hamlin County* Eastern South Dakota, 80 mi/129 km north-northwest of Sioux Falls

1873 Hamlin County formed; **1880** town founded as county seat; **1907** incorporated as a city; **1916** county courthouse completed.

Hecla *Brown County* See **Aberdeen (1931)**

Highmore *Hyde County* Central South Dakota, 150 mi/241 km northwest of Sioux Falls

1873 Hyde County formed; **1881** Chicago & Northwestern Railroad built; town founded as county seat; **1882** town platted; **1903** incorporated as a city; **1912** county courthouse completed.

Hill City *Pennington County* Western South Dakota, 20 mi/32 km southwest of Rapid City

Feb. 1876 town founded as gold camp by Thomas Harvey, John Miller, and Hugh McCullough, abandoned by May; **1880s** tin mining begins; **1891** Chicago, Burlington & Quincy Railroad reaches town; **1979** Black Hills Institute of Geological Research moves to Hill City, established 1974 at Rapid City; **1990** Black Hills Institute discovers largest, most complete *Tyrannosaurus rex* skeleton, named Sue, put on permanent display at Chicago Field Museum 2000.

Hot Springs *Fall River County* Southwestern South Dakota, 47 mi/76 km south-southwest of Rapid City

1875 Dr. Valentine McGillycuddy possibly first white man to visit hot springs; **Apr. 1876** Charles Metz family, living illegally on land granted to Native Americans, killed by natives at their homestead in Red Canyon; **1879** Col. W. J. Thornby claims town site; **1881** post office established, named Oella, renamed Minnekahta; **1882** town incorporated; Wind Cave to north first discovered by whites; **1883** Fall River County formed; town becomes county seat, renamed Hot Springs; **1889** State Soldiers' Home built, town's first large building constructed of local sandstone; **1890** the Plunge Bath house (Evans Plunge) built at edge of town; **1891** county courthouse built, completed Jan. 1892 in four months; Burlington & Missouri Railroad reaches site; sandstone Union Depot built; **Jan. 9, 1903** Wind Cave National Park established to north; **1911** sandstone Morris Grand Theater built; **1949** Angostura Reservoir formed on Cheyenne River to south; **1974** mammoth bones discovered at Mammoth Spring to west by bulldozer operator George "Porky" Hanson, spring originally named for its large size; **1976** Mammoth Site Museum established.

Howard *Miner County* Eastern South Dakota, 50 mi/80 km northwest of Sioux Falls

1873 Miner County formed; **1881** Chicago, Milwaukee, St. Paul & Pacific Railroad built; town founded as county seat; **1886** Howard Public Library established; **1910** incorporated as a city; **1938** county courthouse built.

Huron *Beadle County* East central South Dakota, 93 mi/150 km northwest of Sioux Falls

1873 Beadle County formed; **1879** town founded as county seat on James River; **1880** Chicago & Northwestern Railroad reaches town, establishes division headquarters; **1883** town incorporated; Huron Public Library founded, Carnegie library opened 1909, new building opened 1966; **1884** humorist Charles Partlow "Chic" Sale born (died 1936); **1885** first Dakota Republican Party convention held; South Dakota State Fair first held, held every other year until 1905; **Oct. 4, 1890** suffragette, U.S. Sen. Gladys Pyle born (died 1989); **1898** Huron University established, merges with Si Tanka College (established 1973) at Eagle Butte 2001 to become Si Tanka Huron University; **1922** county courthouse built; **1933–1934** heavy dust storms devastate region; **July 12, 1951** actress Cheryl Ladd born.

Igloo   *Fall River County*   *Southwestern South Dakota, 70 mi/113 km south-southwest of Rapid City*

1941 site chosen by Congress for Black Hills Ordnance Depot; **1941** depot built, ordnance arrives; town site named Igloo at suggestion of 14-year-old boy in reference to dome-shaped storage buildings; population peaks at 4,000; **1964** curtailment of government appropriations closes depot; **1970s** last of privately owned businesses closed; **1983** proposal to use site for nuclear waste dump defeated; **1993** environmentalists block use of site as garbage dump.

Ipswich   *Edmunds County*   *Northern South Dakota, 175 mi/282 km northwest of Sioux Falls*

1873 Edmunds County formed; **1885** area settled by German immigrants; **1886** county organized; town founded as county seat on Chicago, Milwaukee, St. Paul & Pacific Railroad, named for Ipswich, Massachusetts; **c.1890** town becomes shipping point for buffalo bone during mass buffalo extermination by whites; **1908** incorporated as a city; **1934** county courthouse built; **Oct. 25, 1999** Learjet plunges to earth near Mina to east, lost pressurization after leaving Naples, Florida, pro golfer Payne Stewart, four others killed early in flight, drifted pilotless across country.

Jefferson   *Union County*   *Southeastern South Dakota, 12 mi/19 km northwest of Sioux City, Iowa*

1859 Catholic Irish settlers arrive during Irish potato famine; **1867** Father Pierre Boucher arrives to minister to community; **1861** Fourteen Mile House built by Francis Reandeau, closed 1872; town of Willow founded; **1869** town renamed Adelscat; **1873** new town of Jefferson founded; **1874–1875** grasshopper plague devastates area; **May 1876** Father Bouchard leads pilgrimage, plants three crosses to mark deliverance from plague; **1984** incorporated as a city.

Kadoka   *Jackson County*   *Southern South Dakota, 70 mi/113 km southwest of Pierre*

1883 Jackson County first formed, later absorbed by Mellette and Washabaugh counties; **1907** Chicago, Milwaukee, St. Paul & Pacific Railroad built from Chamberlain; town founded; **1915** Jackson County reformed; town becomes county seat; **1916** county courthouse built.

Kennebec   *Lyman County*   *Southern South Dakota, 40 mi/64 km south-southeast of Pierre*

1890 Lyman County formed; **1891** Oacoma becomes county seat; **1907** Chicago, Milwaukee, St. Paul & Pacific Railroad built; **1909** town incorporated; **1922** county seat moved to Kennebec; **1925** county courthouse built.

Keystone   *Pennington County*   *Southwestern South Dakota, 16 mi/26 km southwest of Rapid City*

1885 general store opened, kept by four generations of Halley family; mining party names Mt. Rushmore for attorney Charles Rushmore; **1891** town founded; **1894** Holy Terror Gold Mine established, revived 1940s after flooding closed mine; **1924** sculptor Gutzon Borglum, 56, invited by State Historian Doane Robinson to carve monument at Mt. Rushmore; **March 3, 1925** Mount Rushmore National Memorial authorized; **1927** Borglum begins work on George Washington's head, dedicated by Pres. Calvin Coolidge; **1939** after working on heads of Jefferson and Lincoln, Borglum unveils head of Theodore Roosevelt; **1941** Borglum dies at age 73, son Lincoln Borglum later finishes project; **1973** incorporated as a city; **1980** Halleys sell general store, modernized by new proprietors.

Lake Andes   *Charles Mix County*   *Southeastern South Dakota, 95 mi/153 km southwest of Sioux Falls*

1858 Yankton Indian Reservation established; **1862** Charles Mix County formed, with Yankton Reservation occupying eastern half of county; **1904** town founded in Yankton Reservation at south end of Lake Andes, lake originally named Handy's Lake; **1916** county seat moved from Wheeler; **1917** county courthouse built.

Lead   *Lawrence County*   *Western South Dakota, 32 mi/51 km northwest of Rapid City*

1876 Homestake gold ore vein discovered by Canadian brothers Mose and Fred Manuel; town founded, named Lead City; **1877** George Hearst, future U.S. senator, father of newspaper publisher William Randolph Hearst, buys interest in Homestake Mine; **1879** Hearst builds company store; **1881** Hearst builds railroad spur to Homestake Mine; **1883** fire in boardinghouse kills 11; **1890** town incorporated, renamed Lead ("leed"); **March 8, 1900** fire destroys four-block business area, sparing only Hearst's brick store; **March 25, 1907** timber supports in Homestake Mine catch fire, mine flooded to put out fire, gradually restored; **June 1907** incorporated as a city; **1937** city hall built; **1947** Terry Peak Ski Area established; **1989** Homestake Mine taps new gold vein, ceases operations Dec. 2001.

Leola   *McPherson County*   *Northern South Dakota, 185 mi/298 km northwest of Sioux Falls*

1873 McPherson County formed, named for Union Gen. James Birdseye McPherson; **1884** Russian and German immigrants begin arriving; **1885** county organized; town founded as county seat, named for Leola Haynes, daughter of pioneer family; **1889** prairie fire destroys all but 12 of town's 100 buildings, school, and courthouse; **1907** town incorporated; **1928** county courthouse completed; **1978** bison reintroduced at Ordway Prairie preserve.

Madison *Lake County Eastern South Dakota, 37 mi/60 km north-northwest of Sioux Falls*

1873 county formed; **1875** town founded as county seat; **1878** town platted; **1880** town incorporated; **1881** Chicago, Milwaukee, St. Paul & Pacific Railroad reaches town; Madison State Normal School established, becomes Dakota State University; **1890** Grandview Hotel built, burned 1946; **1935** second county courthouse built; **Nov. 8, 1951** TV personality Mary Hart born; **1961** Prairie Village living museum established to west.

Manchester *Kingsbury County See* **De Smet** (1884)

Martin *Bennett County Southwestern South Dakota, 110 mi/177 km southwest of Pierre*

1903 Bennett County formed; **1912** town founded as county seat, named for U.S. Cong. Eben Martin; **1918** county courthouse built; **1926** town incorporated; **1935** Lacreek National Wildlife Refuge established to southeast, refuge for sandhill cranes, other migratory fowl; **Feb. 18, 2002** hundreds of Lakota march into town on President's Day to protest racial profiling by Sheriff's Department.

Marvin *Grant County Northeastern South Dakota, 120 mi/193 km north of Sioux Falls*

1880 Chicago, Milwaukee, St. Paul & Pacific Railroad built; town founded on railroad, named Grade Siding; **1882** post office established; town renamed, suggested by citizen who notices Marvin brand safe at railroad office, calls it a "safe name"; **Apr. 17, 1886** fire set to clear brush traps Betsy Dalager, her five children, and mother in barn, children escape, Mrs. Dalager crippled, mother dies; **1917** incorporated as a town; **1950** Blue Cloud Catholic Monastery built.

McIntosh *Corson County Northern South Dakota, 117 mi/188 km north-northwest of Pierre*

1878 Standing Rock Indian Reservation established, comprising all of future Corson County, South Dakota, and Sioux County, North Dakota, named for rock formation in Missouri River; **Dec. 15, 1890** Sitting Bull murdered by James McLaughlin and his band of Indian police; **1909** Corson County formed; town founded as county seat, named for McIntosh brothers, surveyors for Chicago, Milwaukee, St. Paul & Pacific Railroad; **1910** town incorporated; county courthouse built; **Feb. 17, 1936**

lowest temperature ever recorded in South Dakota reached, −58°F/−50°C.

Milbank *Grant County Northeastern South Dakota, 116 mi/187 km north of Sioux Falls*

1873 Grant County formed; **1878** area settled by Dutch immigrants; **1880** Chicago, Milwaukee, St. Paul & Pacific Railroad built; town founded and incorporated, named for railroad director Jeremiah Milbank; Big Stone City chosen as county seat by popular vote, county records stolen, brought to Milbank; **1883** county seat moved to Milbank after second election; **1886** windmill built by Henry Holland, used as grist mill until 1907; **1915** county courthouse built.

Miller *Hand County Central South Dakota, 130 mi/209 km northwest of Sioux Falls*

1873 Hand County formed; **1880** Chicago & Northwestern Railroad built; town founded as county seat, named for first settler Henry Miller; **1910** town incorporated; **1926** county courthouse built; **1948** Millerdale Hutterite colony established.

Mission *Todd County Southern South Dakota, 75 mi/121 km south-southwest of Pierre*

1885 St. Francis Mission founded on Rosebud Indian Reservation; **1909** Todd County formed; town founded as county seat in Rosebud Reservation; **1924** Father Eugene Buechel completes *Lakota Bible History*, followed in 1939 by 30,000-word *Lakota Grammar*; **1971** Sinte Gleska University established, named for Sioux leader Sinte Gleska.

Mitchell *Davison County Southeastern South Dakota, 65 mi/105 km west of Sioux Falls*

1873 Davison County formed; **1879** town founded as county seat on Chicago, Milwaukee, St. Paul & Pacific Railroad, named for railroad president Alexander Mitchell; **1880** at age four, sculptor James Earle Fraser arrives with family from Winona, Minnesota, designed U.S. buffalo nickel (died 1953); blizzard leaves town stranded for 16 weeks; **1881** incorporated as a town; Presbyterian Church built; **1883** Dakota University established by Methodist Church, later renamed Dakota Wesleyan University; **1889** university destroyed by fire, rebuilt; **1892** incorporated as a city; first Corn Palace built entirely of multicolored ears of corn, center of first Corn Belt Exposition, held annually since 1902; **1902** Carnegie Library built; **1903** town builds capitol building in anticipation of state capital move from Pierre, 1904 election retains Pierre as capital; **1921** present Corn Palace built; **1936** county courthouse completed; **May 10, 1936** TV personality Gary Owens born; **1939** Friends of the Middle Border Museum founded.

Mobridge *Walworth County* *Northern South Dakota, 83 mi/134 km north of Pierre, on Missouri River*

1804 Lewis & Clark Expedition discovers rock formation in Missouri River, sacred to Native Americans, which they name Stone Idol; **1812** St. Louis fur trader Manuel Lisa builds Fort Manuel to north, near present day Kenel; **Dec. 23, 1812** Sacajawea (Sakakawea) dies at Fort Manuel, served as guide for Lewis and Clark Expedition 1805 (born c.1788); **March 5, 1813** Fort Manuel burned by Yankton Sioux during War of 1812; **May 30, 1823** party of 100 men under Gen. William Hayes Ashley of Rocky Mountain Fur Company camp at Ashley Island, attacked by Arikaras as they begin traveling by land, 12 killed, 11 wounded; Arikara village later attacked by forces of Col. Henry Leavenworth; **c.1831** Sitting Bull born across Missouri River near mouth of Grand River; **Nov. 20, 1862** Fools Soldier Band, group of 11 young Lakotas friendly to whites, trade all they own in exchange for 2 white women, 7 children taken captive in Dakota Conflict in Minnesota, deliver released captives to Fort Pierre at high risk to their own safety [see Slayton, Minnesota]; **1873** Stone Idol rock formation renamed Standing Rock; **1890** tumbleweeds block streets and bury up to 30 homes, introduced by Ukrainian Mennonites with their flax seed in 1873; **Dec. 15, 1890** Sitting Bull murdered by James McLaughlin and his band of Indian police, first buried at Fort Yates, North Dakota, later reburied across river near birthplace; **1900** Leavenworth Monument erected; **1906** bridge built on Missouri River by Chicago, Milwaukee, St. Paul & Pacific Railroad; town founded at eastern end of bridge, hence name "Mo-bridge"; **1908** town incorporated; **1909** monument erected to Fools Soldier Band, **1929** Sacajawea Monument erected.

Mound City *Campbell County* *Northern South Dakota, 95 mi/153 km north of Pierre*

1873 Campbell County formed; **1884** county organized; La Grace becomes county seat; town founded, incorporated; **1885** post office established; **1888** county seat moved to Mound City; **1962** county courthouse built.

Murdo *Jones County* *Southern South Dakota, 37 mi/60 km southwest of Pierre*

1823 fur trader James Clyman leads his men to watering hole, saving them from dehydration; **1905** town founded on Texas Cattle Trail; **1907** Chicago, Milwaukee, St. Paul & Pacific Railroad reaches town; Murdo McKenzie ships several trainloads of Texas longhorns, prompting railroad to name town for him in full, last name later dropped; **1908** incorporated as a city; **1916** Jones County formed; town becomes county seat; **1976** county courthouse built.

North Sioux City *Union County* *Southeastern South Dakota, 7 mi/11.3 km northwest of Sioux City, Iowa*

1855 Paul Pacquette establishes ferry across Big Sioux River to Iowa, first ferry in Dakota Territory; competing ferry established by Henry Ayotte at mouth of Big Sioux River; town of Stevens founded; **1863** Camp Cook established following Sioux uprising (Dakota conflict); **1872** Dakota Southern Railroad built; **1950** incorporated as a city, renamed North Sioux City; **1990** Gateway Computer Company moves from Sioux City, Iowa, established 1985.

Oacoma *Lyman County* *Southern South Dakota, 133 mi/214 km west of Sioux Falls, on Missouri River*

Sept 16-17, 1804 Lewis and Clark camp on west shore of Missouri River, north of Corvus Creek; **Aug. 28, 1806** Lewis and Clark return to site on return from Oregon; **1882** Fort Kiowa built to north; **1890** Lyman County formed; **1891** town platted as county seat; **1893** pontoon bridge built; **1905** incorporated as a town; first train of Chicago, Milwaukee, St. Paul & Pacific Railroad crosses bridge from Chamberlain; **1922** county seat moved to Kennebec; **1925** highway bridge built; **1950s** new railroad and highway bridges built over rising waters of Lake Francis Case.

Olivet *Hutchinson County* *Southeastern South Dakota, 52 mi/84 km southwest of Sioux Falls*

1862 Hutchinson County formed; **1871** town founded as county seat; **1878** Methodist church built of sod, doubles as county courthouse; **1881** county courthouse built; **1896** incorporated as a town.

Onida *Sully County* *Central South Dakota, 27 mi/43 km northeast of Pierre*

1600s sophisticated villages built by Arikara people on Missouri River, occupied through 1700s; **1863** Alfred Sully Expedition camps on Missouri River c.25 mi/40 km to west; **1866** Fort Sully established; **1877** Sully County formed; **1880** town founded as county seat by settlers from New York state, misspelling of home town of Oneida; **1883** town incorporated; **1894** fort abandoned; **c.1897** black gold miners arrive from Black Hills led by Norval Blair; **1912** county courthouse completed; **1954** descendants of black settlers dispersed with creation of Lake Oahe reservoir.

Parker *Turner County* *Southeastern South Dakota, 22 mi/35 km southwest of Sioux Falls*

1871 Turner County formed, named for territorial official John W. Turner; **1879** town founded as county seat; **1883** incorporated as a city; **Jan. 12, 1888** temperature plummets 70°F/38.9°C with 60-mi/97-km winds driving heavy snow at victims, c.200 killed in southeastern South Dakota and adjoining states; **1904** county courthouse completed.

Parmelee *Todd County* *Southern South Dakota,*
80 mi/129 km south-southwest of Pierre

Sept. 19, 1906 Ben Reifel born, U.S. congressman, first
Lakota Sioux to seek public office (died 1990); **1916** town
founded on Rosebud Indian Reservation, originally
named Cut Meat, changed to Wososo, Sioux term for
"cut meat"; **1921** town renamed in honor of settler Dave
Parmelee.

Philip *Haakon County* *Central South Dakota,*
70 mi/113 km west-southwest of Pierre

1907 town founded on extension of Chicago &
Northwestern Railroad, named for James "Scotty"
Philip who gained grazing rights to large portion of
reservation land through marriage to part-Native
American Sarah Larabee, died 1911 [see Fort Pierre];
1908 incorporated as a city; **1914** Haakon County formed;
named for Norwegian King Haakon VII; town designated
county seat; **1924** Silent Guide Monument erected,
replaces marker made by sheep herders marking reliable
water source; **1930** county courthouse built; **1989** Lasting
Legacy Memorial dedicated to local heritage.

Pickstown *Charles Mix County* *Southeastern*
South Dakota, 96 mi/155 km southwest of Sioux Falls

1794 schoolmaster Jean Baptiste Truteau settles in area,
sent by Missouri Company of St. Louis to negotiate trade
agreements with Native Americans; **1856** Fort Randall
established on west side of Missouri River by Brig. Gen.
William S. Harney, named for deputy paymaster Col.
Daniel Randall; **1875** military volunteers build church of
chalk stone; **1892** fort abandoned, monastery-like church
left standing; **1946** construction begins on Fort Randall
Dam on Missouri River, completed 1956; town founded
as construction center; **1953** church restored by U.S.
Corps of Engineers.

Pierre *Hughes County* *Central South Dakota,*
190 mi/306 km west-northwest of Sioux Falls, on Missouri
River

1831 Fort Pierre established as trading post on west side of
Missouri River; **1863** Fort Sully established near Farm
Island to east, moved 36 mi/58 km upriver 1866; **1873**
Hughes County formed; **1874** Protestant mission established by Rev. Thomas L. Riggs; **1878** town founded,
named Mato, Lakota word for "bear"; **1880** county
organized; town becomes county seat; shipment made
from Bismarck by J. D. and Anson Hilger, refers to
destination as "Pierre, on east side Missouri River,
opposite Fort Pierre," Pierre (pronounced "peer")
adopted as new name; Chicago & Northwestern
Railroad arrives; **1883** incorporated as a city; Pierre
loses bid for capital of Dakota Territory to Bismarck;
1887–1888 blizzards in successive years incur heavy losses;
Nov. 2, 1889 South Dakota enters Union as 40th state;
1883 Pierre University established, moved to Huron 1898,
becomes Huron University; **1890** Pierre wins campaign

against Huron for state capital; Pierre Indian Learning
Center founded; **1904** election favors Pierre after Mitchell
wages hard campaign for state capital; **1907** railroad
extended west from Pierre; **1910** state capitol building
dedicated; **1923** Center Monument erected marking center
of state, considered approximate center of North America
until 1931 when U.S. Geological Survey put Rugby,
North Dakota, at continent's center; **1926** highway bridge
built across Missouri River; airfield built to east to receive
Charles Lindbergh's *Spirit of St. Louis*, becomes Pierre
Regional Airport 1938; **1932** Soldiers' and Sailors' World
War Memorial completed; **1934** county courthouse built;
1937 Governor's Mansion completed; **1943** devastating
flooding occurs along Missouri River, reoccurs 1944; **1950**
state office building built; construction begins on Oahe
Dam, on Missouri River north of Pierre, largest earthen
dam in world, completed 1964; **1952** devastating floods hit
area; **1989** South Dakota Cultural Heritage Center
opened.

Pine Ridge *Shannon County* *Southwestern South*
Dakota, 80 mi/129 km south-southeast of Rapid City

1875 Shannon County formed, administered from Fall
River County to west; **1883** Washington County formed
to north, merged with Shannon 1943; **1888** Holy Rosary
Mission founded to north; **1917** artist Andrew Standing
Soldier born, painted murals in public buildings in
Dakotas, Nebraska, Idaho (died 1967); **June 30, 1938**
Billy Mills born, won gold medal in 10,000-meter run at
1964 Tokyo Olympics; **1982** Pine Ridge Heritage Center
opens.

Plankinton *Aurora County* *Southeastern South*
Dakota, 78 mi/126 km west of Sioux Falls

1879 Aurora County formed; **1880** Chicago, Milwaukee,
St. Paul & Railroad built; town founded, named for
railroad director, Milwaukee meat packer John H.
Plankinton; **1881** town incorporated, becomes county
seat; **1884** Charles B. Clark homesteads with year-old
Badger Clark, son becomes South Dakota's first poet
laureate (died 1957); **1891** corn palace built, precedes corn
palace in nearby Mitchell, abandoned 1892; **1949** county
courthouse built.

Rapid City *Pennington County* *Western South*
Dakota, 145 mi/233 km west of Pierre

1852 Lakota accounts tell of flash flood of such great
magnitude that buffalo were exterminated from Black
Hills; **1855** Gen. W. S. Harney leads military expedition
into Black Hills; **1875** Pennington County formed; **Feb.**
1876 town founded, named Hay Town, or Hay Camp;
Aug. 23–24, 1876 town abandoned after killing of five
settlers by Native Americans; **late 1876** sawmill established; settlers begin returning; new town named for swift-
flowing Rapid Creek which exits Black Hills; **1878** county
seat moved to Rapid City; *Rapid City Journal* newspaper
founded; **1882** incorporated as a city; **1883** flash flooding
from Black Hills damages area; **1885** South Dakota School

of Mine and Technology established; **1886** Fremont, Elkhorn & Missouri Valley Railroad reaches town; **1890** railroad extended to Deadwood in Black Hills, requiring over 100 trestles over 50 mi/80 km along Rapid Creek; **1897** Sioux Indian Sanatorium established; **1903** Rapid City Public Library built; **1907** flash flooding again damages area; **July 10, 1907** Chicago & Northwestern Railroad edges out Chicago, Milwaukee, St. Paul & Pacific Railroad in reaching town, first train arriving two days ahead of its competitor; **1922** county courthouse built; **1927** Pres. Calvin Coolidge's visit to Black Hills considered beginning of area's tourist industry, establishes summer office at local high school; **1928** 11-story Alex Johnson Hotel built; **1930s** Dinosaur Park created by archaeologist Dr. C. C. O'Harra; **1934** National Guard Headquarters established; **1938** O'Harra Stadium built; **1941** Rapid City Army Air Base established to east, becomes Ellsworth Air Force Base after World War II; **1949** Rapid City Regional Airport established to southeast; **Oct. 9, 1971** helicopter crash near Ellsworth Air Force Base kills six; **June 9, 1972** over 15 in/38 cm of rain causes collapse of Canyon Lake Dam on Rapid Creek, flash flood kills 238; **Oct. 1974** Dahl Fine Arts Center opened.

Redfield   *Spink County   East central South Dakota, 128 mi/206 km northwest of Sioux Falls*

June 1857 Abigail Gardner, 13, rescued, held hostage by Dakota led by Inkpaduta following Spirit Lake Massacre, Iowa, March 13, two women killed in captivity, a third rescued by Christian Indians; **Aug. 27, 1870** Peter Norbeck born, first native South Dakota governor, U.S. senator (died 1936); **1873** Spink County formed; Ashton becomes county seat; **1880** town platted on Chicago & Northwestern Railroad, named for railroad official; voters decide to move county seat to Redfield, seat remains at Ashton; **Oct. 17, 1880** severe blizzard hits area, leads to winter-long survival struggle; **1883** incorporated as a city; **1884** second election reaffirms county seat move, excessive vote count leads to "Spink County War," armed Ashton group threatens Redfield after records are smuggled, gunmen hired to enforce injunction; **1886** county seat formally moved to Redfield; **Aug. 27, 1890** stage director Hallie Flanagan born (died 1969); **1902** Carnegie Library built; **1908** farmer H. A. Hagman releases 25 Chinese ring-necked pheasants, multiply to become prized hunting commodity and South Dakota state bird; **1926** county courthouse built.

Rockerville   *Pennington County   Southwestern South Dakota, 10 mi/16 km southwest of Rapid City*

1876 gold rush brings instant prosperity to area; town founded; **1878** gold rush subsides; **1880** Ambrose Bierce invents 17-mi-27-km flume to provide jet stream of water for breaking apart ore deposits; **July 28, 1934** first launch of helium balloon for upper atmospheric testing from site called Stratosphere Bowl, lands near Holdredge, Nebraska; **Nov. 11, 1935** second balloon launch delivers solar and atmospheric data from altitude of 13 mi/21 km.

Rosebud   *Todd County   Southern South Dakota, 58 mi/93 km south-southwest of Pierre*

c.1830 Spotted Tail, Sioux name Sinte Gleska, born, Dakota leader who signed 1868 treaty creating Great Sioux Reservation, shot to death 1881, Sinte Gleska University at Mission named for him; **1878** Rosebud Indian Agency established; **1909** Todd County formed, with no county seat, administered from Tripp County to east.

Salem   *McCook County   Southeastern South Dakota, 35 mi/56 km west-northwest of Sioux Falls*

1873 county formed, named for Civil War Gen. Edwin S. McCook, shot to death in South Dakota same year by a personal enemy; **1878** county organized; Bridgewater becomes county seat; **1880** town founded, named for postmaster O. S. Pender's home town in Massachusetts; Salem residents steal county records from Bridgewater, armed conflict narrowly averted; **1885** town incorporated; **1934** county courthouse built.

Selby   *Walworth County   Northern South Dakota, 80 mi/129 km north of Pierre*

1873 Walworth County formed; **1883** county organized; Scranton becomes county seat; **1884** county seat moved to Bangor; **1899** Chicago, Milwaukee, St. Paul & Pacific Railroad built; town founded as new county seat, named for railroad official; **1908** county seat moved to Selby; **1909** incorporated as a city; **1911** county courthouse built.

Sioux Falls   *Minnehaha and Lincoln counties   Southeastern South Dakota, 162 mi/261 km north of Omaha*

1839 French explorer Jean Nicollet visits area; **1844** army expedition ascends Big Sioux River and camps near falls; **1857** town founded by Dr. J. M. Staples of Dubuque, Iowa; squatters hired by Staples arrive from Sioux City; fort built; **1862** Minnehaha County formed; Judge Joseph Amidon and hunchbacked son William killed by Native Americans while baling hay; town abandoned; **1865** Fort Dakota built; town refounded; **1868** county reorganized; town becomes county seat; **1870** Richard Pettigrew persuades U.S. Congress to open lands for settlement; **1873** quarrying of local pink quartzite begins; grist mill built; **1874** grasshopper plague forces many to leave region; **1877** incorporated as a village; **1878** first of seven railroads reaches town; **1879** seven-story Queen Bee Flour Mill built; **1880** State School for the Deaf founded; **1880s** city becomes known for its easy divorce laws; **1881** *Argus* newspaper founded; state penitentiary established; **1883** incorporated as a city; University of Sioux Falls established; *Leader* newspaper founded; **1887** *Argus-Leader* newspaper founded through merger; **1889** Calvary Episcopal Cathedral built; **1890** county courthouse built, becomes museum 1996; **1893** State Children's Home established; **1900** Populist Party convention selects William Jennings Bryan as candidate for president; **1903**

Carnegie Library opened; **1908–1910** Thomas O. Fawick builds five Fawick Flyer automobiles, billed as America's first four-door car; **1909** John Morrell & Company opens meatpacking plant; **1918** St. Joseph Catholic Cathedral built; Augustana College moved from Canton, established in Chicago 1860; **1926** Pettigrew Museum established; **1927** Ku Klux Klan holds march, efforts aimed against Catholics for lack of black people in city; **March 3, 1934** thieves purportedly of John Dillinger gang rob bank, use hostages standing on running boards as cover, are never caught; **Dec. 31, 1936** explosion at Larson Hardware breaks windows throughout city, linked to double murder; **1938** Foss Field airport established to north, becomes Army Air Corps training base 1941, returned to city 1946, becomes Sioux Falls Regional Airport 1955; **1944** veterans hospital built; **1950** North American Baptist Seminary built; Crippled Children's Hospital and School built; **1963** Great Plains Zoo opened; **1966** Sioux Falls Symphony founded, renamed South Dakota Symphony 1985; **1968** Southeast Technical Institute (2-year college) established; **1973** new public library opened; Carnegie Library becomes Fine Arts Center; **1984** Delbridge Museum of Natural History opened; **1996** new county courthouse built.

Sisseton   *Roberts County*   *Northeastern South Dakota, 147 mi/237 km north of Sioux Falls*

1864 Fort Wadsworth established to west following Native American raids; Wadsworth Trail built from St. Cloud, Minnesota; **1868** Sisseton Agency established; **1876** post renamed Fort Sisseton; **1883** Roberts County formed; Travare becomes county seat; **1884** county seat moved to Wilmot; **1889** county seat moved to Sisseton; fort abandoned; **1892** Chicago, Milwaukee & St. Paul Railroad reaches site; incorporated as a city; 600,000 ac/243,000 ha opened to settlement; **1902** county courthouse built; **1950** six fires destroy 11 businesses, including Stavig Brothers department store.

Spearfish   *Lawrence County*   *Western South Dakota, 42 mi/68 km northwest of Rapid City*

1876 Centennial Party composed of 14 men arrive from Iowa to search for gold; town founded on Spearfish Creek; **1877** J. C. Ryan of St. Joseph, Missouri, opens store; hotel and sawmill established; **1878** U.S. Marshall Seth Bullock pays ranch hands to squat land claims not legally surveyed, acquires vast amounts of grazing land, first to introduce alfalfa to plains; **1883** Black Hills Teachers College established, becomes Black Hills State University 1989; **1884** lumber industry flourishes with five sawmills; **1887** Thoen Stone discovered by Louis Thoen, inscription dated 1834 by sole survivor of seven gold miners attacked by Native Americans, skeptics consider it fake; **1888** incorporated as a city; **1889** *Queen City Mail* newspaper founded; **Dec. 1890** Fremont, Elkhorn & Missouri Valley Railroad links town with Deadwood; **1899** D. C. Booth U.S. Fish Hatchery established; **1906** Matthews Opera House built; **1910** citizens build road south into Spearfish

Canyon; **1917** Homestake Mining Company diverts water from Little Spearfish Creek to its gold mine turning Spearfish Falls dry; **1936** Black Hills Airport established; **1938** Black Hills Passion Play first held.

Springfield   *Bon Homme County*   *Southeastern South Dakota, 75 mi/121 km southwest of Sioux Falls*

1862 town founded on Missouri River; **1869** town platted by Gov. John A. Burbank; *Springfield Times* newspaper founded by Burbank; **1872** incorporated as a village; **1873** St. Mary's Mission founded; **1881** incorporated as a city; Southern State Teachers' College established, opened 1897, becomes University of South Dakota at Springfield 1971, closed 1984, campus converted to Durfee Medium Security Correctional Center.

Stephan   *Hyde County*   *Central South Dakota, 45 mi/72 km east of Pierre*

1886 Immaculate Conception (Stephan) Mission founded by Msgr. J. A. Stephan; **1887** mission school built, destroyed by fire 1896, rebuilt; **1900** mission church built, destroyed by fire 1916, rebuilt; **1924** tornado destroys church, again rebuilt; **1943** fire destroys mission's farm buildings, main buildings spared; **Oct. 19, 1965** all five on board private plane from Jackson, Mississippi, killed in crash; **1971** mission school turned over to Crow Creek Sioux tribe.

Sturgis   *Meade County*   *Western South Dakota, 25 mi/40 km northwest of Rapid City*

1857 Lakotas meet at sacred Bear Butte to discuss resistance against whites; **Dec. 1875** Ben Ash blazes Bismarck Trail to Black Hills as lumber supply route; **1878** John D. Hale brings 3,000 head of sheep to area, starting region's sheep industry; Camp Sturgis established by Lt. Gen. Phil Sheridan, named for Maj. Samuel D. Sturgis; town founded; **1879** toll road built to mines at Deadwood; **1884** Sheep Breeders and Wool Growers Association formed; **1888** town incorporated; **1889** Meade County formed; town becomes county seat; **1933–1935** Fort Meade serves as Civilian Conservation Corps camp; **1941** first Black Hills Motorcycle Classic held, attracts 50,000 participants every August; **1944** Fort Meade converted to German prisoner of war camp; Veterans Administration Hospital opened; **1945** Cheyenne leaders gather at Bear Butte to pray for end to World War II, meet for same purpose in 1951 during Korean War; **1948** Black Hills National Cemetery created at Fort Meade; **1965** county courthouse built.

Timber Lake   *Dewey County*   *Northern South Dakota, 83 mi/134 km north-northwest of Pierre*

1883 Dewey County formed, with neighboring Ziebach County to west, comprises Cheyenne River Indian Reservation; **1907** branch of Chicago, Milwaukee, St. Paul & Pacific Railroad built; town founded as county seat; **1911** incorporated as a city; **1959** county courthouse built; **1978** railroad abandoned.

Trail City   *Dewey and Corson counties*   *Northern South Dakota, 78 mi/126 km north-northwest of Pierre*

1900 The Strip created between Standing Rock and Cheyenne River Indian reservations, right-of-way 6-mi/ 9.7-km wide, 80-mi/129-km long used for driving cattle east to Chicago, Milwaukee, St. Paul & Pacific Railroad, terminus on eastern shore of Missouri River, pontoon bridge built for cattle to cross river; **1907** two branches of Milwaukee Road Railroad built southwest from Mobridge, rendering The Strip obsolete, relegated to trail; town founded at junction of two branch rail lines; **1912** town renamed Trail City, reflecting new function of The Strip; **1978** railroad abandoned.

Tyndall   *Bon Homme County*   *Southeastern South Dakota, 70 mi/113 km southwest of Sioux Falls*

1862 Bon Homme County formed; **1879** town founded as county seat; named by Dr. O. Richmond for popular British scientist John Tyndall; town incorporated; **1914** county courthouse built.

Vermillion   *Clay County*   *Southeastern South Dakota, 55 mi/89 km south-southwest of Sioux Falls*

1804 Lewis and Clark visit Spirit Mound, a natural formation, to verify reports of 18-in/46-cm devils with human forms, none found; **1835** Fort Vermillion trading post established on Missouri River; **1845–1846** Mormons winter over here; **1858** first settlers August and Josephine Bruyer homestead to east; **1859** town founded; **1860** Catholic church built on land donated by Bruyer; **1862** Clay County formed; town becomes county seat; University of South Dakota established; **1863** settlers arrive with passage of Homestead Act; **1872** Dakota Southern Railroad reaches town; **Jan. 1875** fire destroys nearly all of town; **1878** town incorporated; **March 1881** two-thirds of town destroyed by flooding of Missouri River, relocated to bluffs; **1906** county courthouse built, completed 1913.

Wall   *Pennington County*   *Southwestern South Dakota, 50 mi/80 km east of Rapid City*

900 AD earliest known inhabitants occupy parts of Badlands; **1830** first reports of large fossils in area; **1843** Alexander Culbertson hauls wagonload of fossils out of Badlands; **1853** Dr. Ferdinand V. Hayden visits Badlands for more detailed investigation, later maps wide part of West; **1907** Chicago, Milwaukee, St. Paul & Pacific Railroad built; town founded, named for the wall formed by Badlands to south; **1908** town incorporated; **1931** pharmacist Ted Hustead and wife Dorothy open Wall Drug store; **1936** the Husteads boost business by offering free ice water to motorists, spread billboards across prairie, business grows to occupy full city block; **1939** Badlands National Monument established, reclassified Badlands National Park 1978; Cedar Park Lodge built in the Badlands.

Wallace   *Codington County*   *See* **Watertown (1911)**

Watertown   *Codington County*   *Eastern South Dakota, 95 mi/153 km north-northwest of Sioux Falls*

1874 James P. Warner settles at outlet of Big Sioux River from Lake Kampeska; Kampeska City founded, abandoned with grasshopper plague; **1876** Ben Lovejoy and O. S. Jewell settle at site; hotel established by Lovejoy; **1877** Codington County formed; **1878** Winona & St. Peter Railroad reaches site; town platted as county seat; **1880** artist John Banvard (1815–1891) moves to town, invents "panoramic paintings" 1841, scrolled canvases up to three miles long simulating moving scenery, becomes rage; **1883** Mellette House built by Arthur C. Mellette, last territorial governor; **1884** *Daily Public Opinion* newspaper founded; **1885** town incorporated; **1889** Sisseton Indian Reservation opened to white settlement; **May 27, 1911** U.S. Sen. from Minnesota, Vice Pres. Hubert H. Humphrey born at Wallace to northwest (died 1978); **1928** county courthouse built; **1937** Municipal Airport built; **1960** Mother of God Monastery established; **1964** Lake Area Institute (2-year college) established.

Webster   *Day County*   *Northeastern South Dakota, 130 mi/209km north-northwest of Sioux Falls*

1868 trading post established on Waubay Lake to northeast; **1875** Day County formed; **1880** Chicago, Milwaukee, St. Paul & Pacific Railroad built; town founded as county seat, named for early settler J. B. Webster; **1895** incorporated as a city; **Feb. 6, 1940** newscaster Tom Brokaw born; **1963** county courthouse built.

Wessington Springs   *Jerauld County*   *Central South Dakota, 100 mi/161 km west-northwest of Sioux Falls*

1863 settler named Wessington tortured to death by natives; **1876** town founded as Wessington, later Wessington Springs; **1887** Wessington Springs College (2-year) established, becomes high school 1964; **1893** town incorporated; balloonist attempts entertainment act from trapeze, parachute fails to release from bar, man and balloon disappear into atmosphere, returns unharmed; **1903** Milwaukee Railroad reaches town; **1930** county courthouse built.

White River   *Mellette County*   *Southern South Dakota, 60 mi/97 km south-southwest of Pierre*

1909 Mellette County formed; **1911** town settled, founded as county seat on Little White River; **1912** incorporated as a city; **1965** county courthouse built.

Whitewood *Lawrence County* *Western South Dakota, 33 mi/53 km northwest of Rapid City*

1876 first settlers arrive on Centennial Prairie; **1877** town site purchased by Powersite Land Company; **1888** Chicago & Northwestern Railroad built; town platted, incorporated; **1889** flour mill opens; **1890** Fremont, Elkhorn & Missouri Valley Railroad reaches town; **1907** Danish American Creamery opened, closed 1954; **1932** Whitewood Bank held up, $25,000 taken, robbers apprehended, bank forced to close a few years later; **1985** Whitewood Creek, polluted with cyanide and raw sewage from Homestake Mine, restored as fishing stream with introduction of trout.

Winner *Tripp County* *Southern South Dakota, 73 mi/117 km south-southeast of Pierre*

1893 Tripp County formed; **1907** Lamro platted as county seat 2 mi/3.2 km to west; **1908** county opened to white settlement; **1910** town founded as new county seat when Chicago & Northwestern Railroad misses Lamro, named Winner for this good fortune; first county courthouse built, destroyed by fire Jan. 15, 1911; **1911** incorporated as a city; **1920** new county courthouse built.

Woonsocket *Sanborn County* *East central South Dakota, 85 mi/137 km northwest of Sioux Falls*

1883 Sanborn County formed; town founded as county seat at junction of two Chicago, Milwaukee, St Paul & Pacific Railroad lines; **1884** C. W. Post attempts to persuade town to donate land for cereal factory, is refused, builds at Battle Creek, Michigan, instead; **1888** town incorporated; **1908** county courthouse completed.

Wounded Knee *Shannon County* *Southwestern South Dakota, 78 mi/126 km southeast of Rapid City*

Dec. 29, 1890 more than 150 members of Big Foot's Minniconjou band of Native Americans massacred by U.S. 7th Cavalry under Col. James Forsyth, 25 soldiers killed; **Feb. 27, 1973** siege of post and church, elderly hostages taken by American Indian Movement wanting congressional hearings on failed treaties, ends May 8; **Dec. 1991** members of Lakota tribe ride Chief Big Foot's route to Wounded Knee, perform ceremonies honoring those who died in 1890.

Yankton *Yankton County* *Southeastern South Dakota, 57 mi/92 km southwest of Sioux Falls*

1822 fur trading post established on Missouri River at mouth of James River by Joseph LaFramboise; **1858** fur trader George D. Fiske becomes first settler; **1859** town founded; **1861** Dakota Territory established; town becomes territorial capital; *Weekly Dakotan* newspaper founded, becomes *Press and Dakotan* 1875; **1862** Yankton County formed; town becomes county seat; ferry established by J. S. Presho; stockade built during Dakota Conflict; **1869** incorporated as a town; **1873** Dakota Southern Railroad reaches town; Mennonites from Ukraine arrive, tumbleweed now common in West introduced by accident in flax seed brought from their homeland [see Mobridge]; **Dec. 1876** following trial, Jack McCall hanged for Aug. 2 shooting Wild Bill Hickok at Deadwood; **1878** Yankton State Hospital opened; **1881** Yankton College established, closed 1984; **March 1881** Missouri River floods follow blizzards destroying buildings and steamboats; **1883** territorial capital moved to Bismarck; **1897** Sacred Heart Catholic Cathedral built; **1902** Carnegie Library opens; **1904** county courthouse built; **1915** Garden Terrace Theatre opens; **1924** Meridian Highway Bridge built across Missouri River; **1927** Lawrence Welk's band, stranded in blizzard on way to New Orleans, auditions at radio station WNAX, remains under contract for nine years; **1936** Mount Marty College established; **1953** incorporated as a city; **1956** Gavin's Point Dam completed on Missouri River, begun 1952; **1973** Yankton Community Library opened; **1975** Yankton County Courts Center completed.

Tennessee

East central U.S. Capital: Nashville. Major cities: Memphis, Nashville, Knoxville.

In 1784, the state of Franklin was declared in the northeastern corner of Tennessee, but ended 1788 without being formally recognized. The area was ceded by North Carolina, becoming part of the Territory South of the Ohio May 26, 1790. Tennessee became the 16th U.S. state July 1, 1796. It seceded from the Union February 1, 1861, as a Confederate state and was readmitted July 25, 1866.

Tennessee is divided into 95 counties. Municipalities have no official classification but refer to themselves informally as towns or cities. There are no townships. See Introduction.

Alamo *Crockett County* *Western Tennessee, 70 mi/113 km northeast of Memphis*

1824 area first settled; **1847** store established by Isaac M. Johnson and Lycurgus Cage; town founded, named Cageville; **1871** Crockett County formed, named for former resident David Crockett; town becomes county seat, renamed for fortress at San Antonio, Texas, where David Crockett was killed fighting the Mexicans March 6, 1836; **1855** town incorporated; **1874** county jail built; **1875** county courthouse built; **1879** county asylum established.

Altamont *Grundy County* *Southern Tennessee, 80 mi/129 km southeast of Nashville*

1844 Grundy County formed, named for U.S. Sen. Felix Grundy; town founded as county seat; **1853** town incorporated; **1995** county courthouse built.

Ashland City *Cheatham County* *Northern Tennessee, 17 mi/27 km northwest of Nashville*

1856 Cheatham County formed; town founded as county seat on Cumberland River; **1858** county courthouse built, used as hotel after 1869; **1859** town incorporated; **1868** Sycamore Powder Mills established to north, remnants of Confederate mill at Augusta, Georgia, purchased and moved here, closed 1904; **1869** second county courthouse built, addition built 1985; **1957** Cheatham Lake formed on Cumberland River by Cheatham Dam.

Athens *McMinn County* *Southeastern Tennessee, 53 mi/85 km southwest of Knoxville*

1819 McMinn County formed; Calhoun becomes first county seat; **1821** town founded on land owned by William Lowry; **c.1822** Cleage House built by Samuel Cleage; **1823** county seat moved to Athens; **1829** town incorporated; **1835** postmaster forced to surrender abolitionist papers just arrived, bonfire created, law passed banning publication of antislavery materials; **1851** Hiawassee Railroad built; **1867** Tennessee Wesleyan College established; **1903** incorporated as a city; **1966** county courthouse built.

Blountville *Sullivan County* *Northeastern Tennessee, 100 mi/161 km east-northeast of Knoxville*

c.1765 area first settled; **1779** Sullivan County formed, named for Revolutionary Gen. John Sullivan; **1784** Washington, Sullivan and Greene counties organized into unofficial state of Franklin, state dissolved 1788; **1790** county organized; county seat located at various residences; **1795** town founded as county seat, named for William Blount, first governor of Territory South of the Ohio; **1806** Jefferson Academy founded; **c.1810** Pearson House built; **1825** county courthouse built, burned 1863 by Union forces, rebuilt 1866 using original brick walls; **1837** Female Academy founded; **1966** Northeast State Technical Community College established.

Bolivar *Hardeman County* *Southwestern Tennessee, 62 mi/100 km east of Memphis*

1822 Brooks Place plantation house built by early settler Col. Ezekiel Polk; **1823** Hardeman County formed, named for Col. Thomas J. Hardeman; town founded as county seat, named Hatchie; **1824** one-room courthouse built, still standing; **1825** town renamed for Simon Bolivar; **1827** incorporated as a town; **1828** The Pillars mansion built; **1853** Bolivar Presbyterian Church built; **1862** thousands of black slaves descend upon General Grant's troops seeking refuge, delaying march on

TENNESSEE

Vicksburg, camps formed allowing them to raise crops on abandoned farms, selling crops for profit; **1870** St. James Episcopal Church built; **1882** incorporated as a city; **1955** third county courthouse built.

Briceville   *Anderson County*   See **Clinton** (**1892, 1911**)

Bristol   *Sullivan County*   *Northeastern Tennessee, 110 mi/177 km northeast of Knoxville*

1770 Rocky Mount built by William Cobb 17 mi/27 km to south, one of oldest houses in Tennessee; **1771** Fort Shelby built by Col. Isaac Shelby; **1779** fort used as gathering point for troops in Shelby's campaign against Chickamauga people near present day Chattanooga; **1784** iron works founded by Rev. James King, hires Englishman John Smith as manager; **1852** Joseph R. Anderson plans town on railroad right of way, names town for English industrial city; **1856** Virginia & Tennessee Railroad completed; incorporated as a town; neighboring town of Goodson, Virginia, also incorporated; **1867** Kings College established; **1890** incorporated as a city; Goodson, Virginia, incorporated as a city, renamed Bristol, creating two adjoining cities of same name; **Feb. 13, 1919** singer, TV personality Tennessee Ernie Ford born (died 1991); **1936** McKellar Airport built by WPA, later renamed Tri-Cities Regional Airport, serves Bristol, Kingsport and Johnson City; **1993** Tennessee Ernie Ford Parkway dedicated.

Brownsville   *Haywood County*   *Western Tennessee, 55 mi/89 km northeast of Memphis*

1819 town founded; **1823** Haywood County formed; town founded as county seat; **1824** town incorporated, becomes county seat; **1845** fourth county courthouse built; **Sept. 1878** yellow fever epidemic decimates population.

Byrdstown   *Pickett County*   *Northern Tennessee, 100 mi/161 km east-northeast of Nashville*

Oct. 2, 1871 Cong. Cordell Hull born, secretary of state under Pres. Franklin D. Roosevelt, instrumental in organizing United Nations (died 1955); **1879** Pickett County formed; town founded as county seat; **1917** town incorporated; **1935** county courthouse built; **1997** Cordell Hull Birthplace State Park and Museum established.

Camden   *Benton County*   *Western Tennessee, 77 mi/124 km west of Nashville*

1835 post office established; **1836** Benton County formed; town incorporated, becomes county seat near Tennessee River; **Nov. 4, 1864** observation post established at Pilot Knob by Confederate Gen. Nathan B. Forrest during attack on Union forces at Johnsonville, six Federal gunboats sunk; **1899** incorporated as a city; **1944** Kentucky Lake formed on Tennessee River by Kentucky Dam in Kentucky near its mouth on Ohio

River, extends almost entire width of Tennessee; **March 5, 1963** country singer Patsy Cline, 30, killed in plane crash; **1972** fifth county courthouse built.

Carthage   *Smith County*   *North central Tennessee, 47 mi/76 km east of Nashville*

1789 William Walton becomes first settler; **1799** Smith County formed; **1804** town founded as county seat on Cumberland River; **1808** *Carthage Gazette* newspaper founded by William Moore; **1879** second county courthouse built; **1887** town incorporated; **1906** Cordell Hull Bridge built across Cumberland River; **1973** Cordell Hull Lake formed by dam to east on Cumberland River.

Castalian Springs   *Sumner County*   *Northern Tennessee, 32 mi/51 km northeast of Nashville*

1769 Isaac and Anthony Bledsoe build cabin to west on creek that bears their name; **1778** Thomas Sharp Spencer settles here, called "Big Foot" by Native Americans for his large feet, killed by natives 1794; **1800** town founded; **1802** Cragfont mansion built by Gen. James Winchester; **1828** Castalian Springs Tavern (Wynnewood Inn) built; **Nov. 5, 1858** Cong. Edward Ward Carmack born, assassinated 1908 in Nashville by opponents of his prohibitionist stand.

Celina   *Clay County*   *Northern Tennessee, 66 mi/106 km northeast of Nashville*

1834 area first settled; town founded on Cumberland River, at mouth of Obey River, named for daughter of educator Moses Fisk; **1863** all but four houses destroyed by Union forces; **1870** Clay County formed; town becomes county seat; county courthouse built; **1891** future Secretary of State Cordell Hull opens law office here; **1909** town incorporated; **1943** Dale Hollow Lake formed by dam on Obey River built to east by Army Corps of Engineers.

Centerville   *Hickman County*   *Central Tennessee, 48 mi/77 km southwest of Nashville*

1807 Hickman County formed; Vernon becomes first county seat; **1823** town founded as new county seat; county courthouse physically moved to new seat; **1830s** iron industry established in county, last furnace closed c.1940; **1911** town incorporated; **Oct. 25, 1912** comedian Minnie Pearl born (died 1996); **1926** fifth county courthouse built.

Chapel Hill   *Marshall County*   See **Lewisburg** (**1821**)

Charlotte   *Dickson County*   *Central Tennessee, 32 mi/51 km west of Nashville*

1793 Cumberland Iron Furnace built by Gen. James Robertson, made cannonballs for Battle of New Orleans; **1803** Dickson County formed; **1804** town founded as county seat; **1828** town incorporated; **1833** county courthouse built; **Feb. 1862** Confederates retreating from Fort Donelson take refuge at iron works; **1899** town of Dickson becomes shared county seat with Charlotte; **1920** iron furnace closes; **1927** Charleston reinstated as sole county seat following bitter rivalry; **May 30, 1830** tornado destroys much of town; **1933** Dickson County Library founded.

Chattanooga *Hamilton County* Southeastern
Tennessee, 118 mi/190 km southeast of Nashville

1540 area explored by Hernando de Soto; **1750s** French build trading post in area on Tennessee River in competition with English; **1760s** arrival of Anglo-Saxon immigrants drives out French; **1779** Col. Evan Shelby's expedition burns Native American village of Chickamauga forcing them to establish new towns at Lookout Mountain; **1794** Maj. James Ore leads Nickajack Expedition to rid region of threat from Chickamaugas and white outlaws; **1803** John Brown establishes ferry and tavern at Williams Island to west; **c.1810** trading post established, named Ross' Landing after 1815 for Scotch-Cherokee family managers of post; **1817** Brainerd Mission established, closed 1838 with Native Americans forced move to west; **1819** Hamilton County formed; Dallas becomes first county seat; **1835** first permanent white settlers arrive at town site; **1837** post office established; **1838** town platted, renamed Chattanooga, Creek term for "rock rising to a point," reference to Lookout Mountain; *Hamilton Gazette*, later *Chattanooga Gazette*, newspaper founded by F. A. Parham; **1839** incorporated as a town; **1840** county seat moved to Harrison; **c.1840** Shepherd House built to east by Col. Lewis Shepherd, becomes Frankstone Inn; Kennedy-Nottingham House built; **1849** Western & Atlantic Railroad reaches town from Atlantic coast; **1851** incorporated as a city; **1854** Nashville & Chattanooga Railroad completed, extended to Knoxville 1855; **1857** Memphis & Charleston Railroad completed to Memphis; **Apr. 1862** Union Gen. Don Carlos Buell advances on Chattanooga from Battle of Shiloh attempting to keep Memphis & Charleston Railroad open as supply line, plans thwarted by constant Confederate attacks on line; **Sept. 9, 1863** Gen. William Rosecrans takes Chattanooga for Union, driven back at Chickamauga by Confederates under Gen. Braxton Bragg Sept. 20, total 18,000 Confederates casualties, 16,000 Union casualties; **Oct. 27-28, 1863** in Battle of Wauhatchie, Gen. Joseph Hooker drives Confederates under Gen. James Longstreet from Wauhatchie Valley; **Nov. 24, 1863** Battle Above the Clouds, Gen. Hooker takes Lookout Mountain from Gen. Walthall's Confederates under cover of fog; **Nov. 25, 1863** General Sherman and General Thomas force Bragg to retreat to Dalton, Georgia, in Battle of Missionary Ridge; **1867** citizens organize against vigilante committees ruling city since end of Civil War; smallpox epidemic ravages city; **1870** county seat moved to Chattanooga; **1873** cholera epidemic strikes city; **1878** Adolph Ochs transforms *Times* newspaper into major publication; **1883** second smallpox epidemic strikes city; **1886** University of Tennessee at Chattanooga

established; **Aug. 19, 1890** Chickamauga and Chattanooga National Military Park established, extends into Georgia; **Apr. 15, 1894** African-American singer Bessie Smith born (died 1937); **Nov. 1895** Incline Railroad opened to Lookout Mountain; **1904** Fort Oglethorpe founded as U.S. Army training camp; **1913** county courthouse built; **1917** bascule bridge built across Tennessee River (State Highway 8); **1919** bankrupt James County (formed 1871) absorbed by Hamilton County; International Harvester purchases Newell Sanders' plow factory; **1920** railroad lift bridge built across Tennessee River; **1926** Red House Hotel built; **1930** Lovell Field airport established, becomes Chattanooga Metro Airport 1985; **1935** Tennessee Valley Authority hydroelectric scheme boosts economy, opens river to navigation; **1937** U.S. post office and courthouse built; **Nov. 24, 1938** African-American basketball player Oscar Robertson born; **1940** Chickamauga Lake formed by Chickamauga Lock & Dam to northeast, part of TVA project; **1952** Hunter Museum of American Art opened in mansion built 1904 by George Thomas Hunter; **1965** Chattanooga State Technical Community College established; **1972** National Knife Museum established; **July 5, 1980** first phase of Sequoyah Nuclear Power Plant opened 10 mi/16 km to northeast; **1981** first Riverbend Festival held; **Dec. 8, 1981** coal mine accident, 13 killed; **1985** Chattanooga Convention Center opened; **1992** Tennessee Aquarium opened; **1998** Max Finley Stadium completed.

Clarksville *Montgomery County* Northern
Tennessee, 40 mi/64 km northwest of Nashville

1780 explorer Moses Renfro and party arrive here; **1784** first settlers arrive; town founded on Cumberland River, named for Gen. George Rogers Clark; **1788** stone blockhouse built by Col. Valentine Sevier; **Nov. 11, 1794** Native American attack repulsed at blockhouse by Sevier and William Snyder; **1796** Montgomery County formed; town becomes county seat; **1808** *Clarksville Leaf Chronicle* newspaper founded; **1819** incorporated as a town; **1855** incorporated as a city; **1875** Southwestern Presbyterian University established, moved to Memphis 1925; **1878** county courthouse built, burned 1900, restored, renovated 1960s, damaged by tornado 1999, rebuilt; **Oct. 17, 1886** virologist Ernest Goodpasture born in rural Montgomery County (died 1960); **1922** Confederate monument erected; **1927** Austin Peay State University established; **Jan. 1937** flooding isolates town, more than 600 people driven from homes; **1942** Camp Campbell military base established to northwest, becomes Fort Campbell Military Reservation 1950.

Cleveland *Bradley County* Southeastern
Tennessee, 25 mi/40 km east-northeast of Chattanooga

1836 Bradley County formed; town founded as county seat; **1838** incorporated as a town; thousands of Cherokee begin long walk to Indian Territory on Trail of Tears; **1842** incorporated as a city; **1880** Hardwick Woolen Mills established; **1912** two hydroelectric dams built to east on

Ocoee River; **1918** Lee University established; **1924** county courthouse built; **1933** Bob Jones University moved from College Point, Florida, established 1927 by evangelist Bob Jones, moved to Greenville, South Carolina, 1947; **1967** Cleveland State Community College established.

Clinton *Anderson County* *Eastern Tennessee, 15 mi/24 km northwest of Knoxville*

1761 area first explored by Virginians; **1787** first settlers arrive; **1801** Anderson County formed; town founded on Clinch River as county seat, named Burrville in honor of Aaron Burr; **1809** town renamed to honor Gov. De Witt Clinton of New York; **1835** town incorporated; **1860** county bitterly divided over secession issue; **1869** railroad reaches town and area's coal fields; **1892** coal miners at rural Briceville to northwest battle use of convict lease labor in mines, loss of jobs; **1895** Clinch River mussel pearl industry begins, ends abruptly with TVA project 1930s; **Dec. 9, 1911** coal mine explosion at Cross Mountain Mine, Briceville, 84 killed; **1966** third county courthouse built.

Columbia *Maury County* *Central Tennessee, 40 mi/64 km south-southwest of Nashville*

1807 Maury County formed; town settled, founded as county seat; **1811** *Western Chronicle* newspaper founded by James Walker; Duck River floods town; **1816** Samuel Polk House built; **1817** town incorporated; **1820** Mercer Hall mansion built by Dr. William Heacock, once owned by James K. Polk; **1832** Clifton Place built to south by Gen. Gideon Pillow; **1834** *Columbia Observer* newspaper founded; **1852** Beechlawn plantation house built; **1854** Mayes-Hutton Place built by Samuel Mayes; **Jan. 1861** county votes to remain in Union, changes allegiance with President Lincoln's call to arms; **1862** *Columbia Herald* newspaper founded; **1882** *Maury Democrat* newspaper founded; **1904** third county courthouse built; Columbia Military Academy founded; **1966** Columbia State Community College established; **June 26, 1977** fire at county jail kills 34 prisoners, 8 visitors, 16-year-old inmate charged with arson.

Cookeville *Putnam County* *Central Tennessee, 75 mi/121 km east of Nashville*

1842 Putnam County formed, voided 1845; **1854** county reestablished; town founded as county seat; **1855** town incorporated; **1856** Jarred House built; **1890** Tennessee Central Railroad reaches town; **1900** county courthouse built; **1915** Tennessee Technological University established; **1939** Putnam County Library founded.

Cornersville *Marshall County* *See* **Lewisburg (1844)**

Covington *Tipton County* *Western Tennessee, 38 mi/61 km north-northeast of Memphis*

1823 Tipton County formed; town founded as county seat; **1826** town incorporated; **1890** third county courthouse built; **Aug. 20, 1942** singer Isaac Hayes born.

Crossville *Cumberland County* *East central Tennessee, 65 mi/105 km west of Knoxville*

1855 Cumberland County formed; **1856** town founded as county seat, named for juncture at Nashville-Knoxville and Kentucky-Chattanooga roads; **1901** town incorporated; **1905** county courthouse built; **1921** Cumberland Mountain School founded by Methodist Episcopal Church; **Dec. 1933** Cumberland Homesteads built to rehabilitate "stranded families," miners, farmers, timber workers affected by hard times of the Depression.

Cumberland Gap *Claiborne County* *Northeastern Tennessee, 47 mi/76 km north-northeast of Knoxville*

1750 pass in Cumberland Mountains explored by Dr. Thomas Walker; **1775** Daniel Boone blazes Wilderness Road through gap; **1803** town of Cumberland Gap founded; **May 1861** fort built by Gen. Felix K. Zollicoffer to stop Union army from invading Eastern Tennessee, driven out by Union Gen. George Morgan in June; **1863** General Burnside's Union troops force General Stephenson's Confederates into retreat, hold gap until end of war; **1903** town incorporated; **June 11, 1940** Cumberland Gap National Historical Park authorized, extends into Virginia and Kentucky.

Dandridge *Jefferson County* *Eastern Tennessee, 24 mi/39 km east of Knoxville*

1783 first whites settle in area near French Broad River; town founded, named for Martha Dandridge Washington; **1785** Hopewell Presbyterian Church established; **1792** Jefferson County formed; town becomes county seat; **1804** McSpadden House built to north by Samuel McSpadden; **1843** town incorporated; **1844** Hynds House built; **1845** county courthouse built, still in use; **1850** Branner Grist Mill built; **Jan. 16, 1864** Confederates under General Longstreet push Union forces under General Granger back to Knoxville; **1869** Glenmore House completed by John Bramer; **1943** Douglas Lake formed on French Broad River by Cherokee Dam, part of TVA project.

Dayton *Rhea County* *East central Tennessee, 60 mi/97 km southwest of Knoxville*

1807 Rhea County formed; **1809** young Sam Houston arrives at Cherokee village at Hiwassee Island, Tennessee River, after running away from home at Maryville, remains three years; **1820** town founded as county seat by W. H. Smith of New England; **1885** town incorporated;

1891 county courthouse built, restored 1978; **Dec. 5, 1901** soprano Grace Moore born at Slabtown to northeast, killed Jan. 26, 1947, in plane crash in Denmark; **July 24, 1925** John T. Scopes fined $100 for teaching evolution in high school, Clarence Darrow defense attorney, prosecuting attorney William Jennings Bryan, Bryan dies July 26; **1930** William Jennings Bryan College established; **1937** Cherokee mounds, village site at Hiwassee Island excavated ahead of TVA inundation; **1940** Chickamauga Lake formed by dam on Tennessee River, part of TVA project; **1947** first Tennessee Strawberry Festival held.

Decatur *Meigs County* *Southeastern Tennessee, 45 mi/72 km northeast of Chattanooga*

1836 Meigs County formed; **1847** town founded as county seat near Tennessee River; **1848** town incorporated; **1849** county courthouse built, burned 1869; **1929** third county courthouse built after second courthouse burned 1927.

Decaturville *Decatur County* *Western Tennessee, 88 mi/142 km southwest of Nashville*

1827 log Cumberland Presbyterian Church built to west; **1845** Decatur County formed; **1847** town founded as county seat; town and county named for Commodore Stephen Decatur of Tripolitan War; **1854** Methodist Church built; **1928** county courthouse built; **Aug. 9, 1930** highest temperature ever recorded in Tennessee reached at rural Perryville to northeast, 113°F/45°C; **1943** Decatur County Public Library founded.

Dickson *Dickson County* *Central Tennessee, 35 mi/56 km west of Nashville*

1862 town founded by Union Army, originally named Sneedville; **1868** town platted; **1869** town incorporated, renamed Dickson; **1896** Ruskin Cooperative Colony moved to site to northwest, founded 1894 at Greensburg, Ohio, by J. A. Wayland and 17 followers, fails 1901; **1899** town reincorporated; town becomes shared county seat with Charlotte; county courthouse built; **1927** county reverts to single county seat at Charlotte following bitter dispute.

Dover *Stewart County* *Northwestern Tennessee, 65 mi/105 km northwest of Nashville*

1803 Stewart County formed; **1806** town founded on Cumberland River as county seat; **c.1810** iron mining becomes important; **1836** town incorporated; **1861** Fort Donelson and Fort Henry built by Confederates to west on Tennessee River; **1862** town burned by Union forces; **Feb. 6, 1862** Fort Henry falls to General Grant's forces; **Feb. 16, 1862** General Buckner surrenders Fort Donelson to General Grant; **1867** Fort Donelson National Cemetery established; **1870** fourth county courthouse built; **1873** iron furnaces reopen following war, production ends by 1900; **March 28, 1926** Fort Donelson National Military Park established, becomes National Battlefield Aug. 1985; **1927** flooding inundates area.

Dresden *Weakley County* *Northwestern Tennessee, 113 mi/182 km northeast of Memphis*

1820s area settled by German immigrants; **1823** Weakley County formed; **1825** town founded as county seat; **1827** town incorporated; **1950** county courthouse built.

Dunlap *Sequatchie County* *East central Tennessee, 23 mi/37 km north of Chattanooga*

1857 Sequatchie County formed; **1858** town founded on Sequatchie River as county seat; **1899** Dunlap Coal Mine opened, closed 1927; **1909** town incorporated; **1911** county courthouse built; **1941** incorporated as a city.

Dyersburg *Dyer County* *Western Tennessee, 74 mi/119 km north-northeast of Memphis*

1823 Dyer County formed; **1825** town founded as county seat; **1850** town incorporated; **1912** county courthouse built; **1942** Dyersburg Army Air Station established, closed 1945; **1969** Dyersburg State Community College established; **1972** Interstate Highway 155 Bridge built across Mississippi River to Caruthersville, Missouri.

Elizabethton *Carter County* *Northeastern Tennessee, 102 mi/164 km east-northeast of Knoxville*

1772 settlers from Virginia and North Carolina arrive; Watauga Association formed here by people living along Watauga River to form organized government with own constitution, short-lived, no surviving documentation; **1775** Fort Watauga built; **1796** Carter County formed, named for Landon Carter; **1797** town founded as county seat, named for Carter's wife; Landon Carter House built; **1799** town incorporated; **1819** Alfred Moore Carter House built; **Aug. 6, 1819** Union Gen. Samuel Powhatan Carter born (died 1891); **1852** county courthouse built, burned Nov. 1932, shell reused, addition built 1987; **July 31, 1875** former Pres. Andrew Johnson dies at Daniel Stover house; **1882** covered bridge built on Doe River by E. E. Hunter, only local bridge to survive flood of May 1901.

Erin *Houston County* *Northwestern Tennessee, 52 mi/84 km west-northwest of Nashville*

1863 town founded as Erin Station; **1867** town founded; **1871** Houston County formed; Arlington becomes first county seat, site 2 mi/3.2 km from Erin, later absorbed by Erin; town becomes county seat; **1872** incorporated as a city; **1878** county seat moved to Erin; **1940s** county library founded; **1956** third county courthouse built.

Erwin *Unicoi County* *Northeastern Tennessee, 88 mi/142 km east-northeast of Knoxville*

c.1775 area first settled; **Oct. 10, 1788** John Sevier arrested by John Tipton for treason against state of North Carolina in role as governor of unofficial state of Franklin, ending its existence; **c.1830** town founded as Greasy Cove, renamed Unaka 1836, Longmire 1840,

TENNESSEE

Vanderbilt 1876; **1875** Unicoi County formed; town founded as county seat; **1879** town renamed Erwin, misspelling of landowner D. J. N. Ervin; **1893** Carolina, Clinchfield & Ohio Railroad reaches town; **1903** town incorporated; **Sept. 12, 1916** Mary the circus elephant kills her trainer at Kingsport, brought to Erwin next day, executed by hanging from derrick rail car; **1975** third county courthouse built.

Fayetteville   *Lincoln County   Southern Tennessee,*
72 mi/116 km south of Nashville

1809 Lincoln County formed; town founded as county seat; **1813** Fayetteville Inn built, later renamed Jackson Court; **1889** town incorporated; **1972** county courthouse completed.

Franklin   *Williamson County   Central Tennessee,*
18 mi/29 km south of Nashville

1780 Edward Swanson builds first house, settles here c.1790 after spending time at Fort Nashborough (Nashville); **1799** Williamson County formed; town founded as county seat; **1815** town incorporated; Carnton Plantation Home built; **c.1830** St. Paul's Episcopal Church built; Carter House built; **1831** St. Paul's Episcopal Church built; **c.1853** Cheairs estate house built to south; **1858** third county courthouse built; **Nov. 30, 1864** in Battle of Franklin, about 1,500 men killed in four hours in one of bloodiest battles of Civil War when Confederate General Hood's forces attack General Schofield's Union forces in their advance on Nashville; **1889** Battleground Academy founded.

Friendsville   *Blount County   Eastern Tennessee,*
18 mi/29 km south-southwest of Knoxville

1793 John Sevier musters 300 militia at Ish's Fort to oppose 1,000 Native Americans, defeating them, thwarting threat of attack on Knoxville; **1796** area settled by Quakers from North Carolina and Virginia; **1802** Gillespie's Armored House built by brothers James and Isaac Gillespie; **1852** town founded; **1857** Friendsville Academy founded.

Gainesboro   *Jackson County   Central Tennessee,*
67 mi/108 km east-northeast of Nashville

1770 area explored by Uriah Stone hunting party; **1801** Jackson County formed; town founded as county seat on Cumberland River, named for Edmund Gaines; **1814** Abraham Hannaniah Lincoln, grandfather of Pres. Abraham Lincoln, killed by natives at Seven Sisters Bluffs; **1817** town incorporated; **1928** county courthouse built; Austin Peay Bridge built across Cumberland River, replaced 1994.

Gallatin   *Sumner County   Northern Tennessee,*
24 mi/39 km northeast of Nashville

1786 Sumner County formed; **1798** Spencer's Choice residence built by Col. David Shelby on parcel claimed by settler Thomas Spencer, killed by Native Americans 1794; **1802** town founded as county seat, named for U.S. secretary of treasury Albert Gallatin; **1803** Duncruzin house built to southwest; **1815** town incorporated; **1825** Foxland Hall mansion built by Thomas Baker; **1828** Rosemont House built; **1832** Fairvue mansion built by Isaac Franklin; **1837** First Presbyterian Church built; **1843** First United Methodist Church built; **1913** Palace Theatre built; **1939** county courthouse built; **1970** Volunteer State Community College established.

Gatlinburg   *Sevier County   Eastern Tennessee,*
28 mi/45 km southeast of Knoxville

1862 Cherokees build road through Newfound Gap for Confederates enabling saltpeter to be hauled into North Carolina from Tennessee for manufacture of gunpowder; **Feb. 6, 1930** Great Smoky Mountains National Park established; **1930s** town founded as resort center at west entrance to national park; **1945** town incorporated; **1986** Dollywood theme park opened at Pigeon Forge by country singer Dolly Parton, born at nearby Sevierville.

Greeneville   *Greene County   Northeastern Tennessee, 63 mi/101 km east-northeast of Knoxville*

1783 Greene County formed; town founded as county seat, town and county named for Revolutionary Gen. Nathanael Greene; **Dec. 1874** unofficial state of Franklin formed; **March 1785** Franklin legislature moved from Jonesborough; **1787** Franklin legislature meets for final time, government collapses 1788; **1794** Greeneville College established; **1795** incorporated as a town; **1818** Tusculum College founded; **1825** Andrew Johnson arrives from North Carolina with mother and stepfather; **May 17, 1827** future Pres. Andrew Johnson (1808–1875) marries Eliza McCardle; **1829** Johnson enters politics, elected alderman; **1851** Andrew Johnson House completed; **1868** Greeneville College merges into Tusculum College; **Sept. 4, 1864** Confederate Gen. John Morgan, escaped from Ohio State Penitentiary Nov. 27, 1863, found shot to death; **1875** incorporated as a city; **1912** First Presbyterian Church built, replacing 1780 structure; **Aug. 29, 1935** Andrew Johnson National Monument authorized, redesignated National Historic Site 1963, includes Andrew Johnson National Cemetery, president's 1875 burial site.

Harrogate   *Claiborne County   Northeastern Tennessee, 46 mi/74 km north-northeast of Knoxville*

early 1800s town founded near Cumberland Gap as summer mountain resort, named for Harrogate, England, by Lord and Lady Pauncefort; **1888** resort declines; coal mining begins; **1889** Southern Railroad reaches town from Knoxville; **1891** post office established; **1897** Lincoln Memorial University established, repository of one of largest collections of Lincoln manuscripts and memorabilia; **June 11, 1940** Cumberland Gap National Historical Park authorized, extends into Virginia and Kentucky; **1996** Cumberland Gap Highway Tunnel completed.

Hartsville *Trousdale County* *Northern Tennessee, 40 mi/64 km northeast of Nashville*

1795 area settled; town founded, originally named Damascus; **1807** post office established; **1833** town incorporated; **Dec. 7, 1862** in Battle of Hartsville, Confederates under Brig. Gen. John H. Morgan disguised as Union troops surround Col. Absalom B. Moore's army forcing surrender, 58 Union killed, 204 wounded, 139 Confederates killed or wounded; **1870** Trousdale County formed; town becomes county seat; **1876** county courthouse built.

Henderson *Chester County* *Southwestern Tennessee, 85 mi/137 km east-northeast of Memphis*

1857 Gulf, Mobile & Ohio Railroad built; town founded; **1860** first store built; **1862** Union troops capture town and railroad; Confederate Gen. Joe Wheeler's Tennessee cavalry overwhelms Union force, many taken prisoner, supplies burned; **1869** Freed-Hardeman University established; **1879** Chester County formed; town becomes county seat; **1901** town incorporated; **1913** county courthouse built; **May 15, 1918** country singer Eddy Arnold born.

Henning *Lauderdale County* *Western Tennessee, 46 mi/74 km north-northeast of Memphis*

1682 Fort Prudhomme built by La Salle party on Mississippi River at uncertain location, named for Pierre Prudhomme, La Salle's armorer; **1863** Fort Pillow built on Mississippi River at mouth of Cole Creek by Union, garrisoned by black soldiers and Tennesseans sympathetic to Union; **Apr. 12-13, 1864** Battle of Fort Pillow, Confederate Gen. Nathan B. Forrest's troops surround Fort Pillow, later accused of massacre in effort to take fort, 350 of 500 African-American defenders killed; **1873** town founded by Dr. D. M. Henning; **1883** town incorporated; **Sept. 1921** author Alex Haley (born Ithaca, New York, 1921, died 1992) spends boyhood here through 1929, grandmother's tales basis of his writings; **1979** Alex Haley State Historic Site opened, author buried here 1992.

Hohenwald *Lewis County* *Central Tennessee, 57 mi/92 km southwest of Nashville*

c.1806 first white settlers arrive on new Natchez Trace post road; **Oct. 11, 1809** explorer Meriwether Lewis dies of gunshot wounds at inn, possibly self-inflicted (born 1774); **1843** Lewis County formed; Gordonsburg becomes first county seat; **1848** county seat moved to Newburgh; **1881** town founded by Swiss immigrant from Illinois, Hohenwald is German term for "high forest"; **1897** county seat moved to Hohenwald; **1911** town incorporated; **Feb. 6, 1925** Meriwether Lewis National Monument proclaimed to southeast, became part of Natchez Trace Parkway (National Park) Aug. 10, 1961; **1939** county courthouse built; **1959** Elephant Sanctuary founded to protect endangered animal species.

Huntingdon *Carroll County* *Western Tennessee, 112 mi/180 km northeast of Memphis*

1821 Carroll County formed; **1824** town founded; second county courthouse built; **1950** town incorporated; **1931** fifth county courthouse built; **1977** Municipal Building built.

Huntsville *Scott County* *Northern Tennessee, 45 mi/72 km northwest of Knoxville*

1849 Scott County formed; **c.1850** town founded as county seat; **1948** fourth county courthouse completed; **March 23, 1959** nine miners killed in gas explosion at Robbins Coal Mine to southwest; **1965** town incorporated.

Jacksboro *Campbell County* *Northeastern Tennessee, 30 mi/48 km north-northwest of Knoxville*

1795 area settled; town founded, originally named Walnut Grove; **1806** Campbell County formed; town becomes county seat; **1819** town renamed Jacksonboro for Andrew Jackson; **1829** name shortened to Jacksboro; **1926** fourth county courthouse built; **1936** Norris Dam built on Clinch River to southeast forming Norris Lake, part of TVA project; **1968** town incorporated.

Jackson *Madison County* *Western Tennessee, 80 mi/129 km northeast of Memphis*

1819 first white settlers arrive; town founded, named for Gen. Andrew Jackson; **1821** Madison County formed; **1822** town becomes county seat; **1823** town incorporated; Union University established; **1824** *Jackson Gazette* newspaper founded, becomes the *Truth Teller* 1830; **1840** cotton depot established; **c.1840** Edgewood mansion built by John R. Campbell; **1845** incorporated as a city; **1858** Illinois Central Railroad reaches city; **1861** Mobile & Ohio Railroad built through city; **1862** Confederate General Beauregard establishes headquarters here; **June 1862** Union General Grant's troops capture city, use it for supply depot through March, 1863, recaptured by Confederate Gen. Nathan B. Forrest's forces; **1875** Union University established; **1880** Lane College established for black students; **1883** *Forked Deer Blade* newspaper founded; **1899** Bemis Brothers Bag Company founded by Judson Bemis; **May 1900** train engineer Casey Jones buried, killed while saving 12 cars of passengers in train collision near Vaughan, Mississippi (born 1864 near Cayce, Kentucky); **1903** Carnegie Library opened; **1924** Lambuth University established; **1963** county courthouse built; **1967** Jackson State Community College established; **Jan. 19, 1999** tornadoes strike area, eight killed; **June 3, 2001** plane crash kills seven prominent business leaders and friends from Malden, Missouri.

Jamestown   *Fentress County*   *Northern Tennessee, 66 mi/106 km northwest of Knoxville*

1823 Fentress County formed; **1827** town founded as county seat on site of Cherokee village; courthouse plans drawn by resident John M. Clemens, father of Samuel L. Clemens (Mark Twain); town and county named for state legislator James Fentress; **1835** county's witchcraft trials include case of Joseph Stout thought to have power to pass through keyholes and cast spells, case dismissed; **1837** town incorporated; **1860** Jamestown Academy founded; **1908** third county courthouse built; **1927** Alvin C. York Agricultural Institute founded; **1928** Tennessee Central Railroad reaches town, abandoned 1954; **1955** Jamestown Public Library founded; **March 7, 1974** Big South Fork National River and Recreation Area authorized to northeast, extends into Kentucky.

Jasper   *Marion County*   *Southeastern Tennessee, 20 mi/32 km west of Chattanooga*

1817 Marion County formed; Cheekville becomes county seat; **1820** town founded as new county seat; **1824** Sam Houston Academy built; **1913** Hale's Bar Dam built to east on Tennessee River, purchased 1930s by TVA; **1924** county courthouse built; **1959** incorporated as a city; **1967** Nickajack Lake formed by dam on Tennessee River to south, built by TVA.

Jefferson City   *Jefferson County*   *Eastern Tennessee, 26 mi/42 km northeast of Knoxville*

1772 The Maples house built by Christopher Haynes; **1810** iron smelter established; **c.1840** town founded, named Mossy Creek; woolen mill, cotton mill, ax handle factory established; **1851** Carson-Newman College established; **1868** Glenmore Mansion built; **1901** town incorporated, renamed; **1942** Cherokee Lake formed by Cherokee Dam on Holston River to northwest, part of TVA project.

Jellico   *Campbell County*   *Northeastern Tennessee, 45 mi/72 km north-northwest of Knoxville*

c.1795 town founded, originally named Smithburg; **1880** railroads built to haul coal; **1882** Falls Branch Coal Mine established; **1883** town renamed for angelica root used to brew local drink; **1885** town incorporated; **Dec. 5, 1901** opera singer Grace Moore born, died June 26, 1947, plane crash in Denmark.

Johnson City   *Washington County*   *Northeastern Tennessee, 93 mi/150 km east-northeast of Knoxville*

1760 Daniel Boone carves inscription in tree telling of bear he killed, Boone Bear Tree blew down 1916; **1769** William Bean builds cabin on Boone Creek, builds first grist mill in Tennessee c.1772; **1777** David Jobe becomes first settler on Watauga River; **1784** Tipton-Haynes House built by John Tipton, site of Battle of Franklin, 1788, skirmish between supporters of state of Franklin and North Carolina loyalists; **1854** Henry Johnson arrives, builds store; town founded; **1859** East Tennessee & Virginia Railroad reaches town; **1869** town incorporated; Johnson serves as first mayor; **1879** charter revoked, reincorporated 1885; **1881** Milligan College established to east; **1903** U.S. Soldiers' Home established; **1911** East Tennessee State University established; **1936** McKellar Airport built to north, later renamed Tri-Cities Regional Airport, serves Johnson City, Kingsport, and Bristol; **1969** Johnson City Symphony Orchestra founded; Tennessee Association of Dance organized; **1974** Freedom Hall Civic Center opened.

Jonesborough   *Washington County*   *Northeastern Tennessee, 85 mi/137 km east-northeast of Knoxville*

1777 Washington County formed, first county in Tennessee, then part of North Carolina, first county in U.S. to be named for George Washington; **1779** town founded as county seat, oldest town in Tennessee, named for North Carolina politician Willie Jones; **1779** town incorporated; **Dec. 14, 1784** state of Franklin established; first legislative sessions held here; **1785** Franklin legislature moved to Greeneville, state collapses 1788; **1786** frontiersman, U.S. Cong. David Crockett born at Limestone to southwest, died defending the Alamo, San Antonio, Texas, March 6, 1836; **1798** Chester Inn built; **Oct. 4, 1810** Eliza McCardle Johnson, wife of Pres. Andrew Johnson, born at Leesburg to west (married 1827, died 1876); **1850** First Presbyterian Church dedicated; **1912** county courthouse built.

Kingsport   *Sullivan County*   *Northeastern Tennessee, 88 mi/142 km northeast of Knoxville*

1750 Dr. Thomas Walker explores area; **1761** Fort Robinson built on Holston River; area first settled by whites; **1769** Daniel Boone blazes his Wilderness Road; **1774** Col. James King builds grist mill and iron works on Reedy Creek; town of Kingsport founded; **1775** Fort Patrick Henry built at site of previous fort; **1776** Battle of Island Flats eliminates Cherokee threat; **1811** Netherland Inn (The Old Tavern) built; **1818** Rotherwood house built by Frederick A. Ross; **1822** incorporated as a town; **Dec. 13, 1864** Union forces capture Confederate force after day-long battle; **1885** brick and tile plant founded; **1909** Carolina, Clinchfield & Ohio Railroad reaches town; **1910** General Shale Plant founded; **1917** incorporated as a city; **c.1917** hosiery factory founded; Mead Corporation pulp mill established; **1922** *Kingsport Press* newspaper founded; **1927** Kingsport Foundry established; **1936** McKellar Airport built by WPA, later renamed Tri-Cities Regional Airport, serves Kingsport, Bristol and Johnson City; **Jan. 8, 1959** Southeast Airlines plane crash kills all 10 on board; **Oct. 4, 1960** chemical plant explosion kills 10, injures 60.

Kingston   *Roane County   Eastern Tennessee, 35 mi/ 56 km west of Knoxville*

1792 South Westport Fort built on Tennessee River by John Sevier, maintained until 1807; **1799** town founded on Tennessee River, at mouth of Clinch River; **1801** Roane County formed; town becomes county seat; **c.1810** Morgan House built by Col. Gideon Morgan; **c.1830** Harvey House built; **Jan. 6, 1882** Texas Cong. Sam Rayburn born, Speaker of the House 1939–1961 (died 1961); **1920** town incorporated; **1942** Watts Bar Lake formed on Tennessee River by Watts Bar Dam to south, part of TVA project; **1973** county courthouse built.

Knoxville   *Knox County   Eastern Tennessee, 165 mi/266 km east of Nashville, on Tennessee River*

1783 area explored by James White, Robert Love, and F. A. Ramsey; **1785** treaty with Cherokees allows settlers onto land; unofficial state of Franklin established, Sevier and Caswell counties formed, site of Knoxville in latter county, state collapses 1788; **1786** first settler James White builds cabin, small fort; **1788** Adair's Blockhouse built to north by John Adair; **1790** town founded, named for Gen. Henry Knox; **1791** incorporated as a town; *Knoxville Gazette* newspaper founded; **1792** Knox County formed; town becomes county seat and capital of Territory South of the Ohio; Blount Mansion built by Gov. William Blount; Chisholm's Tavern built by Capt. John Chisholm; **1793** ferry established on Tennessee River; **1794** Blount College established, becomes University of Tennessee; **June 1, 1796** Tennessee becomes 16th state; town becomes first state capital; **1797** Ramsey House built by Col. F. A. Ramsey to east; **1798** Park House built; **1800** Jackson House built; **July 5, 1801** Adm. David G. Farragut born at Lowe's Ferry Landing on Tennessee River to southwest (died 1870); **1812** state capital moved Nashville; **1820** Hunter-Kennedy House built; **c.1825** John Williams House built, later used for State School for the Deaf, Negro Division; **1830** original section of Dickinson-Atkins House built; **1833** Scott House built by James Scott; **1855** East Tennessee & Georgia Railroad completed from Chattanooga; **1858** East Tennessee & Virginia Railroad completed from Bristol; **1861** Confederates establish East Tennessee headquarters here; **1863** Knoxville National Cemetery founded; **Sept. 1863** Union forces under General Burnside occupy city while Confederates are involved at Chattanooga; **Nov.–Dec. 1863** siege by Confederates fails to end Union occupation; **July 12, 1865** Supreme Court Justice Edward Terry Sanford born (died 1930); **1869** Appalachian Marble Company quarry opened to east originally by U.S. Government; **1871** Lyric Theatre built by Peter Staub; **1875** Knoxville College established; **1876** incorporated as a city; **1885** county courthouse built, renovated 1989; **1886** *Knoxville Sentinel* newspaper founded; **Nov. 25, 1893** author Joseph Wood Krutch born (died 1970); **1897** Market House built; **1900** Standard Knitting Mills open; **1901** First Presbyterian Church built; **Nov. 27, 1909** writer, playwright James Agee born (died 1955); **1917** Lawson McGhee Library built; **Apr. 1917** city limits greatly expanded; **1921** *Knoxville News* newspaper founded; **1925** yards of Southern Railway built to east; **1926** *Sentinel* purchased by *News*, becomes *News-Sentinel*; **May 22, 1926** Great Smoky Mountains National Park established to southeast; **March 2, 1930** actor John Cullum born; **July 14, 1930** actress Polly Bergen born; **1933** Tennessee Valley Authority (TVA) river development project establishes headquarters here; Dempster brothers begin the manufacture of trash hauling equipment; **1934** Norris Dam (TVA) built on Clinch River to north; **1937** McGhee Tyson Airport built by WPA; **1943** Fort Loudoun Dam (TVA) built on Tennessee River to southwest; **July 6, 1944** railroad accident at High Bluff, 35 killed; **May 8, 1954** actor David Keith born; **1961** Museum of Art founded; **May 13, 1972** collision of Greyhound bus, tractor-trailer truck kills 14, injures 15; **1974** Pellisippi State Technical Community College established; **1982** World's Fair held.

La Follette   *Campbell County   Northeastern Tennessee, 32 mi/51 km north-northwest of Knoxville*

1875 town founded, named Big Creek Gap; **1897** railroad reaches town; incorporated as a city, renamed for Henry M. La Follette of Indiana, organizer of La Follette Coal, Iron, & Railway Company; **1936** Norris Lake formed to south by Norris Dam on Clinch River; **1937** walkout at Washington Shirt Factory lasts six months, workers ordered reinstated by National Labor Relations Board; **May 5, 1943** coal mine accident, 10 killed.

Lake City   *Anderson County   Northeastern Tennessee, 22 mi/35 km northwest of Knoxville*

1853 first settlers arrive; **1856** town founded near Clinch River as coal mining center, originally named Coal Creek; **1867** railroad reaches town; **Aug. 13, 1892** for a third time, coal miners strike in protest of state's leasing of prison inmates to work the mines, convicts freed by miners, guerilla fighting leaves several killed, convict lease system later abolished; **May 19, 1902** coal mine accident, 184 killed; **1936** Norris Dam built to east creating Lake Norris, part of TVA project; **1939** town incorporated, renamed Lake City; economy shifts from coal to tourism.

Lawrenceburg   *Lawrence County   Southern Tennessee, 55 mi/89 km south-southwest of Nashville*

1817 Lawrence County formed; **1819** town founded as county seat, named for War of 1812 hero Capt. James Lawrence; **1825** town incorporated; **1870** German Catholic Homestead Association acquires farmland thought to be worthless, transforms land to productivity; **1944** three Amish families migrate to county from Southern Mississippi; **Aug. 20, 1952** actor Michael Jeter born (died 2003); **1970s** third county courthouse built.

Lebanon *Wilson County* *Central Tennessee, 30 mi/ 48 km east of Nashville*

1799 Wilson County formed; **1802** town founded as county seat; **1818** Sam Houston begins legal practice here; **1819** town incorporated; **c.1835** Camp Bell house built by Col. Benjamin Seawell for his daughter; **1842** Cumberland University established; **c.1850** Robert Caruthers House built; **1871** Tennessee & Pacific Railroad reaches town; **1902** Castle Heights Military Academy founded; **1968** fifth county courthouse completed.

Leesburg *Washington County* See **Jonesborough**

Lewisburg *Marshall County* *Southern Tennessee, 50 mi/80 km south of Nashville*

July 13, 1821 Confederate Gen. Nathan Bedford Forrest born at Chapel Hill to north (died 1877); **1836** Marshall County formed; town founded as county seat; **1837** town incorporated; **Aug. 26, 1844** John William Burgess born at rural Cornersville to south, "Father of Political Science" (died 1931); **Apr. 4, 1902** flooding Duck River destroys mills and bridges; **1929** county courthouse built.

Lexington *Henderson County* *Western Tennessee, 103 mi/166 km east-northeast of Memphis*

1818 first white settlers arrive following Chickasaw Treaty; **1821** Henderson County formed; town founded as county seat; **1835** town incorporated; **1863** Battle of Parker's Crossroads, Col. Bob Ingersoll captured by Gen. Nathan B. Forrest's cavalry in 12-hour skirmish; **1896** fourth county courthouse built.

Limestone *Washington County* See **Jonesborough** **(1786)**

Linden *Perry County* *Central Tennessee, 72 mi/ 116 km southwest of Nashville*

1819 Perry County formed; Perryville becomes first county seat; **1845** town founded as new county seat on land donated by David R. Harris; **1848** town incorporated; **1868** county courthouse built.

Livingston *Overton County* *Northern Tennessee, 72 mi/116 km east-northeast of Nashville*

1806 Overton County formed; **July 19, 1806** author Josiah Gregg born in rural Overton County (died 1850); **1821** Alpine Institute mountain school founded to east by John Dillard of South Carolina; **1814** town founded, named for Edgar Livingston, secretary of state under President Jackson; **1824** town incorporated; **1835** county seat moved from Monroe; **1869** county courthouse completed.

Loudon *Loudon County* *Eastern Tennessee, 30 mi/ 48 km southwest of Knoxville*

1756 Fort Loudoun built 12 mi/19 km to southeast; **1828** area first settled; town founded on Tennessee River, originally named Blair's Landing; **1839** John Blair House built; **1852** town incorporated; **1870** Loudon County formed; town becomes county seat; **1872** county courthouse built; **1874** Tennessee Military Institute founded; **1927** incorporated as a city; **1943** Fort Loudoun Lake formed by dam on Tennessee River to northeast, part of TVA; **1979** Tellico Lake formed to south by Tellico Dam to east on Little Tennessee River, part of TVA.

Lynchburg *Moore County* *Southern Tennessee, 67 mi/107 km south-southeast of Nashville*

1833 town incorporated; **1866** Jack Daniel Distillery begins making its famous Old No. 7 whiskey, new distillery later operated by nephew; **1869** post office established; **1871** Moore County formed; town becomes county seat; **1885** county courthouse completed.

Madisonville *Monroe County* *Eastern Tennessee, 40 mi/64 km southwest of Knoxville*

1756 Fort Loudoun built to northeast on Tellico River, near its mouth on Little Tennessee River by British as defense against French; **Feb. 1760** Cherokee attack fort, defenders withstand attack for five months; **1819** Monroe County formed; town founded as county seat; **1846** Guilford Cannon House built; **1847** Hiwassee Junior College established; **1865** town incorporated; **1897** county courthouse built; **July 26, 1903** U.S. Sen. Estes Keefauver born (died 1963).

Manchester *Coffee County* *Southern Tennessee, 63 mi/101 km southeast of Nashville*

c.80 AD Old Stone Fort built as ceremonial site by early Native Americans; **c.1790** town founded as cotton milling center; **1836** Coffee County formed, named for Gen. John Coffee; incorporated as a town, becomes county seat; **1871** county courthouse built; **1905** incorporated as a city; **Oct. 3, 2001** passenger on Greyhound bus cuts driver's throat causing bus to veer off highway, six passengers and assailant killed.

Maryville *Blount County* *Eastern Tennessee, 15 mi/24 km south of Knoxville*

1785 Fort Craig built by John Craig; **1790** Barclay McGhee House built; **1795** Blount County formed, named for Gov. William Blount; town founded as county seat, named for Gov. Blount's wife; **1807** Sam Houston arrives from Virginia, teaches school before moving to Missouri, later Texas; **1819** Southern and Western Theological Seminary founded, becomes Maryville College 1842; **1837** incorporated as a town; **1844** yellow fever epidemic strikes town, pond on Pistol Creek drained; **1864** town burned by Confederates to rout Union occupiers; **1868** Knoxville & Charleston Railroad reaches town; **1874** woolen mill established; **1886** Jackson House Hotel built; **1907** fifth county courthouse built; **1913** aluminum reduction plant built on north side of town by Alcoa; **1927** incorporated as a city.

Maynardville   *Union County*   Northeastern
Tennessee, 21 mi/34 km north-northeast of Knoxville

1850 Union County formed; town founded as county seat, named for Cong. Horace Maynard, avowed Unionist; **Sept. 15, 1903** country singer Roy Acuff born (died 1992); **1958** town incorporated; **1974** county courthouse built.

McMinnville   *Warren County*   Central Tennessee,
68 mi/109 km southeast of Nashville

1800 town founded; **1807** Warren County formed; town becomes county seat; **1810** town incorporated; **1838** John Lusk dies at age 104, soldier fought against British on Plains of Abraham, Quebec City, 1759; **1897** county courthouse built; **1929** Southern School of Photography founded by W. S. Lively, later destroyed by fire.

Memphis   *Shelby County*   Southwestern Tennessee,
205 mi/330 km southwest of Nashville

c.1000 BC community established near Mississippi River by Choctaw people; **May 21, 1541** Hernando de Soto stops here on his exploration of Mississippi River; **1682** La Salle builds Fort Prudhomme on First Chickasaw Bluff; **1763** east side of river ceded to British by French; **1785** land grant made by North Carolina to John Rice and John Ramsey; **1797** U.S. Fort Adams established; **1801** Fort Pickering built, city section now called Pickering; **1812** steamboat *New Orleans* first to visit town; **1818** U.S. purchases West Tennessee from Native Americans; **1819** Shelby County formed; town platted as county seat at mouth of Wolf River by Andrew Jackson, Marcus Winchester, and John Overton; Bell Tavern built; **1826** incorporated as a city; **1827** Nashoba plantation established near Wolf River to east by Frances Wright; *Advocate and Western District Intelligencer* newspaper founded; **1830** Belle Meade mansion built to west, later destroyed by fire, replaced 1853; **1830s** Magevney House built by Eugene Magevney; **1834** *Memphis Gazette* newspaper founded; **1835** Robertson Topp mansion built; **1843** telegraph service established to New Orleans; St. Peter's Catholic Church built; **1844** Gayoso Hotel opens; Calvary Episcopal Church built; **1846** U.S. Navy Yard built, site of Jones and Laughlin Steel plant; **1848** Rhodes College established; **1851** St. Agnes College established; **1857** Memphis & Charleston Railroad completed; **June 6, 1862** city captured by Union forces under Gen. Charles Henry Davis; **Sept. 23, 1863** civil rights leader Mary Church Terrell born (died 1954); **Aug. 1864** brief raid on city made by Confederate Gen. Nathan B. Forrest; **Apr. 27, 1865** steamboat *Sultana* explodes in Mississippi River killing 1,450; **1869** Beale Street Baptist Church completed; **1870** St. Mary's Catholic Church completed; **1871** Christian Brothers University established; Le Moyne College established for black students, later becomes Le Moyne-Owen College; **1873** Cotton Exchange founded; **1878** major yellow fever epidemic, worst of series (1867, 1873), kills thousands, city falls into total lawlessness; **1879** city charter revoked; **1880** *Memphis Scimitar* newspaper founded; **1886** First Methodist Church built; **1891** city regains its charter; **1892** first railroad bridge across Mississippi River south of St. Louis built; **1893** Cossitt Library built; **1906** *Memphis Press* newspaper founded; **1907** Goodwyn Institute founded; **1909** W. C. Handy writes and performs "The Memphis Blues" on Beale Street; Harahan Bridge built across Mississippi River, rebuilt 1916; **1910** county courthouse completed; **June 19, 1910** Supreme Court Justice Abe Fortas born (died 1982); **1912** University of Memphis established, originally West Tennessee State Teachers College; **1913** Wolf River diverted past downtown Memphis to juncture with Mississippi to ensure stable harbor; **1915** Brooks Memorial Art Gallery built; **1916** Brooks Museum of Art founded; **1920** Sterrick Building completed; **Sept. 29, 1920** dancer, choreographer John Butler born (died 1993); **1925** Southwestern Presbyterian University, founded 1875, moved from Clarksville, renamed Southwestern College of the Mississippi Valley; **1926** St. Mary's Episcopal Church built; Doughboy Monument erected to honor World War I soldiers; **1928** Rust Cotton Picker Plant founded; **1930** Museum of Natural History and Industrial Arts opened; **June 20, 1930** actor Ellis Rabb born; **1935** actor George Hearn born; **Jan.–Feb. 1937** flooding produces over 50,000 refugees from surrounding areas; **June 2, 1937** actor Morgan Freeman born; **1939** Graceland Mansion built; **Aug. 12, 1939** actor George Hamilton IV born; **Oct. 15, 1941** baseball player Tim McCarver born; **March 25, 1942** singer Aretha Franklin born; **Nov. 26, 1942** actress Olivia Cole born; **Jan. 10, 1948** actor William Sanderson born; **June 28, 1948** actress Kathy Bates born; **1949** railroad bridge built across Mississippi River; **Dec. 18, 1949** actress, model Cybill Shepherd born; **1952** Memphis Symphony Orchestra founded; Kemmons Wilson founds Holiday Inn motel chain; **May 24, 1955** country singer Roseanne Carter Cash born, daughter of Johnny Cash; **June 10, 1955** actor Andrew Stevens born; **1958** Elvis Presley purchases Graceland Mansion; **1959** Chucalissa Museum and Indian Village established to southwest, ancient Choctaw village excavation site near Mississippi River; first Liberty Bowl football classic held; **Apr. 6, 1968** civil rights leader Rev. Dr. Martin L. King Jr. assassinated at Lorraine Motel, James Earl Ray later convicted; **March 10, 1969** James Earl Ray pleads guilty to killing Martin Luther King Jr., gets 99 years; **1970** Shelby State Community College established; **1972** Interstate Highway 40 Bridge built across Mississippi; **Aug. 16, 1977** Elvis Presley dies at his Graceland Mansion; **July 1–4, 1978** firefighters' strike allows 400 fires to go unchecked; **Jan. 13, 1983** shootout between police and black cult leaves seven cult members dead, captive officer beaten to death; **1991** National Civil Rights Museum opened at former Lorraine Motel; **1992** The Pyramid 32-story arena opened; **Aug. 9-17, 1997** 30,000 gather at Graceland for

Elvis Week, 20th anniversary of Presley's death; **2002** Cook Convention Center opened.

Morristown *Hamblen County* *Northeastern Tennessee, 40 mi/64 km northeast of Knoxville*

1783 brothers Gideon, David, and Absalom Morris become first settlers; town founded; **1825** paper mill built on Holston River; **1833** post office established; **1855** incorporated as a town; **1858** East Tennessee & Virginia Railroad completed; **1870** Hamblen County formed; town becomes county seat; **1874** county courthouse built; **1903** incorporated as a city; **1909** Morristown Normal and Industrial College (2-year) established; **1942** Cherokee Lake formed by dam on Holston River to west; **Apr. 20, 1971** small bus hit by freight train, all seven on bus killed.

Mountain City *Johnson County* *Northeastern Tennessee, 127 mi/204 km east-northeast of Knoxville*

1770 James Robertson settles at Roan Creek, later founds Nashville (1780); **1794** Roan Creek Baptist Church organized; **1836** Johnson County formed, named for Cave Johnson, Postmaster General under President Polk; town founded as county seat; **1854** Tennessee's first county school system created; **1895** second county courthouse built; **1905** town incorporated; **Dec. 30, 1917** lowest temperature ever recorded in Tennessee reached, −32°F/−36°C.

Murfreesboro *Rutherford County* *Central Tennessee, 32 mi/51 km southeast of Nashville*

1803 Rutherford County formed; **Sept. 4, 1803** Sarah Childress Polk, wife of Pres. James Polk, born (married Jan. 1, 1824, died 1891); **1811** town founded as county seat, named Cannonsburg for Gov. Newton Cannon; **c.1807** Marymont house built; **1817** incorporated as a city; **1819** state capital moved from Nashville, returned to Nashville 1826; **1835** county seat moved from Jefferson (Old Jefferson); **c.1840** town renamed for Col. Hardy Murfree, Revolutionary War hero, political opponent of Andrew Jackson; **1859** county courthouse built; **March 21, 1861** meteorologist, pioneer forecaster Henry Helm Clayton born (died 1946); **Dec. 31, 1862–Jan. 3, 1863** in Battle of Stones River to northwest, Confederate General Bragg pushed back by Union General Rosecrans, Union advance on Chattanooga delayed, total 23,000 casualties; **1867** Stone's River National Cemetery established, over 6,000 soldiers buried; **Nov. 8, 1880** sportswriter Grantland Rice born (died 1954); **1911** Middle Tennessee State University established; **March 3, 1927** Stones River National Military Park established, changed to National Battlefield 1960.

Nashville *Davidson County* *Central Tennessee, on Cumberland River*

1767 long hunters from Eastern Tennessee return from Cumberland Valley speaking in glowing terms about its fertility; **1770** Kasper Mansker leads party of long hunters to area in search of settlement sites; **1779** large land grant given to hunter and surveyor James Robertson, arrives Christmas Day with family; **Aug. 24, 1780** party of about 30 flatboats arrives led by Col. John Donelson; Fort Nashborough one of seven forts built; **1783** Davidson County formed, named for Gen. William Davidson of Mecklenburg, North Carolina; **1784** town founded as Nashville; **1787** *Tennessee Gazette* newspaper founded; **June 1, 1796** Tennessee enters Union as 16th state; Knoxville becomes first state capital; **1802** first cotton mill opened by George Poyzer; **c.1805** Two Rivers Farm house built to east by William Harding; **1806** incorporated as a city; James Ridley House built to east; **1807** Natchez Trace post road completed to Natchez, Mississippi; **Nov. 15, 1807** pioneer, California Gov. Peter Hardeman Burnett born (died 1895); **1812** McKendree Methodist Church built; **1812** state capital moved to Nashville; **1817** state legislature moves to Murfreesboro, moves back to Nashville 1825; **1818** first steamboat arrives; **1821** Andrew Jackson builds his home, The Hermitage, to east, rebuilt 1835 after fire; **1836** Melrose house built by Alexander Barrow of Louisiana; **1838** First Lutheran Church completed; First Presbyterian Church built on site of two previous structures (1816, 1832) both destroyed by fire; **1843** Nashville made permanent state capital; **June 8, 1845** former Pres. Andrew Jackson dies at The Hermitage, age 78; **1847** St. Mary's Catholic Church completed; **1850** suspension bridge built across Cumberland River; Westview House built; **June 3, 1850** Southern Convention gathers to discuss preservation of rights of Southern states while staying in Union, reconvenes Nov. 11 to argue against compromise proposed by federal government; **1854** Nashville, Chattanooga & St. Louis Railroad reaches town; **1855** state capitol building completed; the South's first public school opens; **1857** Glen Leven house built by John Thompson; John Bell Home built; **1859** Maxwell House hotel begun by Col. John Overton, later lends its name to Maxwell House brand coffee, originally made in Nashville; **May 6, 1861** Tennessee secedes from Union; **1862** Fort Negley built by Union, restored 1937; **Feb. 16, 1862** Fort Donelson to northwest falls to Union, Gen. D. C. Buell's Union troops overrun city Feb. 24; **March 1862** Andrew Johnson appointed military governor; **Dec. 15–16, 1864** Confederate Gen. John Bell Hood's troops suffer devastating defeat by Union Maj. Gen. George H. Thomas; **1866** Fisk University established for black students; cholera epidemic stops nearly all business activity; **May 1868** carpetbag city government driven north following exposure of corrupt activities; **1873** Vanderbilt University established; thousands leave city during second cholera outbreak, 1,000 die; **1876** Vine Street Hebrew Reformed Temple built; **1881** First Christian Science Church completed, begun 1856; U.S. customhouse completed; **Aug. 17, 1887** Roman Catholic Cardinal Samuel Alphonsus Stritch born (died 1958); **1888** Watkins Institute opened; **1891** David Lipscomb University established; **1892** Christ Episcopal Church completed; **1893** county asylum opened; **1894** Ryman Auditorium built by

Tom Ryman as religious tabernacle; **1897** replica of Parthenon built in Centennial Park; President McKinley opens Centennial Exposition; **1901** Trevecca Nazarene University established; **1904** Carnegie Library built; **May 12, 1907** *The Nashville Tennessean* newspaper founded; **1908** U.S. Cong. Edward Ward Carmack assassinated by Robin and Duncan Cooper, opponents of his prohibitionist politics; **1912** Tennessee State University established; **1913** Ward-Belmont College established; **May 6, 1914** poet Randall Jarrell born (died 1963); **1916** fire destroys part of East Nashville; **July 9, 1918** two-train collision, 101 killed; **Aug. 30, 1919** country singer Kitty Wells born; **1924** Scarritt College moved from Kansas City; **1925** radio station WSM takes to the air; War Memorial Building built; **Nov. 1925** Grand Ole Opry music show begins broadcasting over station WSM; **Nov. 15, 1925** Cong. Howard Henry Baker, Jr. born; **1930** Colemere house built, designed by Russell Hart; **1933** Oak Hill mansion built; **1937** county courthouse completed; City Market completed; **1937** Berry Field airport opened, becomes Nashville Municipal Airport 1945, Nashville International Airport 1988; **May 18, 1938** Natchez Trace Parkway established by National Park Service; **Jan. 14, 1940** civil rights leader, Cong. Julian Bond born; **Jan. 21, 1942** singer Edwin Starr born (died 2003); **1943** Grand Ole Opry opens at Ryman Auditorium; **May 1, 1945** singer Rita Coolidge born; **Dec. 7, 1947** singer Gregg Allman born; **1951** Belmont University established; **Oct. 28, 1952** actress Annie Potts born; **Apr. 1, 1963** city, other municipalities consolidate with Davidson County to form Metropolitan Government; **Apr. 8–10, 1967** rioting following eviction of black man from restaurant injures 17; **1969** Percy Priest Dam completed on Stones River to southeast; **1970** Nashville State Technical Community College established; **Apr. 1972** Grand Ole Opry moves from its beloved music hall to new Opryland USA complex; **March 17–19, 1978** thousands protest participation of South Africa in Davis Cup championship at Vanderbilt University; **June 9, 1981** former Gov. Ray Blanton convicted of conspiracy, extortion, fraud; **1985** 30-story Third National Financial Center opened; **1987** 35-story Stouffer Hotel completed; 27-story Nashville City Center completed; **1997** Tennessee Titans football team opens first season, formerly Houston Oilers; **Apr. 16, 1998** tornadoes kill 11; **1999** Adelphia Coliseum opened.

New Market *Jefferson County* *Eastern Tennessee, 23 mi/37 km northeast of Knoxville*

1788 area first settled; town founded; **1815** Friends (Quaker) Meeting House organized; **1819** Tucker's Tavern built; **1832** Brazelton House built by Quaker William Brazelton; **1862** 450 unarmed men leave to join Union army, captured by Confederates, held at Tuscaloosa, Alabama, until close of Civil War; **1865** Hodgson-Burnett House built; **Sept. 4, 1904** two Southern Railway passenger trains collide, 56 killed; **1977** town incorporated.

Newport *Cocke County* *Eastern Tennessee, 42 mi/68 km east of Knoxville*

1789 area on French Broad River settled by Pennsylvania Germans, named Dutch Bottom; **1797** Cocke County formed; **1799** town founded as county seat; **1812** town incorporated; **1867** Southern Railway built; town site moved; **1931** county courthouse built; **1943** Douglas Lake formed to east by Cherokee Dam on French Broad River, part of TVA project; **July 8, 1964** United Viscount airplane crashes, killing all 39 on board.

Oak Ridge *Anderson and Roane counties* *Eastern Tennessee, 20 mi/32 km west of Knoxville*

1942 Clinton National Laboratory and town founded in secret near Clinch River by U.S. Government; laboratory research devoted to development of atomic bomb with participation of such noted scientists as Albert Einstein and Edward Teller; **1945** existence of town and laboratory revealed; **1948** laboratory and town renamed Oak Ridge; laboratory research emphasis shifts to development of peacetime atomic reactors; **1959** incorporated as a city.

Old Hickory *Davidson County* *Central Tennessee, 7 mi/11.3 km northeast of Nashville*

1798 Andrew Jackson ("Old Hickory") takes up residence at Hunter's Hill, remains through 1804; **1821** Jackson builds Hermitage residence to south; **1917** site at Hadley's Bend, Cumberland River, purchased by U.S. Government for gunpowder plant, living quarters for 35,000, built 1918; **1919** production ceases with World War I armistice; **1924** E. I. du Pont de Nemours & Company purchases town, builds rayon thread production plant; town named Old Hickory; **1946** workers given option to purchase their homes; **1951** community facilities sold to private interests.

Paris *Henry County* *Northwestern Tennessee, 130 mi/209 km northeast of Memphis*

1821 Henry County formed; **1823** town founded as county seat; town incorporated; **1897** third county courthouse built; **1899** Crete Opera House built; **1992** new Paris Landing Bridge built across Tennessee River to northeast.

Perryville *Decatur County* See **Decaturville (1930)**

Petros *Morgan County* *East central Tennessee, 32 mi/51 km west-northwest of Knoxville*

1893 Brushy Mountain State Prison established; **1895** town founded; post office established; **June 10, 1977** James Earl Ray, convicted of killing Dr. Martin Luther King Jr., flees Brushy Mountain State Prison with three others, captured June 13, others June 14; **June 4, 1981** James Earl Ray stabbed 22 times by members of Black Panther group at Brushy Mountain Penitentiary; **Apr. 23, 1998** James Earl Ray, 70, dies.

TENNESSEE

Pikeville   *Bledsoe County   East central Tennessee, 78 mi/126 km west-southwest of Knoxville*

1807 Bledsoe County formed; **1811** Madison becomes first county seat; **1816** town founded on Sequatchie River; county seat moved to Pikeville; **1830** town incorporated; **1910** third county courthouse built; **1917** Herbert Domain, State Training and Agricultural School for Delinquent Negro Boys established to west; **1939** Fall Creek Falls State Park established to west; **1952** Pikeville Library founded, new facility opened 1992.

Pulaski   *Giles County   Southern Tennessee, 65 mi/ 105 km south-southwest of Nashville*

1807 town founded; **1809** Giles County formed; town becomes county seat; **1812** Clifton Place estate built by Englishman Tyree Rodes; **1819** town incorporated; **1825** Ballantine House built by Andrew Ballantine; **1840s** Colonial Hall mansion built by Dr. William Batte; **1850** town incorporated; **Nov. 27, 1863** Sam Davis, 19, hanged by Union troops for being spy for Confederates; **May 1866** Ku Klux Klan organized by Judge T. M. Jones and son Calvin, forced to disband 1869 for its excessive practices; **1870** Martin College (2-year) for women established; **1887** fire destroys buildings in town square; **Apr. 30, 1888** poet John Crowe Ransom born (died 1974); **1906** Sam Davis monument erected; **1909** fifth county courthouse built; **June 17, 1928** singer James Brown born.

Ripley   *Lauderdale County   Western Tennessee, 52 mi/84 km north-northeast of Memphis*

1811 Open Lake formed to west in former channel of Mississippi River by New Madrid Earthquake; **1835** Lauderdale County formed; **1836** town founded as county seat; **1838** town incorporated; **1901** town reincorporated after repeal of its original charter; **1936** county courthouse built; **1984** first annual Tomato Festival held.

Rockwood   *Roane County   East central Tennessee, 45 mi/72 km west of Knoxville*

1813 Post Oak Christian Church organized to east; **1816** Revolutionary War hero Gen. John Brown builds cabin on land awarded him for his military service; town founded; coal and iron deposits discovered; **1865** iron furnaces built by Gen. John T. Wilder; **1868** experienced iron workers from Pennsylvania brought here to work mines by Union Gen. John T. Wilder's Lightning Brigade; **Jan. 6, 1882** Sam Rayburn, Speaker of the House under Presidents Roosevelt, Truman, Eisenhower, and Kennedy born in rural Roane County, family relocates to Windom, Texas, 1887 (died 1961); **1895** town incorporated; **1920** iron mills closed; **1929** flash flood to west kills scoutmaster, seven scouts on camping trip.

Rogersville   *Hawkins County   Northeastern Tennessee, 60 mi/97 km northeast of Knoxville*

1772 first settlers arrive; **1780** Thomas Amis builds stone house; **1781** Amis establishes store, blacksmith shop, distillery, grist mill, and hotel; **1785** Irish immigrant Joseph Rogers arrives, acquires land, marries Amis' daughter; **1786** Hawkins County formed, named for U.S. Sen. Benjamin Hawkins; town founded as county seat; **1806** McMinn Academy founded; **1824** Hale Springs Inn built; **1835** town incorporated; **1836** county courthouse built.

Rutledge   *Grainger County   Northeastern Tennessee, 32 mi/51 km northeast of Knoxville*

1796 Grainger County formed, named for Mary Grainger, wife of Gov. William Blount; mill built at Buffalo Springs; **1801** town founded as county seat, named for Gen. George Rutledge; **1927** town incorporated; **1942** Cherokee Dam built on Holston River to south, part of TVA project, forming Cherokee Lake; **1949** county courthouse completed.

Saint Bethlehem   *Montgomery County   Northern Tennessee, 40 mi/64 km northwest of Nashville*

1830 Woodstock house built, birthplace of Caroline Goodlett and niece Dorothy Dix; **Nov. 3, 1833** Caroline Goodlett born, founder of Daughters of the Confederacy (died 1914); **c.1845** saltpeter mined at Dunbar Cave for manufacture of gunpowder; **Nov. 18, 1861** writer Elizabeth Gilmer born, pen name Dorothy Dix (died 1951).

Savannah   *Hardin County   Southern Tennessee, 105 mi/169 km east of Memphis*

1819 Hardin County formed; Hardinsville becomes county seat; Savannah founded on Tennessee River at Rudd's Ferry; **1827** county seat moved to Savannah; **c.1830** Cherry Mansion built by David Robinson; **1833** town incorporated; **Apr. 6–7, 1862** Battle of Shiloh, bitterly fought battle between General Grant's forces and Confederates under Gen. Albert Johnston, killed in the action, and Gen. P. G. T. Beauregard, though a draw, prepares way for Grant to reach Vicksburg largely unopposed; **1866** Shiloh National Cemetery established, over 3,600 soldiers buried; **Dec. 27, 1894** Shiloh National Military Park established to southwest; **1938** Pickwick Lake formed to south on Tennessee River by Pickwick Landing Dam, part of TVA project, lake extends into Mississippi and Alabama; **1952** fifth county courthouse built; **1980** U.S. Highway 64 bridge built across Tennessee River, replaces earlier structure.

Selmer   *McNairy County   Southwestern Tennessee, 85 mi/137 km east of Memphis*

1823 McNairy County formed; Purdy becomes first county seat; **1825** town founded as new county seat; **1891** county courthouse built; **1901** town incorporated.

Sevierville *Sevier County* *Eastern Tennessee, 21 mi/34 km east-southeast of Knoxville*

March 1785 Sevier County originally formed as part of short-lived state of Franklin, ended 1788; **1794** Sevier County reformed; **1795** town founded as county seat, named for John Sevier, state's first governor; **1887** town incorporated; **Jan. 1892** White Caps organized, similar to Ku Klux Klan, disbanded Jan. 1898 following community opposition to group's murders and harassment; **1896** county courthouse built; **Feb. 6, 1930** Great Smoky Mountains National Park established to south, extends into North Carolina; **Jan. 19, 1946** country singer Dolly Parton born.

Shelbyville *Bedford County* *Southern Tennessee, 52 mi/84 km south-southeast of Nashville*

1807 Bedford County formed; **1810** town founded as county seat, named for Col. Isaac Shelby, led force against British at Battle of King's Mountain, South Carolina; **1819** incorporated as a town; **1915** incorporated as a city; **1935** county courthouse built; **May 28, 1947** actress Sondra Locke born; **1966** Argee Cooper Public Library founded.

Signal Mountain *Hamilton County* *Southeastern Tennessee, 5 mi/8 km north-northwest of Chattanooga*

1863 communications station established here by Union Army; **1878** cholera epidemic in Chattanooga brings refugees to Waldens Ridge; **1911** area settled; **1913** Signal Mountain Inn built by Charles E. James; **1919** town incorporated; **1970** Signal Mountain Library founded; **1972** Signal Mountain Playhouse established; **1979** town hall built.

Slabtown *Cocke County* *See* **Dayton (1901)**

Smithville *De Kalb County* *Central Tennessee, 58 mi/93 km east-southeast of Nashville*

c.1815 area first settled by whites; **1827** town founded; **1837** De Kalb County formed; town becomes county seat **1843** town incorporated; **1890** county courthouse built; **1949** Center Hill Lake formed by dam on Caney Fork River.

Smyrna *Rutherford County* *Central Tennessee, 20 mi/32 km southeast of Nashville*

c.1850 town founded; **1852** post office established; **1869** town incorporated; **1942** Smyrna Air Force Base opened, closed 1970; **1983** Nissan automobile plant completed; **1988** city hall built; **July 12, 2000** three employees of Captain D's seafood restaurant killed by robbers.

Sneedville *Hancock County* *Northeastern Tennessee, 57 mi/92 km northeast of Knoxville*

1844 Hancock County formed; town founded as county seat on Clinch River; **1929** county courthouse built; **1953** town incorporated.

Somerville *Fayette County* *Southwestern Tennessee, 40 mi/64 km east of Memphis*

1814 town founded; **1824** Fayette County formed; **1825** town becomes county seat; **1836** town incorporated; **1911** Magnolia Place mansion built; **1925** county courthouse built.

Sparta *White County* *Central Tennessee, 80 mi/129 km east-southeast of Nashville*

1785 Knoxville-Nashville Road built; **c.1800** area first settled; **1806** White County formed; Rock Island becomes county seat; **1809** town founded as new county seat; **1833** town incorporated; **1975** county courthouse built.

Spencer *Van Buren County* *Central Tennessee, 82 mi/132 km southeast of Nashville*

c.1830 first white settlers arrive; **1840** Van Buren County formed; town founded as county seat, named for long hunter (long distance hunter) Thomas Sharpe Spencer; **1904** county courthouse built; **1909** town incorporated.

Springfield *Robertson County* *Northern Tennessee, 25 mi/40 km north-northwest of Nashville*

1796 town founded; **1819** town incorporated; **1837** Robertson County formed, named for James Robertson, founder of Nashville; town becomes county seat; **1842** St. Michael's Catholic Church built, oldest continually used Catholic church building in state; **1857** Henderson & Edgefield Railroad reaches town; **1861** Camp Cheatham Confederate training base established to west near Cedar Hill; **1879** third county courthouse built, clock tower added 1930.

Tazewell *Claiborne County* *Northeastern Tennessee, 40 mi/64 km north-northeast of Knoxville*

1796 Old Springdale Church organized to south; **1801** Claiborne County formed; town founded as county seat; **1810** Greystone Inn built; **1830** town incorporated; **1939** county courthouse built; **Nov. 5, 1977** President Carter vetoes $80 million appropriation for Clinch River nuclear breeding reactor to spare endangered snail darter fish species.

Tiptonville *Lake County* *Northwestern Tennessee, 93 mi/150 km north-northeast of Memphis*

1811-1812 Reelfoot Lake formed by New Madrid Earthquake in former channel of Mississippi River; **1852** town founded between Reelfoot Lake and Mississippi River; **1870** Lake County formed; **1882–1884** repeated flooding enlarges lake; **1900** town incorporated; **1907** county courthouse completed; **1908** fishermen send night-riders to oppose promoters of scheme to drain Reelfoot Lake to sell land at cheap rate; **May 26–27, 1917** tornado strikes Lake County, one of series in Tennessee, six other states, total 70 killed; **1925** Reelfoot Lake State Fish and Game Preserve established, becomes National Wildlife Refuge.

Trenton   *Gibson County   Western Tennessee, 88 mi/ 142 km northeast of Memphis*

1821 town founded by Thomas Gibson, named Gibson Port; **1823** Gibson County formed; town becomes county seat; **1825** town renamed; **1826** town incorporated; David Crockett elected to House of Representatives, serves two terms, departs for Texas 1835; **1862** Union troops surprised by attack of Gen. Nathan B. Forrest's Confederates who take town; **1885** Trenton Mills cloth factory founded, destroyed by fire 1929, rebuilt; **1901** county courthouse built.

Tullahoma   *Coffee County   Southern Tennessee, 66 mi/ 106 km south-southeast of Nashville*

c.1850 town founded; **1852** town incorporated; **Jan. 1863** Gen. Braxton Bragg's Confederate troops winter over here following bloody battle at Stone's River; **1903** town reincorporated; **1949** Arnold Engineering Development Center established to east, aeronautical testing center; **1969** Motlow State Community College established.

Union City   *Obion County   Northwestern Tennessee, 108 mi/ 174 km north-northeast of Memphis*

1811–1812 Reelfoot Lake formed to west by New Madrid Earthquake, former channel of Mississippi River; **1823** Obion County formed; Troy becomes first county seat; **1854** town founded; **1867** town incorporated; **1890** county seat moved by force to Union City; fourth county courthouse built; **1954** Dixie Gun Works Museum founded.

Wartburg   *Morgan County   East central Tennessee, 40 mi/ 64 km west-northwest of Knoxville*

1817 Morgan County formed; Montgomery becomes county seat; **1845** settled by German-Swiss immigrants;

town founded; Frederic Beneike establishes piano factory; **1870** county seat moved to Wartburg; **1904** county courthouse built; **1968** town incorporated; **Oct. 12, 1976** Obed Wild and Scenic River authorized by National Park Service.

Waverly   *Humphreys County   Central Tennessee, 60 mi/ 97 km west of Nashville*

1809 Humphreys County formed; **1812** Reynoldsburg becomes county seat; **1836** town of Waverly founded as new county seat, named for Sir Walter Scott's *Waverly* novels; **1837** town incorporated; **1935** county courthouse built; **Feb. 24, 1978** propane tank railroad cars derail, explode, 21 killed, 145 injured.

Waynesboro   *Wayne County   Southern Tennessee, 82 mi/ 132 km southwest of Nashville*

1819 Wayne County formed, named for Gen. Anthony Wayne; **1821** town founded as county seat; **1827** town incorporated; **1973** fifth county courthouse built.

Winchester   *Franklin County   Southern Tennessee, 80 mi/ 129 km south-southeast of Nashville*

1807 Franklin County formed; **1814** town founded as county seat; **Feb. 10, 1818** Confederate Gov., Sen. Isham Green Harris born (died 1897); **1821** town incorporated; **1847** Cumberland Mountain Tunnel completed to east for Nashville, Chattanooga & St. Louis Railroad after two years, use of 400 black slaves and Irish laborers, 2,220-ft/ 677-m long; **1892** crimson clover production begun by John Ruck; **1900** Hundred Oaks Monastery established by Catholic Paulist Fathers; **1910** Winchester Creamery founded; **March 1, 1917** TV personality Dinah Shore born (died 1994); **1937** county courthouse built; **1970** Tims Ford Lake formed by Tims Ford Dam on Elk River to west.

Woodbury   *Cannon County   Central Tennessee, 48 mi/ 77 km southeast of Nashville*

1836 Cannon County formed, named for Gov. Newton Cannon (1835–1839); town founded as county seat; **1843** town incorporated; **1936** county courthouse built.

Texas

Southern U.S. Capital: Austin. Major cities: Dallas, Fort Worth, Houston, San Antonio.

The northern extremity of Texas including the Panhandle was acquired by the U.S. with the Louisiana Purchase 1803. The Republic of Texas was declared March 2, 1836. Texas was admitted to the Union as the 28th state December 29, 1845. It seceded February 1, 1861, as a Confederate state and was readmitted March 30, 1870.

Texas is divided into 254 counties. Its municipalities are classified as towns and cities. There are no townships. See Introduction.

Abbott *Hill County* See **Hillsboro (1933)**

Abilene *Taylor and Jones counties* *West Central Texas, 135 mi/217 km west of Fort Worth*

1858 Taylor County formed; **1878** county organized; Buffalo Gap becomes county seat; **1881** Texas & Pacific Railroad built; town founded, named for Abilene, Kansas, at northern end of Chisholm Trail cattle route; **June 17, 1881** *Abilene Reporter-News* newspaper begins publication; **1883** incorporated as a town; county seat moved to Abilene; **1891** Hardin-Simmons University established; **1901** Abilene State Hospital founded; **1906** Abilene Christian University established; **1908** Hotel Grace built, becomes Drake Hotel 1930s, opened as Grace Museum 1985; **1911** incorporated as a city; **1923** McMurry University established; **1937** Lake Fort Phantom Hill formed by dam on Elm Creek to north; **1943** Dyers Air Force Base established; **Jan. 1951** Abilene Philharmonic Orchestra founded; **1965** Abilene Zoo established; **1972** county courthouse built; **1987** Abilene Ballet Company founded.

Albany *Shackelford County* *North central Texas, 31 mi/50 km northeast of Abilene*

1856 Shackelford County formed; **1867** Fort Griffin established 25 mi/40 km to northwest; **1873** county organized; **1874** land donated for town by Henry Jacobs; town founded; county seat moved from Fort Griffin; **Dec. 1881** Texas Central Railroad reaches town; **1883** *Albany News* begins publishing; county courthouse built; **1913** incorporated as a city; **1926** Cook Oil Pool discovered; **1976** Georgia monument erected to honor volunteer Georgia Battalion that helped Texas win its independence in 1836, most of them killed in Goliad massacre; **1980** Old Jail Art Center opened.

Alice *Jim Wells County* *Southern Texas, 40 mi/64 km west of Corpus Christi*

1888 San Antonio & Aransas Pass Railroad built; town founded, originally named Bandana; **1904** incorporated as a town, renamed for Alice King Kleberg, daughter of a founder of King Ranch; **1909** fire destroys business district; **1911** Jim Wells County formed; **1912** town becomes county seat; incorporated as a city; county courthouse built; **1930s** oil discovered, splitting local economy between petroleum and ranching; **1982** naphthaline and penanthene discovered in town drinking water, pollutants linked to oil industry.

Alpine *Brewster County* *Western Texas, 185 mi/298 km southeast of El Paso, in Big Bend region*

1882 Texas & New Orleans (Southern Pacific) Railroad built; town founded, originally named Osborne; **1883** town platted, renamed Murphyville; **1885** Brewster County formed; **1887** county organized; town becomes county seat; **1888** incorporated as a town, renamed Alpine for Del Norte Mountains to east; county courthouse built; **1918** incorporated as a city; **1920** Sul Ross State University established; **May 27, 1978** flash flood in nearby canyon kills three.

Amarillo *Potter and Randall counties* *Northwestern Texas, 300 mi/483 km northwest of Fort Worth*

1887 Fort Worth & Denver Railroad built; town founded, Spanish name refers to yellow clay in area; **1889**

incorporated as a town; **1899** incorporated as a city; **1902** Chicago, Rock Island & Gulf Railroad reaches city; Amarillo Public Library founded; **1905** Amarillo Livestock Auction established; **1909** *Amarillo News* first published; **1918** natural gas discovered; **1921** oil discovered; **March 8, 1921** dancer Cyd Charisse born; **1924** Tri-State Fairgrounds established; **1924** *Amarillo Globe* newspaper first published; **1926** *News-Globe* formed by merger of two newspapers; **1929** Amarillo College (2-year) established; **1931** county courthouse built; **July 12, 1957** astronaut Rick D. Husband born, killed with six other astronauts in breakup of space shuttle *Columbia* over eastern Texas Feb. 1, 2003 [see Nacogdoches]; **Aug. 31, 1965** Alibates Flint Quarries National Monument established to north, site quarried by pre-Columbian Native Americans for 10,000 years; **1972** Amarillo Art Center founded; **Feb. 10, 1998** TV talk show host Oprah Winfrey defeats ranchers' lawsuit over statement about consumption of beef causing mad cow disease.

Anahuac *Chambers County* *Southeastern Texas, 40 mi/64 km east of Houston, on Galveston Bay*

1816 first settled by Col. Henry Perry around Spanish fortress, named Perry's Point; **1825** town renamed Chambersia; **1831** Fort Anahuac established by Mexicans, built by prisoners; **1832, 1835** during Anahuac Disturbances, Mexicans defeated by U.S. settlers in sequence of clashes; **1858** Chambers County formed; Wallisville becomes county seat; **1859** post office opened; **1862** Fort Chambers established by Confederates; **1870** present name adopted, Aztec term meaning "plain near water"; **1907** town platted; **1908** county seat moved to Anahuac; **1935** oil discovered at nearby Mason City and Turtle Bayou, boosting economy; **1936** county courthouse built; **1948** incorporated as a city; **1963** Anahuac National Wildlife Refuge established to southeast; **1989** first annual Gatorfest held.

Anderson *Grimes County* *East Central Texas, 60 mi/97 km northwest of Houston*

1834 town founded by Henry Fanthorp on La Bahia Road; Fanthorp Inn built, wayside for visiting Texas notables; **1846** Grimes County formed; town becomes county seat; **1852** St. Paul's College established; **1861–1865** local arms factory supplies arms during Civil War; **1867** incorporated as a town; **1879** town disincorporated; **1894** county courthouse completed; **1900s** branch of Missouri Pacific Railroad reaches town, abandoned 1944.

Andrews *Andrews County* *Western Texas, 33 mi/53 km north of Odessa*

1876 Andrews County formed; **1908** general store built; **1910** county organized; town founded as county seat, named for Richard Andrews, first soldier to die in Texas Revolution, at Battle of Concepción 1835; **1917–1918** destructive drought affects area; **1929** oil discovered in county; **1937** incorporated as a city; **1939** county courthouse built.

Angleton *Brazoria County* *Southeastern Texas, 40 mi/64 km south of Houston, near Gulf or Mexico*

1836 Brazoria County formed; town of Brazoria becomes county seat; **1890** town founded, named for developer George W. Angle; **1897** county seat moved to Angleton; old county courthouse built, becomes museum and library 1940; **1912** town incorporated; **Aug. 31, 1923** last legal hanging in Texas takes place; **1939** oil discovered, economy remains based on agriculture; **1940** county courthouse built; **1966** Brazoria National Wildlife Area established.

Anson *Jones County* *West central Texas, 23 mi/37 km north-northwest of Abilene*

1858 Jones County formed; **1881** county organized; town founded as county seat, named for Dr. Anson Jones, last president of Republic of Texas; **1885** first Cowboy's Christmas Ball held; **1890** Texas & Pacific Railroad rerouted, missing Anson; **1904** incorporated as a city; **1910** county courthouse completed; **1926** oil discovered to southwest.

Archer City *Archer County* *Northern Texas, 22 mi/35 km south of Wichita Falls*

1858 Archer County formed; site on Wichita Falls & Southern Railroad designated as county seat; **1878** post office established; **1880** county organized; **1910** incorporated as a town; **1912** first producing oil wells bolster economy; **1925** incorporated as a city; **1926** county courthouse built; **1971** movie *The Last Picture Show* filmed here, based upon novel by Texas author Larry McMurtry; **1989** another McMurtry-based film, *Texasville*, filmed here.

Arlington *Tarrant County* *Northern Texas, 17 mi/27 km west of Dallas, 13 mi/21 km east of Fort Worth*

1843 Bird's Fort established, first white settlement in Caddoan territory; **1845** trading post established at Mary le Bone Springs; **1876** Texas & Pacific Railroad built; **1877** town moved 3 mi/4.8 km south to rail line, renamed for Robert E. Lee's hometown in Virginia; **1883** incorporated as a town; **1895** Arlington State College established, becomes University of Texas at Arlington 1965; **1896** incorporated as a city; **1902** interurban trolley extended to Fort Worth and Dallas; **1933** Arlington Downs Race Track opened, closed 1936; **1951** General Motors plant built; **1961** Six Flags Over Texas theme park opened; **1971** Washington Senators baseball team becomes Texas Rangers; **1972** Arlington Stadium built, home of Texas Rangers; **1994** The Ballpark at Arlington replaces Arlington Stadium.

Aspermont *Stonewall County* *Northwest central Texas, 55 mi/89 km north-northwest of Abilene*

1876 Stonewall County formed; **1888** county organized; **1889** town platted on land donated by A. L. Rhomberg, site previously called Sunflower Flat, renamed Latin term for "rough hill"; **1890** selection of Aspermont over Rayner as county seat leads to bitter feud; **1898** county seat dispute resolved in favor of Aspermont; Rayner abandoned; **1909** Stamford & Northwestern Railroad reaches town; **1910** town incorporated; **1983** county courthouse built.

Athens   *Henderson County*   *Eastern Texas, 65 mi/ 105 km southeast of Dallas*

1846 Henderson County formed; Buffalo becomes first county seat; **1848** county seat moved to Centerville; **1850** town founded as new county seat, originally named Alvin; **1856** incorporated as a town; **1857** pottery industry begins; **1880** Cotton Belt Railroad reaches town; **1885** *Athens Review* newspaper founded; **1900** Texas & New Orleans Railroad arrives; **1902** incorporated as a city, renamed Athens; **1913** county courthouse built; **1920s** oil discovered in area; **1946** Trinity Valley Community College established.

Austin   *Travis and Williamson counties*   *South central Texas, 42 mi/68 km northeast of San Antonio*

1838 settlement of four families founded, called Waterloo; site selected for Texas capital; **1839** construction begins on state government buildings; incorporated as a town, renamed to honor Stephen F. Austin, "Father of Texas"; government archives and other effects shipped from Houston; **1840** Travis County formed; town becomes county seat; French Embassy built; **July 4, 1845** Texas approves annexation by U.S.; **Dec. 19, 1845** Texas becomes 28th state to enter Union; **1853** first state capitol completed; **1856** governor's mansion built; **1871** *Austin Statesman* newspaper founded; **1876** Huston-Tillotson College (2-year) established; **1883** University of Texas at Austin established; **1885** St. Edward's University established; **1888** second state capitol completed; **1891** incorporated as a city; **1893** Austin Dam built on Colorado River; **1914** *Austin American* newspaper founded; **1924** *American-Statesman* newspaper created in merger; **Jan. 20, 1925** Miriam (Ma) Ferguson becomes governor, days after Nellie Ross of Wyoming becomes first woman governor in U.S.; **1926** Austin Public Library opened; **1930** county courthouse built; Robert Mueller Municipal Airport dedicated; **Jan. 3, 1932** TV actor Dabney Coleman born; **1942** Lake Travis formed on Colorado River to west by Marshall Ford Dam; Bergstrom Army Air Base opened, becomes Air Force Base 1948, closed 1973; **1943** Austin Museum of Art (Laguna Gloria Art Museum) founded on estate of Clara Driscoll; **1971** Lyndon Johnson Presidential Library dedicated; **1972** Austin Community College (2-year) established; **May 25, 1981** flooding kills at least 10; **1982** National Wildflower Research Center founded by Lady Bird Johnson; 32-story One American Center built; **1984** PC's Limited founded by Michael S. Dell, becomes Dell Computer Corporation 1987; **1987** 30-story One Congress Plaza built; **1999** Austin-Bergstrom International Airport opened at former air base; **Apr. 17, 2000** Gary Paul Karr, 52, gets life for extorting $600,000 from atheist Madalyn Murray O'Hair; she, son Jon,

daughter Robin missing since 1995; **Nov. 15, 2001** tornadoes, flash flooding kills eight.

Baird   *Callahan County*   *Northern Texas, 10 mi/ 16 km east of Abilene*

1858 Callahan County formed; **1875** Matthew Baird, director of Texas & Pacific Railroad, drives first stake into new rail line; **1878** county organized; Callahan (Belle Plain) becomes county seat; **1880** town founded on railroad; **1883** county seat moved to Baird; **mid 1883** fire destroys much of town, rebuilds within year; **1888** incorporated as a town; **1890** Schwartz Opera House built; **1891** incorporated as a city; *Baird Star* newspaper founded; **1929** county courthouse built; **1993** Texas Legislature recognizes town as Antique Capital of West Texas for its 20 antique malls.

Bakersfield   *Pecos County*   See **Fort Stockton** (1973)

Ballinger   *Runnels County*   *West central Texas, 36 mi/58 km northeast of San Angelo, on Colorado River*

1858 Runnels County formed, named for legislator Hiram G. Runnels; **1880** county organized; Runnels City becomes county seat; **1886** town platted on Gulf, Colorado & Santa Fe Railroad as new county seat, named for District Attorney William Pitt Ballinger; **1889** county courthouse built, renovated 1941; **1892** incorporated as a city; **Apr. 27, 1896** baseball pitcher Rogers Hornsby born at Winters to north (died 1963); **1909** Carnegie Library built; **1993** The Cross, 100-ft/30-m tall, 70-ft/21-m wide metal cross, erected by Jim and Doris Studer in field to southeast.

Bandera   *Bandera County*   *South central Texas, 40 mi/64 km northwest of San Antonio*

1852 cypress shingle camp established; **1854** town founded by Mormons, named for Mexican General Bandera; sawmill built; **1855** Polish immigrants arrive to work the mill; **1856** Bandera County formed; town becomes county seat; **1890** county courthouse built; **1964** incorporated as a city; **1978** Medina River flooding causes extensive damage.

Bastrop   *Bastrop County*   *South central Texas, 23 mi/37 km east-southeast of Austin, on Colorado River*

1829 town settled, named Mina; **1832** town platted; **1836** Bastrop County formed; town destroyed during Runaway Scrape, evacuation ordered during Mexican assault; **1837** town incorporated, becomes county seat, renamed for Felipe Enrique Neri, Baron de Bastrop, Dutch impostor wanted in Holland for tax embezzlement, became negotiator for Stephen Austin's government; **1851** *Colorado Reveille* newspaper founded, becomes *Bastrop Advertiser* 1853; **1889** Bastrop Opera House built; **1923** county courthouse built; **1942** Camp Swift Army base opened, closed 1945.

Bay City *Matagorda County* *Southeastern Texas,* *62 mi/100 km southwest of Houston, near Colorado River*

1836 Matagorda County formed; town of Matagorda becomes county seat; **1894** town founded as county seat; **1901** Cotton Belt Railroad reaches town; **1902** incorporated as a city; **1904** oil discovered; **1914** rice production becomes important; **1965** county courthouse built; **1988** South Texas Nuclear Plant begins operation to south.

Baytown *Harris and Chambers counties* *Southeastern Texas, 20 mi/32 km east of Houston*

1822 Nathaniel Lynch establishes Lynchburg Ferry across San Jacinto Bay; **1824** town founded; **1864** Confederates establish shipyard at mouth of Goose Creek; **1916** oil discovered in area; **1917** Morgan's Point Ferry established on Tabbs Bay; **1934** Lee College (2-year) established; **1948** towns of Goose Creek and Pelly merge to form Baytown; incorporated as a city; **1954** La Porte-Baytown Tunnel completed under Houston Ship Channel, eliminating ferry.

Beaumont *Jefferson County* *Southeastern Texas,* *75 mi/121 km east-northeast of Houston*

1825 first settlers arrive; **1836** Jefferson County formed; town platted by Henry Millard; **1838** incorporated as a town; county seat moved from town of Jefferson; **1845** John Jay French builds home and trading post; **1865** Union army occupies town; **1881** incorporated as a city; **Jan. 10, 1901** Anthony Lucas' oil well gushes at 10 A.M., beginning of world's first oil boomtown; population of village of Spindletop to southeast jumps to 30,000 in one month; **Sept. 17, 1907** actress Helen Vinson born (died 1999); **1908** McFaddin-Ward mansion completed; **1916** Neches River shipping channel built from Port Arthur, 15 mi/24 km to southeast, deepened 1927; **March 15, 1916** bandleader Harry James born (died 1983); **1923** Lamar University established; **1932** county courthouse built; **Aug. 31, 1935** baseball player Frank Robinson born; **Feb. 3, 1963** tanker *Marine Sulphur Queen* vanishes after leaving Beaumont for Norfolk, 39 presumed dead; **1970s** area's petrochemical industry becomes important; **1990** Texas Energy Museum opened.

Beeville *Bee County* *Southern Texas, 50 mi/80 km north-northwest of Corpus Christi*

1830s area settled; **1857** Bee County formed; **1858** Beeville founded as county seat, named for Bernard E. Bee, Minister of Texas Republic to U.S.; **1859** new town of Maryville founded, named for Mary Heffernan, only survivor of family massacred by Native Americans in 1830s; **1860** county seat moved to Maryville, renamed Beeville with abandonment of original Beeville; **1886** *Bee* newspaper founded; **1886** San Antonio & Aransas Pass Railroad completed; **1888** Gulf & West Texas Railroad extended to town; **1890** incorporated as a town; *Picayune* newspaper founded, becomes *Bee-Picayune* through merger 1928; **1908** incorporated as a city; **1912** county

courthouse built; **1943** Chase Naval Air Field opened, closed 1946; **1965** Bee County College (2-year) established, becomes Coastal Bend College.

Bellville *Austin County* *South central Texas,* *52 mi/84 km west-northwest of Houston*

1836 Austin County formed; San Felipe becomes county seat; **1838** Thomas B. Bell first to settle in area; **1846** town founded as new county seat; **1848** town platted; **1881** Gulf Coast & Santa Fe Railroad arrives; **1911** county courthouse built; **1915** oil discovered in county; **1927** incorporated as a town; **Jan. 1929** incorporated as a city.

Belton *Bell County* *Central Texas, 7 mi/11.3 km* *west-southwest of Temple*

1850 Bell County formed; town founded as county seat, named Nolanville; **1851** town renamed Belton; **1856** town incorporated; **1860s** Ku Klux Klan develops strong presence; **1866** jailed Union sympathizers accused of murder lynched by mob; **1879** town's first cotton gin established; **1884** incorporated as a city; county courthouse built; **1886** University of Mary Hardin-Baylor moved from Independence, established 1845; Belton Academy founded, closed 1916; **1887** Central Hotel opened.

Ben Ficklin *Tom Green County* *Western Texas,* *5 mi/8 km southwest of San Angelo*

1874 Tom Green County formed; **1875** town founded as county seat, named for Pony Express rider whose route went through area; **Feb. 1882** county courthouse completed; **Aug. 24, 1882** in Ben Ficklin Flood, Middle Concho River completely destroys town, damages other communities, 65 killed; **1883** county seat moved to San Angelo.

Benjamin *Knox County* *Northern Texas, 75 mi/* *121 km west-southwest of Wichita Falls*

1858 Knox County formed; **1884** town founded, named for son of landowner Hilory H. Bedford; **1886** county organized; town becomes county seat; **1928** incorporated as a city; **1938** county courthouse completed.

Big Lake *Reagan County* *Western Texas, 60 mi/* *97 km west-southwest of San Angelo*

1903 Reagan County formed; Stiles becomes county seat; **1911** landowner blocks Orient Railroad from building through Stiles; **1912** railroad completed; town founded; **1923** oil pool discovered at Santa Rita No. 1 well, remains active until 1990; **1923** incorporated as a city; **1925** county seat moved to Big Lake; **1927** county courthouse built.

Big Spring *Howard County* *West central Texas,* *100 mi/161 km west of Abilene*

1849 expedition led by Capt. Randolph Marcy reaches large spring on Sulphur Draw; **1876** Howard County formed; **1880** Texas & Pacific Railroad built through county; **1882** county organized; town founded as county seat; **1905** opera house opens; **1907** incorporated as a city; **1927** oil discovered in area; **1942-1945** Army Air Corps operates Big Spring Bombardier School during World War II; **1945** Howard College (2-year) established; **1951** Webb Air Force Base established, closed 1977; **1953** county courthouse built; **1964** Big Spring State Hospital established.

Boerne *Kendall County* *South central Texas, 30 mi/48 km north-northwest of San Antonio*

1849 town platted, originally named Tusculum; **1851** German settlers arrive; town renamed in honor of German political writer Ludwig Boerne; **1862** Kendall County formed; town becomes county seat; **1909** incorporated as a city; third county courthouse built.

Bonham *Fannin County* *Northeastern Texas, 63 mi/101 km northeast of Dallas, near Red River*

1837 Fannin County formed, named for military hero James Walker Fannin, Jr.; town platted, named Bois d'Arc by Bailey Inglish; **1838** county organized; (Old) Warren becomes county seat; **1843** town renamed for James Bonham, who died at the Alamo; **1845** county seat moved to Bonham; **1848** incorporated as a town; **1888** county courthouse built, burned Dec. 31, 1929, remodeled 1964; **1900** Texas & Pacific Railroad depot built; cotton mill established; **1901** Bonham Public Library founded; **Sept. 19, 1943** baseball player Joe Morgan born; **1947** incorporated as a city.

Borger *Hutchinson County* *Northwestern Texas, 40 mi/64 km northeast of Amarillo, near Canadian River*

1925 Panhandle Oil Field discovered; **1926** town founded, named for promoter A. P. Borger; **Nov. 1927** fire destroys Dixon Creek Oil Refinery; **1929** oil boom dwindles, lingering bad element requires state militia; **1930** incorporated as a city; **1948** Frank Phillips College (2-year) established; **1965** Lake Meredith formed by dam on Canadian River to west; **Oct. 16, 1972** Lake Meredith National Recreation Area established; **1976** Lake Meredith Aquarium opened.

Boston *Bowie County* *Northeastern Texas, 20 mi/ 32 km west of Texarkana*

1840 Bowie County formed; **1841** town founded as county seat; **1846** post office established; **1869** Texas & Pacific Railroad built 3 mi/4.8 km to north; town of New Boston founded on railroad; **1890** county courthouse built, burned by arsonist 1987; **1987** new county courthouse built at New Boston; Boston remains official county seat.

Brackettville *Kinney County* *Southwestern Texas, 29 mi/47 km east of Del Rio*

1850 Kinney County formed, named for Sen. Henry L. Kinney; **1852** Fort Clark established; town founded, named Brackett for landowner Oscar Brackett; **1876** county organized; town becomes county seat; **1878** St. Mary Magdalene Catholic Church built; **1880** town renamed Brackettville; flooding damages town, again in 1899; **1910** county courthouse built; **1930** incorporated as a city; **1944** Fort Clark deactivated.

Brady *McCulloch County* *Central Texas, 70 mi/ 113 km east-southeast of San Angelo*

1830 battle at Calf Creek to southwest between Tawakonis and band led by brothers James and Rezin Bowie, Bowie group fights their way out of it; **1856** McCulloch County formed, named for Confederate Gen. Benjamin McCulloch; **1876** county organized; town founded as county seat, named for county surveyor Peter Brady; **1899** county courthouse built; **1904** Fort Worth & Rio Grande Railroad reaches town; **1906** incorporated as a city.

Brazoria *Brazoria County* *Southeastern Texas, 15 mi/24 km northwest of Freeport, in Brazosport area*

1828 town founded; **1832** town separates from San Felipe, incorporated as a town, serves as capital of Austin's colony; **Apr. 22, 1836** in Runaway Scrape, during Santa Anna's invasion of Texas, all colonists evacuate as Mexican Gen. José Urrea burns town; **Dec. 1836** Brazoria County formed; town becomes county seat; **1897** county seat moved to Angleton; **1912** new town platted; **1939** oil and sulfur deposits discovered; **1945** incorporated as a city.

Breckenridge *Stephens County* *North central Texas, 90 mi/145 km west of Fort Worth*

1858 county formed, named Buchanan County for Pres. James Buchanan; **1876** county organized, renamed for Confederate Alexander H. Stephens; town founded as county seat, named for John C. Breckenridge, vice president under President Buchanan; **1916–1917** oil discovery in neighboring Eastland County boosts economy; **March 1918** oil discovered locally; **1919** incorporated as a city; **1920** oil boom reaches peak, town's population jumps from 1,500 to 30,000 in one year, boom ends 1921; **1926** county courthouse built; **1962** Hubbard Creek Reservoir formed to northwest.

Brenham *Washington County* *South central Texas, 70 mi/113 km west-northwest of Houston*

1836 Washington County formed; Washington-on-the-Brazos becomes county seat; **1844** town founded as new county seat, named for Texas patriot Dr. Richard Brenham, died in Mexico 1843; **1858** town incorporated; **1860** Houston & Texas Central Railroad reaches town; **1860s** town government disbanded; wave of German immigrants settles in area; **1865** Federal military post built; military rule begins; **1866** town reincorporated; **Aug. 1867** feud between Federal troops and citizens leads to burning of town; **1869** military rule lifted; **1881** first annual Maifest held; **1883** Blinn College (2-year) established; **1895** *Banner Press* newspaper founded; **1910** carousel built in Fireman's Park, rare surviving example of manufacturer C. W. Parker; **1911** Brenham Creamery founded, renamed Blue Bell 1930; **1939** county courthouse built; **1967** Somerville Lake reservoir completed to northwest on Yegua River.

Brownfield *Terry County* *Western Texas, 35 mi/ 56 km southwest of Lubbock*

1876 Terry County formed from Bexar County, named for Confederate Col. Benjamin Franklin Terry; **1903** town platted, named for ranchers A. M. and M. V. Brownfield; **1904** county organized; town chosen as county seat over Gomez; **1917** Santa Fe Railroad reaches area; **1920** incorporated as a city; **1925** county courthouse built.

Brownsville *Cameron County* *Southern Texas, 125 mi/201 km south of Corpus Christi, on Rio Grande*

1519 Spanish explorer Alonso Alvarez de la Piñeda explores lower Rio Grande; **1846** Fort Texas established by Gen. Zachary Taylor; **May 8, 1846** in Battle of Palo Alto, first action of Mexican War, forces of Mexican Gen. Mariano Arista overwhelmed by artillery of General Taylor; fort later renamed for Maj. Jacob Brown, killed in action; **1848** Cameron County formed; town founded by Charles Stillman; **1849** town becomes county seat; **1850** incorporated as a town; **Nov. 1863** Brownsville occupied by forces of Union Maj. Gen. N. P. Banks; **Nov. 5, 1863** steamer *Nassau* lost in military action in Brazos Pass; **May 12-13, 1865** Confederate forces of Col. John S. Ford capture Federal force at Palmito Hill Ranch month following Lee's surrender at Appomattox, unaware of the news; **1906** raid on town by black American soldiers stationed at Fort Brown results in dishonorable discharges for 127, decision reversed 1972; **1911** Brownsville & Matamoros Bridge opened to Matamoros, Mexico; **1912** county courthouse built; **1926** Texas Southmost College (2-year) established; **1936** Port of Brownsville opened, 17 mi/27 km ship channel built from Gulf of Mexico; **June 22, 1936** singer, actor Kris Kristofferson born; **1944** Fort Brown deactivated; **1952** incorporated as a city; **1973** University of Texas at Brownsville established; **Nov. 10, 1978** Palo Alto National Battlefield established (dedicated 1993); **Aug. 8, 1980** Hurricane Allen brings flooding to lower Rio Grande, 200,000 evacuated.

Brownwood *Brown County* *Central Texas, 62 mi/ 100 km southeast of Abilene*

1856 Brown County formed; **1857** town founded as county seat; **1876** incorporated as a town; **1884** incorporated as a city; **1889** Howard Payne University established; **May 15, 1890** novelist Katherine Anne Porter born at Indian Creek to south (died 1980); **1917** county courthouse built; **1920** oil discovered, boom lasts until 1927; **1933** Lake Brownwood formed by dam on Pecan Bayou to north; **1942** U.S. Army Camp Bowie opened, closed 1946; **1953** Poage Pecan Field Station established for development of new pecan varieties; **1963** Brownwood Coliseum built.

Bryan *Brazos County* *East central Texas, 85 mi/ 137 km northwest of Houston, twin city of College Station*

1821 Stephen Austin's colonists settle in area; **1841** Brazos County formed; Boonville becomes county seat; **1859** Houston & Texas Central Railroad built; town platted, named for Austin's nephew William Joel Bryan, donated land to railroad; **1861** county seat moved to Bryan; **1869** *Bryan Eagle* newspaper founded; **1872** incorporated as a town; **1903** Carnegie Library built, new library opened 1969; **1917** incorporated as a city; **1957** county courthouse built.

Burkburnett *Wichita County* *Northern Texas, 12 mi/19 km north-northwest of Wichita Falls, on Red River*

1867 area settled by pioneers D. P. McCracken and H. C. Ackers; **1907** town surveyed, named for Burke Burnett, whose 6666 Ranch President Theodore Roosevelt stayed at to hunt wolves 1905, town site located on ranch; *Burkburnett Star* newspaper founded; **1912** Burkburnett Oil Field discovered to west; **1913** incorporated as a town; **July 29, 1918** large oil gusher brings boom to area; **1923** incorporated as a city; **c.1929** oil boom ends.

Burleson *Johnson County* *See* **Fort Worth (1910)**

Burnet *Burnet County* *Central Texas, 45 mi/72 km northwest of Austin*

1849 Fort Croghan established; **1852** Burnet County formed; town founded as county seat, named Hamilton; **1858** town renamed Burnet (BURN-it); **1882** Texas & New Orleans (Southern Pacific) Railroad built from Austin; **1883** town incorporated; **1934** Lake Buchanan formed by dam to west on Colorado River; **1936** county courthouse built.

Caldwell *Burleson County* *South central Texas, 65 mi/105 km east-northeast of Austin*

1830 Mexicans establish Fort Tenoxtitlan to counteract intentions of American colonists, Mexican commander sides with Texans, signs Texas Declaration of Independence; **1840** town founded, named for Matthew "Old Paint" Caldwell, signer of Texas Declaration of Independence; **1846** Burleson County formed; town becomes county seat; **1880** Gulf, Colorado & Santa Fe Railroad reaches town; **1891** incorporated as a city; **1927** county courthouse built.

Cameron   *Milam County*   *Central Texas, 45 mi/ 72 km south of Waco, on San Gabriel River*

1836 Milam County formed, comprises one-sixth of Texas; Nashville-on-the-Brazos becomes county seat; **1846** Burleson County formed from Milam County; town founded as new Milam County seat, named for Scotsman Capt. Ewen Cameron, fought in Texas Revolution, shot by Mexicans 1843; **1856** county land area greatly reduced; **1881** Gulf, Colorado & Santa Fe Railroad reaches town; **1889** incorporated as a city; **1892** county courthouse built.

Camp Verde   *Kerr County*   *South central Texas, 50 mi/80 km northwest of San Antonio*

1855 Camp Verde established on Verde Creek for Army camel experiment for use across Southwestern desert; **1856** 80 camels headquartered at camp; **1857** general store opened, in continuous operation; camp used as base against Mormons in Utah; **March 31, 1862** post taken by Confederates; **March 1864** post recaptured by Union forces, temporarily left unused; **1865** post regarrisoned by Federal troops; **1869** post abandoned; **1947** post office closed.

Canadian   *Hemphill County*   *Northwestern Texas, 90 mi/145 km northeast of Amarillo*

1876 Hemphill County formed; **1887** county organized; town founded on Canadian River as county seat; **1888** Panhandle & Western Railroad extended through town; first rodeo in Texas held; **1904** Canadian Academy founded (closed 1912); **1908** town incorporated; **1909** county courthouse built.

Canton   *Van Zandt County*   *Northeastern Texas, 52 mi/84 km east-southeast of Dallas*

1848 Van Zandt County formed, named for Isaac Van Zandt, member of Texas legislature; Grand Saline becomes county seat; **1850** town platted as new county seat; **1873** Texas & Pacific Railroad built, misses town by 10 mi/16 km; county seat moved to Wills Point; **1877** Canton residents reclaim county seat by obtaining county records by force at Wills Point, state militia quells violence; **1919** incorporated as a city; **1937** county courthouse built.

Canyon   *Randall County*   *Northwestern Texas, 18 mi/29 km south of Amarillo*

1874 Battle of Palo Duro Canyon to east, last Native American battle in Texas, cavalry of Col. Ranald Mackenzie rout large band of Comanches, burn their shelters, kill 1,400 of their horses, forcing them to return to Oklahoma; **1876** Randall County formed; **1878** expansive T Anchor Ranch established, headquarters at town site; **1887** town founded by L. G. Conner, named Canyon City; **1889** county organized; town becomes county seat; **1898** Pecos & Northern Railroad reaches town; **1906** incorporated as a city; **1908** county courthouse built; **1909** West

Texas A & M University established; **1910** city renamed Canyon; **1927** Randall County Library opened; **1932** Panhandle Plains Museum founded; **1965** perennial musical drama *Texas* first performed at Palo Duro Canyon State Park to east.

Carrizo Springs   *Dimmit County*   *Southern Texas, 100 mi/161 km southwest of San Antonio*

1858 Dimmit County formed; **1865** town founded; **1880** county organized; town becomes county seat; **1884** the *Javelin* newspaper founded; **1890** first farmers settle in county in competition with ranchers; **1910** spur of San Antonio, Uvalde & Gulf Railroad built; town incorporated; **1926** county courthouse built.

Carthage   *Panola County*   *Eastern Texas, 140 mi/ 225 km east-southeast of Dallas, near Sabine River*

1846 Panola County formed; Pulaski becomes county seat; **1848** town founded as county seat; **1874** incorporated as a town; **1888** Texas, Sabine Valley & Northwestern Railroad reaches town; **Jan. 12, 1905** country singer Tex Ritter born at Murvaul to south (died 1974); **Aug. 20, 1923** country singer Jim Reeves born at Galloway to southeast (died 1964); **1947** Panola College (2-year) established; **1948** incorporated as a city; **1953** county courthouse built.

Castroville   *Medina County*   *South central Texas, 24 mi/39 km west of San Antonio, on Medina River*

Sept. 1844 town founded by group of Alsatian immigrants led by Henri Castro, main settlement of Castro's colony; **1848** Medina County formed; town becomes county seat; **1853** land donated for county courthouse, completed 1855; **1854** rock dam and grist mill built; **1868–1870** St. Louis Catholic Church built; **1879** county courthouse built; **1880** Southern Pacific Railroad reaches town; **1892** county seat moved to Hondo; **1948** incorporated as a city.

Centerville   *Leon County*   *East central Texas, 70 mi/113 km east-southeast of Waco*

1846 Leon County formed from Robertson County; Leona becomes county seat; **1850** town founded, originally named Centreville; **1851** county seat moved to Centerville; **1887** county courthouse completed; **1915** black man accused of murder of white man lynched; **1930** town incorporated; **1937** first annual Black Eyed Pea Festival held.

Channing   *Hartley County*   *Northwestern Texas, 40 mi/64 km northwest of Amarillo*

1876 Hartley County formed; town of Hartley becomes county seat; **1888** Fort Worth & Denver City Railroad built; **1891** town founded, named for George Channing Rivers, railroad paymaster; **1903** county seat moved to Channing; **1906** county courthouse completed; **Sept. 6, 1931** fire destroys downtown buildings; **1960** incorporated as a city.

Childress   *Childress County*   *Northwestern Texas, 103 mi/166 km southeast of Amarillo, near Red River*

1876 Childress County formed; **1887** county organized; Fort Worth & Denver City Railroad reaches site; town founded as county seat, named for George C. Childress, an author of the Texas Declaration of Independence; **1887** incorporated as a town; **1917** incorporated as a city; **1939** county courthouse built; **May 1942** Childress Army Air Base established, deactivated Dec. 1945.

Cisco   *Eastland County*   *North central Texas, 50 mi/ 80 km east of Abilene*

1851 area settled; **1860s** promoter J. J. Cisco brings Houston & Texas Central Railroad to area; **1881** town founded at junction of Texas & Pacific Railroad; **1893** tornado strikes town, 28 killed; **1893** *Cisco Round-Up* newspaper founded; **1916** Mobley Hotel built, purchased by Conrad Hilton 1919, first in his hotel chain; **1917** Ranger Oil Pool discovered; **1919** incorporated as a city; **1920** Cisco & Northeastern Railway completed, abandoned 1943; **Dec. 23, 1927** "Santa Claus" bank robbery followed by gun battle, four killed, six wounded; **1940** Cisco Junior College established.

Clarendon   *Donley County*   *Northwestern Texas, 55 mi/89 km east-southeast of Amarillo*

1876 Wegefarth County formed; **1878** county renamed Donley County for Stockton P. Donley of Texas Supreme Court; colony established by Methodist minister Lewis Carhart, named for his wife Clara, intended to be a "sobriety settlement," an oasis among the rowdy Texas boom towns, referred to as "Saints Roost" by outsiders; **1882** county organized; town founded as county seat; **1887** Fort Worth & Denver City Railroad reaches site; town relocates to railroad; **1891** county courthouse built; **1898** Clarendon College established, closed 1927; **1901** town incorporated.

Clarksville   *Red River County*   *Northeastern Texas, 57 mi/92 km west of Texarkana*

Sept. 20, 1816 Englishwoman Jane Chandler Gill dies, buried here (born Jan. 1, 1782), one of first white burials in Texas; **1834** town founded by Capt. James Clark; **1836** Red River County formed; **1837** county organized; La Grange (Madras) designated as county seat, county court held at Clarksville instead by Judge John M. Hansford; incorporated as a town; **1850** Clarksville becomes county seat; **Nov. 22, 1868** U.S. Cong. John Nance Garner born at Detroit to west, vice president under Pres. Franklin D. Roosevelt (died 1967); **1885** county courthouse completed, clock tower "Old Red" operates smoothly until 1961, converted to electricity; **1956** incorporated as a city.

Claude   *Armstrong County*   *Northwestern Texas, 26 mi/42 km east-southeast of Amarillo*

1876 Armstrong County formed; **1887** Fort Worth & Denver City Railroad built; town founded; **1890** county

organized; town becomes county seat; **1909** town incorporated; **1912** county courthouse built.

Cleburne   *Johnson County*   *Northern Texas, 27 mi/ 43 south of Fort Worth*

1854 Johnson County formed; Buchanan becomes county seat; **1862** Camp Henderson established by Confederates; **1867** town founded as new county seat, named for Confederate Gen. Pat Cleburne; **1871** incorporated as a town; **1904** Carnegie Library opens; **1907** incorporated as a city; **1913** county courthouse built.

Coldspring   *San Jacinto County*   *Eastern Texas, 60 mi/97 km north of Houston*

1841 post office established, originally named Coonskin; **1847** town founded, renamed Fireman's Hill; **1850** town renamed Cold Spring; **1869** San Jacinto County formed; town becomes county seat; **1894** town renamed Coldspring; **1917** county courthouse completed; **1945** oil discovered to southeast; **1969** incorporated as a city.

Coleman   *Coleman County*   *Central Texas, 45 mi/ 72 km south-southeast of Abilene*

1854 area first settled; **1858** Coleman County formed; **1876** county organized; town of Coleman founded as county seat, named for Robert M. Coleman, signer of Texas Declaration of Independence; **1877** town incorporated; **1884** county courthouse built, remodeled 1952; **1886** Santa Fe Railroad reaches town; **1897** *Coleman Democrat-Voice* newspaper published; **1903** oil discovered to southeast; **1941** Coleman Field Army Air Base established, closed 1944.

College Station   *Brazos County*   *East central Texas, 82 mi/132 km northwest of Houston twin city of Bryan*

1876 Texas A & M College established, becomes University 1963; **1885** post office opens; **1938** incorporated as a city; **Nov. 18, 1999** log tower built for pep rally bonfire at Texas A & M University collapses, 12 killed, 27 injured.

Colorado City   *Mitchell County*   *Western Texas, 65 mi/105 km west of Abilene, on Colorado River*

1876 Mitchell County formed, named for Eli Mitchell, fought in Battle of Gonzales; **1877** site established as camp of Texas Rangers; **1880** town founded; **1881** county organized; town becomes county seat; Texas & Pacific Railroad reaches town; **1907** incorporated as a city; **1920s** oil discovered; **1924** county courthouse built; **1994** D. W. John Wallace medium security prison for men completed.

Columbus   *Colorado County*   *South central Texas, 70 mi/113 km west of Houston, on Colorado River*

1823 members of Austin's colony settle on site of Native American village called Montezuma; **1835** town founded; **1836** Colorado County formed; Alley Log Cabin built;

1837 county organized; town becomes county seat; **1839** Col. Robert Dumfries builds castle with moat, damaged by flood 1869, razed 1873; **1883** water tower built of 400,000 bricks; **1886** Stafford Opera House built; **1891** county courthouse built; **1927** incorporated as a city.

Comanche   *Comanche County*   *Central Texas, 75 mi/121 km southeast of Abilene*

1856 Comanche County formed; Cora becomes county seat; **1858** town founded by John Duncan, who offers it for county seat; **May 1859** county seat moved to Comanche; **1873** town incorporated; **1939** county courthouse built.

Comfort   *Kendall County*   *South central Texas, 45 mi/72 km northwest of San Antonio, on Guadalupe River*

1854 town founded by German immigrants, named Camp Comfort; **1856** Kerr County formed; Kerrville becomes county seat; **1860** Kerr County seat moved to Comfort; **1862** Kendall County separates from Kerr County; Kerr County seat moved back to Kerrville; group of 68 Germans led by Fritz Tegener, sympathetic toward Union, flee area, attacked by Confederates, 19 killed, 15 executed, remainder reach Mexico, return after war, monument built 1865; **1880** Comfort Common Inn built; **1930** art deco Comfort Theater built, used for Hill Country Opry.

Conroe   *Montgomery County*   *Southeastern Texas, 40 mi/64 km north of Houston*

1837 Montgomery County formed, named for settler Andrew Montgomery; town of Montgomery becomes county seat; **1880** town founded on Gulf, Colorado & Santa Fe Railroad, named for sawmill owner Capt. Isaac Conroe; **1885** incorporated as a town; **1889** county seat moved to Conroe; **1904** incorporated as a city; **Dec. 1931** Conroe Oil Field discovered to southeast; **1936** county courthouse built; **1995** Montgomery College (2-year) established.

Cooper   *Delta County*   *Northeastern Texas, 75 mi/121 km northeast of Dallas*

1870 Delta County formed; **1874** town platted, founded as county seat, named for Sen. L. W. Cooper; **1881** incorporated as a town; **1887** incorporated as a city; **1900** Texas & Midland Railroad built; **1925** Miller Drug store established, still in business with its original soda fountain and Wurlitzer juke box; **1940** county courthouse built.

Corpus Christi   *Nueces County*   *Southern Texas, 130 mi/209 km southeast of San Antonio, on Gulf of Mexico*

1519 bay explored by Spaniard Alonzo Alvarez de Piñeda on day of Feast of Corpus Christi; **c.1765** San Petronilla

Ranch founded by Blas María de la Garza Falcón; **1832** Col. Henry L. Kinney settles in area; **1839** trading post established by Kinney; **1846** Nueces County formed; town becomes county seat; **1852** incorporated as a city; **1883** *The Caller* newspaper founded; **1907** Corpus Christi Public Library founded; **1911** *The Times* newspaper founded; **1914** county courthouse built; **1919** hurricane devastates city; **1926** Intracoastal Waterway, barge shipping channel paralleling Gulf coast, completed; **1929** *Caller* and *Times* newspapers merge; **1935** Del Mar College (2-year) established; **1940** Centennial Museum opened; **1941** sea wall completed; **1947** Texas A & M University, Corpus Christi Campus, established; **Feb. 2, 1947** actress Farrah Fawcett born; **1959** Nueces Bay Bridge completed; **1960** Corpus Christi International Airport opened to west; **Apr. 6, 1968** Padre Island National Seashore established to south; **Aug. 4, 1970** Hurricane Celia hits Texas coast, 12 killed; **1972** Art Museum of South Texas opened in former Centennial Museum, becomes part of South Texas Institute for the Arts 1997; **Aug. 10, 1980** Hurricane Allen moves north, 108 killed in Caribbean and Gulf; **March 31, 1995** Mexican-American singer Selena found shot to death in motel, Yolanda Saldivar convicted Oct. 23; **1990** Texas State Aquarium opened; Greyhound Race Track established.

Corsicana   *Navarro County*   *East central Texas, 48 mi/77 km south-southeast of Dallas*

1846 Navarro County formed; **1848** town founded as county seat, incorporated; **1849** McKinney Inn established by Hampton McKinney of Illinois; **1854** Corsicana Female Literary Institute established (closed 1870); **1871** Houston & Texas Central Railroad reaches town; **1872** incorporated as a city; **1894** oil discovered while drilling for water; **1896** Collin Street Bakery begins marketing its "Deluxe" fruitcake, Corsicana Fruit Cake now world famous; **1897** first Texas oil refinery built; **1906** Carnegie Library built, new library opened 1967; **March 3, 1928** country singer Lefty Frizzell born (died 1975); **1946** Navarro College (2-year) established; **1975** county government center dedicated.

Cotulla   *La Salle County*   *Southern Texas, 80 mi/129 km southwest of San Antonio*

1852 Fort Ewell established on Nueces River; **1858** La Salle County formed; **1862** Polish immigrant Joseph Cotulla becomes first settler; **1879** International-Great Northern Railroad built; **1880** county organized; town founded as county seat; **1910** town incorporated; **1931** county courthouse built; **1937** Cotulla Public Library built.

Crane   *Crane County*   *Western Texas, 30 mi/48 km south of Odessa*

1887 Crane County formed; **1926** oil discovered in county; **1927** county organized; town founded as county seat, named for Texas educator William Carey Crane; **1933** town incorporated; **1948** county courthouse built.

TEXAS

Crawford   *McLennan County*   *Central Texas,
17 mi/27 km west of Waco*

1867 town founded as stop on stage line; **1871** post office established; **1881** Gulf, Colorado & Santa Fe Railroad built 2 mi/3.2 km to west; town relocated; **1897** incorporated as a town; **2001** Pres. George W. Bush establishes "Texas White House" at his ranch 8 mi/12.9 km to northwest.

Crockett   *Houston County*   *Eastern Texas, 105 mi/
169 km north of Houston*

1836 Col. David Crockett and his group of men camp at spring on way to fateful battle at the Alamo in San Antonio; **1837** county formed, land donated at town site for county seat; **1837** incorporated as a town; **1839** area first settled; log county courthouse built; **1840** post office established; **1865** courthouse and most of county records burned; **1872** Houston & Texas Central Railroad built; **1886** Mary Allen Junior College for Negroes established (closed c.1942); **1899** oil discovered, produced commercially 1934; **1939** county courthouse built; **1960** incorporated as city.

Crosbyton   *Crosby County*   *Western Texas, 35 mi/
56 km east of Lubbock*

1876 Crosby County formed; area settled; **1886** county organized; Estacado becomes county seat; **1891** county seat moved to Emma; **1908** town platted; Crosbyton Inn opened; **1911** Crosbyton Cut-Off railroad built; **1912** county seat moved to Crosbyton; **1914** county courthouse built; **1917** town incorporated; **1975** Crosbyton Municipal Airport opened; **1976** federal grant awarded to Texas Technical University for development of solar power project to south.

Crowell   *Foard County*   *Northern Texas, 65 mi/
105 km west of Wichita Falls*

1860 in Battle of Pease River, Cynthia Parker and 2-year-old daughter Prairie Flower rescued, both die within four years, she was mother of Quanah Parker, last great Comanche chief [see Groesbeck, 1836]; **1891** Foard County formed, named for Maj. John Robert Foard; town founded as county seat, named for landowner George T. Crowell; **1901** incorporated as a town; **1908** Kansas City, Mexico & Orient Railroad reaches town; incorporated as a city; **1910** county courthouse built; **Apr. 27, 1942** tornado strikes town, 10 killed, 125 injured.

Crystal City   *Zavala County*   *Southern Texas,
95 mi/153 km southwest of San Antonio*

1858 Zavala County formed; **1884** county organized; Batesville becomes county seat; **1907** town founded on Cross S Ranch; **1910** incorporated as a city; **1927** county seat moved to Crystal City; **1930** spinach production begins with aid of irrigation; **1932** vegetable processing plant opened; **1937** Popeye statue erected in honor of local spinach industry; **1942** Alien Internment Camp estab-

lished, includes Japanese nationals, closed 1947; **1970** county courthouse built.

Cuero   *De Witt County*   *Southern Texas, 75 mi/
121 km east-southeast of San Antonio, near Guadalupe River*

1846 De Witt County formed; Daniel Boone Friar opens store; town founded, named Friar's Store; post office established as Cuero; **1850** Clinton becomes county seat after four county seat moves; **1873** Galveston, West Texas & Pacific Railroad built; post office moved 4 mi/6.4 km south to railroad, retains name of Cuero; incorporated as a city; *Weekly Star* newspaper founded; **1876** county seat moved to Cuero; **1886** refugees arrive from Indianola, destroyed by hurricane; **1897** county courthouse built; **1912** first annual Cuero Turkey Trot held.

Daingerfield   *Morris County*   *Northeastern Texas,
45 mi/72 km southwest of Texarkana*

1840 S. R. Shaddick becomes first settler; **1841** town founded as seat of short-lived Paschal County, named for Capt. London Daingerfield, killed fighting Native Americans here; **1846** post office established; **1870** Chapel Hill College established; **1875** Morris County formed; town becomes county seat; **1881** county courthouse built, used as museum 1973; **1913** town incorporated; **1928** fire destroys part of business district, again in 1953; **1973** new county courthouse built.

Dalhart   *Dallam and Hartley counties*
Northwestern Texas, 70 mi/113 km northwest of Amarillo

1876 Dallam County formed; **1882** XIT Ranch granted to Capitol Freehold Land & Investment Company of London, England, over three million acres (1,215,000 ha), as payment for work on state capitol in Austin, largest ranch in world at the time [see Farwell]; **1891** county organized; Texline becomes county seat; **1893** Chicago, Rock Island & Pacific Railroad; town founded as new county seat, named Twist; **1901** Fort Worth & Denver City Railroad built forming junction; town renamed Dalhart; **1902** incorporated as a town; *Dalhart Texan* newspaper founded; **1904** incorporated as a city; **1923** county courthousecounty courthouse built; **1930** Rita Blanca National Grassland established to north; **1934** area used for three wind erosion control demonstrations; **1942** Dalhart Army Air Field established (closed 1946).

Dallas   *Dallas, Kaufman, Collin, and Denton
counties*   *Northern Texas, on Trinity River*

1841 John Neely Bryan of Tennessee founds trading post at ford on Trinity River; **1842** *Dallas Morning News* newspaper founded; **1843** Bryan builds first log cabin; **1844** town platted, namesake unknown; **1846** Dallas County formed; **1850** county organized; town becomes county seat; **1856** incorporated as a town; **1871** incorporated as a city; **1872** Houston & Texas Central Railroad reaches city; **1873** Texas & Pacific Railroad arrives, forms junction; **1886** Texas State Fairgrounds established; **1888** Dallas Zoo established; **1893** county courthouse (Old Red) completed, now vacant; **Sept. 23, 1899** Supreme Court Justice Tom C. Clark born (died 1977); **1900** Dallas Symphony Orchestra founded; **1907** Nieman-Marcus retail store founded; **1911** Southern Methodist University established; **1913** criminal courts building opened; **1917** Love Field Airport opened; **1922** Dallas Historical Society founded; **Oct. 17, 1923** actress Linda Darnell born (died 1965); **Dec. 18, 1927** Ramsey Clark born, Attorney General under Pres. Lyndon Johnson; **1928** Braniff Airlines established by Paul R. Braniff, filed for bankruptcy 1989, went out of business 1992; **Apr. 22, 1928** movie producer Aaron Spelling born; **Oct. 2, 1928** actor George "Spanky" McFarland born (died 1993); **1930s** oil boom in East Texas brings oil companies to Dallas; **1936** Museum of Natural History founded; Texas Centennial Exposition draws over six million visitors; **May 15, 1937** singer Trini Lopez born; **1938** Camp Estate of architect John Staub completed, later becomes Dallas Arboretum; **Dec. 1, 1939** golfer Lee Trevino born; **1941** Dallas Naval Air Station established; Dallas Texans hockey team established; **Jan. 24, 1943** actress Sharon Tate born, murdered by Charles Manson followers Aug. 9, 1969, in Los Angeles; **June 8, 1944** singer Boz Scaggs born; **Jan. 3, 1945** singer Stephen Stills born; **Feb. 3, 1950** actress Morgan Fairchild born; **1952** Big Tex cowboy statue, 52 ft/16 m tall, erected at entrance to state fairgrounds; **1955** University of Dallas established at Irving to northwest; **Jan. 21, 1956** actor Robby Benson born; **1957** Dallas Market Center built, beginning of multi-building complex; Dallas Opera founded; **1959** Dallas Theater Center opened, designed by Frank Lloyd Wright; **1960** Dallas Cowboys NFL team established; **1961** Texas Rangers baseball team moves to Dallas, formerly Washington Senators; **Nov. 22, 1963** Pres. John F. Kennedy fatally shot by Lee Harvey Oswald while riding in motorcade, dies later at hospital, Texas Gov. John Connally seriously wounded; **Nov. 24, 1963** Lee Harvey Oswald shot to death by Jack Ruby as he is escorted from county jail, seen live on television; **1964** 50-story Republic Bank Tower built; Dallas Aquarium established at Fair Park; **March 14, 1964** businessman Jack Ruby (Rubenstein) convicted of murdering Oswald; **Sept. 30, 1964** actress Crystal Bernard born; **1965** 52-story Elm Place building completed; Dallas Baptist University moved from Decatur; **1966** El Centro College (2-year) established; Dallas Arboretum and Botanical Garden founded; **Jan. 3, 1967** Jack Ruby, 55, killer of Kennedy assassin Lee Harvey Oswald, dies of blood clot while serving sentence; **1970** Mountain View College (2-year) established; **1971** Texas Stadium, home of football Cowboys, opens at Irving, to northwest; **1974** Dallas-Fort Worth Airport opens at Irving, replaces Love Field as primary airport; **1978** Art Institute of Dallas founded; **1982** county administration building opened; 50-story Thanksgiving Tower building completed; **1984** 50-story Trammel Crow Center completed; 50-story First City Center completed; Dallas Museum of Art opened; Dallas Sidekicks soccer team established; **1985** 72-story Bank of America Plaza completed; **Aug. 2, 1985** 136 of 160

on board Delta L-1011 Tristar killed when it crashes while landing at Dallas-Fort Worth Airport, one motorist killed; **1986** 60-story Fountain Place built; **1987** 56-story Renaissance Center built; 55-story Chase Texas Plaza built; 60-story Bank One Center built; **1989** Morton H. Meyerson Symphony Center completed, designed by architect I. M. Pei; **1993** Dallas Stars hockey team joins NHL.

Decatur *Wise County* *Northern Texas, 37 mi/ 60 km north-northwest of Fort Worth*

c.1850 area settled; **1856** Wise County formed, named for Confederate Gen. Henry A. Wise; **1857** town founded as county seat, named Taylorsville for Zachary Taylor; **1858** town renamed for Stephen Decatur, naval hero in War of 1812; **1862** Peace Party trial results in hanging of five Union sympathizers; **1873** incorporated as a city; **1892** Decatur Baptist College established, moved to Dallas 1965; **1896** county courthouse completed.

Del Rio *Val Verde County* *Southwestern Texas, 145 mi/233 km west of San Antonio, on Rio Grande*

1808 Mexicans hold Catholic religious services at site; **1868** town founded, named for San Felipe del Rio (St. Philip of the River); **1885** Val Verde County formed, named for Civil War Battle of Val Verde, New Mexico; town becomes county seat; **1911** town incorporated; **1915** second county courthouse built; **1929** *Del Rio News Herald* founded; **1943** Laughlin Army Air Base established to east, becomes Air Force Base 1952; **1960** U.S. and Mexico agree to jointly build the Amistad Dam and Reservoir on Rio Grande; **Nov. 11, 1965** Amisted National Recreation Area established (administered with Mexico); **Aug. 24, 1998** Tropical Storm Charley inundates drought-stricken southern Texas and northern Mexico with 18 in/46 cm of rain, 16 killed, 30 missing in flooding of Rio Grande.

Denison *Grayson County* *Northern Texas, 65 mi/ 105 km north of Dallas, near Red River*

1858 Butterfield Overland Mail Route established through area; **1872** town founded as railhead on Missouri, Kansas & Texas Railroad, named for railroad vice president George Denison; **1873** incorporated as a city; **Oct. 14, 1890** Dwight David Eisenhower, 34th President, born (died March 28, 1969); **1896** interurban electric rail service to Sherman begins; **1909** Katy Depot built; **Dec. 30, 1932** actor John Hillerman born; **1944** Denison Dam completed, forms Lake Texoma on Red River, on Texas/ Oklahoma boundary; **1964** Grayson County Junior College established.

Denton *Denton County* *Northern Texas, 35 mi/ 56 km north-northeast of Fort Worth*

1846 Denton County formed; **1857** town founded, named for pioneer John B. Denton killed in Native American attack; county seat moved from Alton; **1866** incorporated as a town; **1890** University of North Texas established; **1896** county courthouse completed; **1901** Texas Woman's University established; **1914** incorporated as a city.

Dickens   *Dickens County   Northwestern Texas, 60 mi/97 km east of Lubbock*

1876 Dickens County formed; **1889** Charles O'Neal becomes one of first settlers; **1890** first cotton planted in area; **1891** county organized; Espuela becomes county seat; **1892** post office established; town founded as county seat, named for J. Dickens, defender of the Alamo; **1893** county courthouse built; **1934** incorporated as a city.

Dimmitt   *Castro County   Northwestern Texas, 55 mi/89 km south-southwest of Amarillo*

1891 Castro County formed; town founded as county seat and terminus of Fort Worth & Denver City Railroad, named for promoter Rev. W. C. Dimmitt; **1928** Forth Worth & Denver South Plains Railroad reaches town; incorporated as a city; **1940** county courthouse completed.

Dublin   *Erath County   North central Texas, 70 mi/113 km southwest of Fort Worth*

1854 area settled; **1856** town founded by A. H. Dobkins, named Doublin for practice of "doubling in" wagons during Native American raids; **1881** town moved 4 mi/6.4 km to new Texas Central Railroad; town name spelling altered; **1889** town incorporated; **1891** first Dr. Pepper soft drink plant opened; **Aug. 13, 1912** golf legend Ben Hogan born (died 1997).

Dumas   *Moore County   Northwestern Texas, 45 mi/72 km north of Amarillo*

1876 Moore County formed, named for Commodore Edwin W. Moore of Texas Navy; **1892** county organized; town founded as county seat, named for businessman Louis Dumas; **1904** North Plains & Santa Fe Railroad reaches town; **1918** cotton production begins in area; **1926** oil discovered nearby; **1930** incorporated as a city; county courthouse built; **July 29, 1956** fire sweeps through Shamrock-McGee refinery, 19 killed, including 10 firemen.

Eagle Pass   *Maverick County   Southwestern Texas, 52 mi/84 km south-southeast of Del Rio, on Rio Grande*

1849 settlement founded around Camp Eagle Pass; **1850** Fort Duncan established as defense against Mexicans and Native Americans; town platted by John Twohig; **1856** Maverick County formed, named for Cong. Samuel Maverick; **1861** Confederates occupy Fort Duncan; **1868** U.S. reoccupies fort; **1871** county organized; town becomes county seat; **1872** St. Joseph's Academy established; **1885** county courthouse built; **1910** incorporated as a town; **1916** Fort Duncan closed; **1918** incorporated as a city; **1942** Eagle Pass Army Airfield opened (closed 1945).

Eastland   *Eastland County   North central Texas, 50 mi/80 km east of Abilene, on Leon River*

1858 Eastland County formed; **1873** county organized; Merriman becomes county seat; **1875** town founded as new county seat; **1882** incorporated as a town; **1891** incorporated as a city; **1897** county courthouse built; legend of Rip the Frog tells of frog sealed in courthouse cornerstone, found in catatonic state in 1928, died one year later; **1910s** cotton becomes important crop; **1917** oil discovered, boom lasts until 1922; **1928** new county courthouse built.

Edinburg   *Hidalgo County   Southern Texas, 50 mi/80 km west-northwest of Brownsville*

1852 Hidalgo County formed; town of Hidalgo becomes county seat; **1890** town founded, named Chapin for promoter D. B. Chapin; **1908** county seat moved to Chapin; **1911** town renamed for Edinburgh, Scotland, former name of town of Hidalgo; **1919** town incorporated; **1925** Edinburg Junior College established; **1927** Southern Pacific Railroad reaches town; University of Texas, Pan American Campus, established; **1956** county courthouse built.

Edna   *Jackson County   Southern Texas, 93 mi/150 km southwest of Houston*

1824 land granted to Robert Guthrie by Mexican government; **1836** Jackson County formed, named for Andrew Jackson; Texana becomes county seat; **1882** New York, Texas & Mexico Railroad completed; town founded, named for daughter of railroad builder; Lone Star Hotel opened by Mrs. Lucy Flourney; **1883** county seat moved to Edna; **1898** incorporated as a town; **1926** incorporated as a city; **1954** county courthouse built.

El Paso   *El Paso County   Western Texas, on Rio Grande, opposite Mexico, near New Mexico*

1598 Juan de Oñate expedition passes through area; **1681** Corpus Christi de la Isleta established, Texas' oldest mission; Ysleta del Sur founded, oldest community in Texas, now part of El Paso; **1827** settlers led by Juan María Ponce de León arrive; **1848** Fort Bliss army post established to solidify U.S. claim to area; **1850** El Paso County formed; San Elizario becomes county seat; **1868** flooding destroys many homes along Rio Grande; **1873** incorporated as a city; county seat moved to El Paso; **1881** Texas & New Orleans Railroad reaches city; *El Paso Herald* newspaper founded; **1913** University of Texas at El Paso established; **1922** *The Post* newspaper founded; **1928** El Paso International Airport established, dedicated by Charles Lindbergh; **March 26, 1930** Supreme Court Justice Sandra Day O'Connor born; **1931** *Herald-Post* newspaper created by merger; **Aug. 19, 1931** jockey Bill Shoemaker born at Fabens to southeast (died 2003); **Apr. 1, 1932** actress Debbie Reynolds born; **March 11, 1934** newscaster Sam Donaldson born; **Jan. 1, 1935** first Sun Bowl football game held, renamed John Hancock Bowl

1989 for its corporate sponsor; **July 19, 1941** singer Vikki Carr born; **Sept. 4, 1951** actress Judith Ivey born; **1959** El Paso Museum of Art opened; **1963** Sun Bowl Stadium completed; **Nov. 1967** El Chamizal, enclave of scrub on north side of Rio Grande claimed by Mexico, created by shifting river, transferred to Mexico; **1969** El Paso Community College (2-year) established; **Apr. 22, 1973** gas explosion at apartment building kills seven; **1991** county courthouse built.

Eldorado *Schleicher County* *Western Texas, 40 mi/64 km south of San Angelo*

1887 Schleicher County formed; **1895** town founded; **1901** county organized; town becomes county seat; *Eldorado Paper* newspaper founded; **1924** county courthouse built; **1926** town incorporated; **1929** town reincorporated.

Emory *Rains County* *Northeastern Texas, 58 mi/ 93 km east-northeast of Dallas*

1848 area first settled by Emory Rains; mill built on Sabine River; **1870** Rains County formed; town founded as county seat; **1908** county courthouse built; **1929** incorporated as a town; **1985** incorporated as a city.

Fabens *El Paso County* *See* **El Paso (1931)**

Fairfield *Freestone County* *East central Texas, 80 mi/129 km south-southeast of Dallas*

1849 area settled; town founded, named Mount Pleasant; **1850** Freestone County formed; town becomes county seat, renamed Fairfield; **1859** Fairfield Academy established, closed 1861–1865, closed permanently 1889; **1862** Sibley's Brigade, Confederates from Fairfield, lead futile effort to rout Federal troops from New Mexico; **1902** tornado heavily damages town; **1903** cotton crops destroyed by boll weevil infestation; **1911** fire destroys business district; Fairfield Lake formed by dam to east on Trinity River; **1919** county courthouse built; **1933** incorporated as a city.

Falfurrias *Brooks County* *Southern Texas, 55 mi/ 89 km southwest of Corpus Christi*

1881 Mexican faith healer Don Pedritos arrives, stays 25 years, reportedly healed thousands; **1883** town founded by Edward Lasater, Spanish name for wildflower called "heart's delight"; **1903** town moved 3 mi/4.8 km to San Antonio & Aransas Pass Railroad; **1906** *Falfurrias Facts* newspaper founded; **c.1910** Lasater converts ranch to dairy farm, beginning local dairying industry; **1911** Brooks County formed; **1912** town becomes county seat; **1914** county courthouse built; **1920s** irrigation systems introduced, impetus to fruit, truck farming; **1948** incorporated as a city.

Farwell *Parmer County* *Northwestern Texas, 85 mi/137 km northwest of Lubbock, at New Mexico state line*

1876 Parmer County formed, named for Martin Parmer, signer of Texas Declaration of Independence; **1902** William F. Franklin starts business at town site; **1905** town founded by Franklin, named for Farwell brothers, who received land grant in parts of 10 counties for role in building state capitol in Austin [see Dalhart]; **1907** county organized; town becomes county seat; **1916** county courthouse built; **1947** incorporated as a town; **1951** incorporated as a city.

Floresville *Wilson County* *Southern Texas, 29 mi/ 47 km southeast of San Antonio, on San Antonio River*

1832 Canary Islander Don Francisco Flores de Abrego establishes ranch; **1833** town site donated by Flores; **1860** Wilson County formed, named for legislator James C. Wilson; Sutherland Springs becomes county seat; **1867** county seat moved to Lodi; **1885** county seat moved to Floresville; county courthouse built; **1886** San Antonio & Aransas Pass Railroad reaches town; **1890** town incorporated; **c.1915** peanut production becomes important; **Feb. 27, 1917** Gov. John Bowden Connally, Jr. born, wounded in Kennedy assassination, Dallas, Nov. 22, 1963 (died 1993).

Floydada *Floyd County* *Northwestern Texas, 40 mi/64 km northeast of Lubbock*

1876 Floyd County formed; **1890** county organized; town founded as county seat, named Floyd City for Dolfin Ward Floyd, defender of the Alamo; **Sept. 1890** post office opened; town renamed in part for postmaster Ada Price; **1909** town incorporated; **1910** Santa Fe Railroad arrives; **1918** influenza epidemic kills 18; **1950** county courthouse built.

Fort Davis *Jeff Davis County* *Western Texas, 165 mi/266 km southeast of El Paso*

1850 Presidio County formed; **1854** Fort Davis established as trading post on Butterfield Overland Route, at junction Chihuahua Trail; **1871** county organized; town becomes county seat; **1885** county seat moved to Marfa; **1887** Jeff Davis County formed from Presidio County; town becomes county seat; **1891** Fort Davis decommissioned; **1910** county courthouse built; **1912** Limpia Hotel built; **1932** McDonald Observatory of University of Texas built to northwest; **July 4, 1963** Fort Davis National Historic Site established; **Apr. 27, 1997** "Republic of Texas" separatists kidnap couple, held at "embassy" shack, six kidnappers surrender May 2–3, one shot dead May 5 after escaping.

Fort Stockton *Pecos County* *Western Texas, 70 mi/115 km south-southwest of Odessa*

1534 Spaniard Cabeza de Vaca explores area; **1859** Fort Stockton established on Butterfield Overland Mail Route, at intersection of San Antonio Road and Comanche War Trail; Zero Stone erected as point of origin for early surveys; **1868** town founded adjacent to fort, named St. Gall; **1871** Pecos County formed; **1875** county organized; town becomes county seat; **1877** irrigation project begins on Pecos River, one of earliest in Texas; **1881** town renamed Fort Stockton; **1886** fort abandoned; **1899** Annie Riggs Hotel built; **1910** incorporated as a city; **1911** county courthouse built; **March 7, 1973** truck and Greyhound bus collide at Bakersfield to east killing 7, injuring 23.

Fort Worth *Tarrant County* *Northern Texas, 30 mi/48 km west of Dallas*

1843 first settlers arrive; **1849** Tarrant County formed, named for Gen. Edward H. Tarrant, served in Mexican War; Birdville becomes county seat; Fort Worth army post established by Gen. Winfield Scott, named for Gen. William Jenkins Worth (1794–1849), served in Mexican War; **1860** county seat moved to Fort Worth; **1873** incorporated as a city; Texas Christian University established; **1876** Texas & Pacific Railroad reaches city, establishing it as major cattle shipping point; **1879** *Star-Telegram* newspaper founded; **1890** Texas Wesleyan University established; **1893** Fort Worth Stockyards established, closed 1992; **1895** county courthouse built; **1909** Fort Worth Zoo established; **Feb. 4, 1912** golf pro Byron Nelson, Jr. born; **1919** oil discovered to west; **Dec. 22, 1922** U.S. Cong., Speaker of the House James Claude Wright, Jr. born; **1925** Meacham Field Airport established to north, now Meacham International Airport; **Aug. 16, 1925** actor Fess Parker born; **Oct. 2, 1928** film critic Rex Reed born; **1930** businessman C. R. Smith merges more than 80 small airlines to form American Airways, renamed American Airlines 1934; **1935** Fort Worth Botanic Gardens opened; **1936** Will Rogers Memorial Center (Coliseum) opened; **Jan. 2, 1936** singer Roger Miller born (died 1992); **July 3, 1947** actress Betty Buckley born; **Nov. 22, 1963** President Kennedy addresses Fort Worth Chamber of Commerce before making fateful journey to nearby Dallas; **1961** Fort Worth Ballet founded, becomes Fort Worth-Dallas Ballet 1994; **1967** Tarrant County College (2-year) established; **1974** 37-story Bank One Tower built; Dallas-Fort Worth Airport opens to northeast; **1982** 40-story UPR (Continental) Plaza built; 33-story Chase Texas Tower built; **1983** 40-story Burnett Plaza built; **1984** 38-story City Center Tower built; **1996** National Cowgirl Hall of Fame moved from Hereford, established 1975; **Sept. 15, 1999** gunman Larry Ashbrook kills seven then himself at Baptist church service; **March 28, 2000** two tornadoes hit downtown, 4 killed, 100 injured.

Franklin *Robertson County* *East central Texas, 55 mi/89 km southeast of Waco*

1837 Robertson County formed, named for Texas legislator Sterling C. Robertson; (Old) Franklin becomes county seat; **1850** county seat moved to Wheelock, to Owensville 1856, to Calvert 1870; **1871** International & Great Northern Railroad built; new town founded, named Morgan; **1879** county seat moved from Calvert; **1880** town incorporated as Franklin; **1880s** mineral springs transform town into popular resort; **1883** county courthouse completed; **c.1890** *Franklin Weekly* newspaper founded; **1912** incorporated as a city; **1914** Carnegie Library built.

Fredericksburg *Gillespie County* *South central Texas, 65 mi/105 km west of Austin*

May 1846 120 German immigrants led by John O. Meusebach settle at edge of Comanche territory; town founded, named for Frederick the Great of Prussia; **1847** Meusebach-Comanche Treaty brings enduring peace to community; **1848** Gillespie County formed; town becomes county seat; Fort Martin Scott established, first Federal fort built in Texas; **c.1850** traditional Easter Fires story started by unknown pioneer mother about Easter rabbit tending fires to boil Easter eggs, inspired by Comanche fires used as peace signals; **1852** Nimitz Hotel built, operated by grandfather of Admiral Nimitz; **1853** fort abandoned; **1876** Fredericksburg College established (closed 1884); **1882** county courthouse built; **Feb. 24, 1885** Adm. Chester W. Nimitz born, Commander of Pacific fleet in World War II (died 1966); **1914** San Antonio, Fredericksburg & Northern Railroad reaches town; **1928** incorporated as a city; **1939** new county courthouse built; old courthouse becomes Pioneer Memorial Library.

Freeport *Brazoria County* *Southeastern Texas, 55 mi/89 km south of Houston, on Gulf of Mexico*

1822 area settled by members of Stephen Austin's first colony, establish seaport of Quintana, now part of Freeport; **1912** town founded by the Townsite Company, sulfur mining interest from New York; **1817** incorporated as a town; **1939** Dow Chemical Company plant built; **1949** incorporated as a city; Intracoastal Waterway, paralleling Gulf Coast, completed; **1955** new port facilities opened; **1957** Velasquez, one of oldest towns in Texas, annexed by Freeport; **Feb. 1, 1972** tanker *V. A. Hogg* sinks in Gulf of Mexico 32 mi/51 km to south, all 39 on board lost.

Gail *Borden County* *Northwestern Texas, 57 mi/92 km south-southeast of Lubbock*

1876 Borden County formed; **1890** county organized; **1891** town founded as county seat, county and town named for Gail Borden, Jr., surveyor and editor, inventor of condensed milk, founder of Borden Foods and Baylor University; **1902** area experiences ranch land boom; new farmers purchase former grazing lands; **1939** county courthouse built.

Gainesville   *Cooke County   Northern Texas, 60 mi/ 97 km north-northwest of Dallas*

1845 Fort Fitzhugh established; **1848** Cooke County formed; **1850** town founded as county seat on California Trail, named for Edmund Gaines, veteran of War of 1812; **Oct. 1862** in Great Gainesville Hanging, 39 publicly hanged by Confederates for their part in Peace Party movement sympathetic to Union; **1873** town incorporated; **March 17, 1884** explorer, wild animal collector Frank Buck born (died 1950); **1886** Santa Fe Railroad reaches town; **1911** county courthouse built; **1924** North Central Texas College (2-year) established; **1930** first annual Gainesville Community Circus held; **1942** Camp Howze Army Training Center established, closed 1946.

Galloway   *Panola County   See* **Carthage** (1923)

Galveston   *Galveston County   Southeastern Texas, 48 mi/68 km southeast of Houston, on Gulf of Mexico*

1528 Spanish explorer Cabeza de Vaca becomes shipwrecked; **1817** pirate Jean Laffite visits area; **1830s** first settlers arrive; **1836** town founded, named for Spanish colonial leader Bernardo de Gálvez (1746–1786); post office established; **1838** Galveston County formed; town becomes county seat; **1839** incorporated as a town; **Apr. 11, 1842** *Galveston News* newspaper first published; **1862** town temporarily occupied by Union forces; **1867** yellow fever epidemic kills 20 people per day; **March 31, 1878** African-American heavyweight boxer Jack Johnson born (died 1946); **1891** University of Texas, Galveston Medical Branch, established; **1894** Grand Opera House built, restored 1980s; **Feb. 8, 1894** movie director King Vidor born (died 1982); **Sept. 8–9, 1900** hurricane followed by tidal wave kills 6,000, leaves $20 million in damage; **Aug. 17, 1915** hurricane and tidal wave leave 275 dead; **1924** gambling allowed on Galveston Island until State's Attorney crackdown 1957; **July 5, 1934** actress Katherine Helmond born; **1939** incorporated as a city; **Sept. 3, 1943** actress Valerie Perrine born; **Sept. 12, 1944** singer Barry White born (died 2003); **Sept. 12, 1961** Hurricane Carla causes flooding, tornado spawned, 6 killed, 60 injured; **1962** Texas A & M University at Galveston established; **1966** county courthouse built; **1967** Galveston College (2-year) established; **1972** Container Ship Terminal opened; **Aug. 18, 1983** Hurricane Alicia pounds Texas coast, eight killed in Galveston.

Garland   *Dallas, Rockwall and Collin counties Northern Texas, suburb 12 mi/19 km northeast of Dallas*

1887 Missouri, Kansas & Topeka Railroad built; town founded; **1891** incorporated as a city, named for Augustus Garland, Attorney General under President Cleveland; **May 9, 1927** tornado strikes city, 17 killed; **1933** Garland

Public Library opened; **1971** Amber University established.

Gatesville   *Coryell County   Central Texas, 35 mi/ 56 km west-southwest of Waco*

1849 Fort Gates military post established; town founded; **1854** County formed, town becomes county seat; **1873** incorporated as a city; **1882** spur of St. Louis Southwestern Railroad reaches town; **1889** Gatesville State School for Boys established, becomes Mountain View School 1962; **1897** county courthouse built; **1972** rail spur abandoned.

George West   *Live Oak County   Southern Texas, 55 mi/89 km northwest of Corpus Christi*

1856 Live Oak County formed; Oakville becomes county seat; **1913** town founded on San Antonio, Uvalde & Gulf Railroad by rancher George Washington West; **1919** county seat moved to George West; county courthouse built; **1946** town incorporated.

Georgetown   *Williamson County   Central Texas, 25 mi/40 km north of Austin, on San Gabriel River*

1841 town founded, named for landowner George Washington Glasscock; **1848** Williamson County formed; town becomes county seat; **1866** incorporated as a town; **1870** Southwestern University established; **1871** incorporated as a city; **1877** *Williamson County Sun* newspaper founded; **1878** International-Great Northern Railroad reaches town; **1904** Georgetown & Granger Railroad completed from Austin; **1911** county courthouse built; **1996** large Sun City Georgetown retirement complex built by Del Webb; **May 27, 1997** tornado strikes Jarrell to north, 27 killed.

Giddings   *Lee County   South central Texas, 45 mi/ 72 km east of Austin*

1871 Houston & Texas Central Railroad built; **1872** town founded, named for railroad stockholder Jabez D. Giddings, town settled by Wends from Slovakia; **1874** Lee County formed; town becomes county seat; **1890s** cotton becomes important; **1894** Concordia Lutheran College established; **1899** octagonal county courthouse completed, identical design to Comal County courthouse at New Braunfels; **1913** town incorporated; **1980s** oil boom begins.

Gilmer   *Upshur County   Northeastern Texas, 103 mi/166 km east of Dallas*

1846 Upshur County formed, named for U.S. Secretary of State Abel P. Upshur; **1848** town founded as county seat, named for Thomas Gilmer of U.S. Navy; **1854** Gilmer Female Academy established (closed 1861); **1860s** area settled by Slavic Wend people; **1890** sweet potatoes introduced, become major crop; **1902** town incorporated; **1930s** county benefits from East Texas oil boom; **Oct.**

1935 first annual East Texas Yamboree held in honor of sweet potato; **1937** county courthouse completed; **July 22, 1947** singer Don Henley born; **1997** civic center completed.

Glen Rose *Somervell County* *North central Texas, 40 mi/64 km southwest of Fort Worth*

1849 Barnard's Mills trading post established; town develops at post; **1870** town renamed by Thomas Jordan; **1875** Somervell County formed; town becomes county seat; **1894** county courthouse built; **1926** incorporated as a city; **Apr. 3, 1990** Comanche Peak Nuclear Power Plant completed at Squaw Creek Lake reservoir to north.

Goldthwaite *Mills County* *Central Texas, 78 mi/126 km west of Waco*

1885 Gulf, Colorado & Santa Fe Railroad built; town founded, named for railroad official Joseph G. Goldthwaite; **1887** Mills County formed; town becomes county seat; **1888** old jail built; **1907** incorporated as a city; **1913** county courthouse built; **1935** oil discovered.

Goliad *Goliad County* *Southern Texas, 83 mi/134 km southeast of San Antonio*

1749 Mission Espírito Santo and Presidio La Bahía established at Native American village of Santa Dorotea; **1829** La Bahía declared a town, renamed Goliad, anagram for (H)idalgo; **1834** cholera epidemic destroys most of populace; **1836** Goliad County formed; town becomes county seat; **March 27, 1836** in Goliad Massacre, Capt. James W. Fannin and 342 Texans surrender March 20 to Mexicans in good faith, then executed under orders from Santa Anna; **1839** incorporated as a town; **1886** Texas & New Orleans Railroad reaches town; **1894** county courthouse built, clock tower destroyed in 1924 storm; **May 18, 1902** tornado destroys over 100 buildings, 115 killed, 230 injured; **1925** incorporated as a city; **1961** La Bahía Downs horse race track opened.

Gonzales *Gonzales County* *South central Texas, 65 mi/105 km east of San Antonio, on Guadalupe River*

1825 town founded by Green C. DeWitt of Missouri, named for Col. Rafael Gonzales, provisional governor of Mexican combined state of Coahuila and Texas; town becomes county seat; **July 1825** settlement burned in Native American raid; **1827** town relocated on Guadalupe River; **1832** town platted; **Oct. 2, 1835** in Battle of Gonzales, Texans resist Mexican troops sent to take town's cannon, first battle of Texas Revolution; **1836** Gonzales County formed; **March 1836** Sam Houston orders town burned, evacuated in face of advancing Mexicans, beginning of Runaway Scrape; **1837** county organized; town becomes county seat; **1874** spur of Galveston, Harrisburg & San Antonio Railroad reaches town; **1880** incorporated as a city; **1887** county jail built, used until 1975; **1894** county courthouse built.

Graham *Young County* *Northern Texas, 72 mi/116 km west-northwest of Fort Worth*

1856 Young County formed, named for Col. William C. Young of Texas Infantry; **1871** Gustavus and Edwin Graham of Kentucky become first settlers; **1872** town founded on Wichita Falls & Southern Railroad; Graham Brothers Salt Works established; **1874** county organized; town becomes county seat; **1876** incorporated as a city; **1902** Chicago, Rock Island & Gulf Railroad reaches site; **1932** county courthouse built.

Granbury *Hood County* *North central Texas, 34 mi/55 km southwest of Fort Worth, on Brazos River*

1854 town founded by Thomas Lambert, named for Gen. Hiram B. Granbury; **1866** Hood County formed; town becomes county seat; **1873** incorporated as a town; Granbury College established (closed 1886); **1887** Fort Worth & Rio Grande Railroad reaches town; **1890** county courthouse built; **1925** incorporated as a city; **1969** Lake Granbury formed by dam on Brazos River; **Apr. 1990** Comanche Peak Nuclear Power Plant begins operations to southwest.

Grand Saline *Van Zandt County* *Northeastern Texas, 60 mi/97 km east of Dallas, near Sabine River*

1845 John Jordan becomes first settler; town founded on site of prehistoric salt works, named Jordan's Saline; **1848** town becomes county seat; **1850** county seat moved to Canton; **1873** Texas & Pacific Railroad reaches town; town renamed Grand Saline; **1875** first salt well dug; **1890** Grand Saline Salt Company established, acquired by Morton Salt 1920; **1895** incorporated as a city; **Nov. 22, 1898** aviator Wiley Hardeman Post born, killed with humorist Will Rogers in plane crash at Barrow, Alaska, Aug. 15, 1935; **1936** Salt Palace built of salt blocks, rebuilt 1975.

Greenville *Hunt County* *Eastern Texas, 45 mi/72 km northeast of Dallas*

1843 first house built; **1846** Hunt County formed; town founded as county seat; **1860** Greenville Academy founded; **1862** incorporated as a town; **1874** incorporated as a city; **June 20, 1924** Audie Murphy born at Kingston to north, most decorated World War II veteran, died May 28, 1971, in plane crash in Virginia; **1929** county courthouse built.

Groesbeck *Limestone County* *East central Texas, 36 mi/58 km east of Waco*

1834 Fort Parker established; **1836** Comanches overrun fort, kill five of James Parker family, kidnap five others, including nine-year-old Cynthia Ann Parker [see Crowell, 1860]; **1846** Limestone County formed; Springfield becomes county seat; **1870** town founded on Houston & Texas Central Railroad, named for railroad director Abram Groesbeck; **1871** incorporated as a town; **1873** county seat moved to Groesbeck; **1880** incorporated as a city; **1924** county courthouse built; **Feb. 12, 1936** actor Joe Don Baker born.

Groveton   *Trinity County*   *Eastern Texas, 85 mi/ 137 km north of Houston*

March 19, 1687 Robert Cavelier, Sieur de la Salle, killed in Trinity River region to southwest by his own men; **1850** Trinity County formed; Sumpter becomes county seat; **1872** county seat moved to Trinity, to Pennington 1874; **1881** town founded in grove of blackjack trees; **1883** county seat moved to Groveton; **1900** lumber milling becomes important through 1920s, revived 1980s; **1914** county courthouse built; **1919** town incorporated.

Guthrie   *King County*   *Northern Texas, 85 mi/ 137 km north-northwest of Abilene*

1876 King County formed; **1891** county organized; town founded as county seat, named for W. H. Guthrie, stockholder in Louisville Land and Cattle Company; **1904** post office opened; **1914** county courthouse built.

Hallettsville   *Lavaca County*   *South central Texas, 70 mi/113 km southeast of Austin, on Lavaca River*

1831 John Hallett becomes one of first settlers; **1836** town founded by Czech and German immigrants; **1846** Lavaca County formed; **1852** town becomes county seat following violent feud with Petersburg; **1870** incorporated as a town; **1888** incorporated as a city; **1899** county courthouse completed; **1913** town called "13 city" by *Ripley's Believe It or Not!* for the 13 letters in its name, 1,300 population, 13 newspapers, 13 churches, and 13 saloons.

Hamilton   *Hamilton County*   *Central Texas, 60 mi/ 97 km west of Waco*

1855 area first settled; **1858** Hamilton County formed; town founded as county seat; **c.1860** schoolteacher Anne Whitney killed while protecting her students during raid by Comanches; **1899** many homes destroyed by flooding of Pecan Creek; **1908** Stephenville, North & South Texas and St. Louis & Southwestern railroads reach town, abandoned 1934 and 1940 respectively; **1911** town incorporated; **1931** county courthouse completed.

Harlingen   *Cameron County*   *Southern Texas, 23 mi/37 km northwest of Brownsville*

c.1850 Paso Real Stagecoach Inn built; **1901** Lon C. Hall moves to area; **1904** town founded by Hall; railroad reaches site; **1910** incorporated as a city; **1920** Rialto Theatre opened, closed 1993; **1928** Municipal Auditorium opened; **1941** Bougainvillea Trail established, tour route to plantations and noteworthy homes; **1942** Harlingen Army Air Field established, closed 1946, reopened as Harlingen Air Force Base 1952, closed 1962; **1963** Rio Grande Valley International Airport established at former air base; **1967** Texas State Technical College (2-year) established; **Sept. 24, 1967** Hurricane Beulah makes

landfall, city hard hit by flooding; **1989** hard freeze devastates grapefruit crop.

Haskell   *Haskell County*   *Northern Texas, 48 mi/ 77 km north of Abilene*

1858 Haskell County formed; **1879** Thomas F. Tucker builds first house; **1882** town founded; **1885** county organized; town becomes county seat; **1907** town incorporated; **1892** county courthouse built; **1950s** Lake Stamford formed by dam on Paint Creek to southeast.

Hebbronville   *Jim Hogg County*   *Southern Texas, 55 mi/89 km east-southeast of Laredo*

1881 Texas-Mexican Railroad built; **1883** town founded on railroad by W. R. Hebbron; **1913** Jim Hogg County formed, named for Gov. James J. Hogg; town becomes county seat; **1895** post office established; **1913** county courthouse built; **1930s** oil discovered, becomes town's economic mainstay.

Helena   *Karnes County*   *Southern Texas, 50 mi/ 80 km southeast of San Antonio, on San Antonio River*

1852 town of Alamita founded by Mexicans on Chihuahua Trail, later renamed for Helena Owens, friend of county founder Thomas Ruckman; **1854** Karnes County formed; town becomes county seat; **1873** county courthouse built; **1884** Emmett Butler, son of rancher Col. William Butler, killed in saloon shootout, father vows to "kill the town that killed my son," lures railroad away from Helena by giving away land establishing Karnes City, called the "Helena Deal"; **1886** San Antonio & Aransas Pass Railroad bypasses town; **1893** county seat moved to Karnes City.

Hemphill   *Sabine County*   *Eastern Texas, 50 mi/ 80 km east of Lufkin, near Sabine River*

1837 Sabine County formed; Milam becomes county seat; **1858** town founded as county seat, named for Judge John Hemphill; **1906** county courthouse built; **1912** Lufkin, Hemphill & Gulf Railroad reaches town, abandoned 1938; **1939** incorporated as a city; **1968** large Toledo Bend Reservoir formed by dam on Sabine River to east.

Hempstead   *Waller County*   *Southeastern Texas, 50 mi/80 km west-northwest of Houston, near Brazos River*

1853 Liendo Plantation built by Leonard Groce, father Jared Groce was one of largest landowners in Texas, named for Justo Liendo, Spaniard responsible for the 67,000-ac/27,135-ha land grant, occupied by family of sculptress Elisabet Ney 1873–1911; **1856** town founded on Houston & Texas Central Railroad, named for Dr. S. B. Hempstead; **1858** incorporated as a town; **1873** Waller County formed, named for Texas government official Edwin Waller; town becomes county seat; **Apr. 24, 1905** U.S. Cong. John Pinckney, his brother, two others shot to death inside courthouse while meeting with prohibitionists; **1935** incorporated as a city; **1955** third county courthouse built.

Henderson   *Rusk County*   *Northeastern Texas, 120 mi/193 km east-southeast of Dallas*

1843 Rusk County formed, named for Texas statesman Thomas J. Rusk; town founded as county seat; **1844** incorporated as a town; **1855** Howard-Dickinson House built, first brick house in county, by relatives of Sam Houston; **Aug. 1860** most of business district destroyed by fire; **1877** Missouri Pacific Railroad reaches town; **1908** Arnold Outhouse built, first such structure in Texas to be designated a historic site; **1911** incorporated as a city; **1929** county courthouse completed; **1930** discovery of oil boosts economy; **Feb. 20, 1946** actress Sandy Duncan born.

Henrietta   *Clay County*   *Northern Texas, 85 mi/ 137 km northwest of Fort Worth*

1857 Clay County formed; **1860** first settlers arrive; town founded; **1865** settlers driven out by Native American attacks; **1873** county organized; Cambridge becomes county seat; town reoccupied; **1881** town incorporated; **1882** Fort Worth & Denver City Railroad reaches town; county seat moved to Henrietta; **1884** county courthouse built.

Hereford   *Deaf Smith County*   *Northwestern Texas, 40 mi/64 km southwest of Amarillo*

1876 Deaf Smith County formed, named for Erastus "Deaf" Smith, commander of Sam Houston's scouts at Battle of San Jacinto; **1883** cowboys successfully strike against ranchers for higher wages; **1898** general store opened by N. E. Gass; town founded; **1899** county organized, town becomes county seat; **1902** Henrietta College established (closed 1910); **1903** town incorporated; **1910** county courthouse built; **Sept. 17, 1930** astronaut Edgar Dean Mitchell born; **1975** National Cowgirl Hall of Fame opened, moved to Fort Worth 1996.

Hidalgo   *Hidalgo County*   *Southern Texas, 5 mi/ 8 km south of McAllen, on Rio Grande*

1774 site first settled opposite Reynosa, Mexico; **1852** Hidalgo County formed; town founded as county seat, named Edinburg by John Young for Edinburgh, Scotland; **1885** town renamed Hidalgo by post office for Mexican Revolution leader Miguel Hidalgo y Costilla; **1886** county courthouse built; **1908** county seat moved to Chapin (renamed Edinburg 1911); **1926** suspension bridge built to Reynosa replacing ferry; **1959** incorporated as a city.

Higgins   *Lipscomb County*   *Northwestern Texas, 115 mi/185 km northeast of Amarillo*

1886 Santa Fe Railroad reaches site; town founded; **1898** humorist Will Rogers, 19, gains employment at Ewing Ranch; **1908** incorporated as a city; **Apr. 9, 1947** tornado

damages town, 10 killed, 40 injured locally, total 181 killed, part of series of tornadoes in Texas, Oklahoma, Kansas; **1962** first annual Will Rogers Day celebration held.

Hillsboro   *Hill County*   *North central Texas, 31 mi/ 51 km north of Waco*

1853 Hill County formed, named for Cong. George Washington Hill; town founded as county seat; **1856** post office established; **c.1860** *Hillsboro Express* newspaper founded; **1881** Missouri, Kansas & Texas Railroad reaches town; incorporated as a town; **1923** Hill Junior College established; **1928** county courthouse built, destroyed by fire 1993; **May 6, 1930** tornadoes kill 41; **Apr. 30, 1933** country singer Willie Nelson born at Abbott to south; **Aug. 18, 1935** Olympic track and field star Rafer Johnson born; **1962** incorporated as a city; **1999** new county courthouse built.

Hondo   *Medina County*   *Southwestern Texas, 37 mi/60 km west of San Antonio*

1848 Medina County formed; Castroville becomes county seat; **1881** Galveston, Harrisburg & San Antonio Railroad reaches site; town founded, named for Hondo Creek; **1892** county seat moved to Hondo; county courthouse built, expanded 1943; **1942** incorporated as a city; Hondo Army Air Field established, closed 1945.

Houston   *Harris, Fort Bend and Montgomery counties*   *Southeastern Texas, near Gulf of Mexico*

1836 Harris County formed; Harrisburg becomes county seat; **Aug. 1836** town founded by J. K. and A. C. Allen, named for Sam Houston; county seat moved to Houston; **1837** incorporated as a city; **1853** Houston & Texas Central Railroad built from Galveston; **July 26, 1858** diplomat Col. Edward Mandell House born, adviser to President Wilson (died 1938); **1876** work begins on Houston Ship Channel through Galveston Bay and Buffalo Bayou; **Feb. 1, 1880** *Houston Post* newspaper founded; **Oct. 14, 1901** *Houston Chronicle* newspaper founded; **Dec. 24, 1905** reclusive financier Howard Hughes born (died 1976); **1909** Museum of Natural Science founded; **1910** county courthouse built; **1912** Rice University established; **1913** Houston Symphony Orchestra founded; **1914** Houston Ship Channel completed; **May 12, 1918** cosmetics entrepreneur Mary Kay Ash born (died 2001) **Apr. 12, 1919** actress Ann Miller born (died 2004); **1922** Houston Zoo founded at Hermann Park; **1923** Miller Outdoor Theater built in Hermann Park, new facility opened 1968; **1924** Museum of Fine Arts (Bayou Bend Collection) opened; **1927** University of Houston established; **Apr. 28, 1930** James Addison Baker III born, secretary of state under Pres. George H. W. Bush; **Feb. 21, 1936** African-American U.S. Cong. Barbara Jordan born (died 1996); **1937** William P. Hobby Airport established to southeast; **Aug. 21, 1938** singer, actor Kenny Rogers born; **Nov. 1, 1941** actor Robert Foxworth born; **1942** Ellington Field airport established to southeast; **Aug. 7, 1942** singer B. J. Thomas born; **Sept. 7, 1943** fire at the Gulf Hotel kills 55; **1945** Texas Medical Center organized; **Sept. 9, 1946** singer Billy Preston born; **1947** University of St. Thomas established; Texas Southern University established; **Oct. 26, 1947** TV actress Jaclyn Smith born; **June 17, 1948** TV actress Phylicia Rashad born; **Dec. 6, 1948** actress Jo Beth Williams born; **Dec. 25, 1948** country singer Barbara Mandrell born; **July 7, 1949** actress Shelley Duvall born; **Jan. 16, 1950** actress Debbie Allen born; **Aug. 17, 1950** country singer Rodney Crowell born; **Oct. 1, 1950** actor Randy Quaid born; **Apr. 1, 1953** actress Annette O'Toole born; **Apr. 9, 1954** actor Dennis Quaid born; **Aug. 18, 1954** actor Patrick Swayze born; **June 1, 1956** actress Lisa Hartman born; **Nov. 1, 1957** singer Lyle Lovett born in suburban Klein; **Dec. 19, 1959** Walter Williams, 117, dies, last surviving Civil War veteran, served Confederacy in General Hood's Texas Brigade, buried at Franklin, Texas; **1960** Houston Baptist College established; **Feb. 4, 1962** country singer Clint Black born at Katy to west; **1965** Astrodome opened, first enclosed professional sports stadium, home of Astros baseball team until 2000; Houston Arboretum and Botanical Gardens opened; **1969** Bush Intercontinental (Houston International) Airport opened 23 mi/37 km to north; **1970** 50-story One Shell Plaza built; **1971** University of Texas-Houston Health Science Center established; Houston Community College system established; **1972** North Harris College (2-year) established; **Oct. 30, 1972** robbers of Alexandria, Virginia, bank hijack plane in Houston, force it to Cuba with 40 passengers; **Aug. 7, 1973** Elmer Hensley, 17, David Brooks, 18, charged with sex-torture killings of 27 young men over three year period; **1974** 53-story Houston Industries Plaza built; University of Houston, Downtown Campus, established; San Jacinto College North Campus (2-year) established; **Apr. 5, 1976** Howard Hughes, 70, dies of kidney failure en route from Acapulco to Houston for medical treatment, leaves estate of $1.5 billion; **1978** Art Institute of Houston founded; **1979** San Jacinto College South Campus (2-year) established; **1980** 55-story Southwest Bank of Texas built; **1981** 75-story Chase Tower built; **1982** 52-story Chevron Tower built; **1983** 50-story Enron Tower built; 56-story Bank of America built; 64-story Williams Tower built; 71-story Wells Fargo Plaza built; **May 20, 1983** flooding, tornadoes hit area, 10 killed; **Aug. 18, 1983** area hit by Hurricane Alicia, 17 killed, $1 billion in damage; **1984** 54-story 1600 Smith Street office building built; **1987** George R. Brown Convention Center opens; 53-story Texaco Heritage Center built; **1996** Holocaust Museum established; **Dec. 20, 1998** octuplets born to Nigerian U.S. citizens, smallest dies Dec. 27; **2000** Enron Field baseball stadium replaces Astrodome as home of Astros; Buffalo Soldiers National Museum opened; **June 10, 2001** 20 killed as tropical storm delivers 20-in/51-cm rainfall; **June 20, 2001** Andrea Yates, 37, drowns her five children in bathtub, sentenced to life in prison March 15, 2002; **Dec. 2001** Enron Corporation, energy commodities trading firm, files for bankruptcy over $10 billion Dynegy lawsuit, largest business collapse U.S. history; **2002** Houston Texans NFL team launches first season; Hobby Center for the Performing Arts opened; Enron Field baseball stadium renamed Minute Maid Park; **2004** Enron Tower office building purchased by Chevron/Texaco.

Humble *Harris County*   *Southeastern Texas, suburb 17 mi/27 km north of Houston*

1886 town founded, named for P. S. Humble, Justice of the Peace; **1902** post office established, P. S. Humble, Postmaster; **1904** oil discovered; **1909** feed store owner Ross Sterling founds Humble Oil Company, now Exxon Corporation; **1912** artesian water found, used in bathhouses for oil workers; **Dec. 13, 1922** railroad accident, 22 killed; **1933** incorporated as a city.

Huntsville *Walker County*   *East central Texas, 65 mi/105 km north of Houston*

1836 trading post established; town founded; **1845** incorporated as a town; **1846** Walker County formed, named for Cong. Robert J. Walker of Mississippi, who introduced resolution admitting Texas as a state; town becomes county seat; **1847** Texas State Prison established; **1863** honoree of county name changed from pro-Union Robert J. Walker to Samuel H. Walker, killed in Mexican War; **July 26, 1863** Sam Houston dies (born 1840), buried at Oakwood Cemetery; **1867** yellow fever epidemic kills 10 percent of population; **1872** Huntsville Bend Railroad built; **1879** Sam Houston State University established; **Sept. 29, 1924** actor Steve Forrest born; **1967** Huntsville Public Library opened; **1968** incorporated as a city; **1970** county courthouse built; **Aug. 3, 1974** escape attempt at state prison leads to deaths of two hostages and two inmates, apparent suicides; **Dec. 7, 1982** Charles Brooks, charged with murder, first person to be executed by lethal injection, sixth execution since ban was lifted 1976; **Feb. 3, 1998** Karla Faye Tucker, 38, first woman executed in Texas in 135 years, convicted of two murders with pickax.

Indian Creek *Brown County*   *See* **Brownwood (1890)**

Indianola *Calhoun County*   *Southern Texas, 70 mi/113 km north-northeast of Corpus Christi, on Gulf of Mexico*

1687 French explorer Rene Robert Cavalier, Sieur de la Salle, sets foot near town site; **1840s** German immigrants arrive led by Prince Carl of Solms-Braunfels; **1844** town founded; **1846** Calhoun County formed; (Port) Lavaca becomes county seat; **1849** county seat moved to Indianola; **1850s** army depot established; **1853** town incorporated; **1855** two shipments of camels arrive as part of Army desert experiment led by Jefferson Davis; **Nov. 1863** Union forces seize town, remain through 1864; **1866** tropical storm severely damages town; **Sept. 15, 1875** with spectators drawn to trial of Sutton-Taylor feud, massive hurricane destroys town, kills 300 in town, c.900 total, 8 buildings remain; **Aug. 19, 1886** hurricane destroys

TEXAS

rebuilt town leaving few survivors; county seat returned to Port Lavaca.

Irving *Dallas and Tarrant counties Northern Texas, suburb 9 mi/14.5 km northwest of Dallas*

1902 town founded by watermelon farmers J. O. Schulze and Otis Brown, named for author Washington Irving; **1906** Chicago, Rock Island, and Gulf Railroad depot and switching yard built; **1914** incorporated as a town; **1952** incorporated as city; **1955** University of Dallas established; **1971** Dallas Cowboys football team's Texas Stadium opens; **1974** Dallas-Fort Worth International Airport opened to northwest; **1977** North Lake College (2-year) established; **1980s** Las Colinas Urban Center developed by magnate Ben Carpenter, includes people mover system.

Jacksboro *Jack County Northern Texas, 55 mi/ 89 km northwest of Fort Worth*

1855 town founded, originally named Lost Creek, later renamed Mesquiteville; **1856** Jack County formed, named for Texas revolutionaries William III and Patrick C. Jack; **1858** town becomes county seat, renamed Jacksborough; **1867** Fort Richardson established; **May 18, 1871** in Salt Creek Massacre, Kiowa raiders kill 7 of 12 teamsters, 41 mules stolen, chiefs Satanta and Big Tree sentenced to hang, changed to life for fear of retribution; **1875** incorporated as a town; **1878** fort abandoned; **1898** Chicago & Rock Island Railroad reaches town; **1899** incorporated as a city, name shortened; **1910** Gulf, Texas & Western Railroad reaches city; **1920s** oil discovered; **1940** county courthouse built.

Jacksonville *Cherokee County Eastern Texas, 100 mi/161 km southeast of Dallas*

Oct. 5, 1838 Killough Massacre to northwest, 18 members of Isaac Killough family killed by Cherokees, worst case of Native American depredation in eastern Texas; **1847** town founded; **1872** International & Great Northern Railroad built; town relocated 3 mi/4.8 km to railroad; town incorporated; **1873** Lon Morris College (2-year) established; **1899** Jacksonville Baptist College established; **1913** Jacksonville Public Library founded; **1930s** town becomes Texas' "Tomato Capital"; **1971** Blackburn Crossing Dam built on Neches River to northwest, forms Lake Palestine.

Jarrell *Williamson County See Georgetown (1997)*

Jasper *Jasper County Eastern Texas, 110 mi/ 177 km north-northeast of Houston*

1824 area settled; **1836** Jasper County formed; **1838** town founded as county seat by John Bevil, named for Sgt. William Jasper (1750–1779), American Revolution hero; **1851** Jasper Collegiate Institute established (closed 1908); **1865** *Jasper News-Boy* newspaper founded; **1926** incorporated as a city; **1960** county courthouse built; **June 7, 1998** African-American James Byrd, Jr. dragged to death by pickup truck driven by three white supremacists; **Feb. 23, 2000** John William King, 25, one of three accused of dragging death in 1998, sentenced to death.

Jayton *Kent County Northern Texas, 70 mi/ 113 km northwest of Abilene*

1876 Kent County formed; **1886** post office granted to Daniel M. Jay; named Jay Flat; **1892** county organized; Clairemont becomes county seat; **1907** Stanford & Northwestern Railroad built; town moved to rail line, renamed Jayton; **1910** town incorporated; **1954** county seat moved to Jayton; **1857** county courthouse built.

Jefferson *Marion County Northeastern Texas, 14 mi/23 km north of Marshall, on Big Cypress Bayou*

1830s area settled, **1837** Jefferson County formed; town founded as county seat on Big Cypress Bayou, at junction of Texas & Pacific and Louisiana & Arkansas railroads; **1838** county seat moved to Beaumont; **1846** Cass County formed; town becomes county seat; **1852** county seat moved to Linden; **1850** Freeman Plantation house built to west; **1858** Excelsior Hotel built, guest book includes Oscar Wilde and Presidents Grant and Hayes; **1860** Marion County formed; town becomes county seat; **1866** incorporated as a city; fire destroys many of town's businesses; **1873** world's first ammonia refrigerated ice plant established; removal of log jam (Red River Raft) in Louisiana's Red River lowers level of Big Cypress Bayou, ending navigation; **1907** Carnegie Library opened; **1912** county courthouse built.

Johnson City *Blanco County Central Texas, 40 mi/64 km west of Austin, on Pedernales River*

1856 first members of Johnson family, ancestors of Pres. Lyndon B. Johnson, build log cabin; **1858** Blanco County formed; town of Blanco becomes county seat; **1867** grandfather and great-uncle of President Johnson establish ranch; **1879** town site selected on Johnson Ranch over barbecue; **1891** county seat moved to Johnson City; **1916** county courthouse built; **1944** incorporated as a city; **Dec. 2, 1969** Lyndon B. Johnson National Historical Park established 14 mi/22.5 km to west; **Jan. 23, 1973** Pres. Lyndon B. Johnson, 64, dies of heart attack at his ranch, buried there.

Jourdanton *Atascosa County Southern Texas, 34 mi/55 km south of San Antonio*

1856 Atascosa County formed; **1858** Pleasanton becomes county seat; **1909** town founded by Jourdan Campbell and T. H. Zanderson; **1910** county seat moved to Jourdanton; **1911** town incorporated; **1912** county courthouse built.

Junction *Kimble County West central Texas, 100 mi/161 northwest of San Antonio, on Llano River*

1858 Kimble County formed; **1876** county organized; town founded as county seat, originally named Denman; **1877** town renamed Junction City; Texas Rangers establish headquarters here; **1894** town name shortened to Junction; **1919** *Eagle* newspaper begins publication; **1928** town incorporated; **1929** county courthouse built.

Karnack *Harrison County* See **Marshall (1912)**

Karnes City *Karnes County* *Southern Texas, 50 mi/80 km southeast of San Antonio*

1854 Karnes County formed; Helena becomes county seat; **1885** town founded on land of rancher William Butler to spite town of Helena where his son was killed in barroom shooting 1884; town named for Capt. Henry Karnes, officer of Texas Republic; **1894** county seat moved to Karnes City; county courthouse built; **1914** town incorporated.

Katy *Fort Bend, Harris, and Waller counties* See **Houston (1962)**

Kaufman *Kaufman County* *Northeastern Texas, 30 mi/48 km east-southeast of Dallas*

1848 Kaufman County formed, named for U.S. Cong. David S. Kaufman; **1851** town founded as county seat; **1860** Cedar Grove Methodist Institute established; **1872** town incorporated; **1955** county courthouse completed.

Kenedy *Karnes County* *Southern Texas, 57 mi/ 92 km southeast of San Antonio*

1886 San Antonio & Aransas Pass Railroad built; town founded, named Kenedy Junction for rancher Mifflin Kenedy, partner of Richard King of King Ranch; **1887** town name shortened; **1910** town incorporated; **1915** Hot Wells Hotel and Bath House opened; **1942** Kenedy Alien Detention Camp established, prisoner of war camp, closed 1945.

Kermit *Winkler County* *Western Texas, 40 mi/ 64 km west of Odessa, near New Mexico state line*

1887 Winkler County formed, named for Judge C. M. Winkler; **1910** county organized; town founded as county seat, named for Kermit Roosevelt, son of Pres. Theodore Roosevelt, who hunted deer at T Bar Ranch; **1926** discovery of oil launches Permian Basin oil boom; **1927** attempt to move county seat to Wink unsuccessful; **1928** branch of Texas & Pacific Railroad reaches town; **1929** county courthouse built; **Apr. 23, 1936** singer Roy Orbison born at Wink to southwest (died 1988); **1938** town incorporated; **1966** Moorhead Derrick, cable-tool type derrick, ceases operation.

Kerrville *Kerr County* *South central Texas, 55 mi/ 89 km northwest of San Antonio*

1846 area first settled; **1856** Kerr County formed, named for Texas statesman James Kerr; town founded as county seat; **1860** county seat moved to Comfort, returned to Kerrville 1862; **1880** Charles Schreiner founds Y. O.

Ranch, by 1900 covers 600,000 ac/243.000 ha; **1887** San Antonio & Aransas Pass Railroad reaches town; **1889** incorporated as a town; **1923** Schreiner University established; **1926** county courthouse built; **1929** singer Jimmie Rodgers (1893–1933) arrives from Mississippi to alleviate his tuberculosis; **1935** Kerrville State Sanatorium opened, becomes state hospital 1951; **1942** incorporated as a city; **1985** Cowboy Artists of America Museum founded.

Kilgore *Gregg and Rusk counties* *Eastern Texas, 110 mi/177 km east-southeast of Dallas*

1850s area settled by plantation owners; **1872** International-Great Northern Railroad built; town founded, named for Constantine Kilgore (1835–1897), Civil War veteran and state senator; **1930** discovery of oil leads to boom, over 1,200 oil derricks located in city limits; **1931** incorporated as a city; **1935** Kilgore College (2-year) established.

Killeen *Bell County* *Central Texas, 45 mi/72 km southwest of Waco*

1872 town founded, named Palo Alto; **1882** Gulf, Colorado & Santa Fe Railroad built; town renamed for railroad engineer Frank Killeen; **1893** incorporated as a town; **Jan. 19, 1905** publisher Oveta Culp Hobby born (died 1995); **1942** Camp Hood established, becomes Fort Hood Army Base 1950; **1948** incorporated as a city; **1967** Central Texas College (2-year) established; **1973** American Technological University established, becomes University of Central Texas 1989; **Oct. 25, 1992** gunman kills 23 at Luby's Cafeteria.

Kingston *Hunt County* See **Greenville (1924)**

Kingsville *Kleberg County* *Southern Texas, 35 mi/ 56 km southwest of Corpus Christi*

1853 King Ranch, largest ranch in U.S., established by Capt. Richard King, purchases 75,000 ac/30,375 ha, expands to 825,000 ac/334,125 ha; **1904** St. Louis, Brownsville & Mexico Railroad reaches site; town founded at center of King Ranch; **1911** incorporated as a city; **1913** Kleberg County formed; town becomes county seat; **1914** county courthouse built; **1920** oil discovered in area; **1925** Texas A & M University, Kingsville Campus, established; **1942** Naval Auxiliary Station established, becomes Naval Air Station 1951; **1944** Celanese Plant established to north.

Kountze *Hardin County* *Southeastern Texas, 25 mi/40 km north-northwest of Beaumont*

1858 Hardin County formed; town of Hardin founded 2 mi/3.2 km to southwest as county seat; **1881** Sabine & East Texas Railroad built by Herman and Augustus Kountze; new town founded; **1882** post office established; **1887** county seat moved to Kountze; **1902** town incorporated; **1950s** oil discovered in area; **1959** county courthouse built.

La Grange *Fayette County* *South central Texas, 55 mi/89 km east-southeast of Austin, on Colorado River*

1819 trading post established; **1831** town founded; **1837** Fayette County formed; **1838** county organized; town becomes county seat; **1849** La Grange Collegiate Institute founded, becomes Emory College 1860, later University; **1850** town incorporated; **1880s** Missouri, Kansas & Texas Railroad reaches town; **1891** county courthouse built.

Lamesa *Dawson County* *Northwestern Texas, 55 mi/89 km south of Lubbock*

1876 Dawson County formed; **1905** county organized; town founded as county seat; post office established; **1911** Panhandle & Santa Fe Railroad reaches town; **1917** incorporated as a city; county courthouse built, addition built 1950; **Oct. 16, 1940** actor Barry Corbin born; **1942** Lamesa Army Air Field established (closed 1944).

Lampasas *Lampasas County* *Central Texas, 60 mi/97 km north-northwest of Austin*

1854 town founded, originally named Burleson; **1856** Lampasas County formed; town becomes county seat, renamed Lampasas, Spanish for "water lily"; Keystone Hotel opened; **1857** post office established; **1870** Star Hotel opened; **1873** incorporated as a town; **1882** Gulf, Colorado & Santa Fe Railroad reaches town; **1883** county courthouse built; **1910** Houston & Texas Central Railroad built; **1927** incorporated as a city.

Lancaster *Dallas County* *Northeastern Texas, suburb 11 mi/18 km south of Dallas*

1844 area settled, named Pleasant Run; **1852** town platted, renamed Lancaster; **1855** Rawlins Homestead built; **1862** local pistol factory produces the large Colt .44 Dragoon revolver; **1887** incorporated as a city; **1887** *Lancaster Herald* newspaper founded; **1888** Missouri, Kansas & Texas Railroad reaches town; **1896** Randlett House built; **1911** Waco-Dallas International Raceway built; **1977** Cedar Valley College (2-year) established.

Langtry *Val Verde County* *Southwestern Texas, 50 mi/80 km northwest of Del Rio, on Rio Grande*

1879 Judge Roy Bean declares himself "the law west of the Pecos"; **1883** town founded at junction of Southern Pacific and Galveston, Harrisburg & San Antonio railroads; **1885** Bean becomes Justice of the Peace; **1896** Judge Bean stages Maher-Fitzsimmons boxing match in middle of Rio Grande, illegal both in U.S. and Mexico; **Apr. 1904** Judge Bean dies, born in Kentucky c.1825.

Laredo *Webb County* *Southern Texas, 130 mi/229 km west-southwest of Corpus Christi*

1755 town founded by Thomas Sanchez; **1767** town platted; **1775** Nuevo Laredo, Mexico, founded; **1848** Webb County formed; town becomes county seat; Fort McIntosh established; **1852** incorporated as a city; **1880**

Laredo Seminary established; **1881** International-Great Northern and Texas-Mexican railroads reach town; **1887** Mexican National Railroad reaches Nuevo Laredo from Mexico City; **1889** International Bridge built, rebuilt 1922 and 1954; **1898** onion industry introduced; **1905** town partly destroyed by tornado; **1908** natural gas discovered; **1909** county courthouse built; **1920** fire destroys business district; **1921** oil discovered; **1922** Azteca Theater opened; **1936** highway completed to Mexico City; **1942** Laredo Army Air Field established, becomes Air Force Base 1952, closed 1973; **1946** Laredo Community College (2-year) established; Fort McIntosh deactivated; **1969** Texas A & M International University at Laredo established; **Nov. 11, 1971** 32 first graders killed when car crashes into school.

Leakey *Real County* *Southwestern Texas, 75 mi/121 km west-northwest of San Antonio*

1857 cabin built by John Leakey; **1858** Edwards County formed; **1883** county organized; town (LAY-kee) platted as county seat; **1891** county seat moved to Rocksprings; **1913** Real (ray-AL) County formed from Edwards County; town becomes county seat; **1917** county courthouse built; **1951** incorporated as a city.

Levelland *Hockley County* *Northwestern Texas, 30 mi/48 km west of Lubbock*

1876 Hockley County formed, named for George Washington Hockley; **1906** cereal magnate C. W. Post purchases Oxsheer Ranch; **1912** Post plats model community of Hockley City; **1921** county organized; town becomes county seat; **1922** town renamed for level terrain; **1925** Santa Fe Railroad reaches town; **1926** incorporated as a city; **1927** county courthouse built; **1958** South Plains College (2-year) established; **1968** South Plains Museum established.

Liberty *Liberty County* *Southeastern Texas, 40 mi/64 km northeast of Houston*

1818 settled by Americans, one of oldest settled areas in Texas; **1830** American squatters attempt (unsuccessfully) to join Austin's colony; **1831** town platted, named Villa de la Santísima Trinidad de la Libertad; José Francisco Madero grants first land titles; town renamed Liberty; **1836** Liberty County formed; **1837** town incorporated, becomes county seat; **1855** *Liberty Gazette* newspaper founded; **1925** oil production begins; **1931** county courthouse built.

Linden *Cass County* *Northeastern Texas, 30 mi/48 km south-southeast of Texarkana*

1846 Cass County formed; Jefferson becomes county seat; **1848** town founded, incorporated; **1852** Texas & Pacific Railroad reaches town; town platted; county seat moved to Linden; **1866** county courthouse built, oldest functioning courthouse in Texas; **1875** *Cass County Sun* newspaper founded.

Lipscomb *Lipscomb County* *Northwestern Texas, 107 mi/172 km northeast of Amarillo*

1876 Lipscomb County formed, named for Abner S. Lipscomb, Texas Supreme Court Associate Justice; **1886** town founded; **1887** county organized; town becomes county seat; **1888** coal discovered; **1916** county courthouse built.

Littlefield *Lamb County* *Northwestern Texas, 35 mi/56 km northwest of Lubbock*

1876 Lamb County formed, named for Lt. George A. Lamb; **1887** world's tallest windmill (132 ft/40 m high) built on XIT Ranch, blown down in storm Thanksgiving Day, Nov. 25, 1926; **1908** county organized; Olton becomes county seat; **1912** town platted on XIT Ranch, named for rancher George Washington Littlefield; **1913** Panhandle & Western Railroad reaches town; **1915** *Lamb County Leader* published; **1924** incorporated as a city; **June 15, 1937** country singer Waylon Jennings born (died 2003); **1946** county seat moved to Littlefield; **1953** county courthouse built.

Livingston *Polk County* *Eastern Texas, 70 mi/113 km north-northeast of Houston*

1838 town site surveyed; **1839** Moses Choate becomes first settler; **1846** Polk County formed; town founded as county seat, named by Choate for home town of Livingston, Alabama; **1850s** Alabama-Coushatta Indian Reservation created; **1858** Livingston Academy established; **1902** town incorporated; three blocks of business district destroyed by fire; **1903** *Polk County Enterprise* newspaper founded; Livingston & Southeastern Railway built, abandoned 1913; **1923** county courthouse built; **1940s** oil discovered; **1968** Lake Livingston formed by dam on Trinity River to north.

Llano *Llano County* *Central Texas, 65 mi/105 km northwest of Austin*

1855 town founded on Llano Estacado plateau; **1856** Llano County formed; town becomes county seat; **1880s** mining boom begins; **Aug. 5, 1873** raids and horse stealing by Apaches ends with the Packsaddle Mountain Fight, three Native Americans killed, four whites wounded; **1892** incorporated as a city; **1893** county courthouse completed; **1901** incorporated as a city; **1950s** granite quarrying reaches peak; **Dec. 20, 1991** Llano River floods in heavy rains, 18 killed.

Lockhart *Caldwell County* *South central Texas, 27 mi/43 km south of Austin*

Aug. 12, 1840 Texas troops defeat Comanches at Battle of Plum Creek; **1848** Caldwell County formed; town founded as county seat, named for landowner Byrd Lockhart; **1850** Lockhart Academy established; **1852** incorporated as a town; **1856** Emanuel Episcopal Church built, one of oldest Protestant churches in Texas; **1870** incorporated as a city; **1870s** town serves as south terminus of Chisholm Trail;

1874 Southern Pacific Railroad reaches town; **1893** cottonseed gin established; **1894** county courthouse built; **1899** Dr. Eugene Clark Library built.

Longview *Gregg and Harrison counties* *Eastern Texas, 115 mi/185 km east of Dallas*

1830s area first settled; **1850s** wave of settlers arrive from Southern states; **1870** Texas & Pacific Railroad built; town founded; **1871** incorporated as a town; **1873** Gregg County formed; town becomes county seat; **1919** Longview Race Riot sparked by murders of jailed black men, months of unrest called the Red Summer; **1923** incorporated as a city; **1929** Heritage Hotel built, closed 1976; **1930s** oil discovered, population triples; **1932** county courthouse built; **1946** Le Tourneau College, now University, established; **July 15, 1961** actor Forest Whitaker born.

Lubbock *Lubbock County* *Western Texas, 260 mi/418 km west-northwest of Fort Worth*

1690s Spanish explorers pass through Yellow House Canyon; **1876** Lubbock County formed, named for Col. Thomas Lubbock, signer of Texas Declaration of Independence, organized Texas Rangers; **1877** final clash between Native Americans and white buffalo hunters takes place in canyon; **1879** area settled by Quakers; **1890** town of Monterey founded south of canyon by W. E. Rayner; Lubbock founded north of canyon by F. E. Wheelock; **1891** county organized; towns merge as Lubbock, becomes county seat; **1900** *The Leader* newspaper founded, renamed *The Avalanche* 1908; **1909** incorporated as a city; **1923** *Plains Journal* newspaper founded; Texas Technical University established; **1926** newspapers merge as *The Avalanche-Journal*; **1929** Lubbock Municipal Airport established, becomes International Airport 1966; **Sept. 7, 1936** rock and roll icon Buddy Holly born, killed in plane crash at Mason City, Iowa, 1959; **Jan. 21, 1942** singer Mac Davis born; **1946** Lubbock Symphony Orchestra founded; **1949** Reese Air Force Base established to west, closed 1995; **1950** county courthouse built; **1957** Lubbock Christian University established; **1969** Lubbock Ballet founded; **May 11, 1970** tornado kills 21, injures 500; **1995** Buddy Holly Museum opened.

Luckenbach *Gillespie County* *South central Texas, 55 mi/89 km north-northwest of San Antonio*

c.1850 town founded by Germans (LOO-ken-bahk); **1971** entire town purchased by humorist Hondo Crouch; **1977** town made popular by smash country hit by Willie Nelson and Waylon Jennings; **July 4, 1995** first annual Willy Nelson's Fourth of July Picnic held.

Lufkin *Angelina County* *Eastern Texas, 115 mi/185 km north-northeast of Houston*

1846 Angelina County formed; Marion becomes county seat; **1854** county seat moved to Jonesville, then to Homer

(Angelina) 1858; **1882** Houston, East & West Railroad reaches site; town founded, named for railroad surveyor E. P. Lufkin; **Nov. 1885** lot sale complemented with Texas barbecue, excursion trains from Houston, Shreveport, and Tyler; **1890** incorporated as a city; timber industry begins in surrounding Piney Woods region, through 1920s; **1891** county seat moved to Lufkin; **1894** county courthouse built; **1968** Angelina College (2-year) established.

Luling   *Caldwell County   South central Texas, 40 mi/64 km south of Austin, on San Marcos River*

1874 town established on Chihuahua Trail as terminus of Southern Pacific Railroad, named for wife of H. P. Pierce, railroad president; **1875** incorporated as a city; **1889** San Antonio & Aransas Pass Railroad reaches city; **Aug. 9, 1922** discovery of Luling Oil Field transforms cow town into boom town; **1929** Luling Foundation established for advancement of agricultural programs; **1953** first annual Watermelon Thump celebration held.

Madisonville   *Madison County   East central Texas, 87 mi/140 km north-northwest of Houston*

1853 Madison County formed; **1854** town founded as county seat by P. W. Kittrell; town and county named for Pres. James Madison; **1912** incorporated as a city; **1970** fifth county courthouse built.

Marfa   *Presidio County   Western Texas, 170 mi/ 274 km southeast of El Paso*

1833 Fort D. A. Russell established; **1850** Presidio County formed; **1871** county organized; Fort Davis becomes county seat; **1881** Texas & New Orleans Railroad built; town founded, named for character in Dostoyevsky's *The Brothers Karamazov*; **1883** glowing orbs first reported by rancher Robert Ellison, Marfa mystery lights most often seen east on U.S. Highway 90; **1885** county seat moved to Marfa; **1886** county courthouse completed; **1887** town incorporated; **1928** El Paisano Hotel built; **1977** solar powered regional office of U.S. Border Patrol built.

Marlin   *Falls County   East central Texas, 23 mi/ 37 km southeast of Waco*

1836 Fort Marlin built by John Marlin; **1850** Falls County formed, named for falls of Brazos River; **1851** town founded; county seat moved from Viesca; **1867** town incorporated; **1871** Houston & Texas Central Railroad comes to town; **1890s** hot artesian wells discovered, developed as resort; **1901** International-Great Northern Railroad reaches town; **1939** county courthouse built; **1989** William P. Hobby Correction Unit established.

Marshall   *Harrison County   Eastern Texas, 137 mi/ 220 km east of Dallas*

1839 Harrison County formed; area first settled; **1841** town founded; **1842** county organized; town becomes county seat; **1844** town incorporated; **1850** Masonic Female Institute founded (closed 1901); **1861** pro-Confederate Missouri government-in-exile makes Marshall its capital; **1870** Maplecroft mansion built; **1873** Wiley University established; **1896** pottery manufacturing begins, becomes major industry; **1912** East Texas Baptist University established; **Dec. 22, 1912** Claudia Alta Taylor "Lady Bird" Johnson born at Karnak to northeast, wife of Pres. Lyndon B. Johnson (married Nov. 17, 1934); **Oct. 24, 1926** New York Giants football player Y. A. Tittle born; **Jan. 10, 1945** boxing champion George Foreman born; **1964** county courthouse built; **1985** Michelson Museum of Art established.

Mason   *Mason County   Central Texas, 85 mi/ 137 km southeast of San Angelo*

c.1850s area settled by Germans; **1851** Fort Mason established; town founded; **1858** Mason County formed; **1861** town becomes county seat; **1869** Fort Mason abandoned; **1880s** 17-room Seaquist House built; **1909** county courthouse built; **1945** town incorporated; **1951** cattle herds continue to use well at town square.

Matador   *Motley County   Northwestern Texas, 120 mi/193 km north-northwest of Abilene*

1876 Motley County formed, named for Dr. Junius W. Mottley [sp]; **1879** Matador Ranch established; **1886** post office established; **1891** county organized; town founded as county seat on Matador Ranch by manager Henry H. Campbell; **1912** town incorporated; **1913** Short Line Railroad reaches town; **1948** county courthouse built.

McAllen   *Hidalgo County   Southern Texas, 50 mi/ 80 km west-northwest of Brownsville, near Rio Grande*

1904 town founded on St. Louis, Brownsville & Mexico Railroad, named for Scottish landowner John McAllen; **1906** irrigation systems introduced, essential to citrus industry; **1911** incorporated as a city; **1927** first bridge to Mexico built, collapses 1938; **1935** adobe Quinta Mazatlan house built by Jason and Marcia Mathews; **1941** second bridge built to Mexico, replaced 1967; **1946** civic center built; **1952** Miller Airport opened, becomes McAllen Miller International Airport 1999; **Sept. 21, 1989** school bus hit by truck at Alton to west, 21 children killed, 60 injured.

McKinney   *Collin County   Northern Texas, 30 mi/ 48 north-northeast of Dallas*

1836 Collin McKinney, signer of the Texas Declaration of Independence, builds house; **1845** town settled; **1846** Collin County formed; Buckner becomes county seat; **1848** county seat moved to McKinney; **1859** incorporated as a town; **1908** Texas Electric Railway reaches town, ends 1948; **1913** incorporated as a city; **1927** county courthouse built; **May 3, 1948** tornado strikes town, 3 killed, 43 injured; **1985** Collin County Community College established.

Memphis   *Hall County*   *Northwestern Texas, 75 mi/ 121 km east-southeast of Amarillo*

1876 Hall County formed, named for Texas statesman Warren D. C. Hall; **1887** Fort Worth & Denver City Railroad built; **1889** town founded on railroad; **1890** county organized; town becomes county seat; post office opened; Memphis becomes county seat; **1906** town incorporated; **1923** county courthouse built.

Menard   *Menard County*   *West central Texas, 55 mi/89 km southeast of San Angelo*

1751 Spanish presidio built to protect mission Santa Cruz de San Saba; **March 16, 1758** refusal of occupants to abandon mission at recommendation of presidio commander culminates in Comanche attack, only a few escape; **1769** presidio finally abandoned; **1852** Fort McKavett established to west, abandoned 1859; **1858** Menard County formed, named for Michel B. Menard, signer of Texas Declaration of Independence; town of Menardville founded; **1868** Fort McKavett reoccupied by Col. Ranald Mackenzie, abandoned 1883; **1871** county organized; town becomes county seat; **1880** Australia Hotel opened by Australian William Saunders; **1899** Ben Ficklin Flood severely damages town; **1911** Fort Worth & Rio Grande Railroad reaches town; town renamed Menard; **1931** county courthouse built.

Mentone   *Loving County*   *Western Texas, 19 mi/ 31 km north of Pecos*

1887 Loving County formed, named for Indian fighter Oliver Loving, killed 1866; **1893** county organized; town of Mentone founded as county seat 2 mi/3.2 km to southwest, abandoned 1896; **1925** new county seat platted, named Ramsey; **1930** Wheat Oil Pool discovered; **1931** town renamed Mentone; **1936** county courthouse built.

Meridian   *Bosque County*   *Central Texas, 40 mi/ 64 km northwest of Waco*

1850s last of Tawakoni peoples leave area; **1854** Bosque County formed; town founded as county seat, named for its location on 100th meridian; **Dec. 16, 1865** Cleng Peerson dies at age 83, founded over 30 Norwegian settlements from Wisconsin to Texas, town of Norse to south the final part of his legacy; **1874** town incorporated; county courthouse built; **1881** Santa Fe Railroad arrives just north of town; **1909** Meridian College established, closed 1927.

Mertzon   *Irion County*   *Western Texas, 25 mi/ 40 km southwest of San Angelo*

1889 Irion County formed, named for statesman Robert Anderson Irion; Sherwood becomes county seat; **1908** town founded, named for railroad director M. L. Mertzon; **1911** Kansas City, Mexico & Orient Railroad completed; **1936** county seat moved to Mertzon; oil discovered; **1937** town incorporated; county courthouse built.

Mexia   *Limestone County*   *East central Texas, 39 mi/63 km east-northeast of Waco*

1797 expedition of Philip Nolan finds peaceful Tehuacana peoples farming in hills; **1830** attack on Tehuacanas by Cherokees destroys much of tribe; **1852** Tehuacana Academy established, nucleus for Trinity University, San Antonio; **1871** town founded, named for Gen. José Antonio Mexia, rebelled against Santa Anna; Houston & Texas Central Railroad reaches town; **1889** Confederate Reunion Grounds established, used until 1946; **1893** incorporated as a city; **1912** natural gas field discovered; **1921** oil boom begins, state militia called to maintain order.

Miami   *Roberts County*   *Northwestern Texas, 73 mi/117 km northeast of Amarillo*

1876 Roberts County formed; **1887** town founded as construction camp on Santa Fe Railroad by E. H. Eldridge; town named for Miami peoples; **1889** county organized; Parnell becomes county seat; **1898** county seat moved to Miami; **1913** county courthouse built; **1937** incorporated as a city.

Midland   *Midland County*   *Western Texas, 140 mi/ 225 km west-southwest of Abilene*

1885 Midland County formed; town founded as county seat; **1905** blacksmith Johnny Pliska begins building airplane two years after Wright Brothers' flight; **1906** incorporated as a city; **1912** Pliska makes one of earliest airplane flights in Texas; **1923** oil discovered; **1927** Sloan Field airport established; **1930** county courthouse built; **1931** Midland Army Air Field opened, closed 1947, becomes Midland International Airport 1950; **Nov. 4, 1946** Laura Welch Bush born, wife of Pres. George W. Bush (married Nov. 1977); **1950** future Pres. George H. W. Bush settles here with family, including sons Jeb and George W., enters oil business; **1957** Confederate Air Force Flying Museum begins collection of vintage aircraft; **July 23, 1961** TV actor Woody Harrelson born; **1965** Permian Basin Petroleum Museum founded; **1969** Midland College (2-year) established; **2002** Scharbauer Sports Complex completed.

Mineral Wells   *Palo Pinto and Parker counties*   *Northern Texas, 45 mi/72 km west of Fort Worth*

1877 Judge J. W. Lynch builds log cabin; **1881** town platted; water in natural springs found to have medicinal qualities; **1882** town incorporated; stage line opens to Millsap connecting with Texas & Pacific Railroad; **1885** Waters of Crazy Well turns area into popular health resort; **1897** Hexagon House Hotel opened; **1913** Famous Water Company founded by Edward P. Dismuke; **1940** Camp Wolters military base established, recommissioned 1952.

TEXAS

Mission   *Hidalgo County   Southern Texas, 5 mi/ 8 km west of McAllen, near Rio Grande*

1824 Oblate Fathers establish mission to south; **1901** post office established; town named Mission; **1907** Missouri Pacific Railroad arrives; first irrigation canals built; **1910** William Jennings Bryan purchases land, spends two winters here; town incorporated; troops sent to guard against raids by Mexican bandit Pancho Villa; citrus growing begins; **Feb. 11, 1921** U.S. Sen. Lloyd Bentsen, Jr. born; **Sept. 11, 1924** football player, Dallas Cowboys coach Tom Landry born (died 2000); **c.1930** grapefruit industry established; **1930s** oil discovered; **1932** first annual Citrus Fiesta held.

Monahans   *Ward County   Western Texas, 35 mi/ 56 km west-southwest of Odessa*

1880 John Monahans digs first water well; **1881** town founded on Texas & Pacific Railroad; **1887** Ward County formed, named for Thomas William Ward of land office; **1892** county organized; Barstow becomes county seat; **1900** Monahans Hotel opened; **1928** town incorporated; oil storage facility built, converted to Million Barrel Museum 1987; **1937** carbon black plant opens; **1938** county seat moved to Monahans; **1940** county courthouse built.

Montague   *Montague County   Northern Texas, 64 mi/103 km north-northwest of Fort Worth*

1857 Montague County formed, named for Daniel Montague, Texas commander in Mexican War; **1858** town founded as county seat; post office established; first store opened by Joseph Cox; **1878** *Montague News* weekly newspaper founded; **1886** town incorporated; **1900** town disincorporated; **1912** county courthouse built.

Morton   *Cochran County   Northwestern Texas, 55 mi/89 km west of Lubbock*

1870 Cochran County formed; **1922** town founded by Morton Smith; **1924** county organized, town becomes county seat; post office established; **1926** county courthouse built; **1933** incorporated as a city; **1936** oil discovered.

Mount Pleasant   *Titus County   Northeastern Texas, 105 mi/169 km east-northeast of Dallas*

1846 Titus County formed; town founded as county seat; **1882** Texas & St. Louis Railroad reaches town; **1900** incorporated as a city; **1908** resort develops around red mineral springs; **1912** Dellwood Resort Hotel built by W. H. Florey; **1913** Martin Theater built, later home of weekly (Saturdays) Pleasant Jamboree; **1915** mineral springs resorts close; **1940** county courthouse built; **1985** Northeast Texas Community College established.

Mount Vernon   *Franklin County   Northeastern Texas, 90 mi/145 km east-northeast of Dallas*

1830 area first settled by Joshua T. Johnson; **1848** land for town donated by Stephen and Rebecca Keith, named Lone Star; **1858** pottery enterprise begins; **1875** Franklin County formed; town becomes county seat; **1887** St. Louis, Arkansas & Texas Railroad reaches town; **1910** town incorporated, renamed; **1912** county courthouse built.

Muleshoe   *Bailey County   Northwestern Texas, 65 mi/105 km northwest of Lubbock*

1876 Bailey County formed; **1913** North Texas Railway reaches site; town founded; **1919** county organized; town becomes county seat; **1925** county courthouse built; **1926** town incorporated; named for nearby Muleshoe Ranch; **1935** Muleshoe National Wildlife Refuge founded to south; **May 15, 1955** actor Lee Horsley born; **July 4, 1965** National Mule Memorial established as tribute to the mule, unsung heroes in development of modern society.

Murvaul   *Panola County   See Carthage (1905)*

Nacogdoches   *Nacogdoches County   Eastern Texas, 130 mi/209 km north-northeast of Houston*

1000 BC–1500 AD Caddoan people build ceremonial mounds; **1687** region explored by La Salle; **1691** El Camino Real (Kings Highway) built by Domingo Terán de los Ríos; **1716** Spanish mission founded; **1779** Spanish presidio (Old Stone Fort) built; **1813** Texas' first newspapers published, *Gaceta de Tejas* and *El Mejicano*; Gutiérrez-Magee Expedition passes through region, Spanish forces destroy town, response to Mexican revolt; **1819** provisional government of Republic of Texas established, defeated; **1820** Republic of Fredonia declared, suppressed; **1821** municipal government established by Mexicans; **1828** Sterne-Hoya home built by Adolphus Sterne, a founder of Texas Republic, site of Sam Houston's baptism into Catholic faith 1854; **Aug. 2–3, 1832** Battle of Nacogdoches, forces of James Bullock and Vicente Cordova prevent Mexican Col. José de los Piedras from crossing Angelina River, 45 Mexicans killed; **1836** Nacogdoches County formed, 20 counties later formed from it; town becomes county seat; **1837** town incorporated; **Aug. 1838** Córdova Rebellion leads to expulsion of remaining Native Americans from East Texas; **1852** Baptist church built, established 1835; **1858** Nacogdoches University established; **1859** some of state's first oil wells drilled in area; **Sept. 1866** L. T. Barrett drills Texas' first productive oil well, delivers 10 barrels a day; **1923** Stephen F. Austin State University established; **1959** county courthouse built; **Feb. 1, 2003** space shuttle *Columbia* breaks apart over eastern Texas 16 minutes ahead of scheduled landing at Cape Canaveral, Florida, spreading debris from Fort Worth to western Louisiana, astronauts Rick D. Husband, William C. McCool, Michael A. Anderson, David M. Brown, India-born woman Kalpana Chawla, Laurel Clark, and Israeli Ilan Ramon killed.

Navasota *Grimes County* *East central Texas, 60 mi/97 km northwest of Houston*

1687 Robert Cavalier, Sieur de la Salle, murdered by one of his own men near here while in search of mouth of Mississippi River; **1822** area settled; **1831** town founded by Daniel Arnold of Georgia, named Cross Roads; **1854** post office opened; town renamed Navasota; **1859** Houston & Texas Central Railroad reaches town; **1865** Gulf, Colorado & Pacific Railroad built; **c.1865** Ku Klux Klan develops large presence in area; **1866** incorporated as a city; **1867** yellow fever epidemic cuts population by half; **1900** International & Great Northern Railroad built.

New Boston *Bowie County* *See* **Boston**

New Braunfels *Comal County* *South central Texas, 30 mi/48 km northeast of San Antonio*

1845 area settled by German immigrants led by eccentric Prince Carl von Solms-Braunfels; town founded on Guadalupe River; **1846** county formed; town becomes county seat; **1847** town incorporated; **1855** New Braunfels Academy established; **1890** *Herald* newspaper first published; **1899** octagonal county courthouse built, identical design of Lee County courthouse at Giddings; **July 5, 2002** heavy rains, flooding destroys property, eight killed.

Newton *Newton County* *Eastern Texas, 55 mi/89 km north-northeast of Beaumont*

1846 Newton County formed, named for Revolutionary War hero Cpl. John Newton; Quicksand Creek becomes county seat; **1848** county seat moved to Burkeville; **1853** county seat moved to Newton; **1889** W. H. Ford Male and Female College established (closed 1906); **1902** county courthouse built; **1906** Orange & Northeastern Railroad reaches town; **1935** town incorporated.

Odessa *Ector and Midland counties* *Western Texas, 18 mi/29 km southwest of Midland*

1886 town founded on Texas & Pacific Railroad, named by immigrants for resemblance to region around Odessa, Ukraine; **1887** Ector County formed; **1891** county organized; town becomes county seat; **1892** depression discovered to southwest by rancher Julius D. Henderson, identified as meteor crater 1922 by geologist Elias Sellards; **1927** incorporated as a city; oil boom begins in Penn Oil Field; **1930** Camden Oil Field discovered; **1938** county courthouse built; **1940s** city becomes major Permian Basin oil producer; **1946** Odessa College (2-year) established; **1957** Odessa Petrochemical Complex completed; **1969** University of Texas of the Permian Basin established.

Orange *Orange County* *Southeastern Texas, 20 mi/32 km north-northeast of Port Arthur, on Sabine River*

c.1800 area settled; **1836** town founded, named Green's Bluff; **1840** town renamed Madison for Pres. James Madison; **1852** county formed; town becomes county seat; **1858** town incorporated, renamed Orange; **1860** Texas & New Orleans Railroad reaches town; **1877** Lutcher-Moore Lumber Company established, closed 1930; **1881** incorporated as a city; **1894** Victorian W. H. Stark mansion built; **1897** Kansas City Southern Railroad reaches town; **1901** Orange & Northeastern (Missouri Pacific) Railroad reaches town; **1913** Orange Oil Field discovered to west; **1916** channel in Sabine River dredged giving city deepwater access to Gulf of Mexico; **1937** county courthouse built; **1938** Rainbow Bridge built across Neches River to south; **1950s** area's petrochemical industry developed; **1969** Lamar University, Orange Campus, established; **1991** Veterans Bridge (cable-stayed) built across Neches River.

Ozona *Crockett County* *Western Texas, 65 mi/105 km southwest of San Angelo*

1855 Fort Lancaster established by U.S. on San Antonio-El Paso Road; **1861** fort abandoned at start of Civil War; **1875** Crockett County formed; **1891** town founded; **1892** county organized, town becomes county seat; **Apr. 1928** oil discovered; **1930** county courthouse built; **1954** flood destroys half of town, 16 killed.

Paducah *Cottle County* *Northwestern Texas, 100 mi/161 km west of Wichita Falls*

1876 Cottle County formed; **1885** area settled; **1892** county organized; town founded as county seat, named for home town in Kentucky of county surveyor; **1893** *Paducah Post* newspaper founded; **Dec. 25, 1909** Quanah, Acme & Pacific Railroad completed; **1910** town incorporated; **1930** county courthouse built.

Paint Rock *Concho County* *West central Texas, 30 mi/48 km east of San Angelo, on Concho River*

1858 Concho County formed; **1879** county organized; town founded as county seat, named for Native American petroglyphs (rock paintings) in area; **1886** county courthouse built; **1968** town incorporated.

Palestine *Anderson County* *Eastern Texas, 92 mi/148 km southeast of Dallas*

1833 Pilgrim Church built, probable first Protestant church in Texas; **1846** Anderson County formed; town founded as county seat; **1872** International-Great Northern Railroad reaches town; **1898** first fruit cakes produced at Eilenberger's Butternut Baking Company; **1903** salt first mined; **1914** county courthouse completed; Carnegie Public Library built; **1915** school built, becomes

Museum of East Texas Culture 1982; **1928** oil discovered to east.

Palo Pinto *Palo Pinto County* *North central Texas, 55 mi/89 km west of Fort Worth*

1856 Palo Pinto County formed; **1857** town founded as county seat, originally named Golconda; **1858** town renamed Palo Pinto; **1876** *Palo Pinto Star* newspaper founded; **1940** county courthouse built.

Pampa *Gray County* *Northwestern Texas, 50 mi/ 80 km east-northeast of Amarillo*

1876 Gray County formed; **1888** Panhandle & Santa Fe Railroad built; town founded; **1902** county organized; Lefors becomes county seat; **1912** incorporated as a city; **1927** carbon black industry established; **1928** county seat moved to Pampa; county courthouse built; **1932** Fort Worth & Denver and Clinton & Oklahoma railroads reach town.

Panhandle *Carson County* *Northwestern Texas, 27 mi/43 km east-northeast of Amarillo*

1876 Carson County formed from Bexar County; **1887** Panhandle & Santa Fe Railroad built; town founded as rail terminus, named Panhandle City; *Panhandle Herald* first published; **1888** county organized; town becomes county seat, renamed Panhandle; **1897** Methodist pastor George E. Morrison accused of poisoning wife, sensational trial results in his being hanged at Vernon 1899; **1909** town incorporated; **1920s** oil boom begins; **1934** first Southwest Race Meet and Agricultural Fair held; **1950** third county courthouse built.

Paris *Lamar County* *Eastern Texas, 95 mi/153 km northeast of Dallas*

1824 area settled; **1839** town founded; **1840** Lamar County formed; **1841** county organized; **1844** town becomes county seat following two temporary locations; **1845** town incorporated; **1876** Texas & Pacific Railroad arrives; **1887** St. Louis & San Francisco and Gulf, Colorado & Santa Fe railroads reach town; **1916** fire destroys most of town; **1917** county courthouse built; **1924** Paris Junior College established.

Pasadena *Harris County* *Southeastern Texas, suburb 10 mi/16 km east-southeast of Houston*

Apr. 1836 Santa Anna captured in Battle of San Jacinto; **1893** town founded by John H. Burnett; **1894** La Porte, Houston & Northern Railroad reaches town; **1895** incorporated as a town; **c.1900** strawberry growing industry established by Clara Barton; **1928** incorporated as a city; **1936-1939** San Jacinto Monument built, 570-ft/ 174-m tall; **1979** San Jacinto Junior College, South Campus, established.

Pearsall *Frio County* *Southern Texas, 50 mi/80 km southwest of San Antonio*

1858 Frio County formed; **1871** county organized; Frio Town becomes county seat; **1880** International & Great Northern Railroad built; town founded, named for railroad vice-president Thomas W. Pearsall; **1883** county seat moved to Pearsall; **1904** county courthouse built; **1909** town incorporated; **c.1932** oil discovered in area; **May 1, 1952** country singer George Strait born.

Pecos *Reeves County* *Western Texas, 75 mi/ 121 km west-southwest of Odessa, on Pecos River*

1881 town founded on Texas & Pacific Railroad; named Pecos City for settler Pecos Calahan; **1883** Reeves County formed; **1884** county organized, town becomes county seat; first annual rodeo in U.S. established; *Pecos City News* newspaper founded; **1891** Pecos River Railroad built north into New Mexico; **1903** town incorporated, renamed Pecos; **1911** Pecos Valley Southern Railroad built to south; **1920** Ira Bell makes area's first oil strike; **1937** county courthouse built; **1942** Pecos Army Air Field opened, closed 1945, becomes municipal airport 1950.

Perryton *Ochiltree County* *Northwestern Texas, 94 mi/151 km northeast of Amarillo, near Oklahoma*

1876 Ochiltree County formed; **1889** town of Ochiltree becomes county seat; **1919** Panhandle & Santa Fe Railroad completed; town founded as new county seat, named for settler George M. Perry; **1920** incorporated as a town; **1928** county courthouse built; **1951** incorporated as a city.

Pittsburg *Camp County* *Northeastern Texas, 195 mi/169 km east-northeast of Dallas*

1854 town founded, named Pittsburgh; **1874** Camp County formed; town becomes county seat; **1876–1877** two narrow gauge railroads reach town; **1891** town incorporated; **1893** post office alters spelling; **1902** preacher builds Ezekiel Airship flying contraption based upon Biblical reference, said to have flown briefly, destroyed in train wreck en route to 1904 St. Louis World's Fair; **1915** *Pittsburg Gazette* newspaper founded; **1928** county courthouse built.

Plains *Yoakum County* *Western Texas, 60 mi/ 97 km southwest of Lubbock*

1876 Yoakum County formed; **1906** post office established; **1907** county organized; town founded as county seat; **1910** *Yoakum County News* newspaper founded by Neil H. Bigger; **1939** oil discovered in southern part of county; **1949** third county courthouse built; **1952** incorporated as a town; **1954** incorporated as a city.

Plainview *Hale County* *Northwestern Texas,*
40 mi/64 km north of Lubbock

1876 Hale County formed; **1880s** area first settled; **1887**
town founded; **1888** county organized; town becomes
county seat; **1906** Pecos & Northern Texas Railroad
reaches town; **1907** incorporated as a city; **1909** Wayland
Baptist College (University) established; **1910** county
courthouse built; **Aug. 10, 1928** country singer Jimmy
Dean born; **July 15, 1978** hundreds of Mexican-Americans
protest three separate killings since 1973 by police.

Plano *Collin and Denton counties* *Northern*
Texas, suburb 17 mi/27 km north-northeast of Dallas

1845 area settled; **1848** town founded, named Fillmore for
Pres. Millard Fillmore; **1852** town renamed; **1872**
Houston & Texas Central Railroad reaches town; **1873**
incorporated as a town; **1874** *Plano News* first published;
1881 52 buildings destroyed by fire; **1895** fire destroys
many businesses; **1908** Texas Electric Railway interurban
line begins service, discontinued 1940s; **1962** incorporated
as a city; **1980s** television series "Dallas" filmed at
Southfork Ranch.

Port Arthur *Jefferson County* *Southeastern*
Texas, 85 mi/137 km east of Houston, on Gulf of Mexico

1840 town founded, originally named Aurora; **Sept. 8,
1863** Union forces suffer defeat in Battle of Sabine Pass
[see Sabine Pass]; **1890** town abandoned; **1894** new town
founded by Arthur E. Stilwell as terminus of Kansas City
Southern Railroad; **1895** incorporated as a town; **1898**
incorporated as a city; **1899** shipping channel completed;
1900 mansion built by Isaac Ellwood, the "Barbed Wire
King," introduced the valued commodity to region; **1901**
oil discovered at Beaumont to northwest leads to
economic boom; **1906** Rose Hill Manor mansion built;
1909 Lamar University, Port Arthur Campus, established;
June 26, 1914 Olympic athlete Babe Didrikson Zaharias
born (died 1956); **Oct. 22, 1925** artist Robert
Rauschenberg born; **1938** Rainbow Bridge built over
Neches Shipping Channel to north; **Jan. 19, 1943** rock
icon Janis Joplin born (died 1970); **1987** Texas Artists
Museum opened; **1991** Veterans Bridge (cable-stayed)
built over Neches Shipping Channel; **1992** Museum of the
Gulf Coast opened.

Port Isabel *Cameron County* *Southern Texas,*
22 mi/35 km northeast of Brownsville, on Gulf of Mexico

1770 area settled by Mexican ranchers; **1820** cattle herds
taken to Padre Island to hide them from raiders; **1846–
1848** supply base established for Gen. Zachary Taylor's
troops during Mexican War; **1848–1849** as westernmost
U.S. Atlantic port, town serves as embarkation point for
California Gold Rush; **1849** cholera epidemic strikes
town; **1853** Port Isabel Lighthouse built, decommissioned
1905; **May 30, 1863** Union forces destroy all ships in
harbor; **1871** Rio Grande Railroad completed; **1928** town
incorporated; **1936** deepwater channel completed; **1950s**

Intracoastal Waterway completed parallel to Gulf Coast;
1954 Queen Isabella Causeway built across Laguna
Madre to South Padre Island, second span built 1974;
1966 Hurricane Beulah destroys most of town; **Sept. 15,
2001** barges knock out section of Queen Isabella
Causeway sending cars plunging into water, eight killed.

Port Lavaca *Calhoun County* *Southern Texas,*
70 mi/113 km northeast of Corpus Christi, on Gulf of
Mexico

1685 Sieur de la Salle thought to have first landed in Texas
here; **1840s** area settled, named Lavaca; **1842** town
platted; **1846** Calhoun County formed; town becomes
county seat; **1849** county seat moved to Indianola; **1858**
Halfmoon Reef Lighthouse built on Matagorda Bay,
reactivated 1868; **1886** county seat moved back to Lavaca,
renamed Port Lavaca; **1907** incorporated as a city; **1920**
sea wall built; **1934** natural gas discovered; **1935** oil
discovered; **1942** lighthouse damaged in storm, kept
operating, moved to Point Comfort from bombing
range, relocated 1979 to Chamber of Commerce; **1959**
county courthouse built; **1965** Matagorda Ship Channel
completed.

Post *Garza County* *Northwestern Texas, 40 mi/*
64 km southeast of Lubbock

1876 Garza County formed; **1907** county organized; town
founded as county seat by cereal magnate C. W. Post, part
of idealistic economic scheme, named Post City; **1909** *Post*
City Post newspaper founded; **Nov. 1910** Panhandle &
Santa Fe Railroad completed; **1910–1913** elaborate series
of rainmaking experiments undertaken, includes use of
explosives in upper atmosphere; **1914** town renamed Post
after suicide of C. W. Post, May 9; **1920** Garza Theatre
opened, closed 1957, reopened 1988; **1923** county courthouse built.

Presidio *Presidio County* *Western Texas, 190 mi/*
306 km southeast of El Paso, on Rio Grande

1684 Spanish mission founded; **1848** adobe Fort Leaton
built by Ben Leaton as post on Chihuahua and San
Antonio roads; **1864** town founded; **1868** post office
established; **1930** Kansas City, Mexico & Orient Railroad
reaches town; **1981** town incorporated; **1988** Big Bend
Ranch State Park (now State Natural Area) established to
east.

Quanah *Hardeman County* *Northern Texas,*
75 mi/121 km west-northwest of Wichita Falls, near Red
River

Aug. 15, 1824 John Simpson Chisum born, called "Cattle
King of America" for his 100,000 head of cattle in Texas
and New Mexico (died 1884); **1858** Hardeman County
formed, named for statesman Thomas J. Hardeman; **1885**
county organized; Margaret (Argarita) becomes county
seat; **1886** town founded on Quanah, Acme & Pacific
Railroad, named for Quanah Parker, last great Comanche

chief, son of Cynthia Ann Parker [see Groesbeck]; **1887** incorporated as a town; **1890** county seat moved to Quanah; **June 4, 1891** storm dumps 14 in/35 cm of rain on area destroying town; **1908** county courthouse built; mission-style Quanah Depot built; **1919** incorporated as a city.

Quitman   *Wood County   Northeastern Texas, 75 mi/121 km east of Dallas*

1840s area settled; town founded, named for Cong. John A. Quitman of Mississippi, advocate of annexation of Texas by U.S.; **1850** Wood County formed, named for Texas Gov. George T. Wood, 1847–1851; town becomes county seat; **1859** *Quitman Clipper* founded, one of Texas' earliest newspapers, folds 1869; **1873** *Clipper News* founded by James Hogg; **1898** first annual Old Settlers Reunion held; **1925** county courthouse built; **1941** town incorporated; oil discovered; **Dec. 25, 1949** actress Sissy Spacek born.

Ranger   *Eastland County   North central Texas, 77 mi/124 km west-southwest of Fort Worth*

Oct. 1880 settlement built around Texas Rangers camp, named Ranger Camp Valley; **1881** town founded; **1883** name shortened to Ranger; **Oct. 1917** McKlesky No. 1 Well delivers gusher, oil boom begins; **1919** incorporated as a city; **Apr. 6, 1919** fire destroys two city blocks; **1920** Ku Klux Klan attains dominance in area, declines after 1924; **1926** Ranger Junior College established; **1982** Roaring Ranger Museum opened, depicts oil boom years.

Rankin   *Upton County   Western Texas, 55 mi/ 89 km south of Midland*

1887 Upton County formed; Upland becomes county seat; **1911** Kansas City, Mexico & Orient Railroad built; F. E. Rankin discovers source of water, badly needed for ranching; town founded; **1921** county seat moved to Rankin; **1926** county courthouse built; **1927** Yates Hotel built, now museum; **1928** town incorporated.

Raymondville   *Willacy County   Southern Texas, 43 mi/69 km north-northwest of Brownsville*

1904 town platted on St. Louis, Brownsville & Mexico Railroad; **1911** original Willacy County formed; Sarita becomes county seat; **1921** town incorporated; Willacy County renamed Kenedy County; new Willacy County formed from southern strip of old county and northern parts of Cameron and Hidalgo counties; Willacy County seat moved to Raymondville; Sarita becomes seat of new Kenedy County; **1922** county courthouse built, annex built 1977.

Refugio   *Refugio County   Southern Texas, 35 mi/ 56 km north of Corpus Christi*

1795 Mission Nuestra Señora del Refugio established; **1834** town founded; **1836** Refugio County formed; **March**

1836 in Battle of Refugio, José Urrea captures town, soldiers under William Ward and Anson King taken captive, executed in Goliad Massacre; **1837** county organized; Aransas City becomes county seat; town of Refugio incorporated; **1842** town reincorporated; **1846** county seat moved to Refugio; **1905** St. Louis, Brownsville & Mexico Railroad reaches town; **1917** county courthouse built; **1928** oil discovered, boom continues into 1960s; **Jan. 31, 1947** hall of fame baseball pitcher Nolan Ryan born.

Richardson   *Dallas and Collin counties   Northern Texas, suburb 13 mi/21 km north of Dallas*

1850s town founded as Breckenridge; **1872** Houston & Texas Central Railroad reaches town; town renamed for A. J. Richardson, railroad official; **1886** train accident kills one person, residents walk away with buckets of sugar from railcar; **1925** incorporated as a town; **1956** incorporated as a city; **1969** University of Texas at Dallas established.

Richmond   *Fort Bend County   Southeastern Texas, 27 mi/43 km west-southwest of Houston*

1821 Fort Bend established on Brazos River; **1822** town founded by members of Stephen F. Austin's Old Three Hundred colony; **1837** Fort Bend County formed; town incorporated, becomes county seat; **Sept. 8, 1900** Galveston hurricane severely damages town, 84 killed locally; **1930s** oil production begins; **1908** county courthouse completed.

Rio Grande City   *Starr County   Southern Texas, 37 mi/60 mi west-northwest of McAllen, on Rio Grande*

1753 first settled by José de Escandon; **1847** town founded, named Rancho Davis; **1848** Starr County formed, named for Texas official James Harper Starr; town becomes county seat; town renamed; Fort Ringgold established by Gen. Zachary Taylor; **1888** the Rio Grande Riot pits Mexican locals against sheriff's department, culmination of growing ethnic tensions; **1899** La Borde House built, home of French merchant, converted to hotel 1930s; **1926** Missouri Pacific Railroad built; town incorporated; **1939** county courthouse built; **1944** Fort Ringgold deactivated.

Robert Lee   *Coke County   Central Texas, 28 mi/ 45 km north of San Angelo*

1852 Fort Chadbourne built to northeast; **1889** Coke County formed; Hayrick becomes county seat; town founded on Colorado River by L. S. Harris and R. E. Cartlege, named for Gen. Robert E. Lee; **1891** county seat moved from Hayrick (abandoned); most residents, businesses move with county seat; **1929** town incorporated; **1956** county courthouse built; **1969** E. V. Spence Reservoir formed by dam on Colorado River to west.

666

Roby *Fisher County* *Central Texas, 42 mi/68 km northwest of Abilene*

1876 Fisher County formed, named for Samuel Rhoads Fisher, signer of Texas Declaration of Independence; **1885** town platted near Clear Fork Brazos River, named for developers D. C. and M. L. Roby; **1886** county organized; town becomes county seat after struggle with town of Fisher; **1910** wheat and cotton become important industries; **1915** Roby & Northern Railroad built, abandoned 1942; town incorporated; **1972** county courthouse built.

Rockport *Aransas County* *Southern Texas, 26 mi/ 42 km northeast of Corpus Christi, on Gulf of Mexico*

1802 area settled; **1867** town founded as meat packing center; Orleans Hotel built; **1871** Aransas County formed; town becomes county seat; incorporated as a city; **1888** San Antonio & Aransas Pass Railroad built; **1935** Marine Biological Laboratory established; **1940s** shrimp harvesting becomes major industry; **1956** county courthouse built.

Rocksprings *Edwards County* *Southwestern Texas, 61 mi/98 km northeast of Del Rio*

1858 Edwards County formed; **1883** county organized; Leakey becomes county seat; **1887** area settled; **1891** town founded J. R. Sweeney; county seat moved to Rocksprings; county courthouse built; **1897** tornado damages town, 27 killed; s**1924** town incorporated; **Apr. 12, 1927** tornado destroys town, 74 killed.

Rockwall *Rockwall County* *Northeastern Texas, 21 mi/334 km northeast of Dallas*

1851 natural rock wall formation discovered, associated with Balcones Fault system; **1854** town founded; **1857** town platted; **1873** Rockwall County formed; town becomes county seat; **1874** town incorporated; **1886** Missouri, Kansas & Texas Railroad reaches town; **1894** Rockwall College established; **1940** county courthouse built.

Roma *Starr County* *Southern Texas, 50 mi/80 km west of McAllen, on Rio Grande*

1751 mission established; **1765** town founded as part of José de Escandon's colony; **1854** bell tower at Our Lady of Refuge Church built by Father Pierre Keralum; **1886** steamboats begin taking cotton downstream; **1927** suspension bridge built on Rio Grande to Mexico, historic landmark in both countries; **1937** town incorporated; **1951** town used as setting for movie *Viva Zapata* starring Marlon Brando, Anthony Quinn; **1953** Falcon Dam built on Rio Grande.

Rosenberg *Fort Bend County* *Southeastern Texas, 30 mi/48 km west-southwest of Houston*

1830 site established as cattle shipping point; **1883** Gulf, Colorado & Santa Fe Railroad; town platted, named for Henry Rosenberg, railroad president 1874–1877; R. T. Malichy moves here, founds many businesses earning him distinction "Father of Rosenberg"; **1895** *Fort Bend Reporter* newspaper founded, begins temporarily as the *Silver X-Ray*; **1902** incorporated as a city; **1913** town severely damaged by flooding; **1920s** oil discovered in county.

Round Rock *Williamson and Travis counties* *Central Texas, 17 mi/27 km north of Austin*

1834 town founded as Brushy; **1839** Kenney's Fort trading post built; **1854** town renamed for large rock in Brushy Creek; **1876** International-Great Northern Railroad built, bypasses town to northeast; town gradually moves to railroad; **July 18, 1878** outlaw Sam Bass wounded in shootout with Texas Rangers during raid on bank, dies two days later; **1896** *Round Rock Leader* newspaper founded; **1906** Trinity Lutheran College founded, merges with Lutheran College of Seguin 1929; **1912** incorporated as a city; **1928** cheese factory opened (closed 1968).

Rusk *Cherokee County* *Eastern Texas, 40 mi/ 64 km south of Tyler*

1846 Cherokee County formed; town founded as county seat, named for Thomas Jefferson Rusk, signer of Texas Declaration of Independence; **1848** Cherokee Academy established (closed 1851); **1858** incorporated as a town; **1861** footbridges built 546 ft/166 m across valley for use during heavy rains; **1878** Rusk State Prison established; **1887–1888** iron dome for state capitol built by prisoners; **1904** incorporated as a city; **1918** prison converted to Rusk State Hospital, closed 1948; **1920** Rusk Baptist College established (closed 1928); **1941** county courthouse built.

Sabine Pass *Jefferson County* *Southeastern Texas, 8 mi/12.9 km south of Port Arthur, on Gulf of Mexico*

1836 town platted by Sam Houston and Philip A. Sublett, called Sabine City; **1839** town renamed Sabine Pass; **1849** lighthouse built at entrance to pass, kept dark during Civil War to aid blockade runners; **1861** town incorporated; **Sept. 8, 1863** Battle of Sabine Pass, Union attempt to invade Texas from sea, 65 Union soldiers killed, 315 taken prisoner; Confederates, fighting from only earthen defenses, take no casualties; **1886** hurricane devastates town; **1900** hurricane destroys Galveston, other coastal towns **1902** oil pumping plant established by Sun Oil from Spindletop Oil Field near Beaumont; **1915** hurricane hits Louisiana, deals final blow to pass area; **1927** Sun Oil Company discontinues operating its pumping plant; **1952** lighthouse ceases operation; **1978** city of Port Arthur annexes town.

San Angelo   *Tom Green County   Western Texas, 175 mi/282 km northwest of San Antonio*

1864 cattle ranching introduced; **1867** Fort Concho established; town founded; **1874** Tom Green County formed, named for Gen. Thomas Green of Mexican War; town of Ben Ficklin becomes county seat; **1877** first sheep herd driven from California; **1881** barbed wire fencing first used; **1883** Ben Ficklin destroyed by flood 1882; county seat moved to San Angelo, **1884** in wire-cutting wars, open range threatened by new types of fencing, conflict with landowners leads to sabotage; **1888** Santa Fe Railroad arrives; **1889** fort deactivated; **1903** incorporated as a city; **1909** Kansas City, Mexico & Orient Railroad reaches town; **1928** county courthouse built; Angelo State University established; **1942** San Angelo Army Air Base opened, closed 1946, reopened 1947 as Goodfellow Air Force Base.

San Antonio   *Bexar County   South central Texas, 185 mi/298 km west-southwest of Houston*

1601 Spanish troops hold mass on San Antonio River, name of Native American campsite changed from Yanaguana to San Antonio de Padua; **1718** Native American village founded around mission San Antonio de Valero (The Alamo), made capital of Spanish province of Texas; fort San Antonio de Bexar built to protect mission; **1731** first civil settlement established; Mission Concepción built, completed 1755; **1738** foundation laid for San Fernando Cathedral by Canary Islanders; **1749** Spanish governor's palace built; **1755** Alamo mission built; **1800s** large groups of German settlers arrive in Texas hill country; **1821** San Antonio comes under Mexican rule; **Dec. 1835** Alamo captured by Texans; **1836** Bexar (BAY-har) County formed, 128 counties later created from it; town becomes county seat; **Feb. 23–March 6, 1836** siege of Alamo by Santa Anna's Mexican forces leads to surrender, David Crockett and W. B. Travis among defenders killed; **1837** incorporated as a city; **1840** attack on Comanche peoples result in many killed in the "council house fight"; **1842** city briefly retaken by Mexican forces; **1852** St. Mary's University of San Antonio established; **Sept. 27, 1865** *San Antonio Express* newspaper founded; **1876** Fort Sam Houston established; **1877** first railroad reaches city; **1881** University of the Incarnate Word established; **1895** Our Lady of the Lake University of San Antonio established; **1896** county courthouse built; **1898** St. Philip's College (2-year) established; **1902** Trinity University moved from Tehuacana, founded in 1869; **March 23, 1908** actress Joan Crawford born (died 1977); **1913** Spoetzl Brewery founded by Bavarian immigrant Kosmos Spoetzl; **1914** San Antonio Zoo founded; **1916** Kelly Army Air Base established, closed 1993; **1918** Brooks Army Air Field established, becomes Air Force Base after World War II; **Sept. 4, 1918** *San Antonio News* newspaper founded; **1928** Stinson Municipal Airport established; **1929** 30-story Tower Life Building built; **1930** Randolph Army Air Base established to northeast, becomes Air Force Base

1948, closed 1992; **Nov. 14, 1930** astronaut Edward White II born, killed Jan. 27, 1967, in *Apollo* disaster; **1930s** Riverwalk built; **June 6, 1932** astronaut David Scott born; **Apr. 26, 1933** comedian Carol Burnett born; **March 21, March 4, 1939** actress Paula Prentiss born; **Oct. 7, 1943** government official Col. Oliver North born; **1945** Lackland Air Force Base established to southwest; **1946** San Antonio International Airport established to north; **1947** South Texas Medical Center established; **1950** Joe Freeman Coliseum opened; McNay Art Museum founded, opened 1954; **Dec. 6, 1955** singer Tish Hiñojosa born; **1968** Institute of Texas Cultures and Tower of the Americas built for World's Fair (Hemisfair); Henry B. Gonzalez Convention Center opened; **1969** University of Texas at San Antonio established to north-west; **June 21, 1970** Navy jet crashes into residential area, 7 killed, 12 injured; **Nov. 24, 1970** single-engine plane crashes to northeast killing all seven on board; **July 2, 1971** Navy deserter Robert Lee Jackson hijacks plane to Buenos Aires; **1981** San Antonio Museum of Art opened; **Apr. 1, 1983** San Antonio Missions National Historical Park established; **1987** Pope John Paul celebrates mass at San Fernando Cathedral; Palo Alto College (2-year) established; **1988** 32-story Weston Centre built; 38-story Marriott Rivercenter built; **Dec. 20, 1991** flash flooding kills 18; **2002** Brooks Air Force Base becomes first city-owned base with U.S. as tenant.

San Augustine   *San Augustine County   Eastern Texas, 48 mi/77 km east-northeast of Lufkin*

1716 Spanish mission Señora de los Dolores de los Ais established, abandoned 1719; **1721** mission restored, used as headquarters of Zecatecan missions; **1756** fort built; **1773** fort and mission abandoned; **1794** Antonio Leal builds house; **1801** American settlers arrive; **1833** town platted; **1836** San Augustine County formed; **1837** county organized; town incorporated, becomes county seat; **1860** slave labor used to dig 27-ft/8-m town well; **1890** fire destroys much of town; **1901** Gulf, Beaumont & Great Northern Railroad built; **1927** county courthouse built.

San Diego   *Duval County   Southern Texas, 50 mi/80 km west of Corpus Christi*

1858 Duval County formed; **c.1865** first ranches established following Civil War; **1876** county organized; town founded as county seat; **1878** 2,000 Federal troops called out to protect region from Native American and Mexican raiders; **1879** Corpus Christi, San Diego & Rio Grande Railroad reaches town; **Dec. 20, 1907** Democratic leader John Cleary assassinated, beginning of county political machine rule; **1916** county courthouse built; **1935** town incorporated.

San Felipe   *Austin County   Southeastern Texas, 45 mi/72 km west of Houston*

1823 town founded, serves as headquarters of Stephen A. Austin's colony; **1832–1833** Texas Convention held here; **1835** Consultation of 1835 held, meetings lead to

Declaration of Independence; **1836** Austin County formed; town burned and occupied by Santa Anna's forces; **1837** town incorporated, becomes county seat; **1848** county seat moved to Bellville; **1847** J. J. Josey Store built, now museum; **1940** Stephen A. Austin State Historic Park established.

San Marcos   *Hays County*   *South central Texas, 45 mi/72 km northeast of San Antonio*

1755 San Xavier Mission established, abandoned 1776; **1847** first settlers arrive; town founded; **1848** Hays County formed; town becomes county seat; **1851** town platted; **1877** incorporated as a city; **1881** International-Great Northern Railroad reaches town; **1899** Southwest Texas State University established; **1906** San Marcos Academy for boys founded; **1908** county courthouse built; **1942** San Marcos Air Force Base established.

San Patricio   *San Patricio County*   *Southern Texas, 25 mi/40 km west of Corpus Christi*

1830 town founded by John McMullen and James McGloin; **1836** San Patricio County formed; **Feb. 27, 1837** Battle of San Patricio fought, Texas forces under F. W. Johnson and Dr. James Grant, overwhelmed by Mexican forces under José Urrea, 10 Texans killed, 18 taken prisoner; **1837** county organized; town becomes county seat; **1845** county reorganized; town remains county seat; **1848** post office established; **1853** town incorporated; **1893** county seat moved to Sinton; **1901** town disincorporated; **1972** town reincorporated to block annexation by Corpus Christi.

San Saba   *San Saba County*   *Central Texas, 55 mi/89 km west of Killeen*

1854 town settled, founded on San Saba River; **1856** San Saba County formed; town becomes county seat; **1857** post office established; **1896** *San Saba Lancet* newspaper begins publication; **1911** Gulf, Colorado & Santa Fe Railroad reaches town; county courthouse built; **1940** town incorporated; **Sept. 15, 1946** actor Tommy Lee Jones born.

San Ygnacio   *Zapata County*   *Southern Texas, 38 mi/61 km south of Laredo, on Rio Grande*

1830 Fort Trevino built; **1876** post office established; **1890** Mexican revolutionaries conduct raids from here; **Jan. 15, 1916** Mexican troops raid town, clash with U.S. Cavalry; **1951** petition drive spares town's condemnation for Falcon Reservoir; movie *Viva Zapata* with Marlon Brando filmed here; **1953** Falcon Reservoir completed.

Sanderson   *Terrell County*   *Western Texas, 115 mi/185 km south of Odessa*

1881 railroad roundhouse built; **1882** Texas & New Orleans Railroad comes to town; **1905** Terrell County formed, named for legislator Alexander Watkins Terrell; town becomes county seat; *Sanderson Times* newspaper founded; **1906** county courthouse built; **June 11, 1965** flash flooding destroys most of town, 24 killed.

Sarita   *Kenedy County*   *Southern Texas, 45 mi/72 km south-southwest of Corpus Christi, near Gulf of Mexico*

1904 town founded, named for Sarita Kenedy, granddaughter of Mifflin Kenedy, partner of Richard King of King Ranch, largest cattle ranch in U.S; **1907** post office established; **1911** Willacy County formed from Cameron and Hidalgo counties; town becomes county seat; **1917** county courthouse built; **1921** Kenedy County formed from Willacy County; town becomes Kenedy County seat; Raymondville becomes Willacy County seat.

Seguin   *Guadalupe County*   *South central Texas, 33 mi/53 km east-northeast of San Antonio*

1838 town founded by Mathew Caldwell's Gonzales Rangers, named Walnut Springs; **1839** renamed (SEG-win) for Col. Juan N. Seguin, leader of only Texas-born Mexican division in Battle of San Jacinto; **1846** Guadalupe County formed; town becomes county seat; **1853** town incorporated; **1891** Texas Lutheran College, now University, established; **1920s** oil discovery boosts economy; **1935** county courthouse built.

Seminole   *Gaines County*   *Northwestern Texas, 75 mi/121 km southwest of Lubbock*

1836 Seminole peoples moved from Florida; **1876** Gaines County formed; **1905** county organized; town founded as county seat; **1906** county courthouse built; **1918** Midland & Northwestern Railroad reaches town; **Feb. 8, 1933** lowest temperature ever recorded in Texas reached, −23°F/−31°C; **1935** oil discovered; **1936** incorporated as a city; **May 2, 1948** country singer Larry Gatlin born; **Oct. 10, 1958** country singer Tanya Tucker born.

Seymour   *Baylor County*   *Northern Texas, 45 mi/72 km southwest of Wichita Falls*

1858 Baylor County formed; **1878** town settled on California Trail, at crossroads of trail to Dodge City; **1879** county organized; town becomes county seat; **1881** feud between ranchers and farmers, the latter comprised of mainly new settlers, culminates in shooting death of Judge G. R. Morris during meeting; **1884** county courthouse built; **1906** town incorporated; **Aug. 12, 1936** highest temperature ever recorded in Texas reached, 120°F/49°C.

Shamrock   *Wheeler County*   *Northwestern Texas, 85 mi/137 km east of Amarillo*

1890 post office established in dugout home of rancher George Nichels; **1879** county organized; Mobeetie becomes county seat; **1901** town settled; **1902** Chicago, Rock Island & Gulf Railroad arrives; **1903** town named by railroad in consideration for Irish settler George Nichels; *Wheeler County Texan* newspaper founded; **1906** county seat moved from to Shamrock, **1907** county seat moved to Wheeler, at center of county; **1911** town incorporated; **c.1920** Reynolds Hotel opens, now Pioneer West Museum; **1926** oil discovered in area; **1950s** natural gas discovered.

Sherman   *Grayson County*   *Northern Texas, 58 mi/ 93 km north of Dallas*

1835 first settlers arrive; **1846** Grayson County formed; town founded as county seat; **1849** incorporated as a town; **1858** incorporated as a city; **1872** Houston & Texas Central Railroad reaches town; **1875** two fires destroy town south of square; **1876** Austin College moved from Huntsville, established 1849; **Sept. 29, 1907** Western singer Gene Autry born at Tioga to southwest (died 1972). **Aug. 12, 1929** country singer Buck Owens born; **May 9, 1930** black man jailed for killing white woman burned to death in cell by mob; **1936** county courthouse built; **1941** Perrin Army Air Field established, becomes Air Force Base 1948, closed 1970; **1964** Grayson County College (2-year) established.

Sierra Blanca   *Hudspeth County*   *Western Texas, 80 mi/129 km southeast of El Paso*

Dec. 15, 1881 silver spike joins Texas & New Orleans and Texas & Pacific railroads into transcontinental rail line southeast of Sierra Blanca Mountain; town founded; **1882** Fort Hancock established, abandoned 1895; **1917** county organized, town becomes county seat; **1920** adobe county courthouse completed; **1992** 225 tons of treated New York City sewage dumped here per day in 90,000-ac/36,720-ha landfill.

Silverton   *Briscoe County*   *Northwestern Texas, 55 mi/89 km south-southeast of Amarillo*

1876 Briscoe County formed; **1892** county organized, town founded as county seat; stone jail built; **March 6, 1905** country singer, musician Bob Wills born at town of Turkey to east, the "King of Western Swing" (died 1975); **1927** county courthouse built; **1928** incorporated as a city; **May 15, 1957** tornado strikes town, 21 killed.

Sinton   *San Patricio County*   *Southern Texas, 19 mi/31 km north-northwest of Corpus Christi*

1836 San Patricio County formed; town of San Patricio becomes county seat; **1885** San Antonio & Aransas Pass Railroad built; town founded, named for David Sinton, partner in the Coleman-Fulton Pasture Company; **1893** county seat moved to Sinton; **1907** St. Louis, Brownsville & Mexico Railroad reaches town; **1916** incorporated as a town; **1928** county courthouse built; **1930s** oil and natural gas discovered; **1966** incorporated as a city.

Snyder   *Scurry County*   *Northwestern Texas, 70 mi/ 113 km west-northwest of Abilene*

1876 Scurry County formed, named for Confederate Gen. William R. Scurry; **1877** area settled by W. H. "Pete" Snyder; **1882** town platted by Snyder; **1884** county organized; town becomes county seat; **1907** incorporated as a city; **1908** Roscoe, Snyder & Pacific Railroad built; **1911** Panhandle & Santa Fe Railroad reaches city; county courthouse built; **1950** Canyon Reef Oil Field discovered; **1969** Western Texas College (2-year) established.

Sonora   *Sutton County*   *Western Texas, 62 mi/ 100 km south of San Angelo*

1879 area first settled; **1887** Sutton County formed, named for Indian fighter John S. Sutton; town founded; **1890** county organized; town becomes county seat; **1893** county courthouse built; **Sept. 12, 1902** fire destroys half of business district; **1915** Texas Ranch Experiment Station established; **1917** incorporated as a city; **1931** Panhandle & Santa Fe Railroad reaches city; **1960s** wool production gains importance.

Spearman   *Hansford County*   *Northwestern Texas, 80 mi/129 km north-northeast of Amarillo*

1876 Hansford County formed; **1889** county organized; Hansford becomes county seat; **1917** town founded, named for North Texas & Santa Fe Railroad executive Thomas C. Spearman; **1920** railroad completed; **1921** incorporated as a town; **1922** fire destroys business district; **1928** county seat moved to Spearman; **1931** county courthouse built.

Stanton   *Martin County*   *Western Texas, 18 mi/ 29 km east-northeast of Midland*

1876 Martin County formed, named for Texas patriot Wylie Martin; **1881** town settled by German Catholics, named Marienfeld; Texas & Pacific Railroad built; **1884** county organized, town becomes county seat; **1885** Carmelite monastery opened; **1886** drought, blizzard force many settlers to leave; **1890** Protestant settlers arrive, town renamed for Edwin M. Stanton, secretary of war under President Lincoln; **1894** monastery converted to convent; **1904** *Stanton Courier* founded; **1925** town incorporated; **1951** Stanton Oil Field begins production; **1975** county courthouse built.

Stephenville   *Erath County*   *North central Texas, 60 mi/97 km southwest of Fort Worth*

1854 first permanent settlers arrive; town founded, named for landowner John Stephens; **1856** Erath County formed; town becomes county seat; **1859** incorporated as a town; **1869** Victorian cottage built, part of Historical House Museum; **c.1885** coal mining begins; **1889** Fort Worth & Rio Grande Railroad built; incorporated as a city; **1892** county courthouse built; **1893** Tarleton State College (University) established; **1918** oil boom begins, ends 1920.

Sterling City *Sterling County* *Western Texas,
40 mi/64 km northwest of San Angelo*

1891 Sterling County formed, named for first settler Capt.
W. S. Sterling; **1891** town founded as county seat on
North Concho River; **1910** Santa Fe Railroad reaches
town; **1938** county courthouse built; **1955** town incorporated.

Stinnett *Hutchinson County* *Northwestern Texas,
35 mi/56 km north-northeast of Amarillo*

1864 in First Battle of Adobe Walls, troops of Col. Kit
Carson, in his last battle, narrowly succeeds in defeating
Kiowas and Comanches; **1874** Second Battle of Adobe
Walls, Comanches led by Quanah Parker and Lone Wolf
attack buffalo hunters' camp, party of 29 surrounded,
facing defeat, Cheyenne appear on second day in support
of Comanches, Billy Dixon's famous shot kills Native
American a mile away, shocks natives into withdrawal;
1876 Hutchinson County formed; **1899** Isaac McCormick
House built by first settler; **1901** county organized;
Plemons becomes county seat; **1926** town founded as
county seat; **1927** town incorporated; **1928** county courthouse completed.

Stonewall *Gillespie County* *South central Texas,
55 mi/89 km west of Austin*

1870 area settled; **1875** post office established, originally
named Millville; **1882** post office moved to present town
site, town renamed; **Aug. 27, 1908** Lyndon Baines
Johnson, 36th President, born (died Jan. 22, 1973).

Stratford *Sherman County* *Northwestern Texas,
75 mi/121 km north of Amarillo, near Oklahoma*

1876 Sherman County formed from Bexar County; **1885**
area settled; **1889** county organized; Coldwater becomes
county seat; **1901** town founded on Chicago, Rock Island
& Gulf Railroad on land donated by Walter Colton; **July
1901** Stratford succeeds Coldwater as county seat after
bitter dispute requiring state militia intervention; **1907**
incorporated as a city; **1922** county courthouse built; **1928**
Panhandle & Santa Fe Railroad built.

Sulphur Springs *Hopkins County* *Northern
Texas, 70 mi/113 km northeast of Dallas*

1843 David Hopkins family arrives from Indiana, become
county's first white settlers; **1846** Hopkins County formed;
Tarrant becomes county seat; **1859** town founded, named
Bright Star; **1870** incorporated as a town, renamed for
mineral springs; **1871** county seat moved to Sulphur
Springs; **1881** Central College established, becomes
Eastman College 1895; **1894** county courthouse completed; **1917** incorporated as a city; **1920s** dairying
industry established.

Sweetwater *Nolan County* *Western Texas, 40 mi/
64 km west of Abilene*

1876 Nolan County formed; **1877** town founded by Billy
Knight; **1881** county organized; town becomes county
seat; **1882** Texas & Pacific Railroad built; town moved
2 mi/3.2 km northwest; *Advance* newspaper founded; **Feb.
1883** saloon acting as informal bank raided, leads to 11
murder indictments against bandits; **1884** incorporated as
a town; **1902** incorporated as a city; **1970** Texas State
Technical College (2-year) established; **1977** county courthouse built.

Tahoka *Lynn County* *Northwestern Texas, 30 mi/
48 km south of Lubbock*

1876 Lynn County formed, named for George
Washington Lynn, killed at the Alamo; **1903** county
organized; town founded, named for nearby natural lake,
Native American name for clear or fresh water; **1906** town
becomes county seat; **1915** town incorporated; **1916**
county courthouse built; **1940s** cotton production begins
in area.

Tascosa *Oldham County* *See **Vega***

Temple *Bell County* *Central Texas, 60 mi/97 km
north-northeast of Austin*

1880 town established on Gulf, Colorado & Santa Fe and
Missouri, Kansas & Texas railroads; **1882** incorporated as
a town; **1884** incorporated as a city; **1926** Temple College
(2-year) established; **Feb. 6, 1931** actor Rip Torn born
(died 1999); **1989** city designated "Wildflower Capital of
Texas."

Terlingua *Brewster County* *Western Texas,
180 mi/290 km southwest of Odessa*

1860 first mercury claims staked; **1890** first productive
mercury claim discovered; **1893** Chisos Quicksilver Mine
opened; **1905** post office established; population peaks at
2,000; **June 20, 1935** Big Bend National Park established
to east; **1945** Chisos Mine closed; **Nov. 1967** first annual
Terlingua Chili Cookoff held.

Texarkana *Bowie County* *Northeastern Texas,
160 mi/257 km east-northeast of Dallas, near Red River*

1542 Spaniards led by Hernando Cortez explore region;
1840 first settlers arrive; **1850s** town founded; **c.1860**
steamboat *Texarkana* makes trips on Red River; **Nov.
24, 1868** ragtime composer Scott Joplin born in rural Cass
County to southwest (died 1917); **1873** Texas & Pacific
Railroad reaches state line from west; **Dec. 1873** town
platted on Texas side of state line by railroad; **Jan. 1874**
Cairo & Fulton Railroad reaches state line from Arkansas;
town platted on Arkansas side of state line; **1876**
Texarkana, Texas, incorporated as a town; **1880**
Texarkana, Arkansas, incorporated as a town; **Oct. 5,
1908** playwright Joshua Logan born (died 1988); **1909** U.S.

District Courthouse built, later used as Regional Arts Center; **1924** the Saenger Theatre opened, now Perot Theatre; **1927** Texarkana College (2-year) established; **1929** Union Station built; **June 27, 1930** businessman, presidential candidate H. (Henry) Ross Perot born; **1971** Texas A & M University, Texarkana Campus, established.

Texas City *Galveston County* *Southeastern Texas, 35 mi/56 km southeast of Houston, on Gulf of Mexico*

1893 town founded as Shoal Point; shipping channel dredged; **Sept. 8, 1900** town damaged by Galveston Hurricane; **1911** incorporated as a city, renamed Texas City; **1913** U.S. Army establishes camp, staging point during Mexican Revolution; **1915** camp destroyed in hurricane, nine killed, moved to San Antonio; **1934** oil refinery established; **1940** tin processing plant opened; **Apr. 16, 1947** ship loaded with nitrate explodes at pier causing fires in dock area and city, 576 killed; **1967** College of the Mainland (2-year) established; **May 30, 1978** oil refinery explosion kills 4, injures 11.

Throckmorton *Throckmorton County* *Northern Texas, 60 mi/97 km southwest of Wichita Falls*

1858 Throckmorton County formed from Fannin County, named for early settler Dr. William E. Throckmorton; **1879** county organized, town founded as county seat; **1890** county courthouse built; **1917** town incorporated.

Tilden *McMullen County* *Southern Texas, 65 mi/105 km south of San Antonio, on Frio River*

1858 McMullen County formed, named for colonist John McMullen; **1877** county organized; town founded as county seat, named for 1876 Democratic presidential candidate Samuel J. Tilden; **1879** ferry established; **1930** county courthouse built; **1982** Choke Canyon Lake formed by dam on Frio River to east.

Tioga *Grayson County* See **Sherman (1907)**

Tulia *Swisher County* *Northwestern Texas, 45 mi/72 km south of Amarillo*

1876 Swisher County formed; **18887** town founded by W. G. Connor, named for Tule [sp] Creek; **1890** town becomes county seat; **1909** incorporated as a city; county courthouse built, sheathed in brick fascia 1962.

Turkey *Hall County* See **Silverton (1905)**

Tyler *Smith County* *Eastern Texas, 90 mi/145 km east-southeast of Dallas*

1846 Smith County formed, named for Gen. James Smith, served under Sam Houston; town founded as county seat, named for Pres. John Tyler; **1850** incorporated as a town; **1859** Goodman-Le Grand Home built by wealthy

bachelor Gallatin Smith; **1860s** Camp Ford used as Union prisoner of war camp; **1874** Houston & Great Northern Railroad reaches town; **1907** incorporated as a city; **1916** first East Texas Fair held; **1926** Tyler Junior College established; **1930s** East Texas oil boom boosts economy; **Oct. 1933** first annual Texas Rose Festival held; **1938** Caldwell Zoo established; **1954** county courthouse built; **Nov. 7, 1962** con man Billie Sol Estes, friend of Vice-Pres. Lyndon B. Johnson, convicted to eight years for swindling, theft, antitrust violations; **1971** University of Texas at Tyler established.

Uvalde *Uvalde County* *South central Texas, 75 mi/121 km west-southwest of San Antonio*

1790 Capt. Juan de Ugalde of Mexican Army suppresses Native Americans in region; **1850** Uvalde County formed, named for Capt. Ugalde [sp]; **1853** area settled; **1855** town founded, named Encina; **1856** town renamed Uvalde; **Nov. 22, 1868** John Nance Garner born, vice president under Pres. Franklin D. Roosevelt (died 1967); **1888** incorporated as a town; **1891** Grand Opera House built; **Oct. 31, 1912** actress Dale Evans born, wife of cowboy star Roy Rogers (died 2001); **1921** incorporated as a city; **1927** county courthouse built; **1946** Southwest Texas Junior College established.

Van Horn *Culberson County* *Western Texas, 110 mi/177 km southeast of El Paso*

1859 town founded at Van Horn Wells on California Trail, named for Col. J. J. Van Horn; **1911** Culberson County formed; **1912** county organized, town becomes county seat; **1945** town incorporated; **1965** county courthouse built.

Vega *Oldham County* *Northwestern Texas, 35 mi/56 km west of Amarillo*

1870s area settled; **1876** Oldham County formed from Bexar County, named for Confederate statesman Williamson S. Oldham; **1880** county organized; Tascosa becomes county seat; **1900** Chicago, Rock Island & Gulf Railroad built; town founded; **1915** county seat moved to Vega; county courthouse built; **1927** town incorporated; **1939** Maverick Boys' Ranch for underprivileged youths established at old courthouse at Tascosa to north by businessman Cal Farley.

Vernon *Wilbarger County* *Northern Texas, 45 mi/72 km west-northwest of Wichita Falls*

1858 Wilbarger County formed, named for Mathias and Josiah Wilbarger, latter scalped by Native Americans while surveying 1833, survived 12 years; **1870s** Western Trail extended through area; **1877** trading post established at Condon Springs; **1880** town founded, named Eagle Flats; **1881** county organized; town becomes county seat; **1885** Fort Worth & Denver City Railroad reaches town; **1889** incorporated as a city, renamed; **Aug. 20, 1905** jazz trombonist Jack Teagarden born (died 1964); **1928** county courthouse built; **1941** Victory Field Army Air Base opened (closed 1944); **1970** Vernon Regional Junior College established; **Apr. 10, 1979** 12 killed locally in series of tornadoes.

Victoria *Victoria County* *Southern Texas, 100 mi/ 161 km southeast of San Antonio*

1824 Don Martín de León founds town with 41 Spanish families, named for Gen. Guadalupe Victoria (1789–1843), Mexico's first president 1824; **1836** Victoria County formed; **March 20, 1836** Battle of Coleto Creek to west, Col. James W. Fannin surrenders to Mexicans on offer of Gen. José Urrea to intercede on his behalf, Santa Anna overrules him, all 342 of Fannin's men executed March 27 at Goliad; **1837** county organized; town becomes county seat; **1839** town incorporated; **May 1846** *The Advocate* newspaper founded; **1858** first Gulf Coast Fair held, suspended 1862, resumed 1875; **1861** San Antonio & Pacific Railroad reaches town, destroyed by Union forces 1863, rebuilt 1866; **1892** county courthouse built; **1893** opera house opened; **1925** Victoria College (2-year) established; **1932** Nave Museum built by widow of painter Royston Nave (1886–1931); **1957** Victoria Regional Airport established; **1962** Victoria Barge Canal completed; **Jan. 18, 1972** private jet hits utility pole, all nine killed; **1973** University of Houston, Victoria Campus, established; **May 14, 2003** 18 illegal immigrants from Mexico found suffocated in panel truck.

Waco *McLennan County* *Central Texas, 87 mi/ 140 km south of Dallas, on Brazos River*

1542 remnant members of De Soto expedition travel through area; **1837** Fort Fisher built for Texas Rangers; **1845** Neil McLennan arrives with family, build first house; **1849** more white settlers arrive; town founded, named for Waco peoples; **1850** McLennan County formed; town becomes county seat; **1856** town incorporated; **1858** Earle-Harrison mansion built; **1870** suspension bridge built across Brazos River on Chisholm Trail; **1871** Waco & Northwestern Railroad reaches town; **Aug. 19, 1877** U.S. Sen. Tom Connally born (died 1963); **1880s** St. Louis-Southwestern and Missouri, Kansas & Texas railroads reach town; **1885** soft drink Dr. Pepper first blended; **1886** Baylor University moved from Independence, established 1845; **1902** county courthouse built; **Sept. 19, 1905** lawyer, 1973 Watergate scandal prosecutor Leon Jaworski born (died 1982); **1920s** Ku Klux Klan gains control of city affairs; **Apr. 14, 1945** comedian Steve Martin born; **1948** Connally Air Force Base established, closed 1966; **May 11, 1953** tornado destroys city, 114 killed, 145 injured; **1958** Lake Waco dam built on Bosque River; **1965** Texas State Technical College (2-year), Waco-Marshall Campus, established; McLennan College (2-year) established; **1976** Texas Ranger Hall of Fame opened; **1993** Cameron Park Zoo opened; **Feb. 28, 1993** 4 agents killed, 16 injured in shootout at Branch Davidian cult compound, 2 cult members killed, standoff begins; **Apr. 19, 1993** siege at compound ends as agents move in, apparent self-started fire destroys compound killing 72 cult members, including leader David Koresh.

Washington-on the-Brazos *Washington County* *South central Texas, 60 mi/97 km northwest of Houston*

1822 Brazos River ferry established; **1825** settlers begin arriving; **1834** town founded; **Nov. 1, 1835** Texas declares independence from Mexico; **1836** Washington County formed; town becomes county seat; **March 2, 1836** Texas Declaration of Independence ratified; **Sept. 5, 1836** Sam Houston chosen as first Texas president; **1837** Texas capital located at Houston; **June 1837** incorporated as a town; **Dec. 1837** incorporated as a city; **1839** capital moved to Austin; **1842** town becomes capital; **1844** county seat moved to Brenham; **Dec. 29, 1845** Texas enters U.S. as 28th state; Houston becomes state capital; **1855** anti-Catholic Know-Nothing Party becomes active; **1858** Houston & Texas Central Railroad bypasses town; **c.1880** town falls into decline; **1912** last of town's structures destroyed by fire; **1936** Washington-on-the-Brazos State Historical Park established; **1970** Star of the Republic Museum opened.

Waxahachie *Ellis County* *Northern Texas, 17 mi/ 27 km south of Dallas*

1846 town settled; **1849** Ellis County formed; **1850** town becomes seat; **1871** Waxahachie Tap Railroad built; incorporated as a town; **1887** Missouri, Kansas & Texas Railroad reaches town; **1896** county courthouse completed; **1905** Nicholas P. Sims Public Library built; **1906** Burlington & Rock Island Railroad built; **1911** interurban train service begins to Dallas and Waco, ends 1948; **1933** incorporated as a city; **1942** Southwestern Bible Institute founded; **Oct. 19, 1993** Congress halts work on Superconducting Supercollider (SSC) atom smashing unit.

Weatherford *Parker County* *North central Texas, 27 mi/43 km west of Fort Worth*

1855 Parker County formed; Oliver Loving, "Dean of the Texas Trail Drivers," settles here from Kentucky; **1856** town founded as county seat, named for Jefferson Weatherford, member of Texas Senate; **1858** town incorporated; **1867** Loving wounded in Native American attack while on cattle drive, travels five days without food before dying at Fort Sumner, New Mexico, his son travels 600 mi/966 km to bury him at Weatherford; **1869** Weatherford Institute established, becomes Weatherford College (2-year) 1884; **May 1880** Texas & Pacific Railroad begins service; **1886** fourth county courthouse built; **1887** Santa Fe Railroad reaches town; **1900** watermelon production becomes important; **Dec. 1, 1913** actress Mary Martin born (died 1990); **Sept. 21, 1931** TV actor Larry Hagman born.

Wellington *Collingsworth County* *Northwestern Texas, 90 mi/145 km east-southeast of Amarillo*

1876 Collingsworth County formed, named for James Collinsworth [sp]; **1890** county organized; town founded as county seat on Rocking Chair Ranch, called "Nobility Ranch" by locals for English owners Sir Dudley Coutts Marjoribanks and John Campbell Hamilton Golden; town named for Arthur Wellesley, Duke of Wellington (1769–1852); **1891** post office established; **1902** cotton gin established; *Wellington Times* newspaper founded; **1910** incorporated as a city; **1910** Wichita Falls & Northwestern Railroad reaches town; **1931** county courthouse built.

West Columbia *Brazoria County* *Southern Texas, 45 mi/72 km south-southwest of Houston*

1823 town of Marion founded east of Brazos River, becomes East Columbia; **1826** West Columbia founded by Josiah Hughes west of river; **Sept.-Dec. 1836** town briefly serves as capital of Texas Republic; **Oct. 22, 1836** Sam Houston inaugurated as Texas Republic's first president; **Dec. 27, 1836** Stephen F. Austin, the "Father of Texas," secretary of state, dies (born 1793); **1840** Bethel Presbyterian Church built; **Jan. 15, 1918** oil gusher at Tyndall-Hogg No. 2 Well produces 600 barrels a day, marks discovery of West Columbia Oil Field; **1938** incorporated as a city.

Wharton *Wharton County* *Southern Texas, 55 mi/89 km southwest of Houston*

1846 Wharton County formed, named for William H. and John A. Wharton; **1847** town founded as county seat; **1881** New York, Texas & Mexico Railroad reaches town; **1890** *Wheeler Independent* newspaper founded; **1890s** Swedish, German and Czech immigrants settle in area; **1894** Sheriff Hamilton B. Dickson killed while pursuing murder suspect, monument built; **1899** Gulf, Colorado & Santa Fe Railroad arrives; **1902** incorporated as a city; **Oct. 31, 1931** newscaster Dan Rather born; **1935** county courthouse built; **1946** Wharton County Junior College established.

Wheeler *Wheeler County* *Northwestern Texas, 85 mi/137 km east-northeast of Amarillo, near Oklahoma*

1875 Fort Elliott established; **1876** Wheeler County formed, named for Royal T. Wheeler of Texas state supreme court; **1879** Mobeetie becomes county seat; **1880s** town founded; **1890** fort abandoned; **1906** county seat moved temporarily to Shamrock; **1907** county seat moved to Wheeler; **1920s** oil discovered in county; **1925** town incorporated; county courthouse built; **March 15, 1930** astronaut Alan Bean born.

Wichita Falls *Wichita County* *Northern Texas, 105 mi/169 km northwest of Fort Worth*

1858 Wichita County formed; **1870s** area settled; **1876** town platted; **1882** county organized; town becomes county seat; Fort Worth & Denver City Railroad reaches town; **1886** flood on Wichita River destroys parts of town and the falls (54 ft/16 m high) for which town was named; **1889** incorporated as a city; **1904** *Times* newspaper founded; **1916** county courthouse built; **1919** oil boom begins; **1922** Midwestern State University established; **June 3, 1936** author Larry McMurtry born; **1937** second oil boom begins; **Feb. 28, 1939** actor Tommy Tune born; **1941** Sheppard Army Air Field established, becomes Air Force Base 1948; **Apr. 3, 1964** 7 killed, 100 injured as tornado strikes city; **1966** Lake Arrowhead formed by dam on Little Wichita River to southeast; **Apr. 10, 1979** tornado destroys much of city, 41 killed, 9 unconfirmed dead; **1987** Wichita River falls recreated at Lucy Park.

Wink *Winkler County* See **Kermit (1936)**

Winters *Runnels County* See **Ballinger (1896)**

Woodville *Tyler County* *Eastern Texas, 50 mi/80 km north-northwest of Beaumont*

1846 Tyler County formed, named for Pres. John Tyler; **Jan. 1847** town founded as county seat, named for Gov. George T. Wood; **1850s** Alabama-Coushatta Indian Reservation established; **1880s** Texas & New Orleans Railroad extended to town; **1891** county courthouse built; **c.1900** sawmilling becomes dominant industry, through 1940s; **1929** incorporated as a city; **Oct. 11, 1974** Big Thicket National Preserve established to west, south and east.

Zapata *Zapata County* *Southern Texas, 45 mi/72 km south of Laredo, on Rio Grande*

1750 settlement founded by José Vázquez Borrego, named Hacienda Dolores; **1770** town settled by people from Revilla, Guerrero, Mexico, named for pioneer Antonio Zapata; **1852** Fort Drum military post established; **1858** Zapata County formed; town becomes county seat; **1870s** town made duty free zone, eliminated 1903; **1953** International Falcon Reservoir formed by Falcon Dam on Rio Grande; town relocated; county courthouse built.

Utah

West central U.S. Capital and major city: Salt Lake City.

The Mormons established the state of Deseret in 1849, which extended into present-day Nevada. Utah Territory was created by Congress September 9, 1850, with Brigham Young as first governor. Nevada separated from Utah in 1861. Utah entered the Union as the 45th state January 4, 1896.

Utah is divided into 29 counties. Municipalities are classified as towns and cities. There are no townships. See Introduction.

American Fork *Utah County   North central Utah, 25 mi/40 km south of Salt Lake City, near Utah Lake*

1820s trappers Etienne Provost and his men enter area; **1850** town founded on American Fork River; **1853** town incorporated; **1873** Utah Southern (Union Pacific) Railroad reaches town; **1882** Denver & Rio Grande Western Railroad reaches town; **Oct. 14, 1922** Timpanogos Cave National Monument established to northeast; **1968** American Fork Public Library built; **1993** American Fork Symphony founded.

Bagley *Box Elder County   See **Ogden (1944)***

Beaver *Beaver County   Southwestern Utah, 172 mi/ 277 km south-southwest of Salt Lake City*

1856 Beaver County formed; area settled by Mormons from Parowan at request of Brigham Young; town founded as county seat; **1860s** woolen mill founded; **Apr. 13, 1861** outlaw Robert Leroy Parker (Butch Cassidy) born, dies in shootout in Bolivia Nov. 7, 1908; **1867** town incorporated; Cove Fort built to north in Millard County as Native American defense, closed 1900; **1876** John D. Lee convicted here, leader of Mountain Meadow Massacre near Enterprise 75 mi/121 km to southwest, executed by shooting at massacre site 1877; **1882** county courthouse built; **Aug. 19, 1906** Philo T. Farnsworth born, inventor of television, in log cabin near Indian Creek built by his grandfather (died 1971).

Bingham Canyon *Salt Lake County   North central Utah, 20 mi/32 km southwest of Salt Lake City*

1848 Mormons Thomas and Sanford Bingham establish farm here; town founded; **1863** rich deposits of gold and silver discovered; **1868** Clay brothers strike it rich at Clay Bar Gold Mine; **1873** Bingham & Camp Floyd Railroad reaches town; **1896** first copper shipment made; **1903** Utah Copper Company organized, plant built 1904; **1915** Kennecott Copper Corporation acquires interest in Utah Copper, acquires company 1936; **c.1950** expansion of mining forces abandonment of town site.

Blanding *San Juan County   Southeastern Utah, 150 mi/241 km southeast of Salt Lake City*

c.825 AD Anasazi people occupy area, through c.1220; **1880s** area first settled by whites; **1897** site visited by Mormon brothers Walter C. and Joseph Lyman; **1905** irrigation water delivered from Abajo Mountains through efforts of Walter Lyman; town founded, originally named Grayson; **Apr. 16, 1908** Natural Bridges National Monument established to west; **May 30, 1910** Rainbow Bridge National Monument established near Colorado River c.85 mi/137 km to southwest; **1915** town incorporated, renamed in exchange for offer of library by Easterner Thomas W. Bicknell, named for wife's maiden name (Utah town of Thurber also accepted offer, renamed Bicknell); **Oct. 27, 1972** Glen Canyon National Recreation Area established to west, surrounds large Lake Powell, formed by Glen Canyon Dam at Page, Arizona, recreation area extends into Arizona; **1978** Edge of Cedars State Park established, preserves Anasazi ruins; College of Eastern Utah, San Juan Campus, established.

Bluff *San Juan County   Southeastern Utah, 168 mi/ 270 km southeast of Salt Lake City*

c.1300 AD area occupied by Basket Maker and Cliff Dweller cultures; **1879** survey party sent into region by Mormon Church; **1880** town founded on San Juan River; **1886** livestock herds replace failed efforts to farm area;

675

March 2, 1923 Hovenweep National Monument established to east, extends into Colorado.

Bluffdale   *Salt Lake County*   *See* **Draper (1926)**

Bountiful   *Davis County*   *Northern Utah, 8 mi/ 12.9 km north of Salt Lake City, near Great Salt Lake*

1847 area first settled by Mormon named Perrigrine Sessions; town founded, named Sessions Settlement; **1855** town renamed; region invaded by grasshoppers, most crops destroyed overnight; **c.1860** Mormon First Ward Chapel built; **1892** town incorporated; **1976** Performing Arts Center established; **May 1983** flooding and mudslides damage town, also nearby Farmington and Salt Lake City, total 32 killed; **1994** LDS Temple completed.

Brigham City   *Box Elder County*   *Northern Utah, 36 mi/58 km north of Salt Lake City*

1851 town founded near Bear River by Mormon settlers, named Box Elder; **1853** Lorenzo Snow brings 50 Mormon families to area, establishes cooperative community; **1855** peaches introduced as new crop; **1856** Box Elder County formed; town becomes county seat, renamed for Mormon leader Brigham Young; **1857** county courthouse completed; **1864** Brigham City Mercantile established by Lorenzo Snow; **1869** town incorporated; **1877** Brigham Young delivers final public speech here; **1879** financial failures lead co-op to sell interests; **1928** Bear River Migratory Bird Refuge established to west; **1957** Thiokol Chemical Corporation plant built.

Castle Dale   *Emery County*   *Central Utah, 115 mi/ 185 km south-southeast of Salt Lake City*

1875 Orange Seely becomes area's first settler; town founded on Cottonwood Creek, branch of San Rafael River, originally named Orangeville; **1880** Emery County formed; town becomes county seat; **1889** Emery Stake Academy founded, sold 1922; **1890s** area plagued by Robbers Roost, nearby haven for Butch Cassidy's gang; **1892** county courthouse built; **1900** town incorporated; **1937** highway bridge built across San Rafael River opening areas to south; **1939** county courthouse built; **1956** Emery County Reclamation Project begun; **1966** Joe's Valley Reservoir completed to west on San Rafael River; **1978** completion of Hunter Power Plant leads to reopening of coal mines.

Cedar City   *Iron County*   *Southwestern Utah, 220 mi/354 km south-southwest of Salt Lake City*

1851 town settled by English, Scottish and Welsh miners to work coal and iron mines; town founded; **1852** large group of Mormons arrive; **1858** foundry closed; **1868** town incorporated; **1897** Southern Utah University established, originally Branch Normal School; **1923** Union Pacific Railroad reaches town; **1930** Cedar City Mormon Chapel built; **Aug. 22, 1933** Cedar Breaks

National Monument established to east; **1961** first Utah Shakespearean Festival held.

Clearfield   *Davis County*   *Northern Utah, 27 mi/ 43 km north of Salt Lake City, near Great Salt Lake*

1869 Utah Central Railroad reaches site; **1877** town founded by Mormon settlers, originally named Sandridge; **1884** East Canyon Dam completed to west for water supply; **1892** Woods Cross Canning Co-op established; **1905** Bamberger Electric Railroad arrives from Salt Lake City; **1922** town incorporated; **1940** Hill Army Air Base established, become Air Force Base 1948; **1942** Clearfield Navy Depot established, closed 1962.

Coalville   *Summit County*   *Northern Utah, 28 mi/ 45 km east-northeast of Salt Lake City*

1854 Summit County formed; **1858** town founded as county seat by William H. Smith; **1859** first coal mine opened by Thomas Rhodes; **1867** town incorporated; **1904** county courthouse completed; **1940s** most coal mines closed.

Corinne   *Box Elder County*   *Northern Utah, 57 mi/ 92 km north of Salt Lake City, near Great Salt Lake*

1869 Union Pacific Railroad built; town founded on Bear River by Mark A. Gilmore and five other "gentiles," declared "off limits" to Mormons, named for daughter of Gen. J. A. Williamson; **1870** town incorporated; Methodist Church built, first non-Mormon church in Utah; town becomes "Gentile Capital of Utah"; **1872** diphtheria epidemic kills hundreds; **1876** many residents leave after Native Americans raid town; **1877** Mormon settlers begin to move in.

Delta   *Millard County*   *Central Utah, 102 mi/164 km south-southwest of Salt Lake City*

1906 Melville Irrigation Project organized; town founded on Sevier River, named Melville; alfalfa production begins on irrigated land; **1911** town incorporated, renamed Delta; **1917** Utah Sugar Company established, beet sugar refinery built; **1940s** fluorspar mining begins; **Sept. 1942** Topaz Japanese Internment Camp established, closed Aug. 1945.

Draper   *Salt Lake and Utah counties*   *North central Utah, 15 mi/24 km south of Salt Lake City*

1849 Ebenezer Brown becomes first settler; **1854** town founded on Jordan River, named Draperville for Mormon elder William Draper III; **1926** Camp Williams Military Reservation established to southwest near Bluffdale, summer training base for Utah National Guard; **1930s** town becomes major egg producer for Utah, last egg farm razed 1990s; **1940** Utah State Prison moved from Salt Lake City to new facility at Point of Mountain; **1978** incorporated as a city.

Duchesne *Duchesne County Northeastern Utah, 86 mi/138 km southeast of Salt Lake City*

1861 Uintah Indian Reservation established by President Lincoln; **1904** town founded in large Uintah and Ouray Indian Reservation; **1915** Duchesne County formed from Wasatch County; town becomes county seat; **1917** incorporated as a city; **1970** Starvation Reservoir formed by dam to west on Strawberry River; **1997** county courthouse built.

Echo *Summit County Northern Utah, 25 mi/40 km northeast of Salt Lake City*

1847 Mormons enter Utah through Echo Canyon from Wyoming; **1854** town founded on Weber (WEE-ber) River; **1857** in Echo Canyon War, Mormons erect defenses against Federal troops sent to suppress perceived Mormon Rebellion, troops pass through peacefully 1858; **1866** grasshopper plague devastates crops; **1869** Union Pacific Railroad reaches town; **1871** flour mill built; **1931** Echo Reservoir formed by dam on Weber River to south.

Enterprise *Washington County Southern Utah, 237 mi/381 km south-southwest of Salt Lake City*

Sept. 11, 1857 Mormons led by John D. Lee massacre 120 non-Mormons from Arkansas, sparing 17 children under seven years old, at Mountain Meadows to south; **1862** town of Hebron founded as stock-raising center; **1891** settlers arrive to build Enterprise Reservoir on Shoal Creek; **1893** new town of Enterprise founded; **Nov. 17, 1902** earthquake damages Hebron, residents move to Enterprise; **1912** Ward Meeting House built; **1913** incorporated as a city.

Ephraim *Sanpete County Central Utah, 96 mi/155 km south of Salt Lake City*

1853 area settled by Danish Mormons; **1854** town founded; **1866** town plays important role in defense of settlers during Black Hawk War; **1868** incorporated as a city; **1872** Mormon Tabernacle built; **1883** Snow College (2-year) established; **1976** first Scandinavian Festival held.

Escalante *Garfield County Southern Utah, 203 mi/327 km south of Salt Lake City*

1876 town founded by Mormon settlers, named for Spanish explorer Father Francisco Silvestre Velez de Escalante; **1903** incorporated as a town; **June 10, 1963** truck carrying Boy Scouts plunges down embankment killing 12, including a woman reporter; **Sept. 18, 1996** Pres. Bill Clinton establishes by proclamation Grand Staircase-Escalante National Monument, 1,700,000 ac/688,500 ha, stops Kaiparowits Plateau coal mining activities.

Eureka *Juab County Central Utah, 55 mi/89 km south-southwest of Salt Lake City*

1870 silver mining begins in Tintic Valley; town founded; **1878** Utah Southern Railroad built; **1885** *Eureka Reporter* newspaper founded; **1891** Denver & Rio Grande Western Railroad reaches town; **1892** incorporated as a city; **1899** city hall built; **1908** new silver boom begins, smelter built at nearby Knightsville; **1957** last major silver mine closed.

Farmington *Davis County Northern Utah, 18 mi/29 km north of Salt Lake City, on Great Salt Lake*

1848 area settled by Mormons; town founded by Hector C. Haight, named North Cottonwood; **1850** Davis County formed; town becomes county seat, renamed Farmington; **1892** incorporated as a city; **1896** Mormon Farmington Rock Chapel built; Lagoon Resort developed by Simon Bamberger; **1898** county courthouse built; **1923** flash flood descends from Wasatch Range, seven killed, again 1930; **May 1983** flooding causes mudslides, also in Bountiful and Salt Lake City, 32 killed total.

Farr West *Weber County Northern Utah, 6 mi/9.7 km northwest of Ogden*

1858 town founded, named for pioneers Lorin Farr and Chauncey West; first irrigation canal built; **1891** LDS Church built, destroyed by fire 1944; **1896** Union Pacific Railroad reaches town; **1898** sugar beet production introduced with irrigation systems; **1980** incorporated as a city. [see also Far (Farr) West, Missouri]

Fillmore *Millard County Central Utah, 125 mi/201 km south-southwest of Salt Lake City*

1850 Utah Territory created, replacing state of Deseret established by Mormons; **1851** town founded as territorial capital by Brigham Young; **1852** Millard County formed; town becomes county seat; **Oct. 26, 1853** topographical survey team led by John W. Gunnison attacked by Pahvant Utes, seven killed; **1855** first wing of statehouse completed, used only for 1855–1856 session; **1856** territorial capital moved to Salt Lake City; **June 3, 1863** U.S. Sen. William H. King born (died 1949); **1867** incorporated as a city; **1919** county courthouse built.

Fort Duchesne *Uintah County Northeastern Utah, 108 mi/174 km east-southeast of Salt Lake City*

1832 fort built to east by Antoine Robidoux, destroyed by Native Americans 1844; **1861** Uintah and Ouray Indian Reservation established by President Lincoln for Ute peoples; town founded as reservation headquarters; **1886** Fort Duchesne established, site chosen by Gen. George Crook; **Sept. 1912** fort closed.

Green River *Emery County Southeastern Utah, 150 mi/241 km southeast of Salt Lake City*

1869 John Wesley Powell expedition departs from Green River, Wyoming, to north, makes its way down Green

River to Colorado River, thence through Grand Canyon; **1878** town founded on Green River; **1882** Denver & Rio Grande Western Railroad beaches town; **1911** incorporated as a city; **1917** area's melon-growing industry begins.

Gunnison *Sanpete County* *Central Utah, 108 mi/ 174 km south of Salt Lake City*

1861 town founded, named for Capt. John W. Gunnison, U.S. topographical engineer; **1863** sawmill established; **1893** incorporated as a town; **1864–1865** raids on whites called Black Hawk War conducted by Utes in retaliation for smallpox epidemic; **1911** Jewish cooperative colony established to west, disbanded by 1920; **1990** Central Utah Correctional Facility established.

Heber City *Wasatch County* *North central Utah, 30 mi/48 km southeast of Salt Lake City*

1859 town founded, originally named Heber; **1862** Wasatch County formed; town becomes county seat; **1889** incorporated as a town; Denver & Rio Grande Railroad reaches town; Wasatch Stake Tabernacle, presented to city for use as city hall beginning 1987; **1901** incorporated as a city; **1968** county courthouse completed.

Helper *Carbon County* *Central Utah, 88 mi/ 142 km southeast of Salt Lake City*

1870 Teancum Pratt arrives with his two wives to prospect for coal; **1883** Denver & Rio Grande Western Railroad built; town founded, named Pratt's Siding; **1892** town renamed for "helper" engines used to boost trains over Soldier Summit and other steep grades; **1907** town incorporated; **March 8, 1924** three explosions rock Castle Gate Coal Mine to north, 171 killed; **1939** Helper Art Gallery founded; **Dec. 16, 1963** coal mine explosion kills nine miners.

Huntington *Emery County* *Central Utah, 108 mi/ 174 km south-southeast of Salt Lake City*

1877 settled by Mormons called by Latter-day Saints Church; **1878** town founded, named for explorer William Huntington; **1891** town incorporated; **1909** Mohrland Coal Camp established, closed 1938 with increase of commuting miners; **Dec. 19, 1984** fire in Wilberg Coal Mine, 27 killed.

Huntsville *Weber County* *Northern Utah, 35 mi/ 56 km north of Salt Lake City*

1825 trapper Peter Skene Ogden arrives in area; **1856** cattle introduced to Ogden Valley; **1860** toll road built east into Wasatch Range from Ogden for access to building materials, becomes free road 1882; town founded by Brigham Young, named for settler Jefferson Hunt; **1896** dynamite explosions kill five workers on Ogden Waterworks Conduit; **1903** town incorporated; **1924** town reincorporated; **1936** Pineview Reservoir built on Ogden River; **1947** Abbey of Our Lady of the Holy Trinity Trappist monastery founded to southeast.

Hurricane *Washington County* *Southwestern Utah, 255 mi/410 km south-southwest of Salt Lake City*

1893 Hurricane Canal Company organized for irrigation, canal completed 1904; **1906** town founded, named for Hurricane Hill, named by Erastus Snow as strong gust of wind tore his wagon cover while lowering wagon down the hill; **1983** town incorporated.

Junction *Piute County* *South central Utah, 172 mi/ 277 km south of Salt Lake City*

1865 Piute County formed; **1877** town founded as county seat on Sevier River; **1903** county courthouse built; **1913** town incorporated.

Kanab *Kane County* *Southern Utah, 255 mi/ 410 km south of Salt Lake City*

700 AD Anasazi people reach cultural peak, abandon area c.1300; **1864** Kane County formed, named for Thomas L. Kane, friend of the Mormons; **1869** Fort Kanab built by Jacob Hamblin; **1870** Mormons led by elder Levi Stewart settle here; **1871** telegraph line reaches town; **1874** town founded as county seat, Paiute term for "willow"; **1885** incorporated as a city; **1982** county courthouse completed; **Sept. 18, 1996** Grand Staircase-Escalante National Monument established to east.

Kaysville *Davis County* *Northern Utah, 21 mi/ 34 km north of Salt Lake City, on Great Salt Lake*

1849 town founded by Mormon settlers led by Hector C. Haight, named Kay's Fort; **1851** Blood Family House built, birthplace of Gov. Henry H. Blood; **1868** town incorporated, renamed Kaysville; **Oct. 1, 1872** Gov. Henry Hooper Blood born (died 1942); **1938** Clover Club Potato Chip Company established.

Lehi *Utah County* *North central Utah, 25 mi/40 km south of Salt Lake City, near Utah Lake*

1848 area first settled; **1850** town founded on Jordan River, at its outflow from Utah Lake, named for character in Book of Mormon; **1852** town incorporated; **1884** Saratoga Springs Resort established on Utah Lake, burned 1968, rebuilt; **1890** Utah Sugar Company beet sugar refinery established.

Lewiston *Cache County* *Northern Utah, 58 mi/ 93 km north of Salt Lake City*

1870 town founded by Mormon settlers, named for first settler William Lewis; **1870s** July frosts, heavy snows retard development of region; **1873** first irrigation canal dug near Worm Creek; **1879** grasshopper plague damages crops; **1904** incorporated as a town; **1904** beet sugar factory established; **1913** incorporated as a city; **1915** Lewiston-Bear Lake Irrigation Company organized.

Loa *Wayne County* *Southern Utah, 160 mi/257 km south of Salt Lake City*

1878 town founded, named by Mormon missionary Franklin W. Young for Mauna Loa volcano, Hawaii; **1892** Wayne County formed; town becomes county seat; **1909** Latter-day Saints Tabernacle dedicated; **1911** fresh water pipeline completed; **1919** town incorporated; public library built; **1939** county courthouse completed, remodeled 1988.

Logan *Cache County* *Northern Utah, 47 mi/76 km north of Salt Lake City*

1824 fur trappers enter area, cache their furs in Cache Valley; **1847** exploration survey arrives under direction of Mormon leader Brigham Young; **1855** Mormons drive their cattle into valley during grass shortage near Great Salt Lake; first cabins built; **1856** Cache County formed; Maughan's Fort (Wellsville) becomes county seat; **1859** valley resettled after being temporarily abandoned under threat of Col. Albert Johnston's army; town founded on Logan River; incorporated as a town; first irrigation channel dug; **1860** county seat moved to Logan; **1866** incorporated as a city; **1867** telegraph line reaches city; **1874** Utah Northern Railroad reaches city; **1875** United Order cooperative system established among Mormons, fails within ten years; **1878** Mormon Tabernacle completed; **1883** county courthouse built; **1884** LDS Temple completed, begun 1877; **1888** Utah State Agricultural College established, becomes Utah State University; **July 10, 1897** actor John Gilbert (Jack Pringle) born (died 1936); **1916** Logan Public Library founded; **1917** Chinchilla Farm established by M. F. Chapman; **1973** Willow Park Zoo established; **Feb. 1, 1985** lowest temperature ever recorded in Utah reached at Peter's Sink to northeast, −69°F/−56°C.

Manila *Daggett County* *Northeastern Utah, 112 mi/180 km east-northeast of Salt Lake City*

1898 town founded at time when Spanish were defeated by U.S. at Manila, Philippines; **1918** Daggett County formed; town becomes county seat; **1958** town incorporated; **1963** Flaming Gorge Dam completed to east on Green River creating large reservoir; **1968** Flaming Gorge National Recreation Area established by U.S. Forest Service around Flaming Gorge Reservoir, lake and recreation area extend into Wyoming; **1978** county courthouse built.

Manti *Sanpete County* *Central Utah, 102 mi/ 164 km south of Salt Lake City*

1849 town founded by Mormons, name derived from Book of Mormon; **1850** Sanpete County formed; town becomes county seat; **1851** town incorporated; **1854** Patten House built; **Apr. 1865** smallpox epidemic spreads to Ute peoples, begin series of bloody raids on whites in retaliation, referred to as "Black Hawk War"; **1888** Mormon Temple completed, work begun 1877; Sanpete Stake Academy founded, becomes Snow College 1923;

1889 Sanpete Valley towns experience summer floods due to overgrazing, through c.1965; **1937** county courthouse completed.

Midvale *Salt Lake County* *North central Utah, 6 mi/9.7 km south of Salt Lake City*

1852 first settlers arrive; towns of East Jordan and Brigham Junction founded on Jordan River; **1909** town incorporated with merger of two towns, renamed Midvale; **1924** United States Smelting and Refining Plant built; **May 25, 2000** lightning strikes Midvalley Elementary School killing one student, injuring six.

Moab *Grand County* *Eastern Utah, 195 mi/314 km southeast of Salt Lake City, near Colorado River*

1855 mission established to east in La Sal Mountains by Mormon Church; **1876** ranching begins with introduction of 400 head of cattle by George and Silas Green; **1879** post office established; town named for Biblical land of Moab; **1881** ferry service established on Colorado River; **1890** Grand County formed; town becomes county seat; **1891** steamboat *Major Powell* launched, unsuccessful attempt to establish service to Green River; **1903** incorporated as a town; **1912** highway bridge replaces ferry; **Apr. 12, 1929** Arches National Monument established to northeast, becomes National Park Nov. 12, 1971; **1936** incorporated as a city; **1937** county courthouse built; **1951** uranium mining boom begins, through 1950s; **1957** oil discovered, boom continues into 1960s; **1963** potash plant established; **Aug. 27, 1963** potash mine explosion kills 18; **Sept. 12, 1964** Canyonlands National Park established to southwest.

Monticello *San Juan County* *Southeastern Utah, 138 mi/222 km southeast of Salt Lake City*

1879 cabin built by Patrick O'Donnell; **1880** San Juan County formed; Bluff becomes county seat; **1887** town founded by five Mormon families called to settle here, named for Thomas Jefferson's home in Virginia (mon-ti-SEL-lo); **1895** county seat moved to Monticello; **1903** agricultural experimental station established by Utah State Agricultural College; **1910** incorporated as a city; **1915** *San Juan Record* newspaper founded; **1927** county courthouse completed; **1941** vanadium processing mill opened by U.S. Government, privatized 1949; **Sept. 12, 1964** Canyonlands National Park established to northwest; **1990s** hazardous waste cleanup undertaken at vanadium mill.

Morgan (Morgan City) *Morgan County* *Northern Utah, 22 mi/35 km north-northeast of Salt Lake City*

1852 Mormon settlers led into area by Morgan J. Thurston; **1860** town of South Morgan founded by Mormon settlers; **1861** North Morgan founded; **1862** Morgan County formed, named for Jedediah Morgan Grant; **1868** Union Pacific Railroad reaches site; two towns merge as Morgan, becomes county seat; town incorporated; **1904** pea cannery founded; **1959** city and county building replaces courthouse.

Murray   *Salt Lake County*   *North central Utah, 4 mi/6.4 km south of Salt Lake City*

1849 area first settled by Mormons; **1869** area's first silver smelter established; **1881** New Granite Paper Mill built to east; **1890s** town founded on Jordan River, named for Eli H. Murray, Territorial Governor 1880–1886; **1897** Stairs Power Plant built to east; **1902** town incorporated; American Smelting and Refining Plant founded, closed 1950.

Nephi   *Juab County*   *Central Utah, 72 mi/116 km south of Salt Lake City*

1851 town founded by Mormon settlers, named for patriarch in Book of Mormon; **1852** Juab County formed; **1854** Ute Chief Walker and Brigham Young make peace at site near here; **1879** Union Pacific Railroad reaches town; **1882** county organized; town becomes county seat; **1883** county courthouse built, addition built 1937; **1889** town incorporated; **1893** Nebo Salt Company established, closed 1925; **1900** dry farming techniques transform area; **1917** flour mill established, destroyed by fire 1991.

Ogden   *Weber County*   *Northern Utah, 37 mi/60 km north of Salt Lake City, near Great Salt Lake*

c.1825 trapper Peter Skene Ogden of Hudson's Bay Company leads expedition into area; **1844** Miles Goodyear of Connecticut builds first cabin; **1847** area settled by Mormons; Goodyear sells property to Capt. James Brown, moves to California; town founded, named Brownsville; **1849** town renamed Ogden; grist mill built by Lorin Farr of Vermont; **1850** Weber County formed; town becomes county seat; **1851** incorporated as a city; **1852** irrigation canal built from Weber River; **1853–1854** fortifications built during Native American troubles; **1854–1855** grasshopper plague devastates crops; **1855** adobe Robert Chapman House built; **1870** Utah Central Railroad reaches town from Salt Lake City; **1870** adobe Francis A. Brown House built; **1870s** smallpox epidemic sweeps area; **1882** Broom Hotel built; **1889** Weber Stake Academy founded, becomes Weber State University; **Jan. 11, 1897** editor, novelist Bernard De Voto born (died 1955); **1903** Southern Pacific Railroad builds Lucin Cutoff, rail causeway extending west across Great Salt Lake to far shore, eliminating 40 mi/64 km from original route completed 1869; Carnegie Library built; **1926** Ogden Livestock Coliseum built; **1934** first Pioneer Rodeo held; **1937** Mount Ogden Game Preserve established to east; Ogden Japanese Buddhist Temple established; **1940** Hill Army Air Base established to south, becomes Air Force Base 1948; city hall built; county courthouse built; **Sept. 15, 1940** hall of fame football player, commentator, TV actor Merlin Olsen born; **1944** Mayor Kent Braswell keeps political promise to clean up 25th Street district, himself hit with bribery scandal 1954; **Dec. 31, 1944** troop

train rear ended by mail train at Bagley 17 mi/27 km to west, 48 killed, 39 injured; **Dec. 9, 1957** singer Donny Osmond born; **Oct. 13, 1959** singer Marie Osmond born; **1993** Dinosaur Park and Museum opened.

Ophir   *Tooele County*   *North central Utah, 33 mi/53 km southwest of Salt Lake City*

1865 first gold and silver claims made by Army personnel; town founded; **1870** Ophir Mining District established; town incorporated; town hall built; **1871** Community Methodist Church founded; **c.1873** population peaks at 6,000; **1930** tailings mill built; **1990** population dwindles to 25.

Orem   *Utah County*   *Northern Utah, 32 mi/51 km south of Salt Lake City, on Utah Lake*

1861 town founded, originally named Provo Bench; **1919** town incorporated, renamed for Walter C. Orem, president of Salt Lake & Utah Railroad; **1941** Utah Valley State College (2-year) established.

Panguitch   *Garfield County*   *Southern Utah, 200 mi/322 km south of Salt Lake City*

1864 town founded by Mormons led by Jens Nielsen, Paiute term for "big fish"; **Apr. 10, 1865** three settlers killed by Native Americans during Utah's Black Hawk War, **1867** town abandoned; **1871** town resettled; **1882** Garfield County formed; town becomes county seat; **1899** town incorporated; **1907** county courthouse built, addition built 1984; **June 8, 1923** Bryce Canyon National Monument proclaimed to southeast, becomes Bryce Canyon National Park 1928; **Oct. 24, 1947** United Airlines DC-6 catches fire, crashes over Bryce Canyon, 52 killed; **1954** sawmill established.

Park City   *Summit County*   *North central Utah, 20 mi/32 km east-southeast of Salt Lake City*

1869 silver discovered by three soldiers; **1870** soldiers open Flagstaff Silver Mine, starting silver boom; town founded; **1881** Salt Lake & Park City Railroad (narrow gauge) reaches town; Utah Central and Union Pacific railroads reach town later in year; **1884** incorporated as a city; **1898** fire destroys Main Street district, rebuilt within three months; **1907** all gambling halls ordered closed by mayor, reopened 1909; **c.1960** silver mining ceases; **1962** first ski trails built; **Feb. 2002** Salt Lake City Winter Olympics skiing competitions held here.

Parowan   *Iron County*   *Southwestern Utah, 203 mi/327 km south-southwest of Salt Lake City*

1850 Iron County formed; **Dec. 1850** town founded as county seat by Mormon settlers led by George A. Smith, first major Mormon colonizing expedition in Utah; **1874** incorporated as a city; **1974** county courthouse built.

Peter's Sink   *Cache County*   See **Logan (1985)**

Point of Mountain *Salt Lake County* See Draper, Salt Lake City (1940)

Price *Carbon County* *Central Utah, 95 mi/153 km southeast of Salt Lake City*

1869 Mormon bishop William Price leads exploration party into Spanish Fork Canyon; **1878** coal discovered; **1879** area along Price River first settled by farmers; irrigation canals built; **1882** Denver & Rio Grande Western Railroad built; town founded; **1888** Castle Gate Coal Mine established; **1892** town incorporated; **1894** Carbon County formed; town becomes county seat; **1915** Price (Carnegie) City Library built, new building built 1957; **1937** College of Eastern Utah (2-year) established; **1940** Price Art Gallery opened; **Jan. 1960** county courthouse completed.

Promontory *Box Elder County* *Northern Utah, 70 mi/113 km north-northwest of Salt Lake City*

May 10, 1869 golden spike driven at 12:47 P.M. joining Central Pacific Railroad (the *Jupiter*) from west with Union Pacific Railroad (No. 119) from east between opposing engines, north of Promontory Point, peninsula on north shore of Great Salt Lake; **1901** engine *Jupiter* scrapped; **1903** Southern Pacific Railroad builds Lucin Cutoff from Ogden across Great Salt Lake, across tip of Promontory Point, eliminating 40 mi/64 km from original route; engine No. 119 scrapped; **1943** Golden Spike Monument dedicated; **Apr. 2, 1957** Golden Spike National Historic Site established.

Provo *Utah County* *North central Utah, 38 mi/61 km south-southeast of Salt Lake City, on Utah Lake*

1776 Spanish priests Silvestre Escalante and Francisco Dominguez become probable first white men to enter Utah Valley; **1825** French-Canadian trapper Etienne Provot (pro-VOH) enters valley; **1849** town founded by John S. Higbee and 30 Mormon families; Fort Utah built; first irrigation canals built; **1850** Utah County formed; town becomes county seat; skirmishes with Utes lead to their defeat; **1851** incorporated as a city; carding mill established; **1858** U.S. troops sent to quell Mormon insurrection, Mormons move south; **1873** Utah Southern Railroad reaches city; **1875** Brigham Young University established; **1878** Utah & Pleasant Valley Railroad built to mines at Scofield; **1880** Utah Mental Hospital completed; **1881** Denver & Rio Grande Western Railroad reaches city from Salt Lake City; **Sept. 11, 1884** physicist Dr. Harvey Fletcher born, pioneered in research for hard of hearing, invention of stereophonic equipment (died 1981); **1924** Columbia Steel Plant established; **1926** county courthouse completed, begun 1919.

Randolph *Rich County* *Northern Utah, 72 mi/116 km north-northeast of Salt Lake City*

1864 Richland County formed, named for Mormon apostle Charles Coulson Rich; **1868** county name shortened to Rich County; **1870** Mormon settlers arrive led by Randolph H. Stewart; **1871** town founded by Brigham Young as county seat, located on Bear River; **1905** town incorporated; **1942** county courthouse completed.

Richfield *Sevier County* *Central Utah, 135 mi/217 km south of Salt Lake City*

1864 town founded by Mormons led by George W. Bean on orders of apostle George A. Smith; **1865** Sevier County formed; town becomes county seat; **March 21, 1867** three settlers killed by natives, area evacuated; **1868** Black Hawk Treaty ends hostilities with Utes begun in 1865, retaliation for smallpox epidemic blamed on whites; **1871** settlers return; **1878** incorporated as a city; **1975** second county courthouse built.

Richmond *Cache County* *Northern Utah, 55 mi/89 km north of Salt Lake City*

1855 John Bair establishes ferry on Bear River; **1859** Agrippa Cooper becomes first settler; **1859** log fort built; town founded by Mormons; **1860** sawmill and grist mill built; **1868** incorporated as a city; **1896** Utah Plow Factory established; **1903** Benson Stake Tabernacle built, closed by earthquake 1962, rebuilt 1964; **1904** first Holstein cows brought in, beginning of area's dairying industry; Sego Milk Products plant built; **1913** Richmond Holstein Show organized; first annual Black and White Day celebration held to promote Holstein dairying.

Saint George *Washington County* *Southwestern Utah, 265 mi/426 km south-southwest of Salt Lake City*

1852 Washington County formed; New Harmony becomes county seat; **1861** experimental cotton-growing project begun by Mormons; town founded, consisting entirely of wagons lined on both sides of "street"; town named for pioneer leader George A. Smith; **1862** town incorporated before first house is built; **1863** county seat moved to St. George; Angus Cannon House built; **1865** Jed Gates House completed; **1870** first county courthouse built, still standing; **1871** Mormon tabernacle built; **1875** Erastus Snow House built; **1877** Mormon temple completed; **1910** St. George City Library founded; **1911** Dixie Normal School established, becomes Dixie State College (2-year); **1981** county courthouse built; **July 5, 1985** highest temperature ever recorded in Utah reached, 117°F/47°C.

Salt Lake City *Salt Lake County* *North central Utah, near Great Salt Lake, at mouth of Jordan River*

July 24, 1847 Mormons arrive in Great Salt Lake Valley on Mormon Trail under the leadership of Brigham Young; **late 1847** Osmyn Deuel House built; **1849** settlement serves as supply point to pioneers heading for California; settlers saved from cricket plague by sea gulls; city platted by Capt. Howard Stansbury, named Great Salt Lake City; **1850** Utah Territory created; Salt Lake County formed; town becomes county seat; University of

Utah established; **1851** incorporated as a city; old Mormon Tabernacle completed; Mormon Tabernacle Choir organized; **1853** work begins on Mormon Temple; **1854** penitentiary built on Canyon Creek southeast of city, becomes state prison 1896; **1855** Beehive House built; Emprey House built; **1856** Lion House built, housed some of Brigham Young's 26 wives; Utah State Fair first held; **1858** U.S. troops enter city greeted by deserted streets in "Utah War"; **1860–1861** Pony Express station established; **1861** telegraph reaches city; **1862** Fort Douglas built to east, later becomes U.S. Army reservation; Salt Lake Theater opened; **Jan. 10, 1862** Mormon leader, U.S. Sen. Reed Smoot born (died 1941); **1864** work begins on Mormon Tabernacle, completed 1867; **1868** "Great" dropped from city name; **Feb. 4, 1869** mineworkers' labor leader William Dudley Haywood born (died 1928); **May 1869** first transcontinental railroad completed north of Great Salt Lake; **1870** Utah Central Railroad built north to main line; cornerstone laid for St. Mark's Episcopal Church; **Feb. 12, 1871** Utah becomes first territory allowing women right to vote; **Apr. 15, 1871** *Salt Lake Tribune* newspaper founded; **Oct. 2, 1872** Brigham Young arrested for "lewd and lascivious cohabitation"; **Nov. 11, 1872** stage actress Maude Adams born (died 1953); **1873** Utah Southern Railroad built to Provo; **1874** Utah Northern Railroad built to Logan; **1875** Westminster College (Presbyterian) established; St. Mary of the Wasatch Catholic girls school founded; **Aug. 29, 1877** Brigham Young dies, drawing 25,000 mourners; **1886** Denver & Rio Grande Western Railroad completed to Denver; **1887** Edmunds-Tucker Act passed compelling Mormon leaders to be more accommodative to national norms in running Utah's affairs, polygamy violators go into hiding; **1889** Ambassador Hotel built; **Jan. 10, 1889** cartoonist John Held, Jr. born (died 1958); **1891** First Congregational Church built; **1893** Mormon Temple completed after 40 years construction; **1894** city and county building completed; **Apr. 23, 1894** movie director Frank Borzage born (died 1962); **Jan. 4, 1896** Utah admitted to Union as 45th state; city becomes state capital; **1897** Brigham Young monument dedicated; **Aug. 14, 1897** writer, editor Whit Burnett born (died 1973); **1898** Saltair Resort built of Moorish design near shore of Great Salt Lake, destroyed by fire 1925, rebuilt on elevated concrete base; public library founded; **1899** illuminated Salt Palace built, burned 1910; **1900** Cathedral of the Madeleine (Catholic) completed; **1904** Thomas Kearns Mansion built, becomes governor's mansion 1937; **1905** Royal Crystal Salt Plant established on Great Salt Lake, acquired by Morton Salt 1928; **1911** Hotel Utah built; **Jan. 6, 1913** actress Loretta Young born (died 2000); **May 7, 1913** engineer Simon Ramo born, developed guided missile system; **1914** state capitol completed; **1920** Woodward Field airport established, becomes Salt Lake City International Airport 1968; **Feb. 15, 1923** actor Keene Curtis born; **1924** Mountain Dell Reservoir built on Parleys Creek to east; **1927** Masonic Temple completed; **1931** Hogle Zoo established in Liberty Park to east; Pony Express monument erected; **1932** KSL radio transmitter and twin towers built near Great Salt Lake; **Sept. 27, 1934** TV actor Wilford Brimley born; **1938** Utah Art Center opened; **1940** Utah Symphony Orchestra founded; Utah State Prison built at Point of Mountain to south; **1948** Salt Lake Community College established; **1952** Ballet West founded; **Nov. 3, 1952** TV actress Roseanne Arnold born; **1963** Utah Museum of Natural History established, opened 1969; **1965** Hansen Planetarium opened; **Nov. 11, 1965** United 727 airplane crashes while landing, killing 42 of 90 on board; **1972** 30-story Latter-day Saints Church Office Building built; **Jan. 17, 1977** Gary Gilmore executed by firing squad at Utah State Prison for murder of hotel manager, ending 10-year U.S. moratorium on capital punishment; **June 9, 1978** Latter-day Saints Church drops 148-year policy banning black priests; **1979** Utah Jazz NBA basketball team moved from New Orleans, established 1974; **Dec. 2, 1982** Jarvik artificial heart, operated by compressor, implanted into patient Dr. Barney Clark by Dr. William DeVries at University of Utah Medical Center, Clark dies March 23, 1983, after 112 days; **May 18–23, 1983** flooding in city area causes mudslides, sandbags used to channel water through streets, 32 killed; **Dec. 1986** county government centre completed; **1991** Salt Palace Convention Center and Arena opened; **c.1995** rising waters of Great Salt Lake surround venerable Saltair Resort; **1998** 36-story American Stores Center built; **Dec. 11, 1998** investigation into bribes paid for choosing Salt Lake City as 2002 site of Olympic Games implicates Olympic Chairman Marc Hodler of Switzerland; **Feb. 2002** 17-day Winter Olympics held with ski competitions at Park City, Heber City and Ogden; **June 5, 2002** Elizabeth Smart, 15, abducted from bedroom launching massive manhunt, found unharmed March 12, 2003, at traffic stop in suburban Sandy to south, drifter Brian David Mitchell and companion Wanda Barzee held; **Apr. 2003** Hansen Planetarium opened.

Santa Clara   *Washington County*   Southwestern *Utah, 265 mi/426 km south-southwest of Salt Lake City*

1854 town founded by Mormons led by Jacob Hamblin; **1855** area's first cotton grown; **1861** Swiss immigrants arrive; **1862** flash flood destroys town, rebuilt; Jacob Hamblin House built; **1874** Martin Bauman House built; **1914** incorporated as a town; **1916** Shivwits (Shebit) Indian Reservation established to west; **1979** incorporated as a city.

Springville   *Utah County*   Central Utah, 42 mi/ *68 km south-southeast of Salt Lake City, near Utah Lake*

1849 area settled by Mormons; town founded by Aaron Johnson Company; **1853** town incorporated; **July 1853** Walker War begins against Ute peoples, ends with negotiations between Ute Chief Walkara and Brigham Young 1854 at Nephi; **Nov. 22, 1860** sculptor Cyrus Edwin Dallin born (died 1944); **1878** railroad built from coal mines at Scofield, becomes Denver & Rio Grande Railroad 1882; **1902** Pioneer Mother monument erected;

1910 Utah State Trout Hatchery founded; **1916** Federal Fish Hatchery founded; **1937** Springville Art Gallery built.

Syracuse   *Davis County   Northern Utah, 25 mi/ 40 km north of Salt Lake City, on Great Salt Lake*

1877 town founded as farming community; **1884** water diversion canal completed; **1898** Syracuse Cannery established; **1914** first influx of Japanese immigrants arrive; **1935** incorporated as a town; **1950** incorporated as a city; **1969** causeway, 7.25 mi/11.7 km long, completed west to Antelope Island State Park in Great Salt Lake, causeway submerged by rising lake waters 1985, rebuilt 1993 as toll road.

Tooele   *Tooele County   North central Utah, 27 mi/ 43 km southwest of Salt Lake City*

1849 town founded by Mormons (pronounced too-WIL-a), named for Tooele peoples; **1850** Tooele County formed; town becomes county seat; **1853** town incorporated; **1909** lead smelter established, closed 1972; **1923** Combined Metal Reduction Plant founded; **1937** construction of Elton Tunnel begun to east to drain mines, providing irrigation to Tooele Valley, completed 1942; **1973** county courthouse built; **1983** gold mining begins; smelter reopened.

Vernal   *Uintah County   Northeastern Utah, 123 mi/ 198 km east-southeast of Salt Lake City*

1776 Fathers Francisco Dominguez and Silvestre Escalante enter region; **1879** town founded, named Ashley Center; **1880** Uintah County formed; town becomes county seat; **1890s** Butch Cassidy's "Wild Bunch" gang establish Browns Hole 50 mi/80 km to north as base of operations; **1893** town renamed Vernal; **1897** town incorporated; **Oct. 4, 1915** Dinosaur National Monument established to east, extends into Colorado; **1919** Bank of Vernal built, bricks mailed in packages of seven bricks each to circumvent freight rates, post office deluged with packages of bricks inspiring U.S. Post Office to impose limit on pounds-per-day delivered to addressees; **1948** oil discovered; **1958** county courthouse built; **1959** Utah Field House of Natural History opened, second phase opened 1983; **1964** Flaming Gorge Dam built on Green River to north; **1968** Flaming Gorge National Recreation Area established to north, extends into Wyoming.

Washington   *Washington County   Southwestern Utah, 262 mi/422 km south-southwest of Salt Lake City*

1857 town founded by Mormons; first cotton plantations established, called "Utah's Dixie"; **1866** cotton factory established; **1870** town incorporated; **1870s** native grapes used to make wine, Brigham Young orders end to practice; **1873** silkworm project begun, discontinued 1896; **1893** Washington Fields Dam completed on Virgin River for irrigation; **1900** cotton production ceases; **July 31, 1909** Mukuntuweap National Monument established to east, redesignated Zion National Monument 1918; **Nov. 19, 1919** Zion National Monument proclaimed Zion National Park; **Jan. 22, 1937** new Zion National Monument established, absorbed by National Park 1956.

Wendover   *Tooele County   Northwestern Utah, 110 mi/177 km west of Salt Lake City*

1827 Jediediah Strong Smith crosses Great Salt Lake Desert with two other trappers on return from California, first known crossing; **1845** John C. Fremont crosses desert with guide Kit Carson; **1846** Donner-Reed emigrant party crosses desert toward ill-fated winter in Sierra Nevada; **1907** Western Pacific Railroad completed from Salt Lake City; town founded on Nevada border; **1914** Bonneville Speedway opened to northeast; world land record of 141 mph/227 kph set by driver Teddy Tetzleff; **1931** driver Sir Malcolm Campbell sets record of 301 mph/484 kph on Speedway; **1941** Wendover Army Air Field established, becomes Air Force Base 1947, deeded to town for use as airport 1977; **Aug. 4, 1945** "Fat Man" high explosive test completed five days before being dropped on Nagasaki, Japan ("Little Boy" dropped on Hiroshima Aug. 6); **1950** incorporated as a town; **1982** incorporated as a city.

West Valley City   *Salt Lake County   North central Utah, 6 mi/9.7 km southwest of Salt Lake City*

1848 area first settled by Joseph Harker; **1980** communities of Bacchus, Brighton, Granger, Hunter, Redwood, and Pleasant Green merge, incorporated as a city; **1990** becomes Utah's second most populous city.

Vermont

Northeastern U.S. One of the six New England states. Capital: Montpelier. Largest city: Burlington.

Vermont entered the U.S. as part of the state of New York, one of the 13 colonies which adopted the Declaration of Independence July 4, 1776. Vermont separated from New York to become the 14th state on March 4, 1791.

Vermont is divided into 14 counties with weak governments. The counties are divided into townships, called towns, which have strong governments. Municipalities are classified as villages, which remain part of their respective towns when they incorporate, and cities, which are formed from one or more former towns. See Introduction.

Alburg *Grand Isle County* *Northwestern Vermont, 33 mi/53 km north-northwest of Burlington*

1731 first French settlers arrive at this site on large peninsula of Lake Champlain, extending south from Canada; **Sept. 3, 1776** Benedict Arnold anchors at Windmill Point; **Sept. 6, 1776** landing party attacked by natives, three killed, six wounded; **1781** town chartered; **1782** first permanent settlers found town; **1808** smuggling across Canadian border becomes important industry following embargo; **1823** The Stone House built, originally Motte's Inn tavern; **1858** Windmill Point Lighthouse built on Lake Champlain; **1916** Alburg incorporated as a village; **1937** highway bridge built across Richelieu River at its exit from Lake Champlain, near Quebec, replacing ferry to Rouses Point, New York; **1938** highway bridge east across Lake Champlain's east channel to Swanton, Vermont, completed.

Arlington *Bennington County* *Southwestern Vermont, 37 mi/60 km south-southwest of Rutland*

1761 town chartered by New Hampshire; **1763** town first settled; **1764** grist mill and sawmill established by Remember Baker; **1765** land patented by New York, named Princeton; **1777** town clerk Isaac Bisco, a Tory, hides town records, flees to Canada, records never recovered; Thomas Chittenden, Seth Warner other Vermont revolutionary leaders arrive here; **1781** town chartered by New Hampshire; **1830** St. James Church built; **1852** Bridge at the Green (covered) built, spans Batten Kill; **1870** Chiselville Covered Bridge built on Roaring Branch stream; **1939** artist Norman Rockwell takes up residence here, through 1953, uses townspeople as models for paintings.

Barnet *Caledonia County* *Eastern Vermont, 24 mi/39 km east of Montpelier, on Connecticut River*

1763 town chartered by New Hampshire; town center named Stevens Village; **1770** first settler arrives; **1771** Colonel Hurd builds mill at falls; **1774** Scottish company begins settling town; **1776** Scotsmen Stevenson and Cross club bear to death; **1807** post office established; **1838** Vermont Historical Society established, moved to Montpelier 1851; **1920** French oceanographer Jacques Cousteau (1910–1997) begins skin diving at age 10 at Harvey's Lake at West Barnet.

Barre *Washington County* *Central Vermont, 7 mi/11.3 km southeast of Montpelier*

1781 town settled, chartered as Wildersburgh; **1808** Congregationalist Church built; **1814** Paddock House built; **c.1815** granite quarrying begins; **1825** Wheelock House completed; **1833** Joshua Twing establishes foundry; **1833–1837** granite hauled to Montpelier by ox-drawn wagon sled for construction of state capitol; **1863** Green Mountain Central Institute established, becomes Goddard Junior College 1929; **1875** Central Vermont Railway reaches town; **1880s** granite quarrying reaches peak; **1895** incorporated as city of Barre, separates from Town of Barre; **1899** Robert Burns statue dedicated; **1915** Barre Historical Society founded; **Nov. 3–4, 1927** flooding Winooski River destroys town, 84 killed in general flooding in Vermont, including Lt. Gov. S. Hollister Jackson; **1935** East Barre Dam completed on Winooski River; **June 2002** Vermont History Center opened by Vermont Historical Society.

Bellows Falls *Windham County* *Southeastern Vermont, 42 mi/68 km southeast of Rutland*

1785 first bridge across Connecticut River built by Col. Enoch Hale; **1792** construction begins on canal circumventing falls, completed 1802, used until c.1840; **1802** one of first paper mills in Vermont established by Bill Blake, founded in nearby Alstead, New Hampshire, 1799; **1829** Rockingham Hospital built; **1831** Adams' Grist Mill built; **1833** village of Bellows Falls founded within town of Rockingham; **1851** Boston & Maine Railroad tunnel 275-ft/84-m long, built through town; **1867** Immanuel Episcopal Church built; **1869** mill established by William A. Russell, first successful attempt to make paper from pulp, goes on to become first president of International Paper Company; **1870s** paper milling industry becomes established; **1876** Vermont Academy established at village of Saxtons River to west, becomes boys' school 1931; **1881** extensive paper mill complex built; **1883** Rockingham Canal House built, originally named Hotel Rockingham; **1887** Rockingham Town Hall built; **1898** power house built at falls; **1904** Old Fire House built; **1905** steel bridge across river completed above falls; **1927** flooding damages town; **1928** Bellows Falls Hydroelectric station built; **1937** Polish American Club built; **1942** Bellows Falls Diner opened; **1982** fish ladder built to allow salmon to move past power house at falls.

Bennington *Bennington County* *Southwestern Vermont, 50 mi/80 km south-southwest of Rutland*

1749 first town chartered west of Connecticut River by New Hampshire; named for Gov. Benning Wentworth **1761** Samuel Robinson leads six families from Hardwick, Massachusetts, to settle here; **1763** Jedediah Dewey House built; **1766** Walloomsac Inn opens; **1770** Green Mountain Boys organized by Seth Warner and Ethan Allen to free Vermont from New York control; **1771** first skirmish between Green Mountain Boys and New York authority leads to retreat by sheriff and posse to Albany; **May 20, 1776** Canadian fur trader Simon Fraser born (died 1862); **Aug. 16, 1777** Col. John Stark and the Green Mountain Boys defeat the Hessian forces in Battle of Bennington; **1778** David Redding becomes first person publicly hanged in Vermont; **1779** Bennington County organized; town becomes county seat; **1805** Old First Church built; **1806** First Congregational Church built; **1821** Old Academy Library built; **Apr. 1, 1834** stock market speculator James Fisk born (died 1872); **c.1840** Henry Covered Bridge built across Walloomsac River; Paper Mill Covered Bridge built across Walloomsac, rebuilt 2000; **1891** Bennington Battlefield Monument dedicated; **1936** county courthouse built.

Bethel *Windsor County* *Central Vermont, 22 mi/35 km northeast of Rutland*

1779 town chartered; **1780** town first settled; Fort Fortitude built for protection against Native Americans; **1781** Bethel Mills, sawmill and grist mill, established, sawmill remains in operation, grist mill destroyed 1927;

1809 Gen. Stephen Thomas born, hero at Cedar Creek, Virginia, 1864 (died 1903); **1810** McKinstry House built; **1820** Old Church built; **1925** town's last quarries close; **1824** Baptist Church built at East Bethel; **c.1830** Hexagonal Schoolhouse built, also at East Bethel; **1927** great flood destroys mills, bridge.

Bloomfield *Essex County* *Northeastern Vermont, 57 mi/92 km northeast of Montpelier, on Connecticut River*

1759 Rogers Rangers follow Nulhegan River to the Connecticut River pursued by natives, having destroyed Native American village of St. Francis, Quebec, split into smaller bands to better chances of survival; **1762** town chartered by New Hampshire, originally named Minehead; **1830** town renamed, possibly in honor of Revolutionary War hero Joseph Bloomfield; **Dec. 30, 1933** lowest temperature ever recorded in Vermont reached, −50°F/−46°C.

Bradford *Orange County* *Eastern Vermont, 28 mi/45 km southeast of Montpelier, on Connecticut River*

1760s area first settled; **1770** town chartered; **1777** Ellis Bliss Farmhouse built; **1795** Congregational Church built, still standing, current church built 1876; **1796** Low House mansion built; **1804** seaman William Trotter arrives following career as commercial shipper, first to fly U.S. flag in ports of South America; **1812** cartographer James Wilson becomes first in U.S. to produce globes; **1835** American Legion Hall built by Asa Low; **Aug. 10, 1843** Spanish American War naval officer Charles Edgar Clark born (died 1922); **1847** grist mill built by Asa Low; **1849** Methodist Church built; **1890** Boston & Maine train station built; **1894** Bradford Academy founded.

Brandon *Rutland County* *Western Vermont, 13 mi/21 km north-northwest of Rutland*

1759 Crown Point Military Road built from Charlestown, New Hampshire, to Crown Point, New York; **1761** town chartered, named Neshobe; **1777** Native American attack destroys all homes, many prisoners taken; **1784** town renamed Brandon; **1790** Farrington House built, owned by Farrington family from 1808; **1810** John Conant discovers bog iron at Neshobe Falls, builds iron furnace; **Apr. 23, 1813** Stephen A. Douglas born, senator from Illinois, Abraham Lincoln's political rival during 1850s (died 1861); **1831** Congregational Church built; **1832** Baptist Church built; **1834** Thomas Davenport invents electric motor; **1849** Burlington-Rutland Railroad built; **c.1860** Ebenezer Ormsbee House built; **1861** town hall built; **1863** Episcopal Church built; **1875** Churchill House Inn built; **1876** Methodist Church built; **1892** Brandon Inn built, replaces tavern built 1796, destroyed by fire 1890; **1910** Brandon Free Library opened; **1919** Brandon National Bank built, incorporated 1863; **July 1922** fire destroys block of downtown buildings.

Brattleboro   *Windham County*   *Southeastern Vermont, 55 mi/89 km south-southeast of Rutland*

1716 land on Connecticut River sold to citizens of Connecticut for a farthing per acre; **1724** Fort Dummer established by Massachusetts to protect town of Northfield to south, first white settlement in Vermont, dismantled 1763; **1753** town charter granted by New Hampshire, named for William Brattle, Jr., title owner who never visited town; **1791** Hayes Tavern built in West Brattleboro; **Sept. 3, 1811** utopian communities founder John Humphrey Noyes born (died 1886); **March 31, 1824** painter William Morris Hunt born (died 1842); **1836** Brattleboro Retreat for mentally retarded established; **1842** Center Congregational Church built; **1846** Brattleboro Hyrdropathic Establishment founded at mineral springs here, remained fashionable destination for cures until 1871; **1869** fire devastates town, again in 1877; **1892** Rudyard Kipling marries native Caroline Balestier, lived here until 1896; **1888** fire hydrants installed, supplied by Chestnut Hill Reservoir; **1912** Austine School for the Deaf founded.

Brighton   *Essex County*   *See* **Island Pond**

Bristol   *Addison County*   *Western Vermont, 24 mi/ 39 km south-southeast of Burlington*

1762 German John Broadt arrives a supposed fugitive, thinking he had killed his neighbor in a fight in Unadilla, New York; town chartered by New Hampshire, originally named Pocock for Adm. Sir George Pocock; **1784** surveyors discover German John Broadt living here by himself, is able to return upon finding out his neighbor is still alive; **1789** town renamed Bristol; **1819** First Baptist Church built; **1884** town hall built; **1891** Lord's Prayer Rock chiseled by Joseph C. Greene; **1893** Lawrence Memorial Library founded, built 1911 by patron William Lawrence.

Burlington   *Chittenden County*   *Northwestern Vermont, 127 mi/204 km north-northeast of Albany, New York*

1609 Samuel de Champlain discovers Lake Champlain; **1763** Town of Burlington chartered by New Hampshire, named for Burling family, prominent land owners; **1772** first locally-built vessel, the *Liberty*, launched on Winooski River; **spring 1775** many volunteers head for Bennington to join Ethan Allen at beginning of Revolution; **1783** settlers return at end of Revolution; **1787** Chittenden County organized; town becomes county seat; **Nov. 1791** University of Vermont established; **1796** first jail built, Levi Allen, brother of Ethan Allen, dies here 1801, imprisoned for debt; **Nov. 11, 1808** Cyrus Dean, operated smuggling vessel *Black Snake*, hanged in front of 10,000 spectators; **June 1809** the *Vermont* sets out on its first voyage, to Whitehall 150 mi/241 km to south; **1812** First Calvinistic Church built, burned 1839, rebuilt 1842; **June 13, 1813** three British ships begin offensive against town, are beaten back; **1816** Unitarian Church built; **1823**

Champlain Canal completed to Hudson River; **Oct. 1826** Champlain Transportation Company establishes steamship service on Lake Champlain; **1832** St. Paul's Episcopal Church built; **Apr. 1, 1848** *Burlington Free Press* becomes Vermont's first daily newspaper; **Dec. 18, 1849** Rutland & Burlington Railroad beats Central Vermont Railroad in extending first line from Boston to Burlington; **Oct. 20, 1859** educator John Dewey born (died 1952); **1860s** town becomes third most important lumber center in U.S., through 1870s; **1865** town of South Burlington separates from town of Burlington, remainder of town incorporated as City of Burlington; **1870** Van Ness Hotel built; **1874** Mount St. Mary's Academy moves from Manchester, New Hampshire; **1878** Champlain College established; **Jan. 3, 1879** Grace Anne Goodhue Coolidge, wife of President Coolidge, born (married Oct. 4, 1905, died July 8, 1957); **Apr. 28, 1884** librarian William Isaac Fletcher born, developed periodical index (died 1917); **1901** St. Joseph's Catholic Church completed; **1902** land acquired for Ethan Allen Park; **1904** Cathedral of Immaculate Conception completed; **Oct. 10, 1924** radio station WCAX (University of Vermont) begins broadcasting; **1925** Trinity College of Vermont established; **1926** city hall built; **1927** Church of Christ Scientist built; Fletcher Free Library opened, new structure built 1981; **July 22, 1928** actor Orson Bean born; **1930** Flynn Theatre built; **Dec. 6, 1970** National Guard plane from Rhode Island crashes in snow squall on takeoff, killing five; **1981** Flynn Center for the Performing Arts founded; **fall 2002** Firehouse Center for the Visual Arts opened.

Cabot   *Washington County*   *Northeastern Vermont, 16 mi/26 km northeast of Montpelier*

1778 Hazen Military Road built by Gen. Moses Hazen; **1781** town chartered; **1783** Benjamin Webster settles here, uncle of Daniel Webster; **1789** sawmill built by Thomas Lyford; **1792** first schoolhouse built; **1806** Congregational Church built; **c.1810** potash production begins; **1822** Methodist Church built; **1896** Cabot Library founded; **1901** Old Home Week custom established, part of statewide program begun earlier; **1919** Cabot Farmers Creamery established; **1921** Willey Memorial Hall community center built; **1928** Cabot United Church formed, structure built 1849.

Calais   *Washington County*   *North central Vermont, 10 mi/16 km north-northeast of Montpelier*

1781 town chartered; **1824** Old West Church built, uses included meeting house of Millerite sect; **1838** Wareham Chase invents an electrical motor, eccentric who lived to almost 100, stayed within 30 miles his entire life; **c.1840** general store opened at East Calais; **Dec. 31, 1843** citing Scriptural proof, William Miller, leader of Millerite sect, packs church with believers, having predicted the world would end that night, within ten minutes, the house emptied and the sect thereby ended; **July 18, 1864** band of 14 Confederates led by William Collins enter U.S. from New Brunswick, attempt raid on bank, Collins, 3 of his men killed; **1900** Maple Corner General Store opened; **1922** president of General Electric visits Historical Society Museum in Montpelier, declares Chase's motor more perfect than motor invented by Davenport; **Apr. 1935** Adamant Village Coop organized, first rural cooperative in Vermont.

Cambridge *Lamoille County Northwestern Vermont, 20 mi/32 km northeast of Burlington*

1781 town chartered; **1783** town first settled; **1808** Humphrey Homestead built; **1827** village of Jeffersonville, in north part of township, named for Thomas Jefferson by popular vote; **1858** Community House built at South Cambridge; **1887** Poland Covered Bridge built over Lamoille River; **1897** Jeffersonville incorporated as a village; Gates Covered Bridge built on Seymour River; Cambridge incorporated as a village.

Castleton *Rutland County Western Vermont, 10 mi/16 km west of Rutland*

1761 town chartered; **1770** first settlers arrive; **May 1775** Seth Thomas, Ethan Allen, others, meet at Remington's Tavern to plan their successful attack on Fort Ticonderoga; **c.1785** cobbler shop established by Enos Merrill; **1787** Rutland County Grammar School established, later becomes Castleton State College; **1810** Northrup House built; **1818** Castleton Medical College, first medical school in Vermont, established at Castleton State, closed 1862; **1833** Federated Church built; Cale House built by Thomas Dake.

Cavendish *Windsor County Southeastern Vermont, 23 mi/37 km southeast of Rutland*

Aug. 1754 natives raid Johnson homestead, carry seven captives to Canada, Mrs. Johnson gives birth, names child Captive; **1761** town chartered by New Hampshire; **1769** town first settled by Capt. John Coffin on Crown Military Road; **1800** post office established; **1812** Cavendish Academy founded; **1844** Universalist Church built; **1907** village of Proctorsville incorporated, disincorporated 1987; **1927** flooding Black River tears gorge through town.

Chelsea *Orange County Central Vermont, 19 mi/31 km south-southeast of Montpelier*

1781 Orange County organized; town chartered as Turnersburgh by New Hampshire; **1784** town first settled, becomes county seat; **1788** town renamed Chelsea; **1847** county courthouse built; **1892** Chelsea Library built after fire destroys previous structure; **1897** Chelsea Clock Factory established by Joseph H. Eastman.

Chimney Point *Addison County Western Vermont, 32 mi/51 km south-southwest of Burlington*

July 30, 1609 Samuel de Champlain crosses lake named for him, arrives at Chimney Point after defeating Iroquois on west side; **1730** French establish settlement, build Fort

de Pieux at Chimney Point; **1759** French evacuate fort and settlement, site raided by Mohawks 1760; fort taken by British; **1775** Seth Warner and Green Mountain Boys capture fort from British without a fight; **1929** Lake Champlain Bridge opened.

Cornwall *Addison County Western Vermont, 25 mi/40 km north-northwest of Rutland*

1761 town chartered by New Hampshire; **1774** settlement begins, interrupted by Revolution; **1785** 30 families from Connecticut arrive to resume settlement; Congregational Church built; **Jan. 28, 1814** Henry Norman Hudson born, Shakespearean critic (died 1886); **1856** Station Covered Bridge built on Otter Creek; **1915** Sampson Memorial Library built, new building opened 1985, original structure used for town hall.

Danville *Caledonia County Northeastern Vermont, 23 mi/37 km east-northeast of Montpelier*

1784 town settled; **1786** town chartered, named for French Admiral D'Anville; **1792** Caledonia County formed; town becomes first county seat; **Apr. 4, 1792** Congressman from Pennsylvania, abolitionist Thaddeus Stevens born (died 1868); **1805** Vermont General Assembly meets at courthouse; **1830s** town becomes center of Vermont anti-Masonic movement; **1856** county seat moved to St. Johnsbury; **1886** Green Bank Hollow Covered Bridge built on Joes Brook.

Dorset *Bennington County South central Vermont, 25 mi/40 km south of Rutland*

1761 town chartered by New Hampshire; **1773** Cephas Kent Tavern built; **1775–1776** four conventions held in tap room of Kent Tavern; Vermont independence proclaimed; **1785** Isaac Underhill opens first commercial marble quarry in U.S. at South Dorset; **c.1790** John Gray builds tavern, building later serves as Dorset Memorial Library; **1852** hotel built at East Dorset; **1911** Congregational Church completed; **1918** Squire House built; **1929** Dorset Theater built.

Dummerston *Windham County Southeastern Vermont, 50 mi/80 km south-southeast of Rutland*

1752 first settler John Kathan builds house; **1753** town chartered, named Fullam, later unofficially changed to Dummerston; **1760** town organized; **1779** Windham County formed; town becomes county seat; **1787** county courthouse built; **1817** Rutherford and Sophia Hayes emigrate to Ohio five years before birth of future president Rutherford B. Hayes; **1825** county seat moved to Newfane; **1872** West Dummerston Covered Bridge built on West River, longest in Vermont (280 ft/85 m); **1937** town renamed Dummerston.

Enosburg Falls *Franklin County* *Northwestern Vermont, 35 mi/56 km north-northeast of Burlington*

1780 Town of Enosburg chartered to Gen. Rogers Enos; village of Enosburg Falls becomes town's administrative and commercial center; early settler Isaac Farrar employs use of spouts for tapping sap from maple trees; **1875** Hopkins Covered Bridge built on Trout River; **1886** Enosburg Falls incorporated as a village.

Essex *Chittenden County* *Northwestern Vermont, 8 mi/12.9 km east of Burlington*

1763 town chartered by New Hampshire; **1783** town first settled; **1867** Drury Brick and Tile Company begins operating; **1871** Memorial Hall built; **1893** village of Essex Junction incorporated in western part of town of Essex; **1894** Fort Ethan Allen Military Reservation established, closed 1960; **1904** St. Michael's College established; **1905** trolley extended to fort from Burlington; **1965** Essex Community Players founded, venue at Memorial Hall; **1987** Congregational Church converted to Essex Library.

Fair Haven *Rutland County* *Western Vermont, 15 mi/24 km west of Rutland*

1779 town chartered; **c.1780** town first settled; **1783** Irish immigrant Matthew Lyon arrives, builds sawmill, grist mill, iron forge, and meeting house, serves as congressman, moves on to Kentucky in 1801, then Arkansas, is elected to congress in both of those states; **1803** First Congregational Church established, built 1812; **1839** slate quarries begin production; **1850s** town serves as station on Underground Railway, giving haven to fleeing slaves from South.

Fairfax *Franklin County* *Northwestern Vermont, 16 mi/26 km north-northeast of Burlington*

1763 town charter granted by New Hampshire; **1783** town settled; **1849** Baptist Church dedicated; **1853** New Hampton Institute moves here from New Hampton, New Hampshire (closed c.1905); **1865** Maple Street Covered Bridge built on Mill Brook; **1872** St. Luke's Catholic Church completed; **1873** Bellows Free Academy founded, campus rebuilt 1942; **1933** Fairfax Creamery established.

Fairfield *Franklin County* *Southern Vermont, 25 mi/40 km north-northeast of Burlington*

1763 land granted for town by New Hampshire; **1787** first settlers arrive; **1790** town organized; **Oct. 5, 1830** Chester Alan Arthur, 21st President, born (died Nov. 18, 1886); **June 3, 1851** historian George B. Adams born (died 1925); **1903** state monument to President Arthur erected.

Franklin *Franklin County* *Northwestern Vermont, 37 mi/60 km north-northeast of Burlington*

1789 town first settled, named Huntsburg; **1812–1815** embargo imposed during War of 1812, smuggling becomes major industry in this border town; **1817** town renamed Franklin; **Dec. 25, 1835** Union Gen. Orville Babcock born (died 1884); **1866** Fenians of Ireland enter Canada here and at other points in armed attempt to wrest Canada from British; U.S. makes mass arrests to quell movement; **1870** Fenians make second attempt with force of 2,000 to divert attention from main thrust at Ogdensburg, New York, U.S. rounds up conspirators, releases them short time later.

Georgia *Franklin County* *Northwestern Vermont, 17 mi/27 km north of Burlington*

1763 Town of Georgia chartered by New Hampshire, organized following Revolutionary War; **1800** Baptist Church built, used later as town hall; **1808** mill established on Stone Bridge Brook; **Oct. 20, 1820** Union Gen. George J. Stannard born (died 1886); **1896** Georgia Public Library founded.

Glover *Orleans County* *Northeastern Vermont, 36 mi/58 km north-northeast of Montpelier*

1783 town chartered; **1797** town settled, named for Gen. John Glover; **c.1800** the Old House built, only structure to survive Runaway Pond disaster; **June 6, 1810** Long Pond collapses, manmade catastrophe caused by digging of trench to divert water to new mills, houses and mills destroyed, citizens spared by riders warning of encroaching torrent, renamed Runaway Pond; **1827** Clark's Tavern established by Silas Clark; **1846** Union House built, served as stagecoach hotel; **1910** monument erected to commemorate Runaway Pond disaster.

Groton *Caledonia County* *Eastern Vermont, 19 mi/31 km east of Montpelier*

1789 town chartered; **1790** first store built; **1839** William Scott born, sentenced to be shot for sleeping on duty near Potomac River during Civil War, pardoned by Lincoln, died in action April 16, 1862, at Lee's Mill, Virginia; **1843** Old Lake House built, served as boarding house for lumberjacks; **1919** Groton State Forest established to west.

Guildhall *Essex County* *Northeastern Vermont, 53 mi/85 km east-northeast of Montpelier, on Connecticut River*

1761 town chartered by New Hampshire; **1764** town settled; **1787** grist mill built by Ward Bailey; **1792** Essex County formed; town becomes county seat; **1795** county courthouse and Guild Hall are built; **1828** Margaret Fuller House built; **1844** Guildhall United Church built; **1851** second county courthouse built; county office building built; **1865** Methodist Episcopal Church built, razed 1942;

1878 county jail built, closed 1969; **1901** Guildhall Library opened.

Guilford   *Windham County   Southeastern Vermont, 57 mi/92 km south-southeast of Rutland*

1754 town granted by New Hampshire; **1772** residents vote town into Cumberland County, New York; **1776** local civil war waged over town's legal jurisdiction, questioning 1772 decision, continues until Vermont's admission as a state, 1791; **1783** Ethan Allen arrives with Green Mountain Boys, declares town part of Vermont, establishes martial law; **1784** factional disputes disrupt town's way of life, through 1791; **1870** Green River Covered Bridge built.

Hardwick   *Caledonia County   North central Vermont, 20 mi/32 km north-northeast of Montpelier*

1781 town chartered; **1797** town first settled by Capt. John Bridgam; **1810** post office established; **1820** French Meeting House built by settler Samuel French; **June 27, 1823** public official Dorman Eaton born, instrumental in toppling New York City's Boss Tweed political machine (died 1899); **1837** religious sect, the New Lights, use meeting house during their short-lived existence; **c.1840** sawmill begins operation; **1868** Henry R. Mack begins quarrying granite, becomes major industry; **1867** town renamed Hardwick.

Hartford   *Windsor County   See **White River Junction***

Hartland   *Windsor County   Eastern Vermont, 28 mi/45 km east of Rutland, on Connecticut River*

1759 during retreat of Rogers' Rangers, party struggles to get rafts past rapids at North Hartland after being nearly swept to their deaths at White River Falls upstream; **1761** town chartered as Hertford by New Hampshire; **spring 1782** town renamed to eliminate confusion with Hartford, Vermont, to north; **1786** group of some 30 men prevent county court from convening here, force of 600 men from Windsor keep rebellion under control; **1804** Sumner-Steele House built by wealthy businessman David Sumner; **1881** Martins Mill Covered Bridge built at Lull's Brook.

Highgate   *Franklin County   Northwestern Vermont, 33 mi/53 km north of Burlington*

1763 town chartered by New Hampshire; **1787** town first settled by group of Hessian troops brought to fight for British who decided to remain in U.S. following Revolutionary War; **June 2, 1816** poet John Godfrey Saxe born (died 1887); **Nov. 12, 1877** U.S. Sen. Warren Austin born (died 1877); **1943** Missisquoi National Wildlife Refuge established; **1994–1995** two Grateful Dead concerts in successive summers draw total 120,000 "Dead Heads."

Hubbardton   *Rutland County   Western Vermont, 12 mi/19 km northwest of Rutland*

1764 town chartered by New Hampshire, granted to Thomas Hubbard; **July 7, 1777** Battle of Hubbardton, German troops assist British in turning tide against Americans fighting under Seth Warner; **1779** Fort Hubbardton built to defend northern frontier; **1937** Hubbardton Battlefield State Historic Site established, visitor's center opened 1970.

Hyde Park   *Lamoille County   North central Vermont, 30 mi/48 km east-northeast of Burlington*

1781 town chartered, granted to Jedediah Hyde; **1787** first settlers arrive; **1835** Lamoille County organized; Hyde Park becomes county seat; **1836** county courthouse built; **Apr. 17, 1910** 20 buildings destroyed by fire, including courthouse; **1912** opera house built; **1916** Lanpher Memorial Library opened; new county courthouse completed.

Island Pond   *Essex County   Northeastern Vermont, 50 mi/80 km northeast of Montpelier*

1781 originally chartered as Town of Random; **1820** area settled; village of Island Pond becomes administrative and commercial center for town; **1830** first sawmill built by John Currier; **1832** town renamed Brighton; **1852** First Congregational Church built; **1853** Atlantic & St. Lawrence (Grand Trunk) Railroad reaches town; **1858** Catholic Church built; **1878** Grace Methodist Church built; **1890** Island Pond incorporated as a village; **1899** Fitzgerald Lumber Company established; **July 28, 1901** singer Rudy Vallee born (died 1986); **1904** railroad station built.

Isle La Motte   *Grand Isle County   Northwestern Vermont, 28 mi/45 km north-northwest of Burlington*

1666 Fort Ste. Anne built on western shore by Capt. de La Motte as protections against Mohawks, first European settlement in Vermont; **Sept. 1776** Benedict Arnold anchors on west side of island prior to Battle of Valcour Island; **1779** Town of Isle la Motte chartered; **Sept. 1814** British Captain Pring lands here to protect loading operation prior to Battle of Plattsburg Sept. 11; **1880** Isle La Motte Lighthouse built on Lake Champlain, deactivated 1933.

Jericho   *Chittenden County   Northwestern Vermont, 10 mi/16 km east of Burlington*

1763 town chartered by New Hampshire; **1774** Joseph Brown family become first settlers; **1780** Brown family captured in Native American raid ordered by British, taken to Montreal, held until 1783; **1790** Rawson House built; **c.1800** Blackman's Store built; **1810** Blacksmith Shop established; **1825** Congregational Church built; **1828** Jericho Academy founded, closed 1845; **1855** Red Mill built; **1857** Calvary Episcopal Church built; **1858** Methodist Church built; **Feb. 9, 1865** Wilson A. Bentley born, the "Snowflake King" amassed collection of 5,300 microphotos of snowflakes during his 45 years here (died 1931).

Johnson   *Lamoille County   North central Vermont, 25 mi/40 km north-northwest of Montpelier*

1782 land grant given to William Samuel Johnson; **1784** Samuel Eaton founds town; **1836** Lamoille County Grammar School established, becomes State Normal School 1867, later Johnson State College; **1842** Johnson Woolen Mill established; **1846** local artist Julian Scott born (died 1901); **1855** Masonic Temple built; **c.1870** School Street Covered Bridge built on Gihon River; **c.1890** Hotel Sinclair built; **1989** Julian Scott Gallery established.

Londonderry   *Windham County   Southern Vermont, 26 mi/42 km south-southeast of Rutland*

1770 town chartered in state of New York as Kent; **1778** charter confiscated by Tory proprietors; **1780** town charter regranted by state of Vermont, renamed Londonderry; **1877** Ogdensburgh & Portland Railroad completed, becomes St. Johnsbury & Lake Champlain Railroad 1880, abandoned 1992; **1927** flooding of West River damages West River Railroad, Vermont's only state-owned rail line, cost of repairs puts line out of business by 1930s.

Lyndonville   *Caledonia County   Northeastern Vermont, 32 mi/51 km northeast of Montpelier*

1780 town of Lyndon chartered to Dr. Jonathan Arnold, names it for his son, Josias Lyndon Arnold; **1788** Daniel Cahoon, Jr. settles here; **1805** William Cahoon House completed; **1839** Schoolhouse Covered Bridge built; **1866** Boston & Maine Railroad reaches town; **1869** Sanborn Covered Bridge built **1878** Millers Run Covered Bridge built; **1880** incorporated as a village; **1881** Chamberlin Covered Bridge built; **1911** Lyndon State College established.

Manchester   *Bennington County   Southwestern Vermont, 30 mi/48 km south of Rutland*

1761 town chartered by New Hampshire; **c.1764** town settled; **1769** Hoyt House built; **1777** Vermont Council of Safety meets here, serves as interim government until election of state government 1778; **1780** Timothy Mead builds grist mill; **1784** town platted; **1790** Old Tavern built; **1856** Orvis Company founded, maker of fishing gear; **1902** Hildene house built by Robert Todd Lincoln, eldest son of Pres. Abraham Lincoln, Lincolns occupy home until 1975.

Marlboro   *Windham County   Southern Vermont, 52 mi/84 km south-southeast of Rutland*

June 26, 1748 Capt. Humphrey Hobbs and 40 men attacked by Native American forces under half-breed Sackett, many dead or wounded on both sides; **1751** town

chartered by New Hampshire as Marlborough, rechartered 1761; **c.1773** Whetstone Inn built; **1778** Congregational Church built on Town Hill, rebuilt 1819, destroyed by fire 1931; **1814** Newton House built; **1822** Town House built; **1947** Marlboro College established; **1951** Marlboro Music Festival organized; **1936** Southern Vermont Museum of Natural History founded; **1969** town office building built.

Middlebury   *Addison County   Western Vermont, 30 mi/48 km south of Burlington*

1761 town chartered by New Hampshire; **1766** first white settlers arrive in area; **1773** Benjamin Smalley builds first log house; **1778** other settlers arrive, are forced to evacuate by raids from alliance of Native Americans and Tories; **1783** settlers return; town founded by Gamaliel Painter and John Chapman; **1785** Addison County organized; **1792** Middlebury becomes county seat; **1796** Exhibition Hall built for Addison County Fair, used as first courthouse; **1797** Addison County Grammar School founded; **1800** Middlebury College established; **1803** extensive marble quarrying begins; **1807** educator Emma Hart Willard assumes charge of Middlebury Female Academy; Wainwright House built; **1809** Congregational Church completed; **1810** Old Jail built; Waybury Inn built; **1827** Middlebury Inn built; **1829** Sheldon Art Museum founded; **1831** *Middlebury Register* newspaper founded, becomes *Addison County Independent* 1946; **1874** Shard Villa mansion built by Columbus Smith; **1936** Dog Team Tavern built; **1995** county courthouse built.

Montpelier   *Washington County   Central Vermont, 34 mi/55 km east-southeast of Burlington*

1781 town chartered; **1788** Col. Jacob Davis clears land, builds cabin, names town for city in France; **May 4, 1791** Vermont admitted as 14th state of the Union; **1799** first bridge built over Winooski River; **1805** town founded on Winooski River as Vermont state capital; **1807** Pavillion Hotel built; **1808** general assembly moves from Windsor, previously met in fourteen different towns; **1809** first state capitol built; **1810** Jefferson County organized, renamed Washington County 1814; **1811** town becomes county seat; **Nov. 12, 1823** painter Thomas Waterman Wood born (died 1903); **1827** granite quarrying becomes important; **1834** Montpelier Seminary established, becomes branch of Norwich University, finally named Vermont College; **1836** second state capitol built, burned 1857; **Dec. 23, 1837** Adm. George Dewey born, figured in Battle of Manila Bay 1898 (died 1917); **1843** county courthouse built, burned 1844, rebuilt, burned 1880, rebuilt; **c.1845** Athenwood chalet-style mansion built; **1850** National Life Insurance Company founded; **1851** Vermont Historical Society moved from Barnet; **1859** present state capitol completed; **1867** Bethany Congregational Church built; **1875** fire destroys business district; **1876** Pavillion Hotel rebuilt; **1895** incorporated as a city; Wood Art Gallery established; Kellogg-Hubbard Library founded; **1918** supreme court building built; **Nov. 1927** flood waters of

Winooski River reach second-floor level, devastating town; **1935** Wrightsville Dam built on Winooski River; **1936** flooding reoccurs, damage lessened by dams at Montpelier and Barre built 1935; **1954** Bailey Avenue Bridge built; **1971** Vermont State Library founded in Pavillion Building.

Newbury   *Orange County   Eastern Vermont, 27 mi/ 43 km east-southeast of Montpelier, on Connecticut River*

1761 earliest interments made at Ox-Bow Cemetery at South Newbury; **1763** town chartered by New Hampshire; **1775** Col. Thomas Johnson House built; **1790** Isaac Bayley House built by Jacob Bayley; **1794** Congregational Church completed; **1829** Methodist Church built; **1839** Town House built; Methodist Bible Institute founded, becomes important stop on Underground Railway, provided safe havens for escaped slaves from South; **1894** Wildwood Hall Mansion (The Castle) built by George H. Moore; **1896** Tenney Memorial Library built.

Newfane   *Windham County   Southeastern Vermont, 45 mi/72 km south-southeast of Rutland*

1753 town chartered by New Hampshire, originally named Fane; **1779** Windham County organized; **1787** county seat (shire town) moved from West Dummerstown; **1793** Newfane Inn built; **1800** Martin Field, graduate of Dartmouth College, among early settlers; **1811** post office established; **1825** county court-house built; **1832** Union Church built, later becomes town hall; **1839** Congregational Church built; **c.1845** Windham County Hotel built; **1880** Brattleboro & Whitehall Railroad reaches town; **1882** town renamed Newfane; **1898** Moore Free Library founded.

Newport   *Orleans County   Northern Vermont, 50 mi/80 km north-northeast of Montpelier*

1759 Rogers' Rangers pass through here following raid on St. Francis village, Quebec; **1792** Orleans County organized; **1793** Deacon Martin Adams builds first house; **1800** eleven families arrive in new settlement; town becomes county seat; **1802** town chartered as Duncanborough; **1816** town renamed Newport; **1899** Goodrich Library opened; **1903** county courthouse built; **1917** incorporated as a city.

North Hero   *Grand Isle County   Northwestern Vermont, 24 mi/39 km north-northwest of Burlington, on Lake Champlain*

Oct. 10–11, 1776 British fleet emerges from channel north of island, surprised by size of Benedict Arnold's American fleet waiting for him, battle of Valcour Island follows; **1779** town chartered; **1783** Enos Wood, two others become first settlers; **1802** Grand Isle County formed; **1803** North Hero Tavern and Hotel built by Jed Ladd; **1804** town becomes county seat; **1824** county courthouse built; **1867** jail built; **1891** North Hero House Inn built.

Northfield   *Washington County   Central Vermont, 8 mi/12.9 km south-southwest of Montpelier*

1781 town of Northfield chartered; **1785** town first settled; **1855** Village of Northfield incorporated; **1867** Norwich University, founded 1819, moves from Norwich; **1872** Lower and Upper Cox Covered Bridges built; Slaughter House Covered Bridge built on Dog River; Station Covered Bridge built; **1878** Dickinson Memorial Library founded; **1899** Moseley Covered Bridge built on Stony Brook; **1910** U.S. Weather Bureau station established.

Orwell   *Addison County   Western Vermont, 20 mi/ 32 km northwest of Rutland, near Lake Champlain*

1763 town chartered by New Hampshire; **1775** fort built on Mt. Independence, bluff on Lake Champlain opposite Fort Ticonderoga; pontoon bridge built connecting two forts; **July 6, 1777** as Americans evacuate Fort Ticonderoga, a blazing house on Vermont side foolishly set by Colonials illuminates retreat, aids in British victory; **1810** Baptist Church built, later used as town hall; **1842** First Congregational Church built; **1860** St. Paul's Catholic Church built.

Panton   *Addison County   Northwestern Vermont, 23 mi/37 km south-southwest of Burlington*

1761 town chartered on Lake Champlain by New Hampshire; **Jan. 24, 1776** Benjamin Franklin, 70, spends night here on way to Canada in effort to persuade it to join colonies; **Oct. 1776** Benedict Arnold, under pursuit by British, runs aground in flagship *Congress*, four other boats, following Battle of Valcour Island, giving British victory, but delaying their advance for a year; **1778** town burned by British under Burgoyne; **1783** townspeople return following Revolution; **1812** Fort Cassen built to keep British from reaching Vergennes; **Apr. 14, 1814** British forces repulsed in attack on Fort Cassen, sparing Macdonough's fleet under construction; **1827** Old Brick House built.

Pittsford   *Rutland County   Central Vermont, 7 mi/ 11.3 km north-northwest of Rutland*

1761 town chartered; **1769** town first settled; **1774** earliest interments at Old Cemetery; **1781** Fort Vengeance built by state in Otter Valley for defense of settlers; **1840** Depot Covered Bridge built on Otter Brook; **1841** Gorham Covered Bridge built on Otter Brook; **1843** Hammond Covered Bridge built on Otter Brook, pushed one mile downstream during flood of 1927; **1849** Cooley Covered Bridge built on Furnace Brook.

Plymouth   *Windsor County   Central Vermont, 13 mi/21 km east-southeast of Rutland*

1761 town chartered by New Hampshire, originally named Saltash; **1775** Fort Vengeance built to protect against invasions from Canada during Revolution; **1797** town renamed; **July 4, 1872** John Calvin Coolidge, 30th President, born; **Aug. 3, 1923** Vice President Coolidge sworn in as president at parents' home upon learning of President Harding's death; **Jan. 5, 1933** former President Coolidge dies of heart attack in Massachusetts, buried at Plymouth.

Poultney *Rutland County* *Western Vermont, 14 mi/23 km west-southwest of Rutland*

1761 town chartered by New Hampshire; **1771** town settled by Thomas Ashley and Ebenezer Allen, cousin of Ethan Allen; **c.1790** Eagle Tavern built; **1791** Union Academy founded; **1805** Baptist Church completed; **Aug. 16, 1811** George Jones born, cofounder of *New York Times* newspaper (died 1891); **1836** Green Mountain Junior College established as Troy Conference Academy; **1841** Stonebridge Inn built; **1851** slate quarrying begins at North Poultney; **1854** Melodeon Factory built; **July 3, 1876** philosopher Ralph Barton Perry born (died 1957); **1899** Welsh Poultney Chapel built; **1988** Poultney Historical Society founded; St. David's Society founded to preserve local Welsh culture.

Pownal *Bennington County* *Southwestern Vermont, 58 mi/93 km south-southwest of Rutland*

1720s Dutch squatters make short-term attempt to settle here; **1760** town chartered by New Hampshire; **1766** pioneers from Rhode Island become first settlers; **1790** pottery making begins; **Aug. 30, 1790** George Washington rides through town on way to confer with Gov. Moses Robinson concerning Vermont's admission to Union; **1833** Oak Grove Seminary established, U.S. presidents James A Garfield and Chester A. Arthur both taught here.

Proctor *Rutland County* *Central Vermont, 4 mi/6.4 km northwest of Rutland*

1767 John Sutherland settles here, builds several mills; village founded within Town of Rutland, named Sutherland Falls; **1836** marble first quarried in area; **1867** 32-room Wilson Castle built; **1880** Redfield Proctor assumes control of Sutherland Falls Marble Quarry, later becomes Governor of Vermont, 1878–1880; **1882** village renamed Proctor; **1885** post office established; **1886** town of Proctor chartered, separates from Rutland and Pittsford.

Putney *Windham County* *Southeastern Vermont, 48 mi/77 km south-southeast of Rutland*

1753 town chartered; **1740** town first settled; Fort Putney built at Great Meadow, on Connecticut River, as defense against French and Native Americans; **1753** settlement resumes; **1755** new fortress built around dwellings; **1838** John Humphrey Noyes, cousin of Pres. Rutherford B. Hayes, attracts following to his communal society based on religion and free love, called Complex Marriage; **1847** Noyes arrested for group's sexual practices, jumps bond, flees with followers to Oneida, New York; **1935** summer drama school forced to move because members insist on wearing shorts in public; Putney School, private experi-

mental institution, founded; **Oct. 10, 1997** Jody Williams wins Nobel Peace Prize for her role in starting and coordinating of International Campaign to Ban Land Mines.

Randolph *Orange County* *Central Vermont, 21 mi/34 km south of Montpelier*

1781 town chartered; Experience Davis builds first house at South Randolph; **c.1782** Native American raids plague town; **1791** Duke of Kent spends night at Davis' house; **1795** Justin Morgan brings colt to Randolph, establishes first pure breed of American horse; **1804** Maple Grove built, served as parish house; **1805** Montpelier chosen over Randolph as state capital; **1806** Orange County Grammar School opened; **c.1850** railroad reaches town; **1852** first Agricultural Fair held; **1866** Vermont Technical College (2-year) established; **1903** Kimball Public Library built; **1904** Braley, Gifford and Hyde covered bridges built on Second Branch White River; **1905** Gifford Sanatorium founded, later becomes Gifford Medical Center; **1910** Vermont State School of Agriculture established at site of Grammar School; **1927** flooding destroys town center; **1967** Interstate Highway 89 built; **Dec. 26, 1991** fire destroys two downtown city blocks; **Jan. 27, 1992** city block destroyed by fire; **July 8, 1992** third block fire strikes business district.

Richford *Franklin County* *Northern Vermont, 47 mi/76 km north-northeast of Burlington*

1780 town chartered; **March 1795** town settled by Hugh and Mary Miller family; **1797** grist mill and sawmill built at new dam; **1800** first bridge built on Missisquoi River; **1820** Union House built, later used as Catholic rectory; **1866** Lillian "Queen Lil" Miller builds three-story house on international border, operates bar, related services; **1871** Advent Church built, later remodeled into town hall; **1873** Southeastern and Central Vermont railroads reach town; **1890** grain elevator built by Canadian Pacific Railroad; **1895** A. A. Brown Public Library opens; **1927** flooding severely damages powerhouse at Stevens Mills village, destroys Main Street Bridge.

Richmond *Chittenden County* *Northwestern Vermont, 11 mi/18 km east-southeast of Burlington*

1775 town first settled by Amos Brownson and John Chamberlain; **1794** town incorporated; **1813** Old Round Church built with sixteen sides "so Satan can't hide," used by five denominations; **Feb. 1, 1828** Sen. George F. Edmunds born, helped override Johnson veto of 1866 Civil Rights Act (died 1899); **1908** fire destroys Richmond village's entire business district; **1918** first annual pilgrimage to Round Church held; **1927** flooding of Winooski River damages town, sweeps away bridges; **1936** flooding occurs at higher levels than in 1927, damaging town.

Rockingham   *Windham County*   *Southeastern Vermont, 36 mi/58 km southeast of Rutland*

1704 240 natives camp here returning from raid on Greenfield, Massachusetts, with 112 prisoners, including Rev. John Williams; **1752** town chartered by New Hampshire; **c.1753** town settled; **1787** Rockingham Congregational Meeting House built, one of oldest churches in Vermont; **1868** Worrals Covered Bridge built on Williams River; **1870** Bartonsville Covered Bridge built on Williams River; **c.1870** Hall Covered Bridge built on Saxon River.

Royalton   *Windsor County*   *Central Vermont, 25 mi/40 km northeast of Rutland*

1769 town chartered by New York; **Aug. 1780** garrison moved to Bethel following Native American raid there; **Oct. 1780** unprotected town raided, burned by 300 natives; **1792** Cascadnac Inn built; **Dec. 23, 1805** Joseph Smith born, founder of Mormon Church, killed June 27, 1844, by mob at Carthage, Illinois.

Rutland   *Rutland County*   *Central Vermont, 60 mi/ 97 km south-southeast of Burlington*

1730 James Cross gives first description of falls on Otter Creek; **1761** town chartered by New Hampshire to John Murray of Rutland, Massachusetts; **c.1770** area settled; **1775** Fort Rutland built; **1778** Fort Ranger built for state troops; **1781** Rutland County formed; **1784** county seat moved from Tinmouth; **1789** Gookin House built; **c.1793** Pioneer Home built; **1794** *Rutland Herald* newspaper founded; **May 9, 1797** clergyman, writer Walter Colton born (died 1851); **Feb. 7, 1804** farm machinery inventor John Deere born (died 1886); **1812** Temple House built; **1844** marble quarrying begins at West Rutland; William Ripley establishes sawmill; **1849** Rutland & Burlington Railroad completed; **1860** Congregational Church built; **1871** county courthouse built; **1886** Rutland Free Library founded; **1889** Jewish Synagogue built; **1892** incorporated as a city, separates from Rutland Township; **1896** Rutland Regional Medical Center founded; **1927** flooding on Otter Creek washes away railroad bridge, damages highway bridge; **1929** Church of Christ the King completed; **1933** federal building built; **Jan. 8, 1973** fire destroys historic hotel, five killed.

Saint Albans   *Franklin County*   *Northwestern Vermont, 23 mi/37 km north of Burlington*

1763 British take control of area from French, included in New Hampshire grants; town chartered by New Hampshire; **1774** Jesse Welden arrives from Connecticut, becomes first settler; **1785** Welden returns to area after disappearing during Revolution; other settlers arrive; **1788** town organized; **1807** town becomes center for smuggling to Canada on Lake Champlain until War of 1812; **Sept. 11, 1814** town's militia joins other Vermont towns in Battle of Plattsburgh, New York, decisive victory for Lt. Thomas Macdonough's Vermont troops; **1837** during Papineau War, French-Canadians use St. Albans and Swanton as safe havens, drawing threat of invasion from British; **Oct. 1850** Central Vermont Railway reaches town; **1859** incorporated as a village; **Oct. 19, 1864** in St. Albans Raid, 21 Confederate soldiers make way north to town, rob all banks of $200,000, one man killed, others wounded, escape to Canada where they are tried and acquitted, leading to international flap; **June 1866** large numbers of Irish Fenians arrive to join attempt to overtake Canada; Pres. Andrew Johnson sends troops to uphold U.S. neutrality; **1867** Railroad Station completed; **1874** county courthouse built; **1883** Northwestern Medical Center founded, originally named St. Albans Hospital; **1897** incorporated as a city; **1930** Bellows Free Academy built, chartered 1878.

Saint Johnsbury   *Caledonia County*   *Northeastern Vermont, 30 mi/48 km east-northeast of Montpelier*

1786 town charter granted to Jonathan Arnold, who arrives with other settlers from Rhode Island; **1796** Caledonia County formed; **1798** Century House built; **1820** Paddock Mansion built; **1830** Thaddeus Fairbanks invents first lever (platform) scales, leads to development of town's first industry; **1842** St. Johnsbury Academy established; **1852** Octagon House built; **1856** county seat moved from Danville; county courthouse built, addition built 2000; **1871** The Atheneum built; **1891** Fairbanks Museum of Natural Science and Planetarium presented as gift by Col. Franklin Fairbanks; **1910** first airplane flight in Vermont made at County Fair; **1914** Government Fishery Station established.

Salisbury   *Addison County*   *Western Vermont, 20 mi/32 km north of Rutland*

1761 town chartered by New Hampshire; **1774** Amos Story becomes town's first settler, killed by falling tree prior to arrival of his family; wife Ann takes on challenge of raising the children and working the farm, house burned in Native American raid; **1813–1819** Dunmore Glass made at Lake Dunmore, also in 1832–1839; **June 14, 1853** Gov. John Weeks born, also served as U.S. Congressman (died 1949); **1905** monument erected in memory of Mrs. Ann Story.

Shelburne   *Chittenden County*   *Northwestern Vermont, 6 mi/9.7 km south of Burlington*

1763 town chartered by New Hampshire to Jesse Hallock, others; **1768** two Hessian men settle here, harvest timber for nearby Canada; **1778** two settlers slain by marauding British and Native Americans; garrison burned, barrel of beer used to extinguish fire; **1811** first Merino sheep introduced to area; **1814** Macdonough's fleet winters here on Lake Champlain during War of 1812; **1870s** region's fruit orchards established; **1886** Shelburne Farms Estate established by Dr. Seward and Lila (Vanderbilt) Webb; **1947** Shelburne Museum founded by Electra Havemeyer Webb.

Shoreham *Addison County* *Western Vermont,*
25 mi/40 km northwest of Rutland, near Lake Champlain

1761 town chartered by New Hampshire; **1766** town settled by Ephraim Doolittle and 14 others; **May 10, 1775** Ethan Allen and Green Mountain Boys cross Lake Champlain, capture Fort Ticonderoga, New York, from British; **1823** first store built by John Larrabee and Samuel Holly; **May 16, 1824** Levi P. Morton born, vice president under Benjamin Harrison (died 1920); **1846** Congregational Church built; **1852** Universalist Church built; **1873** St. Genevieve Catholic Church built.

South Hero *Grand Isle County* *Northwestern Vermont, 12 mi/19 km northwest of Burlington*

1779 town chartered, created from Hero along with Middle Hero and North Hero; **1783** Ebenezer Allen, cousin of Ethan Allen, lands at south end of Grand Isle, in Lake Champlain, becomes South Hero's first settler; Ebenezer Allen establishes ferry; **Feb. 10, 1789** Ethan Allen, leader of Green Mountain Boys, comes here to collect load of hay, dies on way home after evening of drinking rum (born 1737); **1819** Phelps-Reade House built; **1829** Old Stone Inn built.

Springfield *Windsor County* *Southeastern Vermont, 31 mi/50 km southeast of Rutland*

1752 Abnaki peoples joined by white social outcast John Nott; **1759** Crown Point Military Road built from Crown Point, New York; **1761** town chartered by New Hampshire; **1774** William Lockwood buys land at falls of the Black River, builds sawmill, dam, and bridge; **1785** Eureka Schoolhouse built, oldest in Vermont; **1808** Isaac Fisher arrives from Charlestown, New Hampshire, establishes foundry, cotton and woolen mills, machine shop; **1829** sheep shearing equipment shop established; **1833** Congregational Church built; **1870** Baltimore Covered Bridge built; **1871** Slack Clothing Mill established; **1888** National Hydraulic Company moves to Springfield, founded 1829; **1897** Springfield Terminal Railway built, only electric railroad in northern New England, abandoned 1956; **1903** Hartness House Observatory built by Gov. James Hartness; **1909** St. Trinity Greek Orthodox Church built; **1910** Hartness Telescope installed at observatory, 240-ft/73-m long; **1917** Falls Bridge built; **1920** Hartness State Airport established; **Aug. 1920** Russell W. Porter begins manufacture of telescopes; **Dec. 7, 1923** Springfield Telescope Makers hold first meeting, become Stellafane Society 1926; **1930** Catholic Church completed; **1956** Springfield Art and Historical Society founded; **1964** American Precision Museum founded; **1982** first annual Vermont Apple Festival held.

Stowe *Lamoille County* *North central Vermont, 25 mi/40 km east of Burlington*

1763 town chartered by New Hampshire; **1794** town settled; **1833** Green Mountain Inn built; **Apr. 27, 1843** Catholic missionary Ira Bruno Dutton born (died 1888), succeeded Father Damien as head of leper colony at Kalawao, Molokai, Hawaii; **1848** town of Mansfield annexed by Stowe; **1861** school built, becomes Stowe Free Library 1981.

Swanton *Franklin County* *Northwestern Vermont, 30 mi/48 km north of Burlington*

c.1695 French Jesuits build first church within boundaries of present-day Vermont; **c.1700** French establish settlement; **1759** village destroyed by Rogers' Rangers in retaliation for Native American raids on various Vermont localities; **1763** town chartered by New Hampshire; **1765** lumber mill established; **1779** John Hilliker becomes first permanent white settler; **Aug. 1813** British land at village of Maquam on Maquam Bay, burn Colonists' barracks at Swanton; **1835** French-Canadian rebels take refuge here and at St. Albans during Papineau War, creating threat of invasion by English Canadians; **1877** fire destroys Merchants Row, again in 1878; **1914** Swanton State Fish Hatchery established.

Thetford *Orange County* *Eastern Vermont, 34 mi/ 55 km south-southeast of Montpelier, on Connecticut River*

1761 town chartered by New Hampshire; **1787** Old Congregational Church built at Thetford Hill, oldest church in continuous use in Vermont; **1777** local hero Richard Wallace volunteers hazardous mission of swimming naked at night across Lake Champlain, through British blockade to deliver messages to Fort Ticonderoga; **1819** Thetford Academy established; **1837** Methodist Church at Union Village built; **1877** Latham Memorial Library founded, becomes Latham-Peabody Library 1972; **1936** flooding from Connecticut River inundates village of North Thetford.

Tunbridge *Orange County* *Eastern Vermont, 25 mi/40 km south of Montpelier*

1761 town chartered by New Hampshire; **Oct. 1780** town attacked by 300 Native Americans led by British Lt. Horton, two settlers killed, many prisoners taken; **1845** Flint Covered Bridge built; **1879** Howe Covered Bridge built; **1883** Cilley Covered Bridge built; **1902** Larkin Covered Bridge built; **2000** Mill Covered Bridge built.

Vergennes *Addison County* *Western Vermont, 20 mi/32 km south of Burlington*

1766 first settled by Colonel Reid of New York, claims land; **1733** New Yorkers settle on Reid's claim, Green Mountain Boys burn their dwellings; **1772** Reid dispossessed by New Hampshire; **1788** incorporated as a city from parts of New Haven, Panton, and Ferrisburgh towns, named for Count de Vergennes, French foreign affairs minister; **1790s** city becomes known for its iron works; **1793** General Strong House built; **July 1794** city government organized; **1812–1815** city produces 177 tons of cannonballs for War of 1812; **1814** Thomas

Macdonough builds flagship *Saratoga*, fleet of smaller ships in 40 days for attack on Plattsburgh, New York; **1828** U.S. arsenal established.

Vernon   *Windham County*   *Southeastern Vermont, 62 mi/100 km south-southeast of Rutland*

1672 Northfield land grant made by Massachusetts; **1753** town chartered by New Hampshire, named Hinsdale; **1802** town renamed Vernon by Vermont; **July 4, 1911** highest temperature recorded in Vermont reached, 105°F/41°C; **1968** Vernon Historians incorporated; **1972** Vermont Yankee Nuclear Power Plant begins production.

Vershire   *Orange County*   *Eastern Vermont, 23 mi/37 km southeast of Montpelier*

1779 town settled by Lenox Titus, originally named Ely; **1781** town chartered, renamed Vershire, amalgam of Vermont and New Hampshire; **c.1840** sheep raising becomes important; **1854** Vermont Copper Mining Company established, later becomes Ely Copper; **1876** Ely-Goddard Mansion built; **1880** Ely Copper Mines ship three million lb (1,360,777 kg) of copper; **July 1883** in Ely War, rioting miners demanding back pay, threaten to dynamite town and neighboring West Fairlee, threat broken by National Guard troops, miners paid, mines permanently closed.

Waterbury   *Washington County*   *Central Vermont, 10 mi/16 km northwest of Montpelier*

1763 town chartered by New Hampshire; **1783** town settled by James Marsh; **1816** Carpenter House built; **1824** Congregational Church built; Church of Christ built; **1826** Stagecoach Inn built; **1830s** sheep raising boom begins, through 1870; **1833** Waterbury Center Community Church built; **1850** Vermont Central Railroad Station built, rebuilt 1875; **1865** Waterbury Inn opened, burned 1953; **1869** Baptist Green Mountain Seminary founded; **1870s** dairying becomes important; **c.1890** Waterbury Opera House opened, burned 1985; **1896** Vermont State Hospital established; **1927** flooding devastates town, 20 killed, leads to construction of Little River Dam; **1960** Interstate Highway 89 opened; **1970** Community College of Vermont established; **1980s** Waterbury State Office Complex built.

Westminster   *Windham County*   *Southeastern Vermont, 45 mi/72 km southeast of Rutland*

1735 land grant issued for town on Connecticut River; sawmill and first house built; **1740** settlement, now called New Taunton, abandoned with exclusion from Massachusetts; **1752** town chartered as Westminster by New Hampshire; settlement begins again; **1772** courthouse built for then Cumberland County, New York; **March 13, 1775** courthouse seized by armed men dissatisfied with New York's sovereignty over Vermont in Westminster Massacre, one killed, several wounded by sheriff's men; **Jan. 15, 1777** Vermont declares itself a separate state at convention here; **1778** state's first printing office established by Judah Spooner and Timothy Green, found state's first newspaper, *The Vermont Gazette*, 1781; **1923** Community Hall built.

White River Junction   *Windsor County*   *Eastern Vermont, 32 mi/52 km east of Rutland, on Connecticut River*

1764 Hartford Township settled by families from Lebanon, Connecticut, including Joseph March, first lieutenant governor of Vermont; village of White River Junction becomes town's commercial center; **1803** bridge built across Connecticut River by Elias Lyman; **Jan. 21, 1815** dentist Dr. Horace Wells born, among first to apply laughing gas (nitrous oxide) during tooth extractions (died 1848); **1847** Vermont Central and Connecticut River railroads reach village; **1895** White River Paper Company established; **1907** Gates Memorial Library founded; **1910** Vermont Central Railroad Bridge built; **1912** First National Bank of White River Junction built; **1924** Coolidge Hotel built; **1950** Wilder Dam built on Connecticut River by New England Power Company; **1955** Polka Dot Restaurant opened.

Whitingham   *Windham County*   *Southern Vermont, 55 mi/89 km south of Rutland*

1770 town chartered by New York to Col. Nathan Whiting; **June 1, 1801** Mormon leader Brigham Young born (died 1877); **1850** Baptist Church built; **1924** Harriman Dam completed on Deerfield River, forms Harriman Reservoir, also called Lake Whitingham.

Williston   *Chittenden County*   *Northwestern Vermont, 7 mi/11.3 km east of Burlington*

1763 town chartered by New Hampshire, named for grantee Samuel Willis; **1774** town settled; **1776** home of Thomas Chittenden completed, first governor of Vermont, destroyed by fire c.1933; **1786** town incorporated; **1828** Williston Academy founded, closed 1883, building burned 1949; **c.1812** Eagle Tavern built by Benjamin Going, burned 1850; **1832** Congregational Church built; **1842** Thomas Chittenden Memorial Town Hall built; **1860** Universalist Church built; covered bridge built on Winooski River; **1876** cold storage plant built by Smith Wright; **1896** Chittenden Monument erected; **1905** Williston Public Library founded, renamed Dorothy Alling Memorial Library 1960.

Windsor   *Windsor County*   *Southeastern Vermont, 30 mi/48 km east-southeast of Rutland*

1761 charter granted by New Hampshire; **1764** Col. Nathan Stone becomes first settler; **1765** 16 families arrive at settlement; **1772** second grant given by New York to Colonel Stone; Old Constitution House built as tavern, site of state constitutional convention; **July 2, 1777** convention held to form independent state, Vermont constitution adopted July 8; **1781** Windsor County organized; town becomes county seat; **1783** *Vermont Journal and Advertiser* newspaper begins publication; **1786** county seat shared with Woodstock; Inn at Windsor built; **1791** Green House built, used later as Masonic Lodge; **1794** Woodstock becomes sole county seat; **1796** first local bridge built across Connecticut River, replacing ferry; **1798** Old South Church built; **1800** Asahel Hubbard arrives from Connecticut, patents hydraulic pump 1828; **1805** state capital moved to Montpelier; **1834** Ascutney Mill Dam built on Old Mill Brook; **1807** Vermont State Prison established; **1811** second bridge built, first to charge tolls; **1829** National Hydraulic Company founded; **1846** Robbins and Lawrence Armory built; **1858** manufacture begins on locally developed sewing machine; **1866** covered toll bridge built across Connecticut River to Cornish, New Hampshire; **July 5, 1867** astronomer, dendrochronologist Andrew Douglass born, originated tree ring dating method (died 1962); **1882** Windsor Public Library founded, building opened 1904.

Winooski   *Chittenden County*   *Northwestern Vermont, 2 mi/3.2 km north of Burlington*

1772 Fort Frederick founded; **1787** village settled on Winooski River by Ira Allen and Remember Baker; **c.1825** grist mill built, destroyed by flood 1830, rebuilt 1852; **1835** Burlington Woolen Mill established at falls, beginning of town's industrial growth; **1849** Central Vermont Railroad reaches town; **1850s** Irish immigrants arrive; **1866** incorporated as a village; **1880** Colchester Woolen Mill built; **1892** Chace Cotton Mill built; **1896** Winooski Worsted Mill built; **1904** St. Michael's College established; **1912** Champlain Woolen Mill built; **1921** incorporated as a city, separates from Colchester Township; **1927** flooding destroys Main Street bridge.

Woodstock   *Windsor County*   *Eastern Vermont, 22 mi/35 km east of Rutland*

1761 town chartered by New Hampshire; **1765** Harvard graduate Timothy Knox becomes first settler; **1781** Windsor County organized; **1786** town shares county seat with Windsor; **1792** Richardson's Tavern by Capt. Israel Richardson, later becomes Eagle Hotel; **1794** town becomes sole county seat; Hutchinson House built; **1808** Old White Meeting House built; **1824** Alvin Adams establishes railroad express shipping service, evolves into worldwide Adams Express Company; **1827** medical school established, closed 1856; **1830** Shiretown Inn built; **1846** first Windsor County Fair held, discontinued 1932; **1848** Green Mountain Liberal Institute established at South Woodstock (closed); **1855** county courthouse completed; **1871** Billings Mansion built by railroad entrepreneur Frederick Billings; **1885** Norman Williams Library built; **1892** Woodstock Inn built, replaces Eagle Hotel; **1973** Pentangle Council of the Arts founded; **June 1998** Marsh-Billings-Rockefeller National Historical Park established.

Virginia

Eastern U.S. Capital and largest city: Richmond.

Virginia was one of the 13 colonies which adopted the U.S. Declaration of Independence July 4, 1776. It became the 10th state to ratify the U.S. Constitution June 25, 1788. In 1801, Virginia ceded Arlington County to the District of Columbia, but it was returned to Virginia in 1846. Virginia seceded from the Union as a Confederate state April 17, 1861, with the Confederate capital at Richmond. West Virginia separated from Virginia as a Union state June 20, 1863. Virginia was readmitted to the Union January 26, 1870.

Virginia is divided into 95 counties. In addition to the counties are 40 independent cities that are separate from their surrounding counties. Municipalities are classified as towns and cities. In 1902, the Virginia Constitution obligated municipalities to separate from their counties when they reincorporate as a city in addition to those cities that had done so prior to that year. Also, the term "independent city" was first officially applied. The cities of Virginia Beach, Chesapeake, Suffolk, Hampton, and Newport News were formerly counties. Many independent cities are county seats for their surrounding counties. Besides independent cities, other municipalities are classified as towns. There are no townships. See Introduction.

Abingdon *Washington County* *Southwestern Virginia, 121 mi/195 km west-southwest of Roanoke*

1748 land granted to Dr. Thomas Walker; **1760** Great Road built by William Byrd; **c.1765** town founded, named Wolf Hills; **1774** Black's Fort built by Joseph Black; **1776** Washington County formed; town becomes county seat; **1778** town incorporated, renamed Abingdon; **Oct. 1780** 200 volunteers march south to Battle of Kings Mountain, South Carolina; **Apr. 12, 1791** journalist Francis Preston Blair born (died 1876); **1832** Francis Preston Mansion built, becomes Martha Washington Inn; **Dec. 14–15, 1864** Gen. George Stoneman's 10,000 Union troops burn town; **1867** county courthouse built; **1869** Stonewall Jackson Institute, Presbyterian school for girls, founded, closed 1932; **1967** Virginia Highlands Community College established.

Accomac *Accomack County* *Eastern Virginia, 70 mi/113 km north-northeast of Norfolk, near Atlantic Ocean*

1634 Accomac County formed, boundary defined 1662; **c.1645** Mount Custis house built; **1660** Bowman's Folly house built by Edmund Bowman; **c.1685** Hill Farm house built by Capt. Richard Hill; **1750** Drummond House built; **1786** county seat moved from Onancock; town platted, named Drummond; **Dec. 3, 1806** Henry Wise born, governor of Virginia 1856–1860 (died 1876); **1838** St.

James' Church built; **1893** town renamed Accomac; **1899** county courthouse built; **1940** county name altered, changed to Accomack; **1944** town incorporated.

Alberta *Brunswick County* *Southern Virginia, 55 mi/89 km south-southwest of Richmond*

1720 Brunswick County formed; Alberta, to southwest, becomes county seat; **1732** county courthouse built; **1746** county seat moved to Warfield to east with creation of Lunenburg County out of Brunswick; **1928** incorporated as a town; **1970** Southside Virginia Community College established.

Alexandria *Alexandria City* *Northern Virginia, 7 mi/11.3 km south-southwest of Washington, D.C.*

1608 Capt. John Smith ascends Potomac to falls; **1669** land grant made to Robert Howsing; **1675** Native Americans cross Potomac to drive out settlers in Susquehannock War; **1713** first plantations established in area; **1740** ferry established to Frazier's Point, Maryland; **1742** Fairfax County formed; **1748** town founded on Potomac River, named for landowning family; **1752** county seat moved from Vienna; Gadsby's Tavern built; Carlyle House built; **1773** Christ Church completed; **1779** town incorporated; **Feb. 5, 1784** the *Virginia Journal and Alexandria Advertiser* newspaper founded, becomes the *Gazette* 1861; **1790** Presbyterian

Meeting House built, replaced after 1835 lightning strike, closed 1886; Fendall House built; **1792** Bank of Alexandria founded, first bank in Virginia; **1793** Hallowell School built; **1795** St. Mary's Catholic Church built; **1801** town included with section of Fairfax County ceded to District of Columbia, serves as county seat for District's Alexandria County; Fairfax County seat moved to town of Fairfax; **1816** Lord Fairfax House built; **1817** city hall built, burned 1871, rebuilt 1873; **1823** Protestant Episcopal Seminary founded; **1824** fire damages city; **1836** Lt. Robert Randolph, dismissed by President Jackson for defrauding government, punches Jackson in nose, is arrested but not punished; **1839** Lyceum Hall built; **1847** Alexandria County returned to Virginia; **1852** incorporated as a city; **1861** Fort Ward built, part of Washington defense perimeter; **1863** city serves as capital of Restored Government of Virginia, includes several counties remaining under Federal control; **1898** Alexandria County seat moved to Clarendon; **1902** becomes an independent city; **1918** Torpedo Factory opened, closed 1945; **1920** Alexandria County renamed Arlington County; **1922** George Washington Masonic National Memorial built; **March 7, 1934** TV personality Willard Scott born; **Nov. 10, 1959** singer MacKenzie Phillips born; **1969** Public Broadcasting Service founded; **1974** Torpedo Factory Art Center founded.

Amelia Court House   *Amelia County*   *Central Virginia, 31 mi/50 km southwest of Richmond*

1735 Amelia County formed; **1762** St. John's Episcopal Church built; **March 25, 1845** poet John Bannister Tabb born (died 1909); **1855** St. John's Church built to north; **1924** county courthouse built; **1905** Confederate monument erected.

Amherst   *Amherst County*   *Central Virginia, 15 mi/ 24 km north of Lynchburg*

1761 Amherst County formed; **1810** county seat moved from Clifford; **c.1835** Sweet Briar House built; **1910** incorporated as a town; **1871** county courthouse built; **1901** Sweet Briar College established; **1964** Amhurst Public Library founded; **1973** history museum founded.

Annandale   *Fairfax County*   *Northern Virginia, 12 mi/19 km southwest of Washington, D.C.*

1685 Ravensworth Estate acquired by Col. William Fitzhugh; **1730** Ossian Hall house built, destroyed by fire 1959; **1779** Oak Hill mansion built by Maj. Henry Fitzhugh; **1796** Ravenswood Mansion built, burned 1925; **1846** Annandale Chapel built; **1965** Northern Virginia Community College (Fairfax Campus) established.

Appomattox   *Appomattox County*   *Central Virginia, 77 mi/124 km west-southwest of Richmond*

1845 Appomattox County formed; **c.1845** brick tavern built by county surveyor John Patterson; **1846** county courthouse built on Clover Hill; **Sept. 9, 1865** Confederate Gen. Robert E. Lee surrenders to Gen. Ulysses S. Grant with his 27,000 troops at 8:30 A.M. at courthouse, ending Civil War; **1895** county courthouse built at new location, previous structure destroyed by fire 1892; town founded; **1925** town incorporated; **June 18, 1930** Appomattox Battlefield Site authorized, designated as Appomattox Court House National Historical Park Apr. 15, 1954.

Arlington   *Arlington County*   *Northern Virginia, 2 mi/3.2 km southwest of Washington, D.C.*

1791 area surveyed as part of new District of Columbia for national capital; **1801** Alexandria County formed from Fairfax County, includes town of Alexandria, ceded to newly formed District of Columbia, one of two counties of D.C. (Columbia County on Maryland side); **1802** Arlington House begun by playwright George Washington Parke Custis, completed c.1815; **May 31, 1837** Confederate Gen. William Henry Fitzhugh Lee born (died 1891); **1847** Alexandria County returned to Virginia with Alexandria as county seat; **c.1861** Fort Whipple established, name changed to Fort Myer 1881, becomes U.S. army military base; **June 1864** Arlington National Cemetery established by Department of the Army; **1898** county courthouse completed; **1912** three prominent orange steel towers built near Potomac by Naval Radio Station, demolished 1941 with opening of National Airport; **1920** county renamed Arlington County to end confusion with city of Alexandria; entire county remains unincorporated city of Arlington; **Nov. 11, 1921** Unknown Soldier of World War I buried here, tomb dedicated 1931; **1932** Arlington Memorial Bridge completed across Potomac River from Washington; **1941** Washington National Airport opened, renamed Ronald Reagan International Airport 2001; **1943** The Pentagon building completed; **1950** Marymount University established; **Apr. 16, 1956** astronaut David M. Brown born, killed in *Columbia* shuttle disaster over Texas Feb. 1, 2003; **Nov. 2, 1965** war protester Norman Morrison, 31, immolates himself in front of Pentagon with one-year-old daughter Emily in his arms, drops child without harming her; **Aug. 25, 1967** American Nazi Party leader George Lincoln Rockwell shot dead at laundromat, aide held as suspect; **1997** Women in Military Service for America Memorial dedicated; **Sept. 11, 2001** American Airlines Boeing 757, Flight 77 Dulles Airport to Los Angeles, hijacked by suicide terrorists operating for Osama bin Laden's Al-Qaeda terrorist network out of Afghanistan, plane flown deliberately into Pentagon, killing all 64 on board, 125 Pentagon workers, plus the 4 hijackers, effort coordinated with dual suicide hijackings flown into World Trade Center,

New York, and foiled airline attack crashed in woods near Shanksville, Pennsylvania [see Somerset].

Ashland   *Hanover County*   *East central Virginia, 15 mi/24 km north of Richmond*

1734 Hickory Hill house built, rebuilt 1875 after fire; **1848** land purchased by Edwin Robinson, president of Richmond, Fredericksburg & Potomac Railroad, establishes Slash Cottage health resort; **1855** town name chosen for Henry Clay's Kentucky home; **1858** town incorporated; **1868** Randolph-Macon College, established 1830, moves here from Boydton; **Oct. 19, 2002** 37-year-old man shot, injured while exiting a Ponderosa Steakhouse, 12th victim of "D.C. Sniper," random shooting spree began Oct. 3 in Maryland, suspects captured in Maryland Oct. 24.

Austinville   *Wythe County*   *Southwestern Virginia, 61 mi/98 km southwest of Roanoke, on New River*

1756 lead deposits discovered by Col. John Chiswell; **1772** Fincastle County formed, extends into present-day Kentucky and Tennessee; settlement called The Lead Mines becomes county seat; **Oct. 1776** lagging lead production leads governor to order continuation of mining for Revolutionary War needs; **Dec. 1776** Fincastle County eliminated, Montgomery and Washington counties and "County of Kentucky" created from it; **1784** Moses Austin of Connecticut founds Austinville as headquarters of his mining interests; **1790** Wythe County formed from Montgomery County; Wytheville becomes county seat; **Nov. 3, 1793** Stephen Austin, founding father of Texas, born to Moses Austin, father and son move to Missouri lead district 1798 (died 1836); **1820** lead shot tower built to north.

Bassett   *Henry County*   *See* **Martinsville (2002)**

Bedford   *Bedford City*   *West central Virginia, 25 mi/40 km east-northeast of Roanoke*

1753 Bedford County formed; New London becomes first county seat; **1754** town founded; **1781** Campbell County separates from Bedford County; county seat moved from New London to new settlement of Liberty, founded on land donated by William Downey and Joseph Fuqua; **1839** town of Liberty incorporated; **1890** town renamed Bedford City; **1900** Bedford Public Library founded; **1902** Elk National Home for aged founded; **1912** town name shortened; **1930** county courthouse built; **1968** incorporated as an independent city; name shortened; **June 6, 2001** granite Victory Arch dedicated at National D-Day Memorial, site honors all soldiers who gave their lives on D-Day, June 6, 1944, at Normandy, France, site chosen for the high percentage, 21 of 35, of Bedford servicemen who died that day.

Bensley   *Chesterfield County*   *East central Virginia, 7 mi/11.3 km south of Richmond*

c.1732 Ampt Hill estate built by Henry Cary, Jr. (1675–1750), inherited by Archibald Cary 1749 (1719–1787); **1862** Fort Darling built atop Drewry's Bluff, on James River; **May 16, 1862** Union fleet, including ironclad *Monitor*, beaten back by units at fort; **July 23, 1863** Confederate naval school established on board the *Patrick Henry*; **1927** Du Pont Plant established, manufacturer of synthetic fibers, cellophane; **1929** Ampt Hill house moved to Richmond for Du Pont factory construction.

Berryville   *Clarke County*   *Northern Virginia, 56 mi/90 km west-northwest of Washington, D.C.*

1762 Daniel Morgan builds Soldier's Rest residence; **c.1770** Fairfield House built to north by Warner Washington; **1790** Annefield house built to southwest; **1798** town platted on land owned by Benjamin Berry; **c.1799** The Nook house built; **1809** Battlefield Inn built; **1836** Clarke County formed from Frederick County, separating Clarke's large landowners in east from Frederick's German and Scotch-Irish; **1841** town becomes county seat; county courthouse built; **1861–1864** several minor skirmishes take place in area during Civil War; **1870** town incorporated.

Bland   *Bland County*   *Southwestern Virginia, 70 mi/113 km west-southwest of Roanoke*

1861 Bland County formed, named for patriot Richard Bland; town founded as county seat, originally named Seddon; town renamed Bland later same year; **1874** county courthouse built.

Bluefield   *Tazewell County*   *Southwestern Virginia, 73 mi/117 km west of Roanoke*

1777 area settled by John Davidson and Richard Bailey; **1863** state of West Virginia separates from Virginia; **1883** town of Harman, Virginia, founded adjacent to Bluefield, West Virginia; coal mining begins in area; **1884** Norfolk & Western Railroad built; town renamed Graham for railroad surveyor Thomas Graham; **March 13, 1884** explosion at Laurel Coal Mine at Pocahontas to west, 112 killed; **1921** incorporated as a town; **1922** Bluefield College established; **1924** town renamed Bluefield to agree with its West Virginia neighbor; governors of West Virginia and Virginia hold hand-shaking ceremony at state boundary, pledge cooperation between two states and twin towns.

Bowling Green   *Caroline County*   *East central Virginia, 36 mi/58 km north of Richmond*

1667 Bowling Green House (the Old Mansion) built by Maj. Thomas Hoomes; first horse racetrack in America built by Hoomes; **c.1699** New Hope Tavern built; **1728** Caroline County formed; first county seat established at site 2 mi/3.2 km to north; **1764** first of two breeding stud horses brought from England; **1794** Hoomes donates property from his Bowling Green estate for new county seat; **1803** county seat moved to present site; **c.1800** horse racing declines; **1804** St. Asaph Methodist Church built; **1835** county courthouse built; **1837** incorporated as a town; **1868** The Home School founded by Alice Scott Chandler, moves to Buena Vista 1901; **1890s** Bullard's Opera House opens; **1941** Fort A. P. Hill army base established; **1989** first Harvest Festival held.

Boydton   *Mecklenburg County   Southern Virginia, 80 mi/129 km southwest of Richmond*

1764 Mecklenburg County formed from Lunenburg County; **1790** Boyd Tavern built; **1812** town founded by Alexander Boyd, becomes county seat; **1830** Randolph-Macon College established, moved to Ashland 1868; **1832** Randolph-Macon College established, moved to Ashland 1868; **1834** incorporated as a town; **c.1840** St. James Episcopal Church built; **1842** county courthouse built; **1953** John H. Kerr Dam built on Roanoke (Staunton) River, forming large reservoir on Virginia-North Carolina boundary.

Bristol   *Bristol City   Southwestern Virginia, 133 mi/ 214 km west-southwest of Roanoke*

1749 land surveyed by John Buchanan; **Aug. 1, 1770** explorer William Clark born, of Lewis and Clark Expedition 1804, governor of Missouri Territory (died 1838); **1771** Col. Evan Shelby and Isaac Baker, Sr. of Maryland build first homes; **1803** compromise temporarily settles Virginia-North Carolina boundary dispute; **1856** Virginia & Tennessee Railroad extended to town, at North Carolina boundary; town incorporated as Goodson, for landowner Col. Samuel Goodson; adjacent Bristol, Tennessee, also incorporated; **1870** Sullins College founded, campus rebuilt after 1915 fire, closed 1977; **1890** incorporated as a city; name changed to Bristol; **July 24, 1893** sociologist Charles Spurgeon Johnson born (died 1956); **1897** Virginia-North Carolina boundary dispute rekindled, settled 1903 by U.S. Supreme Court; **1902** becomes an independent city; **1910** Virginia Intermont College, founded 1884, moved from Glade Spring.

Brookneal   *Campbell County   South central Virginia, 28 mi/45 km southeast of Lynchburg*

1736 area first settled; **c.1742** log Hat Creek Presbyterian Church built; **1790** tobacco inspection station established on property owned by Brooke and Neal families; **1796** Patrick Henry moves into Red Hill house after living part-time for two years at Long Island, to west; **June 6, 1799** Patrick Henry dies at Red Hill (born 1736); **1802** town established; **1848** Staunton Hall mansion built to east by Charles Bruce; **1908** incorporated as a town; **May 13, 1986** Red Hill-Patrick Henry National Memorial authorized.

Buckingham   *Buckingham County   Central Virginia, 35 mi/56 km east-northeast of Lynchburg*

1761 Buckingham County formed from Albemarle County; town of Maysville founded as county seat; **c.1800** Buckingham Hotel built, later becomes Moseley House hotel, razed 1963; **1818** town chartered; **1822** second county courthouse built, designed by Thomas Jefferson, destroyed by fire 1869; **c.1830** Maysville Hotel built, later becomes Pearson Hotel; **1833** third county courthouse built; **1852** incorporated as a town; **1906** town renamed Buckingham.

Buena Vista   *Buena Vista City   Northwestern Virginia, 47 mi/76 km northeast of Roanoke*

1880 Norfolk & Western Railroad built; **1889** town founded by Benjamin C. Moomaw; becomes paper industry boomtown; **c.1890** Green Forest house built by Arthur Glasgow; **1890** incorporated as a town; **1892** incorporated as a city; **1901** Alice Chandler's Home School, established in 1868, moves from Bowling Green; **1902** becomes an independent city.

Cape Charles   *Northampton County   Eastern Virginia, 32 mi/51 km north-northeast of Norfolk*

1861 Federal troops occupy cape and entire Delmarva Peninsula during Civil War; **1884** New York, Philadelphia & Norfolk Railroad extended to site on Chesapeake Bay 10 mi/16 km north of end of peninsula, embarkation point of train ferry to Norfolk; town founded; **1886** incorporated as a town; **1933** first automobile ferries begin operating to Norfolk; **1950** ferry terminal relocated south of town; **1964** ferry service ends with opening of Chesapeake Bay Bridge-Tunnel to Norfolk; **1996** Cape Charles Museum founded.

Chancellorsville   *Spotsylvania County   North central Virginia, 55 mi/89 km southwest of Washington, D.C.*

Jan. 14, 1806 Matthew Maury born to east, founder of U.S. Naval Observatory (died 1873); **May 2, 1863** Union General Hooker attempts to surround General Lee, Gen. Stonewall Jackson's troops surround Hooker's forces, Jackson accidentally wounded by own troops, Hooker pushed back May 4; **May 10, 1863** Gen. Jackson dies of wounds; **Feb. 14, 1927** Fredericksburg and Spotsylvania National Military Park established.

Charles City   *Charles City County   Eastern Virginia, 25 mi/40 km southeast of Richmond, on James River*

1634 Charles City County formed, one of Virginia's eight original counties; **1726** Berkeley mansion built to west; Benjamin Harrison born at Berkeley mansion, Virginia governor, signer of Declaration of Independence, father of Pres. Benjamin Harrison (died 1791); **1730** county courthouse built; **c.1730** Sherwood Forest house built to east, home of President Tyler from 1842 until his death 1862; **Oct. 19, 1748** Martha Wayles Jefferson, wife of Pres. Thomas Jefferson, born (married Jan. 1, 1772, died Sept. 6, 1782); **Feb. 9, 1773** William Henry Harrison, 9th President, born at Berkeley Plantation (died April 4, 1841); **c.1789** Greenway House built by John Tyler, father of Pres. John Tyler; **March 29, 1790** John Tyler, 10th President, born (died Jan. 18, 1862); **1902** county clerk's office built; **Jan. 18, 1960** Colombian Curtiss C-46 airliner crashes at village of Holdcroft to east killing 50.

Charlotte Court House   *Charlotte County*
South central Virginia, 38 mi/61 km southeast of Lynchburg

1730 Greenfield house built to east by Isaac Read; **1764** Charlotte County formed; village founded as county seat; **1788** first county courthouse burned by arsonist; **March 4, 1799** Patrick Henry delivers political campaign oratory against opponent John Randolph at courthouse, Henry's last public appearance, died at nearby Red Hill June 6, 1799; **1823** third county courthouse built; **1874** incorporated as a town.

Charlottesville   *Charlottesville City   Central Virginia, 65 mi/105 km northwest of Richmond*

1735 Abraham Lewis and Nicholas Meriwether receive land grants; **1737** Peter Jefferson, father of Thomas Jefferson, is among first four settlers; **c.1741** Shadwell House built to east, burned 1770; **Apr. 13, 1743** Thomas Jefferson, 3rd President, born at Shadwell house (died July 4, 1826, same day as Pres. John Adams); **1744** Albemarle County formed; **Nov. 19, 1752** Gen. George Rogers Clark born in rural Albemarle County (died 1818); **Dec. 7, 1754** patriot Capt. John Jouett born, became "Paul Revere of the South" as he rode through outskirts of Richmond June 1781 with Lord Cornwallis at his heels (died 1822); **1761** land donated for courthouse; **1762** town incorporated; county seat moved from Scottsville; **c.1770** Farmington house built to west by Francis Jerdone, converted to hotel and country club 1929; **1773** Swan Tavern built; **Aug. 18, 1774** explorer Meriwether Lewis, of Lewis and Clark Expedition (1804–1806), born at Locust Hill house to west (died 1809); **1775** first part of Thomas Jefferson's home Monticello completed; **1779** prison camp established to northwest by Continental Congress to ward captives of Battle of Saratoga; **1784** Michie Tavern built; **Dec. 15, 1786** abolitionist, Illinois Gov. Edward Coles born in rural Albermarle County (died 1868); **1798** first part of James Monroe's home Ash Lawn completed; **c.1799** Franklin house built; **1801** town incorporated; **1803** county courthouse built, expanded 1860; **1819** University of Virginia established by Thomas Jefferson; **1848** Virginia Central Railroad reaches town; **1862** Buena Vista house built to northeast, near birthplace of George Rogers Clark; **1868** Charlottesville Woolen Mill founded; **1888** incorporated as a city; **Oct. 15, 1888** writer S. S. Van Dine born (died 1939); **1895** Monticello Guard Armory built; **1902** becomes an independent city; **1920** McIntire

Public Library built; **1921** George Rogers Clark Memorial erected; **1944** Institute of Textile Technology established; **Oct. 30, 1959** Piedmont Airlines DC-3 crashes killing 26, one person survives; **March 17, 1964** actor Rob Lowe born; **1972** Piedmont Virginia Community College established; **1986** Virginia Discovery Museum opened.

Chatham   *Pittsylvania County   Southern Virginia, 43 mi/69 km south of Lynchburg*

1767 Pittsylvania County formed, named for William Pitt, Earl of Chatham; Callands becomes county seat; **June 15, 1767** Rachel Donelson Robards born, wife of Pres. Andrew Jackson (married 1791; died 1828) **1777** town becomes new county seat; **1852** incorporated as a town; **1885** county courthouse built; **1894** Chatham Hall school for girls founded; **1909** Hargrave Military Academy for boys established.

Chesapeake   *Chesapeake City   Southeastern Virginia, 2 mi/3.2 km south of Norfolk, on Elizabeth River*

1728 Col. William Byrd describes Dismal Swamp while surveying state boundary with North Carolina; **1919** South Norfolk incorporated as a town; **1950** South Norfolk incorporated as an independent city; **1963** Norfolk County merges with independent city of South Norfolk becoming independent city of Chesapeake, extending city boundary to North Carolina state line; **1989** city hall completed; **1997** Chesapeake Conference Center built.

Chester   *Chesterfield County   East central Virginia, 15 mi/24 km south of Richmond*

1611 Sir Thomas Dale digs channel called Dale's Dutch Gap across bend in James River; Dale founds Henricopolis on James River; **1619** iron foundry built at Henricopolis; **1625** area settled by Capt. Thomas Osborne; **March 1622** massacre by Chief Opechancanough wipes out Henricopolis; **1748** tobacco warehouses built; **Dec. 9, 1775** Colonial forces defeat British in first encounter on Virginia soil; **Apr. 27, 1781** Benedict Arnold burns 25 British vessels here; **1802** Salem Baptist Church founded; **May 10, 1864** Union forces destroy railroad tracks; **1936** Osborne's Wharf dredging project begun on James River, revival of Dale's project; **1967** John Tyler Community College established.

Chesterfield   *Chesterfield County   East central Virginia, 11 mi/18 km south of Richmond*

1748 Chesterfield County formed from Henrico County; village becomes county seat; **1776** Castlewood house built by Charles Poindexter; **1778** explorer, fur trader William Hayes Ashley born (died 1838); **1780–1781** British destroy first courthouse; **Apr. 3, 1867** explosion at Bright Hope Coal Mine at Winterpock to west, 69 killed; **1889** county clerk's office built; **1903** Chesterfield County Library founded; **1917** county courthouse built.

Chincoteague   *Accomack County   Eastern Virginia, 92 mi/148 km north-northeast of Norfolk*

1662 Chincoteague Island, barrier island on Atlantic Ocean, granted to William Whitington by Gingo Teague peoples; **1908** incorporated as a town; **1924** Pony Penning Day established, roundup of wild ponies, descended from Colonial times, from Chincoteague barrier island, driven across channel, auctioned to prevent overpopulation of island; **1943** Chincoteague Island National Wildlife Refuge established; **Sept. 21, 1965** Chincoteague and Assateague islands become Assateague Island National Seashore; **Feb. 12, 1983** coal freighter *Marine Electric* sinks off coast, killing 33.

Christiansburg   *Montgomery County*

Southwestern Virginia, 23 mi/37 km west-southwest of Roanoke

1776 Montgomery County formed; Fort Chiswell becomes first county seat; **1789** county seat moved to Christiansburg with separation of Wythe County from Montgomery; **1792** town platted on land donated by Col. James Craig; **June 1, 1806** Confederate Gen. John Buchanan Floyd born, secretary of war under President Buchanan (died 1863); **1866** Christiansburg Industrial Institute for black students founded; **1916** incorporated as a town.

Clifton Forge   *Clifton Forge City   Western Virginia, 38 mi/61 km north of Roanoke*

1861 Chesapeake & Ohio Railroad extended to site, shops and terminal built; town founded; **1867** railroad extended to west; **1876** Buchanan & Clifton Forge Railroad built from terminus of James River & Kanawha Canal; **1880** town founded; **1884** incorporated as a town; **1906** incorporated as an independent city; **1964** Dabney S. Lancaster Community College established; **1979** county courthouse completed.

Clintwood   *Dickenson County   Southwestern Virginia, 136 mi/219 km west-southwest of Roanoke*

1816 "Fighting Dick" Colley builds cabin at Sand Lick; **1880** Dickenson County formed; **1882** town becomes county seat, renamed Clinton; county courthouse built; **1894** incorporated as a town.

Colonial Beach   *Westmoreland County   Eastern Virginia, 58 mi/93 km north-northeast of Richmond*

1650 Spence Monroe, banished from Scotland after fighting in Battle of Preston, arrives and patents Monrovia estate near Potomac River; **Apr. 28, 1758** Pres. James Monroe born at Monrovia estate to south (died July 4, 1831); **1892** incorporated as a town; **1940** ferry from Morgantown, Maryland, replaced by highway bridge at Dahlgren, to north.

Colonial Heights   *Colonial Heights City Eastern Virginia, 20 mi/32 km south of Richmond*

1770 Violet Bank residence built near Appomattox River, burned 1810, rebuilt, named for nearby violet-covered hill; **1781** Lafayette establishes headquarters at Violet Bank; **June–Sept. 1864** Gen. Lee establishes headquarters at Violet Bank during siege of Petersburg; **1926** incorporated as a town; **1948** incorporated as an independent city.

Courtland   *Southampton County   Southeastern Virginia, 60 mi/97 km south-southeast of Richmond*

1748 Southampton County formed; town founded as county seat, originally named Jerusalem; **1791** incorporated as a town; **Oct. 2, 1800** slave insurrection leader Nat Turner born in rural Southampton County (died 1831); **July 31, 1816** Union Gen. George Thomas born in rural Southampton County (died 1870); **1825** third county courthouse built; Charlie's Hope Plantation house built to north; **Aug. 22, 1831** black preacher Nat Turner sees halo around sun as sign from God, leads slaves on Nat Turner's Rebellion, 57 whites killed, hundreds of blacks killed by militia, Turner hanged for his activities Nov. 11; **1888** town renamed Courtland; **1970** Southampton Academy founded.

Covington   *Covington City   Western Virginia, 36 mi/58 km north of Roanoke*

1746 land purchased by Peter Wright; **1819** town platted, named for its eldest citizen; **1822** Alleghany County formed from parts of Bath, Botetourt, and Monroe (West Virginia) counties; town becomes county seat; **1855** incorporated as a town; **1857** Humpback Covered Bridge built on Dunlap Creek to west; **1876** railroad reaches town; **1891** Covington Iron Furnace established; **1911** county courthouse built; **1952** incorporated as independent city; **1978** Lake Moomaw reservoir built to north on Dunlap Creek.

Culpeper   *Culpeper County   North central Virginia, 62 mi/100 km southwest of Washington, D.C.*

1748 Culpeper County formed; **1759** town founded; **1775** Culpeper Minutemen organized, volunteers from Culpeper, Orange, and Fauquier counties; **Nov. 9, 1825** Confederate Gen. Ambrose Powell Hill born (died 1865); **Aug. 9, 1862** Battle of Cedar Mountain to south, Stonewall Jackson's 23,000 troops defeat General Banks' 9,000 troops; **1862-1863** Confederate troops winter at nearby camp, officers stay at Virginia Hotel; **June 9, 1863** Battle of Brandy Station to east, heaviest engagement of Civil War involving 10,000 troops on each side over several hours, Gen. Alfred Pleasonton's Union troops attack Gen. J. E. B. Stuart's Confederates, although forced to retreat, are able to protect Lee's northward movement, 936 Federals killed, 523 Confederates killed; **Apr. 1864** General Grant stays at Virginia Hotel; **1870** county courthouse built; **1898** incorporated as a town; **1926** Culpeper Public Library founded.

Cumberland *Cumberland County* *Central Virginia, 44 mi/71 km west of Richmond*

1749 Cumberland County formed; town becomes county seat; **1750** Tar Wallet Church built; **1766** Robert Routledge shot to death at Effingham Tavern by Col. John Chiswell, latter committed apparent suicide in Williamsburg; **1818** county courthouse built; **c.1840** Ca Ira Church built by French refugees to west.

Dale City *Prince William County* *Northern Virginia, 24 mi/39 km south-southwest of Washington, D.C.*

1697 village built on Neabsco Creek; **c.1725** Rippon Lodge house built by Col. Richard Blackburn; **1734** Neabsco Iron Foundry established by John Tayloe; **c.1740** Bel Air house built by Maj. Charles Ewell; **January 29, 1756** Henry "Lighthorse Harry" Lee born, governor of Virginia (died 1818), father of Confederate Gen. Robert E. Lee; **Jan. 21, 1994** Lorena Bobbitt acquitted of mutilation charge for cutting off penis of husband John Bobbitt on grounds he sexually abused her.

Danville *Danville City* *Southern Virginia, 58 mi/93 km southeast of Roanoke, on Dan River*

1793 town founded as inspection point for Piedmont tobacco planters; incorporated as a town; **c.1820** Roanoke Navigation Company completes canal to Albemarle Sound; **1823** Oak Hill house built by Samuel Hairston; **1830** incorporated as a city; **1858** Confederate Memorial Mansion built, final meeting of Jefferson Davis and cabinet held here Apr. 4, 1865; **1859** Averett College established; **Apr. 3-10, 1865** Confederate Pres. Jefferson Davis retreats to Danville following Union victory over the South, making Danville temporary capital of Confederacy during its final days; **1881** Riverside Mill begins founded; **1882** Dan River Incorporated established, leading textile manufacturer, became Dan River Mills 1909; **1902** becomes an independent city; **1920** Danville Military Institute founded; **1928** Danville Public Library founded; **1930** Stratford College (2-year) for women established; **1967** Danville Community College established.

Dinwiddie *Dinwiddie County* *Southern Virginia, 31 mi/50 km south-southwest of Richmond*

May 1607 members of Jamestown colony reach falls of Appomattox River; **1646** Fort Henry built, becomes trading post; town founded; **1752** Dinwiddie County formed; town becomes county seat; **July 13, 1786** Gen. Winfield Scott born, fought in War of 1812 and Mexican War (died 1866); **1851** county courthouse built, remodeled 2002; **1860s** county records destroyed during Civil War; **March 29, 1865** General Sheridan's forces occupy town, are driven back by Gen. Fitzhugh Lee and Gen. George Pickett March 31, Confederates retreat under threat of Union reinforcements.

Eastville *Northampton County* *Eastern Virginia, 40 mi/64 km north-northeast of Norfolk, near Atlantic Ocean*

1620 Accawmacke Plantation established on Chesapeake Bay, one of first settlements on Eastern Shore; **1663** Northampton County formed; **1664** Accawmacke Plantation becomes county seat (renamed Town Fields 1680); **1677** county seat moved to Eastville; **1715** town incorporated; **c.1765** Taylor Tavern (Eastville Inn) built; **1796** Kendall Grove house built; **c.1800** Elkington house built; **1815** Cessford house built to north; **1828** Christ Church built; **1886** Eastville Manor house built; **1899** third county courthouse built.

Edom *Rockingham County* *Northwestern Virginia, 107 mi/172 km northeast of Roanoke*

Jan. 6, 1776 Thomas Lincoln, father of Pres. Abraham Lincoln, born at Lincoln Homestead on Linville Creek to Abraham and Beersheba Lincoln, family moved to Kentucky 1782; **1794** Dr. Jesse Bennett performs Cesarean section on his wife, saving lives of both mother and child; **1798** Mennonite musician Joseph Funk settles with wife Bathsheba in Mountain Valley to west, establish music school, rename valley Singer's Glen; **1800** Lincoln Homestead enlarged by Capt. Jacob Lincoln; **1847** Funk and wife establish music printing house.

Emporia *Emporia City* *Southern Virginia, 60 mi/97 km south of Richmond, on Meherrin River*

1710 Hicksford (South Emporia) founded on south side of Meherrin River; **1781** Greensville County formed; town becomes county seat; county courthouse built; **Apr. 18, 1790** statesman John Y. Mason born to northeast, U.S. Attorney General (died 1859); **1798** town of Belford (North Emporia) founded on north side of river; **Dec. 10, 1864** advancing Union General Warren encounters Gen. Wade Hampton's forces guarding railroad bridge, Warren repulsed, retreats north to Petersburg; **1892** two towns merge, incorporated as town of Belford; **1967** incorporated as an independent city, renamed Emporia; **1974** Virginia Folk Festival founded; **Apr. 27, 1994** Timothy Spencer, accused of rape and killing of four women in 1987, first person to be convicted and executed on DNA evidence.

Ewing *Lee County* *Southwestern Virginia, 200 mi/322 km west-southwest of Roanoke*

1760s area settled; **1769** Daniel Boone explores Cumberland Gap through Cumberland Mountains; **Sept. 1773** Daniel Boone, his wife and 8 children leave North Carolina with 40 other settlers, camp here; **Oct. 10, 1773** James Boone, oldest son of Daniel Boone, Henry Russell, and a son of Captain Drake killed at this site; **June 11, 1940** Cumberland Gap National Historical Park (Virginia, Kentucky, Tennessee) authorized.

Fairfax *Fairfax County* *Northern Virginia, 15 mi/ 24 km west-southwest of Washington, D.C.*

c.1700 area first settled; **1742** Fairfax County formed; **1800** county seat moved from Alexandria with annexation of Alexandria by District of Columbia; site informally called Fairfax Court House; Antonia Ford House built; **1805** town of Providence incorporated; **Nov. 19, 1835** Confederate Gen. Fitzhugh Lee born (died 1905); **c.1855** Blenheim Estate built, includes Union soldier graffiti on outside walls; **June 1, 1861** Capt. John Quincy Marr becomes first Confederate officer killed in action; **1875** town renamed Fairfax; **1938** Fairfax Federal Art Gallery opens; **1957** George Mason University established; **1961** incorporated as an independent city; **1982** judicial center built.

Fairfield *Rockbridge County* *Western Virginia, 57 mi/92 km northeast of Roanoke*

c.1720 valley first settled by Ephraim McDowell (1673–1780), died at age 107, buried in McDowell Burying Ground; **1756** Timber Ridge Presbyterian Church built; **Nov. 11, 1771** surgeon Ephraim McDowell born, pioneer in abdominal surgery (died 1830); **March 2, 1793** Sam Houston born, President of Republic of Texas, first governor of state of Texas (died 1863); **1795** James McDowell born, governor of Virginia (died 1851).

Falls Church *Falls Church City* *Northern Virginia, 8 mi/12.9 km west of Washington, D.C.*

1690s area first settled; **1734** original Falls Church (Anglican) built, rebuilt 1769, abandoned 1890; **1840** Leesburg Turnpike built, toll gate used until 1872; **1850s** Star Tavern established, used as post office through 1870s; **1861** Taylor's Battery built by Union troops next to Taylor's Tavern, part of Civil War defense perimeter around Washington; **1869** Dulin United Methodist Church built; **1870** Tallwood residence built, home of Dr. Milton Eisenhower 1938–1943; **1875** incorporated as a town; **1882** Jefferson Institute school built, closed 1956, razed 1958; **1884** Falls Church Presbyterian Church built; **1897** trolley service from Washington begins; **1899** Mary Styles Public Library founded; **1948** incorporated as an independent city; **Oct. 14, 2002** woman CIA worker shot, killed outside Home Depot store, 11th victim of "D.C. Sniper" random shooting spree.

Falmouth *Stafford County* *Northern Virginia, 47 mi/76 km south-southwest of Washington, D.C.*

1608 Capt. John Smith lands here in search of gold, with Native American Mosco as his guide, erects cross; **1727** town founded on Rappahannock River; **1732** iron foundry established by Augustine Washington, George Washington's father; **1743** at age six, George Washington sent to Augustine Washington's Ferry Farm estate following death of George's father, George and Mary remain here until 1772; **1748** Ellerslie house built by Dr. Michael Wallace; **1761** Belmont house built; **1765**

Chatham house built by Col. William Fitzhugh; **1786** *Falmouth Advertiser* newspaper founded; **1813** bridge replaces ferry; **1862** town serves as headquarters for Federal troops during Battle of Fredericksburg, Dec. 11–15; **Apr. 29, 1863** first balloon message launched by T. C. S. Lowe, Chief of Aeronauts for Federal Army.

Farmville *Prince Edward County* *South central Virginia, 55 mi/89 km west-southwest of Richmond*

1741 Georgia Gov. George Walton born, delegate to Constitutional Convention (died 1804); **1754** Prince Edward County formed from Amelia County; town of Worsham becomes first county seat; **1798** town founded; **Feb. 3, 1807** Confederate Gen. Joseph Eggleston Johnson born (died 1891); **Sept. 20, 1809** Confederate Gen. Sterling Price born in rural Prince Edward County (died 1867); **1839** Longwood College established, originally State Teachers' College for women; **March 1, 1841** Reconstruction Era Sen. Blanche Kelso Bruce born (died 1898); **Apr. 6, 1865** General Lee's Confederate troops attacked from rear by General Sheridan's Union forces at Sailor's Creek three days before Lee's surrender to Grant at Appomattox; **1872** county seat moved to Farmville; **1873** county courthouse built; **1890** incorporated as a town; **1959** in Massive Resistance Movement, Prince Edward County schools close in defiance of court-ordered desegregation, inspires similar actions elsewhere, county holds out longest, finally reopening 1964.

Fincastle *Botetourt County* *Western Virginia, 15 mi/24 km north of Roanoke*

1770 Botetourt County formed; **1772** large part of county separates to form Fincastle County; town founded as county seat of remainder of Botetourt County; **1776** Fincastle County eliminated, subdivided into several new counties; **1821** incorporated as a town; **1832** Fincastle Presbyterian Church built; **1856** county courthouse built.

Floyd *Floyd County* *Southwestern Virginia, 32 mi/ 51 km south-southwest of Roanoke*

1831 Floyd County formed; town founded as county seat; town and county named for John Floyd, governor of Virginia (1830–1834); **1832** town chartered, originally named Jacksonville; **1845** county courthouse built; **Aug. 18, 1846** Adm. Robley "Fighting Bob" Evans born, hero in Battle of Santiago 1898 (died 1912); **1876** incorporated as a town; **1896** town renamed Floyd; **1913** Floyd Country Store built, converted to county music center 1983.

Franklin *Franklin City* *Southeastern Virginia, 38 mi/61 km southwest of Norfolk*

1850 Camp brothers establish sawmills; **1876** incorporated as a town; **1887** Camp Manufacturing assumes control of sawmills, begins paper milling 1937, becomes Union-Camp company 1958, merges with International Paper 1999; **1961** incorporated as an independent city; **1971** Paul D. Camp Community College established.

Fredericksburg *Fredericksburg City* *Northern Virginia, 50 mi/80 km south-southwest of Washington*

1608 Capt. John Smith visits area; **1671** land grant patented to John Buckner, Robert Bryan, and Thomas Royston; **1676** Maj. Lawrence Smith builds fort near falls of the Rappahannock River to southeast; **1722** ferry established on Rappahannock; **1725** Spotswood's Iron Furnace established to west by Alexander Spotswood; **1727** town founded; **c.1750** Rising Sun Tavern built by John Gordon; **1752** Kenmore Plantation house built; **1758** James Monroe Law Office built, used by Monroe 1786–1790; **1772** Mary Washington's house built; **1781** incorporated as a town; **1805** "alleged" John Paul Jones House built, legendary Jones died 1792; **Jan. 16, 1806** Matthew Fontaine Maury born, father of oceanography (died 1873); **1807** overturned candle at funeral starts fire that destroys half of town; **1813** city hall built; **July 13, 1815** Confederate Gen., Cong. James Alexander Seddan born (died 1880); **1833** Presbyterian Church built; **1837** Brompton House built by John Lawrence Marye; **August 30, 1837** Ellen Lewis Herndon Arthur, wife of President Chester A. Arthur, born (married 1850, died 1880); **1844** Salem Baptist Church built to west; **1849** St. George's Church built; **1852** county courthouse built; **Dec. 13, 1862** Union Gen. Ambrose Burnside repulsed by 75,000 troops of Confederate Generals Lee, Longstreet, and Jackson; **1865** Fredericksburg and Spotsylvania National Cemetery, over 15,000 Civil War dead, only 3,000 identified; **1879** incorporated as a city; **1902** becomes an independent city; **1908** Mary Washington College established; **1911** Wallace Library opens; **Feb. 14, 1927** Fredericksburg and Spotsylvania National Military Park established; **1929** George Rogers Clark Memorial erected; **Oct. 4, 2002** woman shot, injured by "D.C. Sniper," 7th random shooting victim, spree began Oct. 3 in Maryland, suspects caught Oct. 24, also in Maryland; **Oct. 11, 2002** "D.C. Sniper" shoots, kills man pumping gas, random shooter's 10th victim.

Front Royal *Warren County* *Northern Virginia, 65 mi/105 km west of Washington, D.C.*

1732 land grant near Shenandoah River patented to William Russell; **1736** ferry established by Thomas Chester; **1754** site purchased by Peter Lehew; town founded, named Lehewtown; **1788** incorporated as a town, renamed Front Royal; **1836** Warren County formed; town becomes county seat; **May 23, 1862** Gen. Stonewall Jackson captures three-fourths of General Banks' Union troops, betrayed by Belle Boyd, hostess of officers' ball; **1864** two of Mosby's guerillas hanged, five shot by General Custer's Union troops, Mosby retaliates by executing seven of Custer's men; **1892** Randolph-Macon Academy established; **1894** Royal Power Company electrical plant built; **1935** Shenandoah National Park established to south; **1936** county courthouse completed; **1939** American Viscose Corporation plant founded, closed 1988; **1989** Virginia Inland Port established on Shenandoah River.

Galax *Galax City* *Southwestern Virginia, 70 mi/113 km southwest of Roanoke, near New River*

1903 town platted on proposed rail line, originally named Cairo; **1904** Norfolk & Western Railroad extends line to site; town founded as Bonaparte; **1905** town renamed for local galax, mountain evergreen used as timber source; **1906** incorporated as a town; Galax Furniture Company founded, destroyed by fire 1914; **1920s** town's furniture industry expanded; **1953** incorporated as an independent city; **Oct. 2002** first Leaf and String Festival held.

Gate City *Scott County* *Southwestern Virginia, 155 mi/249 km west-southwest of Roanoke*

1770s first settlers arrive; **c.1781** blockhouse built at rendezvous point on Wilderness Road; **c.1785** town founded; tavern established by Elisha Faris; **1791** Faris family slain by part-Native American Benge and his antiwhite followers; **1814** Scott County formed, named for Gen. Winfield Scott, hero of War of 1812; **1851** county seat moved from Big Moccasin Gap (site to east); **1876** county courthouse built; **1888** incorporated as a town.

Glasgow *Rockbridge County* *West central Virginia, 21 mi/34 km northwest of Lynchburg*

Dec. 1742 Capt. John McDowell and his seven men, sent to end pillaging of settlers, killed in clash with Native Americans; **1810** Glasgow Manor built by Joseph Glasgow; **1816** sluice navigation used to circumvent Balcony Falls on James River; **c.1840** James River Canal opens beyond falls after 50 years of construction; **1881** railroad extended to town; **1890** town established on James River by promotion company with Gen. Fitzhugh Lee participating; **1892** incorporated as a town; **July 15, 1954** highest temperature ever recorded in Virginia reached, 110°F/43°C, at Balcony Falls.

Glendale *Henrico County* *See **Richmond** (1862)*

Gloucester *Gloucester County* *Eastern Virginia, 54 mi/87 km east of Richmond, near Chesapeake Bay*

1644 first settlers arrive; **1651** Gloucester County formed; **c.1667** Toddsbury House built on North River by Thomas Todd to east; **c.1700** Ware Church built to east; **1723** Poplar Spring Church begun to west, completed 1751, destroyed by fire c.1850; **c.1725** Long Bridge Ordinary built; **c.1732** Marlfield house built to west; **c.1745** debtors' prison built; **1766** county courthouse built; **1769** town founded around courthouse, becomes county seat; Hotel Botetourt built; **Dec. 13, 1851** Dr. Walter Reed born, discovered cause of yellow fever (died 1902); **1940** Virginia Institute of Marine Science established at Gloucester Point by College of William and Mary.

Goochland   *Goochland County*   *Central Virginia,*
25 mi/40 km west-northwest of Richmond, on James River

1727 Goochland County formed from Henrico County; town founded as county seat; **c.1731** Rock Castle house built; **Sept. 4, 1793** Thomas Bates born at Belmont, Attorney General under President Lincoln (died 1869); **1826** county courthouse built; **c.1833** county jail built; **Apr. 10, 1872** political leader Edward Carrington born (died 1938).

Greenville   *Augusta County*   See **Staunton (1907)**

Grundy   *Buchanan County*   *Southwestern Virginia,*
120 mi/193 km west of Roanoke

c.1827 area first settled; **1858** Buchanan County formed; town becomes county seat; **1876** incorporated as a town; **1905** county courthouse built; **1930** U.S. Highway 460 completed; **Apr. 22, 1938** Keen Mountain coal mine explosion, 45 killed; **1995** Appalachian School of Law founded, first commencement May 2000; **Jan. 16, 2001** Nigerian student Peter Odighizuwa, 43, shoots and kills three, injures three at law school day after learning he was flunking.

Hague   *Westmoreland County*   *Eastern Virginia,*
60 mi/97 km northeast of Richmond, near Potomac River

1659 Bushfield Estate acquired by Richard Bushrod; **1666** Matholic house built, destroyed by fire 1729; **1670** Banqueting House built; Pecatone house built, destroyed by fire 1888; **1670s** Wilmington House built; **1680** Glebe House built for Cople Parish; **1685** Wilton House built; **c.1720** Lee Hall house built by Thomas Lee; **c.1752** Nomini Hall residence built by Robert "King" Carter for his son; **June 5, 1762** U.S. Supreme Court justice Bushrod Washington born (died 1829); **1886** Mount Pleasant house built by Thomas Lee; **1929** Linden House built.

Halifax   *Halifax County*   *Southern Virginia, 48 mi/*
77 km south-southeast of Lynchburg

1752 Halifax County formed; **1767** county seat moved from Peytonsburg, part of new Pittsylvania County formed same year; **1827** Episcopal Church built; **c.1830** Masonic temple built; **1839** county courthouse built; **Dec. 16, 1854** soap manufacturer Joseph Fels born (died 1914); **1875** town incorporated as Banister; **1890** railroad extended to town, renamed Houston for railroad executive, who promised to bring industries to town, retracted offer over inadvertent mispronunciation of his name at New York social function; **1920** town renamed Halifax.

Hampton   *Hampton City*   *Southeastern Virginia,*
12 mi/19 km north-northwest of Norfolk

1607 Sir Christopher Newport passes through area to exchange greetings with Kecoughtan peoples; **1609** settlers at Jamestown, to northwest, build Fort Algernourne here; **1610** town founded; **1619** Buck Roe Plantation founded; **1630** fort rebuilt and renamed Fort Point Comfort by Col. Samuel Mathews; **1633** tobacco inspection warehouses established; **1634** Elizabeth City County formed; Syms Academy founded; **1659** Eaton Academy founded; **1680** town founded; **1700** customs collector Peter Heyman killed in ten-hour battle with pirates; **1730** Fort George replaces old fort; **1749** brick Fort George destroyed by "strong gust of wind"; **1755** 1,100 Acadians arrive from Nova Scotia, allowed to remain until spring for deportation; **1805** Syms and Eaton academies merge to form Hampton Academy; **June 1813** town attacked by British; **1819** construction of Fort Monroe begins, completed 1823; **1832** Chief Black Hawk held prisoner at fort following Black Hawk War in northern Illinois; **1849** town incorporated; **Aug. 1861** locals burn entire town to prevent occupation by Union troops; **March 1863** captured Union ironclad *Merrimack*, converted to the *Virginia* by Confederates, battles Union ironclad *Monitor* to a draw; **Feb. 2, 1865** steamship carrying President Lincoln anchors here for peace conference with Confederate Vice Pres. Alexander Stephens; **1868** Hampton Institute established for black students, becomes Hampton University; **1876** county courthouse built; **1882** railroad reaches town; **1884** fire destroys 33 buildings along Queen Street; **1908** incorporated as an independent city; **1912** American Theatre built; **1917** Langley Army Air Base established, oldest air base in U.S.; **1930** Hampton Veterans' Facility established; **1952** Elizabeth City County absorbed by City of Hampton; **1957** Hampton Roads Bridge-Tunnel completed to Norfolk, replacing ferry; **1966** ECPI College of Technology (2-year) established; **1968** Thomas Nelson Community College established; **Jan. 1970** Hampton Coliseum dedicated.

Hanover   *Hanover County*   *East central Virginia,*
20 mi/32 km north-northeast of Richmond

1720 Hanover County formed from New Kent County; village becomes county seat; **c.1723** Hanover Tavern built; **1735** county courthouse completed; **May 29, 1736** patriot Patrick Henry born at Studley Plantation to southeast (died 1799); **Dec. 1, 1763** lawyer Patrick Henry pleads Parsons' Case on behalf of clergy suing for payment of tobacco debts, salaries owed in tobacco, gains Henry's first rise to fame; **1897** Virginia Manual Labor School founded, reformatory for Negro boys; **1915** Virginia Industrial School for delinquent Negro girls founded to south.

Harrisonburg   *Harrisonburg City*   *Northwestern Virginia, 103 mi/166 km northeast of Roanoke*

1739 Thomas and Sarah Harrison settle here; **1778** Rockingham County formed; **1780** town chartered, becomes county seat; **1779** land ceded to county by Thomas Harrison for county courthouse, completed 1781; **c.1790** Warren Hotel built; **1818** Caverns of Melrose discovered to north by David Harrison; **1822** *Rockingham Register* newspaper founded, folded 1922; **c.1845**

Smithland House built; **1849** incorporated as a town; **June 6, 1862** Brig. Gen. Turner Ashby killed, shot during bayonet charge on Pennsylvania Infantry; **1897** fifth county courthouse built; **1908** State Normal and Industrial School for Women established, became Madison College 1938, renamed James Madison University 1977; **1916** incorporated as an independent city; **1917** Eastern Mennonite University established.

Heathsville *Northumberland County Eastern Virginia, 62 mi/100 km northeast of Richmond*

1645 Northumberland County formed, formally named 1648; village becomes county seat; **c.1740** The Tavern built; **1795** Mantua house built; **1828** Springfield house built by William Harding; **1851** county courthouse built.

Henricopolis *Chesterfield County See* **Chester**

Hillsville *Carroll County Southwestern Virginia, 56 mi/90 km southwest of Roanoke*

1842 Carroll County formed; **1878** town founded as county seat; **1900** incorporated as a town; **March 12, 1912** trial of Floyd Allen, arrested for freeing two Allen clan members jailed for disturbing a church service, trial disrupted by other clan members who enter courthouse, shoot and kill judge, prosecutor, sheriff, and jury foreman, wound court clerk, two raiders sentenced to death, two sent to prison, others pardoned; **1999** county courthouse completed.

Hopewell *Hopewell City East central Virginia, 19 mi/31 km south-southeast of Richmond*

1613 plantation granted to Sir Thomas Dale; **1619** town of City Point founded; **March 22, 1622** Native American attack decimates town; **1636** Appomattox Manor house built; **June 2, 1773** statesman John Randolph born in rural Prince George County to southeast (died 1833); **1913** Du Pont munitions plant built; town refounded, renamed Hopewell; **1916** incorporated as an independent city; **1926** city annexes City Point; **Dec. 22, 1935** bus plunges through opened Appomattox River Drawbridge, 14 killed; **1975** toxic insecticide kepone banned, used since 1966 in ant and roach traps, blamed for decline in James River fish populations; **1990** Heritage Mural dedicated, painted by Jay Bohannon.

Hot Springs *Bath County See* **Warm Springs (1912)**

Independence *Grayson County Southwestern Virginia, 80 mi/129 km southwest of Roanoke*

1765 William and Rosamond Bourne become town's first settlers; **1793** Grayson County formed, named for Sen. William Grayson; Oldtown becomes first county seat; **1842** county seat moved to Independence; **1850** incorporated as a town; **1981** third county courthouse built.

Isle of Wight *Isle of Wight County Southeastern Virginia, 24 mi/39 km west of Norfolk*

1608 Capt. John Smith purchases 14 barrels of corn from Native Americans here; **1619** area first settled; **1634** Isle of Wight County formed; Smithfield becomes first county seat; **1800** county seat moved to village of Isle of Wight; **1804** county jail built, rebuilt 1902; **1822** existing building converted into county courthouse, remodeled 1903.

Jamestown *James City County Southeastern Virginia, 35 mi/56 km northwest of Norfolk, on James River*

May 13, 1607 first permanent English settlement established by Capt. John Smith and 105 others, arrive on three ships, the *Sarah Constant*, *Goodspeed*, and *Discovery*; becomes capital of Virginia Colony; first Jamestown church built; **1619** Dutch deliver first shipment of slaves to New World; House of Burgesses established as first legislature in America; **1639** fifth structure of Jamestown Church built; **1676** Nathaniel Bacon and 23 followers protest taxes; town burned; Bacon dies suddenly, followers are executed; **1698** town destroyed again by fire; **1699** capital of Virginia Colony moved to Williamsburg; **c.1710** Jacquelin-Ambler House built, destroyed by fire 1895; **July 1781** Cornwallis crosses James River here in retreat from pursuing Lafayette; **1901** sea wall built to protect Jamestown Island from storm surges on James River estuary; **1907** Jamestown Monument erected; **1925** Jamestown-Scotland Ferry established; **July 3, 1930** Colonial National Monument authorized, becomes Colonial National Historical Park 1936.

Jonesville *Lee County Southwestern Virginia, 180 mi/290 km west-southwest of Roanoke*

1768 Joseph Martin leads settlers to site, builds Martin's Fort; **1793** town founded as county seat; **Nov. 1781** religious dissenters called Separate Baptists led by Rev. Lewis Craig arrive, continue west with soldiers, livestock; **1792** Lee County formed, named for Gov. Henry Lee; **1873** incorporated as a town; **1933** county courthouse built.

King and Queen Court House *King and Queen County Eastern Virginia, 35 mi/56 km east-north-east of Richmond*

1691 King and Queen County formed; first county seat established south of Mattaponi River; **1701** King William County formed; site chosen for new county seat; **c.1710** Newington house built, birthplace of Carter Braxton (1736–1797), signer of Declaration of Independence, destroyed 1865; **Jan. 23, 1765** Supreme Court Justice Thomas Todd born (died 1826); **March 1864** community and courthouse destroyed by Kilpatrick's Federal troops in retaliation for killing of Col. Ulrich Dahlgren; **c.1866** county courthouse built; **1997** new county courthouse completed.

King George *King George County* *Eastern Virginia, 54 mi/87 km north-northeast of Richmond*

1720 King George County formed; village founded as county seat; **1729** Cleve mansion built to southwest; **1769** Lamb's Creek Church built to west; **1830** Powhatan house built by Edward Tayloe; **1915** county courthouse built.

King William *King William County* *Eastern Virginia, 27 mi/43 km northeast of Richmond*

1702 King William County formed from King and Queen County; village founded as county seat; **1725** county courthouse built, one of oldest continuous use courthouses in U.S.; **1732** Acquinton Church built; **1767** Chericoke house built by Carter Braxton on Pamunkey River to southwest; **1885** county clerk's office and jail built.

Kiptopeke *Northampton County* *Eastern Virginia, 28 mi/45 km northeast of Norfolk, on Atlantic Ocean*

Apr. 26, 1607 three English ships of the London Company sail into Chesapeake Bay, name northern cape for prince who later became King Charles I; **1608** Capt. John Smith travels out from Jamestown and visits cape where he meets with hospitable Native Americans; **1612** Lt. William Craddock and 20 men arrive on nearby Smith Island to manufacture salt and harvest fish for colonists under directive from Governor Dale; **1629** Fishing Point Church built; **1676** Arlington estate built by John Custis II, ancestral home of Daniel Parke Custis, first husband of Martha Custis Washington; **1861** Federal troops occupy Cape Charles through Civil War; **1964** Chesapeake Bay Bridge/Tunnel completed across Chesapeake Bay entrance from Cape Charles to Norfolk, 17.6 mi/ 28.3 km long.

Lancaster *Lancaster County* *Eastern Virginia, 58 mi/93 km east-northeast of Richmond*

1652 Lancaster County formed; village becomes county seat; **c.1685** Verville house built by Dr. James Madison near Corotoman River; **1848** White Marsh Church built to east; **1860** county courthouse completed; **1957** Mary Ball Washington Museum and Library founded.

Lawrenceville *Brunswick County* *Southern Virginia, 58 mi/93 km south-southwest of Richmond*

1714 Fort Christanna built to south by Governor Spotswood; **1720** Brunswick County formed; **1732** county organized; Cochran to northwest becomes county seat; **1746** county seat moved to Thomasburg; **1783** county seat moved to Lawrenceville; **1814** town platted on land donated by Col. James Rice; **1854** county courthouse built; **1874** town incorporated; **1875** Church Home for Disabled and Infirm Negroes founded, remained open until last patient died 1912; **1888** St. Paul's College established, originally St. Paul's Normal and Industrial School for Negro boys.

Lebanon *Russell County* *Southwestern Virginia, 121 mi/195 km southwest of Roanoke*

1786 Russell County formed, named for Gen. William Russell; **1816** county seat moved from Dickensonville; **1818** county courthouse built; **1819** town founded; **1835** incorporated as a town; **1873** town reincorporated.

Leesburg *Loudoun County* *Northern Virginia, 33 mi/53 km west-northwest of Washington, D.C.*

1731 Raspberry Plain house built to north by Joseph Dixon; **1733** Goose Creek Chapel built; **1749** town settled near Potomac River; **1757** Loudoun County formed; town becomes county seat; Conrad's Ferry established on Potomac River to northeast, becomes White's Ferry 1828; **1758** town incorporated, named for landowners Francis and Philip Lee; **1803** Oatlands plantation house completed to south, built by George Carter; **1822** Rockland House built; **1823** Oak Hill mansion completed, built by Pres. James Monroe near Oatlands; **1825** Monroe retires to Oak Hill, stays until 1830; **c.1840** Springwood House built; **Oct. 21, 1861** Federal troops under Gen. George B. McClellan lose nearly 200 men in Confederate raid at Battle of Ball's Bluff; **Dec. 1865** Ball's Bluff National Cemetery founded; **1894** county courthouse built; **1900** Selma House built; **c.1900** Morven Park built, home of Gov. Westmoreland Davis (1918–1922); **1922** Loudoun Airport (Godfrey Field) founded; Thomas Balch Library founded; **June 13, 1947** Pennsylvania Central Airlines DC-4 crashes in thunderstorm, killing 50; **1984** Ball's Bluff Regional Park created.

Lexington *Lexington City* *Western Virginia, 45 mi/72 km northeast of Roanoke*

1739 Gilbert Campbell acquires land, builds house; **June 1763** Pontiac War launched to rid region of white settlers; **July 17, 1763** Native American raid kills 12 in at Kerr's Creek, raiders pursued and killed; **1777** Rockbridge County formed; town platted as county seat; **1780** Washington and Lee University moves here, founded 1749 at Augusta as Augusta Academy; **1785** Old Blue Tavern built; **1796** town destroyed by fire; **1801** *Lexington Gazette* newspaper founded, originally *The Rockbridge Repository*; **Feb. 15, 1809** Cyrus Hall McCormick born in rural Rockbridge County, invented the reaper (died 1884); **c.1830** Goose Creek Bridge built to east; **1839** Virginia Military Institute established; **1841** incorporated as a town; **June 10, 1864** Union Gen. David Hunter bombards town, many buildings burned; **1896** county courthouse built; **March 22, 1930** evangelist Pat Robertson born; **1965** incorporated as an independent city.

Louisa *Louisa County* *Central Virginia, 45 mi/72 km northwest of Richmond*

1742 Louisa County formed; town founded as county seat; **May 1765** Patrick Henry begins legal career in case against "loan office" cover-up scheme devised by Colonial Treasurer John Robinson; **Dec. 14, 1829** African-

American educator, diplomat John Mercer Langston born (died 1897); **June 11–12, 1864** Battle of Trevilians Station, Union General Sheridan sent to cut Lee's line of communication, overtaken by Gen. Wade Hampton; **1873** incorporated as a town; **Jan. 1888** fire destroys east side of Main Street; **1905** county courthouse built.

Lovingston   *Nelson County   Central Virginia, 78 mi/126 km west of Richmond*

1794 Woodson's Mill built to west near village of Lowesville; **1807** Nelson County formed; **1809** town platted; town becomes county seat; **Feb. 1810** county courthouse completed; **1972** Nelson Memorial Branch Library founded.

Lunenburg   *Lunenburg County   Southern Virginia, 60 mi/107 km southwest of Richmond*

1746 Lunenburg County formed; **1750s** area settled; village becomes county seat; **1803** country inn founded; **1816** town incorporated as Lewiston; **1826** county courthouse built; town renamed for county; **1861** county citizens declare tentative Old Free State out of impatience for Virginia's delay in seceding from Union.

Luray   *Page County   Northern Virginia, 80 mi/ 129 km west of Washington, D.C.*

1729 Jacob Stover receives land grant; **1746** road built across Massanutten Mountain to west; **1770** Mill Creek Baptist Church built; **1791** Locust Grove house built; **1812** town platted; **1831** Page County formed, named for Gov. John Page; town becomes county seat; **1833** county courthouse built; **1871** incorporated as a town; **1878** Luray Caverns discovered; **1930s** Ida Valley Homesteads built by Resettlement Administration; **2002** new Page Public Library opened.

Lynchburg   *Lynchburg City   Central Virginia, 45 mi/72 km east-northeast of Roanoke, on James River*

1757 John Lynch establishes ferry; oldest house in Lynchburg built; **c.1784** Lynch builds first tobacco warehouse; **1786** town founded; **c.1795** Quaker Memorial Presbyterian Church built; **1797** Sandusky House built; **1805** incorporated as a town; **1806** Thomas Jefferson builds his hexagonal retreat Poplar Forest, completed 1812; **1837** James River & Kanawha Canal reaches town from Richmond; **1852** incorporated as a city; Virginia & Tennessee Railroad reaches city; **Jan. 4, 1858** Sen. Carter Glass born, father of Federal Reserve System (died 1946); **June 17–18, 1864** in Battle of Lynchburg, Confederates under Gen. Jubal Early attacked by forces of Gen. David Hunter, Hunter withdraws to West Virginia, 900 casualties; **1870** manufacture of shoes begins; **1875** Lynchburg Female Orphan Asylum founded; **1880s** textiles and steel manufacturing become important; **1888** Virginia Theological Seminary and College for blacks established; **1893** Randolph-Macon Women's College established; **1898** Confederate statue erected; **1902** becomes an independent city; **1903** Lynchburg College established; **1909** Jones Memorial Library opens; **1911** State Colony for Epileptics and Feebleminded opened; **1930** Little Theater opened; **1936** Lynchburg Federal Art Gallery established; **1966** Central Virginia Community College established; **1971** Liberty University established.

Madison   *Madison County   North central Virginia, 75 mi/121 km northwest of Richmond*

c.1740 Hebron Lutheran Church built to north; Eagle House tavern built; **1792** Madison County formed; town becomes county seat; **1823** Harrison House built; **1829** second county courthouse built; **1832** Piedmont Episcopal Church built; **1834** Washington Hotel built; **1852** Lewis House built, used as Madison Public Library 1967; **1875** incorporated as a town; **1930s** Madison County Homesteads built by Resettlement Administration; **1992** first Taste of the Mountains Festival held.

Manassas   *Manassas City   Northern Virginia, 27 mi/43 km southwest of Washington, D.C.*

1731 Prince William County formed; county seat established at George Mason's ferry landing (Woodbridge); **1743** county seat moved to Brentsville (Brent Town); **1759** county seat moved to Dumfries; **July 21, 1861** in Battle of Bull Run, General McDowell faces Confederate Gen. Thomas (Stonewall) Jackson, Federal troops flee in panic next day, 2,708 killed; **Aug. 26, 1862** General Jackson destroys Union General Pope's supply depot in Second Battle of Bull Run; **Aug. 30, 1862** major battle ensues on Warrenton Pike, Jackson and Longstreet force Pope into retreat; **1873** incorporated as a town; **1893** county seat moved to Manassas; county courthouse built; **May 10, 1940** Manassas National Battlefield Park designated; **1964** Manassas Regional Airport established; **1975** incorporated as an independent city; **Oct. 9, 2002** man pumping gas shot, killed by "D.C. Sniper," 9th random shooting victim Oct. 3–24.

Manassas Park   *Manassas Park City   Northern Virginia, 25 mi/40 km southwest of Washington, D.C.*

1956 town founded; **1957** incorporated as a town; **1975** incorporated as an independent city; **1991** American Military University established.

Marion   *Smyth County   Southwestern Virginia, 93 mi/150 km west-southwest of Roanoke*

1831 town founded, named for "Swamp Fox" Francis Marion; **1832** Smyth County formed; town becomes county seat; **1835** incorporated as a town; **1849** county courthouse built; **1873** Marion Junior College established by Lutheran Church; **1887** Southwestern State Hospital founded.

Markham *Fauquier County* *Northern Virginia,*
54 mi/87 km west of Washington, D.C.

1670 John Lederer passes through Manassas Gap in Blue Ridge to west; **1761** Gap surveyed by George Washington and John Wood; **1764** The Hollow house built by Thomas Marshall; **c.1780** Cool Spring Church built to east, rebuilt 1838; **1811** Manassas Gap Turnpike built; **1828** Confederate Brig. Gen. Turner Ashby born (died 1862); **Dec. 30, 1848** surgeon, Arctic explorer James Ambler born (died 1881); **Dec. 1, 1974** TWA 727 jet crashes near secret government installation in heavy rainstorm, killing 92 at Upperville to north.

Martinsville *Martinsville City* *Southwestern Virginia, 42 mi/68 km south of Roanoke*

1774 Gen. Joseph Martin, Indian fighter, arrives in area; **1776** Henry County formed from Franklin and Patrick counties; **1793** town founded, named for Joseph Martin; town becomes county seat; **1873** incorporated as a town; **1928** incorporated as an independent city; **1947** Martinsville Speedway established; **1962** Patrick Henry Community College established; **1996** new county courthouse built; **Aug. 15, 2002** Jennifer Short, nine, abducted from home at Bassett to northwest, parents found shot to death at home, girl's body found at Madison, North Carolina, Sept. 25.

Mathews *Mathews County* *Eastern Virginia, 65 mi/195 km east of Richmond, near Chesapeake Bay*

1676 Hesse House built; town founded on East River; **c.1750** Poplar Grove house built to south; **c.1760** Clifton Manor house built to north; **1791** Mathews County formed; town becomes county seat; **1795** county courthouse completed; county jail built; **c.1815** Tompkins Cottage built; **1833** Capt. Sally L. Tompkins born, served in Robinson Hospital, Richmond, cared for over 1,300 injured Confederate soldiers (died 1916); **1859** county clerk's office built.

Mechanicsville *Hanover County* *East central Virginia, 8 mi/12.9 km northeast of Richmond*

1656 Chief Totopotomoi killed in battle while assisting Colonials in fighting Native Americans; **1729** Slash Church built; **Apr. 12, 1777** Sen. Henry Clay born at Clay Spring to north (died 1852); **1792** Totomoi house built by Tinsley family; **June 26, 1862** Confederate General Lee begins Seven Days' Battles, McClellan retreats to Gaines Mill to southeast, Lee pursues McClellan June 27, assaults Federal troops at Gaines Mill; **June 3, 1864** General Grant attacks Lee's positions near Chicahominy (Old Cold Harbor, to southeast), Grant's forces suffer heavy losses.

Middletown *Frederick County* *Northern Virginia, 70 mi/113 km west of Washington, D.C.*

1753 Harmony Hall house built; **1771** Gen. Isaac Zane builds mill on Cedar Creek to west; **1794** Belle Grove mansion built to west by Maj. Isaac Hite, Jr.; **1796** town incorporated by Dr. Peter Senseny, originally named Senseny Town; **1797** Wayside Inn built; **1817** early threshing machine demonstrated here; **1845** Long Meadows house built; **Oct. 19, 1864** in Battle of Cedar Creek, Union General Sheridan defeats Gen. Jubal Early for third time in 30 days, part of Sheridan's victorious ride through the Shenandoah Valley; **1969** Lord Fairfax Community College established.

Monterey *Highland County* *Western Virginia, 82 mi/132 km north of Roanoke*

c.1745 area first settled; **1758** Henry Seybert settles to north, one of four children survivors of massacre at Fort Seybert, West Virginia, in which 40 settlers were tomahawked to death by Shawnee people; **1774** Samuel Black builds cabin; **1838** Staunton & Parkersburg Turnpike built; town founded; **1847** Highland County formed; town becomes county seat; **1848** incorporated as a town; county courthouse built; **1872** Seybert Hills house built.

Montross *Westmoreland County* *Eastern Virginia, 53 mi/85 km northeast of Richmond*

1653 Westmoreland County formed; **1674** town founded; **c.1680** John Minor's Ordinary (tavern) built; **1716** property purchased by Col. Thomas Lee; **1729** Lee begins construction of Stratford Hall estate; **Oct. 14, 1734** Continental Congress delegate Francis Lightfoot Lee born, signer of Declaration of Independence (died 1797); **Apr. 28, 1758** James Monroe, 5th President, born in northwestern Westmoreland County (died July 4, 1831); **Jan. 19, 1807** Confederate Gen. Robert E. Lee born at Stratford Hall estate to north (died 1870); **1817** third county courthouse built, expanded 1936; **1850** St. James Episcopal Church built; **1852** incorporated as a town; **1932** Robert E. Lee Memorial Foundation purchases of Stratford Hall; **1939** Westmoreland County Museum and Library founded.

Mount Vernon *Fairfax County* *Northern Virginia, 12 mi/19 km south-southwest of Washington, D.C.*

Apr. 1669 John Washington, grandfather of George Washington, receives land patent on Potomac River; **1730s** Belvoir Estate founded by George William Fairfax; **1735** Augustine Washington arrives with 3-year-old son George, builds house; **1741** Lord Fairfax builds his estate Belvoir to west, destroyed by fire 1783; **1743** George's half-brother Lawrence inherits Hunting Creek property, builds house, names it for Adm. Edward Vernon, his commander in British Navy; **1752** Lawrence Washington dies; **1754** George Washington buys rights to Mount Vernon property; **1759** George brings his bride Martha to estate; **1770** Washington restores Lawrence's grist mill; **1773** third floor added; **Dec. 23, 1782** George Washington returns here to work on memoirs; **1787** Washington presides over Continental Congress; **1789** George Washington becomes 1st U.S. President; **1797**

Washington retires to Mount Vernon; **Dec. 14, 1799** George Washington dies; **May 22, 1802** Martha Washington dies; **1805** nearby Woodlawn Mansion designed by Dr. William Thornton, restored 1902; **1853** Ann Pamela Cunningham of South Carolina launches effort to restore Mount Vernon; **1860** estate acquired by Mount Vernon Ladies' Association of the Union.

New Castle *Craig County Southwestern Virginia, 18 mi/29 km north-northwest of Roanoke*

1756 fort established by Gov. Dinwiddie; town of New Fincastle founded, name later shortened; **1851** Craig County formed; town becomes county seat; **1911** incorporated as a town; **1921** county courthouse built.

New Kent *New Kent County Eastern Virginia, 27 mi/43 km east of Richmond*

1654 New Kent County formed; original county seat located at Brick House, town site near Plum Point to east; **1691** county reduced in size; county seat moved from Brick House; **1703** St. Peter's Church completed; **c.1725** Poplar Grove House built by Col. William Chamberlayne; **June 2, 1732** Martha Dandridge Custis Washington born, wife of Pres. George Washington (married Jan. 6, 1759; died 1802); **1787** county clerk's office burned by British; **November 12, 1790** Letitia Christian Tyler, first wife of Pres. John Tyler, born to west in rural (died 1842); **1820** Hampstead House built; **1906** county courthouse built; **1907** county jail built, becomes county museum 1998.

New Market *Shenandoah County Northern Virginia, 90 mi/145 km west-southwest of Washington, D.C.*

1761 inn and store established by John Sevier, becomes governor of short-lived State of Franklin, then governor of Tennessee; **1785** town platted; **1796** town incorporated; **1806** Henkel Press established by Ambrose Henkel; **1817** New Market Academy established; **1821** Lutheran Seminary established; **c.1822** Court Manor house built to south; **1834** Stanley Hall house built by Dr. John Rice; **May 15, 1864** Battle of New Market, Confederate troops under Gen. John Breckinridge attack Gen. Franz Sigel's troops, driving them northward with aid of young cadets of which 10 are killed, 47 wounded; **1879** Endless Caverns discovered by Reuben Zirkle's dog while chasing a rabbit.

Newport News *Newport News City Southeastern Virginia, 12 mi/19 km northwest of Norfolk*

1607 Sir Christopher Newport arrives to start colony; **June 1610** starving colonists from Jamestown encamp on Mulberry Island intending to return to England, supplies and new colonists arrive next morning; **1611** Robert Salford and son settle at Salford Creek; **1634** Warwick River County formed; **1643** county renamed Warwick; Denbigh becomes first county seat; **c.1695** Jones House built on Mulberry Island; **1759** Endview Plantation house built; **1848** Lee Hall mansion built; **1873** incorporated as a town; county seat moved to Newport News; **1882** railroad completed from Richmond; town platted; slum area called Hell's Half Acre develops near tracks; **1886** Newport News Shipbuilding and Dry Dock Company organized; **1896** incorporated as a city, limits exclude slums; county seat reverts back to Denbigh; **1902** becomes an independent city; **1906** Virginia State School for Colored Deaf and Blind Children founded; **1915** Fort Eustis established on Mulberry Island; **March 29, 1918** singer Pearl Bailey born (died 1990); **Apr. 25, 1918** singer Ella Fitzgerald born (died 1996); **1919** Victory Arch built of wood, rebuilt of granite 1962; **June 11, 1925** novelist William Styron born; **1927** trackside slums razed by railroad; **1928** James River Bridge built; public library built; **1930** Mariners' Museum built; **1930s** Newport News Homesteads for black residents built; **1947** Peninsula Airport established at former Camp Patrick Henry, becomes Patrick Henry Airport (Newport News/Williamsburg International); **1958** Warwick County merges with Newport News city; **1960** Christopher Newport University established; **Sept. 24, 1960** nuclear powered aircraft carrier USS *Enterprise* launched, at 1,100 ft/335 m, world's largest ship; **1962** Peninsula Fine Arts Center opened; **1969** U.S. Army Transportation Museum opened; **1985** Peninsula Junior Nature and Science Center opened, renamed Virginia Living Museum 1987.

Norfolk *Norfolk City Southeastern Virginia, 80 mi/129 km southeast of Richmond, on Chesapeake Bay*

Apr. 28, 1607 ship *Sarah Constant* anchors in Willoughby Bay carrying first colonists led by Sir Christopher Newport; **1636** land grant made to Capt. Thomas Willoughby; ferry service inaugurated on Elizabeth River to Portsmouth; **1641** first St. Paul's Church built, rebuilt 1739; **1680** town founded, named Norfolk Town; **1682** incorporated as a town; **1691** Norfolk County formed from Lower Norfolk County; **1705** name Norfolk adopted; **1728** Norfolk Academy founded; **1739** Old St. Paul's Church built, only surviving structure from 1776 fire; the Naval Shipyard is founded at neighboring Portsmouth; **Jan. 1, 1776** two-thirds of town destroyed by British bombardment in attempt to eradicate Colonial occupiers; **1784** Tazewell Manor house built; **1787** U.S. Marine Hospital founded; **1790** county courthouse built; **1791** Meyer House completed; **1794** Fort Norfolk built; refugees fleeing insurrection in Santo Domingo arrive in great numbers; **1799** town destroyed by fire; **June 22, 1813** British repulsed by Colonial forces at Fort Norfolk and Fort Nelson; **1814** Dismal Swamp Canal opened providing inland boat passage to North Carolina; **Nov. 6, 1821** Confederate naval officer John Wilkinson born (died 1891); **1830** construction of Fort Calhoun begun on manmade island in Hampton Roads channel, renamed Fort Wool after capture by Union forces May 9, 1862; **1832** steam ferry established; **1845** incorporated as a city; **1850** Norfolk Courthouse completed; **1853** free school for Negroes established; **Feb. 2, 1854** inventor Stephen Horgan born, developed photoengraving process (died 1941); **1855** yellow fever epidemic ravages town; **1857**

VIRGINIA

U.S. customhouse built; **1856** St. Vincent de Paul Hospital founded; **May 10, 1862** Union forces under Gen. John Ellis Wool capture Norfolk; **March 8, 1862** Union battleships *Congress* and *Cumberland* destroyed by Confederates, three others grounded, including *Monitor* ironclad vessel; **1865** *The Virginian* (*Virginian-Pilot*) newspaper founded; **Feb. 3, 1865** President Lincoln and Secretary of Interior Seward meet with Confederates on vessel to discuss terms of surrender, Confederates reject national authority; **1870** Norfolk Public Library founded; **1875** Masonic hall built; Elizabeth City & Norfolk Railroad established to Elizabeth City, North Carolina, becomes Norfolk & Southern; **1876** *The Ledger* (*Ledger-Star*) newspaper founded; **1879** Chinese Baptist Church built; **Jan. 10, 1883** bandleader Francis X. Bushman born (died 1966); **1902** becomes an independent city; **Feb. 21, 1892** actress Margaret Sullivan born, died of drug overdose Jan. 1, 1960; **1902** becomes an independent city; **1904** First Baptist Church built; **1906** Norfolk annexes Berkley; **1907** Confederate monument completed, begun 1889; **July 4, 1917** Norfolk Naval Base dedicated; **1919** Crispus Attucks Theatre opened; **1922** U.S. Marine Hospital built; **Feb. 21, 1922** U.S. dirigible *Roma* crashes, killing 24; **1930** Old Dominion University established, originally a branch of College of William and Mary; **1935** Norfolk State University established, originally a branch of Virginia State University; **March 9, 1935** singer Keely Smith born; **1938** Norfolk International Airport founded; **Apr. 3, 1942** singer Wayne Newton born; **Dec. 19, 1944** actor Tim Reid born; **1955** ferry service discontinued, began 1636; **1957** Hampton Roads Bridge-Tunnel completed to Hampton across Hampton Roads, James River entrance to Chesapeake Bay; **1961** Virginia Wesleyan College established; **1963** Norfolk County merges with South Norfolk to form independent city of Chesapeake, eliminating city's role as county seat; **Jan. 1964** Gen. Douglas MacArthur Memorial opened in former city hall, MacArthur died Apr. 1964, was scheduled to attend formal opening Memorial Day, May 1964; **1968** Tidewater Community College established; **1971** Scope convention center opened; **1973** Greater Virginia Medical School established; **1975** Virginia Opera founded; **May 26, 1981** crash of jet fighter on carrier USS *Nimitz* kills 14; **May 28, 1985** John Walker and son, seaman Michael Walker on USS *Nimitz*, charged with spying, son Arthur charged May 29; **1994** National Marine Center opened; **1998** Armed Forces Memorial dedicated.

Norton   *Norton City   Southwestern Virginia, 150 mi/241 km southwest of Roanoke*

1787 town settled by William Prince, named Prince's Flats; **1874** incorporated as a town; **1883** post office established, renamed Eolia; **1889** town platted by Louisville & Nashville Railroad, renamed for railroad president Eckstein Norton; **1894** incorporated as a town; **1920** Hotel Norton built; **1954** incorporated as an independent city.

Nottoway Court House   *Nottoway County   Southern Virginia, 45 mi/72 km southwest of Richmond*

1788 Nottoway County formed from Amelia County; site selected as county seat; **1837** Old Brick Church built; **1840** county courthouse completed; **1870** Mann House built by Gov. William Hodges Mann.

Oak Grove   *Westmoreland County   Eastern Virginia, 53 mi/85 km north-northeast of Richmond*

Dec. 3, 1664 John Washington builds house near Potomac River; **1713** Washington's Mill built by Nathaniel Pope, purchased by Augustine Washington; **c.1725** Wakefield house built by Augustine Washington; **Feb. 22, 1732** George Washington, first president of the U.S., born at family home of Wakefield (died Dec. 14, 1799); **Dec. 25, 1780** Wakefield house destroyed by fire; **Jan. 23, 1930** George Washington Birthplace National Monument established.

Onancock   *Accomack County   Eastern Virginia, 68 mi/109 km north-northeast of Norfolk, near Atlantic Ocean*

1621 John Pory invited as guest of Ekeeks, king of Onancock peoples, given feast of oysters and potatoes; **1655** Accomack County formed; **1680** town founded as port of entry, county seat moved from Pungoteague; **1779** Kerr Place house built; **Nov. 30, 1782** Battle of the Barges, Commodore Whaley's forces pursue British in four barges, Whaley killed by own gunpowder; **1786** county seat moved to Accomac (Accomack); **c.1799** Kerr Place house built, becomes historical museum 1960; **1874** incorporated as a town; **2000** Blue Crab Music Festival established.

Orange   *Orange County   North central Virginia, 60 mi/97 km northwest of Richmond*

1722 Bloomsbury house built; **1734** Orange County formed; **1748** Culpeper county separates from Orange County; Orange county seat moved to central location after being shifted among various localities; **c.1760** original section of Montpelier estate built to west by James Madison, father of Pres. James Madison; **May 25, 1783** Supreme Court Justice Philip Pendleton Barbour born (died 1841); **Nov. 24, 1784** Zachary Taylor, 12th President, born at rural Gordonsville to south (died July 9, 1850); **c.1810** town settled; **c.1825** Greenfield House built; **1833** St. Thomas' Church built; **June 28, 1836** Pres. James Madison buried at his Montpelier estate to west (born 1751), monument erected 1856; **1855** incorporated as a town; Meadow Farm house built, site of earlier house belonging to Zachary Taylor, grandfather of Pres. Zachary Taylor; **1858** county courthouse built; **Jan. 23, 1903** actor Randolph Scott born in Orange County (died 1987); **1947** Grymes Memorial School (academy) founded.

Palmyra *Fluvanna County* *Central Virginia, 50 mi/80 km west-northwest of Richmond*

1777 Fluvanna County formed, name means "Anne River"; Columbia becomes first county seat; **1828** county seat moved to Palmyra; **1830** county courthouse completed.

Pearisburg *Giles County* *Southwestern Virginia, 43 mi/69 km west of Roanoke*

1782 ferry established on New River by Capt. George Pearis; **1806** Giles County formed; **1808** town founded, becomes county seat; **1836** county courthouse built; **1914** town incorporated; **1939** Celanese Corporation of America plant established; **Jan. 22, 1985** lowest temperature ever recorded in Virginia reached, −30°F/−34°C, at Mountain Lake Biological Station 10 mi/16 km to east.

Petersburg *Petersburg City* *Eastern Virginia, 22 mi/35 km south of Richmond, on Appomattox River*

1665 Fort Henry built at falls of Appomattox River; trading post established; **1676** Native Americans driven from village during Bacon's Rebellion; **1735** Blandford Church built; **1748** town platted, incorporated; **c.1775** Lee's Mill built to south; **1781** British forces under generals Benedict Arnold and William Phillips destroy stores, pillage town; **1784** towns of Blandford and Pocahontas merge with Petersburg; **June 13, 1786** Union Gen. Winfield Scott born (died 1866); **March 15, 1809** Joseph Jenkins Roberts born, became first president of Liberia 1847, African republic founded by returned slaves (died 1876); **1815** fire damages city, again in 1826; Trapezium Place house built; **1817** Farmers Bank built; **1823** Centre Hill Mansion built; **1825** Golden Ball Tavern built; **1839** exchange building built; **1850** incorporated as a city; **June 14–15, 1864** Union General Grant marches on Petersburg, imposes siege on town June 15–18, total 8,000 casualties; **July 30, 1864** Pennsylvania Volunteers, led by General Grant, dig tunnel under Confederate defenses, explosion creates large depression, Battle of the Crater leads to 900 Union casualties; **Apr. 2–3, 1865** Union troops push through enemy defense lines, Confederates evacuate city; **1866** Poplar Grove National Cemetery established; **1879** Old Market Place built; **1880** Cary's Methodist Church built to south on site of revival held 1787; **1882** Virginia State University established; **1884** Bishop Payne Divinity School (Episcopal) founded; **1885** Central State Hospital moved here, established 1870 in Richmond; **1888** John Mercer Langston elected as first black Congressman from Virginia; **1902** becomes an independent city; **May 15, 1905** actor Joseph Cotten born (died 1994); **1909** Massachusetts monument erected to honor Union soldiers killed in Virginia; **July 3, 1926** Petersburg National Battlefield established; **1961** Richard Bland College of College of William & Mary (2-year) established; **Aug. 6, 1993** tornado hits town, four killed.

Poquoson *Poquoson City* *Southeastern Virginia, 20 mi/32 km north of Norfolk, on Chesapeake Bay*

1631 first known land grant patented to Christopher Calthorpe; **1726** patriot George Wythe born, first American law professor, signer of Declaration of Independence (died 1806); **c.1812** seafood industry begins; **1858** town founded; **June 10, 1861** Battle of Big Bethel to west, 5,000 Federal troops attack 1,400 defending forces, retreat to Hampton, casualties light; **1952** incorporated as a town; **1975** incorporated as an independent city.

Port Conway *King George County* *Eastern Virginia, 49 mi/79 km north-northeast of Richmond*

March 16, 1751 James Madison, 4th President, born at Conway House (died June 28, 1836); **c.1830** Belle Grove mansion built by John Bernard; **c.1840** Emanuel Church built; **Apr. 23, 1865** John Wilkes Booth, fleeing Washington after assassinating President Lincoln, spends night at Rollins House, ferries across Rappahannock River Apr. 24, reaches Port Royal.

Port Royal *Caroline County* *Eastern Virginia, 47 mi/76 km north-northeast of Richmond*

1725 Gay Mont house built; town founded on Rappahannock River; **1744** town founded; **c.1800** Hazelwood house built by John Taylor, conducts experiments in crop rotation and soil improvement; **1817** John Taylor organizes Agricultural Society of Virginia; **1829** incorporated as a town; **Apr. 26, 1865** John Wilkes Booth mortally shot in burning barn of Garrett Farm after pursuit following assassination of President Lincoln, accomplice Herold surrenders.

Portsmouth *Portsmouth City* *Southeastern Virginia, 2 mi/3.2 km west of Norfolk, on James River*

1664 plantation acquired by Capt. William Carver, confiscated after his participation in Bacon's Rebellion 1676 for which he was hanged; **1691** Norfolk County formed from Lower Norfolk County; **1716** land regranted to Col. William Crawford; **1738** Portsmouth Naval Shipyard established; **1752** town founded, platted by Crawford, named Portsmouth; **1762** Trinity Church built; **1776** town occupied by Dunmore's Tories following burning of Norfolk; **1779** British burn Fort Nelson; exclusive Centennial House hotel built; **c.1784** Ball House built; **1799** first ship built by U.S., the *Chesapeake*; Watt's House built; **1801** government purchases Gosport Navy Yard, becomes Norfolk Navy Yard; **1812** Dismal Swamp Canal opened; **1821** fires sweeps through town; **1822** steam ferry established to Norfolk; **1826** Naval Hospital built on site Fort Nelson; **1837** Portsmouth & Roanoke Railroad completed; **1846** county courthouse completed; **1852** incorporated as a town; **1855** yellow fever epidemic takes over 1,000 lives; **1858** incorporated as a city; **c.1900** city begins wharf extension; **1902** becomes an independent city; **1963** Norfolk County merges with Chesapeake city; **1966** Virginia Sports Hall of Fame organized.

Powhatan *Powhatan County* *Central Virginia, 25 mi/40 km west of Richmond*

1777 Powhatan County formed from Cumberland County; **1778** village established, originally named Scottsville for Gen. Charles Scott; **1836** town renamed Powhatan; **1848** third county courthouse built.

Prince George *Prince George County* *Southeastern Virginia, 24 mi/39 km south-southeast of Richmond*

1616 John Martin becomes one of first landowners; **1702** Prince George County formed; **1785** county seat moved from Fitzgerald's, previously located successively at City Point (annexed by Hopewell 1926), Jordan's Point, and Merchant's Hope Plantation near Brandon; **Sept. 1864** in Great Cattle Raid, Confederates under Gen. Wade Hampton rustle herd of 3,000 Union cattle to sustain troops; **1884** old county courthouse built; **1917** Camp Lee established, becomes Fort Lee military base 1950; **1990** new county courthouse built.

Pulaski *Pulaski County* *Southwestern Virginia, 49 mi/79 km west-southwest of Roanoke*

1839 Pulaski County formed; Newbern becomes first county seat; **1877** coal discovered to northwest; rail stop established, named Martin's Station; **1884** Maple Shade Inn built by Norfolk & Western Railroad; **1886** town incorporated, renamed; **1888** Pulaski Iron Company established; **1896** county seat moved to Pulaski; county courthouse built; **Oct. 1918** Spanish flu epidemic strikes town, 92 killed; **1937** Jefferson Textile Mill opened.

Quantico *Prince William County* *Northern Virginia, 31 mi/50 km south-southwest of Washington, D.C.*

1654 first land patents made; town founded; **1874** incorporated as a town; **1918** Quantico U.S. Marine Corps Base established, tract later extended west into three counties; **Nov. 1932** Federal Bureau of Investigation's (FBI) Criminological Laboratory established; **June 22, 1948** Prince William Forest Park established to west by National Park Service; **May 1972** FBI Academy established; **1983** Quantico National Cemetery opened.

Radford *Radford City* *Southwestern Virginia, 35 mi/56 km west-southwest of Roanoke, on New River*

1750 first settlers arrive; **1756** town founded; **1762** Ingles Ferry established on New River; **1883** Norfolk & Western Railroad establishes division center; **1887** incorporated as a town; **1892** incorporated as a city; **1902** becomes an independent city; **1910** Radford University established; **1939** Clay Lake reservoir built to south on New River.

Reston *Fairfax County* *Northern Virginia, 18 mi/29 km west-northwest of Washington, D.C.*

1927 property acquired by A. Smith Bowman; **1934** distillery established by Bowman; **1961** New York developer Robert E. Simon purchases 6,750 ac (2,734 ha) for planned community from sale of family property in New York for Carnegie Hall; **1962** community master plan adopted, includes parklands, named for Robert E. Simon (RESton); **1974** U.S. Geological Survey headquarters established; **1997** Reston Museum founded.

Richmond *Richmond City* *Eastern central Virginia, 98 mi/158 km south-southwest of Washington*

1607 party of captains John Smith and Christopher Newport ascend James River, cross erected at falls; **1610** Lord Delaware expedition reaches falls in vain search for minerals; **1634** Henrico County formed; town becomes county seat; **1637** trading post established by Thomas Stegg; **1645** Fort Charles built; **1686** Edgar Allen Poe house built, oldest building in Richmond; **c.1712** Tuckahoe House built to west by Thomas Randolph; **1737** town platted; **1741** St. John's Episcopal Church built; **1742** incorporated as a town; **1771** town rebuilt following disastrous floods; **March 23, 1775** Second Virginia Conference held at St. John's Episcopal Church at which Patrick Henry makes famous quote "Give me liberty or give me death!"; **1780** state capital moved from Williamsburg; **Jan. 1781** city burned by British under Benedict Arnold, Lafayette arrives in Apr. to rescue town; **1782** incorporated as a city; **1792** state capitol completed; **March 17, 1804** Western trapper, trader James Bridger born, "King of the Mountain Men" (died 1881); **May 22, 1807** Aaron Burr, arrested in Mississippi, stands trial for treason, acquitted Sept. 1; **1813** governor's mansion built; **1814** Monumental Church built; **1823** state library founded, building completed 1892, new library opened 1997; **Jan. 25, 1825** Confederate Gen. George Edmund Pickett born (died 1875); **1828** Branch's Baptist Church organized; **1830** University of Richmond established; **1836** Richmond, Fredericksburg, & Potomac Railroad completed; **1838** Virginia Commonwealth University established; **1840** James River & Kanawha Canal opens; **1845** St. Paul's Episcopal Church dedicated; **1850** *Times-Dispatch* newspaper founded; **1858** Washington monument erected; **Apr. 19, 1861** Virginia secedes from Union; **June 30–July 1, 1862** in Seven Days' Battles, Gen. Stonewall Jackson is stopped by Union troops at White Oak Swamp near Glendale, 15 mi/24 km to southeast; General Lee is held off at Frayser's Farm; Confederates suffer 5,000 casualties in Federal bombardment of Malvern Hill; **May 11, 1864** Union Gen. Philip Sheridan defeats Confederate Gen. J. E. B. Stuart in Battle of Yellow Tavern 5 mi/8 km to east, Stuart is wounded, dies May 12; **Apr. 2–3, 1865** Confederates evacuate Richmond, burning storehouses full of cotton, tobacco to prevent use by Union troops; **1867** Virginia Union University for blacks opens; **Apr. 27, 1872** floor in state supreme court building collapses, 61 killed, 120 injured; **Apr. 22, 1874**

author Ellen Glasgow born (died 1945); **May 25, 1878** tap dancer Bill Robinson born (died 1949); **Nov. 20, 1878** actor Charles Sidney Gilpin born (died 1930); **Apr. 14, 1879** author James Cabell born (died 1958); **Sept. 6, 1882** composer, pianist John Powell born (died 1963); **1883** Maggie Walker House built for African-American bank entrepreneur, becomes National Historic Site 1978; **1893** Confederate museum opened, residence built 1818 by John Brockenbrough, used as Confederate Executive Mansion 1861; **1895** Jefferson Hotel built; **1896** county courthouse built; *News Leader* newspaper founded; **May 5, 1899** entertainer Freeman F. Gosdon, "Amos" of Amos and Andy, born (died 1982); **1902** becomes an independent city; **1906** Cathedral of the Sacred Heart built; **1924** Richmond Public Library opened; **1927** Byrd Field (Richmond International Airport) established, chartered 1948; **1928** ACCA Theatre (The Mosque) built; **1930** Valentine Museum opens; **Jan. 17, 1931** Gov. L. (Lawrence) Douglas Wilder born, served 1990–1994, first black governor of a Southern state; **March 2, 1931** author Tom Wolfe born; **1934** Virginia Museum of Fine Arts opens; **Apr. 24, 1934** actress Shirley MacLaine born; **March 2, 1936** Richmond National Battlefield Park authorized; **March 30, 1937** actor Warren Beatty born; **1939** Richmond Deepwater Terminal completed to southeast on James River; **Feb. 3, 1940** football player Fran (Francis) Tarkenton born; **July 10, 1943** tennis player Arthur Ashe born (died 1993); **Nov. 8, 1961** Imperial Airlines Constellation crashes killing 77, including 74 Army recruits; **1972** J. Sargeant Reynolds Community College established; **Jan. 10, 1972** city school district ordered to merge with Chesterfield and Henrico county districts to achieve integration; **1974** county government center built to northwest, near suburban Laurel; **1977** Science Museum of Virginia dedicated; **1984** Lewis Ginter Botanical Gardens founded; **1987** Virginia Aviation Museum founded; **1988** Museum of the Confederacy founded; **1991** Black History Museum opened.

Roanoke *Roanoke City* *Southwestern Virginia, 140 mi/225 km west of Richmond, on Roanoke River*

1740 first settlers arrive; **1768** Belmont house built by Dr. William Fleming; **c.1800** Raleigh Tavern built; **1820** Elmwood Park house built by Jonathan Tosh; **1828** Zion Lutheran Church built; **1834** town founded, named Gainsborough; **1838** Roanoke County formed; Salem becomes county seat; **1842** Hollins University established; **1852** Virginia & Roanoke Railroad builds depot here; **1874** incorporated as a town; **1882** town renamed Roanoke, Native American term for "shell money"; **1884** incorporated as a city, **1885** municipal market established; **1886** *The Times* newspaper founded; **1889** *World-News* newspaper founded; **1902** becomes an independent city; **1906** Virginian Railroad arrives; **Sept. 5, 1908** Henry Fowler born, secretary of treasury under Pres. Lyndon Johnson (died 2000); **May 23, 1912** actor John Payne born (died 1989); **1917** American Viscose Corporation Plant opens; **1933** Woodrum Field established, becomes Roanoke Regional Airport 1977; **1966**

Virginia Western Community College established; **May 28, 1971** Audie Murphy, 46, most decorated U.S. veteran of World War II, then actor, dies in plane crash.

Rocky Mount *Franklin County* *Southwestern Virginia, 20 mi/32 km south of Roanoke*

1750 area first settled; **1774** Washington Iron Works founded by Col. John Donelson, closes 1779; **1786** Franklin County formed; town becomes county seat; **1805** adjoining town of Mount Pleasant founded; **Nov. 3, 1816** Gen. Jubal A. Early born in rural Franklin County, led advance on Washington 1864 (died 1894); **c.1858** African-American educator Booker T. Washington born to northeast in rural Franklin County (died 1915), family moved to Malden, West Virginia, 1864; **1873** incorporated as a town, annexes rival village of Mount Pleasant; **c.1900** railroad reaches town; **1909** third county courthouse built; **Apr. 2, 1956** Booker T. Washington National Monument established.

Rustburg *Campbell County* *Central Virginia, 10 mi/16 km south-southeast of Lynchburg*

1736 area first settled; **1781** Campbell County formed from Bedford County, named for Gen. William Campbell, hero of Battle of King's Mountain fought same year; **1783** town established as county seat on land of Jeremiah Rust; **Apr. 1786** Fountain Hotel opened by Bernard Finch; **c.1790** Rustburg Inn established; **1848** county courthouse built.

Salem *Salem City* *Southwestern Virginia, 5 mi/8 km west of Roanoke*

1768 land grant given to Andrew Lewis; **1802** town platted on Great Road by James Simpson; **1836** incorporated as a town; **1838** Roanoke County formed; town becomes county seat; **1847** Roanoke College moved from Augusta County, established 1842; **June 21, 1864** Union Gen. David Hunter encounters Confederate Gen. John McCausland in Battle of Hanging Rock, 30 Union killed, minor Confederate losses; **1909** Catawba Sanatorium founded in Catawba Valley to northwest; **1923** Lakeside Amusement Park established; **1953** South Salem annexed; **1960** third county courthouse built; **1967** incorporated as an independent city; **1992** Salem Museum opened.

Saluda *Middlesex County* *Eastern Virginia, 48 mi/77 km east of Richmond*

1640 first settlers arrive; **1649** Rosegill house built; **1669** Middlesex County formed from Lancaster County; Urbanna becomes county seat; **1714** Christ Church completed to east; **1852** county seat moved to Saluda; county courthouse built, burned during Civil War, rebuilt; **1860s** county clerk hides records in Dragon Rum Swamp during Civil War.

Smithfield   *Isle of Wight County*   *Southeastern Virginia, 21 mi/34 km west-northwest of Norfolk*

1633 tobacco warehouse established; **1634** Isle of Wight County formed; **c.1640** George Hardy builds Hardy's Mill, later Wrenn's Mill, to north on Pagan River; **1737** St. Luke's Church built; **1750** county organized; town becomes county seat; county courthouse built; **1752** incorporated as a town; **1800** county seat moved to Isle of Wight village; **1812** Fort Boykin built to north during War of 1812; **2000** Smithfield Community Center opened.

South Boston   *Halifax County*   *Southern Virginia, 50 mi/80 km south-southeast of Lynchburg*

1796 town chartered; **1830s** Berry Hill antebellum mansion built to west by James Coles Bruce; **1884** incorporated as a town; **1960** incorporated as an independent city; **July 1995** independent city reverts to town status.

Spotsylvania   *Spotsylvania County*   *East central Virginia, 60 mi/97 km south-southwest of Washington, D.C.*

1720 Spotsylvania County formed; **c.1782** Spotsylvania Tavern established; **1832** Orange County separates from Spotsylvania County; county seat moved from Germanna; town founded as new county seat; **May 5–6, 1864** in Battle of the Wilderness, first battlefield encounter of Union General Grant and Confederate General Lee, Confederates routed, rally with arrival of General Longstreet's forces, but Longstreet is wounded by friendly fire, confrontation between Grant and Lee continues for 11 months until Confederate surrender at Appomattox; **May 8–9, 1864** in Battle of Spotsylvania, Gen. J. E. B. Stuart's emplacements attacked by Grant's Union army, Grant prevented from reaching Richmond, 2,725 Union killed, 13,000 wounded, Confederate casualties unknown, Grant counterattacks May 10; **May 12, 1864** Gen. Francis Bartow takes Spotsylvania in Third Wilderness Campaign, includes Battle of Bloody Angle, 27,812 Union soldiers killed, Confederate General Stuart dies from wounds; **1870** county courthouse built, replacing structure burned 1864; **Feb. 14, 1927** Fredericksburg and Spotsylvania National Military Park established.

Stafford   *Stafford County*   *Northern Virginia, 40 mi/64 km south-southwest of Washington, D.C.*

1613 at Native American village of Patawomeke, at Marlborough Point to east, Pocahontas is kidnapped by English; **1664** Stafford County, the "Mother of Counties," formed; **1680** Marlborough becomes county seat; **1688** Parson Waugh's Tumult begins when John Waugh spreads false story of Catholic plot against Protestants; **1715** county seat moved to Stafford; **Apr. 24, 1784** Supreme Court Justice Peter Vivian Daniel born (died 1860); **1834** Anthony Burns born, fugitive slave reached Boston, central figure in abolitionist movement (died 1862); **1922** county courthouse built.

Stanardsville   *Greene County*   *North central Virginia, 75 mi/121 km northwest of Richmond*

1798 town founded on land owned by William Stanard; **1838** Greene County formed, named for Gen. Nathanael Greene; town becomes county seat; county courthouse built; **1858** Stanardsville Methodist Church built; **1901** Grace Episcopal Church built; **1921** incorporated as a town; **1938** county office building completed.

Staunton   *Staunton City*   *North central Virginia, 78 mi/126 km northeast of Roanoke*

1732 area settled, town founded as Mill Place by John Lewis; Bellefont house built by Lewis; **c.1737** Kalorama house built; **1738** Augusta County formed; town becomes county seat; **c.1742** frontiersman Benjamin Logan born in rural Augusta County (died 1802); **c.1775** fur trader, mountain man John Colter born (died 1813); **1791** Stuart House built; **1801** incorporated as a town; **March 20, 1811** painter George Caleb Bingham born in rural Augusta County (died 1879); **1818** Folly house built by Joseph Smith to south; **1825** Western State Hospital founded as Western Lunatic Asylum; **1838** Virginia School for the Deaf and Blind founded; **1842** Mary Baldwin College established; **1843** Stuart Hall preparatory school for girls founded; **1846** Woodrow Wilson's Birthplace built as manse for Presbyterian Church; **1854** Virginia Central Railroad reaches town; **1855** Old Trinity Church built; **Dec. 28, 1856** Thomas Woodrow Wilson, 28th President, born (died Feb. 3, 1924); **1859** Staunton Military Academy founded; **1871** incorporated as a city; **1901** county courthouse built; **1902** becomes an independent city; **May 1, 1907** singer Kate Smith born at rural Greenville to south (died 1986); **1986** Frontier Culture Museum established.

Stuart   *Patrick County*   *Southwestern Virginia, 55 mi/89 km south-southwest of Roanoke*

c.1780 George Taylor granted land on North Mayo River for his Revolutionary War service; **1791** Patrick County formed; town founded on land deeded by Eliphaz Shelton, becomes county seat, originally named Patrick Court House; **Feb. 6, 1833** Confederate Gen. J. E. B. Stuart born in rural Patrick County, died May 12, 1864, at Battle of Yellow Tavern; **1852** county courthouse built; **1884** incorporated as a town; **1938** Pinnacles Hydroelectric Development completed at Pinnacles of Dan, mountain formation to west.

Suffolk   *Suffolk City*   *Southeastern Virginia, 18 mi/ 29 km southwest of Norfolk, on Nansemond River*

1608 Capt. John Smith explores Nansemond River; **1618** Edward Waters becomes first settler; **1637** Upper Norfolk County formed from Norfolk County; **1646** county renamed Nansemond; **1738** Glebe Episcopal Church built; **1741** town founded; **1750** county seat moved to Suffolk from Jarnigan's (Cohoon's) Bridge; **May 13, 1779** town burned by British General Matthews; **1808** incorporated as a town; **1840** county courthouse completed; **May 12, 1862** Union forces capture town; **Jan. 15, 1897** author Stringfellow Barr born (died 1862); **1910** incorporated as an independent city; **1912** Planters Peanut and Chocolate Company established by Italian immigrant Amedro Obici; **Sept. 1907** Supreme Court Justice Lewis Franklin Powell, Jr. born (died 1998); **1928** Ruritan National organized at Holland village by J. J. Gwaltney and T. V. Downing as agricultural and civic improvement group for Virginia and the Carolinas; **1966** Nansemond-Suffolk Academy founded; **1974** Nansemond County merges with city of Suffolk.

Surry *Surry County* *Southeastern Virginia, 45 mi/72 km southeast of Richmond, near James River*

1609 Smith's Fort built by John Smith; **1652** Surry County formed; county seat established at Ware Neck, moved to Troopers 1754; Rolfe (Warren) House built near site of Smith's Fort; **1665** Bacon's Castle house built to southeast by Arthur Allen, originally called Allen's Brick House, never lived in by rebel leader Nathaniel Bacon; **c.1775** Surry Inn tavern established; **1797** county seat moved to Surry; **1923** county courthouse built; **1928** incorporated as a town; **1972** Surry Nuclear Power Plant begins operation on James River to east.

Sussex *Sussex County* *Southeastern Virginia, 45 mi/72 km south-southeast of Richmond*

1605 area settled; **1754** Sussex County formed from Surrey County; town becomes county seat; **1802** Dillard House built by C. H. Bailey, used as county records office; **1828** county courthouse built; **1924** county clerk's office built.

Tangier *Accomack County* *Eastern Virginia, 70 mi/113 km north of Norfolk, in Chesapeake Bay*

1608 Capt. John Smith discovers Pocomoke peoples living on Tangier and Watt Islands; **1686** John Crockett and his eight sons become first white settlers; **1813** British use islands as headquarters for defense of Chesapeake Bay; **1915** incorporated as a town.

Tappahannock *Essex County* *Eastern Virginia, 50 mi/80 km northeast of Richmond*

1680 town founded on Rappahannock River; county seat of former Rappahannock County moved from Caret; **1682** trading post established by Jacob Hobbs; **1692** Essex County formed; town becomes county seat; **c.1750** Ritchie House built; **Apr. 21, 1809** Confederate Gen., Cong. Robert M. T. Hunter born in rural Essex County (died 1887); **Dec. 1814** British bombard town during War of 1812; **1848** county courthouse built; **1914** incorporated as a town; **1927** Downing Bridge built on Rappahannock River, replaced 1963; **1995** Essex County Museum established.

Tazewell *Tazewell County* *Southwestern Virginia, 88 mi/142 km west of Roanoke*

1750 area visited by Dr. Thomas Walker, mentions coal reserves; **1767** Daniel Boone builds cabin-fort for hunting expedition; **1769** area settled; **1772** Wynne's Fort house built by William Wynne; **1799** Tazewell County formed; **c.1800** Witten's Mill built by Thomas Witten, Jr.; town founded as county seat; **July 1863** Molly Tynes makes 40-mi/60-km ride on horseback to warn Wytheville of approaching Union forces; **1866** incorporated as a town; **c.1887** railroad reaches town; coal production expanded; **2001** county courthouse completed.

Upperville *Fauquier County* See **Markham (1974)**

Vienna *Fairfax County* *Northern Virginia, 15 mi/24 km west of Washington, D.C.*

1742 Fairfax County formed; town founded as county seat; **1752** county seat moved to Alexandria; **1890** incorporated as a town; **1966** Vienna Community Center opened; **Oct. 15, 1966** Wolf Trap Farm Park for the Performing Arts established by National Park System; **1971** Patrick Henry Library opened; Filene Center opened at Wolf Trap Farm, destroyed by fire Apr. 1982, rebuilt 1984.

Virginia Beach *Virginia Beach City* *Southeastern Virginia, 17 mi/27 km east of Norfolk, on Atlantic Ocean*

Apr. 26, 1607 English party on three ships—*Sarah Constant, Goodspeed,* and *Discovery*—led by Capt. John Smith lands at Cape Henry, at entrance to Chesapeake Bay; **1634** Adam Thoroughgood House built; **1691** Princess Anne County formed; Lynnhaven becomes county seat; **1751** county seat moved to New Town; **1753** Francis Thorowgood House built; **1760** Woodhouse Plantation Home built; **1773** Horatio Cornick House built; **1778** county seat moved to Kempsville (Kemp's Landing); **1791** Cape Henry Lighthouse built, rebuilt 1879; Green Hill House built; **1888** Princess Anne Hotel built; **1903** old Coast Guard Station built, decommissioned 1969; **1906** incorporated as a town; **1912** Camp Pendleton Military Reservation established; **1913** Fort Story Military Reservation established; **1915** U.S. Coast Guard Station established; **1927** Cavalier Hotel built; **Nov. 12, 1928** British steamship *Vestris* sinks off Virginia coast killing 113; **1941** Oceana Naval Air Station opened; **1952** incorporated as an independent city; **1960** Christian Broadcasting Network (CBN) founded by evangelist Pat Robertson; **1963** Princess Anne County consolidates with city of Virginia Beach; **1964** Chesapeake Bay Bridge-Tunnel completed, crosses Chesapeake Bay entrance to Kiptopeke (Cape Charles), 17.6-mi/28.3-km long; **1966** ECPI College of Technology (2-year) established; **1973** first annual month-long Neptune Festival held; **1978** CBN University established by Pat Robertson, renamed Regent University 1990; **1986** Virginia Science Museum opened; **1988** Old Coast Guard Station museum opened.

Warm Springs   *Bath County   Western Virginia, 55 mi/89 km north of Roanoke*

1732 John and Margaret Lyon Lewis become first settlers; **c.1750** Fort Dinwiddie built on Jackson River to west as protection against Native Americans; first tourists begin arriving at county's mineral springs; **1765** Homestead Hotel built by Thomas Bullitt at Hot Springs to south, used as hospital during Civil War, partially destroyed by fire 1901, rebuilt; **1766** Warm Springs' first hotel built; **1791** Bath County formed; county seat established at Fassifern Farm to west; **1842** county seat moved to Warm Springs; first county courthouse built, converted to Warm Springs Inn 1907; **1908** second county courthouse built; **May 27, 1912** golfer Sam Snead born at Hot Springs to south.

Warrenton   *Fauquier County   Northern Virginia, 45 mi/72 km west-southwest of Washington, D.C.*

1712 first settlers arrive; **1718** Thomas Lee receives land grant here; Leeton Forest house built to south, home of Charles Lee, U.S. Attorney General 1795–1801; **1746** Clovelly house built by Peter Kemper; **Sept. 24, 1755** U.S. Supreme Court Justice John Marshall born at rural Midland (died 1835); **1759** Fauquier County formed; town becomes county seat; **1773** North Wales house built by William Allison; **1808** old jail built; **1810** incorporated as a town; **1819** Thaddeus Norris builds Norris Tavern; **1845** Smith House built; **June 11–Aug. 17, 1849** Virginia assembly meets at White Sulphur Springs to southwest; **1850s** railroad reaches town; **1876** Warren Green Hotel built; **1890** sixth county courthouse built; **1959** John Marshall statue erected; **1974** county office complex completed.

Warsaw   *Richmond County   Eastern Virginia, 50 mi/80 km northeast of Richmond*

1689 Bladensfield mansion built for John Jenkins by Nicholas Rochester; **1692** Richmond County formed; Naylors becomes county seat; **1720** county reduced in area; **1730** county seat moved to present site, named Richmond Court House; **c.1730** Sabine Hall mansion built by Landon Carter; **1749** county courthouse built; **1758** Mount Airy estate built by Col. John Tayloe; **1831** town renamed Warsaw for its Polish heritage; **1948** incorporated as a town.

Washington   *Rappahannock County   Northern Virginia, 65 mi/105 km west-southwest of Washington, D.C.*

Aug. 4, 1749 town platted by George Washington; **1796** town organized, named for George Washington; **1833** Rappahannock County formed, separates from Culpeper County; town becomes county seat; **1871** county courthouse built; **1894** incorporated as a town.

Waynesboro   *Waynesboro City   Northwestern Virginia, 86 mi/138 km northwest of Richmond*

1669 John Lederer becomes first white man to view Shenandoah Valley; **1736** tavern opened by John Tees; town founded, named Teesville; **1797** town renamed for Gen. "Mad" Anthony Wayne; **1813** Thomas Jefferson, James Monroe, James Madison, and John Marshall meet at nearby Mountain Top Tavern, select Charlottesville as site of University of Virginia; **1834** incorporated as a town; **1856** Rockfish Gap Tunnel of Virginia Central Railroad completed to east; **March 2, 1865** Jubal Early defeated by Union General Custer in one of final engagements of Civil War; **1869** Basic City founded on east, merges with Waynesboro 1924; **1879** Fishburne Military School established; **1895** oil hoax leaves investors with worthless stock, new source of water; **1912** Waynesboro Public Library founded; **1920** Fairfax Hall College (2-year) established; **1948** incorporated as an independent city.

West Point   *King William County   Eastern Virginia, 37 mi/60 km east of Richmond, on York River*

1646 Gov. William Berkeley leads soldiers against chief Opechancanough, responsible for massacres of settlers in 1622 and 1644; **1653** estate patented to William Claiborne, builds Romancoke House, current structure succeeded antebellum house that burned 1925; **1691** town founded as West Point; **1705** incorporated as a "free borough," renamed Delaware, for Thomas West, third Lord Delaware; **c.1710** Chelsea house built; **c.1720** Sweet Hall house built to west; **c.1730** Eltham house built by Col. William Bassett, who married Martha Washington's sister, Anna Maria, house destroyed by fire 1876; **1732** St. John's Church built to northwest; **1861** railroad reaches town from Richmond; town name reverts to West Point; **1870** incorporated as a town; **1982** first annual Crab Carnival held.

Williamsburg   *Williamsburg City   Southeastern Virginia, 37 mi/60 km northwest of Norfolk*

1608 area first settled by English; **1622** after massacre by natives, palisade built to protect residents; **1632** Middle Plantation established within palisade; **1634** James City County formed; **1637** Kingsmill estate patented by Richard Kingsmill; **1644** massacre at Middle Plantation prompts construction of new fortifications; **1693** College of William and Mary established, second-oldest college in U.S. after Harvard; **1695** Christopher Wren Building built, oldest public building in U.S.; **1699** town platted, renamed; capital of Virginia Colony moved from Jamestown; governor's palace built; **1705** colonial capitol completed, burned 1747, rebuilt, burned again 1832, restoration begun 1929; **1715** Bruton Parish Church completed; **1722** incorporated as a town; **1730** William Parks establishes first printing press in Virginia; **c.1740** Raleigh Tavern built; **1744** Virginia's first paper mill founded; **1751** Carters Grove estate built; **1755** Wythe House built; **1765** Patrick Henry compels burgesses to repeal Stamp Act; **1771** county courthouse built; **1773** public gaol (jail) built; Eastern State Hospital opens; **1774** burgesses call first Continental Congress; **1780** state capital moved to Richmond; **1785** county seat moved from Jamestown; **May 5, 1862** Battle of Williamsburg, Union General Hooker attacks Confederate forces of General Longstreet, victory for Longstreet, later repulsed by Union General Hancock; **1884** incorporated as a city; **1902** becomes an independent city; **1917** munitions factory opens; **1926** John D. Rockefeller, Jr. spearheads city's restoration; **July 3, 1930** Colonial National Monument established, becomes National Historical Park 1936; **1972** Anheuser-Busch Brewery opened; **1975** Busch Gardens theme park opened; **1967** second county courthouse built.

Winchester *Winchester City   Northern Virginia, 65 mi/105 km west-northwest of Washington, D.C.*

1732 Joist Hite leads 16 families into Shenandoah Valley, settle at village of Opequon (o-PECK-un); **1738** Frederick County formed; **1744** James Wood plats town as county seat, named Fredericktown; **c.1745** Isaac Parkins House built; **1748** 16-year-old George Washington arrives to begin first job as surveyor; **1752** town platted, renamed Winchester; **1754** Abram's Delight (Hollingsworth House) built; **1755** Washington placed in command of frontier forces; **1756** Fort Loudoun built; **1759** Hopewell Friends Meeting House built to north; **1764** Winchester Academy founded, becomes Shenandoah Valley Military Academy; **1779** incorporated as a town; **c.1783** Red Lion Tavern built; **c.1790** Taylor Hotel built, closed 1905; First Presbyterian Church built; **1794** Glen Burnie House built; **Dec. 7, 1804** Supreme Court Justice Noah Haynes Swayne born (died 1884); **1829** Christ Church built; **1836** Winchester & Potomac Railroad built; **1840** county courthouse built; **1862** Star Fort built by Federal troops; **March 23, 1862** Gen. Stonewall Jackson loses to Union forces in Battle of Kernstown to south; **May 25, 1862** Confederate Gen. Stonewall Jackson gains victory in First Battle of Winchester; **June 14, 1863** in Second Battle of Winchester, Gen. Jubal Early captures several thousand of Union Gen. R. H. Milroy's forces; **June 15, 1863** in Battle of Stephenson's Depot to north, General Lee's troops capture 4,000 of General Milroy's forces; **Sept. 19, 1864** Gen. Jubal Early defeated by Union General Sheridan in Third Battle of Winchester; **1874** incorporated as a city; **1875** Shenandoah University established; **Oct. 25, 1888** polar explorer Richard E. Byrd born (died 1957); **1900** city hall built; **1902** becomes an independent city; **1913** Handley Library opened; **1921** Winchester & Western Railroad completed to Wardensville, West Virginia, steep-grade section to Wardensville abandoned 1934; **1924** George Washington Hotel built, closed 1970s; **Sept. 8, 1932** country singer Patsy Cline born at Gore to west (died 1963); **1984** county government center completed.

Winterpock *Chesterfield County   See **Chesterfield** (1867)*

Wise *Wise County   Southwestern Virginia, 148 mi/238 km southwest of Roanoke*

1792 Richard Wells becomes first settler; town founded as Big Glades, renamed Gladesville; **1856** Wise County formed, named for Henry A. Wise, governor of Virginia; town becomes county seat; **1858** log county courthouse built, burned 1864 by Union forces; **1865** county courthouse built; **1870** Beaty's Store established; **1874** incorporated as a town; **1879** coal discovered in county, mining reaches peak 1970s; **1924** town renamed Wise; **Oct. 18, 1927** actor George C. Scott born (died 1999); **1954** Clinch Valley College of University of Virginia established.

Woodstock *Shenandoah County   Northern Virginia, 80 mi/129 km west of Washington, D.C.*

1752 area settled by German immigrants; **1756** land granted to Jacob Mueller; town of Muellerstadt platted; **1761** town chartered by George Washington, renamed Woodstock; **1772** Dunmore County formed; town becomes county seat; **Jan. 28, 1776** Lutheran minister John Muhlenberg sheds vestments to reveal uniform, quotes Ecclesiastes "a time of war, a time of peace"; **1778** county renamed Shenandoah; **1795** county courthouse completed; **1803** mill built on Narrow Passage Creek, closed 1883; **1817** *Shenandoah Herald* newspaper founded; **1822** Liberty Iron Furnace built to southwest; **1872** incorporated as a town; **1899** Massanutten Military Academy established.

Wytheville *Wythe County   Southwestern Virginia, 68 mi/109 km west-southwest of Roanoke*

1745 German and Scottish-Irish settlers arrive; **1790** Wythe County formed, named for George Wythe, first Virginian to sign Declaration of Independence; **1792** town founded as county seat, named Evansham; **1839** incorporated as a town, renamed; **1843** St. Mary's Catholic Church completed; **1851** St. John's Lutheran Church built; **July 1863** home guard repel Union troops intent on destroying railroad; **1867** Villa Maria Academy founded; **October 15, 1872** Edith Bolling Galt Wilson born, second wife of Pres. Woodrow Wilson (married Dec. 18, 1915, died Dec. 28, 1961); **1900** county courthouse built; **1950s** polio epidemic affects all families; **1967** Wytheville Community College established.

Yorktown *York County   Southeastern Virginia, 58 mi/93 km southeast of Richmond, on Chesapeake Bay*

1631 town settled; **1634** Charles River County formed; town becomes county seat; **1642** county renamed York; **1691** town platted; **1697** Grace Episcopal Church built; **1699** Sheild House built by Thomas Sessions; **1706** Custom House built; **1710** Lightfoot House built; **1720** Swan Tavern built, destroyed 1862 in courthouse munitions explosion; **Dec. 26, 1738** patriot Thomas Nelson born, signer of Declaration of Independence (died 1789); **1741** Nelson House (York Hall) mansion built by William

Nelson; **c.1745** Moore House built; **Oct. 19, 1781** Battle of Yorktown, British General Cornwallis surrenders to American and French forces at Moore House in final stages of Revolutionary War; **1862** Federal troops take town from Gen. John Magruder; Federal munitions stored in courthouse explode destroying structure; **1875** county courthouse built; **1880** second Swan Tavern built, destroyed by fire 1915, rebuilt 1934; **1917** Yorktown Navy Base established, now U.S. Naval Weapons Station; **July 3, 1930** Colonial National Monument established, redesignated Colonial National Historical Park 1936; **1952** Coleman Memorial Bridge built across York River, new bridge completed 1996; **1976** Yorktown Victory Center museum opened; **1981** Watermen's Museum founded, dedicated to Chesapeake fishing industry, new building opened 1988.

Washington

Northwestern U.S. Capital: Olympia. Major cities: Seattle, Tacoma, Spokane.

The region was acquired by the U.S. in 1843, and was organized as part of Oregon Territory August 14, 1848. Washington Territory separated from Oregon March 2, 1853. Washington entered the Union as the 42nd state November 11, 1889.

Washington is divided into 39 counties. Its municipalities are classified as towns and cities. There are no townships. See Introduction.

Aberdeen *Grays Harbor County* *Western Washington, 67 mi/108 km west-southwest of Tacoma*

1792 Capt. Robert Gray sails into large bay later named for him; **1867** Samuel Benn of Ireland arrives, becomes first settler; **1870** fish cannery founded by Scotsman George R. Hume; **1875** town founded by James W. Stewart and Alexander Young at mouth of Chehalis River, eastern end of Grays Harbor, named for Aberdeen, Scotland; **1879** schooner *Kate and Ann* begins regular service to Columbia River communities; **1881** logging operations begin along Chehalis River; **1884** town platted; **1886** *Herald* newspaper founded; **1887** Samuel Benn House built; **1889** *Aberdeen Weekly Bulletin* newspaper founded, later becomes *The World*; **1890** town incorporated; telegraph service arrives; **1895** Northern Pacific Railroad reaches town, extended to Hoquiam 1898; **1899** first ship launched from town's shipyard; **1930** Grays Harbor College (2-year) established; **1903** fire destroys large part of town; **1906** channel dredged, shallow areas filled in establishing Port of Grays Harbor; **1935** logging operators strike, requiring call-out of National Guard; **1936** Strand Fisheries Company opened; **1950** suspension bridge built across Wishkah River.

Anacortes *Skagit County* *Northwestern Washington, 63 mi/101 km north-northwest of Seattle*

1876 town founded on Strait of Georgia at north end of Fidalgo Island, first settled by Amos Bowman; town named for Bowman's wife Anna Cortes; **1891** town incorporated; **1910** Carnegie Library built; **Apr. 1922** ferry service established to Sidney, British Columbia; **1935** Deception Pass Bridge built to Whidbey Island to south; **Apr. 14, 1995** singer Burl Ives dies at age 85 (born 1909).

Asotin *Asotin County* *Southeastern Washington, 93 mi/150 km south-southeast of Spokane, on Snake River*

1881 ferry established on Snake River by J. J. Kanawyer at mouth of Asotin Creek; town of Asotin founded; sawmill built by Frank Curtis; **1883** Asotin County formed; town becomes county seat; *Asotin County Sentinel* newspaper founded; **1890** town incorporated; **1907** county courthouse built, remodeled 2002.

Auburn *King County* *Western Washington, suburb 21 mi/34 km south-southeast of Seattle*

1855 area first settled; **Oct. 28, 1855** nine members from Brannon, King, and Jones families killed in their homes by Native Americans in White River Massacre; **1887** Northern Pacific Railroad built, extended east to Stampede Pass, tunnel completed 1888; town founded by settler Dr. Levi W. Ballard, named Slaughter for Lt. W. A. Slaughter, killed during Indian Wars; **1891** incorporated as a town; **1893** town renamed Auburn, from line in Goldsmith's "Deserted Village"; **1914** incorporated as a city; Carnegie Library built; **1923** Masonic temple built; **1962** Federal Aviation Administration air traffic control center established; **1965** Green River Community College established.

Bainbridge Island *Kitsap County* *Western Washington, 9 mi/14.5 km west of Seattle, on Puget Sound*

1792 Capt. George Vancouver arrives at Bainbridge Island, across Puget Sound from site of Seattle; **1841** Charles N. Wilkes identifies land as an island, with narrow passages separating it from Kitsap Peninsula, named for Capt. William Bainbridge, commander of USS *Constitution*; **1853** one of first sawmills on Puget Sound built at Port Gamble at southern end of island; **1902** Hall Brothers Shipyard moved from Port Blakeley on northern end of island to Eagle Harbor, on eastern side; **1905** Eagle Harbor renamed Winslow; **1910** Fort Ward established at southern end of island; **1957** Winslow incorporated as a town; **1990** incorporated as a city; **1991** city renamed Bainbridge Island.

Bellevue *King County* *Western Washington, suburb 5 mi/8 km east of Seattle, on Lake Washington*

1869 William Meydenbauer becomes first settler; **1886** town founded; **1892** ferry service begins on Lake Washington to Seattle; **1903** Northern Pacific Railroad reaches town; **1925** Bellevue Public Library founded; **1940** Lacey V. Murrow Floating Bridge built on Lake Washington; **1953** incorporated as a city; **1963** Evergreen Point Floating Bridge built on Lake Washington; **1966** Bellevue Community College established; **1990** Murrow Bridge sinks in rough weather, rebuilt 1993.

Bellingham *Whatcom County* *Northwestern Washington, 80 mi/129 km north of Seattle*

1792 party led by Joseph Whidbey sent by George Vancouver to explore coastline; **1846** international boundary fixed at 49° north latitude, opening area to settlement; **Dec. 1852** Capt. Henry Roeder and Russell V. Peabody arrive from California; **1853** lumber mill built on Bellingham Bay, Strait of Georgia, by Roeder and Peabody; town founded, originally named Whatcom; **1854** Whatcom County formed; town becomes county seat; **1855** Lummi Indian Reservation established to northwest; **1856** Fort Bellingham built by Capt. George Pickett; **1858** Fraser River gold rush brings boom to area; Sehome Mine opened; *Northern Light* newspaper founded; **c.1858** George Pickett House built; **c.1860** John Bennett establishes region's fruit-growing industry; **1871** town of Sehome platted adjacent to Whatcom; **1878** Sehome mine closed; **1880** town of New Whatcom founded by 600 emigrants from Kansas; **1881** fish cannery opened, fails within few years; **1883** fourth town of Fairhaven founded by Dan Harris; **1892** Ella Higginson House built; **1893** Western Washington College of Education established, becomes Western Washington University; **1900** Fairhaven merges with New Whatcom; **1903** Sehome and Whatcom annexed by New Whatcom, renamed Bellingham; incorporated as a city; **1907** bulb farming begins; **1908** Carnegie Public Library built, replaced 1951; **1911** Port of Bellingham organized; **1924** poultry industry established; **1940** city hall built; **1940s** defense industry brings boom to area; **1970** Whatcom Community College established; **1994** county courthouse built.

Blaine *Whatcom County* *Northwestern Washington, 98 mi/158 km north of Seattle, on Strait of Georgia*

1858 tent community established during Fraser River Gold Rush; **1884** town founded at Canada border, named Concord; **1885** town renamed for 1884 Republican presidential candidate James G. Blaine; **1890** incorporated as a town; **1891** incorporated as a city; **1910** Point Roberts Light erected to west in U.S. enclave isolated from mainland by Boundary Bay, ending smuggling trade; **Sept. 6, 1921** International Peace Arch dedicated on Canada-U.S. border.

Bremerton *Kitsap County* *Western Washington, 15 mi/24 km west of Seattle, on Puget Sound*

1888 German immigrant, real estate agent William Bremer arrives; **1891** town founded by Bremer; site selected by U.S. Navy for shipyard; **1901** incorporated as a town; **1908** Bremerton City Library founded; **Nov. 24, 1917** TV actor Howard Duff born (died 1990); **1919** last of three drydocks completed; **1940** federal shipbuilding programs bring surge of prosperity to city; **1946** Olympic College (2-year) established.

Buckley *Pierce County* *Western Washington, 34 mi/55 km south-southeast of Seattle*

1855 Connell Prairie Blockhouse built as protection against Native American attacks; **1886** White River Shingle Mill built; Northern Pacific Railroad built; town renamed White River Siding; **1888** town platted on White River by Alexander Wickersham, renamed for railroad divisional superintendent; *Banner* newspaper founded; **1890** incorporated as a town; **1894** incorporated as a city; **1939** Washington State Custodial School built by WPA.

Bucoda *Thurston County* *Western Washington, 33 mi/53 km south-southwest of Tacoma*

1854 Aaron Webster settles here, builds sawmill on Skookumchuck River; town founded, named Seatco; **1873** Northern Pacific Railroad built; coal mining begun by John D. David, John M. Buckley, and Samuel Coulter; first territorial prison founded; convict labor used in coal mines; **1887** scandal over convict labor forces prison to be moved to Walla Walla; **1891** town renamed, combination of Buckley, Coulter, and David; **1910** town incorporated.

Camas *Clark County* *Southwestern Washington, 14 mi/23 km northeast of Portland, Oregon*

1846 Jacob Hunsacker builds sawmill on Lacamas Lake to north; **1860** town founded, named for wild camas root eaten by Native Americans; **1884** paper mill built on Lacamas Lake, destroyed by fire 18 months later, rebuilt; **1906** town incorporated; **Sept. 18, 1933** singer Jimmy F.

Rodgers born four months after singing legend Jimmie C. Rodgers died.

Castle Rock   *Cowlitz County   Southwestern Washington, 96 mi/155 km south-southwest of Tacoma*

1883 Eliza and William Huntingdon become first settlers; **1888** town platted on Cowlitz River; **1890** town incorporated; **May 18, 1980** snowcapped Mt. St. Helens volcano to east erupts following weeks of preliminary activity sending pyroclastic flow, mixture of glacial meltwater and volcanic ash, down Toutle and Cowlitz rivers, leveling forests, 57 killed; **1989** Mount St. Helens National Volcanic Monument established to east.

Cathlamet   *Wahkiakum County   Southwestern Washington, 84 mi/135 km southwest of Tacoma*

1805-1806 Lewis and Clark Expedition mentions village of "Cathlamah" in their records; **1825** Wahkiakum and Cathlamet peoples struck by epidemics, wander aimlessly through forests for years; **1846** trading post established on Columbia River; **1854** Wahkiakum County formed; town founded as county seat; **1907** town incorporated; Bradley House built by lumber baron; **1923** third county courthouse completed, addition built 1994.

Centralia   *Lewis County   Southwestern Washington, 42 mi/68 km south-southwest of Tacoma*

1850 J. G. Cochran of Missouri arrives with Negro slave George Washington, adopts him as son, sells his claim to him 1852; **1852** town founded, platted by Washington on Skookumchuck River; **1855** Borst Blockhouse built; **1873** Northern Pacific Railroad built; **1886** incorporated as a town; **1892** incorporated as a city; **Nov. 11, 1919** in Centralia Massacre, shooting in front of International Workers of the World (the "Wobblies") labor hall as American Legion parade marches by, four legionnaires killed, suspect later lynched; **1925** Centralia College (2-year) established.

Chehalis   *Lewis County   Southwestern Washington, 47 mi/76 km south-southwest of Tacoma*

1845 Lewis County formed; **1850** Marys Corner (Jackson Prairie) becomes county seat; **1852** county seat moved to Claquato; **1859** O. B. McFadden House built, later serves as post office; **1873** Northern Pacific Railroad built; town founded on Chehalis River, originally named Saundersville for landowner S. S. Saunders; **1874** county seat moved to Saundersville; **1879** town renamed to Chehalis; **1883** incorporated as a town; **1884** Church of the Epiphany built; **1890** incorporated as a city; **1927** county courthouse built.

Cheney   *Spokane County   Eastern Washington, 14 mi/23 km southwest of Spokane*

1858 Spokane County formed; **Sept. 1, 1858** at Battle of Four Lakes, Col. George Wright's force of 700 soldiers soundly defeats attack of 5,000 allied Native Americans, heavy Native American casualties, no soldiers killed; **1879** county reestablished; **1880** town founded as county seat, named for Benjamin P. Cheney, railroad board member; **1881** Northern Pacific Railroad reaches town; **1882** Eastern Washington University established; **1883** incorporated as a city; **1886** county seat moved to Spokane Falls (Spokane); **1898** *Cheney Free Press* newspaper founded.

Cle Elum   *Kittitas County   West central Washington, 72 mi/116 km southeast of Seattle*

1870 prospector Thomas L. Gambel becomes first white settler; **1884** coal discovered; town founded on Yakima River, name derived from Native American term for "swift water"; **1886** Northern Pacific Railroad reaches town; **1887** forest fire ruins timber industry; **1889** discovery of new coal deposits revitalizes economy; **1893** fire destroys town, town immediately rebuilt; **1902** town incorporated; **1933** Cle Elum Lake formed to northwest by dam on Cle Elum River; **May 19, 1939** astronaut Francis. R. "Dick" Scobee born, killed Jan. 28, 1986 in *Challenger* space shuttle disaster.

Colfax   *Whitman County   Southeastern Washington, 54 mi/87 km south of Spokane*

1870 J. A. Perkins becomes first settler; town founded on Palouse River, named Belleville; **1871** Whitman County formed; town becomes county seat; **1873** town incorporated, renamed for U.S. Vice Pres. Schuyler Colfax, served under President Grant; **c.1890** wheat growing supplants cattle raising as major industry; **1955** county courthouse built.

Colville   *Stevens County   Northeastern Washington, 65 mi/105 km north-northwest of Spokane*

1826 Fort Colville trading post founded by Hudson's Bay Company; **1859** new Fort Colville built by U.S. Army on Mill Creek to northeast; town of Pinckney City founded adjacent to fort; **1863** Stevens County formed; Pinckney City becomes county seat; **1871** fort abandoned; **1882** town of Colville founded on Colville River; **1890** town incorporated; **1921** county seat moved to Colville; **1938** county courthouse built, addition built 1970s.

Concrete   *Skagit County   Northwestern Washington, 70 mi/113 km north-northeast of Seattle*

1890 Magnus Miller becomes first settler; town founded by Miller on Skagit River at mouth of Baker River; town originally named Baker; **1892** post office established; **1900**

Great Northern Railroad reaches town; **1901** Baker Lumber Company builds shingle mill; **1905** Washington Portland Cement plant built; town renamed Cement City; **1908** Superior Portland Cement plant built, closed 1967; **1909** town incorporated, renamed Concrete; **1919** historic Henry Thompson Bridge built across Baker River; **1927** Lake Shannon formed by Baker Dam on Baker River; **1959** Upper Baker Dam built on Baker River to north forming Baker Lake; **1972** State Highway 20 Bridge built across Baker River, highway completed east across Cascade Range to Winthrop; **1996** railroad tracks razed.

Coulee City   *Grant County   Central Washington, 142 mi/229 km east of Seattle*

1881 first log cabin built; **1890** town founded in Grand Coulee, former channel of Columbia River; **1907** incorporated as a city; **1910** Sunset Highway built through town, designated U.S. Highway 2 during 1920s; **1949** Dry Falls Dam built in Grand Coulee forming Banks Lake from water diverted from Grand Coulee Dam on Columbia River to north.

Coupeville   *Island County   Northwestern Washington, 45 mi/72 km north-northwest of Seattle*

c.1300 Skagit peoples settle in area; **1845** Col. Isaac Ebey of Missouri becomes first settler; **1852** retired Capt. Thomas Coupe takes donation claim, offer of free land to homesteaders; town founded on Whidbey Island, Puget Sound; **1853** Island County formed; town becomes county seat; Capt. Thomas Coupe House built; **1855** Alexander's Blockhouse built by John Alexander; Thomas Dow (Waterworth) House built; old county courthouse built; Crockett Blockhouse built, restored 1938; Jacob Ebey Blockhouse built by son of Isaac Ebey; **1857** Isaac Ebey killed by natives in revenge for death of chief; **1860** First Methodist Church built, new structure built 1933; **1891** new county courthouse built; **1901** Admiralty Head Lighthouse built; **1910** incorporated as a town; **1943** Coupeville Outlying Landing Field established; **Nov. 10, 1978** Ebey's Landing National Historical Reserve established.

Dallesport   *Klickitat County   Southern Washington, 70 mi/113 km east of Portland, Oregon, on Columbia River*

1860 Klickitat County formed; town of Rockland founded as county seat; **1878** county seat moved to Goldendale; **1880** Baptist Rev. Orson D. Taylor arrives with scheme to create large boom town, arrested 1895 for fraud; **1895** town renamed Granddalles, named for the Dalles cascades of Columbia River; **1908** Spokane, Portland & Seattle Railroad reaches town; **1912** town renamed Grand Dalles; **1932** town renamed Northdalles for its location opposite city of The Dalles, Oregon; n**1937** town renamed Dallesport; **1957** The Dalles Dam completed on Columbia River.

Davenport   *Lincoln County   Eastern Washington, 35 mi/56 km west of Spokane*

1878 site at Cottonwood Springs used as camp by Native Americans and traders; **1880** store established by J. C. Davenport; town founded; **1883** Lincoln County formed; **1884** Sprague becomes county seat; **1890** town incorporated; **1896** county seat moved to Davenport following 12-year dispute; **1897** county courthouse built.

Dayton   *Columbia County   Southeastern Washington, 96 mi/155 km south-southwest of Spokane*

May 1806 Lewis & Clark Expedition stops at Patit Creek on return journey; **1836** Capt. Benjamin de Bonneville stops here; **1855** H. M. Chase becomes first settler; **1871** town founded on Touchet River by Jesse N. Day; **1875** Columbia County formed; town becomes county seat; **1876** incorporated as a town; **1881** incorporated as a city; Oregon Railway reaches town; **1887** county courthouse completed, oldest functioning courthouse in state; **1907** Weinhard Mansion built by brewer Jacob Weinhard; **1934** Blue Mountain Pea Cannery established.

Edmonds   *Snohomish County   Western Washington, 14 mi/23 km north of Seattle, on Puget Sound*

1868 settler Pleasant H. Elwell builds first cabin; **1872** town founded as timber milling center by George Brackett, later becomes mayor; **1890** incorporated as a city; **1891** Great Northern Railroad reaches town; **1923** ferry established to Kingston across Puget Sound; **1948** Port of Edmonds established.

Ellensburg   *Kittitas County   Central Washington, 93 mi/150 km southeast of Seattle*

1867 trading post established on Yakima River by outlaw named Wilson, later named Robber's Roost; **1872** town founded by John Shoudy, named for wife Mary Ellen; **1883** Kittitas County formed; town incorporated as a city, becomes county seat; **1886** Northern Pacific Railroad built; **1887** county courthouse built; **July 4, 1889** fire destroys most of business district; **1892** Central Washington University established; **1907** Chicago, Milwaukee, St. Paul & Pacific Railroad reaches town; **1923** first annual Ellensburg Rodeo held.

Enumclaw   *King County   Western Washington, 32 mi/51 km south-southeast of Seattle*

1856 Muckleshoot Indian Reservation established; **1857** Klickitat peoples, having retreated from Seattle one year earlier, are driven out of area by Col. Silas Casey's forces; **1874** reservation boundary redefined; **1879** Frank and Mary Stevenson become first settlers; **1885** Northern Pacific Railroad built; town founded by Danish settlers near White River, named for nearby mountain; **1888** Stampede Pass Tunnel completed on Northern Pacific Railroad across Cascade Range to east; **1890s** *Enumclaw*

Evergreen newspaper founded; **1905** Enumclaw-Rochdale Cooperative Store founded; **1913** incorporated as a city; **1948** Mud Mountain Lake formed by dam to south on White River.

Ephrata   *Grant County   Central Washington, 103 mi/166 km west-southwest of Spokane*

1882 Egbert brothers settle here for its abundant springs; **1892** town founded, name taken from Old Testament site noted for its wells; **1901** town platted; **Apr. 1906** about 2,400 wild horses rounded up in Big Bend region's last great horse roundup, moved to South Dakota Badlands; **1909** Grant County formed; incorporated as a city, becomes county seat; **1917** county courthouse built; **1918** first irrigation projects planned for Columbia Basin; **1933** Grand Coulee Dam project begins on Columbia River to north, water diverted through Grand Coulee, former river channel.

Everett   *Snohomish County   Western Washington, 26 mi/42 km north of Seattle, on Puget Sound*

1792 George Vancouver sails into Possession Sound; **1861** Snohomish County formed; Mukilteo becomes county seat; **July 1861** county seat moved to Snohomish; **1862** Dennis Brigham becomes first settler; **1890** town founded at mouth of Snohomish River by brothers Bethel J. and Wyatt J. Rucker, named for son of eastern capitalist Charles L. Colby, financed town founding; **1891** Great Northern Railroad reaches town; **1892** Puget Sound Pulp and Paper Company opened; department store opened by Wisconsin merchant John Hudson Clark; **1893** incorporated as a city; **1894** Everett Public Library founded; **1895** Bell-Nelson Sawmill opened; **1897** county seat moved to Everett; flooded Snohomish River inundates town; **1900** *Everett Telegraph* newspaper founded; **1902** Weyerhauser Timber Company begins operations; **1904** Washington Brewing Company founded; town boasts more than 30 saloons; **1909** county courthouse damaged by fire, rebuilt 1910; **1915** Vancouver's Landing Monument erected; **1908** Norwegian Lutheran College established, becomes Columbia Lutheran College, closed 1925; **May 31, 1912** U.S. Sen. Henry Morton Jackson born (died 1983); **1921** Trinity Episcopal Church completed; **1926** Our Lady of Perpetual Help Catholic Church built; **1930** city hall built; **1934** public library completed, new facility built 1989; **1941** Everett Community College established; civic auditorium built; **Jan. 17, 1947** singer Kenny Loggins born; **Sept. 22, 1957** Lee Crary, 8, kidnapped, $10,000 ransom paid, boy escapes three days later, George Collins arrested, convicted.

Friday Harbor   *San Juan County   Northwestern Washington, 71 mi/114 km north-northwest of Seattle*

1859 American Camp established at south end of San Juan Island in dispute over sovereignty of island; English Camp established on western side of island; tensions rise during "Pig War" precipitated by shooting English-owned pig found rooting through American-owned potato patch, reciprocation over county tax levy on English-owned sheep previous year; **1872** island granted to U.S. through arbitrator led by King William I of Germany; **1873** San Juan County formed comprising San Juan Islands; town founded as county seat on eastern shore of San Juan Island; **1907** county courthouse completed, annex built 1997; **1909** town incorporated; **1922** Friday Harbor Public Library founded, new library opened 1988; **Sept. 9, 1966** San Juan Island National Historical Park authorized preserving sites involved in determining international boundary; **1979** Whale Museum opened in former Odd Fellows Hall built 1892.

Goldendale   *Klickitat County   Southern Washington, 88 mi/142 km east-northeast of Portland, Oregon*

1860 Klickitat County formed; Rockland (Dallesport) becomes county seat; **1863** John J. Golden becomes first homesteader; town founded; **1878** county seat moved to Goldendale; **1879** incorporated as a city; **1941** county courthouse built; **1973** Goldendale Observatory established to house one of largest amateur telescopes ever built, becomes Goldendale Observatory State Park 1981.

Grand Coulee   *Grant County   Central Washington, 72 mi/116 km west-northwest of Spokane*

1933 construction on Grand Coulee Dam begins on Columbia River, named for Grand Coulee, dry valley formed to southwest by former river channel, used in conjunction with dam project for water diversion; town founded; **1935** incorporated as a city; **1942** Grand Coulee Dam completed forming large Franklin D. Roosevelt Lake; **Dec. 18, 1946** Coulee Dam National Recreation Area authorized, comprises all of reservoir almost to Canadian border.

Hoquiam   *Grays Harbor County   Western Washington, 70 mi/113 km west-southwest of Tacoma*

1792 Capt. Robert Gray sails into large bay of Pacific Ocean later named for him; **1859** John R. James becomes first settler; **1860** town founded on Grays Harbor, at mouth of Hoquiam River, Native American term for "hungry for wood"; **1869** post office established; **Nov. 1873** Quinault Indian Reservation established to northwest; **1879** transport service to Columbia River communities established by schooner *Kate and Ann*; **1881** logging begins on Chehalis River; **1884** hotel built; **1885** town platted; **1885** *Grays Harbor News* newspaper founded; **1887** town's shipbuilding industry begins; **1890** incorporated as a city; telegraph service begins; plank road built to Aberdeen 4 mi/6.4 km to east; **1895** Northern Pacific Railroad reaches town; **1901** Hoquiam Carnegie Library built; **1906** improvements made to shipping channel and docking facilities; Port of Grays Harbor established; **1927** Grays Harbor Pulp and Paper Mill established by E. M. Mills; **1935** logging strike tensions prompt call-out of National Guard; **1939** Olympic Stadium built.

Ice Harbor Dam   *Franklin and Walla Walla counties*   See **Pasco** (1961)

Ilwaco   *Pacific County*   *Southwestern Washington, 100 mi/161 km southwest of Tacoma*

1848 Capt. James Johnson arrives at land claim; **1849** town of Pacific City founded near Cape Disappointment; **1851** new town of Ilwaco founded on Pacific Ocean, north of entrance to Columbia River; **1852** original town taken by U.S for military base; **1856** Cape Disappointment Lighthouse built; **1864** Fort Canby built; **1884** gillnet wars pit net fishermen against trappers for fishing rights, continues through 1910; **1889** narrow gauge Ilwaco & Shoalwater Bay Railroad reaches town; **1890** incorporated as a town; **1930** railroad abandoned; **1987** incorporated as a city.

Kalama   *Cowlitz County*   *Southwestern Washington, 37 mi/60 km north of Portland, Oregon, on Columbia River*

1830 Hawaiian-born John Kalama settles here with Nisqually peoples; **1853** Ezra Meeker builds cabin at mouth of Kalama River; **1854** Colwlitz County formed; Monticello becomes county seat; **1870** Northern Pacific Railroad reaches site; train ferry established to Goble, Oregon; **1871** town founded as temporary rail terminus; **1872** county seat moved to Kalama following 1867 floods at Monticello; **1873** Northern Pacific Railroad extended north to Tacoma; **1890** incorporated as a city; **1920** Port of Kalama organized; **1922** county seat moved to Kelso.

Kelso   *Cowlitz County*   *Southwestern Washington, 79 mi/127 km south-southwest of Tacoma*

1847 Scottish surveyor Peter Crawford makes first land claim; **1854** Cowlitz County formed; Monticello (Longview) becomes county seat; **1872** county seat moved to Kalama; **1873** Northern Pacific Railroad reaches site; **1884** town platted by Crawford on Cowlitz River, near confluence with Columbia River, named for Kelso, Scotland; **1889** incorporated as a city; **1922** county seat moved to Kelso; **1923** county courthouse built; **1975** county hall of justice built; courthouse converted to county administrative center.

Kennewick   *Benton County*   *Southern Washington, 130 mi/209 km southwest of Spokane, on Columbia River*

1892 town founded by Northern Pacific Irrigation Company; **1904** incorporated as a city; **1911** Kennewick Public Library founded, new Mid Columbian Library opened 1999; **1942** large Hanford Atomic Energy Commission Site established to northwest; **1954** U.S. Highway 395 Bridge ("The Blue Bridge") built across Columbia River to Pasco; **1988** Ed Hendler Memorial Bridge (State Highway 397; cable-stayed) built across Columbia River.

Kent   *King County*   *Western Washington, suburb 17 mi/27 km south of Seattle, near Puget Sound*

1850s area settled by whites; original settlement named Titusville; **1878** hops growing introduced to area; **1888** town founded by Ezra Meeker, named for Kent, England; **1889** Carnation Condensed Milk Company plant built; **1890** incorporated as a city; **1906** area flooded by White and Green rivers; **1920s** truck farming becomes important with lettuce as leading crop; **1980s** area becomes highly urbanized.

Kettle Falls   *Stevens County*   *Northeastern Washington, 71 mi/114 km north-northwest of Spokane*

1826 grist mill built by Hudson's Bay Company; **1872** new grist mill built by Americans on land owned by L. C. Meyers; town of Meyers Falls founded on Columbia River; **1889** new town of Kettle Falls founded 4 mi/6.4 km to south; **1892** incorporated as a city; **1938** under threat of inundation from Franklin D. Roosevelt Lake, formed by Grand Coulee Dam, town effects move by annexing Meyers Falls, retaining name while abandoning town site.

Kirkland   *King County*   *Western Washington, suburb 8 mi/12.9 km northeast of Seattle, on Lake Washington*

1880 town founded by English millionaire Peter Kirk, envisions "Pittsburgh of the West" with discovery of iron ore on Snoqualmie River, mining venture ends 1893; **1892** wool mill established to provide woolen goods for Yukon Gold Rush; **1905** incorporated as a city; **1917** Lake Washington Ship Canal opened to Puget Sound; **1949** Lake Washington Technical College (2-year) established; **1968** Houghton annexed; **1974** Totem Lake community annexed.

Longview   *Cowlitz County*   *Southwestern Washington, 80 mi/129 km south-southwest of Tacoma*

1846 warehouses built on Columbia River by Hudson's Bay Company; **1849** Americans Jonathan Durbee and H. D. Huntington become first settlers; **Nov. 1852** Monticello Convention held advocating creation of Columbia Territory from Oregon Territory; **1854** Cowlitz County formed; Monticello becomes county seat; **1866–1867** flooding destroys town; **1872** county seat moved to Kalama; **1920** town of Longview founded as a model community by R. A. Long at site of old Monticello; **1924** incorporated as a city; **1926** Community Church completed; **1930** Lewis and Clark (Longview) Bridge built across Columbia River to Oregon; **1934** Lower Columbia College (2-year) established.

Montesano   *Grays Harbor County*   *Western Washington, 58 mi/93 km west-southwest of Tacoma*

1852 Isaiah Scammon becomes first settler; **1854** Chehalis County formed; town founded on Chehalis River; **1860** town becomes county seat; **1872** store opened by John

Esmond; **1881** shingle mill established; first hotel built; **1883** town incorporated; *Chehalis County Chronicle* newspaper founded; **1889** Northern Pacific Railroad reaches town; **1911** county courthouse built; **1915** county renamed Grays Harbor County; **1936** Blue Mountain Pea Cannery built.

Monticello   *Cowlitz County*   See **Longview**

Moses Lake   *Grant County*   *Central Washington, 95 mi/153 km west-southwest of Spokane*

1829 Native American Chief Sulkstalkscosum born, called "Chief Moses" by Presbyterian missionaries (died 1899); **1897** town founded, originally named Neppel; **1938** incorporated as a city, renamed Moses Lake; **1942** Moses Lake U.S. Army Field established, becomes Air Force Base after World War II, closed 1965; **Dec. 20, 1952** U.S. Air Force C-124 aircraft crashes killing 87; **1962** Big Bend Community College established; **May 1980** city covered with 4–6 in/10–15 cm of volcanic ash from Mt. St. Helens eruption.

Mount Rainier National Park   *Pierce and Lewis counties*   See **Paradise**

Mount Vernon   *Skagit County*   *Northwestern Washington, 56 mi/90 km north of Seattle, near Puget Sound*

1870 fur trading post established; **1877** town founded on Skagit River; **1883** Skagit County formed; La Conner becomes county seat; **1884** county seat moved to Mount Vernon; **1890** incorporated as a city; **1922** county courthouse built; **1926** Skagit Valley College (2-year) established; **1972** Mount Vernon Orchestra founded.

Neah Bay   *Clallam County*   *Western Washington, 120 mi/193 km northwest of Seattle, on Pacific Ocean*

1791 Spanish frigate *Princesa* brings first group of settlers to present-day Washington; **1851** Samuel Hancock builds trading post; town founded on Strait of Juan de Fuca, at entrance to Pacific Ocean, at Cape Flattery; **1855** Neah Bay Treaty concluded by Gov. Isaac Stevens and 14 tribes and bands of Native Americans; **1857** lighthouse built on Tatoosh Island off cape; **Nov. 4, 1875** U.S. steamship *Pacific* sinks off Cape Flattery after collision with another ship, 236 killed.

Newport   *Pend Oreille County*   *Northeastern Washington, 40 mi/64 km north-northeast of Spokane*

c.1885 first settlers arrive; town of Newport founded on Pend Oreille (pahnd-oh-ray) River on Idaho side of border; **1890** town of New Port, Washington, founded; Idaho town referred to as Old Town; **1892** Great Northern Railroad built; **c.1897** Old Town abandoned; **1903** incorporated as a town; **1906** first bridge built across river; **1911** Pend Oreille County formed; town becomes

county seat; **1915** county courthouse built; **1926** Interstate Bridge built (river crosses state line at angle); **1970** incorporated as a city.

Okanogan   *Okanogan County*   *Northern Washington, 112 mi/180 km northwest of Spokane*

1886 trading post established on Okanogan River by F. J. "Pard" Cummings; **1888** Okanogan County formed; Conconully becomes county seat; **1906** town of Okanogan founded; irrigation from Conconully Lake reservoir to northwest brings agriculture to area; **1907** incorporated as a city; bridge built across river; **1915** Great Northern Railroad reaches city; county seat moved to Okanogan; county courthouse built.

Olympia   *Thurston County*   *Western Washington, 47 mi/76 km south-southwest of Seattle, on Puget Sound*

1846 fisherman Edmund Sylvester and divinity student Levi Smith assume land claims, become first settlers; town of Smithfield founded on Budd Inlet, southern extremity Puget Sound; **1850** town platted, renamed Olympia; **1851** U.S. customhouse established, first on Puget Sound; **1852** Thurston County formed; town becomes county seat; *Columbian* newspaper founded; **1853** town becomes territorial capital; **1854** Catholic church built; **1856** Sylvester House built; **1859** incorporated as a city; **Nov. 11, 1889** Washington admitted to Union as 42nd state; city becomes state capital; **1891** Northern Pacific Railroad reaches town; **1893** old state capitol built; **1912** deepwater port built in slough of Budd Inlet; **1914** Carnegie Library built, replaced by new library 1978; **1921** Temple of Justice built, first facet of capitol group of state buildings; **1926** Port of Olympia Terminal built; **1927** state capitol completed; Olympian Airport established to south; **1933** state appropriates funds for feasibility study for canal from Puget Sound to Columbia River via Grays Harbor, furthered 1936, later abandoned; **1941** state capitol museum established; **Apr. 13, 1949** 7.1 magnitude earthquake destroys many downtown buildings, eight killed; **1954** state supreme court reaffirms Olympia as state capital; **1963** Port of Olympia organized; **1967** Evergreen State College established; **1970** South Puget Sound Community College established; **1977** county courthouse built; **Feb. 28, 2001** 6.8 magnitude earthquake strikes area, centered to northeast, damaging State Capitol, other government buildings, 250 injured.

Paradise   *Pierce and Lewis counties*   *Western Washington, 45 mi/60 km southeast of Tacoma*

1792 Mt. Rainier viewed from Puget Sound by George Vancouver, named by him for Peter Rainier of British Navy; **1833** Dr. William Fraser Tolmie of Hudson's Bay Company explores Mt. Rainier; **Aug. 17, 1870** Gen. Hazard Stevens and P. B. Van Trump successfully reach summit, 14,410 ft/4,301 m; **March 2, 1899** Mount Rainier National Park established; **1917** Paradise Inn built; **June 21, 1981** ice avalanche kills 11 climbers on Mt. Rainier.

Pasco *Franklin County   Southern Washington, 127 mi/204 km southwest of Spokane, on Columbia River*

1883 Franklin County formed; Ainsworth becomes county seat; **1886** Northern Pacific Railroad built; town founded as county seat near mouth of Snake River 3 mi/ 4.8 km northwest of Ainsworth, named Pasco for mining city in Peru; **1891** incorporated as a city; **1913** county courthouse completed; **1955** Columbia Basin College (2-year) established; **1954** U.S. Highway 395 Bridge ("The Blue Bridge") built across Columbia River to Kennewick; **1956** McNary Dam completed on Columbia River 25 mi/ 40 km to southwest; **Aug. 5, 1961** highest temperature recorded in Washington reached, 118°F/48°C, at Ice Harbor Dam to east; **1962** Ice Harbor Dam completed on Snake River forming Lake Sacajawea; **1988** Ed Hendler Memorial Bridge (cable-stayed) built across Columbia River to Kennewick.

Pomeroy *Garfield County   Southeastern Washington, 82 mi/132 km south of Spokane*

1864 John M. Pomeroy arrives from Ashtabula, Ohio, becomes first settler; **1878** town founded; **1880** newspaper *East Washington* founded; **1881** Garfield County formed; nearby Pataha becomes county seat; **1882** county seat moved to Pomeroy; **1886** incorporated as a city; **1901** county courthouse built; **1970** Little Goose Dam built on Snake River to northwest; **1975** Lower Granite Dam on Snake River to northeast.

Port Angeles *Clallam County   Western Washington, 60 mi/97 km northwest of Seattle*

1791 Capt. Francisco de Eliza explores coastline, names harbor Port of Our Lady of the Angels; **1854** Clallam County formed; New Dungeness becomes county seat; **1861** customs house established on Strait of Juan de Fuca; town founded; **1865** Ediz Hook Lighthouse built on small peninsula forming harbor, rebuilt 1908; customs house moved to Port Townsend; **1890** county seat moved to Port Angeles; **Jan. 1890** incorporated as a town; **Dec. 1890** incorporated as a city; **1897** Olympic Forest Reserve established to south; **March 2, 1909** Mount Olympus National Monument proclaimed to south, becomes Olympic National Park 1938; **1915** county courthouse completed, becomes museum 1980; **1919** Port Angeles Public Library founded; **1924** Coho Ferry established to Victoria, British Columbia, taken over by Black Ball Transit 1959; **1980** new county courthouse built.

Port Orchard *Kitsap County   Western Washington, 16 mi/26 km west-southwest of Seattle, on Puget Sound*

1792 George Vancouver names harbor for H. M. Orchard of his ship *Discovery*; **1854** sawmill built by William Renton and Daniel Howard; town platted by Sidney Stevens, originally named Sidney; **1857** Kitsap County formed comprising most of Kitsap Peninsula; **1861** Port Madison becomes county seat; **1871** Puget Sound Naval Station established on Port Orchard Bay; **1890** incorporated as a city; **1893** town renamed Port Orchard, becomes county seat; **1924** Kitsap Regional Library founded; **1930** county courthouse built.

Port Townsend *Jefferson County   Western Washington, 40 mi/64 km northwest of Seattle*

1792 George Vancouver visits harbor, names it Port Townsend; **1851** Alfred A. Plummer and Charles Bacheller become first settlers; town founded on Strait of Juan de Fuca; **1852** Jefferson County formed; town becomes county seat; **1860** incorporated as a city; **1890** Port Townsend & Southern Railroad built to Quilcene, soon abandoned; **1892** county courthouse built; **1893** many ships anchor in bay with economic panic, remain until 1897; **1902** Fort Worden military base established, becomes Navy base 1953, closed 1970s; **1913** Point Wilson Lighthouse built, automated 1960s; **1927** Crown Zellerbach paper and pulp mill opened; **1981** Port Townsend Marine Science Center established.

Prosser *Benton County   Southern Washington, 147 mi/237 km southwest of Spokane*

1880 James Kinney becomes first settler; **1881** Col. William Prosser opens trading post; town founded on Yakima River, originally named Yakima Falls; **1883** town renamed Prosser Falls; **1887** Prosser Flour Mill built; **1889** incorporated as a town; **1894** power station built at falls; **1899** incorporated as a city; **1905** Benton County formed; town becomes county seat; **1926** county courthouse built; **1960s** wine industry developed in area.

Pullman *Whitman County   Southeastern Washington, 65 mi/105 km south of Spokane*

c.1878 cattleman Bolin Farr becomes first settler; **1882** town founded on South Palouse River; town originally named Three Forks; **1884** town renamed for George Pullman, inventor of railroad sleeping car; **1885** Oregon (Union Pacific) Railroad reaches town; **1888** incorporated as a city; branch of Northern Pacific Railroad arrives; **1890** Washington Agricultural College established, later becomes Washington State University.

Redmond *King County   Western Washington, suburb 10 mi/16 km east-northeast of Seattle*

1871 Luke McRedmond becomes first settler, also first postmaster; **1881** town founded, originally named Salmonburg; **1888** Seattle, Lake Shore & Eastern (Northern Pacific) Railroad reaches town; incorporated as a town, renamed for Luke McRedmond, donated land for rail depot; **1912** incorporated as a city.

Renton *King County   Western Washington, suburb 10 mi/16 km south-southeast of Seattle*

1853 Henry and Diana Tobin become first settlers; **1873** William Renton establishes large scale coal operations;

town founded at southern end of Lake Washington; **1901** incorporated as a city; **1905** Pacific Iron Foundry established; **1909** Chicago, Milwaukee, St. Paul & Pacific Railroad completed with building of Snoqualmie Pass tunnel through Cascade Range; **1914** Carnegie Library built, replaced 1966; **1942** Renton Technical College (2-year) established.

Republic *Ferry County* *Northern Washington, 91 mi/146 km northwest of Spokane*

1896 gold discovered on Granite Creek by John Welty; town founded North Fork Sanpoil River; *Republic Pioneer* newspaper founded; **1899** Ferry County formed; town becomes county seat; **1900** incorporated as a city; town boasts 28 saloons; **1936** county courthouse built.

Richland *Benton County* *Southern Washington, 131 mi/211 km southwest of Spokane, on Columbia River*

1892 Benton Land and Water Company established; town founded at mouth of Yakima River, named Benton; **1905** post office established; town renamed Richland; **1910** incorporated as a city; **1942** large Hanford Atomic Energy Commission Site established to north; **1980s** nuclear waste disposal begins at Hanford Site amid controversy; **June 27, 2000** fiery auto crash ignites wildfire, burns 190,000 ac/76,950 ha of brush including half of Hanford Nuclear Reservation, 20 homes destroyed; **Aug. 6, 2000** Hanford Reach National Monument proclaimed to northwest.

Ritzville *Adams County* *Eastern Washington, 58 mi/93 km southwest of Spokane*

1878 Philip Ritz becomes first settler; town founded; **1883** Adams County formed; town becomes county seat; **1889** Northern Pacific Railroad built; **1890** incorporated as a town; **1905** third county courthouse built; **1906** incorporated as a city; **May 18, 1980** city covered by 3-6 in/8-15 cm of volcanic ash by Mt. St. Helens eruption.

Roslyn *Kittitas County* *West central Washington, 67 mi/108 km southeast of Seattle*

1880 Johnson House built by "Cayuse" Johnson; **1886** Northern Pacific Railroad built; railroad begins mining coal as fuel for trains; town founded on Cle Elum River; **1888** black workers brought in as strike breakers; **1889** incorporated as a city; **May 1892** coal mine explosion, 45 killed; **Oct. 1909** second coal mine explosion kills 10; **1930s** most coal mining ceases; town declines; **1933** Cle Elum Lake formed by dam to northwest on Cle Elum River.

Seattle *King County* *Western Washington, on Puget Sound*

1851 town founded at mouth of Duwamish River, named for Suquamish Chief Sealth (Seattle) who befriended settlers; **1852** King County formed; first steam-powered sawmill on Puget Sound established by Henry Yesler; town platted, becomes county seat; **1855** two blockhouses built as Indian defense; **1858** Fraser Gold Rush in Canada brings influx of transients and settlers; **1861** University of Washington established; **1863** *Seattle Gazette* newspaper founded, later becomes *Post-Intelligencer*; **1864** group of unmarried women brought to area by Asa Mercer to ease town's bachelor population; **1865** incorporated as a city; **Dec. 7–12, 1880** two earthquakes shake area, second accompanied by large fireballs in north near Bellingham, possible meteorite; **1883** Columbia & Puget Sound Railroad reaches town; **1886** attempt by mob to deport 100 Chinese brings out Seattle Rifles militia to Pioneer Square; **1889** fire destroys downtown; **1891** Seattle University established; Seattle Pacific University established; Seattle Public Library opened; **1893** Great Northern Railroad reaches city; **1894** Rainier Brewing Company established; **1896** *Seattle Times* newspaper founded; **1897–1898** Klondike Gold Rush brings stream of people through city; **1898** steamship *Portland* arrives with first shipment—one ton—of Yukon gold; **1899** Woodland Park Zoo established; **1902** Meadows Race Track built, site at south end of King County Airport; **1903** Seattle Symphony Orchestra organized; **June 23, 1905** actress Mary Livingstone born, wife of Jack Benny (died 1983); **Feb. 8, 1906** physicist Chester F. Carlson born, invented xerography (died 1968); **1907** Pike Place Public Market established; St. James Cathedral built; **1908** Temple de Hirsch synagogue built; **1909** Chicago, Milwaukee, St. Paul & Pacific Railroad reaches city; first Alaska-Yukon-Pacific Exposition held; **May 15, 1910** actress Constance Cummings born; **1911** Duwamish Waterway created in south part of city greatly adding to port capacity; Museum of History and Industry founded, opened 1915; **June 8, 1911** actress Gypsy Rose Lee (Rose Hovick) born (died 1970); **June 21, 1912** novelist Mary McCarthy born (died 1989); **Sept. 21, 1912** Looney Tunes animator Chuck Jones born (died 2002) **Dec. 1, 1912** architect Minora Yamasaki born (died 1986); **1914** 42-story Smith Tower building completed; **Feb. 15, 1914** actor Kevin McCarthy born; **1916** Lake Washington Canal completed; city-county building built; **1917** canal and locks linking Lake Washington to Puget Sound opened; **1919** general strike of city's labor force cripples economy; **Feb. 24, 1922** actor Steven Hill born; **Jan. 31, 1923** actress Carol Channing born; **1924** Sand Point Naval Air Station established, closed 1990s; **March 23, 1926** actress Martha Wright born; **1927** civic auditorium opened; **Oct. 5, 1927** astronaut Richard Gordon born; **1928** King County Airport (Boeing Field) established; **1929** 27-story Northern Life Tower building completed; **1931** county courthouse completed; St. Mark's Episcopal Cathedral completed; **1932** U.S Marine Hospital built; federal building completed; **1937** Colman Street Ferry Terminal built; **1939** Sick's Seattle Stadium built; **May 1, 1939** singer Judy Collins born; **1940** Lacey V. Murrow Pontoon Bridge built east across Lake Washington to Bellevue; **1940s** World War II defense industry boosts economy; **1944** Seattle Philharmonic Orchestra established; **1949** Seattle-Tacoma (Sea-Tac) Airport built to south, replaces King County Airport as primary airport;

1950 Alaskan Freeway opened; **Nov. 10, 1950** actress Ann Reinking born; **1951** Washington State Ferry system established in Puget Sound, becomes permanent 1959 when legislature rejects proposal to build series of cross-sound bridges; **Oct. 28, 1955** William Gates born, computer innovator and founder of Microsoft Corporation; **Aug. 29, 1956** dancer, choreographer Mark Morris born; **Apr. 21, 1962** Century 21 Exposition opens for six-month run, includes Space Needle and monorail; **Sept. 10, 1962** Air Force KC-135 jet tanker aircraft crashes killing all 44 on board; **1963** Evergreen Point Pontoon Bridge built east across Lake Washington to Bellevue; **1964** Shoreline Community College established; Seattle Opera founded; **1966** Seattle Central Community College established; **1967** Seattle Super Sonics NBA basketball team established; **1969** 50-story Fourth Avenue Plaza built; Seattle Pilots American League baseball team established, become Milwaukee Brewers 1970; **1970** North Seattle Community College established; South Seattle Community College established; **March 20, 1970** hotel fire kills 19; **Apr. 25, 1971** apartment fire kills 12, injures 9; **1972** Daybreak Star Indian Cultural Center founded in Discovery Park; **Aug. 18, 1972** hijacker shot, captured by FBI, commandeered plane at Reno; **Sept. 1976** Seattle Seahawks NFL football team begin first season; **1977** Seattle Mariners American League baseball team established; 42-story Security Pacific Bank built; **1980** Nordic Heritage Museum founded; **1981** Rainier Symphony founded; 42-story Seafirst Fifth Avenue Plaza built; **1982** Art Institute of Seattle (2-year college) established; **1983** 48-story Wells Fargo Center built; **1985** 76-story Bank of America Center built; **1988** 55-story Washington Mutual Tower built; **1989** 44-story Pacific First Center built; 56-story Two Union Square built; **1990** Lacey V. Murrow Floating Bridge sinks into Lake Washington in storm, rebuilt 1993; 62-story Key Tower built; **1991** first annual Shakespearean Festival held; **Apr. 8, 1994** Kurt Cobain, 27, lead singer rock group Nirvana, dies of self-inflicted gunshot; **July 1999** SAFECO Field stadium opened; **March 26, 2000** King Dome baseball stadium imploded, $125 million in debt; **Feb. 27, 2001** Mardi Gras celebrations in Pioneer Square area lead to violence, 70 injured, hundreds arrested; **Feb. 28, 2001** earthquake centered between Tacoma and Olympia strikes area, 6.8 magnitude, causing widespread damage, especially historic Pioneer Square, 250 injured; **Dec. 5, 2001** Gary Leon Ridway, 52, charged with murder of 4 women, believed to be Green River Killer responsible for deaths of 49 women since 1980s; **May 27, 2002** race horse Seattle Slew dies at age 28.

Sedro Woolley *Skagit County Northwestern Washington, 62 mi/100 km north of Seattle*

1884 town of Sedro (SEE-dro) founded on Skagit River by Mortimer Cook, Spanish for "cedar"; **1886** shingle mill built; **1889** junction formed by Great Northern and Northern Pacific railroads to north; **1890** new town of Woolley founded, named for Phillip A. Woolley; **1898** two towns consolidate, incorporated as a city; **1912** Northern State Hospital opened; **1949** Ross Dam built on Skagit River 55 mi/89 km to east forming Ross Lake; **Oct. 2, 1968** two units of North Cascades National Park established to east; Ross Lake National Recreation Area established to east.

Sequim *Clallam County Western Washington, 51 mi/82 km northwest of Seattle*

1853 John Dunnell becomes first white settler; **1857** New Dungeness Lighthouse built, sheathed 1927; town founded by John Bell near Strait of Juan de Fuca, named Seguin; **Sept. 1868** Tsimshian Native American migrant workers attacked by Clallam Native Americans, 19 killed, 1 wounded; **1907** town renamed Sequim ("skwim"); **1913** incorporated as a city.

Shelton *Mason County Western Washington, 31 mi/50 km west of Tacoma, on Puget Sound*

1853 David Shelton becomes first settler; **1854** Mason County formed; Oakland, town site 2 mi/3.2 km to north, becomes county seat; **1884** town platted, originally named Sheltonville; **1886** Northern Pacific Railroad reaches town from south; **1888** town renamed Shelton; county seat moved to Shelton; **1889** town incorporated; **1926** county courthouse built; **1927** Rayonier Pulp Plant founded, company's first mill; **1930s** under threat of losing pulp mill, citizens compensate oyster fishers for damage to oyster beds caused by sulphite waste pollution of Oakland Bay.

Skykomish *King County Western Washington, 45 mi/72 km east-northeast of Seattle*

1899 town founded on South Fork Skykomish River by John Maloney and wife; **1900** Stevens Pass Tunnel, 3-mi/4.8-km long, completed to east on Great Northern Railroad in Cascade Range; **1909** town incorporated; **March 1, 1910** avalanche buries two Great Northern trains at Wellington to east, at western portal of Stevens Pass Tunnel, 96 killed; **1929** Cascade Tunnel, 8-mi/12.9-km long, completed to east, replaces Stevens Pass Tunnel.

Snohomish *Snohomish County Western Washington, 24 mi/39 km north-northeast of Seattle*

1853 town founded on Snohomish River with construction of military road north to Fort Bellingham; **1861** Snohomish County formed; Mukilteo becomes first county seat; **July 1861** county seat moved to Snohomish; **1864** logging operations begin; **1866** first sawmill built; **1867** shipyards launch first boat, steamer *Ruby*; **1873** Atheneum Society founded; **1888** Seattle, Lake Shore & Eastern Railroad reaches town; **1890** incorporated as a city; **1897** county seat moved to Everett; **1910** Carnegie Library built, replaced by new library 2003.

South Bend   *Pacific County*   *Southwestern Washington, 72 mi/116 km southwest of Tacoma*

c.1850 first oyster reserves on Pacific Coast discovered at Willapa Bay; **1851** Pacific County formed; **1855** Oysterville becomes county seat; **1869** first sawmill established; **1889** town founded on Willapa Bay; **1890** incorporated as a city; **1892** county seat moved to South Bend, citizens of Oysterville refuse to yield county records; **Jan. 1893** South Bend residents forcibly remove county records from Oysterville; **1895** Northern Pacific Railroad reaches town; **1911** county courthouse built; **Aug. 6, 1927** comedian Pat Paulsen born.

Spokane   *Spokane County*   *Eastern Washington, 230 mi/370 km east of Seattle, on Spokane River*

1805 Lewis & Clark Expedition passes through area; **1810** Spokane House trading post established on Spokane River by Finan McDonald and Joco Finlay for North West Fur Company, closed 1826 by Hudson's Bay Company; **1838** mission established 25 mi/40 km to northwest by Rev. Cushing Eells and Rev. Elkanah Walker, abandoned 1847 following Whitman Massacre at Waiilatpu (Walla Walla); **1858** Spokane County formed; **Sept. 5, 1858** Coeur d'Alene, Palouse, and Spokane peoples stage uprising in response to plans to build Mullan Road from Missouri River, suppressed by Col. George Wright's forces; **1860** county organized; Pinckney City becomes county seat; **1862** Mullan Road completed; **1864** Spokane County annexed by Stevens County; Colville becomes county seat; **1871** sawmill established by Richard M. Benjamin at falls of Spokane River; town founded, named Spokane Falls (spo-KAN); **1872** James Nettle Glover and J. N. Matheny arrive from Salem, Oregon, purchase mill, open store; post office established; **1877** Nez Perce peoples go on warpath, troops sent to thwart potential threat; **1878** town platted by Glover; *Spokane Times* newspaper founded; **1880** Spokane County reestablished; Cheney becomes county seat; **1881** incorporated as a city; *Daily Chronicle* newspaper founded; Globe Theater opened; **1882** Joy's Opera House built; **1883** Northern Pacific Railroad reaches city; **1884** Annie Wright Seminary founded; **1886** county seat moved to Spokane Falls; Spokane Interstate Fair established; **1887** Gonzaga University established; **1888** St. Paul and Tacoma Lumber Plant built; **1889** city renamed Spokane; **Aug. 4, 1889** fire destroys 32 blocks of business district; **1890** Whitworth College established; Tacoma Theater built; **1893** Great Northern Railroad reaches city; **1894** Fort George Wright military base established; **1895** county courthouse completed; **1903** Union Pacific Railroad reaches city; College of Puget Sound established; **1904** Spokane Public Library built, new library opened 1994; **1908** Our Lady of Lourdes Catholic Cathedral completed; **1909** federal building built; **1910** 15-story Old National Bank built; **Aug. 25, 1913** entertainer Bob Crosby born, brother of Bing Crosby (died 1993); **June 2, 1912** sociologist Bernard Berelson born (died 1979); **1915** Metropolitan Performing Arts Center built; **1920** Sunset Field (later Spokane International Airport) established to west; **May 7, 1922** actor Darren McGavin born; **May 14, 1925** soprano Patrice Munsel born; **March 6, 1929** U.S. Sen. Thomas Foley born; **Apr. 1935** Playfair Race Track opened; **1945** Spokane Symphony founded; **Apr. 4, 1946** actor Craig Nelson born; **1949** Episcopal Cathedral of St. John the Evangelist completed; **1950** Joe Albi Stadium built; **1963** Spokane Community College established; **1967** Spokane Falls Community College established; **1974** Spokane World's Fair held; Spokane Convention Center opened; Spokane Opera House built.

Steilacoom   *Pierce County*   *Western Washington, 9 mi/14.5 km southwest of Tacoma, on Puget Sound*

1846 grazing rights granted to Hudson's Bay Company; **1849** Thomas M. Chambers assumes donated land claim, though ordered to leave, instead invites other settlers; **1851** town founded by Lafayette Balch; **1852** Pierce County formed; town becomes county seat; Church of Immaculate Conception founded, first Catholic church in Washington, built 1867; **1854** town incorporated, first incorporated place in Washington; **1855** Fort Steilacoom established; Peter Judson House built; **1858** County Jail built; **1867** fort abandoned; **1873** Northern Pacific Railroad reaches town; **1881** county seat moved to Tacoma; **1920** Deep Sea Aquarium established by retired sea captain Ed Bair, closed 1942.

Stevenson   *Skamania County*   *Southwestern Washington, 38 mi/61 km east-northeast of Portland, Oregon*

1854 Skamania County formed; First Cascades (Cascades) becomes county seat; **1856** Fort Rains built on Columbia River; **1880** Stevenson family of Missouri settles near Cascades; **1893** town of Stevenson founded; county seat moved from Cascades; **1894** flooding destroys old town, county records spared by move previous year; **1907** incorporated as a city; **1908** Spokane, Portland & Seattle Railroad reaches town; **1926** Bridge of the Gods built across Columbia River to Cascade Locks, Oregon, named for legendary natural stone bridge that spanned river, subject of 1890 novel *Bridge of the Gods* by Frederick Homer Balch (1861–1891); **1927** replica of fort built; **1940** deck of Bridge of the Gods raised to allow for rising waters of Bonneville Dam; **1948** county courthouse built.

Tacoma   *Pierce County*   *Western Washington, 25 mi/40 km south of Seattle, on Puget Sound*

1833 Fort Nisqually built to southwest near Du Pont; **1852** Pierce County formed; Steilacoom becomes county seat; town founded by Swede Nicholas De Lin; sawmill built; **1864** Job Carr builds cabin at Point Defiance; **1869** town chosen as timber milling site; **1873** Northern Pacific Railroad reaches town from Columbia River; *Pacific Tribune* newspaper moved from Olympia, founded 1861 as *The Press*; St. Peter's Episcopal Church built; **1875** coal mining begins in area; **1881** county seat moved to Tacoma; **1884** incorporated as a city; Chinese community removed from city limits; **1888** University of Puget Sound established; **1890** Pacific Lutheran University established; **1896** St. Leo's Catholic Church built, destroyed by fire 1921; **1903** Carnegie Library built, replaced by new library 1951; **May 2, 1904** actor, singer Harry "Bing" Cosby born (died 1977); **1905** Point Defiance Zoo and Aquarium opened; **1911** railroad station built; **Sept. 3, 1914** woman biologist, Gov. Dixy Lee Ray born (died 1994); **1917** Fort Lewis Military Base established to south; **Sept. 16, 1922** actress Janis Paige born; **1925** Talmud Torah Synagogue built; First Presbyterian Church completed; **1931** Tacoma (Hong Wanji) Buddhist Temple built; **1933** Browns Point Lighthouse built on east side of Commencement Bay, automated 1963; **1934** Fort Nisqually moved to Point Defiance Park; **May 24, 1935** George Weyerhauser, 9, son of paper company magnate, kidnapped, $200,000 ransom paid, returned safely June 1, kidnaper gets 20–60 years in prison; **Dec. 27, 1936** Charles Mattson, 10, kidnapped, $28,000 ransom misses connection, boy found dead Jan. 11, 1937; **Jan. 4, 1937** actress Dyan Cannon born; **1938** McChord Army Air Field established, becomes Air Force Base after World War II; **Nov. 7, 1940** storm destroys Narrows Bridge months after its completion; **1941** new Narrows Bridge built across The Narrows of Puget Sound; **1949** Seattle-Tacoma (Sea-Tac) Airport built to north; **1951** Tacoma Public Library built; **Apr. 1959** county-city building dedicated; **Aug. 25, 1964** actress Blair Underwood born; **1967** Pierce College (2-year) established; **1983** Tacoma Dome stadium opened; **Feb. 28, 2001** 6.8 magnitude earthquake centered to south heavily damages Puget Sound region, 250 injured.

Tumwater   *Thurston County*   *Western Washington, 2 mi/3.2 km south of Olympia*

1845 town founded on Deschutes River by Col. Michael T. Simmons, first permanent American settlement in Northwest; originally named Newmarket; **1846** grist mill built; **1850** new town of Olympia platted immediately to north; **1855** Fort Eaton built to east; **1863** town renamed for Native American term for waterfalls on Deschutes River; **1869** incorporated as a city; **1896** Olympia Brewing Company established, acquired by Pabst Brewing 1980s.

Union Gap   *Yakima County*   See **Yakima**

Vancouver   *Clark County*   *Southwestern Washington, 10 mi/16 km north of Portland, Oregon, on Columbia River*

1792 William Broughton of George Vancouver expedition visits site; **Nov. 1805** Lewis and Clark Expedition reaches mouth of Columbia River, camps here on return journey 1806; **1824** Fort Vancouver built by Hudson's Bay Company, replacing trading post at Astoria; **1826** sawmill established by Dr. John McLoughlin; **1829** fort relocated; **1832** first American settlers arrive; **1838** Catholic mission established; **1844** Clark County formed; **1845** town founded as county seat, named by Henry Williamson for George Vancouver; Covington House built; **1846** area ceded to U.S.; **1848** town platted; **1854** saloon opened by Peter Fulkerson; **1857** incorporated as a city; **1874** Northern Pacific Railroad reaches town from north; **1885** St. James Catholic Church built; **1886** State School for the Deaf built; **June 1889** suspicious fires destroy business district; **1910** public library built; first railroad bridge built across Columbia River; **1912** Vancouver Port Commission organized; **1917** Interstate Bridge completed; **1925** Pearson Field airport established; **1933** Clark College (2-year) established; **1938** State School for the Blind built; **1941** county courthouse built, concrete exterior left exposed when money runs out for brick facia, form marks remain; **1942** Kaiser Shipyard built; **1949** Carborundum Company plant built; **1927** General Grant memorial erected; **1950** Aluminum Company of America (ALCOA) plant built; **1955** I-5 Bridge built from Portland; **1981** I-205 Bridge built.

Walla Walla   *Walla Walla County*   *Southeastern Washington, 117 mi/188 km south-southwest of Spokane*

1818 Fort Walla Walla built; **1836** Waiilatpu mission founded by Dr. Marcus Whitman; first white women to cross plains reach fort with husbands Dr. Whitman and Rev. H. H. Spalding; **1847** in Whitman Massacre, Dr. Whitman, wife, 12 others killed by Cayuse Native Americans; **1854** Walla Walla County formed; **1856** Steptoeville founded; Fort Walla Walla becomes military fort; **1858** town renamed Walla Walla; **1859** town becomes county seat; post office established; Whitman College established; **1861** town serves as staging area for Idaho gold rush; *Washington Statesman* newspaper founded, merged with *Walla Walla Union* 1914; **1862** town platted, incorporated as a city; **1865** vigilante groups formed to enforce laws, hangings become routine; **1870** St. Paul's Episcopal Church built, replaced 1902; St. Patrick's Catholic Church built, rebuilt following 1916 fire; **1875** Walla Walla & Columbia Railroad completed west to Columbia River; **Aug. 23, 1883** World War II Gen. Jonathan Mayhew Wainwright born (died 1953); **1905** Carnegie Public Library built; **1916** county courthouse completed; **1917** Liberty Theater built; **1925** Pioneer Methodist Church built, organized 1859; **June 29, 1936** Whitman Mission National Monument authorized, becomes National Historic Site 1963; **1949** airline terminal completed at city-county airport; **1967** Walla Walla Community College established; **1970** new library dedicated, Carnegie facility becomes Carnegie Art Center.

Wallula   *Walla Walla County*   *Southern Washington, 130 mi/209 km southwest of Spokane, on Columbia River*

1818 Fort Walla Walla built on Columbia River for North West Fur Company; **1856** Fort Walla Walla military post established at site of old fort; **1875** Walla Walla & Columbia Railroad built from Walla Walla by Dr. D. S. Baker; town founded at mouth of Walla Walla River as rail-to-river transfer point (name Native American term for "abundant water"); **1882** town platted; Oregon-Washington and Union Pacific railroads reach town; **1953** new town platted away from rising waters of Umatilla Reservoir (Lake Wallula); **1958** container plant established by Boise Cascade Company.

Waterville *Douglas County Central Washington, 105 mi/169 km east of Seattle*

1883 Douglas County formed; **1884** town founded as county seat, originally named Okanogan City; **1886** county seat moved to Douglas for lack of water supply; new town of Waterville platted with building of well; **1887** county seat moved to Waterville; post office established; **1890** town incorporated; **1905** county courthouse built.

Wellington *King County See* **Skykomish (1910)**

Wenatchee *Chelan County Central Washington, 95 mi/153 km east of Seattle, on Columbia River*

1811 fur traders for North West Fur Company enter region; **1860** gold discovered by miners returning from Fraser River Gold Rush in Canada; **1863** mission established by Father Respari; **1888** town founded by Don Carlos Corbett near mouth of Wenatchee River; **1889** post office established; **1892** Great Northern Railroad reaches town; incorporated as a city; **1899** Chelan County formed; town becomes county seat; **1903** Highline Irrigation Canal built; **1908** Columbia River bridge built, replaced 1950; **1924** county courthouse built; **1939** Wenatchee Valley College (2-year) established; **1962** Rocky Reach Dam built to north on Columbia River forming Lake Entiat.

Winthrop *Okanogan County Northern Washington, 115 mi/185 km northeast of Seattle*

1883 area first settled; **1891** town founded on Methow River; **1928** town incorporated; **Dec. 30, 1968** lowest temperature ever recorded in Washington reached, −48°F/−44°C, record shared on same date with Mazama to northwest; **1972** State Highway 20 completed west across Cascade Range to Skagit Valley.

Yakima *Yakima County Southern Washington, 110 mi/177 km southeast of Seattle*

1847 St. Joseph's Mission established; **1851** first irrigation in area undertaken by Catholic priests; **Nov. 9, 1855** U.S. troops under Maj. Gabriel Rains open fire on Yakimas, driving them into Naches Canyon to west; **1861** Fielding M. Thorpe and wife become first settlers; town founded on Yakima River as Yakima City; **1865** Yakima County formed; town becomes county seat; **1870** region's first orchard planted by John W. Beck; **1883** town incorporated; **1884** Northern Pacific Railroad reaches town; town of North Yakima founded; **1886** North Yakima incorporated as a city; county seat moved to North Yakima; **1889** St. Michael's Episcopal Church completed; **1903** *Yakima Republic* newspaper founded, becomes *Herald-Republic* 1970; **1905** Sunnyside Irrigation Project built; **1907** Carnegie Library built; **1912** Rimrock Irrigation Project completed; **1917** Yakima Valley Museum established; Washington Dehydrated Food Company plant built; **1918** North Yakima renamed Yakima; Yakima City renamed Union Gap; **1928** Yakima Valley Community College established; **1931** 11-story Larson Building built; **1942** U.S. Army Yakima Training Center established to northeast; **1947** 14-story Aluminum Hotel built; **1961** county courthouse built; **May 18, 1980** eruption of Mt. St. Helens to west blankets city with great drifts of ash, 57 killed.

West Virginia

Eastern U.S. Capital and largest city: Charleston.

West Virginia was originally part of Virginia, one of the 13 colonies which adopted the U.S. Declaration of Independence July 4, 1776. Virginia seceded from the Union as a Confederate state April 17, 1861. West Virginia, with primarily pro-Union sentiments, separated from Virginia June 20, 1863, as the 35th state of the U.S. It consisted of 40 counties at the time of separation.

West Virginia today is divided into 55 counties. Municipalities are classified as villages, towns, and cities. There are no townships. See Introduction.

Addison   *Webster County*   *See* **Webster Springs**

Alderson   *Greenbrier and Monroe counties*
Southern West Virginia, 70 mi/113 km southeast of Charleston

1777 area on Greenbrier River first settled by Rev. John Alderson, Baptist minister and ferry operator; **1781** Alderson builds Baptist church; **1871** town incorporated; **1872** Chesapeake & Ohio Railroad built; **1885** Greenbrier Seminary founded, closed 1890s; **1888** Alderson Collegiate Institute founded, closed 1925; **1901** Alderson Baptist Academy founded, merged with Broaddus College at Philippi 1932; **1926** Federal Industrial Institution for Women established.

Barboursville   *Cabell County*   *Western West Virginia, 9 mi/14.5 east of Huntington*

1809 Cabell County formed; **1813** incorporated as a town, named for James Barbour, governor of Virginia; **1814** county seat moved from Guyandotte; **c.1840** town becomes important river port; **1854** second county courthouse built; **1887** county seat moved to Huntington; **1888** county courthouse converted to Barboursville College, renamed Morris-Harvey College 1901, moved to Charleston 1935, becomes University of Charleston 1978.

Bartley   *McDowell County*   *See* **Welch (1940)**

Bath   *Morgan County*   *See* **Berkeley Springs**

Beckley   *Raleigh County*   *Southern West Virginia, 47 mi/76 km south-southeast of Charleston*

1836 Gen. Alfred Beckley settles here with dreams of founding grain and livestock center; **1838** town chartered; **1850** Raleigh County formed; town becomes county seat; blacksmith shop becomes town's first business; **1853** post office established; Raleigh Baptist Church built; **May 19, 1863** town shelled by Union troops; **1872** incorporated as a town; **1873** Chesapeake & Ohio Railroad built through area, misses town 10 mi/16 km to east, branch extended to town 1901; **1900** Beckley Seminary opened, later renamed Beckley Institute; **1907** Winding Gulf coal vein becomes major producer; **1909** Virginian Railroad built to Chesapeake Bay; **Apr. 14, 1912** fire destroys 20 buildings; **Apr. 28, 1914** accident at Eccles coal mine to west, 183 killed; **March 8, 1926** coal mine disaster, 19 killed; **1927** incorporated as a city; **1932** Soldiers and Sailors Memorial Building built; **1933** The College of West Virginia established as Beckley College; **1938** county courthouse built; **1962** Beckley Exhibition Coal Mine opened; **1976** Raleigh County Library opened; **Aug. 1976** National Mine Health and Safety Academy opened.

Benwood   *Marshall County*   *See* **Wheeling (1924)**

Berkeley Springs (Bath)   *Morgan County*
Northeastern West Virginia, 94 mi/151 km east of Morgantown

March 18, 1748 George Washington surveys area, speaks favorably of warm springs here; **1756** land grant around springs made to colony of Virginia by Lord Fairfax for public use; **1772** Berkeley County formed; **Oct. 1776** town chartered as Bath by George Washington, remains its official name; town becomes county seat; **1777** town platted; **c.1783** The Sign of General Washington Inn opened by John Hunter, replaced by brick hotel 1938; **1784** James Rumsey experiments with steam-powered boats on Potomac; **c.1799** Allen House built; **1814** Robert Bailey opens the Old Coffee House, later becomes Fairfax Inn; **1820** Morgan County formed from Berkeley County; town remains county seat; **1836** work begins on Paw Paw Tunnel of Chesapeake & Ohio Railroad to southwest, 3,118 ft/950 m long, completed 1850, walls lined with six million bricks; **1844** fires sweeps through several boarding houses and hotels; **1847** arrival of Baltimore & Ohio Railroad at nearby Hancock, Maryland, boost to resort town; **1850** Strother House built by William Duckwell; **1861–1865** Civil War brings series of bloody skirmishes; **1887** bathhouse built, now Berkeley Springs State Park; Castle Mansion built by Judge S. T. Soult; **1907** county courthouse built.

Beverly   *Randolph County*   *East central West Virginia, 50 mi/80 km south of Morgantown*

1754 town site settled by Robert Files family, within months all but one boy massacred by natives; **1772** fort built by six Westfall brothers; **1787** Randolph County formed; **1790** town founded as county seat; **1790** incorporated as a town; **July 11, 1861** Battle of Rich Mountain, Confederates routed by Gen. George McClellan's Union forces; **1873** Chenoweth Covered Bridge built on Tygarts Valley River by Lemuel Chenoweth, dismantled 1954; **1900** county seat moved to Elkins; **1933** Tygarts Valley Homesteads built to south by federal government.

Bethany   *Brooke County*   *Northern West Virginia, 52 mi/84 km northwest of Morgantown*

1792 construction of Campbell House begun by Alexander Campbell, completed in stages until 1940; **1811** Brush Run Meeting House (Disciples of Christ) built; town founded; **1827** post office established; **1830** Disciples of Christ denomination founded by Alexander Campbell; **1840** Bethany College established by Campbell of Disciples of Christ church; **1847** town platted by Campbell; **1852** Bethany Meeting House built; **Apr. 1853** incorporated as a town.

Blennerhassett   *Wood County*   *Northwestern West Virginia, 65 mi/105 km north of Charleston*

1770 George Washington observes long island in his diary while traveling down Ohio River; **1797** Harman Blennerhassett, wealthy Irish immigrant, acquires part of island, builds mansion 1800; **May 1805** Aaron Burr and Harman Blennerhassett leave island at night with plan to establish a southwestern empire around Natchez, island property confiscated, both declared traitors by Thomas Jefferson, arrested at Natchez, later released; **1811** fire destroys mansion; **1970s** mansion rebuilt as historic site.

Bluefield   *Mercer County*   *Southern West Virginia, 77 mi/124 km south-southeast of Charleston*

1777 settled by John Davidson and Richard Bailey; **1791** Davidson family attacked by natives, three children killed, wife kidnapped, Davidson killed in separate attack 1793; **1811** Davidson House built; **1883** Norfolk & Western Railroad completed; first coal mines opened; **1889** incorporated as a city; **1895** Bluefield State College established; **1902** Bluefield Sanitarium founded, becomes Bluefield Community Hospital 1979, Bluefield Regional Medical Center 1990; **1921** neighboring Graham, Virginia, renamed Bluefield; **1924** governors of Virginia and West Virginia shake hands at state boundary, pledge cooperation between two states and twin towns; **1956** municipal auditorium opened.

Buckhannon   *Upshur County*   *Central West Virginia, 47 mi/76 km south-southwest of Morgantown*

1773 cabin built to west by Schoolcraft family, killed or taken captive by Native Americans in 1780; **c.1805** Jacob Lorentz drives 937 hogs to market at Richmond, Virginia, 265 mi/426 km away; **1806** site purchased by Elizabeth Cummings Jackson; **1815** town platted by Col. Edward Jackson, grandfather of Gen. Stonewall Jackson; **1851** Upshur County formed; town becomes county seat; **1856** Methodist Episcopal Church built; **1890** West Virginia Wesleyan College established; **1901** county courthouse built; **1933** incorporated as a town.

Cameron   *Marshall County*   *Northern West Virginia, 36 mi/58 km northwest of Morgantown*

1788 blockhouse built by Joseph, Christopher, and John Hime, successful at making peace with the Native Americans; **1852** Baltimore & Ohio Railroad extended to town; **1853** Methodist Episcopal Church built; **1879** incorporated as a town; **1895** town destroyed by fire, rebuilt by 1896; **1901** Patterson Glass Company established; **1907** Eljer Pottery Company established; **1914** Cameron Glass Company established; **1926** Perfect Glass Company established.

Charles Town   *Jefferson County*   *Northeastern West Virginia, 12 mi/19 km southeast of Martinsburg*

1755 Braddock's Well dug by troops of General Braddock to southwest; **1769** St. George's Episcopal Chapel built; **1770** Col. Charles Washington, younger brother of George Washington, acquires land; **1774** Mordington house built, home of Charles Washington; **1786** town platted; first Charles Town horse race held; **1787** incorporated as a town; Charles Town Academy for Boys founded, female academy founded c.1790; **1793** Altona Farm house built by Col. Abram Davenport; **c.1798** Wheatlands house built to south by Henry Smith Turner; **1801** Jefferson County formed; town becomes county seat; **1803** jail built, housed John Brown in 1859, razed 1922; **1805** George Washington Hall built, later called the Market House; **March 6, 1812** African-American leader

Martin Robinson Delaney born (died 1885); **1819** Zion Episcopal Church built, rebuilt 1849 but destroyed by fire soon after, rebuilt again 1859; **1820** Clamont Court mansion built by Bushrod Corbin Washington, grandnephew of George Washington; Blakely House built by John Augustine Washington; **c.1835** Cassillis House built by Andrew Kennedy; **1836** second county courthouse built; Rion Hall house built; **Dec. 2, 1859** abolitionist John Brown hanged for leading raid on U.S. arsenal at Harpers Ferry; **1863** courthouse and market house damaged by Union shelling; **1865** county seat moved to Shepherdstown; **1871** annexation of Jefferson and Berkeley counties by West Virginia embitters town; county seat returned to Charles Town; **1910** opera house built; **c.1940** Charles Town Races (horse racing) established.

Charleston   *Kanawha County   Central West Virginia, on Kanawha River*

1775 Col. Thomas Bullitt stakes land claim; **1789** Kanawha County formed; Fort Lee built by Col. George Clendenin, settlement founded adjacent to fort; town becomes county seat; **1789** rough riding Ann Bailey makes three-day ride to Fort Savannah at Lewisburg to resupply Fort Lee during Native American attack; **1792** Daniel Boone moves into cabin with wife Rebecca, serves one term in state legislature, moves to Kentucky 1795; **1794** town incorporated as Charles Town; **Nov. 11, 1799** fur trader Charles Bent born, governor of New Mexico Territory (died 1847); **1815** Holly Grove house built, home of David Ruffner; **1817** David Ruffner begins using coal burning furnaces to produce salt, method introduced to Kanawha Valley 1797 by Elisha Brooks, industry reaches peak 1846; **1818** town renamed Charleston; **1824** dredging opens Kanawha River to navigation; **Sept. 1862** only Civil War battle fought here, skirmish between Gen. W. W. Loring's Confederate troops and Union forces of Gen. Joseph Lightburn; **June 20, 1863** West Virginia separates from Virginia; **1870** Charleston becomes state capital, records brought by boat from Wheeling; incorporated as a city; **1873** *Charleston Gazette* founded, becomes *Kanawha Chronicle* 1898; **1875** state capital moved back to Wheeling; **1885** state capital returned to Charleston by popular vote; development of oil, coal and natural gas begins; **1891** West Virginia State College established for black students at Institute to west, originally West Virginia Colored Institute; **1892** county courthouse built; **1904** Kelley Axe and Tool Works founded; **1909** Charleston Public Library organized; **1914** Kanawha Valley chemical industry begins with production of chlorine and caustic acid for World War I; **1917** Libbey-Owens Flat Glass Company plant opened; **1925** governor's mansion completed; **1929** Charleston Municipal Airport (Wirtz Field) established to west; **1932** new state capitol completed, designed by Cass Gilbert; **1935** Morris Harvey College moved from Barboursville, becomes University of Charleston 1978; **1939** municipal auditorium built; **March 28, 1943** actress Conchata Ferrell born; **1947** Yeager (Kanawha) Airport established to northeast;

1961 Sunrise Art Museum founded; **July 19, 1961** flooding Kanawha River kills 19; **Dec. 18, 1975** Gov. Archie Moore indicted for extorting $25,000 from bank financier, acquitted May 5, 1976.

Clarksburg   *Harrison County   Northern West Virginia, 32 mi/51 km southwest of Morgantown*

1764 hunting camp built by trapper John Simpson; **c.1770** first settlers arrive; **1772** Nutters Fort built; **1773** Daniel Davisson assumes land claim; **1774** Richards Fort built by Arnold Richards; **1781** town founded, named for George Rogers Clark; **1784** Harrison County formed; town platted, becomes county seat; **1795** incorporated as a town; **1810** *By-Stander* newspaper founded; **Jan. 21, 1824** Confederate Gen. Thomas Jonathan (Stonewall) Jackson born, died from wounds May 10, 1863, at Chancellorsville, Virginia; **1835** Lee House built by Judge George H. Lee; **1856** Baltimore & Ohio Railroad arrives; **1861** Federal troops establish major supply base here; **1876** Broaddus College moved from Winchester, Virginia, founded 1871, moved to Philippi 1909; **1910s** glass industry becomes important; **March 27, 1917** Cyrus Vance born, secretary of state under President Carter (died 2002); **1930** public library established; **1931** county courthouse built; **Apr. 25, 1963** explosion kills 26 coal miners at Clinchfield Mine at Dola to northwest; **1995** FBI Criminal Justice Information Service complex completed; **1999** federal building completed.

Clay   *Clay County   Central West Virginia, 30 mi/48 km east-northeast Charleston*

1774 Philip Hammond becomes Clay County's first settler; **1813** Jacob Summers builds cabin on Elk River; town founded, originally named Henry; **1858** Clay County formed; town becomes county seat, renamed; town and county both named for statesman Henry Clay; **1895** incorporated as a town; **1978** county courthouse built.

Dola   *Harrison County   See Clarksburg (1963)*

Eccles   *Raleigh County   See Beckley (1914)*

Elizabeth   *Wirt County   Northwestern West Virginia, 52 mi/84 km north-northeast of Charleston*

1796 William Beauchamp becomes first settler; **1803** grist mill built by Beauchamp; site named Beauchamp's Mill; **1822** incorporated as a town, renamed for Beauchamp's wife; **1848** Wirt County formed; town becomes county seat; **1859** oil discovered at Burning Spring; **May 9, 1863** Confederate Cavalry under Gen. William E. Jones burns town and oil storage tanks; **1911** county courthouse built.

Elkins   *Randolph County   Northeast central West Virginia, 50 mi/80 km south of Morgantown*

1774 Wilson's Fort built by Capt. Benjamin Wilson; **1787** Randolph County formed; **1823** post office established, originally named Leadsville; **1889** Western Maryland

Railroad reaches town; town platted; **1890** incorporated as a town, renamed for U.S. Sen. Stephen Benton Elkins; **1899** county seat moved from Beverly; **1905** Coal and Coke Railroad built from Charleston; **1904** Davis and Elkins College established; **1908** county courthouse built.

Everettville *Monongalia County* *See* **Morgantown (1927)**

Fairmont *Marion County* *Northern West Virginia, 14 mi/23 km southwest of Morgantown*

late 1770s area first settled; **1793** Jacob Paulsley builds town's first house; **1819** town of Middletown founded on road midway between Clarksburg and Morgantown; **1820** incorporated as a town; **1838** neighboring town of Palatine incorporated; **1842** Marion County formed; Middletown becomes county seat; **1843** Middletown and Palatine merge to become Fairmont; Governor Pierpont House built, razed 1934; **Jan. 1852** Baltimore & Ohio Railroad reaches town; **1854** area's first coal mine opens; **Apr. 29, 1863** cavalry division of Confederate Gen. William Ezra Jones raids town, takes 260 prisoners, destroy railroad bridge, attack Pierpont home; **1865** Fairmont State College established as Fairmont State Normal School **Apr. 2, 1876** fire destroys business district; **1890** railroad built from Clarksburg; area experiences oil and natural gas boom; **1892** town of West Fairmont incorporated; **1899** Fairmont incorporated as a city; West Fairmont annexed; **1900** county courthouse completed; **1910** estate built by coal magnate James Watson, Sr.; **Nov. 20, 1968** explosion at Consolidated Coal Mine at Farmington to west, 78 of 99 miners killed.

Fayetteville *Fayette County* *South central West Virginia, 35 mi/56 km southeast of Charleston*

1818 town settled by Abraham Vandal, named Vandalia; **1831** Fayette County formed; Ansted becomes county seat; **1837** town renamed; county seat moved to Fayetteville; **May 19, 1863** Union forces under Col. Carr B. White shelled by Gen. John McCausland's Confederates; **1883** town incorporated; **1895** county courthouse built.

Franklin *Pendleton County* *Eastern West Virginia, 76 mi/122 km south-southeast of Morgantown*

1766 McCoy's Mill built to south by Ulrich Conrad, acquired by Gen. William McCoy 1800; **1769** area first settled by Francis (Frank) Evick; town founded, named Frankford; **1788** Pendleton County formed; **1794** town becomes county seat; town incorporated, renamed Franklin; **1850** Anderson House built; **1924** county courthouse built; fire destroys most of town's older buildings.

Glenville *Gilmer County* *Central West Virginia, 62 mi/100 km northeast of Charleston*

1845 Gilmer County formed; town founded as county seat, originally named Hartford; **1856** town renamed Glenville; **1871** incorporated as a town; **1872** Glenville Normal School established, later renamed Glenville State College; **1929** county courthouse built; **1950** first annual West Virginia State Folk Festival held, one of oldest folk festivals in U.S.; **2002** Glenville Federal Correctional Center established.

Grafton *Taylor County* *Northern West Virginia, 20 mi/32 km south of Morgantown*

1844 Taylor County formed; Pruntytown becomes first county seat; **1852** Baltimore & Ohio Railroad reaches site; town founded; **1856** incorporated as a town; **1889** county seat moved to Grafton; **1890** county courthouse built; **1937** Tygart Lake formed by dam on Tygart Valley River.

Grantsville *Calhoun County* *Central West Virginia, 50 mi/80 km northeast of Charleston*

1856 Calhoun County formed; **1866** town platted by Simon P. Stump, named for Gen. Ulysses S. Grant; **1869** county seat moved from Arnoldsburg after bitter rivalry; incorporated as a town; **1901** oil first discovered at Yellow Creek; **1910** carbon black plant built; **1941** fourth county courthouse built.

Hamlin *Lincoln County* *Western West Virginia, 27 mi/43 km west of Charleston*

802 land patented to David Stephenson, builds log cabin; **1833** town founded, originally named Hamline for Methodist Episcopal Bishop Leonidas L. Hamline; **1853** town incorporated, "e" dropped from town name; **1867** Lincoln County formed; town becomes county seat; **1910** county courthouse built after fire destroys previous structure 1909, all county records destroyed; **1964** new county courthouse built.

Harpers Ferry *Jefferson County* *Northeastern West Virginia, 50 mi/80 km northwest of Washington, D.C.*

1734 Robert Harper purchases log cabin from Peter Stephen; **1747** Harper establishes ferry on Potomac River; town founded; **1753** town damaged by Pumpkin Flood, thousands of Indian pumpkins washed away; **1763** incorporated as a town; **1775** Harper House built; **1801** U.S. Arsenal established by Thomas Jefferson; **1827** village of Virginius established on Herr's Island, Shenandoah River, thrived during Civil War, washed away in flood of 1870; **1830** St. Peter's Roman Catholic Church built; **1833** St. John's Episcopal Church built, rebuilt 1896; **1836** first bridge across Potomac built by Casper W. Wever, Y-shaped covered bridge for road and railroad traffic; **1840** Chesapeake & Ohio Canal opened, closed after 1924 floods; **1850** Lutheran Church built; **Oct. 16–18, 1858**

abolitionist John Brown's party raids U.S. Arsenal, 10 of Brown's men, including 2 sons, killed, 4 others killed, Brown arrested for treason; **Apr. 18, 1861** after destruction of U.S. arsenal by Stonewall Jackson's Confederates, Union army recaptures town, driven out by another Confederate thrust, regained by Union Feb. 1862, lost again in Sept. with surrender of 12,500 troops to Jackson; **1869** Storer College for black men established; **June 30, 1944** Harpers Ferry National Monument established, becomes National Historical Park 1963; **1972** first Mountain Heritage Arts and Crafts Festival held.

Harrisville *Ritchie County* *Northwestern West Virginia, 68 mi/109 km northeast of Charleston*

1822 town platted on land owned by Thomas Harris; **1843** Ritchie County formed; town becomes county seat, named Ritchie Court House; **1844** county courthouse built; **1860-1863** oil boom brings rush of drillers; **1869** incorporated as a town; **1892** town renamed for Gen. Thomas M. Harris, son of founder.

Hillsboro *Pocahontas County* *See* **Marlinton** **(1892)**

Hinton *Summers County* *Southern West Virginia, 63 mi/101 km southeast of Charleston*

1831 town platted by John Hinton; **1871** Summers County formed; town becomes county seat; Chesapeake & Ohio Railroad reaches town after major construction project through New River Gorge; **1875** county courthouse built; **1880** incorporated as a town; **1913** Confederate monument erected; **1927** Avis and Bellepoint annexed by Hinton; **1948** Bluestone Dam built on New River at confluence of Greenbrier River forming Bluestone Lake.

Huntington *Cabell County* *Western West Virginia, 45 mi/72 km west of Charleston, on Ohio River*

1749 party of Capt. de Bienville claims area for France; **1772** large land tract granted to soldiers following French and Indian War; **1796** Thomas and Jonathan Buffington become first settlers; **1802** Thomas Buffington establishes ferry on Ohio and Guyandotte rivers; **1809** Cabell County formed; Guyandotte becomes county seat; **1814** county seat moved to Barboursville; **1821** James Holderby acquires farm; **1830** James River and Kanawha Turnpike opens; **1837** Marshall University established; **Nov. 1861** Confederate raid takes 100 prisoners; town burned by Union troops for raising Confederate flag at start of Civil War; **1863** county seat moved back to Guyandotte, returned to Barboursville 1865; **1870** city of Huntington platted at Holderby's Landing by Chesapeake & Ohio Railroad owner Collis P. Huntington; **1871** incorporated as a city; **Jan. 1873** Chesapeake & Ohio Railroad reaches city; **1887** county seat moved to Huntington; **1891** Central City platted, incorporated 1893; **1901** county courthouse completed; **1902** Huntington Public Library built with Carnegie

grant, new library opened 1980; **1909** Central City annexed; *Herald-Dispatch* newspaper founded; **1911** Guyandotte annexed by Huntington; **1923** International Nickel Company plant opened; **March 30, 1927** TV actor Peter Marshall born; **1937** Ohio River flood inundates most of city; **1938** construction of flood wall begins; **1940s** Tri-State Airport (Walker Long Field) established; **1950s** Huntington Museum of Art founded; **1956** Cabell-Huntington Hospital opened; **1970s** civic arena built; **Nov. 14, 1970** Southern Airways DC-9 crashes into mountains near airport killing 75, including 43 from Marshall University football team.

Institute *Kanawha County* *See* **Charleston (1891)**

Keyser *Mineral County* *Northeastern West Virginia, 55 mi/89 km east-southeast of Morgantown*

1802 town settled on Potomac River by Patrick McCarthy, named Paddys Town; **1852** Baltimore & Ohio Railroad reaches town; town renamed New Creek; **Nov. 1864** Confederates capture town, Union's Fort Fuller and railroad destroyed; **1866** Mineral County formed; town becomes county seat; **1868** county courthouse built; **1874** town incorporated, renamed for railroad vice pres. William Keyser; **1901** Potomac State College (2-year) established.

Kingwood *Preston County* *Northern West Virginia, 18 mi/29 km southeast of Morgantown*

c.1800 first few settlers arrive; **1811** town founded; **1818** Preston County formed; **1841** Preston Academy founded; **1853** incorporated as a town; **1857** Preston County Inn built as residence, became inn 1932; **1903** soldiers memorial erected; **1934** third county courthouse built.

Layland *Fayette County* *See* **Mount Hope (1915)**

Lewisburg *Greenbrier County* *Southeastern West Virginia, 75 mi/121 km southeast of Charleston*

1751 Andrew Lewis camps here while surveying with his father for Greenbrier Land Company; **1755** Lewis builds Fort Savannah under orders from General Braddock, later renamed Fort Union; **1769** area resettled following French and Indian War; **1778** Greenbrier County formed; Fort Union becomes county seat; **1782** incorporated as a town, renamed Lewisburg; **1796** Old Stone Presbyterian Church built, replaces 1783 structure; **1798** General Lewis Hotel built; **1800** Lewisburg Hotel built; Morlunda estate built by Col. Samuel McClung; **1810** Lewisburg Academy founded, becomes Greenbrier College 1925; **1837** county courthouse built; **1855** first Greenbrier County Fair held, becomes West Virginia State Fair 1941; **c.1855** John Wesley Methodist Church built; **1890** Greenbrier Military School founded; **Dec. 30, 1917** lowest temperature ever recorded in West Virginia reached, −37°F/−38°C.

Logan   *Logan County*   *Southwestern West Virginia, 40 mi/64 km south-southwest of Charleston*

1765 Aracoma, oldest daughter of Chief Cornstalk, arrives with white husband Bolling Baker, establishes small tribe on island in Guyandotte River; **1780** Aracoma fatally wounded in battle with settlers; **1824** Logan County formed; **1827** town becomes county seat, originally named Lawnsville; **1862** courthouse burned by Union forces; **1882** Hatfield and McCoy feud develops at town of Omar to south when Johnse Hatfield elopes with Rosanna McCoy; **1884** incorporated as a town, renamed Aracoma; **1896** last incident in Hatfield-McCoy feud involves fatal shooting of Cap Hatfield by John Rutherford, a McCoy relative [see also Williamson]; **1904** railroad reaches town; coal mining begins; **1907** town renamed Logan; **Jan. 31, 1923** actress Joanne Dru born (died 1996); **1926** Jack Dempsey loses heavyweight title to Gene Tunney, bout staged here; **March 8, 1960** 18 coal miners killed when trapped in fire; **1965** county courthouse completed; **Feb. 26, 1972** flooding on Buffalo Creek kills 118.

Madison   *Boone County*   *West central West Virginia, 23 mi/37 km south-southwest of Charleston*

1847 Boone County formed; town founded as county seat; **1906** incorporated as a town; **1923** county courthouse completed, begun 1919; **Nov. 7, 1980** methane gas explosion at Ferrell Mine kills five coal miners.

Malden   *Kanawha County*   *Central West Virginia, 5 mi/8 km east-southeast of Charleston, on Kanawha River*

1775 Van Bibbers discovers Burning Spring, that would burn when lit; **1797** first salt furnace built by Elisha Brooks; **1815** about 30 salt furnaces in operation; town founded as Tera Salis, or Kanawha Salines; **1817** salt producers' trust established using black slave labor; **1843** large natural gas deposit discovered at salt wells; **1850** salt production reaches peak; **1876** only one salt furnace remains in operation.

Marlinton   *Pocahontas County*   *Eastern West Virginia, 85 mi/137 km east of Charleston*

1749 first settlers Stephen Sewell and Jacob Marlin share cabin, Sewell walks out after quarrel, lives in hollowed tree, tree remains standing until 1930; town originally called Marlin's Bottom; **1755** Andrew Lewis builds stockade; **1821** Pocahontas County formed; Huntersville becomes first county seat; **1887** town renamed; **1891** county seat moved to Marlinton; **June 26, 1892** author Pearl S. Buck born at Hillsboro to south (died 1973); **1895** county courthouse built; **1900** Chesapeake & Ohio Railroad reaches town; incorporated as a town.

Martinsburg   *Berkeley County*   *Northeastern West Virginia, 110 mi/177 km east of Morgantown*

1732 area first settled by German and English immigrants; town founded; **c.1740** Tuscarora Presbyterian Church built to south; **1755** Big Spring house built by John Evans on site of Fort Evans, to south; **1772** Berkeley County formed; town becomes county seat; **1774** Lemen House built; **June 30, 1792** post office established, oldest in West Virginia; **1812** Boydville estate built by Elisa Boyd; **1832** St. John's Lutheran Church completed; **1837** Baltimore & Ohio Railroad reaches town; **May 9, 1843** actress Belle Boyd born, imprisoned 1862 as Confederate spy, released 1865 (died 1900); **1855** county courthouse built; **1859** incorporated as a town; **June 1861** Confederate Gen. J. E. B. Stuart's cavalry raids town, burns new railroad bridge; **Dec. 3, 1871** Newton Diehl Baker born, secretary of war under President Wilson (died 1937); **1877** railroad strike leads to mob action, Federal troops called out by President Hayes; **Jan. 10, 1887** Virginia Sen. Henry Floyd Byrd born (died 1966); **1890s** woolen and knitting mills built; **1910** incorporated as a city; **July 10, 1936** highest temperature recorded in West Virginia reached, 112°F/44°C.

Matewan   *Mingo County*   *Southwestern West Virginia, 58 mi/93 km south-southwest of Charleston*

1790s first settlers occupy Tug River Valley; **c.1830** John and Richard Ferrell settle at town site; **1890** Norfolk & Western Railroad reaches site; town platted, named for Mattawan, New York, home of railroad official Erskine Hazard; **1895** incorporated as a town; **May 19, 1920** the Matewan Massacre, shootout between United Mine Workers and mine security agents, nine killed, leads to killing of Sheriff Sid Hatfield by agents, protest march by miners; **Apr. 4, 1977** worst flood in town's flood-prone history; **1984** town suffers 33rd flood in 35 years.

Middlebourne   *Tyler County*   *Northwestern West Virginia, 90 mi/145 km north-northeast of Charleston*

1814 Tyler County formed, named for Virginia Gov. John Tyler (1747–1813), father of Pres. John Tyler; **1813** town founded; **1816** town becomes county seat; **1871** incorporated as a town; **1874** county jail built; **1923** county courthouse built; **1976** public library built.

Monongah   *Marion County*   *Northern West Virginia, 18 mi/29 km southwest of Morgantown*

1768 Capt. James Booth becomes first settler on this part of West Fork Monongahela River; **June 16, 1778** Booth killed in Native American ambush; **1880s** coal deposits discovered; town founded, named Briartown; **1891** incorporated as a town, renamed short form of Monongahela; **Dec. 6, 1907** explosions at Consolidated Coal Mines 6 and 8, 362 killed, leave 250 widows, 1,000 fatherless children, worst mining disaster in U.S. history.

Moorefield *Hardy County* *Northeastern West Virginia, 67 mi/108 km southeast of Morgantown*

Oct. 7, 1747 pioneer Ebenezer Zane born (died 1812); **1777** area first settled by Conrad Moore; town founded on Moore's land; incorporated as a town; **1786** Hardy County formed; town becomes county seat; **1788** Old Stone Inn built; **1818** Willow Hall house built by Capt. Daniel McNeill, base of operations for McNeill's Confederate Rangers; **Aug. 7, 1864** Union forces under Gen. William W. Averill attacks Confederate cavalry under Gen. John McCausland, 530 casualties; **1913** county courthouse built; **1938** Moorefield Public Library founded.

Morgantown *Monongalia County* *Northern West Virginia, 130 mi/209 km northeast of Charleston*

1758 settlers led by Thomas Decker reach site, establish village on Monongalia River, destroyed by Delaware and Mingo Native Americans following year; **1767** resettled by Zackquill Morgan, others; **1769** Fort Pierpont built to northeast by John Pierpont; **1772** Fort Morgan established; **1776** Monongalia County formed; **1781** town platted; **1783** town becomes county seat; **1785** incorporated as a town; **1790** town's iron industry begins; McCleery House built; **c.1812** Old Stone House built; **Jan. 25, 1814** Gov. Francis H. Pierpont born, "Father of West Virginia" (died 1899); Monongalia Academy founded; **Apr. 29, 1826** first steamboat *Reindeer* reaches town; **1834** Henry Clay Iron Furnace built to northeast, one of four built by Leonard Lamb, closed 1847; **1838** Waitman Willey House built; **1840** John Rogers House built; **1852** Baltimore & Ohio Railroad reaches town; **1858** Woodburn Female Seminary founded; **1860** Alexander Wade House built; **1867** West Virginia University established on seminary site; **1889** oil fields open nearby; **1891** county courthouse built; **1896** abundance of natural gas leads to opening of glass factories; Seneca Glass Plant moved from Fostoria, Ohio; **1905** incorporated as a city; **1910s** glass industry reaches peak; **July 21, 1924** TV actor Don Knotts born; **Apr. 20, 1927** explosion in Federal Mine No. 3 at Everettville to southwest, 97 killed; **1937** Morgantown Airport (Hart Field) established, opened 1940; **May 12, 1942** explosion at Christopher No. 3 Coal Mine at Osage to west, 56 killed.

Moundsville *Marshall County* *Northern West Virginia, 47 mi/76 km northwest of Morgantown*

1771 area on Ohio River first settled by Joseph, Samuel, and James Tomlinson, build cabin near Grave Creek Mound; **1772** town founded, named Grave Creek; **1798** town platted by Joseph Tomlinson, Jr., renamed Elizabethtown for his wife; **1831** Simon Purdy establishes Mound City adjacent to first town; **1835** Marshall County formed; Elizabethtown becomes county seat; **1865** two towns merge, incorporated as Moundsville; **1866** West Virginia State Penitentiary built, completed 1876; **1876** county courthouse built; **1907** Grave Creek Mound State Park established, mounds of Adena people date to c.1000

BC; **1917** Moundsville Public Library founded; **1995** West Virginia Penitentiary closed.

Mount Hope *Fayette County* *South central West Virginia, 40 mi/64 km southeast of Charleston*

1805 William Blake, Sr. becomes first white settler; **c.1870** town founded as coal mining center; **1873** Chesapeake & Ohio Railroad completed; **1894** production begins of "smokeless coal" with low volatility; **1895** incorporated as a town; **March 24, 1910** town destroyed by fire; **1915** Mount Hope Presbyterian Church built; **March 2, 1915** explosion at Layland No. 3 Coal Mine to east, 115 killed; **1917** New River Coal Company headquarters established.

New Cumberland *Hancock County* *Northern West Virginia, 71 mi/114 km northwest of Morgantown*

1784 Fort Chapman built on Ohio River; town founded, named Cuppytown for founder John Cuppy; **1839** town platted, renamed New Cumberland; **1848** Hancock County formed; nearby New Manchester becomes county seat; **1850** county seat moved to New Cumberland; **1852** county seat moved back to New Manchester; **1872** incorporated as a town; **1884** county seat moved final time back to New Cumberland; **1921** county courthouse built.

New Martinsville *Wetzel County* *Northern West Virginia, 100 mi/161 km north-northeast of Charleston*

1780 land on Ohio River granted to Edward Doolin; **1782** Doolin killed by natives, wife and baby unharmed; **1810** Presley Martin buys Doolin property, settles here 1811; **1838** town platted and incorporated, named Martinsville; **1846** Wetzel County formed; town becomes county seat, renamed New Martinsville; **1902** county courthouse completed; **1972** Hannibal Lock & Dam built on Ohio River.

Omar *Logan County* *See* **Logan (1882)**

Osage *Monongalia County* *See* **Morgantown (1942)**

Parkersburg *Wood County* *Northwestern West Virginia, 65 mi/105 km north of Charleston, on Ohio River*

1773 Robert Thornton makes "tomahawk claim" by making notches in trees, sells to Alexander Parker 1783; **1785** James Neal builds Fort Neal; town founded at mouth of Kanawha River, named Neal's Station; **1790** Native American attack kills all settlers living outside fort; **1798** Wood County formed; **1800** Tavenner House built; **1801** new town founded as county seat, named Stokelyville for landowner John Stokely, renamed Parkersburg 1809; **1812** Stratford Hotel built; **1820** incorporated as a town; **1833** *Republican* newspaper founded; Oakland house begun, completed 1843; **1857** Baltimore & Ohio Railroad reaches town; **1860** oil discovered; **1863** incorporated as a city; **Sept. 21, 1885**

cartoonist H. T. Webster born (died 1952); **1899** county courthouse built; **1937** last oil refinery closes; **1971** West Virginia University at Parkersburg (2-year) established.

Parsons   *Tucker County   Northeastern West Virginia, 40 mi/64 km south-southeast of Morgantown*

1774 brothers Thomas, Jr. and James Parsons become first settlers; **Apr. 1781** settlers John Minear, Daniel Cameron and Jacob Cooper massacred by Native Americans; **1856** Tucker County formed; St. George becomes first county seat; **July 13, 1861** in Battle of Corrick's Ford, Union forces claim victory over Confederates; **1880s** area experiences lumber boom; **1893** incorporated as a town; county seat moved to Parsons; **1900** county courthouse built.

Petersburg   *Grant County   Northeastern West Virginia, 64 mi/103 km southeast of Morgantown*

c.1745 town settled by German immigrants, named Petersburg; Jacob Peterson opens first store; **1825** Mount Zion Church built, destroyed by Union forces in Civil War; **1833** post office established, town renamed Lunice Creek since there already was a Petersburg in Virginia; **1845** incorporated as a town; **1863** West Virginia separates from Virginia; **1866** Grant County formed; town becomes county seat; **1910** town reincorporated; **1914** town renamed Petersburg; **1978** county courthouse built.

Philippi   *Barbour County   Northern West Virginia, 34 mi/55 km south of Morgantown*

1780 town first settled on Tygart Valley River by Richard Cottrill and Charity Talbott, named Anglin's Ford; **1787** Daniel Booth arrives, establishes ferry; **c.1800** town renamed Booth's Ferry; **1843** Barbour County formed; town becomes county seat, renamed for Philip Pendleton Barbour, also county's namesake; **1852** Philippi Covered Bridge built by Lemuel Chenoweth; **June 1861** Union troops under Col. B. F. Kelley rout Confederate forces of George A. Porterfield, forcing them into retreat; **July 10, 1861** in Battle of Laurel Hill, 555 Confederate soldiers under Gen. Robert S. Garnett surrender to Gen. George McClellan's forces; **1871** incorporated as a town; **1903** county courthouse built; **1909** Broaddus College moves from Clarksburg, becomes Alderson-Broaddus College 1931.

Pineville   *Wyoming County   Southern West Virginia, 53 mi/85 km south of Charleston*

1840 town founded, originally named Rock View; **1850** Wyoming County formed; Oceana (Cassville) becomes county seat; **1871** incorporated as a town; **1880** town renamed Pineville; **1907** county seat moved to Pineville; **1916** county courthouse built.

Point Pleasant   *Mason County   Western West Virginia, 45 mi/72 km northwest Charleston, on Ohio River*

1749 French explorer Capt. Peter Joseph Celeron visits site; **1770** George Washington camps at mouth of Kanawha River, names site; **1774** Fort Blair built, followed by Fort Randolph in 1776; **Oct. 10, 1774** Battle of Point Pleasant fought between Long Knives Native Americans under Gen. Andrew Lewis and Shawnee under Chief Cornstalk; **1797** Mansion House built; **1804** Mason County formed; town becomes county seat; **1833** town incorporated; **1857** county courthouse built; **1909** Battle of Point Pleasant monument erected; **1928** Silver Bridge built across Ohio River to Kanauga, Ohio; **Dec. 15, 1967** Silver Bridge collapses into river, 46 killed; **1969** new Silver Memorial Bridge built.

Princeton   *Mercer County   Southern West Virginia, 75 mi/121 km south-southeast of Charleston*

1826 town settled, named for Revolutionary Battle of Princeton in which Gen. Hugh Mercer was killed; **1837** Mercer County formed; incorporated as a town; **1839** town becomes county seat; **May 1, 1862** courthouse burned by retreating Confederate troops; **1865** county seat moved to Athens by Judge Nathaniel Harrison, disliked in Princeton; **1869** county seat moved back to Princeton after citizens seize county records; **1908** first passenger train reaches town on Virginian Railroad; **1930** county courthouse built, rebuilt 1931 following arson fire shortly after its completion.

Ripley   *Jackson County   Western West Virginia, 32 mi/51 km north of Charleston*

1768 area first settled by William John and Lewis Rogers; **1830** Rev. Harry Ripley drowns in Big Mill Creek; **1831** Jackson County formed; **1832** town established as county seat; incorporated as a town; **Oct. 1877** first annual Jackson County Fair held at Evans Fairground; **1887** Staats Mill Covered Bridge built; **1889** Sarvis Creek Covered Bridge built; **1920** third county courthouse built; **1949** Jackson County Library founded, new library built 1973.

Romney   *Hampshire County   Northeastern West Virginia, 68 mi/109 km east-southeast of Morgantown*

1738 Job and John Pearsall become first settlers; town of Pearsall Flats founded; **1753** Hampshire County formed; town becomes county seat; **1756** Fort Pearsall built as protection against raids led by Chief Killbuck, surrenders claims 1761; about 100 of George Washington's men killed and scalped by Native Americans at Capon Bridge to east; **1762** new town founded as county seat; **Dec. 1762** incorporated as a town; one of two oldest towns in West Virginia (with Shepherdstown); **1771** Mytinger House built; **June 11, 1861** Confederate troops stationed here attacked by Gen. Lew Wallace's Union forces; **1870** State

Schools for Deaf and Blind established; **1922** county courthouse built.

Saint Albans *Kanawha County* *Central West Virginia, 11 mi/18 km west of Charleston, on Kanawha River*

1787 area settled by Lewis and John Tackett, build Fort Tackett; **1790** most inhabitants of fort killed in Native American attack; **c.1792** Stephen Teays becomes first permanent settler; **1799** ferry established by Teays; **1832** Riverlawn residence built as tavern; **1861** Teays' Tavern destroyed by floods; **July 17, 1861** Confederates under Gen. Henry A. Wise win first victory in Kanawha Valley, then driven back by Union forces; **1868** incorporated as a city.

Saint Marys *Pleasants County* *Northwestern West Virginia, 76 mi/122 km north-northeast of Charleston*

1790 French immigrants Isaac and Jacob La Rue settle on Ohio River; **1834** land purchased by Alexander H. Creel, has vision of Virgin Mary while watching steamboat pass; **1849** town founded by Creel; **1851** Pleasants County formed; town becomes county seat; **1872** incorporated as a town; **1925** county courthouse built.

Shepherdstown *Jefferson County* *Northeastern West Virginia, 8 mi/12.9 km east of Martinsburg*

c.1730 town founded on Potomac River by Germans from Pennsylvania, named Mecklenburg; **1732** town platted by Thomas Shepherd; **1762** incorporated as a town, with Romney, one of two oldest towns in state; **1769** Wyncoop Tavern built, acquired by Cornelius Wyncoop 1781; **July 17, 1775** Berkeley Riflemen of Virginia Volunteers gather at Morgan's Spring, march east toward Washington's troops, arrive in Boston 26 days later; **1780** log Presbyterian Church built, replaced 1787, again in 1836; **Dec. 3, 1787** James Rumsey's steam-powered boat makes repeated half-mile runs on Potomac to delight of spectators; **1790** George Washington considers site for national capital; **1798** town renamed for Thomas Shepherd; **c.1799** Bellevue house built; **1810** Thomas James Tavern built; **1812–1815** British prisoners held at Entler Tavern during War of 1812; **1825** Riflemen hold 50th reunion at Morgan's Grove; **c.1830** Falling Springs house built my Jacob Morgan; **1840s** Chesapeake & Ohio Canal completed; **1859** Trinity Episcopal Church built; **1865** county seat moved from Charles Town, returned 1871; **1871** Shepherd College established; **1880s** Shepherdstown Flour Mill built; **1915** Rumsey Monument erected.

Shinnston *Harrison County* *Northern West Virginia, 25 mi/40 km southwest of Morgantown*

1778 Levi Shinn becomes first settler; **1802** son Jonathan Shinn builds house; **1815** town founded, named Shinn's Town; **1852** incorporated as a town; **1870s** coal deposits discovered; **1877** town renamed Shinnston; **Jan. 23, 1944** tornado damages town, one of series of tornadoes, 60 killed, 116 killed in state; **1998** incorporated as a city.

Spencer *Roane County* *West central West Virginia, 35 mi/56 km north-northeast of Charleston*

1812 first settlers Samuel Tanner, his wife and child live in cave, build first cabin; settlement named Tanners Cross Roads; **c.1817** more settlers arrive; **1849** town founder Raleigh Butcher stops here on way to California, gets no further; town named New California; **1856** Roane County formed; town becomes county seat; **1858** town chartered, renamed for Judge Spencer Roane; **1893** Spencer State Hospital opens, closed 1989; **1964** county courthouse built.

Summersville *Nicholas County* *Central West Virginia, 43 mi/69 km east of Charleston*

1818 Nicholas County formed; **1824** town founded as county seat; **1860** incorporated as a town; **July 1861** town burned, Union Captain Starr's forces captured in attack initiated by Confederate spy Nancy "Peggy" Hart; **Sept. 10, 1861** in Battle of Carnifex Ferry, smaller force of Confederates under Gen. John B. Floyd engage 5,000 Union troops under William S. Rosecrans in several hours of fighting; **1898** county courthouse completed; **1965** dam built on Gauley River to form Summersville Lake.

Sutton *Braxton County* *Central West Virginia, 55 mi/89 northeast of Charleston*

c.1800 pioneer John O'Brien lives here for several years in hollowed-out sycamore tree; **1810** town first settled by John D. Sutton; **1826** incorporated as a town, originally named Suttonville; **1836** Braxton County formed; town becomes county seat; **1861** entire town burned by Confederate guerillas led by Capt. Jack Tuning; **1889** town reincorporated as Sutton; **1960** county courthouse completed; Sutton Lake formed by dam to east on Elk River.

Switchback *McDowell County* *See Welch (1908)*

Union *Monroe County* *Southern West Virginia, 80 mi/129 km southeast of Charleston*

1774 area settled by James Alexander; **1786** Rehoboth Church built, oldest Methodist church west of Allegheny Mountains; **1799** Monroe County formed; **1802** hotel established by Charles Friend; **1823** resort at Salt Sulphur Springs opens to south; **c.1838** Elmwood Mansion built by Hugh Caperton; **1868** incorporated as a town; **1881** county courthouse built; **1903** Indian Creek Covered Bridge built; **1911** Laurel Creek Covered Bridge built.

Wayne *Wayne County* *Western West Virginia,*
45 mi/72 km west-southwest of Charleston

1842 Wayne County formed, named for Gen. "Mad" Anthony Wayne; first white settlers arrive; town founded as county seat, named Trout's Hill, later Fairview; **1860** town chartered; **1882** incorporated as a town; **1911** town renamed Wayne; **1924** third county courthouse completed.

Webster Springs (Addison) *Webster County*
Central West Virginia, 72 mi/116 km east of Charleston

1785 spring discovered by Abram Meirs; **1860** Webster County formed; town founded as county seat by Polly Arthur, named for Addison McLaughlin, donated land for first courthouse; Webster Springs becomes preferred name; **c.1890** 300-room Webster Springs Hotel built by U.S. Sen. Johnson N. Camden; **1892** incorporated as a town, officially remains Addison; **1896** county courthouse built, rebuilt 1901 after fire; **1926** hotel destroyed by fire.

Weirton *Hancock and Brooke counties* *Northern West Virginia, 65 mi/105 km northwest of Morgantown*

1790s town founded on Ohio River; **1909** town's first steel mill built by Ernest T. Weir and J. R. Phillips, Weirton Steel Company formed, beginning of town's growth; **1926** Mary H. Weir Public Library opened; **1947** incorporated as a city, previously unincorporated; **March 1982** under threat of closing, employees purchase steel mill; **1990** Veterans Memorial Bridge (U.S. Highway 22) built across Ohio River to Steubenville, Ohio.

Welch *McDowell County* *Southern West Virginia, 65 mi/105 km south of Charleston*

1820s William Fletcher becomes first settler; **1858** McDowell County formed; **1880** store built by Squire W. G. Hunt; **1885** town founders I. A. Welch, J. H. Bramwell, and J. H. Juring purchase site from John Henry Hunt; **1891** Norfolk & Western Railroad reaches town; **1892** county seat moved from English (Perryville); **1893** town platted; **1894** incorporated as a town; **1895** county courthouse built; **Dec. 29, 1908** explosion at Long Branch Coal Mine at Switchback to southeast, 51 killed; **Jan. 12, 1909** second Long Branch Mine explosion, 67 killed; **March 26, 1912** Jed (Havaco) Coal Mine explosion to south kills 83 miners; **Jan. 10–12, 1940** explosion at Pond Creek Coal Mine at Bartley to southwest, 91 killed; **Jan. 15, 1946** explosion at Havaco No. 9 Mine, 15 killed, 30 injured.

Wellsburg *Brooke County* *Northern West Virginia, 57 mi/92 km northwest of Morgantown, on Ohio River*

1772 Jonathan, Israel, and Friend Cox build cabin; **1788** Charles Prather purchases land from Cox brothers, starts ferry service; **1790** town platted; **1791** town incorporated as Charles Town; **1797** Brooke County formed; town becomes county seat; area becomes known for its distilleries; **1798** Miller's Tavern built; **1813** town's first glass plant founded by Isaac Duval; **1816** town renamed Wellsburg; **1829** flood walls built, first flood-prevention project on Ohio River; **1835** paper manufacturing begins; **1845** temperance movement forces closing of last distillery; **1849** second county courthouse built; **1879** Riverside Glass Works established, closed 1907.

West Union *Doddridge County* *Northern West Virginia, 50 mi/80 km southwest of Morgantown*

1787 land patented to James Caldwell; **1808–1810** Lewis Maxwell purchases land, sells parcels to settlers; **c.1820** town founded as Lewisport; store established by John Chaney; post office established; **1845** Doddridge County formed; town becomes county seat; **1850** incorporated as a town, renamed West Union; **1856** Baltimore & Ohio Railroad reaches town; **1890s** oil and natural gas industry developed in county; **1903** county courthouse completed.

Weston *Lewis County* *Central West Virginia, 50 mi/80 km south-southwest of Morgantown*

1784 Henry Flesher becomes first settler; settlement on West Fork Monongahela River originally named Preston, later Flesherville; **1816** Lewis County formed; **1818** town founded as county seat; **1820** town renamed Weston; **1847** Staunton-Parkersburg Turnpike built by Irish laborers; **1859** Trans-Allegheny Asylum founded, becomes Weston State Hospital, closed 1994; **1888** third county courthouse completed; **1890s** oil and natural gas boom begins; **1913** incorporated as a town; **1986** Stonewall Jackson Lake formed by dam on West Fork Monongahela River.

Wheeling *Ohio County* *Northern West Virginia, 50 mi/80 km northwest of Morgantown, on Ohio River*

Aug. 1749 French explorer de Bienville stops here while descending Ohio River; **1755** English map shows Wheeling Island and adjacent Wheeling Creek; **1769** site first settled by brothers Col. Ebenezer, Silas, and Jonathan Zane; **1774** Fort Fincastle built as defense against Native American uprising after murder of Chief Logan's family; **1776** Ohio County formed; fort renamed Fort Henry for Patrick Henry; **Sept. 1782** British and Native Americans attack fort, withdraw after two-day siege; **1793** town platted by Ebenezer Zane, named Zanesburg; Linsly Institute of Technology founded; **1795** incorporated as a town, renamed Wheeling; **1797** county seat moved from West Liberty; **1807** Old Stone Presbyterian Church built; **1818** National Road completed to Wheeling; **May 24, 1825** first steamboat *Herald* docks at Wheeling Wharf; **1836** incorporated as a city; wooden bridge built from Wheeling Island to Ohio side of river; **1840** M. Marsh and Sons cigar factory established; **1848** Mount de Chantal Academy for women founded; **1849** first complete bridge built across river, destroyed by storm 1854; **1852** Baltimore & Ohio Railroad completed; **1853** Washington Hall office building built; **1854** customhouse built; **1856** new bridge built; **1861** convention held at Washington Hall by western and northern Virginia counties to discuss creation of new state; **June 20, 1863** West Virginia separates from Virginia as 35th state; Wheeling becomes first state capital; **1870** state capital moved to Charleston, returned to Wheeling 1875; **1876** capitol building built, becomes city-county building 1885; **1879** Bloch Brothers Tobacco Plant founded; **1885** state capital moved permanently to Charleston; **1900** Oglebay Mansion built for iron industry leader Earl W. Oglebay, completed 1905; **Sept. 1, 1907** steel industry labor leader Walter Reuther born (died 1970); **1910** Wheeling Public Library built, established 1859; **1911** Upper Market House built; **Apr. 28, 1924** explosion at Benwood Coal Mine to south, owned by Wheeling Steel Corporation, kills 119; **1930** Museums of Oglebay Institute established at mansion; **1933** Jamboree USA established by George W. Smith at Capitol Music Hall, built 1928; **1937** Wheeling Downs horse racetrack opened; **Apr. 23, 1949** actress Joyce Dewitt born; **1954** Wheeling Jesuit University established; **1972** West Virginia Northern Community College established; **1990** Women's History Museum founded.

White Sulphur Springs   *Greenbrier County*
Southeastern West Virginia, southeast of Charleston

c.1750 Nathaniel Carpenter becomes first settler; **1772** invalid woman carried to spring, cured of rheumatism, beginning of site's popularity; **c.1790** town founded; **1808** tavern built by James Caldwell; **1830s** resort gains notoriety among Southern social elite; **1854** White Sulphur Springs Hotel ("Old White") built; **1864** Union Gen. David Hunter dissuaded from burning hotel, used as barracks; **1909** incorporated as a town; **1913** old hotel demolished, Greenbrier Hotel built in its place, expanded 1931; **1958** secret bunker built beneath Greenbrier Resort by U.S. government as shelter for officials in event of nuclear attack; **1995** nuclear bunker decommissioned.

Williamson   *Mingo County*   *Southwestern West Virginia, 58 mi/93 km southwest of Charleston*

Jan. 1, 1888 home of Randolph McCoy burned by members of Hatfield clan, wife injured, two children killed [see Logan]; **1891** Norfolk & Western Railroad reaches site; town founded; **1892** incorporated as a town; **1895** Mingo County formed; town becomes county seat; **1905** incorporated as a city; **1920** coal miners' strike attended by colorful labor activist Mother Jones; **1937** Coal House built entirely of coal; **1940s** proliferation of coal mines in county earns it the designation Billion Dollar Coal Field; **1966** county courthouse completed.

Williamstown   *Wood County*   *Northwestern West Virginia, 75 mi/121 km north of Charleston, on Ohio River*

1770 Joseph Tomlinson and son Samuel make land claim; **1787** Isaac Williams, Revolutionary veteran, settles here; **1809** Tomlinsons build log cabin; **1831** Henderson House built; **1839** Tomlinson House built by Joseph Tomlinson III; **1907** Fenton Art Glass Company established by Frank L. Fenton; **1977** Fenton Art Glass Museum founded.

Winfield   *Putnam County*   *Western West Virginia, 20 mi/32 km northwest of Charleston, on Kanawha River*

1818 ferry established by Charles Brown; town founded, named for Gen. Winfield Scott; **1848** Putnam County formed; town becomes county seat; **1868** incorporated as a town; **1900** county courthouse built; **1937** Lock & Dam No. 1 completed on Kanawha River; **1997** judicial center completed.

Wisconsin

Northern U.S. Capital: Madison. Major city: Milwaukee.

Wisconsin became part of the U.S. with creation of the Northwest Territory July 13, 1787. It became part of Indiana Territory January 11, 1805. Michigan Territory, including Wisconsin, was established on January 11, 1805. Wisconsin Territory was established January 26, 1837, the same date that Michigan became a state. Wisconsin entered the Union as the 30th state May 29, 1848.

Wisconsin is divided into 72 counties. The counties are divided into townships, also called towns, with governments having broad powers. Municipalities are classified as villages and cities. See Introduction.

Alma *Buffalo County Western Wisconsin, 75 mi/ 121 km southeast of St. Paul, Minnesota, on Mississippi River*

1852 town founded; **1853** Buffalo County formed; **1860** county seat moved from Fountain City; **1885** incorporated as a village; **1891** large landmark rock outcrop falls from atop Twelve Mile Bluff; **1962** county courthouse built.

Antigo *Langlade County Northern Wisconsin, 72 mi/116 km northwest of Green Bay*

1878 town founded by Swiss immigrant Francis Augustine Deleglise; **1877** Deleglise House built; **1879** Langlade County formed, named for fur trader Charles Michel de Langlade; town becomes county seat; **1885** incorporated as a city; **1897** Antigo Public Library founded; **1905** second county courthouse built; Carnegie Library opened, replaced by new structure 1997; **1922** Kraft-Phoenix cheese factory established by William and J. L. Kraft, becomes Antigo Cheese Company 1992; **1930** cooperative creamery built.

Appleton *Outagamie and Calumet counties Eastern Wisconsin, 90 mi/145 km north-northwest of Milwaukee*

1847 Lawrence University established on land donated by Amos A. Lawrence; **1848** town founded on Fox River, near Lake Winnebago; **1851** Outagamie County formed; town becomes county seat; **1853** incorporated as a village; **1857** incorporated as a city; **1882** escape artist Harry Houdini brought to Appleton at age 4, born March 24, 1878, in Budapest, Hungary (died 1926); nation's first Edison system hydroelectric plant built; **Sept. 30, 1886** Heathstone mansion built for Henry J. Rogers, first to be electrically lighted; **1886** state's first streetcar system installed; **Nov. 14, 1908** Sen. Joseph R. McCarthy born at Grand Chute, now part of Appleton, headed committee investigating alleged American Communists 1950–1954 (died 1957); **1942** county courthouse built; **July 22, 1955** actor Willem Dafoe born; **1965** Outagamie County Airport opened; **March 12, 1970** firebombs damage college and high school, part of dissident bombing campaign across U.S.; **1974** Tri-County Ice Arena opened; **1987** Paper Valley Hotel opened.

Ashland *Ashland County Northern Wisconsin, 62 mi/100 km east of Duluth, Minnesota, on Lake Superior*

1659 Pierre Esprit, Sieur Radisson and Medard Chouart, Sieur de Groseiliers, become first white men to enter Chequamegon Bay; small fort built; **1665** French mission established by Father Claude Allouez, assumed by Father Marquette 1669, closed 1671; **1854** Asaph Whittlesey builds cabin; town founded by Whittlesey; Bad River (La Pointe) Indian Reservation established to east; **1860** Ashland County formed; town becomes county seat; **1872** first sawmill built; **1877** Wisconsin Central Railroad reaches town from Lake Michigan; Chequamegon Hotel opened; **1880s** lumber milling becomes important; brownstone quarrying begins; **1882** Milwaukee, Lake Shore & Western (Chicago & Northwestern) Railroad built to Ironwood, Michigan; **1886** iron ore mining boom begins in Gogebic Range; **1887** incorporated as a city; **1888** Vaughn Public Library established; **1892** Northland College established; **1894** federal building built, later used as city hall; **1900** forest reserves depleted; **1910** county courthouse built; **Sept. 26, 1970** Apostle Islands National Lakeshore established to north; **1978** first Bay Day Festival held.

Baraboo   *Sauk County   Southern Wisconsin, 32 mi/ 51 km north-northwest of Madison*

early 1700s French trader Jean Baribault (Baribeau) builds post on Wisconsin River; **1837** Winnebago peoples cede land to U.S.; **1840** Sauk County formed; town founded as county seat; **1866** incorporated as a village; **1882** incorporated as a city; **1882** Charles, Otto, Albert, John, and Alfred Ringling organize Ringling Brothers Circus, brothers Henry and August opt out, give first performance at Mazomanie; **1906** county courthouse built.

Barron   *Barron County   Western Wisconsin, 67 mi/ 108 km northeast of St. Paul, Minnesota*

1859 Dallas County formed; **1869** county organized, renamed Barron County; **c.1871** town founded; **1874** town becomes county seat after several short-term moves; **1878** sawmill built; **1884** Minneapolis, St. Paul & Sault Ste. Marie Railroad built through town; flour mill, second sawmill built; **1887** incorporated as a city; **1902** Barron Cooperative Creamery Company organized; **1959** Barron County Library established; **1964** county courthouse built.

Belmont   *Lafayette County   Southwestern Wisconsin, 54 mi/87 km southwest of Madison*

1827 Maj. John H. Rountree becomes first settler; town founded; **Apr. 1836** Wisconsin Territory created; **Oct. 1836** town serves as territorial capitol for 46 days; **Dec. 1836** capital moved to Madison; **1837** town goes out of existence; **c.1847** new Belmont founded; **1894** incorporated as a village; **1924** territorial capitol restored as state historical site.

Beloit   *Rock County   Southern Wisconsin, 42 mi/ 68 km south-southeast of Madison*

1824 trading post established on Rock River by French Canadian Joseph Thibault; **1832** during Black Hawk War, militia captain Abraham Lincoln camps on Rock River, carves inscription on boulder; **1837** land bought by Dr. Horace White of New England Emigrating Company; first settlers arrive from Colebrook, New Hampshire; **1846** incorporated as a village; Beloit College established; **1856** incorporated as a city; **1858** Beloit Iron Works founded; **1859** on campaign tour, Abraham Lincoln revisits his 1832 camp site; **Jan. 26, 1884** explorer Roy Chapman Andrews born (died 1960); **1887** Berlin Machine Works founded, becomes Yates-American Machine Company; **1889** Charles Morse founds Fairbanks-Morse Company, maker of Diesel motors; **1895** Beloit Public Library founded, new building opened 1972; **1953** Beloit Symphony founded, later Beloit-Janesville Symphony; **1967** Beloit Airport established.

Black River Falls   *Jackson County   Western Wisconsin, 112 mi/180 km northwest of Madison*

1819 one of first sawmills in Wisconsin built at falls of Black River; **1839** town founded by Jacob Spaulding; **1840s** Mormons from Nauvoo, Illinois, among first settlers; **1853** Jackson County formed; town becomes county seat; **1860** town destroyed by fire; **1867** incorporated as a village; **1878** county courthouse built; **1883** incorporated as a city.

Boscobel   *Grant County   Southwestern Wisconsin, 67 mi/108 km west of Madison, on Wisconsin River*

1846 town founded; **1864** incorporated as a village; **1873** incorporated as a city; **1898** Gideons Bible Society founded to promote distribution of Bibles in hotel rooms and ship staterooms; **1930s** Boscobel Municipal Airport established.

Cassville   *Grant County   Southwestern Wisconsin, 85 mi/137 km west-southwest of Madison, on Mississippi River*

1831 Glendower Price becomes first settler, opens general store; **1836** town platted by Lucius Lyon and Garrett V. Dennison; Nelson Dewey, first Governor of Wisconsin (1848–1852), settles here, builds farmstead, mansion destroyed by fire 1873; Dennison House built to house legislature in town's unsuccessful bid for state capitol; Cassville Ferry established to Iowa; **1882** incorporated as a village; **1885** Chicago, Burlington & Quincy Railroad reaches town; **1893** vegetable cannery established; **1937** Lock & Dam No. 10 built on Mississippi River.

Cedar Grove   *Sheboygan County   See* **Sheboygan (2002)**

Chilton   *Calumet County   Eastern Wisconsin, 70 mi/113 km north-northwest of Milwaukee*

1836 Calumet County formed; **1842** county organized; **1843** Stockbridge becomes first county seat; **1847** town founded on east shore of Lake Winnebago by Moses "Elder" Stanton and his wife; **1856** county seat moved from Stockbridge; **1877** incorporated as a village; Trinity Presbyterian Church built; **1914** county courthouse built.

Chippewa Falls   *Chippewa County   Western Wisconsin, 83 mi/134 km east of St. Paul, Minnesota*

1766 explorer Jonathan Carver, working for British, passes through area; **1836** Jean Brunet establishes sawmill; **1837** town founded on Chippewa River; **1845** Chippewa County formed; town becomes county seat; **1853** incorporated as a village; **1869** incorporated as a city; **1910** Carnegie Library built, replaced 1969; **1918** county courthouse built.

Columbus *Dodge and Columbia counties* *South central Wisconsin, 25 mi/40 km northeast of Madison*

1839 Maj. Elbert Dickson returns from Indian wars, builds first house, sawmill; town founded; **1840s** hotel and grist mill built; **1859** Kurth Brewery established, destroyed by fire 1916; **1864** incorporated as a village; **1874** incorporated as a city; **1877** Columbus Public Library founded, built 1912; **1892** city hall built; **1919** Farmers' and Merchants' Union Bank building built, designed by Louis H. Sullivan.

Crandon *Forest County* *Northern Wisconsin, 86 mi/138 km northwest of Green Bay*

1885 Forest County formed; **1887** town founded as county seat on Lake Metonca, named for railroad official F. P. Crandon; **1898** incorporated as a village; **1902** sawmill built, burned 1923; **1909** incorporated as a city; **1910** county courthouse completed; **1920s** series of forest fires destroys much of town's lumber and woodworking industries.

Danbury *Burnett County* See **Siren** (1922)

Darlington *Lafayette County* *Southern Wisconsin, 46 mi/74 km southwest of Madison*

1846 Lafayette County formed; Shullsburg becomes first county seat; **1848** town founded, originally named Hamilton; **1851** town renamed Darlington; **1857** county seat moved to Avon; **1861** county seat moved from Avon; **1877** incorporated as a city; **1905** county courthouse built.

De Pere *Brown County* *Northeastern Wisconsin, 5 mi/8 km south of Green Bay, on Fox River*

1671 St. Francis Xavier Mission established by Father Claude Allouez; **1676** Father Allouez transferred to Kaskaskia, Illinois, to replace Father Marquette who died 1675; **1687** mission burned by Fox peoples, later reopened; **1717** Fort La Baye built; mission closed; **1818** Brown County formed; Shantytown becomes first county seat; **1821** Native American-born missionary Eleazar Williams homesteads with Oneida and Stockbridge peoples from New York; **1825** county seat moved to Menomineeville; **1836** De Pere Dam built on Fox River; **1837** town founded as new county seat; **1838** county courthouse built; **1847** flash flood washes dam away, inundates town; **1849** De Pere Dam rebuilt; **1854** county seat moved to Green Bay; **1857** incorporated as a village; **1890** West De Pere merges with De Pere; **1883** incorporated as a city; **1898** St. Norbert College established; **1933** Claude Allouez Bridge built across Fox River.

Dodgeville *Iowa County* *Southwestern Wisconsin, 38 mi/61 km west of Madison*

1827 future governor Henry Dodge settles illegally on Native American land, begins lead mining; town founded; **1829** Iowa County formed; Mineral Point becomes first county seat; **1858** incorporated as a village; **1859** county courthouse built; **1861** county seat moved to Dodgeville; county courthouse built; **1889** incorporated as a city; **1900** Dodgeville Public Library founded.

Durand *Pepin County* *Western Wisconsin, 60 mi/97 km east-southeast of St. Paul, Minnesota*

1856 town founded on Chippewa River by Myles Durand Prindle; **1858** Pepin County formed; **1861** town becomes county seat; **Feb. 7, 1867** author Laura Ingalls Wilder born at town of Pepin to southwest (died 1957); **Nov. 5, 1881** county deputy sheriff killed in shootout with notorious outlaws Ed and Lon Maxwell; **1882** county courthouse built; **1887** incorporated as a village.

Eagle River *Vilas County* *Northern Wisconsin, 116 mi/187 km northwest of Green Bay*

1855 area's first logging camp established; **1856** trading post established; **1883** Chicago & Northwestern Railroad reaches site; Eagle Waters Resort established at site of logging camp; **1885** town founded; **1893** Vilas County formed, named for U.S. Sen. William Freeman Vilas; town founded becomes county seat; **1923** incorporated as a village; **1936** county courthouse built; **1937** incorporated as a city; **1980** railroad abandoned.

Eau Claire *Eau Claire and Chippewa counties* *Western Wisconsin, 78 mi/126 km east of St. Paul*

1784 French trapper Le Duc becomes first white man to live in area; **1822** logging begins on Chippewa River; **1842** Jeremiah Thomas and Stephen S. McCann become first permanent white settlers; **1856** Eau Claire County formed; town founded as county seat on Chippewa River; **1860** proposal to build dam on river meets with vigorous opposition by town of Chippewa Falls upstream, Eau Claire wins court battle; **1870** railroad reaches town; **1872** incorporated as a city; **1873** county courthouse built; **1904** Carnegie Library built, new L. E. Phillips Memorial Library opened 1976; **1912** Chippewa Valley Technical College (2-year) established; **1916** University of Wisconsin, Eau Claire Campus, established; **1943** Eau Claire Municipal Airport established; **1973** new county courthouse built.

Elkhorn *Walworth County* *Southeastern Wisconsin, 40 mi/64 km southwest of Milwaukee*

1836 Walworth County formed; **1837** town founded as county seat; **1842** town platted; **1852** incorporated as a village; **1856** Milwaukee & Mississippi Railroad reaches town; **1897** incorporated as a city; **1918** Frank Holton Musical Instrument Company moves from Chicago; **1924** Band Shell built, relocated to Courthouse Square 1963; **1952** town used as setting for "March of Time" television series; **1958** Chicago artist Cecille Johnson creates six Christmas cover illustrations for *Ford Times* magazine using town as setting; **1960** county courthouse completed.

Ellsworth *Pierce County Western Wisconsin, 33 mi/53 km east-southeast of St. Paul, Minnesota*

1853 Pierce County formed; Prescott becomes first county seat; **1861** town founded; county seat officially moved from Prescott leading to protracted struggle; **1869** Prescott yields county seat to Ellsworth; **1887** incorporated as a village; **1890** Omaha Railroad reaches town; **1905** county courthouse built; **1908** Milton Dairy Company established.

Ephraim *Door County Northeastern Wisconsin, 61 mi/98 km northeast of Green Bay, on Lake Michigan*

1853 town founded on Green Bay, Lake Michigan, by group of Moravian immigrants on land purchased 1849 by Norwegian Nils Otto Tank; **1858** Moravian Church built; **1858** Anderson's General Store built; **1919** incorporated as a village; **1926** Village Hall built; **Nov. 27, 1930** Chief Simon Onanguisse Kahquados dies (born 1851), last descendant of Potawatomi Chief Onanguisse; **1949** Ephraim-Gibraltar Airport established.

Florence *Florence County Northeastern Wisconsin, 100 mi/161 km north of Green Bay*

1879 town founded near Menominee River; **1881** Florence County formed; town becomes county seat; **1889** county courthouse built.

Fond du Lac *Fond du Lac County Eastern Wisconsin, 58 mi/93 km north-northwest of Milwaukee*

1785 Laurent Ducharme establishes trading post at south end of Lake Winnebago; **1835** Judge James Duane Doty purchases land here; site considered for state capital; **1836** Fond du Lac County formed; town founded as county seat at southern end of Lake Winnebago by Colwert and Edwin Pier; **1840s** sawmill and grist mill built; **1850s** lumber milling becomes chief industry; **1847** incorporated as a village; **1852** incorporated as a city; **1853** Milwaukee, Lake Shore & Western (Chicago & Northwestern) Railroad reaches town from East Waupun, completed to Chicago 1859; **1877** Fond du Lac Library founded; **1887** St. Paul's Roman Catholic Cathedral built; **1936** Marian College at Fond du Lac established; **1967** Moraine Park Technical College (2-year) established; **1982** county courthouse completed.

Fort Atkinson *Jefferson County Southern Wisconsin, 46 mi/74 km west of Milwaukee*

1832 Gen. Henry Atkinson stops here while pursuing Chief Black Hawk during Black Hawk War, builds stockade on Rock River, at mouth of Bark River; **1836** first settler Dwight Foster builds house near abandoned fort; town founded; **1860** incorporated as a village; **1878** incorporated as a city; **1885** *Hoard's Dairyman* publication founded by William D. Hoard, later becomes governor; **1949** National Dairy Shrine built to honor dairying industry.

Friendship *Adams County Central Wisconsin, 67 mi/108 km north-northwest of Madison*

1848 Adams County formed; **1856** town founded as county seat near Wisconsin River; **1860** Wisconsin Central Railroad built through Adams to south; **1907** incorporated as a village; **1914** county courthouse built.

Genoa *Vernon County Southwestern Wisconsin, 100 mi/161 km west-northwest of Madison*

1827 in "Red Bird War," Winnebago Chief Red Bird and men kill farmer and farmhand in retaliation of murder of two of their own, Chief Red Bird dies months later in prison, others pardoned; **Aug. 1–2, 1832** in Battle of Bad Axe, many of Chief Black Hawk's band of Sauk, including women and children, are killed while attempting to cross into Minnesota, Black Hawk captured later, ending Black Hawk War; **1848** town founded on Mississippi River by Italian fisherman and farmers; **1935** incorporated as a village; **1937** Lock & Dam No. 8 built on Mississippi River.

Grand Chute *Outagamie County See Appleton* (1908)

Green Bay *Brown County Northeastern Wisconsin, 103 mi/166 km north of Milwaukee, on Lake Michigan*

1634 Jean Nicolet lands at end of Green Bay, large arm of Lake Michigan, probably at Red Banks to east, in search of Northwest Passage to Pacific Ocean; **1669** Jesuit mission founded at La Baye by Claude Allouez; **1673** Father Marquette and Louis Joliet explore Fox River; **1684** Fort La Baye and trading post built as headquarters for Nicolas Perrot, regional commissioner; **1703** Fox Indian wars begin; **1733** new fort established; **1740** French fur trading resumes; **1761** fort occupied by British; town of Green Bay founded at fort, at mouth of Fox River; **1787** Northwest Territory becomes part of U.S.; **1808** American Fur Company established by John Jacob Astor, controls most of trade; **1816** Fort Howard built at Astor's demand; **1818** Brown County formed; Shantytown (Allouez) becomes first county seat, seat moved to Menomineeville 1825, to De Pere 1837; **1829** Daniel Whitney plats town of Navarino at north end of east Fox River bank, now downtown Green Bay; **Dec. 1833** *Green Bay Intelligencer* newspaper founded, first newspaper in Wisconsin; **1835** town of Astor platted at south end of east bank by John Jacob Astor; Astor Hotel built; **1838** Oneida Indian Reservation established to west through Oneida Treaty; **c.1838** Morgan L. Martin House built; **1850s** German, Dutch, Belgian, and Scandinavian immigrants arrive; **1854** incorporated as a city; county seat moved from De Pere; **1857** Astor Hotel burns; **Sept. 25, 1905** sports announcer Red Smith born (died 1982); **1910** county courthouse built; **1919** Green Bay Packers NFL team organized; **1925** city stadium built, later becomes Green Bay Packer Stadium; **1949** Austin Straubel International Airport established; **1957** Lambeau Field built, replacing Packer Stadium; **1968** University of Wisconsin, Green Bay Campus, established.

Green Lake   *Green Lake County   East central Wisconsin, 76 mi/122 km northwest of Milwaukee*

1844 town founded on northern shore of Green Lake; **1858** Green Lake County formed; town becomes county seat; **1871** incorporated as a village; **1899** county courthouse built; **1962** incorporated as a city.

Hayward   *Sawyer County   Northwestern Wisconsin, 60 mi/97 km southeast of Duluth, Minnesota*

1873 Lac Court Oreilles Indian Reservation established to southeast for Chippewa people; **1881** town founded on Namekagon River; **1883** Sawyer County formed, named for lumber magnate Philetus Sawyer; town platted, becomes county seat; **1885** county courthouse built; **1904** Hayward Carnegie Library founded; **1915** incorporated as a village; **1934** Camp Hayward founded by state Public Welfare Department to house transients left homeless during Depression, was last welfare camp to close 1940; **Oct. 2, 1968** St. Croix National Scenic Riverway authorized.

Hudson   *Saint Croix County   Western Wisconsin, 15 mi/24 km east of St. Paul, Minnesota*

1838 French-Canadian Louis Massey builds dugout, dwelling dug out of embankment; town founded on St. Croix River; **1840** St. Croix County formed; original county seat Brown's Warehouse, now Hastings, Minnesota; **1846** part of county granted to Minnesota, county seat moved to Stillwater (now Minnesota); **1853** present St. Croix County boundaries established; town becomes county seat; **1856** incorporated as a city; **1900** county courthouse built.

Hurley   *Iron County   Northern Wisconsin, 173 mi/ 278 km northwest of Green Bay*

1882 Milwaukee, Lake Shore & Western (later Chicago & Northwestern) Railroad reaches town; **1884** town founded on Montreal River opposite Ironwood, Michigan; **1886** iron ore boom brings thousands of miners to Gogebic Range; Carey Mine opened; **1893** Iron County formed; town becomes county seat; county courthouse completed; **c.1910** town's boom era ends; **1918** incorporated as a village; **1930** town boasts 80 taverns among its 115 businesses.

Janesville   *Rock County   Southern Wisconsin, 33 mi/53 km south-southeast of Madison*

1835 first white settlers arrive; **1836** Rock County formed; settler Henry F. Janes arrives, plats town; **1837** Janes establishes ferry on Rock River, builds tavern; town founded; **1839** Janes and family move away from growing population; **1842** Milton House built; **1844** Stone House built; **1853** incorporated as a city; **1855** mob gathers for lynching of David F. Mayberry, murdered lumberjack who had given him a ride, next day hanging tree is hacked to pieces by souvenir hunters; **Aug. 11, 1862** songwriter Carrie Jacobs Bond born (died 1946); **1892** George Parker founds Parker Pen Company; **1919** General Motors acquires Janesville Machine Company plant, begins manufacture of tractors, replaces tractor works with Fisher Body and Chevrolet plants 1922; **1953** Beloit-Janesville Symphony Orchestra founded; **1955** county courthouse built; **1968** Blackhawk Technical College (2-year) established.

Jefferson   *Jefferson County   Southern Wisconsin, 45 mi/72 km west of Milwaukee*

1836 Jefferson County formed; town founded by Easterners as county seat on Rock River, at mouth of Crawfish River; **1840s** German immigrants begin arriving in large numbers, through 1850s; **1856** chair factory established; **1866** woolen mill built; **1868** shoe factory built; **1878** incorporated as a city; **1966** county courthouse built.

Juneau   *Dodge County   Southern Wisconsin, 47 mi/ 76 km northwest of Milwaukee*

1836 Dodge County formed; **1845** town founded as county seat, originally named Victory; **1848** county courthouse built; **1865** incorporated as a village, renamed for Milwaukee founder Solomon Juneau; **1887** incorporated as a city.

Kaukauna   *Outagamie County   Eastern Wisconsin, 90 mi/145 km north-northwest of Milwaukee, on Fox River*

1793 area settled by Dominique Ducharme; brother Paul Ducharme begins trading business; **1818** property acquired by Augustin Grignon; Grignon family builds grist mill, sawmill at Grand Kakalin ("long rapids"); town founded; **1839** Grignon Mansion, completed, occupied until 1933; **1850** town platted by George W. Laws; **1862** Chicago & Northwestern Railroad reaches town; **1880s** construction of five electricity plants leads to nickname "Electric City"; **1885** incorporated as a city; village of Ledyard annexed; **1933** cold pack method of cheese making invented.

Kenosha   *Kenosha County   Southeastern Wisconsin, 32 mi/51 km south of Milwaukee, on Lake Michigan*

1835 first families arrive at new town founded at mouth of Pike Creek by Western Emigration Company of Hannibal, New York; town named Pike Creek; **1837** town renamed Southport; **1841** incorporated as a village; **1842** wharf built; **1847** Carthage College established; **1848** soldiers' monument dedicated; **1850** Kenosha County formed; town becomes county seat; incorporated as a city, renamed Kenosha, Native American term for "pike" or "pickerel"; **1855** Lake Shore Railroad completed; **1861** Kemper Hall school for girls built; Durkee Mansion built;

1866 Kenosha Lighthouse erected; **1870** Simmons Company founded, maker of bedding; **1884** harbor improvements made; **1885** shipping activity dwindles; **1886** Chicago Brass Company locates here; **1893** Chicago and Rockford Hosiery Company moves to Kenosha; **1900** Simmons Library opened; **May 31, 1908** actor Don Ameche born (died 1993); **1911** Gateway Technical College (2-year) established; **1915** Nash-Kelvinator Plant founded, maker of refrigerators; **May 6, 1915** actor Orson Welles born (died 1985); **June 24, 1919** actor Al Molinaro born; **1925** county courthouse opened; **1968** University of Wisconsin, Parkside Campus, established; **1990** Dairyland Greyhound Park race track opened.

Keshena *Menominee County* *Northeastern Wisconsin, 41 mi/66 km northwest of Green Bay*

1836 Menominee people move inland after ceding territory on Lake Michigan and Menominee River to whites; **1846** Corpus Christi Parsonage established by Father Theodore Van Den Broeck, land held until 1960; **1848** additional lands on Wolf and Wisconsin rivers to south ceded to white interests; **1854** Menominee Indian Reservation settled with assistance of Father Florimond T. Bonduel; **1856** smaller Stockbridge Indian Reservation founded to west in Shawano County by Stockbridge (Mohican) peoples from Lake Winnebago [see Stockbridge], originally from New England; Chief Reginald Oshkosh (died 1858) establishes trading post on Wolf River in southern part of Menominee Reservation; town founded; **1857** post office established; **1871** Gautier Place tavern built to north; **1892** Soo Line Railroad built through reservation; **1894** outlaw Raymond Holzse holds up stagecoach to north, empties two pistols, killing two passengers, sentenced to life; **1908** Menominee Indian Reservation officially established; **1961** Menominee County formed, boundaries coincide with reservation; town becomes county seat (has no county courthouse).

Kewaunee *Kewaunee County* *Northeastern Wisconsin, 102 mi/164 km north-northeast of Milwaukee*

1634 explorer Jean Nicolet passes site traversing Lake Michigan shoreline; **1795** trading post established on Lake Michigan by Jacques Vieau of North West Company; **1836** rumors of gold deposits brings short-lived boom; prospectors turn to timber harvesting; town founded; **1843** John Volk consolidates several sawmills to produce lumber under U.S. government contract, strips timber reserves by 1860 well beyond his holdings; **1852** Kewaunee County formed; town becomes county seat; **1871** large Peshtigo forest fire stops at town's edge; **1872** U.S. Coast Guard Station established; **1873** incorporated as a village; county courthouse built; **1883** incorporated as a city; **1891** Green Bay & Western Railroad reaches town; **1892** ferry service established to Frankfort (Elberta), Michigan, suspended 1982; **1898** business district destroyed by fire; **1906** Kewaunee Free Library founded; **1912** Kewaunee

Lighthouse built; **March 7, 1974** Kewaunee Nuclear Power Station begins production.

Kohler *Sheboygan County* *Eastern Wisconsin, 2 mi/3.2 km southwest of Sheboygan, near Lake Michigan*

1899 Kohler foundry, maker of plumbing fixtures, founded in Sheboygan 1873, moves to settlement of Riverside; **1912** incorporated as a village, renamed Kohler; **1954** bitter labor strike begins against Kohler Company, ends 1960.

La Crosse *La Crosse County* *Western Wisconsin, 105 mi/169 km northwest of Madison*

1841 Nathan Myrick of New York builds log hut and trading post on Mississippi River; town founded; **1844** logs floated down Black River from north, floated in rafts down Mississippi to St. Louis; Mormons settle in valley named Mormon Coulee; **1848** Winnebago people are removed to Minnesota by U.S. government clearing way for white settlement; **1851** La Crosse County formed; town becomes county seat; **1852** Baptist and Congregational churches organized; **1855** German settlers organize their *Turnverein*, men's organization promoting physical exercise and forum for deliberating issues; **1856** incorporated as a city; **1857** G. Heileman Brewing Company founded by Gottlieb Heileman; **1858** La Crosse & Milwaukee Railroad completed from Milwaukee; **1860s** Civil War revitalizes town's economy, serving as vital river and rail center; **Apr. 1865** mob, enraged by Lincoln assassination, moves to lynch pro-South editor Mark M. Pomeroy, mob stops at brewery to quench their thirst, fail to carry out threat; **1866** offices and shipyard of Northwestern Union Packet Company established; **1869** first Norwegian and German singing societies organized; **1870s** five railroads converge on town; **1872** St. Rose Catholic Chapel begun, completed 1906; **1876** railroad bridge built across Mississippi River; **1888** La Crosse Public Library opened; **1890** farm implement plant built, taken over by Allis Chalmers 1929; Viterbo College established; **1897** La Crosse Rubber Mills established; **1909** La Crosse State Normal School established, later becomes University of Wisconsin-La Crosse; **1911** La Crosse Continuation and Adult School established, becomes Western Wisconsin Technical College; **1939** U.S. Highway 14/61 bridge built across Mississippi River, replaces municipal bridge built 1891; **1940** Lock & Dam No. 7 completed on Mississippi River north of city; **1965** county courthouse built; **1967** I-90 Bridge built to La Crescent, Minnesota; **1997** new county courthouse and law enforcement center built; old courthouse becomes administration center.

La Pointe *Ashland County* *Northern Wisconsin, 65 mi/105 km east of Duluth, Minnesota, on Lake Superior*

1665 Jesuit mission established at west end of Madeline Island, Lake Superior, by Claude Allouez; **1693** French trading post built, abandoned 1698; **1718** Fort La Pointe reestablished by French; **1727** dock and mill built; **1733** copper mining begun by Louis Denis, Sieur de la Ronde, halted 1740 due to outbreak between Sioux and Chippewa; **1759** French withdraw from fort; **1765** English fur trader Alexander Henry arrives; **1832** Protestant mission established; **1854** treaty signed moving Chippewa to reservations in area; **1890s** first summer visitors begin arriving, called "cottagers"; **1858** La Pointe Township formed; **1958** Madeline Island State Historical Museum opened.

Ladysmith   *Rusk County   Northern Wisconsin, 103 mi/166 km northeast of St. Paul, Minnesota*

1900 E. D. Smith selects site for branch factory of Menasha Wooden Ware Company; town founded on Flambeau River, named for E. D. Smith's wife; **1901** Rusk County formed; town becomes county seat; **1902** county courthouse built; **1905** incorporated as a village; **July 25, 1906** in "Battle of Cameron Dam," John Dietz and family members, angry over flooding of farm by logging company in 1904, hold off six sheriff's men near Thornapple River to northeast in Sawyer County, Dietz remains at large until his surrender 1910; **1907** Ladysmith Carnegie Library built; **1962** Mount Senario College established, closed 2002; **Sept. 2, 2002** tornado damages large part of town.

Lake Geneva   *Walworth County   Southeastern Wisconsin, 40 mi/64 km southwest of Milwaukee*

1840 resort town founded at eastern end of Lake Geneva as stagecoach stop between Kenosha (then Southport) and Beloit; **1844** incorporated as a village; **Oct. 8, 1871** many wealthy Chicagoans, including mayor, take refuge here during and after Great Chicago Fire; **1883** incorporated as a city; **1910** Green Gables home built for William Wrigley, Jr. (1861–1932), razed 1955; **1912** Hotel Geneva-on-the-Lake built, designed by Frank Lloyd Wright.

Lancaster   *Grant County   Southwestern Wisconsin, 70 mi/113 km west-southwest of Madison*

1836 Grant County formed; **1837** town founded as county seat; **1856** incorporated as a village; **1878** incorporated as a city; **1922** city hall built; **1976** county courthouse built.

Madison   *Dane County   Southern Wisconsin, 75 mi/121 km west of Milwaukee*

1836 Wisconsin Territory organized; Dane County formed; town founded by Judge James Duane Doty on isthmus between lakes Mendota and Monona as territorial capital and county seat; Plow Inn built; first white family, Eben and Rosaline Peck, settles here, open Madison House hostelry; **Dec. 1836** territorial capital moved from Belmont; **1838** *Wisconsin Enquirer* newspaper founded; American Hotel opened; **1839** Protestant Episcopal parish organized; *Madison Express* newspaper founded; **1842** *Wisconsin Democrat* newspaper founded; **1846** incorporated as a village; State Historical Society of

Wisconsin founded; **1848** Wisconsin admitted to Union as 30th state; town becomes state capital; state capitol completed; University of Wisconsin established; Fauerbach Brewery opened; **1849** Milwaukee businessman Leonard J. Farwell arrives to make major improvements to town; Catfish, now Yahara, River linking lakes Mendota and Monona channelized; Tibbets and Gordon Brewery founded; **1851** David Atwood House built; Vilas House built by Levi B. Vilas; **1854** first railroad reaches town; St. Raphael's Catholic Church built; **June 14, 1855** Sen. Robert M. LaFollette born in rural Dane County, leader of Progressive Movement (died 1925); **1856** incorporated as a city; **1858** city hall built; Grace Episcopal Church built; Pierce House built; **1861** Fairgrounds become Camp Randall, Union training camp during Civil War; **1863** Turner Hall built, destroyed by fire Nov. 1940; former Schaare Shomain (Gates of Heaven) Synagogue built; **1865** Dudley House completed; **1867** *City of Madison* steamboat begins excursions on Lake Mendota; **1871** Park Hotel built; **1876** Madison Public Library established; **1881** Edgewood Academy for girls founded; **1885** county courthouse built; Gisholt Machine Plant founded; **1890** Fuller Opera House opened; **1894** Madison Park and Scenic Drive Association organized to improve scenic quality of city's lake margins; **1895** Lamp House built by Robert Lamp, designed by Frank Lloyd Wright; **Apr. 17, 1897** playwright, novelist Thornton Wilder born (died 1957); **Oct. 20, 1900** Oregon Sen. Wayne Morse born (died 1974); **1904** fire partially destroys state capitol; **1906** Frank Lloyd Wright's Airplane House built; **1910** U.S. Forest Products Laboratory established; Wisconsin Foundry and Machine Plant built; **1911** Madison Area Technical College (2-year) established; **1912** Memorial Arch erected to honor Civil War soldiers; **1917** new state capitol completed, started 1906; **1924** Wisconsin General Hospital built; **1926** Madison Symphony Orchestra founded; **1927** Edgewood College established; **1930** First Congregational Church dedicated; **1932** first phase of capitol annex completed; **1938** Truax Field airport established, military reservation until 1959, becomes Dane County Regional Airport; **Feb. 21, 1947** actress Tyne Daly born; **1949** governor's mansion purchased by state, built 1927; **June 14, 1958** Olympic speed skater Eric Heiden born; **1963** city-county building completed; **Dec. 10, 1967** singer Otis Redding killed in plane crash at age 26; **Sept. 29, 1969** Father James Groppi jailed for contempt, charges stemming from welfare march Milwaukee to Madison by 1,000 demonstrators; **Aug. 24, 1970** Army Mathematics Research Center damaged by blast, young scientist killed, four anti-Vietnam War activists charged Sept. 2; **1980** Madison Civic Center opened.

Manitowish Waters   *Vilas County   Northern Wisconsin, 130 mi/209 km northwest of Green Bay*

1884 town founded; canoe flotillas deliver log rafts to mills; **1927** incorporated as a village, named Spider Lake; **1934** John Dillinger's gang engage in shootout with law enforcement at hideout to southeast, one G-man killed,

Dillinger and men escape; **1940** village renamed Manitowish Waters; **1946** cranberry farming begins on Wild Rice Lake.

Manitowoc   *Manitowoc County   Eastern Wisconsin, 75 mi/121 km north of Milwaukee, on Lake Michigan*

1795 trading post established on Lake Michigan; **1835** town founded with land boom; **1836** Manitowoc County formed; town becomes county seat; **1840s** German, Norwegian, and Polish immigrants arrive; **1847** Rahr Malting Company founded; schooner *Citizen* first ship built at Manitowoc; **1848** German freethinker Carl von Brause arrives, harsh conditions lead to death of his delicate wife, local legend evolves over her apparition being seen on cold winter nights; **1850** whitefish industry flourishes on Lake Michigan; **summer 1850** cholera epidemic claims many lives, reoccurs 1854; **1851** incorporated as a village; **1860** shipbuilding becomes important industry; **1870** incorporated as a city; **1890** car ferry service begins on Lake Michigan to Ludington, Michigan; **1896** car ferry established to Frankfort (Elberta), Michigan, suspended 1973; **1902** Manitowoc Equipment Works founded, maker of heavy construction machinery; **1918** Manitowoc Lighthouse built; **1940s** 28 submarines built here during World War II; **1952** SS *Badger* begins ferry service to Ludington, Michigan, suspended 1990, reactivated 1992 by Ludington businessman, only remaining trans-lake ferry remaining on Lake Michigan, formerly eight routes in 1960s; **1968** Manitowoc Maritime Museum founded; **Apr. 5, 1972** flash fire at home for elderly in rural town of Rosecrans kills 10, injures 3.

Marinette   *Marinette County   Northeastern Wisconsin, 45 mi/72 km north-northeast of Green Bay*

1795 trading post built by Stanislaus Chappu of American Fur Company on Menominee River, near its mouth on Green Bay, Lake Michigan; **1822** trapper William Farnsworth begins competing with Chappu, marries Marinette Chevalier, daughter of Menominee chief; **1831** dam and sawmill built by Farnsworth and partner Charles R. Brush; **1858** town platted; timber man Isaac Stephenson arrives, promotes Menominee Timber Boon, later donates library to city; **1870** Merryman Mansion built; **1879** Marinette County formed; town founded as county seat; **1887** incorporated as a city; **1917** last log drive made on Menominee River; **1929** Interstate Bridge built across Menominee River from Menominee, Michigan, replaces Middle Bridge built 1867; **1931** last sawmill closed; **1942** county courthouse built.

Marshfield   *Wood and Marathon counties   Central Wisconsin, 110 mi/177 km west of Green Bay*

1868 Louis and Frank Rivers arrive, establish tavern to serve railroad construction workers; town founded; **1870s** sawmills established; **1872** Wisconsin Central Railroad reaches site; **1883** incorporated as a city; **1887** fire caused by spark from locomotive destroys most of town; **c.1890** town rebuilt; economy turns to dairying and cheese making; **1901** Marshfield Public Library opened.

Mauston   *Juneau County   Central Wisconsin, 60 mi/97 km northwest of Madison*

1840 Gen. M. M. Maugh establishes lumber mill; town founded, originally spelled Maughston; **1856** Juneau County formed; town becomes county seat; **1883** incorporated as a city; **1938** county courthouse built.

Medford   *Taylor County   Northern Wisconsin, 125 mi/201 km west-northwest of Green Bay*

1874 town founded; **1875** Taylor County formed; town becomes county seat; county courthouse built at site determined by Milwaukee Central Railroad; **1889** incorporated as a city; **1903** Francis L. Simek Library founded, new library opened 1998; **1914** county courthouse built; **Jan. 3, 1918** popular psychic Jeane Dixon born (died 1997).

Menasha   *Winnebago, Calumet counties   Eastern Wisconsin, 86 mi/138 km north-northwest of Milwaukee*

1836 sawmill built for Menominee peoples by U.S. government; Native Americans move away same year; **1840** town founded on Fox River, at its outflow from Lake Winnebago; **1849** locks and dam built on Fox River; wooden pail factory built; **1857** town becomes known for its hardwood products; **1874** incorporated as a city; **1896** Menasha Public Library founded, new building opened 1969; **1933** University of Wisconsin, Fox Valley Campus (2-year), established.

Menomonie   *Dunn County   Western Wisconsin, 57 mi/92 km east of St. Paul, Minnesota*

1822 lumber mill built by Harding Perkins; **1854** Dunn County formed; Dunnville becomes first county seat; **1859** town founded on Red Cedar River; **1861** county seat moved to Menomonie after courthouse in Dunnville burns 1838 and several county seat moves; **1870s** town becomes major timber processing center; **1882** incorporated as a city; **1890s** ornate Opera House built; **1891** Stout Institute established, later becomes University of Wisconsin-Stout Campus; **1959** county courthouse built; **1986** Menomonie Public Library opened.

Merrill   *Lincoln County   Northern Wisconsin, 96 mi/155 km northwest of Green Bay*

1843 trading post built to south; **1847** Andrew Warren, Jr. becomes first settler, builds sawmill, burned 1899; town founded, originally named Jenny Bull Falls; **1874** Lincoln County formed; town becomes county seat; Wisconsin Valley Railroad reaches town; **1881** Chicago, Milwaukee, St. Paul & Pacific Railroad reaches town; town renamed for railroad general manager S. S. Merrill; **1883** incorporated as a city; **1889** area boasts 20 shingle mills; **1890s**

town prospers as lumber milling center; **1902** county courthouse built.

Middleton   *Dane County   Southern Wisconsin, suburb 6 mi/9.7 km west of Madison, on Lake Mendota*

1832 trading post established on northwestern shore of Lake Mendota by Michael St. Cyr; **1847** Stamm House built; **1852** German Lutheran Church established, built 1876; **1856** railroad reaches town; **1858** Palmer House built; **1860s** town founded as lumber milling center on western end of Lake Mendota; **Jan. 19, 1900** fire destroys business district; **1905** incorporated as a village; **1963** incorporated as a city.

Milwaukee   *Milwaukee County   Southeastern Wisconsin, 83 mi/134 km north of Chicago, on Lake Michigan*

1673 Father Jacques Marquette visits site; **1795** North West Company establishes fur trading post; **1818** town founded at mouth of Milwaukee River by French fur trader Solomon Juneau, originally named Juneautown; **1836** Milwaukee County formed; town becomes county seat; *Advertiser* newspaper founded; **1838** incorporated as a village, formed by merger of several settlements including rival Kilbourntown, renamed Milwaukee; **1844** first German-language newspaper *Das Wiskonsin Banner* founded; brewery founded by Johann Braun, bought by Valentine Blatz after Braun's death 1851, Blatz Brewery sold to Miller Brewing 1961; brewery founded by Jacob Best, half interest purchased by Frederick Pabst leading to establishment of Pabst Brewing Company in 1889; Plankinton Packing Plant established by John Plankinton; **1846** incorporated as a city; "Bridge War" erupts between two wards, former rival settlements, over payment for Milwaukee River bridges, settled 1845 when state orders equal ward financing of bridges; Charles Best founds brewery, reorganized as Miller Brewery by Fred Miller; **1848** German immigrants begin arriving in large numbers; **1849** August Krug establishes Krug Brewery, reorganized 1874 as Joseph Schlitz Brewery, sold to Stroh Brewing 1982; first cholera epidemic strikes city; **1850s** city becomes important shipbuilding center; **1851** state's first railroad completed to Waukesha; **1853** St. John's Cathedral completed, destroyed by fire 1935, rebuilt; **1854** escaped slave Joshua Glover arrested, freed by angry mob, transported to Canada; abolitionist editor Sherman Booth arrested under Fugitive Slave Act; **1855** Miller Brewing Company founded by Frederick J. Miller; **1857** St. Aloysius Academy founded, forerunner of Marquette University; **Sept. 1859** Abraham Lincoln delivers speech at Wisconsin State Fair; **1867** Joseph L. Leinenkugel Brewing Company founded; Knights of St. Crispin shoe workers union organized; Wisconsin Soldiers' Home opened; **1870** old county courthouse built in Cathedral Square, demolished 1939; **1876** car ferry service begins to Ludington, Michigan, suspended 1980, resumed 1984, suspended again 1990; **1881** Marquette University established; Victor L. Berger arrives, leads city into his

Social Democratic political movement during 1890s as mayor and U.S. Congressman, convicted with four others for espionage 1919, freed 1922; *Milwaukee Journal* newspaper founded; Milwaukee County Zoo founded; **Jan. 10, 1883** fire destroys Newhall Hotel, 71 killed; **1886** state troops fire on strikers at North Chicago Rolling Mills, Bay View, five killed, four injured; **1887** Alverno College established; **1888** Layton Art Gallery opened; **1891** Wisconsin Club founded, originally the Deutscher Club; **1892** Wisconsin State Fair permanently located at suburban West Allis, founded 1851 at Janesville, made several moves; **Oct. 28, 1892** fire destroys 16 city blocks between Milwaukee River and Lake Michigan; **1895** city hall completed; Pabst Theater built; Milwaukee-Downer College established; **1898** Milwaukee Public Library built; St. Josaphat's Basilica (Roman Catholic) built; **1899** Milwaukee Conservatory of Music founded; **Nov. 11, 1899** actor Pat O'Brien born (died 1983); **Apr. 5, 1900** actor Spencer Tracy born (died 1967); **1903** Milwaukee School of Engineering established; car ferry service begins on Lake Michigan from Muskegon, Michigan, suspended 1982; **Feb. 16, 1904** diplomat George Frost Kennan born; **1907** Harley-Davidson Motor Company established; **March 13, 1908** philanthropist Walter H. Annenberg born; **1909** Milwaukee Auditorium built; **1910** Milwaukee-Downer Congregational Seminary founded; **1911** St. Benedict the Moor Mission founded in inner city; **Oct. 14, 1912** former Pres. Theodore Roosevelt shot and wounded by "demented man"; **1913** Mount Mary College established; **May 16, 1913** jazz musician Woody Herman born (died 1987); **May 3, 1915** sculptor Richard Lippold born (died 2002); **June 15, 1916** economist Herbert Simon born, Nobel Prize 1978 (died 2001); **1918** Milwaukee Art Institute founded; **1919** Prohibition era ruins city's brewing industry; **May 16, 1919** pianist Liberace (Wladziu Valentino Liberace) born at West Allis to southwest (died 1987); **1925** Sewage Disposal Plant built on Jones Island, once popular fishermen's haunt; **1926** Milwaukee Vocational School built; **Apr. 22, 1926** actress Charlotte Rae born; **1927** General Mitchell Airport founded, became International Airport 1986; **Oct. 22, 1929** car ferry *City of Milwaukee* sinks 25 mi/40 km to east on Lake Michigan, 53 killed; **Jan. 12, 1930** singer Glenn Yarborough born; **1931** county courthouse built; **June 11, 1933** comic actor Gene Wilder born; **Jan. 26, 1935** TV personality Bob Uecker born; **1936** South Shore Yacht Club built; **1937** Cardinal Stritch University established; **July 21, 1938** Cong. Les Aspin born (died 1995); **March 12, 1940** singer Al Jarreau born; **Oct. 31, 1948** actress Deirdre Hall born; **1953** County Stadium completed, home of new Braves baseball team, formerly Boston Braves; **1956** University of Wisconsin, Milwaukee Campus, established; **1957** Milwaukee Art Museum formed by merger of Art Institute and Layton Gallery; **1959** Milwaukee Symphony Orchestra established; **1965** Milwaukee Braves move to Atlanta; **1970** Milwaukee Brewers baseball team established; Milwaukee Ballet company inaugurated; **1971** 42-story Firstar Bank Center built, becomes US Bank Center 2002; **Sept. 6, 1985** Midwest Express DC-9 airliner crashes after takeoff, all 31 killed; **1986** Henry Maier

Festival Grounds established on Lake Michigan; **1989** 37-story 100 East Wisconsin Street Building completed; **Aug. 1991** Jeffrey Dahmer arrested for cannibalistic slayings of 15 boys since 1978, sentenced to 936 years in prison, murdered in prison Nov. 28, 1994; **1998** Midwest Exposition Center opened; **2001** Miller Park Stadium opened, home of Milwaukee Brewers baseball team.

Mineral Point *Iowa County* *Southwestern Wisconsin, 42 mi/68 km west-southwest of Madison*

1827 lead mining begun to north by future first Governor Henry Dodge; **1828** Nat Morris begins lead mining at town site; town founded, settled by Southern prospectors; **1829** Iowa County formed; **1830** town becomes county seat; **1832** Cornish immigrants arrive to work the mines; **1836** Mineral Point Bank chartered; Walker Hotel built; **1837** incorporated as a village; **1838** *Miner's Free Press* newspaper founded; **1844** second county courthouse built; **1845** Trinity Methodist Church built, rebuilt 1871; **1857** incorporated as a city; Mineral Point Railroad built; **1861** county seat moved to Dodgeville; **1868** Gundry House built; **1882** Mineral Point Zinc Company established, closed 1979.

Monroe *Green County* *Southern Wisconsin, 35 mi/56 km south-southwest of Madison*

1835 first settlers arrive; **1836** Green County formed; **1839** town founded as county seat; **1853** first county fair held; **1857** Milwaukee & Mississippi Railroad built through town; **1859** incorporated as a village; **1870s** area's cheese and dairying industries grow rapidly; **1882** incorporated as a city; **1891** county courthouse built; **1914** first annual Cheese Day observed; **1926** Swiss Colony mail order cheese company established.

Montello *Marquette County* *Central Wisconsin, 88 mi/142 km northwest of Milwaukee*

1836 Marquette County formed; village of Marquette becomes first county seat; **1849** town founded as county seat on Fox River, at east end of Buffalo Lake; **1850** post office established; **1859** county seat moved to Montello; **1880** Montello Granite Company quarry opened; **1938** incorporated as a village; **1968** county courthouse built.

Neenah *Winnebago County* *Eastern Wisconsin, 85 mi/137 km north-northwest of Milwaukee*

1835 town founded on Lake Winnebago at outflow of Fox River, twin town to Menasha; **1849** locks and dam built on Fox River; sawmill and grist mill built; **1856** incorporated as a village; **1866** paper mill built; **1872** Kimberly-Clark Paper Company established; **1873** incorporated as a city; **1945** Neenah Lighthouse built, donated by J. C. Kimberly.

Neillsville *Clark County* *Central Wisconsin, 130 mi/209 km west of Green Bay*

1844 town founded as lumber milling center on Black River; **1853** Clark County formed; **1855** town platted, becomes county seat, named for James O'Neill; **1878** Winnebago Indian Mission School founded by Rev. Jacob Hauser; **1882** incorporated as a city; **1897** old jail built; **1965** third county courthouse built.

New Glarus *Green County* *Southern Wisconsin, 22 mi/35 km southwest of Madison*

1845 town founded by Swiss immigrants Judge Nicholas Duerst and blacksmith Fridolin Streiff from Glarus Canton, followed by 193 fellow immigrants from same canton, of which 108 survive journey and ordeal of finding town site; **1858** cheese factory opened by Nickolaus Gerber; **1860s** farmers turn to dairying, discover widespread market for their Swiss cheese; **1870s** cheese and dairying industries spread rapidly through Green County, other areas; **1901** incorporated as a village; **1938** Swiss Historical Village established; **1970** Hall of History museum opened.

Oconto *Oconto County* *Northeastern Wisconsin, 27 mi/43 km north of Green Bay, on Lake Michigan*

Dec. 1669 French Mission of St. Francis Xavier established on Green Bay, Lake Michigan, at mouth of Oconto River by Father Claude Allouez; **1685** Nicolas Perrot establishes fortified trading posts here and other parts of Wisconsin; **c.1825** trading post established by Astor Fur Company; **c.1850** first white settlers arrive; **1851** Oconto County formed; **1852** town founded as county seat and lumber milling center; **1859** incorporated as a village; **1869** incorporated as a city; **1886** Christian Scientist meeting house built; **1891** second county courthouse built.

Oshkosh *Winnebago County* *Eastern Wisconsin, 75 mi/121 km north-northwest of Milwaukee*

1670 Father Claude Allouez performs mass to Native Americans on western shore of Lake Winnebago; **1818** area at entrance to Fox River settled by whites; **1833** George Johnson establishes trading post on south bank Fox River; town of Algoma founded; ferry established by James Knaggs; **1837** town of Athens founded on north bank Fox River; **1839** sawmill built in Algoma by Conrad Coon; **1840** Winnebago County formed; post office established at Athens, renamed Oshkosh for Menominee chief; **1844** steamship *Manchester* begins passenger service on Lake Winnebago and Fox River; **1847** incorporated as a village, becomes county seat; **1850** several new industries established including brewery, foundry, tannery; **1853** incorporated as a city; Algoma annexed; **1859** first railroad arrives; **1870** one of first yacht clubs in the West established; **1870s** lumber milling becomes dominant; **1871** State Normal School established, becomes University of Wisconsin, Oshkosh Campus; **1872** Northern Hospital for the Insane established, becomes

Winnebago Mental Health Institute; **1875** worst of several fires destroys downtown, leads to use of brick and stone materials; **1883** Grand Opera House opened; **1890s** immigrants from Germany and Eastern Europe swell population; **1895** Oshkosh B'Gosh Overalls Company established; **1898** woodworkers strike to abolish woman and child labor; **1909** Rockwell Lighthouse built; **1911** final spring lumber drive brought down Fox River; **1914** Carl Schurz Monument dedicated to German American liberal figure; **1924** Oshkosh Public Museum founded; **1927** Menominee Chief Oshkosh reburied at lakefront Menominee Park; **1938** county courthouse completed; **1947** Wittman Regional Airport established; **1970** first Experimental Aircraft Association Fly-In Convention held, museum opened 1983.

Pepin   *Pepin County*   See **Durand (1867)**

Peshtigo   *Marinette County*   *Northeastern Wisconsin, 40 mi/64 km north of Green Bay, near Lake Michigan*

1852 town founded on Peshtigo River, named Clarksville; **1858** town renamed Peshtigo; **1865** incorporated as a village; **Oct. 8, 1871** forest fire destroys town and surrounding villages killing 1,200, 600 in Peshtigo, exceeds death toll of Great Chicago Fire, occurred same day; **1903** incorporated as a city; **1951** monument to Great Fire dedicated.

Phillips   *Price County*   *Northern Wisconsin, 145 mi/233 km northwest of Green Bay*

1872 logging activities begin; **1874** town founded, named for president of Wisconsin Railroad; **1876** town platted; incorporated as a village; **1879** Price County formed; town becomes county seat; **1880** county courthouse built; **1891** incorporated as a city; **1894** fire destroys most of town, leaving only 13 buildings standing, 13 killed; **1895** town rebuilt; **1983** first annual Czechoslovakian Festival held.

Platteville   *Grant County*   *Southwestern Wisconsin, 60 mi/97 km west-southwest of Madison*

1827 town founded by Maj. John H. Rountree; **1854** Rountree House built on town's outskirts by Rev. Samuel Mitchell, later lived in by Major Rountree; **1866** Platteville State Teachers College established, first normal school in state, becomes University of Wisconsin, Platteville Campus; **1876** incorporated as a city; **1907** Wisconsin Institute of Technology founded; **Feb. 3, 1925** actor John Fiedler born.

Port Washington   *Ozaukee County*   *Eastern Wisconsin, 25 mi/40 km north of Milwaukee, on Lake Michigan*

1835 town founded by Gen. Worcester Harrison, originally named Washington; **1848** Old Pebble House built by Edward Dodge using pebbles collected on Michigan lakeshore by his wife; **1849** town renamed Ozaukee; first

Port Washington Lighthouse built, replaced 1860, again 1934; **1853** Ozaukee County formed; town becomes county seat; **1856** steamship *Niagara* burns within sight of harbor, over 60 killed, including John B. Macy, Chicago railroad promoter, jumps from ship with gold-laden money belt, capsizes lifeboat, drowning himself and occupants; **1854** Friedens Evangelical Church founded; **Nov. 10, 1862** protestors, many newly arrived immigrants, riot against military conscription for Civil War effort; **1873** Milwaukee, Lakeshore & Western Railroad reaches town; **1879** town renamed Port Washington; **1881** Port Washington Malt Company established; **1882** incorporated as a city; **1899** Niederkorn Public Library founded, built 1908; **1902** county courthouse built; **1982** city marina completed.

Portage   *Columbia County*   *Central Wisconsin, 32 mi/51 km north of Madison, on Wisconsin River*

1828 Fort Winnebago built on Fox River; **1832** Indian Agency House built at fort; **1836** town founded at portage between Wisconsin and Fox rivers (Mississippi and Great Lakes watersheds); **1846** Columbia County formed; town becomes county seat; **1851** Portage Canal nearly completed between the two rivers, financial difficulties prevent total completion until 1872, **1854** incorporated as a city; **Nov. 14, 1861** historian Frederick Jackson Turner born (died 1932); **1903** levee built along Wisconsin River to prevent flooding; **1962** county courthouse built.

Prairie du Chien   *Crawford County*   *Southwestern Wisconsin, 90 mi/145 km west of Madison*

1686 Fort St. Nicolas built on Mississippi River by Nicolas Perrot; **1781** French settlers arrive; town founded; **1814** Fort Shelby built by Americans; **1815** Brisbois House built by Michel Brisbois; **1816** Fort Crawford built by Brevet Brig. Gen. Thomas A. Smith, abandoned 1856; **1817** John Jacob Astor's fur company begins doing business here; **1818** Crawford County formed; **1829** Dr. William Beaumont investigates human digestive processes on young patient who survived gunshot through stomach, work started 1822 at Mackinac Island, Michigan; **1835** trading post built by Joseph Rolette, rents building to American Fur Company 1842; **1836** ferry established to McGregor, Iowa, by Alexander McGregor; **1843** Villa Louis mansion built by Hercules L. Dousman, agent for John Jacob Astor; **1857** railroad reaches town; **1864** Dousman House hotel built; Diamond Jo Steamship Line Warehouse built; **1865** Crawford Military Hospital built; **1867** county courthouse built; **Oct. 19, 1871** physiologist Walter Bradford Cannon born (died 1945); **1872** incorporated as a city; **1874** railroad pontoon bridge built to Marquette, Iowa, dismantled 1961; **1895** freshwater pearl button industry becomes important; **1932** highway bridge built to Marquette, Iowa, replaced 1974 by Marquette-Joliet Bridge; **1938** Lock & Dam No. 9 completed to north on Mississippi River.

WISCONSIN

Racine   *Racine County*   *Southeastern Wisconsin, 22 mi/35 km south of Milwaukee, on Lake Michigan*

1673 Louis Joliet visits town site; **1834** town founded by Capt. Gilbert Knapp, named Port Gilbert; **1836** Racine County formed; town becomes county seat; Horlick Mill built by William See; **1841** incorporated as a village, renamed Racine; **1842** Knight House built; **1844** J. I. Case begins manufacture of threshing machines, makes Pierce-Racine automobiles 1899; harbor improvements built eliminating hazardous Racine Reef; **1846** Herrick House built; **1848** incorporated as a city; Hunt House built; **1851** First Presbyterian Church built; **1853** Taylor House built; **1855** Racine & Mississippi Railroad reaches city; **1860** Bohemian newspaper *Slovan Amerikansky* founded; **1877** Horlick Malted Milk Company founded by William and James Horlick; **1880** Wind Point Lighthouse built to north; **March 18, 1889** Catholic Bishop Francis Joseph Hass born (died 1953); **Aug. 31, 1897** actor Fredric March born (died 1975); **1906** Sporer House built, designed by Frank Lloyd Wright; **June 3, 1913** actress Ellen Corby born (died 1999); **1923** Racine Zoo established; **1925** Nash Motors Company takes over Mitchell Company factory, wagon maker turned automobile manufacturer; **1931** county courthouse built; **1939** Research Tower office building completed at S. C. Johnson and Son Company, designed by Frank Lloyd Wright; **1941** Horlick-Racine Airport established, renamed John H. Batten International Airport 1989; **1967** Golden Rondelle Theatre opened.

Rhinelander   *Oneida County*   *Northern Wisconsin, 105 mi/169 km northwest of Green Bay*

1857 logging operations begin; town founded, named Pelican Rapids; **1881** town renamed for Shore Line Railroad president Frederic W. Rhinelander; **1882** town platted; Milwaukee, Lake Shore & Western Railroad reaches town; **1885** Oneida County formed; town becomes county seat; **1886** Soo Line Railroad reaches town; **1894** incorporated as a city; **1896** piglet-sized spiny creature called a hodag "discovered" by Gene Shepard, fake animal displayed at county fairs before believing audiences, becomes part of local folklore; **1903** Rhinelander Paper Company established; **Oct. 4, 1905** fire destroys city's north side; **1911** county courthouse built; **1916** timber reserves depleted; town turns to pulp milling; **Apr. 1923** final timber drive conducted on Pelican River; **1932** Logging Museum founded; **1947** Rhinelander-Oneida County Airport established; **1968** Nicolet Area Technical College (2-year) established.

Rice Lake   *Barron County*   *Northwestern Wisconsin, 75 mi/121 km northeast of St. Paul, Minnesota*

1854 Sioux people sign treaty relinquishing last of their Wisconsin lands to white settlement; **1872** town founded on small Rice Lake, on Red Cedar River; **1887** incorporated as a city; **1941** Wisconsin Indianhead Technical College, Rice Lake Campus (2-year), established.

Richland Center   *Richland County*   *Southwestern Wisconsin, 55 mi/89 km west-northwest of Madison*

1842 Richland County formed; **1849** settled by immigrants from Norway and British Isles; town founded as county seat; **1851** town platted; **1866** incorporated as a village; **June 8, 1867** architect Frank Lloyd Wright born (died 1959); **1873** Park Hotel built; **1882** several housewives organize suffrage movement in secret, expand effort statewide; **1887** incorporated as a city; town suffragettes fail to have women's rights clause written into city charter; **1889** county courthouse built; **1918** Simon Brothers' Grocery Warehouse built, designed by Frank Lloyd Wright.

Ripon   *Fond du Lac County*   *Eastern Wisconsin, 72 mi/116 km northwest of Milwaukee*

1844 town founded by followers of Socialist Francois Fourier; town named Ceresco for Ceres, Roman goddess of agriculture; Warren Chase organizes stock company called Wisconsin Phalanx; **1850** Phalanx disbanded; new town of Ripon founded; **1853** incorporated as a village; **Feb. 28, 1854** U.S. Republican Party established by group of Whigs, Anti-Nebraska Democrats, and Free Soilers; **1858** incorporated as a city; **Jan. 9, 1859** feminist leader Carrie Chapman Catt born (died 1947); **1860** antislavery demonstration staged during "Booth's War" after townspeople aid escape of abolitionist Sherman M. Booth; **1868** fire destroys block of business district, second block destroyed 1869.

River Falls   *Pierce County*   *Western Wisconsin, 23 mi/37 km east-southeast of St. Paul, Minnesota*

1848 Joel Foster of Connecticut becomes first settler in Kinnikinnick Valley; town founded, named Greenwood, soon renamed Kinnikinnick; **1858** town renamed River Falls; **1870** Hinckley's Military Academy founded; **1874** University of Wisconsin, River Falls Campus, established; **1885** incorporated as a city; **1876** fire destroys business district; **1894** flooding Kinnikinnick River inundates town; **1923** River Falls Public Library founded, new facility opened 1997.

Saint Nazianz   *Manitowoc County*   *Eastern Wisconsin, 68 mi/109 km north of Milwaukee*

1854 town founded by 113 communist Christian followers from Baden, Germany, led by Father Ambrose Oschwald; **1873** Father Ambrose dies; control of community taken over by Roman Catholic Church, followed by lawsuits from society members; **1896** community stops accepting new members, declines.

Shawano   *Shawano County*   *Northeastern Wisconsin, 35 mi/56 km northwest of Green Bay*

1840 town founded on Wolf River; **1843** Samuel Farnsworth builds first sawmill; **1853** Shawano County formed; town becomes county seat; **1874** incorporated as a city; **1914** Shawano (Carnegie) Library built, replaced 1960; **1958** county courthouse built.

760

Sheboygan *Sheboygan County* *Eastern Wisconsin, 50 mi/80 km north of Milwaukee, on Lake Michigan*

1835 sawmill built at falls of Sheboygan River to west; **1836** Sheboygan County formed; **1840s** German immigrants begin farming in area; **1844** town founded on Lake Michigan, at mouth of Sheboygan River, becomes county seat; **1845** pier improvements made; **1846** incorporated as a village; **1847** steamship *Phoenix* burns offshore just short of delivering Dutch immigrants, 163 killed, 46 rescued; **1853** incorporated as a city; J. J. Vollrath begins manufacture of engines and farm implements; **1856** German Bank founded; **1860** Sheboygan & Mississippi Railroad reaches town; city boasts 20 flour mills; Concordia Society founded as one of several singing societies; **1862** Lakeland College established; **1864** first cheese factory built; **1873** Kohler foundry established by Walter J. Kohler, moved to suburb of Kohler 1899; **1874** J. J. Vollrath introduces enamelware, originated in Germany; **1875** city boasts 45 cheese factories; **1880s** German immigration peaks; **1897** Mead Public Library founded; **1915** Sheboygan Lighthouse erected; **June 9, 1931** comedian Jackie Mason born; **1933** county courthouse built; **Oct. 11, 2002** fiery pileup of 38 vehicles on Interstate 43 near Cedar Grove to south caused by Lake Michigan fog, 10 killed, 34 injured.

Shell Lake *Washburn County* *Northwestern Wisconsin, 72 mi/116 km south of Duluth, Minnesota*

1880 town founded; **1883** Washburn County formed; town becomes county seat; **1908** incorporated as a village; **1961** incorporated as a city; **1989** county courthouse built.

Siren *Burnett County* *Northwestern Wisconsin, 65 mi/105 km north-northeast of St. Paul, Minnesota*

1856 Burnett County formed; Grantsburg becomes first county seat; **1870** town founded, Swedish term for "lilac"; **1895** post office established; Soo Line Railroad reaches town; **Jan. 24, 1922** lowest temperature ever recorded in Wisconsin reached at Danbury to north, −54°F/−48°C; **1948** incorporated as a village; **1982** county seat moved to Siren; **1984** county government center completed; **June 18, 2001** tornado kills 3, injures 16, damages 200 homes.

Sparta *Monroe County* *Western Wisconsin, 93 mi/ 150 km northwest of Madison*

1850 Frank Petit becomes first settler; town founded on La Crosse River; **1852** logging begins; **1854** Monroe County formed; town becomes county seat; **1857** incorporated as a village; **1865** man creates "oil well" with buried oil drums, convinces stockholders to part with $50,000, swindler disappears; **1883** incorporated as a city; **1885** State Public School founded; **1896** county courthouse built; **1935** Snow and Ice Cave opened to public to southwest.

Spring Green *Sauk County* *Southern Wisconsin, 35 mi/56 km west of Madison, on Wisconsin River*

1854 town founded as agricultural shipping point; post office established; **1869** incorporated as a village; **1911** architect Frank Lloyd Wright acquires grandfather Richard Lloyd-Jones' property to south, designs and builds Taliesin house, damaged by fire 1914; **1915** Taliesin II built, destroyed by fire 1924; **1925** Taliesin III built; **1933** Taliesin Fellowship established to serve apprentice architects under tutorship of Frank Lloyd Wright.

Stevens Point *Portage County* *Central Wisconsin, 80 mi/129 km west of Green Bay*

1836 Portage County formed; **1839** George Stevens of St. Louis establishes supply depot to supplement his sawmills at Wausau; town founded; **1844** Plover becomes county seat; **1847** town platted; public square created from land donation by Mathias "Big Mitch" Mitchell; **1857** first Polish immigrants arrive; **1858** incorporated as a city; **1869** county seat moved to Stevens Point; **1894** University of Wisconsin, Stevens Point Campus, established; **1942** Stevens Point Municipal Airport established; **1959** third county courthouse completed.

Stoughton *Dane County* *Southern Wisconsin, 14 mi/23 km southeast of Madison*

1838 land purchased by Daniel Webster; **1847** Luke Stoughton acquires land from Webster; settlers arrive from New England; town founded; **1853** railroad reaches town; **1865** T. G. Mandt Wagon Factory established, closes 1889; **1882** incorporated as a city; **Feb. 6, 1892** physician William Perry Murphy born, shared Nobel Prize 1934 (died 1987); **1896** Mandt Vehicle Company established, becomes Moline Plow Company 1902; **1901** city auditorium opened, later renamed Stoughton Opera House; **1926** Highway Trailer Company established in former plow factory.

Sturgeon Bay *Door County* *Northeastern Wisconsin, 38 mi/61 km northeast of Green Bay*

1673 Father Marquette becomes first white man to stop here; **Nov. 1680** four survivors of Native American mutiny at Fort Crevecoeur, Illinois River, reach Sturgeon Bay, saved by Potawatomi people; **1831** Potawatomi peoples of Door Peninsula evicted even though eviction treaty was signed with Menominees only; **1835** town settled as lumbering center on Sturgeon Bay, arm of Lake Michigan; **1851** Door County formed; **1857** county seat moved from Baileys Harbor; **Oct. 8, 1871** forest fire creates tornado-like whirlwind killing 61 of 77 residents of Williamsonville to west; **1874** incorporated as a village; **1878** canal built across mid-section of Door Peninsula; **1882** Pier Head Lighthouse erected at canal entrance; **1883** incorporated as a city; **1893** first cherry orchard plantings, sheltered from harsh winters by lake effect; **1975** Miller Art Museum established; **1991** county courthouse completed.

Sun Prairie *Dane County* *Southern Wisconsin, 10 mi/16 km northeast of Madison*

1837 first settler Charles H. Bird arrives, happy to see sunshine after traveling for days in rain, names site Sun Prairie; **1839** town founded by Bird; **1863** Sacred Heart Catholic Church built; **1868** incorporated as a village; **Nov. 15, 1885** painter Georgia O'Keeffe born (died 1986); **1901** Sun Prairie Public Library founded; **1958** incorporated as a city.

Superior *Douglas County* *Northwestern Wisconsin, 4 mi/6.4 km southeast of Duluth, Minnesota*

1662 two Frenchmen, Pierre Esprit, Sieur Radisson, and Medard Chouart, Sieur de Groseilliers, camp at town site; **1667** Father Allouez establishes mission; **1679** trading post established by Daniel Greysolon, Sieur du Lhut; **1787** fur trading post founded by North West Fur Company, replaced 1816 by John Jacob Astor's fur trading company; **1853** town founded on St. Louis Bay, Lake Superior; first settlers arrive from Kentucky; **1854** Douglas County formed; town becomes county seat; **1858** incorporated as a village; **1862** stockades built during Indian scare; **Dec. 1881** Northern Pacific Railroad reaches Superior; **1882** Northern Pacific Ore Docks built; **1885** town of West Superior platted; **1886** Great Northern Elevator built; **1889** incorporated as a city; West Superior annexed; West Superior Iron and Steel established, closed 1910; **1892** Great Northern Ore Docks built; **1893** University of Wisconsin, Superior Campus, established; **1926** Arrowhead Bridge built across St. Louis Bay to Duluth; **1920** county courthouse completed; **Dec. 1927** Cathedral of Christ the King (Catholic) opened; **1936** half of Douglas County burned in forest fire; **1949** adjoining municipality Village of Superior incorporated; **1957** Blatnik Bridge (I-535) built across harbor.

Tomah *Monroe County* *Central Wisconsin, 85 mi/137 km northwest of Madison*

1855 town founded, named for Menominee Chief Tomau; **1883** incorporated as a city; **1905** Camp McCoy Military Reservation established to west, redesignated Fort McCoy 1974; **1927** Camp Douglas National Guard Base established to southeast, renamed Volk Field 1957 for pilot Jerome A. Volk killed in Korean War; **1937** Central Wisconsin Farms established by U.S. Resettlement Administration for betterment of 72 "worthy" farm families.

Two Rivers *Manitowoc County* *Eastern Wisconsin, 80 mi/129 km north-northeast of Milwaukee*

1836 Lake Michigan commercial whitefish industry begins here; town founded; sawmill built; **1850** shipbuilding begins, flourishes through 1875; **1856** chair factory established; **1857** pail factory established; **1858** incorporated as a village; **June 12, 1859** Montana Sen. Thomas Walsh born (died 1933); **1878** incorporated as a city; **1880** Hamilton Manufacturing Company founded by James E. Hamilton, makes wooden type for printing; **1881** ice

cream sundae invented here; **1891** Three Rivers Public Library opened; **1895** German immigrant Joseph Koenig begins making aluminum products, merges 1909 with competitor to become Aluminum Goods Manufacturing Company; **Nov. 2, 1970** Manitowoc Nuclear Power Plant begins production; **1973** Lighthouse Inn (Carlton on the Lake) established.

Viroqua *Vernon County* *Southwestern Wisconsin, 83 mi/134 km west-northwest of Madison*

1850 town platted by Samuel McMichael; first settlers arrive; **1851** Bad Axe County formed; town founded as county seat; **1862** county renamed Vernon County, original name had been scaring away settlers; **1881** county courthouse; **1885** incorporated as a city; **1905** Carnegie Library built.

Voree *Walworth County* *Southeastern Wisconsin, 30 mi/48 km south-southwest of Milwaukee*

1844 Mormons led by James Jesse Strang establish colony called Garden of Peace following their expulsion from Nauvoo, Illinois; **1847** Strang leads Mormons to Beaver Island, Lake Michigan, founds new colony; **1849** Voree colony abandoned; **June 1856** Strang slain by Michigan mainlanders, is buried here.

Washburn *Bayfield County* *Northern Wisconsin, 60 mi/97 km east of Duluth, Minnesota, on Lake Superior*

1845 Bayfield County formed; **1884** Chicago, St. Paul, Minnesota & Omaha Railroad purchases town site; **c.1888** coal loading docks built; **1892** town founded, named by railroad for Gov. Cadwallader C. Washburn; **1894** county seat moved from Bayfield; county courthouse built; **1904** incorporated as a village.

Washington *Door County* *Northeastern Wisconsin, 70 mi/113 km northeast of Green Bay*

1679 La Salle expedition lands on Washington Island, off tip of Door Peninsula, in vessel *Griffon*; **c.1830** island settled by fishermen, joined by Danish and Norwegian farmers; town founded; **1835** fishermen settle on Rock Island to northeast; **1837** Potawatomi Lighthouse built on Rock Island, rebuilt 1858; **1852** David Kennison dies at Rock Island, age 116, oldest survivor of Boston Tea Party 1773; **1870** first group of Icelandic settlers arrives.

Watertown *Jefferson and Dodge counties* *Southern Wisconsin, 54 mi/87 km west-northwest of Milwaukee*

1836 town founded by New Englanders; **1849** incorporated as a village; **1850** toll plank road reaches town from Milwaukee; **1853** incorporated as a city; **1854** Octagon House built; **1855** political reformer Carl Schurz (1829–1906) arrives, having fled revolution in Germany, becomes Minister to Spain under President Lincoln; **1856** Mrs. Margarethe (Meyer) Schurz establishes first kindergarten in America; **1865** Northwestern College established by

Lutheran Church; **1875** first factory in U.S. making brick cheese established by Swiss immigrant John Jossie, closed 1943.

Waukesha   *Waukesha County   Southeastern Wisconsin, 15 mi/24 km west of Milwaukee*

1833 lands ceded by Potawatomi people; **1834** Alonzo and Morris Cutler arrive, build sawmill; town founded; **1840s** German immigrants arrive; **1844** *American Freeman* abolitionist newspaper founded, folds 1848; **1846** Waukesha County formed; town becomes county seat; Carroll College established; **1857** State Industrial School established; **1869** Col. Richard Dunbar develops town's natural springs; **1874** Fountain Springs Hotel built; **1896** incorporated as a city; **1905** Metropolitan Church Association (Shakers) converts Fountain Springs Hotel into national headquarters; **1959** county courthouse built; **1966** University of Wisconsin, Waukesha Campus (2-year), established.

Waupaca   *Waupaca County   Central Wisconsin, 55 mi/89 km west-southwest of Green Bay*

June 1849 first white settlers arrive; **1851** Waupaca County formed; town founded as county seat; **1852** post office established; **1857** incorporated as a village; **1875** incorporated as a city; **1990** county courthouse built.

Wausau   *Marathon County   Northern Wisconsin, 87 mi/140 km west-northwest of Green Bay*

1836 Robert Wakely canoes up Wisconsin River to rapids here; **1839** St. Louisan George Stevens arrives, builds several sawmills; town founded, named Big Bull Falls; **1850** Marathon County formed; town becomes county seat, renamed Wausau; **1867** village president August Kickbush travels to Germany, returns with 702 immigrants; **1872** incorporated as a city; **1874** Wisconsin Valley Railroad reaches city; logging industry begins; **1906** forest reserves depleted; town turns to manufacture of wood products, cheese, electrical motors; **1911** Wausau Insurance Company founded; **1912** Northcentral Technical College (2-year) established; **1955** fifth county courthouse built.

West Allis   *Milwaukee County   See* **Milwaukee** **(1919)**

West Bend   *Washington County   Eastern Wisconsin, 30 mi/48 km north-northwest of Milwaukee*

1836 Washington County formed; **1845** town founded on bend in Milwaukee River by Dr. E. B. Wolcott of Milwaukee; stone brewery built; **1868** incorporated as a village; **1873** Chicago & Northwestern Railroad reaches town; **1885** incorporated as a city; **1889** county courthouse built; **1901** West Bend Public Library founded; **1961** town of Barton to north merges with West Bend; **Apr. 4, 1981** tornado kills 6, injures 100, $15 million in damage.

West Salem   *La Crosse County   Western Wisconsin, 102 mi/164 km northwest of Madison*

1851 Thomas Leonard becomes first settler; **1856** Palmer-Gullickson Octagon House built; **1858** town founded on La Crosse River by Norwegian immigrants; **Sept. 14, 1860** author Hamlin Garland born (died 1940); **1891** cooperative creamery established; **1893** incorporated as a village; **1911** fire destroys business district, ignited by passing train.

Whitehall   *Trempealeau County   Western Wisconsin, 96 mi/155 km east-southeast of St. Paul, Minnesota*

1854 Trempealeau County formed; **1855** town founded as county seat; **1873** Green Bay & Western Railroad reaches town; **1887** incorporated as a village; **1941** incorporated as a city; **1956** county courthouse built.

Whitewater   *Walworth, Jefferson counties   Southeastern Wisconsin, 42 mi/68 km southwest of Milwaukee*

1839 mill built on Whitewater Creek; town founded; **1852** Milwaukee & Mississippi Railroad reaches town; **1857** George Easterly moves his reaper factory from La Grange, Illinois, moves to Minneapolis 1893; **1868** University of Wisconsin, Whitewater Campus, established; **1885** incorporated as a city; **Dec. 6, 1953** actor Tom Hulce born.

Wisconsin Dells   *Columbia County   Central Wisconsin, 42 mi/68 km north-northwest of Madison*

1844 *Maid of Iowa* becomes first steamboat to sail up Wisconsin River to The Dells rock formations; **1850** first bridge built across river; **June 1856** town platted, named Kilbourn City; **1858** Chicago, Milwaukee, St. Paul & Pacific Railroad built; **1873** steamboat pleasure excursions offered on *Dell Queen*; **1908** power dam built improving navigability through Upper Dells; **1925** incorporated as a city; **1931** town renamed Wisconsin Dells; **July 13, 1936** highest temperature ever recorded in Wisconsin reached, 114°F/46°C; **1946** surplus amphibious duck military vehicles introduced by Mel Flath to transport tourists; **1950s** amusement parks and attractions built during tourism boom.

Wisconsin Rapids   *Wood County   Central Wisconsin, 93 mi/150 km north-northwest of Madison*

1839 town of Grand Rapids founded on east bank of Wisconsin River; town of Centralia founded on west bank; **1842** first store built at Centralia; **1856** Wood County formed; Grand Rapids becomes county seat; **1869** Grand Rapids incorporated as a city; **1874** Centralia incorporated as a city; **1900** Grand Rapids annexes Centralia; **1917** Mid-State Technical College (2-year) established; **1920** city renamed Wisconsin Rapids; **1956** county courthouse built.

Wyoming

West central U.S. Capital and largest city: Cheyenne.

Most of Wyoming was acquired by the U.S. with the Louisiana Purchase of 1803. The southwestern part was acquired in 1848 from Mexico. Wyoming Territory was created July 25, 1868. Wyoming was admitted as the 44th state July 10, 1890.

Wyoming is divided into 23 counties. Municipalities are classified as towns and cities. There are no townships. See Introduction.

Alcova   *Natrona County*   *Central Wyoming, 25 mi/ 40 km southwest of Casper, on North Platte River*

1812 Robert Stuart discovers large boulder to west, becomes travelers' landmark, named Independence Rock by William Sublette, July 4, 1830; **July 28, 1888** S. Morris Waln of Philadelphia and C. H. Strong of New York City murdered by guide Thomas O'Brien, imprisoned for stealing, never charged in murders; **1891** town founded by Eastern syndicate seeking to establish hot springs resort, project fails; **1938** Alcova Reservoir formed on North Platte River.

Almy   *Uinta County*   *Southwestern Wyoming, 278 mi/447 km west of Laramie*

1852 coal deposits indicated here on map drawn by Capt. Howard Stansbury; **1868** coal mining begun by Union Pacific Railroad for new line under construction; town founded on Bear River; **1869** town prospers with completion of railroad and high price of coal; **March 4, 1881** coal mine explosion kills 38; **Jan. 1886** coal mine explosion, 13 killed; **March 20, 1895** Red Canyon coal mine explosion kills 60; **1900** remaining coal mines closed.

Alpine   *Lincoln County*   *Western Wyoming, 235 mi/ 378 km west of Casper*

1812 Robert Stuart party camps in Star Valley, build rafts to sail down Snake River, ridding themselves of Native Americans that had pursued them for hundreds of miles; **1882** Mormons retreat to Star Valley to evade Edmunds Anti-Polygamy Act, Wyoming authorities uncooperative with Act enforcement; **1907** town founded; **1920s** bridge built across Snake River; **1957** Palisades Reservoir formed by dam on Snake River in Idaho; **1989** town incorporated.

Basin   *Big Horn County*   *Northern Wyoming, 135 mi/217 km northwest of Casper*

1890 Big Horn County formed; **1896** town founded on Bighorn River, named Basin City for its location in Big Horn Basin; town wins designation of county seat over town of Otto; **July 12, 1900** highest temperature ever recorded in Wyoming reached, 114°F/46°C; **1902** town incorporated; **1906** Chicago, Burlington & Quincy Railroad reaches town; **1910** Carnegie Library built; **1917** county courthouse built; **1927** state tuberculosis sanitarium established.

Buffalo   *Johnson County*   *Northern Wyoming, 105 mi/169 km north of Casper*

1866 Fort Phil Kearney established to north, abandoned 1868; Capt. H. E. Palmer builds sod hut, forced to return to Montana at insistence of Cheyenne peoples; **1875** Johnson County formed; **Dec. 21, 1866** Capt. W. J. Fetterman and 80 men killed in ambush by 200 Native Americans led by Chief Crazy Horse; **1879** Fort McKinney established; town founded as county seat; **1884** town incorporated; county courthouse built; **1886–1887** many ranchers placed ruined by hard winter; **1903** Wyoming Soldiers and Sailors Home founded at old Fort McKinney; **1920s** oil boom boosts economy.

Canyon Junction   *Park County*   *Northwestern Wyoming, 242 mi/389 km northwest of Casper*

March 1, 1872 Yellowstone National Park established; **Aug. 25, 1877** party of 10 tourists attacked by band of Nez Perce led by Chief Joseph, one killed, another captured, purchases his freedom with gold watch and $160; **1903** Chittenden Bridge built across Yellowstone River, replacing ferry; **Aug. 24, 1908** stagecoach holdup yields $2,000 in tourist money; **1911** Canyon Hotel built, adjoins previous structure built 1886; **1957** Canyon Village built; **Aug. 1960** Canyon Hotel, scheduled for demolition, destroyed by fire; **1992** Canyon Lodge built.

Casper   *Natrona County   Central Wyoming,*
140 mi/225 km northwest of Cheyenne, on North Platte River

1812 Robert Stuart's party passes through area representing John Jacob Astor's fur trading company; **1842** first train of prairie schooners led by Elijah White reaches town site, beginning of migration of pioneers over Oregon Trail along Platte River Valley; **June 1847** Brigham Young's Mormons arrive; ferry established by Mormons; **1859** Platte Bridge built of cedar logs by John Richaud, replacing ferry; **1863** military post established at bridge; **July 26, 1865** Cheyenne attack wagon train after it leaves Platte Bridge Station, 6 soldiers killed, including Lt. Caspar Collins, for whom fort was renamed; Battle of Red Buttes fought same day to southwest, 38 soldiers killed as they approach Platte Bridge; **1876** first herd of cattle trailed into area by Judge Joseph M. Carey; **1877** Goose Egg Ranch House built to southwest, setting for Owen Wister's *The Virginian*; **1887** Fremont, Elkhorn & Missouri Valley Railroad extended from Douglas; **1888** Natrona County formed; town founded on Judge Carey's land; **1889** incorporated as a city; **1890** town becomes county seat; oil discovered in Salt Creek Field to north; **1895** first oil refinery in Wyoming built by Pennsylvania Oil and Gas Company; **1905** railroad extended west to Lander; **c.1908** Irish Park Oil Field (Teapot Dome) to north first exploited by oil companies; **1910** President Taft sets aside Teapot Dome as U.S. Petroleum Reserve No. 3 for Navy Department; **1913** Chicago, Burlington & Quincy Railroad reaches town; **1914** Standard Oil Refinery built; **1922** Secretary of Interior Albert B. Hall leases Petroleum Reserve to Harry F. Sinclair's Mammoth Oil Company, leads to Teapot Dome Oil Lease Scandal, all leases invalidated; **Sept. 27, 1923** railroad accident, 37 killed; **1938** Fort Caspar reconstructed; **1939** county courthouse built; **1941** Casper Army Air Base established, becomes Natrona County International Airport 1952; **1967** Nicolayson Art Museum opened; **1970** Werner Wildlife Museum opened; **1977** Casper College (2-year) established; **1980** Tate Mineralogical Museum opened.

Cheyenne   *Laramie County   Southeastern Wyoming, 90 mi/145 km north of Denver, Colorado*

1831 Blackfeet and Crow peoples converge on each other in pursuit of same buffalo herd, all 160 Blackfeet killed, 40 Crow killed; **1865** Maj. Gen. Grenville M. Dodge's troops camp at Crow Creek; **1867** Laramie County formed, part of Dakota Territory; site chosen as division point for Union Pacific Railroad by chief engineer Grenville M. Dodge; town founded, *Daily Leader* newspaper founded; telegraph line extended from Colorado; Fort D. A. Russell established, renamed Fort Francis E. Warren 1930, becomes U.S. Air Force Base 1949; **1867** incorporated as a city; **July 25, 1868** Wyoming Territory created;

1869 city becomes territorial capital and county seat; Dale Creek Bridge completed to west by Union Pacific Railroad, 135 ft/41 m above gorge, highest railroad bridge in world at the time; first herds of cattle driven from Texas; **Dec. 10, 1869** Wyoming passes women's suffrage legislation; **1870s** region develops as major cattle district; **1872** Wyoming Stock Growers Association organized; **1887** Colorado & Southern Railroad reaches city; **1890** state capitol completed; **July 10, 1890** Wyoming enters Union as 44th state; city becomes state capital; **1895** Wyoming State Museum founded; **1897** first annual Frontier Days celebration held; **1905** governor's mansion completed; **1909** St. Mary's Cathedral completed; **1919** county courthouse built; **Jan. 5, 1925** Nellie Ross becomes first woman governor in U.S., succeeding her late husband; **1926** air mail service inaugurated to Denver and Pueblo, Colorado; **1927** Cheyenne Municipal Airport established; **1929** Robert Burns statue erected; **1937** supreme court building built; **1968** Laramie County Community College established.

Cody   *Park County   Northwestern Wyoming, 177 mi/285 km northwest of Casper*

1807 trapper John Colter discovers springs here; **March 1, 1872** Yellowstone National Park established to west, first national park in U.S.; **1885** Charles de Maris homesteads at springs, later named De Maris Springs; **March 30, 1891** Shoshone National Forest created by Pres. Benjamin Harrison, first national forest in U.S.; **1895** town founded on Shoshone River, named for Buffalo Bill Cody, whose popular show was traveling the area at the time; **1902** town incorporated; **1909** Park County formed; town becomes county seat; Shoshone Cave National Monument established (closed 1939); **1910** Buffalo Bill Reservoir formed by dam to west on Shoshone River, part of large irrigation project; **1912** county courthouse built; **Jan. 28, 1912** painter Jackson Pollock born, died Aug. 11, 1956, auto accident in East Hampton, New York; **Sept. 1913** Buffalo Bill Cody's final big game hunt held at "Camp Monaco" to northwest with Prince Albert I of Monaco among notables (Cody died 1917 at Denver); **1924** Buffalo Bill Cody statue erected, sculpted by Gertrude Whitney; **1927** Buffalo Bill Museum founded; **1938** first annual Cody Nite Rodeo held; **1959** Whitney Gallery of Western Art established; Buffalo Bill Historical Center established, museum completed 1969.

Daniel   *Sublette County   Western Wyoming, 187 mi/301 km west of Casper*

1824 first gathering of trappers in annual Green River Rendezvous, social and business event essential to fur trapping; **1828** trapper Pinckney Sublette killed by unknown assailant, remains discovered 1897, shipped to St. Louis for verification; **1835** with fur trading at its zenith, Rendezvous attended by reverends Dr. Marcus Whitman and Samuel Parker, who represented advent of settlers which would bring end to fur trading; **July 5, 1840** Father Pierre Jean de Smet practices first High Mass in

Wyoming at Prairie de la Masse; **c.1891** general store established by T. P. Daniel; **1900** town founded on Green River; **1909** Daniel Hotel built; **1917** Daniel Fish Hatchery established; **1922** Sargent's Inn built; **July 4, 1936** remains of Pinckney Sublette returned to area, reburied at Prairie de la Masse.

Douglas *Converse County* *East central Wyoming, 48 mi/77 km east of Casper, on North Platte River*

1867 Fort Fetterman built by Maj. William M. Dye, abandoned 1882; **1882** Hog Ranch established by Jack Saunders and John Lawrence as gambling and dance resort; **1883** Sheriff Malcolm Campbell arrests Alfred Packer at Hog Ranch for killing and cannibalizing five prospectors snowbound with him in Colorado Rockies 1874; **1886** Fremont, Elkhorn & Missouri Valley Railroad proposed; town founded, nicknamed Tent Town; **May 1886** first church services held in saloon; **June 1886** railroad falls 10 mi/16 km short of town site, town moved; **1887** incorporated as a city; **1888** Converse County formed; city becomes county seat; **Oct. 1903** in Lightning Creek Battle, Sheriff Billy Miller of Newcastle, Deputy Louie Falkenberg, Chief Eagle Feather, Chief Black Kettle, two other Native Americans killed in gun battle over Native American hunting rights; **1905** Wyoming State Fairgrounds established; **1976** county courthouse built.

Encampment *Carbon County* *Southern Wyoming, 62 mi/100 km west of Laramie*

1851 fur trappers hold large rendezvous; **1897** copper discovered by Ed Haggarty; town founded, named Grand Encampment in reference to trappers' rendezvous; smelter built by George Emerson; **1901** town incorporated; **1908** smelter closed; **Feb. 9, 1933** lowest temperature recorded in Wyoming reached at Riverside to east, −66°F/−54°C.

Evanston *Uinta County* *Southwestern Wyoming, 275 mi/443 km west of Laramie*

Nov. 23, 1868 first settler Harvey Booth pitches tent, opens restaurant, saloon, hotel; **Dec. 1868** Union Pacific Railroad completed; town founded on Bear River; **1869** Uinta County formed; **1870** town becomes county seat; **1871** roundhouse built, demolished 1912; **1873** incorporated as a town; **1874** county courthouse built; **1887** Wyoming State Hospital completed; **1888** incorporated as a city; **1906** Carnegie Library opened; **1907** federal building completed; **1912** Hotel Evanston built; **Jan. 13, 1939** Ah Yuen, "China Mary," dies between age 104 and 110, one of first residents of Evanston's Chinatown; **Nov. 12, 1951** railroad accident at Wyuta Ranch to south, 17 killed.

Fort Bridger *Uinta County* *Southwestern Wyoming, 245 mi/394 km west of Laramie*

1834 cabin built by trapper John Robertson; rendezvous held by Robertson attracting mountain men from all over

to share stories, information, to dine on woodland fare; **1843** Fort Bridger established by traders Jim Bridger and Louis Vasquez; **1853** Mormons take control of fort driving out Bridger; **1857** Mormons flee Fort Bridger and Fort Supply to south in face of Col. Albert Johnston's army; **1858** Fort Bridger rebuilt as military outpost; **1890** fort abandoned.

Fort Laramie *Goshen County* *Southeastern Wyoming, 75 mi/121 km north-northeast of Cheyenne*

1834 Fort William trading post (first Fort Laramie) built on North Platte River, at mouth of Laramie River, by Robert Campbell and William L. Sublette; Sutler's Store built; **1841** Fort Platte built by rival trappers; **1843** first emigrants pass on Oregon Trail; **1845** Fort John (second Fort Laramie) built by John B. Sarpy of American Fur Company; Fort Platte abandoned; **1868** Sioux treaty signed by Red Cloud at Sutler's Store; **1876** iron bridge built on North Platte River; **July 16, 1938** Fort Laramie National Monument established, becomes national historic site 1960.

Fort Washakie *Fremont County* *West central Wyoming, 128 mi/206 km west of Casper*

1868 Wind River Indian Reservation established for Shoshone people; Camp Augur established, renamed Fort Brown 1869; **1871** Indian agency transferred to village of Wind River to south; **1878** renamed Fort Washakie for Shoshone Chief Washakie, refused to fight white men; **1889** Shoshone Mission Board School founded; **1899** fort abandoned; **Feb. 20, 1900** Chief Washakie dies (born c.1804); **1933** irrigation project initiated by Public Works Administration.

Gillette *Campbell County* *Northeastern Wyoming, 106 mi/171 km north-northeast of Casper*

1891 Chicago, Burlington & Quincy Railroad built; town founded, named for engineer Edward Gillette; town incorporated; **1911** Campbell County formed; town becomes county seat; **1970s** coal mining begins, reaches peak 1980 (some 30 burning coal mines in existence, fires glow through fissures); **1971** county courthouse built.

Glenrock *Converse County* *East central Wyoming, 22 mi/35 km east of Casper, on North Platte River*

July 2, 1852 Indiana emigrant A. H. Unthank buried along Oregon Trail, members of party carve names in sandstone ridge above grave; **1857** Deer Creek Station established by Mormons, becomes military post 1861; **1904** town founded; **1909** town incorporated; **1916** Hotel Higgins opened; **1919** Big Muddy Oil Field to west reaches maximum production; **1994** Glenrock Paleontological Museum established.

Green River   *Sweetwater County*   *Southwestern Wyoming, 200 mi/322 km west of Laramie*

1862 Overland Trail stage route crosses Green River near here; **1867** Carter County formed, renamed Sweetwater County 1869; South Pass becomes county seat; **1868** Union Pacific Railroad built, shops and roundhouse located here; town founded at Green River crossing; **May 29, 1869** John Wesley Powell expedition heads down Green and Colorado rivers, completed Aug. 30; **1872** county seat moved to Green River; **1891** town incorporated; **1913** Lincoln Highway reaches town; **July 31, 1919** announcer Curt Gowdy born; **1922** first highway bridge built across Green River; **1963** Flaming Gorge Reservoir formed to south on Green River, Flaming Gorge Dam located in northeastern Utah; **Oct. 1, 1968** Flaming Gorge National Recreation Area established to south by U.S. National Forest Service.

Guernsey   *Platte County*   *Southeastern Wyoming, 76 mi/122 km north of Cheyenne, on North Platte River*

1842 earliest known inscription made at Register Cliff, contains thousands of travelers' carved signatures, c.700 are legible; Lt. John C. Fremont camps at Warm Spring, called Emigrant's Laundry Tub, used by pioneers; **1860–1861** Pony Express station founded; **1880** rancher, mining promoter Charles A. Guernsey arrives; **1881** copper discovered to north at Hartville; town founded; **1899** iron deposits discovered at Sunrise to north; **1900** Chicago, Burlington & Quincy Railroad reaches town; **1902** town incorporated; **1927** Guernsey Reservoir formed on North Platte River.

Jackson   *Teton County*   *Northwestern Wyoming, 225 mi/362 km west-northwest of Casper*

1807 John Colter explores Jackson Hole; **1883** first settlers arrive on Snake River; **1898** summit of Grand Teton mountain (13,771 ft/4,197 m) first reached by climbers; **1900** town platted; **1901** cattlemen kill 300 sheep on Mosquito Creek during "sheep wars"; **1912** National Elk Refuge established; **1916** dam built on Snake River at outflow of natural Jackson Lake to north raising lake; **1914** incorporated as a town; Church of the Transfiguration built on Jackson Lake; **1921** Teton County formed; town becomes county seat; **Feb. 26, 1929** Grand Teton National Park established to north; **1930** Jackson Hole Airport established; **1968** county courthouse built; **Aug. 25, 1972** John D. Rockefeller, Jr. Memorial Parkway established by National Park Service to north between Grand Teton and Yellowstone national parks; **1985** first Fall Arts Festival held; **1994** National Wildlife Art Museum founded.

Kaycee   *Johnson County*   *North central Wyoming, 60 mi/97 km north of Casper*

1828 several buildings erected by Portuguese trader Antonio Mateo on South Fork Powder River; **1860** German Lutheran mission founded by missionaries from Iowa; **July 1865** Fort Connor established, renamed Fort Reno, abandoned 1868; **Apr. 9, 1892** cattlemen's group the Regulators shoot and kill two suspected cattle rustlers Nate Champion and Nick Ray of Red Sash Gang at K C Ranch, later brought to surrender following standoff with Sheriff Red Angus, Home Defenders citizens' corps, and 6th Cavalry; **1900** town founded; **1913** incorporated as a town.

Kemmerer   *Lincoln County*   *Southwestern Wyoming, 253 mi/407 km west-northwest of Laramie*

1822 earliest legible inscription on Names Hill to northeast, collection of names left by emigrants to area, includes "James Bridger–1844"; **1881** Union Pacific Railroad built; first coal mine opened; **1890** specimen hunters begin blasting rocks of Fossil Cliffs to west in search of fossil fish, alligators, birds; **1897** coal mining company organized by Mahlon Kemmerer; town founded; **1899** town incorporated; **1902** James Cash Penney's Golden Rule Store opens, first of what would become J. C. Penney retail chain; **1911** Lincoln County formed; town becomes county seat; **July 1919** Anna Richey accused of rustling 32 head of cattle, poisoned after release from prison; **Aug. 14, 1923** explosion at Frontier Coal Mine, 99 killed; **1925** county courthouse built; **1964** Fontenelle Reservoir formed on Green River to northeast; **Oct. 23, 1972** Fossil Butte National Monument established to west.

Lander   *Fremont County*   *West central Wyoming, 120 mi/193 km west of Casper*

1868 Camp Augur established to west, renamed Fort Washakie 1878; **1872** area opened to white settlement; town founded; **1884** Fremont County formed, named for John C. Fremont; town becomes county seat; oil and coal discovered in area; first oil well in Wyoming drilled; **1890** town incorporated; **1914** Pioneer Museum opened; **1917** Noble Hotel built; **1956** second county courthouse built; **1965** National Outdoor Leadership School established.

Laramie   *Albany County*   *Southeastern Wyoming, 42 mi/68 km west-northwest of Cheyenne*

c.1820 French-Canadian trapper Jacques La Ramie works in region, killed by Native Americans near Laramie River; **1860s** road ranches established along Overland Trail as supply points for hay, wood; **1866** Fort John Buford (Fort Sanders) built; **1868** Albany County formed; Union Pacific Railroad built; town founded on Laramie River as county seat; town incorporated, later revoked; first herds of cattle introduced to Laramie Valley; **1874** town reincorporated; **1876** territorial prison built, closed 1900, 12 years after prison at Rawlins opened; **Aug. 30, 1876** Jack McCall arrested for shooting Wild Bill Hickok in Deadwood, South Dakota, Aug. 2; **1877** outlaw Jesse James jailed as stagecoach robbery suspect, freed before his identity is made known; **1881** *Boomerang* newspaper founded by Edgar "Bill" Nye, becomes well-known humorist; **1886** University of Wyoming established; **1932** second county courthouse completed; **Oct. 6, 1955** United

Airlines DC-4 crashes in Medicine Bow Mountains to west, killing 66.

Lovell   *Big Horn County*   *Northern Wyoming, 170 mi/274 km northwest of Casper*

1900 Mormons settle in region; town founded; **1906** Chicago, Burlington & Quincy Railroad reaches town; town incorporated; **1909** irrigation system built; sugar beet production begins; **1916** Great Western Sugar Factory founded; **Oct. 15, 1966** Bighorn Canyon National Recreation Area established on Bighorn River to east, extends into Montana.

Lusk   *Niobrara County*   *Eastern Wyoming, 110 mi/ 177 km north-northeast of Cheyenne*

1868 Hat Creek Station established to north on Sage Creek by soldiers under orders to build station at Hat Creek, Nebraska, mistakenly went too far west; **1875** stagecoach driver "Stuttering" Brown fatally shot by outlaw Persimmons Bill Chambers over stolen horses; **1876** Black Hills freight wagons attacked by 500 Native Americans, saved by Captain Eagan's cavalry; **Aug. 1877** outlaw Frank Towle shot and killed by stagecoach guards Boone May and John Zimmerman, Boone takes Towle's severed head in bag to Cheyenne for reward, learns reward had been withdrawn; **1886** town founded, named for settler Frank Lusk; **1898** town incorporated; **1911** Niobrara County formed; town becomes county seat; **1918** oil discovered at Buck Creek Dome to north; **1919** county courthouse built.

Medicine Bow   *Carbon County*   *Southern Wyoming, 50 mi/80 km northwest of Laramie*

1868 Union Pacific Railroad built; town founded on Medicine Bow River; **1885** author Owen Wister arrives, spends 15 years riding with Two Bar cattle outfit, publishes novel *The Virginian* 1902; **1901** The Virginian Hotel built; **1909** town incorporated; **1913** Lincoln Highway reaches town; **1939** Owen Wister monument erected.

Newcastle   *Weston County*   *Northeastern Wyoming, 188 mi/303 km north-northeast of Cheyenne*

1875 Jenney Stockade built; **1889** town founded near Cambria coal mining center, named for English coal city on North Sea; incorporated as a city; **1890** Weston County formed; town becomes county seat; **1892** Mondell House built by Frank W. Mondell; **1903** Diamond L. "Slim" Clifton hanged for brutal murder of law-abiding John Church and his pregnant wife Luella; **1910** county courthouse built; **1928** coal mining at Cambria ceases.

Old Faithful   *Teton County*   *Northwestern Wyoming, 247 mi/398 km northwest of Casper*

1870 Old Faithful Geyser named by Washburn-Langford-Doane Expedition for regularity of its eruption (64.5 min-utes); **March 2, 1872** Yellowstone National Park established; **1904** Old Faithful Inn completed; **1959** earthquake alters regularity of Old Faithful Geyser's eruptions.

Pinedale   *Sublette County*   *Western Wyoming, 177 mi/285 km west of Casper*

1878 first white settlers arrive; **1895** Charles A. Petersen family moves into abandoned trapper cabin in Pine Creek Flat; **1904** town founded; Sprague Hotel built; **1912** town incorporated; **1921** Sublette County formed; town becomes county seat; **1931** county courthouse built; **1985** Museum of the Mountain Man established, opened 1990.

Powell   *Park County*   *Northern Wyoming, 178 mi/ 286 km northwest of Casper*

1890s town planned by Department of Interior as headquarters for Shoshone Reclamation Project; **1900** Mormon pioneers settle in area; **1906** first natural gas wells drilled in area; Garland Canal irrigation project leads to production of alfalfa, wheat, sugar beets; **1908** town founded on Shoshone River, named for explorer John Wesley Powell; **1910** town incorporated; **1915** oil discovered at Elk Basin to north; **1946** Northwest College (2-year) established.

Rawlins   *Carbon County*   *Southern Wyoming, 90 mi/145 km west-northwest of Laramie*

1867 spring discovered by Gen. John A. Rawlins; **1868** Carbon County formed; Union Pacific Railroad built; town founded on railroad as county seat; **1874** shipment from Rawlins' red paint mines used on new Brooklyn Bridge, New York; **June 1878** posse leaders Tip Vincent and Ed Widdowfield shot dead by "Big Nose George" Parrot and "Dutch Charlie" Burris, the men they were pursuing, bandits found in Montana one year later, returned and hanged; **1886** incorporated as a city; **1903** Frontier State Prison opened, closed 1982; **1940** county courthouse completed.

Riverside   *Carbon County*   *See* **Encampment (1933)**

Riverton   *Fremont County*   *Central Wyoming, 103 mi/166 km west of Casper*

1884 St. Stephen's Mission established; **1905** part of Shoshone Indian Reservation opened to white settlement; **1906** town founded on Wind River as center for irrigation project; settlers begin arriving; incorporated as a city; **1924** Pilot Butte Power Plant built; **1966** Central Wyoming College (2-year) established.

Rock River   *Albany County*   *Southeastern Wyoming, 35 mi/56 km north-northwest of Laramie*

1868 Union Pacific Railroad built; **1877** Como Bluff Dinosaur Graveyard discovered to north, renowned fossil beds; **1878** town of Rock Creek founded on railroad

11 mi/18 km to east at junction of cattle trail from Fort Fetterman; **June 2, 1899** train robbed to west by two gunmen, $60,000 in unsigned bank notes taken, act attributed to Butch Cassidy and "Flat Nose" George Currie; **1900** route of Union Pacific altered; new town of Rock River founded; irrigation systems introduced; **1909** incorporated as a town; **1916** two cowboys discover cache of gold coins in glass jars in abandoned basement at Rock Creek town site, apparently hidden there by German-born innkeeper.

Rock Springs *Sweetwater County   Southwestern Wyoming, 187 mi/301 km northwest of Laramie*

1861 springs discovered by Pony Express rider detouring hostile natives; **1862** stage station founded on Overland Trail; **1866** Archie and Duncan Blair build trading post at Rock Spring; town founded; **c.1860** coal mining begins; **1875** Chinese immigrants hired to break coal miners' strike, by 1885 become largest ethnic group at 1,200; **1885** mob burns Chinatown, 30 Chinese killed; state troops quell violence, remain until 1898; **1888** town incorporated; **July 17, 1891** 1,200 kegs of blasting powder ignited by two drunken men, four killed; **1924** first annual International Night held to celebrate town's ethnic diversity; **1959** Western Wyoming Community College established.

Sheridan *Sheridan County   Northern Wyoming, 137 mi/220 km north-northwest of Casper*

Aug. 2, 1867 in Wagon Box Fight to south, two woodcutter camps guarded by Maj. James Powell's troops attacked by Lakota Sioux under Chiefs Red Cloud and Crazy Horse, defeated by Army's new breech-loading Springfield rifles, 3 troops killed, 50–60 Sioux killed; **1868** Father De Smet visits area, preaches to large gathering of Crow people; **1873** Martha Canary dubbed "Calamity Jane" by Capt. Pat Egan after rescuing injured officer during Native American raid; **1878** trapper Jim Mason builds cabin; **1881** Mason cabin converted to store by Harry Mandel; **1882** town founded by John D. Loucks, named for Union Gen. Philip Sheridan; **1884** incorporated as a town; **1887** *Sheridan Post* and *Sheridan Enterprise* newspapers founded; **1888** Sheridan County formed; town becomes county seat; **1892** Chicago, Burlington & Quincy Railroad reaches town; **1893** lavish Sheridan Inn built by Buffalo Bill Cody; **1898** Fort Mackenzie military post built, abandoned 1918; **1903** Carnegie Library built, replaced by new library 1974; **1905** county courthouse built; **1907** incorporated as a city; **1914** Trail End mansion completed, built by Sen. John B. Kendrick, the "Cowboy Senator"; **1922** Veterans Administration Hospital established at old Fort Mackenzie; **1925** Wyoming Girls' School established; **1939** citizens unhappy with Wyoming patronage system declare state of Absaroka, includes area north of North Platte River, never put to a vote; **1948** Sheridan College (2-year) established.

Shoshoni *Fremont County   Central Wyoming, 92 mi/148 km west-northwest of Casper*

July 4, 1874 troops of Capt. Alfred Bates, accompanied by 100 Shoshone, attack Arapaho encampment to northeast, 4 soldiers killed, 40 wounded, heavy Native American losses on both sides; **1880s** Birdseye Stage Station established to north, remains in service through 1890s; **1905** part of Shoshone Indian Reservation opened to whites; town founded near Bighorn River; **1906** incorporated as a town; **1908** Boysen Reservoir formed on Bighorn River, dam rebuilt 1948.

Sinclair *Carbon County   Southern Wyoming, 83 mi/134 km west-northwest of Laramie*

1843 explorer John C. Fremont camps near site of Fort Steele, attacked by Cheyenne and Arapaho, peace pipe smoked after realization that Fremont party were not enemy tribe; **1868** Union Pacific Railroad built; Fort Steele built to east to protect rail line; **1886** fort abandoned; **1913** Pathfinder Reservoir formed on North Platte River to north; **1923** Parco Oil Refinery built, completed 1926; town founded as Parco; **1925** incorporated as a town; **1939** Seminoe Reservoir formed on North Platte River to north, upstream from (south of) Pathfinder Reservoir; **1943** town renamed for Sinclair Oil Company; **1950** Kortes Dam built on North Platte River between Pathfinder and Seminoe reservoirs.

South Pass City *Fremont County   West central Wyoming, 125 mi/201 km west-southwest of Casper*

1812 South Pass on Continental Divide discovered by Robert Stuart; **July 4, 1836** Dr. Marcus Whitman, H. H. Spalding, and their wives stop to rest at Pacific Springs, dedicate The West as "home of American mothers and the Church of Christ"; **1842** gold discovered near source of Sweetwater River; town founded; **1855** most gold diggings played out, last mines close 1861; **1867** placer gold discovered in streams; **1868** Idaho House hotel built; **1870** Esther Hobart Morris becomes justice of the peace, goes on to support women's suffrage; **1880s** town declines.

Sundance *Crook County   Northeastern Wyoming, 145 mi/233 km northeast of Casper*

1875 Crook County formed; **1879** town founded as county seat; **1887** incorporated as a town; **Sept. 24, 1906** Devils Tower National Monument established to northwest, first national monument in U.S.; **1967** county courthouse built.

Ten Sleep *Washakie County   Northern Wyoming, 98 mi/158 km north-northwest of Casper*

1882 first settlers arrive; **1889** town founded; **1903** "sheep wars" feud between cattlemen and sheepmen results in killings of sheep herders and their sheep; **Apr. 2, 1909** in Ten Sleep Raid, cattleman turned sheepman Joe Emge and Joe Allemand shot to death by 20 masked men, 3,000 sheep killed; **1933** incorporated as a town.

Thermopolis *Hot Springs County* *Central Wyoming, 110 mi/177 km northwest of Casper*

1807 trapper John Colter becomes first known white man to enter Big Horn Basin; **1871** J.D. Woodruff builds first house in basin; first settlement established 6 mi/9.7 km from present town site; **1879** first cattle trailed into Big Horn Basin from Oregon by Charles Carter; **1897** town founded on Bighorn River, named for hot springs, largest hot springs in world; **1899** incorporated as a town; **1906** Chicago, Burlington & Quincy Railroad reaches town; **1911** Hot Springs County formed; **1916–1917** Grass Creek Oil Field discovered to northwest; **1938** county courthouse built.

Torrington *Goshen County* *Southeastern Wyoming, 72 mi/116 km northeast of Cheyenne*

Aug. 19, 1854 Lt. John Grattan and his men attempt arrest of Sioux for killing settler's cow at Lingle to west, all 29 men and Lt. Grattan killed after refusing chief's offer to bring accused to fort, several Sioux killed; **1889** post office established; **1900** Chicago, Burlington & Quincy Railroad reaches site; town founded; **1908** incorporated as a town; **1911** Goshen County formed; town becomes county seat; **1913** county courthouse built; **1926** beet sugar refinery established; **1936** efforts undertaken to check further erosion in dust bowl area to south known as Goshen Hole, once prolific wheat-growing district; **1948** Eastern Wyoming College (2-year) established.

Wheatland *Platte County* *Southeastern Wyoming, 60 mi/97 km north of Cheyenne*

1885 town founded by on Chugwater River; **1887** Colorado & Southern Railroad built; **1905** town incorporated; **1911** Platte County formed; town becomes county seat; **1918** county courthouse built.

Worland *Washakie County* *Northern Wyoming, 113 mi/182 km northwest of Casper*

1900 Charles H. "Dad" Worland establishes stage stop in dugout, dwelling dug from side of hill, builds house 1904; **1903** Big Horn Basin irrigation project begun; town founded on Bighorn River; **1906** Chicago, Burlington & Quincy Railroad reaches town; town incorporated; **1911** Washakie County formed; town becomes county seat; **1913** State Industrial School for Boys established; **1918** Worland Ranch built by Dad Worland; **1937** county courthouse built.

Wyuta *Uinta County* *See* **Evanston (1951)**

Index

INDEX

INDEX

INDEX

Boyden, Charles, 607
Boyden, Seth, 311
Boydton, Va., 702
Boyer, Charles S., 445
Boyle, Kay, 359
Boyle, Peter, 583
Boyle County, Ky., 247, 251, 257
Boys Town, Nebr., 410
Bozeman, John M., 402
Bozeman, Mont., 402
Brach, Amy Mary, 434
Brach, Moses, 102
Bracken, Eddie, 489
Bracken County, Ky., 245
Brackett, George, 726
Brackett, Oscar, 641
Brackett, Theophilus, 323
Brackettville, Tex., 641
Bradbury, John, 392
Bradbury, Ray, 190
Bradbury, William, 290
Braddock, Edward, Gen., 584
Braddock, James, 301
Braden, Joseph, Dr., 118
Bradenton, Fla., 118
Bradford, Augustus, Gov., 293
Bradford, David, 588
Bradford, Gov., 593
Bradford, Pa., 569
Bradford, Richard, Capt., 132
Bradford, Vt., 686
Bradford, William, 311, 452
Bradford County, Fla., 132
Bradford County, Pa., 587
Bradley, Bill, Sen., 382
Bradley, Ed, 583
Bradley, Edward, Col., 129
Bradley, Eugene M., Lt., 103
Bradley, H.J., 66
Bradley, Jonathan, 430
Bradley, Milton, 287
Bradley, Omar, Gen., 391
Bradley, Samuel, 430
Bradley, Thomas, 61
Bradley, William O., Gov., 252
Bradley County, Tenn., 623–624
Bradstreet, John, Col., 486
Brady, Craig, 569
Brady, James, 114
Brady, James Buchanan "Diamond Jim," 479
Brady, John, 123
Brady, John, Capt., 580
Brady, Matthew B., 475
Brady, Samuel, 531
Brady, Tex., 641
Brady, William, Sheriff, 459
Brady, William Aloysius, 70
Bragg, Braxton, Gen., 140, 142, 147, 248, 505, 511, 623, 632, 636
Bragg, Thomas, 504, 511
Brahan, Robert, 6
Braidwood, Ill., 171
Brainerd, Minn., 348–349
Braintree, Mass., 307
Brame, Judge, 369
Bramer, John, 624
Bramwell, J.H., 746
Branch, L. O'Bryan, Gen., 507
Branch County, Mich., 331
Brand, Christopher C., 99
Brand, Leslie C., 56
Brand, Neville, 210
Brandeis, Louis Dembitz, Justice, 252

Brandenburg, Ky., 245
Brandenburg, Solomon, Col., 245
Brando, Marlon, 417, 667, 669
Brandon, Gerard, 364, 375
Brandon, Miss., 364
Brandon, Vt., 686
Braniff, Paul R., 647
Brannan, Charles Franklin, 82
Brannan, Samuel, 70, 78, 287
Branson, David, 201
Branson, Mo., 379
Branson, Reuben S., 379
Brant, Joseph, 470, 474, 491, 577
Brantley County, Ga., 150
Braswell, Benjamin, 149
Braswell, Kent, Mayor, 680
Brattle, William, Jr., 687
Brattleboro, Vt., 687
Braun, Johann, 757
Braun, Werner von, 8
Braxton, Carter, 709
Braxton County, W. Va., 745
Brazelton, William, 633
Brazil, Ind., 194
Brazill, Nathaniel, 134
Brazoria, Tex., 641
Brazoria County, Tex., 638, 641, 650, 674
Brazos County, Tex., 642, 644
Breathitt County, Ky., 251
Breaux, Firmin, 265
Breaux, Scholastique Picou, 265
Breaux Bridge, La., 265
Breckenridge, Colo., 80
Breckenridge, John C., 641
Breckenridge, Minn., 349
Breckenridge, Tex., 641
Breckinridge, John, 249, 252, 264, 349, 713
Breckinridge County, Ky., 246, 249
Bremer, Arthur, 298
Bremer, Edward, 359
Bremer, Fredrika, 225
Bremer, William, 724
Bremer County, Iowa, 225
Bremerton, Wash., 724
Brenham, Richard, Dr., 641
Brenham, Tex., 641–642
Brennan, Eileen, 60
Brennan, Walter, 324
Brennan, William Joseph, Jr., Justice, 451
Brenner, David, 583
Brenton, Peter, 203
Breton, Francois Azor, 394
Brevard, Ephraim, Dr., Col., 498
Brevard, N.C., 498
Brevard County, Fla.
  Cape Canaveral, 119
  Cocoa, 119
  Melbourne, 126
  Port Canaveral, 130
  Titusville, 134
Brewer, James, 408
Brewer, John, Col., 279
Brewer, Maine, 279
Brewer, Teresa, 541
Brewer, Wilson C., 225
Brewster, Nebr., 410
Brewster, N.Y., 467
Brewster, Walter, 467
Brewster County, Tex., 637, 671
Brewton, Ala., 3–4
Breyer, Stephen Gerald, Justice, 71
Brice, Fanny, 480
Briceville, Tenn., 622

Brick, Riley A., 449
Brickell, William, 126
Bridgam, John, Capt., 690
Bridgeport, Ala., 4
Bridgeport, Calif., 52
Bridgeport, Conn., 92
Bridgeport, Nebr., 410–411
Bridger, James, 404, 716, 767, 768
Bridges, Beau, 57
Bridges, Edmund, 314
Bridges, Jeff, 60
Bridges, Lloyd, 57, 60, 72
Bridges, Todd, 71
Bridgeton, N.J., 444–445
Bridgewater, Mass., 307
Bridgman, George W., 330
Bridgman, Mich., 330
Bridgman, Percy William, 308
Briggs, Elias, 565
Briggs, George D., Cong., 303
Brigham, Dennis, 727
Brigham City, Utah, 676
Bright, James H., 122
Bright, John, Capt., 259
Brighton, Clarence Crane, 103
Brighton, Colo., 80
Brighton, Vt., 687
Brill, John, 510
Brimley, Wilford, 682
Bringhurst, William, 425
Brink, Hazelwood, 189
Brink, J.W. "Doc," 410
Brinkley, Christie, 341
Brinkley, David, 512
Brisbois, Michel, 759
Briscoe, Walter, 150
Briscoe County, Tex., 670
Brisebois, Danielle, 484
Bristol, Fla., 118
Bristol, Maine, 279
Bristol, Pa., 569
Bristol, R.I., 592
Bristol, Tenn., 622
Bristol, Va., 702
Bristol, Vt., 687
Bristol, William, 470
Bristol Bay Borough, Alaska, 19–20
Bristol City, Va., 702
Bristol County, Mass.
  Attleboro, 304
  Dartmouth, 309–310
  Easton, 310
  Fairhaven, 311
  Fall River, 311
  New Bedford, 317
  North Attleboro, 318
  Norton, 318
  Rehoboth, 320
  Somerset, 322
  Swansea, 324
  Taunton, 324
Bristol County, R.I., 591–592, 597
Bristow, Gwen, 604
Britton, John, 130
Britton, Nathaniel Lord, 492
Britton, S.Dak., 608
Broadt, John, 687
Broadus, Mont., 402
Broadus, C.A., Col., 405
Broadwater County, Mont., 408
Brock, Isaac, Gen., 332
Brockenbrough, John, 717
Brockton, Mass., 307

Broder, David, 175
Broderick, David, Sen., 70
Broderick, Matthew, 483
Brodhead, Daniel, 587
Broken Bow, Nebr., 411
Brolin, James, 60
Bromfield, Louis, 534
Bronck, Jonas, 467
Bronson, Fla., 118
Bronx County, N.Y., 467–468
Bronx (The Bronx), N.Y., 467–468
Brook, Preston, Cong., 118
Brooke, Edward, II, 569
Brooke, Edward William, Sen., 112
Brooke, John Mercer, 133
Brooke County, W. Va., 738, 746
Brookfield, Ill., 171
Brookfield, Mass., 307
Brookhaven, Miss., 364
Brookings, S.Dak., 608
Brookings County, S.Dak., 608
Brookline, Mass., 307
Brooklyn, N.Y., 468–469
Brooklyn Supreme, 494
Brookneal, Va., 702
Brooks, Albert, 51
Brooks, Alfred H., 15
Brooks, Avery, 196
Brooks, Charles, 655
Brooks, David, 655
Brooks, Elisha, 739, 742
Brooks, Garth, 557
Brooks, Gwendolyn, 240
Brooks, Isaac, 509
Brooks, John, Gov., 315
Brooks, Joseph, Rev., 41
Brooks, Marin Gowen, 315
Brooks, Mel, 482
Brooks, Peter Chardon, 526
Brooks, Preston S., Cong., 151, 602
Brooks County, Ga., 151
Brooks County, Tex., 649
Brooksville, Fla., 118
Brooksville, Ky., 245
Brookville, Ind., 194
Brookville, Pa., 569
Broom, Jacob, 109
Broome County, N.Y., 467, 472
Broomfield, Colo., 80
Broomfield County, Colo., 80
Broson, Silas, 102
Brothers, Joyce, Dr., 482
Broughton, Thomas, 604
Broughton, William, 562, 734
Broward County, Fla., 121–122, 130
Browder, Earl Russell, 242
Brown, A.A., 693
Brown, Barnum, 405
Brown, Basil, 569
Brown, Ben, 562
Brown, Blair, 113
Brown, Charles, 747
Brown, Cleyson L., 227
Brown, David M., 119, 662, 700
Brown, Ebenezer, 676
Brown, Edmund Gerald "Jerry," Gov., 71
Brown, Edmund Gerald "Pat," Gov., 70
Brown, F.B., Gen., 390
Brown, Francis A., 680
Brown, Frank E., 67
Brown, George R., 655
Brown, H. Rap, 293, 294, 484
Brown, Harold C. "Old Wayside," 500

Brown, Henry Billings, Justice, 314
Brown, Henry Newton, 236
Brown, Jacob, Maj., 642
Brown, James, 634
Brown, James, Capt., 680
Brown, James V., 589
Brown, J.H., 418
Brown, Jim, 153
Brown, John, 45, 66, 102, 214, 224, 234, 237,
    323, 332, 391, 433, 476, 523, 532, 539,
    570, 571, 623, 738, 739, 741
Brown, Joseph, 352, 360, 690
Brown, Lawrence, 381
Brown, Margaret Tobin, 385
Brown, Nicholas, 595
Brown, Nicole, 61, 74
Brown, Paul, 537
Brown, Peleg, 101
Brown, Ray, 584
Brown, Ronald H., 113
Brown, Ruth, 546
Brown, Samuel, 361, 488
Brown, "Stuttering," 769
Brown, Thomas, 383, 569
Brown, William, Capt., 160
Brown, W.K., 77
Brown County, Ill., 183–184
Brown County, Ind., 202
Brown County, Kans., 232, 239
Brown County, Minn., 356
Brown County, Nebr., 409
Brown County, Ohio, 531, 539
Brown County, S.Dak., 607, 611
Brown County, Tex., 642, 655
Brown County, Wis., 751–753
Browne, Abraham, 324
Browne, Roscoe Lee, 454
Brownell, Herbert, Jr., 418
Brownfield, A.M., 642
Brownfield, M.V., 642
Brownfield, Tex., 642
Brownie, Ky., 245
Browning, Mont., 402
Brownrigg, Richard, 501
Brownson, Amos, 693
Brownstown, Ind., 194
Brownsville, Ky., 245
Brownsville, Pa., 569
Brownsville, Tenn., 622
Brownsville, Tex., 642
Brownville, Maine, 279
Brownville, Nebr., 411
Brownwood, Tex., 642
Brubeck, Dave, 53
Bruce, Blanche Kelso, 706
Bruce, Charles, 702
Bruce, James Cole, 718
Bruguier, Theophile, 223
Brule, Edward F., 26
Brule, Etienne, 345, 541
Brule County, S.Dak., 609
Bruner, John, 12
Bruner, Ulrich, 586
Brunet, Jean, 750
Brunswick, Ga., 138–139
Brunswick, Maine, 279–280
Brunswick, Mo., 379
Brunswick County, N.C., 510
Brunswick County, Va., 699, 710
Brush, Charles R., 756
Brutscher, Sebastian, 563
Bruyer, August, 618
Bruyer, Josephine, 618

Bryan, John Neely, 646
Bryan, Ohio, 525
Bryan, Robert, 707
Bryan, Tex., 642
Bryan, William Jennings, 180, 188, 387, 415,
    616, 625, 662
Bryan, William Joel, 642
Bryan County, Ga., 145, 151–152
Bryan County, Okla., 547–549
Bryant, Anita, 126
Bryant, Cyrus, 187
Bryant, James, 306
Bryant, William Cullen, 312
Bryantsville, Ky., 245
Bryn Athyn, Pa., 569–570
Bryn Mawr, Pa., 570
Bryson, N.C., 499
Buchanan, Franklin, 292
Buchanan, Ga., 139
Buchanan, James, 571, 577, 579, 641
Buchanan, John, 702
Buchanan County, Iowa, 217
Buchanan County, Mo., 395
Buchanan County, Va., 708
Buchman, Ira, 474
Buchwald, Art, 478
Buck, Frank, 651
Buck, Jack, 313, 396
Buck, Pearl S., 742
Buckeye, Ariz., 26
Buckhannon, W.Va., 738
Buckingham, Thomas, 97
Buckingham, Va., 702
Buckingham County, Va., 702
Buckley, Betty, 650
Buckley, John M., 724
Buckley, Wash., 724
Buckley, William F., Jr., 482
Bucklin, A.J., 331
Bucklin, Earl, Mayor, 348
Bucknall, Stephen, 102
Buckner, Aylette H., 249
Buckner, John, 707
Buckner, Simon, Gen., 244, 249, 255
Bucks County, Pa.
    Bristol, 569
    Doylestown, 572
    Levittown, 578
    Morrisville, 580
    Newtown, 580
    Washington Crossing, 588
Bucksport, Maine, 280
Buckwalter, Francis, Rev., 583
Bucoda, Wash., 724
Bucyrus, Ohio, 525
Buechel, Eugene, Father, 613
Buell, Don Carlos, Gen., 257, 534, 623, 632
Buell, Elijah, 212
Buell, James T., Lt. Col., 386
Buena Vista, Ga., 139
Buena Vista, Va., 702
Buena Vista City, Va., 702
Buena Vista County, Iowa, 223
Buffalo, Minn., 349
Buffalo, Mo., 379
Buffalo, N.Y., 469–470
Buffalo, Okla., 547
Buffalo, S.Dak., 608
Buffalo, Wyo., 765
Buffalo County, Nebr., 413–414
Buffalo County, S.Dak., 611
Buffalo County, Wis., 749
Buffington, Jonathan, 741

INDEX

INDEX

INDEX

INDEX

Duplin County, N.C., 504
Duplun, J.L., 575
du Pont, Amy, 105
du Pont, E.I., 195, 633
du Pont, Henry, 105
du Pont, Irene, 105
Dupree, S.Dak., 610
Dupris, Frank, 610
du Puis, Hypolite, 355
du Puy, Louis, 84
Duquesne, Pa., 572
du Quoigne, Jean Baptiste, 177
Du Quoin, Ill., 177
Durand, Wis., 751
Durango, Colo., 83
Durant, Okla., 549
Durant, W.C., 343
Durant, Will, 318
Durant, William, 306, 334
Durante, Jimmy, 480
Durbee, Jonathan, 728
Durfee, E. H., Comdr., 407
Durfee, Joseph, Col., 311
Durham, Bartlett, Dr., 501
Durham, Conn., 93
Durham, Maine, 281
Durham, N.C., 501
Durham, N.H., 432
Durham County, N.C., 501
Durocher, Leo Ernest, 325
du Ru, Father, 275
Duryea, Charles, 171, 323
Duryea, Frank, 323
Duryea, Rulief, 191
Duson, C.C., 266
Dussault, Nancy, 130
Dustin, Hannah, 313
Dutchess County, N.Y.
    Beacon, 467
    Hyde Park, 474
    Poughkeepsie, 488
    Red Hook, 489
    Tivoli, 492–493
Dutch Harbor, Alaska, 17
Dutton, Charles S., 292
Dutton, Edward Payson, 435
Dutton, Ira Bruno, 695
Duval, Isaac, 746
Duval County, Fla., 123
Duval County, Tex., 668
Duvall, Robert, 69
Duvall, Shelley, 655
Duveneck, Frank, 247
Duxbury, Mass., 310
Dye, William M., Maj., 767
Dyer County, Tenn., 625
Dyersburg, Tenn., 625
Dykes, B.B., 140
Dylan, Bob, 350
Dysart, Richard, 278

E

Eads, Colo., 83
Eads, James, 200, 271, 396
Eagan, James, 383
Eager, Ariz., 27
Eager, John, 27
Eagle, Alaska, 17
Eagle, Colo., 83–84
Eagle County, Colo., 83–84, 90
Eagle Grove, Iowa, 215
Eagle Pass, Tex., 648
Eagle River, Mich., 333

Eagle River, Wis., 751
Eagleton, Thomas, 396
Eagletown, Okla., 549
Eames, Charles, 396
Earhart, Amelia, 122, 126, 228
Earibault, Jean Baptiste, 355
Earl, Lyman T., 227
Earle, Alice Morse, 593
Earle, Ralph, 326
Earlsboro, Okla., 549
Early, Jubal, Gen., 112, 296, 570, 588, 589,
    711, 712, 717, 720, 721
Early County, Ga., 138
Earp, Wyatt, 32, 183
East Baton Rouge Parish, La., 264, 273–274
East Brunswick, N.J., 446
East Carroll Parish, La., 269
East Chicago, Ind., 196
Easterly, George, 763
East Feliciana Parish, La., 265, 268
East Granby, Conn., 93
East Grand Forks, Minn., 350
East Greenwich, R.I., 593
East Haddam, Conn., 94
Eastham, Mass., 310
Easthampton, Mass., 310
East Hampton, N.Y., 472
East Hartford, Conn., 94
East Haven, Conn., 94
Eastin, Lucian J., Gen., 393
Eastlake, Samuel, 157
Eastland, James Oliver, Sen., 368
Eastland, Tex., 648
Eastland County, Tex., 644, 648, 666
East Lansing, Mich., 333
East Liverpool, Ohio, 530
Eastman, Charles Alexander, 357
Eastman, Ebenezer, 430
Eastman, Ga., 143
Eastman, George, 490, 494
Eastman, Joseph H., 688
Eastman, Max, 470
East Moline, Ill., 177
Easton, Mass., 310
Easton, Md., 296
Easton, Pa., 572–573
Easton, Rufus, Col., 169
Easton, William, Capt., 280
East Orange, N.J., 446
East Peoria, Ill., 177
Eastport, Maine, 281
East Providence, R.I., 593
East Rutherford, N.J., 446
East Saint Louis, Ill., 177
Eastville, Va., 705
East Windsor, Conn., 94
Eastwood, Clint, 71
Eaton, Dorman, 690
Eaton, James, 247
Eaton, John, 440
Eaton, John Henry, Sen., 503
Eaton, Josiah, Capt., 121
Eaton, Ohio, 530
Eaton, Samuel, 691
Eaton, William, 143, 530
Eaton County, Mich., 330, 334, 338–339
Eaton Rapids, Mich., 334
Eatonton, Ga., 143
Eatonville, Fla., 121
Eatop, Silas, 94
Eau Claire, Wis., 751
Eau Claire County, Wis., 751
Ebenburg, Pa., 573

Eberhart, Richard, 348
Ebert, Roger, 190
Ebey, Isaac, Col., 726
Ebey, Jacob, 726
Ebsen, Buddy, 170
Eccles, W.Va., 739
Echo, Utah, 677
Echols County, Ga., 154
Echota, Ga., 143
Eckstine, Billy, 584
Ector County, Tex., 663
Eddy, Charles B., 456
Eddy, John, 456
Eddy, Mary Baker, 289, 303, 306, 323, 430
Eddy, Nelson, 596
Eddy County, N.Dak., 520
Eddy County, N.Mex., 456, 463
Eddystone, Pa., 573
Eddyville, Ky., 247–248
Edelman, Herb, 468
Eden, Barbara, 33
Eden, Charles, Gov., 501
Eden, Colo., 84
Eden, Robert, 291, 296
Edenborn, William, 267
Edenton, N.C., 501
Edgar County, Ill., 185
Edgard, La., 266
Edgartown, Mass., 310
Edgecombe County, N.C., 508–510
Edgefield, S.C., 602
Edgefield County, S.C., 602
Edgeley, N.Dak., 517
Edgemont, S.Dak., 610
Edgerton, Sidney, 401
Edina, Mo., 382
Edinburg, Tex., 648
Edison, Thomas, 122, 343, 369, 449, 454, 480,
    536, 587
Edmond, Okla., 549
Edmonds, Wash., 726
Edmonson County, Ky., 245
Edmonton, Ky., 248
Edmunds, George F., Sen., 693
Edmunds, Jacob, 323
Edmunds County, S.Dak., 612
Edmundson, William, 503
Edna, Tex., 648
Edom, Va., 705
Edrington, William B., 44
Edward, Cliff (Ukelele Ike), 385
Edwards, Anthony, 73
Edwards, Blake, 557
Edwards, Douglas, 545
Edwards, Edwin, Gov., 264
Edwards, Isaac, 504
Edwards, Jonathan, 94, 318, 323
Edwards, Larkin, 274, 275
Edwards, Louis, Mayor, 477
Edwards, Miss., 366
Edwards, Ninian, Gov., 170
Edwards, Ralph, 463
Edwards, Stephen, 264
Edwards County, Ill., 169
Edwards County, Kans., 234
Edwards County, Tex., 667
Edwardsville, Ill., 177
Eells, Cushing, Rev., 733
Effingham, Ill., 177
Effingham, N.H., 432
Effingham County, Ga., 154
Effingham County, Ill., 177
Egan, Pat, Capt., 770

INDEX

Gooding, Frank R., Sen., 165
Gooding, Idaho, 165
Gooding County, Idaho, 165
Goodland, Kans., 232
Goodlett, Caroline, 634
Goodman, Benny, 174, 285
Goodman, John, 396
Goodman, Moses, 102
Goodman, Paul, 481
Goodnow, Mary, 313
Goodpasture, Ernest, 623
Goodrich, Benjamin, F., Dr., 523
Goodrich, Elizur, Rev., 93
Goodrich, Samuel Griswold, 100
Goodsill, Napoleon, 520
Goodson, Samuel, Col., 702
Goodwin, Hannibal, Rev., 451
Goodwin, Joseph, Capt., 92
Goodwin, Moses, 564
Goodwin, Nat, 305–306
Goodyear, Charles, 92, 98
Gookin, Daniel, 326
Gorbachev, Mikhail, Soviet Pres., 384
Gordon, Gail, 481
Gordon, George, 111
Gordon, James, 140
Gordon, John, 155, 707
Gordon, Joseph, 525
Gordon, Max, 480
Gordon, Richard, 731
Gordon, Robert, 363
Gordon, Ruth, 320
Gordon, W.W., 153
Gordon County, Ga., 139, 143, 150, 152
Gore, Albert Arnold, Vice Pres., 113, 121, 122, 127, 133, 134
Gorges, Ferdinand, Sir, 289, 290
Gorges, Robert, 315
Gorham, Ill., 179
Gorham, John, 592
Gorham, Maine, 282
Gorham, Nathaniel, 305, 487
Gorham, N.H., 433
Gorin, John, 249
Gorman, Margaret, 443
Gorme, Edie, 468
Gormley, John, 411
Gorshin, Frank, 584
Gorton, Samuel, 597
Gosdon, Freeman F. "Amos," 717
Goshen, Conn., 95
Goshen, Ind., 198
Goshen, N.Y., 473
Goshen County, Wyo., 767, 771
Gosnold, Bartholomew, 285, 308, 310, 317, 320
Gosnold, Mass., 312
Gosper County, Nebr., 412
Gosport, Ind., 198
Gossett, Louis, Jr., 468–469
Gottlieb, Adolph, 481
Gottschalk, Louis, 271
Gould, Abram, 495
Gould, Elliott, 469
Gould, Harold, 491
Gould, Jay, 44
Gould, Morton, 489
Goulding, Francis R., Rev., 152
Goulet, Robert, 314
Grady, Henry, 136, 139
Grady County, Ga., 139
Grady County, Okla., 548
Grafton, N.Dak., 518

Grafton, W.Va., 740
Grafton County, N.H.
    Ashland, 429
    Bath, 429
    Bethlehem, 430
    Campton, 430
    Enfield, 432
    Franconia, 432
    Hanover, 433
    Haverhill, 433
    Holderness, 434
    Lisbon, 435
    North Woodstock, 437
    Orford, 437
    Plymouth, 438
    Rumney, 439
Graham, Billy, 500
Graham, Edwin, 652
Graham, Frank Porter, Sen., 502
Graham, George, Capt., 500
Graham, Gustavus, 652
Graham, Harrison, 352
Graham, Isaac, 63
Graham, J. D., Col., 108
Graham, Katharine, 481
Graham, Martha, 584
Graham, Mary, 390
Graham, N.C., 502
Graham, Tex., 652
Graham, Thomas, 701
Graham, Virginia, 174
Graham, William A., 502, 505, 509
Graham County, Ariz., 31–32
Graham County, Kans., 232, 237
Graham County, N.C., 509
Graham Otto, 190
Grainger, Mary, 634
Grainger County, Tenn., 634
Grambling, La., 267
Gramm, Phil, Sen., 141
Granada, Colo., 85
Granbury, Hiram B., 652
Granbury, Tex., 652
Grand Canyon, Ariz., 27–28
Grand Chute, Wis., 752
Grand Coulee, Wash., 727
Grand County, Colo., 85
Grand County, Utah, 679
Grand Detour, Ill., 179
Grand Forks, N.Dak., 518
Grand Forks County, N.Dak., 518
Grand Gulf, Miss., 367
Grand Haven, Mich., 335
Grand Island, Nebr., 413
Grand Island, N.Y., 473
Grand Isle, La., 267
Grand Isle County, Vt., 685, 690, 692, 695
Grand Junction, Colo., 85
Grand Marais, Mich., 335
Grand Marais, Minn., 351
Grand Portage, Minn., 352
Grand Rapids, Mich., 335
Grand Rapids, Minn., 352
Grand Saline, Tex., 652
Grand Traverse County, Mich., 337, 346
Granger, Farley, 72
Granger, Francis, 470
Granger, Gen., 624
Granger, Madison Gideon, 101
Grangeville, Idaho, 165
Granite City, Ill., 179
Granite County, Mont., 406
Granite Falls, Minn., 352

Grant, Alexander, 453
Grant, James, Dr., 669
Grant, Jedediah Morgan, 679
Grant, John F., 403
Grant, Julia Dent, 395
Grant, Lee, 482
Grant, Nebr., 413
Grant, Ulysses S., 41, 178, 182, 246, 256, 265, 266, 269, 366, 367, 368, 372, 373, 375, 381, 386, 395, 429, 432, 449, 457, 479, 480, 531, 621, 625, 634, 700, 704, 712, 715, 718, 740
Grant City, Mo., 384
Grant County, Ind., 197, 201
Grant County, Kans., 241
Grant County, Ky., 260
Grant County, Minn., 350
Grant County, N.Dak., 516
Grant County, Nebr., 414
Grant County, N.Mex., 456, 462
Grant County, Okla., 552
Grant County, Oreg., 560, 565
Grant County, S.Dak., 608, 613
Grant County, W.Va., 744
Grant County, Wash., 726–727, 729
Grant County, Wis., 750, 755, 759
Grant Parish, La., 265
Grants, N.Mex., 458
Grants Pass, Oreg., 562
Grantsville, W.Va., 740
Granville, Ohio, 531
Granville County, N.C., 508
Grass, Daniel, 204
Grasso, Ella T. Gov., 103
Gratiot County, Mich., 327–328
Grattan, John, Lt., 771
Grattan, John L., Lt., 414
Grau, Shirley Ann, 272
Grauman's Chinese Theatre, 57
Grave County, Ky., 260
Graveraet, Robert, 340
Graves, John, 385
Graves, Peter, 355
Graves County, Ky., 254
Gray, Alice, 203
Gray, Edmund, 158
Gray, Edwin, 424
Gray, Elisha, 327
Gray, Ga., 145
Gray, Henry Judd, 482
Gray, James, 107, 145
Gray, John, 211, 525, 570, 688
Gray, Linda, 74
Gray, Maine, 282
Gray, Robert, Capt., 559, 723, 727
Gray County, Kans., 229, 237
Gray County, Tex., 664
Grayling, Mich., 335
Grays Harbor County, Wash., 723, 727–729
Grayson, Kathryn, 513
Grayson, Ky., 249
Grayson, Robert Col., 249
Grayson County, Ky., 252
Grayson County, Tex., 647, 670, 672
Grayson County, Va., 709
Graziano, Rocky, 482
Great Barrington, Mass., 312
Great Bend, Kans., 232
Great Falls, Mont., 404
Great Falls, S.C., 603
Greaves, Clinton, Corp., 456
Greb, Harry, 584
Greco, Buddy, 583

INDEX

INDEX

Jones, Willie, 628
Jonesboro, Ga., 147
Jonesboro, Ill., 180
Jonesboro, La., 268
Jonesborough, Tenn., 628
Jones County, Ga., 145
Jones County, Iowa, 210
Jones County, Miss., 366, 369
Jones County, N.C., 511
Jones County, S.Dak., 614
Jones County, Tex., 637–638
Jonesville, Va., 709
Jong, Erica, 482
Joplin, Harris G., Rev., 387
Joplin, Janis, 61, 665
Joplin, Mo., 387
Joplin, Scott, 397, 671
Joques, Isaac, Father, 475, 476
Jordan, Barbara, Cong., 654
Jordan, Jim, 186
Jordan, John, 652
Jordan, Michael, 469
Jordan, Mont., 405
Jordan, Thomas, 652
Jordan, Vernon, 137
Joseph, Chief, 402, 406, 408, 561, 765
Josephine County, Oreg., 562
Josey, J.J., 669
Joslin, Daniel R., 335
Jossie, John, 763
Jouett, John, Capt., 703
Jourdanton, Tex., 656
Joy, Caroline, 416
Joy, James, 438
Joyner, Daniel, 500
Joynter, Isaac, 473
Juab County, Utah, 677, 680
Juaniata County, Pa., 579
Juarez, Cayetano, 63
Judah, Theodore, 55, 68
Judd, Ashley, 61
Judd, Naomi, 61, 243
Judd, Wynonna, 243
Judith Basin County, Mont., 407
Judson, Asa, 353
Judson, Davis, 101
Judson, Edward G., 67
Judson, Peter, 733
Julesburg, Colo., 85–86
Jump, Gordon, 530
Junalaska, Chief, 509
Junction, Tex., 656–657
Junction, Utah, 678
Junction City, Kans., 233
Junction City, Ky., 251
Juneau, Alaska, 18–19
Juneau, Joe, 18
Juneau, Wis., 753
Juneau County, Wis., 756
Jupiter, Fla., 124
Juring, J.H., 746
Justis, John, 108
Justison, Andrew, 109

K

Ka'ahumanu, Queen, 159
Kaczynski, David, 405
Kaczynski, Theodore ("Unabomber"), 68, 405, 445
Kadoka, S.Dak., 612
Kael, Pauline, 66
Kahn, Herman, 444
Kahn, Madeline, 306

Kahoka, Mo., 387
Kahoolawe, Hawaii, 160
Kahquados, Simon Onanguisse, Chief, 752
Kailua, Hawaii, 160
Kailua-Kona, Hawaii, 160–161
Kakaako, Hawaii, 161
Kake, Alaska, 19
Kalakaua, David, 160
Kalama, John, 728
Kalama, Wash., 728
Kalamazoo, Mich., 338
Kalamazoo County, Mich., 338
Kalaniopau, Chief, 159
Kalaupapa, Hawaii, 161
Kalawao, Hawaii, 161
Kalawao County, Molokai island, 161
Kaline, Al, 292
Kalispell, Mont., 405
Kalkaska, Mich., 338
Kalkaska County, Mich., 338
Kamal, Ali Abu, 484
Kamehameha, King, 159, 161, 162
Kampan, Dan, 410
Kamuela (Waimea), Hawaii, 161
Kanab, Utah, 678
Kanabec County, Minn., 356
Kanaly, Steve, 52
Kanawha County, W. Va., 739, 741–742, 745
Kanawyer, J.J., 723
Kandiyohi County, Minn., 361
Kane, Carol, 528
Kane, Thomas L., 213, 678
Kane County, Ill.
    Aurora, 169–170
    Batavia, 170
    Elgin, 177
    Geneva, 179
    Saint Charles, 188
    West Dundee, 190
Kane County, Utah, 678
Kaneohe, Hawaii, 161
Kankakee, Ill., 180
Kankakee County, Ill., 171, 180
Kannapolis, N.C., 504
Kansas, 227–242
Kansas City, Kans., 233–234
Kansas City, Mo., 387–388
Kantor, MacKinlay, 225
Karnack, Tex., 657
Karnes, Henry, Capt., 657
Karnes City, Tex., 657
Karnes County, Tex., 657
Karpis, Alvin, 359
Karr, Gary Paul, 639
Karras, Alex, 198
Karshner, J.F., 20
Karstens, Harry, 17
Kasaan, Alaska, 19
Kasem, Casey, 333
Kaskaskia, Ill., 180–181
Kasson, Minn., 353
Kate, Fannie, 604
Kathan, John, 688
Katy, Tex., 657
Kauai County, Kauai island, 159, 161–162
Kauai County, Niihau island, 162
Kaufman, David S., Cong., 657
Kaufman, George S., 584
Kaufman, Tex., 657
Kaufman County, Tex., 646–647, 657
Kaukauna, Wis., 753
Kavner, Julie, 60
Kay, James K., 132

Kaycee, Wyo., 768
Kay County, Okla., 547, 553, 555
Kaye, Danny, 468
Kaye, Sammy, 533
Kayenta, Ariz., 28
Kaysville, Utah, 678
Kazan, Lainie, 483
Kazin, Alfred, 468
Keach, Stacy, 153
Kealakekua, Hawaii, 161
Kean, John, Sen., 448
Keansburg, N.J., 448
Kearney, Mo., 388
Kearney, Nebr., 414
Kearney, Philip, 594
Kearney, Stephen W., 55, 63, 89, 462
Kearney County, Kans., 234
Kearney County, Nebr., 415–416
Kearns, Thomas, 682
Keaton, Buster, 242
Keaton, Diane, 73
Kedzie, William, 332
Keefauver, Estes, Sen., 630
Keeler, Timothy, 100
Keene, Benjamin, Sir, 435
Keene, N.H., 435
Keeney, Jonathan, 566
Keeshan, Bob (Captain Kangaroo), 490
Keewatin, Minn., 353
Keillor, Garrison, 348
Keim, Jacob, 443
Keimer, Samuel, 581
Keith, Brian, 444
Keith, David, 629
Keith, Josiah, 310
Keith, Rebecca, 662
Keith, Stephen, 662
Keith County, Nebr., 417
Keller, Helen, 5, 13, 323
Keller, W.H., 195
Keller, William, 5
Kellerman, Sally, 59
Kelley, Addison, 533
Kelley, B.F., Col., 744
Kelley, Datus, 532
Kelley, De Forest, 137
Kelley, Ellsworth, 485
Kelley, Florence, 582
Kelley, Irad, 532
Kelleys Island, Ohio, 532–533
Kellogg, Dorr, 341
Kellogg, Frank Billings, Sen., 488
Kellogg, Idaho, 165
Kellogg, John Harvey, Dr., 328
Kellogg, Noah, 165
Kellogg, Will, 328
Kellogg, W.K., 66
Kelly, Charles T., 213, 215
Kelly, Emmett, 239, 386
Kelly, Gene, 584
Kelly, Grace, 583
Kelly, Joseph, 212
Kelly, William, 251, 584
Kellyville, Okla., 551
Kelso, Wash., 728
Kemmerer, Wyo., 768
Kemmler, William, 466
Kemp, Jack, Sen., 60
Kemper, Peter, 720
Kemper County, Miss., 366
Kenai, Alaska, 19
Kenai Peninsula Borough, Alaska, 18–19, 22–23
Kenan, James, Col., 504

Kingford, E.G., 338
King George, Va., 710
King George County, Va., 710, 715
Kingman, Ariz., 28
Kingman, Kans., 234
Kingman County, Kans., 234
King of Prussia, Pa., 576–577
King Salmon, Alaska, 19
Kingsbury, Cyrus, Rev., 547
Kingsbury, Elisha, 429
Kingsbury, Ephraim, 429
Kingsbury, George W., 609
Kingsbury County, S.Dak., 609–610, 613
Kings County, Calif., 56
Kings County, N.Y., 468–469
Kingsford, Mich., 338
Kingsland, Ark., 41
Kingsley, Zephaniah, 123
Kingsmill, Richard, 720
Kings Mountain, N.C., 504
Kingsport, Tenn., 628
Kingston, Mo., 388
Kingston, N.H., 435
Kingston, N.Y., 475
Kingston, Ohio, 533
Kingston, R.I., 594
Kingston, Tenn., 629
Kingston, Tex., 657
Kingstree, S.C., 603
Kingsville, Tex., 657
King William, Va., 710
King William County, Va., 710, 720
Kingwood, W.Va., 741
Kinkaid, Thomas Casson, 433
Kinkel, Kipland, 565
Kinney, Abbott, 76
Kinney, Henry L., 641, 645
Kinney, James, 730
Kinney, John, Judge, 410
Kinney, Joseph, Capt., 383
Kinney County, Tex., 641
Kino, Eusebio Francisco, 29, 32, 33
Kinsey, Stephen A., 425
Kinsley, Kans., 234
Kinsman, Ohio, 533
Kinston, N.C., 505
Kiowa, Colo., 86
Kiowa County, Colo., 83, 89
Kiowa County, Kans., 232
Kiowa County, Okla., 551
Kipling, Rudyard, 449, 687
Kipp, James, 407
Kiptopeke, Va., 710
Kirby, Durwood, 247
Kirby-Smith, Edmund, 131, 269
Kirk, Jesse, 388
Kirk, Jesse, Mrs., 388
Kirk, Peter, 728
Kirkland, Lane, 600
Kirkland, Wash., 728
Kirkparick, J.C., 570
Kirkpatrick, Jeanne, 549
Kirkpatrick, Judson, Maj. Gen., 502
Kirksville, Mo., 388
Kirkwood, James P., 388
Kirkwood, Mo., 388–389
Kirtland, Ohio, 533
Kirtland, Philip, 314
Kirwan, Michael J., 539
Kirwin, Joseph, 185
Kirwin, Kans., 234
Kissimmee, Fla., 124
Kit Carson County, Colo., 80

Kitsap County, Wash., 723–724, 730
Kittanning, Pa., 577
Kittery, Maine, 283
Kittinger, Joe W., 280
Kittinger, Joseph, Capt., 455
Kittitas County, Wash., 725–726, 731
Kittredge, Thomas, 318
Kittrell, P.W., 660
Kittrell, Solomon, 393
Kittson, Norman, 352, 521
Kittson County, Minn., 352
Kitty Hawk, N.C., 505
Klaas, Polly, 66
Klamath County, Oreg., 560–562
Klamath Falls, Oreg., 562
Klaus, Anton, 518
Kleberg, Alice King, 637
Kleberg County, Tex., 657
Klebold, Dylan, 87
Klein, Calvin, 483
Klein, Chuck, 199
Klein, Robert, 483
Klickitat County, Wash., 726–727
Kline, Franz, 589
Kline, Kevin, 396
Kling, Marin Luther, 175
Klock, Johannes, 490
Kluckhohn, Clyde, 219
Klugman, Jack, 583
Knapp, Gilbert, Capt., 760
Knapp, John H., 216
Knapp, John H, 569
Kneisel, Franz, Dr., 279
Knife, Dull, Chief, 410
Knight, Billy, 671
Knight, Gladys, 137
Knight, Newt, 366, 369
Knight, Sarah Kemble, 305
Knight, Ted, 101
Knoell, Ernie, 476
Knoph, Alfred Abraham, 480
Knott, W.H., 207
Knott County, Ky., 251
Knotts, Don, 743
Knox, Charles, 475
Knox, Henry, 218, 288, 305, 629
Knox, Ind., 199
Knox, J.D., 347
Knox, Philander Chase, Sen., 569
Knox, Timothy, 697
Knox County, Ill., 178
Knox County, Ind., 206
Knox County, Ky., 243, 247
Knox County, Maine
  Camden, 280
  Rockland, 287
  Rockport, 287
  Saint George, 287
  Thomaston, 288
  Union, 289
  Warren, 289
Knox County, Mo., 382
Knox County, Nebr., 411, 416, 419
Knox County, Ohio, 531, 536
Knox County, Tenn., 629
Knox County, Tex., 640
Knoxville, Ga., 147
Knoxville, Iowa, 218
Knoxville, Tenn., 629
Knyphause, Gen., 449
Knyphausen, Gen., 571
Kocherthal, Joshua, 485
Kodiak, Alaska, 19–20

Kodiak Island Borough, Alaska, 19–20
Koekuk County, Iowa, 223
Koenig, Joseph, 762
Koepfli, Caspar, Dr., 179
Kohala, Hawaii, 161
Kohler, Walter, J., 761
Kohler, Wis., 754
Kokomo, Ind., 199–200
Koloa, Hawaii, 161
Kona, Hawaii, 161
Konkapot, Chief, 312
Koochiching County, Minn., 353
Koon, Stacey, Sgt., 61
Kootenai County, Idaho, 164
Kopechne, Mary Jo, 310
Kopell, Bernie, 482
Koresh, David, 673
Korman, Harvey, 174
Kornberg,Arthur, 468
Kosciusko, Miss., 369
Kosciusko, Thaddeus, 207
Kosciusko County, Ind., 207
Kosciuszko, Thaddeus, 471, 583
Kossuth, Louis, 209
Kossuth County, Iowa, 209
Kosygin, Alexei, 447
Kotto, Yophet, 482
Kotzebue, Alaska, 20
Kotzebue, Otto von, 20
Koufax, Sandy, 468
Kountze, Tex., 657
Kraft, J.L., 749
Kraft, William, 749
Kramer, Jack, 425
Kramer, Stanley, 481
Krebs, Okla., 551
Krist, Gary, 137
Kristofferson, Kris, 642
Kroeber, Alfred Louis, 448
Kronholm, Gunnar, 359
Krug, August, 757
Krupa, Gene, 174
Krutch, Joseph Wood, 629
Kubrick, Stanley, 468
Kuhlman, Kathryn, 381
Kuhn, Bowie, 333
Kuhn, Walt, 468
Kulm, N.Dak., 518
Kunitz, Stanley, 326
Kupreanof Island, Alaska, 19
Kuralt, Charles, 512
Kurtz, Swoosie, 417
Kuskof, Ivan, 51, 58
Kuskokwim Bay, Alaska, 21
Kuskokwim River, Alaska, 16
Kuttawa, Ky., 251
Kuyper, Lucille, 222
Kuyper, Peter, 222
Kyle, Robert B., Col., 7
Kyn, Joran, 571

L

La Balme, Auguste de, Col., 195
La Bathe, Joseph, 360
La Bell, Fla., 125
LaBelle, Patti, 583
Labette County, Kans., 238
Lacey, Lewis, 340
Lackawanna, N.Y., 475
Lackawanna County, Pa., 586–587
Lackawaxen, Pa., 577
Laclede, Mo., 389

Lansing, Robert, 69, 494
Lantana, Fla., 125
Lanyon, Robert, 238
La Paz County, Ariz., 30–31
Lapeer, Mich., 339
Lapeer County, Mich., 339
La Place, La., 269
La Plata, Md., 298
La Plata County, Colo., 83, 85
La Pointe, Wis., 754–755
La Porte, Ind., 200
Laporte, John, 577
Laporte, Pa., 577
La Porte County, Ind., 200–201
Lapwai, Idaho, 165
Larabee, Sarah, 615
La Ramie, Jacques, 768
Laramie, Wyo., 768
Laramie County, Wyo., 766
Lardner, Lynford, 567
Lardner, Ring (Ringgold Wilmer), 342
Laredo, Ruth, 333
Laredo, Tex., 658
Largo, Fla., 125
Larimer, William, Gen., 82
Larimer County, Colo., 84, 87
Lariviere, Philips, 84
Larkin, Thomas O., 63
Larned, Kans., 234
Larrabee, John, 288, 695
Larroquette, John, 272
Larson, Faye, Mrs., 524
La Rue, Isaac, 745
La Rue, Jacob, 745
Larue County, Ky., 251, 256
Larwill, Joseph, 543
Larwill, William, 543
La Salle, Ill., 181
La Salle, Robert de, 469, 476
La Salle County, Ill.
  La Salle, 181
  Norway, 185
  Ottawa, 185
  Peru, 186
  Streator, 189
  Troy Grove, 189
La Salle County, Tex., 645
La Salle Parish, La., 268
Las Animas, Colo., 86
Las Animas County, Colo.
  Delagua, 82
  Hastings, 85
  Las Animas, 86
  Ludlow, 87
  Primero, 88
  Trinidad, 89
Lasater, Edward, 649
Las Cruces, N.Mex., 459
Lassen County, Calif., 75–76
Lasser, Louise, 483
Lasuen, Fermin, Padre, 56
Las Vegas, Nev., 425–426
Las Vegas, N.Mex., 459
Latah County, Idaho, 166
Latham, James, 181
Lathrop, John, 180
Lathrop, Julia Clifford, 187
Latimer, Lewis Howard, 308
Latimer County, Okla., 558
Latrobe, Benjamin, Jr., 577
Latrobe, Pa., 577
Lauder, Estee, 481
Lauderdale, William, Maj., 121

Lauderdale County, Ala., 6–7, 9
Lauderdale County, Miss., 370–371
Lauderdale County, Tenn., 627, 634
Laughlin, Nev., 426
Laughlin, W.C., 562
Laughton, Marie Ware, 438
Lauper, Cyndi, 483
Laurel, Del., 106
Laurel, Md., 298
Laurel, Miss., 369
Laurel, Nebr., 414
Laurel, Stan, 136
Laurel County, Ky., 253
Laurel Run, Pa., 577
Lauren, Ralph, 468
Laurens, Henry, 604
Laurens, S.C., 604
Laurens County, Ga., 143
Laurens County, S.C., 604
Laurie, Piper, 333
Laurinburg, N.C., 505
Laurium, Mich., 339
Lauter, Ed, 477
Lavaca County, Tex., 653
La Vasseur, Noel, 171
Lavin, Linda, 286
Law, Bernard, Cardinal, 307
Law, John, 35, 178, 187, 363
Lawrence, Alexander, 550
Lawrence, Amos A., 234, 313, 749
Lawrence, Ariel, 98
Lawrence, E.O., 609
Lawrence, Isaac, Capt., 92
Lawrence, Jacob, 443
Lawrence, James, Capt., 147, 181, 445, 449,
  629
Lawrence, John, 767
Lawrence, Kans., 234
Lawrence, Mass., 313–314
Lawrence, Steve, 468
Lawrence, Vicki, 57
Lawrence, William, 252, 687
Lawrenceburg, Ind., 200
Lawrenceburg, Ky., 252
Lawrenceburg, Tenn., 629
Lawrence County, Ala., 10–11
Lawrence County, Ill., 181
Lawrence County, Ind., 194, 201
Lawrence County, Ky., 253
Lawrence County, Miss., 371
Lawrence County, Mo., 391
Lawrence County, Ohio, 532
Lawrence County, Pa., 580
Lawrence County, S.Dak., 610, 612, 617, 619
Lawrence County, Tenn., 629
Lawrenceville, Ga., 147
Lawrenceville, Ill., 181
Lawrenceville, N.J., 449
Lawrenceville, Va., 710
Laws, George W., 753
Lawson, Ernest, 70
Lawson, John, 507, 510
Lawson, Roger, 148
Lawton, Okla., 552
Lay, Elza, 166
Laycock, S.G., Dr., 264
Layland, W.Va., 741
Lazarus, Emma, 479
Lea, Albert, Col., 347
Lea, Margaret, 9
Lea, Pleasant, 389
Leachman, Cloris, 215
Lea County, N.Mex., 458–460

Lead, S.Dak., 612
Leadville, Colo., 86–87
Leahy, Frank, 417
Leahy, William Daniel, Adm., 217
Leake, Walter, Gov., 365, 369
Leake County, Miss., 365
Leakesville, Miss., 369
Leakey, John, 658
Leakey, Tex., 658
Lear, Norman, 98
Learned, Michael, 113
Lease, Mary Elizabeth, 585
Leathers, A.J., 425
Leaton, Ben, 665
Leavenworth, Henry, 235, 355, 552, 614
Leavenworth, Ind., 200
Leavenworth, Kans., 235
Leavenworth County, Kans., 234–235
Leavitt, Daniel, 89
Leavitt, Henrietta Swan, 313
Lebanon, Conn., 96
Lebanon, Ill., 181
Lebanon, Ind., 200
Lebanon, Kans., 235
Lebanon, Ky., 252
Lebanon, Mo., 389
Lebanon, Ohio, 533
Lebanon, Oreg., 562–563
Lebanon, Pa., 577
Lebanon, Tenn., 630
Lebanon, Va., 710
Lebanon County, Pa., 577
Lebec, Calif., 58
Lebecque, Peter, 58
le Bone, Mary, 638
Le Center, Minn., 353
Leche, Richard, Gov., 264
le Claire, Antoine, 214, 218
Le Claire, Iowa, 218
Lecompte, Samuel D., 235
Lecompton, Kans., 235
Lecon, William, 101
Ledbetter, Huddle William (Lead Belly), 270
Lederberg, Joshua, 449
Lederer, John, 712, 720
le Duc, trapper, 751
le Duc, William Gates, Gen., 352
Ledyard, William, Lt. Col., 95
Lee, Ann, Mother, 494
Lee, Brenda, 137
Lee, Charles, 720
Lee, Euel, 302
Lee, Fitzhugh, 294, 570, 705, 706, 707
Lee, Francis Lightfoot, 712
Lee, George H., Judge, 739
Lee, Gypsy Rose (Hovick, Rose), 731
Lee, Harper, 10
Lee, Henry (Lighthorse Harry), 147, 448, 705,
  709
Lee, Isaac James, 9
Lee, Jason, 386, 563, 565
Lee, Jeremiah, Col., 315
Lee, John D., 29, 675, 677
Lee, L.N., 229
Lee, Mass., 314
Lee, Michelle, 60
Lee, Peggy, 518
Lee, Robert E., Gen., 154, 155, 297, 299, 301,
  574, 575, 638, 666, 700, 704, 705, 712,
  718
Lee, Samuel, 322
Lee, Spike, 137
Lee, Stephen D., 365

Lynn Canal estuary, Alaska, 22
Lynn County, Tex., 671
Lyon, David, 200
Lyon, Henry W., Rear Adm., 288
Lyon, John E., 438
Lyon, Lucius, 750
Lyon, Matthew, 689
Lyon, Nathaniel, Gen., 222, 378, 395, 397
Lyon County, Iowa, 222
Lyon County, Kans., 231
Lyon County, Ky., 247–248, 251
Lyon County, Minn., 354–355, 360
Lyon County, Nev., 427–428
Lyons, Ga., 148
Lyons, Kans., 235
Lyons, N.Y., 477
Lyons, William, Col., 365

M

MacArthur, Arthur, 323
MacArthur, Douglas, 41, 332, 714
MacArthur, James, 60
Macclenny, Fla., 125
MacDonald, Gerald, 407
MacDonald, Jeannette, 583
MacDonald, Robert, 407
MacDonald, Ross, 60
MacDonough, Thomas, 108, 149, 182, 694, 695–696
MacDowell, Andie, 602
MacDowell, Edward, 438, 480
MacGahan, J.A., 537
MacGregor, John, 283
Machias, Maine, 284
MacIntosh, Sheriff, 369
Mack, Connie, 307
Mack, Henry R., 690
Mack, Ted, 85
MacKage, Wallace, 480
Mackenzie, Ranald, Col., 643, 661
Mackinac County, Mich., 339, 344
Mackinac Island, Mich., 339
Mackinaw City, Mich., 340
Mackle, Barbara Jane, 137
Mackley, Charles, 33
MacLaine, Shirley, 717
Maclay, William, 587
Maclot, John N., 385
Maclure, William, 202
MacMillan, Donald, 320
MacMurray, Fred, 180
MacNeil, Cornell, 355
Macomb, Alexander, 182, 335
Macomb, Ill., 182
Macomb, J.N., Capt., 88
Macomb County, Mich., 341, 345–346
Macon, Ga., 148–149
Macon, Miss., 370
Macon, Mo., 390
Macon, Nathaniel, 148, 502
Macon County, Ala., 11, 13
Macon County, Ga., 136, 149, 151
Macon County, Ill., 176
Macon County, Mo., 390
Macon County, N.C., 502
Macoupin County, Ill., 172, 183
MacRae, Gordon, 446
Macy, Anne Mansfield Sullivan, 323
Macy, John B., 759
Macy, Nebr., 415
Macy, Thomas, 303
Madden, John, 348

Maddocks, Luther, 279
Maddox, Lester, 137
Maddy, Joseph E., 346
Madero, Jose Francisco, 658
Madill, George A., 552
Madill, Okla., 552
Madison, Conn., 96
Madison, Dorothea (Dolly) Payne, 502
Madison, Fla., 125
Madison, Ga., 149
Madison, Guy, 50
Madison, Ind., 200–201
Madison, James, 149, 201, 267, 291, 470, 502, 582, 663, 709, 710, 714, 715, 720
Madison, Minn., 354
Madison, Nebr., 415
Madison, N.J., 449
Madison, S.Dak., 613
Madison, Va., 711
Madison, Wis., 755
Madison, W.Va., 742
Madison County, Ala., 8, 11
Madison County, Fla., 125
Madison County, Ga., 142
Madison County, Idaho, 167–168
Madison County, Ill.
  Alton, 169
  Collinsville, 176
  Edwardsville, 177
  Granite City, 179
  Highland, 179–180
Madison County, Ind., 193, 196
Madison County, Iowa, 225
Madison County, Ky., 244, 258
Madison County, Miss., 364–365, 368–369
Madison County, Mo., 383
Madison County, Mont., 408
Madison County, N.C., 506
Madison County, Nebr., 415–416
Madison County, N.Y., 486, 493
Madison County, Ohio, 534
Madison County, Tenn., 627–628
Madison County, Tex., 660
Madison County, Va., 711
Madison Parish, La., 266, 275
Madisonville, Ky., 254
Madisonville, Tenn., 630
Madisonville, Tex., 660
Madonna (Ciccone), 329
Madras, Oreg., 563
Madrid, N.Mex., 460
Magevney, Eugene, 631
Magnolia, Ark., 42
Magnolia, Miss., 370
Magoffin, Beriah, Gov., 258
Magofin County, Ky., 258
Magruder, Jeb, 114
Magruder, John, Gen., 722
Mahaska County, Iowa, 221
Mahnomen, Minn., 354
Mahnomen County, Minn., 354
Mahoney, Edward L., 299
Mahoning County, Ohio, 543
Maiden, N.C., 505
Maier, Henry, 757
Mailer, Norman, 449
Maine, 277–290
Maine Prairie, Minn., 354
Maitland, Fla., 125
Maitland, William S., Capt., 125
Major County, Okla., 550
Majors, Lee, 346
Malad City, Idaho, 166

Malamud, Bernard, 468
Malcolm, Dorothy, 150
Malcolm, Roger, 150
Malcolm X (Little, Malcolm), 417, 484
Malden, Karl, 174
Malden, Mass., 315
Malden, W.Va., 742
Maldonado, Lucas, Father, 455
Malheur County, Oreg., 566
Malibu, Calif., 61
Malichy, R.T., 667
Mallory, Peter, 102
Malone, Dorothy, 174
Malone, Edmund, 477
Malone, N.Y., 477
Malone, Vivian, 13
Maloney, John, 732
Malta, Mont., 406
Malvern, Ark., 42
Malvo, John Lee, 297
Manassa, Colo., 87
Manassas, Va., 711
Manassas City, Va., 711
Manassas Park, Va., 711
Manassas Park City, Va., 711
Manatee County, Fla., 118
Manby, A.R., 463
Manchester, Iowa, 219
Manchester, Ky., 254
Manchester, Melissa, 468
Manchester, N.H., 435–436
Manchester, N.Y., 477
Manchester, S.Dak., 613
Manchester, Tenn., 630
Manchester, Vt., 691
Mancini, Henry, 528
Mandan, N.Dak., 519
Mandel, Harry, 770
Mandeville, La., 269
Mandrell, Barbara, 655
Mandt, T.G., 761
Mangione, Chuck, 490
Mangum, Okla., 552
Manhattan, Kans., 235–236
Manhattan, N.Y., 477
Manheim, Pa., 578
Manila, Utah, 679
Manilow, Barry, 483
Manistee, Mich., 340
Manistee County, Mich., 328, 340
Manistique, Mich., 340
Manitou Springs, Colo., 87
Manitowish Waters, Wis., 755–756
Manitowoc, Wis., 756
Manitowoc County, Wis., 756, 760, 762
Mankato, Kans., 236
Mankato, Minn., 354
Manley, Frank, 20
Manley Hot Springs, Alaska, 20
Mann, Herbie, 482
Mann, James Robert, Cong., 170
Mann, John, 437
Mann, Thomas, 437
Mann, William Hodges, Gov., 714
Manning, N.Dak., 519
Manning, Richard, 287
Manning, S.C., 604
Manny, J.L., 187
Manofff, Dinah, 483
Mansfield, Jared, 534
Mansfield, La., 269
Mansfield, Mike, Cong., 481
Mansfield, Ohio, 534

INDEX

INDEX

Owings, Thomas, Col., 256
Owingsville, Ky., 256
Ownsley, William, 252
Owosso, Mich., 342
Owsley County, Ky., 244
Owyhee County, Idaho, 166
Oxford, Conn., 99
Oxford, Ga., 151
Oxford, Ind., 203
Oxford, Mass., 319
Oxford, Miss., 371–372
Oxford, N.C., 508
Oxford, Ohio, 538
Oxford County, Maine
  Bethel, 279
  Fryeburg, 282
  Paris, 285
  Rumford, 287
  South Paris, 288
  Waterford, 289
Oxnard, Calif., 65
Oyster Bay, N.Y., 487
Ozark, Ala., 11
Ozark, Ark., 44
Ozark, Mo., 392
Ozark County, Mo., 384
Ozaukee County, Wis., 759
Ozona, Tex., 663

P

Pabst, Frederick, 757
Paca, William, 291
Pace, C.G., 375
Pacheco, Salvio, 53
Pacific County, Wash., 728, 733
Pacino, Al, 483
Pack, Edward, 109
Packard, J. Ward, 542
Packard, Ky., 256
Packer, Alfred, 767
Packwood, Bob, Sen., 564
Packwood, George H., 125
Pacoima, Calif., 65
Pacquette, Paul, 614
Padilla, Juan, 28
Paducah, Ky., 256–257
Paducah, Tex., 663
Paduke, Chickasaw Chief, 256, 257
Page, A. Frank, 499
Page, Ariz., 29
Page, David, 435
Page, Geraldine, 388
Page, Patti, 548
Page, Walter Hines, 499
Page County, Iowa, 212
Page County, Va., 711
Pagosa Springs, Colo., 88
Paige, Satchel, 9
Paine, Francis, 320
Paine, John Knowles, 286
Paine, Robert T., 305, 324
Paine, Thomas, 581, 593
Paineville, Ohio, 538
Painter, Gamaliel, 691
Paint Rock, Tex., 663
Paintsville, Ky., 257
Palatine Bridge, N.Y., 487
Palatka, Fla., 129
Palestine, Tex., 663–664
Palisade, Nev., 426
Palm Beach, Fla., 129
Palm Beach County, Fla.
  Belle Glade, 118

  Boca Raton, 118
  Jupiter, 124
  Lantana, 125
  Palm Beach, 129
  West Palm Beach, 134
Palmer, Alaska, 21
Palmer, Ambrose E., 329
Palmer, Arnold, 577
Palmer, Betsy, 196
Palmer, D.D., 214
Palmer, Dennison, 339
Palmer, Dudley, 101
Palmer, Edward, 487
Palmer, H.E., Capt., 765
Palmer, Potter, Mrs., 132
Palmer, William, Gen., 81, 87
Palm Springs, Calif., 65
Palmyra, Mo., 392
Palmyra, N.Y., 487
Palmyra, Va., 715
Palo Alto, Calif., 65
Palo Alto County, Iowa, 215
Palo Pinto, Tex., 664
Palo Pinto County, Tex., 661, 664
Palos, Ala., 11
Palo Verde, Ariz., 29
Pamlico County, N.C., 498
Pampa, Tex., 664
Panama City, Fla., 129
Panguitch, Utah, 680
Panhandle, Tex., 664
Panola County, Miss., 363, 374
Panola County, Tex., 643, 651, 662
Panton, Vt., 692
Paola, Kans., 238
Paoli, Ind., 203
Paoli, Pa., 581
Paoli, Pasquale, Gen., 581
Papillion, Nebr., 418
Papp, Joseph, 468
Papst, Rudolph, 328
Paradise, Wash., 729
Paragould, Ark., 44
Paramore, J. W., 44
Paramus, N.J., 451
Parham F.A., 623
Paris, Ark., 44
Paris, Idaho, 166
Paris, Ill., 185
Paris, Ky., 257
Paris, Maine, 285
Paris, Mo., 393
Paris, Tenn., 633
Paris, Tex., 664
Parish, Cople, 708
Parish, David, 486
Parish, John, 329
Park, George S., Col., 235, 393
Park City, Ky., 257
Park City, Utah, 680
Park County, Colo., 81, 84
Park County, Mont., 404, 406
Park County, Wyo., 765–766, 769
Parke County, Ind., 204
Parker, Alexander, 743
Parker, Ariz., 30
Parker, Asa, 576
Parker, Bonnie, 264
Parker, Charles, 234, 536
Parker, C.W., 642
Parker, Cynthia, 547, 646, 652, 666
Parker, Fess, 650
Parker, Francis Wayland, 429

Parker, George, 753
Parker, Isaac, Judge, 39
Parker, James, 308, 652
Parker, Jameson, 292
Parker, Jean, 403
Parker, John, 161
Parker, Lyon, 50
Parker, Marian, 60
Parker, Mary E., 556
Parker, Peter, Sir, 295
Parker, P.P., 516
Parker, Quanah, Comanche Chief, 547, 646, 665, 671
Parker, Robert Leroy, (Butch Cassidy), 675
Parker, Samuel, 766
Parker, S.Dak., 614
Parker, Walter, 271
Parker, W.B., 259
Parker County, Tex., 661, 673
Parkersburg, W.Va., 743–744
Park Hills, Mo., 393
Parkhurst, Charlotte, 74
Parkin, Ark., 44
Parkin, Walter, 58
Parkin, William, 44
Parkins, Isaac, 721
Park Rapids, Minn., 357
Park Ridge, Ill., 186
Parks, Benjamin, 142
Parks, George, 21
Parks, Rosa, 10, 13
Parks, William, 720
Parkville, Mo., 393
Parmelee, Dave, 615
Parmelee, S.Dak., 615
Parmer, Martin, 649
Parmer County, Tex., 649
Parowan, Utah, 680
Parr, Charles, 212
Parr, Jack, 525
Parrant, Pierre "Pig's Eve," 358
Parrot, "Big Nose George," 769
Parshall, N.Dak., 520
Parsons, Elizabeth, 219
Parsons, Elsie Clews, 480
Parsons, Estelle, 315
Parsons, James, 744
Parsons, Kans., 238
Parsons, Levi, 238
Parsons, Samuel, 102
Parsons, Thomas, Jr., 744
Parsons, William, 572
Parsons, W.Va., 744
Parton, Dolly, 626, 635
Pasadena, Calif., 65–66
Pasadena, Tex., 664
Pascagoula, Miss., 372
Pasco, Wash., 730
Pasco County, Fla., 120
Pasquotank County, N.C., 501
Passaic, N.J., 451
Passaic County, N.J., 451–453
Pass Christian, Miss., 372
Pastor, Tony, 479
Pataki, George E., Gov., 487
Patch, Dan (race horse), 359
Paterson, N.J., 451–452
Paterson, William, Gov., 451
Patinkin, Mandy, 174
Patrick, Daniel, 95
Patrick, Samuel, 470
Patrick County, Va., 718
Patterson, Floyd, 509

INDEX

INDEX

INDEX

Saint Paul, Nebr., 418–419
Saint Peter, Minn., 359
Saint Petersburg, Fla., 132
Saint Simons Island, Ga., 153
Saint Tammany Parish, La., 266, 269, 275
Sajak, Pat, 174
Saks, Gene, 482
Salamanca, N.Y., 490–491
Salameh, Mohammed, 448
Salas, Juan Pablo, 124
Salazar, Ruben, 61
Saldivar, Yolanda, 645
Sale, Charles Partlow "Chic," 612
Salem, Ark., 45
Salem, Ill., 188
Salem, Ind., 204
Salem, Mass., 321
Salem, Mo., 397
Salem, N.H., 439
Salem, N.J., 453
Salem, Ohio, 539
Salem, Oreg., 565
Salem, S.Dak., 616
Salem, Va., 717
Salem City, Va., 717
Salem County, N.J., 452–453
Salford, Robert, 713
Salida, Colo., 88–89
Salina, Kans., 239
Salina, Okla., 555
Salinas, Calif., 68
Saline County, Ill., 179
Saline County, Kans., 239
Saline County, Mo., 377–378, 390
Saline County, Nebr., 412, 420
Salinger, J.D., 481
Salisbury, Mass., 321
Salisbury, Md., 301
Salisbury, N.C., 509
Salisbury, N.H., 439
Salisbury, Vt., 694
Salk, Jonas, 69, 481
Salle, Sieur de la, 395
Sallier, Charles, 269
Sallisaw, Okla., 555
Salmon, Idaho, 167
Saltiel, Emanuel H., 82
Salt Lake City, Utah, 681–682
Salt Lake County, Utah
  Bingham Canyon, 675
  Bluffdale, 676
  Draper, 676
  Midvale, 679
  Murray, 680
  Point of Mountain, 681
  Salt Lake City, 681–682
  West Valley City, 683
Saluda, S.C., 606
Saluda, Va., 717
Saluda County, S.C., 606
Salvi, John, 306
Salyers, Sam, Cong., 258
Salyersville, Ky., 258
Sampras, Pete, 114
Sampson, William T., 487
Sampson County, N.C., 498, 500, 507
Samuelson, Anthony Paul, 197
San Andreas, Calif., 68
San Angelo, Tex., 668
San Antonio, Tex., 668
San Augustine, Tex., 668
San Augustine County, Tex., 668
San Benito County, Calif., 57

San Bernardino, Calif., 68
San Bernardino County, Calif.
  Barstow, 51
  Colton, 53
  Loma Linda, 58
  Needles, 63–64
  Ontario, 65
  Redlands, 67
  San Bernardino, 68
  Twentynine Palms, 76
  Victorville, 77
Sanborn, Franklin B., 433
Sanborn, William, 429
Sanborn County, S.Dak., 619
San Bruno, Calif., 69
San Buenaventura, Calif., 69
Sanchez, Gil, 63
Sanchez, Thomas, 658
San Clemente, Calif., 69
Sandburg, Carl, 178
Sanders, Harland T., 247
Sanders, Newell, 623
Sanders County, Mont., 407–408
Sanderson, Tex., 669
Sanderson, William, 631
Sandersville, Ga., 153
San Diego, Calif., 69
San Diego, Tex., 668
San Diego County, Calif.
  Chula Vista, 52–53
  Coronado, 53–54
  El Cajon, 55
  Escondido, 55
  La Jolla, 58
  Oceanside, 64
  San Diego, 69
Sandoval County, N.Mex., 456, 459
Sandoz, Mari, 418
Sand Point, Alaska, 22
Sandpoint, Idaho, 167
Sands, Robert, 468
Sandusky, Mich., 345
Sandusky, Ohio, 539–540
Sandusky County, Ohio, 531
Sandwich, Mass., 321
Sandy Hook, Ky., 258
San Felipe, Tex., 668–669
Sanford, Aaron, 100
Sanford, Charles O., Col., 509
Sanford, Edward Terry, Justice, 629
Sanford, Fla., 132
Sanford, Henry R., Gen., 132
Sanford, Isabel, 481
Sanford, John, Gen., 149
Sanford, Maine, 287
Sanford, N.C., 509
Sanford, Peleg, 287
San Francisco, Calif., 69–71
San Francisco County, Calif., 69–71
San Gabriel, Calif., 71
Sangamon County, Ill., 189
Sanger, Margaret, 471
Sangerville, Maine, 287
Sanilac County, Mich., 331, 345
San Jacinto, Nev., 427
San Jacinto County, Tex., 644
San Joaquin County, Calif., 58, 75
San Jose, Calif., 71–72
San Juan Capistrano, Calif., 72
San Juan County, Colo., 89
San Juan County, N.Mex., 456, 458, 462
San Juan County, Utah, 675–676, 679
San Juan County, Wash., 727

San Juan Pueblo, N.Mex., 461
San Leandro, Calif., 72
San Luis, Calif., 89
San Luis, Colo., 89
San Luis Obispo, Calif., 72
San Luis Obispo County, Calif., 72–73
San Marcos, Tex., 669
San Mateo, Calif., 72
San Mateo County, Calif.
  Belmont, 51
  Daly City, 54
  Montara, 63
  Redwood City, 67
  San Bruno, 69
  San Mateo, 72
San Miguel County, Colo., 89
San Miguel County, N.Mex., 459–461
San Patricio, Tex., 669
San Patricio County, Tex., 669–670
San Pedro, Calif., 72
Sanpete County, Utah, 677–679
San Rafael, Calif., 72–73
San Saba, Tex., 669
San Saba County, Tex., 669
San Simeon, Calif., 73
Sanson, Nicholas, 532
Santa Ana, Calif., 73
Santa Anna, 668
Santa Barbara, Calif., 73
Santa Barbara County, Calif., 58–59, 73
Santa Carla Pueblo, N.Mex., 461
Santa Clara, Calif., 73
Santa Clara, Utah, 682
Santa Clara County, Calif.
  Cupertino, 54
  Gilroy, 56
  Milpitas, 62
  Palo Alto, 65
  San Jose, 71–72
  Santa Clara, 73
  Saratoga, 74
  Sunnyvale, 75
Santa Clarita, Calif., 73
Santa Claus, Ind., 204
Santa Cruz, Calif., 73–74
Santa Cruz County, Ariz., 29, 32
Santa Cruz County, Calif., 73–74, 77
Santa Fe, N.Mex., 462
Santa Fe County, N.Mex., 457, 460, 462
Santa Monica, Calif., 74
Santa Paula, Calif., 74
Santa Rita, N.Mex., 462
Santa Rosa, Calif., 74
Santa Rosa, N.Mex., 462
Santa Rosa County, Fla., 124, 127
Santee, Nebr., 419
San Ygnacio, Tex., 669
Sappington, William B., 378
Sapulpa, Jim, 555
Sapulpa, Okla., 555
Saranac Lake, N.Y., 491
Sarandon, Susan, 483
Sarasota, Fla., 132
Sarasota County, Fla., 132
Saratoga, Calif., 74
Saratoga County, N.Y., 466–467, 491, 494
Saratoga Springs, N.Y., 491
Sarber, Jesse, Sheriff, 533
Sardis, Miss., 374
Sargent, James, 183
Sargent County, N.Dak., 517
Sarita, Tex., 669

INDEX

Stoddard, Richard, 313
Stoddard County, Mo., 378
Stoddert, Benjamin, 293
Stoeckel, Carl, 98
Stokely, John, 743
Stokes, Anson Phelps, 423
Stokes, Carl Burton, 528
Stokes, Edward, 480
Stokes, John, Col., 501
Stokes County, N.C., 501
Stone, Billy Ray, 374
Stone, David, 409
Stone, Eber, 494
Stone, Edward Durell, 38
Stone, Fred, 87
Stone, Lucy Blackwell, 307
Stone, May, 251
Stone, Oliver, 483
Stone, Sharon, 579
Stone, Thomas, 300
Stone, Uriah, 626
Stone, W. Clement, 174
Stone, William, 258, 291
Stone County, Miss., 375
Stone County, Mo., 384
Stoneman, George, Gen., 148, 699
Stone Mountain, Ga., 154
Stonewall, Tex., 671
Stonewall County, Tex., 638–639
Stoney, George, 600
Stonington, Conn., 101
Stookey, Paul, 292
Storber, Frank, 229
Storey, Adam, 486
Storey County, Nev., 427–428
Storm Lake, Iowa, 223
Storr, Augustine, 432
Storr, Richard, 542
Storrs, Conn., 101
Story, Amos, 694
Story, Joseph, Justice, 315
Story County, Iowa, 210, 220
Stott, David, 332
Stoughton, Shem, 94
Stoughton, William, Judge, 305
Stoughton, Wis., 761
Stout, Joseph, 628
Stover, Daniel, 625
Stover, Jacob, 711
Stover, Russell, 221, 227
Stowe, Calvin, 317
Stowe, Harriet Beecher, 96, 280, 304, 317
Stowe, Madeleine, 60
Stowe, Vt., 695
Strafford County, N.H.
  Dover, 431–432
  Durham, 432
  Farmington, 432
  Rochester, 439
  Somersworth, 439
Strait, George, 664
Strand, Paul, 480
Strang, James Jesse, 344, 762
Strange, Tubal E., 386
Strasberg, Susan, 482
Strasburg, N.Dak., 521
Stratford, Conn., 101
Stratford, Tex., 671
Stratham, Lady, 440
Stratham, N.H., 440
Stratton, Charles S., 92
Stratton, J.F., 212
Stratton, Sherwood S., 92

Straubel, Austin, 752
Straus, Lazarus, 155
Strauss, Levi, 70
Strauss, Peter, 483
Streator, Ill., 189
Street, Elnathan, 94
Streiff, Fridolin, 758
Streight, A.D., Col., 3, 152
Streisand, Barbra, 469
Stricker, John, Gen., 299
Strickland, William, 368
Stringfield, William W., 511
Stritch, Elaine, 332
Stritch, Samuel Alphonsus, Cardinal, 632
Strode, John, 261
Strode, Woody, 60
Strong, C.H., 765
Stroud, Jacob, Col., 587
Stroudsburg, Pa., 587
Strub, Charles, 50
Strunk, Harry, 419
Struthers, Sally, 564
Stuart, A. O., 46
Stuart, Elijah, 46
Stuart, Fla., 132–133
Stuart, Gilbert, 593
Stuart, Homer H., Jr., 133
Stuart, James E.B., Gen., 571, 574, 716, 718, 742
Stuart, Robert, 765, 766
Stuart, Va., 718
Stubblefield, Nathan B., 255
Stuck, Hudson, 17
Studebaker, Clement, 205, 574
Studebaker, Henry, 205
Studebaker, John, 524
Stumbo, James L., 412
Stump, Simon P., 740
Sturdy, W.A., 318
Sturgeon Bay, Wis., 761
Sturgis, James, 366
Sturgis, Samuel D., Maj., 617
Sturgis, S.Dak., 617
Sturgis, William, 211
Stutsman County, N.Dak., 518
Stuttgart, Ark., 46
Stuyvesant, Peter, 106, 109, 465, 475, 479
Styron, William, 713
Sublett, Philip A., 667
Sublette, Andrew, 88
Sublette, Kans., 240
Sublette, Pinckney, 766
Sublette, William, 240, 765
Sublette, William L., 259, 767
Sublette County, Wyo., 766–767, 769
Sudbury, Mass., 323
Sudik, Mary, 553
Suffield, Conn., 101
Suffolk, Va., 718–719
Suffolk City, Va., 718–719
Suffolk County, Mass., 305–308, 320
Suffolk County, N.Y.
  East Hampton, 472
  Greenport, 473–474
  Montauk, 477–478
  Riverhead, 489
  Southhampton, 491–492
  Westhampton, 494
Sugden, Richard, 323
Suit, Samuel Taylor, 302
Suitland, Md., 302
Sullivan, Barry, 481
Sullivan, Ed, 481

Sullivan, Frank, 491
Sullivan, Ill., 189
Sullivan, Ind., 205
Sullivan, James, Gen., 472
Sullivan, John, 306, 368, 432, 437, 474, 621
Sullivan, Louis, 212, 305, 357, 396, 469, 540, 751
Sullivan, Margaret, 714
Sullivan, Mo., 398
Sullivan, Stephen, 398
Sullivan, Susan, 483
Sullivan County, Ind., 196, 205
Sullivan County, Mo., 391
Sullivan County, N.H., 430–431, 437, 440
Sullivan County, N.Y., 478
Sullivan County, Pa., 577
Sullivan County, Tenn., 621–622, 628
Sullivant, Lucas, 528
Sully, Alfred, 517, 518, 519, 611, 614
Sully, Vin, 482
Sully County, S.Dak., 614
Sulphur, La., 275
Sulphur, Okla., 556
Sulphur Springs, Tex., 671
Summer, Benjamin, 295
Summer, Donna, 306
Summerall, David, 138
Summers, Jacob, 739
Summers, Jonathan, 535
Summers County, W. Va., 741
Summersville, W.Va., 745
Summerville, Ga., 154
Summit County, Colo., 80
Summit County, Ohio
  Akron, 523
  Barberton, 524
  Cuyahoga Falls, 529
  Hudson, 532
  Huron, 532
Summit County, Utah, 676–677, 680
Sumner, Charles, Sen., 305, 602
Sumner, David, 690
Sumner, E.V., Gen., 458
Sumner, James Batcheller, 308
Sumner, Miss., 374
Sumner, Mo., 398
Sumner County, Kans., 241
Sumner County, Tenn., 622, 626
Sumter, S.C., 606
Sumter, Thomas, Gen., 136, 603, 606
Sumter County, Ala., 9
Sumter County, Fla., 118–119
Sumter County, Ga., 136, 151
Sumter County, S.C., 606
Sunbury, Ga., 154–155
Sunbury, Pa., 587
Sundance, Wyo., 770
Sunday, William Ashley "Billy," 210
Sunflower County, Miss., 366, 368
Sunnyvale, Calif., 75
Sun Prairie, Wis., 762
Sun Valley, Idaho, 168
Superior, Ariz., 32
Superior, Mont., 407
Superior, Wis., 762
Surratt, Mary, 295
Surrey County, Va., 719
Surry, Va., 719
Surry County, N.C., 501, 506
Susanville, Calif., 75–76
Susquehanna County, Pa., 579
Sussex, Va., 719
Sussex County, Del.

INDEX

Telluride, Calif., 89
Telluride, Colo., 89
Tempe, Ariz., 32
Temple, John, 59
Temple, Shirley, 74
Temple, Tex., 671
Tenen, Gary, 25
Tennessee, 621–636
Tennille, Toni, 10
Tensas Parish, La., 274
Ten Sleep, Wyo., 770
Terhune, Albert, 451
Terhune, John, 447
Terlingua, Tex., 671
Terrbonne Parish, La., 268
Terre Haute, Ind., 205–206
Terrell, Alexander Watkins, 669
Terrell County, Ga., 142
Terrell County, Tex., 669
Terry, Alfred H., Gen., 407
Terry, Benjamin Franklin, Col., 632
Terry, Bill, 137
Terry, David S., Justice, 70
Terry, Eli, 101, 102
Terry, Gen., 404
Terry, Mont., 407
Terry County, Tex., 642
Terryville, Conn., 101
Tesson, Louis, 220
Teton, Idaho, 168
Teton County, Idaho, 164
Teton County, Mont., 402–403
Teton County, Wyo., 768–769
Tetzleff, Teddy, 683
Texarkana, Ark., 46
Texarkana, Tex., 671–672
Texas, 637–674
Texas City, Tex., 672
Texas County, Mo., 386
Texas County, Okla., 551
Thacker, Charles B., 461
Tharp, Twyla, 203
Thatcher, Ariz., 32
Thatcher, Daniel Cunningham, 187
Thatcher, Moses, 32
Thatcher, S.D., 64
Thatcher, W.L., 64
Thaw, Henry, 481
Thaxter, Celia Leighton, 439
Thayer, John M., Gen., 413, 416
Thayer County, Nebr., 414
The Dalles, Oreg., 565
Thedford, Nebr., 420
Theobald, Harriet B., 367
Thermopolis, Wyo., 771
Theroux, Paul, 316
Thetford, Vt., 695
Thibault, Joseph, 750
Thibodaux, Henry Schuyler, 275
Thibodaux, La., 275
Thief River Falls, Minn., 360
Thoen, Louis, 617
Thomas, B.J., 655
Thomas, Clarence, Justice, 153
Thomas, Danny, 332, 333
Thomas, Eleazer, Dr., 76
Thomas, George H., Gen., 229, 259, 523, 632, 704
Thomas, Henry "Gold Tom," 82
Thomas, Isaiah, 305, 326
Thomas, Jack, 252
Thomas, Jay, 272
Thomas, Jean, 243, 246

Thomas, Jeremiah, 751
Thomas, Jesse Brooks, 194
Thomas, Jett, Gen., 155
Thomas, Lowell, 532
Thomas, M. Carey, 570
Thomas, Marlo, 333
Thomas, Martha Carey, 570
Thomas, Norman, 535
Thomas, Richard, 483
Thomas, Robert Bailey, 325
Thomas, Seth, 101, 102, 103, 228, 403, 688
Thomas, Stephen, 686
Thomas, Thomas, 365
Thomas County, Ga., 155
Thomas County, Kans., 229
Thomas County, Nebr., 420
Thomaston, Conn., 101
Thomaston, Ga., 155
Thomaston, Maine, 288
Thomasville, Ga., 155
Thomasville, N.C., 511
Thompson, Albert S., 172
Thompson, Augustin, 289
Thompson, Benjamin, Sir, 326
Thompson, David, 405, 406, 407, 439
Thompson, Dorothy, 469
Thompson, Edgar J., 156
Thompson, Edward Herbert, 326
Thompson, Eliza Jane, 532
Thompson, George, 78
Thompson, Henry, 726
Thompson, Ida, 370
Thompson, James, Capt., 500
Thompson, John, 256, 632
Thompson, Lea, 358
Thompson, Orrin, 94
Thompson, Sada, 215
Thompson, Samuel, 529
Thompson, Stephen, 94
Thompson, William, 32, 78, 223, 306, 374, 544
Thompson Falls, Mont., 407–408
Thomson, Ga., 155–156
Thoreau, Henry David, 309, 326
Thornburg, T.T., Maj., 82
Thornby, W.J., Col., 611
Thorndike, Ebenezer, 323
Thorndike, Lynn, 315
Thornton, Mary Shorter, 6
Thornton, Matthew, 432
Thornton, Robert, 743
Thornton, William, 111, 432, 713
Thoroughgood, Adam, 719
Thorowgood, Francis, 719
Thorpe, Fielding M., 735
Thorpe, Jim, 558, 576
Thorpe, Owen, 194
Thorton, James, 3
Three Forks, Mont., 408
Three Rivers, Calif., 76
Throckmorton, Tex., 672
Throckmorton, William E., Dr., 672
Throckmorton County, Tex., 672
Throop, Pa., 587
Thumb, Tom, Gen., 92
Thurber, James, 528
Thurmond, R.J., Col., 373
Thurmond, Strom, Sen., 602
Thurmont, Md., 302
Thurston, Morgan J., 679
Thurston County, Nebr., 415, 418, 420–421
Thurston County, Wash., 724, 729, 734
Tibbe, Henry, 399
Tibbets, Eliza, 67

Tibbs, Casey, 610
Ticonderoga, N.Y., 492
Tiernan, Frances Fisher (Christian Reid), 509
Tierney, Gene, 468
Tierney, Lawrence, 468
Tierra Amerilla, N.Mex., 463
Tiffany, Louis Comfort, 240, 479
Tiffin, Edward, 540
Tiffin, Ohio, 540
Tift, Asa, 124
Tift, Bessie, 144
Tift, Henry H., 156
Tift, Nelson, Col., 135
Tift County, Ga., 156
Tifton, Ga., 156
Tilden, Samuel J., 672
Tilden, Tex., 672
Tilghman, Lloyd, Gen., 257
Tillamook, Oreg., 565
Tillamook County, Oreg., 565
Tillett, William Smith, 500
Tillinghast, Pardon, 595
Tillis, Mel, 133
Tillman, Benjamin R., Sen., 602
Tillman, B.R., Gov., 602
Tillman County, Okla., 550, 557
Tillotson, Neil, 431
Timber Lake, S.Dak., 617–618
Times Beach, Mo., 398
Tingle, William, 387
Tinker, Robert, 188
Tiny Tim (Khaury, Herbert), 482
Tioga, Tex., 672
Tioga County, N.Y., 487, 489
Tioga County, Pa., 569, 588
Tionesta, Pa., 587
Tippah County, Miss., 373
Tippecanoe County, Ind., 194, 200, 207
Tipton, Ind., 206
Tipton, Iowa, 224
Tipton, John, 195, 625, 628
Tipton, Okla., 557
Tipton County, Ind., 206
Tipton County, Tenn., 624
Tiptonville, Tenn., 635–636
Tishler, Max, 306
Tishomingo, Okla., 557
Tishomingo County, Miss., 368
Tittle, Y.A., 660
Tituba, West Indian woman, 321
Titus, Henry T., Col., 134
Titus, H.T., Col., 234
Titus, Jonathan, 587
Titus, Lenox, 696
Titus County, Tex., 662
Titusville, Fla., 134
Titusville, Pa., 587
Tiverton, R.I., 596
Tivoli, N.Y., 492–493
Tobias, Channing Heggie, 138
Tobin, Diana, 730
Tobin, Henry, 730
Toccoa, Ga., 156
Todd, John, 224, 334
Todd, Thomas, 707, 709
Todd County, Ky., 248–249
Todd County, Minn., 354
Todd County, S.Dak., 613, 615–616
Toklas, Alice B., 70
Tok (Tok Junction), Alaska, 23
Toledo, Ill., 189
Toledo, Iowa, 224
Toledo, Ohio, 541

INDEX

INDEX

Whalley, Edmund, 312
Wharton, Edith, 480
Wharton, John A., 674
Wharton, Joseph, 444
Wharton, Richard, 289
Wharton, Tex., 674
Wharton, William H., 674
Wharton County, Tex., 674
Whatcom County, Wash., 724
Wheatland, Wyo., 771
Wheatland County, Mont., 404
Wheaton, Henry, 595
Wheaton, Ill., 191
Wheaton, Jesse, 191
Wheaton, Minn., 361
Wheaton, Warren, 191
Wheaton, Wil, 52
Wheeler, Benjamin Ide, 320
Wheeler, Burton Kendall, 313
Wheeler, Cordelia Hinds, 441
Wheeler, Frank H., 205
Wheeler, Joe, Gen., 627
Wheeler, John, 123, 507
Wheeler, Joseph, Cong., 137
Wheeler, Moses, 101
Wheeler, Royal T., 674
Wheeler, Tex., 674
Wheeler, William Almon, 477
Wheeler County, Ga., 135
Wheeler County, Nebr., 409–410
Wheeler County, Oreg., 561
Wheeler County, Tex., 669–670, 674
Wheeling, W.Va., 746–747
Wheelock, F.E., 659
Wheelock, Gersham, 322
Wheelock, John, 96
Wheelwright, John, 432
Whelan, Thomas, Mayor, 448
Whellock, Eleazar, 103
Whidbey, Joseph, 724
Whidden, James, Capt., 277
Whipple, Abraham, 595
Whipple, Cullen, 596
Whipple, Eva Dalton, 236
Whipple, Fred Lawrence, 222
Whipple, George Hoyt, 429
Whipple, Henry, Bishop, 351
Whipple, William, 283
Whistler, James, 314
Whistler, John, Maj., 197
Whitaker, Forest, 659
Whitaker, William, 132
Whitchill, Clarence Eugene, 219
Whitcomb, F.W., 610
White, Andrew, Father, 300
White, Barry, 651
White, Benjamin, 312
White, Betty, 185
White, Byron, 84
White, C., 260
White, Carr B., Col., 740
White, Delos, Dr., 470
White, E.B., 478
White, Edward, 119, 275, 668
White, Elijah, 92, 766
White, Horace, 750
White, James, 220, 254, 512, 629
White, James Larkin, 456
White, Jesse, 469
White, John, 152, 506
White, Josh, 603
White, Morrison Remick, Justice, 99
White, Peregrine, 320

White, Stanford, 474, 479, 481
White, Stewart Edward, 335
White, Theodore H., 306
White, Vanna, 604
White, Walter Francis, 137
White, William Allen, 231
White Castle, La., 276
White Cloud, Mich., 346
White County, Ga., 140
White County, Ill., 172
White County, Ind., 201
White County, Tenn., 635
Whitehall, Wis., 763
Whitehead, Ralph, 495
Whiteley, William, 540
Whitely City, Ky., 260
Whitely County, Ky., 256, 260
Whiteman, Paul, 82
White Oak, Ga., 158
White Pine County, Nev., 424–425, 427
White Plains, N.Y., 495
White River, S.Dak., 618
White River Junction, Vt., 696
Whitesburg, Ky., 260
Whiteside County, Ill., 183, 189
White Springs, Fla., 134
White Sulphur Springs, Mont., 408
White Sulphur Springs, W.Va., 747
Whiteville, N.C., 512
Whitewater, Wis., 763
Whitewood, S.Dak., 619
Whitfield, Nathan, Gen., 5
Whitfield County, Ga., 142
Whitford, Joseph, 351
Whiting, Leonard, 319
Whiting, Margaret, 332
Whiting, Nathan, Col., 696
Whitingham, Vt., 696
Whitley, William, 260
Whitley County, Ind., 195
Whitley County, Ky., 247
Whitlock, Ambrose, Maj., 195
Whitman, Clair, 119
Whitman, Marcus, 734, 766, 770
Whitman, Sarah, 596
Whitman, Walt, 445, 583
Whitman County, Wash., 725, 730
Whitney, Ann, 653
Whitney, Anne, 324
Whitney, Asa, 95, 324
Whitney, Daniel, 752
Whitney, Eli, 95, 153, 157, 325
Whitney, J.D., 59, 318
Whitney, Joel, 326
Whitney, William Collins, 309
Whitney, William Dwight, 309
Whittaker, Charles Evans, Justice, 241
Whittemore, Amos, 326
Whittemore, Betsy, 431
Whittemore, John, 431
Whittier, Alaska, 23
Whittier, John Greenleaf, 23, 309, 313, 316, 433
Whittington, Granville, 43
Whittington, William, 704
Whittlesey, Asaph, 749
Whittmore. Gideon, 346
Wiard, Thomas, 466
Wibaux, Mont., 408
Wibaux, Pierre, 408
Wibaux County, Mont., 408
Wichita, Kans., 242
Wichita County, Kans., 235

Wichita County, Tex., 642, 674
Wichita Falls, Tex., 674
Wickenburg, Ariz., 33
Wickenburg, Henry, 33
Wickersham, Alexander, 724
Wickersham, George, 584
Wickersham, James, Judge, 21
Wickford, R.I., 598
Wickliffe, Ky., 260
Wicks, John, 180
Wicomico County, Md., 301
Widdowfield, Ed, 769
Wiener, Norbert, 381
Wiest, Dianne, 388
Wiggin, Thomas, Capt., 431
Wiggins, Benjamin, 434
Wiggins, Kate D., 582
Wiggins, Miss., 375
Wilbarger, Josiah, 672
Wilbarger, Mathias, 672
Wilbarger County, Tex., 672–673
Wilber, Nebr., 420
Wilbur, Curtis Dwight, Justice, 211
Wilbur, Richard Purdy, 482
Wilburn, Aaron O., 461
Wilcox, Eliza, 410
Wilcox, H.K., 97
Wilcox, Horace H., 57
Wilcox, James, 182
Wilcox, J.F., 213
Wilcox, Joseph M., Lt., 4
Wilcox, Orlando B., Gen., 33
Wilcox County, Ala., 4
Wilcox County, Ga., 135
Wilder, Almanzo, 609
Wilder, Douglas, 717
Wilder, Gene, 757
Wilder, John T., 255, 634
Wilder, Laura Ingalls, 609, 751
Wilder, Thornton, 755
Wildman, Zalmon, 540
Wiliams, Ben Ames, 370
Wilkes, Charles, Lt., 162
Wilkes, John, 157, 589
Wilkes-Barre, Pa., 589
Wilkesboro, N.C., 512
Wilkes County, Ga., 157
Wilkes County, N.C., 507, 512
Wilkie, Wendell L., 196
Wilkin, Alexander, Col., 349
Wilkin County, Minn., 349
Wilkins, Collie Leroy, Jr., 8
Wilkins, Roy, 359, 396
Wilkinson, James, Gen., 5, 9, 248, 270, 486
Wilkinson, Jemima, 322, 592
Wilkinson, John, 713
Wilkinson County, Ga., 146
Wilkinson County, Miss., 376
Willacy County, Tex., 666
Willamsport, Ind., 207
Willard, Emma, 91, 691
Willard, Frances, 178
Willard, Samuel, Capt., 434
Willard, Simon, 309
Will County, Ill., 171, 180, 182, 184
Willcox, Ariz., 33
Willcox, Mark, Gen., 135
Willemsen, Thunis, 106
Willett, Thomas, 479
Willey, Gordon Randolph, 212
Willey, Waitman, 743
Willey House, N.H., 441
William, Prince of Orange, 221, 451